THE OXFORD HANDBOOK OF CRIMINOLOGY

Third Edition

EDITED BY

MIKE MAGUIRE
ROD MORGAN
AND
ROBERT REINER

OXFORD
UNIVERSITY PRESS

OXFORD

UNIVERSITY PRESS

Great Clarendon Street, Oxford OX2 6DP

Oxford University Press is a department of the University of Oxford.
It furthers the University's objective of excellence in research, scholarship,
and education by publishing worldwide in

Oxford New York

Auckland Bangkok Buenos Aires Cape Town Chennai
Dar es Salaam Delhi Hong Kong Istanbul Karachi Kolkata
Kuala Lumpur Madrid Melbourne Mexico City Mumbai Nairobi
São Paulo Shanghai Taipei Tokyo Toronto

Oxford is a registered trade mark of Oxford University Press
in the UK and in certain other countries

Published in the United States
by Oxford University Press Inc., New York

British Library Cataloguing in Publication Data

Data available

Library of Congress Cataloging in Publication Data

Data available

ISBN 0–19–925609–8
ISBN 0–19–924937–7 (pbk.)

5 7 9 10 8 6 4

Typeset in Adobe Minion
by RefineCatch Limited, Bungay, Suffolk
Printed in Great Britain by
Ashford Colour Press Ltd,
Gosport, Hampshire

OUTLINE CONTENTS

PART 4 FORMS OF CRIME

PART 5 REACTIONS TO CRIME

DETAILED CONTENTS

PART 2 THE SOCIAL CONSTRUCTION OF CRIME AND CRIME CONTROL

PART 3   DIMENSIONS OF CRIME

PART 4 FORMS OF CRIME

PART 5 REACTIONS TO CRIME

NOTES ON CONTRIBUTORS

ANDREW ASHWORTH is Vinerian Professor of English Law at the University of Oxford, and a Fellow of All Souls College, Oxford.

BEN BOWLING is Reader in Criminology and Criminal Justice in the School of Law, King's College, London.

ANTHONY E. BOTTOMS is Wolfson Professor of Criminology at the University of Cambridge, and Visiting Professor of Criminology at the University of Sheffield.

DAVID DOWNES is Professor of Social Administration at the London School of Economics.

CLIVE EMSLEY is Professor of History at the Open University.

DAVID P. FARRINGTON is Professor of Psychological Criminology at the University of Cambridge.

JANET FOSTER is in the Department of Sociology at the London School of Economics.

DAVID GARLAND is Arthur T. Vanderbilt Professor of Law and Professor of Sociology at New York University.

LORAINE GELSTHORPE is Senior Lecturer in Criminology in the Institute of Criminology, University of Cambridge, and a Fellow of Pembroke College, Cambridge.

FRANCES HEIDENSOHN is Professor of Social Policy at Goldsmiths College, University of London.

CLIVE R. HOLLIN is Professor of Criminological Psychology in the Centre for Applied Psychology, University of Leicester.

BARBARA HUDSON is Professor of Law at the Lancashire Law School, University of Central Lancashire.

NICOLA LACEY is Professor of Criminal Law at the London School of Economics, and Adjunct Professor of Social and Political Theory, Research School of Social Sciences, Australian National University.

MICHAEL LEVI is Professor of Criminology in the School of Social Sciences, Cardiff University.

IAN LOADER is Reader in Criminology in the Department of Criminology, Keele University.

MIKE MAGUIRE is Professor of Criminology and Criminal Justice in the School of Social Sciences, Cardiff University.

ROD MORGAN is Professor Emeritus of Criminal Justice, University of Bristol, and HM Chief Inspector of the Probation Service for England and Wales.

DAVID NELKEN is Distinguished Professor of Legal Institutions and Social Change, University of Macerata, Italy, and Distinguished Research Professor of Law at Cardiff University.

TIM NEWBURN is Joseph Rowntree Foundation Professor of Urban Social Policy, and Director of the Public Policy Research Unit, Goldsmiths College.

KEN PEASE is Visiting Professor of Crime Science at the Jill Dando Institute, University College, University of London.

JILL PEAY is Reader in the Department of Law, London School of Economics and Political Science.

CORETTA PHILLIPS is Lecturer in the Department of Social Policy, London School of Economics.

PETER RAYNOR is Professor of Applied Social Studies in the School of Social Sciences and International Development, University of Wales Swansea.

ROBERT REINER is Professor of Criminology in the Law Department, London School of Economics.

PAUL ROCK is Professor of Social Institutions in the Department of Sociology, London School of Economics.

ANDREW SANDERS is Professor of Criminal Law and Criminology at the University of Manchester.

DAVID J. SMITH is Professor of Criminology at the University of Edinburgh.

NIGEL SOUTH is Professor in the Department of Sociology, University of Essex.

RICHARD SPARKS is Professor in Criminology in the Department of Criminology, Keele University.

PAUL WILES is Director of Research, Development, and Statistics, Home Office.

JOCK YOUNG is Professor of Sociology at the Centre for Criminology, Middlesex University.

RICHARD YOUNG is Lecturer in Criminal Justice and Assistant Director at the Centre for Criminological Research, University of Oxford.

LUCIA ZEDNER is Reader in Criminal Justice in the Law Faculty, University of Oxford, and a Fellow of Corpus Christi College, Oxford.

INTRODUCTION TO THE THIRD EDITION

Mike Maguire, Rod Morgan, and Robert Reiner

This is the third edition of *The Oxford Handbook of Criminology*. The first edition was prepared in 1992–3 and published in 1994. The second edition, which had a much shorter gestation, was prepared in 1996 and appeared in 1997. Our authors wrote their chapters for this edition during the summer, autumn, or early winter of 2001 (some of them engage in brinkmanship more than others), and we delivered the text to Oxford University Press at the beginning of January 2002. We would like to thank all our contributors for producing chapters of such a high standard while meeting such a demanding schedule. The fact that they will be available to students eight months later is a credit to everyone involved in the project at Oxford University Press.

In 1994 we said that we hoped the *Handbook* would meet a teaching and research need. The success of the enterprise suggests that it has. The *Handbook* is now widely acknowledged as the leading British text in its field and we conclude that our editorial rationale, explained in the Introduction to the first edition, has been vindicated. We therefore see no need to change our basic strategy. However, for this new edition we have not only ensured that all material has been thoroughly updated, but have also added some new chapters and made substantial changes in the coverage of others. This has entailed some changes in authorship (including bringing in some 'new blood'), but the great majority of the current contributors have been with us from the beginning. Sadly, one change of authorship was forced upon us by the untimely death of Ian Taylor. We shall greatly miss Ian, and we remain very grateful for the high-quality contributions he made to both the previous editions.

We came to this venture in the early 1990s as three long-serving members of British universities with a wide variety of teaching and research experience in the broad area of criminology and criminal justice. The initial stimulus came from our strong feeling that there was no single comprehensive textbook covering sufficient ground in enough depth to build a general criminology course around it. There were (and are still) many excellent texts on most *specific* areas of crime and criminal justice, such as the criminal justice process, the penal system, policing, victims, gender, and race. There were also a number of well-established and stimulating texts on the theoretical development of criminology. However, reading lists for courses intending to cover theoretical and substantive issues had to use a variety of different references (books and articles) for each topic. Reading lists had become dauntingly elephantine, and increasingly unfriendly to students with limited resources in time and money. This is the gap we originally set out to fill, and do so again with the third edition. The *Handbook* aims to provide students with authoritative overviews of the major issues that most criminology courses cover, whether taught in schools of law or social science, to undergraduates, postgraduates, or practitioners.

As described at some length in the Introductions to the previous editions, criminology is a field that has experienced a huge and continuing expansion, as well as a major 'fragmentation' (Ericson and Carriere 1994) in terms of substantive areas of specialization and epistemological, methodological, and political orientations. It is no longer possible, as once it was, for individuals to keep abreast of all this activity and output. Scores of research monographs and general texts of a criminological nature are published each year. At least a dozen British publishing houses carry a substantial list of criminology titles, and many university centres have in-house monograph series. The *British Journal of Criminology* and the *Howard Journal* now compete with several other British-based academic journals in more specialized areas of criminology—*Theoretical Criminology, Punishment and Society* and *Criminal Justice* are among those that have recently joined the pack—and with journals on substantive areas like policing, victimology, and probation. In addition, most of the general social science and law journals regularly publish articles of a criminological character.

Rather than attempt to write about all of these areas ourselves, we set out to assemble a collection of state-of-the-art reviews by leading academics covering, as nearly as possible, the full range of issues addressed by criminology, and representing the diverse array of viewpoints in criminological discourse. To make this already highly ambitious task more manageable, we have since the beginning maintained a fairly strong focus on issues and material of particular interest to British criminologists and their students, but this does not by any means exclude reference to major international developments and literature. For this third edition, we commissioned thirty-two British scholars (two of them based overseas) to provide reviews of thirty-one major topics, most as single but some as joint authors. We asked them to refer to relevant theory and recent research, to point to policy developments, and to highlight those aspects of current debate of which students, teachers, and practitioners should be aware. We also asked them to provide a short guide to further reading and include comprehensive bibliographies so that students can follow up topics in greater detail. All the feedback we have received on the previous editions suggests that these bibliographical resources are a valuable feature of the *Handbook* for students and teachers alike.

We have for each edition selected contributors recognized for their research and scholarship, usually, though not always, in the topic areas about which we asked them to write. However, we have never stipulated the theoretical approach they should adopt, and have deliberately approached scholars representing different perspectives. The *Handbook* remains unashamedly a collection of different voices.

The result will not please everyone. We recognize that our commitment to non-dogmatic inclusiveness carries with it the pitfall that a way of seeing is also always a way of not seeing (Burke 1989). Editorial inclusion, however wide-ranging and non-partisan, always entails exclusion, and our claims to be non-dogmatic are to some extent necessarily disingenuous. A few of the chapters in this collection are contributed by fairly obvious authors who could not easily be replaced. But most topics could have been covered by equally worthy others. Our choice of collaborators has inevitably been shaped by our circles of acquaintanceship, our disciplinary origins and affiliations, and our theoretical orientations.

CHANGES TO THE LAST EDITION

As in the past, we have tried to ensure that all the principal topics ordinarily included in criminology and criminology-related courses are covered. Clearly, criminology is a rapidly changing field, which responds to new ideas in other academic fields as well as to developments in crime policy and politics. Since the last edition, there have been some important shifts in direction, and the changes we have made to the structure of the book reflect these to some extent.

In addition to updating—itself a major exercise—the principal changes in this third edition are intended to rectify gaps and weaknesses evident to us from our own discussions and the feedback provided by colleagues and collected by Oxford University Press. We think that the coverage of substantive topics achieved in the first and second editions was broadly adequate, and the enhanced discussion of contemporary theoretical developments achieved in the second edition a great improvement compared to the first. However, we concluded that two additions, in particular, would be beneficial.

First, we have sought further to strengthen the place of contemporary theory in the collection, by inviting five of the contributors to the 'symposium' of short essays on 'Frontiers of Criminological Theory' in the second edition—Loraine Gelsthorpe, Barbara Hudson, Nicola Lacey, David Nelken, and Richard Sparks (joined now by Ian Loader)—to expand their chapters to full length. Another symposium author, Jock Young, has taken over the territory previously covered by the late Ian Taylor, that of social inequality and crime.

Secondly, we have sought to acknowledge more than in previous editions the contribution made by psychology, and psychologically-oriented approaches, to the field of criminology. There is no doubt that sociology (and the related discipline of social policy) has had a dominant influence on the British criminological scene over the past thirty years—and, we concede, has dominated the academic links and theoretical orientations of we three editors—but psychology has also always occupied an important place within criminology. In recent years, psychological approaches to crime have become increasingly prominent in both academic criminology and public policy, on both sides of the Atlantic. We have therefore considerably expanded our coverage of such approaches, which are now reflected primarily in the chapters by Clive Hollin (on the contribution of psychological theory to criminology over the years), David Farrington (on developmental criminology), David Smith (on crime and the life course), and Peter Raynor (whose chapter on community penalties includes a substantial discussion of the growing use of cognitive-behavioural programmes and the neo-rehabilitative orientation of the 'What Works' movement).

Lastly, in shuffling the structure of the book and the topic coverage of individual chapters, we have had to make some difficult decisions about authorship. On the one hand, we are very pleased to welcome seven new contributors, who will not only bring fresh ideas and approaches, but who will between them bring down the average age of the *Handbook* authors: Ben Bowling, Janet Foster, Clive Hollin, Ian Loader, Coretta Phillips, Peter Raynor, and Richard Young. On the other hand, we are at our limits of space for one volume, and have inevitably had to lose a small number of highly valued contributors to previous editions. We would like to express our sincere thanks to all of them for their past contributions.

References

BURKE, K. (1989), *On Symbols and Society*, Chicago, Ill.: Chicago University Press.

ERICSON, R., and CARRIERE, K. (1994), 'The Fragmentation of Criminology', in D. Nelken (ed.), *The Futures of Criminology*, 89–109, London: Sage.

PART I

CRIMINOLOGY: HISTORY AND THEORY

1

OF CRIMES AND CRIMINALS
THE DEVELOPMENT OF CRIMINOLOGY IN BRITAIN

*David Garland**

INTRODUCTION: THE CONTINGENT CHARACTER OF CONTEMPORARY CRIMINOLOGY

This chapter presents an interpretation of the historical development of criminology in Britain. Any such history is inevitably a contentious undertaking, entailing theoretical choices and rhetorical purposes as well as the selection and arrangement of historical materials. Whether they acknowledge it or not, histories of the discipline necessarily come up against fundamental issues—What is 'criminology'? What are its central features? How are its conceptual and historical boundaries identified? In what institutional, political, or cultural contexts should it be situated? It may therefore be useful to begin by outlining some of the theoretical assumptions that underpin the interpretation offered here.

I take criminology to be a specific genre of discourse and inquiry about crime—a genre that has developed in the modern period and that can be distinguished from other ways of talking and thinking about criminal conduct. Thus, for example, criminology's claim to be an empirically grounded, scientific undertaking sets it apart from moral and legal discourses, while its focus upon crime differentiates it from other social scientific genres, such as the sociology of deviance and control, whose objects of study are broader and not defined by the criminal law. Since the middle years of the twentieth century, criminology has also been increasingly marked off from other discourses by the trappings of a distinctive disciplinary identity, with its own journals, professional associations, professorships, and institutes. One of the concerns of this essay will be to try to explain how such a discipline came to exist as an accredited specialism, supported by universities and governments alike.

My broad historical argument will be that modern criminology grew out of the

* I am grateful to the following friends and colleagues for their help with this essay and its subsequent revisions: Stanley Cohen, Mitchell Duneier, Gretchen Feltes, James B. Jacobs, Aaron Kupchik, Dorothy Nelkin, Robert Reiner, Paul Rock, and Peter Young. Research for this project was assisted by the Lindsay Bequest Fund of the Edinburgh University Law Faculty and by the Filomen D'Agostino and Max E. Greenberg Research Fund of the New York University School of Law.

convergence of two quite separate enterprises—'the governmental project' and 'the Lombrosian project'—which together provided a social and an intellectual rationale for the subject. By talking about a 'governmental project' I mean to refer to the long series of empirical inquiries, which, since the eighteenth century, have sought to enhance the efficient and equitable administration of justice by charting the patterns of crime and monitoring the practice of police and prisons. This tradition of inquiry was eventually to become a major part of the criminological enterprise and to provide criminology with its central claim to social utility. The 'Lombrosian project', in contrast, refers to a form of inquiry which aims to develop an etiological, explanatory science, based on the premise that criminals can somehow be scientifically differentiated from non-criminals.[1] Although each of these projects underwent important revisions during the twentieth century, and the situation of criminology has been significantly altered by its entry into the universities, I will suggest that the discipline continues to be structured by the sometimes competing, sometimes converging, claims of these two programmes. One pole of the discipline pulls its practitioners towards an ambitious (and, I have argued elsewhere—Garland 1985b—deeply flawed) theoretical project seeking to build a science of causes. The other exerts the pragmatic force of a policy-oriented, administrative project, seeking to use science in the service of management and control. Criminologists have sometimes sought to overcome this tension by rejecting one project in favour of the other—either giving up the search for causes in favour of a direct policy orientation, or else disengaging from governmental concerns in the name of a pure (or a critical) science. However, the combination of the two projects seems essential to criminology's claim to be sufficiently useful and sufficiently scientific to merit the status of an accredited, state-sponsored, academic discipline.

The coming together of these two projects was by no means inevitable. The historical record suggests that it took several decades for criminal justice officials to accept that the Lombrosian search for the causes of crime had any relevance to their administrative tasks, and, in fact, Lombroso's criminology had to be extensively modified before it could be of service to policy-makers and state authorities. Beyond that, the very idea of a science devoted to 'the criminal' seems in retrospect to have been something of an historical accident, originally prompted by a claim that was quickly

---

[1] I use the concept of a 'project' here to characterize an emergent tradition of inquiry that, despite a degree of variation, shares a cluster of aims and objectives. The 'governmental' project refers to those inquiries that direct their attention to the problems of governing crime and criminals. Studies which fall within this tradition are not necessarily official, state-sponsored studies, although, from the nineteenth century onwards, the state came to dominate work of this kind. Nor are these inquiries necessarily focused upon state practices (such as criminal laws, police, prisons, etc.), since the governance of crime and criminals also occurs through 'private' institutions such as the family, boys' clubs, settlement houses, and so on. As I discuss later, the study of crime and criminal justice practices was not at first separate from a much broader concern with the rational governance of the population in all its aspects. (On the concept of governmentality, see Foucault 1979; Burchell et al. 1991; Garland 1997.) The 'Lombrosian' project refers to that tradition of inquiry, begun by Lombroso, which aims to differentiate the criminal individual from the non-criminal. By naming the etiological project in this way I wish to emphasize the continuity in scientific objective which runs from Lombroso to the present, rather than to suggest a continuity of method or of substantive analysis: most etiological studies of the twentieth century de-emphasized the biological determinants which Lombroso took to be fundamental.

discredited: namely, that 'the criminal type' was an identifiable anthropological entity. Were it not for the contingency of that intellectual event there might never have been any distinctive criminological science, or any independent discipline. As an historical counterfactual, it is perfectly plausible to imagine that crime and criminals could have remained integral concerns of mainstream sociology and psychiatry, and that 'criminological' research undertaken for government purposes could have developed without the need of a university specialism of that name. If this is so, and criminology has a contingent rather than a necessary place in the halls of science, then its history becomes all the more relevant to an understanding of the discipline.

In the light of the assumptions and arguments I have outlined here, history becomes essential to an understanding of the modern criminological enterprise. If we are to understand the central topics that criminology has marked out as its own, if we are to understand the discipline's relation to institutional practices and concerns, if we are to understand some of the key terms and conceptions that structure the discourse, then we will have to ask genealogical questions about the constitution of this science and examine the historical processes that led to the emergence of an accredited disciplinary specialism. Moreover, the kind of historical inquiry required is one that is sensitive to context and contingency, and to the relation between intellectual developments and the social practices out of which they emerge. If my claim is correct, and criminology is a product of the convergence of certain ideas and interests, in a particular institutional context, then its history cannot be treated, as it so often is, as the gradual unfolding of a science that was always destined to appear. Such is the prevalence of this kind of history that it may be worth discussing the shortcomings of received accounts, before going on to sketch an alternative approach.

TEXTBOOK HISTORIES

Criminology's history is most often presented in the form of a preface. It appears, usually in a few compressed and standardized pages, as the opening section of a book or article, introducing the reader to the subject and placing the author's text within a longer tradition. Sometimes the prefatory history has a job to do, providing the reader with enough historical understanding to appreciate the significance and provenance of the text that follows. At other times it is merely decorative—a routine flourish with little real purpose beyond getting started in a way that has come to be expected of authors. Ironically, this routine repetition of conventional historical wisdom can have an influence quite out of keeping with its value as scholarship. The telling and retelling of the standard historical tale is a most effective way of persuading the discipline's recruits that whatever else may be contested, this much, at least, can be taken for granted.

Occasionally, textbooks, research monographs, or critical studies make a feature of their historical introductions, offering a more extensive (and usually more tendentious) account of the subject's history, which acts as a kind of framing device for subsequent arguments.[2] On these occasions, history becomes a way of conducting

---

[2] See, e.g., the historical introductions to the following: Taylor, Walton, and Young 1973; Morris 1957; Matza 1964.

theoretical debate by other means. The recovery of a lost theoretical tradition, the reinterpretation of the subject's early history, claims and counter-claims about the true 'founders' of the discipline, or critical summaries of previous patterns of thought, are all ways in which the subject's history gets drafted into current controversies and made to do duty for one side or the other.[3]

The history of the discipline has, on a few occasions, formed the central subject matter for a book or an article. Most of these excursions into historical criminology are minor attempts to attribute importance to a particular author whose influence upon the subject is felt to have been slighted,[4] but some historical writings have more ambitious intentions. Books such as Mannheim's *Pioneers in Criminology* (1960), or Radzinowicz's *Ideology and Crime* (1966)—both published by leading figures in the process of discipline-building—played an important role in shaping the contours and self-consciousness of the discipline, and sought to enhance its status by invoking a distinguished Enlightenment past and a progressive scientific mission.[5] The collection entitled *The History of British Criminology* (Rock 1988a)—edited by one of the sociologists who helped remake British criminology in the 1960s and 1970s—professes similar discipline-forming ambitions, aiming to introduce new generations of criminologists to a revised history more in keeping with contemporary interests and understandings. It is not just the textbooks that have to be adjusted when a discipline changes; history must also be rewritten.

The received history of the discipline, often simplified into a tale of icons and demons (Beccaria, Lombroso, Burt, Radzinowicz . . .), a few key distinctions (classicism, positivism, radicalism . . .), and an overarching narrative in which ideological error is gradually displaced by the findings of science (e.g., the myth of the born criminal and its subsequent debunking), plays a small but significant role in shaping the horizons and reference points of contemporary criminology. A discipline's practitioners work with a sense of where their subject has come from and where it is going, which issues are settled and which are still live, who are the exemplars to imitate and who are the anathemas to be avoided. Perhaps most importantly, the received history provides practitioners with a standard-issue kit of collective terms and shared values. Thus, for example, anyone who learned about the discipline's history from the textbooks of the 1970s and 1980s would find it hard to identify with the methods and aspirations of 'positivism', even though this term was broad enough to include

---

[3] Laub and Sampson 1991 is a good example. The authors of this article develop a sophisticated historical account that aims to explain the disappearance of the work of Sheldon and Eleanor Glueck from the canon of contemporary criminology. Their revisionist historical account serves to reassert the importance of the Gluecks' contribution and its central themes (age and crime; criminal careers and longitudinal research; stability of crime and deviance; social control and the family). In doing so, it operates as a corrective to the historical record, but also as a prolegomenon to a major work of Laub and Sampson that builds upon the Gluecks' research findings. See Sampson and Laub 1993.

[4] See, e.g., Savitz *et al.* 1977; also Lyell 1913, Levin and Lindesmith 1937.

[5] For a discussion of the rhetorical, discipline-building character of Radzinowicz's *Ideology and Crime*, see Garland 2002.

virtually the whole discipline prior to the rise of 'labelling' theories and the associated anti-positivist critiques.[6]

The standard textbook account of criminology's history begins with the writings of criminal law reformers in the eighteenth century, particularly Beccaria, Bentham, Romilly, and Howard. These writers are said to have characterized the offender as a rational, free-willed actor who engages in crime in a calculated, utilitarian way and is therefore responsive to deterrent, proportionate penalties of the kind that the reformers preferred. This 'classical school of criminology', as it is usually called, was subsequently challenged, in the late nineteenth century, by writers of the 'positivist school' (Lombroso, Ferri, and Garofalo are usually cited) who adopted a more empirical, scientific approach to the subject, and investigated 'the criminal' using the techniques of psychiatry, physical anthropology, anthropometry, and other new human sciences. The positivist school claimed to have discovered evidence of the existence of 'criminal types' whose behaviour was determined rather than chosen and for whom treatment rather than punishment was appropriate. Subsequent research refuted or modified most of the specific claims of Lombroso, and restored the credibility of some of the 'classicist' ideas he opposed, but the project of a scientific criminology had been founded, and this enterprise continues, in a more diverse and sophisticated way, today.

This standard textbook history is, of course, broadly accurate—it would be very surprising if it were not. But the broad sweep of its narrative and the resounding simplicity of its generic terms can be profoundly misleading if they are taken as real history, rather than as a kind of foundational myth, developed not for historical purposes but for heuristic ones.

MISLEADING CATEGORIES

A problematic feature of these histories is their uncritical use of key terms that then subsequently enter into standard criminological discourse in an equally unselfconscious way. The term 'classicism', to take an important example, is used as a generic term to denote the criminology of Beccaria and Bentham, and eighteenth-century thought more generally. It is also used, by extension, to describe modern theories that affirm the rational, free-willed character of offenders' decision-making processes (see Roshier 1989). But, despite this conventional usage, it actually makes little sense to claim that these eighteenth-century thinkers possessed a 'criminology', given that they made no general distinction between the characteristics of criminals and non-criminals, and had no conception of research on crime and criminals as a distinctive form of inquiry. To use the term 'classical criminology' to characterize eighteenth-century thought seriously misrepresents the nature of these writings and forcibly assimilates them to a project that was not invented until a century later.

---

[6] See, e.g., the discussions of 'positivism' in Taylor, Walton, and Young 1973 and in Matza 1964. The tradition of 'positivist criminology' has been re-evaluated and reaffirmed in the USA (see Gottfredson and Hirschi 1987), and in Britain, some of its sternest critics have modified their views and realigned themselves with some of its central concerns. For a discussion of the changing relationship between 'radical criminology' and 'positivism', see Young 1988.

The notion that these various writers all maintained the same view of the offender (as a rational, free-willed actor) is also a distortion, derived from the polemics of late nineteenth-century positivists rather than from a reading of the eighteenth-century texts. There are, for example, quite major differences between authors such as Bentham and Howard on the questions of human nature and freedom of choice; and Beccaria, as a good Lockean empiricist, viewed human character and conduct as shaped by sense impressions and habit as well as by free will and reason.[7] Other eighteenth-century writers on crime approached the question from a quite different perspective, stressing the social conditions that shaped individual conduct and using a deterministic language to describe the process of becoming criminal.[8] The notion of 'classicism' thus tends to dissolve under close scrutiny, deriving any coherence it has not from the facts of intellectual history but from the careless habits of contemporary criminological teaching.

'Positivism' holds up little better as a descriptive term, although, unlike classicism, it at least has the merit of having been the self-description of a school of criminologists. The use of this word to describe the specific claims of Lombroso and his *scuola positiva* in the late nineteenth century (the born criminal, the constitutional and hereditary roots of criminal conduct, criminal types, etc.), and also to describe the huge and diverse range of criminological work which has been carried out within an empiricist framework (i.e., using 'theory-neutral' observation as a basis for inductive propositions, stressing measurement, objectivity, etc.), has been a source of great confusion in the discipline. Potted histories entrench this muddle whenever they talk indiscriminately about a 'positivist era' which stretched from the 1870s to the 1960s.

THE OBJECT OF INQUIRY

One of the most problematic issues to be addressed by any intellectual history is the question of criteria for inclusion and exclusion. If one is writing the history of criminology, what is to count as relevant? Where does the subject start and where does it stop? Textbook histories generally avoid the issue and simply begin with Beccaria, the arbitrariness of this decision being concealed by the fact that this is by now the traditional place to start. But one can see the problem much more clearly on those occasions when criminology's intellectual history is the subject of a whole article or series of chapters. Thus, for instance, Israel Drapkin's essay in the *Encyclopedia of Crime and Justice* (Drapkin 1983)—like the more historically oriented textbooks by Bonger (1936) and Vold (1958)—seeks to provide a more serious, scholarly account of the subject's historical development. Drapkin traces criminology's intellectual history back through the early modern period, the Middle Ages, and the classical period to the ancient world and 'prehistoric times'. The problem here is that the selection criteria are unargued and hopelessly broad. Criminology's history becomes the history of everything that has ever been said, or thought, or done in relation to

---

[7] On the differences between Howard and Bentham, see Ignatieff 1978. On Beccaria as a Lockean empiricist, see Zeman 1981.

[8] See the discussion of writers such as Henry Dagge and Mannasseh Dawes in Green 1985.

law-breakers, and the links between this amorphous past and the particular present remain vague and unspecified. Worse still, the writings of ancient and medieval authors are ransacked in search of 'criminological' statements and arguments, as if they were addressing the same questions in the same ways as modern criminologists, and we are introduced to anachronistic creatures such as 'early modern criminology' and St Thomas Aquinas' analysis of 'criminogenic factors' (Drapkin 1983: 550).

This criminology-through-the-ages style of history is objectionable on a number of grounds. First of all, it distorts the meaning of earlier writers and conceals the fact that their statements are structured by assumptions and objectives—not to mention institutional contexts and cultural commitments—which are quite different from those of modern criminology.[9] Secondly, it gives the false impression that criminology is our modern response to a timeless and unchanging set of questions that previous thinkers have also pondered, though with notably less success. Criminology is seen as a science that was waiting to happen, the end point of a long process of inquiry that has only recently broken through to the status of true, scientific knowledge. This progressivist, presentist view of things fails to recognize that criminology is, in fact, a socially constructed and historically specific organization of knowledge and investigative procedures—a particular style of reasoning, representing, and intervening[10]—which is grounded in a particular set of institutions and forms of life. It is a 'discipline', a regime of truth with its own special rules for deciding between truth and falsity, rather than the epitome of right thought and correct knowledge. To adopt this fallacious way of thinking about the discipline's history is to cut off from view the other 'problematizations' (as Foucault would call them) that the historical record reveals, and to forget that our own ways of constituting and perceiving 'crime' and 'deviance' are established conventions rather than unchallengeable truths.[11] An important purpose of writing history is to help develop a consciousness of how conventions are made and remade over time, and thus promote a critical self-consciousness about our own questions and assumptions. The myth of an emergent criminological science, progressing from ancient error to modern truth, does little to improve our understanding of the past or of the present.

My remarks up to now have been directed against criminology's history as told by criminologists to criminologists. But in recent years our historical understanding of the subject has been considerably advanced by the work of 'outsiders' who owe no allegiance to the discipline and whose work is driven by quite different historical and critical concerns. The writings of Michel Foucault (1977), Robert Nye (1984), Daniel Pick (1989), Martin Wiener (1990), Marie-Christine Leps (1992), and others have, in their different ways, situated criminological discourse on a wider canvas, showing how this form of knowledge was grounded in quite specific institutional practices, political movements, and cultural settings. None of these authors provide an overall account of criminology's development, each one being concerned to understand the

---

[9] The classic discussion of this problem in the history of ideas is contained in Skinner 1969.

[10] For an elaboration of the conception of scientific practice suggested here, see Hacking 1983.

[11] For an account of how our ways of thinking and acting upon crime have recently been transformed, see Garland 2001.

criminological ideas prevailing in a particular period or setting, rather than to produce a genealogy of the discipline. But the analyses of these and other writers are of great importance for the understanding of criminology's past, and their work adds breadth and depth to the somewhat narrower, diachronic account which the present paper sets out. Similarly valuable is the recent work done in the newly developed field of the history of the human sciences by authors such as Nikolas Rose (1988), Roger Smith (1988), Kurt Danziger (1990), and Ian Hacking (1990). These writers have set out important methodological and theoretical guidelines for work in this area— guidelines that I have tried to follow in the present essay. They have also developed cogent historical analyses of disciplines such as psychology and statistics that are of great relevance for any account of criminology's development.[12]

ORIENTATIONS: A HISTORY OF THE PRESENT

I begin with the clear assumption that the phenomenon to be explained is a present-day phenomenon—the modern discipline of criminology—and that my task is to trace its historical conditions of emergence, identify the intellectual resources and traditions upon which it drew, and give some account of the process of its formation and development. This explicit concern to write a history of the present acknowledges that our contemporary problems and practices are quite distinct from those of the past; but equally, it recognizes that our present arrangements were constructed out of materials and situations that existed at earlier points in time. The present is continuous with the past in some respects, and discontinuous in others. It is the historian's job to identify the processes of transmutation which characterize change and, in particular, the generation of those differences which constitute our modernity.

Modern criminology, like any other academic specialism, consists of a body of accredited and systematically transmitted forms of knowledge, approved procedures and techniques of investigation, and a cluster of questions which make up the subject's recognized research agendas. These intellectual materials and activities are loosely organized by means of a 'discipline'—the standard form of academic organization. The discipline establishes and enforces appropriate norms of evidence and argument, evaluates and communicates research findings and other contributions to knowledge, fixes and revises the canon of theoretical and empirical knowledge, supervises the training of students, and distributes professional status and authority among accredited practitioners. These disciplinary functions are carried out, more or less effectively, by means of a variety of institutions—professional journals and associations, institutes and university departments, professional appointments, processes of peer review, letters of recommendation, training courses, textbooks, conferences, funding agencies, and so on—that make up the material infrastructure of the

---

[12] The history of anthropology also contains many suggestive parallels with that of criminology; see, e.g., Darnell 1974.

enterprise.[13] One has only to describe these taken-for-granted features explicitly to demonstrate that the modern discipline of criminology is indeed 'modern', and to pose the question of how such an institutional structure came to form itself around an intellectual specialism of this kind.

Modern criminology is a composite, eclectic, multidisciplinary enterprise. The subject is typically located in departments of law, sociology, or social policy, and training in criminology is normally at the postgraduate level, following on a first degree in a more basic field of study—though some British universities now offer undergraduate degrees in criminology and several have established centres for criminological research. In their research and teaching, criminologists draw upon a variety of other disciplines, most notably sociology, psychology, psychiatry, law, history, and anthropology—indeed, one of the major dynamics of modern criminology is the incessant raiding of other disciplines or ideologies for new ideas with which to pursue (and renew) the criminological project. Criminologists also address themselves to a wide range of research topics which somehow or other relate to crime and its control. Major areas of work include research on the incidence and distribution of criminal behaviour, inquiries about the causes or correlates of criminal conduct, clinical studies of individual delinquents and ethnographies of deviant groups, penological studies, victim studies, the monitoring and evaluation of criminal justice agencies, the prediction of future criminal conduct, crime prevention studies, research on criminal involvement, careers, and desistance, the study of processes of social reaction, and historical work on changing patterns of crime and control. The list of 'central' topics is long and diverse, and each topic breaks down further into numerous sub-topics and specialisms. When one considers that these substantive areas have been approached using a variety of quantitative and qualitative methods, drawing upon the whole gamut of theoretical perspectives (psychoanalysis, functionalism, interactionism, ethnomethodology, Marxism, feminism, critical race theory, econometrics, systems theory, postmodernism, etc.) and ideological concerns (the implicit welfarism of most twentieth-century criminology, the radicalism of the 1970s, abolitionism, left realism, etc., etc.), it becomes apparent that modern criminology is highly differentiated in its theoretical, methodological, and empirical concerns.

The diverse character of the modern subject makes the question of its historical emergence and identity seem even more puzzling. How did this vast, eclectic bundle of disparate approaches, theories, and data come to acquire the status of a distinct academic specialism? At one level, the answer to this has already been set out above: the subject derives whatever coherence and unity it has from the exertions of its discipline-forming institutions. The danger of an exploding, unmanageable chaos of concerns is held in check by textbooks and teaching and a pattern of professional judgements that draw the subject together and establish its *de facto* boundaries. But this response necessitates a set of prior questions, such as: Why has there emerged a discipline of this kind? And what makes it possible and desirable to have a distinctive, specialist discipline of criminology in the first place? It seems to me that an answer to these questions can be formulated if one has regard to the basic problem-structures or

[13] On scientific disciplines and their development, see Lemaine *et al.* 1976.

projects of inquiry that underlie these disparate investigations. My argument will be
that criminology is structured around two basic projects—the governmental and the
Lombrosian—and that the formation and convergence of these projects can be traced
by studying the texts and statements which constitute criminology's historical archive.
Criminology, in its modern form and in its historical development, is oriented
towards a scientific goal, but also towards an institutional field; towards a theoretical
project, but also towards an administrative task. Whatever fragile unity the discipline
achieves emerges from the belief that these two projects are mutually supportive
rather than incompatible, that etiological research can be made useful for administrative purposes, and that the findings of operational research further the ends of theoretical inquiry. Occasionally, criminologists lose this faith, and when they do, their
arguments cast doubt on the very viability of the discipline.[14]

As with most 'human sciences', criminology has a long past but a short history.[15]
Discourses about crime and punishment have existed, in one form or another, since
ancient times, but it is only during the last 120 years that there has been a distinctive
'science of criminology', and only in the last sixty or seventy years has there been in
Britain an established, independent discipline organized around that intellectual
endeavour. My account of the emergence of the modern British discipline will be
divided into four parts:

1. a brief discussion of what I will call 'traditional' representations of crime and
   criminals;

2. an outline of the empirical analyses that were brought to bear upon crime and
   criminal justice in the eighteenth and nineteenth centuries, and which began the
   tradition of inquiry which I call the governmental project;

3. an account of the emergence of a positive, specialist 'science of the criminal'—
   the Lombrosian project—in the late nineteenth century, both in continental
   Europe and in Britain;

4. an account of how these two projects converged in a way and to an extent which
   facilitated the formation of a criminological discipline in Britain in the middle
   years of the twentieth century.

This order of exposition implies a certain developmental pattern, and to some
extent that seems appropriate. Criminological thought and practice have developed,
at least in some respects, in a scientific direction, and the analysis presented here is
concerned precisely to chart this evolution and to reconstruct the events and developments which played a role in that transmutation. The chronology of events is
constructed in order to show how our particular ways of organizing thought and
research have come into existence. But it needs to be emphasized that no overall
process of progressive development is being asserted here, and there are no exclusive

---

[14] See, e.g., the debates surrounding the development of a radical criminology that aimed to disengage
from the policy goals of the state—a development which, for some writers, came to imply the dissolution of
criminology as a discipline. See Bankowski *et al.* 1976, Hirst 1975. See also the reflections on the relationship
between criminology and criminal justice policy by Petersilia 1991 and Bottoms 1987.

[15] For a theoretical discussion addressing this issue in the history of psychology, see Smith 1988.

boundaries neatly separating the thought of one period from the thought of another. Some residues of the 'traditional' ideas to be found in the seventeenth century still circulate today in the form of common sense and moral argument. Forms of thought and inquiry that flourished in the eighteenth and early nineteenth centuries were rediscovered in the late twentieth century and adapted to serve contemporary purposes. Conversely, certain ideas and arguments that appeared progressive and persuasive to criminologists at the start of the twentieth century have since come to seem pseudo-scientific and faintly absurd.

Criminology's history is not one of steady progress and refinement, although whenever a framework of inquiry has endured for a long enough time, such refinements have taken place. Instead, it is a story of constant reformulation in response to shifting political pressures, changes in institutional and administrative arrangements, intellectual developments occurring in adjacent disciplines, and the changing ideological commitments of its practitioners. The very fact that a basic orientation of the discipline links it to a field of social problems and to administrative efforts to govern that field imparts a certain instability to the subject and constantly transforms its objects of study. As a discipline criminology is shaped only to a small extent by its own theoretical object and logic of inquiry. Its epistemological threshold is a low one, making it susceptible to pressures and interests generated elsewhere.

TRADITIONAL REPRESENTATIONS OF CRIME

Social rules and the violation of them are intrinsic aspects of social organization, a part of the human condition. Discourse about crime and criminals—or about sin, villainy, roguery, deviance, whatever the local idiom—is thus as old as human civilization itself. Wherever generalized frameworks developed for the representation and explanation of human conduct—whether as myths, cosmologies, theologies, metaphysical systems, or vernacular common sense—they generally entailed propositions about aberrant conduct and how it should be understood.

As we have seen, some writers have taken this recurring concern with law-breakers as sufficient licence to talk about a 'criminology' which stretches back to the dawn of time. But rather than see such writings as proto-criminologies struggling to achieve a form which we have since perfected, it seems more appropriate to accept that there are a variety of ways in which crime can be problematized and put into discourse, and that 'criminology' is only one version among others. The propositions about crime and criminals that appear in the writings of ancient and medieval philosophers, the theologies of the Church of Rome and the Protestant Reform tradition, the mythico-magical cosmologies of the Middle Ages, and the legal thought of the early modern period, were not aspiring criminologies, even though their subject matter sometimes bears a resemblance to that which criminology seeks to explain. These broad resemblances begin to appear less compelling when one looks in detail at what were the conceptual elements of these discourses and their implicit assumptions about the world. Entities such as fate and demons, original sin and human depravity, temptation, lust, and avarice are the products of mental frameworks and forms of life rather different from our own.[16]

The differences between these mentalities and our own can be quite instructive, pointing up some of the peculiarities of our accustomed ways of thinking about crime. It is significant, for example, that the major tradition of Western thought—Christianity, in all its variants—did not separate out the law-breaker as different or abnormal, but instead understood him or her as merely a manifestation of universal human depravity and the fallen, sinful state of all mankind.[17] 'There but for the grace of God go I' is an understanding of things quite alien to much of the criminology that was written in the late nineteenth and early twentieth centuries. In the same way, the explicitly moral and spiritual terms in which the Christian tradition discusses individual wrongdoing, the lack of reference to systematically controlled empirical evidence, the invocation of the Devil, or divine intervention to account for human action, and the appeal to scriptural authority as proof for propositions, are all reminders of the rather different rules governing modern criminological discourse.

But traditional accounts of crime—Christian and otherwise—are not entirely remote from modern thinking about the subject. Scattered around in the diverse literature of the early modern period, in criminal biographies and broadsheets, accounts of the Renaissance underworld, Tudor rogue pamphlets, Elizabethan dramas and Jacobean city comedies, the utopia of Thomas More and the novels of Daniel Defoe,[18] one can discover rudimentary versions of the etiological accounts that are used today to narrate the process of becoming deviant. Stories of how the offender fell in with bad company, became lax in his habits and was sorely tried by temptation, was sickly, or tainted by bad blood, or neglected by unloving parents, became too fond of drink or too idle to work, lost her reputation and found it hard to get employment, was driven to despair by poverty, or simply driven to crime by avarice and lust—these seem to provide the well-worn templates from which our modern theories of crime are struck, even if we insist upon a more neutral language with which to tell the tale and think that a story's plausibility should be borne out by evidence as well as by faith or intuition.[19] Indeed, Faller's research (Faller 1987) suggests that what was lacking in these seventeenth- and eighteenth-century accounts was not secular or materialist explanations of the roots of crime, which were present in abundance alongside the spiritual explanations proffered by the church. What was lacking was a developed sense of differential etiology. Crime was seen as an omnipresent temptation to which all humankind was vulnerable, but when it became a question of why some succumbed and others resisted, the explanation trailed off into the unknowable: resorting

[16] For a wide-ranging discussion, see Jean Delumeau's account (Delumeau 1990) of sin and fear in thirteenth- to eighteenth-century Europe.

[17] For developments of this point, see Zeman 1981; and also Faller 1987.

[18] On criminal biographies and broadsheets, see Faller 1987; Sharpe 1985. On crime and criminals in Tudor rogue pamphlets and Jacobean city comedies, see Curtis and Hale 1981. For descriptions of the Elizabethan underworld, see Judges 1930; Salgado 1972.

[19] Matza (1969) analyses the recurring narratives of everyday discourse and shows how, in a slightly adapted form, these come to comprise the basic explanatory structures of contemporary criminological theory.

to fate, or providence, or the will of God. When, in the late nineteenth century, the science of criminology emerged, one of its central concerns would be to address this issue of differentiation and subject it to empirical inquiry.

'Traditional' ways of thinking about crime did not disappear with the coming of the modern, scientific age, though they may nowadays be accorded a different status in the hierarchy of credibility. These older conceptions—based upon experience and ideology rather than systematic empirical inquiry—have not been altogether displaced by scientific criminologies, and we continue to acknowledge the force of moral, religious, and 'common-sensical' ways of discussing crime. Expert, research-based knowledge about crime and criminals still competes with views of the subject which are not 'criminological' in their style of reasoning or their use of evidence. Judges, moralists, religious fundamentalists, and populist leader-writers still offer views on criminological subjects that are quite innocent of criminological science or research findings. Unlike physics, or even economics, which have established a degree of monopoly over the right to speak authoritatively about their subjects, criminology operates in a culture that combines traditional and scientific modes of thought and action. Intuitive, 'instinctive', common-sense views about crime and criminals are still more persuasive to many—including many in positions of power and authority—than are the results of carefully executed empirical research.

THE SCIENTIFIC ANALYSIS OF CRIME IN THE EIGHTEENTH AND NINETEENTH CENTURIES

In most criminological histories, the true beginnings of modern criminological thought are seen in writings of the eighteenth and early nineteenth centuries. Radzinowicz's monumental *History* (1948) begins in 1750, as does his historical essay on *Ideology and Crime* (1966). Mannheim's earliest 'pioneer' is Beccaria, whose *Of Crimes and Punishments* first appeared in 1764. Even *The New Criminology* (Taylor, Walton, and Young 1973), the radical and immensely influential textbook of the 1970s, begins its account with Beccaria and 'the classical school of criminology'. There are good grounds for choosing to emphasize the role of these eighteenth-century writings in the formation of criminology, but, as I suggested earlier, the connections are not as straightforward as is usually assumed. I have already argued that the writings of Beccaria, Bentham, and the others did not constitute a 'criminology'. But despite this, they did establish and develop some of the key elements and conditions necessary for the subsequent development of the subject in its modern form. They are quite properly a part of criminology's genealogy, having been a direct source for some of the subject's basic aims and characteristics, as well as having produced a stock of propositions and arguments which would feature prominently in the criminological discourse which developed in the twentieth century.

There are several genealogical strands that link certain eighteenth- and early nineteenth-century writers with the criminology that followed. Most importantly, Enlightenment writers such as Beccaria, Bentham, and Howard wrote secular,

materialist analyses, emphasizing the importance of reason and experience and deni-
grating theological forms of reasoning. They viewed themselves as proceeding in a
scientific manner and dealing objectively with an issue that had previously been
dominated by irrational, superstitious beliefs and prejudices. Members of the *scuola
positiva* would later disparage the 'classical school' for its 'unscientific' reliance upon
speculative reasoning rather than observed facts, but this is not how these writers
viewed themselves. Indeed, it was the 'classicists' who first established the claim that
crime and its control could be studied in a neutral, scientific manner.

Another important connection between the literature of the reformers and the
criminology that followed was that the reformers of the late eighteenth and early
nineteenth centuries were writing about a set of legal institutions which were becoming (partly through those reformers' efforts) recognizably modern. The institutional
concerns which animated the writings of Beccaria, Bentham, Howard, and the rest
are, in an important sense, modern concerns—about the systematic arrangement of
criminal laws and procedures in order to promote social policy goals; about the
sentencing choices of magistrates; about the organization and conduct of professional
police; about the design and purposes of prison regimes. The questions of interest to
these writers—the psychology of offending, the nature of criminal motivation, the
possibilities of deterrence and reform, and the most appropriate way for state
institutions to regulate individual conduct—are also questions which were to
become quite central to later criminology. These issues gripped the imagination of
eighteenth-century thinkers because they lived in a world caught up in the dynamics
of modernization. This was the period which saw the emergence of the centralized
administrative state, a national economy and a population increasingly subject to
governance, an autonomous, secular legal system, the political relations of liberalism,
and institutional enclosures like the prison and the asylum with their reformative,
disciplinary regimes. The writings of Beccaria, Bentham, and Howard—like those of
Benjamin Rush in America—were the first soundings of a modernist discourse about
crime. As intellectual responses to the challenge of crime in a newly urbanized market
society, they were addressing problems of a novel type, quite unfamiliar to traditional
social thought. This new social and institutional environment, modified in certain
ways, also formed the background against which the science of criminology would
subsequently emerge, and in that respect there is a broad continuity of reference
which makes eighteenth-century discourse 'modern' in a way that earlier writing is
not. (Indeed, it is precisely because the reformist discourse of Beccaria *et al.* and the
scientific discourse of Lombroso share a common institutional context that they are
able to be viewed as 'opposites'. Each one entails a programme for directing the
modern field of criminal justice.)

If one widens the lens to look beyond Beccaria and Bentham to some of the other
discourses on crime and criminals dating from this period, one can detect other lines
of affiliation. Patrick Colquhoun and Henry Fielding, as well as a large number of
Parliamentary and private committees of the late eighteenth and early nineteenth
centuries, used empirical evidence to situate and measure the extent of various crime
problems ('the late increase in robbers', the relation between 'indigence' and crime,
'the alarming increase in juvenile delinquency', the 'police of the metropolis', and so

on).[20] As Leon Radzinowicz (1956) and Robert Reiner (1988) have pointed out, these inquiries formed part of a wider 'science of police' which flourished in this period, concerned not just with crime or criminals, but with the regulation and maintenance of the whole population in the interest of economy, welfare, and good governance (see also Foucault 1979; Pasquino 1991). John Howard's investigation of the state of the prisons was undertaken as a work of charity and reform, but his methods were doggedly empirical, and his study laid much stress on measurement and systematic observation as a basis for its findings.[21] Howard's work in the 1770s sparked the beginnings of a line of empirical penological inquiry that, from the 1830s onwards, became an increasingly important element in what was to become the British criminological tradition.

By the middle years of the nineteenth century this 'scientific' style of reasoning about crime had become a distinctive feature of the emergent culture of amateur social science. The papers delivered by Rawson W. Rawson, Joseph Fletcher, and John Glyde to the Statistical Society of London used judicial statistics and census data to chart the distribution and demography of crime, and to match up crime rates with other social indices—just as A.M. Guerry and Adolphe Quetelet had been doing in France and Belgium.[22] On the basis of carefully calculated correlations, they drew conclusions about the moral and social causes that influenced criminal conduct and presented their findings as instances of the new statistical science and its social uses. Henry Mayhew, writing in the middle years of the nineteenth century, was essentially a journalist concerned with 'the social question' and the problem of the poor. But unlike the moralists of a century earlier, his journalism was grounded in empirical research, using ethnographic and survey methods as well as life histories and statistical data; and his analyses of London Labour and the London Poor (1861–2) offered a series of empirically supported claims about the patterns and causes of professional crime in the city.[23]

Another line of inquiry which flourished in this period, and whose advocates would later be seen as progenitors of criminology, centred not upon the population and its governance by a well-ordered state, but instead upon individuals and their ability (or lack of ability) to govern themselves. As early as the 1760s and 1770s, Henry Dagge and Mannasseh Dawes argued that the law's notions of a free-willed offender were often enough fictions in the face of real social and psychological circumstances that limited choice and shaped human conduct, and they drew upon the new materialist psychologies of the time to explain how it was that causal processes could be acknowledged without entirely destroying the belief in man's free will (see Green 1985). Indeed, both Thomas Zeman (1981) and Piers Beirne (1993) have shown that

---

[20] See Colquhoun 1797, 1800, 1806, 1814; Fielding 1751; and the discussion of the Parliamentary and private committees of inquiry of this period in Radzinowicz 1956.

[21] See Howard 1973 [1777], 1973 [1789] and the discussion of his work in Ignatieff 1978.

[22] See the discussion of the work of Rawson, Fletcher, and Glyde in Morris 1957. Beirne (1993) provides detailed discussions of the work of Guerry and Quetelet and their place in the development of criminological thought.

[23] For a discussion of Mayhew's work and its relation to subsequent criminological analyses, see Morris 1957.

Cesare Beccaria's account of human conduct is shaped not by metaphysical assumptions about the freedom of the will, but instead by John Locke's empiricist psychology and the new 'science of man' developed by the thinkers of the Scottish Enlightenment.

During the nineteenth century this reconceptualization of human character and conduct was taken up and developed in the field of medicine, especially psychological medicine. The art of 'physiognomy'—which, it was claimed, enabled its practitioners to judge character and disposition from the features of the face and the external forms of the body—had been known since the seventeenth century, but the essays of J.C. Lavater purported to give a scientific foundation to this useful skill (Lavater 1792).[24] The craniometry and phrenology of F.J. Gall and J.C. Spurzheim made similar claims in the early nineteenth century, this time focusing upon the shape and contours of the human skull as an external index of character.[25] By the 1830s physiognomy and phrenology had lost much of their scientific credibility and had become the obsession of a few enthusiastic publicists, but the quest to uncover the links between physical constitution and psychological character was continued in a different and more important line of research: the new science of psychiatry.

The emergence of a network of private asylums in the eighteenth century led to the development of a new quasi-medical specialism which was at first called alienism and subsequently came to be known as psychological medicine or psychiatry. The writings of asylum managers about their patients—about their conduct, the antecedents of their madness, and the forms of treatment to which they responded—formed the basis for a major tradition of scientific investigation, and one that would subsequently be an important source of criminological data and ideas.

Attempts to link psychological characteristics to physical constitutions formed an abiding concern of this new discipline, but equally significant for our purposes is its intense focus upon the insane individual—a focus permitted and encouraged by the long-term confinement of asylum patients under the daily gaze of the alienist (see Porter 1987). The new psychiatry produced an extensive scientific literature concerned with the description of different mental types, case histories and causal analyses of how their madness developed, and detailed accounts of how they responded to various forms of 'moral' and medical treatment. What was developing here was a new kind of empirical psychology, concentrating upon pathological cases and their rational management. And because many of these cases involved criminal conduct (whether of a minor or a serious kind), one of the offshoots of this enterprise was a developing diagnostic and prognostic literature claiming to give a scientific account of certain kinds of individual criminals. Particularly after the Lunacy Acts of the mid-nineteenth century, when the asylum network was expanded to house the country's poor as well as the well-to-do, the new psychiatric profession had more and more to say about conditions such as 'moral imbecility', 'degeneracy', and 'feeblemindedness' that were deemed to be prevalent among the populations dealt with by the

---

[24] Richard Sennett (1977) provides an interesting account of various nineteenth-century efforts to judge character by outward appearance and describes the cultural predicament that prompted these concerns.

[25] On phrenology and its links to subsequent criminological studies, see Savitz et al. 1977. More generally, see Cooter 1981.

poor-houses and the prisons. Consequently, when a science of the criminal began to develop in the last decades of the century, there already existed a tradition of work the concerns of which ran in parallel with its own and from which it could draw a measure of support and encouragement. Indeed, for about fifty years after the publication of Lombroso's *L'Uomo Delinquente* (1876) the journals of the psychiatric profession were virtually the only ones in Britain that took a serious interest in Lombroso's project.

If one were reviewing all of the ideas and undertakings of the eighteenth and early nineteenth centuries that bore a resemblance to elements which later appeared within the discipline of criminology, there would be other stories to tell. The various forms of charitable and social work with the poor, the societies for the care of discharged convicts, the management of workhouses, inquiries about the causes and extent of inebriety, investigations into the labour market, the employment and treatment of children, education, the housing of the poor, the settlement and boys' club movements, could all be identified as the roots of particular ingredients in the modern criminological mix. But one needs to recall that the ideas and forms of inquiry set out here did not add up to an early form of criminology for the simple reason that they did not 'add up' at all; nor could they until the later emergence of a form of inquiry centred upon the criminal which drew together these various enterprises under the umbrella of a specialist criminological discipline. In their own time, they were discrete forms of knowledge, undertaken for a variety of different purposes, and forming elements within a variety of different discourses, none of which corresponded exactly with the criminological project that was subsequently formed. Beccaria, for example, developed his arguments about the reform of the criminal law within the broader context of a work on political economy. Colquhoun's writings about crime and police were, for him, one aspect of a treatise on government in which he addressed the changing problems of governance thrown up by the emergence of urbanized market society and the baleful effects of trade and luxury upon the manners of the people. Physiognomists, phrenologists, and psychiatrists were attempting to understand the physical and mental roots of human conduct rather than to develop a particular knowledge of offenders and offending. Like the utilitarian psychology developed by Bentham, these were attempts to capture the springs of human action in general, not to single out the criminal for special and exclusive attention. None of these discourses was struggling to create a distinctive criminological enterprise, though once such a subject was created, each formed a resource to be drawn upon, usually in a way which wrenched its insights about crime apart from the framework which originally produced them.

Certainly, if one looks back from the perspective of the present, one can glimpse the outlines of the governmental project and the Lombrosian project gradually taking shape in this period. Empirical studies of the police, of prisons, of crime rates, and of the deterrent effects of criminal laws—the very stuff of criminology's governmental concerns—were already underway, conducted at first by amateurs but later by state officials utilizing the elementary tools of scientific method. However, these studies were not, at the time, viewed as distinct from other inquiries, into the market, morals, workhouses, or poverty. The underlying theme animating all of these studies was a concern with governance and the use of empirical data and scientific methods to improve government's grip on the population. Only with the later professionalization and specialization of the various state agencies—and with the invention of 'criminology'—did the study of governance in criminal matters come to be viewed as distinct from the governance of the population in general. Similarly, one can see in the work of the nineteenth-century phrenologists and psychiatrists a concern to understand human conduct in scientific terms, to identify character types, and to trace the etiologies of pathological behaviours. But at this historical moment there was no focus upon the criminal as a special human type and no felt need for a specialism built around this entity. The splitting off of criminological studies—both in the administrative field and in the clinic—was a late nineteenth-century event that significantly changed the organization of subsequent thought and action.

Since the formation of criminology, criminologists have repeatedly identified what they take to be their 'roots'—the various lines of descent which link their present practice to work done a century and more before. But this is perhaps the wrong way to look at things. A more accurate account might suggest that at the end of the nineteenth century the idea of a specialist criminological science emerged—centred, as it happens, on the figure of the 'criminal type'—and that, after a process of struggle, adaptation, and convergence, this programmatic idea led to the establishment, in a rather different form, of an independent criminological discipline. Since the discipline was characterized by an eclectic, multidisciplinary concern to pursue the crime problem in all its aspects, the subject has continually expanded to embrace all of the ways in which crime and criminals might be scientifically studied; and in so doing, it has constantly created new predecessors for itself. The connection between eighteenth- and twentieth-century discourse about crime is not a matter of tenacious traditions of thought which have survived continuously for 200 years. Rather, it is a matter of a certain broad similarity between forms of inquiry and institutional arrangements which prevailed in the eighteenth and the twentieth centuries, together with the tendency of the modern discipline to embrace everything that might be scientifically said about crime and criminals. Each time a new element is added to the criminological armoury—be it radical criminology, ecological surveys, sociological theory, or situational crime prevention—someone sooner or later discovers that eighteenth- and nineteenth-century writers were doing something similar, and that this new approach should therefore be considered a central feature of the criminological tradition, albeit one that was temporarily (and inexplicably) forgotten. But this recurring 'recovery of tradition' is perhaps better understood as a bid for intellectual respectability and disciplinary centrality than as a serious claim about the development of the subject. After all, the crucial requirement of a genealogy is continuity of descent, and it is precisely this continuity which is missing wherever 'traditions' have to be 'rediscovered'.[26]

---

[26] For an historical account that seeks to explain the disappearance and subsequent reappearance of a set of criminological themes, see Garland 2000. This article analyses why ideas that would now be described as being about 'situational crime prevention' dropped out of criminological discourse for close to 200 years before reappearing in the 1970s.

If this account is accurate, and if criminology is a specific organization of knowledge which first emerged in the late nineteenth century, then the key problem is to try to describe its particularity and to explain the historical transmutation which produced this new form of enterprise. It has to be shown how the project of a specialized science emerged out of some other project or set of projects, and how it marked itself off from what went before. It is to that task that I now turn.

THE EMERGENCE OF A POSITIVE SCIENCE OF THE CRIMINAL

FROM CRIMINAL ANTHROPOLOGY TO THE SCIENCE OF CRIMINOLOGY

The idea of a specialist science of the criminal was born out of the interaction of a specific intellectual endeavour and a certain social context. As is often the case, a transmutation was produced in the history of ideas when a particular set of ideas and inquiries was found to have relevance to a field that had previously been regarded as quite separate. Ironically enough, the scientific work which led Cesare Lombroso to found a specialist 'science of the criminal'—a key ingredient in the formation of the modern discipline of criminology—was not, in fact, criminological in any sense that we would recognize. Lombroso's criminal science grew, somewhat accidentally, out of an anthropological concern to study humanity and its natural varieties, using the methods of anthropometry and craniometry to measure the physical features of human subjects. Influenced by the physical anthropology of Paul Broca and a Darwinian concern with species and their evolution, Lombroso's study of Italian army recruits and asylum and prison inmates was an attempt to identify different racial types and to subject them to scientific scrutiny and categorization (see Gould 1981). By the 1870s, however, the science of 'racial anthropology', like the science of degeneracy developed by Morel, had begun to overlap with potent social concerns, as is shown by its identification of 'types' such as the genius, the epileptoid, and the insane which were patently derived from social policy interests rather than evolutionary processes. Thus Lombroso's 'pioneering' inquiries were actually extending a line of research that was already well established: his 'discovery' of the 'criminal type' merely restated, in a more vivid form, an observation that had already been made by psychiatrists such as Maudsley and prison doctors such as J. Bruce Thomson.

But if Lombroso's discovery was old news, the significance he gave to it was altogether novel. For him, the apparent distinctiveness of the criminal type prompted an idea that no one had imagined before: the idea of a distinctive science of the criminal. His conception of the criminal as a naturally occurring entity—a fact of nature rather than a social or legal product—led Lombroso to the thought of a natural science which would focus upon this entity, trace its characteristics, its stigmata, its abnormalities, and eventually identify the causes which make one person a criminal and another a normal citizen. And the startling thing about this Lombrosian project for the scientific differentiation of the criminal individual was that, despite its dubious scientific credentials, it immediately met with a huge international response. In the twenty years following the appearance of *L'Uomo Delinquente* in 1876, this strange new science came to form the basis of a major international movement, manifesting itself in an outpouring of texts, the formation of new associations, international congresses, specialist journals, national schools of thought, and interested officials in virtually every European and American state. At the same time, Lombroso himself became something of a household name, featuring in the fiction of Tolstoy, Musil, Bram Stoker, and Conan Doyle, as well as in countless journalistic essays and scientific reports.[27]

In the years immediately following the publication of Lombroso's sensational claims a group of talented disciples gathered around him and a journal, *La Scuola Positiva*, was founded to publicize the new research and its practical implications. But disciples such as Enrico Ferri and Raffaele Garofalo were not content merely to repeat the master's formulations, and even the early work of this Italian school showed a considerable diversity and eclecticism, widening out the analysis to examine the social and legal aspects of criminality as well as its 'anthropological' embodiment. This process of differentiation within the research enterprise was amplified by the formation of rival schools of inquiry, notably the 'French school' which emphasized the sociological and environmental determinants of crime and played down the role of fixed constitutional attributes, and the 'German school' which included the study of criminalistics and the development of new forensic techniques and procedures.[28] A series of highly publicized international congresses, beginning in 1883, aired these disputes at length, with much acrimony on all sides, and resulted in the modification of most of Lombroso's original claims, particularly on the subject of the 'born criminal' and the fatalistic implications this notion was seen to have for the treatment and reform of offenders.

What eventually emerged from this process—especially in the writings of important second-generation figures like Prins, Saleilles, and Von Hamel—was a scientific movement which was much more eclectic and much more 'practical' than the original criminal anthropology had been (see Garland 1985a; Wetzell 2000). One indication of the process of revision and modification whereby Lombroso's original formulations were reworked into a more acceptable form was the adoption of the term 'criminology', which came into general use in the 1890s. The term was originally used not as an exact synonym for criminal anthropology, but as a neutral, generic term which avoided the partisanship implicit in the original term and others—such as 'criminal sociology', 'criminal biology', and 'criminal psychology'—which competed with it.

This new science of criminology, as it developed in the last decades of the

---

[27] On the spread of the criminological movement at the end of the nineteenth century, see Garland 1985a; Nye 1984. On Lombroso in contemporary fiction, see Pick 1989; Gould 1981; Leps 1992. On the development of criminal anthropology in the USA, see Rafter 1992 and 1997. On the reception of Lombroso's work in Britain, see Radzinowicz and Hood 1986, which also provides the most detailed account of the indigenous traditions of thinking about crime in the nineteenth century.

[28] On the development of German criminology, see Wetzell 2000. On the place of criminalistics in the history of criminology, see Valier 1998.

nineteenth century, was characterized by a number of distinctive features.[29] It was an avowedly scientific approach to crime, concerned to develop a 'positive', factual knowledge of offenders, based upon observation, measurement, and inductive reasoning, and rejecting the speculative thinking about human character which had previously informed criminal justice practices. In keeping with its Lombrosian origins, it focused its attentions upon the individual criminal, and in particular upon the characteristics which appeared to mark off criminals as in some way different from normal, law-abiding citizens. It assumed that scientific explanation amounted to causal explanation and therefore set itself the task of identifying the causes of crime, though it should be added that the notion of 'cause' was understood in a wide variety of ways, some of which were more 'determinist' than others, and the kinds of cause identified ranged from innate constitutional defects to more or less contingent social circumstances. Lastly, it addressed itself to the investigation of a new, pathological phenomenon—'criminality'—which it deemed to be the source of criminal behaviour and which, in effect, became the subject's *raison d'être* and the target of its practical proposals.

This concern to produce a differential diagnosis of the individual criminal and the etiology of his or her offending behaviour was in turn linked to a definite programme of practical action, quite at odds with the legal principles which had previously underpinned criminal justice practice. The notion of the offender's free will was attacked as a metaphysical abstraction, as was the concept of legal responsibility. Uniformity of sentencing was viewed as a failure to differentiate between different types of offender, and the principle of proportionate, retrospective punishment was rejected in favour of a flexible system of penal sanctions adapted to the reformability or dangerousness of the specific individual. Criminal justice was to cease being a punitive, reactive system and was to become instead a scientifically informed apparatus for the prevention, treatment, and elimination of criminality. It was to be a system run by criminological experts, concerned to maximize social defence, individual reform, and measures of security rather than to uphold some outdated and overly legalistic conception of justice.

That such a radical programme of research and reform could be developed and become influential is testimony to the extent to which the new criminology resonated with the concerns and preoccupations of the political and cultural milieux in which it emerged.[30] The popularity of Lombroso's work is probably explicable in terms of the extent to which his conception of the criminal type chimed with deep-rooted cultural prejudices and offered scientific respectability to middle-class perceptions of the 'criminal classes' forming in the growing cities (see Sennett 1977). But the viability of the criminological movement, and the fact that it so quickly became an international phenomenon, are indications that it was a programme of thought and action which successfully meshed with the social policies and institutional practices which were becoming established at the time. The increasing involvement of experts and scientists

[29] For an analysis of the science of criminology and its early development, see Garland 1985b.
[30] For a detailed account of the British cultural milieu in which the new criminological science took hold, see Wiener 1990.

in the administration of social problems in the late nineteenth century, and the related development of statistical data as a resource for governing, are relevant background conditions. So too is the developing concern on the part of governments, Poor Law administrators, police, and local authorities to classify and differentiate the populations they dealt with, seeking to identify and separate out dangerous elements while shoring up the social attachments of the 'deserving poor' and the 'respectable' working classes. In this specific context, the criminological programme offered certain regulatory and legitimatory possibilities that made it attractive to late nineteenth-century governments and administrators.

The regulatory advantages of the new criminology lay in its rejection of the formal egalitarianism that had previously shaped the practices of criminal law and its enforcement. As against the principle that everyone should be treated equally, criminology offered to differentiate between constitutional and accidental criminality, thus identifying the real sources of social danger and marking out the contours of the criminal class in a scientific rather than a moralistic way. Criminology also promised to provide a more extensive and a more effective form of intervention and regulation. Concerned to diagnose an individual's level of dangerousness rather than to judge whether or not he or she had yet broken the law, criminology offered the prospect of a system of control in which official measures need not wait for an offence to occur, or be limited by any principle of proportionality. At the same time, this more interventionist system could also claim to be more humane, in so far as its rationale was the promotion of individual and social welfare and not merely the infliction of retributive punishment (see Garland 1985a; Wiener 1990).

Finally, as is by now well documented, the new criminology met with extensive interest and social support because it was closely linked to the new prisons which had, by the late nineteenth century, become a prominent feature of all Western societies. As Michel Foucault (1977) has shown, the disciplinary, reformative practices of the penitentiary prison acted as a practical 'surface of emergence' for the individualizing, differentiating discourse of criminology. What Lombroso invented was a science of individual differences; but the data and social arrangements necessary for the production of this science, as well as the practical context in which such a knowledge would be practically useful, were already inscribed in the architecture and regimes of the disciplinary prison. In the prison setting inmates were arranged in individual cells, and subjected to constant, individual surveillance for long periods of time, their behaviour and characteristics being continually monitored in order that disciplinary measures could be adjusted to deal with individual reactions and peculiarities. The systematic and differentiating knowledge of offenders to which this gave rise formed the basis for the new science of criminology, which slowly fed back into the practices of imprisonment, refining the prison's classifications and techniques, and enhancing the authorities' understanding of the individuals who were held in custody (see Garland 1985a). The widespread use of disciplinary imprisonment in late nineteenth-century Europe and America thus provided a ready-made setting through which criminology could emerge and establish itself as a useful form of knowledge. As Sir Evelyn Ruggles-Brise (1924) put it, '*la science penitentiaire* develops gradually into the science of the discovery of the causes of crime—the science of criminology'.[31] Lombroso's project was thus propelled not just by its own scientific logic but by a combination of institutional and cultural dynamics, a set of forces which were to sustain this form of inquiry long after Lombroso's own reputation was utterly destroyed.

THE DEVELOPMENT OF CRIMINOLOGY IN BRITAIN

As was often pointed out at the time, British intellectuals and criminal justice officials played very little part in the early development of this European criminological movement. Most of the relevant research and publication took place in Italy, France, and Germany, and the British were notable absentees at the international congresses held to debate the claims and counter-claims of the various schools. It was not until the Geneva Congress of Criminal Anthropology in 1896 that Britain first sent an official delegate—the prison inspector Major Arthur Griffiths—and Griffiths returned with a critical report (see Griffiths 1904) that reinforced the scepticism with which British officials viewed the claims of the new criminologists. Griffiths was later to write the first entry to appear on 'Criminology' in the *Encyclopaedia Britannica* (1910–11) in which he attacked the theory of criminal types, but went on to show a cautious interest in the penological ideas which were by then emerging from the movement.

The arm's-length attitude of the British penal establishment to the new criminology was something of a surprise to individual enthusiasts such as Havelock Ellis and William Douglas Morrison, both of whom did much to introduce continental ideas into this country. Ellis published a book entitled *The Criminal* in 1890 which was, in effect, a summary of the major ideas of criminal anthropology, and he regularly reviewed foreign criminological publications for the *Journal of Mental Science* from 1890 to 1919. Morrison established and edited 'The Criminology Series', which published translations of works by Lombroso (1895), Ferri (1895) and Proal (1898), as well as publishing a number of his own works, including *Juvenile Offenders* (1896). One cause of this surprise was that many of the new criminologists, including Lombroso himself, pointed to earlier work published in Britain which appeared to contain the kinds of ideas which would later become central to the criminological movement. Thus, in the 1860s the psychiatrist Henry Maudsley and the prison medical officer J. Bruce Thomson had written about 'the genuine criminal' and 'the criminal class', describing these individuals as 'morally insane', 'degenerate', 'defective in physical organisation . . . from hereditary causes' and 'incurable' in a way that appeared to be altogether 'Lombrosian' before Lombroso.[32]

---

[31] On the prison as a 'surface of emergence' for criminological knowledge, see Foucault 1977; also Garland 1992.

[32] Maudsley (1863: 73) refers to 'the criminal' as a 'fact in nature' and to criminals as 'if not strictly a degenerate species, certainly . . . a degenerate variety of the species'. Thomson (1867: 341) states that 'all who have seen much of criminals agree that they have a singular family likeness or caste . . . Their physique is coarse and repulsive; their complexion dingy, almost atrabilious; their face, figure and mien, disagreeable. The women are painfully ugly; and the men look stolid, and many of them brutal, indicating physical and moral deterioration. In fact there is a stamp on them in form and expression which seems to me the heritage of the class.' For a discussion of these debates, see Garland 1988; also Radzinowicz and Hood 1986.

But to describe Maudsley and Thomson as criminologists before the fact was misleading. Maudsley was engaged in a distinctively psychiatric endeavour (the development and application of typologies dealing with various mental disorders and pathologies) and Thomson's concern was to assess the impact of prison discipline upon the bodies and minds of prisoners (see Thomson 1867). Neither of them for a moment imagined that there was any justification for a distinctive scientific specialism centered upon the criminal. More importantly, during the 1870s and 1880s British medical and psychiatric opinion had shifted away from earlier attempts to characterize 'criminals' in such indiscriminate, pathological terms. From the 1870s onwards, prison doctors such as David Nicolson and John Baker set about redefining 'the morbid psychology of criminals', so as to differentiate a range of conditions rather than a single type. Nicolson (1878–9) emphasized that professional observation made it plain that only a minority of criminals were in any sense mentally abnormal, and he forcibly rejected any suggestion that offenders were generally 'incurable' or beyond the reach of prison reformation. During the same years, the nascent British psychiatric profession was learning that criminal courts would not tolerate psychiatric evidence that contradicted basic legal axioms about individual free will and responsibility, and psychiatrists gradually developed a *modus vivendi* that aimed to minimize conflict between psychiatry and law. By the 1880s, leading figures of the new profession such as Needham, Hack Tuke, Nicolson, and Maudsley were taking pains to distance themselves from the embarrassing claims made by psychiatrists (Maudsley among them) in earlier years— claims that were now being taken up again by criminologists with their talk of 'born criminals', 'the criminal type', atavism, and so on (see Nicolson 1878–9; Maudsley 1889; Tuke 1889; Needham 1889; Baker 1892; Nicolson 1895; Garland 1988).

The relationship between the new continental movement and the studies of criminals carried out in Britain by prison doctors and psychiatrists is a complex one, and the assumption (made by Ellis and others) that the two were continuous is a simplification which glosses over important differences. Unlike Lombroso's anthropology, British psychiatry was not concerned to isolate discrete human 'types' and classify them by means of racial and constitutional differences. Instead, it was a therapeutically oriented practice based upon a system of classifying mental disorders which, like the disease model of nineteenth-century medicine, discussed the condition separately from the individual in whom it might be manifested. Within the classification schemes of morbid psychology there was a variety of conditions which criminals were said to exhibit, including insanity, moral insanity, degeneracy, and feeblemindedness. But generally speaking, the criminal was not conceived of as a distinct psychological type.

More important than this theoretical difference was the way in which British psychiatry contrasted with Lombrosian anthropology in its practical commitments and its relationship to the institutions of criminal justice. In his early publications, Lombroso claimed that his ideas had great relevance for criminal law and penal policy, but, as his critics soon pointed out, he was not particularly well informed about the practical realities of crime and punishment.[33] In consequence, his penology was not just radical

---

[33] See, for instance, the review by Arthur St John (1912) of Lombroso's work, in which he contrasts Lombroso's naivety with the experienced practical understanding of a prison doctor such as James Devon.

and at odds with current practices; it was also naive and distorted, lacking a close familiarity with the normal range of offenders and the institutions that dealt with them. Lombroso's conception of the criminal type had emerged from the theoretical hypotheses of physical anthropology rather than from extensive penological experience, and only gradually did he modify his views to bring them more into line with the way legal institutions worked. In contrast, the scientific thinking about the criminal which developed in British psychiatric and medico-legal circles was closely tied into professional tasks such as the giving of evidence before courts of law, or the decisions as to classification, diagnosis, and regimen that prison medical officers made on a daily basis. This practical experience was crucial in shaping the psychiatric approach to 'criminological' issues, because it ensured that psychiatrists and prison doctors were well acquainted with the day-to-day realities of criminal justice and with the need to bring psychiatric propositions into line with the demands of courts and prison authorities.

The British tradition that was closest to the criminology developing on the continent—penal and forensic psychiatry—was thus also somewhat hostile to it. The scientific studies conducted by British prison doctors and psychiatrists were, from an early stage, situated within an institutional framework that shaped their purposes and constrained their findings. In consequence, these studies were generally modest in their claims and respectful of the requirements of institutional regimes and legal principles. As far as most prison doctors and experienced psychiatrists were concerned, the majority of criminals were more or less normal individuals; only a minority required psychiatric treatment, and this usually involved removing them from the penal system and putting them into institutions for the mentally ill or defective. And although the diagnostic and therapeutic claims of psychiatry changed over time, from an early stage it was recognized that, for the majority of offenders, the normal processes of law and punishment should apply. Compared to the sweeping claims of criminal anthropology, the British medico-legal tradition was, by the 1890s, somewhat conservative, and generally dismissive of Lombrosian ideas. Senior psychiatric figures such as Maudsley and Conolly Norman referred publicly to the 'puerilities of criminal anthropology' and the 'lamentable extravagances' of the new theories (Norman 1895; Maudsley 1895). Sir Horatio Bryan Donkin, the first Medical Commissioner of Prisons, gave clear expression to the difference between the two traditions when he defined 'criminology', properly so-called, as the investigations undertaken by 'persons concerned in some way with the prison authorities who strive to discover just principles on which to base their work', and distinguished this from the newer 'doctrine and debate on the causation of crime' which he condemned as 'theories based on preconceived assumptions regardless of fact' (Donkin 1917).

So scientific research on individual criminals in Britain stemmed from a rather different root than did continental criminology, and inclined towards a more pragmatic, institutionalized approach to its subject. But, as I noted earlier, the international criminological movement tended to become more eclectic, more moderate, and more practical over time, gradually dissociating itself from extremist claims and adapting to the basic demands of the institutions it sought to influence. And as it became more respectable and more firmly established, the initial hostility of Britain's scientific and penological circles tended to fade. From the mid-1890s onwards, the English and Scottish Prison Commissions began to take an active interest in the movement, as did the leading psychiatric periodicals. Even the influential Gladstone Committee Report gave passing approval to the 'learned but conflicting theories' which subjected 'crime, its causes, and treatment' to 'scientific inquiry' (Gladstone Committee 1895: 8). What seems gradually to have happened in Britain in the years before the First World War is that 'criminology' ceased to be exclusively identified with its European anthropological origins and instead became used as a general term to describe scientific research on the subject of crime and criminals. Grudgingly at first, but more and more frequently, prison officials, psychiatrists, and doctors began to refer to their researches as 'criminological', until this became the accepted name for a new scientific specialism. The irony is that, in Britain at least, criminology came to be recognized as an accredited scientific specialism only when it began to rid itself of the notion of the distinctive 'criminal type'—the very entity that had originally grounded the claim that a special science of the criminal was justified.

Most of the early British work which identified itself as criminological was actually a continuation of the older medico-legal tradition of prison research, now opened out to engage with an expanding criminological literature imported from Europe and North America. It is, for example, almost exclusively within the Reports of the Medical Commissioner of Prisons and of the various prison medical officers that one will find any official discussion of criminological science in the first few decades of the twentieth century, and most of the major scientific works on crime written in Britain before the 1930s were written by doctors with psychiatric training and positions within the prison service.[34] The first university lectures in 'criminology' delivered in Britain—given at Birmingham by Maurice Hamblin Smith in 1921—were directed at postgraduate medical students within a course entitled 'Medical Aspects of Crime and Punishment'. And long before Hermann Mannheim began teaching at the London School of Economics in 1935, there were courses on 'Crime and Insanity' offered at London University by senior prison medical officers such as Sullivan and East.[35] In the absence of any specialist periodicals devoted to criminology, criminological articles and reviews appeared chiefly in the *Journal of Mental Science*, *The British Journal of Medical Psychology*, and the *Transactions of the Medico-Legal Association* (from 1933 *The Medico-Legal and Criminological Review*), although the *Howard Journal* also carried some reviews, as did the *Sociological Review*.

The institutionally based, medico-legal criminology which predominated in Britain for much of the nineteenth century and the first half of the twentieth century was, by its nature, an evolving, adaptive tradition. The criminological texts that it generated grew out of practical contexts that were forever changing, since institutions continually redefined their operations and took on new concerns, and also because new methods, theories, and techniques became available to the professionals who

---

[34] See, amongst others, Sutherland 1908; Quinton 1910; Devon 1912; Smith 1922; Sullivan 1924; East 1927.

[35] According to his own account, Cyril Burt had regularly given lectures on juvenile delinquency at Liverpool University between 1906 and 1914, but these had occurred in the context of a psychology class rather than one devoted to 'criminology'. See Mannheim 1957.

administered them. Many of the criminological texts written in the nineteenth century focused upon the problems of classifying particular offenders—as psychiatric rather than criminal cases, as morally insane, feebleminded, and so on—and of course these problems had a direct bearing upon the practices of penal institutions. As the penal system diversified in the early part of the twentieth century, developing specialist institutions for the inebriate, habitual offenders, the feebleminded, and for juveniles, and becoming more refined and differentiated in the classification of adult prisoners, the criminological literature similarly began to address itself to these new diagnostic and classificatory problems.[36] Thus, although this line of research came close to the concerns of the Lombrosian project in its focus upon individuals and their differential classification, it lacked the scientific ambition and theory-building concerns of the latter, being almost exclusively focused upon knowledge that was useful for administrative purposes.

In 1919, the emphasis upon individual character and specialized treatment prompted by the Gladstone Committee Report—together with concerns about large numbers of shell-shocked and mentally disturbed men returning from the war—led the Birmingham Justices to establish a permanent scheme for the clinical examination of untried adult offenders. Previously such work had been done on an occasional, ad hoc basis, and depended upon the skill and interest of the local prison doctor. By appointing Hamblin Smith and W.A. Potts, both psychiatrically trained prison doctors, and charging them with these new duties, the Justices effectively created a new specialism of applied criminology. Before long, Potts and Hamblin Smith were adapting the standard mental tests for use in this area, publishing the results of their clinical studies, and writing extensively about the need for this kind of investigation and its implications for the treatment and prevention of crime. In *The Psychology of the Criminal* (1922b) and in a series of articles in the *Journal of Mental Science*, the *Howard Journal*, and elsewhere, Smith emphasized the importance of criminological study, though for him this meant the clinical examination of individual offenders for the purpose of assessment and diagnosis. As Britain's first authorized teacher of 'criminology', and as the first individual to use the title of 'criminologist', it is significant that Smith, like Donkin and Ruggles-Brise before him, rejected the search for 'general theories' in favour of the 'study of the individual'. It is also significant that the centres for criminological research and teaching which he proposed were envisaged as places where 'young medical graduates' would be trained to become expert in the medico-psychological examination and assessment of offenders (Smith 1922a).

Hamblin Smith was also one of the first criminological workers in Britain to profess an interest in psychoanalysis, which he used as a means to assess the personality of offenders, as well as a technique for treating the mental conflicts which, he claimed, lay behind the criminal act. In this respect Smith met with much official opposition, particularly from W. Norwood East; but there were others, outside the prisons establishment, who were more enthusiastic. In the winter of 1922–23, Dr Grace Pailthorpe

---

[36] Works on alcoholism by W.C. Sullivan (1906), on recidivism by J.F. Sutherland (1908), and on the psychology of the criminal by M. Hamblin Smith (1922) and H.E. Field (1932) are significant examples of research derived from the developing penal-welfare complex.

assisted Smith in the psychoanalytic investigation of female offenders in Birmingham, and went on to complete a five-year study at Holloway, funded by a grant from the Medical Research Council. Her report (Pailthorpe 1932), which was completed by 1929 but held back by the Council until 1932, claimed that crime was generally a symptom of mental conflict that might be psychoanalytically resolved. This radical approach met with some consternation in official circles (see East 1936: 319), but it excited the interest of a number of analysts and medical psychologists who formed a group to promote the Pailthorpe report and its approach. Out of their meetings emerged the Association for the Scientific Treatment of Criminals (1931), which, in 1932, became the Institute for the Scientific Treatment of Delinquency (ISTD) (see Glover 1960).

Most of the founder members of this group were involved in the new outpatient sector of psychiatric work, made possible by a developing network of private clinics, which included the Tavistock (1921) and the Maudsley (1923), the new child guidance centres, and, in 1933, the ISTD's own Psychopathic Clinic (which in 1937 was moved and renamed the Portman Clinic). This new field of practice gave rise to its own distinctive brand of criminological theory. The early publications of the ISTD emphasize the clinical exploration of individual personality, and in that sense are continuous with much previous work. But they also manifest a new preventive emphasis, which reflected the fact that the new clinics operated outside the formal penal system and could deal with individuals before their disturbed conduct actually became criminal.[37] Eventually, the ISTD's emphasis upon psychoanalysis, and its open hostility to much official penal policy, ensured that it remained essentially an outsider body, operating at arm's length from the Home Office and the Prison Commission. This outsider status forms an important background to the later decision of the Home Office to support the establishment of a criminological institute at Cambridge, rather than under ISTD auspices in London, for although 'the formation of such a body was one of the original aims of the ISTD' (Glover 1960: 70), and the claims of the organization were canvassed to the Home Secretary in 1958, the Home Office appears not to have seriously considered such an option (see Radzinowicz 1988: 9).

Despite its subsequent neglect, the medico-legal work of W. Norwood East— particularly *An Introduction to Forensic Psychiatry in the Criminal Courts* (1927) and *The Medical Aspects of Crime* (1936)—better represents the mainstream of British criminology in the 1920s and 1930s. East was a psychiatrically trained prison medical officer who became a leading figure in the 1930s as Medical Director on the Prison Commission and President of the Medico-Legal Society, and his views dominated official policy-making for a lengthy period. East was himself a proponent of a psycho- logical approach to crime, but he considered its scope to be sharply delimited, and

---

[37] As the editors of the *British Journal of Delinquency* put it in the first issue: 'the activities of the "institutional" criminologist have been rather overshadowed in recent years by the expansion of what might be called the "ambulant" approach to delinquency, i.e. the application of diagnostic and, where necessary or possible, therapeutic methods to early cases attending Delinquency Clinics, Child Guidance and Psychiatric Centres, etc. . . . And to the extent that the Delinquency Clinic bridges the gap between the "non-delinquent" and the "recidivist", it is inevitable that the ambulant system should provide the most fruitful field for research into causes and methods of prevention' ('Editorial', *British Journal of Delinquency*, 1/1 (1950/1): 4).

consistently warned against the dangers and absurdities of exaggerating its claims. Instead of theoretical speculation and scientific ambition he stressed the importance of 'day-to-day administration', and the practical impact of theoretical ideas. (Hence his criticism of deterministic ideas, which he thought promoted 'mental invalidism' instead of trying to build up a sense of 'social responsibility' (East 1931: 2).) In 1934 he established an extended experiment at Wormwood Scrubs prison, whereby those offenders deemed most likely to respond to psychological therapy—particularly sex offenders and arsonists—were subjected to a period of investigation and treatment. At the end of five years, East and Hubert's Report on *The Psychological Treatment of Crime* (1939) reaffirmed East's view that while 80 per cent of offenders were psychologically normal, and would respond to routine punishment, a minority might usefully be investigated and offered psychological treatment. The Report proposed a special institution to deal with such offenders—a proposal that was immediately accepted but not put into effect until the opening of Grendon Underwood prison in 1962. East and Hubert also recommended that this institution should function as a centre for criminological research, and it is significant that when a criminological centre was here proposed for the first time in an official report, it should be envisaged as part of a psychiatric institution, dealing only with a small minority of pathological offenders.

An important departure from this British tradition of clinically based psychiatric studies was *The English Convict: A Statistical Study*, published in 1913 by Dr Charles Goring under the auspices of the Home Office and the Prison Commission. This work was made possible by institutional routines, in so far as anthropometric methods were used in prisons for the identification of habitual offenders during the 1890s, and in fact one of its starting points was a desire to measure the impact of prison diet and labour upon the inmates' physiques. But the issues addressed by the final report went far beyond these institutional matters and engaged, for the first time in an official publication, with the theoretical claims of scientific criminology.

The analysis and tabulation of the vast quantity of data collected by the study were carried out in Karl Pearson's Biometrical Laboratory at the University of London—an unusual location for prison research but one which was well suited to the statistical and eugenic themes which dominated the final report. As its sponsors intended, the study gave a definitive refutation of the old Lombrosian claim that criminals exhibited a particular physical type, thus confirming the position which the British authorities had held all along. However, the significance of Goring's study went far beyond this negative and somewhat out-of-date finding. In fact, Goring's analysis began by *assuming* that there was no criminal type, and although it was not much noticed at the time, his study is chiefly notable for inventing a quite new way of differentiating criminals from non-criminals.

In the early part of the book, Goring set out extensive theoretical and methodological arguments which insisted that criminality should be viewed not as a qualitative difference of type, marked by anomaly and morbidity, but instead as a variant of normality, differentiated only by degree. Following the arguments of Manouvrier and Topinard, Goring pointed out that so-called criminal 'anomalies' are only 'more or less extreme degrees of character which in some degree are present in all men'.

Moreover, he made it clear that his use of statistical method necessarily presupposed this idea of a criminal characteristic which is a common feature of all individuals, and he went on to name this hypothesized entity 'the criminal diathesis'. This conception of criminality as normal, rather than morbid or pathological, implied a new basis for criminological science, which Goring vigorously set forth. From now on, criminology would no longer depend on the clinical gaze of a Lombroso and its impressionistic identification of anomalies. (Goring had, in any case, provided a devastating critique of this 'anatomico-pathological method'.) Instead it must be a matter of large populations, careful measurement, and statistical analysis, demonstrating patterns of differentiation in the mass that would not be visible in any specific individual nor apparent to the naked eye unaided by statistical analysis.

Goring's own application of these methods purported to reveal a significant, but by no means universal, association between criminality and two heritable characteristics, namely low intelligence and poor physique, and suggested that 'family and other environmental conditions' were not closely associated with crime. From these findings he drew a series of practical, eugenic conclusions, declaring that 'crime will continue to exist as long as we allow criminals to propagate' and that government should therefore 'modify opportunity for crime by segregating the unfit' and 'regulate the reproduction of those constitutional qualities—feeblemindedness, inebriety, epilepsy, deficient social instinct, insanity, which conduce to the committing of crime' (Goring 1913). Here, as so often in subsequent studies, we see Lombroso's specific claims rejected, only to find that his basic assumptions and project are being reasserted in some new, revised form.

Although *The English Convict* had a considerable impact abroad, and especially in the USA, in Britain it received a much more muted response. On the one hand, Goring's attack had been centred upon theoretical positions that had little support in this country, other than from maverick outsiders such as Havelock Ellis. On the other, it appeared to have policy implications—particularly the possibility that inherited traits would render reformative prison regimes impotent—which were not altogether welcome in official circles. The Prison Commissioners, while supporting the study's publication as a Blue Book, refused to endorse its conclusions (see Garland 1985a), and Sir Bryan Donkin (1919) distanced himself from the book altogether, arguing that 'even correct generalisations . . . concerning criminals in the mass are not likely to be of much positive value in the study or treatment of individuals'. In much the same way W.C. Sullivan, the medical superintendent at Broadmoor, argued in *Crime and Insanity* (1924) that clinical rather than statistical methods were the only reliable means of obtaining useful, policy-relevant knowledge.

These exchanges are revealing because they show the extent to which British criminology up to this point was shaped by the interests and assumptions of official policy-makers and the institutions that they served. In the years before the First World War, the medico-legal assessment of individual offenders played an explicit role in the trial process and in the disposition of offenders after conviction, so the promised benefits of clinical research were readily apparent in a way that was not true of statistical studies. Later on, when criminal justice officials came to realize how they could use the results of actuarial calculations—in predicting response to treatment, deploying police resources, calculating crime rates, making parole decisions, and so on—the balance of interest shifted the other way. Though he did not live to see it (having died in 1919), Goring's argument for the importance of statistical method and mass data in criminological research was the one which was ultimately most persuasive to the British authorities. By the end of the 1930s, the Prison Commission and the Home Office had each embarked upon large-scale, statistically based projects, subsequently published as East (1942) and Carr-Saunders et al. (1942), and such studies became a characteristic form of government-sponsored research in the years after 1945.

If East's work exemplified the mainstream British tradition of medico-psychiatric criminological research (with the ISTD's more radical clinical studies forming an important tributary), and Goring inaugurated a new stream of statistical studies, there was also another significant line of inquiry which influenced criminological work in the post-war period. This third stream is best represented by the eclectic, multifactorial, social-psychological research of Cyril Burt. When later criminologists such as Mannheim and Radzinowicz looked back upon their predecessors, they spent little time discussing the merits of The English Convict or The Medical Aspects of Crime. Instead, they invariably picked out Cyril Burt's 1925 study, The Young Delinquent, as the first major work of modern British criminology and as an exemplar for the discipline that they were helping to create.[38] Like most criminological texts in this period, The Young Delinquent emerged from a specific field of practice—it was not until the 1960s that research took off from an academic base—but in marked contrast to the work of East, Hamblin Smith, Sullivan, and company, this field of practice was outside the penal system rather than central to it. In his post as educational psychologist to the London County Council, Burt was responsible for the psychological assessment and advice of London's schoolchild population, which involved him in examining thousands of individual problem cases, many of them behavioural as well as educational, and making recommendations for their treatment. Consequently, his criminological study was built upon a wider than usual population, dealing mostly with 'pre-delinquents' rather than convicted offenders, and it was not constrained by the narrowly penal concerns that affected most contemporary studies. Rather than inquire about specific classifications or distinctions, Burt was interested to specify all the possible sources of individual psychological difference, and thereby to identify the causal patterns that precipitate delinquency and non-delinquency.

The Young Delinquent was based upon the detailed clinical examination of 400 schoolchildren (a delinquent or quasi-delinquent group and a control group), using a battery of techniques that included biometric measurement, mental testing, temperament testing, and psychoanalytic and social inquiries, together with the most up-to-date statistical methods of factor analysis and correlation. Its findings were expansively eclectic, identifying some 170 causative factors that were in some way associated with delinquency, and showing, by way of narrative case histories, how each factor might typically operate. From his analysis, Burt concluded that certain

---

[38] See Mannheim (1949: 11); also Radzinowicz (1961: 173–6): 'it may be said that modern criminological research in England dates only from Sir Cyril Burt's study of The Young Delinquent, first published in 1925.'

factors, such as defective discipline, defective family relationships, and particular types of temperament, were highly correlated with delinquency, while the influence of other factors, such as poverty or low intelligence, though not altogether negligible, had been seriously overstated in the past. His major proposition was that delinquency was not the outcome of special factors operating only on delinquents, but was rather the result of a combination of factors—typically as many as nine or ten—operating at once upon a single individual. In consequence, the study of criminality must be, above all, multicausal in scope, while its treatment must be tailored to fit the needs of the individual case. The influence of Burt's work, and especially its eclectic, multifactorial search for the correlates of individual delinquency, was to become something of a hallmark of British criminology in the mid-twentieth century, though ironically enough (in view of Burt's modern reputation as a proponent of genetically-based intelligence) his most immediate impact was to shift attention away from the purported intellectual deficiencies of delinquents towards questions of temperament and emotional balance.

The scientific criminology that developed in Britain between the 1890s and the Second World War was thus heavily dominated by a medico-psychological approach, focused upon the individual offender and tied into a correctionalist penal-welfare policy. Within this approach there were a number of important variants and the enterprise was differently understood by different practitioners; but compared to the subject which exists today, criminology operated within rather narrow parameters. Sociological work, such as that developed by Durkheim in France at the turn of the century, or in Chicago in the 1920s and 1930s (which treated crime rates as social facts to be explained by sociological methods), was virtually absent. Instead the 'social dimension' of crime was conceived of as one factor among many others operating upon the individual—a good example of how the criminological project transforms the elements which it 'borrows' from other disciplines. Nor was the radicalism of foreign criminologists such as Enrico Ferri and Willem Bonger much in evidence here; indeed, if British criminology can be said to have developed radical analyses during this period, they were inspired by Sigmund Freud rather than by Karl Marx.[39]

The major topics of scientific interest were those thrown up as problems for the courts, the prisons, and the Borstal system—such as the mentally abnormal offender, recidivists, and especially juvenile delinquents—and the central purpose of scientific research was not the construction of explanatory theory but instead the more immediate end of aiding the policy-making process. The governmental project dominated, almost to the point of monopolization, and Lombroso's science of the criminal was taken up only in so far as it could be shown to be directly relevant to the governance of crime and criminals. Such a pragmatic, correctionalist orientation was, of course, hardly surprising when one recalls that the authors of pre-war criminological research in Britain were, virtually without exception, practitioners working in the state penal system or else in the network of clinics and hospitals which had grown up around it. In Britain, before the mid-1930s, criminology as a university-based, academic discipline simply did not exist.

[39] See, for instance, the works by Glover (1941, 1960), Aichhorn (1951), and Friedlander (1947).

THE ESTABLISHMENT OF A CRIMINOLOGICAL DISCIPLINE IN BRITAIN

The transformation of British criminology from a minor scientific specialism—the part-time activity of a few practitioners and enthusiasts—into an established academic discipline took place comparatively late, occurring some time between the mid-1930s and the early 1960s. Even then, it was by no means an inevitable or necessary development. Indeed, had it not been for the rise of Nazism in Germany, and the appointment of three distinguished European emigrés, Hermann Mannheim, Max Grunhut, and Leon Radzinowicz, to academic posts at elite British universities, British criminology might not have developed sufficient academic impetus to become an independent discipline during that period. But however contingently, the process of discipline formation did take hold in the post-war years, and its symbolic culmination occurred in October 1961 with the inauguration of a postgraduate course for the training of criminological researchers and teachers at the new Institute of Criminology at Cambridge. In the intervening years, the other concomitants of disciplinary status had gradually come into being, initially as the result of private initiatives, and then, in the late 1950s, with the support and funding of government.

Criminology teaching in the universities began to expand from the late 1930s onwards, catering to the needs of the fast-growing social work and probation professions and attracting a first generation of research students (such as John Spencer, Norval Morris, Tadeuz Grygier, and John Croft) who would go on to become important figures in the new discipline.[40] Cambridge University established a Department of Criminal Science in 1941, which sponsored research projects as well as a book series, and eventually formed the base upon which the Institute of Criminology was built. In 1950, Britain's first specialist criminology journal, the *British Journal of Delinquency* (renamed the *British Journal of Criminology* in 1960), was established as 'the official organ of the ISTD' and set about the task of moulding a coherent discipline out of the scores of small-scale research efforts dotted around the country. Editorials by Mannheim and his co-editors Edward Glover and Emmanuel Miller identified key aspects of an emerging research programme, and the journal carried extensive discussions of methodology and data sources as well as acting as a kind of bulletin board through which researchers could keep abreast of activities in the expanding field. In 1953, the ISTD also established the Scientific Group for the Discussion of Delinquency Problems, which acted as a forum for discussion for several years until younger members of the group—some of them with newly-created university posts in criminology—grew dissatisfied with the clinical and psychoanalytical emphasis

[40] According to the results of a survey carried out by Mannheim in the mid-1950s, twenty-one British universities claimed that criminology formed a part of their teaching curriculum, whether for undergraduate students or as a part of extension courses and diplomas taken by trainee social workers and probation officers (Mannheim 1957). From 1938 onwards, the ISTD was a centre for the University of London four-year Diploma Course in Social Studies, an evening course, of which the fourth year was devoted to criminology. Mannheim himself taught 'criminology as a separate subject in all its aspects' at the LSE from 1935 onwards.

of leading figures such as Glover and split off to found the more academically oriented British Society of Criminology. In 1956, Howard Jones published the first British criminology textbook, *Crime and the Penal System*, a work much influenced by the teachings of Mannheim at the London School of Economics. In its emphasis upon penological issues and its assumption of a reforming, welfarist stance it encapsulated an important and continuing strand of British criminological culture. (Such was the pace of change in this, the discipline's take-off phase, that the third edition of the book, appearing only nine years later in 1965, was described by an otherwise sympathetic reviewer as 'sadly out of date' (Taylor 1968).)

The Criminal Justice Act of 1948 provided for the regular allocation of Treasury funds for the purposes of criminological research, but in the years that followed only a tiny annual budget was actually made available. However, the 1950s saw the emergence of an explicit and continuing commitment by the British government to support criminological research, both as an in-house activity and as a university-based specialism. This, in effect, marked the point of convergence between criminology as an administrative aid and criminology as a scientific undertaking—the consolidation of the governmental and Lombrosian projects—and it represents a key moment in the creation of a viable, independent discipline of criminology in Britain. This new and closer relationship between government and criminological science not only endorsed criminology's claim to be a useful form of knowledge; it also gave official and financial backing to criminology's claim to scientific status and university recognition. Thus the Home Office proceeded to set up not just an infrastructure for policy-led research—which it did in 1957 with the opening of the Home Office Research Unit (see Lodge 1974)—but also an academic institute, the Cambridge Institute of Criminology, sited in a prestigious university, with the explicit task of undertaking scientific research and training recruits for the newly-founded discipline of criminology (see Radzinowicz 1988). As the 1959 White Paper *Penal Policy in a Changing Society* announced, 'the institute should be able, as no existing agency is in a position to do, to survey with academic impartiality . . . the general problem of the criminal in society, its causes, and its solution' (Home Office 1959).

This new-found compatibility between traditions which had often pulled in different directions had a number of sources. In part it was testimony to the degree to which the scientific strand of criminological research had modified its ambitions and adapted its terms to fit the institutional realities and policy concerns which so heavily influenced the market place of criminological ideas. In part it was attributable to the fact that research concerned to differentiate criminals from non-criminals, and especially those who would recidivate from those who would not, was thought to be important for the development of effective sentencing decisions (especially Borstal allocations) and decisions regarding early release. Thus, for example, the prediction research that claimed so much attention in the late 1950s could appear to satisfy both the needs of administration and the ends of science, in so far as these studies sought to identify offender characteristics that were highly correlated with subsequent offending. (In the event, the most effective prediction tables made little use of clinical information about the offender, and actually discredited to some extent the whole project of etiological research.) One might also suggest, however, that this convergence between the search for useful knowledge and the search for scientific truth was actually more apparent than real, because, in the event, the research agenda pursued by the Cambridge Institute, at least in the early years, was heavily influenced by immediate policy needs. Indeed, for the most part, it was scarcely distinguishable from the in-house research of the Home Office—a fact that did not go uncriticized at the time.

If the emergence of a criminological discipline was the coming together of traditions of inquiry that had once been more distinct, it was also, and more immediately, the achievement of a few key individuals, backed by an alliance of interested organizations. These discipline-builders had to struggle with all sorts of resistance, but their decisive advantage was that they acted in a context in which government ministers and officials had become receptive to the idea that policy-making could be enhanced by the availability of systematic research and trained expertise. The shrewd political skills and institution-building energies of Leon Radzinowicz were particularly important (not least in persuading the Wolfson Foundation to fund the British discipline's first chair and provide the Cambridge Institute with the resources to become one of the world's leading centres of criminological work),[41] as was the influential teaching of Hermann Mannheim and the proselytizing work that he and the other ISTD members conducted in academic and practical circles. Similarly, the impressive body of research publications produced by these authors and others, such as Burt, Bowlby, Grunhut, Sprott, Mays, and Ferguson, created a strong case for the value of criminology as an academic subject.

The practical and educational benefits to be derived from establishing institutes and university departments of criminology were also canvassed by a number of influential political figures and associations. Senior government officials such as Alexander Paterson, Sir Lionel Fox, Sir Alexander Maxwell, and Viscount Templewood made public declarations about the need for criminology; Margery Fry and George Benson MP made representations to the Home Office to this effect; and at various times the Howard League, the Magistrates' Association, the British Psychological Society, the National Association for Mental Health, the Royal Medico-Psychological Association, and the United Nations European Seminar on Crime all added their weight to the campaign to obtain government sponsorship and university recognition for the subject (see Radzinowicz 1988, 1999). In the event, criminology's most influential supporter was R.A. Butler, who as Home Secretary in the late 1950s took a personal interest in the development of the subject, and who was instrumental in extending government funding for criminological research and in setting up the Cambridge Institute (see Butler 1974; Radzinowicz 1988, 1999).

The government's interest in sponsoring the creation of a viable criminological

---

[41] For Radzinowicz's own account of this period, see Radzinowicz 1999. It is worth pointing out that the standard claim made by those who canvassed the British government to support the development of criminology—namely, that the UK was trailing far behind other countries in the pursuit of criminological research—was subsequently shown to be quite false. Radzinowicz's empirical survey of the state of criminology around the world suggested that, with the establishment of the Cambridge Institute and the Home Office Research Unit, British criminology probably enjoyed more official support than that of any other country, with the possible exception of the USA. See Radzinowicz 1961.

enterprise was a combination of immediate penological concerns and broader conceptions of how the policy-making process ought to be organized. In the years immediately preceding the Second World War, a concern about increasing rates of juvenile offending prompted the Home Office to arrange a series of conferences and research projects in order to estimate the extent of the problem and identify its social and psychological roots. When, in the post-war years, the high wartime rates of delinquent behaviour failed to decline, the problem attracted extensive political and press attention and provided a compelling rationale for the promotion of criminological research. (In the years that followed, juvenile delinquency was to become a central topic in British criminology.) Similarly, the gradual development of a penal philosophy of 'treatment and training', centred upon the Borstal system and relying for its effectiveness upon accurate assessment and classification procedures, led to a growing demand for criminological knowledge and advice. More generally, the wartime experience of operational research and the utilization of expertise in various forms of strategic planning, together with the growing professionalization of administration and social work in the new welfare state, gradually convinced post-war governments of the value of research and expertise as a basis for social policy.[42] The same governmental mentality that looked to Beveridge and Keynes to solve the social and economic problems of the nation came to recognize criminology as a form of knowledge that should be integrated into the institutions of government. Criminology thus became an integral part of the process of 'social reconstruction', a small element in the post-war settlement which sought to secure stability and capitalist growth by means of welfare provision and social democratic management (see Mannheim 1946; Taylor 1981).

One might add that this tendency to appeal to expert, 'scientific' knowledge as a source of solutions to social and personal problems was increasingly apparent not just in government but also in the wider culture. As the prestige of the traditional moral and religious codes continued to wane, the new figure of the 'popular expert' began to appear more regularly on the radio and in the Press, teaching a mass audience how 'modern science' thought about age-old problems, including crime and delinquency.[43]

Once set in place, the component parts of the emergent discipline proceeded to establish the range of issues and research questions that was to characterize the subject. In hindsight, this research agenda is easily regarded as narrow and consensual, reflecting broad agreement about the importance of correctionalist aims and positivist methods and a traditional British bias against theoretical or sociological work (see Cohen 1981; Wiles 1976). However, there was actually a good deal of conflict and disagreement regarding the appropriate research agenda for the subject, and rather

---

[42] For a contemporary discussion of these developments, see National Association for Mental Health 1949. Ten years later, Barbara Wootton's review of the social sciences and their role in policy-making was severely critical of criminology's achievements in this respect (Wootton 1959). For a retrospective account, see Wiles 1976.

[43] See the transcripts of the BBC radio series on the causes of crime in *The Listener* of 1929 and 1934, especially the broadcasts by Cyril Burt on 'The Psychology of the Bad Child' (6 February 1929) and on 'The Causes of Crime' (2 May, 1934).

more diversity in intellectual style and policy orientation than the textbook histories have suggested. The major institutions in the newly created discipline—the Cambridge Institute and the Home Office Research Unit—were each, to differing degrees, tied into a framework of government-sponsored research which quickly assumed a distinctive pattern, although the Institute was home to other work as well, most notably Radzinowicz's monumental *History of English Criminal Law and its Administration* (1948–86), and was careful to maintain its claim to academic independence. Neither organization concerned itself closely with the development of clinical studies of the causes of crime or with the task of theory-building, preferring instead to pursue knowledge which would be more readily obtained and more immediately accessible to the policy process. As Radzinowicz argued in 1961, 'the attempt to elucidate the causes of crime should be put aside' in favour of more modest, descriptive studies which indicate the kinds of factors and circumstances with which offending is associated. Using an interdisciplinary approach and a diversity of methods, research was to be focused upon 'descriptive, analytical accounts of the state of crime, of the various classes of offenders, of the enforcement of criminal law [and] of the effectiveness of various measures of penal treatment' (Radzinowicz 1961: 175).

This approach, well characterized by George Vold (1958) as 'administrative criminology', attracted harsh criticism at the time from those more attached to criminology's scientific and explanatory ambitions, particularly the psychoanalysts at the ISTD and the group of sociological criminologists that was forming around Mannheim at the LSE—just as it would later be criticized again in the 1970s, this time by a new generation of criminologists more attracted to critical and sociological theory. But to figures such as Radzinowicz, trying to establish a fledgling and still precarious discipline, the concern was to produce useful knowledge and produce it quickly, rather than risk the failure of a more ambitious programme of etiological research, a programme which, in any case, would depend on the production of a more accurate and wide-ranging description of criminal phenomena (Radzinowicz 1988).

This pragmatic vision of the criminological enterprise was echoed by the 1959 White Paper, which argued that etiological research 'is confronted with problems which are immense both in range and complexity', that 'there are no easy answers to these problems and progress is bound to be slow', and that consequently emphasis should be placed instead upon 'research into the use of various forms of treatment and the measurement of their results, since this is concerned with matters that can be analysed more precisely' (Home Office 1959: 5). The Home Office Research Unit began its work squarely within this newly constructed framework of science-for-government, using the methodologies of social science to measure and improve the effectiveness of penal treatments and trying to harness the concepts and classifications of academic criminology to the work of administering criminal justice institutions. Nor was it surprising that the paradigmatic study which shaped much of the Unit's research in the first decade of its existence should be a prediction study—precisely the kind of work that formed a junction point between criminology's scientific and governmental concerns—and one, moreover, that focused on the Borstal, the British institution which more than any other embodied the correctionalist ideals of a scientific penology. The distinctive mixture of advanced statistical technique,

correctionalist classificatory concerns, and obvious policy relevance which characterized Mannheim and Wilkins' *Prediction Methods in Relation to Borstal Training* (1955)
came to be the hallmark of the Research Unit's work throughout the 1950s and 1960s
(see Clarke and Cornish 1983).

EPILOGUE

By the 1960s, then, one could say with confidence that a discipline of criminology had
come into existence in Great Britain. Centred on the core institutions at Cambridge
and London, but increasingly building a significant presence in universities and colleges throughout the country, the subject was well placed to benefit from the rapid
expansion of higher education that occurred during this decade, and in the space of a
few years criminology took on, rather suddenly, the character of a well-established
discipline (see Rock 1988b). Indeed, such was the success of the new discipline in
becoming a part of the academic scheme of things that many of its younger members
seemed not to be aware of just how recently the battle for recognition had been won.
Thus, in the critical writings that emerged in the late 1960s and 1970s, in which a new
generation of criminologists mounted a radical assault on all that had gone before,
one gets the sense that what is being attacked is a very powerful criminological
establishment, rather than a *parvenu* and somewhat precarious subject still in the
process of constituting itself.[44]

Gaining a secure place in the institutions of higher education had a major and
unanticipated impact upon the discipline, so that no sooner had it become 'established' than it began to transform itself in significant ways. Many of the developments
of the 1960s and 1970s—particularly the reassertion of theoretical ambition, the
emergence of a strongly critical discourse, and a widespread dissatisfaction with criminology's relationship to correctionalist policies—are explicable in terms of a discipline adjusting to its new situation, pulled between the demands of policy relevance
and the aspiration for academic credibility. Thus the discipline became not only more
diversified, more specialized, more professional, and more self-critical in these years, it
also became bitterly divided between those who sought to pursue the 'traditional'
criminological agenda (in either its etiological or its administrative variant) and those
associated with the National Deviancy Conference, founded at York in 1968, who were
deeply critical of the medico-psychological assumptions, social democratic politics,
and atheoretical pragmatism of what they termed 'positivist criminology' (see Cohen
1981; Wiles 1976).

---

[44] For examples of the radically self-critical criminology of this period, see Cohen 1971; Taylor and Taylor
1973; Taylor, Walton, and Young 1973; Taylor *et al.* 1975. In the context of these polemics—through which
contemporary readers too often interpret the past—it is easy to forget that criminological writings had never
been wholly uncritical of official practices. Most British criminological work has been framed by an amelior-
ist, social democratic politics, often sharply critical of state policies. Opposition to the death penalty was, for
instance, a central concern for many criminologists in the period up to the 1960s. On the complex relationship of criminological knowledge to state power, see Garland 1992.

In those years, during which university funding seemed more secure than it would subsequently, and academic criminology momentarily enjoyed a degree of autonomy from government greater than at any time before or since, one of the repeated refrains of theoretical writing was that criminology had no epistemological warrant and that analytical considerations demanded that the discipline be dissolved into the broader concerns of sociology or social psychology. That such claims could be made, and made so forcefully, was a stark reminder of just how contingent was criminology's existence as a scientific subject. That they altogether failed to disturb the discipline and its continued expansion is perhaps a measure of the social and institutional forces that continue to underwrite the existence of British criminology.

Selected further reading

The history of criminology is probably too complex to be captured in a single text, however compendious, but two collections— *The Origins and Growth of Criminology*, edited by Piers Beirne (Dartmouth: Aldershot, 1994) and *The History of Criminology*, edited by Paul Rock (Dartmouth: Aldershot, 1994)—do a good job of suggesting the main lines of descent and development. Other worthwhile collections include Paul Rock (ed.), *A History of British Criminology* (Oxford: Oxford University Press, 1988), which features essays on the formation and contemporary character of the discipline; and the still useful *Pioneers in Criminology*, edited by H. Mannheim (London: Stevens, 1960).

Piers Beirne's *Inventing Criminology: Essays on the Rise of Homo Criminalis* (Albany: State University of New York Press, 1993) rescues Beccaria, Quetelet, Guerry, Tarde, and Goring from the condescension of textbook caricatures. Despite decades of revisionist work of this kind, Leon Radzinowicz's essay *Ideology and Crime: A Study of Crime and its Social and Historical Context* (London: Heinemann, 1966) remains an illuminating introduction to the subject for undergraduates, and of course Radzinowicz's five-volume *History of the English Criminal Law and its Administration* (vols 1–4, London: Stevens; vol. 5, co-authored with Roger Hood, Oxford: Oxford University Press) is an indispensable source for anyone doing serious research in this field.

A number of studies follow the lead of Michel Foucault's classic work *Discipline and Punish* (London: Allen Lane, 1977) in analysing criminology as an apparatus of power/ knowledge, linked into disciplinary and governmental institutions. Pasquale Pasquino's essay 'The Invention of Criminology: Birth of a Special Savior' (in G. Burchell, C. Gordon, and P. Miller (eds), *The Foucault Effect: Studies in Governmentality*, London: Harvester Wheatsheaf, 1991) and my article 'The Criminal and his Science' (*British Journal of Criminology* (1985), 25: 109–37) focus upon the emergence of the criminal delinquent as a new object of science and administration in nineteenth-century Europe; while my book *Punishment and Welfare: A History of Penal Strategies* (Aldershot: Gower, 1985) shows how a developing criminological discourse spiralled in and out of the penal-welfare institutions that emerged in Britain at the start of the twentieth century. The Foucauldian account of criminology's history and its relation to power is reconsidered in my later article 'Criminological Knowledge and its Relation to Power: Foucault's Genealogy and Criminology Today' (*British Journal of Criminology* (1992), 32/4: 403–22) which argues for a more differentiated account of power, of criminology, and of the various ways in which they relate to one another.

There are several useful accounts of the institutional history of criminology in Britain, often written by insiders who played a key part in the development of the subject. Radzinowicz's memoir *Adventures in Criminology* (London: Routledge, 1999) is a hugely enjoyable read. Other accounts include Radzinowicz's history of *The Cambridge Institute of Criminology: Its Background and Scope* (London: HMSO, 1988), and *Crime Control in Britain: A Review of Policy Research*—a review of the development of Home Office edited by R.V.G. Clarke and Derek B. Cornish (Albany: State University of New York, 1983). Stanley Cohen, himself an important insider in a different strand of British criminology, offers a sociological analysis of post-war developments in 'Footprints on the Sand: A Further Report on Criminology and the Sociology of Deviance in Britain', in M. Fitzgerald, G. McLennan, and J. Pawson (eds), *Crime and Society: Readings in History and Theory* (London: Routledge, 1981), and reflects upon the institutional and intellectual tensions that structured the field in the 1960s and 1970s. *The Sociology of Deviance: An Obituary* by Colin Sumner (Buckingham: Open University Press, 1994) is an extended essay on the history of 'the sociology of deviance', a form of analysis that bears an oblique and often critical relationship to criminology. Many of the theoretical and political concerns themes that animate contemporary criminological research in Britain are discussed in David Nelken (ed.), *The Futures of Criminology* (London: Sage, 1994), and in Simon Holdaway and Paul Rock (eds), *Thinking About Criminology* (London: UCL Press, 1998).

Lastly, there are several works of social and intellectual history which explore particular aspects of criminology's past. The most important of these are Daniel Pick's *Faces of Degeneration: A European Disorder, c.1848–c.1918* (Cambridge: Cambridge University Press, 1989); Robert Nye's *Crime, Madness and Politics in Modern France: The Medical Concept of National Decline* (Princeton: Princeton University Press, 1984); Simon Cole's *Suspect Identities: A History of Fingerprinting and Criminal Identification* (Cambridge, Mass: Harvard University Press, 2001); and Martin Wiener's *Reconstructing the Criminal: Culture, Law and Policy in England, 1830–1914* (Cambridge: Cambridge University Press, 1990).

References

AICHHORN, A. (1951), *Wayward Youth*, London: Imago.

BAKER, J. (1892), 'Some Points Connected With Criminals', *Journal of Mental Science*, 38: 364.

BANKOWSKI, Z., MUNGHAM, G., and YOUNG, P. (1976), 'Radical Criminology or Radical Criminologist?', *Contemporary Crises*, 1/1: 37–51.

BECCARIA, C. (1963 [1764]), *Of Crimes and Punishments*, Indiana: Bobbs-Merill. First published in Italian as *Dei Delitti e Delle Pene*.

BEIRNE, P. (1993), *Inventing Criminology: The Rise of 'Homo Criminalis'*, Albany, NY: State University of New York Press.

BONGER, W. (1936), *An Introduction to Criminology*, London: Methuen.

BOTTOMS, A.E. (1987), 'Reflections on the Criminological Enterprise', *Cambridge Law Journal*, 46/2: 240–63.

BURCHELL, G., GORDON, C., and MILLER, P. (eds) (1991), *The Foucault Effect: Studies in Governmentality*, London: Harvester Wheatsheaf.

BURT, C. (1925), *The Young Delinquent*, London: University of London Press.

—— (1929), 'The Psychology of the Bad Child', *The Listener*, 6 February.

—— (1934), 'Causes of Crime', *The Listener*, 2 May.

BUTLER, R.A. (1974), 'The Foundation of the Institute of Criminology at Cambridge', in R. Hood (ed.), *Crime, Criminology and Public Policy*, London: Heinemann.

CARR-SAUNDERS, A., MANNHEIM, H., and RHODES, E.C. (1942), *Young Offenders*, Cambridge: Cambridge University Press.

CLARKE, R.V.G., and CORNISH, D.B. (1983), *Crime Control in Britain: A Review of Research*, Albany: State University of New York Press.

COHEN, S. (ed.) (1971), *Images of Deviance*, Harmondsworth: Penguin.

COHEN, S. (1981), 'Footprints on the Sand: A Further Report on Criminology and the Sociology of Deviance in Britain', in M. Fitzgerald, G. McClennan, and J. Pawson (eds), *Crime and Society*, London: Routledge.

COLQUHOUN, P. (1797), *Treatise on the Police of the Metropolis*, 4th edn, London: J. Mawman.

—— (1800), *Treatise on the Commerce and Police of the River Thames*, London: J. Mawman.

—— (1806), *Treatise on Indigence*, London: J. Mawman.

—— (1814), *Treatise on the Wealth, Power and Resources of the British Empire*, London: J. Mawman.

COOTER, R. (1981), 'Phrenology and British Alienists, 1825–1845', in A. Scull (ed.), *Madhouses, Mad-Doctors and Madmen: The Social History of Psychiatry in the Victorian Era*, London: Athlone Press.

CURTIS, T.C., and HALE, F.M. (1981), 'English Thinking about Crime, 1530–1620', in L.A. Knafla (ed.), *Crime and Criminal Justice in Europe and Canada*, Waterloo Ontario: Wilfred Laurier University Press.

DANZIGER, K. (1990), *Constructing the Subject: The Historical Origins of Psychological Research*, Cambridge: Cambridge University Press.

DARNELL, R. (1974), *Readings in the History of Anthropology*, New York: Harper & Row.

DELUMEAU, J. (1990), *Sin and Fear: The Emergence of a Western Guilt Culture 13th-18th Centuries*, New York: St Martin's Press.

DEVON, J. (1912), *The Criminal and the Community*, London: John Lane.

DONKIN, Sir H.B. (1917), 'Notes on Mental Defect in Criminals', *Journal of Mental Science*, 63.

—— (1919), 'The Factors of Criminal Action', *Journal of Mental Science*, 65: 87–96.

DRAPKIN, I. (1983), 'Criminology: Intellectual History', in S. Kadish (ed.), *Encyclopedia of Crime and Justice*, ii, 546–56, New York: Free Press.

EAST, W. NORWOOD (1927), *An Introduction to Forensic Psychiatry in the Criminal Courts*, London: J.A. Churchill.

—— (1931–2), 'Report of the Medical Commissioner', in *Report of the Commissioners of Prisons and Directors of Convict Prisons, 1930,*' PP 1931–2 (Cmd 4151), xii.

—— (1936), *The Medical Aspects of Crime*, London: J.A. Churchill.

—— (1942), *The Adolescent Criminal: A Medico-Sociological Study of 4,000 Male Adolescents*, London: J.A. Churchill.

EAST, W. NORWOOD, and HUBERT, W.H. DE B. (1939), *Report on the Psychological Treatment of Crime*, London: HMSO.

ELLIS, H. (1890), *The Criminal*, London: Walter Scott.

FALLER, L. (1987), *Turned to Account: The Forms and Functions of Criminal Biography in Late Seventeenth and Early Eighteenth Century England*, Cambridge: Cambridge University Press.

FERRI, E. (1895), *Criminal Sociology*, London: Fisher Unwin.

FIELD, H.E. (1932), 'The Psychology of Crime: The Place of Psychology in the Treatment of Delinquents', *British Journal of Medical Psychology*, 12: 241–56.

FIELDING, H. (1988 [1751]), *An Enquiry into the Causes of the Late Increase of Robbers . . . and Other Related Writings*, M.R. Zircar (ed.), Oxford: Oxford University Press.

FOUCAULT, M. (1977), *Discipline and Punish*, London: Allen Lane.

—— (1979), 'On Governmentality', *Ideology and Consciousness*, 6: 5–23.

FRIEDLANDER, K. (1947), *The Psychoanalytical Approach to Juvenile Delinquency*, London: Kegan Paul.

GARLAND, D. (1985a), *Punishment and Welfare*, Aldershot: Gower.

—— (1985b), 'The Criminal and his Science', *British Journal of Criminology*, 25/2: 109–37.

—— (1988), 'British Criminology before 1935', in P. Rock (ed.), *A History of British Criminology*, Oxford: Oxford University Press.

—— (1992), 'Criminological Knowledge and its Relation to Power: Foucault's Genealogy and Criminology Today', *British Journal of Criminology*, 32/4: 403–22.

—— (1997), 'Governmentality and the Problem of Crime: Foucault, Criminology, Sociology', *Theoretical Criminology* 1:2, 173–214.

—— (2000), 'Ideas, Institutions and Situational Crime Prevention', in A. von Hirsch, D. Garland, and A. Wakefield (eds), *Ethical and Social Perspectives on Situational Crime Prevention*, Oxford: Hart Publishing.

—— (2001), *The Culture of Control: Crime and Social Order in Contemporary Society*, Oxford: Oxford University Press.

—— (2002), 'Ideology and Crime: A Further

Chapter', in M. Tonry (ed.), *Ideology, Crime and Criminal Justice: A Symposium in Honour of Sir Leon Radzinowicz*, London: Willan Publishing.

GLADSTONE COMMITTEE (1895), *Report of the Departmental Committee on Prisons*. PP 1895, lvi.

GLOVER, E. (1941), *The Diagnosis and Treatment of Delinquency*, London: ISTD.

—— (1960), *The Roots of Crime*, London: Imago.

GORING, C. (1913), *The English Convict: A Statistical Study*, London: HMSO.

GOTTFREDSON, M.R., and HIRSCHI, T. (eds) (1987), *Positive Criminology*, Newsbury Park, Ca.: Sage.

GOULD, S.J. (1981), *The Mismeasure of Man*, New York: Norton.

GREEN, T.A. (1985), *Verdict According to Conscience: Perspectives on the English Trial Jury, 1200–1800*, Chicago: University of Chicago Press.

GRIFFITHS, A.G.F. (1904), *Fifty Years of Public Service*, London: Cassell.

—— (1910–11), 'Criminology', in *Encyclopaedia Britannica*, 11th edn, London: Encyclopaedia Britannica.

HACKING, I. (1983), *Representing and Intervening: Introductory Topics in the Philosophy of Natural Science*, Cambridge: Cambridge University Press.

—— (1990), *The Taming of Chance*, Cambridge: Cambridge University Press.

HIRST, P.Q. (1975), 'Marx and Engels on Law, Crime and Morality', in Taylor *et al.* (eds), *Critical Criminology*, London: Routledge and Kegan Paul.

HOME OFFICE (1959), *Penal Practice in a Changing Society: Aspects of Future Development* (Cmnd 645), London: HMSO.

HOWARD, J. (1973 [1777]), *The State of the Prisons in England and Wales*, Montclair, NJ: Paterson Smith. First published Warrington: W. Eyres.

—— (1973 [1789]), *An Account of the Principal Lazarettos of Europe*, Montclair, NJ: Paterson Smith. First published Warrington: W. Eyres.

IGNATIEFF, M. (1978), *A Just Measure of Pain: The Penitentiary and the Industrial Revolution*, London: Macmillan.

JONES, H. (1956), *Crime and the Penal System*, London: University Tutorial Press.

JUDGES, A.V. (ed.) (1930), *The Elizabethan Underworld*, London: Routledge (repr. 1965).

KING, P. (1998), 'The Rise of Juvenile Delinquency in England 1780–1840: Changing Patterns of Perception and Prosecution', *Past and Present*, 160: 116–66.

LAUB, J.H., and SAMPSON, R.J. (1991), 'The Sutherland-Glueck Debate: On the Sociology of Criminological Knowledge', *American Journal of Sociology*, 96: 6, 1402–40.

LAVATER, J.C. (1792), *Essays on Physiognomy, Designed to Promote the Knowledge and Love of Mankind*, London: J. Murray.

LEMAINE, G., MACLEOD, R., MULKAY, M., and WEINGERT, P., (eds) (1976), *Perspectives on the Emergence of Scientific Disciplines*, Paris: Maison des Sciences de l'Homme.

LEPS, M.-C. (1992), *Apprehending the Criminal: The Production of Deviance in Nineteenth Century Discourse*, Durham, N.C.: Duke University Press.

LEVIN, Y., and LINDESMITH, A. (1937), 'English Ecology and Criminology of the Past Century', *Journal of Criminal Law, Criminology and Police Science*, 27/6: 801–16.

LODGE, T.S. (1974) 'The Founding of the Home Office Research Unit', in R. Hood (ed.), *Crime, Criminology and Public Policy*, London: Heinemann.

LOMBROSO, C. (1876), *L'Uomo Delinquente*, Turin: Fratelli Bocca. (No English translation was ever published, but see G. Lombroso-Ferrero, *Criminal Man: According to the Classification of Cesare Lombroso*, New York: Putnam, 1911; repr. Montclair, NJ: Paterson Smith, 1972.)

—— (1895), *The Female Offender*, London: Fisher Unwin.

LYELL, J.H. (1913), 'A Pioneer in Criminology: Notes on the Work of James Bruce Thomson of Perth', *Journal of Mental Science*, 59.

MANNHEIM, H. (1946), *Criminal Justice and Social Reconstruction*, Oxford: Oxford University Press.

—— (1949), Contribution to the Proceedings of the Conference, in National Association for Mental Health, *Why Delinquency? The Case for Operational Research*, London: NAMH.

—— (1957), 'Report on the Teaching of Criminology in the United Kingdom', in UNESCO, *The University Teaching of Social Sciences: Criminology*, Lausanne: UNESCO.

—— (ed.) (1960), *Pioneers in Criminology*, London: Stevens.

—— and WILKINS, L. (1955), *Prediction Methods in Relation to Borstal Training*, London: HMSO.

MATZA, D. (1964), *Delinquency and Drift*, New York: Wiley.

—— (1969), *Becoming Deviant*, Englewood Cliffs, NJ: Prentice-Hall.

MAUDSLEY, H. (1863), 'Review of A Prison

Matron's *Female Life in Prison*', *Journal of Mental Science*, 9: 69.

—— (1889), 'Remarks on Crime and Criminals', *Journal of Mental Science*, 34: 159, 311.

—— (1895), 'Criminal Responsibility in Relation to Insanity', *Journal of Mental Science*, 41: 657.

Mayhew, H. (1861–2), *London Labour and the London Poor*, London: Griffin, Bohn & Co.

Morris, T. (1957), *The Criminal Area*, London: Routledge and Kegan Paul.

Morrison, W.D. (1896), *Juvenile Offenders*, London: Fisher Unwin.

National Association for Mental Health (1949), *Why Delinquency? The Case for Operational Research*, London: NAMH.

Needham, D. (1889), 'Comments on Maudsley's "Remarks on Crime and Criminals"', *Journal of Mental Science*, 34: 311.

Nicolson, D. (1878–9), 'The Measure of Individual and Social Responsibility in Criminal Cases', *Journal of Mental Science*, 24: 1, 249.

—— (1895), 'Crime, Criminals and Criminal Lunatics: The Presidential Address to the Medico-Psychological Association', *Journal of Mental Science*, 41: 567.

Norman, D.C. (1895), 'Comments on Dr Nicolson's Presidential Address', *Journal of Mental Science*, 41: 487.

Nye, R. (1984), *Crime, Madness and Politics in Modern France*, Princeton: Princeton University Press.

Pailthorpe, G.W. (1932), *Studies in the Psychology of Delinquency*, London: HMSO.

Pasquino, P. (1978), 'Theatrum Politicum: The Genealogy of Capital, Police, and the State of Prosperity', in G. Burchell, C. Gordon, and P. Miller (eds), *The Foucault Effect: Studies in Governmentality*, London: Harvester Wheatsheaf, 105–18.

—— (1991), 'The Invention of Criminology: Birth of a Special Savior', in G. Burchell, C. Gordon, and P. Miller (eds), *The Foucault Effect: Studies in Governmentality*, London: Harvester Wheatsheaf.

Petersilia, J. (1991), 'Policy Relevance and the Future of Criminology: The American Society of Criminology 1990 Presidential Address', *Criminology*, 29/1: 1–15.

Pick, D. (1989), *The Faces of Degeneration*, Cambridge: Cambridge University Press.

Porter, R. (1987), *Mind-Forg'd Manacles: A History of Madness in England from the Restoration to the Regency*, Cambridge, Mass.: Harvard University Press.

Proal, L. (1898), *Political Crime*, London: Fisher Unwin.

Quinton, R.F. (1910), *Crime and Criminals 1876–1910*, London: Longmans, Green.

Radzinowicz, L. (1948–86), *A History of the English Criminal Law and its Administration, from 1750*, 5 vols (Vol. 5 with R. Hood), London: Stevens.

—— (1961), *In Search of Criminology*, London: Heinemann.

—— (1966), *Ideology and Crime*, London: Stevens.

—— (1988), *The Cambridge Institute of Criminology: Its Background and Scope*, London: HMSO.

—— (1999), *Adventures in Criminology*, London: Routledge.

Rafter, N.H. (1992), 'Criminal Anthropology in the United States', *Criminology*, 30/4: 525–45.

—— (1997), *Creating Born Criminals*, Urbana, University of Illinois Press.

Reiner, R. (1988), 'British Criminology and the State', in P. Rock (ed.), *A History of British Criminology*, Oxford: Oxford University Press.

Rock, P. (ed.) (1988a), *A History of British Criminology*, Oxford: Oxford University Press.

—— (1988b), 'The Present State of Criminology in Britain', in P. Rock (ed.), *A History of British Criminology*, Oxford: Oxford University Press.

Rose, N. (1988), 'Calculable Minds and Manageable Individuals', *The History of the Human Sciences*, 1/2: 179–200.

Rosen, F. (1999), 'Crime, Punishment and Liberty', *History of Political Thought*, XX, 1: 173–85.

Roshier, B. (1989), *Controlling Crime: The Classical Perspective in Criminology*, Chicago: Lyceum Books.

Ruggles-Brise, Sir E. (1924), *Prison Reform at Home and Abroad: A Short History of the International Movement since the London Conference, 1872*, London: Macmillan.

Salgado, G. (1972), *Cony-Catchers and Bawdy Baskets*, Harmondsworth: Penguin.

Sampson, R.H. and Laub, J.H. (1993), *Crime in the Making: Pathways and Turning Points Through Life*, Cambridge, Mass: Harvard University Press.

Savitz, L., Turner, S.H., and Dickman, T. (1977), 'The Origin of Scientific Criminology: Franz Gall as the First Criminologist', in R.F. Meier (ed.), *Theory in Criminology*, Beverly Hills: Sage.

Sennett, R. (1977), *The Fall of Public Man*, London: Faber.

Sharpe, J.A. (1985), '"Last Dying Speeches": Religion, Ideology and Public Execution in

Seventeenth Century England', *Past and Present*, 107: 144–67.

SKINNER, Q. (1969), 'Meaning and Understanding in the History of Ideas', *History and Theory*, 8/1: 3–53.

SMITH, M.H. (1922a), 'The Medical Examination of Delinquents', *Journal of Mental Science*, 68.

—— (1922b), *The Psychology of the Criminal*, London: Methuen.

SMITH, R. (1988), 'Does the History of Psychology have a Subject?', *The History of the Human Sciences*, 1/1: 147–78.

ST JOHN, A. (1912), 'Criminal Anthropology and Common Sense', *Sociological Review*, 5: 65–7.

SULLIVAN, W.C. (1906), *Alcoholism*, London: J. Nisbet.

—— (1924), *Crime and Insanity*, London: Edward Arnold.

SUTHERLAND, J.F. (1908), *Recidivism: Habitual Criminality and Habitual Petty Delinquency*, Edinburgh: William Green & Sons.

TAYLOR, I. (1981), *Law and Order: Arguments for Socialism*, London: Macmillan.

—— and TAYLOR, L. (eds) (1973), *Politics and Deviance: Papers from the National Deviancy Conference*, Harmondsworth: Penguin.

——, WALTON, P., and YOUNG, J. (1973), *The New Criminology*, London: Routledge and Kegan Paul.

—— et al. (eds) (1975), *Critical Criminology*, London: Routledge and Kegan Paul.

TAYLOR, R.S. (1968), 'Review of Jones' *Crime and the Penal System*, 3rd edn', *Howard Journal*, 12/3.

THOMSON, J.B. (1867), 'The Effects of the Present System of Prison Discipline on the Body and Mind', *Journal of Mental Science*, 12.

TUKE, H. (1889), 'Comments on Maudsley's "Remarks on Crime and Criminals"', *Journal of Mental Science*, 34: 311.

VALIER, C. (1998), 'True Crime Stories: Scientific Methods of Criminal Investigation, Criminology and Historiography', *British Journal of Criminology*, 38/1: 88–105.

VOLD, G.B. (1958), *Theoretical Criminology*, New York: Oxford University Press.

WETZELL, R.F. (2000), *Inventing the Criminal: A History of German Criminology, 1880–1945*, Chapel Hill: University of North Carolina Press.

WIENER, M. (1990), *Reconstructing the Criminal: Culture, Law and Policy in England, 1830–1914*, Cambridge: Cambridge University Press.

WILES, P. (1976), 'Introduction', in *The Sociology of Crime and Delinquency in Britain*, ii, Oxford: Martin Robertson.

WOOTTON, B. (1959), *Social Science and Social Pathology*, London: Allen and Unwin.

YOUNG, J. (1988), 'Radical Criminology in Britain: The Emergence of a Competing Paradigm', in P. Rock (ed.), *A History of British Criminology*, Oxford: Oxford University Press.

ZEMAN, T. (1981), 'Order, Crime and Punishment: The American Criminological Tradition', Ph.D. thesis, University of California at Santa Cruz.

2

SOCIOLOGICAL THEORIES
OF CRIME

Paul Rock

INTRODUCTION

The Oxford English Dictionary defines sociology as 'the study of social organization and institutions and of collective behaviour and interaction, including the individual's relationship to the group'. That is a catholic definition which encompasses almost every situation in which individuals or groups can influence one another. Sociological theories of crime are themselves correspondingly catholic: they extend, for example, from an examination of the smallest detail of street encounters between adolescents and the police to comparative analyses of very large movements in nations' aggregate rates of crime over centuries, and it is sometimes difficult to determine where their boundaries should be drawn.

There is no one, royal way to lay out the sociology of crime: some have classified its component theories by their supposed political leanings (liberal, conservative, and radical, for instance); some by their attentiveness or inattentiveness to gender; some by their alleged foundational assumptions about the character of the social world (classical, positivist, 'social constructionist', and the like); some by their chronology; some by the great men and women who propounded them; and others by schools of thought.

In an empirically-driven sub-discipline where the frontiers between theories and parent disciplines are frequently frail and deceptive, where formally different theories often contend with the same problems in very much the same way, as useful a procedure as any is to identify and describe a number of broad families of theories that share some big idea or ideas in common. The organization of this chapter will therefore follow intellectual themes more closely than chronologies or hierarchies of thought in an attempt to convey some small part of the present preoccupations and environment of sociological criminology.

I shall take it that those themes, in their turn, seem quite commonly to take the form of different combinations of ideas about the key issues of control, signification, and order. Crime, after all, is centrally bound up with the state's attempts to impose its will through law; with the meanings of those attempts to law-breaker, law-enforcer, observer, and victim; and with concomitant patterns of order and disorder. Criminologists differ about the weights and meanings that should be attached to those attributes: some, and control theorists in particular, would wish to be what Matza once called 'correctionalist', that is, to use knowledge about crime to suppress it. Others would look upon the exercise of control more critically. But they all feed off one another's ideas even if their practices and politics diverge. The attributes are visible features of the discipline's landscape, and I shall employ them to steer a more or less straight route through Durkheimian and Mertonian theories of *anomie*; control theories; rational choice theory; routine activities theory; the work of the 'Chicago School'; studies of the relations between control and space, including Newman's 'defensible space', and more recent ideas of risk and the marshalling of dangerous populations; radical criminology and left realism; functionalist criminology; and 'labelling theory' and cultural and subcultural analyses of crime as meaningful behaviour. I shall take it that such a grand tour should take in most of the major landmarks which criminologists would now consider central to their field.

What this chapter cannot do, of course, is provide much context, history, criticism and detail. That would be impossible in a short piece. I can hope at best to select only a few illustrative ideas that are of current or recent interest, as well as discussing some of the older arguments that informed them.

Further, like any scheme of classification, this chapter will inevitably face problems of anomaly and overlap, not only internally but also with other chapters in the *Handbook*. If the study of crime cannot be severed from the analysis of control, the state, or gender, there will always be such problems at the margins. But the chapter should furnish the larger contours of an introductory map of contemporary sociological theories of crime.

CRIME AND CONTROL

ANOMIE AND THE CONTRADICTIONS OF SOCIAL ORDER

I shall begin by describing *anomie* theory, one of the most enduring and, for a while, hard-researched of all the ideas of criminological theory, and one that still persists in disguised form.

At heart, many theories take it that crime is a consequence of defective social regulation. People are said to deviate because the disciplines and authority of society are so flawed that they offer few restraints or moral direction. The idea is a very old one, antedating the emergence of sociology itself, but its formal birth into theory is linked indissolubly with *anomie* and the French sociologist, Émile Durkheim.

Durkheim awarded two rather different meanings to *anomie*, or normlessness. In *The Division of Labour in Society*, published in 1893, and in *Suicide*, published in 1897, he asserted that French society was in uneasy transition from one state of solidarity or integration to another. A society without an elaborate division of labour rested on what he called (perhaps misleadingly) the mechanical solidarity of people who not only reacted much alike to problems, but who also saw that everyone about them reacted alike to those problems, thereby lending objectivity, scale, and solidity to moral response, and bringing a potential for massive disapproval and repression to bear on the deviant. Such a social order was conceived to lie in the simpler past of pre-industrial society. The future of industrial society would be distinguished by a state of organic solidarity, the solidarity appropriate to a complex division of labour. People would then be allocated by merit and effort to very diverse positions, and they would not only recognize the legitimacy of the manner in which rewards were distributed, but also acknowledge the indispensability of what each did in his or her work for the other and for the common good. Organic solidarity would thus have controls peculiar to itself: 'Sheerly economic regulation is not enough . . . there should be moral regulation, moral rules which specify the rights and obligations of individuals in a given occupation in relation to those in other occupations' (Giddens 1972: 11). People might no longer think wholly in unison, their moral response might not be substantial and unanimous, but they should be able to compose their differences peaceably by means of a system of restitutive justice that made amends for losses suffered.

Durkheim's distinction between the two forms of solidarity and their accompanying modes of control was anthropologically suspect, but it was in his analysis of the liminal state between them that criminologists were most interested. In that transition, where capitalism was thought to impose a 'forced division of labour', people acquiesced neither in the apportionment of rewards nor in the moral authority of the economy or state. They were obliged to work and act in a society that not only enjoyed little legitimacy but also exercised an incomplete control over their desires. In such a setting, it was held, 'man's nature [was to be] eternally dissatisfied, constantly to advance, without relief or rest, towards an indefinite goal' (Durkheim 1952: 256). Moral regulation was relatively deficient and people were correspondingly free to deviate. That is the first meaning Durkheim gave to *anomie*. His second will be visited below.

Given another, distinctively American, complexion by Robert Merton, *anomie* became a socially-fostered state of discontent and deregulation that generated crime and deviance as part of the routine functioning of a society which promised much to everyone but actually denied them equal access to its attainment (Merton 1938). People might have been motivated to achieve in the United States, but they confronted class, race, and other social differences that manifestly contradicted the myth of openness. It was not easy for a poor, inner-city adolescent to receive sponsorship for jobs, achieve academic success, or acquire capital. In a society where failure was interpreted as a sign of personal rather than social weakness, where failure tended to lead to guilt rather than to political anger, the pressure to succeed could be so powerful that it impelled people thus disadvantaged to bypass legitimate careers and take to illegitimate careers instead: 'the culture makes incompatible demands . . . In this setting, a cardinal American virtue—"ambition"—promotes a cardinal American vice—"deviant behavior"' (Merton 1957: 145).

Merton's *anomie* theory was to be modified progressively for some thirty years. In the work of Richard Cloward and Lloyd Ohlin, for example, his model was elaborated to include *illegitimate* routes to success. Their *Delinquency and Opportunity* (1960) described the consequences of young American men (in the 1950s and 1960s the criminological gaze was almost wholly on the doings of young American men) not only being pushed into crime by the difficulties of acquiring money and position in conventional ways, but also being pulled by the lure of lucrative and unconventional criminal careers. There would be those who were offered an unorthodox path in professional or organized crime, and they could become thieves, robbers, or racketeers. There would be those for whom no path was available, and they could become members of conflict gangs. And there were those who failed to attain admission to either a law-abiding or a law-violating group, the 'double failures', who would, it was conjectured, give up and become drug-users and hustlers. Each of those modes of adaptation was, in effect, a way of life, supported by a system of meanings or a subculture, and Cloward and Ohlin provided one of the bridges between the structural and the interpretive models of crime which will be discussed at the end of this chapter.

In the work of Albert Cohen, *anomie* was to be synthesized with the Freudian idea of 'reaction formation' in an effort to explain the manifestly expressive and 'non-rational' nature of much delinquency. The prospect of failure was depicted as bringing about a major psychological rejection of what had formerly been sought, so that the once-aspiring working-class adolescent emphatically turned his back on the middle-class world that spurned him and adopted a style of behaviour that was its systematic inversion. The practical and utilitarian in middle-class life was transformed into non-utilitarian delinquency; respectability became malicious negativism; and the deferment of gratification became short-run hedonism. Again, in the work of David Downes, conducted in London in the early 1960s to explore how far beyond America *anomie* theory might be generalized, the ambitions of English adolescents were found to be so modulated by what was then a stable and legitimated system of social stratification that working-class youth did not seem to undergo a taxing guilt or frustration in their failure to accomplish middle-class goals. They neither hankered after the middle-class world nor repudiated it. Rather, their response was 'dissociation'. Where they *did* experience a strong dissatisfaction, however, was in their thwarted attempts to enjoy leisure, and their delinquencies were principally hedonistic, focused on drinking, fighting, and malicious damage to property, rather than instrumentally turned towards the accumulation of wealth. And that theme—of the part played by the adolescent 'manufacture of excitement' and the courting of risk—was to be echoed repeatedly in the empirical and theoretical work of criminologists. Making 'something happen' in a world without significant cultural or material resources could easily bring about a drift into delinquency (see Matza 1964; Corrigan 1979; and Cusson 1983).

ANOMIE AND SOCIAL DISORGANIZATION

The second reading of *anomie* stemming from Durkheim touched on moral regulation that was not so much flawed as in a critical or chronic state of near collapse. People, he argued, are not endowed at birth with fixed appetites and ambitions. On the contrary, their purposes and aspirations are shaped by the generalized opinions and reactions of others, by a collective conscience, that can appear through social ritual and routine to be externally derived, solid, and objective. When society is disturbed by rapid change or major disorder, however, that semblance of solidity and objectivity can itself founder, and people may no longer find their ambitions subject to effective social discipline. It is hard to live outside the reassuring structures of social life, and the condition of *anomie* was experienced as a 'malady of infinite aspiration' that was accompanied by 'weariness', 'disillusionment', 'disturbance, agitation and discontent'. In extreme cases, Lukes observed, 'this condition would lead a man to commit suicide and homicide' (1967: 139).

Durkheim conceived such anomic deregulation to be a matter of crisis, innately unstable and short-lived. Disorganization could not be tolerated for very long before a society collapsed or order of a sort would be restored. Indeed, sociologists are generally ill-disposed towards the term, believing that it connotes a want of understanding and perception on the part of the observer (see Anderson 1976; Katz 1997; and Whyte 1942). They would hold that, even in Sierra Leone, Bosnia, or Rwanda at their most devastated, people were able to sustain a measure of organization within disorganization. Yet, on both the small and the large scale, there are clear examples of people living in conditions where informal control and cooperativeness are only vestigial; where formal control is either absent or erratic; where others are, or are seen to be, predatory and dangerous; where life is unpredictable; and where, as cause and consequence, there is little personal safety, much anxiety, and abundant crime. Take William Julius Wilson's description of life in the poorest areas of the American city: 'broken families, antisocial behavior, social networks that do not extend beyond the ghetto environment, and a lack of informal social control over the behavior and activities of children and adults in the neighborhood' (1996: xvi). On some housing estates in Paris, London (see Genn 1988), Nottingham (Davies 1998), and St Louis (Rainwater 1970), social groupings have been portrayed as so lacking in cohesion that they enjoyed no shared trust, neighbour preyed on neighbour, and joint defensive action was virtually impossible.

Rampant *anomie* has been well documented (Erikson 1994). Consider Davis's half-prophetic description of MacArthur Park, one of the poorest areas of Los Angeles, as 'feral' and dangerous, 'a free-fire zone where crack dealers and street gangs settle their scores with shotguns and Uzis' (1992a: 6). Consider, too, Turnbull's description of the condition of the Ik of northern Uganda, a tribe that had been moved to a mountainous area after their traditional hunting grounds had been designated a national park. They could no longer live, cooperate, and work as they had done before; familiar patterns of social organization had become obsolete; and the Ik were portrayed as having become beset by 'acrimony, envy and suspicion' (1973: 239), 'excessive individualism, coupled with solitude and boredom' (ibid.: 238), and the victimization of the weak: 'without killing, it is difficult to get closer to disposal than by taking the food out of an old person's mouth, and this was primarily an adjacent-generation occupation, as were tripping and pushing off balance' (ibid.: 252).

A number of criminologists and others are beginning to prophesy a new apocalypse in which *anomie* will flourish on such a massive scale that entire societies will dissolve into chaos and lawlessness. There are parts of the world whose political structures are so radically disordered that it becomes difficult to talk about legitimate governments operating effectively within secure national boundaries at all (see Bayart, Ellis, and Hibou 1999). So it was that Kaplan wrote graphically about the road-warrior culture of Somalia, the anarchic implosion of criminal violence in the Ivory Coast, and Sierra Leone, which he depicted as a lawless state that had lost control over its cities at night, whose national army was a 'rabble', and which was reverting to tribalism. The future for many, he luridly predicted, would be a 'rundown, crowded planet of skinhead Cossacks and *juju* warriors, influenced by the worst refuse of Western pop culture and ancient tribal hatreds, and battling over scraps of overused earth in guerilla conflicts . . .' (1994: 62–3). So, too, Martin van Creveld analysed what he called the ubiquitous growth of 'low-intensity conflict' waged by guerillas and terrorists who threatened the state's conventional monopoly of violence: 'Should present trends continue, then the kind of war that is based on the division between government, army, and people, seems to be on its way out. . . . A degree of violent activity that even as late as the 1960s would have been considered outrageous is now accepted as an inevitable hazard of modern life . . .' (1991: 192, 194). If Kaplan and van Creveld are even partially gifted with foresight (and much of their argument is quite stark), the trends they foretell will be of major consequence to criminology. Without a viable state legislature, laws, and law enforcement, without adequate state control over the distribution of violence, how can one write intelligently about a discrete realm of crime at all? Crime, after all, is contingent on a state's ability clearly to define, ratify, and execute the law. When the police of a state are massively and routinely corrupt (as they appear to be in Mexico); when, for example, the Colombian president's aeroplane was found to be carrying large quantities of cocaine in September 1996 (see the *New York Times*, 22 September 1996); when the President of Liberia has been accused of cannibalism (*The Times*, 2 November 1999); it is not difficult to acknowledge the disarray to which Stan Cohen pointed when he asked whether it was possible any longer to distinguish firmly between crime and politics. There has been, Cohen asserted, a widespread decline of the myth that the sovereign state can provide security, law, and order; a decline in the legitimacy of the state through corruption scandals; a growth of international crime and a rise of criminal states such as Chechnya; and, in Africa particularly, the emergence of barbarism, horror, and atrocity. In some settings, he remarked, 'lawlessness and crime have so destroyed the social fabric that the state itself has withdrawn' (1996: 9).

CONTROL THEORY

A second, large cluster of theories centres loosely around the contention that people seek to commit crime because it is profitable, useful, or enjoyable for them to do so, and that they will almost certainly break the law if they can. Even if that contention, with its covert imagery of feral man (and woman), is not strictly 'correct', control theorists would argue that it certainly points enquiry in a helpful direction. They are interested less in the fidelity of description than in its yield for policy intervention and prediction in concrete situations. Theirs is a theory of practical rather than of observational truths, and the practical is thought to suggest that more will be learned by exploring a few, uncomplicated factors that seem to *prevent* people from offending than by investigating all the complicated motives, meanings, and antecedents of their actions. Travis Hirschi put the issue baldly: 'The question "Why do they do it?" is simply not the question the theory is designed to answer. The question is, "Why don't we do it?"' (1969: 34). Such a doctrine is a recognizably close neighbour of *anomie* theories in its focus on the regulation of potentially unbridled appetites; and, indeed, it is occasionally very difficult to distinguish one set of ideas from the other.

Earlier variants of control theory, compiled in the 1960s and 1970s, proceeded by drafting lists of the constraints which could check the would-be offender, an offender who, it was assumed for analytic purposes, could be much like you, me, or anyone. Thus, arguing against subcultural theory, and grounded in a Freudian conception of human impulses that required taming, Hirschi claimed that 'delinquent acts result when the individual's bond to society is weak or broken' (1969: 16). Four chief elements were held to induce people to comply with rules: attachment, commitment, involvement, and belief. Attachment reflected a person's sensitivity to the opinions of others; commitment flowed from an investment of time, energy, and reputation in conformity; involvement stemmed from engrossment in conventional activity; and belief mirrored a person's conviction that he or she should obey legal rules. There is tautology and repetition in that formulation, but Hirschi nevertheless usefully directed the criminological mind towards answering his one big question, 'why *don't* we do it?'.

Later, with Gottfredson, Hirschi developed control theory by turning to self-control and impulsivity. Crime, they claim, flows from low self-control: it provides a direct and simple gratification of desires that is attractive to those who cannot or will not postpone pleasure. In the main, it requires little skill or planning. It can be intrinsically enjoyable because it involves the exercise of cunning, agility, deception, or power. It requires a lack of sympathy for the victim. But it does not provide medium- or long-term benefits equivalent to those that may flow from more orthodox careers. In short, it is, they say, likely to be committed by those who are 'impulsive, insensitive, physical . . . Risk-taking, short-sighted, and non-verbal . . . ' (1990: 90).

David Matza would not have called himself a control theorist, but in *Delinquency and Drift* he did effectively straddle theories of control, *anomie* and signification, and he did portray delinquents and delinquency in a manner that control theorists would find complementary. It was indeed he who later wrote an eloquent case for what he called an appreciative criminology (Matza 1969). Delinquents are not very different from us, he argued. Most of the time they are conventional enough in belief and conduct, and it is difficult to predict who will conform and who will not. But there are occasions when the grip of control loosens, adolescents fatalistically experience themselves as if they were object and effect rather than as subject and cause, as if they were no longer morally responsible for their actions, and they will then find themselves released to drift in and out of delinquency. What eases that process of disengagement are widely-circulating accounts or 'techniques of neutralization' (an idea that he had developed earlier with Gresham Sykes (Sykes and Matza 1957)) which enable people methodically to counter the guilt and offset the censure they might experience when offending. Matza claimed that delinquents could be fortified in their resolve by their ability to condemn their condemners (by asserting that police and judges were themselves corrupt and invalid critics, for instance); to deny injury (by asserting that no significant harm was done); to deny the victim (by asserting that the victim was of no consequence, or deserved what happened); or to appeal to higher loyalties (a noble motive could be cited for an ignoble deed).

Steven Box attempted to take analysis yet further by reconciling Hirschi's emphasis on social bonds with Matza's conception of drift. He compiled his own new alliterative list of variables that were held to affect control: secrecy (the delinquent's chances of concealment); skills (a mastery of knowledge and techniques needed for the deviant act); supply (access to appropriate equipment); social support (the endorsement offered by peers and others); and symbolic support (the endorsement offered by accounts available in the wider culture) (1971: 150). The greater the access to requisite skills, secrecy, supplies, and social and symbolic support, the greater would be the likelihood of offending.

Perhaps one of the most telling and economical contributions to control theory was supplied by Harriet Wilson. Examining 'socially deprived' families in Birmingham, England, she was to conclude that what most sharply differentiated families with delinquent children from those with none was simply what she called the exercise of 'chaperonage' (1980). Parents who acted as chaperons effectively prevented their children from offending: they were so convinced that the neighbourhood in which they lived was dangerous and contaminating that they sought to protect their children by keeping them indoors or under close supervision, escorting them to school, and prohibiting them from playing with others defined as undesirable.

Control theory has also been applied with effect to the problem of gender differences in offending. Apart from age, no other demographic feature at present so powerfully discriminates between offenders and non-offenders. At one time, however, scant criminological attention was paid to female crime because there was so very little of it. As Lemert once said, like Custer's men, criminologists rode to the sound of the guns, and there were few female guns indeed firing. By contrast, what made male offending appear so interesting was its sheer seriousness and scale.

However, when feminist criminologists and others began to ask Travis Hirschi's central question (without actually citing Hirschi himself), female offending became analytically transformed precisely *because* it was so rare. There was the new and intriguing riddle of the conforming woman, and the riddle was answered, in part, by reference to the effects of differentials in control. In particular, John Hagan and his colleagues put it that deviation as a form of fun and excitement was more commonly open to males than to females because daughters are more frequently subject to intense, continual, and diffuse family control in the private, domestic sphere. That control, by extension, not only removed girls from the purview of agents of formal social control, the criminal justice system, and the possibility of public identification as criminal; it also worked more effectively because it rested on the manipulation of emotional sanctions rather than the imposition of physical or custodial controls. Shaming strategies and the withdrawal of affection are seemingly more potent than fines, probation, or prison. It followed that the more firmly structured and hierarchical the family, the sharper the distinction drawn between male and female roles, the more women were confined to private space, the greater would be the disparity between rates of male and female offending (see Hagan *et al.* 1979, 1985, and 1988). Pat Carlen gave that analysis yet another twist by reflecting that female criminals were most likely to emerge when domestic family controls were removed altogether, when what she called the 'gender deal' was broken, young women left home or were taken into the care of the state, and were thereby exposed to controls characteristically experienced by men (1988). The answer to the 'crime problem', Frances Heidensohn once concluded, would have to lie in the feminization of control.

RATIONAL CHOICE THEORY

An increasingly important, but not indispensable, foundation for control theories is 'rational choice theory', a resuscitation of old utilitarian theories that preceded sociology and were once linked with Adam Smith, Jeremy Bentham, Cesare Beccaria, and James Mill. Rational choice theory has recently been re-introduced to criminology through the medium of a revived economics of crime, and it brings with it the convenient fiction of economic man, a fiction which has an immediate affinity with the criminal man (or woman) of control theory. Economic man, deemed to be continually looking about him for opportunities, making amoral and asocial choices to maximize his personal utility, may not be an empirically-grounded or well-authenticated entity, but, it is argued, he does help to simplify model-making, strip away what rational choice theorists conceive to be unessential theoretical and descriptive clutter, and aim directly at what are conceived to be practically useful policy questions (see Clarke and Cornish 1985). Economic man in his (or her) criminal guise does not have a past, complex motives, rich social life, or, indeed, a recognizable social identity (a 'disposition' is how Ron Clarke would put it (1992)). He or she does not need to have any of those attributes. Indeed, he or she may not be perfectly rational, muddling through, as we all do, on the basis of imperfect information and the presence of risks and uncertainty. He or she is very much like any one of us or, better still, like some Everyman who stands abstractly and plainly for all of us. He or she needs no such complexity, because what weighs in control theory is the piecemeal theoretical analysis of discrete instances of disembodied offending behaviour conducted by people making decisions about the issues of risk, effort, and reward (Clarke and Cornish 2000: 7) in the settings in which they may take place (see introduction to Clarke and Felson 1993).

In Ron Clarke's particularly influential formulation, the rate of crime was held to vary in response to three broad configurations of factors. The first grouping revolved around increasing the effort Everyman would have to expend in committing a crime, and that entailed what was called 'target hardening' (by defending objects and people by shields and other devices); 'access control' (and that involved making it difficult for predators to approach targets); deflecting offenders (by encouraging them, for example, to act in a legitimate rather than an illegitimate manner through the provision of graffiti boards, litter bins, and spittoons); and 'controlling facilitators' (through gun control or checks on the sales of spray cans, for instance). The second revolved around increasing the risks of offending through the screening of people (by means of border searches, for example); formal surveillance by police, security guards, and others; surveillance by employees such as bus conductors, concierges, and janitors; and 'natural surveillance' (aided by lowering or removing obstacles such as hedges and shrubs, installing closed circuit television cameras, lighting the interiors of stores, and enhanced street lighting). The final grouping was 'reducing the rewards' of crime, itself composed of 'target removal' (using electronic transactions to reduce the number of cash payments, and thus the accumulation of cash in single places, for instance); property identification; removal of inducements (by the rapid cleaning of graffiti or repair of vandalized property); and rule setting (through income tax returns, customs declarations, and the like) (taken from Clarke 1992: 13). A pursuit of those common-sense, sometimes indistinguishable, but nevertheless practical ideas allowed research officers at the Home Office to undertake a long chain of illustrative studies, discovering, for example, that compact, old school buildings on small sites were a third as likely to be burgled as large, sprawling, modern buildings with their many points of access and weak possibilities of surveillance (see Hope 1982); or that there was some twenty times as much malicious damage on the upper than on the lower decks of 'one man', double-decker buses whose drivers' powers of surveillance were confined to one level only (Mayhew *et al.* 1976: 26).

   None of those variables touched on conventional sociological questions about who offenders might be, what they think, and how they act (and for that rational choice theorists have been criticized (see Wright and Decker 1997)). They concentrated instead on the imagined impact of different forms of control on Everyman or Everywoman abroad in space, and from that it was but a short step to extend control theory to an analysis of the disciplines that are built into everyday social practices, on the one hand, and into the social uses of space, on the other.

ROUTINE ACTIVITIES THEORY

Ron Clarke, the situational control theorist, and Marcus Felson, the theorist of crime and routine activities, agreed that they shared ideas in common (see Clarke and Felson 1993) as well as ideas apart (thus situational control theory is microscopic, routine activities theory largely macroscopic in its application (Clarke and Cornish, undated 25)). Clarke and his colleagues had asked what prevented specific criminal incidents from occurring in specific situations. Felson asked how such incidents originate or are checked in the routine activities of mundane social life (1994). Just as Clarke and others had emphasized how, for explanatory purposes, it was convenient to assume that offenders were little different from anyone else, so Felson and his colleagues argued that most criminals are unremarkable, unskilled, petty, and nonviolent people much like us. Just as control theorists made use of a tacit version of original sin, so routine activities theory adopted a series of presuppositions about basic human frailty, the importance of temptation and provocation, and the part played by idleness ('We are all born weak, but . . . we are taught self-control', Felson claimed (1994: 20)).

   The routine activities criminologist would argue that the analysis of predatory crime does not necessarily require weighty causes. Neither does it demand that the theorist commit the 'like-causes-like' fallacy which covertly insists that a 'pathological' phenomenon such as crime must be explained by a pathological condition such as alienation, poverty, family dysfunction, or oppression. Crime was taken to be embedded in the very architecture of everyday life. More precisely, it was to be found in the convergence in space of what were called motivated offenders, suitable targets, and capable guardians (see Cohen and Felson 1979): being affected by such matters as the weight, value, incidence, and distribution of stealable goods (the growth in the quantity of portable, high-cost goods such as video-recorders will encourage more theft, for instance); the impact of motor cars (they aid rapid flight, permit the discreet transportation of objects, and give rise to a geographical dispersal of the population which dilutes surveillance); habits of leisure (adolescents now have larger swathes of empty time than did their predecessors, time in which they can get up to mischief); habits of work (when all members of a household are in employment, there will be no capable guardians to protect a home); habits of residence (single people are less effective guardians of property than are larger households); the growth of technology (telephones, for instance, amplify the public's ability to report crime); and so on. It is an uncomplicated enough theory but again, like its near neighbour, control theory, it does ask empirically productive questions.

CRIME, CONTROL, AND SPACE

THE CHICAGO SCHOOL

Routine activities theory and control theory both talk about convergence in space, and space has always been analytically to the fore in criminology. Indeed, one of the earliest and most productive of the research traditions laid down in criminology was the social ecology and urban mapping practised by the sociology department of the University of Chicago in the 1920s and beyond (see Park 1925; Thrasher 1927; and Landesco 1968).

As cities grow, it was held, so there would be a progressive and largely spontaneous differentiation of space, population, and function that concentrated different groupings in different areas. The main organizing structure was the zone, and the Chicago sociologists discerned five principal concentric zones shaping the city: the central business district at the very core; the 'zone in transition' about that centre; an area of stable working-class housing; middle-class housing; and the outer suburbia.

The zone in transition was marked by the greatest volatility of its residents. It was an area of comparatively cheap rents, weak social control, internal social differentiation, and rapid physical change. It was to the zone in transition that new immigrant groupings most frequently came, and it was there that they settled into what were called 'natural areas', small communal enclaves that were relatively homogeneous in composition and culture. Chicago sociologists plotted the incidence of social problems on to census maps of the city, and it was the zone in transition that was found repeatedly to house the largest proportions of the poor, the illegitimate, the illiterate, the mentally ill (see Faris and Dunham 1939), juvenile delinquents (Shaw and McKay

1942), and prostitutes (Reckless 1933). The zone in transition was virtually co-extensive with what was then described as social pathology. Not only were formal social controls held to be at their weakest there (the zone in transition was, as it were, socially dislocated from the formal institutions and main body of American society (see Whyte 1942)); but informal social controls were eroded by moral and social diversity, rapid population movement, and a lack of strong and pervasive local institutions: 'contacts are extended, heterogeneous groups mingle, neighborhoods disappear, and people, deprived of local and family ties, are forced to live under . . . loose, transient and impersonal relations' (Wirth 1964: 236).

A number of the early Chicago sociologists united social ecology, the study of the patterns formed by groups living together in the same space, with the fieldwork methods of social anthropology, to explore the traditions, customs, and practices of the residents of natural areas. They found that, while there may well have been a measure of social and moral dislocation between the zone in transition and the wider society, as well as within the zone in transition itself, those natural areas could also manifest a remarkable coherence and persistence of culture and behaviour that were reproduced from generation to generation and from immigrant group to immigrant group within the same terrain over time. Delinquency was, in effect, not disorganized at all, but a stable attribute of social life, an example of continuity in change: 'to a very great extent . . . traditions of delinquency are preserved and transmitted through the medium of social contact with the unsupervised play group and the more highly organized delinquent and criminal gangs' (Shaw and McKay 1971: 260). Cultural transmission was to be the focus of the work pursued by a small group of second generation Chicago sociologists. Under the name of 'differential association', it was studied as a normal process of learning motives, skills, and meanings in the company of others who bore criminal traditions (see Sutherland and Cressey 1955).

That urban research was to prepare a diverse legacy for criminology: the spatial analysis of crime; the study of subcultures (which I shall touch on below); the epidemiology of crime; crime as an interpretive practice (which I shall also touch on); and much else. Let me turn first to some examples of spatial analysis.

CONTROL AND SPACE: BEYOND THE CHICAGO SCHOOL

The Chicago sociologists' preoccupation with the cultural and symbolic correlates of spatial congregations of people was to be steadily elaborated by criminologists. For instance, Wiles, Bottoms, and their colleagues, originally working at the University of Sheffield, added two important observations. They argued first that, in a then more tightly regulated Britain, social segregation did not emerge, as it were, organically with unplanned city growth, but with the intended and unintended consequences of policy decisions taken by local government departments responsible for housing a large proportion of the population in municipal accommodation. Housing allocation was an indirect reflection of moral judgements about tenants that resulted, or were assumed to result, in the concentration of criminal populations (see Bottoms *et al.* 1989). Further, and partly in accord with that argument, the reputations of natural areas themselves became a criminological issue: how was it that the moral meanings attached to space by residents and outsiders affected people's reputations, choices, and action? One's very address could become a constraining moral fact that affected not only how one would be treated by others in and about the criminal justice system (see Damer 1974), but also how one would come to rate oneself as a potential deviant or conformist (see Gill 1977).

Secondly, Bottoms and his colleagues argued, while the Chicago sociologists may have examined the geographical distribution of offenders, it was instructive also to scrutinize how offending itself could be plotted, because the two measures need not correspond (Baldwin and Bottoms 1976). Offending has its maps. Indeed, it appears to be densely concentrated, clustered around offenders' homes, areas of work and recreation, and the pathways in between (Brantingham and Brantingham 1981–2). So it was that, pursuing routine activities theory, Sherman and his colleagues surveyed all calls made to the police in Minneapolis in one year; and they discovered that a few 'hot spots' had exceptional densities of crime: only 3 per cent of all places produced 50 per cent of the calls; all robberies took place in only 2.2 per cent of places, all rapes in 1.2 per cent of places, and all car thefts in 2.7 per cent of places (Sherman *et al.* 1989; see also Roncek and Maier 1991).

DEFENSIBLE SPACE

If offending has its maps, so does social control; and criminologists and others have become ever more interested in the fashion in which space, conduct, and control intersect. One forerunner was Jane Jacobs, who speculated about the relations between city landscapes and informal controls, arguing, for example, that dense, busy thoroughfares have many more 'eyes on the street' and opportunities for witness reporting and bystander intervention, than sterile pedestrian zones or streets without stores and other lures (Jacobs 1965).

The idea of 'defensible space', in particular, has been borrowed from anthropology and architecture, coupled with the concept of surveillance, and put to work in analysing formal and informal responses to different kinds of terrain. 'Defensible space' itself leans on the psychological notion of 'territoriality', the sense of attachment and symbolic investment that people can acquire in space. Territoriality is held by some to be a human universal, an imperative that leads people to wish to guard what is their own. Those who have a stake in a physical area, it is argued, will care for it, police it, and report strangers and others who have no apparent good purpose to be there.

What is quite critical is how space is marked out and bounded. The prime author of the idea of defensible space, Oscar Newman (1972), claimed that, other things being equal, what induces territorial sentiments is a clear demarcation between private and public areas, even if the demarcations are only token. The private will be protected in ways that the public is not, and the fault of many domestic and institutional buildings is that separations and segregations are not clearly enough inscribed in design. Alice Coleman and others took it that improvements to the physical structures of built space could then achieve a significant impact on crime: above all, she insisted on restricting access to sites; reducing the interconnections between buildings; and emphasizing the distinction between public and private space and minimizing what

Oscar Newman called 'confused space', the space that was neither one nor the other (Coleman 1985, 1986). She has been roundly faulted, both methodologically and analytically, for her neglect of dimensions other than the physical, but she and New-man have succeeded in introducing an analytic focus on the interrelations between space and informal control that was largely absent before. Only rarely have criminologists such as Shapland and Vagg enquired into the informal practices of people as they observe, interpret, and respond to the ambiguous, the deviant, and the non-deviant in the spaces around them (1988). It is Shapland and Vagg's contention that there is a continuous, active, and often informed process of surveillance transacted by people on the ground; a process which is so discreet that it has escaped much formal notice, and which meshes only haphazardly with the work of the police.

CRIME, POWER, AND SPACE

Surveillance has not always been construed as neutral or benign, and there are current debates about what its newest forms might portend. Even its sponsors in government departments and criminal justice agencies have spoken informally about their anxiety that people are being encouraged to become unduly fearful of crime and to retreat into private fastnesses. It began to be argued, especially by those who followed Michel Foucault, that a 'punitive city' was in the making, that, in Stan Cohen's words, there was 'a deeper penetration of social control into the social body' (1979: 356).

Some came to claim not only that there had been a move progressively to differentiate and elaborate the distribution of controls in space, but also that there had been a proliferating surveillance of dangerous areas, often conducted obliquely and with an increasingly advanced technology. Michel Foucault's (1977) dramatic simile of Jeremy Bentham's model prison, the Panopticon, was to be put to massive use in criminology. Just as the Panopticon, or inspection house, was supposed to have permitted the unobserved observation of many inmates around the bright, illuminated rim of a circular prison by the few guards in its obscured centre, just as the uncertainty of unobserved observation worked to make the controlled control themselves, so, Foucault and those who followed him wished to argue, modern society is coming to exemplify the perfection of the automatic exercise of power through generalized surveillance. The carceral society was a machine in which everyone was supposed to be caught (even, it seems, the police, who may survey one another as well as the wider population (see *The Times*, 4 November 1999)): it relied on diffuse control through unseen monitoring and the individualization and 'interiorization' of control (Gordon 1972). Public space, it was said, was becoming exposed to ever more perfunctory, distant, and technologically-driven policing by formal state agencies; while control in private and semi-private space (the space of the shopping malls, university campus, and theme park) was itself becoming more dense, privatized, and widespread, placed in the private hands of security guards and store detectives, and reliant on a new electronic surveillance (Davis 1992b: 233).

A paradigmatic case study has been supplied by Shearing and Stenning's ethnography of Disney World as a 'private, quasi-feudal domain of control' (Shearing and Stenning 1985: 347) that was comprehensively, discreetly, and adeptly controlled by employees, extensive surveillance, the encouragement of self-discipline, and the very physical configuration of space. The nature of crime and deviance itself can undergo change in such a transformed environment: they are no longer always and everywhere so markedly affronts to deep values but are, instead, very often breaches of impersonal, morally-neutral, technical controls (see Lianos and Douglas 2000: 270–71).

What also underlies much of that vision is a new, complementary stress on the sociology of risk, a focus linked importantly with the work of Ulrich Beck (although he did not himself write about crime (1992)). It has been argued that people and groups are becoming significantly stratified by their exposure to risk and their power to neutralize harm. The rich can afford private protection, the poor cannot, and a new ecology emerges (Simon 1987). Phrased only slightly differently, and merged with the newly-burgeoning ideas about the pervasiveness of surveillance by machine and person (Gordon 1986–7 and Lyon 1994), those theories of risk suggest that controls are being applied by state and private organizations not on the basis of some moralistic conception of individual wrong-doing, but on a foundation of the identification, classification, and management of groups categorized by their perceived dangerousness (Feeley and Simon 1992; Simon and Feeley 1995). Groups are becoming ever more rigidly segregated in space: some (members of the new dangerous classes or under-class) being confined to prison, semi-freedom under surveillance, or parole in the community; others (the more affluent) retreating into their locked and gated communities, secure zones, and private spaces. There are new bifurcations of city space into a relatively uncontrolled 'badlands' occupied by the poor and highly-controlled 'security bubbles' inhabited by the rich. Geographical and social exclusion thereby conspire to corral together populations of the unprotected, victimized and victimizing—the mentally disordered, the young, and the homeless—reinforcing both their vulnerability and their propensities to offend (Carlen 1996; Hagan and McCarthy 1998).

RADICAL CRIMINOLOGY

So far, control has been treated without much direct allusion to the power, politics, and inequalities that are its bedfellows. There was to be a relatively short-lived but active challenge to such quiescence from the radical, new, or critical criminologies of the late 1960s and 1970s, criminologies that claimed their mandate in Marxism (Taylor, Walton, and Young 1973), anarchism (Kittrie 1971; Cohen 1985), or American populism (Quinney 1970), and whose ambitions pointed to political activism or praxis (Mathiesen 1972).

Crime control was said to be an oppressive and mystifying process that worked through legislation, law-enforcement, and ideological stereotyping to preserve unequal class relations (Chambliss 1976; Box 1983). The radical political economy of crime sought chiefly to expose the hegemonic ideologies that masked the 'real' nature of crime and repression in capitalist society. Most mundane crime, it was argued, was

actually less politically or socially consequential than other social evils such as alienation, exploitation, or racism (Scraton 1987). Much proletarian offending could be
redefined as a form of redistributive class justice, or as a sign of the possessive individualism which resided in the core values of capitalist society. Criminal justice itself
was engineered to create visible crowds of working-class and black scapegoats who
could attract the public gaze away from the more serious delicts of the rich and the
more serious ills of a capitalism that was usually said to be in terminal crisis. If the
working class reacted in hostile fashion to the crime in their midst then they were, in
effect, little more than the victims of a false consciousness which turned proletarian
against proletarian, black against black, inflated the importance of petty problems,
and concealed the true nature of bourgeois society. So construed, signification, the act
of giving meaning, was either manipulative or misconceived, a matter of giving and
receiving incorrect and deformed interpretations of reality. Indeed, it was in the very
nature of subordination in a capitalist society that most people must be politically
unenlightened about crime, control, and much else, and the task of the radical
criminologist was to expose, denounce, and demystify.

It was concluded variously that crime was not a problem which the poor and their
allies should actually address (there were more important matters for socialists to
think about: Hirst 1975); that the crime which *should* be analysed was the
wrong-doing of the powerful (the wrong crimes and criminals were being observed:
Chapman 1967; Reiman 1990); or that crime and its problems would shrivel into
insignificance as a criminogenic capitalism gave way to the tolerant diversity of socialism (Taylor, Walton, and Young 1973). The crime and criminals that chiefly warranted
attention were those exceptional examples of law-breaking that seemed to represent
an incipient revolt against the state, and they demanded cultivation as subjects of
study, understanding, and possible politicization. Black prisoners, in particular, were
sometimes depicted, and depicted themselves, as prisoners of class or race wars
(Cleaver 1969). Prisons were the point of greatest state repression, and prison riots a
possible spearhead of revolution.

In its early guise, radical criminology withered somewhat under a quadruple-
barrelled assault. In some places, and in America especially (where it had never been
firmly implanted), it ran foul of university politics, and some criminology departments, such as that of the University of California at Berkeley, were actually closed
down. More often, radical criminology did not lend itself to the government-funded,
policy-driven, 'soft money', empiricist research that came to dominate schools of
criminology in North America in the 1970s and 1980s.

Second was the effect of the publication of mass victim surveys in the 1970s and
1980s (Hough and Mayhew 1983) which disclosed both the extent of working-class
victimization and the manner in which it revolved around intra-class, rather than
inter-class, criminality. It was evident that crime *was* a manifest problem for the poor,
adding immeasurably to their burdens, and difficult to dismiss as an ideological
distraction (David Downes called it a regressive tax on the poor). Two prominent
radical criminologists came frankly to concede that they had believed that 'property
offences [were] directed solely against the bourgeoisie and that violence against the
person [was] carried out by amateur Robin Hoods in the course of their righteous

attempts to redistribute wealth. All of this [was], alas, untrue' (Lea and Young 1984: 262).

Third was the critique launched from within the left by a new generation of feminist scholars, who asserted that the victimization of women was no slight affair or ideological diversion, and that rape, sexual assault, child abuse, and domestic violence should be taken very seriously indeed (Smart 1977). Not only had the female criminal been neglected, they said, but so had the female victim, and it would not do to wait until the revolution for matters to be put right. Once more, a number of radical criminologists gave ground. There had been, Jones, Maclean, and Young observed, 'a general tendency in radical thought to idealize their historical subject (in this case the working class) and to play down intra-group conflict, blemishes and social disorganization. But the power of the feminist case resulted in a sort of cognitive schizophrenia amongst radicals . . . ' (Jones *et al.* 1986: 3). The revitalized criminology of women is the subject of Chapter 4 in this handbook.

Fourthly, there was a critique launched belatedly from non-feminist criminologists who resisted the imperious claims of radical criminology to be *the* lone fully social theory of crime (Downes and Rock 1979; Inciardi 1980). Marxist and radical theories of crime, it was argued, lacked a comparative emphasis: they neglected crime in 'non-capitalist' and 'pre-capitalist' societies and crime in 'socialist' societies. There was a naivety about the expectation that crime would wither away as the state itself disappeared after the revolution. There was an irresponsibility about radical arguments that 'reformism' would only strengthen the grip of the capitalist system.

'Left realism' was to be the outcome, and it was represented by Jock Young, one of its parents, as a novel fusion of analyses of crime in the vein of *anomie* theory and symbolic interactionist analyses of the reactions which crime evokes (Young 1997: 484). It was 'realist' because, refusing to accept the so-called 'left idealists'' dismissal of crime as an ideological trick, it acknowledged the practical force of crime in society and its especially heavy impact on the poor, minority ethnic people and women. It was 'left' because it focused descriptively and politically on the structural inequalities of class, race, and gender. Its project was to examine patterns of crime and control as they emerged out of what Young came to call the 'square of crime', a field of forces dominated by the state, the victim, the offender, and the public.

Left realism was to follow the earlier radical criminologist's injunction to act, but action was now as much (if not more) in the service of more effective and practical policing and crime reduction strategies as in the cause of revolution. Left realists joined the formerly disparaged 'administrative criminologists' working in and for the state to work on situationally-based projects to prevent crime and the fear of crime. They designed new and confusing configurations of streets to make it more difficult for 'kerb-crawlers' to cruise in search of prostitutes. They explored the impact of improved street lighting on the fear of crime. They assisted in the rehabilitation of delapidated housing estates. Were it not for their theoretical preambles, it was at times difficult to distinguish between the programmes of the Home Office Research Unit or the Ministry of the Solicitor General of Canada, on the one hand, and of left realism, on the other.

If left realism was radical criminology's *praxis*, its more scholarly current continued to evolve, and it evolved in diverse directions. A number of criminologists began to turn away from analyses of causation towards studies of current (Cohen 1985; Simon 1993) and historical forms of social control (see Scull 1979), originally under the influence of E.P. Thompson and Eric Hobsbawm and latterly under that of Michel Foucault. Others responded to the wider theories that began to dominate sociology proper in the 1980s and 1990s, incorporating them to write about crime, post-modernism (or late modernity), and globalization, and producing what was, in effect, the 'fully social theory' promised by the new criminologists back in 1973. Above all, that promise was fulfilled by books published in 1999 by two of the original troika of new criminologists: Ian Taylor's *Crime in Context* and Jock Young's *The Exclusive Society*.

  Crime in Context catalogues a series of crises flowing from transitions in the political and economic structures of society, and the manner in which they bear down upon poverty, class, gender, race, and the family to affect the national and trans-national environments of crime and control. *The Exclusive Society* is subtitled 'Social Exclusion, Crime and Difference in Late Modernity', and its focus is more narrow but nevertheless effective, concentrating upon the social and political consequences of vast increases in crime in the West. Crime is held by Young to be no longer regarded as abnormal, the property of a pathological few who can be restored therapeutically to the security of a moral community at one with itself, but *normal*, the actions of a significant, obdurate minority of Others who are impatiently excluded and demonized in a world newly insecure, fractured, and preoccupied with problems of risk and danger.

FUNCTIONALIST CRIMINOLOGY

Another, apparently dissimilar but substantially complementary, theory presented deviance and control as forces that worked discreetly to maintain social order. Functionalism was a theory of social systems or wholes, developed at the beginning of the twentieth century within a social anthropology grown tired of speculative accounts of the origins and evolution of societies which lacked the written history to support them, and dedicated to what was seen to be the scientific pursuit of intellectual problems. It was argued that the business of a social science necessitated moving enquiry beyond the reach of common sense or lay knowledge to an examination of the unintended, objective consequences of action that were visible only to the trained eye.

  There were three clear implications. First, what ordinary people thought they were doing could be very different from what they actually achieved. The functionalist was preoccupied only with objective results, and people's own accounts of action held little interest. Secondly, the functionalist looked at the impact made by institution upon institution, structure upon structure, in societies that were remarkable for their capacity to persist over time. Thirdly, those consequences, viewed as a totality, consti-tuted a system whose parts were thought not only to affect one another and the whole, but which also affected them in return. To be sure, some institutions were relatively detached, but functionalists would have argued that the alternative proposition—that social phenomena lack all influence upon one another, that there was no functional reciprocity between them—was conceptually insupportable. Systemic interrelations were an analytic *a priori*, a matter of self-evidence so compelling that Kingsley Davis could argue that 'we are all functionalists now' (Davis 1959).

There have been very few dedicated functionalist criminologists. Functionalists tend to deal with the properties of whole systems rather than with empirical fragments. But crime and deviance did supply a particularly intriguing laboratory for thought-experiments about social order. It was easy enough to contend that religion or education shaped social cohesion, but how much harder it would be to show that *crime* succeeded in doing so. After all, 'everyone knew' that crime undermined social structures. It followed that functionalists occasionally found it tempting to try to confound that knowledge by showing that, to the contrary, the seemingly recalcitrant case of crime could be shown scientifically to contribute to the working of the social system. From time to time, therefore, they wrote about crime to demonstrate the potency of their theory. Only one functionalist, its grand master, Talcott Parsons, ever made the obvious, and therefore unsatisfying, point that crime could be what was called 'dysfunctional' or injurious to the social system as it was then constituted (Parsons 1951). Everyone else asserted that crime actually worked mysteriously to support it.

The outcome was a somewhat miscellaneous collection of papers documenting the multiple functions of deviance: Kingsley Davis showed that prostitution shored up monogamy by providing an unemotional, impersonal, and unthreatening release for the sexual energy of the promiscuous married male (Davis 1937) (Mary McIntosh once wondered what the promiscuous married female was supposed to do about her sexual energy); Ned Polsky made much the same claim for pornography (Polsky 1967); Daniel Bell showed that racketeering provided 'queer ladders of success' and political and social stability in the New York dockside (1960); Émile Durkheim (1964) and George Herbert Mead (1918) contended that the formal rituals of trial and punishment enhanced social solidarity and consolidated moral boundaries; and, more complexly, Mary Douglas (1966), Kai Erikson (1966), Robert Scott (1972), and others argued that deviance offered social systems a dialectical tool for the clarification and management of threats, ambiguities, and anomalies in classification systems. The list could be extended, but all the arguments tended to one end: what appeared, on the surface, to undermine social order accomplished the very reverse. A sociological counterpart of the invisible hand transmuted deviance into a force for cohesion.

Functionalism was to be discarded by many criminologists in time: it smacked too much of teleology (the doctrine that effects can work retrospectively to act as the causes of events); it defied rigorous empirical investigation (see Cotterrell 1999: 75); and, for some liberal and radical criminologists, it represented a form of Panglossian conservatism that championed the *status quo*. But its ghost lingers on. Any who would argue that, contrary to appearances, crime and deviance buttress social order; any who argue for the study of seamless systems; any who argue that the sociologist should mistrust people's own accounts of their actions; any who insist that social science is the study of unintended consequences; all these must share something of the functionalist's standpoint. *Anomie* theories that represented crime as the system-stabilizing, unintended consequence of strains in the social order are one example (see Merton 1995): deviance in that guise becomes the patterned adjustments that defuse an otherwise disruptive conflict and reconcile people to disadvantage (although, as I have argued, the theories can also envisage conditions in which crime becomes 'system-threatening'). Some versions of radical criminology provide another example. More than one criminologist has argued that crime, deviance, and control were necessary for the survival of capitalism (Stinchcombe 1968). For instance, although they did not talk explicitly of '*function*', the neo-Marxists, Hall (1978), Pearce (1976), and Reiman (1990), *were* recognizably functionalist in their treatment of the criminal justice system's production of visible and scapegoated roles for the proletarian criminal, roles that attracted public anxiety and outrage, deflected anger away from the state, and thereby emasculated political opposition. Consider, for example, Ferrell and Sanders's observation that 'the simplistic criminogenic models at the core of . . . constructed moral panics . . . deflect attention from larger and more complex political problems like economic and ethnic inequality, and the alienation of young people and creative workers from confining institutions' (1995: 10).

SIGNIFICATION

LABELLING THEORY

Perhaps the only other outstanding big idea is signification, the interpretive practices that order social life. There has been an enduring strain of analysis, linked most particularly to symbolic interactionism and phenomenology, which insists that people do not, and cannot, respond immediately, uncritically, and passively to the world 'as it is'. Rather they respond to their *ideas* of that world, and the business of sociology is to capture, understand, and reproduce those ideas; examine their interaction with one another; and analyse the processes and structures that generated them. Sociology becomes the study of people and practices as symbolic and symbolizing processes.

   Central to that idea is reflectivity, the capacity of consciousness to translate itself into its own object. People are able to think about themselves, define themselves in various ways, toy with different identities, and project themselves imaginatively into any manner of contrived situation. They can view themselves vicariously by inferring the reactions of 'significant others', and, in so 'taking the role of the other', move symbolically to a distance outside themselves to inspect how they might appear. Elaborating action through 'significant gestures', the symbolic projection of acts and identities, they can anticipate the likely responses of others, and tailor their own prospective acts to accommodate them (Mead 1934). In all this, social worlds are compacted symbolically into the phrasing of action, and the medium that makes that possible is language.

Language is held to objectify, stabilize, and extend meaning. Used conversationally in the anticipation of an act, it permits people to be both their own subject and object, speaker and thing spoken about, 'I' and 'me', opening up the mind to reflective action. Conferring names, it enables people to impart moral and social meanings to their own and others' motives (Mills 1940; Scott and Lyman 1970), intentions, and identities. It will matter a great deal if someone is defined as eccentric, erratic, or mad; a drinker, a drunk, or an alcoholic; a lovelorn admirer or a stalker. Consequences will flow from naming, consequences that affect not only how one regards oneself and one's position in the world, but also how one may be treated by others. Naming creates a self.

Transposed to the study of crime and deviance, symbolic interactionism and phenomenology gave prominence to the processes by which deviant acts and identities are assembled, interpreted, judged, and controlled (Katz 1988). A core pair of articles was Howard Becker's 'Becoming a Marihuana User' and 'Marihuana Use and Social Control' (1963), both of which described the patterned sequence of steps that could shape the experience, moral character, and fate of one who began to smoke marihuana. Becoming a marihuana user was a tentative process, developing stage by stage, which required the user satisfactorily to learn, master, and interpret techniques, neutralize forbidding moral images of use and users, and succeed in disguising signs of use in the presence of those who might disapprove. It became paradigmatic.

Deviance itself was to become more generally likened to a moral career consisting of interlocking phases, each of which fed into the next; each of which presented different existential problems and opportunities; each of which was populated by different constellations of significant others; and each of which could distinctively mould the self of the deviant. However, the process was also assumed to be contingent. Not every phase was inevitable or irreversible, and deviants could often elect to change direction. Luckenbill and Best provide a graphic description:

Riding escalators between floors may be an effective metaphor for respectable organizational careers, but it fails to capture the character of deviant careers. A more appropriate image is a walk in the woods. Here, some people take the pathways marked by their predecessors, while others strike out on their own. Some walk slowly, exploring before moving on, but others run, caught up in the action. Some have a destination in mind and proceed purposively; others view the trip and enjoy it for its own sake. Even those intent on reaching a destination may stray from the path; they may try to shortcut or they may lose sight of familiar landmarks, get lost, and find it necessary to backtrack [1981: 201].

What punctuates such a career is acts of naming, the deployment of language to confer and fix the meanings of behaviour, and symbolic interactionism and phenomenology became known within criminology as 'labelling theory'. One of the most frequently cited of all passages in sociological criminology was Becker's dictum that 'deviance is not a quality of the act the person commits, but rather a consequence of the application by others of rules and sanctions to an "offender". The deviant is one to whom that label has successfully been applied; deviant behavior is behavior that people so label' (1963: 9).

Labelling itself is contingent. Many deviant acts are not witnessed and most are not reported. People may well be able to resist or modify deviant designations when attempts *are* made to apply them: after all, we are continually bombarded by attempts to label us and few succeed. But there are special occasions when the ability of the self to resist definition is circumscribed; and most fateful of all may be an encounter with agents of the criminal justice system, because they work with the power and authority of the state. In such meetings, criminals and deviants are obliged to confront not only their own and others' possibly defensive, fleeting, and insubstantial reactions to what they have done, their 'primary deviation', but also contend publicly with the formal reactions of others, and their deviation can then become a response to responses, 'secondary deviation': 'When a person begins to employ his deviant behavior or a role based upon it as a means of defense, attack, or adjustment to the overt and covert problems created by the consequent societal reaction to him, his deviation is secondary' (Lemert 1951: 76).

What is significant about secondary deviation is that it will be a symbolic synthesis of more than just the meanings and activities of primary deviation. It will also incorporate the myths, professional knowledge, stereotypes, and working assumptions of lay people, police officers, judges, medical practitioners, prison officers, prisoners, policy-makers, and politicians. Drug-users (see Schur 1963), mental patients (Goffman 1968; Scheff 1966), homosexuals (Hooker 1963), and others may be obliged to organize their significant gestures and character around the public symbols of their behaviour. Who they are and what they do may then be explained as much by the symbolic incorporation of a public response as by any set of original conditions. Control will be inscribed into the very fabric of a self.

What is also significant is that secondary deviation entails confrontations with new obstacles that foreclose future choice. Thus, Gary Marx has listed a number of the ironic consequences that can flow from forms of covert social control such as under-cover policing and the work of *agents provocateurs*: they include generating a market for illegal goods; the provision of motives and meanings for illegal action; entrapping people in offences they might not otherwise have committed; the supply of false or misleading records; retaliatory action against informers, and the like (Marx 1988: 126–7). Once publicly identified as a deviant, moreover, it becomes difficult for a person to slip back into the conventional world, and measures are being taken with increasing frequency to enlarge the visibility of the rule-breaker. In the United States, for instance, 'Megan's Law' makes it mandatory in certain jurisdictions for the names of sex offenders to be publicly advertised, possibly reducing risk but certainly freezing the criminal as a secondary deviant. An answering response to the dangerously amplified problems of the outlawed deviant is the increasing adoption by states of strategies of restorative justice, based largely on the work of Braithwaite (1989), which attempt to unite the informal control of shaming by significant others with rituals of reintegration that work against the alienating consequences of secondary deviation.

Borrowing its ideas from Durkheim and labelling theory and its procedures from a number of forms of dispute resolution, but from Maori practice in particular, Braithwaite took it that shaming is at its most effective when it is practised by those whose opinions matter to the deviant—his or her 'significant others'; and that it would work only to exclude and estrange the deviant unless it was accompanied by rituals of reparation and restoration, effected, perhaps, by the tendering and acceptance of a public apology. Reintegrative shaming is currently one of the 'big ideas' underpinning criminal justice policy across the Western world, but also in South Africa and elsewhere, where it is seen to be a return to the practices of aboriginal justice.

CULTURE AND SUBCULTURE

Meanings and motives are not established and confirmed by the self in isolation. They are a social accomplishment, and criminology has paid sustained attention to signification as a collaborative, subcultural process. Subcultures themselves are taken to be exaggerations, accentuations, or editings of cultural themes prevalent in the wider society. Any social group which has permanence, closure, and common pursuits is likely to engender, inherit, or modify a subculture; but the criminologist's particular interest is in those subcultures that condone, promote, or otherwise make possible the commission of delinquent acts. A subculture was not conceived to be utterly distinct from the beliefs held by people at large. Neither was it necessarily oppositional. It was a *sub*culture, not a discrete culture or a counterculture, and the analytic stress has tended to be on dependency rather than conflict or symbolic automony.

The materials for subcultural theory are to be found across the broad range of criminology, and they could be combined in various proportions. *Anomie* theory supplied the supposition that social inequalities generate problems that may have delinquent solutions, and that those solutions, in their turn, could be shared and transmitted by people thrown together by their common disadvantage. Albert Cohen, the man who invented the phrase 'delinquent subculture', argued: 'The crucial condition for the emergence of new cultural forms is the existence, in effective interaction with one another, of a number of actors with similar problems of adjustment' (1957: 59). The social anthropology of the Chicago school, channelled for a while into differential association theory, supplied an emphasis upon the enduring, intelligible, and locally-adapted cultural traditions shared both by professional criminals and by boys living, working, and playing together on the crowded streets of morally-differentiated areas. Retaining the idea of a 'subculture of delinquency', David Matza and a number of control theorists pointed to the manner in which moral proscriptions could be neutralized by invoking commonly-available extenuating accounts. Strands of 'Left realism' could be described as little more than early subcultural theory in a new guise. And symbolic interactionism supplied a focus on the negotiated, collective, and processual character of meaning. In all this, an argument ran that young men (it was almost always young men), growing up in the city, banded together in groups or 'near-groups' (Yablonsky 1962) in the crowded public life of the streets, encountering common problems, exposed to common stereotypes and stigmas, subject to similar formal controls, setting themselves against common Others who are used to define who they are, are likely to form joint interpretations that are sporadically favourable to delinquency. Subcultural theory and research were to dominate explanations of delinquency until they exhausted themselves in the 1960s.

Subcultural theory lent itself to amalgamation with radical criminology, and particularly that criminology which was preoccupied with the reproduction of class inequalities through the workings of ideology. In Britain, there was to be a renaissance of *anomie*-derived subcultural theory as a group of sociologists centred around Stuart Hall at the University of Birmingham gave special attention to the existential plight of young working-class men about to enter the labour market. The prototype for that work was Phil Cohen's analysis of proletarian cultures in London: young men responded to the decline of community, loss of class cohesion, and economic insecurity by resurrecting in subcultural form an idealized and exaggerated version of working-class masculinity that 'express[ed] and resolve[d], albeit "magically," the contradictions which remain hidden or unresolved in the parent culture' (1972: 23). Deviance became a form of symbolic resistance to tensions perceived through the mists of false consciousness. It was doomed to disappoint because it did not address the root causes of discontent, but it did offer a fleeting release. There was a contradiction within that version of subcultural theory because it was not easy to reconcile a structural Marxism which depicted adolescent culture as illusory with a commitment to understanding meaning (Willis 1977). But it was a spirited and vivid revival of a theory that had gone into the doldrums in the 1960s, and it continues to influence theorizing (see Ferrell 1993). Indeed, interestingly, there are strong signs of a *rapprochement* between critical cultural studies and symbolic interactionism (see Becker and McCall 1990).

CRIMINOLOGY AS AN ECLECTIC DISCIPLINE

It would be misleading to conclude that criminology can easily be laid out as an array of discrete clumps of theory. On the contrary, it has continually borrowed ideas from other disciplines, and has compared, contrasted, amalgamated, reworked, and experimented with them to furnish an eclectic discipline marked by an abundance of theoretical overlaps, syntheses, and confusions.

There are exchanges and combinations of criminological ideas within disciplines. For instance, sociological criminologists are exposed to changes in intellectual fashion in their parent discipline, and the result has been that almost every major theory in sociology has been fed in some form into criminology at some time, undergoing adaptation and editing in the process, and occasionally becoming very distant from its roots. Indeed, one of the distinctive properties of that process is that criminology can sometimes so extensively rework imported ideas that they will develop well beyond their original limits in sociology, becoming significant contributions to sociological theory in their own right. *Anomie*, the symbolic interactionist conception of the self and its others, and feminism are examples of arguments that have grown appreciably in scale and sophistication within the special environment of criminology.

There are exchanges and combinations between disciplines. Criminology is what David Downes would call a *rendez-vous* discipline that is defined principally by its attachment to an empirical area. The study of *crime* gives unity and order to the enterprise, not adherence to any particular theory or social science. It is in the examination of *crime* that psychologists, statisticians, lawyers, economists, social anthropologists, sociologists, social policy analysts, and psychiatrists meet and call themselves criminologists, and in that encounter, their attachments to the conventions and boundaries of their parent disciplines may weaken. So it is that sociological criminologists have confronted arguments born and applied in other disciplines and, from time to time, they have domesticated them to cultivate new intellectual hybrids. Stan Cohen (1972) and Jock Young (1971) did so in the early 1970s when they married the symbolic interactionism of Edwin Lemert (1951) and Howard Becker (1963) to the statistical theory of Leslie Wilkins (1964). Wilkins had argued that deviant events fall at the poles of normal distribution curves, that knowledge about those events will be distorted by the ensuing social distance, and that patterns of control and deviant responses are likely to become ever more exaggerated as they are affected by those distortions. That concept of deviance amplification married well with interactionist ideas of secondary deviation.

Thus constituted, the development of sociological criminology is at once marked by discontinuities and continuities. It may be represented as a staggered succession of interchanges with different schools and disciplines which do not always sit well together. It is evident, for instance, that the feminist may entertain a conception of theory and the theorist very unlike that of the functionalist or rational choice theorist. Yet there are also unities of a kind. All competent criminologists may be presumed to have a rough working knowledge of the wide range of theory in their discipline; theory once mastered is seldom forgotten or neglected entirely, and there is a propensity for scholars overtly and covertly to weave disparate ideas together as problems and needs arise. Quite typical was an observation offered in the author's introduction to a work on the lives of urban street criminals in Seattle, Washington: 'I link . . . ethnographic data to criminological perspectives as a *bricoleur* seeking numerous sources of interpretation. Had I selected just one criminological perspective to complement these ethnographic data, the value of these firsthand accounts would be constrained . . .' (1995: 5). Scholars thus tend frequently to be more accommodating in practice than in principle, and if there *is* an ensuing gap between a professed purity of theory and an active pragmatism of procedure, it may well be masked by the obliteration of sources or the renaming of ideas. Seemingly distinct sociological theories are open to continual merging and blurring as the practical work of criminology unfolds, and in that process may be found opportunities for theoretical innovation.

PROSPECTS FOR THE FUTURE

What is uncertain, and what has always been uncertain, is how those criminological theories may be expected to evolve in the future. Very few would have predicted the rapid demise of radical criminology, a brand of theorizing that once seemed so strong that it would sweep all before it, at least in large parts of Europe, Canada, and Australasia. Few would have predicted the resurgence of utilitarian theories of rational choice—they seemed to have been superseded forever by a sociology that pointed to the part played by social and moral contexts in the shaping of meaning and action.

What may certainly be anticipated is a continuation of the semi-detached relations between criminology and its parent disciplines, and with sociology above all. The half-life of sociological theories is brief, often bound up with the duration of intellectual generations, and sociological theory is itself emergent, a compound of the familiar and the unfamiliar. It is to be assumed that there will always be something new out of sociology, and that criminology will almost always respond and innovate in its turn.

Other matters are also clear. First, criminology remains a substantively-defined discipline, and it tends not to detain the intellectual system-builders. Those who would be the sociological Newtons, the men and women who would explain the great clockwork of society, are often impatient with the limitations imposed by analysing the mere parts and fragments of larger totalities. Almost all the grand theorists have made something of a mark on criminology, but they, or their disciples, have rarely stayed long. Their concern is with the wider systemic properties of society, not the surface features of empirical areas. Thus the phenomenologist, Phillipson, once remarked that '[we should] turn away from constitutive and arbitrary judgements of public rule breaking as deviance towards the concept of rule itself and the dialectical tension that ruling is, a subject more central to the fundamental practice of sociology . . .' (1974: 5). And Marxists (Bankowski *et al.* 1977) and feminists (Smart 1989) have said much the same about the relations between their theories and the sub-discipline of criminology.

Secondly, criminology will probably persist in challenging economics as a contender for the title of the dismal science. Criminologists are not professionally optimistic. A prolonged exposure to the pain of crime, rates of offending that (until very recently at least) had seemed prone inexorably to rise, frequent abuses of authority, misconceived policies, and 'nothing' or very little appearing to work, seems to have fostered a propensity amongst the larger thinkers to infuse their writing with gloom and to argue, in effect, that all is really not for the best in the best of all possible worlds. Stan Cohen once confessed that 'most of us—consciously or not—probably hold a rather bleak view of social change. Things must be getting worse' (1979: 360). Prophecies of a criminological future will still be tinged at the margins with the iconography of Mad Max, Neuromancer and Blade Runner.

Thirdly, there is the growing influence of government and government money in shaping criminological work. Policies and politics have conspired to make restorative justice and rational choice theory, the criminological anti-theory, particularly attractive to criminal justice agencies. Restorative justice is new, modest in its reach, and it seems to 'work'. Rational choice and control theories lay out a series of neat, inexpensive, small-scale, practicable, and noncontroversial steps that may be taken to 'do something' about crime. Moreover, as theories that are tied to the apron strings of economics, they can borrow something of the powerful intellectual authority that economics wields in the social sciences.

Fourth is the persistence of a feminist influence. Crime is clearly gendered, the intellectual yield of analysing the connections between gender and crime has not yet been fully explored, and women are entering the body of sociological criminology in ever greater numbers (although, to be sure, some feminists, like Carol Smart, are also emigrating and absolute numbers remain small). Criminological feminisms and feminist criminologies (Gelsthorpe and Morris 1988) will undoubtedly sustain work on gender, control, and deviance and, increasingly, on masculinity. After all, if crime is largely a male preserve, criminology should ask what it is about masculinity that seems to have such an affinity with offending. Connell (1987), not himself a criminologist, has sketched the possibilities of an answer in his writing on 'hegemonic masculinity'—the overriding ideology of male power, wealth, and physical strength—that lends itself to exploit, risk-taking, and aggression. Messerschmidt (1997), Bourgois (1995), and Polk (1994) have pursued that model of masculine behaviour into criminology, Bourgois exploring the work done to maintain 'respect' by cocaine-dealing Latin Americans on the streets of New York, and Polk describing how the defence of masculine conceptions of honour and face can precipitate homicide.

A role will continue to be played by the sociological criminology that attaches importance to the ethnographic study of signifying practices. Symbolic interactionism and phenomenology have supplied an enduring reminder of the importance of reflectivity; the symbolically-mediated character of all social reality; and the sheer complexity, density, and intricacy of the social world. And, lastly, one would hope that criminology will continue to contribute its own distinct analysis of the wider social world, an analysis that can take it beyond the confines of a tightly-defined nexus of relations between criminals, legislators, lawyers, and enforcement agents. A criminology without a wider vision of social process would be deformed. A sociology without a conception of rule-breaking and control would be an odd discipline indeed.

Selected further reading

There is no substitute for the original works, some of the more important of which are Howard Becker's *Outsiders* (1963); John Braithwaite's *Crime, Shame and Reintegration* (1989); Richard Cloward and Lloyd Ohlin's *Delinquency and Opportunity* (1960); David Matza's *Delinquency and Drift* (1964); Ian Taylor, Paul Walton, and Jock Young's *The New Criminology* (1973); and Jock Young's *The Exclusive Society* (1999). Among the secondary texts are David Downes and Paul Rock's *Understanding Deviance* (1998), and John Tierney's *Criminology: Theory and Context* (1996).

References

AKERLOF, G., and YELLEN, J. (1994), 'Gang Behavior, Law Enforcement, and Community Values', in H. Aaron *et al.* (eds.), *Values and Public Policy*, Washington DC: Brookings Institute.

ANDERSON, E. (1976), *A Place on the Corner*, Chicago: University of Chicago Press.

BALDWIN, J., and BOTTOMS, A. (1976), *The Urban Criminal*, London: Tavistock.

BANKOWSKI, Z. *et al.* (1977), 'Radical Criminology or Radical Criminologist?', *Contemporary Crises*, 1.

BAUMAN, Z. (1989), *Modernity and the Holocaust*, Cambridge: Polity Press.

BAYART, J.-F., ELLIS, S., and HIBOU, B. (1999), *The Criminalization of the State in Africa*, Bloomington: Indiana University Press.

BECK, U. (1992), *Risk Society*, London: Sage.

BECKER, G. (1968), 'Crime and Punishment: An Economic Approach', *The Journal of Political Economy*, 76.

BECKER, H. (1963), *Outsiders*, New York: Free Press.

—— and McCALL, M. (eds) (1990), *Symbolic Interaction and Cultural Studies*, Chicago: University of Chicago Press.

BELL, D. (1960), 'The Racket-Ridden Longshoremen', in *The End of Ideology*, New York: Collier.

BOTTOMS, A. *et al.* (1989), 'A Tale of Two Estates', in D. Downes (ed.), *Crime and the City*, Macmillan: Basingstoke.

—— and WILES, P. (1996), 'Crime and Insecurity in the City', in C. Fijnaut *et al.* (eds), *Changes in Society, Crime and Criminal Justice in Europe*, The Hague: Kluwer.

BOURGOIS, P. (1995), *In Search of Respect*, Cambridge: Cambridge University Press.

BOX, S. (1971), *Deviance, Reality and Society*, London: Holt, Rinehart, and Winston.

—— (1983), *Power, Crime and Mystification*, London: Tavistock.

BRAITHWAITE, J. (1989), *Crime, Shame and Reintegration*, Cambridge: Cambridge University Press.

BRANTINGHAM, P., and BRANTINGHAM, P. (1981–2), 'Mobility, Notoriety, and Crime', *Journal of Environmental Systems*, 11(1).

CARLEN, P. (1988), *Women, Crime and Poverty*, Milton Keynes: Open University Press.

—— (1996), *Jigsaw: a political criminology of youth homelessness*, Buckingham: Open University Press.

CHAMBLISS, W. (1976), 'The State and Criminal Law', in W. Chambliss and M. Mankoff (eds), *Whose Law, What Order?*, New York: Wiley.

CHAPMAN, D. (1967), *Sociology and the Stereotype of the Criminal*, London: Tavistock.

CLARKE, R. (1992), *Situational Crime Prevention*, New York: Harrow and Heston.

—— (1999), 'Situational Prevention', paper delivered at the Cambridge Workshop on *Situational Crime Prevention—Ethics and Social Context*, 14–16 October.

—— and CORNISH, D. (undated), 'Rational Choice', unpublished paper.

—— and —— (1985), 'Modeling Offenders' Decisions', in M. Tonry and N. Morris (eds), *Crime and Justice*, 6, Chicago: University of Chicago Press.

—— and —— (2000), 'Analyzing Organized Crime', unpublished paper.

—— and FELSON, M. (eds) (1993), *Routine Activity and Rational Choice*, New Brunswick: Transaction.

CLEAVER, E. (1969), *Post-Prison Writings and Speeches*, London: Cape.

CLOWARD, R., and OHLIN, L. (1960), *Delinquency and Opportunity*, New York: Free Press.

COHEN, A. (1957), *Delinquent Boys*, Glencoe: Free Press.

COHEN, L., and FELSON, M. (1979), 'Social Change and Crime Rate Trends', *American Sociological Review*, 44.

COHEN, P. (1972), 'Working-Class Youth Cultures in East London', *Working Papers in Cultural Studies*, Birmingham, 2.

COHEN, S. (1972), *Folk Devils and Moral Panics*, London: Paladin.

—— (1979), 'The Punitive City: Notes on the Dispersal of Social Control', *Contemporary Crises*, 3.

—— (1985), *Visions of Social Control*, Cambridge: Polity.

—— (1996), 'Crime and politics: spot the difference', *British Journal of Sociology*, 47.

COLEMAN, A. (1985), *Utopia on Trial*, London: Hilary Shipman.

—— (1986), 'Dangerous Dreams', *Landscape Design*, 163.

CONNELL, R. (1987), *Gender and Power*, Cambridge: Polity.

CORRIGAN, P. (1979), *Schooling the Smash Street Kids*, London: Macmillan.

COTTERRELL, R. (1999), *Émile Durkheim: Law in a Moral Domain*, Stanford: Stanford University Press.

CUSSON, M. (1983), *Why Delinquency?*, Toronto: University of Toronto Press.

DAMER, S. (1974), 'Wine Alley: The Sociology of a Dreadful Enclosure', *Sociological Review*, 22.

DAVIES, N. (1998), *Dark Heart: The Shocking Truth about Hidden Britain*, London: Vintage.

DAVIS, K. (1937), 'The Sociology of Prostitution', *American Sociological Review*, 2.

—— (1959), 'The Myth of Functional Analysis as a Special Method in Sociology and Anthropology', *American Sociological Review*, 24.

DAVIS, M. (1992a), 'Beyond Blade Runner', *Open Magazine Pamphlet*, New Jersey.

—— (1992b), *City of Quartz*, New York: Vintage.

DOUGLAS, M. (1966), *Purity and Danger*, London: Pelican.

Downes, D. (1966), *The Delinquent Solution*, London: Routledge and Kegan Paul.

—— and Rock, P. (eds) (1979), *Deviant Interpretations*, Oxford: Martin Robertson.

—— and —— (1998), *Understanding Deviance*, Oxford: Oxford University Press.

Durkheim, É. (1952), *Suicide*, London: Routledge and Kegan Paul.

—— (1964), *The Division of Labour in Society*, New York: Free Press.

Erikson, K. (1966), *Wayward Puritans*, New York: Wiley.

—— (1994), *A New Species of Trouble*, New York: Norton.

Faris, R., and Dunham, H. (1939), *Mental Disorders in Urban Areas*, Chicago: University of Chicago Press.

Feeley, M. (1996), 'The Decline of Women in the Criminal Process', in *Criminal Justice History*, 15, Westport, Ct.: Greenwood Press.

—— and Simon, J. (1992), 'The New Penology', *Criminology*, 30.

Felson, M. (1994), *Crime and Everyday Life*, California: Pine Forge.

—— and Clarke, R. (1998), *Opportunity Makes the Thief*, Police Research Series Paper, London: Home Office.

Ferrell, J. (1993), *Crimes of Style*, Boston: Northeastern University Press.

—— and Sanders, C. (1995), *Cultural Criminology*, Boston: Northeastern University Press.

Fleisher, M. (1995), *Beggars and Thieves*, Madison, Wisconsin: University of Wisconsin Press.

Foucault, M. (1977), *Discipline and Punish*, Harmondsworth: Penguin.

Gelsthorpe, L., and Morris, A. (1988), 'Feminism and Criminology in Britain', *British Journal of Criminology*, 28.

Genn, H. (1988), 'Multiple Victimisation', in M. Maguire and J. Pointing (eds), *Victims of Crime: a New Deal?*, Milton Keynes: Open University Press.

Giddens, A. (1972), *Émile Durkheim: Selected Writings*, Cambridge: Cambridge University Press.

—— (1991), *Modernity and Self-Identity*, Cambridge: Polity Press.

Gill, O. (1977), *Luke Street: Housing Policy, Conflict and the Creation of the Delinquent Area*, London: Macmillan.

Gluckman, M. (1955), *The Judicial Process Among the Barotse of Northern Rhodesia*, Manchester: Manchester University Press.

Goffman, E. (1968), *Asylums*, Harmondsworth: Penguin.

Gordon, C. (ed.) (1972), *Power/Knowledge*, Brighton: Harvester Press.

Gordon, D. (1986–7), 'The Electronic Panopticon', *Politics and Society*, 15.

Gottfredson, M., and Hirschi, T. (1990), *A General Theory of Crime*, Stanford, Calif.: Stanford University Press.

Hagan, J. *et al.* (1979), 'The Sexual Stratification of Social Control', *British Journal of Sociology*, 30.

—— (1985), 'The Class Structure of Gender and Delinquency: Toward a Power-Control Theory of Common Delinquent Behavior', *American Journal of Sociology*, 90.

—— (1988), *Structural Criminology*, Cambridge: Polity Press.

Hagan, J. and McCarthy, B. (1998), *Mean Streets: Youth Crime and Homelessness*, Cambridge: Cambridge University Press.

Hall, S. *et al.* (1978), *Policing the Crisis*, London: Macmillan.

Hillier, W. (1973), 'In Defence of Space', *RIBA Journal*, November.

—— (1986), 'City of Alice's Dreams', *Architecture Journal*, 9.

Hirschi, T. (1969), *The Causes of Delinquency*, Berkeley: University of California Press.

Hirst, P. (1975), 'Marx and Engels on Law, Crime and Morality', in I. Taylor *et al.* (eds), *Critical Criminology*, London: Routledge and Kegan Paul.

Hooker, E. (1963), 'Male Homosexuality', in N. Farberow (ed.), *Taboo Topics*, New York: Prentice-Hall.

Hope, T. (1982), *Burglary in Schools*, London: Home Office.

Hough, M., and Mayhew, P. (1983), *The British Crime Survey*, London: HMSO.

Inciardi, J. (ed.) (1980), *Radical Criminology: the Coming Crises*, Beverly Hills: Sage.

Jacobs, J. (1965), *The Death and Life of Great American Cities*, Harmondsworth: Penguin.

Jones, T. *et al.* (1986), *The Islington Crime Survey*, Aldershot: Gower.

Kaplan, R. (1994), 'The Coming Anarchy', *The Atlantic Monthly*, February.

Katz, J. (1988), *Seductions of Crime*, New York: Basic Books.

—— (1997), 'Ethnography's Warrants', *Sociological Methods and Research*, 25: 4.

KITTRIE, N. (1971), *The Right to be Different*, Baltimore: Johns Hopkins Press.

KORNHAUSER, R. (1978), *Social Sources of Delinquency: An Appraisal of Analytic Models*, Chicago: University of Chicago Press.

KUMAR, R. (1993), *The History of Doing*, New Delhi: Kali for Women.

LANDESCO, J. (rep. 1968), *Organized Crime in Chicago*, Chicago: University of Chicago Press.

LEA, J., and YOUNG, J. (1984), *What is to be Done about Law and Order?*, London: Penguin Books.

LEMERT, E. (1951), *Social Pathology*, New York: McGraw-Hill.

LIANOS, M., with DOUGLAS, M. (2000), 'Dangerisation and the End of Deviance: the Institutional Environment', *British Journal of Criminology*, Spring, 40: 2.

LLEWELLYN, K., and HOEBEL, A. (1941), *The Cheyenne Way: Conflict and Case Law in Primitive Jurisprudence*, Norman: University of Oklahoma Press.

LUCKENBILL, D., and BEST, J. (1981), 'Careers in deviance and respectability', *Social Problems*, 29.

LUKES, S. (1967), 'Alienation and Anomie', in P. Laslett and W. Runciman (eds), *Philosophy, Politics and Society*, Oxford: Blackwell.

LYON, D. (1994), *The Electronic Eye*, Cambridge: Polity Press.

MARTINSON, R. (1974), 'What Works? Questions and Answers about Penal Reform', *Public Interest*, 35.

MARX, G. (1988), *Under Cover*, Berkeley: University of California Press.

MATHIESEN, T. (1974), *The Politics of Abolition*, London: Martin Robertson.

MATZA, D. (1964), *Delinquency and Drift*, New York: Wiley.

—— (1969), *Becoming Deviant*, New Jersey: Prentice-Hall.

MAYHEW, P. *et al.* (1976), *Crime as Opportunity*, London: Home Office.

McROBBIE, A., and GARBER, J. (1976), 'Girls and Subcultures', in S. Hall and T. Jefferson (eds), *Resistance through Ritual*, London: Hutchinson.

MEAD, G. (1918), 'The Psychology of Punitive Justice', *American Journal of Sociology*, 23.

—— (1934), *Mind Self and Society*, Chicago: University of Chicago Press.

MERTON, R. (1938), 'Social Structure and Anomie', *American Sociological Review*, 3.

—— (1957), *Social Theory and Social Structure*, Glencoe: Free Press.

—— (1995), 'Opportunity Structure: The Emergence, Diffusion and Differentiation of a Sociological Concept, 1930s–1950s', in F. Adler and W. Laufer (eds), *The Legacy of Anomie Theory*, New Brunswick: Transaction.

MESSERSCHMIDT, J. (1997), *Crime as Structured Action: Gender, Race, Class, and Crime in the Making*, Thousand Oaks, Cal.: Sage.

MILLS, C. (1940), 'Situated Actions and Vocabularies of Motive', *American Sociological Review*, 5.

MORRIS, T. (1958), *The Criminal Area*, London: Routledge and Kegan Paul.

NEWBURN, T., and STANKO, E. (eds) (1994), *Just Boys Doing Business: Masculinity and Crime*, London: Routledge.

NEWMAN, O. (1972), *Defensible Space: People and Design in the Violent City*, London: Architectural Press.

NORRIS, C., and ARMSTRONG, G. (1999), *The Maximum Surveillance Society*, Oxford: Berg.

O'MALLEY, P. (1992), 'Risk, power and crime prevention', *Economy and Society*, August 1992, 21.

PARK, R. (1915), 'The City: Suggestions for the Investigation of Human Behavior in the City Environment', *American Journal of Sociology*, 20.

—— (1925), 'Community Organization and Juvenile Delinquency', in R. Park and R. Burgess (eds), *The City*, Chicago: University of Chicago Press.

PARSONS, T. (1951), *The Social System*, London: Routledge and Kegan Paul.

PEARCE, F. (1976), *Crimes of the Powerful*, London: Pluto.

PHILLIPSON, M. (1974), 'Thinking Out of Deviance', unpublished paper.

POLK, K. (1994), *When Men Kill*, Cambridge: Cambridge University Press.

POLSKY, N. (1967), *Hustlers, Beats and Others*, Chicago: Aldine.

QUINNEY, R. (1970), *The Social Reality of Crime*, Boston, Mass: Little Brown.

RAINWATER, L. (1970), *Behind Ghetto Walls*, Chicago: Aldine.

RECKLESS, W. (1933), *Vice in Chicago*, Chicago: University of Chicago Press.

RECKLESS, W. *et al.* (1957), 'The Good Boy in a High Delinquency Area', *Journal of Criminal Law, Criminology, and Police Science*, 48.

REIMAN, J. (1990), *The Rich Get Richer and the Poor Get Prison*, New York: Macmillan.

RONCEK, D., and MAIER, P. (1991), 'Bars, Blocks, and Crimes Revisited: Linking the Theory of Routine Activities to the Empiricism of "Hot Spots"', *Criminology*, 29.

RORTY, R. (1991), *Objectivity, Relativism, and Truth*, Cambridge: Cambridge University Press.

SCHEFF, T. (1966), *Being Mentally Ill*, London: Weidenfeld and Nicolson.

SCHUR, E. (1963), *Narcotic Addiction in Britain and America*, London: Tavistock.

SCOTT, M., and LYMAN, S. (1970), 'Accounts, Deviance and Social Order', in J. Douglas (ed.), *Deviance and Respectability*, New York: Basic Books.

SCOTT, R. (1972), 'A Proposed Framework for Analyzing Deviance as a Property of Social Order', in R. Scott and J. Douglas (eds), *Theoretical Perspectives on Deviance*, New York: Basic Books.

SCOTTISH CENTRAL RESEARCH UNIT (1999), 'The Effect of Closed Circuit Television on Recorded Crime Rates and Public Concern about Crime in Glasgow', Edinburgh: The Scottish Office.

SCRATON, P. (ed.) (1987), *Law, Order, and the Authoritarian State: Readings in Critical Criminology*, Milton Keynes: Open University Press.

SCULL, A. (1979), *Museums of Madness: the Social Organization of Insanity in Nineteenth-century England*, New York: Allen Lane.

SEMPLE, J. (1993), *Bentham's Prison: a Study of the Panopticon Penitentiary*, Oxford: Clarendon Press.

SHAPLAND, J., and VAGG, J. (1988), *Policing by the Public*, Oxford: Clarendon Press.

SHAW, C., and McKAY, H. (1942), *Juvenile Delinquency and Urban Areas*, Chicago: University of Chicago Press.

—— (1971), 'Male Juvenile Delinquency and Group Behavior', in J. Short (ed.), *The Social Fabric of the Metropolis*, Chicago: University of Chicago Press.

SHEARING, C., and STENNING, P. (1985), 'From the Panopticon to Disney World: The Development of Discipline', in A. Doob and E. Greenspan (eds), *Perspectives in Criminal Law*, Aurora: Canada Law Book.

SHERMAN, L. *et al.* (1989), 'Hot Spots of Predatory Crime: Routine Activities and the Criminology of Place', *Criminology*, 27.

SHORT, E., and DITTON, J. (1998), 'Seen and Now Heard: Talking to the Targets of Open Street CCTV', *British Journal of Criminology*, 38: 3.

SHORT, J., and STRODBECK, F. (1967), *Group Process and Gang Delinquency*, Chicago: University of Chicago Press.

SIMON, J. (1987), 'The Emergence of a Risk Society', *Socialist Review*.

—— (1993), *Poor Discipline: Parole and the Social Control of the Underclass*, Chicago: University of Chicago Press.

—— and FEELEY, M. (1995), 'True Crime: The New Penology and Public Discourse on Crime', in T. Blomberg and S. Cohen (eds), *Punishment and Social Control*, New York: Aldine de Gruyter.

SMART, C. (1977), *Women, Crime and Criminology*, London: Routledge and Kegan Paul.

—— (1989), *Feminism and the Power of Law*, London: Routledge.

SMITH, D. (2000), 'Changing Situations and Changing People', in A. von Hirsh, D. Garland, and A. Wakefield (eds), *Ethical and Social Perspectives on Situational Crime Prevention*, 147–74, Oxford: Hart Publishing.

STEPHENS, J. (1976), *Loners, Losers and Lovers*, Seattle: University of Washington Press.

STINCHCOMBE, A. (1968), *Constructing Social Theories*, New York: Harcourt Brace and World.

SUTHERLAND, E., and CRESSEY, D. (1955), *Principles of Criminology*, Chicago: Lippincott.

SUTTLES, G. (1972), *The Social Construction of Communities*, Chicago: University of Chicago Press.

SYKES, G., and MATZA, D. (1957), 'Techniques of Neutralization', *American Sociological Review*, 22.

TAYLOR, I. (1999), *Crime in Context: A Critical Criminology of Market Societies*, Cambridge: Polity Press.

TAYLOR, I., WALTON, P., and YOUNG, J. (1973), *The New Criminology*, London: Routledge and Kegan Paul.

THRASHER, F. (1927), *The Gang*, Chicago: University of Chicago Press.

TIERNEY, J. (1996), *Criminology: Theory and Context*, London: Prentice-Hall.

TURNBULL, C. (1973), *The Mountain People*, London: Paladin.

VAN CREVELD, M. (1991), *The Transformation of War*, New York: Free Press.

WHYTE, W. (1942), *Street Corner Society*, Chicago: University of Chicago Press.

WILKINS, L. (1964), *Social Deviance*, London: Tavistock.

WILLIS, P. (1977), *Learning to Labour*, Farnborough, Hants: Gower.

WILSON, H. (1980), 'Parental Supervision: A Neglected Aspect of Delinquency', *British Journal of Criminology*, 20.

WILSON, W. (1996), *When Work Disappears: The World of the New Urban Poor*, New York: Alfred Knopf.

WIRTH, L. (1964), 'Culture Conflict and Misconduct', in *On Cities and Social Life*, Chicago: University of Chicago Press.

WRIGHT, R., and DECKER, S. (1997), *Armed Robbers in Action: Stickups and Street Culture*, Boston: Northeastern University Press.

YABLONSKY, L. (1962), *The Violent Gang*, London: Pelican.

YOUNG, J. (1971), *The Drugtakers*, London: Paladin.

—— (1997), 'Left Realist Criminology', in M. Maguire *et al.* (eds), *The Oxford Handbook of Criminology*, 2nd edn, Oxford: Oxford University Press.

—— (1998), 'From inclusive to exclusive society: nightmares in the European Dream', in V. Ruggiero *et al.* (eds), *The New European Criminology*, London: Routledge.

—— (1999), *The Exclusive Society*, London: Sage.

3

CONTEMPORARY LANDSCAPES OF CRIME, ORDER, AND CONTROL
GOVERNANCE, RISK, AND GLOBALIZATION

Ian Loader and Richard Sparks

INTRODUCTION

Our aim in this chapter is to outline certain challenges and prospects for criminological thinking in seeking to address in timely and relevant fashion the world it confronts in the early years of a new century. This review is necessarily partial and personal in its choice of topics and sketchy in its coverage of any of them. It also consciously leaves many large issues—such as the many varieties of 'gender-trouble' and the ways in which relations between genders and the reshaping of our sexed subjectivities might inform the agenda of contemporary criminology—to others (see Chapters 4 and 15 by Gelsthorpe and Heidensohn in this volume). We seek simply to raise for discussion a number of sightings on the changing landscape of crime, order, and control that seem to us to require (and in many cases to be at least beginning to receive) some response from criminological theory and research.

In summary form our argument is that as the landscape of crime, order, and control shifts and changes so the shape of criminology as a field of study cannot but be revised. Our sense of which topics command the most serious attention, of which theoretical resources and empirical materials best advance contemporary analysis, of how to contribute most pertinently to public debates about crime and its control; these need, or so we contend, to be fully attuned to the changing contours of the world we inhabit. Among the features of that world which strike us as significant, and which we pursue here, are: contemporary shifts in the character of the governance of crime; the changing postures and capacities of the state; the intensity of public sensibilities towards criminal justice matters; the shifting boundaries between the public and private realms in providing 'security'; the social consequences of risk; and the place of crime and social order in public culture. What in our view connects up these various topics is a series of questions to do with the contemporary reconfiguration—

and possible futures—of the nation state: can the modern sovereign state—considered for some two centuries to be pivotal to the production of social order—any longer remain the sole, or even pre-eminent, guarantor of civil peace and public tranquillity? What effects are current transformations of the state—perhaps even its displacement from a once pivotal place in the field of crime control—likely to have on the politics of (in)security?

With this in mind, we organize the discussion that follows under the three main headings that figure in our title and which seem to us to summarize some of the main points of intersection between criminological work and the wider domains of social and political inquiry: governance, risk and globalization. We conclude with some remarks on the ways in which criminological research and reflection may—under the altered conditions we set out—hope to inform public discussion and intervention.

GOVERNANCE

Governance blurs the distinction between state and civil society. The state becomes a collection of interorganizational networks made up of governmental and societal actors with no sovereign actor able to steer or regulate [Rhodes 1997: 57].

The field of crime control was—up until some three decades ago—characterized by what seemed an entrenched assemblage of institutions and ideas. It was, most fundamentally, dominated by a set of state institutions (police, courts, prisons, and so on) that had since the advent of modernity come to assume a pivotal place in the production of order and security. These institutions, in turn, had over the early and middle decades of the twentieth century become progressively infused with, and shaped by, some specific ways of thinking and acting in relation to crime and its control. The resultant complex of institutional sites, dispositions, and practices—what Garland (2001a: chapter 2) has termed 'the penal-welfare state'—was orchestrated around the following mutually reinforcing axioms:

1. *A conception of crime as conceptually unproblematic ('we know what it is') and geographically and socially delimited ('we know where it happens and the kinds of people who do it').* The attendant official focus was on identifying and re-assimilating the individual 'delinquent'; a task that—against a political and cultural backdrop in which crime was neither a bone of electoral contention nor a staple of media discourse—seemed relatively 'obvious, clear cut and uncontested' (Young 1999: 4).

2. *A causal theory that understood crime as a presenting symptom of more deep-seated social problems.* The ensuing policy focus here was on social welfare measures (public housing, social security, family support, etc.) aimed at tackling the 'roots' of offending, coupled with 'correctionalist' treatment programmes oriented to returning individual offenders to the fold of social democratic citizenship. This, in turn, formed part of a strategy of economic and social government oriented to securing a range of basic citizen needs (education,

work, home, health, etc.), one underpinned by 'a civic narrative of inclusion' (Garland 2001a: 46; see generally, Hobsbawm 1994: chapter 9; Hay 1996: chapters 2–4).[1]

3. *An attachment to the idea of crime control policy as the province of 'experts' and 'expert knowledge'*—a sphere of government in which a coterie of civil servants and senior practitioners could (and should) determine the direction of policy, with relatively little direct input from politicians, and at some remove from the interest or supervision of citizens (Windlesham 1987). It was a style of policy formation in which criminological research (especially that conducted in the Home Office Research and Planning Unit and Cambridge Institute of Criminology) came to occupy a prominent and influential place (see Lodge 1974; Radzinowicz 1999: chapters 8–9).

Since the 1970s, this field of control institutions and philosophies has been quite profoundly called into question and transformed—undone by a combination of at least the following three factors. First, a massive escalation in post-war recorded crime rates (see Chapter 11 by Maguire), one that has seen criminal victimization move from the margins of social life to 'become a routine part of modern consciousness, a standing possibility that is constantly to be "kept in mind"' (Garland 2001a: 106). This, according to Jock Young (1999: 35), represents 'the central motor of change' in post-war criminal justice and crime control—something that has exposed the limitations of simple social democratic accounts of crime causation (wherein better social conditions should mean less crime); seen the 'discovery' of hitherto hidden offences and unknown victims (domestic violence, sexual and physical abuse of children, stalking, environmental pollution . . .); and given the crime question (and crime imagery) a prominent, noisy, and hotly disputed place in everyday life and political discourse (cf. Young 1996; Hope and Sparks 2000; Garland 2001a: chapter 6).

Secondly, some significant shifts in the pattern of economic, social, and cultural relations—transitions profound enough for social theorists and criminologists to speak of the advent of 'late' (Giddens 1990; Young 1999; Garland 2001a) or 'post' (Harvey 1989; Bauman 1992; Reiner 1992) modernity. These include: (i) transformations in capitalist production and exchange (e.g., the creation of core, secondary, and peripheral labour markets, the rise of consumerism); (ii) changes in family structure (e.g., the proliferation of dual career households, rising divorce rates) and the ecology of cities (e.g., suburbanization); (iii) the proliferation of electronic mass media; and (iv) a 'democratization' of everyday life—as witnessed in altered relations between men/women, parents/children, etc. and a marked decline in unthinking adherence towards authority. Each of these can plausibly be said to have contributed to new opportunities and motivations for crime, to intensified demands for 'something to done' about it, and to heightened levels of popular scrutiny of criminal justice agencies (Taylor 1999; Young 1999; Garland 2001a).

Thirdly, and more contingently, the effects of the New Right governments that

---

[1] This governmental project exhibited, in these respects, a certain affinity with the *sociological* criminologies—social disorganization, *anomie*, etc.—outlined in Chapter 2 by Paul Rock.

ruled in Britain, the USA, Australia, and New Zealand throughout much of the 1980s and 1990s. These administrations strove explicitly to break with the economic and social consensus of the post-war decades. They thus embarked on a sustained assault on the institutions and 'social insurance' logics of the welfare state and public provision; seeking to replace 'dependence' on the state with private enterprise and individual responsibility ('standing on one's own two feet'). The resultant formation of 'market societies' in which social solidarity atrophied and social inequalities deepened (Taylor 1999) has had profound ramifications not only on levels of, and responses to, crime and disorder (Currie 1997), but also in fuelling an overt politicization of questions of crime and punishment.[2]

We cannot in this chapter consider these transformations and their effects in any serious depth. Neither can we hope to determine the weight that ought properly to be accorded to each of the aforementioned explanations (cf. Young 1999; O'Malley 1992, 1999; Garland 2001a). What can be claimed with some warrant, however, is that these factors, taken together, have served to make 'crime-related' anxieties and public demands for order pervasive—if differentially felt and articulated—features of late modern societies. This has not merely rendered untenable the quiet, elitist, ameliorative styles of crime management that held sway until the 1970s; it has also, more profoundly, called into doubt—even undermined—the sovereign state's claim to be able to offer security to its citizens (Garland 2001a: chapter 5). But what effects are these mutations and realizations having? What institutions and styles of control are emerging in their wake?

The landscape here is volatile, uneven, and contradictory. On the one hand, there exists ample evidence of governments seeking to (re)assert their sovereign authority over the terrain of crime, policing, and punishment—to, in Jonathon Simon's (1997) nice phrase, 'govern through crime'. In Britain and the US especially, the last decade or so has seen the emergence of emotionally-charged and (ostensibly) punitive lay sensibilities and media discourses towards crime, and of governments that aim not to temper and tame such sentiments, but to give voice and—legislative—effect to them (Windlesham 1996, 1998, 2001). Record levels of imprisonment (Christie 1993; Garland 2001b); 'boot camps' (Simon 1995); minimum mandatory sentences (Schichor and Sechrest 1996); new controls on sex offenders (Levi 2000; Kemshall and Maguire 2001); teenage curfew provisions, and zero-tolerance policing (Dennis 1997; Stenson 2000) all—to varying degrees—attest to this. So too do the rhetorics of condemnation—what Garland (2001a: 184–6) terms a 'criminology of the other'— that now routinely surround such measures. However we are to understand these phenomena—as 'the flexing of the muscles of the displaced state' (Bauman 1999: 50; Garland 2001a: chapter 5), or as manifestations of an antique conservatism within the neo-liberal project (O'Malley 1999)—they clearly represent significant structuring properties of the contemporary crime control field.

This, however, is not the only game in town, nor the only story to be told. We can also discern in the present signs of some quieter, less prominent, but also more

---

[2] On 'law and order' in British politics, see Hall *et al.* (1978); Brake and Hale (1992); Downes and Morgan (Chapter 10 of this volume). A cogent account of the US experience can be found in Beckett (1997).

conceptually novel, shifts in the architecture and technologies of control, figurations that may turn out to be far-reaching in their effects. It is in this context that criminologists and social theorists have begun to speak of, and analyse, a shift from *government* to *governance*. Two main strands of enquiry are relevant here. For some—taking their cue from Foucault's (1991) essay on 'governmentality'—investigation has centred on the *multiplicity* of strategies, techniques, and rationalities that are today deployed to govern 'economic activity, social life and individual conduct' (Rose and Miller 1992: 174).[3] Others, working more straightforwardly within political science, emphasize the emergence of a 'differentiated polity' (Rhodes 1997: 3), wherein government institutions become less concerned with 'rowing' (delivering actual services on the ground) and oriented more towards 'steering' (establishing overall policy frameworks), and one sees the formation—in policy domains once dominated by the unitary state—of interorganizational *networks* of public, commercial, and voluntary agencies.[4]

There are some important differences between these two bodies of work (the latter, for instance, retains an institutional focus that governmentality scholars generally take to be outmoded). But they share in common a concern with the fragmentation and diffusion of power, the emergence of new sites of social authority, the deployment of new rationalities and technologies of rule, and the advent of new professional actors and expert knowledges. With this in mind, let us try to discern the broad contours of what we might call the *new governance of crime* and, in so doing, offer some brief remarks on its likely implications and effects.

REFIGURING POLICING AND PREVENTION

To speak of the emergence of governance is not to suggest that the state has ceased to be a key institutional actor in the field of crime control. Rather, it is to highlight the ways in which the objectives of state criminal justice institutions, their organizational logics and cultures, their working relations with other agencies, and their modes of accountability are each being reconfigured in potentially significant ways. Three—overlapping—aspects of this are worthy of note here. First, the tendency—especially pronounced among government officials and senior practitioners—to emphasize the limits of the police and criminal justice in controlling crime, and to seek to inculcate correspondingly more 'realistic' public expectations of what state criminal justice agencies can accomplish. We might call this process—wherein organizations like the police have become less confident of their ability to produce positive 'outcomes' in the external world, and increasingly preoccupied with internally deliverable 'outputs'

---

[3] For general statements and empirical exemplars of work on 'governmentality', see Dean (1999), Rose (1999), and the essays collected in Burchill *et al.* (1991) and Barry *et al.* (1996). For more specific analyses of crime control, see Stenson (1993); Garland (1997); Smandych (1999); Rose (2000). The recent work of O'Malley (1992, 2001) and Shearing (1996, 2001) also draws upon themes from the governmentality perspective, though without ever being fully 'signed-up' to it.

[4] On 'governance' thus conceived, see Kooiman (1993); Rhodes (1997). The nautical metaphor was first developed by Osborne and Gaebler (1992). It has been utilized in the analysis of policing and crime prevention by Shearing (1996); Crawford (1997); Walker (1999); and Loader (2000).

(Garland 2001a: 119–20)—the *de-centring* of the criminal justice state. Secondly, the rise, since the early 1980s, of a new political rationality—*managerialism* (Clarke and Newman 1997)—that has subjected the police, courts, probation, and prisons to a regime of efficiency and value-for-money, performance targets and auditing, quality of service and consumer responsiveness (Jones 1993; McLaughlin and Murji 2001). This has represented an explicit—neo-liberal—attempt to inject into public criminal justice agencies private sector 'disciplines' and ways of doing things; one that has sought to fence-in the autonomy of justice professionals by means of national standards/objectives, more robust systems of financial accountability, and greater external scrutiny. Thirdly, the emergence at a local level of crime prevention *partnerships* (Crawford 1997). Attendant upon the realization that the police alone can have only modest effects upon crime levels, we have seen since the 1980s a thickening of 'community safety' networks, comprising not only formal cooperative arrangements between the police, local government, and cognate criminal justice/social service agencies,[5] but also instances of public authorities contracting with commercial actors to deliver closed-circuit television (CCTV) systems and 'police' patrols (see below).

We are, in short, witnessing a reconfiguration of the local field of policing and prevention. Unfolding largely beyond the glare of the media, and often in the shadow of their punitive scripts, an altered landscape of control is coming into view—one made up of new institutional actors (e.g., local government, the Audit Commission, the Inspectorate of Constabulary, Nacro, Crime Concern); professional specialisms (community safety practitioners, crime prevention consultants, evaluation researchers); modes of criminological knowledge (audits, inspections, evaluations) and legitimating discourses (currently: 'what works'—see Raynor, in Chapter 31). Making sense of these often opaque, self-corroborating networks of local crime governance, and of the questions of effectiveness, equity, and political accountability they raise, amounts to a pressing challenge for contemporary criminological and socio-legal enquiry (cf. Crawford 1997: chapters 7–8; Loader 2000).

'RESPONSIBILIZING' CITIZENS

The new governance of crime has, we have argued, been in large measure the outcome of an occupationally-grounded recognition of the limits of the sovereign state, and of neo-liberal politics bent on 'decollectivizing' social risks whose management had up until the 1970s come to be viewed as the legitimate province of government (O'Malley and Palmer 1996; Rose 1999: chapter 7). One further aspect of these discursive shifts has been a relocation of responsibility for crime prevention into the hands of individual citizens—figures who have in recent years been re-imagined not as mere

---

[5] The Crime and Disorder Act 1998 (ss 5–7) placed this collaboration—which had unfolded somewhat haltingly and unevenly since the 1980s—on a legal footing by imposing a joint statutory responsibility on police and local authorities, together with probation and health authorities, to establish local 'crime and disorder reduction partnerships'. These are tasked with responsibility for undertaking a local crime *audit*, *consulting* locally on the results of that audit, and drawing up a crime and disorder reduction *strategy*, a process that has to be repeated on a three-year cycle (see Crawford 1998).

recipients of state policing and criminal justice, but as self-calculating, risk-monitoring actors with important parts to play in the 'co-production' of order and security. This, in general terms, has taken the form of encouraging individuals, communities, and organizations to think about their everyday and/or working lives in terms of crime prevention and to act accordingly—guidance that has been aimed as much at small business, town planners, schools, and hospitals as at 'ordinary citizens'. More specifically, it has entailed: (i) eliciting people's direct participation in anti-crime activity, whether by joining a local crime prevention panel, responding to a *Crimestoppers* appeal, or participating in some form of 'watch' scheme (neighbourhood-, street-, pub-, shop-, farm-, etc.); (ii) schooling people in the importance of forming preventative habits and routines, such as locking car doors, maintaining a tight grip on one's bags, avoiding 'dangerous' locations, and not walking home alone after dark;[6] and (iii) encouraging people to deploy their judgement and means as consumers in order to secure in the market place the kinds of protection of person and property they find desirable—a process increasingly fuelled by the inducements and stipulations of the insurance industry (O'Malley 1991). By such means has the state to varying degrees sought in the crime prevention field to govern 'at a distance' *through* the exercise of freedom by self-activating individuals and 'communities' (O'Malley 1992).

There is, of course, much in these 'responsibilization strategies' (Garland 2001a: 124–7) that makes good sociological sense—order and security ultimately depend not on formal agencies of criminal justice, but on informal social controls exercised within civil society. There may, in addition, be sound normative reasons why democratic societies should seek to enhance citizen participation in crime control. In their current form, however, these trajectories—which amount to a form of 'privatized prudentialism' (O'Malley 1992: 261)—possess a number of potentially troubling elements. In terms of democracy, they introduce some subtle but important shifts in the meanings of 'responsibility' and 'accountability', these terms coming to denote within governmental discourse either: (i) the *responsibility* of individuals and organizations to manage their own crime risks (and to assume a proportion of the blame should they fail so to do), and/or (ii) the *responsiveness of* commercial security providers to their *paying* consumers—a form of contractual (rather than political) accountability that tends to efface a number of wider, public interest considerations. In terms of equity, the encouragement of market-based and citizen-initiated prevention tends to effect a re-allocation of policing services and security hardware in favour of the (already) advantaged at the expense of the disadvantaged (Shearing 1996). It serves, in particular, to harden divisions between those consumers and communities who are well placed to become active risk managers and those (generally more 'at risk' groups) who lack the economic and social capital required to provide for their own individual and collective safety. It is these cleavages in the distribution of security

---

[6] As Stanko (1990) points out in her critique of these modes of address, much of this 'advice' is directed at women. So too, one might add, is the marketing that aims to promote products that have little ostensibly to do with security—such as mobile phones, or the services of certain motoring organizations—in terms of safety.

benefits and burdens that responsibilization strategies presently threaten to entrench and exacerbate.

PRIVATE SECURITY AND PRIVATE ORDERS

A closely connected dimension of this shift in responsibility for security from state to citizen has been the significant expansion of commercial involvement in the provision of policing services and security technology, and a corresponding growth in the size of the private security industry (Jones and Newburn 1998: chapters 3–4; Kempa *et al.* 1999).[7] The key developments here may be categorized thus:

1. The commercial supply of guarding and patrol services, something that has included deployment by government organizations and corporations of either 'in-house' or 'contracted-in' security; the use of private security in shopping malls, office complexes, and other sites of 'mass private property' (Shearing and Stenning 1983); and citizens clubbing together to employ commercial patrols to keep watch over their neighbourhood—a development more pervasive in the US (Davis 1992: chapter 4; Blakely and Snyder 1997), though not unknown in Britain (Noaks 2000).

2. Burgeoning markets in the supply of security hardware and technology. This includes locks, bars, grilles, gates, and alarms—things that have become an increasingly visible (and audible) feature of the urban landscape in Britain in recent years. But it also encompasses the installation and running of CCTV and cognate security systems, as well as more 'sophisticated' monitoring, surveillance, and data-processing technologies (Lyon 2001).[8]

3. The increasingly rapid entry of commercial security into the policing of 'new social spaces' (Manning 2000), such as cyberspace, industrial espionage, the protection of multinational corporations, and military conflict (Kempa *et al.* 1999; Johnston 2000).

Policing and security have, in short, become a fragmented, plural, and commodified phenomenon, the distribution of which is being increasingly determined by people's capacity and willingness to pay.

---

[7] It has now become commonplace to observe—notwithstanding the difficulties entailed in seeking accurately to gauge the size of the private security industry—that the number of operatives employed by the private sector in Britain, the US, and Canada exceed those employed by state police forces. Jones and Newburn (1998: chapter 3) note, for instance, that the numbers employed in the 'security services and equipment' sector alone (182, 596) are approximate to the total numbers (civilians included) serving in all 43 police forces in England and Wales.

[8] CCTV has—since it was first introduced in public space in 1985—become all-pervasive in Britain, with in excess of 5,000 schemes now in operation (Norris *et al.* 1998; Norris and Armstrong 1999). It has also—notwithstanding the many vexing questions it raises—come to be very much taken for granted, with such unease and opposition to surveillance cameras as exists taking a largely inchoate, pre-political form (Girling *et al.* 2000: chapter 7). As such, CCTV offers a telling instance of how control techniques influenced by rational choice theory, routine activities theory, and other 'criminologies of everyday life' (Garland 2001a: 182–3) are today becoming embedded in the physical and social fabric of urban life in ways that tend to efface their ineluctably ethico-political dimensions (cf. von Hirsch *et al.* 2000).

Various analytic frameworks have been mobilized to make sense of these developments, the preponderance of which have centred on shifts in the character of governance (O'Malley and Palmer 1996; Shearing 1996); transitions to late- or post-modernity (Reiner 1992; Jones and Newburn 1998: chapter 8), and the efforts of anxious citizens to satisfy their demands for order (Loader 1997, 1999). We cannot deal here with the respective merits and lacunae of each of these explanatory efforts. Instead, let us wrap up our reflections on governance by briefly setting out two posited consequences of fragmented, commodified security, and considering—in the form of urgent, but as yet unanswered, questions—some of the issues it raises.

The commodification of security appears, first of all, to be creating commercial and residential spaces in which an exclusive, particularistic order comes to be defined and enforced. The sanitized, consumer-friendly realm offered by shopping malls represents important instances of the former; so too—according to Shearing and Stenning (1996)—does Disneyland. In respect of the latter, walled, gated, privately policed enclaves—of the kind evident in Southern California and elsewhere in the US (Davis 1992: chapter 4), though also apparent (in embryonic forms) in parts of Britain— serve cognately as means of physical protection, as marks of 'distinction' (Loader 1999), and as vehicles for upholding the value of economic capital.[9] *But what new forms of solidarity, identification and affiliation are being forged in such places? Is the commodification of policing and security operating to cement (sometimes literally) and deepen social and spatial inequalities generated elsewhere? Are we witnessing the formation of a tribalized, 'neo-feudal' world of private orders in which social cohesion and common citizenship are strained to the point of collapse?*

We appear, secondly and relatedly, to be witnessing the advent of new modes of 'private government'—'the proliferation of corporate loci devoted to governing security in ways that sometimes resonate with, and at other times stand in contradistinction to, those of the state in general, and of criminal justice in particular' (Shearing and Wood 2000: 458). Policing, it seems, is being de-coupled from the state and relocated in diverse networks of agents and agencies that are coming to perform what has for some two centuries been regarded as a constitutive task of government— the production of order (Walker 1999). It is not merely—against this backdrop—that the state is ceasing, in Osborne and Gaebler's (1992) terms, to 'row' when it comes to policing. There are also increasingly good grounds for thinking that it lacks the effective capacity to 'steer' (Loader and Walker 2001). *What though are the likely implications of all this? How—against the backdrop of fragmentation and pluralization—can the idea of effective, equitable, and democratic policing be sustained? How might 'security networks' ground their claims to authority and legitimacy? Does the state still have a viable and justifiable role to play in the delivery or governance of security?*

---

[9] Such enclosures are of course predicated on the existence of, and danger posed by, a hostile wider environment, an environment that provides a constant, and potentially debilitating, reminder of the self-limiting, costly, and contingent quality of the version of security to which such market-based, exclusionary solutions subscribe. It is in this deep sense that the very concept of *private* security may be considered oxymoronic (Loader 1997).

RISK

In the responses of criminologists and other social observers to the stew of developments sketched above, one term seems to recur with increasing insistence and frequency (and hence, arguably, with less and less dependability as to the consistency and precision of its uses)—risk. In our attempts to grasp the peculiar features of the present—whether on the levels of states' actions in choosing to 'govern through crime'; or that of private corporations selling 'security'; or of local criminal justice agencies engaging in 'partnerships' to *audit* and *manage* losses and threats to individuals, households, and businesses; or indeed of people's everyday practices and decisions about housing, consumption, and leisure—this protean and seemingly limitlessly adaptable notion presses itself on our attention.

In the last twenty years or so risk has moved from the periphery to the core of criminological theorizing and crime control practice. Until quite recently it held a relatively specialized and limited, though respectable, place somewhere on the margins of criminological research and policy discussion. For those who explicitly used the term at all, it arose in the context of certain determinate and particular questions—Could early intervention reduce the chances of 'at-risk' youth embarking on criminal careers? Was the extended incarceration of some individuals on grounds of 'dangerousness' justified? Were parole boards good enough at predicting future behaviour? Did deterrence have any measurable bearing on crime rates?

In some cases of its use the increasing centrality of 'risk' just means in essence that such discussions have become more intensive and more technically sophisticated. In that process, long-standing professional concerns with judgements about ways of anticipating and forestalling future harms (concerns that have their origin in nineteenth-century preoccupations with 'moral statistics' and twentieth-century innovations in preventive detention, among other places) have evolved and extended to incorporate new methods, statistical models, and the availability of previously unimagined computational power. Such extensions of technology and technique, however, arguably change the character of the crime control apparatus in more pronounced ways than might at first appear. Far from merely furnishing better data about, and more advanced and exhaustive analyses of, the same topics and questions (while leaving its basic purposes unchanged), the refocusing of the theory and practice of crime control in terms of risk actually serves to reconfigure its objects of attention and intervention, its intellectual and institutional connections with other domains, and its cultural and political salience and sensitivity in potentially fundamental fashion. The intrusion of risk into criminal justice thus carries a certain inherent irony in that the enhanced role attributed to anticipation and prevention restructures the field in unanticipated (and apparently unpreventable) ways. Here we can do no more than sketch some of the key aspects of this restructuring and, in particular, point to certain connections between the growth of risk-based practices and techniques and the larger contours of change that are our main concern in this chapter.

It is important to note that in criminal justice as in other domains (industrial safety, pollution and environmental policy, food hygiene, fire prevention, medicines management—this list could go on, and on), attention to risk assessment and risk management does not arise arbitrarily. The ascendancy of risk-based reasoning derives in large measure from the fact that probabalistic models based on large data samples do provide more efficient and pragmatic guides to intervention in many spheres of activity than previous methods did. Just as we no longer expect the licensing of, for example, new pharmaceuticals to proceed without rigorous testing, numerous contemporary fields of criminological enquiry (such as, classically, criminal careers research and attempts to scale the probability of reconviction after release from prison; but also, especially latterly, attempts to estimate the risks of victimization experienced by given categories of people or those living in particular localities) are increasingly unimaginable without reference to such methods.

Yet this is very far from being the whole story. On one hand, the fact that risk-management in crime control bears such close technical similarity to other fields and practices of governance, poses the question of how far specifically *criminological* varieties of expertise can remain immune from colonization by new cadres of versatile technician-managers for whom crime is just one species of manipulable risk among others. In this respect the stage is set for various as yet unresolved struggles for predominance between risk-based reasoning and other resources of knowledge, influence, and prestige (for example, between judicial wisdom and actuarial prediction in sentencing; between clinical judgement and algorithmic scaling in parole decisions; and between 'personalist' social work values and 'craft' skills versus numericized risk inventories in probation). In other words, 'risk' may be seen as a 'cognitive habit' (Brown and Pratt 2000: 3) whose origins lie outwith the criminological field as such but which gradually infiltrates its every nook and cranny. The expression 'actuarial justice', famously coined by Feeley and Simon (1992) in their account of the rise of the 'new penology', nicely and deliberately expresses some of the internal tensions that result.

On the other hand, the very fact that every one of the fields that 'actuarial' thinking enters is already occupied by existing practitioners and their associated specialist discourses conversely suggests that we should not expect 'risk' always to emerge pristine and unadulterated from the encounter. Rather, we should expect to see new hybrid or compromise formations ('effort-bargains' as they are sometimes called) between 'actuarial' reasoning properly so-called and other priorities and commitments. In this respect 'risk' may be the paradigm case of rational decision-making or resource-allocation *de nos jours*, but it is remarkable how commonly actual practices depart from their prototypical models (see further O'Malley 2000; Kemshall and Maguire 2001; Sparks 2001; Robinson 2002).

Moreover, and of more pressing concern for us here, the term 'risk' cannot feasibly be restricted only to what happens in specialist, technical arenas (even if one of its chief properties is precisely that of bringing into being many new arenas of quasi-technical intervention). Rather, risk 'seeps out' from such protected spaces to become part of the very idiom of our contemporary moral and political conversations. Increasingly, and undoubtedly at much cost in terms of precision as to when it is or is not being used appositely, risk is part of the common currency of cultural exchange (creeping into the language of everything, from weather forecasting to the control of bovine diseases). For this reason Mary Douglas wonders at the 'innocence' of those professional risk analysts who evince surprise when the increasing sophistication of their collective wisdom fails to put an end to public controversy over nuclear power, or biotechnology, or indeed crime, policing, and public safety. Quite the reverse: when we speak now of risk in relation to crime we are plumb in the middle of our topic in this essay, namely how theory and research speak to the moral aspects of the governance of our contemporary insecurities. A risk, Douglas observes, is not a 'thing' but a way of thinking—not just the probability of an event 'but also the probable magnitude of its outcome, and everything depends on the value that is set on the outcome' (1992: 31). Douglas's 'cultural theory of risk' thus brings into special focus the way in which the identification of particular sources of threat and danger (and by extension whom we blame for them) refracts a given community's dispositions towards order and authority: 'There is no way of proceeding with analysing risk perception without typifying kinds of communities according to the support their members give to authority, commitment, boundaries and structure' (Douglas 1992: 47).

The presentiment of risk, therefore, is inherently political: it galvanizes action and prompts discourse. But studying the connections between risk, fear, and blame can never be solely an activity of quantitatively cataloguing dangers and assorting responses to risk into boxes marked 'rational' and 'irrational' (Sparks 1991).

In principle this suggests a daunting and exciting research agenda for criminologists, one that is today being pursued quite vigorously, especially in relation to the vexed issue of the 'fear of crime' (Sparks 1992; Hollway and Jefferson 1997; Walklate 1998; Girling *et al.* 2000; Hope and Sparks 2000). Such an agenda would draw attention to the weight that attaches to the dangers of crime, and to some crimes rather than others, in the social and political conversations that go on in particular times and places—the social construction of their differential visibility (see further, Pavarini 1997). It also gives a clue as to why, amidst the proliferation of technical means of risk assessment in the administrative culture of modern societies (the generic 'probabilization' of which Hacking speaks (1991)), the social discourse of crime and punishment still 'falls into antique mode' (Douglas 1992: 26) and refuses to shed 'its ancient moral freight' (ibid.: 35).

Douglas here nails a point that in some degree clarifies a number of the diverse developments already noted in this chapter. Crime and punishment have consequences both for the very texture of personal life and for some embedded features of social organization. And they are Janus-faced phenomena—they have both novel and archaic dimensions (cf. Garland 1990). A number of social theorists have concluded that the identification and management of risks have become structuring principles of contemporary organizational and political life. Once they have been named and identified, risks demand responses from the responsible bodies, even though it may exceed their powers substantially to control, let alone to abolish them. Thus, for Beck (1992) as for Giddens (1990, 1991), thinking about danger *in terms of risk* is a pervasive feature of contemporary life. For Giddens, we live in a world of 'manufactured uncertainty', and it is characteristic of such a 'risk-climate' that its institutions become *reflexive*—endlessly monitoring, adjusting, and calculating their behaviour in the face of insatiable demands for information and pressures for accountability. For Beck (1992: 21): 'Risk may be defined as a systematic way of dealing with hazards and insecurities induced and introduced by modernization itself. Risks, as opposed to older dangers, are consequences which relate to the threatening force of modernization and to its globalization of doubt.'

In Beck's view the 'risk society' is characterized by ambivalence: between faith in progress and nostalgia (or what Giddens elsewhere terms 'reactive traditionalism'); between demands for technical information and suspicion of experts, and hence between authority and withdrawal of legitimacy; between local particularism and the utopian image of a world society; between indifference and hysteria. Nor does he doubt that such a society has authoritarian potentialities, arising in part from the accumulation of expert knowledge in the hands of elites (1992: 80) and in part from the formation of solidarities based in fear and given to scapegoating (1992: 75).

In this respect the term 'risk' increasingly does not just denote what happens within specialized expert-systems designed to anticipate and manage harm or loss (or the tendency for the familiar institutions of criminal justice to be reconfigured into risk-managing agencies of this kind). Rather, it also concerns the often fevered politics that swirl around questions of risk and the battles that determine which risks are selected for particular attention, which categories of person and which places come to be regarded as bearers or containers of intolerable levels of risk, and so on. At the same time the problem of risk is critical to the restructuring of the criminal justice state that we have sketched above. It does appear that in certain senses the state has latterly tended to lose some of its former centrality and authority, and that power leeches out and passes to other actors. Yet in other respects this very process engenders a refocusing on certain 'core' activities and a more heated politics of crime and punishment, precisely because the state's capacity to deliver 'security' is so much in question. To this extent there is a narrowing of the grounds on which the state can claim legitimacy, and every failure of propriety or competence in risk management is potentially a scandal. Two primary consequences result. First, risk is never the dry, technocratic matter that it initially appears. Instead each system of risk management creates as its counterpart a *blaming* system (see further, Sparks 2000, 2001; Garland 2001a). Secondly, the 'minimal state' of neo-liberalism—the state which is, as we shall shortly see, in some degree 'hollowed out' by globalization—is also a *penal* state in ways that are often more intense and more politically central than was the case for its predecessor 'state regimes' of the post-war period (Hay 1996; Wacquant 1999; Young 1999).

GLOBALIZATION

While the nation state still looks imposing in its shiny uniform, and people's bodies and souls are still routinely tortured around the world, information flows bypass, and sometimes overwhelm, the state; terrorist wars criss-cross national boundaries; and communal turfs exhaust the law and order patrol. The state still relies on violence and surveillance, but it does not hold its monopoly any longer, nor can it exercise them from its national enclosure [Castells 1997: 303].

The advent of 'global figuration' is, according to Zygmunt Bauman (2001: 11), 'by far the most prominent and seminal feature of our times'. Globalization has, as such, come to the forefront of analysis across the social sciences, as well as assuming a visible and sharply contested place within media and political discourse. A term barely known beyond academia but a decade or so ago is today a staple of public conversation—its existence, benefits, and costs routinely tussled over by politicians, commentators, corporate executives, and social movements. But what—beyond some commonly uttered platitudes concerning the planetary reach of the likes of Nike and McDonald's, or the onset of the Internet and satellite TV—is signified by the idea of 'globalization'? How is this process—or, better, processes—most adequately understood? And what interest or relevance does it have for those concerned—in one small corner of the global woods—with the social analysis of crime, order, and the institutions of 'sovereign' crime control?

Let us start with some attempts at definition. For Beck (2000: 11) globalization refers to 'the processes through which sovereign national states are criss-crossed and undermined by transnational actors with varying prospects of power, orientations, identities and networks'. In a similar spirit, Giddens (1990: 64) suggests that 'globalization can thus be defined as the intensification of worldwide social relations which link distant localities in such a way that local happenings are shaped by events occurring many miles away and vice versa'. While, in a recent synthesis, David Held and his colleagues conceptualize globalization in the following terms:

A process (or set of processes) which embodies a transformation in the spatial organization of social relations and transactions—assessed in terms of their extensity, intensity, velocity and impact—generating transcontinental or interregional flows and networks of activity, interaction, and the exercise of power [Held *et al.* 1999: 16].

A number of helpful pointers can be distilled from these formulations, four of which we wish to pursue further. They suggest, first, that relations between states and societies (and the economic and political systems within which they are embedded) have altered in ways that rob analyses of 'societies' as distinct entities with clear boundaries of much of their purchase, and bring to the fore the issue of *networks* and *flows*—movements of capital, goods, people, symbols, and information across formerly separate national contexts (Castells 1996; Urry 2000). Secondly, they indicate that *local* social relations, and the fate of particular *places*, are being reconfigured in ways that contemporary social—and criminological—enquiry is only beginning to get to grips with (Lash and Urry 1994; Bottoms and Wiles 1995). Thirdly, they alert us to the possibility (should that be fact?) that *sovereign authority* is no longer merely territorial, the sole prerogative of nation states, but has instead escaped national enclosures in a fashion that creates new sites of power beyond the state and calls radically into doubt some entrenched theories of accountability, legitimacy, and democracy (Held 1995; Sassen 1996). Lastly, in respect of each of these overlapping domains, they draw attention both to some emergent social *cleavages, insecurities and inequalities* (of affluence and destitution, access and exclusion, mobility and fixity) sparked by globalization, and to the *contradictory political responses* (old fundamentalisms and violent protectionism on the one hand, new international social movements and cosmopolitan possibilities on the other) that globality has ushered forth (Giddens 1990; Bauman 1998; Beck 2000). Let us elaborate a little on each of these themes, paying particular attention to their intersections with questions of crime, security, and control.

CRIMINAL NETWORKS AND CROSS-BORDER CRIME FLOWS

In their attempt to steer a course between those they coin 'hyperglobalizers' (e.g., Albrow 1996) and those they term 'sceptics' (e.g., Hirst and Thompson 1996), Held *et al.* (1999) emphasize that there is nothing historically unprecedented about processes of globalization. Phases of global interconnectedness can, they acknowledge, be traced back over centuries (ibid.: 16–20). They nonetheless maintain—persuasively in our view—that processes of change in political, military, economic, and cultural domains amount today to a distinct and novel form of globalization, a form that can be registered in terms of the extensity, intensity, velocity, and impact of global networks and flows.

This connects closely with one 'type of anxiety' (Nelken 1997: 253) found in contemporary accounts of the globalization of crime (see also, Ruggiero 2000). This centres upon how globalizing processes are creating new opportunities for transnational corporate and organized crime—opportunities that territorially-bound state criminal justice agencies are poorly placed to stem.[10] The category 'transnational crime' generally includes the cross-border smuggling of drugs, weapons, radioactive materials, information, art, cars, and other stolen goods; trafficking in illegal immigrants, women and children (often to work in the sex industry), and body parts; counterfeiting, international fraud, and other financial crime; and espionage, terrorism, extortion, and kidnapping (Castells 1998: 168–80)—modes of illicit action that depend crucially upon 'money laundering by the hundreds of billions (maybe trillions) of dollars' (ibid.: 167; cf. Sheptycki 2000a; Levi, in Chapter 24 of this volume). These activities are, moreover, taken to be the work of local and regional criminal networks—networks that effectively couple (pre-modern) local identities and kinship affiliations with (post-modern) entrepreneurial organization and know-how (Karstedt 2000)—whose operations routinely whirl across national borders. These include (the list appears well-known): the Sicilian Mafia, Colombian and Mexican drugs cartels, Nigerian crime networks, the Yakuza in Japan, Chinese and Taiwanese Triads, and an array of post-soviet Russian *Mafiyas* (Sterling 1994; Ruggiero 1996; Ruggerio *et al.* 1998: Pt III).

All this, Castells (1998: 166) contends, 'is a new phenomenon that profoundly affects international and national economies, politics, security, and, ultimately, societies at large'. It does so in several ways. Illegal activity—generally pursued in close combination with forms of legitimate enterprise—contributes in significant (if difficult to estimate) measure to the size and functioning of the global economy

---

[10] It should of course be noted that transnational criminal activities are not merely an *effect* of globalization; these activities serve in turn as a *causal agent* in deepening and extending globalizing processes (Nelken 1997: 261–62).

(Nordstrom 2000: 37–8). Criminal networks operate ruthless protection and enforcement systems that challenge directly 'an essential component of state sovereignty *and legitimacy*: its ability to impose law and order' (Castells 1998: 203; emphasis in original). Such networks become appealing cultural idols for many dispossessed young males who see no other obvious route out of poverty, as well as having more diffuse effects at the level of popular culture. And in many states across the world (Italy, Colombia, Bolivia, Russia, Afghanistan, large swathes of Africa), 'shadow' enterprises deploy some variant of bribery, extortion, political funding, assassination, or armed combat as a means to undermine the governing capacities and political authority of weak or 'failed' states (Job 1992; Goldsmith 2001).[11] Such networks have, in short, assumed a key role in setting the basic terms of existence across many parts of the globe; something that calls into question many received—criminological—wisdoms about the locus of effective, sovereign crime control:

Shadow networks forge economic policies, they operate within political realms, they fashion foreign policy. These networks have developed dispute resolution systems and systems of enforcement. They have code of conduct and rules of behaviour set in social and cultural systems. They are not states, but they share these attributes with states. And perhaps they share the status of sovereignty—a social sovereignty in this case—as well [Nordstrom 2000: 51].

'LOCAL' CRIME AND RESPONSES TO CRIME

Giddens (1991) stresses that globalization is not merely an 'out-there' phenomenon, a process impacting only on distant occurrences and relations between states. Its effects, he points out, are also experienced *by* and felt *within* localities that can no longer insulate themselves from events and processes happening elsewhere. Global flows of capital and culture today powerfully shape the texture of local social relations and the fate of particular neighbourhoods, towns, and cities, altering people's sense of what it means to live 'here' as against there, of who 'we' are and where we feel 'at home' (Robertson 1995). None of this means that 'place' ceases to matter—although global trends appear in some respects to be eroding the distinctiveness of particular places. Rather, it is to point to a process of 'divergent modernization' that produces not 'sameness' but new 'particularities' and 'hybridizations' (ibid.). It thus, in a global economy, makes a fatal difference to one's life chances *who* one is (in terms of one's skills and 'social capital') and *where one lives* (a 'sunrise zone' or 'rust-belt city', a 'gentrifying suburb' or an 'impacted ghetto'). In these respects, the notoriously widening income dispersions in many major economies, and the creation of structurally widening sub-populations within them, are the key properties of capitalist globalization.

This could hardly be of greater import to criminology. In part this has to do with

---

[11] Such states tend to respond in kind (and self-defence) with a retrenchment of democratic rights and institutions and a resort to xenophobic rhetoric and measures. As Goldsmith (2001: 18) notes, police violence and human rights abuses are often an expression not of a state's strength, but of its *weakness*: '*despotic* police power is often a substitute for *infrastructural* state power' (ibid.: 23; emphases in original).

the fact that the forms of transnational crime just alluded to are themselves global and local, registering their effects (unevenly) on social relations in Medellin and Palermo *and* in the Bronx and Birkenhead (on 'glocal' organized crime, see Hobbs and Dunnighan 1998). But this is far from all. Criminologists interested in the ecology of urban crime have also done much of late to flesh-out empirically the social impact of current macro-economic transformations. They have, in the first place, indicated how the differential 'urban fortunes' (Logan and Molotch 1987) of late modernity are profoundly interlaced with both the distribution and effects of victimization-risks and the contemporary forms and meanings of urban crime and violence. In respect of the former, such concerns have given rise not just to a microscopically-detailed 'criminology of place' (Sherman *et al.* 1989; Eck and Weisburd 1996), but also to a criminological concern with the spatial dynamics of inequality in the contemporary city, especially in the forms of 'white flight', 'ghettoization', 'disrepute', and so on (Taub *et al.* 1984; Skogan 1990; Hagan and Petersen 1995; Hope 2001). In terms of the latter, one can point to a clutch of powerfully-observed ethnographies oriented to documenting the—often violent, criminal—street cultures formed in urban localities washed-up on the tide of global capitalism, and to making sense of these formations in ways that make explicit their englobement within transnational circuits of capital and culture (Sullivan 1988; Nightingale 1993; Bourgois 1995; cf. Hagan 1994: chapter 3).

Secondly, mention can be made of certain 'local' lay responses to crime and the closely connected topic of the renewed politicization of order and penality seen in at least some nation states (Beckett 1997; O'Malley 1999; Garland 2001a). These appear—under global conditions—to be deeply entangled with the inability of individuals to protect established identities from a 'generalized risk climate' (Giddens 1991: 126) and with the erosion of state sovereignty. Bauman has written provocatively in this regard of how the economic precariousness and existential insecurity attendant upon globalization generates 'withdrawal into the safe haven of territoriality' and condensed anxieties about—and social demands for—safety (1998: 117). Supporting warrants for such a proposition appear to abound. We have, for instance (in collaboration with our colleague Evi Girling), striven to make sense of the demands for order found among residents of one—relatively prosperous, low-crime—town in 'Middle England' very much in these terms (Girling *et al.* 2000). The aforementioned mushrooming of private security patrols, gating, and related measures designed to create 'bubbles of security' (whether in Los Angeles (Davis 1990), São Paulo (Caldeira 2000), or elsewhere) is at least partly explicable in such ways (Bottoms and Wiles 1995). So too, arguably, are the fears stirred up in many states of western Europe by real and imagined migrants—fears that in some places (Britain and Germany for instance) have given rise to racialized violence directed by young, dispossessed males towards asylum-seekers and guest-workers.[12] Bauman notes

[12] The explosion of ethnic violence and warfare in the former Yugoslavia in the 1990s has also been interpreted by some theorists in something approaching these terms—as either stoked by apprehended threats to established borders and identities (what Bauman calls 'globalization-induced wars'), or—as in the case of Kosovo—waged in the name of an incipient international community (what he terms 'globalizing wars') (Bauman 2001; cf. Kaldor 1999; Delanty 2001). Criminologists have also recently begun to turn their attention to the issues raised by the return of war to Europe (Nikolic-Ristanovic 1998; Jamieson 1998).

further how state governments (in their now diminished role as administrators of what he terms 'over-sized police precincts' (1998: 120)) eagerly concur with and encourage the translation of citizen insecurities into the question of 'law and order'; not least because it enables them—often to great electoral advantage—practically and rhetorically to deploy those levers over which they appear to retain some control—to wit, the punishment of law-breakers (Garland 2001b; Hudson, in Chapter 8 of this volume). An adequate account of the febrile politics of order that obtain today across many liberal democracies (notably the US and UK) cannot but make some reference to such considerations (cf. Garland 2001a: chapters 5–6).

Yet we must also take care not to read the emerging—global—landscape too flatly. For while the prospects of particular places (towns, cities, regions, nations) and their citizens *are* today structured by events and processes happening quite elsewhere, we ought not to disregard the ways in which the levels and meanings of crime, and public and official responses to it, remain constituted—at least in part—within the national political cultures and local 'structures of feeling' of different societies. This—or, to be more precise, the demands, refusals, and resistances that attend the reception of CCTV, commercial security, and the like into one particular place—we took to be an abiding lesson of our researches in Macclesfield (Girling *et al.* 2000: chapter 8). It is also something that recent comparative enquiry in criminology has nicely and importantly documented (Nelken 1994, 2000; Pavarini 1997; Åkeström 1998; Lacey and Zedner 1998; Karstedt and Bussmann 2000: Pt III; Sparks 2001). We shall briefly revisit these issues—which seem to us to entail some thorny problems pertaining to the notion of 'culture'—by way of conclusion below.

TRANSNATIONAL CRIME CONTROL

The second—and opposite—'type of anxiety' (Nelken 1997: 253) one encounters in the criminological literature on globalization concerns the slow, halting, but nonetheless discernible advent of networks and institutions of crime control at the transnational level. The attendant concern here is that, far from rebuilding the capacity of states to deal in effective *and* accountable ways with transnational organized crime, the fears of such crime are, instead, being 'exploited with a view to cutting normative corners and eroding civil rights' (Ruggiero 2000: 195). More of such concerns in a moment. First, let us briefly sketch the contours of this unfolding landscape.

The most extensive developments in this field lie in the realm of policing (Sheptycki 2000b). These reach back to the formation of Interpol, which was originally set up in 1923, in its current guise in 1949 (Anderson 1989). While still a significant actor in international policing, Interpol has, however, been eclipsed of late: first, by US efforts to extend and coordinate law enforcement beyond its borders (in actions against Colombian drugs cartels, in securing an increasingly militarized US-Mexican border, in training police forces in post-communist eastern Europe—Nadelman 1993); and, secondly, by the building of an enhanced police and criminal justice capacity within the European Union (Anderson *et al.* 1995; den Boer and Wallace 2001; Walker 2001). These latter developments have included: (i) the extension—following the creation under the 1992 Maastricht Treaty of a Third Pillar of EU competence in 'justice and home affairs'—of forms of intergovernmental activity and supranational policy-making in areas of police cooperation, efforts to tackle organized crime, and measures concerning immigration, asylum policy, and other matters pertaining to the 'free movement of persons';[13] (ii) the onset of institutions, networks, and training programmes aimed at furthering the exchange of information and know-how among Europe's police officers, prosecutors, and judges (e.g., Europol, Eurojust, the Operational Task Force of European Police Chiefs, an incipient European Police College); and (iii) new modes of ground-level cooperation between national police forces, whether through the auspices of Europol liaison officers (Bigo 2000a), under programmes 'twinning' EU forces with their counterparts in east European 'accession states', or in respect of new security 'hotspots' such as the Channel Tunnel (Sheptycki 1996) and the post-Schengen French–German 'border zone' (Nogala 2001).[14]

The future direction of these developments is hard to anticipate. It is certainly true that some obstinate professional interests and entrenched national sentiments litter the path towards further transnationalization; not least because policing and criminal justice stand as powerful icons of sovereign statehood (Loader 2002). Yet under conditions of globalization events and processes seem likely to exert a continuing pressure to thicken and extend forms of cross-border crime control—witness the calls made, following the violent disorders at the Genoa G8 summit in July 2001, for the setting-up of a 'European riot police' (*Guardian*, 6 August 2001).[15] In this context a series of concerns arise about the consequences (for effective policing, for human rights, for democratic accountability) of these emergent developments. Given the uncertain state of the field, and the limits of our present knowledge, they are best posed—and left hanging—in the shape of questions: *Are we witnessing a steady erosion of the distinction between 'internal' and 'external' security and, with it, the demise of sovereign nation states as principal guarantors of social order* (Bigo 2000b)? *Is transnational cooperation between governmental and criminal justice elites unfolding in ways that are inimical to democratic rights and liberties? If so, how must our ideas of democracy and citizenship adapt to these new global realities?*

[13] In what is perhaps a telling indicator of the speed and direction of policy activity, at the 1999 European Justice Council in Tampere, Finland, EU interior ministers agreed a 'programme of work' equivalent in scale to that which led up to the formation of the single market in 1992 (den Boer and Wallace 2001: 517).

[14] The EU, it should be said, far from exhausts contemporary developments in transnational policing. In particular, one must take account of the growing involvement of 'global commercial security' (Johnston 2000) in efforts to, among other things, regulate cyberspace, protect multinational enterprise, and wage low-intensity warfare (Kempa *et al.* 1999; Manning 2000).

[15] Mention might additionally be made here of the ways in which 'national' crime policies are—under global conditions—both reflexively open to scrutiny occasioned by knowledge of how 'things are done' elsewhere, and prone to 'travel' across jurisdictions—witness the diffusion of discourse and policy initiative surrounding such matters as zero-tolerance, 'problem-oriented' policing, mandatory minimum sentences, wars on drugs, community notification of sex offenders, and restorative conferencing (for what it is worth, our own personal favourite is neighbourhood watch in Buenos Aires!). This raises a number of puzzles: What does and does not get exported? How, under what conditions, and by whom (the media, politicians, justice professionals, criminologists)? With what effects in the country of import? Criminologists have only just started to reflect upon and investigate these (Newburn and Sparks 2002).

SOME GLOBAL PROBLEMS AND PROSPECTS

The prognosis offered by social theorists and criminologists in the face of globalization is, on the whole, rather gloomy. Not, arguably, without good reason. Transnational crime networks routinely overrun the efforts of control agencies to contain
them and often decisively undercut the capacity of 'sovereign' governments to govern.
The generally authoritarian responses such struggling states make in the face of their
impotence serve merely to compound the misery and violence. The free flight of
capital investment from one place to another forges widening material inequalities
within and between states, and creates new insecurities and anxieties among
citizens—these often presenting as demands for 'law and order'. New sites of transnational crime control emerge that outstrip the capacity of territorially-rooted legal
and democratic institutions to bring them effectively to account. The creation of
'Fortress Europe', and the devising of more robust, militarized responses to those who
protest against globalization in its neo-liberal forms, continue apace (Ericson and
Doyle 1999; Mathieson 2000). These are all, indeed, deeply worrying components of
the 'runaway world' we inhabit.

But the picture is by no means uniform, or uniformly bleak. Some more constructive, hopeful sightings can also be detected on the global landscape. One might, for
instance, point to a burgeoning international consciousness and related citizen mobil-
izations around crimes against the environment (see Bierne and South 1998 on 'green
criminology'), and to social movements campaigning against state crime and abuses
of human rights (Amnesty, Helsinki Human Rights Watch, and so on) (Cohen 1993).
One might mention the advent in 1998 of a permanent International Criminal Court
in The Hague and the stripping from the Milosovics and Pinochets of this world of
immunity from prosecution (McGoldrick 1999). And one might cite the role played
by inter- or supra-national bodies (the Council of Europe, the European Union) and
international treaties and conventions (the UN Declaration of Fundamental Human
Rights, the African Charter of Rights, the European Convention on Human Rights) in
constraining what states can do to their citizens, and serving as focuses for international pressure and citizen action (Evans and Morgan 1999; Coyle and van Zyl Smit
2000; Girling 2001). The cosmopolitan global governance of—among other things—
crime, organized violence, and law enforcement may remain some distance off. But it
no longer seems quite so absurdly utopian (Held 1995; Archibugi et al. 1998; Delanty
2000).

CONCLUSION: CRIMINOLOGY, 'CULTURE', AND PUBLIC LIFE

One might be forgiven for concluding that the import of the social transformations
we have surveyed in this chapter is that criminology should henceforth concern itself
primarily with things that are big—the global, the geo-political, the transnational. In
fact this is by no means our thesis. We have indeed suggested—it has been our central,

organizing claim—that questions of security and order (and regimes of governance and the position of the state) are currently being rapidly and radically altered in some fairly fundamental ways and towards no very certain destination. In order to speak to these conditions in a properly contemporary and relevant fashion, criminology certainly does need to think anew about its relations with social theory (and political sociology, and international relations, and . . .) and really cannot rest content only with doing the old work in the old way (cf. Garland and Sparks 2001). Equally, however, criminology's topics and themes always have been caught up irredeemably in the grander movements of social and political change. This is not in itself new, even if at times it has appeared possible to conduct research (somewhat in the way that Kuhn calls 'normal science') as if this could be bracketed off. Yet, in common with all the other social sciences, criminology itself is originally a child of another era of massive upheavals, namely the industrial and scientific revolutions of the nineteenth century. And equally it always has been possible to look at criminology's involvements with social, political, and technological change from either end of the telescope; from far off or from up close. As C. Wright Mills (1959) wrote long ago, the sociological imagination addresses 'the place where history and biography meet'.

A concern with the implications of macro-level developments for criminological theory and research, therefore, is not now (any more than at any other time) simply a licence for preferring the novel and the fashionable, and for sweeping over the grounded, the empirical, and the local; nor for disengaging from intricate and detailed problems of policy and politics wherever we happen to encounter them. One can readily make these points in respect of each one of the issues that we have sketched above. We may need to remind ourselves more sharply than we often do that new structures and regimes of *governance* are not just models dreamed up by management consultants (though they often *are* this), but also introduce significant changes to the conditions and pressures under which people work, or the ways in which they receive (as 'customers') the services that organizations deliver. When we speak of changes in the delivery and consumption of 'security', in respect, for example, of the electronic surveillance of public space, we are dealing with developments that alter the mundane experiences of shopping, travelling, working, and 'going out' in important respects, and that indeed are generally *designed* to do so. Surveillance techniques, therefore, are in no sense abstract matters; rather, they form part of the infrastructure of the environment in which they operate and hence of the everyday habitat of the people using those spaces. But we cannot know just how this infiltrates our subjective worlds or affects our daily routines, and with what consequences for the participation of some and the exclusion of others, unless we study these matters *in situ* and in detail.

Similarly, when we speak of *risk* we are not generally alluding only to the calculation of probabilities *stricto sensu*. We are talking also about ways of *representing* risky topics, people, and places, and this generally suggests an active and often impassioned disposition towards them. We select the risks that we want to calculate and manage in large measure because of the ways in which they alarm and disconcert us. For these reasons the ways in which we perceive, depict, magnify, displace, deny, or indeed seek out risky things are inherent to what they are for us. Lastly, *globalization*, as we have been at pains to point out here and elsewhere, is not some 'out-there' phenomenon that strips 'place' and 'locality' of all contemporary significance. Far from it. Rather, it continues to matter greatly—to one's opportunities, access to resources, chances of becoming a crime victim, and so forth—*where* one happens to reside, and criminological research has much to contribute to public understanding of these spatial inequalities and their effects. It is also precisely under globalizing conditions that people's *sense of place*—and of *differences* between 'here/there', 'inside/outside', 'us/them'—takes on renewed force as a structuring feature of social relations and culture; questions of crime, danger, safety, and order often today figuring pivotally in how the quotidian life of particular neighbourhoods, towns, cities, and nations is experienced, imagined, and defended.

We can see then that—in the midst of some potentially far-reaching transformations in the world we inhabit—there remains much to be said for research strategies that continue to attend to such things as experience, beliefs, values, sensibilities, and feeling; and, furthermore, that there is much to be gained from seeking to grasp aspects of global social and political change *microscopically*—through ethnography, and observation, and talking to people about the lived texture of their everyday lives. Those dimensions of social life denoted by the idea of 'culture' continue, in short, to matter and ought properly to command criminological attention.

They matter because macro-level social change of the kind we have been concerned with here filters into the lives, experiences, and dispositions of individuals and social groups (become, as it were, features of *mundane culture*) in ways that are uneven and never entirely predictable, and which cannot simply be 'read off' from the texts and tenets of social theory—they stand, in other words, in need of patient empirical investigation. In part, this points to the renewed significance of that rich body of enquiry concerned with how crime, order, justice, and punishment are represented through print and an increasingly bewildering and diverse array of electronic media; this being one of the principal routes through which the profane meanings of notions such as security, risk, and danger are encoded and passed into cultural circulation. The criminological gaze might also fruitfully turn (further) here towards the ways in which crime and social order figure in the lived, and always in some part local, social relations of differently-situated citizens—towards what it *means*, in the altered conditions of the present, to be a jobless teenager, or parent, or asylum-seeker, or to have property to protect or a neighbourhood to defend, or to be a computer-hacker, or community safety practitioner, or Europol liaison officer. One might suggest, in addition, that this is unlikely to be fully accomplished without due attention being afforded to the *feelings* and *passions* that continue to animate the politics of crime, policing, and punishment; something that requires human emotion—anger, fear, shame, resentment, pleasure, and so on—to be located somewhere near to the heart of contemporary criminological enquiry (deHaan and Loader 2002). And it signals, lastly, the importance of paying close *comparative* attention not merely to the *uneven* ways in which the crime question is represented and acted upon in different locations across the globe, but also to the intersections that exist between the often affectively-charged demands of citizens for security and the volatile dynamics and popular-punitive tone of much contemporary 'law and order' politics and governmental practice.

This brings us, in turn, to a bundle of questions pertaining to aspects of *political culture*, and, in particular, to the ways in which criminological research and reflection might (or should?) strive to connect with wider forms of cultural and political disputation concerning 'its' subject matter (Garland and Sparks 2001). Criminology has since its inception been for the most part a consciously 'applied' undertaking (both in its 'official' and in various 'radical' guises), concerned to participate in, and make effective contributions to, the realm of politics and practical affairs. Throughout much of the twentieth century it seemed relatively clear what this entailed and how it might be effected (even if 'success' was never guaranteed). For some, it meant presenting to government and policy-makers scientifically legitimate knowledge that could inform rational policy-making—a stance that Roger Hood (2001) has recently sought to defend and rehabilitate. For others, of more 'radical' political persuasions, the appropriate stance of the 'criminologist' was never the pursuit of 'relevance' (as defined by the policy-audience), but rather that of sceptic and problem-raiser, someone whose knowledge and skills were to be placed—if anywhere at all—at the service of pressure groups and new social movements (Cohen 1988). The implication of our argument in this chapter is that things have, in ways that disturb the coherence of both of these outlooks, become murky and distinctly less clear-cut. When the criminal justice state has become but one node within a diverse network of security actors; when crime and crime control whirl above our heads at the transnational level; when policing and punishment seem shaped less by hard-won knowledge and reasoned deliberation than by punitive passions and short-term political calculation; when judgements concerning crime 'risks' are no longer the province of a cosy coterie of 'experts'—what under these conditions does it mean for criminological knowledge to make effective, intelligible contributions in the public sphere? And within what settings, by what means, and to what ends might such contributions plausibly be made?

These are pressing questions for which there are no instant, off-the-shelf answers, and we are certainly not in the business here of trying to proselytize on behalf of any one of the contending candidates. Suffice it then, by way of conclusion, merely to repeat and re-emphasize our view that criminology cannot today simply go on 'doing the old things in the old ways'. An intellectually serious, worldly criminology for the twenty-first century will be one that comes to terms with and seeks—conceptually, empirically, and normatively—to make sense of the emergent landscapes of crime, order, and control we have started to sketch here. It will be one that operates with a sociologically-informed grasp of mundane and political cultures in which questions of crime and social order have come to assume a prominent, emotively-charged place. And it will be one that is alive to the fact that this is at least in part the case because crime and justice are ineluctably entangled with the properly political question of what—today—would constitute the 'good society'.

Selected further reading

Probably the best 'way into' many of the issues we have been concerned with in this chapter is to consult two recently published edited collections: Kevin Stenson's and Robert Sullivan's

Crime, Risk and Justice (2001), and Tim Hope's and Richard Sparks's *Crime, Risk and Insecurity* (2000). More extended treatments of the same broad themes can be found in Ian Taylor's *Crime in Context* (1999), Jock Young's *The Exclusive Society* (1999), and David Garland's *The Culture of Control* (2001). While these texts cover some of the same substantive ground, the authors develop distinct lines of argument around their subject matter in ways that—in each case—repay careful attention.

Readers might, in addition, usefully refer to the following texts on aspects of the ground we have covered here. There are now two extensive readers on the intersections between governmentality and crime control (Smandych 1999) and crime and risk (O'Malley 1998). Les Johnston's *Policing Britain: Risk, Security and Governance* offers a thoughtful overview of many of our themes as they impact upon policing (1999); Ericson and Haggerty's *Policing the Risk Society* (1997) provides a cognate theoretical and empirical 'application' of the risk problematic. Our take on globalization has been most obviously informed by Zygmunt Bauman's little polemic, *Globalization: The Human Consequences* (1998), a text that also has some important things to say about safety and security. Interested readers could do a lot worse than begin here.

In general, the best advice to anyone who wishes to keep abreast of current thinking is to keep their eye on the journals, especially *Theoretical Criminology*, *Punishment and Society*, *Social and Legal Studies*, and *The British Journal of Criminology*.

References

ÅKESTRÖM, M. (1998), 'The Moral Crusade on Violence in Sweden: Moral Panic or Material for Small-Town Indignation?', in V. Ruggiero, N. South, and I. Taylor (eds), *The New European Criminology: Crime and Social Order in Europe*, London: Routledge.

ALBROW, M. (1996), *The Global Age*, Cambridge: Polity.

ANDERSON, M. (1989), *Policing the World: Interpol and the Politics of International Police Cooperation*, Oxford: Clarendon.

—— BOER, M. DEN, CULLEN, P., GILMORE, W., RAAB, C., and WALKER, N. (1995), *Policing the European Union: Theory, Law and Practice*, Oxford: Clarendon.

ARCHIBUGI, D., HELD, D., and KÖHLER, M. (eds) (1998), *Re-Imagining Political Community: Studies in Cosmopolitan Democracy*, Cambridge: Polity.

BARRY, A., OSBORNE, T., and ROSE, N. (eds) (1996), *Foucault and Political Reason: Liberalism, Neoliberalism and Rationalities of Government*, London: University College London Press.

BAUMAN, Z. (1992), *Intimations of Postmodernity*, London: Routledge.

—— (1998), *Globalization: The Human Consequences*, Cambridge: Polity.

—— (1999), *In Search of Politics*, Cambridge: Polity.

—— (2001), 'Wars of the Globalization Era', *European Journal of Social Theory*, 4/1: 11–28.

BECK, U. (1992), *Risk Society*, London: Sage.

—— (2000), *What is Globalization?*, Cambridge: Polity.

BECKETT, K. (1997), *Making Crime Pay: Law and Order in Contemporary American Politics*, Oxford: Oxford University Press.

BIERNE, P., and SOUTH, N. (eds) (1998), *Special Issue of Theoretical Criminology on 'For a Green Criminology'*, 2/2.

BIGO, D. (2000a), 'Liaison Officers in Europe: New Officers in the European Security Field', in J. Sheptycki (ed.), *Issues in Transnational Policing*, London: Routledge.

—— (2000b), 'When Two Become One: Internal and External Securitisations in Europe', in M. Kelstrup and M. Williams (eds), *International Relations Theory and the Politics of European Integration: Power, Security and Community*, London: Routledge.

BLAKELY, E., and SNYDER, M. (1997), *Fortress*

America: Gated Communities in the United States, Washington DC: Brookings Institution Press.

BOER, M. DEN, and WALLACE, W. (2001), 'Justice and Home Affairs: Integration Through Incrementalism?', in H. Wallace and W. Wallace (eds), *Policy-Making in the European Union*, 4th edn, Oxford: Oxford University Press.

BOTTOMS, A., and WILES, P. (1995), 'Crime and Insecurity in the City', in C. Fijnaut, J. Goethals, T. Peters, and L. Walgrave (eds), *Changes in Society, Crime and Criminal Justice in Europe*, 1, The Hague: Kluwer.

BOURGOIS, P. (1995), *In Search of Respect: Selling Crack in El Barrio*, Cambridge: Cambridge University Press.

BRAKE, M., and HALE, C. (1992), *Public Order and Private Lives*, London: Routledge.

BROWN, M., and PRATT, J. (2000), 'Introduction', in M. Brown and J. Pratt (eds), *Dangerous Offenders: Punishment and Social Order*, London: Routledge.

BURCHILL, G., GORDON, C., and MILLER, P. (eds), (1991), *The Foucault Effect: Studies in Governmentality*, Hemel Hempstead: Harvester Wheatsheaf.

CALDEIRA, T. (2000), *City of Walls: Crime, Segregation and Citizenship in São Paulo*, Berkeley: University of California Press.

CASTELLS, M. (1996), *The Information Age: Economy, Society and Culture: Vol. I—The Rise of the Network Society*, Oxford: Basil Blackwell.

—— (1998), *The Information Age: Economy, Society and Culture: Vol. III—End of Millennium*, Oxford: Basil Blackwell.

CHRISTIE, N. (1993), *Crime Control as Industry: Towards Gulags Western-Style*, London: Routledge.

CLARKE, J., and NEWMAN, J. (1997), *The Managerial State*, London: Sage.

COHEN, S. (1988), *Against Criminology*, New Brunswick, NJ: Transaction Books.

—— (1993), 'Human Rights and Crimes of the State: The Culture of Denial', *Australian and New Zealand Journal of Criminology*, 26/2: 97–115.

COYLE, A., and ZYL SMIT, D. VAN (eds) (2000), *Special Issue of Punishment and Society on 'The International Regulation of Punishment'*, 2/3.

CRAWFORD, A. (1997), *The Local Governance of Crime: Appeals to Partnerships and Community*, Oxford: Clarendon.

—— (1998), 'Community Safety and the Quest for Security: Holding Back the Dynamics of Social Exclusion', *Policy Studies*, 19 (3/4): 237–53.

CURRIE, E. (1997), 'Market, Crime and Community', *Theoretical Criminology*, 1/2: 147–72.

DAVIS, M. (1990), *City of Quartz: Excavating the Future in Los Angeles*, London: Vintage.

DEAN, M. (1999), *Governmentality: Power and Rule in Modern Society*, London: Sage.

DEHAAN, W., and LOADER, I. (eds) (2002), *Special Issue of Theoretical Criminology on 'Crime, Punishment and the Emotions'*, 6/3.

DELANTY, G. (2000), *Citizenship in a Global Age: Society, Culture, Politics*, Buckingham: Open University Press.

—— (2001), 'Cosmopolitanism and Violence: The Limits of Global Civil Society', *European Journal of Social Theory*, 4/1: 41–52.

DENNIS, N. (ed.) (1997), *Zero Tolerance: Policing a Free Society*, London: Institute of Economic Affairs.

DOUGLAS, M. (1992), *Risk and Cultural Theory*, London: Routledge.

ECK, J., and WEISBURD, D. (eds) (1995), *Crime and Place*, Monsey, New York: Criminal Justice Press.

ERICSON, R., and HAGGERTY, K. (1997), *Policing the Risk Society*, Oxford: Clarendon.

—— and DOYLE, A. (1999), 'Globalization and the Policing of Protest: The Case of APEC 1997', *British Journal of Sociology*, 50/4: 589–608.

EVANS, M., and MORGAN, R. (1999), *Preventing Torture*, Oxford: Oxford University Press.

FEELEY, M., and SIMON, J. (1992), 'The New Penology', *Criminology*, 30/4: 449–74.

FOUCAULT, M. (1991), 'Governmentality', in G. Burchell *et al.* (eds), *The Foucault Effect Studies in Governmentality*, Hemel Hempstead: Harvester Wheatsheaf.

GARLAND, D. (1990), *Punishment and Modern Society: A Study in Social Theory*, Oxford: Clarendon.

—— (1997), 'Governmentality and the Problem of Crime: Foucault, Criminology, Sociology', *Theoretical Criminology*, 1/2: 173–214.

—— (2001a), *The Culture of Control: Crime and Social Order in Contemporary Society*, Oxford: Clarendon.

—— (ed.) (2001b), *Mass Imprisonment: Social Causes and Consequences*, London: Sage.

—— and SPARKS, R. (2001), 'Criminology, Social Theory and the Challenge of Our Times', in D. Garland and R. Sparks (eds), *Criminology and Social Theory*, Oxford: Clarendon.

GIDDENS, A. (1990), *The Consequences of Modernity*, Cambridge: Polity.

—— (1991), *Modernity and Self-Identity: Self and Society in the Late Modern Age*, Cambridge: Polity.

GIRLING, E. (2001), 'Will the Next President be a Killer? The US Death Penalty Under the European Gaze', paper presented to the joint meetings of the Research Committee on the Sociology of Law (ISA) and American Law and Society Association, Central European University, Budapest, Hungary, July.

——, LOADER, I., and SPARKS, R. (2000), *Crime and Social Change in Middle England: Questions of Order in an English Town*, London: Routledge.

GOLDSMITH, A. (2001), 'Police, States and Fear', paper presented to the joint meetings of the Research Committee on the Sociology of Law (ISA) and American Law and Society Association, Central European University, Budapest, Hungary, July.

HACKING, I. (1991), *The Taming of Chance*, Cambridge: Cambridge University Press.

HAGAN, J. (1994), *Crime and Disrepute*, Thousand Oaks: Pine Forge Press.

—— and PETERSEN, R. (eds) (1995), *Crime and Inequality*, Stanford, Cal.: Stanford University Press.

HALL, S., CLARKE, J., CRITCHER, C., JEFFERSON, T., and ROBERTS, B. (1978), *Policing the Crisis: Mugging, Law and Order and the State*, London: Macmillan.

HARVEY, D. (1989), *The Condition of Postmodernity*, Oxford: Basil Blackwell.

HAY, C. (1996), *Re-stating Social and Political Change*, Buckingham: Open University Press.

HELD, D. (1995), *Democracy and the Global Order: From the Modern State to Cosmopolitan Governance*, Cambridge: Polity.

——, McGREW, A., GOLDBLATT, D., and PERRATON, J. (1999), *Global Transformations: Politics, Economics and Culture*, Cambridge: Polity.

HIRST, P., and THOMPSON, G. (1996), *Globalization in Question: The International Economy and the Possibilities of Governance*, Cambridge: Polity.

HOBBS, D., and DUNNGHAM, C. (1998), 'Glocal Organized Crime', in V. Ruggiero, N. South, and I. Taylor (eds), *The New European Criminology: Crime and Social Order in Europe*, London: Routledge.

HOBSBAWM, E. (1994), *The Age of Extremes: The Short Twentieth Century 1914–1991*, London: Michael Joseph.

HOLLWAY, W., and JEFFERSON, T. (1997), 'The Risk Society in an Age of Anxiety: Situating the Fear of Crime', *British Journal of Sociology*, 48/2: 255–66.

HOOD, R. (2001), 'Penal Policy and Criminological Challenges in the New Millennium', *Australian and New Zealand Journal of Criminology*, 34/1: 1–16.

HOPE, T. (2001), 'Crime Victimisation and Inequality in Risk Society', in R. Matthews and J. Pitts (eds), *Crime, Disorder and Community Safety*, London: Routledge.

—— and SPARKS, R. (eds) (2000), *Crime, Risk and Insecurity: Law and Order in Political Discourse and Everyday Life*, London: Routledge.

JAMIESON, R. (1998), 'Towards a Criminology of War in Europe', in V. Ruggiero, N. South, and I. Taylor (eds), *The New European Criminology: Crime and Social Order in Europe*, London: Routledge.

JOHNSTON, L. (1999), *Policing Britain: Risk, Security and Governance*, Harlow: Longman.

—— (2000), 'Transnational Private Policing: The Impact of Commercial Security', in J. Sheptycki (ed.), *Issues in Transnational Policing*, London: Routledge.

JOB, B. (ed.) (1992), *The Insecurity Dilemma: National Security of Third World States*, Boulder, Col.: Lynne Reinner.

JONES, C. (1993), 'Auditing Criminal Justice', *British Journal of Criminology*, 33/3: 187–202.

JONES, T., and NEWBURN, T. (1998), *Private Security and Public Policing*, Oxford: Clarendon.

KALDOR, M. (1999), *New and Old Wars: Organized Violence in a Global Age*, Cambridge: Polity.

KARSTEDT, S. (2000), 'Knights of Crime: The Success of "Pre-Modern" Structures in the Illegal Economy', in S. Karstedt and K.-D. Bussmann (eds), *Social Dynamics of Crime and Control: New Theories for a World in Transition*, Oxford: Hart.

—— and BUSSMANN, K.-D. (eds) (2000), *Social Dynamics of Crime and Control: New Theories for a World in Transition*, Oxford: Hart.

KEMPA, M., CARRIER, R., WOOD, J., and SHEARING, C. (1999), 'Reflections on the Evolving Concept of "Private Policing"', *European Journal of Criminal Policy and Research*, 7: 197–223.

KEMSHALL, H., and MAGUIRE, M. (2001), 'Public Protection, Partnership and Risk Penality: The Multi-Agency Management of Sex and Violent Offenders', *Punishment and Society*, 3/2: 237–64.

KOOIMAN, J. (ed.) (1993), *Modern Governance: New Government-Society Interactions*, London: Sage.

LACEY, N., and ZEDNER, L. (1998), 'Community in German Criminal Justice: A Significant Absence?', *Social and Legal Studies*, 7/1: 7–25.

LASH, S., and URRY, J. (1994), *Economies of Signs and Space*, London: Sage.

LEVI, R. (2000), 'The Mutuality of Risk and Community: The Adjudication of Community Notification Statutes', *Economy and Society*, 29/4: 578–601.

LOADER, I. (1997), 'Private Security and the Demand for Protection in Contemporary Britain', *Policing and Society*, 7/3: 143–62.

—— (1999), 'Consumer Culture and the Commodification of Policing and Security', *Sociology*, 33/2: 373–92.

—— (2000), 'Plural Policing and Democratic Governance', *Social and Legal Studies*, 9/3: 323–45.

—— (2002), 'Policing, Securitization and Democratization in Europe', *Criminal Justice*, 2/2: 125–53.

—— and WALKER, N. (2001), 'Policing as a Public Good: Reconstituting the Connections Between Policing and the State', *Theoretical Criminology*, 5/1: 9–35.

LODGE, T. (1974), 'The Founding of the Home Office Research Unit', in R. Hood (ed.), *Crime, Criminology and Public Policy*, London: Heinemann.

LOGAN, J., and MOLOTCH, H. (1987), *Urban Fortunes: The Political Economy of Place*, Berkeley: University of California Press.

LYON, D. (2001), *Surveillance Society: Monitoring Everyday Life*, Buckingham: Open University Press.

MANNING, P. (2000), 'Policing New Social Spaces', in J. Sheptycki (ed.), *Issues in Transnational Policing*, London: Routledge.

MATHIESON, T. (2000), 'Toward an Integrated Surveillance System in Europe', in P. Green and A. Rutherford (eds), *Criminal Policy in Transition*, Oxford: Hart.

McGOLDRICK, D. (1999), 'The Permanent International Criminal Court: An End to the Culture of Impunity?', *Criminal Law Review*, 627–55.

McLAUGHLIN, E., and MURJI, K. (2001), 'Lost Connections and New Directions: Neo-Liberalism, New Public Managerialism and the "Modernization" of the British Police', in K. Stenson and R. Sullivan (eds), *Crime, Risk and Justice: The Politics of Crime Control in Liberal Democracies*, Cullompton: Willan Publishing.

NADELMAN, E. (1993), *Cops Across Borders: The Internationalization of US Criminal Law Enforcement*, Philadelphia: Pennsylvania State University Press.

NELKEN, D. (1994), 'Whom can you Trust?: The Future of Comparative Criminology', in D. Nelken (ed.), *The Futures of Criminology*, London: Sage.

—— (1997) 'The Globalization of Crime and Criminal Justice: Prospects and Problems', *Current Legal Problems*, 50: 251–77.

—— (ed.) (2000), *Contrasting Criminal Justice: Getting From Here to There*, Aldershot: Dartmouth.

NEWBURN, T., and SPARKS, R. (eds) (2002), *Special Issue of Criminal Justice on 'How Does Crime Policy Travel?'*, 2/2.

NIGHTINGALE, C. (1993), *On the Edge*, New York: Basic Books.

NIKOLIC-RISTANOVIC, V. (1998), 'War and Crime in the Former Yugoslavia', in V. Ruggiero, N. South, and I. Taylor (eds), *The New European Criminology: Crime and Social Order in Europe*, London: Routledge.

NOAKS, L. (2000), 'Private Cops on the Block: A Review of the Role of Private Security in Residential Communities', *Policing and Society*, 10/2: 143–62.

NOGALA, D. (2001), 'Policing Across a Dimorphous Border: Challenge and Innovation at the French–German Border', *European Journal of Crime, Criminal Law and Criminal Justice*, 9/2: 130–43.

NORDSTROM, C. (2000), 'Shadows and Sovereigns', *Theory, Culture and Society*, 17/4: 35–54.

NORRIS, C., and ARMSTRONG, G. (1999), *The Maximum Surveillance Society: The Rise of CCTV*, Oxford: Berg.

—— and MORAN, J. (eds) (1998), *Surveillance, Closed Circuit Television and Social Control*, Aldershot: Ashgate.

O'MALLEY, P. (1991), 'Legal Networks and Domestic Security', *Studies in Law, Politics and Society*, 11: 171–90.

—— (1992), 'Risk, Power and Crime Prevention', *Economy and Society*, 21/3: 251–68.

—— (ed.) (1998), *Crime and the Risk Society*, Aldershot: Ashgate.

—— (1999), 'Volatile and Contradictory Punishment', *Theoretical Criminology*, 3/2: 175–96.

—— (2000), 'Risk Societies and the Government of Crime', in M. Brown and J. Pratt (eds), *Dangerous Offenders: Punishment and Social Order*, London: Routledge.

—— (2001), 'Policing Crime Risks in the Neo-Liberal Era', in K. Stenson and R. Sullivan (eds),

Crime, Risk and Justice: The Politics of Crime Control in Liberal Democracies, Cullompton: Willan Publishing.

—— and PALMER, D. (1996), 'Post-Keynesian Policing', *Economy and Society*, 25/2: 137–55.

OSBORNE, D., and GAEBLER, T. (1992), *Re-Thinking Government*, Harmondsworth: Penguin.

PAVARINI, M. (1997), 'Controlling Social Panic: Questions and Answers About Security in Italy at the End of the Millennium', in R. Bergalli and C. Sumner (eds), *Social Control and Political Order*, London: Sage.

RADZINOWICZ, L. (1999), *Adventures in Criminology*, London: Routledge.

REINER, R. (1992), 'Policing a Postmodern Society', *Modern Law Review*, 55/6: 761–82.

RHODES, R. (1997), *Understanding Governance: Policy Networks, Governance, Reflexivity and Accountability*, Buckingham: Open University Press.

ROBERTSON, R. (1995), 'Glocalization: Time-Space and Homogeneity-Heterogeneity', in M. Featherstone, S. Lash, and R. Robertson (eds), *Global Modernities*, London: Sage.

ROBINSON, G. (2002), 'Exploring Risk Management in Probation Practice: Contemporary Developments in England and Wales', *Punishment and Society*, 4/1: 5–26.

ROSE, N. (1999), *Powers of Freedom: Reframing Political Thought*, Cambridge: Cambridge University Press.

—— (2000), 'Government and Control', in D. Garland and R. Sparks (eds), *Criminology and Social Theory*, Oxford: Clarendon.

—— and MILLER, P. (1992), 'Political Power Beyond the State: Problematics of Government', *British Journal of Sociology*, 43/2: 173–205.

RUGGIERO, V. (1996), *Organized Crime and Corporate Crime in Europe*, Aldershot: Ashgate.

—— (2000), 'Transnational Crime: Official and Alternative Fears', *International Journal of the Sociology of Law*, 28: 187–99.

——, SOUTH, N., and TAYLOR, I. (eds) (1998), *The New European Criminology: Crime and Social Order in Europe*, London: Routledge.

SASSEN, S. (1996), *Losing Control?: Sovereignty in an Age of Globalization*, New York: Columbia University Press.

SCHICHOR, D., and SECHREST, D. (1996), *Three Strikes and You're Out: Vengeance as Public Policy*, Thousand Oaks, Cal.: Sage.

SHEARING, C. (1996), 'Reinventing Policing:

Policing as Governance', in O. Marenin (ed.), *Changing Police: Policing Change*, New York: Garland.

—— (2001), 'Punishment and the Changing Face of Governance', *Punishment and Society*, 3/2: 203–20.

—— and STENNING, P. (1983), 'Private Security: Implications for Social Control', *Social Problems*, 30/5: 493–506.

—— and —— (1996), 'From the Panoptican to Disneyworld: the Development of Discipline', in J. Muncie, E. McLaughlin, and M. Langan (eds), *Criminological Perspectives: A Reader*, London: Sage.

—— and WOOD, J. (2000), 'Reflections on the Governance of Security: A Normative Enquiry', *Police Practice*, 1/4: 457–76.

SHEPTYCKI, J. (1996), 'Police Co-operation in the English Channel Region 1968–1996', *European Journal of Crime, Criminal Law and Criminal Justice*, 6/3: 216–35.

—— (2000a), 'Policing the Virtual Launderette: Money Laundering and Global Governance', in J. Sheptycki (ed.), *Issues in Transnational Policing*, London: Routledge.

—— (2000b), *Issues in Transnational Policing*, London: Routledge.

SHERMAN, L., GARTIN, P., and BUERGER, M. (1989), 'Hot Spots of Predatory Crime: Routine Activities and the Criminology of Place', *Criminology*, 27/1: 27–55.

SIMON, J. (1995), 'They Died With Their Boots on: The Boot Camp and the Limits of Modern Penality' *Social Justice*, 22/2: 25–48.

—— (1997), 'Governing Through Crime', in L. Friedman and G. Fisher (eds), *The Crime Conundrum: Issues in Criminal Justice*, Boulder, Co.: Westview Press.

SKOGAN, W. (1990), *Disorder and Decline: The Spiral of Decay in American Neighborhoods*, New York: Oxford University Press.

SMANDYCH, R. (ed.) (1999), *Governable Places: Readings in Governmentality and Crime Control*, Aldershot: Dartmouth.

SPARKS, R. (1991), 'Reason and Unreason in Left Realism: Some Problems in the Constitution of the Fear of Crime', in R. Matthews and J. Young (eds), *Issues in Realist Criminology*, London: Sage.

—— (1992), *Television and the Drama of Crime: Moral Tales and the Place of Crime in Public Life*, Buckingham: Open University Press.

—— (2000), 'Risk and Blame in Criminal Justice

Controversies: British Press Coverage and Official Discourse on Prison Security (1993–6)', in M. Brown and J. Pratt (eds), *Dangerous Offenders: Punishment and Social Order*, London: Routledge.

—— (2001), 'Degrees of Estrangement: The Cultural Theory of Risk and Comparative Penology', *Theoretical Criminology*, 5/2: 159–76.

STANKO, E. (1990), 'When Precaution is Normal: A Feminist Critique of Crime Prevention', in L. Gelsthorpe and A. Morris (eds), *Feminist Perspectives in Criminology*, Buckingham: Open University Press.

STENSON, K. (1993), 'Community Policing as Governmental Technology', *Economy and Society*, 22: 373–89.

—— (2000), 'Some Day My Prince Will Come: Zero-Tolerance Policing and Liberal Government', in T. Hope and R. Sparks (eds), *Crime, Risk and Insecurity: Law and Order in Political Discourse and Everyday Life*, London: Routledge.

—— and SULLIVAN, R. (eds) (2001), *Crime, Risk and Justice: The Politics of Crime Control in Liberal Democracies*, Cullompton: Willan Publishing.

STERLING, C. (1994), *Thieves' World: The Threat of the New Global Network of Organized Crime*, New York: Simon and Schuster.

SULLIVAN, M. (1988), *Getting Paid: Youth, Crime and Work in the Inner City*, Ithaca, NY: Cornell University Press.

TAUB, R., TAYLOR, D., and DUNHAM, J. (1984), *Paths of Neighborhood Change*, Chicago: University of Chicago Press.

TAYLOR, I. (1999), *Crime in Context: A Critical Criminology of Market Societies*, Cambridge: Polity.

URRY, J. (2000), *Sociology Beyond Societies: Mobilities for the Twenty-First Century*, London: Routledge.

VON HIRSCH, A., GARLAND, D., and WAKEFIELD, A. (eds) (2000), *Ethical and Social Perspectives on Situational Crime Prevention*, Oxford: Hart.

WACQUANT, L. (1999), *Les Prisons de Miseres*, Paris: Editions Liber-Raisons d'Agir.

WALKER, N. (1999), 'Decoupling Police and State', in E. Bort and R. Keat (eds), *The Boundaries of Understanding: Essays in Honour of Malcolm Anderson*, Edinburgh: International Social Sciences Institute.

—— (2000), 'Transnational Contexts', in F. Leishman, B. Loveday, and S. Savage (eds), *Core Issues in Policing*, 2nd edn, Harlow: Longman.

WALKLATE, S. (1998), 'Excavating the Fear of Crime: Fear, Anxiety or Trust?', *Theoretical Criminology*, 2/4: 403–18.

WINDLESHAM, L. (1987), *Responses to Crime—Volume 1: Ministering to a Gentler Age*, Oxford: Clarendon.

—— (1996), *Responses to Crime—Volume 3: Legislating with the Tide*, Oxford: Clarendon.

—— (1998), *Politics, Punishment and Populism*, Oxford: Oxford University Press.

—— (2001), *Responses to Crime—Volume 4: Dispensing Justice*, Oxford: Clarendon.

WRIGHT MILLS, C. (1959), *The Sociological Imagination*, Harmondsworth: Penguin.

YOUNG, A. (1996), *Imagining Crime*, London: Sage.

YOUNG, J. (1999), *The Exclusive Society: Social Exclusion, Crime and Difference in Late Modernity*, London: Sage.

4

FEMINISM AND CRIMINOLOGY

Loraine Gelsthorpe

INTRODUCTION

Feminists engaging with criminology in the twenty-first century might be forgiven for looking back with a certain envy at the diversity of the projects outlined by their predecessors.[1] These predecessors set out to question some of the gender-blind assumptions within criminology and to create a space for women's voices and experiences. It might be supposed that today there are few silences left to articulate and that the 'classic masculine discourse' of criminology (Collier 1998) has been well and truly (if paradoxically) 'penetrated' by feminism. This is not the case. Doubts are still expressed in conference halls, institutional corridors and class rooms (if not in academic papers) as to whether there *is* such a thing as feminist criminology, let alone its present, past, and future. But reports of its death or non-existence have been greatly exaggerated. The chief aim of this chapter is to alert readers to key precepts and issues which are relevant to an understanding of the importance of feminist contributions to criminology, and to reflect on their overall relationship.

This chapter thus offers an overview of the critical insights provided or prompted by feminism which might be said to have transgressed both the theory and politics of research and action in criminology. But, first, what is meant by 'feminism and criminology'? In 1988, Allison Morris and I attempted to describe something of the relationship between feminism and criminology by reviewing early feminist achievements to address criminologists' 'amnesia' of women, and by giving something of an overview of the impact or potential impact of feminism on the broad parameters of criminology (Gelsthorpe and Morris 1988). But we recorded then, as I reiterate now, that any discussion of the relationship between feminism and criminology would need to recognize complexities in the relationship. For there is no *one* feminism and no *one* criminology. Despite some serious doubts as to whether a single feminist criminology

---

[1] It is important to recognize some of the early work which challenged criminology. The work of Marie Andrée Bertrand (1969) and Frances Heidensohn (1968, 1970), for example, drew attention both to the neglect of women in the study of crime and to the tendency to distort images and understandings of female offenders in the work which *did* manage to feature women in any shape or form. While this early work might be described as pre-feminist, it is perhaps no less important than the work of Carol Smart (1976) and others which is more self-consciously feminist in intent.

could exist because it could not do justice to the differences and tensions that exist within the field, we acknowledged, however, that it was still possible to talk of feminist criminologies or, better still, of feminist perspectives in criminology.

Yet it is important to speak of different feminist perspectives, and of different criminologies. The chapters in this text provide ample evidence of this. There is no one relationship, but a myriad of relationships between feminism and criminology. Moreover, the criminology of the 1970s, which prompted Carol Smart's 1976 critical text *Women, Crime and Criminology*, one of the first openly feminist critiques of criminology in Britain, is not the criminology of today. The criminology of today seems much more diverse. Whether it is sufficiently diverse or open enough to accommodate some of the critical precepts of feminisms remains a matter for debate. There are feminists who have made a strong case for abandoning criminology (Smart 1990), or who, because of resistance to a feminist transformation of the discipline of criminology, see fundamental incompatibilities between feminism and criminology (Stanko 1993; A. Young 1994). In a percipient conclusion to her 1976 text, Smart commented:

Criminology and the sociology of deviance must become more than the study of men and crime if it is to play any significant part in the development of our understanding of crime, law and the criminal process and play any role in the transformation of existing social practices [Smart 1976: 185].

Her concern was that criminology, even in its more radical form, would be 'unmoved' by feminist critiques. By 1990, she viewed criminology as the 'atavistic man' in intellectual endeavours and wished to abandon it because she could not see what it had to offer feminism. But whereas the abandonment of criminology once seemed a logical response to criminological intransigence, there is arguably good reason to pause before pursuing this option given recent signs of critical thinking in criminology.

There have been several serious explorations of the relationship between feminism and criminology over the years (Daly and Chesney-Lind 1988; Gelsthorpe and Morris 1990; Morris and Gelsthorpe 1991; Heidensohn 1997; A. Young 1994; Rafter and Heidensohn 1995; and Naffine 1995, 1997). A key question which has perplexed some of these writers is whether key substantive and political and epistemological and methodological projects make what might be described as the 'criminological project' untenable in and of itself (see also Heidensohn, in Chapter 15 of this volume). So, what is it about feminist work that might make criminological work untenable?

When we speak of feminism, we are not speaking of something which is obvious or can be taken for granted (Delmar 1986). In a powerful exposition of feminist thinking, Rosemarie Tong (1989) illuminates some of the key differences between different feminist perspectives. While her catalogue of feminisms and history of feminist thought is not the only one that might be produced (see Oakley 1981; Evans 1995, for example), Tong (1989) identifies and elaborates six main kinds of feminism:

1. *Liberal feminism.* This involves a commitment to reforms concerning equal civil rights, equality of opportunity, and the recognition of women's rights in welfare, health, employment, and education.

2. *Marxist feminism.* This involves describing the material basis of women's oppression and the relationship between the modes of production and women's status, and applying theories of women and class to the role of the family.

3. *Socialist feminism.* This involves beliefs that women are treated as second-class citizens in patriarchal capitalism, and that we need to transform the ownership of the means of production *and* women's social experience because the *roots* of women's oppression lie in the total economic system of capitalism. As Walklate (2001) describes, socialist feminism is an outgrowth of Marxist feminist dissatisfaction with the gender-blind concept of class.

4. *Existential feminism.* Existentialism is a philosophical theory which argues that individuals are free and responsible agents able to transcend their social roles and determine their own development. Feminist existentialism is perhaps epitomized by Simone de Beauvoir's (1949) *The Second Sex*, in which she argues that women are oppressed because they are 'Other' to man's 'Self', and that as 'Other' they are 'not man'. Man is taken to be the 'Self', the free, self-determining agent who defines his own existence, while woman remains the 'Other', the object, whose meaning is determined by what she is not.

5. *Psychoanalytical feminism.* Psychoanalysis was invented by Freud (see Strachey 1953–74) to refer to his theory of the psyche and the methods and techniques he applied to understanding it. While psychoanalysis has come under attack because of its seemingly inherent sexism (emphasizing biology over social relations and taking masculine characteristics as the norm), a feminist psychoanalysis has been developed to show how prevailing norms of gender are imposed and structure the human mind. Feminist psychoanalysis is sometimes referred to as gender theory.

6. *Postmodern feminism.* Drawing on the general features of postmodernism as a major cultural phenomenon in the arts, architecture, philosophy, and economics, and amongst other things rejecting the idea of single explanations or philosophies, feminist postmodernism involves opposition to essentialism (the belief that differences between men and women are innate rather than socially/experientially constructed)[2] and a belief in more plural kinds of knowledge. Some of the roots of postmodern feminism are found in the work of Derrida (1978, 1981), Lacan (1995) and Simone de Beauvoir (1949), whose critical exploration of women as the 'Other' has been turned on its head so that the condition of 'Otherness' is celebrated in all its diverse forms. Emphasis on the positive side of 'Otherness' is a major theme in the associated deconstructionist approaches and in the celebration of a plurality of knowledges. 'Otherness' thus symbolizes plurality, diversity, difference, and openness. The so-called rationality and objectivity of contemporary science also comes under attack in feminist postmodernism (Harding 1986; Benhabib 1992), and there are attempts to create fluid, open terms and language which more closely reflect women's

---

[2] To expand, essentialism is a form of analysis in which social phenomena are understood not in terms of the specific conditions of their existence, but in terms of some presumed essence or interest (Hindess 1977).

experiences. There is a further dimension to feminist postmodernism here in the creation of a new language, *écriture féminine* (Cixous 1976; Irigaray 1977).[3]

To these types of feminism I would add *Black feminist thought*, which consists of ideas produced by Black women that clarify a standpoint of and for Black women. It is assumed that Black women possess a unique standpoint on, and experiences of, historical and material conditions (Lorde 1984; Hill-Collins 2002). It is further claimed that Black women's experiences uniquely provide an 'outsider-within' perspective on self, family, and society which in turn serves to establish a distinctive standpoint vis-à-vis sociology's paradigmatic facts and theories.

It is also important to acknowledge the notion of 'global' feminisms, by which we must recognize similarities and differences between feminisms in the West, East, North, and South, and the differential attention given to class, racial, ethnic, and imperial tensions in different economic, technological, sexual, reproductive, ecological, and political contexts (Bulbeck 1998; Smith 2000). This is particularly important if we wish to understand something of international feminist perspectives in criminology and accommodate difference and diversity away from westernized concepts of crime and justice.

There are many sophisticated explorations of the different feminist positions, detailed examination of which lies beyond the scope of this chapter (see Carrington 1994; Evans 1995; Daly 1997; and Jackson and Scott 2002). These different positions collectively illustrate men's material interest in the domination of women and the different ways in which men construct a variety of institutional arrangements to sustain this domination. Feminists argue the case for the economy to be fully transformed and aim to 'make visible the invisible' by bringing into focus the gender structure of society (Rowbotham 1973; Mitchell 1984; Mitchell and Oakley 1986; Humm 1992, 1995). Feminists have challenged the political, ontological, and epistemological assumptions that underlie patriarchal discourses as well as their theoretical contents. They have developed both an anti-sexist stance, and a stance which involves the construction of alternative models, methods, procedures, discourses, and so on. Put simply, feminists have a normative commitment to revealing, and attempting to negate, the subordination of women by men.

Such summaries do not do justice to the concepts and theories involved in feminisms, but they do illustrate some of the key challenges to criminology. There are crucial theoretical, conceptual, and methodological distinctions within these feminist perspectives, and such ideas are not mutually exclusive (see, for example, Hirsch and Keller 1990); different theorists subscribe to different strands of thought within each group of theories. Equally, the various feminisms are not always rigorously discrete. But from the summaries it is possible to see how feminist challenges to criminology

---

[3] Postmodern feminism is perhaps perceived to have the most difficult relationship with the broad project of feminism (Tong 1989; Nicholson 1990; Carrington 1994, 1998), largely because of beliefs that feminism itself may be misconceived in assuming that it is possible to provide *overarching* explanations for women's oppression and identify steps towards its resolution. At the same time, it is arguable that feminist criminologists have been open to debates in this area and that this has been important in terms of developing the epistemological project that I have mentioned.

have been informed in a multiplicity of ways. I will elaborate some of these challenges
later in the chapter.

THE INTELLECTUAL INHERITANCE
OF CRIMINOLOGY

What does the intellectual endeavour involved in these feminisms mean for criminology? Large sections of this and previous editions of *The Oxford Handbook of Criminology* alone are testament to the dominant intellectual history of criminology,
though it has been the subject of much debate and critique elsewhere too (Rock 1988,
1994; Cohen 1988; Garland 1992, 1994; J. Young 1994; Naffine 1997, for example).
What is beyond dispute, however, is that criminology was traditionally conceived as
the scientific study of the causes of crime, and the 'scientific endeavour' involving
'methods, techniques or rules of procedure', more than substantive theory or perspective (Gottfredson and Hirschi 1987: 10), is possibly 'healthier and more self-assured'
than hitherto (ibid.: 18). The strident belief in an objective, external reality capable of
measurement, and a fascination with causal and correlational factors—whether they
be situational opportunities, low self-control, or relative deprivation—is reflected in
the pages of new and old textbooks alike.

The essentials are that mainstream criminology has been dominated by a persistent
commitment to what Garland (see Chapter 1 of this volume) describes as 'the Lombrosian project' and 'the governmental project'. By the former he means a form of
inquiry 'which aims to develop an etiological, explanatory science, based on the
premise that criminals can somehow be scientifically differentiated from non-
criminals'—essentially a 'science of causes'. The 'governmental project' involves a
long series of empirical inquiries which 'have sought to enhance the efficient and
equitable administration of justice by charting the patterns of crime and monitoring
the practice of police and prisons'—essentially what might be described as 'conservative administrative criminology'. In examining developments in criminology, Naffine
(1997) describes how the logic of conventional 'scientific criminology' looms large
and presses on through the 1980s, 1990s, and into the 2000s.

There have been important intellectual/sociological starts along the way. Sociological insights are evident in the history of the sociology of crime and deviance,
though women and 'gender' are absent from analyses (Millman 1975; Smart 1976;
Scraton 1990). Picking on one particular 'progressive' criminology as an example,
the *New Criminology* (Taylor, Walton, and Young 1973) attempted to eschew the
scientific orthodoxy and instead illustrate how crime was socially constructed
through the capacity of state institutions to define and confer criminality on others.
But the authors do this in an 'ungendered' way (Sumner 1994; Naffine 1997). In this
progressive conception of events, crime is not simply an act, but a reflection of a
political process. The new criminologists took note of the new deviancy theorists'
work on social reaction (see, for example, Becker 1963), seeing the application of a
label of deviance as part of a broader context of social, political, economic, and

cultural relations. In developing an agenda for a social theory of deviance, they connected the established influences of social interaction with a Marxist perspective which prioritized structural relations. But there was a neglect of gender in their analysis.

Another example concerns Left Realist theoretical propositions (J. Young 1994) which have given attention to the social and political context of crime and crime control and, importantly, to victims. There is 'essentialism' in the thinking (see Brown and Hogg 1992; Carlen 1992, for example) because of the partial or misconceived recognition of gender (women's fear of crime is recognized, but not in a direct way, for women's fear of crime is generally women's fear of men). Left Realism's analytical framework looks at the links between social order and social justice, and its critical stance involves the development of a whole raft of interventionist policies to deal with the realities of crime (including the experiences of victims). But this is inadequate when it comes to women's experiences.[4] Overall, Left Realists do no more than offer a sophisticated version of a scientific paradigm—a paradigm which is largely ungendered.

Foucauldian insights in criminology have also been of crucial importance—this time in directing attention to power and knowledge and to the discursive practices of control. However, as Sumner (1990), for one, has pointed out, while Foucauldian thought addresses issues of discrimination, the deeper, structural condition of hegemonic masculinity is not addressed. The gendered character of disciplinary power is ignored (Diamond and Quinby 1988).

Thus, though these intellectual/sociological challenges to mainstream criminology have offered some exciting critical insights, none has been adequate in conceptualizing gender; there has been no fundamental shift in gear to address feminists' questions about criminological knowledge. Feminists' challenges to criminology have come from different directions—not always in forms that make the theoretical lineage apparent, but in forceful and unmistakable ways that question the epistemological basis and methodological processes of criminology.

FEMINISM WITHIN AND WITHOUT CRIMINOLOGY: A REVIEW OF INTERCONNECTIONS BETWEEN FEMINISM AND CRIMINOLOGY

Eschewing the internecine arguments about who or what is feminist (see Delmar 1986; Morris 1987; Daly and Chesney-Lind 1988; Gelsthorpe and Morris 1988, 1990, for example; and Heidensohn, in Chapter 15 of this volume), we can identify a broad range of feminist work which questions criminology:

1. an early critique of criminological theory and of criminal justice practices: that is, a substantive and political project;

---

4 Other criticisms are identified by contributors to Matthews and Young (1992).

2. a more discursive questioning of the epistemological and methodological contours of the discipline;

3. international feminist perspectives; and

4. theoretical work on gender leading to developments in masculinity theory.

THE EARLY CRITIQUE

Drawing generally from the feminist positions outlined above, one of the first tasks was to develop a comprehensive critique of the discipline. The early critique has been well rehearsed elsewhere (see, for example, Morris 1987); suffice to say here that it has frequently focused on the two main themes of amnesia or neglect and distortion (Smart 1976; Heidensohn 1985). It is indisputable that women account for a very small proportion of all known offenders (cf. Greenwood 1981), despite recently recorded increases (Home Office 2000), and yet there has been relatively little attention given to female offenders. The neglect of women's criminality by a predominantly male profession is one of criminology's determining features. The majority of studies of crime and delinquency prior to the 1980s were of men's crime and delinquency (Leonard 1982; Scraton 1990). The discipline was dominated by men studying other men. A second theme in the critique is that, even when women were recognized, they were depicted in terms of stereotypes based on their supposed biological and psychological nature. While the 'new criminology' challenged the assumptions of positivism in explaining men's crime, it neglected to acknowledge how such assumptions remained most prevalent in academic and popular conceptions of women's crime. Similarly, while analyses of class structure, state control, and the political nature of deviance gained credibility, the study of women's crime remained rooted in notions of biological determinism and an uncritical attitude towards the dominant sexual stereotypes of women as passive, domestic, and maternal (Smart 1976; cf. Brown 1986). Tracing the continuance of sexist assumptions from Lombroso to Pollak and beyond, Smart (1976) examined how assumptions of the abnormality of female offenders came to dominate both theory and criminal justice policy—despite evidence of more critical thinking in relation to men and men's crime. Eileen Leonard usefully summarized mainstream criminological theory by stating:

Theories that are frequently hailed as explanations of human behaviour are, in fact, discussions of male behaviour and male criminality . . . We cannot simply apply these theories to women, nor can we modify them with a brief addition or subtraction here and there [1982: 181].

Women were ignored, or marginalized, or distorted, both in their deviancy and conformity, and the exposure of criminology as the criminology of men marked the starting point of feminists' attempts to find alternative modes of conceptualizing the social worlds of deviance and conformity, punishment and control.

The focus of this general critique, however, was limited. Some writers naively assumed that a remedy to criminological and criminal justice deficiencies could be sought by appropriating existing criminological theories and 'inserting' women: for example, by discovering girl gangs (Velimesis 1975) and considering girls in relation to subcultural theory (McRobbie 1980; Shacklady Smith 1978). Rafter and Natalizia (1981) presented the message in a different way, suggesting that 'women only' studies should strive to produce a body of information as extensive as that which existed for men.

In criminal justice practice there were strivings for 'equality' (that is, for women to be treated like men), though this early, undoubtedly unthinking and limited, liberal feminist position gradually came to be challenged by those who questioned the meaning and nature of equality (e.g., MacKinnon 1987a, 1987b; Fudge 1989; Smart 1990). Some of these feminist claims and assertions now seem naive, but the significance of the critique as a starting point for reflection and for changes in criminal justice practice should not be underestimated. Moreover, feminist contributions soon moved beyond a critique.

Dominant strands in the development of feminist perspectives in criminology have included empirical illuminations about discriminatory practices. For example, imprisoned women have been shown to be likely to experience the promotion and enforcement of a domestic role in penal regimes. Subject to petty and coercive systems of control, they are also more likely to be defined as in need of medical or psychological treatment than as simply criminal (Morris 1987; Carlen and Worrall 1987; Dobash, Dobash, and Gutteridge 1986). The treatment of women in the courts suggests that the widely assumed concept of 'chivalry' is misplaced, and that women who do not occupy the appropriate gender role may be seen by the court as 'doubly deviant' (see, for example, Edwards 1984; Eaton 1986; Gelsthorpe 1989; Gelsthorpe and Loucks 1997; Worrall 1990). New ways of conceptualizing matters—the different ways in which conformity is produced for instance—were also developed. Heidensohn (1985) concluded her review of women, crime, and criminal justice by arguing for a return to the sociology of gender and for the use of insights from other studies of women's oppression. Such a redirection helped to expose the explicit and informal controls exercised over women—in the home and at work—and, above all, focused on the rather peculiar notion of 'normal behaviour'. Smart and Smart (1978), Hutter and Williams (1981), Klein and Kress (1976), and Allen (1987), along with Cain (1989) and Howe (1994), have all made apparent the correspondences between the policing of everyday life and policing through more formal mechanisms of social control. And a large body of empirical work drew attention to the experiences of female victims of crime and to female victims' and offenders' experiences of criminal justice processes (see, for example, Stanko 1985, 1990; Dobash and Dobash 1992; Mawby and Walklate 1994; Lees 1997; Carlen 1998; Walklate 1989, 1992, 2001). Indeed, some of the focus on women and criminal justice developed from important feminist work in this area. Other writers focused on women's role in social control (Zimmer 1986; Jones 1986; Heidensohn 1989, 1992; Brown and Heidensohn 2000). Heidensohn (1992), for example, gave particular attention to gender and policing and the ways in which female police officers survive in a predominantly masculine occupation. Such themes are elaborated upon in Brown and Heidensohn (2000). (For an overview of new empirical evidence, see Heidensohn, in Chapter 15 of this volume.)

TRANSFORMING THE DISCIPLINE?: DISCURSIVE QUESTIONINGS OF THE EPISTEMOLOGICAL AND METHODOLOGICAL TERRAIN OF CRIMINOLOGY

In working towards a transformed discipline, feminist perspectives in criminology have moved through stages which resemble a 'Hegelian dialectic' of thesis, antithesis, and synthesis. To translate this into the language of feminism, these stages represent a critique of masculinist criminology, a deconstruction of mainstream portrayals of crime and criminality, and, lastly, steps towards reconstructing adequate theoretical formulations. These three stages do not necessarily follow sequentially throughout the discipline; they are recursive and ongoing. However, the transformation (or need for a transformation) has been depicted in a number of different ways, which are worth repeating here as illustration of the broad body of work which has constituted feminist challenges to criminology.

Daly and Chesney-Lind (1988) raise two key questions in relation to criminological theory. First, can theories generated to describe men's or boys' offending apply to women and girls (what they call the 'generalizability problem')? Secondly, why do women commit less crime than men (what they term the 'gender ratio problem')? In other words, they express concern about '*gender*', the implication being that theories of crime must be able to take account of both men's and women's (criminal) behaviour, and that they must also be able to highlight factors which operate differently on men and women. But more than this, they draw attention to the crucial problematization of gender in different feminist perspectives. This leads to a sophisticated notion of gender relations in which gender is seen not as a natural fact, but as 'a complex, historical, and cultural product . . . related to, but not simply derived from, biological sex difference and reproductive capacities' (ibid.: 504). Thus complex gender codes are internalized in a myriad of ways to regulate behaviour. In other words, criminologists could learn a great deal from looking at feminist insights in relation to gender. Daly and Chesney-Lind also urge criminologists to read first-hand of women's experiences rather than relying on distorted, received wisdom about women, for these accounts of experience have not only enriched feminist thought, but have also become a central part of feminist analyses and epistemological reflections. There is also encouragement for criminologists to reflect on the ethnocentricity inherent in mainstream criminological thinking: the fact that the questions posed by criminologists are generally those of white, economically privileged men. Lastly, Daly and Chesney-Lind indicate the potentialities of points of congruence between feminist perspectives and other social and political theories, and consequently between feminist theories and 'alternative to mainstream' theoretical trajectories in criminology (critical and Marxist criminologies, for example).

In *Feminist Perspectives in Criminology* (Gelsthorpe and Morris 1990), it was similarly noted that creative feminist contributions to criminology go well beyond critique. The contributors to this book both illustrated the hegemonic masculinity of most criminological work and clarified the foundations for future gender-conscious work. To develop this latter point, particular attention was given to the ways in which feminist insights changed the questions relating to violence against women. Whereas conventional theorists focused on the pathological and structural aspects of violent individuals to explain their violence in particular situations, feminists attempted to explain why men *as a group* generally direct their violence towards women. Similarly, while conventional writers focused on the reasons why a woman might stay in an abusive relationship (perhaps signifying that there is something wrong with her), feminist writers asked 'what factors inhibit women's opportunity to leave violent men?'. In this sense, the book was part of a reconstructive moment in criminology, though there were different views as to the nature of this reconstruction. Some contributors, as previously indicated, spelt out a wish to abandon criminology altogether —Carol Smart being one.

Smart's (1990) distinctive contribution is to question whether the focus on female lawbreakers is a proper concern for feminism, and whether a feminist criminology is theoretically possible or politically desirable. She draws attention to the rich variety of feminist scholarship and contrasts it with the limited horizons of criminology. In focusing on the continuing 'marriage' of criminology to (unacknowledged) positivist paradigms and criminologists' pursuit of grand and totalizing theories, she highlights criminology's isolation from some of the major theoretical and political questions which are engaging feminist scholarship in criminology and elsewhere. Indeed, she suggests that feminist criminologists are risking something of a 'marginalized existence—marginal to both criminology and to feminism' (ibid.: 71)—because of their continued engagement with the project of modernism, within which criminology is nurtured and sustained. While feminists outside criminology are increasingly influenced by postmodern reappraisals of knowledge forms and scientific approaches to knowledge (indeed, are leading the way in such appraisals), and are questioning the notion of a universal reality (Weedon 1987; Harding 1986, 1987; Fraser and Nicholson 1988; Gunew 1990; Oakley 2000), many criminologists are perhaps stuck in the conventional mode of seeking 'the truth' through scientific, empirical endeavours— holding fast to the notion of referential finalities. Even critical criminologies such as Left Realism, she argues, are flawed because the work is anchored within positivist paradigms and displays a belief that it is still possible objectively to uncover both the causes of and solutions to 'crime'. Smart claims:

the core enterprise of criminology is problematic, that feminist attempts to transform criminology have only succeeded in revitalising a problematic enterprise, and that, as feminist theory is increasingly engaging with and generating postmodern ideas, the relevance of criminology to feminist thought diminishes. [Smart 1990: 70]

As Smart puts it, this gives rise to questions as to whether an association with criminology is desirable:

. . . for a long time, we have been asking 'what does feminism have to contribute to criminology (or sociology)?'. Feminism has been knocking at the door of established disciplines hoping to be let in on equal terms. These disciplines have largely looked down their noses (metaphorically speaking) and found feminism wanting. Feminism has been required to become more objective, more substantive, more scientific, more anything before a grudging entry could be granted. . . . It might be that criminology needs feminism more than the converse [1990: 83–84].

I shall return to this call for the abandonment of criminology in due course.

I want now to give attention to the feminist epistemological and methodological project that I have foreshadowed. In the same volume (*Feminist Perspectives in Criminology*), Kelly, Hudson, and Gelsthorpe (1990) focus on the processes of knowledge production and reflect research experiences and research methodologies—exploring some of the challenges presented by feminism and its core principles of relating research to practice; engaging with 'the researched', recognizing their subjectivity in a non-hierarchical way; and using sensitive research methods which maximize opportunities to reflect more accurately the experiences of 'the researched'. While feminist research practices have been the focus of much debate in recent years (Clegg 1975; Stanley and Wise 1983; Roberts 1981; Cook and Fonow 1986; Cain 1986; Hammersley *et al.* 1992), myths abound. For example, the oft-quoted phrase from sociologists Stanley and Wise that feminist research must be 'on, by and for women' (1983: 17), is often misunderstood. What they actually said indicates that they are *questioning* this dictum, as have a number of feminist writers in criminology (Cain 1986; Gelsthorpe and Morris 1988; Gelsthorpe 1990; Stanko 1993). Close reading of many feminist discussions about research methods (Reinharz 1979; Roberts 1981; Bowles and Duelli Klein 1983; Gelsthorpe 1990; Oakley 1999, for example) ultimately reveals no fixed 'absolutes' beyond the need for sensitivity in the research task, for personal reflexivity—to reflect on the subjectivities of all involved—and commitment to make the research relevant to women.[5]

There is a crucial focus on 'experience' in feminist research, but not in simplistic ways. The focus on women's 'experiences' (with democratic insistence that women should be 'allowed to speak for themselves') has been used both to make women visible and to link feminist ontology (beliefs about the nature of the world) with feminist epistemology (beliefs about what counts as appropriate knowledge). Feminist beliefs about reality, for example, revolve around the idea that reality is constituted by various sets of structural constraints which subordinate and oppress women. From this, appropriate knowledge is that which allows women to speak for themselves, rather than knowledge about men's worlds which so often presumes itself to be about women's worlds too. As Maureen Cain (1990a) puts it, strategies for the transformation of criminology involve reflexivity, de-construction and re-construction, and a clear focus on women—particularly on 'women only' studies. This is not as a corrective to traditional criminology which has excluded or marginalized women, but for 'women's unspeakable "experiences" to be captured, experienced, named and tamed' (ibid.: 9) without using men and their experiences as a yardstick against which women's experiences must be compared. Along with Smart (1990), Cain also exhorts feminists to locate themselves outside the narrow boundaries of criminology. As she reflects:

Only by starting from outside, with the social construction of gender, or with women's experiences of their total lives, or with the structure of the domestic space, can we begin to

---

[5] There are exceptions to this. See, for example, Belenky *et al.* (1986), and Crawford and Gentry (1989). The authors in both these texts argue that there are distinctive gender-based ways of knowing, and therefore that distinctive methodological methods apply. They suggest that qualitative methods reflect women's experiences and ways of knowing more accurately than other methods.

make sense of what is going on. Feminist criminology must now start from outside [1990a: 10].

Thus Cain proposes a focus on the construction of gender, on discourses which lie beyond criminology, and on the sites which are relevant to women. The questions are about women, she emphasizes, not about crime. This is not to suggest that men are irrelevant to the task, far from it. Cain's claims for serious consideration of gender include men: 'We shall fall into essentialism if we exclude men from our analyses, even if we may wish to exclude them from much of our field research' (1990a: 11). Similarly, she encourages us to learn from the world of women's political struggle:

We must record those forms of resistance to censure and policing which have been effective. This construction of an analytic dossier of women's political struggles, repression and resistance will have a moral function, will save us from continually having to reinvent the wheel, and will drive the creative political enterprise which has brought us this far [1990a: 14].

This concern to place women's experiences, viewpoints, and struggles at the centre of projects has led to the development of what Sandra Harding (1987) has called 'feminist standpointism': that is, a commitment to try to understand the world from the perspective of the socially subjugated—to see things through women's eyes. Citing Longino (1993), Naffine (1997) helpfully outlines the position:

'feminist standpointism' takes many forms, ranging 'from the romantic idea that women come, by nature or social experience, to be better equipped to know the world than are men to the more modest proposal that a social science adequate for women must proceed from a grasp of the forms of oppression women experience' [Longino 1993: 201, *cited in* Naffine 1997: 46].

While there are debates about the nature of women's 'shared' experience and different experiences, and about assumptions that women's realities are somehow 'more real' or produce 'better knowledge' than those discerned from traditional methodologies (Cain 1986), there are no fixed views. Indeed, there is increasing recognition of ontological complexities which both justifies the focus on women's direct/first-hand 'experiences' and raises questions about the usefulness of standpointism. The implication that there is perhaps only 'one experience' or one standpoint is clearly very difficult. There has been a strong tendency to conflate women in feminist theory; different voices (standpoints) have sometimes assumed a false commonality, a false unity. In particular, race and class differences have been underplayed and the relational character of identity has been ignored. At the same time, the notion of 'feminist standpointism' has encouraged both theoretical and personal reflexivity in relation to knowledge and the processes of knowledge production through research: this can help to overcome some of the problems of conventional methodologies associated with mainstream criminology.[6]

---

[6] Maureen Cain (1990b) develops the notion of standpointism using insights from philosophical realism (see Keat and Urry 1975) to argue for a 'successor science' (a way of gaining both transitive and intransitive understandings of the world, and questioning those understandings at the same time) as an alternative to orthodox scientific values and research approaches, but there is not space here to more than float her ideas.

Feminist writers have reflected long and hard on the research methodologies they employ and there are methodological preferences within feminist criminology. However, early dismissals of anything tainted with positivism have (rightly, in my view) given way to critical reflections on the need to use research methods appropriate to the nature of the task (Eichler 1980; Kelly 1990; Oakley 1999). There is no longer anything to suggest that the ideas of feminist writers in criminology are fundamentally antithetical to those of criminologists, though the former might urge the latter in general to be more reflexive and to question the epistemological bases of knowledge. In the wake of feminist concerns to place women's experiences at the centre of research (often exemplified through an exclusively qualitative methodological approach), and criticisms of such feminist concerns, we have witnessed an expansion of interest in the study of lived experience taking place within the social sciences generally.[7] It would be hard to sustain a claim that some of the challenges to conventional research methodologies are distinctively 'feminist'. The most that might be said is that feminist writers have perhaps reflected on the issues more than conventional criminologists, and can lay claim to a concern with doing 'good' research which is not automatically and unthinkingly driven by positivist paradigms and processes.

If we characterize the first two main developments in feminist criminology as *feminist empiricism* (as evidenced in the wide-ranging criminological research on women, crime, control, and justice to counterbalance the absence of women from conventional work) and *feminist standpointism* (drawing attention to the need to place women's experience at the centre of knowledge), the third is best described as *feminist deconstructionism* (Naffine 1997) since it draws on postmodern insights. Deconstructionism involves the problematizing of language and concepts, with authors in this field coming under the influence of key writers such as Foucault (1970, 1972) and Derrida (1978, 1981), and critical understandings of the constitution of perspective. This is a theme evident in the work of Alison Young (1994) and Adrian Howe (1994).

In counterpoising feminism and criminology, Alison Young (1994) outlines the mismatching of a dominant masculinist culture reflected in criminology along with the insouciant parochialism of criminological practitioners, and the aims of feminism to consciously revindicate representations of the feminine and women by and of women themselves. She argues that postmodern insights empower the feminist critic of criminology to 'resist the master-narratives' of criminology (1994: 71). 'Criminology', she suggests, 'as pre-eminent modernist science, exists in continual suppression of Woman as unpresentable, as Other. Postmodernism, for a feminist critic, can expose this act of suppression and can work to reveal the organisation and

---

[7] See, for example, Gluck and Patai (1991); Hollway and Jefferson (2000); Goodey (2000); Chamberlayne *et al.* (2000); Cosslett *et al.* (2000); Plummer (2001); and Roberts (2002), for a detailed account of this interest as well as description of methods. Although it has to be acknowledged that this new interest takes place against a background of concern that too few social scientists are numerate (Major 2001). This may be a case of developments within the academe and interests which revolve around the governmental project being out of alignment (though, arguably, one sort of skill should not replace the other; many would claim that both developments are needed in the social sciences).

self-representation of criminology in binary oppositions' (ibid.: 74). Giving examples of criminology's deployment of binary combinations (the 'normal' and the 'criminal', 'male' and 'female' criminals, for example, thus creating a criminological semantic rectangle), Young suggests that feminist interventions in criminology have hitherto been bound by such a rectangle, and that only a postmodern feminism can effect an escape from such constraints and analytical limitations. Naffine (1997), however, identifies the feminist problem of working both within and without existing frames of reference and the limiting preoccupation with unravelling textual meaning, leaving untouched:

The economic, political and legal structures that help to keep . . . traditional meaning in place and make it appear natural and inevitable . . . alone it [deconstruction] is insufficient to undo the institutional systems that have been built upon, and that help to sustain, the economic and political power of men over women [1997: 89].

Naffine's approach is to build on feminist insights thus gained to argue that we *can* challenge the constitution of meanings in criminological discourse *if* we recognize that meanings can change. In other words, instead of accepting the recalcitrance and intransigence of categories of meaning (woman, crime, rape, and so on), we should realize the 'referential, "relational" and metaphorical nature of meaning' more fully (ibid.: 98). In this way, the fixed, negative categories and tight interpretations of meaning identified through deconstructionist approaches can become fluid—changing their meaning. Naffine acknowledges that such a position bears testament to standpoint feminism (and to its ideas of conscious knowledge production from specific sites and experiences). I would add that we can see traces of Giddensian thinking in this creative combination of deconstructionism and standpointism. In trying to move away from a natural science model for sociology and to reconcile some elements of both the newer interpretative forms of sociology with the more traditional 'structural' forms (what he calls 'institutional analysis'), Giddens (1986) identifies a 'duality of structure'. That is, rather than recognizing two separate and opposed phenomena (structuralism—functionalism and so on, on the one hand, and interpretation—subjectivity and the like on the other), we should recognize that social practices comprise both action and structure. Structure is not 'external' to action; it is perhaps more 'internal' to the flow of action which constitutes the practices in question. In the same way, Naffine is promoting the concept of 'agency'—stemming from standpointism —to counteract some of the claims of feminist deconstructionists, and in this way is recognizing a 'duality' in the creation of knowledge.

Thus Naffine (1997) is exploring some creative possibilities for effecting change in the epistemological assumptions that bind conventional criminology. As illustration, she looks at different ways in which understandings of the sexes (and thereby the logic of explanations) within the context of a major crime (rape) can be approached using insights of deconstructionism and feminist standpointism (1997: 98–119). In a further analysis of a particular genre of feminist crime fiction, Naffine illustrates very clearly how images, meaning, and interpretation *can* change. The hard-boiled male detective as the central character in plots which involve women as vulnerable sexual sirens or sexual victims is transposed into something quite different—a female, often overtly feminine, expert who solves corporate crimes and not just crimes against women. Further, the offenders are very often ordinary men, like 'real' (not media portrayed) killers. In this way, stereotypical notions of powerful men, female victims, and glamorized sexual crimes are challenged, and meanings and understandings are reshaped for us in fiction. There is potential for learning from fiction in the sense that fiction might be translated into reality, though Howe (2000) is rather more pessimistic and argues that the desires, concerns, and methodologies of feminist postmodernism and criminology are so antagonistic as to be irreconcilable.

INTERNATIONAL FEMINIST PERSPECTIVES

I now consider the impact of feminist perspectives more broadly. There have been widely published debates about whether a feminist jurisprudence is possible and/or desirable in different parts of the world, for instance. Boyle (1985) in Canada, Dahl (1987) in Norway, MacKinnon (1987a) and Smart (1989) in England, Redcar (1990) in Australia, and Fineman and Thomadsen (1991) in the USA, for example, all contribute to discussions here. One of the first combined attempts to address feminist perspectives regarding criminology on an international basis, however, took place in Quebec in 1991, when Marie-Andrée Bertrand, Kathleen Daly, and Dorie Klein organized an international feminist conference on Women, Law, and Social Control (Bertrand *et al.* 1992). There have been subsequent discussions of global feminist perspectives—particularly at British Society of Criminology and American Society of Criminology conferences (in 1993 and 1994 respectively, for example). But it is Nicole Hahn Rafter's and Frances Heidensohn's (1995) edited collection of essays, *International Feminist Perspectives in Criminology*, which notably first attempted to provide an international picture of developments in feminist thinking in criminology. The contributors collectively question the extent to which the 'macho criminology' (so characterized by Meda Chesney-Lind) can become 'engendered', and they identify a number of themes which reflect feminist interests which are central to theoretical, methodological, and pedagogical developments and policy in criminology. On the positive side, such themes include a unifying focus on the gendered nature of victimhood, and the authors provide evidence of changes in understandings of rape and the abuse of children in theory, policy, and practice. On the negative side, there are stories of the continued marginalization of feminism, feminist scholars, and female students within the academy, and of an intellectual and political backlash against feminism. Individual authors identify tensions too, where feminist concerns seem marginal to broader political concerns. Through Monica Platek's (1995) poignant description of the development of feminism in Poland, we learn that women there in the early 1990s were reluctant to fight for, or take on, any 'rights' that might deplete their energies further. This debate rightly problematizes wider concerns about women's failure to enjoy equal human rights (Bahar 2000).

The authors of *International Feminist Perspectives in Criminology* do not simply celebrate feminist developments and challenges to criminology. They critically reflect on the nature and scope of the intersections between feminism and criminology. This involves some characterization of criminology in the different countries. There was, in the mid-1990s, a rather depressing picture of a dominant right realist and positivistic criminology in South Africa, a psycho-medical—but fortunately ineffectual—criminology in Italy, and a general sense that criminology is so often detached from central political and practical concerns relating to crime and justice. At the same time, there were pockets of hope. In Australia, for example, we learn from Alder (1995) that feminist scholars in criminology were able to work collaboratively with feminist women in government bureaucracies. In South Africa, Hansson (1995) described that by the mid-1990s there was a new receptivity to a critical criminology which, at that time, was at least partially gendered.

These developments apart, there is certainly evidence of feminist activism in a number of countries (Smith 2000). When apartheid was overthrown in South Africa in the 1990s, for example, women had hard-won political experience and diasporic connections with black activists on other continents. Prompted by warnings from the curtailed women's rights movements that followed on the heels of other national liberation movements' success (Mangaliso 1997), South African women were prepared to make demands and ensure their recognition as full citizens by the various parties involved in post-apartheid South Africa. The new constitution of South Africa reflects their insistent efforts. There is also much evidence of transnational feminist activity with regard to racism (Twine and Blee 2001) and legal reform with regard to offences against women (see, for example, Morris 1993; Kelly and Regan 2000). But in other regards, and especially with regard to other forms of crime and criminal justice, the activity of feminist criminologists, as such, remains somewhat unclear or, some would say, parochial. That this may reflect a contemporary detachment of criminology as a whole from such issues, is clearly no answer.

Since the Second World War, the number of people killed globally in wars of liberation or in civil, ethnic, or inter-state wars has, according to various newspaper accounts, passed the fifty million mark. Some have described a twentieth-century descent into 'barbarism' to encapsulate the incidence and ferocity of wars and ethnic conflicts (Mestrovic 1993; Hobsbawm 1994). It is estimated that these wars, and the accompanying rape and violence, have disproportionately impacted on women (Stiglmayer 1994; Nikolic-Ristanovic 1996a, 1996b; Amnesty International 1995; Turpin and Lorentzen 1996). A number of feminist writers in the past twenty-five years have turned their attention to the idea that war crimes such as rape or mass rape are an expression of the gender order or of a militarized masculinity (Enloe 1993; Mackinnon 1994; Nikolic-Ristanovic 1996a, 1996b). Other feminists have focused on the sexual victimization of women in wartime and its relation to pornography (Brownmiller 1975; Mackinnon 1994, for instance). Recent notable exceptions to this include Nikolic-Ristanovic's (1998) concerns with war and crime in the former Yugoslavia, and Pickering's (2000) discussion of women's resistance in Northern Ireland in which she focuses on women's experiences of house raids by security forces. Nevertheless, it is striking how little attention has been given to gender issues in the context of war. Drawing on the important work of Jamieson (1998), there is a need to focus both on women's *and* men's sexual victimization in war settings, the impact of the militarization of masculinity on women (and the sexual and other crimes which ensue), and the concomitant sexual regulation and policing of women *by* women in such contexts.

DOING GENDER: WORK ON MASCULINITY

Although the 'maleness of crime' has traditionally been acknowledged within main-stream criminology (indeed, sex along with age has long been recognized as one of the most important predictors of crime), it has not, in most mainstream texts, been regarded as problematic. The sociology of masculinity, however, emerged from feminist work on gender, and from men's involvement in feminism, as well as the growing field of gay and lesbian studies. A vital change came in asking what it is about men, 'not as working-class, not as migrants, not as underprivileged individuals but *as men*, [that] induces them to commit crime' (Grosz 1987). Feminist criminologists were interested in this question from the outset. Cain (1990a), for instance, argued that feminist criminology must consider what it was in the social construction of maleness that was so criminogenic.

The literature on masculinity has increased markedly in the last few years (see, for example, Tolson 1977; Connell 1987, 1995; Segal 1990; Hearn and Morgan 1990; Morgan 1992; Messerschmidt 1993; Jefferson 1997; Collier 1998; Hood-Williams 2001). While early feminist work focused on the need to acknowledge women in all areas of criminological debate (see, for example, Heidensohn 1968 and Smart 1976), later work introduced a more critical consideration of the concept of gender (Cain 1990a; Daly 1997; Walklate 2001). There is little doubt that some of the work by feminists in the area of gender therefore contributed to the recognition of mascu-linities as critical to an understanding of crime and victimization (Newburn and Stanko 1994; Collier 1998). But it is also fair to say that some sociological thinking about gender was prompted by the rather one-dimensional images of men's domin-ance presented by radical feminist work on gender (for example, the notion that all men are rapists). Some of the problems with the early sociological engagements with masculinity theory have been well documented (Naffine 1997; Walklate 2001). The failure to address the larger issues of social structure in understanding men's power was a major problem—all crime was regarded as an individual phenomenon. This overwhelming focus on men as the 'norm' within criminological discourse served to pathologize the individual 'deviant', obscuring what men (as men) may share. A key shift came with the introduction of a gender paradigm based on the idea that gender was socially constructed, where encultured sex roles were ascribed to bodily differ-ence. Gender became an essential dimension to progressive feminist politics: the idea of the social construction of gender supporting women's rights to claim equality in spite of bodily differences. Connell's (1987) use of the notion of 'categorical theory' (which depends on the key concepts of patriarchy, domination, oppression, and exploitation through which men are deemed the powerful and women the 'other') at once draws together differing feminist perspectives on gender and puts the contest-ation of power at the centre of his analysis of masculinities.[8] Connell's work has been hugely important for the development of theory into multiple masculinities and in locating different practices of gender within structures of power. The focus on

---

[8] This has had the effect of challenging feminist explanations for violence against women which reflected assumptions about men's power over women amongst other things, and neutralized issues of unequal power relations: see Walklate (2001) for a detailed discussion.

masculinity was thus transformed into an understanding of multiple masculinities which were primarily either 'hegemonic', or 'subordinated'.

Connell's notion of hegemonic masculinity has been used by several scholars to address ways of conceptualizing relations among men, especially where a power differential exists. In fact the concept of 'hegemonic' masculinity is useful in suggesting the power of potential cultural influences. As Connell points out, hegemonic masculinity was not intended to be regarded as corresponding to actual masculinities as they are lived, since 'what most men support is not actually what they are' (1987: 72). It influences, but does not determine what they do. Thorne (1993: 106) elaborates upon this in the following way: 'individuals and groups develop varied forms of accommodation, reinterpretation, and resistance to ideologically hegemonic patterns'. At its core is the Gramscian notion of hegemony, a concept which invokes the constantly contested definition of power. Thus for Connell, the gender structure is always being reproduced and reconstituted. This leads to a more sensitive appreciation of the situational and diverse notions of how the concept of hegemonic masculinity can and should be used.

These intentions, however, have become clouded by varying usage of the term 'hegemonic masculinity'. Collier, for instance, has indicated that the term is used 'on the one hand as referring to a certain set of characteristics or traits, which are then meant to signify "the masculine" in particular contexts; and on the other, as explaining, the *cause* of, the crimes of men' (1998: 19). Hegemonic masculinity is thus expected to explain a vast array of (almost always negative) male behaviours and criminal activities. The concept then becomes overused and potentially tautological (Walklate 1995). For Collier, the use of 'hegemonic masculinity' is untenable since it imposes an 'a priori theoretical/conceptual frame on the psychological complexity of men's behaviour' (1998: 22).

Other commentators have been moved to criticize theoretical developments in a different way. McMahon (1993), for instance, suggests that 'masculinity' is becoming an explanatory cliché in many academic and popular accounts of men, in the same way that sex-role theory did in earlier accounts:

Masculinity is abstract, fragile, insecure, unemotional, independent, non-nurturant and so on. All the attributes of man discussed in the literature are spoken of as aspects of masculinity. It is remarkable how seldom writers on masculinity explicitly indicate what kind of concept they take masculinity 'to be' [1993: 690].

Indeed, recent accounts often leave us with many problems, not least how 'masculine' qualities relate to what men do in concrete and material ways. These analyses also leave unanswered questions of the relationship of masculinity to the individual and the 'embodied social selves' of men. They also fail to help us understand the dimensions of the unities and differences among men. Hood-Williams (2001: 39) proposes that: 'the radical question to be asked here is whether the term "masculinities" adds anything to the analysis of criminal events or is it an empty tautology signifying nothing more than (some of) the things men and boys do'.

Messerschmidt's (1993) analysis has been the most extensive attempt to apply Connell's framework to the study of crime. He draws heavily on Connell's (1987) notions of multiply structured fields of gender relations—those of hegemonic and subordinated masculinities—and on Sylvia Walby's (1990) feminist theory of gender, which revolves around six patriarchal structures. Borrowing also from phenomeno-logical approaches, Messerschmidt develops the idea of gender as a 'situational accomplishment' and of crime as a means of 'doing gender' (West and Zimmerman 1987). Following in Connell's wake, he addresses race and class alongside gender in his theorization of these categories as 'structured action' (1997). The idea is that masculinity can be seen as a crucial point of intersection of different forms of power, stratification, desire, and subjective identity formation. Yet this work is clearly problematic in terms of the way the world is divided up into 'structures'—these 'structures' omit age and disability, for instance (Mac an Ghaill 1994). In short, it is suggested that there is more complexity to these relationships than is presupposed. Hood-Williams (2001) questions whether or not it is actually possible to know and accomplish 'class', for example, in any systematic way.

To add to the complexity, Bob Connell (1995) notes that the concept of masculinity is bound up with modern notions of individuality and self. Although Connell's work is sensitive to the problems of understanding identity, Jefferson (1997) develops these ideas in greater depth. He calls for a more sophisticated understanding of individual identities, and pulls together post-structuralist thinking with psychoanalytic theory to provide a more contextualized account of individuals and crime. He asks:

How do subjects, for example, come to take up (desire/identify with) one (heterosexual) rather than another (homosexual) subject position within the competing discourses of masculinity? This route makes unavoidable a reengagement with the split, contradictory subject of psychoanalysis, if Connell's 'practice' is to be fully understood [1997: 540].

Following post-structuralist theory, Jefferson (1997) has used a conception of dis-course rather than a general notion of 'structures', and has placed the importance of the psyche in the foreground of the investigation.

Needless to say, problems with the notion of 'hegemonic masculinities' have prompted negative attention (in much the same way as there were problems with early feminist theories regarding assumptions about women's shared experiences). Some of the work reveals 'essentializing tendencies'—as did early feminist work (see Hood-Williams 2001; Walklate 2001, for overviews). Neither is it entirely clear where sophisticated theories about masculinity leave us in terms of comprehending crime. In many respects they make the task infinitely more complex, particularly the new 'puzzles' suggested to us by questions of subjectivity (Collier 1998; Hood-Williams 2001). But what should not be underestimated is the importance of feminist work on theorizing about gender relations and expressions of masculinity.

Hood-Williams's (2001: 54) conclusion, that 'criminology knows about gender, confidently goes out to find it and does indeed discover it. Analytic work on the other hand, raises the difficult question of just exactly what is to count as masculinity', lays bare the unresolved difficulties and the relationship between masculinity theory and crime. One of the challenges that Jefferson (1997) throws out at the end of his excellent introduction to masculinity theory is the utility of Jack Katz's (1988) 'seduc-tions of crime' in terms of understanding the lived reality of crime. This is a work, he tells us, that challenges what a gendered dimension of understanding actually contributes. Katz has been admired by critical criminologists as posing an important postmodern challenge to the project of positivistic explanations of crime causation. By focusing on the 'foreground factors' of the exprience of crime and its 'moral emotions', he has perhaps brought us closer to understanding the lived reality of crime. His analysis of 'excitement' and 'seduction' is free from any sustained attempt to perceive or analyse these emotions as masculine elements of identity. What such work suggests is that at the moment of desire, pleasure, and risk-seeking, a specifically masculine identity may not be the most important element in engagement in crime. Thus, crucially, we return to feminist precepts regarding reality as 'lived experience'. The foregrounding of agency goes straight to the heart of the feminist enterprise.

My intention in this section has been to highlight some of the theoretical reasoning regarding masculinity and masculinities studies promoted, at least in part, by feminist insights. It is arguable, though, that neither the work on masculinities nor the work on women, sex, and gender, has yet fully explicated links with crime and victimization. As Walklate indicates, 'a gendered lens certainly helps us see some features of the crime problem more clearly; but how and under what circumstances is that clarity made brighter by gender or distorted by it?' (2001: 186). Moreover, there is much work to be done with regard to recognizing the state as a gendered institution, and identifying how and under what circumstances the state acts as a gendered institution (in combination with considerations of race and class). Yet it is clear that some of the emergent work on masculinities owes a debt to pioneering feminist work on gender theory, and that without it sociological and criminological work would be impoverished.

TOWARDS A CONCLUSION

The discussion in this chapter serves as a comment on the impact of feminism on criminology and adds to the various published accounts already referred to in preceding pages (see in particular, Gelsthorpe and Morris 1988; Daly and Chesney-Lind 1988; Gelsthorpe and Morris 1990; Morris and Gelsthorpe 1991; Rafter and Heidensohn 1995; Naffine 1997; and Heidensohn and Rock, in Chapters 15 and 2 of this volume). Yet Heidensohn, amongst others, has from time to time pointedly asked 'Has anyone been listening?' Without wishing to add to Rock's picture of criminology as a rather pessimistic profession, the answer is necessarily mixed. There are awakenings in some quarters of criminology, and this fact is reflected in theory, research, teaching, and policy developments. In other quarters there is what I term 'selective deafness', and theory, research, teaching, and policy remain unreconstituted.

According to Naffine (1997), criminology remains a male-dominated discipline principally about academic men studying criminal men. It is certainly the case that, over the past decade, there has been a considerable decline in the mass base of feminist activism, as well as a popular backlash against feminism. It is arguable, moreover, that this backlash has impinged upon the academic world of criminology. But as Rock indicates in Chapter 2 of this volume, criminology, as a profession, is not optimistic, and since there is much to value in the inroads that feminists have made within criminology, I choose not to dwell in a discourse of perpetual disappointment. It is worth noting that lively feminist debates and intellectual advances in criminology abound in the Women's Division of the American Society of Criminology (the ASC). And at the beginning of the new millennium, as the British Society of Criminology reviews its structure and functioning, there are early signs that subject or themed divisions to mirror the structure of the ASC may emerge. A division on women and crime has already been strongly mooted. More than this, there is evidence of an impact of feminism on criminological research, policy, and practice (see, for instance, Lacey 2001; ESRC Violence Programme 1998; Prison Reform Trust 2000), at least in the kinds of questions asked if not in the end result (though Carlen (1998) rightly points out that the questions have to be rehearsed again, and again, and again). It is also heartening that there is currently a Home Office gender network involving academics, as well as policy-makers and practitioners from statutory and voluntary agencies (Fawcett Society 2001). Beyond this, we might pause for a moment to look at the debate on the most-cited scholars and works of criminologists, for there is perhaps more here to signify impact than might first be imagined.

There has recently been much interest (however misguided; Levi 1998) in producing studies to identify the most-cited scholars and works in criminology and criminal justice journals (see, for example, Cohn and Farrington 1994; Wright and Cohen 1996). In these studies, few female scholars emerge with high scores—which might easily be taken to mean that they have had limited impact on criminology as a whole. By extending the analysis beyond the usual range of journals chosen for such analyses (to include 'women and crime' and 'women and criminal justice' journals), however, Wright and Sheridan (1997) note how frequently feminist authors are cited, and come to the conclusion that 'women and crime' literature is neglected outside 'women and crime' and 'women and criminal justice' publications.[9] But their key point is that lists of the most-cited scholars and works are no more representative of a discipline than the publications that researchers choose to analyse. If the protagonists of citation counts were to include a wider range of journals (Wright and Sheridan note that Cohn and Farrington, for instance, analyse mostly quantitative journals), the overall conclusions might be rather different. Though clearly it is willingness to *engage with* feminist work which is most required, and not simply citations.

Unsurprisingly, however, feminist work in criminology has drawn criticism. Leaving aside the fallacious, but significant, inferences of some criminological writers that feminist work is somehow just ideological reasoning or irrelevant to criminological tasks (Bottomley and Pease 1986; Walker 1987), Marcia Rice (1990), for example, forcefully and rightly takes early feminist writers to task because Black women were noticeably absent from their early discourse. Indeed, she argues that feminists have

---

[9] This is not to suggest that all work by female scholars, or all work on women and crime, is feminist, but we can assume that much of it is. On a related but separate point, a notable special edition of the *British Journal of Criminology* (2000) 40/2, devoted to Criminology and Social Theory, was disappointing in its lack of attention to feminist theoretical advances.

failed to notice that traditional machocentric criminology was constructed on *racist* and sexist ideologies, and that feminist work is equally ethnocentric.

Further, what Pat Carlen (1992) calls the 'theoreticist, libertarian, separatist and gender-centric tendencies' in feminist writings in general, and the strong 'abandon criminology' position of Carol Smart (1990) in particular, have come under attack. In a searching and important paper, which is part of a collection of papers appraising Left Realism, Pat Carlen (1992) identifies an unwillingness on the part of some feminists to link theoretical struggles with political struggles, because of assumptions that theoretical rigour and discourse will be subsumed or lost within engagement with politics and practice.[10] She also identifies a libertarian (and short-sighted) tendency in feminist thinking which is reflected in scepticism that involvement in criminal justice policy directed towards the reduction of crime cannot be without an element of interference and 'social engineering'. I agree with her that this would be to abandon women caught up in the criminal justice system. Under the same heading of 'libertarian tendencies', Carlen focuses on what she believes to be mistaken feminist 'glorification' in 'allowing women to speak for themselves' (1992: 63), though while Carlen believes that feminists are suggesting this as a distinctly 'feminist' pursuit, and a pursuit which involves only women, it may be that this is merely identified and celebrated by feminists as 'good social science' and as a strategy which should be used with men too (Gelsthorpe 1990; Cain 1986).[11]

Continuing in critical vein, Carlen suggests that the separatist tendency in feminist writings on crime and justice reflects a feminist reluctance (or even refusal) to acknowledge theoretical advances in criminology, so that theories continue to be hailed as 'malestream' or termed in some other cryptic, negative way. There is some validity in this claim, and I shall return to it in the conclusion. A more obvious criticism relating to 'separatism', however, might be directed at ideas relating to the development of a feminist jurisprudence (Mackinnon 1987b; Smith 1993; Olsen 1995; Bottomley 1996) because of the impracticability of the proposal, though Carlen suspends such criticism when it comes to her own agenda (I discuss this point further below).

The criticism of a 'gender-centric' tendency, and the privileging of gender over race and class in feminist approaches, undoubtedly hits hard. But debates have begun to acknowledge this tendency in a constructive way (Hammersley *et al.* 1992), and there

---

[10] It is arguable that Smart is eminently 'engaged' in the field of law and politics and sexuality, outside criminology (Smart 1995); but Carlen's point is valid even if the direction in which it is offered is slightly awry.

[11] Moreover, there is clearly evidence of women not being allowed to speak for themselves. For example, with regard to domestic violence, some feminist commentators argue for the increased criminalization and penalization of violent men (see, for example, Kelly 1999), yet there are indications that when women call the police because of domestic violence, they do so for many reasons which may or may not include wanting their partner arrested. Many simply want the violence to stop. In Hoyle's (1998) sample of 33 victims, for example, only a third wanted their partner arrested, and many of these women did not want the police to proceed further: they wanted immediate protection, but not necessarily prosecution. Morris and Gelsthorpe (2000), amongst others, support moves towards restorative justice, and suggest that criminologists and feminists alike should listen more carefully to victims. That is, they should *really* allow women (and men) to speak for themselves.

is clear evidence that such issues are pressing within feminist approaches to criminology (Daly 1994; Daly and Stephenson 1995). Moreover, some of the important
theoretical developments regarding 'doing gender' include race and class issues
(Jefferson 1997). This is an important theme which, amongst others, contributors to
Daly and Maher's (1998) review of the crossroads and intersections of criminology
and feminist work on crime and justice, highlight. But Pat Carlen's criticism of
gender-centricism is a rather different criticism from the earlier comments of Marcia
Rice (1990) and, more recently, of Pat Connell (1995) on the neglect of Black perspectives. While the privileging of gender is now commonly questioned, Rice and Connell
both make the case for a specifically Black feminist perspective within criminology.
Rafter and Heidensohn (1995) present *International Feminist Perspectives in Criminology* as a genuine attempt to deal with such issues by offering a multi-cultural collection of papers. Nevertheless, there is a difference between genuinely multi-cultural
analysis and multi-cultural representations, as Daly (1994) has noted, and it is not
clear that this point is dealt with.

   Turning to postmodern developments, Carlen (1992) suggests that feminists do not
need to abandon criminology to employ the critical precepts of a deconstructionist
approach and to work through some of the theoretical contradictions of knowledge
and political strategy. She outlines her own agenda for a feminist realist approach to
criminology which involves the deconstruction and re-theorization of the problematic relation between 'women and crime' and justice for women. Carlen's agenda thus
involves deconstruction of what is already known about women lawbreakers via a
'bricolage' of concepts appropriated from a variety of theoretical discourses and
research, from the empirical investigation of the different contexts (ideological, economic, political) in which women break the law and their routes through various
welfare and penal networks, and from the investigation of the ideological discourses
within which women's law-breaking is known. She also thinks there is scope for
investigation of the utility of feminist jurisprudence along with more detailed analysis
of social justice (1992: 65–6). Her political agenda, however, is conceptually broad in
arguing that:

... the aim should be to 'ensure that the penal system of female law-breakers does not
increase their oppression as unconventional women, as black people and as poverty-stricken
defendants still further; and to ensure that the penal regulation of law-breaking men is not
such that it brutalises them and makes them behave even more violently or oppressively
towards women in the future [1992: 66].

Many feminist writers in criminology would support this approach.

   So, despite criticisms of Left Realism for its positivistic, essentializing, deterministic, and popularizing tendencies, Carlen holds fast to Left Realism's critical attempts
to overcome the 'impossibilism' of earlier critical criminologies and their political/
practical focus. While we cannot assume that feminists would wish to pin feminist
perspectives in criminology to Left Realism, I do not believe Pat Carlen is alone in
being concerned that the abandonment of criminology could be seen as the abandonment of people to their fate in existing criminal justice practices. Indeed, if we
can recognize a *political* project in criminology as well as a feminist project, then it is

surely worth sticking within criminology. Some of the moral and political dimensions of criminology are thoroughly defensible, even if certain epistemological assumptions are highly questionable. By all means, let us view the criminological tasks both within and without, but let us not cut off criminology's political nose to spite its face.

THE HALLMARKS OF FEMINISM

The hallmarks of contemporary feminism and feminist approaches to criminology include a focus on *gender* as a central organizing principle for contemporary life, recognition of the importance of *power* in shaping social relations, a sensitivity to the way that the social *context* shapes human relations, recognition that all social reality must be understood as a *process*, and recognition that research methods should take all this into account. There is also political commitment to *social change* as a critical part of feminist scholarship and practice—hence a strong *political project*. Of crucial importance, too, is the *epistemological and methodological project*, the epistemological questioning and creative thinking about the production of knowledge and processes of knowledge production, and the emphasis on personal and theoretical reflexivity. Some difficult issues remain unresolved in this, and there is much scope for further development so that feminism embraces humanism, without committing to the humanistic paradigms so criticized by Foucault, for example (Soper 1990). In this way, feminists could deal with the potential to close off and be self-referential. Also, while borrowed postmodern insights enhance the epistemological and methodological project, by challenging and deconstructing the constitution of meaning in criminological discourse, I am not sure that there are useful postmodern insights regarding concrete practices and knowledges which could replace current ones. Postmodernists have very little to say about visions of justice, for example, or about the ways in which difference can be accommodated in notions of justice. Yet this is vital to the broad feminist political project (Flax 1992; Hudson 2000). To summarize, however, I would argue that there is an unmistakable openness in feminist thinking, and a willingness to engage with tough epistemological issues. Feminism has not escaped the epistemological crisis facing the social sciences; rather, it has embraced it and is working creatively within it.

THE HALLMARKS OF CRIMINOLOGY

At the beginning of this chapter, I claimed that the criminology of the 1990s and twenty-first century was arguably more diverse (and more plural) than the criminology of the 1970s and 1980s. But I sense that there is a qualitative difference in some of the criminologies of today too. A great deal of what we see in criminology continues to be empiricist/positivist and is tied to the Lombrosian and governmental projects (Garland, in Chapter 1 of this volume). But I also note new ways of thinking about the social world in general and about criminology in particular. We need to acknowledge these advances. We can discern greater theoretical reflexivity than hitherto (Nelkin 1994; Morrison 1994; Muncie *et al.* 1996; Henry and Milovanovic

1996; MacLean and Milovanovic 1997); a re-enchantment with the social—those very phenomena (emotions, intuition, personal experience, and mystical experience, for example) which were once outlawed by modernist projects—including criminology (Katz 1988; Braithwaite 1989; Garland 1992, 1994); and an interest in intertextuality (Redhead 1995; Stanley 1996; Davis 1990, for example).[12] Significantly, too, there is evidence that criminology is participating in the blurring of disciplinary boundaries (Ericson and Carriere 1994), a phenomenon which renders moves to abandon criminology as something of an empty gesture. Finally, we can discern an interest in 'alterity' (Nelkin 1994)—an interest in the significance of the 'other' and the constitution of identity within modern intellectual and cultural life. While these interests do not mirror feminist insights from empirical work, standpointism, and deconstructionism, and while the heartlands of criminology remain untouched by feminism, there is something to encourage optimism. There is possibly scope to see more fluid/sensitive/gender aware criminologies on the horizon. At least some elements of the criminological project are in transition.

As well as drawing attention to the positive contributions of feminism to criminology, this review of the relationship between feminism and criminology rehearses a number of problems which inhere in feminist efforts to engage with criminology. The range of feminist work is extremely wide—from empirical studies which are undertaken in the name of feminist criminology, to theoretical developments on gender and deconstructionist approaches. Criticisms of feminist work within criminology abound, but neither criticisms of incompatability between feminism (as it develops and engages with postmodern thought) and criminology (Carrington 1998), nor criticisms of continuing empiricism (Howe 1997) necessarily cast feminists struggling to work within criminology into the intellectual shadows. On the contrary, there is much evidence of a liveliness and spiritedness in these debates. The main problem perhaps remains one of ideological resistance to feminism from within the heartlands of criminology. Feminism may not now be 'the great unspoken' in criminology, but in certain quarters it remains 'the great unheard'. Yet, overall, I believe that there is good reason to share Daly's (1994) proposition that feminists 'work within and against criminology' (see also Comack 1999) and to join Naffine in her appeal to the ethical senses of criminologists to 'bring women (and other exiles) in from the cold' (1997: 153). As she says, 'We must let the exile bear witness' (ibid.). Feminists have done much to question masculinist viewpoints of criminology and to alter their thinking. A broad and generous reading of criminology suggests that there may now be a convergence of interests between feminism and criminology, at least in some quarters, and thus scope for positive dialogue. With this is mind, feminist criminologies have as many possible futures as they have pasts.

[12] Such stylistic innovations potentially have the same impact as Naffine's (1997) 'crime fictions' which turn on their head the meanings attached to crime, men and women, and so on.

Selected further reading

Naffine's *Feminism and Criminology* (Cambridge: Polity Press, 1997) offers an excellent synthesis of ideas relating to the relationship between feminism and criminology. Walklate's *Gender, Crime and Criminal Justice* (Cullompton, Devon: Willan Publishing, 2001) also provides an excellent introduction to empirical work on gender and to issues pertinent to the impact of feminism on criminology.

There are three main collections of essays which provide critical overviews of the relationship between feminism and criminology: Gelsthorpe's and Morris's *Feminist Perspectives in Criminology* (Buckingham: Open University Press, 1990) covers three broad areas: the feminist critique of criminology and its theoretical parameters; attempts to transform criminology through research methodologies; and the relationship between feminism, politics, and action. Rafter's and Heidensohn's *International Feminist Perspectives in Criminology* (Buckingham: Open University Press, 1995) describes the impact of feminism on criminology in a wide range of countries. Daly's and Maher's *Criminology at The Crossroads: Feminist Readings in Crime and Justice* (Oxford: Oxford University Press, 1998) contains key works in criminology and law by feminist scholars on the construction of women in feminist, legal, and criminological discourses; the blurred boundaries of victimization and criminalization; masculinities and violence; and the crossroads and intersections of class-race-gender, politics, and justice.

The area of feminist epistemology and methodology is vast, but the following provide a useful starting point: Fonow's and Cook's *Beyond Methodology* (Indiana: Indiana University Press, 1991); Lennon's and Whitford's *Knowing the Difference: Feminist Perspectives in Epistemology* (London: Routledge, 1994); and Oakley's *Experiments in Knowing: Gender and Methods in the Social Sciences* (Cambridge: Polity, 2000).

References

ALDER, C. (1995), 'Feminist Criminology in Australia', in N.H. Rafter and F. Heidensohn (eds), *International Feminist Perspectives in Criminology*, Buckingham: Open University Press.

ALLEN, H. (1987), *Justice Unbalanced: Gender, Psychiatry and Judicial Decisions*, Milton Keynes: Open University Press.

AMNESTY INTERNATIONAL (1995), 'Women: "Invisible victims of human rights violations"', 8 March, news release.

BAHAR, S. (2000), 'Human Rights Are Women's Right', originally published in *Hypatia*, 11/1, 1996, reproduced in B. Smith (ed.), *Global Feminisms Since 1945*, London: Routledge.

BECKER, H. (1963), *Outsiders*, Glencoe, NY: Free Press.

BELENKY, M., CLINCHY, B., and GOLDBERGER, N. (1986), *Women's Ways of Knowing*, New York: Basic Books.

BENHABIB, S. (1992), *Situating the Self: Gender, Community and Postmodernism in Contemporary Ethics*, Cambridge: Polity.

BERTRAND, M. (1969), 'Self-Image and Delinquency: A Contribution to the Study of Female Criminality and Women's Image', in *Acta Criminologica*, II: 71–144.

——, DALY, K., and KLEIN, D. (eds) (1992), *Proceedings of the International Feminist Conference on Women, Law, and Social Control*, Mont Gabriel, Quebec, 18–21 July 1991.

BOTTOMLEY, A (ed.) (1996), *Feminist perspectives on the foundational subjects of law*, London: Cavendish Publishing.

BOTTOMLEY, K., and PEASE, K. (1986), *Crime and Punishment: Interpreting the Data*, Milton Keynes: Open University Press.

BOWLES, G., and DUELLI KLEIN, R. (eds) (1983), *Theories of Women's Studies*, London: Routledge and Kegan Paul.

BOYLE, C. (1985), *A Feminist Review of Criminal Law*, Canada: Ministry of Supply and Services.

BRAITHWAITE, J. (1989), *Crime, Shame and Reintegration*, Cambridge: Cambridge University Press.

BROWN, B. (1986), 'Women and crime: the dark figures of criminology', *Economy and Society*, 15/3: 355–402.

BROWN, D., and HOGG, R. (1992), 'Law and order politics—left realism and radical criminology: a view from down under', in R. Matthews and J. Young (eds), *Issues in Realist Criminology*, London: Sage.

BROWN, J., and HEIDENSOHN, F. (2000), *Gender and Policing*, Basingstoke: Macmillan/Palgrave.

BROWNMILLER, S. (1975), *Against Our Will*, New York: Simon and Schuster.

BULBECK, C. (1998), *Re-orienting western feminisms: women's diversity in a post colonial world*, Cambridge: Cambridge University Press.

CAIN, M. (1986), 'Realism, feminism, methodology, and law', *International Journal of the Sociology of Law*, 14/3: 255–67.

—— (ed.) (1989), *Growing Up Good. Policing the Behaviour of Girls in Europe*, London: Sage.

—— (1990a), 'Towards transgression: new directions in feminist criminology', *International Journal of the Sociology of Law*, 18: 1–18.

—— (1990b), 'Realist philosophy and standpoint epistemologies or feminist criminology as a successor science', in L. Gelsthorpe and A. Morris (eds), *Feminist Perspectives in Criminology*, Buckingham: Open University Press.

CARLEN, P. (1992), 'Criminal women and criminal justice: the limits to, and potential of, feminist and left realist perspectives', in R. Matthews and J. Young (eds), *Issues in Realist Criminology*, London: Sage.

—— (1998), *Sledgehammer*, Basingstoke: Macmillan/Palgrave.

—— and WORRALL, A. (eds) (1987), *Gender, Crime and Justice*, Milton Keynes: Open University Press.

CARRINGTON, K. (1994), 'Postmodernism and Feminist Criminologies: Disconnecting Discourses?', *International Journal of the Sociology of Law*, 22: 261–77.

—— (1998), 'Postmodernism and Feminist Criminologies: Disconnecting Discourses', in K. Daly and L. Maher (eds), *Criminology at the Crossroads*, New York: Oxford University Press.

CHAMBERLAYNE, P., BORNAT, J., and WENGRAF, T. (eds) (2000), *The Turn to Biographical Methods in Social Science*, London: Routledge.

CIXOUS, H. (1976), 'The laugh of the medusa', *Signs*, 1/4: 875–93.

CLEGG, S. (1975), 'Feminist methodology — fact or fiction?', *Quality and Quantity*, 19: 83–97.

COHEN, E., and FARRINGTON, D. (1994), 'Who Are the Most-Cited Scholars in Major American Criminology and Criminal Justice Journals?', *Journal of Criminal Justice*, 22: 517–34.

COHEN, S. (1988), *Against Criminology*, New Brunswick, NJ: Transaction Books.

COLLIER, R. (1998), *Masculinities, Crime and Criminology*, London: Sage.

COMACK, E. (1999), 'New possibilities for a feminism "in" criminology? From dualism to diversity', *Canadian Journal of Criminology*, April: 161–70.

CONNELL, P. (1995), 'Black, British and Beaten? Understanding Violence, Agency and Resistance', paper presented to the British Criminology Conference, Loughborough, 1995.

CONNELL, R. (1987), *Gender and Power*, Cambridge: Polity Press.

—— (1995), *Masculinities*, Cambridge: Polity Press.

COOK, J., and FONOW, M. (1986), 'Knowledge and women's interests: issues of epistemology and methodology in feminist sociological research', *Sociological Inquiry*, 56: 1–29.

COSSLETT, T., LURY, C., and SUMMERFIELD, P. (eds) (2000), *Feminism and Autobiography. Text, Theories, Methods*, London: Routledge.

CRAWFORD, M., and GENTRY, M. (eds) (1989), *Gender and Thought*, New York: Springer Verlag.

DAHL, T. (1987), *Women's Law. An Introduction to Feminist Jurisprudence*, Oslo: Norwegian University Press.

DALY, K. (1994), 'Criminal Law and Justice System Practices as Racist, White and Racialised', *Washington and Lee Law Review*, 15/2: 431–64.

—— (1997), 'Different Ways of Conceptualising Sex/Gender in Feminist Theory and Their Implications for Criminology', *Theoretical Criminology*, 1/1: 25–51.

—— and CHESNEY-LIND, M. (1988), 'Feminism and Criminology', *Justice Quarterly*, 5/4: 498–538.

—— and MAHER, L. (1998), *Criminology at the Crossroads. Feminist Readings in Crime and Justice*, Oxford: Oxford University Press.

—— and STEPHENSON, D. (1995), 'The "Dark Figure" of Criminology: Toward a Black and Multi-Ethnic Feminist Agenda for Theory and Research', in N.H. Rafter and F. Heidensohn (eds), *International Feminist Perspectives in Criminology*, Buckingham: Open University Press.

DAVIS, M. (1990), *City of quartz: excavating the futures of Los Angeles*, London: Verso.

DE BEAUVOIR, S. (1949), *Le Deuxième Sexe*, Paris: Gallimard.

DELMAR, R. (1986), 'What is Feminism?', in J. Mitchell and A. Oakley (eds), *What is Feminism?*, Oxford: Blackwell.

DERRIDA, J. (1978), 'Structure, Sign and Play in the Discourse of the Human Sciences', in *Writing and Difference*, Chicago: Chicago University Press.

—— (1981), *Positions*, Chicago: University of Chicago Press.

DIAMOND, I., and QUINBY, L. (eds) (1988), *Feminism and Foucault*, Boston: Northeastern University Press.

DOBASH, R.E., and DOBASH, R.P. (1992), *Women, Violence and Social Change*, London: Routledge.

——, —— and GUTTERIDGE, S. (1986), *The Imprisonment of Women*, Oxford: Blackwell.

EATON, M. (1986), *Justice for Women?*, Milton Keynes: Open University Press.

ECONOMIC AND SOCIAL RESEARCH COUNCIL (ESRC) (1998), *Research Programme on Violence*, Swindon: ESRC.

EDWARDS, S. (1984), *Women on Trial*, Manchester: Manchester University Press.

EICHLER, M. (1980), *The Double Standard: A Feminist Critique of Feminist Social Science*, London: Croom Helm.

ENLOE, C. (1983), *Does Khaki Become You? The Militarisation of Women's Lives*, London: Pluto.

ERICSON, R., and CARRIERE, K. (1994), 'The Fragmentation of Criminology', in D. Nelken (ed.), *The Futures of Criminology*, London: Sage.

EVANS, J. (1995), *Feminist Theory Today*, London: Sage.

FAWCETT SOCIETY (2001), *Gender and Justice Policy Network* (minutes of meetings), London: Fawcett Society.

FINEMAN, M., and THOMADSEN, N. (eds) (1991), *At the Boundaries of Law*, New York: Routledge.

FLAX, J. (1992), 'Beyond equality: gender, justice and difference', in G. Bock and S. James (eds), *Beyond Equality and Difference*, London: Routledge.

FOUCAULT, M. (1970), *The Order of Things: An Archaeology of the Human Sciences*, London: Tavistock.

—— (1972), *The Archaeology of Knowledge*, London: Tavistock.

FRASER, N., and NICHOLSON, L. (1988), 'Social criticism without philosophy: an encounter between feminism and postmodernism', *British Journal of Law and Society*, 7: 215–41.

FUDGE, J. (1989), 'The effect of entrenching a Bill of Rights upon political discourse: feminist demands and sexual violence in Canada', *International Journal of the Sociology of Law*, 17/4: 445–63.

GARLAND, D. (1992), 'Criminological Knowledge and its Relation to Power: Foucault's Genealogy and Criminology Today', *British Journal of Criminology*, 32/4: 403–22.

—— (1994), 'Of Crimes and Criminals: The Development of Criminology in Britain', in M. Maguire, R. Morgan, and R. Reiner (eds), *Oxford Handbook of Criminology*, 1st edn, Oxford: Oxford University Press.

GELSTHORPE, L. (1989), *Sexism and the female offender: an organizational analysis*, Aldershot: Gower.

—— (1990), 'Feminist methodologies in criminology: a new approach or old wine in new bottles?', in L. Gelsthorpe and A. Morris (eds), *Feminist Perspectives in Criminology*, Buckingham: Open University Press.

—— and MORRIS, A. (1988), 'Feminism and Criminology in Britain', *British Journal of Criminology*, 28/2: 93–110.

—— and —— (eds) (1990), *Feminist Perspectives in Criminology*, Buckingham: Open University Press.

—— and LOUCKS, N. (1997), 'Magistrates' explanations of sentencing decisions', in C. Hedderman and L. Gelsthorpe (eds), *Understanding the Sentencing of Women*, Home Office Research Study 170, London: Home Office.

GIDDENS, A. (1986), *The Constitution of Society. Outline of the Theory of Structuralism*, Cambridge: Polity.

GLUCK, S., and PATAI, D. (eds) (1991), *Women's Words: The Feminist Practice of Oral History*, London: Routledge.

GOTTFREDSON, M., and HIRSCHI, T. (eds) (1987), *Positive Criminology*, Newbury Park: Sage.

GREENWOOD, V. (1981), 'The myth of female crime', in A. Morris and L. Gelsthorpe (eds), *Women and Crime*, Cambridge: Institute of Criminology.

GROSZ, E. (1987), 'Feminist theory and the challenge to knowledge', *Women's Studies International Forum*, 10/5: 208–17.

GUNEW, S. (ed.) (1990), *Feminist Knowledge. Critique and Construct*, London: Routledge.

HAMMERSLEY, M., RAMAZANOGLU, C., and GELSTHORPE, L. (1992), 'Debate: Feminist Methodology, Reason and Empowerment', *Sociology*, 26/2: 187–218.

HANSSON, D. (1995), 'Agenda-ing gender: feminism and the engendering of academic criminology in South Africa', in N.H. Rafter and F. Heidensohn (eds), *International Feminist Perspectives in Criminology*, Buckingham: Open University Press.

HARDING, S. (ed.) (1986), *The Science Question in Feminism*, Milton Keynes: Open University Press.

—— (1987), *Feminism and Methodology*, Milton Keynes: Open University Press.

HEARN, J., and MORGAN, D. (eds) (1990), *Men, Masculinities and Social Theory*, London: Unwin Hyman.

HEIDENSOHN, F. (1968), 'The Deviance of Women: A Critique and Enquiry', *British Journal of Sociology*, 19/2: 160–75.

—— (1970), 'Sex, Crime and Society', in G. Harrison (ed.), *Biosocial Aspects of Sex*, Oxford: Blackwell.

—— (1985), *Women and Crime*, London: Macmillan.

—— (1989), *Women and Policing in the USA*, London: Police Foundation.

—— (1992), *Women in Control? The Role of Women in Law Enforcement*, Oxford: Oxford University Press.

—— (1997), 'Gender and Crime', in M. Maguire, R. Morgan, and R. Reiner (eds), *Oxford Handbook of Criminology*, 2nd edn, Oxford: Oxford University Press.

HENRY, S., and MILOVANOVIC, D. (1996), *Constitutive Criminology*, London: Sage.

HILL-COLLINS, P. (2002), 'Learning From The Outsider Within. The sociological significance of Black feminist thought', in S. Jackson and S. Scott (eds), *Gender. A Sociological Reader*, London: Routledge.

HINDESS, B. (1977), *Philosophy and Methodology in the Social Sciences*, Brighton: Harvester.

HIRSCH, M., and KELLER, E. (eds) (1990), *Conflicts in Feminism*, New York: Routledge.

HOBSBAWM, E. (1994), 'Barbarism: A User's Guide', *New Left Review*, 206: 44–54.

HOLLWAY, W., and JEFFERSON, T. (2000), *Doing Qualitative Research Differently*, London: Sage.

HOME OFFICE (2000), *Criminal Statistics in England and Wales*, London: HMSO.

HOOD-WILLIAMS, J. (2001), 'Gender, masculinities and crime: From structures to psyches', *Theoretical Criminology*, 5/1: 37–60.

HOWE, A. (1994), *Punish and Critique: Towards a Feminist Analysis of Penality*, London: Routledge.

—— (1997), 'Criminology Meets Postmodern Feminism (and Has a Nice Day)', in B. MacLean and D. Milovanovic (eds), *Thinking Critically About Crime*, Vancouver: The Collective Press.

—— (2000), 'Postmodern Criminology and its Feminist Discontents', *The Australian and New Zealand Journal of Criminology*, 33/2: 221–36.

HOYLE, C. (1998), *Negotiating Domestic Violence: Police, Criminal Justice and Victims*, Oxford: Oxford University Press.

HUDSON, A. (1990), '"Elusive subjects": researching young women in trouble', in L. Gelsthorpe and A. Morris (eds), *Feminist Perspectives in Criminology*, Buckingham: Open University Press.

HUDSON, B. (2000), 'Criminology, Difference and Justice: Issues for Critical Criminology', *The Australian and New Zealand Journal of Criminology*, 33/2: 168–82.

HUMM, M. (ed.) (1992), *Feminisms: A Reader*, New York: Harvester Wheatsheaf.

—— (1995), *The Dictionary of Feminist Theory*, New York: Prentice Hall.

HUTTER, B., and WILLIAMS, G. (eds) (1981), *Controlling Women: The Normal and the Deviant*, London: Croom Helm in association with Oxford University Women's Studies Committee.

IRIGARAY, L. (1977), *Ce sexe qui n'en est pas un*, Paris: Editions de Minuit.

JACKSON, S., and SCOTT, S. (2002), *Gender. A Sociological Reader*, London: Routledge.

JAMIESON, R. (1998), 'Towards a criminology of war in Europe', in V. Ruggiero, N. South, and I. Taylor (eds), *The New European Criminology*, London: Routledge.

JEFFERSON, T. (1997), 'Masculinities and Crimes', in M. Maguire, R. Morgan, and R. Reiner (eds), *Oxford Handbook of Criminology*, 2nd edn, Oxford: Oxford University Press.

JONES, S. (1986), *Policewomen and Equality*, London: Macmillan.

KATZ, J. (1988), *Seductions of crime: moral and sensual attractions in doing evil*, New York: Basic Books.

KEAT, R., and URRY, J. (1975), *Social Theory as Science,* London: Routledge and Kegan Paul.

KELLY, L. (1990), 'Journeying in reverse: possibilities and problems in feminist research on sexual violence', in L. Gelsthorpe and A. Morris (eds), *Feminist Perspectives in Criminology,* Buckingham: Open University Press.

—— (1999), *Domestic Violence Matters: An Evaluation of a Developmental Project,* Home Office Research Study No. 193, London: Home Office.

—— and REGAN, L. (2000), *Stopping the Traffic: exploring the extent of, and responses to, trafficking in women for exploitation in the UK,* Home Office: Police Research Series 125.

KLEIN, D., and KRESS, J. (1976), 'Any Woman's blues: a critical overview of women, crime and the criminal justice system', *Crime and Social Justice,* 5: 34–49.

LACAN, J. (1996), 'A theoretical introduction to the functions of psychoanalysis in criminology', *Journal for the Psychoanalysis of Culture and Society,* 1/2: 13–25.

LACEY, N. (2001), 'Beset by Boundaries. The Home Office Review of Sex Offences', *Criminal Law Review* (January), 3–14.

LEES, S. (1997), *Ruling Passions,* London: Sage.

LEONARD, E. (1982), *Women, Crime and Society: a Critique of Criminology Theory,* New York: Longman.

LEVI, M. (1998), 'She's giving me no citations: the return of the Cambridge blues', British Society of Criminology Newsletter No. 30, April.

LONGINO, H. (1993), 'Feminist Standpoint Theory and the Problems of Knowledge', *Signs,* 19/1: 201–12.

LORDE, A. (1984), *Sister Outsider,* Trumansburg, NY: Crossing Press.

MAC AN GHAILL, M. (1994), *The Making of Men: Masculinities, Sexualities and Schooling,* Buckingham: Open University Press.

MACKINNON, C. (1987a), *Feminism unmodified: discourses on life and law,* Cambridge, Mass: Harvard University Press.

—— (1987b), 'Feminism, Marxism, Method and The State: Toward Feminist Jurisprudence', in S. Harding (ed.), *Feminism and Methodology,* Milton Keynes: Open University Press.

—— (1994), 'Rape, Genocide, and Women's Human Rights', in A. Stiglmayer (ed.), *Mass Rape, The War Against Women in Bosnia-Herzegovina,* Lincoln: University of Nebraska Press.

MACLEAN, B., and MILOVANOVIC, D. (eds) (1997), *Thinking Critically About Crime,* Vancouver: The Collective Press.

MAGUIRE, M., MORGAN, R., and REINER, R. (eds) (1994; 1997), *Oxford Handbook of Criminology,* Oxford: Oxford University Press.

MAJOR, L. (2001), 'Don't count on us', *Guardian,* 6 February.

MANGALISO, Z. (1997), 'Gender and nation-building in South Africa', in L. West (ed.), *Feminist Nationalism,* London: Routledge.

MATTHEWS, R., and YOUNG, J. (1992), 'Questioning left realism', in R. Matthews and J. Young (eds), *Issues in Realist Criminology,* London: Sage.

MAWBY, R., and WALKLATE, S. (1994), *Critical Victimology,* London: Sage.

MCMAHON, A. (1993), 'Male readings of feminist theory: the psychologisation of sexual politics in the masculinity literature', *Theory and Society,* 22/5: 675–96.

MCROBBIE, A. (1980), 'Settling accounts with subcultures', in S. Hall and T. Jefferson (eds), *Resistance Through Rituals,* London: Hutchinson.

MESSERSCHMIDT, J. (1993), *Masculinities and Crime: Critique and Reconceptualisation of Theory,* Lanham, MD: Rowman and Littlefield.

—— (1997), *Crime As Structured Action. Gender, Race, Class and Crime in the Making,* Thousand Oaks, Cal.: Sage.

MESTROVIC, S. (1993), *The Barbarian Temperament,* London: Routledge.

MILLMAN, M. (1975), 'She Did it All for Love: a feminist view of the sociology of deviance', in M. Millman and R.M. Kanter (eds), *Another Voice: Feminist Perspectives on Social Life and Social Science,* New York: Anchor Books.

MITCHELL, J. (1984), *Women: The Longest Revolution,* London: Virago.

—— and OAKLEY, A. (1986), *What is Feminism?,* Oxford: Blackwell.

MORGAN, D. (1992), *Discovering Men,* London: Routledge.

MORRIS, A. (1987), *Women, Crime and Criminal Justice,* Oxford: Blackwell.

—— (1993), 'Law Reform Initiatives on Violence Against Women: successes and pitfalls'. A Paper presented at the International Conference of Women Judges held to celebrate the centenary of women's suffrage in New Zealand. Wellington, NZ: Institute of Criminology, Victoria University of Wellington.

—— and GELSTHORPE, L. (1991), 'Feminist Perspectives in Criminology: Transforming and

Transgressing', *Women & Criminal Justice*, 2/2: 3–26.

MORRISON, W. (1994), *Theoretical Criminology*, London: Cavendish Publishing.

MUNCIE, J., McLAUGHLIN, E., and LANGAN, M. (eds) (1996), *Criminological Perspectives. A Reader*, London: Sage in association with the Open University.

NAFFINE, N. (ed.) (1995), *Gender, Crime and Feminism*, Dartmouth: Aldershot.

—— (1997), *Feminism and Criminology*, Cambridge: Polity.

NELKIN, D. (ed.) (1994), *The Futures of Criminology*, London: Sage.

NEWBURN, T., and STANKO, E. (eds) (1994), *Just Boys Doing Business? Men, Masculinities and Crime*, London: Routledge.

NICHOLSON, L. (ed.) (1990), *Feminism/Postmodernism*, New York: Routledge.

NIKOLIC-RISTANOVIC, V. (1996a), 'Domestic Violence Against Women in the Conditions of War', in C. Sumner, M. Israel, M. O'Connell, and R. Sarre (eds), *International Victimology*, Canberra: Australian Institute of Criminology.

—— (1996b), 'War and Violence Against Women', in J. Turpin and L. Lorsentzen (eds), *The Gendered New World Order: Militarism, Development and the Environment*, New York: Routledge.

—— (1998), 'War and crime in the former Yugoslavia', in V. Ruggiero, N. South, and I. Taylor (eds), *The New European Criminology*, London: Routledge.

OAKLEY, A. (1981), *Subject Women*, Oxford: Martin Robertson.

—— (1999), 'People's ways on knowing: gender and methodology', in S. Hood, B. Mayall, and S. Oliver (eds), *Critical Issues in Social Research. Power and Prejudice*, Buckingham: Open University Press.

—— (2000), *Experiments in Knowing. Gender and Method in the Social Sciences*, Cambridge: Polity.

OLSEN, F. (1995), *Feminist Legal Theory*, Aldershot: Dartmouth.

PICKERING, S. (2000), 'Women, the Home and Resistance in Northern Ireland', *Women & Criminal Justice*, 11/3: 49–82.

PLATEK, M. (1995), 'What it's like for women: criminology in Poland and Eastern Europe', in N.H. Rafter and F. Heidensohn (eds), *International Feminist Perspectives in Criminology*, Buckingham: Open University Press.

PLUMMER, K. (2001), *Documents of Life 2*, London: Sage.

PRISON REFORM TRUST (2000), *Justice for Women: The Need for Reform*, The Report of the Committee on Women's Imprisonment, chaired by Professor Dorothy Wedderburn, London: Prison Reform Trust.

RAFTER, N.H., and NATALIZIA, E. (1981), 'Marxist feminism: implications for criminal justice', *Crime and Delinquency*, 27: 81–98.

—— and HEIDENSOHN, F. (eds) (1995), *International Feminist Perspectives in Criminology*, Buckingham: Open University Press.

REDCAR, R. (ed.) (1990), *Dissenting Opinions*, Sydney: Allen & Unwin.

REDHEAD, S. (1995), *Unpopular Cultures: The Birth of Law and Popular Culture*, Manchester: Manchester University Press.

REINHARZ, S. (1979), *On Becoming a Social Scientist: From Survey Research and Participant Observation to Experimental Analysis*, San Francisco: Jossey-Bass.

RICE, M. (1990), 'Challenging orthodoxies in feminist theory: a black feminist critique', in L. Gelsthorpe and A. Morris (eds), *Feminist Perspectives in Criminology*, Buckingham: Open University Press.

ROBERTS, B. (2002), *Biographical Research*, Buckingham: Open University Press.

ROBERTS, H. (ed.) (1981), *Doing Feminist Research*, London: Routledge and Kegan Paul.

ROCK, P. (ed.) (1988), *A History of British Criminology*, Oxford: Oxford University Press.

—— (1994), 'The Social Organization of British Criminology', in M. Maguire, R. Morgan, and R. Reiner (eds), *Oxford Handbook of Criminology*, 1st edn, Oxford: Oxford University Press.

ROWBOTHAM, S. (1973), *Women's Consciousness, Man's World*, Harmondsworth: Penguin.

SCRATON, P. (1990), 'Scientific knowledge or masculine discourses? Challenging patriarchy in criminology', in L. Gelsthorpe and A. Morris (eds), *Feminist Perspectives in Criminology*, Buckingham: Open University Press.

SEGAL, L. (1990), *Slow Motion: Changing Masculinities, Changing Men*, London: Virago.

SHACKLADY SMITH, L. (1978), 'Sexist assumptions and female delinquency: an empirical investigation', in C. Smart and B. Smart (eds), *Women, Sexuality and Social Control*, London: Routledge and Kegan Paul.

SMART, C. (1976), *Women, Crime and Criminology*, London: Routledge and Kegan Paul.

—— (1989), *Feminism and the Power of Law*, London: Routledge.

—— (1990), 'Feminist approaches to criminology or postmodern woman meets atavistic man', in L. Gelsthorpe and A. Morris (eds), *Feminist Perspectives in Criminology*, Buckingham: Open University Press.

—— (1995), *Law, crime and sexuality: essays on feminism*, London: Sage.

—— and SMART, B. (eds) (1978), *Women, Sexuality and Social Control*, London: Routledge and Kegan Paul.

SMITH, B. (ed.) (2000), *Global Feminisms Since 1945*, London: Routledge.

SMITH, P. (ed.) (1993), *Feminist Jurisprudence*, New York: Oxford University Press.

SOPER, K. (1990), 'Feminism, humanism and postmodernism', *Radical Philosophy*, 55: 11–17.

STANKO, E. (1985), *Intimate Intrusions: Women's Experience of Male Violence*, London: Virago.

—— (1990), *Danger Signals*, London: Pandora.

—— (1993), 'Feminist Criminology: An Oxymoron?', paper presented to the British Criminology Conference, Cardiff, 1993.

STANLEY, C. (1996), *Urban Excess and the Law: capital, culture and desire*, London: Cavendish Publishing.

STANLEY, L., and WISE, S. (1983), *Breaking Out: Feminist Consciousness and Feminist Research*, London: Routledge and Kegan Paul.

STIGLMAYER, A. (ed.) (1994), *Mass Rape: The War Against Women in Bosnia-Herzegovina*, Lincoln: University of Nebraska Press.

STRACHEY, J. (ed.) (1953–74), *The Standard Edition of the Complete Psychological Works of Sigmund Freud*, 24 vols, London: Hogarth Press.

SUMNER, C. (1990), 'Foucault, gender and the censure of deviance', in L. Gelsthorpe and A. Morris (eds), *Feminist Perspectives in Criminology*, Buckingham: Open University Press.

—— (1994), *The Sociology of Deviance: An Obituary*, Buckingham: Open University Press.

TAYLOR, I., WALTON, P., and YOUNG, J. (1973), *The New Criminology*, London: Routledge and Kegan Paul.

THORNE, B. (1993), *Gender Play: Girls and Boys in School*, New Brunswick, NJ: Rutgers University Press.

TOLSON, A. (1977), *The Limits of Masculinity*, New York: Harper and Row.

TONG, R. (1989), *Feminist Thought*, London: Unwin Hyman.

TURPIN, J., and LORENTZEN, L. (eds) (1996), *The Gendered New World Order: Militarism, Development and Environment*, New York: Routledge.

TWINE, F.W., and BLEE, K. (eds) (2001), *Feminism and Antiracism. International Struggles for Justice*, New York: New York University Press.

VELIMESIS, M. (1975), 'The female offender', *Crime and Delinquency Literature*, 7/1: 94–112.

WALBY, S. (1990), *Theorizing Patriarchy*, Oxford: Blackwell.

WALKER, N. (1987), *Crime and Criminology. A Critical Introduction*, Oxford: Oxford University Press.

WALKLATE, S. (1989), *Victimology*, London: Unwin Hyman.

—— (1992), 'Appreciating the Victim: Conventional, Realist or Critical Victimology?', in R. Matthews and J. Young (eds), *Issues in Realist Criminology*, London: Sage.

—— (1995), *Gender & Crime. An Introduction*, Hemel Hempstead, Herts.: Prentice Hall/Harvester Wheatsheaf.

—— (2001), *Gender, Crime and Criminal Justice*, Cullompton, Devon: Willan Publishing.

WEEDON, C. (1987), *Feminist Practice and Poststructuralist Theory*, Oxford: Blackwell.

WEST, C., and ZIMMERMAN, D. (1987), 'Doing Gender', *Gender and Society*, 1/2: 125–51.

WORRALL, A. (1990), *Offending Women*, London: Routledge.

WRIGHT, R., and COHEN, E. (1996), 'The Most-Cited Scholars in Criminal Justice Textbooks, 1989–1993', *Journal of Criminal Justice*, 24: 459–67.

—— and SHERIDAN, C. (1997), 'The Most-Cited Scholars and Works in Women and Crime Publications', *Women & Criminal Justice*, 9/2: 41–60.

YOUNG, A. (1994), 'Feminism and the Body of Criminology', in D. Farrington and S. Walklate (eds), *Offenders and Victims: Theory and Policy*, London: British Society of Criminology and ISTD. (British Criminology Conference Selected Papers, vol. 1.)

YOUNG, J. (1994), 'Incessant Chatter: Recent Paradigms in Criminology', in M. Maguire, R. Morgan, and R. Reiner (eds), *Oxford Handbook of Criminology*, 1st edn, Oxford: Oxford University Press.

ZIMMER, L. (1986), *Women Guarding Men*, Chicago: University of Chicago Press.

5

CRIMINOLOGICAL PSYCHOLOGY

Clive R. Hollin

INTRODUCTION

The current vogue in psychology in Britain is to use the term 'forensic psychology' when referring to any topic even remotely connected with crime. Blackburn has commented on this etymological inaccuracy, noting of the word 'forensic' that 'Its established English meaning is hence "pertaining to or used in courts of law", and that is how it has been understood by the public in general and lawyers in particular' (1996: 4). Indeed, this sense of psychology applied to legal decision-making is the way in which forensic psychology is properly understood elsewhere (Hess 1999). It is difficult, however, to arrive at a straightforward term that accurately describes the application of psychological theory and research to antisocial conduct, criminal behaviour, and law. For many years The British Psychological Society (the professional body for psychologists in Britain) used the term 'Criminological and Legal Psychology' rather than 'Forensic Psychology' to describe this specialist area of psychological knowledge and practice. The British Psychological Society maintains this terminology in the title of its academic journal, *Legal and Criminological Psychology*.

The topic of legal psychology, the application of psychological knowledge and methods to the process of law, has become a speciality in its own right (e.g., Bartol and Bartol 1994; Bull and Carson 1995; Gudjonsson and Hayward 1998; Hess and Weiner 1999; Kagehiro and Laufer 1992; Kapardis 1997; Roesch, Corrado, and Dempster 2001). However, the focus of this chapter is on *criminological* psychology: that is, the application of psychological theory and investigation to understanding (and attempting to change) criminal behaviour. It is important at the onset to emphasize the point that criminological psychology is concerned with the use of psychology to help explain criminal behaviour. It follows, therefore, that criminological psychology represents a meeting of psychology and criminology. The juxtaposition of psychology and criminology has been a constant issue for both disciplines. One way to understand the interplay between the disciplines, and hence the aetiology and changing emphases of criminological psychology, is to consider the historical highs and lows of this cross-discipline relationship. Adopting an historical perspective allows a picture to emerge of the theoretical points of contact and departure of the two disciplines. As this chapter is concerned with psychology, the perspective here is from a psychological viewpoint; doubtless a similar exercise could be carried out from a criminological perspective.

THE GROWTH OF PSYCHOLOGY

Criminological psychology is a specialist branch of what might be called mainstream psychology, that is the assembly of knowledge and theory about human functioning. To understand the evolution of criminological psychology it is helpful to set this against the development of psychology as an academic discipline and a profession.

PSYCHOLOGY AS AN ACADEMIC DISCIPLINE

It is generally taken that the founding of the first psychological laboratory at Leipzig in 1879 by Wilhelm Wundt (1832–1920) signalled the beginning of psychology as a scientific, experimental discipline. (Although another school of thought gives that particular credit to William James (1842–1940) at Harvard.) After the 1870s, the spread of experimental psychology (with the attendant growth in sophisticated statistical techniques) to universities in Britain and the United States quickly followed. Thus, by the early 1900s, psychology had become an established academic discipline in its own right across the university system (Richards 1996). The empirical, scientific approach adopted by the early experimental psychologists was in marked contrast to the strong European style of psychology heavily influenced by philosophy and intellectual analysis, as seen for example in psychoanalysis and Gestalt Psychology.

The subject matter of these two approaches (Anglo-American versus European) to psychology also differed markedly. Early British psychology, heavily influenced by the theories of Charles Darwin (1809–82) and by intellectual figures of the time such as Sir Francis Galton (1822–1911), looked primarily to the study of individual differences. The empirical search by psychologists for individual differences in psychological constructs, such as intelligence, incorporated biological as well as psychological variables.

Early American psychology, as seen most clearly in the writings of John B. Watson (1878–1958), eschewed the inner world and focused on overt behaviour as the proper subject matter for psychological investigation. Indeed, Watson's 1913 paper, 'Psychology as the Behaviourist Views it', has been called a 'manifesto paper' (Richards 1996: 47) for the later development of behavioural psychology. Two trademarks of this emergent behavioural approach were an implicit assumption of the link between behaviour and biological structures; and a belief in the scientific legitimacy of the use of animals in experimental research. In both instances the influence of the major physiologists of the time, such as the Nobel Prizewinner Ivan Pavlov (1849–1936), is clearly discernible.

THE BEHAVIOURAL TRADITION

From the 1930s onwards, the growth of an empirical literature with a specific focus on behaviour saw a profusion of theoretical concepts and associated theoretical positions under the general theme of 'behavioural' (O'Donohue and Kitchener 1999). The work of B.F. Skinner (1904–90) is undoubtedly the most influential within the behavioural tradition (Skinner 1938, 1974). Briefly, Skinner was concerned to show empirically the nature of the relationship between behaviour and its environmental setting and consequences. Over time, a body of experimental evidence accrued to show that the environment provides settings for particular behaviours to occur that are likely to produce predictable environmental effects. Thus, the environment is said to *operate* on the individual to increase or decrease the frequency of a given behaviour. Thus, the concept of *operant* learning was developed, with a growing understanding of how behaviour is acquired and maintained through the force of the environment.

Simply, behaviour that produces consequences that the individual finds rewarding is likely to be repeated, a process termed *positive reinforcement*; behaviour that produces the consequence of avoiding an outcome that the individual finds aversive is, similarly, likely to be repeated, which is termed *negative reinforcement*. On the other hand, behaviour that produces directly aversive consequences is likely to decrease in frequency, termed *positive punishment*; while behaviour with the consequence of losing something of value is similarly likely to decrease in frequency, termed *negative punishment*. (In operant theory the term 'punishment' is used in a technical sense: behaviour that is decreasing in frequency is said to be punished. Punishment in this technical sense is not value-laden, nor specifically about physical chastisement; the term simply refers to the nature of the relationship between a behaviour and its consequences.) This deceptively straightforward theory is underpinned by complex and controversial philosophical arguments about the very substance of human nature (Nye 1992).

The behavioural approach, with its emphasis on the role of the environment, challenged the widespread orthodoxy that the origins of behaviour are to be found inside the person. There is a long history of theorizing, both within and outwith psychology, that sees inner forces as the causes of an individual's behaviour. Such inner forces have at various times been portrayed as spiritual, or biological, or, as most notably articulated by Sigmund Freud (1859–1939) in the European tradition, psychic in origin. In the history of psychology, Freud's work is of huge importance in its critical influence on generations of theorists (Brown 1961).

As psychological theories grew in sophistication so, inevitably, they were applied to offer explanations of a range of human conditions. One application of psychological theories was to attempt to provide an explanation for criminal behaviour.

PSYCHOLOGY AND CRIMINOLOGY: EARLY ACCORD

THEORY AND CRIME

With its concern focused on the individual, the first psychological theories of criminal behaviour variously applied what was known of genetics, intelligence, and psychic functioning. It is difficult, however, to distinguish the concerns of some of the early schools of psychology and those of the similarly emergent discipline of criminology. For example, the study of genetics and individual differences was of interest to psychologists, as seen in the first empirical studies of intelligence (e.g., Spearman 1927). In early criminology there are similar interests to be found. Famously, Cesare Lombroso (1835–1909) advanced theories of criminal behaviour based primarily on the hereditability of criminogenic traits (Lombroso 1876). Charles Goring (1870–1919) studied large numbers of prisoners, using anthropological methods and measures, and arrived at the view that criminals were characterized by defects in intelligence (Goring 1913). This concern with the interplay between genetic influences and physical and psychological conditions in explaining criminal behaviour occupied notable criminologists such as Raffaele Garofalo (1852–1934) and Enrico Ferri (1856–1929), as well as eminent psychologists such as Sir Cyril Burt (1883–1971). (For further discussion, see Garland, in Chapter 1 of this volume.)

In a parallel stream of theorizing, Freud's psychodynamic ideas were also being used to explain criminal behaviour. Freud himself had remarkably little to say about criminal behaviour, but the concepts drawn from his theory were steadily applied to criminal behaviour by several of the post-Freudians. For example, Aichhorn (1925/1955) developed a view of delinquency that saw juvenile crime as a consequence of a psychological disposition which was called 'latent delinquency'. Based on the Freudian notion of a 'pleasure principle'—the supposed hedonistic basis of behaviour—Aichhorn took the view that a failure of socialization and emotional development allowed the latent delinquency to become overt behaviour. There are other examples to be found, such as Healy and Bronner's (1936) application of the psychoanalytic concept of *sublimation* (the channelling of unsatisfied psychological impulses into action, typically linked with emotional ties with a parent) as an explanation for antisocial behaviour.

Within the study of delinquency, perhaps the most influential of the psychodynamic theories was developed by John Bowlby (1907–90). As explained in a string of texts (e.g., Bowlby 1944, 1951; Bowlby and Slater-Ainsworth 1965), the 'maternal deprivation' thesis was developed on the basis of clinical study. This influential theory holds that the emotional impact on the child of separation from and rejection by his or her mother can provide a means by which to explain problems during childhood, including persistent delinquency, and later development.

Applying theory

As theory develops, so its applications to real world issues will be explored. As practitioners, the early applied psychologists followed theory and so naturally gravitated towards arenas in which the focus was on the individual. Thus, the emerging areas of professional psychological practice became the selection of personnel, including military personnel during wartime (Capshew 1999), and an alignment with the psychiatric profession in the treatment of individual distress and dysfunction. Consequently, many of the early practitioners applying psychological theory approached the task of working with offenders with an implicit understanding of criminal behaviour as a result of an individual failing or dysfunction. As early psychological theories, perhaps particularly the psychodynamic theories, were concerned with abnormal development, so explanations for criminal behaviour were couched in terms of defect and disorder. Indeed, given the historical association between mental illness and crime (Long and Midgely 1992), it would have been in keeping with the times to account for criminal behaviour in terms of psychopathology.

The solution for criminal behaviour favoured by practitioners, naturally, was to 'put right' the dysfunction 'causing' the criminal behaviour by the application of psychological methods of bringing about change. The methods employed to bring about such change were steeped in a quasi-medical, clinical tradition as seen with psychotherapy, counselling, group therapy, and so on. The thesis underpinning this approach is straightforward: criminal behaviour is a consequence of individual dysfunction; correct the dysfunction and the individual will no longer be criminal. Thus the treatment ideal was born.

The notion of treating offenders found its place alongside the liberal reforms of the early twentieth century when the broader notion of rehabilitation of offenders had taken hold. The rehabilitative movement held that a range of measures, encompassing social welfare and educational improvements, was required in order to reduce crime.

Thus, in the beginning, the association between criminology and psychology was evident: as Tierney (1996: 55) notes: 'By the late 1930s, mainstream criminology was linking criminal behaviour to a range of psychological and social factors, against the backdrop of a continuing debate about the relative importance of genetic endowment'. Similarly, Tierney comments that 'by the time we reach World War Two psychology was clearly in pole position within criminological discourses' (ibid.). The focus of this discourse was the interplay between heredity and environment, in the sense of criminal behaviour as the product of a predisposition to crime interacting with inadequate social conditions.

These early attempts both to understand and treat criminal behaviour, as Jeffery (1960) notes, implicitly hold the three assumptions of *determinism, differentiation,* and *pathology.* Deterministic in holding that factors outside the individual's control— such factors might be biological, psychological, social, or some combination of these three—directly cause criminal behaviour. Following determinism is the assumption of differentiation: that criminals are in some way (biologically, psychologically, or socially) different to non-criminals. Lastly, the difference between criminals and non-criminals (whatever it may be) is manifest in a pathology evinced by criminal behaviour: this pathology, with clear medical overtones, necessitates treatment.

It is clear that these early assumptions form the basis of some contemporary criminological criticisms of psychological theory. For example, Siegal (1986: 175–6) comments: 'Psychological theories are useful as explanations of the behaviour of deeply disturbed, impulsive, or destructive people. However, they are limited as general explanations of criminality. For one thing, the phenomenon of crime and delinquency is so widespread that to claim that all criminals are psychologically disturbed is to make that claim against a vast majority of people'. Hopkins Burke (2001: 94–95) voices similar sentiments in commenting that the implication of psychological theories 'is that there is such a thing as the criminal mind or personality . . . the causes are dysfunctional, abnormal emotional adjustment or deviant personality traits formed in early socialisation and childhood development'.

The accuracy of these statements from a contemporary perspective will be discussed in due course; however, as we move through the 1930s and beyond so tensions begin to appear in the relationship between psychology and criminology.

PSYCHOLOGY AND CRIMINOLOGY: THE PARTING OF THE WAYS

THE CHICAGO SCHOOL

The beginnings of the split between criminology and psychology are often traced back to the influence of the Chicago School of Criminology, particularly reflected in the work of Ernest Burgess, Clifford Shaw, and Henry McKay (see Rock, in Chapter 2 of this volume). Briefly, the force of the Chicago School's research was to shift the focus of the study of crime away from the individual (i.e., psychology) and towards social structure (i.e., sociology). The theoretical impact of the Chicago School was to instigate a movement away from the notion that the study of criminal behaviour entailed the study of the individual. Rather, it was argued, a richer understanding of criminal behaviour could be found in the study of the social structures that shaped, influenced, and defined the social ecology. Lilly, Cullen, and Ball (1995: 39) capture the essence of the force of the Chicago School in saying, 'It was only a short leap for them to believe that growing up in the city, particularly the slums, made a difference in people's lives. In this context crime could not be seen simply as an individual pathology, but made more sense when viewed as a social problem.'

In a series of seminal studies, Shaw and McKay illustrated how the development and persistence of delinquent behaviour is associated with social deprivation, disorganization, and disadvantage (e.g., Shaw and McKay 1942). Further, Shaw and McKay ventured that the process by which delinquency was transmitted across generations was via the loosening of social controls. If the social and institutional forces that bind society—the church, the family, the educational system—are starved of resources then their influence weakens, leaving young people free to act in a delinquent way. Further, if weak social bonds create the conditions for delinquency, then ready association with delinquent peers provides the stimulus for persistent offending.

It follows that if social conditions create the setting for crime then environmental not individual change is required to reduce crime. Social policies to alleviate poverty and disadvantage were the way ahead, a message with a ready audience during the Progressive era of American political thought.

DIFFERENTIAL ASSOCIATION THEORY

The environmental focus evident in criminology (particularly in America) during the 1930s and 1940s is most clearly seen in the formulation of differential association theory by the American criminologist Edwin H. Sutherland (1853–1950). Influenced by the work of the Chicago group, of which he was briefly a member, Sutherland placed a sociological emphasis on the forces that define crime and the types of environment in which crime occurs most frequently. In formulating the principles of differential learning theory, Sutherland advanced nine propositions (Sutherland 1947). The key principles, in which Sutherland demonstrated a keen anticipation of contemporary behavioural research, were hinged around the proposition that against a social backdrop, criminal behaviour is a *learned* behaviour. This explanatory stance immediately raises a number of questions. First, how does learning occur: what are the processes by which behaviour is acquired? Secondly, what exactly is learned? Thirdly, what is the substance of learned behaviour? Sutherland's answers to these questions, bounded by the knowledge of his time, speculated that learning occurs in close social groups (not necessarily delinquent groups), and hence behaviour is acquired through such contacts. The product of learning is not only the skills needed to commit a crime, but also the attitudes that outweigh conformist attitudes and so are conducive to breaking the law. While not articulating the exact mechanisms by which behaviour is acquired, Sutherland made the critical statement that as a learned behaviour, criminal behaviour is no different in nature to any other learned behaviour.

From a psychological perspective there is nothing at all startling about the ideas expressed by the Chicago School. Indeed, as American psychology was setting itself for the paradigm shift of behaviourism, in which the clear focus would be the power of the environment in shaping behaviour, a parallel steam of theorizing in another discipline might well be seen as a stimulus for collaboration. Ironically, Sutherland's theory failed to attract any substantial attention from psychologists, particularly behavioural psychologists, interested in explanations of crime. Psychological research maintained a focus on the individual offender, with studies of the relationship between physical physique and crime becoming particularly popular (Sheldon, Hartl, and McDermott 1949). Thus, at a key point psychology failed to connect with criminology and the opportunity for a genuine academic alliance slipped away.

Criminology continued along the line of moving away from the study of the individual and increasingly focusing on the environment, particularly in terms of social process and social structure. Nonetheless, it is possible to see instances where there are obvious points of contact between the two disciplines and where fruitful connections could be made. For example, the concept of drift draws on cognitive processes ('techniques of neutralization' such as denial of harm or responsibility) and suggests that in daring to become delinquent the individual has *learned* to play a social role (Matza 1964, 1969).

DIFFERENTIAL REINFORCEMENT THEORY

The most overtly psychological theory of criminal behaviour of the period, again formulated by a criminologist, that clearly draws on the theoretical advances in behavioural psychology is to be found in differential reinforcement theory (Jeffery 1965). As with Sutherland's differential association theory, Jeffery also suggested that learning plays a fundamental part in understanding criminal behaviour. Thus, Jeffery (ibid.) refined the principles inherent in differential association theory by incorporating theoretical constructs from operant learning theory. Jeffery suggested, following Sutherland's criminological lead and Skinner's behavioural research, that criminal behaviour is operant behaviour: in other words, criminal behaviour is a function of the consequences it produces for the individual concerned. It follows, therefore, that an understanding of criminal behaviour relies on a comprehension of the consequences of the act for the individual concerned. For example, a substantial number of crimes produce material and financial gain; such gains are, in learning theory terms, positively reinforcing the offending. Alternatively, if the gains from theft help to avoid the effects of poverty then (again in learning theory terms) the criminal behaviour would be negatively reinforced. Of course, the rewards from crime can be social as well as material, as with gains in social approval and status following offending. The aversive consequences of criminal behaviour—including prison, a probation order, family problems—can have a punishing effect (in the sense of decreasing the frequency of the behaviour).

As Jeffery (ibid.: 295) notes:

The theory of differential reinforcement states that a criminal act occurs in an environment in which in the past the actor has been reinforced for behaving in this manner, and the aversive consequences attached to the behaviour have been of such a nature that they do not control or prevent the response.

Thus, from this theoretical perspective, the individual's history of reinforcement and punishment can be used to explain his or her criminal behaviour. The defining characteristic of this approach, as with behavioural theory in general, is that each person *must* be considered as an individual: depending on their social environment, some individuals will have gained rewards for criminal behaviour, others will have suffered aversive consequences. Thus, patterns of reinforcement and punishment are unlikely to be constant either between individuals, or for the same person over time. Within even similar social and cultural groups, differences in experience across individuals will exist in terms of peer group interactions, family functioning, education, and so on. It is axiomatic to this approach that for individuals living within comparable environments there will be some people who become criminal while others do not. Individuals will have complex learning histories, leading to intricate theoretical accounts of the development and maintenance of criminal behaviour (Gresswell and Hollin 1992).

Thus, as we move through the 1950s and into the 1960s, behaviourism continued to be the main paradigm influencing mainstream psychological research. The advances in learning theory were utilized by criminologists, but criminological psychology failed to make the connection. Nonetheless, there was potential for a fruitful association between criminology and psychology; but any common ground slipped away as the next phase of development unfolded in the aetiology of the two disciplines.

PSYCHOLOGY AND CRIMINOLOGY: LITTLE COMMON GROUND

PERSONALITY AND CRIME

The study of personality has a long tradition in psychology, but the use of increasingly sophisticated methodological and statistical techniques gave a new impetus to its scientific study (Cattell 1965). Drawing on his own theory of personality, Hans Eysenck (1916–90) began to develop during the 1960s what is perhaps to date the most complete *psychological* theory of crime (Eysenck 1964). Drawing on theoretical developments and empirical research, Eysenck continued to refine his theory of crime over the next decade (Eysenck 1970, 1977, 1984, 1987, 1996; Eysenck and Gudjonsson 1989). As Eysenck's theory is a widely cited example of what psychological theory has to offer in explaining crime, with a substantial associated research literature, it is worth considering in some detail. However, its reception by the most influential criminology text of the time provides a perfect example of disciplines that have moved so far apart as to have little to say to each other.

Eysenck's theory is expansive in that it seeks to offer an explanation of crime based on an interaction of biological, social, and individual factors. The foundation of the theory lies in the proposition that through genetic inheritance there are individual differences in the functioning of the cortical and autonomic nervous systems. These physiological differences are associated with individual differences in the ability to learn from, or more properly to *condition* to, environmental stimuli.

In his early research, Eysenck (1959) defined two dimensions of personality, *extraversion* (E) and *neuroticism* (N). In later research (Eysenck and Eysenck 1968) a third personality dimension, *psychoticism* (P), was described. Eysenck conceives these three personality dimensions (E, N, and P) in terms of a continuum: most people fall at the centre of the continuum with, it follows, fewer individuals at the extremes. Extraversion runs from high (extravert) to low (introvert); similarly, neuroticism runs from high (neurotic) to low (stable); as also does psychoticism.

The interrelationship between extraversion and neuroticism is shown in Figure 5.1. It can be seen that there are four combinations of the two personality dimensions (it can be understood that P adds another dimension across all the quadrants), and the physiological differences between those at the extreme corners of quadrants begins to form the basis of Eysenck's theory.

In terms of physiological functioning, Eysenck describes the extravert as cortically *under*-aroused, therefore seeking stimulation to increase cortical arousal to an optimal level. Thus, the extravert personality is characterized by impulsivity, risk-taking, and thrill-seeking. On the other hand, the introvert is cortically *over*-aroused and so

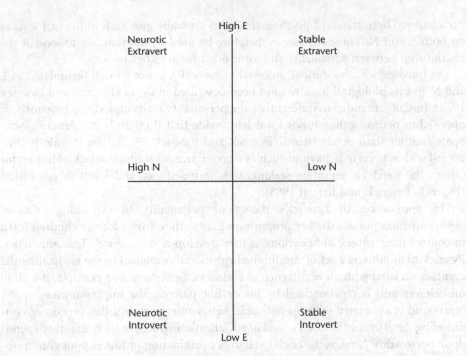

Fig. 5.1 Representation of the relationship between E and N

avoids stimulation to hold arousal at a comfortable, optimal level. The introvert personality is characterized by a quiet, reserved demeanour, avoiding excitement and high levels of stimulation. In terms of conditioning, that is learning by Pavlovian conditioning or association (i.e., classical conditioning rather than operant learning), Eysenck's theory maintains that extraverts condition less efficiently than introverts.

Neuroticism, or emotionality, is held to be related to the functioning of the autonomic nervous system (ANS). Individuals at the high end of the N continuum are characterized by a highly labile ANS, giving strong reactions to any unpleasant or painful stimuli: High N individuals are characterized by irritable, anxious behaviour. Conversely, those at the lower end of the neuroticism continuum have a highly stable ANS, showing calm, even-tempered behaviour even when under stress. As with E, N is also related to conditionability: High N is associated with poor conditioning because of the disruptive effects of anxiety; Low N leads to efficient conditioning. As conditionability is related to levels of *both* E and N (see Figure 5.1 for the four combinations), it is further suggested that stable introverts (Low N–Low E) will condition best; stable extraverts (Low N–High E) and neurotic introverts (High N–Low E) will be at some mid-level; while neurotic extraverts (High N–High E) will condition least well.

These individual differences in conditionability lead to varying levels of socialization. An individual's stable pattern of behaviour, influenced by both biological and social factors, thus flows from that person's *personality*. Through the development of psychometric tests such as the Eysenck Personality Inventory, Eysenck was able to provide a simple and straightforward means by which to assess and measure personality. These standard psychometric tests typically give each individual a score on both E and N. These scores can therefore be used in research, say to look at the relationship between personality and some other form of behaviour.

The third personality dimension, psychoticism (P), is not so well formulated as E and N and its biological basis has not been described in detail (Eysenck and Eysenck 1976). Initially intended to differentiate the personality traits underlying psychosis, as opposed to neurosis, the proposal was later made that P might better denote psychopathy rather than psychoticism (Eysenck and Eysenck 1972). The P scale is concerned with aspects of behaviour such as a preference for solitude, a lack of feeling for others, the need for sensation-seeking, toughmindedness, and levels of aggression (Eysenck, Eysenck, and Barrett 1985).

The application of Eysenck's theory of personality to explaining criminal behaviour incorporates the key proposition that as they grow older so children learn to control their antisocial behaviour as they develop a 'conscience'. The conscience, Eysenck maintains, is a set of conditioned emotional responses to the environmental events associated with an occurrence of antisocial behaviour. For example, if a child misbehaves and is reprimanded by his or her parents, the unpleasantness of the reprimand is associated with the antisocial behaviour: over time this process of conditioning determines the child's level of socialization which, in turn, mainly depends upon personality. Now, as the High E–High N combination produces poor conditionability, so individuals with this particular combination of personality traits will have weak control over their behaviour and therefore, the theory predicts, will be over-represented in offender populations. Conversely, the Low E–Low N personality configuration leads to effective socialization, so that this type of individual would be predicted to be under-represented among offender groups. The remaining two combinations, High E–Low N and Low E–High N, would be at a mid-level and would be found in both offender and non-offender groups. Psychoticism (P) is also seen to be related to criminal behaviour, particularly with regard to offences that involve aggression.

In summary, Eysenck (1977: 58) suggests that 'in general terms, we would expect persons with strong antisocial inclinations to have high P, high E, and high N scores'.

Testing Eysenck's theory

Given the possibility of measurement of personality and the testability of the predictions, Eysenck's theory of crime has generated a substantial body of empirical research. The reviews of the literature up to 1980 (e.g., Bartol 1980; Feldman 1977) suggest that there is strong support for the prediction that offenders will score highly on P and on N. However, the findings are varied for E: some studies support the theory (i.e., high E scores in offenders); other studies report no difference in the E scores of offender and non-offender samples; while a small number of studies report *lower* E scores in offender groups. The general pattern for P, E, and N is similar with both young and adult offender groups.

To explain the variation in findings for E, Eysenck and Eysenck (1971) suggested that E might be divided into two components, sociability and impulsiveness, with only the latter related to criminal behaviour. A study by Eysenck and McGurk (1980) provided evidence in support of this hypothesis, showing that an offender sample scored higher than a non-offender sample only on impulsiveness but not sociability.

One of the criticisms of the pre-1980 studies is that they looked at the personality traits singly, rather than in combination as originally suggested by the theory. A study by McGurk and McDougall (1981) used cluster analysis to look at the patterns of P, E, and N scores in delinquent and non-delinquent samples. McGurk and McDougall reported that there were four personality clusters in each sample: both samples contained the Low E–High N and High E–Low N combinations, but the combinations predicted to be related to criminal behaviour—High E–High N and High P–High E–High N—were found only in the delinquent sample. The highly socialized Low E–Low N combination was, as predicted, found only in the non-delinquent group. Several subsequent studies attempted to replicate the McGurk and McDougall study, with varying degrees of exactness of match with the original theory (McEwan 1983; McEwan and Knowles 1984). It is the case that contemporary research still produces findings testing Eysenck's theory (e.g., Kirkcaldy and Brown 2000); however, it is also true to say that as personality theory has waned generally in mainstream psychology, so has research testing Eysenck's theory.

Overall, there is empirical evidence in favour of Eysenck's theory, leading one influential criminological psychologist to state that the 'Eysenckian personality dimensions are likely to make a useful contribution to the explanation of criminal behaviour' (Feldman 1977: 161). Nonetheless, there are reservations, as Eysenck acknowledges, such as the need firmly to establish the relationship between classical conditioning and socialization. Further, Eysenck's theory is specifically a trait theory of personality, an approach that is not without its critics in mainstream psychology (Mischel 1968). However, these points are mere quibbles when set against the criticism delivered by the new criminologists.

NEW CRIMINOLOGY AND PERSONALITY

The key text that heralded a sea change in thought in criminology, certainly in Britain, was *The New Criminology* by Taylor, Walton, and Young (1973). Tierney (1986: 157) suggests that this text represented 'an ambitious attempt to develop a Marxist theory of deviance ... Whatever the merits of *The New Criminology*, it stands as a supreme example of criminological work nurtured by the twin influences of the New Left and the counter culture'.

Eysenck is heavily cited in the first part of the text and there is a concerted criticism of his theory. The criticisms delivered by Taylor *et al.* clearly reject Eysenck's approach to understanding criminal behaviour. To appreciate the differences between Taylor *et al.* and Eysenck, is to see how that at that time there could be no point of contact between the new criminology and mainstream psychology (of which Eysenck was a leading figure).

The first point of departure is to be seen in Taylor *et al.*'s analysis of positivism which, they suggest, characterizes Eysenck's work (as well as other researchers, including some criminologists). The key attribute of positivism 'is its insistence on the unity of scientific method' (Taylor *et al.* 1973: 11). (Certainly this is one characterization of

positivism, although Halfpenny (1982/1992) identified no fewer than twelve positiv-
isms, not all of which would concord with the centrality of the scientific method.)
Thus, Taylor *et al.* continue, to promote a positivistic approach is implicitly to seek to
measure and quantify behaviour, to proclaim the objectivity of the scientist, and to see
human action as determinate and law-governed. A positivistic approach is to be
found in the work of the early criminologists, but it is Eysenck as a *biological* positivist
who is placed in the critical spotlight.

Eysenck is clear in his understanding of human nature: through conditioning,
influenced by biological factors (and hence personality), we become socialized in the
sense that we learn to control our impulses and actions. Taylor *et al.* are forthright in
their views on Eysenck's model of human functioning:

Therefore man's voluntary, rational activity comes to be seen as being solely concerned with
the satisfaction of his individual and pre-social ideas . . . The model of learning is Darwinian
in its mindlessness . . . The conscience is a passive reflex which unthinkingly checks those
hedonistic impulses by virtue of autonomic distress [1973: 49].

Thus, on the one hand there is the basic philosophical stance, exemplified by
Eysenck, of a world in which behaviour is rule-governed and determinate. It follows
that once the basic science has been completed and the rules properly understood, the
intellectual problem will be solved (and practical solutions might well follow). On the
other hand, Taylor *et al.* express an altogether different perspective. They do not seek
to deny the role of biological factors in understanding human behaviour: 'The central
and autonomic nervous systems are undoubtedly involved in the learning process—to
deny this would be to deny that man has a body' (ibid.: 51). However, Taylor *et al.*
view the interaction between the biological individual and society not as something
which is fixed and measurable, but as a dynamic, shifting process: 'His definitions of
himself evolve not as a determinate result of the addition of social factors on to a
biological substratum but rather as a *praxis*, as the meaningful attempt by the actor to
construct and develop his own self-conception' (ibid.: 56).

Taylor *et al.* repeatedly make a point regarding the centrality of meaning in their
understanding of human nature. Thus, the reactions of society to criminal behaviour
are not an automatic delivery of positive or negative consequences, but 'are meaningful attempts of the powerful to maintain and justify the status quo' (ibid.: 52). Again,
the different behaviour of extraverts and introverts is not a product of poor conditionability and socialization, but represents 'meaningful behaviour by individuals
which is judged by others, in this case the psychological testers, to be undesirable'
(ibid.: 56). Yet further, Taylor *et al.* note that even if it were true that behaviour was
biologically driven, this would not explain deviant behaviour: 'To explain social phenomena demands social analysis involving the meaning that behaviour has to the
actor' (ibid.: 60).

The point being made by Taylor *et al.* with regard to meaning is fundamental and,
in truth, is a basic philosophical issue: is human behaviour determined (by whatever
means), or are we active, rational agents shaping and interpreting our own destiny?
This is an issue that has been played out in debate within the recent history of
criminology, as seen in the discussion generated by classical criminology (Roshier

1989), and in psychology around the notion of consciousness (Dennett 1991). On an altogether grander historical stage, the issue of free will versus determinism has been pondered by philosophers through the ages (Honderich 1993; Russell 1961). Despite attempts to square the circle (e.g., Alper 1998), it is a solid academic wager that the issue is not about to be resolved.

Taylor *et al.* turn next to the matter of the scientist as the objective recorder of human behaviour. The matter they raise is not one of technicalities, of the finer points of Eysenck's use of psychometrics and statistics (although others have criticized Eysenck in this regard). Rather they ask a bigger question: if Eysenck sees all behaviour as the product of mindless learning, how can understanding of the process of learning be put to work for the common good?

But who, then, are to be the far-seeing, 'unnatural' men who are able to transcend utilitarian natures and act rationally for society in general? Presumably the psychologists—but, if this is true, it would demand that Eysenck's paradigm of behaviour does not apply to all men [Taylor *et al.* 1973: 54].

The point is well made by Taylor *et al.*: in the human sciences, can the scientist ever be objective and detached? The issue being raised here hinges around ideas of measurement, another of the basic issues Taylor *et al.* raised regarding this style of psychological research and theory. Is it possible to measure intangible constructs such as personality in a way that is value free and valid? As Richards (1996: 110) notes: 'For Psychology, quantifying the phenomena that it studies has been a perennial problem. For many thinkers, like Kant, it was the apparent impossibility of doing so that excluded Psychology from natural science'. It is probably true to say that many contemporary psychologists would have sympathy with the view that it is difficult to separate the research from the researcher (or vice versa).

Taylor *et al.* move on to perform a similar critical analysis of the work of Gordon Trasler, whose theories are perhaps more all-encompassing than Eysenck's in terms of an inclusion of a wide range of psychological and social factors (e.g., Trasler 1962). However, the line was drawn and there could be no point of contact between the criminologist and the psychologist because 'the positivist conception of science as exemplified in the work of Eysenck, is a conception of science which denies any meaning to the action taken outside the consensus and thereby the established social order itself' (Taylor *et al.* 1973: 61).

PSYCHOLOGY AND CRIMINOLOGY: NOT ON SPEAKING TERMS

It is fair comment to suggest that Eysenck's research is a reasonably representative example of mainstream academic psychology during the 1960s, 1970s, and into the 1980s. This is not to say that all psychological research was of this nature, but the predominant approach was empirical and experimental. There were a minority of psychologists engaged in research on criminal behaviour who were working in a style which would have meshed with Taylor *et al.*, but this work was the exception rather than the norm. In particular, the early work of Kevin Howells, influenced by Kelly's (1955) personal construct theory, sought to understand criminal acts in terms of the meaning they held for the individual (Howells 1978, 1979). Within the field of psychology and crime there are examples to be found of work that directly continues in this tradition (e.g., Houston 1998), and those which seek to ask similar questions (e.g., Elmer and Reicher 1995); although it is also the case that biological research continues apace (Ciba Foundation 1996).

As we move out of the 1970s and into the 1980s, mainstream criminology developed further its political ideas with the advent of Left Realist Criminology (Young 1997) and became increasingly occupied with a feminist critique of criminology (Gelsthorpe, in Chapter 4 of this volume). Critical criminology offered an alternative political stance, while postmodernism made an impact (Hopkins Burke 2001). However, as mainstream psychology began to enter its next theoretical phase, the focus did not follow criminology in moving outwards to look for social accounts for behaviour, but rather turned inwards to search for cognitive explanations for human action. It becomes increasingly difficult to find any point of contact between psychology and criminology.

COGNITION AND CRIME

As reflected in the title of Baars's (1986) text, *The Cognitive Revolution in Psychology*, the shift from a behavioural to a cognitive perspective in mainstream psychology seemed to happen almost overnight. It is true, of course, that psychologists had always been interested in cognition: for example, there is a long history of psychological research into aspects of cognition such as intelligence, mathematical problem-solving, and the strategies used by high-level chess players. The cognitive revolution saw a resurgence of interest not only in these traditional topics, but also in what came to be called social cognition. Ross and Fabiano (1985) have helpfully drawn the distinction between *im*personal cognition, such as solving mathematical puzzles, and *inter*personal cognition that is concerned with the style and content of our thinking about ourselves and our relationships with other people. During the 1980s and into the 1990s, a clutch of studies appeared which were concerned with various aspects of cognition, but primarily interpersonal cognition, in offender groups. The contribution that came to be made by this cognitive slant was to reframe some existing theoretical concepts in cognitive terms and to introduce some fresh ideas. Some examples drawn from the cognitive literature are given below.

A lack of *self-control*, at times leading to impulsive behaviour, has a long history in explanations of crime (Wilson and Hernstein 1985), and figures in at least one major theory of crime (Gottfredson and Hirschi 1990). Brownfield and Sorenson (1993) have suggested several different ways by which low levels of self-control may be related to criminal behaviour, including inability to defer gratification, a lack of concern about other people, and impulsivity. In keeping with the mood of the times, Ross and Fabiano (1985: 37) have offered a cognitive perspective on impulsivity, which they view 'as a failure to insert between impulse and action a stage of reflection, a cognitive analysis of the situation'.

The notion of *locus of control* refers to the degree to which an individual believes that his or her behaviour is under his or her personal control. Individuals high on *internal* control believe that what happens to them is under their own control; while individuals high on *external* control believe that forces such as luck or authority figures influence their behaviour (Rotter 1966). A number of studies have found that offenders tend to external control: that is, they explain their behaviour as controlled by outside influences beyond their personal control (e.g., Hollin and Wheeler 1981; Kumchy and Sayer 1980).

As we mature as individuals we develop the ability, variously termed *empathy*, or *perspective-taking*, or *role-taking*, to 'see things from the other person's point of view'. The cognitive processes underpinning empathy probably have two related components: first, the thinking skills that allow comprehension of the other person's situation; secondly, an emotional capacity to 'feel for' the other person. As empathy develops across the life-span, so we learn to adjust our own behaviour to account for how we judge our actions will affect others. Several studies have suggested that some offenders tend to view life principally from their own perspective, not taking the other person into account, as seen in low scores by offenders as compared to non-offenders on measures of empathy and perspective-taking ability (e.g., Ellis 1982; Feshbach 1989; Kaplan and Arbuthnot 1985).

Moral reasoning is another aspect of social cognition associated with criminal behaviour. The process of socialization is related to moral development in the theories of both Piaget (1932) and Kohlberg (1964, 1978). Kohlberg, like Piaget, takes the view that as the individual attains maturity so moral reasoning develops in a sequential manner. Kohlberg describes three levels of moral development, with two stages at each level. As shown in Box 5.1, at the lower stages moral reasoning is concrete in orientation, becoming more abstract as the stages progress to involve abstract ideas such as 'justice', 'rights', and 'principles'.

Offending, Kohlberg argues, is associated with a delay in the development of moral reasoning: when the opportunity for offending presents itself, the individual does not have the reasoning that would allow him or her to control and resist temptation. A number of reviews have examined this basic premise with respect to the empirical evidence, and the generally accepted position is that offenders do typically show lower levels of reasoning, i.e., Kohlberg's immature stages (1 and 2), than non-offenders (e.g., Blasi 1980; Nelson, Smith, and Dodd 1990).

Social problem-solving skills are the complex cognitions we all use to deal effectively with the interpersonal struggles that are part of life. Specifically, social problem-solving skills necessitate the ability first to understand the situation, then to envisage potential courses of action, then to consider and evaluate the outcomes that might follow the various actions, and finally to decide on a course of action and plan its execution to achieve a desired outcome.

A number of studies have shown that compared to non-delinquents, offenders, both male and female, give less socially competent responses to social problems than

> ### Box 5.1 LEVELS AND STAGES OF MORAL JUDGEMENT IN KOHLBERG'S THEORY
>
> LEVEL 1: PRE-MORALITY
>
> *Stage 1.* Punishment and obedience: moral behaviour is concerned with deferring to authority and avoiding punishment.
>
> *Stage 2.* Hedonism: the concern is with one's own needs irrespective of others' concerns.
>
> LEVEL 2: CONVENTIONAL CONFORMITY
>
> *Stage 3.* Interpersonal concordance: moral reasoning concerned with general conformity and gaining social approval.
>
> *Stage 4.* Law and order: commitment to social order for its own sake, and hence deference to social and religious authorities.
>
> LEVEL 3: AUTONOMOUS PRINCIPLES
>
> *Stage 5.* Social contract: acknowledgement of individual rights and the role of the democratic process in deriving laws.
>
> *Stage 6.* Universal ethical principles: moral judgement determined by justice, respect, and trust, and may transcend legal dictates.

non-offenders (e.g., Freedman *et al.* 1978; Higgins and Thies 1981; Palmer and Hollin 1996).

Cognitive connections?

There are two points that arise from this body of research: first, how, if at all, do the various aspects of cognition connect to each other?; secondly, what is the overall model that explains the dynamics of cognition?

The search for an answer to the first point brings us to the forefront of current research. For example, the evidence suggests an association between antisocial behaviour and moral development as seen in immature, hedonistic, self-centred, moral judgements. However, as Gibbs (1993) notes, moral reasoning does not function in a vacuum: Gibbs argues that the relationship between moral development and cognitive distortions provides a more complete theoretical picture (ibid.; Goldstein, Glick, and Gibbs 1998). In this context, the term 'cognitive distortions' is used to mean 'nonveridical attitudes or beliefs pertaining to the self or one's social behaviour' (Gibbs 1993: 165).

Gibbs suggests that cognitive distortions can function directly to support the attitudes consistent with sociomoral developmental delay, and can also act to reduce any dissonance. An example of self-centred moral reasoning is seen in the view that 'if I want it, I take it': Gibbs terms this type of reasoning a *primary distortion*. The distorted secondary cognitions associated with such a primary distortion will serve to rationalize or mislabel the behaviour. To follow the example, the primary cognitive distortion evident in the reasoning 'I want it, I take it', might be rationalized (secondary cognitive distortion) by blaming other people: thus, if car owners leave their cars unlocked then they 'deserve to have them stolen'; or victims of physical assault got what they deserved because 'they were asking for it'. Similarly, the secondary cognitive distortion seen in mislabelling is evident in a biased view of one's behaviour: for example, car theft is 'just a laugh', or 'nothing serious'; victims of assault 'could have had it worse' and 'no real damage was done' (Gibbs 1996). This style of distorted thinking is seen as both socially supported and reinforced by the offender's peer group. Some of the most recent work in this area attempts to look for complex relationships between aspects of cognition such as sociomoral reasoning, perception of own parenting, and attribution of intent (Palmer and Hollin 2000, 2001).

Social information processing

While appreciation of the content of some aspects of cognition may provide some understanding of offending, an overall model of cognitive functioning is clearly required. In this regard, criminological psychologists have borrowed the notion of *social information processing* from mainstream cognitive psychology. There are several models of social information processing, but one of the most influential in criminological psychology has been developed by Nicki Crick and Kenneth Dodge (e.g., Crick and Dodge 1994, 1996). As shown in Box 5.2, the model of social information processing proposed by Crick and Dodge has six related stages. It should be noted that this is not a model of abnormal or deviant behaviour, but a general model of human functioning.

The first two stages are concerned with the encoding and interpretation of social cues: the focus here lies in the way the individual is actively perceiving and attending to the words and actions of other people, and seeking to make sense of a given social interaction within a given situational context. At the third stage the person attempts to set or select a goal or some desired endpoint for the situation. At the fourth stage the individual judges how best to respond to the situation, in the main by relying on previous experience, although novel situations may necessitate a new way of acting. The fifth stage, response decision, requires a range of cognitive skills and abilities, including generating a range of alternative responses, considering the consequences of different courses of action, and planning what needs to be done to achieve the differ-

---

BOX 5.2 SIX STAGES OF SOCIAL INFORMATION PROCESSING

1. Encoding of Social Cues.
2. Interpretation of Social Cues.
3. Clarification of Goals.
4. Response Access or Construction.
5. Response Decision.
6. Behavioural Enactment.

ent outcomes. This type of cognitive activity obviously overlaps most closely with social problem-solving. Lastly, the individual needs the physical social skills, both verbal and non-verbal, to perform the actions he or she has decided are best suited to gaining the outcome he or she wants in that social situation.

In summary, the model proposed by Crick and Dodge encompasses three fundamental questions central to human psychology: (1) How do we perceive and make sense of our social world?; (2) How do we effectively solve the problems our social world sets for us?; (3) What social skills do we need to respond to social situations and achieve the goals we value? These are basic psychological questions, but the specific query within criminological psychology is whether there is anything characteristic about the social information-processing of offenders. The main weight of research in this respect has been devoted to aggressive and violent offenders, particularly young offenders. A brief overview of this research shows how the model can be applied to generate more comprehensive models of offending.

Applying the model

The first part of the cognitive sequence involves the individual in perceiving and interpreting situational cues. There is some research evidence to suggest that aggressive individuals search for and perceive fewer social cues than non-violent people (e.g., Dodge and Newman 1981). It also appears to be the case that violent people are more likely to interpret cues in a hostile fashion (Slaby and Guerra 1988). This hostile interpretation of social cues may be a fundamental component in a general understanding of some forms of violent behaviour.

In the next part of the model, social problem-solving, the aggressive person will make decisions on how best to respond to the situation as he or she sees matters. Thus, given a restricted perception of the situation and a hostile interpretation of events, the individual must judge what outcome he or she wants and what action he or she needs to take to gain this outcome. There is some evidence to suggest that violent people generate fewer solutions to interpersonal conflicts—remembering that the violent person may be perceiving hostility when others may not—and hence consider fewer consequences of their actions (Slaby and Guerra 1988).

Finally, the individual must act to respond to the situation. There are two issues to consider with regard to violent acts. The first point is that the violent individual may see his or her violent behaviour as an acceptable form of conduct, a legitimate response in a hostile world (Slaby and Guerra 1988). The second point is that the violent person may lack the social, interpersonal skills to behave in a less aggressive manner. There is research evidence to suggest that some violent people may be characterized by inappropriate assertive skills, so that they resort to violence to solve interpersonal problems (Howells 1986).

As mainstream psychology concentrated its efforts on events inside the skin, so to speak, so the topic of emotion once more returned to the attention of researchers and theorists. For example, in understanding violence, the relationship between emotional arousal and cognitions such as perception, attribution, and problem-solving may be important.

The role of emotion

The work of the social psychologist Raymond Novaco has shown that there can be reciprocal relationships between environmental events, both physical and social, cognitive processes, and the emotion of anger (e.g., Novaco 1975, 1994; Novaco and Welsh 1989). In his model of violence, Novaco suggests that situational events can trigger angry thoughts; these angry thoughts heighten emotional (including physiological) arousal, in turn intensifying the hostile, angry thoughts. This reciprocity between cognition and emotional arousal may then increase the likelihood of the individual acting in a violent manner. This model has much in common with Crick and Dodge in that, for example, Novaco and Welsh (1989) identified several information-processing biases in individuals prone to anger: these biases are all concerned with the cognitive encoding of external and internal cues, and the interpretation and cognitive representation of those cues. For example, Novaco and Welsh (ibid.) explain that the process of *attentional cueing* refers to the tendency of individuals who are prone to anger to see hostility and provocation in the words and actions of other people (cf. Dodge *et al.* 1990).

As the cognitive revolution gathered momentum, so the associated research base grew and the theoretical models became increasingly complex. Could there ultimately be a cognitive model of criminal behaviour? With regard to this question, Andrews and Bonta (1998: 190) are clear where they stand:

Moral reasoning, egocentrism and empathy are just some of the cognitive factors that play a role in the development of delinquency. They are, however, not *necessary* factors: simply being unempathic, self-centered and functioning at Stage 2 of moral reasoning does not automatically result in antisocial behaviour. Sometimes other personal characteristics such as sensation-seeking ... and negative family socialization experiences are needed. Nevertheless, these cognitive abilities appear to be mild risk factors for delinquency.

The important point here is that psychologists are beginning to move to complex models which, while seeing a role for psychological variables, seek to locate these in a broader social context. For example, Nietzel, Hasemann, and Lynam (1999) have provided a model of violence based on four sequential stages across the life span. First, there are distal antecedents to violence: Nietzel *et al.* suggest that these are *biological precursors*, including genetic transmission and ANS lability; psychological predispositions, including impulsivity and deficient problem-solving; and environmental factors, such as family functioning and the social fabric of the neighbourhood. Secondly, there are early indicators of violence in childhood, including features of childhood such as conduct disorder and poor emotional regulation. Thirdly, as the child matures through adolescence so developmental processes associated with the escalation of violent behaviour are evident: these processes include school failure, association with delinquent peers, and substance abuse. Finally, as the adolescent moves into adulthood, there is a stage at which maintenance variables come into force. These maintaining variables include continued reinforcement for violent conduct, association with criminal peers, and social conditions.

In summary, the cognitive revolution that swept through mainstream psychology also shifted the focus of psychological research into criminal behaviour. Nonetheless, there was always an awareness that cognitive factors were not in and of themselves, going to offer a full explanation for offending (cf. Andrews and Bonta 1998). However, before moving to the current concerns in criminological psychology, it is worth taking a detour to another development in the cognition and crime literature.

THE REASONING CRIMINAL

In terms of style of explanation, it is evident that most psychological (and some criminological) research takes a 'dispositional' approach to criminal behaviour. Thus, with varying degrees of emphasis, criminal behaviour is seen as the consequence of an interaction between individual, social, cultural, and legal variables which act to dispose the person towards an offence. A contrary approach, with overtones of classical theory (Roshier 1989), took shape during the 1970s and 1980s.

The beginnings of this new approach are seen in research concerned with the environmental conditions in those parts of cities that seem to attract crime. The link between specific environmental conditions and patterns of crime was seen, for example, in the rise in frequency of burglary and more empty houses as increasing numbers of family members leave to go to work, or a greater incidence of street violence in poorly-lit areas of towns and cities. Cohen and Felson's (1979) routine activities theory drew this research together, suggesting that a crime will occur when three elements combine: these three elements are a specific situation (i.e., a time and a place), a target, and the absence of effective guardians. The combination of these elements gives the *opportunity* for successful offending, and the idea of 'crime as opportunity' took hold. Thus, a crime occurs when the environmental circumstances present the opportunity; the criminal is the individual who seizes the chance. While one line of work looked more closely at aspects of this approach such as the distinctiveness of a target (Bottoms and Wiles, Pease, in Chapters 18 and 26 respectively of this volume), another line focused on the individual.

Closer to economic rather than psychological theory, the view was advanced that, motivated by self-interest, the basis of human action lies in the 'expected utility' from a criminal act. Van Den Haag (1982: 1,026–1,027) provides an example of this approach:

I do not see any relevant difference between dentistry and prostitution or car theft, except that the latter do not require a license . . . The frequency of rape, or of mugging, is essentially determined by the expected comparative net advantage, just as is the rate of dentistry and burglary. The comparative net advantage consists in the satisfaction (produced by the money or by the violative act itself) expected from the crime, less the expected cost of achieving it, compared to the net satisfaction expected from other activities in which the offender has the opportunity to engage. Cost in the main equals the expected penalty divided by the risk of suffering it.

Thus, like an accountant with a balance sheet, the individual reckons his or her likely net gains and losses and enters the criminal market place intending to make a profit. Lilly *et al.* (1995) have dryly described this approach as offering a model of the criminal as a calculator. However, implicit within this approach was the notion that the offender does not act in a random or in a disorganized manner. Rather, the individual makes rational choices about whether to obey or break the law: the offender is a rational decision-maker, a 'reasoning criminal'.

A key text in the further development of this approach was *The Reasoning Criminal: Rational Choice Perspectives on Offending*, edited by Cornish and Clarke (1986). The thesis unpinning this approach, as articulated by Cornish and Clarke, is that personal benefit is the prime motivation for crime. In pursuit of personal gain, individuals make decisions and choices that, to a greater or lesser degree, are rational in nature. Social factors, including family and peer group, play a background role in an individual's development in growing up with an association with crime. However, the rational 'event decision' at the point of committing the offence is predominant. For example, circumstances such as the presence of a hidden entrance, an open window, or sight of expensive goods will all influence the offender's thinking with respect to committing a burglary. Similarly, the rational choice model has been applied to other offences including shoplifting, robbery, and drug use (Clarke 1992; Cornish and Clarke 1986).

Akers (1990) argues that it is questionable whether development of the idea of rational choice is a radical new development in criminology. Nonetheless, the point was made that the frequency of crime is associated with increased opportunity: further, when confronted with opportunity, offenders do make rational choices about their behaviour.

PSYCHOLOGY AND CRIMINOLOGY: RETURN TO CORDIALITY?

As the 1980s became the 1990s, and into the new millennium, criminological psychologists became sufficiently confident in their subject to begin to produce a string of textbooks on the topic of psychology and crime (e.g., Ainsworth 2000; Andrews and Bonta 1994; Bartol 1999; Blackburn 1993; Hollin 1989, 1992). As part of this growing confidence, some psychologists challenged directly what they perceived to be a criminological bias against psychology. For example, Andrews (1990) chastised the report of the Canadian Sentencing Commission for the criminological bias that led to its failure to utilize psychological research in setting its policies. Andrews and Wormith (1989) coined the term 'knowledge destruction' to describe what they saw as the fraudulent and spurious dismissal of psychological research and theory by criminologists. This theme of knowledge destruction was expounded by Andrews (1989) in his paper on the spurious tactics used by critics to destroy evidence on the effectiveness of correctional treatment.

However, as Lilly *et al.* (2002) suggest, during the 1990s criminology itself was revisiting theories of crime with a focus on the individual offender.

CRIMINOLOGY REDISCOVERS THE INDIVIDUAL

Lilly *et al.* (2002) suggest several strands of thinking, and a supporting weight of psychological research (including Eysenck's research), within American conservative criminology that have led criminologists to resurrect the study of the individual offender. The first reason Lilly *et al.* raise is the return to popularity of biological theories, fuelled partly by technological developments that allowed much better observation and measurement, and partly by a growing weight of empirical data (some psychological). Secondly, the popularity of texts such as *Crime and Human Nature* (Wilson and Herrnstein 1985) which seek to explain crime primarily by recourse to constitutional and other biosocial factors. Thirdly, a cluster of developments that placed the individual at centre stage: these include a return by criminologists to the primacy of psychological factors such as intelligence (Herrnstein and Murray 1994); the spate of publications around the notion of a 'criminal mind' (Samenow, 1984); the growth of research around the notion of the 'reasoning criminal' (see above); and the formulation of explanations for crime framed in terms of the offender's 'moral poverty' (Bennett *et al.* 1996).

While there is some overlap between American and British developments, it is possible to see another two lines of research which have led to increased harmony between criminologists and psychologists in Britain. The first unifying theme stems from the accumulation of research focused on Developmental Criminology (see Farrington, in Chapter 19 of this volume) and the associated Life-Course Criminology (Moffitt 1993; Smith, in Chapter 20 of this volume). The force of this work is to show empirically that complex models, involving a wide range of individual and social factors, must be developed to have any degree of explanatory power.

The second area of research to stimulate discussion between criminologists and psychologists comes from the meta-analyses of the effects of treatment on offenders. This particular line of enquiry will be considered in detail.

'WHAT'S WORKING'?

As documented in a string of publications (e.g., Gendreau 1996; Gendreau and Andrews 1990; Hollin 1993, 1994; Lipsey 1995; Lösel 1996), a reasonable consensus has developed in the literature regarding the components of interventions that are effective in reducing offending. In Britain this treatment initiative has coalesced around the theme of 'What Works' (McGuire 1995), a phrase borrowed from the title of Martinson's (1974) paper which is generally taken as implying that 'nothing works'. The broader details of the What Works initiative and offender treatment are discussed elsewhere in this text (see Raynor, in Chapter 31), but the theoretical issues it raises are germane to the current discussion.

The 'What Works' literature has looked at interventions in terms of their effects on offending and has presented issues of treatment management, treatment focus, and the types of treatment that characterize effective treatment. Treatment management and focus have been discussed elsewhere (Hollin *et al.* 1995), but there are points to be made about theory. The meta-analyses show that effective interventions will address the offender's behaviour but will also include a cognitive component to address the 'attitudes, values, and beliefs that support anti-social behaviour' (Gendreau and Andrews 1990: 182). The interweaving of behaviour and cognition in interventions can be traced directly to cognitive-behavioural treatment and, indeed, it is this particular approach to treatment that has been identified by the meta-analyses as having the greatest likelihood of success (see also Lipsey *et al.* 2001).

Cognitive-behavioural theory

This focus on the effectiveness of cognitive-behavioural treatment has, naturally, led to an upsurge in interest in cognitive-behavioural explanations for criminal behaviour. At face value cognitive-behavioural theory provides a ready meeting point for criminology and psychology. Within criminology there is a history of theories that include learning, behaviour, and cognition (e.g., differential association theory and differential reinforcement theory), and these concepts are central to behavioural learning theories (e.g., operant theory) and cognitive theories (e.g., social information-processing). However, a theoretical difficulty comes about when we look for a common understanding of the term 'cognitive-behavioural theory'.

In its traditional form, as exemplified by the work of Skinner (see above), behavioural theory concentrated on the relationship between the environment and observable behaviour. However, within mainstream psychological theory the significant development was in terms of social learning theory which, while maintaining its behavioural origins, incorporated cognition and emotion into a theoretical account of human behaviour (Bandura 1977, 1986). As social learning theory precipitated interest in the role of cognition within an overarching behavioural framework, the term cognitive-behavioural slipped into popular usage. In particular, the term became increasingly used by practitioners, and cognitive-behavioural treatment became popular for a range of groups, including offenders (Hollin 1990). However, with its varied background, from the standpoint of both research and practice, it is difficult to give a sound definition of cognitive-behavioural theory and practice.

Kendall and Bacon (1988) have previously commented on the problems in attempting to define cognitive-behaviour therapy and to indicate precisely how it relates to traditional theory. Indeed, they suggest that it is preferable to see a cognitive-behavioural approach to practice as a general perspective rather than as a single unified theory. Thus, McGuire (2000) is able to show with clarity the strands in the evolution of cognitive-behavioural therapies, but can be far less certain about an agreed definition of cognitive-behavioural theory.

Consequently, rather than the purist sequence of a theory leading to the design of an intervention, so producing outcome evidence by which to amend theory and practice, 'What Works' has started from a quite different position. The meta-analyses have brought together a disparate batch of treatment outcome studies and distilled their effective components. In an about turn, the position has been arrived at whereby positive treatment outcome data have outstripped theory. As noted elsewhere (Hollin 1999), one of the tasks following the meta-analyses is to make theoretical sense of their findings. To date this theoretical clarity is sorely missing in the literature.

It might, briefly, be interesting to speculate what such theory might look like and how it might offer a bridge for psychological and criminological research. It seems likely that a cogent account of criminal behaviour would seek to blend cognitive, behavioural, and environmental factors, probably drawing on basic principles of learning. This is a complex task, requiring genuine cross-disciplinary collaboration, but the basic theoretical structures are probably available. One might venture that social learning theory—which in itself has crossed the divide between psychology and criminology (Akers 1985, 1999)—has the potential to be the springboard for such an ambitious journey into theory.

In this light it is interesting that psychologists and criminologists are making essentially the same points regarding theory and practice in light of 'What Works'. Hollin (1999: 369) makes the following observation:

It is important that 'what works' develops as practice evolves, as the research base increases, and as other complementary models of effective practice unfold ... Clearly, treatment will never eliminate crime, but if effective work with offenders can reduce the human and financial costs of victimization then the effort is surely worthwhile.

While from a criminological perspective, Crow (2001: 78–79) writes as follows:

Programmes for the individual offender need to be seen as part of a broader attack on the conditions that give rise to crime. Programmes for offenders rightly take many forms and include economic and social provision, including education, training, jobs and housing. But unless they take place in circumstances which favour good educational, training and job prospects their impact may be no greater than that of Sispyhus rolling a rock uphill.

The points made in the above two quotations are similar in emphasis. First, there are no grandiose claims for the benefits of treatment; secondly, that the 'What Works' style of treatment needs to be connected to other styles of effective practice (see Hollin 2001); thirdly, this must all be set against a backdrop that includes victims, financial costs, and social conditions.

CONCLUDING COMMENT

Finally, it is time to put to rest the question of pathology, that psychological theories are only fit for explanation of abnormal states. Of course there are mentally disordered offenders, and a substantial theoretical and practical literature has accumulated in this specialist field (e.g., Blumenthal and Lavender 2000; Howells and Hollin 1993). (Although it is interesting that a meta-analysis of prediction of recidivism in mentally disordered offenders (Bonta *et al.* 1998) suggested that 'criminological predictors' such as offence history out-performed 'mental disorder' predictors such as diagnosis.) However, psychological theories such as operant learning, social information-processing, and social learning theory, have been developed in mainstream psychology to generate theories of human behaviour in general, not abnormal or pathological behaviour. These psychological theories may be applied to abnormal states, but are not restricted to that context. (For discussion in relation to violent crime, see Levi with Maguire, Chapter 22 of this volume.) If that point is taken and a connection can be made between criminological theory and psychological theory then, with informed collaboration, significant theoretical advances will be possible. A strong criminology-psychology theory that provides a solid platform for a coordinated multi-component crime prevention programme would be progress of the highest order.

Selected further reading

The texts listed below have been selected as giving reviews and informed commentary across the broad field of psychology and criminal behaviour. Inevitably, some stray into legal psychology, although it is useful to see the two topics together to appreciate their similarities and differences.

Curt Bartol's text, *Criminal Behaviour: A Psychosocial Approach* (Upper Saddle River, NJ: Prentice-Hall, 1999) is now in its 5th edition and offers a considered view of the field. A more assertive view of the role of psychology in explaining crime can be found in the book *The Psychology of Criminal Conduct* (Cincinnati, OH: Anderson Publishing, 1994) by Don Andrews and James Bonta. Clive Hollin's books *Psychology and Crime: An Introduction to Criminological Psychology* (London: Routledge, 1989) and *Criminal Behaviour: A Psychological Approach to Explanation and Prevention* (London: Falmer Press, 1992) were written primarily for an undergraduate audience; Ron Blackburn's text *The Psychology of Criminal Conduct: Theory, Research and Practice* (Chichester: Wiley, 1993) reaches a more advanced readership. For a detailed exposition of personality theories, *The Causes and Cures of Criminality* (New York: Plenum Press, 1989) by Hans Eysenck and Gisli Gudjonsson is available.

Peter Ainsworth's book, *Psychology and Crime: Myths and Realities* (London: Longman, 2000) gives an eclectic mix of topics; while *Behaviour, Crime and Legal Processes: A Guide for Forensic Practitioners* (Chichester: John Wiley, 2000), edited by James McGuire, Tom Mason, and Aisling O'Kane, cuts across criminological psychology, legal psychology, and practice. A comprehensive recent overview of theory and practice with regard to treatment issues can be found in Clive Hollin's edited book, *Handbook of Offender Assessment and Treatment* (Chichester: John Wiley, 2001).

References

AICHHORN, A. (1955), *Wayward Youth* (trans.), New York: Meridian Books. Original work published 1925.

AINSWORTH, P.B. (2000), *Psychology and Crime: Myths and Reality*, London: Longman.

AKERS, R.L. (1985), *Deviant Behavior: A Social Learning Approach*, 3rd edn, Belmont, Ca.: Wadsworth.

—— (1990), 'Rational Choice, Deterrence, and Social Learning Theory in Criminology: The Path Not Taken', *Journal of Criminal Law and Criminology*, 81: 653–76.

—— (1999), *Social Learning and Social Structure: A General Theory of Crime and Deviance*, Boston, Mass.: Northeastern University Press.

ALPER, J.S. (1998), 'Genes, Free Will, and Criminal Behavior', *Society, Science, and Medicine*, 46: 1599–1611.

ANDREWS, D.A. (1989), 'Recidivism is Predictable and Can Be Influenced: Using Risk Assessments to Reduce Recidivism', *Forum on Corrections Research*, 1: 11–18.

—— (1990), 'Some Criminological Sources of Anti-Rehabilitation Bias in the Report of The Canadian Sentencing Commisssion', *Canadian Journal of Criminology*, 32: 511–24.

—— and BONTA, J. (1994), *The Psychology of Criminal Conduct*, Cincinnati, OH: Anderson Publishing.

—— and —— (1998), *The Psychology of Criminal*

Conduct, 2nd edn, Cincinnati, OH: Anderson Publishing.

—— and WORMITH, J.S. (1989), 'Personality and Crime: Knowledge Destruction and Construction in Criminology', *Justice Quarterly*, 6: 289–309.

BAARS, B.J. (1986), *The Cognitive Revolution in Psychology*, New York: Guilford Press.

BANDURA, A. (1977), *Social Learning Theory*, Englewood Cliffs, NJ: Prentice Hall.

—— (1986), *Social Foundations of Thought and Action: A Social-cognitive Theory*, Englewood Cliffs, NJ: Prentice Hall.

BARTOL, C.R. (1980), *Criminal Behavior: A Psychological Approach*, Englewood Cliffs, NJ: Prentice Hall.

—— (1999), *Criminal Behavior: A Psychological Approach*, 5th edn, Upper Saddle River, NJ: Prentice Hall.

—— and BARTOL, A.M. (1994), *Psychology and Law*, 2nd edn, Pacific Grove, Cal.: Brooks/Cole.

BENNETT, W.J., DILULIO, J.J. Jr, and WALTERS, J.P. (1996), *Body Count: Moral Poverty and How to Win America's War Against Crime and Drugs*, New York: Simon and Schuster.

BLACKBURN, R. (1993), *The Psychology of Criminal Conduct: Theory, Research and Practice*, Chichester: Wiley.

—— (1996), 'What *is* Forensic Psychology?', *Legal and Criminological Psychology*, 1: 3–16.

BLASI, A. (1980), 'Bridging Moral Cognition and Moral Action: A Critical Review', *Psychological Bulletin*, 88: 1–45.

BLUMENTHAL, S., and LAVENDER, T. (2000), *Violence and Mental Disorder: A Critical Aid to the Assessment and Management of Risk*, London: Jessica Kingsley Publishers.

BONTA, J., LAW, M., and HANSON, R.K. (1998), 'The Prediction of Criminal and Violent Recidivism Among Mentally Disordered Offenders: A Meta-analysis', *Psychological Bulletin*, 123: 123–42.

BOWLBY, J. (1944), 'Forty-four Juvenile Thieves', *International Journal of Psychoanalysis*, 25: 1–57.

—— (1951), *Maternal Care and Mental Health*, Geneva: World Health Organisation.

—— and SALTER-AINSWORTH, M.D. (1965), *Child Care and the Growth of Love*, Harmondsworth: Penguin.

BROWN, W.C. (1961), *Freud and the Post-Freudians*, Harmondsworth: Penguin.

BROWNFIELD, D., and SORENSON, A.M. (1993), 'Self-control and Juvenile Delinquency: Theoretical Issues and an Empirical Assessment of Selected Elements of a General Theory of Crime', *Deviant Behavior*, 14: 243–64.

BULL, R., and CARSON, D. (eds) (1995), *Handbook of Psychology in Legal Contexts*, Chichester: Wiley.

CAPSHEW, J.H. (1999), *Psychologists on the March: Science, Practice, and Professional Identity in America 1929–1969*, Cambridge: Cambridge University Press.

CATTELL, R.B. (1965), *The Scientific Analysis of Personality*, Harmondsworth: Penguin.

CIBA FOUNDATION (1996), *Ciba Foundation Symposium 194. Genetics of Criminal and Antisocial Behaviour*, Chichester: Wiley.

CLARKE, R.V. (ed.) (1992), *Situational Crime Prevention: Successful Case Studies*, New York: Harrow and Heston.

COHEN, L.E., and FELSON, M. (1979), 'Social Change and Crime Rate Trends: A Routine Activities Approach', *American Sociological Review*, 44: 588–608.

CORNISH, D.B., and CLARKE, R.V.G. (eds) (1986), *The Reasoning Criminal: Rational Choice Perspectives on Offending*, New York: Springer-Verlag.

CRICK, N.R., and DODGE, K.A. (1994), 'A Review and Reformulation of Social Information-processing Mechanisms in Children's Social Adjustment', *Psychological Bulletin*, 115: 74–101.

—— and —— (1996), 'Social Information-processing Mechanisms in Reactive and Proactive Aggression', *Child Development*, 67: 993–1002.

CROW, I. (2001), *The Treatment and Rehabilitation of Offenders*, London: Sage Publications.

DENNETT, D.C. (1991), *Consciousness Explained*, London: Allen Lane.

DODGE, K.A., and NEWMAN, J.P. (1981), 'Biased Decision-making Processes in Aggressive Boys', *Journal of Abnormal Psychology*, 90: 375–9.

——, PRICE, J.M., BACHOROWSKI, J.-A., and NEWMAN, J.P. (1990), 'Hostile Attributional Biases in Severely Aggressive Adolescents', *Journal of Abnormal Psychology*, 99: 385–92.

ELLIS, P.L. (1982), 'Empathy: A Factor in Antisocial Behavior', *Journal of Abnormal Child Psychology*, 2: 123–33.

ELMER, N., and REICHER, S. (1995), *Adolescence and Delinquency: The Collective Management of Reputation*, Oxford: Blackwell.

EYSENCK, H.J. (1959), *Manual of the Maudsley Personality Inventory*, London: University of London Press.

—— (1964), *Crime and Personality*, London: Routledge and Kegan Paul.

—— (1970), *Crime and Personality*, 2nd edn, London: Granada Press.

—— (1977), *Crime and Personality*, 3rd edn, London: Routledge and Kegan Paul.

—— (1984), 'Crime and Personality', in D.J. Muller, D.E. Blackman, and A.J. Chapman (eds), *Psychology and Law*, Chichester: Wiley.

—— (1987), 'Personality Theory and the Problems of Criminality', in B.J. McGurk, D.M. Thornton, and M. Williams (eds.), *Applying Psychology to Imprisonment: Theory & Practice*, London: HMSO.

—— (1996), 'Personality and Crime: Where Do We Stand?', *Psychology Crime & Law*, 2: 143–52.

—— and EYSENCK, S.B.G. (1968), 'A Factorial Study of Psychoticism as a Dimension of Personality', Special issue of *Multivariate Behavioural Research*: 15–31.

—— and —— (1976), *Psychoticism as a Dimension of Personality*, London: Hodder & Stoughton.

—— and GUDJONSSON, G.H. (1989), *The Causes and Cures of Criminality*, New York: Plenum Press.

EYSENCK, S.B.G., and EYSENCK, H.J. (1971), 'Crime and Personality: Item Analysis of Questionnaire Responses', *British Journal of Criminology*, 11: 49–62.

—— and —— (1972), 'The Questionnaire Measurement of Psychoticism', *Psychological Medicine*, 2: 50–55.

——, —— and BARRETT, P. (1985), 'A Revised Version of the Psychoticism Scale', *Personality and Individual Differences*, 6: 21–29.

—— and McGURK, B.J. (1980), 'Impulsiveness and Venturesomeness in a Detention Centre Population', *Psychological Reports*, 47: 1299–1306.

FELDMAN, M.P. (1977), *Criminal Behaviour: A Psychological Analysis*, Chichester: Wiley.

FESHBACH, N.D. (1984), 'Empathy, Empathy Training and the Regulation of Aggression in Elementary School Children', in R.M. Kaplan, V.J. Konečni, and R.W. Novaco (eds), *Aggression in Children and Youth*, 192–208, The Hague: Martinus Nijhoff.

FREEDMAN, B.J., ROSENTHAL, L., DONAHOE, C.P., SCHLUNDT, D.G., and McFALL, R.M. (1978), 'A Social-behavioral Analysis of Skills Deficits in Delinquent and Non-delinquent Adolescent Boys', *Journal of Consulting and Clinical Psychology*, 46: 1448–62.

GENDREAU, P. (1996), 'Offender Rehabilitation: What We Know and What Needs to be Done', *Criminal Justice and Behavior*, 23: 144–61.

—— and ANDREWS, D.A. (1990), 'What the Meta-analyses of the Offender Treatment Literature Tells Us About "What Works"', *Canadian Journal of Criminology*, 32: 173–84.

GIBBS, J.C. (1993), 'Moral-cognitive Interventions', in A.P. Goldstein and C.R. Huff (eds), *The Gang Intervention Handbook*, Champaign, Ill.: Research Press.

—— (1996), 'Sociomoral Group Treatment for Young Offenders', in C.R. Hollin and K. Howells (eds), *Clinical Approaches to Working with Young Offenders*, 129–149, Chichester: Wiley.

GOLDSTEIN, A.P., GLICK, B., and GIBBS, J.C. (1998), *Aggression Replacement Training* (rev. edn), Champaign, Ill.: Research Press.

GORING, C. (1913), *The English Convict*, London: Methuen.

GOTTFREDSON, M.R., and HIRSCHI, T. (1990), *A General Theory of Crime*, Paulo Alto, Cal.: Stanford University Press.

GRESSWELL, D.M., and HOLLIN, C.R. (1992), 'Towards a New Methodology for Making Sense of Case Material: An Illustrative Case Involving Attempted Multiple Murder', *Criminal Behaviour and Mental Health*, 2: 329–41.

GUDJONSSON, G.H., and HAYWARD, L.R.C. (1998), *Forensic Psychology: A Guide to Practice*, London: Routledge.

HALFPENNY, P. (1982/1992), *Positivism and Sociology: Explaining Social Life*, London: George Allen & Unwin/Aldershot, Hants: Gregg Revivals.

HEALY, W., and BRONNER, A.F. (1936), *New Light on Delinquency and Its Treatment*, New Haven, Conn.: Yale University Press.

HERRNSTEIN, R.J., and MURRAY, C. (1994), *The Bell Curve: Intelligence and Class Structure in American Life*, New York: Free Press.

HESS, A.K. (1999), 'Defining Forensic Psychology', in A.K. Hess and I.B. Weiner (eds), *The Handbook of Forensic Psychology*, 24–47, New York: Wiley.

—— and WEINER, I.B. (eds) (1999), *The Handbook of Forensic Psychology*, New York: Wiley.

HIGGINS, J.P., and THIES, A.P. (1981), 'Social Effectiveness and Problem-solving Thinking of Reformatory Inmates', *Journal of Offender Counselling Services and Rehabilitation*, 5: 93–8.

HOLLIN, C.R. (1989), *Psychology and Crime: An Introduction to Criminological Psychology*, London: Routledge.

—— (1990), *Cognitive-behavioral Interventions With Young Offenders*, Elmsford, NY: Pergamon Press.

—— (1992), *Criminal Behaviour: A Psychological Approach to Explanation and Prevention*, London: Falmer Press.

—— (1993), 'Advances in the Psychological Treatment of Criminal Behaviour', *Criminal Behaviour and Mental Health*, 3: 42–57.

—— (1994), 'Designing Effective Rehabilitation Programmes for Young Offenders', *Psychology, Crime, & Law*, 1: 193–99.

—— (1999), 'Treatment Programmes for Offenders: Meta-analysis, "What Works", and Beyond', *International Journal of Law and Psychiatry*, 22: 361–72.

—— (ed.) (2001), *Handbook of Offender Assessment and Treatment*, Chichester: Wiley.

——, EPPS, K., and KENDRICK, D. (1995), *Managing Behavioural Treatment: Policy and Practice With Delinquent Adolescents*, London: Routledge.

—— and WHEELER, H.M. (1982), 'The Violent Young Offender: A Small Group Study of a Borstal Population', *Journal of Adolescence*, 5: 247–57.

HONDERICH, T. (1993), *How Free Are You? The Determinism Problem*, Oxford: Oxford University Press.

HOPKINS BURKE, R. (2001), *An Introduction to Criminological Theory*, Cullompton, Devon: Willan Publishing.

HOUSTON, J. (1998), *Making Sense with Offenders: Personal Constructs, Therapy and Change*, Chichester: Wiley.

HOWELLS, K. (1978), 'The Meaning of Poisoning to a Person Diagnosed as a Psychopath', *Medicine, Science and the Law*, 18: 179–84.

—— (1979), 'Some Meanings of Children for Pedophiles', in M. Cook and G. Wilson (eds), *Love and Attraction*, Oxford: Pergamon Press.

—— (1986), 'Social Skills Training and Criminal and Antisocial Behaviour in Adults', in C.R. Hollin and P. Trower (eds), *Handbook of Social Skills Training, Volume 1: Applications Across the Life Span*, 185–210, Oxford: Pergamon Press.

—— and HOLLIN, C.R. (eds) (1993), *Clinical Approaches to the Mentally Disordered Offender*, Chichester: Wiley.

JEFFERY, C.R. (1960), 'The Historical Development of Criminology', in H. Mannheim (ed.), *Pioneers in Criminology*, 364–94, London: Stevens.

—— (1965), 'Criminal Behavior and Learning Theory', *Journal of Criminal Law, Criminology and Police Science*, 56: 294–300.

KAGEHIRO, D.K., and LAUFER, W.S. (eds) (1992), *Handbook of Psychology and Law*, New York: Springer-Verlag.

KAPARDIS, A. (1997), *Psychology and Law: A Critical Introduction*, Cambridge: Cambridge University Press.

KAPLAN, P.J., and ARBUTHNOT, J. (1985), 'Affective Empathy and Cognitive Role-taking in Delinquent and Non-delinquent Youth', *Adolescence*, 20: 323–33.

KELLY, G.A. (1955), *The Psychology of Personal Constructs*, New York: Norton.

KENDALL, P.C., and BACON, S.F. (1988), 'Cognitive Behavior Therapy', in D.B. Fishman, F. Rotgers, and C.M. Franks (eds), *Paradigms in Behavior Therapy: Present and Promise*, 141–67, New York: Springer.

KIRKCALDY, B.D., and BROWN, J.M. (2000), 'Personality, Socioeconomics and Crime: An International Comparison', *Psychology, Crime, & Law*, 6: 113–25.

KOHLBERG, L. (1964), 'Development of Moral Character and Moral Ideology', in M. Hoffman and L. Hoffman (eds), *Review of Child Development Research*, Vol. 1, 383–431, New York: Russell Sage Foundation.

—— (1978), 'Revisions in the Theory and Practice of Mental Development', in W. Damon (ed.), *New Directions in Child Development: Moral Development*, 83–97, San Francisco, Cal.: Jossey-Bass.

KUMCHY, C., and SAYER, L.A. (1980), 'Locus of Control and Delinquent Adolescent Populations', *Psychological Reports*, 46: 1307–10.

LILLY, J.R., CULLEN, F.T., and BALL, R.A. (1995), *Criminological Theory: Context and Consequences*, 2nd edn, Thousand Oaks, Cal.: Sage.

——, —— and —— (2002), *Criminological Theory: Context and Consequences*, 3rd edn, Thousand Oaks, Cal.: Sage.

LIPSEY, M.W. (1995), 'What Do We Learn From 400 Studies on the Effectiveness of Treatment With Juvenile Delinquents?', in J. McGuire (ed.), *What Works: Reducing Reoffending*, 63–78, Chichester: Wiley.

——, CHAPMAN, G.L., and LANDENBERGER, N.A. (2001), 'Cognitive-behavioral Programs for Offenders', *Annals of The American Academy of Political and Social Science*, 578: 144–57.

LOMBROSO, C. (1876), *L'Uomo Delinquente*, 5th edn, Turin: Bocca. First pub. Milan: Hoepli.

LONG, C.G., and MIDGELY, M. (1992), 'On the Closeness of the Concepts of the Criminal and the Mentally Ill in the Nineteenth Century: Yesterday's Professional and Public Opinions Reflected Today', *Journal of Forensic Psychiatry*, 3: 63–79.

LÖSEL, F. (1996), 'Working With Young Offenders: The Impact of the Meta-analyses', in C.R. Hollin and K. Howells (eds), *Clinical Approaches to Working With Young Offenders*, 57–82, Chichester: Wiley.

MARTINSON, R. (1974), 'What Works? Questions and Answers About Prison Reform', *The Public Interest* 35: 22–54.

MATZA, D. (1964), *Delinquency and Drift*, New York: Wiley.

—— (1969), *Becoming Deviant*, Englewood Cliffs, NJ: Prentice Hall.

McEWAN, A.W. (1983), 'Eysenck's Theory of Criminality and the Personality Types and Offences of Young Delinquents', *Personality and Individual Differences*, 4: 201–4.

—— and KNOWLES, C. (1984), 'Delinquent Personality Types and the Situational Contexts of Their Crimes', *Personality and Individual Differences*, 5: 339–44.

McGUIRE, J. (ed.) (1995), *What Works: Reducing Reoffending*, Chichester: Wiley.

—— (2000), *Cognitive-behavioural Approaches: An Introduction to Theory and Research*, London: Home Office.

McGUIRE, J., MASON, T., and O'KANE, A. (2000) (eds), *Behaviour, Crime and Legal Processes: A Guide for Forensic Practitioners*, Chichester: John Wiley.

McGURK, B.J., and McDOUGALL, C. (1981), 'A New Approach to Eysenck's Theory of Criminality', *Personality and Individual Differences*, 2: 338–40.

MISCHEL, W. (1968), *Personality and Assessment*, New York: Wiley.

MOFFITT, T.E. (1993), 'Adolescence-Limited and Life-Course-Persistent Antisocial Behavior: A Developmental Taxonomy', *Psychological Review*, 100: 674–701.

NELSON, J.R., SMITH, D.J., and DODD, J. (1990), 'The Moral Reasoning of Juvenile Delinquents: A Meta-analysis', *Journal of Abnormal Child Psychology*, 18: 709–27.

NIETZEL, M.T., HASEMANN, D.M., and LYNAM, D. R. (1999), 'Behavioral Perspective on Violent Behavior', in V.B. Van Hasselt and M. Hersen (eds), *Handbook of Psychological Approaches with Violent Offenders: Contemporary Strategies and Issues*, 39–66, New York: Kluwer Academic/Plenum.

NOVACO, R.W. (1975), *Anger Control: The Development and Evaluation of an Experimental Treatment*, Lexington, Mass.: D.C. Heath.

—— (1994), 'Anger as a Risk Factor for Violence Among the Mentally Disordered', in J. Monahan and H. Steadman (eds), *Violence and Mental Disorder: Developments in Risk Assessment*, 21–59, Chicago, Ill.: University of Chicago Press.

—— and WELSH, W.N. (1989), 'Anger Disturbances: Cognitive Mediation and Clinical Prescriptions', in K. Howells and C.R. Hollin (eds), *Clinical Approaches to Violence*, 39–60, Chichester: Wiley.

NYE, R.D. (1992), *The Legacy of B.F. Skinner: Concepts and Perspectives, Controversies and Misunderstandings*, Pacific Grove, Cal.: Brooks/Cole Publishing Company.

O'DONOHUE, W., and KITCHENER, R. (1999) (eds), *Handbook of Behaviorism*, San Diego, Cal.: Academic Press.

PALMER, E.J., and HOLLIN, C.R. (1996), 'Assessing Adolescent Problems: An Overview of the Adolescent Problems Inventory', *Journal of Adolescence*, 19: 347–54.

—— and —— (2000), 'The Interrelations of Sociomoral Reasoning, Perceptions of Own Parenting and Attributions of Intent with Self-reported Delinquency', *Legal and Criminological Psychology*, 5: 201–18.

—— and —— (2001), 'Sociomoral Reasoning, Perceptions of Parenting and Self-reported Delinquency in Adolescents', *Applied Cognitive Psychology*, 15: 85–100.

PIAGET, J. (1932), *The Moral Judgement of the Child*, London: Kegan Paul.

RICHARDS, G. (1996), *Putting Psychology in its Place: An Introduction from a Critical Historical Perspective*, London: Routledge.

ROESCH, R., CORRADO, R.R., and DEMPSTER, R. (eds) (2001), *Psychology in the Courts: International Advances in Knowledge*, London: Routledge.

ROSHIER, B. (1989), *Controlling Crime: The Classical Perspective in Criminology*, Milton Keynes: Open University Press.

ROSS, R.R., and FABIANO, E.A. (1985), *Time to Think: A Cognitive Model of Delinquency Prevention and Offender Rehabilitation*, Johnson City, Tenn.: Institute of Social Sciences and Arts.

ROTTER, J.B. (1966), 'Generalized Expectancies for Internal Versus External Control of Reinforcement', *Psychological Monographs*, 80 (Whole No. 609).

RUSSELL, B. (1961), *A History of Western Philosophy*, 2nd edn, London: George Allen & Unwin.

SAMENOW, S.E. (1984), *Inside the Criminal Mind*, New York: Times Books.

SHAW, C.R., and McKAY, H.D. (1942), *Juvenile Delinquency in Urban Areas*, Chicago, Ill.: Chicago University Press.

SHELDON, W.H., HARTL, E.M., and McDERMOTT, E. (1949), *Varieties of Delinquent Youth: An Introduction to Constitutional Psychiatry*, New York: Harper.

SIEGAL, L.J. (1986), *Criminology*, 2nd edn, St Paul, Minn.: West Publishing.

SKINNER, B.F. (1938), *The Behavior of Organisms: An Experimental Analysis*, New York: Appleton-Century-Crofts.

—— (1974), *About Behaviorism*, London: Jonathon Cape.

SLABY, R.G., and GUERRA, N.G. (1988), 'Cognitive Mediators of Aggression in Adolescent Offenders: 1. Assessment', *Developmental Psychology*, 24: 580–88.

SPEARMAN, C. (1927), *The Nature of Intelligence and the Principles of Cognition*, London: Macmillan.

SUTHERLAND, E.H. (1947), *Principles of Criminology*, 4th edn, Philadelphia, Pa. Lippincott.

TAYLOR, I., WALTON, P., and YOUNG, J. (1973), *The New Criminology: For a Social Theory of Deviancy*, London: Routledge & Kegan Paul.

TIERNEY, J. (1996), *Criminology: Theory & Context*, London: Prentice Hall.

TRASLER, G. (1962), *The Explanation of Criminality*, London: Routledge & Kegan Paul.

VAN DEN HAAG, E. (1982), 'Could Successful Rehabilitation Reduce the Crime Rate?', *Journal of Criminal Law and Criminology*, 73: 1,022–1,035.

WATSON, J.B. (1913), 'Psychology as the Behaviourist Views It', *Psychological Review*, 20: 158–77.

WILSON, J.Q., and HERRNSTEIN, R.J. (1985), *Crime and Human Nature*, New York: Simon and Schuster.

YOUNG, J. (1997), 'Left Realist Criminology: Radical in its Analysis, Realist in its Policy', in M. Maguire, R. Morgan, and R. Reiner (eds), *The Oxford Handbook of Criminology*, 2nd edn, 473–98, Oxford: Oxford University Press.

6

COMPARING CRIMINAL JUSTICE

David Nelken

Do we really need a separate chapter on comparative criminal justice? An objection which has been raised to the continued inclusion of this chapter in this *Handbook* is that every chapter in a reference work of criminology worthy of its name should already incorporate a comparative dimension. Putting comparison in the title of only one chapter smacks of tokenism. On the other hand, some reviewers of earlier editions of the *Handbook* complained about what they saw as the British, Anglo-American, or English language parochialism of many of the chapters.

Even the best of current English-language theorizing about crime and crime control *does* take much of its sense and point from background assumptions and developments which are most at home in what continentals call 'Anglo-American' legal culture. For example, Garland's influential analysis of the way 'the state' is currently seeking to offload some of its responsibilities on to the 'community' (Garland 1996), has less application to the state-centred societies of Continental Europe. Here, in many respects, it is only now that the responsibility of the state to protect its citizens from street crime and burglary, rather than to maintain 'public order' as such, is beginning to be emphasized. His more recent analysis of the 'modern' culture of crime control (Garland 2001) likewise has little to say about variation in the sources and consequences of the growing fear of crime in Continental Europe. Much the same can be said for many of the main arguments in Young's eloquent analysis of what he calls the 'exclusive society' (Young 1999). Most of his worries concern the danger of the UK going down the road taken by the USA. But his description of the strengths and weaknesses of alternative, more inclusive types of approach to criminal justice would surely be enriched by more consideration of Continental Europe. Despite the many similarities at the level of practice brought about by the homogenizing and converging influences of the European Union, the debate over solidarity versus exclusion takes rather different forms depending on whether it is the representatives of the state or rather the members of civil society who are allocated the main role in creating an integrated sense of identity and community (Favell 1998). As Garland himself has persuasively shown us, 'penality' is as much a matter of cultural meaning as of instrumental effectivity (Garland 1990). But it is obvious that such meaning will vary from culture to culture (as well as within cultures). Indeed, it is fair to say that many of the important points made by these leading scholars are in fact comparative observations, but ones which are limited to the similarities and the differences they notice within Anglo-American societies.

How to proceed beyond this point is not obvious. Even the above criticisms, like the rest of this chapter, could be accused of being too Eurocentric. There is still little agreement on how best to pursue the comparative study of crime and criminal justice (P. Roberts 2002). The options range from, on the one hand, seeking comparative evidence so as to ensure that criminological hypotheses have cross-cultural validity to, on the other, trying to use such research in order to undermine such pretensions. This chapter will discuss issues of rationale, method, and approach in addressing the following questions: Why should we study criminal justice comparatively? What methods can we use to gather our data? What type of theoretical approaches are equal to the task of comparing criminal justice systems? It concludes with an illustrative case study intended to suggest how the pursuit of the different goals of comparative research can and should be reconciled.

WHY STUDY CRIMINAL JUSTICE COMPARATIVELY?

Interest in learning more about different systems of criminal justice can be shaped by a variety of goals of explanation, understanding, and reform. For many scholars the major contribution of comparative work lies in the way it could advance the agenda of a scientific criminology aimed at identifying the correlates of crime as anti-social behaviour. These writers use cross-national data so as to test claims about the link between crime and age, crime and social structure, crime and modernization, and so on. Much the same could be done in constructing arguments about variations between types of crime and social reaction (Black 1997).

By contrast, evidence of differences in the relationship between crime and criminal justice may be sought in order to excavate the positivist worm at the core of criminology. When 'crime' is treated as a social construct, a product of contrasting social and political censures, criminology is obliged to open out to larger debates in moral philosophy and the humanities as well as in the social sciences themselves. By posing fundamental problems of understanding the 'other' it challenges scholars to overcome ethnocentrism without denying difference or resorting to stereotypes. Engaging in comparative criminology thus has the potential to make criminologists become more reflexive (Nelken 1994a), for example learning to avoid the common error of treating the modern Anglo-American type of 'pragmatic instrumental' approach to law as if it were universal. Setting out to describe other countries' systems of criminal justice in fact often leads to rival accounts proposed by criminologists of the countries concerned (see, for example, Downes 1988, 1990; Franke 1990; Clinard 1978; Balveg 1988; Killias 1989). The debates that follow, painful and replete with misunderstanding as they sometimes tend to be, are fundamentally healthy for limiting the pretensions of a discipline which too often studies the powerless.

One result of studying the way crime is defined and handled in different jurisdictions by legislatures, criminal justice agencies, and the media (and others) is to discover—yet again—the crucial need to relate the study of crime to that of criminal justice. But it also demonstrates the difficulty of distinguishing criminal justice from social control more broadly. The exceptionally low crime rates in Switzerland and Japan, for example, can only be understood in terms of such interrelationships. Like-wise, if Italian courts send to prison only one-tenth of the youngsters who end up there in England and Wales (and one-hundredth of those in California), this may in part be explained by differences in the type and level of offences carried out by young people. But it will also have to do with the way Italian juvenile court judges and social workers feel they can (and should) defer to family social controls—given that children generally live at home at least until their late twenties, and often rely on family help to find work. On the other hand, cross-national data may on occasion also show that criminal behaviour is relatively uninfluenced by legal and social responses. There is evidence that even when different nation states change their drug laws at different times and in different directions, the patterns of national drug use (and drug over-dose) seem to be less affected by this than by international developments in supply and demand.

But we should not limit our interest in comparative criminal justice only to its effects on levels of crime. We can also study it in its own right. This sort of compara-tive enquiry has as one of its chief concerns the effort to identify the way a country's types of crime control resonate with other aspects of its culture. Why is it that countries like UK and Denmark, who complain most about the imposition of Euro-pean Union law, also maintain the best records of implementation? What does this tell us about the centrality of enforcement as an aspect of law in different soci-eties? Why, in the United States and the UK, does it often take a sex scandal to create official interest in doing something about corruption, whereas in Latin countries it takes a major corruption scandal to excite interest in marital unfaithfulness? What does this suggest about the way culture conditions the boundaries of law and the way criminal law helps shape those self-same boundaries?

Many claims about crime control which purport to be universal turn out to take their sense and limits of applicability from such cultural connections. Much British writing on the police, for example, takes it for granted that nothing could be more ill-advised than for the police to risk losing touch with the public by relying too much on military, technological, or other impersonal methods of crime control. The results of this, it is claimed, could only be a spiral of alienation which would spell the end of 'policing by consent'. In Italy, however, two of the main police forces are still part of the military, and this insulation from the pressures of local people is actually what inspires public confidence. Britain, like most English-speaking countries, adopts a preventive style of responding to many white-collar offences which is sufficiently different to be characterized as a system of 'compliance' as compared to 'punishment' (Nelken, in Chapter 23 of this volume). This is often justified as the only logical way of proceeding given the nature of the crimes and offenders involved. But in Italy such a contrast is much less noticeable. Enforcement is guided by the judiciary, who do their best to combat pollution, the neglect of safety at work, etc. using the normal techniques of criminal law and punishment.

As these examples illustrate, the interest in how criminal justice is organized elsewhere is often (some would say predominantly) guided by practical and policy goals. Perceived differences, such as the continued use of the death penalty in the United States, as well as its relatively high rate of imprisonment, may be used to reassure us about the superiority of our own institutions. But, more commonly, scholars cite evidence from abroad in an attempt to challenge and improve the way we do things at home. The concern for reform is manifest not only in the long-standing Anglo-American search for better means of controlling the police. Many descriptive or explanatory cross-cultural exercises are often shaped by a more or less hidden normative agenda, or finish by making policy recommendations. Would it necessarily be counter-productive for Italy to try to make its police forces more approachable? What is it that really prevents the adoption in Britain of methods to deal with business crime more similar to those used against ordinary crime? The same obviously applies to involvement in action–research abroad (Cain 2000a). Even cross-national victim surveys are deployed as much as a tool for change as in a search for understanding variability (Van Dyke 2000).

The search for patterned differences in law and practice also raises the question what it could mean to affirm (either as a sociological or a normative claim) that a country has the system it 'requires'. What price might a society have to pay to introduce 'reintegrative shaming'? What are the costs of pursuing 'zero tolerance'? If the Italian criminal process can effectively de-criminalize most cases involving juvenile delinquency (with the important exceptions of cases involving young immigrants or gypsies), could we and should we do the same (Nelken 2000b)? If prosecutors in Japan succeed in keeping down the level of cases sent to court, could we and should we follow their example (Johnson 2000)? Policy-led research can itself produce interesting descriptive and explanatory findings. But cultural variability in ideas and values means that it can also be tricky. Is it safe, for example, to assume that 'all criminal justice systems have to handle the "built-in-conflict" of how to maximise convictions of the guilty at the same time as maximising the acquittal of the innocent' (Feest and Murayama 2000)? What would it mean to shift our focus from 'taking or leaving' single elements of other systems in favour of a broader effort to rethink practices as a whole in the light of how things are done elsewhere (Hodgson 2000)?

The search to find convincing, plausible interpretations of systems of criminal justice at the level of the nation state, as in accounts of 'Japanese criminal justice' or descriptions of 'French criminal procedure', continues to be an ambition of comparative researchers. But, in an era of globalization, there is increasing recognition of the difficulties of drawing boundaries between systems of criminal justice. Many current changes in political systems and boundaries, such as those following the implosion of the ex-Soviet Union, or the menace posed by terrorist groups in some Islamic countries, are producing a different focus for research. Attempts to deal with a host of perceived international or transnational threats such as (amongst others) organized crime, terrorism, corruption, illegal dumping of waste, computer crime, money laundering, and tax evasion raise the problem of how far it is possible or advisable to harmonize different systems of criminal justice. The weakness of current national and international efforts to combat transnational crimes is no secret. Cultural differences, practical difficulties, and political factors (including turning a blind eye, or even colluding with crime) inhibit collaboration between states (Nelken 2002d).

Globalization is a name for complex and contradictory developments. It should not be reduced simply to the opportunities it opens up for organized crime or for terrorism (Nelken 1997c, 2003b). It also leads to greater borrowing of models of criminal justice, as well as to processes of ideological homogenization that help produce more world-wide fear of 'ordinary crimes' such as mugging or burglary. Neither should we underestimate the significance of the International Courts dealing with war crimes (with their mixed civil and common law criminal procedures), nor the way the line between crime and war has likewise been blurred by recent terrorist attacks and the response to them. It should be remembered, though, that even before the climactic events of September 2001, countries in the European Union, individually and collectively, had already developed a 'fortress' mentality, intent on finding ways to prevent an influx of immigrants from less economically-favoured countries. In sum, students of comparative criminal justice need to be concerned not only with the growth of transnational crimes, but also with the implications of transnational policing (Nelken 1997c, 2003b; Sheptycki 1995).

In the realm of criminal justice, moreover, many of the phenomena allegedly connected to globalization have a long history. It is enough to think of the spread of Beccaria's ideas about punishment, or the flurry of international exchange visits in the nineteenth century to compare styles of prison building. Thus an important issue for policy in many societies involves deciding when and how to borrow foreign ideas and practices in criminal justice, and which ones are likely to be most appropriate. It is tempting to judge the likely success of such legal 'transplants' or transfers in terms of their 'fit' to existing features of society and culture. But it should not be forgotten that in many cases legal transfers are as much about changing as about preserving existing patterns of society and culture. Some societies hope to transform their political and economic conditions through borrowing legal institutions from other societies, even if this aspiration may often have something 'magical' about it (Nelken 2001a, 2001b, 2001c, 2002a). Conversely, economically more developed societies can and do borrow ideas about criminal justice institutions, such as mediation and other forms of dispute processing, from less economically-developed societies. Comparative lawyers argue that the choice of what to borrow (where there is a choice about this) depends as much on the acceptability and prestige or the source of the borrowing as it does on the likelihood of the new institution matching its new context. Social scientists have hardly begun to develop their theories about such matters.

ON METHODS OF COMPARATIVE RESEARCH

In the past, a common but unsatisfactory way of trying to reach out to the experience of other systems was by what can be called 'comparison by juxtaposition'. The resulting texts, whether produced by one hand or many hands, often had the merits of

offering careful accounts of different systems of criminal justice in their legal, historical, and political settings. But they rarely brought into sharp enough focus what such
comparisons were designed to achieve. The standard textbooks in comparative criminal justice still tend to base themselves directly or indirectly on national reports from
'experts' in different countries, rather than asking contributors to address the assumptions which lie behind their descriptions and interpretations—and this is in any case a
difficult matter to do without the experience of collaboration. Merely juxtaposing
descriptions of various aspects of the criminal process in different cultures does little
to advance the goal of explanation or understanding, and provides an unsound basis
for policy-making. It even begs too many questions simply to assume that the
Anglo-American idea of 'criminal justice', conceived as a series of interconnected
decisions by decision-makers, exists as such in other cultures. Our guiding problem
must be: how can we be sure that we are comparing 'like with like', both in terms of
the distinctive elements of the criminal process and in terms of its place in the larger
culture?

Many US textbooks aimed at undergraduates set out to provide summary descriptions of a large variety of national systems. But these accounts are often out of date,
and are usually much less well-informed about the 'law in action' than about the 'law
in books'. Even in the better texts the urge to classify, as in so much work by comparative lawyers, often stands in for a concern to explain or understand. The organizing
typologies chosen, framed in terms of alternatives such as justice or welfare, or crime
control versus due process, too easily present American dilemmas as if they were
cultural universals (Reichel 1999). The American literature is also patchy, revealing
deeper knowledge of Japanese criminal justice practices than of those in Europe (or
elsewhere). But increasingly, English language writing about criminal justice, crime
prevention, and criminology in European Union countries and elsewhere is slowly
becoming available (see, for example, Crawford 1998: chapter 7; Downes 1988;
Harding et al. 1995; Findlay and Zvekic 1992; Fionda 1995; Heidensohn and Farrell
1991; King 1989; Muncie and Sparks 1991; Ruggiero et al. 1995; Ruggiero et al. 1998;
Vagg 1994; Van Swaaningen 1998, 1999). Historically informed comparisons of
criminal justice systems offer important background knowledge (Mawby 1990).
Comparative interview data (Hamilton and Sanders 1992) and international self-report
or victim surveys (e.g., Junger Tass 1994; Van Dyke 2000) provide information about
those on the receiving end of criminal justice agencies. There are even valuable attempts
to pool knowledge from all the above sources, as well as to relate to it the challenges
posed by transnational crimes (Newman 1999). Collections in other languages (e.g.,
Robert and Van Outrive 1993) should not be overlooked, and where possible studies in
the local language of the culture concerned should always be consulted.

With rare exceptions, however, most texts about comparative criminal justice contain relatively little about the actual process of doing cross-cultural research in criminal justice. At best this question is addressed by the editors rather than by the
contributors themselves (e.g., Cole et al. 1995; Fields and Moore 1996; Heiland,
Shelley, and Katoh 1992). There is never only one ideal research method, and choice of
method is inseparably linked to the objectives being pursued. But the point to note
here is how often the questions posed in comparative work are more ambitious than

the methodologies adopted. It is one thing for 'Anglo-American' comparative scholars to enquire obsessively whether the Continental instructing judge really does control the action of the police, hoping in this way to find a solution to their own unresolved problem of police discretion (Frase 1990). It is another matter if the comparativist is tempted by explanatory questions such as 'could there be a relationship between the mildness or severity of a penal climate and an inquisitorial or an accusatorial system of justice?' (Fennell *et al.* 1995: xvi); it is interesting that Fennell *et al.* then add immediately afterwards 'or is the question absurd'. Methodological issues loom still larger when comparative enquiries seek to tackle fundamental problems such as 'how do different societies conceive "disorder"?', how do 'differences in social, political, and legal culture inform perceptions of crime and the role of criminal agencies in responding to it?', or 'what factors underlie the salience of law and order as a political issue?' (Zedner 1996). Only long and intimate familiarity with a society could even begin to unravel such complex puzzles.

How, then, are we to acquire sufficient knowledge of another culture for such purposes? Either we can rely mainly on cooperation with foreign experts, or we can go abroad to interview legal officials and others, or we can draw on our direct experience of living and working in the country concerned. These three possible strategies I have elsewhere dubbed as 'virtually there', 'researching there', or 'living there' (Nelken 2000a).

The first of these methods allows for a variety of focused forms of international collaboration in comparative research. Feest and Murayama, for example, describe the result of a 'thought experiment' which starts from a careful description of the actual case of an American student arrested and tried in Spain on a false charge of participating in an illegal squatting demonstration. The authors then discuss what would have been the likely outcome given the same sequence of events in Germany and Japan, the countries whose criminal justice systems they know best (Feest and Murayama 2000). Other scholars set out to explain past and possible future trajectories in various aspects of the work of police, courts, or prisons. Thus Field and Brants ask how different jurisdictions have responded to the rise of covert and proactive policing— and why (Field and Brants 2000). These authors are constantly worried about the dangers of not comparing like with like, and they draw attention to the continuing difficulties of reaching shared meanings between experts in different legal cultures even after long experience of cooperation. Such collaboration, they say, requires a high degree of mutual trust and involves 'negotiating' mutually acceptable descriptions of legal practice in each of their home countries. The lesson they seek to drive home is that correct interpretation of even the smallest detail of criminal justice organization requires sensitivity to 'broader institutional and ideological contexts'.

Given these difficulties it is not suprising to find that many scholars advocate going to the research site in person. Immersion in another social context gives the researcher invaluable opportunities to become more directly involved in the experience of cultural translation. On the basis of his regular visits to France, Crawford, for example, offers a sophisticated reading of the contrasting meanings of mediation in two different settings (Crawford 2000). In France the move to introduce mediation can be seen as part of a project of 'bringing law to the people' both by making the criminal justice response more immediate in time and also by subtly transforming its referent. But it is not about involving the 'community' in the actual delivery of criminal justice. For this conception of the 'community' has a meaning and appeal which is strongly tied to the Anglo-American type of political and social order. In France it has historically been the role of the state to represent the larger community, and its social institutions have it as their fundamental task to lead those who are not yet part of the *polis* into becoming *bona fide* French citizens. 'Researching there' also provides the chance for 'open-ended' enquiry which can lead to the discovery of new questions and new findings about the 'law in action'. Some things are never written down because they belong to 'craft rules of thumb'. Other matters are considered secrets which should not be written down, for example, because theory and practice do not coincide, and so on (Hodgson 2000).

Short research visits, however, usually involve considerable reliance on local experts and practitioners. Indeed obtaining their views is very often the whole point of the exercise. But care must be taken in drawing on such insiders as the direct or indirect source of claims about other cultures. Who count as experts, and how do *they* know? What are the similarities and differences between academics and practitioners? If experts and practitioners are in agreement, could this be because experts themselves get their information from practitioners? In all cultures descriptions of social and legal ideas carry political implications, in some cases even issuing directly from particular political or social philosophies. When we think of experts in own culture we will normally, without much difficulty, be able to associate them with 'standing' for given political or policy positions. But what about this factor when we rely on experts from abroad? In much of the comparative criminal justice literature there seems to be little recognition, and less discussion, of the extent to which those describing the aims or results of local legal practices or reforms are themselves *part* of the context they are describing, in the sense of being partial to one position rather than another. In Italy, for example, some academics and practitioners are notoriously pro-judges, others are anti-judges. In France some commentators are strongly against importing ideas from the common law world, others are less antagonistic. It can be misleading to rely on the opinions or work of members of different camps without making allowance for this fact.

Moreover, cultural variability means that the problem faced here is not always the same. There are some cultures (Italy and Latin America, for example) where many consider it quite appropriate for academics—and even for judges and prosecutors—to identify and to be identified as members of a faction. In playing the role of what Gramsci called an 'organic intellectual' your prime duty is understood, both by your allies and by your opponents, to be the furtherance of a specific group ideal. In consequence, in such societies the question of social and political affiliation is one of the first questions raised (even if not always openly) in considering the point and validity of academic criticisms of current practices and of corresponding proposals for reform. In other cultures, however, the approved practice is to do one's best to avoid such identification. In some cases this just makes the process of establishing affiliation more elusive. Alternatively, the extent of political consensus, or of admiration for allegedly neutral criteria based on 'results' or 'efficiency', may be such that academics are indeed less pressed to take sides. Or intellectuals may simply count for less politically! The point again is that without knowledge about their affiliations, and an understanding of role responsibilities in the culture under investigation, it can be hard to know what credit to give to the arguments of any expert about criminal justice.

Even if we assume that our sources are not 'partial' (or, better still, if we try to make proper allowance for this) there still remains the problem that experts and practitioners are undoubtedly part of their own culture. This is after all why we consult them. But this also means that they do not necessarily ask or answer questions based on where the researcher is 'coming from' (and may not even have the basis for understanding such questions). In a multitude of ways both their descriptions and their criticisms will also belong to their culture. In Italy, a principled but inefficient system will regularly be attacked by local commentators on grounds of principle; in England and Wales, a system highly influenced by managerial considerations will be criticized for its remaining inefficiencies.

Longer-term involvement in another culture does offer, amongst other things, a better route to grasping the intellectual and political affiliations of insiders. Through everyday experience of another culture, 'observant participation' (Nelken 2000a), rather than merely 'participation observation' in a given research site, the researcher can begin to fill in the 'taken-for-granted' background to natives' views and actions. Direct experience and involvement with what is being studied can also help give the researcher's accounts the credibility that comes from 'being there'. But actually moving to a research site—for shorter or longer periods—does not guarantee that the researcher comes to see things as a native. Our 'starting points' (Nelken 2000b) play a vital role in what we set out to discover. Our own cultural assumptions continue to shape the questions we ask or the answers we find convincing. Much of the voluminous American research on the specificity of Japanese criminal justice, for example, can be criticized for seeking to explain what is distinctive about Japanese legal culture in contrast to familiar American models without recognizing how much it derived from the civil law systems of Continental Europe from which Japan borrowed.

Similarities and differences come to life for an observer when they are exemplified by 'significant absences' in relation to past experience. A good example is provided by Lacey's and Zedner's discussion of the lack of any reference to 'community' in discourse about crime prevention in Germany (Lacey and Zedner 1995, 1998). But the vital question of starting points is often left begging, especially in research based on short visits, because of the implicit collusion between the writer and her audience which *privileges what the audience wants to know as if it is what it should want to know*. The long-stay researcher, by contrast, is engaged in a process of being slowly re-socialized. He or she will increasingly want to re-formulate the questions others back home wish to address to the foreign setting. As important, he or she may even begin to doubt whether they ever really understood their own culture of origin. The comparative researcher, like Simmels' 'stranger', is thus *obliged* to move between worlds, never entirely 'at home' in either (cf. S. Roberts 1998). Sometimes the researcher will try to see things like a native insider, at other times he or she will try to do 'better' than the natives. The ability to look at a culture with new eyes is, after all, the great strength of any outsider.

This said, the heavy investment required by 'observant participation', or by sustained ethnography, may not always be necessary or feasible. The choice to follow any particular approach to data-gathering is linked to the many considerations which influence the feasibility of a given research project; not least the time available, whether one is able to visit the country concerned, and with what sort of commitment. Depending on its purposes, collaboration with experts or a limited period of interviewing abroad may even have some advantages as compared with living and working in a country. There are the usual trade-offs amongst methodologies. It is possible to cover a large number of cases with questionnaires or interviews only by dispensing with in-depth observation. And the short-termer can also pretend to a useful naivety which the long-term researcher must abandon, since that is part of what it means to become an insider/outsider. In practice, even the insider/outsider or 'observant participant' cannot possibly experience everything at first hand. So all three approaches have to face, to some extent, similar problems in knowing who to trust, and then conveying credibility. However findings are (re)presented, they are always in large part the result of interviews and consultation of experts and practitioners, and the resident scholar may often obtain these in ways which are less systematic and representative than those followed by the other approaches. The main advantage of 'full immersion' in another society for this purpose is that enquiry becomes more fruitful when you have enough cultural background to identify the right questions to ask. But there may be more than one way of acquiring such background.

APPROACHES TO COMPARISON

Within the social sciences, some argue that *all* sociological research is inherently comparative. The aim is always the same: the explanation of 'variation' (Feeley 1997). But explicitly comparative work does have to face special difficulties. These range from the technical, conceptual, and linguistic problems posed by the unreliability of statistics, lack of appropriate data, meaning of foreign terms, etc., to the complications of understanding the differences in other languages, practices, and world views which make it difficult to know whether we are comparing like with like. Indeed often it is that which becomes the research task. Others claim that for these and other reasons comparative work is near impossible. Legrand, for example, argues that what he calls 'legal epistemes' are incommensurable and certainly never the same matter for those who have been socialized in the culture being studied and those who are merely researching into it (Legrand 2001; but see Nelken 2002c). Cain, who prefers a form of active collaboration with the subjects of her research, insists that comparison faces the allegedly unavoidable dangers of 'occidentalism'—thinking that other societies are necessarily like ours—or 'orientalism'—assuming that they are inherently different from us. Her advice is to 'avoid comparison, for it implies a lurking occidentalist standard and user, and focuses on static and dyadic rather than dynamic and complex relations' (Cain 2000b: 258).

These reservations about comparison are given added point by the current processes of globalization. In a globalized world there is no archimedian point of comparison from which to understand distinct nations or traditions. Within anthropology the process of producing accounts of other cultures has become increasingly contested (Clifford and Marcus 1986). The very idea of 'culture' becomes highly problematic, no more than a label to be manipulated by elements within the culture concerned or by outside observers (Kuper 1999). Cultures are influenced by global flows and trends; the purported uniformity, coherence, or stability of given national cultures will often be no more than ideological projection or rhetorical device. The links between societies and individuals have been so extended and transformed that it makes little sense to look for independent legal cultures. Hence 'all totalising accounts of society, tradition and culture are exclusionary and enact a social violence by suppressing contingent and continually emergent differences' (Coombe 2000).

For all this, however, at any given time there continue to be important and systematic differences in criminal justice, whether this be regarding the relationship between law and politics, the role of legal and lay actors, levels of leniency, degrees of delay, and so on (Nelken 2002b, 2003a). And most scholars (including the above authors!) continue to offer competing proposals for which approach to comparison to adopt. Typically, disagreements over the right way to approach comparative criminology and criminal justice play themselves out with regard to a series of interconnected (though not necessarily isomorphic) dichotomies. To some extent choices must be made between searching for explanation or for other forms of understanding, emphasizing similarities or differences, giving attention to the specificities of local culture or noting the effects of globalization, cultivating elegant theorizing or practical knowledge.

My argument in this chapter is that it is important to be alive to these differences but a mistake to use the challenges of comparative research merely as occasions for 're-enacting' theoretical battles. Different approaches to comparative work may be more or less useful for achieving the various possible goals of comparative research indicated at the outset. We may want to distinguish, for example, between research that sets out:

1. to test and validate explanatory theories of crime or social control (which we may, at some risk of oversimplification, call the approach of 'behavioural science' or 'positivist sociology');

2. to show how the meaning of crime and criminal justice is embedded within changing, local and international, historical and cultural contexts (an approach which we will call 'interpretivist');

3. to classify and learn from the rules, ideals, and practice of criminal justice in other jurisdictions (which we can call the approach followed by 'legal comparativists' and 'policy researchers').

I shall say something more about each of these approaches and then suggest how (and how far) their strengths may be combined.

Even amongst behavioural scientists there are different points of view about the role of comparative work. For some writers, taking the model of science seriously means that comparative work must show that cultural variability is as irrelevant to social laws as it is to physical laws. Gottfredson and Hirschi argue that failure to recognize this has meant that up until now 'cross national research has literally not known what it was looking for and its contributions have rightfully been more or less ignored' (Gottfredson and Hirschi 1990: 179). Some of the most influential American explanations of crime, such as Merton's *anomie* theory and Cohen's sub-cultural theory of delinquency, do seem almost deliberately ethnocentric in the sense that the explanation is designed to fit variables found in American society. Yet *anomie* theory was first developed in France, and only afterwards was it reworked in the United States with particular reference to the American dream of egalitarianism and the cultural emphasis on success as measured in money. It has since been applied with advantage in very different cultural contexts; for example, in Italy to explain the growth of political corruption in the 1980s (Magatti 1996), and in Japan to account for the relative lack of crime there (Miyazawa 1997). Is the same theory being employed? How and why does this matter?

For Gottfredson and Hirschi the fact that Cohen's account of the frustrations of American lower-class children is hardly likely to be applicable to the genesis of delinquency in an African or Indian slum, spells its doom. Rather than assume that every culture will have its own crime with its own unique causes, which need to be sought in all their specificity, the object of criminological theorizing must be to transcend cultural diversity in order to arrive at genuine scientific statements (Gottfredson and Hirschi 1990: 172–3). In this search for a universal criminology Gottfredson and Hirschi define crimes as 'acts of force or fraud undertaken in pursuit of self interest'. For them, different cultural settings cannot influence the causes of crime except by affecting the opportunities and the ease with which crimes can occur. They are therefore comforted by apparent cross-cultural consistency in correlations between crime involvement and age and sex differences, urban–rural differences, and indices of family stability. A similar approach is—or could be—followed by those scholars who seek to establish general laws about judicial institutions. Shapiro's classic study of appeal courts sets out to demonstrate that higher courts always function primarily as agents of social control, whatever other political and legal differences may characterize the systems in which they are found, and whatever other legitimating ideologies they may themselves employ (Shapiro 1981). Gottfredson and Hirschi, however, just *assume* that the agencies which apply criminal law have the universal task of reminding people both of their own long-term interests and of those of other people.

Cain seems to give credit to the universalizing approach of Hirschi and Gottfredson, even when criticizing their substantive claims (Cain 2000a). Drawing on her long-term research in the West Indies, she complains that standard criminological textbooks (which are also used in the West Indies) wrongly present the alleged relationship between youth and crime as if it were a cultural universal. But it is not clear whether her point is that Western criminology has got it wrong, or merely that it is wrong for the West Indies. If it is the first, by seeking to demonstrate that Gottfredson and Hirschi have proposed a *falsely universal* claim Cain's critique presupposes the universalizability of criminology. Other authors suggest that comparative research actually undermines the possibility of scientific criminology by showing how the same causes can have opposite effects in different contexts (Ruggiero 2000). But the fact that given variables do not hold true universally does not undermine the positivist approach to explanation. We would not necessarily want to doubt the influence of inequality on crime in Britain just because this correlation may not hold true also in India or Africa. Cain's findings about the relationship between age and crime in the West Indies would be welcomed by many positivist criminologists in the same way that they are interested in evidence that the relationship between single families and crime patterns is different in Northern and Southern Europe, or in the finding that, whatever happens elsewhere, in Switzerland at least school failure is not correlated with criminality.

Most behavioural scientists are less concerned than Gottfredson and Hirschi with finding cultural universals. Some, it is true, do place their emphasis on displaying underlying, unexpected similarities. Setting out to demonstrate that all higher courts play an essential and less than independent role in ensuring governmental social control becomes a provocative argument if the cultures surveyed are as different as Muslim, Chinese, French, and British (Shapiro 1981). Likewise, there are intriguing implications for criminal justice in the evidence being gathered by Feeley, which suggests that all across Europe in the late eighteenth century there was apparently a precipitous decline in the proportion of women in the criminal statistics. But many behavioural scientists simply see comparative work as offering special opportunities to enlarge the range of variables to use in explanations of crime or criminal justice. What matters is the *implicit* generalizability of the variables, not whether they actually do apply universally. For theories which link crime and industrialization, for example, it is strategically important to investigate apparent counter-instances such as Switzerland (Clinard 1978) or Japan (Miyazawa 1997), both so as to test existing hypotheses and to uncover new ones. Similarly, we can ask about variations in the patterns of policing, courts, or prisons in terms of the patterns found in different cultures or historical periods. If the Dutch prison-rate could, at least until recently, be kept so much lower than that of other countries in Europe, this is important not only because it shows that there is no inevitable connection between crime rates and prison rates but also because it challenges us to look for the particular variables that explain the Dutch case (Downes 1988).

On the other hand, many scholars of comparative criminal justice are more fascinated by difference than by similarity. But the point of compiling differences, apart from its value as description or in correcting ethnocentrism, is not always made as clear as it might be. Certainly, the assumption that all economically-advanced countries would be expected to have exactly similar ideas and practices for dealing with crime seems far-fetched. What then is a difference? And when does a difference make a difference? It is here that the interpretivist approach(es) to comparative criminal justice come into play. Such approaches seek to uncover the inner meaning of the facts which positivist social scientists take as the starting or finishing points of their comparisons. The strength of the interpretivist approach is the way it recognizes that data such as crime or prosecution statistics used in behavioural science explanations are themselves cultural products the interpretation of which requires considerable preliminary knowledge of the society concerned. Even the technical definition of crime varies between legal systems, so that in Japan, for example, assaults that result in death are classified as assault, not murder; and in Greece the definition of 'rape' includes lewdness, sodomy, seduction of a child, incest, prostitution, and procuring (Kalish 1988). Less obviously, there is considerable variation in the stress which legislatures, justice agencies, or the media put on responding to different sorts of behaviour as crime. In Germany or Italy, until recently, the police and the mass media kept a remarkably low profile regarding most street crime or burglary, at least by British or American standards (Zedner 1995; Nelken 2000b).

It would be wrong to take too extreme a stand on the idea of crime as a cultural construction. This could lead to a relativism by which comparative criminology would become implausible (Beirne 1983), and this could be simply countered by the argument that if understanding 'the other' was really that difficult then even social science research into different social worlds at home would be impossible (Leavitt 1990). As noted, criminal justice cultures are in any case less and less sealed off from each other for them not to have some common language in which to express their concerns. Far from being relativist, the interpretivist approach in fact actually presupposes the possibility of producing cross-cultural comparisons, even if it does seek to display difference more than demonstrate similarity.

The search for difference only really becomes interesting when the attempt is made to show how differences in criminal justice are linked to other differences (e.g., in types of political culture). If the positivist approach operationalizes 'culture' (or deliberately simplified aspects of it) to explain variation in levels and types of crime and social control, this second approach tends more to use crime and criminal justice as themselves an 'index' of culture. Grasping the 'other' requires the willingness to put our assumptions in question: the more so the greater the cultural distance. Some of the most exciting current work in comparative criminal justice sets out to interpret what is distinctive in the practice and discourse of a given system of criminal justice by drawing an explicit or implicit contrast with another system, usually that of the scholar's culture of origin (e.g., Crawford 1996; Zedner 1995). In an important study, Whitman seeks to explain the relative harshness of the treatment of criminals in the USA in comparison to that reserved for them in the countries of Continental Europe. His argument is that whereas France and Germany 'levelled up' their treatment of criminals, on the basis of long-standing more respectful treatment for higher status prisoners, in America criminals suffered from a general levelling-down process which presupposed status equality (Whitman forthcoming).

But interpretative approaches are not without their own problems (Nelken 1995a). One difficulty is knowing who or what can speak for the culture (especially when matters are controversial). Very different results will be obtained by analysing texts and documents, testing public attitudes, or relying on selected informants such as criminologists or public officials: the drawbacks of exclusive reliance on these last sources have already been discussed. Because the interpretative approach is so labour-intensive it does not allow for large-scale, cross-cultural comparison. Much therefore depends on which other system is taken as the yardstick of comparison—and how this is to be justified. Taking criminal justice discourse in England as our starting point may reveal that France works with one model of 'mediation' whereas we have several (Crawford 2000). If we compare England with Germany, on the other hand, we may find that Germany seems to have several ideas of 'community' where we have just one (Lacey and Zedner 1995, 1998). But what exactly is the significance of such findings?

Care also needs to be taken in assuming that a given feature of the practice or discourse of criminal justice necessarily indexes, or 'resonates' with, the rest of a culture. Specific ideals and values of criminal justice may not always be widely diffused in the culture. In many societies there is a wide gulf between legal and general culture, as where the criminal law purports to maintain principles of impersonal equality before the law in polities where clientilistic and other particularistic practices are widespread. It is also not easy to get the balance right between identifying relatively enduring features as compared to contingent aspects of other cultures. Relying on ideas of national character would make it difficult to reconcile the defiance of law in Weimar Germany as compared to the over-deference to law of the Fascist period. What are taken to be entrenched cultural practices in the sphere of criminal justice can be overturned with remarkable rapidity. The Dutch penal system was rightly celebrated for its 'tolerance', from the 1960s on, keeping its proportionate prison population well below that of its European neighbours (Downes 1988). But shortly after gaining such praise, the criminal justice elite who pioneered the 'Utrecht' approach were sidelined by the pressures of gaining popular political consensus in the face of Holland's growing drug problem (Downes 1996). Holland engaged in a massive programme of prison building which took it back towards the levels of the 1950s, a period when its relative level of incarceration was comparable to the rest of Europe.

The third approach, that followed by comparativists, is particularly sensitive to the fact that criminal justice and procedure will often not 'mirror' wider features of social structure and culture. This is explained as the consequence of the extent to which they have been shaped by processes of borrowing, imitation, or imposition from elsewhere. The approach's historico-legal classifications of systems in terms of families is a poor starting point for socio-legal research; but it does provides some corrective to explanations which start and finish with the nation state. Another advantages lies in the way its language and concerns connect directly to those used by many of the legal actors themselves whose behaviour is being interpreted (Nelken 1995b). It must be relevant to pay attention to rules and ideals to which actors are obliged at least to pay lip-service but which they may well take as guides for much of the time. The evolution of the discourse used by criminal justice actors may also be better understood, even for sociological purposes, when related to its own forms rather than simply translated into sociological language.

Research carried out by comparative lawyers is sufficiently different from comparative social science for both to have something to gain from the other's approach. Although comparative lawyers rely mainly on historical, philosophical, and juridical analyses they are well aware that legal and other rules are not always applied in practice, and that legal outcomes do not necessarily turn out as planned. But the sociological significance of such evidence is usually ignored in favour of processing it normatively, as an example of deviance or 'failure', to which the solution is typically a (further) change in the law. The weaknesses of this approach, which are the converse of its strengths, thus come from its tendency to share rather than understand or criticize the self-understanding of the legal perspective. Because the terms it uses are legal and normative it will not capture many of the organizational or personal sources of action which shape what actors are trying to do, still less the influences of which actors are not aware.

Social scientists, on the other hand, are more interested in what does happen than in what should happen, looking beyond written rules and documents to the structures which shape the repeated patterns of everyday action. Their approach has the opposite drawbacks. The determination to take practice more seriously than protestations of ideals can sometimes lead to an underestimation of the role law plays in many cultures as a representation of values, including 'counterfactual' values (Van Swaaningen 1998, 1999) which are all the more important for not being tied to existing practice. And the importance given to the present, rather than to the past or future of law, can block an appreciation of law's character as a bearer of tradition which makes 'the past live in the present'.

Each of these three approaches to comparison tends to be associated, in its pure form, with a distinctive epistemology, respectively (predictive) explanation, 'understanding by translation', and categorization-evaluation. The standard way of deciding which approach to choose is to ask: are we trying to contribute to the development of explanatory social science, or to improve existing penal practice? Confusion, it is said, is caused by combining such different enterprises (Feeley 1997). Influential comparative sociologists recommend a division of labour in which the legal comparativists (with their strong interest in reform) stick to legal doctrine while the sociologist goes beyond this so as to explain the 'law in action' and other aspects of the 'legal infrastructure' which cannot be read out of legal texts (Blankenburg 1997; Nelken 1997b). While these recommendations do make sense, the danger of taking them too seriously is that social scientists can lose touch with rather than capture those nuances of legal culture which bring the comparative exercise to life. For effective comparison is as much a matter of good translation as it is of successful explanation. We may need, for example, to understand how and why 'diversion' from criminal justice is treated as intrinsic to the criminal process in Holland, but as somehow extrinsic to it in the UK (Brants and Field 2000). And this will require considerable historical, juridical, and linguistic analysis.

In practice these three approaches are rarely found in their pure form. Sociologists—especially those interested in legal culture and ideology—need to know about law and legal procedures (and sometimes get it wrong); comparative lawyers often make sociologically questionable assumptions about what a system is trying to do and how it actually operates. Debates within, as well as between, comparative law and sociological criminology turn on mixed questions of explanation and evaluation, so that it is not the choice of one or other of these aims which guarantees either insight or confusion. Within the field of comparative law, Goldstein and Marcus, who reported that there was little America could learn from Europe in order to reform its pre-trial procedures, used sociological-type arguments based on the attempt to see how the rules actually worked in practice (Goldstein and Marcus 1977). But those who claimed that this understanding of Continental procedure was superficial were able to show how the very desire for generalizable explanation reinforced American ethnocentrism (Langbein and Weinberg 1978). On the other hand, Downes's sociological study of the role of prosecutors in keeping down prison rates in Holland clearly had a practical purpose aimed at changing the situation in Britain, but it was not (or at least not for that reason) unsuccessful in illuminating the Dutch situation.

Key conceptual building blocks for comparing criminal justice, such as the term 'legal culture' (Nelken 1997a), figure in each of the three approaches even if they are often employed with competing meanings. Another heuristic idea, used both by social scientists and by comparative lawyers, is that of 'functional equivalence'. One comparative law textbook tells us to assume that other societies will often meet a given legal 'problem' by using unfamiliar types of law and legal techniques (Zweigert and Kotz 1987). Likewise, Feest and Murayama, in their study of criminal justice in Spain, Germany, and Japan, demonstrate that each jurisdiction has some (but not necessarily the same) crucial pre-trial and post-trial filters to distinguish the innocent from the guilty, while others are more formalistic and typically presuppose that the required critical attention has or will be given at another stage. They come close to suggesting that there are 'functional equivalents' in each system for legitimizing even unsound cases of police arrests, and that systems 'self correct' to reach rather similar outcomes (Feest and Murayama 2000).

But assumptions of functional equivalence can also be misleading. At a minimum we shall also need to extend our analysis to the role of non-legal institutions, alternatives to law, and competing professional expertises as well as to other groupings within civil society such as the family or patron–client networks. Moreover, in some cultures, some problems may simply find no 'solution'—especially, but not only, if the 'problem' is not perceived as such. Cultures have the power to produce relatively circular definitions of what is worth fighting for and against, and their institutions and practices can express genuinely different histories and distinct priorities (Nelken 1996c). Often matters are 'problematized' only when a society is exposed to the definition used elsewhere. In the 1980s, for example, the appearance of league tables of relative levels of incarceration may have induced Finland to move towards the norm by reducing its prison population—and apparently influenced Italy to do the opposite!

THE CONTROL OF PROSECUTION DISCRETION IN ITALY: A CASE STUDY

If the short-cut of functional equivalents may sometimes lead us astray we shall need to find other ways of drawing on the indications offered by these different approaches so as to guide us towards our goals. The following case study discusses the constitutionally entrenched rule regarding mandatory prosecution in Italy. This is a rule which purports to limit prosecution discretion so tightly that unjustifiable failure to prosecute is itself a ground for prosecution! I shall seek to draw on all three of the approaches to comparative research described so far in order to resolve the following puzzle. How can this rule, which in comparative terms is so strict in limiting prosecutor's autonomy, have allowed, and even helped, Italian prosecutors to achieve their remarkable recent successes in driving from power the entire class of governing politicians (Nelken 1996a, 1996b, 1997d)?

From a theoretical point of view the question is of interest because it requires us not merely to study the ways the 'law in action' differs from the 'law in books', but also how and why rules which require what surely must be considered a sociological impossibility (given the limits on prosecution resources) are nonetheless enacted and maintained. A better understanding of the criminal process in Italy is also of some practical interest because its procedures represent, on paper, an extreme version of the 'legality principle' characteristic of many Continental European countries. This alternative method of controlling the rectitude of the pre-trial process, as compared to the safeguards employed in Anglo-American systems, has for many years been a central topic of enquiry for comparative law scholars of criminal justice. It was looked into— and once again rejected—by the Royal Commission on Criminal Justice in the UK (Leigh and Zedner 1992), though they considered the procedures in France and Germany only.

The aptness of this example for present purposes can best be seen, however, from the difficulty of describing the research task here. When I first talked about researching prosecution *discretion* in comparative perspective, this immediately drew the harsh criticism from some scholars that this could not possibly provide a sound basis for sociological work across cultures. As Feest put it, in commenting on the initial presentation of this research, 'if the term "discretion" is used in a technical-legal way then it is not translatable to begin with. But if it is used in a non-technical way then it has the disadvantage of being identical with a technical-juridical term of the English language which makes it confusing, at least to non English speakers' (Feest 1996). His proposed solution, in line with one of the standard approaches I have described, would be to look for a more universal sociological language for conducting such investigations, by talking about 'decision-making', or 'the power to define deviant conduct'. As he argues, sociological terms such as 'social control' or 'total institutions' have proved their worth in the sociology of deviance despite not being part of anyone's everyday language—or rather just for this very reason. Feest's argument rightly highlights the difficulties of doing comparative research into discretion, though the issue probably goes beyond the question of comparative methodology (thus some sociologists claim that any investigation of discretion is futile because official behaviour is socially rather than legally rule-governed; see Baumgartner 1990). But I remain convinced that attempting to study prosecution *decision-making* while avoiding using the term *discretion* risks jettisoning the baby with the bath water. The problem is rather how best to illuminate one in the light of the other.

How can we explain the mandatory rule of prosecution in Italy, and what is there about it to explain? We could ask how the rule got to be what it is—noting, for instance, how it emerged in the immediate post-Second World War period when it was unclear to the political parties who would be in command in the Ministry of Justice and who the use of discretion might therefore favour. We might then also trace how later developments have taken Italy increasingly further from the patterns found in the rest of Continental Europe (Guarnieri 1993, 1997). Beyond this, however, if we are interested in making sense of their decision-making behaviour we will want to explore what Italian prosecutors actually do in their everyday work, how this fits into the system as a whole, and how all this is affected by the mandatory rule regulating their discretion.

One strategy we could follow would be to assume that all criminal justice systems of a certain complexity must face similar operational problems of coping with overload and the efficient throughput of cases. Certainly, the Italian criminal justice system faces similar, or even worse, problems of management to other comparable systems. The criminal law has enormous reach and is expected to deal with many matters which in Anglo-American systems are dealt with by civil law, or administrative bodies, or even political machinery. In addition to ordinary crime, the criminal courts are expected to process high levels of regulatory contraventions, fiscal crimes, administrative malpractice, white collar and organized crimes. A function of legally permitted discretionary decision-making is that it makes it easier to manage problems of priorities: we would therefore expect to find that where prosecution discretion is heavily restricted there would be 'functional equivalents' to discretion, either or both in the prosecutor's office and elsewhere in the system.

We can in fact identify numerous features of the Italian criminal process which do provide the chance to filter out cases or exercise priorities even in a regime of legally mandated prosecution. The threshold decision whether there is enough evidence to take a case to trial, or whether instead to opt for what is called *archiviazione*, does provide or require opportunity for exercise of choice. In practice, some heavy dossiers—the fruit of months, or even years, of preliminary investigation—can end up simply being disposed of in this way. A good example concerns the proceedings started with reference to *Gladio*. This was an allegedly illegal, underground, post-Second World War military organization created by the Italian secret service, with CIA finance. Though purportedly set up to repel external invasion, the allegations made were that it was really secretly intended to deal with the threat that the Italian Communist Party might come legally to power. The fact that the case was dismissed through *archiviazione* says more about the political sensitivity of these proceedings than about the lack of evidence for a trial. More prosaically, Italy also uses methods comparable to the Prosecutor fine in France and Germany to deal with less serious offences.

Discretion also comes in elsewhere. Decision-making in other parts of the criminal justice system is always somehow much less controversial than the actual decision to prosecute. There is virtually no questioning of what Anglo-American writers call low-visibility operational police discretion; the so-called 'judicial' police are just presumed to be following the prosecutors' instructions, or to be acting in an executive rather than judicial capacity. Nor is there much agonizing over judicial sentencing. Avoidance of punishment is made possible through the use of difficult to meet prescription periods; post-sentence flexibility through government amnesties, pardons, and the institution of *condono*. More generally, the interpretation and application of rules of evidence, both in pre-trial and sentencing decision-making, in code-based systems without binding precedents, provide considerable scope for interpretative disagreement. Another sort of (somewhat random) flexibility is provided by competing and overlapping jurisdictions of types of law and courts, multiple supreme courts, and the three stages of trial. Not all of this is likely to be labelled as 'discretion', and rightly so. But, as Feest notes, for the sociologist it is important to discover how flexibility is built into the system and not merely how it is labelled.

But we should be cautious in going too far in searching for 'functional equivalents' in Italy, as if every system is predestined to reach a certain level of efficiency. Even if we stay with functional language, it is not easy to determine what is functional and for whom. Some left-wing prosecutors believe the courts are left dealing with an overload of low-level regulatory and fiscal contraventions so as to keep them from pursuing more politically sensitive matters. Even apparently minimal functional operating requirements are not met. The apparently irrational distribution of courts around the country is explained mainly by political pressure not to lose the courthouse as a sign of local prestige. Formalities and complicated division or overlapping of responsibilities help produce enormous delays; some criminal cases can take up to ten years to go through all their stages; civil cases even longer; other administrative and other bureaucratic proceedings can take what the Italians call 'Biblical periods'. Italy has been regularly condemned for this by the Court of Human Rights at Strasbourg (Nelken 2003a). The language of functionalism is especially misleading if it suggests that all criminal justice systems operate with a managerial vision of their purposes. For this is itself a cultural variable.

The Italian criminal justice system thus has some functional equivalents of discretionary decision-making, though not necessarily where they would be found in other systems. But they do not always serve the same (or any?) function. The argument that the term 'discretion', unlike 'decision-making', does not have a common behavioural referent across cultures may also be correct. But then it is exactly this variability which needs exploring. Research into discretion is not just about explaining variation in similar phenomena amongst different cultures, but also about appreciating the variation in what each takes to be the phenomenon. If ideas about discretion are embedded in a specific political and cultural context, its significance depends on appreciating the role it plays in this wider context rather than just trying to extract its behavioural kernel in the actual decision-making behaviour of prosecutors. Research on discretion can, for example, be connected to the way attempts to control legal decision-making reflect and help constitute the trustworthiness attributed to different social actors (Bankowski and Nelken 1981; Nelken 1994b). And the lack of concern over police discretion in Italy may need to be explained not only by alleged functional requirements, but also by seeking to understand how, in Continental Europe, 'the idea of the administration of law belongs to a lower and more flexible order of things' (Goldstein and Marcus 1977: 281).

In each culture the meaning of discretion is coloured by its place in wider discourses. In Italy the term carries strong overtones of inevitable arbitrariness, favouritism, and potential corruption. Acknowledging discretion is seen as abandoning the 'impersonal' ideal of the state and its 'rule of law'. It is only by adhering strictly to this vision that a bulwark can be maintained against the pressures of a highly factionalized and personalized society, where the 'public interest' has little meaning and where many fear that legalizing the discretion to prosecute would lead to impossible pressures being placed on decision-makers. It is relevant that there are no exact linguistic (and conceptual) equivalents for terms like 'enforcement' or 'policy'; even the Italian word for 'compromise' carries pejorative overtones, and to be 'pragmatic' means lacking principle rather than representing the 'practical' British virtue of 'muddling through'. In Anglo-American political and legal discourse, by contrast, discretion carries overtones of potentially unruly decision-making which can be, and needs to be, exercised reasonably, and in the public interest. It can and must be kept within bounds by mechanisms of accountability. In Holland, to take yet another example, prosecutors direct away from trial well over 50 per cent of the cases that come before them. Here the use of the positively weighted term 'beleid' (Blankenburg 1994) reflects and underpins the faith in prosecutors' ability to exercise good judgement and act in ways which meet the public interest.

Even when we have gained a better sense of the larger context, we cannot dispense with careful examination of the way specific cultural definitions and debates about discretion interact with actual decision-making. Patterns of behaviour cannot simply be deduced from normative (legal and cultural) rules, but ignoring the contribution such rules make to shaping practical action means that we easily slip up on the banana skin of presumed functional equivalence. It may be, as Goldstein and Marcus argue, that the Continental 'principle of legality' has only limited influence over everyday police and prosecutor behaviour. It may even be something of a myth. But if we want to understand a culture, what could be more important than a myth?

In any case, the effects of the mandatory rule of prosecution in Italy are certainly not limited to the level of the symbolic. One illustration is provided by a newspaper account of a case which occurred in a small town in Central Italy. A man had separated from his first wife but the divorce had not finally come through (this is something that can take more than five years in Italy, though in this case it was apparently a matter of waiting weeks rather than months). In the meantime his new companion, with whom he had been living since his separation, was diagnosed as having an incurable cancer, and to give her some comfort in the days before she died he decided that they should get married. This exposed him to a prosecution for bigamy—which duly took place. From the news report it was impossible to tell whether there could have been some special reason for prosecution; the case was presented simply as one resulting from the rule of mandatory prosecution.

Research which does not rely only on newspaper reports also confirms that this rule can and does have effects at the everyday level—mainly by reinforcing bureaucratic formalism in the definition of the prosecutor's role. Obligatory prosecution goes hand in hand with other legal (and in-house) rules about how to deal with cases within set periods so as to avoid cases becoming time-bound. Thus one lower court prosecutor I interviewed decided that she wanted to establish some priority in the thousands of cases on her desk, most of which involved minor contraventions. Rather than merely limiting herself to classifying the legal strengths of the cases referred to her, and then passing them on down the line, she wanted to exercise judgement on their priority. In particular, she wanted to devote more time to the careful preparation of witnesses and technical evidence in the more serious cases of manslaughter connected with unsafe working conditions, and the industrial pollution cases, which she thought were otherwise likely to fail when they eventually came to trial some years later (perhaps in front of not particularly well-informed lawyers serving as deputy judges). But the head of her office refused to allow this and threatened her with disciplinary proceedings, or even legal action, if she allowed any of the thousands of minor cases on her desk to become time-bound.

The most remarkable consequences of the rule of mandatory prosecution, however, are not to be found in its effects on everyday routines but in the way, in certain historical moments, it can help to *increase* prosecutors' freedom to make politically crucial and sensitive decisions. To start with it is necessary to recall that in Italy, as in some other Continental European countries, prosecutors are part of the judicial profession and receive similar university-based training. But Italy stands out for the ease with which it is possible to move between these two somewhat different roles; both judges and prosecutors enjoy the same constitutional guarantees, the same automatic career progression, and the same self-governing body for matters of discipline. Thus the outstanding feature of Italian prosecutors and prosecution offices, as compared to other civil law countries, is their autonomy from hierarchical bureaucratic control (Guarnieiri 1993, 1997). They are not subject to instructions from the Ministry of Justice, and coordination of the different prosecution offices is rudimentary except where it is a case of dealing with organized crimes and terrorism.

With this guaranteed autonomy comes the possibility—in the right circumstances—of exercising *much more* freedom of choice than would be found in an Anglo-American system. In the 1970s, left-wing prosecutors, the so called 'judges of assault', consciously tried to use prosecution to improve worker safety and to attack pollution. In the 1990s, the target of some prosecutors' offices, above all that of the Milan pool of *Mani Pulite* prosecuting judges, was political corruption. Italy is a society formally governed by innumerable laws, many of which are in fact unenforced, or at least under-enforced. Hence a strategy of prosecution starting from small cases, or easy to prove crimes, such as illegal financing of political parties, or abuse of official duties, could be used as a lever, as in the *Tangentopoli* anti-corruption investigations, to remove from power many of those at the highest levels of society (Nelken 1996a, 1996b). The rule of mandatory prosecution acted as no bar to such heavily loaded decisions, provided only that there was some minimal evidence of a crime having been committed. If anything, it provided a marvellous shield to protect prosecutors against important political and business defendants who would otherwise certainly have insisted that it was not in the public interest that their cases be proceeded with. Paradoxically, therefore, a limit on discretion was ultimately transformed into the opposite.

What about the policy implications? For many observers *Tangentopoli* has magnificently underlined the value of the rule of mandatory prosecution in Italy. But, for others (especially those holding different political views), the events of these past years only demonstrate all too clearly how the rule helps to conceal the too-wide powers available to independent prosecutors. The fact that there is no way that such momentous prosecution initiatives can be institutionally regulated by those outside the judiciary, has for some time been a bane to those politicians and scholars critical of the present system who argue that Italy should be brought more in line with other civil law countries (Di Federico 1989). For them this means separating the careers of prosecutors and judges and (ultimately) returning the prosecutors to some form of effective, central, hierarchical control. This is very much the legislative programme that the current Berlusconi government will attempt to implement, though the rule of mandatory prosecution itself has not (yet) been put in question.

Being an 'observant participant' helped me to separate out some of the many layers of these events as well as to identify some of the interests and ideals being fought over. But it also drew me—if only very marginally—into becoming part of the events themselves. As an Anglo-American criminologist transplanted to Italy just as the *Tangentopoli* investigations took off, it mattered to insiders to discover—or decide— whether I was 'for' or 'against' the judges. After writing some articles about *Tangentopoli* for English-speaking readers, I wrote a chapter in Italian about it which I thought (and still think) was relatively pro the judges (Nelken 1997d). But any attempt to set *Tangentopoli* against the wider background of struggles for power between politicians and judges (in which rules such as that concerning mandatory prosecution become expedients) was enough to encourage the politicians under attack to seek whatever help they could get. Thus my chapter was praised in Parliament by a notoriously anti-judge deputy, which made me cringe with embarrassment. I refused an invitation from lawyers defending a businessman facing extradition from the States, who enquired whether I would act as an expert witness explaining to the American courts that the crimes uncovered by *Tangentopoli* should be considered 'political'. And I was interviewed on the foreign broadcasting station of Italian State Radio about whether I thought the judges had planned a *coup*—as had recently been sustained in a CIA/*Forza Italia*-authored book—and rather cut short the discussion by exclaiming 'No way!'.

Now that the previously under-emphasized problem of street crime is increasingly hitting the headlines, it is again difficult to disentangle developments in criminal justice from the political uses made of the crime problem. A number of distinctive elements are influencing the trend towards a more populist approach to crime. On the one hand, there is the fear and dislike of immigrants, who are identified as the source of such crimes. On the other, there is the potentially democratic bottom-up demand that central and local government should take more action to protect citizens' personal safety. This is itself fuelled by the worldwide growth in an individualist, consumer-based approach to politics and law which in Italy is slowly undermining the previously solidaristic ideologies of Catholicism and communism. The political battle lines, however, do not allow for such over-determination. These tend to be drawn rather sharply between those, on the one hand, who see rising concern over street crime as a justification for introducing packages of criminal justice measures so as to defuse public anxiety, and those, on the other, who treat such concern and the reaction to it as an excuse for ill-concealed racism and a means of deflecting attention from more serious issues of political corruption and organized crime.

Whatever was achieved during *Tangentopoli* (and the anti-corruption campaign is now past history), for the time being ordinary penal administration continues to be bogged down in procedural guarantees and formalistic bureaucratic requirements—in which the rule of mandatory prosecution certainly plays its part. Various changes have been made to try to reshape Italian criminal procedure more towards the Anglo-American model. Starting with the reforms of the new Code of Criminal Procedure of 1989, the possibility of greater flexibility has been introduced through alternatives to normal trial proceedings and schemes of plea bargaining, which are justified in part in the name of 'speed' and expediency. But things are changing slowly; few lawyers opt for the alternatives to normal trial, given the advantages of procrastination and the good possibilities of arriving at 'prescription'. Some judges and, even more, many lawyers and academics are also uneasy about what the new procedures represent. Those scholars who dislike these changes say that the trend towards embracing the Anglo-American pre-trial process, based as it is on confession and plea discounts, threatens the replacement of 'legality' by 'administration', consecrating as an ideal the type of 'pragmatic' methods used by the anti-corruption prosecutors (behind the screen of mandatory prosecution) in a moment of political emergency. In practice, however, adding a rigorous interpretation of the guarantees required by the accusatorial process to those which characterized the older inquisitorial procedures means that many petty crimes can end up being handled, in various stages, by up to eight professional judges!

This case study provides partial support for the proposition that globalization is cancelling particularity and bringing about homogenization towards an Anglo-American model of criminal justice. But it also shows that there is still much that is singular about the theory and practice of prosecution discretion in Italy. Far from the judicial activity in *Tangentopoli* being a foreign import, it served instead as an inspiration (or warning) to judges in other societies, such as France, Spain, and Portugal. But the point of this chapter is not to argue that those who want to bring about a more equal society in Britain, or elsewhere, can or should immediately opt for the Italian rule of mandatory prosecution and its associated legal and political arrangements. Even the Italian system achieved the effects it did only during an exceptional period of political transition—though it is also fair to add that the judges themselves played an important part in bringing about that transition. What can be learned at a practical level has more to do with the different possible meanings of prosecutorial constraint and prosecutorial independence, and their social and political preconditions and consequences. Beyond this, however, whatever the policy implications, even such a brief (and partial) examination of the Italian prosecution process should have shown the possibility and need of combining different approaches to the study of criminal justice. Close examination of foreign criminal justice practices suggests that it is above all the certainties buried in universalizing approaches to explanation, such as the claim that all systems find ways of relieving case-load pressures, or that criminal law must always serve the interests of the powerful, which turn out to be cultural rather than scientific truisms. Understanding must come before as well as after explanation.

Selected further reading

The student of comparative criminal justice will need to sample literatures which touch on many different disciplines. For example, a lot of the running in anything to do with judges is made by political scientists. Likewise, works inspired by the positivist, interpretative, and comparative law approaches do not communicate much, though this is slowly beginning to change. Many textbooks on comparative law and comparative criminal justice are little more than guides to classification. But Damaska's typology of hierarchical and coordinate forms of justice is still an important starting point for the attempt to theorize differences in criminal justice in civil law and common law countries (M. Damaska, *The Faces of Justice and State Authority*, New Haven: Yale University Press, 1986). And G. Newman (ed.), *Global Report on Crime and Justice* (Oxford: OUP, 1999) is a valuable recent overview, though it pays for its comprehensiveness by being subject to the problems discussed in the above chapter regarding the variable quality of the sources it draws on.

The best way to get deeper into the subject is to read monographs and articles about one or two specific societies, for example D. Downes, *Contrasts in Tolerance* (Oxford: Clarendon Press, 1988), or V.L. Hamilton and J. Sanders, *Everyday Justice: Responsibility and the Individual in Japan and the United States* (New Haven: Yale University Press, 1992). Explorations of the concept of legal culture will be found in D. Nelken (ed.), *Comparing Legal Cultures* (Aldershot: Dartmouth, 1997). Methodological reflections on ways of contrasting criminal justice are collected in D. Nelken (ed.), *Contrasting Criminal Justice* (Aldershot: Dartmouth, 2000). R. Van Swaaningen's *Critical Criminology in Europe* (London: Sage, 1998) is good on different national styles of criminology.

References

BALVIG, F. (1988), *The Snow White Image: The Hidden Reality of Crime in Switzerland*, Scandinavian Studies in Criminology 17, Oslo: Norwegian University Press, Scandinavian Research Council for Criminology.

BANKOWSKI, Z., and NELKEN, D. (1981), 'Discretion as a Social Problem', in M. Adler and S. Asquith (eds), *Discretion and Welfare*, 247–69, London: Heinemann.

BAUMGARTNER, M.P. (1992), 'The Myth of Discretion', in K. Hawkins (ed.), *The Uses of Discretion*, 129–63, Oxford: Clarendon Press.

BEIRNE, P. (1983), 'Cultural Relativism and Comparative Criminology', *Contemporary Crises*, 7: 371–91.

BLACK, D. (1997), *The Social Structure of Right and Wrong*, New York: Academic Press.

BLANKENBURG, E. (1997), 'Litigation Rates as Indicators of Legal Cultures', in D. Nelken (ed.), *Comparing Legal Cultures*, 41–69, Aldershot: Dartmouth.

—— and BRUINSMA, F. (1994), *Dutch Legal Culture*, 2nd edn, Amsterdam: Kluwer.

BRAITHWAITE, J. (1989), *Crime, Shame and Integration*, Cambridge: Cambridge University Press.

BRANTS, C., and FIELD, S. (2000), 'Legal Culture, Political Cultures and Procedural Traditions: Towards a Comparative Interpretation of Covert and Proactive Policing in England and Wales and the Netherlands', in D. Nelken (ed.), *Contrasting Criminal Justice*, 77–116, Aldershot: Dartmouth.

CAIN, M. (2000a), 'Through Other Eyes. On the Limitations and Value of Western Criminology for Teaching and Practice in Trinidad and Tobago', in D. Nelken (ed.), *Contrasting Criminal Justice*, 265–94, Aldershot: Dartmouth.

—— (2000b), 'Orientalism, Occidentalism and the Sociology of Crime', *British Journal of Criminology*, 40: 239–60.

CLIFFORD, J., and MARCUS, G. (1986), *Writing Culture: The Poetics and Politics of Ethnography*, Berkeley: University of California Press.

CLINARD, M.B. (1978), *Cities with Little Crime*, Cambridge: Cambridge University Press.

COLE, G.F. *et al.* (eds) (1987), *Major Criminal*

Justice Systems: A Comparative Survey, Beverly Hills, California: Sage.

COOMBE, R.J. (2000), 'Contingent Articulations: Critical Studies of Law', in A. Sarat and T. Kearns (eds), *Law in the Domains of Culture*, Ann Arbor: University of Michigan Press.

CRAWFORD, A. (1998), *Crime Prevention and Community Safety*, Harlow: Longman.

—— (2000), 'Contrasts in Victim/Offender Mediation and Appeals to Community in Comparative Cultural Contexts: France and England and Wales', in D. Nelken (ed.), *Contrasting Criminal Justice*, 205–29, Aldershot: Dartmouth.

DI FEDERICO, G. (1991), 'Obbligatorietà dell'azione penale, coordinamento delle attività del pubblico ministero e loro rispondenza alle aspettative della comunità', *La Giustizia Penale*, XCVI, March 1991: 148–71.

DOWNES, D. (1988), *Contrasts in Tolerance*, Oxford: Clarendon Press.

—— (1990), 'Response to H. Franke', *British Journal of Criminology*, 30/1: 94–6.

—— (1996), 'The Buckling of the Shields: Dutch Penal Policy 1985–1995', unpublished paper presented at the Onati Workshop on *Comparing Legal Cultures*, April 1996.

FAVELL, A. (1998), *Philosophies of Integration, Immigration and the Idea of Citizenship in France and England*, Basingstoke: Macmillan.

FEELEY, M. (1997), 'Comparative Law for Criminologists: Comparing for what?', in D. Nelken (ed.), *Comparing Legal Cultures*, 93–105, Aldershot: Dartmouth.

FEEST, J. (1996), written comments on D. Nelken's paper 'The Rule of Mandatory Prosecution in Italy and its relevance for Comparative Criminal Justice', presented and distributed at the conference of the Law and Society Association, Glasgow, July 1996.

—— and MURAYAMA, M. (2000), 'Protecting the Innocent through Criminal Justice: A Case Study from Spain, Virtually compared to Germany and Japan', in D. Nelken (ed.), *Contrasting Criminal Justice*, 205–29, Aldershot: Dartmouth.

FENNELL, P., SWART, B., JORG, N., and HARDING, A. (1995), 'Introduction', in C. Harding, P. Fennell, N. Jorg, and B. Swart (eds), *Criminal Justice in Europe: A Comparative Study*, xv–xix, Oxford: Clarendon Press.

FIELDS, C.B., and MOORE, R.H. (eds) (1996), *Comparative Criminal Justice*, Prospect Heights, Ill.: Waveland Press.

FINDLAY, M., and ZVEKIC, U. (eds) (1993), *Alternative Policing Styles*, Kluwer: Deventer.

FIONDA, J. (1995), *Public Prosecutors and Discretion: A Comparative Study*, Oxford: Clarendon Press.

FRANKE, H. (1990), 'Dutch Tolerance: Facts and Fallacies', *British Journal of Criminology*, 30/1: 81–93.

FRASE, R.S. (1990), 'Comparative Criminal Justice as a Guide to American Law Reform', 79, *California Law Review*: 539.

GARLAND, D. (1990), *Punishment and Modern Society*, Oxford: Oxford University Press.

—— (1996), 'The Limits of the Sovereign State: Strategies of Crime Control in Contemporary Society', *British Journal of Criminology*, 36/(4): 445–71.

—— (2000), *The Culture of Control*, Oxford: Oxford University Press.

GOLDSTEIN, A., and MARCUS, M. (1977), 'The Myth of Judicial Supervision in Three Inquisitorial Systems: France, Italy and Germany', 87, *Yale LJ*: 240.

GOTTFREDSON, M., and HIRSCHI, T. (1990), *A General Theory of Crime*, Stanford: Stanford University Press.

GUARNIERI, C. (1993), *Magistratura e Politica: Pesi senza Contrappesi*, Bologna: Il Mulino.

—— (1997), 'Prosecution in two civil law countries: France and Italy', in D. Nelken (ed.), *Comparing Legal Cultures*, 183–95, Aldershot: Dartmouth.

HAMILTON, V.L., and SANDERS, J. (1992), *Everyday Justice: Responsibility and the Individual in Japan and the United States*, New Haven: Yale University Press.

HARDING, C., FENNELL, P., JORG, N., and SWART, B. (eds) (1995), *Criminal Justice in Europe: A Comparative Study*, Oxford: Clarendon Press.

HEIDENSOHN, F., and FARRELL, M. (1991), *Crime in Europe*, London: Routledge.

HEILAND, H.G., SHELLEY, L.I., and KATOH, H. (eds) (1992), *Crime and Control in Comparative Perspectives*, Berlin: de Gruyter.

HODGSON, J. (2000), 'Comparing Legal Cultures: The Comparativist as Participant Observer', in D. Nelken (ed.), *Contrasting Criminal Justice*, 139–56, Aldershot: Dartmouth.

JOHNSON, D. (2000), 'Prosecutor Culture in Japan and USA', in D. Nelken (ed.), *Contrasting Criminal Justice*, 157–204, Aldershot: Dartmouth.

JUNGER-TAS, J. (1994), *Delinquent Behaviour*

among Young People in the Western World, Amsterdam: Kugler.

KALISH, C. (1988), *International Crime Rates*, Washington DC: Bureau of Justice Statistics, US Department of Justice.

KILLIAS, M. (1989), book review (of Balvig) in *British Journal of Criminology*, 29: 300–305.

KING, M. (1989), 'Social Crime Prevention à la Thatcher', in D. Nelken (ed.), *Criminal Justice on the Margin*, special issue of *Howard Journal of Criminal Justice*: 291–312.

LACEY, N., and ZEDNER, L. (1995), 'Discourses of Community in Criminal Justice', *Journal of Law and Society*, 22/1: 301–20.

—— and —— (1998), 'Community in German Criminal Justice: A Significant Absence?', 7, *Social and Legal Studies*: 7–25.

LANGBEIN, J., and WEINREB, L. (1978), 'Continental Criminal Procedure: Myth and Reality', 87, *Yale LJ*: 1549.

LEAVITT, G. (1990), 'Relativism and Cross-Cultural Criminology', *Journal of Crime and Delinquency*, 27/1: 5–29.

LEGRAND, P. (2001), 'What "Legal Transplants?"', in D. Nelken and J. Feest (eds), *Adapting Legal Cultures*, 1–55, Oxford: Hart Publishing.

LEIGH, L., and ZEDNER, L. (1992), *Royal Commission on Criminal Justice: Research Study No. 1*, London: HMSO.

MAGATTI, M. (1996), *Corruzione Politica e Società Italiana*, Bologna: Il Mulino.

MAWBY, R. (1990), *Comparative Policing Issues*, London: Unwin Hyman.

MIYAZAWA, S. (1997), 'The Enigma of Japan as a Testing Ground for Cross Cultural Criminological Studies', in D. Nelken (ed.), *Comparing Legal Cultures*, 195–215, Aldershot: Dartmouth.

MUNCIE, J., and SPARKS, R. (1991), *Imprisonment: European Perspectives*, Milton Keynes: Open University Press.

NELKEN, D. (1994a), 'Reflexive criminology', in D. Nelken (ed.), *The Futures of Criminology*, 7–43, London: Sage.

—— (1994b), 'Whom can you trust? The future of comparative criminology', in D. Nelken (ed.), *The Futures of Criminology*, 220–44, London: Sage.

—— (1995a), 'Disclosing/Invoking Legal Culture', in D. Nelken (ed.), *Legal Culture, Diversity and Globalization*, special issue of *Social and Legal Studies*, 4/4: 435–52.

—— (1995b), 'Can there be a sociology of legal meaning?', in D. Nelken (ed.), *Law as Communication*, 107–29, Aldershot: Dartmouth.

—— (1996a), 'The Judges and Corruption in Italy', in M. Levi and D. Nelken (eds), 'The Corruption of Politics and the Politics of Corruption', *Journal of Law and Society*, 23/1: 95–113.

—— (1996b), 'Stopping the judges', in M. Caciagli and D. Kertzer (eds), *Italian Politics: The Stalled Transition*, 186–204, Boulder, Colorado: Westview Press.

—— (1996c), 'Law without Order: A letter from Italy', in V. Gessner, A. Hoeland, and C. Varga (eds), *European Legal Cultures*, 355–58, Aldershot: Dartmouth.

—— (ed.) (1997a), *Comparing Legal Cultures*, Aldershot: Dartmouth.

—— (1997b), 'Puzzling out Legal Culture: A comment on Blankenburg', in D. Nelken (ed.), *Comparing Legal Cultures*, 69–93, Aldershot: Dartmouth.

—— (1997c), 'The Globalisation of Crime and Criminal Justice: Prospects and Problems', in M. Freeman (ed.), *Law at the Turn of the Century*, 251–79, Oxford: Oxford University Press.

—— (1997d), 'Il Significato di Tangentopoli: La Risposte Giudiziaria alla Corruzione e i Suoi Limiti', in L. Violante (ed.), *Storia d'Italia 14: Legge, Diritto e Giustizia*, 597–627, Turin: Einaudi.

—— (ed.) (2000a), *Contrasting Criminal Justice*, Aldershot: Dartmouth.

—— (2000b), 'Telling Difference: Of Crime and Criminal Justice in Italy', in D. Nelken (ed.), *Contrasting Criminal Justice*, 233–64, Aldershot: Dartmouth.

—— and FEEST, J. (eds) (2001a), *Adapting Legal Cultures*, Oxford: Hart Publishing.

—— (2001b), 'Towards a Sociology of Legal Adaptation', in D. Nelken and J. Feest (eds), *Adapting Legal Cultures*, 1–55, Oxford: Hart Publishing.

—— (2001c), 'Beyond the Metaphor of Legal Transplants?: Consequences of Autopoietic Theory for the Study of Cross-Cultural Legal Adaptation', in J. Priban and D. Nelken (eds), *Law's New Boundaries: The Consequences of Legal Autopoiesis*, 265–302, Aldershot: Dartmouth.

—— (2002a), 'Changing Legal Cultures', in M.B. Likosky (ed.), *Transnational Legal Processes*, London, Butterworth.

—— (2002b), 'Comparative Sociology of Law', in M. Travers and R. Benakar (eds), *Introduction to Law and Social Theory*, Oxford: Hart Publishing.

—— (2002c), 'Comparatists and Delocalisation', in P. Legrand and R. Munday (eds), *Comparative Legal Studies: Traditions and Transitions*, Cambridge: Cambridge University Press.

—— (2002d), 'Corruption in the European Union', in M. Bull and J. Newell (eds), *Corruption and Scandal in Contemporary Politics*, London: Macmillan.

—— (2003a), 'Comparing Legal Cultures', in A. Sarat (ed.), *The Blackwell Handbook to Law and Social Science*, Oxford: Blackwell.

—— (2003b), 'Crime's Changing Boundaries', in P. Cane and M. Tushnet (eds), *The Oxford Handbook of Legal Studies*, Oxford: Oxford University Press.

NEWMAN, G (ed.) (1999), *Global Report on Crime and Justice*, Oxford: Oxford University Press.

REICHEL, P.L. (1999), *Comparative Criminal Justice Systems: A Topical Approach*, 2nd edn, New Jersey: Prentice Hall.

ROBERT, P., and VAN OUTRIVE, L. (eds) (1993), *Crime et Justice en Europe*, Paris: L'Harmattan.

ROBERTS, P. (2002), 'The Ascent of Comparative Criminal Justice', *Oxford Journal of Legal Studies*, 2002.

ROBERTS, S. (1998), 'Against Legal Pluralism: Some Reflections on the Contemporary Enlargement of the Legal Domain', *Journal of Legal Pluralism*, 42: 95–106.

RUGGIERO, V. (1996), *White Collar and Organised Crime*, Aldershot: Dartmouth.

—— (2000), *Crime and Markets*, Cambridge: Cambridge University Press.

——, RYAN, M., and SIM, J. (eds) (1995), *Western European Penal Systems*, London: Sage.

——, SOUTH, N., and TAYLOR, I. (1998), *The New European Criminology*, London: Routledge.

SHAPIRO, M. (1981), *Courts*, Chicago: Chicago University Press.

SHEPTYCKI, J. (1995), 'Transnational Policing and the Makings of a Postmodern State', *British Journal of Criminology*, 35: 613.

VAGG, J. (1994), *Prison Systems*, Oxford: Oxford University Press.

VAN DYKE, J. (2000), 'Implications of the International Crime Victims survey for a victim perspective', in A. Crawford and J. Goodey (eds), *Integrating a Victim Perspective within Criminal Justice: International Debates*, 97–124, Ashgate: Dartmouth.

VAN SWAANINGEN, R. (1998), *Critical Criminology in Europe*, London: Sage.

—— (1999), 'Reclaiming Critical Criminology: Social Justice and the European Tradition,' *Theoretical Criminology*, 3/1: 5–29.

WHITMAN, J. (forthcoming), *Degradation and Mercy: Paths of Punishment in America and Europe*, Oxford: Oxford University Press.

YOUNG, J. (1999), *The Exclusive Society*, London: Sage.

ZEDNER, L. (1995), 'In Pursuit of the Vernacular: Comparing Law and Order Discourse in Britain and Germany', in D. Nelken (ed.), *Legal Culture, Diversity and Globalisation*, special issue of *Social and Legal Studies*, 4/4: 517–35.

—— (1996), 'German Criminal Justice Culture', unpublished paper presented at the Onati Workshop on Changing Legal Cultures, 13–14 July.

ZWEIGERT, K., and KOTZ, H. (1987), *An Introduction to Comparative Law*, Oxford: Oxford University Press.

7

THE HISTORY OF CRIME AND CRIME CONTROL INSTITUTIONS

Clive Emsley

INTRODUCTION

Until the 1970s, historians discussing developments in the area of crime control institutions in Britain tended to take a perspective formulated in Whig notions of progress and drawing on a positivist approach to crime and criminals. Crime tended to be seen as an absolute: it was largely understood in terms of theft and, to a lesser extent, violence; it was something perpetrated by 'criminals' on the law-abiding majority of the population. Improvements in the control mechanisms had been brought about by a progressive humanitarianism and the sensible, rational responses of reformers to abuses and inefficiences. Since the 1970s these perspectives and interpretations have been subjected to critical examination by a new generation of social historians. These historians began to work on court records in the hopes of penetrating the lives of the poor and socially disadvantaged; they have tended to concentrate on periods of social and economic upheaval such as the late sixteenth and early seventeenth centuries, or the years of industrialization and urbanization in the late eighteenth and early nineteenth centuries. The initial focus was on property crime, seen by some as a kind of 'protest' offence by the poor during periods of economic upheaval and privation. More recently, partly as a result of social historians' growing interest in gender issues, the focus has shifted towards violent offences, with important research addressing domestic violence and child abuse (D'Cruze 1998; Jackson 2000). All of these historians have sought to relate crime and the control of crime to specific economic, social, and political contexts; all have acknowledged that crime is something defined by the law, and that the law was changed and shaped by human institutions.

This chapter seeks to provide a synthesis of the recent research into the history of crime and its control in Britain from the late eighteenth century until the end of the Second World War. The period constitutes a long but nevertheless coherent unit, beginning with calls for reform in punishments and for improvements in the policing of the metropolis, and ending with police and prisons poised for the major reorganizations of the 1960s and with crime beginning its dramatic post-Second World War increase. The chapter begins with an assessment of the scale of crime across the period, followed by a discussion of the changes in the way that crime and the offender were perceived and understood by contemporaries and by subsequent historians. The focus then shifts to the solutions developed in response to these problems. A discussion of the origins of the police and their subsequent development is followed by a survey of the changes in the courts and the system of prosecution. The final section explores the different means deployed to remove the offender from society and to punish and/or reform him or her. Of necessity, given the research which has been done, the main focus of the essay is England and Wales; unfortunately, as yet, there has been little detailed research into the developments within the independent Scottish legal system, while much of the work on Irish 'crime' has tended to concentrate on its manifestations within English cities.

THE EXTENT OF CRIME

Acknowledging that a crime is an action defined by the law and which, if detected, will lead to some kind of sanction being employed against the perpetrator, enables the historian to draw some conclusions about a society's priorities and its attitudes towards social groups, individuals, and property. But the problem which commonly affects contemporaries, and which has much vexed the new generation of historians of crime, is estimating the scale of crime. There are no official statistics for crime in England before 1805. Historians of the eighteenth century and earlier have sought to construct figures from court records, particularly the indictments for assizes and quarter sessions. Recognizing that such figures cannot give any precise picture of the incidence of crime, it has, nevertheless, been forcefully argued that they can give an idea of the pattern. In 1810, the government determined to start collecting criminal statistics annually; the first collection went back to 1805, but in the early years the statistics only registered committals. The system was refined during the first half of the nineteenth century, notably with a reorganization into six main types of offence in 1834:

1. offences against the person (ranging from homicide to assault);
2. offences against property involving violence (robbery, burglary);
3. offences against property without violence;
4. malicious offences against property (arson, machine breaking, etc.);
5. offences against the currency;
6. miscellaneous offences (including riot, sedition, and treason).

Twenty-two years later an appendage to the County and Borough Police Act established the tripartite division of:

1. indictable offences reported to the police;
2. committals for trial both on indictment and before summary jurisdiction;
3. the number of persons convicted and imprisoned.

There has been considerable debate over the value of these statistics for histor. Some have maintained that because we cannot be sure why crimes were reported and prosecuted, and because of variations in recording practices across police jurisdictions, the figures are worthless for serious historical analysis (Tobias 1972a: 18–25; Sindall 1990: 16–28). Others have insisted that careful use of the figures can permit the construction of useful, hypothetical graphs for the pattern of crime, and also enable conclusions to be drawn about the nature of crime and perceptions of criminality (Beattie 1981; Gatrell 1980; Philips 1977). The most recent historical criticism of the statistics is that, rather than reflecting any patterns of crime, they owe more to financial constraints on the criminal justice system and to police manipulation (Taylor 1998a and 1998b), yet the conclusive evidence of significant Treasury interference remains unproven.

The pattern that can be drawn from the statistics shows a steady increase in crime, particularly property crime, in the late eighteenth century, becoming much sharper from the first decade of the nineteenth century until about 1850 when the pattern levels out, except, most noticeably, for the offence of burglary. After the First World War a steady, accelerating increase began again; it momentarily checked during the Second World War and the following decade, but then began to rise sharply once again. This pattern tends to make some sense when deployed alongside other social data. The eighteenth-century increase coincides with major shifts in the economy, with population growth and with fears for the social order; the sharp upturn in the first part of the nineteenth century corresponds with the aggravation of these problems and new concerns generated by the example of the French Revolution and by the seemingly uncontrollable squalor of the new industrial cities. The question must remain as to whether these problems caused more crime *per se*, or whether they simply made people more sensitive to offences and prompted them to report and/or prosecute any crimes committed against them. The steady plateau of the second half of the nineteenth century coincides with what one historian dubbed the Victorian 'age of equipoise' (Burn 1964); it was a period of confidence and of faith in progress. Moreover, the growth of international markets and reductions in the price of food, meant that problems in the home market were more easily off-set by both employers and employees than in the earlier years of the century; the necessity of stealing to survive consequently became less pressing as problems in primary production became less interrelated with production elsewhere in the economy. Burglary was one of the few offences which did not follow the general pattern in the second half of the nineteenth century. But the greater incidence of burglary itself may, in large measure, be a reflection of greater prosperity and the fact that ordinary people had more possessions in their homes. Both World Wars witnessed a slight reduction of crime in the judicial statistics: this could be explained by the fact that the police had a myriad of other tasks with which to contend and therefore relegated ordinary crime on their list of priorities; but also the needs of war shifted many of the young men often prone to committing criminal offences out of the country, and subjected many of those who remained to new and stricter forms of control through the military. The steady increase of crime during the inter-war period might arguably reflect both the difficulties generated by the Depression as well as the temptations offered by the first manifestations of the consumer society; it was during the inter-war years that motor vehicle ownership began to be widespread, and that motor vehicle offences congested the magistrates' courts.

But even if the statistical pattern makes some sense deployed against one set of social criteria, caution remains necessary. The late eighteenth and early nineteenth centuries which witnessed an increase in the statistics of crime, were also the key period for Britain becoming an urbanized society with an economy rooted in industrial capitalism. Most contemporaries believed that the burgeoning towns were much more prone to crime than the countryside, but the evidence for this is difficult to come by. Of course there were different opportunities for theft in the towns, and the goods stolen could be very different between town and country. But some poaching gangs were urban based and drew their members from the urban working class; moreover, John Glyde, studying crime in mid nineteenth-century Suffolk, concluded that while one third of the county's inhabitants were urban dwellers, they were responsible for only about a fifth of the crime (Glyde 1856a: 146–47; Glyde 1856b: 102–106). The interrelationship between the growth of property crime and the growth of capitalism was a popular area of analysis for the first serious historians of crime. This work often began on the premise that the thefts of poor men might be seen as resistance to capitalism and new work discipline. There were examples of judicial bias where employers sat as magistrates and passed verdicts on members of their workforce (Godfrey 1999b). But the studies of the 'perks' taken by workers from the raw materials with which they did their work reveal a situation far more complex than a simple class-struggle model might suggest. There were times when the purchaser, rather than the employer, was the victim of workplace fraud; and while the employer might, in such circumstances, have had some concern for the reputation of his business, this can scarcely be construed as an aspect of the struggle between capital and labour. It is possible that many workers preferred the steady wage which they earned under the capitalist system to a more traditional form of payment part in kind and part in wage; the continuing appropriation of goods, even in capitalizing textile industries, is therefore less clearly a protest against new systems of payment and conditions of work. Employers did not always prosecute the appropriation of perks. There continued to be a variety of other sanctions which they could employ; and occasionally they even took perks and fiddles into account when calculating pay rates (Davis 1989; Emsley 1996a: chapter 5; Godfrey 1999a and 1999c; Randall 1990). Furthermore, any simple equation that economic hardship prompted the working class to crime must confront the fact that there does not appear to have been anything other than a steady growth of offending during the inter-war period in spite of the acute depression in many of the largest and traditional centres of industrialization. A more profitable line of enquiry delineating an interrelationship between capitalism and crime has been the exploration of the enormous scale of business and financial fraud during the nineteenth and early twentieth centuries (Robb 1992). This style of offending netted profits for some far beyond the dreams of any non-fiction Bill Sikes.

Overall, the statistics suggest that property crime was the most common form of offence. Court records reveal that most thefts involved objects of relatively little monetary value. In the eighteenth and early nineteenth centuries drying sheets were taken from washing lines or where they were stretched over hedges or fences; tools were stolen from fellow workmen; furniture, cutlery, plates, and mugs were taken from lodgings and inns. The proceeds of such thefts were often pawned for a small amount of ready cash. In the long run the changes in the economy resulted in people having more disposable income; and as more people had more moveable property, and as shops and warehouses had more goods for consumers, so the style of theft changed and the opportunities became greater. Yet, perhaps paradoxically, in spite of the growing opportunities for illicit appropriation in wealthy Victorian Britain, overall the statistics of theft declined, and always very many of the victims were relatively poor people.

Statistically violence also declined over the same period. But the suggestion, largely based on figures for homicide, that there has been a general decline in interpersonal violence since the Tudor period has excited a lively debate (Cockburn 1991; Sharpe 1985; Stone 1983, 1985). The wife- and child-beater was increasingly demonized during the second half of the nineteenth century and was perceived as a phenomenon rooted in the poorest of the working class along with other vices. In the same period the growing delineation of the respectable standards expected from men in marriage pressed both by feminists and conservative moralists may have contributed to a diminution of overbearing and aggressive male behaviour. Yet assessing the scale of domestic abuse, especially when the construction of the idea of the family as a safe haven was at its peak and when the police were discouraged from involving themselves in private affairs, remains extremely difficult. Overall, however, the evidence suggests that from the late eighteenth century at least, a high proportion of the victims of violence appear to have known their assailants, or were related to them in some way; the major exception here was the police officer who, from the origins of the new police, was found in disproportionate numbers among assault victims (Gatrell 1980).

THE OFFENDER

Yet whatever the statistics suggest about the predominance of petty theft and the scale of, and profits from, financial fraud, it was violent crime which frightened people and which newspaper editors knew sold their papers and vicariously enthralled their readers. The newspapers could contribute significantly to periodic scares by the way in which they chose to emphasize particularly horrific crimes either for the sake of sales, or for some crusading, legislative purpose. The image of Jack the Ripper is a good example of the former. There is no conclusive evidence that the appalling murders committed in Whitechapel towards the end of 1888 were all committed by the same individual; and while only the most pathetic women in one very small district of East London appear to have been at risk, the panic about the Ripper spread far and wide, both geographically and socially. The garotting panic of 1862 provides an example of the Press, and particularly the influential *The Times*, building on concerns about 'criminals' released on licence and manufacturing a scare from a few street robberies to encourage the passage of legislation authorizing harsh penalties against violent offenders (Sindall 1990). There has been no systematic survey of crime reporting in the Press from the mid-eighteenth to the mid-twentieth centuries, but it is clear that even before the advent of cheap newspapers towards the end of the Victorian period, the reading public were being fed on cases of 'orrible murder and outrage perpetrated by members of a criminal class outside of, and at war with, society.

The idea of a criminal subgroup was not new. Vagrants and beggars were perceived as such, and legislated against, at least as far back as the Tudor and Stuart periods. The members of the criminal class portrayed in the writings of those interested in crime from the mid-eighteenth to the mid-nineteenth century had much in common with the Tudor 'sturdy beggar': he would not do a honest day's work because he sought a life of luxury and ease (Fielding 1751: 169; Hanaway 1772: 38; Colquhoun 1796: 33). Yet events led to a significant shift in the perceptions of crime and criminality, particularly in the first half of the nineteenth century. The wars against Revolutionary and Napoleonic France had severely limited access to foreign grain markets at a time when a series of bad harvests had led to food shortages, with resulting outbreaks of popular disorder and the need to increase poor rates. At the same time the war forced the propertied to dig deeply into their pockets for war taxes required by the national government, as well as for increased poor rates to assist the wives and children of poor men serving in the armed forces. For a variety of reasons the restoration of peace in 1815 did not bring an end to these escalating poor rates. The new national crime statistics, the first decade of which coincided with the last decade of the wars, while they only demonstrated an increase in committals and prosecutions, were taken as proof positive of a serious increase in crime. During the eighteenth century a crime was an individual action which the law sought to penalize; but against the background of the new statistics and resentment at increasing poor rates which a harsh reading of Malthusian theory deemed unnecessary, crime increasingly acquired a symbolic meaning as a kind of disease within society and a new stress was put on the pathological nature of the offender. By the 1840s the offender had become a member of the 'dangerous classes' lurking in the urban rookeries and slums; by the early 1860s the term the 'criminal classes' was rather more popular (Stevenson 1983: 32, n 4).

Social commentators like Henry Mayhew made forays into the rookeries of these so-called 'criminal classes'. The stigmatizing label, however, says more about these commentators and their readers than about the social group that they were studying. Those labelled as the 'criminal class' were generally the poorest sections of the working class who eked out their existence in the uncertain casual labour market. Given their hard lives, their poor living conditions, and inadequate diets, it is not surprising that members of this 'criminal class' often died young. With their poor diet and shabby clothing they also looked different from those in steady work; in particular, they looked different from members of the growing middle class. The intrepid social investigators emphasized the differences by categorizing and describing the 'criminal classes' as if they were members of strange tribes in far-away lands; the physical differences also chimed well with Victorian notions that the face portrayed the character (Emsley 1996a: 68–75).

The 'criminals' of the 'criminal class' portrayed by Victorian commentators were essentially working-class and male. Statistically, offences by women were always fewer than those committed by men; moreover, the percentage of women prosecuted in the principal courts from the late seventeenth through to the early twentieth century declined steadily. Single women living alone in towns and employed as domestic servants appear to have been more criminal than their sisters in the country; and while they were always far fewer than their male equivalents, their age of offending appears to have declined much more slowly. The explanation is probably to be found in the greater degree of family support and male protection available in the rural districts, but above all in the vulnerability of women in the uncertain, casual labour market of the town. This latter may also account for the fact that, while the proportion of female offenders before the courts was smaller than that of males, the percentage of female recidivists was higher; it appears to have been more difficult for a woman to shake off the stigma of prison than a man (Beattie 1975; Feeley and Little 1991; Zedner 1991; King 1996). For Victorian commentators, the female equivalent of the male criminal was the prostitute. Even sympathetic observers described the prostitute as entering her trade for the same kind of reasons that men became criminals, notably idleness and the love of luxury; only very low on the list came the most probable spur to most prostitution, poverty. In her gaudy clothes and with her effrontery in propositioning potential clients, the archetypal prostitute was the antithesis of the ideal of Victorian womanhood. She was also much easier to apprehend than many male criminals. The notorious Contagious Diseases Acts, passed in the middle of the nineteenth century in an attempt to reduce venereal disease in the armed forces, assumed that prostitutes were readily detectable, but they inadvertently made thousands of ordinary working-class women the victims of officious and suspicious policemen (McHugh 1980; Walkowitz 1980).

The levelling out of the crime statistics, which implied a degree of success in the mechanisms of crime control, Social Darwinism, and the advent of social science led to changing perceptions of the criminal classes. Criminals might still be described as those who shunned hard work and enjoyed the vagrant life, but they were also increasingly understood as individuals who turned to crime because of mental and physical, as well as moral, degeneracy: defects assumed to be passed on through heredity. Crime ceased to be seen as the work of a semi-organized criminal or dangerous class, and more that of, on the one hand, a small core of hardened professionals, and, on the other, a much larger group of socially and mentally inadequate individuals who indulged in petty offences. This perception led to increasingly careful categorization and separation as experts differentiated between the young and the habitual offender, the necessitous and the incorrigible, the opportunist, and the professional (Wiener 1990).

The judicial statistics commonly revealed a large number of young offenders as responsible for the mass of petty crime. These offenders were not always perceived as part of the criminal class; from the early nineteenth century at least, they were regarded as a group in need of protection, both from immoral and uncaring parents and from hardened recidivists in prisons. Once the problem was identified a variety of expedients were tried either to reform the juvenile offender—industrial schools and reformatories—or to offer healthy alternatives—youth clubs and organizations—and thus prevention. The increase in juvenile offending during the First World War, attributed by contemporaries to a weakening of parental control, with fathers at the front and more mothers at work, prompted further attempts to foster such alternatives (Bailey 1987: 11; Gillis 1975; Shore 1999).

Mayhew had categorized his criminals by their various crafts—possibly taking the argot verb for a particular offence and transforming it into a noun (Emsley 1996a: 73). The garotting panic led some to assume that street robbers were professionals who specialized in a particular 'science of garotting' (Anon 1863). By the early twentieth century, criminal archetypes specializing in particular offences were commonly constructed in the Press and by moral entrepreneurs: in the inter-war period there was the bag-snatcher, the motor bandit, and the razor gang; the Second World War saw the black-marketeer 'spiv'; in the aftermath of the war came the cosh-boy. Of course there were individuals who perpetrated each and every one of these offences, and in the inter-war period it is possible to find something of an organized underworld involved in sexual vice, like the Messina family in London's Soho, and the gangs involved in gambling on the race tracks and at boxing matches, notably the Darby Sabini gang and the Brummagen Boys. This underworld could be vicious, but its members generally fought amongst themselves over territory (Bean 1981; Jenkins and Potter 1988; Samuel 1981). But even including these gangs, it is unlikely that more than a very few offenders were 'professionals' for whom crime was the principal source of income. The creation of the archetype often clouded the understanding of the offence, and serious difficulties arose (particularly for the police) when policy was made with reference to the archetype rather than the problem; such was the case with, for example, the Contagious Diseases Acts and much anti-gambling legislation (Dixon 1991: 37; Gatrell 1990: 306–10; Pearson 1983; Petrow 1994).

Since the eighteenth century at least, politicians and jurists claimed that all English men and women were equal before the law. This, it has been argued, was a trick in Hanoverian England which enabled the ruling, propertied elite to run the country without a police force. The occasional example of an individual like Lord Ferrers, executed in 1760 for the murder of his steward, ensured the lower orders' faith in the law which, for most of the time, was concerned with reinforcing and upholding an unequal division of property (Hay 1975). This argument has not gone unchallenged, and nineteenth-century governments became increasingly sensitive to accusations of class law. Yet the limited work which has been done on police practice and the sentencing policies of the courts suggests that the perception of stereotypes influenced both. Police, magistrates, and judges weighed up offenders according to their class, gender, and respectability and how they conformed with the accepted social mores; they then acted accordingly (Conley 1991; Zedner 1991). At the same time, while financial fraud was widespread—one estimate has it that as many as one sixth of the company promotions during the nineteenth century were fraudulent—the law was feeble in this area, the police were not geared up to pursuing such offenders, and such men who were convicted of major fraud were generally treated leniently in comparison with offenders from the 'criminal class' (Robb 1992: chapter 7). It was the quantity of petty crime and fears about violent crime which focused definitions, and treatment, of the offender.

THE POLICE

The traditional, Whig historians of the English police accepted fairly uncritically the notion that crime was increasing significantly at the end of the eighteenth and beginning of the nineteenth centuries. They also accepted, again uncritically, the claims of the early police reformers that the old system of parish constables and watchmen was inefficient and had quite outgrown its usefulness. The development of the new police, beginning with the creation of the Metropolitan Police in London in 1829, was therefore the logical solution of far-sighted men to a real and serious problem (Ascoli 1979; Critchley 1978; Reith 1938, 1943).

There were problems with the old system of policing. Some parish constables were inefficient and reluctant to act. Constables were chosen in a variety of different ways from among the respectable members of local communities. Usually they were expected to serve for a year; the tasks were neither permanent nor full-time and constables continued their trade or profession while they served. Some town watchmen, who were recruited by local authorities and paid to patrol the streets after dark, were also inefficient. But while the 'policemen' of Hanoverian England still await thorough historical investigation, it is becoming ever more clear that the situation was by no means as bleak as has been traditionally portrayed. There was an increasing number of professional constables who served permanently as substitutes for the men selected. At the same time, significant improvements were being made to some of the urban watches.

The chief focus of concerns over crime and public order during the eighteenth century was London. It was the largest city in Europe, comprising both the cities of London and Westminster, and spreading out into the counties of Middlesex, Surrey, and Kent. It was a booming commercial centre as well as the seat of government. Contemporaries viewed it with pride for its obvious prosperity; but they were also anxious about its slums and the temptations which its wealth offered to those who lived in the slums. The parish watches in the metropolis began to be reorganized and improved early on in the century (Reynolds 1998). Private thief-takers established themselves to investigate offences for victims; they took rewards from victims for the return of stolen property, and they also cashed in on the rewards offered by government for the apprehension of offenders leading to conviction. Several unsavoury characters installed themselves in the entrepreneurial role of thief-taker, organizing both the theft and the apprehension of the offender (Howson 1970; Paley 1989a). Alongside these developments a new kind of magistrate—the trading justice— emerged in the metropolis and on its fringes. Trading justices have received almost as bad a press as the entrepreneurial thief-takers, yet they were not all bad and, sitting regularly in their offices, they provided a much-needed service for the increasing numbers who wanted legal problems solved quickly and easily and who were prepared to pay the justices' fees (Landau 1984: 184–90). A marked step forward was made in the middle of the century when, under Henry Fielding and his blind half-brother Sir John Fielding, the magistrate's office in Bow Street became a model of how the trading justice might function. The Fieldings were supported by government money, which enabled them to keep their fees low; equally significant was their organization of half a dozen constables, the celebrated Bow Street thief-takers or 'Runners', and their experiment with night patrols organized to watch the main roads of the metropolis (Palmer 1988: 78–9).

The Gordon Riots of 1780, when the variety of civil powers in the metropolis showed themselves unable to cope with major disorder, prompted some to contemplate a centralized, professional system of policing. Indeed, in 1785 such a body was proposed in a Bill presented to Parliament. But the Bill was poorly drafted, poorly presented, and provoked the fury of the powerful City of London which objected to losing its authority over its own police. The Bill fell, though the system outlined in it was subsequently established in the city of Dublin. Seven years later a new Bill was introduced to improve the policing of London, but rather than creating a centralized body of horse and foot answerable to government-appointed commissioners, this proposed only the creation of seven police offices along the lines of that in Bow Street. Each office was to be staffed by three stipendiary magistrates and six constables; the City of London was omitted from the proposal and continued with its own independent system. Over the next thirty years government and private initiative built on the system successfully established by the Middlesex Justices Act of 1792. By 1828 the policing of London was in the hands of some 300 patrolmen working out of the Bow Street Office, about eighty men in the Thames River Police (set up by West India merchants in 1798), the twenty-four stipendiaries and their constables, the two City of London Marshals and their constables and patrol, and the dozens of parish constables and nightwatchmen of the individual metropolitan parishes (Palmer 1988: 117–19, 143–7, 171–2; Rumbelow 1971: 104–105). The effectiveness and honesty of these different policemen varied from district to district depending on pay, recruitment policies, and the effectiveness of supervision. Some nightwatchmen were young and fit, and worked relatively short beats which they got to know well and policed conscientiously. But even the much-lauded Bow Street Police succumbed to the kinds of corruption present among the old thief-takers, as a sucession of scandals in the aftermath of the Napoleonic wars revealed (Emsley 1996a: 223 and 243, n 18).

The argument for sweeping aside such a motley system appeared a logical and forcible one to the traditional Whig historians of the police, especially since they considered that most parish constables and watchmen were useless. Yet for contemporaries there were strong arguments for maintaining the system: there was concern that a centralized police was something peculiarly foreign, worst of all French, and that it would be a threat to liberty; there was even greater concern about central government encroaching on the rights of local government. The police offices and the Bow Street patrols had been increasingly coordinated by the Home Office; but the Metropolitan Police, established in 1829, was a significant development in central government control.

The prime mover in the creation of the Metropolitan Police was the Home

Secretary, Sir Robert Peel. He first came to the Home Office in 1822, and during the mid-1820s he had embarked on a major rationalization of the criminal law; in Peel's mind police reform had always been central to his law reforms. He brought with him to the Home Office his experience of Ireland, where he had served as Chief Secretary from 1812 to 1818 and where he had been instrumental in improving the police system. Manifestations of public disorder were different in the two countries. Ireland was overwhelmingly a peasant society; its Catholic minority was dominated by an Anglo-Irish gentry which was largely Protestant. In 1798 and again in 1803 there had been rebellions, and peasant guerrilla war spluttered on in the countryside. The magistracy was often reluctant to act in the face of disorder. Peel had created the Peace Preservation Force to help resolve these problems; one of his successors, Henry Goulburn, developed the force further in 1822 by legislation which established a French-style gendarmerie, the Irish Constabulary (Palmer 1988: 193–276). Peel remained in close touch with Goulburn throughout the latter's preparation of the Constabulary Bill, and while he recognized that the problems of the new industrial society in England were different, that magistrates were often active, that local authorities were jealous of their independence, and that there would be ferocious hostility to a French-style military police, he nevertheless believed that some kind of national police system was desirable. Neither was he alone among the Tory cabinet in this belief. Concerns about public order were probably central in ministers' minds. While the duration and scale of the Gordon Riots had never been equalled, there had been sporadic disorders in the metropolis and in the provinces both during and after the wars against revolutionary and Napoleonic France. Yet it was not on the issue of maintaining public order that Peel chose to argue the need for a police, but on the problem of increasing crime; and it is possible that Peel's reforms of the criminal law, which made it easier to prosecute offenders and which reduced the amount of time lost by victim-prosecutors and their witnesses in the courts, had themselves inflated the crime figures for the metropolis.

From the beginning in 1829 the constables of the new Metropolitan Police were informed that their first duty was the prevention of crime. It is arguable whether they were any more efficient at this than the more competent of the watches which preceded them, especially since they could be less numerous on the ground (Paley 1989b: 114–17). But the new policemen did constitute a sizeable body which could be deployed across the metropolis to clear away street people and to suppress popular tumult. In their early years also, Metropolitan Police officers and constables were commonly deployed in the provinces as a kind of national riot squad (Emsley 1996b: 31, 42, 46, 54–6).

The Metropolitan Police provided a new model for consideration by those advocating police reform in the provinces. In the aftermath of the Napoleonic wars, fear of disorder and of increasing crime prompted a variety of developments in provincial policing. Some local Associations for the Prosecution of Felons organized private police; some towns improved their watches either through private Acts of Parliament or, after 1833, by taking advantage of the Lighting and Watching Act of that year. The Municipal Corporations Act of 1835 sought to establish uniformity among the chartered boroughs by requiring each elected municipality to appoint a watch committee, and each watch committee to appoint a police force. In 1829 the County of Cheshire established, by Act of Parliament, a constabulary of paid professionals whose task it was to supervise the existing parish constables and to liaise with the developing police in the towns of the county and its neighbours. Yet these reforms were generally found wanting by the Royal Commission on a Rural Constabulary which deliberated between 1836 and 1839; and it was the conclusions of this Royal Commission that informed the Whig police histories.

Three men served on the Royal Commission: Colonel Charles Rowan, one of the first two commissioners of the Metropolitan Police; Charles Shaw-Lefevre, a Whig MP and country gentleman; and Edwin Chadwick, the dynamic Benthamite reformer who had earlier played a key role in drafting the Poor Law Commissioners' Report of 1834. Chadwick's enthusiasm for a centralized system was controlled by the other two commissioners, but it is clear that Chadwick was primarily responsible for drafting the Constabulary Commissioners' Report, and in so doing he underplayed the extent to which developments were taking place in the provinces and ignored the wishes of the majority of the magistrates in the different quarter sessions who were opposed to the kind of sweeping changes which he favoured. The Whig government too was opposed to the extent of the changes proposed by the Report, if for no other reason than that it recognized the impossibility of getting Parliament to agree to a national police force in which the control of local magistrates—then the unchallenged decision-makers for, and administrators of, the provinces through the medium of county quarter sessions—would be all but dispensed with. Instead the government introduced legislation which enabled county magistrates to establish county police forces if they so wished, with the Home Office playing only a distant supervisory role (Philips and Storch 1999).

It is difficult fully to assess the extent to which the County Police legislation was adopted across England and Wales; twenty-four counties appear to have adopted it during the first two years of its existence; another eleven did so over the next fifteeen years, but nine of these seem to have appointed a constabulary for only parts of their jurisdiction. The causes of adoption varied, as did assessments of the success of the new constabularies. In the early 1840s there was considerable agitation in several counties that the new forces be abolished, particularly because of their expense. In those counties which did not adopt the legislation there were new experiments to improve the existing system of parish constables, particularly by appointing profes-sional superintending constables to oversee and organize their activities. Kent took the lead in these developments, yet when a parliamentary select committee investi-gated policing across the country in 1852 and 1853, no witnesses were called from that county.

The main fault with the superintending constable system seems to have been the way in which some magistrates sought to tie these policemen to petty sessions divi-sions and were jealous of requests that they be allowed to assist elsewhere in their county. By the early 1850s there was a dominant view in government circles that the county was the natural unit of local government, and Lord Palmerston, first as Home Secretary and then as Prime Minister, was keen to see a national system of county-based police forces, with only the larger towns maintaining their own independent police under watch committees. His initial ideas foundered on the hostility of the smaller boroughs, but in 1856 his Home Secretary, Sir George Grey, successfully negotiated the County and Borough Police Act through Parliament. This legislation made the creation of a police force obligatory on all counties of England and Wales and on all incorporated boroughs (even as late as this some small boroughs had not complied with the requirements of the Municipal Corporations Act). The Treasury was to pay one quarter of the pay and clothing costs of efficient forces, and 'efficiency' was to be assessed by three new Inspectors of Constabulary whose duty it was to inspect each force annually and report to Parliament.

The Metropolitan Police remained separate from the new legislation. It continued to be answerable not to any representatives of local government but to the Home Secretary, and the Metropolitan Police Commissioner himself made an annual report to Parliament. In the provinces, however, the system established by the 1856 Act largely survived for the next hundred years. Borough police forces were answerable to their watch committees; in some instances these committees took a close interest in the day-to-day operations of their men, giving precise administrative and operational directives to their head constables. The chief constables of counties had more autonomy both by statute and since the police committees of quarter sessions met far less frequently than watch committees. This greater autonomy was maintained when the magistrates' police committees were replaced, under the local government reorganization of 1888, by standing joint committees made up equally of magistrates and elected members of the new county councils.

Parallel with developments in England and Wales, a similar system of policing emerged in Scotland. Towns were establishing their own forces by private legislation at the end of the eighteenth and beginning of the nineteenth centuries; the first public enactment came in 1833, with further legislation fourteen years later. At least twelve out of the twenty-eight Scottish counties had set up some form of police by 1839 when an Act authorized them to levy an additional Rogue Money assessment to create a constabulary. Lanarkshire was the only county of any significance which had not taken advantage of this legislation when an Act of 1857 required burghs and counties to establish police (Carson 1984, 1985; Carson and Idzikowska 1989).

While the form of local control over the police established under the 1856 and 1857 Police Acts and the 1888 Local Government Act remained in place for the next hundred years, the reality of this control was gradually undermined by the steady encroachment of the state. The Treasury grant to efficient provincial police forces was increased to half the cost of pay and clothing in 1874, specifically to give the Home Office a greater measure of control. Yet, overall, there was nothing conspiratorial in the steady encroachment of the state; rather, it was the logical development of the increasing perception of policemen, by Home Office functionaries and by the police themselves, as the professionals and experts in the job of 'policing'. This prompted a succession of circulars and Acts of Parliament by which central government required specific administrative duties to be undertaken by the police without reference to their local police committees. More dramatic, and more noticeable in their impact on the links between senior police officers and civil servants, were the central government's concerns about managing national emergencies, notably strikes, subversion, and world wars. During the 1830s and 1840s squads of Metropolitan policemen had been deployed across the country to combat industrial disorder, agitation against the new Poor Law, Chartist demonstrations, and the Rebecca troubles in South Wales. But the Home Office became increasingly reluctant to commit London policemen in this way and urged magistrates that they should establish their own police. Initially, as county forces developed, there was some doubt about the extent to which they might be moved out of their jurisdiction to assist another force, though by the last quarter of the nineteenth century such concerns had faded, and by the last decade of the century the Home Office was urging all police forces to enter into mutual aid agreements. The strike wave before the First World War witnessed an active Home Secretary, Winston Churchill, ordering both police and troops around the country to assist local forces against striking dockers, miners, and railwaymen. In Churchill's eyes, even where these were not national strikes (as in the case of the South Wales coal strike), they nevertheless threatened national security and supply, and consequently they needed a national response. Churchill's more grandiose proposals for organizing police during strikes were defeated, and he himself moved from the Home Office in 1911, but the outbreak of war in 1914 brought about new links between central government and local police (Emsley 1996b: 54–6, 68–9, and 112–19; Morgan 1987: chapters 3 and 6; Weinberger 1991: chapters 3 and 4).

The spy scares before the war had brought the provincial police forces into close contact with the embryonic secret service. The war itself strengthened these developments as the police were ordered first to watch out for German spies and saboteurs, then for subversives who had taken German gold to undermine the war effort. The Russian Revolution produced a new kind of subversive in the mind of the authorities, the Bolshevik agitator, and fear of this creature lasted long after the war. A few chief constables, notably in South Wales, had major confrontations with their standing joint committees when they equated Labour Party membership and industrial unrest with Communism and Bolshevism: the Home Office backed the chief constables. Local police committees were bypassed by the Home Office as it prepared to confront widespread industrial unrest and communicated directly with chief constables. The Emergency Powers Act of 1920 was a key element in these changes, enabling the Home Secretary to deploy up to 10 per cent of a police force outside its own jurisdiction, not necessarily for mutual aid (Emsley 1996b: chapter 6; Weinberger 1991: chapter 8).

Other developments, contemporaneous with the growing links between the police forces and the Home Office, further strengthened the idea of a single police service and undermined the local nature of the police. Towards the end of the nineteenth century the notion of policing as a skilled, professional trade, practised by men of similar origins with similar problems across the whole of the United Kingdom as well as in the Empire, began to emerge. These ideas were fostered by newspapers aimed at a police audience, and by campaigns to establish proper pension schemes and a weekly rest day. While both of these latter campaigns were successful, there were many police officers who believed that a national police union was the best means of ensuring a permanent voice for the rank and file in matters of pay, promotion, and discipline. The National Union of Police and Prison Officers was established in December 1913. The wartime pressures on the police, including longer hours and pay falling well below the level of inflation, encouraged recruitment to the union which conducted a successful strike over pay and conditions in London in August 1918. A second strike, a year later, involving Birmingham and Liverpool as well as London, was a disaster for the union. All the strikers were dismissed, and the union itself was banned and replaced by a Police Federation to which all men belonged up to and including the rank of inspector. The Federation was refused the right to strike. The establishment of the Police Federation was among the recommendations of the committee appointed under Lord Desborough in the wake of the first police strike. Among the other proposals that it made, and which were accepted by the government, were that the pay and conditions of the police should be standardized and that half the total cost of the police, and not simply half the cost of pay and clothing, should be borne by the Treasury. Legal arguments, particularly Justice H.A. McCardie's controversial ruling in the case of *Fisher v Oldham* in 1930 ([1930] 2 KB 364), tended further to undermine local authority over the police. Yet local independence remained sufficiently strong thoughout the inter-war years to check any hint of nationalization and, in particular, to prevent the forcible amalgamations of the smallest forces with their larger neighbours. It was the national emergency of the Second World War which provided the opportunity for central government to pass legislation enabling the Home Secretary to enforce amalgamations. The Labour government which came to power in 1945 was sufficiently impressed by temporary wartime amalgamations to introduce legislation abolishing forty-five borough forces, which, together with four voluntary amalgamations, reduced the number of police forces in England and Wales to 131 by the end of 1947.

The argument for amalgamation and the abolition of the smaller forces was generally that such rationalization promoted efficiency. Yet police efficiency has always been notoriously difficult to estimate. The first Metropolitan Police constables were told that their principal task was the prevention of crime; and this instruction was taken up in the orders issued to the constables in provincial forces. The measurement of prevention is, of course, impossible; arrest statistics, however, are tangible. The new police were able to demonstrate their efficiency to watch committees, magistrates' police committees, and standing joint committees by arresting drunks, prostitutes, street sellers, and anyone else whose behaviour was offensive in a public place to Victorian perceptions of morality. Their presence may have had some impact on petty theft, particularly in public places, and may, in consequence, have contributed in some measure to the levelling out of the crime statistics in the second half of the nineteenth century. Of course they did catch some offenders, but their methods were not particularly sophisticated. They appear to have accepted the notion of the criminal class and to have concentrated their efforts on containing stigmatized areas and the groups which lived in them; to paraphrase the explanation of one of the first commissioners of the Metropolitan Police to a parliamentary select committee, they guarded the elegant areas of St James by watching the slums of St Giles. Practices changed little in the first half of the twentieth century. The use of scientific and technological developments depended on the awareness and determination of a chief constable and what he was able to persuade his police committee to finance. But even when neighbouring forces were equipped with radios, local pride and independence meant that they might not share frequencies. Detectives had been viewed with suspicion in the early nineteenth century as the man in plain clothes was feared as a spy; furthermore, the early commissioners of the Metropolitan Police appear to have been wary of detective policemen since they were much more difficult to control and supervise than the uniformed constable patrolling a regular beat at a steady two-and-a-half miles an hour. A Home Office Committee was appointed in 1933 to investigate detective policing and, after deliberating for five years and investigating the situation elsewhere, particularly in North America, it concluded that England lagged far behind in training and the deployment of scientific aids. The Committee's report led to significant developments in training, the exchange of information between forces, and the awareness of scientific aids; but the scale of the backwardness is demonstrated by the fact that even at the beginning of the Second World War, some county forces, let alone the smaller borough forces, had no CID.

A lack of sophistication, however, was one of the main attributes of the image of the British Bobby as it developed during the nineteenth and early twentieth centuries. By the middle of the Victorian period at least he was perceived as solid and dependable; his ability to pull himself up by hard work and diligence from constable third class to superintendent—or, in some of the smaller borough forces, to head constable—made him, in the perception of the Victorian middle class, a working-class role model in Samuel Smiles's self-help mould. At the same time the Bobby was seen as a mainstay of the British constitution, which Victorians liked to think of as a model for the rest of the world; politicians, journalists, and senior policemen commonly declared the British police to be the best in the world. There were occasions when this image crumbled, and probably it was never particularly strong among the poorer sections of the working class. Furthermore, as the ownership of private motor vehicles increased during the inter-war period, so, for the first time, the police were brought more and more into direct confrontation with 'respectable' members of society.

PROSECUTION AND THE COURTS

Just as policing increasingly became the preserve of experts and professionals from the mid-eighteenth century, so too did the system of prosecution and the activity within the courtroom. The eighteenth century has been called 'the golden age of discretionary justice' in England and Wales (King 2000: 355). Discretion ran through all elements of the criminal justice process, from the decision to prosecute to the decision of the jury and the sentence passed. The decision to prosecute an offender was generally taken by the victim, or by the victim's relations or friends. In Scotland, by the beginning of the century, the procurators-fiscal, subordinated to the Lord Advocate, had largely taken over the prosecution of all serious crimes. But in England representatives of the central government rarely intervened; the occasional exceptions were coining cases commonly prosecuted by the Treasury Solicitor, and those few cases of treason or sedition which threatened the state and which were conducted by the Attorney General.

One of the problems in the English system was the expense; the prosecutor had to find fees and pay for a variety of legal documents. This appears often to have encouraged the victim to settle with the offender outside of the courtroom, though compounding a felony with a monetary payment was itself an offence. The expense of prosecution also prompted men of property to organize themselves into subscription insurance clubs, known as Associations for the Prosecution of Felons, which met any prosecution costs that a member might incur (King 1989; Philips 1989). Legislation of 1752 authorized the payment of expenses to poor prosecutors in felony cases when the accused was convicted, and sixteen years later this payment was extended to all prosecutors. Peel's Criminal Justice Act of 1826 extended the provision to witnesses, and permitted such payment in some misdemeanour cases, notably assaults. These developments probably contributed to the increase in the number of prosecutors who came forward with charges, but well into the nineteenth century some victims still refused to prosecute, sometimes through fear, sometimes because of anxiety about the loss of time from work, or because the whole procedure seemed inconvenient. In the case of sexual offences, embarrassment, and the oppressive climate of Victorian morality which had little time for women who could not demonstrate their adherence to the expected norms of female behaviour, probably dissuaded many women from reporting, let alone prosecuting, an offence.

The Scottish system had its advocates in nineteenth-century England, but the idea of a public prosecutor was perceived as European, and French in particular; it was lumped together with political police, and was regarded as alien to English common law and constitutional traditions. However, it is apparent that, as the nineteenth century wore on, the new police increasingly took on the role of prosecutor, though under the continuing official insistence that the English system was one of private prosecution. In the beginning the police assumption of this role was, at least in some instances, partly to uphold their own authority; but they also appear to have acted when no one else came forward, or because the victim was poor or a woman. The pattern of police involvement as prosecutors varied between the different force jurisdictions. Nevertheless, by the last quarter of the nineteenth century prosecutors seem invariably to have been policemen, and the senior officers of municipal forces were often formally presenting cases to the courts, much to the fury of another growing body of professionals—the lawyers (Emsley 1996a: 190–3; Emsley 1996b: 234–5; Hay 1989: 36–47).

Criminal prosecutions were heard in three different kinds of court, each developing its distinctive style of practice between the mid-eighteenth and the mid-twentieth centuries. The most serious cases went before the county assize courts, which generally met only twice a year, at Lent and in the Summer, until the early twentieth century. In London these cases were heard at the Old Bailey, more properly known as the Central Criminal Court after 1834; but the pressure of business in the metropolitan area meant that the courts here met far more frequently. County quarter sessions met four times a year and heard felony cases, but, unlike the judges at the assizes, the magistrates of the county bench did not have the authority to hear capital offences. Less serious offences went before the summary jurisdiction of magistrates meeting in petty sessions. During the eighteenth century new legislation had permitted more and more cases to be heard summarily; the trend increased in the following century, particularly with the Juvenile Offenders Acts 1847 and 1850, which empowered magistrates to try summarily any juvenile charged with simple larceny, the Criminal Justice Act 1855, and the Prevention of Crime Act 1879. It has been estimated that by 1900, 80 per cent of indictable offences were tried summarily (Bentley 1998: 20). The courts of petty sessions became more and more formal as the century progressed and, in consequence of their growing workload and greater formality, the role of the quarter sessions declined. The formal petty sessions were increasingly known as police courts, something which concerned members of the legal profession and others, who were worried that this implied some linkage between the police and the courts.

In both the assize courts and the courts of quarter sessions, cases were heard before juries. However, one of the most significant developments over the period was the way in which the jury shifted from being an active participant in a trial, with its members interrupting, asking questions, and using their perceptions of the defendant and the offence in shaping their verdict, to becoming an audience whose task was simply to reach a verdict after watching the adversarial contest between professional lawyers. The process was gradual. It was not the result of any legislation or key legal rulings; rather, it was the corollary of the growing authority of the legal profession. At the beginning of the eighteenth century it was rare for a man with legal training to prosecute, still less defend, in a run-of-the-mill criminal case. However, by the 1730s prosecution counsel were appearing in increasing numbers, and defence counsel to a slightly lesser extent. It is not clear why the development occurred, especially since counsel increased the costs of a case markedly, but by the 1840s the lack of prosecuting counsel at an assize could provoke caustic comments from the presiding judge. Poor defendants had problems with this system; not only could they not give evidence on oath until after 1898, but there was no provision for legal aid until the Poor Prisoner's Defence Act 1903. During the nineteenth century any defendant seeking a professional defence could get cheap counsel through the 'Dock Brief' system by which, for the fee of a guinea, he or she could obtain the services of a barrister without the mediation of a solicitor, but the services obtained in this way were rarely of much quality (Beattie 1986: 352–62; Emsley 1996a: 193–6).

The shift to summary jurisdiction may have speeded up the process between arrest, trial, and verdict, but it also brought anxieties. The legal profession complained about the impact on the fees, and consequently on the livelihood, of its members. More seriously, there was disquiet about the fact that an increase in summary trials meant a decrease in the number of defendants who had their cases heard before that keystone of the British constitution—the jury. The latter concern was compounded, first by the fear that magistrates, as men of property, might adjudicate in their own interest, and secondly, by the fact that so many magistrates were laymen with no formal training in the law. In a few instances some magistrates did hear cases when they themselves were involved; but such practice was frowned upon and always provoked critical comment. It was much more common for a magistrate to step down from the bench if he was involved in a case; but this, of course, did not always ensure an unbiased verdict since magistrates were appointed from the same social class. No government contemplated instituting the requirement of legal training for the men appointed as magistrates; it was simply accepted that they could take the advice of their clerks, who had legal training. Furthermore, increasingly in the nineteenth century, magistrates were bolstered by recorders, who were barristers, and by stipendiaries, who were also trained in the law. Indeed the pressure of business meant that the police courts in the cities came to be dominated by stipendiaries.

Tangentially it should be noted that the increasing shift to summary jurisdiction and the development of professional, bureaucratic police forces contributed to a significant change in the role of the magistrate. During the eighteenth century he (women were not eligible to serve until 1918) had an administrative as well as a judicial role. The former was reduced by the development of elected local government, in the boroughs by the Municipal Corporations Act 1835 and in the counties by the Local Government Act 1888. It was further reduced as the new police assumed more and more responsibility for making decisions in suppressing instances of disorder and riot.

PUNISHMENT

It used to be popular to think in terms of a steady amelioration in the punishment of offences from the notorious 'Bloody Code' of the eighteenth century, with over 200 capital statutes, to the final abolition of the death penalty in 1965, going hand in hand with a steady recognition of the need to reform the offender manifested by the development of the prison. Unfortunately historical processes have rarely moved in such a convenient linear fashion, and the changes in punishment and the reformation of offenders are no exceptions.

The number of capital statutes increased in the eighteenth century; but consolidation and codification were alien to the English legal tradition, and consequently there were now 200 completely distinct offences for which persons could be executed: often separate statutes covered virtually the same offence, but referred to a separate part of the country, or tidied up an outstanding problem left over from an earlier law. Furthermore, even though the number of capital statutes increased, the number of executions declined over the century. Since the second half of the seventeenth century judges had been exercising their discretion to ensure that convicted offenders were not all executed. The Transportation Act 1718, which authorized the sending of offenders to the American colonies, provided the best alternative means of avoiding execution and getting rid of offenders. As the eighteenth century wore on, only those offences deemed to be the most aggravated were likely to be punished by death. This punishment was to be a terrible example to others. As a consequence, while sensibilities decreed that fewer should hang, the need for terrible examples, following concerns about violent crime in London in the middle of the century, led to the passage of the 1752 Murder Act which, in order to deter potential offenders, instructed that the bodies of convicted murderers be delivered to surgeons for dissection, or, at the judge's discretion, be hanged in chains; furthermore, while there were usually two or three weeks between sentence and execution, under the Murder Act sentence was to be carried out the next day but one.

The shifting sensibilities which questioned the reliance on the death penalty seem to have been linked with developing arguments about the nature of God. The traditional view assumed links between God assessing sinners on the Day of Judgement and judges assessing offenders in the courts; as one cleric explained in 1739, there would be great 'confusion' in the state, 'where men only stand in awe of them that can kill the body, and trouble not at the displeasure of that Almighty Being, who after he hath killed, hath power to cast into hell!'. However, increasingly during the eighteenth century, God, rather than being the God of wrath and vengeance, was understood as the benevolent Creator; He had never intended barbarous punishments, and consequently, far more appropriate than the gallows was the prison conducted on humane principles to encourage the offender's reformation (McGowen 1988).

Prisons were not a new departure. From Tudor times petty offenders, vagrants, and prostitutes could have found themselves sentenced to a period in a Bridewell or House of Correction; and those awaiting trial on an indictment for felony were kept in prison, often for several months, awaiting trial. The use of imprisonment to punish simple felonies had been largely abandoned after the Transportation Act 1718. Interest was revived during the 1760s and early 1770s, at least in part because the combination of the occasional example on the gallows and transportation did not appear to be deterring crime effectively. The outbreak of the American War of Independence forced the issue; the courts might still sentence felons to transportation, but now there was nowhere that the sentence might be carried out. By the end of the 1780s the government had settled on the colony of New South Wales as its receptacle for felons; however, by then moves for creating prisons where the offender might be reformed were already under way, partly through local initiative but also with significant moves on the part of central government.

Pinpointing the reasons behind the growth of the prison has given rise to considerable debate. On one level there are the arguments which tie its development in with an interrelationship between forms of knowledge and the shifting strategies and institutions through which power is exercised; thus the prison becomes interlinked with the new expertise of medicine and psychiatry and with a new, enclosing, and restricting orientation to the body (Foucault 1977). For others the emergence of the prison ties in with the needs of a new industrial order and its desire for a controllable, disciplined workforce (Ignatieff 1978). On a more prosaic level there were obvious, practical difficulties which fostered change and reform. Typhus broke out in crowded gaols made still more crowded by the temporary halt to transportation. The periodic baccanalia at Tyburn not only threatened order, but also suggested that the traditional argument behind this kind of punishment, that it served to deter, was unconvincing; such suspicions fused with the changing view of God and the Enlightenment's perception of man as a rational being who could, through reason, be taught good behaviour. In 1767, Cesare Beccaria's *Dei Delitti e delle Pene*, already widely praised on the Continent, appeared in English translation; it was warmly received for its criticisms of the barbaric punishments of the past and its exhortation to create a rational system within which punishment was certain and fitted the crime. Ten years later John Howard published his detailed and depressing account of *The State of the Prisons in England and Wales*. Rather than changing men's minds, both of these books probably crystallized thoughts and ideas already in motion. In 1779 Parliament passed the Penitentiary Act providing for the construction of two prisons in the metropolis, one for 600 men and the other for 300 women who, instead of transportation, were to be reformed and taught the habits of industry. However, financial retrenchment following the war against the American colonists and the enormous expense of the Revolutionary and Napoleonic wars slowed and constrained national developments along these lines. Millbank, the first national penitentiary, was not begun until 1812 and not opened until 1816.

The Revolutionary and Napoleonic wars compelled the government to take on the management of large numbers of prisoners. On the one hand there were the felons, held in increasing numbers on aged, dismasted warships (known as the hulks) because of the difficulties which war imposed on their shipment to Australia; on the other, there were the large numbers of prisoners of war who had to be accommodated— the prison at Princeton on Dartmoor was opened in 1809 for 6,000 such. At the same time the chorus of demands for reform of the system of punishment became ever more shrill, driven by determined individuals, like Sir Samuel Romilly, and by Evangelical reformist bodies such as, most notably, the Society for the Improvement of Prison Discipline and the Reformation of Juvenile Offenders which was established in 1815. Parliament, by no means the diehard reactionary institution it is sometimes portrayed as for this period, responded by reducing the number of capital statutes and by limiting the opportunities for graft and corruption among prison governors and their turnkeys. During the 1820s, Peel successfully reformed and rationalized the criminal law; though whether this was the result of humanitarianism, or the desire to shore up a system creaking under the weight of increased prosecutions and convictions, remains a moot point (Gatrell 1994). In 1833, a body of Criminal Law Commissioners was appointed to establish a rational system of punishment whereby the punishment was to fit the crime; but their attempts foundered on the sheer complexity of the task.

Prison reform reached a climax in the 1830s, with debates between the advocates of the separate system (wherein convicts were separated from each other in the belief that, in the quiet of their solitary cells, with their Bibles, the exhortation of the chaplain, and their work at a hand crank, they would reach a realization of their wrongdoing and consequent repentence) and those of the silent system (wherein a strict discipline of silence would bring the prisoner to a similar recognition). The former, urged by William Crawford, a member of the Society for the Improvement of Prison Discipline, and by the Rev. Whitworth Russell, the chaplain of Millbank, who were both appointed to a new inspectorate of prisons in 1835, resulted in the opening of Pentonville in 1842. Pentonville was a bleak, dehumanizing establishment from which, in its early years, an annual toll of between five and fifteen of the 450 inmates were taken away to the asylum; and others sought escape through suicide. But while the separate and silent systems were experimented with in varying degrees across the country, the majority of prisons remained under the control of local authorities, and developments here were constrained by local government finance and the pressures from ratepayers.

It was also during the 1830s that the number of offenders who were transported reached a peak of about 5,000 a year. There had always been debate about the effectiveness of transportation. During the eighteenth century there were a few who protested that, rather than punishing the offender, transportation gave him or her an undeserved opportunity to start a new life. By the early nineteenth century it was being alleged that some individuals were committing crimes deliberately so as to get themselves transported to a pleasant environment where the shortage of labour promised opportunity for profit and advancement. In reality the convict settlements in Australia could be harsh and cruel, yet the very fact that such allegations could be made in itself served to undermine the deterrence of the punishment. Furthermore, as free settlers and the children of the convicts began to form the majority of citizens in the Australian colonies, so their opposition grew to the mother country foisting its dregs upon them. Dissatisfaction with transportation, both in Britain and in the colonies, brought about a steady reduction from the 1840s until, in 1857, it was abolished as a judicial sentence (though a handful of offenders continued to be sent to Western Australia until 1867).

The Annual Criminal Statistics reveal that, by the 1860s, over 90 per cent of those convicted of indictable offences were being sentenced to terms of imprisonment, and the gradual end of transportation confirmed the prison as the principal form of punishment. But the same period witnessed increasing fears about what to do with offenders once they were released from gaol. In many respects the popular assumptions about a separate 'criminal class' tended to undermine the notions of moral reformation which were central to prison policy during the second quarter of the century. Individuals stamped with the stigma of a prison term often found it difficult to find work, and this could be aggravated by the police marking them out as 'known offenders'. The Penal Servitude Act 1853 attempted to address some of the problems. It extended sentences and toughened the discipline in prisons in lieu of transportation; it also formally introduced the ticket of leave system, whereby convicts could be released on licence following good behaviour. A succession of Acts followed, seeking to fine-tune the system; but penal servitude, while it remained on the statute book until 1948, was never precisely defined, and the problems for the police in supervising those on tickets of leave, not to mention the threat which this supervision suspended over an ex-convict's head, were enormous.

It was popularly assumed that the garotting attacks of the 1850s and early 1860s were the work of members of the criminal class on tickets of leave. The panic prompted a further hardening of penal discipline with the 'Garotter's Act' of 1863; this also introduced flogging as a punishment for street robbery in addition to a prison term, and, like penal servitude, this provision remained on the statute book until 1948. The recommendations of a Lords' Select Committee chaired by Lord Carnarvon, also in 1863, led to a further tightening of discipline within the national convict prisons; long-term prisoners sentenced to penal servitude now spent an initial nine months in solitary confinement in Millbank or Pentonville, before being moved to one of the public works prisons of Chatham, Dartmoor, Portland, or Portsmouth.

The Scottish equivalent of these institutions was the General Prison in Perth, begun in 1840, opened in 1843, and completed in 1859. But in Scotland, as well as in England and Wales, the majority of gaols continued to be not these national institutions but smaller, local ones. Only in 1877 did legislation sweep away local management and, in consequence, begin to reduce the number of prisons. The Prisons Act of that year appointed prison commissioners, responsible to the Home Secretary, who were to superintend all prisons and submit annual reports to Parliament.

Centralization under the prison commissioners brought a uniform system of punishment across the country, which had been the aim of many reformers at least since the early nineteenth century; and punishment was now to be in private—not for the Victorians the public spectacle to deter potential offenders. Floggings and, after 1868, executions were to be carried out behind prison walls. But no sooner was the uniformity of punishment achieved than it began to be queried, as the authorities sought to come to terms with the individuals who did not fit the criminal stereotype for whom the prison system had been designed—notably juveniles, women, and offenders from the higher social classes, such as some of the Irish Nationalists and the gentlemen convicted of various forms of commercial fraud or embezzlement. At the same time the number of recidivists committed to prison was increasing, and while the decline of first offenders and the levelling out of the crime statistics suggested that the Victorian war against crime was a success, the recidivists were regarded as evidence of the prisons' overall failure to deter or to reform criminals. The problem became linked to the changing perception of professional criminals less as a 'class' and more as a small hard core, bolstered by a much larger number of social inadequates who constituted that part of the population least able to cope with the pressures of modern life, especially modern urban life. This changing perception increasingly worked its way into sentencing policy and policy-making in general, notably with the report of the Gladstone Committee in 1895 and the direction pursued by the second chairman of the prison commissioners, Evelyn Ruggles-Brise. Alternatives were sought for incarceration, and, rather than seeking to eradicate the evil habits of a class, the treatment of offenders began to be geared, more and more, to what were perceived as the needs of particular individuals. Probation was introduced for first offenders in 1887 and was put on a more general footing twenty years later, with social workers, in the form of probation officers, seeking to help the inadequate, petty criminal member of society to adjust to the community without being taken from that community. Borstals were developed for young offenders, and these particularly—but also in some degree the conventional prisons—were encouraged to employ what were, in contemporary parlance, scientific systems of therapeutics (Weiner 1990: chapters 8 and 9).

The amelioration of the prison system during the inter-war period was gradual. The Victorian prison uniform with its broad arrows, the silence rule, and the punitive labour, were all mitigated in the 1920s. But the food and living conditions of prisoners remained poor and provoked a serious 'mutiny' among the inmates of Dartmoor in 1932. The policy of reducing incarceration and the search for alternatives were maintained, and the overall success of the system appeared to be underlined by the prison commissioners' ability to continue closing prisons but, at the same time, to maintain a surplus capacity. In 1951, the chairman could boast that it had been necessary to build only two institutions since the beginning of the century: Camp Hill on the Isle of Wight, and Lowdham Grange Borstal (Fox 1952: 98). In many respects the Criminal Justice Act 1948, which swept away most of the severe vestiges of the Victorian system, was the climax of the shift towards rehabilitating individual offenders. It showed something of a liberal consensus between Labour and Conservative politicians, the penal reform lobby, and the professionals working in the system. The Act abolished corporal punishment; it provided preventive detention for the worst recidivists, but 'corrective training' for others; detention centres were created for young offenders who were felt to require something stiffer than probation, but not as severe as Borstal; and attendance centres were established for a variety of petty offenders of all ages who could be required to attend in their free time and participate in a variety of activities not necessarily of their own choosing (Bailey 1987: 302–305).

SHIFTS AND CONTEXTS

The 200 years surveyed here witnessed a shift from crime control mechanisms which were essentially local, personal, and—since constables, thief-takers, justices, and gaolers took fees from clients and charges—entrepreneurial, to crime control institutions which were bureaucratic, largely impersonal, and increasingly centralized. This shift took place against the background of a move from a predominantly agrarian-based economy with a largely rural population, to an industrial, capitalist economy, with, from about 1850, a majority of people living in towns. The growing economy resulted in more moveable possessions owned by a greater variety of individuals, and this provided new and probably greater opportunities and temptations for theft; and while not necessarily accepting arguments about *anomie* leading to crime, the more complex, impersonal nature of towns probably also offered greater opportunities and temptations for crime. The question remains, however, what, if anything, was the relationship between economic and social change and the developing institutions of crime control?

Exploring the institutional developments in the light of the economic and social changes has been illuminating: clearly, economic and social ideas influenced the understanding of offences and offenders; the growth of London and other big cities, together with fears about the new urban population, contributed to the creation of police forces; parallels can be detected between the nature of, and the supporters and advocates of, the prison, the new workhouse, and the factory. Yet the development of crime control institutions has not been unique to liberal capitalist societies like Britain. Where Britain has been unique is in the perception of the state. During the nineteenth century, unlike the most influential and powerful of its continental neighbours, the British state acquired an aura of stability, success and, above all, benevolence. It remains a moot point the extent to which this state acted in the interests of a new capitalist class; certainly businessmen as tax and ratepayers were often reluctant to provide the money for new police and prisons, and government, both central and local, often disappointed reformers by not raising the money necessary for their cherished projects. Yet the Victorian state and its successors did grow; and, in the name of greater efficiency and rationalization which, it was claimed, would benefit the population as a whole, it centralized. The people driving this growth—reformers, politicians, and civil servants—believed in progress and their own humanitarianism; the gradual amelioration of the penal system from the late nineteenth century, in itself, is an indication of the power of these beliefs. The same world view also influenced the first historians of these institutions and celebrated the police and prison systems as the achievements of a benificent, progressive state and society. A more cynical, more pessimistic age is also more critical of its institutions, and the contemporary historians of crime and crime control cannot so readily share such an explanation for the changes they explore.

Selected further reading

The five volumes of Leon Radzinowicz, *A History of English Criminal Law and its Administration from 1750* (London: Stevens, 1948–86) are an invaluable, though daunting and rather Whiggish, reference work for the eighteenth and nineteenth centuries. Those looking for a gentler introduction to the subjects discussed above could usefully turn to the following:

J.M. Beattie, *Crime and the Courts in England 1660–1800*, Oxford: Clarendon Press, 1986. A scholarly but highly readable exploration of the way that the English courts dealt with crime during the period of the Bloody Code. The main focus is on Surrey and Sussex.

Clive Emsley, *Crime and Society in England, 1750–1900*, 2nd edn, London: Longman, 1996. A basic text pulling together recent research.

Clive Emsley, *The English Police: A Political and Social History*, 2nd edn, London: Longman, 1996. A reassessment of the development of the English Police which draws on several largely unexplored, provincial, archival collections as well as the better-known Parliamentary and Metropolitan Police records.

David J.V. Jones, *Crime and Policing in the Twentieth Century. The South Wales Experience*, Cardiff: University of Wales Press, 1996. The only historical study of crime and policing in the twentieth century. It draws usefully on the hitherto unused archives of the South Wales Police.

Peter King, *Crime, Justice and Discretion in England 1740–1820*, Oxford: Oxford University Press, 2000. An important, cogently argued account of the judicial process in eighteenth-century England, how it was used by different social groups, and how offenders were processed through it.

Martin J. Wiener, *Reconstructing the Criminal: Culture, Law and Policy in England 1830–1914*, Cambridge: Cambridge University Press, 1990. An important and illuminating assessment of how shifts in the understanding of human nature shaped the development of criminal policy.

Lucia Zedner, *Women, Crime, and Custody in Victorian England*, Oxford: Clarendon Press, 1991. This has to be the starting point for any historical research on women and crime in the modern period.

References

ANON (H.W. HOLLAND) (1863), 'The Science of Garrotting and Housebreaking', *Cornhill Magazine*, 7: 79–92.

ASCOLI, D. (1979), *The Queen's Peace: The Origins and Development of the Metropolitan Police 1829–1979*, London: Hamish Hamilton.

BAILEY, V. (ed.) (1981), *Policing and Punishment in Nineteenth-Century Britain*, London: Croom Helm.

—— (1987), *Delinquency and Citizenship: Reclaiming the Young Offender 1914–1918*, Oxford: Clarendon Press.

BEAN, J.P. (1981), *The Sheffield Gang Wars*, Sheffield: D and D Publications.

BEATTIE, J.M. (1975), 'The criminality of women', *Journal of Social History*, 8: 80–116.

—— (1981), 'Judicial Records and the Measurement of Crime in Eighteenth-Century England', in L.A. Knafla (ed.), *Crime and Criminal Justice in Europe and Canada*: Waterloo, Ontario: Wilfred Laurier University: 127–45.

—— (1986), *Crime and the Courts in England 1660–1800*, Oxford: Clarendon Press.

BENTLEY, D.J. (1998), *English Criminal Justice in the Nineteenth Century*, London: Hambledon Press.

BURN, W.L. (1964), *The Age of Equipoise: A Study of the Mid-Victorian Generation*, London: Allen and Unwin.

CARSON, W.G. (1984), 'Policing the Periphery: The Development of Scottish Policing 1795–1900', Part I, *Australian and New Zealand Journal of Criminology*, 17: 207–32.

—— (1985), 'Policing the Periphery: The Development of Scottish Policing 1795–1900', Part II, *Australian and New Zealand Journal of Criminology*, 18: 3–16.

—— and IDZIKOWSKA, H. (1989), 'The Social Production of Scottish Policing, 1795–1900', in D. Hay and F. Snyder (eds), *Policing and Prosecution in Britain 1750–1850*, Oxford: Clarendon Press.

COCKBURN, J.S. (1991), 'Patterns of Violence in English Society: Homicide in Kent 1560–1985', *Past and Present*, 131: 70–106.

COLQUHOUN, P. (1796), *A Treatise on the Police of the Metropolis*, 3rd edn, London: C. Dilly.

CONLEY, C.A. (1991), *The Unwritten Law: Criminal Justice in Victorian Kent*, New York: Oxford University Press.

CRITCHLEY, T.A. (1978), *A History of Police in England and Wales*, 2nd edn, London: Constable.

DAVIS, J.S. (1984), '"A Poor Man's System of Justice." The London Police Courts in the Second Half of the Nineteenth Century', *Historical Journal*, 27: 309–35.

—— (1989), 'Prosecutions and their Context: The Use of the Criminal Law in Later Nineteenth-Century London', in D. Hay and F. Snyder (eds), *Policing and Prosecution in Britain 1750–1850*, Oxford: Clarendon Press.

D'CRUZE, S. (1998), *Crimes of Outrage: Sex, violence and Victorian working women*, London: UCL Press.

DE LACY, M. (1986), *Prison Reform in Lancashire, 1700–1850. A Study in Local Administration*, Manchester: Manchester University Press.

DIXON, D. (1991), *From Prohibition to Regulation: Bookmaking, Anti-Gambling and the Law*, Oxford: Clarendon Press.

EMSLEY, C. (1996a), *Crime and Society in England 1750–1900*, 2nd edn, London: Longman.

—— (1996b), *The English Police: A Political and Social History*, 2nd edn, London: Longman.

FEELEY, M.M., and LITTLE, D.H. (1991), 'The vanishing female: The decline of women in the criminal process, 1687–1912', *Law and Society Review*, 25: 719–57.

FIELDING, H. (1751), *An Enquiry into the Late Increase of Robbers*, London: A. Millar.

FORSYTHE, W.J. (1987), *The Reform of Prisons, 1830–1900*, London: Croom Helm.

—— (1991), *Penal Discipline, Reformatory Projects and the English Prison Commission, 1895–1939*, Exeter: University of Exeter Press.

FOUCAULT, M. (1977), *Discipline and Punish: The Origins of the Prison*, London: Allen Lane.

FOX, Sir L. (1952), *The English Prison and Borstal Systems*, London: Routledge and Kegan Paul.

GATRELL, V.A.C. (1980), 'The Decline of Theft and Violence in Victorian and Edwardian England', in V.A.C. Gatrell, B. Lenman, and G. Parker (eds), *Crime and the Law: The Social History of Crime in Western Europe since 1500*, 238–370, London: Europa.

—— (1990), 'Crime, Authority and the Policeman State', in F.M.L. Thompson (ed.), *The Cambridge Social History of Britain 1750–1950*, 3: 243–310, Cambridge: Cambridge University Press.

—— (1994), *The Hanging Tree: Execution and the English People 1770–1868*, Oxford: Oxford University Press.

GILLIS, J.R. (1975), 'The Evolution of Juvenile Delinquency in England, 1890–1914', *Past and Present*, 67: 96–126.

GLYDE, J. (1856a), *Suffolk in the Nineteenth Century: Physical, social, moral, religious and industrial*, London.

—— (1856b), 'Localities of Crime in Suffolk', *Journal of the Statistical Society*, 19: 102–106.

GODFREY, B (1999a), 'Law, Factory Discipline and "Theft": The Impact of the Factory on Workplace Appropriation in Mid to Late Nineteenth-Century Yorkshire', *British Journal of Criminology*, 39: 56–71.

—— (1999b), 'Judicial impartiality and the use of the criminal law against labour: the sentencing of workplace appropriators in Northern England, 1840–1880', *Crime, histoire & sociétés/Crime, history & societies*, 3: 57–72.

—— (1999c), 'Workplace appropriation and the gendering of Factory "Law": West Yorkshire, 1840–1880', in M. Arnot and C. Usborne (eds), *Gender and Crime in Modern Europe*, London: UCL Press.

HANAWAY, J. (1772), *Observations on the Causes of the Dissoluteness which reigns among the lower Classes of People: the Propensity of some to Petty Larceny: and the Danger of Gaming, Concubinage, and an excessive Fondness for amusement in high life*, London: J. and F. Rivington.

HAY, D. (1975), 'Property, Authority and the Criminal Law', in D. Hay, P. Linebaugh, E.P. Thompson *et al.*, *Albion's Fatal Tree: Crime and Society in Eighteenth-Century England*, 17–63, London: Allen Lane.

—— and SNYDER, F. (eds.) (1989), *Policing and Prosecution in Britian 1750–1850*, Oxford: Clarendon Press.

HOWSON, G. (1970), *Thief-taker General: The Rise and Fall of Jonathan Wild*, London: Hutchinson.

IGNATIEFF, M. (1978), *A Just Measure of Pain: The Penitentiary in the Industrial Revolution 1750–1850*, London: Macmillan.

INNES, J., and STYLES, J. (1986), 'The Crime Wave: Recent Writing on Crime and Criminal Justice in Eighteenth-Century England', *Journal Of British Studies*, 25: 380–435.

JACKSON, L. (2000), *Child Sexual Abuse in Victorian England*, London: Routledge.

JENKINS, P., and POTTER, G.W. (1988), 'Before the Krays: Organised Crime in London, 1920–1960', *Criminal Justice History: An International Annual*, 9: 209–30.

JONES, D.J.V. (1982), *Crime, Protest, Community and Police in Nineteenth-Century Britain*, London: Routledge and Kegan Paul.

—— (1992), *Crime in Nineteenth-Century Wales*, Cardiff: University of Wales Press.

KING, P.J.R. (1989), 'Prosecution Associations and their Impact in Eighteenth-Century Essex', in D. Hay and F. Snyder (eds), *Policing and Prosecution in Britain 1750–1850*, Oxford: Clarendon Press.

—— (1996), 'Female offenders, work and life-cycle change in late-eighteenth-century London', *Continuity and Change*, 11: 61–90.

KING, P. (2000), *Crime, Justice and Discretion in England 1740–1820*, Oxford: Oxford University Press.

LANDAU, N. (1984), *The Justices of the Peace 1679–1760*, Berkeley, Cal.: University of California Press.

McCONVILLE, S. (1981), *A History of English Prison Administration, vol. 1, 1750–1877*, London: Routledge and Kegan Paul.

McGOWEN, R. (1988), 'The Changing Face of God's Justice: The Debates over Divine and Human Punishment in Eighteenth-Century England', *Criminal Justice History: An International Annual*, 9: 63–98.

McHUGH, P. (1980), *Prostitution and Victorian Social Reform*, London: Croom Helm.

MORGAN, J. (1987), *Conflict and Order: Labour Disputes in England and Wales 1900–1939*, Oxford: Clarendon Press.

PALEY, R. (1989a), 'Thief-takers in London in the Age of the McDaniel Gang, c.1745–1754', in D. Hay and F. Snyder (eds), *Policing and Prosecution in Britain 1750–1850*, Oxford: Clarendon Press.

—— (1989b), '"An Imperfect, Inadequate and Wretched System"? Policing London before Peel', *Criminal Justice History: An International Annual*, 10: 95–130.

PALMER, S.H. (1988), *Police and Protest in England and Ireland 1780–1850*, Cambridge: Cambridge University Press.

PEARSON, G. (1983), *Hooligan: A History of Respectable Fears*, London: Macmillan.

PETROW, S. (1994), *Policing Morals: The Metropolitan Police and the Home Office 1870–1914*, Oxford: Clarendon Press.

PHILIPS, D. (1977), *Crime and Authority in Victorian England: The Black Country 1835–1860*, London: Croom Helm.

—— (1989), 'Good Men to Associate and Bad Men

to Conspire: Associations for the Prosecution of Felons in England, 1760–1860', in D. Hay and F. Snyder (eds), *Policing and Prosecution in Britain 1750–1850*, Oxford: Clarendon Press.

—— and STORCH, R.D. (1999), *Policing Provincial England, 1829–1856: The Politics of Reform*, London: Leicester University Press.

RADZINOWICZ, L. (1948–86), *A History of the English Criminal Law and its Administration from 1750*, 5 vols: 1 (1948), *The Movement for Reform*; 2 (1956), *The Clash between Private Initiative and Public Interest in the Enforcement of the Law*; 3 (1956), *Cross-Currents in the Movement for the Reform of the Police*; 4 (1968), *Grappling for Control*; 5 (with R. Hood) (1986), *The Emergence of Penal Policy in Victorian and Edwardian England*, London: Stevens and Sons.

RANDALL, A.J. (1990), ' "Peculiar perquisites and pernicious practices": Embezzlement in the West of England Woollen Industry c. 1750–1840', *International Review of Social History*, 35: 193–219.

REITH, C. (1938), *The Police Idea*, Oxford: Oxford University Press.

—— (1943), *British Police and the Democratic Ideal*, Oxford: Oxford University Press.

REYNOLDS, E. (1998), *Before the Bobbies: The Night Watch and Police Reform in Metropolitan London, 1720–1830*, London: Macmillan.

ROBB, G. (1992), *White-Collar Crime in Modern England: Financial Fraud and Business Morality 1845–1929*, Cambridge: Cambridge University Press.

RUMBELOW, D. (1971), *I Spy Blue: The Police and Crime in the City of London from Elizabeth I to Victoria*, London: Macmillan.

SAMUEL, R. (1981), *East End Underworld: Chapters in the Life of Arthur Harding*, London: Routledge and Kegan Paul.

SHARPE, J.A. (1985), 'The History of Violence in England: Some Observations', *Past and Present*, 108: 206–15.

SHORE, H. (1999), *Artful Dodgers: Youth and Crime in Early Nineteenth-Century London*, Woodbridge: Royal Historical Society/Boydell Press.

SINDALL, R. (1990), *Street Violence in the Nineteenth Century: Media Panic or Real Danger?*, Leicester: Leicester University Press.

STEVENSON, S.J. (1983), 'The "criminal class" in the mid-Victorian City: A study of policy conducted with special reference to those made subject to the provisions of 34 & 35 Vict. c. 112 (1871) in Birmingham and East London in the early years of registration and supervision', D. Phil., University of Oxford.

STONE, L. (1983), 'Interpersonal Violence in English Society, 1300–1980', *Past and Present*, 101: 22–33.

—— (1985), 'A Rejoinder', *Past and Present*, 108: 216–24.

STORCH, R.D. (1989), 'Policing Rural Southern England before the Police: Opinion and Practice, 1830–1856', in D. Hay and F. Snyder (eds), *Policing and Prosecution in Britain 1750–1850*, Oxford: Clarendon Press.

TAYLOR, H. (1998a), 'The politics of the rising crime statistics of England and Wales, 1914–1960', *Crime, histoire & sociétés/Crime, history & societies*, 2: 5–28.

—— (1998b), 'Rationing Crime: The Political Economy of Criminal Statistics since the 1850s', *Economic History Review*, 51: 569–90.

TOBIAS, J.J. (1972), *Crime and Society in the Nineteenth Century*, Harmondsworth: Penguin.

WALKOWITZ, J.R. (1980), *Prostitution and Victorian Society: Women, class and the state*, Cambridge: Cambridge University Press.

WEINBERGER, B. (1991), *Keeping the Peace? Policing Strikes in Britain 1906–1926*, Oxford: Berg.

WIENER, M.J. (1990), *Reconstructing the Criminal: Culture, Law and Policy in England, 1830–1914*, Cambridge: Cambridge University Press.

ZEDNER, L. (1991), *Women, Crime and Custody in Victorian England*, Oxford: Clarendon Press.

PART II

THE SOCIAL CONSTRUCTION OF CRIME AND CRIME CONTROL

8

PUNISHMENT AND CONTROL

Barbara Hudson

INTRODUCTION: CRIMINOLOGY, PUNISHMENT, AND CONTROL

This chapter will present an overview of the body of criminological work which has examined the nature of *punishment and control* in modern societies. Major themes to be covered are:

— the relationship between crime and control;
— the nature of punishment and control;
— transformations in strategies of punishment and control;
— the relationship between punishment, control, and other societal characteristics;
— the punishment and control of women.

These themes recur throughout the development of sociological and criminological work on punishment and control, albeit in slightly different formulations as they are reproduced in the terminology and theoretical orientations of different periods. This chapter is organized more or less chronologically; its division into sections reflects both developments and transitions in the nature of punishment and control (the development of the modern prison; the growth of alternatives to custody; the emergence of contemporary mass imprisonment), and the theoretical perspectives in currency at any particular time (progressivist, Marxist, Foucauldian, and post-structuralist, etc.). The exception to this thematic continuity is the punishment and control of women. This is largely absent in the mainstream work on punishment and control in all eras, and is dealt with in a more or less separatist literature which often has little connection with theorizing in other fields of criminology and penology, and is often detached from any political–penological context. A separate section on the control and punishment of females is therefore included here, although there is some reference to gender issues in the other sections.

Key writers whose work will be discussed include Pat Carlen, Stanley Cohen, Michel Foucault, David Garland, and Jonathan Simon, and important concepts which will be introduced and explained include *discipline; panopticism; crime and governance; inclusion and exclusion; new penology; penal populism; legitimation; penal modernism and postmodernism; risk and control; punishment as an aspect of culture*; and *mass imprisonment*.

Punishment, in criminology, is punishment for crime, imposed by the judiciary in accordance with penal law, and administered by penal institutions such as prisons and the probation service. Other types of 'punishment', such as detention of pupils by teachers, beatings or community expulsions of criminals by vigilantes and lynch mobs, are usually excluded (Hudson 1996: 2). It is essential to the definition of punishment in this context that it is inflicted because of behaviour which transgresses the criminal law, and that the pain or hardship involved is intentional, not just a coincidental or accidental outcome. The criminology of punishment is conceived as the study of *penality*, a term associated with Michel Foucault (1977), which indicates a complex of theories, institutions, practices, laws, professional roles, and political–public attitudes which are concerned with the sanctioning of criminals (Garland and Young 1983: 14).

Just as criminology's concern with punishment does not include all the usages of the term in everyday life, the discipline has generally adopted a more restricted definition of control than the wider sociological concept of 'social control'. It has followed the American sociological tradition of designating processes designed to produce conforming behaviour, such as education, religion, broadcasting, etc., as 'socialization', concerning itself with those institutions of control—law, police, courts, prisons, etc.—which provide 'the repertoire of organized social responses to deviance' (Blomberg and Cohen 1995: 3). This definition allows for further differentiation into, for example, state-sponsored and non state-sponsored responses to deviance; responses to crime and responses to other forms of deviance such as mental illness or 'alternative lifestyles'; socially inclusive and socially exclusive strategies of control.

At various times, criminology has dealt with punishment and control as separate phenomena or as one phenomenon, and at different times it has merged 'crime control' within a generalized study of social control, or has focused on crime control without much reference to wider fields of control. However close the focus on crime as opposed to other forms of deviant behaviour, and however close the focus on punishment rather than more general strategies of crime control, it is usually necessary to utilize the insights of wider aspects of social control, and of broader traditions of social theory, to understand particular facets of punishment and control which criminologists wish to study (Garland and Sparks 2000; Loader and Sparks, in Chapter 3 of this volume). Two of the most important strands in the criminology of punishment and control have been investigations of the balance between conformity-producing and deviance-repressing modes of control (or the balance between informal social control and repressive penal control), and of the ways in which punishment and control are reflections of more general cultural trends (for example, the 'civilizing' and 'de-civilizing' of punishments).

Criminology is itself part of the apparatus of control in modern societies, as well as being concerned with the study of control. It is a body of knowledge developed to help the day-to-day work of police, courts, prison governors and medical officers, probation officers, social workers, and forensic psychiatrists, as well as to inform legislators and policy-makers. Much criminology, often referred to as mainstream or administrative criminology (Young 1988 *inter alia*), contents itself with the unre-flexive production of technicist information for legislators, criminal justice planners, and practitioners. Such literature is not my concern here. More critical criminologies have sought to interrogate and understand the nature of punishment and control in modern societies, and it is this body of work which is discussed in what follows. This focus also excludes work which—although it may be critical and analytical—is concerned primarily with describing the detail of imprisonment, community penalties, or crime prevention programmes (Morgan, in Chapter 30 of this volume; Pease, in Chapter 26 of this volume; Raynor, in Chapter 31 of this volume; Matthews and Francis 1996; Brownlee 1998; Worrall 1997).

Another body of work, which has bearing on criminological understanding of punishment and control, is the legal-philosophical writing on punishment. This is in many ways analogous to the wider sociology (theories of modernism and late-modernism, for example) that control studies draw on. From time to time such work becomes especially important, as for example when the theory of 'just deserts' became prominent in the 1980s and influenced the institutions and practices of punishment and control in many countries (Cohen 1985; Hudson 1987). Generally, though, this legal-philosophical work is a separate discursive enterprise and proceeds in parallel to, but not as part of, the criminology of punishment and control.

MODERNISM AND THE RISE OF THE PRISON

THE LABOUR MARKET HYPOTHESIS

A major, perhaps *the* major, stimulus to the socio-criminological study of punishment has been penal change: change in the use of imprisonment; abolition of the death penalty; the changing nature of penal goals and regimes. The first big penological project of sociological criminology was understanding the emergence of a new form of penality with the industrial revolution. The 200 years from the middle of the eighteenth century (approximately) to the beginning of the third quarter of the twentieth century (approximately) is seen as a distinct period of *penal modernism*, a period characterized by two linked phenomena:

1. emergence of imprisonment as the main form of punishment for routine crimes;

2. a penal goal of bringing about change in the offender, and the use of the emergent human/social sciences to that end.

A common starting point of social-historical analysis of the development of penal systems in the modern industrial state is to note that as nations industrialized they moved from the arbitrary infliction of physical punishments (execution, mutilation, the stocks) to punishments aimed at the mentalities, making bad people good. Prisons ceased to be primarily places where people were held awaiting processing (trial, sentence, execution, deportation, payment of debts) and became a place for the serving of sentences. Although remand functions continued, the use of imprisonment as punishment grew massively and rapidly with the coming of the industrial revolution. In every country that industrialized, imprisonment emerged as the main form of punishment.

Imprisonment was seen by the first sociologists of penality simply as penal progress. The rise of the prison was thought to be progressive in two senses: first, it was more lenient than previous forms of punishment;[1] secondly, it was developed around a rationale of reforming offenders. The clearest theoretical expression of the progressive idea comes in Durkheim's *Two Laws of Penal Evolution* (1984, first published 1902). Durkheim's two laws are, first, that punishments will become less intense as societies modernize; and, secondly, that imprisonment will become the main sanction, replacing death and torture. He argues that in less-developed societies power is concentrated in an absolute sovereign (be that a king, a theocracy, or a small oligarchy). Such an authority will present itself as representing the divine, or embodying the sacred spirit of the society, so that crime will not only be an act against fellow-citizens, but will be against the highest authority; crime will have a sacrilegious quality and thus demand severe, sacrificial penalties. As societies modernize, governments become more democratic and citizens more equal and inter-dependent, crime takes on a more secular aspect and does not demand such severe penalties. Offenders also evoke more sympathy, according to Durkheim, because of the networks of solidarity such societies engender.

Durkheim allows for occasional penal regression if modern societies experience periods of absolutism, but sees such reversions as 'blips' in a general progression towards more humane punishments. He cites evidence of penal progress from ancient Egypt onwards, noting, for example, that Athens in its most democratic periods resorted to torture less than under previous regimes; that penalties of the *Ancien Régime* in France were more brutal than those of post-revolutionary regimes.[2] In modern democratic, industrial societies death without mutilation yields to imprisonment with hard labour, and then to imprisonment without additional burdens.

By the mid-1970s, this story of penal progress dropped out of criminological favour. With hindsight, we can see this as part of a general disillusionment with the idea of penal progressiveness. The idea of rehabilitation was falling out of favour with criminal justice professionals and their academic critics, and the idea of penal failure was more in keeping with the spirit of the times than the idea of penal progress. So-called 'revisionist' accounts of the development of modern penal systems appeared which linked the rise of imprisonment as a mass punishment not to humanitarianism, but to the needs of capitalist economies, and saw modern systems not as more humane, but as more sophisticated.

The first of these 'labour market' accounts was Rusche and Kirchheimer's

---

[1] It needs to be remembered that imprisonment at this time was introduced as an alternative to execution or (for a limited time in the imperial nations) transportation, rather than, today, being an alternative to probation, community service, and other community penalties.

[2] The torture, death and mutilation of Wallace depicted in the film *Braveheart* provides a good illustration of pre-democratic punishment.

Punishment and Social Structure (1968), first published in 1939 but re-published in 1968, when it was more in keeping with the mood of the times. This book demonstrated that historically, fluctuations in the severity of punishment were linked to changes in the value of labour. At times when demand for labour outstripped supply, and labour was therefore valuable, punishments became less severe; and when supply outstripped demand, they became harsher. Rusche, who sets out the basic principles of the labour market hypothesis in the first half of the book, explains that in times of high demand, forms of punishment which include forced labour and which return offenders to the labour market will be preferred to forms such as execution which remove them from it. Rusche also described a principle of *less eligibility*. This principle provides that in order to deter the 'reserve army of labour' from crime, conditions inside the prison must be worse than anything the 'free' labourer is likely to encounter outside the prison.

Critics charge that even if there is a fit between labour market statistics and punishment statistics, Rusche and Kirchheimer oversimplify the connection; correlations do not mean that penal change can be 'reduced to' changes in the demand for labour. Nonetheless, it has generally been accepted among criminologists that there is a strong connection between demand for labour and harshness of punishments. In more recent times, labour market studies have concentrated on fluctuations in the use of imprisonment, seeing rates rise in times of high unemployment and fall in times of full employment (Greenberg 1977; Jankovic 1977; Box and Hale 1982; Melossi 1985; Barlow *et al.* 1993).

Both Durkheim and Rusche and Kirchheimer raise, but do not adequately answer, the question 'why prison?'. Explaining rises and falls in penal severity is not the same as explaining why prison became the major form of punishment. For Rusche and Kirchheimer, the answer was that prison labour supplemented the supply of free labour at the same time as allowing for the transformation of criminals into labourers, but it is not inevitable that the form of punishment which supplied labour should be imprisonment. They perhaps provide an answer as to why prisoners are made to work, but not why penalized workers should work in prison. In modern times we have seen the introduction of community service as an alternative form of penal labour, and it is not immediately obvious why something like bonded labour should not have developed rather than imprisonment.[3]

Melossi and Pavarini focus on the question 'why prison?', rather than a generalized argument about penal severity and leniency. They ask: 'Why is it that in every industrial society, this institution has become the dominant punitive instrument to the extent that prison and punishment are commonly regarded as almost synonymous?' (1981: 1). They find their answer in the work of the Marxist theorist Pashukanis, who suggests that the precondition for development of imprisonment as the major form of

---

[3] Analysts of the growth of imprisonment and the functions of prison labour in the USA have argued that prison labour replaced slave labour after the abolition of slavery, as a source of cheap labour used for the building of the infrastructure of the spread of capitalism throughout the country: building railroads which opened up the west and the south, for example (Hawkins 1986). This does not answer the 'why prison' question for non-slave European nations.

punishment was the development of wage labour as the major economic form. Wage labour is measured in units of time (so much per hour, so much per annum), and imprisonment is also measured in units of time—'do the crime, do the time'.

Even if this Marxist account is no longer as simplistic as the earlier versions, it set the tone for a decidedly functionalist approach to penality. Again, this is congruent with the disillusionment with penal systems that was setting in as crime rates rose in the affluent and relatively tolerant and lenient 1960s and early 1970s (Taylor 1981). Prison, it was widely held, failed to control crime, yet it persisted as a social institution: its real function must therefore be something else.

Other functionalist accounts of the prison concentrated on the need of capitalist industrialism to have a geographically stable labour force, and highlighted the prison's role in controlling vagrancy (Rothman 1971). Another theme was the prison as a visible symbol to the poor of what awaited them if they refused to accept the discipline of factory labour (Reiman 1979). The prisons of the 'great incarceration' of the Victorian era were built in working-class areas and were visible from the rows of back-to-back houses built for workers—Strangeways, Walton, and Pentonville are among English examples.

Melossi and Pavarini developed the functionalist approach and the idea of the equivalence of prison and wage labour, by focusing on the concept of *discipline*. The essence of factory work, they point out, is that workers accept the discipline of time and place—they are in the factory at the designated times. This requirement for a disciplined populace is paralleled in all the institutions developed in the era of industrial capitalism, especially in schools and prisons (Melossi and Pavarini 1981).

DISCIPLINE AND THE ECONOMY OF ILLEGALITIES

These studies of the development of modern penal systems did not pay attention to their economic function alone, but also to their overall and defining characteristics, and to their role in the project of modern governance. The social histories of the prison established that there was no simple relationship between crime and punishment; rises and falls in use of the most severe punishments available at the time did not correlate closely with rises and falls in crime rates. These works established that there was a consistency between modes of punishment and modes of production; and further, that there was a *cultural consistency* between punishment and other social institutions. A key aspect of this cultural consistency is that the institutions of control developed in modernity—schools, prisons, factories—were *disciplinary*. They were disciplinary in two senses: they imposed discipline on those who were within them; and they enlisted the emergent disciplines of psychology, pedagogy, and sociology for control and reform.

Michel Foucault's *Discipline and Punish* (1977) is a hugely influential book, which has dominated the criminology of punishment since its publication. Foucault's central theme is discipline and the disciplines. His conception of discipline is very similar to that of Melossi and Pavarini, and although he, too, sees the influence of modes of production, Foucault departs a long way from the orthodox labour market analysis of punishment. He opens his account by contrasting a public execution in pre-revolutionary France with the regime of an institution for young offenders, eighty years later. Foucault does not show us the steps by which the one regime of punishment evolved into the other, but uses the two punitive moments to illustrate two different penalities, with different political and economic imperatives, different control strategies, and different theoretical underpinnings. What he shows us is two different modes of exercising power: a *sovereign* mode, designed to demonstrate the power of the ruler over the ruled; and a *disciplinary* mode, aimed at producing the right-thinking, lawfully-acting, conformist-behaving, 'docile bodies' needed by modernist economies, and constrained by the necessity of using strategies of power which will be regarded as legitimate in modern democratic-industrial societies.

Foucault's descriptions of the modernist institution reveal discipline and surveillance (the French title of the book is *Surveiller et Punir*) governing every moment of the inmate's life. The day is full of activity—work, education, and, as the modern penal regime developed, treatment and therapy—and even when the prisoner is alone in the cell, surveillance is a constant presence. 'The disciplinary gaze' is the essence of modern punishment as described by Foucault:

The perfect disciplinary apparatus would make it possible for a single gaze to see everything constantly. A central point would be both the source of light illuminating everything, and a locus of convergence for everything that must be known; a perfect eye that nothing would escape and a centre towards which all gazes would be turned. [Foucault 1977: 173]

This essence is encapsulated by the 'panopticon prison', a design blue-print put forward by Jeremy Bentham. In a panopticon prison, rows of cells radiate from a circular central control area, so that a guard in the centre can look down the rows. In the original design, there were arrangements of periscopes and mirrors in the cells, so that the guard could look into the cell, although the prisoner could not see the centre and know whether, at any particular moment, he was being looked at or not. He had, therefore, best assume that he was being looked at, and so behave according to the rules even in his cell. There was thus no privacy, and the restraint that prisoners were induced to impose on their behaviour made for realization of the ideal of discplinary society: the fusion of external control and self-control.[4]

The functionalism of the accounts of the rise of imprisonment produced in the 1970s and 1980s is evident in Foucault's analysis. He points out that prisons, far from reforming offenders, encourage recidivism, as inmates form a subculture with loyalties to each other and further alienation from authority. Rather than seeing this as a failure which must surely lead to the prison's demise, Foucault says that we should ask what is served by the failure of the prison. The answer he gives is that prison classifies and organizes crime and delinquency into that which can be tolerated and that which must be repressed, laying down the limits of social tolerance, revealing criminals to other sections of the poor (who might otherwise be sympathetic to them) as dangerous, wicked, and as those against whom the 'respectable' poor need protection:

---

[4] Bentham's blue-print was never fully implemented in the Victorian era. Now, however, CCTV cameras are installed in some cells, where the most difficult and disturbed prisoners are kept under constant surveillance.

... perhaps one should reverse the problem and ask oneself what is served by the failure of the prison; what is the use of these different phenomena that are continually being criticized; the maintenance of delinquency; the encouragement of recidivism, the transformation of the occasional offender into a habitual delinquent, the organization of a closed milieu of delinquency ... Penality would then appear to be a way of handling illegalities, of laying down the limits of tolerance, of giving free rein to some, of putting pressure on others, of excluding a particular section, of making another useful, of neutralizing certain individuals and of profiting from others. In short, penality does not simply 'check' illegalities; it differentiates them, it provides them with a general economy. [Foucault 1977: 262]

These themes of prison (and modern penality) functioning not so much to control crime as to repress and divide the poor; serving the needs of the economy by containing unwanted labour in times of surplus, and training and moralizing criminals in times of labour shortage; and ideologically performing the task of demonstrating which rules are important and which transgressions are too damaging not to be taken seriously, have been constant in theorizing about prisons and punishment since then, reappearing in slightly different forms, with slightly different balances of emphasis between the elements. The critical criminology of punishment is concerned above all with the exercise of power against the economically unwanted, the marginalized, alien, and dispossessed (Mathiesen 1974; Reiman 1979; Wacquant 2001).

Some analysts have objected to the functionalism of these accounts, especially Foucault's. Prison, they say, really is a failure, and the reason it survives is that nothing else has proved effective in controlling crime (Ignatieff 1983; Mathiesen 1990). Foucault's account has also been criticized for concentrating too closely on penality as a strategy for the exercise of power so that it substitutes a will-to-power reductionism for economic reductionism (Garland 1990); for empirical deficiencies in describing when and where transformative penal events occurred (Spierenburg 1984); and for over-emphasizing the disciplinary aspects of modern penality while under-emphasizing the purely punitive (Pasquino 1991; Howe 1994).

These 'revisionist' theorists of punishment (Foucault, Ignatieff, Melossi and Pavarini, Rusche and Kirchheimer) also incorporated other aspects of the sociology of modernization, especially those which stressed the growth of the power and functions of the state, and they drew upon Weber's account of the progression of bureaucratic-rationalization (Spitzer 1983). While they may differ in emphasis, these revisionist accounts of the development of modern strategies of control share many of the same concerns and assumptions:

... scepticism about the professed aims, beliefs and intentions of the reformers; concern with the analysis of power and its effects; curiosity about the relationships between intentions and consequences; determination to locate the reform enterprise in the social, economic and political contexts of the period. The problem of maintaining the social order—in the case of crime, so obvious; in the case of mental illness less so, but still traceable ... becomes dominant. [Cohen and Scull 1983: 2]

These histories established that modes of punishment reflected economic relations; that they utilized the available knowledges and technologies of their time; that there were continuities between the punishment of crime and the control of other deviant populations. Punishment and other social control processes, were, on these accounts, part of the apparatus of a governance aimed at producing a geographically stable, docile, workforce imbued with the capitalist work ethic; they were conducted according to the rule-following parameters of bureaucratic rationality, where power inheres in the office not the person; where the power attaching to any office, including the highest, is limited; where power is exercised for purposes and by means accorded legitimacy by the population.

MODALITIES OF CONTROL

PUNISHMENT AND WELFARE

Although the prison is at the centre of Foucault's study, his analysis moves out of the institution and looks at the character of control as it operates throughout society. He sees that all members of modern societies are subject to disciplinary surveillance, and may be subject to punitive partial suspension of rights short of the total deprivation of the right to liberty that imprisonment involves (disqualification from driving; supervision orders prescribing attendance at probation centres at certain times; curfews and injunctions, for example). Punitive discipline is *dispersed* from the prison, so that not only does formal punishment and control take place in many tiny 'theatres of punishment' throughout society, but all social relations become relationships of control, infused with disciplinary power. Foucault is saying much more than Melossi and Pavarini, and Rusche and Kirchheimer here, because he is not merely pointing out the similarities and symmetries between prisons and factories, but proposing that there is no essential difference between them—they are all examples of the same power principle.

Foucault famously says that modernist prisons and other sanctions form not a less severe instance of the same social institution as pre-modern punishment, but are elements of a different structure of moral ordering. He claims that the shift from a penality of corporal punishments to a penality of suspended rights signified a new objective:

to make of the punishment and repression of illegalities a regular function, coextensive with society; not to punish less, but to punish better; to punish with an attenuated severity perhaps, but in order to punish with more universality and necessity; to insert the power to punish more deeply into the social body. (1977: 82)

The task that he sees this dispersed disciplinary complex engaged in is *normalization*: the task of making all the people in the modern state into well-controlled, well-behaved, hard-working, right-thinking citizens. Through his work on mental illness, sexuality and penology, Foucault shows how the human and social sciences, and their deployment by power in the exercise of governance, produce dichotomies of the healthy and the sick, the sane and the insane, the proper and the perverted, the

law-abiding and the criminal (1973, 1977, 1978, 1986). He shows the modern individual caught up in a web of control, with self-control, informal control, and formal
control forming a seamless whole, one stepping in where the other fails. The humanities and social sciences constitute the subjectivity and the mode of being of the
citizen of modernity, and are brought into play across the different modes of control
to describe, to diagnose, to reform, to coerce the reluctant and the deviant. In describing normalization, Foucault is describing a continuous process, dispersed throughout
the social body.[5]

Dichotomies of normality and deviance produced by the human sciences are
reproduced through the working of power as the characteristics of the rough and the
respectable, the dangerous and the imperilled, the rational citizen and the irrational
outsider. The task modernity sets itself is to make the entire populace approximate to
the standards of normality: this is of course an impossible task. Normalization, therefore, as well as being dispersed is forever incomplete, which is why a crucial sub-
division among the deviant is between the curable and the incurable, the corrigible
and the incorrigible. Much of mainstream criminology, and the policies and practices
of criminal justice and punishment, are constitutively concerned with this division:
producing the diagnostic or factorial criteria for classification, devising and
implementing programmes for rehabilitation of the corrigible, lengthy or permanent
exclusion of the incorrigible.

Normalization involved the establishment of a wide spectrum of institutions to
enable, encourage, and enforce the required mentalities. A penal-welfare complex
system developed, becoming progressively more diffuse and far-reaching as the disciplines provided the classifications and technologies to deal with an ever-wider range of
abnormalities. This *penal welfarism* (Garland 1985) put counsellors as well as guards
into prisons, but also meant that welfare problems of juveniles were dealt with by
court orders, supervision, and sometimes even incarceration. The balance between the
penal system and the welfare system changes over time, under the influence of different fashions in penal theory and other political–social shifts. At times, the welfare-
disciplinary overwhelms the penal-juridical (females and young people dealt with as
sick, maladjusted, 'in moral danger', or 'in need of care and protection' rather than as
perpetrators of minor, routine crimes); and at other times the penal overwhelms the
welfarist (the addicted, the mentally disordered, the homeless, refugees being
imprisoned rather than given treatment, help, or cash). There has been a great deal of
analysis of these changes, particularly in relation to juveniles (Cohen 1979; Donzelot
1980; Newburn, in Chapter 16 of this volume).

That there are links between punishment and other modes of control is common
ground between control theorists. Control of deviant populations such as the elderly,
the mentally ill and handicapped, sufferers from contagious diseases, youthful
delinquents, and adult criminals uses the same techniques and principles: diagnosis,
labelling, segregation. Concepts such as *less eligibility* (Rusche 1978; Melossi 1985)—
the idea that conditions inside an institution should be worse than anything the

---

[5] Foucault's idea of normalization thus reconnects punishment to other forms of control, echoing Ross's
earlier conception of social control as all the processes producing conformist behaviour (Coser 1982).

potential inmate is likely to encounter on the outside— occur in relation to prison and to workhouses. Less eligibility is proposed as a deterrent both to crime and to idleness, and acts as a limit to prison reform; it is also evident, for example, in current policy limiting housing benefit for the unemployed to the cost of a bed-sitting room or room in a shared house, not allowing for rent or mortgage payments for a whole house or flat, and in restriction of benefits for asylum seekers.

FROM THE PRISON TO THE COMMUNITY (AND BACK AGAIN): DECARCERATION, DEINSTITUTIONALIZATION AND TRANSCARCERATION

Rusche and Kirchheimer, Melossi and Pavarini, and Foucault were writing about the rise of imprisonment. They took as their subject the transformation of control from torture and execution to imprisonment; from the whim of individuals to the performance of scheduled procedures by state officials; from exclusion by death or banishment to inclusion through reform and rehabilitation. What was common to the control of different dimensions of deviance in the period of rapid industrialization in the late eighteenth and nineteenth centuries, was the building of institutions to segregate and then to socialize recruits to the labour force and to isolate or normalize the deviant: schools, workhouses, asylums, and sanatoriums were institutions which had much in common, both architecturally and socially, with prisons.

The period in which these works appeared and became influential in criminology, however, was a period in which the institutional response to deviance was subject to sustained critique, and during which total institutions appeared to be becoming less central to control strategies. Mental hospitals, for example, had begun to close following the Mental Health Act 1959 in England and Wales; the Children and Young Persons Act 1969 introduced supervision orders for young people, which were meant to lead to fewer young people being committed to children's homes for either delinquency or welfare reasons; community service and suspended sentences were introduced as alternatives to custody for offenders; and the use of probation was extended.

Three of the key writers on control in the era of decarceration are David Greenberg (1975, 1977), Andrew Scull (1977, 1983), and Stanley Cohen (1979, 1985). These authors have produced critiques of the move away from institutional corrections to community corrections that have used many of the ideas and theoretical perspectives of the historians of the prison-building era.

During the 1960s and early 1970s, community corrections, such as work with adolescents designed to prevent the onset of delinquency (alternative schooling; neighbourhood projects in high-delinquency areas; placement of 'at risk' youngsters on social work caseloads; removal of children of single parents, or supposedly inadequate parents, to children's homes; treatment of 'hyperactive' children with drugs and/or counselling, in much the same way that children are being diagnosed as having attention deficit disorder and prescribed ritalin today), proliferated to general approval. Similarly, in the field of mental illness, it was taken as axiomatic that treatment in the community was preferable to treatment in hospital. To proponents of such policies, community corrections and treatments were regarded as incontrovertibly both more humane and more effective than institutional measures.

David Greenberg (1975) challenged some of the assumptions behind community corrections, saying that they were not necessarily more humane, more effective, or less costly than institutional sanctions. Andrew Scull (1977) extended a similar analysis to the treatment of the mentally ill. Their thesis was that community treatment often amounted to malign neglect, with people left to fend for themselves, unsupported or inadequately supported in a rejecting, uncaring environment; receiving patchy, untested treatment/corrections; and that the move from the institution to the community might represent cost savings for the central state, which paid the costs of care in institutions, but represented additional costs to local authorities or voluntary agencies, who paid for community corrections and care. Only if central state institutions were closed down, and income transferred from central to local government, might there be cost savings. There was usually, it was pointed out, a trade-off between humanity, effectiveness, and cheapness: the provision of benign, effective community control and care is expensive.

Greenberg and Scull identified an apparent 'decarceration era' of the 1970s. What had occurred, they argued, was that the expanding demand for labour of the prosperous 1960s, which had encouraged the spread of rehabilitative sanctions designed to fit offenders and other deviants for the labour market, had encountered the fiscal crisis of the 1970s, triggered by rises in world oil prices. As states were trying to rein back their public expenditure, recession led to mounting unemployment, so that the imperative of reducing money spent on deviant populations became stronger than the need to fit as many people as possible for the labour force.

A paradox of the decarceration period was that although there appeared to be a reduction in the incarceration of deviants, more and more people were being brought into the social control net. This apparent paradox has been explored most comprehensively by Cohen (1977, 1979, 1985), who demonstrated that the extension of community corrections seemed to fit Foucault's model of 'dispersed discipline'.

Cohen documented the increasing number of people cautioned and convicted; he chronicled the strengthening of supervisory punishments; he observed the recruitment of friends, relatives, and neighbours into surveillance, and the development of contracts and curfews. Phrases such as net-widening (more people subject to control), net-strengthening (sanctions such as probation and social work supervision having added requirements), and blurring of the boundaries (between liberty and confinement, friend and controller) became part of the academic discourse of criminologists and the professional discourse of criminal justice practitioners. Cohen's (1985) analysis seemed to show that good intentions often had bad, unintended consequences, and that the 'deeper structures' of control meant that whatever might seem to be happening in the direction of greater tolerance of diversity, normalization through the established mixture of socialization and repression would continue.

By the late 1980s, decarceration of the criminal seemed to be going into reverse, while deinstitutionalization of the mentally ill and of other 'problem populations' proceeded (children's homes and homes for the elderly continue to close, for example). Instead of following the same trajectories, as the meta-analyses of control such as those of Cohen and Foucault had anticipated, the control of crime and of other forms of deviance seemed to be reversals of each other. In the case of crime and delinquency, the criticism of reformers and others today is that the mechanisms of community control have proliferated while the number of prisons and young offender institutions has also expanded; in the case of the mentally disordered, the criticism is that hospitals and asylums have closed, but have not been replaced by community care facilities (Hudson 1993).

Exploration of these different control trends, amounting to major revision of the decarceration thesis, is provided in a volume of essays which claims that what happened was not *de*carceration, but *trans*carceration (Lowman, Menzies, and Palys 1987). Rather than moving from institutions to the community, the authors argue, people were experiencing an institutionally mobile deviant career. They were moving between jails/local prisons, half-way houses, sheltered accommodation, and in some cases on to federal penitentiaries/dispersal prisons and/or to large state mental hospitals. Whether they were in an institution within the penal system or within the health/welfare system could vary not with their actual behaviour but according to the exigencies of funding, to the relative strength and weakness of these sub-systems, and to ideological circumstances which render behaviour likely to be labelled as ill or criminal. Chapters in the collection thus comment on the 'criminalization' of mental illness and homelessness, as well as on the substitution of penal policy for social policy which has occurred in recent years (see also Hudson 1993: chapter 3). Examples of shifts between penal and medical/welfare constructions of deviant behaviour in recent years include, importantly, the moves between responding to drug addiction as sickness, needing treatment and harm-reduction responses, or as crime, needing punitive responses.

Understanding of changes in the balance between repressive and rehabilitative, coercive and socializing, exclusive and inclusive modes of control has been enhanced by the work of Stuart Hall (1980), Phil Scraton (1987), and others who have analysed the 'legitimation crisis' brought about by economic recession. If conformity cannot be secured by offering rewards to all or most of those who lead a law-abiding, orderly, and industrious life then it must be obtained—and dissent and disorder discouraged—by increased repression. For this to be accepted by the majority of the population as legitimate, blame must be seen to be due to the deviants, rather than to the socio-economic system itself.

The result of this has been described as 'authoritarian populism', whereby people who either fail to be economically successful by legitimate means, or who challenge the system, are constituted as 'enemies within', worthy only of punishment and exclusion. Criminals, the homeless, strikers, refugees, and the unemployed are seen as forming an unemployable, crime-prone and crime-tolerant, feckless and dangerous underclass, from whom the respectable must be protected both economically and physically, as they walk the streets. They are economically excluded by restrictions on benefits; excluded from concern by new conventions for counting the unemployed; and excluded from society by new rules on immigration and by increasing use of imprisonment and youth custody. Thus, even in times of economic hardship, increasing expenditure on punishment and other forms of repressive control is justified and even demanded.

POST-SOCIAL CONTROL

GOVERNANCE, RISK, AND ACTUARIALISM

From the mid-1980s onwards, criminology seemed to have retreated from concern with wider fields of deviancy and control, and to once again be focusing more exclusively on crime and punishment. The emergence of the 'left realist' paradigm, associated in England with the work of Jock Young (1986, 1987, 1988) and his colleagues, and in America with the work of Elliott Currie and others (1985), is illustrative of this reconcentration on crime. As well as urging fellow radical criminologists to take crime seriously, they were trying to produce a counter-agenda which would be as attractive to policy-makers as the right-realist recommendations of James Q. Wilson (1975), Charles Murray (1984, 1986), and John DiIulio (1991).

By the end of the century, however, punishment was being reconnected with the wider field of control. This was partly because of the analytic utility of wider socio-political and cultural contexts for understanding punishment, but also because of the appearance of new modes of control, which appear to dissolve some of the distinctions between coercive and non-coercive, penal and social, control. Closed-circuit television in city centres, security patrols in shopping malls, strengthened asylum and immigration policies, and expansion of electronic data collection, all catch in the control net the innocent as well as the guilty, and operate on distinctions such as member/non-member, resident/non-resident, creditworthy or non creditworthy, as much as on criminal/non-criminal. In the venues of late twentieth-century England and America, the dress code was as important as the criminal code (Shearing and Stenning 1985).

Much of the emerging analysis of these new modes of control is utilizing the Foucauldian framework to ask whether the ubiquitousness of the electronic eye denotes the arrival of the *panopticon society*, where social control is everywhere and becomes so pervasive that the distinction between external control and self-control disappears (Lyon 1994; Poster 1990). It would appear that these developments signify further progress in the dispersal of discipline, but that the essential project of power identified by Foucault—that of normalization—has been abandoned. The objective of the new strategies of control is identification of the different and the dangerous so as to exclude them—from the club, from the apartment building, from the estate, from the shopping mall, and even from the country.

Theorists working with Foucault's ideas have drawn increasingly upon his later works, in particular his essay on 'Governmentality', where he looks at the project of government in modern society in a way which brings all the various facets of normalcy/deviancy together, and comments on the interrelationships of the different forms of power, their strategies, and their technologies (Foucault 1991). This work has provided the template for analyses of new forms of control which highlight the devolution of power from the central state to local and individual modes of governance, from public to private, from long-term to short-term.

Most of the new forms of control are operated by and on behalf of private individuals and institutions, individually and in cooperation: cars, shops, clubs, buildings, neighbourhoods. Terms like *state* and *social* have come to be replaced by *individual* and *community*, reflecting arguments made by Rose and others about 'the death of the social' (Rose 1996; Stenson 1995). The new associations of control signify a loss of confidence in the state to provide solutions to problems of crime and other aspects of degeneration of communal life, and a general lack of trust in expert systems that social theorists see as one of the key characteristics of late-modernity (Giddens 1990).

Critical accounts of the development of these control strategies have questioned the sort of communities being created by partnerships and initiatives formed to counter crime and the fear of crime. Crawford (1997), for example, highlights the elevation of business interests over individual interests. These 'policy communities', or 'issue networks', become more important than states in some respects (Braithwaite 2000). In particular, they have no accountability to the people they target, only to their members, and little statutory regulation over their activities.[6]

Others argue that crime is by its nature a divisive issue, rather than one which brings communities together, and that community crime control is easier to establish in neighbourhoods that are already cohesive than in those which are not (Abel 1995). While in affluent communities, used to associations such as resident groups and parent-teacher groups, associations to control crime might be easy to establish and might be another forum to bring people together, in less favoured areas they may be harder to establish, leaving residents without protection if policing is increasingly carried out on behalf of (through associations employing private police) or in conjunction with (as in ideals of community policing) local groups. They can also be divisive, directing neighbourhood hostility towards individuals or groups perceived as different, dangerous, or simply as newcomers.[7]

The more apocalyptically-minded have found a new dystopia in the communities described by Mike Davis (1990), with the affluent living in gated housing developments, working in secure buildings, and shopping in patrolled malls; and with the poor increasingly barred from 'public' property by defensive street and park furniture ('bum-proof seats', which are little more than tubes of metal, in place of the traditional park bench, for example), barred from public transport by express routes which no longer stop at supposedly dangerous locations, and barred from places of shopping and entertainment by bouncers and security guards.

These new control strategies have been described as forming an 'actuarial regime' by Jonathan Simon, a regime which has given up on normalization as a strategy of maximizing inclusion. Changing people, which is difficult and expensive, he says has been abandoned in favour of the simpler task of restricting people's possibilities of

---

[6] CCTV schemes, for example, are regulated, if at all, by 'good practice' codes, rather than by legislation.

[7] Demonstrations against, and harassment and aggression towards, asylum seekers, suspected paedophiles, hostels for the mentally disordered or ex-offenders, are examples.

movement and action, through exclusion from general and particular locations and from opportunities to obtain goods and services, and through exclusion from participation in various activities:

> Disciplinary practices focus on the distribution of behaviour within a limited population . . . This distribution is around a norm, and power operates with the goal of closing the gap, narrowing the deviation, and moving subjects towards uniformity . . . Actuarial practices seek instead to maximise the efficiency of the population as it stands. Rather than seeking to change people ('normalize them', in Foucault's apt phrase) an actuarial regime seeks to manage them in place. (Simon 1988: 773)

Feeley and Simon (1992) identified a *new penology* based on actuarial techniques for identifying probable persistent offenders, using risk calculation to allocate penalties and to design preventive projects. 'Criminal career research' and studies associated with persistence and desistence were made central to criminal justice policy and planning, and the 'selective incapacitation' of persistent offenders was a prominent theme (Greenwood 1983). This policy was attractive to politicians because it rested on the widely held idea that a small number of highly active criminals are responsible for a great deal of crime: sentencing them to long, incapacitative prison terms therefore offers the prospect of crime reduction without increased public expenditure, since non-persistent offenders and those not predicted to become persistent can be dealt with by short prison terms or community penalties. This strategy has been subject to criticism on moral, theoretical, and empirical grounds (Zimring and Hawkins 1995), but understandably remains in favour with politicians and policy-makers.

The idea of 'new penology' connects with the governmentality approach because it is clear that though techniques may be statistical, and although it is a strategy of governance in its objectives of regulating populations and providing security through management of risk, new penology is operating in a context where people are no longer willing to share risks. What it is describing is essentially a move from social to private insurance. The contemporary mode of insurance is *private prudentialism* (O'Malley 1992) rather than collective protection. Individuals come together in temporary, shifting alliances because they perceive some personal benefit (policing targeted at one's own concerns; businesses in a shopping precinct sharing the costs of CCTV; lower house insurance costs if home-owners are members of neighbourhood watch schemes, for example).

This *post-social control* is, more than anything, a recognition of the limits of the state in controlling crime, and the new strategies are based on potential victims taking responsibility for their own safety while demanding of the state that it effectively exerts its power over those who do offend (Garland 1996). Theorists analysing these new forms of control in late modernity[8] have attempted to rethink the nature,

---

[8] Most commentators, including Garland (1995), refer to the state of contemporary society as 'late modernity'. Pratt (2000), however, argues that the latest penal innovations represent the emergence of a postmodern turn in penality. He cites the public nature of new penalties, such as clearing graffiti in front of an audience, convict labourers wearing uniforms, and the re-emergence of 'shame' as an important motif, as evidence of the beginning of the end of modernist reasoning and sentiments in penality.

functions, and interrelationships of the state, of the community, and of the individual (Garland 1995, 1996; Lacey and Zedner 1995; Melossi 1990; O'Malley 1992, 1996; Loader and Sparks, in Chapter 3 of this volume).

GOVERNING THROUGH CRIME: THE POPULIST AGENDA

Contemporary accounts that seek to characterize the nature of late modernity's strategies towards crime, have brought the sociologies of punishment and wider forms of control close together again. Theorists in the 1990s drew upon the ideas of authoritarian populism and legitimation crisis developed in the 1980s and mentioned above, refracting them through the analytic prism of 'governmentality' and adding in a focus on 'risk'.

Two key concepts which have emerged from this work are *penal populism* (Bottoms 1995) and *governing through crime* (Simon 1997). Penal populism is used to describe government's promotion of hard-line penal policies because it believes them to be popular, as distinct from implementing policies derived from public opinion. As Bottoms describes it, penal rationalism is from time to time undermined by outbreaks of penal populism. This may come about because political parties fear electoral disadvantage in maintaining liberal law and order policies. Examples are Bill Clinton's authorizing an execution in his capacity as governor of Arkansas during his presidential campaign, after the electoral damage that was thought to have been done to the Democratic Party by candidate Dukakis's reluctance to endorse the death penalty in the Willie Horton case in the previous election, and Tony Blair's adoption of the slogan 'tough on crime, tough on the causes of crime' to dispel Labour's image as a party soft on crime. Penal populism is also invoked to maintain popularity in the face of public and media outcries in the wake of crimes seen as especially terrible (the Polly Klaas killing in California; the James Bulger killing in Liverpool), or following 'moral panics' about particular kinds of crime, again usually illustrated by individual cases which are made much of by the media (the sexual assault and murder of Megan Kanka in the USA, and of Sarah Payne in England, for example). The closely related idea of 'governing through crime' shows how, in the era of distrust in governments and their experts, which presents continuous legitimation dilemmas for governments, the fear and outrage aroused by crime lead to public calls for more governmental power and resources, and thereby relegitimate governmental sovereignty.

Beck (1992) and Giddens (1990), in their descriptions of late modernity, claim that the western democracies are now 'risk societies' in the sense that their citizens are preoccupied with risk and its avoidance. These authors point out that some risks are politicized, and are highlighted as the risks that are to be controlled above all others.

Explaining why crime is promoted as the risk of all risks, theorists of 'governance through crime' draw upon ideas associated with the perspective of neo-liberalism. Like authoritarian populism, this explanation of penal change sees that the neo-liberal political orthodoxy of the 1980s, which persists in only slightly attenuated form at the beginning of the twenty-first century, prescribed very strictly reduced expenditure on welfare benefits, job protection, and similar social interventions. This hands-off political ideology poses dilemmas for politicians such as Margaret Thatcher and Tony Blair who wish to project themselves as strong leaders (Gamble 1994). Crime is the area where popular fears mandate strong action, and where this does not run counter to economic doctrines of non-interference with markets and business cycles.

The demands and constrictions of neo-liberalism are basic to most explanations of punishment and control policies emerging in the 1980s and 1990s; and with hindsight, the era of so-called 'penal rationalism' evidenced by just desert-oriented sentencing reforms, from the Criminal Justice Act 1982 to the Criminal Justice Act 1991 and their counterparts in other countries, was inevitably short-lived. Policies based on ideas of fairness to offenders, proportionate punishment, and limitation of imprisonment could not survive the politicization of the risk of crime of the magnitude that has taken place in the Reagan/Thatcher, Bush/Major, and Clinton/Blair times.

MASS IMPRISONMENT IN THE
TWENTY-FIRST CENTURY

CULTURE AND CRISIS

Understanding one's own times, lacking the 20:20 vision of hindsight and not knowing how things turned out, is always more difficult than understanding the (fairly recent) past, and in the final quarter of the last century rival explanations jostled for influence. Were we seeing the emergence of a new 'master pattern' (Cohen 1985) of control, an actuarial 'new penology' which would lead to less emphasis on the symbolic functions of punishment in apportioning moral blame on individuals, and more emphasis on rational risk-management strategies with 'smart sentencing' based on risk-assessment? Would this mean that the prison moved from the centre to the periphery of punishment and control strategies? Would crime prevention become much more important than punishment, with the criminal justice system coming to be seen as 'an anachronism whose agents serve only to shoot the wounded after the battle is over'? (Marx 1995: 227).

Whatever doubts there may have been about the strength and pace of decarceration, in the mid-1970s many people assumed that the prison, even if it did not disappear altogether, would become a less central institution. It was supposed that the introduction of enhanced probation, intermediate treatment, and above all community service (and equivalents in other jurisdictions) would mean that the proportion of offenders punished by imprisonment would dwindle. Imprisonment, it was thought, would decline, dealing with only the most serious crimes and the most dangerous criminals. Later, it was also thought that falling crime rates, brought about by rising levels of employment as well as by effective crime prevention policies, would take the political heat out of law-and-order issues. Further, some thought that the democratic nature of the new control strategies would reduce the distance between offenders and non-offenders (Marx 1995).

By the end of the twentieth century, however, criminological analysis of punishment and control was looking at a new upturn in imprisonment; at a degradation of regimes; at the return of hard labour; and at the reintroduction of shaming techniques, such as the wearing of uniforms while on labour assignments in the community and the name-and-shame publication of offenders' names, community notification schemes for sex offenders, and the like. As well as referring back to the predictions of the decentring of the prison and the democratization of control and asking 'why did we get it so wrong?', criminologists and social theorists are asking 'what do present trends represent?'.

With both of the questions, the answer is that earlier analysts relied too much on rational assessments of penal effectiveness, market conditions, and fiscal concerns—in other words, the functional aspects of punishment and control—and that understanding present trends necessitates moving investigation of the cultural meanings and contexts of penality from the margins to become the focus of attention. Reductionist arguments about the failure of the prison to reform have been finessed by changing the goal of imprisonment from reform to secure containment; rises in imprisonment in the 1990s took place at a time of falling crime rates and rising employment rates, thus showing that the labour market theory was no longer a much more adequate explanation even than the public/political assumption that punishment is simply a response to crime explanation; since the 1980s, prisons have been built on a scale not seen since the 'great incarceration' of the eighteenth and nineteenth centuries despite a political climate of reduced public expenditure.

David Garland inserted a specifically cultural theme into the study of penality in *Punishment in Modern Society* (1990: chapters 9–11). Garland builds on what he says is a 'banal' observation' (ibid.: 200) that penal practices will imitate or reflect wider cultural forms, highlighting the cultural resources on which penal policy-makers and practitioners draw—ideas about justice, humanitarian and religious ideals, for example. He then uses the work of Norbert Elias (1978, 1982) on the 'civilizing process' to explain how the development of modern sensibilities has turned the infliction of pain, the carrying out of bodily functions, the acting out of drives and aggressions, into behaviours and emotions which should be repressed if possible, and carried out in private rather than public if they are unavoidable. Spierenburg, too, has emphasized the decline of the 'spectacle of suffering' in modern punishments, drawing on Elias's work (Spierenburg 1984).

To say that punishment and control became more civilized is not to slip back into the barbarism-to-humanitarianism progress mode; it is to point out that whatever the aims of punishment (both instrumental and symbolic), they will be pursued in ways consistent with the mentalities and sensibilities (beliefs, ideals, fears, manners) of the time. One of the most prominent themes in the cultural study of contemporary penal trends is to say that the last twenty or so years have exhibited a 'decivilizing' trend (Pratt 1998). This is manifested through the resumption of executions in the USA;[9] incarceration for long periods in 'life-trashing' prisons, and strategies of punishment and control which exhibit vengeance and cruelty rather than the carefully-graduated, partial suspension of rights of a rational, justice-oriented culture (Sarat 1997; Simon 2001; von Hirsch 1995).

---

[9] There was a 'moratorium' on use of the death penalty during the 1970s.

During the 1990s, Garland produced a series of articles investigating what he terms the 'cultural pre-conditions' of these penal trends. He synthesizes the various elements produced by the writers mentioned above—preoccupation with risk; distrust of government and professional elites; neo-liberal political ideology—and adds the important fact of high crime rates becoming accepted as the normal state of affairs. Falls in crime rates, he points out, tend to be reversed, and in any case are not of such a scale as to bring a return to the lower rates of previous eras.

These ideas are brought together and developed further by Garland in his review of penal change from the 1970s to the end of the twentieth century (2001a). In this important book, Garland brings the theme of culture together with that of *crisis*. Crisis is a recurrent theme in the literature on punishment and control: labour shortage or over-supply; fiscal crisis, legitimation crisis, crisis of overcrowding, crisis of trust (Cavadino and Dignan 1997; Sparks 1994, *inter alia*). Garland argues that penal change comes about because of some order of crisis, but that the responses to this crisis will depend on cultural resources available, and that choices from within the repertoire of resources will reflect particular cultural configurations at the time the crisis occurs.

In the last quarter of the twentieth century, he says, there was a sense of perpetual crisis, creating a demand for perpetual penological innovation. The cultural elements influencing the choices of punishment and control strategy and tactics that will be preferred include patterns of allocation of risk and blame; hyper-individualism and distrust of large and remote power groupings; the impact of mass media; the social effects of migration; the dominance of economic rather than social reasoning.

Garland says that responses to crises are of three types: adaptation; denial; and acting out. Adaptive responses recognize the impossibility of controlling crime and of the insatiable nature of demands for total control. Non-recording of crimes with little prospect of clear-up, non-prosecution of offences such as possession of small amounts of drugs, community crime prevention schemes, adoption of values of consistency, fairness, and proportionality in punishment rather than more ambitious values of reform and crime reduction, are all examples of adaptive policies which seek to make the crime problem seem manageable, to do what realistically can be done. Denial responses are demonstrated when politicians, police, and criminal justice professionals make grandiose claims of effectiveness, announcing 20-point plans, 'prison works', 'zero tolerance', and the like. 'Acting out' responses are policies introduced with little thought, responding to sudden public demands—for example, Megan's Law and sexual predator legislation in response to outcries about sexual offending; the introduction of 'no treats for offenders' regimes, and the like.

Garland addresses the question of why liberal elites, especially those working in criminal justice, have not been more strongly supportive of adaptive responses and have themselves promoted, or at least gone along with, acting-out responses. One effect of high crime rates, he explains, is that liberal elites are not so distanced from crime: they too feel the necessity to fit burglar and car alarms, and live in a state of constant awareness of crime that erodes their traditional sympathy for offenders (1996, 2000).

THE TWO-MILLION PRISONER SOCIETY

The analyses of punishment and control discussed so far have tended to treat the USA, UK, Australia, and other western countries as examples of a single phenomenon. All these societies have witnessed rising imprisonment rates, a spread of community penalties and crime prevention schemes, and the axiom that what happens in California happens in the rest of America next month and the rest of the western world next year, appears to be apposite. Three-strikes laws spread from California throughout the US, and have been echoed in the UK and elsewhere. Even states with traditionally low incarceration rates, such as The Netherlands, have seen rises in imprisonment (Downes 2001). The prospect of the US prison population exceeding two million for the first time, however, has prompted a more focused look at America as a unique case, a revival of the idea of 'American exceptionalism'. US imprisonment rates are five times larger than in 1972 and six to ten times higher than in most European countries.

The phenomenon of mass imprisonment in the USA is examined in a special edition of the journal *Punishment and Society*, subsequently published in book form (Garland 2001b). In his editorial introduction, Garland proposes two defining features of mass imprisonment: (1) that the rate of imprisonment and the size of the prison population is markedly above the historical and comparative norm for societies of the same type; (2) that the excessive imprisonment is concentrated on certain groups among the population. Both of these conditions apply in the USA at the present time.

Studies of US mass imprisonment are turning again to the familiar themes of repressing the poor, substituting penal policy for social and economic policy according to the dictates of new right, neo-liberal politics, and acting out populist sentiments of vengeance towards the poor and the criminal. Beckett and Western (2001) note the relationship between welfare spending and imprisonment: those states that spend least on welfare have the highest imprisonment rates. They echo the transcarceration thesis, saying that welfare and penal institutions have come to form a single policy regime for controlling marginalized groups.

Much of the rise in prison rates has been ascribed to the so-called 'war on drugs', and it has been pointed out that this war has been conducted against African-Americans and other minority groups (Tonry 1995). The war has been waged principally against the drugs of the minority poor—crack cocaine—and this selectivity reveals that it is more sensibly understood as containment of minorities rather than as a rational policy to curb a drug menace. In a very powerful chapter, Loic Wacquant (2001) talks about the brutal penal repression as a way of controlling and warehousing the surplus minority populations, whose labour is unwanted in a situation where economic recovery after the recession of the 1980s has been a recovery in profits and dividends rather than a recovery in jobs yielding a living wage. Wacquant recasts the idea of the equivalence of the prison and the factory by talking of the merging of the prison and the ghetto. As the proportion of black Americans in prison rises, prisons become ghettoes, with prisoners associating within ethnic groups and racial stratification displacing any possibility of general inmate solidarity. On the outside, aggressive policing, degenerated physical and social environments, purposeless and hopelessness make minority neighbourhoods like prisons. As Wacquant describes, penal strategies targeted against minorities, and their disproportionate presence in prisons and on probation case-loads, confirm a white stereotype of minorities as criminals: prisons are part of the construction of black Americans as criminals.

The contributors to the volume on mass imprisonment in the USA share the cultural analysis of the importance of political manipulation in the selection of which risks should be robustly controlled; of the links between neo-liberal politics and aggressive punishment and control policies, and the race war being waged through supposed crime-control policies. Most also refer to the factor of cultural sensibilities: record levels of execution, mass-imprisonment with ultra-long sentences in austere and degraded regimes, the return of chain gangs, these happen only because society no longer has inhibitions about imposing pain (Mauer 2001). Certain risks are attractive because they allow for the blaming of certain groups of people (Simon 2001), and risks of being killed in drive-by shootings, being robbed for the price of a hit of crack, allow the blaming of black Americans.[10] The criminalization and penalization of the minority underclass has come about because they are regarded with 'fear and loathing' (Simon 2001); there is no longer a public mood of inclusion, but a preferred tactic of elimination and exclusion.

Whether Europe and other western countries will allow their imprisonment rates to rise to something approaching US levels is open to question, and the signs are mixed. In the UK, new prisons continue to be built, but at the same time renewed emphasis is being put on community penalties. Whether the US itself will continue with its penal repression is also open to question: there are some signs of a falling-off in public support for the death penalty, and even conservative criminologists like DiIulio have moved from saying 'Let 'em Rot', to 'Two Million Prisoners Are Enough' (1994, 1999).

THE PUNISHMENT AND CONTROL OF WOMEN

WOMEN AND THE SOCIAL HISTORY OF PUNISHMENT

The histories and sociologies of control by Foucault, Melossi and Pavarini, and Garland discussed above largely ignored the control of women. These histories are formulated in class terms—control of the working class and the underclass or lumpenproletariat by the bourgeoisie or elite—or in terms of power—the strategies adopted by power to fulfil the tasks of governance and establish itself as legitimate— but little, if any, attention is paid to gender. During the 1970s and 1980s, however, studies of the control of women appeared which, had they been taken into account, would have greatly enriched the understanding of punishment and control (Hudson 1996).

---

[10] Wacquant explains that the distinctions between African-Americans, Hispanic-Americans, Asian-Americans and such have lost their point: non-white Americans are collectively regarded as 'blacks' in apartheid America.

Adrian Howe (1994), in her critique of the neglect of women in the history of punishment, points out that most of the labour market studies have not considered the relationship between females, use of imprisonment, and economic recession. One of the few that has, she reports, finds that women's imprisonment, unlike that of men, declines during periods of economic recession. Howe suggests that this is because women's importance for keeping families together, and men under control, is more crucial than ever in times of economic hardship. This idea is consistent with findings that lenient treatment of women correlates with their presenting themselves as conventional women: good mothers (Farrington and Morris 1983; Eaton 1986). Howe's suggestion is also consistent with the widespread finding that the control of women is such as to uphold conventional gender and familial roles, as much as to penalize and control criminality (Carlen 1983; Edwards 1984).

Foucault's hypothesis of the disciplinary nature of control, and Cohen's refinement of the idea of the dispersal of discipline, have been challenged by, for example, Bottoms (1983), who argues that since the most common penalty for crime is the fine, it cannot be held that disciplinary forms are the most pervasive. This is a sound argument in relation to the punishment of men convicted of routine crimes, but looking at the penalization of adult men, women, and juveniles would reveal that for women and juveniles, welfare-disciplinary responses are more pervasive than for men. Foucault's example of the disciplinary regime is taken from an institution for juveniles; many of Cohen's examples are also drawn from programmes for dealing with young offenders.

Studies of the control of women demonstrate extensive use of normalizing strategies: for example, Carlen's (1983, 1985) studies of women prisoners, and Worrall's (1990) analysis of discursive constructions of female offending, show the operation of stereotypes of conventionality and techniques of normalization. Research on young women showed that they were being subjected to normalizing, disciplinary techniques in a way which made them more vulnerable to committal to an institution than young men on grounds such as 'being in need of care and control', rather than having committed any serious offence, or often, any offence at all (Cain 1989; Gelsthorpe 1989). The analysis developed by Foucault and Cohen would, therefore, have been much enhanced, allowing for a more nuanced view of the limits and applications of disciplinary control, if its variable application to women and men had been considered (Hudson 1996).

The control of women also illuminates the transcarceration thesis, as studies show the continuum of regulation of their lives through the penal system, the health/welfare system, and informal social controls (Cain 1989; Hutter and Williams 1981; Smart 1995). Women are more readily assigned to the psychiatric realm than are men (Allen 1987), while men—especially poor, black men—are more vulnerable to penalization without help or treatment (Carlen 1993). Zedner (1991) has shown women 'disappearing' from criminal processes in the Victorian era—in the midst of the 'great incarceration'—to become the client group of the burgeoning social work and psychiatric professions.

WOMEN AND CONTEMPORARY PENAL POLICY

In the current great incarceration, women's imprisonment rates are rising along with men's, and in the UK at least, proportionately faster than men's. The largest increase has been in sentences of under six months (Halliday 2001). These sentences are given for the sort of non-violent property offences that the just desert-oriented sentencing theories that were influential in the 1980s (culminating in the Criminal Justice Act 1991) sought to keep out of prison. They are also the sort of offences, committed by the sort of women, which in the decarceration era would have led to probation orders rather than terms of imprisonment. Carlen's (1998) study of women's imprisonment in the 1990s demonstrates that more women with children, more women with addictions, more women with histories of abuse were being imprisoned, and that they were still being imprisoned for shoplifting, prostitution, fine default, and offences of a similar order. As in the US, the reason for rising female imprisonment given by officials is usually that more women are being convicted of drugs offences; as in the US, the women who are being caught up in this war on drugs are impoverished, minority women.

Studies of sentencing provide evidence for greater leniency *and* greater severity compared to male offenders (Heidensohn, in Chapter 15 of this volume). What seems to make the difference to whether women are treated with greater leniency or severity is the degree to which they conform to stereotypes of approved femininity, and also whether they can plausibly be constructed (by sympathetic lawyers or probation officers) as not wholly to blame for their offending. If they can construct themselves as victims to some degree (of poverty, of addictions, of abusive men) then they will receive sentences which offer help and attenuated punishment (Daly 1994; Hudson 1998). Their demeanour as women, their plausibility in claiming victimization, will influence whether circumstances such as having responsibility for children, being desperately short of money, being independent or faithful to a long-term partner, will be construed as aggravating or mitigating factors (Hudson 2002). Empirically, black women, young women who present themselves as defiant, women whose self-presentation is not that of a caring, gentle, 'feminine' woman, will have their constrained life chances regarded as demonstrating need for punishment; for women who appear feminine, docile, and remorseful, the same circumstances will be seen as demonstrating need for help.

Work on sentencing and imprisonment of women shows that law is essentially male in its reasoning, and that it both thinks within a masculine perspective and treats women in the way that men treat women (MacKinnon 1989). Equality of treatment means treating women the same as men, whether or not this is appropriate to the circumstances surrounding their offending and the resources and treatments they may need to help them avoid re-offending. Further, the male of legal reasoning is white and middle-class (Naffine 1990). Feminist criminologists have called for legal processes to admit bearers of specifically feminist viewpoints as expert witnesses in order to correct this masculinist construction of offenders and their offences (O'Donovan 1993; Valverde 1996). What is called for is a 'feminist penality' which has as its basic requirements:

1. That the penal regulation of female-lawbreakers does not increase their oppression as women still further.
2. That the penal regulation of law-breaking men does not brutalize them and make them even more violently or ideologically oppressive towards women in the future.
(Carlen 1990: 114)

Although the punishment and control of women demonstrate less close correlation with fashions in penal theory and with the cultural conditions governing punishment and control generally, these contexts obviously exert some influence. Few studies, however, utilize these cultural/social/political frameworks when studying females. Daly's *Gender, Crime and Punishment* (1994) and Carlen's *Sledgehammer* (1998) are exemplary works that locate sentencing and imprisonment of women in penological and political contexts. Kelly Hannah-Moffat has analysed the imprisonment of women in Canada in terms of neo-liberalism and governmentality, showing the way that constructions of risk are giving a morally pejorative twist to older notions of need, and looking at the way neo-liberal notions of responsibilization and feminist notions of empowerment are interacting in the governance of women prisoners (Hannah-Moffat 1999, 2000).

More studies in which feminist perspectives and insights are brought together with the paradigms which have been established to understand punishment and control, are needed to test the generalizability of the theories of penality and social control. Daly and Chesney-Lind's questions 'Do theories of men's crime apply to women? Can the logic of such theories be modified to include women?' (1988: 514) have scarcely been considered in relation to society's response to crime. Although the full impact of get tough law and order policies, the replacement of the reform rationale with the revenge rationale, has been vented primarily upon males, women are being imprisoned in greater numbers; women are being sent to prisons where appropriate treatment is unavailable; women are being penalized for crimes of survival, both through excessive punishment for property offences and minor drug-trafficking, and through the persistence of male reasoning and world-views when considering wounding or killing abusive partners. Studying women's punishment and control is therefore important in its own right. Additionally, consideration of females in work which purports to be non-gendered would illuminate the interactions of race, gender, and class in the development and change of strategies of punishment and control.

CONCLUSION: THE FUTURE OF CONTROL

It is clear that predicting trends in punishment and control is extremely difficult. From the vantage point of the present, it is impossible to know which innovations will be long-lasting; whether current changes are temporary disruptions to a long-term trend, or manifestations of a new trend. For the moment, innovations in punishment and control seem to be constant, and they seem to be, as O'Malley describes, 'volatile and contradictory' (1999). Even in the short term, it is difficult to tell whether the dominant trend will be in the direction of a return to inclusionary penalties, or in the direction of even greater exclusion. Both tendencies are apparent in contemporary western societies: social divisions manifested through spatial segregation within and between communities may make for greater moral distance between offenders and non-offenders, the risky and the fearful; on the other hand, the glimmerings of a revival of rehabilitative programmes and the introduction of restorative justice may represent a movement in the other direction, with communities instinctively sensing that social divisions (in the UK and USA at least) may be reaching the point where they become more of a threat to social order than they are a contribution to community safety. And more broadly, whether changes we are seeing now represent the penality of late modernity or the emergence of a postmodern penality, it is too soon to know.

Even a year ago, I might have expected to be writing about the influence of human rights legislation, and the coming to dominance of a human rights discourse. The response to the terrorist attacks on the USA on 11 September 2001 has shown that in the country (the USA) with the most entrenched and elaborated rights discourse, and in one where incorporation of the European Convention on Human Rights into domestic legislation has been late and reluctant (the UK), abrogation of some human rights provision has been announced with little public opposition.

What is clear is that punishment is linked not just to economic upturns and downturns, but also to changes in the degree of cohesiveness and divisiveness in societies. It seems to be clear that scales of inequality and feelings of belonging to the same community are basic to the apportionment of blame, the extent to which risks are seen as shared, and whether or not the principal modes of punishment and control will be inclusionary or exclusionary. Punishment and control are not merely reflections of crime rates but are also reflections of the political climate, feelings of solidarity and division, atmospheres of welcome or hostility to strangers; and that strategies for dealing with crime, disorder, and difference will reflect both technological and cultural possibilities available to those with power.

Selected further reading

Michel Foucault's *Discipline and Punish: the Birth of the Prison* (London: Allen Lane, 1977) and Dario Melossi's and Massimo Pavarini's *The Prison and the Factory: Origins of the Penitentiary System* (Basingstoke: Macmillan, 1981) are probably the most important books of the 'revisionist' and 'political economy' body of literature on social control. Together they build the account of the links between capitalism and social control, the emergence of 'disciplinary' control and the spread of the control network, discussed in the chapter above.

Stanley Cohen's *Visions of Social Control: Crime, Punishment and Classification* (Cambridge: Polity Press, 1985) brings a predominantly Foucauldian perspective to bear on developments in the mid-twentieth century. Scull's work, *Decarceration: Community Treatment and the Deviant—A Radical View* (Englewood Cliffs, NJ: Prentice-Hall, 1977), is closer to the Marxist tradition of linking shifts in control to economic cycles. David Garland's *The Culture of Control* (Oxford: Oxford University Press, 2001a) provides a similarly wide-ranging analysis of developments between 1970 and 2000, emphasizing responses to a perpetual crisis of legitimacy brought about by persistent high crime rates and the cultural conditions of late-modernity.

David Garland's *Punishment and Modern Society* (Oxford: Oxford University Press, 1990) and Barbara Hudson's *Understanding Justice: An introduction to ideas, perspectives and controversies in modern penal theory* (Buckingham: Open University Press, 1996) provide clear and critical accounts of the work on social control by Durkheim, Foucault, and Melossi and Pavarini. Garland argues for the necessity of incorporating the insights of Durkheim and Weber, and the political economy of writers such as Melossi and Pavarini, alongside those of Foucault to provide a full account of punishment. He develops a strong synthesis of these different perspectives to demonstrate punishment as an expression of culture. Hudson criticizes the work of Foucault, Melossi and Pavarini, and the other 'revisionist historians' for their neglect of the social control of women. She introduces feminist challenges to Marxist theory, and discusses feminist jurisprudence. Hudson also includes the legal-philosophical debates about the justifications for punishment.

Blomberg's and Cohen's edited collection *Punishment and Social Control: Essays in Honor of Sheldon L. Messinger* (New York: Aldine de Gruyter, 1995) contains a range of essays which link the established issues of penality with emergent themes in contemporary control strategies. The essays by Pat Carlen, David Garland, and Jonathan Simon are particularly relevant to issues of control in the postmodern era. Stenson's and Sullivan's *Crime, Risk and Justice* (Cullompton: Willan Publishing, 2001) is a collection of essays covering a range of topics concerning the growing influence of risk considerations on punishment and control.

Maureen Cain (ed.), *Growing Up Good: Policing the Behaviour of Girls in Europe* (London: Sage, 1989); Pat Carlen, *Sledgehammer: Women's Imprisonment at the Millennium* (Basingstoke: Macmillan, 1998); Carol Smart, *Law, Crime and Sexuality: Essays in Feminism* (London: Sage, 1995); and Anne Worrall, *Offending Women: Female Offenders and the Criminal Justice System* (London: Routledge, 1990), between them encompass many of the issues that have arisen in the study of the control of women. All are concerned with the control of women through constructions of feminity; through power imbalances between women and men; through issues of sexuality and motherhood. Cain's volume focuses on the control of young women; Carlen shows that impoverished, addicted, black and marginal women continue to be imprisoned for crimes which are neither very serious nor very dangerous; Smart's collection of essays explores the control of women through civil as well as criminal law, discusses feminist constructions of masculinity, and engages with the challenges of postmodernism for the analysis of women and social control; Worrall's book describes and analyses the discursive constructions of women that are made by criminal justice professionals.

Michael Tonry's *Malign Neglect* (New York: Oxford University Press, 1995) shows the consequences of war-on-drugs policies on African-Americans, policies which have led to their mass imprisonment. David Garland's collection *Mass Imprisonment:*

Social Causes and Consequences (London: Sage, 2001b) contains a number of essays analysing the rise of mass imprisonment in present-day USA. The essays draw on a range of perspectives, and provide a good example of critical engagement with issues which have urgent moral and political importance.

References

ABEL, R. (1995), 'Contested Communities', *Journal of Law and Society*, 22: 113–26.

ALLEN, H. (1987), *Justice Unbalanced: Gender, Psychiatry and Judicial Decisions*, Milton Keynes: Open University Press.

BARLOW, D.E., BARLOW, M.H., and CHIRICOS, J.G. (1993), 'Long Economic Cycles and the Criminal Justice System in the US', *Crime, Law and Social Change*, 19: 143–69.

BECK, U. (1992), *Risk Society: Towards a New Modernism*, London: Sage.

BECKETT, K., and WESTERN, B. (2001), 'Governing Social Marginality: Welfare, Incarceration and the Transformation of State Policy', in D. Garland (ed.), *Mass Imprisonment: Social Causes and Consequences*, London: Sage.

BLOMBERG, T.G., and COHEN, C. (eds) (1995), *Punishment and Social Control: Essays in Honor of Sheldon L. Messinger*, New York: Aldine de Gruyter.

BOTTOMS, A. (1983), 'Neglected Features of Contemporary Penal Systems', in D. Garland and P. Young (eds), *The Power to Punish*, London: Heinemann.

—— (1995), 'The Philosophy and Politics of Punishment and Sentencing', in C.M.V. Clarkson and R. Morgan (eds), *The Politics of Sentencing Reform*, Oxford: Clarendon Press.

BOX, S., and HALE, C. (1982), 'Economic Crisis and the Rising Prisoner Population', *Crime and Social Justice*, 17: 20–35.

BRAITHWAITE, J. (2000), 'The New Regulatory State and the Transformation of Criminology', *British Journal of Criminology*, 40/2: 222–38.

BROWNLEE, I. (1998), *Community Punishment: A Critical Introduction*, Harlow: Addison, Wesley, Longman.

CAIN, M. (ed.) (1989), *Growing Up Good: Policing the Behaviour of Girls in Europe*, London: Sage.

CARLEN, P. (1983), *Women's Imprisonment: A Study in Social Control*, London: Routledge and Kegan Paul.

—— (ed.) (1985), *Criminal Women*, Cambridge: Polity Press.

—— (1990), *Alternatives to Women's Imprisonment*, Milton Keynes: Open University Press.

—— (1993), 'Gender, Class, Racism and Criminal Justice', in G. Bridges and M. Myers (eds), *Inequality, Crime and Social Control*, Toronto: Westview.

—— (1998), *Sledgehammer: Women's Imprisonment at the Millennium*, Basingstoke: Macmillan.

CAVADINO, M., and DIGNAN, J. (1997), *The Penal System: An Introduction*, 2nd edn, London: Sage.

COHEN, S. (1977), 'Prisons and the Future of Control Systems', in M. Fitzgerald *et al.* (eds), *Welfare in Action*, London: Routledge and Kegan Paul.

—— (1979), 'The punitive city: notes on the dispersal of social control', *Contemporary Crises*, 3: 83–93.

—— (1985), *Visions of Social Control: Crime, Punishment and Classification*, Cambridge: Polity Press.

—— and SCULL, A. (eds) (1983), *Social Control and the State*, Oxford: Martin Robertson.

COSER, L. (1982), 'The notion of control in sociological theory', in J.P. Gibbs (ed.), *Social Control: Views from the Social Sciences*, Beverly Hills, Cal.: Sage.

CURRIE, E. (1985), *Confronting Crime: An American Challenge*, New York: Basic Books.

DALY, K. (1994), *Gender, Crime and Punishment*, New Haven, Conn.: Yale University Press.

—— and CHESNEY-LIND, M. (1988), 'Feminism and Criminology', *Justice Quarterly*, 5/4: 498–538.

DAVIS, M. (1990), *City of Quartz*, London: Vintage.

DIIULIO, J.J. (1991), *No Escape: The Future of American Corrections*, New York: Basic Books.

—— (1994), 'Let 'em Rot', *The Wall Street Journal*, 26 January.

—— (1999), 'Two Million Prisoners Are Enough', *The Wall Street Journal*, 12 March.

DONZELOT, J. (1981), *The Policing of Families*, London: Hutchinson.

DOWNES, D. (2001), 'The macho penal economy', *Punishment and Society*, 3/1: 61–80.

DUFF, R.A. (1986), *Trials and Punishments*, Cambridge: Cambridge University Press.

DURKHEIM, E. (1984), 'Two Laws of Penal Evolution', in S. Lukes and A. Scull (eds), *Durkheim and the Law*, Oxford: Basil Blackwell.

EATON, M. (1986), *Justice for Women? Family, Court and Social Control*, Milton Keynes: Open University Press.

EDWARDS, S. (1984), *Women on Trial*, Manchester: Manchester University Press.

ELIAS, N. (1978), *The Civilizing Process: vol. 1 The History of Manners*, Oxford: Blackwell, first published 1939.

—— (1982), *The Civilizing Process: vol. 2 State Formation*, Oxford: Blackwell, first published 1939.

FARRINGTON, D., and MORRIS, A. (1983), 'Sex, sentencing and reconviction', *British Journal of Criminology*, 23/3: 229–48.

FEELEY, M., and SIMON, J. (1982), 'The new penology: notes on the emerging strategy of corrections and its implications', *Criminology*, 30/4: 449–75.

FOUCAULT, M. (1973), *The Birth of the Clinic*, trans. A. Sheridan, London: Tavistock.

—— (1977), *Discipline and Punish: the Birth of the Prison*, London: Allen Lane.

—— (1978), *The History of Sexuality, vol. 1 An Introduction*, trans. R. Hurley, New York: Random House.

—— (1986), *The History of Sexuality, vol. 2 The Use of Pleasure*, trans. R. Hurley, New York: Random House.

—— (1991), 'Governmentality', in G. Burchill, C. Gordon, and P. Miller (eds), *The Foucault Effect: Studies in Governmentality*, Chicago: University of Chicago Press.

GAMBLE, A. (1994), *The Free Economy and the Strong State: the Politics of Thatcherism*, 2nd edn, Basingstoke: Macmillan.

GARLAND, D. (1985), *Punishment and Welfare: A History of Penal Strategies*, London: Gower.

—— (1990), *Punishment and Modern Society*, Oxford: Oxford University Press.

—— (1995), 'Penal Modernism and Postmodernism', in T. Blomberg and S. Cohen (eds), *Punishment and Social Control*, New York: Aldine de Gruyter.

—— (1996), 'The Limits of the Sovereign State: Strategies of Crime Control in Contemporary Society', *British Journal of Criminology*, 36/4: 445–71.

—— (2001a), *The Culture of Control*, Oxford: Oxford University Press.

—— (2001b), *Mass Imprisonment: Social Causes and Consequences*, London: Sage.

—— and SPARKS, R. (2000), 'Criminology, Social Theory and the Challenge of Our Times', *British Journal of Criminology*, 40/2: 189–204.

—— and YOUNG, P. (1983), 'Towards a Social Analysis of Penality', in D. Garland and P. Young (eds), *The Power to Punish: Contemporary Penality and Social Analysis*, London: Heinemann.

GELSTHORPE, L. (1989), *Sexism and the Female Offender*, Aldershot: Gower.

GREENBERG, D. (1975), 'Problems in Community Corrections', *Issues in Criminology*, 19: 1–34.

—— (ed.) (1977), *Corrections and Punishment*, Beverly Hills: Sage.

GREENWOOD, P. (1983), 'Controlling the Crime Rate through Imprisonment', in J.Q. Wilson (ed.), *Crime and Public Policy*, San Francisco: Institute for Contemporary Studies.

HALL, S. (1980), *The Drift to a Law and Order Society*, London: Cobden Trust.

HALLIDAY, J. (2001), *Making Punishments Work: A Review of the Sentencing Framework for England and Wales*, London: Home Office.

HANNAH-MOFFAT, K. (1999), 'Moral agent or actuarial subject: Risk and Canadian women's imprisonment', *Theoretical Criminology*, 3/1: 71–94.

—— (2000), 'Prisons that Empower: Neo-Liberal Governance in Canadian Women's Prisons', *British Journal of Criminology*, 40/3: 510–31.

HAWKINS, D.F. (1986), 'Trends in Black–White Imprisonment: Changing Patterns of Race or Changing Patterns of Social Control', *Crime and Social Justice*, 24: 187–209.

HOWE, A. (1994), *Punish and Critique: Towards a Feminist Analysis of Penality*, London: Routledge.

HUDSON, B.A. (1987), *Justice through Punishment: A critique of the 'justice' model of corrections*, London: Macmillan.

—— (1993), *Penal Policy and Social Justice*, Basingstoke: Macmillan.

—— (1996), *Understanding Justice: An Introduction to Ideas, Perspectives and Controversies in Modern Penal Theory*, Buckingham: Open University Press.

—— (1998), 'Doing Justice to Difference', in A. Ashworth and M. Wasik (eds), *Fundamentals of Sentencing Theory*, Oxford: Clarendon Press.

—— (2002), 'Gender issues in penal policy and penal theory', in P. Carlen (ed.), *Women and Punishment: the Struggle for Justice*, Cullompton: Willan Publishing.

HUTTER, B., and WILLIAMS, G. (eds) (1981), *Controlling Women: the Normal and the Deviant*, London: Croom Helm.

IGNATIEFF, M. (1983), 'State, Civil Society and Total Institutions: A Critique of Recent Social Histories of Punishment', in S. Cohen and A. Scull (eds), *Social Control and the State*, London: Martin Robertson.

JANKOVIC, I. (1977), 'Labour Market and Imprisonment', *Crime and Social Justice*, 8: 17–31.

LACEY, N., and ZEDNER, L. (1995), 'Locating the Appeal to Community in Contemporary Criminal Justice', *Journal of Law and Society*, 22/3: 301–25.

LOWMAN, J., MENZIES, R.J., and PALYS, T.S. (eds) (1987), *Transcarceration: Essays in the Sociology of Social Control*, Aldershot: Gower.

LYON, D. (1994), *The Electronic Eye*, Cambridge: Polity Press.

MACKINNON, C.A. (1989), *Toward a Feminist Theory of the State*, Cambridge, Mass: Harvard University Press.

MARX, G. (1995), 'The Engineering of Social Control: The Search for the Silver Bullet', in J. Hagan and R. Peterson (eds), *Crime and Inequality*, Stanford, Ca.: Stanford University Press.

MATHIESEN, M. (1990), *Prison on Trial*, London: Sage.

MATHIESEN, T. (1974), *The Politics of Abolition*, London: Martin Robertson.

MATTHEWS, R., and FRANCIS, P. (eds) (1996), *Prisons 2000*, Basingstoke: Macmillan.

MAUER, M. (2001), 'The causes and consequences of prison growth in the USA', in D. Garland (ed.), *Mass Imprisonment: Social Causes and Consequences*, London: Sage.

MELOSSI, D. (1985), 'Punishment and Social Action: Changing Vocabularies of Motive within a Political Business Cycle', *Current Perspectives in Social Theory*, 6: 169–97.

—— (1990), *The State of Social Control*, Cambridge: Polity Press.

—— and PAVARINI, M. (1981), *The Prison and the Factory: Origins of the Penitentiary System*, Basingstoke: Macmillan.

MURRAY, C. (1984), *Losing Ground*, New York: Basic Books.

—— (1996), 'The Underclass', in J. Muncie, E. McLaughlin, and M. Langan (eds), *Criminological Perspectives: A Reader*, London: Sage/Open University Press.

NAFFINE, N. (1990), *Law and the Sexes: Explorations in Feminist Jurisprudence*, Sydney: Allen and Unwin.

O'DONOVAN, K. (1993), 'Law's Knowledge: the Judge, the Expert, the Battered Woman, and Her Syndrome', *Journal of Law and Society*, 20/4: 427–37.

O'MALLEY, P. (1992), 'Risk, Power and Crime Prevention', *Economy and Society*, 21: 252–75.

—— (1996), 'Post-Social Criminologies: Some Implications of Current Political Trends for Criminological Theory and Practice', *Current Issues in Criminal Justice*, 8: 26–38.

—— (1999), 'Volatile and Contradictory Punishments', *Theoretical Criminology*, 3: 175–96.

PASQUINO, E.B. (1991), 'Criminology: the birth of a special knowledge', in G. Burchell, C. Gordon, and P. Miller (eds), *The Foucault Effect: Studies in Governmentality*, Chicago: University of Chicago Press.

POSTER, M. (1990), *The Mode of Information*, Cambridge: Polity Press.

PRATT, J. (1998), 'Towards the 'Decivilizing' of Punishment', *Social and Legal Studies*, 7/4: 487–516.

—— (2000), 'The Return of the Wheelbarrow Men: Or, the Arrival of Postmodern Penality?', *British Journal of Criminology*, 40: 127–45.

REIMAN, J. (1979), *The Rich Get Richer and the Poor Get Prison*, New York: John Wiley.

ROSE, N. (1996), 'The death of the social? Refiguring the territory of government', *Economy and Society*, 25/3: 327–56.

ROTHMAN, D. (1971), *The Discovery of the Asylum*, Boston: Little Brown.

RUSCHE, G. (1978), 'Labour market and penal sanction: thoughts on the sociology of punishment', *Crime and Social Justice*, 10: 2–8.

—— and KIRCHHEIMER, O. (1988), *Punishment and Social Structure*, New York: Russell and Russell.

SARAT, A. (1997), 'Vengeance, Victims and the Identities of Law', *Social and Legal Studies*, 6/2: 163–90.

SCRATON, P. (ed.) (1987), *Law, Order and the Authoritarian State*, Milton Keynes: Open University Press.

SCULL, A. (1977), *Decarceration: Community Treatment and the Deviant—A Radical View*, Englewood Cliffs, NJ: Prentice-Hall (revised edition, 1984).

—— (1983), 'Community corrections: panacea, progress or pretence?', in D. Garland and P. Young (eds), *The Power to Punish*, London: Heinemann.

SHEARING, C.D., and STENNING, P.C. (1985), 'From the Panopticon to Disneyworld: The Development of Discipline', in A.N. Doob and E.L. Greenspan (eds), *Perspectives in Criminal Law*, Aurora, Ontario: Canada Law Books Inc.

SIMON, J. (1988), 'The ideological effects of actuarial practices', *Law and Society Review*, 22/4: 772–800.

—— (1997), 'Governing through Crime', in L.M. Friedman and G. Fisher (eds), *The Crime Conundrum: Essays on criminal justice*, Boulder, Co: Westview.

—— (2001), 'Fear and loathing in late modernity', in D. Garland (ed.), *Mass Imprisonment: Social Causes and Consequences*, London: Sage.

SMART, C. (1995), *Law, Crime and Sexuality: Essays in Feminism*, London: Sage.

SPARKS, R. (1994), 'Can Prisons be Legitimate?', *British Journal of Criminology*, 34: 14–28.

SPITZER, S. (1983), 'The Rationalization of Crime Control in Capitalist Society', in S. Cohen and A. Scull (eds), *Social Control and the State*, Oxford: Martin Robertson.

STENSON, K. (1995), 'Communal Security as Government—the British Experience', in W. Hammerschick, I. Karazman-Moraewetz, and W. Stangl (eds), *Jahrbuch fur Rechts und Kriminalsoziologie*, Baden-Baden: Nomos.

—— and SULLIVAN, R.R. (eds) (2001), *Crime, Risk and Justice: The politics of crime control in liberal democracies*, Cullompton: Willan Publishing.

TAYLOR, I. (1981), *Law and Order. Arguments for Socialism*, London: Macmillan.

TONRY, M. (1995), *Malign Neglect: Race, Crime and Punishment in America*, New York: Oxford University Press.

VALVERDE, M. (1996), 'Social Facticity and the Law: A Social Expert's Eyewitness Account of Law', *Social and Legal Studies*, 5/2: 201–18.

VON HIRSCH, A. (1995), 'The Future of the Proportionate Sentence', in T. Blomberg and S. Cohen (eds), *Punishment and Social Control*, New York: Aldine de Gruyter.

WACQUANT, L. (2001), 'Deadly Symbiosis: When ghetto and prison meet and merge', in D. Garland (ed.), *Mass Imprisonment: Social Causes and Consequences*, London: Sage.

WILSON, J.Q. (1978), *Thinking About Crime*, New York: Basic Books (2nd edn, 1983).

WORRALL, A. (1990), *Offending Women: Female Offenders and the Criminal Justice System*, London: Routledge.

—— (1997), *Punishment in the Community: the Future of Criminal Justice*, Harlow: Addison, Wesley, Longman.

YOUNG, J. (1986), 'The Failure of Criminology: the Need for a Radical Realism', in R. Matthews and J. Young (eds), *Confronting Crime*, London: Sage.

—— (1987), 'The Tasks of a Realist Criminology', *Contemporary Crises*, 11: 337–56.

—— (1988), 'Radical Criminology in Britain: the Emergence of a Competing Paradigm', *British Journal of Criminology*, 28/2: 289–313.

ZEDNER, L. (1991), *Women, Crime and Custody in Victorian England*, Oxford: Oxford University Press.

ZIMRING, F., and HAWKINS, G. (1995), *Incapacitation: Penal Confinement and the Restraint of Crime*, New York: Oxford University Press.

9

LEGAL CONSTRUCTIONS
OF CRIME

Nicola Lacey

To anyone other than a specialist, the proposition that the intellectual concerns of criminology are intimately connected with those of criminal law would probably seem obvious to the point of banality. Yet within the institutional construction of disciplines, such common sense is often effaced by the development of theoretical frameworks which illuminate particular aspects of a practical terrain while obscuring their links with others. This (in some ways productive) blindness is one to which lawyers are probably more prone than criminologists. Both the professional auton-omy of legal practice and the technical nature of legal argumentation have lent them-selves to the construction of relatively rigid disciplinary boundaries. By contrast, the status of criminology as a discrete discipline has always been contested, and crimino-logical research is inevitably informed by the methods and insights of the social sciences in general—insights which continue to have a rather fragile position within legal scholarship (Nelken 1987b; Sumner 1994). It is nonetheless almost as rare to find a criminology text which concerns itself with the scope and nature of criminal law as it is to find a criminal law text which addresses criminological questions (Lacey and Wells 1998; Bronitt and McSherry 2001).

In this chapter, I shall examine the relationship between legal constructions of crime (criminal law) on the one hand and social constructions of crime and criminal-ity (the core subject matter of criminology and criminal justice studies) on the other. Focusing initially on criminal law, I shall consider two aspects of the contemporary legal construction of crime: its conceptual form and its substantive scope. I shall then set this analysis in social and historical perspective, thereby illustrating the links between legal and social constructions of crime—and hence between criminal legal and criminological/criminal justice inquiry. On the basis of this preliminary analysis, the latter part of the paper will consider two further issues. First, what can students of criminal law learn from the study of criminal justice? What questions might a degree of criminological insight prompt a criminal lawyer to ask? Secondly, what do crimino-logists need to know about criminal law? And what might they learn from criminal law scholarship?

The main burden of my argument will be that an adequate grasp of the two fields may best be attained by conceptualizing them as interlocking spaces within a broader conceptual frame: that of 'criminalization' (Lacey 1995). The framework of criminalization, as I shall argue, keeps the close relationship of the criminal legal and criminological/criminal justice practices firmly in view, while avoiding a synthesis which would lose sight of their specificity. Such a framework is, moreover, implicit in some of the most intellectually persuasive recent contributions to criminal law scholarship (Farmer 1996a, 1996b; Loveland (ed.) 1995; Norrie 2001; Wells 2001). In what follows, I shall assume that the reader is a student of criminal justice who may not have studied criminal law.

THE RELATIONSHIP BETWEEN CRIMINAL LAW, CRIMINOLOGY, AND CRIMINAL JUSTICE STUDIES

Within the academy in the United Kingdom, the study of the various social practices associated with 'criminal justice' is currently divided into two main blocks. These blocks are themselves marked by a combination of disciplinary tools and institutional objects. Let us call these two blocks the legal and social construction of crime (though 'legal' and 'extra-legal' might be more accurate, given that legal constructions of crime are, evidently, themselves social phenomena). Study of the social construction of crime itself divides into two broad fields—criminology and criminal justice— brought together in this particular volume. Criminology concerns itself with social and individual antecedents of crime and with the nature of crime as a social phenomenon: its disciplinary resources come mainly from sociology, social theory, psychology, history, and, though more rarely, economics and political science. Criminologists raise a variety of questions about patterns of criminality and its social construction, along with their historical, economic, political, and social conditions of existence. While, as Garland's contribution to this volume suggests (see Chapter 1), the dynamic social construction of crime gives reason for scepticism about criminology's discreteness as a discipline, it continues to hold a distinctive institutional position in the academy. Criminal justice studies, which have a variety of legal, historical, sociological, and other focuses, deal with the specifically institutional aspects of the social construction of crime: with criminal processes such as policing, prosecution, plea bargaining, sentencing and punishment, and with normative questions about the principles around which a criminal justice system worth the name ought to be organized (Ashworth 1998; Lacey 1994).

Criminal law, by contrast, concerns itself with the formally established norms according to which individuals or groups are adjudged guilty or innocent. These norms are of several kinds, arguably mapping on to the core related functions of criminal law. For criminal law encompasses not only substantive rules of conduct addressed to citizens, but also rules determining how liability should be attributed and how breaches of criminal norms should be graded—rules which are arguably more plausibly seen as addressed to officials than to potential offenders (Robinson 1997). Contemporary criminal lawyers tend to be concerned not so much with the historical development or changing scope of these norms—matters which would be of obvious interest to the criminologist—as with their conceptual structure and

judicial interpretation in particular cases or sets of cases. Criminal lawyers are therefore also concerned with the doctrinal framework of 'general principles' within which
that interpretive practice and—though more tenuously—legislative development
purportedly proceed (Ashworth 1999; Clarkson and Keating 1999; Williams 1983).
The rules of evidence and procedure which have an important bearing on the application and historical development of criminal law tend to find only a small place in
criminal law studies in the UK, and are often dealt with in specialist, optional courses,
or relegated to interstitial treatment in criminal justice or legal methods courses.
Within degree courses in law, only criminal law is regarded as a 'core' part of the
curriculum.

   While the organization of research conforms less rigidly to this division, it nonetheless bears a close relationship to the different areas of expertise claimed by scholars
within the field. This partitioning of the intellectual terrain is, it should be noted, both
historically and culturally specific. To Continental European eyes, for example, the
Anglo-American separation of criminal law and criminal procedure, and indeed of
criminal law and sentencing, appears extraordinary (Cole *et al.* 1987; Fletcher 1978).
And although a superficially similar division has characterized the British approach
for much of this century, the rationale underlying the three branches of 'criminal
science' of the 1920s and 1930s was rather different from that underlying today's
division (Radzinowicz and Turner 1945; Kenny 1952: ch 1, Pt II).

   What is the significance of the contemporary partition between study of legal and
social constructions of crime; between criminal law on the one hand and criminology
and criminal justice on the other? Is it not merely a common-sense division of labour
based both on distinctive expertise and the distinctive roles of legal and social factors
in the construction of crime? While there is some truth in this, I would argue that the
prevailing division is likely to obscure our view of certain crucially important issues.
For example, criminological insights about patterns of 'deviance' pose important
questions about the working of criminal justice institutions such as police and courts.
The practice of legal interpretation takes place within a particular social context and
in relation to criminal laws which are themselves the product of a political process
which is surely relevant to their application and enforcement. Practices of punishment take place against the background of prevailing concerns about patterns of
criminality, and of attitudes to the vitality of social norms thought to be embodied in
criminal law and of beliefs about the legitimacy of state power. The problems of
legitimation and coordination faced by systems of criminal law vary according to both
the institutional frameworks within which criminal law is enforced—policing, prosecution, trials, penal practices—and the shifting range of social tasks which the
criminal law is expected to fulfil. Furthermore, the very edifice of criminalization as a
relatively discrete object of enquiry is itself a porous one, given that criminal justice
practices exist alongside and relate in an intimate, albeit complex, way to a variety
of other—political, economic, moral, religious, educational, familial—normative,
labelling, and sanctioning practices (Lacey and Wells 1998: chapter 1).

   While it would clearly be impossible to address all criminal justice concerns within
a single research project or course, there is a real risk that questions which transcend
the prevailing boundaries marking off the three areas may be lost from view. For

example, the relevance of the political context or of particular features of the criminal process to the development of legal doctrine in a series of appeal cases may be excluded from a criminal law course, while criminal justice or criminology courses may ignore the bearing of legal developments upon practices of prosecution and punishment. In short, a legitimate focus on the issues raised both within particular disciplines and in relation to particular institutional practices may serve to obscure broader questions about the assumptions on which those disciplines and practices are based. What are lawyers' implicit ideas about the nature of crime and of offenders? What assumptions do criminologists make about the nature of criminal law? And who, within the prevailing division of intellectual labour, is to study these important matters?

CRIMINAL LAW

As I have already suggested, a certain discreteness of both subject matter and disciplinary framework is much more firmly established in relation to criminal law than in relation to the extra-legal processes contributing to the construction of crime which form the object of criminological and criminal justice enquiry. In this section, I shall focus specifically on the distinguishing features of criminal law—substantive and formal—so as to examine the degree to which these pretensions to disciplinary autonomy are justified. Of course, many criminal law scholars have concerned themselves with sociology and history and with questions about the criminal process: indeed, this socio-legal leaning has probably been more marked in criminal law than in other fields of legal scholarship over the last forty years (Hall 1960; Packer 1967). The objection to socio-legal approaches to criminal law has always been, however, that they underestimate or obscure the specificity of legal techniques and legal argumentation, reducing legal regulation to the exercise of political or economic power, and assuming legal decision-making to be explicable in terms of some crude set of personal, economic, or political causes. Furthermore, it has been argued that socio-legal scholars often ask the wrong kinds of questions about criminal law—questions which assume that law is to be judged in terms of its instrumental functions rather than its symbolic dimensions or its discrete logic. These problems are probably best exemplified by American Legal Realism and Chicago-style law and economics, reductive approaches in which legal decision-making is explained, respectively, in terms of judicial actors' policy preferences and their concern to maximize economic efficiency (Farmer 1995, 1996a; Nelken 1987b). In the context of the debate about the proper balance between autonomy and openness in criminal law scholarship, the development over the last fifteen years of 'critical' approaches is worthy of particular attention (for a general review, see Nelken 1987a; Norrie 1992). For, as I shall try to show, they promise to combine a focus on legal specificity without obscuring broader questions about the historical, political, and social conditions under which the apparently discrete and technical practices of modern criminal law flourish.

THE SUBSTANCE AND SCOPE OF CRIMINAL LAW

One obvious reason why criminologists and criminal justice scholars might be interested in studies of criminal law would be to get a picture of the extent and shape of the formally articulated rules which in some sense provide the jumping-off point for all other criminal justice practices—crime prevention, reporting, investigation, prosecution, punishment. More than this, the criminal justice scholar might expect criminal lawyers to deliver some overall and coherent conception of the aims and functions of criminal law: a conception which would explain or rationalize why the legal order deals with certain kinds of conduct as a criminal rather than a civil or private matter; as calling for state prosecution and punishment rather than privately initiated litigation and compensation. The social scientist would also be interested in the shifting boundaries of this overall conception: in the changing contours of criminal law over time and space; in the changing balance between not only different kinds of legal regulation, but also between legal and informal, social modes of governance; and in the implications of these changes for our understanding of how societies are organized.

In pursuing these questions, the criminal justice scholar would not be entirely disappointed in criminal law commentaries. In almost all of them, he or she would be greeted with a discussion of the aims and functions of criminal law and of the rationale of punishment. From his or her understanding of criminal justice more generally, the scholar would already be familiar with the way in which two rather different visions of the rationale of criminal law compete for dominance in most accounts. On the one hand, criminal law is understood—as distinct from civil law— as being concerned with *wrongdoing* in a quasi-moral sense. On this view, crime is conduct judged to be sufficiently seriously in violation of core social or individual interests, or shared values, that it is appropriate for the state to proscribe and punish its commission. This is a view which sits naturally with a retributive approach to punishment and with a strong emphasis on the symbolic, expressive dimensions of criminal justice. On the other hand, criminal law is understood in more neutrally instrumental terms as a particular kind of regulatory system: as attaching costs, through sanctions, to certain kinds of conduct which it is in the overall public interest to reduce. This second view sits naturally with a deterrent or otherwise utilitarian view of punishment. The obvious question arises, of course, as to how these competing views are to be reconciled as rationalizations of contemporary criminal law.

Two attempted resolutions are of interest in this context. At a philosophical level, H.L.A. Hart's account, which builds on the liberal utilitarianism of J.S. Mill (Hart 1963, 1968; Mill 1859), argues that, while the general justifying aim of criminal law is a utilitarian one of crime reduction through deterrence, the state is justified in invoking its coercive criminalizing power only as against conduct for which an individual is responsible and which is harmful to others or (in Hart's modified, social-democratic version of Mill's 'harm principle'), in certain conditions, to oneself. This account provides a less moralistic version of the nature of crime than is characteristic of the quasi-moral, retributive conception already discussed, while nonetheless providing an account of why criminal law is of special moral significance. It has difficulty, however, in generating an adequately specified concept of harm: does, for example, the offence felt by people who disapprove of certain kinds of behaviour—such as homosexual conduct or public displays of nudity—count as 'harm'? Secondly, at the level of legal doctrine, the usual solution is to divide the terrain of criminal law as between the 'moral core' of 'real crime'—theft, homicide, assault, rape, and so on—and the 'quasi-criminal' 'regulatory offences'—licensing offences, driving offences, tax offences, pollution offences, and so on. In other words, it is accepted that criminal law has not one but two rationales; and their co-existence is enabled by a functional differentiation between offences. This functional differentiation is then, so the argument goes, mapped on to legal doctrine (see below).

This pragmatic reconciliation, however, leaves many questions of interest to the social scientist unaddressed. How is the division between 'quasi-moral' and 'regulatory' crimes defined, and is the boundary a clear one? How does it change over time? Under what kinds of social, political, and institutional conditions does such a criminal law system emerge, and what broader governmental or ordering roles, if any, does it pursue? These are questions, however, in which contemporary criminal lawyers are relatively uninterested: as we shall see in the next section, their rationalization of criminal law moves on quickly from the very sketchy substantive conceptions mentioned above to a more elaborated, technical account of the specific form which criminal liability must take. The reason for this is relatively clear. In a system in which criminal law is regarded as a regulatory tool of government and in which (as in the UK) there are very weak constitutional constraints on what kinds of conduct can be criminally proscribed—a world in which everything from terrorism through dumping litter to licensing infractions and 'raves' can be criminalized—there is little which can be said by way of substantive rationalization of the nature of criminal law. This, however, is a contingent matter. If we look back, for example, to the legal commentaries of the mid-eighteenth century (Blackstone 1765–69), or even the late nineteenth century (Stephen 1883), we will find a richer and more confident assertion of a substantive rationale for criminal law: of the interests and values which criminal law sets out to express and protect. In Blackstone's *Commentaries*, the account is organized around groups of offences threatening these interests— offences against God and religion; offences against the state; offences against the person; offences against property. This works well enough for a very circumscribed system of criminal law. But over the last 200 years, in tandem with the growing diversity of the nation state's governmental concerns, the scope and functions of criminal law have increased dramatically. The expansion of criminal law's scope has entailed a fragmentation of its rationale and, as we shall see in the next section, has gone along with an intensification of focus, among legal commentaries, on the formal conditions of criminal liability. This change in the way in which criminal law is organized and thought about is of enormous significance to criminal justice scholars, because it gives us, as we shall see, a real clue to the way in which criminal law resolves the changing legitimation and coordination problems thrown up by its environment.

THE CONCEPTUAL FRAMEWORK OF CRIMINAL LAW

Contemporary codes and commentaries on criminal law in both the common and the civilian traditions tend to be organized around a core framework which sets out the general conditions under which liability may be established. This core framework is often known as the 'general part', or 'general principles', of criminal law—in other words, the set of rules and doctrines which applies across the whole terrain of criminal law rather than to specific offences. In the UK, this framework consists of four main elements: capacity, conduct, responsibility, and (absence of) defence.

Capacity

Only those who share certain basic cognitive and volitional capacities are regarded as the genuine subjects of criminal law. For example, one might regard defences such as insanity as defining certain kinds of people as simply outwith the system of communication embodied by criminal law. Since law operates in terms of general standards, the line between criminal capacity and criminal incapacity is a relatively crude one from the point of view of other disciplines. For instance, almost every criminal law system exempts from criminal liability people under a certain age, whatever their actual capacities.

Conduct

Criminal conviction is founded, secondly, in a certain kind of conduct specified in the offence definition: appropriating another person's property in the case of theft; causing a person's death in the case of homicide; having sexual intercourse with a person without his or her consent in the case of rape; driving with a certain level of alcohol in one's blood in the case of driving while intoxicated. Though there are exceptions in this country's criminal law doctrine, it is generally asserted that mere thoughts, being of a certain status rather than doing an act, and—in the absence of a specific duty to act—omitting to do something rather than acting positively, are insufficient to found criminal liability.

Responsibility/fault

Criminal liability is generally said to depend, thirdly, on the capable subject being in some sense responsible for or at fault in committing the conduct specified in the offence definition: we do not hold people liable, to put it crudely, for accidents. Responsibility or fault conditions generally consist of mental states or attitudes such as intention, recklessness, knowledge, belief, dishonesty, and negligence. To revert to the examples above, the relevant conditions consist in a dishonest intention permanently to deprive in the case of theft; an intention to kill or cause some less serious kind of harm, or gross negligence in relation to these results, in the case of homicide; recklessness as to the victim's lack of consent in the case of rape. The fourth example —driving while intoxicated—provides an exception to what is generally represented as the general principle that a discrete responsibility element must be proven by the prosecution: only the driving and the blood alcohol level need be established by the prosecution. Notwithstanding their 'exceptional' status, however, these offences of so-called 'strict' liability are in fact empirically dominant in English criminal law today. This division between offences of 'strict' liability and offences requiring proof of fault is the way in which the division between the 'quasi-moral' and 'instrumental/ regulatory' terrains of criminal law is purportedly mapped on to legal doctrine. However, as the example of driving while intoxicated—an offence which thirty years ago was regarded as a quintessentially regulatory offence, yet which today carries a marked moral stigma—illustrates, this line is in fact far from clear.

Defences

Even where a capable subject has committed the relevant conduct with the requisite degree of fault, a range of defences may operate to preclude or mitigate his or her liability. For example, if the defendant has committed a theft while under a threat of violence, she may plead the defence of duress; if a person kills, intentionally, in order to defend himself against an immediate attack, he may plead self-defence; and if that person kills under provocation, he may be convicted of a lesser degree of homicide. These 'general defences' apply not only to crimes which require proof of responsibility, but also to those of strict liability. Hence, for example, a person who drives while intoxicated because of duress, whether in the form of a threat or in the form of highly compelling circumstances, may be able to escape liability.

Defences are often thought to fall into three main groups—*exemptions*, *justifications*, and *excuses*—each relating to the other three components of liability already mentioned. The defence of insanity, for example, arguably operates to recognize that the defendant's *incapacity exempts* him or her from the communications of criminal law; the defence of self-defence may be seen as amounting to a claim that the *conduct* in question was, in the circumstances, *justified* and hence not the sort of conduct which criminal law sets out to proscribe; the defence of duress may be viewed as *excusing* the defendant on the basis that the conditions under which she formed the relevant *fault* condition—in cases of duress, this would generally be intention—are such that the usual inference of *responsibility* is blocked. One might, in short, see the defences as a mechanism which fine-tunes, along adequately contextualized and morally sensitive lines, the presumptive inferences of liability produced by the first three elements.

At one level, this conceptual framework is analytic: it simply provides a set of building blocks out of which legislators and lawyers construct criminal liability. On the other hand—as the description of the framework as a set of 'general principles' suggests— it contains an implicit set of assumptions about what makes the imposition of criminal liability legitimate. The ideas, for example, that there should be no punishment for mere thoughts, or that defendants should not be convicted unless they were in some sense responsible for their conduct, or in circumstances in which some internal incapacity or external circumstance deprived them of a fair opportunity to conform to the law, express a normative view of criminal law not merely as an institutionalized system of coercion but rather as a system which is structured around certain principles of justice or morality. This normative aspect of the 'general part' of criminal law becomes yet clearer in the light of two broad procedural standards which characterize most modern systems. The first of these is the *principle of legality* or *rule of law*—the idea that criminal law must be announced clearly to citizens in advance of its imposition. Only those who know the law in advance can be seen as having a fair opportunity to conform to it. Principles such as clarity and non-retroactivity are therefore central tenets of the liberal ideal of the rule of law. The second procedural doctrine is the *presumption of innocence*—the idea that a crime must be proven by the prosecution (generally the state, and hence far more powerful than the individual defendant) to a very high standard. Criminal law is therefore implicitly justified not only in terms of its role in proscribing, condemning, and (perhaps) reducing conduct which causes or risks a variety of harms, but also in treating its subjects with respect, as moral agents whose conduct must be assessed in terms of attitudes and intentions, and not merely in terms of effects. And underlying this normative framework is a further set of assumptions about the nature of human conduct: about voluntariness, will, agency, capacity as the basis for genuine human personhood and hence responsibility.

The various assumptions underlying the conceptual framework within which criminal liability is constructed should be of great interest to criminological and criminal justice scholars. First, they give us insight into the processes of interpretation in the courtroom—one key moment in the process of criminalization. Thus, secondly, they also provide some interesting points of both contrast and similarity when compared with the assumptions on the basis of which other practices within the criminal process are founded. Are the assumptions of responsible subjecthood that constitute the core of criminal law thinking the same as, or even consistent with, those that underpin the development of policing strategy, sentencing decision-making, probation practice, or prison regimes? If not, does it matter? And what does it signify?

'GENERAL PRINCIPLES' OF CRIMINAL LAW: A CRITICAL ASSESSMENT

The need to bring criminal justice and criminal law analyses into relation with one another is therefore clear. However, it is equally clear that criminal justice scholars ought to be wary of taking the 'general principles' of criminal law on lawyers' terms. For the fact is that the 'general principles of criminal law' are honoured in many systems, and certainly in the UK, as much in the breach as in the observance—a fact which suggests that they are as much an ideological as an 'actual' feature of criminal law's operations. In this respect, the criminal justice scholar will get some enlightenment from the more critical genre of criminal law scholarship that has been emerging over the last twenty years, and which has subjected the 'general principles' of criminal law to a searching examination. Early examples of critical criminal law scholarship, notably the work of Mark Kelman (1981), were closely associated with the American 'critical legal studies' movement. The movement embraced a group of scholars who sought to expose the 'politics of law' by means of a close examination of doctrinal principles and categories.

Conventional criminal law scholars, as we have seen, generally provide a brief resumé of the moral/retributive, regulatory/deterrent aspects of criminal justice. They go on to give a terse statement of the competing concerns of fairness and social protection, due process and crime control which are taken to inform the development and implementation of criminal law in liberal societies. From this point on, they take the idea of 'crimes' as given by acts of law-creation. In this way both political and criminological issues are quietly removed from the legal agenda. In contrast, critical criminal lawyers assume that the power and meaning of criminal laws depend on a more complex set of processes and underlying factors than the mere positing of prohibitory norms to be enforced according to a particular procedure. Most obviously, they assume that the influences of political and economic power permeate the practice of doctrinal interpretation. Yet their view is not the reductive, instrumental one of Realism or the Chicago School. Rather, critical criminal lawyers argue that judicial practice is shaped by tensions between competing values whose power infuses all social practices, and which cannot be reconciled by either legislative reform or feats of rationalizing interpretation. From this critical perspective, further links between the legal and social construction of crime appear. For it seems, *a priori*, likely that the evaluative and pragmatic tensions which shape the development of criminal law will also manifest themselves, albeit to different degrees and in different ways, in other criminal justice practices.

The primary aim of early critical criminal law scholarship was to develop an internal or 'immanent' critique of the doctrinal framework within which different areas of law have been taken to be organized. Taking a close interest in the way in which criminal liability is *constructed* within legal discourse, critical scholars took as their focus the structure of 'general principles' which are usually taken to underpin criminal law in liberal societies. These included not only the liberal ideals about the fair terms under which criminal punishment may be imposed upon an individual agent, which we considered above, but also the aspirations of neutrality, objectivity, and determinacy of legal method which are associated with the rule of law (Norrie 2001). For example, Kelman's work scrutinized the basis of the responsibility/fault doctrine which purports to structure and justify the attribution of criminal responsibility to the free individual *via* the employment of standards of fault such as intent and recklessness. He showed that fault requirements veer in an unprincipled way between 'subjective' standards, in which attributions of responsibility depend on what the defendant actually intended or contemplated, and 'objective' standards such as negligence, which impute to the defendant the state of mind of the 'reasonable man'. Following from this, Kelman emphasized the fact that criminal law doctrine evinces no consistent commitment to either a free-will or a determinist model of human behaviour (Kelman 1981).

Furthermore, Kelman and others demonstrated the manipulability and indeterminacy of the generally accepted doctrinal framework according to which criminal liability is constructed in terms of the four elements discussed above: capacity, conduct, responsibility or fault, and absence of defence. For example, critical scholars pointed out that the issue of mistake could be conceptualized with equal doctrinal propriety as matter pertaining to the existence of the conduct or fault elements of a crime, or to the existence of a defence (Lacey and Wells 1998: chapter 1). A person who assaults another person in the mistaken belief that that other person is in the process of committing an assault on a third party could, in other words, be regarded as having a defence (of mistaken self-defence), or as lacking the conduct (no 'unlawful' act) or (in certain circumstances) fault/responsibility (no relevant intention) elements of a crime. Since these conceptualizations sometimes affect the outcome of the legal analysis, this entails that doctrinal rules are not as determinate as the conventional theory of legal reasoning assumes. Moreover, critical analysis illustrated the fact that the outcome of legal reasoning is contingent upon factors such as the time frame within which the alleged offence was set. For example, whether or not a person is regarded as negligent, in the sense of having failed to reach a reasonable standard of care or awareness, may well depend on what range of conduct the court is able to examine. What appears an unreasonable lapse judged in itself may look more reasonable if evidence about its history can be admitted. This broadening of the time frame or context is precisely what the defences often effect. How far the time frame is expanded, however, also depends on interpretive and evidential factors: on whether, for example, evidence of a history of domestic violence is seen as relevant to the establishment of the defence of provocation or self-defence. Yet the influence of the framing process is not acknowledged within the doctrinal structure, which accordingly fails to regulate judicial interpretation in the way which is generally supposed.

The critical enterprise here is to hold criminal law up to scrutiny in terms of the standards which it professes to instantiate; and in doing so, to reveal that, far from consisting of a clear, determinate set of norms, based on a coherent set of 'general principles', it rather exemplifies a contradictory and conflicting set of approaches which are obscured by the superficial coherence and determinacy of legal reasoning. By scrutinizing carefully the form which criminal legal reasoning takes, it becomes possible to reveal that practice as having important ideological dimensions, rationalizing and legitimating a system which serves a variety of powerful interests by representing criminal law as a technical and apolitical sphere of judgement (Norrie 2001). An important part of this process is the (re)reading of cases not merely as exercises in formal legal analysis, but also as texts whose rhetorical structure is at least as important as their superficial legal content (Goodrich 1986). In this kind of reading, critical scholars emphasize the significant symbolic aspect of the power of criminal law, along with the implicit yet powerful images of wrongdoing and rightful conduct, normal and abnormal subjects, guilt and innocence which legal discourse draws upon and produces (Lacey 1993).

The early critical focus on the intricacies of doctrinal rationalization and the exposure of conflicts which such rationalization obscures has, however, gradually been supplemented by a further set of questions suggested by the process of immanent critique. If critical criminal law was not to remain a set of observations about the apparent irrationality of legal doctrine, the question of the deeper logics underpinning legal discourse had to be addressed (Norrie 2001). Hence questions about the broad socio-political conditions under which a particular doctrinal framework arises and 'works', and about the historical conditions of existence of particular doctrinal systems of classification (taken as 'given' within conventional scholarship) have begun to claim the attention of criminal law scholars (Norrie 1992; Lacey 1998a, 2001a, 2001b).

RELATING FORM TO SUBSTANCE: PERSPECTIVES FROM HISTORY AND THE SOCIAL SCIENCES

This development, which might be conceptualized as 'external' critique, illuminates some important links between criminal law scholarship and socio-legal and sociological work on the criminal process. For as critical scholars sought to understand the deeper political and historical logics underpinning the logical defects of criminal law doctrine, and to grasp precisely how doctrinal ideology serves to obscure apparently obvious political questions about criminal law, new issues began to force themselves on to the research agenda. These include questions about the ways in which a focus on certain portions of substantive criminal law, and a lack of attention to others—notably the so-called 'regulatory' offences—serves to perpetuate the myth of coherent 'general principles', and about the ways in which this selectivity relates to prevailing understandings of what constitutes 'real crime', the imperatives of 'law and order' politics, and the deeper factors underpinning the governmental and judicial need to represent criminal law as just and as politically 'neutral'. They also include questions about the way in which a certain model of criminal procedure—that of trial by jury—plays a legitimating role which can be maintained only by diverting attention away from the exceptional nature of jury trials and the prevalence of lay justice, diversion from the criminal process and practices such as plea bargaining.

While earlier examples of critical criminal law scholarship were primarily concerned with the form of criminal legal reasoning, later examples have begun to examine the substantive patterns of criminal legislation and judicial interpretation, and the relationship between shifts in these frontiers of criminality and the broader social meaning of the practice of criminal justice (Loveland (ed.) 1995). Striking examples during the 1980s include the development of criminal law in the area of serious fraud (Weait 1995) and the debate about homicide doctrine following a number of unsuccessful 'corporate manslaughter' prosecutions consequent upon incidents which would until recently have been regarded as fatal 'accidents' (Wells 1995, 2001). Similarly, socio-legal work on patterns of enforcement in the so-called 'regulatory' offences have revealed that, in the context of limited resources, specialist regulatory enforcement agencies often fall back on criminal law-like notions of fault such as negligence or recklessness in selecting cases for prosecution—hence disrupting the doctrinal distinction between regulatory and fault-based offences, between 'real' crime and 'quasi-'crime discussed above (Richardson 1987).

It is not only socio-legal analysis of crime and criminal enforcement which provides material for a re-assessment of the 'general principles' of criminal law, however. Further purchase on the contemporary significance of those general principles can be achieved by taking a longer-term, historical perspective on the substantive development of criminal law and of the institutional framework within which it is interpreted and enforced. As we noted above, 200 years ago, English criminal law was far less extensive than it is today, and was more readily rationalized in terms of a set of core interests and values. Of course, this does not mean that there was no social or value conflict, or that criminal law was not already being used for what today we would think of as 'regulatory' purposes. But with rapid urbanization and industrialization in the early nineteenth century, and with the growth of the nation state's governmental capacities and ambitions, the conditions under which criminal law operated changed markedly (Lacey 2001a).

Social mobility and fragmentation also had direct implications for the environment which shaped the extent of social reliance on criminal law, as opposed to informal or private dispute resolution. The first institutional responses to these developments were the reforms of the policing, prosecution, trial, and penal processes of the nineteenth century (Lacey 2001b), with a professionalization of enforcement and legal practice and a regularization of penal practice consonant with an emerging, rationalist, modernist, and (potentially) liberal conception of the rationale of criminal law. In this country, the obvious counterpart in the substantive law—full-scale codification —never materialized. But the successive attempts at codification, along with the changing conditions under which criminal trials went forward—a developed set of rules of evidence, legal representation of defendants, the slow emergence of an appellate system—conduced to the incremental development and to the judicial and scholarly articulation of more general principles of criminal law (Smith 1998). Such general principles were important not only in rationalizing criminal law power in the context of an increase in democratic sentiments, and hence within an emerging liberal understanding of the legitimation problems of the system, but also—crucially—in focusing the legitimation narrative on the form of criminal law rather than on its substance, hence managing the substantive fragmentation and diversification of criminal law occasioned by its rapid expansion. Furthermore, these doctrinal developments spoke to the resolution of what we may call criminal law's coordination problem: the changing problems of gathering and validating knowledge—the facts on the basis of which a criminal conviction is arrived at via the application of legal norms—in an increasingly centralized system in which reliance on the local knowledge of jurors and justices of the peace, characteristic of the early modern criminal law, was no longer feasible.

One striking feature which illustrates further connections between criminal law developments and broader social and intellectual developments here is the gradual formalization of principles of criminal responsibility around mental concepts such as intention, knowledge, belief, and recklessness, as opposed to the overtly evaluative concepts such as malice and wilfulness which had characterized the common law for centuries. This development played a crucial role in criminal law's legitimation, because it shifted the focus of justified liability from an overt evaluation (malice) to a factual, psychological state (intention), hence (apparently) distancing controversial moral and political judgements from the court room. This shift from older ideas of 'fault' to a more empirically based conception of 'responsibility' was made possible by the growth of what we would now call psychology, itself premised on a certain understanding of the mind–body distinction and of the idea of the mental as a discrete object of social knowledge. But the criminal law development could not have occurred had it not been for the further belief that the factual question of what is going on in someone's mind when he or she is acting can be an object of investigation, and indeed proof, in a criminal court (Smith 1981). This in turn depended on institutional developments in the trial process, and particularly in the law of evidence (Lacey 2001b).

These examples suggest that the full implications of legal analysis can be realized only once they are set in the context of a broader set of historical, political, and social questions about the conditions of existence and efficacy of particular doctrinal arrangements. These questions are not legal questions, neither do they detract from the importance of a specifically legal analysis. What they do is to give that analysis a far greater significance than it would otherwise have, both by relating it to a wider set of social-theoretic questions and by suggesting links with normative (typically philosophical) thinking about the conditions under which the criminal process might operate in less unjust, undemocratic, and oppressive ways. It is in this sense that criminal law scholarship has begun to open up a new agenda for cross-institutional and interdisciplinary study. This agenda, as I shall argue below, may best be understood within the framework of 'criminalization'.

CONTEXTUALIZING CRIMINAL LAW: CRIMINOLOGICAL PERSPECTIVES

It follows from what has been said in the last section that criminological thinking, broadly understood, brings important insights to the study of criminal law. Since the specific practices of both legislation and legal interpretation take place within the context of broader social processes, which shape not only the range and definition of criminal laws but also the particular subjects in relation to whom the courts apply their legal techniques, that context is an important factor in understanding the dynamics of legal interpretation. Ideas and principles which are central to criminal law doctrine and its broader accompanying framework, the ideal of the rule of law, begin to take on a different colour once we appreciate, as criminology helps us to do, the partiality and selectivity of their enforcement.

As an overtly coercive state practice within societies which think of themselves as liberal—as composed of self-determining individuals whose rights and freedoms must be respected—criminal law confronts a serious challenge of legitimation. The challenge is accentuated by the increasing scope and diversifying functions which characterize the development of criminal law since the early nineteenth century, and by the value pluralism and social conflict which characterize late modern societies (Garland 2001). Criminal law seeks to meet this challenge by making a number of normative claims which relate both to the substance of legal norms and to the process through which they are enforced. In relation to the former, criminal law legitimates itself in two main ways. First, it does so by appealing to the normative, purportedly 'objective' status of the standards which it applies. Yet, as we have seen, this poses problems of reconciliation, both with the vast range of actual criminal laws and the political manipulation of the frontiers of criminality by legislative changes and executive decisions which criminalize hitherto lawful activities or remove criminal sanctions from formerly prohibited conduct. Secondly, criminal law legitimates itself by appealing to the basis of its standards in common, shared understandings or commitments. This is difficult to reconcile with pervasive social conflict in relation to the existence or interpretation of particular criminal norms. Instructive contemporary examples include not only obvious disagreements about the propriety of criminalizing certain forms of sexual behaviour and commercial conduct, but also dissensus about the proper standard of fault to be applied in the key offence of homicide (Lacey 1993).

In relation to procedure and enforcement, criminal law legitimates itself as the fair and even-handed application of rules to subjects conceptualized in terms of their formal capacities for understanding and self-control. Yet how is this claim to be reconciled with the statistics on disparate patterns of enforcement along lines of race or ethnicity, gender, socio-economic status, age, place of residence? Criminal law claims legitimacy by appealing to the detached and even-handed application of its standards to all who come before it. How is this claim to be reconciled with the pervasiveness of practices such as plea-bargaining, which are driven by the relative power relations of particular actors within the process and by managerialist concerns about the cost-efficient disposal of cases? Criminal law prides itself on its application of a standard of proof beyond reasonable doubt and on its tailoring of liability requirements to the particular individual before the court. How is this to be reconciled with extensive plea-bargaining, or with the indeterminacy of fault/responsibility standards? Evidently, these legitimating strategies are heavily dependent on criminal law's capacity to sustain the aura of its separateness from the politics and practicalities of the criminal process. Many principles which are central to the 'common sense' of doctrinal criminal law come to look somewhat fragile as that separateness is eroded by a little knowledge of criminal justice. This realization itself propels the sorts of questions discussed above on to the consciousness of the criminal law scholar.

THE DOCTRINAL STRUCTURE OF CRIMINAL LAW: QUESTIONS FOR THE SOCIAL SCIENCES

The idea that criminological insight can sharpen the perspective of criminal lawyers will probably be accepted by anyone who has chosen to study criminology. The converse idea—that criminologists or students of criminal justice ought to concern themselves with criminal law—may be less intellectually digestible. For some students of criminology this has to do with a (not entirely unjustified) scepticism about the relative importance of law in determining social practices of labelling and punishment which are seen in broader sociological and political terms. For others it may have to do with a crude understanding of criminal law received from 'black-letter' positivist scholarship. The legal positivist approach views laws as the products of legislative or judicial decision, that operate straightforwardly as rules which are applied in a deductive way to cases coming before the courts. From a criminological perspective, legal positivism entails, once again, that the interesting questions are not legal ones but rather social and political ones, having to do with the factors shaping the selection of cases coming before the courts and the influences upon legislative changes in the scope and contours of criminal prohibitions. This, however, is to miss out on the significance of law as an interpretive practice which plays a central role in the legitimation of the state's penal power. I shall suggest, therefore, that at least four aspects of critical criminal law scholarship are likely to generate important insights from a criminological point of view.

First, the critical criminal lawyer's focus on shifting boundaries of criminal law provides one important part of the broader criminal justice jigsaw. While changes in the legislative content of criminal law are themselves highly significant as both political and legal events, the subsequent process of judicial interpretation is what shapes both the meaning and (to some degree) the social efficacy of new criminal laws. Judicial interpretations which, for example, render criminal laws very difficult to enforce will have both knock-on effects for future prosecution policy and implications for the symbolic meaning of the relevant law. An excellent example is the law on incitement to racial hatred, the strict interpretation of which has arguably rendered it virtually unenforceable and which is regarded by some as a *de facto* legitimation of racial abuse (Fitzpatrick 1987). Furthermore, long-standing aspects of the doctrinal framework of criminal law may facilitate or inhibit the movement of the boundaries of criminality in directions aspired to by political institutions and other groupings. One good example here is the inchoate move towards imposing criminal liability on corporations—a development which continues to be inhibited by the association of the 'mens rea' framework with the mental states of individual human agents (Wells 2001). Another example is the debate about how to administer the law of rape so as more even-handedly to recognize the sexual integrity of rape victims and defendants. This project is hindered by the doctrinal shape of the rape offence. Proof of rape turns on the victim's lack of consent—something which continues to be judged (notwithstanding legislative attempts to change the position: Youth Justice and Criminal Evidence Act 1999, s 41; *R v A* [2001] 3 All ER 1) in relation to broad evidence about the victim's (as opposed to the defendant's) sexual or other experience. This legal arrangement is widely recognized to invite prejudicial stereotypes about certain kinds of victim into the courtroom. Liability for rape also depends on proof of a subjective standard of responsibility. This entails that even a grossly unreasonable mistake about the victim's consent can, in principle, exonerate the defendant—hence giving legal force to the defendant's (as opposed to the victim's) understanding of the encounter. These problems are reinforced by an adversarial court procedure in which the best defence strategy is almost invariably to attack the victim's character (Temkin 1987, 2000; Smart 1995; Lacey 1998b: chapter 4).

Secondly, the critical criminal lawyer's focus on the specificities of legal reasoning sheds light on the ways in which power at one stage of the criminal process is both exercised and legitimated. Notwithstanding their relative infrequency, trial by jury and criminal appeals play a central role in the legitimation of the entire criminal process. A close appreciation of how these stages work—one which pays attention to the particularities of legal discourse—is therefore of central importance to any integrated understanding of criminal justice. For example, critical scholarship has generated important insights into the ways in which the power of law depends on the capacity of legal discourse to construct itself as generating 'truths' which are impervious to critical scrutiny from other perspectives (Smart 1989). This in turn sheds light on processes by which other knowledges introduced as evidence in criminal trials—sociological or psychological knowledges, for example—are subtly invalidated or else modified in the course of 'translation' into the terms of legal discourse. A good example here is the slow and partial legal recognition of evidence about the effects of long-term violence in 'domestic' homicide cases. While recent cases have begun to accept such evidence as relevant, its force was initially limited by the need to shape it to fit the conceptual straitjackets of legal defences such as provocation, self-defence, and diminished responsibility (Lacey 1998b: chapter 7). For instance, the legal requirement that, to qualify as provocation or self-defence, a violent response must follow immediately upon provocative or threatening conduct posed difficulties in several cases in which defendants (most of them women) who had been subject to 'domestic' violence killed their abusers, yet in which there was no immediate relation between the ultimate killing and a particular attack (Nicolson and Bibbings (eds) 2001). The result was that defence lawyers were forced to reconstruct the relevant evidence in psychiatric terms which accorded with a diminished responsibility defence, which misrepresented the defendant's position. Such transformations of non-legal knowledges in the legal process have generally been invisible to conventional legal analysis, and until recently received only partial recognition and understanding in socio-legal scholarship.

This is not to imply a reductive, sociological reading of the criminal trial or the criminal appeal: neither is it, conversely, to deny the importance of interpretive questions about the meaning of the rituals and architecture of the trial as a public event. It is rather to assert that the images of subject and society, of guilt and innocence, of responsibility and non-responsibility, of the autonomy and independence of legal power, and of the objectivity and political neutrality of judgment which are produced within legal reasoning are discrete objects of criminal justice knowledge. While the ultimate direction of my argument is that these legal specificities have meanings which are systematically obscured by the structure of legal doctrine, these meanings cannot be grasped without a close analysis of the practices of legal argumentation themselves, along with their historical development and place within particular professional institutions. Hence the critical criminal lawyer's approach of taking the doctrinal framework seriously in itself, but of simultaneously reading it as a clue to broader socio-political factors, sheds light on matters of central concern to the criminologist. The alleged autonomy or 'closure' of legal reasoning has to be identified, and its *modus operandi* understood, before it can take its place as one of the objects of interpretation within any general attempt to understand the nature of crime and the criminal process.

Thirdly, historical shifts in the patterns of 'general principles' which purportedly structure legal doctrine, and indeed in the degree of insistence on any such structure, are themselves significant from a criminological point of view. Let us take, for example, the fact that today's focus on fault/responsibility as the central doctrinal problem in legitimizing criminal liability emerged only during the nineteenth century, and reached its current predominance only in the second half of the twentieth century (Lacey 1997). Before this, as discussed above, the organizing framework for doctrine was focused on the types of conduct proscribed rather than the basis on which individuals could fairly be held responsible for that conduct. As we have seen, this shift relates to a number of social developments of direct relevance to criminalization: a changing conception of the subject as an individual and of his or her relation to the polity and to government (Wiener 1990); a shifting view of the legitimation problems posed by the criminal justice system occasioned by, among other things, the diffusion of liberal-democratic expectations (Lacey 2001a, 2001b); a changing view of the role of criminal law as one form of social ordering among others, the latter driven by significant transformations in the shape and variety of criminal procedure over the last 150 years (Farmer 1996b: chapter 3). While these developments have been central to the social history of crime, and relate directly to the shift from substance to form in the rationalization of criminal law (Norrie 2001), their significance and its relation-ship with changes in the organizing framework of criminal law doctrine have largely been ignored. Hence a promising avenue of enquiry into the developing nature of crime and criminal justice has been closed off by the current organization of disciplines.

Lastly, critical criminal law scholarship generates a finely tuned analysis of the shape of particular criminal laws and their interpretation over time. From a criminological or criminal justice point of view, it is all too easy to take 'criminal law' as a unitary, undifferentiated body of norms which are straightforwardly applied by the courts. Yet a close reading of cases and statutes reveals an enormous diversity among criminal laws: in terms of the style of their drafting; their scope; their construction of their subjects and objects; their assumptions about responsibility; their procedural requirements. Careful micro-level analysis of legal discourse illuminates assumptions about human nature, and about the status of various kinds of conduct, which structure legal reasoning yet which may not appear on the face of legal arrangements. Good examples are the close feminist readings of criminal laws dealing with sexual offences, and with rape in particular (Temkin 1987, 2000; Lacey and Wells 1998: chapter 4; Lacey 1998b: chapter 4; Duncan 1996; Zedner 1995), which reveal a troubling set of assumptions about male and female sexuality and about the reliability of female witnesses. Similarly, the readings of criminal law's construction of homosexuality within queer legal theory (Moran 1996; Stychin 1998) reveal a situation which is substantially at odds with the (relatively) liberal approach which appears on the surface of criminal laws. And critical readings of the property offences have generated a wealth of insights about their assumptions about honesty and propriety, their construction of the fragile lines between 'enterprise' and 'dishonesty', and the ways in which this construction shifts as between different kinds of property offence (Lacey and Wells 1998: chapter 3; Hall 1952). Such analysis of individual criminal laws or areas of criminal law generates an enormous amount of material which can illuminate the broad social meaning of criminalization. It also reveals a multi-directional process in which both legislature and courts are involved in reflecting, interpreting, and shaping the social attitudes and norms upon which the efficacy and legitimacy of criminal justice depends.

FROM CRITICAL CRIMINAL LAW
TO CRIMINALIZATION

My suggestion, then, is that criminology, broadly understood, and criminal law scholarship of a critical temper are complementary, albeit distinctive, tasks within the general intellectual enterprise of working towards an understanding of the diverse social practices associated with criminal justice. I have argued that the term 'criminalization' constitutes an appropriate conceptual framework within which to gather together the constellation of social practices which form the subject matter of criminal law on the one hand and criminal justice and criminological studies on the other (Lacey 1995; see also Farmer 1996a). Escaping the notion of crimes as 'given', the idea of criminalization captures the dynamic nature of the field as a set of interlocking practices in which the moments of 'defining' and 'responding to' crime can rarely be completely distinguished and in which legal and social (extra-legal) constructions of crime constantly interact. It accommodates the full range of relevant institutions within which those practices take shape and the disciplines which might be brought to bear upon their analysis; it allows the instrumental and symbolic aspects of the field to be addressed, as well as encompassing empirical, interpretive, and normative projects. It embraces questions about offenders and victims, individuals and collectivities, state and society.

Within the framework of criminalization, we may therefore accommodate the relevant practices of a variety of social actors and institutions: citizens, the media, the police, prosecution agencies, courts, judges and lawyers, social workers, probation officers and those working in the penal and mental health systems, legislators, and key members of the executive. We are also able to acknowledge the relevance of a wide variety of disciplines to the analysis of these institutions: sociology, psychology, political science, economics, legal studies, moral and political philosophy, and anthropology, to name only the most obvious. This we can do without collapsing the study of criminalization into a chaotic mass which escapes rigorous analysis, and without falling prey to fantasies about the possibility of a unitary synthesis of different approaches. Doubtless the study of criminalization is less intellectually tidy than the all-encompassing 'theories of criminal justice' which have been academically fashionable since the 1960s (Hall 1960; Packer 1968; Gross 1979). This seems an eminently worthwhile sacrifice if it enables us to define a field of scholarship which is sufficiently open to identify the intersecting issues which, as I argued earlier, are all too often lost from view in the prevailing division of labour within the field.

Selected further reading

Readers interested in the debate about 'critical criminal law' should consult the important early papers by Mark Kelman, 'Interpretive Construction in the Substantive Criminal Law' (1981), *Stanford Law Review*, 33: 591, and David Nelken, 'Critical Criminal Law' (1987), *Journal of Law and Society*, 14: 105. Alan Norrie's *Crime, Reason and History* (2nd edn, London: Butterworths, 2001) provides an extended application of critical method to criminal law, and pushes the critical approach forward by exploring the historical context in which criminal law doctrine has developed (see in particular chapter 1) and the relationship between criminal law doctrine and sentencing practice (see chapter 10). An assessment of the relationship between developments in political culture, criminal justice institutions, and criminal law doctrine is attempted in Nicola Lacey's 'In Search of the Responsible Subject' (2001), *Modern Law Review*, 64: 350, and 'Responsibility and Modernity in Criminal Law' (2001), *Journal of Political Philosophy*, 9: 249.

The interaction between the three fields distinguished in this chapter is explored in greater detail in N. Lacey and C. Wells, *Reconstructing Criminal Law* (2nd edn, London: Butterworths, 1998), chapter 1; S. Bronitt and B. McSherry, *Principles of Criminal Law* (Pyrmont, NSW: Law Book Company, 2001); N. Lacey, 'Contingency and Criminalisation', in I. Loveland (ed.), *Frontiers of Criminality* (London: Sweet and Maxwell, 1995); and in Donald Nicolson and Lois Bibbings (eds), *Feminist Perspectives on Criminal Law* (London: Cavendish, 2001). Lindsay Farmer's *Criminal Law, Tradition and Legal Order* (Cambridge: Cambridge University Press, 1996) provides another useful exposition of critical method in the criminal law field, and a fascinating case study of the interaction between national politics, criminal law, and criminal procedure in nineteenth-century Scotland: see in particular chapters 1 and 3.

References

ASHWORTH, A. (1998), *The Criminal Process: An Evaluative Study*, 2nd edn, Oxford: Oxford University Press.

—— (1999), *Principles of Criminal Law*, 3rd edn, Oxford: Clarendon Press.

BLACKSTONE, WILLIAM (1765–69), *Commentaries on the Laws of England*, Chicago, Ill.: University of Chicago Press.

BRONITT, S., and McSHERRY, B. (2001), *Principles of Criminal Law*, Pyrmont, NSW: Law Book Company.

—— (1995), *Principles of Criminal Law*, 2nd edn, Oxford: Clarendon Press.

CLARKSON, C., and KEATING, H. (1998), *Criminal Law: Text and Materials*, 4th edn, London: Sweet and Maxwell.

COLE, G.F., FRANKOWSKI, S.J., and GERTZ, M.G. (eds) (1987), *Criminal Justice Systems: A Comparative Survey*, 2nd edn, London: Sage.

DUNCAN, S. (1996), 'The Mirror Tells its Tale: Constructions of Gender in Criminal Law', in A. Bottomley (ed.), *Feminist Perspectives on the Foundational Subjects of Law*, London: Cavendish: 173.

FARMER, L. (1995), 'Bringing Cinderella to the Ball: Teaching Criminal Law in Context', *Modern Law Review*, 58: 756.

—— (1996a), 'The Obsession with Definition', *Social and Legal Studies*, 5: 57.

—— (1996b), *Criminal Law, Tradition and Legal Order*, Cambridge: Cambridge University Press.

FITZPATRICK, P. (1987), 'Racism and the Innocence of Law', *Journal of Law and Society*, 14: 119.

FLETCHER, G. (1978), *Rethinking Criminal Law*, Boston and Toronto: Little, Brown & Co.

GARLAND, D. (2001), *The Culture of Control*, Oxford: Oxford University Press.

GOODRICH, P. (1986), *Reading the Law*, Oxford: Blackwell.

GROSS, H. (1979), *A Theory of Criminal Justice*, Oxford: Oxford University Press.

HALL, J. (1952), *Theft, Law and Society*, New York: Bobbs-Merrill.

—— (1960), *General Principles of Criminal Law*, 2nd edn, Indianapolis and New York: Bobbs-Merrill.

HART, H.L.A. (1963), *Law, Liberty and Morality*, Oxford: Oxford University Press.

—— (1968), *Punishment and Responsibility*, Oxford: Clarendon Press.

KELMAN, M. (1981), 'Interpretive Construction in the Substantive Criminal Law', *Stanford Law Review*, 33: 591.

KENNY, C.S. (1952), *Outlines of Criminal Law*, 16th edn (ed. J.W.C. Turner), Cambridge: Cambridge University Press.

LACEY, N. (1993), 'A Clear Concept of Intention: Elusive or Illusory', *Modern Law Review*, 56: 621.

—— (1994), 'Making Sense of Criminal Justice', in N. Lacey (ed.), *Criminal Justice: A Reader*, 1, Oxford: Oxford University Press.

—— (1995), 'Contingency and Criminalization', in I. Loveland (ed.), *Frontiers of Criminality*, chapter 1, London: Sweet & Maxwell.

—— (1998a), 'Contingency, Coherence and Conceptualism: Reflections on the Encounter between "Critique" and "Philosophy of the Criminal Law"', in A. Duff (ed.), *Philosophy and the Criminal Law*, Cambridge: Cambridge University Press.

—— (1998b), *Unspeakable Subjects: Feminist Essays in Legal and Social Theory*, Oxford: Hart Publishing.

—— (2001a), 'In Search of the Responsible Subject', *Modern Law Review*, 64: 350.

—— (2001b), 'Responsibility and Modernity in Criminal Law', *Journal of Political Philosophy*, 9: 249.

—— and WELLS, C. (1998), *Reconstructing Criminal Law: Critical Perspectives on Crime and the Criminal Process*, 2nd edn, London: Butterworths.

LOVELAND, I. (ed.) (1995), *Frontiers of Criminality*, London: Sweet & Maxwell.

MILL, J.S. (1859), *On Liberty*, Harmondsworth: Penguin, 1974.

MORAN, L. (1996), *The Homosexual(ity) of Law*, London: Routledge.

NELKEN, D. (1987a), 'Critical Criminal Law', *Journal of Law and Society*, 14: 105.

—— (1987b), 'Criminal Law and Criminal Justice: Some notes on their irrelation', in I. Dennis (ed.), *Criminal Law and Justice*, 139, London: Sweet & Maxwell.

NICOLSON, D., and BIBBINGS, L. (eds) (2001), *Feminist Perspectives on Criminal Law*, London: Cavendish.

NORRIE, A. (1992), 'Criminal Law', in I. Griggs Spall and P. Ireland (eds), *The Critical Lawyer's Handbook*, 76, London: Pluto Press.

—— (2001), *Crime, Reason and History*, 2nd edn, London: Butterworths.

PACKER, H. (1968), *The Limits of the Criminal Sanction*, Stanford, Cal.: Stanford University Press.

RADZINOWICZ, L., and TURNER, J.W.C. (1945), 'The Meaning and Scope of Criminal Science', in *The Modern Approach to Criminal Law*, Cambridge: Cambridge University Press.

RICHARDSON, G. (1987), 'Strict Liability for Regulatory Crime: the Empirical Research', *Criminal Law Review*, 295.

ROBINSON, P.H. (1997), *Structure and Function in Criminal Law*, Oxford: Clarendon Press.

SMART, C. (1989), *Feminism and the Power of Law*, London: Routledge.

—— (1995), *Law, Crime and Sexuality*, London: Sage.

SMITH, K.J.M. (1998), *Lawyers, Legislators and Theorists*, Oxford: Clarendon Press.

SMITH, R. (1981), *Trial by Medicine*, Edinburgh: Edinburgh University Press.

STEPHEN, J.F. (1893), *A History of the Criminal Law of England*, London: Macmillan.

STYCHIN, C.F. (1995), *Law's Desire: Sexuality and the Limits of Justice*, London and New York: Routledge.

SUMNER, C. (1994), *The Sociology of Deviance: An Obituary*, Buckingham: Open University Press.

TEMKIN, J. (1987), *Rape and the Legal Process*, London: Sweet & Maxwell.

—— (2000), 'Prosecuting and Defending Rape: Perspectives from the Bar', *Journal of Law and Society*, 219.

WEAIT, M. (1995), 'The Serious Fraud Office: Nightmares (and Pipe Dreams) on Elm Street', in I. Loveland (ed.), *Frontiers of Criminality*, chapter 4, London: Sweet & Maxwell.

WELLS, C. (1995), 'Cry in the Dark: Corporate Manslaughter and Cultural Meaning', in I. Loveland (ed.), *Frontiers of Criminality*, chapter 5, London: Sweet & Maxwell.

—— (2001), *Corporations and Criminal Responsibility*, 2nd edn, Oxford: Clarendon Press.

WIENER, M. (1990), *Reconstructing the Criminal: Culture, Law and Policy in England, 1830–1914*, Cambridge: Cambridge University Press.

WILLIAMS, G. (1983), *A Textbook of Criminal Law*, 2nd edn, London: Stevens.

ZEDNER, L. (1995), 'Regulating Sexual Offences within the Home', in I. Loveland (ed.), *Frontiers of Criminality*, chapter 8.

10

THE SKELETONS IN THE CUPBOARD

THE POLITICS OF LAW AND ORDER AT THE TURN OF THE MILLENNIUM[1]

David Downes and Rod Morgan

INTRODUCTION

This chapter concerns the public contestation of the dynamics of crime and disorder—that is, debates about which phenomena should be defined as such, how crime and disorder events are interpreted, and, above all, how they are reacted to. The key players in this matrix are: the major political parties, in particular successive Home Secretaries and their ministerial and Opposition teams; senior civil servants who, despite their non-political role, bear crucial advisory responsibilities; pressure and interest groups in the criminal justice field; and the mass media. The private, off-stage, often confidential, and even secretive processes of discussion, negotiation, and exchange, which provide the ingredients of public utterance and action, remain implicit rather than spelt out. Further, when we employ terms such as 'the Conservative Party', we do not mean to propagate the fallacy of misplaced concreteness: these terms are necessary abbreviations for the welter of possible responsibilities for actions and policies that may be the work of many thousands of individuals. Neither, in quoting the words of ministers or other politicians, do we assume that perfect comprehension can be achieved—if it ever can be—without much more detail about timing, context, and much else. Our purpose is limited—to demonstrate a point rather than to convey some total reality.

Compared with the contested party politics of the economy, foreign affairs, defence, health, housing, and education, those of 'law and order' are of remarkably recent origin: they emerged in the mid-1960s, and came decisively to the fore in the 1979 election. This absence from party political discourse and contention seems now to be surprising. At the beginning of the twenty-first century we think of law and order as highly emotive and fundamentally political issues: over the past quarter of a century

---

[1] Part of this chapter was earlier published as an article: Downes, D., and Morgan, R. (2002), 'The British General Election 2001: the Centre-Right Consensus', *Punishment and Society*, 4/1: 81–96.

we have got used to the fact that they arouse passionate political debate. But it was not always so. That law and order were relatively insulated from the realm of party politics for so long testifies perhaps to the strength of belief that crime, like the weather, is beyond political influence; and that the operation of the law and criminal justice should be above it. This is not to deny that criminal law reform has long been regarded as the prerogative of Parliament. But once laws are enacted, the liberal doctrine of the separation of powers holds that their enforcement is the preserve of the police and the judiciary. Hence, bipartisanship was the rule rather than the exception in the twentieth century on such matters as the response to crime, the nature of policing, sentencing policy, and so on. Even at the fringes of political life, few challenges were made to this profound consensus. This bipartisan approach was largely abandoned in the 1970s and 1980s, though in the 1990s we began to witness a return to some underlying agreement. The party political squabbles now are largely about relative levels of expenditure on law and order services, police numbers, and the like. Moreover, campaigns today typically involve one or more competitively expressive gestures about what should be done with some particular group of deviants—predatory psychopaths or paedophiles, for example—recently the high-profile subject of outrage or scandal. But closer analysis of party statements reveals that this sound and fury masks substantial agreement that the incidence of volume crime—common property crime and public disorder—is not easily reduced by legislation or the manner in which the law is applied, and that responsibility for reasserting control must be more widely dispersed.

The reasons for the change from a broadly bipartisan to a sharply contested, and now a more twin-track, politics of law and order, are central to our concerns in this chapter. The prelude to the change was deeply significant because the nature of the bipartisanship was both complex and far from apolitical. This was a politics more of nuance and inflection than of explicit difference. The politics of law-breaking are not necessarily those of order-defiance (Elder 1984), and the latter has a far more developed history, particularly in the realm of industrial conflict (Dixon and Fishwick 1984). Friction over public order legislation and its enforcement has throughout the period been far more evident than that concerning straightforward criminality. It was the achievement of 'Thatcherism' to blur the difference between the two, and even to fuse them symbolically to political effect. And the consequences of the change have been more than a simple matter of the major parties taking up starkly opposing stances across the range of relevant issues. Despite new, overt differences, a species of second-order consensus has emerged to replace former orthodoxies. Moreover, the politics of law and order are not confined to the party sphere. Extra-parliamentary processes have often been more vigorous than those within the confines of Westminster, and developments at local government level, or formulations by pressure groups and lobbies, have frequently been the stimulus for national attention. Lastly, the eruption of particular scandals and concerns, via a rapidly changing media framework, have consistently proved catalysts for changing policies. In what follows, we shall address these topics in turn.

BRITISH GENERAL ELECTIONS AND 'LAW AND ORDER' 1945–2001

In earlier versions of this chapter (Downes and Morgan 1992, 1997) we examined in some detail (by analysing party manifestos and drawing on the rigorous Nuffield studies of successive election campaigns and voting patterns conducted by David Butler and his colleagues) how law and order issues figured in the fourteen General Elections which took place from 1945 to 1992 inclusive. We refer those of our readers interested in that detail to those earlier versions. For present purposes it is necessary only to summarize what those analyses demonstrated as a prelude to a close examination of the 1997 and 2001 Elections when the Labour Party, or rather New Labour as it preferred to style itself, wrested power from the Conservatives and retained it for a second term.

FROM GAITSKELL TO THATCHER AND MAJOR: THE POST-WAR MANIFESTOS AND CAMPAIGNS

In 1945 Britain 'was a society both exhausted and exhilarated' (Morris 1989: 13). The awesome task of post-War reconstruction led the three main parties to contend overwhelmingly about the priorities of rebuilding the economy and constructing the 'welfare state'. Despite fundamental ideological differences, out of this period was evolved a form of consensus, usually known as 'Butskellism', which set limits to the scope of political conflict. Full employment, core welfare rights in health, housing, and income maintenance, and education and economic growth based on Keynesian assumptions, were broadly accepted as shared goals, as was a mixed economy—though strong differences persisted over the nature of the mix. Crime and criminal justice were minor, taken-for-granted aspects of this consensus.

Except for minor issues such as legal aid and betting and gaming law, none of the major political parties said anything in their manifestos about law and order in the five post-War elections from 1945 to 1959, nor did such issues figure in their campaigns. The exhaustive Nuffield studies of each campaign bear this out.

During the 1960s the mood began subtly to change. Law and order issues began to creep into manifesto statements. In the face, since the mid-1950s, of steeply rising recorded crime rates, all three major parties began to make statements indicating that they would pursue policies which would more effectively combat crime, but without—and this is important to note—suggesting that the level or form of crime was itself attributable to the politics and policies of the party in government.

All that changed in the 1970s. The Conservative Party started the trend, albeit in a restrained fashion. In their 1970 election manifesto they argued that 'the Labour government cannot entirely shrug off responsibility for the present situation', the 'situation' being 'the serious rise in crime and violence' and increased fear of both: in particular the government was accused of having restricted police recruitment (Conservative Party 1970). In the same document the Conservatives also began to connect crime with the disorders associated with industrial disputes. The law needed to change to deal with offences 'connected with public order—peculiar to the *age of demonstration and disruption*' (ibid.: 25, emphasis added). Labour responded that it was the first duty of government to protect the citizen and prosecute the fight against 'vandals and law breakers', but decried the breakdown of bipartisanship about crime: 'Nothing could be more cynical than the current attempts of our opponents to exploit for Party political ends the issue of crime and law enforcement' (Labour Party 1970).

The chords struck in 1970 grew more insistent in the two elections of 1974, and reached a crescendo in 1979. The victory which the Conservatives won under Margaret Thatcher in 1979 set the tone for the 1980s and ushered in eighteen years of continuous Conservative administration. By 1979 the Conservative Party had fused the issues of law-breaking and order-defiance, and in doing so attacked not just the policies but also the integrity of the Labour government. The Conservatives refashioned their traditional claim to be the natural party of government, representing the order of established authority (Honderich 1990). They successfully pinned to Labour responsibility for the alleged 'ungovernability' of Britain and capitalized on widespread public fears about: national decline; loss of economic competitiveness (the forced loan from the International Monetary Fund); bad industrial relations (apparent to everyone during the strike-ridden 1978–9 'Winter of Discontent'); declining public morals (the great 'permissive society' debate on homosexual and abortion law reform, and the end of censorship by the Lord Chamberlain at the end of the 1960s had generated unease along with emancipation); fear of crime, inner city decay, and the extravagances of youth fashion and street protests.

During the four elections of 1966, 1970, and 1974 (in both February and October), neither the Labour or Liberal parties made much of a response to the raised 'law and order' stakes of the Conservatives: it was not a topic which they appeared willing to contest. But this self-restraint was abandoned in 1979. Knowing that it was to be attacked on its law and order record, the Labour Party devoted more space to these issues in its 1979 manifesto and campaign than ever before, but it stuck to its traditional objective of creating 'one nation' by attacking 'the social deprivation which allows crime to flourish'. The Party continued to put its faith in the welfare state. Thus most of Labour's 'law and order' policy was implicitly to be found elsewhere in its manifesto, in its social and economic policies. By contrast, the Conservatives made restoring the 'rule of law', which they claimed that the Labour Party 'in government as in opposition . . . have undermined', one of their five major tasks; and they undertook to do so by implementing a whole raft of specific 'law and order' policies (Conservative Party 1979). These undertakings included spending more on law and order services (police, courts, and prisons) while they economized elsewhere, and introducing tougher sanctions for criminals. Any lingering doubts about there being a bipartisan consensus on 'law and order' was finally dispelled.

The evidence suggests that the stance developed by the Conservative Party during the 1970s was to the great detriment of Labour. 'Maintaining law and order' moved from sixth to fourth in the list of 'biggest failures of the present government' in Gallup polls during 1975–8 (Butler and Kavanagh 1980: 37–8). Across a range of policy issues tested by MORI polls between August 1978 and April 1979, no policy placed the Conservatives so far ahead of Labour as 'law and order' (ibid.: 163).

The ground staked out by the Conservatives in 1979 set the tone for the early 1980s. The Conservatives stuck to their tough stance: they would give a high priority to law and order expenditure, and were prepared to grant the police and the courts the additional powers which they maintained would bring crime and disorder under control. This was a bravura stance given that the first half of the 1980s witnessed not just a continuing rise in recorded crime, but also a rash of inner-city disorders unmatched in their ferocity in recent history and the bitter, year-long Miners' Strike of 1984–5. Both events acquainted the public, for the first time in mainland Britain, with television images of the police in serried ranks, NATO-helmeted and wielding long batons, drawn up behind flame-proof shields, doing battle with rioters and protesters. In response the Labour Party stuck initially to their 'one nation' position, focusing on 'healing the wounds' brought about by unemployment and the Conservative cuts in public expenditure. They also promised to repeal some of the police powers granted by the Police and Criminal Evidence Act 1984 and undertook to make the police more accountable by amending the constitutional arrangements for their governance. By contrast the Liberal Party (variously Liberal/SDP Alliance, and subsequently Liberal Democrats) took a more radically reformist position, arguing for structural changes in the law (a Bill of Rights incorporating the European Convention on Human Rights) and the organization of criminal justice and crime prevention (the creation of a Ministry of Justice, getting local authorities to set up crime prevention units, and so on).

In the 1987 and 1992 elections, however, significant changes began to emerge in the positions taken by the main parties. Both Conservatives and Labour began to display greater realism and restraint. For the Conservatives this meant no longer implicitly claiming that their policies would reduce the incidence of crime: crime prevention was now a task for everyone because the origins of crime lie 'deep in society'. For its part, the Labour Party dropped its opposition to the new police powers and assured voters, vis-à-vis the governance of the police, that police responsibility for operational matters would not be tampered with. However, the Labour Party also began playing the Conservatives at their own game: in the 1987 election the continued steep rise in recorded crime was attributed to Conservative policies, though not necessarily those on 'law and order'. In 1992 it seemed as if the Labour Party intended pressing home this attack; the Party produced a criminal justice policy document, *Seven Steps to Justice*, which represented its most ambitious thinking on crime and criminal justice for more than two decades. But in the event, somewhat anti-climactically, Labour chose to fight the 1992 election on a smaller front and fewer issues than any since 1945. The Home Secretary, Kenneth Baker, called Labour 'soft and flabby on crime', but apart from his Shadow, Roy Hattersley, calling for improved police strength and social measures to stem the unprecedented rise in recorded crime in 1990–91, Labour disengaged from the fight. Even more strikingly than in 1983 and 1987, it was a case of 'the dog that did not bark'. Six weeks before the election, the Conservative Party capitalized on Labour's silence by unveiling a poster depicting a policeman with one hand tied behind his back. The accompanying slogan was: 'Labour's soft on crime'. It was to the repudiation of this label that the Labour Party dedicated itself in the period up to 1997, a process we examine in detail later in this chapter.

THE 1997 AND 2001 ELECTIONS AND THE ASCENDANCE OF NEW LABOUR

In neither the 1997 nor the 2001 Elections were law and order issues prominent. In their manifestos all three major political parties devoted what has in recent years become the required high proportion of space to community safety, policing, and criminal justice issues. In 2001, coverage of immigration and political asylum questions was added to this mix. However, these were not the issues that flared during the campaigns. In both elections it was the management of the economy, the future shape of taxation, Britain's place in Europe, constitutional issues (devolution in 1997 and the political consequences of possible British entry to the Euro-zone in both 1997 and 2001), and the general quality of public services given particular taxation commitments which assumed the greatest importance (Butler and Kavanagh 1997). The last topic encompassed law and order, particularly in relation to police numbers. Further, the charges and counter-charges made during the campaigns were remarkably similar.

In 1997, New Labour castigated the Conservative Government for presiding over unprecedented rises in recorded crime and failing to provide promised additional police officers, both of which trends it undertook to reverse (Labour Party 1997: 22–3). In their defence the Conservatives asserted that since 1992 recorded crime had fallen by 10 per cent—the biggest fall since records began—and police spending had substantially increased (Conservative Party 1997: 34). In 2001, both the Conservatives and the Liberal Democrats attacked Labour for its broken promises on police numbers, an accusation which Labour attempted to rebut with recent evidence of police recruitment. In its defence Labour proudly proclaimed that recorded crime had during the period 1997–9 fallen by 10 per cent. All three parties engaged in an auction regarding the additional police officers they would ensure were provided in future. The implication was that the incidence of crime is directly related to police numbers, which, of course, it is not (Reiner 2000: 77–8).

The party manifestos of 1997 and 2001 were not short on law and order attacks and defences of the governments' records, or detailed undertakings about what each party would deliver if elected. On the contrary, such material was provided in abundance. But there were striking similarities. In 1997, for example, all three major parties undertook to get tough with persistent young offenders, including those engaged in petty crime and disorder: all said that they would ensure that the parents of offending children were made to face up to their parental responsibilities, and all promised to do more for the victims of crime. The latter refrain, geared up now to give victims greater voice in court proceedings and more rights to information, appeared again in 2001.

Which is not to say that there were no differences between the parties. In 2001, for example, the Conservatives accused the Labour government of having, through the Home Detention Curfew Scheme, an early release programme for short- and medium-term prisoners, permitted crimes to be committed which would otherwise have been prevented (for a detailed evaluation, see Dodgson *et al.* 2001).

The Conservatives claimed that more such crimes would be prevented if, as they proposed, there were 'honesty in sentencing so that the sentence handed down in court is the one served by the criminal' (Conservative Party 2001: 12). This attack, however, was little more than the legacy of the policies they pursued while in office—the provisions for the abolition of parole in the Crime (Sentences) Act 1997—and which Labour refused to implement. Moreover, the challenges offered by the Liberal Democrats served to emphasize what they saw as the common ground between their principal opponents. The Liberal Democrats bewailed the fact that Labour in 1997–2001, echoing the Tory record from 1992–7, had unduly concentrated resources on prison building rather than on primary crime prevention: they believed there was 'more scope for the use of community sentences which are proven to work' (Liberal Democrats 2001: 7). Labour, meanwhile, displayed its laurels, but was careful not to rest on them. Like the Tories in their 1997 manifesto, Labour was not complacent about law and order: much remained to be done. But its 1997 manifesto commitment on crime—'We will be tough on crime and tough on the causes of crime'—a slogan first enunciated by Tony Blair in 1993—'and halve the time it takes persistent juvenile crime to come to court' (Labour Party 1997), had, it proclaimed, been delivered:

The British Crime Survey shows that overall crime fell by 10 per cent from 1997 to 1999. Investment is now rising. The time from arrest to sentence for persistent young offenders is down from 142 days to 89 days—on track to halve the time within the five years promised in 1997 [Labour Party 2001: 44].

None of these detailed messages attracted much press comment or inspired high-profile inter-party argument during the campaigns, however. Even the Conservatives' attempt to label Labour as soft on 'bogus' asylum seekers, thereby stimulating a flood of them to enter the country—a flood that the Conservatives would stem by detaining all asylum seekers in specially created institutions—failed to capture the imagination of either the media or the electorate. It was 'the economy, stupid', and everything else—including the effective management of crime—appeared derivative. As a result of the September 1993 debacle of 'Black Wednesday' and British withdrawal from the exchange rate mechanism, bitter Party in-fighting over British membership of the European Community and entry to the Euro-zone, and the moral failings of significant Party figures—represented by their opponents as 'sleaze'—the Conservatives had by 1997 lost their reputation for governmental competence and party discipline. By contrast, Labour had, during the final years of its long period in the political wilderness, re-branded itself. Through an assiduous programme of modernization, New Labour had established itself as a credible party to take up the reins of government; and during its first administration, proved it could run the economy to the satisfaction of the majority of the electorate—particularly its new voters occupying the prosperous middle ground. Labour was now:

a broad-based movement for progress and justice . . . in strong communities . . . but we have liberated those values from outdated dogma or doctrine . . . On crime, we believe in personal responsibility and in punishing crime . . . different from the Labour approach of the past [Labour Party 1997: 2–3].

That is, Labour claimed now to be the party of 'law and order'. By its failure to criticize Conservative proposals while in Opposition, and by its legislation and other initiatives while in government, it was the 'tough on crime' part of Labour's slogan that it emphasized. It was not that it was unable in 2001 to point to policy initiatives which addressed the 'causes of crime' and diminished 'social exclusion', but the latter policies were noticeably less hard-hitting than the ones being pursued against criminals. After four years in office Labour was convincingly able to claim to be managing crime. The Conservatives fired their best shots, but they were unable effectively to resurrect the old adage that Labour was 'soft': it was manifestly not the case. This metamorphosis was to prove but one aspect of the re-launching of Labour as 'New Labour'.

FROM OLD TO NEW LABOUR

Frank Parkin argued over three decades ago that the principal strength of the Conservative Party was its claim to oneness with the bastions of traditional British sovereignty: the monarchy, the aristocracy, property ownership, the City of London, the armed forces, the ancient universities, the land, and the law (Parkin 1967). The only countervailing force to this ruling-class ideology was that of the Labour Party as representative of the working-class labour movement and its trade union organization. Yet this constituency was always deviant with respect to the core values and most cherished allegiances of British traditionalism. The Labour Party could flourish only in its industrial heartland, most typically in a single-occupation, one-class, urban area like a mining town. Against the Tory Party's keystone value of what Macpherson (1962) termed 'possessive individualism', the Labour Party rested on an appeal to the alternative morality of redistributive social justice and community.

These ideological differences translated readily into quite distinct post-1945 policy choices. The Conservative preference for owner-occupation in housing contrasted sharply and successfully with Labour's emphasis on large-scale, estate-based, municipal, rented accommodation. On the other hand, Labour's development of the National Health Service commanded far more widespread support than the system of private medicine it largely replaced. On taxation, Labour supported the steeply progressive direct taxation of income and wealth; the Conservatives favoured lower direct and more indirect, regressive taxation on spending. On education, Labour came to back comprehensive, neighbourhood schooling; the Conservatives more selective, specialist education with a large private sector. Despite these differences, enough overlap and compromise prevailed for three decades after 1945 for some reality to be granted to the notion of a consensus. It was only from the mid-1970s until the mid-1990s that sharper conflicts prevailed with the rise of New Right policies.

This shift itself needs to be explained in the context of the unique character of post-War political developments in Britain. From 1945–51, the Labour government under Clement Attlee constructed the 'Welfare State' in conditions of post-War hardship and economic crisis, an outstanding achievement recaptured in Peter Hennessey's *Never Again* (1992), a title which dramatically registers the determined seizure of an historic and never-to-be-repeated opportunity. But the Labour Party, unlike all other left-wing parties in Europe, was unable to capitalize on the era of rapidly growing post-War prosperity that, in the 1950s, succeeded austerity and severe constraint. Forced in part by British involvement in the Korean war of 1949–51 to postpone the end of rationing, Labour lost office to the Conservatives in 1951, whose succeeding thirteen years in government coincided with the post-War boom that Harold Macmillan, Prime Minister from 1957–63, termed the 'Never Had It So Good' era. As a result, the association of Conservative government and affluence became cemented, to the point where their aura was that of the 'natural' party of government. No other right-wing party in Europe was so fortunately enabled to evade the negative associations of post-War austerity and to capitalize on the positive associations of post-War prosperity. As a result, even when Labour regained office, its tenure seemed provisional and counter-intuitive. Thus was created the bogey which the 2001 Election has exorcized.

It was this aura of 'Old Labour', as the party of austerity rather than affluence, of economic crisis rather than stability, that Tony Blair and Gordon Brown sought to dispel with the creation of 'New Labour'. They were undoubtedly assisted by two key aspects of 'Thatcherism'. First, the rigours of marketization weakened the hold of the Conservative Party over some of their traditional constituencies. For example, the ancient universities resented controls over higher education expenditure, and Oxford University famously refused Mrs Thatcher an honorary degree. Secondly, the Tories became increasingly schizoid about European Union terms of membership and policy, just as Labour came to realize that far from being simply a rich man's club, the trend of Union policy was firmly Social Democratic. Nevertheless, given this background, the Labour majorities of 1997 and 2001 were achievements of real magnitude. The question is: were they bought at too great a cost of abandoning Labour's defining principles and past achievements, even to the point of metamorphosis into a party of the Centre Right rather than the Centre Left—an extension of 'Thatcherism' by other means? In almost all fields, New Labour has embraced policies and principles associated with neo-liberal rather than social democracy, of the Right rather than the Left. It has refused, for example, to increase direct taxation, even on annual incomes over £100,000, but has increased indirect, regressive taxes on spending, most contentiously on fuel. It has pursued public–private partnerships in hospital and school building, the management of prisons and failing schools, the management of the rail system, the London Underground network, and air traffic control. Moreover, by imposing strict limits on public expenditure in its first two years of office, 1997–9, New Labour ended its first term by lowering rather than raising spending on public services as a proportion of GDP, which remains almost the lowest in Europe (see, for example, Elliott 2001). There are, of course, counter-balancing components to such developments: the substantial reduction in unemployment; the introduction of the minimum wage; the New Deal for the unemployed; reductions in family and child poverty by the Working Families Tax Credit and rises in child benefit; and commitments to greater spending on public services over the next three years. But, on balance, Labour's policies have more in common with recent Conservative than with past Labour governments. How far do its policies on 'law and order' fit that pattern?

THE NEW CONSENSUS ON LAW AND ORDER

The character of Conservative policy on law and order from the mid-1980s until 1993 was in key respects a remarkably liberal departure from Tory orthodoxy. The 1979 Election, which marked the beginning of eighteen years in government, was won on the most radically tough law and order ticket the Conservatives had ever produced. They would restore the 'rule of law' which the Labour government had 'undermined'. They would spend more money on law and order services while 'we economize elsewhere'. There would be more police, and more powers for them to use. There would be 'short, sharp shock' sentences for young 'hooligans' and 'tough sentences . . . for violent criminals and thugs' (Conservative Party 1979). By the late 1980s the Conservative tone had changed, however. Their 1987 election manifesto maintained that fighting crime was a task for 'all of us'. The worsening crime rate was a problem 'not just in Britain but in most other societies too'. Its origins lay 'deep in society' (Conservative Party 1987). Further, David Faulkner, a senior Home Office civil servant, was given an unusually free hand to develop criminal justice and penal policy afresh (Rutherford 1996: 86–7). Drawing on the work of penal reform pressure groups, academic criminology, and in-house research, he fashioned a programme for decarceration which, over several years, was widely canvassed and to some extent 'sold' to the judiciary, partly on the basis of successful developments in community alternatives to custody for young offenders from the early 1980s (Cavadino and Dignan 1997: chapter 9). Perhaps the most striking index of its success was the fall in the prison population from 50,000 in 1987–8 to 42,500 in 1991. This was done in parallel with the passage of the Criminal Justice Act 1991, which sought, among other things, to adopt a minimalist 'just deserts' basis for sentencing—a measure aimed at diverting from custody those petty, persistent offenders jailed more for their persistence than for the seriousness of their crimes (see Ashworth, in Chapter 29 of this volume).

The fateful twist to this ambitious but well-formulated programme lay in the character of the 1987 election victory of the Conservatives, which was fuelled by a pre-election consumer boom engineered by the then Chancellor, Nigel Lawson. When boom turned to bust after the election, with soaring inflation and unemployment reaching three million by 1992, the crime rate soared with it, by some 50 per cent between 1989 and 1992. Despite these monumental failures, the Conservatives, under a new Prime Minister, John Major, still managed to win the 1992 Election, only to have their image as the party of economic good management finally destroyed by the forced devaluation of 'Black Wednesday' in October 1992. By this point, the new Shadow Home Secretary, Tony Blair, had begun decisively to change the grounds of opposition to Conservative policy on crime. Not only would Labour press home criticism of the costs in crime terms of economic mismanagement leading to high unemployment, it would also attack the key provision of the 1991 Criminal Justice Act—the emphasis on just deserts for the current offence rather than for previous convictions. Labour's longstanding but largely ineffective project to nail the weakness of the Conservative position—the refusal to link crime with social and economic policies they themselves had promoted—was now to be renewed, and linked implicitly with undue leniency in sentencing.

In his celebrated phrase summarizing Labour's 'law and order' policy—'tough on crime, tough on the causes of crime'—Blair resonated with public fear of, and anger about, rising crime in several respects. First, crime would be tackled more 'toughly', but the phrase neatly avoided dissonance with past Labour policy by making the subject 'crime' rather than the 'criminal'. Secondly, a variety of interpretations, which included being tough on the criminal, were neatly embraced; it was certainly not ruled out. Thirdly, 'tough on the causes of crime' captured the traditional Labour position to perfection, strengthening the sinews by linking an attack on poverty, inequality, joblessness, and pursuit of the whole Labour pantheon of their opposites, with crime prevention. Fourthly, by introducing the very notion of the 'causes of crime', Blair implicitly condemned the Conservatives for having failed to make those connections over the past decade and a half in government.

Having hit on this phrase, thereby illustrating the immense potency of symbolic language in politics, Labour was now positioned to extract maximum advantage from the fact that the Tory government had presided over four years of steeply rising crime from 1989–1993. Alarmed by their deteriorating position in public opinion polls, both in general and on crime, the Conservatives rapidly cast their previous, and long-germinated, penal policy to the winds and sought to reoccupy lost terrain. First Kenneth Clarke, then Michael Howard, as the new Conservative Home Secretaries after 1992, quickly dropped the key reforming clauses of the 1991 Act: unit fines (which linked the level of fines to disposable incomes) and the need normally to disregard previous convictions in sentencing. Michael Howard's notorious 'Prison Works' speech to the Tory Party Conference in 1993 was the climax to this somewhat panic-stricken shift. However much it might appal the liberal reformers in his own party, Howard was determined to deal with the Labour challenge by recreating its image as a party 'soft on crime'. By 1997 the prison population had risen to 65,000, some 50 per cent higher than it had been less than a decade earlier.

But if Howard thought he could shake off Labour's newfound embrace of 'tough' penal policies, he was badly mistaken. This was no longer the Labour Party of the 1970s and early 1980s when, in response to Conservative assaults on its law and order record and the Conservative fusion of law-breaking and order-defiance (notably in relation to labour disputes), Labour initially failed to respond and later maintained an almost passive 'one nation' response. First Blair, then Straw, not only dogged Howard's heels; they became his doppelganger, even his caricature. They beat him to the punch on several fronts. They trumpeted their admiration for the 'zero tolerance' policing in New York, the need to crack down on 'incivilities', 'squeegee merchants', and beggars. The punitive measures in the 1994 Criminal Justice and Public Order Bill went unopposed by Labour, as did proposals for mandatory sentencing. Labour reneged on its pre-1992 support for the reforms of the 1991 Act, criticizing the Conservatives for their promotion of lenient sentencing. For the first time since law and order became a partisan issue in the 1970s, an effective bi-partisanship in 'toughness' now prevailed in the contest for leadership (Dunbar and Langdon 1998). A major irony was that the forced devaluation of sterling in 1992 inaugurated an economic recovery which steadily reduced unemployment levels and, at least in part, the rate of crime. Yet the Conservatives were ideologically unable to link crime reduction with economic factors: that would be to render their previous responsibility for soaring crime admissible. But neither was Labour prepared to give the Conservatives credit for having reduced crime by better economic management. Both locked themselves in to the position of defining undue leniency as the prime cause of high crime rates. The politics of law and order had now become inherently and increasingly punitive. They were to shape the character of New Labour's policies between 1997 and 2001, as well as the remnant of Conservative rule until that point. Looking back, it is more accurate to see Kenneth Clarke and Michael Howard as the prisoners of Blair and Straw's agenda, rather than—as is conventionally assumed—the reverse (Downes 1998; Cohen 2001).

THE REDISCOVERY OF THE CRIMINAL

Labour's mantra—'tough on crime, tough on the causes of crime'—was notable for more than contriving to get the word 'tough' twice into a single phrase (Newburn 2000a). It cloaked implications and difficulties none too apparent at the point of utterance. First, the agenda for being 'tough on crime' was immediate, that for tackling the 'causes of crime' much more long-term (Downes 1998). The scope for tensions and goal displacement in this dual agenda was soon to surface. For example, commenting on incidents of soccer hooliganism in France by Britons in the summer of 1998, Blair asserted that anyone convicted for such offences should lose their job, a statement blatantly at odds with the government's emphasis on work training as a means of crime prevention, as well as civil liberties. Moreover, the 'long term' lengthened even further with the acceptance of Tory spending limits for the first two years of office, a self-imposed restriction that stretched to cover the entire first term of four years. In practice, that meant reduced spending on the major public services and no core funding to support the local government crime prevention 'partnership' responsibilities created by the Crime and Disorder Act 1998.

Secondly, while liberal reformers had interpreted 'tough on crime' to mean target hardening and other forms of situational crime prevention, and 'tough on the causes of crime' to mean tackling poverty, unemployment, and inequality, in reality it largely meant being tough on the criminal (Pease 1998). A string of largely punitive measures, announced in discussion papers in Opposition and mostly enacted in office, in the Crime and Disorder Act 1998 and other statutes, were designed to meet the 'tough on crime' agenda. These included Anti-social Behaviour Orders, a new device to curtail 'neighbours from hell' which invoked the resort to civil rather than criminal law criteria of proof; the activation of minimum mandatory sentencing for repeat burglary, drug trafficking, violence, and sexual offending; curfews for juveniles; electronic monitoring of offenders on early release; ending *doli incapax*, a measure in effect reducing the age of full criminal responsibility to ten, while simultaneously punishing parents of young offenders—a form of double jeopardy for families (see Newburn, in Chapter 16 of this volume); extending grounds for the disclosure of offending histories to employers to virtually all offences; and depriving offenders in breach of community penalties of benefits; all measures that would hardly have been countenanced by Labour before 1992.

The political effect of these policies was to neutralize any claim by the Conservatives that New Labour was 'soft on crime'. Having ceded this ground to Labour, the Conservatives were drawn into frankly silly attempts to outdo it in toughness, as in the Shadow Home Secretary, Ann Widdecombe's proposal in 2001, endorsed by William Hague, that simple possession of cannabis be grounds for 'on the spot' fines of £100. This proposal was contemptuously rejected by the police and, by implication, by several Shadow Cabinet colleagues, who instantly 'confessed' to smoking pot in their youth.

Yet Labour hegemony on law and order was not translated, in the 2001 Election, into policies that sought to retrieve what had been Labour's position in the 1980s and early 1990s. With crime rates down by 20 per cent during 1995–9 (Kershaw *et al.* 2000) despite a minor fall in police numbers, with prisons bulging and criminal justice practitioners under strain, this could have been the ideal moment to signal the resumption of decarceration (Young 2001). Instead, Labour's new term of office was heralded by announcements that the first year would contain yet more 'tough on crime' legislation: the confiscation of criminal assets (again using civil rather than criminal evidential bases); stepping up penalties for persistent offenders, however petty their crimes; and targeting the 100,000 offenders allegedly responsible for committing 50 per cent of crime. Predictions seemed to be borne out that, once in the grip of 'populist punitiveness' (Bottoms 1995), once addicted to the rhetoric of 'zero tolerance' (Newburn 2001b), once bought into the logic of 'prison works' (Downes 2001), there is every prospect of self-confirming penal expansionism at the expense of due process and civil liberties. Moreover, in the wake of the destruction of the World Trade Centre, Manhattan, in September 2001, Labour introduced an anti-terror Bill which went way beyond that considered necessary by many observers, including the House of Lords, who trimmed back its proposals.

There are some compensating measures to weigh against the above, in particular: the incorporation into domestic law of the European Convention on Human Rights in the Human Rights Act 1998; the Macpherson Report (1999) on the Stephen Lawrence case, which has led to a tightening up of procedures for policing racist violence and, more contentiously, to proposals to remove the double jeopardy obstacle in cases of murder; the new system of Youth Offending Teams (YOTs) to plan a programme of action for young offenders in the community; the proposal to reduce the age of consent for male homosexual relations to sixteen; and the development of restorative justice measures for youthful offending. It remains to be seen how far the YOTs will improve community supervision schemes if the core services they wish to 'join up' remain under-resourced, and how far restorative justice will extend beyond the margins of criminal sentencing practice. On balance, however, the overall impact of this welter of legislative innovation tends so far to be at the punitive end of the scale.

THE SKELETONS IN THE CUPBOARD

In previous analyses of why Labour challenges to the Tories on law and order were either muted or unsuccessful, despite Labour's record of being their equal or even superior on that front, we argued (Downes and Morgan 1994, 1997) that Labour suffered from its traditional links with four key constituencies: trade unionism and the Labour movement; the most deprived working class and ethnic minorities; supporters of civil disobedience; and libertarian causes. For over two decades, from the late 1960s until the early 1990s, these associations were a source of vulnerability to Tory claims that Labour was 'soft on crime' and weak in upholding the rule of law. After 1992, however, New Labour moved swiftly to dump these 'hostages to fortune': by distancing the Party from the militant wing of trade unionism; by a sequence of policy papers heralding a crackdown on incivilities, hooliganism, and crime in general; by not opposing the 1994 Act legislating against travellers, hunt saboteurs, and 'ravers'; and by forbidding any discussion by shadow ministers of changes to the drugs laws, even to the point of reprimanding those who sought to re-open discussion on decriminalizing cannabis.

During Labour's first period of office after 1997, the 'hostages to fortune' were even more decisively dumped, to the point where they could more accurately be termed 'the skeletons in the cupboard'. First, moderate unionism was granted its primary demands: the minimum wage; the right of workers at GCHQ (the MI5 'factory') to regain union membership; and UK signature of the Social Charter of the European Union (not accepting that the Charter had been John Major's compromise to keep the Tory Party from open hostility over the terms of continued EU membership). The trade unions were thus kept 'on board' despite wishing for stronger rights regarding such questions as company stakeholding. The guarantee of union rights within the EU enabled New Labour surgically to remove any hint of association with militant trade unionism and its municipal socialist bases. Ken Livingstone's candidacy for the new mayoralty of London was openly and vehemently opposed by Blair and Brown in person, and Livingstone was expelled from the Party for standing as an Independent following the selection of another official candidate for the Labour Party, Frank Dobson. Livingstone's resounding victory certainly embarrassed the New Labour leadership, but they had taken the precaution of denying the new mayoralty any substantial powers or funding. At national level, militant unionism's potential to embarrass New Labour was greatly reduced by Arthur Scargill's creation and leadership of the Socialist Labour Party, a rump with negligible electoral appeal. However, the signs are that even moderate unions will strongly resist extending new forms of privatization to the public sector heartlands of the health and education services.

Secondly, on the issue of crime, delinquency, and disorder, especially on the worst hit housing estates, Labour has repositioned the Party from regarding such problems as largely symptomatic of underlying social and economic distress, and therefore remediable by social and economic programmes. A more condemnatory and morally censorious view has been adopted. *No More Excuses* (1997) was the telling title of a White Paper aiming, in David Garland's (1996, 2001) phrase, for the 'responsibilisation' of delinquents and their parents. A great deal was made of the inefficiencies of the youth justice system, especially following a series of reports by the Audit Commission on *Misspent Youth* (1996, 1998, 1999), which concluded that swifter and more efficient justice could be delivered by 'final warnings' replacing second or more cautions and other procedural reforms to youth justice. The Audit Commission's reports have themselves been audited, and found seriously flawed in both their data and reasoning (Jones 2001), but they nonetheless proved a basis for much of New Labour's thinking on youth crime. More recent initiatives involve the tracking of 2,500 persistent young offenders and the targeting of the 100,000 most persistent offenders who allegedly commit half of all crime (Labour Party 2001: 32). The skewed character of offending has long been known (see, for example, Shaw 1931; Wolfgang, Figlio, and Sellin 1972) and provides many clues to the underlying causes of crime. But to regard the skew as an identifiable and fixed population of constant offenders is to mistake the nature of the problem, and risks joined-up labelling of a small minority as innately criminal.

If zero tolerance is the basis for tackling the criminal, social exclusion is New Labour's definition of the main underlying problem. The New Deals, the Social Exclusion Unit at 10 Downing Street, and British versions of Welfare to Work have emerged as key policies to address it, but on terms which, as Ruth Levitas (1998) has stressed, preclude any hint of the need to address inequality, whether at work or in terms of income and wealth. New Labour has thereby fashioned a strategy for crime reduction which shifts the need for intervention and control from structural to community and family levels. In this respect, it has converged with the trend of Conservative policies (Crawford 1997). Labour has alleviated poverty more than the Conservatives would have done (Piachaud and Sutherland 2001), but, by refusing to impose extra taxation even on the very rich, it has allowed income and wealth inequalities to proliferate even more than under the Conservatives. And it is this fount of polarization in inequality which classical social theories of crime see as far more criminogenic than absolute deprivation. Indeed the inequalities are arguably more potent sources of influence today, because modern mass media have made them so much more 'in your face'.

Thirdly, New Labour is more removed from the world of civil disobedience than at any point in Party history. To capture the centre ground, Labour has distanced itself from the ruck of street demonstrations, marches, and unticketed public meetings. Smooth corporate management is the New Labour style rather than noisy public assemblies. This fits the global trend, with management at all levels far more at home in air-conditioned, smoke-free pods than in the sweaty, smoke-filled rooms of yore, of which the younger generation of elite politicians have no direct experience. The centre also occupies ground on which scope for the genuine contestation of issues is narrowed to a small segment of the spectrum of acceptable opinion. Hence, the proliferation of single-issue pressure groups, who feel themselves unrepresented in the party political process, and the rise of what might be termed the super-issue networks, concerned with globalization, genetic engineering, and global warming, immense problems which governments are slowly wheeling round to confront. This stalemate produces a sense of disenfranchisement combined with disengagement from formal political processes. It generates the street politics of Seattle, Prague, and Gothenberg, where at the turn of the century world trade and finance conferences were disrupted by concerted protest groups. The forces of economic globalization, largely driven by vast corporate capitalist interests, are as yet unregulated by any Wellsian form of world governance. Nation states are far from ceding their sovereignty to supra-national bodies, but defer to the power of corporate capital to shift their investments around the globe to seek maximum profit (Held 2001). International institutions are seen as either unable to cope (the United Nations and its myriad agencies), or as cloaking and reinforcing the problems (the World Bank, the World Trade Organization, etc.). This matrix is suffused with conflicts of interest which will inevitably explode into future direct action. The danger is that governments will simply insulate themselves by tighter security against the unsightly disturbances that might challenge the 'business as usual' atmosphere of high-level conferencing.

Over the past four years, the Labour government has proved adept, and somewhat fortunate, in coping with various nasty surprises on the civil disobedience front. The anti-fuel tax protest of summer 2000 proved unsustainable against threats of prosecution and removal of participants' licences to operate. Just before the 2001 Election, Asian (largely Muslim community) youth attacked white shops and fought with the police in Oldham. The disturbances were soon traced back to extreme right-wing British National Party (BNP) provocation from outside the town. However, other outbreaks of white–ethnic minority Asian clashes in Bradford and Leeds could not be so readily explained away. The drift of schooling, housing, and community towards segregated patterns opens up the prospect of a US-style ghettoization that is replete with signs of future trouble (Home Office 2001a, 2001b).

An even more difficult situation to resolve was the outbreak of community violence against those suspected locally of involvement in the sexual violation of children. The 'anti-paedophile' protests were sparked off by the abduction and murder of a young girl, Sarah Payne; and her parents called for a comparable law to that in the United States known as 'Megan's Law', which followed a similarly shocking crime. That law compelled the police to 'name and shame' known offenders against children and to inform local communities of their movements. Failing Home Office agreement to do so, the editor of the Sunday tabloid, the *News of the World*, began to publish a weekly list of names. It was persuaded to drop this strategy by the Home Office, following police, probation, and penal reform resistance to the scheme. American experience had shown no fall in rates of sexual assaults against children, and every danger that known offenders would 'go underground' and be too fearful to take part in the therapeutic programmes that alone offered hope of lasting desistance. This refusal by the Home Office to copy an American populist demand and to work in conjunction with advice offered by the main agencies was more the exception than the rule, however, in regard to 'zero tolerance' imports (Newburn 2001a).

Fourthly, one of the most symbolic acts concerning libertarian issues in New Labour's first term of office was that of the Home Secretary, Jack Straw, taking his son to the police following his involvement in a cannabis deal set up by a tabloid newspaper reporter. The whole episode revealed the exploitative character of the seedier media regarding the debate on illicit drug control. Straw gained much sympathy for avoiding any hint of special pleading for his son and for his principled handling of what could have been a scandal in the making. But the episode also had the effect of reinforcing his refusal to countenance any hint of movement away from a prohibitionist stance on drugs control. One of the first acts of the government in 1997 had been to appoint a drugs 'czar', Keith Halliwell, a Chief Constable who had pronounced with some of his colleagues on the counter-productive aspects of government policy on drugs but, subsequent to his appointment, ceased to do so. The very notion of a drugs czar was an import from the USA, whose prohibitionist policies have been notoriously repressive and a major reason for the rise of mass incarceration there (Gainsborough and Mauer 2000). Labour has never been particularly progressive on drugs. Straw's peremptory rejection of the authoritative Police Foundation Report *Drugs and the Law* (2000) echoed a previous Labour Home Secretary James Callaghan's outright dismissal of the report on cannabis for the Advisory Council on Drug Dependence by Barbara Wootton (1968), which had also recommended its decriminalization. However, after three decades of failed policies, with heroin use rising one hundred-fold, and other European countries beginning to experiment with heroin maintenance programmes similar to those once termed 'the British system', the chance to begin a fresh debate was scorned. As illicit drug-use drives a great deal of crime, including its more complex, highly organized forms, such as money laundering, this was a wasted opportunity.

PRESSURE-GROUP AND INTEREST-GROUP POLITICS

Prior to the first party political stirrings of the law and order pot in the 1970s, the business of generating policy was largely left to permanent or temporary expert bodies with memberships broadly representative of the key criminal justice decision-making agencies. It was government on the 'inner circle', by the 'great and good', exercised to a substantial extent behind the scenes. If the principal political parties did not promise in their manifestos to adopt new approaches to such issues as policing or sentencing, neither did they come to government with a programme ready to implement. The Labour Party's 1964 statement, *Crime, A Challenge To Us All*, was the exception that proved the rule. New criminal justice statutes were introduced seldom, and their formulation and gestation were mostly left to non-political processes and specialists. The Advisory Council on the Treatment of Offenders (1944–64) (ACTO), shadowed within the Home Office by the Departmental Committee on the Treatment of Offenders, was the acme of this tradition. It comprised judges, magistrates, academics, and prominent reformers. During its life it considered everything from corporal punishment to prisoner after-care. It was replaced by the other favoured policy-making forum, the Royal Commission, a mechanism which in 1960–2 was also used to formulate the arrangements, adopted in the Police Act 1964, for the governance of the police. In retrospect the ill-fated Royal Commission on the Penal System (1964–6) might be considered a foretaste of the controversies to come: it was disbanded, the only Royal Commission ever not to report, because its members could not agree on fundamental aspects of their task. However, such was the strength of the traditional reliance on policy-making by professionals, that the government response was to revert to the *modus quo ante*: an Advisory Council on the Penal System (ACPS) was created which, until killed off by Margaret Thatcher's so-called Quango axe of 1980, produced a series of reports on, amongst other things, detention centres, prison regimes, reparation by offenders, and sentences of imprisonment.

The final years of the ACPS coincided with the rise of the interest or pressure groups, an emerging phenomenon across the whole range of British politics, but given momentum in the law and order field by the apparently inexorable rise of the crime rate from the mid-1950s onwards, despite growing prosperity and the creation of a fairly comprehensive welfare safety net. Policy formation and electoral behaviour was more capable of being altered by short-term, single issues which could 'only with difficulty be forced within the straitjacket of the old, class-based, two-party system' (Gamble 1990: 353).

Within the criminal justice field, moreover, the reformists were dismayed by the manner in which the Conservatives were dominating the policy agenda, with Labour showing little inclination to formulate a systematic one of its own. Further, the most influential lobbies within the law and order arena, the staff unions—the Police Federation and Prison Officers' Association, for example—and the professional associations—the Magistrates' Association, the Law Society, and so on—were usually less than progressive and often downright reactionary. In this particular sphere there was no close alliance between Old Labour and the trades unions, quite the contrary.

THE PENAL PRESSURE GROUPS AND CONSORTIA

It is perhaps because law and order issues and personnel never fitted the left–right straitjacket to any marked extent, that the criminal justice pressure groups have very different pedigrees, some of them much older than the Thatcher decade. The oldest, the Howard League for Penal Reform, emerged in 1921 from the amalgamation of the original Howard Association, founded in 1866, and the more militant Penal Reform League, formed in the wake of the suffragette movement in 1907 (see Ryan 1978). It has counterparts in many Commonwealth countries. Until the foundation of the National Association for the Care and Resettlement of Offenders (NACRO) in 1966, it had no real contenders in the field of penal reform. From the late 1960s, however, new pressure groups flourished: Radical Alternatives to Prison (RAP) in 1969; the Legal Action Group (LAG) in 1971; and, within the Labour Party, the Labour Campaign for Criminal Justice in 1978. JUSTICE had, however, preceded even NACRO: founded by Tom Sargent, it was a remarkably successful pressure group in its highly focused pursuit of legal reform. On occasion, alliances between two or more of these groups enhanced their effectiveness, as with the battle of the Howard League, JUSTICE, and NACRO to expunge certain classes of ex-offender records in the Rehabilitation of Offenders Act 1974 (ibid.: 60–63). Inquest (founded 1981) and the Prison Reform Trust (founded 1982) were more clearly the reactive product of Thatcher's tough talking policing and penal agenda of 1979.

It was the illiberal penal policy climate of the early 1980s, combined with the proliferation of criminal justice pressure groups, which led to the concept of the campaigning consortium. This was successfully adopted between 1978 and 1983, when New Approaches to Juvenile Crime—a grouping of NACRO and the principal social work and probation practitioner organizations—did much to foster the views leading to the dramatic decline in the use of custody for juvenile offenders in the 1980s. The group used all the informational techniques which have made NACRO a force to be reckoned with: briefing papers and associated press releases were regularly produced; deputations to ministers were arranged; meetings with magistrates were held; and regular parliamentary briefings were organized. It was Lady Faithful, the group's organizer, who, against government wishes, introduced amendments to the Bill which became the custody criteria for young offenders in the Criminal Justice Act 1982, s 1: this measure led to greatly reduced use of custody. Moreover, though cause and effect can never precisely be established, there seems little doubt that New Approaches to Juvenile Crime did much to counter the rhetoric of the early 1980s in support of the experimentally punitive 'short, sharp shock' regimes in detention centres—the courts used these centres less rather than more—and helped to lay the foundation whereby the DHSS funded more than 100 intermediate treatment programmes from 1983 onwards.

More recent pressure groupings are: the Penal Affairs Consortium, a lobbying collective which comprised thirteen organizations when it was formed in 1989 and now comprises forty, ranging from the Prison Governors' and the Prison Officers' Associations to NACRO, the Prison Reform Trust, the Howard League, and Liberty—a previously unthinkable combination; and the Alliance for Reducing Offending (ARO), a consortium of thirteen organizations, created in Spring 2001, with the specific aim of raising the priority given by the Prison and Probation Services to the resettlement of prisoners. By contrast, some single-issue pressure groups, such as the National Campaign for the Abolition of the Death Penalty (1955), rise and fall as the issue around which they are built waxes and wanes.

The extent and breadth of contemporary pressure group activity can be gauged from the (by no means exhaustive) catalogue of such groups listed as having given evidence to the 1990 Woolf Inquiry into the prison disturbances of April that year. They included sixty-five groups in all, as well as professional associations, public service unions and ministries, and agencies of central and local government (Woolf 1991). More recently, the Home Office review of the sentencing framework, *Making Punishments Work* (the Halliday Report), deliberated with the assistance of an 'External Reference Group' with a membership of more than forty, including the Directors or Chairs of JUSTICE, the Penal Affairs Consortium, the Federation of Prisoners' Families Support Group, Drugscope, Payback, the Prison Reform Trust, DIVERT, and Victim Support. Combining these pressure group activists with representatives of the major government departments and agencies and criminal justice professionals, represented an attempt at corporate consensus building with regard to an aspect of policy, sentencing, notoriously prone to founder (Home Office 2001c: appendix 1).

The sheer proliferation of pressure groups in the law and order field is striking, but less salient than the impressive professionalization of the larger organizations. A good many do not merely campaign, they provide extensive services and undertake evaluative research. This makes them a formidable counter to Home Office senior advisers, who increasingly, as we have seen, seek representation from them when it comes to undertaking major stock-takes. Their challenge, if the government pursues policies of which they disapprove, is high profile: some of their leading spokespersons gather as much media attention, and are as widely known, as junior Home Office ministers. NACRO's Paul Cavadino, for example, achieved such prominence, and became such a *bête noire* for Conservative Home Secretary Michael Howard in the mid-1990s, that NACRO decided it was politic to give him a more backroom role for a while. This example illustrates a broader trend.

Before 1970, the date assigned by Bailey (1987) to the final break-up of the post-War consensus on delinquency, pressure-group activity metaphorically sought to influence policy by a well-informed word in the ministerial ear. From that date, reformers increasingly began to beat on the ministerial door in a far more public, confrontational way, albeit one which was, if anything, even more highly informed. Douglas Hurd, Home Secretary from 1984 to 1988, remarked that such clamour was counter-productive. However, this metaphor should not be allowed to obscure the growth, from the 1980s onwards, of myriad links between the Home Office and the pressure groups. This was partly because some groups, of which NACRO is the prime example (their website claims that the organization currently provides services to 25,000 offenders per annum), had developed a network of local contacts, services, and experience which matched that available to senior civil service policy-makers. In conferences, media debates, seminars, and the regular call for expert evidence on penal matters in particular, opportunities abounded for pressure groups to inform penal policy-making processes. None of these processes, either singly or in total, however, equalled the kind of unforced insider access that the Howard League enjoyed in its heyday of close, informal (as well as formal) contact with the Home Office (see Ryan 1978), or the strong role for criminological expertise, which in the early days was thin on the ground, provided by the ACTO and ACPS before 1980.

That inside track had, of course, carried the danger that research might uphold punitive measures, and inhibit challenge to government policy, as in the example of Max Grunhut's long gestation of a project which eventually reported in favour of detention centres, to the detriment of the Howard League's stance on the issue (Ryan 1978: 83–4). Further, in its final years, the ACPS produced more and more lengthy reports—on *Young Adult Offenders* in 1974 and *Sentences of Imprisonment* in 1978— which attracted critical academic judgement as well as ministerial impatience (see Morgan 1979). In the 1980s the government largely replaced advice from Royal Commissions and standing advisory bodies with official inquiries set up whenever a need was perceived.

It was partly this decline in government reliance on officially organized advice that stimulated the emergence of more professional pressure groups, most of them, even when beneficiaries of government funding—as NACRO has always been—more or less critical of government policy. The pressure groups have generally favoured: explanations of crime which stress economic inequality, social exclusion, and individual vulnerability; use of social policy in general rather than criminal justice policy in particular to prevent or control crime; and scepticism as to the value of police powers and punitive methods (particularly imprisonment) as crime control measures—indeed, they generally stress the discriminatory and unjust consequences of such methods for repressing already oppressed minorities (Ryan 1978, 1983). Thus though there are substantial differences between these groups regarding their ideological commitments, constitutional form, access to policy-makers, and credibility with government, they have a good deal in common. They are generally perceived as left of centre, generally have allegiances with Liberal or Labour rather than Conservative politicians (though NACRO and the Prison Reform Trust are always careful to involve politicians of all parties on their councils), and tend, in spite of the consortia arrangements referred to above, also to have fragile relationships with the practitioner sectional groups, such as the Prison Officers' Association, the Police Federation, the Association of Chief Police Officers (ACPO), and the Magistrates' Association. The latter tend to adopt policies emphasizing the 'thin blue line' and the importance of their members' powers to safeguard the community from crime.

Given these dissonances, it is notable how much interchange occurred between the groups and the government from the 1980s on. In other fields of social policy, such as education, where pressure groups of comparable expertise are largely lacking, ideologically driven changes since 1979 arguably met with less resistance, despite strong interest-group and practitioner unease or hostility. Given the immense imbalance of power between the groups and the Home Office, the latter could be said to have little to lose and much to gain from such contacts. The pressure groups provide positive feedback services for governments in furnishing early warnings of probable trouble, in canvassing feasible reforms, and in heightening the legitimacy of the governmental process itself. In a complex society, pressure-group and interest-group activities are the major avenues for active citizen participation in democratic decision-making. In the 1980s, pressure groups also fitted the ideological predispositions of the Thatcher administrations to accord client-based and consumerist agencies a better hearing, albeit at the expense of local government (which still harboured socialist residues) and the trade unions. Quangos and Royal Commissions were seen as stifling government and citizen initiative. The Woolf Inquiry of 1990 was a model of democratic participation by an informed citizenry (by comparison with, say, the average Royal Commission), holding seminars at which the views and evidence of different groups were debated rather than simply presented *seriatim*—though the views of prisoners were separately canvassed and, to that extent, somewhat devalued (Morgan 1991; Sim 1993). This consultative model was subsequently adopted by the Committee of Inquiry into *Complaints about Ashworth Hospital* in 1991–2, with similarly radical impact (Blom-Cooper Report 1992; see also Richardson 1993), and is now regarded as almost standard procedure (both the Halliday review of sentencing (Home Office 2001c) and the Auld review of the criminal courts (Auld Report 2001) employed a range of consultative arrangements—posting ideas on websites, employing advisory groups, and holding consultative seminars).

Even so, the huge imbalance of power remains a political reality. When 'pressured', the Home Office can brush aside any protest, as exemplified by the recent acceleration of prison privatization, a policy opposed vehemently by all the groups cited as well as by the Prison Officers' and Prison Governors' Associations. The Conservative government, in its drive to cut the cost of public services and expose them to the allegedly beneficial rigours of market competition, increasingly viewed the practitioner–representative organizations as little more than vested interests resisting any challenge to the inefficient monopolistic services within which they shelter. Thus the consultative instincts of senior judges, like Woolf, asked to undertake official inquiries, have seldom characterized ministerial policy initiatives. The early 1990s, for example, saw a series of initiatives regarding policing policy in which real consultation was lacking. Changes in the rank structure and proposals radically to alter the basis of police pay— changes recommended by the 1992 Sheehy Inquiry (Sheehy Report 1993)—and major amendments to the constitutional framework for the governance of the police— amendments first set out in the 1991 White Paper on *Police Reform* and implemented in the Police and Magistrates' Courts Act 1994—were taken speedily and in spite of the views of practitioners, local government associations, and the overwhelming majority of informed commentators. Likewise, both Conservative and Labour administrations have resisted change widely called for. It was successive governments' refusal to institute a review of the drugs laws which led the Police Foundation, a small interest group founded in 1979 to promote police-related research, to set up in 1997 an independent inquiry under Lady Runciman, the next best thing to a Royal Commission. The exercise was funded by the Princes Trust, and the membership of the inquiry, which included two chief constables and senior academic experts, was not dissimilar to that which might have been expected of a Royal Commission, whose methods and typical timescale were also adopted. The resulting report (Police Foundation 2000) was authoritative, measured, and far from radical, but the government, to the increasingly public irritation of Lady Runciman, took almost a year to respond to the recommendations, and then only to say that it was not inclined to make the legislative changes proposed. This particular stone wall cracked, however, when some leading Conservatives, following their disastrous defeat in June 2001, suggested that it might be time to reconsider current drugs legislation. In the following Autumn, the new Labour Home Secretary, David Blunkett, announced that there were to be changes in the use of police discretion, which virtually decriminalized possession of small amounts of cannabis.

THE THINK TANKS

This last example illustrates a new trend. The government's drive to effect change in law and order services in the face of practitioner opposition prompted the Labour Party to move closer to the slighted practitioner organizations and distance itself from the pressure groups whose liberal credentials and 'soft' image had themselves become hostages to fortune in the struggle for the political middle ground. As a consequence the pressure groups did not quite enjoy the direct contacts and influence with either the world of Whitehall or Westminster in the 1990s which they achieved in the 1980s. They have to some extent been displaced, particularly with New Labour, by the think tanks.

It was the free marketeers who first established think tanks. Their function was to promote a political and economic philosophy. The Institute of Economic Affairs (IEA), founded in 1955, and the Adam Smith Institute, founded in 1977, were the precursors of the Thatcherite revolution, advocating deregulation, privatization, and, as part of that exercise, trades union reform. Keen advocates of prisons privatization and private security provision on the grounds that state monopolistic provision is inefficient and has failed to deliver, their core ideas have to a substantial extent been incorporated in New Labour's mixed economy programme now advocated by the

Institute for Political and Policy Research (IPPR), founded in 1988, and Demos, founded in 1993. What the IEA and the Adam Smith Institute did for the Conservatives in the years preceding 1979, the IPPR and Demos did for New Labour in the run-up to its electoral victory in 1997. They defined New Labour's 'modernizing government' agenda. This comprised a mixed economy of provision, private finance partnerships and, within the state services, an emphasis on managerial techniques developed in the private sector—that is SMART objectives and planning processes combined with measurable outputs and outcomes and regular reviews of achievement.

The ascendancy of New Labour and its landslide victory in June 2001 has currently put the IEA and the Adam Smith Institute very much in the shade. But the IPPR and Demos have in many observers' eyes become extensions of the Cabinet Office, flying kites for ministers to see how the wind of public or elite opinion blows. Law and order issues figure relatively prominently in this arrangement. In 2000, for example, IPPR established a Criminal Justice Forum, and in early 2000 it commissioned a piece of 'blue skies' work on the future of the lay magistracy (Sanders 2001) at the same time as the Home Office commissioned research on the same topic (Morgan and Russell 2000), all designed to feed into and influence the Auld review of the criminal courts (Auld 2001).

THE ROLE OF THE MASS MEDIA AND THE POLICY-MAKING PROCESS

The pressure groups are finding it more of a struggle to get their views across, and their voices heard, in a media world increasingly dominated by the think tanks and governmental public relations spin. In response to being held more at arm's length, they have subdued their critical stance and 'kept their powder dry' for a support role in backing up such heavyweight players as the Lord Chief Justice, Lord Woolf, and the former Chief Inspector of Prisons, Sir David Ramsbotham, both outspoken critics of key trends in Home Office policy: the erosion of judicial autonomy (by minimum mandatory sentencing) and the uneven momentum of prison reform (as represented in the dire state of some prisons). Otherwise, especially where they depend substantially on governmental funding, they tend to be scripted, if not incorporated, into Home Office scenarios. The IPPR is more likely to host seminars attended by NACRO than the reverse. Professional groups have become more constrained by central directives and reorganization, better coordinated but less autonomous professionally. Nevertheless, some individual voices retain their critical force: for example, Harry Fletcher (of NAPO—the National Association of Probation Officers) and Paul Cavadino (of NACRO), both of whom spoke out knowledgeably against the 'naming and shaming' of former 'paedophile' offenders. Overall, however, the media skills which made NACRO and other pressure groups such a force to be reckoned with in the 1980s and early 1990s have now been upstaged by governmental strategists. Moreover, the resort to comparative European examples, once so telling for its placing of the UK at or near the top of the prison population league table, has been displaced by the apparent success of the USA in dramatically reducing crime rates. That may come under increasing challenge as the full penal, political, economic, and social cost of mass imprisonment in the United States gains wider currency (see, especially, Garland 2001).

The micro-politics of law and order are intimately bound up with the processes whereby the goals and agendas set by ministers are translated into policies and specific directives by civil servants. They are also creatively authored in key respects by senior civil servants, whose briefings and policy formulations have a distinct part to play in formal policy-making. As Rock (1995) has shown, policy formation within the Home Office is typically a matter of written argument developing 'crescively'. For example, the 1991 Criminal Justice Act was the outcome of a decade-long process of casting about for the most appropriate means of reducing the level of the prison population without either eroding judicial independence, or offending the more reactionary wing of the Conservative Party (see Rutherford 1996 for his analysis of the leading role played by David Faulkner in that process). By their creation of a 'symbolic environment' (Edelman 1971) and by their active refinement of issues and arguments culled from such diverse gatherings as international conferences and informal discussion groups, it is possible, even in Britain, for senior civil servants such as Faulkner and, in an earlier period, Morrell (in connection with the Children and Young Persons Act 1970), to energize the field (see also Rock 1986; Bottoms 1974; King and McDermott 1995: chapter 1). They are far from being passive bureaucrats.

Other relevant processes can be found in the Select Committee stages of drafting legislation, which can be the site for its profound amendment or effective termination by delay. For example, the Police and Criminal Evidence Act 1984 was a vastly different affair from the 1983 Bill which lapsed on the calling of the 1983 General Election (Ryan 1983). Such major transformations due to detailed Parliamentary scrutiny are, however, increasingly the exception rather than the rule. Within four months of the implementation of the Criminal Justice Act 1991, the then Home Secretary, Kenneth Clarke, conceded, in the face of criticisms from the judiciary and the media, and polls showing a new-found public preference for Labour over the Conservatives on 'law and order', that some key provisions required amendment. Two in particular, on unit fines and the constraints on basing sentences in part on previous convictions, were scrapped. Critics argued that a policy of decarceration that had taken a decade to construct was despatched with indecent haste, partly because of shoddy drafting and too little Parliamentary scrutiny (this was the Act that made a pudding out of a principle: 'just desserts' slipped through uncorrected). More recently, the reconstituted House of Lords threw out or amended for re-scrutiny in the Commons a record number of Bills on criminal justice, again in part due to over-hasty drafting and the over-use of three-line whips to bulldoze controversial laws through despite a huge majority. For example, private prisons have now survived two U-turns: the first under Douglas Hurd in 1987, the second by Jack Straw in 1998. Both Home Secretaries accepted in practice what they had previously denounced in principle. Another example was the repeated attempts by Labour in 2000–2001 to bludgeon the Lords into accepting the restricted right to jury trial by defendants in 'triable either way' cases. In sum, despite the occasional instance of Parliamentary scrutiny bearing innovatory discussion on criminal justice and penal policy, many important policy developments are preceded by virtually no public debate, Parliamentary or otherwise (see Richardson 1993).

Despite the exceptional, landmark Police and Criminal Evidence Act 1984, the history of policing is redolent with major changes effected without Parliamentary debate. Policing policy underwent a sea-change in the late 1970s and early 1980s, with the creation of Special Patrol Groups, whose activities involved the killing of Blair Peach in Southall in 1978 and sparked the major riot in Brixton in 1981 (Hall 1978; Scarman 1981); the increased reliance on mutual aid between forces, sometimes under the direction of the National Reporting Centre (Spencer 1985); the deployment of new paramilitary equipment and techniques (Jefferson 1990; Waddington 1991); and the adoption of neighbourhood crime prevention strategies (Bennett 1990; Rosenbaum 1988), all without the benefit of research, public, or Parliamentary debate.

It is because so much policy is made and implemented without adequate public debate on its implications that many analysts of criminal justice and penal policy insist that statutes should, in future, state more precisely what objectives agencies should pursue and what specific powers decision-makers should have, and provide for procedural rights for those citizens—suspects, prisoners, and mental hospital patients—caught up in the system (Richardson 1993). Ideally, accountability should begin with Parliament and end with the day-to-day answerability of practitioners. And yet, despite the endless evaluations and managerial reorganizations of the 'Audit Society' (Power 1997), the exigencies of the politics of law and order (or of education, health, or public transport, etc.) increasingly mean that 'the buck', to adapt Harry Truman's phrase, no longer 'stops here', or indeed anywhere, but is endlessly recycled.

MATTERS OF SCANDAL AND CONCERN

The remaining variable is the unpredictable realm of scandal and concern. For all their pretensions, both Parliamentary and extra-Parliamentary groupings can be utterly outpaced by events which explode in such a way that unusual responses are called for by 'public opinion'—a phenomenon for which media attention is often taken to be the proxy. In the penal realm, for example, three types of events seemingly dwarf all others in their impact on the 'public': prison escapes, appalling murders, and riotous assemblies. The examples, several of which have already been mentioned, are legion.

The escapes of Ronald Biggs and George Blake in 1965–6, and the break-outs from the high-security prisons at Whitemoor and Parkhurst in 1994–5, radically changed the emphasis on security in the Prison Service. The rioting at Strangeways, Manchester, and other prisons in 1990 led to a major inquiry conducted by Lord Justice Woolf, the outcome of which appeared, initially, to set a new agenda for prisons but which the security lapses of 1994–5, combined with a rising prison population, have in turn knocked off course (see Morgan, in Chapter 30 of this volume). In 1993, in the wake of the horrific murder of two-year-old James Bulger by two juveniles, and a sustained police campaign regarding offences committed, particularly by juveniles, while on bail, custodial measures were introduced for serious juvenile offenders which contravened principles only just implemented in the Criminal Justice Act 1991 and which research suggested were ill-advised (see Ashworth, in Chapter 29 of this volume). The massacre by Thomas Hamilton of schoolchildren and their teacher at Dunblane in 1996 stimulated the government and Opposition literally to vie with each other over the extent to which gun control and, subsequently, control of other offensive weapons should be tightened. The ownership of certain handguns, including those held purely for competitive sporting events, was banned (Taylor 1999). The aftermath of the recent running battles against paedophiles, which in 2000 flared across Britain in the wake of Sarah Payne's murder (see above), is being played out as we write (December 2001). The immediate compromise response to the call for 'Sarah's Law' to 'name and shame paedophiles', was a provision in the Criminal Justice and Court Services Act 2000 whereby victims of sexual and other violent crimes for which the offender was sentenced to more than one year's imprisonment, were given the right to be consulted about the conditions, though not the timing, of their release. However, the conviction of Roy Whiting, a repeat child sexual offender, for Sarah's murder has stimulated a new clamour for longer sentences and tighter restrictions than already exist: the government is already indicating its willingness to consider mandatory life sentences for allegedly 'dangerous offenders' in cases where a life sentence is currently discretionary.

Issues of law enforcement in relation to race and ethnicity have provided examples of both short- and long-fuse responses since New Labour assumed office in 1997, with mixed results. The murder of Stephen Lawrence, a black British teenager, in 1993, came to symbolize both the character of violent racism (Bowling 1999) and the inadequacy of policies to address it. The hugely bungled investigation by the Metropolitan Police led to a lengthy campaign, sustained by Stephen Lawrence's parents, for a public inquiry into the case. This was resisted by the Conservative Home Secretary, Michael Howard, but his Labour successor, Jack Straw, made it one of his first priorities. The inquiry, chaired by a senior judge, Lord Macpherson, generated immense public interest and media coverage, not least due to the cross-examination of the five main suspects, young white men associated with extreme racist views, two of whom had been tried and acquitted for the murder on grounds of insufficient evidence. The police investigation, that 'could most kindly be described as deeply flawed' (Morris 2001: 372), was judged by the Macpherson Report to be the outcome of 'institutional racism', broadly and contentiously defined as the failure of any institution to meet ethnic minority needs.

The Report contained seventy recommendations for urgent reform of the recruitment, training, conduct, and accountability of police officers, all but six of which were claimed to be immediately acted on by the Home Secretary. Some have already led to distinct improvements in awareness of racial issues, the reporting and recording of racist violence, steps to recruit more ethnic minority officers, and to the Race Relations (Amendment) Act 2000, which extended the coverage of the Commission for Racial Equality (CRE) to the police, prisons, local authorities, and the National Health Service. The Macpherson Report thus 'caused turmoil in the force and soul-seeking

among organisations of all kinds' (Toynbee and Walker 2001: 172). Critics of the
Report pointed out that the very vagueness of the term 'institutional racism' could be
counter-productive: for example, it may enable individuals to deny personal responsibility; it may engender 'impotence at best and resentment at worst' if individuals feel
guilty of the unchallengeable charge of 'unconscious' racism, however they behave; and
it may raise unfulfillable expectations of reform which mar the criminal justice system
as forever racist (Fitzgerald 2001). Moreover, one of the main planks of the case that the
police used their 'stop and search' powers discriminatingly—the disproportionate
ratio of young black male suspects compared to white—disappears when the school-
age population is used as the basis for comparison rather than all ages (ibid.).

Nevertheless, two subsequent cases in 2000–2001 which seemed to bear out key
aspects of the 'institutional racism' charge were the killings of a ten-year-old Nigerian
boy, Damilola Taylor, in Peckham, London; and of Zahid Mubarek, a 19-year-old
Asian prisoner who was placed with, and brutally murdered by, a white cellmate
known for his violent racist beliefs, in Feltham Young Offenders Institution. In the
case of Damilola, the only link with 'institutional racism' was the very broad failure of
society to protect a young innocent boy from being set upon and killed in broad
daylight on a bleak stairwell in a rundown estate. However, white families too are
consigned to live in such surroundings. Institutional racism appeared far more clearly
evident in the case of Zahid. The white prison officers responsible for his cell assign-
ment must have known about the character of his cellmate: it was at best a colossal
failure of elementary crime prevention, at worst a set-up. These cases show how
racism intensifies and complicates flaws of long standing in institutional arrangements and their implementation.

The same could be said of the immigration services, whose handling of the sharp
increase in numbers applying for entry into the UK—or seeking entry illegally, due to
the war-zone character of so many post-Soviet, post-Tito, and post-colonial states—
fell lamentably short of humane standards. Faced in 2000 with a large back-log of
adjudications, Labour introduced a set of measures designed to deter 'bogus' applications. Applicants for entry were given vouchers, not cash, for bare living expenses; and
fourteen days to complete in English a twenty-page document about their application.
Even such sympathetic critics of New Labour as Polly Toynbee commented, 'it was a
test of New Labour's decency—one many subsequently felt they failed . . . gross delay,
sub-poverty benefits and petty harassment caused the worst injustice' (Toynbee and
Walker 2001: 170–71). Reception point local authorities, Dover in particular, pressed
the Home Office for relief, which eventually came in the form of a dispersal policy
whereby would-be immigrants were dispatched to various points, usually rundown
estates, far from the key centres of immigration processing. Friction between the
newcomers and established residents led to aggressive flare-ups and at least one murder. Following Labour's re-election in 2001, these policies were reviewed, yet it
remains to be seen if the blanket tendency to stigmatize all asylum-seekers as 'bogus'
until proved otherwise will be effectively reversed. Confidence in Britain as a relatively
tolerant and liberal state, which can all too easily tip into self-deluding complacency,
was also shaken by the riots among the supposedly settled Asian communities in
Oldham and Bradford, referred to above.

PUBLIC DISCOURSE ABOUT POLICING

The conventional wisdom about policing tends to the apocalyptic. Things have fallen apart since the Golden Age of policing in the 1950s, embodied in the folk hero, PC George Dixon, the linchpin of the community in the long-running TV serial 'Dixon of Dock Green'. Nowadays, the image of the police constable is more like Robocop, a barely human presence in a technological armour, holding a seething mob at bay with advanced weaponry (see Reiner 2000: chapter 5). The real story is more complex and less sensational. The Golden Age of policing was a myth based upon blind faith in authority and ignorance of actual police work at a time of relatively harmonious community relations. Declining public confidence in the police is due to rates of crime that have soared for social, economic, and cultural reasons that affect, but hardly originate in, policing; the exposure of forms of corruption that were customary rather than novel; and the growth of problems such as terrorism and drug trafficking which are unparalleled this century in their scale and viciousness. We are only now coming to grips with age-old problems that defy short-term solutions. The police are almost certainly now in a healthier state than before, but look worse because far more is known about their shortcomings, thanks to a mixture of fly-on-the-wall media exposure, scandals, research, and the gradual move towards more stringent forms of both legal and political accountability (Morgan and Newburn 1997). For example, in the public order realm, the 1981 Brixton riots (Scarman 1981), and those at Broadwater Farm Estate in 1985 (Gifford 1986), far transcended other disturbances in evoking profound unease. The Scarman Report on the events at Brixton led to the development of formal police–community consultation, which arguably has played a role in defusing conflictual situations at the outset or containing them when they do arise.

The three cases which came to dramatize public concerns about policing most vividly were those of the Guildford Four, the Maguire Seven, and the Birmingham Six. In all three cases, Irish suspects were convicted of causing explosions that killed multiple victims. Outrage, as expressed through the media, placed immense pressure on the police to get 'results'. Sentences of life imprisonment were accompanied by recommendations that at least twenty years be served in several cases. Fifteen to seventeen years later, after tireless campaigning, the verdicts were declared 'unsafe' and the prisoners freed. These and other cases of similar magnitude so eroded public confidence in the police and the courts, as shown by opinion polls, that a Royal Commission on Criminal Justice was appointed in 1991, the first Royal Commission for fourteen years, to enquire into the procedural issues involved and suggest remedies.

These cases exemplify the tendency for matters of notoriety to originate in taken-for-granted practices that are exposed as a result of unusual degrees of pressure or modes of scrutiny, rather than being exceptional instances of individual pathology—a 'few bad apples'. 'Constructing the suspect' by embellishing the evidence against him or her and ignoring countervailing evidence is standard police practice (McBarnet 1981; McConnville, Leng, and Sanders 1991). Once socialized into an occupational culture which affirms such practices as a necessary evil and a professional skill, designed ultimately to secure conviction in the ornate adversarial exchanges in open

court, it is a small step for the police officer to fabricate evidence and 'lose' counter-
evidence. The appeal of such procedures is the greatest when the suspect has 'previous' and is 'overdue' for conviction. The logic of methodical suspicion casts certain
groups more readily into the suspect role than others. The moral economy of police
work reinforces these images of deviance, certain groups being seen as 'slag', 'rubbish',
and 'police property' (Reiner 1992). If such variables as age, sex, ethnicity, demeanour,
degrees of cooperation with the police, and the reputation of areas are consequential
in routine offending, how much larger they loom when intense pressures for a 'result'
are generated. Another example of unusual modes of enquiry bringing new focus to
established practices was Roger Graef's 1982 TV documentary series on the Thames
Valley police. The public outcry at the merciless grilling by officers of a female rape
victim led to rapid changes in the procedures for the processing of similar cases. The
impetus had also led to the heightened awareness and changing practices in cases of
domestic violence.

The last four years have seen the continuing struggle of the police to contend with
the rapid proliferation of new forms of crime technology and opportunity. The Internet and the processes of globalization are opening up new channels for money laundering, drug trafficking, electronic fraud, and the like. At the same time, the old, staple
forms of crime have maintained their high volume. The principal source of pressure
has become the normalization of illicit drug use for millions who are otherwise non-
criminal, especially the rising adolescent generation. 'Crimes without victims' now
dwarf those of victimization, in the sense that whatever the protestation of the authorities that they are 'victims', nonetheless drugtakers actively collude in the criminalized
processes of drug supply. By contrast, householders hardly invite burglars into their
homes, any more than car-owners supply car thieves with the key, or victims of fraud
knowingly supply fraudsters with their credit card details. Yet because the supply of
drugs remains illicit, crimes with victims spin off from the trade: money laundering is
big business; gangs fight for territorial hold over clubs and custom; officialdom is
subject to corruption; and drug-related crime to feed the habit has become a standard
component of the crime rate. Yet one government after another acts as if 'prohibition', like prison, 'works', a state of denial that, if we have learnt anything at all from
the history of comparative criminology, not just fails to work but is potently criminogenic. The police, ironically, are now playing a lead role in persuading the government
to modify prohibitionist drug laws.

NORTHERN IRELAND AND ITS IMPACT

The context for the most notorious recent miscarriages of justice is of course the
political quagmire of Northern Ireland and its ramifications for the control of terrorism in Britain. Since 1969, 'nearly 3,000 people have died because of political violence
in Northern Ireland. The conflict has often spilled outside the borders of the region,
leading to the deaths of approximately 200 people in Great Britain, the Republic of
Ireland, and sites elsewhere in Europe, ranging from Gibraltar to Western Germany'
(O'Leary and McGarry 1993). Three thousand dead may seem a relatively small toll
over two decades. 'However, scale matters. The population of Northern Ireland in the

1981 census ... was estimated as 1,488,077. If the equivalent ratio of victims to population had been produced in Great Britain in the same period some 100,000 people would have died, and ... in the USA ... over 500,000, or about ten times the number of Americans killed in the Vietnam War' (ibid.: 2). Comparatively speaking, 'the death-toll in Northern Ireland alone made the UK absolutely the most violent liberal democracy during the same time-span' (ibid.: 4). Close to one in fifty of the population have suffered serious injuries over the period. The costs in law enforcement, paramilitary measures, compensation, and legal processes have been huge. One audit in 1985 estimated the annual direct costs of violence in Northern Ireland at £1,194 million per annum (ibid.: 22). The costs in terms of negative effects on public trust in British political institutions have been incalculable. The granting of strong emergency powers to the legal authorities under the regularly renewed Emergency Provisions Act in Northern Ireland, and the Prevention of Terrorism Act throughout the UK, has meant that departures from traditional English legal procedures have become normal in Northern Ireland and spill over into aspects of crime control in Britain (as, for example, in the short-lived 'control units' for recalcitrant prisoners in two English prisons in the 1970s, whose regimes paralleled forms of sensory deprivation used in Northern Ireland). 'Since 1973 no-jury single-judge courts have presided over cases arising from "scheduled offences", i.e. "terrorist offences", on the grounds that jury-trials are not safe from perverse verdicts or the intimidation of jurors and witnesses. Confessions are admissible as the sole basis for conviction on charges "of this kind"' (O'Leary and McGarry 1993: 24). The rise and discrediting of 'supergrass' evidence in the 1980s (Greer 1994); the abandonment of the 'right of silence' in 1988; the regular delay of several years in holding inquests on persons killed by the security forces (Amnesty International 1978); and the violation of the European Convention on Human Rights on a number of fronts concerning interrogation and time held in custody; all have severely eroded the belief, both nationally and internationally, in the impartiality of British justice. They also provided the context within which routine police practices for constructing the suspect escalated into 'the greatest twentieth century crisis of confidence in the administration of justice in Great Britain' (ibid.). In the event, the 1991–3 Royal Commission proved unequal to the task of tackling such deep-rooted problems.

In the past four years, Northern Ireland has nevertheless proved the site for 'the most surprising co-achievement of the New Labour government': the 1998 Belfast Agreement, more widely known as the 'Good Friday Agreement' (O'Leary 2001: 449). While Blair was the legatee of the foundations laid by others, he gave the process momentum, setting in motion such highly charged measures as the prisoner release scheme and the Patten Report on the Royal Ulster Constabulary. While the peace process flourished under Mowlam and stalled under Mandelson, the role of the UK government has throughout been formidably constrained by the nature of the entrenched interests of the various groups and parties to the Agreement (see O'Leary for the complex field of force involved). At the time of writing, the decommissioning of arms issue has proved a critical obstacle, but any prevention of meltdown will entail a reactivation of Patten's key proposals for the reform of policing in Northern Ireland.

POLICY IMPLICATIONS

However, not all scandals translate into calls for reform or change: for example, the so-called Moors Murders of the early 1960s, in which several children were fatal victims of sadistic sexual practices, were the source of heightened moral fears, but also of sheer bafflement. As Bottoms and Stevenson argue (1992: 23–4):

It is a fact well known to students of social policy that reforms of the system often take place not so much because of careful routine analysis by ministers and civil servants in the relevant Department of State, nor even because of a critique or exposé, by an outside journalist or pressure group, but because one or more individual incident(s) occurs, drawing public attention to some underlying imperfections of policy in a dramatic way which seems to demand change. Very often an inquiry is set up after such incidents, and it is the report of the inquiry that sets the agenda for subsequent reforms; but the reforms would not have taken place without the public attention created by the original incident.

It is worth embellishing this point a little. Such incidents tend to generate change only when they discredit institutions so drastically and dramatically that their credibility and effectiveness—and, by extension, those of the government and the state—risk serious erosion unless changes are made. The damage is not simply symbolic, a matter of reputation and belief, though declining public confidence carries grave implications for the agencies of control and the caring professions. The authority of the modern state rests heavily on its claims to expertise (Giddens 1984). Practical effects include the predictable increase in, for example, escape attempts in the wake of successful break-outs, and increasing dismissal rates in courts where juries no longer unquestioningly accept police evidence. As the latter point suggests, scandals can and should result in improved policy and practice. The abolition of capital punishment is arguably an example of 'things going right' in criminal justice and penal policy after a series of executions that caused public disquiet. Much hinges on the character of the response; and the trend has recently been towards specific and limited rather than wide-ranging and searching modes of enquiry. Nor are scandals randomly scattered throughout the system: the police and the prisons have produced far more than, for example, probation and after-care.

CONCLUSIONS

The politics of law and order since 1945 have been shaped by the responses to the almost continuous rise in recorded crime and to the unforeseen explosion of illicit drug-taking and politically inspired terrorism. Three phases can be discerned in the party political sphere. First, until 1970 a consensus prevailed the terms of which, heavily influenced by 'liberal progressive' ideology, implicitly rested on the non-partisan character of crime and on the merit of gradual shifts towards rehabilitative policies for its control. This consensus was not shared, other than for a range of juvenile offenders, by the judiciary, who continued to adhere to broadly retributive and deterrent principles of sentencing, except for a small minority of clinically diagnosed mentally ill offenders. Governments of both left and right shared a strong reluctance to intrude into the judicial realm.

The 1970 Election was a watershed which, by 1979, had swept away the main supports of non-partisanship. The second phase, of sharp and growing contention between the parties for the 'law and order' terrain, saw the Conservative Party emerge relatively unscathed from Labour's tentative attempts to link rising crime with the social and economic effects of growing inequality and unemployment: the 'hostages to fortune' which the Labour Party traditional attachments to the trade unions and to libertarian causes entail, initially led its leaders to seek to neutralize, rather than sharply contest, the Conservative hegemony on this issue.

After the 1992 Election a third phase began. Rebranding itself in opposition, 'New Labour' distanced itself from the trades unions, the penal pressure groups, and libertarian causes. The Conservatives, bent on the further restructuring of public services to achieve cuts in public expenditure while simultaneously pursuing tough populist penal measures, prejudiced their traditional support base with the judiciary, the police, and prison personnel. In the run-up to the 1997 Election, the tables now being reversed, 'New Labour' was coy about opposing Conservative 'law and order' legislation, on several occasions sought to out-tough Conservative legislative proposals, and, following its electoral victory, implemented Conservative measures that Labour would a decade earlier have anathematized.

The past four years have seen New Labour reinforced in power, mainly on the strength of its perceived competence in economic management, but at least in part due to its shedding of the unwarranted image that it was 'soft on crime'. Its newfound and more justified image, that it is 'tough on crime', has been bought at a considerable cost in terms of civil liberties and the humane justice and penal policies that Labour espoused in the 1980s. There appears now to be a new and uneasy 'second-order consensus'.

The major political parties are agreed, for example, that victims must be given more information about proceedings against 'their' offenders and greater voice; they favour an 'active community' or the reconstruction of 'civil society'; prolific and dangerous offenders should be targeted; the parents of juvenile offenders should be held more accountable; restorative justice is a good thing; communitarian crime reduction initiatives should be pursued; there is considerable scope for privatizing, voluntarizing, or civilianizing policing and penal services. They do not always agree about the means for achieving these objectives. The Labour Party, for example, has always placed greater emphasis on the role of local authorities as the linchpin of crime prevention. The Conservatives have preferred alternative self-help and agency frameworks—neighbourhood watch and Crime Concern, the catalyst organization that they created and funded in the early 1990s. But Crime Concern continues, and is now the principal national adviser of local authority crime prevention partnerships into most of which neighbourhood watch groups are now woven. There is arguably more fusion than faction.

The establishment of this second-order consensus means that there is constant jockeying for party political advantage to both left and right of the agreed central ground. In Autumn 2001, for example, the Conservatives opposed, on the grounds

that they threaten civil liberties, the government's emergency anti-terrorism legislative proposals introduced in the wake of the Manhattan Twin Towers attack. By
contrast, Labour's Home Secretary, David Blunkett, has cut through the increasingly
discredited log-jam created by his predecessor by virtually decriminalizing the small-
scale possession and personal use of cannabis. The new realism on drugs, suddenly
acknowledged as good sense on all fronts, reflects New Labour's 'law and order'
confidence and appears to be the foundation from which the government will attempt
what the Conservatives failed to achieve in the 1980s—radical operational reform of
the police and the criminal courts and tighter managerial control of their budgets
(Home Office 2001d; Auld Report 2001).With respect to both these proposals and
others relating to sentencing (Halliday Report 2001), we can confidently predict that
in the months and years ahead that government and Opposition will battle for the
high ground as to who best promotes public safety, effective policing, and law
enforcement. In reaction, the law and order practitioner associations, the Police Federation, the Magistrates' Association, ACPO, and the Law Society and Bar Council,
etc., will seek to secure party political support for their vested interests, or what they
will claim to be the public interest or human rights. How far the traditional liberal
bastions—now paradoxically embodied in certain core members of the judiciary,
the House of Lords, and the pressure groups—can hold the line against the
ever-tightening 'culture of control' (Garland 2001) remains to be seen.

Selected further reading

There have been few studies of the part played by 'law and order' in British political life.
Philip Norton's *Law and Order and British Politics* (Gower, 1984) and Mike Brake's and
Chris Hale's *Public Order and Private Lives: the Politics of Law and Order* (Routledge, 1992),
the latter a highly critical account of the Thatcher years, are exceptions. David Downes's
edited collection, *Unravelling Criminal Justice* (Macmillan, 1992), contains relevant essays,
particularly those by Bottoms and Stevenson on the extent and difficulties of the liberal
consensus, and McBarnet on the burgeoning field of tax avoidance and evasion. Roger
Hood's collection, *Crime, Criminology and Public Policy: Essays in Honour of Leon Radzinowicz* (Heinemann, 1974), provides detailed scrutiny of the public policy issues of the mid-
period, and Terence Morris's *Crime and Criminal Justice in Britain since 1945* (Blackwell,
1989) covers the entire period with shrewd political insight. Some recent developments are
well reviewed in: a special edition of *Policy Studies* (December 1998), 'New Directions in
Criminal Justice: Labour's Crime Policy Examined', edited by A.K. Bottomley, G. Johnstone,
and J. Penn; R. Mathews and J. Pitts (eds), *Crime, Disorder and Community Safety*
(Routledge, 2001); and A. von Hirsch, D. Garland, and A. Wakefield, *Ethical and Social
Perspectives on Situational Crime Prevention* (Hart, 2000, for an excellent exploration of the
subject and its political implications). K. Stenson and R. Sullivan (eds), *Crime, Risk and
Justice: The politics of crime control in liberal democracies* (Willan, 2001) provide good coverage of key issues on both sides of the Atlantic.

   Brendan O'Leary and John McGarry (*The Politics of Antagonism: Understanding Northern
Ireland*, Athlone, 1993) are sure guides to the complexities of Northern Ireland, without
which some key developments are lost. In *Beyond Law and Order: Criminal Justice Policy into*

the 1990s (Macmillan, 1991), Robert Reiner and Malcolm Cross have collected a set of papers on most of the key aspects of criminal justice policy, with their editorial chapter spelling out the political context. Lastly, Mick Ryan (*The Politics of Penal Reform*, Longman, 1983) is a political scientist in criminology who documents the micro-politics of penal reform in the wider political economy of Britain.

References

ADVISORY COUNCIL ON THE PENAL SYSTEM (1974), *Young Adult Offenders*, London: HMSO.

—— (1978), *Sentences of Imprisonment*, London: HMSO.

AUDIT COMMISSION (1996), *Misspent Youth*, Abingdon: Audit Commission.

—— (1998), *Misspent Youth*, Abingdon: Audit Commission.

—— (1999), *Misspent Youth*, Abingdon: Audit Commission.

AULD REPORT (2001), *Review of the Criminal Courts of England and Wales*, London: Stationery Office.

BAILEY, V. (1987), *Delinquency and Citizenship: Reclaiming the Young Offender 1914–1948*, Oxford: Clarendon Press.

BENNETT, T. (1990), *Evaluating Neighbourhood Watch*, Farnborough: Gower.

BLOM-COOPER REPORT (1992), *Report of the Committee of Inquiry into Complaints About Ashworth Hospital* (Cm 2028), London: HMSO.

BOTTOMS, A.E. (1974), 'Reflections on the Renaissance of Dangerousness', *Howard Journal*, 16: 70–96.

—— (1995), 'The Philosophy and Politics of Punishment and Sentencing', in C. Clarkson and R. Morgan (eds), *The Politics of Sentencing Reform*, Oxford: Clarendon Press.

—— and STEVENSON, S. (1992), 'What Went Wrong? Criminal justice policy in England and Wales 1945–70', in D. Downes (ed.), *Unravelling Criminal Justice*, London: Macmillan.

BOWLING, B. (1999), *Violent Racism*, Oxford: Clarendon Press.

BUTLER, D., and KAVANAGH, D. (1980), *The British General Election 1979*, Basingstoke: Macmillan.

—— and —— (1992), *The British General Election 1991*, Basingstoke: Macmillan.

—— and —— (1997), *The British General Election 1997*, Basingstoke: Macmillan.

CAVADINO, M., and DIGNAN, J. (1997), *The Penal System: An Introduction*, 2nd edn, London: Sage.

COHEN, N. (2001), 'A Cruel Reckoning', *Observer*, 24 June.

CONSERVATIVE PARTY (1970), *A Better Tomorrow*, London: Conservative Party.

—— (1979), *The Conservative Manifesto*, London: Conservative Party.

—— (1987), *Our First Eight Years: The Next Moves Forward*, London: Conservative Party.

—— (1997), *You Can Only Be Sure with the Conservatives*, London: Conservative Party.

—— (2001), *Time for Common Sense*, London: Conservative Party.

CRAWFORD, A. (1997), *The Governance of Crime*, Oxford: Clarendon Press.

DIXON, D., and FISHWICK, E. (1984), 'The Law and Order Debate in Historical Perspective', in P. Norton (ed.), *Law and Order and British Politics*, Aldershot: Gower.

DODGSON, K., GOODWIN, P., HOWARD, P., LLEWELLYN-THOMAS, S., MORTIMER, E., RUSSELL, N., and WEINER, M. (2001), *Electronic monitoring of released prisoners: an evaluation of the Home Detention Curfew scheme*, Home Office Research Study No. 222, London: Home Office.

DOWNES, D. (1998), 'Toughing It Out: From Labour Opposition to Labour Government', *Policy Studies*, 19, 3(4): 191–8.

—— (2001), 'The macho penal economy', *Punishment and Society*, 3(1): 61–80.

—— and MORGAN, R. (1994), ' "Hostages to Fortune"?: The Politics of Law and Order in Post-War Britain', in M. Maguire, R. Morgan, and R. Reiner (eds), *The Oxford Handbook of Criminology*, 1st edn, Oxford: Oxford University Press.

—— and MORGAN, R., (1997), 'Dumping the "Hostages to Fortune"?: The Politics of Law and Order in Post-War Britain', in M. Maguire *et al.* (eds), *The Oxford Handbook of Criminology*, 2nd edn, Oxford: Oxford University Press.

DUNBAR, I., and LANGDON, A. (1998), *Tough Justice: Sentencing and Penal Policies in the 1990s*, London: Blackstone Press.

EDELMAN, M. (1971), *Politics as Symbolic Action*, Chicago, Ill.: Markham.

ELDER, N.C.M. (1984), 'Conclusion', in P. Norton (ed.), *Law and Order and British Politics*, Aldershot: Gower.

ELLIOTT, L. (2001), 'Labour Underspends Tories', *Guardian*, 24 April.

FITZGERALD, M. (2001), 'Ethnic minorities and community safety', in R. Matthews and J. Pitts (eds), *Crime, Disorder and Community Safety*, London: Routledge.

GAINSBOROUGH, J., and MAUER, M. (2000), *Diminishing Returns: Crime and Incarceration in the 1990s*, Washington DC: The Sentencing Project.

GAMBLE, A. (1990), 'The Thatcher Decade in Perspective', in P. Dunleavy, A. Gamble, and G. Peele (eds), *Developments in British Politics*, London: Macmillan.

GARLAND, D. (1996), 'The Limits of the Sovereign State: Strategies of Crime Control in Contemporary Society', *British Journal of Criminology*, 64(4): 445–71.

—— (2001), *The Culture of Control: Crime and Social Order in Contemporary Society*, Oxford: Oxford University Press.

GIDDENS, A. (1984), *The Constitution of Society*, Cambridge: Polity.

GIFFORD, Lord (1986), *The Broadwater Farm Inquiry*, London: Karia Press.

GREER, S. (1995), *Supergrasses*, Oxford: Clarendon Press.

HALL, S., CRITCHER, S., JEFFERSON, T., CLARKE, J., and ROBERTS, B. (1978), *Policing the Crisis: Mugging, the State and Law and Order*, London: Macmillan.

HELD, D. (2001), 'Regulating Globalisation? The Reinvention of Politics', in A. Giddens (ed.), *The Global Third Way Debate*, Cambridge: Polity.

HONDERICH, T. (1990), *Conservatism*, London: Hamish Hamilton.

HENNESSEY, P. (1992), *Never Again*, London: Cape.

HETHERINGTON, P. (2001), 'Scots and Welsh face subsidy axe', *Guardian*, 24 April.

HOME OFFICE (White Paper) (1997), *No More Excuses*, London: Home Office.

—— (2001a), *Community Cohesion: A Report of the Independent Review Team*, London: Home Office.

—— (2001b), *Building Cohesive Communities: A Report of the Ministerial Group on Public Order and Community Cohesion*, London: Home Office.

—— (The Halliday Report) (2001c), *Making Punishments Work: Report of a Review of the Sentencing Framework for England and Wales*, London: Home Office.

—— (2001d), *Police Reform*, London: Home Office.

JEFFERSON, T. (1990), *The Case Against ParaMilitary Policing*, Milton Keynes: Open University Press.

JONES, D. (2001), '"Misjudged Youth": A Critique of the Audit Commission's Reports on Youth Justice', *British Journal of Criminology*, 41(2): 362–80.

KERSHAW, C., BUDD, T., KINSHOTT, G., MATTINSON, J., MAYHEW, P., and MYHILL, A. (2000), *The 2000 British Crime Survey: England and Wales*, Statistical Bulletin 18/00, London: Home Office.

KING, A. (1993), *Britain at the Polls 1992*, New Jersey: Chatham House.

KING, R.D., and McDERMOTT, C. (1995), *The State of Our Prisons*, Oxford: Clarendon Press.

LABOUR PARTY (1970), *Now Britain's Strong—Let's Make It Great To Live In*, London: Labour Party.

—— (1992), *Seven Steps To Justice*, London: Labour Party.

—— (1997), *New Labour—Because Britain Deserves Better*, London: Labour Party.

—— (2001), *Ambitions for Britain: Labour's Manifesto 2001*, London: Labour Party.

LEVITAS, R. (1998), *The Inclusive Society? Social Exclusion and New Labour*, Basingstoke: Macmillan.

LIBERAL DEMOCRATIC PARTY (1997), *Make the Difference*, London: Liberal Democratic Party.

—— (2001), *Freedom, Justice, Honesty: Manifesto for a Liberal and Democratic Britain—General Election 2001*, London: Liberal Democratic Party.

MACPHERSON, C.B. (1962), *The Political Theory of Possessive Individualism*, Oxford: Oxford University Press.

MACPHERSON REPORT (1999), *The Stephen Lawrence Inquiry: Report of an Inquiry by Sir William Macpherson of Cluny* (Cm 4262-I), London: Stationery Office.

McCONVILLE, M., SANDERS, A., and LENG, R. (1991), *The Case for the Prosecution*, London: Routledge.

MORGAN, R. (1979), *Formulating Penal Policy: The Future of the Advisory Council on the Penal System*, London: NACRO.

—— (1991), 'Woolf: In Retrospect and Prospect', *Modern Law Review*, 54: 713–25.

—— and NEWBURN, T. (1997), *The Future of Policing*, Oxford: Oxford University Press.

—— and RUSSELL, N. (2000), *The Judiciary in the Magistrates' Courts*, London: Home Office.

MORRIS, T. (1989), *Crime and Criminal Justice in Britain since 1945*, Oxford: Blackwell.

—— (2001), 'Crime and Penal Policy', in A. Seldon (ed.), *The Blair Effect: The Blair Government 1997–2001*, London: Little, Brown.

NEWBURN, T. (2001a), 'Atlantic Crossings', Inaugural Lecture, Goldsmiths College, London.

—— (2001b), '"Policy Transfer" and Crime Control: Some Reflections on Zero Tolerance', paper presented at the Mannheim Centre, London School of Economics, 13 June.

O'LEARY, B. (2001), 'The Belfast Agreement and the Labour Government', in A. Seldon (ed.), *The Blair Effect: The Blair Government 1997–2001*, London: Little, Brown.

—— and McGARRY, J. (1993), *The Politics of Antagonism: Understanding Northern Ireland*, London: Athlone.

PARKIN, F. (1967), 'Working-Class Conservatives: A Theory of Political Deviance', *British Journal of Sociology*, 18/3: 278–90.

PEASE, K. (1998), 'Crime, Labour and the Wisdom of Solomon', *Policy Studies*, 19, 3(4): 255–66.

PIACHAUD, D., and SUTHERLAND, H. (2001), 'Child poverty—aims, achievements and prospects for the future', *New Economy*, 8, 2: 71–6.

POLICE FOUNDATION (Runciman Report) (2000), *Drugs and the Law*, London: Police Foundation.

POWER, M. (1997), *The Audit Explosion*, Oxford: Oxford University Press.

REINER, R. (2000), *The Politics of the Police*, 3rd edn, Oxford: Oxford University Press.

RICHARDSON, G. (1993), *Law, Process and Custody: Prisoners and Patients*, London: Weidenfeld and Nicholson.

ROCK, P. (1986), *A View From the Shadows: The Ministry of the Solicitor General of Canada and the Justice for Victims of Crime Initiative*, Oxford: Clarendon Press.

—— (1995), 'The Opening Stages of Criminal Justice Policy Making', *British Journal of Criminology*, 35: 1–6.

ROSENBAUM, D. (1988), 'A Critical Eye on Neighbourhood Watch: Does it Reduce Crime and Fear?', in T. Hope and M. Shaw (eds), *Communities and Crime Reduction*, London: HMSO.

RUTHERFORD, A. (1996), *Transforming Criminal Policy*, Winchester: Waterside.

RYAN, M. (1978), *The Acceptable Pressure Group— Inequality in the Penal Lobby: A Case Study of the Howard League and PAP*, Farnborough: Saxon House.

—— (1983), *The Politics of Penal Reform*, London: Longman.

SANDERS, A. (2001), *Community Justice— Modernising the Magistracy in England and Wales*, London: IPPR.

SCARMAN REPORT (1981), *The Brixton Disorders 10–12 April 1981*, London: HMSO.

SHAW, C. (1931), *The Natural History of a Delinquent Career*, Chicago, Ill.: University of Chicago Press.

SHEEHY REPORT (1993), *Report of the Inquiry into Police Responsibilities and Rewards* (Cm 2281), London: HMSO.

SIM, J. (1993), 'Reforming the Penal Wasteland?: A Critical Review of the Woolf Report', in E. Player and M. Jenkins (eds), *Prisons After Woolf: Reform Through Riot*, London: Routledge.

SMITH, D. (1999), 'Less Crime Without More Punishment', *Edinburgh Law Review*, 3: 294–316.

SPENCER, S. (1985), *Called To Account*, London: National Council for Civil Liberties.

TAYLOR, I. (1999), 'Respectable, Rural and English: the Lobby Against the Regulation of Firearms in Great Britain', in P. Carlen and R. Morgan (eds), *Crime Unlimited: Questions for the 21st Century*, Basingstoke: Macmillan.

TOYNBEE, P., and WALKER, D. (2001), *Did Things Get Better? An Audit of Labour's Successes and Failures*, Harmondsworth: Penguin.

WADDINGTON, P.A.J. (1991), *The Strong Arm of the Law*, Oxford: Oxford University Press.

WOLFGANG, M.E., FIGLIO, R.M., and SELLIN, T. (1972), *Delinquency in a Birth Cohort*, Chicago: University of Chicago Press.

WOOLF REPORT (1991), *Prison Disturbances April 1991: Report of an Inquiry by the Rt Hon. Lord Justice Woolf (Parts I and II) and His Honour Judge Stephen Tumim (Part II)* (Cm 1456), London: HMSO.

WOOTTON COMMITTEE (1968), *Cannabis: Report by the Advisory Committee on Drug Dependence*, London: HMSO.

YOUNG, J. (2001), 'Winning the Fight Against Crime? New Labour, Populism and Lost Opportunities', University of Middlesex: unpublished.

11

CRIME STATISTICS
THE 'DATA EXPLOSION' AND ITS IMPLICATIONS

Mike Maguire

INTRODUCTION

This chapter explores a number of interrelated questions regarding the state of our knowledge about 'crime levels', 'crime patterns', and 'crime trends'. These range from what may sound like (but are not) straightforward empirical and methodological questions, such as 'How much crime is there?', 'How is it changing?', and 'How do we find out?', to broader questions about the relationships between, on the one hand, the kinds of data which are collected and published about crime and, on the other, public perceptions of 'the crime problem' and developments in criminological thought and criminal justice policy. A key message throughout is that statements about crime numbers or trends should always be approached in a critical frame of mind. This is an area of shifting sands, where one has always to be aware of the creation of new offences, or changes in legal definitions or counting rules and practices. More than this, though, the possibility must be faced that the concept of a 'true' total of crimes has no useful meaning. Criminal offences may be carefully defined in law, but they are also *socially* defined and constructed: whether people perceive a particular action or event as a crime, let alone whether they report it as such to anyone else (including the police, or a survey interviewer), can vary according to their own knowledge, awareness, or feelings about crime, which in turn may be influenced by the general public 'mood' or the preoccupations of politicians and the media. Moreover, the collection and presentation of data themselves play a dynamic part in the crime construction process, both influencing and being influenced by current social concerns. It is nevertheless worth emphasizing that recognition of these issues does not mean that we have to adopt the extreme relativist position, espoused by many criminologists in the 1970s, that quantitative data (and especially the official crime statistics) tell us *nothing* about crime and that they should therefore be abandoned or ignored. On the contrary, they can tell us a great deal: the trick is to approach them critically, with a full understanding of how, why, and for what purposes they were produced.

Most of the data and examples presented here relate to England and Wales, but the questions they raise are pertinent to all jurisdictions in which attempts are made to 'measure' crime. Since the last edition of the *Oxford Handbook of Criminology* in 1997, there have been some significant developments in this country affecting the official crime statistics. These include various technical changes which together have considerably inflated the official totals of recorded crime: for example, the upgrading of 'common assault' and other minor offences to the status of 'notifiable offences', thus widening the range of behaviours included in the published statistics. Another development has been a doubling of the sample size of the British Crime Survey (BCS), which will for the first time provide survey data at the level of individual police force areas, thus enhancing the role of the BCS (which has also moved to an annual cycle) as a directly comparable 'rival' to the police-generated crime statistics. Potentially most important for the longer term, however, have been proposals from the Home Office for a radical revision of its traditional approaches to the collection and presentation of crime data, the main aim of which is to produce a 'picture of crime' of more practical use to policy-makers. The proposals include combining data from a wider range of sources, providing more information about contextual factors (such as the locations of offences and the extent of damage or loss suffered), and, more controversially, a move from 'offences recorded by the police' to 'calls for service' as the basic building blocks of official statistics. All these developments and their implications will be discussed in more detail later in the chapter.

The chapter is set out as follows. The first main section explores some of the major changes that occurred during the last quarter of the twentieth century in the collection and presentation of information about crime. It is demonstrated that a major 'data explosion' occurred, greatly widening the range of 'knowledge' about crime, especially about offences which had previously remained largely hidden from view, about the physical circumstances of offences, and the differential risks of victimization among different types of area and individual. The production of (and investment in) new kinds of knowledge, it is argued, is dynamically linked to major changes that have taken place in public, political, and media perceptions and representations of the 'crime problem' and how to deal with it—developments themselves associated with wider social and economic changes which have helped to elevate crime to a central position on the political agenda. The next two sections take a close look at statistics based on police crime records, and at data from the BCS, which are fast replacing the former as the key 'official' source of statistics used in policy-making, planning, and performance measurement, as well as research. This is followed by a brief discussion of the 'Simmons Report' (Home Office 2000), which sets out a vision for a radically new approach to the collection and presentation of crime data. Its recommendations, it is argued, have far-reaching implications, both nationally and locally, for how crime 'problems' and 'risks' are conceptualized, analysed, prioritized, and responded to. The penultimate section examines the relatively neglected topic of data about offenders (as opposed to offences), including a brief look at the pictures which emerge from self-report studies in comparison with police, court, and prison records. Lastly, some concluding remarks are made about the broad implications of all these changes.

THE 'DATA EXPLOSION'

The rapid development of electronic data storage in the last quarter of the twentieth century has fuelled what might be called a 'data explosion' in almost every area of public and private life. This is certainly true of crime and justice, most obviously in policing, where the collection and use of information has always been 'core business' (see, for example, Ericson and Haggerty 1997). What is most interesting about this phenomenon is not simply the volume of data being gathered and stored, but the extensive range of aspects of the 'crime problem' that are now being carefully 'measured'. An examination of these provides a useful illustration of the two-way relationship between developments in the information field and changes in thinking about crime and justice.

Let us begin with a brief and broad comparison between the kinds of information that were available to criminologists in, say, the middle of the last century and those that they can draw upon now. The focus here is upon systematically gathered (and mainly quantitative) data, although it should be remembered that 'knowledge' about crime is influenced by information from many other sources, including personal experience, anecdote and gossip, political rhetoric, and media reports of individual cases, not to mention fictional representations in books and films (Sparks 1992; Reiner, in Chapter 12 of this volume): indeed, it is likely that many of these have a stronger immediate influence on public perceptions. However, the more systematic kinds of data directly inform policy-making and 'seep through' into the public consciousness via political debate and media reports, where they are used to support or counter claims based on more anecdotal evidence.

THEN AND NOW

In the 1940s and 1950s, virtually the only sources of substantial and systematic information about crime in England and Wales were the annually published *Criminal Statistics*, and the results of research by the small number of criminologists (most of whom had a psychological or psychiatric background) working in academic or clinical settings. *Criminal Statistics*, as now, presented national compilations of records produced at local level by the police and the courts: most importantly, the totals of notifiable offences recorded by the police, and of offenders found guilty of or cautioned for criminal offences. Research data were more diverse, but most commonly were based upon detailed records of the personal characteristics and social backgrounds of incarcerated offenders (see, for example, Bowlby 1944, 1953; Burt 1944).

In the intervening years, the numbers of people engaged in data collection and research have expanded dramatically. There has been a significant growth in the research capacity of the Home Office, as well as a rapid expansion of criminology in universities: there are now several hundred lecturers and researchers working countrywide (many in specialist 'Centres' attracting substantial research funds), and a flourishing market for publications.[1] A wide variety of new data sources have been created and exploited, and numerous new fields of enquiry have been opened up, in many cases challenging the basic pictures of crime presented by the official statistics or studies of the characteristics of convicted offenders.

Among the most important new sources, of course, are massive electronic data sets, including the results of large-scale victim surveys (notably the BCS), national data-bases of offenders (e.g., the Offenders Index) or offences (e.g., the Homicide Index), and a host of local record systems maintained by the police, criminal justice agencies, and other statutory and voluntary organizations, many of which will eventually be brought together for combined analysis in regional and national 'data warehouses' (Home Office 2000). Other large data sets—many of them accessible for secondary analysis through the ESRC data archive at Essex University—have been produced by major funded research projects, including longitudinal 'cohort' studies, local crime surveys, and self-report surveys. There have also been significant advances in the analytical tools available, such as computer packages for multivariate analysis and statistical modelling (Hair *et al.* 1998) and, more recently, detailed 'mapping' of the locations of offences and the identification of so-called 'hot-spots', using postcodes or map references (Read and Oldfield 1995; Longley *et al.* 2001). Last but not least, there has been a whole raft of more qualitative research, using methods ranging from formal interviews to participant observation.

In terms of the production of new kinds of 'knowledge', the following are among the most important developments:

1. *Unreported and unrecorded offences.* Before the 1980s, very little data had been systematically collected in England and Wales on offences not reported to, or recorded by, the police. However, in 1982, following the lead set in the United States a decade earlier, the Home Office carried out the first British Crime Survey (BCS), a survey of households across England and Wales, which clearly demonstrated that only a minority of incidents that are recognized as 'crimes' by their 'victims' end up in the official statistics (Hough and Mayhew 1983). The BCS has since been repeated many times and has become as important as—if not more important than—police-generated statistics for the analysis and pre-sentation of patterns and trends in crime. It has also been complemented by a variety of local surveys and a periodic international crime survey (Van Kesteren *et al.* 2000). Recently, too, other sources of systematic information about unreported crime, such as questions to assault victims attending Accident and Emergency departments, are being actively explored (Home Office 2000).

2. *Circumstances of offences.* Much more detailed information is now collected (in the BCS, from police records, and elsewhere) on, for example, where, when, and how offences take place, how far offenders travel to offend, and what kinds of

---

[1] It is worth remembering that, in the 1950s, academic criminology boasted only a few lone scholars and one research institute of any size. For useful accounts of the growth of the subject up to the late 1980s, see Rock's (1988) edited Special Issue of the *British Journal of Criminology*. Were these papers to be revised now, they would show even greater growth in the 1990s, including the establishment of many specialist undergraduate and postgraduate degrees.

loss or damage victims suffer. The spatial aspects of this kind of information have attracted particular attention, which has led to the growth of a flourishing new branch of the subject, usually referred to as 'environmental criminology' (see Bottoms and Wiles, in Chapter 18 of this volume).

3. *Specificity and sub-classification.* Following on from the previous comments, it is clear that, unlike in the 1950s, we no longer perceive, analyse, and discuss types of crime in terms of a few broad legal categories. Instead, they tend to be sub-classified into a myriad of highly specific forms of behaviour (a list, moreover, which grows frequently as offenders devise new ways of stealing property, or as the police or media discover a new 'crime threat'). For example, it would be unusual nowadays to find an analysis of 'robbery': writers or researchers are more likely to examine a more specific problem such as 'street robbery' (as opposed to, say, bank or building society robbery, or security van robbery), or even something as narrow as the forcible theft of mobile phones (Harrington and Mayhew 2001).

4. *Hidden types of crime.* More and more kinds of 'private' criminal activity which formerly lay largely hidden from public view—and which remain even now greatly under-represented in recorded crime figures—have not only become familiar subjects in television programmes and newspaper articles, but have been studied, described, and analysed in systematic fashion. Prominent among these are some intra-household offences (such as domestic violence and child sex abuse), 'white-collar' and corporate offences, and crimes between consenting parties (notably the supplying of drugs), none of which attracted any sustained attention in the 1950s.

5. *Hidden offenders.* In the 1940s and 1950s, people who committed crime tended to be represented as a fairly small and discrete category, substantially different from the 'normal' population: in essence, the young, male, socially deprived, and often psychologically damaged perpetrators of offences such as burglary and petty theft, who make up much of the prison population. However, it is now well known that criminal behaviour is by no means restricted to this group. Self-report studies have consistently indicated that a *majority* of the population have committed criminal offences at some time in their lives; and analysis of the Offenders Index shows, for example, that one-third of all males born in 1953 had acquired at least one criminal conviction for an indictable offence by the age of forty-six (Prime *et al.* 2001).[2] It has also become clear that 'middle class' offending goes well beyond trivial indiscretions: research has established, for example, that child sex abuse (Baker and Duncan 1985), domestic violence (Dobash and Dobash 1992), football hooliganism (Murphy *et al.* 1990), work-

---

[2] Cohort studies trace the progress of a given group of people over a long period of time, in some cases from birth to adulthood. The best known in criminology include cohorts traced and interviewed at regular intervals by the Gluecks (1950) and by West and Farrington (1969, 1973; see also Farrington 1995, 2002). The Home Office study on convictions is carried out retrospectively at intervals using official records. It is interesting to note that, despite the high figure for males, only 9 per cent of females were found to have acquired a criminal conviction.

place theft (Ditton 1977; Mars 1982), and drug offences (Pearson 1987; South, in Chapter 25 of this volume) are committed by people from all social classes. On the other hand, there has been little evidence to dent the view that crime is predominantly a *male* preserve (see Heidensohn, in Chapter 15 of this volume).

6. *Victim perspectives and public views.* Much more information is now available—mainly from the BCS, local crime surveys, interview studies, and analysis of police incident records—about crime from the perspective of the victim or potential victim. This includes detailed knowledge about the emotional and financial impact of different kinds of offence (e.g., Shapland *et al.* 1985; Maguire and Corbett 1987); calculations of the relative risks among different social groups of falling victim to particular kinds of crime (see Zedner, in Chapter 13 of this volume); public and victim attitudes towards offenders and the criminal justice system (Mattinson and Mirrlees-Black 2000); ratings of the seriousness of different types of crime (Pease 1988); and regular measures of 'fear of crime'.[3]

EXPLAINING THE CHANGES

In trying to explain why the kinds and volume of data collected now are so different from fifty years ago, it is important to look not just at technological advances (which have obviously played an important part), but at general differences in ways of thinking about and responding to crime. Many theorists have identified a broad shift in 'penality' associated with the transition of western societies, during the last quarter of the twentieth century, from the conditions of 'modernity' into those of 'late modernity' (see, for example, Foucault 1977; Feeley and Simon 1992; Garland 1995, 1996, 2001; Loader and Sparks, and Hudson, in Chapters 3 and 8 respectively of this volume). In simple terms, the 'modern' period corresponded with the growth and consolidation of the power of centralized and bureaucratic nation states, while late modernity is characterized above all by globalized economies, the dispersal of many of the functions of central government, and the breakdown of many of the relative certainties (e.g., long-term employment and stable communities) associated with the previous era. 'Modern' governments, it has been argued, established control over their populations primarily by efforts to 'transform' offenders and potential offenders into obedient citizens through a complex net of disciplinary and reformative institutions and practices, organized around the meticulous classification and collection of knowledge about individuals. By contrast, reflecting the prevailing sense of insecurity and impermanence characteristic of late modernity, we are now seeing the emergence of new forms of penality, organized increasingly around the assessment and management of 'risk', and the dispersal of responsibility for crime control to local agencies, communities, and individual citizens (Garland 1996, 2001).

Criminologists (and still less, government statisticians) clearly do not stand in isolation from the rest of society, and it is possible to explain their central preoccupations—and the kinds of data they collect and analyse—in terms of the

---

[3] The last, based on standard BCS questions, are even to be used as performance indicators for the police and crime and disorder partnerships.

dominant penality of their time. Thus Garland (2001, and in Chapter 1 of this volume) argues that the aims of criminology in the first two-thirds of the last century can be broadly understood as the pursuit of two parallel 'projects' reflecting key aspects of modern penality: the 'governmental' and the 'Lombrosian'. He describes the aims of the former as to 'enhance the efficient and equitable administration of justice by charting the patterns of crime and monitoring the practice of police and prisons' (Garland, in Chapter 1 of this volume: p. 2), aims easily understood in the context of growth of central bureaucracies in 'modern' states. The Lombrosian project he describes as attempts to 'develop an etiological, explanatory science, based on the premise that criminals can somehow be scientifically differentiated from non-criminals' (ibid.). Here he is referring to the continuing dominance of the 'positivist' tradition among British criminologists,[4] with its focus on understanding and explaining the 'criminality' of particular individuals (especially the predominantly male, lower-class recidivists who populated the prisons and were convicted of a limited range of relatively visible predatory property crimes).[5] As Garland (2001: 43) neatly expresses it, for many at the time 'the *crime* problem came to be viewed as a *criminal* problem'. The two main sources of crime-related data produced in the middle of the twentieth century—regularly repeated statistical series based on police and court records, and research on the characteristics of prisoners—fit neatly into this framework. The former can clearly be seen as part of the wider 'governmental' project, and the latter as part of the 'Lombrosian' project.

Equally, the production of many new kinds of data and knowledge can be linked to broad changes in thinking, attitude, and practice (or 'penality') which have accompanied the transition to late modernity. We identify a number of such changes below, as well as some more specific factors which have stimulated new research. There is space here only for brief discussion of some of these.

Heightened concern and the politicization of crime

Clearly, the huge increases in production of new information would not have occurred without major increases in government investment in data collection and research. These in turn would not have been sanctioned without the emergence of crime (as evidenced in opinion polls and elsewhere) as one of the areas of greatest public concern and as a key issue on the national political agenda. While it has always attracted considerable attention, its prominence and degree of 'politicization' over the last decade or so is probably unprecedented (Downes and Morgan, in Chapter 10 of this volume). Explanation of this phenomenon is beyond the scope of this chapter, but it is clear that rising official crime rates, growing intolerance and fear of crime

---

[4] Positivism as a distinct, self-proclaimed 'school' is principally associated with the work of Italian scholars such as Ferri (1913) and Garofalo (1914), who had a major influence in the institutionalization of criminology in the USA in the early years of the twentieth century.

[5] Few criminologists at the time showed any interest in the surrounding circumstances or geographical distribution of offences, and still less to other, more 'hidden' forms of crime, particularly those practised by more powerful social groups. Although Edwin Sutherland's ground-breaking book on white-collar crime (Sutherland 1949) had considerable impact in the USA, British criminologists appear to have paid it little heed at this time.

among the public, sensationalist media reporting, and exploitation of the subject by politicians have all combined to produce a general perception that crime is 'getting out of control'. At a deeper level, this has been fuelled by the above-mentioned sense of insecurity and heightened awareness of risk associated with life in the globalized economies of 'late modernity' (Bottoms 1995; Garland 2001; Loader and Sparks, and Hudson, in Chapters 3 and 8 respectively of this volume).

A specific sign of the heightened sensitivity to crime—and a factor driving searches for new information—is the growing frequency with which examples of 'deviancy amplification' (Young 1971) or 'moral panics' (Cohen 1972) have been observable. These tend to be triggered by newspapers reporting cases of what appears to be a new variety of criminal behaviour, thereby sparking off a general media trawl for similar events and 'uncovering' (or, from another perspective, 'creating') a significant new 'crime problem'. A new name may be coined, enhancing the sense of a new kind of threat: for example, two successful neologisms in the 1990s were 'road rage' and 'lager louts'. The extra publicity often leads more people to report instances to the police (and perhaps more people to engage in the behaviour themselves), researchers begin to seek grants to investigate its 'scale' in a more systematic way, policy-makers ask agencies to keep new kinds of records, and politicians call for government action to respond to what is now judged to be a mounting problem.[6] Such situations tend to involve a 'self-fulfilling prophecy' as the different elements of the process feed off each other, and it becomes extremely difficult to disentangle them in subsequent analyses of what happened—not least, to determine whether there ever was a 'real' increase of any significance in the relevant behaviour.

Some writers—among the best known being Hall *et al.* (1978)—have claimed that 'crime waves' are deliberately manufactured by governments (with assistance from the police and the media) during economic recessions, when their popularity is low and/or the legitimacy of the class structure is weakened. Hall *et al.*'s main example was the 'mugging' scare in the early 1970s, which was created, they claimed, to focus public hostility upon, and justify greater social control over, the unemployed young black populations of inner cities. They pointed out that 'mugging' is a term which does not correspond to a legal offence category, and that the racially differentiated statistics issued by the Metropolitan Police which fuelled the scare were highly unreliable (see Levi and Maguire, in Chapter 22 of this volume). Types of behaviour which various government ministers 'talked up' during the 1990s as meriting a stronger response included illegal immigration, 'benefit fraud', 'youth disorder', trespass by 'squatters', 'travellers', or 'rave' party-goers, and even the activities of 'aggressive beggars' and 'squeegee merchants' (Home Secretary Jack Straw's phrase for people who demand money for cleaning car windscreens at traffic lights). In some cases, the rhetoric was accompanied by controversial legislation creating new criminal offences (and hence new 'criminals') in areas of behaviour which had previously been

---

[6] More recently, the campaign by the *News of the World* for a 'Sarah's law' to force the police to notify the public of the whereabouts of convicted 'paedophiles', though failing in its main aim, has resulted in a statute (Criminal Justice and Court Service Act 2000) compelling annual publication of the numbers of registered sex offenders in each police force area (see Kemshall and Maguire 2002).

regulated only by civil law.[7] Most of those targeted by such legislation were from socially marginalized groups, and doubtless an updated version of Hall *et al.*'s thesis could be applied to the governments' actions—though to what extent these represented cynical political manoeuvring and to what extent the driving forces were public experiences and concerns, remains a matter for debate.

Lastly, increases in the level of effort devoted to recording and publishing new information have also been brought about through the persistence of groups campaigning or lobbying to get a particular form of behaviour taken more seriously by the police and criminal justice system. For example, the pioneering work of feminist writers and campaigners in the 1970s generated numerous surveys of the extent of 'domestic violence'. Almost certainly, by pressing police to arrest perpetrators rather than simply give advice, it also had the effect of creating more official records of its incidence.

The focus on risk

As noted earlier, one of the main themes driving contemporary criminal justice policy and practice—and one closely associated with the uncertainties of life in conditions of late modernity—is that of assessing and managing 'risk'. Indeed, it is not uncommon for contemporary penality to be described as 'risk penality' (see, for example, Pratt 1995; Ericson and Haggerty 1997; Kemshall and Maguire 2001; Loader and Sparks, in Chapter 3 of this volume). This relates both to risks of offending and risks of victimization. Where offenders are concerned, calculation of risk by means of assessment and prediction instruments such as 'OASys' is becoming a routine part of decisions about allocation to particular programmes or interventions (Raynor, in Chapter 31 of this volume) or, in the case of sex offenders, about the degree of monitoring to be carried out (Kemshall and Maguire 2001). This is leading to the collection of huge new amounts of data about individuals, much of it stored centrally for the purpose of obtaining evidence about 'what works'—for example, by comparing predicted with actual reconvictions (Raynor, *op. cit.*; Hollin, in Chapter 5 of this volume).

Where risks of victimization are concerned, one of the most important developments is the statutory requirement on crime and disorder partnerships (i.e. partnerships between police and local authorities in the 376 local authority areas in England and Wales) to carry out regular 'crime audits' to map levels of risk of different crimes across their areas, often down to ward level. Increasingly, the findings from these audits are being collated by the ten 'Regional Crime Reduction Directors' appointed to oversee the process, in order to identify high-risk areas across each region and to distribute resources to reduce their predicted levels of crime. This involves the collection and amalgamation of numerous sets of data, produced by a wide variety of

---

[7]   An important example was the Criminal Justice and Public Order Act 1994, which created the new crime of 'aggravated trespass', aimed mainly at travellers who camped on farmland; this law also had the effect of criminalizing many of the activities of politically active groups such as road protesters and hunt saboteurs, with obvious implications for civil liberties. The Crime and Disorder Act 1998 introduced the anti-social behaviour order, which could be imposed on people who had not committed any criminal offence, but allowed substantial terms of imprisonment for breaching its conditions. For more detailed discussion of these developments, see Downes and Morgan, in Chapter 10 of this volume.

organizations, and is aimed at the identification of areal 'risk factors' which can be addressed by multi-agency teams. In terms of the production of new kinds of knowledge about crime, and their translation into new kinds of crime policy, the cumulative impact over the next few years could be considerable.

The perspective from the victim

One of the most important changes in focus came about in the early to mid-1980s, which saw a rapid growth in attention to crime victims. This perspective, which had already been prominent for over ten years in the USA, rapidly began to affect the thinking of large numbers of British criminologists and policy-makers, informing debates about, *inter alia*, the relative rights of victims and offenders, policing policy, crime prevention, court processes, mediation, racial harassment, and male oppression of women (for overviews, see Zedner, in Chapter 13 of this volume; Maguire and Pointing 1988; Walklate 1989; Heidensohn 1989; Maguire 1991; Davis *et al.* 1997). More important for our purposes here, it had the general effect of focusing attention much more upon the *offence* than on the *offender*, including the production of large amounts of detailed information about where, when, how, and against whom different types of crime are (or are likely to be) committed.

An early British example of a victim-focused study was Maguire and Bennett's (1982) work on residential burglary.[8] The researchers described it as a 'crime specific' study: a detailed look at one particular form of crime, the circumstances under which it is committed, the motives and behaviour of those committing it, and the experiences of its victims. They mapped every burglary recorded by the police over various periods in three separate areas, and conducted 'in depth' interviews with as many of the victims as possible about the precise circumstances of the incident. A number of recurrent patterns were found: burglaries tended to be clustered either in poorer housing areas, or in more expensive properties close to main roads on the edges of towns; and individual houses were more likely to be burgled if situated near road junctions, or if they offered good cover (e.g., high hedges or fences) or access (e.g., rear or side alleys) to potential offenders. These patterns were tentatively explained in terms of interactions between, on the one hand, variations in the attractiveness of targets and in the risks and opportunities they offered and, on the other, the aims, thought processes, and behaviour patterns of different types of offender (juvenile and adult, local and travelling, and so on). Findings of this kind, which also emerged from other studies of burglary in the UK (e.g., Winchester and Jackson 1982; Bennett and Wright 1984) and North America (Reppetto 1974; Waller and Okihiro 1978; Brantingham and Brantingham 1975), contributed to a more general and growing theoretical interest in crime patterns as, for example, the product of 'opportunity' (Mayhew *et al.* 1976) or as a by-product of 'routine activities' (Cohen and Felson 1979). They also helped to stimulate attention to the decision-making processes of

---

[8] Several North American studies, illustrating the value of attempting to understand crime through detailed information from or about victims, had been carried out considerably earlier. These include Von Hentig's (1948) classic *The Criminal and his Victim*, Wolfgang's (1959) work on criminal homicide, and Amir's (1971) controversial study of forcible rape.

potential offenders in response to differential opportunities to steal, which later found theoretical expression in, among other approaches, 'rational choice theory' (Cornish and Clarke 1986), as well as informing new approaches to crime prevention.

New thinking about crime prevention

Another driving factor in the shift of focus towards the offence rather than the offender—and hence in the production of new forms of knowledge and data about crime—was the growing disillusionment among influential policy-makers with the idea that crime can be controlled solely, or even principally, through the actions of the police and criminal justice system (cf. Brody 1976; Clarke and Hough 1984). Faced with the apparent failure of the police, courts, and prisons to stem rising crime rates, the Home Office Research Unit, under the leadership of Ronald Clarke, took a firm decision in the late 1970s to concentrate research efforts on 'primary' forms of crime prevention (see Pease, in Chapter 26 of this volume): that is, upon ways of altering the physical environment in order to reduce the opportunities for crime. This led eventually to the formation of a separate research unit, the Home Office Crime Prevention Unit.

The distinctive contribution of Home Office research during the early and mid-1980s was the development of 'situational crime prevention'. Eschewing any interest in what Clarke (1980) called 'dispositional' theories of crime (i.e. that certain people have a predisposition to offend, and hence that the key to crime prevention lies in changing them), it set out to use detailed crime pattern analysis to pinpoint areas of the environment which could be altered in such a way as to make it less easy or less attractive for potential offenders to commit particular types of crime. The alteration might be through any of a variety of initiatives, including extra physical security, new design of buildings or vehicles, increased surveillance, and the marking of property (for overviews and examples, see Clarke and Mayhew 1980; Heal and Laycock 1986; Pease, *op. cit.*). This 'targeting' approach necessitated detailed knowledge about the prevalence, geographical and temporal patterning, as well as the physical 'mechanics', of particular offences, thus stimulating the Home Office to fund much more empirical research in these areas.

As noted earlier, a more recent development is the statutory formation under the Criminal Justice Act 1998 of crime and disorder partnerships in every local authority area in England and Wales. These each have a duty to prepare a comprehensive 'crime audit' of their area every three years, for which relevant data are collected from a variety of local agencies (see Hough and Tilley 1998). This requirement has given a major boost to data collection and analysis, including the employment of many new data analysts and the expanded use of analytical techniques such as geographical 'mapping' (Longley *et al.* 2001).

Managerialism and the rise of the performance culture

Since the early 1980s, when the government introduced the concept of the 'three Es' (efficiency, economy, and effectiveness) as a guiding principle for the public services, criminal justice agencies have become increasingly subject to inspection, audit, evaluation, and other means of testing their 'performance' against defined criteria. Reliable data with which to measure performance have become a prime requisite of these processes, which have led to huge improvements in both the coverage and the quality of record-keeping systems, at the same time providing rich new veins of data for use by researchers. Where the police are concerned, a good illustration is the current development of computerized 'incident' data, i.e. details of calls to the police reporting incidents of crime or disorder, together with additions indicating the police response and its outcome. Largely developed as part of improvements to management information systems to monitor levels and types police activity, they provide a useful new research tool and are increasingly seen by policy-makers as offering a more complete picture of offences and their contexts than is obtainable from the recorded crime figures.

The legacy of labelling theory

Lastly, although the 'labelling' and 'deviancy' theorists of the 1960s and early 1970s are not normally associated with what we have here called the 'data explosion'—indeed, the latter were largely responsible for a period in British criminology (spanning most of the 1970s) when the climate in the discipline was generally *anti*-statistical—they undoubtedly played an important part in steering criminologists away from traditional statistics towards new and creative approaches to the collection and understanding of crime data.

The main argument of the American 'labelling' theorists (e.g., Becker 1963; Kitsuse 1964; see also Rock, in Chapter 2 of this volume) was that 'crime' (or 'deviance') is not an independently existing phenomenon, but simply a label attached for a variety of reasons to diverse forms of behaviour. In the words of Erikson (1964): 'Deviance is not a property inherent in certain forms of behaviour, it is a property conferred upon those forms by the audience which directly or indirectly witness them.'

In Britain, the 'deviancy' theorists (e.g., Rock 1973; Cohen 1974) and their more radical successors built upon such ideas to initiate a broad shift in the focus of inquiry of explanation, away from 'the pathology of the criminal' towards 'the social construction of crime'—the social and political processes that determine which particular activities and people become defined as 'crimes' or 'criminals'. This entailed looking on the one hand at the nature and scope of criminal law and the processes shaping it, and on the other at the routine social interactions which 'create' crime day by day (for further discussion, see Lacey, and Rock, in Chapters 9 and 2 respectively of this volume). In this framework, police and court records are regarded not as the product of a neutral fact-collecting process, but of one geared first and foremost to organizational (primarily police) aims and needs. Hence they do not reflect the 'reality' of crime: they are part of its creation. Indeed, the statistics may tell us more about the organization which produced them than about the activities they are used to describe.

This line of argument led some writers to conclude that there was no point in analysing crime figures for the purpose of finding out anything about the extent of any kind of illegal behaviour—if, indeed, it made any sense to speak of 'real' crime rates at all. For them, crime rates were simply 'indices of organisational processes' (Kitsuse and Cicourel 1963) or 'an aspect of social organisation' (Black 1970), worthy of study only to help one understand the agency producing them.[9] This '*institutionalist*', as opposed to 'realist', approach was broadly the starting position adopted by Bottomley and Coleman (1981) in a major empirical study of crime-recording processes in police stations which revealed the importance of police practices and attitudes in shaping the official statistics—although victims (the initial source of most crime records) were also found to have a major influence.

Although the growing scepticism about the value of information from official sources led many criminologists away from these kinds of data, it had the parallel effect of raising awareness of the rich potential of alternative sources of knowledge about crime, especially qualitative research, but also victim surveys, offender self-report studies, and data from agencies other than the police. Importantly, too, studies began to appear of previously neglected and largely hidden areas of 'deviant' and/or 'criminal' activity, such as drugtaking, workplace 'fiddles', corporate crime, domestic violence, and sexual violence against women (examples being, respectively, Young 1971; Ditton 1977; Levi 1981; Dobash and Dobash 1979; Hanmer and Saunders 1984). In the 1980s, when attention began to shift again, this time towards victims and situational crime prevention, this habit of looking beyond the official statistics towards alternative sources of information about the context of crimes and the inter-actions between offenders and victims, proved well suited to the new data demands.

RECORDED CRIME

Having given a general overview of some of the major changes that have been occur-ring in the production of knowledge about crime, and of the reasons behind them, it is time to take a closer and more detailed look at some of the key data sources and the kinds and status of the 'pictures' of crime they produce. Before coming to the 'new kids on the block', we begin with a critical examination of the source which reigned almost unchallenged for over a century as the authoritative voice on the state of crime in England and Wales.

Criminal Statistics England and Wales, the annual Home Office compilation of data derived from police and court records, dates back to 1876. Despite the warnings of criminologists and government statisticians alike, these statistics are still treated by many politicians and journalists as an accurate 'barometer' of crime, and any sizeable rise in the figures they produce tends to receive widespread publicity and spark off arguments about police or government ineffectiveness or the need for sentencing changes (falls, conversely, tend to be largely ignored). The figures are also used a great deal at a local level to inform the distribution of police resources[10] and, increasingly, the preparation of crime 'audits' and crime reduction plans, as well as the measure-ment of police and crime reduction partnerships' 'performance' in comparison with targets and with other areas (see below and Pease, in Chapter 26 of this volume). While

[9] An alternative view was put forward by Taylor, Walton, and Young (1975), who argued that the statistics could be usefully analysed to reveal truths about the importance attached to various forms of property under a capitalist economy.

[10] Both between districts and between different crime problems. They also form part of national formulae for the allocation of funds to police force areas (Carr-Hill 2000).

alternative sources—not least police 'incident logs', records from other agencies, and the expanded BCS—are developing fast, it will be some time before the basic crime statistics are knocked off their perch as the central component of these exercises.

Let us begin with some brief preliminary comments about the limitations of police-generated crime statistics and some of the main difficulties they pose for analysis and the drawing of conclusions. First of all, decisions as to which kinds of offence to include or not to include in the official statistics, and what counting rules to apply, can make a huge difference to the published totals and hence to the impressions given to the public about the levels of crime in society. However, the problems of police crime statistics are by no means restricted to questions about formal rules. Not only do the figures (obviously) not include offences known to the public which fail to come to police notice, but the police have always possessed a great deal of discretion about whether and how to record possible offences which do come to their notice. Reports from the public—which are the source of over 80 per cent of all recorded crimes (McCabe and Sutcliffe 1978; Bottomley and Coleman 1981)—may be disbelieved, or considered too trivial, or deemed not to constitute a criminal offence, with the result that they are either not recorded at all, or are officially 'no crimed' later. They may also be excluded ('cuffed') for less defensible reasons, such as to avoid work or to improve the overall clear-up rate (Bottomley and Coleman 1981).[11] Calculations from BCS data indicate that at the time of writing about 40 per cent of 'crimes' known to victims and reported to the police do not end up in the official statistics, for good or bad reasons (Kershaw *et al.* 2001: 992).[12] However, it is possible that the situation will change significantly as the result of the introduction, from April 2002, of a National Crime Reporting Standard, which is designed to remove much of this traditional discretion and establish an 'ethical' or 'prima facie' approach whereby victims largely determine the recording of offences (see below and Simmons 2000, 2001).

The numbers of offences 'discovered' by the police themselves—either in the course of patrols or observation, or through admissions by arrested offenders—are also subject to major fluctuation. For example, planned operations against a particular type of offence will usually result in a considerable increase in arrests and the uncovering and recording of many new offences. This is particularly true of operations against 'victimless' crimes: for example, a pop festival is almost guaranteed to generate a sudden dramatic boost in an area's recorded drug offences. Conversely, numbers may fall owing to a withdrawal of police interest in a particular type of crime, as in the late 1950s and early 1960s when, pending anticipated legislation to legalize homosexuality, most forces turned a blind eye to instances of 'indecency between males' and the recorded total of such offences declined to half the level previously regarded as 'normal' (Walker 1971). The current rapid development of 'crime management' and

[11] The more 'hopeless' cases, in terms of their potential for detection, that are omitted from the figures, the higher the proportion detected (the clear-up rate) is likely to be. If a division's or force's clear-up rate is exceptionally low, officers (especially those in the CID) can expect criticism from management as well as, in some cases, the media. There is thus some incentive to 'massage' local crime statistics to avoid such criticism (for a first-hand account of police behaviour in this respect, see Young 1991).

[12] Over the various sweeps of the BCS, this figure has varied between 38 and 45 per cent for the comparable subset of police and BCS offences (Kershaw *et al.* 2001: 50). It should be noted that the rate varies considerably between offence types (see the section on the BCS for further discussion).

'proactive' policing systems based on the selective use of surveillance and informants to 'catch offenders in the act' (Audit Commission 1993; Maguire and John 1996, 1996a) is also likely to have a significant impact upon the patterns of offences which come to light through police activity.

NUMBERS OF CRIMES

The latest official figures available at the time of writing (Home Office 2001) indicate that the total number of 'notifiable offences' recorded by the police in England and Wales in the financial year 2000/2001[13] was just under 5.2 million. Although this is the global figure referred to in most public debates about the extent of crime, it has to be emphasized that, even as a record of criminal offences officially known to the authorities, it is anything but complete. Notifiable offences are largely, though not fully, coterminous with 'indictable' offences, i.e. those which may be tried in a Crown Court (Home Office 2001: 244).[14] This means that a large number of summary offences (i.e. those triable only in magistrates' courts) do not appear in the figures. No records are kept of the totals of such offences, although statistics are available on the numbers of people officially sanctioned for them. For example, in 2000, well over a million people were convicted or formally cautioned for summary offences: a total, it is worth noting, over double that of people convicted or cautioned for indictable offences.[15]

In addition, the 'official crime figures' do not include many of the offences recorded by police forces for which the Home Office is not responsible, notably most of those recorded by the British Transport Police, Ministry of Defence Police, and UK Atomic Energy Authority Police, who between them record about 80,000 notifiable offences annually.[16] Neither, more significantly in terms of numbers, do they include numerous cases of tax and benefit fraud known to agencies such as the Inland Revenue, Customs and Excise, and the Benefits Agency, which have investigative and prosecutional functions but which deal with the vast majority of cases by using their administrative powers to impose financial penalties (Levi 1993). Again, such agencies keep internal records of the numbers of people dealt with in these ways, or of the total amounts of revenue saved, but not of the total numbers of 'offences' coming to their notice—a task which, given that a single offender may repeat the same kinds of fraud numerous times over a period, would require complex counting rules.

It might be argued that, for practical purposes, it is perfectly adequate to judge the

---

[13] Before 1997, criminal statistics were presented on the basis of calendar years, but have since moved to accord with the financial year (April to March).

[14] 'Indictable' is used here as shorthand for offences which are either 'triable only on indictment' (i.e. in Crown Court) or 'triable either way' (i.e. in either Crown Court or magistrates' court) under the 1977 Criminal Law Act.

[15] More than half of the summary offences were motoring offences, but even excluding these, more people were convicted or cautioned for summary offences (578,800) than for indictable offences (476,400) (Home Office 2001: 98–9).

[16] These agencies have published separate totals of notifiable offences since 1989. A number of these, in fact, overlap with offences recorded by the police, owing to joint operations or joint processing of cases. Moreover, local police forces now tend to include in their own records the most serious offences recorded by the British Transport Police, as well as many of those which are cleared up (Kershaw et al. 2001: 91).

size and shape of 'the crime problem' by means of the notifiable offences recorded by the police, on the grounds that these embrace the most serious crimes, for which the vast majority of prison sentences are passed. However, they also include large numbers of incidents which it is difficult to claim are any more serious than some of the offences dealt with administratively, referred to above. For example, among the largest categories of notifiable offences, together making up around two-fifths of the total recorded, are theft from a vehicle, criminal damage, and theft from shops: most cases in these categories involve relatively small amounts of loss or damage (indeed, unsuccessful attempts to commit some kinds of notifiable offences are counted along with completed crimes). At the same time, many of the uncounted and unprosecuted tax and benefit frauds involve considerable sums of money (admittedly, of course, much of this is recovered through administrative penalties). There are also some quite serious summary offences which are still not counted—for example, driving after consuming alcohol or drugs—despite a major effort to clear up such anomalies in 1998 (see below).

Debates about the logic of the notification rules and the seriousness or otherwise of particular kinds of offence have periodically led the Home Office to change its instructions about what to include in the official crime totals. For example, prior to 1977, offences of criminal damage of £20 or less—which were not indictable—were not counted, but since that date they have been defined as notifiable and included. This decision immediately raised the 'total volume of crime' by about 7 per cent.[17] In 1998, too, ostensibly for the purpose of producing a more 'truthful' picture of the more serious kinds of crime, a number of quite common summary offences were added to the published totals of notifiable offences, again boosting the overall totals and making comparisons with previous years more difficult. The most important of these numerically were common assault and assault on a constable, which between them significantly increased the numbers of recorded offences of 'violence against the person'. This has created the impression among those unaware of the technical issues, of a major 'rise in violent crime'—interestingly, during a period when the BCS indicates that incidents of violence have seen a significant and sustained fall (Kershaw et al. 2001: 30).

In addition to the issue of which categories of offence are included, there are important questions to ask about how individual crimes are *counted*. Some kinds of offence tend to be repeated many times within a short period, to the extent that, though there may be several separate actions or people involved, they could be considered to form part of one, concerted criminal incident. For example, a thief may go through twenty trouser pockets in a changing-room, or try the doors of a whole row of cars, or steal a cheque card and use it many times to obtain goods or cash. Equally, a large affray—for example, at a demonstration or a football match—may involve numerous assaults by many people on many others; or a man may assault his partner virtually every night for a period of months or years.

---

[17] This is recognized in *Criminal Statistics* when comparisons are required between pre- and post-1977 figures, adjustments being made to the relevant tables. However, such comparisons are further complicated by the problem of inflation.

Prior to 1968, there was little consistency between police forces on how many offences to record when events of these kinds came to their notice. Following the recommendations of the Perks Committee in 1967, clearer 'counting rules' were established (Home Office 1971), which tidied up some of the discrepancies between forces, but at the same time appeared fairly arbitrary and inconsistent in some respects and clearly understated the relative frequency of some offences. These rules were revised again in 1980 and in 1998. The latest counting rules certainly have the merit of greater simplicity (although police officers have not always found them easy to apply in practice). The basic rule is that, wherever possible, the statistics should now reflect the *number of victims*, rather than the number of criminal acts. Where one person reports having been victimized by the same offender in a number of different ways (e.g., assaulted, defrauded, and robbed on a number of occasions), only the most serious offence is counted.[18] In the above examples, then, the changing-room thief and the cheque fraudster, who would previously have produced only one offence each, would now produce several (depending upon how many victims can be identified). The spouse abuser, as in the past, is likely to be credited with only one offence, while the affray (again, as before the changes) may produce quite a large number of offences. The biggest impact of the changes numerically has been upon the recording of fraud and forgery offences, especially cheque and credit card fraud, where one offender can defraud a large number of individuals or businesses with a single card or chequebook.

Criminal Statistics estimates that the joint impact of the above changes in coverage and counting rules was to elevate the total number of recorded offences between 1997/8 and 1998/9 by as much as 14 per cent (Home Office 2001: 28).

It can already be seen from the above few examples that there is no 'perfect' answer to the question of how to count crimes. Indeed, they begin to raise the question of whether it is sensible, let alone possible, to try to 'count' some kinds of offences at all. In other words, it should already be clear that statements about the 'total volume of crime' have to be hedged about with qualifications, even when they purport only to describe crimes officially known to state agencies: when different notification or counting rules are adopted (let alone new offences being created by legislation), the total can be raised or lowered significantly at a stroke.

TYPES OF CRIME

There are about 100 different categories of notifiable offences recorded by the police, each of them assigned a Home Office classification number. They are currently grouped by *Criminal Statistics* under nine broad headings, namely: 'offences of violence against the person'; 'sexual offences'; 'robbery'; 'burglary'; 'theft and handling stolen goods'; 'fraud and forgery'; 'criminal damage'; 'drug offences'; and 'other notifiable offences'. Most of these groups contain a considerable variety of offences, but most are dominated numerically by just one or two categories. Thus the category 'violence against the person' includes offences as diverse as murder, causing death by

---

[18] Though if a *new report* is made later by the same victim about the same offender, a new offence is recorded! This is the so-called 'finished incident rule' (Home Office 2001: 245).

reckless driving, and concealment of birth, but over 80 per cent of its total is accounted for by the (generally less serious) offences of 'harassment', 'common assault', and 'assault occasioning actual bodily harm'. Similarly, 'sexual offences' range from rape to bigamy to indecency between males, but over half consist of indecent assault on a female. In other words, a relatively small number of offence categories play a major part in determining both the overall crime total and the size of each offence group in relation to the others. Moreover, trends in these dominant offence types tend to disguise countertrends in less prolific offences.

Table 11.1 shows in simplified form the contributions of the main offence groups to the total number of offences recorded by the police in 2000/2001. It also separates out 'autocrime' (the theft or unauthorized taking of, or theft from, motor vehicles) from other forms of theft.

If one looks at the figures as a whole, the picture of the 'crime problem' which emerges is one dominated by property offences. The 'theft and handling' group as a whole, with about 2,145,000 recorded offences, constitutes well over 40 per cent of the sum total, with 'autocrime' its largest sub-category. Criminal damage makes up another fifth, and burglary—primarily a property offence, though with the added (and often disturbing) element of trespass—another sixth. Even after the increases since 1998 created by the inclusion of common assault (as explained above), the numbers of violent and sexual offences appear small in comparison.

The fact that offences against the person make up a relatively small proportion of all recorded crime has quite often been quoted in a reassuring tone, especially to support the argument that the popular media focus too strongly upon violence and distort its importance within the overall crime picture (see Reiner, in Chapter 12 of this volume). However, the statistics can be misleading without an acknowledgement

Table 11.1 Notifiable offences recorded by the police, 2000/2001

Offence group	Number (to the nearest 1,000)	Per cent
Theft of/from vehicles	968,000	19
Other theft/handling	1,177,000	23
Criminal damage	960,000	19
Burglary	836,000	16
Violence against person	601,000	12
Fraud and forgery	319,000	6
Drug offences	114,000	2
Robbery	95,000	2
Sexual offences	37,000	<1
Other	63,000	1
Total	5,171,000	100

Source: Criminal Statistics England and Wales 2000, London: Home Office, 2001.

of the relative importance of violent offences judged by criteria other than sheer numbers: for example, in terms of public concern, the effects upon victims, or the number and length of prison sentences they attract. Sexual assaults, robberies, and woundings have been found to have a profound emotional impact on much higher proportions of victims than is the case with offences of theft (Maguire and Corbett 1987). Fear of violence also severely restricts the social lives of many people (Maxfield 1984; Zedner, in Chapter 13 of this volume). Importantly, too, on any one day, around a third of the total population of sentenced prisoners will be found to be serving sentences for violent or sexual offences. By contrast, people sentenced for the much more common offences of theft and handling (who tend to attract considerably lighter sentences) together make up under 10 per cent of the population (Elkins and Olagundaye 2001: 2).[19]

Related comments can be made about fraud, where—again despite the changes in 1998—both the frequency and seriousness of offences known to the authorities are undoubtedly far greater than the published police figures suggest. First of all, the counting rules still allow a great number of repetitive fraudulent acts, for example those involving false entries in accounts, to be recorded as only one or two 'sample' offences. Secondly, many fraudulent tax or benefit offences are dealt with administratively by the Inland Revenue, Customs and Excise, or Benefits Agency, rather than as 'crimes'. Thirdly, if one measures the importance of property offences in terms of the value stolen, rather than the quantity of incidents, fraud comes out as of enormously greater significance than other categories. For example, Levi (1993) points out that the minimum criterion for cases to be accepted for investigation by the Serious Fraud Office is a fraud of £5 million, and that in April 1992 the Frauds Divisions of the Crown Prosecution Service were supervising cases involving nearly £4 billion. By contrast, the combined costs of the prolific offences of 'autocrime' and burglary for 1990 were estimated by the Association of British Insurers at under £1.3 billion. (Levi also points out that the alleged fraud in any one of several major cases—Barlow Clowes, Guinness, Maxwell, BCCI, Polly Peck—alone exceeded the total amount stolen in thefts and burglaries recorded by the police.)

GEOGRAPHICAL DISTRIBUTION

Criminal Statistics does not include detailed breakdowns of the distribution of recorded crime across the country, but basic figures are supplied separately for each of the forty-three police forces in England and Wales. Of course, some forces are much larger than others, and in order to afford a ready means of comparison, crime rates are expressed for each in terms of numbers of recorded offences per 100,000 population. This is by no means a fully satisfactory way of compensating for the differences, as it takes no account of possible difference in the compositions, as opposed to the sizes, of the relevant populations. As Bottomley and Pease (1986: 11–12) point out in relation to changes in one area over time:

---

[19] It should be noted that the proportion of violent offenders among receptions into prison (the other main statistic used to monitor trends in the use of imprisonment) is considerably lower: their prominence among the population reflects the disproportionate length of their sentences.

We should beware of easily reaching the conclusion that 'people commit crime, therefore more people can be expected to commit more crime' so that if the ratio between crime and population is unchanged then there can be nothing which requires an explanation. It can be seen at once that underlying such an assumption is an emergent theory about rates of offending, and possibly about rates of victimization, which leaves itself wide open to a series of supplementary questions such as whether all members of a population are equally 'at risk' of offending . . . what significance should be attached to the gender composition of the population . . . [and] given the change in the pattern of criminal opportunities, should one adjust for social changes like the number of cars registered.

It should also be noted that the rates provided may not reflect important differences between areas *within* forces. Nevertheless, they do offer some fairly consistent patterns. Table 11.2 shows the police forces with the highest and the lowest recorded

Table 11.2 Notifiable offences per 100,000
population: selected police force areas, 2000/2001

Offences per 100,000 population	
1. *Forces with rates above 10,000 per 100,000 population*	
Greater Manchester	14,104
West Midlands	13,892
MPS (London)	13,761
Nottinghamshire	13,547
Humberside	12,513
West Yorkshire	12,239
Cleveland	11,576
Merseyside	10,174
2. *Forces with rates below 7,000 per 100,000 population*	
Dyfed-Powys	4,760
Surrey	5,874
Wiltshire	5,989
Hertfordshire	6,157
Cheshire	6,441
Devon & Cornwall	6,552
Suffolk	6,569
Essex	6,600
Cumbria	6,684
North Yorkshire	6,895
West Mercia	6,970

Adapted from Table 2.6, *Criminal Statistics England and Wales 2000*,
London: HMSO, 2001.

crime rates per 100,000 population in 2000/2001. It is clear that most of those with the highest rates include major metropolitan and/or industrial areas within their boundaries, while those with the lowest rates are predominantly rural in character. One of the most interesting forces in this table is Nottinghamshire, a county force whose figures match those of some of the major metropolitan areas. This has been a familiar situation for many years: indeed, in 1995 Nottinghamshire returned the highest *per capita* crime rate in the country. The apparent anomaly has long been an object of curiosity and has been held up as a prime example of the potentially misleading nature of official statistics. Farrington and Dowds (1985) published a detailed study of police recording practices in the county, from which they concluded that its apparently huge crime rate relative to its neighbouring counties of Leicestershire and Staffordshire (which are socially not dissimilar to Nottinghamshire) was a function of (a) a much greater number and proportion of recorded crimes originating directly from offenders' admissions to the police (25 per cent, compared to 4 and 8 per cent in the other forces), (b) a greater number and proportion of recorded crimes involving property of little value (48 per cent valued at £10 or under, compared with 29 and 36 per cent), and (c) a somewhat higher 'true' crime rate (or, more accurately, a higher crime rate as measured by public surveys). The researchers stated:

It is reasonable to conclude that between two-thirds and three-quarters of the difference in crime rates . . . reflected differences in police reactions to crime, while the remaining one-third reflected differences in criminal behaviour . . .

The research shows once again the difficulties of interpreting official statistics. Almost certainly, Nottinghamshire has never been the most criminal area in the country. [Farrington and Dowds 1985: 70–71]

Interestingly, Nottinghamshire fell from its top place in the national table in 1981 to fifth place in 1982, a change which, Farrington and Dowds (*op. cit.*) claimed, 'is almost certainly attributable to changes in police policies for recording offences, which may have been caused partly by this research project'.

The foregoing discussion provides us with two messages about the value of the official statistics as a means of comparing crime rates between areas. On the one hand, some confidence can be drawn from the fact that the broad pattern they indicate—i.e. of higher crimes in more densely populated parts of the country, and particularly the metropolitan areas—is consistent with the differences one would expect according to most sociological theories of crime causation, as well as from ordinary experience. On the other hand, as the Nottinghamshire example shows, variations in recording practices can have such a great effect on the totals produced as to render 'face value' comparisons almost meaningless. This underlines once again the necessity to treat all police figures with caution, as well as the point that they can nevertheless yield valuable insights when one probes closely into the practices which generate them.

CONTEXT AND RELATIVE RISK

A long-standing criticism of the presentation of official statistics (see, for example, McLintock and Avison 1968) has been that they do not give a clear picture of the social or situational context of crimes, or of the likelihood of different kinds of people becoming victims. For example, 'robbery' includes actions as diverse as an organized bank raid, the theft at knifepoint of the contents of a shopkeeper's till, and a drunken attempt to snatch a handbag from a woman in the street. Knowing that 95,000 robberies were recorded in 2000/2001, or that this represented an increase of 13 per cent over the previous year, tells us very little about the events, or whether different styles of robbery against different kinds of victim are declining or becoming more prevalent. Until recently, the only offences for which any attempt was made in *Criminal Statistics* to illustrate the context were homicide and offences involving firearms.[20] Information is regularly provided in homicide cases about the age and sex of the victim, the relationship between the principal suspect and the victim, and the method of killing used. For example, in 2000/2001 (as in most years) the highest victimization rate, expressed in terms of deaths per million population in each age group, was found among children under the age of one year (82 per million, against 15 per million overall); or, again, 42 per cent of female victims were killed by a current or former spouse, cohabitant or lover, most commonly by means of strangulation or a sharp instrument (Home Office 2001: 75–7).

The importance of providing 'context' has been increasingly recognized by the Home Office over recent years, and forms a key plank of the Simmons proposals, which will be discussed later. An important point to flag up here, however, is that with the development of sophisticated computer systems (such as 'STORM') for recording 'incidents', or 'calls for service' (i.e. mainly messages received by telephone or radio in police command and control centres), statistical analysts and researchers are beginning to look towards these, rather than *crime* records, as the key police source of information about the context or circumstances of offences.

TRENDS

Although graphic references to the frequency of offences (e.g., 'A burglary every 20 seconds') are not uncommon, the kinds of statistic most likely to feature in newspaper headlines are those referring to apparent *trends* in crime (e.g., 'Burglary up 20 per cent'). This makes it particularly important to understand issues relating to the measurement of change over time.

In many cases, figures wrongly presented as 'trends' refer only to a rise or fall

---

[20] There was, however, an experimental analysis of data (from a small number of forces) on offences of violence against the person in 1988 and 1989. For example, assaults recorded in 1988 and 1989 were classified into 'street brawls' (the largest group among offences in which the victim was male), 'pub brawls', 'attacks on a public servant', and 'domestic violence' (the largest group for female victims). Again, analysis of assaults recorded in 1990–92 indicated that 52 per cent of violent attacks on women (but only 19 per cent of those on men) took place in their own or the offender's home. In addition, members of both sexes were several times more likely to be assaulted if they were between the ages of sixteen and twenty-four than if they were over forty. While there are considerable doubts about the factual accuracy of these data (let alone the question of how much they reflect police decision-making and how much victim reporting), their publication in *Criminal Statistics* at least helped to draw wider attention to important questions about the relationships between gender, age, and violence (for further discussion of this topic, see the chapters by Heidensohn, and by Levi and Maguire, in this volume).

relative to the previous year, paying no attention to earlier years. Sometimes, too— a practice which, if used deliberately, is simply dishonest—commentators refer to a percentage fall or increase since a particular year, selecting as their baseline year one in which the official total had deviated significantly from the underlying trend. To take a concrete example, if one had stated at the end of 1992 that, 'Recorded burglaries have risen by 65 per cent since 1988', this would be factually correct, but it would be misleading not to point out that 1988 had produced one of the lowest recorded totals of burglary for many years and that, for example, the figure had risen by only 45 per cent since 1986.

To represent trends properly, then, it is necessary at the very least to use figures produced at regular intervals over a sufficient period of time. However, if we move to the other extreme and look at changes in recorded offences over a very long period, another set of problems associated with trend measurement comes into clearer view. Let us start by examining such changes over the full period during which official statistics have been collected, namely 1876–2001. As is shown in Figure 11.1, the broad picture indicated is one of little change until the 1930s, a clear rise up to and through the War, small falls in the early 1950s, then a sharp and sustained increase from the mid-1950s until the early 1990s, replaced since then by another period of mainly modest falls. (As will be explained later, the last three years in the Figure were affected by significant changes in coverage and counting rules.) The recent falls, however, should not obscure the central 'message' from the official statistics, that during the second half of the twentieth century there was a dramatic and unprecedented increase in crime in England and Wales—a message, it is important to note, similar to that which emerges from the official crime statistics in most other western democracies.[21]

To underline the apparent scale of this change, it is worth making some direct comparisons between the picture of crime painted by the official figures in the early 1950s and at the turn of the millennium. First of all, the annual totals of recorded offences are now more than ten times greater: over five million, compared with around half a million.[22]

The composition and patterning of the picture have also changed significantly. For example, thefts of or from motor vehicles, relatively rare in the 1950s when there were few cars on the roads, now make up almost a fifth of the total;[23] offences of criminal damage, then an almost negligible category, now make up nearly another fifth;[24] and crimes of violence against the person, although still one of the smaller categories, have greatly outstripped in growth other important groups such as sexual

[21] An interesting exception was Switzerland, which produced such low crime rates that a distinguished American criminologist (Clinard 1978) wrote a book attempting to explain why.

[22] The total number of notifiable offences recorded in 2000/2001 was 5,170,800. Even when the growth in population is taken into account, the increase has been well over eightfold, from 1.1 offences per 100 population in 1950 to 9.8 per 100 in 2000/2001.

[23] Between 1950 and 1954, thefts of or from vehicles averaged under 45,000 per year, around 9 per cent of all recorded offences. In 2000/2001 they totalled 968,400.

[24] Between 1950 and 1954, the average annual recorded total of 'malicious injuries to property' was just over 5,000. In 2000/2001, recorded offences of criminal damage totalled 960,100.

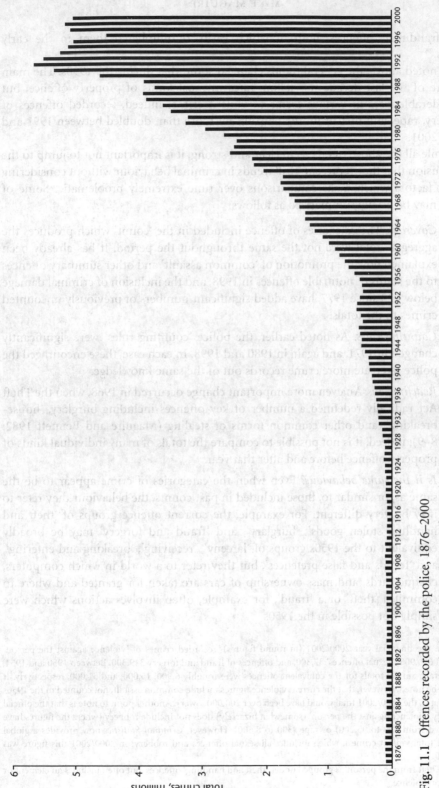

Fig. 11.1 Offences recorded by the police, 1876–2000

Source: Criminal Statistics, England and Wales 2000 (Home Office 2001)

Notes: From 1997 onwards, the Figure is based on statistics for each financial year (i.e. April to March). New counting rules and offence coverage changes have applied since 1998.

and fraudulent offences, both of which easily outnumbered them in the early 1950s.[25]

As noted above, the general trends changed somewhat during the 1990s. The main feature of the last decade was falling rates in most kinds of property offence, but considerable rises in various forms of violent crime. Indeed, recorded offences of robbery, rape, and theft from the person[26] all more than doubled between 1991 and 2000/2001.

While all the above trends seem clear and strong, it is important not to jump to the conclusion that they represent 'real' trends in criminal behaviour without considering many factors which make comparisons over time extremely problematic. Some of these may be briefly summarized as follows:

1. *Coverage.* The categories of offence included in the 'count' which produces the aggregate total were not the same throughout the period. It has already been explained how the promotion of 'common assault' and other summary offences to the status of notifiable offences in 1998, and the inclusion of criminal damage below £20 since 1977, have added significant numbers of previously uncounted crimes to the totals.

2. *Counting rules.* As noted earlier, the police 'counting rules' were significantly changed in 1971, and again in 1980 and 1998. In each case, these encouraged the police to create more crime records out of the same knowledge.

3. *Redefinitions.* An even more important change occurred in 1968, when the Theft Act radically redefined a number of key offences including burglary, 'house-breaking', and other common forms of stealing (Maguire and Bennett 1982: 8–9): indeed, it is not possible to compare the totals of many individual kinds of property offence before and after that year.

4. *Is it the same behaviour?* Even when the categories of crime appear to be the same as, or similar to, those included in past counts, the behaviour they refer to may be very different. For example, the current offence groups of 'theft and handling stolen goods', 'burglary', and 'fraud and forgery' may be broadly equivalent to the 1950s groups of 'larceny', 'receiving', 'breaking and entering', and 'frauds and false pretences', but they refer to a world in which computers, cheque cards, and mass ownership of cars are taken for granted and where to commit a 'theft' or a 'fraud', for example, often involves actions which were simply not possible in the 1950s.

[25] In the financial year 2000/2001 (in round figures), recorded crimes of 'violence against the person' totalled 600,900, 'sexual offences' 37,300, and offences of fraud and forgery 319,300. Between 1950 and 1954, the average annual totals for the equivalent offences were roughly 6,900, 15,000, and 31,000, respectively. It should be noted, however, that the current violence figures include common assault, not counted in the 1950s (without it, the 2000/2001 total would have been over 200,000 lower). Another point to note is that the official category 'violence against the person' (somewhat bizarrely) does not include robbery (where the figures have increased from 900 to 95,200) or rape (300 to 8,600). However, *Criminal Statistics* now provides a global figure ('total violent crime'), which includes all sexual offences and robbery: in 2000/2001 this figure was 733,400.

[26] 'Theft from the person' is grouped under 'theft and handling' offences, but often includes an element or threat of violence.

5. *Recording rates.* Even during periods when the 'counting rules' do not change, the actual behaviour of the police when receiving information about a pos sible crime may change markedly over time, thus raising or lowering the 'recording rate' (i.e. the percentage of such incidents which end up being recorded as crimes). This applies to how control-room staff deal with calls from the public, and how officers respond to incidents that they witness themselves, as well as to subsequent decision-making in crime management units. Such changes are often unintentional and unnoticed, but some observers have suggested that trends in crime figures are also subject to deliberate manipulation by the police (acting alone, or with the encouragement of others) in order, for example, to support arguments for more resources, justify changes in criminal justice policy, or divert attention from other social problems.[27] In an attempt to combat this problem, a new National Crime Recording Standard has been introduced in England and Wales from April 2002. This essentially asks police forces to adopt a 'prima facie' approach to reports of offences from the public, that is, to take at face value what the person reports, even if there is no sound evidence that an offence occurred. Simmons (2001) calculates that the change will lead to an artificial increase in crime rates of several percentage points, thus making trend measurement more difficult for some time.

6. *Reporting rates.* Changes in the 'reporting behaviour' of the public can have an even greater impact on crime trends. Decisions on whether or not to report possible offences to the police are influenced by a huge variety of factors, including views about the police and expectations of their response, the ease with which reports can be made (to which, for example, the spread of mobile telephones has made a difference), the number of victims with insurance policies (reporting being necessary to support a claim), levels of public tolerance of particular kinds of behaviour, and the break-up of traditional communities (both the last making people more inclined to call in the police rather than 'sort the problem out' themselves). All of these can change significantly over time (for further discussion, see Zedner, in Chapter 13 of this volume; Coleman and Moynihan 1996).

7. *At risk populations.* The size of the population 'at risk' of either offending or becoming a victim can change significantly over time. For this reason, *Criminal Statistics* presents many tables in the form of 'rates per 100,000 population'. Even so, as discussed earlier, it cannot simply be assumed that crime levels 'should' rise or fall in direct relation to rises or falls in population.

Awareness of these kinds of issues is a necessary starting point for interpreting trend data, as it assists one to begin to look for and make judgements about possible

---

[27] One advocate of this view, the American criminologist, Hal Pepinsky, showed how significant increases in crime could be created simply by assiduously recording every trivial offence that comes to light: for example, in a small unpublished study in one subdivision of a British city he showed that almost half the year's 'increase in crime' had been produced by the police recording every admission by a single offender who frequently stole milk bottles from doorsteps (see Pepinsky 1976 for similar research in the USA). On a wider scale, Selke and Pepinsky (1984) claimed that rises (and occasional falls) over time in crime figures in Indiana could be shown to coincide closely with shifts in the political needs of the party in power.

alternative explanations for particular changes. For example, the rising trend in recorded offences of rape referred to earlier might be partly explained by improvements in the treatment of victims and a greater willingness on the part of police officers to believe their accounts (see Zedner, in Chapter 13 of this volume)— developments which may have affected both reporting and recording behaviour. In order to investigate this possibility further, of course, it is necessary to seek evidence from other kinds of research.

More generally, it should be clear from the discussion throughout this section that the use of police-generated crime statistics to try to say virtually anything definite about crime—including its overall incidence, patterns, and trends—is a pursuit fraught with pitfalls. Such data are collected by busy people for a variety of purposes, not by researchers setting out to answer specific questions in a systematic way. And even aside from problems of validity, crime statistics simply do not contain some of the most important kinds of information that are now in strong demand by criminologists, researchers, policy-makers, crime analysts, members of crime and disorder partnerships, and others: notably, information about the 'context' of events that result in crime, and about the distribution of risks of victimization among different social groups. In the next section, we begin to look at alternative sources of knowledge, in particular the BCS.

CRIME SURVEYS

During the 1970s, in particular, it was a commonly held view among British criminologists that the continuing rise in crime figures was to a large extent an artefact of changes in reporting and recording practices. Indeed, as outlined earlier, a strong legacy of the 'deviancy' school was a deep scepticism about the value of *any* institutionally produced statistics. The extreme 'institutionalist' view was that there is anyway no such thing as an empirically measurable quantity of crime (for discussions of this view, see Coleman and Moynihan 1996; Bottomley and Coleman 1981).

Others maintained that that there may be a real (and in principle discoverable) 'dark figure' of criminal offences, and that trends do exist in the 'true' volume of crime, but that nothing can be deduced about these matters by looking at recorded offences. Even so, for many years these kinds of issues did not attract much interest outside the ranks of a few academics and statisticians.[28] In the final analysis, they were not considered very important: policy-makers, practitioners, and, indeed, many less theoretically-minded criminologists, would simply acknowledge the problem of the so-called 'dark figure' of crime, but then proceed as though it did not matter. However, as discussed earlier in the chapter, from the mid-1980s onwards the greatly increased attention paid to crime by politicians and the media made it more and more difficult for criminologists simply to ignore the apparently 'soaring' official crime rates: to make a useful contribution to wider debates, they had to find new ways of investigating and representing the 'crime situation'. Equally, major policy changes in

---

[28] On occasion, however, the 'institutionalist' argument was temporarily adopted by politicians and civil servants, who found it a useful way of deflecting criticism of the ineffectiveness of crime prevention policies!

relation to crime prevention, victims, and the management of criminal justice (also outlined earlier) contributed to a situation in which the quest for new, more detailed and better quality data took on increasingly high priority. A clear indication of the strength of these needs is the high status and success achieved by—and the level of investment in—crime surveys, the subject to which we now turn.

NATIONAL SURVEYS

In the mid-1960s, the first serious attempts were made to assess the extent of the 'dark figure' of crimes which were either not reported to the police or, having been reported, were not officially recorded by the police. Two substantial experimental surveys were conducted in the USA (Ennis 1967; Bidermann and Reiss 1967), wherein members of a random sample of households were asked whether anyone in the house had been the victim of a crime within the previous year and, if so, whether the matter had been reported to the police. A similar experiment was carried out in three areas of London in the early 1970s (Sparks, Genn, and Dodd 1977).

In both countries, despite the many methodological problems identified by the researchers, governments were sufficiently persuaded of the value of such surveys to invest considerable sums of money in running them officially on a large scale. In the USA, the Department of Justice funded regular surveys at both a national and a local level from 1972, while the first British Crime Survey (BCS) was undertaken by the Home Office in 1982 (Hough and Mayhew 1983). Many other European countries have followed suit. Indeed, since 1988 there have been several *international* crime victim surveys, in which similar questions are asked simultaneously of respondents in several different countries (see van Dijk *et al.* 1990; Mayhew *et al.* 1993; Van Kesteren *et al.* 2000).

Further 'sweeps' of the BCS (the radar metaphor consistently used by its authors) were conducted in 1984, 1988, 1992, 1994, 1996, 1998, 2000, and 2001. It is now an annual survey, and the size of the interview sample has been greatly increased—to 40,000 a year—in order to allow analysis of the results at the level of police force areas, rather than just at a national level. The main rationale for the survey—and, particularly, for its regular repetition—is that, by asking samples of the public to describe crimes committed against them within the past twelve months, the vagaries of crime reporting behaviour and police recording behaviour are neatly avoided, and the responses can be grossed up into a 'fuller' and hence, by implication, more 'valid' picture of crime and its trends in Britain.

To comment sensibly on the status of knowledge about crime derived from the BCS, it is necessary to know something about how its data are collected and compiled. The complex sampling techniques used[29] are aimed at producing representative cross-sections of (a) all private households in England and Wales, and (b) all individuals aged sixteen and over living in them. The basic format of the questionnaire, and the

[29] For the first three surveys, the households were selected from the Electoral Register, but since 1992 the Postcode Address File (PAF) has been used as the sampling frame, it being argued that this produces a better representation of the population: the Electoral Register may significantly under-represent young people, the unemployed, ethnic minorities, and those living in rented accommodation (Mayhew *et al.* 1993: 149–51).

framework for presenting the results, were established in the 1982 survey and have changed surprisingly little since. The interviews (which last on average around fifty minutes) are designed, first, to establish whether the respondents, or anyone else in their household, have been the victim of any of a list of specified crimes (described to them in ordinary language) within the past twelve months.[30] If any positive answers are received, interviewers complete a detailed 'Victim Form' for each incident.[31] The results are analysed to produce estimated national totals of both 'household offences' (such as burglary) and 'personal offences' (such as assaults), based on calculations using, respectively, the total number of households and the total adult population of England and Wales.[32] Finally, in addition to being asked about offences to which they have fallen victim, respondents currently answer questions from one of four 'Follow Up Modules', which elicit their views or attitudes on a variety of topics; and all those aged sixteen to fifty-nine are asked to complete 'self-interviewing questionnaires' directly on to a computer screen (which is not seen by the interviewers) on sensitive topics such as their own knowledge and use of illicit drugs, or their experience of domestic violence. Unlike the victim forms (which are used to measure trends as precisely as possible), the numbers of follow up forms, and the topics they cover, have changed significantly between different 'sweeps' of the BCS.

Relationships between police and BCS data

The offence categories produced by the BCS are shown in Table 11.3. The first important point to note is that by no means all are co-terminous with police categories. In fact, when making direct comparisons of 'official' and 'BCS' crime rates, only about three-quarters of the BCS-generated 'offences' can justifiably be used—the so-called 'comparable subset' (Kershaw et al. 2001).[33] Similarly, there are many categories of offence covered in the police-derived statistics which are not measured by the BCS. These include crimes against commercial or corporate victims (notably shop-lifting, burglary, and vandalism), fraud, motoring offences, and so-called 'victimless' crimes such as the possession of or dealing in drugs. In addition, sexual offences have so far been reported to BCS interviewers so infrequently that no reliable estimates of their

[30] In order to facilitate comparison with the previous year's official crime figures, the survey used to be conducted between January and April, people being asked to recall incidents within the previous calendar year. However, now that the police-generated figures cover the financial year (April to March), the need for this has disappeared and the BCS has moved to a 'rolling' programme of interviews in which people are asked simply about incidents occurring during the past twelve months. It should be noted that the analysis in this chapter is based only upon data collected in the 'old way' (i.e. on January–April interviews referring to the calendar year): in 2001, which was the 'changeover' year, the survey used both methods in order to test any differences in the results. In fact, it appears from early analysis that the methodological change has not significantly affected them (see Kershaw et al. 2001: 2 and Appendix B).

[31] Up to a maximum of six separate incidents. However, if the respondent reports a number of similar events involving the same offender, these may be treated as one 'series incident'.

[32] As the total interview sample deliberately includes an over-representation of households from denser urban areas (to maximize the chances of finding 'victims' to interview), the calculated victimization rates are weighted to take account of this (see Kershaw et al. 2001: 89). For the latest technical report on the BCS as a whole, see Bolling et al. 2002.

[33] Those not directly comparable are 'other household thefts' and 'other personal thefts'. The same used to apply to 'common assaults', but these have been included in police statistics since 1998 and are now therefore comparable.

Table 11.3 Estimated totals of offences in England and Wales 2000, as derived from the British Crime Survey and *Criminal Statistics*

	[BCS] N	[% of comparable offences]	[% of all BCS offences]	Police[1] N	[% of comparable offences]	[% of all recorded offences]
Comparable offences:						
Theft of/from vehicles	2,619,000	(27)	(20)	937,000	(37)	(18)
Vandalism private property	2,608,000	(26)	(20)	481,000	(19)	(9)
Burglary dwelling	1,063,000	(11)	(8)	409,000	(16)	(8)
Assault/wounding	2,307,000	(23)	(18)	388,000	(16)	(7)
Robbery	276,000	(3)	(2)	78,000	(3)	(1)
Theft from person	629,000	(6)	(5)	87,000	(3)	(2)
Bicycle theft	377,000	(4)	(3)	119,000	(5)	(2)
Subtotals	9,879,000	(100)	(77)	2,501,000	(100)	(48)
BCS offences not covered by/comparable with police data:						
Other household theft	1,616,000	***	(13)	***		
Other personal theft	1,404,000	***	(11)	***		
Subtotals	3,020,000	***	(23)	***		
Police-recorded offences not covered by/comparable with BCS:						
Other theft	***			917,000	***	(18)
Vandalism public/commercial property	***			481,000	***	(9)
Burglary not dwelling	***			440,000	***	(9)
Fraud and forgery	***			319,000	***	(6)
Other theft of/from vehicles[2]	***			148,000	***	(3)
Other violence/robbery[3]	***			146,000	***	(3)
Sex offences	***			37,000	***	(1)
Other	***			255,000	***	(5)
Subtotals	***			2,706,000	***	(52)
Totals	12,899,000		(100)	5,207,000		(100)

Adapted from Kershaw *et al.* (2001) and *Criminal Statistics England and Wales 2000*. All figures are rounded to the nearest 1,000.

[1] The figures shown in this column refer to offences recorded by the police in the financial year 2000/2001. They include approximately 36,000 offences recorded by the British Transport Police (BTP), which were not included in the officially published statistics. The totals of 'comparable' police-recorded offences reflect adjustments outlined by Kershaw *et al.* (2001: Appendix C) which involve, on the one hand, adding relevant BTP offences and, on the other, making reductions to allow for attempted thefts in which nothing was stolen and for cases where the victim was either an organization or institution, or was under 16 years old (i.e. types of offence not measured by the BCS). About 27,000 of the BTP offences were deemed to be comparable with BCS offences.

[2] Mainly thefts of and from commercial vehicles, and attempted thefts.

[3] Mainly assaults, robberies, and snatch thefts where the victim was under sixteen.

prevalence or incidence have been possible (although this may be remedied by the recent inclusion of self-completion forms on sexual attacks and 'stalking'). The main BCS schedule also excludes offences against victims under sixteen years old (though the 1992 'sweep' was designed to generate more information about these).

In other words, as their designers have always freely admitted (see, for example, Hough and Mayhew 1985: chapter 1), national surveys are much less successful in obtaining information about some types of incident than others. They do not produce an overall figure purporting to represent the 'total volume of crime', but concentrate instead upon selected categories of offence which are usually discussed individually or in sub-groups. The BCS, therefore, it cannot be too heavily stressed, provides *an alternative, rather than a directly comparable, overall picture of crime to that offered by police statistics*: it is 'fuller' than the latter in some respects, but 'narrower' in others.

Let us look first at the areas where the two data sets do overlap and then at the BCS 'picture of crime' in the round. The authors of the initial BCS (Hough and Mayhew 1983: 10) summarized the results of this exercise as follows:

Only for one category—thefts from motor vehicles—were the figures similar. For instance, the survey indicated twice as many burglaries as were recorded by the police; nearly five times as much wounding; twelve times as much theft from the person; and thirteen times as much vandalism (or criminal damage) . . . The overall ratio *for incidents which had been compared* was one in four. [emphasis added]

It will be noted from the first section of Table 11.3 that, though the proportions have changed somewhat, the general thrust of this statement also holds for the results of the 2001 survey. In 2000/2001, the total of notifiable offences recorded by the police in categories covered by the BCS was around two and a half million, whereas the BCS produced evidence to suggest that nearly 10 million offences of these kinds had been committed in the same year.

There is a strong temptation to interpret such figures as showing that there is 'four times as much crime' as the official records suggest: a trap into which many people have duly fallen. The problem lies in the wide variations between offences in terms of their reporting and (to a lesser extent) recording rates. For example, whereas an estimated 75 per cent of all 'burglaries with loss' that are reported to BCS interviewers end up in the official crime statistics, this is the case for only 10 per cent of 'common assaults' (Kershaw *et al.* 2001: Table 2.1). Such variations mean that the choice of offence groups to include in any comparison can significantly affect the overall ratio between the survey figures and the police figures. Indeed, if the comparison included survey data covering some of the offences in the final section of Table 11.3—let us say, estimates of instances of shoplifting or pilfering from work or cheque frauds, derived from surveys of employers or shopkeepers or bank employees—where the proportions which end up in police records are known to be tiny,[34] the overall 'dark figure' would emerge as a very much larger one. In this context, it is worth noting that the overall 'dark figure' estimated by Sparks *et al.* (1977) in their pioneering victim survey was one of *eleven* times the police figure, unlike the 'four times' estimate of the BCS. This is partly explained by the nature of the area surveyed and the particular

---

[34] See, for example, Martin (1962) and Levi (1993).

methodology used, but also by the different spread of offences covered. These remarks are highly pertinent to the difference between the 'image' of crime presented by the BCS and that presented by some *local* surveys, which will be discussed in the next section.

How, then, can we summarize the main picture of crime that has emerged from the BCS? First, the central message sent out by its authors during the initial passage of its results into the public domain was, in essence: the bad news is that there is a lot more crime than we thought, the good news is that most of it is not very serious. Their remark about 'the petty nature of most law-breaking' (Hough and Mayhew 1983: 33) was designed to deflect a possible moral panic in reaction to the huge amount of 'new' crime revealed by the survey, but it also reflected the key finding—supported by all surveys conducted since—that unreported crimes generally involve much lower levels of financial loss, damage, and injury than those reported to the police.[35]

Secondly, the series of 'sweeps' of the BCS, like most surveys in the USA, together suggest that, overall, increases in crime have been less dramatic than police figures suggest. Between 1981 and 2000, among the sub-set of offences which are comparable, the number of recorded crimes increased by 52 per cent, while those uncovered by the BCS rose by 22 per cent.

Thirdly, despite the above difference, the *basic shapes of the trends* displayed by both BCS and official crime statistics are roughly similar—that is, an increase to a peak in the early to mid-1990s, followed by some falls in the second half of the decade (see Figure 11.2). Indeed, a statistical analysis by Farrington and Langan (1998) of the

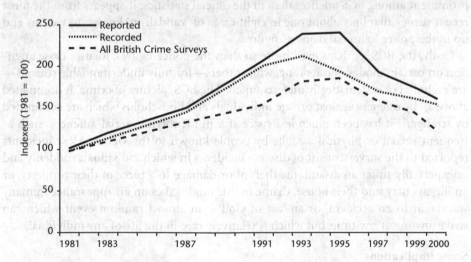

Fig. 11.2 Indexed trend in comparable crime, 1981 to 2000
Source: Kershaw *et al.* (2001).

---

[35] This message has been sent out less loudly latterly as the media and the public have become more used to the idea that there is a great deal of unrecorded crime. At the same time, the idea that 'minor' crime is of little importance has become less easy to sell to the public as the general level of tolerance for petty theft, vandalism and disorders appears to have fallen significantly since the early 1990s.

relationship between the two sets of data from 1981–1996 found that they were closely correlated in relation to all four categories of crime examined (vehicle theft, burglary, robbery, and assault). This is an important finding, which increases confidence in both sources of data.[36] At the same time, however, Figure 11.2 indicates some important differences which suggest that caution should be exercised in identifying short-term trends. Between 1987 and 1991, the increase in police-recorded crimes accelerated markedly, while that in the BCS-derived offences continued at its previous rate; interestingly, this position reversed itself over the next four years, to the extent that, between 1993 and 1995, the two sets of figures moved in opposite directions for the first time, the police totals falling while BCS figures rose. Based purely on the evidence of the table, the main reasons seem to be (a) a considerable increase during the late 1980s and early 1990s in the *reporting rate,* and (b) in the early to mid-1990s, a significant fall in the police *recording rate* (for more details, see Kershaw *et al.* 2001: 15–22). However, why these changes in victim and police behaviour should have occurred, is not easy to explain.

Fourthly, aside from the much larger totals of offences, the BCS produces a basic picture of crime not wildly dissimilar to that projected by police records: for example, both sets of figures are dominated by 'autocrime' and both indicate low levels of violent offences in relation to property offences. Of course, as emphasized above, there are many kinds of offence (notably those against organizations, as well as 'victimless' crimes) which do not appear in the BCS figures at all, but most of these constitute only small proportions of the totals of police-recorded crime. The main difference where directly comparable offences are concerned is that vandalism is more prominent among BCS offences than in the official statistics: it appears from the most recent survey that only about one in eight cases of 'vandalism' known to victims end up in the police 'criminal damage' figures.

Lastly, the BCS, perhaps even more so than the police figures, focuses close attention on certain modes of offending, while others—for fully understandable reasons—are excluded or systematically undercounted. The BCS 'picture of crime' is dominated above all by offences against private individuals and households which are committed by strangers: it has been much less successful in identifying 'serial' offences, such as frequent sexual or physical assaults by people known to the victim. Most incidents reported to the survey consist of discrete incidents in which individuals suddenly and unexpectedly suffer an assault, the theft of or damage to a piece of their property, or an illegal entry into their house. Crime in this mode takes on an appearance in many ways akin to an accident, or an 'act of God'—an almost random event which can strike anyone at any time, but which is relatively rare in the life of any individual.

Some implications

As noted above, the BCS findings on trends in crime have broadly supported the general message from the official crime statistics, that crime levels first rose and then fell back somewhat over the last two decades of the last century, albeit at more modest

---

[36] By contrast, however, a similar analysis of American data found much weaker correlations and, where assault was concerned, no systematic relationship at all between official and survey figures.

rates than those suggested by the police figures. One effect of the advent of the survey has been that few criminologists now take the extreme line that the inexorable 'increases in crime' indicated by official statistics up to the early 1990s were entirely an artificial creation of data collection processes. Most agree, at least, that the incidence of certain forms of criminal behaviour measured by the BCS did increase over this period: on the whole, visible predatory 'crimes of the poor' such as burglary and petty theft. This may not seem a surprise now, but it was a major step for many radical criminologists to take, and writers such as Jock Young, who developed the 'left realist' movement in the 1980s (see, for example, Matthews and Young 1986; Rock, in Chapter 2 of this volume), had to fight some major polemical battles with others on the left to establish his view that long-term increases in these kinds of crime were not only 'real' but had created a very serious social problem for the residents of deprived areas.

At the same time, however, BCS findings have at times diverged sufficiently far from police-generated statistics to reinforce continuing scepticism about the value of indications that either give of *short-term* trends in crime. Indeed, the implications of the divergence between them in the early 1990s, when considered alongside political developments at the time, could lead one to question very seriously whether the dramatic increases in recorded crime between 1990 and 1992—which helped to justify some major changes in criminal justice policy and sentencing practice, leading to a rapid increase in the prison population—ever 'really' happened.

Local surveys and the radical critique

While the BCS has achieved widespread respect among academics, as well as policy-makers, it has also attracted criticism. In the 1980s, especially, concerns about a tendency to distort 'real' experiences of crime—especially those of women, ethnic minorities, and the very poor—were raised by several critics, particularly those writing from a left realist or feminist perspective (see, for example, Matthews and Young 1986; Young 1988a; Stanko 1988; Genn 1988; Dobash and Dobash 1992). Such concerns also strongly influenced the design of a number of local crime surveys, funded mainly by left-leaning local authorities in inner-city areas.[37] These aimed to uncover areas of criminal behaviour not seriously touched by the BCS and, equally important, to examine and emphasize the extent to which victimization is unequally distributed among the population (see, for example, Kinsey 1984; Hanmer and Saunders 1984; Jones *et al.* 1986, 1987; Crawford *et al.* 1990).

By focusing chiefly upon inner-city districts, local crime surveys brought out much more vividly than the BCS the extent to which crime is concentrated in some small areas—predominantly those blighted by poverty—and, moreover, how particular forms of crime are suffered disproportionately by particular social groups within those areas. For example, the first Islington Crime Survey (Jones *et al.* 1986) indicated that a third of all households had been touched by burglary, robbery, or sexual assault within the previous twelve months: a situation quite different from that of the notional

---

[37] Since then, however, local surveys have been carried out in some different kinds of environment, including rural areas (Koffman 1996).

'statistically average' person referred to in the first BCS.[38] It also found that young, white females in the area were twenty-nine times more likely to be assaulted than white females aged over forty-five. As Young (1988b: 171) observed, such massive differences between subgroups illustrate 'the fallacy of talking of the problem of women as a whole, or of men, blacks, whites, youths, etc.'. Rather, he insisted, criminological analysis should 'start from the actual subgroups in which people live their lives'.

To be fair to the BCS, some aspects of the distribution of risk were considered from the start, and the very first report noted that council properties were more vulnerable than owner-occupied dwellings (Hough and Mayhew 1983). However, more prominence was given in the early reports to the findings that younger males, and people who frequently went out drinking, faced the highest risks of being assaulted. From these findings the Home Office authors concluded that the fears of street violence expressed by both women and the elderly (which were greater than those of young men) were to some extent 'irrational'. One of their main critics, Jock Young (1988b: 173–5) pointed out that such a conclusion, like their argument that fears are exaggerated because much crime is 'trivial' in terms of loss or injury, obscures the fact that what are 'objectively' similar events can have enormously different meanings and consequences for different people:

People differ greatly in their ability to withstand crime . . . The 'same' punch can mean totally different things in different circumstances . . . Violence, like all kinds of crime, is a social relationship. It is rarely random: it inevitably involves particular social meanings and occurs in particular hierarchies of power. Its impact, likewise, is predicated on the relationship within which it occurs . . . The relatively powerless situation of women—economically, socially and physically—makes them more unequal victims than men.

As the BCS authors admitted (Mayhew and Hough 1988; Percy and Mayhew 1997), later BCS 'sweeps' and reports benefited from such criticisms, and much more attention has since been paid to differential patterns of victimization. For example, 'booster' samples have been interviewed to explore the experiences of ethnic minorities (e.g., Mayhew et al. 1989).

Another major strand of criticism concerned the extent to which some forms of crime still remained largely 'hidden' to the BCS, even though questions were asked which apparently covered them. Efforts to put this right were central to the design of many local crime surveys. Particular efforts were made to find ways of obtaining more information about sexual and other assaults on women. These included less restrictive wording of questions, and emphasis on sensitive approaches to these topics in the training and selection of interviewers. The results stand in considerable contrast to the BCS findings: in the Islington survey, for instance (Jones et al. 1986), significantly

---

[38] In the first BCS report, it was calculated that a 'statistically average' person aged sixteen or over could expect to fall victim to: a robbery once every five centuries (excluding attempts); an assault resulting in injury (even if slight) once every century; a family car stolen or taken by joyriders once every sixty years; a burglary in the home once every forty years. The authors added that 'These risks can be compared with the likelihood of encountering other sorts of mishaps: the chances of burglary are slightly less than the chances . . . of a fire in the home; the chances a household runs of car theft are smaller than the chances . . . of having one of its members injured in a car accident' (Hough and Mayhew 1983: 15).

higher levels of sexual assault were found, while over one-fifth of reported assaults were classified as 'domestic'—more than twice the BCS proportion. Moreover, questions were asked about incidents which would not necessarily be classified by the police as 'crime' but may be experienced as serious by victims, namely sexual and racial 'harassment'. It was found, for example, that over two-thirds of women under the age of twenty-four had been 'upset by harassment' in the previous twelve months.

Various surveys of women, mainly conducted by feminist researchers, also found high levels of actual or threatened sexual violence. For example, Hanmer and Saunders (1984) found that 59 per cent of 129 women surveyed in Leeds had suffered some form of threat, violence, or sexual harassment within the previous year, and Hall (1985) and Radford (1987) produced even more startling figures. Among the most challenging of all was a survey by Painter (1991), based on a representative sample of over 1,000 married women, which suggested that 14 per cent had been raped by their husbands at some time during their marriage—over 40 per cent of them perceiving the incident as 'rape' at the time.[39]

Again, the BCS designers have made efforts to improve their results in such areas, and since 1994 computer-assisted self-interviewing forms have been used to ask about sensitive topics such as sexual attacks, domestic violence (Mirrlees-Black 1999), and stalking (Budd and Mattinson 2000), although it is likely that they do not gain the confidence of all respondents.

Lastly, an important illustration of the limitations of crime surveys of all kinds was provided by Hazel Genn (1988), in an exploration of the problem of 'multiple victimization'. Genn, who had been involved in a major pilot survey in some deprived areas of London (Sparks *et al.* 1977), later revisited (and temporarily lived with) some of the female respondents who had claimed to have been victimized many times. She gives an eye-opening account of the way that the lives of these women were blighted by frequent sexual and physical assaults, thefts, burglaries, and other forms of mistreatment, many of them from people with whom they had some sort of continuing relationship. Yet this kind of crime, she notes, is lost from view in most surveys, partly because they tend to impose artificial limits upon the number of crimes that can be counted for any one victim, and partly because such victims may be less likely than others to respond to the survey or to admit their victimization to interviewers. (Similar comments could be made about other marginalized groups—the homeless, the mentally ill, those who drift from bed-sitter to bed-sitter, and so on—whose voice is not often heard in the large surveys but who may also be subject to exceptionally high levels of victimization.) At the same time, Genn raises fundamental questions, touched on earlier in this chapter, about how meaningful it is to 'count' certain crimes at all. She writes:

In asking respondents about their experiences of crime, victim surveys have tended to use an approach which Skogan has termed 'the events orientation': that which conceptualizes

---

[39] The question used was 'Have you ever had sex with your present husband (or previous husband) against your will, when you had clearly insisted that you did not want to and refused your consent?'. This is a legal definition of rape, though despite court decisions which mean that a man can be convicted of raping his wife, it is unlikely that many police officers would arrest on allegations of refused consent by a wife living with her husband, without evidence of violence.

crime as *discrete incidents*. This ... can be traced back to one of the original primary objectives of victim surveys: the estimation of the 'dark figure' of unrecorded crime for direct comparison with police statistics. In order to accomplish this ... information obtained from victims had to be accommodated within a rigid 'counting' frame of reference. *Although isolated incidents of burglary, car theft or stranger attacks may present few measurement problems, for certain categories of violent crime and for certain types of crime victim, the 'counting' procedure leads to difficulties. It is clear that violent victimization may often be better conceptualized as a process rather than as a series of discrete events.* This is most evident in cases of prolonged and habitual domestic violence, but there are also other situations in which violence, abuse and petty theft are an integral part of victims' day-to-day existence. (1988: 91, emphasis added)

NEW DIRECTIONS: THE IMPLICATIONS OF THE SIMMONS REPORT

In July 2000, the Home Office published a wide-ranging and far-reaching discussion document by Jon Simmons, a manager from its Performance and Strategy Unit. Entitled *Review of Crime Statistics*, this sets out a vision, first of all, for 'police statistics of much greater depth and variety than in the past', combined with greater quality in the collection, analysis, and presentation of data (Home Office 2000: i). However, it goes beyond this to a much wider vision of a 'modernization' process, '[a revision of] the philosophy underlying the production of statistics', which has major implications for the future of crime data. In this, '19th century' aims and practices are replaced by 'a more flexible view of information—one where we first define the problems requiring solution and then develop the information needed to better understand those problems ... rather than rely on the routine statistics supplied in summary form by the police' (ibid.: ii).

The annual *Criminal Statistics*, Simmons recommends, should be discontinued, and replaced by an annual *Picture of Crime in England and Wales* incorporating data from a range of sources including police crime and incident data, the BCS, research studies, and information from other agencies and institutions. (There would be a parallel 'picture of the criminal justice system' to replace the court-based section of *Criminal Statistics*.) The traditional priority given to the measurement of 'trends in recorded crime' through the maintenance of long-running series of identical statistical tables would disappear. The central focus on legally-defined offences would also be weakened, more attention being given to social definitions of crime (through, for example, 'prima facie' approaches to recording—see below) and to non-crime events which cause concern to the public.

This document does not merely represent the author's personal views; it was the result of wide consultation and encapsulates much of current government and Home Office thinking about the role of statistical information in research, policy-making, and practice. It is therefore worth looking in a little more detail at some of the changes in aims and practices it envisages, drawing out their implications. Due to space limitations, we shall focus on just two areas: the possible end of the existing statistical series on notifiable offences; and the elevation of 'incident' data to a central plank of crime data.

THE END OF STATISTICAL SERIES?

The Simmons proposals aim to cut the cord that, for over a hundred years, has bound the annual collection and presentation of crime statistics to a standard list of 'notifiable offences' to which only occasional changes have been made. The main rationale for keeping change to a minimum has been the perceived need to ascertain 'trends' in crime by measuring, as far as possible, the 'same thing' year by year. However, as Simmons points out, the list of offences is simply a historical legacy which, looked at through contemporary eyes, seems rather arbitrary in character, excluding some offences that are arguably more serious, or cause more public concern, than some of those included. It has also to be asked whether there is any useful meaning attached to the aggregate total which is arrived at by simply adding together all the offences, serious and trivial, from each category in this diverse list—and hence whether an overall rise or fall in 'recorded crime' tells us anything useful about criminal behaviour, or about the performance of the police or government in tackling crime.

To replace the current list, Simmons recommends the introduction of a new 'national index' of crime, focusing on a much smaller set of offences (chosen after consultation with, among others, 'independent academics' and 'members of the media'). This, he suggests, should focus on 'the most serious crimes and the main high volume crimes', and should also avoid crimes such as drug offences which mainly originate from police activity rather than reports from the public. Its main purpose would be to allow a more realistic annual judgement of the government's and others' 'performance' in their crime reduction efforts.

Attractive as this idea may sound, it raises a number of questions. Whether the straightforward addition of all offences in a new index would produce a total any more 'meaningful' than the current system, is open to doubt (after all, changes in 'volume' offences would, as now, 'swamp' changes in more serious, but less numerous, offences).[40] More important, the smaller the list of offences that are used to measure

---

[40] This problem of minor offences 'counting' the same as major offences was recognized many years ago by Sellin and Wolfgang (1964), who devised a weighted index, based on the notional gravity of each recorded offence. Simmons (op. cit.: 63–4) toys with a similar idea, but the evidence from this earlier experiment is not greatly encouraging. Sellin and Wolfgang argued that weighting would allow more realistic comparisons of the seriousness of the crime problem, either over time or in different cities, states, or countries. They attached a different score to each category of crime, based upon ratings of seriousness derived from interviews with random samples of the population. They were encouraged to discover a fair degree of agreement among raters, both about the order in which they placed offences and the degree of difference in 'seriousness' between them. Various comparisons were carried out in the USA between changes in officially recorded crime rates and changes in 'crime rates' as measured by the Sellin-Wolfgang index. Some interesting results emerged—for example, Normandeau (1969) found some contrary trends in robbery in Philadelphia, as measured by the index and by the official Uniform Crime Rates—but at the end of the day, most criminologists abandoned it as both of dubious validity and dubious utility. Lesieur and Lehman (1975), for example, doubted whether seriousness is 'one kind of thing' that can be ordered along a scale as on a ruler, let alone whether adding up the scores would produce a total which had any meaning at all (see also Nettler 1978).

crime totals or trends, the more obvious it becomes that questions need to be asked about the reasons for including or excluding particular types. Clearly, the creation of such an index would have a powerful influence on the levels of attention and resources devoted by the police and other agencies to different kinds of crime, with major consequences for victims and offenders: if (to take an unlikely example) street violence was included but domestic violence was not, it is likely that more effort would be put into preventing the former, while more victims of domestic violence would be neglected. For this reason, it would be essential to ensure that the choices made accorded with general views about priorities. Simmons's criteria for selection, and his suggestions on who should be involved in the decisions, do not seem to have any strong logic to them, beyond the need to show that the government is not manipulating the choices for political reasons. To create public confidence in an index, it would have to be constructed on the basis of more transparent and principled criteria, such as degree of 'seriousness' or level of 'harm'—though even then it would be difficult to achieve consensus. For example, would it include various forms of 'white-collar' crime, which currently receive relatively little police attention but are arguably much more serious than some 'volume' offences such as shoplifting and theft from vehicles?

THE RISE OF INCIDENT DATA

The Simmons Report advocates the use of incident data as a baseline measure of criminal activity, to be 'read' in conjunction with figures on recorded crime. The author looks forward, somewhat ambitiously, to a time when the police 'ensure that *every* incident relating to crimes, allegations of crimes and also disorder that is brought to their attention is recorded as an incident (or "call for service")' (Home Office 2000: 19, original emphasis). Reports of incidents, he argues, should be treated on the 'prima facie' principle: that is, the victim's understanding of the incident should be 'completely and accurately reflected' in the original incident record, rather than allowing the police to decide that the report was mischievous or mistaken and should therefore be discounted (the 'evidential' principle). There should also be a traceable link in police records between every incident log and any crime record relating to the same incident, so that the degree of 'attrition' can be measured: that is, it can be seen how many allegations of crimes were, and were not, eventually recorded as crimes (and, if thought necessary, the reasons for the pattern can be investigated). Certainly, if achievable, this would go a long way to solving a major problem which presently blights comparisons of recorded crime rates between areas: the unknown differences in the kinds and degrees of police discretion used. However, the practical difficulties, first of all, of achieving 100 per cent recording of alleged incidents (particularly of those reported in person or observed by patrol officers, rather than reported by telephone) and then of linking them with crime records, are not to be underestimated (see Burrows *et al.* 2000).

A second major role that Simmons envisages for incident data is in the provision of fuller *contextual* information of practical use to policy-makers, both at central level and within local crime and disorder partnerships. He notes that *Criminal Statistics* has rarely (with the major exception of homicide data) moved beyond furnishing simple counts of broad offence types. To remedy this, he advocates the development of information systems which allow incidents to be broken down easily into socially (rather than just legally) meaningful categories and which provide information of the 'where, when, and how?' kind. He suggests a number of types of information that should be routinely recorded and analysed, including whether assaults were carried out by a stranger or an acquaintance, whether robberies were of personal or commercial property, and victims' views of the offender's motives and of the seriousness of the offence. He also encourages current developments in recording the postcodes or grid references of the locations of incidents, which can be used to 'map' crimes in order to identify 'hot spots' and differential risks of victimization. He does not see such analysis as limited to incidents involving 'crime' in the formal sense, but as including incidents of 'disorder' or other forms of non-criminal behaviour which create 'public concern'.

Lastly, Simmons looks forward to the implementation of systems of data collection in which a common incident record format is used by every police force, and records or part-records of *individual cases*, as opposed to simple statistical summaries, can be transferred electronically to the Home Office, hence allowing much more analysis to be undertaken centrally. This kind of process, incidentally, is already beginning to occur at a regional level, where electronic 'data warehouses' are being created from records provided not just by police forces but by other partner agencies.

SOME COMMENTS

Although they are still in their infancy, the above developments provide good illustrations of the theme explored in the early part of this chapter, that decisions about how to collect and present crime data do not occur in a vacuum: they have to respond to the changing demands of the 'consumers' of the information and to the dominant preoccupations of the day. In the rapidly changing and insecure societies of late modernity, there is no longer any strong demand for a crude general 'barometer' of the level of crime, constructed from simple counts of recorded offences (the fact that such figures are not reliable indicators of short-term trends is hardly a secret any more, and they are beginning to lose their sting as a political weapon). Instead, the demand at central government level now tends to be for more malleable and contextualized forms of information with which to assess and respond quickly to the new and highly specific 'problems' and 'risks' which emerge at frequent intervals to preoccupy the public, politicians, and media. And as the dispersal of responsibilities for crime control accelerates, especially through the development of multi-agency crime and disorder partnerships, demands are growing for more detailed information about small local areas rather than the country (or even police force areas) as a whole. Equally, in the managerialist culture which now pervades the public sector, precise information is demanded for monitoring the performance of agencies against increasingly specific targets. Some important questions about the long-term implications of these changes will be raised at the end of the chapter.

THE OFFENDER POPULATION

Throughout this chapter we have looked at crime mainly from the point of view of those who experience it and of those who chart its incidence, the focus being upon how often, where, and against whom it is known and perceived to occur. Of course, what is glaringly absent from the discussion so far is information about the perpetrators of all these crimes. While it is important to conclude our account with some comments on this topic, these will be kept to a minimum, partly to avoid trespassing too much upon the territory of other authors in this volume, and partly because the collection of data about offenders has been relatively neglected as the focus of attention has shifted towards victims and offence patterns.

ADJUDICATED OFFENDERS

Just as the annual statistics compiled by the police produce an 'official' account of the extent of crime, the statistics compiled from court records and police cautioning records produce a picture of all those officially held responsible for recorded offences.

In looking at all those convicted of or cautioned for indictable offences in any given year, the first point to note is that their total is very much lower than the total of offences recorded. In 2000, for example, about 325,000 people were sentenced in court and a further 151,000 were cautioned—small figures compared with the recorded crime total of over five million offences. Even taking into account that some offenders are held responsible for more than one crime, this means that only around one in ten offences recorded by the police that year resulted in a caution or conviction: in other words, in the vast majority of cases, nothing was officially known about those responsible. Of course, if one uses BCS results to bring into the picture crimes which are not reported to the police, the 'attrition rate' becomes even more striking: for example, based on data from 1997, it has been estimated that only about three in 100 crimes against individuals or their property lead to an offender being convicted or cautioned for the offence (Barclay and Tavares 1999: 29).

Such findings caused a considerable amount of political and media concern when they were first published, questions being asked about the effectiveness of the police and others in bringing offenders to justice. However, we are more interested here in their implications for our knowledge about offenders. Obviously, with such a large 'unknown', it cannot simply be assumed that the characteristics of 'offenders' as a whole can be inferred from those of adjudicated offenders—a central point to which we shall return in a moment. First, though, let us look at the official figures.

Among the 476,000 offenders convicted or cautioned for indictable offences in 2000, 80 per cent were male, and 41 per cent were under the age of twenty-one. The 'peak age' of offending—that is, the age at which people had the highest risk of acquiring a conviction or caution—stood at eighteen for males and fifteen for females (Home Office 2001: 104). While 42 per cent of males convicted of a standard list offence were first offenders, at the other extreme 17 per cent were highly 'recidivist' offenders, having been convicted ten or more times previously.

Another, more detailed, picture of adjudicated offenders—in this case, the sub-group thought to have offended seriously enough to warrant detention in a custodial institution—is provided by analysis of information held in prison records. The most obvious characteristic of the prison population is its 'maleness': despite rapid increases in the numbers of women imprisoned in the 1990s, they still made up only 94 per cent of the average daily prison population in 2000 (see Morgan, in Chapter 30 of this volume).

The most detailed breakdown of the social characteristics of the custodial population was provided by the National Prison Survey (Walmsley *et al.* 1992). This sampled 10 per cent of all male, and 20 per cent of all female, prisoners over the age of seventeen held in custodial institutions in England and Wales in early 1991.[41] Like the sentenced and cautioned population, the prison population was shown to be predominantly young: excluding juveniles in both cases, 62 per cent of inmates were aged below thirty, compared with 25 per cent of the general population. Disproportionate numbers of prisoners were also found to come from ethnic minorities: 15 per cent of male prisoners and as many as 23 per cent of female prisoners described themselves as black or Asian.[42] Where social class was concerned, 41 per cent of males had had unskilled or partly skilled jobs, compared with 18 per cent of the general population.

Other striking findings included the revelation that over a quarter of prisoners had at some time been in local authority care (compared with an estimated 2 per cent of the general population); 40 per cent of male prisoners had left school before the age of sixteen (compared with 11 per cent of all British males); and 13 per cent had been 'of no fixed abode' before coming into prison (for further details, see Morgan, in Chapter 30 of this volume).

Taken overall, these data clearly illustrate that the social characteristics of people who are arrested and processed by the criminal justice system—and particularly of offenders who are eventually sent to prison—present a very different pattern from that found in the general population. There are many more males, young people, black people, poor people, poorly-educated people, and people with disturbed childhoods than one would find in a random sample.

SELF-REPORT STUDIES

Of course, as pointed out above, if only about 3 per cent of known crimes end in a conviction or caution, it is important to ask whether the other 97 per cent are likely to have been committed by a similarly skewed section of the population (or, indeed, by the very same people). This is the province of self-report studies—the technique by which samples of the population are asked in confidence whether they have

---

[41] The survey included remand prisoners as well as those convicted, so was not strictly speaking a sub-group of all adjudicated offenders (a relatively small proportion will subsequently have been found not guilty).

[42] For a full discussion of the massive over-representation of black people in prisons in the USA and England and Wales, see Tonry (1994). Hood (1992), Smith (1997), and Bowling and Phillips (this volume) provide more general discussions of the disproportionate black–white ratios, and the probable extent of racial bias, at each stage of the criminal justice process.

committed crimes, including those for which they have not been caught. On the one hand, these suggest that crime is committed by a much larger proportion of the population than is officially held responsible for it. On the other hand, survey respondents who have previously been in trouble with the law tend to admit to both more serious and more frequent offending behaviour than people who have never been convicted.

Depending upon the age, sex, and other social characteristics of those questioned, as well as upon the wording of the questions, self-report studies have generally found that between 40 and almost 100 per cent will admit to having committed at least one criminal offence during their lifetime. Most such studies have used samples of young males, often schoolchildren or students. For example, in one of the best early studies, Elmhorn (1965) found that 92 per cent of a random sample of teenage schoolboys in Stockholm admitted to at least one offence, while 53 per cent admitted to at least one 'serious' offence (roughly the equivalent of an indictable crime in Britain), principally theft. More recently, the first international self-report survey indicated that consistently high proportions of young people across a range of developed countries had committed at least one criminal offence (Junger-Tas *et al.* 1994). Self-report studies of adults—particularly studies with a sound methodology—are rarer, although there are some useful data from a sample of twenty-two to twenty-five-year-olds which was included in the British version of the international survey, conducted by the Home Office (Graham and Bowling 1995), as well as from the cohort used in the long-term studies of delinquency carried out by Cambridge University. Farrington (1989) reported that 96 per cent of the Cambridge cohort—which, it should be stressed, contains a higher than average proportion of working-class urban males—admitted to having committed at least one criminal offence by the age of thirty-two. The Home Office survey found that nearly a third of twenty-two to twenty-five-year-old males (though only 4 per cent of females) admitted to committing a criminal offence within the previous year (Graham and Bowling 1995: 25). Moreover, these figures exclude drug offences, which would have increased them considerably.

However, the authors of the above studies, like most other researchers in the field (e.g., Short and Nye 1958; Christie *et al.* 1965; Huizinga and Elliott 1986; see also Farrington 1973), found that much smaller proportions of respondents admitted to large numbers of offences, or frequent offending. Thus, for example, Graham and Bowling (1995) found that over a quarter of all offences admitted by fourteen- to twenty-five-year-olds were committed by just 3 per cent of offenders. Equally, when one looks at the more serious offences, the numbers admitting to participation fall substantially.[43]

In sum, the general conclusion reached over twenty years ago by Hood and Sparks (1970: 51), after a summary of results of self-report studies from several countries, seems to remain valid today: 'While it may be correct to say that to commit one or two delinquent acts is "normal behaviour" for boys, to be involved in frequent criminal acts is apparently relatively rare.' An important qualification, however, is that self-report

---

[43] In the British self-report survey, for example, only 7 per cent of males aged fourteen to twenty-five admitted to having committed, within the past year, any of a sub-set of the most serious offences asked about (car theft, bag snatching, burglary, robbery, fighting, arson, assault and wounding).

studies have generally covered a limited range of offences, chiefly the less serious forms of street crime. Many, too, have included vaguely defined 'delinquent' or 'anti-social' acts, such as 'defying parents' authority' or 'a fist fight with one other person' (Short and Nye 1958), which would be unlikely to qualify as crimes if reported to the police. These features of their methodology have played a part in one of the most controversial issues surrounding the results of self-report studies, that of the social class of offenders.

Social class

The argument was started in earnest by the publication of Short and Nye's (1958) study, which indicated that middle-class boys were as likely as lower-class boys to be involved in delinquent acts, despite the fact that adjudicated offenders are predomin-antly working-class. This finding, supported by some (but contradicted by other) subsequent studies, suggested that there must be some major form of class bias in the processes of arrest and prosecution by which offenders come to official notice. A lively debate ensued over many years, focusing particularly on the reliability of the research methodologies employed. Questions were raised about the representativeness of the samples used, the suitability of the method of administering the questions (for example, self-completion questionnaires, as opposed to face-to-face interviews, may elicit a fuller response from middle-class than working-class people), the doubtful status as 'crime' of many of the acts asked about, the possibility of respondents telling lies, and, indeed, the definition of 'lower class'—including the possible significance of differences between the urban and the rural working classes (for more detailed accounts of these problems and the related arguments, see Hood and Sparks 1970; Braithwaite 1979; Bottomley 1979; Hindelang *et al.* 1979, 1981; Bottomley and Pease 1986; Coleman and Moynihan 1996).

One of the most thorough reviews of the evidence was provided by Braithwaite (1979), who analysed forty-one self-report studies as well as over 250 other studies concerning the relationship between social class and crime. He concluded that, although the evidence was often contradictory and confusing, although police bias probably exaggerates the relative extent of working-class delinquency, and although self-report studies tend to exaggerate the relative extent of middle-class delinquency, the following statements may be made with some confidence:

1. Lower-class adults commit *those types of crime which are handled by the police* at a higher rate than middle-class adults.
2. Adults living in lower-class areas commit *those types of crime which are handled by the police* at a higher rate than adults who live in middle-class areas.
3. Lower-class juveniles commit crime at a higher rate than middle-class juveniles.
4. Juveniles living in lower-class areas commit crime at a higher rate than juveniles living in middle-class areas. (Braithwaite 1979: 62, emphasis added)

The use of the phrase '*those types of crime which are handled by the police*' is telling here. Braithwaite's care with words underlines the point that the offences covered in the studies to which he refers are chiefly the common and visible predatory street offences like burglary and 'autocrime'—almost by definition the 'crimes of the poor'—which occupy a high proportion of police attention, rather than the more hidden kinds of crime which happen within the private spheres of the commercial world or within the household. In this case, it might be unsurprising that surveys reveal them to be committed more often by poorer people!

The most recent British contribution to the debate is the Home Office survey mentioned above, which confirmed the common finding—at least, among surveys based on self-completion questionnaires—of no significant association between social class and admissions to offending as a whole, but of a strong association, for both males and females, between social class and admissions of more serious offending (Graham and Bowling 1995: 33–5).

Race and gender

There is insufficient space here to do justice to debates about the complex and controversial issue of race and crime, which is tackled by Bowling and Phillips in Chapter 17 of this volume (see also Smith 1997). It will merely be noted in passing that perhaps the most interesting finding on this topic from a methodological (as well as sociological) point of view is that, despite the relatively high proportions of black people who are prosecuted and imprisoned, there tend to be few differences between black and white respondents in terms of offences admitted to self-report studies: to what extent this reflects 'reality' (and hence biases in the criminal justice system) and to what extent it arises from the unreliability of the self-report method, remains unclear.[44] However, we shall examine a little more closely what is perhaps the most interesting phenomenon of all to emerge from statistics on offenders, no matter what their source: the overwhelming preponderance of males over females.

This imbalance seems to be a universal feature of the criminal justice records of all modern countries, enduring over time, and confirmed by self-report studies and other research methods (Heidensohn 1985 and in Chapter 15 of this volume). It happens, for example, that the male–female ratio of convictions was almost precisely the same in 1992 as in 1892 (Home Office 1993)—although the picture changed a little over the 1990s, with a disproportionate increase in female convictions and, particularly, imprisonment (Heidensohn, and Morgan, in Chapters 15 and 30 respectively of this volume). Gender differences are also apparent when one looks at the types of offence for which males and females are convicted. For example, 66 per cent of all females convicted in England and Wales in 1994 had been charged with theft or handling stolen goods, compared with 39 per cent of males; on the other hand, convictions for burglary or drugs offences were relatively infrequent among female defendants (Home Office 1995: 115).[45]

[44] For discussion and evidence on this issue, see Smith (1997); Bowling and Phillips, this volume; Graham and Bowling (1995); and Hindelang et al. (1981). The last study caused considerable debate through its finding that black males were three times less likely than white males to admit (to researchers) having committed offences which they were already 'known' (from official records) to have committed. This involved a technique known as a 'reverse record check', which is used to test the memory of survey respondents and/or their willingness to admit to crime.

[45] The equivalent proportions for burglary were 2 per cent compared with 11 per cent, and for indictable drugs offences they were 7 per cent compared with 15 per cent.

The argument that the official statistics grossly distort the 'true picture' and that a huge amount of female crime remains 'hidden' finds little evidence to support it. Where 'traditional' property crime is concerned, the Home Office self-report survey found, for example, that males were, respectively, eight, six, and four times more likely than females to admit to having committed burglary, car theft, and theft from vehicles (Graham and Bowling 1995: 13). Moreover, as Heidensohn (1989: 87) rightly points out:

There is little or no evidence of a vast shadowy underworld of female deviance hidden in our midst like the sewers below the city streets. As we have become increasingly aware in modern times, *quite the opposite is true*. There is a great deal of crime which is carefully hidden from the police, from families, friends and neighbours. Much of this takes the form of domestic violence, the abuse of children both physically and sexually, incest and marital rape. *The overwhelming majority of such cases involve men*, usually fathers and husbands injuring or abusing their wives and children. (emphasis added)

Similar points can be made about another major area of crime which remains largely unrevealed by both police statistics and conventional crime surveys, that of corporate crime. As few women are in the high-level positions from which markets can be manipulated or business frauds perpetrated, it is safe to assume that this genre of crime, too, is overwhelmingly a male province.

Discussion

To sum up, there now appears to be relatively little dispute about the broad validity of the general picture, as reflected in the official statistics, of the relative 'contribution' as offenders of males and females; but there is much more argument about the relative contributions of other major social groups, particularly black people and white people, and people from different social classes. Where the persistent commission of common predatory street offences is concerned, it is true, both 'official' and 'self-reported' offenders emerge with a broadly similar profile (partly, one may presume, because few persistent burglars or car thieves succeed in escaping conviction entirely). However, this does not alter the vital point that, just as victim surveys are vastly more effective in revealing 'hidden' instances of some kinds of crime than of others, so the perpetrators of different kinds of offence are not equally well 'revealed' through the medium of self-report studies. Thus, while respondents tend to be asked in great detail about the relatively visible kinds of anti-social activity which are associated with the court appearances of adolescents, they are not often asked whether they have assaulted their partners or sexually abused their children, nor whether they have perpetrated a significant financial fraud. In many of the studies conducted, of course, there would have been little point in asking such questions, as the samples were drawn from groups of young males rather than being representative of the population as a whole. If a way could be found of overcoming the methodological and ethical problems of expanding self-report studies into such sensitive areas, the results might well support the indications from some (also methodologically problematic) victim surveys, that the perpetrators of intra-family violence and abuse are much more evenly distributed throughout the population (see, for example, Morgan 1988; Morgan and

Zedner 1992; Dobash and Dobash 1992; though for scepticism on this point, see Levi and Maguire, in Chapter 22 of this volume). And without doubt, they would confirm that the social class distribution of people involved in business fraud is skewed in a different direction to that of burglary and street robbery.

SUMMING UP

This chapter has covered a great deal of ground, and it may be helpful to finish by drawing together some of the key themes that have emerged. These can be grouped as six main points:

1. The last twenty or so years have seen a 'data explosion' in the crime field. The high levels of interest and investment that have made this possible can be explained in a variety of ways, but are clearly linked with the emergence of crime (and fear of crime) as a key issue of public, media, and political concern in late modern societies around the world. The high media profile of the 'crime problem', together with significant changes in perceptions and understandings of how and by whom it should be responded to, have created major demands, not just for more data, but for new and different kinds of data. As they are produced, these new data feed back into the process, creating new concerns and demands.

2. Driven to some extent by the growth of policy interest in victims and in situational crime prevention, as well as by the continuing dispersal of responsibility for crime control and by managerialist demands for information to help monitor agencies' 'performance', the main focus of attention (and hence of data collection and analysis) has shifted away from offenders towards the circumstances of offences, from the national to the local, and from the general to the specific.

3. The traditional source of crime data associated with the 'modern' period—the standard statistical series of notifiable offences published in *Criminal Statistics*—has become increasingly irrelevant to this changed environment and new demands. Not only are police-generated crime statistics increasingly viewed as too vulnerable to the vagaries of reporting and recording behaviour to produce reliable 'pictures' of crime and trends in crime, but they consist of simple counts of large heterogeneous categories of offences, about which they provide little or no contextual information. Furthermore, the purpose and value of regularly quoting to the public largely meaningless global figures of recorded crimes are beginning to be seriously doubted. The Simmons Report proposes their replacement by a new 'national index', composed of a relatively small number of selected offence types, to act as both the main 'headline' measure of crime and as a key indicator of performance in crime reduction. A question to ponder here is whether such a move might replace one measuring rod which is too inflexible with another that can be too easily bent into a particular shape. In particular, might it lead eventually to the 'problem of crime' being perceived

in essence as one narrow band of offence types, and to particular groups of offenders being targeted ever more intensively? If so, the focus would most likely be on various kinds of 'street crime' and their generally socially deprived perpetrators, while other, more hidden—but arguably more damaging—criminal activities became increasingly ignored.

4. Other developments which offer potentially richer sets of data for the presentation of information about crime include the expansion of the BCS to allow it to measure crime (and hence police 'performance') at police force level; more systematic recording of police 'incident' data (or 'calls for service'), which are seen as a better reflection than recorded crime of the kinds of incident which the public perceive as criminal behaviour worthy of police attention; and data from other agencies such as hospitals (for alternative measures of the incidence of assaults) or fire services (for better data on arson). These help to distinguish between different types of behaviour covered by a broad legal category (e.g., street as opposed to post office robbery), and allow analysis as well as mere description. The amount and sophistication of analysis will also grow as data from different sources are increasingly combined in 'data warehouses', 'mapped' via grid references, and so on—developments being actively encouraged by the new regional 'crime reduction directors' who have been appointed to facilitate the work of local crime and disorder partnerships.

5. Most of this 'data explosion' has occurred in relation to offences rather than offenders. Knowledge about offending behaviour itself, about how offenders understand and exploit criminal opportunities, about the interactions between offenders, about how they perceive and respond to risk, and indeed—despite occasional self-report surveys—about the size and composition of the 'offender population' and 'hidden' offending by people not convicted, remains patchy, much of it gleaned through small-scale qualitative research projects. There has been little investment in research into these kinds of areas since the 1970s: at present, most funded offender-based research is concerned with whether reconvictions are reduced by particular interventions, which, though useful for guiding policy, tells us little about the 'reality' of criminal behaviour.

6. Overall—particularly as represented in the Simmons Report—it seems that thinking about the collection and presentation of 'official' crime data is moving away from the traditional focus on strict *legal* definitions of offences (as in the statistics on recorded offences) towards more flexible, pragmatic, and policy-driven approaches and a willingness to work with *social* definitions of crime. This is encapsulated in the encouragement of a '*prima facie*' as opposed to 'evidential' approach to the recording and counting of crime incidents (Burrows *et al.* 2000; Home Office 2000): in other words, if the victim perceives an act as robbery then the incident is (and remains) recorded as a robbery. It is also to be seen in the instruction to police forces following the Stephen Lawrence case, that they should record an offence as 'racially motivated' if the victim states a belief that it was so motivated, even if there is no evidence of this. In a slightly different form, it is seen in suggestions (again in the Simmons Report) that the police

should record and count incidents (such as loutish behaviour) about which members of the public express concern, even if no crime has been committed. If 'incident' data, rather than recorded crime, eventually come to be regarded as the primary police source of statistics about the level of crime, the widespread adoption of this principle could have a major impact upon how 'crime' is perceived and responded to.

Selected further reading

Understanding Crime Data, by Clive Coleman and Jenny Moynihan (Buckingham: Open University Press, 1996), is the best recent British textbook on the subject, and covers in more depth several of the main issues discussed in this chapter. It has the added advantage of accessibility and a light and humorous touch. Despite their much greater age, both *Understanding Crime Rates*, by Keith Bottomley and Clive Coleman (Farnborough: Saxon House, 1981) and *Crime and Punishment: Interpreting the Data*, by Bottomley and Ken Pease (Milton Keynes: Open University Press, 1986) are theoretically informed and illuminating books of high quality. *Interpreting Crime Statistics*, edited by Monica Walker (Oxford: Oxford University Press, 1995) contains some useful chapters on specialized data such as prison statistics and homicide.

The annual publication, *Criminal Statistics England and Wales*, published by the Home Office, should still be required reading for all students who wish to start exploring the subject. It is not simply a list of tables, but contains succinct and informative commentary on a wide range of topics. I also strongly recommend Gordon Barclay's and Cynthia Tavares's *Digest of Information on the Criminal Justice System in England and Wales* (4th edn, London: Home Office, 1999), which provides an excellent 'user friendly' summary of key statistics, using coloured graphs, bar charts, and pie charts, and is excellent as a quick reference source. A key discussion of the future of criminal statistics, to which extensive reference has been made in this chapter, is the *Review of Criminal Statistics: A Discussion Document*, by Jon Simmons (London: Home Office, 2000).

The other essential reading, of course, is the summary reports of findings from the British Crime Survey, the most recent at the time of writing being *The 2001 British Crime Survey* (Home Office Statistical Bulletin 18/01), by Chris Kershaw and others. In addition to the main reports, there are many other reports based on analysis of particular parts of the BCS. Interesting examples include the findings from computer-assisted self-interviewing forms, covering sensitive topics such as domestic violence (see Mirrlees-Black 1999) and stalking (Budd and Mattison 2000). The international crime survey (Van Kesteren *et al.* 2000) adds another dimension. One of the most interesting self-report studies is John Graham's and Ben Bowling's *Young People and Crime* (London: Home Office, 1995), while the first international self-report survey is also worth a look (Junger-Tas *et al.* 1994). More generally, the Home Office website is now a mine of information on crime-related statistics of all kinds, and most of its main publications can be downloaded.

References

AMIR, M. (1971), *Patterns in Forcible Rape*, Chicago, Ill.: University of Chicago Press.

AUDIT COMMISSION (1993), *Tackling Crime Effectively*, London: Audit Commission.

BAKER, A., and DUNCAN, S. (1985), 'Child Sexual Abuse: A Study of Prevalence in Great Britain', *Child Abuse and Neglect*, 9: 457–67.

BARCLAY, G., and TAVARES, C. (1999), *Digest 4—Information on the Criminal Justice System in England and Wales*, London: Home Office.

BECKER, H.S. (1963), *Outsiders: Studies in the Sociology of Deviance*, London: Macmillan.

BENNETT, T., and WRIGHT, R. (1984), *Burglars on Burglary*, Aldershot: Gower.

BIDERMANN, A.D., and REISS, A.J. (1967), 'On Explaining the "Dark Figure" of Crime', *Annals of the American Academy of Politics and Social Science*, November.

BLACK, D.J. (1970), 'The Production of Crime Rates', *American Sociological Review*, 35, 4: 733–48.

BOLLING, K., CLEMENS, S., LOYD, R., SMITH, P., and TURTLE, J. (2002), *2001 British Crime Survey England and Wales: Technical Report*, London: BRMB.

BOTTOMLEY, A.K. (1979), *Criminology in Focus*, London: Martin Robertson.

—— and COLEMAN, C.A. (1981), *Understanding Crime Rates*, Farnborough: Saxon House.

—— and PEASE, K. (1986), *Crime and Punishment: Interpreting the Data*, Milton Keynes: Open University Press.

BOTTOMS, A.E. (1995), 'The Philosophy and Politics of Punishment and Sentencing', in C. Clarkson and R. Morgan (eds), *The Politics of Sentencing Reform*, Oxford: Clarendon Press.

BOWLBY, J. (1944), 'Forty-four juvenile thieves', *International Journal of Psychoanalysis*, 25: 1–57.

—— (1953), *Childcare and the Growth of Love*, Harmondsworth: Penguin.

BRAITHWAITE, J. (1979), *Inequality, Crime and Public Policy*, London: Routledge and Kegan Paul.

BRANTINGHAM, P.J., and BRANTINGHAM, P.L. (1975), 'The spatial patterning of burglary', *Howard Journal*, 14, 2: 11–23.

BRODY, S. (1976), *The Effectiveness of Sentencing*, Home Office Research Study No. 35, London: HMSO.

BUDD, T., and MATTINSON, J. (2000), *The Extent and Nature of Stalking: Findings from the 1998 British Crime Survey*, Research Study No. 210, London: Home Office.

BURROWS, J., TARLING, R., MACKIE, A., LEWIS, R., and TAYLOR, G. (2000), *Review of Police Forces' Crime Recording Practices*, Home Office Research Study No. 204, London: Home Office.

BURT, C. (1944), *The Young Delinquent*, London: University of London Press.

CARR-HILL, R. (2000), 'Developing a robust resource allocation formula for police', *Policing and Society*, 10: 235–61.

CHRISTIE, N., ANDENAES, J., and SKIRBEKK, S. (1965), 'A Study of Self-reported Crime', in K.O. Christiansen (ed.), *Scandinavian Studies in Criminology*, London: Tavistock.

CLARKE, R.V.G. (1980), 'Situational Crime Prevention: Theory and Practice', *British Journal of Criminology*, 20: 136–47.

—— and HOUGH, M. (1984), *Crime and Police Effectiveness*, Home Office Research Study No. 79, London: HMSO.

—— and MAYHEW, P. (eds) (1980), *Designing Out Crime*, London: HMSO.

CLINARD, M. (1978), *Cities with Little Crime*, Cambridge: Cambridge University Press.

COHEN, L.E., and FELSON, M. (1979), 'Social Change and Crime Rate Trends: a Routine Activity Approach', *American Sociological Review*, 44: 588–608.

COHEN, S. (1972), *Folk Devils and Moral Panics*, London: Paladin.

—— (1974), 'Criminology and the Sociology of Deviance in Britain', in P. Rock and M. McIntosh (eds), *Deviance and Social Control*, London: Tavistock.

COLEMAN, C., and MOYNIHAN, J. (1996), *Understanding Crime Data*, Buckingham and Philadelphia, Pa.: Open University Press.

CORNISH, D.B., and CLARKE, R.V.G. (1986), 'Situational Prevention, Displacement of Crime and Rational Choice Theory', in K. Heal and G. Laycock (eds), *Situational Crime Prevention: From Theory into Practice*, London: HMSO.

CRAWFORD, A., JONES, T., WOODHOUSE, T., and YOUNG, J. (1990), *Second Islington Crime Survey*, London: Middlesex Polytechnic.

DAVIS, R., LURIGIO, A., and SKOGAN, W. (eds) (1997), *Victims of Crime*, New York: Sage.

DITTON, J. (1977), *Part-time Crime*, London: Macmillan.

DOBASH, R.E., and DOBASH, R.P. (1979), *Violence against Wives*, London: Tavistock.

—— and —— (1992), *Women, Violence and Social Change*, London: Routledge.

ELKINS, M., and OLAGUNDAYE, J. (2001), *The Prison Population in 2000: A Statistical Review*, Findings 154, London: Home Office.

ELMHORN, K. (1965), 'Study in Self-reported Delinquency Among School Children in Stockholm', in K.O. Christiansen (ed.), *Scandinavian Studies in Criminology*, London: Tavistock.

ENNIS, P. (1967), *Criminal Victimization in the United States: A Report of the National Survey*, Washington, DC: US Government Office.

ERICSON, R., and HAGGERTY, K. (1997), *Policing the Risk Society*, Oxford: Oxford University Press.

ERIKSON, K.T. (1964), 'Notes on the Sociology of Deviance', in H.S. Becker (ed.), *The Other Side: Perspectives on Deviance*, New York: Free Press.

FARRINGTON, D.P. (1973), 'Self-reports of Deviant Behaviour: Predictive and Stable?', *Journal of Criminal Law and Criminology*, 64: 99–110.

—— (1989), 'Self-reported and Official Offending from Adolescence to Adulthood', in M.W. Klein (ed.), *Cross-national Research in Self-reported Crime and Delinquency*, Dordrecht: Kluwer.

—— (1995), 'The development of offending and antisocial behaviour from childhood: Key findings from the Cambridge Study in Delinquent Development', *Journal of Child Psychology and Psychiatry*, 36: 929–64.

—— (2002), 'Key findings from the first 40 years of the Cambridge Study in Delinquent Development', in T.P. Thornberry and M.D. Krohn (eds), *Longitudinal Research in the Social and Behavioural Sciences*, New York: Kluwer/Plenum.

—— and DOWDS, E.A. (1985), 'Disentangling Criminal Behaviour and Police Reaction', in D.P. Farrington and J. Gunn (eds), *Reaction to Crime: The Public, The Police, Courts and Prisons*, Chichester: John Wiley.

—— and LANGAN, P. (1998), *Crime and Justice in the United States and in England and Wales 1981–96*, Washington DC: Bureau of Justice.

FEELEY, M., and SIMON, J. (1992), 'The New Penology', *Criminology*, 39, 4: 449–74.

FERRI, E. (1913), *The Positive School of Criminology*, Chicago, Ill.: C.H. Kerr.

FOUCAULT, M. (1977), *Discipline and Punish: The Birth of the Prison*, London: Allen Lane.

GARLAND, D. (1995), 'Penal Modernism and Postmodernism', in T. Blomberg and S. Cohen (eds),

Punishment and Social Control, New York: Aldine de Gruyter.

—— (1996), 'The Limits of the Sovereign State: Strategies of Crime Control in Contemporary Society', *British Journal of Criminology*, 36, 4: 445–71.

—— (2001), *Punishment and Control*, Oxford: Oxford University Press.

GAROFALO, R. (1914), *Criminology*, Boston, Mass.: Little, Brown.

GENN, H. (1988), 'Multiple Victimization', in M. Maguire and J. Pointing (eds), *Victims of Crime: A New Deal?*, Milton Keynes: Open University Press.

GRAHAM, J.G., and BOWLING, B. (1995), *Young People and Crime*, Home Office Research Study No. 145, London: HMSO.

HAIR, J., ANDERSON, R., TATHAM, R., and BLACK, W. (1998), *Multivariate Data Analysis*, New York: Prentice Hall.

HALL, R. (1985), *Ask Any Woman: A London Enquiry into Rape and Sexual Assault*, Bristol: Falling Wall Press.

HALL, S., CUTCHER, C., JEFFERSON, T., and ROBERTS, B. (1978), *Policing the Crisis*, London: Macmillan.

HANMER, J., and SAUNDERS, S. (1984), *Well-founded Fear*, London: Hutchinson.

HARRINGTON, V., and MAYHEW, P. (2001), *Mobile Phone Theft*, Home Office Research Study No. 235, London: Home Office.

HEAL, K., and LAYCOCK, G. (eds) (1986), *Situational Crime Prevention: From Theory into Practice*, London: HMSO.

HEIDENSOHN, F.M. (1985), *Women and Crime*, London: Macmillan.

—— (1989), *Crime and Society*, London: Macmillan.

HINDELANG, M., HIRSCHI, T., and WEIS, J. (1979), 'Correlates of Delinquency: the Illusion of Discrepancy between Self-report and Official Measures', *American Sociological Review*, 44: 995–1014.

——, —— and —— (1981), *Measuring Delinquency*, Beverly Hills, Cal.: Sage.

HOME OFFICE (1971), *Instructions for the Preparation of Statistics Relating to Crime*, London: HMSO.

—— (1993), *Criminal Justice Statistics 1882–1892*, Home Office Statistical Findings 1/93, London: Home Office Research and Statistics Department.

—— (1995), *Digest 3: Information on the Criminal Justice System in England and Wales*, London: Home Office Research and Statistics Department.

—— (2000), *Review of Criminal Statistics: A Discussion Document*, London: Home Office, 2000.

—— (2001), *Criminal Statistics in England and Wales 2000*, Cmnd 5312, London: Home Office.

HOOD, R. (1992), *Race and Sentencing: A Study in the Crown Court*, Oxford: Clarendon Press.

—— and SPARKS, R. (1970), *Key Issues in Criminology*, London: Weidenfeld and Nicolson.

HOUGH, J.M., and MAYHEW, P. (1983), *The British Crime Survey*, Home Office Research Study No. 76, London: HMSO.

—— and —— (1985), *Taking Account of Crime: Key Findings from the Second British Crime Survey*, Home Office Research Study No. 85, London: HMSO.

HOUGH, M., and TILLEY, N. (1998), *Auditing Disorder: Guidance for Local Partnerships*, Crime Detection and Prevention Series No. 91, London: Home Office.

HUIZINGA, D., and ELLIOTT, D.S. (1986), 'Reassessing the Reliability and Validity of Self-report Measures', *Journal of Quantitative Criminology*, 2: 293–327.

JONES, T., MACLEAN, B., and YOUNG, J. (1986), *The Islington Crime Survey: Crime, Victimization and Policing in Inner City London*, Aldershot: Gower.

——, LEA, J., and YOUNG, J. (1987), *Saving the Inner City: The First Report of the Broadwater Farm Survey*, London: Middlesex Polytechnic.

JUNGER-TAS, J., TERLOUW, G., and KLEIN, M. (1994), *Delinquent Behaviour Among Young People in the Western World: First Results of the International Self-Report Delinquency Study*, Amsterdam: Kugler.

KEMSHALL, H., and MAGUIRE, M. (2001), 'Public Protection, Partnership and Risk Penality: The Multi-Agency Risk Management of Sexual and Violent Offenders', *Punishment and Society: The International Journal of Penology*, 5, 2: 237–64.

—— and —— (2002), 'Community Justice, Risk Management and the Role of Multi-Agency Public Protection Panels', *Journal of Community Justice*, 1.

KERSHAW, C., CHIVITE-MATTHEWS, N., THOMAS, C., and AUST, R. (2001), *The 2001 British Crime Survey*, Home Office Statistical Bulletin 18/01, London: Home Office.

KINSEY, R. (1984), *Merseyside Crime Survey: First Report*, Liverpool: Merseyside Metropolitan Council.

KITSUSE, J.I. (1964), 'Societal Reactions to Deviant Behavior: Problems of Theory and Method', in H.S. Becker (ed.), *The Other Side: Perspectives on Deviance*, New York: Free Press.

—— and CICOUREL, A.V. (1963), 'A Note on the Uses of Official Statistics', *Social Problems*, 11: 131–9.

KOFFMAN, L. (1996), *Crime Surveys and Victims of Crime*, Cardiff: University of Wales Press.

LESIEUR, H.R., and LEHMAN, P.M. (1975), 'Remeasuring Delinquency: a Replication and Critique', *British Journal of Criminology*, 15: 69–80.

LEVI, M. (1981), *The Phantom Capitalists: The Organization and Control of Long-Firm Fraud*, London: Heinemann.

—— (1993), *The Investigation, Prosecution and Trial of Serious Fraud*, Research Report No. 14, London: Royal Commission on Criminal Justice.

—— and PITHOUSE, A. (1992), 'The Victims of Fraud', in D. Downes (ed.), *Unravelling Criminal Justice*, Basingstoke: Macmillan.

LONGLEY, P., GOODCHILD, M., MAGUIRE, D., and RHIND, D. (2001), *Geographic Information Systems and Science*, New York: John Wiley & Sons.

McCABE, S., and SUTCLIFFE, F. (1978), *Defining Crime: A Study of Police Decisions*, Oxford: Blackwell.

McLINTOCK, F., and AVISON, N.H. (1968), *Crime in England and Wales*, London: Heinemann.

MAGUIRE, M. (1991), 'The Needs and Rights of Victims of Crime', in M. Tonry (ed.), *Crime and Justice: a Review of Research*, 14: 363–433, Chicago, Ill.: University of Chicago Press.

—— in collaboration with BENNETT, T. (1982), *Burglary in a Dwelling: The Offence, the Offender and the Victim*, London: Heinemann Educational Books.

—— and CORBETT, C. (1987), *The Effects of Crime and the Work of Victims Support Schemes*, Aldershot: Gower.

—— and JOHN, T. (1996), *Intelligence, Surveillance and Informants: Integrated Approaches*, Police Research Group Crime and Prevention Series, Paper No. 64, London: Home Office.

—— and —— (1996a), 'Covert and Deceptive Policing in England and Wales: Issues in Regulation and Practice', *European Journal of Crime, Criminal Law and Criminal Justice*, 4: 316–34.

—— and PONTING, J.E. (eds) (1988), *Victims of Crime: A New Deal?*, Milton Keynes: Open University Press.

Mars, G. (1982), *Cheats at Work*, London: Allen and Unwin.

Martin, J.P. (1962), *Offenders as Employees*, London: Macmillan.

Matthews, R., and Young, J. (eds) (1986), *Confronting Crime*, London: Sage.

Mattinson, J., and Mirrlees-Black, J. (2000), *Attitudes to Crime and Justice: Findings from the 1998 British Crime Survey*, Home Office Research Study No. 200, London: Home Office.

Maxfield, M.G. (1984), *Fear of Crime in England and Wales*, Home Office Research Study No. 78, London: HMSO.

Mayhew, P., Clarke, R.V.G., Sturman, A., and Hough, J.M. (1976), *Crime as Opportunity*, Home Office Research Study No. 34, London: HMSO.

——, Elliott, D., and Dowds, L. (1989), *The 1988 British Crime Survey*, Home Office Research Study No. 111, London: HMSO.

—— and Hough, J.M. (1988), 'The British Crime Survey: Origins and Impact', in M. Maguire and J. Pointing (eds), *Victims of Crime: A New Deal?*, Milton Keynes: Open University Press.

—— and Aye Maung, N. (1992), *Surveying Crime: Findings from the 1992 British Crime Survey*, Home Office Research and Statistics Department, Research Findings No. 2, London: HMSO.

——, —— and Mirrlees-Black, C. (1993), *The 1992 British Crime Survey*, Home Office Research Study No. 132, London: HMSO.

Mirrlees-Black, C. (1999), *Domestic Violence: Findings from a new British Crime Survey Self-Completion Questionnaire*, Home Office Research Study No. 191, London: Home Office.

Morgan, J. (1988), 'Children as Victims', in M. Maguire and J. Pointing (eds), *Victims of Crime: A New Deal?*, Milton Keynes: Open University Press.

—— and Zedner, L. (1992), *Child Victims: Crime, Impact and Criminal Justice*, Oxford: Oxford University Press.

Murphy, P., Williams, J., and Dunning, E. (1990), *Football on Trial: Spectator Violence and Developments in the Football World*, London: Routledge.

Nettler, G. (1978), *Explaining Crime*, New York: McGraw-Hill.

Normandeau, A. (1969), 'Trends in Robbery as Reflected by Different Indexes', in T. Sellin and M.E. Wolfgang (eds), *Delinquency: Selected Studies*, New York: Wiley.

Painter, K. (1991), *Wife Rape, Marriage and the Law: Survey Report*, Manchester: Faculty of Economic and Social Science, University of Manchester.

Pearson, G. (1987), *The New Heroin Users*, Oxford: Blackwell.

Pease, K. (1988), *Judgements of Offence Seriousness: Evidence from the 1984 British Crime Survey*, Research and Planning Unit Paper No. 44, London: Home Office.

Pepinsky, H. (1976), 'Police patrolmen's offence reporting behaviour', *Journal of Research in Crime and Delinquency*, 13: 33–47.

Percy, A., and Mayhew, P. (1997). 'Estimating Sexual Victimization in a National Crime Survey: A New Approach', *Studies in Crime and Crime Prevention*, 6, 2: 125–50.

Pratt, J. (1995), 'Dangerousness, Risk and Technologies of Power', *Australian and New Zealand Journal of Criminology*, 29: 236–54.

Prime, J., White, S., Liriano, L., and Patel, K. (2001), *Criminal careers of those born between 1953 and 1978*, Statistical Bulletin 4/01, London: Home Office.

Radford, J. (1987), 'Policing Male Violence', in J. Hanmer and M. Maynard (eds), *Women, Violence and Social Control*, London: Macmillan.

Read, T., and Oldfield, D. (1995), *Local Crime Analysis*, Crime Detection and Prevention Series, Paper 65, London: Home Office.

Reppetto, T. (1974), *Residential Crime*, Cambridge, Mass.: Ballinger.

Rock, P. (1973), *A Sociology of Deviance*, London: Hutchinson.

—— (ed.) (1988), 'The History of British Criminology', Special Issue of the *British Journal of Criminology*.

Selke, W., and Pepinsky, H. (1984), 'The Politics of Police Reporting in Indianapolis 1948–78', in W.J. Chambliss (ed.), *Criminal Law in Action*, New York: Wiley.

Sellin, T., and Wolfgang, M.E. (1964), *The Measurement of Delinquency*, New York: Wiley.

Shapland, J., Willmore, J., and Duff, P. (1985), *Victims in the Criminal Justice System*, Aldershot: Gower.

Short, J.F., and Nye, F.I. (1958), 'Extent of Unrecorded Juvenile Delinquency', *Journal of Criminal Law, Criminology and Police Science*, 49: 296–302.

Simmons, J. (2000), *Review of Crime Statistics: A Discussion Document*, London: Home Office.

—— (2001) *An Initial Analysis of Police Recorded Crime Data to end of March 2001 to Establish the Effects of the Introduction of the ACPO National Crime Recording Standard*, London: Home Office website.

SMITH, D. (1997), 'Ethnic origins, crime and criminal justice', in M. Maguire, R. Morgan, and R. Reiner (eds), *The Oxford Handbook of Criminology*, 2nd edn, Oxford: Oxford University Press.

SPARKS, R. (1992), *Television and the Drama of Crime*, Buckingham: Open University Press.

——, GENN, H., and DODD, D. (1977), *Surveying Victims*, Chichester: John Wiley.

STANKO, E. (1988), 'Hidden Violence against Women', in M. Maguire and J. Pointing (eds), *Victims of Crime: A New Deal?*, Milton Keynes: Open University Press.

SUTHERLAND, E.H. (1949), *White-collar Crime*, New York: Holt, Rinehart and Winston.

TAYLOR, I., WALTON, P., and YOUNG, J. (1975), *The New Criminology*, London: Routledge and Kegan Paul.

TONRY, M. (1994), 'Racial Disproportion in US Prisons', in R. King and M. Maguire (eds), *Prisons in Context*, Oxford: Oxford University Press.

VAN DIJK, J.J.M., MAYHEW, P., and KILLIAS, M. (1990), *Experiences of Crime Across the World: Key Findings of the 1989 International Crime Survey*, The Hague: Ministry of Justice.

VAN KESTEREN, J., MAYHEW P., and NIEUWBEERTA, P., (2000), *Criminal Victimisation in Seventeen Industrial Countries*, The Hague: WODC.

VON HENTIG, H. (1948), *The Criminal and his Victim*, New Haven, Conn.: Yale University Press.

WALKER, M. (ed.) (1995), *Interpreting Crime Statistics*, Oxford: Oxford University Press.

WALKER, N.D. (1971), *Crimes, Courts and Figures: An Introduction to Criminal Statistics*, Harmondsworth: Penguin.

WALKLATE, S. (1989), *Victimology: The Victim and the Criminal Justice System*, London: Unwin Hyman.

WALLER, I., and OKIHIRO, N. (1978), *Burglary: the Victim and the Public*, Toronto: University of Toronto Press.

WALMSLEY, R., HOWARD, L., and WHITE, S. (1992), *The National Prison Survey 1991: Main Findings*, Home Office Research Study No. 128, London: HMSO.

WEST, D.J., and FARRINGTON, D.P. (1969), *Present Conduct and Future Delinquency*, London: Heinemann.

—— and —— (1973), *Who Becomes Delinquent?*, London: Heinemann.

WINCHESTER, S., and JACKSON, H. (1982), *Residential Burglary*, Home Office Research Study No. 74, London: HMSO.

WOLFGANG, M. (1959), *Patterns in Criminal Homicide*, Philadelphia, Pa.: University of Pennsylvania Press.

YOUNG, J. (1971), *The Drugtakers*, London: Paladin.

—— (1986), 'The Failure of Radical Criminology: The Need for Realism', in R. Matthews and J. Young (eds), *Confronting Crime*, London: Sage.

—— (1988a), 'Radical Criminology in Britain: The Emergence of a Competing Paradigm', *British Journal of Criminology*, 28, 2: 289–313.

—— (1988b), 'Risk of Crime and Fear of Crime: a Realist Critique of Survey-based Assumptions', in M. Maguire and J. Pointing (eds), *Victims of Crime: A New Deal?*, Milton Keynes: Open University Press.

YOUNG, M. (1991), *An Inside Job*, Oxford: Clarendon Press.

12

MEDIA MADE CRIMINALITY

THE REPRESENTATION OF CRIME IN THE MASS MEDIA

Robert Reiner

CRIME IN THE MEDIA: SUBVERSION, SOCIAL CONTROL, OR MENTAL CHEWING GUM?

Mass media representations of crime, deviance, and disorder have been a perennial cause of concern. Two competing anxieties can be discerned in public debate, and both are reflected in a large research literature. On the one hand the media are often seen as fundamentally subversive, on the other as a more or less subtle form of social control.

Those who see the media as subversive see media representations of crime themselves as a significant cause of offending. This has been a constantly recurring theme of that 'history of respectable fears' which Geoffrey Pearson has traced back through the last few centuries (Pearson 1983). At the end of the eighteenth century, for example, the Middlesex magistrate Patrick Colquhoun claimed that crime was rising because 'the morals and habits of the lower ranks in society are growing progressively worse' (Radzinowicz 1956: 275). He attributed this in part to an alleged wave of bawdy ballad singers who went around entertaining in pubs. He regarded suppression of these as counter-productive, so he urged the government to sponsor rival groups of wholesome ballad singers. He was confident that these eighteenth century precursors of Sir Cliff Richard and Dame Vera Lynn would soon supplant their bawdy brethren in popularity and influence.

A different concern about media representations of crime has worried liberals and radicals (Wykes 2001). To them the media are the cause not of crime itself but of exaggerated public alarm about law and order, generating support for repressive solutions. A fundamental theme of the radical criminologies of the 1960s and 1970s was the power of the mass media to foment fears about crime and disorder (Cohen 1972; Cohen and Young 1973; Hall *et al.* 1978). Within the field of media studies the influential 'Cultural Indicators' project has for three decades monitored the damaging consequences of media representations of violence for democratic institutions (Gerbner 1970, 1995).

In their ideal-typical form these perspectives are polar opposites, sharing in common only their demonization of the media, whether as a subversive threat to law, order, and morality, or as an insidious form of social control paving the way to authoritarianism by cultivating exaggerated fears about criminality. Each has generated huge research industries conducting empirical studies of media content, production, and effects (Leishman and Mason 2002).

Because of the difficulties in rigorously establishing straightforward causal relationships between images and effects, some researchers tacitly imply that media images of crime do not have significant implications. This often provokes the canard that media researchers are blinkered by libertarian prejudices. For example, Melanie Phillips has claimed that 'for years, media academics have pooh-poohed any link between violence on screen and in real life' (1996: 2). She denounced the supposed 'cultural studies orthodoxy that media images have no direct influence on behaviour . . . such images merely provide "chewing gum for the eyes" '(ibid.). It is of course a non sequitur to move from the denial of a *direct* influence to the assertion of *no* influence, and this portrait of media studies 'orthodoxy' is a caricature. Nonetheless it does point uncomfortably to the way some opponents of censorship have interpreted the complexity of the relationship between images and behaviour as a warrant for implying that there is none at all.

This chapter reviews the broad contours of empirical research, theorization, and policy debates about crime and the media. It is organized in terms of three interrelated issues that have been the primary foci of research: the *content, consequences*, and *causes* of media representations of crime. Each has been the basis for a voluminous literature attempting to analyse the content, effects, and sources of media images of crime. These are phases of an intertwined process that can only be separated artificially. Analysis of content always presupposes criteria of relevance in interpreting and coding aspects of communication. The categories of content are chosen because of an implicit assumption that they are significant because of their effects. Creators of media products, whether their primary motives are commercial, political, moral, or aesthetic, hope to achieve some audience response. The consequence of media images depends on how content is interpreted by different audience sections, and this often involves attempting to assess the meaning of the text intended by authors.

Texts, audiences, and authors are interdependent. The organization of this chapter into the three main sections of causes, content, and consequence should be taken as a presentational convenience rather than implying hermetically sealed areas. I will begin with a review of the vast literature on the content of representations of crime. I will then look at the extensive research attempting to assess the consequences of media images in terms of audience attitudes and behaviour. Following this I will turn to the attempts to understand content by studying production processes. In the concluding section I will assess the implications of the detailed research for the alternative views of the significance of the mass media representation of crime that were outlined earlier.

THE CONTENT OF MEDIA IMAGES OF CRIME

PROBLEMS OF CONTENT ANALYSIS

Most analyses of the content of mass media have been within a positivist paradigm. As defined by one leading practitioner: 'content analysis is a method of studying and analyzing communications in a systematic, objective, and quantitative manner for the purpose of measuring certain message variables' (Dominick 1978: 106). While 'content analysis' so-called has been colonized by this positivist and quantitative approach, it may be distinguished from the more general project of the analysis of content. The claim made for traditional content analysis is that it 'provides for an objective and quantitative estimate of certain message attributes, hopefully free of the subjective bias of the reviewer' (ibid.: 106–7). Dominick goes on to concede that 'inferences about the effects of content on the audience are, strictly speaking, not possible when using only this methodology. More importantly, the findings of a particular content analysis are directly related to the definitions of the various content categories developed by the researcher. The validity of these definitions is an important consideration in the evaluation of any content analysis' (ibid.).

There are major problems with the claim that traditional content analysis is 'objective'. While the categories used to quantify 'certain message attributes' may be free of 'subjective bias' they are neither randomly plucked out of thin air, nor do they miraculously reflect a structure of meaning objectively inherent in the texts analysed. They always embody some theoretical presuppositions by the researcher about criteria of significance. Moreover, while content analysis indeed cannot justify 'inferences about the effects of content on the audience', the categories selected for quantification tacitly presuppose some theory about likely consequences. There would be little purpose in studying media texts without a presupposition that the meanings conveyed by them have an impact on audience beliefs, values, or practices. The common tactic in content analyses (e.g., Pandiani 1978; Surette 1998: 47–51, 69–70) of contrasting the pattern of media representations of crime and criminal justice with the 'real world' picture (supposedly conveyed by official statistics), is only of interest on the assumption that this 'distortion' leads to problematic consequences such as excessive fearfulness or support for vigilantism. Meticulously counting units of 'violence' is not a form of train-spotting for sadists but motivated by concern that exposure to these images carries risks such as desensitization, or heightened anxiety. Thus the 'objectivity' of traditional content analysis lies in the precision of the statistical manipulation of data, but the categories used necessarily presuppose some theory of meaning, usually about likely consequences (Sparks 1992: 79–80).

There is a further fundamental problem with traditional content analyses. They collate 'message attributes' according to characteristics set *a priori* by the observer. But what in the abstract may seem to be the 'same' image may have very different meanings within particular narrative genres and contexts of reception. How viewers interpret images of 'violence', for example, is not just a function of the amount of blood seen or number of screams heard. The same physical behaviour, for instance a shooting, means different things to any viewer depending on its placement in different genres, say whether it is news, a Western, a war film, or a contemporary cop show. It will be interpreted differently if the violence is perpetrated on or by a character constructed in the narrative as sympathetic. How audiences construe violence will vary according to their own position vis-à-vis the narrative characters, quite apart from any preferred reading intended by the creators or supposedly inscribed in the narrative (Livingstone *et al.* 2001). For example, to black audiences, Rodney King, whose beating by Los Angeles police officers was captured on an amateur videotape, was a victim of police racism, while to many white police officers he appeared to be a threatening deviant who invited the beating (Lawrence 2000: 70–73).

This does not mean that quantification is necessarily misleading. Any reading of content, even an avowedly qualitative one, implies some quantification, contrasting observed behaviour with an assumed norm, for example reading a character as 'brave' or 'strong'. Nor should the statistical manipulation of such categories be ruled out. The questions raised are about the claims of positivist content analysis to quantify in a value-free way aspects of a supposed objective structure in texts. Counting features of texts should be self-consciously seen as based on the observer's frame of reference, according to explicit criteria. Results must be interpreted reflexively and tentatively as one possible reading. As such, they can yield valuable insights and questions about the significance of trends and patterns.

CONTENT ANALYSIS: A REVIEW OF RESULTS

Most analyses of the content of media representations of crime have focused on news—print and broadcast—although there are also many studies of fiction. Crime and criminal justice have long been sources of popular spectacle and entertainment, even before the rise of the mass media. This is illustrated by the genre of criminal biography and pre-execution confessions and apologias, of various degrees of authenticity, which flourished in the seventeenth and eighteenth centuries (Faller 1987; Rawlings 1992; Durston 1996). Similar accounts continue to the present day, filling the 'true crime' shelves of bookshops (Rawlings 1998; Peay 1998; Wilson 2000: chapter 4), and they have been joined by the many volumes retelling the exploits of legendary cops as if they were fictional sleuths (e.g., Fabian 1950, 1954). On the side of overtly fictional crime narratives, ultra-realism (often a quasi-documentary style of presentation) has been common (using such devices as voice-overs giving precise dates and locations, and acknowledgements to the files of Scotland Yard and similar legendary police organizations as the source of stories).

The fact/fiction distinction has become more fluid in recent years, with the emergence of what is usually referred to as 'reality' television or 'infotainment' (Fishman and Cavender 1998; Surette 1998: 70–80; Beckett and Sasson 2000: 111–16; Leishman and Mason 2002: chapter 7). There has been the growth of programming such as *Crimewatch UK* that recreates current cases, often with an avowed purpose of solving them (Dobash *et al.* 1998). Fly-on-the-wall footage of actual incidents has proliferated in documentaries like Roger Graef's pioneering 1981 Thames Valley Police series (Gregory and Lees 1999), and entertainment programming based on real cops in action, for example *Cops* (Doyle 1998; Kooistra *et al.* 1998). Live newscasts of particular occurrences are increasingly common, such as the O.J. Simpson car chase and subsequent trial. Film footage of criminal events in process are frequently used in news broadcasts, like the amateur video capturing the beating by Los Angeles police of Rodney King (Lawrence 2000), or the CCTV shots of Jamie Bulger being led away by his killers. The police in turn resort to the media as a part of criminal investigations (Innes 1999, 2001), as well as to cultivate support more generally (Mawby 1998, 1999, 2001, 2002). The media and criminal justice systems are penetrating each other increasingly, making a distinction between 'factual' and 'fictional' programming ever more tenuous (Manning 1998; Ferrell 1998; Tunnell 1998). The implications will be explored further in the conclusions, but I will turn next to a consideration of the results of content analyses.

Deviant news

Crime narratives and representations are, and have always been, a prominent part of the content of all mass media. Many studies have provided estimates of what proportion of media content consists of images of crime, sometimes comparing this across media, or over time.

The proportion of media content that is constituted by crime items clearly will depend on the definitions of 'crime' used. Probably the widest definition was that adopted by Richard Ericson and his colleagues in their penetrating study of newsmaking in Toronto (Ericson *et al.* 1987, 1989, 1991). Their concern was 'social deviance and how journalists participate in defining and shaping it' (Ericson *et al.* 1987: 3). Deviance was defined very broadly as 'the behaviour of a thing or person that strays from the normal . . . not only . . . criminal acts, but also . . . straying from organisational procedures and violations of common-sense knowledge' (ibid.: 4). When defined so broadly deviance is the essence of news; 'deviance is *the* defining characteristic of what journalists regard as newsworthy' (ibid.). Stories about crime in the narrower sense of violations of criminal law are a more limited proportion of all news, varying between outlets according to their medium (e.g., radio, TV, or print journalism) and market (e.g., 'quality' or 'popular' journalism).

Unsurprisingly, given their broad definition, Ericson *et al.* found that a high proportion of news was about 'deviance and control'. This ranged from 45.3 per cent in a quality newspaper to 71.5 per cent on a quality radio station (Ericson *et al.* 1991: 239–42). Both medium and market influenced the proportion of news related to deviance. Contrary to most other studies, they found that 'quality' broadcasting outlets had more deviance stories, because of 'their particular emphasis on deviance and control in public bureaucracies' (ibid.).

Ericson *et al.* adopted a broad concept of 'violence' in which ' "state violence" and "state terrorism" were conceptualised in the same way as various acts of violence by individual citizens' (ibid.: 244). They included stories, for example, about 'harms to health and safety such as impaired driving, unsafe working environments, and unsafe living environments' (ibid.). This covered concerns that are more characteristic of 'quality' than 'popular' news outlets, but nonetheless Ericson *et al.* find that in each medium more attention is paid to violence by popular than by quality journalism.

Broadcast news gave more prominence to stories of violence than print (ibid.: 244–7).

Ericson *et al.* adopted an equally wide-ranging concept of 'economic' deviance. This included not only property crimes but also 'questionable business practices . . . legal conflict over property . . . and social problems related to economic matters' (ibid.: 247). 'The reporting of economic *crimes* was rare in all news outlets . . . Much more common in all news outlets were reports of violation of trust, with or without criminal aspects or criminal charges being laid' (ibid.). Their data contradict the conventional finding of limited news coverage of business crime (Marsh 1991: 73). But the reporting of white-collar crime tends to be concentrated in 'quality' newspapers and is often restricted to specialist financial pages, sections, or newspapers (Stephenson-Burton 1995: 137–44), and is framed in ways that mark it off from 'real' crime (Tombs and Whyte 2001; Levi 2001).

Overall, Ericson *et al.* found that stories of deviance and control constituted the majority of items in most news outlets. 'Popular' media focused overwhelmingly more often on 'interpersonal' conflicts and deviance (ibid.: 249–50), but 'quality' ones included many items on such official deviance as rights violations, or on policy debates about criminal justice or corporate conduct. The pattern of reporting about deviance and control varied in complex ways according to media and markets, but deviance in a broad sense is the staple, defining feature of newsworthiness across the board.

The extent of crime in the news

Most analyses of the content of media representations of crime have focused more narrowly on a legally defined category of crime, not the broad sociological concept of deviance adopted by Ericson *et al.* Some studies look only at stories about specific criminal incidents, but others include stories, articles, or editorials about the state of crime generally, about criminal justice, and about criminal law violations related to political and social conflict, such as terrorism. The proportion of crime stories varies according to medium and market, and between different times and places. 'Because of this variability, estimates of the proportion of total news that is devoted to crime coverage range from 5 to 25% ' (Sacco 1995: 142[1]).

The lower estimates tend to come from earlier research (such as Harris 1932; Swanson 1955; Deutschmann 1959). More recent American studies have found higher proportions of crime-related items, in most media and markets. Graber found that crime and justice topics accounted for 22 to 28 per cent of stories in the newspapers she studied, 20 per cent on local television news, and 12 to 13 per cent on network television news (Graber 1980: 24). A literature review of thirty-six American content analyses of crime news conducted between 1960 and 1980 found considerable variation in the proportion of crime: from 1.61 per cent to 33.5 per cent (Marsh 1991: 73).

The first study of crime news in Britain came to similar conclusions (Roshier 1973). This looked at reporting for September 1938, 1955, and 1967 in a range of

---

[1] Other useful reviews of this literature are: Dominick 1978; Garofalo 1981; Marsh 1991; Surette 1998: chapter 3; Howitt 1998: chapter 3; Beckett and Sasson 2000: chapter 5.

newspapers. In the national dailies the proportion of total news space devoted to crime varied according to market position. In September 1967 the percentage of crime news was 5.6 per cent in the *Daily Mirror*, 4.4 per cent in the *Daily Express*, 2.4 per cent in the *Daily Telegraph* (and 2 per cent in the *Newcastle Journal*). The *News of the World* gave crime much more prominence: 11 per cent of news space. There was no clear trend over time. In the dailies the proportion of crime news in 1967 was virtually the same as in 1938, but it had been higher in 1955 in the *Daily Mirror* and *Daily Express*. The *News of the World* showed a similar U-shaped pattern: crime was 17.8 per cent of news in 1938, 29.1 per cent in 1955, and 11 per cent in 1967 (ibid.: 45).

In Britain, more recent studies find higher proportions of crime news than Roshier's average of 4 per cent for 1938–67. For example, a study of six Scottish newspapers in 1981 found that an average of 6.5 per cent of space was given to crime news (Ditton and Duffy 1983: 161; see also Smith 1984; Schlesinger *et al.* 1991: 411–15). This rise was confirmed by a later study comparing coverage of crime in ten national daily newspapers for four weeks from 19 June 1989 (Williams and Dickinson 1993). 'On average, 12.7% of event-oriented news reports were about crime' (ibid.: 40). The proportion of space devoted to crime was greater the more 'downmarket' the newspaper. The smallest proportion of crime news was 5.1 per cent in the *Guardian*; the largest was 30.4 per cent in the *Sun* (ibid.: 41).

Broadcast news in general devotes even more attention to crime reports than most newspapers (Cumberbatch *et al.* 1995: 5–8). There are similar variations in the proportion of news items concerning crime between different media operating in different markets. Commercial radio and television broadcast a higher proportion of crime news stories overall than the BBC, although the latter carried more reports about crime in general or criminal justice. Crime news is more frequent than any other category for every medium at each market level (ibid.: 7).

Given that different studies work with vastly different concepts of crime, and have ranged over many different newspapers and places, it is not possible to conclude from a literature review whether there is a trend for a greater proportion of news to be about crime. Although later studies predominantly find higher proportions of crime stories than earlier ones, they have also adopted broader concepts of crime, so the increase may well be a result of the measurement procedures used rather than a reflection of change in the media.

A recent study I conducted with Sonia Livingstone and Jessica Allen examined a random sample of issues of *The Times* and the *Mirror* for each year between 1945 and 1991 (Reiner *et al.* 2000a and 2000b; Reiner 2001). We found a generally upward (albeit fluctuating) trend in the proportion of stories focused on crime in both newspapers (from under 10 per cent in the 1940s to over 20 per cent in the 1990s). The sharpest increase occurred during the late 1960s, when the average annual proportion of crime stories almost doubled, from around 10 per cent to around 20 per cent in both papers. The percentage of crime stories overall, and *a fortiori* the proportion which is specifically about criminal activities as distinct from criminal justice, is almost always slightly higher in the *Mirror*. In both papers the proportion of stories about the criminal justice system, as distinct from the commission of criminal offences, has clearly increased since the Second World War. Criminal justice stories were on average 2 per cent of all stories in the *Mirror* between 1945–51, and 3 per cent in *The Times*. By 1985–1991 the average had increased to 6 per cent in the *Mirror*, and 9 per cent in *The Times*. This is probably a reflection of the politicization of law and order policy in this period (Downes and Morgan, in Chapter 10 of this volume).

In conclusion, estimates of the extent of news devoted to crime are highly sensitive to the varying definitions adopted by different researchers. They are also variable according to differences between media, markets, and over time. Deviance and control in a broad sense are the very stuff of news. However, stories about the commission of particular offences are more common in 'popular' news outlets (although for official or corporate crime the reverse is true). The proportion of news devoted to crime, and even more so the proportion about criminal justice, has increased over the last half-century.

The pattern of crime news

Content analyses have found systematic differences between the pattern of offences, victims, and offenders represented by the news and in official crime statistics or crime surveys. The last two sources are usually taken as representing the 'real' world of crime, ignoring the many pitfalls in interpreting the meaning of such statistics (Maguire, in Chapter 11 of this volume).

Although many studies do recognize the problems of inferring effects on audiences from analyses of media content, there is usually at least an implicit assumption that the gap between media representations of crime and the actuality supposedly disclosed by official statistics causes significant problems. Most commonly, the media are accused of exaggerating the risks of crime, cultivating an image of the world that is 'scary' and 'mean' (Gerbner and Gross 1976; Carlson 1985; Howitt 1998: chapter 4). Fear of crime and the coping strategies it leads to (such as not venturing out at night) are deemed disproportionate to the actual risks, and thus irrational and problematic in themselves (Sparks 1992 gives a cogent critique of this 'realist' conception of fear). Furthermore, media misrepresentation of crime risks is said to increase political support for authoritarian solutions to the supposed 'crisis' of law and order (Hall *et al.* 1978; Sasson 1995; Beckett 1997: chapters 5, 6).

Whatever its consequences, crime news does exhibit remarkably similar patterns in studies conducted at many different times and places. From the earliest studies (e.g., Harris 1932) onwards, analyses of news reports have found that crimes of violence are featured disproportionately compared to their incidence in official crime statistics or victim surveys. Indeed a general finding, emphasized originally in a pioneering study of Colorado newspapers, has been the lack of relationship between patterns and trends in crime news and crime statistics (Davis 1952).

Marsh reviewed thirty-six content analyses of crime news in the USA published between 1960 and 1988, and twenty studies in fourteen other countries between 1965 and 1987 (Marsh 1991). These all found an over-representation of violent and interpersonal crime, compared to official statistics, and an under-reporting of property offences. In America 'the ratio of violent-to-property crime stories appearing in the surveyed newspapers was 8 to 2; however, official statistics reflected a property-to-violent crime ratio of more than 9 to 1 during the survey period' (ibid.: 73). A similar pattern is found in the content analyses reviewed for other countries (ibid.: 74–6).

Reiner et al.'s historical study of two British newspapers since the Second World War found that homicide was by far the most common type of crime reported, accounting for about one-third of all crime news stories throughout the period. Other violent crimes were the next most common. However, there were significant shifts in the proportion of stories featuring other sorts of crime. In particular there was a marked decline in the proportion of stories featuring 'volume' property crimes such as burglary in which no violence occurred. These are of course the overwhelming majority of crimes according to official statistics and crime surveys (Maguire, in Chapter 11 of this volume). During the 1940s and 1950s they also featured frequently in news stories, but after the mid-1960s they were hardly ever reported unless some violence ensued from them. On the other hand, some offences began to feature prominently in news stories only after the mid-1960s, notably drug offences, which by the 1990s accounted for about 10 per cent of all crime stories (Reiner et al. 2000a and 2000b; Reiner 2001).

Studies conducted in the 1990s continue to show the same pattern of over-representation of violent and interpersonal (especially sex) crimes (Chiricos et al. 1997; Beckett and Sasson 2000: chapter 5). In some respects this tendency is increasing. Between 1951 and 1985 the number of rape trials in Britain increased nearly four times, from 119 to 450. In the same period, the number of rape cases reported in the Press increased more than five times, from 28 to 154. The percentage of rape cases reported in the Press jumped from 23.5 per cent in 1951 to 34.2 per cent in 1985 (Soothill and Walby 1991: 20–22).

The proportion of news devoted to crime of different types, and the prominence with which it is presented, varies according to market and medium. In one month of 1989, 64.5 per cent of British newspaper crime stories dealt with personal violent crime, while the British Crime Survey found that only 6 per cent of crimes reported by victims were violent (Williams and Dickinson 1993: 40). The percentage of stories dealing with crimes involving personal violence, and the salience they were given (as measured by where they appeared in the layout and the extent of pictures accompanying them), increased considerably the more downmarket the newspaper studied (ibid.: 40–43).

The pattern of offences reported varies according to medium as well as market. In Britain, the proportion of violent crimes relative to other crimes reported in television news broadcasts is closer to the tabloid figure than the quality or mid-market Press, especially for local rather than national bulletins. A study of crime news in January–March 1987 found that the proportion of reports about non-sexual violence against the person in 'quality', 'mid-market', and 'tabloid' newspapers respectively was 24.7 per cent, 38.8 per cent, and 45.9 per cent. On national news bulletins it was 40 per cent, while on local bulletins violent crime stories were 63.2 per cent of all crime news. There was no significant difference between ITV (43.5 per cent) and BBC1 (42.3 per cent), but Channel 4 was more like the quality Press (18.2 per cent; Schlesinger et al. 1991: 412–15). Similar patterns are found for other offence categories: there are some 'market' differences between broadcast news channels, but on the whole the proportion of different offences portrayed on television news is closer to tabloid than broadsheet print journalism.

Violent crimes in general figure disproportionately in British broadcast news, although there are substantial variations according to medium and market. In one study, over 40 per cent of crime news items concerned death and murder on nearly all BBC Radio stations. On television, murder and death accounted for 53 per cent of all crime stories on Sky News, 42 per cent on ITN, and 38 per cent on BBC1 (Cumberbatch *et al.* 1995: 25).

A further indirect consequence of the pattern of offences reported by news stories is an exaggeration of police success in clearing-up crime (resulting largely from Press reliance on police sources for stories). As summed-up in a review of fifty-six content analyses in fifteen different countries between 1960 and 1988, 'the over-representation of violent crime stories was advantageous to the police . . . because the police are more successful in solving violent crimes than property crimes' (Marsh 1991: 73). A historical study of British crime news stories found that although the overwhelming majority report crimes that are cleared up by the police, this is declining. The clear-up rate for stories in *The Times* fell from 80 per cent in 1945–64 to 64 per cent in 1981–91, and from 75 per cent to 70 per cent in the *Mirror* in the same period (Reiner 2001).

There is a clear pattern to news media portrayal of the characteristics of offenders and victims. Most studies find that offenders featuring in news reports are typically older and higher-status offenders than those processed by the criminal justice system (Roshier 1973: 45–6; Graber 1980; Reiner 2001). This finding needs some qualification, however, in the light of the problems of official statistics (cf. Maguire, in Chapter 11 of this volume). The profile of offenders dealt with by the criminal justice system is likely to be biased misleadingly towards lower-status offenders. In this respect the socio-economic characteristics of offenders in media stories may actually be closer to the—ultimately unknowable—'real' pattern than the official statistics which are based on the small proportion of offenders who are the losers of the criminal justice lottery. The over-representation of higher-status offenders is primarily confined to national news media. There is contradictory evidence about whether news reports disproportionately feature ethnic minority offenders (Graber 1980; Garofalo 1981: 324; Marsh 1991: 74; Sacco 1995: 143). Crime reports in local newspapers or broadcasting clearly focus more on ethnic minority and lower-status group suspects (Dussuyer 1979; Garofalo 1981: 324; Beckett and Sasson 2000: 79). 'Reality' TV programmes also present a marked variation to national news reports in terms of the demography of the offenders portrayed, concentrating on stories with young, ethnic minority suspects (Oliver and Armstrong 1998; Kooistra *et al.* 1998). The one demographic characteristic of offenders which is overwhelmingly congruent in news stories and in all other data sources on crime is their gender: 'both crime statistics and crime news portray offending as predominantly a male activity' (Sacco 1995: 143).

Studies assessing the profile of victims in news stories are fewer in number than analyses of the representation of offenders, although there is a clear trend for victims to become the pivotal focus of news stories in the last three decades (Reiner 2001). This parallels the increasing centrality of victims in criminal justice and criminology (see Zedner, in Chapter 13 of this volume). Victims have also become the focal point for crime fiction narratives (as shown in Reiner *et al.* 2000a and 2000b). News stories exaggerate the risks faced by higher status, white, female adults of becoming victims of crime (Graber 1980; Garofalo 1981: 324; Mawby and Brown 1983; Chermak 1995; Chiricos *et al.* 1997; Beckett and Sasson 2000: 79–80), although child victims do feature prominently (Reiner 2001). The most common victims of violence according to official crime statistics and victim surveys are poor, young, black males. However, they figure in news reporting predominantly as perpetrators.

Another consistent finding of studies of content is the predominance of stories about criminal incidents, rather than analyses of crime patterns or the possible causes of crime. As summed up in one survey of the literature, 'crime stories in newspapers consist primarily of brief accounts of discrete events, with few details and little background material. There are very few attempts to discuss causes of or remedies for crime or to put the problem of crime into a larger perspective' (Garofalo 1981: 325; see also Marsh 1991: 76; Sasson 1995; Barlow 1998; Beckett and Sasson 2000: 80–81). Although an aspect of the more general event-orientation that is part of the 'eternal recurrence' of news (Rock 1973), the 'mass media provide citizens with a public awareness of crime . . . based upon an information-rich and knowledge-poor foundation . . . Anyone interested in learning about crime from the mass media is treated to examples, incidents, and scandals but at such a level of description that it is impossible for them to develop an analytical comprehension of crime' (Sherizen 1978: 204).

An important example of the concentration on events rather than exploration of underlying causes is the reporting of child sex abuse, which has systematically excluded issues of gender and focused primarily on the alleged excesses or failures of social workers in particular cases (Nava 1988; Skidmore 1995). Reporting of rape and other sex crimes is another area where issues of power and gender disappear in the fascination with the demonization of individual offenders or victims (Soothill and Walby 1991; Lees 1995; Gregory and Less 1999).

The tendency to exclude analysis of broader structural processes or explanations is also evident in stories about political disorder (Halloran *et al.* 1970; Hall 1973: 232–43; Sumner 1982; Tumber 1982; Cottle 1993). The portrayal of political conflict such as riot or terrorism is often in terms of sheer criminality, echoing the discourse of conservative politicians (Clarke and Taylor 1980; Hillyard 1982; Iyengar 1991: 24–46). This has been evident again in the overall media coverage of the events of 11 September 2001. However, the pattern varies according to different phases in the reporting of such conflicts (Wren-Lewis 1981/2). After the initial reporting of events such as the 1981 Brixton riots, which tends to be in terms of criminality, there is often a later phase of analysis of possible causes, especially if there is an official inquiry like Lord Scarman's (Murdock 1982).

There are also variations between different media and markets. Print journalism, especially 'quality' newspapers and editorial pages, will often have more analysis, with radio news having the least, and television intermediate (Ericson *et al.* 1991; Cumberbatch *et al.* 1995: 7). Newspapers and quality broadcasting channels are more likely to carry points of view critical of the actions of the authorities, giving some voice to those campaigning against officials. There is a tendency in recent years for critical and campaigning groups to have more access to the media. This is partly because of the sheer growth in the space for news in all outlets, partly because of the increasing politicization of law and order (Schlesinger and Tumber 1994; Lawrence 2000; Downes and Morgan, in Chapter 10 of this volume).

Although critical stories exposing wrongdoing by the police or other criminal justice officials are regularly published, and an aspect of the high news-value attached to uncovering scandals amongst the powerful, this 'watchdog' function does not necessarily undermine the legitimacy of criminal justice institutions. Corruption and other police deviance stories have traditionally been set within the 'one bad apple' framework, whereby the exposure of individual wrongdoing is interpreted as a testimony to the integrity of the system which dealt with it (Chibnall 1977: chapter 5). As the volume of police deviance stories has increased in recent years (Reiner 2001), the 'one bad apple' story becomes harder to recycle. An alternative frame, in which malpractice is often revealed within a damage limitation narrative, is by presenting it as a story of institutional reform. This acknowledges the problems of previous practices but safeguards the legitimacy of the institution as one that is already putting things right (Schlesinger and Tumber 1994: chapter 7).

An earlier literature review concluded 'a typical metropolitan paper probably devotes around 5–10% of its available space to crime news. Further, the type of crime most likely reported is individual crime accompanied by violence. Less than 5% of available space is devoted to covering the general issue of crime: its causes, remedies etc.' (Dominick 1978: 108). This pattern remains recognizable, but there have been changes over time (Reiner 2001). The proportion of crime news is higher, and there is more about criminal justice. Increasing attention is paid to the effects of crime on individual victims. While reports of violent crime still predominate, there are many stories about other types of deviance and control. More critical and analytic pieces have increased in frequency. The representation of crime in the news clearly varies between different media, markets, and historical periods.

THE CONTENT OF CRIME FICTION

Some social scientists have conducted quantitative content analyses of film and television crime fiction.[2] More commonly, however, crime fiction—in print, the cinema, or on television—has been analysed using a variety of qualitative techniques and theoretical perspectives drawn from literary, film, and social theory.[3] The pattern of

[2] Gerbner 1970; Gerbner et al. 1980; Dominick 1978; Pandiani 1978; Gunter 1985; Carlson 1985; Lichter et al. 1994; Powers et al. 1996; Surette 1998: chapter 2; Allen et al. 1998.

[3] McArthur 1972; Shadoian 1977; Rosow 1978; McCarty 1993; Clarens 1997; Hardy 1997, 1998; Rubin 1999; Chibnall and Murphy 1999 and Rafter 2000 are just a few of the many studies of gangster and crime movies. Haycraft 1941; Watson 1971; Cawelti 1976; Palmer 1978; Knight 1980; Porter 1981; Benstock 1983; Most and Stowe 1983; Mandel 1984; Bell and Daldry 1990; Thompson 1993; and Clarke 2001 are some of the numerous texts on literary detective stories. Everson 1972; Tuska 1978; Meyers 1981, 1989; Parrish and Pitts 1990a offer histories of detective films and television shows. Reiner 1978, 1981, 1994, 2000a and 2000b; Park 1978; Hurd 1979; Kerr 1981; Clarke 1983, 1986, 1990; Dove 1982; Dove and Bargainnier 1986; Inciardi and Dee 1987; Buxton 1990; Parrish and Pitts 1990b; Laing 1991; Winston and Mellerski 1992; Sparks 1992: chapter 6, 1993; Eaton 1996; Hale 1998; King 1999; Wilson 2000; Gitlin 2000: chapters 11–14 examine police stories. Nellis and Hale 1982; Mason 1996; Cheatwood 1998 are studies of prison films.

representation of crime in fictional stories, in all media, resembles the results of content analyses of crime news.

The frequency of crime fiction

Respectable fears about waves of excessive media focus on crime are perennial, just as they are about crime in reality (Pearson 1983). (Recent examples include Medved 1992; Powers *et al.* 1996: chapter 5.) However, while there have been important changes over time in *how* crime is represented in fictional narratives, crime stories have always been a prominent part of popular entertainment.

Stories of crime and detection have been staples of modern literature since the early days of the novel, as the works of Defoe, Fielding, and Dickens illustrate (Ousby 1976; Durston 1996). Some authors have sought to trace the ancestry of the detective story as far back as possible. 'We find sporadic examples of it in Oriental folk-tales, in the Apocryphal Books of the Old Testament, in the play-scene in *Hamlet*; while Aristotle in his *Poetics* puts forward observations about dramatic plot-construction which are applicable today to the construction of a detective mystery' (Sayers 1936: vii). This was clearly an attempt to emphasize the 'snobbery' rather than the 'violence' of the classic ratiocinative detective story (Watson 1971). The dominant style of crime fiction has varied from the classic puzzle mystery exemplified by Sayers and Agatha Christie, to the tougher private eye stories pioneered by Dashiell Hammett and Raymond Chandler, and the police procedurals of Ed McBain, Joseph Wambaugh and others (accessible histories include Symons 1972, Binyon 1989, and Ousby 1997).

In the heyday of the 'Golden Age' detective story, the 1930s, crime novels were about 25 per cent of the popular fiction titles available through the W.H. Smith subscription library service (Watson 1971: 31). One estimate suggests that 'between a quarter and a third of total paperback output could probably be put into the category of "thriller" of one kind or another . . . since 1945, at least 10,000 million copies of crime stories have been sold world-wide' (Mandel 1984: 66–7).

Crime stories have also been a perennially prominent genre in the cinema, the dominant mass medium of the first half of the twentieth century (Rafter 2000). As with its successors, television and video, the cinema has been haunted by respectable fears about its portrayal of crime and violence (Barker 1984; Mathews 1994; Miller 1994). The proportion of films about crime has fluctuated cyclically since the Second World War, but there is no long-term increase or decrease in crime films (Allen *et al.* 1997). In most years, around 20 per cent of all films are crime movies, and around half of all films have significant crime content.

Radio was the main broadcasting medium of the first half of the twentieth century. Stories about crime and law enforcement were a popular part of radio drama, in Britain and North America, although never as dominant as they subsequently became on television (Shale 1996). In the USA it has been calculated that the proportion of evening radio programming taken up by crime stories was 4 per cent in 1932, 5 per cent in 1940, 14 per cent in 1948, and 5 per cent in 1956, by which time there was significant competition from television (Dominick 1978: 112–3).

Stories about crime and law enforcement have been prominent on television ever since it became the leading broadcasting medium in the 1950s. In the early to mid-1950s, the proportion of prime-time television devoted to shows about crime and law enforcement hovered just under 10 per cent (Dominick 1978: 114). But by 1959 over one-third of prime-time television was crime shows. Since then there have been cyclical fluctuations, but in most years at least 20 per cent of prime-time is given to crime shows, and in a few years nearly 40 per cent (ibid.). Crime shows are just as much a staple of British television. In most years since 1955 around 25 per cent of the most popular television shows in Britain have been crime or police series. While there are sharp cyclical fluctuations, there is no long-term trend (Reiner *et al.* 2000a and 2000b).

Thus crime fiction, like crime news, is a prominent part of all types of mass medium, usually accounting for about 25 per cent of output. Whereas there was some tendency for the proportion of news space devoted to crime to increase in the last half-century, this was not true of fiction. Crime stories seem to have been a staple of popular entertainment throughout the modern period. While concern about crime in fiction appears to have been a constant, there have been changes in *how* crime and criminal justice are represented. The overall pattern of fictional representations of crime is similar to that in news stories—and shows similar discrepancies from the picture conveyed by official crime statistics.

The pattern of crime in fiction

Murder and other violent crimes feature predominantly in crime fiction, vastly more frequently than other offences that are much more common in official statistics. In a recent study (financed by ESRC grant no. L/210/25/2029), Jessica Allen, Sonia Livingstone, and I analysed in detail the crime films that have done best at the British box office since the Second World War (Allen *et al.* 1998; Reiner *et al.* 2000a and 2000b). Murder was the primary crime (the McGuffin of the plot, in Hitchcock's terminology) in the overwhelming majority of films throughout the period. However, property offences provided the McGuffin in a significant minority of films up to the late 1960s, though seldom thereafter. Sexual and drug offences began to appear as central aspects of narratives only after the late 1960s. Up to the mid-1960s, most films did not feature any crimes which were not directly related to the McGuffin. After that they begin to portray a world which is full of contextual crimes, unrelated to the central crime animating the narrative (to the point where characters like the eponymous Dirty Harry cannot go for a hamburger without coming across a bank robbery in progress). Up to the mid-1960s, crime was represented usually as an abnormal, one-off intrusion into a stable order. Thereafter images of an all-pervasive, routinized threat of crime become more common. Linked to this is the increasing prevalence in films of police heroes. This signifies that crime has become sufficiently routine to provide employment for a large bureaucracy, not just a diversion for enthusiastic amateurs at country house weekends (Reiner 1978, 1980, 2000b; Allen *et al.* 1998: 67–8; King 1999; Rafter 2000: chapter 3; Wilson 2000).

The representation of violence has become increasingly graphic throughout the period since the Second World War. Up to the early 1970s, hardly any films in our sample showed more than a minor degree of pain or damage to the victim (beyond the fact of the murder itself!). Since then there has been an increasing number of films depicting severe suffering by victims, who are often depicted as severely traumatized (see also Powers *et al.* 1996: 104–106). There is an even more marked increase in the extent of violence shown in contextual crimes, as well as a growing frequency of violence not strictly necessary for the achievement of instrumental objectives (such as escaping arrest).

On television also, fictional narratives have always featured violent crimes more prominently than other offences, but are focusing on them to an increasing extent. Studies of American television suggest that about two-thirds of crime shown on prime-time shows consists of murder, assault, or armed robbery (Dominick 1973: 245; Garofalo 1981: 326; Sparks 1992: 140; Lichter *et al.* 1994; Beckett and Sasson 2000: chapter 6).

A recent historical content analysis of 620 randomly selected prime-time TV shows broadcast between 1955 and 1986 demonstrated the growing preponderance of violent crime in television fiction (Lichter *et al.* 1994: chapter 8). It found that 'television violence has far outstripped reality since the 1950s. In the first decade of our study, there were seven murders for every one hundred characters seen on the screen. This was more than 1,400 times the actual murder rate for the United States during the same time period' (ibid.: 275; the measure of 'reality' is taken to be the FBI *Uniform Crime Reports*, which of course suffer from the same limitations as other official crime statistics).

Violent crimes apart from homicide also featured prominently.

Other violent crimes accounted for one crime in eight on TV during the decade 1955 to 1964. Violent crimes short of murder occurred at a rate of 40 for every 1,000 characters. At that time the real-world rate was only 2 in every 1,000 inhabitants . . . During the second decade of our study, covering 1965 to 1975, crime rose both on TV and in the wider world. In the real world the rate for serious offences doubled to 25 for every 1,000 inhabitants, according to FBI statistics. Despite this increase in crime rates around the country, the television crime rate remained more than five times that of the real world, at 140 crimes per 1,000 characters. The FBI-calculated rate for violent crimes also doubled to 3 incidents per 1,000 inhabitants. The TV rate for violent crimes, at 114 incidents per 1,000 characters, was more than 30 times greater. [Lichter *et al.* 1994: 276]

The victimization studies that began in the late 1960s in the USA reveal far more crime of all kinds than the FBI statistics, but the 'television rate for violent crimes was still fifteen times higher than estimates from victimisation surveys' (ibid.).

In the third decade covered by Lichter *et al.*'s historical content analysis, television and the world of statistically recorded crime converge slightly. On the one hand, broadcasting standards were altered in 1975 to create 'Family Viewing Time', which led to reduced levels of television violence. 'The rate for serious crimes on television fell 3 percent to a "low" of 110 crimes per 1,000 characters. The rate for violent crimes also dropped almost 3 percent, to 86 incidents in every 1,000 characters . . . Thus, television and reality have moved closer together in terms of the overall crime rate, but television continues to present far more violent crimes than occur in real life' (ibid.: 278). The drop in the television violence rate was more than compensated for by the appearance of serious crimes which hitherto had hardly featured in genre crime fiction: prostitution and other organized vice such as pornography, and drug-related offences. On American television there was a fifteenfold increase in prostitution offences and a tenfold rise in drug-related crime between 1975 and 1985 (ibid.: 285).

Ironically, in relation to property crime risks television has become safer than the world presented in official statistics. Between 1955 and 1964 and 1975 and 1984, the average annual rate for serious property offences in the USA increased from ten to fifty incidents per 1,000 people according to the FBI data. Victimization studies show the rate increasing from about 50 per 1,000 between 1965 and 1974 to 100 for every 1,000 inhabitants in 1975–84. However, on television 'the rate for serious property crimes has remained steady at 20 incidents per 1,000 characters over the thirty years of our study' (ibid.: 284). Thus between 1955 and 1964 the television property crime rate exceeded the official statistics, but since then it has fallen far behind them, and *a fortiori* behind the picture presented by victimization surveys. There is also a trend for the cinema (and newspapers) to understate the risks of property crime (Allen *et al.* 1998: 65; Reiner 2001: 5).

The portrayal of crime on television and in other fiction presents it as predominantly violent, contrary to the picture in official statistics. Apart from statistical frequency, the *qualitative* character of crimes depicted in fiction is vastly different from the officially recorded pattern. While most 'real' murders are extensions of brawls between young men, or domestic disputes, in fiction murder is usually motivated by greed and calculation (Dominick 1973: 250; Garofalo 1981: 326–7; Lichter *et al.* 1994: 279; Allen *et al.* 1998: 69). Rape is also presented in opposite ways in fiction and criminal justice statistics. In reality most reported rapes are perpetrated by intimates or acquaintances, not strangers (Barclay and Tavares 1999: 16). On television and in other fiction, although rarely shown (and virtually never before the early 1960s) rape is usually committed by psychopathic strangers and involves extreme brutality, often torture and murder ('5% of the murders on TV result from rape', Lichter *et al.* 1994: 279–80).

While crime fiction presents property crime less frequently than the reality suggested by crime statistics, the crimes it portrays are far more serious than most recorded offences. Official statistics and victim surveys concur in calculating that the overwhelming majority of property crimes involve little or no loss or damage, and no physical threat or harm to the victim—indeed, there is usually no contact at all with the perpetrator. In fiction, however, most property crimes involve tightly planned, high value, project thefts, and are frequently accompanied by violence (Garofalo 1981: 326; Lichter *et al.* 1994: 284).

Related to the disproportionate emphasis on the most serious end of the crime spectrum is the portrayal of the demographic characteristics of offenders and victims presented by crime fiction. Offenders in fiction are primarily higher-status, white, middle-aged males (Pandiani 1978: 442–7; Garofalo 1981: 326; Lichter *et al.* 1994: 290–5; Reiner *et al.* 2000a and 2000b). Interestingly, the new genre of 'reality' infotainment cop shows such as *Cops* differs from this pattern, primarily presenting offenders as non-white, underclass youth (Fishman and Cavender 1998; Beckett and Sasson 2000: 113). The social characteristics of fictional victims are similar, but a higher proportion are female. Apart from gender, the demographic profile of offenders and victims in fiction is the polar opposite of criminal justice statistics (Surette 1998: 47 calls this 'the law of opposites'). (See also Pandiani ibid.; Garofalo ibid.; Lichter *et al.* ibid.; Barclay and Tavares 1999: chapters 2 and 3. Sparks 1992: 140–45 offers a qualitative analysis.)

A final important feature of fictional crime is the high clear-up rate. This is paralleled by crime news, but completely different from the picture presented by official statistics. In fiction the cops usually get their man (Dominick 1973: 246; Garofalo 1981: 327; Lichter *et al.* 1994: chapter 9; Powers *et al.* 1996: chapter 5). Although crime fiction concentrates on the kind of serious violent crimes that have the highest clear-up rates in reality, the media have always exaggerated this. In Allen *et al.*'s sample of movies since 1945, there was no film before 1952 in which criminals escaped capture, and hardly any up to the early 1970s. Thereafter, offenders get away with their crimes in an increasing number of films, albeit still a minority (Allen *et al.* 1998: 185; Reiner *et al.* 2000a and 2000b). Trends on television are similar, with the overwhelming majority of crimes cleared up by the police, but an increasing minority where they fail (Lichter *et al.* ibid.).

The police and criminal justice system are thus overwhelmingly portrayed in a positive light in popular fiction, as the successful protectors of victims against serious harm and violence. This continues to be so, although with increasing questioning of police success and integrity (Reiner 2000b). Although the majority of police characters in films and television shows are represented as sympathetic, honest, and just, there is an increasing portrayal of police deviance. Corrupt, brutal, and discriminatory police officers have become more common since the mid-1960s in films (Powers *et al.* 1996: 113–6; Allen *et al.* 1998: 185–6) and television (Lichter *et al.* 1994: chapter 9), as has acceptance of routine police violation of due process legal restraints (Dominick 1978: 117; Garofalo 1981: 327; Sparks 1992: chapter 6).

A major shift in media crime fiction is the increasingly prominent representation of victims. Victims have moved from a shadowy and purely functional role in crime narratives to a pivotal position. Film and television stories increasingly focus on the plight of victims, whose suffering is portrayed more graphically and often constitutes the driving force of the story (Allen *et al.* 1998; Reiner *et al.* 2000a and 2000b). This is paralleled by their treatment in news stories (Reiner 2001). Support for law and enforcement and criminal justice is increasingly constructed in narratives by presenting them as defenders or avengers of victims with whose suffering the audience is invited to identify.

THE MEDIA REPRESENTATION OF CRIME: A SUMMARY

The review of analyses of the content of media representations of crime suggests the following conclusions:

1. News and fiction stories about crime are prominent in all media. While there is evidence of increasing attention to crime in some parts of the media, overall this fascination has been constant throughout media history.

2. News and fiction concentrate overwhelmingly on serious violent crimes against individuals, albeit with some variation according to medium and market. The proportion of different crimes represented is the inverse of official statistics.

3. The demographic profile of offenders and victims in the media is older and higher status than those processed by the criminal justice system.

4. The risks of crime as portrayed by the media are both quantitatively and qualitatively more serious in the media than the official statistically recorded picture, although the media underplay the current probabilities of victimization by property crimes.

5. The media generally present a very positive image of the success and integrity of the police, and criminal justice more generally. However, in both news and fiction there is a clear trend to criticism of law enforcement, both in terms of its effectiveness and its justice and honesty. While in the past the unbroken media picture was that *Crime Does Not Pay* (the title of a series of short films produced by MGM between 1935 and 1947), this is increasingly called into question in contemporary media news and fiction.

6. Individual victims and their suffering increasingly provide the motive force of crime stories.

The next section will discuss the possible implications of this pattern of representation.

THE CONSEQUENCES OF MEDIA IMAGES OF CRIME

This section offers an overview and analysis of the huge research literature assessing the impact of media images of crime. Much of the inspiration (and dollars) for empirical evaluations of media effects derives from the broader, apocalyptic concerns of subversion or hegemony. However, in practice most research has sought to measure two possible consequences of media representations (which are not mutually exclusive): criminal behaviour (especially violence); and fear of crime. I will first consider the way that the media feature in the most common social theories of crime, and then assess the empirical research evidence. (For detailed critical surveys of theories and research evidence on the media and crime causation, see Surette 1998: chapter 5; Howitt 1998: chapters 1, 5–8, 10–11.)

THE MEDIA AND CRIMINOLOGICAL THEORY

The media play at least a subordinate role in all the major theoretical perspectives attempting to understand crime and criminal justice (see Rock, in Chapter 2 of this volume). To illustrate this the predominant theories of crime can be assembled in a simple model. For a crime to occur there are several logically necessary preconditions, which can be identified as: labelling; motive; means; opportunity; and the absence of controls. The media potentially play a part in each of these elements, and thus can affect levels of crime in a variety of ways.

Labelling

For an act to be 'criminal' (as distinct from harmful, immoral, anti-social, etc.) it has to be labelled as such. This involves the creation of a legal category. It also requires the perception of the act as criminal by citizens and/or law enforcement officers if it is to be recorded as a crime. The media are an important factor in both processes, helping to shape the conceptual boundaries and recorded volume of crime.

The role of the media in helping to develop new (and erode old) categories of crime has been emphasized in most of the classic studies of shifting boundaries of criminal law within the 'labelling' tradition. Becker's seminal book *Outsiders* analysed the emergence of the Marijuana Tax Act in the USA in 1937, emphasizing the use of the media as a tool of the Federal Bureau of Narcotics and its moral entrepreneurship in creating the new statute (Becker 1963: chapter 7). Jock Young showed that media representations amplified the deviance of drug-takers (Young 1971). Stan Cohen coined the influential concept of 'moral panic' in his study of the part played by the media together with the police in developing a spiral of respectable fear about clashes between 'mods' and 'rockers' (Cohen 1972). Hall *et al.*'s wide-ranging analysis of the development of a moral panic about a supposedly new type of robbery, 'mugging', emphasized the crucial part played by the media. Newspapers stimulated public anxiety, producing changes in policing and criminal justice practice which appeared to confirm the initial reports by processing more offenders: a self-fulfilling spiral of deviancy amplification (Hall *et al.* 1978).

Since these pioneering works many other studies have illustrated the crucial role of the media in shaping the boundaries of deviance and criminality, by creating new categories of offence, or changing perceptions and sensitivities, leading to fluctuations in apparent crime. For example, Roger Graef's celebrated 1982 fly-on-the-wall documentary about the Thames Valley Police was a key impetus to reform of police treatment of rape victims (Gregory and Lees 1999; 'TV that changed the world', *Radio Times*, 24–30 November 2001). This also contributed, however, to a rise in the proportion of victims reporting rape, and thus an increase in the recorded rate. Many other studies document media-amplified 'crime waves' and 'moral panics' about law and order.[4]

What all these studies illustrate is the significant contribution of the media to determining the apparent level of crime. Increases and (perhaps more rarely) decreases in recorded crime levels are often due in part to the deviance construction and amplifying activities of the media (Barak 1994; Ferrell and Sanders 1995; Surette 1998: chapter 7).

---

[4] E.g., Fishman 1981; Christensen *et al.* 1982; Best and Horiuchi 1985; Nava 1988; Altheide 1993; Orcutt and Turner 1993; Skidmore 1995; Lees 1995; Brownstein 1995; Beckett 1997; Beckett and Sasson 2000: chapters 4, 5, 7.

Motive

A crime will not occur unless there is someone who is tempted, driven, or otherwise motivated to carry out the 'labelled' act. The media feature in many of the most commonly offered social and psychological theories of the formation of criminal dispositions. Probably the most influential sociological theory of how criminal motives are formed is Merton's version of *anomie* theory (Merton 1938; echoes of which are found in more recent work such as Lea and Young 1984; Dahrendorf 1985; Young 1999; and Messner and Rosenfeld 2000). The media play a key role in these accounts of the formation of anomic strain generating pressures to offend. The media are pivotal in presenting for universal emulation images of affluent life-styles, which accentuate relative deprivation and generate pressures to acquire ever higher levels of material success regardless of the legitimacy of the means used.

Psychological theories of the formation of motives to commit offences also often feature media effects as part of the process. It has been claimed that the images of crime and violence presented by the media are a form of social learning, and may encourage crime by imitation or arousal effects. Others have argued that the media tend to erode internalized controls by disinhibition or desensitization through witnessing repeated representations of deviance (for detailed discussion of such theories, see Bailey 1993; Carey 1993; Wartella 1995: 309–11; Livingstone 1996: 308).

Means

It has often been alleged that the media act as an open university of crime, spreading knowledge of criminal techniques. This is often claimed in relation to particular *causes célèbres* or horrific crimes, for example during the 1950s' campaign against crime and horror comics (Barker 1984; Nyberg 1998). A notorious case was the allegation that the murderers of Jamie Bulger had been influenced by the video *Child's Play 3* in the manner in which they killed the unfortunate toddler (Morrison 1997). A related line of argument is the 'copycat' theory of crime and rioting (Tumber 1982; Howitt 1998: 75–84; Surette 1998: 137–52). Despite a plethora of research and discussion, the evidence that this is a major source of crime remains weak.

Opportunity

The media may increase opportunities to commit offences by contributing to the development of a consumerist ethos, in which the availability of tempting targets of theft proliferates. They can also alter 'routine activities', especially in relation to the use of leisure time, which structure opportunities for offending (Cohen and Felson 1979). The domestic hardware and software of mass media use—TVs, videos, radios, CDs, personal computers, mobile phones—are the common currency of routine property crime, and their proliferation has been an important aspect of the spread of criminal opportunities.

Absence of controls

Motivated potential offenders, with the means and opportunities to commit offences, may still not carry out these crimes if effective social controls are in place. These might be *external*—the deterrent threat of sanctions represented in the first place by the police—or *internal*—the still, small voice of conscience—what Eysenck has called the 'inner policeman'.

A regularly recurring theme of respectable anxieties about the criminogenic consequences of media images of crime is that they erode the efficacy of both external and internal controls. They may undermine external controls by derogatory representations of criminal justice, for example ridiculing its agents, a key complaint at least since the days of Dogberry, resuscitated in this century by the popularity of comic images of the police, from the Keystone Cops onwards. Serious representations of criminal justice might undermine its legitimacy by becoming more critical, questioning, for example, the integrity and fairness, or the efficiency and effectiveness of the police. Negative representations of criminal justice could lessen public cooperation with the system, or potential offenders' perception of the probability of sanctions, with the consequence of increasing crime.

Probably the most frequently suggested line of causation between media representations and criminal behaviour is the allegation that the media undermine internalized controls, by regularly presenting sympathetic or glamorous images of offending. In academic form this is found in the psychological theories about disinhibition and desensitization, which were referred to in the section above on the formation of motives (Wartella 1995: 309–12; Surette 1998: 119–30 are succinct evaluations).

In sum, there are several possible links between media representations of crime and criminal behaviour which are theoretically possible, and frequently suggested in criminological literature and political debate. In the next section I will review some of the research evidence examining whether such a link can be demonstrated empirically.

CRIMINOGENIC MEDIA? THE RESEARCH EVIDENCE

In a comprehensive review of the research literature, Sonia Livingstone noted that 'since the 1920s thousands of studies of mass media effects have been conducted' (Livingstone 1996: 306). She added that even listing the references to research in the previous decade would exhaust the space allocated to her article (some twenty pages).[5] But 'despite the volume of research, the debate about media effects—whether it can be shown empirically that specific mass media messages . . . have specific, often detrimental effects on the audiences who are exposed to them remains unresolved' (ibid.). Reviews of the literature regularly recycle the apotheosis of agnosticism represented by the conclusion of one major study from the 1960s: 'for some children, under some conditions, some television is harmful. For some children under the same conditions, or for the same children under other conditions, it may be beneficial. For most children, under most conditions, most television is probably neither particularly harmful nor particularly beneficial' (Schramm *et al.* 1961: 11).

This meagre conclusion from the expenditure of countless research hours and dollars is primarily a testimony to the limitations and difficulties of empirical social science. The armoury of possible research techniques for assessing directly the effects

---

[5] Other useful overviews of the evidence about media effects in relation to crime and violence include Bailey 1993; Carey 1993; Wartella 1995; Surette 1998: chapter 5; Howitt 1998: chapters 1–2, 5–11.

of media images on crime is sparse, and suffers from evident and long-recognized limitations.

The primary technique used by such research has been some version of the classic experiment. The archetypal form of this is to show a group of subjects a media stimulus—say a film, or TV programme, or extract—and measure the response, in terms of behaviour or attitudes compared to before the experiment. In a characteristic example, children of four to five were shown a five-minute film in the researcher's office, and then taken to a room with toys and observed for twenty minutes through a one-way mirror (Bandura *et al.* 1961, 1963). The children were randomly assigned to watch one of three films, enacting scenarios in which a boy who attacked another boy and some toys was depicted as either being rewarded, punished, or neither. The children (especially the boys) who saw the film about the boy rewarded for his attack by getting all the toys to play with, were observed to carry out twice as much imitative aggression as the other groups, but no more non-imitative aggression.

This example shows all the problems of inferring conclusions about links between media and violence from laboratory-style experiments. Are the results a Hawthorn effect arising from the experimental situation itself? For instance, were the more aggressive children who saw a film in which aggression was rewarded influenced by their perception that the experimenter approved of such behaviour? How far can results from one context of viewing be extrapolated to others? Do experimental results exaggerate the links in the everyday world by picking up short-term effects of media exposure that rapidly evaporate? Or do they underestimate the long-term cumulative effects of regular, repeated exposures by measuring only one-off results? To some the artificiality of such experiments fatally compromises them (Surette 1998: 122–3). Others point out that 'laboratories' (or more typically researchers' offices or other convenient campus locations) are social situations 'whose particular dynamics and meanings must be considered . . . and generalisability depends on how far these same factors may occur or not in everyday life' (Livingstone 1996: 310).

Given the huge number of such experimental studies (using different forms of stimuli and different types of measures of response, for different sorts of subjects, at many different times and places) it is hardly surprising that there are considerable variations in the extent of effect shown, if any. However, most studies do show *some* effect, and the few that conducted follow-ups over time found that while effects diminished by about 25 per cent over the fortnight or so after an experiment, they do not disappear (Livingstone 1996: 309–10). There are many suggestions in the experimental literature about what determines the degree of effect caused by media exposures. These include the perceived realism of the representation, whether violence or deviance was seen as justified, punished, or rewarded, whether the viewers identified with the perpetrator, the variable vulnerability or susceptibility of the viewer, and so on (ibid.).

Typically, however, the effects of exposure to media stimuli in experimental situations are small. Interestingly, most of the research has looked at supposed negative effects of media, such as violence. The few studies that have examined the effects of 'prosocial' images suggest that these are much larger. One meta-analysis of 230 studies of media effects estimated that overall they showed that a single exposure to violent or stereotyped content was followed by about an extra 20 per cent of 'anti-social' responses, compared to an extra 50 per cent of 'prosocial' responses after viewing positive images (Hearold 1986; Livingstone 1996: 309). All of this has to be qualified, however, by the above caveats about how far such findings can be extrapolated to 'natural' contexts of viewing, and long-term effects in ordinary life (Wartella 1995: 306).

Given the limitations of laboratory experiments, some studies have tried to assess the effects of media exposure in more or less 'natural' everyday situations. One method has been by looking at the introduction of some form of medium (usually television) in an area where it did not exist before. This was most frequently done in the 1950s, when the spread of television ownership, first in the USA, then in the UK, provided the opportunity of a once-and-for-all natural experiment. One study of matched sets of thirty-four US cities in the early 1950s found that larceny increased by about 5 per cent in those cities where television was introduced for the first time, compared to cities without TV or those that had been receiving it for some time (Hennigan *et al.* 1952). However, British research in the same period does not find similar effects on deviance (Himmelweit *et al.* 1958; Livingstone 1996: 312–3). Since the virtually universal availability of television, such natural experiments are seldom possible. One recent example found that children's verbal and physical aggression increased in a Northern Canadian town after television, was introduced, compared to two towns with established television (Williams 1986). While such natural experiments do not suffer from the artificiality of their laboratory counterparts, they are of course less completely controlled: the possibility can never be ruled out that differences between experimental and control areas were due to factors other than television which changed at the same time.

The same issue arises in comparing the natural viewing habits of people who differ in their attitudes or behaviour concerning crime. Several studies have compared the viewing patterns of known offenders and (supposed) non-offenders. Some studies have concluded that more exposure to television is related to greater aggressiveness (see Belson 1978, and the other examples in Wartella 1995: 307–9); others that the viewing preferences of delinquents are remarkably similar to the general pattern for their age (Hagell and Newburn 1994). Neither conclusion is free from the possibility of other, unmeasured factors explaining either the association or the lack of it.

There is also some evidence that abuses of power by police and other criminal justice agents may be affected by media representations. A study of 'reality' TV programmes such as *Cops* suggests that the police may adopt forms of entrapment or illicit punishment of offenders to ensure good video footage for such shows (Doyle 1998: 110–12).

The big fix: the media–crime connection

A reading of any of the recent reviews of the research literature on possible links between media and criminal behaviour refutes the canard that libertarian wishful thinking has blinded researchers to the harm done by violent or deviant images. As one such survey found, 'current reviews conclude that there is a correlation between violence viewing and aggressive behaviour, a relationship that holds even when a variety of controls are imposed' (Wartella 1985: 306). However, the overall negative effects of media exposure seem to be small compared to other features in the social experience of offenders. Thus 'the question that remains is not whether media violence has an effect, but rather how important that effect has been, in comparison with other factors, in bringing about major social changes such as the postwar rise in crime' (ibid.: 312).

The problem with most of the effects debate and research is that it has often been directed at a rather implausible notion. What has been at issue is the will o' the wisp of a 'pure' media effect. The implicit model behind much popular anxiety, which was imported into the research agenda (especially in earlier work), was of the media as an autonomous and all-powerful ideological hypodermic syringe, injecting ideas and values into a passive public of cultural dopes.

It is far more plausible that media images affect people, who are not passive recipients but active interpreters, in a complex process of interaction with other cultural and social practices. Changes in media representations do not come fully formed from another planet and produce changes in behaviour patterns *ex nihilo*. They are themselves likely to reflect on-going changes in social perceptions and practices. Changing media images will then be interpreted by different audience sections in various ways, which may reinforce or alter emerging social patterns. The relationship between developments in the media and in the wider society is a dialectical one. While this makes the isolation and measurement of pure media effects chimerical, it certainly does not imply that media representations have no significant consequences.

As Sonia Livingstone concluded:

Most media researchers believe that the media have significant effects, even though they are hard to demonstrate, and most would agree that the media make a significant contribution to the social construction of reality. The problem is to move beyond this platitude . . . Part of the continued concern with media effects (aside from the occasional moral panics engendered around key issues) . . . is a concern with changing cultural understandings and practices . . . The study of enculturation processes, which work over long time periods, and which are integral to rather than separate from other forms of social determination, would not ask how the media make us act or think, but rather how the media contribute to making us who we are. [Livingstone 1996: 31–2]

Most of the research on the consequences of media representations of crime has concerned their possible impact on offending. In the last thirty years, however, another policy and research issue has come to the fore: the impact of the media on public fear of crime, and the consequences of this.

THE MEDIA AND FEAR OF CRIME

In recent years policy debates have focused increasingly on fear of crime as an issue potentially as serious as crime itself (Ditton and Farrell 2000; Hope and Sparks 2000). Concern is not just about the unnecessary pain of excessive anxiety, nor even the damage done to trust and social relations by fear and the prevention strategies it encourages. In the 'cultivation analysis' tradition which Gerbner and his associates have been developing for thirty years, media images of crime and violence are a threat to democracy.

Fearful people are more dependent, more easily manipulated and controlled, more susceptible to deceptively simple, strong, tough measures and hard-line postures—both political and religious. They may accept and even welcome repression if it promises to relieve their insecurities and other anxieties. That is the deeper problem of violence-laden television [Signorielli 1990: 102].

'Cultivation analysis' is derived from an on-going project of annual 'violence profiles': an elaborate content analysis of one week's prime-time television in an American city (Gerbner 1970, 1995). When reel-world violence is compared to real-world crime as measured by official statistics, it appears that the media images exaggerate the probability and severity of danger. This is said to 'cultivate' a misleading view of the world based on unnecessary anxiety about levels of risk from violent crime. The content analyses of programmes is the basis for construction of a set of 'television answers' to survey questions: the views about crime and violence which would be given by respondents 'if all we knew is what we saw' (Pandiani 1978). The closeness of fit of actual survey respondents' answers to these questions is then analysed according to their pattern of television consumption. The general finding is that 'heavier' television viewing is associated with world-views closer to the 'television answer' (Carlson 1985; Signorielli 1990: 96–102). There has been extensive criticism of the empirical and theoretical validity of these claims (Sparks 1992: chapter 4 is a penetrating and detailed review of these arguments).

The empirical debates have centred on two broad issues (Howitt 1998: chapter 4 is a useful review). How much of the association between measures of exposure to the media and of fearfulness survives the introduction of other control variables such as class, race, gender, place of residence, and actual experience of crime (Doob and MacDonald 1979; Gunter 1987; Chadee 2001; Roberts 2001)? Could any association between viewing and fearfulness result from the opposite causal process to that suggested by Gerbner and his associates, i.e. do more fearful viewers watch more TV rather than vice versa? More generally, it appears that 'cultivation' does not export well. British attempts to replicate the Gerbner findings have failed to do so, possibly because American television has a much higher violence profile (Wober 1978). This means that 'the British *heavy* viewer may see less television violence than American *light* viewers' (Gunter 1985: 250).

Gerbner and his colleagues have replied by various developments of their perspective, most significantly the concept of 'mainstreaming' (Gerbner *et al.* 1980). This is the argument that television views are all-pervasive, constituting the cultural mainstream, and this dampens down the measurement of distinct effects. To a large extent 'cultivation' through heavy viewing reinforces widespread images in the dominant television-formed world-view. In order to rescue this plausible argument from untestability, subsequent research in the tradition has tried to measure mainstreaming by calculating the extent of 'the sharing of common outlooks among the heavy viewers in those demographic groups whose light viewers hold more divergent views' (Signorielli 1990: 88).

Although the debate about the empirical validity of the cultivation hypothesis continues, there is evidence from other studies to confirm the plausible idea that exposure to media images is associated with fear of crime. A recent British study, for example, concluded after extensive multi-variate analysis that there was a significant relationship between reading newspapers with more emphasis on violent crime and measures of fearfulness expressed in a survey (Williams and Dickinson 1993). This association survived control by a number of demographic variables, such as socio-economic status, gender, and age. However, this association was not found with behavioural concomitants of fear, such as going out after dark. Neither could the study rule out the possibility that fear led to heavier readership of newspapers with more crime, rather than vice versa. On the empirical issue, while it remains a reasonable hypothesis that much public fear of crime is created or accentuated by media exposure, the research evidence remains equivocal about the strength, or even existence, of such a causal relationship (Sacco 1995: 151).

As with the research on media and criminal behaviour, much of this inconclusiveness is rooted in the theoretical limitations of positivist content analysis (Sparks 1992: chapter 4). In Gerbner's violence profiles, for instance, items of violence are collated according to operational definitions used by observers, without reference to the narrative contexts within which they are embedded. As shown earlier, it remains the case that most narratives have conclusions in accordance with Miss Prism's celebrated definition of fiction: 'The good ended happily, and the bad unhappily' (Oscar Wilde, *The Importance of Being Earnest*, Act II). Although there is a trend towards the incorporation of more critical perspectives and greater ambivalence and ambiguity, most crime stories still have an underlying emphasis on just resolutions of conflict and violence (Zillman and Wakshlag 1987; Reiner *et al.* 2000a and 2000b). It is not obvious that exposure to high degrees of violence en route to a happy ending has a fear-enhancing effect. 'When suspenseful drama featuring victimisation is known to contain a satisfying resolution, apprehensive individuals should anticipate pleasure and enjoyment' (Wakshlag *et al.* 1983: 238). Neither do counts of disembodied acts of violence distinguish between representations which are perceived as more or less 'realistic', and their differing impact.

Above all, quantitative assessments of the relationship between 'objectively' measured units of media content and survey responses cannot begin to understand the complex and dynamic inter-dependence of the differential experiences of crime, violence, and risk of different social groups and their subjective interpretations of the meaning of texts. The subtle intertwinings of differential social positions and life experiences with the reception of media texts is only beginning to be addressed by studies of content and interpretation. These use qualitative methods and ways of reading that seek to be sensitive to the complexities of analysing meaning (Sparks 1992, 2000, 2001; Schlesinger *et al.* 1992; Livingstone *et al.* 2001). As with the issue of the effects of media images on criminality, so too with fear, the issue is not whether media representations have consequences. Hardly anyone would deny this. The agenda is the unravelling of the complex interrelationship of media content and other dimensions of social structure and experience in shaping offending behaviour, fear of crime, and the politics of law and order (Sasson 1995; Beckett

1997; Girling *et al.* 2000; Stenson and Sullivan 2000; Hope and Sparks 2000; Garland 2001).

Having examined the content and consequences of media representations of crime, the next section will consider the causes of these images. What processes and priorities produce the pattern of representation of crime?

THE CAUSES OF MEDIA REPRESENTATIONS OF CRIME

Until recently, accounts of the production of crime news were primarily based on inferences drawn from content analyses and the political economy of the media, and valuable studies of this kind continue (e.g., Hall *et al.* 1978; Sherizen 1978; Tunnell 1998; Green 2000; Lawrence 2000). Other research has used interviews with reporters and other creative personnel or the police (e.g., Chibnall 1977; Fishman 1981; Ross 1998; Mawby 1998, 1999, 2001, 2002; Innes 1999, 2001). It is only relatively recently, however, that studies based on observation of the production process itself have been conducted (Ericson *et al.* 1987, 1989, 1991; Schlesinger *et al.* 1991; Schlesinger and Tumber 1992, 1993, 1994; Chermak 1995, 1998; Skidmore 1996; Doyle 1998).

CRIME NEWS AS HEGEMONY IN ACTION

Most of the earlier studies supported a version of the dominant ideology model. The immediate source of news content was the ideology of the reporter, personal and professional. However, a variety of organizational and professional imperatives exerted pressure for the production of news with the characteristics identified by content analyses. The sources of news production were seen as threefold:

1. The political ideology of the Press.
2. The elements of 'newsworthiness'.
3. Structural determinants of news-making.

The political ideology of the Press

The majority of newspapers have a more or less overtly C/conservative political ideology, and individual reporters are aware of this whatever their personal leanings. The broadcasting media, especially the BBC, are characterized by an ethic of political neutrality and professional objectivity in performing a public service of providing news information. In practice, however, this becomes a viewpoint which takes for granted certain broad beliefs and values, those of moderate, middle-of-the-road majority opinion—what Stuart Hall succinctly called a 'world at one with itself' (Hall 1970). The master concepts of this world-view include such notions as the 'national interest', the 'British way of life', and the 'democratic process' as epitomized by Westminster. In political or industrial conflict situations these are seen as threatened by 'mindless militants' manipulated by extremist minorities seeking 'anarchy' and subversion, with only the 'thin blue line' to save the day for law and order (Chibnall 1977: 21). Political conflict is assimilated to routine crime; both are portrayed as pathological conditions unrelated to wider social structures (Clarke and Taylor 1980; Hillyard 1982; Iyengar 1991; Beckett 1997: 38; Lawrence 2000: 57–60).

Traditional crime reporters explicitly saw it as their responsibility to present the police and the criminal justice system in as favourable a light as possible. As a crime reporter put it: 'If I've got to come down on one side or the other, either the goodies or the baddies, then obviously I'd come down on the side of the goodies, in the interests of law and order' (Chibnall 1977: 145). This of course did not mean that even the most pro-police crime reporter would not pursue stories of police malpractice as assiduously as possible. But it generated a tendency to present these within a 'one bad apple' framework (ibid.: chapter 5). However, the characteristics of crime reporting were more immediately the product of a professional sense of news values rather than any explicitly political ideology.

The elements of 'newsworthiness'

News content is generated and filtered primarily through reporters' sense of 'newsworthiness', what makes a good story that their audience wants to know about, rather than any overtly ideological considerations. The core elements of this are immediacy, dramatization, personalization, titillation, and novelty (Chibnall 1977: 22–45; Hall *et al.* 1978; Ericson *et al.* 1989). The value of novelty means that most news is about deviance in some form (Ericson *et al.* 1987). The primacy of these news values explains the predominant emphasis on violent and sex offences, and the concentration on higher-status offenders and victims, especially celebrities. It also accounts for the tendency to avoid stories about crime in general, or explanation of criminal trends and patterns.

These news values also encourage the presentation of political violence or disorder in terms of individual pathology rather than ideological opposition; as discrete criminal events, not manifestations of structural conflict (Lawrence 2000: chapter 3). This was shown in a detailed study of the reporting of the 27 October 1968 anti-Vietnam War demonstration in Grosvenor Square (Halloran *et al.* 1970). The media constructed their reporting around the issue of violence, crystallized in a photo showing a policeman being held and kicked by demonstrators, which appeared prominently on most front pages the day after the event (Hall 1973). The overall peacefulness of the occasion, let alone the broader issues of Vietnam, were subordinated to the emphasis on one dramatic but isolated incident of anti-police brutality. Most of the features of news reporting are not the result of ideology—political or professional—but are unintended consequences of a variety of structural and organizational imperatives of news-gathering.

Structural determinants of news-making

A variety of concrete organizational pressures underlying news production have unintended consequences, bolstering the law and order stance of most crime reporting. For example, concentrating personnel at institutional settings like courts, where newsworthy events can be expected to recur regularly, is an economic use of reporting resources. But it has the unintended consequence of concentrating on cleared-up cases, creating a misleading sense of police effectiveness.

The need to produce reports to fit the time schedules of news production contributes to their event orientation, the concentration on specific crimes at the expense of analysis of causal processes or policies (Rock 1973: 76–9; Lawrence 2000: chapter 8). Considerations of personal safety and convenience lead cameramen covering riots typically to film from behind police lines, which unintentionally structures an image of the police as vulnerable 'us' threatened by menacing 'them' (Murdock 1982: 108–109).

The police and criminal justice system control much of the information on which crime reporters rely, and this gives them a degree of power as essential accredited sources. The institutionalization of crime reporters as a specialist breed itself becomes a self-reinforcing cause of regular crime news. Crime reporters tend to develop a symbiotic relationship with the contacts and organizations they use regularly, especially the police (Chibnall 1977: chapters 3 and 6). According to one influential account of news production, this means that such institutional sources as the police become the 'primary definers' of crime news, which tends to be filtered through their perspective. The structural dependence of reporters on their regular sources 'permits the institutional definers to establish the initial definition or *primary interpretation* of the topic in question. This interpretation then "commands the field" in all subsequent treatment and sets the terms of reference within which all further coverage of debate takes place' (Hall *et al.* 1978: 58; Lawrence 2000: chapter 3).

In recent years the production of crime news (like news in general) has been transformed by a decline in the use of specialist reporters, including court and crime correspondents. This is due partly to the increasing news emphasis on celebrities, to a point where even sensational murders and other crime stories may be squeezed out unless there is also a celebrity element (as was present in the Jill Dando murder, for example). The decline of specialist reporting is also a result of the increasingly commercial orientation of the multimedia conglomerates that own most news outlets, which has restricted editorial budgets severely. Many crime and criminal justice stories, cases, and issues now fail to get aired prominently or perhaps at all, even in the sensationalist manner that used to be a core news staple (Davies 1999).

In sum, this account of news production within the hegemonic model sees news content as the largely unintended but determined consequence of the structure and political economy of news production. As one recent text summarizes it, 'journalists are not *necessarily* biased towards the powerful—but their bureaucratic organisation and cultural assumptions make them conduits of that power' (McNair 1993: 48).

CRIME NEWS AS CULTURAL CONFLICT

Observational studies of the crime news production process suggest that the deterministic implications of the hegemonic model require qualification (Ericson *et al.* 1987, 1989, 1991; Schlesinger *et al.* 1991; Schlesinger and Tumber 1992, 1993, 1994; Skidmore 1996). They do not overthrow its fundamental implications, however.

Ericson *et al.* confirm earlier accounts of the structuring of news-gathering and presentation around a sense of news values, criteria leading to the selection of particular types of stories and perspectives. These constitute a 'vocabulary of precedents': not hard and fast rules, but 'what previous exemplars tell them should be done in the present instance' (Ericson *et al.* 1987: 348). This leaves room for flexibility and judgement; the newsroom is not characterized by normative consensus but by negotiation and conflict between reporters, editors, and sources. News stories vary in character. Many are routine fillers, where a clearly-established paradigm is followed, albeit with new names, dates, and details each time. What usually makes a story newsworthy at all is some departure from expected norms, an element of freakishness or an opportunity to explore everyday moral dilemmas (Katz 1987). But the big stories are ones where novelty is a high value, and there is more room for negotiation of angles and priorities.

There is always a tension between two contradictory pressures. The highest journalistic accolade is the 'scoop', reporting a high news value story that has not yet been reported. This exerts pressure to be ahead of the pack, to seek out sources that no rivals have yet found. However, the worst possible scenario is to miss important information that everybody else has. This generates a tendency to hunt with the pack, mining the same sources as rivals. The fear of failure usually prevails over the lure of the scoop, on minimax principles, which is why front pages tend to be so similar.

There are also systematic variations between news stories in different media and markets (Ericson *et al.* 1991). This is partly because they have different variants of political and professional journalistic ideology according to patterns of ownership (state *versus* private, for example) and perceived audience (business or policy elites, other opinion leaders, liberal professionals, or a mass public seeking entertainment; local or national). These are interconnected with differences in technological resources, budgetary limitations, and the different 'grammars' of written and spoken language, still and moving pictures.

Observation also alerts analysts to the ever-present role of contingency and cock-ups (Ericson *et al.* 1991: 93–4). 'We know that at the level of production news is more procedure-related than content-related' (ibid.), and procedures can be disrupted for all sorts of random reasons.

Detailed study reveals not only that there is more diversity, negotiation, and contingency within news organizations than the hegemony model implies, but also in the sources used. These now range far beyond the accredited agencies of the formal criminal justice institutions (Schlesinger and Tumber 1994; Lawrence 2000). Groups critical of the establishment (such as penal reform or civil liberties groups) *are* given a voice, depending in part on their organizational and presentational skills, and their hold on interesting knowledge; and partly on medium and market differences. This is also a process which has gathered pace over time with the politicization of law and order (Downes and Morgan, in Chapter 10 of this volume). The news values of dramatization, personalization and titillation often lead to inputs from individual victims, offenders, witnesses, or their families and friends. The hegemonic model over-emphasizes the capacity of official viewpoints to monopolize the news.

While more detailed analyses of news production in action do emphasize its contingency and fluidity compared to the determinism suggested by earlier accounts, they do not fundamentally change the picture of the role of crime news. While news may be a competitive arena of conflicting viewpoints, it is one which is culturally and structurally loaded (Schlesinger 1989: 82). For all the fluidity and contingency which can be observed in the process of production, in the final analysis 'the news media are as much an agency of *policing* as the law-enforcement agencies whose activities and classifications are reported on' (Ericson *et al.* 1991: 74). They reproduce order in the process of representing it.

Although there have been many studies of the production of crime news, there has been no comparable research on fiction. All we have are memoirs of writers, directors, and other creators of crime fiction, and fan-oriented biographies or accounts of the making of particular films or programmes. The only exception is an interview study of Hollywood writers, directors, and producers of TV shows and cinema films (Lichter *et al.* 1994: Part IV; Powers *et al.* 1996: chapter 3). The interviews suggest that the contemporary Hollywood elite sees itself as having a mission. In essence the members of this are an example of the 1960s radicals' long march through the institutions. Their ideology is a combination of acceptance of the economic and political institutions of America to which they owe their status and privileges, and the libertarian stance on issues of personal and sexual morality that they have carried since their youth. They feel a mission to put as much of this into their work as is compatible with the overriding priority of keeping the audience ratings high and the networks happy. How this expressed ideology translates into actual creative and production practices has not been studied, however, in any research analogous to that on crime news.

OBSERVERS OR PLAYERS? THE MEDIA AND CRIME IN POSTMODERNITY

In the introduction to this chapter two competing concerns about media representations of crime were outlined: the 'respectable fear' that they were subversive and desubordinating (e.g., Medved 1992); and the radical anxiety that they were a means of social control and discipline (e.g., Wykes 2001). The review of research suggests that there is a complex interplay between media representations of crime, criminal behaviour, and criminal justice.

With variations according to medium and market, mass media news and entertainment are saturated with stories about crime. These disproportionately feature the most serious and violent crimes, but strip them from any analytic framework. The emphasis is on crime as the product of individual choice and free-floating evil, diverting attention from any links to social structure or culture (Sasson 1995). There is strong evidence that media images *can* influence criminal behaviour, but overall their direct effect is small relative to other factors. This is largely because people vary in their interpretation of representations according to demographic, generational, and other life-course factors (Livingstone *et al.* 2001). There is a variety of ways suggested by different criminological perspectives in which media representations could influence crime rates and patterns. For example, the overall volume of property crime is likely to be affected by media portrayals of material success as the acme of the good life in a context of structural inequalities of opportunity, as Mertonian strain theories suggest. It is unlikely to be an accident that the remorseless rise of volume property crime after the mid-1950s in Britain coincided with the advent of commercial television. But such connections are much harder to test by the quasi-experimental methods that have dominated the research on media effects.

The disciplinary role of media stories about crime, reproducing as well as representing order, is supported more clearly by the research. This is due to what Surette has called 'the law of opposites': the pattern of crime in the media is in most respects the reverse of what official statistics suggest (Surette 1998: 47). (Surette himself says the media show 'the opposite of what is true', but this formulation begs the questions about the truth of the picture conveyed by the official statistics, discussed by Maguire in Chapter 11 of this volume.) Media representations tend to exaggerate the threat of crime and to promote policing and punishment as the antidote. This is likely to accentuate fear, and thus support for law and order policies. Because of organizational exigencies as much as ideological reasons, the media present viewpoints on crime and criminal justice policy which—though not monolithic—are loaded towards official perspectives.

The present trends indicate a growing symbiosis between media images, criminality, and criminal justice. In Simon Lee's words, 'The media are no longer, if they ever were, observers of the scene, they are players in the game' (cited in Peay 1998: 8). This accentuates past patterns to an extent amounting to a qualitatively new stage. The insecure borderline between purportedly factual and fictional narratives is eroding. A growing variety of criminal justice lobbies and pressure groups seek to influence, if not construct, the news. At the same time technological developments interact with cultural changes to produce more 'reality' broadcasting (Fishman and Cavender 1998).

The current stage of development reflects the impact of the more general features of 'postmodernity' on the relationship between media, crime, and criminal justice. The space–time distanciation between criminal cases and their reporting in the media, and the reciprocal feedback of images on practice, are eroding rapidly (Giddens 1984; Thompson 1995). Increasing numbers of criminal justice events, such as the 1992 LA riots or the O.J. Simpson case, are broadcast around the world literally as they are happening. An ever-wider range of participants in the criminal justice process are not only seeking to influence representations but are creating events specifically for the media. 'We live in a dramatised world' (Ericson 1991: 235), where the media are participants in the processes they represent. Criminal justice agencies tailor their activities to public relations, how their activities will play on the news. Police investigate (sometimes instigate) all the crimes fit to print. Crimes and legal processes are not only reflected in reporting with greater rapidity, they may be created for news stories. Offences have been incited by law enforcement agencies in order to have the successful investigation televised (as in the Azscam entrapment case analysed by Altheide 1993). Since the 1960s, protesters and police act with self-conscious awareness that 'the whole world is watching' (Gitlin 1980; Della Porta and Reiter 1998). The tragedy of 11 September 2001 is simply the most vivid and dramatic example of these developments to date, when thousands of people were murdered in front of the eyes of TV audiences around the globe, in a way calculated to achieve the maximum possible media impact.

The mass media are important not only because of their ideological significance. Media technology plays an increasingly direct role in social control, above all through the growth of CCTV (Norris and Armstrong 1999), as the cover of this edition illustrates. Media technology can also be used to control the controllers, to make authorities more accountable, as the use of CCTV and other recording devices in police stations shows (Newburn and Hayman 2001). The proliferation of cheap, portable cameras contributes to this too, as the Rodney King case indicated (Lawrence 2000). Mass media technologies make the model of contemporary social control a Synopticon (Mathiesen 1997): they provide the means for the many to see the few, offsetting the Benthamite paradigm of the few observing the many. However, this reciprocal process of surveillance between elites and masses is highly unbalanced. The greater vulnerability of the powerful to exposure and scandal does not fundamentally change structures of power and advantage. Indeed Mathiesen argues plausibly that the illusion of intimacy, with elites provided by contemporary media surveillance of their activities, gives people a misleading sense of empowerment which acts as a more complex process of discipline than traditional forms of legitimation. It is possible, he argues, 'that the control and discipline of the "soul", that is, the creation of human beings who control themselves through self-control and thus fit neatly into a so-called democratic capitalist society, is a task which is actually fulfilled by modern Synopticon' (Mathiesen 1997: 215).

The growing interdependence of media representation and social 'reality' raises the spectre of 'a media spiral in which the representations of crime and the fear of crime precisely constitute . . . the hyperreal' (Osborne 1996: 36). Certainly these developments vastly complicate the vexed question of how images and narratives that are felt to be undesirable can be regulated or influenced. Perhaps hope lies precisely in the greater openness of the media to a diversity of inputs and influences (Ericson 1991; Schlesinger and Tumber 1994). Past experience, however, suggests the more pessimistic prediction that although contemporary mass communications present 'an appreciably open terrain for struggles for justice' (Ericson 1991: 242), the dice are loaded in favour of dominant interests—even if they have to struggle harder for their hegemony.

Selected further reading

Richard Sparks' *Television and the Drama of Crime* (Buckingham: Open University Press, 1992) is a theoretically sophisticated critique of content analyses of crime fiction, and their relationship to fear of crime. Classic studies of crime news that remain valuable are S. Cohen and J. Young (eds), *The Manufacture of News* (London: Constable, 1973) and S. Chibnall, *Law-and-Order News* (London: Tavistock, 1977). Two illuminating studies of the production and content of crime news are the trilogy by R. Ericson, P. Baranek, and J. Chan, *Visualising Deviance, Negotiating Control,* and *Representing Order* (Milton Keynes: Open University

Press, 1987, 1989, 1991 respectively); and P. Schlesinger and H. Tumber's *Reporting Crime* (Oxford: Oxford University Press, 1994). Useful reviews of the research on media effects can be found in: S. Livingstone, 'On the Continuing Problem of Media Effects', in J. Curran and M. Gurevitch (eds), *Mass Media and Society* (London: Arnold, 1996), and D. Howitt, *Crime, The Media and the Law* (London: Wiley, 1998). A valuable text on crime and media is R. Surette, *Media, Crime and Justice* (2nd edn, Belmont: Wadsworth, 1998). K. Beckett and T. Sasson, *The Politics of Injustice* (Thousand Oaks: Pine Forge, 2000) offers an excellent critique of media representations of crime, and their impact on policy. M. Fishman and G. Cavender (eds), *Entertaining Crime* is a valuable collection of papers on 'reality television'. Very useful edited volumes offering a rich diversity of research papers on media and crime are: R. Ericson (ed.), *Crime and the Media* (Aldershot: Dartmouth, 1995); D. Kidd-Hewitt and R. Osborne (eds), *Crime and the Media: The Post-Modern Spectacle* (London: Pluto, 1996); F. Bailey and D. Hale (eds), *Popular Culture, Crime and Justice* (Belmont: Wadsworth, 1998); and the recent special issue of *Criminal Justice Matters* on 'Crime and the Media' (No. 43, Spring 2001, Centre for Crime and Justice Studies, Kings College, London). Two recent valuable edited collections looking at contemporary relationships between risk and crime control policy that include discussions of the role of the media are: K. Stenson and R. Sullivan (eds), *Crime, Risk and Justice* (Cullompton: Willan, 2000); and T. Hope and R. Sparks (eds), *Crime, Risk and Insecurity* (London: Routledge, 2000).

References

ALLEN, J., LIVINGSTONE, S., and REINER, R. (1997), 'The Changing Generic Location of Crime in Film', *Journal of Communication*, 47, 4: 1–13.

—— (1998), 'True Lies: Changing Images of Crime in British Postwar Cinema', *European Journal of Communication*, 13, 1: 53–75.

ALTHEIDE, D. (1993), 'Electronic Media and State Control: The Case of Azscam', *The Sociological Quarterly* 34, 1: 53–69.

BAILEY, F., and HALE, D. (eds) (1998), *Popular Culture, Crime and Justice*, Belmont: Wadsworth.

BAILEY, S. (1993), 'Fast Forward to Violence: Violent Visual Imaging and Serious Juvenile Crime', *Criminal Justice Matters*, 11, Spring: 6–7.

BANDURA, A., ROSS, D., and ROS, S.A. (1961), 'Transmission of Aggression Through Imitation of Aggressive Models', *Journal of Abnormal and Social Psychology*, 63, 3: 575–82.

BARAK, G. (ed.) (1994), *Media, Process, and the Social Construction of Crime*, New York: Garland.

BARCLAY, G., and TAVARES, C. (1999), *Information on the Criminal Justice System in England and Wales: Digest 4*, London: Home Office.

BARKER, M. (1984a), *A Haunt of Fears*, London: Pluto.

—— (1984b), *The Video Nasties: Freedom and Censorship in the Media*, London: Pluto.

—— and PETLEY, J. (eds) (2001), *Ill Effects: The Media/Violence Debate*, 2nd edn, London: Routledge.

BARLOW, M.H. (1998), 'Race and the Problem of Crime in Time and Newsweek Cover Stories, 1946–1995', *Social Justice*, 25: 149–83.

BECKER, H. (1963), *Outsiders*, New York: Free Press.

BECKETT, K. (1997), *Making Crime Pay*, New York: Oxford University Press.

—— and SASSON, T. (2000), *The Politics of Injustice*, Thousand Oaks: Pine Forge Press.

BELL, I.A., and DALDRY, G. (eds) (1990), *Watching the Detectives*, London: Macmillan.

BELSON, W. (1978), *Television Violence and the Adolescent Boy*, Westmead: Saxon House.

BENSTOCK, B. (ed.) (1983), *Essays on Detective Fiction*, London: Macmillan.

BEST, J., and HORIUCHI, G.T. (1985), 'The Razor Blade in the Apple: The Social Construction of Urban Legends', *Social Problems*, 32, 5: 488–99.

BINYON, T.J. (1989), *Murder Will Out: The Detective in Fiction*, Oxford: Oxford University Press.

BROWNSTEIN, H. (1995), 'The Media and the Construction of Random Drug Violence', in J. Ferrell and C.R. Sanders (eds), *Cultural Criminology*, 45–65, Boston, Mass.: Northeastern University Press.

BUXTON, D. (1990), *From The Avengers to Miami Vice: Form and Ideology in Television Series*, Manchester: Manchester University Press.

CAREY, S. (1993), 'Mass Media Violence and Aggressive Behaviour', *Criminal Justice Matters*, 11, Spring: 8–9.

CARLSON, J.M. (1985), *Prime-Time Law Enforcement: Crime Show Viewing and Attitudes to the Criminal Justice System*, New York: Praeger.

CAWELTI, J.G. (1976), *Adventure, Mystery and Romance*, Chicago: Chicago University Press.

CHADEE, D. (2001), 'Fear of Crime and the Media: From Perceptions to Reality', *Criminal Justice Matters*, 43: 10–11.

CHEATWOOD, D. (1998), 'Prison Movies: Films About Adult, Male, Civilian Prisons: 1929–1995', in F. Bailey and D. Hale (eds), *Popular Culture, Crime and Justice*, 209–31, Belmont: Wadsworth.

CHERMAK, S.M. (1995), *Victims in the News: Crime in American News Media*, Boulder: Westview.

—— (1998), 'Police, Courts, and Corrections in the Media', in F. Bailey and D. Hale (eds), *Popular Culture, Crime and Justice*, 87–99, Belmont: Wadsworth.

CHIBNALL, S. (1977), *Law-and-Order News*, London: Tavistock.

—— and MURPHY, R. (eds) (1999), *British Crime Cinema*, London: Routledge.

CHIRICOS, T., ESCHHOLZ, S., and GERTZ, M. (1997), 'Crime, News and Fear of Crime', *Social Problems*, 44, 3: 342–57.

CLARENS, C. (1997), *Crime Movies*, New York: Da Capo.

CLARKE, A. (1982), *Television Police Series and Law and Order* (Popular Culture Course Unit 22), Milton Keynes: Open University.

—— (1983), 'Holding the Blue Lamp: Television and the Police in Britain', *Crime and Social Justice*, 19: 44–51.

—— (1986), 'This is Not the Boy Scouts: Television Police Series and Definitions of Law and Order', in T. Bennett, C. Mercer, and J. Woollacott (eds), *Popular Culture and Social Relations*, 219–32, Milton Keynes: Open University Press.

—— (1992), '"You're Nicked!" Television Police Series and the Fictional Representation of Law and Order', in D. Strinati and S. Wagg (eds), *Come On Down? Popular Media Culture in Post-War Britain*, 232–53, London: Routledge.

—— and TAYLOR, I. (1980), 'Vandals, Pickets and Muggers: Television Coverage of Law and Order in the 1979 Election', *Screen Education*, 36: 99–112.

CLARKE, J. (2001), 'The Pleasures of Crime: Interrogating the Detective Story', in J. Muncie and E. McLaughlin (eds), *The Problem of Crime*, 2nd edn, 71–106, London: Sage.

COHEN, L., and FELSON, S. (1979), 'Social Change and Crime Rate Trends: A Routine Activities Approach', *American Sociological Review*, 44: 588–608.

COHEN, S. (1972), *Folk Devils and Moral Panics*, London: Paladin.

—— and YOUNG, J. (eds) (1973), *The Manufacture of News*, London: Constable.

COTTLE, S. (1993), *TV News, Urban Conflict and the Inner City*, Leicester: Leicester University Press.

CUMBERBATCH, G. (1989), *A Measure of Uncertainty: The Effects of Mass Media*, Broadcasting Standards Council Research Monograph 1, London: John Libbey.

——, WOODS, S., and MAGUIRE, A. (1995), *Crime in the News: Television, Radio and Newspapers: A Report for BBC Broadcasting Research*, Birmingham: Aston University, Communications Research Group.

DAHLGREN, P. (1988), 'Crime News: The Fascination of the Mundane', *European Journal of Communication*, 3, 1: 189–206.

DAHRENDORF, R. (1985), *Law and Order*, London: Sweet and Maxwell.

DAVIS, J. (1952), 'Crime News in Colorado Newspapers', *American Journal of Sociology*, 57: 325–30.

DELLA PORTA, D., and REITER, H. (eds) (1998), *Policing Protest*, Minneapolis: University of Minnesota Press.

DEUTSCHMANN, P. (1959), *News Page Content of Twelve Metropolitan Dailies*, Cincinnati, Ohio: Scripps-Howard Research Centre.

DITTON, J., and DUFFY, J. (1983), 'Bias in the Newspaper Reporting of Crime News', *British Journal of Criminology*, 23, 2: 159–65.

—— and FARRALL, S. (eds) (2000), *The Fear of Crime*, Aldershot: Dartmouth.

DOBASH, R.E., SCHLESINGER, P., DOBASH, R., and WEAVER, C.K. (1998), '"Crimewatch UK": Women's Interpretation of Televised Violence', in M. Fishman and G. Cavender (eds), *Entertaining Crime*, 37–58, New York: Aldine De Gruyter.

DOMINICK, J. (1978), 'Crime and Law Enforcement

in the Mass Media', in C. Winick (ed.), *Deviance and Mass Media*, 105–28, Beverly Hills, Cal.: Sage.

DOOB, A., and MACDONALD, G. (1979), 'Television Viewing and the Fear of Victimisation: Is the Relationship Causal?', *Journal of Personality and Social Psychology*, 37, 1: 170–79.

DOVE, G. (1982), *The Police Procedural*, Bowling Green, Ohio: Bowling Green Popular Press.

—— and BARGAINNIER, E. (eds) (1986), *Cops and Constables: American and British Fictional Policemen*, Bowling Green, Ohio: Bowling Green Popular Press.

DOYLE, A. (1998), '"Cops": Television Policing As Policing Reality', in M. Fishman and G. Cavender (eds), *Entertaining Crime*, 95–116, New York: Aldine De Gruyter.

DURSTON, G. (1997), *Moll Flanders: Analysis of 18th Century Criminal Biography*, Chichester: Barry Rose.

DUSSUYER, I. (1979), *Crime News: A Study of 40 Toronto Newspapers*, Toronto: University of Toronto Centre of Criminology.

EATON, M. (1995), 'A Fair Cop? Viewing the Effects of the Canteen Culture in *Prime Suspect* and *Between the Lines*', in D. Kidd-Hewitt and R. Osborne (eds), *Crime and the Media: The Post-Modern Spectacle*, London: Pluto.

ELTON, B. (1996), *Popcorn*, London: Simon and Schuster.

ERICSON, R. (1991), 'Mass Media, Crime, Law, and Justice', *British Journal of Criminology*, 31, 3: 219–49.

—— (ed.) (1995), *Crime and the Media*, Aldershot: Dartmouth.

——, BARANEK, P., and CHAN, J. (1987), *Visualising Deviance*, Milton Keynes: Open University Press.

——, —— and —— (1989), *Negotiating Control*, Milton Keynes: Open University Press.

——, —— and —— (1991), *Representing Order*, Milton Keynes: Open University Press.

EVERSON, W. (1972), *The Detective in Film*, New York: Citadel.

FABIAN, R. (1950), *Fabian of the Yard*, London: Naldrett.

—— (1954), *London After Dark*, London: Naldrett.

FALLER, L. (1987), *Turned to Account: The Forms and Functions of Criminal Biography in Late Seventeenth and Early Eighteenth Century England*, Cambridge: Cambridge University Press.

FERRELL, J. (1998), 'Criminalising Popular Culture',

in F. Bailey and D. Hale (eds), *Popular Culture, Crime and Justice*, 71–84, Belmont: Wadsworth.

—— and SANDERS, C.R. (eds) (1995), *Cultural Criminology*, Boston, Mass.: Northeastern University Press.

FISHMAN, M. (1981), 'Police News: Constructing An Image of Crime', *Urban Life*, 9, 4: 371–94.

—— and CAVENDER, G. (eds) (1998), *Entertaining Crime: Television Reality Programs*, New York: Aldine De Gruyter.

GARLAND, D. (2001), *The Culture of Control*, Oxford: Oxford University Press.

GAROFALO, J. (1981), 'Crime and the Mass Media: A Selective Review of Research', *Journal of Research in Crime and Delinquency*, 18, 2: 319–50.

GERBNER, G. (1970), 'Cultural Indicators: The Case of Violence in Television Drama', *Annals of the American Academy of Political and Social Science*, 338, 1: 69–81.

—— (1972), 'Violence in Television Drama: Trends and Symbolic Functions', in G. Comstock and E. Rubinstein (eds), *Television and Social Behaviour Vol. 1: Content and Control*, 28–187, Washington, DC: US Government Printing Office.

—— (1995), 'Television Violence: The Power and the Peril', in G. Dines and J. Humez (eds), *Gender, Race and Class in the Media*, 547–57, Thousand Oaks, Cal.: Sage.

—— and GROSS, L. (1976), 'Living With Television: The Violence Profile', *Journal of Communication*, 26, 1: 173–99.

——, ——, MORGAN, M., and SIGNORIELLI, N. (1980), 'The Mainstreaming of America: Violence Profile No 11', *Journal of Communication*, 30, 1: 19–29.

——, ——, —— and —— (1984), 'Political Correlates of Television Viewing', *Public Opinion Quarterly*, 48, 2: 283–300.

——, ——, —— and —— (1986), 'Living With Television: The Dynamics of the Cultivation Process', in J. Bryant and D. Zillman (eds), *Perspectives on Media Effects*, 17–40, Hillside, NJ: Lawrence Erlbaum.

GIDDENS, A. (1984), *The Constitution of Society*, Cambridge: Polity Press.

GIRLING, E., LOADER, I., and SPARKS, R. (2000), *Crime and Social Change in Middle England*, London: Routledge.

GITLIN, T. (1980), *The Whole World Is Watching*, Berkeley: University of California Press.

—— (2000), *Inside Prime Time*, revised edn, Berkeley: University of California Press.

GRABER, D. (1980), *Crime News and the Public*, New York: Praeger.

GREEN, P. (2000), 'American Television, Crime and the Risk Society', in K. Stenson and R. Sullivan (eds), *Crime, Risk and Justice*, 214–27, Cullompton: Willan.

GREGORY, J., and LEES, S. (1999), *Policing Sexual Assault*, London: Routledge.

GUNTER, B. (1981), 'Measuring Television Violence: A Review and Suggestions for a New Analytic Perspective', *Current Psychological Research*, 1, 1: 91–112.

—— (1985), *Dimensions of Television Violence*, Aldershot: Gower.

HAGELL, A., and NEWBURN, T. (1994), *Young Offenders and the Media*, London: Policy Studies Institute.

HALE, D.C. (1998), 'Keeping Women in their Place: An Analysis of Policewomen in Videos, 1972–1996', in F. Bailey and D. Hale (eds), *Popular Culture, Crime and Justice*, 159–79, Belmont: Wadsworth.

HALL, S. (1970), 'A World At One With Itself', *New Society*, 18 June: 1056–8.

—— (1973), 'The Determination of News Photographs', in S. Cohen and J. Young (eds), *The Manufacture of News*, 226–43, London: Constable.

—— (1979), *Drifting Into A Law and Order Society*, London: Cobden Trust.

——, CRITCHLEY, C., JEFFERSON, T., CLARKE, J., and ROBERTS, B. (1978), *Policing the Crisis*, London: Macmillan.

HALLORAN, J., ELLIOTT, L., and MURDOCK, G. (1970), *Demonstrations and Communication*, London: Penguin.

HARDY, P. (1997), *The BFI Companion to Crime*, London: Cassell.

—— (1998), *Gangsters*, London: Aurum.

HARRIS, F. (1932), *Presentation of Crime in Newspapers*, Minneapolis, Minn.: Minneapolis Sociological Press.

HAYCRAFT, H. (1941), *Murder For Pleasure*, New York: Appleton Century.

HEAROLD, S. (1986), 'A Synthesis of 1043 Effects of Television on Social Behaviour', in G. Comstock (ed.), *Public Communications and Behaviour Vol. 1*, 65–133, New York: Academic Press.

HENNIGAN, K.M., DELROSARIO, M.L., HEATH, L., COOK, J.D., and CALDER, B.J. (1982), 'Impact of the Introduction of Television Crime in the United States: Empirical Findings and Theoretical Implications', *Journal of Personality and Social Psychology*, 42, 3: 461–77.

HILLYARD, P. (1982), 'The Media Coverage of Crime and Justice in Northern Ireland', in C. Sumner (ed.), *Crime, Justice and the Mass Media*, 36–54 (Cropwood Papers 14), Cambridge: Institute of Criminology.

HIMMELWEIT, H., OPPENHEIM, A.N., and VINCE, P. (1958), *Television and the Child*, London: Oxford University Press.

HOPE, T., and SPARKS, R. (eds) (2000), *Crime, Risk and Insecurity*, London: Routledge.

HOWITT, D. (1998), *Crime, The Media and The Law*, London: Wiley.

HURD, G. (1979), 'The Television Presentation of the Police', in S. Holdaway (ed.), *The British Police*, London: Edward Arnold.

INCIARDI, J., and DEE, J.L. (1987), 'From the Keystone Cops to Miami Vice: Images of Policing in American Popular Culture', *Journal of Popular Culture* 21, 2: 84–102.

INNES, M. (1999), 'The Media as an Investigative Resource in Murder Enquiries', *British Journal of Criminology*, 39, 2: 268–85.

—— (2001), '"Crimewatching": Homicide Investigations in the Age of Information', *Criminal Justice Matters*, 43: 42–3.

IYENGAR, S. (1991), *Is Anyone Responsible? How Television Frames Political Issues*, Chicago, Ill.: Chicago University Press.

KATZ, J. (1987), 'What Makes Crime "News"?', *Media, Culture and Society*, 9, 1: 47–75.

KERR, P. (1981), 'Watching the Detectives: American Television Crime Series 1949–81', *Prime-Time*, 1, 1: 2–6.

KIDD-HEWITT, D., and OSBORNE, R. (eds) (1996), *Crime and the Media: The Post-modern Spectacle*, London: Pluto.

KING, N. (1999), *Heroes in Hard Times: Cop Action Movies in the US*, Philadelphia: Temple University Press.

KNIGHT, S. (1980), *Form and Ideology in Crime Fiction*, London: Macmillan.

KOOISTRA, P.G., MAHONEY, J.S., and WESTERVELT, S.D. (1998), 'The World of Crime According to "Cops"', in M. Fishman and G. Cavender (eds), *Entertaining Crime*, 141–58, New York: Aldine De Gruyter.

LAING, S. (1991), 'Banging in Some Reality: The Original "Z-Cars"', in J. Corner (ed.), *Popular Television in Britain: Studies in Cultural History*, 125–43, London: British Film Institute.

LAWRENCE, R.G. (2000), *The Politics of Force: Media and the Construction of Police Brutality*, Berkeley: University of California Press.

LEA, J., and YOUNG, J. (1984), *What is to Be Done About Law and Order?*, London: Penguin.

LEES, S. (1995), 'Media Reporting of Rape: The 1993 British "Date Rape" Controversy', in D. Kidd-Hewitt and R. Osborne (eds), *Crime and the Media*, 107–30, London: Pluto.

LEISHMAN, F., and MASON, P. (2002), *Policing and the Media: Facts, Fictions and Factions*, Cullompton: Willan.

LEVI, M. (2001), 'White-Collar Crime in the News', *Criminal Justice Matters*, 43: 24–5.

LICHTER, S.R., LICHTER, L.S., and ROTHMAN, S. (1994), *Prime Time: How TV Portrays American Culture*, Washington: Regnery.

LIVINGSTONE, S. (1996), 'On the Continuing Problem of Media Effects', in J. Curran and M. Gurevitch (eds), *Mass Media and Society*, 305–24, London: Arnold.

——, ALLEN, J., and REINER, R. (2001), 'Audiences for Crime Media 1946–91: A Historical Approach to Reception Studies', *Communication Review*, 4, 2: 165–92.

MANDEL, E. (1984), *Delightful Murder: A Social History of the Crime Story*, London: Pluto.

MANNING, P. (1998), 'Media Loops', in F. Bailey and D. Hale (eds), *Popular Culture, Crime and Justice*, 25–39, Belmont: Wadsworth.

MARSH, H.L. (1991), 'A Comparative Analysis of Crime Coverage in Newspapers in the United States and Other Countries From 1960–1989: A Review of the Literature', *Journal of Criminal Justice*, 19, 1: 67–80.

MASON, P. (1996), 'Prime Time Punishment: The British Prison and Television', in D. Kidd-Hewitt and R. Osborne (eds), *Crime and the Media*, 185–205, London: Pluto.

MATHEWS, T.D. (1994), *Censored*, London: Chatto and Windus.

MATHIESEN, T. (1997), 'The Viewer Society: Michel Foucault's "Panopticon" Revisited', *Theoretical Criminology*, 1, 2: 215–34.

MAWBY, R.C. (1998), 'The Changing Image of Policing in Television Drama 1956–96', *Journal of the Police History Society*, 13: 39–44.

—— (1999), 'Visibility, Transparency, and Police-Media Relations', *Policing and Society*, 9, 3: 263–86.

—— (2001), 'Promoting the Police? The Rise of Police Image Work', *Criminal Justice Matters*, 43: 44–5.

—— (2002), *Policing Images: Policing, Communication and Legitimacy*, Cullompton: Willan.

MAWBY, R.I., and BROWN, J. (1983), 'Newspaper Images of the Victim', *Victimology*, 9, 1: 82–94.

MCARTHUR, C. (1972), *Underworld USA*, London: Secker and Warburg.

MCCARTY, J. (1993), *Hollywood Gangland*, New York: St Martin's Press.

MCNAIR, B. (1993), *News And Journalism in the UK*, London: Routledge.

MEDVED, M. (1992), *Hollywood vs. America*, London: HarperCollins.

MERTON, R. (1938/1957), 'Social Structure and Anomie', *American Sociological Review*, 3: 672–82. Reprinted in R. Merton, *Social Theory and Social Structure*, Glencoe, Ill.: Free Press, 1957; revised edn, 1963.

MESSNER, S.F., and ROSENFELD, R. (2000), *Crime and the American Dream*, 3rd edn, Belmont: Wadsworth.

MEYERS, R. (1981), *TV Detectives*, San Diego, Cal.: Barnes.

—— (1989), *Murder on the Air*, New York: The Mysterious Press.

MILLER, F. (1994), *Censored Hollywood: Sex, Sin and Violence on Screen*, Atlanta, Ga.: Turner.

MORRISON, B. (1997), *As If*, Cambridge: Granta.

MOST, G., and STOWE, W. (1983), *The Poetics of Murder*, New York: Harcourt, Brace and Jovanovich.

MURDOCK, G. (1982), 'Disorderly Images', in C. Sumner (ed.), *Crime, Justice and the Mass Media*, 104–23 (Cropwood Papers 14), Cambridge: Institute of Criminology.

NAVA, M. (1988), 'Cleveland and the Press: Outrage and Anxiety in the Reporting of Child Sexual Abuse', *Feminist Review*, 28: 103–21.

NELLIS, M., and HALE, C. (1982), *The Prison Film*, London: Radical Alternatives to Prison.

NEWBURN, T., and HAYMAN, S. (2001), *Policing, CCTV and Social Control*, Cullompton: Willan.

NORRIS, C., and ARMSTRONG, G. (1999), *The Maximum Surveillance Society: The Rise of CCTV*, Sussex: Berg.

NYBERG, A.K. (1998), 'Comic Books and Juvenile Delinquence: A Historical Perspective', in F. Bailey and D. Hale (eds), *Popular Culture, Crime and Justice*, 61–70, Belmont: Wadsworth.

OLIVER, M.B., and ARMSTRONG, G.B. (1998), 'The

Color of Crime: Perceptions of Caucasians' and African-Americans' Involvement in Crime', in M. Fishman and G. Cavender (eds), *Entertaining Crime*, 19–36, New York: Aldine De Gruyter.

ORCUTT, J.D., and TURNER, J.B. (1993), 'Shocking Numbers and Graphic Accounts: Quantified Images of Drug Problems in the Print Media', *Social Problems*, 40, 2: 190–206.

OSBORNE, R. (1996), 'Crime and the Media: From Media Studies to Post-modernism', in D. Kidd-Hewitt and R. Osborne (eds), *Crime and the Media*, 25–48, London: Pluto.

OUSBY, I. (1976), *Bloodhounds of Heaven: The Detective in English Fiction From Godwin to Doyle*, Cambridge, Mass.: Harvard University Press.

PALMER, J. (1978), *Thrillers*, London: Edward Arnold.

PANDIANI, J. (1978), 'Crime Time TV: If All We Knew Is What We Saw . . .', *Contemporary Crises*, 2: 437–58.

PARK, W. (1978), 'The Police State', *Journal of Popular Film*, VI, 3: 229–38.

PARRISH, R., and PITTS, M. (1990a), *The Great Detective Pictures*, Metuchen, NJ: Scarecrow.

—— and —— (1990b), *The Great Cop Pictures*, Metuchen, NJ: Scarecrow.

PEARSON, G. (1983), *Hooligan: A History of Respectable Fears*, London: Macmillan.

PEAY, J. (1998), 'The Power of the Popular', in T. Newburn and J. Vagg (eds), *Emerging Themes in Criminology*, Loughborough: British Society of Criminology.

PHILLIPS, M. (1996), *The Observer Review*, 8 December: 2.

PORTER, B. (1981), *The Pursuit of Crime*, New Haven, Conn.: Yale University Press.

POWERS, S.P., ROTHMAN, D.J., and ROTHMAN, S. (1996), *Hollywood's America: Social and Political Themes in Motion Pictures*, Boulder: Westview.

RADZINOWICZ, L. (1956), *A History of English Criminal Law*, Vols. 2/3, London: Stevens.

RAFTER, N. (2000), *Shots in the Mirror: Crime Films and Society*, New York: Oxford University Press.

RAWLINGS, P. (1992), *Drunks, Whores, and Idle Apprentices: Criminal Biographies of the Eighteenth Century*, London: Routledge.

—— (1998), 'Crime Writers: Non-Fiction Crime Books', in T. Newburn and J. Vagg (eds), *Emerging Themes in Criminology*, Loughborough: British Society of Criminology.

REINER, R. (1978), 'The New Blue Films', *New Society*, 43, 808: 706–708.

—— (1981), 'Keystone to Kojak: The Hollywood Cop', in P. Davies and B. Neve (eds), *Politics, Society and Cinema in America*, 195–220, Manchester: Manchester University Press.

—— (1994), 'The Dialectics of Dixon: The Changing Image of the TV Cop', in S. Becker and M. Stephens (eds), *Police Force, Police Service*, 11–32, London: Macmillan.

—— (2000a), *The Politics of the Police*, 3rd edn, Oxford: Oxford University Press.

—— (2000b), 'Romantic Realism: Policing and the Media', in F. Leishman, B. Loveday, and S. Savage (eds), *Core Issues in Policing*, 52–66, London: Longman.

—— (2000c), 'Crime and Control in Britain', *Sociology*, 34, 1: 71–94.

—— (2001), 'The Rise of Virtual Vigilantism: Crime Reporting Since World War II', *Criminal Justice Matters*, 43: 4–5.

——, LIVINGSTONE, S., and ALLEN, J. (2000a), 'Casino Culture: Media and Crime in a Winner-Loser Society', in K. Stenson and R. Sullivan (eds), *Crime, Risk and Justice*, 175–93, Cullompton: Willan.

——, —— and —— (2000b), 'No More Happy Endings? The Media and Popular Concern About Crime Since the Second World War', in T. Hope and R. Sparks (eds), *Crime, Risk and Insecurity*, 107–25, London: Routledge.

ROBERTS, J.V., and STALANS, L.J. (2000), *Public Opinion, Crime and Criminal Justice*, Boulder: Westwood.

ROBERTS, M. (2001), 'Just Noise? Newspaper Crime Reporting and Fear of Crime', *Criminal Justice Matters*, 43: 10–11.

ROCK, P. (1973), 'News As Eternal Recurrence', in S. Cohen and J. Young (eds), *The Manufacture of News*, 64–70, London: Constable.

ROSHIER, B. (1973), 'The Selection of Crime News By the Press', in S. Cohen and J. Young (eds), *The Manufacture of News*, 40–51, London: Constable.

ROSOW, E. (1978), *Born to Lose*, New York: Oxford University Press.

ROSS, J.I. (1998), 'The Role of the Media in the Creation of Public Police Violence', in F. Bailey and D. Hale (eds), *Popular Culture, Crime and Justice*, 100–10, Belmont: Wadsworth.

RUBIN, M. (1999), *Thrillers*, Cambridge: Cambridge University Press.

SACCO, V.F. (1995), 'Media Constructions of Crime',

The Annals of the American Academy of Political and Social Science, 539: 141–54.

SASSON, T. (1995), Crime Talk: How Citizens Con struct A Social Problem, New York: Aldine De Gruyter.

SAYERS, D. (ed.) (1936), Tales of Detection, London: Dent.

SCHLESINGER, P., DOBASH, R., DOBASH, R., and WEAVER, C. (1992), Women Viewing Violence, London: British Film Institute.

——, —— and MURDOCK, G. (1991), 'The Media Politics of Crime and Criminal Justice', British Journal of Sociology, 42, 3: 397–420.

—— and TUMBER, H. (1992), 'Crime and Criminal Justice in the Media', in D. Downes (ed.), Unravelling Criminal Justice, 184–203, London: Macmillan.

—— and —— (1993), 'Fighting the War Against Crime: Television, Police and Audience', British Journal of Criminology, 33, 1: 19–32.

—— and —— (1994), Reporting Crime, Oxford: Oxford University Press.

SCHRAMM, W., LYLE, J., and PARKER, E.B. (1961), Television in the Lives of Our Children, Stanford, Cal.: Stanford University Press.

SHADOIAN, J. (1977), Dreams and Dead Ends, Cambridge, Mass.: MIT Press.

SHALE, S. (1996), 'Listening to the Law: Famous Trials on BBC Radio 1934–69', Modern Law Review, 59, 6: 813–44.

SHERIZEN, S. (1978), 'Social Creation of Crime News: All the News Fitted to Print', in C. Winick (ed.), Deviance and Mass Media, 203–24, Beverly Hills, Cal.: Sage.

SIGNORIELLI, N. (1990), 'Television's Mean and Dangerous World: A Continuation of the Cultural Indicators Perspective', in N. Signorielli and M. Morgan (eds), Cultivation Analysis: New Directions in Media Effects Research, 85–106, Newbury Park: Sage.

—— and MORGAN, M. (eds) (1990), Cultivation Analysis: New Directions in Media Effects Research, Newbury Park: Sage.

SKIDMORE, P. (1995), 'Telling Tales; Media Power, Ideology and the Reporting of Child Sexual Abuse in Britain', in D. Kidd-Hewitt and R. Osborne (eds), Crime and the Media, 78–106, London: Pluto.

SKLAR, R. (1975), Movie-Made America, New York: Vintage.

SMITH, S. (1984), 'Crime in the News', British Journal of Criminology, 24, 3: 289–95.

SOLOMONS, S. (1976), Beyond Formula: American Film Genres, New York: Harcourt, Brace, Jovanovich.

SOOTHILL, K., and WALBY, S. (1991), Sex Crime in the News, London: Routledge.

SPARKS, R. (1992), Television and the Drama of Crime, Buckingham: Open University Press.

—— (1993), 'Inspector Morse', in G. Brandt (ed.), British Television Drama in the 1980s, Cambridge: Cambridge University Press.

—— (2000), '"Bringin' It All Back Home": Populism, Media Coverage, and the Dynamics of Locality and Globality in the Politics of Crime Control', in K. Stenson and R. Sullivan (eds), Crime, Risk and Justice, 194–213, Cullompton: Willan.

—— (2001), 'The Media, Populism, Public Opinion and Crime', Criminal Justice Matters, 43: 6–7.

STENSON, K., and SULLIVAN, R. (eds) (2000), Crime, Risk and Justice: The Politics of Crime Control in Liberal Democracies, Cullompton: Willan.

STEPHENSON-BURTON, A. (1995), 'Through the Looking-Glass: Public Images of White Collar Crime', in D. Kidd-Hewitt and R. Osborne (eds), Crime and the Media, 131–63, London: Pluto.

SUMNER, C. (1982), '"Political Hooliganism" and "Rampaging Mobs": The National Press Coverage of the Toxteth "Riots"', in C. Sumner (ed.), Crime, Justice and the Mass Media, 25–35, Cropwood Papers 14, Cambridge: Institute of Criminology.

SURETTE, R. (1998), Media, Crime and Criminal Justice: Images and Realities, 2nd edn, Belmont: Wadsworth.

SWANSON, C. (1955), 'What They Read in 130 Daily Newspapers', Journalism Quarterly, 32, 4: 411–21.

SYMONS, J. (1972), Bloody Murder, London: Penguin.

THOMPSON, J. (1993), Fiction, Crime and Empire: Clues to Modernity and Postmodernity, Urbana, Ill.: University of Illinois Press.

THOMPSON, J.B. (1995), The Media and Modernity: A Social Theory of the Media, Cambridge: Polity Press.

TOMBS, S., and WHYTE, D. (2001), 'Reporting Corporate Crime Out of Existence', Criminal Justice Matters, 43: 22–23.

TUMBER, H. (1982), Television and the Riots, London: British Film Institute.

TUNNELL, K.D. (1998), 'Reflections on Crime,

Criminals, and Control in Newsmagazine Tele-
vision Programs', in F. Bailey and D. Hale (eds),
Popular Culture, Crime and Justice, 111–22,
Belmont: Wadsworth.

TUSKA, J. (1978), *The Detective in Hollywood*, New
York: Doubleday.

WAKSHLAG, J., VIAL, V., and TAMBORINI, R. (1983),
'Selecting Crime Drama and Apprehension
About Crime', *Human Communication Research*,
10, 2: 227–42.

WARTELLA, E. (1995), 'Media and Problem
Behaviours in Young People', in M. Rutter and
D. Smith (eds), *Psychological Disorders in Young
People*, 296–323, London: Wiley.

WATSON, C. (1971), *Snobbery With Violence: English
Crime Stories and Their Audience*, London: Eyre
Methuen.

WILLIAMS, P., and DICKINSON, J. (1993), 'Fear of
Crime: Read All About It? The Relationship
Between Newspaper Crime Reporting and Fear
of Crime', *British Journal of Criminology*, 33, 1:
33–56.

WILLIAMS, T.M. (ed.) (1986), *The Impact of*

*Television: A Natural Experiment in Three
Communities*, New York: Academic Press.

WILSON, C.P. (2000), *Cop Knowledge: Police Power
and Cultural Narrative in Twentieth-Century
America*, Chicago: University of Chicago Press.

WINSTON, R., and MELLERSI, N. (1992), *The Public
Eye: Ideology and the Police Procedural*, London:
Macmillan.

WOBER, M. (1978), 'Televised Violence and Paranoid Perception: The View From Great Britain',
Public Opinion Quarterly, 42, 3: 315–21.

WREN-LEWIS, J. (1981/2), 'TV Coverage of the
Riots', *Screen Education*, 40: 15–33.

WYKES, M. (2001), *News, Crime and Culture*,
London: Pluto.

YOUNG, J. (1971), *The Drug-Takers*, London:
Paladin.

—— (1999), *The Exclusive Society*, London: Sage.

ZILLMAN, D., and WAKSHLAG, J. (1987), 'Fear of
Victimisation and the Appeal of Crime Drama',
in D. Zillman and J. Bryant (eds), *Selective
Exposure to Communication*, Hillsdale, NJ:
Erlbaum.

PART III

DIMENSIONS OF CRIME

13

VICTIMS

*Lucia Zedner**

INTRODUCTION

Victims, once on the margins of criminology research, are now a central focus of academic research. Victim surveys, both national and local, and qualitative studies of the impact of crime and of victim needs have permanently altered the criminological agenda. Victims complicate the old triumvirate of crimes, criminals, and their control. And criminologists have been obliged to recognize that crime has consequences more painful than once acknowledged. Academic research on victims has been mirrored and encouraged by the growth of influential interest groups, cross-party political concern, and international recognition. As a result, the victim has moved from being a 'forgotten actor' to become a key player in the criminal justice process. The promotion of victims' interests at both national and international level has prompted debate about victims' rights and the setting of standards of service. For victims are now the subject of political as much as criminological attention.

This chapter traces the genesis of 'victimology' and the development of victim surveys. It examines fear of crime, constraints on lifestyle, and the impact of crime on its victims. It surveys the harms suffered by victims; their consequent needs, together with the victims' movement's responses and the provision of services. It examines the place of the victim in the criminal justice process and attempts made specifically to limit his or her 'secondary victimization' by that process. Lastly, it explores the rise of restorative justice, its philosophical bases and its implications for the place of victims within criminal justice. Reorientation of criminal justice towards the victim connotes a shift in penological thinking that challenges the prevailing paradigm of retributive punishment. The chapter will conclude by examining the prospects for restorative justice and its limitations.

* In preparing this edition, I would like to thank Carolyn Hoyle, Mike Maguire, Declan Roche, and Richard Young for their valuable comments.

CLASSICAL STUDIES IN VICTIMOLOGY

Interest in victims has a long history. The term 'victimology' appears to have been coined first in 1949 by the American psychiatrist, Frederick Wertham, who called for 'a science of victimology' (Wertham 1949). It is, however, von Hentig, *The Criminal and his Victim* (von Hentig 1948), which is now widely regarded as the seminal text in developing victim studies. Highly critical of the traditional offender-oriented nature of criminology, von Hentig proposed a dynamic, interactionist approach that challenged conceptions of the victim as passive actor. This focused both on those characteristics of victims which precipitated their suffering and on the relationship between victim and offender. He argued, 'The law . . . makes a clear-cut distinction between the one who does and the one who suffers. Looking into the genesis of the situation, in a considerable number of cases, we meet a victim who consents tacitly, co-operates, conspires or provokes' (von Hentig 1948, quoted in Fattah 1989: 44). By classifying victims into typologies based on psychological and social variables, he suggested that certain individuals were 'victim-prone'.

Others took up these notions of victim-precipitation and victim-proneness. Mendelsohn drew on explanations of accident causation in attempting to quantify the victim's 'guilty contribution to the crime' (Mendelsohn 1956). His approach went beyond merely designating victim typologies to assign degrees of culpability. His classification is highly moralistic, with categories ranging from the 'completely innocent' to the 'most guilty victim'. This form of 'victim blaming' later attracted considerable criticism, but Mendelsohn's intent was less to exculpate the offender than to devise an explanatory model on which preventive programmes might be built to reduce the extent and severity of victimization.

Not until Wolfgang's classic study *Patterns in Criminal Homicide* (1958) were von Hentig's ideas systematically empirically tested. Wolfgang defined victim-precipitated offences as those 'in which the victim is a direct, positive precipitator in the crime' (Wolfgang 1958). Examining police records of 588 homicides in Philadelphia (from 1948 to 1952), he calculated that 26 per cent of known homicides resulted from victim-initiated resort to violence. His conclusion that some crime was victim-precipitated inspired many subsequent studies replicating his approach (for example, by Amir, Hindelang, Gottfredson, and Garafalo). While these studies were as concerned to develop victim typologies as to assess victim precipitation, it is this latter aim, with its emotive connotations of victim blaming, that continues to attract criminological attention.

Perhaps the most controversial application of Wolfgang's model of victim precipitation is Amir's *Patterns of Forcible Rape* (1971). Amir analysed 646 forcible rapes recorded by the police in Philadelphia, and concluded that 19 per cent were victim-precipitated. Amir's study provoked considerable disquiet and has been criticized both on methodological and ideological grounds. His definition of precipitation is broad and vague, encompassing all those instances in which 'the victim actually—or so it was interpreted by the offender—agreed to sexual relations but retracted . . . or did not resist strongly enough when the suggestion was made by the offender. The term also applies to cases in which the victim enters vulnerable situations charged sexually' (Amir 1971: 262). This shift, from recognizing victim–offender interaction as a precipitating factor to re-ascribing blame to the victim in rape cases, was heavily criticized by the newly emergent feminist movement. Since only a small proportion of rapes is reported (Temkin 1987: 9), Amir's reliance on police records necessarily presents a very partial picture. Moreover, reports in police files are problematic accounts: arguably they reveal as much about police attitudes to rape victims as they do about the etiology of the crime. The chief difficulty with Amir's study (and others, which followed its model) is that it conflates analysis of the dynamics of crime with the attribution of responsibility to the victim. In so doing, it moves from examining the correlates of victimization to victim blaming. In short, it seems to suggest 'that victims of assault have no one except themselves to blame if they deliberately walk in dark alleys after dark' (Anttila 1974: 7).

Fattah has defended the idea of victim-precipitation, arguing that in a rigorously pursued, value-free social science there is no reason why it should entail victim blaming. Although it has been used carelessly in the past, he argues it is a sound explanatory tool (Fattah 1991). Understood not as victim-precipitation but as the recognition that crime is a transaction in which both offender and victim play a role, this approach might lead to a fuller understanding of crime. Unfortunately, however, the tendency for victim-precipitation studies to lead to victim blaming has undermined its potential explanatory power and attracted only criticism (Morris 1987: 173–4; Walklate 1989: 4–5). The concentration of early victim studies on reassigning responsibility for crime offered few new, coherent theoretical insights (Rock 1986: 72–3) and produced little by way of empirical findings other than that *some* victims bear *some* responsibility for *some* crimes (Miers 1989: 15; though see Edgar and O'Donnell 1998). As such, it is perhaps not surprising that, throughout the 1960s and much of the 1970s, mainstream criminology remained firmly wedded to offender-oriented studies. More recently, 'radical' and 'critical' victimologists challenged these strictures by engaging in analysis of the wider political, economic, and social context of victimization, in political analysis of the rights of victims, and in cross-cultural analysis of the development of victims' movements (Mawby and Walklate 1994; Walklate 2000).

VICTIMIZATION SURVEYS

One of the most important factors in regenerating criminological interest in victims was the development of the victim survey. In America, in the 1960s, mass victimization surveys sought to uncover the unreported 'dark figure' of crime. Pilot studies carried out on behalf of the US President's Crime Commission 1967 (Ennis 1967; Reiss 1967) were followed up by annual National Crime Surveys (NCSs) (now National Crime Victimization Surveys, NCVSs) carried out by the Bureau of Justice Statistics. The core findings of the annual NCVS have been characterized as follows: 'that the bulk of events uncovered by the surveys are relatively trivial, that criminal victimization of the types measured is relatively rare, and that there is a large amount of repeat victimization' (Gottfredson 1986: 251). Only as a consequence of later studies on the impact of victimization were these sanguine conclusions revised. In Britain, the first major survey was carried out in London by Sparks, Genn, and Dodd (Sparks *et al.* 1977). It sought to ascertain the extent and nature of unreported crime, and asked about victims' perceptions of crime and attitudes to the criminal justice system. In so doing, it set the agenda for many subsequent surveys and smaller-scale, qualitative studies.

In Britain national victim surveys have been funded and administered by the Home Office. The first British Crime Survey (BCS), conducted in 1982, drew on a representative sample of over 10,000 people over the age of fifteen. In addition to crime itself, it collected data on 'factors predisposing people to victimization; the impact of crime on victims; fear of crime; victims' experiences of the police; other contacts with the police; and self-reported offending' (Hough and Mayhew 1983). It has been replicated several times (Hough and Mayhew 1985; Mayhew *et al.* 1989; Mayhew 1993; Mayhew *et al.* 1994; Mirrlees-Black *et al.* 1996; Mirrlees-Black *et al.* 1998; Kershaw *et al.* 2001). From 2001 the BCS moved to an annual cycle. The first Scottish Crime Survey was carried out in 1983 (Chambers and Tombs 1984) and has also been repeated, most recently in 2000 (MVA Consultancy 2000). National surveys have also been carried out in many other countries, including Australia, Canada, The Netherlands, and Switzerland. These large-scale surveys seek to gain a better picture of victimization than that supplied by police records, and to identify the social, economic, and demographic characteristics of the victim population (on their range and methodology, see Maguire, in Chapter 11 of this volume).

Successive BCSs have found that while the chance of being a victim of a minor offence is high, the risk of suffering a more serious offence is small. In providing a snapshot of national trends, the BCS tends to gloss over major geographical, social, and economic differences. Risk of victimization generally is closely related to geographical area, and risk of personal victimization correlated with age, sex, and patterns of routine activity, such as going out in the evenings and consuming alcohol. In respect of burglary, risk is much higher in inner-city areas, particularly those with high levels of physical disorder, and in rented accommodation rather than owner-occupied homes. Households with lower levels of disposable income, with single-adult, young, or unemployed heads of households, are also at greater risk (Kershaw *et al.* 2000: 20; Budd 1999). Crimes of violence also correlate closely with specific variables. Data from the 1999 BCS shows that age is the key determinant of being the victim of violence: young men between the ages of 16 and 24 are most at risk (Kershaw *et al.* 2000: 37). The unemployed, single parents, and single people generally are those next most at risk, followed by those living in the private rented sector and those visiting a pub or club three or more times per week. Men are victims in 64 per cent of muggings and 80 per cent of stranger assaults, whereas women are the victims in 74 per cent of domestic incidents of violence.

For many types of crime, both Afro-Caribbeans and Asians tend to be more at risk than whites. In part this may be because they are over-represented in social and age groups particularly prone to crime. Members of ethnic minority groups are disproportionately likely to be council tenants, or to live in younger households in socially disadvantaged areas. Pakistanis appeared to be most vulnerable to racially motivated crimes, reporting that nearly a third of all incidents had been racially motivated compared to 18 per cent of crimes against Indians and 14 per cent against Afro-Caribbeans (Fitzgerald and Hale 1996: 2). Assaults, threats, and vandalism are those offences most often thought to be committed for racial reasons.

Many methodological problems with victim surveys have been identified both by independent commentators (see Maguire, this volume) and by the surveyors themselves: not least it seems likely that non-respondents suffer higher victimization rates than respondents. Obviously, victim surveys enumerate only those incidents for which individuals are able and willing to identify themselves as victims. For this reason they tend to concentrate on physical and sexual assaults (though even these may not be readily revealed to an interviewer) and personal or household property crime. The BCS does not include crimes against those aged under sixteen, the commercial and public sector (such as company fraud, fare dodging, and tax evasion), those in institutions, and the homeless (Kershaw *et al.* 2000: 2). Neither does it measure crimes in which the victim is complicit (such as drug and alcohol misuse, gambling, and prostitution), 'victimless' crimes (like motoring and environmental offences), and murder and manslaughter. Crimes in which the victim and offender are known to each other are less likely to be reported to the interviewer, especially if the offender is a relative or a member of the household, or present when the interview takes place. As a consequence this 'hidden violence' (Stanko 1988) is likely to be significantly undercounted. Recognizing that sexual offences are probably under-reported, the BCS has introduced 'computer-aided self-interviewing' (CASI) in an attempt to increase response rates (Mirrlees-Black 1999: 91).

BCS data reveal that victimization falls unequally on particular individuals and groups (Trickett *et al.* 1995). Analysing the distribution of victimization is complicated by the fact that educated, middle-class respondents appear more willing and able to report offences. Further down the social scale, respondents may be so regularly exposed to crime that they fail to recognize activities as criminal, cannot distinguish between repeated offences, or have difficulties in recalling all those offences perpetrated against them. Where the period under survey is more than a few months, problems of recall arise. Victims may forget less serious incidents, or fail to remember whether a distant occurrence fell within the specified period. Moreover, 5 to 10 per cent of incidents reported to the BCS are discounted by interviewers on the grounds that the details given do not suggest genuine crimes, or would not have been recorded as such by the police. Mayhew gives the example of some forms of harassment, which may be unpleasant or even frightening but do not meet the legal criteria of a crime (Mayhew 2000: 101).

Aside from domestic crime surveys, an important source of comparable data has been developed through the International Crime Victimization Survey programme (ICVS). This was responsible for standardized surveys in about twenty industrialized countries in 1989, 1992, and 1996 (Mayhew and van Dijk 1997). Other surveys have been carried out in over fifty developing and transitional states under the auspices of the United Nations (Mayhew 2000: 92). Together they are an important means of creating comparable data on victimization (van Dijk 2000).

LOCAL SURVEYS

By narrowing their geographical focus, local victim surveys document the uneven distribution of risk, showing that certain age or social groups and particular residential areas are far more frequently subjected to crime than others (see Maguire, in Chapter 11 of this volume). They set crime in its broader social context by including questions about racial and sexual harassment, drug abuse, and other forms of anti-social behaviour (Crawford *et al.* 1990: 4). They also ask victims about their perceptions of police priorities and service delivery, and their opinions concerning the control and accountability of police forces. Other questions address the role of agencies like local authority social services, housing departments, and Victim Support schemes in responding to crime.

Early local victim surveys focused on areas of dense population (Merseyside, Islington, Hammersmith and Fulham, and Edinburgh), reflecting the presumption that crime is primarily an urban problem. They sought to reveal the higher levels of crime prevailing in socially deprived inner-city areas; to highlight the disproportionate victimization of women, of members of ethnic minority groups, and of those lower down the social scale. They also appear to have been more sensitive than national surveys in revealing incidents of sexual assault. In their sensitivity both to local variation and to the feelings of victims, local victim surveys have had greater success in revealing differential patterns of victimization and have prompted changes also to the BCS (Percy and Mayhew 1997). Recognition that some crimes are highly prevalent in rural areas has led researchers to conduct rural victim surveys (Koffman 1996: 89–114). The Aberystwyth Crime Survey (ACS) 1993 was a direct attempt to remedy the paucity of information about victimization in rural areas.

'Differential victimization' has been studied with reference not only to geographic, social, and economic variables, but also with reference to age, sex, and race. Securing sufficient numbers of other victim groups such as the elderly, the young, the disabled, or those subject to domestic violence, requires dedicated surveys directed, for example, at residential homes, schools, or refuges. Another rarely considered example is victimization in prisons (O'Donnell and Edgar 1998). Concern that women's experiences of crime were less readily documented by mass victimization surveys led researchers to study personal crimes against women (Dobash and Dobash 1980; Hanmer and Saunders 1984; Stanko 1988). More recent research by Painter and Farrington based on a sample of 1,000 married women found, for example, that 24 per cent of married women and 59 per cent of divorced or separated women had been hit by their spouses (Painter and Farrington 1998). Research on domestic violence among ethnic minority communities has revealed that Pakistani women are particularly inhibited from reporting their plight because of cultural pressures, linguistic difficulties, lack of information, and fear of deportation (Choudry 1996). Several surveys have suggested levels of sexual crime against women far higher than those revealed by national victim surveys, and much higher than those indicated by police records (Hanmer and Saunders 1984; Radford 1987). Hall, for example, found that only 8 per cent of those respondents alleging rape and 18 per cent of those alleging sexual assault had reported their victimization to the police (Hall 1985). The chief difficulty with these studies is that differences in approach, wording, and categorization of responses have generated widely differing estimates of the extent of victimization. The wide variation in their findings highlights the difficulty of ascertaining the true extent and nature of sexual victimization (Morris 1987: 165). The degree of variation is such that Mayhew has concluded, perhaps harshly, 'that comparisons between them are, frankly, fruitless' (Mayhew 2000: 97).

One reason why some victims fail not only to report crimes but even to recognize themselves as victims is that media reporting of crime creates and reinforces stereotypes of those who may legitimately claim that status. Prevailing assumptions about rape, for example, foster self-blame, which also inhibits victims from reporting (Soothill and Walby 1991). As a consequence, the sensitivity of survey questions and the approach and demeanour of the interviewer may dramatically alter response rates. Another important issue is which offences respondents remember and which, and for what reasons, are simply forgotten. The conclusion by Reiss that 10 per cent of crimes reported to the police in the United States are not reported to those conducting victim surveys must make us wary of seeing the findings of victim surveys as in any way representing the 'true' figure of crime (Reiss 1986; see also Maguire, in Chapter 11 of this volume).

In switching attention from offenders to victims, it is arguable that victim surveys did no more than suggest a new subject area for positivist criminology. Yet victim surveys have typically gone beyond the counting of unreported offences to ask questions about perceptions and reactions to crime and policing. In so doing, they provide the basis for a new agenda focusing on the attributes of crime victims, societal attitudes to crime, and the effects of crime on the community.

FEAR OF CRIME

Interest in fear of crime originated in the United States in the 1960s, during a period of race riots and growing urban violence. But it was the victim survey that, by providing data about the extent and severity of such fear, pinpointed a new area for criminological enquiry (Maxfield 1984; Garafalo 1979; Skogan 1986a and 1986b). Fear of crime is now recognized as a distinct social problem, extending well beyond those who have actually been victimized to affect the lives of all those who perceive themselves to be at risk. Moreover, although fear of crime is closely related to levels of crime, and tends to increase as crime rises, it cannot be seen as a mere function of crime rates (Farrall *et al.* 2000; Pantazis 2000; Zedner 2000: 200). Recognition of fear of crime as a distinct area of enquiry raises theoretical problems about what it is we mean by the term (Hollway and Jefferson 2000; Farrell *et al.* 2000). To what exactly is it a reaction? What are its social correlates? Who is most vulnerable to fear, when, and why (Hale 1996)? Ironically, carrying out victim surveys increases sensitivity to the risks of crime. Situating questions about fear within a survey may consequently elicit higher levels of anxiety than would otherwise be the case.

Generally, 'fear of crime' has been used to refer to perceived threats to personal safety rather than threats to property or generalized perceptions of risk (Maxfield 1984: 3). One problem is how to control for variations in respondents' willingness to admit to such fears. Socialization tends to make men less willing to admit fear than women (Stanko and Hobdell 1993; Walklate 2001: 77–104). Another methodological difficulty is how to phrase questions so as to identify the nature and level of fear without importing other anxieties (Hale 1996: 84–94). Questions in victim surveys typically ask 'How safe do you feel walking in your neighbourhood alone at night?' Phrased this way, the question elicits answers relating to a given neighbourhood, fear of the dark, respondents' feelings of weakness or other anxieties that may, or may not, be crime-related.

Historically, victim surveys have produced problematic data that suggested a weak correspondence between fear and risk (Hough 1995). Young working-class men who spend a great deal of leisure time outside the home, particularly those who habitually visit pubs, are most at risk but admit to little fear. By contrast, women and the elderly commonly express profound anxiety despite lower levels of risk. The 'risk-fear para-dox', namely that the two appear to be poorly correlated (or even inverted), has been the subject of close criminological attention (Crawford *et al.* 1990; Pain 1995; Bannister *et al.* 1997; Hollway and Jefferson 2000). Suspicious that characterizing fear as irrational was an administrative attempt to downplay the costs of crime, researchers have attempted to identify the social structural causes of people's fear (Crawford *et al.* 1990: 40); other factors that render 'disproportionately' high levels of fear rational (Hale 1996: 94–112); and the manner in which external risks are mediated through individual characteristics and personal histories (Hollway and Jefferson 2000).

Demographic factors, not least age and sex, are key determinants of fear (Walklate 1997; though see Brogden and Nijhar 2000). The 1999 BCS found, for example, that in respect of every category of crime (except theft of or from a car) women consistently expressed greater worry than men, and that older women were most fearful (Kershaw *et al.* 2000: 47–8). Since crimes against women, particularly sexual offences and assaults occurring within the home, are least susceptible to discovery, women may suffer far higher levels of victimization than are revealed even by victim surveys. The assumed 'irrationality' of women's fears, when judged against that level of risk known to the surveys, may be all too rational a reflection of 'hidden violence' (Stanko 1988: 40). Nor does a straight tally of offences take account of the differential impact of actual or potential violation. Women and the elderly are 'unequal victims', in that the physical, psychological, or economic costs of crime are greater for them than for more robust or affluent individuals (Crawford *et al.* 1990: 70; Walklate 2001: 86–95). The lower risks faced, if indeed they are lower, are more than offset by greater vulnerability to the impact of crime (Pantazis 2000).

Fear of crime varies also by ethnic minority group (Fitzgerald and Hale 1996). Asians are more likely to feel unsafe than Afro-Caribbeans, who actually feel safer than any other group alone on the street at night. In general ethnic minorities are far more concerned than whites about the possibility of racial attack, with Asians again expressing greater concern than black respondents. Assessing the impact of racial harassment on levels of fear is hindered by the difficulty, even for the victim, of identifying whether crime is racially motivated or not. Other important correlates of fear include personal experiences of crime, living in inner-city areas, perceived levels of disorder, lack of neighbourhood cohesion, and racial or sectarian tensions. 'Local incivilities', such as poor street lighting, vandalism, boarded-up buildings, youths loitering on street corners, drunks, and other signals of a hostile environment, have all been found to increase fear (Crawford *et al.* 1990: 82). A more diffuse sense of insecurity may be exacerbated by media portrayal of crime, which itself has changed significantly in the post-war period (Reiner *et al.* 2000). Ironically, crime prevention efforts, whether by individuals, the police, government, or media campaigns, may raise perceptions of risk and so stimulate feelings of insecurity (Zedner 2000).

These findings have led criminologists to consider the ways in which individuals' lifestyles are altered and life choices constrained by concern about crime. Several models of fear-related behaviour have been identified (see, for example, Skogan 1986a). To the extent that they consider risks unacceptable, some individuals withdraw from social life. Others assess the costs and benefits of modifying their behaviour to achieve a reasonable level of risk and delimit their lifestyle accordingly. Yet here again behavioural responses are not tied solely or exactly to risk (Ewald 2000). The wealthy may be no more at risk, and in many situations are arguably less so, but they have the resources to take precautionary measures such as installing burglar alarms or taking taxis in preference to public transport. A prime example is the development of Neighbourhood Watch schemes in settled 'affluent suburban areas, high-status non-family areas and in areas of modern family housing with higher incomes' (Mayhew *et al.* 1989: 52), areas known to be less vulnerable to crime. The geographical spread of these schemes illustrates the way in which alleviating fear is correlated to income rather than risk. One of the underlying purposes of Neighbourhood Watch is to enable communities to develop a sense of control over crime and so enjoy increased security and lower levels of fear. Interpreting the success of Neighbourhood Watch is complicated by the fact that those joining, often as a result of having been burgled in the past, tend to be more anxious initially than non-scheme members. There is even evidence that rather than reducing fear, membership of Neighbourhood Watch increases it by heightening sensitivity to risk.

LIFESTYLE

The relationship between fear of crime and quality of life is also problematic. Victim surveys have typically attempted to assess damage to quality of life by asking whether fear prevented respondents from going out alone at night or not. Their findings have been very varied. Of respondents to the Second Islington Crime Survey, nearly two-thirds gave fear of crime as a reason for not going out, and 41 per cent gave it as a considerable part of the reason. They also mentioned other factors such as physical disabilities, financial restrictions, having nowhere to go, or preferring to stay at home in the evenings with friends or family (Crawford *et al.* 1990: 59). By contrast, of respondents to the most recent BCS, only 19 per cent gave fear of crime as the reason, whereas 57 per cent said that they did not go out for simple lack of inclination (Kershaw *et al.* 2000: 50). Interestingly, the authors of the BCS suggest that a 'certain level of concern or wariness is actually beneficial in encouraging people to take measures to reduce their risk of victimization'. Their approach is consistent with the 'responsibilization' strategies, identified by Garland, by which government seeks to displace responsibility for crime from its own shoulders to those of the public (Garland 2001: 124). The ultimate logic of this counsel is that people must accept limitations on their freedom of movement (avoiding high-risk places and poorly-lit routes) and develop strategies for avoiding or deflecting potential violations (by going out only if accompanied, or avoiding use of public transport). The authors of the Second Islington Crime Survey concluded that the avoidance strategies of women in particular 'limits their participation in public, to the extent of a virtual curfew' (Crawford *et al.* 1990: 91). The effects of crime and racial harassment against members of the ethnic minorities are also often profound. Many victims of racial harassment and their families 'end up living like prisoners in their homes or being forced to move away from a familiar environment; children are unsettled and both their education and social life suffer; women are scared to go about the normal tasks . . . and also feel insecure in their own homes' (Cooper and Pomeyie 1988: 85). Such evidence raises the question of whether adjustments to lifestyle and mobility should be seen as sensible precaution or as a further cost of crime.

In order to elicit subjective assessments of the impact of crime, the BCS now asks respondents how much their quality of life is affected by fear of crime. In 2000, just over half (55 per cent) reported that fear of crime had no more than a minimal impact, and a further 38 per cent said the impact was moderate. Only 6 per cent considered that their quality of life was greatly affected (Kershaw *et al.* 2000: 51). The problem with these gross figures is that they mask substantial differences in the impact of crime upon different groups. Moreover, by focusing on lifestyle choices outside the home, they obscure the poor quality of life suffered by those whose primary source of fear lies within it.

IMPACT OF VICTIMIZATION

Victim surveys provide important information about the extent, frequency, and nature of victimization; they are less informative about its impact, not least because their respondents include very small numbers of serious crime victims and much larger populations of victims of petty infractions. As a consequence, aggregate results 'tend to wash or attenuate the overall effect of crime' (Lurigio 1987: 454). To rectify this tendency, qualitative research has focused on particular types of crime or specific victim groups. Studies have been carried out, for example, on burglary victims (Maguire and Corbett 1987), on victims of violence (Shapland *et al.* 1985; Stanko 1988), on rape victims (Burgess and Holstrom 1974; Chambers and Millar 1983; Allen 2002), on child victims (Morgan and Zedner 1992a; Anderson *et al.* 1992; Hartless *et al.* 1995), and on the elderly (Brogden and Nijhar 2000). These studies, by concentrating on more serious offences, have highlighted the acute stress and adverse physical, practical, or financial effects suffered by many victims.

The vast majority of victims suffer in some way in the immediate aftermath of crime. Early research by Lurigio in the United States found that most 'crime victims suffer from adverse, short-term psychological consequences as a result' (Lurigio 1987: 464). Overall, the BCS found that 84 per cent of respondents were affected emotionally (Maguire and Kynch 2000b: 3). In Britain, Maguire and Bennett found that 83 per cent of burglary victims experienced strong reactions on discovering that their homes had been invaded, and that 65 per cent suffered some continuing impact four to ten weeks later (Maguire 1982: 126–31). When asked about the worst aspect of burglary, only 32 per cent spoke of loss or damage, while 41 per cent cited feelings of intrusion, and 19 per cent of emotional upset.

Personal crimes such as physical and sexual assault commonly entail longer-term effects. Shapland *et al.* studied 300 victims of assault, robbery, or rape and found that 75 per cent were affected at the 'outcome interview' two and a half years after the offence (Shapland *et al.* 1985: 98–9). Rape victims and victims of sexual abuse during childhood have been found to suffer persisting effects for many years afterwards (Burgess and Holstrom 1974; Morgan and Zedner 1992a: 44–5). Resick found that rape victims experienced profound distress for several months after the crime and that 'many continue to experience problems with fear, anxiety, and interpersonal functioning for years after the event' (Resick 1987: 474). Unsurprisingly, sexual assault victims recover more slowly than victims of other types of crime, suffering emotional disturbance, sleeping or eating disorders, feelings of insecurity or low self-esteem, or troubled relationships for months or years after the event (Maguire and Corbett 1987; Smith 1989a; Kelly 1988).

The types of effect victims suffer vary according to the crime. Assaults may entail physical injury, shock, loss or damage to property, time off work, and financial losses (Shapland *et al.* 1985: 97). The impact of burglary is more likely to be emotional (involving feelings of shock, insecurity, violation, etc.), financial, or practical (loss of property, disruption, mess, broken doors or windows) (Maguire 1982). Child sexual abuse may inflict few visible or tangible injuries but induce profound feelings of 'fear, revulsion, shame and guilt' (Morris 1987: 191). In the long term, child abuse victims may suffer impaired self-esteem, school learning problems, withdrawal, and regressive behaviour (Finkelhor 1986: 152–63). While reactions are highly crime-specific, most studies suggest that psychological distress is the dominant reaction. At its most severe, this has been formally recognized by psychologists as 'post-traumatic stress disorder'—a clinical condition the symptoms of which include anxiety, depression, loss of control, guilt, sleep disturbance, and obsessive dwelling on the crime (Burgess and Holstrom 1978; Jones *et al.* 1987).

Studies of the differential impact of victimization seek to understand why some victims of apparently similar crimes are more severely affected than others (*British Journal of Criminology* 1995). Skogan identified as key factors in determining differential impact: isolation, resources, vulnerability, and previous experience (Skogan 1986b: 140–43). Those living alone, with few friends or no close family, tend to fear crime and feel its impact more acutely than those who are well supported (Maguire 1980). Criminal damage, theft, and burglary place heavier burdens on those with fewer financial resources, particularly because they are least likely to be insured against loss. General feelings of vulnerability among women, ethnic minorities, and the poor also increase the impact of crime. The BCS identified the 'very poor and uninsured', the 'very poor with restricted mobility', single parents, the 'intimidated' (or harassed), and the 'relatively housebound' as 'exceptionally vulnerable' groups (Maguire and Kynch 2000b: 6). Lack of ability to resist or to defend oneself against an attacker may amplify pre-existing feelings of vulnerability. For children, a burglary of the family home may entail trauma quite out of proportion to the physical damage or loss of property incurred (Morgan and Zedner 1992a: 63–4). Apart from feelings of vulnerability, actual physical weakness may result in victims suffering more serious injuries or taking longer to recover from assaults than those who are more robust (Garafalo 1979). This said, the tendency to associate victimization with vulnerability obscures the fact that men also suffer as victims. Expectations of masculinity also inhibit them from expressing their reactions to victimization (Stanko and Hobdell 1993; Goodey 1997; Gradey 2002; Allen 2002). Similarly, it is unclear whether the recent BCS finding that the very elderly living alone do not report greater impact or increased needs than other respondents implies greater resilience than expected, or a tendency to understate their needs to strangers (Maguire and Kynch 2000b: 6).

Multiple or series victimization compounds the impact suffered with each repeated occurrence. One study suggests that 4 per cent of victims experience 44 per cent of all crimes (National Board for Crime Prevention 1994). A minority is so repeatedly victimized that it becomes virtually impossible to distinguish the impact of discrete crimes from the generally impoverished quality of their life (Genn 1988; Hope 2001; Hope *et al.* 2001). Racial harassment is an important example here (Bowling 1998: 223). Bowling suggests that violent racism is best seen as a 'process' that the mere counting of individual incidents cannot capture (ibid.: chapter 5). For those who suffer continual 'name-calling and racial insults and abuse, graffiti . . . and racial violence varying from slapping, punching, jostling, and assault to maiming', the cumulative impact is far greater than any account of each individual incident would suggest (Commission for Racial Equality 1988: 7). Aside from previous crimes, other non-crime related life experiences also influence the experience of victimization. The death of a relative, divorce, separation, or other family trauma, illness, or pre-existing psychological problems can amplify or be amplified by the impact of crime.

Just as factors external to the crime may be relevant in determining its impact, so the consequences of crime extend beyond the incident itself. Considerable expenses may be incurred in replacing uninsured property, in medical care, counselling, or funeral costs. Some victims are driven to move house as a consequence of a traumatic burglary, or to escape continuing attacks, harassment, or stalking. Some lose earnings, or even risk their jobs, after missing time from work for court attendance or due to crime-related illness or depression (Shapland *et al.* 1985: 104–5; Resick 1987). Crime may place considerable stress on family relations, and even lead to their break up. The consequent dislocation not only affects those who are the direct victims, but also impinges on those other members of the household who are its 'indirect victims'— most commonly children (Morgan and Zedner 1992a: 28–31).

The wider impact of crime on secondary or indirect victims is increasingly recognized. The most telling example is that of the families of murder victims (Rock 1998). Although not primary victims, they suffer the profound trauma of bereavement, often compounded by the viciousness of the attack or the senselessness of the killing. For those who witness homicide or other non-fatal assaults, the shock or guilt for failing to intervene may be profound (Victim Support 1991). The mass of other, less serious offences may also create indirect victims. For example, over a third of the 400,000 households burgled every year include children (Morgan and Zedner 1992a). At its worst, the impact of crime on those who are witnesses or obliged to live with its consequences is such that they should properly be recognized as victims in their own right.

The impact of corporate or business crime upon its victims is also important. Most victims of fraud are, by its very nature, unaware that they have been victimized at all, or unwilling to recognize that they have been duped (Box 1983: 17). Criminal negligence leading to workplace injuries and deaths is rarely recognized as crime. Large-scale incidents involving loss of life tend not to be popularly perceived as crimes but as disasters—witness Piper Alpha, Zeebrugge, and Bhopal. Only with the intense media coverage of high-profile fraud cases, such as those involving Barings Bank, BCCI, the Maxwell pension fund, and Guinness, has attention been drawn to the plight of those who are their victims and the financial and emotional impact upon them (Levi and Pithouse 1992 and forthcoming). The remote consequences of corporate crime may extend to employees, tenants, and consumers (Young 2000: 230). In turn, much crime is committed against corporations: businesses, local authorities, government agencies, and charitable or religious foundations. Given the limitations of the stereotypical image of the individual victim, Young argues for 'a multi-victim perspective' that recognizes that 'a crime typically involves a range of harms to multiple victims, affecting individuals, groups, communities and society as a whole' (Young 2000: 234–5).

VICTIMS' NEEDS

The relationship between impact of crime and need is problematic. Those suffering the worst harm or loss do not necessarily have correspondingly high needs. They may enjoy a supportive environment, be innately resilient, or are otherwise able to overcome the effects of victimization. Victims suffering objectively less serious crimes may require greater support if they are vulnerable or isolated. Criminological understanding of victims' needs is largely reliant on views expressed by victims themselves—a source that is necessarily problematic (Maguire 1991: 403–406). Vocal, determined, or well-connected victims may express their needs forcibly, ironically at the expense of those whose needs are greatest but whose very vulnerability or inability to ask for help ensures their silence. Educated, informed, and resourceful individuals are better placed to seek out help, be it practical assistance, information, or advice on future crime prevention. For these reasons, Shapland and colleagues argue that needs as expressed by victims are no more than subjective assessments (Shapland *et al.* 1985: 112).

Victims' expressions of need are determined in part by cultural background, expectations, and knowledge of what services may be available to them. Those ignorant of the existence of available help may express only a vague need for emotional support, whereas others specifically identify their desire for voluntary or professional counselling. The provision of services, too, plays a part in determining victims' needs.

Expert-led innovations in the provision of support in turn drive victim expectations. Maguire and Kynch distinguish between 'assessed needs' as determined by an observer or practitioner, 'expressed needs' voiced by victims, and needs 'negotiated' between victims and those offering help (Maguire and Kynch 2000b: 8; see also Maguire 1991).

While most attention has focused on emotional impact and psychological needs, victims also often need practical help, information, and financial support. In response to the 1998 BCS, 18 per cent expressed a need for someone to talk to, 14 per cent information from the police, 13 per cent protection from further victimization, and 9 per cent advice on security (Maguire and Kynch 2000b: 8). Practical needs tend to be short term and relatively easily satisfied. The mending of windows, replacement of keys, or broken locks following a burglary are obvious examples (Maguire 1982). Longer-term practical help may be required following the most serious offences (Newburn 1994): transportation to and from hospital for the treatment of injuries (Shapland *et al.* 1985), help with child-care following rape (Morgan and Zedner 1992a), or refuge from domestic violence (Smith 1989b). While many victims' needs are met by family and friends, almost 40 per cent of respondents to the BCS expressed needs which were not met by any source (Maguire and Kynch 2000b: 12). Information commonly sought by victims includes advice on crime prevention, insurance, and compensation claims. For more serious crimes, the progress of police investigations, prosecution decisions, and the dates and outcome of any trial are all likely to be a source of considerable interest and concern. Studies by Maguire and Corbett (1987), Shapland *et al.* (1985), and Newburn and Merry (1990) reveal the importance attached by victims to being kept informed of the progress of 'their case'. Largely as a result of these research findings, the Home Office has made progressive attempts to improve the ways in which victims are kept informed by police and prosecutors (HO Circular 20/1988; Home Office 1990, 1996b; Hoyle *et al.* 1999a)—of which more below.

THE VICTIM MOVEMENT

In the United States, a strongly rights-based victim movement emerged in the 1960s and 1970s. Largely conservative in outlook, often seeking a more punitive response to offenders, it was in some states associated with demands for the retention or reintroduction of the death penalty. Dissatisfied with the existing responses to victims, the movement demanded a reorientation of the criminal justice system to take account of the needs and the rights of victims. Although it has become more variegated, with groups like 'Parents of Murdered Children' eschewing political involvement, many groups like 'Families and Friends of Murder Victims' engage in high-profile political lobbying.

In Britain, the central organ of the victim movement, Victim Support (formerly the National Association of Victim Support Schemes, NAVSS), has a very different history. Beginning life as a local initiative in Bristol in 1974, Victim Support grew dramatically in the following decades (Rock 1990). Its affiliated schemes now cover the entire country, calling on the services of over 17,000 volunteers who offer help to over a million victims a year (Reeves and Mulley 2000). Funding to Victim Support from the Home Office rose from £5,000 in 1979–80 to over £17 million in 1999–2000, an extraordinary increase at a time of financial retrenchment in other areas of public service. Traditionally, Victim Support has maintained a relatively low-key political profile, partly to maximize its pool of volunteers, of potential donors, and cross-party political support, and partly to preserve its charitable status. Where it sought legislative change, it avoided overt political lobbying, preferring to work behind the scenes to bring pressure to bear on issues such as services to victims by the police, compensation, and provision for the victim in court (Rock 1990, 1991; Maguire and Corbett 1987). More recently, however, Victim Support adopted a proactive role promoting rights for victims. Noting that 'offenders have clear rights in our system of justice but victims have no enforceable rights under the law', Victim Support demanded that victims should have the right to be heard, to be kept informed about the progress of 'their case', to provide information, to be protected by law enforcement agencies, and to receive compensation and 'respect, recognition and support' (Victim Support 1995). Whether so-called rights such as these can in practice be provided is debatable, and as such it is debatable whether the language of rights is misleading (Fenwick 1995).

The main thrust of Victim Support's endeavour remains in the provision of services to individual victims at a local level. Its chief difficulty lies in balancing the need to offer help as widely as possible, to reach those in greatest need and ensure their needs are met, and leave as many victims as possible feeling better (Maguire and Kynch 2000b: 13). Given the considerable problems of identifying those most badly affected, local schemes operate an 'outreach' service. This takes the form of 'crisis intervention' by volunteers contacting victims direct to offer emotional support, practical services, and information. The means of contacting victims varies between sending letters or leaflets (69 per cent), doorstep visits (13 per cent), or more rarely telephone calls. In the main, letters and calls do not lead to subsequent visits, though follow-up contact appears to double the number of visits. Of all victims contacted, about a quarter are subsequently visited. Fifty-eight per cent of victims contacted rate the service as very or fairly helpful (this rises to 80 and 69 per cent respectively for those visited or telephoned); and even of those receiving letters or leaflets alone, 46 per cent found this helpful.

Each local scheme operates under the guidance of a management committee; a central paid coordinator liaises with the police to collect details of victims on a daily basis and makes decisions about who should receive offers of help and how. Provision of support is increasingly determined by national policy, not least ensuring equal access to services and harmonization of provision across the country. But there remains considerable diversity of local policy and practice, particularly as between inner-city and rural areas. The availability of volunteers also determines the level of service a scheme is able to offer; particularly since inner-city areas with the highest crime rates tend to furnish the fewest recruits. In rural areas, on the other hand, volunteers have to travel considerable distances to visit victims. In total, in 1998, Victim Support made contact with between 30 and 45 per cent of victims of all 'BCS comparable' personal and household offences recorded by the police (Maguire and Kynch 2000b: 18). Outreach is more expensive in terms of volunteers' time and scheme resources, so Victim Support now encourages 'self-referral' by victims, not least via the national telephone help-line (Victim Supportline).

Originally, Victim Support focused mainly on 'conventional' victims of burglary, robbery, and theft, crimes generally committed by strangers. Later it expanded its remit to victims of sexual and violent crime, often committed by those known to them, and the families of murder victims. Work with these victims tends to be of a very different nature from the general pattern of short-term crisis intervention, involving instead long-term support, often by a pair of specially trained volunteers over months or even years. Formally, Victim Support is now committed to providing services to all victims of crime: in practice it is obliged to balance this ideal with the targeting of limited resources to those most in need.

The Women's Refuge Movement is another important source of support for victims of domestic violence. It grew out of the women's movement of the late 1960s and 1970s, with the first refuge for battered women established at Chiswick by Erin Pizzey in 1972 (Pizzey 1974). It was quickly emulated across the country as small, under-funded refuges proliferated, clearly fulfilling an unmet need in providing emergency accommodation, as well as outreach support, for women fleeing from abusive partners. There are now some 250 projects running 400 safe houses and offering support, advice, information, help with legal proceedings, financial arrangements, and housing to abused women and their children. Most local and regionally based services are coordinated through the Women's Aid Federation (founded in 1974). In 2000, refuges in England took in 54,000 women and children, 145,000 contacted them for support, and over 35,000 called the National Domestic Violence Helpline for advice or support (and BT recorded over 100,000 attempted calls). Funding of refuges is piecemeal and precarious, coming from rents (paid through housing benefit), local authority housing and social services departments, housing associations, and other ad hoc sources. As a consequence, provision is very variable, heavily reliant on voluntary support, and often in very poor quality accommodation (Dobash and Dobash 1998).

'Rape Crisis' centres developed out of the same wave of re-emergent feminism in the 1970s, on a similar model to that of refuges. Rape crisis centres were first opened in London in 1976 and in Birmingham in 1979. By 1988 there were forty such centres in operation, offering emotional support and legal and medical advice to women who have been sexually assaulted or raped (Anna T. 1988). With few funded posts, reliant mainly on the work of volunteers, rape crisis centres offer a twenty-four-hour telephone helpline and provide face-to-face counselling. Committed also to educating and informing the public about rape, these centres have been loath to use the term 'victim'. They object that 'using the word "victim" to describe women takes away our power and contributes to the idea that it is right and natural for men to "prey" on us' (London Rape Crisis Centre 1984: ix). Using the term 'survivor' instead, rape crisis campaigners have deliberately differentiated their response from that of the rest of the victim movement (Kelly 1988). Although based upon diverse feminist beliefs, the general commitment of rape crisis centres to radical feminism and their deep suspicion of police attitudes to rape have limited the interplay between their work and that of other voluntary and criminal justice agencies (Anna 1988). The Rape Crisis Federation, founded in 1996, is an umbrella organization for local rape crisis groups which acts as a referral service, provides advice, information, and training to local groups, and campaigns on issues of sexual violence.

New lobby groups promoting victims' interests continue to proliferate. The mid-1990s saw the launch of many new, single-issue groups. The Zito Trust, which campaigns for victims of mentally disordered offenders; the tiny pressure group 'Justice for Victims', campaigning on behalf of the families of homicide victims; Support After Murder and Manslaughter (SAMM), which primarily provides support after homicide; and Victim's Voice (a relaunch of the Suzy Lamplugh Trust), were all launched in the mid-1990s. While groups like Victim Support, SAMM, and the Zito Trust work with government for the advancement of victims' interests, others, notably Justice for Victims, are more confrontational and exigent in their promotion of victims' interests, and less mindful of the need to balance these against the rights of offenders (Rock 1998). As such they represent a new and, in some cases, disturbing direction for the victim movement.

Victim Support, women's refuges, rape crisis centres, and the newer victims' interest groups are far from enjoying coherence of outlook, organization, or method. The 'victim movement' is ideologically diverse. Relations between the various groups range from close cooperation to outright hostility (Rock 1998: 206–77). Despite, or perhaps because of, this heterogeneity, the combined impact of their endeavours has been enormous.

VICTIMS IN THE CRIMINAL JUSTICE PROCESS

The victim is now recognized as a key player in the criminal justice process (JUSTICE 1998). Without the cooperation of the victim in reporting crime, furnishing evidence, identifying the offender, and acting as a witness in court, most crime would remain unknown and unpunished. The reliance of the criminal justice system on the victim has proved a powerful bargaining tool in the recognition of victims' interests. Much criminological research into victims has been funded, promoted, and in many cases instigated, by central or local government. And providing for victims has become a central plank of criminal justice policy (Crawford and Goodey 2000).

That victims became a focus for political concern has been related to the profound and growing sense of disillusionment across the political spectrum with the ability of the criminal justice system to 'do anything' about crime. By contrast, concern for the victim promised relatively easy, high public relations benefits (Rock 1990). The *Victim's Charter*, first published in 1990 (Home Office 1990), signified an important advance in the recognition of victims' interests, though it has been criticized for offering little by way of enforceable standards (Reeves and Mulley 2001: 131). Its message was reinforced by the publication of several other statements of standards of service for victims, including the Crown Prosecution Service 'Statement on the

Treatment of Victims and Witnesses' (1993), the 'Court Users' Charter' (1994), and Report of the Royal Commission on Criminal Justice (1993). Taken together these recommendations seek to ensure that victims get better information about the progress of their case, that their views are obtained and considered, and that witnesses receive proper facilities and assistance in court. A Victim's Helpline set up in 1994 allows victims to contact prison authorities if they are concerned about unwanted contact from an offender or the arrangements for an offender's release. These developments were followed up in 1996 by a second *Victim's Charter* (Home Office 1996b), which set twenty-seven standards of service which the various agencies of the criminal justice system are to deliver in four broad areas: provision of information to victims, taking victims' views into account, treating them with respect and sensitivity at court, and providing them with support.

In common with all charters, however, the Victim's Charter has no legal status: its provisions encourage rather than bind, and as such it is questionable whether it can be said to furnish rights in any meaningful sense. Accordingly, it is perhaps better seen as a formulation of standards rather than as the provider of justiciable rights (Fenwick 1995). And it is significant that the report of the JUSTICE committee on 'Victims in the Criminal Justice System' (JUSTICE 1998) uses the language of standards and of 'legitimate expectations' rather than rights (Shapland 2000: 151–3). It is noteworthy also that the European Convention on Human Rights (ECHR), incorporated through the Human Rights Act 1998, lacks any clear statement of victim's rights (Ashworth 2000a: 188), although it is has been established that articles relating to the protection of life, liberty, and security of a person may be invoked in relation to victims.

Pressure for the recognition of victims' rights has a long history. In 1985, the General Assembly of the United Nations adopted a 'Declaration of the Basic Principles of Justice for Victims of Crime and Abuse of Power'. The Declaration lays down basic standards for the treatment of victims, including the right to information and fair treatment, consideration of their views, restitution and compensation, and the provision of victim services. Likewise, the Council of Europe 'Convention on State Compensation' for victims of violent crime (1983) paved the way for many subsequent international agreements and recommendations on the role of the victim in the criminal law and criminal process, on assistance to victims, and on crime prevention. In the prevailing 'rights culture', the balancing of victims' rights against the right of the defendant to a fair trial under Article 6 ECHR will no doubt be a source of continuing academic debate and court jurisprudence (Ashworth 2000a; Sanders and Young 2000: 741–9).

It has long been recognized that, at best, prosecution, conviction, and sentence may have a powerful cathartic effect in relieving victims' feelings of complicity and guilt (Adler 1988: 140). Depending on the sanction meted out, victims may benefit from compensation for their losses and harms suffered, or enjoy feelings of increased security when an offender is incarcerated. On the other hand, insensitive questioning by police, inadequate provision of information, delays, or unexplained decisions by the prosecution service to drop a case each entail further suffering. At worst, the impact of the criminal process is tantamount to secondary victimization (Maguire and Pointing 1988: 11). Failure to recognize the burdens placed upon victims can also lead them to withdraw from the criminal process and limit its ability to pursue cases effectively (Cretney and Davis 1997; Hoyle and Sanders 2000).

As the first point of contact with the criminal justice system, the police play an important role in shaping the victim's experience. Shapland *et al.* found that while initial levels of satisfaction with the police were generally high, these tended to decline steadily as the case progressed (Shapland *et al.* 1985: 83–9; see also Newburn and Merry 1990). Dissatisfaction arose from police failure to keep victims informed, perceived inefficiency, unhelpfulness, or unfairness. Disillusionment was a product, therefore, of a growing feeling that 'the police did not care and were not doing anything' (Shapland *et al.* 1985: 85). In a bid to respond to such criticisms, the Home Office introduced regular surveys of public satisfaction with police services; police forces issue 'Statements of Policing Standards'; and the Victim's Charter stipulates standards for police response to reports of crime by victims (Home Office 1996b). Paradoxically, the BCS found that victims' satisfaction with the police declined from 67 per cent in 1994 to 57 per cent in 2000 (Sims and Myhill 2001).

Particular efforts have been made to improve the police response to victims of sexual assault. Special interview suites in police stations, specially trained women officers or 'chaperones', and joint interviewing with social workers in child abuse cases (Metropolitan Police and Bexley Social Services 1987) are just a few of the innovations introduced in recent decades. Despite these initiatives, lack of resources and enduring cultural resistance has limited the ability of the police to respond sensitively to sexual assault victims (Temkin 1999). In the case of these and other serious offences, victims look for sensitivity in the conduct of interviews, in the collecting of forensic evidence, in the handling of identification procedures, and for information about developments in the investigation. For the mass of property crimes where a suspect is never located, there is often little more the police can do than inform the victim of the reasons for ceasing their enquiries (Newburn and Merry 1990).

INNOVATIONS UNDER THE VICTIM'S CHARTER

Under the Victim's Charter 1996, the Home Office introduced two innovations: the so-called 'One Stop Shop' (OSS), and Victim Statements. Both were piloted in six police force areas. The OSS initiative attempts to ensure that victims are kept informed by making the police a single source of information throughout the case. Victims choosing to opt into the OSS initiative are kept informed by the police about whether a suspect is cautioned or charged, whether the charge is altered, the date of trial, verdict, and sentence. Initially, the scheme applies only to crimes of domestic burglary, grievous bodily harm and attempted murder, robbery, sexual assault, criminal damage over £5,000, arson, and racially motivated offences. It is a welcome move toward ensuring that the difficulties faced by victims in obtaining information from several different sources are overcome. In the pilot study, just under half of eligible victims opted into the scheme: of those who did, almost two-thirds considered that the police dealt with their cases well, and a much higher proportion of them felt better about being victims when their cases were over than those who had opted out (Hoyle *et al.* 1999a: 41–2). About one-fifth did not get the information they wanted, and about one-third said that it came too late. The OSS is open to other criticisms: many serious crimes (including domestic violence) have been excluded from the scheme, as have decisions relating to remands and bail conditions, and the police are not able to explain decisions made. In recognition of this last deficit, the Glidewell Review of the Crown Prosecution Service (CPS) proposed that the CPS take responsibility for the OSS, informing victims of their decisions and explaining them in person where requested (Glidewell 1998), and this is now being carried out on an experimental basis.

The second innovation under the Victim's Charter 1996 was the introduction of Victim Statements (VSs), initially on a pilot basis. The term 'victim' statement rather than 'impact' statement was deliberately chosen to distance the initiative from those in America where victims are given some say over sentence (Morgan and Sanders 1999: 1). In the pilot study victims were invited to state what physical, financial, psychological, social, or emotional effects the offence had on them or their family (Hoyle *et al.* 1999b). Information was gathered either by a police officer taking a free-form statement, or by victims recording their statement on a pro forma. Criminal justice officials could then use this information in making prosecution, bail, and sentencing decisions. About a third of victims invited to give statements in the pilot did so. They gave a variety of expressive, instrumental, and procedural reasons for doing so. Those who did not participate either failed to understand what they were being asked to do, or refused because they wanted to forget about the crime, felt it was not sufficiently serious, or feared reprisals. Of those who did participate, about one-third felt better, about 18 per cent were upset by the process, and the remainder were indifferent. It is not clear, therefore, that VSs successfully fulfil an expressive role. And it is arguable that by raising victims' expectations unrealistically, both the OSS and VSs lead to lower levels of satisfaction than expected. Criminal justice practitioners generally welcomed VSs, but were split whether they should influence sentencing decisions, not least because information so provided was regarded as potentially irrelevant, exaggerated, or unverifiable (Hoyle *et al.* 1999b: 3). It is unclear whether the fact that VSs appear seldom to influence sentencing decisions is a product of resistance by criminal justice professionals to victims' influence (Erez 1999; Erez and Rogers 1999), or because they are 'misconceived in principle and unsatisfactory in practice' (Sanders *et al.* 2001). Other difficulties arise in regard to the timing of the statement and whether it should be updated at the time of trial; the problem of multiple victims or multiple offenders; and, not least, contested evidence. Despite considerable reservations enumerated by the researchers evaluating the VS pilots, the government introduced what is now called the 'Victim Personal Statement Scheme' nationwide in October 2001(Home Office 2001). It was swiftly followed by a Practice Direction by the Lord Chief Justice limiting the role that it was to be permitted to play: '. . . the court must pass what it judges to be the appropriate sentence having regard to the circumstances of the offence and of the offender taking into account, so far as the court considers it appropriate, the consequences to the victim. The opinions of the victim or the victim's close relatives as to what the sentence should be are not therefore relevant, unlike the consequences of the offence upon them' (LCJ 2001).

VICTIMS AS WITNESSES

Unlike jurisdictions such as France or Germany, where victims have considerable rights to participate in the prosecution or to present civil claims within the criminal process (Jones 1994; Kury *et al.* 1994), in Britain victims have traditionally had little role other than as a source of evidence (Joutsen 1994). Limited regard for victims' interests is shown at various stages in the criminal justice process. Since 1994, the police have been under a duty to consult with the victim before cautioning the offender in place of prosecution (though curiously, not when they decide to take no further action). Relieving victims from cross-examination at trial is one consideration in plea-bargaining, though significantly victims are not consulted when a lesser charge is agreed in return for a guilty plea. In reaching the decision to prosecute, the Victim's Charter requires the CPS to have regard to the loss, damage, or injury suffered by the victim, and their fears of further victimization. Trial dates are in theory set at as convenient a date as possible for witnesses, and victims' views are routinely sought in respect of bail decisions. At trial, prosecutors are supposed to introduce themselves to witnesses (in order to make the experience less intimidating), explain the outcome, ensure compensation is considered, and challenge unjust claims put forward in mitigation by the defence. The victim as witness remains in a position of some vulnerability—at the mercy of questioning by defence counsel *and* prosecution alike. Guidance for local agencies dealing with witnesses is provided in the National Standards of Witness Care (Trials Issues Group 1996): for example, on the need to minimize waiting times, to make special provision for vulnerable witnesses, and to avoid the reading out in court of witnesses' addresses (Reeves and Mulley 2001: 132).

The predicament of victims called as witnesses is most starkly illustrated by the plight of rape victims and the extent to which they, quite as much as the defendant, are placed on trial (Temkin 1987: 6–8; Soothill and Soothill 1993). Other vulnerable witnesses include children, the elderly, and those with learning difficulties. Recognition of their plight has led to innovations in court procedure and changes in the rules of evidence. Where children are witnesses, judges have long removed wigs and robes or come down from the bench; barristers have derobed; quietly spoken victim/witnesses are provided with microphones; and provision has been made for the use of screens, of live video-links and pre-recorded video-taped interviews, all intended to reduce the stress to victims (Morgan and Zedner 1992a: 128–44, and 1992b; Spencer *et al.* 1990; Keenan *et al.* 1999). The needs of vulnerable and intimidated witnesses were specifically addressed in the government report *Speaking up for Justice* (Home Office 1998), and plans for its implementation set out in *Action for Justice* (Home Office 1999). These led to the Youth Justice and Criminal Evidence Act 1999, Pt II of which contains several provisions for the protection of witnesses (Ashworth 2000a: 190–91). The Act provides for vulnerable or intimidated witnesses to be screened in court, or to give evidence by live link or in camera; for the removal of gowns and wigs; for the admissibility of video-recorded evidence-in-chief and cross-examination; and for the examination of witnesses through an intermediary (Birch 2000). It provides also for the protection of certain witnesses from cross-examination by the accused in person; and restricts the cross-examination of rape complainants about their sexual history. These provisions go a considerable way toward protecting witnesses from secondary victimization at the hands of the court, though their successful implementation relies also upon changes in attitude by criminal justice professionals (Sanders and Young 2000: 749–55) and adequate resources.

The Witness Service, run by Victim Support, funded by the Home Office, and modelled on American victim-witness assistance programmes, seeks to provide information and counsel to those called as witnesses in court. Established in 1990, the Service now covers all Crown Court centres and magistrates' courts in England and Wales. For witnesses obliged to wait in crowded, inhospitable areas often for lengthy periods, the presence of Witness Service volunteers has been recognized as 'comforting and congenial, a symbolic end to their solitary and pariah status' (Rock 1991). The Witness Service not only provides advice, information, and support to help witnesses through the stress of a court appearance, it also seeks to ensure better facilities, such as separate waiting areas for victims and their families, and special provisions, such as 'fast-tracking' of cases involving child witnesses (Parliamentary All Party Penal Affairs Group 1996: 14). Although there has been a significant change in attitudes towards witnesses, as well as in the facilities and services offered, there are continuing deficiencies, for example, in respect of the provision of information and protection from intimidation (Shapland and Bell 1998). Most importantly, all these services do little to mitigate the continuing ordeal of cross-examination in the witness box (Riding 1999).

In an attempt to judge whether the various innovations in respect of victims and witnesses are appreciated by them, the first national witness satisfaction survey was conducted in 2000. It found that 76 per cent of witnesses were fairly or very satisfied with their overall treatment within the criminal justice system, but nearly a fifth were intimidated by the process of giving evidence, and almost 40 per cent said they would not be happy to be a witness again (Whitehead 2001). The experience was likely most painful for that minority of victims and witnesses (about 8 per cent) who suffer direct intimidation by the offender, his family, or friends (Tarling *et al.* 2000). Clearly, more could be done to improve facilities, support, and protection for witnesses and victims, to prepare them for cross-examination and to limit its rigours (Ashworth 2000a: 192; JUSTICE 1998: 51–5).

COMPENSATION

Of disposals available to the court the most obviously victim-centred is the compensation order. Arguably the initial impetus to both offender and state compensation was negative, spurred on by the feeling that if punishment was failing to deter or to rehabilitate then some limited good might be achieved by compensating victims for the wrongs suffered. Compensation payable by the offender was introduced in the Criminal Justice Act 1972: this gave the courts powers to make an ancillary order for compensation in addition to the main penalty in cases where 'injury, loss, or damage' had resulted. The Criminal Justice Act 1982 made it possible to order compensation as the sole penalty, and required that in cases where fines and compensation orders were given together, the payment of compensation should take priority over the fine. These developments signified a major shift in penological thinking, reflecting the growing importance attached to reparation over the more narrowly retributive aims of conventional punishment. The Criminal Justice Act 1988 furthered this shift by requiring courts to consider making a compensation order in every case of death, injury, loss, or damage; and, where such an order was not given, imposed a duty on the court to give reasons for not doing so. It also extended the range of injuries eligible for compensation. The Criminal Justice Act 1991 increased the maximum sum to be ordered by magistrates' courts from £2,000 to £5,000 per offence, so allowing a larger total sum to be awarded and, incidentally, encouraging the retention of a larger number of cases by magistrates' courts (Wasik and Taylor 1991). Payment of compensation is now deducted at source from state income support, and the attachment of compensation orders to suspended sentences is encouraged.

Figures for the use of compensation orders suggest that the need for the criminal justice system to respond to the harms suffered by victims has firmly established itself in the minds of sentencers. Difficulties remain in determining what constitute reasonable grounds for failing to make an order. Where an order is made, problems arise in determining the degree of harm caused and, therefore, the level of compensation payable. In 1999, 43 per cent of offenders sentenced in magistrates' courts for offences of violence, 27 per cent for burglary, 45 per cent for robbery, 31 per cent for fraud and forgery, and 51 per cent for criminal damage were ordered to pay compensation (Home Office 2000). In the Crown Court, the figure was much lower, partly because compensation orders are not normally combined with custodial sentences. In 17 per cent of offences of violence, 4 per cent of burglary, 12 per cent of fraud and forgery, and 16 per cent of criminal damage, a compensation order was made. In 1999 the average value of a compensation order was £1,338. Most compensation orders are paid in full within twelve months, not least because the courts have wide powers to enforce payment, including ultimately imprisonment.

Compensation is also made through the state-funded Criminal Injuries Compensation Scheme (CICS) (Miers 1991; Zedner 1996). This was set up in 1964 and makes discretionary payments to victims of unlawful violence. It is debatable whether state-funded compensation is premised on the recognition that crime represents a failure of the state obligation to maintain law and order; a cynical 'buying off' of victim co-operation; or an expression of public sympathy (Newburn 1989). The government's own line is that payments reflect 'society's sense of responsibility for and sympathy with the blameless victims of crimes of violence' but explicitly not any liability (CICA 2000: 3).

The original scheme was modified in 1969, 1979, 1990, 1995—when a new tariff scheme was introduced under the Criminal Injuries Compensation Act 1995 in an attempt to curb the spiralling cost of payments and improve administrative efficiency (Zedner 1996: 188–9)—and in 2001 (Miers 2001b). The minimum award is set at £1,000 (effectively denying compensation to the mass of victims of minor assaults and robberies). The tariff groups injuries of comparable severity into twenty-five bands, each receiving a standard fixed payment (from £1,000 to £250,000). For those who are incapacitated as a result of their injury for twenty-eight weeks or more, a separate payment for loss of earnings (or potential earnings) and for the cost of any necessary special care is available. This leaves those unable to work for periods of less than twenty-eight weeks without compensation. Compensation to the arguably derisory figure of £7,500 is payable to the family in cases of fatal injury. The tariff scheme has been criticized for unduly limiting maximum awards, for excluding consideration of the complexities of individual cases, for failing to take full account of loss of earnings, and for removing parity between state compensation payments and civil awards (Zedner 1996: 189). Compensation continues to be available only to victims of violence, though why they should be singled out for help denied to other victims has long been a matter of debate (Ashworth 1986; Duff 1987).

Earlier provisions allowing the Criminal Injuries Compensation Board to take into account the victim's character and way of life have been abolished. However, the new Criminal Injuries Compensation Authority retains discretion to have regard to previous unspent criminal convictions, even those having no causal relation to the injury which is the subject of a claim. Where an applicant can be seen to have attracted assault through his own provocative conduct, or where he has convictions for serious offences, however unconnected with the offence in question, then compensation will generally be withheld. It is less clear, however, why those who have committed a minor, non-violent offence should be denied compensation when they are later violently assaulted.

The police play a significant role as gate-keepers; in deterring would-be recipients from applying, failing to inform those they consider inappropriate claimants about CICS, or giving information to the Authority which calls into question the legitimacy of claims (Newburn and Merry 1990). Without a strategy for ensuring that victims are routinely informed of the existence of CICS, the police (and Victim Support schemes) may deprive victims of access to compensation. In contrast to this unregulated exclusion of 'undeserving victims', those who fulfil the stereotypical picture of a worthy or deserving recipient receive awards more readily than those who do not. Despite research evidence on the relative rarity of elderly women being violently robbed or assaulted, the 'poor, innocent, little old lady' continues to represent the 'ideal victim' in the mind of the state (Newburn 1989: 15; Christie 1986).

Victim recourse to the CICS has increased dramatically over the years. The number of applications rose from 22,000 in 1979–80 to 78,000 in 1999–2000 (CICA 2000: 6). In 1990–91, £109.3 million was paid out to victims, by 1994–5 this had risen to £175 million. Thanks to the limiting effects of the tariff scheme, payments fell to £116 million by 1999–2000, paid out to some 40,000 victims. Concern about the limitations of the scheme (Home Office 1999) led to the introduction of revisions in 2001; these include an increase in the level of awards, an increase in the formula for multiple injuries, the extension of eligibility for awards in the case of fatalities to same-sex partners, and revisions to the tariff itself to make it easier for victims to use.

OTHER DEVELOPMENTS

Legislative recognition of victims' interests can also be found in the Protection from Harassment Act 1997, which principally deals with stalking but also addresses domestic abuse, racial harassment, and neighbour disputes (Harris 2000). The Crime and Disorder Act 1998 also contains important measures relating to victims; not least, provision for restorative conferences under the auspices of the new youth offending teams (s 39) and the introduction of reparation orders (s 67) which require young offenders to make reparation as specified in the order to the victim of an offence or 'a person otherwise affected by it' (Wasik 1999). Section 68 provides that the victim's views must first be sought. Where the victim does not want reparation, it may be made to the community at large. The types of reparation envisaged by the government include 'writing a letter of apology, apologising to the victim in person, cleaning graffiti or repairing criminal damage'. It is a matter of debate how far these provisions will further the aims of restorative justice (of which more below) (Dignan 1999; Morris and Gelsthorpe 2000). The government is now considering expanding the scope of the Victim's Charter and placing it on a statutory basis, and introducing a Victim's Ombudsman (Home Office *et al.* 2001). It remains open to question whether the increased involvement of victims within the criminal justice process is really about securing their rights or meeting their needs, or whether it is aimed rather at promoting the system's own efficiency and goals (JUSTICE 1998; Erez 1999; Edwards 2001).

Post-sentence, there is arguably less scope for victim involvement. Since 1990, the probation service has been under an obligation to contact the victims of life-sentenced prisoners, and since 1995 victims of other categories of prisoner, to ascertain if they have concerns about the conditions attached to the offender's release (HM Inspectorate of Probation 2000; Crawford and Enterkin 2001). Again, it is a matter of controversy whether victims' interests should be in any way determinative of offenders' release or conditions imposed thereafter.

Arguments in favour of increased victim participation in the criminal justice process include: recognition of their status as a party to the dispute (Christie 1977); reduced risk of inflicting further psychological harm on the victim; greater victim co-operation, and thereby the improved efficiency of the system; and better information about harms suffered, and thereby closer proportionality in sentencing (von Hirsch and Jareborg 1991; Wasik 1998). Arguments against allowing victims a greater say include: the intrusion of private views into public decision-making; limitations on prosecutorial discretion; the danger that the victim's subjective view undermines the court's objectivity; disparity in sentencing of similar cases depending on the resilience or punitiveness of the victim (Ashworth 1993); and, lastly, that to increase their involvement may entail further burdens on victims while raising their expectations unrealistically (Parliamentary All Party Penal Affairs Group 1996: 12; JUSTICE 1998; Williams 1999; Reeves and Mulley 2001: 138).

THE RISE OF RESTORATIVE JUSTICE

The proliferation of research about victims has raised larger questions about the very purpose of criminal justice and the place of the victim within it. Victim surveys have consistently revealed that victims are no more punitive than the general public, and many are willing to engage in direct mediation, or to receive monetary or other compensation from their offender (Mattinson and Mirrlees-Black 2000: 41).

Academics, policy-makers, and criminal justice professionals seeking an alternative paradigm to that of punishment have advocated various models of restitution, or reparative or restorative justice with increasing success (Barnett 1977; Wright 1991, 1995; Marshall 1999; Braithwaite 1999). Restorative justice (as it is now predominantly called) is an umbrella term for a variety of theories concerned with the restoration of victim, offender, and community. Other terms used in broadly the same sense include community justice, positive justice, reintegrative justice, relational justice, and transformative justice (Braithwaite 1989; Marshall 1999: 7).

A BRIEF HISTORY OF RESTORATIVE JUSTICE

The idea of restorative justice has several historical roots. An important precursor was experiments with victim-offender mediation and reconciliation carried out in America and Britain in the 1970s. Mediation seeks to resolve disputes without recourse to the courts, allowing both parties to retain control and to voice their grievances under the supervision of a mediator, whether a trained professional or lay volunteer (Davis 1992; Davis *et al.* 1987; Marshall 1991). The mediator makes no decisions and any resolution is reached by the mutual agreement of the two parties. In practice, mediation has varied considerably from operating as a direct alternative to adjudication; through pre- and post-sentence schemes; to meetings between victims and offenders already in custody (Launay 1985). In 1996, twenty-five initiatives were in operation, including fifteen fully-fledged schemes bringing victims and offenders together on a one-to-one basis, or in groups, to hold regular discussions. Their aims are similarly various: from providing victims with tangible reparation and offenders with the hope of a reduced sentence; through providing a conduit for communication; to allowing both parties to understand one another better and, possibly, to resolve their conflict. Although mediation has obvious attractions, sceptics have questioned whether it can really operate 'in the shadow of the court'. Victim Support has warned of the additional burdens, in terms of time, goodwill, and energy, it may place on the victim (Reeves 1984). This said, Home Office research published in 1990 found that 80 per cent of victims and 86 per cent of offenders were satisfied by the process (Parliamentary All Party Penal Affairs Group 1996: 15). While mediation has been quite successful in respect of crimes of low-level seriousness, it is doubtful whether it could substitute for formal adjudication in the case of serious crime (Hudson 1998).

Another important root of restorative justice is the academic argument for reorientation of the criminal justice system toward the victim. This was founded on the argument that crime is not only a wrong against society but often represents also a private wrong done by the offender to a specific victim. Historically, it is argued, the state has stolen the dispute from the hands of victims and offenders (Christie 1977), and, in so doing, has usurped the right of the victim to seek recompense for harms suffered (Wright 1991: 1–9). 'Making good', it has been argued, should be the primary aim of the criminal justice system (Barnett 1977; Wright 1991; Davis 1992). To quote Barnett: 'Justice consists of the culpable offender making good the loss he has caused . . . Where we once saw an offense against society, we now see an offense against an individual' (Barnett 1977: 287–8). This, it is claimed, would reduce reliance on negative, solely punitive disposals, and institute in their place positive attempts to rectify the specific harm caused by crime. In practice, these reparative principles have historically been incorporated somewhat awkwardly into the existing punitive framework (Zedner 1994; Dignan and Cavadino 1996). The stigmatizing and deterrent qualities of punishment are retained, but alongside traditional punishments provision is made for compensation and reparation to identifiable victims. The problems entailed in reorienting the criminal justice system towards the victim in this way have not passed unobserved (Ashworth 1986; Duff 1988; Miers 1992). Objections include: that it has no penal character; that to secure reinstatement to the victim is no more than the enforcement of a civil liability; and that by focusing on harm, it fails to take sufficient account of the offender's culpability (Ashworth 1986: 97).

More recently, restorative justice has been strongly influenced by models of community justice in use in non-Western cultures, particularly the indigenous populations of North America (Native American Sentencing Circles) and New Zealand (Maori justice) (Marshall 1999: 7; Braithwaite 1999). These have inspired experiments in family group conferencing, restorative conferencing, restorative cautions, and community conferencing, most notably in New Zealand, Australia, the United States, and Britain (Miers *et al.* 2001). Academic writings by John Braithwaite, Mark Umbreit, and Howard Zehr, among others, have also been highly influential in promoting restorative justice and have been the driving force behind many of these experiments (Braithwaite 1989; Umbreit 2001; Zehr 1990).

RESTORATIVE JUSTICE IN PRACTICE

Restorative justice initiatives have developed across the world—in Australia, Canada, New Zealand, and South Africa, as well as in Britain (Young 2001; Hoyle and Young 2002). Typically, they are intended to involve offenders, their families, victims, other interested members of the community, and a facilitator (often a youth justice co-ordinator, social worker, or police officer). The United Nations defines restorative justice as a process 'in which the victim, the offender and/or any other individuals or community members affected by a crime participate actively together in the resolution of matters arising from the crime' (United Nations 1999b). In contrast to mediation, therefore, bi- or tri-partite resolution is replaced with a meeting of all those involved, however tangentially. The group discusses the offence, the circumstances underlying it, its effects on the victim, and how relationships have been affected by it. The principal purpose is to share information and, collectively, 'to formulate a plan about how best to deal with the offending' (Morris and Maxwell 2000: 209).

In principle the victim is a central actor in restorative justice. In practice, levels of victim participation in restorative justice schemes, in Britain at least, are very low. For example, the Youth Justice and Criminal Evidence Act 1999 set up youth offender panels governed by restorative principles. In 2000–2001, less than 7 per cent of panels were attended by victims: a very low figure even bearing in mind that many of the offences were 'victimless' (Newburn *et al.* 2001: 19; see also Miers *et al.* 2001). Given that responses to the 1998 BCS suggested that 41 per cent of victims were willing to meet with their offender (Mattinson and Mirrlees-Black 2000), it is possible that the problem lies with inadequacies in the means by which victims are involved. In New Zealand, by contrast, victims attended about half of all family group conferences (reasons given for non-attendance included that they were not invited, the time arranged was unsuitable, or inadequate notice was given) (Morris and Maxwell 2000: 211). And rates of victim attendance in Australia are even higher: 73 per cent at conferences in New South Wales and up to 89 per cent for crimes of personal violence in the RISE experiments in Canberra. Aside from actual attendance, victims can have an input to restorative programmes (through victim statements, for example), or benefit from reparative work done for them. Moreover, to judge the success of restorative justice schemes by reference to victim participation rates might encourage wholly undesirable pressure upon victims to take part. But on current evidence it is far from clear that restorative justice is centrally, or even principally, about victims. A review of restorative justice programmes in twelve European countries found that only one country (Denmark) claimed to be victim-oriented; a further five are offender-oriented; in two countries the orientation varies with the particular programme; and in the remaining four the orientation is mixed (Miers 2001a: 79).

The question then arises: how much is restorative justice really about victims? There is some evidence that restorative justice works in the sense of reducing reconviction rates in respect of serious offenders undergoing intensive, long-term intervention (though there is little evidence of success in respect of lesser offenders with whom contact is short and superficial) (Miers *et al.* 2001). But does it serve victims' interests as well? Is there a danger that victims are being used to promote ends that have little to do with their own interests? Ashworth has warned of the dangers of 'victim prostitution' (Ashworth 2000a: 186). In restorative cautioning panels, for example, emphasis is on diversion or reducing re-offending among offenders rather than on the value of the process for victims (Young and Goold 1999). Like victim–offender mediation before them, restorative justice conferences and panels may entail pressure upon victims to participate; burdens upon their time and goodwill; and possible psychological costs inherent in meeting with their offender and talking again about the crime and its impact. Victims may feel responsible for the outcome faced by their offender, such that they feel obliged to cooperate and to accept any apology offered, even when they doubt its sincerity. And a small but significant minority of victims report feeling worse after involvement in a restorative justice conference (Braithwaite 1999: 22).

Fundamental questions remain unresolved: can and should restorative justice challenge the prevailing paradigm of punishment, or should restorative justice remain ancillary to the proper purposes of punishment? How far are developments in restorative justice based on a coherent view of the rights and responsibilities of victim, offenders, and the state? Do they offer sufficient procedural safeguards to victims and offenders? Can they ensure substantive fairness (if, for example, a particular victim is forgiving or vengeful)? What are the implications of restorative justice for the mass of 'victimless' crimes, or for crimes where there is not one victim but many (Young 2001)?

Alongside the rise of restorative justice, recent decades have witnessed a very

different trend in criminal justice towards increasingly punitive policies. Prison populations have burgeoned in both America and, to a lesser extent, Britain. Although the
victims' movement in general has been careful to avoid political involvement in penal
policy, certain victims' organizations have been vociferous in their demand for greater
severity in sentencing (Rock 1998: 218). More generally, the idea of the victim has
been invoked as a potent rhetorical device or symbolic tool to lever up punitiveness in
what Ashworth calls 'victims in the service of severity' and Garland describes as 'the
projected, politicized, image of "the victim" . . . as an all-purpose justification for
measures of penal repression' (Ashworth 2000a: 186; Garland 2001: 143). Similarly, the
naming of criminal laws and penal measures after individual victims (for example,
'Megan's Law' in America, and the campaign for 'Sarah's Law' in Britain) uses the
plight of the victim to legitimate more extensive controls and new punitive measures.
The power of restorative justice to counter, or even to displace, these punitive tendencies remains to be seen (Levrant *et al.* 1999; Sanders and Young, in Chapter 28 of this
volume).

CONCLUSION

Victims now attract an unprecedented level of interest, both as a subject of criminological enquiry and as a focus of criminal justice policy. Far from being simply a
compartmentalized topic, victim research has had an impact upon every aspect of
criminological thinking and has profoundly altered our picture of crime by uncovering a vast array of hidden offences, many against the most vulnerable members of
society. Political pressure, too, has raised the victim's profile, ensuring recognition of
victim needs and the importance of victim services. It has greatly expanded the role
of compensation, provision of services, and information, and has allowed victims'
interests to inform key decisions in the criminal justice process. At a time when the
impulse to punish dominates, the growing commitment to restorative justice is an
important countertrend. Whether, and how far, restorative justice is about serving the
interests of victims is a separate question entirely.

Selected further reading

On the development of victimology from its early origins, see Walklate (1989), *Victimology*,
or Mawby and Walklate (1994), *Critical Victimology*. A good overview of the victim survey
in all its forms is provided in Koffman (1996), *Crime Surveys and Victims of Crime* (and on
its methodology in Mayhew (2000)); while Kershaw *et al.* (2000), *The 2000 British Crime
Survey* gives the latest findings from the BCS. A good survey of the literature on fear of crime
and its impact is Hale (1996), 'Fear of Crime: A Review of the Literature' in the *International
Review of Victimology*. For discussion of the impact of victimization and the needs of
victims, the classic work is Shapland *et al.* (1985), *Victims and the Criminal Justice System*,
which spawned later studies such as those by Maguire and Corbett (1987) and Morgan and

Zedner (1992). On the development of services into a victims' movement, see Rock (1990), *Helping Victims of Crime: The Home Office and the Rise of Victim Support in England and Wales*. The role of the victim in the criminal justice system is an area of lively debate. Classic texts are Barnett (1977), 'Restitution: A New Paradigm of Criminal Justice' in *Ethics*; and Christie (1977), 'Conflicts as Property' in the *British Journal of Criminology*. More recent contributions include Braithwaite (1999), 'Restorative Justice; Assessing Optimistic and Pessimistic Accounts', in M. Tonry (ed.), *Crime and Justice*; Strang and Braithwaite (eds) (2000), *Restorative Justice: Philosophy to Practice*; and Crawford and Goodey (eds) (2000), *Integrating a Victim Perspective within Criminal Justice*. Lastly, essential documents on the place of victims within the system are Home Office (1996), *Victim's Charter* and JUSTICE (1998), *Victims in Criminal Justice*.

References

ADLER, Z. (1988), 'Prosecuting Child Sexual Abuse: A Challenge to the Status Quo', in M. Maguire and J. Pointing (eds), *Victims of Crime: A New Deal?*: 138–46, Milton Keynes: Open University Press.

ALLEN, S. (2002), 'Developing a Typology of Male Victims of Rape', in C. Hoyle and R. Young (eds), *New Visions of Crime Victims*, Oxford: Hart Publishing.

AMIR, M. (1971), *Patterns of Forcible Rape*, Chicago, Ill.: University of Chicago Press.

ANDERSON, S., GROVE SMITH, C., KINSEY, R., and WOOD, J. (1990), *The Edinburgh Crime Survey: First Report*, Edinburgh: Scottish Office.

——, KINSEY, R., LOADER, I., and SMITH, C. (1992), *Cautionary Tales—A Study of Young People and Crime in Edinburgh*, Edinburgh: University of Edinburgh.

ANNA T. (1988), 'Feminist Responses to Sexual Abuse: The Work of the Birmingham Rape Crisis Centre', in M. Maguire and J. Pointing (eds), *Victims of Crime: A New Deal?*, Milton Keynes: Open University Press.

ANTTILA, I. (1974), 'Victimology: a New Territory in Criminology', *Scandinavian Studies in Criminology*, 5: 3–7.

ASHWORTH, A. (1986), 'Punishment and Compensation: Victims, Offenders and the State', *Oxford Journal of Legal Studies*, 6: 86–122.

—— (1993), 'Victim Impact Statements and Sentencing', *Criminal Law Review*: 498–509.

—— (2000a), 'Victims' Rights, Defendants' Rights and Criminal Procedure', in A. Crawford and J. Goodey (eds), *Integrating a Victim Perspective within Criminal Justice*, Aldershot: Ashgate Dartmouth.

—— (2000b), 'Restorative Justice and Victims' Rights', *New Zealand Law Journal*: 84–88.

BALL, C. (2000), 'The Youth Justice and Criminal Evidence Act 1999. Part I: A significant move towards restorative justice, or a recipe for unintended consequences?', *Criminal Law Review*: 211–22.

BANNISTER, J., FARRALL, S., DITTON, J., and GILCHRIST, E. (1997), 'Questioning the measurement of the fear of crime', *British Journal of Criminology*, 37, 4: 658–79.

BARNETT, R.E. (1977), 'Restitution: A New Paradigm of Criminal Justice', *Ethics*, 87: 279–301.

BIRCH, D. (2000), 'The Youth Justice and Criminal Evidence Act 1999. A Better Deal for Vulnerable Witnesses?', *Criminal Law Review*: 223–49.

BOWLING, B. (1998), *Violent Racism Victimization, Policing and Social Context*, Oxford: Clarendon Press.

BOX, S. (1983), *Power, Crime and Mystification*, London: Routledge.

BRAITHWAITE, J. (1989), *Crime, Shame and Reintegration*, Cambridge: Cambridge University Press.

—— (1999), 'Restorative Justice; Assessing Optimistic and Pessimistic Accounts', in M. Tonry (ed.), *Crime and Justice: A Review of Research*, Chicago, Ill.: Chicago University Press.

British Journal of Criminology (1995), 'Symposium on Repeat Victimization', 35, 3.

BROGDEN, M., and NIJHAR, P. (2000), *Crime, Abuse and the Elderly*, Cullompton: Willan.

BUDD, T. (1999), *Burglary of Domestic Dwellings: Findings from the British Crime Survey HO Statistical Bulletin 4/9*, London: Home Office.

BURGESS, A.W., and HOLSTROM, L.L. (1978), *Rape: Victims of Crisis*, Bowie, Md.: Brady.

CAVADINO, M., and DIGNAN, J. (1997), 'Reparation, Retribution, and Rights', *International Review of Victimology*, 4: 233–53.

CHAMBERS, G., and MILLAR, A. (1983), *Investigating Sexual Assault*, Edinburgh: HMSO.

—— and TOMBS, J. (1984), *The British Crime Survey Scotland*, Edinburgh: Scottish Office.

CHOUDRY, S. (1996), 'Pakistani Women's Experience of Domestic Violence in Great Britain', *HORS Research Findings No. 43*, London: HMSO.

CHRISTIE, N. (1977), 'Conflicts as Property', *British Journal of Criminology*, 17: 1–15.

—— (1986), 'The ideal victim', in E. Fattah (ed.), *From Crime Policy to Victim Policy*, London: Macmillan.

COMMISSION FOR RACIAL EQUALITY (1988), *Learning in Terror: A Survey of Racial Harassment in Schools and Colleges*, London: Commission for Racial Equality.

COOPER, J., and POMEYIE, J. (1988), 'Racial Attacks and Racial Harassment: Lessons from a Local Project', in M. Maguire and J. Pointing (eds), *Victims of Crime: A New Deal?*, Milton Keynes: Open University Press.

CRAWFORD, A. (2000), 'Salient Themes Towards a Victim Perspective and the Limitations of Restorative Justice', in A. Crawford and J. Goodey (eds), *Integrating a Victim Perspective within Criminal Justice*, Aldershot: Ashgate Dartmouth.

—— and GOODEY, J. (eds) (2000), *Integrating a Victim Perspective within Criminal Justice: International Debates*, Aldershot: Ashgate Dartmouth.

—— and ENTERKIN, J. (2001), 'Victim Contact Work in the Probation Service: Paradigm Shift or Pandora's Box?', *British Journal of Criminology*, 41, 4: 707–25.

—— JONES, T., WOODHOUSE, T., and YOUNG, J. (1986), 'The Ideal Victim', in E.A. Fattah (ed.), *From Crime Policy to Victim Policy*, London: Macmillan.

——, ——, —— and —— (1990), *Second Islington Crime Survey*, Middlesex: Middlesex Polytechnic.

CRETNEY, A., and DAVIS, G. (1997), 'Prosecuting Domestic Assault: Victims Failing Courts, or Courts Failing Victims?', *Howard Journal of Criminal Justice* 36, no. 2: 146–57.

CRIMINAL INJURIES COMPENSATION AUTHORITY (2000), *Annual Report and Accounts 1999/2000*, Edinburgh: The Stationery Office.

CROWN PROSECUTION SERVICE (1993), *Statement on the Treatment of Victims and Witnesses*, London: HMSO.

DALY, K. (2000), 'Revisiting the Relationship between Retributive and Restorative Justice', in H. Strang and J. Braithwaite (eds), *Restorative Justice: Philosophy to Practice*, Aldershot: Ashgate Dartmouth.

DAVIS, G. (1992), *Making Amends: Mediation and Reparation in Criminal Justice*, London: Routledge.

——, BOUCHERAT, J., and WATSON, D. (1987), *A Preliminary Study of Victim Offender Mediation and Reparation Schemes in England and Wales*, Home Office RPU Paper 42, London: HMSO.

DAVIES, R.C., LURIGIO, A.J., and SKOGAN, W.G. (1999), 'Services for Victims: A Market Research Study', *International Review of Victimology*, 6: 101–15.

DIGNAN, J. (1999), 'The Crime and Disorder Act and the Prospects for Restorative Justice', *Criminal Law Review*: 48–60.

—— and CAVADINO, M. (1996), 'Towards a Framework for Conceptualising and Evaluating Models of Criminal Justice from a Victim's Perspective', *International Review of Victimology*, 4: 153–82.

DOBASH, R., and DOBASH, R. (1980), *Violence against Wives: A Case Against Patriarchy*, New York: Open Books.

—— (1998), *Rethinking Violence Against Women*, London: Sage.

DUFF, P. (1987), 'Criminal Injuries Compensation and "Violent" Crime', *Criminal Law Review*: 219–30.

—— (1988), 'The "Victim Movement" and Legal Reform', in M. Maguire and J. Pointing (eds), *Victims of Crime: A New Deal?*, Milton Keynes: Open University Press.

EDGAR, K., and O'DONNELL, I. (1998), 'Assault in Prison', *British Journal of Criminology*, 38, 4: 635–50.

EDWARDS, I. (2001), 'Victim Participation in Sentencing; The Problems of Incoherence', *Howard Journal of Criminal Justice*, 40, 1: 39–54.

ELLINGWORTH, D., FARRELL, G., and PEASE, K. (1995), 'A Victim is a Victim is a Victim?', *British Journal of Criminology*, 35, 3: 360–65.

ENNIS, P.H. (1967), *Criminal Victimization in the United States: A Report of a National Survey*, Washington, DC: US Department of Justice.

EREZ, E. (1999), 'Who is Afraid of the Big Bad Victim? Victim Impact Statements as Victim

Empowerment and Enhancement of Justice,' *Criminal Law Review.* 545–56.

—— (2000), 'Integrating a Victim Perspective in Criminal Justice Through Victim Impact Statements', in A. Crawford and J. Goodey (eds), *Integrating a Victim Perspective within Criminal Justice*, Aldershot: Ashgate Dartmouth.

—— and ROGERS, L. (1999), 'Victim Impact Statements and Sentencing Outcomes and Processes', *British Journal of Criminology*, 39, 2: 216–39.

EWALD, U. (2000), 'Criminal Victimisation and Social Adaptation in Modernity', in T. Hope and R. Sparks (eds), *Crime, Risk and Insecurity*, London: Routledge.

FARRALL, S., BANNISTER, J., DITTON, J., and GILCHRIST, E. (1997), 'Questioning the Measurement of "Fear of Crime"', *British Journal of Criminology*, 37, 4: 658–79.

——, ——, —— and —— (2000), 'Social Psychology and the Fear of Crime', *British Journal of Criminology*, 40, 3: 399–413.

FATTAH, E. (ed). (1986), *From Crime Policy to Victim Policy*, London: Macmillan.

—— (1989), 'Victims and Victimology: The Facts and the Rhetoric', *International Review of Victimology*, 1: 43–66.

—— (1991), *Understanding Criminal Victimization*, Scarborough, Ontario: Prentice-Hall.

FENWICK, H. (1995), 'Rights of Victims in the Criminal Justice System', *Criminal Law Review.* 843–53.

—— (1997), 'Procedural "Rights" of Victims of Crime: Public or Private Ordering of the Criminal Justice Process?', *Modern Law Review*, 60: 317–33.

FINKELHOR, D. (1986), *A Sourcebook on Child Sexual Abuse*, New York: Sage.

FITZGERALD, M., and HALE, C. (1996), 'Ethnic Minorities Victimisation and Racial Harassment', *HO Research Study*, London: HMSO.

GARAFALO, J. (1979), 'Victimization and the Fear of Crime', *Journal of Research in Crime and Delinquency*, 16: 80–97.

GARLAND, D. (2001), *The Culture of Control: Crime and Social Order in Contemporary Society*, Oxford: Oxford University Press.

GENN, H. (1988), 'Multiple Victimization', in M. Maguire and J. Pointing (eds), *Victims of Crime: A New Deal?*, Milton Keynes: Open University Press.

GLIDEWELL, I. (1998), *The Review of the Crown Prosecution Service: A Report* (Cmnd. 3960), London: HMSO.

GOODEY, J. (1997), 'Boys Don't Cry: Masculinities, Fear of Crime and Fearlessness', *British Journal of Criminology*, 37, 3: 401–18.

GOTTFREDSON, M.R. (1984), *Victims of Crime: The Dimensions of Risk*, HORS No. 81, London: HMSO.

—— (1986), 'Substantive Contributions of Victimization Surveys', *Crime and Justice*, 7: 251–87.

GRADY, A. (2002), 'Female-on-Male Domestic Abuse: Uncommon or Ignored?', in C. Hoyle and R. Young (eds), *New Visions of Crime Victims*, Oxford: Hart Publishing.

HALE, C. (1996), 'Fear of Crime: A Review of the Literature', *International Review of Victimology*, 4: 79–150.

HALL, R. (1985), *Ask Any Woman*, Bristol: Falling Wall Press.

HANMER, J., and SAUNDERS, S. (1984), *Well Founded Fear*, London: Hutchison.

HARRIS, J. (2000), *The Protection from Harassment Act 1997—An evaluation of its use and effectiveness*, HO Research Findings No. 130, London: Home Office.

HARTLESS, J., DITTON, J., NAIR, G., and PHILLIPS, S. (1995), 'More Sinned Against than Sinning: A study of young teenagers' experience of crime', *British Journal of Criminology* 35, 1: 114–33.

HINDELANG, M., GOTTFREDSON, M.R., and GARAFALO, J. (1978), *Victims of Personal Crime: An Empirical Foundation for a Theory of Personal Victimization*, Cambridge, Mass.: Ballinger.

HM INSPECTORATE OF PROBATION (2000), *The Victim Perspective: Ensuring the Victim Matters*, London: Home Office.

HOLLWAY, W., and JEFFERSON, T. (2000), 'The Role of Anxiety in Fear of Crime', in T. Hope and R. Sparks (eds), *Crime, Risk and Insecurity*, London: Routledge.

HOME OFFICE (1990), *Victim's Charter: A Statement of the Rights of Victims*, London: HMSO.

—— (1993), *Compensating Victims of Violent Crime*, London: HMSO.

—— (1996a), *Protecting the Public: The Government's Strategy on Crime in England and Wales*, London: HMSO.

—— (1996b), *Victim's Charter*, London: HMSO.

—— (1998), *Speaking Up for Justice*, Report of the Interdepartmental Working Group on the Treatment of Vulnerable or Intimidated Witnesses in the Criminal Justice System, London: Home Office.

—— (1999), *Action for Justice: Implementing the Speaking Up for Justice Report*, London: Home Office.

—— (2000), *Criminal Statistics 1999–2000*, London: Home Office.

—— (2001), *The Victim Personal Statement Scheme: Guidance Note for Practitioners or Those Operating the Scheme*, London: Home Office.

——, LORD CHANCELLOR'S DEPARTMENT AND THE ATTORNEY-GENERAL (2001), *A Review of the Victims' Charter*, London: Home Office.

HOPE, T. (2001), 'Crime victimization and inequality in risk society', in R. Matthews and J. Pitts (eds), *Crime, Disorder and Community Safety*, London: Routledge.

HOPE, T., BRYAN, J., TRICKETT, A., and OSBORN, D. (2001), 'The Phenomena of Multiple Victimization: The Relationship between Personal and Property Crime Risk', *British Journal of Criminology* 41, 4: 595–617.

HOUGH, M. (1995), 'Anxiety about Crime: Findings from the 1994 British Crime Survey', *HORS Research Findings No. 25*, London: HMSO.

—— and MAYHEW, P. (1983), *The British Crime Survey: First Report*, London: HMSO.

—— (1985), *Taking Account of Crime: Key Findings from the Second British Crime Survey*, London: HMSO.

HOWARTH, G., and ROCK, P. (2000), 'Aftermath and the Construction of Victimisation', *Howard Journal of Criminal Justice*, 39, 1: 58–78.

HOYANO, L. (2000), 'The Youth Justice and Criminal Evidence Act 1999: Variations on a Theme by Pigot; Special Measures for Child Witnesses', *Criminal Law Review*: 250–73.

HOYLE, C. (1998), *Negotiating Domestic Violence; Police, Criminal Justice and Victims*, Oxford: Oxford University Press.

—— and SANDERS, A. (2000), 'Police Response to Domestic Violence: From Victim Choice to Victim Empowerment?', *British Journal of Criminology*, 40, 1: 14–36.

—— and YOUNG, R. (2002), *Proceed with Caution: An Evaluation of the Thames Valley Police Initiative in Restorative Cautioning*, York: Joseph Rowntree Foundation.

—— and —— (eds) (2002), *New Visions of Crime Victims*, Oxford: Hart Publishing.

——, CAPE, E., MORGAN, R., and SANDERS, A. (1999a), *Evaluation of the 'One Stop Shop' and Victim Statement Pilot Projects*, London: Home Office.

——, MORGAN, R., and SANDERS, A. (1999b), *The Victim's Charter: An Evaluation of Pilot Projects*, HO Research Findings No. 107, London: Home Office.

HUDSON, B. (1998), 'Restorative Justice: The Challenge of Racial and Sexual Violence', *Journal of Law and Society*, 25: 237–56.

JOHNSTONE, D. (2002), *Restorative Justice: Ideas, Values, Debates*, Cullompton: Willan.

JONES, D., PICKETT, J., OATES, M.R., and BARBOR, P. (1987), *Understanding Child Abuse*, Basingstoke: Macmillan Education.

JONES, R.L. (1994), 'Victims of Crime in France', *Justice of the Peace*: 795–6.

JONES, T., MACLEAN, B., and YOUNG, J. (1986), *The Islington Crime Survey*, Aldershot: Gower.

JOUTSEN, M. (1987), *The Role of the Victim of Crime in European Criminal Justice Systems: A Cross-national Study of the Role of the Victim*, Helsinki: Heuni.

—— (1994), 'Victim Participation in Proceedings and Sentencing in Europe', *International Review of Victimology*, 3: 57–67.

JUSTICE (1998), *Victims in Criminal Justice*, Report of the JUSTICE Committee on the Role of Victims in Criminal Justice, London: JUSTICE.

KAISER, G., KURY, H., and ALBRECHT, H.-J. (1991), *Victims and Criminal Justice: Victimological Research: Stocktaking and Prospects*, Freiburg: Max Planck Institute.

KEENAN, C., DAVIS, G., HOYANO, L., and MAITLAND, L. (1999), 'Interviewing Allegedly Abused Children with a View to Criminal Prosecution', *Criminal Law Review*: 863–73.

KELLY, L. (1988), *Surviving Sexual Violence*, Oxford: Polity Press.

KERSHAW, C., BUDD, T., KINSHOTT, G., MATTINSON, J., MAYHEW, P., and MYHILL, A. (2000), *The 2000 British Crime Survey. Home Office Statistical Bulletin 18/00*, London: Home Office.

——, CHIVITE-MATTHEWS, A., THOMAS, C., and AUST, R. (2001), *The 2001 British Crime Survey. Home Office Statistical Bulletin 18/01*, London: Home Office.

KINSEY, R. (1984), *Merseyside Crime Survey: First Report*, Liverpool: Merseyside County Council.

—— (1985), *Merseyside Crime and Police Surveys: Final Report*, Liverpool: Merseyside County Council.

KOFFMAN, L. (1996), *Crime Surveys and Victims of Crime*, Cardiff: University of Wales Press.

Kury, H., Kaiser, M., and Teske, R. (1994), 'The Position of the Victim in Criminal Procedure—Results of a German Study', *International Review of Victimology*, 3: 69–81.

Launay, G. (1985), 'Bringing Victims and Offenders Together: A Comparison of Two Models', *The Howard Journal*, 24, 3: 200–212.

Lees, S. (1997), *Carnal Knowledge: Rape on Trial*, Harmondsworth: Penguin.

Levi, M., and Pithouse, A. (1992), 'The Victims of Fraud', in D. Downes (ed.), *Unravelling Criminal Justice*, London: Macmillan.

—— (forthcoming), *Victims of White-Collar Crime*, Oxford: Oxford University Press.

Levrant, S., Cullen, F.T., Fulton, B., and Wozniak, J.F. (1999), 'Reconsidering Restorative Justice: The Corruption of Benevolence Revisited', *Crime and Delinquency*, 45.1: 3–27.

London Rape Crisis Centre (1984), *Sexual Violence: The Reality for Women*, London: LRCC.

Lord Chief Justice (2001), *Practice Direction: Victim Personal Statements*, London: Court Service.

Lurigio, A.J. (1987), 'Are All Victims Alike? The Adverse, Generalized, and Differential Impact of Crime', *Crime and Delinquency*, 33: 452–67.

——, Skogan, W.G., and Davis, R.C. (eds) (1997), *Victims of Crime*, London: Sage.

MacCormick, N., and Garland, D. (1998), 'Sovereign States and Vengeful Victims', in A. Ashworth and M. Wasik (eds), *Fundamentals of Sentencing Theory*, Oxford: Clarendon Press.

Maguire, M. (1980), 'The Impact of Burglary upon Victims', *British Journal of Criminology*, 20, 3: 261–75.

—— in collaboration with Bennett, T. (1982), *Burglary in a Dwelling*, London: Heinemann.

—— (1985), 'Victims' Needs and Victims' Services', *Victimology*, 10: 539–59.

—— (1991), 'The Needs and Rights of Victims of Crime', in M. Tonry (ed.), *Crime and Justice: A Review of Research*, 14: 363–433, Chicago, Ill.: Chicago University Press.

—— and Corbett, C. (1987), *The Effects of Crime and the Work of Victim Support Schemes*, Aldershot: Gower.

—— and Kynch, J. (2000a), *Victim Support: Findings from the 1998 British Crime Survey*, HO Research Findings No. 117, London: HMSO.

—— and —— (2000b), *Public Perceptions and Victims' Experiences of Victim Support: Findings from the 1998 British Crime Survey*, HO Occasional Paper, London: Home Office.

—— and Pointing, J. (eds) (1988), *Victims of Crime: A New Deal?*, Milton Keynes: Open University Press.

Marshall, T. (1984), *Reparation, Conciliation and Mediation*, London: HMSO.

—— (1991), 'Victim–Offender Mediation', *HORS Research Bulletin No. 30*: 9–15, London: HMSO.

—— (1996), 'The Evolution of Restorative Justice in Britain', *European Journal of Criminal Policy and Research*, 4, 4: 21–43.

—— (1999), *Restorative Justice: An Overview*, London: Home Office.

Mattinson, J., and Mirrlees-Black, C. (2000), *Attitudes to Crime and Criminal Justice: Findings from the 1998 British Crime Survey*, Home Office Research Study 200, London: Home Office.

Mawby, R., and Walklate, S. (1994), *Critical Victimology*, London: Sage.

Maxfield, M.G. (1984), *Fear of Crime in England and Wales*, HORS 78, London: HMSO.

Mayhew, P. (2000), 'Researching the State of Crime: Local, National, and International Victim Surveys', in R.D. King and E. Wincup (eds), *Doing Research on Crime and Justice*, Oxford: Oxford University Press.

—— and Aye Maung, N. (1992), 'Surveying Crime: Findings from the 1992 British Crime Survey', *HORS Research Findings No. 2*, London: HMSO.

—— (1993), *The 1992 British Crime Survey*, London: HMSO.

——, Elliot, D., and Dowds, L. (1989), *The 1988 British Crime Survey*, London: HMSO.

——, Mirrlees-Black, C., and Aye Maung, N. (1994), 'Trends in Crime: Findings from the 1994 British Crime Survey', *HORS Research Findings No. 14*, London: HMSO.

—— and van Dijk, J.J.M. (1997), *Criminal Victimisation in Eleven Industrialised Countries: Key Findings from the 1996 International Crime Victimisation Survey*, The Hague: Ministry of Justice, Dept of Crime Prevention.

Mendelsohn, B. (1956), 'Une nouvelle branche de la science bio-psycho-sociale: Victimologie', *Revue internationale de criminologie et de police technique*: 10–31.

Metropolitan Police and Bexley Social Services (1987), *Child Sexual Abuse: Joint Investigative Programme: Final Report*, London: HMSO.

Miers, D. (1989), 'Positivist Victimology: A Critique,' *International Review of Victimology*, 1: 3–22.

—— (1991), *Compensation for Criminal Injuries*, London: Butterworths.

—— (1992), 'The Responsibilities and the Rights of Victims of Crime', *Modern Law Review*, 55, no. 4: 482–505.

—— (2001a), *An International Review of Restorative Justice, Home Office CRRS 10*, London: Home Office.

—— (2001b), 'Criminal Injuries Compensation: The New Regime', *Journal of Personal Injuries Law*, 4: 371–95.

——, MAGUIRE, M., GOLDIE, S., SHARPE, K., HALE, C., NETTEN, A., UGLOW, S., DOOLIN, K., HALLAM, A., ENTERKIN, J., and NEWBURN, T. (2001), *An Exploratory Evaluation of Restorative Justice Schemes*, Home Office Crime Reduction Research Series 9, London: Home Office.

MIRRLEES-BLACK, C. (1999), *Domestic Violence: Findings from a New British Crime Survey Self-Completion Questionnaire*, HORS 191, London: HMSO.

——, MAYHEW, P., and PERCY, A. (1996), *The 1996 British Crime Survey*, London: HMSO.

——, BUDD, T., PARTRIDGE, S., and MAYHEW, P. (1998), *The 1998 British Crime Survey, Home Office Statistical Bulletin 21/98*, London: Home Office.

MORGAN, J., and ZEDNER, L. (1992a), *Child Victims: Crime, Impact, and Criminal Justice*, Oxford: Oxford University Press.

—— (1992b), 'The Victim's Charter: A New Deal for Child Victims?', *The Howard Journal*: 294–307.

MORGAN, R., and SANDERS, A. (1999), *The Uses of Victim Statements*, London: Home Office.

MORRIS, A. (1987), *Women, Crime and Criminal Justice*, Oxford: Blackwell.

—— and GELSTHORPE, L. (2000), 'Something Old, Something Borrowed, Something Blue, but Something New? A comment on the prospects for restorative justice under the Crime and Disorder Act 1998', *Criminal Law Review*: 18–30.

—— and MAXWELL, G. (2000), 'The Practice of Family Group Conferences in New Zealand', in A. Crawford and J. Goodey (eds), *Integrating a Victim Perspective within Criminal Justice*, Aldershot: Ashgate Dartmouth.

—— and YOUNG, W. (2000), 'Reforming Criminal Justice: The Potential of Restorative Justice', in H. Strang and J. Braithwaite (eds), *Restorative Justice: Philosophy to Practice*, Aldershot: Ashgate Dartmouth.

MVA CONSULTANCY (2000), *The 2000 Scottish Crime Survey*, Edinburgh: The Scottish Executive.

NATIONAL BOARD FOR CRIME PREVENTION (1994), *Wise after the Event: Tackling Repeat Victimisation*, London: Home Office.

NEWBURN, T. (1989), *The Settlement of Claims at the Criminal Injuries Compensation Board*, HORS No. 112, London: HMSO.

—— (1994), 'The Long-term Needs of Victims of Crime: A Review of the Literature', *HORPU Paper No. 80*, London: HMSO.

—— and MERRY, S. (1990), *Keeping in Touch: Police–Victim Communication in Areas*, HORS No. 116, London: HMSO.

—— et al. (2001), *The introduction of referral orders into the youth justice system: second interim report, RDS Occasional paper no. 73*, London: Home Office.

O'DONNELL, I., and EDGAR, K. (1998), 'Routine Victimisation in Prisons', *Howard Journal of Criminal Justice*, 37, 3: 266–79.

PAIN, R.H. (1995), 'Elderly Women and Fear of Violent Crime: The Least Likely Victims?', *British Journal of Criminology*, 35, 4: 584–98.

PAINTER, K., and FARRINGTON, D. (1998), 'Marital Violence in Great Britain and its relationship to Marital and Non-Marital Rape', *International Review of Victimology*, 5: 257–76.

PANTAZIS, C. (2000), ' "Fear of Crime", Vulnerability and Poverty: Evidence from the British Crime Survey', *British Journal of Criminology*, 40, 3: 414–36.

PARLIAMENTARY ALL PARTY PENAL AFFAIRS GROUP (1996), *Increasing the Rights of Victims of Crime*, London: Parliamentary Paper.

PERCY, A., and MAYHEW, P. (1997), 'Estimating Sexual Victimization in a National Crime Survey: A New Approach', *Studies in Crime and Crime Prevention*, 6: 125–50.

PHILLIPS, C., and SAMPSON, A. (1998), 'Preventing Repeated Racial Victimization', *British Journal of Criminology*, 38, 4: 124–44.

PIZZEY, E. (1974), *Scream Quietly or the Neighbours Will Hear*, London: IF Books.

POLLARD, C. (2000), 'Victims and the Criminal Justice System: A New Vision', *Criminal Law Review*: 5–17.

RADFORD, J. (1987), 'Policing Male Violence', in J. Hanmer and M. Maynard (eds), *Women, Violence and Social Control*, London: Macmillan.

REEVES, H. (1984), 'The Victim and Reparation' *Probation Journal*, 31: 136–9.

—— and MULLEY, K. (2000), 'The New Status of Victims in the UK: Opportunities and Threats', in A. Crawford and J. Goodey (eds), *Integrating a Victim Perspective within Criminal Justice*, Aldershot: Ashgate Dartmouth.

REINER, R., LIVINGSTONE, S., and ALLEN, J. (2000), 'No more happy endings? The media and popular concern about crime since the Second World War', in T. Hope and R. Sparks (eds), *Crime, Risk and Insecurity*, London: Routledge.

REISS, ALBERT J. (1967), *Studies in Crime and Law Enforcement in Major Metropolitan Areas*, Washington, DC: US Department of Justice.

—— (1986), 'Official Statistics and Survey Statistics', in E. Fattah (ed.), *From Crime Policy to Victim Policy*, London: Macmillan.

RESICK, P.A. (1987), 'Psychological Effects of Victimization: Implications for the Criminal Justice System', *Crime and Delinquency*, 33, no. 4: 468–78.

RIDING, A. (1999), 'The Crown Court Witness Service: Little Help in the Witness Box', *Howard Journal of Criminal Justice* 38, no. 4: 411–20.

ROCK, P. (1986), *A View from the Shadows*, Oxford: Oxford University Press.

—— (1988), 'The Present State of Criminology in Britain', *British Journal of Criminology*, 28, 2: 188–99.

—— (1990), *Helping Victims of Crime: The Home Office and the Rise of Victim Support in England and Wales*, Oxford: Oxford University Press.

—— (1991), 'The Victim in Court Project at the Crown Court at Wood Green', *The Howard Journal of Criminal Justice*, 30, 4: 301–10.

—— (1998), *After Homicide*, Oxford: Clarendon Press.

ROYAL COMMISSION ON CRIMINAL JUSTICE (1993), *Report*, London: HMSO.

SANDERS, A. (1999), *Taking Account of Victims in the Criminal Justice System: a Review of the Literature*, Edinburgh: Scottish Office.

—— *et al.* (1997), *Victims with Learning Disabilities: Negotiating the Criminal Justice System*, Oxford: Centre for Criminological Research.

—— and YOUNG, R. (2000), *Criminal Justice*, London: Butterworths.

—— HOYLE, C., MORGAN, R., and CAPE, E. (2001), 'Victim Impact Statements: Don't Work, Can't Work', *Criminal Law Review*: 447–58.

SARAT, A. (1997), 'Vengeance, Victims and the Identities of Law', *Social and Legal Studies*, 6, 2: 163–89.

SEBBA, L. (1996), *Third Parties: Victims and the Criminal Justice System*, Columbus: Ohio State University Press.

SHAPLAND, J. (2000), 'Victims and Criminal Justice; Creating Responsible Criminal Justice Agencies', in A. Crawford and J. Goodey (eds), *Integrating a Victim Perspective within Criminal Justice*, Aldershot: Ashgate Dartmouth.

——, WILLMORE, J., and DUFF, P. (1985), *Victims and the Criminal Justice System*, Aldershot: Gower.

—— and BELL, E. (1998), 'Victims in the Magistrates' Court and Crown Court', *Criminal Law Review*: 537–46.

SIMS, L., and MYHILL, A. (2001), *Policing and the Public: Findings from the 2000 British Crime Survey, HO Research Findings No. 136*, London: Home Office.

SKOGAN, W.G. (1986a), 'The Fear of Crime and its Behavioural Implications', in E. Fattah (ed.), *From Crime Policy to Victim Policy*, London: Macmillan.

—— (1986b), 'The Impact of Victimization on Fear', *Crime and Delinquency*, 33: 135–54.

SMITH, L.J. (1989a), *Concerns about Rape*, HORS No. 106, London: HMSO.

—— (1989b), *Domestic Violence: An Overview of the Literature*, HORS No. 107, London: HMSO.

SOOTHILL, K., and SOOTHILL, D. (1993), 'Prosecuting the Victim? A Study of the Reporting of Barristers' Comments in Rape Cases', *Howard Journal of Criminal Justice*, 32, no. 1: 12–24.

—— and WALBY, S. (1991), *Sex Crime in the News*, London: Routledge.

SPARKS, R., GENN, H., and DODD, D.J. (1977), *Surveying Victims*, London: Wiley.

SPENCER, J. (1990), *Children's Evidence in Legal Proceedings: An International Perspective*, Cambridge: University of Cambridge, Faculty of Law.

STANKO, E.A. (1988), 'Hidden Violence Against Women', in M. Maguire and J. Pointing (eds), *Victims of Crime: A New Deal?*, Milton Keynes: Open University Press.

—— (2000), 'Victims R Us: The life history of "fear of crime" and the politicization of violence', in T. Hope and R. Sparks (eds), *Crime, Risk and Insecurity*, London: Routledge.

—— and HOBDELL, K. (1993), 'Assault on Men: Masculinity and Male Victimization', *British Journal of Criminology*, 33, 3: 400–415.

STRANG, H., and BRAITHWAITE, J. (eds) (2000),

Restorative Justice: Philosophy to Practice, Aldershot: Ashgate Dartmouth.

TARLING, R., DOWDS, L., and BUDD, T. (2000), *Victim and Witness Intimidation: Findings from the British Crime Survey, HO Research Findings No. 124*, London: Home Office.

TEMKIN, J. (1987), *Rape and the Legal Process*, London: Sweet and Maxwell.

—— (1999), 'Reporting Rape in London: A Qualitative Study', *Howard Journal of Criminal Justice*, 38, 1: 17–41.

TRIALS ISSUES GROUP (1996), *Statement of the National Standard of Witness Care in the Criminal Justice System*, London: Home Office.

TRICKETT, A., ELLINGWORTH, D., HOPE, T., and PEASE, K. (1995), 'Crime Victimization in the Eighties', *British Journal of Criminology*, 35, 3: 343–59.

UMBREIT, M. (2001), *The Handbook of Victim/ Offender Mediation: An Essential Guide to Practice and Research*, San Francisco: Josey Bass.

UNITED NATIONS (1999a), *Handbook on Justice for Victims*, New York: UN.

—— (1999b), *Draft Declaration on Basic Principles on the Use of Restorative Justice Programmes in Criminal Matters*, New York: UN.

VAN DIJK, J. (2000), 'Implications of the International Crime Victims Survey for a Victim Perspective', in A. Crawford and J. Goodey (eds), *Integrating a Victim Perspective within Criminal Justice*, Aldershot: Ashgate Dartmouth.

VAN KESTEREN, J., MAYHEW, P., NIEUWBEERTA, P., and VAN DIJK, J. (2001), *Criminal Victimisation in seventeen industrialized countries: Key Findings from the 2000 International Crime Victims Survey*, The Hague: Ministry of Justice.

VICTIM SUPPORT (1991), *Supporting Families of Murder Victims*, London: Victim Support.

—— (1993), *Compensation for Victims of Crime*, London: Victim Support.

—— (1995), *The Rights of Victims of Crime*, London: Victim Support.

—— (1996a), *Women, Rape and the Criminal Justice System*, London: Victim Support.

—— (1996b), *Children in Court: Research Report*, London: Victim Support.

VON HENTIG, H. (1948), *The Criminal and his Victim*, New Haven, Conn.: Yale University Press.

VON HIRSCH, A., and JAREBORG, N. (1991), 'Gauging Criminal Harm: A Living-Standard Analysis', *Oxford Journal of Legal Studies*, 11, 1: 1–38.

WALBY, S., and MYHILL, A. (2001), 'New Survey Methodologies in Researching Violence against Women', *British Journal of Criminology*, 41, 3: 502–22.

WALKLATE, S. (1989), *Victimology*, London: Unwin Hyman.

—— (1990), 'Researching Victims of Crime: Critical Victimology', *Social Justice*, 17, 2: 25–42.

—— (1997), 'Risk and Criminal Victimization: A Modernist Dilemma?', *British Journal of Criminology*, 37, 1: 35–45.

—— (2000), 'Researching Victims', in R.D. King and E. Wincup (eds), *Doing Research on Crime and Justice*, Oxford: Oxford University Press.

—— (2001), 'The Victim's Lobby', in M. Ryan, S. Savage, and D. Wall (eds), *Policy Networks in Criminal Justice*, Basingstoke: Palgrave.

WASIK, M. (1998), 'Crime Seriousness and the Offender–Victim Relationship in Sentencing', in A. Ashworth and M. Wasik (eds), *Fundamentals of Sentencing Theory*, Oxford: Clarendon Press.

—— (1999), 'Reparation: sentencing and the victim', *Criminal Law Review*: 470–79.

—— and TAYLOR, R. (1991), *Blackstone's Guide to the Criminal Justice Act 1991*, London: Blackstone Press.

WERTHAM, F. (1949), *The Show of Violence*, New York: Vintage.

WHITEHEAD, E. (2001), *Key findings from the Witness Satisfaction Survey 2000, HO Research Findings No. 133*, London: Home Office.

WILLIAMS, B. (1999), 'The Victim's Charter: Citizens as Consumers of Criminal Justice Services', *Howard Journal of Criminal Justice*, 38, 4: 384–96.

WOLFGANG, M. (1958), *Patterns in Criminal Homicide*, Philadelphia, Penn.: University of Pennsylvania Press.

WRIGHT, M. (1991), *Justice for Victims and Offenders*, Buckingham: Open University Press.

—— (1995), 'Victims, Mediation and Criminal Justice', *Criminal Law Review*: 187–99.

—— (1999), *Restoring Respect for Justice*, Manchester: Waterside Press.

YOUNG, R. (2000), 'Integrating a Multi-Victim Perspective into Criminal Justice Through Restorative Justice Conferences', in A. Crawford and J. Goodey (eds), *Integrating a Victim Perspective within Criminal Justice*, Aldershot: Ashgate Dartmouth.

—— (2001), 'Just Cops Doing "Shameful" Business?: Police-Led Initiatives in Restorative Justice and the Lessons of Research', in A. Morris and G. Maxwell (eds), *Restorative Justice for Juveniles*, Oxford: Hart.

—— and GOOLD, B. (1999), 'Restorative Police Cautioning in Aylesbury—From Degrading to Reintegrative Shaming Ceremonies?', *Criminal Law Review*: 126–38.

ZAUBERMAN, R. (2000), 'Victims as Consumers of the Criminal Justice System?', in A. Crawford and J. Goodey (eds), *Integrating a Victim Perspective within Criminal Justice*, Aldershot: Ashgate Dartmouth.

ZEDNER, L. (1994), 'Reparation and Retribution: Are They Reconcilable?', *Modern Law Review*, 57: 228–50.

—— (1996), 'Reparation in Criminal Law', in A. Eser and S. Walther (eds), *Wiedergutmachung im Kriminalrecht: Internationale Perspektiven*: 109–227, Freiburg: Max Planck Institute.

—— (2000), 'The Pursuit of Security', in T. Hope and R. Sparks (eds), *Crime, Risk and Insecurity*, London: Routledge.

ZEHR, H. (1990), *Changing Lenses*, Scottdale, PA: Herald Press.

14

CRIME AND SOCIAL EXCLUSION

Jock Young

The problem of social exclusion is a central concern within the European Union; it is a key term in the policies of New Labour and, although less frequently used in North America, parallel discourses are present in the major arenas of social policy. It is a term which is flexible and somewhat amorphous in use, yet there are core features which separate it out from previous notions such as poverty or marginalization. First, it is multi-dimensional: social exclusion can involve not only social but also economic, political, and spatial exclusion, as well as lack of access to specific desiderata such as information, medical provision, housing, policing, security, etc. These dimensions are seen to interrelate and reinforce each other: overall they involve exclusion in what are regarded as the 'normal' areas of participation of full citizenship (Percy-Smith 2000; Perri 6 1997). Secondly, social exclusion is at root a social, not an individual, problem. It contrasts with earlier post-war notions which viewed marginality as a problem of isolated dysfunctional individuals. Rather it is a collective phenomenon, hence its association with a posited underclass. Indeed, it has more in common with the dangerous classes of Victorian times than the dysfunctional families of the welfare state of the 1950s and 1960s. Thirdly, that such exclusion has global roots rather than being a restricted local problem. It is a function of the impact of the rapid changes in the labour market, the decline of manufacturing industries, the rise in a more fragmented service sector, the creation of structural unemployment in particular areas where industry has shut down. It is thus a *systemic* problem: global in its causes, local in its impact (see Byrne 1999). Fourthly, the concept of social exclusion carries with it the imperative of inclusion; it is not happy with the excluded being outside of the ranks of citizenship and seeks to generate opportunities, whether by changing the motivation, capacity, or available openings for the socially excluded.

This being said, there are important differences and political, divergent interpretations of social exclusion. These revolve around the issue of 'agency', namely whether social exclusion is seen as self-imposed or socially imposed. John Veit-Wilson (1998) makes the distinction between 'weak' and 'strong' conceptions of social exclusion. The weak version emphasizes the individual's self-handicapping characteristics which inhibit his or her integration into society; the strong version emphasizes the role of those doing the excluding (see Byrne 1999). Let me finesse this further: there would seem to be three basic positions on agency:

1. That which basically blames the individuals concerned for their lack of motivation and their self-exclusion from society as a whole, although the ultimate responsibility for this is placed at the doors of the welfare state which is seen as engendering a state of 'dependency' where, for example, even if the jobs are available out there, the underclass does not want to take them. That is, it is a product of ill-conceived social policies which give rise to collections of individuals who are unwilling to work or take responsibility. The classic example of this position is the work of Charles Murray, starting with the influential *Losing Ground* (1984) and epitomized in *The Emerging British Underclass* (1990) (but see also the work of Lawrence Mead 1986, 1992, 1997).

2. That which sees the problems as a sort of hydraulic failure of the system to provide jobs, which leads to a situation of 'social isolation' wherein people lose not so much the motive to work as the capacity to find work because of lack of positive role models, coupled with a spatial isolation from job opportunities. Here direct exclusion, for example, because of racism, is explicitly ruled out as a primary reason for social exclusion. The classic texts here are the work of William Julius Wilson: *The Truly Disadvantaged* (1987) and *When Work Disappears* (1996); but note also his earlier *The Declining Significance of Race* (1980).

3. Lastly, there is a commentary which stresses the active rejection of the underclass by society: through the downsizing of industry, the stigmatization of the workless, and the stereotyping of an underclass as criminogenic and drug-ridden with images which are frequently racialized and prejudiced. The work of Foucauldians such as Nikolas Rose (1999) fits this bill, as does *Lockdown America*, the brilliantly written, neo-Marxist account of Christian Parenti (2000), as does the prolific postmodernist work of Zygmunt Bauman (see particularly 1998b, 2000a).

In the first instance, then, there is self-exclusion, albeit socially engendered; in the second the structure unintentionally excludes by leaving behind pockets of incapacitated actors; in the last instance it is the structure which actively excludes. In the first instance agency refuses opportunity; in the second opportunities are few and far between and the agent does not have the capacity to take them up; in the third opportunities are actively blocked. The weak thesis is the realm of the first and the strong of the third, whereas the notion of social isolation involves the arena between them. Let me say at this juncture that although parts of all these elements (motivation, capacity and opportunity) are part of the process of social exclusion—they are after all the fundamental components of the relationship between agency and structure— the weak thesis which puts almost total emphasis on inadequacies of motivation and capacity is palpably ideological in nature. To put it bluntly, it blames social exclusion on the excluded. As Bauman maintains: 'In the process of exclusion, the excluded themselves are cast as the principal, perhaps the sole, agency. Being excluded is presented as an outcome of social *suicide*, not a social *execution*' (2000: 25). Thus structure and agency have been reversed, and what starts out as a problem *of* society becomes a problem *for* society (see Colley and Hodgkinson 2001). Furthermore, it should be noted that it is the weak thesis which has by far the widest political currency. I want to illustrate this by describing the use of social exclusion by New Labour, particularly in its relationship to the explanation of crime, and then turn to a wider critique of the concept of social exclusion as a whole—whether based in the weak or the strong thesis. But let us first of all place social exclusion within the changing terrain of late modernity.

FROM INCLUSIVE TO EXCLUSIVE SOCIETY

The last third of the twentieth century witnessed a remarkable transformation in the lives of citizens living in advanced industrial societies. The Golden Age of the post-war settlement, with high employment, stable family structures, and consensual values underpinned by the safety net of the welfare state, was replaced by a world of structural unemployment, economic precariousness, a systematic cutting of welfare provisions, and the growing instability of family life and interpersonal relations. And where there once was a consensus of value, there was now burgeoning pluralism and individualism (see Hobsbawm 1994). A world of material and ontological security from cradle to grave was replaced by precariousness and uncertainty; and where social commentators of the 1950s and 1960s berated the complacency of a comfortable 'never had it so good' generation, those of today talk of a risk society where social change becomes the central dynamo of existence and where anything might happen. As Anthony Giddens put it, 'to live in the world produced by high modernity has the feeling of riding a juggernaut' (1991: 28; see also Beck 1992; Berman 1983).

Such a change was brought about by market forces which have systematically transformed both the sphere of production and consumption. This shift from Fordism to post-Fordism involves the unravelling of the world of work where the primary labour market of secure employment and 'safe' careers shrinks, and the secondary labour market of short-term contracts, flexibility, and insecurity increases, as does the growth of an underclass of the structurally unemployed. It results, in Will Hutton's catchphrase, in a '40:30:30 society' (1995), where 40 per cent of the population are in tenured secure employment, 30 per cent in insecure employment, and 30 per cent marginalized, idle, or working for poverty wages.

Market forces generate a more unequal and less meritocratic society, market values encourage an ethos of every person for themselves; together these create a combination which is severely criminogenic. Such a process is combined with a decline in the forces of informal social control, as communities are disintegrated by social mobility and left to decay as capital finds more profitable areas to invest and develop. At the same time, families are stressed and fragmented by the decline in communities' systems of support, the reduction of state support, and the more diverse pressures of work (see Currie 1997; Wilson 1996). Thus, as the pressures which lead to crime increase, the forces which attempt to control it decrease.

Changes in the market place (both in the spheres of production and consumption) give rise to an increase in levels of crime and disorder, and also a problematization of order itself. Rules are more readily broken, but also more regularly questioned. Civil society becomes more segmented and differentiated: people become more wary and appraising of each other because of ontological insecurity (living in a plural world where individual biographies are less certain) and material insecurity (a world of risk and uncertainty). Exclusion in the market gives rise to exclusions and divisions within civil society, which give rise to quantitative and qualitative changes in the exclusion imposed by the state. And, finally, the responses of the state have repercussions in reinforcing and exacerbating the exclusion of civil society and the market place. The strange anthropoemic machine of late modernity generates a resonance of exclusion throughout its structure, with the main motor being the rapidly developing pitch of market relations. Such changes are rooted in the market place, yet their impact is mediated by how they are experienced by human actors.

Having set the scene, let us now examine New Labour policies which explicitly recognize and endeavour to tackle social exclusion.

NEW LABOUR: NEW INCLUSIONISM

At the very heart of the British Labour Party's thinking is the notion of social inclusion. Thus we have a Welfare to Work programme, a New Deal for teenagers, lone parents, and communities, and a core think tank, the Social Exclusion Unit, established by Peter Mandelson in the Summer of 1997, whose task has been to tackle the problems of bringing truants back into school and single mothers to work, of reducing the dole queues, rescuing the sink estates, and rehabilitating teenage mothers (see Mandelson 1997; Social Exclusion Unit 1999a, 1999b). In the area of crime control the focus on inclusionism is most marked: the Crime and Disorder Act 1998 crucially views crime and all sorts of sub-criminal disorder (noisy neighbours, vandals, teenagers on the street late at night, etc.) as the very antithesis of community, and their reduction as a central aspect of the process of inclusion. Curfews are therefore to be set by local authorities to control local youth, 'hotspots' of crime are to be identified, focused upon, and eliminated, and crime audits set up across the country by local authorities and backed by an intricate system of performance indicators (see Hough and Tilley 1998).

The inclusionary project of New Labour represents a response to the new and difficult social terrain of late modernity. It directly acknowledges the exclusionary problems on the level of the market and community: the rise of structural unemployment, the decay of community, the breakdown of family, the fears of crime, and the intrusions of disorder. Yet its attempts to counteract the emergence of an exclusive society are, ironically for a party committed to modernization, surprisingly nostalgic. Father (and mother) is at work, the children are at school, the truant officers scour the streets, the teenage curfew begins at dark, the nuclear family is shored up (the positive virtues of marriage are introduced to the national curriculum), the criminal effectively punished, and disorderly individuals curbed and neighbourhoods tidied up. Every now and then the images of the old Labour Party, the paternalistic world post-1945 of Herbert Morrison, Clement Attlee, and Sir Stafford Cripps, seems to peep through the veneer, yet the problems are distinctly late modern and the emergence of a politics of nostalgia, or backward-looking discourse, perfectly understandable in terms of the new times that we find ourselves in. A comparison with the neo-liberal responses of the Conservative Administrations which preceded New Labour underscores this, for here we have a contrasting response to the same newly-emerged problems. For, at risk of exaggeration, if New Labour attempts to roll back the exclusive society, neo-liberalism accedes to, or even encourages, it. Famous of all the pronouncements—a *frisson noir* to the ears of all progressive commentators the world over—was Thatcher's 'there is no such thing as society only individuals and their families'. The atomization of society into a series of exclusive units was in this axiom elevated to an accurate depiction of reality and, by implication, the inclusive society portrayed as an illusion, an interference in the market relations between free-standing individuals. And the divisions between people are augmented by the divisions between classes. The economic divisions within society were actively widened during the Conservative Administration, partly by tax-benefit policies, so that between 1979 and 1994/5, the poorest 10 per cent had a cut of 8 per cent on real income, whereas the top 10 per cent had an increase of 42 per cent (Lister 1998). Unemployment soared, casting whole neighbourhoods into a limbo of poverty and worklessness, while the recorded crime rate more than doubled between 1979 and 1991. In one year alone, 1991, the increase in recorded crime was one and a quarter times that of all the total rate in 1950. The response to this, far from inclusion, was, if anything, a defensive exclusion. The central ethos, for example, of the Home Office moved from notions of rehabilitation to that of 'situational crime prevention'. Seeking to understand the causes of crime and the motivation of the offender was deemed a nonsensical task: almost anyone would commit crime if the opportunities arose. What was necessary was to prevent crime, by interposing locks and bolts, physical barriers, and closer surveillance to cut down the opportunities for offending (Young 1994; Clarke 1980). The Home Office produced booklets on crime prevention strongly reminiscent of the civil defence booklets of two decades earlier: a middle-class, detached house, where arrows marked possible weaknesses and points of entry, targets to be hardened, doors and windows to be made safe; the enemy was without, and the family home a place of safety and tranquillity (see Radford and Stanko 1991).

Thatcher's neo-liberalism, then, involved a deregulation of industry, a further commodification of labour, the advocacy of self-sufficiency and individualism, the emergence of structural unemployment, and the notion of defence against crime rather than the rehabilitation of the offender. All in all, a programme which went with the tide of exclusion and actually egged it on. But New Labour has reacted, on one level, in the opposite direction. It is intent on reversing the trend, and of achieving an inclusive society; it engages in an almost postmodern bricollaging of the past in order to depict its ideal, yet the past is somehow just around the corner and the means to get there a mere change of management or effort of will.

Yet the move from neo-liberalism to New Labour is not as revolutionary as it might seem, for paradoxically the core mechanism which is identified as creating the problem was shared by both neo-liberals and New Labour: that is the notion of an underclass of weak and dysfunctional families immersed in a dependency culture generated by an over-generous welfare state.

THE WELFARE STATE: NOT THE SOLUTION BUT THE PROBLEM

In the inclusive society of the post-war period, the welfare state, particularly in Europe, was seen as the main instrument of the state to *include* citizens. It reached out to those who were marginal and ensured that they had the minimal benefits of economic citizenship. In the 1980s and early 1990s, a critique of this position occurred from libertarians and neo-liberals of the right. They completely reversed the social democratic nostrum. For they argued that the welfare state generated a dependency culture which, far from ensuring the integration of the marginal into society, was the prime force in creating an underclass who excluded themselves from society (see, for example, Murray 1984).

In their analysis, the benefits system was a disincentive to entering the world of work and normal economic behaviour; furthermore, the dependency culture created a situation where those permanently on benefits were not only unwilling but eventually also unable to meet the disciplines and punctualities necessary to function in the workaday world. By the 1990s the administrations of Clinton and of Blair took on board much of this thinking. In particular, the change in direction of New Labour was most astonishing, because, instead of returning to some new Fabianism bent on seeking out the poor and bestowing upon them welfare rights, benefits, and empowerment, they began to argue that the welfare state 'as we know it' did not correspond to present-day realities and compounded the problems of the poor, while the poor themselves, because of welfare dependency, lost their sense of responsibility as citizens.

THE LABOUR PARTY AND CRIME

In 1993, in an article in *The New Statesman* entitled 'Why Crime is a Socialist Issue', Tony Blair first presented his famous couplet 'tough on crime, tough on the causes of crime', which suggested two things. First of all, a criminal justice policy which was tough on offenders in opposition to what was seen as the previously 'soft', 'liberal' policies of rehabilitation and prison reductionism, and which thus had an exclusionary rather than an inclusionary aspect. Indeed 'tough' policies, particularly with respect to the more widespread use of imprisonment, were enacted. Secondly, that Labour tackling the causes of crime, coupled with the heading 'Crime as a Socialist Issue', would suggest that an attempt to tackle the deep, structural causes of crime (the 'strong thesis' of social exclusion) would be implemented. The word 'socialism' soon, of course, disappeared from Blair's vocabulary, and structural causes became transmuted, as Jayne Mooney (2002) has shown, to problems within the family and then the inadequate family sited within the underclass. Poverty did not lead to crime, as Jack Straw, who was then Home Secretary, pointed out at a conference on social exclusion and the Third Way (1998). Poor families with good parenting led to law-abiding behaviour; it was inadequate families which gave rise to crime.

The three theoretical influences constituting the 'big idea' for New Labour all came from the United States: from Charles Murray, the maverick anti-state libertarian; John DiIulio (1995), the right-wing advocate of US prison expansion; and James Q. Wilson, an adviser to Nixon, Reagan, and Bush. Thus the vocabulary of underclass and social exclusion came to dominate New Labour discourse. Crime was the provenance of a small minority of excluded; the realm of dependency was occupied by single mothers, pregnant teenagers, dysfunctional families, the work shy, and the substance abuser. The solution was to drum them into work, regiment benefits, etc. From Charles Murray, New Labour took the view of the underclass as those unwilling to work, rather than the social democratic version of William Julius Wilson, i.e. those cut off from work. From DiIulio they absorbed the notion that a small number of young people—sited in the underclass—committed a large proportion of street crime and that the task of government was to target them. So it was claimed that 6 per cent of young males committed 50 per cent of all delinquencies.

John Birt, the ex-governor of the BBC—bizarrely drafted into the Home Office in 1998 as a 'crime czar'—focused his attention on these 'super-predators' as a technical fix to the delinquency problem. Such claims have become a key part of New Labour's policy. Thus Tony Blair, in a speech delivered on 30 May 2001, set out the government's crime reduction plans in its second term:

We will take further action to focus on the 100,000 most persistent offenders. They are responsible for half of all crime. They are the core of the crime problem in this country. Half are under 21, nearly two-thirds are hard drug users, three quarters are out of work and more than a third were in care as children. Half have no qualifications at all and 45% are excluded from school . . . Spending on the police will be an extra £1.6 billion per year by 2003–2004. And we are pledged to recruit another 6,000 police officers . . .

Let us note that these figures are as hypothetical as they are politically convenient. They ignore the fact that a large proportion of young people commit crime, that only a few are caught, and that generalization about their background from these few is grossly unreliable. Further, that the number of crimes committed is based on police interviews with apprehended young offenders, who are encouraged to exaggerate in order to boost the clear-up figures; and that even given this, only one-quarter of offences are cleared up, so that for four million uncleared offences we do not have the faintest idea of the identity of the offenders. Furthermore, that for youth offences such as burglary and robbery the clear-up rate is even lower, 18 per cent and 13 per cent respectively, and the culprits even more unknown and indescribable (*Criminal Statistics, England and Wales 1999*). Lastly, that even in those instances where a small number of youths are involved in crime, it is not the same youths every time. Four muggers may commit most of the street robberies in a locality in a month, but with such an amateurish crime it is different people from one month to the next.

Via DiIulio and James Q. Wilson, New Labour adopted the metaphor of the war against crime and against drugs, and incarceration as the key weapon in this war. From Wilson they took the concept of zero-tolerance, the idea that we best tackle crime through dealing with incivilities. Indeed, at times Blair's recent pronouncements on crime look like literal transcriptions from J.Q. Wilson's *Thinking About*

Crime (1975). Thus, on 5 December 2000, Blair suggested curfews and a zero-tolerance campaign to stamp down hard on petty criminals, drunken yobs, and juvenile delinquents. In an exclusive interview with the *Daily Express*, the Prime Minister said:

If you are tolerant of small crimes, and I mean vandalism and the graffiti at the end of the street, you create an environment in which pretty soon the drug dealers move in, and then after that the violent people with their knives and their guns and all the rest of it, and the community is wrecked.

I am not suggesting, of course, that Tony Blair or Jack Straw have any direct acquaintance with these commentators. Merely that it is their ideas, filtered through the lens of policy advisers and speech writers, which greatly influenced New Labour's policy on law and order. What is important to note here is that the ideas imported from the US were not those of liberal criminology; they were not the ideas of Elliott Currie, William Julius Wilson, or Frank Cullen, but those of the highly contested American right.

NEW LABOUR, SOCIAL EXCLUSION AND CRIME

Numerous authors (e.g., Giddens 2001: 323; Byrne 1999) suggest that the idea of social exclusion has superseded that of the underclass. Far from it: although the phrase might suggest otherwise, in particular its 'weak' and politically dominant version is wedded to the notion of underclass. It is clear from the above that New Labour adopted a 'weak thesis' version of social exclusion, with the emphasis for the problem placed upon the excluded themselves. It is obvious also that the government has adopted both intensive inclusionary and exclusionary strategies towards crime. These two seemingly contradictory processes of exclusion and inclusion—the source of the frisson in the 'tough on crime, tough on the causes of crime' couplet—make sense in terms of the position of crime in this discourse. Crime is a product of exclusion; it must, therefore, be tackled at a fundamental level by policies of inclusion which will in time bring down crime rates; but crime *in the here and now* disintegrates communities, it undermines the forces of inclusion, it must therefore be combated strongly where it arises. Let us summarize at this point the posited relationship between social exclusion and crime.

1. Although crime is widespread, a small number of offenders commit a large proportion of these offences.

2. That these offenders are clustered within a socially excluded underclass.

3. That the social disorganization and drug use endemic in these areas permit and sustain crime.

4. That the cause of social exclusion lies in lack of motivation and capability, itself a product of a dependency culture.

5. That such disorganized communities produce and perpetuate inadequate families, particularly those with a high proportion of single mothers, often in their teenage years.

6. That such inadequate families are criminogenic, reproducing disorganization over generations and perpetuating dependency.

7. That the policy solution is inclusionary, back-to-work programmes to tackle the 'causes', backed up with a forceful criminal justice system to deal with the problems of the present.

Having outlined the particular approach to social exclusion taken by New Labour, I wish to move on to a more general critique of the concept, *as it is presently used*, both in its 'weak' and in its 'strong' thesis.

THE SOCIAL EXCLUSION PARADIGM

In *The Exclusive Society* (1999) I contrasted the inclusive world of the post-war period of the 1950s and 1960s with the more exclusionary social order of late modernity in the last third of the twentieth century and beyond. For whereas the Golden Age granted social embeddedness, strong certainty of personal and social narrative, and a desire to assimilate the deviant, the immigrant, the stranger, late modernity generated both economic and ontological insecurity, a discontinuity of personal and social narrative, and an exclusionary tendency towards the deviant.

In my research I started from the most immediate and apparent manifestations of social exclusion in late modern societies. I sub-divided these exclusions into three layers: the labour market, civil society, and the state. Corresponding to this exclusion from the labour market was the exclusion from civil society: an underclass left stranded by the needs of capital on housing estates either in the inner-city, or on its periphery; those who because of illiteracy, family pathology, or general disorganization were excluded from citizenship, whose spatial vistas were those of constant disorder and threat, and who were the recipients of stigma from the wider world of respectable citizens. The welfare 'scroungers', the immigrants, the junkies and crack heads: the demons of modern society. And lastly, such a second-class citizenship was demonstrated and exacerbated by the focus of the criminal justice system, by their existence in J.A. Lee's (1981) graphic phrase as 'police property' and by the extraordinarily disproportionate presence of the immigrant and the poor within the penal system (see Mooney and Young 2000).

Such a dualism is captured by John Galbraith's (1992) contrast between the 'contented majority' and an underclass of despair, with respectability on the one hand and stigma on the other, a world of civility and tranquillity over against that of crime and mayhem. It underscores much of the contemporary usage of the phrase 'social exclusion'. But it soon became clear to me that such a dualism was fundamentally misconceived. It echoed the conventional wisdoms of the subject, to be sure, but it did not adequately grasp the social and spatial terrain of the late modern city, nor the dynamics of the actors who traverse it. It rightly suggests barriers and divisions, but wrongly exaggerates their efficacy and solidity: it mistakes rhetoric for reality, it attempts to impose hard lines on a late modern city of blurred demarcation and crossovers.

Furthermore, it neither captures the intensity of the exclusion—the vindictiveness—nor the passionate resentment of the excluded, while painting a far too calm picture of the fortunate citizens—the included.

Let us first examine the components of the social exclusion thesis:

1. *The binary*: that society can be divided into an inclusive and largely satisfied majority and an excluded and despondent minority.

2. *Moral exclusion*: that there exists a vast majority with good habits of work, virtuous conduct between citizens, and stable family structures, and a minority who are disorganized, welfare dependent, criminal and criminogenic, who live in unstable and dysfunctional families.

3. *Spatial exclusion*: that the excluded are isolated from the included, that stronger and stronger barriers occur between them, and that these borderlines are rarely crossed. Furthermore, that the fortunate classes create gilded ghettos within which systematically to exclude the poor.

4. *The dysfunctional underclass*: that the underclass is a residuum which is dysfunctional to itself and to society at large, both in its cost in taxes and in its criminogenic nature. It is the 'dangerous classes' of the Victorians underwritten by the taxes of the welfare state.

5. *Work and redemption*: that the provision of work will transform the underclass, changing their attitudes of mind, habits of dependency, cultures of hedonism, criminal tendencies and dysfunctional families, and transport them into the ranks of the contented and the law abiding.

This thesis is held by writers of various theoretical and political dispositions: whether it is the 'social isolation' of William Julius Wilson (1987), the 'hyperghettoization' of Lois Wacquant (2001), the warnings of 'Indian style reservations' by Richard Herrnstein and Charles Murray (1994), 'the New Bantustans' of Mike Davis (1990), the language and rhetoric of New Labour's Social Exclusion Unit (1999a), 'the dual city' of Manuel Castells (1994), 'the geographies of exclusion' of David Sibley (1995), or the New York of nightmares and dreams portrayed in Tom Wolfe's *Bonfire of the Vanities* (1988). And parallel to the segregation of the poor is the self-imposed isolation of the middle classes, whether it is in 'the gated communities' of Los Angeles, so well publicized by Mike Davis (1990), or 'the fortress city' of Susan Christopherson (1994), or 'the hyper-anaesthetized play zones' which are the 'flip side narrative of the "jobless ghetto"' (2000: 91) of Christian Parenti.

I wish to contest this thesis not from a perspective that there are no widescale disparities in late modern society, nor that areas of the city are not particularly blighted by crime and that their inhabitants experience social exclusion and stigmatization. Surely all of this is true and should be a target and priority of any progressive policy. But the construction of the problem in a binary mode obfuscates the issue, while the notion of social exclusion ironically exaggerates the degree of exclusion whilst underestimating the gravity of the problem.

BLURRING THE BINARY VISION

The Binaries of Social Exclusion

Society at Large	The Underclass
The Unproblematic	The Problem
Community	Disorganization
Employment	The Workless
Independence	Welfare Dependency
Stable Family	Single Mothers
The Natives	The Immigrants
Drug Free	Illicit Drug Use
Victims	Criminals

The danger of the concept of social exclusion is that it carries with it a series of false binaries: it ignores the fact that problems occur on both sides of the line, however much one has clusters in one area rather than another, and, more subtly, it conceals the fact that the 'normality' of the majority is itself deeply problematic.

Thus in the first respect, unemployment, poverty, and economic insecurity are scarcely unknown outside the designated areas—indeed, quantitatively they are over-all more prevalent in the supposedly secure majoritarian heartlands of society than they are in the selected minority of 'excluded' areas. And the same, of course, is true of illicit drug use, community disorganization, unstable family structures, etc. In the case of the notion of 'the normal majority' it assumes that, in this world, class differentials are somehow insignificant, that paid work is an unambiguous benefit, that 'stable' family life is unproblematic, licit psychoactive drug use is less a problem than illegal drug 'abuse', etc. Furthermore, it assumes that the transition from the social excluded to the majority via the vehicle of work will miraculously solve all these problems.

But we can go further than this, for there is widespread evidence that the culture of contentment—which John Galbraith (1992) talks of—a 'contented majority' who are all right thank you, doing fine, and sharing little in common or concern for the excluded minority—is a myth. Note, first of all, Will Hutton's figures, 40:30:30, where the secure primary labour market is reduced itself to a minority, and it would be foolish to suggest that even this island of seeming certainty was secure, serene, or self-satisfied. The demands for a more and more flexible labour force, coupled with the leaps forward in automation and the sophistications of computer software, caused great reverberations of insecurity throughout the employment structure. Redundancy, short-term contracts, and multiple career structures have become the order of the day. Furthermore, as the recent Joseph Rowntree Foundation Report, *Job Insecurity and Work Intensification* (Burchell 1999), discovered, redundancy not only causes chronic job insecurity, but the workers who remain have to work longer hours and expand their skills to cover the areas of those dismissed (ibid.: 60). For those in work the length of the working day increases: it is, of course, easier for the employer to ask for more and more time when security of employment is uncertain. *The market does not compete in hard places, it goes for the soft tissue of time and vulnerability.* Moreover, while in the past the income of one wage earner was sufficient to maintain a family, the dual career family has now become a commonplace where both partners are immersed in the labour market. And if in the economic sphere precariousness and uncertainty are widespread, so too in the domestic sphere: divorce, separation, and single parenthood are endemic, with the pressures of work merely adding to the instability of the late modern family.

BULIMIA: NOT EXCLUSION BUT INCLUSION/EXCLUSION

There is a strange consensus in recent writings about the underclass. Both writers of the right and of the left concur that what one has is not a separate culture of poverty, as earlier conservative and radical writers presumed (e.g., Edward Banfield 1968 on the right; or Michael Harrington 1963 on the left), but rather a breakdown of culture. Thus William Julius Wilson (1987) in his influential 'social isolation' thesis points to the way in which whole areas of the inner-city, having been formed around the previous needs of the manufacturing industry, are left stranded as capital wings its way to find more profitable dividends elsewhere in the country or abroad. While the middle and respectable working classes escape to the suburbs, the less skilled remain behind bereft of work and, indeed, role models who display work discipline and the values of punctuality and reliability. The loss of work, in turn, leads to a lack of 'marriageable men' who can earn a family wage, and engenders the rise of single mothers in the ghetto—and the role model of the family, parallel to that of work, is likewise diminished.

Charles Murray (1984), writing from the opposite political perspective, comes to surprisingly similar conclusions. His causal sequences are, of course, very different: it is not lack of work that causes the problem but lack of willingness to work, engendered by an 'over generous' welfare state which creates 'dependency' amongst the poor. Such a dependency manifests itself in a lack of motivation to work and single mothers. Thus the effects on attitudes to work and the family are similar, and the perceived consequences—a high rate of crime and incivilities—identical.

All of these assessments of the morals of the poor are those of *deficit*: in the recent writers' eyes they lack our values; in the earlier writers' eyes they have different values which are seen as deficient. And, as it is, all of them describe a fairly similar value system or lack of it, namely short-term hedonistic, lacking in restraint, displaying unwillingness to forgo present pleasures, aggressiveness, and willingness to use violence to achieve desired goals. In short, a spoilt, petulant, immature culture at the bottom of the social structure.

In *The Exclusive Society*, I set out to examine this picture of mores at the bottom of the social structure. I decided to look at the American black underclass as a test case, for surely, if this thesis were true, it would be amongst these supposed outcasts of the American Dream that this distinct, localized, and anomic deficit culture would be found. In particular I looked at Carl Nightingale's (1993) brilliant ethnography of the black ghetto of Philadelphia, *On the Edge*. What Nightingale discovered confounded such an image. Instead, the ghetto was the apotheosis of America. Here is full immersion in the American Dream: a culture hooked on Gucci, BMW, Nikes, watching television eleven hours a day, sharing the mainstream culture's obsession with violence, backing (at the time of the study) Bush's involvement in the Gulf War, lining up outside the cinemas, worshipping success, money, wealth, and status—even sharing in a perverse way the racism of the wider society. The problem of the ghetto was not so much the process of its being simply excluded, but rather one where it was all too strongly included in the culture but then systematically excluded from its realization. All of this is reminiscent of Merton, but where, in a late modern context, the implosion of the wider culture on the local is dramatically increased. We have a process which I likened to bulimia of the social system: a society which choruses the liberal mantra of liberty, equality, and fraternity yet systematically, in the job market, on the streets, in the day-to-day contacts with the outside world, practices exclusion. It brands as 'losers' those who had learnt to believe that the world consisted of 'winners' and 'losers'.

CROSSING THE BORDERLINE: THE DUAL CITY THESIS

Thus the underclass is constructed as an Other, as a group with defective norms who contrast with the normal majority. And here in this region lie all sorts of crime and incivilities. From this perspective of essentializing the other, the demand is to locate the problem areas: where exactly *are* the demons, so to speak? The powerful seek, in Todd Gitlin's poignant phrase, 'to purge impurities, to wall off the stranger' (1995: 233). Thus the underclass is said to be located within the clear-cut ghettos of the inner city sink estates, or in the long-lost satellite slums at the cities' edge (see Byrne 1999). But in fact there is no such precision here: the poor are not as firmly corralled as some might make out. Thus, as Gerry Mooney and Mike Danson write in their critique of the 'dual city' concept, based on their research in Glasgow—a city, some would say, of extreme cultural and economic contrasts:

The conclusion which is drawn from the analysis of poverty and deprivation in contemporary Glasgow presented here is not one which lends support to the dual city model. . . . This is not to deny however, that there is an uneven distribution of poverty in the city or that poverty is concentrated in certain areas. What is being contested is the usefulness of the dual city argument for our understanding of such distributions and the processes which contribute to it. . . .

   The language of the two city/dual city argument is one which is seriously flawed by definitional and conceptual difficulties. Despite the continuing use of concepts such as polarisation, underclass, exclusion and marginalisation, we are little clearer about the underlying factors which are viewed as contributing to such processes. In this respect the dual city perspective and its implicit arguments about growing socio-spatial polarisation are plagued by ambiguity and vagueness.

   In discussions of the emerging 'tale of two cities' in Glasgow, the attention which the peripheral estates received does not relate directly to the levels and proportions of poverty to be found there. In part this is a consequence of reluctance to define adequately the areas or social groups concerned. Further *within* peripheral estates there is a marked differentiation between the various component parts in terms of unemployment, poverty and deprivation. This is almost completely neglected in the dominant picture of these estates which has emerged in recent years which stereotypes the estates as homogeneous enclaves of 'despair' or 'hopelessness'. (1997: 84–5)

Maybe urban geographers of all political persuasions would like more of a clear-cut cartography than is healthy but, in reality, the contours of late modernity always blur, fudge, and cross over.

Manuel Castells (1994) advocates the concept of dual city as the fundamental urban dualism of our time, creating a division between the information-rich keyed into global networks and the information poor. In this conception the rich live in late modernity, whereas the poor are trapped in locality, tribalism, and the past. Such a notion tied to that of a class divide based on information fails to grasp the cultural penetration of globalization. For as John Tomlinson points out:

those marginalized groups for whom 'locality is destiny' experience a *transformed* locality into which the wider world intrudes more and more. They may in all sorts of ways be the 'losers' in globalisation, but this does not mean that they are excluded from its effects, that they are consigned to cultural backwaters out of the mainstream of global modernity. Quite to the contrary, it seems to me that the poor and marginalized—for example those living in inner-city areas—often find themselves daily closest to some of most turbulent transform- ations, while it is the affluent who can afford to retire to the rural backwaters which have at least the appearance of a preserved and stable 'locality'. [1999: 133–4]

Thus, in terms of mass communication the 'poor and marginalized' are exposed to messages and commodities from all over the world, while the inner-city areas in which they live become multi-ethnic and diverse due to labour immigration. They are exposed to what Dick Hebdidge (1990) calls a 'mundane cosmopolitanism' just as real as, or perhaps more significant than, that of the rich tourist who travels the world in a fairly sanitized fashion from chain hotel to chain hotel, from airport lounge to airport lounge. And cultures of distant places, either through the media or on the streets, become incorporated in the local cultures, particularly of the youth (see Young 2001; Back 1996).

THE FUNCTIONAL UNDERCLASS

What is not accepted, and indeed is little mentioned, is that the underclass is integrally a part of the larger economic process and, more importantly, that it serves the living standard and the comfort of the more favored community . . . The economically fortunate, not excluding those who speak with greatest regret of the existence of this class, are heavily dependent on its presence.

The underclass is deeply functional; all industrial countries have one in greater or lesser measure and in one form or another. As some of its members escape from deprivation and its associated compulsions, a resupply becomes essential. But on few matters, it must be added, is even the most sophisticated economic and social comment more reticent. The picture of an economic and political system in which social exclusion, however unforgiv- ing, is somehow a remediable affliction is all but required. Here, in a compelling fashion, the social convenience of the contented replaces the clearly visible reality. [Galbraith 1992: 31–2]

In contrast to Galbraith, it is common to portray the underclass as not wanted, as a social residuum. They are the people who were left behind in the urban hinterlands as capital winged its way to places where labour was cheaper; they are those whose labour is no longer required and who, furthermore, are 'flawed consumers', as Zygmunt Bauman (1998b) would have it, whose income is insufficient to render them of any interest to those selling the glittering commodities of late modern society. They are the casualties of globalization and the new technology: they are the useless class, a segment of society which has become detached and irrelevant. As Ralf Dahrendorf (1985: 20) put it: 'They are, if the cruelty of the statement is pardonable, not needed. The rest of us could and would quite like to live without them.' They are not simply of little use because their presence has dysfunctions for the rest of society: they have no uses but great costs. These dysfunctions take two forms: first, the underclass is a source of crime and incivilities, it is viewed as a dangerous class; secondly, the residuum is costly, an ever-increasing burden on the hard-pressed taxpayer. Such a notion of dysfunction reinforces the dual city thesis: they are simply not part of the same social system. Thus Zygmunt Bauman writes of Washington DC:

One difference between those 'high up' and those 'low down' is that the first may leave the second behind—but not vice versa. Contemporary cities are sites of an 'apartheid à rebours': those who can afford it, abandon the filth and squalor of the regions that those who cannot afford the move are stuck to. In Washington DC . . . there is an invisible border stretching along 16th Street in the west and the Potomac river in the north-west, which those left behind are wise never to cross. Most of the adolescents left behind the invisible yet all-too-tangible border never saw downtown Washington with all its splendours, ostentatious elegance and refined pleasures. In their life, that downtown does not exist. There is no talking over the border. The life experiences are so sharply different that it is not clear what the residents of the two sides could talk to each other about were they to meet and stop to converse. As Ludwig Wittgenstein remarked, 'If lions could talk, we would not understand them'. [1998a: 86]

This eloquent expression of the dual city thesis is wrong, not in its sense of division, but in its sense of borders. For the borders are regularly crossed and the language spoken on each side is remarkably similar. The most obvious flaw in the argument is that of gender: maids, nurses, and clerical staff move across into work everyday. Women, as William Julius Wilson argues in *When Work Disappears* (1996), are more acceptable to the world outside of the ghetto than their male counterparts. It is after all 'home boys' who stay at home. But bellhops, taxi drivers, doormen, and maintenance men regularly make their way across the invisible borders of Washington DC. It is not, therefore, just through television that the sense of relative deprivation of the poor is heightened, it is in the direct and often intimate knowledge of the lives of the affluent.

David Rieff, in *Los Angeles: Capital of the Third World* (1993), writes of the close physical proximity of the professionals and the underclass in Los Angeles; of their interdependence yet of the chasm that separates their lives. Frank Webster captures this well when he comments:

Illustrations of this are easy to find. On the one hand, maids are an essential element of the professionals' lifestyles, to cook, to clean, to look after children, to prepare for the dinner parties held in the gaps found in the frenetic work schedules of those deep into careers in law, corporate affairs, trading and brokerage. The maids, generally Hispanics, ride the infamously inadequate public transit buses to points in the city where their employers may pick them up in their cars to bring them home to clean up breakfast and take the children off to school. On the other hand, visitors are often struck by how verdant are the gardens of those living in the select areas of LA. Often they make the assumption that 'anything grows here in this wonderful sunshine'. But they are wrong: Los Angeles is a desert and gardens need most intensive care to bloom. They get it from an army of mainly Chicano labourers which arrives on the back of trucks very early in the mornings to weed, water and hoe—for a few dollars in wages, cash in hand.

   In spite of this dependence, which obviously involves a good deal of personal interaction, the lives of the two groups are very far apart. Of course this is largely because they occupy markedly different territories, with members of the poor venturing out only to service the affluent on their terms as waiters, valets, shop assistants and the like whilst the underclass also inhabit areas which the well-to-do have no reason (or desire) to visit. [1995: 205–206]

   The dual city where the poor are morally segregated from the majority and are held physically apart by barriers is a myth. The borderlines are regularly crossed, the underclass exists on both sides anyway, but those who are clustered in the poorer parts of town regularly work across the tracks to keep the well-off families functioning. *The work poor keep the work rich going: indeed, it is only the availability of such cheap 'help' that enables the dual career families to continue.* The situation of the dual income family and their need for support is well documented in Nicky Gregson's and Michelle Lowe's *Servicing the Middle Classes* (1994). The class relations of this emergent form were well summarized by the Hunts when they wrote:

Hired help on a single family basis involves a category of workers that must be paid out of the take home earnings of the nuclear unit. Consequently, the dual-career family is premised upon the increased use of a class of workers locked into a standard of living considerably lower than their employers . . . it would provide the 'liberation' of one class of women by the continued subjugation of another. [Hunt and Hunt 1977: 413]

Neither are the poor excluded morally; they are far from socially isolated, the virtues of work and the stable nuclear family are daily presented to them. For not only do they actually directly physically experience them in their roles as nannies, kitchen help, as waiters in restaurants, and as cleaners and bell boys in hotels, they receive from the mass media a daily ration of these virtues—indeed one that is in excess of that consumed by those who work in the primary labour market.

REDEMPTION THROUGH LABOUR

Work is central to the Government's attack on social exclusion. Work is the only route to sustained financial independence. But it is also much more. Work is not just about earning a living. It is a way of life . . . Work helps to fulfil our aspirations—it is the key to independence, self-respect and opportunities for advancement . . . Work brings a sense of order that is missing from the lives of many unemployed young men. . . . [The socially excluded] and their families are trapped in dependency. They inhabit a parallel world where: income is derived from benefits, not work; where school is an option not a key to opportunity; and where the dominant influence on young people is the culture of the street, not the values that bind families and communities together. There are some estates in my constituency where: the common currency is the giro; where the black economy involves much more than moonlighting—it involves the twilight world of drugs; and where relentless anti-social behaviour grinds people down . . . [a speech by Harriet Harman, then Minister for Social Security, at the opening of the Centre for the Analysis of Social Exclusion at the London School of Economics, 1997]

The worker . . . feels only outside of work, and during work he is outside himself. He is at home when he is not working and when he is working he is not at home. His work, therefore, is not voluntary, but coerced *forced labour*. It is not the satisfaction of a need but only a *means* to satisfy other needs. Its alien character is obvious from the fact that as soon as no physical or other pressure exists, labour is avoided like the plague. . . . Finally the external nature of work for the worker appears in the fact that it is not his own but another person's, that in work he does not belong to himself but to some one else . . . It is the loss of his own self. [Karl Marx, *Economic and Philosophic Manuscripts*, 1844 (1967: 292)]

To suggest that any work is better than no work, and that work has this essential redeeming quality, is bizarre in the extreme. Work, as John K. Galbraith so wryly commented in *The Culture of Contentment* (1992), is largely repetitive and demeaning; the use of 'work' by the 'contented classes' to describe their highly-paid, creative, and self-fulfilling activities in the same breath as the low-paid, oppressive chores of the working poor is a fraud of the first order. And to add to this the notion of the majority of work as an act of redemption, a liberation of the self and a role model to one's children, as our New Labour politicians and their Democratic cousins would maintain, is to add insult to injury.

Even for the working majority, the main virtues of work are the coffee break, the wage packet, and the weekend. In fact the inherently boring and tedious nature of work seems to many people to be precisely the reason that one is paid to do it. It is what you *definitely* would not do if you were not being paid. Yet provided the hours are not too long and the wages high enough, a deal of some sort is being made, based much more on the perceived obdurate, difficult, and unchanging nature of reality than on any ideas of redemption. There is always the teenagers' Saturday night, the forty-somethings' house and car, the 'real' world of home, kids, and television. But such a *realpolitik* of desire is far from redemption. The confusion arises, of course, as Galbraith points out, that for the contented classes work is indeed precisely that:

[it is] enjoyable, socially reputable and economically rewarding. Those who spend pleasant, well compensated days say with emphasis that they are 'hard at work', thereby suppressing the notion that they are a favored class. They are, of course, allowed to say that they enjoy their work, but it is presumed that such enjoyment is shared by any *good* worker. In a brief moment of truth, we speak, when sentencing criminals, of years at 'hard labor'. Otherwise we place a common gloss over what is agreeable and what, to a greater or lesser extent, is endured or suffered. [1992: 33]

The élite workers of stage, screen and song, the sportsmen and women, and the sizeable segment of the contented middle classes for whom the day is never long enough—for all of these, their identity is based upon work. Take work away from them and they flounder hopelessly: their ontology *is* work. But if one part of society defines work as what they are, the other very definitely defines it as what they are not.

Below the contented top of society lies the broad mass of people who are, if anxious about job security, reconciled to the wage deal. But below that, for the working poor the deal breaks down, the equivalence of selling time and buying leisure is frayed and insubstantial. To take family life as an example: the politicians' rhetoric about work sustaining the family and providing role models for the children is hollow, if not downright cruel. For, in fact, the type of work available to many of the poor leaves little time for stable family relationships, either with partners or with children, and has wide repercussions for community instability. As Elliott Currie puts it, 'less often discussed [than lack of work] but not less important, is the effect of *overwork* in poorly-paid jobs on the capacity of parents to provide a nurturing and competent environment for childrearing and on the capacity of communities for self-regulation and the maintenance of networks of mutual support and care' (1997: 155).

To force people to work long and anti-social hours undermines the very 'basic' morality of family and community which the politicians of all persuasions are constantly harping on about. The way in which, for example, single mothers are forced into work at rates which scarcely makes affordable the childcare which long hours at work necessitates, suggests ideology at work rather than any genuine care for people. The single mother looking after her children is dependent; the same mother paid to look after your children is by some miracle independent and resourceful. The true motive—the reduction of the tax burden of the well-off—is, as Galbraith suggests, thinly concealed by the rhetoric. Furthermore, the notion that such work provides role models for the children of the neighbourhood is implausible: much more likely is that they make crime and the illicit markets of drug dealing all the more attractive. If there are indeed 'seductions of crime', as Jack Katz (1988) suggests, then these seductions are all the more sweet given the misery of the alternatives.

INCLUDING THE EXCLUDED

What I am suggesting is that both the unemployed and the working poor—what one might call the overemployed—experience exclusion from social citizenship. The first because they are denied a basic economic substratum concomitant with the widespread expectations of what citizenship implies; the second because they experience the nature of their work, the hours worked and the remuneration, as unfair, as being outside of the norms of the wage deal—a fair day's work for a fair day's pay. They are, of course, part of the labour market but they are not full citizens. The dragooning, therefore, of people from one category of exclusion to another ('getting the people to work', as the Social Exclusion Unit (1999a) put it with its cheerless *double entendre*) is experienced all too frequently not as inclusion but as exclusion, not as the 'free' sale of labour but as straightforward coercion. The 'New Deal', therefore, is not the solution but the problem; it is not inclusion but palpable exclusion; the solution to the New Deal is engaging in the hidden economy, drug dealing, becoming a single mother: the solution is what the aptly named Social Exclusion Unit sets out as the problem (see Willis 2000: 89–91).

BOUNDARIES OF BULIMIA

Physical, social, and moral boundaries are constantly crossed in late modernity. As we have seen, they are transgressed because of individual movement, social mobility, the coincidence of values and problems both sides of any line, and the tremendous incursion of the mass media which presents citywide (and indeed global) images to all and sundry while creating virtual communities and common identities across considerable barriers of space. Boundaries are crossed, boundaries shift, boundaries blur and are transfixed.

The socially excluded do not, therefore, exist in some 'elsewhere' cut off spatially, socially, and morally from the wider society. To suggest this is not to say that physical barriers do not occur. Traffic is often scheduled so as to cut off parts of town, transport systems leave whole tracts of the city dislocated from the rest, and gated communities occur both in the fortunate and unfortunate parts of the city. It is not to deny that a characteristic of late modern society is the setting up of barriers, of exclusion. Neither is it to suggest that cultural divisions are set up with society propelled by misconception and prejudice. Indeed the discourse about social exclusion with its binary structure is itself part of such an attempt to construct moral barriers and distinctions. Rather, it is to say that such physical parameters are exaggerated, that the virtual communities set up by the mass media easily transcend physical demarcations, and that values are shared to a much greater extent than social isolation theorists would suggest. Of course subcultural variations exist within society, but that is what they are—*sub*cultural—variations in accentuation of core values rather than deficits or differences in value.

The binary language of social exclusion fundamentally misunderstands the nature of late modernity. Here is a world where borders blur, where cultures cross over, hybridize and merge, where cultural globalization breaks down, where virtual communities lose their strict moorings to space and locality. The late modern city is one of blurred boundaries; it was the Fordist city of modernity which had a segregated structure, a division of labour of specialized areas, a Chicago of concentric rings. Now the lines blur: gentrification occurs in the inner city; deviance occurs in the suburbs. It is a world of globalization, not separation; of blurring, not strict lines of demarcation. It is culturally a world of hybrids, not of pedigrees; of minor, not major, differences. The very decline in the physical community and rise of its virtual counterpart means that it is impossible for an underclass to exist separately.

Once again, none of this is to suggest that considerable forces of exclusion do not occur, but the process is not that of a society of simple exclusion which I originally posited. Rather it is one where both inclusion and exclusion occur concurrently—

a *bulimic society* where massive cultural inclusion is accompanied by systematic structural exclusion. It is a society which has both strong centrifugal and centripetal currents: it absorbs and it rejects.

Let us note first of all the array of institutions which impact the process of inclusion: the mass media, mass education, the consumer market, the labour market, the welfare state, the political system, the criminal justice system. Each of these carries with it a notion of universal values, of democratic notions of equality and reward and treatment according to circumstance and merit. Each of them has expanded throughout the past century and has been accompanied by a steady rise in the notion of citizenship encompassing greater and greater parts of the population in terms of age, class, gender, and race. And within the period of late modernity the mass media, mass education, and the consumer and labour markets have, in particular, increased exponentially. Each of these institutions is not only a strong advocate of inclusive citizenship, it is also paradoxically the site of exclusion. The consumer markets propagate a citizenship of joyful consumption, yet the ability to spend (and sometimes even to enter) within the mall is severely limited; the labour market incorporates more and more of the population (the entry of women into paid work being the prime example), yet, as André Gorz (1999) has so astutely stressed, precisely at the time when work is seen as a prime virtue of citizenship, well paid, secure, and meaningful work is restricted to a tiny minority. The criminal justice system is on paper a paragon of equal rights. The British Police and Criminal Evidence Act 1984, for example, governs amongst other things the powers of stop and search. It is a veritable cameo of neo-classicist notions of equality of citizens in the face of the law and the need for 'democratic' suspicion, yet on the streets, in practice, policing is indisputably biased in terms of race and class (see Mooney and Young 2000). Politics is an hourly interjection of radio and television, the mass media speak on our part for 'the common good' and 'the average' man and woman—they even parade and interview Joe Public with regularity—yet the vast majority of people feel manifestly excluded from political decision-making. Indeed, even the tiny minority of active party members often feel impotent and uninfluential. Mass education is the major transmission belt of meritocratic ideas, it is the nursing ground of equal opportunity, yet, as subcultural theorists from Albert Cohen to Paul Willis have pointed out, its structures serve to reproduce class divisions and to exacerbate resentment. Lastly, the mass media have a pivotal role. They have grown immensely and occupy a considerable part of waking life; in 1999, for example, the average person in England and Wales watched twenty-six hours of television and listened to nineteen hours of radio every week, and read, on top of that, mass circulation newspapers and magazines. That is, 40 per cent of one's waking life is spent in watching TV or listening to the radio, rising to 60 per cent of your free time if you are lucky enough to be in work. The lower down the class structure—the more socially excluded the citizen, if you want—the more mass media are consumed. Thus, paradoxically, cultural inclusion is the inverse of structural inclusion. The media carry strong notions of the universal citizen and they, of course, depict the other institutions: the world of consumption, work, education, politics, and criminal justice. Yet despite this overall commitment to social order the very stuff of news is the opposite: disorder, breakdown, mayhem, injustice (see Young 1981). To take the criminal justice system as an example: crime and police stories are a staple of both factual and fictional mass media, and the miscarriage of justice is a major theme. From the murder of Stephen Lawrence to the Cincinnati riots, from the Guildford Four to Rodney Hill, police prejudice, corruption, and incompetence are paraded daily. The mass media present a spectacular noticeboard of exclusion which it has all the characteristics of a bulimic narrative: it stresses order, justice, and inclusion (the backcloth of the news) yet it highlights disorder, injustice, and exclusion (the foreground).

The contrast between a bulimic society and an exclusive society can be seen if one compares Western liberal democracies (and perhaps the new South Africa) with an explicitly exclusive society, the South Africa of Hendrik Verwoerd and P.W. Botha. Here one had explicit spatial and social exclusion, a multi-culturalist apartheid based on racist distinctions, a controlled mass media which refused (on the whole) to report police brutality and which extolled divisions. It was both exclusivist culturally and exclusivist structurally (see Dixon 2001).

The phenomenon of cultural globalization fundamentally ratchets up this process of bulimia. Television drama, news, and advertisement contain not only plot, story, and product but also a background of expectancies and assumptions. First world culture permeates the globe and carries with it notions of equality, meritocratic values, and civil liberties; it proselytizes not only expectancies of standard of living, but also notions of freedom and citizenship.

I want to suggest that it is the bulimic nature of late modern societies which helps to explain the nature and tenor of the discontent at the bottom of the social structure. It is rooted quite simply in the contradiction between ideas which legitimate the system and the reality of the structure which constitutes it. But the tensions between ideals and reality exist only because of the general and manifest awareness of them. Both the punitive anger of the righteous and the burning resentment of the excluded occur because the demarcation lines are blurred, because values are shared and space is transfixed, because the same contradictions of reward and ontology exist throughout society, because the souls of those inside and those outside the 'contented minority' are far from dissimilar, sharing the same desires and passions, and suffering the same frustrations, because there is no security of place or certainty of being and because differences are not essences but mere intonations of the minor scales of diversity.

The very intensity of the forces of exclusion is a result of borders which are regularly crossed rather than boundaries which are hermetically sealed. No caste-like social order would be as transfixed with crime, or so ready to demonize and pillory the other. For it is an altogether unsatisfactory exclusion: borders and boundaries are ineffective; they create resentment but do not achieve exclusivity. The 'excluded' regularly pass across the boundaries, whether physically or virtually; they sense injustice, they *know* about inequality: whereas those 'lucky' enough to be 'included' are not part of the 'culture of contentment' which John Galbraith famously alludes to; rather, they are unsure about their good fortune, unclear about their identity, uncertain about their position on the included side of the line. But to understand the nature of the forces of exclusion, the barriers set up to man the social structure, we must go further and look at the predicament of the 'included'.

THE PRECARIOUSNESS OF INCLUSION

We have discussed in the process of bulimia how the excluded are included in the norms and social world of the wider society. But we can blur the binaries further, for we must now understand how the social predicament and experience of the insiders parallel those of the outsiders and how this process is the key to understanding some of the most fundamental antagonisms within late modern society.

In order to understand this we must first of all distinguish the two basic facets of social order within advanced industrial societies. First of all, the principle that rewards are allocated according to merit, that is a meritocratic notion of distributive justice. Secondly, that people's sense of identity and social worth is respected by others, that is justice of recognition. When the first is infringed we speak of relative deprivation, and when the second is violated we talk of misrecognition and ontological insecurity (see Young 2001; Fraser 1997). If we examine the terrain of late modernity in these key areas of distributive justice and justice of recognition we find a high degree of uncertainty. My assessment is that in both these areas late modernity brings with it a sense of randomness: a chaos of reward and a chaos of identity.

To take distributive justice first of all, the unravelling of the labour markets and the lottery of who finds themselves in each sector, the rise of a service industry consisting of diverse and disparate units, the seemingly random discontinuities of career, the profligate and largely unmerited rewards in the property market and in finance, all give a sense of rewards which are allocated by caprice rather than by the rules of merit. My suggestion is that a generation which has been extensively instructed in the values of meritocracy are confronted with chaos in the market of rewards, and this engenders a feeling of relative deprivation which does not have the easy comparative points of position in industry within standardized careers characteristic of Fordism, mass manufacturing industry, and the Golden Age, but is instead more individualistic in its envy, more internecine in its rivalry.

Secondly, in the area of recognition, of sense of worth and place, of ontology, there has been a parallel chaos. This is fuelled very largely by the widespread discontinuities of personal biography both in the world of work and within the family, coupled with the undermining of a sense of locality—of physical place of belonging (see Young 2001). This disembeddedness (see Giddens 1991) creates an ontological insecurity— an identity crisis—the most ready response to this being the evocation of an essentialism which asserts the core, unchanging nature of oneself and others. This consists of two stages: first, an insistence of some essential and valued qualities (whether cultural or biological) which are associated with the individuals in question (whether of masculinity, 'race', class, religion, or ethnicity); and, secondly, the denigration of others as essentially lacking these virtues (see Young 1999). Furthermore, that such a process of mobilizing negative essences with regard to others creates prejudices, exclusions, and stereotypes within society which further fuel the feelings of ontological insecurity of others.

Both crime and punishment are areas greatly affected by these uncertainties. Relative deprivation, especially when coupled with misrecognition and disparagement, can readily lead to crime. The classic instance is economic marginalization of a group accompanied by police harassment. But relative deprivation can also occur where someone higher in the class structure looking down can see undeserved rewards unmatched with the disciplines of work and restraint. Further, just as the relative deprivation of the poor can lead to crime, the deprivation of the more wealthy can lead to feelings of punitiveness.

THE FOCUS UPON THE UNDERCLASS

As we have seen, the hard working citizen of the majority perceives a world where rewards seem allocated in a chaotic fashion. These rewards have become so diffuse that it is difficult to see rhyme or reason in society at large; hostility at this chaos of rewards tends to focus on the very rich, or on those at the bottom of the structure. That is, those who are very obviously paid too much for the amount of work they do and those who are paid for doing no work. It fastens on the more obvious violators of meritocratic principle, namely, the super rich and the underclass. The antagonism towards the idle rich and, for example, members of the Royal Family or company directors who allocate themselves incommensurate rewards, I have documented elsewhere (see Young 1999).

The underclass, although in reality a group heterogeneous in composition and ill-defined in its nature, is a ready target for resentment (see Gans 1995: 2; Bauman 1998b: 66–7). Reconstituted, rendered clear-cut and homogenous by the mass media, it became a prime focus of public attention in the sense of stereotypes—'the undeserving poor', 'the single mother', 'the welfare scrounger', etc.—and an easy focus of hostility. Such stereotypes derive their constitution from the process of essential-izing, so prevalent because of the prevalent crisis of identity. That is, of negative images, the very opposite of the 'virtues' of the included, thus casting the social world into the binary mould which I have discussed previously. Thus if the chaos of reward creates ready hostility towards the underclass, the chaos of identity grasps upon them as a phantasmagoric Other with all the opposite characteristics of the world of honest, hardworking citizens and a ready prop to ontological security.

But note the paradox here: an underclass which is, in fact, very similar to the rest of society, generates antagonism and distancing. The poor become more like the wealthy at the same time as they are 'othered' by them; the degree to which the poor become more like the rest, the more they resent their exclusion. Indeed, as we shall see, it is the narrowing of cultural differences which allows resentment to travel both ways along this two-way street. Thus, Zygmunt Bauman insightfully notes how it is the very similarity of aspiration which the underclass has which exacerbates the dislike of those above them, just as it is this self-same aspiration, thwarted, which creates discontent amongst the excluded. In his critique of Laurence Mead he writes:

The underclasses offend all the cherished values of the majority while clinging to them and desiring the same joys of consumer life as other people boast to have *earned*. In other words, what Americans hold against the underclass in their midst is that its dreams and the model of life it desires are so uncannily similar to their own.

Further, and the other side of the coin:

it is logic of consumer society to mould its poor as unfulfilled consumers [yet] consumer lifestyles are becoming increasingly inaccessible to those on low incomes. However, it is precisely that inaccessibility of consumer lifestyles that the consumer society trains its members to experience as the most powerful of deprivations [1998b: 73].

CRIME AND THE NARROWING OF DIFFERENCES

Feelings of discontent, of unfairness both in terms of material reward and recognition, are experienced either when cultural differences diminish or when those that were once similar begin to be regarded differently. That is because discontent relates to relative, not to absolute, deprivation (see Runciman 1966). Thus discontent rises when migrants are assimilated or when lower classes are granted citizenship, or when ethnic groups, once separate, become part of the mainstream, coupled with blockages of social mobility, limited access to privileged labour markets, and public prejudice and denigration—in short, an incomplete meritocracy. The importance, then, of the ethnographies of Carl Nightingale on the black underclass of Philadelphia and Philippe Bourgois on the Puerto Ricans of the East Harlem barrio of New York City, is that they root discontent in the *narrowing* of cultural differences. In the first case, Nightingale traces how much of African-American culture of the South is lost in the assimilated generation growing up in the Northern cities; and in the second case, Bourgois shows that it is the second generation Puerto Rican immigrants becoming more 'American' who experience the greatest discontent.

Thus the breakdown of spatial and social isolation in late modernity, which I have documented—a consequence of globalization, the mass media, the consumer market, mass education—leads to a diminishing of cultural differences and a rise in discontent, both within nations and between nations.

TOWARDS A SOCIOLOGY OF VINDICTIVENESS

Relative deprivation downwards, a feeling that those who work little or not at all are getting an easy ride on your back and your taxes, is a widespread sentiment. Thus whereas the 'contented' middle classes may well feel sympathy towards the underclass, and their 'relative satisfaction' with their position translates into feelings of charity, those of the much larger constituency of discontent are more likely to demand welfare to work programmes, stamping down on dole 'cheats', etc. Such a response, whatever its rationality, is not in itself punitive: it is at most authoritarian, but it is not necessarily vindictive. But tied to such a quasi-rational response to a violation of meritocratic principles is frequently a much more compelling subtext which seeks not only to redress a perceived reluctance to work, but also to go beyond this to punish, demean, and humiliate. (See Pratt 2000; Hallsworth 2000.)

The key features of such resentment are disproportionality, scapegoating, and stereotyping. That is, the group selected is seen to contribute to the problems of society quite disproportionally to its actual impact (e.g., teenage mothers, beggars, immigrants, drug users), and its members are scapegoated and depicted as key players in the creation of social problems. Their portrayal is presented in an extraordinarily stereotypical fashion which bears little relationship to reality. Thus in *The Exclusive Society* I note how there seems to be a common narrative about such depictions of late modern folk devils which is common from 'single mothers' to 'drug addicts' (see Young 1999: 113).

Svend Ranulf, in his pathbreaking book *Middle Class Psychology and Moral Indignation* (1938), was intrigued by the desire to punish those who do not directly harm you. Such 'moral indignation', he writes, is 'the emotion behind the disinterested tendency to inflict punishment [and] is a kind of disguised envy' (1964: 1). He explores this emotion using the concept of 'resentment', which was first used by Nietzsche in his condemnation of the moral basis of Christian ethics and developed by Max Scheler in his 'Das Ressentiment im Aufbau der Moralen' (1923). Resentment has within it the impulse, as Merton put it, to 'condemn what one secretly craves' (1957: 156). Ranulf's innovation was to locate resentment sociologically and to tie the source of envy to restraint and self-discipline. Thus he writes: 'the disinterested tendency to inflict punishment is a distinctive characteristic of the lower middle class, that is, of a social class living under conditions which force its members to an extraordinarily high degree of restraint and subject them to much frustration of natural desires' (1964: 198).

It cannot be an accident that the stereotype of the underclass—with its idleness, dependency, hedonism, and institutionalized irresponsibility; with its drug use, teenage pregnancies, and fecklessness—represents all the traits which the respectable citizen has to suppress in order to maintain his or her lifestyle. Or as Albert Cohen famously put it (1965: 7): 'The dedicated pursuit of culturally approved goals, the eschewing of interdicted but tantalizing goals, the adherence to normatively sanctioned means—these imply a certain self-restraint, effort, discipline, inhibition. What effect does the propinquity of the wicked have on the peace of mind of the virtuous?' Such a social reaction is moral indignation rather than moral concern. The demons are not the fallen and the pitiful which fixate the philanthropist, rather they, at once, attract and repel: they are the demons within us which must daily be renounced. Thus the stereotype of minorities is not a wholly negative identity, for as Homi Bhabha reminds us, in a telling phrase, it is a 'complex, ambivalent, contradictory mode of representation as anxious as it is assertive' (1993: 70).

The rigours of late modernity extend such restraints and insecurities far beyond a narrow class band. A large part of the population is subject to relative deprivation and ontological uncertainties, and on top of this the pressures and restraints necessary to function exacerbate these even further. To survive in the late modern world demands a great deal of effort, self-control, restraint. Not only is the job insecure and poorly paid, the hours worked are long—extra hours are expected as a sign of commitment and responsibility; children are often not seen for long after the weary commute home; people talk of 'quality time' as a euphemism for 'little'; the weekends seem short and enjoyment has to be snatched, often with the liberal aid of alcohol. The dual career family more and more becomes a norm, with the planning both of adults' and children's schedules that this entails.

Let us summarize the restraints:

- increased working hours (see Schor 1992; Gorz 1999)

- increased intensity of work (see Burchell 1999)

- increased commuting (see Knox 1995)

- dual career family (see Taylor 1999; Gregson and Lowe 1994).

It is the experience of restraint and sacrifice which turns simple displeasure (a sense of unfairness) into vindictiveness. Furthermore, as the climate of work pressure and job uncertainty pervades a wide swathe of the class structure, it is not restricted to the lower middle classes—which Ranulf pinpointed, in line with much of the thinking at the time with its concerns about the rise and social basis of fascism (see also Luttwak 1995). Moreover, this climate of restraint exists on the top of the problems of job security and fairness of rewards and the crises of identity. We thus have a three-layered process, each layer contributing to the process of the demonization of the underclass:

1. *Sense of economic injustice*: the feeling that the underclass unfairly lives on our taxes and commits predatory crime against us fuels the dislike and fear of the underclass.

2. *Crisis of identity*: the underclass readily become a site for establishing identity by asserting the binary them and us, where 'us' is normal, hardworking, and decent, and 'them' is a lack of these essential qualities. It is such essentialism which demonizes the underclass, constituting it as a homogenous, clear-cut, dysfunctional entity.

3. *The situation of restraint*: it is the projection of all the problems of restraint that supplies the *content* of the demonization; the various supposed facets of under-class life—teenage pregnancy, single mothers, substance abuse, criminogenic cultures, highly racialized (immigrants, asylum seekers).

Such a process is, of course, not that of simple envy. The lawyer does not want to be a junkie, the professional woman certainly did not want to be a teenage mother, the bank manager could not countenance being a street beggar, the life of the New Wave traveller does not instantly draw the careful couple from Croydon. Certainly not: for both real and imagined reasons, the lives of such disgraced 'Others' are impoverished and miserable. No one would want to swap places with them. But their very existence, their moral intransigence, somehow hits all the weak spots of our character armour. Let us think for one moment of the hypothetical day of the hypothetical 'included' citizen on the advantaged side of the binary: the traffic jam on the way to work; the hours which have been slowly added to the working day; the crippling cost of housing and the mortgage which will never end; the need for both incomes to make up a family wage; the delay in having children so that the woman's career can get established; the fear of biological timeclocks and infertility; the daily chore of getting the children to school across the crowded city; the breakdown of locality and community; the planning of the day of two careers and two children (thank God for the mobile 'phone!); the lack of time with the children and the fear of missing out ('they've grown up before you knew it'); the temptations and fears of the abuse of alcohol as a means of enjoyment, in the time slots between the rigours of work . . .

It is surely not difficult to see how the members of an underclass who, at least in stereotype, are perceived as having their children irresponsibly early, hanging around all day with their large families, having public housing provided almost free, living on the dole, staying up late drinking and taking exotic, forbidden substances, and on top of all that committing incivilities and predatory crimes against the honest citizen, are an easy enemy. They set off every trigger point of fear and desire.

We live in a world, therefore, of intense anxieties and conflicts. Social inclusion, as it has been widely formulated, merely reproduces the exclusions it attempts to remedy, and in doing so replays the resentments which underlie the deep social divisions within late modern society. To conclude I wish to outline a transformative politics which would allow us to move beyond the repeated reaffirmation of the status quo.

AFFIRMATIVE AND TRANSFORMATIVE INCLUSION

Nancy Fraser, in *Justice Interruptus* (1997), develops an extremely useful typology of the politics of reform based on the two dimensions of redistribution and recognition. Reform, she argues, must recognize the necessity of changes in both these areas, assuaging both the failings of distributive justice and misrecognition and devaluation. But to this dichotomy she adds a further distinction—between the politics of affirmation and the politics of transformation. Affirmative politics merely involve the surface transfer of resources without changing the basic underlying divisions; whereas transformative politics seek to eliminate the basic underlying structures of injustice (see Young 1999; Mooney 2000). Thus in the area of redistribution affirmative remedies involve, for example, coercing the underclass into the labour market at extremely low wages. Their underclass position is merely reproduced, this time within the lower reaches of the market place (see Levitas 1996). This movement of people from one category of exclusion to another is experienced, as I have argued above, not as inclusion but as exclusion. Relative deprivation would, of course, not be solved by such 'inclusionary' politics, and the sources of discontent which are liable to generate high crime rates would be unabated. Transformative redistribution, on the other hand, would involve such measures as retraining so that jobs could be gained and then rewarded on a meritocratic basis, thus putting a genuine element of equality into equal opportunity policies, the recognition of non-paid work (e.g., child rearing, caring for ageing parents) as of vital importance for social reproduction, the creation of viable childcare infrastructures for women with children, and the enforcement of a minimum wage on a level which allows the individual an existence which is neither demeaning nor severely straitening in circumstance. Above all it would not make a fetish of paid work—it would not view such work as the vital prerequisite for full citizenship, for acceptance and inclusion in society.

An affirmative politics of recognition does not question the various essentialisms of difference. That is, in the case of conventional multiculturalism, what is stressed is the need for the positive recognition of various groups on equal terms, for example: Irish, African-Caribbean, gays, women, etc. In contrast, transformative politics seek to break down and destabilize the categories by questioning the very notion of fixed identity and essence. Thus the invented notion of tradition is challenged, the overlapping, interwoven nature of what are supposedly separate cultures stressed, and the ambiguity and blurred nature of boundaries emphasized. Diversity is encouraged and, where non-oppressive, celebrated, but difference is seen as a phenomenon of cultures in flux, not essences which are fixed.

In the case of crime and punishment, the critique of essences both in criminal victimization and in punishment is a high priority. The category of hate crimes must be widened out in the realization that a considerable proportion of acts of violence involve vocabularies of motive which debase and dehumanize the victim (see I. Young 1990). Thus not only crimes against gays and blacks, but also those against women, the elderly, the poor, etc. In terms of our response to crime it is vital that the essentialism which runs through the discourses about crime and its causes is thoroughly debunked. Important, here, is to confront and shatter the triptych which locates crime spatially and socially in three loci—the underclass, the drug user, and the immigrant. Such a combination, portrayed as interdependent and very frequently racialized, is presented as the major source of crime and disorder in our society.

Against this we must emphasize that crime occurs throughout the structure of society and that its origins lie not in a separate aetiology but in the structure of society and its core values. The identification of a distinct criminal class is an endeavour bound to failure. Politicians forget this at their peril. Tony Blair roundly castigates drunken hooligans one week and calls for robust legislation to bring them under control, when in the next week his own sixteen-year-old son is arrested for drunkenness in Central London. A year previously, the then Home Secretary, Jack Straw, famous for his tough on crime approach and the appointment of a drug czar, is awakened from sleep by a telephone call from the police to inform him that his son has been arrested for selling drugs. As the perceptive journalist Joan Smith put it:

The Government's responses are off the cuff and authoritarian . . . Again and again it reveals an us-and-them mentality as though there are only two Britons: decent God-fearing folk whose only transgression is the occasional parking ticket and a violent, anti-social sub-class whose members habitually exploit drugs and alcohol and go out deliberately looking for trouble. (2000: 13)

THE CHANGING MEANING OF SOCIAL INCLUSION

At the start of this chapter I discussed the journey into late modernity. It is necessary to examine the terrain, choose our means of travel, and be clear as to our destination. We have seen that the terrain has changed dramatically: employment, family, community—the structure of society—has become less secure, boundaries blur, identities are less and less fixed, place and social category become less determinate in prescribing behaviour, vocabularies of motive lose their mooring in discrete parts of the structure—we have entered the period of what Bauman (2000b) graphically calls 'liquid modernity'. And this terrain has become a more risky place, both in terms of crime and disorder and in terms of demonization and scapegoating.

The terrain has changed and, of course, with it the available means of change. Thus as Hans Hofman (1996) pointed out, the worthy social democratic critiques of society which link crime and punitiveness to lack of stable employment, community, and family life assume that we can nostalgically bring these entities of the 1960s back into existence by an act of political will. In the case of community, this is an implausible dream possible only for a minority. Artificially created communities, such as Disney's new town 'Celebration' in central Florida (Ross 1999), are the exceptions which prove this rule. But this is true of the other institutional areas. Take paid work as an example, an important site both of distributive justice and identity. Herein, as André Gorz trenchantly puts it:

is an enormous fraud. There is not and never will be 'enough work' (enough paid, steady, full-time employment) for everyone any longer, but society (or, rather, capital), which no longer needs everyone's labour, and is coming to need it less and less, keeps on repeating that it is not society which needs work (far from it!), but you who need it . . .

Never has the 'irreplaceable', 'indispensable' function of labour as the source of 'social ties', 'social cohesion', 'integration', 'socialization', 'personalization', 'personal identity' and meaning been invoked so obsessively as it has since the day it became unable any longer to fulfil *any* of these functions . . . Having become insecure, flexible, intermittent, variable as regards hours and wages, employment no longer integrates one into a community, no longer structures the daily, weekly or annual round, or the stages of life, and is no longer the foundation on which everyone can base his/her life project.

The society in which everyone could hope to have a place and a future marked out for him/her—the 'worked-based society', in which he/she could hope to have security and usefulness—is dead. Work now retains merely a phantom centrality: phantom in the sense of phantom limb from which an amputee might continue to feel pain . . . (1999: 57–8)

Work in the sense of that which involves self-realization and creativity is not, of course, dead, but secure, paid, full-time employment for life is considerably diminished and where it exists does not have this quality. Hence Gorz's title 'Reclaiming Work'. Work, like the community and the family, needs to be reformulated if we are to seek to provide the basis of identity and social worth.

But the direction in which we are going has also dramatically altered. Social inclusion as a goal has changed meaning from the Golden Age of the post-war period.

Whereas inclusion once meant lifetime stabilities of work, family and locality embedded in a culture of homogeneity, inclusion must now entail re-assessment and change
in all these spheres and the creation of narratives which can cope with instabilities and
uncertainties of biography and the problems of identity in a diverse society. The
fundamental flaw in the present discourse about social exclusion is that its terms of
reference are inclusion into a world that is fast disappearing.

TOWARDS A NEW POLITICS OF INCLUSION

The central fault line in modern post-industrial society is that between the winners and the
losers in the global marketplace. The lion's share of the extraordinary productivity gains
associated with the current capitalist renaissance has gone to the owners of capital, to a new
techno-managerial elite and to a handful of stars in the increasingly global entertainment
industries . . . Confronting them are the losers: the anxious middle classes, threatened by
proletarianisation; the increasingly casualised working class; and the burgeoning underclass.
That fault line runs through the new Labour coalition. No project for social inclusion will
work unless it captures some of the winners' gains and redirects them to the losers. The
notion . . . that the workfare state can turn the trick all by itself, that a mixture of training,
education and moral suasion can transform the entire society into winners, and that this can
be done at nil cost to those who have already won, is an illusion . . . the losers' interests are
bound to differ from those of the winners, and it is self-deception to pretend otherwise.
(Marquand 1998: 85)

We live increasingly in a consensus of broken narratives: jobs lost, relationships ended,
neighbourhoods left, and localities transformed beyond recognition. The contrast in
the post-war Golden Age between the mass of workers in steady jobs and the tiny
minority of unemployed has gone, as has the division between stable families and a
minority of broken homes, all-embracing organic communities and the few nooks
and crannies of *anomie* and disintegration. As we have seen, the discourse about social
exclusion has nostalgically sought to resurrect this Golden Age; it has attempted to
construct solidarity in terms which few in our society—let alone the poor—could
seek to emulate. What ironically the mass of us have in common is exactly what this
discourse disparages. Yet there is a considerable measure of potential solidarity on
such issues, especially looking across the fissure which David Marquand so clearly
demarcates—between the minority who have profited so well out of late modernity,
both in terms of income and recognition, and the vast majority outside of this privileged orbit. Similarly, we live now in an increasingly diverse society in terms both of
cultures of origin and those lifestyles which we have chosen to develop. Whereas the
Golden Age saw inclusion as meaning assimilation into a massive, homogeneous
culture, today inclusion means the recognition of our mutual diversity. Here again
this shared diversity is something which can unite us. It is difficult to talk of 'them'
and 'us' when there are numerous 'thems' and various 'us's. The emergence of cities
where people of great diversity live in close proximity is, however unintended, one of
the great achievements of late modernity. It is this frisson of diversity which, as Iris

Young (1990) reminds us, makes for the great excitement of the city and its attraction for so many.

But such politics which seek to transform the distribution of reward and celebrate diversity are counterposed against that which involves the internecine resentment of the fairly well-off against the poor, and where uncertainties of identity are shored up by stigmatizing and 'othering' vulnerable groups within the population. The discourse of social exclusion as presently constituted feeds into this latter regressive process. What we need is a reconceptualization of inclusion to embrace a politics which enhances social justice and welcomes diversity.

Selected further reading

My book, *The Exclusive Society* (London: Sage, 1999) provides a background to the transition into late modernity and the nature of the exclusionary tendencies in contemporary society. The latter part has a detailed discussion of transformative politics and the policies necessary to combat social exclusion.

A wide-ranging analysis of the economic processes underwriting social exclusion is presented in David Byrne's *Social Exclusion* (Buckingham: Open University Press, 1999), while a useful examination of the various policy initiatives is J. Percy-Smith's *Policy Responses to Social Exclusion* (Buckingham: Open University Press, 2000). Two exceptional articles critical of the concept of social exclusion are R. Levitas's 'The Concept of Social Exclusion and the New Durkheimian Hegemony', *Critical Social Policy* (1996), 16(1): 5–20, and R. Lister, 'From equality to Social Inclusion', *Critical Social Policy* (1998), 18(2): 215–25.

For classic statements of social exclusion from differing political and theoretical perspectives, read: Charles Murray, *The Emerging British Underclass* (London: Institute of Economic Affairs, 1990); Social Exclusion Unit, *Bringing Britain Together* (London: The Stationery Office, 1999); W.J. Wilson, *When Work Disappears* (New York: Knopf, 1996).

References

BACK, L. (1996), *New Ethnicities and Urban Culture*, London: UCL Press.

BANFIELD, E. (1968), *The Unheavenly City*, Boston: Little Brown.

BAUMAN, Z. (1998a), *Globalization*, Cambridge: Polity Press.

—— (1998b), *Work, Consumerism and the New Poor*, Buckingham: Open University Press.

—— (2000a), 'Social uses of Law and Order', in D. Garland and R. Sparks (eds), *Criminology and Social Theory*, Oxford: Oxford University Press.

—— (2000b), *Liquid Modernity*, Cambridge: Polity Press.

BECK, U. (1992), *Risk Society*, London: Sage.

—— (2000), *The Brave New World of Work*, Cambridge: Polity Press.

BERMAN, M. (1983), *All That's Solid Melts Into Air*, London: Verso.

BHABHA, H. (1993), *The Location of Culture*, London: Routledge.

BLAIR, T. (1993), 'Why Crime is a Socialist Issue', *New Statesman*, 29 January: 27–8.

BOURGOIS, P. (1995), *In Search of Respect*, Cambridge: Cambridge University Press.

BURCHELL, B. (1999), *Job Insecurity and Work Intensification*, York: Joseph Rowntree Foundation.

BYRNE, D. (1999), *Social Exclusion*, Buckingham: Open University Press.

CASTELLS, M. (1994), 'European Cities, the Informational Society, and the Global Economy', *New Left Review* (March–April), 204: 19–35.

CHRISTOPHERSON, S. (1994), 'The Fortress City: Privatized Spaces, Consumer Citizenship', in A. Amin (ed.), *Post-Fordism*, Oxford: Blackwell.

CLARKE, R. (1980), 'Situational Crime Prevention', *British Journal of Criminology*, 20(2): 136–47.

COHEN, A. (1965), 'The Sociology of the Deviant Act: Anomie Theory and Beyond', *American Sociological Review*, 30: 5–14.

COLLEY, H., and HODGKINSON, P. (2001), 'Problems with "Bridging the Gap": the Reversal of Structure and Agency in Addressing Social Exclusion', *Critical Social Policy*, 21(3): 335–59.

CURRIE, E. (1997), 'Market Society and Social Disorder', in B MacLean and D. Milovanovic (eds), *Thinking Critically About Crime*, Vancouver: Collective Press.

DAHRENDORF, R. (1985), *Law and Order*, London: Stevens.

DAVIS, M. (1990), *City of Quartz*, London: Verso.

DiIULIO, J. (1995), 'Crime in America: It's Going to Get Worse', *Readers Digest* (August): 57.

DIXON, W. (2001), *Exclusive Societies: Towards a Critical Criminology of Post-Apartheid South Africa*, Institute of Criminology, University of Capetown.

FRASER, N. (1997), *Justice Interruptus: Critical Reflections on the Post-Socialist Condition*, New York: Routledge.

GALBRAITH, J.K. (1992), *The Culture of Contentment*, London: Sinclair-Stevenson.

GANS, H. (1995), *The War Against the Poor*, New York: Basic Books.

GARLAND, D. (2001), *The Culture of Control*, Oxford: Oxford University Press.

GIDDENS, A. (1991), *Modernity and Self-Identity*, Cambridge: Polity Press.

—— (2001), *Sociology*, 4th edn, Cambridge: Polity Press.

GITLIN, T. (1995), *Twilight of Common Dreams*, New York: Henry Holt.

GORZ, A. (1999), *Reclaiming Work: Beyond the Wage-Based Society*, Cambridge: Polity Press.

GREGSON, N., and LOWE, M. (1994), *Servicing the Middle Classes*, London: Routledge.

HALLSWORTH, S. (2000), 'Rethinking the Punitive Turn', *Punishment and Society*, 2(2): 145–60.

HARRINGTON, M. (1963), *The Other America*, New York: Macmillan.

HEBDIDGE, D. (1990), 'Fax to the Future', *Marxism Today* (January): 18–23.

HERRNSTEIN, R., and MURRAY, C. (1994), *The Bell Curve*, New York: Free Press.

HOBSBAWM, E. (1994), *The Age of Extremes*, London: Michael Joseph.

HOFMAN, H. (1996), 'Krilische Criminologie en Preventie in Let Licht van een Postmoderne Conditie', *Tijdschrift voor Sociale Wesenschappen*, 41(2): 109–205.

HOME OFFICE (2001), *Criminal Justice: The Way Ahead* (Cm5074), London: The Stationery Office.

HOUGH, M., and TILLEY, N. (1998), *Auditing Crime and Disorder*, London: Home Office.

HUNT, J., and HUNT, L. (1977), 'Dilemmas and Contradictions of Status: The Case of the Dual-Career Family', *Social Problems*, 24: 407–16.

HUTTON, W. (1995), *The State We're In*, London: Cape.

KATZ, J. (1988), *The Seductions of Crime*, New York: Basic Books.

KNOX, P. (1995), *Urban Social Geography*, 3rd edn, Harlow: Longman.

LEE, J.A. (1981), 'Some Structural Aspects of Police Deviance in Relations with Minority Groups', in C. Shearing (ed.), *Organisational Police Deviance*, Toronto: Butterworth.

LEVITAS, R. (1996), 'The Concept of Social Exclusion and the New Durkheimian Hegemony', *Critical Social Policy*, 16(1): 5–20.

LISTER, R. (1990), *The Exclusive Society: Citizenship and the Poor*, London: Child Poverty Action Group.

—— (1998), 'From Equality to Social Inclusion: New Labour and the Welfare State', *Critical Social Policy*, 18(2): 215–25.

LUTTWAK, E. (1995), 'Turbo-Charged Capitalism and Its Consequences', *London Review of Books*, 17(21), 2 November: 6–7.

MANDELSON, P. (1997), *Labour's Next Steps: Tackling Social Exclusion*, Pamphlet 581, London: The Fabian Society.

MARQUAND, D. (1998), *The Unprincipled Society: New Demands and Old Politics*, London: Fontana.

MARX, K. (1844 [1967]), *Economic and Philosophic Manuscripts*, in L. Easton and K. Guddat (eds), *Writings of the Young Marx on Philosophy and Society*, New York: Anchor Books.

MATTHEWS, R. (2002), 'The Revolving Door: Penality and Community in Late Modernity', in R. Matthews (ed.), *The New Politics of Crime and Punishment*, Cullompton, Devon: Willan.

MEAD, L. (1986), *Beyond Entitlement. The Social*

Obligations of Citizenship, New York: The Free Press.

—— (1992), *The New Politics of Poverty*, New York: Basic Books.

—— (1997), *From Welfare to Work*, London: Institute for Economic Affairs.

MERTON, R. (1957), *Social Theory and Social Structure* (rev. edn), Glencoe: Free Press.

MOONEY, G., and DANSON, M. (1997), 'Beyond Culture City: Glasgow as a Dual City', in N. Jewson and S. MacGregor (eds), *Transforming Cities*, London: Routledge.

MOONEY, J. (2002), 'It's the Family Stupid: New Labour and Crime', in R. Matthews (ed.), *The New Politics of Crime and Punishment*, Cullompton, Devon: Willan.

—— and YOUNG, J. (2000), 'Policing Ethnic Minorities', in B. Loveday and A. Marlow (eds), *Policing After the Stephen Lawrence Inquiry*, Lyme Regis: Russell House.

MUNCIE, J. (1999), 'Institutionalised Intolerance: Youth Justice and the 1998 Crime and Disorder Act', *Critical Social Policy*, 19(2): 147–75.

MURRAY, C. (1984), *Losing Ground*, New York: Basic Books.

—— (1990), *The Emerging British Underclass*, London: Institute of Economic Affairs.

NIGHTINGALE, C. (1993), *On the Edge*, New York: Basic Books.

PARENTI, C. (2000), *Lockdown America*, London: Verso.

PECK, J. (1999), 'New Labourers? Making a New Deal for the "Workless Class"', *Environment and Planning C Governmental Policy*, 17: 345–72.

PERCY-SMITH, J. (2000), 'The Contours of Social Exclusion', in J. Percy-Smith (ed.), *Policy Responses to Social Exclusion*, Buckingham: Open University Press.

PERRI 6 (1997), 'Social Exclusion; Time to be Optimistic', in *The Wealth and Poverty of Networks*, London: DEMOS.

PRATT, J. (2000), 'Emotive and Ostentatious Punishment: Its Decline and Resurgence in Modern Society', *Punishment and Society*, 2(4): 417–40.

RADFORD, J., and STANKO, B. (1991), 'Violence Against Women and Children', in K. Stenson and D. Cowell (eds), *The Politics of Crime Control*, London: Sage.

RANULF, S. (1964/1938), *Moral Indignation and Middle Class Psychology*, New York: Schocken.

RIEFF, D. (1993), *Los Angeles: Capital of the Third World*, London: Phoenix/Orion.

ROSE, N. (1999), *Powers of Freedom: Reframing Political Thought*, Cambridge: Cambridge University Press.

ROSS, A. (1999), *The Celebration Chronicles*, New York: Balantine.

RUNCIMAN, W. (1966), *Relative Deprivation and Social Justice*, London: Routledge and Kegan Paul.

SCHELER, M. (1923), 'Das Ressentiment im Aufbau der Moralem', in *Van Umsturz der Werte* I, Leipzig.

SCHOR, J.B. (1992), *The Overworked American*, New York: Basic Books.

SIBLEY, D. (1995), *The Geographies of Exclusion*, London: Routledge.

SMITH, J. (2000), 'The Two Britains', *Guardian*, 17 September: 12–13.

SOCIAL EXCLUSION UNIT (1999a), *Bringing Britain Together*, London: The Stationery Office.

—— (1999b), *Teenage Pregnancy*, London: The Stationery Office.

STEPNEY, P., LYNCH, R., and JORDAN, B. (1999), 'Poverty, Exclusion and New Labour', *Critical Social Policy*, 19(1): 109–27.

STRAW, J. (1998), 'Social Exclusion and the Third Way', speech to the Nexus Conference on the Third Way, Kings College, London.

TAYLOR, I. (1999), *Crime in Context*, Oxford: Polity Press.

TOMLINSON, J. (1999), *Globalization and Culture*, Cambridge: Polity Press.

VEIT-WILSON, J. (1998), *Setting Adequacy Standards*, Bristol: Policy Press.

WACQUANT, L. (1996), 'The Comparative Structure and Experience of Urban Exclusion in Chicago and Paris', in K. McFate, R. Lawson, and W.J. Wilson (eds), *Poverty, Inequality and the Future of Social Policy*, New York: Russell Sage Foundation.

—— (2001), 'Deadly Symbiosis: When Ghetto and Prison Meet and Merge', *Punishment and Society*, 3(1): 95–134.

WEBSTER, F. (1995), *Theories of the Information Society*, London: Routledge.

WILLIS, P. (2000), *The Ethnographic Imagination*, Cambridge: Polity Press.

WILSON, J.Q. (1975), *Thinking About Crime*, New York: Basic Books.

WILSON, W.J. (1980), *The Declining Significance of*

Race, 2nd edn, Chicago: Chicago University Press.

—— (1987), *The Truly Disadvantaged*, Chicago: Chicago University Press.

—— (1996), *When Work Disappears*, New York: Knopf.

WOLFE, T. (1988), *The Bonfire of the Vanities*, New York: Bantam Books.

YOUNG, I. (1990), *Justice and the Politics of Difference*, Princeton: Princeton University Press.

YOUNG, J. (1981), 'Beyond the Consensual Paradigm', in S. Cohen and J. Young (eds), *The Manufacture of News*, London: Constable.

—— (1994), 'Incessant Chatter', in M. Maguire, R. Morgan, and R. Reiner (eds), *The Oxford Handbook of Criminology*, 1st edn, Oxford: Oxford University Press.

—— (1999), *The Exclusive Society*, London: Sage.

—— (2001), 'Identity, Community and Social Exclusion', in R. Matthews and J. Pitts (eds), *Crime, Disorder and Community Safety*, London: Routledge.

15

GENDER AND CRIME

Frances Heidensohn

The associations between gender and crime are profound, persistent, and paradoxical. For as long as observation of offending has been made, it has been noted that men and women differ in their offence rates and patterns, and in their experiences of victimization. As Braithwaite put it, listing it as the first of his key points about crime, '[it] is committed disproportionately by males' (1989: 44). In the twenty-first century this statement can be analysed and qualified in several ways. Moreover, the considerable body of work flowing from the statement has had some major effects on criminological thinking and on criminal justice policies. The purpose of this chapter is to indicate the range and significance of this work and outline its impact.

Most social enquiry is concerned with issues both of sex and of gender, although the second term is used more often because it covers both aspects of innate and acquired characteristics and the interaction between them and society. In the case of crime there is an elision made between the two forms of categorization which has considerable salience for the study of this field. For as long as systematic records of crime have been kept, the sex of offenders has been noted. Indeed sex has sometimes had significance as a legal category in relation to criminal acts. While criminal law broadly applies equally to women and to men, there have been, and still are, some exceptions. Male homosexual acts have at certain times been defined as criminal in most western countries, while lesbian acts have not. Criminal codes often treat prostitute activities of males and females differently. Under English common law, women charged with a felony committed in the presence of their husbands (except murder and treason) could rely on the presumption that they acted under compulsion (Mannheim 1965: 691–3) until this was abolished in 1925.

The sex of offenders also needed to be known for routine criminal justice purposes, especially once segregation was practised in prisons (Smith 1962; Zedner 1991). Obviously, only the sex of known offenders can be registered, and thus data on this topic are subject to even more limitations than those considered in general elsewhere in this volume (see, for example, Maguire, in Chapter 11 of this volume). Despite these reservations, certain trends and patterns in female criminality as compared with male have long been observed. In summary these are:

1. that women commit a small share of all crimes;
2. that their crimes are fewer, less serious, more rarely professional, and less likely to be repeated;

3. in consequence, women formed a small proportion of prison populations.

The attentive reader will see that I have moved from discussing the question of sex and gender to a focus on *women*, or women compared with men. This shift reflects what has happened historically in the history of criminology, although, as I shall argue later in this chapter, masculine gender and its relation to crime became an area of increasing interest in the late twentieth century. There is a marked contrast between this situation and that which obtained during what can be described as the prehistory of this subject. A grasp of this history is important in understanding more recent developments.

THE EARLY HISTORY OF GENDER AND CRIME

It has often been asserted that the subject of women and crime suffered from criminological neglect until the late twentieth century. While this statement is broadly true, it needs some qualification. Female criminality was *relatively* neglected and was treated in certain very specific ways.

Accounts of female criminality published during the nineteenth and early twentieth century can usefully be divided into two groups: practical criminologies; and essays on theory which were frequently characterized by their psychological or biological reductionism. By practical criminologies I mean that range of mainly Victorian studies which dwelt on women's social and moral position, and especially their vulnerability to 'falling' into crime and deviance. They were written by prison chaplains (Horsley 1887), doctors (Acton 1857), journalists (Mayhew 1861), lawyers (Pike 1876), and amateur social scientists concerned with 'denouncing casinos and dancing saloons as sources of female corruption' (cited in Zedner 1991: 61). As Zedner points out, many of these descriptions locate the origins of female crime in the same sources as those of male: variously poor urban conditions and moral weakness (*op. cit.*). Most, however, she notes, regarded women as more vulnerable because their 'purity', and hence their whole moral being, could be at risk.

Later in the nineteenth century, women criminals became, as did their male counterparts, the subjects of enquiry of positivist criminology. Lombroso and Ferrero's *The Female Offender* (1895) is the best-known example of this trend and the only one generally cited. Their study does deal, albeit crudely, with the sex/crime ratio. They failed to find the numbers of 'born female criminals' marked by physical, atavistic traits which they had anticipated. They argued that all women were less evolved than men, and thus closer to primitive types, but also that natural selection had bred out the criminal tendencies among women, since more 'masculine' women did not find sexual partners. Most of the flaws in positivism, and the inadequacies of Lombroso's methods, are represented in this work.

Lombroso and Ferrero's work is notable, however, for several features. First, it has frequently been used to represent psychological and bio-determinist theories of female crime. Secondly, it survived and was cited as a convincing commentary on female criminality (Mannheim 1965) long after comparable work on males had been rejected (Heidensohn 1985), and has, it has been argued, cast a long shadow over women's penal treatment (Dobash *et al.* 1986; but see Rock 1996 for a critique). Key problems of gender and crime are tackled in Lombroso's *La Donna Delinquente*, but it is characteristic of so much of this literature and other, related types, that such issues are not discussed in studies of male offenders. Another feature of Lombroso's work was that, as modern scholarship has demonstrated, it was a contribution to a range of complex debates about criminality and social control at the turn of the century in Europe (Beirne 1988; Garland 1985). Lombroso was subject to serious challenge. What is fascinating is that, while the force of some of these criticisms had been overestimated (see, for instance, Beirne's appraisal of *The English Convict* as unsuccessful (1988)), evaluations of Lombroso and Ferrero have been much more neglected. Frances Kellor, an American sociologist, conducted comparative studies which did not substantiate Lombroso's findings, and indeed showed social and environmental factors to be much more important.

The consequence of this was a scenario reminiscent of *Sleeping Beauty*. Whereas the rest of the criminological world moved on from positivism, embracing in particular a series of sociological theories of crime and deviance, female crime was cut off from most of this as though by thickets of thorn (Smart 1977; Leonard 1982). Those few studies which did appear in the first half of the twentieth century seem isolated and to lack a base. Pollak's treatise (1950), for example, I have characterized as curiously outside and unrelated to all the fervour of work at the time on 'strain' theory and subcultures (Heidensohn 1996). It exists in an ahistoric limbo in which women, as domestic servants and full-time housewives, commit *more* crime than men, but keep this hidden through devious means and by exploiting men's innate chivalry. This relative neglect and isolation in research on female crime was a major target of criticism for the many, and many varieties of, feminist criminologists, who were to transform work on this subject in the late twentieth century. Their primary focus was on women and crime, and thus their central theme is that in ignoring women's experiences of crime as both perpetrator and victim, the subject was impoverished (Smart 1977; Heidensohn 1968, 1985). This criticism also extends to the limitations of all studies of crime which do not address questions of gender. In order to demonstrate how central these questions are we shall now look in detail at evidence and analysis of the configurations of gender in several key areas. Given the emphases in past and recent studies, the main focus will be on women, but comparisons will also be made between women and men, and the importance of gender to each topic will also be addressed.

WOMEN, MEN, AND CRIME

'Women commit much less crime than men do' is a statement that has achieved the status of a truth universally acknowledged. Closer examination leads, however, to some qualification. On most comparisons, the differences are remarkable, robust, and, as we shall see, appear to be valid. The overall female share of recorded crime appears to be fairly stable. In England and Wales in 1984, 84 per cent of known offenders were male. In 1999 the figure was 83 per cent. Of the population born in 1953, 34 per cent of men, but only 8 per cent of women, had a conviction for an indictable or other serious offence by the age of forty (Barclay 1995: 20).

Remarkably similar figures for the female proportion of arrests are shown in one US survey (Poe-Yamagata 1996). The authors of this study emphasize the shift in the gender ratio over the period, although this is of three percentage points. Yet in another review, of a much longer time period, Steffensmeier concludes that, for 'trends in female crime: it's still a man's world' and that 'overall, the pattern of change was similar for both sexes', although he does note increases in women's share of larceny, fraud, drug offences, and assault (1995).

One effect of the growth of wider gender awareness in criminal justice studies is that we can now review much more *information* from official records and reports, and have a far fuller range of research with which to analyse such material. In an earlier account, I described these developments as the *recognition* and *expansion* of the field (Heidensohn 1996: xiii). In Britain, the Home Office now regularly publishes *Statistics on Women and the Criminal Justice System* (1999, 2000), and there are numerous American reports, e.g., NCJRS (1998), Richie *et al.* (2000). From these sources, which tend to focus on questions of the sex/crime ratio, we learn that while, as noted above, most 'known' offenders are male, with a ratio of about 6:1 in 1999, 'self report studies show that fewer females than males admit ever committing an offence' but that the differences are less, with a ratio of around 3:1, over the age of seventeen (Home Office 2000: 3). The female share of crime does appear to be increasing, if slightly, in Britain, up from 7:1 in the 1950s to 6:1 in 1999. In the USA there have been marked shifts, with women representing 13 per cent of arrests in 1975 and 19 per cent in 1995 (NCJRS 1998). Breaking down these totals by type of offence, we can see that, between 1989 and 1999 there was a 4 per cent increase in the numbers of women cautioned for or found guilty of violence, but a decrease of 22 per cent for men over the same period. Gelsthorpe and Morris (2002) point out that 'the bulk of violence offences are made up of those categorised as less serious and it is in these that there has been the biggest increase'; they also stress that, of the rise in drug offences committed by women (from 5 to 12 per cent of their offences between 1989 and 1999), 'almost all (96 per cent) related to unlawful possession rather than to the more serious offences such as the sale of controlled drugs and 90 per cent of the possession offences involved class B drugs' (ibid.).

Using an innovative methodology to examine the impact of domestic violence on police and public services in the UK, Betsy Stanko found the following figures from an audit of one day's calls to police:

... using the Home Office definition which specifies partners or former partners as the victim of domestic violence:

- 86% are female victims attacked by male perpetrators
- 8% are male victims attacked by female perpetrators
- 2% are female victims attacked by female perpetrators

- 4% are male victims attacked by male perpetrators

[this] demonstrates that the requests for assistance in domestic violence are dominated by female victims of heterosexual partner/former partnership violence. [Stanko 2001: 219–20]

Stanko comments on the differences between these figures and both the 2000 British Crime Survey, which reported an incidence of 74 per cent women to 26 per cent men, and the self-completion survey which indicates that equal proportions of men and women (4.2 per cent) 'said they had been assaulted by a current or former partner in the last year' (Mirrlees-Black 1999: vii). Over their lifetimes, 23 per cent of women and 15 per cent of men said that they had experienced domestic assault. 'Virtually all incidents against women reported to the survey were committed by men (99%), 95% of those against men were by women' (ibid.: ix). However, none of the men in the study defined the incidents as crime, but 39 per cent of 'chronic' female victims did so (ibid.: 47). Even in this study, 64 per cent of all the assailants were male, 36 per cent female (ibid.: Table 6.1) (and see Walby and Myhill 2001 for an analysis of domestic violence survey methods).

In the USA, where rates of intimate murder declined steadily amongst most victim groups from the 1970s onwards, Fox, in an analysis of US Homicide Reports of over 50,000 intimate murders between 1976 and 1996, notes that about six in ten spouse murder victims were women, and two-thirds of ex-spouse murder victims were too (Fox 1998).

Women who commit serious crimes, especially those involving violence, are often subject to considerable media attention which distracts from the more mundane nature of most female offending. Several writers have commented on the moral panics this can generate. Chesney-Lind outlines this in relation to girls' violence in US cities in the 1990s, especially to reports of gang and street violence by African American and Hispanic girls. 'Gang has become a code word for *race*', she argues (Chesney-Lind 1997: 57). Arrest rates for girls in the US increased more rapidly than those for boys in the last two decades of the twentieth century. Between 1981 and 1995 they rose by over 100 per cent for all violent crime, by over 160 per cent for aggravated assault, and by nearly 200 per cent for weapons offences (Poe-Yamagata 1996). The *numbers* of boys involved were far greater. Reviewing gendered patterns of law-breaking in the USA during the 1990s, Kathy Daly notes an increase in the female share of all arrests from 10 to 20 per cent, but finds considerable continuity in overall trends. 'In general', she concludes, 'as offences increase in seriousness, the gender gap widens for both prevalence and incidence' (Daly 1998). In England and Wales, most known female offending is at the minor end of the spectrum: in 1999, 33 per cent related to indictable offences. For males the percentage was lower, 30 per cent, but the numbers much greater—over half a million males, but under 100,000 females found guilty or cautioned (Home Office 2000: Table 2.1). Among these, theft and handling were the most common activities (59 per cent), followed by drugs (12 per cent) and violence against the person (9 per cent).

In their review of trends in Britain, Gelsthorpe and Morris reach a similar conclusion to Daly: 'It remains the case that women commit relatively few offences, although they are now committing more offences than ten years ago. There has only, however,

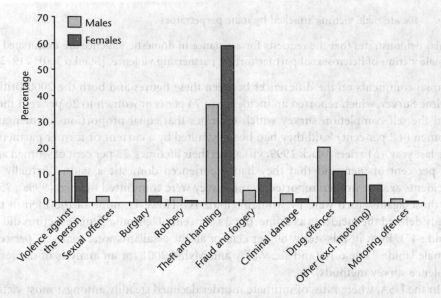

Fig. 15.1 Persons found guilty at all courts or cautioned for indictable offences, 1999

Source: Statistics on Women and the Criminal Justice System 2000 (Home Office).

been a slight change in the nature of women's offending, mainly with respect to offences involving drugs' (Gelsthorpe and Morris 2002).

Such differences seem to be common across a variety of nations and cultures. In surveying material on Europe, I found that 'crime is still an activity over-whelmingly dominated by men in all European countries. In France in 1986 . . . of persons . . . dealt with in criminal proceedings 81.27% were male and 18.73% female . . . in Germany . . . 79.5% were male and 20.5% female'. Similar, or lower, shares can be found in The Netherlands and Scandinavia (Heidensohn and Farrell 1991; Ministry of Justice 2000), and in nations as diverse as Brazil and India (Lemgruber 2001; Patkar 2001). This apparently consistent pattern has led some commentators to suggest that women offenders are 'only 10% of the trouble'. Considering different types of offence and changes over time, a more complex and qualified picture emerges. Women contribute to all types of offending, but their share varies considerably.

Arguments about whether female crime was rising at a faster rate than male, and that thus the female share was going up, have been a highly contended criminological issue since the 1970s. Indeed, this is one of the few topics to do with women and crime to excite widespread attention (Heidensohn 1989: chapter 5). The issue was first raised by Freda Adler (and in a more modified form by Rita Simon) who argued:

1. that female crime rates had been rising more rapidly in the late 1960s and early 1970s;

2. women offenders were changing their patterns of offending to more 'masculine' styles, becoming more aggressive and violent; and

3. that this was due to the growth of the modern women's movement. 'Liberation', in short, 'causes crime' (1975).

These contentions have been much discussed and analysed. Two aspects of the thesis need to be distinguished: that of rising female crime rates; and that of the influence of feminism. As to the first, no very clear picture emerges and, given what we know of the limitations of such data (see Maguire, in Chapter 11 of this volume), great caution is necessary. Smart, for instance, taking long time-series for England and Wales, finds that female crime rates were already rising at a faster rate than male long before the advent of the modern Women's movement (1979), although Austin is critical of some of her interpretation (1981). Austin has also argued that male and female crime rates will eventually converge (1993). Smart pointed out too the dangers which interpretations of figures on female criminality are *additionally* subject to: because numbers are so small they are highly susceptible to shifts in policing, recording, and other policies. Further, measuring percentage changes may give an exaggerated view—an increase from five to ten cases is 100 per cent.

All of this work represents a focus on *equity*, the first and most widely-debated theme in this field. Its basis is the assumption that female offending needs to be compared with male, and that the significant issues are what the size of the gender gap is, and whether it is narrowing or may even disappear. Questions which have scarcely ever been considered, yet could be equally valid, are why males are not more like females, and how the sex/crime ratio could be altered from their perspective (Heidensohn 1996). 'Female share' studies have many limitations: we only know the gender of 'known' offenders, who are a small percentage of those who contribute to recorded crime; and self-report studies measure individuals' responses to questionnaires, not encounters with law enforcement. The continued importance of this topic in criminology derives from its status as an 'enigma'—why are women so deviant by being conformist? It also provides a defining test (the 'generalizability' problem—see Daly and Chesney-Lind 1988) of criminological theories which claim to explain all criminality. They have also been used in discussions about women's experiences in the criminal justice system (see below). As Downes and Rock put it, this discipline 'can only benefit from addressing more creatively the question of why the oppression of women has not led to rates of crime as high as those of males' (1998: 325). However, much the most interesting work inspired by the recognition of gender as a key aspect of crime can be found in areas where 'women's perspectives within criminology [have] significantly reoriented the field . . . [and] revitalized existing perspectives' (ibid.). In the twenty-first century there is an immense amount of such material to consider; there follow some major examples.

GENDER, CRIME, AND HISTORY

Modern historical work on crime has experienced a renaissance, and studies of women offenders have been one offshoot of this. They enrich, and also complicate, the patterns of crime we are trying to unravel. Writing of Britain in the eighteenth century, McLynn says that 'Only 12 per cent of the accused in the home counties in 1782–7 were female' (1989: 128). Nonetheless, Feeley and Little (1991), taking a sample of Old Bailey cases tried between 1687 and 1912, found that 45 per cent of defendants were women. Others have pointed out, though, that women participated in food riots in the pre-modern period (Beattie 1975). Figures for these, and earlier, periods need to be treated with even more circumspection than those from today. In particular, they record such phenomena as 'The Criminal Classes'. Zedner notes that: 'Overall there was a considerable decline in those designated as the "criminal classes". Over the period 1860–90 they fell by more than half. The number of women fell at roughly the same rate as men, remaining at around a fifth of the total in this category over the period' (Zedner 1991: 20). She concludes that this relatively low rate was due to the exclusion of prostitutes, vagrants, and tramps. In terms of convictions, Zedner notes, 'overall, women's crimes made up a steady 17 percent of all summary convictions' (ibid.: 34), with drunkenness, assault, and larceny the commonest types of offence. In contrast to the steady state in summary jurisdiction, 'over the second half of the nineteenth century, women formed a declining proportion of those proceeded against by indictment . . .' (from 27 per cent of the total in 1867 to only 19 per cent by 1890) (ibid.: 36). Zedner's detailed work on nineteenth-century data confirms on the whole the 'modest share' view of female crime as compared with male. She also notes some reporting of a decline in convictions of women for serious offences by the end of the century (ibid.: 23).

Other writers have asserted that women's share of criminality declined relatively in certain modern periods (Mannheim 1965). Boritch and Hagan (1990), taking the period 1850 to 1950 in Toronto, document such a trend and claim that this was due to the success of moral entrepreneurs of the first wave of feminism, who provided diversion from criminality and stigma through non-punitive interventions in women's lives. Jones also records a fall in female crime: 'The mid Victorian years witnessed a concerted campaign against the crime and violence associated with "women of the streets" and a sustained fall in reported female attacks on property and persons, especially by the very young' (1982: 7).

Several historians are both more cautious or rely either on changed practices of recording, controlling, and classifying crime and misdemeanours (Walkowitz 1980), or 'chivalry' arguments (McLynn 1989), or views about the changed nature of femininity in Victorian Britain (Zedner 1991), or on combinations of all three.

While gendered, historical accounts of crime and the criminal justice system are important in their own right, it is for the contribution to contemporary discourse that they have most salience for criminology. Wiener's view of the 'vanishing female' in Victorian crime figures is that this was partly due to the increasing prominence and visibility of the male criminal. Just as private and informal social control withdrew women from the public sphere (and public record), so antisocial violent male behaviour was increasingly proscribed and punished (1998). In his analysis of male and female workplace appropriation (embezzlement) in mid nineteenth-century Yorkshire, Godfrey (1999) provides support for modern arguments which attribute female conformity to greater levels of social control and the harsh effects of punishment (Heidensohn 1996).

Women clearly faced many disincentives to appropriate workplace materials, ranging from the physical and the supervisory structures of the factory, to the deterrence of punishments which were particularly severe for women—the loss of children and future employment . . . foremen and employers preferred to use informal punishments [Godfrey 1999: 147].

He also contributes to the debates on leniency, or chivalry, towards women in the criminal justice system, finding that, although the evidence is mixed, courts were *perceived* by manufacturers to excuse women. King reviews evidence from court records over an earlier period, 1791–1822: '[t]he Old Bailey data on verdicts indicate clearly that female property offenders awaiting trial in London had much better prospects than their male counterparts. The majority of men (61%) were convicted. The majority of women were not (44%)' (King 1999: 46). He goes on to claim that there was an 'apparent continuity of relatively lenient trial outcomes in cases involving females accused for major property crimes from the late sixteenth century to the early nineteenth century' (ibid.: 59).

In a study of street violence in the late nineteenth century in Manchester and Salford, Davies describes how 'young working-class women on occasion fought each other, and assaulted men (including police officers) in the streets' (1999: 87). He also found evidence of gender discrimination in sentencing and of the use of informal controls. This case study, like a number of others, adds more material to the case for women's agency in both criminal activity and in relation to the law and the courts. All these examples illustrate the ways in which gendered historical perspectives on crime both illuminate their subject matter and inform current debates.

EXPOSING DOMESTIC 'SECRETS'

Our understanding of other features of the gender ratio has not, in any case, remained static. The subject of victimization, and the contributions of feminists, amongst others, to its 'discovery', are covered elsewhere in this volume (see Zedner in Chapter 13). It is important to note how the focus on the 'private' harms perpetrated within the home in domestic violence, and physical and sexual abuse of children, alter the gender ratio adversely for men, since they are largely, though not exclusively, the offenders in such crimes. While measures of incidence are shadowy, victim surveys do suggest that there are low reporting rates for such offences and yet a high rate of distress (Jones *et al.* 1986; Hamner and Saunders 1984; Stanko 1990). Serious sexual crimes such as rape also have low reporting rates because of women's fear of shame and of police and court procedures. Koss (1988), for instance, found that 25 per cent of women in her research had been victims of rape or attempted rape. Using a description which matched the legal definition of the act, she found that fewer than 30 per cent of these women thought of themselves as victims. Of her sample of male respondents, one in twelve had carried out acts meeting the criteria for legally-defined rape or attempted rape, yet the vast majority did not define their actions as rape. Some attempts have been made to redress the gender 'imbalance' in such private and personal crimes. Dobash and Dobash (1992: 258 *et seq.*) review family violence research in the US which seeks to show that there is an equivalence in violence between spouses, with husbands more likely to be victims than wives. The Dobashes also review that they call 'violence-against-women research', and conclude that empirical studies conclusively support an asymmetric view which further imbalances the gender ratio.

Two Home Office studies provide useful counterpoints on domestic violence. Mirlees-Black (1995) considers the complexities of its incidence, noting the 1992 British Crime Survey estimate of 'one in ten women who have lived with a partner have at some time experienced physical violence'. Bush and Hood-Williams describe an ethnographic study of a London housing estate where 'domestic violence . . . may even be seen as part of ordinary life. The climate of acceptance ensures that few will seek the assistance of statutory agencies and that those who do will first have to overcome the conviction that they brought the violence on themselves' (1995: 11).

Other, related topics have also been considered in this way. Child sexual abuse by women, including mothers, has been the subject of some concern, even though the proportion of women carrying out such acts is still acknowledged to be very small. Research on abuse of children in the home by the British National Society for the Prevention of Cruelty to Children (Creighton and Noyes 1989) is significant in that their data enable comparisons to be made of the relative risks to which children are exposed with parents, step-parents, etc. This study, based on some 8,274 children on NSPCC registers, indicates the *suspected* abusers. In the period covered (1983–7) natural mothers were implicated in 33 per cent and natural fathers in 29 per cent of the physical injury cases. When the figures were adjusted to take account of which parent the child lived with then the natural fathers were implicated in 61 per cent and mothers in 36 per cent of cases. Moreover, these figures, as the authors point out, make no allowance for time spent with children, and especially not of time alone with them. Such findings, based as they are on observations and not on police evidence or court verdicts, may be even less robust than official crime records. Whether they record assumptions rather than acts, there is perhaps some significance in their consistency with all the other material noted in this section.

GENDER AND POLICING

The nature and tasks of modern policing have been much discussed both in academic and public debate (Reiner 2000; and Bowling and Foster, in Chapter 27 of this volume). In particular, the culture of police agencies and the impact this has on their activities have been anatomized as based on macho values, stressing aggression, sexism, and racism, and giving status to serious crime work (Smith and Gray 1983; Chan 1997). There are differing views on how far attitudes derived from such values affect police in their work with citizens (Waddington 1999).

Police operate within a very considerable range of discretion, processing only a proportion of incidents and citizens through to a full criminal charge (and being limited at that stage by the Crown Prosecution Service). How women fare in such encounters is another considerably contested area, and one on which it is much harder to reach conclusions than on criminal behaviour. No record exists of all police–public encounters. However, there are significant sex differences in reported contacts. Thus in the PSI survey of policing in London, more men than women (63 per cent compared to 51 per cent) had had recent contacts with the police. Class and race complicated the issue: 87 per cent of unemployed men, but only 16 per cent of Asian women reported direct encounters. Surveys do show that frequent contact with the police lowers the esteem in which the police are held, and this may help to explain women's slightly greater support for the police. It is particularly their treatment of *men* from ethnic minorities (including the Irish) that has been linked to the cop culture discussed above.

Women, it has been argued by many writers, benefit from the values the police canteen culture gives rise to (Morris 1987: 80–81). They are seen as in need of protection not punishment, and they are accorded the respect of chivalry. Indeed this view was long adduced in explanation of lower rates of recorded female crime (Mannheim 1965). More recent work suggests a more complex picture in which 'demeanour' (Piliavin and Briar 1964) is a key factor in determining police reactions, as well as seriousness and recidivism. Gender appears to be only one factor in determining police decisions: 'to be older, apologetic and "respectable" is as advantageous for men as for women and gender is only one of many variables to consider in the complex process of police arresting behaviour' (Harris 1992: 95). However, there does not appear to be a neatly constructed demonology from least to most deviant, cross-tabulated by sex, demeanour, and aggression. If there were, as Visher noted (1983:19), then violent women offenders would be at one extreme, yet they do not seem so to feature (and see Allen 1987).

Some female offenders complain of especially harsh treatment by the police. Prostitutes have long complained, and more recently campaigned, as have others on their behalf, about such treatment. Høigård and Finstad, in their study (1992) of street prostitution in Norway, describe the women's fear of police brutality, sexual advances, and their failure to offer protection against dangerous clients. McLeod outlines a somewhat different pattern in Britain. Harassment and entrapment were reported, but also a degree of accommodation (1982: 106).

While street prostitutes are one, untypical group of women who have frequent contact with the police, the converse is true of the other deviant women who make complaints about how the police treat them. The militant suffragettes were among the first political protestors to object to police manhandling of them, a tradition carried on by the Greenham Common women and other demonstrators (Strachey 1978; A. Young 1990). These accounts are unlike those of most white men, in that they often allege sexual abuse and humiliation. These are yet more marked in the episodes recounted by lesbian, Irish, and black women (e.g., Natzler *et al.* 1989).

Discussions of these issues are often based on the sexist notion that all police officers are male, and on the stereotyped one that 'the police' are a unified body with common aims and procedures. Women's entry into policing in the UK and the USA, and in some European nations and Australia, was promoted in the late nineteenth century and early twentieth century precisely to provide protection to female and juvenile offenders and victims which, it was felt, they did not receive from an all-male force (Carrier 1988; Feinman 1986). For more than fifty years, until integration in the 1970s, small numbers of female officers worked in this fashion in both systems.

A considerable body of recent research has applied gender perspectives to law enforcement. Studies of police culture have arguably always had masculinity at their core (Reiner 1985) because of the nature of that culture. As Waddington somewhat provocatively puts it:

the core of the police's oral tradition lies in the glorification of violence over which they hold the legitimate monopoly . . . Nor is it surprising that this celebration is generalized to a 'cult of masculinity', for the exercise of coercive authority is not just something that just anybody can do. It is traditionally the preserve of 'real men' who are willing and able to fight [1999: 298].

Other writers have made harsher judgements and challenged, for instance, the notion, implicit in the above quotation, that such a cop culture is inevitable or immutable, let alone desirable (Young 1991; Heidensohn 1992).

Findings from studies with a gender perspective throw light on the role and position of women in law enforcement, reconstruct the notion of police culture, and form part of the basis for 'modernization' in many agencies around the world. In the first major study of female officers, Martin (1980) claimed that her Washington DC subjects divided between *Police* women and Police *Women*, the former being 'defeminized' women who compete directly with their male colleagues, and the latter 'deprofessionalized' women who accept subordinate roles, routine tasks in the station house, and who do not compete. Jones, reporting her 'Medshire' study in Britain, described 'traditional' and 'modern' types of woman officer. Heidensohn (1992) compared British and American policewomen and found that they constructed their work identities around a series of key concepts; in relation to the management of public order situations, they adopted tactics similar to those of their male colleagues. However, they were very different in the manner they presented themselves and dealt with violent and threatening encounters, developing 'ways to construct "presences" and demonstrate them in challenging situations' (Heidensohn 1994a: 300).

In a later project, Brown and Heidensohn (2000) compared the experiences of an international sample of policewomen and found, as had all the earlier studies, widespread evidence of a macho cop culture, manifested in sexual discrimination and sexual harassment of women officers by their male colleagues. The authors developed a comparative framework for this study, grouping police organizations around the world into four categories of cops, colonials, transitionals, and gendarmeries. They noted the relationship between these models, the impact of police culture on women officers, and the attitudes to the victimization of women (ibid.: Table 15.1).

GENDER, JUSTICE, AND SENTENCING

We have already observed that gender has its greatest impact on recorded patterns of offending. With some important exceptions, it is the differences to which this gives rise which are reflected in sentencing patterns. Most notably, the numbers of women in prison are relatively small at any one time. Moreover, they form a very small percentage of the total population which is overwhelmingly male: the ratio is around 20:1. However, the numbers of women sentenced to immediate imprisonment in England and Wales grew faster than comparable figures for males for much of the

Table 15.1 Policing models, reported impact on police women and women's victimization

Type of police organization	Sex discrimination	Sexual harassment	Women's victimization
Cops	high	high	High levels of awareness, policy developed, variable interventions: inter agency, service based and/or punitive
Colonial history	low	high	Moderate awareness, policy developed, ambivalent implementation
Transitionals	high	low	Low levels of awareness, little policy development and negative practice
Gendarmes	low	low	Variable policy development and practice

Source: Brown and Heidensohn (2000), reproduced with permission of Palgrave.

1980s, although there was a fall for both from 1987–90. Since 1993, the average female population has grown by over 100 per cent, the male by only 30 per cent. Many women in prison are there as untried or unsentenced prisoners, and it has been argued, since many of the former are not subsequently imprisoned, that women are subject to 'punitive remands' (Heidensohn 1985). Whereas nearly 20 per cent of males convicted of indictable offences go to prison, only 5 per cent of females do so.

Much modern research on women and crime is marked by its engagement with debates from the past. This is nowhere more true than in relation to women's experiences of the criminal justice and penal systems. One old and commonly-held view of why women's crime rates were so low was that the police, the courts, and other agencies extended 'chivalry' towards them. As a result they were protected from the full rigours of the law (Mannheim 1965). Of course, we have already seen that the sex/crime ratio differential is related more to a smaller 'pool' on which agencies may draw. Nevertheless, discussions have focused around this topic, and a series of concepts which modify the notion of chivalry have been advanced and discussed. These include the notions of double deviance and double jeopardy, of stigma, and of the importance of formal and informal controls in the lives of women.

CHIVALRY

Several authors have reviewed and/or researched the respective treatment of women and men by the courts. Smith (1988), reviewing the British literature, was unable to come to a clear-cut conclusion about whether men and women were treated in different ways by the courts, although the proposal of systematic chivalric bias is supported by Allen's study (1987) which showed violent women offenders receiving more sympathetic and individualized justice for serious crimes for which men got no comparable understanding. Other British researchers have found a more complex pattern in which courts appear to have somewhat conventional and stereotyped views of gender roles which they then reinforce with conviction and sentencing decisions. Farrington and Morris (1983) found that apparent court leniency towards women was due to their lesser criminal records, while Eaton (1986) noted that men *and* women conforming to conventional roles were better treated than those, such as homosexuals or single mothers, who did not. She stresses that gender expectations differed, and that women were supposed to take much more responsibility for home-making and for domestic morality. Carlen (1983) also found Scottish sheriffs distinguishing between 'good' and 'bad' mothers and being prepared to sentence them accordingly. Worrall (1990) discerned a still more complex situation in which various agents and agencies contrived to play down and almost to 'lose' female offenders in the system.

In the USA, Daly (1989a) found that it was children and the family, rather than women themselves, who were the focus of chivalry, or 'judicial paternalism', as the courts sought to support and conserve the fabric of society. In marked contrast, Player, studying crime in an inner-city area, found that black women were more likely to be stopped and questioned than white women, and that the police had different perceptions of them (1989). Daly, using a sample of matched pairs, in a study of a New Haven felony court, concluded that men and women were not sentenced differently for like crimes (1994: 259).

DOUBLE DEVIANCE, DOUBLE JEOPARDY, AND STIGMA

Women's low share of recorded criminality is so well-known that it has significant consequences for those women who do offend. They are seen to have transgressed not only social norms but gender norms as well. As a result they may, especially when informal sanctions are taken into account, feel that they are doubly punished. Carlen (1983, 1985) notes the prevalence of informal punishment of women by their partners. Several observers have stressed that concern over the anomalous position of deviant women leads to excessive zeal in their treatment, in remands in custody for reports and more medicalized interventions (Heidensohn 1981; Edwards 1984). Such approaches are particularly marked towards young girls, whose minor sexual misdemeanours seem consistently to be more harshly handled than those of boys (Webb 1984; Cain 1990; see also Newburn, in Chapter 16 of this volume). Such bias is not, as Gelsthorpe emphasizes (1989: 147), the sole determining factor in the way young people are handled by agencies. Other variables, such as organizational features, are important as well. Much evidence has accumulated to suggest that women suffer especially from the stigma associated with deviance. I have discussed the negative and positive forces that affect this (Heidensohn 1996).

Much of the sense of injustice felt by women who come before the courts stems from their perceptions of such agencies as male-dominated and unsympathetic (Heidensohn 1986). Such feelings have been much increased by the greater publicity now given to crimes, especially violent crimes against women, and what are often perceived as inappropriate reactions to them (Edwards 1989). The reactions are by no means consistent. They vary by age, ethnic background, and social class, and whether a woman has herself been a victim (Schlesinger *et al.* 1992). What research does make clear is the considerable effect victimization can have on women's world views (Stanko 1990; Walklate 1989). Such was the concern about public reaction to these issues that the Home Office published a research paper reviewing evidence regarding the claim 'that the criminal justice system in England and Wales routinely discriminates against women', concluding 'that the weight of evidence is against this claim' (Hedderman and Hough 1994: 1).

The rise in the number of women in prison at the turn of the millennium has prompted a major rethink. In Britain, the female prison population and the incarceration rate fell to such an extent during the twentieth century that the Home Office was able to contemplate ending female imprisonment by 2000. Yet as the century drew to a close the massive growth of overall rates of imprisonment in both the USA and the UK, despite the decline in recorded crime, led analysts to point to a new penality as part of a wider culture of control (Garland 2001: 14).

A Home Office study suggests that the interaction of three factors has led to this phenomenon:

1. an increase in the number of women appearing before the courts;
2. an increase in the proportion of those women receiving a custodial sentence;
3. an increase in the length of prison sentences being imposed on women.

Its conclusions are that the causes of the rise in women in custody are complex and differ over time. For example, in 1996–7, 95 per cent of the increase was due to more women coming before the courts, whereas earlier 50 per cent of it was due to greater use of custody for women. Convictions for drug offences explain a significant part of the growth since they attract longer sentences (Woodbridge and Frostega 1998).

Carlen uses a series of interviews with prisoners and staff to illustrate her argument that:

the steep increases in the numbers of women received into British prisons in the 1990s can best be explained by the increased numbers of women in the social categories of economic need and social deprivation who have traditionally been more vulnerable to imprisonment ... and by the increased punitiveness of the courts towards female offenders in general [1999: 56].

Gelsthorpe and Morris, however, are more cautious in their analysis of the reasons for increased penality towards women. They argue that:

[t]here is some evidence of increased punitiveness because a greater proportion of women are being sentenced to imprisonment and more women are being received into prison for short periods, although the 'type' of woman imprisoned remains much the same. . . . However, . . . there is little evidence of an increased punitiveness *solely* towards women [2002].

They find no argument entirely convincing, despite a spate of statistical studies in the 1990s (see Prison Reform Trust 2000: 3). The paradox remains that women's relatively minor offending, and distinctive 'troubled' rather than 'troublesome' status as offenders (Gelsthorpe and Loucks 1997), have led to what is widely seen as a dramatic and extraordinary increase.

The rise in receptions into women's prisons in Britain at the end of the twentieth century had its parallel in the USA. There the numbers tripled in the 1980s and continued to grow in the 1990s. As in Britain, the *rate* of increase was greater than for males: between 1984 and 1994, the numbers of women in federal prisons (generally for more serious offences) jumped by 258 per cent, compared to 169 per cent for men. Between 1984 and 1994, the proportion of the US gaol prisoners comprising women rose from 7 to 10 per cent (Chesney Lind 1997: 146). Concern about these twin developments has prompted a range of research studies and policy-related reports. These have covered gender and sentencing, women's prisons, and penal and criminal justice reform in respect of women. Taken together, these constitute an example of the impact of gendered perspectives on criminology and criminal justice policy. The impact, however, has so far been only at the level of debates and policy-making structures; concrete achievements remain elusive. Strong claims for examples of good practice in Great Britain have already been made; the issues are more to do with strategies and their implementation (Scottish Office 1998; HM Inspectorate of Prisons 2000; Donnegan 2002).

The same phenomenon in the USA is beset by similar paradoxes. In an extensive review of research on sex effects and sentencing, Daly and Bordt concluded: '[o]f the fifty cases of gender and sentencing, half found sex effects favouring women; one quarter each showed mixed effects or no effects' (1995: 158). This was a much higher proportion than in studies of race effects, where whites were favoured in 9 per cent of cases (ibid.).

American commentators have pointed to some factors which resemble those cited in Britain—for example, the 'war on drugs', the growth of drug offences and greater penalties for them (Chesney Lind 1997: 149). More significant, however, has been the impact of 'gender blind' mandatory sentences and sentencing guidelines:

Section 5HI.10 of the sentencing guidelines decrees that sex is not relevant in the determination of a sentence. Ironically, such legislated gender equality appears to have back-fired against women, since the current male-based sentencing model defies any attempt to develop a rational sentencing policy for nonviolent female offenders [Raeder 1995: 157].

In Britain, considerably more judicial discretion remains (see Ashworth, in Chapter 29 of this volume). The Halliday Review of the Sentencing Framework put 'crime reduction and reparation' and the reduction of re-offending as its first recommendation, rather than the reduction of the prison population (Home Office 2001b: ii). However, it also proposes that new guidelines should recognize 'justifiable disparity, for example, in cases where the offender has young dependant children' (ibid.: iv).

FEMINIST APPROACHES TO CRIMINOLOGY

I have already suggested that there was a pre-history to the study of this field. Its modern cultivation can be said to have started in the late 1960s as one of the by-products of modern second wave feminism. Definitions of feminism abound (Mitchell and Oakley 1986; Stanley and Wise 1984) and will not be rehearsed here. Being 'woman-centred' and stressing the importance of gender in social structures and relations are at least two key components. As far as criminology is concerned, there are, if anything, greater problems. Gelsthorpe and Morris (1988) seek to define a canon of work which has certain core features, although in a later account (1990) they suggest a diversity of perspectives, while Smart doubts either the possibility or validity of such an enterprise (1990). I am sceptical about an 'add and stir' approach, simply mixing feminism into criminology. I do recognize that there have been considerable contributions made by scholars who would accept a feminist label to the field, and that this may be one way of defining it (Heidensohn 1985, 1989).

Precise demarcations may elude us. Of the changes in assumptions, above all in this part of the subject, and of the massive contribution to the literature, there can be no question. Scholars from other perspectives began to write much more extensively about gender at the very end of the twentieth century. Mainstream texts, for example, started to include gender as a key theme (Braithwaite 1989; Hagan 1987). What is striking, however, is that they did so *in response* to the criticisms raised by feminists and the sheer volume and range of work which they had produced. I therefore make no apology for starting with these perspectives, and will include other contributions within that framework.

PIONEERING

It is useful, if arbitrary, to divide feminist criminological studies into two phases: pioneering and consolidation. The pioneers defined the agenda for the study of gen-der, which remains broadly unaltered. Consolidation has seen a range of studies produced in response to that agenda. It is now possible to suggest what the future might possibly hold too.

In articles published in the late 1960s, Marie Andrée Bertrand (1969) and I (Heidensohn 1968) drew attention to the neglect of women in the study of crime, and to the stereotyped distortions which were imposed on their female subjects by those few authors who did address this topic. There was a widespread tendency, for example, to sexualize all female deviance and to ignore any rational or purposive part to it. It was the gender ratio problem which provided the stimulus for these critiques: 'the patterns . . . of male and of female deviance were long ago observed, . . . nevertheless, the focus of research has been very much away from this particular area' (Heidensohn 1968: 160–61).

It was this lack which was emphasized in all the early pioneer work. Two aspects were stressed:

Orthodox, control-oriented criminology . . . has virtually ignored the existence of female offenders. . . . An important consequence of this lack of development has been the total neglect of any critical analysis of the common-sense perceptions of female criminality informing classical . . . and contemporary studies [Smart 1977: 3]

In short, *absence* of women in the literature and/or *distortion* of their experiences when present were the accusations levelled at criminologists.

Successive studies from this phase filled out this picture. Leonard (1982) examined major theorists in detail, showing how their ideas failed to deal with the gender gap and urging that women be fitted back in again. Millman (1982) analysed in depth the appreciative stance of labelling theorists such as Becker (1963). Central to Becker's approach was to take the perspective of the deviant as social critic, yet in discussing jazz musicians' wives it was the men's viewpoint alone which he quoted.

IMPACT OF FEMINIST PERSPECTIVES

Reviewing British criminological research of the past decade, Jefferson and Shapland declared:

feminism was the growth area in criminology . . . and now has a very powerful presence in the field. . . . However . . . one can argue that *despite* the massive growth about women, crime, law and criminal justice . . . the experience of women remained marginal to the *criminological* enterprise [1994: 282].

This judgement challenges the notion that feminist work has greatly influenced criminology. Yet the body of this work is now so great that readers should refer to summaries and their extensive bibliographies and reviews (Gelsthorpe and Morris 1990; Rafter and Heidensohn 1995; Heidensohn 1996; Rafter 2000). Here I shall outline developments in relation to three major themes:

1. *Women and crime*—in what ways gender affects criminal activity.

2. *Women and justice*—how women (as compared with men) experience the criminal justice and penal systems.

3. *Key concepts*—the concepts and approaches which have been developed to provide theories of the relationships of gender to crime and criminology.

WOMEN AND CRIME

In the 1970s, Smart (1977) suggested that women's crimes had been ignored because they did not constitute a major social problem. She was concerned about the consequences of possible exposure, fearful of what I later called the 'Falklands factor', the dire consequences of moving from the periphery to the centre of world attention. Many aspects of female offending have been studied since then. Female criminals have found their own voices (see Carlen 1985; Reynolds 1991), or observers have presented the perspectives of women who murder their husbands (Browne 1987), who are prostitutes (McLeod 1982; Miller 1986), are members of violent gangs (Campbell 1981, 1984), take crack cocaine (Maher 1990), or are involved in other serious forms of offending (Daly 1994). Many of these studies give offending women a voice and are small-scale and ethnographic in approach. Several large-scale studies of female offenders have been conducted in the USA, notably on homicide (Jurik and Gregware 1992). Three characteristics are attributed to female offending in these studies. They suggest that women do act purposively, and sometimes distinctively. They also contribute to the (re)discovery of female iniquity.

AGENCY

Much of the 'prehistoric' work on women cited above stressed the irrational nature of their actions. Women's behaviour was said to be determined by their physiology or instincts. Such ideas have not been absent from more modern debate, for example, in relation to the effects of menstruation (Dalton 1980), although caution is expressed now (Vanezis 1991). In contrast, the majority of modern studies have emphasized how rational and purposive were the women offenders studied.

Carlen, for example, in a series of ethnographic studies of convicted women in the UK, has shown how they are caught in two constricting structures, the gender bind and the class bind, and yet how their choosing to offend and the type of offence was often made on the basis of carefully weighed consideration: 'Property crime was *chosen* because certain types (e.g. shoplifting and cheque fraud) were seen to be so "easy" and because women, most women expressed inhibitions about engaging in prostitution' (1988: 34). She stresses also the variety of the offending patterns and the short-term nature of their rewards (1988: 45). Such emphasis is found in other kinds of deviant activities too. Many social researchers have sought to challenge the view of drug users as 'dope fiends', helpless addicts, hooked after one shot or smoke and at the mercy of evil pushers (Pearson 1987; MacGregor 1989). While women drug users have been studied far less often, the same notion of at least initial choice occurs: 'In analysing the career of the woman addict, I found her career is inverted and that is the essence of its social attraction' (Rosenbaum 1981: 11). Maher, using her field research amongst young crack-cocaine users in New York, is highly critical of the official response which defines pregnant women who use crack as irresponsible and criminal (1990). She argues that many of them manage their lives well and, in most cases, deliver healthy infants.

In a similar vein, McLeod (1982) and Miller (1986) suggest that prostitution is one kind of reasonable, if restricted and ultimately destructive, choice made by some women whose other options are very restricted. Even grave violence, such as homicide, has been depicted as the 'last option' when no others exist in battering relationships, when, it is argued, 'women . . . are extremely knowledgeable about the patterns of violence in their relationships' (Browne 1987: 184). Such views are supported by several appraisals of historical material on violence perpetuated by women which shows that they were, even in the eighteenth century and nineteenth century, able to make skilful use of conventions about femininity to obtain leniency (McLynn 1989; Hartman 1977; Jones 1982; Heidensohn 1991).

Contributions from all these sources suggest the development of what Daly has termed the 'leading scenario' for a typical entry, based on constrained choices due to poverty, poor education, and so on, for women into a career of petty crime. Daly, however, has suggested that it is possible to find a variety of 'pathways' into criminality which are distinctive for women: 'Street women; harmed and harming women; battered women; drug connected women; other' (Daly 1994: 47–8). Though Daly found these pathways paralleled in the lives of male offenders, they also included a significant category she labelled 'costs and excesses of masculinity' (ibid.: 67–8).

THE (RE)DISCOVERY OF INIQUITY

The study of female offenders has undergone various phases since the 1960s. During one of these far more attention was devoted to women as victims than as perpetrators of crime. This was true at both an academic level (Stanko 1984, 1990; Hammer and Saunders 1984; Dobash and Dobash 1979, 1992) and a practical, policy level where refuges for victims of domestic violence were set up (Pizzey 1974), rape crisis centres founded, and help lines for victims of sexual abuse instituted (Parton 1991). For many observers, the latter contributions remain the most important made by modern feminism to criminology and criminal justice (Lupton and Gillespie 1994), and are credited by Young as a key factor in the shaping of left realism (J. Young 1986).

Crucial though these developments were (see also Zedner, in Chapter 13 of this volume), they meant in effect that offending by women was less the focus of enquiry. In the late 1980s and 1990s, however, this changed. A variety of female crime, especially violence, was explored more fully. This was again partly stimulated by a confrontation with older debates, now re-emerging in new forms. The notion of the especially evil woman, the 'witch' of mythology, had stalked the texts of earlier writers such as Lombroso and Ferrero and Pollak. Adler and Simon advanced the notion of a new, ruthless, female criminal. The new factors lay in the approach taken, for example, by the American 'Family violence' school, who argued (Dobash and Dobash 1992) that, contrary to the arguments of many researchers in the field of domestic violence, as many women abused their husbands or partners as *vice versa*. Several notable court cases, including the trial of a female serial killer and a notorious child death in New York, focused attention on aspects of female offending and posed questions about women's acceptance of, or collusion in, the abuse of children (Johnson 1991). The prominence of child abuse and child sexual abuse cases also led, as Parton pointed out (1991), to a focus on family interactions and the roles played by mothers. Several thorough journalistic studies covered women's involvement in international terrorism (Macdonald 1991), homicide (Jones 1991; Reynolds 1991), and a spate of books appeared covering aspects of female violence (Lloyd 1993; Krista 1993). These texts did not, for the most part, attempt to theorize women's participation in violence, although one approach did suggest that gender roles in the use of legitimate violence were important in understanding women's low share of such actions (Heidensohn 2000).

PRISON FOR WOMEN

Research on the imprisonment of women has tended to focus on a series of critical issues:

1. Are women 'too few to count' in the prison system?
2. Do regimes for women have special characteristics?
3. Do women respond differently to imprisonment?
4. Are their pains of imprisonment greater?

Women have historically been subject to broadly the same prison system as men, but with distinctive variations introduced from time to time. Welfare objectives have sometimes been to the fore, especially in the nineteenth century and in relation to women said to be in moral danger. Rafter has catalogued the history of one such institution in the USA and noted how the lofty intentions of its founders led it to becoming additionally repressive of its female inmates who were infantilized by middle-class maternalism (1985).

Zedner describes the parallel history of two schemes in Britain primarily designed for women. Like the US example, these had aims which were thought especially appropriate for women: diversion from the penal system, care and welfare of offenders, and moral protection. In the first programme from 1898–1914, a number of inebriate reformatories for habitual female drunkards were founded. The official assumption was 'that the female inebriate was the greatest problem and must therefore, be the main focus of their work' (Zedner 1991: 233), the purpose being 'quite simply, to create of the enfeebled and degraded drunk a model of healthy, domesticated femininity' (ibid.: 237). A special system was set up with much emphasis on fresh air, clean living, and close supervision. The experiment failed.

Having defined the female inebriate primarily as a moral offender, reformatories operated on the premise that, by providing a sufficiently propitious environment and benign moral influences her cure could be achieved. Finding, instead, women resiliently resistant to the intentions of the regime, or so feeble-minded as to be irredeemable, the very momentum of the endeavour collapsed [ibid.: 263].

This initiative was followed by another in which assumptions about female deviance had changed and centred on a switch to 'feeble mindedness' as a prime cause of female crime and deviance, and, indeed, wider social evils (Simmons 1978). Because of their reproductive role, women were again the especial focus of such policies, their containment being emphasized (Zedner 1991: 296). It was the undermining of its key assumptions which irreparably damaged this approach, although not before many women had been institutionalized.

As Zedner points out, such case histories are highly instructive. They show that when women are the subjects of special penal treatment, it frequently results in the development of benevolently repressive regimes which emphasize dependency and traditional femininity and fail to provide the skills which could aid rehabilitation. Secondly, such programmes tend to be determined by the assumed characteristics and needs of women, rather than well-explored evidence. Such examples are not just historical. The rebuilding of Holloway Prison, London, in the 1970s was based on views about women offenders being physically or mentally sick, or both, and thus needing a therapeutic environment. The case was not proven, and the design of the prison proved unsatisfactory and controversial (RAP 1969; Heidensohn 1975). Ironically, it was its lack of adequate psychiatric facilities for treating disturbed women which was the focus of most concern (Carlen 1985; Padel and Stevenson 1988). Paul Rock's detailed reconstruction of the politics behind the new Holloway provides unparalleled insight into this topic (Rock 1996).

Research in women's prisons in Britain in the 1980s and 1990s stressed both the distresses and discomforts common to men and women, and certain features largely suffered by the latter. Women in prison are still less likely to receive good education, training and job opportunities, and are more likely to have to carry out domestic tasks. This is, however, part of a wider policy which tends to define criminal women as doubly deviant, needing additional pressures to conform and be rehabilitated (Carlen 1983; Dobash and Dobash 1986). Petty modifications—no uniforms and better décor—soften the contours of the women's system but do not alter its basic shape. Despite all these factors, Eaton has presented women's survival strategies after imprisonment, noting their skill and resourcefulness (1993).

WOMEN'S RESPONSES TO IMPRISONMENT

The early prison studies focused largely on institutions for men (Sykes 1956; Cressey 1961), and the vast literature on responses to imprisonment is dominated by studies of men. There are, to oversimplify, two major areas of interest: the process of prisonization; and the existence of inmate subcultures (see Morgan, in Chapter 30 of this volume). By the first is meant how far prisoners adapt to their incarceration and are thus unable to cope with the outside world (Sykes 1956). Two kinds of explanation are offered for this phenomenon. Sykes's 'pains of imprisonment' argument (1956) was that prisoners responded to the losses they felt in prison—of liberty, security, privacy, sex, etc.—by setting up compensating structures and roles. Irwin and Cressey (1962), on the other hand, favour external influences as causative, insisting that prisoners bring their (pre)prison criminal values with them.

Much research on prisons for women in the USA has used the now rather dated features of such studies to explore women's reactions. Some important sex differences are found in responses to imprisonment, especially in subcultures. The pioneering US studies of women in this area noted the salience of sexual and emotional relations in female correctional establishments, and insisted that the penal life of women, largely because of their small numbers and restricted provision, was distinctive. Female felons in the USA were said to feel the pains of imprisonment (the loss of family and home) more acutely and therefore set up alternative sexual relationships one with another, or formed 'pseudo families' to replace their missing kin (Ward and Kassebaum 1965; Giallombardo 1966)). Several studies found women's commitment to inmate codes to be less than men's (Tittle 1969; Kruttschmitt 1981).

In Scotland, Carlen (1983) found little evidence of inmate solidarity, or indeed the presence of subcultures. One of the paradoxical conclusions of a review of research on female subcultures is that they are weaker and more diffuse than male (Pollock Byrne 1990) yet, certainly in Britain, women perceive the pains of imprisonment as sharper and react with greater vehemence against them (Heidensohn 1975, 1981; Casale 1989; Mandaraka-Sheppard 1986; Carlen 1985). A higher proportion of women are charged with disciplinary offences, tranquillizers are more frequently prescribed, and there is a significantly greater incidence of self-mutilation.

A new generation of women's prison studies provides both confirmation and challenge to the earlier accounts. Owen's ethnographic study of a Californian women's prison on the whole supports a gendered and importational view of female experiences of imprisonment. She observed three critical areas of life: '(1) negotiating the prison world (2) styles of doing time and involvement in the "mix"' (Owen 1998: 167). The 'mix' comprises a number of problems *inside* the prison—drugs, homosexuality, fighting. Avoiding trouble meant keeping out of these. Kruttschmitt *et al.* compared two other women's prisons (CIW and VSP), also in California. They did not find the same responses from women in both institutions. While 'how women at CIW talked about their experiences . . . [had] important similarities, including diverse styles of adaptation, the importance placed on primary group relationships, and the absence of serious violence or racial conflict . . . women's adaptations at VSP— anomic, suspicious and detached' were quite different (2000: 712). They attributed these differences to the quite distinct institutional features of the two institutions. VSP represented the new, harsher penology, and CIW an historic, maternal, therapeutic culture. Their conclusion

is that women's adaptations to prison may not be as fundamentally structured by gender in many of the ways traditionally assumed . . . The adaptations described in so many other studies of women in prison are likely as much or more a product of the nature of women's corrections at a particular time and place as they are a product of the nature of women themselves. [ibid.: 713]

Bosworth's (1999) study of power relations in three women's prisons in Britain also found distinctive responses. Her subjects resist the regime imposed on them and construct new identities.

While scholars may differ on how distinctively gendered is women's experience of imprisonment, there is a growing policy consensus in Britain that women offenders should be differentially treated. Carlen argues that this is essential because of the nature and the context of female offending: they are already more severely sentenced and subject to a double form of regulation (Carlen 1998: 153). She is clearly linking back to earlier debates about double deviance, double jeopardy, and stigma. Building on the findings of an international comparative study of provision for women, Carlen and her fellow authors offer a range of examples of how successful, gender-specific policies can be achieved.

A series of reports on women's establishments in Britain by the Chief Inspector of Prisons, including a highly critical *Thematic Review* (HMCIP 1997), described the shortcomings of the system. On one unannounced visit to Holloway Prison, London, he and his team were so shocked by what they found that they walked out, thus creating a great deal of adverse publicity (HMCIP 2000). In 1998, the Prison Reform Trust (PRT) set up an inquiry, led by Dorothy Wedderburn, on women's imprisonment. The resulting report identified key problems already outlined here and presented them as the basis for change. They argued that: 'the criminal justice and prison system is so dominated by the handling of men that it is failing to provide for the particular needs of women' (PRT 2000: xii). They instance four distinctive characteristics of women:

1. their different patterns of offending from men and lower levels of risk to the public;
2. their role as mothers and primary carers and the resulting higher costs of their imprisonment;
3. their histories of psychiatric illness and earlier abuse;
4. the 'Cinderella' factor of small numbers [ibid.].

Among their key recommendations are the formation of a National Women's Justice Board, on the lines of the Youth Justice Board, and a network of local Women's Supervision, Rehabilitation and Support Centres, linked to small, local custodial units, to replace the existing women's system.

This sounds close to Carlen's 'Womenwise' model, yet it would be wise to enter a note of caution about creating specific models of penal treatment for women. Zedner and Rafter's accounts of historical examples which failed, or which resulted in benign but oppressive regimes, are apposite. A more recent example is that of Canada where a series of well-intentioned reforms appear not to have been wholly successful (Shaw 1991; Hannah-Moffat 2002). British policy-makers have been convinced by aspects of these arguments and have issued two documents on their approach to women offenders (Home Office 2000, 2001c). Their emphasis is on crime reduction, the specific needs of women offenders, and the high costs, individual and social, of their offences. The second report announced the development of the *Women's Offending Reduction Programme: 2002–2005* (Home Office 2001c).

GENDER AND CRIME IN LATE MODERNITY

Criminology is protean: the early twenty-first century sees it being subjected to another series of reviews about its character, its position in conditions of 'late modernity', and its relationships vis-à-vis the 'new' forms of regulation and control in contemporary society (Garland and Sparks 2000; Braithwaite 2000; Garland 2001; J. Young 1999; Heidensohn 2000; and Rock, in Chapter 2 of this volume). This process reflects true paradigm shifts which, unlike the new sociology of deviance of the 1960s and 1970s, have their source largely outside the discipline. The growth of the regulatory state and new forms of social control in particular have effected these changes (Braithwaite 2000). As with all shape-shifting, there is a striking change in *vocabulary*, reflecting new key *concepts* and concerns. Among these new concepts are those of risk, insecurity, responsibility, regulation, exclusion, and control. Defining and using them are complex and contentious tasks (J. Young 1999). Garland and Sparks describe what has happened thus:

From the point of view of politicians, crime and punishment become too important to leave to criminologists. The primary themes of the new penal policies—the expression of punitive sentiment, concern for victims, public protection, exclusion, enhanced control—are grounded *in a new collective experience from which they draw their meaning* and their strength . . . The mobile and insecure world of late modernity has given rise to new practices of control and exclusion that seek to make society less open and less mobile: to fix identities, immobilize individuals, quarantine whole sections of the population, erect boundaries, close off access [2000: 200, emphasis added].

In another account, Garland has noted that 'older social welfare criminology . . . which views criminality as the dispositional outcome of social deprivation now compete with two new criminologies—of "everyday life" and "the other"' (Garland 2001: 182–4). These are contrasting views, he contends:

the first purposes the piecemeal development of a network of unobtrusive situational controls, retrofitted to modify existing routines . . . The other exerts an excess of control . . . from the outside in the form of legal threats and moral exhortations [ibid.: 186].

Putting aside the validity of Garland's delineation, and its relevance for Britain compared to the USA, he omits from his taxonomy a third criminology represented by his own work. Braithwaite calls this the scholarship of new regulation (2000: 234). What I am describing is more than this. It focuses on the twin phenomena of the new culture of control and its reflections in criminological thought.

How do gender perspectives fit into/alongside the new paradigms? This is a vital question; their introduction and spread in criminology has been one of the main discipline stories of the late twentieth century (Downes and Rock 1998; Heidensohn 1996, 2000: chapter 6). As a result, gender and feminist issues have formed part of the cutting edge of criminology, central and open to 'theoretical and methodological innovation' (Daly 1997: 42). Can this position be maintained and enhanced, or is there a danger that 'despite the massive growth about women, crime, law and criminal justice . . . the experience of women [remains] marginal to the criminological enterprise' (Jefferson and Shapland 1994: 282)?

The review of the various accounts listed at the beginning of this section is not encouraging. This is less to do with the rather perfunctory references to gender (see, for example, J. Young 1999: 139; Heidensohn 2000: 4–5; although Young's is much the most positive of this group). Rather, it is the depressing amnesia with regard to the lessons which gendered studies have to offer.

An initial critique is provided by Maureen Cain's contribution to the *British Journal of Criminology* special issue. Cain's paper stands out because she provides a nuanced account of the politics of gender and social control in the Caribbean, which challenges many of the key assumptions of the new social control: that it is global, irresistible, exportable, or even effective in another context (Cain 2000). We can also draw on a wider range of recent work to illustrate three key themes which should really be integrated into these new studies: agency, identity, and resistance.

Most of the 'new' control studies present the citizen as subject in a passive, helpless way. Rose's is the most dystopian picture in this gallery: 'Control society is one of constant and never ending *modulation* . . . One is always in continuous training, lifelong learning, perpetual assessment . . . Surveillance is "designed in" to the flows of everyday existence' (2000: 325). Few examples of actual surveillance are cited in this piece. What is also missing, and from much of the rest of this body of work, is any consideration of the possibility of *resistance* to such controls or of *agency*, whether of the controlled or the controllers. Young rebuffs this approach in a robust fashion: 'some theories . . . focus on "social control" as if it were autonomous of what was being controlled . . . nearly all tend to regard social control as, somehow, separate from the public, as if control and social discipline were something unilaterally imposed upon people' (J. Young 1999: 58).

Some of the best examples of resistance to control come from recent feminist studies which describe the resourcefulness of some of the most marginal and oppressed subjects, deviant women and girls who are conventionally seen as passive and submissive. Lisa Maher, in her award-winning study of gender, race, and resistance in a Brooklyn drug market, describes 'the tactics women use to resist and contest the constraints that shape their occupational lives' (1997: 199). In an entirely different setting, Sharon Pickering provides:

a perspective on women's resistance in Northern Ireland by focussing on their experience of house raids . . . [she] argues that women have become increasingly politicised and organised in their resistance to repeated incursions into the home by security forces . . . [she] suggests the coercive agents of the state have played a significant role in both the individual and collective resistance of women. Paradoxically . . . the security forces have become agents of change [2000: 49].

A British study of the meaning girls give to violence in their lives (Burman *et al.* 2001), and Miller's (1998) account of women's participation in street robbery, both address the question of the *agency* of women who have few channels of expression yet find their own.

At a quite different level, a substantial range of work presents the ways in which several past generations of women reformers took part in, and sometimes took over, or invented, forms of social control (Brown and Heidensohn 2000; Appier 1998; Schulz 2000). While these are not appraisals of the current control situation, I have tried elsewhere to suggest how 'gender transformations' (Walby 1997) can be achieved and what lessons can be applied from experiences of the past (Heidensohn 2000).

In some respects the new culture of control resembles its predecessors: it lacks gendered dimensions. The future of criminology and of criminal justice surely lies most securely in inclusiveness, integration, and innovation.

CONCEPTS AND CONTINUING THE CRITIQUE

The title of my first contribution to this field was '*The Deviance of Women: A Critique and an Enquiry*' (Heidensohn 1968, emphasis added). My enquiry concerned the lack of interest in sex differences in recorded criminality and in female deviance in itself. My critique was of the limitations of existing explanations of these two matters. These two points still serve as useful guides for considering the considerable range of conceptual studies which have appeared since then. If one interrogates bibliographies and databases, there is much to consider of an explanatory kind. However, it is still vital to engage in a dialogue with mainstream criminology, especially about the assimilation of ideas about gender.

This area has been one of the most fruitful and dynamic in the whole of criminology. It is not surprising, then, that its theoretical development has been subject to considerable challenge and debate. In the section that follows I shall outline, in summary, some of the key contributions and also indicate how they are part of a continuing debate. As in all such debates, there has never been full, clear discussion of every issue; there is no great masterscript covering all roles and perspectives.

One summary of work in feminist criminology divided its conceptual concerns into the *gender gap* and the *generalizability* problem (Daly and Chesney-Lind 1988). Some theorists have attempted to deal with these issues, however. The most significant work of feminist theorists is to be found in *explanations of female criminality*. Because of problems in developing such approaches and because of wider difficulties and developments, there is another, and growing, category of criminological *feminist sceptics* who proffer no answers but ask more profound questions.

THE GENDER GAP AND GENERALIZABILITY

We have already noted the main contributors to theories about the gender gap: the so-called 'liberation causes crime' theorists (Adler 1975; Simon 1975) and the consequent debates about their views. This approach is one of the few perspectives on female crime to have been subjected to thorough empirical testing and to have been disproved (Box and Hale 1983; Austin 1993; Smart 1979; Steffensmeier 1995). The 'liberation hypothesis' was not a single coherent theory. Indeed Adler and Simon differ in key aspects of their approaches, although both see increased equality for women as a key variable in causing their changing patterns of criminal behaviour. However, Adler contended that the battle to emancipate women had been won by the mid-1970s, and thus male and female behaviour was converging, with females more and more resembling males by becoming aggressive and violent. Simon, on the other hand, suggested an opposite situation and outcome. Women's opportunities had not yet expanded very much; when they did so, their violence would diminish and, with growing opportunity, their property crimes increase. Both approaches fail when tested because they do not fit statistical trends. Criminal women are amongst those least likely to be affected by feminism (and those most affected by it, middle-class white women, are the least likely to be criminal). Moreover, criminal women tend to score highly on 'femininity' scores, whereas 'masculine' scoring women are less delinquent (Naffine 1987). These ideas are not supported, then, by the evidence. 'Yet ironically it is around this theme that a considerable debate has focused, putting female criminality into mainstream discussion' (Heidensohn 1989: 95).

The initial critique of criminology's failure to address the issues of gender and of women was mostly directed at the limits of conventional theories. They could not for the most part account for the gender gap, and broke down when applied to women as well as men, usually because they overpredicted female crime. Some critics went on to suggest that some criminological theories could be applied to women with success if only they were developed or modified (Leonard 1982; Morris 1987). Indeed this was a criticism made of feminist criminologists: they merely wished to add women back in. In practice it is hard to find examples of this, although Smith and Paternoster (1987) have suggested that 'general-neutral' theories of delinquency should be developed and try to do this in a study of marijuana use. They take factors from classic theories of male delinquency and conclude 'factors that influence participation decisions and the frequency of marijuana use are similar for males and females' (ibid.: 156).

This does not, however, explain the differences in recorded or self-reported narcotic offences. Neither does it explain why many other researchers find gender-specific theories important in just such areas (Rosenbaum 1981).

GENDER THEORIES

In the early days of work on women, Carol Smart issued a warning:

In the movement towards developing a feminist perspective a critique of sexism is vital, but in itself a feminist perspective critique alone cannot constitute a new theoretical approach . . . In particular more research is needed in the area of women and crime [1977: 183].

This has in fact turned out to be the agenda for most of those who have contributed to this field. Once more it will be helpful to adopt a taxonomy within which we can group the work we are reviewing. This would include studies of patriarchy, of social economic marginalization, of control, and lastly there is a group of feminosceptics who have focused on epistemological issues.

Patriarchy

Patriarchy is simply the rule of fathers. But defining it and using it as a concept has not proved at all simple for feminists, who have none the less used it frequently. Many writers have tried to define and refine it (Mitchell and Oakley 1986; Walby 1989), and have subjected it to rigorous criticisms (Pollert 1996). Quite often it appears to signify the rule of men or the power of men, and especially the use of these against women. On the whole patriarchy, or male power, is not much used in direct explanations of female crime. The concept is nevertheless employed in at least two important ways: to explain women's experience of the criminal justice system; and the gendered nature of much criminal victimization, especially from violence and abuse within the home. Indeed, it is from concern about women's treatment as victims in the processes of the criminal justice system and their experience of 'family law' that much of the evidence comes which has led, as Dobash and Dobash put it, to:

some feminist activists and scholars [arguing] that it is impossible to use the law and legal apparatus to confront patriarchal domination and oppression when the language and pro-cedures of these social processes and institutions are saturated with patriarchal beliefs and structures [1992: 147].

Victims and victimization are topics covered fully elsewhere in this volume. It is only the elision of the issues which I wish to discuss here. Susan Edwards, whose earlier work did emphasize sexist aspects of criminal justice (1984), puts this view forcefully:

A consideration of patriarchy has been central to an understanding of sex/gender division within the law . . . the criminal justice process . . . and policing . . . it is the precise juncture of bourgeois and male interest which constitutes the corner-stone of women's experience and corresponding oppression. In everyday experience women's need for protection, women's voice as victims of crime, as criminal offenders and as victims of the law has been totally eclipsed [1989: 13].

Carol Smart has gone furthest in arguing that 'it is important to think of non-legal strategies and to discourage resort to law as if it holds the key to unlock women's oppression' (1989: 5). Boldly she concludes:

a main purpose of this book has been to construct a warning to feminism to avoid the siren call of law. But of equal importance has been the attempt to acknowledge the power of feminism to construct an alternative reality to the version which is manifested in legal discourse [ibid.: 160].

Howe has extended Smart's discussion and insisted on its relationship with Carlen's apparently more pragmatic approach (1994: 213–15 *et passim*). In the 1980s there was widespread discussion of the work of Carol Gilligan (1982, 1987) who argued that men and women differ in their approaches to moral questions, with men stressing 'justice' as an independent concept and women focusing more on a relational notion of caring.

I used Gilligan's dichotomy as the basis of an ideal-type model of two types of justice system—the *Portia*, rational, judicial, and masculine; and the *Persephone*, relational, informal, and feminine—and explored what the effects of using such an alternative system might be. The conclusion was that such approaches had been adopted at certain times and had not always been beneficial (1986). Daly, in a review of this and other applications of Gilligan's difference discourse, disagrees with this approach and concludes:

in canvassing feminist scholarship for ways to rethink the problem of justice for men and women accused of crime, I find little guidance. . . . I would like to see a feminist conception of criminal justice which maintains a focus on women's lives and on redressing harms to women, but which does not ignore those men who have been crippled by patriarchal, class and race relations [1989b].

These comments could serve as the basis for the whole of this series of perspectives. What these studies amount to is a sophisticated critique of the administration of justice and the structures in which it operates. Clearly, there are certain gender-specific forms of discrimination rife within it. However, as Gelsthorpe (1989: 137–45) goes to great lengths to point out, it is impossible to try to demonstrate the existence of a conspiracy behind such practices. It is even more difficult to relate them, aetiologically, to women's crime. Although women can be shown to be more socially and economically oppressed than men, their experience of the system as perpetrators, rather than as victims, is far less. Where links can be made it is through social construction theories which actually deconstruct the meanings of concepts such as rape (Rafter 1990) or, as in Zedner's work quoted above, those of 'inebriation' and 'feeble mindedness' as applied to women. As Zedner's studies show, redefinitions of female deviance can diminish their apparent deviance or increase it (1991). This is not, of course, solely due to the operation of the criminal justice system. On the contrary, many other features of the Zeitgeist contribute: culture, values, changes in medical science. Politics and the media have also played crucial roles in such developments, as Young, for example, shows in her analysis of the media reactions to the women protesters at the Greenham Common Airbase in Britain in the 1980s. She argues that the criminal justice system and the media rely on each other's definitions of deviance (1990).

This set of approaches informs much writing on women and crime. It leads us to question some of the most basic assumptions about law, justice, and punishment in our society and to raise queries about unstated 'patriarchal' values. However, it is also then essential to question all the other implicit parts of the system, and we are likely, as Daly points out, to need to raise at least as many points about what happens to men, especially if they are young, poor, and come from minorities, as we do about women.

Marginalization

Economic explanations of criminal behaviour go back at least as far as Bonger and, albeit implicitly, to Marx (Taylor *et al.* 1975). More recently, critical criminologists insisted on the criminogenic capacities of capitalist societies (ibid.). *Critical Criminology* omits all consideration of gender, yet this is surely a crucial test for such theories since women are generally poorer than men in most, especially capitalist, societies, and have suffered more in modern recessions (Millar and Glendinning, 1989). Some writers researching female crime have put forward a variation of such approaches in arguing that deviant women are an especially marginalized group.

Part of the purpose of proposing this perspective is to counteract the liberation hypothesis discussed earlier. Chapman (1980) stressed that the rise in female property crime was due to women's poverty, and especially to the problems of single mothers, a growing proportion of the poor. In an empirical study, Jurik (1983) found support for such findings. A series of studies undertaken by Carlen in Britain elaborate on this theme (Carlen 1983, 1985, 1988). She concludes:

the analyses presented here claim only to indicate that, under certain, relatively rare *combinations* of otherwise general economic and ideological conditions, some women are more likely than not to choose to break the law and/or be imprisoned. Such analyses do *not* assume or imply that the women involved have no choice [1988: 162, original emphasis].

Recent work from Europe (Pitch 1995; Platek 1995) and elsewhere (Hansson 1995) suggests parallel concerns, and has also focused much more fully on women of colour (e.g., the special edition of the journal *Women and Criminal Justice*, 1995). Obviously, as Carlen suggests, poverty can be an important factor in the choice of women's criminal careers. It then often reinforces such choices by limiting others. Yet, as Daly showed in her study cited above, other factors, such as abuse in childhood and marriage, or relationships with men with associations with drugs, are also important. None of these offender-based, somewhat positivist approaches can answer certain important queries, however: namely, are the situations of those not convicted of crimes necessarily different? In short, do these explanations fulfil necessary and sufficient conditions of theorizing; or have they, perhaps, not addressed the right questions?

Control and conformity

A quite different approach has been adopted by a number of other writers who have sought to understand female criminality. So-called 'control theory' was developed originally by Hirschi and his colleagues (1969), who sought to explain delinquency by the failure of social bonding processes. The emphasis shifted from deviance and what caused it to conformity and what impaired it. Hirschi's work has been much criticized, notably for its weak theoretical base, although it appears to have empirical support from large survey studies (for a review, see Downes and Rock 1998). In various modified forms, control theories have been applied to women because 'an examination of female criminality and unofficial deviance suggests that we need to move away from studying infractions and look at conformity instead, because the most striking thing about female behaviour ... is how notably conformist to social mores women are' (Heidensohn 1996: 11).

In the same book I suggested that women were subject to a series of pressures and rewards to conform to which men were not. Informal sanctions discourage women and girls from straying far from proper behaviour: parents will disapprove or impose sanctions, as will gossip, ill-repute, and male companions. Fear of crime, harassment, and stigma all aid this process. A range of other commitments—to children, family, and community—occupy women much more fully than they do men. Lastly, public images and culture encourage daring deviance in men, but suggest that deviant women are punished (ibid.: chapters 5 and 9). Hagan and colleagues have also offered gender-specific versions of their general control theory, arguing that girls are much more subject to controls within the family than are boys (1979). Extensive empirical testing of various related hypotheses produced somewhat inconclusive results. Hagan found more informal control of girls, more formal of boys in his Canadian study, and some predictive value for his hypothesis. Others, however, found that while greater social bonds among girls (and women) explained some of the sex/crime ratio differences, they did not do so fully (Mawby 1981; Norland et al. 1981). Further, some of the differences were not in the expected direction. Thus girls who were 'masculine' in their identification in the last study were *less* delinquent than indeterminate or 'feminine' girls.

These approaches do at least try to account for the gender gap and to present a generalizable theory of a kind, even though it seems to have only limited explanatory power since the operation of the bonds is not fully theorized (though Hagan (1987) does attempt this in another text). Naffine is especially critical of such approaches. They depict females as essentially passive (1987: 68–70), whereas male delinquency is glorified as active and defiant. She misses, I think, the rising tide of comment on women's own contribution to social control, especially of their own sex. In *Women and Crime* I discussed this issue at some length, noting women's higher investment in conformity and stability. More recently a spate of studies have focused on women's role as social control agents, both historically (Carrier 1988; Boritch and Hagan 1990; Daly 1988) and in modern times (Jones 1986; Heidensohn 1989, 1992). In a complex analysis, Worrall has suggested that women offenders do act within the criminal justice system to alter their own fates, although they are able to do so only because as women they confront *two* systems of social control: 'They are effectively offered a contract which promises to minimize the consequences of their criminality by rehabilitating them within the dominant discourses of feminity (that is, domesticity, sexuality and pathology). Despite these programmes of feminization, such women it is argued, attempt to resist such construction by exploiting the contradictions of official discourses' (1990: 163).

Almost all the empirical testing of control theories has been conducted with juvenile subjects. Measures of delinquency often include relatively minor infractions such as truancy and under-age drinking. This limits the value of such studies where adults and more serious crimes are concerned. Gender-specific social control is, nevertheless, a widely-cited component of most efforts to discuss women and crime. There is also scope within such an approach to ask about many further issues: the control of males, for instance, or the role of women in control.

In reviewing theories of female criminality advanced in recent times, Pollock Byrne makes a succinct if gloomy point: 'Unfortunately feminist criminology has not offered any comprehensive theory to supplement those it has criticized' (1990: 25). It is hard to disagree with this. Despite a considerable body of work in the field, theoretical crocks of gold have failed to appear. What has developed is a much more sustained and sophisticated critique, and several important conceptual contributions which have some scope in application. The debate is for the most part still with older and existing theories and the development of second-order constructs. This does not merely reflect poverty of imagination. Something of an epistemological crisis has affected social science and feminism, and studies of crime are implicated. There are, however, pitfalls in these approaches, as I have argued in a review of my own research experiences with 'deviant' women (Heidensohn 1994b).

Feminist sceptics

Much modern feminist debate in social science has focused on methodological issues. How should women be studied? What is feminist analysis? Many articles and books have sought to respond to these questions, and several scholars have applied the answers to the study of gender and crime. These debates are complex, subtle and arcane, and are beyond the scope of this chapter. I wish to draw attention to the proposals made by several scholars who have tackled the epistemological crisis. What characterizes them all, to some degree, is their scepticism about either the past or the future of this field. Smart mounts the most devastating attack on criminology: 'It is very hard to see what criminology has to offer feminism' (1990: 83–4). This contrasts with what she sees as the value and influence of feminist postmodernism on analyses of women's experiences. It is also in contrast to other possible approaches such as feminist empiricism and what is termed 'standpointism'. The latter is based in experience and on the argument that only a shared perspective with the subject gives a researcher adequate insight and knowledge. Smart favours the deconstruction of everything, insisting that no meanings should be taken for granted.

Cain, in the same volume, tries also to describe what she calls the 'successor science' and lays down criteria for its operation (1990b: 125–40). Somewhat confusingly, she calls her approach 'realism'. Rafter (1990) also advocates a ruthless deconstruction of all laws and concepts, as does Bertrand (1994). Once again, the source of this continuing critique is outside criminology, although in these examples it is debates within feminism itself which have fuelled these developments. *La lutte continue*, no doubt, without resolution of the issues, although these developments suggest yet further room for growth and dynamism as advocated by Klein in her spirited call for new approaches to justice (1995).

CONCLUSIONS: *ALICE IN WONDERLAND* AND *THROUGH THE LOOKING GLASS*

An intelligent enquirer who followed the growth of this topic during the late twentieth century may feel that she has moved from the world of *Alice in Wonderland* to that of *Through the Looking Glass*. It is possible to construe all the modern work on women and crime as a great heap of glistening treasure. There is diversity, great range, rich material. It is possible to find the answers to many questions. There are still many puzzles and absurdities, but it is even possible to use key concepts to explain the studied world. Yet one of the main lessons which recurs throughout all the texts, articles, and reports is simple yet stunning in its implications. That is that Alice should be in the other strange place, through the glass where everything is reversed or upside down.

Then it becomes clear that we have to ask different questions. Not what makes women's crime rates so low, but why are men's so high? Such questions are being asked in a few places (Kersten 1996; Newburn and Stanko 1994), but they are the crucial ones, intellectually and politically. There is already a new *policy* agenda for law and order which highlights the gendered nature of much personal crime: domestic violence, rape, child abuse, etc. It is in the impact of such studies that its effect should be found.

There has been a significant shift in the study of crime because of feminist perspectives on it. New ideas have been developed. The most important contribution of all, however, was to see the centrality of gender to crime and to press for that. We know a vast amount about women and crime viewed through the prism of gender. Research on masculinity and crime is a fast-developing area (Messerschmidt 1993; Newburn and Stanko 1994; Jefferson and Carlen 1996) and is likely to provide some very challenging ideas to both criminology and feminist perspectives on crime. As

Nelken has suggested, it is with just such a reflexive synthesis that the futures of criminology are likely to be preoccupied (1994).

In the twenty-first century, the key questions still resemble those first posed decades ago about gender and crime:

- What are the dimensions of the gender gap?
- How can we characterize female (and male) patterns of offending?
- Should criminal justice policies and practices recognize gender differences?

The field has grown. It has gained scholarly recognition and public policy acknowledgement. But this has been a long journey which has not yet taken us very far.

Selected further reading

For more detailed coverage of the topics in this chapter, Frances Heidensohn's *Women and Crime* (2nd edn, Basingstoke: Macmillan/Palgrave, 1996) is the standard work. For comparative historical perspectives, M. Arnot and C. Usborne (eds), *Gender and Crime in Modern Europe* (London: UCL Press, 1999), is a good starting point, while N.H. Rafter and F.M. Heidensohn (eds), *International Feminist Perspectives in Criminology* (Buckingham: Open University Press, 1995) provides modern viewpoints, and N.H. Rafter (ed.), *The Encyclopedia of Women and Crime* (Phoenix, Ariz.: Onyx Press, 2000) is a wide-ranging text. *Statistics on Women and the Criminal Justice System* are published annually by the Research Development and Statistics section of the Home Office. The Prison Reform Trust Report, *Justice for Women: The Need for Reform* (London: PRT, 2000) summarizes key issues and debates, and the journal *Women and Criminal Justice* publishes relevant articles. Tim Newburn and Betsy Stanko's edited collection, *Just Boys Doing Business* (London: Routledge, 1994), remains the best text on masculinity and crime. On gender and justice professions, see S.E. Martin and N. Jurik, *Doing Gender, Doing Justice* (London: Sage, 1995), and on law enforcement, Jennifer Brown and Frances Heidensohn, *Gender and Policing* (Basingstoke: Macmillan/Palgrave, 2000).

References

ACTON, W. (1857), *Prostitution: Considered in its Moral, Social and Sanitary Aspects in London and Other Large Cities and Garrison Towns*, London: Frank Cass.

ADLER, I. (1975), *Sisters in Crime*, New York: McGraw Hill.

ALLEN, H. (1987), *Justice Unbalanced*, Milton Keynes: Open University Press.

APPIER, J. (1998), *The Sexual Politics of Law Enforcement and the LAPD*, Philadelphia, Pa: Temple University Press.

ARNOT, M., and USBORNE, C. (eds) (1999), *Gender and Crime in Modern Europe*, London: UCL Press.

AUSTIN, R.L. (1981), 'Liberation and Female Criminality in England and Wales', *British Journal of Criminology*, 21, 4: 371–4.

—— (1993), 'Recent Trends in Official Male and Female Crime Rates: The Convergence Controversy', *Journal of Criminal Justice*, 21: 447–66.

BARCLAY, G.C. (1995), *Digest 3: Information on the Criminal Justice System In England and Wales*, London: Home Office.

BEATTIE, J.M. (1975), 'The Criminality of Women in Eighteenth Century England', *Journal of Social History*.

BECKER, H.S. (1963), *Outsiders: Studies in the Sociology of Deviance*, London: Macmillan.

BEIRNE, P. (1988), 'Heredity versus Environment', *British Journal of Criminology*, 28, 3: 315–39.

BERTRAND, M.A. (1969), 'Self-image and delinquency: a contribution to the study of female delinquency and women's image', *Acta Criminologica*.

—— (1994), 'From La Donna delinquente to a postmodern deconstruction of the "woman-question" in social control theory', *Journal of Human Justice*, 5, 2: 43–57.

BORITCH, H., and HAGAN, J. (1990), 'A Century of Crime in Toronto: Gender, Class and Patterns of Social Control, 1859 to 1955', *Criminology*, 20, 4: 567–99.

BOSWORTH, M. (1999), *Engendering Resistance: Agency and Power in Women's Prisons*, Aldershot: Ashgate.

BOX, S., and HALE, C. (1983), 'Liberation and Female Criminality in England and Wales', *British Journal of Criminology*, 23, 1: 35–49.

BRAITHWAITE, J. (1989), *Crime, Shame and Reintegration*, Cambridge: Cambridge University Press.

—— (2000), 'The New Regulatory State and the Transformation of Criminology', *British Journal of Criminology*, 40, 2: 222–38.

BROWN, J., and HEIDENSOHN, F. (1996), 'Exclusion Orders', *Policing Today*, September: 20–24.

—— and —— (2000), *Gender and Policing*, Basingstoke: Macmillan/Palgrave.

BROWNE, A. (1987), *When Battered Women Kill*, London: Collier Macmillan.

BURMAN, M., BATCHELOR, S., and BROWN, J. (2001), 'Researching Girls and Violence: Tracing the Dilemmas of Fieldwork', *British Journal of Criminology*, 41, 3: 443–59.

BUSH, T., and HOOD WILLIAMS, J. (1995), *Domestic Violence on a London Housing Estate*, Research Bulletin 37, London: Home Office.

CAIN, M. (ed.) (1990a), *Growing up Good*, London: Sage.

—— (1990b), 'Realist Philosophy and Standpoint Epistemologies or Feminist Criminology as a Successor Science', in L. Gelsthorpe and A. Morris (eds), *Feminist Perspectives in Criminology*, Buckingham: Open University Press.

—— (2000), 'Orientalism, Occidentalism and the Sociology of Crime', *British Journal of Criminology*, 40, 2: 239–60.

CAMPBELL, A. (1981), *Girl Delinquents*, Oxford: Blackwell.

—— (1984), *The Girls in the Gang*, Oxford: Blackwell.

CARLEN, P. (1983), *Women's Imprisonment*, London: Routledge and Kegan Paul.

—— (1985), *Criminal Women*, Oxford: Polity Press.

—— (1988), *Women, Crime and Poverty*, Buckingham: Open University Press.

—— (1990), *Alternatives to Women's Imprisonment*, Buckingham: Open University Press.

—— (1999), *Sledgehammer*, Basingstoke: Macmillan.

—— (ed.) (2002), *Women and Punishment: The Struggle for Justice*, Cullompton: Willan.

CARRIER, J. (1988), *The Campaign for the Employment of Women as Police Officers*, Aldershot: Gower.

CASALE, S. (1989), *Women Inside. The Experience of Women Remand Prisoners in Holloway*, London: Civil Liberties Trust.

CHAN, J. (1997), *Changing Police Culture*, Cambridge: Cambridge University Press.

CHAPMAN, J. (1980), *Economic Realities and the Female Offender*, Lexington: Lexington Books.

CHESNEY-LIND, M. (1997), *The Female Offender*, London: Sage.

CREIGHTON, S. J., and NOYES, P. (1989), *Child Abuse Trends in England and Wales 1983–1987*, London: NSPCC.

CRESSEY, D.R. (ed.) (1961), *The Prison*, New York: Holt, Rinehart and Winston.

DALTON, K. (1980), 'Cyclical Criminal Acts in the Premenstrual Syndrome', *Lancet*, 2: 1070–71.

DALY, K. (1988), 'The Social Control of Sexuality: A Case Study of the Criminalization of Prostitution in the Progressive Era', *Research in Law, Deviance and Social Control*, 9: 171–206.

—— (1989a), 'Rethinking Judicial Paternalism: Gender, Work-Family Relations and Sentencing', *Gender and Society*, 3, 1: 9–36.

—— (1989b), 'Criminal justice ideologies and practices in different voices: some feminist questions about justice', *International Journal of the Sociology of Law*, 17: 1–18.

—— (1994), *Gender, Crime and Punishment*, New Haven: Yale University Press.

—— (1995), 'Gender and Sentencing: What We Know and Don't Know From Empirical Research', *Federal Sentencing Reporter*, 8, 3: 163–8.

—— (1997), 'Different Ways of Conceptualizing Sex/Gender in Feminist Theory and Their Implications for Criminology', *Theoretical Criminology*, 1, 1: 25–51.

—— (1998), 'Gender, Crime and Criminology', in M. Tonry (ed.), *The Handbook of Crime and Punishment*, New York: Oxford University Press.

—— and BORDT, R.L. (1995), 'Sex Effects and Sentencing: An Analysis of the Statistical Literature', *Justice Quarterly*, 12, 1: 141–75.

—— and CHESNEY-LIND, M. (1988), 'Feminism and Criminology', *Justice Quarterly*, 5, 4: 498–538.

DAVIES, A. (1999), '"These Viragoes are No Less Cruel Than The Lads": Young Women, Gangs and Violence in Late Victorian Manchester and Salford', *British Journal of Criminology*, 39, 1: 72–89.

DOBASH, R.E., and DOBASH, R.P. (1979), *Violence Against Wives*, Buckingham: Open University Press.

—— and —— (1992), *Women, Violence and Social Change*, London: Routledge.

——, —— and GUTTERIDGE, S. (1986), *The Imprisonment of Women*, Oxford: Blackwell.

DONNEGAN, K. (2002), 'A Caring Prison: Opportunities For and Limits to Reform', in P. Carlen (ed.), *Women and Punishment: the Struggle for Justice*, Cullompton: Willan.

DOWNES, D., and ROCK, P. (1998), *Understanding Deviance*, 3rd edn, Oxford: Oxford University Press.

EATON, M. (1986), *Justice for Women?*, Buckingham: Open University Press.

—— (1993), *Women After Prison*, Buckingham: Open University Press.

EDWARDS, S.M. (1984), *Women on Trial*, Manchester: Manchester University Press.

—— (1989), *Policing 'Domestic' Violence*, London: Sage.

FARRINGTON, D.P., and MORRIS, A.M. (1983), 'Sex, Sentencing and Reconviction', *British Journal of Criminology*, 23, 3: 229–48.

FEELEY, M., and LITTLE, D. (1991), 'The Vanishing Female: The Decline of Women in the Criminal Process, 1687–1912', *Law and Society Review*, 25, 4: 719–57.

FEINMAN, C. (1986), *Women in the Criminal Justice System*, New York: Praeger.

FOX, J. (1998), 'Analysis of Trends in Intimate Murder, 1976–1996', in L.A. Greenfield (ed.), *Violence by Intimates*, Washington DC: Bureau of Justice Statistics.

GARLAND, D. (1985), *Punishment and Welfare*, Aldershot: Gower.

—— (2001), *The Culture of Control*, Oxford: Oxford University Press.

—— and SPARKS, R. (2000), 'Criminology, Social Theory and the Challenge of Our Times', *British Journal of Criminology*, 4, 2: 189–204.

GELSTHORPE, L. (1989), *Sexism and the Female Offender*, Aldershot: Gower.

—— and LOUCKS, N. (1997), in C. Hedderman and L. Gelsthorpe (eds), *Understanding the Sentencing of Women*, Home Office Research Study No. 170, London: Home Office.

—— and MORRIS, A. (1988), 'Feminism and Criminology in Britain', *British Journal of Criminology*, 28, 2: 223–40.

—— and —— (eds) (1990), *Feminist Perspectives in Criminology*, Buckingham: Open University Press.

—— and —— (2002), 'Women's Imprisonment in England and Wales in the 1990s: A Penal Paradox', *Criminal Justice*, forthcoming.

GIALLOMBARDO, R. (1966), *Society of Women: A Study of a Women's Prison*, New York: Wiley.

—— (1974), *The Social World of Imprisoned Girls*, New York: Wiley.

GIBSON, M., and RAFTER, N. (2003), *Criminal Woman. A new translation of Cesare Lombroso's La Donna Delinquente*, Durham N. Carolina: Duke University Press.

GILLIGAN, C. (1982), *In a Different Voice*, Cambridge, Mass.: Harvard University Press.

—— (1987), 'Moral Orientation and Moral Development', in E. Kittay and D. Meyers (eds), *Women and Moral Theory*, New Jersey: Rowman and Littlefield.

GODFREY, B. (1999), 'Workplace Appropriation and the Gendering of Factory "Law": West Yorkshire, 1840–80', in M. Arnot and C. Usborne (eds), *Gender and Crime in Modern Europe*, London: UCL Press.

HAGAN, J. (1987), *Modern Criminology: Crime, Criminal Behaviour and its Control*, New York: McGraw Hill.

——, SIMPSON, J.H., and GILLIS, A.R. (1979), 'The Sexual Stratification of Social Control: a Gender-based Perspective on Crime and Delinquency', *British Journal of Sociology*, 30.

HANMER, J., and SAUNDERS, S. (1984), *Well-founded Fear*, London: Hutchinson.

HANNAH-MOFFAT, K. (2002), 'Creating Choices? Reflecting on the Choices', in P. Carlen (ed.), *Women and the Struggle for Justice*, Cullompton: Willan.

HANSSON, D. (1995), 'Agenda-ing Gender: Feminism and the Engendering of Academic Criminology in South Africa', in N.H. Rafter and F.M. Heidensohn (eds), *International Feminist Perspectives in Criminology*, Buckingham: Open University Press.

HARRIS, R. (1992), *Crime, Criminal Justice and the Probation Service*, London: Routledge.

HARTMAN, M. (1977), *Victorian Murderesses*, London: Robson Books.

HEDDERMAN, C., and HOUGH, M. (1994), *Does the Criminal Justice System Treat Men and Women Differently?*, Home Office Research Findings No. 10, London: Home Office.

HEIDENSOHN, F.M. (1968), 'The Deviance of Women: A Critique and an Enquiry', in *British Journal of Sociology*, XIX, 2.

—— (1975), 'The Imprisonment of Females', in S. McConville (ed.), *The Use of Imprisonment*, London: Routledge and Kegan Paul.

—— (1981), 'Women and the Penal System', in A. Morris and L. Gelsthorpe (eds), *Women and Crime*, Cambridge: Cropwood Conference Series 13.

—— (1985), *Women and Crime*, London: Macmillan.

—— (1986), 'Models of Justice: Portia or Persephone? Some Thoughts on Equality, Fairness and Gender in the Field of Criminal Justice', *International Journal of Sociology of Law*, 14.

—— (1989), *Crime and Society*, Basingstoke: Macmillan.

—— (1991), 'Women and Crime in Europe', in F. Heidensohn and M. Farrell (eds), *Crime in Europe*, London: Routledge.

—— (1992), *Women in Control? The Role of Women in Law Enforcement*, Oxford: Oxford University Press.

—— (1994a), '"We Can Handle It Out Here". Women Officers in Britain and the USA and the Policing of Public Order', *Policing and Society*, 4, 4: 293–303.

—— (1994b), 'From Bening to Knowing: Some Reflections on the Study of Gender in Contemporary Society', *Women and Criminal Justice*, 6, 1: 13–37.

—— (1995), 'Feminist Perspectives and their Impact on Criminology and Criminal Justice in Britain', in N. Rafter and F. Heidensohn (eds), *International Feminist Perspectives in Criminology*, Buckingham: Open University Press.

—— (1996), *Women and Crime*, 2nd edn, Basingstoke: Macmillan.

—— (2000), *Sexual Politics and Social Control*, Buckingham: Open University Press.

—— and FARRELL, M. (eds) (1991), *Crime in Europe*, London: Routledge.

HIRSCHI, T. (1969), *Causes of Delinquency*, Berkeley, Cal.: University of California Press.

HM CHIEF INSPECTORATE OF PRISONS (1997), *Women in Prison: A Thematic Review*, London: Home Office.

—— (2000), *An Unannounced Follow-up Inspection of HM Prison Holloway*, London: Home Office.

HØIGÅRD, C., and FINSTEAD, L. (1992), *Backstreets Prostitution, Money and Love*, Oxford: Polity.

HOME OFFICE (1999), *Statistics on Women and the Criminal Justice System*, London: Home Office.

—— (2000), *Statistics on Women and the Criminal Justice System*, London: Home Office.

—— (2001a), *The Government's Strategy for Women Offenders*, London: Home Office.

—— (2001b), *Making Punishments Work*, London: Home Office.

—— (2001c), *Women's Offending Reduction Programme: 2002–2005*, London: Home Office.

HORSLEY, J.W. (1887), *Jottings from Jail: Notes and Papers on Prison Matters*, London: T. Fisher Unwin.

HOWE, A. (1994), *Punish and Critique*, London: Routledge.

IRWIN, J., and CRESSEY, D. (1962), 'Thieves, Convicts and the Inmate Culture', *Social Problems*, 10, 3: 145–7.

JEFFERSON, T., and SHAPLAND, J. (1994), 'Criminal Justice and the Production of Order and Control: Criminological Research in the UK in the 1980s', *British Journal of Criminology*, 34, 3, 265–90.

—— and CARLEN, P. (eds) (1996), *Masculinities, Social Relations and Crime*, Special Edition of the *British Journal of Criminology*, 36, 3.

JOHNSON, J. (1991), *What Lisa Knew*, London: Bloomsbury.

JONES, D. (1982), *Crime, Protest, Community and Police in Nineteenth Century Britain*, London: Routledge.

JONES, S. (1986), *Policewomen and Equality*, London: Macmillan.

JONES, T., MACLEAN, B., and YOUNG, J. (1986), *The Islington Crime Survey*, Aldershot: Gower.

JURIK, N. (1983), 'The Economics of Female Recidivism', *Criminology*, 21, 4: 3–12.

—— and GREGWARE, P. (1992), 'A Method for Murder. The Study of Homicides by Women', *Perspectives on Social Problems*, 4: 179–201.

KELLOR, F. (1900), 'Criminal Sociology: Criminality Among Women', *Arena*, 23: 516–24.

KERSTEN, J. (1996), 'Culture, Masculinities and Violence against Women', *British Journal of Criminology*, 36, 3: 381–95.

KING, P. (1999), 'Gender, Crime and Justice in Late Eighteenth Century and Early Nineteenth Century England', in M. Arnot and C. Usborne (eds), *Gender and Crime in Modern Europe*, London: UCL Press.

KLEIN, D. (1995), 'Gender's Prism: Towards a Feminist Criminology', in H.N. Rafter and F. Heidensohn (eds) (1995), *International Feminist Perspectives in Criminology*, Buckingham: Open University Press.

KOSS, M. (1988), 'Hidden Rape: Sexual Aggression and Victimization in a National Sample of Students in Higher Education', in A. Burgess (ed.), *Rape and Sexual Assault*, New York: Garland.

KRISTA, A. (1993), *Deadlier than the Male*, London: Harper Collins.

KRUTTSCHMITT, C. (1981), 'Prison Codes, Inmate Solidarity and Women: A Re-examination', in M. Warren (ed.), *Comparing Female and Male Offenders*, Newbury Park: Sage.

——, GARTNER, R., and MILLER, A. (2000), 'Doing Her Own Time? Women's Response to Prison in the Context of the Old and the New Penology', *Criminology*, 38, 3: 681–717.

LEMGRUBER, J. (2001), 'Women in the Criminal Justice System', in N. Ollus and S. Nevala (eds), *Women in the Criminal Justice System: International Examples and National Responses*, Helsinki: HEUNI.

LEONARD, E.B. (1982), *A Critique of Criminology Theory: women, crime and society*, London: Longman.

LLOYD, A. (1993), *Women and Violence*, Harmondsworth: Penguin.

LOMBROSO, C., and FERRERO, W. (1895), *The Female Offender*, London: T. Fisher Unwin.

LUPTON, C., and GILLESPIE, T. (eds) (1994), *Working with Violence*, Basingstoke: Macmillan.

MACDONALD, E. (1991), *Shoot the Women First*, London: Fourth Estate.

MACGREGOR, S. (ed.) (1989), *Drugs and British Society*, London: Routledge.

McLEOD, E. (1982), *Women Working: Prostitution Now*, London: Croom Helm.

McLYNN, F. (1989), *Crime and Punishment in the Eighteenth Century*, Oxford: Oxford University Press.

MAHER, L. (1990), 'Criminalising Pregnancy—the Downside of a Kinder, Gentler Nation?', *Social Justice*, 17, 3: 111–35.

—— (1997), *Sexed Work*, Oxford: Oxford University Press.

MANDARAKA-SHEPPARD, A. (1986), *The Dynamics of Aggression in Women's Prisons in England*, Aldershot: Gower.

MANNHEINN, H. (1965), *Comparative Criminology*, London: Routledge and Kegan Paul.

MARTIN, S.E. (1980), *Breaking and Entering*, Berkeley, Cal.: University of California Press.

MAWBY, R. (1981), 'Sex and Crime: the Results of a Self Report Study', *British Journal of Criminology*, 31, 4: 525.

MAYHEW, H. (1861), *London Labour and London Poor*, Vols I–IV, London.

MESSERSCHMIDT, J. (1993), *Masculinities and Crime*, Lanham, MD: Rowman and Littlewood.

MILLAR, J., and GLENDINNING, C. (1989), 'Gender and Poverty', *Journal of Social Policy*, 18, 3: 368–83.

MILLER, E. (1986), *Street Women*, Philadelphia, Pa.: Temple.

MILLER, J. (1998), 'Up it Up: Gender and the Accomplishment of Street Robbery', *Criminology*, 36, 1: 37–65.

MILLMAN, M. (1982), 'Images of Deviant Men and Women', in M. Evans (ed.), *The Women Question*, London: Fontana.

MINISTRY OF JUSTICE, SWEDEN (2000), *Principles for the Treatment of Women Sentenced to Imprisonment*, Stockholm.

MIRRLEES-BLACK, C. (1995), 'Estimating the Extent of Domestic Violence: Findings from the 1992 BCS', in C. Byron (ed.), *Home Office Research Bulletin 37*, London: Home Office.

—— (1999), *Domestic Violence: Findings from a New British Crime Survey Self-completion Questionnaire*, Home Office Research Study, London: Home Office.

MITCHELL, J., and OAKLEY, A. (eds) (1986), *What is Feminism?*, Oxford: Blackwell.

MORRIS, A. (1987), *Woman, Crime and Criminal Justice*, Oxford: Basil Blackwell.

NAFFINE, N. (1987), *Female Crime*, Sydney: Allen and Unwin.

NATIONAL CRIMINAL JUSTICE REFERENCE SERVICE (1998), *Women in Criminal Justice: A Twenty Year Update*, Maryland: Rockville.

NATZLER, C., O'SHEA, M., HEAVEN, O., and MARS, M. (1989), all in C. Dunhill (ed.), *The Boys in Blue Women's Challenge to the Police*, London: Virago.

NELKEN, D. (ed.) (1994), *The Futures of Criminology*, London: Sage.

NEWBURN, T., and STANKO, B. (1994), *Just Boys Doing Business*, London: Routledge.

NORLAND, S., WESSEL, R.C., and SHOVER, N. (1981), 'Masculinity and Delinquency', *Criminology*, 19, 3: 421.

OWEN, B. (1998), *'In the Mix': Struggle and Survival in a Women's Prison*, Albany: State University of New York Press.

PADEL, U., and STEVENSON, P. (eds) (1988), *Insiders: Women's Experience of Prison*, London: Virago.

PARTON, N. (1991), *Governing the Family*, Basingstoke: Macmillan.

PATKAR, P. (2001), 'Consolidating Protection against Ever-escalating Violation', in N. Ollus and S. Nevala (eds), *Women in the Criminal Justice System: International Examples and National Responses*, Helsinki: HEUNI.

PEARSON, G. (1987), *The New Heroin Users*, Oxford: Blackwell.

PICKERING, S. (2000), 'Women, the Home and Resistance in Northern Ireland', *Women and Criminal Justice*, 11, 3: 49–82.

PIKE, L. (1876), *A History of Crime in England*, London: Smith Elder.

PILIAVIN, I., and BRIAR, S. (1964), 'Police Encounters with Juveniles', *American Journal of Sociology*, 70: 206.

PITCH, T. (1995), 'Feminist Politics, Crime, Law and Order in Italy', in N.H. Rafter and F.M. Heidensohn (eds), *International Feminist Perspectives in Criminology*, Buckingham: Buckingham University Press.

PIZZEY, E. (1974), *Scream Quietly or the Neighbours Will Hear*, Harmondsworth: Penguin.

PLATEK, M. (1995), 'What its Like for Women: Criminology in Poland and Eastern Europe', in N.H. Rafter and F.M. Heidensohn (eds), *International Feminist Perspectives in Criminology*, Buckingham: Buckingham University Press.

PLAYER, E. (1989), 'Women and Crime in the Inner City', in D. Downes (ed.), *Crime in the City*, Macmillan: London.

POE-YAMAGATA, E. (1996), *A Statistical Overview of Females in the Juvenile Justice System*, Pittsburg Pa.: National Centre for Juvenile Justice.

POLLAK, O. (1950), *The Criminality of Women*, New York: Barnes/Perpetua.

POLLERT, A. (1996), 'Gender and Class Re-visited: or the Poverty of "Patriarchy"', *Sociology*, 304: 639–59.

POLLOCK-BYRNE, J. (1990), *Women, Prison and Crime*, Belmont, Cal.: Wadsworth.

PRISON REFORM TRUST (2000), *Justice for Women: The Need for Reform*, London: PRT.

RAEDER, M. (1995), 'The Forgotten Offender: The Effect of the Sentencing Guidelines and Mandatory Minimums on Women and Their Children', *Federal Sentencing Reporter*, 8, 3: 157–62.

RAFTER, N. (1985), 'Chastizing the Unchaste: Social Control Functions of a Women's Reformatory', in S. Cohen and A. Scull (eds), *Social Control and the State*, Oxford: Blackwell.

—— (1990), 'The social construction of crime and crime control', *Journal of Research in Crime and Delinquency*, 27, 4: 376–89.

—— (ed.) (2000), *Encyclopedia of Women and Crime*, Phoenix, Ariz.: Onyx Press.

—— and HEIDENSOHN, F. (eds) (1995), *International Feminist Perspectives in Criminology*, Buckingham: Open University Press.

RAP (1969), *Radical Alternatives to Prison*, London: Christian Action Publications.

REINER, R. (1985), *The Politics of the Police*, Oxford: Oxford University Press.

REYNOLDS, A. (1991), *Tight Rope*, London: Sidgwick and Jackson.

—— (2000), *The Politics of the Police*, 3rd edn, Oxford: Oxford University Press.

RICHIE, B., TSENIN, K., and SPATZ WIDOM, C. (2000), *Research on Women and Girls in the Justice System*, Washington DC: Office of Justice Programmes.

ROCK, P.E. (1996), *Reconstructing a Women's Prison*, Oxford: Clarendon Press.

ROSE, N. (2000), 'Government and Control', *British Journal of Criminology*, 40, 2: 321–39.

ROSENBAUM, M. (1981), *Women on Heroin*, New Brunswick, NJ: Rutgers University Press.

SCHLESINGER, P., DOBASH, R.E., and DOBASH, R.P. (1992), *Women Viewing Violence*, London: British Film Institute.

SCHRAG, C. (1961), 'A Preliminary Criminal Typology', *Pacific Sociological Review*, 4, 2: 11.

SCHULZ, D.M. (2000), 'Review Essay: Maternal

Justice', *Women and Criminal Justice*, 11, 1: 89–98.

Scottish Office (1998), *Women Offenders—A Safer Way*, Edinburgh: Social Work Services and Prisons Inspectorate for Scotland.

Shaw, M. (1991), *The Federal Female Offender*, Ottawa: Solicitor General of Canada.

Simon, R.J. (1975), *Women and Crime*, Toronto: Lexington.

Simmons, H.G. (1978), 'Explaining Social Policy: The English Mental Deficiency Act of 1913', *Journal of Social History*, 11, 3.

Smart, C. (1977), *Women, Crime and Criminology*, London: Routledge and Kegan Paul.

—— (1979), 'The new female criminal: reality or myth', *British Journal of Criminology*, 19, 1: 50–71.

—— (1989), *Feminism and the Power of Law*, London: Routledge.

—— (1990), 'Feminist Approaches to Criminology', in L. Gelsthorpe and A. Smart (eds), *Feminist Perspectives in Criminology*, Buckingham: Open University Press.

Smith, A.D. (1962), *Women in Prison*, London: Stevens and Sons.

Smith, D., and Gray, J. (1983), *Police and People in London*, Vols I–IV, London: Policy Studies Institute.

—— and Paternoster, R. (1987), 'The Gender Gap in Theories of Deviance: Issues and Evidence', *Journal of Research on Crime and Delinquency*, 24: 140–72.

Smith, L.J.F. (1988), 'Images of Women—Decision-Making in Courts', in A. Morris and C. Wilkinson (eds), *Women and the Penal System*, Cambridge: Cropwood Conference Series.

Stanko, E. (1984), *Intimate Intrusions*, London: Routledge and Kegan Paul.

—— (1990), *Everyday Violence*, London: Pandora.

—— (2001), 'The Day to Count: Reflections on a Methodology to Raise Awareness about the Impact of Domestic Violence in the UK', *Criminal Justice*, 1, 2: 215–26.

Stanley, L., and Wise, S. (1984), *Breaking Out*, London: Routledge and Kegan Paul.

Steffensmeier, D.J. (1995), 'Trends in Female Crime: It's Still a Man's World', in B. Raffel Price and N.J. Sokoloff (eds), *The Criminal Justice System and Women*, New York: McGraw-Hill.

Strachey, R. (1978), *The Cause*, London: Virago.

Sykes, G. (1956), *Society of Captives*, Princeton: Princeton Univ. Press.

Taylor, I., Walton, P., and Young, J. (1975), *Critical Criminology*, London: Routledge and Kegan Paul.

Tittle, C. (1969), 'Inmate Organization: Sex Differentiation and the Influence of Criminal Sub Cultures', *American Sociological Review*, 34: 492–505.

Vanezis, P. (1991), 'Women, Violent Crime and the Menstrual Cycle: A Review', *Medicine, Science and the Law*, 31, 1: 11–14.

Visher, C.A. (1983), 'Gender, police arrest decisions and notions of chivalry', *Criminology* 21: 5–28.

Waddington, P.J. (1999), 'Police (Canteen) Sub-Culture: An Appreciation', *British Journal of Criminology*, 39, 2: 287–309.

Walby, S. (1989), 'Theorising Patriarchy', *Sociology*, 23, 2: 213–34.

—— (1997), *Gender Transformations*, London: Routledge.

—— and Myhill, A. (2001), 'New Survey Methodologies in Researching Violence against Women', *British Journal of Criminology*, 41, 3: 502–22.

Walklate, S. (1989), *Victimology*, London: Unwin Hyman.

Walkowitz, J. (1980), *Prostitution and Victorian Society*, Cambridge: Cambridge University Press.

Ward, D.A., and Kassebaum, G.G. (1965), *Women's Prison*, London: Weidenfeld.

Webb, D. (1984), 'More on Gender and Justice: Girl Offenders on Supervision', *Sociology*, 18.

Wiener, M. (1998), 'The Victorian Criminalization of Men', in P. Spierenburg (ed.), *Men and Violence: Gender, Honor and Rituals in Modern Europe and America*, Columbus, Ohio: Ohio State University Press.

Woodbridge, J., and Frosztega, J. (1998), *Recent Changes in the Female Prison Population*, London: Home Office.

Worrall, A. (1990), *Offending Women*, London: Routledge.

Young, A. (1990), *Femininity in Dissent*, London: Routledge.

Young, J. (1986), 'The future of criminology', in R. Matthews and J. Young (eds), *Confronting Crime*, London: Sage.

—— (1999), *The Exclusive Society*, London: Sage.

Young, M. (1991), *An Inside Job*, Oxford: Oxford University Press.

Zedner, L. (1991), *Women, Crime and Custody in Victorian England*, Oxford: Oxford University Press.

16

YOUNG PEOPLE, CRIME, AND YOUTH JUSTICE

Tim Newburn*

'Youth' is an elastic concept. It means different things, at different times, and in different places. This chapter is about those young people described, often in a very approximate manner, as teenagers, adolescents, or juveniles. More particularly, the focus of the chapter is on youth crime and the shape and operation of the youth justice system. The chapter is divided into four sections. The first looks at the different ways in which deviance (whether criminal or not) has been viewed and theorized. As such it draws on a broad, primarily sociological literature, from both the United States and Britain, which explores the nature of youthful deviance and, more particularly, examines and seeks to provide an explanation for youth (sub)culture(s). The second section focuses more directly on trends and patterns in youth crime. Using data from a range of sources including the major British surveys—the British Crime Survey (BCS) and the Youth Lifestyles Survey (YLS)—this section explores the prevalence of offending by young people, how these patterns are mediated by sex and ethnicity, and how patterns of youthful offending have changed over time. The last two sections look at youth justice policy and the youth justice system in England and Wales.[1] The origins of the current system are outlined before moving on to consider in some detail the radical changes that have been brought about under New Labour by the Crime and Disorder Act 1998 and subsequent legislation which has attempted to introduce restorative justice practices into youth justice.

* I am grateful to the following for advice and for supplying material during the course of the writing of this chapter: Siobhan Campbell, Adam Crawford, Rod Earle, Kirsten Grace, Simon King, Rod Morgan, John Muncie, and Michael Shiner.

[1] There is not the space here to discuss the very different systems that operate in Northern Ireland and Scotland. A full description of the philosophy and practice of the latter is contained in Kelly, A. (1996), *Introduction to the Scottish Children's Panel*, Winchester: Waterside Press.

IMAGES AND THEORIES OF 'YOUTH'
AND DEVIANCE

Geoffrey Pearson (1983, 1989, 1994) has repeatedly pointed out that all too often academic writing about the problems of youthful misbehaviour and of youth crime is ahistorical in character. He has charted generalized complaints about 'juvenile delinquency' since at least pre-industrial seventeenth-century 'Merrie' England. More distinctively 'modern' forms of complaint about juveniles began to appear during the urban and industrial revolutions of the early nineteenth century. Indeed, although youth cultures in Britain are generally thought of as a post-War phenomenon, they have been observable for far longer. The unhelpful, historical amnesia which tends to characterize the youth question means that 'youth cultures and youth crime assume the appearance of ever-increasing outrage and perpetual novelty' (Pearson 1994: 1168). However, just as we must guard against the assumption that the problems of youth are a peculiarly post-War phenomenon so, having discovered parallels for our modern concerns as far back as the seventeenth century, we must not fall into the trap of thinking that it was ever thus. Both continuity and change are visible, and it is important to pay due regard to each.

THE DISCOVERY OF ADOLESCENCE

In England and Wales no child may be guilty of a criminal offence below the age of ten. Between the ages of ten and eighteen, young offenders are dealt with in what is now referred to as the 'youth court', distinguishable in style and approach from the adult magistrates' courts which, together with the Crown Court, deal with offenders aged eighteen or above. This system reflects, in crude terms, the distinctions made between three life stages: childhood, adolescence, and adulthood. However, just as the system itself is the product of a number of important historical forces, so the categories of childhood, adolescence, and adulthood are socially constructed and have their own history. The French historian Philippe Aries argued that in the Middle Ages childhood was a considerably foreshortened period: 'Children were mixed with adults as soon as they were considered capable of doing without their mothers or nannies, not long after a tardy weaning (in other words at about the age of seven)' (Aries 1973: 395). Society was divided by status which, generally speaking, was not age-related (Stone 1979). However, from the seventeenth century onward, childhood was progressively extended and increasingly separated from adulthood. In Aries' view, it is only since that time that we have become preoccupied with the physical, moral, and sexual development of young people. As childhood as a separate category evolved, so there developed with it the idea that children were a responsibility—that they required protection—and, moreover, that children were creatures with the potential for good and evil, discipline being required to ensure that the former predominated over the latter (Anderson 1980).

Furthermore, as these two phases in the life-cycle were progressively separated and, through restrictions on work and the formalization of education, the transition between the two was extended, so the opportunity for the development of a further, intermediary phase increased. This we have come to refer to as 'adolescence'. The meaning of this term changed considerably during the course of the twentieth century, now representing a longer period than it did even fifty years ago (Coleman and Hendry 1990). What brought this about? In part it was to do with the emergence and development of formal education in schools and, linked with this, significant changes in the family. These changes in family structures were, it is argued, bound up with the development of market capitalism (Shorter 1976) and the growth of individualism in philosophical, political, and religious thought (Stone 1979). The end product was the progressive isolation of the family, changing it into the type of private, domestic unit we know today, and, through the separation of work from domestic life, its transformation from a unit of production into a unit of consumption.

It was in the nineteenth century that the distinctively modern adolescent started to appear. The Factory Acts limited working hours, compulsory education began to develop from the 1870s—albeit slowly—and urban working-class young people were developing what can perhaps be regarded as the first modern youth subcultures (Davis 1990), such as the 'scuttlers' and 'peaky blinders' (Humphries 1981; Pearson 1983). Institutions were developed for delinquents and for those *at risk* of delinquency—the 'perishing classes'—and it was out of these that the modern juvenile justice system grew.

By the turn of the century, young people in the new cities and manufacturing towns were experiencing considerable economic independence and leisure time was expanding. It was at this time that heightened concerns about delinquency and hooliganism emerged (Rook 1899; Booth 1902). Perhaps the key representation of youth in the past century has been to see them as a 'problem'—either as its source, or as being 'at risk' (Griffin 1993). The close association between 'youth' and 'crime' has remained generally undisturbed ever since, and it has been paralleled by a continual nostalgic yearning for a lost 'golden age' of tranquillity and calm (Pearson 1983).

The 'discovery' of 'adolescence' (as understood as a physiological stage triggered by the onset of puberty) is generally associated with the American psychologist G. Stanley Hall. In his model, often referred to as a 'storm and stress' model, adolescence was conceived as a time of 'hormonal turmoil' (Griffin 1993: 16), in which young people required freedom in order to fulfil their potential, and control to instil discipline. Early theories of 'delinquency', such as that associated with Cyril Burt, owed much to Hall's work and shared elements of its biological determinism. Although theories of delinquency broadened in their approach during the course of the last century, the ways in which adolescence is conceived remain heavily influenced by the 'storm and stress' model. Nonetheless, even Burt's predominantly psychological theory of delinquency recognized the secondary influence of the social and cultural environment. Juvenile crime was generally perceived as resulting from deficient self-control and control by others, particularly parents. Poor social conditions and inadequate opportunities for constructive use of leisure were also seen as problematic, and the response to the problem of 'delinquency' was primarily via youth movements which sought to improve the leisure activities of working-class, or more particularly, 'rough' working-class, youth. Most of these movements were voluntary, often attached to churches. This conception of delinquency informed the philosophy and much of the practice of juvenile justice up to the Second World War and beyond.

Most official indicators of the level of juvenile crime suggested that it rose fairly steadily during the 1930s, and rose sharply, though with some ups and downs, during the War. War-time conditions—the black-out, high wages for youth labour, family disruption, the closure of schools and youth clubs—were blamed for much delinquency (Bailey 1987). Indeed, family disruption or dysfunction is one of the few 'factors' that appears with regularity in much of the theorizing about delinquency, including psychoanalytic approaches (Schoenfeld 1971), social control theories (Hirschi 1969), and social learning theories (Bandura 1977). With the end of the War and the advent of the welfare state, there was some expectation that crime would return to its pre-War levels. This proved not to be the case, though for the first decade or so the rate of increase in crime was not sharp. This was a time of broad political consensus (generally referred to as Butskellism) and, after a period in which consumption was held back by rationing and wage-restraint, eventually also a time of optimism and increasing affluence (see Downes and Morgan, in Chapter 10 of this volume).

YOUTH IN POST-WAR BRITAIN

The Butskellite programme of social reconstruction was aided and abetted by a vast army of scientists and professionals—planners, researchers, social workers, teachers —whose task was to support the state in its great endeavour. Considerable autonomy and power were often involved and, as will become clear in connection with the role of social workers in juvenile justice, continued well into the 1960s. Part of this project of reconstruction was the creation and maintenance of a new social order. The causes of disorder were believed to lie in the consequences of the War and in the continuing inequalities of the post-War era, the solutions in successful economic management and the reduction of inequality. Of great concern were the effects of the War on the family and children. If anything, the family became even more central to the understanding of delinquency in the 1950s; such work involving the '"discovery" (and persistent rediscovery)' of the 'problem family' (Clarke 1980: 73), together with the continuing influence of the work of Cyril Burt, that of John Bowlby, the ecological work of Mays, and the beginnings of community studies which identified the family as the 'central transmitting agency of social values and behaviour'.

'Youth' in post-War Britain appeared to transcend class. Although the subcultural styles that developed were, seemingly, distinctly class-based, there was wide concern over youth as a whole, and the development of phrases such as the 'generation gap' gave expression to the prevalent feeling that it was the differences between age groups as opposed to classes that were the more problematic. This received some support in sociological quarters from those who believed that traditional class divisions were being broken down by increasing affluence (Goldthorpe *et al.* 1969). Crucially, 'youth' were perceived to be one of the most striking indications of social change. For the moral entrepreneurs of the period, 'youth' was a problem (Newburn 1991). Most importantly, youth was 'a cornerstone in the construction of understandings, interpretations and quasi-explanations *about* the period' (Clarke *et al.* 1976: 9).

The number of known juvenile offenders began to rise substantially from about 1955, as did public concern about youth in general. Young people were beginning to enjoy a degree of autonomy that was significantly greater than that of previous generations, and at the heart of this was their generally increasing affluence (Abrams 1959; Pinto-Duschinsky 1970). This led to the growth of increasingly spectacular youth styles based around the conspicuous consumption of 'leisure and pleasure' (Frith 1983), linked with the emergence of what became known as 'mass culture' and the development of its most spectacular offshoot, youth culture.

The first of the major post-War subcultures was the 'Teds'. The appearance of rock 'n roll in Britain lit the touch paper of respectable moral outrage (Gillett 1983), and the quiff, 'Duck's Arse', long jackets with velvet collars, bootlace ties, drainpipe trousers, and suede shoes defined the style. Moral concern was focused in the main on the sporadic violence at rock 'n roll movies, on the occasional confrontations between rival groups of 'Teds', and on the so-called 'race riots' of the late 1950s. However, concerns about the general behaviour of young people in post-War British society focused both on sexual and criminal behaviour, and images of juvenile delinquency, and more generalized forms of rebellion or resistance, were closely intertwined. It was not just violence associated with the 'Teds', therefore, but the blatant sexuality of what Melly (1972: 36) called 'screw and smash' music ('a contemporary incitement to arbitrary fucking and mindless vandalism'), which terrified older generations. Though post-War thinking—influenced by Fabianism and positivism—looked for solutions in increasing prosperity, it seemed clear that 'consensus, affluence and consumerism had produced, not the pacification of worry and anxiety—their dissolution in the flux of money, goods and fashion—but their reverse: a profound, disquieting sense of moral unease' (Hall *et al.* 1978: 233). The more liberal atmosphere of the 1960s, illustrated in the reform of the laws on obscenity, abortion, theatre censorship, capital punishment, homosexuality, divorce, and licensing, was counterbalanced, at least in part, by moral campaigns to check the 'permissive revolution' (Newburn 1991; see also Downes and Morgan, in Chapter 10 of this volume).

A succession of white working-class subcultures followed in the wake of the Teds, and with what appeared to be increasing speed. These included 'Mods'—of various sorts—whose style was 'sharp but neat and visually understated' (Hebdige 1976: 88) and broad enough to encompass sharp-suits, parkas, and the seemingly ubiquitous Vespa (Cohen 1972). In opposition, sometimes literally, always stylistically, were the Rockers. Similar to the Teds, in that they originated from lower down the social scale than the Mods (Barker and Little 1964), they were unfashionable, unglamorous, and associated with leather, motor bikes, and an aggressive, often violent, masculinity (Willis 1978). Perhaps the most starkly aggressive of all subcultural styles were the skinheads, who appeared in the late 1960s. The skinheads espoused traditional, even reactionary, values and, through their association with football violence and attacks on ethnic minorities and gays, quickly obtained folk devil status. Their racism, defence of territory, opposition to hippy values, their social origins (unskilled working class) and particular construction of style or 'bricolage' (Clarke 1976b)—

Doc Marten boots, cropped hair, braces—were seen by subcultural theorists as representing 'an attempt to recreate through the "mob" the traditional working class community' (Clarke 1976a: 99).

Subcultural theory grew out of a more generally functionalist sociology of delinquency, the origins of which lay in the Chicago School in the 1920s–1940s (see Rock, in Chapter 2 of this volume). It was not until the late 1960s that a distinctly British school of subcultural theory emerged. Its distinctiveness lay in taking traditional subcultural theory and locating it within cultural and historical time and place. This was in part a response to the perceived shortcomings of *anomie* theory, but also because North American theory was felt inapplicable to the British context in a number of ways (Downes and Rock 1982). As British subcultural theory developed, so its focus moved gradually away from delinquency and increasingly towards leisure and style (the main exceptions being Patrick (1973), Parker (1974), and Gill (1977)). Parker's is a study of criminal subculture in which theft from cars provided a profitable adolescent interlude before the onset of a more respectable adult life or a more serious and long-term criminal career. Both his and Patrick's study—in which the focus was on the machismo of the 'hard man'—brought insights from labelling theory to bear on the study of subcultures. Parker's 'boys' used theft as a means of dealing with some of the problems they faced, dissociating themselves in part from the values of the dominant social order and, like the delinquents in Downes's (1966) study, responding within the physical and material conditions which constrained their range of choice and freedom.

Subcultures emerged not just as a response to the problems of material conditions —their class circumstances, schooling, and so on. They were also taken to represent a symbolic critique of the dominant culture in which 'style' was read as a form of resistance. Subcultures, at least from the viewpoint of the more radical commentators of the 1970s, were essentially oppositional rather than subordinate. It was this opposition, fundamentally, which gave rise to the kinds of societal reaction that Stan Cohen, utilizing interactionism, labelling theory, and the idea of deviancy amplification, first described as 'moral panics', wherein 'a condition, episode, person or group of persons emerges to become defined as a threat to societal values and interests' (1980: 9).

The most recurrent forms of moral panics in Britain since the War have been those surrounding youthful forms of deviance—from subcultural styles, through football hooliganism, to drug use. For their members, subcultures allowed the possibility of providing solutions to material and socio-cultural problems, albeit through solutions that were symbolic. In a seminal essay on working-class youth culture, Phil Cohen (1972: 23) argued that the latent function of subculture was to

express and resolve, albeit 'magically', the contradictions which appear in the parent culture. The succession of subcultures which this parent culture generated can thus all be considered as so many variations on a central theme—the contradiction, at an ideological level, between traditional working-class puritanism and the new hedonism of consumption; at an economic level between a part of the socially mobile elite or a part of the new lumpen proletariat.

The solution, however, is largely expressed through style rather than crime. The style of each subculture involves the creation of identities and images built upon objects appropriated from other cultures and eras. It was at this point that the vocabulary of cultural studies met various strands of the sociology of deviance. Discerning 'the hidden messages inscribed in code on the glossy surfaces of style, to trace them out as maps of meaning' (Hebdige 1979: 18), became the key task.

Though the bulk of youthful styles in the 1960s were of working-class origin, the last years of the decade also saw the development of a middle-class counter-culture which, associated with both permissiveness and drug use, was guaranteed a hostile reaction from 'respectable' society. Brake argues that hippy culture in Britain was made up largely of students and ex-students and 'provided a moratorium for its members of approximately five years in which to consider one's identity and relationship to the world' (1985: 95). Drugs and sex were the focuses of moral concern, and the late 1960s saw significant increases in prosecutions for possession of marijuana and a concerted campaign of prosecutions against the underground press (Palmer 1971; Newburn 1991).

The dominant focus of British subcultural theory in the 1970s was on white, working-class, male culture (Dorn and South 1982). There were, at least in the earliest years of such writing, few attempts to understand either female delinquency or the styles associated with female subcultures, though the work of Angela McRobbie was both an early and a consistent exception to this (McRobbie and Garber 1976; McRobbie 1980, 1991). According to McRobbie and Garber (1976), because of their position within public and private worlds, girls tend to be pushed to the periphery of social activities, and much 'girl culture' becomes a culture of the bedroom rather than the street (see also Frith 1983). It is this, McRobbie (1980: 40) argues, that most subcultural theorists ignore:

in documenting the temporary flights of the Teds, Mods or Rockers, they fail to show that it is monstrously more difficult for women to escape (even temporarily) and that these symbolic flights have often been at the expense of women (especially mothers) and girls. The lads' . . . peer-group consciousness and pleasure frequently seem to hinge on a collective disregard for women and sexual exploitation of girls.

Subcultural theory had little to offer by way of explanation of the involvement of young women in criminal activity. In the 1980s, however, as the youth cultural scene went quiet, so the sociological students of style moved their focus away from youth and towards sexuality and ethnicity (McRobbie 1994a; see also Heidensohn, in Chapter 15 of this volume).

By comparison with the 1960s, the early 1970s were a relatively quiet time on the youth subcultural front, though they did see the blossoming of Afro-Caribbean cultural resistance, in part associated with, and reinforced by, the mugging panic of the mid-1970s (Hall *et al.* 1978). Up to this point there appears to have been no explicit association between black youth and crime. Such an association became firmly established, and the 'view of the blacks as innately criminal, or at least more criminal than the white neighbours whose deprivation they share, which became "common sense" during the early 1970s, is crucial to the development of new definitions of the black problem and new types of racial language and reasoning' (Gilroy 1987: 109). In subcultural terms, Hebdige (1987) argues that as the mood of some black British youth became more angry and bitter, so the central messages of reggae and of Rastafarianism became increasingly relevant (see Cashmore 1983).

In the late 1970s reggae also attracted punks 'who wished to give tangible form to their alienation' (Hebdige 1979: 63). First visible around 1976, punk was visually and verbally violent, but less frequently physically so than was publicly portrayed (Savage 1996). Moreover, with its links with Malcolm McLaren and Vivienne Westwood's King's Road shop, *Sex*, it incorporated a degree of commercialism which some commentators viewed as distinguishing it from previous, more 'authentic' subcultural styles (though for criticisms of this view, see McRobbie 1994b; Thornton 1995). Punk attempted to undermine 'every relevant discourse' (Hebdige 1979: 108). It used bin liners, safety pins, PVC, graffiti, ripped clothing, and bondage gear as a counterpoint to conventional dress style; and its music, dancing, band names, song titles, and language (Laing 1985) provided further shock tactics to reinforce the sought-after outcast status. 'Things were never the same after punk' (McRobbie 1994b: 159), and if hippies were a direct product of the permissive 1960s and early 1970s, and punk was, in part, a reaction to hippy romanticism, youth culture in the 1980s and after was profoundly shaped by the conservatism, economic depression, and the highly individualized consumerism of the times.

YOUTH AT THE *FIN DE SIÈCLE*

Through the late 1970s and into the 1980s, social and economic conditions for many young people became dramatically tougher. The key defining features were unemployment and racism, and it was against this background that African-Caribbean cultural resistance burgeoned and that 'punk' appeared. From the late 1970s onward, youth unemployment became a permanent feature of the social landscape: by the mid-1980s less than three-tenths of sixteen to seventeen-year-olds had full-time jobs (Roberts 1995). In parallel with the precipitous decline in youth employment, especially full-time youth employment, and the withdrawal of entitlement to benefits for most sixteen to seventeen-year-olds, there was also a significant expansion in the late 1980s of youth training schemes, though these have declined once more, and a massive rise in the numbers 'staying on' in education.[2] The major consequence of these structural changes was to extend and complicate the transition from dependent childhood to independent adulthood (Newburn 2002). The developing gap between 'work rich' and 'work poor' families has meant that at least a proportion of young people face considerable difficulties in negotiating the now extended transition into adult life (Wallace 1987; Jones 1995). There is a further, small group about whom relatively little is known. These young people, who are not in education (often having been excluded), training, or work, will disappear from the system altogether. For some this will be temporary, others may be 'permanently lost'; and it is

[2] The activity status of 16 to 17-year-olds illustrates the changes. In 1985, 29 per cent of 16 to 17-year-olds were in a full-time job and 37 per cent in full-time education. By 1992, the respective figures were 13 per cent and 66 per cent.

around these young people that many concerns about future criminal activity coalesce (Hagell and Newburn 1994).

As the world of work has retreated as a realistic prospect for many, so, it is argued, lifestyles dominated by consumption have come closer to the foreground. This was reflected in youth culture in the 1980s which 'became more of an advertising medium than ever before; it was notable not for opposition, but for its role in selling everything from Levi 501 jeans to spot cream' (Redhead 1990: 105). As a consequence, much was made of the supposed 'end of youth culture'. Bottoms and Wiles (1994) suggest that one of the consequences of the increasing dominance of consumption is a gradual relocation of sources of trust in late modern society from groups or collectivities— kin, local community, religious group—to individualized relations. Given the import- ance of collective norms in limiting individual deviant actions, the criminogenic consequences of the relocation of trust are easy to see. Furthermore, they argue, this decline in traditional collectivities has impacted negatively on age-integrated leisure patterns, and this, linked to globalization of aspects of youth culture and consump- tion, is likely to reinforce both age-specific activities and the boundaries between 'youth' and other social groups. In such circumstances, 'respectable fears' about young people become exacerbated. The most recent and most consistent of respect- able fears about youth concern drugs and drug use (Parker *et al.* 1998).

The late 1980s and 1990s saw the emergence of dance-based, drug-associated youth cultural styles, to which the acid house subculture and subsequent rave 'movement' or 'scene' were central. With its origins in Chicago House music and Euro-Pop (the Balearic Beat), acid house enjoyed a brief moment of approbation in the media before its drug connections led to inevitable backlash. Acid house parties and, more particu- larly, the use of ecstasy were the focal point of moral campaigns. Such partying—or 'hedonism in hard times' (Redhead 1993: 4)—was somewhat in contrast with the drabber youth culture of the late 1970s and early 1980s. Where 'punk had rejected such obvious pleasure a decade before . . . youth hedonism was now back, with a vengeance. A fortnight's holiday in the sun became packed into a single weekend— then the next weekend and the next' (McKay 1996: 105).

Rave culture inspired considerable moral indignation—at least in the Press—and was also subject to increasing legislative attention. First of all, Graham Bright MP—a well-known 'moral entrepreneur' associated with previous campaigns such as that against 'video nasties' (Newburn 1991)—introduced a Private Member's Bill further to restrict the holding of 'raves' or large-scale parties. The Entertainments (Increased Penalties) Act 1990 enabled courts to impose fines of up to £20,000, or prison sentences of up to six months, for holding illegal parties. This was followed by the Criminal Justice and Public Order Act 1994, which contained provisions for dealing with raves, together with other forms of 'collective trespass', particularly those associated with 'new age travellers'. In late 1996 a Private Member's Bill—the Public Entertainments (Drug Misuse) Bill—was introduced, with Home Office support, which contained provisions giving local authorities powers to close down clubs where there is evidence of the sale and use of drugs. Arguably, this represents a significantly more repressive set of measures than most previous post-War youth cultures experi- enced. Moreover, as we will see in a later section of this chapter, this was part and parcel of a more authoritarian approach to juvenile offending and deviance in general.

I suggested towards the beginning of this chapter that one of the key representations of youth during the course of the last century has been to see them as a 'problem'. Indeed, Pearson and others have illustrated the historical durability of such concerns. Nonetheless, a distinctive conception of adolescence emerged in the mid- to late nineteenth century, as did a more 'modern' concern about delinquency. In post-War Britain there emerged a more colourful or spectacular array of youth subcultures than had been visible before on the national stage. From the 1970s onwards, as structural circumstances changed and, more particularly, youth unemployment rose, youth cultures fragmented. If anything, this served further to reinforce the view that adolescence was a problematic period in the life-course, and that adolescents themselves were a problem. Though the specific nature of that problem varies by time and place, deviance and, more particularly, delinquency or criminal activity have generally been central to it. It is this connection between young people and crime to which we turn next.

YOUNG PEOPLE AND CRIME

Though the activities of young people are both more visible and more closely policed than those of other age groups (Farrington and Burrows 1993; Pearson 1994; Loader 1996), it is undeniable that a significant proportion of crime is committed by young people (Hirschi and Gottfredson 1983). This, in tandem with adult fears about youthful deviance, leads to young offenders occupying the 'dubiously privileged position', in changing guises, as society's number one folk devil (Muncie *et al.* 1995). Though official statistics can only ever provide a crude estimate, they nevertheless suggest that at least one-quarter of all recorded crime is committed by ten to seventeen-year-olds, and that over two-fifths is committed by those under twenty-one (*Criminal Statistics* 2000). Self-report studies confirm the by now largely accepted point that committing an offence in the teenage years is relatively common. Research conducted by the Home Office in the mid-1990s found that over half of males and almost one-third of females aged between fourteen and twenty-five admitted to committing one or more criminal offences at some point in their lives (Home Office 1995a). Figure 16.1 shows that approximately one-third of young males and just under one-fifth of young females aged fourteen to fifteen, for example, report having committed at least one offence in the past year.

The relationship between age and crime has been the subject of considerable criminological analysis, and Smith (1995: 395), echoing Hirschi and Gottfredson, has suggested that 'probably the most important single fact about crime is that it is committed mainly by teenagers and young adults'. The main evidence for this lies in the rate of recorded offending attributed to offenders of particular ages, and this is generally reinforced by data collected from self-report studies. Generally speaking, the peak age of offending is higher for males than it is for females; currently being

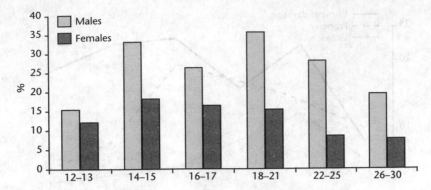

Fig. 16.1 Prevalence of offending (self-reported) in the last year, by age and sex

Source: Flood-Page *et al.* 2000.

eighteen for males and fifteen for females. Official statistics also suggest that the peak age of known male offending has increased; it was fourteen years in 1971, fifteen in 1980, and increased to eighteen by 1990, where it has since remained according to the 2000 *Criminal Statistics*.

The location of the peak age of offending in the mid to late adolescent years has traditionally been taken as indicating that a significant proportion of young people will simply 'grow out of crime' (Rutherford 1992). The first YLS (Graham and Bowling 1995) provided new evidence about the prevalence of offending for different age groups. The data showed that the peak age of offending for males to be fourteen for 'expressive property offences', sixteen for violent offences, seventeen for serious offences, and twenty for drug offences. Among females, the peak age of offending was fifteen for property, expressive, and serious offences, sixteen for violent offences, and seventeen for drug offences. Looking, however, at the proportions of males at different ages who admitted to having committed various offences within a one-year period, Graham and Bowling (ibid.) found that expressive and violent offences were most prevalent among fourteen to seventeen-year-olds, property offences (excluding fraud and theft from work) among eighteen to twenty-one-year-olds, and theft of motor vehicles among twenty-two to twenty-five-year-olds. When fraud and theft from work were included within the property crime category, twenty-two to twenty-five-year-olds had the highest rate of offending. They concluded that, among males, while the rate of participation in offending does not change significantly between the ages of fourteen and twenty-five, it does change markedly in character. Most particularly, they suggested that young men did not appear to be desisting from property offences in their early twenties. They cast some doubt, therefore, on the idea that young people tend to 'grow out of crime'. This thesis was explored again in the second YLS, which had an extended age range (twelve to thirty) and a larger sample size. Though this again found that rates of property offending differed from rates of criminal damage and violence, remaining fairly stable between the ages of eighteen and twenty-five, it found that the proportion declined thereafter (see Figure 16.2), possibly suggesting a somewhat delayed pattern of 'desistance' (Flood-Page *et al.* 2000).

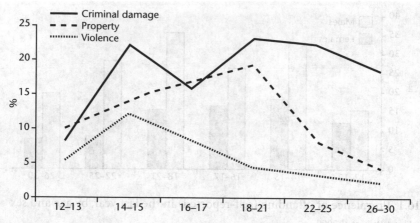

Fig. 16.2 Rates of offending for different types of offences by age (males only)
Source: Flood-Page *et al.* 2000.

THE NATURE OF MALE AND FEMALE OFFENDING

The predominance of property crime among those offences committed by young people is confirmed by official statistics. Juveniles, irrespective of age or sex, are most likely to be cautioned or convicted for theft and handling stolen goods. Burglary is the second most common source of cautions and convictions for male juvenile offenders (see Figure 16.3).

The pattern visible in Figure 16.3 has been relatively stable for some time. Thus, for example, for well over a decade theft and handling stolen goods, followed by burglary and then violence against the person, have, in that order, remained the most common offences for which male juvenile offenders are cautioned or convicted. The most serious offences are relatively uncommon. There has, however, been a rise in recorded drugs offences since 1985, and a significant rise in the recorded rate of violence committed by juveniles since 1987. In his analysis of the official statistics, James (1995) shows that the prevalence of recorded violence against the person by juveniles increased slightly among ten to thirteen-year-olds between 1980–87 and declined

Fig. 16.3 Young offenders found guilty or cautioned by type of offence, age and sex, 2000

slightly among fourteen to sixteen-year-olds. Thereafter, a dramatic change appears to have taken place—though it is possible that this reflects changes in processing rather than actual behaviour. There was a 52 per cent increase in the recorded rate of violent offending among ten to thirteen-year-olds between 1987–93, and a 29 per cent increase in the rate for fourteen to sixteen-year-olds in the same period; overall, an increase of approximately two-fifths in the rate of violent offending by juveniles. This may be compared with the prevalence rates for the most common juvenile offence category of theft and handling stolen goods, where there was a decrease of almost two-fifths between 1987–93. The juxtaposition of these two trends means that violent offences now account for a much larger proportion of recorded juvenile crime than was the case, for example, a decade and a half ago. As a proportion of the overall number of juvenile cautions and convictions, violence against the person rose from 3 to 4 per cent for ten to thirteen-year-olds between 1980 and 1987, and remained stable at 8 per cent for fourteen to sixteen-year-olds. By 1993, violence against the person accounted for 9 per cent of cautions or convictions among the younger age category, and for 13 per cent among the older age category. This rise is all the more startling given the fact that, as we shall see, the number of known juvenile offenders declined markedly in the same period.

According to both criminal statistics and self-report studies, violence by young females remains relatively rare. In 1980, 1,700 females aged ten to sixteen were cautioned or convicted for offences of violence against the person, this representing 5.4 per cent of all cautions and convictions for this age group. Since that time, the number of cautions or convictions for violent offences for female juveniles has been rising; and set against a background of the overall decline in the number of known juvenile offenders, violence also represents an increasing proportion of all offences for which young females are found guilty or cautioned. In terms of participation rates, self-report data suggest that approximately 7 per cent of fourteen to seventeen-year-old females will admit to having committed a violent offence within the previous year (Graham and Bowling 1995; Flood-Page et al. 2000). The most common offences committed by girls aged under fifteen are criminal damage, shoplifting, buying stolen goods, and fighting. Over the age of sixteen, most of these offences decline in frequency, though fraud and buying stolen goods tend to become more common (Flood-Page et al. 2000).

ETHNIC MINORITY YOUTH AND CRIME

A full discussion of ethnicity and youth crime is not within the scope of this chapter (but see Phillips and Bowling, in Chapter 17 of this volume). As was suggested above, it was not until the 1970s that there was any explicit association between black youth and crime. The increased concern arose partly as a result of the 'mugging panic' early in the decade, and other signs of poor or deteriorating relationships between the police and black youth. This was reinforced by the release of statistics by the Metropolitan Police suggesting that crime rates were particularly high among African-Caribbean youth in the capital. Additionally, other sources of data show black youth to be over-represented at all other stages of the criminal justice process: they are, for example, more likely to be prosecuted than are white youth, who are more likely to be cautioned (Landau and Nathan 1983); they are more likely to be charged with offences which must be heard in the Crown Court (Audit Commission 1996); and they are more likely to be remanded in, and sentenced to, custody (Bowling and Phillips, ibid.).

Given the now strong popular association between black youth and crime, it is perhaps surprising how little rigorous, empirical research has been conducted in the area. The most recent, and most useful, exception to this is the first YLS which included a booster sample of 808 young people from ethnic minorities (Graham and Bowling 1995). The data from the study are striking, for they suggest that, in general, white and African-Caribbean youth have similar rates of participation in offending (see Figure 16.4), though these are significantly higher than self-reported participation by South Asian youth.

Though overall levels of participation are similar for whites and blacks, there is significant variation between offence types. Thus, young white males are much more likely to be involved in fraud and theft from the workplace, whereas both African-Caribbean and Indian young people are more likely to steal from schools. White and Pakistani males are more likely to be involved in vandalism than are African-Caribbean young men.

YOUNG PEOPLE, DRUG USE, AND CRIME

There have been close associations between youth subcultures and illicit drug use since at least the hippy counter culture of the 1960s (Young 1971). However, far from being perceived as problematic, 'during the 1960s and 1970s it was fashionable in social science and liberal circles to question whether the prevailing concern about drug use might not be an example of . . . "moral panic"' (Dorn and South 1987: 2).

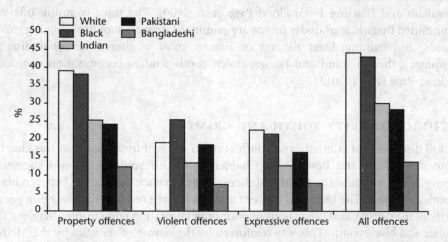

Fig. 16.4 Cumulative participation (self-reported) in offending by young people aged 12–25, by ethnic origin

Source: Graham and Bowling (1995).

This all changed in the late 1970s, and the years 1979–81 were the watershed during which 'the heroin habit' really began to take off and when, for the first time, its use became associated with the young unemployed (Pearson 1987). The number of known addicts trebled between 1979 and 1983, and research in the late 1980s confirmed the impression of a significant spread of heroin use (Parker *et al.* 1988). Public concern about increasing heroin use was followed by fears of a possible 'crack' epidemic, though, in the main, the worst of these fears have not been realized. Research in the 1990s suggests that 'the picture now is one of continuing widespread availability of a great variety of drugs, use being shaped by familiar factors such as local supply, contexts of use, preferred styles of consumption and purpose or intent' (South 1994: 399; see also South, in Chapter 25 of this volume).

Data on the incidence and prevalence of drug use among young people are now available as a result of a number of important surveys (*inter alia* Plant *et al.* 1985; Balding 1994; Measham *et al.* 1994; Mott and Mirrlees-Black 1993; Miller and Plant 1996; Ramsay and Percy 1996; Ramsay *et al.* 2001; Goulden and Sondhi 2001). Prevalence for fifteen to twenty-year-olds varies between approximately 10–35 per cent in the national samples and 5–50 per cent in local samples. The surveys show cannabis to be the most popular drug, though use of LSD, amphetamines, and ecstasy has increased since the late 1980s, as has polydrug use (Parker *et al.* 1995). Drug use and age are clearly linked. Use of illicit drugs is rare in early teenage years, increases sharply in the mid-teens, and is generally shown to peak in the late teens or early twenties (ISDD 1994). It has been the annual surveys conducted by Howard Parker and colleagues since the early 1990s that have probably been most influential in framing contemporary understandings of youth drug use (Measham *et al.* 1994; Parker and Measham 1994; Parker *et al.* 1995; Parker *et al.* 1988, 2000). Conducted in schools in the North West of England, the surveys provide data on use of illicit drugs among samples of children aged approximately fourteen in the first survey through to the age of eighteen. The surveys indicate relatively high prevalence rates of 'lifetime use' reported by over a third (36 per cent) of fourteen-year-olds to almost two-thirds (64 per cent) of eighteen-year-olds (Parker *et al.* 1998).

Both national and local surveys indicate that, at least until recently, drug use by young people appears to have been on the increase. Mott and Mirrlees-Black (1993), for instance, note that the percentage of sixteen to nineteen-year-olds reporting cannabis use more than doubled between 1983 and 1991. The late 1980s and early 1990s witnessed an increase in the use of dance drugs. Though this increase started from a relatively low baseline, by the mid-1990s dance drugs had become an important part of the youth drug scene (Measham *et al.* 1993; Clements 1993). Moreover, according to Parker *et al.* (1995), unlike the situation a decade previously, there were no longer any significant differences in the prevalence of illicit drug use by young men and women, though the authors recognize that in terms of the quantities, the frequency, and the repertoire of drug use, gendered differences may still remain. Parker *et al.* (1995) conclude that the ways in which young people perceive and relate to illicit drugs is changing quite dramatically, and that adolescents now live in a world in which the availability of drugs is unexceptional, even 'a *normal* part of the leisure-pleasure landscape' (1995: 25; though for a critical review see Shiner and Newburn

1997, 1999). The most recent national surveys of youthful drug use (Ramsay *et al.* 2001) suggest that there has been some stabilizing of prevalence rates, though there appears to have been a significant increase in cocaine use since the mid-1990s.

Against the background of rising levels of drug use it is perhaps not surprising that faith in primary prevention diminished and that attention increasingly turned to forms of secondary prevention, particularly the reduction or minimization of harm associated with drug use (Lloyd and Griffiths 1998). Recent years have seen growing attention, both at an official level and academically, paid to levels and types of drug use among 'vulnerable groups' (Lloyd 1998; Lord President of the Council 1998). A growing body of research has highlighted the particularly 'vulnerable' position of young offenders (Collison 1994; Newburn 1998, 1999). The most recent YLS found that three-quarters (74 per cent) of 'persistent offenders' reported lifetime use of drugs, and almost three-fifths (57 per cent) reported having used drugs in the past year (Goulden and Sondhi 2001). In addition to raised general prevalence rates, the survey also suggests that the rates of use of drugs such as crack and heroin are significantly higher among young serious and/or persistent offenders than they are in the general population, a finding reinforced by studies of adult offending populations (Bennett 2000).

YOUNG PEOPLE, VICTIMIZATION, AND THE POLICE

When the words 'youth' and 'crime' are linked, the picture in most minds is generally of the young person as an offender. Given the frequency and prevalence of offending by young people this is perhaps not surprising. Young people, however, are frequently victims of crime. Outside those studies which have focused specifically on child abuse and domestic violence, most criminological studies of victimization have paid scant attention to young people's experiences as victims of crime (though for some exceptions see Morgan and Zedner 1992; Anderson *et al.* 1994; Aye Maung 1995; Hartless *et al.* 1995; Loader 1996; see also Zedner, in Chapter 13 of this volume).

Whereas the first three sweeps of the BCS focused on the experiences of those aged sixteen or older, the fourth included questions for twelve to fifteen-year-olds. The results are illuminating. They show that twelve to fifteen-year-old boys and girls are at least as much at risk of victimization as adults, and for some types of crime, more at risk than adults and older teenagers (Aye Maung 1995). Within a period of little more than half a year one-third of twelve to fifteen-year-olds recall having been assaulted, almost a quarter had had property stolen, and over one in twenty had experienced theft or attempted theft from the person. By contrast, less than one-tenth of sixteen to nineteen-year-olds had been assaulted (the figure was 1 per cent for twenty to fifty-nine-year-olds) and 6 per cent recalled having property stolen. The majority of assaults on twelve to fifteen-year-olds were found to have taken place at or near school, to have generally involved perpetrators of roughly the same age and, in the bulk of cases, not to have been deemed to be terribly serious incidents, though 10 per cent had left the victim feeling 'very frightened'. Incidents of 'harassment' followed a roughly similar pattern. African-Caribbeans generally faced higher risks than young people from other ethnic groups. Only about one in ten incidents were brought to the attention of the police, though the proportion rose to one in five of the more serious incidents experienced. In contrast, one in three members of the sample said that they had had some form of contact with the police in the previous six to eight months. About one-fifth had been stopped and 8 per cent said they had been searched, a higher rate than is the case for older age groups (Aye Maung 1995). Juveniles were also less likely to be told why they were being stopped than were their elders. This, combined with the not infrequent experience for many of being 'moved on', contributed to the apparently paradoxical position in which young people feel both over-controlled and under-protected by the police (Anderson *et al.* 1994; Aye Maung 1995; Hartless *et al.* 1995; Loader 1996).

Despite the often-made assumption that young people are more likely to hold negative views of the police than older people, the 1992 BCS found that 88 per cent of twelve to fifteen-year-olds agreed with the statement 'We need a police force in this country to keep law and order', and 63 per cent thought that the police did a very (10 per cent) or fairly (53 per cent) good job in their area. Less than one-tenth said they felt the police did a very poor job. The most recent YLS (Flood-Page *et al.* 2000) found that over half (53 per cent) of young people aged twelve to eighteen felt that the police did a 'fairly good job', and a further 12 per cent felt they did a 'very good' job. Paralleling the attitudes within the black adult population, the least favourable views of the police were held by young African-Caribbeans, and indeed, the views expressed by young people generally were found to correspond closely with the views expressed by the adults in the same households.[3] The study was not able to explore such links in detail, but nevertheless concluded that 'how the police treat both young people *and* adults may well influence the attitudes the other group holds' (Aye Maung 1995: 57).

RECENT TRENDS IN YOUTH CRIME

Recent trends in recorded youth crime tell us at least as much about the workings of the youth justice system as they do about youthful offending itself. Prevalence increased markedly from the mid-1960s to the mid-1970s, then stalled and dropped slightly in the second half of the 1970s before rising in the mid-1980s to approximately the level of ten years previously. The most significant decreases in the number of known juvenile offenders took place between 1985 and 1989, though the number continued to decline until 1993. In 1985, a total of 172,700 males and 40,700 females aged between ten and seventeen were cautioned for or convicted of indictable offences. By 1993, the respective figures had dropped to100,200 for males and 29,300 for females, and the figure has remained relatively stable since that point (approximately 127,000 young people were found guilty or cautioned in 1998). Within this general picture, the patterns for younger and older juveniles depart slightly. The prevalence of convictions of ten to thirteen-year-olds has generally been in decline throughout the last thirty years, dropping from over 1,800 per 100,000 population in the early 1960s to just over 200 per 100,000 population in the early 1990s. The pattern

---

[3] The 2000 YLS did not find any significant differences in the views of different ethnic groups (Flood-Page *et al.* 2000).

for fourteen to sixteen-year-olds is rather different, with the prevalence of convictions increasing steadily throughout the 1960s and 1970s, then falling throughout the 1980s and particularly sharply in the second half of the decade. In the mid-1980s approximately 60 per cent of the disposals for this age group were convictions, the other 40 per cent being made up of cautions. By 1993, this situation had reversed, with the proportion of convictions dropping to slightly under 38 per cent of the total. For both age groups the use of cautions increased throughout the period until the mid-1980s, and then began to drop. A similar pattern is visible in relation to young females. The prevalence of offending by both younger and older female age groups increased up until approximately 1985, whereupon it began to drop and continued to do so until 1989. The overall movement since that point has been upwards. There is a strong pattern here and Farrington (1992: 155) has noted that 'the sharp decreases in prevalence between 1985 and 1989 apply to convictions and cautions, males and females, and both age groups'.

The most thorough analysis of the downturn in recorded juvenile crime rates in the late 1980s is provided by Farrington (1992). Although he says that 'it is embarrassing to have to admit that there is little hard evidence either about true changes in juvenile delinquency in England and Wales or about the most likely explanations for any such changes' (ibid.: 161), he nonetheless concludes that 'the official figures probably reflect official reactions to delinquency more than juvenile misbehaviour' (ibid.: 155). He suggests that the reverse of the net-widening process that took place in the late 1960s and early 1970s occurred; that an increasing number of juveniles were given unrecorded warnings *rather* than recorded cautions. What, though, of the possibility that offending itself was declining during the late 1980s? Farrington (ibid.: 157) concludes: 'Bearing in mind the very large increases in police-recorded crimes since 1985, it also seems likely that real juvenile offending has continued to increase since then, despite the decline in the official figures, *which is almost certainly an illusion caused by changes in police policies*' (emphasis added).

If Farrington is correct in his analysis that the fall in the number of known juvenile offenders does not reflect a *real* diminution in offending by juveniles—and it seems likely that he is—then it is to the operation of the criminal justice system that we must turn for an explanation. Doing so, however, is not to suggest that the rise and fall in numbers of known juvenile offenders are *merely* a product of the operation of the youth justice system, or that concerns about youth and crime are merely the product of labelling or moral panic. There are solid empirical reasons for the association between youth, particularly male youth, and crime. First, a significant proportion of recorded crime is committed by young offenders. Secondly, in whatever way it is measured, the peak age of offending is found to lie somewhere in mid- to late adolescence. Lastly, self-report studies confirm that offending is relatively common among young people. For almost one hundred years now the focus of responsibility for responding to, or dealing with, that offending has been on the juvenile justice system. It is to the philosophy and practice of that system that we turn now.

THE DEVELOPMENT OF YOUTH JUSTICE

The modern juvenile justice system emerged in roughly the same period as 'adolescence' and 'delinquency' were 'discovered'. Many of the social reformers in the nineteenth century who campaigned to protect children from danger and exploitation demanded that they should be removed from the 'adult' prison system and placed in privately managed, state-funded institutions. The Youthful Offenders Act 1854 provided the basis for reformatories for the 'dangerous classes', and legislation three years later established the industrial schools for the 'perishing classes'. Although initially they were part of the educational system rather than the penal system, they housed children aged between seven and fourteen who had been convicted of vagrancy.

Juvenile courts began to emerge around the turn of the century. However, they were not formally established until after the election of a reformist Liberal government in 1906. The Probation of Offenders Act 1907 provided a statutory basis for the probation service, and in 1908 the Children Act created the juvenile court. It also barred under-fourteens from prison and restricted the imprisonment of fourteen to fifteen-year-olds. The juvenile courts—special sittings of the magistrates' courts in the early years—were empowered to act in criminal cases and in cases of begging and vagrancy, though they remained, in essence, criminal courts. Nonetheless, reflecting the changes that had taken place in the nineteenth century, the Act endorsed 'the conception of the child or juvenile as a special category' (Garland 1985: 222).

Also in 1908, 'borstals' were created to cater for sixteen to twenty-one-year-olds (the 'juvenile-adult category') who 'by reason of his criminal habits and tendencies or associations with persons of such character, it is expedient that he should be subject to detention for such a term and such instruction and discipline as appears most conducive to his reformation and the repression of crime' (quoted in Garland 1985). The welfare principle was further enshrined in the Children and Young Persons Act 1933. The Act prohibited capital punishment for those under the age of eighteen, and reorganized the reformatory and industrial schools, bringing about the creation of 'approved schools' which provided juvenile offenders with education and training, and remand homes which kept remanded juveniles apart from adult prisoners. Between 1938 and 1945 recorded indictable offences rose by 69 per cent, and before long the prison population began to swell, and the increase in juvenile crime exposed the difficulties inherent in a system dependent on accommodation provided by charities and local authorities. A Criminal Justice Bill was introduced in 1947, which was heavily based on recommendations made before the War which 'strongly emphasised the unwisdom of sending young persons to prison' (quoted in Bailey 1987).

The 1948 Act consequently placed a number of restrictions on the use of imprisonment and marked the beginning of a trend restricting the use of custody for juvenile offenders. It also introduced remand centres, attendance centres, support for probation hostels, and abolished corporal punishment. However, the Magistrates' Association renewed their demands for a new short-term custodial sentence, and this was eventually accepted by the government. The detention centre order introduced by the Act was intended to be a short, unpleasant sentence which would combine hard work with the minimum of amusement—a sentence not unlike the 'short, sharp shock' experiment of the early 1980s. In fact, detention centres were not provided until the 1950s, and even then their development was slow. Continuing concern about the 'welfare' of juveniles also found expression in the Children Act 1948. This sought to end the placement of neglected children in approved schools alongside offenders, and set up local authority children's departments with their own resources for residential care—'the first professional social work service exclusively for children' (Harris and Webb 1987).

Levels of recorded crime rose in a generally sustained and sharp way from the mid-1950s on. For the first three decades of the period, the levels of recorded offences by juveniles followed a roughly similar pattern. Thus, there was an increase of approximately 98 per cent in the numbers of juvenile offenders per 100,000 population cautioned or convicted for indictable offences in the period 1961–85. During the same period the number of offences recorded by the police increased by over 150 per cent. Windlesham (1993) has argued that from the early post-War period onwards, 'the twin claws of the pincer that was to hold the development of penal policy fast in its grip were the remorseless increase in the incidence of crime, and the overcrowding in the prisons'.

JUVENILE JUSTICE SINCE THE 1960S

The 1950s closed with the Ingleby Committee, set up in 1956. The major focus of the Committee's deliberations centred around the conflict that it felt existed between the *judicial* and *welfare* functions of the juvenile court. Though its major proposals, including raising the age of criminal responsibility to fourteen, did not become law— the Children and Young Persons Act 1963, by way of compromise, raised the age of criminal responsibility to ten—one author in particular has argued that they were of considerable symbolic importance for later events (Bottoms 1974). Two White Papers, *The Child, the Family and the Young Offender* in 1965 and *Children in Trouble* in 1968, were followed by the Children and Young Persons Act 1969. The Act abolished the system of approved schools, and the remand homes or remand centres for juveniles which existed alongside them, and replaced them with community homes with residential and educational facilities. The juvenile court was retained. Care was preferred over criminal proceedings; the circumstances in which court proceedings were possible were narrowed. The intention was that the juvenile court should become a welfare-providing agency and 'an agency of last resort' (Rutter and Giller 1983), referral happening only in those cases in which informal and voluntary agreement had not been reached between the local authority, the juvenile, and parents (Morris and McIsaac 1978). It was also intended that detention centres and borstals for juveniles be phased out and replaced by a new form of intervention—intermediate treatment. 'This (though) was less a policy of decarceration than a reiteration of the traditional welfare abhorrence of the prison system' (Rutherford 1986b).

For most of the century, and certainly for the whole of the post-War period up to 1970, there existed a consensus the terms of which 'implicitly rested on the non-partisan character of crime and on the merits of gradual shifts towards rehabilitative policies for its control' (see Downes and Morgan 1997: 128). If the 1969 Children and Young Persons Act was the high point of 'welfarism', the general election of 1970 was the watershed for the previously existing political consensus, and perhaps for criminal justice generally (Bottoms and Stevenson 1992). Indeed, as was suggested above, the period has been characterized as one of marked political dissensus and a turn towards authoritarianism (Hall *et al.* 1978). The change of government which the general election brought about put paid to any possibility of full implementation of the 1969 Act, with the consequence that juvenile courts continued to function largely as they had before—criminal proceedings for ten to fourteen-year-olds continued, powers in relation to fourteen to sixteen-year-olds were not restricted, and the minimum age for qualification for a borstal sentence was not increased. Perhaps most significantly, although care proceedings on the commission of an offence were made possible, such powers were used exceedingly sparingly, and the number of custodial sentences rose from 3,000 in 1970 to over 7,000 in 1978 (Rutter and Giller 1983; Cavadino and Dignan 1992).

Against this background of rapidly increasing use of custody, it is worthwhile considering what full implementation of the 1969 Act would have meant. First, it would have abolished prosecution of any child under fourteen for a criminal offence, with the exception of homicide. Secondly, it would have restricted civil care measures for that group as well. Thirdly, wherever possible, the assumption would have been that children would be dealt with outside court. Though fourteen to sixteen-year-olds could have been prosecuted, non-criminal care proceedings would be available and the preferred alternative in most cases. For those prosecuted, there would have been two main disposals available—the care order and the supervision order—both of which would be supervised by social workers given considerable discretion (Bottoms 1974). The intention was that the use of penal custody for offenders aged fourteen to sixteen should be phased out (Nellis 1991). This added up to 'the most developed application of welfare principles to criminal justice ever seen in an English statute' (Bottoms and Stevenson 1992: 36).

Partial implementation, and the consequences which flowed from that, led one group of commentators at the end of the decade to argue that the 'tragedy' of the 1969 Act was that people had 'been persistently led to believe that the juvenile criminal justice system has become softer and softer, while the reality has been that it has become harder and harder' (Thorpe *et al.* 1980, quoted in Muncie 1984). Though only partly implemented, the Act became the major scapegoat for the perceived ills of juvenile crime and juvenile justice in the 1970s, and the 'welfare' model it espoused was replaced by an expanding youth justice system in which the emphasis was increasingly on 'justice' or punishment. The Act was attacked from all sides (Harwin 1982). Within three years of its implementation a sub-committee of the House of Commons Expenditure Committee had been set up to make recommendations for change. While accepting that there was a class of juvenile that required care and support rather than punishment, the Committee argued that it was important to 'hasten the process in the case of certain offenders to deter others from embarking on criminal activities, to contain a hard core of persistent offenders, and to punish some offenders' (House of Commons Expenditure Committee 1975, quoted in Morris and Giller 1987). In response the government issued a White Paper which was equally 'bifurcatory' in its approach. It recommended both a shift away from residential care and towards supervision and fostering, while also articulating considerable concern about what it believed to be the inadequate powers available for dealing with 'serious and persistent offenders' (Home Office *et al.* 1976: para. 3). Bifurcation, or the 'twin-track approach' (Bottoms 1977), is one in which the penalties are simultaneously increased for serious offenders and decreased for less serious offenders. The 1970s witnessed a doubling of the use of custody for juveniles with a concomitant decline in the use of community-based alternatives, while at the same time the use of cautions increased substantially.

Youth justice policy at the end of the 1970s 'bore little resemblance to that proposed in the 1969 Act' (Morris and Giller 1987) and the Conservative manifesto of 1979 promised to strengthen sentencing powers with respect to juveniles and young adults. The 1980 White Paper, *Young Offenders*, included proposals for the reintroduction of a limited number of detention centres with 'tougher' regimes—the so-called 'short, sharp shock' treatment first mooted by William Whitelaw when Shadow Home Secretary (Harwin 1982). This 'experiment' began in two centres—Send and New Hall —in 1980. The Home Secretary announced that life at the centres would 'be conducted at a brisk tempo. Much greater emphasis will be put on hard and constructive activities, on discipline and tidiness, on self-respect and respect for those in authority . . . These will be no holiday camps and those who attend them will not ever want to go back' (quoted in Home Office 1984b). The experiments were quickly found to fail. The Home Office Young Offender Psychology Unit, which evaluated the initiatives, concluded: 'Apparently, the announcement of the policy did not affect crime rates generally: there was no interruption in trends in crime among young people generally, nor in the catchment areas of the two pilot project regimes especially' (Home Office 1984b). Yet Whitelaw's successor, Leon Brittan, remained steadfast in his public support of the new regimes, and announced that they were to be extended to all detention centres (Muncie 1990). 'The political damage was limited', suggests Windlesham (1993: 161), 'but it is hard to avoid the verdict that sound penal administration was made to serve the needs of a defective icon of political ideology'. The Thatcherite rhetoric remained tough. However, the legislation emanating from the Home Office —at least as far as juveniles were concerned—contained countervailing tendencies. Thus, the Criminal Justice Act 1982 aimed to limit the use of custody for young offenders; it shortened the detention centre sentence, and the end of borstals and indeterminate sentences was signalled with the new order for 'Youth Custody' (the institutions becoming known as Youth Custody Institutions). It was against this background that the significant and sustained decline in recorded crime by young people took place in the latter half of the 1980s. The paradox is that 'the decade of "law and order" was also the decade of what has been called "the successful revolution" in juvenile justice' (Rutherford 1986a), and Lord Windlesham, himself a former Home Office minister, described this transformation as 'one of the most remarkable post-War achievements of deliberate legislative enactment' (Windlesham 1993).

THE SUCCESSFUL REVOLUTION?

The 1980s have seen a revolution in the way the juvenile justice system operates in England and Wales. There are few areas of criminal justice practice of which we can be proud but this is an exception ... Many notions, which once seemed totally unrealistic, such as the abolition of juvenile imprisonment, are now viewed as achievable. (Jones 1989: i)

The reason that it was possible to make such a statement lay in the fall in the number of known juvenile offenders already described and in the declining number of fourteen to sixteen-year-olds receiving custodial sentences. The number of male juveniles receiving custodial orders in England and Wales in 1988 was less than half that in 1984, and under 42 per cent of those in 1981 (see Figure 16.5), a decline in the use of custody not seen for other age groups (see Morgan, in Chapter 30 of this volume). Neither was there a similar fall in the numbers of juveniles remanded in care or custody prior to sentence during the period in which the use of immediate custody for juveniles declined.

Several factors must be considered in explaining the remarkable fall in the use of custody for juveniles during the 1980s, and the decline in known juvenile offenders during the second half of that decade. First, there is demographic change. During the period 1981–8 there was approximately an 18 per cent drop in the population of fourteen to sixteen-year-old males. This clearly had an impact on the overall numbers sentenced to immediate custody, but it does not explain the fall in the proportion of fourteen to sixteen-year-old males sentenced to custody, from 12 per cent in 1985 to 7 per cent in 1990.

Secondly, there were the provisions contained in the Criminal Justice Act 1982. The new powers it provided to magistrates to use the determinate sentence of youth custody (rather than commit to Crown Court with a recommendation for borstal training), and the reduction in the minimum length of the detention centre order it brought about, were widely thought to presage an increase in the prison population. However, the Act also contained restrictions on the use of custody and introduced a range of non-custodial penalties. Community service became available for sixteen-year-olds, though reservations were expressed about the appropriateness of the provision on the grounds that it might be used less as an alternative to custody and more as

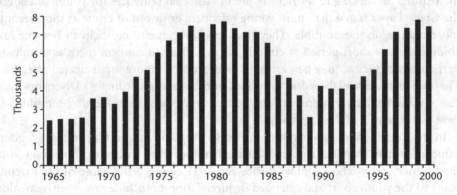

Fig. 16.5 Young offenders sentenced to immediate custody, 1965–2000

an alternative to other non-custodial penalties. Early indications, however, were that this was not the case and that the type of offender receiving community service was not dissimilar to that receiving custody. New requirements that could be added to supervision orders were also introduced and Allen (1991) has argued that, while it is far from conclusive, there is some evidence to suggest that supervision orders were used as an increasingly higher tariff option throughout the 1980s.

Thirdly, there was the increase of intensive intermediate treatment schemes. The term 'intermediate treatment' (IT) first appeared in the White Paper which preceded the Children and Young Persons Act 1969 (Home Office 1968). IT was originally to be one possible requirement of a supervision order under the 1969 Act. However, because of the difficulties existing in juvenile justice in the early 1970s, IT initially made little progress. A number of initiatives followed which aimed 'to relocate inter-mediate treatment at a higher point in the tariff' (Bottoms *et al.* 1990), key amongst which was what later became known as 'systems management' or the 'new orthodoxy' (Jones 1984). The decisive change followed the publication of a circular by the then Department of Health and Social Security, which stressed the importance of multi-agency approaches to the management of serious and persistent offenders, and made available £15 million of seedcorn money to develop IT projects as alternatives to custody and care. One hundred and ten projects offering 3,389 places were set up by voluntary bodies in sixty-two local authority areas between 1983 and 1987 (Allen 1991). Though it is difficult to assess the impact of IT, the decline in the proportionate use of imprisonment for juveniles between 1985 and 1990 suggests that it served as an alternative to custody (though see Parker *et al.* 1989).

Fourthly, there was diversion from court, the most important form of diversion in the period. This, as was shown in Farrington's (1992) analysis of crime trends in the period, appears to be key in understanding the very significant decline in the number of juvenile offenders being formally processed in the latter half of the 1980s. Indeed, so successful was the general cautioning policy in relation to juveniles believed to be that, as early as the 1988 Green Paper *Punishment, Custody and the Community*, the Home Office signalled its intention to transfer the lessons learnt in juvenile justice to policies in relation to offenders more generally, though it recognized that modifica-tions would need to be made (Home Office 1988: paras 2.17–2.19). In emphasizing the reasons for seeking to restrict the use of custodial sentences for young offenders, the Green Paper stated that 'most young offenders grow out of crime as they become more mature and responsible. They need encouragement and help to become law abiding. Even a short period of custody is quite likely to confirm them as criminals, particularly as they acquire new criminal skills from the more sophisticated offenders. They see themselves labelled as criminals and behave accordingly'. Diversion from custody and from court were emphasized and, consequently, cautioning continued to have a central role in this approach.

In the same period, two major new pieces of legislation affecting young offenders came into force. The Children Act 1989 finally removed all civil care proceedings from the juvenile court. The Criminal Justice Act 1991 changed the name of the juvenile court to the youth court and extended its jurisdiction to include seventeen-year-olds. The Act reduced the maximum term of detention in a young offender institution to twelve months, and brought seventeen-year-olds within the ambit of s 53 of the Children and Young Persons Act 1933, which gives the Crown Court the power to order longer terms of detention in respect of certain 'grave crimes'. Again reinforcing lessons learnt from developments in practice over the past decade, the 1991 Act signalled the importance of inter-agency and joint working by giving Chief Probation Officers and Directors of Social Services joint responsibility for making local arrangements ('action plans') for dealing with young offenders, and more generally for providing services to the youth court. Lastly, not only did it represent the final nail in the coffin of the 'welfare' model, but it further reinforced, though temporarily, the pre-eminence of the 'justice' model in juvenile justice.

THE REBIRTH OF POPULIST PUNITIVENESS

In the first half of the 1990s there was a noticeable change in the tenor of official concern about juvenile offending. Concerns were fuelled by one or two very specific factors, including the well-publicized urban disturbances of 1991 (Campbell 1993) and an emergent moral panic about so-called 'persistent young offenders'. The Home Secretary at the time, Kenneth Clarke, in a speech to the Metropolitan Police in 1992, suggested that youth 'are committing a large number of crimes. There is a case for increasing court powers to lock up, educate and train them for their own and everyone else's interest. We will certainly be taking a long hard look at the options which are available to the courts in dealing with serious offenders of this age. If court powers need to be strengthened or new institutions created, then they will be'. Clarke's speech was widely reported and stories of 'persistent juvenile offenders', as they were generally referred to, started to appear on a regular basis in the press (Newburn 1996).

Clarke acted quickly. In March 1993, he announced that the government proposed to introduce legislation that would make a new disposal available to the courts. These 'secure training orders' were to be aimed at 'that comparatively small group of very persistent juvenile offenders whose repeated offending makes them a menace to the community' (*Hansard*, 2 March 1993, col. 139). The new order would apply to twelve to fifteen-year-olds (though this was later amended to twelve to fourteen-year-olds) who had been convicted of three imprisonable offences, and who had proved 'unwilling or unable to comply with the requirements of supervision in the community while on remand or under sentence'.

Public concern might not have reached the pitch it eventually did were it not for the tragic events of 12 February 1993 and their highly publicized aftermath. It was at approximately 3.30 that afternoon that two-year-old James Bulger was abducted from the Strand shopping centre in Bootle, Liverpool. As time passed, and the young boy remained missing, the search spread and intensified. Enhanced still photographic images from the closed-circuit television cameras at the shopping centre were broadcast on national television. These showed James walking with, or being led by, one of two young people with whom witnesses had seen him leaving the shopping centre; pictures which appeared to convey both innocence and, because of what was then already suspected and later confirmed, something much more sinister. Eventually, two days later, James Bulger's battered body was found near a railway line in Liverpool, some two miles from the shopping centre. The abduction and murder of such a young child would always have had a significant public impact. The Bulger case acted as a 'focusing event' (Birkland 1997)—a dramatic, sudden, and indicative illustration of policy failure. The arrest and charging of two ten-year-old boys 'inspired a kind of national collective agony' (Young 1996: 113), and provided the strongest possible evidence to an already worried public that something new and particularly malevolent was afoot.

The trial of the two youngsters accused of James Bulger's murder took place at Preston Crown Court in November 1993 amidst massive national and international media interest. On the day after the verdict, 25 November, the *Daily Mail* carried twenty-four stories about the case, and a total of almost forty stories in the three days after the trial. The broadsheets gave it similar space: the *Guardian* including twenty-two articles, and the *Daily Telegraph* twenty-three articles and two editorials (Franklin and Petley 1996). The tone of most of the coverage—despite the age of the offenders—was harshly punitive. Similarly, politicians of all parties became increasingly punitive in their pronouncements and, the Labour Party's clichéd but resonant soundbite 'tough on crime, tough on the causes of crime' apparently meeting with some success, the new Home Secretary, Michael Howard, used his speech at the Conservative Party conference to announce yet another new 'law and order' package. The choice that Howard made in seeking to bolster his party's and his own fortunes was to employ a strategy of 'populist punitiveness' (Bottoms 1995).

The package of measures that Howard announced involved a reassertion of the central position of custody in a range of sanctions he interpreted as having deterrence as their primary aim. Most famously, he announced that previous approaches which involved attempts to limit prison numbers were henceforward to be eschewed. The new package of measures would be likely to result in an increase in prison numbers, an increase which he appeared to welcome: 'I do not flinch from that. We shall no longer judge the success of our system of justice by a fall in our prison population . . . Let us be clear. *Prison works*. It ensures that we are protected from murderers, muggers and rapists—and it makes many who are tempted to commit crime think twice' (quoted in Newburn 1995, emphasis added). The Criminal Justice and Public Order Act 1994 doubled the maximum sentence in a young offenders institution for fifteen to seventeen-year-olds from one year to two. It introduced the possibility that parents of young offenders could be bound over to ensure that their children carried out their community sentences, and it provided for the introduction of a new 'secure training order' for twelve to fourteen-year-olds. The proposal was that five new secure training centres would be built, each housing approximately forty inmates. The new sentences would be determinate, of a maximum of two years, half of which would be served in custody and half under supervision in the community. There was widespread criticism of, and resistance to, the new provisions for dealing with twelve to fourte-year-olds. Home Office-funded research cast doubt on the likely efficacy of such a policy (Hagell and Newburn 1994), the main voluntary organizations in the field refused to consider becoming involved in the management of the new centres, and planning permission for the building of them was consistently refused by local councils. Though it was originally anticipated that the centres would be up and running in

1995, by the end of 1996 only one of the five contracts had been let and building of the centre had yet to begin. The resistance to secure training centres came mainly from professionals working with young offenders, rather than Opposition politicians. By and large, the secure training order met with relatively little political hostility within Parliament.

After the passage of the 1994 Act, the battle between the Home Secretary and his Shadow for the law and order 'high ground' escalated. A series of leaks from the Home Office announced numerous proposed initiatives. In February 1995, a leaked Prison Service document suggested that the government wished to introduce American-style 'boot camps' for young offenders, one of numerous US imports considered by both major political parties in the period (Newburn 2002). By August 1995, further leaks revealed that the government was to press ahead with the idea of boot camps—the first to be instituted at Thorn Cross near Warrington, though with a far more progressive regime than those associated with US models. Again, pressure delayed the opening until early 1997. Nonetheless, the predictable consequence of such punitive rhetoric was the increasing numbers of children and young people in prison establishments. The number of fifteen to seventeen-year-olds given custodial sentences rose by almost four-fifths (79 per cent) between 1992 and 1998. The number of young people serving custodial sentences more than doubled (122 per cent) between 1993 and 1999.

At the other end of the scale from custody, the cautioning system was also coming in for increased scrutiny and criticism, and Home Office Circular 18/1994 (Home Office 1994) sought to place further limits on its use. The 1990 Circular had stated that 'a previous conviction or caution should not rule out a subsequent one if other factors suggest it might be suitable'. At the launch of the new Circular, the Home Secretary outlined the new approach. He said: 'From now on your first chance is your last chance. Criminals should know that they will be punished. Giving cautions to serious offenders, or to the same person time and again, sends the wrong message to criminals and the public' (quoted in Evans 1994). At around the same time the Labour Party began to publish proposals for reform of youth justice under a future Labour government and, again, overhaul of the cautioning system was central.

THE AUDIT COMMISSION AND THE INFLUENCE OF MANAGERIALISM

Established to promote economy, efficiency, and effectiveness in public services, the Audit Commission became increasingly influential in criminal justice during the course of the 1990s. Though its initial focus was on policing (Morgan and Newburn 1997), by the middle of the decade it had turned its attention to the youth justice system and added its voice to the growing roll-call of commentators calling for increased emphasis on 'criminality prevention' and, in particular, support for those interventions early in life which research suggests hold out the best hope for reducing youth crime (*inter alia* Utting *et al.* 1993; Farrington 1996; Faulkner 1996; Allen 1997). At the same time that the Labour Opposition Home Affairs team were preparing their proposals for youth justice reform, the Audit Commission was engaged in its first major inquiry into young people and crime. The parallels between the Labour Party's pre-election consultation document, *Tackling Youth Crime and Reforming Youth Justice* (Labour Party 1996), and the Audit Commission's hugely influential report, *Misspent Youth* (Audit Commission 1996), are striking—both in terms of the issues covered and the proposals each contained.

The Audit Commission had little of a positive nature to say about the youth justice system and a number of biting criticisms. Its view was that the system in England and Wales was uneconomic, inefficient, and ineffective. There were at least six important ideas or conclusions bound up in the Audit Commission's report. The Commission was critical of the cautioning system, and particularly of 'repeat cautioning'. It argued that first-time cautions were reasonably effective, but that subsequent use became progressively less effective while simultaneously running the risk of bringing the youth justice system into disrepute. At a general level, it was critical of the lack of programmes directed at offending behaviour. While noting that Social Services Departments continued to appear committed to diversion, 'agencies were either opposed in principle to addressing offending behaviour outside the court system or the co-ordination between them was inadequate'. The problem, according to the Audit Commission, was that 'the agencies dealing with young offenders have different views about what they are trying to achieve . . . these different approaches need to be reconciled if agencies are to work together and fulfil their different responsibilities'. Here two critical themes are linked. The first was that different agencies do not necessarily share a consistent or complementary view of youth justice. The second was that, at least in part because of this, agencies were often poor at working together to tackle offending.

According to the Audit Commission, it was not just the approach of youth justice teams that was problematic. The whole court system, it suggested, was becoming less and less efficient. In its most damning indictment it suggested that 'overall, less is done now than a decade ago to address offending by young people. Fewer young people are now convicted by the courts, even allowing for the fall in the number of people aged 10–17 years, and an increasing proportion of those who are found guilty are discharged'. The system, they argued, needed to be streamlined and speeded up.

Lastly, the Audit Commission turned its attention away from the system of youth justice and towards the prevention of offending. Its approach was heavily influenced by the results of longitudinal criminological research that identified the 'risk factors' associated with offending by juveniles. These risk factors may be used to target areas where young people are at particular risk and help identify approaches that may reduce the risks. The Commission's analysis and proposals were predictably managerialist in character. Bottoms (1995) distinguishes between what he takes to be three distinct aspects of managerialism: its *systemic*, *consumerist*, and *actuarial* dimensions. It is the systemic form which is most helpful in making sense of the Audit Commission's approach and for analysing the general thrust of the subsequent reforming legislation, the Crime and Disorder Act 1998. *Systemic managerialism* within criminal justice tends to contain some or all of the following features:

1. An emphasis on inter-agency cooperation in order to fulfil the overall goals of the system.

2. An emphasis on creating an overall strategic plan for criminal policy.

3. The creation of key performance indicators, related to the overall 'mission statement' of each agency.

4. Active monitoring of aggregate information about the system and its functioning.

The emphasis in the Commission's report was on clarity of objectives, consistency of approach, and targeting of resources. Central to this was the aim that resources be shifted from processing to prevention. Its central recommendations emphasized the need for: consistency of aims and objectives in youth justice; improved inter-agency cooperation in meeting these aims and objectives; the creation of appropriate performance indicators for all agencies involved in youth justice; and the monitoring of performance so as to improve the functioning of the system.

NEW LABOUR, NEW YOUTH JUSTICE?

The history of youth justice has been one of competing philosophies, approaches, and ideologies. For much of the twentieth century an uneasy balance existed in the juvenile justice system between welfarism, on the one hand, and a punitive tendency, on the other, that at best mitigated and at worst subverted the more rehabilitative approaches to youth crime (Newburn 1997). In the latter part of the century, in the interstices between the decline of the rehabilitative ideal in the 1960s and 1970s and the rediscovery of authoritarian populism in the 1990s (Newburn 1996), there emerged a 'third way' in youth justice—what John Pratt has termed 'corporatism' (Pratt 1989). Efficient and effective 'management' of the offending population came to the fore, underpinned by the rediscovery that 'something works'. In the late 1990s New Labour, as it had by then become, added a further dose of managerialism, together with its own potent blend of communitarianism and populism (Newburn 1998). The consequence, allegedly, has been the emergence of a 'new youth justice' (Goldson 2000), the 'broad contours' of which 'are easily described' (Pitts 2000). In fact, New Labour's youth justice is somewhat tricky to characterize for, as some commentators have pointed out, one key element of the government's style was to 'talk tough' while behind the scenes enabling sometimes more enlightened practices to be developed and promulgated (Savage and Nash 2001).

The first six months in government were characterized by a frenzy of activity. Within the space of less than two months, six consultation documents on the subject of youth crime were published (Home Office 1997a, 1997b, 1997c, 1997d, 1997e, 1997f),[4] each of which contained considerable discussion of various proposals that had first been outlined in *Tackling Youth Crime, Reforming Youth Justice* (Labour Party

---

[4] Windlesham (2001: 78) observes correctly that because so much of New Labour's discussion of its proposals occurred in the pre-election period, the pre-legislative period is more accurately thought of as 'informative rather than consultative'.

1996). The major proposals eventually found their way, largely unchanged, into the government's flagship legislation, the Crime and Disorder Act 1998. This Act, though followed by others, contains the key elements of Labour's 'new youth justice': the establishment of the Youth Justice Board (YJB); the creation of Youth Offending Teams (YOTs); and the restructuring of the non-custodial penalties available to the youth court. In its White Paper, *No More Excuses* (Home Office 1997d), the government had said that there was:

Confusion about the purpose of the youth justice system and principles that should govern the way in which young people are dealt with by youth justice agencies. Concerns about the welfare of young people have too often been seen as in conflict with the aims of protecting the public, punishing offences and preventing offending.

In an attempt to ameliorate such confusion the reforms contained, for the first time, an overarching mission for the whole youth justice system. Section 37 of the Crime and Disorder Act establishes that, 'It shall be the principal aim of the youth justice system to prevent offending by children and young persons'.

Historically, juvenile justice had a 'broad church' in which considerable variation in service delivery at the local level had existed. Inspired in part by the excoriating criticisms of the extant system by the Audit Commission (1996), New Labour sought, as in so many areas, to impose order from the centre. With an enormous legislative programme envisaged, the new Home Secretary established a youth justice task force in June 1997. Its aims were to maintain the momentum developed in opposition and to provide a continuing formal link with the major agencies involved with young offenders (Windlesham 2001). The chair of the task force was Norman Warner, who had been adviser to Jack Straw in opposition, and its secretary was one of the authors of the Audit Commission report. When, as a result of s 41 of the Crime and Disorder Act, the YJB became a non-departmental public body sponsored by the Home Office, Warner became its chairman, and the Audit Commission author its first chief executive.

The YJB's principal function was to monitor the operation of the youth justice system and the provision of youth justice services, together with monitoring national standards and establishing appropriate performance measures. The 1998 Act also allowed the Home Secretary to expand the Board's role and, from April 2000, the YJB also became the commissioning body for all placements of under-eighteens in secure establishments on remand or sentence from a criminal court. The Comprehensive Spending Review of the secure estate (Home Office 1998a) had concluded that there was 'little positive to say about the current arrangement . . . Regime standards are inconsistent and often poor. Costs vary considerably. There is no effective oversight or long term planning'. The YJB's role was therefore expanded to include commissioning places from Prison Service YOIs, local authority secure units, and secure training centres (STCs). In this connection, the Board advises the Home Secretary, is responsible for planning and setting standards, and accredits establishments that operate according to those standards (see also Morgan, in Chapter 30 of this volume).

The core of New Labour's managerialism was embodied in the creation of the YJB and the YOTs. The arrangements exhibited all four major characteristics of 'systemic managerialism', but it was the need for inter-agency cooperation that underpinned what was arguably the most significant reform introduced by the Crime and Disorder Act—the establishment of YOTs.

Prior to the 1998 Act, youth justice teams, comprised mainly of social workers, had had primary responsibility for working with young offenders subject to non-custodial penalties, and for liaising with other criminal justice and treatment agencies in connection with that work. Stimulated by a concern with efficiency and consistency on the one hand, and by a pragmatic belief in multi-agency working on the other, New Labour's new model YOTs had to include a probation officer, a local authority social worker, a police officer, a representative of the local health authority, and someone nominated by the chief education officer. YOTs have been in operation in all 154 local authority areas since April 2000. Social Services remain the major player in local youth justice, contributing 55 per cent of the YOTs' resources. They are followed by the police (13 per cent), probation (10 per cent), local authority chief executives (9 per cent), education (7 per cent), and health (6 per cent) (Renshaw and Powell 2001).

As Pitts (2001) notes, the constitution of these new teams echoes those of the Multi-Agency Diversion Panels of the 1980s and of the Northampton Diversion Scheme, the latter having been subject to particularly good press by the Audit Commission (Audit Commission 1996). However, whereas the Diversion Schemes were the child of an earlier era—a product of the 1980s 'corporatism' in juvenile justice (Pratt 1989)—YOTs were established not to divert but to intervene. The two primary functions of YOTs are to coordinate the provision of youth justice services for all those in the local authority's area who need them, and to carry out such functions as are assigned to the team in the youth justice plan formulated by the local authority. The Home Office-funded evaluation of the YOT pilots outlined the key assumptions about offending that informed the development of the new structures:

[The Crime and Disorder Act] has a central objective to prevent offending by children and young people and is concerned with addressing offending behaviour; with early interventions on the basis of risk assessments related to known criminogenic factors; with the systematic use of evidence-based practice; with reparation and, therefore, the needs of victims; and with the promotion of crime prevention measures. (Holdaway et al. 2001)

As implied above, the Crime and Disorder Act places a duty on local authorities to formulate and implement annual youth justice plans. In doing this, the authority must consult with the senior offices of the major agencies (police, probation, health) that make up YOTs. Such reports are published and submitted to the YJB, which monitors local provision and advises the Home Secretary. It was originally suggested that there be some further inspection of YOTs, either jointly by the Inspectorates of Constabulary, Probation, and Social Services along with Ofsted, or by the YJB itself (Leng et al. 1998). In practice, neither of these has yet occurred, and the work of YOTs (and arguably the YJB itself) remains one of the significant gaps in performance management in the criminal justice system—an odd situation for bodies that are the product of managerialism.

In addition to new forms of performance management and multi- and inter-agency working, New Labour also promised increased, and earlier, interventions in the lives of young offenders (and those 'at risk' of becoming young offenders). As outlined above, one of the clearest illustrations of the influence of the Audit Commission was New Labour's critique and reform of the cautioning system. The Crime and Disorder Act scrapped the caution (informal and formal) and replaced it with a reprimand (for less serious offences) and a final warning. As the name implies, one of the crucial characteristics of the final warning is that, except in unusual circumstances, it may be used only once. In addition to the change of nomenclature, and the more sparing manner of usage, the new system of reprimands and final warnings also set in motion a set of other activities—such as those previously associated with 'caution plus'— more frequently, and often earlier, than previously had been the case. Under the Act, all young offenders receiving a final warning are referred to a YOT. Offenders are then expected, 'unless they consider it inappropriate to do so', to participate in a rehabilitation programme (in which reparation is expected generally to be present). According to one informed commentator (Dignan 1999: 52), 'this new approach represents a considerable improvement on Michael Howard's much more restrictive plans simply to crack down on repeat cautioning'.

The Criminal Justice and Court Services Act 2000 removed the requirement that a police reprimand or final warning be given to a young offender only at a police station. This introduced the possibility of 'conferences' at which parents, victims, and other adults could be present—what has sometimes been referred to as 'restorative cautioning' (Young and Goold 1999). Though one of the intentions behind the new warnings system may have been to encourage more restorative practices with young offenders, to date there is little evidence that the new system is experienced as a more participative one by young people. Indeed, the Home Office evaluation of the Crime and Disorder pilots (Holdaway *et al.* 2001) raised questions about the appropriateness of some of the change programmes attached to warnings, and the most recent research, conducted in the North West of England (Evans and Puech 2001: 804), concluded that many young offenders and YOT workers saw 'the warning system as arbitrary, unfair and disproportionate'.

One major concern about the putative impact of the new system was that it might lead to a significant increase in proceedings against young people. It is somewhat early to tell precisely what the impact of the reforms will be. Evidence from the YOT pilots evaluation (Holdaway *et al.* 2001) did not suggest that there had been any significant increase in proceedings. Data from the pilot areas, and subsequently from the YJB (Renshaw and Powell 2001), show that just under 30 per cent of those receiving warnings have had one prior formal caution, and 3 per cent have two or three formal cautions recorded. Nonetheless, in the past two years there has been a decline in the number of young offenders being 'cautioned', and a contemporaneous increase in those being found guilty in court (see Figure 16.6).

The Crime and Disorder Act provided the basis for earlier interventions in the lives of young offenders, and for interventions in the lives and the families of those 'at risk'. In doing so it became 'the first piece of criminal justice legislation in England and Wales (at least since the Vagrancy Statutes of the early 19th century) to act explicitly against legal *and* moral/social transgressions' (Muncie 2001). Adopting the new 'what works' paradigm and using the language of risk factors (see Raynor, in Chapter 31 of

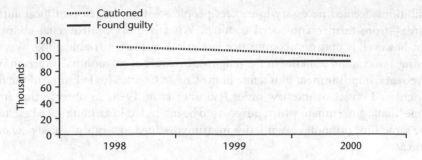

Fig. 16.6 Young offenders found guilty or cautioned, 1998–2000

this volume), New Labour introduced a range of new orders, covering both criminal and civil penalties, that focused not only on criminal activity but also on 'anti-social behaviour' and 'poor parenting'. It contained a number of orders—the child safety order, the anti-social behaviour order, the local child curfew order, and the sex offender order—where there is no necessity for either the prosecution or the commission of a criminal offence. These, together with the abolition of *doli incapax*, represent the most controversial aspects of the 'new youth justice'.

The Labour Party in opposition had been much influenced by the 'Broken Windows' thesis (Wilson and Kelling 1982) and sought to introduce a range of measures that would enable local agencies to tackle 'low-level disorder' or 'anti-social behaviour'. One of these new measures, the child safety order, relates to children aged under ten (i.e. below the age of criminal responsibility). In fact the order, made in a family proceedings court, is aimed at controlling anti-social behaviour rather than protecting a child's welfare, and involves placing a child under supervision usually for a period of three months, though up to a maximum of twelve months. Though the child safety order was subject to criticism in some quarters (Family Policy Studies Centre 1998), it was the anti-social behaviour order which drew the greatest ire. Originally termed the 'community safety order' in Labour's consultation documents, the order was renamed because of the potential for confusion with the proposed 'community protection order' (which became the 'sex offender order') and because the original title was felt not to capture the purpose of the order.

The order was designed specifically to tackle 'anti-social behaviour', defined as 'a matter that caused or was likely to cause harassment, alarm or distress to one or more persons not of the same household'. Prior to the Crime and Disorder Act, much of this behaviour had been dealt with, if at all, under the provisions of the Housing Act 1996, the Noise Act 1996, the Environmental Protection Act 1990, or the Protection from Harassment Act 1997. However, proceedings against juveniles were often problematic under such legislation (Nixon *et al.* 1999). By contrast, anti-social behaviour orders (ASBOs) were clearly designed with juvenile 'anti-social behaviour' in mind.

Applications for an ASBO can be made by the police or the local authority. The orders are formally civil, requiring a civil burden of proof.[5] The order itself consists of

[5] That this is the case was confirmed by the Court of Appeal (*R v Manchester Crown Court ex parte McCann* (2001)).

prohibitions deemed necessary to protect people—within the relevant local authority area—from further anti-social conduct. What is most controversial about the order, however, is that non-compliance is a criminal matter, triable either way and carrying a maximum sentence in the magistrates' court of six months' imprisonment, or five years' imprisonment plus a fine in the Crown Court. This led some of the most distinguished critics of the new order (Gardner *et al.* 1998) to observe that it was strange 'that a government which purports to be interested in tackling social exclusion at the same time promotes a legislative measure destined to create a whole new breed of outcasts'.

Though it initially appeared that there was some reluctance on the ground to use ASBOs, the most recently published information suggests that they are now being sought with increasing regularity. The take-up varies greatly across police force areas, although thirty-nine of the forty-three police forces in England and Wales have now applied for and been granted orders. The numbers of ASBOs applied for by police forces and local authorities have been more or less equal (49 per cent versus 51 per cent). In the first eighteen months of operation (April 1999 to September 2000), a total of 466 ASBOs were made and eighteen were refused (Campbell 2002). Just under three-fifths (58 per cent) were made against juveniles. Three-quarters of those given ASBOs were aged twenty-one or under. Home Office research identified a broad range of behaviours in the files of cases resulting in ASBOs, with the average case citing six different forms of anti-social behaviour. 'Threats' were most commonly cited— occurring in just under half of all cases—followed by 'intimidation' in over a third.

Concerns similar to those voiced about the ASBO were also aimed at the provisions in the Act that allowed local authorities to introduce 'local child curfew schemes'. The introduction of curfews in the UK had been foreshadowed by proposals in the consultation paper, *Tackling Youth Crime* (Home Office 1997b) and the White Paper, *No More Excuses* (Home Office 1997a). The former described the problem thus: 'unsupervised children gathered in public places can cause real alarm and misery to local communities and can encourage one another into anti-social and criminal habits' (1997b: para. 114). The provisions in the Crime and Disorder Act enabled local authorities, after consultation with the police and with support of the Home Secretary, to introduce a ban on children of specified ages (though under ten) in specified places for a period of up to ninety days. Children breaking the curfew were to be taken home by the police, and breach of the curfew would constitute sufficient grounds for the imposition of a child safety order. In practice, there has been remarkable reluctance to use such powers, and no child curfew orders had been made by the end of 2001. Despite such reluctance, and sustained criticism of curfews from some quarters, the government has remained keen on the idea of curfews. Armed with what appeared to be some positive results from an evaluation of a scheme in Hamilton in Scotland (McGallagly *et al.* 1998), new legislation was introduced to extend the reach of curfew powers. The Criminal Justice and Police Act 2001 extends the maximum age at which children can be subject to a curfew, up from ten to 'under 16', and also makes provision for a local authority or the police to make a curfew on an area and not just an individual.

The final element of the Act that drew sustained criticism (*inter alia* Wilkinson

1995) was the abolition of the presumption—rebuttable in court—that a child aged between ten and thirteen is incapable of committing a criminal offence (generally known as *doli incapax*). While the UK has long been out of step with much of the rest of Western Europe with its significantly lower age of criminal responsibility, the principle of *doli incapax* has traditionally protected at least a proportion of children under the age of fourteen from the full weight of the criminal law. However, during the course of the 1990s, spurred in part by the Bulger case, pressure had built up to abolish the principle, and politicians from both major parties were vocal in their criticism of it. In fact the doctrine very nearly disappeared in 1996, when the Divisional Court ruled that *doli incapax* was no longer part of the criminal law. This was, however, later overturned by the House of Lords (*C (A Minor) v DPP* [1996] 1 AC 1, HL), though their Lordships took the view that the law in this area was in need of reform. New Labour worked hard to appear a convincing party of 'law and order', and 'responsibilization'—of parents, of young offenders, and of those below the age of criminal responsibility—was a key part of its approach. The Home Secretary was vehemently critical of the doctrine of *doli incapax*, arguing that it was archaic, illogical, and unfair (Leng *et al.* 1998). He stated his reasons for the reform robustly: 'The presumption that children aged ten to thirteen do not know the difference between serious wrongdoing and simple naughtiness flies in the face of common-sense and is long overdue for reform' (Straw 1998). Though much of New Labour's discourse may have concerned 'what works', this hardly applied to the abolition of *doli incapax*, which had more to do with the government's 'remoralizing' mission and its focus on individual and parental responsibility (Muncie 2000).

Those concerned about the trajectory of New Labour's youth justice have also pointed to its perceived failure to tackle the problem of increasing use of custodial sentences for young offenders. Indeed, in its first term, Labour continued with the previous administration's secure training centre building programme—even arguing that they might be expanded—and introduced a new, generic custodial sentence: the detention and training order (DTO). Available to the courts from April 2000, in a DTO half of the sentence is served in custody and half in the community. Over 500 such orders have been made per month on average since they were introduced. The DTO is a single sentence replacing the secure training order (available for twelve to fourteen-year-olds) and detention in a YOI (available for fifteen to seventeen-year-olds). Long-term detention under s 53 of the Children and Young Persons Act 1933 for 'grave offences' remains an available sentence in the Crown Court. The intention behind the DTO was to create a more 'constructive sentence' (Home Office 1997d) in which a training plan would be drawn up for the custodial phase and where the subsequent period of supervision in the community would be considered an integral part of the sentence.

As such the DTO represents something of an increase in the powers of the youth court to impose custodial sentences. Thus, whereas the maximum period of detention in a YOI for fifteen to seventeen-year-olds had been six months for a single offence, the DTO has a maximum of two years. Similarly, although the secure training order for twelve to fourteen-year-olds already provided for a twenty-four-month maximum, the DTO has the potential to be extended to young offenders below the age of twelve.

In practice, the introduction of the DTO has if anything heightened the existing trend towards increased use of custodial penalties for young offenders. In the first year (April 2000–March 2001) a total of 6,058 DTOs were made. Of these, 617 (10 per cent) involved twelve to fourteen-year-olds, and 455 (7.5 per cent) young women. The numbers increased steadily during the first year of operation, from 1,235 in the first quarter to 1,799 in the fourth quarter. During this period the juvenile-sentenced population in secure establishments rose by 15 per cent, though the remand population fell by 21 per cent. The total number in secure facilities was higher during the course of the year than it was during the previous year. The average daily population was 2,807, compared with 2,611 in 1999—an increase of 7.5 per cent (Renshaw and Powell 2001).

RESTORATIVE JUSTICE AND YOUNG OFFENDERS

The influence of communitarian thinking, which was very visible in the Home Office's consultation documents published immediately after the 1997 general election, found form in the central place accorded to restorative justice in New Labour's youth justice. This was initially most visible in the place given to reparation in the Crime and Disorder Act, and in the support given to experiments such as that with restorative cautioning in Thames Valley (Young and Goold 1999).

Some aspects of the Crime and Disorder Act were based, at least in part, on ideas influenced by restorative justice. In particular, the reformed cautioning system, action plan orders, and reparation orders all sought to promote the idea of reparation and, wherever possible, to seek victims' views. The action plan order was designed to be the first option for young offenders whose offending is serious enough to warrant a community sentence. *No More Excuses* (Home Office 1997d) described the order as 'a short, intensive programme of community intervention combining punishment, rehabilitation and reparation to change offending behaviour and prevent further crime'. The evaluation of the Crime and Disorder pilots found that many YOTs developed standard programmes in order to meet the reparative requirements of the order, and that 'it is common for the same reparative activity to be built in final warning programmes, reparation orders, action plan orders and supervision orders' (Holdaway *et al.* 2001: 42).

The 'reparation order' requires young offenders to make reparation—specified in the order—either to a specified person or persons, or 'to the community at large'. The language of responsibilization was once again central to the underlying rationale. According to the Minister of State at the time (Michael 1998): 'With the restorative approach there is no way for youngsters—or their parents—to hide from their personal responsibilities'. The White Paper (Home Office 1997d) explained the order in the following terms:

Courts will have to consider imposing [this penalty] on young offenders in all cases where they do not impose a compensation order. The order will require reparation to be made in kind, up to a maximum of 24 hours work within a period of three months . . . Of course not all victims would want reparation. The government's proposals will ensure that the victim's

views will be sought before an order is made. Where a victim does not want direct reparation, the reparation may be made to the community at large.

There can be little doubt that there was a concerted effort by New Labour to make
both victims' views and reparation more central aspects of youth justice than previously had been the case. However, Dignan (1999: 58) was undoubtedly correct when
he argued that these 'reforms hardly amount to a "restorative justice revolution", let
alone the "paradigm shift" that some restorative justice advocates have called for'.
Following the implementation of the 1998 Act, the YJB also committed considerable
funds to the stimulation of restorative justice projects for young offenders and,
together with Crime Concern, issued guidance on the establishment of victim–
offender mediation and family group conferencing programmes. Of all New Labour's
restorative youth justice initiatives, arguably the most significant, however, has been
the creation of referral orders as part of the Youth Justice and Criminal Evidence Act
1999.

The referral order is available in the youth court and adult magistrates' courts, and
may be made for a minimum of three and a maximum of twelve months depending
on the seriousness of the crime (as determined by the court). The order is mandatory
for ten to seventeen-year-olds pleading guilty and convicted for the first time by the
courts, unless the crime is serious enough to warrant custody, or the court orders an
absolute discharge. The disposal involves referring the young offender to a youth
offender panel (YOP). The intention is that the panel will provide a forum away from
the formality of the court. As Crawford (2002) argues, the panels draw on at least
three sources: the Scottish children's hearings system (Whyte 2000); the experience of
family group conferencing (Morris and Maxwell 2000); and the history of victim–
offender mediation in England and Wales (Marshall and Merry 1990) and restorative
cautioning (Young 2000). The referral order constitutes the entire sentence for the
offence and, as such, substitutes for action plan orders, reparation orders, and
supervision orders.[6]

The 1999 Act extends the statutory responsibility of YOTs to include the recruitment and training of YOP volunteers, administering panel meetings, and implementing referral orders. Panels consist of one YOT member and (at least) two community
panel members, one of whom leads the panel. One or both parents of a young
offender aged under sixteen are expected to attend all panel meetings in all but
exceptional cases. The offender can also nominate an adult to support him or her. It is
not intended that legal representatives acting in a professional capacity be included in
panel meetings either directly, or as an offender's supporter. To encourage the restorative nature of the process a variety of other people may be invited to attend given
panel meetings (any participation is strictly voluntary). Those who may attend
include: the victim or a representative of the community at large; a victim supporter; a
supporter of the young person and/or anyone else that the panel considers to be

---

[6] However, the referral order may be accompanied by certain ancillary orders, such as orders for costs,
compensation, forfeiture of items used in committing an offence, exclusion from football matches, etc. (s 4(2)
and (3)).

capable of having a 'good influence' on the offender; and signers and interpreters for any of the participants in the process who require them.

The aim of the initial panel meeting is to devise a 'contract' and, where the victim chooses to attend, for them to meet and talk about the offence with the offender. It is intended that negotiations between the panel and the offender about the content of the contract should be led by the community panel members. The contract should always include reparation to the victim or wider community, and a programme of activity designed primarily to prevent further offending. Where possible it is recommended that reparation should have some relation to the offence itself. Early reports from the evaluation of the referral order pilots indicate mixed success. On the positive side, the youth offender panels appear to have established themselves within a year of operation as deliberative and participatory forums in which a young person's offending behaviour can be addressed (Newburn *et al.* 2001b). The informal setting of youth offender panels appears to allow young people, their parents/carers, community panel members, and YOT advisers opportunities to discuss the nature and consequences of a young person's offending, as well as how to respond to this in ways which seek to repair the harm done and to address the causes of the young person's offending behaviour. In addition, the successful integration of a large number of volunteers within the youth justice process provides an opportunity for a potentially powerful new exterior voice to participate and influence this arena.

The major difficulty encountered so far, as in other restorative justice developments (Dignan 2000; Miers *et al.* 2001), concerns the involvement of victims (Newburn *et al.* 2001a, 2001b). During the period of the referral order pilots, the level of victim involvement in panels was very low. There were a number of reasons for this. They appeared to concern issues of implementation rather than problems with the general principles underlying referral orders. The response of all the major participants in the process to date has been largely supportive of the general principles underlying such orders. The introduction of referral orders and youth offender panels and, more especially, the involvement of community panel members, represents a fairly radical departure in youth justice in England and Wales (Crawford and Newburn 2002). However, as a number of authors have noted (Dignan 1999; Crawford 2002; Crawford and Newburn 2002), there are some important tensions between attempts to extend the reach of restorative justice and other aspects of New Labour's approach to youth justice. First, as we have seen, apparent promotion of restorative justice exists alongside the continuing 'incarceration spiral' (Dignan 1999). Secondly, despite the more inclusionary tone associated with restorative justice, much contemporary youth justice discourse remains profoundly punitive. Thirdly, there is a tension between the managerialism at the heart of New Labour's reforms—and its concern with speed, efficiency, cost reductions, and performance measurement—and communitarian appeals to local justice in which there is an expectation that local people will play a central role in the handling of cases in their own local area (Crawford and Newburn 2002). Thus, the growing emphasis on output and outcome measurement puts at risk restorative justice processes, which place greater emphasis on providing a secure forum in which there is room for emotions to be expressed and for sometimes complex negotiations to take place. Most fundamentally, the greatest danger, perhaps as a result of a combination of the above, is that the very idea of restorative justice, 'and the mainly positive image which it has enjoyed thus far, might become subordinated to the more traditional and punitive approaches of the past' (Dignan 1999: 54).

CONCLUSION: WHITHER YOUTH JUSTICE?

The intermediary life-stage between childhood and full adulthood is generally thought of as a period characterized by problems and conflicts, partly because of the continuing dominance of the 'storm and stress' model, but also because young people continue to occupy a dominant position as a source of adult fears and concerns. Adolescence is characterized by physiological and emotional difficulties or pressures. In addition, young people appear to engage disproportionately in anti-social activities, including crime, in their adolescent years. For the majority there is a marked fall in criminal behaviour during early adult life, though a minority continue to persist in their offending 'careers'. In many ways, therefore, in relation to controlling crime, the aim has been the management of this 'problem population'. For the whole of the last century and into this, young offenders have also been seen as a group necessitating an approach different from that employed with adults.

For much of the twentieth century an uneasy tension existed between approaches that were broadly 'welfarist' in conception and intention, and a more punitive model which, in its 1970s incarnation, placed greater emphasis on individual responsibility, due process, and punishment. In the 1980s there emerged a 'third way' in youth justice—'corporatism'—in which juvenile justice specialists played a significant role in increasing the influence of diversionary practices and policies. More recently we have witnessed another significant shift in both the rhetoric and reality of youth justice. In the early 1990s the developing managerialist and actuarialist discourses of the previous decade were joined by the embracing of 'populist punitiveness' by politicians of all hues. As Windlesham (2001: 308) notes, the contemporary politics of youth justice (indeed, criminal justice generally) have become increasingly dominated by 'the fiercely competitive day-to-day struggle for favourable media exposure'. The shape of New Labour's policies was influenced by one further factor: the perception that it was not simply crime but anti-social behaviour, or what one junior Minister once referred to as 'sub-criminal activity' (quoted in Rutherford 2000: 55), that should be the focus of intervention. The consequence is a rather strange 'mélange' of policies and practices (Muncie 2001).

Though there are clear continuities between New Labour and previous administrations (Smith 2000), not least in some of their punitive rhetoric, there are also clear differences. Indeed, even in that regard there have been changes, for some of the populist punitiveness of the pre-1997 period has been toned down or jettisoned altogether. Similarly, the corporatist modernizing agenda, though clearly a descendant of the 1980s version, is also radically different from it. In particular, the rise to prominence of the 'what works' paradigm, and the centralizing managerialist initiatives embodied in the creation of the YJB and YOTs, signal a major departure from

previous arrangements. Criminologists have been somewhat reluctant to acknowledge the positive elements in such developments. It is undoubtedly right to be concerned about the likely impact of increasing 'managerialism'; the pitfalls are well
known and the dangers are real. However, it is important not to lose sight of the fact
that New Labour's 'systemic managerialism' in youth justice has led to the development of an organizationally more creative and coherent environment. The 'new youth
justice' is significantly better funded, and is therefore *potentially* better placed to
deliver necessary services, than the system it replaced.

Yet some significant tensions remain. New Labour youth justice, which combines
the rhetoric and practice of criminality prevention and crime reduction with that of
'what works' and 'evidence-based policy', attempts to concern itself with the causes of
crime and the delivery of justice while simultaneously focusing on probabilistic calculations of risk and harm minimization. There are clear tensions between some of the
inclusionary aspirations of community safety and some of the exclusionary potential
of criminality prevention. Similarly, the restorative justice-influenced reforms offer
the prospect of a more participatory and deliberative form of youth justice, yet may,
inadvertently or otherwise, encourage net-widening and mesh-thinning. Though
'what works' can be made to sound as if it is simply an empirical question, in reality it
is at least as much a question of politics. Perhaps most noticeably, New Labour has
failed even to mitigate the continuing increased use of custody for young offenders,
let alone reverse the trend. Ironically, we find ourselves in a position in which, despite
the fact that for the first time the youth justice system has an over-arching aim, there is
still no clear philosophy or approach governing policy-making or practice in this area.
In such circumstances it should be no surprise that New Labour's message, and in
many ways its record too, is a mixed one. Its modernization project has diverse
tributaries and, at heart, has contained an uneasy mix in which the desire to produce
technically competent, well-resourced, and publicly responsive local systems of delivery has continually been in tension with a strong desire to manage and control from
the centre. The practical resolution of these tensions will determine the shape and
nature of youth justice in the first decade of the twenty-first century.

Selected further reading

Geoffrey Pearson's *Hooligan: A History of Respectable Fears* (London: Macmillan, 1983)
should be the starting point for anyone interested in putting adult concerns about youth
into historical and sociological perspective. Dick Hebdige's *Subculture: The Meaning of Style*
(London: Methuen, 1979) remains the classic text on youth culture, and Howard Parker's
View From the Boys (London: David and Charles, 1974) still sets the standard for sociologists
writing about 'lads'. The changing nature of being young in the twentieth century was
accompanied by a noisy soundtrack, and should be understood in that context. The best
three books in the business are Nik Cohn's *Awopbopaloobop Alopbamboom* (London:
Paladin, 1970), Charlie Gillet's *The Sound of the City* (London: Souvenir Press, 1983), and
Jon Savage's *England's Dreaming: Sex Pistols and Punk Rock* (London: Faber and Faber,
1991). On youth crime and youth justice, John Muncie's *Youth and Crime* (London: Sage,
2000) is the most comprehensive and thoughtful introduction. Little of what has happened

in the past five years can be understood without reading the Audit Commission's *Misspent Youth* (London: Audit Commission, 1996), or the subsequent White Paper *No More Excuses* (London, Home Office, 1997).

References

ABRAMS, M. (1959), *The Teenage Consumer*, London: Routledge and Kegan Paul.

ALLEN, R. (1991), 'Out of jail: The reduction in the use of penal custody for male juveniles 1981–88', *Howard Journal of Criminal Justice*, 30, 1: 30–52.

—— (1997), *Children and Crime: Taking responsibility*, London: IPPR.

ANDERSON, M. (1980), *Approaches to the History of the Western Family 1500–1914*, London: Macmillan.

ANDERSON, S., KINSEY, R., LOADER, I., and SMITH, C. (1994), *Cautionary Tales*, Aldershot: Avebury.

ARIES, P. (1973), *Centuries of Childhood*, Harmondsworth: Penguin.

AUDIT COMMISSION (1996), *Misspent Youth: Young people and crime*, London: Audit Commission.

—— (1998), *Misspent Youth '98*, London: Audit Commission.

AYE MAUNG, N. (1995), *Young people, victimisation and the police: British Crime Survey findings on the experiences and attitudes of 12–15 year olds*, Home Office Research Study No. 140, London: HMSO.

BAILEY, V. (1987), *Delinquency and Citizenship: Reclaiming the young offender 1914–1948*, Oxford: Clarendon Press.

BALDING, J. (1994), *Young people and illegal drugs*, Exeter: Health Education Unit, University of Exeter.

BANDURA, A. (1977), *Social Learning Theory*, Englewood Cliffs, NJ: Prentice Hall.

BARKER, P., and LITTLE, A. (1964), 'The Margate offenders — a survey', *New Society*, 4, 96: 6–10.

BENNETT, T. (2000), *Drugs and Crime: The results of the second developmental stage of the NEW-ADAM programme*, Home Office Research Study No. 205, London: Home Office.

BIRKLAND, T.A. (1997), *After Disaster: Agenda setting, public policy and focusing events*, Washington DC: Georgetown University Press.

BLAIR, T. (1993), 'Why crime is a socialist issue', *New Statesman and Society*, 29 January.

BOOTH, C. (1902), *Life and Labour of the People of London*, London: Macmillan.

BOSWELL, G. (1996), *Young and Dangerous: The backgrounds and careers of section 53 offenders*, Aldershot: Avebury.

BOTTOMLEY, A.K., and PEASE, K. (1986), *Crime and Punishment: Interpreting the data*, Milton Keynes: Open University Press.

BOTTOMS, A.E. (1974), 'On the decriminalisation of the English juvenile courts', in R. Hood (ed.), *Crime, Criminology and Public Policy*, London: Heinemann.

—— (1977), 'Reflections on the renaissance of dangerousness', *Howard Journal*, 16, 2: 70–96.

—— (1995), 'The philosophy and politics of punishment and sentencing', in C.M.V. Clarkson and R. Morgan (eds), *The Politics of Sentencing Reform*, Oxford: Oxford University Press.

——, BROWN, P., McWILLIAMS, B., McWILLIAMS, W., and NELLIS, M. (1990), *Intermediate Treatment and Juvenile Justice: Key findings and implications from a national survey of intermediate treatment policy and practice*, London: HMSO.

—— and STEVENSON, S. (1992), 'What went wrong? Criminal justice policy in England and Wales 1945–1970', in D. Downes (ed.), *Unravelling Criminal Justice*, Basingstoke: Macmillan.

—— and WILES, P. (1994), 'Crime and insecurity in the city', paper presented at the Conference of the International Society of Criminology, Leuven, Belgium.

BOX, S. (1981), *Deviance, Reality and Society*, 2nd edn, London: Holt, Rinehart and Winston.

BRAKE, M. (1980), *The Sociology of Youth Culture and Youth Subcultures*, London: Routledge and Kegan Paul.

—— (1985), *Comparative Youth Culture*, London: Routledge.

CAMPBELL, B. (1993), *Goliath: Britain's Dangerous Places*, London: Methuen.

CAMPBELL, S. (2002), *A Review of Anti-Social Behaviour Orders*, London: Home Office.

CARLEN, P. (1996), *Jigsaw: A political economy of youth homelessness*, Milton Keynes: Open University Press.

CASHMORE, E. (1983), *Rastaman: The Rastafarian Movement in England*, London: Unwin.

CAVADINO, M., and DIGNAN, J. (1992), *The Penal System: An introduction*, London: Sage.

CLARKE, J. (1976a), 'The skinheads and the magical recovery of community', in S. Hall and T. Jefferson (eds), *Resistance Through Rituals*, London: Hutchison.

—— (1976b), 'Style', in S. Hall and T. Jefferson (eds), *Resistance Through Rituals*, London: Hutchison.

—— (1980), 'Social democratic delinquents and Fabian families', in National Deviancy Conference (ed.), *Permissiveness and Control: The fate of sixties legislation*, London: Macmillan.

——, HALL, S., JEFFERSON, T., and ROBERTS, B. (1976), 'Subcultures, cultures and class: A theoretical overview', in S. Hall and T. Jefferson (eds), *Resistance Through Rituals: Youth subcultures in post-war Britain*, London: Hutchison.

—— and JEFFERSON, T. (1976), 'Working class youth cultures', in G. Mungham and G. Pearson (eds), *Working Class Youth Culture*, London: Routledge and Kegan Paul.

CLEMENTS, I. (1993), 'Too hot to handle', *Druglink*, 8.

CLOWARD, R.A., and OHLIN, L.E. (1960), *Delinquency and Opportunity: A theory of delinquent gangs*, New York: Free Press.

COHEN, A.K. (1955), *Delinquent Boys: The culture of the gang*, New York: Free Press.

COHEN, P. (1972), 'Subcultural conflict and working class community', in S. Hall *et al.* (eds), *Culture, Media, Language*, London: Hutchison.

COHEN, S. (1980), *Folk Devils and Moral Panics*, London: Martin Robertson.

COLEMAN, J., and HENDRY, L. (1990), *The Nature of Adolescence*, London: Routledge.

COLLISON, M. (1994), 'Drug offenders and criminal justice: careers, compulsion, commitment and penalty', *Crime, Law and Social Change*, 21: 49–71.

CRAWFORD, A. (2002), 'The prospects of restorative justice for young offenders in England and Wales: A tale of two Acts', in K. McEvoy and T. Newburn (eds), *Criminology and Conflict Resolution*, Basingstoke: Palgrave.

—— and NEWBURN, T. (2002), 'Recent developments in restorative justice for young people in England and Wales: community participation and restoration', *British Journal of Criminology*, 42: 2.

DAVIS, J. (1990), *Youth and the Condition of Britain*, London: Athlone Press.

DIGNAN, J. (1999), 'The Crime and Disorder Act and the Prospects for Restorative Justice', *Criminal Law Review*: 48–60.

—— (2000), *Youth Justice Pilots Evaluation: Interim report on reparative work and youth offending teams*, London: Home Office.

DORN, N., and SOUTH, N. (1982), 'Of males and markets: A critical review of youth culture theory', *Research Paper 1, Centre for Occupational and Community Research*, London: Middlesex Polytechnic.

—— and —— (eds) (1987), *A Land Fit for Heroin? Drug policies, prevention and practice*, Basingstoke: Macmillan.

DOWNES, D. (1966), *The Delinquent Solution*, London: Routledge and Kegan Paul.

—— and MORGAN, R. (1997), 'Dumping the Hostages to Fortune', in M. Maguire, R. Morgan, and R. Reiner (eds), *The Oxford Handbook of Criminology*, 2nd edn, Oxford: Oxford University Press.

—— and ROCK, P. (1982), *Understanding Deviance*, Oxford: Oxford University Press.

EVANS, R. (1994), 'Cautioning: Counting the cost of retrenchment', *Criminal Law Review*: 566–75.

—— and PUECH, K. (2001), 'Reprimands and Warnings: Populist punitiveness or restorative justice?', *Criminal Law Review*: 794–805.

FAMILY POLICY STUDIES CENTRE (1998), *The Crime and Disorder Bill and the Family*, London: Family Policy Studies Centre.

FARRINGTON, D.P. (1977), 'The effects of public labelling', *British Journal of Criminology*, 17: 112–25.

—— (1989), 'Self-reported and official offending from adolescence to adulthood', in M.W. Klein (ed.), *Cross-National Research in Self-Reported Crime and Delinquency*, Dordrecht: Kluwer.

—— (1990), 'Age, period, cohort and offending', in D.M. Gottfredson and R.V. Clarke (eds), *Policy and Theory in Criminal Justice: Contributions in honour of Leslie T. Wilkins*, Aldershot: Avebury.

—— (1992), 'Trends in English juvenile delinquency and their explanation', *International Journal of Comparative and Applied Criminal Justice*, 16, 2: 151–63.

—— (1996), *Understanding and preventing youth crime*, York: Joseph Rowntree Foundation.

—— and BENNETT, T. (1981), 'Police cautioning of juveniles in London, *British Journal of Criminology*, 21, 2: 123–35.

—— and BURROWS, J. (1993), 'Did shoplifting really decrease?', *British Journal of Criminology*, 33: 57–69.

—— and LANGAN, P.A. (1992), 'Changes in crime and punishment in England and America in the 1980s', *Justice Quarterly*, 9: 5–46.

——, OSBORN, S.G., and WEST, D.J. (1978), 'The persistence of labelling effects', *British Journal of Criminology*, 18: 277–84.

FAULKNER, D. (1996), *Darkness and Light: Justice, crime and management for today*, London: The Howard League.

FLOOD-PAGE, C., CAMPBELL, S., HARRINGTON, V., and MILLER, J. (2000), *Youth Crime: Findings from the 1998/99 Youth Lifestyles Survey*, Home Office Research Study No. 209, London: Home Office.

FRANKLIN, B., and PETLEY, J. (1996), 'Killing the age of innocence: newspaper reporting of the death of James Bulger', in J. Pilcher and S. Wagg (eds), *Thatcher's Children: Politics, childhood and society in the 1980s and 1990s*, London: Falmer.

FRITH, S. (1983), *Sound Effects: Youth, leisure and the politics of rock and roll*, London: Constable.

GARDNER, J., VON HIRSCH, A., SMITH, A.T.H., MORGAN, R., ASHWORTH, A., and WASIK, M. (1998), 'Clause 1 — The hybrid law from hell?', *Criminal Justice Matters*, 31 (Spring): 25–7.

GARLAND, D. (1985), *Punishment and Welfare: A history of penal strategies*, Aldershot: Gower.

GELSTHORPE, L. (1984), 'Girls and juvenile justice', *Youth and Policy*, II: 1–5.

—— and MORRIS, A. (1994), 'Juvenile justice 1945–1992', in M. Maguire, R. Morgan, and R. Reiner (eds), *The Oxford Handbook of Criminology*, 1st edn, Oxford: Oxford University Press.

GILL, O. (1977), *Luke Street: Housing policy, conflict and the creation of the delinquent area*, London: Macmillan.

GILLER, H., and TUTT, N. (1987), 'Police cautioning of juveniles: The continuing practice of diversity', *Criminal Law Review*.

GILLETT, C. (1983), *The Sound of the City*, London: Souvenir Press.

GILLIS, J.R. (1974), *Youth and History: Tradition and change in European age relation, 1770–present*, New York: Academic Press.

—— (1975), 'The evolution of juvenile delinquency in England, 1880–1914', *Past and Present*, 67.

GILROY, P. (1987), *There Ain't No Black in the Union Jack*, London: Hutchinson.

GOLDSON, B. (ed.) (2000), *The New Youth Justice*, Lyme Regis: Russell House.

GOLDTHORPE, J., LOCKWOOD, D., BECHOFER, F., and PLATT, J. (1969), *The Affluent Worker in the Class Structure*, Cambridge: Cambridge University Press.

GOULDEN, C., and SONDHI, A. (2001), *At the margins: drug use by vulnerable young people in the 1998/99 Youth Lifestyles Survey*, Home Office Research Study No. 228, London: Home Office.

GRAHAM, J., and BOWLING, B. (1995), *Young People and Crime*, London: Home Office.

GRIFFIN, C. (1993), *Representations of Youth: A study of youth and adolescence in Britain and America*, Cambridge: Polity Press.

HAGELL, A., and NEWBURN, T. (1994), *Persistent Young Offenders*, London: Policy Studies Institute.

HAINES, K., and DRAKEFORD, M. (1998), *Young People and Youth Justice*, Basingstoke: Macmillan.

HALL, S. (1969), 'The hippies: An American moment', in J. Nagel (ed.), *Student Power*, London: Merlin Press.

—— (1980), *Drifting into a Law and Order Society*, London: Cobden Trust.

——, CRITCHER, C., JEFFERSON, T., CLARKE, J., and ROBERTS, B. (1978), *Policing the Crisis. Mugging, the State and Law and Order*, London: Macmillan.

HARDING, C., HINES, B., IRELAND, R., and RAWLINGS, P. (1985), *Imprisonment in England and Wales: A concise history*, Beckenham: Croom Helm.

HARRIS, R., and WEBB, D. (1987), *Welfare, Power and Juvenile Justice*, London: Tavistock.

HARTLESS, J., DITTON, J., NAIR, G., and PHILLIPS, S. (1995), 'More sinned against than sinning: A study of young teenagers' experiences of crime', *British Journal of Criminology*, 35, 1: 114–33.

HARWIN, J. (1982), 'The battle for the delinquent', in C. Jones and J. Stevenson (eds), *The Yearbook of Social Policy in Britain, 1980–81*, London: Routledge and Kegan Paul.

HEBDIGE, D. (1976), 'The Meaning of Mod', in S. Hall and T. Jefferson (eds), *Resistance Through Rituals*, London: Hutchison.

—— (1979), *Subculture: The meaning of style*, London: Methuen.

—— (1987), *Cut 'n Mix: Culture, identity and Caribbean music*, London: Methuen.

HEIDENSOHN, F. (1996), *Women and Crime*, Basingstoke: Macmillan.

HINDELANG, M.J., HIRSCHI, T., and WEIS, J.G. (1979), 'Correlates of delinquency: the illusion of discrepancy between self-report and official measures', *American Sociological Review*, 44: 995–1014.

HIRSCHI, T. (1969), *Causes of Delinquency*, Berkeley, Ca: University of California Press.

—— and GOTTFREDSON, M. (1983), 'Age and the explanation of crime', *American Journal of Sociology*, 89: 552–84.

HOLDAWAY, S., DAVIDSON, N., DIGNAN, J., HAMMERSLEY, R., HINE, J., and MARSH, P. (2001), *New Strategies to Address Youth Offending: The national evaluation of the pilot youth offending teams*, RDS Occasional Paper No. 69, London: Home Office.

HOME AFFAIRS COMMITTEE (1993), *Juvenile Offenders*, Sixth Report, London: HMSO.

—— (1994), *Video Violence and Young Offenders*, Fourth Report, London: HMSO.

HOME OFFICE (1965), *The Child, The Family and the Young Offender*, Cmnd 2742, London: HMSO.

—— (1968), *Children in Trouble*, Cmnd 3601, London: HMSO.

—— (1980), *Young Offenders*, Cmnd 8045, London: HMSO.

—— (1984a), *Cautioning by the Police: A consultative document*, London: Home Office.

—— (1984b), *Tougher Regimes in Detention Centres: Report of an Evaluation by the Young Offender Psychology Unit*, London: HMSO.

—— (1985), *The cautioning of offenders*, Circular 14/1985, London: Home Office.

—— (1988), *Punishment, Custody and the Community*, Cm 424, London: HMSO.

—— (1990), *The cautioning of offenders*, Circular 59/1990, London: Home Office.

—— (1994), *The cautioning of offenders*, Circular 18/1994, London: Home Office.

—— (1995a), *Criminal careers of those born between 1953 and 1973*, Home Office Statistical Bulletin 14/95, London: Home Office Research and Statistics Department.

—— (1995b), *Digest 3: Information on the Criminal Justice System in England and Wales*, London: Home Office Research and Statistics Department.

—— (1996a), *Projections of long-term trends in the prison population to 2004*, Home Office Statistical Bulletin 4/96, London: Home Office Research and Statistics Department.

—— (1996b), *Protecting the Public: The govern-* ment's strategy on crime in England and Wales, Cm 3190, London: HMSO.

—— (1997a), *Community Safety Order: A Consultation Paper*, London: Home Office.

—— (1997b), *Getting to Grips with Crime*, London: Home Office.

—— (1997c), *New National and Local Focus on Youth Crime: A Consultation Paper*, London: Home Office.

—— (1997d), *No More Excuses — A New Approach to Tackling Youth Crime in England and Wales*, Cm 3809, London: Home Office.

—— (1997e), *Preventing Children Offending: A Consultation Document*, London: Home Office.

—— (1997f), *Tackling Delays in the Youth Justice System: A Consultation Paper*, London: Home Office.

—— (1997g), *Tackling Youth Crime: A Consultation Paper*, London: Home Office.

—— (1998a), *Summary of the Response to the Comprehensive Spending Review of Secure Accommodation for Remanded and Sentenced Juveniles*, London: Home Office.

—— (1998b), *The Child Safety Order: Draft Guidance*, London: Home Office.

—— (1998c), *The Parenting Order: Draft Guidance Document*, London: Home Office.

—— and OTHERS (1976), *Children and Young Persons Act 1969: Observations on the eleventh report of the expenditure committee*, Cmnd 6494, London: HMSO.

HUMPHRIES, S. (1981), *Hooligans or Rebels? An oral history of working class childhood and youth, 1889–1939*, Oxford: Basil Blackwell.

ISDD (1994), *Drug Misuse in Britain 1994*, London: ISDD.

JAMES, A., and RAINE, J. (1998), *The New Politics of Criminal Justice*, Harlow: Longman.

JAMES, O. (1995), *Juvenile Violence in a Winner–Loser Culture*, London: Free Association Books.

JEFFERSON, T. (1976), 'Cultural responses of the Teds', in S. Hall and T. Jefferson (eds), *Resistance Through Rituals*, London: Hutchison.

JONES, D. (1989), 'The successful revolution', *Community Care*, 30 March: i–ii.

JONES, G. (1995), *Family Support for Young People*, London: Family Policy Studies Centre.

JONES, R. (1984), 'Questioning the new orthodoxy', *Community Care*, 11 October: 26–29.

KELLY, A. (1996), *Introduction to the Scottish Children's Panel*, Winchester: Waterside Press.

LABOUR PARTY (1996), *Tackling Youth Crime: Reforming youth justice*, London: Labour Party.

LAING, D. (1985), *One Chord Wonders: Power and meaning in punk rock*, Milton Keynes: Open University Press.

LANDALL, S., and NATHAN, G. (1983), 'Selecting delinquents for cautioning in the London metropolitan area', *British Journal of Criminology*, 23, 2: 128–49.

LAYCOCK, G., and TARLING, R. (1985), 'Police force cautioning: Policy and practice', *Howard Journal of Criminal Justice*, 24, 2: 81–92.

LENG, R., TAYLOR, R., and WASIK, M. (1998), *Blackstone's Guide to the Crime and Disorder Act 1998*, London: Blackstone Press.

LLOYD, C. (1998), 'Risk factors and problem drug use: identifying vulnerable groups', *Drugs: Education, Prevention and Policy*, 5, 3: 217–32.

—— and GRIFFITHS, P. (1998), 'Problems for the future: Drug use among vulnerable groups of young people', *Drugs: Education, Prevention and Policy*, 5, 3: 213–16.

LOADER, I. (1996), *Youth, Policing and Democracy*, Basingstoke: Macmillan.

LORD PRESIDENT OF THE COUNCIL (1998), *Tackling Drugs to Build a Better Britain: The Government's Ten-year Strategy for Tackling Drug Misuse*, Cm 3945, London: The Stationery Office.

McGALLAGLY, J., POWER, K., LITTLEWOOD, P., and MEIKLE, J. (1998), *Evaluation of the Hamilton Child Safety Initiative*, Crime and Criminal Justice Research Findings No. 24, Edinburgh: Scottish Office.

McKAY, G. (1996), *Senseless Acts of Beauty: Cultures of resistance since the sixties*, London: Verso.

McROBBIE, A. (1980), 'Settling accounts with subcultures: A feminist critique', *Screen Education*, 39.

—— (1991), *Feminism and Youth Culture: From 'Jackie' to 'Just Seventeen'*, London: Macmillan.

—— (1994a), 'A cultural sociology of youth', in A. McRobbie (ed.), *Postmodernism and Popular Culture*, London: Routledge.

—— (1994b), 'Shut up and dance: youth culture and the changing modes of femininity', in A. McRobbie (ed.), *Postmodernism and Popular Culture*, London: Routledge.

—— and GARBER, J. (1976), 'Girls and subcultures: An exploration', in S. Hall and T. Jefferson (eds), *Resistance Through Rituals*, London: Hutchison.

MARSHALL, T., and MERRY, S. (1990), *Crime and Accountability*, London: HMSO.

MATZA, D., and SYKES, G. (1957), 'Techniques of Neutralization', *American Sociological Review*, 22: 664–70.

—— (1961), 'Juvenile Delinquency and Subterranean Values', *American Sociological Review*, 26: 712–19.

MAY, M. (1973), 'Innocence and experience: the evolution of the concept of juvenile delinquency in the mid-nineteenth century', *Victorian Studies*, 17: 1.

MAYHEW, H. (1861), *London Labour and London Poor*, London: Griffin, Bohn and Co.

MEASHAM, F., NEWCOMBE, R., and PARKER, H. (1993), 'The post-heroin generation', *Druglink*, May/June: 16–17.

—— (1994), 'The normalization of recreational drug use amongst young people in North-West England', *British Journal of Sociology*, 45, 2: 287–312.

MELLY, G. (1972), *Revolt into Style*, Harmondsworth: Penguin.

MERTON, R. (1938), 'Social Structure and Anomie', *American Sociological Review*, 3: 672–82.

MICHAEL, A. (1998), Speech to the Crime Concern Parliamentary Discussion Group, London, 7 July.

MIERS, D., MAGUIRE, M., GOLDIE, S., SHARPE, K., HALE, C., NETTEN, A., UGLOW, S., DOOLIN, K., HALLAM, A., ENTERKIN, J., and NEWBURN, T. (2001), *An Exploratory Evaluation of Restorative Justice Schemes*, Crime Reduction Series Paper 9, London: Home Office.

MILLER, P., and PLANT, M. (1996), 'Drinking, smoking and illicit drug use among 15 and 16 year olds in the United Kingdom', *British Medical Journal*, 17 August: 313, 394–7.

MILLER, W.B. (1958), 'Lower Class Culture as a Generating Milieu of Gang Delinquency', *Journal of Social Issues*, 15: 1.

MORGAN, J., and ZEDNER, L. (1992), *Child Victims: Crime, impact and criminal justice*, Oxford: Oxford University Press.

MORGAN, R., and NEWBURN, T. (1997), *The Future of Policing*, Oxford: Oxford University Press.

MORRIS, A., and GELSTHORPE, L. (1981), 'False clues and female crime', in A. Morris and L. Gelsthorpe (eds), *Women and Crime*, Cropwood Series No. 13, Cambridge: University of Cambridge.

—— and GILLER, H. (1987), *Understanding Juvenile Justice*, Beckenham: Croom Helm.

—— and McISAAC, M. (1978), *Juvenile Justice?*, London: Heinemann.

—— and MAXWELL, G. (2000), 'The practice of

family group conferences in New Zealand: Assessing the place, potential and pitfalls of restorative justice', in A. Crawford and J. Goodey (eds), *Integrating a Victim Perspective Within Criminal Justice*, Aldershot: Ashgate.

MOTT, J., and MIRRLEES-BLACK, C. (1993), *Self-reported Drug Misuse in England and Wales: Main finding from the 1992 British Crime Survey*, London: Home Office.

MUNCIE, J. (1984), *The Trouble with Kids Today*, London: Hutchison.

—— (1990), 'Failure never matters: detention centres and the politics of deterrence', *Critical Social Policy*: 53–66.

—— (2000), 'Pragmatic Realism? Searching for criminology in the new youth justice', in B. Goldson (ed.), *The New Youth Justice*, Lyme Regis: Russell House.

—— (2001), 'A new deal for youth? Early intervention and correctionalism', in G. Hughes, E. McLaughlin, and J. Muncie (eds), *Crime Prevention and Community Safety: New Directions*, London: Sage.

—— (2002), 'A new deal for youth? Early intervention and correctionalism', in G. Hughes, J. Muncie, and E. McLaughlin (eds), *Crime Prevention and Community Safety: New Directions*, London: Sage.

——, COVENTRY, G., and WALTERS, R. (1995), 'The politics of youth crime prevention: developments in Australia and England and Wales', in L. Noaks, M. Levi, and M. Maguire (eds), *Issues in Contemporary Criminology*, Cardiff: University of Wales Press.

MURDOCK, G., and McCRON, R. (1976), 'Consciousness of class and consciousness of generation', in S. Hall and T. Jefferson (eds), *Resistance Through Rituals: Youth subcultures in post-war Britain*, London: Hutchison.

MURRAY, C. (1990), *The Emerging Underclass*, London: Institute of Economic Affairs.

NATHAN, S. (1995), *Boot camps: return of the short, sharp shock*, London: Prison Reform Trust.

NELLIS, M. (1991), 'The last days of "juvenile" justice?', in P. Carter, T. Jeffs, and M. Smith (eds), *Social Work and Social Welfare Yearbook 3*, Milton Keynes: Open University Press.

NEWBURN, T. (1991), *Permission and Regulation: Law and morals in post-war Britain*, London: Routledge.

—— (1995), *Crime and Criminal Justice Policy*, Harlow: Longman.

—— (1996), 'Back to the future? Youth crime, youth justice and the rediscovery of "authoritarian populism"', in J. Pilcher and S. Wagg (eds), *Thatcher's Children? Politics, childhood and society in the 1980s and 1990s*, London: Falmer Press.

—— (1997), 'Youth, Crime and Justice', in M. Maguire, R. Morgan, and R. Reiner (eds), *The Oxford Handbook of Criminology*, 2nd edn, Oxford: Oxford University Press.

—— (1998), 'Young offenders, drugs and prevention', *Drugs, Education, Prevention and Policy*, 5, 3: 233–43.

—— (1999), 'Drug Prevention and Youth Justice: Issues of Philosophy, Politics and Practice', *British Journal of Criminology*, 39, 4: 609–24.

—— (2002), *Disaffected Young People in Poor Communities*, PPRU Paper No. 1, Goldsmiths College: Public Policy Research Unit.

——, CRAWFORD, A., EARLE, R., GOLDIE, S., HALE, C., MASTERS, G., NETTEN, A., SAUNDERS, R., SHARPE, K., and UGLOW, S. (2001a), *The Introduction of Referral Orders into the Youth Justice System*, RDS Occasional Paper No. 70, London: Home Office.

——, CRAWFORD, A., EARLE, R., GOLDIE, S., HALE, C., MASTERS, G., NETTEN, A., SAUNDERS, R., SHARPE, K., UGLOW, S., and CAMPBELL, A. (2001b), *The Introduction of Referral Orders into the Youth Justice System: Second Interim Report*, RDS Occasional Paper No. 73, London: Home Office.

NIXON, J., HUNTER, H., and SHAYER, S. (1999), *The use of legal remedies by social landlords to deal with neighbourhood nuisance: Survey report*, Centre for Regional Economic and Social Research Paper No. H8, Sheffield: Sheffield Hallam University.

PALMER, T. (1971), *The Trials of OZ*, London: Blond and Briggs.

PARKER, H. (1974), *View From The Boys*, London: David and Charles.

——, ALDRIDGE, J., and MEASHAM, J. (1998), *Illegal Leisure: The normalization of adolescent recreational drug use*, London: Routledge.

—— and MEASHAM, F. (1994), 'Pick 'n mix: changing patterns of illicit drug use among 1990s adolescents', *Drugs, Education, Prevention and Policy*, 1, 1: 5–13.

——, —— and ALDRIDGE, J. (1995), *Drug Futures: Changing patterns of drug use amongst English youth*, London: ISDD.

——, NEWCOMBE, R., and BAKX, K. (1988), *Living*

With Heroin: The impact of drugs 'epidemic' on an English community, Milton Keynes: Open University Press.

——, SUMNER, M., and JARVIS, G. (1989), *Unmasking the Magistrates: The 'custody or not' decision in sentencing young offenders*, Milton Keynes: Open University Press.

PARLIAMENTARY ALL-PARTY PENAL AFFAIRS GROUP (1981), *Young Offenders: A strategy for the future*, Chichester: Barry Rose.

PATRICK, J. (1973), *A Glasgow Gang Observed*, London: Methuen.

PEARSON, G. (1983), *Hooligan: A history of respectable fears*, Basingstoke: Macmillan.

—— (1987), 'Social deprivation, unemployment and patterns of heroin use', in N. Dorn and N. South (eds) (1987), *A Land Fit for Heroin? Drug policies, prevention and practice*, Basingstoke: Macmillan.

—— (1989), '"A Jekyll in the Classroom, a Hyde in the Street": Queen Victoria's Hooligans', in D. Downes (ed.), *Crime in the City: Essays in Honour of John Barron Mays*, London: Macmillan.

—— (1994), 'Youth, Crime and Society', in M. Maguire, R. Morgan, and R. Reiner (eds), *The Oxford Handbook of Criminology*, 1st edn, Oxford: Oxford University Press.

PINTO-DUSCHINSKY, M. (1970), 'Bread and circuses? The Conservatives in power 1951–64', in V. Bogdanor and R. Skidelsky (eds), *The Age of Affluence*, London: Macmillan.

PITTS, J. (2000), 'The new youth justice and the politics of electoral anxiety', in B. Goldson (ed.), *The New Youth Justice*, Lyme Regis: Russell House.

—— (2001), 'The new correctionalism: young people, youth justice and New Labour', in R. Matthews and J. Pitts (eds), *Crime, Disorder and Community Safety*, London: Routledge.

PLANT, M., PECK, D., and SAMUEL, E. (1985), *Alcohol, Drugs and School Leavers*, London: Tavistock.

PRATT, J. (1989), 'Corporatism: The third model of juvenile justice', *British Journal of Criminology*, 29(3): 236–54.

RADZINOWICZ, L., and HOOD, R. (1990), *The Emergence of Penal Policy in Victorian and Edwardian England*, Oxford: Clarendon Press.

RAMSAY, M., and PERCY, A. (1996), *Drug Misuse Declared: Results of the 1994 British Crime Survey*, Home Office Research Study 151, London: Home Office.

——, BAKER, P., GOULDEN, C., SHARP, C., and SONDHI, A. (2001), *Drug misuse declared in 2000:*

results from the British Crime Survey, Home Office Research Study 224, London: Home Office.

REDHEAD, S. (1990), *The End of the Century Party: Youth and pop towards 2000*, Manchester: Manchester University Press.

—— (1993), 'The end of the end-of-the-century party', in S. Redhead (ed.), *Rave Off*, Avebury: Aldershot.

RENSHAW, J., and POWELL, H. (2001), *The Story So Far: Emerging evidence of the impact of the reformed youth justice system*, Draft Report, London: Youth Justice Board.

ROBERTS, K. (1983), *Youth and Leisure*, London: George Allen and Unwin.

—— (1995), *Youth and Employment in Modern Britain*, Oxford: Oxford University Press.

ROOK, C. (1899), *The Hooligan Nights*, London: Grant Richards.

ROYAL COMMISSION ON CRIMINAL PROCEDURE (1981), *Report*, London: HMSO.

RUTHERFORD, A. (1986a), *Growing Out of Crime: Society and young people in trouble*, Harmondsworth: Penguin.

—— (1986b), *Prisons and the Process of Justice*, Oxford: Oxford University Press.

—— (1992), *Growing Out of Crime: The New Era*, Winchester: Waterside Press.

—— (2000), 'An elephant on the doorstep: Criminal policy without crime in New Labour's Britain', in P. Green and A. Rutherford (eds), *Criminal Policy in Transition*, Oxford: Hart.

RUTTER, M., and GILLER, H. (1983), *Juvenile Delinquency: Trends and perspectives*, Harmondsworth: Penguin.

—— and SMITH, D.J. (1995a), *Psychosocial Disorders in Young People: Time trends and their correlates*, Chichester: Wiley.

—— and —— (1995b), 'Towards causal explanations of time trends in psychosocial disorders of youth', in M. Rutter and D.J. Smith (eds), *Psychosocial Disorders in Young People: Time trends and their correlates*, Chichester: Wiley.

SAVAGE, J. (1996), *Time Travel, From the Sex Pistols to Nirvana: Pop, media and sexuality 1977–1996*, London: Chatto and Windus.

SAVAGE, S., and NASH, M. (2001), 'Law and order under Blair', in S.P. Savage and R. Atkinson (eds), *Public Policy Under Blair*, Basingstoke: Palgrave.

SCHOENFELD, C.G. (1971), 'A psychoanalytic theory of juvenile delinquency', *Crime and Delinquency*, 17: 479–80.

SHAPIRO, H. (1997), 'Dances with drugs: pop music, drugs and youth culture', in N. South (ed.), *Drugs: Cultures, controls and everyday life*, London: Sage.

SHAW, C.R., and McKAY, H. (1942), *Juvenile Delinquency and Urban Areas*, Chicago, Ill.: University of Chicago Press.

SHINER, M., and NEWBURN, T. (1997), 'Definitely, Maybe Not? The normalization of recreational drug use amongst young people', *Sociology*, 31, 3: 511–29.

—— (1999), 'Taking Tea With Noel: The place and meaning of drug use in everyday life', in N. South (ed.), *Drugs: Cultures, controls and everyday life*, London: Sage.

SHORTER, E. (1976), *The Making of the Modern Family*, London: Collins.

SMITH, D. (2000), 'Corporatism and the new youth justice', in B. Goldson (ed.), *The New Youth Justice*, Lyme Regis: Russell House.

SMITH, D.J. (1994), *The Sleep of Reason: The James Bulger case*, London: Century.

—— (1995), 'Youth crime and conduct disorders', in M. Rutter and D.J. Smith (eds), *Psychosocial Disorders in Young People: Time trends and their correlates*, Chichester: Wiley.

SOUTH, N. (1994), 'Drugs and crime', in M. Maguire, R. Morgan, and R. Reiner (eds), *The Oxford Handbook of Criminology*, 1st edn, Oxford: Oxford University Press.

STONE, L. (1979), *The Family, Sex and Marriage in England 1500–1800*, Harmondsworth: Penguin.

STRAW, J. (1998), Speech to Magistrates' Association, Blackburn, 25 June.

THORNTON, S. (1995), *Club Cultures: Music, media and subcultural capital*, Oxford: Polity Press.

THORPE, D., SMITH, D., GREEN, C., and PALEY, J. (1980), *Out of Care: the community support of juvenile offenders*, London: George Allen and Unwin.

THRASHER, F. (1927), *The Gang*, Chicago, Ill.: University of Chicago Press.

TUTT, N. (1981), 'A decade of policy', *British Journal of Criminology*, 21: 4.

—— and GILLER, H. (1983), 'Police cautioning of juveniles: The practice of diversity', *Criminal Law Review*: 587–95.

UTTING, D., BRIGHT, J., and HENRICSON, C. (1993), *Crime and the Family*, London: Family Policy Studies Centre.

WALKER, M.A. (1995) (ed.), *Interpreting Criminal Statistics*, Oxford: Clarendon Press.

WALLACE, C. (1987), *For Richer, For Poorer: Growing up in and out of work*, London: Tavistock.

WEST, D.J., and FARRINGTON, D.P. (1977), *The Delinquent Way of Life*, London: Heinemann.

WHYTE, B. (2000), 'Between two stools: Youth justice in Scotland', *Probation Journal*, 47, 2: 119–25.

WILKINSON, T. (1995), 'Doli Incapax resurrected', *Solicitors Journal*, 14 April: 338–9.

WILLIS, P. (1978), *Profane Culture*, London: Routledge and Kegan Paul.

WILLMOTT, P. (1966), *Adolescent Boys of East London*, London: Routledge and Kegan Paul.

WILSON, J.Q., and HERRNSTEIN, R. (1985), *Crime and Human Nature*, New York: Simon and Schuster.

—— and KELLING, G. (1982), 'Broken Windows', *Atlantic Monthly*, March, 29–38.

WINDELSHAM, LORD (1993), *Responses to Crime (vol. 2): Penal Policy in the Making*, Oxford: Oxford University Press.

—— (2001), *Responses to Crime (vol. 4): Dispensing Justice*, Oxford: Oxford University Press.

YOUNG, A. (1996), *Imagining Crime: Textual outlaws and criminal conversations*, London: Sage.

YOUNG, J. (1971), *The Drugtakers*, London: Paladin.

YOUNG, R. (2000), 'Integrating a multi-victim perspective into criminal justice through restorative justice conferences', in A. Crawford and J. Goodey (eds), *Integrating a Victim Perspective Within Criminal Justice*, Aldershot: Ashgate.

—— and GOOLD, B. (1999), 'Restorative police cautioning in Aylesbury—from degrading to reintegrative shaming ceremonies?', *Criminal Law Review*: 126–38.

17

RACISM, ETHNICITY, CRIME, AND CRIMINAL JUSTICE

Coretta Phillips and Ben Bowling

Even readers new to this area will probably have heard of the murder of African/
Caribbean[1] teenager Stephen Lawrence in 1993, and of the public inquiry into the
police investigation of his murder (Macpherson 1999). Stephen Lawrence was stabbed
to death in a completely unprovoked attack by one of a gang of white youths who
chased him and his friend Duwayne Brooks shouting racist abuse. The Lawrence
Inquiry addressed many of the issues discussed in this chapter, including racist violence and discrimination in policing and criminal justice practices, all of which
impinge on ethnic minorities as victims of crime, as members of the public calling on
police services, and when suspected of committing offences.

The Lawrence Inquiry shifted the terms of what is commonly referred to as the
'race and crime' debate that had hitherto focused—sometimes to the exclusion of all
other issues—on the consistent pattern of over-representation of African/Caribbean
people in prison in Britain which first became evident in the 1970s. At the end of the
twentieth century, black British nationals formed 10 per cent of the male prison
population in England and Wales and 12 per cent of the female prison population,
while comprising only 2 per cent of the resident population according to the 1991
Census (Home Office 2000a). Until now, the most frequently asked question has been
whether this over-representation results from African/Caribbean people's offending
rates, or because of discriminatory treatment by the criminal justice system. In this
chapter, we aim to move beyond the narrow confines of the traditionally defined 'race
and crime' debate by identifying a range of relatively neglected issues such as racist
violence, deaths in custody, prison racism, and the experiences of ethnic minority
practitioners. We also attempt to go beyond the either/or debate—elevated crime
rates versus discrimination—to ask how official crime rates among specific ethnic
groups become 'elevated' and what explains the disproportionate outcomes in the
criminal justice process, and by attempting to make linkages between crime, criminal
justice practice, and its broader historical and social contexts. We conclude by briefly
mapping out future areas of policy change and research in this field.

---

[1] This is our preferred terminology to describe people of Caribbean (African) origin and African origin
who live in Britain. However, we use the terms used by authors throughout the chapter.

A BRIEF HISTORY OF 'RACE', CRIME, AND ETHNIC MINORITIES IN BRITAIN

A historical perspective is critical to understanding contemporary patterns because it establishes a context for the relationship between ethnicity, racism, crime, and criminal justice. Although bodily differences between groups of people, such as skin colour and hair texture, have been commented on for thousands of years, the 'scientific' ideas of 'race' and racial hierarchies are modern ones, originating in the European Enlightenment with the work of philosophers and physical scientists such as Hume, Kant, de Gobineau, Linne, and Blumenbach (Eze 1997). For thinkers of this period, 'the Age of Reason' and 'civilization' were synonymous with 'white' people and northern Europe, while those considered to be of other 'racial' and cultural origins were regarded as inferior with less rational, moral, and evolutionary potential. In these early narratives, the stereotypes used to describe people of African origin were different from those applied to people from Asia. In his 1853 essay on *The Inequality of Human Races*, de Gobineau referred to 'negroes' in the following way: 'the animal character that appears in the shape of the pelvis is stamped on the negro from birth and foreshadows his destiny . . . mental faculties are dull or even non-existent . . . kills willingly, for the sake of killing . . .'. The 'yellow race', by contrast, had 'little physical energy and inclined to apathy . . . desires are feeble . . . tends to mediocrity in everything . . . his whole desire is to live in the easiest way possible'. De Gobineau described the Aryan race as beautiful, intelligent, and strong, and believed that only where there was Aryan blood could civilization exist (Kleg 1993). Cesare Lombroso, the most influential of the new 'scientific criminologists', also made a direct link between 'race' and crime in his work, *Criminal Man* (1876). He concluded from his research on soldiers, convicts, and lunatics that 'many of the characteristics found in savages, and in the coloured races, are also to be found in habitual delinquents', including low cranial capacity, receding foreheads, darker skin, curly hair, and large or handle-shaped ears. As might be expected, Lombroso considered the white races as the 'triumph of the human species, its hitherto most perfect advancement' (cited in Miller 1996: 184–5).

The idea of white supremacy and the dehumanization of 'racial others' legitimized practices of slavery and indentured labour which were ascendant during this time. Ships left London, Bristol, and Liverpool with commodities such as textiles, brass, and copper made in Britain. In West Africa, these were bartered for black slaves, who were shipped in chains across the notorious 'middle passage' to the West Indies where they were exchanged for sugar, spices, rum, and tobacco which were carried back to British cities and sold. It was on this triangular trade that shipping, manufacturing, and other industries in Britain thrived and grew at the beginning of the factory age.

Although slavery ended in 1833 (1807 in Britain), the themes of racist thinking—what Gilroy (2000) refers to as 'raciology'—became embedded in British imperialism and colonial policies covering parts of Africa, Asia, and the West Indies, and were applied in similar form to the white working class in Ireland and England (Solomos and Back 1996). Racist ideas, born in the Enlightenment period, prompted institutionalized practices in many parts of the world which drew on notions of the superiority of whiteness, racial purification, and systems to exclude the arrival or settlement of 'non whites'. Examples include the White Australia policy, South African apartheid, and Jim Crow racial segregation in the USA. A particularly extreme and horrific manifestation of racial supremacist ideology was the Nazi regime in Germany based on the idea of Aryan superiority, leading to the extermination of a significant proportion of European Jewry.

In the aftermath of the Second World War, international migration to Britain from colonial territories was actively encouraged because of extreme labour shortages as well as economic collapse in many former colonies (Solomos and Back 1996). Nonetheless, the political and public discourses of this time echoed earlier concerns about 'racial degeneration' and the problem of 'bad stock' assimilating into English culture. British 'race relations' research in the 1950s and 1960s documented widespread rejection of people migrating from the Caribbean, Africa, and, somewhat later, from the Indian subcontinent. In some cases this escalated into forms of racist violence, although the racist nature was frequently denied or downplayed by the government and the police (Bowling 1999a).

In the 1960s, the local political climate was hostile to the influx of 'coloured' immigrants. This is best epitomized in the racist campaign platforms used by MPs such as Peter Griffiths in Smethwick and Enoch Powell, who, in a notorious speech in Birmingham in 1968, predicted that 'rivers of blood' would flow as a result of the arrival of people from the Indian subcontinent and the West Indies (Hiro 1992: 247). Powell's doctrine—which included proposals for a Ministry of Repatriation for post-colonial settlers—was based on racist stereotypes and concerns about the 'mixing' of races which overlapped with discussions about crime and policing amidst growing conflict between the police and black communities (Gilroy 1987a, 1987b).

Margaret Thatcher was elected to her first term as Conservative Prime Minister in 1979, publicly sympathizing with white fears of being 'swamped' by 'alien cultures' and promising more law and order reforms to stem a 'rising tide of crime' (Solomos 1988). The relationship between African/Caribbean communities and the police, which had become increasingly fractious by the end of the 1970s—in large part because of perceptions of oppressive policing—collapsed vividly in public disorder in St Paul's, Bristol in 1980, then in Brixton and across the country in 1981, and again in several British cities in 1985. Images of disorderly and riotous African/Caribbean youth became etched in the public imagination and cemented views about 'black criminality'. The Scarman Report (1981) into the disturbances of the early 1980s placed centre-stage the African/Caribbean experience of oppressive policing and the context of social and economic exclusion which beset inner-city ethnic minority communities.

These social and economic conditions are relevant for understanding the current position of ethnic minorities in Britain. The first comprehensive study of the position of ethnic minorities in Britian was carried out in 1966 by Daniel (1968) for the Policy Studies Institute (PSI). He found that black and Asian people were consistently in jobs below the level to which they were qualified. Overwhelmingly in manual work, they were confined to a limited number of industries. This was because some employers flatly refused to employ 'coloureds' (the Metropolitan Police did not recruit its first

African/Caribbean police officer until 1966). Daniel found overt exclusion from public and private sector housing, with properties available only in areas that white people were leaving, and this was the principal cause of a pattern of racial segregation in residential settlement which persists to this day. Daniel also used objective tests in housing and employment—using identical application letters for example, with only the ethnic origin of the applicant changed—which conclusively demonstrated racial discrimination.

The legacy of these patterns is that ethnic minority communities are geographically concentrated in the most deprived neighbourhoods, where housing stock is poorest. This is accounted for partly by preference, but systematic inequalities and discrimination in the provision of public and private housing are significant contributory factors (Smith 1989). In education, the statistical evidence points to lower academic attainment among ethnic minorities, particularly those of African, Caribbean, Pakistani, and Bangladeshi origin, which can partly be explained by discrimination in schools (see, for example, Gillborn 1998). Likewise, exclusions from school show an over-representation of African/Caribbean boys, who are commonly perceived by teachers to be disciplinary problems (DfEE 2000). Studies of work and income consistently reveal higher levels of unemployment among ethnic minorities, and for those in employment, lower mean weekly earnings, leading to many ethnic minority families falling below the poverty threshold (see Home Office 2000b; Bowling and Phillips 2002: 44–51). These patterns of disadvantage also contribute to disproportionate outcomes in criminal justice, and it is to these that we now turn.

REDRAWING THE PARAMETERS OF THE 'RACE AND CRIME' DEBATE: VICTIMIZATION AND OFFENDING

As noted previously, the focus of popular and academic attention in this field has been on whether people from specific ethnic minority communities are more or less likely to be involved in offending compared with white people; and as a consequence, the experience of ethnic minorities as victims of crime has never been at the heart of the 'race and crime' debate. It is significant, however, as former Home Secretary Jack Straw pointed out, that the *cause célèbre* that prompted shifts in criminal justice in the 1990s, was not the overzealous pursuit of an offender or a wrongful conviction, as in the 1970s and 1980s, but the failure to convict the murderers of African/Caribbean teenager, Stephen Lawrence.

RACIST VICTIMIZATION

The racist victimization of ethnic minorities provides an unequivocal example of the impact of direct racism on experiences of crime because individuals are selected as targets as a result of their 'race' or ethnicity. Criminological knowledge about racist victimization and its impact comes from a number of sources, including documentary accounts and the records of local monitoring groups, recorded statistics, victimization surveys, empirical research studies, and public inquiries such as the Macpherson Inquiry (1999). Documentary accounts have been important in bringing to public attention the problem of racist violence and in contextualizing the experience of ethnic minority communities. For example, it was the Bethnal Green and Stepney Trades Council (1978) report into the high levels of violence and harassment against the Bangladeshi community in Tower Hamlets which led to official recognition of a wider problem of racist violence in society (Bowling 1999a).

Extent and nature

Police recorded racist incidents have increased by 525 per cent since figures were first collected, from 4,383 incidents in 1988 to 23,049 incidents in 1998/99 (Home Office 1994, 2000a; Maynard and Read 1997). However, these statistics provide only a partial picture of racist victimization in England and Wales because of under-reporting by victims and variation in police recording patterns. There is speculation as to whether the steep increase in recorded incidents is the result of an increase in racist violence, increased confidence on the part of victims to report incidents to the police, improved recording practices, or changes in the definition of a racist incident following the Macpherson Inquiry (1999).

As might be expected, the volume of recorded incidents is likely to be higher in areas with relatively large ethnic minority populations, simply because there are more potential targets. However, Maynard and Read's (1997) study of police records found that *per capita rates* of racist victimization were highest in three provincial forces in the North of England, in contrast to other police force areas such as London, the West Midlands, and Greater Manchester where ethnic minorities were more heavily concentrated. Brincombe *et al.*'s (2001) analysis of victimization allegations in wards of the London Borough of Newham highlighted the importance of ethnic neighbourhood demographic composition, and supported the hypothesis that attacks cluster where ethnic minorities form a small but growing proportion of the population (see also Smith 1989; Hesse *et al.* 1992; Sampson and Phillips 1992, 1996; Bowling 1999a).[2]

To overcome some of the problems associated with official statistics, victimization surveys have been used to uncover the so-called 'dark figure' of racist victimization; that is, incidents not reported to, or recorded by, the police. Using British Crime Survey (BCS) data for 1995, Percy (1998) found that of a national sample, 4 per cent of blacks, 5 per cent of Indians, and 8 per cent of Pakistanis and Bangladeshis had been the victims of racially motivated offences in the previous year. Recent BCS data show a decline in racist incidents, with prevalence rates half those in 1995 for black (2 per cent) and Pakistani and Bangladeshi (4 per cent) respondents, while 4 per cent of Indians reported being racially victimized in 1999 (Clancy *et al.* 2001). Thus about 98,000 racially motivated incidents against ethnic minorities were estimated for 1999. Comparison of BCS and police figures indicated both increased reporting by victims to the police and increased recording by them.

Although victimization surveys go some way further than official statistics in

---

[2] In contrast, the Nail Bomber David Copeland chose well-known centres of black, Asian, and gay community concentration (Brixton, Brick Lane, and Soho) to attack minority communities.

documenting the extent of racist violence, when it comes to investigating its nature, some conceptual and methodological problems arise which are not easily resolved. Most importantly, surveys do not capture the process of victimization, with its complex and repeated interactions and cumulative impact on the victim (Bowling 1993a, 1999a). As research by Sampson and Phillips (1992) has demonstrated, racist victimization is likely to be of an ongoing nature, with both 'minor' and extreme incidents of violence interwoven in a pattern of harassment and intimidation. Incidents perceived by statutory agencies to be discrete and judged as single, 'one-off' events cannot capture this experience, which can significantly undermine individual victims' and communities' sense of safety (Bowling 1999a). Not surprisingly, then, in the 2000 BCS, 51 per cent of black and 60 per cent of Asian respondents were 'fairly' or 'very worried' about racist assaults (Kershaw *et al.* 2000).

Responses to racist victimization

In response to their victimization, people have been known to move home or school, or to restrict their movements to safe spaces. Situational measures, such as fireproof letterboxes and strengthened glass to protect property, have also been used, while collective self-defence campaigns aimed at physically defending neighbourhoods in the face of official inaction have a long history in Britain. After the racist riots of 1958 in Nottingham and Notting Hill, transport workers organized safe passage for drivers. Organizations such as the Newham Monitoring Project, the Southall Monitoring Group, and the work of the Campaign Against Racism and Fascism (CARF) and Searchlight, have been instrumental in assisting self-defence campaigns, in monitoring racist incidents and the police response to them, and in providing legal assistance to support victims and their families. The statutory response, after a long period of denying the existence of racist victimization as a social problem, has focused on policing, multi-agency approaches, and new legislation.

Research and community accounts have revealed low levels of satisfaction with the police. Victims have reported that the racist element of their victimization has been denied and presented as youthful misbehaviour, drunken pranks, or as neighbour disputes (Graef 1989; Sampson and Phillips 1992; Bjørgo and Witte 1993). The police have blamed victims' culture for the violence directed against them (implying that traditional dress or speaking in a foreign language makes someone both more threatening and more vulnerable to attack). There has also been a consistent pattern of the police failing to record and investigate reported incidents, and ultimately of the criminal justice system failing to bring offenders to justice. The police sometimes even have viewed the victim as a suspect instead. This reflects racist stereotyping on the part of the police, who are more likely to perceive all ethnic minorities with a degree of suspicion and specifically portray African/Caribbean people as violent offenders, and to consider Asian people as devious liars. Evaluations of multi-agency projects to reduce racist victimization have revealed these attitudes in the police service, but also show them to exist in local authorities (Saulsbury and Bowling 1991; Sampson and Phillips 1992; Phillips and Sampson 1998). It is too early yet to assess the impact of the introduction of penalty enhancements for 'racially aggravated' offences under the Crime and Disorder Act 1998.

The Macpherson Inquiry into the investigation of Stephen Lawrence's murder: an exemplar

The racist murder of Stephen Lawrence in south-east London in 1993 and the Macpherson Inquiry (1999) brought the issue of racist violence to the top of the public agenda at the end of the 1990s. The Inquiry concluded that the initial investigation into Mr Lawrence's murder was 'marred by a combination of professional incompetence, institutional racism and a failure of leadership by senior officers' (Macpherson 1999: 46.1). It documented the denial of the racist motive for the murder among at least five police officers, and the racist stereotyping of Duwayne Brooks at the scene, where he was wrongly assumed to be one of the protagonists in a fight between youths rather than a victim of an unprovoked attack (Hall *et al.* 1998). The Report criticized the use of inappropriate and offensive language, and the insensitive and patronizing handling of Mr and Mrs Lawrence (Stephen's parents) throughout the investigation.

Some police union representatives and right-wing commentators have challenged the Inquiry findings, in particular its conclusions concerning institutional racism. Claims have been made that the Report significantly affected police morale, and led to increased street crime as a result of a decline in the use of stop and search powers following criticism of police practice in this area in the Macpherson Report. There is little evidence to support this latter claim, and the modest drop in stop and search rates in 1999/2000 was lower for black than for white people in England and Wales (Home Office 2000c; see also Miller *et al.* 2000).

The government response to the Macpherson Inquiry was to establish a Ministerial Priority for the police service 'to increase trust and confidence in policing amongst minority ethnic communities', as well as a range of other measures focusing on defining, reporting, recording, investigating, and prosecuting racist incidents, training for racism awareness and cultural diversity, police discipline, and enhancing the preventive role of education (Home Office 1999a).

Explaining racist offending

Victims' accounts and case studies indicate that racist offenders are typically white males aged sixteen to twenty-five years, but younger children and older adults are also sometimes involved. Attacks frequently involve groups of offenders, and sometimes include whole families (Percy 1998; Aye Maung and Mirrlees-Black 1994; Sibbitt 1997; Bowling 1999a). Sibbitt's (1997) study of racist perpetrators in two London boroughs found that the perpetrators' racist views were shared by the communities to which they belonged, and offenders saw this as providing legitimacy for their actions, a finding echoed in Ray, Smith, and Wastell's (2001) research in Greater Manchester.

The 'economic scapegoating' of ethnic minorities is one of several theoretical and popular explanations for racist victimization. Both Sibbitt's study in London and Ray, Smith, and Wastell's research in Manchester showed that racist offenders target minority communities because they perceive them as receiving preferential treatment or access to scarce social and economic resources, such as housing, employment, education, and leisure facilities. European and US analyses have focused on the role of the increasing size of the ethnic minority population (Bjørgo and Witte

1993), elements of nationalism in particular cultures (Goldhagen 1996), the consumption of alcohol, and the similarities of belief and ideology among extreme right-wing organizations and ordinary communities across Europe and North America (Kaplan and Bjørgo 1998). This is an underdeveloped area of research which deserves empirical attention.

There have been about 100 racist murders in Britain in the last thirty-five years. Nonetheless, it should be remembered that most crime committed against ethnic minority communities—perhaps 85 per cent—is not racially motivated, and it is this 'ordinary' victimization that we now consider.

VICTIMIZATION AND FEAR OF CRIME

Since the late 1980s, the BCS has included booster samples of ethnic minority respondents to allow robust analyses of how patterns of victimization differ by ethnic origin. The first statistical evidence that ethnic minorities were at a greater risk of victimization relative to their white counterparts came from the 1988 BCS. In the fourteen months prior to the survey, 9.6 per cent of white respondents had been the victim of violent crime compared with 16.1 per cent of Afro-Caribbeans and 14.8 per cent of Asians interviewed (Mayhew, Elliott, and Dowds 1989). This pattern for both property and violent offences has remained in subsequent sweeps of the BCS. However, in the most recent BCS in 2000, household victimization risks for white and black people were more similar, with Indians, Pakistanis, and Bangladeshis at greater risk from household crime. Ethnic minorities were more likely to be victims of burglary and vehicle theft than white respondents, and black respondents experienced the highest levels of personal crimes. The prevalence rates are shown in Table 17.1.

Socio-economic and demographic factors—such as the concentration of minority communities into high crime areas and their younger age structure—explain a significant proportion of the increased risk of victimization that ethnic minorities face. In fact, in contrast to past British Crime Surveys, the 2000 BCS found factors

Table 17.1 Differential risk of victimization by ethnicity (percentage victimized once or more 2000 British Crime Survey): selected offences

	White	Black	Indian	Pakistani/ Bangladeshi
Burglary	4	6	6	5
Vehicle theft	13	17	14	16
All household offences	**25**	**25**	**27**	**29**
Assault	3	3	2	2
Threats	3	3	3	3
Robbery/theft from person	2	4	4	2
All personal offences	**8**	**10**	**7**	**7**

Source: Clancy *et al.* (2001: 12).

such as age, low income, unemployment, inner-city residence, and a lack of academic qualifications were more important in explaining ethnic minorities' higher levels of victimization than ethnicity (Clancy *et al.* 2001). Nonetheless, some of these factors, such as inner-city residence and unemployment, may themselves be partly explained by discrimination in housing and employment.

The increased risk of victimization for ethnic minorities is reflected in their higher levels of fear and concern about crime (Kershaw *et al.* 2000). On the street, and especially at home alone at night, ethnic minorities feel less safe than white people, and that feeling affects their individual freedom of movement. In the 1996 BCS, 13 per cent of white respondents said that they avoided certain places or events (such as football matches, night-clubs, theatres, or pubs) because they feared crime or violence, compared with 29 per cent of black respondents, 27 per cent of Indian respondents, and 22 per cent of Pakistani and Bangladeshi respondents (Percy 1998: 33).

So far our discussion has centred on ethnic minorities as victims of crime. This must be viewed alongside an analysis of patterns of offending by ethnic group, not least because of the overlap between victims and offenders, but also because it is necessary to explore the inter- and intra-ethnic patterns of crime within ethnic minority and white communities.

OFFENDING BY ETHNIC MINORITIES

Deconstructing notions of 'black' and 'Asian' criminality

Racist beliefs and stereotypes depicting African/Caribbean people as criminals have existed for centuries, and were widely and freely expressed in Britain well into the post-War years. This notwithstanding, in the 1970s, a quarter of a century after the onset of mass migration from the West Indies and Indian subcontinent, there was an official consensus that the settler communities offended at lower rates than the majority population. As the House of Commons Select Committee put it: '[t]he conclusions remain beyond doubt: coloured immigrants are no more involved in crime than others; nor are they generally more concerned in violence, prostitution and drugs. The West Indian crime rate is much the same as that of the indigenous population. The Asian crime rate is very much lower' (House of Commons 1972: 71). This position dramatically altered in the mid-1970s in the face of increased conflict between the police and African/Caribbean communities, and the accumulation of police statistics which documented higher arrest rates—particularly for robbery and theft from the person—among African/Caribbean youth in London. Despite methodological weaknesses in these statistical data, views about 'black criminality' and its supposed roots in black culture became entrenched in the public consciousness, and even more so following the media reporting of the disorders of the 1980s (Gilroy 1987b).

The construction of 'Asian criminality' has assumed a very different character from that of black or white 'criminalities'. In general, images of Asian communities are thought of as 'inward looking', 'tightly-knit', self-regulating, passive, and ordered by tradition and with strong family ties. Asian youth were largely absent from debates about urban unrest in the 1980s, and studies two decades later have referred to Pakistani and Bangladeshi young people as 'conformists' who emphasized the desire to avoid bringing shame on the family name (Webster 1997; Wardak 2000) and accepting the traditional strategy of avoiding conflict in the face of racist assault (Desai 1999; Webster 1997). However, these studies have also identified other groups of Asian males who were less conformist, with some active in defending 'Asian territory' from incursions by overtly racist white youth. Linked to this form of behaviour in the public mind was the 'Rushdie Affair', which saw young Asian Muslim men burning copies of the *Satanic Verses*, demonstrating their ties to Islam in a display of militancy and aggression (Desai 1999). The media construction of the 'Asian gang' emphasizing resistance to passive stereotypes of Asian people, was brought to the fore in 1994 by the murder of Richard Everitt in King's Cross by a group of Bangladeshi youths, the disorders in Manningham in Bradford in 1995, and again in the summer of 2001 with disorders in Oldham, Burnley, and Bradford.

Since relatively few people are themselves the victims of crime, the media are central in allaying or confirming public fears. Yet media accounts, sometimes unrepresentative and sensationalist, may bear little relation to the extent of 'actual' offending, while contributing much to the social construction of crime and criminality (see Hall *et al.* 1978; Cohen 1972). Over time, various ethnic groups have been portrayed as inherently criminal, including 'white' ethnic groups such as the Irish, Maltese, Russians, and Jews (Pearson 1983). Today, communities of African, Caribbean, and Asian origin all appear as 'folk devils'; and more recently, refugees fleeing from civil war and genocide and 'asylum seekers' have also become a new source of public anxiety about crime. These images have led authors such as Gilroy (1982, 1987b) to conclude that it is impossible to disentangle the myth of black (and Asian) criminality from its 'reality'. The myth of higher rates of offending by some ethnic minorities inspires the practices of the criminal justice system—as evident in proactive policing and responses to gatherings of African/Caribbean people in public space—which lead to the production of statistics; and this, in turn, feeds the myth. This issue is returned to in the concluding section of this chapter, but for now it is necessary to turn to the criminological evidence about patterns of offending among ethnic minorities, drawing particularly on victimization surveys, self-report offending studies, and official statistics—each with a health warning attached.

Victim reports: violence and robbery

Of course, victims can rarely provide suspect descriptions where there is no personal interaction, as in most property offences, but they may be able to do so in incidents involving personal crimes. There can be problems with the accuracy of victims' descriptions, particularly where incidents occur quickly and the victim suffers shock as a result. Some evidence also points to racist stereotyping playing a part in victims' reporting. Shah and Pease's (1992) analysis of (1982, 1984, and 1988) BCS data found that where no injury was inflicted, victims were more likely to report crimes to the police where the offender was from an ethnic minority (36 per cent) than where the offender was white (25 per cent).[3] Conversely, Shah and Pease found that where injuries were inflicted, victims were more likely to report crimes where the offender was white than where he or she was of ethnic minority origin. For Smith (1997) this amounted to a cancelling out of any differential reporting by victims depending on their ethnic origin. FitzGerald and Hale (1996), using the 1988 and 1992 BCSs, reported that the same pattern as found in Shah and Pease's analysis holds for whites and Pakistanis (where the offender was black), while black people were more balanced in their reporting, and Indians were less likely to report offences involving black offenders.

While victim survey data tell us little about the offending population *per se*, and can only quantify offender ethnic origin in cases where they were identified by the victim, they do show that much, but by no means all, personal crime reported in the surveys is intra-ethnic. Mayhew, Aye Maung, and Mirrlees-Black (1993) found that the vast majority of white victims of violence said that white offenders had been involved (88 per cent), and in most violent offences against ethnic minorities (51 per cent black, 62 per cent Asian) the offenders were also said to be white (see Table 17.2). This is to be expected because the general population is overwhelmingly white and because most people from ethnic minorities live, work, and socialize in areas where white people are the majority. Once victimization by white people is accounted for, the majority of black victims of violence (42 per cent) involved other black people, while for Asians, 19 per cent of violent crime was perpetrated by Asians and 11 per cent by black people.

Part of the explanation for the intra-ethnic pattern of violence can be found in the relationships between Britain's majority and minority populations. The most recent PSI study of *Ethnic Minorities in Britain* estimated that only about 1 per cent of all partnerships in the population as a whole are ethnically 'mixed', with most of these involving white and Caribbean partners (Modood *et al.* 1997). It is likely that domestic violence, therefore, is overwhelmingly intra-ethnic. Since places of entertainment, except in a relatively small number of cosmopolitan urban settings, are to a large extent still *de facto* segregated in Britain (reflecting structurally patterned geographical settlement, employment, family and friendship formation, and different tastes in entertainment and socializing), the intra-ethnic nature of violence is only to be expected.

It is the figures associated with robbery and 'mugging'[4] which have provoked the greatest controversy, heightened most recently by the increase in this crime in the last few years (Kershaw *et al.* 2000),[5] but also because, of all offences, 'mugging' stands out as one which has consistently been portrayed as a 'black crime' (Hall *et al.* 1978; Solomos 1988; McConville and Shepherd 1992). Perhaps unsurprisingly it is also violent offences such as robbery which capture public attention and exacerbate fear,

---

[3] An earlier study of arrests in London by Stevens and Willis (1979) reported the same finding.

[4] 'Mugging' is a criminal label with no formal legal standing, imported to England from the USA in August 1972. It is used in the BCS to comprise robbery, together with a proportion of the thefts from the person.

[5] If 'bullying' incidents involving under-16s are excluded, robbery increased by 2 per cent between 1997 and 1999, and 'mugging' dropped by 7 per cent (Kershaw *et al.* 2000).

Table 17.2 Ethnic origin of offender [1] by ethnic origin of victim: combined 1988 and 1992 British Crime Survey

	White victims	Black victims	Asian victims
	%	%	%
Violence			
White offender	88	51	62
Black offender	3	42	11
Asian offender	1	1	19
Other/mixed group	5	3	7
Unknown	3	3	1
N	628	108	59
Mugging [2]			
White offender	49	16	20
Black offender	32	58	55
Asian offender	1	–	10
Other/mixed group	8	13	8
Unknown	10	13	9
N	103	30	41

Notes:

[1] Based on all cases where the victim could say something about the offender.

[2] This term is used by Mayhew, Aye Maung, and Mirrlees-Black (1993) to include all robbery and 'snatch theft'. See Hall *et al.* (1978), Gilroy (1987a), Keith (1997) for a discussion of the social construction of 'mugging'.

Source: Mayhew, Aye Maung, and Mirrlees-Black (1993: 92).

although such offences made up only 1.8 per cent of notifiable offences in 2000/2001 and 2.8 per cent (including snatch thefts) of those recorded by the BCS (Povey and colleagues 2001; Kershaw *et al.* 2000).

Data from the combined 1988 and 1992 BCSs indicate that half of the white victims surveyed were 'mugged' by other whites (see Table 17.2). However, it is also striking that nearly one in three white victims of 'mugging' said that the offender was black. Among the black respondents who said that they were 'mugged', nearly six out of ten (58 per cent) said that the offence involved another black person, while only 16 per cent said that the perpetrator was white. Among Asians, again more than half of those who said that they had been 'mugged' said that a black person was responsible (55 per cent), while 20 per cent of offences were said to have been committed by whites and 10 per cent by Asians. Overall, around 42 per cent of robbery incidents reported to the BCS were committed by black offenders, a significant over-representation by any standard. In 1999 this figure was lower, at 31 per cent, based on a similarly small total sample size of 203 'mugging' incidents (Clancy *et al.* 2001).

Among the explanations for this elevated rate of offending by black people are those relating to poverty, deprivation and social exclusion, disruptive home lives, peer

pressure and the desire for demonstrating street credibility through branded possessions, and 'revenging' white society, as well as explanations rooted in discriminatory
criminal justice processes such as 'overcharging' by the police. However, the empirical
base for shedding any light on the validity of these explanations is currently weak, as
the few qualitative studies undertaken have been subject to various methodological
weaknesses (see Pratt 1981; Burney 1990; Barker *et al.* 1993; Savill 1994; Miller
forthcoming).

Homicide

Homicide data are generally less prone to the well-documented methodological problems of definition and categorization that afflict other offences.[6] More comprehensive
reporting and recording practices means that they serve as a more reliable measure of
victimization and offending, although detection rates for homicide do vary according
to the ethnicity of the victim.

Ethnic minorities face a higher risk of homicide than would be expected by their
number in the population, and this is most marked for black people. Between 1997
and 2000, there were 2,003 murder victims in England and Wales, of which 1,584 (79
per cent) were white. Of the remainder, 200 homicides involved black victims, 111
victims were Asian, and 108 were of other ethnic origins or their origins were not
known. Ten per cent of homicides recorded by the police involved the killing of a
black person, in comparison with black people's representation of 2 per cent in the
general population, and 6 per cent of victims were Asian compared with their comprising 3 per cent of the general population (Home Office 2000c). Official statistics
confirm that 91 per cent of whites and 67 per cent of both blacks and Asians were
murdered by someone from the same ethnic group in 1997–2000.

It was less common for homicides involving black victims (28 per cent) to be
detected by the police as compared with where the victim was either white or Asian
(11 per cent). Black victims were much more likely to have been shot, and homicides
by shooting are generally much more likely not to have suspects identified (Home
Office 2000c). Such 'black-on-black' violence has been the cause of much concern in
ethnic minority communities, particularly where firearms have been used (see, for
example, *The Voice*, 22 May 2000: 1–3). Although homicide occurs rarely in Britain, it
does appear to be the case that ethnic minorities, particularly black people, suffer a
heightened risk of this intra-ethnic crime.

The attrition process

The most common basis for discussing 'race' or ethnic differences in offending is
official statistics, specifically arrest and imprisonment rates. The problem with using
these data to analyse the characteristics of offenders is that they comprise details of
only a small proportion of offenders who commit crime and are identified by the
criminal justice system. For evidential, legal, and financial reasons, an even smaller
proportion of such offenders end up convicted and sentenced to imprisonment.

---

[6] However, the cases of Michael Menson and Ricky Reel show the potential for disagreement about
whether a death is a suicide, accident, or racist murder (Bowling and Phillips 2002: 95).

Individual offenders are, in effect, 'filtered out' of the process between the commission of a deviant act, its discovery by the victim, reporting to the police, then during charge, prosecution, conviction, and at the point of sentence, and imprisonment.

Home Office figures indicate that 24 per cent of offences reported in the 1998 BCS were recorded by the police; in 23 per cent of these recorded offences a suspect was identified (or the offence 'cleared-up'), with around half of these detected offences resulting in a conviction. The end result was that 2.2 per cent of offences resulted in the conviction of an offender, and 0.3 per cent resulted in a custodial sentence (Home Office 1999b). Both arrest and prison statistics are limited in that, while they show an over-representation of ethnic minorities, particularly black people, they can only tell us about an atypical group who have not been diverted from the 'filtering in' process. There are numerous other points in the criminal justice process where offenders have been 'filtered out' following the decision-making of victims, witnesses, Crown prosecutors, magistrates, juries, and judges. For this reason, official statistics such as arrest and imprisonment rates represent decisions made by criminal justice agencies rather than a measure of 'actual offending' (see Bottomley and Pease 1986; Coleman and Moynihan 1996).

Self-report offending studies

Self-report offending studies have the advantages of being unbiased by the attrition process, or by the limitations of victims' reports. Using this method, respondents are shown a list of dishonest and violent acts and are asked to say which ones they have ever done. Using these data, comparisons can be made of offending among different ethnic groups.

British self-report offending studies paid no attention to the question of ethnicity until the Home Office study *Young People and Crime* (Bowling, Graham, and Ross 1994; Graham and Bowling 1995). Based on a sample of 1,700 fourteen to twenty-five-year-olds and a random sample of 800 young people from ethnic minority communities, this study found that white and black respondents had very similar rates of offending (44 per cent and 43 per cent respectively), while Asian respondents—Indians (30 per cent), Pakistanis (28 per cent), and Bangladeshis (13 per cent)—had significantly lower rates. The pattern was broadly consistent for property, expressive, and violent offences, and was replicated in the second sweep of the survey (Flood-Page *et al.* 2000).

A series of Home Office studies of drug use have produced similar and very consistent findings (Mott and Mirrlees-Black 1995; Leitner, Shapland, and Wiles 1993; Ramsay and Percy 1996; Ramsay and Spiller 1997). Analysis of the 1996 BCS indicated lower levels of drug use by Afro-Caribbeans in both the sixteen to twenty-nine and the thirty to fifty-nine age brackets compared with whites. Based on these results, Ramsay and Spiller conclude that 'irrespective of age group, drug use is in general significantly more widespread on the part of whites than other ethnic groups' (1997: 45).

The self-report technique is obviously limited by the necessity to rely on the honesty of interviewees to reveal their criminal and disorderly behaviour. Further methodological weaknesses include the under-measuring of serious offences, and the under-sampling of groups of people such as the homeless and those in institutions who may be more involved in offending.

Research in the USA and The Netherlands has suggested that ethnic minorities—such as African-Americans and Turkish, Moroccan, and Surinamese—were more likely to 'conceal' their offending than their 'white' counterparts, although these studies themselves have been criticized on conceptual and methodological grounds (see Hindelang, Hirschi, and Weis 1981; Junger 1989, 1990; Bowling 1990). In the UK, it has been found that ethnic minority respondents had generally lower rates of completion of the sections on offending and drug use in the self-report offending surveys (Graham and Bowling 1995; Ramsay and Spiller 1997), although it is not clear how far this affects the validity of the results.

There is clearly a multitude of difficulties which bedevil attempts to discover the 'real' rate of offending among different ethnic groups. Our major sources of data are all flawed in some way: victim reports are available in only a small minority of incidents; self-report studies rely on the honesty of respondents; and the value of official statistics is diluted by the attrition process, and because they are the product of decisions taken by criminal justice agencies. However, despite their limitations, official statistics provide details of who is detected for particular types of offences, who is processed by the criminal justice system, and who become officially labelled as offenders. Criminal justice statistics feature in discussions of policy and practice, and in the media portrayal of crime in England and Wales. For this reason they need to be carefully scrutinized as they contribute to our understanding of the process of criminalization as it affects ethnic minorities. This process begins with the policing of ethnic minority communities.

THE PROCESS OF CRIMINALIZATION: STAGES IN THE CRIMINAL JUSTICE PROCESS

'OVER-POLICING'

Over the past four decades, the relationship between ethnic minorities and the police has often been adversarial, if not in open conflict. One of the earliest community accounts referred to the practice of 'nigger hunting', whereby junior police officers at some police stations allegedly planned to 'bring in a coloured person at all cost' (Hunte 1966: 12). Hunte highlighted issues that would still be at the heart of policing African/Caribbean people thirty-five years later, including racist abuse and a failure to protect ethnic minority communities. Throughout the 1970s and 1980s, other accounts documented the use of oppressive policing techniques, such as mass stop and search operations, the use of riot squads using semi-military equipment, excessive surveillance, unnecessary armed raids, and police use of racially abusive language, particularly in the centres of Britain's African, Caribbean, and Asian communities. Collectively these practices have been referred to as the 'over-policing' of ethnic minority communities (see Bowling and Phillips 2002: 128–9).

Excessive use of force and deaths in custody continue to be a source of tension. Over the years the numbers of deaths in police custody have been disproportionately high for black people compared to both the general and arrest population (Home Office 2000c). In the most recent figures, however, the number of ethnic minority deaths decreased markedly, perhaps influenced by the adverse reaction to such deaths in ethnic minority communities, highlighted by the Macpherson Inquiry (1999).

Police deployment and targeting

It is clear that targeting people from ethnic minorities and trawling for suspects plays a part in producing the over-representation of African/Caribbeans among those arrested by the police. They are less likely to receive the benefits of under-enforcement by the police than other ethnic groups which, alongside the ongoing targeting and heavy police deployment in African/Caribbean communities, means that their offending behaviour is more likely to come to official attention than that of other ethnic groups. Hood's (1992) research in Crown courts in the West Midlands found that 15 per cent of those dealt with for drugs offences – typically for small trades in cannabis – were black compared with only 3 per cent who were of Asian origin and 2 per cent who were whites. These offences came to official attention following proactive policing. Indeed, the most common reason given by police when searching black and Asian people was suspicion of drugs possession, even though self-report studies challenge the perception that they are more likely to use drugs than white people (Home Office 2000c; Ramsay *et al.* 2001).

Stop and search

The history of police use of 'stop and search' powers provides a context for the distrust of the police felt by African/Caribbean and, increasingly, Asian communities. These practices are seen by many people as the most glaring example of an abuse of police powers, hostility to which dates back to the time of 'sus' laws when a person could be arrested under the 1824 Vagrancy Act (s 4 and s 6) for frequenting or loitering in a public place with intent to commit an arrestable offence. Now regulated by the Police and Criminal Evidence Act (PACE 1984), a stop and search can be carried out only when there is 'reasonable suspicion' that stolen property or prohibited articles are being carried.

The national police data for 1999/2000 found, with some force variation, the number of PACE searches of black people to be five times higher than of whites. Rates for Asians were almost always higher than for whites (Home Office 2000c). The same pattern has been observed in the use of other stop and search powers, including stops under s 13 of the Prevention of Terrorism Act 1989, designed specifically to combat terrorism from the IRA. In 1997/8, 7 per cent of these stops were of African/ Caribbeans and 5 per cent were of Asians, a clear example of direct discrimination (Home Office 1998).

It also seems to be the case that the extent of police intrusion and formal action tends to be greater when the suspect is not white. People from ethnic minority communities are more likely to be stopped repeatedly, stops are more likely to result in a search, and searches tend to be more intrusive, including the use of clothing searches and strip searches (Skogan 1990; Newburn and Hayman 2001). Formal action is also more common in stops involving black people compared with other ethnic groups (Norris *et al.* 1992; Bucke 1997).

Methods of calculating stop and search rates have been questioned recently, because they are based on outdated census figures and take no account of the likelihood that many stops may be of individuals who do not live in the area where they are stopped. To address this problem, a recent study has examined 'suspect availability' for being stopped. Using CCTV and street observers, MVA and Miller (2000) assessed the pedestrian and vehicle populations in Hounslow, Greenwich, Ipswich, Chapeltown, and central Leicester. Based on these calculations they conclude that white people were over-represented among those stopped and searched by the police, while Asian people were under-represented when rates were calculated on 'available' rather than 'resident' populations. The findings for black people were mixed, with evidence of both over- and under-representation in different localities.

This research emphasizes the need for caution in assessing disproportionality in stop and search, but it also raises important questions about the 'neutrality of availability'. For example, African/Caribbean pupils may be victims of direct discrimination when they are excluded from school, and racism undoubtedly contributes to unemployment patterns among ethnic minorities; therefore, 'being available' to be stopped and searched by the police may in itself be explained by discrimination. It is also problematic that 'lifestyle factors' such as going out more in the evening should lead African/Caribbean people to be more often the subject of proactive policing than other ethnic groups (Modood *et al.* 1997; Bourne, Bridges, and Searle 1997). Moreover, to the list of factors which arouse police suspicion, Quinton, Bland, and Miller (2000) have added items of clothing (such as baseball caps and hooded jackets), type, make, and cost of cars, and engaging in vaguely defined 'suspicious activity', all of which can be negatively associated with African/Caribbeans and Asians to a lesser extent, and which may contribute to the process of criminalization.

FitzGerald's (1999) study in London has provided an insight into the use of stop and search in the late 1990s. It found that reasonable suspicion was frequently absent in the use of stop and search, and that the power is often not used for the purpose of detection (as justified in PACE) but instead is used for 'intelligence-gathering', 'disruption', and the 'social control' of young people. Until 1997 these practices were institutionalized by the Metropolitan Police who used stop and search as a 'performance indicator' of productivity. Despite a policy shift away from this approach, some operational officers believe it is still used by supervisors to measure performance (see HMIC 2000). In the wake of the Lawrence Inquiry, concerns were expressed about the declining use of stop/search for ethnic minorities. However, Home Office (2000a) statistics show that in 1999/2000 the fall in the number of recorded stops was lower for black people in England and Wales (10 per cent) than it was for other ethnic groups (14 per cent).

Direct discrimination through the negative stereotyping of people of African/ Caribbean origin offers one explanation for these patterns consistently observed over time. Additionally, Jefferson (1993) has pointed to the role of sex, age, and class in explaining the criminalizing experiences of black people (see also FitzGerald 1993;

Reiner 1993). It is certainly to be expected that the police will conduct more stops of younger people than older groups who are less likely to be involved in offending. This is relevant because the age structure of ethnic minority populations is significantly younger than that of whites (FitzGerald 1993). Until recently, BCS analyses have found, nonetheless, that ethnic origin was a predictor of being stopped by the police, after controlling for age, household income, employment status, occupation, type of housing tenure and area, vehicle access, gender, marital status, and age of leaving school (Skogan 1990). In the 2000 BCS, however, ethnic origin was predictive only of car stops for black people and Pakistanis and Bangladeshis, while ethnic origin no longer predicted foot stops (Clancy *et al.* 2001). The authors speculate as to whether this is due to a 'Macpherson effect' following the Inquiry team's criticism of police practices in this area.

As FitzGerald and Sibbitt (1997) note, force objectives, the use of 'intelligence' about local 'villains', and victim reports are also likely to influence stop and search patterns, although each of these factors may be influenced by racial bias. There is official acknowledgement that stop and search powers must be regulated to safeguard the individual's right to privacy and unnecessary intrusion by the state (Home Office 1997). The inherent danger lies in the extent of discretion which such powers allow and the limitations of legal regulation, particularly where concepts such as 'reasonable suspicion' and 'consent' are applied. These notions are vague, open to different understanding and interpretation by police officers, and therefore difficult to operationalize (Young 1994; Dixon, Coleman, and Bottomley 1990; Quinton, Bland, and Miller 2000; Sanders and Young, in Chapter 28 of this volume). Moreover, as Young has observed, stop/searches occur outside the police station and, like many aspects of police work, are outside the purview of supervisory officers where 'the norms and working practices of the street level police officer take priority over outside regulation' (Young 1994: 14).

A key question remains concerning the role of stop and search in explaining the over-representation of black people in arrest and imprisonment statistics. However, official statistics (which do not record 'voluntary' stop/searches and which may under-record other statutory stops) show that only a small minority of stop/searches —8 per cent of all ethnic groups in 1999/2000—led to an arrest (Home Office 2000c). Although this figure is slightly higher for black and Asian people, it is clear that most arrests result from reactive behaviour by the police following notification of an offence by a member of the public (see Mawby 1979; Steer 1980; Bottomley and Coleman 1976). This means that stop and search makes a modest, but significant, contribution to the over-representation of black people in the arrest population.

Nonetheless, the consequences of the abuse of discretionary police powers (such as stop and search and the use of force) and the poor response to racist victimization are wide-ranging. Confidence in the police and cooperation with investigations, for example, in providing information about crime, have undoubtedly been harmed by these negative interactions over the last four decades. Attitudinal and victimization surveys have provided ample evidence to support this, with lower levels of satisfaction with the police among African/Caribbeans compared with white respondents, with mixed findings among Asian respondents (see Bowling and Phillips 2002: 135–8 for a review). It is more than likely that such negative views of the police influence the decision-making of ethnic minority suspects when in police custody under arrest.

Arrest

Under PACE 1984, the police can arrest an individual when they have reasonable grounds for suspicion that he or she has committed an offence. The national aggregated figures for 1999/2000 show that the number of black people arrested was four times higher than would be expected from their numbers in the general population. The arrest rate for Asians was also higher than it was for whites. The breakdown according to offence type mirrors that observed among those imprisoned. As Figure 17.1 shows, the over-representation of blacks was evident in all offence categories, but was most striking in connection with fraud and forgery arrests and drug arrests (these offences accounted for 6 per cent and 2 per cent respectively of recorded notifiable offences in 1999/2000). For robbery there was a significant over-representation of black people in arrest figures (at 28 per cent); and although this is a crime which causes serious public concern, it accounted for only 2 per cent of notifiable offences in 1999/2000 (Home Office 2000c; Povey, Cotton, and Sisson 2000). Asians were over-represented in fraud and forgery arrests.

Once in police custody, opting for legal advice, exercising their right of silence, and denying the offence for which they have been arrested to a greater extent than their white counterparts, all cumulatively disadvantage ethnic minorities in the criminal justice process (see Phillips and Brown 1998; Bucke and Brown 1997). For example, the least punitive outcome of police action following arrest—a caution or reprimand em;can be given only where an offender admits the offence, and this partly explains the lower rates of cautioning for ethnic minorities (Home Office 2000c; Phillips and Brown 1998). There is also some evidence that black juveniles are subtly discriminated against, which contributes to their being 'filtered in' to the criminal justice process rather than being diverted from court. Phillips and Brown (1998) found in their observational survey of over 4,000 police arrests that black juveniles were less likely to have their cases referred to a multi-agency panel which plays a key role in diverting juveniles out of the process, and this held even once admission of the offence had been taken into account. It can be speculated that these decisions derive from ethnic minorities' negative opinions of the police which emerge in attitudinal and victimization surveys, thus further emphasizing the significance of relations between the police and ethnic minorities for how individuals fare in the criminal justice process.

PROSECUTORIAL DECISION-MAKING AND SENTENCING

Following the charge of a suspect by the police, there is a further point at which it is possible for individuals to be diverted from formal action, but this decision-making lies in the hands of the Crown Prosecution Service (CPS). Case files are sent to the CPS who decide whether to proceed to court, or to terminate the case against a suspect so that he or she does not face prosecution. Prosecutors have to consider whether there is a 'realistic prospect of conviction' based on the strength of evidence against the suspect. If the evidence is judged to be strong enough, Crown prosecutors

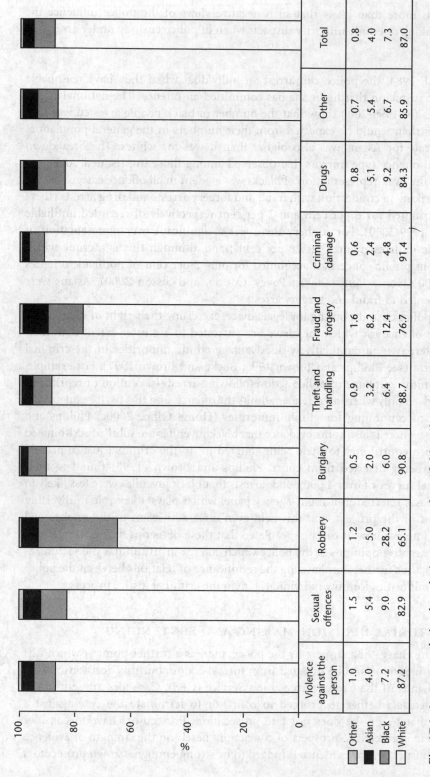

	Violence against the person	Sexual offences	Robbery	Burglary	Theft and handling	Fraud and forgery	Criminal damage	Drugs	Other	Total
Other	1.0	1.5	1.2	0.5	0.9	1.6	0.6	0.8	0.7	0.8
Asian	4.0	5.4	5.0	2.0	3.2	8.2	2.4	5.1	5.4	4.0
Black	7.2	9.0	28.2	6.0	6.4	12.4	4.8	9.2	6.7	7.3
White	87.2	82.9	65.1	90.8	88.7	76.7	91.4	84.3	85.9	87.0

Fig. 17.1 Arrest population by ethnic group and notifiable offences, 1999/2000

Source: Home Office 2000c

then have to decide whether cases should proceed on public interest grounds (CPS 1994). Factors such as the seriousness of the offence, whether the defendant was central or peripheral to the offence, and the willingness of the victim to participate in the prosecution process are considered by the CPS.

Case termination: a break on criminalization?

There are only two empirical research studies which have examined case termination rates to see if they differ according to the ethnic origin of the defendant. In their study of 1,175 defendants, Phillips and Brown (1998) found that 12 per cent of cases against white defendants were terminated compared with 20 per cent of cases against African/ Caribbeans and 27 per cent against Asians. Using multivariate analysis, they found that ethnic origin predicted an increased chance of case termination by the CPS, after controlling for type and seriousness of the offence, and whether the defendant had previous convictions. Higher termination rates for ethnic minorities compared with their white counterparts were also found in more comprehensive research by Mhlanga (1999) with a larger national sample of defendants aged under twenty-two years.

Both studies raise questions about policing practices in relation to ethnic minorities. A presumption of guilt appears to be selectively applied by police officers in the case of some African/Caribbean and Asian suspects, reflecting negative stereotyping and discrimination. The CPS 'break' on criminalizing ethnic minorities might be explained by the fact that case review is a point in the criminal justice process when discretion and subjectivity are at a minimum as Crown prosecutors are guided by the stringent Code for Crown Prosecutors (1994), the reasons for decisions are recorded, and, in most cases, the ethnic origin of the defendant is not known (Phillips and Brown 1998). A second explanation notes the greater ethnic diversity of the CPS compared with other criminal justice agencies such as the police (see Home Office 2000c).

Both studies also highlight the limits to research approaches that study one stage of the criminal justice process in isolation. Phillips and Brown (1998) found that the proportion of white and black suspects charged at the police station was identical at 59 per cent, with slightly fewer Asians (54 per cent) being charged. Differences in outcome became apparent only at the case review stage. This highlights the contingent nature of the criminal justice process which must be taken into account in research in this area.

Pre-sentence processes

The decision to remand a defendant in custody or to bail him or her to appear at court is the next critical decision point in the criminal justice process. Studies have consistently demonstrated that those defendants who are remanded in custody before trial are subsequently more likely to receive a custodial sentence if they are found guilty (Hood 1992), probably because they cannot be presented in a positive light either by demonstrating regular employment, or a smart physical appearance. Commentators such as Hudson (1993) have referred to this as one of the clearest examples of indirect discrimination against ethnic minorities, as research shows that black people are significantly more likely to be remanded in custody before and during their trial, partly because they have an increased risk of being 'of no fixed abode', a key criterion on which courts refuse bail (Walker 1989; Hood 1992; Brown and Hullin 1992). Thus, the apparently neutral legal factor relating to the likelihood of court appearance indirectly discriminates against suspects from ethnic minorities.

Where cases are proceeded with to court, magistrates or juries will consider the guilt of the suspect at trial. A mixed picture emerges in relation to acquittal rates— early studies found little difference in the acquittal rates of white and ethnic minority defendants (Walker 1989; Home Office 1989). However, more recent data, including national ethnic monitoring data for 1999, revealed higher acquittal rates for both black and Asian defendants, which is consistent with the finding of higher levels of case termination by the CPS in cases where ethnic minorities were charged (Home Office 2000c; Barclay and Mhlanga 2000). Rather than indicating the absence of bias, it raises questions about previous actions taken by the police and the CPS in cases involving ethnic minorities (cf. Smith 1997). As the Denman Inquiry (2001: 107) into race discrimination in the CPS concluded, this suggested that the CPS was 'discriminating against ethnic minority defendants by failing to correct the bias in police charging decisions and allowing a disproportionate number of weak cases against ethnic minority defendants to go to trial'.

The writing of pre-sentence reports by probation officers for magistrates to consider before passing sentence presents another opportunity for racial bias to creep in. While much research has been done on this, it is difficult to make definite conclusions because of mixed research findings on the number and quality of reports written and the extent to which specific sentencing recommendations are included when comparing white and ethnic minority defendants (see Bowling and Phillips 2002: 176–9). However, the most recent inspection of the probation service identified 16 per cent of pre-sentence reports written on black offenders and 11 per cent on Asian defendants as reinforcing stereotypical attitudes about race and ethnicity, although the impact on final sentencing was not measured (HMIP 2000).

Statistical and research evidence has consistently documented higher rates of committal to the Crown Court for ethnic minorities, particularly those of African/Caribbean origin. This means that even before sentencing decisions are made, African/Caribbean people face a greater possibility of a more severe sentencing outcome if found guilty than their white counterparts, by virtue of being tried in the Crown Court rather than the magistrates' court. It seems plausible to suggest that the distrust that ethnic minorities have of the police may also affect the prosecution and sentencing process (see Mirrlees-Black 2001). The research is inconclusive as to whether the higher rate of committal to the Crown Court for ethnic minority defendants is because more elect for jury trial, or because magistrates are more likely to decline jurisdiction (Walker 1989; Home Office 1989; Jefferson and Walker 1992; Shallice and Gordon 1990; Brown and Hullin 1992).

SENTENCING

Most studies of sentencing in the magistrates' courts, and the limited statistical evidence that exists, have observed little or no difference in the extent to which white and

African/Caribbean defendants have been sentenced to immediate custody, or in custodial sentence lengths (Crow and Cove 1984; Mair 1986; Walker 1989; Home Office 1989; Shallice and Gordon 1990; Brown and Hullin 1992; cf. Hudson 1989). These studies have been limited in their ability to consider a range of legitimate legal factors which influence sentencing decisions. The first study to use more sophisticated techniques in an attempt to isolate the 'independent' effect of ethnic origin on sentencing was Roger Hood's (1992) pioneering research, conducted in five Crown Courts in the West Midlands in 1989. All male black, Asian, and other ethnic minority defendants found guilty and sentenced in 1989 were compared with an equivalent random sample of male white defendants.

The approach taken by Hood (1992) was to construct a 'Probability of Custody Score', using sixteen variables which best predicted the possibility of a custodial sentence, such as offence seriousness and number of previous convictions. This approach, while significantly improving on previous methods, cannot take account of the extent to which legal factors such as seriousness of the offence and previous convictions are themselves the result of discrimination earlier in the process. Since the police 'over-charge' ethnic minority suspects in some cases, seriousness of the offence may be a factor which is itself dependent on ethnic origin. For this reason, Hood's results must be regarded as a conservative estimate of the effect of racial discrimination.

Overall, Hood estimated that only 479 of the 503 male black defendants should have been sentenced to custody on the basis of legally relevant factors. This amounted to a 5 per cent greater probability of black people being sentenced to custody compared with their white counterparts. Where defendants pleaded not guilty, and once all other factors had been controlled for, Asians, on average, were sentenced to nine months longer and blacks three months longer than whites.

The differences in sentencing occurred most often in the middle range of offence seriousness where judicial discretion was high. In these types of cases, black defendants (68 per cent) were significantly more likely to be sentenced to custody than whites (60 per cent). It was also found that the unequal treatment of black defendants occurred mainly at Dudley Crown Court (and Warwick and Stafford courts, although the numbers were much smaller), but not at the more urban Birmingham Crown Court. Using multivariate analysis too, Mhlanga (1997) reported similar findings, with young African/Caribbean defendants having an increased risk of custody being imposed.

For female defendants in Hood's study, the decision to sentence to immediate custody was accounted for by the seriousness of the offence, albeit that this may not be 'racially neutral' in itself. However, as was the case with males, African/Caribbean females at Dudley Crown Court had higher than expected rates of custody. No differences were found in sentence lengths for custody, or in the pattern of non-custodial sentencing (Hood 1992).

Hood's findings represent a clear example of direct discrimination against people of African/Caribbean origin, which has a clear contributory effect to the higher proportion of African/Caribbean people in prison in England and Wales. However, although this section has concluded the review of research on the criminal justice process up to the point of the oft-cited prison statistics, the process does not end there. The treatment of ethnic minorities in prison must also be considered before looking, more generally, at the impact of criminalization processes on the over-representation of African/Caribbean people in prison.

PRISON AND PROBATION

Prison populations

Ethnic monitoring data on Britain's prison population have been available since 1985. The first statistics revealed a marked over-representation of West Indians, Guyanese, and Africans within prisons among both males and females. The over-representation varied by sex of offender and whether they were sentenced or on remand, but the level of over-representation was in the region of seven times as many in prison compared with their representation in the general population. This is partly explained by the inclusion of non-British nationals (see Morgan, in Chapter 30 of this volume). The discussion that follows focuses on ethnic minorities of British nationality.

Since the mid-1980s the patterns have largely remained unchanged, although there has been a striking increase in the proportion of African/Caribbeans imprisoned, particularly among female prisoners whose actual numbers in prison are much smaller. As Figures 17.2 and 17.3 indicate, the ethnic minority prison population has fluctuated with the rises and falls of the white prison population, but this masks the overall increase in the ethnic minority prison population. While the white male prison population increased by 31 per cent between 1985 and 1999, the black population grew by 101 per cent, the Asian by 80 per cent, and the 'Chinese/other Asian' population increased 106 per cent. For females, the increase has been even more dramatic, at 217 per cent and 188 per cent for the black and 'Chinese/other Asian' female prison populations respectively. In sharp contrast, the number of Asian women in prison has remained consistently low, with only 34 in 1999. A future area of research should be to shed light on the protective factors which assist Asian women in avoiding criminalization.

The impact of more punitive sentencing policies, the younger age structure of the ethnic minority population contributing proportionately more in the group at risk of offending, and the effects of discrimination in the criminal justice process are all possible explanations for the increase in the ethnic minority prison population.

The most recent Home Office statistics show that on 30 June 1999 there were 12,120 people from ethnic minorities held in custody in Prison Service establishments. This amounted to 18 per cent of the male prison population and 25 per cent of the female population, although one-quarter of the male and one half of the female ethnic minority population were of foreign nationality (Home Office 2000a). Table 17.3 gives the percentages by ethnic origin for British nationals, compared against the census population figures, with the final column presenting incarceration rates—the rate per 100,000 of that ethnic group.

These statistics show that rates of incarceration for the Indian, Bangladeshi, and Chinese communities are very low (fewer than 100 per 100,000). This can be

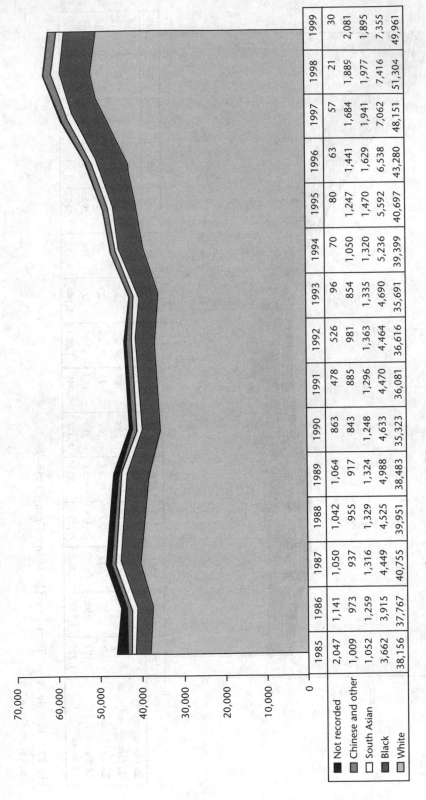

	1985	1986	1987	1988	1989	1990	1991	1992	1993	1994	1995	1996	1997	1998	1999
Not recorded	2,047	1,141	1,050	1,042	1,064	863	478	526	96	70	80	63	57	21	30
Chinese and other	1,009	973	937	955	917	843	885	981	854	1,050	1,247	1,441	1,684	1,889	2,081
South Asian	1,052	1,259	1,316	1,329	1,324	1,248	1,296	1,363	1,335	1,320	1,470	1,629	1,941	1,977	1,895
Black	3,662	3,915	4,449	4,525	4,988	4,633	4,470	4,464	4,690	5,236	5,592	6,538	7,062	7,416	7,355
White	38,156	37,767	40,755	39,951	38,483	35,323	36,081	36,616	35,691	39,399	40,697	43,280	48,151	51,304	49,961

Fig. 17.2 Male Prison Population by Ethnic Group, 1985–99

Source: Home Office 2000a

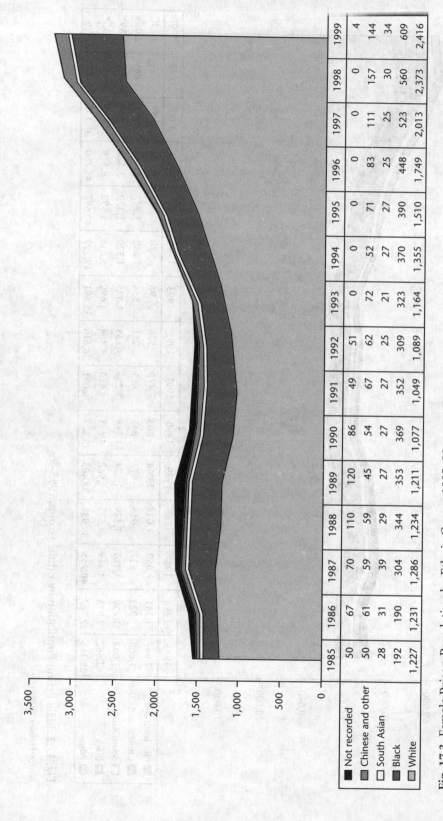

	1985	1986	1987	1988	1989	1990	1991	1992	1993	1994	1995	1996	1997	1998	1999
Not recorded	50	67	70	110	120	86	49	51	0	0	0	0	0	0	4
Chinese and other	50	61	59	59	45	54	67	62	72	52	71	83	111	157	144
South Asian	28	31	39	29	27	27	27	25	21	27	27	25	25	30	34
Black	192	190	304	344	353	369	352	309	323	370	390	448	523	560	609
White	1,227	1,231	1,286	1,234	1,211	1,077	1,049	1,089	1,164	1,355	1,510	1,749	2,013	2,373	2,416

Fig. 17.3 Female Prison Population by Ethnic Group, 1985–99

Source: Home Office 2000a

Table 17.3 Prison population by ethnic origin and sex (1999)

Ethnic Group		Prison Population British Nationals – 1999[1]		Resident Population (Age 15–64)[2]	Incarceration Rates for 1999[3]
		Males	Females	Males and Females	Males and Females
White		86	85	94	184
Black:		10	12	2	1,265
	Caribbean	6	6	1	1,395
	African	1	1	1	713
	Other	3	5	<1	1,399
Asian:		2	1	3	147
	Indian	1	<1	2	93
	Pakistani	1	<1	1	260
	Bangladeshi	<1	<1	<1	74
	Chinese/Other	2	2	1	424[4]

Notes:
[1] *Source: Statistics on Race and the Criminal Justice System* (Home Office 2000c).
[2] *Source:* 1991 Census (OPCS 1993).
[3] *Source: Prison Statistics 1999* (Home Office 2000a).
[4] This figure aggregates incarceration rates for Chinese (44), Other Asian (914), and other ethnic groups (358).
Percentages are rounded to the nearest whole number.

compared with white people (who make up 97 per cent of the population) imprisoned at a rate of 184 per 100,000 and the strikingly high incarceration rate for black people, of over 1,265, amounting to around 1.25 per cent of the black population. The disparate group of those from other Asian origins experience a similarly high incarceration rate.

Experiences in prison

The historical context for understanding 'race relations' for those in prison is one in which there was staunch support for the National Front among many prison officers in the 1970s, alongside incidents of brutality and harassment by prison officers (Gordon 1983), following which 'race relations' policies were introduced in the early 1980s. The *Alexander v Home Office* case was also pivotal in this development. In December 1987, the Court of Appeal ruled in favour of an African/Caribbean inmate who had been discriminated against in being denied a kitchen job. It was shown that comments based on racial stereotype in his assessment and induction reports at Wandsworth prison had led to him being discriminated against. The report opined that, '[h]e displays the usual traits associated with people of his ethnic background, being arrogant, suspicious of staff, anti-authority, devious and possessing a very large chip on his shoulder, which he will find very difficult to remove if he carries on the way he is doing'.

Genders and Player's (1989) study of five prisons in the mid-1980s revealed similar patterns of direct racial discrimination which disadvantaged African/Caribbean prisoners in particular. African/Caribbean prisoners were stereotyped as arrogant, lazy, noisy, hostile to authority, with values incompatible with British society, and as having 'a chip on their shoulder'. These stereotypes explained patterns of work allocations, with prisoners of African/Caribbean origin most often doing the least favoured jobs. Genders and Player (ibid.: 127) concluded that 'racial bias lies at the root of the racial imbalance evidenced in labour allocation'. Black prisoners were also more likely to be disciplined for misbehaviour in prison, and this appeared to be due to a more stringent application of prison disciplinary rules compared with infractions involving white prisoners. Chigwada-Bailey (1997) has drawn attention to the similar way in which African/Caribbean women are perceived in prison, as troublesome and causing disciplinary problems.

A more recent study by the Race Relations Adviser to HM Prison Service Agency uncovered a climate of victimization, the use of inappropriate language, harassment, abuse, and bullying of both ethnic minority staff and prisoners at Brixton prison (Clements 2000). The 'Reflections' regime—which involved loss of association by prisoners—was used disproportionately against prisoners from minority ethnic groups without due process and without the knowledge of senior managers. In November 2000, the Commission for Racial Equality announced a formal investigation into HM Prison Service, focusing on racial discrimination and racial harassment in HMP Brixton and Parc, and HM Feltham young offenders institution.

It was in the last institution that Zahid Mubarek was murdered by his cellmate, despite evidence that prison authorities were aware of the cellmate's violent racist tendencies. Research by Burnett and Farrell (1994) has suggested that racist victimization in prison is a common occurrence, and deaths in prison custody have raised the same concerns as those occurring in police custody. Again, negative stereotyping of African/Caribbean people as 'violent' and 'dangerous' appears to legitimize brutality against them, and allows their mental and physical health needs to be overlooked when in the care of the Prison Service.

Probation

Negative stereotyping of ethnic minorities, particularly African/Caribbeans, has also been noted in studies of probation practice, leading to assumptions that there was less possibility for change among African/Caribbean offenders (Green 1989; Denney 1992). A key issue has been the extent to which probation officers have considered the role of racism in explaining the offending of ethnic minorities (Holdaway and Allaker 1990). Claims have been made that the Probation Service operated a 'colour-blind' approach, with all offenders treated in the same way (see also Mavunga 1993).

In the most recent thematic inspection on racial equality, concerns centred around the quality of supervision of black offenders, particularly in terms of levels of contact during the later stages of probation orders (HMIP 2000). Linked to this has been an acknowledgement that little is known about the needs of ethnic minority probationers, or 'what works' in reducing offending among this group of offenders (Home Office 2001; Lawrence 1996).

In the concluding section of this chapter, we reflect on the influence of 'race' and racism on the criminal justice process taken as a whole, and examine future directions for policy and research. Before this, we consider the role and experiences of ethnic minority practitioners in the criminal justice professions.

THE EXPERIENCE OF ETHNIC MINORITY PRACTITIONERS

Ensuring that the criminal justice organizations have a workforce that reflects the diversity of the communities they serve is substantively important for social justice. It is also considered to be a key element in increasing ethnic minority communities' 'confidence and trust' in the criminal justice system. It is assumed that officers from ethnic minority communities will act in a more even-handed and sensitive way than white officers because of the greater understanding of and respect for ethnic minority citizens that they have. Specific skills, such as being multi-lingual, offer further attributes necessary for policing multi-racial communities. Against this is the view that ethnic minority police officers are 'co-opted' into the police culture, which is all-encompassing, to the extent that the gulf between police officer and citizen is maintained regardless of the ethnicity of the police officer (Cashmore 1991).

Statistics on the representation of ethnic minorities in criminal justice agencies in 2000 show their marked under-representation in the police and prison services, and in the professional magistracy and judiciary (see Table 17.4). In contrast, their representation is proportionate to the general population in the CPS, the courts, the Probation Service, the Parole Board, and the Home Office (although what appears to be an over-representation of ethnic minorities in the Home Office masks the lower than expected level in London where many of the posts are located). In none of these agencies is the representation near client populations. Where data exist on seniority, including police, prisons and the CPS, ethnic minorities are less likely to be employed in the higher grades of the criminal justice agencies (Home Office 2000c; see also Denman Inquiry 2001).

In 1998, the Home Secretary published local or national targets for the increased recruitment, retention, career progression, and senior level representation of ethnic minority operational and non-operational staff in the Home Office, police, prisons, and probation services (Home Office 1999c). The first progress report on meeting these ten-year employment targets revealed a mixed picture with some good progress, although retention and promotion rates still varied across the Home Office and its service areas, and levels of senior representation remained low in most (Home Office 2000d). It seems likely, moreover, that recruitment efforts will continue to be hampered by negative perceptions of certain criminal justice professions, particularly the police and prison services (see, for example, Stone and Tuffin 2000). This is partly because ethnic minorities have often experienced hostile working environments, alienation, and marginalization, punctuated by instances of racially abusive language

Table 17.4 Proportion of ethnic minorities in the criminal justice professions in 2000

Agency		%
Police		2.2
Crown Prosecution Service		9.2
Magistrates' court		4.8
Crown Court		4.6
Magistracy:	Lay	5.0
	Stipendiary	2.1
Solicitors:	On the Roll	8.4
	In private practice	6.0
Judiciary		1.9
Barristers in independent practice		8.8
Prison officers		2.6
Probation officers		9.6
Parole Board		11.1
Home Office		14.8

Notes:
[1] Source: Statistics on Race and the Criminal Justice System (Home Office 2000c).
[2] Excluding the Duchy of Lancaster.

and sometimes victimization or harassment (Holdaway 1993, 1996; Holdaway and Barron 1997; Alfred 1992; McDermott 1990; Mavunga 1993; Reardon 1993; Francis-Spence 1995; HMIP 2000). Recent evidence shows that supervisory and senior police officers still often fail to discourage and discipline racist comments and behaviour by police officers (HMIC 1997). A recent investigation of the CPS similarly found ethnic minorities' experience of unequal treatment by managers and a denial of support for career advancement, including 'acting up' opportunities (Denman Inquiry 2001). This has resulted in increasing numbers of applications to employment tribunals and mounting compensation costs for discriminatory treatment. In all of the criminal justice professions, ethnic minority-run support organizations[7] have been set up to provide support networks and training, and in many cases they have a campaigning and lobbying function (see Bowling and Phillips 2002: chapter 9).

---

[7] For example, the National Black Police Association, the Minority Lawyers Association, Society of Black Lawyers, African, Caribbean and Asian Lawyers Group, Society of Asian Lawyers, The Association of Muslim Lawyers, the National Black Crown Prosecutors' Association, RESPECT in the prison service, Association of Black Probation Officers, National Association of Asian Probation Staff, and the Home Office Ethnic Minority Network.

EXPLAINING DISPROPORTIONATE OUTCOMES

Having documented disproportionate outcomes, we are left with the more difficult task of explaining how racism—as a set of ideas and iniquitous social practices—actually results in racial discrimination in victimization, offending, the criminal justice process, imprisonment, and the experience of ethnic minority practitioners.

The process of criminalization, beginning with the over-policing of neighbourhoods where ethnic minorities, particularly African/Caribbeans, are heavily concentrated, to the end point of incarceration and deprivation of liberty, more readily engulfs people from ethnic minorities compared with their white counterparts. Intensively targeted proactive policing tactics mean that wrongdoing among African/Caribbean people comes to the attention of the police more often than wrongdoing among other ethnic groups. From the point of arrest onwards there is now mounting evidence of both direct and indirect discrimination in police cautioning, juvenile referral to multi-agency panels, case termination by the CPS, remands in custody, acquittals, committals to Crown Court, custodial sentencing, and prison life.

Smith (1994, 1997) argues that it is unhelpful to conceptualize the experiences of people of African, Caribbean, and Asian origin in the criminal justice system as part of a 'generalized racism', pointing out that many Asian communities suffer direct and indirect racial discrimination in many socio-economic spheres such as housing and employment, but they are not over-represented in Britain's prisons. While we concur with the latter point, the patterns of selective enforcement and harsher criminal justice outcomes for African/Caribbeans is consistent with cultural stereotyping and the 'heightened suspicion' of African/Caribbeans that has emerged in empirical studies in the last two decades. This contrasts sharply with the stereotyping of Asians as passive, traditional, and self-regulating with strong family ties. Given the form and nature of these stereotypes it would be surprising if these criminal justice outcomes were otherwise. It also confirms post-structuralist and postmodern positions which reject notions of a uniform, homogeneous, and static understanding of racism, instead emphasizing its historically and spatially specific nature (Solomos and Back 1996).

Figure 17.4 provides an indication of the impact of discrimination at one point in the criminal justice process and its subsequent cumulative effect at a later stage of the process, by comparing arrest rates and prison rates for different ethnic groups, following the approach of studies conducted in the USA (Blumstein 1982, 1993; Langan 1995[8]) and in the UK (Smith 1997).

Arrest rates for 1999/2000 indicate that around four times the number of black people were arrested than would be expected from their numbers in the general population. At the end point of the criminal justice process this has increased to six times the number of black people incarcerated when compared with the resident population. As Figure 17.4 shows, proportionately more whites appear to be filtered out of the criminal justice process following their arrest (87.1 per cent are arrested while 85.7 per cent are incarcerated); the reverse is true for black people (they make

---

[8] Langan used victim report data.

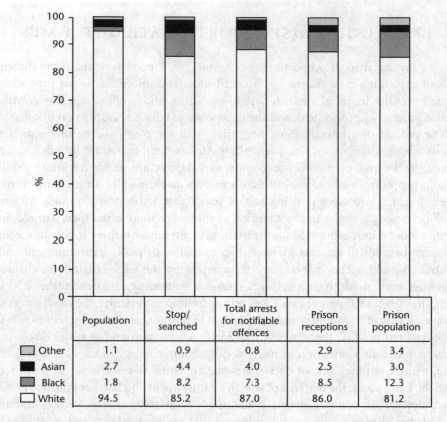

	Population	Stop/ searched	Total arrests for notifiable offences	Prison receptions	Prison population
Other	1.1	0.9	0.8	2.9	3.4
Asian	2.7	4.4	4.0	2.5	3.0
Black	1.8	8.2	7.3	8.5	12.3
White	94.5	85.2	87.0	86.0	81.2

Fig. 17.4 Representation of Ethnic Groups at Different Stages of the Criminal Justice Process

Source: Home Office 2000a

up 7.3 per cent of those arrested but 12.3 per cent of those incarcerated), and the same is true for those from other ethnic origins. The pattern for Asians is similar to that for white people, although the category conflates Indian, Pakistani, and Bangladeshi populations who have very different experiences of crime and criminal justice. While the differences in outcomes at each stage of the process are subtle, these differences are significant for the treatment of ethnic minorities, particularly for a system that purports to be fair (cf. Smith 1997).

Hood (1992) calculated the contribution of direct racial discrimination to be 7 per cent between arrest and incarceration in his sentencing study, although this took no account of police actions prior to arrest. In Figure 17.4 there is an increase of 5 per cent of African/Caribbeans from arrest to prosecution. Criminal justice practice is cyclical. An African/Caribbean individual who is imprisoned, even though the relevant legal factors would indicate that a non-custodial sentence is more appropriate, and who then re-offends, is much more likely to receive a custodial sentence of longer length because his or her previous highest sentence was a custodial one. Moreover, viewed within an historical context of institutionally racist criminal justice practices in the 1970s and 1980s, fewer African/Caribbeans than whites escaped the process of criminalization during that period. Today they are more likely to be targeted by the police because of their previous criminal histories, and thus the cycle is repeated.

The increase in the proportion of black people at subsequent stages of the criminal justice process is magnified in the case of drugs. Self-report studies indicate that 'the most likely drug user is a young white male in AB or C1 socio-economic groups' (ISDD 1997: 5; Ramsay and Spiller 1997; Ramsay *et al*. 2001). Yet stop and search figures show that a black person is much more likely than his white counterpart to be stopped by the police on suspicion of possessing drugs (Home Office 2000c). The stops usually prove to be fruitless. In the 1990s, stop and search hit a nadir in its effectiveness in targeting black drug users, with only one in seventeen suspected drug users actually found in possession. Despite its ineffectiveness, this targeting means that a greater proportion of black drug users will be arrested than their white counterparts. Home Office data show that while at least 95 per cent of drug users in England and Wales are white, they make up 78 per cent of the people imprisoned for drugs offences in 1999/2000. The black population, on the other hand, makes up about 2 per cent of drug users nationally, but account for 16 per cent of British nationals serving a custodial sentence for a drugs offence. A similar picture is true for 'other' ethnic groups, while the pattern for Asians is more complex.

As already discussed here and elsewhere in this volume, there are conceptual and methodological problems associated with these individual sources of data which urge caution in this type of analysis. Without more comprehensive self-report and criminal process data for a variety of comparable offences, it is difficult to determine whether the cumulative impact of discrimination against ethnic minorities explains a large or small part of the over-representation of African/Caribbeans in prison. Some British criminologists, such as Reiner (1993), have argued that this question is unanswerable due to these inherent problems. Others have argued that the extent of disproportionate imprisonment is too great to be explained through reference to discrimination in the criminal justice process (for example, Smith 1997).

Official statistics indicate higher rates of offending of African/Caribbean people. However, they can only examine the results of actions by the criminal justice system. For the small proportion of crime that is interpersonal (violence and robbery), victim reports of offenders highlight its intra-ethnic nature. They point to the greater involvement of African/Caribbeans in robbery and homicide offences. Self-report studies, on the other hand, present a more even distribution of offending between whites and African/Caribbeans, with lower rates of self-reported offending by Asian ethnic groups. Elsewhere we have referred to attempts to uncover the extent of offending by different ethnic groups as a 'methodological dead-end', but on the balance of em;albeit limited—evidence, homicide and robbery may be exceptions (Bowling and Phillips 2002). Using victim reports of offender ethnic origin, along with the more robust data which exist for homicide offences, suggests somewhat 'elevated' rates of offending by African/Caribbeans.

Any explanation for this over-representation, which represents a very small but significant minority of recorded crime, must acknowledge the structural context of life within ethnic minority communities. 'Race' and ethnicity are not ahistorial essences, but are socially constructed categories upon which iniquitous social structures are based. Both historically and in recent times, public officials have used racist notions to exclude or disadvantage ethnic minorities in many areas of social and economic life—such as housing, education, and employment. The consequence of these patterned but dynamic social practices is a set of social and economic conditions that lead to some, but not all, ethnic minority groups (including some 'whites') becoming marginalized and socially excluded. This exclusionary process continues in the monitoring and surveillance of African/Caribbean communities, which will inevitably draw proportionately more into the criminal justice net, and the further criminalizing impact of practices of the criminal justice system which exacerbate and entrench a cyclical pattern of exclusion and criminalization. This cannot be the whole story, as critics of structural theories have long contended. Structural analyses of culture offer a possible way forward, and the 'new ethnicities' literature which stresses the fragmentary and fluid nature of identity must assist this theoretical development (see Bowling and Phillips 2002). However, while African/Caribbean individuals are still viewed largely as 'bad' (Stephen Lawrence and Duwayne Brooks were viewed as protagonists in a fight) or 'mad' (Michael Menson was assumed by police to be a suicide victim) within criminal justice, racism must be central to our explanations of victimization, offending, and imprisonment.

ISSUES FOR POLICY AND FUTURE RESEARCH

Perhaps the most significant issue is the cumulative disadvantage experienced by African/Caribbeans following the application of certain supposedly 'neutral criteria' in criminal justice decision-making, in cautioning, bail decisions, and sentencing. Although there are legal reasons why practices such as sentencing discounts for guilty pleas occur, as Smith (1997: 175) observes, '[t]he use of a criterion that has an adverse effect on a whole ethnic group will be seen as an attack on that group, unless the reasons for adopting it are extremely compelling'. Bearing in mind the critical nature of relations between ethnic minorities and the criminal justice system, the time would seem ripe for reviewing these criteria.

While it is likely that improved data will shed further light on aspects of ethnicity, crime, and criminal justice discussed in this chapter, it seems probable that the answer to one central question—is the over-representation of African/Caribbeans in prison due to their 'elevated' rates of offending, or due to discrimination by the criminal justice system?—will remain out of empirical reach (Gilroy 1987b; Reiner 1993). Future research in this area will need to approach the question of criminal justice processing with a more nuanced and sophisticated analysis than the single-point approach adopted at the moment. To progress both empirical and theoretical crimin-ology, greater qualitative (and quantitative) detail will be required on how decisions are taken and how these impact on later decisions, and on the cyclical nature of criminal justice processing. This should, in addition, explore the effects of a dis-proportionately high (and growing) ethnic minority prison population on other aspects of life within ethnic minority communities, such as patterns of employment, health, and family life. There is also a need to fill our knowledge gaps with qualitative research examining drug use and supply, interpersonal and domestic violence, robbery and other forms of crime within ethnic minority communities, viewed from the perspective of the victims or offenders involved. Most importantly, we need to know how best to support communities themselves to reduce crime and victimization.

Further research attention could usefully focus on assessing the impact of the Race Relations (Amendment) Act 2000, which applies anti-discrimination principles for the first time to public services including the police. It is also likely that new strands of research will emerge using the more detailed 2001 census data when they are available. It is hoped that this will facilitate a careful analysis of the experience and treatment of those of mixed heritage, not least because the over-representation of black people in prison in 1999 was jointly the result of an over-representation of black Caribbeans and the black other group, of whom some are likely to be of mixed heritage. In addition, for socio-economic and demographic reasons, and because of recent accounts of the relationship between young Asian men and the police, this group may well face similar processes of criminalization as black ethnic groups in the coming years. It is also imperative that research explores the changing patterns in criminal justice which are emerging. The chapter has noted recent evidence of proportionate outcomes in relation to deaths in custody, and has reported BCS findings of ethnicity no longer being predictive of victimization (with a few exceptions) or foot stops by the police. While these are signs for optimism, a temporary 'Macpherson effect' cannot yet be discounted.

Selected further reading

This chapter draws extensively on *Racism, Crime and Justice*, by Bowling and Phillips (London: Longman, 2002), which is the first comprehensive critical analysis of racism and the criminal justice process in England from crime and victimization to policing, punishment, prison, and probation. Earlier overviews include *White Law*, by Paul Gordon (London: Pluto, 1983); *Racism and Criminology*, edited by Dee Cook and Barbara Hudson (London: Sage, 1993); *Minority Ethnic Groups in the Criminal Justice System*, edited by Loraine Gelsthorpe (Cambridge: Cambridge Institute of Criminology, 1993); *Ethnic Minorities in the Criminal Justice System*, by Marian FitzGerald (London: Home Office, 1993); and 'Ethnic Origins, Crime and Criminal Justice', by David Smith (in *Oxford Handbook of Criminology*, 2nd edn, Oxford: Oxford University Press, 1997).

Reviews of the US literature can be found in *Unequal Justice*, by Coramae Richey Mann (Bloomington, IN: Indiana University Press, 1993); *The Color of Justice*, by Sam Walker, Cassia Spohn, and Miriam DeLone (Belmont, Ca: Wadsworth, 1996); and *Images of Color, Images of Crime*, edited by Coramae Richey Mann and Marjorie Zatz (Los Angeles, Ca: Roxbury, 1998).

Attempts at comparative analysis can be found in the edited volumes by Ineke Marshall, *Minorities, Migrants and Crime* (London: Sage, 1997), and Michael Tonry, *Ethnicity, Crime and Immigration* (Chicago, Ill.: University of Chicago Press, 1997).

There is now an extensive literature on racist violence: *Racial Violence in Britain*, edited by Panikos Panayi (London: Leicester University Press/Pinter, 1996,) provides an historical perspective; contemporary research studies include *Violent Racism*, by Ben Bowling

(Oxford: Clarendon Press, 1999), *The Perpetrators of Racial Harassment*, by Rae Sibbitt (London: Home Office, 1997), *We Can't All Be White! Racist Victimisation in the UK*, by Kusminder Chahal and Louise Julienne (York: York Publishing Services, 1999); and for an international perspective, see *Hate Crime: International Perspectives on Causes and Control*, by Mark Hamm (Cincinnati, OH: Academy of Criminal Justice Sciences/Anderson, 1993), and *Racist Violence in Europe*, by Tore Bjørgo and Rob Witte (London: Macmillan, 1993).

The research on policing ethnic minority communities is also very extensive. *The Racialisation of Policing*, by Simon Holdaway (London: Macmillan, 1996), covers some key areas, as does *Out of Order? Policing Black People*, by Ellis Cashmore and Eugene McLaughlin (London: Routledge, 1991). The starting point for a theoretical account of racism in policing is *Policing the Crisis*, by Stuart Hall *et al.* (London: Macmillan, 1978), while studies produced by the Institute of Race Relations, such as *Policing Against Black People* (London: IRR, 1987) and *Deadly Silence: Black Deaths in Custody* (London: IRR, 1991), provide a challenging antidote to the overwhelmingly empiricist work in this area. *Entry into the Criminal Justice Process*, by Coretta Phillips and David Brown (London: Home Office, 1998), *Race and Drug Trials*, by Anita Kalunta Crumpton (Aldershot: Avebury, 1999), *Race and Sentencing*, by Roger Hood (Oxford: Oxford University Press, 1992), and *The Colour of English Justice*, by Bonny Mhlanga (Aldershot: Avebury, 1997), are key empirical studies on the criminal justice process; while *Race Relations in Prisons*, by Elaine Genders and Elaine Player (Oxford: Oxford University Press, 1989), remains the most comprehensive study of racism and ethnicity in prison life. To place the study of racism and criminal justice in its wider criminological context, see *Malign Neglect: Race, Crime and Punishment in America*, by Michael Tonry (Oxford: Oxford University Press, 1995), *Search and Destroy*, by Jerome Miller (Cambridge: Cambridge University Press, 1996), and *The Culture of Control*, by David Garland (Oxford: Oxford University Press, 2001).

References

ALFRED, R. (1992), *Black Workers in the Prison Service*, London: Prison Reform Trust.

AYE MAUNG, N., and MIRRLEES-BLACK, C. (1994), *Racially Motivated Crime: A British Crime Survey Analysis*, London: Home Office.

BARCLAY, G., and MHLANGA, B. (2000), *Ethnic Differences in Decisions on Young Defendants Dealt with by the Crown Prosecution Service*, Home Office Section 95 Findings No. 1, London: Home Office.

BARKER, M., GERAGHTY, J., WEBB, B., and KEY, T. (1993), *The Prevention of Street Robbery*, Police Research Group Crime Prevention Unit Paper 44, London: Home Office.

BETHNAL GREEN and STEPNEY TRADES COUNCIL (1978), *Blood on the Streets*, London: Bethnal Green and Stepney Trades Council.

BJØRGO, T., and WITTE, R. (eds) (1993), *Racist Violence in Europe*, London: Macmillan.

BLUMSTEIN, A. (1982), 'On the Racial Disproportionality of United States' Prison Populations', *Journal of Criminal Law and Criminology*, 73: 1259–81.

—— (1993), 'Racial Disproportionality of US Prison Populations Revisited', *University of Colorado Law Review*, 64: 743–60.

BOTTOMLEY, A.K., and COLEMAN, C. (1976), 'Criminal Statistics: the police role in the discovery and detection of crime', *International Journal of Criminology and Penology*, 4: 33–58.

—— and PEASE, K. (1986), *Crime and punishment: interpreting the data*, Milton Keynes: Open University Press.

BOURNE, J., BRIDGES, L., and SEARLE, C. (1997), *Outcast England: How Schools Exclude Black Children*, London: Institute for Race Relations.

BOWLING, B. (1990), 'Conceptual and Methodological Problems in Measuring "Race" Differences in Delinquency: A Reply to Marianne Junger', *British Journal of Criminology*, 30: 483–92.

—— (1993a), 'Racial Harassment and the Process of Victimization: Conceptual and Methodological Implications for the Local Crime Survey', *British Journal of Criminology*, 33, 1, Spring.

—— (1993b), 'Racial harassment in East London', in M.S. Hamm (ed.), *Hate Crime: International Perspectives on Causes and Control*, Academy of Criminal Justice Sciences/Anderson Publications.

—— (1999a), *Violent Racism: Victimisation, Policing and Social Context*, revised edn, Oxford: Oxford University Press.

—— (1999b), 'The Rise and Fall of New York Murder: Zero Tolerance or Crack's Decline?', *British Journal of Criminology*, 39, 4, Autumn: 531–54.

—— (1999c), *Arresting the abuse of police power: review of the Met's report on stop and search*, December 1999, Diversity on Line (**www.diversityonline.org**).

——, GRAHAM, J., and ROSS, A. (1994), 'Self-reported offending among young people in England and Wales', in J. Junger-Tas *et al.*, *Delinquent Behaviour Among Young People in the Western World*, Amsterdam: Kugler.

—— and PHILLIPS, C. (2002), *Racism, Crime and Justice*, London: Longman.

BRINCOME, A., RALPHS, M., SAMPSON, A., and TSUE, H. (2001), 'An Analysis of the Role of Neighbourhood Ethnic Composition in the Geographical Distribution of Racially Motivated Incidents', *British Journal of Criminology*, 41, 2, Spring.

BROWN, I., and HULLIN, R. (1992), 'A Study of Sentencing in the Leeds Magistrates' Courts', *British Journal of Criminology*, 32, 1: 41–53.

BUCKE, T. (1997), *Ethnicity and Contacts with the Police: Latest Findings from the British Crime Survey*, Home Office Research Findings No. 59, London: Home Office.

—— and BROWN, D. (1997), *In Police Custody: Police Powers and Suspects' Rights Under the Revised PACE Codes of Practice*, Home Office Research Study 174, London: Home Office.

BURNETT, R., and FARRELL, G. (1994), *Reported and Unreported Racial Incidents in Prisons*, Occasional Paper No. 14, Oxford: University of Oxford Centre for Criminological Research.

BURNEY, E. (1990), *Putting street crime in its place: a report to the Community/Police Consultative Group for Lambeth*, London: Centre for Inner City Studies, Department of Social Science and Administration, Goldsmiths College.

CASHMORE, E. (1991), 'Black Cops Inc.', in E. Cashmore and E. McLaughlin (eds), *Out of Order?: Policing Black People*, London: Routledge.

CHIGWADA-BAILEY, R. (1997), *Black Women's Experiences of Criminal Justice: Discourse on Disadvantage*, Winchester: Waterside Press.

CLANCY, A., HOUGH, M., AUST, R., and KERSHAW, C. (2001), *Crime, Policing and Justice: the Experience of Ethnic Minorities Findings from the 2000 British Crime Survey*, Home Office Research Study 223, London: Home Office.

CLEMENTS, J. (2000), *Assessment of Race Relations at HMP Brixton* (**www.hmprisonservice.gov.uk/filestore/202_206.pdf**).

COHEN, S. (1972), *Folk Devils and Moral Panics: The Creation of Mods and Rockers*, London: Martin Robertson.

COLEMAN, C., and MOYNIHAN, J. (1996), *Understanding Crime Data: Haunted by the Dark Figure*, Milton Keynes: Open University Press.

CROW, I., and COVE, J. (1984), 'Ethnic Minorities in the Courts', *Criminal Law Review*: 413–17.

CROWN PROSECUTION SERVICE (1994), *The Code for Crown Prosecutors*, London: CPS.

DANIEL, W.W. (1968), *Racial Discrimination in England*, Harmondsworth: Penguin.

DENMAN, S. (2001), *The Denman Report—Race Discrimination in the Crown Prosecution Service*, London: Crown Prosecution Service.

DENNEY, D. (1992), *Racism and anti-racism in probation*, London: Routledge.

DEPARTMENT FOR EDUCATION AND EMPLOYMENT (2000), *Statistics of Education: permanent exclusions from maintained schools in England*, Bulletin Issue No. 10/00, London: Department for Education and Employment.

DESAI, P. (1999), *Spaces of Identity, Cultures of Conflict: The Development of New British Asian Identities*, PhD, Goldsmiths College, University of London.

DIXON, D., COLEMAN, C., and BOTTOMLEY, K. (1990), 'Consent and the Legal Regulation of Policing', *Journal of Law and Society*, 17, 3: 345–59.

EZE, E. (1997), *Race and The Enlightenment: a reader*, Oxford: Blackwell.

FITZGERALD, M. (1993), *Ethnic Minorities in the Criminal Justice System*, Research Study No. 20, Royal Commission on Criminal Justice, London: Home Office.

—— (1999), *Searches in London under Section 1 of the Police and Criminal Evidence Act*, London: Metropolitan Police.

—— and HALE, C. (1996), *Ethnic Minorities: Victimisation and Racial Harassment: Findings from the 1988 and 1992 British Crime Surveys*, Home

Office Research Study No. 154, London: Home Office.

—— and SIBBITT, R. (1997), *Ethnic Monitoring in Police Forces: a Beginning*, Home Office Research Study No. 173, London: Home Office.

FLOOD-PAGE, C., CAMPBELL, S., HARRINGTON, V., and MILLER, J. (2000), *Youth crime: findings from the 1998/99 Youth Lifestyle Survey*, Home Office Research Study No. 209, London: Home Office.

FRANCIS-SPENCE, M. (1995), 'Justice: Do They Mean for Us? Black Probation Officers and Black Clients in the Probation Service', in D. Ward and M. Lacey (eds), *Probation: Working for Justice*, London: Whiting and Birch.

GENDERS, E., and PLAYER, E. (1989), *Race Relations in Prison*, Oxford: Clarendon Press.

GILLBORN, D. (1998), 'Race and Ethnicity in Compulsory Schooling', in T. Modood and T. Acland (eds), *Race and Higher Education: experiences, challenges and policy implications*, London: Policy Studies Institute.

GILROY, P. (1982), 'Police and Thieves', in Centre for Contemporary Cultural Studies, *The Empire Strikes Back*, London: Hutchinson.

—— (1987a), *There Ain't No Black in the Union Jack*, London: Hutchinson.

—— (1987b), 'The Myth of Black Criminality', in P. Scraton (ed.), *Law, Order and the Authoritarian State: readings in critical criminology*, Milton Keynes: Open University Press.

—— (2000), *Between Camps: race, identity and nationalism at the end of the colour line*, London: Allen.

GOBINEAU DE, A. (1853), *The Inequality of Human Races* (transl. 1915), London.

GOLDHAGEN, D.J. (1996), *Hitler's willing executioners: ordinary Germans and the Holocaust*, London: Abacus.

GORDON, P. (1983), *White Law: Racism in the Police, Courts and Prisons*, London: Pluto.

GRAEF, R. (1989), *Talking Blues: The Police in their own words*, London: Collins Harvill.

GRAHAM, J., and BOWLING, B. (1995), *Young People and Crime*, Home Office Research Study No. 145, London: Home Office.

GREEN, R. (1989), 'Probation and the Black Offender', *New Community*, 16, 1: 81–91.

HALL, S., CRITCHER, C., JEFFERSON, T., CLARKE, J., and ROBERTS, B. (1978), *Policing the Crisis: Mugging, the State and Law and Order*, London: Macmillan.

——, LEWIS, G., and McLAUGHLIN, E. (1998), *The Report on Racial Stereotyping* (prepared for Deighton Guedalla, solicitors for Duwayne Brooks, June 1998), Milton Keynes: Open University.

HER MAJESTY'S INSPECTORATE OF CONSTABULARY (1997), *Winning the Race: Policing Plural Communities*, HMIC Thematic Inspection Report on Community and Race Relations 1996/7, London: Home Office.

—— (2000), *Policing London. Winning Consent: A Review of Murder Investigations and Community and Race Relations Issues in the Metropolitan Police Service*, London: Home Office.

HER MAJESTY'S INSPECTORATE OF PROBATION (2000), *Towards Race Equality. Thematic Inspection*, London: Home Office.

HESSE, B., RAI, D.K., BENNETT, C., and McGILCHRIST, P. (1992), *Beneath the Surface: Racial Harassment*, Aldershot: Avebury.

HINDELANG, M., HIRSCHI, T., and WEIS, J. (1981), *Measuring Delinquency*, Beverly Hills: Sage.

HIRO, D. (1992), *Black British White British: a history of race relations in Britain*, London: Paladin.

HOLDAWAY, S. (1993), *The Resignation of Black and Asian Officers from the Police Service*, London: Home Office.

—— (1996), *The Racialisation of British Policing*, London: Macmillan.

—— and ALLAKER, J. (1990), *Race Issues in the Probation Service: a Review of Policy*, Wakefield: Association of Chief Officers of Probation.

—— and BARRON, A. (1997), *Resigners? The Experience of Black and Asian Police Officers*, London: Macmillan.

HOME OFFICE (1989), *The Ethnic Group of Those Proceeded Against or Sentenced by the Courts in the Metropolitan District in 1984 and 1985*, Home Office Statistical Bulletin 6/89, London: Home Office Statistical Department.

—— (1994), *Race and the Criminal Justice System 1994: a Home Office Publication Under section 95 of the Criminal Justice Act 1991*, London: Home Office.

—— (1996), *Taking steps: multi-agency responses to racial attacks and harassment*, The Third Report of the Inter Departmental Racial Attacks Group, London: Home Office.

—— (1997), *Police and Criminal Evidence Act 1984 (s. 66) Code of Practice (A) on Stop and Search*, London: Home Office.

—— (1998), *Statistics on Race and the Criminal Justice System 1998: a Home Office publication under section 95 of the Criminal Justice Act 1991*, London: Home Office.

—— (1999a), *Action Plan. Response to the Stephen Lawrence Inquiry*, London: HMSO.

—— (1999b), *Digest of Criminal Justice Statistics, Digest 4*, London: Home Office.

—— (1999c), *Race Equality—the Home Secretary's Employment Targets: staff targets for the Home Office, the Prison, the Police, the Fire and the Probation Services, a Home Office Publication under section 95 of the Criminal Justice Act 1991*, London: Home Office.

—— (2000a), *Prison Statistics England and Wales 1999*, Cm 4805, London: The Stationery Office.

—— (2000b), *Race Equality and Public Services*, London: Home Office.

—— (2000c), *Statistics on Race and the Criminal Justice System 2000: a Home Office publication under section 95 of the Criminal Justice Act 1991*, London: Home Office.

—— (2000d), *Race Equality—the Home Secretary's Employment Targets: First Annual Report on Progress. Staff targets for the Home Office, the Prison, the Police, the Fire and the Probation Services*, London: Home Office.

—— (2001), *What Works Diversity Issues and Race*, Probation Circular 76/2001, London: Home Office.

HOOD, R. (1992), *Race and Sentencing*, Oxford: Clarendon Press.

HOUSE OF COMMONS (1972), *Select Committee on Race Relations and Immigration Session 1971–2*, Police/Immigration Relations, 1: 471.

HUDSON, B. (1989), 'Discrimination and Disparity: the Influence of Race on Sentencing', *New Community*, 16, 1: 23–34.

—— (1993), *Penal Policy and Social Justice*, Basingstoke: Macmillan.

HUNTE, J. (1966), *Nigger Hunting in England?*, London: West Indian Standing Conference.

INSTITUTE FOR THE STUDY OF DRUG DEPENDENCE (ISDD) (1997), *Drug Misuse in Britain 1996*, London: ISDD.

JEFFERSON, A. (1993), 'The Racism of Criminalization: Police and the Reproduction of the Criminal Other', in L.R. Gelsthorpe (ed.), *Minority Ethnic Groups in the Criminal Justice System*, Cambridge: University of Cambridge Institute of Criminology.

JEFFERSON, T., and WALKER, M.A. (1992), 'Ethnic Minorities in the Criminal Justice System', *Criminal Law Review*, 81, 140: 83–95.

JUNGER, M. (1989), 'Discrepancies between police and self-report data for Dutch racial minorities', *British Journal of Criminology*, 29, 3: 273–84.

—— (1990), 'Studying ethnic minorities in relation to crime and police discrimination: answer to Bowling', *British Journal of Criminology*, 30(4): 493–502.

KAPLAN, J., and BJØRGO, T. (1998), *Nation and Race: The Developing Euro-American Racist Subculture*, New York: NYU Press.

KERSHAW, C., BUDD, T., KINSHOTT, G., MATTINSON, J., MAYHEW, P., and MYHILL, A. (2000), *The 2000 British Crime Survey*, Home Office Statistical Bulletin 18/00, London: Home Office.

KLEG, M. (1993), *Hate prejudice and racism*, Albany: State University of New York Press.

LANGAN, P.A. (1985), 'Racism on Trial: New Evidence to Explain the Racial Composition of Prisons in the United States', *Journal of Criminal Law and Criminology*, 76, 3: 666–83.

LAWRENCE, D. (1996), 'Race, Culture and the Probation Service: Groupwork Programme Design', in G. McIvor (ed.), *Working with Offenders*, Research Highlights in Social Work 26, London: Jessica Kingsley.

LEITNER, M., SHAPLAND, J., and WILES, P. (1993), *Drug usage and drugs prevention: the views and habits of the general public*, London: HMSO.

LOMBROSO, C. (1876), *L'Uomo Delinquente*, Turin: Fratelli Bocca.

MACPHERSON, W. (1999), *The Stephen Lawrence Inquiry*, Report of an Inquiry by Sir William Macpherson of Cluny, advised by Tom Cook, The Right Reverend Dr John Sentamu and Dr Richard Stone, Cm 4262-1, London: The Stationery Office.

MAIR, G. (1986), 'Ethnic Minorities, Probation and the Magistrates' Courts', *British Journal of Criminology*, 26, 2: 147–55.

MAVUNGA, P. (1993), 'Probation: A Basically Racist Service', in L. Gelsthorpe (ed.), *Minority Groups in the Criminal Justice System*, Cambridge: Cambridge University Institute of Criminology.

MAWBY, R. (1979), *Policing the City*, Farnborough: Saxon House.

MAYHEW, P., ELLIOTT, D., and DOWDS, L. (1989), *The 1988 British Crime Survey*, Home Office Research Study No. 111, London: HMSO.

——, AYE MAUNG, N., and MIRRLEES-BLACK, C. (1993), *The 1992 British Crime Survey*, Home Office Research Study No. 132, London: HMSO.

MAYNARD, W., and READ, T. (1997), *Policing*

Racially Motivated Incidents, Police Research Group Crime Detection and Prevention Series, No. 59, London: Home Office.

McConville, M., and Shepherd, D. (1992), Watching Police Watching Communities, London: Routledge.

McCrudden, C., Smith, D.J., and Brown, C. (1991), Racial Justice at Work: The Enforcement of the 1976 Race Relations Act in Employment, London: Policy Studies Institute.

McDermott, K. (1990), 'We Have No Problem: the Experience of Racism in Prison', New Community, 16, 2: 213–28.

Mhlanga, B. (1997), The Colour of English Justice: a Multivariate Analysis, Aldershot: Avebury.

—— (1999), Race and Crown Prosecution Service Decisions, London: The Stationery Office.

Miller, J. (forthcoming), Young Offenders from Different Ethnic Backgrounds: a Qualitative Study, PhD Thesis.

——, Bland, N., and Quinton, P. (2000), The Impact of Stops and Searches on Crime and the Community, Police Research Series Paper 127, London: Home Office.

Miller, J.G. (1996), Search and Destroy: African-American Males in the Criminal Justice System, Cambridge: Cambridge University Press.

Mirrlees-Black, C. (2001), Confidence in the Criminal Justice System: findings from the 2000 British Crime Survey, Research Findings No. 137, London: Home Office.

Modood, T., Berthoud, R., with the assistance of Lakey, J., Nazroo, J., Smith, P., Virdee, S., and Beishon, S. (1997), Ethnic Minorities in Britain: Diversity and Disadvantage, London: Policy Studies Institute.

Mott, J., and Mirrlees-Black, C. (1995), Self-reported drug misuse in England and Wales: Findings from the 1992 British Crime Survey, Research and Planning Unit Paper No. 89, London: Home Office.

MVA and Miller, J. (2000), Profiling Populations Available for Stops and Searches, Police Research Series Paper No. 131, London: Home Office.

Norris, C., Fielding, N., Kemp, C., and Fielding, J. (1992), 'Black and Blue: an Analysis of the Influence of Race on Being Stopped by the Police', British Journal of Sociology, 43, 2: 207–23.

Newburn, T., and Hayman, S. (2001), Policing, Surveillance and Social Control: CCTV and Police Monitoring of Suspects, Cullumpton, Devon: Willan Publishing.

OPCS (1993), 1991 Census: Ethnic Group and Country of Birth (Great Britain), London: Office of Population and Censuses Survey.

Pearson, G. (1983), Hooligan: a history of respectable fears, London: Macmillan.

Percy, A. (1998), 'Ethnicity and Victimisation: Findings from the 1996 British Crime Survey', Home Office Statistical Bulletin 6/98, 3 April, London: Home Office.

Phillips, C., and Brown, D. (1998), Entry into the Criminal Justice System: a Survey of Police Arrests and Their Outcomes, Home Office Research Study No. 185, London: Home Office.

—— and Sampson, A. (1998), 'Preventing Repeat Racial Victimisation: An Action Research Project', British Journal of Criminology, 38, 1: 124–44.

Povey, D., Cotton, J., and Sisson, S. (2000), Recorded Crime Statistics: England and Wales, April 1999 to March 2000, Home Office Statistical Bulletin 12/00, London: Home Office.

—— et al. (2001), Recorded Crime England and Wales, 12 months to March 2001, Home Office Statistical Bulletin 12/01, London: Home Office.

Pratt, M. (1981), Mugging as a social problem, London: Routledge.

Quinton, P., Bland, N., and Miller, J. (2000), Police Stops, Decision-Making and Practice, Police Research Series Paper No. 130, London: Home Office.

Ramsay, M., and Percy, A. (1996), Drug Misuse Declared: Results of the 1994 British Crime Survey, Research Findings No. 33, London: Home Office Research and Statistics Directorate.

—— and Spiller, A. (1997), Drug Misuse declared in 1996: latest results from the British Crime Survey, Home Office Research and Statistics Directorate, Home Office Research Study No. 172, London: Home Office.

——, Baker, P., Goulden, C., Sharp, C., and Sondhi, A. (2001), Drug Misuse Declared in 2000: Results from the British Crime Survey, Home Office Research Study No. 224, London: Home Office.

Ray, L., Smith, D., and Wastell, L. (2001), 'Understanding Racist Violence', Criminal Justice Matters, 43.

Reardon, D. (1993), 'The Reality of Life for Black Professionals in the Criminal Justice System', in D. Woodhill and P. Senior (eds), Justice for Black Young People, Sheffield: Panic Publications.

Reiner, R. (1993), 'Race, Crime and Justice: Models

of Interpretation', in L.R. Gelsthorpe (ed.), *Minority Ethnic Groups in the Criminal Justice System*, Cambridge: University of Cambridge Institute of Criminology.

SAMPSON, A., and PHILLIPS, C. (1992), *Multiple Victimisation: Racial Attacks on an East London Estate*, Police Research Group Crime Prevention Unit Series Paper 36, London: Home Office.

—— and —— (1996), *Reducing Repeat Victimisation on an East London Estate*, Police Research Group Crime Prevention Unit Crime Prevention and Detection Paper 67, London: Home Office.

SAULSBURY, W.E., and BOWLING, B. (1991), *The Multi-Agency Approach in Practice: the North Plaistow Racial Harassment Project*, Home Office Research Study No. 64, London: Home Office.

SAVILL, J. (1994), *Towards understanding the offender profile of a young mugger. A comparison of young offenders in the London Boroughs of Lambeth and Lewisham*, Unpublished thesis, University of Exeter.

SCARMAN, L. (1981), *The Scarman Report*, London: HMSO.

SHAH, R., and PEASE, K. (1992), 'Crime, Race and Reporting to the Police', *Howard Journal*, 31, 3: 192–9.

SHALLICE, A., and GORDON, P. (1990), *Black People, White Justice? Race and the Criminal Justice System*, London: Runnymede Trust.

SHAW, J.W. (1990), 'Institutional Racial Discrimination, Strategic Planning and Training in the Prison Department', *New Community*, 16, 4: 533–50.

SIBBITT, R. (1997), *The Perpetrators of Racial Harassment and Racial Violence*, Home Office Research Study No. 176, London: Home Office.

SIVANANDAN, A. (1982), *A Different Hunger: Writings on Black Resistance*, London: Pluto.

SKOGAN, W.G. (1990), *The Police and the Public in England and Wales: A British Crime Survey*

Report, Home Office Research Study No. 117, London: HMSO.

SMITH, D.J. (1994), 'Race, Crime and Criminal Justice', in M. Maguire, R. Morgan, and R. Reiner (eds), *The Oxford Handbook of Criminology*, 1st edn, Oxford: Clarendon Press.

—— (1997), 'Ethnic Origins, Crime and Criminal Justice', in M. Maguire, R. Morgan, and R. Reiner (eds), *The Oxford Handbook of Criminology*, 2nd edn, Oxford: Oxford University Press.

SMITH, S.J. (1989), *The Politics of 'Race' and Residence: citizenship, segregation and white supremacy in Britain*, Cambridge: Polity.

SOLOMOS, J. (1988), *Black Youth, Racism and the State*, Cambridge: Cambridge University Press.

—— and BACK, L. (1996), *Racism and Society*, London: Macmillan.

STEER, D. (1980), *Uncovering Crime: the police role*, Royal Commission on Criminal Procedure Research Study No. 7, London: HMSO.

STEVENS, P., and WILLIS, C.F. (1979), *Race, Crime and Arrests*, Home Office Research Study No. 58, London: HMSO.

STONE, V., and TUFFIN, R. (2000), *Attitudes of People from Minority Ethnic Communities towards a Career in the Police Service*, Police Research Series Paper 136, London: Home Office.

WALKER, M.A. (1989), 'The Court Disposal and Remands of White, Afro-Caribbean, and Asian Men (London, 1983)', *British Journal of Criminology*, 29, 4: 353–67.

WARDAK, A. (2000), *Social Control and Deviance: A South Asian Community in Scotland*, Aldershot: Ashgate.

WEBSTER, C. (1997), 'The Construction of British "Asian Criminality"', *International Journal of the Sociology of Law*, 25: 65–86.

YOUNG, J. (1994), *Policing the Streets: stops and searches in North London*, Middlesex: Centre for Criminology, Middlesex University.

18

ENVIRONMENTAL CRIMINOLOGY

Anthony E. Bottoms and Paul Wiles

Environmental criminology is the study of crime, criminality, and victimization as they relate, first, to particular *places* and, secondly, to the way that individuals and organizations shape their activities *spatially*, and in so doing are in turn influenced by *place-based* or *spatial* factors.[1] The study of the spatial patterning of crime and criminality has a long and continuous criminological history, and is now entering a new phase with the use of computerized mapping systems by the police and researchers.

Environmental criminology would be of little interest—either to scholars or those concerned with criminal policy—if the geographical distribution of offences, or of victimization or offender residence, were random. In fact this is very far from being the case, and the geographical concentration of crime and criminality parallels other skews in criminological data (for example, the fact that a relatively small number of persistent offenders commit a very disproportionate number of crimes).[2]

It is no accident that environmental criminology was born in the nineteenth century, the century *par excellence* of industrialization and urbanization in most Western societies. Crime seemed, to many observers, to be integrally and obviously linked to these developments in modern society. While there is strong empirical support for a higher crime rate in cities, especially large cities (see, for example, Cressey 1964: chapter 3; Braithwaite 1989: chapter 3), research has not always shown a direct or simple temporal link between urbanization and crime (see, for example, Gillis 1996). Furthermore, a significant group of scholars now argue that the social transformations of the late twentieth century have already projected us from 'modern' to 'late modern' societies, a transformation that may have as profound an influence on social life as the original arrival of industrialization and urbanization. We shall return to this thesis, and its criminological implications, after discussing the more orthodox literature of environmental criminology.

---

[1] 'Place' is not the same as 'space'. The former concept refers to a geographical location, with fairly definite boundaries, within which people may meet, engage in various activities, etc. 'Space' is a much broader concept, but environmental criminologists are interested in it because some social activities have become quite markedly *spatially differentiated* (e.g., the 'zoning' policies of some urban planners); on the other hand, modern transport and telecommunications allow for individuals (and organizations) to bridge spatial separation to a much greater extent than in previous generations.

[2] On this, see David Farrington, in Chapter 19 of this volume.

Traditionally, the two central concerns of environmental criminology have been *explaining the spatial distribution of offences* and *explaining the spatial distribution of offenders*. Hence, sections on these topics will feature prominently in this chapter. These central sections will be preceded by an historical introduction and some methodological comments. They will be followed by a discussion of the relationship between the areal distribution of offences and offenders, and a short theoretical section. Lastly, these 'static' analyses will be supplemented by a review of the relevance of social change for environmental criminology, both at meso and macro levels. For reasons of space, some aspects of environmental criminology will not be covered, in particular a consideration of perceptions of crime and fear of crime at neighbourhood level; and the important, but specialized, topic of design and crime.[3]

ENVIRONMENTAL CRIMINOLOGY: A BRIEF HISTORY

In a chapter of this length there is not the space to discuss the nineteenth-century precursors of environmental criminology.[4] However, because of its major subsequent influence, attention must be paid to the criminological work carried out between the two World Wars from within the Chicago School of Sociology (on which see generally Bulmer (1984) and Kurtz (1984)).

The main Chicagoan criminological contribution came from Clifford Shaw and Henry McKay, whose *magnum opus* on juvenile delinquency in urban areas is still read, more than half a century on (Shaw and McKay 1942). Their main contribution to criminology was empirical, and their research embraced two very different styles, always seen by the authors themselves as complementary. In the first place, they meticulously mapped the residences of juvenile delinquents, first of all in Chicago itself at different points in time, and then also in other American cities. Secondly, they also tried, in the tradition of the Chicago School more generally, to stay close to the life of the people and the communities they were writing about, particularly by producing life histories of offenders and low life in the city[5] (see, for example, Shaw 1930).

For present purposes, we can concentrate on Shaw and McKay's mapping of delinquent residences. In developing this research, they drew upon the more general work in urban sociology of the Chicago School, notably that of Robert E. Park and Ernest W. Burgess, the dominant concept of which was 'human ecology'. Human ecology was seen as the study of the spatial and temporal relations of human beings as affected by the selective, distributive, and accommodative forces of the environment; the

[3] Among the most important literature on design and crime, see Newman (1973), Poyner (1983), Coleman (1985, 1989), Poyner and Webb (1992), Taylor and Harrell (1996), and Department of the Environment (1997).

[4] On this nineteenth-century background, see generally Morris (1957: chapter 3); Radzinowicz (1966: chapter 2); Tobias (1972).

[5] For a discussion of the importance of the life history method and its links to environmental criminology, see Howard S. Becker's introduction to the 1966 edition of Shaw (1930).

concept was derived, by analogy, from the botanical sub-discipline of plant ecology. Shaw and McKay drew only to a limited extent upon the most explicitly quasi-biological elements of Park's urban sociology (see Alihan 1938), but they made quite central use of Burgess's zonal theory of city development. According to this theory, the typical city could be conceptualized as consisting of five main concentric zones. The innermost zone was described as the non-residential central business district (or 'loop'),[6] which was then circled by a 'zone in transition' where factories and poorer residences were intermingled, and lastly by three residential zones of increasing afflu-ence and social status as one moved towards the outer suburbs. New immigrants, it was postulated, would move into the cheapest residential areas of the city (in the 'zone in transition') and then, as they became economically established, migrate outwards. This would be a continuous process, so that the 'zone in transition' would (as its name implies) have a high residential mobility rate and, by implication, a rather hetero-geneous population. In the case of a rapidly expanding city, particular districts which had once been peripheral and affluent might become, in time, part of the zone in transition within the larger metropolis (see, for example, Rex and Moore 1967 on Sparkbrook, Birmingham).

Applying this zonal model to their empirical data, Shaw and McKay made three central discoveries:[7]

First, the rates of juvenile delinquency residence conformed to a regular spatial pattern. They were highest in the 'zone in transition', and then declined with distance from the centre of the city; and this was so not only in Chicago but in other cities as well.

Secondly, the same spatial pattern was shown by many other indices of social problems in the city.

Thirdly, the spatial pattern of rates of delinquency showed considerable long-term stability, even though the nationality make-up of the population in the inner-city areas changed greatly from decade to decade (with successive waves of migration to American cities in the early twentieth century).

In seeking to explain these striking findings, Shaw and McKay focused especially upon the observed *cultural heterogeneity* and the *constant population movements* in the 'zone in transition'. Economic mobility lay at the heart of the process they described, but they did not posit a direct relationship between economic factors and rates of delinquency. Instead, areas characterized by economic deprivation and physical deterioration were seen as transitional zones which were characterized by population instability and cultural fragmentation. It was these factors which especially influenced juvenile delinquency through a process which they called 'social disorganization' (although some later commentators have felt it might have been better described as 'lack of social organization'). In Shaw and McKay's thinking, 'social disorganization exists in the first instance when the structure and culture of a community are incap-able of implementing and expressing the values of its own residents' (Kornhauser

---

[6] So called because the business area in Chicago was within the inner loop of Chicago's elevated transit system—'the El'.

[7] This formulation draws on that of Finestone (1976: 25).

1978: 63); and this was seen as strongly related to the genesis of juvenile delinquency because incoming immigrant communities could not provide for their young people common and clear non-delinquent values and control, given the social fluidity and moral diversity[8] in the area.[9] We will return to the theme of social disorganization later in the chapter.

It is a measure of the standing and achievement of Shaw and McKay that, in the quarter century immediately after the end of the Second World War, there were relatively few major new developments in environmental criminology, despite the publication of some significant individual research monographs (for example, Lander 1954; Morris 1957). However, the 1970s were to see environmental criminology given new impetus, mainly by two fresh developments.

The first of these can be described as the *rediscovery of the offence*. Shaw and McKay's work had been all about *area offender rates* (i.e., the rate of offenders per head of population in each area), but these are not necessarily the same as *area offence rates* (i.e., the rate of offences committed in each area), since we cannot necessarily assume that offenders commit offences close to their homes (see further below). Various different criminological developments combined to re-focus attention on *crimes* rather than *offenders* in the 1970s (see generally P.J. and P.L. Brantingham 1981: Introduction). These included the first large-scale victim surveys (carried out in the US in the late 1960s); the early work of the Home Office Research Unit on 'crime as opportunity' (Mayhew *et al.* 1976), leading in due course to the more sophisticated development of 'situational crime prevention' theory (see Clarke 1995); and the increasing interest of geographers in crime issues (see, for example, Harries 1980; Davidson 1981; Herbert 1982).

The second major development of the 1970s came in the field of explaining offender rates. In his pioneering 1957 book, Terence Morris (1957) showed that the areal rates of offender residence in Croydon did not conform to the Chicago zonal hypothesis. This finding was later confirmed and strengthened by work in Sheffield (Baldwin and Bottoms 1976) that showed that, while there was something of a cluster-ing of high offender rate areas around the central business district, for the city as a whole the data did not display any tidy zonal pattern. In seeking to explain these findings, the Sheffield researchers were drawn increasingly towards the exploration of the *direct and indirect consequences of the operation of the housing market* (see, for example, Bottoms and Wiles 1986). This emphasis on housing markets has been taken up by other researchers, and has been found to be of particular significance when assessing change in offender and offence rates in residential areas (see, for example, Taub, Taylor, and Dunham 1984; Wikström 1991; Hancock 2001).

The *rediscovery of the offence* and the *discovery of the significance of housing markets*

---

[8] The moral diversity arose not only from the presence in the zone in transition of several different immigrant groups, but also from the fact that 'many illegitimate enterprises and deviant moral worlds' (Firestone 1976: 28) found their natural home in this zone of the city.

[9] At various points in their writings, Shaw and McKay also speak of another and rather different theor-etical approach to the explanation of criminality, namely that of *criminal subcultures*, linked to the *cultural transmission of delinquent values*. The precise relationship between these two varied theoretical strands of Shaw and McKay's work was not always made fully clear in their writings (see Kornhauser 1978: chapter 3).

have, between them, done much to revivify environmental criminology in the last twenty years. More recently, the advent of computerized geographical information systems (GIS) has led to an explosion of practitioner interest in 'crime mapping' (for a practitioners' handbook, see Harries 1999). The real importance of this development for the future of environmental criminology is that digital data are not necessarily subject to the same constraints of two-dimensionality as traditional maps, and future advances will depend on our ability to theorize and then analyse interactive effects between more than two geo-coded data sets—e.g., the effects of different population groups on offence rates in *both* time and space. Furthermore, GIS can act as the means of linking together any types of data which are capable of being geo-coded (e.g., health or education data as well as crime data). The current manifestations of the GIS revolution are often more mundane, however; they consist mainly in the rapidly increasing police use of GIS to map crime patterns (see, for example, La Vigne and Wartell 1998/2000), although more academic discussions are also available (see, for example, Weisburd and McEwen 1998; Hirschfield and Bowers 2001).

PRELIMINARY METHODOLOGICAL ISSUES

Before we turn to substantive research findings, four key methodological issues in environmental criminology must be briefly addressed: the offence/offender distinction; the validity of official statistics; the so-called 'ecological fallacy'; and the problem of what denominator to use to express offence rates.

The offence rate/offender rate distinction has already been highlighted above. It is an absolutely central issue in environmental criminology, as will quickly become apparent if one compares a map of offence locations in any given town with a map of offender residences in the same year (see, for example, Baldwin and Bottoms 1976: 58 and 75–6). Interestingly, however, research has shown that if one excludes non-residential areas such as the city centre and industrial districts, there is often a high (but not perfect) correlation between offender and offence rates in residential areas (Mawby 1979).[10]

One should further note (see Bottoms and Wiles 1986: Appendix) that, in any given geographical area, both the offence rate and the offender rate are in principle measurable both by official (police-recorded) data and by research-generated data (namely, victim surveys in respect of offence rates, and self-report surveys in respect of offender rates). In practice, however, self-report studies carried out on an areal basis are rare. One should also be aware that there is an important distinction in principle between an *area offence rate* and an *area victimization rate*. The former measures all offences committed in an area, whether against businesses, individual residents, or individuals who are visiting the area; the latter measures all offences committed

---

[10] Unfortunately, some early research studies did not adequately appreciate the importance of the offence/offender rate distinction, with sometimes confusing results. For a discussion of such studies, see P.J. and P.L. Brantingham (1981: 17).

against a defined population (e.g., respondents to a household victim survey living in a particular residential district), *wherever those offences were committed*. Because of this conceptual difference, particular care must be taken in comparing total police recorded offence rates for an area (which will be geographically bounded, but will include offences against businesses, and against individual visitors to the area) with overall rates generated from a household victim survey carried out in the same area (which will exclude crimes against businesses and individual victims visiting the area, but will include crimes committed against residents of the area when they have ventured outside the district, e.g., to the city centre or their place of work).

These considerations take us straight to the second methodological issue, that of the validity of official criminal statistics in relation to area-based data. There has been a lively debate on this issue, with particular scepticism about the validity of official statistics being expressed during the heyday of labelling theory in the 1970s (for a useful historical overview of the debate, see Mawby 1989). Commenting on this debate in a short space is difficult, but to begin with the uncontroversial, there is now little doubt that, on a large-area basis—for example, as between police forces—the message conveyed by official criminal statistics can be misleading, either because of differential public reporting of offences or (and more probably) because of different police investigative and recording practices (on the latter see, for example, Farrington and Dowds 1985; Burrows *et al.* 2000; and HM Inspectorate of Constabulary 2000).[11] On a smaller-area, within-city basis, however, as Mawby (1989) points out, there are good empirical grounds for believing that differential police-recorded offence and offender rates as between different areas might often express a basically true difference in crime or criminality levels. However, one must always be quite careful in interpreting even such data, especially for offences that are recorded as a result of pro-active policing, such as drug possession or prostitution.

The third preliminary methodological issue to consider is the so-called 'ecological fallacy', discussed mathematically in a famous article by Robinson (1950). This fallacy, which was sometimes unfortunately evident in early studies in environmental criminology (see Baldwin 1979 for some examples), occurs where 'the assumption [is] made that the descriptive characteristics of *areas* having high proportions of offenders resident also [identify] . . . the *individuals* who are likely to commit crimes' (P.J. and P.L. Brantingham 1981: 17). To take a simple example of the fallacy, in the 1960s various British research studies demonstrated that recorded crime and offender rates were highest in areas with a relatively high rate of recent ethnic minority immigration (mostly from the Caribbean and the Indian sub-continent), but research also showed, at that time, that on an individual basis such immigrants had on the whole rather low offending rates (see Baldwin and Bottoms 1976: 37–8, for references relating to this example). While in some cases areal and corresponding individual correlations may move in the same directions (see Janson 1993), nevertheless the wise researcher will always guard against the ecological fallacy when interpreting area-based data.

---

[11] The Association of Chief Police Officers has recently introduced new procedures, which, if successfully implemented, will significantly reduce the extent of recording variation between police forces in England and Wales from 2002.

The last methodological issue concerns the best denominator to use in order accurately to represent offence rates. Resident population might seem to be the obvious choice (and is the universally agreed denominator for offender rates, although where necessary broken down demographically), but it can be seriously misleading when measuring offence rates. For example, the City of London has a very high offence rate per thousand of the resident population, but this is an artefact of very few people being resident in the City, while its crime is largely a product of large numbers travelling to work there. Most city centres will produce a similarly artificial high rate of offences per head of resident population. More generally, careful thought usually needs to be given to what is the appropriate offence rate denominator for different types of crime: for example, for car crime a denominator of numbers of cars, or for burglary the number of households, are both better than population denominators (for a fuller discussion, see Wikström 1991: 193–200).

Having considered these methodological issues, we can now turn to the substantive results of modern environmental criminology.

EXPLAINING THE LOCATION OF OFFENCES

DESCRIPTIVE DATA

We begin with the location of offences. Wikström's (1991) study of police-recorded offences in Stockholm provides one of the best illustrations of the way in which such offences are locationally distributed in a major city.[12] Previous research work (see Baldwin and Bottoms 1976) had shown that offences tend, in traditional cities, to be clustered around the city centre;[13] and the offence data in Wikström's study (see Figure 18.1, (a), (b) and (c)) show this to be especially the case for violence in public, vandalism in public, and theft of and from cars. (Wikström does not present data concerning shoplifting or thefts from the person, but other research studies have shown that these offences also are particularly located in city centres.) However, there is nothing necessarily immutable about such patterns. For example, in cities that develop large shopping or entertainment complexes on peripheral sites, some corresponding modification of this traditional geographical pattern may take place. In Sheffield the development of such a complex (the Meadowhall shopping mall) helped to reduce the proportion of all crime occurring in the city centre from 24 per cent in 1966 to 10 per cent in 1995 (Wiles and Costello 2000: 46).

Turning to offences in residential areas, the distributions of family violence and residential burglaries in Wikström's study are shown in Figure 18.1, (d) and (e). The highest rates of family violence were found in certain outer-city wards, and further

[12] Note that Wikström's study uses different denominators for different kinds of offence rates (see rubric at foot of Figure 18.1).

[13] In fact, in Sheffield in 1966, 24 per cent of recorded offences were committed within a half mile radius of the centre of the city, though this area constituted less than 3 per cent of the total land area in the city (Baldwin and Bottoms 1976: 57).

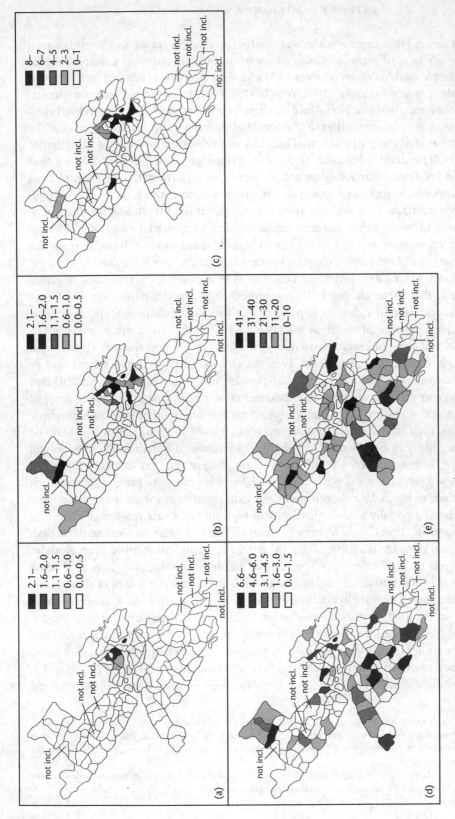

Fig. 18.1 Areal offence rates for selected types of crime, Stockholm, 1982: (a) violence in public per hectare; (b) vandalism in public per hectare; (c) thefts of and from cars per hectare; (d) family violence per 1,000 households; (e) residential burglaries per 1,000 residences

Source: Wikström (1991: 203–206).

analysis showed that there was a strong positive correlation (at an area level) between (i) an area's rates of recorded family violence, and (ii) its score on a factor (derived from a factor analysis of social areas in Stockholm) which was labelled by Wikström as 'problem residential areas' (Wikström 1991: 226). Hence, and perhaps not surprisingly, police-recorded family violence was heavily concentrated in poorer public housing areas. A further inspection of the Stockholm maps indicates, however, that the distribution of offences of residential burglary was substantially different from that of family violence, and additional analysis by Wikström (ibid.: 226–7) showed that recorded residential burglaries tended to occur disproportionately in areas of high socio-economic status, and especially in districts where there were nearby high offender-rate areas. This finding, while not unique in the literature,[14] conflicts with the results of many other research studies, which suggest that rates of residential burglary are greatest in, or in areas close to, socially disadvantaged housing areas (for a summary, see Mawby 2001: chapter 5). We will return to this issue later.

Wikström's study demonstrates, at any rate as regards crimes as measured by police data, first, that there are marked geographical skews in the patterning of offence locations and, secondly, that areal patterns can vary significantly by type of offence. This general message of variation has been heavily reinforced in other research. For example, 'hotspots' of crime research, by Sherman, Gartin, and Buerger (1989), used police call data for Minneapolis for 1985–86, and found (i) that just 3.3 per cent of specific locations in the city generated 50 per cent of crime-related calls, and (ii) that there was considerable variation in the victimization rate (as measured by call data) of specific micro-locations even *within* high-crime rate areas—that is, even high-crime areas have their relatively safe specific locations, as well as their 'hotspots' where the public are likely to be especially vulnerable.[15] Moreover, different kinds of areas will also have different patterns of crime. We have already referred to city centres, but other non-residential areas, such as industrial estates, can have burglary rates much higher than residential neighbourhoods, yet with significant variations which appear to be related especially to their proximity to high offender rate residential areas (see Johnston *et al.* 1994). Again, domestic burglary has a different time pattern than commercial burglary (Ratcliffe 2001), the latter occurring much more often at night. Lastly, even in high offence rate residential neighbourhoods, the chance of being victimized is not random, with some households not being victimized at all in a year, but others being repeatedly victimized. For example, in the worst tenth of areas studied in the 1988 British Crime Survey (BCS), only 28 per cent of respondents reported having been the victim of a property offence in the previous year, but the average number of incidents reported by property crime victims was 4.6, with some having been victimized only once, but others very frequently (Farrell 1995: 526).

The above discussion of offence locations has been primarily descriptive. We need

[14] See, e.g., Baldwin and Bottoms (1976: 63); Winchester and Jackson (1982: 18–19). It should be pointed out that these studies, like Wikström's, are based on data recorded by the police, and it is likely that they proportionately overstate the number of high-value burglaries, since value is known to be related to the decision to report.

[15] See also Sherman's later discussion of 'hot spots' in Sherman (1995). For other similar work see Block and Block (1995), and for an excellent critical review Spelman (1995).

now to attempt to explain the variations discussed, and so we turn to the related concepts of opportunity and routine activities.

OPPORTUNITY THEORY AND ROUTINE ACTIVITIES THEORY

As Clarke (1995) has shown, the concept of opportunity is multifaceted, but in the present context two aspects of opportunity are especially important. The first of these can be described as *target attractiveness*, a concept which includes both value (monetary and/or symbolic) and portability. In terms of the location of offences, the value of property can sometimes be of special importance, both as regards the general affluence of an area (see Wikström's data on residential burglary, above) and as regards the value of a particular target, by comparison with neighbouring potential targets. For example, in the BCS's analysis of car crime, it has been found that, within a given residential area, the cars of the more obviously affluent residents are more likely to be targeted,[16] and Clarke has shown how certain goods are 'hot products' in terms of being targeted for theft (Clarke 1999).

The second main dimension of opportunity might be described as *accessibility*, a concept that includes visibility, ease of physical access, and the absence of adequate surveillance. This dimension of opportunity is well illustrated by an analysis of the rates of autocrime from different multi-storey car parks in Croydon (see table in Bottoms 1994: 603). This showed that three short-stay car parks which were used primarily by shoppers (and which therefore had a constant stream of passers-by providing natural surveillance) had substantially lower crime rates than two long-stay car parks, primarily used by London commuters, which lacked such surveillance.[17] Other (and similar) examples of the importance of accessibility and natural surveillance can also be found in the literature (see, for example, Clarke 1995; Mayhew *et al.* 1976).

The problem with opportunity theory, unless mediated by some other considerations, is that it cannot account for the general distribution of victimization in most cities. As already explained above, while some affluent neighbourhoods, with plenty of attractive targets, do have high offence rates, others do not—and the highest victimization rates are often to be found in the poorest neighbourhoods with low levels of target attractiveness. Partly in an attempt to overcome this defect, opportunity theory is often combined with 'routine activities theory', originally developed by Cohen and Felson (1979) and subsequently elaborated mostly by Marcus Felson and others (see, for example, Felson 1986, 1992, 1995; Eck 1995). The central hypothesis of routine activities theory was originally stated as:

[16] Specifically, in thefts of and from cars from immediately around the house, 'consumerist' households were more likely to be victimized, even when area and type of residence was controlled for (see Mayhew, Aye Maung, and Mirrlees-Black 1993: 140–41). ('Consumerist' households were those owning three or more of five specified electronic consumer products.)

[17] A complicating variable here was that each car on average stayed longer in the commuter car-park (= greater risk availability per vehicle); however, even when the data was calculated as a 'rate per car park space' (in effect controlling for this difference), the commuter car parks had significantly higher autocrime rates.

the probability that a violation will occur at any specific time and place might be taken as a function of the convergence of likely offenders and suitable targets in the absence of capable guardians [Cohen and Felson 1979: 590].

However, of the three elements identified in the above quotation, routine activities theory has in practice concentrated very heavily on the second and third (suitable targets and capable guardians).[18] That being so, the link with opportunity theory is self-evident; but (as we will show later) by largely ignoring the offender dimension, advocates of routine activities theory have closed off a promising approach to the explanation of city-wide victimization rates. Despite this self-imposed limitation, there are nevertheless two features of the routine activities approach which usefully develop and extend the straightforward concept of 'opportunity'. These are as follows:

First, there is a strong interest within routine activities theory in *the day-to-day activities of potential victims of crime, and of those potentially able to offer 'natural surveillance'*. There is therefore seen to be an interdependence between the varied social organisation of daily life patterns (for example, in different decades, and/or in different places, and/or among different social groups in the same area) and the spatial–temporal patterns of illegal activities.

Secondly, routine activities theory has an explicitly spatial dimension, which, while implicitly present in simple opportunity theory, has not always been much developed by writers of that school. Routine activities theory, on the other hand, precisely because of its interest in the everyday lives of potential victims of crime and of potential 'natural guardians', specifically emphasises 'the fundamental human ecological character of illegal acts as *events* which occur at specific locations in *space* and *time*, involving specific persons and/or objects'. (Cohen and Felson 1979: 589, emphasis in original)

In sum, routine activities theory in effect embeds the concept of opportunity within the routine parameters of the day-to-day lives of ordinary people, and in doing so also emphasizes the spatial–temporal features of opportunity.

Once one begins to link the opportunity concept to that of routine activities then other relevant issues in considering the spatial distribution of offences also begin to become apparent. One such issue is that of *self-policing*, as it affects potential offences against the person. Potential victims can respond to possible opportunities for them to be attacked by various kinds of 'avoidance' behaviour. For example, since there is clear empirical evidence of substantially greater harassment of women (especially younger women) in the public spaces of cities (see, for example, Anderson *et al.* 1990: 23–4; Painter 1992), it is hardly surprising that women are likely to engage in 'self-policing' as regards their use of public space (see, for example, Ramsay 1989). Unfortunately, such routine self-policing activities might themselves have further unintended social consequences—such as compounding the fears of other women and undermining the overall quality of urban life (see Painter 1992).

---

[18] See Cohen and Felson (1979: 589): 'Unlike many criminological enquiries, we do not examine why individuals or groups are inclined criminally, but rather we take criminal inclination as given and examine the manner in which the spatio-temporal organisation of social activities helps people to translate their criminal inclinations into action'. Felson has, however, subsequently considered the offender dimension to a limited extent: see, e.g., Felson (1986).

Taking all the evidence of this subsection together, there is not much doubt that 'opportunity' (understood here as incorporating the routine activities approach) powerfully influences crime locations. However, the research literature also suggests that matters are more complex than this. To begin to see why that is so, let us first consider a qualitative study of convicted burglars in a Texas city (Cromwell, Olson, and Avary 1991). These authors found, congruently with opportunity theory, that offenders weighed potential gains, levels of guardianship (e.g., signs of occupancy), and risks of detection at possible sites of residential burglary (see also Bennett and Wright 1984). Hence, it appeared that *active weighing of the opportunity factor at the potential crime site* was a significant factor in the ultimate decision whether or not to commit a particular crime. On the other hand, Cromwell and his colleagues also found that there was individual variation in the degree of planning as between different offenders (or groups of offenders); complex interactive effects within groups of burglars; differences related to whether illicit drugs were used by the offenders; and interactions with fences that could affect the decision processes.

Opportunity theory uses a rational model of decision making, but all too often its exponents have assumed both that the form of rationality is instrumental and that the actual behaviour mirrors the model. The research of Cromwell, Olson, and Avory (1991) suggests a less straightforward empirical reality, and this view has been strongly reinforced by research on burglars' decision making, by Wright and Decker (1994), which shows that decisions to offend can be irrational, arational, or rational; and when rational, are more likely to be affectually rather than instrumentally rational[19] and to be driven by short-term, immediate emotional needs. In so far as targets were instrumentally assessed for degree of risk, Wright and Decker found that because most crimes were committed to satisfy an immediate need (for money, drugs, etc.),[20] they were more often based on existing routine knowledge rather than a calculated process of crime planning prior to the act.

The work of Cromwell and his colleagues, and especially that of Wright and Decker, draws attention to the routine activities of *offenders*. As previously noted, that is a subject about which the proponents of 'routine activities theory' have normally shown rather little interest. We shall return to the question of how offenders use space in a later section on bringing together explanations of offence locations and offender locations; as we shall see, this will provide a more complete picture that helps to provide an improved explanation of the geographical distribution of offences.

[19] 'Affectual' and 'instrumental' rationality are borrowed from Max Weber's terms 'vertrationalitat' and 'zweckrationalitat'. Weber, of course, long ago spelt out the difference between behaviour and action and the different kinds of rational action. He was also at pains to point out that models of rational action are ideal types against which empirical reality has to be compared and understood. See Weber (1949, 1968).

[20] Interestingly, Wright and Decker suggest that their work reveals more about the non-instrumental nature of burglar's actions than earlier studies because they interviewed non-incarcerated subjects. They argue that those in prison are more likely to rationalize the accounts of their previous actions.

EXPLAINING THE LOCATION OF OFFENDER
RESIDENCE

We turn now to the problem of explaining the observed area distribution of offender residence.

As seen in an earlier section, traditionally this subject was heavily dominated by the conceptualizations of the Chicago School; and their explanations were themselves strongly influenced by the facts of stability over time in the zonal distribution of area offender rates, and the nature of land use in different zones of the city, as an outcome of the operation of the property market (Bursik 1986: 61).

Post-Second World War evidence, however, dealt a mortal blow to these underpinning assumptions. As previously indicated, offender rates in post-War British cities have borne little resemblance to the Chicagoan concentric ring pattern. Even in Chicago, careful analysis by Bursik (1986) showed that the old areal regularities have broken down, and that while the areas of the city that underwent the most rapid social change generally experienced considerable increases in delinquency, nevertheless there were some atypical areas where this relationship did not hold (see further Taub, Taylor, and Dunham 1984). Hence, while Shaw and McKay's social disorganization theory is still being supported and developed (see below), no one would now defend—at least in any generalized fashion—the Chicago concentric ring theory and the formulation of urban process that went with it.

In order to see what might replace this approach, it is useful first to consider how, in principle, area of residence and offender rates might be statistically related (this discussion develops that of Wikström 1991: 130).

First, area of residence and offender rates might be related because more or less crime-prone individuals or groups are distributed (by the dynamics of the local housing market) to certain areas. In this kind of correlation, however, the social life of the area itself does not affect the criminality levels of the residents.

Secondly, however, in principle *the social life of the area might itself influence criminal motivation*; and this possible influence is itself of two types. First, acquaintance patterns among local residents, and others who use the area, may lead to one being influenced by others to commit an offence. In such cases, it can be assumed (for the sake of argument) that the relevant social interactions would not have occurred had the offender lived elsewhere; but also that the transaction is a 'one-off' affair, not necessarily affecting the person's general way of living. Secondly, however, the social life of an area might have longer-term effects on a person's daily routines, social activities, thought processes, and even personality, such that his or her overall propensity to commit crime in certain situations is intrinsically affected. This kind of longer-term effect is obviously most likely to be manifested among young residents of an area, but the possibility of its occurring among older residents should not be ruled out.

In describing the first of the above possibilities, we referred to the operations of the local housing market as the key to the distribution of more or less crime-prone individuals to different areas. However, one of our own central contentions is that the housing market is also an important element in understanding the kinds of processes outlined in the second paragraph. We will return to that question after first considering the prior issue of whether neighbourhood effects on offending, of the kind postulated in the preceding paragraph, do in fact exist.

NEIGHBOURHOOD EFFECTS ON OFFENDER RATES

An important recent research study asked the question: 'Do disadvantaged neigh-bourhoods cause well-adjusted children to become adolescent delinquents?' (Wikström and Loeber 2000). This research was conducted, in part, to investigate empirically issues arising from the scepticism expressed by some criminologists (e.g., Wilson and Herrnstein 1985) about the existence of neighbourhood effects on delin-quent careers. The argument of the sceptics is that criminal careers research has uncovered a number of key 'risk factors' in the causation of delinquency which are individual in nature. They continue that criminal careers research shows that persist-ent offenders typically begin to offend early in life, well before communal factors—such as delinquent peers or neighbourhood processes—could play much of a role (Wilson and Herrnstein 1985: 311).[21]

Using data from the Pittsburgh Youth Study (a major longitudinal research project on male criminal careers), Wikström and Loeber divided their sample into those with high risk scores, those with high protective scores (the obverse of individual risk factors), and an intermediate group which was numerically the largest. They also divided the sample into four groups by 'neighbourhood context': these comprised those living in advantaged, middle range, and disadvantaged areas, the last being further sub-divided into areas of public housing and non-public housing. Table 18.1(a) shows the principal results for serious juvenile offending. In the sample as a whole, the proportion of serious offenders rose rapidly as one moved from boys with a high protective score to those with a high risk score (in advantaged and middle-range areas, from less than 10 per cent to over 70 per cent). Among those with high individual risk scores, there was no neighbourhood effect (all areas had rates between 70 and 80 per cent). But for those outside the high risk group, living in a disadvantaged area dominated by public housing significantly increased the probability of offending: for these youths, therefore, there seemed to be a clear neigh-bourhood effect.[22] Further analysis showed, however, that in one respect Wilson and Herrnstein's scepticism was apparently correct: for a first serious offending at the age of twelve or less, no neighbourhood effect was discernible in any of the risk groups.

[21] A number of empirical studies in the United States appear to support the sceptical position, with cumulative effects that 'may appear devastating for theories about the importance of community influences in offending' (Wikström 1998: 277). These studies include Simcha-Fagan and Schwartz (1986), Gottfredson, McNeill and Gottfredson (1991) and Lizotte et al. (1994). These studies, however, can be regarded as largely superseded by the more sophisticated Wikström and Loeber work: for a more detailed discussion, see Wik-ström (1998).

[22] It is also important to note that, in the disadvantaged public housing areas, there was little difference (and no statistically significant difference) in the offender rate by the number of risk or protective factors present. Thus, in these areas, the neighbourhood context appeared to 'swamp' the effects of individual risk factors that were—in other areas—highly significant.

In fact, however, the results shown in Table 18.1(a) almost certainly understate the neighbourhood effects on offending in Pittsburgh. To understand why, Table 18.1(b) should be examined. This shows, in detail, the percentage of research subjects in different types of neighbourhood who were assessed as 'high risk' on each of the six variables in the 'risk-protective score'. As may be seen, the overall risk index (bottom row of table) produced higher scores in the disadvantaged areas, especially those dominated by public housing; and these overall differences were predominately the result of strong area differences in the individual variables of 'low school motivation',

Table 18.1 Key results from the Pittsburgh Youth Study

(a) Per cent having committed serious offence by risk/protective score and neighbourhood context

| | | | Neighbourhood context | | | |
| | | | Disadvantaged | | | |
	Advantaged	Middle-range	Nonpublic	Public	Gamma	N
High Protective Score	11.1	5.1	16.7	37.5	0.23	155
Balanced Risk and Protective Score	27.3	40.1	38.5	60.7	0.23	651
High Risk Score	77.8	71.3	78.3	70.0	n.s.	222
Gamma	0.70	0.74	0.69	n.s.		
N	142	556	188	142		

(b) Per cent of subjects with high risk scores by neighbourhood context

| | | | Neighbourhood context | | | |
| | | | Disadvantaged | | | |
	Advantaged	Middle-range	Nonpublic	Public	Gamma	N
High Hyperactivity-Impulsivity-Attention Problems	13.8	20.9	28.7	20.1	0.15	1,436
Lack of Guilt	19.2	30.0	35.5	46.0	0.26	1,254
Poor Parental Supervision	15.8	22.8	29.1	39.7	0.28	1,414
Low School Motivation	21.9	31.2	44.9	47.6	0.30	1,432
Many Peer Delinquents	17.9	22.9	27.7	29.4	0.15	1,323
Positive Perception of Anti-Social Behaviour	29.2	25.8	19.8	25.9	n.s.	1,431
RISK INDEX	13.3	19.9	28.8	34.9	0.30	1,148

Source: Wikström and Loeber (2000: 1132 and 1130).

'poor parental supervision', and 'lack of guilt'. It is obviously in principle possible that all of these 'individual' factors might, over time, have been influenced by the community context in which the youths had been raised (e.g., parenting styles might have been learned, perhaps years ago, from neighbours; 'lack of guilt' might be influenced by the dominant norms of the local community, etc). Since, however, Table 18.1(a) controls for these 'individual' risk factors, it follows that it might in fact be 'overcontrolling'—that is, in effect discounting the possibility of some indirect neighbourhood effects. This possibility is explicitly recognized by Wikström and Loeber (2000: 1134).[23]

We may, therefore, reasonably conclude that neighbourhood effects on offending can and do exist. In a direct sense, they are weaker than 'individual risk factors', as Table 18.1(a) shows; but these individual risk factors might themselves incorporate significant indirect neighbourhood effects.[24] We may finally note one further interesting feature of the Pittsburgh study, namely that the neighbourhood effect was particularly evident in a set of neighbourhoods defined not only by social disadvantage, but also by their housing tenure (public housing). That leads us to an examination of the role of the housing market in the explanation of offender rates.

THE ROLE OF THE HOUSING MARKET

As indicated in an earlier section, in the 1970s a statistical study of recorded offender rates in Sheffield (Baldwin and Bottoms 1976) strongly suggested that the housing market might be relevant to the spatial distribution of offender rates,[25] over and above the other relevant variables such as the social class distribution of households in the area.[26] Subsequently, Wikström (1991) produced similar results, based on a path model analysis for offender rates in different areas of Stockholm.

To illustrate such effects more concretely, we will focus attention here on a pair of council estates studied in detail in a subsequent stage of the Sheffield research (the following account draws principally upon Bottoms, Mawby, and Xanthos 1989; for a follow-up study of the same areas in the late 1980s, see Bottoms, Claytor, and Wiles 1992). Briefly, the original problem for explanation was that these two small areas (population 2,500–3,000 each, and separated only by a main road), had (i) a 300 per

---

23 For interesting parallel work in psychology, see Bronfenbrenner (1979); the relevance of Bronfenbrenner's work for criminologists is well discussed by Martens (1993).

24 A recent study in Cologne by Oberwittler (2001) suggests that, in a socio-political context where schools draw pupils from a wide range of neighbourhoods, the 'school effect' is stronger than the 'home area effect' for juvenile delinquency. This is an important distinction, not previously much used in the environmental criminology literature because in the past school catchment areas were often co-terminous with the home neighbourhood. The distinction is potentially of considerable importance in contemporary Britain, given the advent of greater parental choice in school placements; it will be very interesting to see whether the Cologne results are replicated in future British studies.

25 This study was based on police-recorded offender rates, but subsequent work (e.g., by Mawby 1979; Bottoms, Mawby, and Walker 1987) suggested that the areal differences shown by these official data were trustworthy.

26 The researchers pursued this line of enquiry because of the then recent work in urban sociology on the concept of 'housing classes' (Rex and Moore 1967).

cent difference in recorded offender rates and a 350 per cent difference in recorded offence rates against individual residents and households, but (ii) no statistically significant differences at all on a set of key demographic variables (namely: sex; age; social class; ethnic origin; average household size; percentage single; percentage male unemployment; age of termination of full-time education; and length of stay in current dwelling). Preliminary research (adult victim and juvenile self-report studies) established that the crime rate differences could not, for the most part, be regarded as artefactual. A further point of interest was that both areas had been built at approximately the same time (in the 1920s), and both had, it seemed clear, begun as 'good', crime-free council areas. One of the estates (Stonewall) had retained this characteristic, but its neighbour (Gardenia) had 'tipped' sometime in the 1940s. Neither, however, was in any sense an 'area in transition'; rather, they were extremely settled, with 60 per cent of the adult residents in both areas having lived in their current dwelling for ten years or more.

The research team was unable to discover retrospectively exactly why Gardenia had tipped in the 1940s (though some speculative suggestions were made). But through detailed analysis of records in the local authority's housing department, plus ethnographic work in the areas, they were able to show that once Gardenia had tipped, the local authority's rules for housing allocation had the unintended effects of maintaining the difference between the two areas,[27] and of ensuring that Gardenia attracted, as new tenants, predominantly those in severe housing need and those who had prior affective links with the area (relatives living on the estate, etc.). To some extent, therefore, housing allocation processes were drawing to the two estates new residents with a differential propensity to offend (i.e., the first possible explanation for differential residential area offender rates discussed earlier). On the other hand, ethnographic work also showed that the second likely explanation also probably applied: the factors involved were very complex, and interactive, but included (in addition to the housing market context): a mild criminal sub-culture in one part of the more criminal estate (Gardenia); the effects of the negative reputation of Gardenia on its residents and on potential residents; possibly a difference relating to the main schools serving the two areas; and some important apparent differences in parental and peer socialization processes (see Bottoms, Mawby, and Xanthos 1989: 67–75, especially 74).

Three points are of special importance about this case study. First, it must be re-emphasized that, in terms of social-class-related demographic variables these two areas were almost identical; hence, the study presents a major obstacle to those who wish to argue that differential area offender rates are simply the product of macro-level aspects of social stratification, worked through to a local level. Secondly, very little in Shaw and McKay's conceptualization helps one in explaining the difference between Gardenia and Stonewall, not least since neither area had high population turnover. And thirdly, the researchers identified the operation of the local housing market as a key to understanding the areas. The operation of the local housing

---

[27] Subsequently, however, there was some convergence between the two areas—but again this could be explained by housing market changes: see Bottoms, Claytor, and Wiles (1992).

market, however, does not work in a stand-alone fashion, or only in relation to the population composition of an area. Rather, the Sheffield researchers stressed that the housing market could have crucial secondary social effects—in terms of, for example, the nature of the relationships that subsequently developed in an area, and responses by outsiders (including social control agents, potential residents, etc.). Subsequently, some of these effects might themselves have the potential to influence the housing market context of the area, for example, by altering the area's perceived desirability, or perhaps by escalating the number of residents wishing to leave. These complex inter-active processes are set out schematically in Figure 18.2 (taken from Bottoms, Claytor, and Wiles 1992). This model has received strong implicit support from later British empirical research (Hope and Foster 1992; Hancock 2001).

If the model in Figure 18.2 is correct, it follows that changes in the macro-level structures of the housing market could have significant effects on the distribution of offender rates in a given city (and possibly even on overall offending levels). In an earlier work, we noted apparently important polarization and residualization pro-cesses that were occurring in British housing markets, including some that developed after the Gardenia–Stonewall research was completed (Bottoms and Wiles 1995; see also Burney 1999). To date, there has been little detailed exploration of the implica-tions of these changes for the distribution of offender rates in British cities; but the issue remains an important one, as we argue in the concluding section of this chapter.

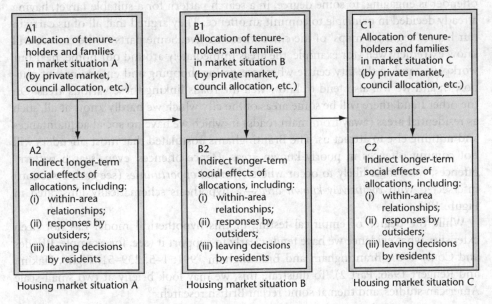

Fig. 18.2 Diagrammatic representation of the relationship between the potential effects of the housing market and residential community crime careers

Source: Bottoms et al. (1992: 120).

BRINGING TOGETHER EXPLANATIONS OF OFFENCE LOCATIONS AND OFFENDER LOCATIONS

We have now examined how offences are distributed in cities and, separately, how the homes of known offenders are distributed. We can therefore turn to the relationship between these two phenomena.

It is a commonplace of criminological textbooks that much crime is committed close to offenders' homes. There are a number of 'crime and distance' studies,[28] which explore detected offenders' distance from home when committing offences. However, this is rather less interesting than the related question of *the relationship of the place of the offence to the offender's habitual use of space.*

Let us first note that there are some purely *opportunist* crimes, where a person responds 'there and then' to a set of attractive environmental cues. For example, a teenage boy calls at a friend's house, finds the back door open and £20 unguarded on the table. Furthermore, there are also some *affectively spontaneous* crimes, where a person commits, say, an assault in the course of a sudden heated argument with an acquaintance. These offences, by definition, must occur in the place where the offender happens to be, as a result of his or her daily life-choices.

However, Patricia L. and Paul J. Brantingham (1981) have proposed that offenders' daily life patterns might influence the location of offending behaviour even when the offender is engaging, to some degree, in a search pattern for a suitable target, having already decided in principle to commit an offence. They argued that all of us carry in our heads 'cognitive maps' of the cities where we live. Some parts of the city we will know extremely well (for example, the areas immediately around our home, near our workplace, and in the city centre where we go for shopping and entertainment pur-poses); and we will also tend to know well the roads linking these various areas. On the other hand, there will be some areas of the city which we hardly know at all, such as residential areas (away from main roads) in which we have no social acquaintances and nothing else to attract us. The Brantinghams postulated that most offenders will not commit offences in poorly-known areas. Hence offences, even 'search pattern' offences, were most likely to occur where *criminal opportunities* (see earlier section) intersected with *cognitively-known areas*—a hypothesis schematically illustrated in Figure 18.3.

While the degree of empirical testing of this hypothetical model has not been extensive, what evidence we have tends clearly to support it (see, for example, Rhodes and Conly 1981; Brantingham and Brantingham 1991: 1–5, 239–51; Figlio, Hakim, and Rengert 1986: Part 2). To illustrate this, we may look briefly at two small-scale American studies, and then at some recent British research.[29]

---

[28] For a review of such studies, see McIver (1981) and Wiles and Costello (2000).

[29] It is also important to note that the Brantinghams' model has been successfully used in police detective work on serial assault cases by reversing the logic of the model, and constructing an algorithm to proximate the offender's likely residential or other familiar area, hence narrowing down the number of possible suspects (for a full discussion, see Rossmo 2000).

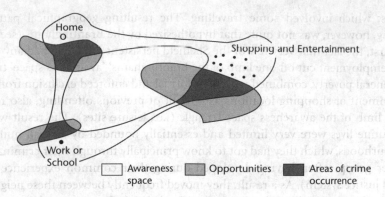

Fig. 18.3 The Brantinghams' hypothetical model of intersection of criminal opportunities with offenders' cognitive awareness space

Source: Brantingham and Brantingham (1984: 362).

Rengert and Wasilchick (2000: chapter 3) carried out an interview study of imprisoned adult burglars from Delaware County, Pennsylvania, and showed that burglary sites were clustered disproportionately in areas closest to the offenders' normal routes to work and recreation. By contrast, a very different directional pattern was observed for the few burglaries in the sample committed not as a result of the offender's own search pattern, but because a secondary source (e.g., a fence) told the offender about an appropriate opportunity for crime. An earlier study in Oklahoma City had found some similar results (Carter and Hill 1979), though because Oklahoma City is a racially divided city, neither black nor white offenders ventured much into residential areas predominantly lived in by the other ethnic group. Based on their findings, Carter and Hill (ibid.: 49) proposed an interesting distinction between 'strategic' and 'tactical' choices in search-pattern property crimes. 'Tactics' refer to 'short-term operational considerations for a specific crime', and may well be influenced by (instrumentally rational) opportunity factors. However, these 'tactical' decisions, Carter and Hill suggest, will be taken only within a limited geographical framework already set by 'strategic' considerations. These 'strategic' considerations relate especially to the issues of familiarity, and are thus more likely to be based on affective factors (e.g., 'areas towards which he has a favorable feeling'; ibid.: 49). Wright and Decker's (1994) findings, discussed earlier, also point to the importance, for some aspects of the process of offending, of this reliance on pre-existing familiarity. These results and suggestions provide a plausible reason why so much offending takes place near offenders' homes, or in other areas in which they routinely and regularly move.

A recent study in Sheffield (Wiles and Costello 2000) found that offenders on average travelled only 1.93 miles from their homes to commit a crime—a finding similar to many other studies. Interviews with Sheffield persistent offenders confirmed that most travel was not in order to offend. Moreover, most offending was not an outcome of criminally instrumental travel: less than a third of burglaries, for example, had involved travelling in order to commit the offence (ibid.: 36). The locations of offences were more usually the outcome of the offender's routine activities, which involved some travelling. The resulting geographical pattern of offending, however, was not quite that hypothesized by the Brantinghams (see Figure 18.3). First, the fact that very few of the Sheffield persistent offenders had any experience of employment cut off one limb of the Brantinghams' 'awareness space' triangle. Their general poverty, combined with their formal and enforced exclusion from some entertainment or shopping locations as a result of previous offending, also reduced another limb of the awareness space triangle (i.e., leisure sites). The result was that their routine lives were very limited and essentially bounded by a small number of neighbourhoods, which they had got to know principally through their criminal peers (the peer groups often having developed during their common experience of the criminal justice system). As a result, they moved frequently between these neighbourhoods, lived precariously, and persistently offended. Another aspect of their routines was a somewhat itinerant lifestyle, which meant that they quite often slept somewhere other than their 'official' home address. One consequence of this was that the average travel distance to commit an offence of household burglary was 2.0 miles if measured from offenders' homes, but this reduced to 1.6 miles if measured from where the offender slept the previous evening.

The Sheffield findings do not mean that the Brantinghams' broad thesis is wrong, just that the routine activities of this group of offenders were more limited than the thesis had assumed. The general hypothesized link between routine activities, awareness space, and the resulting distribution of offending locations remained true. Furthermore, these Sheffield offenders demonstrated the link between routine activities and crime in a slightly different way, for about 80 per cent of out-of-city travelling that involved offending was to places with strong traditional cultural links to Sheffield. Traditions are, of course, a powerful form of routine activity—a point to which we will return in our concluding section.

Using police-recorded data, Wiles and Costello (2000) also carried out an area-based analysis of residential neighbourhoods, categorizing them according to whether they had high, medium, or low offence rates and offender rates. Not all the possible categories were found empirically: residential areas with a high offender rate but low offence rate did not exist, and few areas had a low offender rate but high offence rate. Given the findings on travel just discussed, the first of these results is probably universal, but the latter will depend on either the nearness of low offender rate neighbourhoods to their opposite, or the existence in low offender rate neighbourhoods of powerful attractors for offenders as part of their routine activities.[30] This is possibly why studies of burglary patterns in different cities have come to such conflicting results (see earlier section); the apparently conflicting findings may simply reflect the differing social geographies of the cities in which research has been carried out. BCS burglary victimization data, when analysed by ACORN areas,[31] shows that while most better-off areas have low victimization rates, those which are more likely to be located

<hr/>

[30] One low offender/high offence area in Sheffield (Wiles and Costello 2000: 53) is a fashionable, small inner-suburban shopping and entertainment area surrounded by residential properties; it is likely that the high residential offence rate arises from offenders' familiarity with the area when visiting it for leisure purposes.

[31] A construct to represent demographically different kinds of areas using small area census data.

near to high offender rate areas (such as 'Better-off executives, inner-city areas') do not (Kershaw *et al.* 2001: 58). The extent to which different cities have such better-off areas near to poorer areas with high offender rates will produce differing city maps of offence rate distributions. In other words, the crime maps for a city will reflect the way in which the history of the city has relatively located different social groups and facilities such as shopping centres. Cities with the same degree of social differentiation can, therefore, have very different distributions of offences.

However, the proximity of offenders to offences, and therefore to victims, is not just geographical but also often social. It has been known for some time that for crimes of violence, those who go out frequently at night, especially to certain areas or places of entertainment, have higher risks of victimization arising out of these social activities (see, for example, Gottfredson 1984); and American data suggest that even robbery by acquaintances is far from unknown (Felson, Baumer, and Messner 2000). Evidence is now also beginning to emerge that known offenders have high rates of property crime victimization. A recent study has shown that, for police-recorded burglary, households which contained a known offender had a higher rate of victimization than other households, regardless of the area offence rate, and also that repeat victimization was higher in offender-households. A follow-up interview study suggested that one reason for these high victimization rates was that offender-victims were much more likely than the average burglary victim to be offended against by an acquaintance (Bottoms and Costello 2001). In short, the worlds of offending and victimization are not necessarily separate, and this is part of the explanation as to why high offender rate areas also have high offence rates.

This general picture is further confirmed by research analyses of repeat victimization. We have already seen that in high-victimization areas, many residents report no offences in a year, but others suffer multiple victimizations. An analysis of the BCS data for 1982, 1984, and 1988 by Trickett *et al.* (1992) further showed that the higher an area's victimization prevalence rate,[32] the higher the rate of repeat victimization (for a fuller discussion, see Farrell 1995). Repeats occur disproportionately in the first months after the initial victimization, and there is research evidence (reviewed in Everson and Pease 2001) that much of this is due to the same offender returning. Moreover, we referred in our introduction to the fact that relatively few persistent offenders commit a very disproportionate amount of crimes, and there is now tentative evidence that repeat victimization may be especially carried out by persistent offenders (ibid.). However, most research studies of repeat victimization, especially those based on national victim survey data (such as the BCS), have confined themselves to a twelve-month time-frame, but analyses of recorded crime over a five- or six-year period now show that some second victimizations on the same target occur years after the first offence, but still at a level that is well above chance (Kleemans 2001; Costello and Bottoms 2001). It is implausible that these long-term repeats are predominantly due to the same offender returning, and this focuses attention on the

---

[32] A 'prevalence rate' in a crime victimization survey is the proportion of survey respondents reporting one or more victimizations for the offence(s) in question. For this measurement, therefore, single victims and multiple victims count equally.

possibility—consistent with opportunity theory—that there are some targets that, over time, will be repeatedly attractive to different offenders, acting (unknown to one another) on the same set of cues. The full dimensions of this complex emerging picture of repeat victimization (involving area characteristics, offender characteristics, target characteristics, and differential time-lags) remain to be established, and are an important challenge for the future.

SOCIAL DISORGANIZATION REVISITED

This chapter began with a brief exposition of the work of Shaw and McKay, and it is appropriate at this point to return to them, for two reasons. First, the evidence of the links between high offender and offence rates in certain deprived areas (see previous section) reminds one of the Chicago theorization about 'social disorganization' in the zone in transition. Secondly, recent years have seen an important renaissance of research and writing in the social disorganization tradition (see especially Bursik and Grasmick 1993; Sampson 1995; Sampson and Groves 1989; Sampson, Raudenbush, and Earls 1997).

The commonsense account of the inter-linking of offender residence and victimization is simply that such neighbourhoods are characterized by social deprivation, and this is a sufficient explanation. However, this account is faulty, because the correlation between deprivation indices and either offender or offence rates is not perfect: not all deprived areas have high offender rates, and demographically very similar areas can have markedly different rates (see the Sheffield case study discussed above).

The Chicago School's explanation for high offender rates focused on 'social disorganization', that is (in Kornhauser's (1978) formulation), where the structure and culture of a community are unable to implement and express the values of its own residents, and so do not provide common and clear non-delinquent values and control. As previously noted, economic factors were strongly linked to the social disorganization concept, but the Chicago School did not posit a direct relationship between economic factors and offending levels. One important feature of the social disorganization tradition was Shaw and McKay's highlighting of the 'residential mobility' aspect of the zone in transition, and this led a number of later researchers to emphasize the importance for offending levels of factors like 'sparse friendship networks'.[33] However, a recent empirical study of the black ghettos, by William Julius Wilson (1996), suggests a more complex picture:

. . . what many impoverished and dangerous neighborhoods have in common is a relatively high degree of social integration (high levels of local neighboring while being relatively

---

[33] An obvious problem with this formulation was that many middle-class suburbs have quite low friendship levels, yet they usually also have low offender rates. (For an interesting study of the moral order of an American suburb, see Baumgartner 1988.) This objection was one of the reasons that led researchers like Robert Sampson to abandon the language of 'social disorganization', and to focus instead on 'collective efficacy' (see below).

isolated from contacts in the broader mainstream society) and low levels of informal social control (feelings that they have little control over their immediate environment, including the environment's negative influence on their children). In such areas, not only are children at risk because of the lack of informal social controls, they are also disadvantaged because social interaction among neighbors tends to be confined to those whose skills, styles, orientations, and habits are not as conducive to positive social outcomes (academic success, prosocial behavior, etc.) as are those in more stable neighborhoods. Despite being socially integrated, the residents of Chicago's ghetto neighborhoods shared a feeling that they had little informal social control over their children in their environment. A primary reason is the absence of a strong organizational capacity or an institutional resource base that would provide an extra layer of social organization in their neighborhood. (Wilson 1996: 63–4)

Two points are especially important about this formulation. First, Wilson's account links areal processes much more firmly to wider political and social structural processes than did the original version of Chicago theorization (for a criminological development of this line of thought, see Bursick and Grasmick 1993). Secondly, Wilson implicitly refers to a separate theoretical tradition of writing about 'social capital',[34] as when he speaks of social interaction based on 'skills, styles, orientations and habits . . . conducive to positive social outcomes'. This approach has also recently been developed criminologically by a contemporary Chicago researcher, Robert Sampson, who has argued that high crime neighbourhoods differ from others in that they lack the kinds of social capital which would allow them to define collective goals *and then organize effectively to achieve them*—what he calls a lack of 'collective efficacy' (Sampson, Raudenbush, and Earls 1997).[35] The emphasis here—which is congruent with Shaw and McKay's work, but more theoretically rigorous—is thus not simply on whether communities have non-criminal values, but rather on their capacity to collectively express these values, and effectively enforce them against deviant threats. Most interestingly, Sampson and his colleagues have demonstrated empirically that variations in violent crime rates between Chicago neighbourhoods can in part be explained by the relative possession of the capacity for collective efficacy; or, more technically, 'after adjustment for measurement error, individual differences in neighborhood composition, prior violence and other potentially confounding social processes, [collective efficacy was] a robust predictor of lower rates of violence' (Sampson, Raudenbush, and Earls 1997: 923).

Despite this impressive empirical support for the importance of collective efficacy, two qualifications must be made. First, as Sampson, Raudenbush, and Earls

[34] 'Social capital' must be distinguished from both economic capital (financial resources) and human capital (the resources, especially those derived from formal education and industrial/professional experience, held by particular individuals within a social group). 'Social capital' refers to the potentially positive effects of social interactions (including functioning social institutions such as voluntary organizations) within a given society or sub-society. People living in a particular community may benefit from social capital even if they do not contribute to it: 'if the crime rate in my neighborhood is lowered by neighbors keeping an eye on one another's homes, I benefit even if I personally spend most of my time on the road and never even nod to another resident on the street' (Putnam 2000). See further Coleman (1990).

[35] More specifically, it is argued that 'the neighborhood context of collective efficacy' can be defined in terms of 'the linkage of mutual trust and the willingness to intervene for the common good ["informal social control"]' (Sampson, Raudenbush, and Earls 1997: 919).

themselves put it, 'the image of local residents working collectively to solve their own problems is not the whole picture', and the empirical results in Chicago also demonstrate the importance of structural variables such as 'socio-economic and housing factors linked to the wider political economy'. Hence, 'recognising that collective efficacy matters does not imply that inequalities at the neighborhood level can be neglected' in criminological explanation (ibid.).

Secondly, the concept of collective efficacy remains vulnerable to one of the classic criticisms of social disorganization as a criminological explanation; for just as some crime is the product of organization rather than disorganization, so some criminal gangs are certainly capable of influencing neighbourhoods in a way which demonstrates a degree of 'collective efficacy', but the results are not necessarily unambiguously desirable. A vivid recent demonstration of this point arose in one of the two high-crime areas of Salford studied by Walklate and Evans (1999). In 'Oldtown' (an inner-city area with quite strong family and kinship ties, and a reputation for 'toughness') there was an organized criminal group known as the 'Salford Firm'. This group, while both practising and condoning criminal activity outside the local area, took it upon themselves to police local criminal incidents (such as burglaries) by giving the culprits (mostly local youth) a 'smacking' in a process of self-proclaimed 'street justice' (ibid.: 93). Moreover, 'grassing' by local residents to the police was discouraged by, for example, writing informants' names on a wall in a central location in the area. The researchers report that ordinary people felt intimidated by the presence of the gang and its activities, but also felt that it had at times afforded the community a degree of protection from criminal victimization, protection that was not always provided by the police (for example, the gang had apparently kept hard drugs out of the area). Residents were, as a result, often ambivalent about the area; they recognized that a particular kind of social order was in operation, and 'appreciated the personal advantage it afforded them', but they 'nevertheless worried about their children growing up in such an environment' (ibid.: 95). The complexities of this kind of situation are not adequately encompassed by a unidimensional concept of 'collective efficacy', and this suggests that collective efficacy theory needs to address more specifically some normative dimensions of 'efficacy'.

COMMUNITY CHANGE AND CRIME

So far in this chapter, environmental influences have been described in a somewhat static fashion, although the interactive model shown in Figure 18.2 contains within it the possibility of analysing dynamic changes in the housing market situations of particular areas, and the consequences of such changes. In bringing this chapter to a close, we will focus more explicitly on change, first at an areal (or meso) level, and then at a societal (or macro) level.

MESO-LEVEL CHANGE

In an important essay, Albert Reiss (1986) drew attention to the importance for criminology of changes in local communities, and he suggested that, analogously to the concept of the individual criminal career, one might speak in terms of local areas having 'community crime careers'. This is a concept that we have worked with in the context of the Sheffield study (see Bottoms and Wiles 1986, 1992; Bottoms, Claytor, and Wiles 1992); but, rather than use further Sheffield evidence here, we will consider the 'community crime career' idea using research studies from the United States, some based on offender data and some on offence or victimization data.[36]

Schuerman and Kobrin (1986) carried out a statistical study of juvenile offender rates in different areas of Los Angeles for the period 1950–70. They found evidence for a three-stage process which appeared to underpin the emergence of particular districts as high offender-rate areas, and they were satisfied from the temporal patterning of the data that the causal influences were cumulative, and in the order specified. First, they argued, there were shifts in land use (for example, an increase in renting; an increase in apartment dwellings). Secondly, there were changes in population-related features in areas (for example, a decline in total population; an increase in the proportion of unrelated individuals; or an increase in residential mobility). Thirdly, there were changes in socio-economic status (more unskilled people; a higher proportion unemployed), and also in what they label, perhaps doubtfully, 'subculture variables' (including an increase in the size of ethnic minority populations). These changes were cumulative (for example, limited changes in land use seemed to induce a larger number of demographic changes) and eventually resulted in a shift from low to high offender-rate areas.

This proposed causal model, derived purely statistically from census and offender data, of course fits extremely well with that postulated in the Sheffield study from more on-the-ground fieldwork experience (see Figure 18.2); and it is also congruent with more recent evidence from Hancock's (2001) study in Merseyside. But perhaps of special interest in the Los Angeles research was a further finding, namely that it seemed to be '. . . the speed of structural change, rather than simply the fact of such change that initiates the transition of city neighborhoods from a low to a high-crime status' (Schuerman and Kobrin 1986: 97–8).

This emphasis on the speed of change raises particularly the issue of how areas 'tip' from low-crime to high-crime areas, sometimes quite quickly. This is an issue of some importance, not least since there is evidence from a variety of sources that tipping processes can often begin slowly and then rapidly accelerate.

One criminological theory relevant to tipping processes is the so-called 'broken windows' hypothesis of James Q. Wilson and George Kelling (1982). According to these authors, there is at least a strong likelihood that signs of disorder in an area—such as broken windows, housing abandonment, litter, and graffiti—will undermine the subtle and informal processes whereby communities normally maintain social control. For example, where signs of disorder are prevalent in an area, residents may

---

[36] Although the studies use these different measures, one must remember that *in residential areas* offender rates tend to be positively correlated with offence or victimization rates.

shrink back into their own dwellings, and take no responsibility for what goes on in public spaces. Meanwhile, the increasing dilapidation of the public space means that it may become fair game for plunder and/or destruction, and may also act as an unintended invitation to those engaged in crime of a commercial or semi-commercial nature (drugs, prostitution, etc.) to come and trade in the area.

The researcher who was initially most active in seeking to investigate empirically the 'spiral of decay in American neighborhoods', as he called it, was Wesley Skogan (1986, 1990). Skogan distinguished between physical and social disorders (physical = abandoned or ill-kept buildings, broken streetlights, litter, vermin, etc.; social = public drinking, prostitution, sexual catcalling, etc.: Skogan 1990: 4), but found that, on a neighbourhood basis, the two sorts of disorder were strongly correlated (ibid.: 51). Skogan also showed that, not surprisingly, disorders tended to be highest in areas with low neighbourhood stability, poverty, and a high minority ethnic population. But the real interest of his research, for the purposes of this chapter, lies in his analysis of the consequences of disorder on neighbourhoods (i.e., what Taylor (2001) calls the 'longitudinal ecological' version of the broken windows hypothesis). Reasonable evidence of three impacts of disorder were found, though Skogan was hampered by the fact that his data were cross-sectional rather than longitudinal.

First, 'disorder undermines the mechanisms by which communities exercise control over local affairs' (Skogan 1990: 65). On cross-sectional analyses, there was a negative relationship between the presence of disorder in an area and the extent to which residents were willing to help one another in a neighbourly way; and also in the extent to which residents engaged in simple crime-prevention activities such as property marking, or asking their neighbours to keep an eye on their homes during an absence.

Secondly, 'disorder sparks concern about neighborhood safety, and perhaps even causes crime itself' (ibid.: 65). As we have already seen, Skogan statistically linked disorder to areal poverty, ethnic minority residence, and social instability, and, not surprisingly, such areas tended also to have high crime rates. Disentangling the causal order of these variables is of course very difficult, especially in cross-sectional analyses, but a path model was presented based on thirty areas for which robbery victimization data were available, from which it was suggested that 'there were no significant paths between those social and economic variables and neighborhood crime, except through disorder' (ibid.: 75).

Thirdly, 'disorder undermines the stability of the housing market . . . [it] undercuts residential satisfaction, leads people to fear for the safety of their children, and encourages area residents to move away' (ibid.: 65). Drawing on work in the general field of urban sociology, Skogan suggested that selective out-migration from an area may be the most fundamental source of neighbourhood change. In the areas studied, there was a negative correlation between disorder and residents' degree of commitment to their area; moreover, this was related to moving intentions. Skogan went on to note that these data probably underestimate the impact of disorder on local housing markets, since he had no data on perceptions of areas from anyone except area residents, and 'the stigma associated with high levels of visible disorder probably affects the perceptions and decisions of [potential in-migrants] as well' (ibid.: 84).

Overall, therefore, Skogan's research tended to support Wilson and Kelling's (1982) original 'broken windows' hypothesis, although the support was not conclusive (see also Harcourt 1998). In the light of the Sheffield and Stockholm evidence, the fact that the housing market plays an important role within Skogan's theorization is also of great interest, though unfortunately Skogan made no direct attempt to link his housing market variables to the crime variables. Lastly, Skogan's emphasis on out-migration from areas as an engine of neighbourhood change is undoubtedly of great importance, as the earlier work of Taub, Taylor, and Dunham (1984) had also suggested (see further below).

A more recent research study, based on longitudinal data on neighbourhoods in Baltimore, essentially confirms Skogan's results following a more rigorous longitudinal analysis. Summarizing his empirical findings on the 'longitudinal ecological' version of the broken windows hypothesis, Ralph B. Taylor (2001) indicates that disorders (or 'incivilities' as he terms them) were important for crime changes, social-structural changes, and changes in perceptions of fear of crime. But, Taylor continues, 'incivilities do not matter for as many outcomes as proponents of this thesis have suggested; nor do they matter as consistently as other features of neighborhood fabric, especially [neighbourhood social] status; nor do they matter consistently, regardless of the indicator used' (ibid.: 20). Indeed, generally speaking, initial neighbourhood social status, neighbourhood racial composition, and crime rates were each as important as initial incivilities in shaping later crime changes and social decline (ibid.: 22). The implication, for Taylor (and consistently with Skogan's suggestions about the housing market and out-migration from neighbourhoods), was that research on 'incivilities' and 'broken windows' should break away from the tradition (very evident in some writers) of treating these topics in isolation. Instead, incivilities research 'needs to reconnect more firmly with works in the areas of urban sociology, urban political economy, collective community crime prevention and organizational participation' (ibid.: 20).

An earlier research study that sought to do exactly what Ralph Taylor here recommends was Taub, Taylor, and Dunham's (1984) work on Chicago neighbourhoods. Three key points, from a rather complex argument, are of special interest for the present discussion.

First, the authors conclude that crime levels are an issue for residents and potential residents in judging the quality of an area; however, these judgements are comparative rather than absolute.

Secondly, Taub and his colleagues discuss the ways in which individuals make decisions relevant to neighbourhood decline. They find some empirical evidence for a 'threshold model', which might operate in the following way: early signs of deterioration will lead some residents to move away ('pioneers'); but some (e.g., the elderly) will not move whatever anyone else does ('conservatives'); while others in between these polar groups will be influenced (often strongly so) by opinions and decisions of others in the area. Hence, if significant numbers try to move from the area, this will have a snowball effect, influencing others to do so. The importance of this model for present purposes is twofold. In the first place, it shows clearly how a 'tipping' process in an area can gather speed, and this re-emphasizes the importance of the 'velocity' dimension in Schuerman and Kobrin's results. Moreover, it shows, by implication, that once a tipping process is under way, there is very little that an individual can do to stop it, for an individual acting alone can have very little power to sway other individuals in an accelerating process of this kind. On the other hand, a corporate body can influence the decisions of other individuals, and hence (in principle at least) halt a tipping process.[37] The University of Chicago seems to have achieved this in the Hyde Park-Kenwood district (at least as regards a tipping process into urban decline, and a racial tipping process; though, in this case, the crime rate remained high).

These considerations lead directly on to the third and last main point to be emphasized from Taub, Taylor, and Dunham's research. In their closing chapter, they offer a threefold approach to the understanding of neighbourhood change: such change is, they suggest, always a product of the interaction between (i) ecological facts, (ii) individual decisions, and (iii) corporate decisions. 'Ecological facts' are defined as including the potential employment base for neighbourhood residents, demographic pressures on the local housing market, the age and quality of the housing stock, and external amenities such as attractive physical locations. Taub and his colleagues note that most previous theories of neighbourhood change have concentrated on ecological facts as the main explanatory variable, but they argue that this is an incomplete approach, as shown by some of their area case studies.

Lastly, harking right back to the Chicago School, these authors comment that, with hindsight, one can see only too clearly the central weakness of the urban model adopted. In a nutshell, it '. . . [did] not make a place for the decision rules of individual and corporate actors, [and it led] to the too-simple view that the neighborhoods in a city are somewhat interchangeable parts of a single integrated urban system that operates according to univariate rules of evolution' (Taub, Taylor, and Dunham 1984: 186).

Hence, ultimately, the study of community change and crime leads—just as does the following through of the implications of offence location studies and offender residence studies—to a linking together of macro, meso, and micro social processes. Nothing else will provide an adequate framework for explanation. In the study of change, however, because one's focus is more long-term, it is perhaps easier to see the macro-level and the overtly political processes in operation. Hence it is particularly important to remember, when studying other and more static issues in environmental criminology, that these macro-level and political forces are always present, even if not very visible in a particular piece of local research.

MACRO-LEVEL CHANGE

So far this chapter has been concerned to summarize the existing literature on environmental criminology. Now we turn to the future research agenda of environmental criminology. Our starting point is a recognition that the economically more

---

[37] 'Corporate' bodies in this context do not have to be businesses, but can be any large organization with powerful local influence—be it business, charity, government (local or central), statutory agencies, or a well-organized local community group. The point being that effective corporate action of any kind can alter the social dynamics in an area, and the confidence of individuals to remain in the area.

advanced countries of the world are at the present time undergoing some quite fundamental economic and social changes that will significantly affect the nature and patterning of crime. Environmental criminology needs to understand these trans-formations in order to explain crime in the future. The macro changes we are refer-ring to are usually designated as the change from 'modernity' (basically, the social formations which emerged out of industrialization) to 'late modernity' or, alter-natively, 'postmodernism'. Within the length of this chapter we can do no more than summarize those main areas of change which seem to us to have criminological implications, but for a fuller treatment see Bottoms and Wiles (1995).[38]

First, business and the flows of capital have become increasingly transnational and have created their own transnational orders. The ability of nation states to control this transnational order is not very great, precisely because international corporations do not operate solely within the territory of one nation state. The result is that effective power is being increasingly exercised either at the transnational level, or—with the decline of state power—at the local level,[39] leading to what is often described as the 'hollowing out' of power at the state level. Yet during modernity the nation state has been the prime location for the making of laws against crime, and the control and policing of crime. If the state is being hollowed out in this way, the main definers of crime in the modern period will cede this power both upwards (to transnational capital and political organizations) and downwards (to local areas). We have already seen within Europe the EU taking such a role, and local campaigns and programmes against crime are increasingly common.

Secondly, in a decreasingly manufacturing-based and increasingly services-oriented economy, business decisions are determined less by the supply of raw materials for manufacture and more by new considerations such as the availability of skilled labour, or a pleasant environment to attract such labour. The wealth and prosperity of a city are thus no longer determined by its location relative to the physical resources of material production, and the result is that cities, or regions, can have very uneven and different economic development. The economic structures, which (as we have seen) provide the macro framework for the routine activities which pattern crime, are therefore increasingly uneven and varied. On the one hand, declining traditional industries can leave environmentally blighted cities (or parts of cities), including residential areas—originally built to provide labour for those industries—with high unemployment rates and having lost their most entrepreneurial residents ('rustbelt' areas). On the other hand, new information-based industries may flourish in small towns or semi-rural locations, bringing growth and economic prosperity to these areas.

Thirdly, recent technology means that neither time nor space are as 'fixed' as they

[38] For a general, historical account of how the processes of change can create new crime and social control patterns in a city, see Mike Davis's (1990) study of Los Angeles. For criminological texts focusing on the transformations of late modernity, see Taylor (1999) and Young (1999).

[39] Not only has the state ceded power to the transnational level, but some services must respond to increasingly differentiated local demands, and the state is much less able to provide such services effectively than locally-based institutions and organizations. Hence the state's ability to govern is being attacked both from above and below.

were half a century ago. The result can be globalized cultures, no longer fixed in time or space, from which consumers can choose and indeed make a series of different choices. Yet geographically localized cultures, in the sense of 'community' and spatially fixed institutions (such as families, churches, and community organizations) have been regarded by much criminological theory as the main defences against crime: hence the Chicago School's concern with community 'disorganization' and crime.[40] Furthermore, a globalized market culture of consumer choice is available only to those with the financial ability to participate, and may encourage crime by those who do not possess the (legitimate) resources to exercise such choice. Indeed, as we noted earlier in this chapter, many offenders' lives are lived out in poverty and in very bounded geographical circumstances, notwithstanding the galloping globalization of late modernity. That particular tension may well be central to the environmental criminology of the future.

Fourthly, in our new social world we are increasingly dependent upon reflexively acquired social knowledge rather than tradition, yet this new form of knowledge becomes ever more specialized and, in practice, forces us to take on trust the expertise of others, and the efficacy of abstract systems. This can create various insecurities, one response to which can be the creation of 'security aids' deliberately designed to calm our fears and encourage our trust. Many of these innovations (such as CCTV systems, gated housing areas, and well-protected shopping malls) particularly focus on the insecurities associated with crime or disorder.

Fifthly, our new social world has developed new forms of social differentiation, ranging from changes in gender roles to increasing economic polarization. From a criminological point of view these new forms change the context of the routine activities relating to crime (for example, more working women can mean less occupied and guarded homes during the day: Cohen and Felson 1979). Most importantly, increased economic polarization and the decline of traditional manufacturing industry has created an increasing social exclusion of some sub-groups of the population from effective participation in key areas of social life (ranging from jobs to education and leisure facilities). Where particular groups experience multiple exclusion then the operation of the housing market may well concentrate them in particular residential areas (see Wiles 1992). In the contemporary USA this has especially happened to poor blacks and produced the black ghettos of American rustbelt cities, such as Chicago or Detroit. The ghettos have alarmingly high offence and offender rates, and this has produced a generalized (although statistically largely misplaced) fear of the danger they may represent to the rest of the city, which mirrors the nineteenth-century Victorian concerns about the dangerous classes (see Morris 1994). An acrimonious debate has ensued about the reasons for such high ghetto crime rates (see, for example, Murray 1984; Wilson 1987, 1996), and this American debate about the 'underclass' has since been borrowed to try to explain high crime and lawlessness in some British council estates (see Murray 1990, 1994). More generally, the Canadian criminologist John Hagan (1994: chapter 3) has argued that the economic changes of

---

[40] Of course, this does not mean that local place-based community factors are no longer important in people's lives—they clearly are, but alongside the more globalized influences.

late modernity have created the need for a 'new sociology of crime and disrepute', central to which will be the study of the 'criminal costs of social inequality' (ibid.: 98).

These changes, of course, are not uniform either within or between countries—indeed, that is one of the characteristics of late modernity. Nevertheless, they seem to affect all late modern societies to some degree. Clearly our cities, their surrounding hinterlands, and rural areas are being physically re-modelled by these processes, but this is happening in different ways in different places. The housing tenure map of Britain, for example, is being transformed, and we have already seen how important housing markets have been in environmental criminological explanations. The new housing markets will change areal crime patterns, but how is not yet clear. A shrinking public housing sector could produce increasing residualization of public housing and, at its most extreme, mirror the American problem of ghettos (see Wiles 1992); but alternatively, a more varied housing market could encourage a new social discipline, enforced by housing managers and the civil courts, which reduces residential area crime rates in at least some areas (cf. NACRO 1996). The development of out-of-town shopping centres and leisure facilities is creating attractive new crime targets away from traditional city centres; but because these are often legally privately owned places, they are more likely to be rigorously and privately policed, though in an unobtrusive style of which most of the public approve (see Beck and Willis 1995). The decline of time or space as fixed frameworks for our lives could reduce the commitment to geographical neighbourhood, and so reduce social control at the local level. On the other hand, these changes could mean that we learn successfully to base local control increasingly on the *public* rather than the *parochial* level (see Hunter 1985), or that residential areas become less important and parochial control is instead exercised in the locations where people choose to pursue their varied interests. Increasing social differentiation, combined with the creation of 'security aids', could lead to increased segregation and the exclusion of deviant or threatening groups (for example, the exclusion of certain groups of young people from shopping malls), and to the collapse of a public civic society into a series of private realms (for example, private places with their own private police forces effectively enforcing their private law). Alternatively, increasing lifestyle choices may freely and spatially separate social groups with different interests (for example, by lifestyle activities being provided at different places, or in the same place at different times) and so reduce the potential for inter-group conflicts which produced crime in traditional city centres, especially at weekends.

We can be certain that changes in the geographical patterning of routine activities will alter the pattern of crime, but since such changes are most commonly the outcome of a large number of uncoordinated individual market decisions, the resulting changes in crime patterns will not be easy to predict. Some of the alternative crime outcomes suggested above could be influenced by political choices, although the most important ones will, increasingly, be just as likely to be made at either the transnational or local level as by the state.

The environmental criminology of the future will therefore need to continue to study crime patterns at local levels, but it will necessarily have to situate its explanations within a macro-level understanding of the emerging forces of late modernity.

Selected further reading

Those wishing to delve further into environmental criminology are recommended to begin with two overview chapters by leading scholars in the field, namely Sampson (1995) and Wikström (1998). Each has a slightly different focus than the present chapter, so the three essays complement one another.

The most useful book-length account of the main themes of environmental criminology is probably Wikström (1991), a volume which presents the author's Swedish research in the comparative context of the relevant American and British research literature. Readers will, however, have to be comfortable with quantitative social science research methods to get the most out of this work.

After that, readers are advised to pursue the references listed in the present chapter, in relation to their own particular research or professional requirements. For example, those interested in so-called 'crime mapping' and the GIS revolution should consult Hirschfield and Bowers (2001); those interested in repeat victimization should look at the essays in Farrell and Pease (2001); those concerned with linking offence locations and offender locations could usefully begin with Wiles and Costello (2000); those whose principal preoccupation is 'the broken windows hypothesis' should consult Taylor's (2001) recent work (which contains a full literature review); and those concerned with the social changes of late modernity might begin with our own 1995 essay (Bottoms and Wiles 1995), and then pursue some of the other theoretical references in the text above. Lastly, those who wish to pursue the important but difficult debate on 'social disorganization' and 'collective efficacy' should first ensure that they have mastered Kornhauser's (1978: chapter 3) classic chapter, and then move on to some of the other materials cited in the section of our chapter entitled 'Social Disorganization Revisited', especially Sampson and Groves (1989), and Sampson, Raudenbush, and Earls (1997).

References

ALIHAN, M. (1938), *Social Ecology*, New York: Columbia University Press.

ANDERSON, S., GROVE SMITH, C., KINSEY, R., and WOOD, J. (1990), *The Edinburgh Crime Survey: First Report*, Edinburgh: Scottish Office Central Research Unit Papers.

BALDWIN, J. (1979), 'Ecological and areal studies in Great Britain and the United States', in N. Morris and M. Tonry (eds), *Crime and Justice: An Annual Review of Research*, vol. 1, Chicago, Ill.: University of Chicago Press.

—— and BOTTOMS, A.E. (1976), *The Urban Criminal*, London: Tavistock.

BAUMGARTNER, M.P. (1988), *The Moral Order of a Suburb*, New York: Oxford University Press.

BECK, A., and WILLIS, A. (1995), *Crime and Security: Managing the Risk*, Leicester: Perpetuity Press.

BENNETT, T., and WRIGHT, R. (1984), *Burglars on Burglary*, Aldershot: Gower.

BLOCK, R.L., and BLOCK, C.R. (1995), 'Space, place and crime: hot spot areas and hot places of liquor-related crime', in J.E. Eck and D. Weisburd (eds), *Crime and Place*, Monsey, NY: Criminal Justice Press.

BOTTOMS, A.E. (1994), 'Environmental Criminology', in M. Maguire, R. Morgan, and R. Reiner (eds), *The Oxford Handbook of Criminology*, 1st edn, Oxford: Oxford University Press.

——, CLAYTOR, A., and WILES, P. (1992), 'Housing markets and residential community crime careers: a case study from Sheffield', in D.J. Evans, N.R. Fyfe, and D.T. Herbert (eds), *Crime, Policing and Place: Essays in Environmental Criminology*, London: Routledge.

—— and COSTELLO, A. (2001), 'Offenders as Victims of Property Crimes in a Deindustrialised City', paper presented at the Annual Meeting of the European Society of Criminology, Lausanne, Switzerland.

——, MAWBY, R.I., and WALKER, M.A. (1987), 'A localised crime survey in contrasting areas of a city', *British Journal of Criminology*, 27: 125–54.

——, —— and XANTHOS, P. (1989), 'A tale of two estates', in D. Downes (ed.), *Crime and the City*, London: Macmillan.

—— and WILES, P. (1986), 'Housing tenure and residential community crime careers in Britain', in A.J. Reiss and M. Tonry (eds), *Communities and Crime*, Chicago, Ill.: University of Chicago Press.

—— and —— (1992), 'Explanations of crime and place', in D.J. Evans, N.R. Fyfe, and D.T. Herbert (eds), *Crime, Policing and Place: Essays in Environmental Criminology*, London: Routledge.

—— and —— (1995), 'Crime and insecurity in the city', in C. Fijnaut, J. Goethals, T. Peters, and L. Walgrave (eds), *Changes in Society, Crime and Criminal Justice in Europe*, 2 Vols, The Hague: Kluwer.

BRAITHWAITE, J. (1989), *Crime, Shame and Reintegration*, Cambridge: University Press.

BRANTINGHAM, P.J., and BRANTINGHAM, P.L. (1981), *Environmental Criminology*, Beverly Hills, Ca.: Sage Publications.

—— and —— (1984), *Patterns in Crime*, New York: Macmillan.

—— and —— (1991), *Environmental Criminology* (revised edn), Prospect Heights, Ill.: Waveland Press.

BRANTINGHAM, P.L., and BRANTINGHAM, P.J. (1981), 'Notes on the geometry of crime', in P.J. Brantingham and P.L. Brantingham (eds), *Environmental Criminology*, Beverly Hills, Ca.: Sage Publications.

BRONFENBRENNER, U. (1979), *The Ecology of Human Development*, Cambridge, Mass: Harvard University Press.

BULMER, M. (1984), *The Chicago School of Sociology*, Chicago, Ill.: University of Chicago Press.

BURNEY, E. (1999), *Crime and Banishment: Nuisance and Exclusion in Social Housing*, Winchester: Waterside Press.

BURROWS, J., TARLING, R., MACKIE, A., LEWIS, R., and TAYLOR, G. (2000), *Review of Police Forces' Crime Recording Practices*, Home Office Research Study No. 204, London: Home Office.

BURSIK, R.J. (1986), 'Ecological stability and the dynamics of delinquency', in A.J. Reiss and M. Tonry (eds), *Communities and Crime*, Chicago, Ill.: University of Chicago Press.

—— and GRASMICK, H.G. (1993), *Neighborhoods and Crime*, New York: Lexington.

CARTER, R.L., and HILL, K.Q. (1979), *The Criminal's Image of the City*, New York: Pergamon Press.

CLARKE, R.V.G. (1995), 'Situational crime prevention', in M. Tonry and D. Farrington (eds), *Building a Safer Society*, Chicago, Ill.: University of Chicago Press.

—— (1999), *Hot Products: Understanding, Anticipating and Reducing Demand for Stolen Goods*, Police Research Series No. 112, London: Home Office.

COHEN, L.E., and FELSON, M. (1979), 'Social change and crime rate trends: a routine activities approach', *American Sociological Review*, 44: 588–608.

COLEMAN, A. (1985), *Utopia on Trial: Vision and Reality in Planned Housing*, London: Hilary Shipman.

—— (1989), 'Disposition and situation: two sides of the same crime', in D.J. Evans and D.T. Herbert (eds), *The Geography of Crime*, London: Routledge.

COLEMAN, J.S. (1990), *Foundations of Social Theory*, Cambridge, Mass: Belknap Press.

COSTELLO, A., and BOTTOMS, A.E. (2001), 'Repeat Domestic Burglary Victimisation in North Sheffield 1995–2000', paper presented at the Annual Meeting of the American Society of Criminology, Atlanta, Georgia.

CRESSEY, D. (1964), *Delinquency, Crime and Differential Association*, The Hague: Martinus Nijhoff.

CROMWELL, P.F., OLSON, J.N., and AVARY D'A.W. (1991), *Breaking and Entering: An Ethnographic Analysis of Burglary*, Newbury Park, Ca.: Sage.

DAVIDSON, R.N. (1981), *Crime and Environment*, London: Croom Helm.

DAVIS, M. (1990), *City of Quartz; Excavating the Future of Los Angeles*, London: Vintage.

DEPARTMENT OF THE ENVIRONMENT (1997), *The Design Improvement Controlled Experiment: an evaluation of the impact, costs and benefits of estate remodelling*, London: Department of the Environment.

ECK, J.E. (1995), 'A general model of the geography of illicit retail marketplaces', in J.E. Eck and D. Weisburd (eds), *Crime and Place*, Monsey, NY: Criminal Justice Press.

EVERSON, S., and PEASE, K. (2001), 'Crime Against the Same Person and Place: Detection Opportunity and Offender Targeting', in G. Farrell and K. Pease (eds), *Repeat Victimization*, Monsey, NY: Criminal Justice Press.

FARRELL, G. (1995), 'Preventing Repeat Victimization', in M. Tonry and D. Farrington (eds), *Building a Safer Society*, Chicago, Ill.: University of Chicago Press.

—— and PEASE, K. (2001), *Repeat Victimization*, Monsey, NY: Criminal Justice Press.

FARRINGTON, D.P., and DOWDS, E.A. (1984), 'Disentangling criminal behaviour and police reaction', in D.P. Farrington and J. Gunn (eds), *Reactions to Crime*, Chichester: Wiley.

FELSON, M. (1986), 'Linking criminal choices, routine activities, informal control and criminal outcomes', in D.B. Cornish and R.V.G. Clarke (eds), *The Reasoning Criminal*, New York: Springer-Verlag.

—— (1992), 'Routine activities and crime prevention', *Studies on Crime and Crime Prevention: Annual Review*, 1: 30–34.

—— (1995), 'Those who discourage crime', in J.E. Eck and D. Weisburd (eds), *Crime and Place*, Monsey, NY: Criminal Justice Press.

FELSON, R.B., BAUMER, E.P., and MESSNER, S.F. (2000), 'Acquaintance robbery', *Journal of Research in Crime and Delinquency*, 37: 284–305.

FIGLIO, R.M., HAKIM, S., and RENGERT, G.F. (eds) (1986), *Metropolitan Crime Patterns*, Monsey, NY: Criminal Justice Press.

FINESTONE, H. (1976), 'The delinquent and society: the Shaw and McKay tradition', in J.F. Short, Jr (ed.), *Delinquency, Crime and Society*, Chicago, Ill.: University of Chicago Press.

GILLIS, A.R. (1996), 'Urbanisation, Socio-historical Context and Crime', in J. Hagan, A.R. Gillis and D. Brownfield, *Criminological Controversies: A Methodological Primer*, Boulder, Col.: Westview Press.

GOTTFREDSON, D.C., McNEILL, R.J., and GOTTFREDSON, G.D. (1991), 'Social Area Influences on Delinquency: a Multi-level Analysis', *Journal of Research in Crime and Delinquency*, 28: 197–226.

GOTTFREDSON, M. (1984), *Victims of Crime: The Dimensions of Risk*, Home Office Research Study No. 81, London: HMSO.

HAGAN, J. (1994), *Crime and Disrepute*, Thousand Oaks, Ca.: Pine Forge Press.

HANCOCK, L. (2001), *Community, Crime and Disorder*, Basingstoke: Palgrave.

HARCOURT, B.E. (1998), 'Reflecting on the subject: a critique of the social influence conception of deterrence, the broken windows theory, and order maintenance policing New York style', *Michigan Law Review*, 97: 291–372.

HARRIES, K.D. (1980), *Crime and the Environment*, Springfield, Ill.: Charles C. Thomas.

—— (1999), *Mapping Crime: Principle and Practice*, Washington, DC: Crime Mapping Research Center, US Department of Justice.

HERBERT, D. (1982), *The Geography of Urban Crime*, London: Longman.

HIRSCHFIELD, A., and BOWERS, K. (eds) (2001), *Mapping and Analysing Crime Data: Lessons from Research and Practice*, London: Taylor and Francis.

HM INSPECTORATE OF CONSTABULARY (2000), *On the Record*, London: Home Office.

HOPE, T., and FOSTER, J. (1992), 'Conflicting forces: changing the dynamics of crime and community on a "problem" estate', *British Journal of Criminology*, 32: 488–504.

HUNTER, A.J. (1985), 'Private, Parochial and Public Social Orders; The Problem of Crime and Incivility in Urban Communities', in G.D. Suttles and M.N. Zald (eds), *The Challenge of Social Control: Citizenship and Institution Building in Urban Society*, Norwood, NJ: Abex Publishing.

JANSON, C.-G. (1993), 'Ecological and individual approaches in the study of crime and delinquency', in D.P. Farrington, R.J. Sampson, and P-O.H. Wikström (eds), *Integrating Individual and Ecological Aspects of Crime*, Stockholm: National Council for Crime Prevention.

JOHNSTON, V., LEITNER, M., SHAPLAND, J., and WILES, P. (1994), *Crime on Industrial Estates*, Home Office Crime Prevention Unit Paper No. 54, London: Home Office.

KERSHAW, C., CHIVITE-MATTHEWS, N., THOMAS, C., and AUST, R. (2001), *The 2001 British Crime Survey*, London: Home Office.

KLEEMANS, E.R. (2001), 'Repeat Burglary Victimization: Results of Empirical Research in the Netherlands', in G. Farrell and K. Pease (eds), *Repeat Victimization*, Monsey, NY: Criminal Justice Press.

KORNHAUSER, R.R. (1978), *Social Sources of Delinquency*, Chicago, Ill.: University of Chicago Press.

KURTZ, L.R. (1984), *Evaluating Chicago Sociology*, Chicago, Ill.: University of Chicago Press.

LA VIGNE, N., and WARTELL, J. (1998/2000), *Crime Mapping Case Studies: Successes in the Field*, Washington, DC: Police Executive Research Forum, 2 Vols.

LANDER, B. (1954), *Towards an Understanding of Juvenile Delinquency*, New York: Columbia University Press.

LIZOTTE, A.J., THORNBURY, T.P., KROHN, M.D., CHARD-WIERSCHEM, D.C., and McDOWALL, D. (1994), 'Neighborhood Context and Delinquency', in E.M.G. Weitekamp and H.-J. Kerner (eds), *Cross-National Longitudinal Research on Human Development and Human Behavior*, Dordrecht: Kluwer.

MARTENS, P.L. (1993), 'An ecological model of socialisation in explaining offending', in D.P. Farrington, R.J. Sampson, and P-O.H. Wikström (eds), *Integrating Individual and Ecological Aspects of Crime*, Stockholm: National Council for Crime Prevention.

MAWBY, R.I. (1979), *Policing the City*, Farnborough, Hants: Saxon House.

—— (1989), 'Policing and the criminal area', in D.J. Evans and D.T. Herbert (eds), *The Geography of Crime*, London: Routledge.

—— (2001), *Burglary*, Collompton, Devon: Willan Publishing.

MAYHEW, P., AYE MAUNG, N., and MIRRLEES-BLACK, C. (1993), *The 1992 British Crime Survey*, London: Home Office.

——, CLARKE, R.V.G., STURMAN, A., and HOUGH, J.M. (1976), *Crime as Opportunity*, Home Office Research Unit Study No. 34, London: HMSO.

McIVER, J.P. (1981), 'Criminal mobility: a review of empirical studies', in S. Hakim and G. Rengert (eds), *Crime Spillover*, Beverly Hills, Ca.: Sage Publications.

MORRIS, L. (1994), *Dangerous Classes: The Underclass and Social Citizenship*, London: Routledge.

MORRIS, T.P. (1957), *The Criminal Area: a Study in Social Ecology*, London: Routledge and Kegan Paul.

MURRAY, C. (1984), *Losing Ground*, New York: Basic Books.

—— (1990), *The Emerging British Underclass*, London: Institute of Economic Affairs.

—— (1994), *Underclass: The Crisis Deepens*, London: Institute of Economic Affairs.

NACRO (1996), *Crime, Community and Change: Taking Action on the Kingsmeade Estate in Hackney*, London: NACRO.

NEWMAN, O. (1973), *Defensible Space*, London: Architectural Press.

OBERWITTLER, D. (2001), 'Juvenile Delinquency in Urban Neighborhoods: Do Community Contexts Matter?', paper presented at the Annual Meeting of the European Society of Criminology, Lausanne, Switzerland.

PAINTER, K. (1992), 'Different worlds: the spatial, temporal and social dimensions of female victimization', in D.J. Evans, N.R. Fyfe, and D.T. Herbert (eds), *Crime and Policing: Essays in Environmental Criminology*, London: Routledge.

POYNER, B. (1983), *Design Against Crime*, London: Butterworth.

—— and WEBB, B. (1992), *Crime Free Housing*, Oxford: Butterworth Architecture.

PUTNAM, R.D. (2000), *Bowling Alone: The Collapse and Revival of American Community*, New York: Simon and Schuster.

RADZINOWICZ, L. (1966), *Ideology and Crime*, London: Heinemann.

RAMSAY, M. (1989), *Downtown Drinkers: The Perceptions and Fears of the Public in a City Centre*, Home Office Crime Prevention Unit Paper No. 19, London: Home Office.

RATCLIFFE, J.H. (2001), *Policing Urban Burglary*, Trends and Issues in Crime and Criminal Justice No. 213, Canberra: Australian Institute of Criminology.

REISS, A.J. (1986), 'Why are communities important in understanding crime?', in A.J. Reiss and M. Tonry (eds), *Communities and Crime*, Chicago, Ill.: University of Chicago Press.

RENGERT, G., and WASILCHICK, J. (2000), *Suburban Burglary: A Tale of Two Suburbs*, 2nd edn, Springfield, Ill.: Charles C. Thomas.

REX, J., and MOORE, R. (1967), *Race, Community and Conflict: A Study of Sparkbrook*, London: Oxford University Press.

RHODES, W.M., and CONLY, C. (1981), 'Crime and mobility: an empirical study', in P.J. Brantingham and P.L. Brantingham (eds), *Environmental Criminology*, Beverly Hills, Ca.: Sage Publications.

ROBINSON, W.S. (1950), 'Ecological correlations and the behavior of individuals', *American Sociological Review*, 15: 351–7.

ROSSMO, D.K. (2000), *Geographical Profiling*, Boca Raton, Fla.: CRC Press.

SAMPSON, R.J. (1995), 'The Community', in J.Q. Wilson and J. Petersilia (eds), *Crime*, San Francisco: Institute for Contemporary Studies.

—— and GROVES, W.B. (1989), 'Community structure and crime: testing social disorganisation theory', *American Journal of Sociology*, 94: 774–802.

——, RAUDENBUSH, S.W., and EARLS, F. (1997), 'Neighborhoods and Violent Crime: A Multi-Level Study of Collective Efficacy', *Science*, 277: 918–924.

SCHUERMAN, L., and KOBRIN, S. (1986), 'Community careers in crime', in A.J. Reiss and

M. Tonry (eds), *Communities and Crime*, Chicago, Ill.: University of Chicago, Ill. Press.

SHAW, C.R. (1930), *The Jack Roller*, Chicago, Ill.: University of Chicago Press.

—— and McKAY, H.D. (1942), *Juvenile Delinquency and Urban Areas*, Chicago, Ill.: University of Chicago Press.

SHERMAN, L.W. (1995), 'Hot spots of crime and criminal careers of places', in J.E. Eck and D. Weisburd (eds), *Crime and Place*, Monsey, NY: Criminal Justice Press.

——, GARTIN, P.R., and BUERGER, M.E. (1989), 'Hot spots of predatory crime: routine activities and the criminology of place', *Criminology*, 27: 27–55.

SIMCHA-FAGAN, O., and SCHWARTZ, J.E. (1986), 'Neighborhood and Delinquency: an Assessment of Contextual Effects', *Criminology*, 24: 667–703.

SKOGAN, W.G. (1986), 'Fear of crime and neighborhood change', in A.J. Reiss and M. Tonry (eds), *Communities and Crime*, Chicago, Ill.: University of Chicago Press.

—— (1990), *Disorder and Decline: Crime and the Spiral of Decay in American Neighborhoods*, New York: Free Press.

SPELMAN, W. (1995), 'Criminal careers of public places', in J.E. Eck and D. Weisburd (eds), *Crime and Place*, Monsey, NY: Criminal Justice Press.

TAUB, R., TAYLOR, D.G., and DUNHAM, J.D. (1984), *Paths of Neighborhood Change*, Chicago, Ill.: University of Chicago Press.

TAYLOR, I. (1999), *Crime in Context: A Critical Criminology of Market Societies*, Cambridge: Polity Press.

TAYLOR, R.B. (2001), *Breaking Away from Broken Windows: Baltimore Neighborhoods and the Nationwide Fight against Crime, Grime, Fear and Decline*, Boulder, Col.: Westview.

—— and HARRELL, A.V. (1996), *Physical Environment and Crime*, Washington, DC: National Institute of Justice.

TOBIAS, J.J. (1972), *Urban Crime in Victorian England*, New York: Schocken Books.

TRICKETT, A., OSBORN, D.R., SEYMOUR, J., and PEASE, K. (1992), 'What is different about high crime areas?', *British Journal of Criminology*, 32: 81–9.

WALKLAKE, S., and EVANS, K. (1999), *Zero Tolerance or Community Tolerance?*, Aldershot: Ashgate.

WEBER, M. (1949), *The Methodology of the Social Sciences*, transl. E.A. Shils and H.A. Finch, New York: Free Press.

—— (1968), *Economy and Society: an Outline of Interpretive Sociology 3 Vols*, edited by G. Roth and C. Wittich, New York: Bedminster Press.

WEISBURD, D., and McEWEN, T. (eds) (1998), *Crime Mapping and Crime Prevention*, Monsey, NY: Criminal Justice Press.

WIKSTRÖM, P-O.H. (1991), *Urban Crime, Criminals and Victims: The Swedish Experience in an Anglo-American Comparative Perspective*, New York: Springer-Verlag.

—— (1998), 'Communities and Crime', in M. Tonry (ed.), *The Handbook of Crime and Punishment*, New York: Oxford University Press.

—— and LOEBER, R. (2000), 'Do Disadvantaged Neighborhoods Cause Well-adjusted Children to Become Adolescent Delinquents?: A Study of Male Serious Juvenile Offending, Individual Risk and Protective Factors, and Neighborhood Context', *Criminology*, 38: 1109–42.

WILES, P. (1992), 'Ghettoization in Europe?', *European Journal on Criminal Policy and Research*, 1: 52–69.

—— and COSTELLO, A. (2000), *The 'Road to Nowhere': the Evidence for Travelling Criminals*, Home Office Research Study No. 207, London: Home Office.

WILSON, J.Q., and HERRNSTEIN, R.J. (1985), *Crime and Human Nature*, New York: Simon and Schuster.

—— and KELLING, G. (1982), 'Broken windows', *The Atlantic Monthly* (March), 29–38.

WILSON, W.J. (1987), *The Truly Disadvantaged*, Chicago, Ill.: University of Chicago Press.

—— (1996), *When Work Disappears: The World of the New Urban Poor*, New York: Alfred Knopf.

WINCHESTER, S., and JACKSON, H. (1982), *Residential Burglary*, Home Office Research Study No. 74, London: Home Office.

WRIGHT, R.T., and DECKER, S.H. (1994), *Burglars on the Job: Street Life and Residential Break-ins*, Boston: Northeastern University Press.

YOUNG, J. (1999), *The Exclusive Society: Social Exclusion, Crime and Difference in Late Modernity*, London: Sage Publications.

19

DEVELOPMENTAL CRIMINOLOGY AND RISK-FOCUSED PREVENTION

David P. Farrington

INTRODUCTION

The main aim of this chapter is to review what is known about developmental criminology and risk-focused prevention. The chapter focuses on individual, family, and school risk factors for offending and antisocial behaviour, and on the results of prevention initiatives targeting these risk factors. The emphasis is on offending by males; most research on offending has concentrated on males, because they commit most of the serious predatory and violent offences (for reviews of risk factors for females, see Moffitt *et al.* 2001). The review focuses on research carried out in the United Kingdom (especially), the United States, and in similar Western industrialized democracies.

Within a single chapter, it is obviously impossible to review everything that is known about the development of offending and risk-focused interventions. I will be very selective in focusing on some of the more important and replicable findings obtained in some of the more methodologically adequate studies—especially prospective longitudinal studies of large community samples and randomized experiments to evaluate the impact of prevention techniques.

There are many possible ways of classifying prevention strategies. In the public health sphere (Moore 1995), the most common distinction is between primary prevention (measures targeted on the whole community to prevent the onset of a disease), secondary prevention (measures targeted on persons at high risk of a disease), and tertiary prevention (measures targeted on persons who have contracted a disease). In this scheme, risk-focused prevention spans primary and secondary prevention.

Tonry and Farrington (1995) distinguished four major prevention strategies. *Developmental prevention* refers to interventions designed to prevent the development of criminal potential in individuals, especially those targeting risk and protective factors discovered in studies of human development (Tremblay and Craig 1995). *Community prevention* refers to interventions designed to change the social conditions and institutions (e.g., families, peers, social norms, clubs, organizations) that influence offending in residential communities (Hope 1995). *Situational prevention* refers to interventions designed to prevent the occurrence of crimes by reducing opportunities and increasing the risk and difficulty of offending (Clarke 1995). *Criminal justice prevention* refers to traditional deterrent, incapacitative, and rehabilitative strategies operated by law enforcement and criminal justice system agencies. The term 'risk-focused prevention' is now used more generally than 'developmental prevention', but the two terms have the same meaning.

This chapter is structured as follows. This section introduces the key concepts of developmental criminology and risk-focused prevention, and outlines recent developments in cost–benefit analysis and systematic reviews of criminological interventions, which are important in translating research results into evidence-based policy. This is followed by more detailed discussions of individual, family, and school risk factors for offending, including reviews of possible intervening processes and a description of a larger integrative theory. The next section reviews risk-focused prevention programmes that have been proved to be effective in high-quality evaluation research, and the concluding section outlines recommendations for research and policy.

DEVELOPMENTAL CRIMINOLOGY

Developmental criminology advanced enormously in the 1980s and 1990s, and is concerned with three main issues: the development of offending and antisocial behaviour; risk factors at different ages; and the effects of life events on the course of development (Loeber and LeBlanc 1990; LeBlanc and Loeber 1998). Developmental topics are reviewed only briefly here, as the focus is on risk factors and on risk-focused prevention.

In studying development, efforts are made to investigate the prevalence of offending at different ages, the frequency of offending by offenders, the ages of onset and desistance, and specialization and escalation of offending over time (for reviews of criminal career research, see Farrington 1992a, 1997a). There are many studies of the persistence of offending and characteristics of persistent offenders (e.g., Farrington and West 1993). There is an emphasis on investigating within-individual change over time, for example, when people graduate from hyperactivity at age two to cruelty to animals at six, shoplifting at ten, burglary at fifteen, robbery at twenty, and eventually spouse assault, child abuse and neglect, alcohol abuse, and employment and mental health problems later on in life. Attempts are made to study developmental pathways and sequences over time, for example, where one type of behaviour facilitates or acts as a kind of stepping stone to another (Loeber *et al.* 1993). It is desirable to identify non-criminal behaviours that lead to criminal behaviours, and early indicators of later frequent and serious offending that might suggest opportunities for early prevention.

It seems that offending is part of a larger syndrome of antisocial behaviour that arises in childhood and tends to persist into adulthood (West and Farrington 1977). There is significant continuity over time, since the antisocial child tends to become the antisocial teenager and then the antisocial adult, just as the antisocial adult then tends to produce another antisocial child. Typically, researchers find relative stability (the relative ordering of people on measures of antisocial behaviour is significantly stable) but changing behavioural manifestations over time, as individual capacities, opportunities, and social contexts change (Farrington 1990a). For example, only children at school can truant or be excluded from school, only older people can beat up their spouses, seventy-year-olds have difficulty committing burglaries, and so on. There is a great deal of interest in different types of behavioural trajectories, for example, the distinction between adolescence-limited and life-course persistent antisocial behaviour (Moffitt 1993; Nagin and Tremblay 2001). Also, there is a great deal of interest in intergenerational continuity and explaining why crime runs in families (see later).

Risk factors at different ages are studied, including biological, individual, family, peer, school, neighbourhood, and situational factors. As mentioned, it is only possible to review individual, family, and school factors within the scope of this chapter (for more wide-ranging reviews, see Rutter *et al.* 1998; Farrington 1998, 2001b).

Many risk factors for offending are well established and highly replicable. For example, a systematic comparison of two longitudinal surveys in London and Pittsburgh (Farrington and Loeber 1999) showed numerous replicable predictors of delinquency over time and place, including impulsivity, attention problems, low school attainment, poor parental supervision, parental conflict, an antisocial parent, a young mother, large family size, low family income, and coming from a broken family. Vazsonyi *et al.* (2001) found that the patterns of association between measures of self-control (e.g., impulsivity, risk-taking, getting angry) and measures of antisocial behaviour (e.g., theft, assault, vandalism, drug use) were highly similar across four countries (Hungary, The Netherlands, Switzerland and the United States). Less well established are the causal mechanisms linking risk factors and offending. For example, does large family size predict offending because of the consequent poor supervision of each child, overcrowded households, poverty, or merely because more antisocial people tend to have more children than others?

There is a great deal of interest in the early prediction of later offending, and in risk factors that might form the basis of risk (and needs) assessment devices (e.g., Augimeri *et al.* 2001). Typically, prospective prediction (e.g., the percentage of high-risk children who become persistent offenders) is poor, but retrospective prediction (e.g., the percentage of persistent offenders who were high-risk children) is good. The fact that many children at risk have successful lives inspires the search for protective factors and individual resilience features that might inform prevention techniques. There is a great deal of interest in cumulative, interactive, and sequential effects of risk factors. For example, the probability of becoming a persistent offender increases with the number of risk factors (Farrington 2001a), almost independently of which particular risk factors are included. There are also attempts to study individual development in different neighbourhood and community contexts (Wikström and Loeber 2000).

There are many life events that influence the course of development of offending and antisocial behaviour, including getting married, becoming separated, moving house, joining the military, and getting convicted (Farrington 1977; Osborn 1980; Sampson and Laub 1993; Farrington and West 1995). Life course transitions and turning points are important, for example, when parental influence gives way to peer influence or when people move from school to work. The timing and duration of life events (e.g., parental conflict) is also studied. Researchers have also tried to assess the effects of national contexts and macro events, such as recessions and wars, on individual development. These topics are not reviewed in this chapter.

In researching development, risk factors, and life events, it is essential to carry out prospective longitudinal surveys. I will refer especially to knowledge gained in the Cambridge study in Delinquent Development, which is a prospective longitudinal survey of over 400 London males from age eight to age forty-six (Farrington and West 1990; Farrington 1995, 2002). In general, results obtained in British longitudinal surveys of offending (e.g., Wadsworth 1979; Kolvin *et al.* 1990) are highly concordant with those obtained in comparable surveys in North America (e.g., Capaldi and Patterson 1996; Loeber *et al.* 1998), the Scandinavian countries (e.g., Pulkkinen 1988; Klinteberg *et al.* 1993), and New Zealand (e.g., Fergusson *et al.* 1994; Henry *et al.* 1996), and indeed with results obtained in British cross-sectional surveys (e.g., Hagell and Newburn 1994; Boswell 1995; Graham and Bowling 1995; Flood-Page *et al.* 2000).

RISK-FOCUSED PREVENTION

During the 1990s, there was an enormous increase in the influence of risk-focused prevention in criminology. The basic idea of this approach is very simple: identify the key risk factors for offending and implement prevention methods designed to counteract them. There is often a related attempt to identify key protective factors against offending, and to implement prevention methods designed to enhance them. Typically, longitudinal surveys provide knowledge about risk and protective factors, and experimental and quasi-experimental studies are used to evaluate the impact of prevention and intervention programmes. Thus, risk-focused prevention links explanation and prevention, links fundamental and applied research, and links scholars, policy-makers, and practitioners. The book *Serious and Violent Juvenile Offenders: Risk Factors and Successful Interventions* (Loeber and Farrington 1998) contains a detailed exposition of this approach as applied to serious and violent juvenile offenders.

Risk-focused prevention was imported into criminology from medicine and public health by pioneers such as Hawkins and Catalano (1992). This approach has been used successfully for many years to tackle illnesses such as cancer and heart disease. For example, the identified risk factors for heart disease include smoking, a fatty diet, and lack of exercise. These can be tackled by encouraging people to stop smoking, to have a more healthy, low-fat diet, and to take more exercise. Interventions can be targeted on the whole community, or on persons at high risk. Typically, the effectiveness of risk-focused prevention in the medical field is evaluated using the 'gold standard' of randomized controlled trials, and there has been increasing emphasis in medicine on cost–benefit analyses of interventions. Not surprisingly, therefore, there has been a similar emphasis in criminology recently on high-quality evaluations and on cost–benefit analyses (Sherman *et al.* 1997, 2002; Welsh *et al.* 2001).

Risk factors tend to be similar for many different outcomes, including violent and non-violent offending, mental health problems, alcohol and drug problems, school failure and unemployment. Therefore, a prevention programme that succeeds in reducing a risk factor for offending will in all probability have wide-ranging benefits in reducing other types of social problems as well. Because of the interest in linking risk factors with prevention programmes, risk factors that cannot be changed feasibly in such programmes (e.g., gender and race) are excluded from consideration, except to the extent that they act as moderators (e.g., if the effect of a risk factor is different for males and females).

One methodological problem is that most knowledge about risk factors is based on variation between individuals, whereas prevention requires variation (change) within individuals. It is not always clear that findings within individuals would be the same as findings between individuals. To take a specific example, unemployment is a risk factor for offending between individuals, since unemployed people are more likely than employed people to be offenders (West and Farrington 1977). However, unemployment is also a risk factor for offending within individuals, since people are more likely to offend during their periods of unemployment than during their periods of employment (Farrington et al. 1986). The within-individual finding has a much clearer implication for prevention, namely that a reduction in unemployment should lead to a reduction in offending. This is because it is much easier to demonstrate that a risk factor is a cause in within-individual research. Since the same individuals are followed up over time, many extraneous influences on offending are controlled (Farrington 1988).

A major problem of risk-focused prevention is to establish which risk factors are causes and which are merely markers or correlated with causes (Farrington 2000). It is also desirable to establish mediators (intervening causal processes) between risk factors and outcomes (Baron and Kenny 1986). Ideally, interventions should be targeted on risk factors that are causes; interventions targeted on risk factors that are markers will not necessarily lead to any decrease in offending. The difficulty of establishing causes, and the co-occurrence of risk factors, encourages the blunderbuss approach: interventions that target multiple risk factors. However, there is also evidence that integrated or multi-modal intervention packages are more effective than interventions that target only a single risk factor (Wasserman and Miller 1998).

In principle, a great deal can be learned about causes from the results of intervention experiments, to the extent that the experiments establish the impact of targeting each risk factor separately (Robins 1992). For example, if an intervention that improves school success leads to a decrease in delinquency (Schweinhart et al. 1993), this might be good evidence that school failure has a causal impact on delinquency (assuming that alternative hypotheses can be eliminated). Ideally, intervention experiments need to be designed to test causal hypotheses, as well as to test a particular intervention technology. However, there is a clear tension between maximizing the effectiveness of an intervention (which encourages a multiple component approach) and assessing the effectiveness of each component and hence drawing conclusions about causes (which requires disentangling of the different components).

Risk-focused prevention includes protective factors. Ideally, risk and protective factors should be identified, and then risk factors should be reduced while protective factors are enhanced. However, both the definition and existence of protective factors are controversial. On one definition, a protective factor is merely the opposite end of the scale to a risk factor. Just as a risk factor predicts an increased probability of offending, a protective factor predicts a decreased probability. However, to the extent that explanatory variables are linearly related to offending, researchers may then object that risk and protective factors are merely different names for the same underlying construct.

Another possible definition of a protective factor is a variable that interacts with a risk factor to minimize the risk factor's effects. Such interactive variables are often termed 'moderators' (Baron and Kenny 1986). If poor parental supervision predicted a high risk of offending only for males from low income families, and not for males from high income families, then high income might be regarded as a protective factor counteracting the effects of the risk factor of poor parental supervision. Problems associated with the definition of protective factors may be alleviated by focusing on resilience or psychosocial skills and competencies. More research is needed to identify protective factors, linked to the use of interventions targeted on protective factors.

COST—BENEFIT ANALYSIS

As mentioned, an important development in the 1990s was the increasing use of cost–benefit analysis in evaluating crime prevention programmes. The conclusion from the Perry project (discussed later), that for every dollar spent on the programme, seven dollars were saved in the long term (Schweinhart et al. 1993: xviii), proved particularly convincing to policy-makers. The monetary costs of crime are enormous. For example, Brand and Price (2000) estimated that they totalled £60 billion in England and Wales in 1999. There are tangible costs to victims, such as replacing stolen goods and repairing damage, and intangible costs that are harder to quantify, such as pain, suffering, and a reduced quality of life. There are costs to the government or taxpayer for police, courts, prisons, crime prevention activities, and so on. There are also costs to offenders—for example, those associated with being in prison or losing a job.

To the extent that crime prevention programmes are successful in reducing crime, they will have benefits. These benefits can be quantified in monetary terms according to the reduction in the monetary costs of crime. Other benefits may accrue from reducing the costs of associated social problems such as unemployment, divorce, educational failure, drug addiction, welfare dependency, and so on. The fact that offending is part of a larger syndrome of antisocial behaviour (West and Farrington 1977) is good news, because the benefits of a crime prevention programme can be many and varied. The monetary benefits of a programme can be compared with its monetary costs to determine the benefit:cost ratio. The adequacy of an economic analysis of the monetary benefits and costs of a crime prevention programme depends crucially on the methodological adequacy of the underlying evaluation design.

Surprisingly few cost–benefit analyses of crime prevention programmes have ever been carried out (Welsh and Farrington 2000; Welsh et al. 2001). Existing analyses are difficult to compare, because researchers have taken account of different types of programme costs and programme effects, and have used different methods for calculating monetary costs and benefits. For example, Painter and Farrington (2001) used Home Office estimates of the monetary cost of each type of crime in calculating the benefit:cost ratio of improved street lighting, as a crime prevention measure. There is a great need for a standard how-to-do-it manual to be developed and followed, that specifies a list of costs and benefits to be measured in all studies and their monetary values. The Home Office is carrying out cost–benefit analyses in its Crime Reduction Programme.

SYSTEMATIC REVIEWS OF CRIMINOLOGICAL INTERVENTIONS

The reviews of the effectiveness of interventions by Goldblatt and Lewis (1998) are extremely valuable and informative, but they are not systematic reviews in the modern sense of this term (see Farrington and Petrosino 2000, 2001). Systematic reviews are much more rigorous than more traditional narrative reviews of the literature. Whereas traditional reviews rarely detail the methods they used to search the literature, systematic reviews give full details about all sources searched and all searches carried out. Whereas traditional reviews rarely go beyond easily available journal articles and books in the English language, systematic reviews try to obtain all potentially relevant evaluation reports in all languages, whether published or unpublished. Whereas traditional reviews rarely include detailed information about why studies were included or excluded, giving rise to possible bias in their conclusions, systematic reviews provide explicit and transparent information about the criteria used for including or excluding studies.

Systematic reviews focus on studies that have the highest methodological quality and use the most rigorous methods possible to combine results from different studies statistically to draw conclusions about what works. These reviews contain methods and results sections and are reported with the same level of detail that characterizes high-quality reports of original research. They include detailed summary tables of key features of studies, such as design, sample sizes, and effect sizes.

Following the success of the Cochrane Collaboration in reviewing health care interventions, the Campbell Collaboration was founded in February 2000 to produce systematic reviews of social, educational, and criminological interventions. The aim of the Campbell Collaboration is to make the best knowledge about 'What Works' immediately available electronically (e.g., on the Internet) to all interested persons, including scholars, practitioners, policy-makers, and the general public. Whereas traditional reviews are typically one-off exercises that soon become out of date, systematic reviews for the Campbell Collaboration will be regularly updated. These reviews will be subject to rigorous quality control, will cover research throughout the world, and will be revised in the light of new evaluation studies and cogent criticisms.

Unfortunately, the Campbell Collaboration is still in its infancy, and very few systematic reviews of criminological interventions have been completed. The most common ones are meta-analyses of correctional treatments (e.g., Lipsey and Wilson 1998; Redondo *et al.* 1999). This chapter is not a systematic review. Its aim is to summarize briefly some of the best risk-focused crime prevention programmes whose effectiveness has been demonstrated in high-quality evaluation research. (For a more systematic review of family-based crime prevention, see Farrington and Welsh 1999.)

Within the space available, it is not feasible to present an exhaustive review of risk-focused interventions to reduce crime. In particular, I will not focus on interventions that do not work. Instead, a selection of some of the most effective and best-designed programmes will be described, with special reference to programmes that have carried out a cost–benefit analysis. As far as possible, programme elements will be linked to risk factors, but there is often only a tenuous link between risk factors and prevention programmes. As mentioned, many programmes have multiple components, making it difficult to isolate their 'active ingredients'.

INDIVIDUAL RISK FACTORS

RISK FACTORS

Risk factors are prior factors that increase the risk of occurrence of the onset, frequency, persistence, or duration of offending. Longitudinal data are required to establish the ordering of risk factors and criminal career features. The focus in this chapter is on risk factors for the onset or prevalence of offending; few studies have examined risk factors for persistence or duration. For simplicity, risk factors are reviewed one by one in this chapter. However, many risk factors tend to be inter-related, and it is of course necessary to investigate which factors are independent predictors of offending. This is discussed later in the section on 'Explaining Development and Risk Factors'.

It is difficult to decide if any given risk factor is an indicator (symptom), or a possible cause of offending. For example, are heavy drinking, truancy, unemployment, and divorce symptoms of an antisocial personality, or do they cause people to become more antisocial? Similarly, to the extent that delinquency is a group activity (Reiss and Farrington 1991), delinquents will usually have delinquent friends, and this does not necessarily show that delinquent friends cause delinquency. It is important not to include a measure of the dependent variable (e.g., delinquent friends) as an independent variable in causal analyses, because this will lead to false (tautological) conclusions and an over-estimation of explanatory or predictive power (Amdur 1989).

It is possible to argue that some factors may be both indicative and causal. For example, long-term variations *between* individuals in an underlying antisocial tendency may be reflected in variations in alcohol consumption, just as short-term variations *within* individuals in alcohol consumption may cause more antisocial behaviour during the heavier drinking periods. In other words, heavy drinking may be viewed as a situational trigger rather than a long-term cause. The interpretation of other factors may be easier. For example, being exposed as a child to poor parental child-rearing techniques might cause (or even be a consequence of) the child's antisocial behaviour but would not be an indicator of it.

PERSONALITY

As mentioned, antisocial behaviour is remarkably consistent over time; or, to be more precise, the relative ordering of individuals is remarkably consistent over time (Roberts and del Vecchio 2000). Psychologists assume that behavioural consistency depends primarily on the persistence of underlying tendencies to behave in particular ways in particular situations. These tendencies are termed personality traits, such as impulsiveness, excitement seeking, assertiveness, modesty, and dutifulness. Larger personality dimensions such as extraversion refer to clusters of personality traits.

Historically, the best-known British research on personality and crime was that inspired by Eysenck's theory and personality questionnaires (Eysenck 1996). He predicted that persons high on his dimensions of extraversion (E), neuroticism (N), and psychoticism (P) would tend to be offenders. However, the meaning of the P scale is unclear, and it might perhaps be more accurately labelled as psychopathy.

A review of studies relating Eysenck's personality dimensions to official and self-reported offending concluded that high N (but not E) was related to official offending, while high E (but not N) was related to self-reported offending (Farrington *et al.* 1982). High P was related to both, but this could have been a tautological result, since many of the items on the P scale reflected antisocial behaviour, or were selected in light of their ability to discriminate between prisoners and non-prisoners. In the Cambridge study, those high on both E and N tended to be juvenile self-reported offenders, adult official offenders, and adult self-reported offenders, but not juvenile official offenders (Farrington *et al.* 1982). These relationships held independently of other criminogenic risk factors such as low family income, low intelligence, and poor parental child-rearing behaviour. However, when individual items of the questionnaire were studied, it was clear that the significant relationships were caused by the items measuring impulsiveness (e.g., doing things quickly without stopping to think). Hence, it seems likely that research inspired by the Eysenck theory mainly identifies the link between impulsiveness and offending (see later).

TEMPERAMENT

Temperament is basically the childhood equivalent of personality, although there is more emphasis in the study of temperament on constitutional predisposition and on biological factors (Robinson *et al.* 1992). Modern research on child temperament began with the New York Longitudinal Study of Chess and Thomas (1984). Children in their first five years of life were rated on temperamental dimensions by their parents, and these dimensions were combined into three broad categories of easy, difficult, and 'slow to warm up' temperament. Having a difficult temperament at age three to four (frequent irritability, low amenability and adaptability, irregular habits) predicted poor adult psychiatric adjustment at age seventeen to twenty-four.

Because it was not very clear exactly what a 'difficult' temperament meant in practice, other researchers have used more specific dimensions of temperament. For example, Kagan (1989) in Boston classified children as inhibited (shy or fearful) or uninhibited at age twenty-one months, and found that they remained significantly stable on this classification up to age seven years. Furthermore, the uninhibited children at age twenty-one months significantly tended to be identified as aggressive at age thirteen years, according to self and parent reports (Schwartz *et al.* 1996).

The most important results on the link between childhood temperament and later offending have been obtained in the Dunedin longitudinal study in New Zealand, which has followed up over 1,000 children from age three years into their twenties (Caspi 2000). Temperament at age three years was rated by observing the child's behaviour during a testing session. The most important dimension of temperament was being undercontrolled (restless, impulsive, with poor attention), which predicted aggression, self-reported delinquency and convictions at age eighteen to twenty-one.

EMPATHY

There is a widespread belief that low empathy is an important personality trait that is related to offending, on the assumption that people who can appreciate and/or experience a victim's feelings are less likely to victimize someone. This belief also underlies cognitive-behavioural skills training programmes that aim to increase empathy (see later). However, its empirical basis is not very impressive. The field includes inconsistent results, measures of empathy are not well validated or widely accepted, and there are no prospective longitudinal surveys relating early empathy to later offending.

A distinction has often been made between cognitive empathy (understanding or appreciating other people's feelings) and emotional empathy (actually experiencing other people's feelings). The best studies of the 1990s that have related empathy to offending in relatively large samples are as follows. In Australia, Mak (1991) found that delinquent females had lower emotional empathy than non-delinquent females, but that there were no significant differences in empathy for males. In Finland, Kaukiainen *et al.* (1999) reported that empathy (cognitive and emotional combined) was negatively correlated with aggression (both measured by peer ratings). In Spain, Luengo *et al.* (1994) carried out the first project that related cognitive and emotional empathy separately to (self-reported) offending, and found that both were negatively correlated with offending, as predicted.

IMPULSIVENESS

Impulsiveness is the most crucial personality dimension that predicts offending. Unfortunately, there are a bewildering number of constructs referring to a poor ability to control behaviour. These include impulsiveness, hyperactivity, restlessness, clumsiness, not considering consequences before acting, a poor ability to plan ahead, short time horizons, low self-control, sensation-seeking, risk-taking, and a poor ability to delay gratification.

Many studies show that hyperactivity predicts later offending. In the Copenhagen Perinatal project, hyperactivity (restlessness and poor concentration) at age eleven to thirteen significantly predicted arrests for violence up to age twenty-two, especially among boys experiencing delivery complications (Brennan *et al.* 1993). More than half of those with both hyperactivity and high delivery complications were arrested for violence, compared to less than 10 per cent of the remainder. Similarly, in the Orebro longitudinal study in Sweden, hyperactivity at age thirteen predicted police-recorded violence up to age twenty-six. The highest rate of violence was among males with both motor restlessness and concentration difficulties (15 per cent), compared to 3 per cent of the remainder (Klinteberg et al. 1993).

In the Cambridge study, boys nominated by teachers as lacking in concentration or as restless, those nominated by parents, peers, or teachers as the most daring or risk-taking, and those who were the most impulsive on psychomotor tests at age eight to ten, all tended to become offenders later in life. Daring, poor concentration, and restlessness all predicted both official convictions and self-reported delinquency, and daring was consistently one of the best independent predictors (Farrington 1992c). A combined measure of HIA ('hyperactivity-impulsivity-attention deficit') significantly predicted juvenile convictions independently of conduct problems at age eight to ten (Farrington et al. 1990). Lynam (1996) argued that children with both HIA and conduct problems were at greatest risk of later chronic offending.

The most extensive research on different measures of impulsiveness was carried out in another longitudinal study of males (the Pittsburgh Youth Study) by White et al. (1994). The measures that were most strongly related to self-reported delinquency at ages ten and thirteen were teacher-rated impulsiveness (e.g., 'acts without thinking'), self-reported impulsiveness, self-reported under-control (e.g., 'unable to delay gratification'), motor restlessness (from videotaped observations), and psychomotor impulsiveness (on the Trail Making Test). Generally, the verbal behaviour rating tests produced stronger relationships with offending than the psychomotor performance tests, suggesting that cognitive impulsiveness (based on thinking processes) was more relevant than behavioural impulsiveness (based on test performance). Future time perception and delay of gratification tests were only weakly related to self-reported delinquency.

THEORIES OF IMPULSIVENESS

There have been many theories put forward to explain the link between impulsiveness and offending. One of the most popular suggests that impulsiveness reflects deficits in the executive functions of the brain, located in the frontal lobes (Moffitt 1990). Persons with these neuropsychological deficits will tend to commit offences because they have poor control over their behaviour, a poor ability to consider the possible consequences of their actions, and a tendency to focus on immediate gratification. There may also be an indirect link between neuropsychological deficits and offending which is mediated by hyperactivity and inattention in school and the resulting school failure. In discussing links between executive functions and offending, impulsiveness may be difficult to disentangle from intelligence (see later), although Lynam and Moffitt (1995) argued that they were different constructs.

A related theory suggests that low cortical arousal produces impulsive and sensation-seeking behaviour. Offenders have a low level of arousal according to their low alpha (brain) waves on the EEG, or according to autonomic nervous system indicators such as heart rate, blood pressure, or skin conductance, or they show low autonomic reactivity (Raine 1993). In the Cambridge study, a low heart rate was significantly related to convictions for violence, self-reported violence, and teacher-reported violence, independently of all other explanatory variables (Farrington 1997b). In several regression analyses, the most important independent risk factors for violence were daring, poor concentration, and a low heart rate. Other researchers (Wadsworth 1976; Raine *et al.* 1990) have also identified a low heart rate as an important predictor and correlate of offending.

An important criminological theory focusing on impulsiveness and offending was propounded by Wilson and Herrnstein (1985). This suggested that people differ in their underlying criminal tendencies, and that whether a person chooses to commit a crime in any situation depends on whether the perceived benefits of offending are considered to outweigh the perceived costs. Hence, there is a focus on cognitive (thinking and decision-making) processes.

The benefits of offending, including material gain, peer approval, and sexual gratification, tend to be contemporaneous with it. In contrast, many of the costs of offending, such as the risk of being caught and punished, and the possible loss of reputation or employment, are uncertain and long-delayed. Other costs, such as pangs of conscience (or guilt), disapproval by onlookers, and retaliation by the victim, are more immediate. As in many other theories, Wilson and Herrnstein (1985) emphasized the importance of the conscience as an internal inhibitor of offending, and suggested that it was built up in a social learning process according to whether parents reinforced or punished childhood transgressions.

The key individual difference factor in the Wilson–Herrnstein theory is the extent to which people's behaviour is influenced by immediate as opposed to delayed consequences. They suggested that individuals varied in their ability to think about or plan for the future, and that this was linked to intelligence. The major determinant of offending was a person's impulsiveness. More impulsive people were less influenced by the likelihood of future consequences, and hence were more likely to commit crimes.

In many respects, Gottfredson and Hirschi's (1990) theory is similar to the Wilson–Herrnstein theory. Gottfredson and Hirschi castigated criminological theorists for ignoring the fact that people differed in underlying criminal propensities, and that these differences appeared early in life and remained stable over much of the life course. They called the key individual difference factor in their theory 'low self-control', which referred to the extent to which individuals were vulnerable to the temptations of the moment. People with low self-control were impulsive, took risks, had low cognitive and academic skills, were self-centred, had low empathy, and had short time horizons. Hence, they found it hard to defer gratification and their decisions to offend were insufficiently influenced by the possible future painful consequences of offending. Gottfredson and Hirschi also argued that between-individual differences in self-control were present early in life (by age six to eight), were remarkably stable over time, and were essentially caused by differences in parental child-rearing practices.

COGNITIVE THEORIES

The most popular theory of offending events suggests that they occur in response to specific opportunities, when their subjectively perceived benefits (e.g., stolen property, peer approval) outweigh their subjectively perceived costs (e.g., legal punishment, parental disapproval). For example, Clarke and Cornish (1985) outlined a theory of residential burglary which included such influencing factors as whether a house was occupied, whether it looked affluent, whether there were bushes to hide behind, whether there were nosy neighbours, whether the house had a burglar alarm, and whether it contained a dog. This rational choice theory has inspired situational methods of crime prevention, which are not reviewed here (see Clarke 1997).

Some theories of aggression focus on cognitive processes. Huesmann and Eron (1984) put forward a cognitive script model, in which aggressive behaviour depends on stored behavioural repertoires (cognitive scripts) that have been learned during early development. In response to environmental cues, possible cognitive scripts are retrieved and evaluated. The choice of aggressive scripts, which prescribe aggressive behaviour, depends on the past history of rewards and punishments, and on the extent to which children are influenced by immediate gratification as opposed to long-term consequences. According to Huesmann and Eron, the persisting trait of aggressiveness is a collection of well-learned aggressive scripts that are resistant to change.

There are other cognitive social learning theories that emphasize the role of modelling, thinking processes, and interpersonal problem solving strategies (e.g., Bandura 1977). The individual is viewed as an information processor whose behaviour depends on cognitive processes as well as on the history of rewards and punishments received in the past. Ross and Ross (1995) explicitly linked offending to cognitive deficits, arguing that offenders tended to be impulsive, self-centred, concrete rather than abstract in their thinking, and poor at interpersonal problem solving, because they failed to understand how other people were thinking and feeling.

FAMILY RISK FACTORS

FAMILY FACTORS

Family factors are important predictors of offending. Loeber and Dishion (1983) extensively reviewed risk factors for male offending and concluded that the most important predictors were (in order) poor parental child management techniques, childhood antisocial behaviour, offending by parents and siblings, low intelligence and educational attainment, and separation from a parent. Later, Loeber and Stouthamer-Loeber (1986) completed an exhaustive review of family factors as predictors of offending. They found that the best predictors were (in order) poor parental supervision, parental rejection of children, large family size, low parental involvement with children, parental conflict and antisocial parents.

More recent reviews confirm the importance of family factors. Smith and Stern (1997: 383–4) concluded that:

We know that children who grow up in homes characterized by lack of warmth and support, whose parents lack behavior management skills, and whose lives are characterized by conflict or maltreatment will more likely be delinquent, whereas a supportive family can protect children even in a very hostile and damaging external environment . . . Parental monitoring or supervision is the aspect of family management that is most consistently related to delinquency.

Lipsey and Derzon (1998) systematically reviewed the predictors at age six to eleven of serious or violent offending at age fifteen to twenty-five. The best explanatory predictors (i.e., predictors not measuring some aspect of the child's antisocial behaviour) were antisocial parents, male gender, low socio-economic status of the family, and psychological factors such as daring, impulsiveness, and poor concentration. Other moderately strong predictors were minority race, poor parent–child relations (poor supervision, discipline, low parental involvement, low parental warmth), other family characteristics (parent stress, family size, parental discord), antisocial peers, low intelligence, and low school achievement. In contrast, abusive parents and broken homes were relatively weak predictors. It is clear that some family factors are at least as important as risk factors for offending as are gender and race.

Reviewing these kinds of results reveals the bewildering variety of family constructs that have been studied, and also the variety of methods used to classify them into categories. In this chapter, family factors are grouped into five categories:

1. criminal and antisocial parents;
2. large family size;
3. child-rearing methods (poor supervision, poor discipline, coldness and rejection, low parental involvement with the child);
4. abuse (physical or sexual) or neglect; and
5. parental conflict and disrupted families.

Excluded are socio-economic factors such as low family income, low social class of the family, living in a poor neighbourhood, and the residential mobility of the family.

CRIME RUNS IN FAMILIES

Criminal and antisocial parents tend to have delinquent and antisocial children, as shown in the classic longitudinal surveys by McCord (1977) in Boston and Robins (1979) in St Louis. The most extensive research on the concentration of offending in families was carried out in the Cambridge study. Having a convicted father, mother, brother, or sister predicted a boy's own convictions, and all four relatives were independently important as predictors (Farrington et al. 1996). For example, 63 per cent of boys with convicted fathers were themselves convicted, compared with 30 per cent of the remainder. Same-sex relationships were stronger than opposite-sex relationships, and older siblings were stronger predictors than younger siblings. Only

6 per cent of the families accounted for half of all the convictions of all family members.

Similar results were obtained in the Pittsburgh Youth Study. Arrests of fathers, mothers, brothers, sisters, uncles, aunts, grandfathers, and grandmothers all predicted the boy's own delinquency (Farrington *et al.* 2001). The most important relative was the father; arrests of the father predicted the boy's delinquency independently of all other arrested relatives. Only 8 per cent of families accounted for 43 per cent of arrested family members.

In the Cambridge study, having a convicted parent or a delinquent older sibling by the tenth birthday were consistently among the best age eight to ten predictors of the boy's later offending and antisocial behaviour. Apart from behavioural measures such as troublesomeness, they were the strongest predictors of juvenile convictions (Farrington 1992c). Having a convicted parent or a delinquent older sibling were also the best predictors, after poor parental supervision, of juvenile self-reported delinquency.

There are several possible explanations (which are not mutually exclusive) for why offending tends to be concentrated in certain families and transmitted from one generation to the next. First, there may be intergenerational continuities in exposure to multiple risk factors. For example, each successive generation may be entrapped in poverty, disrupted families, single and/or teenage parenting, and living in the most deprived neighbourhoods. Secondly, the effect of a criminal parent on a child's offending may be mediated by environmental mechanisms. In the Cambridge study, it was suggested that poor parental supervision was one link in the causal chain between criminal fathers and delinquent sons (West and Farrington 1977: 117). Thirdly, the effect of a criminal parent on a child's offending may be mediated by genetic mechanisms (Raine 1993). In a convincing design comparing the concordance of identical twins reared together and identical twins reared apart, Grove *et al.* (1990) found that heritability was 41 per cent for childhood conduct disorder and 28 per cent for adult antisocial personality disorder, showing that the intergenerational transmission of offending is partly attributable to genetic factors. Fourthly, criminal parents may tend to have delinquent children because of official (police and court) bias against criminal families, who also tend to be known to official agencies because of other social problems. At all levels of self-reported delinquency in the Cambridge study, boys with convicted fathers were more likely to be convicted themselves than were boys with unconvicted fathers (West and Farrington 1977: 118). However, this was not the only explanation for the link between criminal fathers and delinquent sons, because boys with criminal fathers had higher self-reported delinquency scores and higher teacher and peer ratings of bad behaviour.

LARGE FAMILY SIZE

Large family size (a large number of children in the family) is a relatively strong and highly replicable predictor of delinquency (Fischer 1984; Ellis 1988). It was similarly important in the Cambridge and Pittsburgh studies, even though families were on average smaller in Pittsburgh in the 1990s than in London in the 1960s (Farrington and Loeber 1999). In the Cambridge study, if a boy had four or more siblings by his tenth birthday, this doubled his risk of being convicted as a juvenile (West and Farrington 1973: 31), and large family size predicted self-reported delinquency as well as convictions (Farrington 1992c). It was the most important independent predictor of convictions up to age thirty-two in a logistic regression analysis; 58 per cent of boys from large families were convicted up to this age (Farrington 1993a).

In the National Survey of Health and Development, Wadsworth (1979) found that the percentage of boys who were officially delinquent increased from 9 per cent for families containing one child to 24 per cent for families containing four or more children. The Newsons in their Nottingham study also concluded that large family size was one of the most important predictors of offending (Newson et al. 1993). A similar link between family size and antisocial behaviour was reported by Kolvin et al. (1988) in their follow-up of Newcastle children from birth to age thirty-three, by Rutter et al. (1970) in the Isle of Wight survey, and by Ouston (1984) in the Inner London survey.

There are many possible reasons why a large number of siblings might increase the risk of a child's delinquency. Generally, as the number of children in a family increases, the amount of parental attention that can be given to each child decreases. Also, as the number of children increases, the household tends to become more overcrowded, possibly leading to increases in frustration, irritation, and conflict. In the Cambridge study, large family size did not predict delinquency for boys living in the least crowded conditions (West and Farrington 1973: 33). This suggests that household overcrowding might be an important intervening factor between large family size and delinquency.

In a study of delinquent boys and girls in Ottawa, Jones et al. (1980) proposed that brothers tended to encourage a boy's delinquency, whereas sisters tended to suppress it. This theory was intended to explain why they found that male delinquents had many more brothers than sisters. However, this result was not obtained in the Cambridge study, where the number of sisters was just as closely related to a boy's delinquency as was the number of brothers (West and Farrington 1973: 32).

Brownfield and Sorenson (1994) reviewed several possible explanations for the link between large families and delinquency, including those focusing on features of the parents (e.g., criminal parents, teenage parents), those focusing on parenting (e.g., poor supervision, disrupted families), and those focusing on economic deprivation or family stress. Another interesting theory suggested that the key factor was birth order: large families include more later-born children, who tend to be more delinquent. Based on an analysis of self-reported delinquency in a Seattle survey, they concluded that the most plausible intervening causal mechanism was exposure to delinquent siblings. In the Cambridge study, co-offending by brothers was surprisingly common; about 20 per cent of boys who had brothers close to them in age were convicted for a crime committed with their brother (Reiss and Farrington 1991: 386).

CHILD-REARING METHODS

Many different types of child-rearing methods predict a child's delinquency. The most important dimensions of child-rearing are supervision or monitoring of children, discipline or parental reinforcement, warmth or coldness of emotional relationships, and parental involvement with children. Parental supervision refers to the degree of monitoring by parents of the child's activities, and their degree of watchfulness or vigilance. Of all these child-rearing methods, poor parental supervision is usually the strongest and most replicable predictor of offending (Smith and Stern 1997; Farrington and Loeber 1999). Many studies show that parents who do not know where their children are when they are out, and parents who let their children roam the streets unsupervised from an early age, tend to have delinquent children. For example, in the classic Cambridge-Somerville study in Boston, poor parental supervision in childhood was the best predictor of both violent and property crimes up to age forty-five (McCord 1979).

Parental discipline refers to how parents react to a child's behaviour. It is clear that harsh or punitive discipline (involving physical punishment) predicts a child's delinquency, as the review by Haapasalo and Pokela (1999) showed. In their follow-up study of nearly 700 Nottingham children, John and Elizabeth Newson (1989) found that physical punishment at ages seven and eleven predicted later convictions; 40 per cent of offenders had been smacked or beaten at age 11, compared with 14 per cent of non-offenders. Erratic or inconsistent discipline also predicts delinquency (West and Farrington 1973: 51). This can involve either erratic discipline by one parent, sometimes turning a blind eye to bad behaviour and sometimes punishing it severely, or inconsistency between two parents, with one parent being tolerant or indulgent and the other being harshly punitive. It is not clear whether unusually lax discipline predicts delinquency. Just as inappropriate methods of responding to bad behaviour predict delinquency, low parental reinforcement (not praising) of good behaviour is also a predictor (Farrington and Loeber 1999).

Cold, rejecting parents tend to have delinquent children, as McCord (1979) found twenty years ago in the Cambridge-Somerville study. More recently, she concluded that parental warmth could act as a protective factor against the effects of physical punishment (McCord 1997). Whereas 51 per cent of boys with cold physically punishing mothers were convicted in her study, only 21 per cent of boys with warm physically punishing mothers were convicted, similar to the 23 per cent of boys with warm non-punitive mothers who were convicted. The father's warmth was also a protective factor against the father's physical punishment.

Low parental involvement in the child's activities predicts delinquency, as the Newsons found in their Nottingham survey (Lewis et al. 1982). In the Cambridge study, having a father who never joined in the boy's leisure activities doubled his risk of conviction (West and Farrington 1973: 57), and this was the most important predictor of persistence in offending after age twenty-one as opposed to desistance (Farrington and Hawkins 1991). Similarly, poor parent-child communication predicted delinquency in the Pittsburgh Youth Study (Farrington and Loeber 1999), and low family cohesiveness was the most important predictor of violence in the Chicago Youth Development Study (Gorman-Smith et al. 1996).

Most explanations of the link between child-rearing methods and delinquency focus on attachment or social learning theories. Attachment theory was inspired by the work of Bowlby (1951; discussed later), and suggests that children who are not emotionally attached to warm, loving, and law-abiding parents tend to become delinquent (Carlson and Sroufe 1995). The sociological equivalent of attachment theory is social bonding theory, which proposes that delinquency depends on the strength or weakness of a child's bond to society (Catalano and Hawkins 1996).

One of the most influential British social learning theories was propounded by Trasler (1962). This suggested that, when a child behaved in a socially disapproved way, the parent would punish the child. This punishment caused an anxiety reaction, or an unpleasant state of physiological arousal. After a number of pairings of the disapproved act and the punishment, the anxiety became conditioned to the act, and conditioned also to the sequence of events preceding the act. Consequently, when the child contemplated the disapproved act, the conditioned anxiety automatically arose and tended to block the tendency to commit the act, so the child became less likely to do it. Hence, Trasler viewed the conscience as essentially a conditioned anxiety response, which might be experienced subjectively as guilt.

Trasler (1962) emphasized differences in parental child-rearing behaviour as the major source of differences in antisocial tendencies or in the strength of the conscience. According to his theory, children were unlikely to build up the link between disapproved behaviour and anxiety unless their parents supervised them closely, used punishment consistently, and made punishment contingent on disapproved acts. Hence, poor supervision, erratic discipline, and inconsistency between parents were all conducive to delinquency in children. It was also important for parents to explain to children why they were being punished, so that they could discriminate precisely the behaviour that was disapproved.

More recent social learning theories (Patterson 1982, 1995) suggest that children's behaviour depends on parental rewards and punishments and on the models of behaviour that parents represent. Children will tend to become delinquent if parents do not respond consistently and contingently to their antisocial behaviour, and if parents themselves behave in an antisocial manner. These theories have inspired the use of parent training methods to prevent delinquency (see later).

CHILD ABUSE AND NEGLECT

Children who are physically abused or neglected tend to become offenders later in life (Malinosky-Rummell and Hansen 1993). The most famous demonstration of this was completed by Widom (1989) in Indianapolis. She used court records to identify over 900 children who had been abused or neglected before age eleven, and compared them with a control group matched on age, race, gender, elementary school class, and place of residence. A twenty-year follow-up showed that the children who were abused or neglected were more likely to be arrested as juveniles and as adults than were the controls, and they were more likely to be arrested for juvenile violence (Maxfield and Widom 1996). Child sexual abuse, and child physical abuse and neglect, also predict adult arrests for sex crimes (Widom and Ames 1994).

Similar results have been obtained in other studies. In the Cambridge-Somerville study in Boston, McCord (1983) found that about half of the abused or neglected boys were convicted for serious crimes, became alcoholics or mentally ill, or died before age thirty-five. In the Rochester Youth Development Study, which is a prospective longitudinal survey of about 1,000 children originally aged twelve to fourteen, Smith and Thornberry (1995) showed that recorded child maltreatment under age twelve (physical, sexual, or emotional abuse or neglect) predicted later self-reported and official delinquency. Furthermore, these results held up after controlling for gender, race, socio-economic status, and family structure.

Numerous theories have been put forward to explain the link between child abuse and later offending. Brezina (1998) described three of the main ones. Social learning theory suggests that children learn to adopt the abusive behaviour patterns of their parents through imitation, modelling, and reinforcement. Attachment or social bonding theory proposes that child maltreatment results in low attachment to parents and hence to low self-control. Strain theory posits that negative treatment by others generates negative emotions such as anger and frustration, which in turn lead to a desire for revenge and increased aggression. Based on analyses of the Youth in Transition study, Brezina found limited support for all three theories.

PARENTAL CONFLICT AND DISRUPTED FAMILIES

Bowlby (1951) popularized the theory that broken homes cause delinquency. He argued that mother love in infancy and childhood was just as important for mental health as were vitamins and proteins for physical health. He thought that it was essential that a child should experience a warm, loving, and continuous relationship with a mother figure. If a child suffered a prolonged period of maternal deprivation during the first five years of life, this would have irreversible negative effects, including becoming a cold 'affectionless character' and a delinquent.

Most studies of broken homes have focused on the loss of the father rather than the mother, because the loss of a father is much more common. In general, it is found that children who are separated from a biological parent are more likely to offend than children from intact families. For example, in their birth cohort study of over 800 children born in Newcastle-upon-Tyne, Kolvin et al. (1988) discovered that boys who experienced divorce or separation in their first five years of life had a doubled risk of conviction up to age thirty-two.

McCord (1982) in Boston carried out an interesting study of the relationship between homes broken by loss of the biological father and later serious offending by boys. She found that the prevalence of offending was high for boys from broken homes without affectionate mothers (62 per cent) and for those from unbroken homes characterized by parental conflict (52 per cent), irrespective of whether they had affectionate mothers. The prevalence of offending was low for those from unbroken homes without conflict (26 per cent) and—importantly—equally low for boys from broken homes with affectionate mothers (22 per cent). These results suggest that it might not be the broken home which is criminogenic but the parental conflict which often causes it. They also suggest that a loving mother might in some sense be able to compensate for the loss of a father.

In the Cambridge study, both permanent and temporary (more than one month) separations before age ten predicted convictions and self-reported delinquency, provided that they were not caused by death or hospitalization (Farrington 1992c). However, homes broken at an early age (under age five) were not unusually crimino-genic (West and Farrington 1973). Separation before age ten predicted both juvenile and adult convictions (Farrington 1992b), and was an important independent pre-dictor of adult social dysfunction and spouse assault at age thirty-two (Farrington 1993a, 1994).

The importance of the cause of the broken home is also shown in the National Survey of Health and Development, which is a survey of over 5,000 children born in one week in England, Scotland, or Wales (Wadsworth 1979). Boys from homes broken by divorce or separation had an increased likelihood of being convicted or officially cautioned up to age twenty-one (27 per cent) in comparison with those from homes broken by death of the mother (19 per cent), death of the father (14 per cent) or from unbroken homes (14 per cent). Homes broken while the boy was under age five especially predicted delinquency, while homes broken while the boy was between ages eleven and fifteen were not particularly criminogenic. Remarriage (which happened more often after divorce or separation than after death) was also associated with an increased risk of delinquency, suggesting a negative effect of step-parents. The meta-analysis by Wells and Rankin (1991) also shows that broken homes are more strongly related to delinquency when they are caused by parental separation or divorce rather than by death.

In the Dunedin study in New Zealand, boys from single parent families dispropor-tionally tended to be convicted; 28 per cent of violent offenders were from single parent families, compared with 17 per cent of non-violent offenders and 9 per cent of unconvicted boys (Henry et al. 1996). Based on analyses of four surveys (includ-ing the Cambridge study), Morash and Rucker (1989) concluded that the combin-ation of teenage child-bearing and a single-parent, female-headed household was especially conducive to the development of offending in children. Later analyses of the Cambridge study showed that teenage child-bearing combined with a large number of children particularly predicted offending by the children (Nagin et al. 1997).

There is no doubt that parental conflict and interparental violence predict anti-social behaviour by a child (Kolbo et al. 1996; Buehler et al. 1997). In the Christchurch Health and Development Study, which is a prospective longitudinal survey of over 1,200 New Zealand children from birth, children who witnessed violence between their parents were more likely to commit both violence and property offences accord-ing to their self-reports (Fergusson and Horwood 1998). The predictability of witness-ing father-initiated violence held up after controlling for other risk factors such as parental criminality, parental substance abuse, parental physical punishment, a young mother, and low family income. Parental conflict also predicted delinquency in both the Cambridge and Pittsburgh studies (Farrington and Loeber 1999).

Explanations of the relationship between disrupted families and delinquency fall into three major classes. Trauma theories suggest that the loss of a parent has a damaging effect on a child, most commonly because of the effect on attachment to the parent. Life course theories focus on separation as a sequence of stressful experiences, and on the effects of multiple stressors such as parental conflict, parental loss, reduced economic circumstances, changes in parent figures, and poor child-rearing methods. Selection theories argue that disrupted families produce delinquent children because of pre-existing differences from other families in risk factors such as parental conflict, criminal or antisocial parents, low family income, or poor child-rearing methods.

Hypotheses derived from the three theories were tested in the Cambridge study (Juby and Farrington 2001). While boys from broken homes (permanently disrupted families) were more delinquent than boys from intact homes, they were not more delinquent than boys from intact high-conflict families. Overall, the most important factor was the post-disruption trajectory. Boys who remained with their mother after the separation had the same delinquency rate as boys from intact low-conflict families. Boys who remained with their father, with relatives, or with others (e.g., foster parents) had high delinquency rates. It was concluded that the results favoured life course theories rather than trauma or selection theories.

SCHOOL RISK FACTORS

SCHOOL FACTORS

It is clear that the prevalence of offending varies dramatically between different secondary schools, as Power *et al.* (1967) showed more than thirty years ago in London. Characteristics of high delinquency-rate schools are well known (Graham, 1988). For example, such schools have high levels of distrust between teachers and students, low commitment to school by students, and unclear and inconsistently enforced rules. However, what is far less clear is how much of the variation should be attributed to differences in school climates and practices, and how much to differences in the composition of the student body.

In the Cambridge study, the effects of secondary schools on offending were investigated by following boys from their primary schools to their secondary schools (Farrington 1972). The best primary school predictor of offending was the rating of troublesomeness at age eight to ten by peers and teachers. The secondary schools differed dramatically in their official offending rates, from one school with twenty-one court appearances per 100 boys per year to another where the corresponding figure was only 0.3. However, it was very noticeable that the most troublesome boys tended to go to the high-delinquency rate schools, while the least troublesome boys tended to go to the low delinquency-rate schools.

All the schools had overlapping catchment areas. The low delinquency-rate secondary schools were over-subscribed, because parents who were most interested in their children's education, who tended to have high-achieving, well-behaved children, were very concerned that their children should go to these schools. Taking account of reports from primary schools, the head teachers of these secondary schools could pick and choose the best children out of all the applicants, leaving the high delinquency-rate schools with lower-achieving, worse-behaved children. Hence, it was clear that most of the variation between schools in their delinquency rates could be explained by differences in their intakes of troublesome boys. The secondary schools themselves had only a small effect on the boys' offending.

The most famous British study of school effects on offending was also carried out in London, by Rutter *et al.* (1979). They studied twelve comprehensive schools, and again found big differences in official delinquency rates between them. High delinquency-rate schools tended to have high truancy rates, low ability students, and low social class parents. However, the differences between the schools in delinquency rates could not be entirely explained by differences in the social class and verbal reasoning scores of the students at intake (age eleven). Therefore, Rutter *et al.* argued that they must have been caused by some aspect of the schools themselves. The main school factors that were related to delinquency were a high amount of punishment and a low amount of praise given by teachers in class. However, it is difficult to know whether much punishment and little praise are causes or consequences of antisocial school behaviour, which in turn is linked to offending outside school.

Another important British study of school effects on student-reported misbehaviour was completed by Heal (1978). He found that schools with large numbers of students, more formal and more severe punishments, tended to have worse-behaved students. There have been no more recent British studies of school effects on delinquency outcomes. However, reviews of American research show that schools with clear, fair, and consistently enforced rules tend to have low rates of student misbehaviour (Gottfredson 2001; Herrenkohl *et al.* 2001).

LOW INTELLIGENCE AND ATTAINMENT

Low intelligence is an important predictor of offending, and it can be measured very early in life. For example, in a prospective longitudinal survey of about 120 Stockholm males, low intelligence measured at age three significantly predicted officially recorded offending up to age thirty (Stattin and Klackenberg-Larsson 1993). Frequent offenders (with four or more offences) had an average IQ of 88 at age three, whereas non-offenders had an average IQ of 101. All of these results held up after controlling for social class. Also, in the Perry pre-school project in Michigan, low intelligence at age four significantly predicted the number of arrests up to age twenty-seven (Schweinhart *et al.* 1993).

In the Cambridge study, one-third of the boys scoring 90 or less on a non-verbal intelligence test (Raven's Progressive Matrices) at age eight to ten were convicted as juveniles, twice as many as among the remainder (Farrington 1992c). Low non-verbal intelligence was highly correlated with low verbal intelligence (vocabulary, word comprehension, verbal reasoning) and with low school attainment at age eleven, and all of these measures predicted juvenile convictions to much the same extent. In addition to their poor school performance, delinquents tended to be frequent truants, to leave school at the earliest possible age, and to take no school examinations.

Low non-verbal intelligence was especially characteristic of the juvenile recidivists (who had an average IQ of 89) and those first convicted at the earliest ages (ten to thirteen). Furthermore, low intelligence and attainment predicted self-reported delinquency almost as well as convictions (Farrington 1992c), suggesting that the link between low intelligence and delinquency was not caused by the less intelligent boys having a greater probability of being caught. Also, measures of intelligence and attainment predicted measures of offending independently of other variables such as family income and family size (Farrington 1990b). Similar results have been obtained in other projects (Wilson and Herrnstein 1985; Moffitt and Silva 1988a; Lynam *et al.* 1993). Delinquents often do better on non-verbal performance tests, such as object assembly and block design, than on verbal tests (Walsh *et al.* 1987), suggesting that they find it easier to deal with concrete objects than with abstract concepts.

Low intelligence and attainment predicted both juvenile and adult convictions (Farrington 1992b). Low intelligence at age eight to ten was also an important independent predictor of spouse assault at age thirty-two (Farrington 1994). Low intelligence and attainment predicted aggression and bullying at age fourteen, and poor reading ability at age eighteen was the best predictor of having a child bully at age thirty-two (Farrington 1989, 1993b). Also, low school attainment predicted chronic offenders (Farrington and West 1993).

The key explanatory factor underlying the link between intelligence and delinquency is probably the ability to manipulate abstract concepts. People who are poor at this tend to do badly in intelligence tests such as the Matrices and in school attainment, and they also tend to commit offences, probably because of their poor ability to foresee the consequences of their offending and to appreciate the feelings of victims (i.e. their low empathy). There has been a great deal of recent interest in the concept of emotional intelligence (e.g., Schutte *et al.* 1998), but this seems to be related to both empathy and impulsiveness. Certain family backgrounds are less conducive than others to the development of abstract reasoning. For example, lower-class, poorer parents tend to talk in terms of the concrete rather than the abstract, and tend to live for the present, with little thought for the future, as Cohen (1955: 96) pointed out many years ago. In some ways, it is difficult to distinguish a lack of concern for future consequences from the concept of impulsivity (discussed earlier).

Low intelligence may be one element of a pattern of cognitive and neuro-psychological deficits. For example, in the Dunedin (New Zealand) longitudinal study, Moffitt and Silva (1988b) found that self-reported delinquency was related to verbal, memory, and visual-motor integration deficits, independently of low social class and family adversity. Neuropsychological research might lead to important advances in knowledge about the link between brain functioning and offending. For example, the 'executive functions' of the brain, located in the frontal lobes, include sustaining attention and concentration, abstract reasoning and concept formation, anticipation and planning, self-monitoring of behaviour, and inhibition of inappropriate or impulsive behaviour (Moffitt 1990). Deficits in these executive functions are conducive to low measured intelligence and to offending. Moffitt and Henry (1989) found deficits in these executive functions especially for delinquents who were both antisocial and hyperactive.

EXPLAINING DEVELOPMENT AND RISK FACTORS

KEY INDEPENDENT PREDICTORS

In explaining the development of offending, a major problem is that most risk factors tend to coincide and tend to be interrelated. For example, adolescents living in physically deteriorated and socially disorganized neighbourhoods disproportionally tend also to come from families with poor parental supervision and erratic parental discipline, and tend also to have high impulsivity and low intelligence. The concentration and co-occurrence of these kinds of adversities make it difficult to establish their independent, interactive, and sequential influences on offending and antisocial behaviour. Hence, any theory of the development of offending is inevitably speculative in the present state of knowledge.

A first step is to establish which factors predict offending independently of other factors. In the Cambridge study, it was generally true that each of six categories of variables (impulsivity, intelligence or attainment, poor parenting, criminal family, socio-economic deprivation, child antisocial behaviour) predicted offending independently of each other category (Farrington 1990b). For example, the independent predictors of convictions between ages ten and twenty included high daring, low school attainment, poor parental child rearing, a convicted parent, poor housing, and troublesomeness (Farrington and Hawkins 1991). Hence, it might be concluded that impulsivity, low intelligence, poor parenting, a criminal family and socio-economic deprivation, despite their interrelations, all contribute independently to the development of delinquency. Any theory needs to give priority to explaining these results.

THE FARRINGTON THEORY

The modern trend is to try to achieve increased explanatory power by integrating propositions derived from several earlier theories (Catalano and Hawkins 1996). My own theory of male offending and antisocial behaviour (Farrington 1986, 1992b, 1996a, 1998, 2001b) is also integrative, and it distinguishes explicitly between the development of underlying antisocial tendencies and the occurrence of antisocial acts. It includes elements of classic delinquency theories (e.g., strain, control, social learning, rational choice, labelling: see Agnew 2002) and is an explicit attempt to integrate developmental and situational theories. The theory suggests that offending is the end result of a four-stage process: energizing, directing, inhibiting, and decision-making.

The main long-term energizing factors that ultimately lead to long-term variations in antisocial tendencies are desires for material goods, status among intimates, and excitement. The main short-term energizing factors that lead to short-term situational variations in antisocial tendencies are boredom, frustration, anger, and alcohol consumption. The desire for excitement may be greater among children from deprived families, perhaps because excitement is more highly valued by lower-class people than by middle-class ones, because deprived children think they lead more boring lives, or because deprived children are less able to postpone immediate gratification in favour of long-term goals (which could be linked to the emphasis in lower-class culture on the concrete and present as opposed to the abstract and future).

In the directing stage, these motivations produce antisocial tendencies if socially disapproved methods of satisfying them are habitually chosen. The methods chosen depend on maturation and behavioural skills; for example, a five-year-old would have difficulty stealing a car. Some people (e.g., children from deprived families) are less able to satisfy their desires for material goods, excitement, and social status by legal or socially approved methods, and so tend to choose illegal or socially disapproved methods. The relative inability of deprived children to achieve goals by legitimate methods could be because they tend to fail in school and tend to have erratic, low status employment histories. School failure in turn may be a consequence of the unstimulating intellectual environment that lower-class parents tend to provide for their children, and their lack of emphasis on abstract concepts.

In the inhibiting stage, antisocial tendencies can be inhibited by internalized beliefs and attitudes that have been built up in a social learning process as a result of a history of rewards and punishments. The belief that offending is wrong, or a strong conscience, tends to be built up if parents are in favour of legal norms, if they exercise close supervision over their children, and if they punish socially disapproved behaviour using love-oriented discipline. Antisocial tendencies can also be inhibited by empathy, which may develop as a result of parental warmth and loving relationships. The belief that offending is legitimate, and anti-establishment attitudes generally, tend to be built up if children have been exposed to attitudes and behaviour favouring offending (e.g., in a modelling process), especially by members of their family, by their friends, and in their communities.

In the decision-making stage, which specifies the interaction between the individual and the environment, whether a person with a certain degree of antisocial tendency commits an antisocial act in a given situation depends on opportunities, perceived costs and benefits, and on the subjective probabilities of the different outcomes. The costs and benefits include immediate situational factors such as the material goods that can be stolen, and the likelihood and consequences of being caught by the police, as perceived by the individual. They also include social factors such as likely disapproval by parents or spouses, and encouragement or reinforcement from peers. In general, people tend to make rational decisions. However, more impulsive people are less likely to consider the possible consequences of their actions, especially consequences that are likely to be long delayed.

The consequences of offending may, as a result of a learning process, lead to changes in antisocial tendencies or in the cost–benefit calculation. This is especially likely if the consequences are reinforcing (e.g., gaining material goods or peer approval) or punishing (e.g., legal sanctions or parental disapproval). Also, if the consequences involve labelling or stigmatizing the offender, this may make it more difficult for offenders to achieve their aims legally, and hence there may be an increase in antisocial tendency. In other words, events that occur after offending may lead to changes in energizing, directing, inhibiting, or decision-making processes in a dynamic system.

Applying the theory to explain some of the key results of developmental criminology, children from deprived families are likely to offend because they are less able to achieve their goals legally and because they value some goals (e.g., excitement) especially highly. Children with low intelligence are more likely to offend because they tend to fail in school and hence cannot achieve their goals legally. Impulsive children, and those with a poor ability to manipulate abstract concepts, are more likely to offend because they do not give sufficient consideration to the possible consequences of offending. Children who are exposed to poor parental child-rearing behaviour, disharmony, or separation are likely to offend because they do not build up strong internal controls over socially disapproved behaviour; while children from criminal families and those with delinquent friends tend to build up anti-establishment attitudes and the belief that offending is justifiable. The whole process is self-perpetuating, in that poverty, low intelligence, and early school failure lead to truancy and a lack of educational qualifications, which in turn lead to low status jobs and periods of unemployment, both of which make it harder to achieve goals legitimately.

The onset of offending might be caused by increasing long-term motivation (an increasing need for material goods, status, and excitement), an increasing likelihood of choosing socially disapproved methods (possibly linked to a change in dominant social influences from parents to peers), increasing facilitating influences from peers, increasing opportunities (because of increasing freedom from parental control and increasing time spent with peers), or an increasing expected utility of offending (because of the greater importance of peer approval and lesser importance of parental disapproval). Desistance from offending could be linked to an increasing ability to satisfy desires by legal means (e.g., obtaining material goods through employment, obtaining sexual gratification through marriage), increasing inhibiting influences from spouses and female partners, decreasing opportunities (because of decreasing time spent with peers), and a decreasing expected utility of offending (because of the lesser importance of peer approval and the greater importance of disapproval from spouses and female partners).

The prevalence of offending may increase to a peak in the teenage years because boys (especially lower-class school failures) have high impulsivity, high desires for excitement, material goods, and social status between these ages, little chance of achieving their desires legally, and little to lose (since legal penalties are lenient and their intimates—male peers—often approve of offending). In contrast, after age twenty, desires become attenuated or more realistic, there is more possibility of achieving these more limited goals legally, and the costs of offending are greater (since legal penalties are harsher and their intimates—wives or girlfriends—disapprove of offending).

RISK-FOCUSED PREVENTION

This section reviews prevention programmes targeted on individual, family, and school risk factors that have been proved to be effective in high-quality evaluation research. Recent British crime prevention initiatives are reviewed in the 'Conclusions'.

SKILLS TRAINING

The most important prevention techniques that target the risk factors of impulsiveness and low empathy are cognitive-behavioural skills training programmes. For example, Ross and Ross (1995) devised a programme that aimed to teach people to stop and think before acting, to consider the consequences of their behaviour, to conceptualize alternative ways of solving interpersonal problems, and to consider the impact of their behaviour on other people, especially victims. It included social skills training, lateral thinking (to teach creative problem solving), critical thinking (to teach logical reasoning), values education (to teach values and concern for others), assertiveness training (to teach non-aggressive, socially appropriate ways to obtain desired outcomes), negotiation skills training, interpersonal cognitive problem-solving (to teach thinking skills for solving interpersonal problems), social perspective training (to teach how to recognize and understand other people's feelings), and role-playing and modelling (demonstration and practice of effective and acceptable interpersonal behaviour).

Ross and Ross (1988) implemented this 'Reasoning and Rehabilitation' programme in Ottawa, and found (in a randomized experiment) that it led to a large decrease in reoffending for a small sample of adult offenders in a short, nine-month follow-up period. Their training was carried out by probation officers, but they believed that it could be carried out by parents or teachers. This programme has been implemented widely in several different countries, and forms the basis of many accredited cognitive-behavioural programmes used in the UK prison and probation services, including the Pathfinder projects (McGuire 2001).

For example, a similar programme, entitled 'Straight thinking on Probation' was implemented in Glamorgan by Raynor and Vanstone (2001). Offenders who received skills training were compared with similar offenders who received custodial sentences. After one year, offenders who completed the programme had a lower reconviction rate than control offenders (35 per cent as opposed to 49 per cent), although both had the same predicted reconviction rate of 42 per cent. The benefits of the programme had worn off at the two-year follow-up point, when reconviction rates of experimentals (63 per cent) and controls (65 per cent) were similar to each other and to predicted rates. However, the reconvicted experimentals committed less serious crimes than the reconvicted controls.

PARENT EDUCATION

Many types of parent education programmes have been implemented to tackle family risk factors such as poor child-rearing and poor parental supervision. In the most famous intensive home-visiting programme, Olds *et al.* (1986) in Elmira (New York) randomly allocated 400 mothers either to receive home visits from nurses during pregnancy, or to receive visits both during pregnancy and during the first two years of life, or to a control group who received no visits. Each visit lasted about one and quarter hours, and the mothers were visited on average every two weeks. The home visitors gave advice about pre-natal and post-natal care of the child, about infant development, and about the importance of proper nutrition and the avoidance of smoking and drinking during pregnancy.

The results of this experiment showed that the post-natal home visits caused a decrease in recorded child physical abuse and neglect during the first two years of life, especially by poor, unmarried teenage mothers; 4 per cent of visited versus 19 per cent of non-visited mothers of this type were guilty of child abuse or neglect. This last result is important, because (as mentioned above) children who are physically abused or neglected tend to become violent offenders later in life. In a fifteen-year follow-up, the main focus was on lower-class unmarried mothers. Among these mothers, those who received pre-natal and post-natal home visits had fewer arrests than those who received pre-natal visits or no visits (Olds *et al.* 1997). Also, children of these mothers who received prenatal and/or postnatal home visits had less than half as many arrests as children of mothers who received no visits (Olds *et al.* 1998).

Several economic analyses show that the monetary benefits of this programme outweighed its costs for the lower-class unmarried mothers. The most important are by Karoly *et al.* (1998) and Aos *et al.* (1999). However, both measured only a limited range of benefits. Karoly *et al.* measured only benefits to the government or taxpayer (welfare, education, employment, and criminal justice), not benefits to crime victims following from reduced crimes. Aos *et al.* measured only benefits to crime victims (tangible, not intangible) and in criminal justice savings, excluding other types of benefits (e.g., welfare, education, and employment). Nevertheless, both reported a benefit:cost ratio greater than 1 for this programme: 4.1 according to Karoly *et al.* and 1.5 according to Aos *et al.*

PARENT TRAINING

Parent training is also an effective method of preventing offending. Many different types of parent training have been used (Barlow 1997; Kazdin 1997), but the behavioural parent management training developed by Patterson (1982) in Oregon is one of the best-known approaches. His careful observations of parent–child inter-action showed that parents of antisocial children were deficient in their methods of child rearing. These parents failed to tell their children how they were expected to behave, failed to monitor their behaviour to ensure that it was desirable, and failed to enforce rules promptly and unambiguously with appropriate rewards and penalties. The parents of antisocial children used more punishment (such as scolding, shouting, or threatening), but failed to make it contingent on the child's behaviour.

Patterson attempted to train these parents in effective child-rearing methods, namely noticing what a child is doing, monitoring behaviour over long periods, clearly stating house rules, making rewards and punishments contingent on behaviour, and negotiating disagreements so that conflicts and crises did not escalate. His treatment was shown to be effective in reducing child stealing and antisocial behaviour over short periods in small-scale studies (Dishion *et al.* 1992; Patterson *et al.* 1982, 1992).

Parent training was shown to reduce childhood antisocial behaviour in an experiment conducted by Scott *et al.* (2001) in London and Chichester. About 140 mainly poor, disadvantaged children aged three to eight referred for aggressive and antisocial behaviour were allocated to experimental (parent training) or control (waiting list) groups. The parent training programme, based on videotapes, was given for two hours a week over thirteen to sixteen weeks, covering praise and rewards, setting limits, and handling misbehaviour. Follow-up parent interviews and observations showed that the antisocial behaviour of the experimental children decreased significantly compared to that of the controls. Furthermore, after the intervention, experimental parents gave their children far more praise to encourage desirable behaviour, and used more effective commands to obtain compliance.

The Montreal longitudinal-experimental study used a multi-modal intervention based on child skills training and parent management training. Tremblay *et al.* (1995) identified disruptive (aggressive/hyperactive) boys at age six, and randomly allocated over 300 of these to experimental or control conditions. Between ages seven and nine, the experimental group received training designed to foster social skills and self-control. Coaching, peer modelling, role playing, and reinforcement contingencies were used in small group sessions on such topics as 'how to help', 'what to do when you are angry' and 'how to react to teasing'. Also, their parents were trained using the parent management training techniques developed by Patterson (1982).

This prevention programme was quite successful. By age twelve, the experimental boys committed less burglary and theft, were less likely to get drunk, and were less likely to be involved in fights than the controls (according to self-reports). Also, the experimental boys had higher school achievement. At every age from ten to fifteen, the experimental boys had lower self-reported delinquency scores than the control boys. Interestingly, the differences in antisocial behaviour between experimental and control boys increased as the follow-up progressed.

PRE-SCHOOL PROGRAMMES

Several pre-school programmes have been designed to enhance cognitive abilities, intelligence, and attainment. The most famous pre-school intellectual enrichment programme is the Perry project carried out in Ypsilanti (Michigan) by Schweinhart and Weikart (1980). This was essentially a 'Head Start' programme targeted on disadvantaged African American children, who were allocated to experimental and control groups. The experimental children attended a daily pre-school programme, backed up by weekly home visits, usually lasting two years (covering ages three to four). The aim of the 'plan–do–review' programme was to provide intellectual stimulation, to increase thinking and reasoning abilities, and to increase later school achievement.

This programme had long-term benefits. Berrueta-Clement *et al.* (1984) showed that, at age nineteen, the experimental group was more likely to be employed, more likely to have graduated from high school, more likely to have received college or vocational training, and less likely to have been arrested. By age twenty-seven, the experimental group had accumulated only half as many arrests on average as the controls (Schweinhart *et al.* 1993). Also, they had significantly higher earnings and were more likely to be home owners. More of the experimental women were married, and fewer of their children were born out of wedlock.

Several economic analyses show that the monetary benefits of this programme outweighed its costs. The benefit:cost ratio was 2.1 according to Karoly et al. (1998) and 1.5 according to Aos et al. (1999), but both of these figures are under-estimates. The estimates of Aos et al. (1999) included only tangible, not intangible, victim costs; their later estimates including intangible victim costs (Aos et al. 2001) were based on a meta-analysis of several programmes rather than analysing each programme individually, so figures are not given for the Perry project alone. The Perry project's own calculation (Barnett 1993) was more comprehensive, including crime and non-crime benefits, intangible costs to victims, and even including projected benefits beyond age twenty-seven. This generated the famous benefit:cost ratio of 7.1 mentioned earlier. Most of the benefits (65 per cent) were derived from savings to crime victims. Desirable results were also obtained in evaluations of other pre-school programmes (Pagani et al. 1998; Webster-Stratton 1998).

SCHOOL PROGRAMMES

One of the most important school-based prevention experiments was carried out in Seattle by Hawkins et al. (1991). This was a multiple component programme combining parent training, teacher training, and child skills training. About 500 first grade children (aged six) in twenty-one classes in eight schools were randomly assigned to be in experimental or control classes. The children in the experimental classes received special treatment at home and school which was designed to increase their attachment to their parents and their bonding to the school. Also, they were trained in interpersonal cognitive problem-solving. Their parents were trained to notice and reinforce socially desirable behaviour in a programme called 'Catch them being good'. Their teachers were trained in classroom management, for example to provide clear instructions and expectations to children, to reward children for participation in desired behaviour, and to teach children prosocial (socially desirable) methods of solving problems.

This programme had long-term benefits. O'Donnell et al. (1995) focused on children in low-income families and reported that, in the sixth grade (age twelve), experimental boys were less likely to have initiated delinquency, while experimental girls were less likely to have initiated drug use. In the latest follow-up, Hawkins et al. (1999) found that, at age eighteen, the full intervention group (receiving the intervention from grades 1–6) admitted less violence, less alcohol abuse, and fewer sexual partners than the late intervention group (grades 5–6 only) or the controls. The benefit:cost ratio of this programme according to Aos et al. (2001) was 4.3.

Another important school-based prevention experiment was carried out by Kolvin et al. (1981) in Newcastle-upon-Tyne. They randomly allocated 270 junior school children (age seven to eight) and 322 secondary school children (age eleven to twelve) to experimental or control groups. All children had been identified as showing some kind of social or psychiatric disturbance or learning problems (according to teacher and peer ratings). There were three types of experimental programmes: (a) behaviour modification-reinforcement with the seniors, 'nurture work' teaching healthy inter-actions with the juniors; (b) parent counselling-teacher consultations with both; and (c) group therapy with the seniors, play groups with the juniors.

The programmes were evaluated after eighteen months and after three years using clinical ratings of conduct disturbance. Generally, the experimental and control groups were not significantly different for the juniors, although there was some tendency for the nurture work and play group children to be better behaved than the controls at the three-year follow-up. For the seniors, those who received group therapy showed significantly less conduct disturbance at both follow-ups, and there was some tendency for the other two programmes also to be effective at the three-year follow-up. Other school-based prevention experiments have also been successful in reducing antisocial behaviour (Catalano *et al.* 1998).

ANTI-BULLYING PROGRAMMES

School bullying, of course, is a risk factor for offending (Farrington 1993b). Several school-based programmes have been effective in reducing bullying. The most famous of these was implemented by Olweus (1994) in Norway. It aimed to increase aware-ness and knowledge of teachers, parents, and children about bullying, and to dispel myths about it. A thirty-page booklet was distributed to all schools in Norway, describing what was known about bullying and recommending what steps schools and teachers could take to reduce it. Also, a twenty-five minute video about bullying was made available to schools. Simultaneously, the schools distributed to all parents a four-page folder containing information and advice about bullying. In addition, anonymous self-report questionnaires about bullying were completed by all children.

The programme was evaluated in Bergen. Each of the forty-two participating schools received feedback information from the questionnaire, about the prevalence of bullies and victims, in a specially arranged school conference day. Also, teachers were encouraged to develop explicit rules about bullying (e.g., do not bully, tell someone when bullying happens, bullying will not be tolerated, try to help victims, try to include children who are being left out) and to discuss bullying in class, using the video and role-playing exercises. In addition, actions were taken to improve moni-toring and supervision of children, especially in the playground. The programme was successful in reducing the prevalence of bullying by half.

A similar programme was implemented in twenty-three Sheffield schools by Smith and Sharp (1994). The core programme involved establishing a 'whole-school' anti-bullying policy, raising awareness of bullying and clearly defining roles and responsi-bilities of teachers and students, so that everyone knew what bullying was and what they should do about it. In addition, there were optional interventions tailored to particular schools: curriculum work (e.g., reading books, watching videos); direct work with students (e.g., assertiveness training for those who were bullied); and playground work (e.g., training lunch-time supervisors). This programme was suc-cessful in reducing bullying (by 15 per cent) in primary schools, but had relatively small effects (a 5 per cent reduction) in secondary schools. The effects of these anti-bullying programmes on later offending need to be investigated.

COMMUNITIES THAT CARE

One of the best ways of achieving risk-focused prevention is through multiple-component community-based programmes, including several of the successful interventions listed above, and *Communities That Care* (CTC) has many attractions (Farrington 1996b). Perhaps more than any other programme, it is evidence-based and systematic: the choice of interventions depends on empirical evidence about what are the important risk and protective factors in a particular community, and on empirical evidence about 'What Works'. It is currently being implemented in twenty sites in England, Scotland, and Wales, and also in The Netherlands and Australia (Communities that Care 1997; Utting 1999; France and Crow 2001). While the effectiveness of the overall CTC strategy has not yet been demonstrated, the effectiveness of its individual components is clear (as reviewed above). If its small-scale implementation in Great Britain proves to be successful, there would be a strong argument for implementing CTC on a much larger scale.

CTC was developed as a risk-focused prevention strategy by Hawkins and Catalano (1992), and it is a core component of the US Office of Juvenile Justice and Delinquency Prevention's (OJJDP's) Comprehensive Strategy for Serious, Violent and Chronic Juvenile Offenders (Wilson and Howell 1993). CTC is based on a theory (the social development model) that organizes risk and protective factors. The intervention techniques are tailored to the needs of each particular community. The 'community' could be a city, a county, a small town, or even a neighbourhood or a housing estate. This programme aims to reduce delinquency and drug use by implementing particular prevention strategies that have demonstrated effectiveness in reducing risk factors or enhancing protective factors. It is modelled on large-scale community-wide public health programmes designed to reduce illnesses such as coronary heart disease by tackling key risk factors (Farquhar 1985; Perry *et al.* 1989). There is great emphasis in CTC on enhancing protective factors and building on strengths, partly because this is more attractive to communities than tackling risk factors. However, it is generally true that health promotion is more effective than disease prevention (Kaplan 2000).

CTC programmes begin with community mobilization. Key community leaders (e.g., elected representatives, education officials, police chiefs, business leaders) are brought together, with the aim of getting them to agree on the goals of the prevention programme and to implement CTC. The key leaders then set up a Community Board that is accountable to them, consisting of neighbourhood residents and representatives from various agencies (e.g., school, police, social services, probation, health, parents, youth groups, business, church, media). The Community Board takes charge of prevention on behalf of the community.

The Community Board carries out a risk and protective factor assessment, identifying key risk factors in that particular community that need to be tackled, and key protective factors that need enhancing. This risk assessment might involve the use of police, school, social or census records, or local neighbourhood or school surveys. After identifying key risk and protective factors, the Community Board assesses existing resources and develops a plan of intervention strategies. With specialist technical assistance and guidance, they choose programmes from a menu of strategies that have been shown to be effective in well-designed evaluation research.

The menu of strategies listed by Hawkins and Catalano (1992) includes pre-natal/post-natal home visiting programmes, pre-school intellectual enrichment programmes, parent training, school organization and curriculum development, teacher training and media campaigns. Other strategies include child skills training, anti-bullying programmes in schools, situational prevention, and policing strategies. The choice of prevention strategies is based on empirical evidence about effective methods of tackling each particular risk factor, but it also depends on what are identified as the particular problems and strengths of the community.

While it may appear to be superficially similar, the CTC approach is quite different from the crime prevention strategy in the Crime and Disorder Act 1998, which requires local authorities, the police, health authorities, police authorities, and probation committees to form partnerships to (a) produce an audit of crime and disorder in the area, and (b) develop a strategy to reduce these problems. As of December 2000, most audits relied mainly on official data, although about half included survey responses on attitudes to crime or fear of crime, and one-fifth included survey responses from young people or from focus groups (Phillips *et al.* 2000). The focus in the audits was on crime and disorder, not on risk and protective factors. However, two areas with similar crime problems could have a very different pattern of risk and protective factors, and hence might require very different intervention programmes.

Most strategies proposed to reduce crime involved raising the awareness of the public, law enforcement approaches, or situational measures. It is not clear how far these proposed strategies were based on evidence about either risk factors or effective interventions: 'since the data in the audits appeared to be largely included on the basis of its availability, it was not possible to deduce from the sources of data cited in the audits which crime types/issues should be prioritised by the partnership for inclusion in their crime and disorder reduction strategies' (Phillips *et al.* 2000: 2). It is important to establish how risk factors influence crime in different community contexts in order to implement risk-focused prevention effectively. It is not clear how far the risk-focused strategy would be effective in the most disadvantaged and unstable communities.

CONCLUSIONS

RESEARCH IMPLICATIONS

A great deal has been learned in the last twenty years, particularly from longitudinal surveys, about risk factors for offending and other types of antisocial behaviour. Offenders differ significantly from non-offenders in many respects, including impulsivity, intelligence, family background, and socio-economic deprivation. These differences are often present before, during, and after criminal careers. More research is needed to elucidate the causal chains that link these factors with antisocial behaviour, the ways in which these factors have independent, interactive, or sequential effects, and developmental sequences leading to persistent offending. Since most is known about risk factors for prevalence and onset, more research is needed on risk factors for frequency, duration, escalation, and desistance.

Existing British longitudinal surveys of offending were often conducted many years ago when social conditions were very different, and results are often based on white males living in cities. New prospective longitudinal surveys are needed to take account of the increasing ethnic diversity of the population, to advance knowledge about risk factors for girls and in non-urban areas, and especially to advance knowledge about protective factors that prevent offending. Ideally, prevention programmes should aim not only to tackle risk factors but also to strengthen protective factors, and both risk and protective factors should be measured and targeted. Particular efforts should be made to investigate the effects of life events on the course of development of offending.

Only recently have longitudinal researchers begun to pay sufficient attention to neighbourhood and community factors, and there is still a great need for them to investigate immediate situational influences on offending (Farrington *et al.* 1993; Wikström *et al.* 1995). Existing research tells us more about the development of criminal potential than about how that potential becomes the actuality of offending in any given situation. Research on immediate situational influences on offending should be included in new longitudinal studies, to link up the developmental and situational approaches.

The risk factor approach should be used more in studying situational influences on crime. Characteristics of places as well as individuals should be investigated. For example, to the extent that victimized places were characterized by low surveillance, an intervention to increase surveillance would be warranted. Before increasing police patrols in crime 'hot-spots' (e.g., Sherman and Weisburd 1995), it would be useful to investigate characteristics of these places and to establish what were the most import-ant risk factors that distinguished them from other places. New studies are also needed to establish characteristics of risky places, situations, and communities, in order to guide intervention efforts.

High-quality experimental and quasi-experimental evaluations of the effectiveness of crime reduction programmes are needed in the United Kingdom. Most knowledge about the effectiveness of prevention programmes, such as cognitive-behavioural skills training, parent training, and pre-school intellectual enrichment programmes, is based on American research.

As mentioned, an important development in the 1990s was the increasing use of cost–benefit analysis in evaluating prevention programmes. Cost–benefit analyses of the effectiveness of prevention programmes should be given some priority, and a standard how-to-do-it manual should be developed.

It is hard to evaluate large-scale crime reduction strategies, and to answer questions about whether it is better (in terms of crimes saved per £ spent, for example) to invest in risk-focused early prevention, in physical or situational prevention, in more police officers, or in more prison cells. Nevertheless, this is of vital importance to govern-ment policy-makers and to the general population. Therefore, research is needed to investigate the cost-effectiveness of risk-focused prevention in comparison with other general crime reduction strategies.

POLICY IMPLICATIONS

There have been many commendable UK crime prevention initiatives in recent years. Following the review of research carried out as part of the Comprehensive Spending Review in 1997 (Goldblatt and Lewis 1998), the Home Office Crime Reduction Programme was established. Most of the initiatives were situational (e.g., focusing on burglary reduction) or probation/prison oriented (focusing on the treatment of offenders) until the *On Track* programme was launched at the end of 1999. This provided services for children aged four to twelve who were identified as at risk of being involved in crime in highly deprived communities. In 2002, the Crime Reduction Programme will be replaced by the Safer Communities Initiative, and ten regional crime reduction directors have been appointed to identify regional problems and decide how to use this new tranche of Home Office money.

The Youth Justice Board was established in 1998 and has been mainly concerned with providing services for offenders aged ten to seventeen, for example through the Youth Offending Teams. However, it has established seventy Youth Inclusion Programmes, each aimed at the fifty young people aged thirteen to sixteen who are most at risk in particular deprived neighbourhoods. The Department for Education and Skills established the *Sure Start* programme for children aged up to 3 in deprived neighbourhoods, and *New Deal for Communities* and neighbourhood renewal funds have been established by the Department for the Environment.

While all of these initiatives are commendable, and all are being evaluated in some sense (at least by means of a process evaluation), what is largely missing in the UK at present is risk-focused primary prevention delivered at an early age and designed to reduce later offending and antisocial behaviour. The Youth Justice Board (2001) currently seems most likely to introduce this kind of initiative, based on *Communities That Care*.

Consideration should be given to implementing a multiple component risk-focused prevention programme such as CTC more widely throughout Great Britain. This integrated programme could be implemented by existing crime and disorder partnerships. However, they would need resources and technical assistance to conduct youth surveys and household surveys to identify key risk and protective factors for both people and places. They would also need resources and technical assistance to measure risk and protective factors, to choose effective intervention methods, and to carry out high-quality evaluations of the effectiveness of programmes in reducing crime and disorder.

The focus should be on primary prevention—offering the programme to all families living in specified areas—not on secondary prevention—targeting the programme on individuals identified as at risk. Ideally, the programme should be presented positively, as fostering safe and healthy communities by strengthening protective factors, rather than as a crime prevention programme targeting risk factors.

Implementing a risk-focused prevention programme on a large scale requires inter-agency cooperation at both local and national levels. The CTC model says a great deal about local cooperation and organization but little about national cooperation and organization. Ideally, several government departments should cooperate in mounting risk-focused prevention, because the intervention strategies and the potential benefits are very wide-ranging. For example, while the Home Office is concerned with reducing crime and drug abuse, the Department of Health is concerned with reducing intentional injuries and mental health problems, the Department for Education and Skills is concerned with reducing truancy, bullying, and school failure, and the Department for the Environment is concerned with reducing urban deprivation. All of these problems tend to be associated in multiple problem families. Even this shortlist of problems makes it clear that several government departments are basically concerned with the same problems and the same people.

Effective intervention strategies include some that might be organized by the Home Office, such as policing strategies, some that might be organized by the Department of Health, such as home visiting just before and just after birth, some that might be organized by the Department for Education and Skills, such as pre-school and school programmes, and some that might be organized by the Department for the Environment, such as improving household security and street lighting. Other intervention strategies could be organized by private industry or business (e.g., improving vehicle security, anti-shoplifting programmes).

Nationally and locally, there is no agency whose primary mandate is the prevention of crime. For example, the very worthwhile intervention programmes being implemented by Youth Offending Teams are overwhelmingly targeted on detected offenders. Therefore, a national agency should be established with a primary mandate of fostering and funding the prevention of crime.

This national agency could provide technical assistance, skills, and knowledge to local agencies in implementing prevention programmes, could provide funding for such programmes, and could ensure continuity, coordination, and monitoring of local programmes. It could provide training in prevention science for people in local agencies, and could maintain high standards for evaluation research. It could also act as a centre for the discussion of how policy initiatives of different government agencies influence crime and associated social problems. It could set a national and local agenda for research and practice in the prevention of crime, drug and alcohol abuse, mental health problems, and associated social problems. National crime prevention agencies have been established in many other countries, such as Sweden (Ministry of Justice 1997; Wikström and Torstensson 1999).

The national agency could also maintain a computerized register of evaluation research and, like the National Institute of Clinical Excellence, advise the government about effective and cost-effective crime prevention programmes. Medical advice is often based on systematic reviews of the effectiveness of health care interventions organized by the Cochrane Collaboration and funded by the National Health Service. Systematic reviews of the evaluation literature on the effectiveness of criminological interventions should be commissioned and funded by government agencies.

Crime prevention also needs to be organized locally. In each area, a local agency should be set up to take the lead in organizing risk-focused crime prevention. In

Sweden, two-thirds of municipalities have local crime prevention councils. The local prevention agency could take the lead in measuring risk factors and social problems in local areas, using archival records and local household and school surveys. It could then assess available resources and develop a plan of prevention strategies. With specialist technical assistance, prevention programmes could be chosen from a menu of strategies that have been proved to be effective in reducing crime in well-designed evaluation research. This would be a good example of evidence-based practice.

Recent promising developments in the UK have clearly been influenced by recent research on risk factors and intervention strategies. The time is ripe to expand these experimental programmes into a large-scale, evidence-based, integrated national strategy for the reduction of crime and associated social problems, including rigorous evaluation requirements.

Selected further reading

Antisocial Behaviour by Young People, by Michael Rutter, Henri Giller, and Ann Hagell (Cambridge: Cambridge University Press 1998), is an excellent text that reviews developmental issues, risk factors, and intervention techniques. Extensive reviews of all three topics can also be found in the two books edited by Rolf Loeber and myself: *Serious and Violent Juvenile Offenders: Risk Factors and Successful Interventions* (Thousand Oaks, Ca: Sage 1998), and *Child Delinquents: Development, Intervention and Service Needs* (Thousand Oaks, Ca: Sage 2001). Turning to developmental criminology, the eighty-page chapter by Marc LeBlanc and Rolf Loeber ('Developmental criminology updated') in *Crime and Justice*, vol. 23 (Chicago, Ill.: University of Chicago Press 1998), sets out many of the key ideas in detail. Several of the most important prospective longitudinal surveys are reviewed in detail in *Taking Stock of Delinquency*, edited by Terence Thornberry and Marvin Krohn (New York: Kluwer/Plenum 2002). Criminal career research is described in *Analysing Offending: Data, Models and Interpretations*, by Roger Tarling (London: HMSO 1993). Of the more specific topics, *Schools and Delinquency* by Denise Gottfredson (Cambridge: Cambridge University Press 2001), and *Costs and Benefits of Preventing Crime* edited by Brandon Welsh, myself, and Lawrence Sherman (Boulder, Col.: Westview Press 2001), can confidently be recommended.

References

AGNEW, R. (2002), 'Crime causation: Sociological theories', in J. Dressler (ed.-in-chief), *Encyclopedia of Crime and Justice*, vol. 1: 324–34, New York: Macmillan.

AMDUR, R.L. (1989), 'Testing causal models of delinquency: A methodological critique', *Criminal Justice and Behaviour*, 16: 35–62.

AOS, S., PHIPPS, P., BARNOSKI, R., and LIEB, R. (1999), *The Comparative Costs and Benefits of Programs to Reduce Crime* (version 3.0), Olympia, Wash: Washington State Institute for Public Policy.

——, ——, —— and —— (2001), *The Comparative Costs and Benefits of Programs to Reduce Crime* (version 4.0), Olympia, Wash: Washington State Institute for Public Policy.

AUGIMERI, L.K., KOEGL, C.J., WEBSTER, C.D., and LEVENE, K.S. (2001), *Early Assessment Risk List for Boys (EARL-20B)*, Version 2, Toronto: Earlscourt Child and Family Centre.

BANDURA, A. (1977), *Social Learning Theory*, Englewood Cliffs, NJ: Prentice-Hall.

BARLOW, J. (1997), *Systematic Review of the Effectiveness of Parent-Training Programmes in Improving Behaviour Problems in Children aged 3–10 Years*, Oxford: Health Services Research Unit.

BARNETT, W.S. (1993), 'Cost–benefit analysis' in L.J. Schweinhart, H.V. Barnes, D.P. Weikart (eds), *Significant Benefits: The High/Scope Perry Preschool Study Through Age 27*, 142–73, Ypsilanti, Mich.: High/Scope Press.

BARON, R.M., and KENNY, D.A. (1986), 'The moderator-mediator variable distinction in social psychological research: Conceptual, strategic and statistical considerations', *Journal of Personality and Social Psychology*, 51: 1173–82.

BERRUETA-CLEMENT, J.R., SCHWEINHART, L.J., BARNETT, W.S., EPSTEIN, A.S., and WEIKART, D.P. (1984), *Changed Lives: The Effects of the Perry Preschool Program on Youths Through Age 19*, Ypsilanti, Mich.: High/Scope Press.

BOSWELL, G. (1995), *Violent Victims: The Prevalence of Abuse and Loss in the Lives of Section 53 Offenders*, London: The Prince's Trust.

BOWLBY, J. (1951), *Maternal Care and Mental Health*, Geneva, Switzerland: World Health Organization.

BRAND, S., and PRICE, R. (2000), *The Economic and Social Costs of Crime*, Home Office Research Study No. 217, London: Home Office.

BRENNAN, P.A., MEDNICK, B.R., and MEDNICK, S.A. (1993), 'Parental psychopathology, congenital factors, and violence', in S. Hodgins (ed.), *Mental Disorder and Crime*, 244–61, Newbury Park, Calif.: Sage.

BREZINA, T. (1998), 'Adolescent maltreatment and delinquency: The question of intervening processes', *Journal of Research in Crime and Delinquency*, 35: 71–99.

BROWNFIELD, D., and SORENSON, A.M. (1994), 'Sibship size and sibling delinquency', *Deviant Behaviour*, 15: 45–61.

BUEHLER, C., ANTHONY, C., KRISHNAKUMAR, A., STONE, G., GERARD, J., and PEMBERTON, S. (1997), 'Interparental conflict and youth problem behaviours: A meta-analysis', *Journal of Child and Family Studies*, 6: 233–47.

CAPALDI, D.M., and PATTERSON, G.R. (1996), 'Can violent offenders be distinguished from frequent offenders? Prediction from childhood to adolescence', *Journal of Research in Crime and Delinquency*, 33: 206–31.

CARLSON, E.A., and SROUFE, L.A. (1995), 'Contribution of attachment theory to developmental psychopathology', in D. Cicchetti and D.J. Cohen (eds), *Developmental Psychopathology, vol. 1: Theory and Methods*, 581–617, New York: Wiley.

CASPI, A. (2000), 'The child is father of the man: Personality continuities from childhood to adulthood', *Journal of Personality and Social Psychology*, 78: 158–72.

CATALANO, R.F., ARTHUR, M.W., HAWKINS, J.D., BERGLUND, L., and OLSON, J.J. (1998), 'Comprehensive community and school based interventions to prevent antisocial behaviour', in R. Loeber and D.P. Farrington (eds), *Serious and Violent Juvenile Offenders: Risk Factors and Successful Interventions*, 248–83, Thousand Oaks, Calif.: Sage.

—— and HAWKINS, J.D. (1996), 'The social development model: A theory of antisocial behaviour', in J.D. Hawkins (ed.), *Delinquency and Crime: Current Theories*, 149–97, Cambridge: Cambridge University Press.

CHESS, S., and THOMAS, A. (1984), *Origins and Evolution of Behaviour Disorders: From Infancy to Early Adult Life*, New York: Brunner/Mazel.

CLARKE, R.V. (1995), 'Situational crime prevention', in M. Tonry and D.P. Farrington (eds), *Building a Safer Society: Strategic Approaches to Crime Prevention*, 91–150, Chicago, Ill.: University of Chicago Press.

—— (ed.) (1997), *Situational Crime Prevention: Successful Case Studies*, 2nd edn., Guilderland, NY: Harrow and Heston.

—— and CORNISH, D.B. (1985), 'Modelling offenders' decisions: A framework for research and policy', in M. Tonry and N. Morris (eds), *Crime and Justice*, vol. 6, 147–85, Chicago, Ill.: University of Chicago Press.

COHEN, A.K. (1955), *Delinquent Boys: The Culture of the Gang*, Glencoe, Ill.: Free Press.

COMMUNITIES THAT CARE (1997), *Communities That Care (UK): A New Kind of Prevention Programme*, London: Communities That Care.

DISHION, T.J., PATTERSON, G.R., and KAVANAGH, K.A. (1992), 'An experimental test of the coercion model: Linking theory, measurement and intervention', in J. McCord and R.E. Tremblay (eds), *Preventing Antisocial Behaviour: Interventions from Birth through Adolescence*, 253–82, New York: Guilford.

ELLIS, L. (1988), 'The victimful–victimless crime distinction, and seven universal demographic correlates of victimful criminal behaviour', *Personality and Individual Differences*, 3: 525–48.

EYSENCK, H.J. (1996), 'Personality and crime: Where do we stand?, *Psychology, Crime and Law*, 2: 143–52.

FARQUHAR, J.W. (1985), 'The Stanford five-city project: Design and methods', *American Journal of Epidemiology*, 122: 323–34.

FARRINGTON, D.P. (1972), 'Delinquency begins at home', *New Society*, 21: 495–7.

—— (1977), 'The effects of public labelling', *British Journal of Criminology*, 17: 112–35.

—— (1986), 'Stepping stones to adult criminal careers', in D. Olweus, J. Block, and M.R. Yarrow (eds), *Development of Antisocial and Prosocial Behaviour: Research, Theories and Issues*, 359–84, New York: Academic Press.

—— (1988), 'Studying changes within individuals: The causes of offending', in M. Rutter (ed.), *Studies of Psychosocial Risk: The Power of Longitudinal Data*, 158–83, Cambridge: Cambridge University Press.

—— (1989), 'Early predictors of adolescent aggression and adult violence', *Violence and Victims*, 4: 79–100.

—— (1990a), 'Age, period, cohort, and offending', in D.M. Gottfredson and R.V. Clarke (eds), *Policy and Theory in Criminal Justice: Contributions in Honour of Leslie T. Wilkins*, 51–75, Aldershot: Avebury.

—— (1990b), 'Implications of criminal career research for the prevention of offending', *Journal of Adolescence*, 13: 93–113.

—— (1992a), 'Criminal career research in the United Kingdom', *British Journal of Criminology*, 32: 521–36.

—— (1992b), 'Explaining the beginning, progress and ending of antisocial behaviour from birth to adulthood', in J. McCord (ed.), *Facts, Frameworks and Forecasts: Advances in Criminological Theory*, vol. 3, 253–86, New Brunswick, NJ: Transaction.

—— (1992c), 'Juvenile delinquency', in J.C. Coleman (ed.), *The School Years*, 2nd edn, 123–63, London: Routledge.

—— (1993a), 'Childhood origins of teenage antisocial behaviour and adult social dysfunction', *Journal of the Royal Society of Medicine*, 86: 13–17.

—— (1993b), 'Understanding and preventing bullying', in M. Tonry and N. Morris (eds), *Crime and Justice*, vol. 17, 381–458, Chicago, Ill.: University of Chicago Press.

—— (1994), 'Childhood, adolescent and adult features of violent males', in L.R. Huesmann (ed.), *Aggressive Behaviour: Current Perspectives*, 215–40, New York: Plenum.

—— (1995), 'The development of offending and antisocial behaviour from childhood: Key findings from the Cambridge study in Delinquent Development', *Journal of Child Psychology and Psychiatry*, 36: 929–64.

—— (1996a), 'The explanation and prevention of youthful offending', in J.D. Hawkins (ed.), *Delinquency and Crime: Current Theories*, 68–148, Cambridge: Cambridge University Press.

—— (1996b), *Understanding and Preventing Youth Crime*, York: Joseph Rowntree Foundation.

—— (1997a), 'Human development and criminal careers', in M. Maguire, R. Morgan, and R. Reiner (eds), *The Oxford Handbook of Criminology*, 2nd edn, 361–408, Oxford: Oxford University Press.

—— (1997b), 'The relationship between low resting heart rate and violence', in A. Raine, P.A. Brennan, D.P. Farrington, and S.A. Mednick (eds), *Biosocial Bases of Violence*, 89–105, New York: Plenum.

—— (1998), 'Predictors, causes and correlates of male youth violence', in M. Tonry and M.H. Moore (eds), *Youth Violence*, 421–75, Chicago, Ill.: University of Chicago Press.

—— (2000), 'Explaining and preventing crime: The globalization of knowledge', *Criminology*, 38: 1–24.

—— (2001a), 'Multiple risk factors for multiple problem violent boys', in R.R. Carrado, R. Roesch, S.D. Hart, and J.K. Gierowski (eds), *Multiproblem Violent Youth*, Amsterdam: IOS Press.

—— (2001b), 'The causes and prevention of violence', in J. Shepherd (ed.), *Violence in Health Care*, 2nd edn, 1–27), Oxford: Oxford University Press.

—— (2002), 'Key findings from the first 40 years of the Cambridge study in Delinquent Development', in T.P. Thornberry and M.D. Krohn (eds), *Taking Stock of Delinquency: An Overview of Findings from Contemporary Longitudinal Studies*, New York: Kluwer/Plenum.

——, BARNES, G., and LAMBERT, S. (1996), 'The concentration of offending in families', *Legal and Criminological Psychology*, 1: 47–63.

——, BIRON, L., and LEBLANC, M. (1982), 'Personality and delinquency in London and Montreal', in J. Gunn and D.P. Farrington (eds), *Abnormal Offenders, Delinquency, and the Criminal Justice System*, 153–201, Chichester: Wiley.

——, GALLAGHER, B., MORLEY, L., ST LEDGER, R.J., and WEST, D.J. (1986), 'Unemployment, school leaving, and crime', *British Journal of Criminology*, 26: 335–56.

—— and HAWKINS, J.D. (1991), 'Predicting participation, early onset, and later persistence in officially recorded offending', *Criminal Behaviour and Mental Health*, 1: 1–33.

——, JOLLIFFE, D., LOEBER, R., STOUTHAMER-LOEBER, M., and KALB, L.M. (2001), 'The concentration of offenders in families, and family criminality in the prediction of boys' delinquency', *Journal of Adolescence*, 24: 579–96.

—— and LOEBER, R. (1999), 'Transatlantic replicability of risk factors in the development of delinquency', in P. Cohen, C. Slomkowski, and L.N. Robins (eds), *Historical and Geographical Influences on Psychopathology*, 299–329, Mahwah, NJ: Lawrence Erlbaum.

——, —— and VAN KAMMEN, W.B. (1990), 'Long-term criminal outcomes of hyperactivity-impulsivity-attention deficit and conduct problems in childhood', in L.N. Robins and M. Rutter (eds), *Straight and Devious Pathways from Childhood to Adulthood*, 62–81, Cambridge: Cambridge University Press.

—— and PETROSINO, A. (2000), 'Systematic reviews of criminological interventions: The Campbell Collaboration Crime and Justice Group', *International Annals of Criminology*, 38: 49–66.

—— and —— (2001), 'The Campbell Collaboration Crime and Justice Group', *Annals of the American Academy of Political and Social Science*, 578: 35–49.

——, SAMPSON, R.J., and WIKSTRÖM, P-O.H. (eds) (1993), *Integrating Individual and Ecological Aspects of Crime*, Stockholm: National Council for Crime Prevention.

—— and WELSH, B.C. (1999), 'Delinquency prevention using family-based interventions', *Children and Society*, 13: 287–303.

—— and WEST, D.J. (1990), 'The Cambridge study in Delinquent Development: A long-term follow-up of 411 London males', in H.-J. Kerner and G. Kaiser (eds), *Criminality: Personality, Behaviour, Life History*, 115–38, Berlin: Springer-Verlag.

—— and —— (1993), 'Criminal, penal and life histories of chronic offenders; Risk and protective factors and early identification', *Criminal Behaviour and Mental Health*, 3: 492–523.

—— and —— (1995), 'Effects of marriage, separation and children on offending by adult males',

in J. Hagan (ed.) *Current Perspectives on Aging and the Life Cycle, vol. 4: Delinquency and Disrepute in the Life Course*, 249–81), Greenwich, Connecticut: JAI Press.

FERGUSSON, D.M., and HORWOOD, L.J. (1998), 'Exposure to interparental violence in childhood and psychosocial adjustment in young adulthood', *Child Abuse and Neglect*, 22: 339–57.

—— HORWOOD, L.J., and LYNSKEY, M.T. (1994), 'The childhoods of multiple problem adolescents: A 15 year longitudinal study', *Journal of Child Psychology and Psychiatry*, 35: 1123–40.

FISCHER, D.G. (1984), 'Family size and delinquency', *Perceptual and Motor Skills*, 58: 527–34.

FLOOD-PAGE, C., CAMPBELL, S., HARRINGTON, V., and MILLER, J. (2000), *Youth Crime: Findings from the 1998/99 Youth Lifestyles Survey*, Home Office Research Study No. 209, London: Home Office.

FRANCE, A., and CROW, I. (2001), *CTC—The Story So Far*, York: Joseph Rowntree Foundation.

GOLDBLATT, P., and LEWIS, C. (eds) (1998), *Reducing Offending: An Assessment of Research Evidence on Ways of Dealing with Offending Behaviour*, Home Office Research Study No. 187, London: HMSO.

GORMAN-SMITH, D., TOLAN, P.H., ZELLI, A., and HUESMANN, L.R. (1996), 'The relation of family functioning to violence among inner-city minority youths', *Journal of Family Psychology*, 10: 115–29.

GOTTFREDSON, D.C. (2001), *Schools and Delinquency*, Cambridge: Cambridge University Press.

GOTTFREDSON, M.R., and HIRSCHI, T. (1990), *A General Theory of Crime*, Stanford, Calif.: Stanford University Press.

GRAHAM, J. (1988), *Schools, Disruptive Behaviour and Delinquency*, Home Office Research Study No. 96, London: HMSO.

—— and BOWLING, B. (1995), *Young people and crime*, Home Office Research Study No. 145, London: HMSO.

GROVE, W.M., ECKERT, E.D., HESTON, L., BOUCHARD, T.J., SEGAL, N., and LYKKEN, D.T. (1990), 'Heritability of substance abuse and antisocial behaviour: A study of monozygotic twins reared apart', *Biological Psychiatry*, 27: 1293–304.

HAAPASALO, J., and POKELA, E. (1999), 'Child-rearing and child abuse antecedents of criminality', *Aggression and Violent Behaviour*, 1: 107–27.

HAGELL, A., and NEWBURN, T. (1994), *Persistent Young Offenders*, London: Policy Studies Institute.

HAWKINS, J.D., and CATALANO, R.F. (1992), *Communities that Care*, San Francisco: Jossey-Bass.

——, ——, KOSTERMAN, R., ABBOTT, R., and HILL, K.G. (1999), 'Preventing adolescent health risk behaviours by strengthening protection during childhood', *Archives of Pediatrics and Adolescent Medicine*, 153: 226–34.

——, VON CLEVE, E., and CATALANO, R.F. (1991), 'Reducing early childhood aggression: Results of a primary prevention programme', *Journal of the American Academy of Child and Adolescent Psychiatry*, 30: 208–17.

HEAL, K. (1978), 'Misbehaviour among school children: The role of the school in strategies for prevention', *Policy and Politics*, 6: 321–32.

HENRY, B., CASPI, A., MOFFITT, T.E., and SILVA, P.A. (1996), 'Temperamental and familial predictors of violent and non-violent criminal convictions: Age 3 to age 18', *Developmental Psychology*, 32: 614–23.

HERRENKOHL, T.I., HAWKINS, J.D., CHUNG, I-J., HILL, K.G., and BATTIN-PEARSON, S. (2001), 'School and community risk factors and interventions', in R. Loeber and D.P. Farrington (eds), *Child Delinquents: Development, Intervention and Service Needs*, 211–46, Thousand Oaks, Calif.: Sage.

HOPE, T. (1995), 'Community crime prevention', in M. Tonry and D.P. Farrington (eds), *Building a Safer Society: Strategic approaches to Crime Prevention*, 21–89, Chicago, Ill.: University of Chicago Press.

HUESMANN, L.R., and ERON, L.D. (1984), 'Individual differences and the trait of aggression', *European Journal of Personality*, 3: 95–106.

JONES, M.B., OFFORD, D.R., and ABRAMS, N. (1980), 'Brothers, sisters and antisocial behaviour', *British Journal of Psychiatry*, 136: 139–45.

JUBY, H., and FARRINGTON, D.P. (2001), 'Disentangling the link between disrupted families and delinquency', *British Journal of Criminology*, 41: 22–40.

KAGAN, J. (1989), 'Temperamental contributions to social behaviour', *American Psychologist*, 44: 668–74.

KAPLAN, R.M. (2000), 'Two pathways to prevention', *American Psychologist*, 55: 382–96.

KAROLY, L.A., GREENWOOD, P.W., EVERINGHAM, S.S., HOUBE, J., KILBURN, M.R., RYDELL, C.P., SANDERS, M., and CHIESA, J. (1998), *Investing in Our Children: What We Know and Don't Know about the Costs and Benefits of Early Childhood Interventions*, Santa Monica, Calif.: Rand Corporation.

KAUKIAINEN, A., BJORKVIST, K., LAGERSPETZ, K., OSTERMAN, K., SALMIVALLI, C., ROTHBERG, S., and AHLBOM, A. (1999), 'The relationships between social intelligence, empathy, and three types of aggression', *Aggressive Behaviour*, 25: 81–9.

KAZDIN, A.E. (1997), 'Parent management training: Evidence, outcomes and issues', *Journal of the American Academy of Child and Adolescent Psychiatry*, 36: 1349–56.

KLINTEBERG, B.A., ANDERSSON, T., MAGNUSSON, D., and STATTIN, H. (1993), 'Hyperactive behaviour in childhood as related to subsequent alcohol problems and violent offending: A longitudinal study of male subjects', *Personality and Individual Differences*, 15: 381–8.

KOLBO, J.R., BLAKELY, E.H., and ENGLEMAN, D. (1996), 'Children who witness domestic violence: A review of empirical literature', *Journal of Interpersonal Violence*, 11: 281–93.

KOLVIN, I., GARSIDE, R.F., NICOL, A.R., MACMILLAN, A., WOLSTENHOLME, F., and LEITCH, I.M. (1981), *Help Starts Here: The Maladjusted Child in the Ordinary School*, London: Tavistock.

——, MILLER, F.J.W., FLEETING, M., and KOLVIN, P.A. (1988), 'Social and parenting factors affecting criminal-offence rates: Findings from the Newcastle Thousand Family Study (1947–1980)', *British Journal of Psychiatry*, 152: 80–90.

——, ——, SCOTT, D.M., GATZANIS, S.R.M., and FLEETING, M. (1990), *Continuities of Deprivation? The Newcastle 1000 Family Study*, Aldershot: Avebury.

LEBLANC, M., and LOEBER, R. (1998), 'Developmental criminology updated', in M. Tonry (ed.), *Crime and Justice*, vol. 23, 115–98, Chicago, Ill.: University of Chicago Press.

LEWIS, C., NEWSON, E., and NEWSON, J. (1982), 'Father participation through childhood and its relationship with career aspirations and delinquency', in N. Beail and J. McGuire (eds), *Fathers: Psychological Perspectives*, 174–93, London: Junction.

LIPSEY, M.W., and DERZON, J.H. (1998), 'Predictors of violent or serious delinquency in adolescence and early adulthood: A synthesis of longitudinal research', in R. Loeber and D.P. Farrington (eds), *Serious and Violent Juvenile Offenders: Risk factors and Successful Interventions*, 86–105, Thousand Oaks, Calif.: Sage.

—— and WILSON, D.B. (1998), 'Effective intervention for serious juvenile offenders: A synthesis of research', in R. Loeber and D. P. Farrington (eds), *Serious and Violent Juvenile Offenders: Risk*

Factors and Successful Interventions, 313–45, Thousand Oaks, Calif.: Sage.

LOEBER, R., and DISHION, T. (1983), 'Early predictors of male delinquency: A review', *Psychological Bulletin*, 94: 68–99.

—— and FARRINGTON, D.P. (eds) (1998), *Serious and Violent Juvenile Offenders: Risk Factors and Successful Interventions*, Thousand Oaks, Calif.: Sage.

——, ——, STOUTHAMER-LOEBER, M., MOFFITT, T.E., and CASPI, A. (1998), 'The development of male offending: Key findings from the first decade of the Pittsburgh Youth Study', *Studies on Crime and Crime Prevention*, 7: 141–71.

—— and LEBLANC, M. (1990), 'Toward a developmental criminology', in M. Tonry and N. Morris (eds), *Crime and Justice*, vol. 12, 375–473, Chicago, Ill.: University of Chicago Press.

—— and STOUTHAMER-LOEBER, M. (1986), 'Family factors as correlates and predictors of juvenile conduct problems and delinquency', in M. Tonry and N. Morris (eds), *Crime and Justice*, vol. 7, 29–149, Chicago, Ill.: University of Chicago Press.

——, WUNG, P., KEENAN, K., GIROUX, B., STOUTHAMER-LOEBER, M., VAN KAMMEN, W.B., and MAUGHAN, B. (1993), 'Developmental pathways in disruptive child behaviour', *Development and Psychopathology*, 5: 101–31.

LUENGO, M.A., OTERO, J.M., CARRILLO-DE-LA-PENA, M.T., and MIRON, L. (1994), 'Dimensions of antisocial behaviour in juvenile delinquency: A study of personality variables', *Psychology, Crime and Law*, 1: 27–37.

LYNAM, D. (1996), 'Early identification of chronic offenders: Who is the fledgling psychopath?', *Psychological Bulletin*, 120: 209–34.

—— and MOFFITT, T.E. (1995), 'Delinquency and impulsivity and IQ: A reply to Block', *Journal of Abnormal Psychology*, 104: 399–401.

——, —— and STOUTHAMER-LOEBER, M. (1993), 'Explaining the relation between IQ and delinquency: Class, race, test motivation, school failure or self-control?', *Journal of Abnormal Psychology*, 102: 187–96.

MAK, A.S. (1991), 'Psychosocial control characteristics of delinquents and nondelinquents', *Criminal Justice and Behaviour*, 18: 287–303.

MALINOSKY-RUMMELL, R., and HANSEN, D.J. (1993), 'Long-term consequences of childhood physical abuse', *Psychological Bulletin*, 114: 68–79.

MAXFIELD, M.G., and WIDOM, C.S. (1996), 'The cycle of violence revisited 6 years later', *Archives of Pediatrics and Adolescent Medicine*, 150: 390–95.

MCCORD, J. (1977), 'A comparative study of two generations of native Americans', in R.F. Meier (ed.), *Theory in Criminology*, 83–92, Beverly Hills, Calif.: Sage.

—— (1979), 'Some child-rearing antecedents of criminal behaviour in adult men', *Journal of Personality and Social Psychology*, 37: 1477–86.

—— (1982), 'A longitudinal view of the relationship between paternal absence and crime', in J. Gunn and D.P. Farrington (eds), *Abnormal Offenders, Delinquency, and the Criminal Justice System*, 113–28, Chichester: Wiley.

—— (1983), 'A forty year perspective on effects of child abuse and neglect', *Child Abuse and Neglect*, 7: 265–70.

—— (1997), 'On discipline', *Psychological Inquiry*, 8: 215–7.

MCGUIRE, J. (2001), 'What works in correctional intervention? Evidence and practical implications', in G.A. Bernfeld, D.P. Farrington, and A.W. Leschied (eds), *Offender Rehabilitation in Practice: Implementing and Evaluating Effective Programmes*, 25–43, Chichester: Wiley.

MINISTRY OF JUSTICE (1997), *Our Collective Responsibility: A National Programme for Crime Prevention*, Stockholm: National Council for Crime Prevention.

MOFFITT, T.E. (1990), 'The neuropsychology of juvenile delinquency: A critical review', in M. Tonry and N. Morris (eds), *Crime and Justice*, vol. 12, 99–169, Chicago, Ill.: University of Chicago Press.

—— (1993), 'Adolescence-limited and life-course-persistent antisocial behaviour: A developmental taxonomy', *Psychological Review*, 100: 674–701.

——, CASPI, A., RUTTER, M., and SILVA, P.A. (2001), *Sex Differences in Antisocial Behaviour*, Cambridge: Cambridge University Press.

—— and HENRY, B. (1989), 'Neuropsychological assessment of executive functions in self-reported delinquents', *Development and Psychopathology*, 1: 105–18.

—— and SILVA, P.A. (1988a), 'IQ and delinquency: A direct test of the differential detection hypothesis', *Journal of Abnormal Psychology*, 97: 330–3.

—— and —— (1988b), 'Neuropsychological deficit and self-reported delinquency in an unselected birth cohort', *Journal of the American Academy of Child and Adolescent Psychiatry*, 27: 233–40.

MOORE, M.H. (1995), 'Public health and criminal justice approaches to prevention', in M. Tonry and D.P. Farrington (eds), *Building a Safer Society: Strategic Approaches to Crime Prevention*, 237–62), Chicago, Ill.: University of Chicago Press.

MORASH, M. and RUCKER, L. (1989), 'An exploratory study of the connection of mother's age at childbearing to her children's delinquency in four data sets', *Crime and Delinquency*, 35: 45–93.

NAGIN, D.S., POGARSKY, G., and FARRINGTON, D.P. (1997), 'Adolescent mothers and the criminal behaviour of their children', *Law and Society Review*, 31: 137–62.

—— and TREMBLAY, R.E. (2001), 'Analysing developmental trajectories of distinct but related behaviours: A group-based model', *Psychological Methods*, 6: 18–34.

NEWSON, J., and NEWSON, E. (1989), *The Extent of Parental Physical Punishment in the UK*, London: Approach.

——, ——, and ADAMS, M. (1993), 'The social origins of delinquency', *Criminal Behaviour and Mental Health*, 3: 19–29.

O'DONNELL, J., HAWKINS, J.D., CATALANO, R.F., ABBOTT, R.D., and DAY, L.E. (1995), 'Preventing school failure, drug use, and delinquency among low-income children: Long-term intervention in elementary schools', *American Journal of Orthopsychiatry*, 65: 87–100.

OLDS, D.L., ECKENRODE, J., HENDERSON, C.R., KITZMAN, H., POWERS, J., COLE, R., SIDORA, K., MORRIS, P., PETTITT, L.M., and LUCKEY, D. (1997), 'Long-term effects of home visitation on maternal life course and child abuse and neglect: Fifteen-year follow-up of a randomized trial', *Journal of the American Medical Association*, 278: 637–43.

——, HENDERSON, C.R., CHAMBERLIN, R., and TATELBAUM, R. (1986), 'Preventing child abuse and neglect: A randomized trial of nurse home visitation', *Pediatrics*, 78: 65–78.

——, ——, COLE, R., ECKENRODE, J., KITZMAN, H., LUCKEY, D., PETTITT, L., SIDORA, K., MORRIS, P., and POWERS, J. (1998), 'Long-term effects of nurse home visitation on children's criminal and antisocial behaviour: 15-year follow-up of a randomized controlled trial', *Journal of the American Medical Association*, 280: 1238–44.

OLWEUS, D. (1994), 'Bullying at school: Basic facts and effects of a school based intervention programme', *Journal of Child Psychology and Psychiatry*, 35: 1171–90.

OSBORN, S.G. (1980), 'Moving home, leaving London, and delinquent trends', *British Journal of Criminology*, 20: 54–61.

OUSTON, J. (1984), 'Delinquency, family background, and educational attainment', *British Journal of Criminology*, 24: 2–6.

PAGANI, L., TREMBLAY, R.E., VITARO, F., and PARENT, S. (1998), 'Does preschool help prevent delinquency in boys with a history of perinatal complications?', *Criminology*, 36: 245–67.

PAINTER, K.A., and FARRINGTON, D.P. (2001), 'The financial benefits of improved street lighting, based on crime reduction', *Lighting Research and Technology*, 33: 3–12.

PATTERSON, G.R. (1982), *Coercive Family Process*, Eugene, Oregon: Castalia.

—— (1995), 'Coercion as a basis for early age of onset for arrest', in J. McCord (ed.), *Coercion and Punishment in Long-Term Perspectives*, 81–105, Cambridge: Cambridge University Press.

——, CHAMBERLAIN, P., and REID, J.B. (1982), 'A comparative evaluation of a parent training programme', *Behavior Therapy*, 13: 638–50.

——, REID, J.B., and DISHION, T.J. (1992), *Antisocial Boys*, Eugene, Oregon: Castalia.

PERRY, C.L., KLEPP, K-I., and SILLERS, C. (1989), 'Community-wide strategies for cardiovascular health: The Minnesota Heart Health Programme youth programme', *Health Education and Research*, 4: 87–101.

PHILLIPS, C., CONSIDINE, M., and LEWIS, R. (2000), *A Review of Audits and Strategies Produced by Crime and Disorder Partnerships in 1999*, Briefing Note 8/00, Policing and Reducing Crime Unit, London: Home Office.

POWER, M.J., ALDERSON, M.R., PHILLIPSON, C.M., SHOENBERG, E., and MORRIS, J.N. (1967), 'Delinquent schools?', *New Society*, 10: 542–43.

PULKKINEN, L. (1988), 'Delinquent development: Theoretical and empirical considerations', in M. Rutter (ed.), *Studies of Psychosocial Risk: The Power of Longitudinal Data*, 184–99, Cambridge: Cambridge University Press.

RAINE, A. (1993), *The Psychopathology of Crime: Criminal Behaviour as a Clinical Disorder*, San Diego, Ca.: Academic Press.

——, VENABLES, P.H., and WILLIAMS, M. (1990), 'Relationships between central and autonomic measures of arousal at age 15 years and criminality at age 24 years', *Archives of General Psychiatry*, 47: 1003–07.

RAYNOR, P., and VANSTONE, M. (2001), 'Straight

thinking on Probation': Evidence-based practice and the culture of curiosity', in G.A. Bernfeld, D.P. Farrington, and A.W. Leschied (eds), *Offender Rehabilitation in Practice: Implementing and Evaluating Effective Programmes*, 189–203, Chichester: Wiley.

REDONDO, S., SANCHEZ-MECA, J., and GARRIDO, V. (1999), 'The influence of treatment programmes on the recidivism of juvenile and adult offenders: A European meta-analytic review', *Psychology, Crime and Law*, 5: 251–78.

REISS, A.J., and FARRINGTON, D.P. (1991), 'Advancing knowledge about co-offending: Results from a prospective longitudinal survey of London males', *Journal of Criminal Law and Criminology*, 82: 360–95.

ROBERTS, B.W., and DEL VECCHIO, W.F. (2000), 'The rank-order consistency of personality traits from childhood to old age: A quantitative review of longitudinal studies', *Psychological Bulletin*, 126: 3–25.

ROBINS, L.N. (1979), 'Sturdy childhood predictors of adult outcomes: Replications from longitudinal studies', in J.E. Barrett, R.M. Rose, and G.L. Klerman (eds), *Stress and Mental Disorder*, 219–35, New York: Raven Press.

—— (1992), 'The role of prevention experiments in discovering causes of children's antisocial behaviour', in J. McCord and R.E. Tremblay (eds), *Preventing Antisocial Behaviour: Interventions from Birth through Adolescence*, 3–18, New York: Guilford.

ROBINSON, J.L., KAGAN, J., REZNICK, J.S., and CORLEY, R. (1992), 'The heritability of inhibited and uninhibited behaviour: A twin study', *Developmental Psychology*, 28: 1030–37.

ROSS, R.R., and ROSS, B.D. (1988), 'Delinquency prevention through cognitive training', *New Education*, 10: 70–5.

—— and ROSS, R.D. (eds) (1995), *Thinking Straight: The Reasoning and Rehabilitation Programme for Delinquency Prevention and Offender Rehabilitation*, Ottawa: Air Training and Publications.

RUTTER, M., GILLER, H., and HAGELL, A. (1998), *Antisocial Behaviour by Young People*, Cambridge: Cambridge University Press.

——, MAUGHAN, B., MORTIMORE, P., and OUSTON, J. (1979), *Fifteen Thousand Hours: Secondary Schools and their Effects on Children*, London: Open Books.

——, TIZARD, J., and WHITMORE, K. (1970), *Education, Health and Behaviour*, London: University of London Press.

SAMPSON, R.J., and LAUB, J.H. (1993), *Crime in the Making: Pathways and Turning Points through Life*, Cambridge, Mass: Harvard University Press.

SCHUTTE, N.S., MALOUFF, J.M., HALL, L.E., HAGGERTY, D.J., COOPER, J.T., GOLDEN, C.J., and DORNHEIM, L. (1998), 'Development and validation of a measure of emotional intelligence', *Personality and Individual Differences*, 25: 167–77.

SCHWARTZ, C.E., SNIDMAN, N., and KAGAN, J. (1996), 'Early childhood temperament as a determinant of externalizing behaviour in adolescence', *Development and Psychopathology*, 8: 527–37.

SCHWEINHART, L.J., BARNES, H.V., and WEIKART, D.P. (1993), *Significant Benefits: The High/Scope Perry Preschool Study Through Age 27*, Ypsilanti, Mich.: High/Scope Press.

—— and WEIKART, D.P. (1980), *Young Children Grow Up: The Effects of the Perry Preschool Programme on Youths Through Age 15*, Ypsilanti, Mich.: High/Scope Press.

SCOTT, S., SPENDER, Q., DOOLAN, M., JACOBS, B., and ASPLAND, H. (2001), 'Multicentre controlled trial of parenting groups for child antisocial behaviour in clinical practice', *British Medical Journal*, 323: 194–6.

SHERMAN, L.W., FARRINGTON, D.P., WELSH, B.C., and MACKENZIE, D.L. (eds) (2002), *Evidence-Based Crime Prevention*, London: Routledge.

——, GOTTFREDSON, D., MACKENZIE, D., ECK, J., REUTER, P., and BUSHWAY, S. (1997), *Preventing Crime: What Works, What Doesn't, What's Promising*, Washington, DC: US Department of Justice.

—— and WEISBURD, D. (1995), 'General deterrent effects of police patrol in crime 'hot spots': A randomized controlled trial', *Justice Quarterly*, 12: 625–48.

SMITH, C. A., and STERN, S.B. (1997), 'Delinquency and antisocial behaviour: A review of family processes and intervention research', *Social Service Review*, 71: 382–420.

—— and THORNBERRY, T.P. (1995), 'The relationship between childhood maltreatment and adolescent involvement in delinquency', *Criminology*, 33: 451–81.

SMITH, P.K., and SHARP, S. (1994), *School Bullying*, London: Routledge.

STATTIN, H., and KLACKENBERG-LARSSON, I. (1993), 'Early language and intelligence development and their relationship to future criminal behaviour', *Journal of Abnormal Psychology*, 102: 369–78.

TONRY, M., and FARRINGTON, D.P. (1995), 'Strategic approaches to crime prevention', in M. Tonry and D.P. Farrington (eds), *Building a Safer Society: Strategic Approaches to Crime Prevention*, 1–20, Chicago, Ill.: University of Chicago Press.

TRASLER, G.B. (1962), *The Explanation of Criminality*, London: Routledge and Kegan Paul.

TREMBLAY, R.E., and CRAIG, W.M. (1995), 'Developmental crime prevention', in M. Tonry and D.P. Farrington (eds), *Building a Safer Society: Strategic Approaches to Crime Prevention*, 151–236, Chicago, Ill.: University of Chicago Press.

——, PAGANI-KURTZ, L., MASSE, L.C., VITARO, F., and PIHL, R.O. (1995), 'A bimodal preventive intervention for disruptive kindergarten boys: Its impact through mid-adolescence', *Journal of Consulting and Clinical Psychology*, 63: 560–68.

UTTING, D. (ed) (1999), *A Guide to Promising Approaches*, London: Communities that Care.

VAZSONYI, A.T., PICKERING, L.E., JUNGER, M., and HESSING, D. (2001), 'An empirical test of a general theory of crime: A four-nation comparative study of self-control and the prediction of deviance', *Journal of Research in Crime and Delinquency*, 38: 91–131.

WADSWORTH, M.E.J. (1976), 'Delinquency, pulse rates, and early emotional deprivation', *British Journal of Criminology*, 16: 245–56.

—— (1979), *Roots of Delinquency: Infancy, Adolescence and Crime*, London: Martin Robertson.

WALSH, A., PETEE, T.A., and BEYER, J.A. (1987), 'Intellectual imbalance and delinquency: Comparing high verbal and high performance IQ delinquents', *Criminal Justice and Behaviour*, 14: 370–79.

WASSERMAN, G.A., and MILLER, L.S. (1998), 'The prevention of serious and violent juvenile offending', in R. Loeber and D.P. Farrington (eds), *Serious and Violent Juvenile Offenders: Risk Factors and Successful Interventions*, 197–247, Thousand Oaks, Calif.: Sage.

WEBSTER-STRATTON, C. (1998), 'Preventing conduct problems in Head Start children: Strengthen parenting competencies', *Journal of Consulting and Clinical Psychology*, 66: 715–30.

WELLS, L.E., and RANKIN, J.H. (1991), 'Families

and delinquency: A meta-analysis of the impact of broken homes', *Social Problems*, 38: 71–93.

WELSH, B.C., and FARRINGTON, D.P. (2000), 'Monetary costs and benefits of crime prevention programmes', in M. Tonry (ed.), *Crime and Justice*, vol. 27, 305–61), Chicago, Ill.: University of Chicago Press.

——, —— and SHERMAN, L.W. (eds) (2001), *Costs and Benefits of Preventing Crime*, Boulder, Col.: Westview Press.

WEST, D.J., and FARRINGTON, D.P. (1973), *Who Becomes Delinquent?*, London: Heinemann.

—— and —— (1977) *The Delinquent Way of Life*, London: Heinemann.

WHITE, J.L., MOFFITT, T.E., CASPI, A., BARTUSCH, D.J., NEEDLES, D.J., and STOUTHAMER-LOEBER, M. (1994), 'Measuring impulsivity and examining its relationship to delinquency', *Journal of Abnormal Psychology*, 103: 192–205.

WIDOM, C.S. (1989), 'The cycle of violence', *Science*, 244: 160–66.

—— and AMES, M.A. (1994), 'Criminal consequences of childhood sexual victimization', *Child Abuse and Neglect*, 18: 303–18.

WIKSTRÖM, P-O.H., CLARKE, R. V., and McCORD, J. (eds) (1995), *Integrating Crime Prevention Strategies: Propensity and Opportunity*, Stockholm: National Council for Crime Prevention.

—— and LOEBER, R. (2000), 'Do disadvantaged neighbourhoods cause well-adjusted children to become adolescent delinquents? A study of male juvenile serious offending, individual risk and protective factors, and neighbourhood context', *Criminology*, 38: 1109–42.

—— and TORSTENSSON, M. (1999), 'Local crime prevention and its national support: Organisation and direction', *European Journal on Criminal Policy and Research*, 7: 459–81.

WILSON, J.J., and HOWELL, J.C. (1993), *A Comprehensive Strategy for Serious, Violent, and Chronic Juvenile Offenders*, Washington, DC: US Office of Juvenile Justice and Delinquency Prevention.

WILSON, J.Q., and HERRNSTEIN, R.J. (1985), *Crime and Human Nature*, New York: Simon and Schuster.

YOUTH JUSTICE BOARD (2001), *Risk and Protective Factors Associated with Youth Crime and Effective Interventions to Prevent It*, YJB Research Note No. 5.

20

CRIME AND THE
LIFE COURSE

David J. Smith

Crime is mostly committed by young people—by adolescents and adults in their twenties. Criminal offending, therefore, is closely linked to the life course. It is one of a number of psychosocial disorders that are characteristic of youth, in the sense that they rise in prevalence or frequency, or reach a peak, in adolescence or early adulthood. Other examples are problem drinking, use of illegal drugs, depression (especially in females), suicide (especially in males), and eating disorders (Rutter and Smith 1995; Smith and Rutter 1995).

Statements about the relationship between age and crime are usually based on a simple count of offences, without taking account of their monetary or symbolic value. It is possible to argue that crimes of the powerful, usually committed by older men, are far more important than their showing in conventional crime statistics. Nevertheless, there is a large body of 'ordinary' crime, some of it serious, some relatively trivial, which undeniably has a major impact on victims, and which indirectly structures people's lives: this is mostly committed by young men.

Any theory of criminal offending should explain how it fits with the course of individual development from infancy to old age, because the relationship between age and offending is so striking. Gottfredson and Hirschi (1990) argued that it is enough to state that there exists an invariant relationship between age and offending. Their argument is unconvincing for several reasons. First of all, the relationship is not invariant: for example, the peak age of offending varies considerably according to the type of offence (Farrington 1986: 199). More important, to state that age 'causes' crime is empty. Gottfredson and Hirschi quoted the analogy of Boyle's Law, which expresses the relationship between the temperature, volume, and pressure of a gas, yet this analogy self-destructs, because Boyle's Law describes a regularity, but does not provide a deeper explanation of the underlying physical processes. Such an explanation was provided later by molecular physics, which interprets heat, temperature, and pressure in terms of the movement of particles in a container. An equally important point is that age is not a personal characteristic but an index of the likely stage that someone has reached in a partly predictable sequence of development, and an indicator of social standing. As Rutter (1989) has argued, the explanation for 'age effects' must therefore lie in the detailed process of development, and in associated social meanings and social roles. For example, there is a fundamental difference between behavioural change arising from maturation (e.g., puberty) and from experience.

The evolution of offending over the life course is a story of both continuity and change. On the one hand, there is considerable stability in the differences between individuals at succeeding stages of the life cycle: the most disruptive child is likely to the most serious and persistent adult offender. On the other hand, the likelihood of offending, and the forms that antisocial behaviour takes, change radically with advancing years, and these striking changes are reflected in the age–crime curve. The predictability and persistence of offending in the same individuals over the years needs to be explained. Because criminal behaviour appears to be dysfunctional for most people, explaining why they persist in it poses a challenge. Possible explanations span constitutional factors, personality, cognitive processes, social interactions, victimization-offending loops, labelling and stigmatization, and constraints imposed by social structure. Equally, the dramatic change in offending over the life course needs to be explained, and it is remarkable that most classic criminological theories have not even tried to explain it. Possible realms of explanation are changing social responses to misbehaviour in people of different ages, changing social bonds and peer influence, changing social roles, activities, and associated opportunities for offending, and changing cultural definitions.

Stability and change over the life course are two of the organizing concepts of this chapter, but before analysing continuity or change in offending, it is necessary to consider whether criminal behaviour is so diverse that generalizations are not possible. After a section reviewing methodological problems in collecting information about offending over the life course, the first main section therefore considers the extent of specialization in offending, and the strength of the evidence that different criminal behaviours are closely linked. Following sections analyse the extent of stability in offending over the life course, and the extent of change. The next two sections then review explanations first for stability, and then for change. The last main section summarizes and reviews Moffitt's (1993; 1997) theory that both stability and change in offending over the life course can be better understood on the assumption that offenders can be divided into those who persist over the life course and those who offend only in adolescence. The conclusion argues that a number of central problems in criminology, such as the explanation for the contrast in offending between males and females, and the influence of the penal system on offending, can be tackled only by further research adopting a life course perspective.

PROBLEMS OF METHOD

The two main sources of information used on offending over the life course are official statistics (usually convictions, occasionally arrests, or police contacts) and self-reports (information that people give about their own offending in personal interviews or self-completion questionnaires). Official records have a special importance because an offence officially recorded against someone's name has a legal, social, and symbolic significance that sets it apart from an offence not known to the authorities. Their severe limitation is that they cover only a small fraction of criminal incidents, because only a minority of offences are reported to the police and recorded by them, and only a minority of recorded offences lead to an arrest or charge. Statistics for England and Wales in 1997 (see Maguire, in Chapter 11 of this volume) show that cases where action was successfully taken against an offender (cautions and convictions) accounted for only 2.97 per cent of offences (estimated from victims' reports in the British Crime Survey) (Barclay and Tavares 1999). Also, official statistics are distorted, because these rates of attrition vary widely between types of offence. From the early 1960s onwards, a huge number of studies have been carried out using self-report methods, and these provide a much more complete account of offending. The criticism that people will generally not admit to having committed offences in a confidential survey has long been disproved: self-report studies reveal far more offences, including serious ones, than are shown in official records (Huizinga 1991; Elliott 1994). A considerable number of studies have tested the validity of self-reports against the criterion of official records, a 'bootstrapping' method of validation, since self-reports aim to improve on official records. These studies generally show a significant correlation between self-reports and official records (e.g., Farrington 1973), but the correlation cannot be high since self-reported offending is so much more common than official offending, and the complex, partly probabilistic processes of the criminal justice system mediate between the two. A particularly thorough study of this kind was carried out by Dunford and Elliott (1984) using five annual sweeps of data from the US National Youth Survey (the subjects were aged eleven to seventeen at the first sweep, and sixteen to twenty-two at the fifth). First, youths were divided into four groups reflecting the level and seriousness of their self-reported delinquency in a given year. Then they were further classified into four groups reflecting the delinquency types they belonged to over the sequence of years: for example, serious career offenders were defined as those who had committed at least three of the more serious[1] offences in two or more consecutive years. The same youths were then classified into comparable groups using official arrest data. The results showed that the proportion who had been arrested in the first three years of the study varied regularly across the four groups, from 1.9 per cent among self-reported non-offenders to 24.3 per cent among self-reported serious career offenders. All of the officially-defined career offenders (serious and non-serious) were also identified as career offenders from self-reports. However, only 14 per cent of the self-reported career offenders had a record of arrest, and among these only 2 per cent were identified as career offenders from their arrest records. This both supports the validity of the self-report measures, and shows that they reveal far more offending and offenders than the arrest records.

As Bowling (1990) has pointed out, a limitation of this form of validation is that the self-reports of those without an official record remain untested, and this is a major limitation because a high proportion of self-reported offenders have no official record. The point was earlier addressed by Farrington (1973), who showed that among youths with no official record, self-reported offending was a good predictor of

---

[1] UCR (Uniform Crime Report) Part 1 offences were the ones regarded as more serious for this purpose.

whether they would acquire an official record in future. This finding also demonstrates that the correlation between self-reports and official records does not arise merely because those without a record are more likely to conceal their offending in answers to survey questions.

The studies mentioned above compared official records and self-reports for the same individuals, but did not try to match particular acts (e.g., the burglary at 12 Beechgrove Crescent on 3 June). Where this has been done, studies have found that offences known to the police are self-reported in 80 to 90 per cent of cases (Huizinga 1991: 60). However, the important finding from this back-check method is that there may be systematic differences between ethnic groups. Huizinga and Elliott (1986) in a US study found that white males reported 84 per cent of their officially recorded offences, whereas black males reported 61 per cent of theirs. Junger (1989) in a Dutch study also found a difference between ethnic groups in level of disclosure, and found a much lower level of disclosure than the American studies. In his review, Huizinga (1991) quotes several other US studies that found a higher level of under-reporting among black males than other groups, and also several that found more under-reporting among males than females.

In broad terms, these findings suggest that the self-report method is the best available for collecting information about criminal offending in the life course. Like other research instruments, it has important defects and limitations, but these are offset in the best studies by combining official records and self-reports, and by collecting information from various informants (parents, teachers, peers) as well as the individual included in the study. The findings on differential disclosure among males and females, and among different ethnic groups, show that self-reports introduce some systematic bias. However, the systematic biases in official records are probably at least as serious.

A different challenge for researchers is obtaining samples that adequately represent serious and persistent offenders, who account for a high proportion of offences, but a small proportion of the population. The problem is that serious and persistent offenders are likely to lead unconventional, unstable lives, and are therefore unlikely, for a variety of reasons, to be included in conventional data collection exercises. For example, they may tend be absent from school when a questionnaire is administered, they may escape selection in a random sample because they often move house or have no fixed abode, they may be in prison when the interviewer calls, and they may often refuse to be interviewed. Some classic studies of offending in the life course have used a sample of institutionalized youths in order to ensure that heavy end offenders are properly studied: the best example is the Gluecks' study in Boston (Glueck and Glueck 1950; Sampson and Laub 1993). Most have simply over-sampled neighbourhoods with high levels of social and economic stress: for example, the Cambridge Study in Delinquent Development (Farrington and West 1990), or the Pittsburgh Youth Study (Loeber et al. 1998). A study by Cernkovich et al. (1985) compared two groups: a sample designed to be representative of all young people aged twelve to nineteen in a US Metropolitan Area; and a sample of the populations of three male juvenile institutions within the same state, together with the entire population of the only female juvenile institution in the state. The same self-reported delinquency questions, based on the US National Youth Survey, were applied to both samples. The group defined as 'high frequency major offenders' accounted for 13.6 per cent of neighbourhood youths but 80 per cent of the institutional sample. When comparisons were confined to this group of chronic offenders, they were found to be far more delinquent among the institutional than among the neighbourhood sample. For example, 41 per cent of the institutional chronic offenders reported breaking and entering more than once a month, compared with none of the neighbourhood chronic offenders at that frequency. The study is far from conclusive, because the sampling method used for the neighbourhood survey may well have been inadequate.[2] Nevertheless it points to a fundamental problem which has not been fully addressed even by the most elaborate recent studies. The problem is even more challenging for the small number of studies that cover mature adults than for the much larger number that concentrate on adolescents.

The method favoured by most contemporary researchers is the prospective longitudinal study. In the best examples, information is obtained regularly (say, once a year) about a cohort of young people from a number of informants (the cohort members, their parents, teachers, friends) and records (school records, police, criminal records). The advantage of this approach is that information is obtained soon after the event, so that sequences in time can be used to establish the priority of cause versus effect. Also, to the extent that many individual characteristics and circumstances remain stable, those few that have changed can be identified as the likely cause of a change in behaviour; or in other words, as longitudinal researchers often put it, individuals act as their own controls. However, these advantages are not as decisive as they seem at first. Supposing that the interval between sweeps of data collection is twelve months, an enormous sequence of interactions will have taken place over that period, for example, between a sixteen-year-old girl and her friends. It will be wholly impossible to establish which came first: the girl's delinquency, or her friends' delinquency. This is because a so-called prospective longitudinal study is actually a series of retrospective surveys, and the period of retrospection is enormously long in relation to the complexity of social interactions in people's lives. It turns out, therefore, that even in longitudinal studies, evidence supporting or contradicting causal explanations is usually indirect, and seldom wholly conclusive.

THE EXTENT OF SPECIALIZATION IN OFFENDING

Criminal offending covers a wide diversity of actions: some serious, others trivial; some direct, overt, symbolically transgressive, others covert, deceptive, avoiding open conflict; some violently aggressive, others (the majority) non-violent; some involving

---

[2] Sampling methods are not fully reported, but it seems that a quota sampling method was used at the final stage. This would have allowed interviewers to carry out interviews with those who were easiest to find. No response rates are quoted, and there is no information about the number of recalls made by interviewers, which suggests that a quota sampling method was used.

special knowledge or complex techniques (safe-blowing, embezzlement, computer fraud), others simple (hand-bag snatching, wife-battering); some involving unusual or abnormal impulses (paedophilia), others (the majority) springing from universal frustrations and needs. A decision to generalize about such a wide variety of behaviours reflects the theoretical position that despite surface differences, there are fundamental similarities beneath. In fact, nearly all research in the developmental tradition takes the generalization further, by treating antisocial behaviour in children as essentially similar to offending in adults. This approach is underpinned by the assumption that the law and a common moral fabric provide a unifying framework. Diverse forms of criminal, antisocial, even unconventional behaviour have in common that they are all infractions of the law, a moral code, or social conventions and expectations. This could mean that these varied forms of behaviour have some common origins. For example, Gottfredson and Hirschi (1990) and Hirschi and Gottfredson (1994) have argued that 'the generality of deviance' encompasses not only criminal offending but also road accidents, which are similarly related to age, and that the common origin is a lack of self-control. Alternatively, it is possible to argue that a wide range of deviant behaviour springs from aggression, even though aggression is often not manifest in the act: a burglar who breaks into an empty house must be prepared to confront the owner if necessary, and there may be an edge of aggression even in the behaviour of a child who refuses to eat his supper.

Although the idea of the generality of deviance is certainly a theoretical position, there is also a considerable weight of evidence to show that offenders are predominantly versatile rather than specialized. Yet there is some degree of specialization, and an important question is whether this tends to increase as the criminal career lengthens.

An important early contribution was Wolfgang and colleagues' pioneering study of a cohort of Philadelphia boys (Wolfgang et al. 1972: the findings on specialization are summarized in Farrington et al. 1988). They classified offences into five broad types, then constructed matrices showing, for example, the probability that a boy who had committed an injury offence at the first arrest would commit another injury offence at the next arrest. The 'average transition matrix' (showing the transitional probabilities from any one arrest to the next one) clearly showed more versatility than specialization: for example, the probability that the next arrest would be for a non-index offence was over .5 regardless of the current offence. There was, however, some specialization superimposed on this versatility: for example, the probability that the next arrest would be for theft was .271 where the current arrest was for theft, but only .128 where the current arrest was for causing injury. A number of further studies in the 1980s produced essentially similar conclusions, but the study by Farrington et al. (1988) considerably developed the analytic approach. It used a far more detailed classification of offences, which is probably required to capture patterns of specialized offending; and it used a statistic, the 'forward specialization coefficient', which is 0 when the next offence type is unrelated to the last one, and 1 when every next offence is of the same type as the last one. Using a database of nearly 70,000 juvenile offenders in Utah and in Maricopa County, Arizona, the study found an average forward specialization coefficient over all offences of .107, which agrees with earlier studies in showing a small degree of specialization. Some of the offences such as 'incorrigibility' would be unrecognizable in other jurisdictions, but confining our attention to recognizable offences, there were notable variations in specialization according to the offence: for example, specialization was relatively high for burglary and motor vehicle theft, and relatively low for trespassing, weapons, and vandalism.

The two major studies mentioned above were of juveniles. A study of a large Danish cohort of 28,884 men demonstrated a modest degree of specialization in violent offending (Brennan *et al.* 1989). The main conclusion (that there is far more versatility than specialization) was confirmed for adults in a study by Stander *et al.* (1989). This time the database was a 10 per cent sample survey of adult males (aged twenty-one and above) under sentence in twenty-one prisons in the south-east of England in 1972 (N = 811). Offences were classified into just six categories (violence, sex, burglary, theft, fraud, other). The transition matrices for this adult sample showed a greater degree of specialization than for the juvenile samples discussed above, but there was still much more versatility than specialization. For example, the probability that a second conviction for violence would follow a first was .221, whereas the probability that a conviction for violence would follow a conviction for a sexual offence was only .075. If there were complete specialization, the first of these probabilities would be 1.00, yet the contrast between the two probabilities illustrates a modest degree of specialization. A Markov chain analysis demonstrated that the transitional probabilities remained constant: that is, the links among offence types between the first and second conviction were the same as between the second and third conviction, between the third and fourth conviction, and so on. On the other hand, a first-order Markov chain analysis did not adequately describe the pattern: for example, the probability of a violent offence on the fourth conviction was not best predicted by the type of offence on the third conviction alone; instead, the prediction was improved by taking account of the type of offence at the second conviction as well. This showed that the best description of specialization involved identifying a sequence of at least three convictions. As in Farrington *et al.* (1988), forward specialization coefficients were also calculated. These ranged between .14 and .21 for theft, violence, burglary, and other offences, but were considerably higher for fraud (.27) and, especially, for sexual offences (.45). These findings confirmed the picture of predominant versatility, but with partial exceptions for certain offences.

In an early review of specialization in juvenile offending, Klein (1984) referred to several studies that made use of self-report data, but these have not analysed the question in the detailed way described above. Most detailed studies of offending patterns have used official data on convictions or arrests. Self-report data could be used in principle, although they carry the limitation that the exact date of the offence is usually not known. In practice, they have generally been used in rather a different way, to investigate how far some 'general deviance factor' will go to explain different forms of deviance or offending. For example, McGee and Newcomb (1992) analysed self-reports of a wide range of behaviours among a cohort of young people studied at four developmental stages: early adolescence (aged around thirteen), late adolescence (aged around seventeen), young adulthood (aged around twenty-one) and adulthood (aged around twenty-five). Factor analysis was used to identify 'latent constructs' underlying the specific items about deviant behaviour. For example, four factors were identified at the young adulthood and adulthood stages: drug use, social conformity, sexual involvement, and criminal behaviour. At each developmental stage, several of the factors were fairly closely correlated, and further analysis showed that the fit of the model could be significantly improved by adding a second-order 'general deviance' factor. This single second-order factor explained 63 per cent of the variance in the first-order factors in early adulthood, and 43 per cent in adulthood. These findings show that there is a general factor underlying not only a wide range of criminal behaviours, but also other deviant, unconventional, and rebellious behaviours as well. They also suggest that the importance of this general factor declines with age, which is equivalent to the idea that criminal specialization increases as the criminal career lengthens. A considerable number of other studies (e.g., Donovan and Jessor 1985) have used factor analysis on self-report data to confirm the existence of a 'general deviance' factor, which usually accounts for about half of the variance in specific forms of deviance or offending. Among the most interesting are those that extend this approach to high-risk juvenile offenders (Dembo *et al.* 1992) and to different time periods and cultural groups (LeBlanc and Girard 1997).

The recent work by Soothill *et al.* (2002) is a new approach to the problem of classifying offending behaviour. The study made use of the Offenders Index, a court-based reporting system of convictions for standard-list offences in England and Wales ('standard-list offences' do not include less serious ones that are not centrally recorded). The data used were for two cohorts of all offenders born in four specified weeks in 1953 and 1958, although most findings quoted here will be from the 1953 cohort (N = 11,402). For most of the analysis, a very detailed offence classification was used (seventy-one separate offences for the 1953 males and twenty-nine for the 1953 females). The task that Soothill and colleagues set themselves was to describe the structure of offending activity in a way that would show how different offence types were related, but allow for changes in the pattern of offending at different points in the criminal career. They approached this problem by finding typologies of criminal activity within *five-year periods* of the offender's criminal history (before the age of 16, age 16–20, 21–25, 26–30, 31–35, 36–40). A form of latent class analysis was used to identify clusters of five-year strips of events (the events being convictions for specific offences). The structure of these clusters was held constant across the whole period up to the age of forty, but an individual was allowed to move from one cluster to another at different stages of the life cycle. Statistical tests established that the definitions of the clusters were fairly robust, and this was checked by repeating the analysis for the 1958 cohort. This produced closely similar clusters for the most part, although the clusters for the 1958 cohort were more detailed, as certain of the clusters identified in the analysis of the 1953 cohort had split into two. A cluster can be described by showing (a) the probability that a strip in that cluster will include each type of offence, and (b) the probability that each type of offence will belong to the cluster. The problem is that a description of this kind is enormously complex. With some inevitable simplification, this can be boiled down to an outline description. For example, the authors provide the following description of cluster D in the analysis of males from the 1953 cohort:

Involved in wounding, assault, and criminal damage. Also those most likely to be in possession of an offensive weapon. 16–25 year olds.
So to sum up: **General violence**

Figure 20.1 shows how male offenders were assigned to clusters, by age group, for the
1953 cohort. Figure 20.2 shows the same for females, and Figure 20.3 adds the results
for females in the 1958 cohort. These latter findings are of interest because the cluster
solution for the 1958 cohort females was more detailed and informative. These figures
immediately demonstrate major differences between the age profiles of offenders
included in the clusters. In the case of the males, for example, cluster B (non-violent
property, especially burglary) is heavily dominated by very young offenders, whereas
cluster C (fraud and general theft) has a much older profile, with a peak between the
ages of twenty-six and thirty. Another interesting contrast is that cluster D (general
violence) is heavily concentrated in two age groups, 16–20 and 21–25, whereas cluster
I (shoplifting) is much more evenly distributed across the full age range. These striking differences in age profiles demonstrate that the clusters mean something. There
are patterns of offending that are related to age, and these become much more evident
when the clustering of offences over a five-year period is taken into account, instead of
considering types of offence individually, as in the later Figure 20.5. The fact that the
clusters make stronger patterns than the individual offence types also demonstrates
that offending is patterned, that is, types of offence do not follow each other randomly, and therefore any theory that sees offending as flowing from a single factor
such as lack of self-control (Gottfredson and Hirschi 1990; Hirschi and Gottfredson
1994) is seriously inadequate. In the case of females, there are only three clusters for
the 1953 cohort and five for the 1958 cohort, and differences between the age profiles
of these clusters are not striking. Hence the analysis reveals far less evidence of patterned or specialized offending for females than it does for males. In the case of
females, the shoplifting cluster is heavily concentrated in the 16–20 age group, and
numbers in this cluster fall off quite rapidly in later age groups. There is also a
shoplifting cluster for males, but this has a much flatter age distribution.

As set out in earlier paragraphs, most discussions of offence specialization have
considered the probability that the next offence will be of the same type as the present
one—a transition matrix methodology. Soothill *et al.* considered and rejected this
approach on the grounds that it was 'simplistic and potentially misleading'. Their
main criticism was that most offenders commit bunches of offences of several types,
so that analysis of a sequence of single offences is inappropriate. If someone commits
a sequence of offences consisting of 'burglary—theft—burglary—theft', etc., he is
clearly showing a pattern of offending confined to burglary and theft, but a transition
matrix approach shows no link between the current and next offence type.[3] A related
problem with this approach is that it uses individual offence types rather than clusters.
If these are broadly defined, as has often been the case, the analysis will not be

---

[3] Strictly this is a criticism of a Markov chain analysis that considers only first-order effects. In the example
quoted, the links between every other offence would show up as a second-order effect in a Markov chain
analysis. Soothill *et al.* would argue that considering nth-order effects in a Markov chain is a cumbersome way
of proceeding, however.

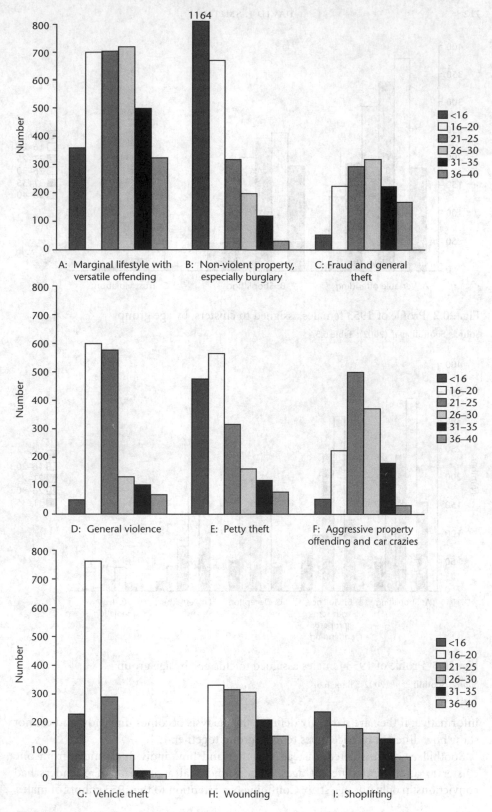

Fig. 20.1 Profile of 1953 males assigned to clusters, by age group

Source: Soothill *et al.* (2002): Table 6.1.

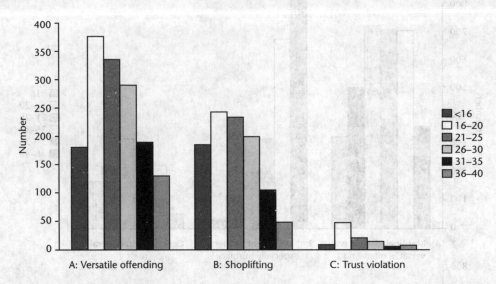

Fig. 20.2 Profile of 1953 females assigned to clusters, by age group
Source: Soothill *et al.* (2002): Table 6.5.

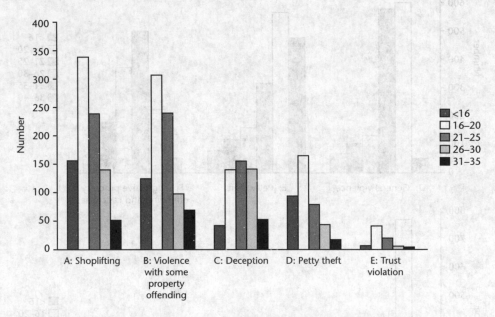

Fig. 20.3 Profile of 1958 females assigned to clusters, by age group
Source: Soothill *et al.* (2002): Table 6.6.

informative. If they are narrowly defined, the analysis becomes unwieldy, and cannot show how different offence types tend to group together.

Soothill *et al.* considered, instead, whether and how individuals move from one cluster to another at different ages. They found that a majority of offenders had convictions in only one age strip. Confining our attention to the 1953 cohort of males,

63.5 per cent had convictions in only one age strip, and a total of 83.0 per cent had convictions in only one or two. It was rare for male offenders to have convictions in all five age strips (.9 per cent) or in five out of the six (2.5 per cent) (Soothill *et al.* 2002: Table 7.1). 'Age-strip recidivism' defined in this way was much rarer still among females. Because most criminal careers were confined to one or two age strips, most offenders could by definition appear in only one or two clusters. In fact, 68.0 per cent of the males in the 1953 cohort appeared in only one cluster, while a further 20.4 per cent appeared in just two, 8.3 per cent in three, and 3.3 per cent in four or more (ibid.: Table 7.2). In one sense this illustrates a high degree of specialization in criminal careers, because it shows that most offenders only ever belong to one cluster. However, this is potentially misleading, since offenders with relatively short criminal careers do not have the opportunity to move between clusters. A more detailed analysis (ibid.: Table 7.3) showed that where offenders had convictions in more than one age strip, it was common for them to move between clusters. This can be illustrated by reference to the statistics for the 1953 cohort of males. One-fifth of the men had convictions in two age strips, and of these, 79.8 per cent were assigned to two different clusters in these two age groups. A further 8.6 per cent had convictions in three age strips, and of these more than half (53.2 per cent) were assigned to three different clusters, 41.4 per cent to two different clusters, and only 5.4 per cent to the same cluster throughout. There were dwindling numbers with convictions in four, five, and six separate age strips, but most of these were assigned to three or more clusters at different stages of their careers.

In order to summarize patterns of switching between clusters, Soothill *et al.* took each age strip in turn and considered the next age strip in which the same individuals had a conviction. In this analysis, individuals who had no later conviction were excluded. The analysis then showed what proportion switched to a different cluster in the next age strip in which they had a conviction (ibid.: Table 7.4). The pattern of switching varied substantially depending on age and the offence cluster at the starting point. For several clusters, there was a clear trend towards increasing specialization with age: examples are 'marginal lifestyle with versatile offending', 'fraud and general theft', 'wounding', and 'shoplifting'. However, there was a trend towards declining specialization with age for some clusters: examples are 'aggressive property offending and car crazies' and 'vehicle theft'. The proportion assigned to the same cluster at the next age strip where they had a conviction seldom rose above 40 per cent, and for many cells it was 10 per cent or lower.

As this discussion has illustrated, analysis of specialization is complicated by the fact that criminal careers may be short or long. Most offenders are active for only a short period of their lives, and clear patterns can be discerned in these short criminal careers, in the sense that offences tend to fall into clusters, and these clusters are strongly related to the life cycle. A minority of offenders are active over a longer period of their lives, and for this group offending patterns tend to be more changeable than stable from one point to another in the life cycle. Increasing specialization with age is a pattern that applies to certain offence clusters but not to others.

On the whole, the evidence suggests that it is fruitful to think of the great diversity of antisocial and criminal behaviour as closely related at a deeper level. This approach is supported by the many studies showing a single factor underlying more specific forms of deviance, and by the widely corroborated finding that arrests and convictions show more versatile than specialized patterns of offending. Specific offences do tend to cluster into patterns within criminal careers, but because those with long careers typically switch between clusters, it is unlikely that clusters of offences correspond to well-defined criminal types.

THE EXTENT OF STABILITY OVER THE LIFE COURSE

Individual differences in antisocial behaviour and criminal offending are relatively stable over the life course. A good illustration of that predictability up to the adolescent years was provided by an article entitled 'How early can we tell?', by White *et al.* (1990), based on analysis of a longitudinal study of a birth cohort of over 1,000 children in Dunedin, New Zealand. The children were divided into three groups on the basis of reports by parents, teachers, and the children themselves at the ages of nine, eleven and thirteen (self-reports at ages eleven and thirteen only). The fifty children designated AD were pervasively antisocial at two of the three age points at least, and as rated by at least two of the three informants; the thirty-seven children designated OD had other diagnoses at age eleven (e.g., attention deficit disorder with no conduct disorder symptoms); the remaining 837 children designated ND were those with no disorder. A total of thirty-three characteristics of the children collected at the ages of three and five were reviewed, and five that were strongly related to this definition of antisocial disorder were identified. A discriminant function analysis was then conducted in which the five selected variables were jointly used to predict the AD and ND cases. This correctly classified 70 per cent of the AD cases and 81 per cent of the ND cases at age eleven. The three strongest predictors were parent-reported behaviour problems at age five, and 'difficult to manage' and 'externalizing behaviour problems' at age three. The other two predictors were a test of motor coordination, and a cognitive test (involving drawing), both at age five. As the authors stated, 'the results . . . suggest that behavioural problems are the best preschool predictors of antisocial behaviour at age 11, and that behavioural problems as early as age 5, especially when rated by parents, can be predictive of future conduct problems' (ibid.: 519).

The analysis was extended to predict delinquency at the age of fifteen. At that age, variety of self-reported delinquency and police contacts were more than twice as high among the AD as among the ND group. Delinquents at age fifteen were defined as those with a high self-report score and at least one police contact, and there were thirty-eight adolescents in this group. Using the five preschool predictors as before, a discriminant function analysis correctly classified 65 per cent of the delinquents and 67 per cent of the non-delinquents. This still showed considerable stability in individual differences from the preschool years, but also indicated a decline a predictability in the adolescent years, which suggests that new causes of delinquency start to be influential at that time.

In interpreting these findings it has to be borne in mind that the AD group is much smaller than the ND group, which means that even though the predictors are powerful, there are many false positives. For example, 19 per cent of the ND cases were wrongly predicted at age eleven, meaning that 159 children were incorrectly predicted to be pervasively antisocial, whereas only fifty children were actually classified as such. This would be a severe limitation on use of the findings for targeted intervention (whether ethical or unethical). Nevertheless, these findings do demonstrate a considerable degree of stability of individual differences in antisocial and delinquent behaviour from a very early age. This confirms findings from a considerable number of other studies (e.g., Robins 1966, 1978; Loeber and Dishion 1983; Robins and Regier 1991; Farrington 1995), some of which show that prediction from an early age continues to be powerful into adulthood.

The stability of aggressiveness and its pervasive influence have been particularly well studied. Reviewing sixteen studies, Olweus (1979) found that the correlation between early aggressive behaviour and later criminality averaged .68. Huesman et al. (1984), in a longitudinal study over a twenty-two-year period, found that early aggressiveness predicted traffic violations, as well as spouse abuse, other criminal behaviour, and self-reported physical aggression. It seems that early aggression is nearly always a precursor of violent offending in adulthood. Farrington (1978) found that seven out of ten males arrested for a violent offence by the age of twenty-one had been rated as highly aggressive between the ages of twelve and fourteen. In spite of the high level of continuity overall, West and Farrington (1977) showed that a minority of adult criminals were free of conduct disturbance during childhood, and that late onset was associated with low social status and criminality of the parents. Again, Magnusson et al. (1983) found that nine out of ten males who had committed violent offences by the age of twenty-six had been rated as highly aggressive between the ages of ten and thirteen. However, Magnusson (1987) later found from the same longitudinal study in Stockholm that the apparent link between aggressiveness in childhood and later criminality arose because there was a group of boys having a combination of characteristics including both aggressiveness and hyperactivity. Boys who were hyperactive and aggressive were likely to become persistent offenders, whereas those who were aggressive but not hyperactive had no more than an average chance of offending later.

THE EXTENT OF CHANGE OVER THE LIFE COURSE

AGE AND CRIME

Just describing the relationship between age and crime is more difficult than might at first appear, because differences between age groups reflect both developmental change and shifts between historical epochs. In more detail, it is possible to distinguish between three effects (Farrington 1986; Rutter 1995). *Age effects* refer to changes that occur with movement through the life cycle regardless of time period or geography. *Period effects* are changes over historic time that affect all individuals equally, regardless of age. *Cohort effects* are ones affecting all individuals sharing a common experience, typically an experience shared by everyone born at about the same time. For example, the risk of death was elevated for young adults who served in the armed forces during the Second World War. Again, Easterlin (1968) hypothesized that competition would be greater, and outcomes less favourable, for members of a 'baby boom' generation.

There are substantial conceptual, and hence mathematical, difficulties in trying to disentangle these three effects. Even if one variable (age or period) is held constant, the resulting trends confound two of the effects. Thus, cross-sectional data hold period constant: they show variations between different age groups in rates of offending at a particular time. This confounds ageing and cohort effects. Longitudinal data compare rates of offending at different stages of the life cycle for the same cohort of individuals born in a given year. This confounds ageing and period effects. For example, crime rates rose rapidly in the 1960s and 1970s across the developed world. This exaggerated the rise in offending among individuals passing from adolescence into adulthood at that time.

In broad terms, cross-sectional data from official records in the second half of the twentieth century show a very sharp peak in offending around the age of fourteen to eighteen both in England (based on cautions and convictions) and in the US (based on arrests). The rise up to this peak, starting from the age of criminal responsibility, is very steep, whereas the decline is steep up to the age of about twenty-four, then flattens into a very long and slow decline from the age of thirty-five continuing indefinitely into old age (Farrington 1986: 192–3). Hirschi and Gottfredson (1983) and Gottfredson and Hirschi (1990) argued that the age–crime curve was a 'constant' in criminology: that it was closely similar at different historical epochs, and among different population groups, such as males and females. Farrington (1986) showed that there had been some shifts in the peak age of offending in England, but his summary statistics suggested that historic change in the shape of the distribution had been rather small between 1938 and 1983. Again, there were detailed differences in the distribution for males and females, although the general shape was rather similar.

Analyses of data for a single age cohort show a broadly similar pattern. Thus Farrington (1990) showed that for his sample of 411 London males, mostly born in 1953, the peak age for convictions was seventeen; there was a sharp decline in convictions between the ages of eighteen and twenty-three, then a level, lower rate up to the age of thirty, when a further slow decline began. Findings for a national cohort of individuals born in 1953 were similar.

As set out earlier, the recent study by Soothill *et al.* (2002) divided histories of recorded convictions into 'strips'. Figure 20.4 shows for the 1953 birth cohort the rate of conviction per 1,000 population within each five-year strip. To facilitate the comparison between males and females, the results have been indexed on the last strip (age 36–40) which is always set to 100. The findings show that when local year-on-year variations are averaged out, there was a sharp rise to a peak between the ages of sixteen and twenty, followed by a steady decline in a straight line thereafter. This pattern applied to males and females, but the peak was less pronounced for females than for males.

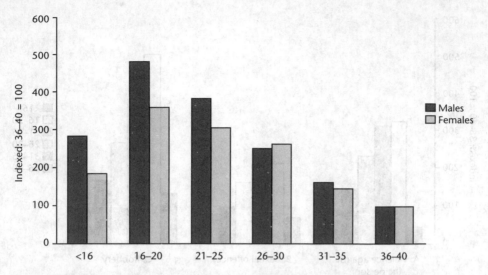

Fig. 20.4 Rate of conviction of 1953 birth cohort by age band: England & Wales

Source: Soothill *et al.* (2002), calculated from Table 3.1 and 3.2.
Convictions expressed per 1,000 population, then indexed.

Figure 20.5, which is confined to males, shows similar graphs for ten broad offence categories. These illustrate sharp differences in the age–crime curve according to the offence. It is striking that the rate of conviction for burglary before the age of sixteen was so high that there was little further rise in the 16–20 age strip, and a very sharp fall thereafter. Both motoring and drug convictions, by contrast, peaked between the ages of twenty-one and twenty-five. Convictions for fraud and forgery also peaked between the ages of twenty-one and twenty-five, but remained almost as high between the ages of twenty-six and thirty. Although the peak is never later than young adult-hood, these findings make it clear that different offences occupy different positions in the developmental cycle. As set out in an earlier section, these contrasts between age groups become stronger when offence clusters are considered, instead of broad offence categories.

PREVALENCE VERSUS FREQUENCY

The statistics shown in Figures 20.4 and 20.5 are based on aggregate crime rates: that is, they relate a count of the total number of convictions to a count of the population. These aggregate crime rates spread offences across the whole population, when in reality some people participate in offending whereas others do not; and among those who do participate, some commit more offences than others. To capture patterns of offending more accurately, it is useful to distinguish between prevalence (the propor-tion of the population who participate in offending) and frequency of offending among active offenders. The exact meaning of prevalence varies according to the period that is taken (one year, five years, lifetime). Frequency of offending among active offenders is often referred to as *lambda* λ to distinguish it from crimes per

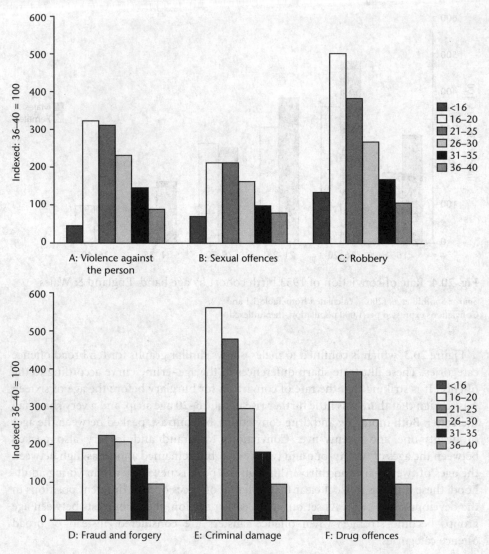

Fig. 20.5 Rate of conviction of 1953 birth cohort (males) by age band: England & Wales

Source: Soothill *et al.* (2002), calculated from Table 3.1.
Convictions expressed per 1,000 population, then indexed.

capita. Gottfredson and Hirschi (1986) argued that 'the true value of lambda would appear to be zero', or in other words that the distinction between prevalence and frequency was worthless. In a comprehensive rebuttal, Blumstein *et al.* (1988) reviewed the evidence for the proposition that ë tends to remain constant over that segment of the individual life course during which a person is involved in offending at all. The Gluecks published data from their longitudinal study in Boston from which it was possible to compute the number of arrests per person arrested at different stages of the life course. This remained constant over four periods (under the age of 14,

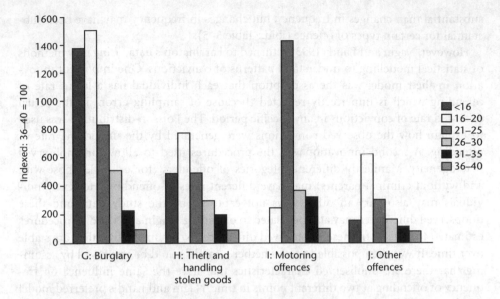

Fig. 20.5 (continued) Rate of conviction of 1953 birth cohort (males) by age band: England & Wales

14–19, 19–24, and 24–29). By contrast, the total number of arrests of cohort members fell from 1,272 between the ages of 14 and 19, to 390 between the ages of 24 and 29 (Blumstein *et al.* 1988: Table 1). The fall in the number of arrests after the peak age of offending was entirely due to a decline in prevalence, as there was no decline in frequency among active offenders.

This conclusion was confirmed by an elaborate analysis of arrest data by Blumstein *et al.* (1986, summarized in Blumstein *et al.* 1988). This identified four annual birth cohorts among a sample of over 5,000 adults arrested in Washington DC in 1973. Multiple cohorts were used in an attempt to overcome the confounding of ageing and period effects. Frequency of arrest was calculated for the periods when individuals were at large and not confined in prison. There was no consistent change in λ attributable to age. Farrington (1983) found for the London cohort that the peak in the number of convictions was primarily affected by prevalence rather than frequency. The limitation of these statistics is that convictions are rather infrequent, and far more infrequent than actual offences; and because of the way the criminal justice system works, it is rare for an individual to have more than two convictions in a single year. Thus convictions are a weak indicator of changes in the actual frequency of offending. Farrington (ibid.) tried to overcome the problem by dividing the period from the age of ten to the age of twenty-four into four phases of three or four years each. Changes in the number of convictions between these phases were mostly a consequence of changes in prevalence (ibid.: Table 3–4). Using self-reports rather than convictions for a similar analysis, it was necessary to make separate comparisons for each type of offence, and it appears that these comparisons ran into problems due to low sample sizes and high sampling errors (although significance tests were not reported). Discounting sampling error problems, it seems that changes in prevalence were more

substantial than changes in frequency, but changes in frequency may have been substantial for certain types of offence (ibid.: Table 3–5).

However, Nagin and Land (1993) returned to Farrington's data, using new methods
of statistical modelling to understand patterns of convictions. One important innovation in their model was the assumption that each individual has a latent rate of
offending which is imperfectly reflected (because of sampling error) in the actual
observed rate of convictions in any specific period. The Poisson distribution was used
to explain how the observed convictions were generated by the underlying rate of
offending. A second innovation was the procedures used to allow for unobserved
heterogeneity. Manifestly different categories of offenders (for example, those with
and without criminal parents) may have different rates of offending. However, individuals may also vary in other ways not captured by the study data, and these
unobserved differences may also be related to offending. Nagin and Land's procedures
estimated the effects of these unobserved differences by assuming that they are stable
over time. It was then possible to test whether a model could be improved by assuming that there are unobserved characteristics that have the same influence on frequency of offending at two different points in time. Nagin and Land's preferred model
divided offenders into three groups: high-rate chronic offenders, adolescence-limited
offenders, and low-rate chronic offenders. Between the ages of ten and thirty, the
estimated λ (frequency of convictions among offenders) rose and fell only gently
among high-rate and low-rate chronic offenders, but rose and fell sharply among
adolescence-limited offenders. These findings are consistent with the earlier conclusion that, overall, changes in prevalence are more influential than changes in frequency, but they suggest that the conclusion does not apply to all groups of offenders.
More specifically, they open the way to Moffitt's theory on the importance of the
distinction between adolescence-limited and lifecourse-persistent offending, which
will be discussed in a later section.

More detailed evidence is still needed from self-reports in longitudinal studies, but
the balance of existing evidence suggests that the age–crime curve largely reflects
changes in participation in offending rather than changes in frequency. On this
account, the sharp rise in crime in the teenage years occurs as new recruits are made
to offending. Two processes are involved as crime levels off and falls after the peak.
First, there is a decline in new recruits as the market begins to become saturated: an
increasing proportion of those with an inclination to crime have already started to
offend, so there is declining scope to make new recruits. Secondly, active offenders
start putting an end to their criminal careers: as the number of offenders in the
market and the length of their careers increase, there is increasing scope for desistance. In these ways, the age–crime curve is produced even though each active offender
tends to maintain a constant rate of offending as long as he or she remains in the
market. Nevertheless, the analysis by Nagin and Land (1993) suggests that this is not
the whole story, and that among the adolescence-limited group there are rises and
falls in frequency during the short period that they are active, which also influence the
overall shape of the age–crime curve.

SUMMING UP ON STABILITY AND CHANGE

There is a considerable degree of stability in individual differences in antisocial and criminal behaviour. The framework of analysis within which this statement is made is the theoretical assumption that different forms of antisocial and criminal behaviour are closely related, or, to use the medical analogy, part of the same syndrome. There is a great weight of evidence to support that theory. In other words, there is good evidence for stable dispositions to offend or not offend, which influence behaviour across all situations, and at all stages of the life cycle. Fairly good predictions can be made as early as the preschool years as to which individuals will have serious offending careers, with the major limitation that there are many false positives, because serious, persistent offending has a low base rate.

At the same time, involvement in offending changes dramatically within the individual life cycle, mostly because active offending tends to be confined to the teenage years and early adulthood. This is not necessarily paradoxical in conjunction with the stability of individual differences. It is possible that there are stable differences in a propensity to offend, but that this propensity is expressed most readily at particular stages of the life cycle. Another possibility, however, is that there are different population groups, with stability dominant in one group, and life cycle change in another. That possibility will be reviewed in a later section.

EXPLAINING STABILITY

To say that there are stable dispositions to offend or not offend may be accurate as a description, but it is certainly useless as an explanation. If we think of behaviour as flexible and adaptive, it is easy to explain why individuals persist in successful behaviour that brings about outcomes they desire. In the terms of social learning theory, they persist in this behaviour because it is reinforced. The problem with explaining stability in criminal offending is that this behaviour appears to be inflexible and maladaptive. This central problem is ignored by some of the classic criminological theories. For example, Merton (1938) argued that crime arises out of blocked opportunity, and that innovators turn to crime as a means of achieving conventional goals by unconventional means. One problem with such a theory is that most criminals are so obviously unsuccessful in conventional terms. Persistent offenders typically persist in crime in spite of low incomes, insecurity, fragile relationships, physical injury, spells of imprisonment, and so on. Although a few offenders, perhaps those who misuse powerful positions in legitimate organizations, successful fraudsters, or leading lights in criminal networks, may achieve wealth, status, and power, most persistent offenders who end up in prison seem to lead miserable lives. That is why, despite the misgivings of criminologists, it is not unreasonable to use the medical language of psychopathology to talk about persistent offending. It is also why an explanation of continuity in offending is required. The explanation needs to move beyond dispositions or propensities to show how maladaptive behaviour is generated and regenerated at different stages of the life course.

THE IDEA THAT OFFENDING CAUSES MORE OFFENDING

As Matsueda and Heimer (1997) have argued, theoretical traditions in criminology that can indeed be used to explain life course continuity in offending are symbolic interactionism and labelling theory. On Lemert's (1967) classic account, everyone performs deviant acts from time to time, but usually they escape formal censure. Even when other people notice and disapprove, the matter is often resolved by negotiation and accommodation on both sides. When a deviant act does lead to formal censure, the offender may choose to stop or conceal the deviant behaviour in future. However, a person stigmatized as deviant may respond by embracing the new role, and may reorganize the self around this new identity. From this point, the person will find new associates, and learn new offending skills and techniques of self-justification. Now each new criminal act will take the person further down a road that leads to more offending, and will make it more and more difficult to return. On this account, offending, in conjunction with the response to offending by other people and institutions, leads to more offending, and this interactive process embeds the individual in a criminal way of life.

If this theory is true, then offending should tend to increase after a first conviction. Farrington (1977) found that boys first convicted between the ages of fourteen and eighteen increased their self-reported delinquency compared with a matched group of unconvicted boys. The same result was obtained in studying the effect of first convictions between the ages of eighteen and twenty-one (Farrington *et al.* 1978). This seems to support labelling theory, but there are two important limitations of the test. First, the matched comparison design may not be good enough to control for all relevant differences between the convicted and unconvicted groups, which may differ on variables not covered by the matching, or not measured by the study at all. Secondly, Lemert's theory proposed a detailed set of mechanisms through which offending and stigmatization may lead to more offending. A more adequate test would examine these mechanisms: for example, it would show whether moral values and definitions of self changed among the convicted but not among the unconvicted boys.

These qualifications are important, because these early findings on the effects of labelling appear to conflict with later analyses of the same dataset. These later analyses do not focus on labelling theory in particular, but are concerned in a completely abstract way with whether offending causes more offending.[4] Nagin and Paternoster (1991) argued that stability in offending could arise from 'persistent heterogeneity'— fixed differences between individuals explained by either known or unknown variables. Alternatively, stability could arise from 'state dependence'—offending now causes further offending in the future, so the future state of the system is dependent on its present state. The innovation introduced by Nagin and Paternoster was a method of estimating the effects of differences between individuals with respect to

---

[4] Nagin and Paternoster (1991) analysed self-reported offending, whereas Nagin and Farrington (1992a, 1992b) analysed convictions. These analyses did not draw attention to the distinction between offending and convictions, and the authors seemed to assume that both were tapping the same underlying construct. There was no discussion of the possible effects of formal stigmatization by the criminal justice system as distinct from the effects of participating in offending itself.

unknown variables not measured in the study. In any longitudinal study with several waves, a statistical model was set up to predict offending at time T2 from a range of individual characteristics and offending at time T1. In such a model, persistent heterogeneity arising from unknown variables was estimated from the correlations between unexplained variations in delinquency at T1 and T2. The logic underlying this procedure is that if there are unknown differences between individuals that cause offending at both times, then unexplained variations in offending during the two periods should be correlated, as they flow from the same unknown stable personal characteristics. In the first analysis of this kind, Nagin and Paternoster (ibid.) used a three-year study of high school students. They found that after allowing for persistent unobserved heterogeneity, and for a large number of observed variables, prior involvement in delinquency was still significantly associated with later delinquency. This was consistent with state dependency.

Nagin and Farrington (1992a, 1992b) carried out further analyses on this and related themes, using West and Farrington's London cohort of 411 males. This dataset was more appropriate, especially because it covered a much longer span (age ten to thirty-two). Both papers used statistical modelling to predict convictions at each of eleven periods between the ages of ten and thirty one, using a small number of explanatory variables that earlier work had shown to be the most powerful ones. Models taking account of persistent unobserved heterogeneity were found to make significantly better predictions than simpler models. When the models included persistent unobserved heterogeneity along with the explanatory variables, prior convictions did not significantly help to predict future convictions. Contrary to the study by Nagin and Paternoster (1991), therefore, these studies were consistent with the theory that offending arises out of fixed dispositions rather than generating and regenerating itself in a dynamic process. Whereas the earlier analyses of the same dataset (Farrington 1977; Farrington et al. 1978) which focused on public labelling suggested that convictions led to more self-reported offending, these later analyses suggested that convictions did not lead to more convictions. The likely explanation of this conflict is that the later, more refined analyses were more successful in allowing for differences between individuals than the earlier matched comparison technique.

This conclusion is strengthened by further analyses in Nagin and Farrington's (1992b) second paper. Farrington (1990) had earlier reviewed evidence showing that early onset of delinquent behaviour is associated with more persistent future offending. Nagin and Farrington (1992b) found that, in a model allowing for persistent unobserved heterogeneity, age of onset no longer had a significant effect on later convictions. This is in harmony with the finding, already discussed, that in such a model prior convictions no longer predict future ones. On balance, therefore, there is little evidence from this analytic tradition to show that offending causes further offending. However, a different approach would be to examine the mechanisms or processes through which offending can lead to further offending. Analysis of that kind may produce different results.

CONSTITUTIONAL FACTORS

There is strong evidence for an important genetic influence on antisocial behaviour. In their review, Carey and Goldman (1997) listed seven twin studies and six adoption studies. Since then, several relevant papers have been published presenting further evidence from the Virginia Twin Study (Silberg *et al.* 1996; Eaves *et al.* 1997). These studies are consistent in showing that in terms of antisocial behaviour identical twins, are more similar than fraternal twins, and that adoptees are similar to their biological relatives. Many different approaches have been taken to defining and measuring crime and antisocial behaviour in these studies, but the finding remains essentially the same. The strong genetic influence is found, for example, for convictions, for self-reported delinquency, and for personality scales of hostility or aggression. The leading problem with the twin design is the assumption that the correlation between the environments of twins is the same whether they are identical or fraternal. This may be violated: for example, identical twins may have more friends in common than fraternal twins. Yet after discounting such factors, for example through studies of twins raised apart, the measured genetic influence remains important. The leading problem with the adoption design is that selective placement may mean that adoptees are placed with adoptive parents having similar attributes to their biological parents. However, a study by Miles and Carey (1997) was able to show that allowing for selective placement only slightly reduced the estimate of the heritability of antisocial behaviour.

All relevant studies show a strong environmental influence as well as a substantial genetic influence. In order to estimate the relative size of these effects, measurement error needs to be taken into account, and this has not often been done. However, from studies that used measures with known properties, Carey and Goldman (1997) estimated that 40 to 50 per cent of the valid variance in these measures must be environmental. The studies summarized above specifically relate to antisocial behaviour and crime, but of course the finding of important genetic and environmental influences on behaviour is much more general. According to Scarr (1992), behavioural genetics shows that for a wide variety of traits, including intelligence, specific cognitive abilities, personality, and psychopathology, heritability is between .40 and .70. However, the focus of current research is not on separate genetic and environmental effects, but on the interactions between genes and environment. Three broad types of interaction can be distinguished: passive, evocative, and active. First, parents' genes make the children's genes, but also help to construct the children's environment, which brings about a passive correlation between the children's genes and their environment. Secondly, people evoke responses from others that are correlated with their own characteristics: for example, a person who behaves aggressively (influenced by a genetic predisposition) evokes aggressive behaviour in others, so that his aggressive nature is correlated with an aggressive microsocial environment. Thirdly, people actively select environments that are correlated with their interests, tastes, and preferences, so that the genotype finds a suitable ecological niche.

The important genetic influence on antisocial behaviour may help to explain its continuity through the life course, although it needs to be demonstrated that the same genetic factors have an influence at difference stages of the life cycle. The appropriate, long-term, genetically sensitive studies of antisocial behaviour have not yet been carried out. At present, the evidence is stronger that gene-environment interaction can help to explain continuity. For example, although an important genetic influence on aggression in children and adolescents is well-established, there is also extensive evidence to show that aggressiveness in the child will tend to be reproduced and enhanced through a sequence of family processes, involving all three kinds of gene-environment interaction.

In themselves, the studies of heritability do not take us very far, because they do not show *what* is inherited that might influence antisocial behaviour. One kind of suggestion is a trait like aggressiveness, but in fact evidence for the heritability of violent behaviour (assault, robbery, rape, homicide) is much less consistent than for the heritability of general deviant and antisocial behaviour, although this could reflect the low power of the studies to detect heritability of violent behaviour because of its low base rate (Carey and Goldman 1997). A different suggestion is that the relevant inherited traits are cognitive. It has long been established that antisocial behaviour is associated with a deficit of about half a standard deviation (eight points) on IQ tests (Rutter *et al.* 1998). The relationship is not spurious, because it remains after controlling for a wide range of other variables, but in his review of the extensive evidence on this topic, Hinshaw (1992) concluded that the mechanisms underlying the association were not well understood. Children with behaviour problems may be less likely to acquire cognitive skills as a consequence; alternatively, poor cognitive skills may lead to behaviour problems, for example because a person finds it difficult to understand and therefore comply with requests. Caspi and Moffitt (1995) emphasized that antisocial behaviour is associated not just with low IQ, but with low verbal IQ in relation to performance IQ. They suggested, following J.Q. Wilson, that low verbal IQ might be related to a present-oriented cognitive style, because self-control involves giving verbal instructions to oneself.

Antisocial behaviour is also associated with a deficit in the brain's executive functions: attention, goal formation, planning, inhibition of unsuccessful behaviours (Caspi and Moffitt 1995). There is a considerable body of evidence to show that hyperactivity or attention deficit disorder, in particular, is related to the development of antisocial behaviour (Magnusson 1987; Moffitt 1990; Soussignan *et al.* 1992; Taylor *et al.* 1996). The evidence is not entirely clear-cut, however, since Fergusson *et al.* (1993) found in their analysis of a large New Zealand cohort (N = 1,265) that there were separate paths from conduct disorder in childhood to offending in adolescence, and from attention deficit disorder in childhood to academic problems later. Because conduct and attention deficit disorders in childhood were related to each other, it might appear that early attention deficit was related to later offending, but a more refined analysis suggested that this was not the case. However, children who show both problem behaviour and attention deficit disorder tend to have much worse outcomes than those who show only one of the two problems (Moffitt 1990). At the same time, there is ample evidence that a large component of hyperactivity is heritable (Levy *et al.* 1997; Sherman *et al.* 1997), and that it is related to a low level of responsiveness by the autonomic nervous system, associated with low adrenalin secretion (Magnusson 1987).

In summary, it is clear that there is an important heritable component in criminal behaviour, and likely that this contributes to its continuity over the life course, but the interesting questions for research are about how the genes and the social environment interact to produce stability at different points in the life cycle. Among the inherited characteristics that may be involved are IQ, and verbal IQ in particular, and a deficit in the brain's executive functions, especially attention deficit disorder.

FAMILY AND PARENTING

A very large number of studies have produced evidence on the relation between family functioning and crime or antisocial behaviour in children. In 1986, Loeber and Stouthamer-Loeber reported the results of a meta-analysis of the many American, British, and Scandinavian studies that had been published at that time; although more have been published since, the main conclusions have not changed. As a method of organizing the data, they distinguished four paradigms of family influences. The first paradigm is neglect, which has two aspects: a lack of supervision; and a lack of involvement. Second is the conflict paradigm, a pattern of escalating conflict involving inadequate, inappropriate, or inconsistent discipline, and rejection (of the child by the parents, or of the parents by the child). The third paradigm concerns deviant behaviours and values. Parents may be criminal themselves, or they may hold attitudes that condone lawbreaking. Fourth is the disruption paradigm. Neglect and conflict may arise because of marital discord, breakup of the marriage with the subsequent absence of one parent, and parental illness.

Variables belonging to all four paradigms were found to be consistently related to conduct problems and delinquency. These relationships tended to be strongest for the neglect paradigm, intermediate for the deviant behaviours and attitudes and the conflict paradigms, and lowest for the disruption paradigm. Broadly speaking, socialization variables (such as parents' involvement with children) were more strongly related than familial background variables (such as the absence of a parent). The familial variables were related to the full range of child problems captured by self-reports of conduct and delinquency and by arrest or court records. The amount of supervision was related (inversely) to the seriousness or amount of delinquency, and the association was stronger for official than for self-reported delinquency. The same was true for several other familial variables. The effect of socialization variables was stronger in longitudinal studies (which relate family process at an earlier time to adolescent behaviour at a later time) than in concurrent studies. This suggested that socialization variables have a sleeper effect which becomes stronger over time.

These findings strongly suggest that family functioning is often the start of a process that leads to continuity of antisocial behaviour, but they do not explain how that continuity is maintained, since the adolescent and young adult gradually moves out of the sphere of influence of the original family. Sampson and Laub (1993), in their reanalysis of the Gluecks' longitudinal data, were able to show that family factors had an important influence on whether the boy was delinquent in adolescence. More important, they also found that the family process variables were related to adult criminality, but that this relationship was entirely mediated by adolescent delinquency (such that if adolescent delinquency was included in a statistical model, family process variables no longer had a significant effect on adult criminality). On the basis of these findings, they suggested that much of the linkage between the childhood family experiences and adult criminality may be due to interactional and cumulative continuity through the responses of other people and institutions, and not to stable dispositions formed in childhood as a result of family experiences.

The most detailed and powerful work on family interactions has been carried out by Gerald Patterson and colleagues at the Oregon Social Learning Center (Patterson *et al.* 1992).[5] The great strength of this programme is that it used a range of methods to describe interactions between parents and children in some detail. Although it used questionnaires to parents and children that incorporate the usual generalizations and over-simplifications, that was combined with many hours of observation in the home, video-taped problem-solving tasks, and standardized tests. This could not provide a blow-by-blow account of specific interactions, but it gave a much more textured description of family interactions than most other research. The team gave close attention to the development of robust measures from several convergent sources. Because this detailed approach was adopted, it was possible to cover only 200 families, which limits the statistical power of the study, and means that only large effects will be measurable.

In theoretical terms, Patterson *et al.* adopted a social learning approach, which places the emphasis on operant conditioning. The central idea is that social exchanges within the family have a few simple structures, and that interactions of a particular kind are repeated a huge number of times if they are reinforced. The participants are not typically aware of what is happening in these interactions so, contrary to Bandura (1986, 1997), Patterson *et al.* argued that self-esteem and self-efficacy are epiphenomena, not causes of behaviour. They defined coercive behaviours as those that are both aversive (unpleasant for others) and contingent (turned on or off depending on the other person's response). Coercive behaviours are often functional for children, and the more often they work, the more often the child uses them. For example, mother refuses to give the child a sweet, the child begins to whine and goes on whining until mother gives in and lets the child have a sweet after all, at which point the whining stops. To quote a more detailed example, mother finds the boy watching television instead of studying, and scolds him. The boy responds that school is boring, and he has no homework anyway. Mother stops scolding, which reinforces the boy's coercive behaviour (coercive because it puts pressure on mother to let him watch television). This increases the likelihood that the boy will argue next time. Also he may escalate the intensity of the attack. Now that mother has stopped scolding him, the boy stops arguing, and behaves in a neutral or positive fashion. This reinforces the mother's withdrawal, and reduces the likelihood that she will do anything in the long term about his school work problems.

Patterson *et al.* argued that in certain families the children effectively receive 'coercion training' as sequences of this kind are frequently repeated. Socially skilled

---

[5] There has been a stream of publications from the team at the Oregon Social Learning Center, but the core findings are contained in the report cited here.

parents learn to halt the sequence at the second stage where the child behaves aversively, for example by ignoring it, or using humour. But Oregon research shows that coercive exchanges are far more common in some families than in others, and that this is strongly connected with the development of antisocial behaviour in the child. In broad terms, the difference between coercive and other families is that in the at-risk families parents and children have roughly equal power, whereas in other families, the balance of power is with the parents. In more detail, parenting in coercive families is characterized by ineffective discipline and monitoring. Effective discipline is defined by accurately tracking and classifying problem behaviours; ignoring trivial coercive events; and using effective back-up consequences when punishment is necessary. Instead, parents with problem children classify too much as deviant; are less likely to ignore coercive behaviour, and more likely to 'natter' or respond coercively (which stimulates further aversive behaviour); and they don't back up their requests, and fail to reward compliance. These ideas first received support from the results of the longitudinal study (Patterson et al. 1992). A later experimental test confirmed that changes in parent discipline practices were associated with reductions in child problem behaviours in the way that Patterson's model had predicted (Dishion et al. 1992).

Patterson et al.'s findings suggest that ineffective parenting contributes to the development of an antisocial trait in the child. It is possible to argue that this antisocial trait then becomes self-sustaining, because it sets in train further interaction sequences that again reinforce coercive behaviour in situations outside the family as well as within it. The key theoretical point is that individual sequences are reinforced, that is, individual coercive acts are functional for the child (and later the adolescent and adult), but the developing pattern of behaviour in the longer term is dysfunctional. The reinforcement mechanism works within a very short time scale on a myriad of short sequences of events. Ineffective parenting allows the development of a pattern of behaviour that is self-sustaining and prevents longer-term costs and benefits from having any impact. Consequently, this theory, and the associated empirical evidence, do constitute an attempt to answer the question why criminal and antisocial behaviour, viewed as maladaptive, should persist over the life course.

Analysis of the London and Pittsburgh cohorts (Farrington et al. 1996; Farrington et al. 2001) has shown close links in terms of convictions or arrests between parents and children, between siblings, and between other relatives, to the extent that 6 per cent of families in the London cohort accounted for half of the convictions. This is not informative about causal mechanisms, or about the importance of genetic influence, but it does show that in one way or another continuity in offending is brought about through the family.

PEERS AS A SOURCE OF CONTINUITY

Some accounts of continuity in antisocial behaviour give an important role to relationships with peers. For example, Patterson et al. (1989) proposed a general model in which ineffective parenting (influenced by the social and economic context) leads to childhood conduct disorders, conduct disorders lead to academic failure and peer rejection, those twin failures lead to depressed mood and involvement in a deviant peer group, and peer group influence leads to chronic delinquency. The plausibility of such a model depends on whether associating with delinquent peers is, in fact, a cause of delinquency. A very large number of studies have found a strong relationship between offending by an individual person and by his or her friends (Rutter *et al.* 1998: 193–99), and also that many criminal activities, particularly among adolescents, are carried out by groups rather than by individuals acting alone (Reiss 1988). However, people tend to associate with others like themselves (for a summary of the evidence on assortative patterns of association, see Caspi and Moffitt 1995). A young person who is already aggressive, antisocial, or delinquent may seek out other, similar companions, and may also be rejected by those who are more peaceable, pro-social, and conformist. From this it has been argued that the strong association between delinquency in a person and his or her friends does not arise from peer influence but merely indicates that 'birds of a feather flock together' (Glueck and Glueck 1950).

Most of psychology and sociology is based on the premise that individuals are influenced by others, hence the concepts of learning, modelling, and socialization. The Gluecks' suggestion that friends and associates do *not* have an influence is therefore implausible. What is more at issue is the strength of this influence. One way of estimating this is to study pairs of friends over time. In a classic study, Kandel (1978) did this with a sample of adolescent pairs of best friends (N = 957) who completed questionnaires at the beginning and end of a school year. Information was therefore obtained independently from each friend on a number of points, including frequency of current marijuana use and minor delinquency. The results showed, for example, that stable pairs of friends became more alike, for example in marijuana use, between time 1 and time 2; that stable pairs were much more alike at time 2 than former friends; and that stable pairs at time 2 were more alike than new friends at time 2. Kandel used a procedure to estimate from the whole pattern of results what proportion of the association between 'ego' and 'alter' was due to selection, and what proportion to influence, and concluded that each accounted for about half of the association. However, many different analytic procedures are possible, and Rowe *et al.* (1994) re-analysing the same data, concluded that 12 per cent of the association was influence, 71 per cent selection, and 16 per cent unexplained. Reviewing a number of other studies that used broadly comparable methods, Rowe *et al.* concluded that they 'support notions of both selection and influence, but selection tends to be the stronger of the two processes' (ibid.: 171). As the raw association between self and friends is typically the largest of all effects found in longitudinal studies, this cautious conclusion still implies that peer influence is likely to be very important.[6] In their review of a large number of studies, Thornberry and Krohn (1997) concluded that the effect of peer influence was generally found to be greater than that of parental supervision and discipline.

A major limitation of nearly all other studies is that information about the delinquency of both self and friends was obtained from the same respondent. The use of a

---

[6] For example, in the current Edinburgh study (Smith and McVie, in press) the correlation found between own and friend's delinquency at age 12 was .724. Furthermore, estimates of peer influence from Kandel's study relate to a period of only 9 months.

common source is likely to inflate the correlation, for example because people can justify their own bad behaviour by ascribing similar behaviour to their friends. Studies of the effects of gang membership (Thornberry *et al.* 1993; Esbensen and Huizinga 1993) have largely overcome this problem, because respondents were not asked about the behaviour of their friends, but rather a series of well-validated questions that establish their membership of a gang. Both of these studies made use of the fact that people tend to belong to gangs for fairly short periods. Both studies showed that prevalence and frequency of offending were considerably higher during years when individuals were gang members than in earlier or later years, although there was a tendency for offending to rise in the year prior to gang membership.

The Oregon study obtained information from peers as well as the study child, and also analysed videotaped exchanges between pairs of boys. Multivariate analyses estimated the effect of peer associations on antisocial behaviour in the context of a range of prior behaviours and characteristics (Dishion and Patterson 1997). These effects were shown to be substantial. Making use of the longitudinal design, the researchers showed that periods of association with delinquents coincided with periods of change in the extent or form of antisocial behaviour. The videotape study showed that pairs of delinquents show approval for each other's talk about delinquent behaviour. A study by Tremblay *et al.* (1995) also obtained information independently from dyads of friends at ages eleven, twelve, and thirteen years. The behaviour of self and best friend were associated at each year, but the best friend's behaviour did not explain the subject's own behaviour the following year. This study was therefore unusual in not showing any influence of best friends on delinquency. Rutter *et al.* (1998) suggested that this could be because of the exclusive focus on best friends, or because of the age group studied.

Many other studies have used multivariate methods to analyse longitudinal data about offending and friends' offending, as reported by the study respondents. These analyses have generally found a large effect of friends' delinquency after allowing for the effect of a wide range of other variables. This remains true when a range of analytic strategies are used, but the major limitation is that information about own and friend's delinquency comes from the same source (Keenan *et al.* 1995; Thornberry *et al.* 1994; Menard and Elliott 1994; for a review, see Thornberry and Krohn 1997).

Although the distinction between peer selection and peer influence is important, selection and influence work together to help maintain the stability of delinquent behaviour through the life course. Individuals who have already started to become delinquent for prior reasons tend to select delinquent friends, or to be selected by them, and these friends then tend to reinforce their prior delinquency. Overall the evidence suggests that this is one of the most important sources of interactional and cumulative continuity.

THE OFFENDING/VICTIMIZATION LOOP

A feature of crime patterns that has been emphasized too little is the tendency for victims and offenders to share some characteristics. For example, both victimization and offending rates are elevated among African Caribbeans in Britain (Smith 1997) and among African Americans in the US (Sampson and Lauritsen 1997) and this is explained by an elevated rate of black-on-black crime. Again, both the perpetrators and victims of assaults tend to be young males (Levi, in Chapter 24 of this volume). A recent report has shown that more than three-quarters of mobile phone robberies are by males on males, although offenders and victims in this case are not alike in terms of age or ethnic group (Harrington and Mayhew 2001).

For some years, there have been scattered indications of a link between victimization and offending, but this is now beginning to receive closer attention. In a current longitudinal study of a cohort of 4,300 young people in Edinburgh, McAra and Smith (forthcoming) found a raw correlation of .414 between crime victimization and a broad measure of self-reported delinquency across fifteen items at the age of thirteen. An ordinal regression model was fitted to predict delinquency at age thirteen from a wide range of contemporary information about the young people. In this model, crime victimization was the strongest predictor of self-reported delinquency: stronger, for example, than impulsivity, parental supervision, spare-time activities, or moral disengagement. Victimization at age twelve also powerfully predicted self-reported delinquency at age thirteen within the context of a multivariate model. Harassment by adults (staring, flashing, following, pressure to 'go along with them') was also strongly related to delinquency, although the size of the effect was about half of that for crime victimization. Experience of being bullied (by other young people) was not significantly related to delinquency.

Although this requires further investigation, McAra and Smith (forthcoming) argued that the link between victimization and offending is partly connected with social circles and situations. In the Edinburgh study, the link between own and friends' delinquency was found to be very strong (raw correlation of .72 at age thirteen), and particularly at that age it is likely that young people tend to commit offences on others in their own social circle, who strongly tend to be delinquent also. Intra-group offences may tend to occur in situations where the group is going out to offend against others, and the same situations (e.g., rowdy behaviour in the street) may provide opportunities for both crime and victimization. The same personal qualities (such as impulsivity and risk-taking) may lead to both offending and victimization, although the multivariate model controlled for known variables that might be common causes. Perhaps most interesting is the possibility that victimization may lead to offending later. Various mechanisms might be involved. One possibility is learning: through being the victim of crime, people may learn that offending is a useful method of achieving objectives, or may learn the techniques required, or acquire the psychological apparatus of self-justification and moral neutralization. Another possibility is trauma: for example, the damage caused by abuse in childhood may cause the victim to become an abuser. A third possibility is retribution: the victim decides to get back at his attacker by committing an offence himself. All of these mechanisms will tend to enhance the continuity of both offending and victimization in close interaction with each other.

IMPULSIVITY OR LACK OF SELF-CONTROL

It is well established that impulsivity, viewed as inability to plan ahead and to defer gratification (Mischel 1983) predicts antisocial behaviour and delinquency (Pulkkinen 1986; Krueger *et al.* 1994). There is evidence that impulsivity is specifically related to aggression and delinquency, and not to 'internalizing' disorders such as anxiety and depression (Krueger *et al.* 1996). In fact, impulsivity is probably the best example of a personality characteristic that can help to explain continuity in antisocial behaviour and delinquency over the life course. It can be argued that, for those who find it difficult to delay gratification, impulsive behaviour is self-reinforcing because by definition it involves achieving immediate gratification. Hence, a pattern of impulsive behaviour, once established, should tend to persist. Building in part on these findings, Gottfredson and Hirschi (1990) put forward a general theory of crime as a lack of self-control, but such a theory goes well beyond the psychological evidence, which shows that many other factors help to predict delinquency after lack of impulse control has been taken into account.

SOCIAL INFORMATION PROCESSING

There is evidence that antisocial persons have different conceptions of themselves and the world from other people, and different beliefs about what kind of behaviour is acceptable and effective in achieving results (for a summary of the evidence on social information processing and self-concepts, see Dodge and Schartz 1997). In particular, aggressive persons tend to believe that aggression will produce tangible rewards, that aggression is a legitimate way of solving problems, that it is a normal and acceptable means of guarding and improving one's reputation, and that victims don't suffer (Caspi and Moffitt 1995: 486). These psychological findings describe something similar to the 'techniques of neutralization' described by Sykes and Matza (1957) and the 'moral disengagement' described by Bandura (1991). These self-concepts and beliefs about the world tend to be self-sustaining, because of certain very general, conservative features of the system for processing social information, that tend to reinforce already existing personal theories of reality. *Primacy effects* give priority to the first impressions that people form of the world; *anchoring bias* makes people cling to their present theory and reluctant to adjust it or change to a new one (similar to Kuhn's (1962) account of the scientific paradigm); *confirmatory bias* means that people seek to confirm and not disprove the theory they have already formed. Dodge (1980; Crick and Dodge 1994; Dodge and Schartz 1997) has developed a more detailed theory of the steps through which social information is processed. In particular, he proposed that aggressive people tend to attribute hostile intent to neutral social signals, to put the worst interpretation on other people's behaviour, and to focus on aggressive cues while ignoring non-aggressive ones. This theory of attribution bias has generated a huge body of research, much of it using experimental methods, and most supporting its main propositions.

This evidence shows that individual differences in social information processing predict differences in antisocial behaviour. At the same time, biased processing is a powerful mechanism through which these differences can be maintained and accentuated. Individuals who wrongly attribute hostility to others will behave aggressively towards them, bringing about this time an actual aggressive response. This in turn will tend to confirm the personal theory of reality that supports the biased processing, and increase the likelihood of wrong attribution of hostility the next time round. Dodge *et al.* (1995) showed from a longitudinal study that similar patterns of social information processing are partly responsible for the linkage between early child abuse and later conduct problems.

SOCIAL STRUCTURE

As detailed elsewhere (Bottoms and Wiles, in Chapter 18 of this volume) there are substantial differences in both offending and victimization between neighbourhoods, and these differences have some relationship to social class composition, levels of deprivation, types of housing, features of the physical environment, and the functioning of communities. Differences in offending between individuals within neighbourhoods are much greater than differences between neighbourhoods, however, so that statistical models that include both neighbourhood and individual characteristics find that neighbourhood characteristics significantly predict offending, but the effects of individual characteristics are much larger (Sampson, Raudenbush, and Earls 1997). Nevertheless, this may under-estimate the importance of neighbourhood differences, because individuals tend to grow up in the same neighbourhood, or type of neighbourhood, and have no prospect during childhood and adolescence of escaping from it. Hence neighbourhood influence is a factor promoting developmental continuity in antisocial or prosocial behaviour. The matter is still more complex, since analysis of the Pittsburgh study has shown that neighbourhood influences are greatest for the *least* vulnerable individuals. Unfortunately, nearly all existing evidence on neighbourhood effects is cross-sectional, and in that type of analysis these effects seem fairly small. However, it is entirely possible that longitudinal studies will eventually show that the cumulative effects on the developmental process of growing up in a particular kind of neighbourhood are larger than shown by cross-sectional studies.

There is a considerable tradition of theorizing and research, starting from Bronfenbrenner (1979), that sees family process as being located within the social ecology of the neighbourhood and larger town or district (Lerner *et al.* 1995). For example, parental supervision will be more effective if other parents in the neighbourhood have concordant attitudes and expectations than if a particular family is trying to swim against the tide. Hence it is likely that the interaction between the individual family and the neighbourhood will have important consequences for child development.

In their reanalysis of the Gluecks' longitudinal study in Boston, Sampson and Laub (1993) showed that social structure factors, such as unemployment or low income, had little direct effect on the development of offending in young people. Instead, they had an important indirect effect, through influencing family functioning. Parents who have insecure employment, low incomes, or poor housing find it much more difficult as a result of these material difficulties to find the time and energy to supervise and control their children, to do things with them, and to discuss their projects and problems. The view that social and economic deprivation has a crucial effect through its influence on family functioning and parenting is supported by a large number of other studies. For example, Dodge *et al.* (1994) found in a longitudinal study of children from pre-school to age eight that socio-economic status at the pre-school stage predicted a range of antisocial behaviour problems, and was also related to a range of parenting practices and styles, including harsh discipline, lack of maternal warmth, and exposure to aggressive adult models. These aspects of parenting in turn predicted later antisocial behaviour in the children. Similarly, Larzelere and Patterson (1990) found in the Oregon Youth Study that the relationship between socio-economic group and delinquency in early adolescence was entirely mediated by parental management skills. Analysis of data from the Oregon Divorce Study extended this finding to single-parent families (Bank *et al.* 1993). Similar results were found for the outcomes of academic competence and socio-emotional adjustment in a study of two-parent African-American families (Brody *et al.* 1994). Two studies by Conger *et al.* (1992, 1993)—one of adolescent boys, the other of girls—developed a structural equation model which showed how family economic pressure because of unstable income, debts, and loss of income, caused depressed mood in both parents, leading to marital conflict, which in turn reduced quality of parenting, causing an increase in behaviour problems among the adolescent girl or boy. Finally, a long-term follow-up in the Newcastle Thousand Study showed that children who grew up in deprived rather than non-deprived families were more at risk of offending during later childhood and beyond (Kolvin *et al.* 1988).

MOFFITT'S THEORY OF OFFENDER TYPES

Moffitt (1993, 1997) has proposed that there are two distinct categories of antisocial behaviour and offending: life-course persistent; and adolescence-limited. According to this taxonomy, life-course persistent antisocial behaviour starts very early, and continues throughout life, but the forms in which it is expressed, the ways it is perceived and described, and the social reactions to it, change at different stages of the life cycle. By contrast, adolescence-limited antisocial behaviour increases rapidly in early adolescence, then declines rapidly after the peak age at around eighteen. The two groups of offenders are hard to distinguish in adolescence from their rates or patterns of offending, but they are entirely different in terms of their past and future offending patterns. The causes of offending are also entirely different in the two groups, and hence the characteristics of the two groups, for example in terms of personality, cognitive style, or family background, are again entirely different.

According to Moffitt's theory, the substantial stability of offending over the life course is entirely due to life-course persistent offenders, whereas the substantial change in rates of offending is entirely due to adolescence-limited offenders. When the two groups are superimposed, as in most statistics, the result is the observed age–crime curve.

One part of the theory is an interpretation of patterns of antisocial behaviour over the life course, whereas the other part is a set of causal explanations for stability in one group, and for change in the other. With regard to the life-course patterns, several studies have shown that early onset of antisocial behaviour predicts persistence over many years. In the London study, age on first conviction was one of the four best predictors of whether boys became 'chronic' offenders with six or more convictions (Blumstein *et al.* 1985). Tolan and Thomas (1995), in an analysis of a subsample of the American National Youth Survey (N = 984), found that early onset predicted frequency and persistence of offending, especially for serious offences. This shows that there is indeed a group who start behaving antisocially at an early age, go on for a long time, and probably also offend at a high frequency. However, the relationship between early onset and persistence is only a tendency, so among those who start early there are some who do not continue to behave antisocially in adolescence and adulthood. From analysis of their New Zealand cohort, Fergusson *et al.* (1996) found that those with severe childhood problem behaviours were sixteen times more likely to have problem behaviours in adolescence, confirming the general drift of Moffitt's ideas. On the other hand, whereas the great majority (92.1 per cent) of those without severe childhood problem behaviours remained without them, among those with severe childhood problem behaviours, 58.1 per cent continued in adolescence, but 41.9 per cent did not. This shows that on the basis of offending patterns alone, the distinction between life-course persistent and adolescence-limited offenders is not clear-cut until after the event. However, findings from the same study also showed that the group whose early problem behaviours remitted in adolescence differed from the group whose early problem behaviours continued in terms of a range of risk factors assessed at an early age. This shows that the life-course persistent group can be clearly defined only by early offending patterns in combination with personal and contextual characteristics.

It is no part of Moffitt's theory that early onset in itself causes offending to persist, or to be more frequent or serious. Hence, her theory is not disturbed by Nagin and Farrington's (1992b) finding that age of onset has no independent effect on later convictions, after allowing for the effects of other variables. (However, it is worth noting that Fergusson *et al.* (1996), using a different dataset and statistical approach, came to the opposite conclusion.) In the terminology introduced by Nagin and Paternoster (1991), life-course persistent offenders are precisely an example of persistent heterogeneity. The idea is *not* that early offending locks these young people into a cycle of re-offending. Instead, the theory is that early onset is an *indication* that these children have a range of *other* characteristics that will cause them to behave antisocially throughout their lives.

It can be concluded that the evidence on patterns of offending broadly fits with the first element of Moffitt's theory. The second element proposes that the causes of offending are different among the two groups. Among life-course persistent offenders, the causes of offending are those factors, discussed in the last section, that may be invoked to explain stability of offending over the life course. Among adolescence-limited offenders, the causes of offending are entirely different, and they must be factors that explain a short burst of offending during the period of transition from childhood to adulthood. What makes the theory tricky in its logical structure is that the two elements (causes and patterns) come together in the *definition* of the two groups. Thus, life-course persistent offenders are defined as those who *will* persist in offending throughout their lives, *and* whose offending has a distinctive set of causes, connected with constitutional factors, personality, cognitive processes, and family functioning. The main doubt about this framework is whether the distinction can be entirely clear-cut. Nagin *et al.* (1995), using the London data, defined four groups of offender: never convicted from age eight to thirty-two; ceased offending by early twenties (adolescence-limited); high-level chronic offenders; and low-level chronic offenders. A refined modelling procedure was used to test whether the four groups differed on a range of risk factors. This showed that adolescence-limited offenders did differ from both groups of chronic offenders, but they also differed from the never-convicted group. Although they had ceased being convicted, they continued (from their self-reports) to commit certain kinds of offence, such as thefts from employers, to use drugs, to drink heavily, and to get involved in fights. This suggests that the adolescence-limited offenders had a number of things in common with the life-course persistent offenders which neither group shared with the non-offenders. Again, the analysis of the New Zealand cohort by Fergusson *et al.* (1996) showed that the adolescence-limited group had scores on a range of risk factors that were intermediate between the non-offenders and the life-course persistent offenders. Given that the *definition* of the groups takes in scores on early risk factors, this does suggest that the distinction between them is somewhat blurred. Moffitt (1997) was explicit in arguing that life-course persistent offending is psychopathology, whereas adolescence-limited offending is normal. The New Zealand findings suggest, instead, that adolescence-limited offenders are mildly pathological where life-course persistent offenders are severely pathological on the same dimensions.

Despite some blurring at the edges, Moffitt's theory provides a useful framework for analysing offending over the life course. It fits many of the facts. Moffitt has shown, for example, that a small group consisting of 5 per cent of boys in the Dunedin cohort who were consistently rated antisocial across seven biennial assessments, accounted for 68 per cent of the stability in antisocial behaviour within the whole cohort (Moffitt 1997: 14). DiLalla and Gottesman (1989) found that childhood aggression and adult crime are heritable, whereas juvenile delinquency is much less so, which fits with the theory that adolescence-limited offending flows from the social and psychological conditions of adolescence and not from constitutional factors. It has been argued that the large secular increase in crime from 1950 to 1980 was associated with changes in youth transitions which raised the level of adolescence-limited offending (Rutter and Smith 1995; Moffitt 1997). Consistently with that theory, the age peak became more extreme in a number of crimes typical of adolescents over this period (Moffitt 1997: 38).

EXPLAINING CHANGE

Adopting Moffitt's framework, we are left with the problem of explaining why offending rises to a peak at age eighteen then falls among a large group of young people who for the most part do not share the disadvantages and problems of life-course persistent offenders. One theoretical tradition explains this by changes over the life course in the strength of social bonds (Sampson and Laub 1990, 1993). From the perspective of social control theory, reciprocal relationships lock people into conventional society, and restrain them from committing deviant acts. Children have very strong bonds with the adults who are responsible for them, and are utterly dependent on them and more or less effectively controlled by them. Conventional adults have bonds to a spouse, children, employer, friends. Adolescence is the period when young people loosen the bonds with family and school, and before the time when they have formed a new set of adult relationships and acquired new commitments. People are therefore less constrained during the period of adolescence than at any other time of their lives, and hence more likely to be involved in crime and deviance.

The clearest support for explanations in terms of social control theory come from longitudinal studies that examine changes in social bonds in relation to patterns of offending. For example, Quinton *et al.* (1993) found that offenders who formed a supportive cohabiting relationship in early adulthood were more likely to desist from crime than those who did not. Sampson and Laub (1990, 1993) found that commitment to steady employment was strongly related to desistance from offending. A much broader argument for social control theory draws attention to secular change in the nature of adolescence (Rutter and Smith 1995). At the beginning of the twentieth century, young people normally left school at about age twelve, to work often in mixed-age groups. Although sexual maturity, financial independence, and forming an independent household followed after several years, young people were locked into reciprocal relationships with adults from a fairly early age, and spent much of their time with adults. In the second half of the twentieth century, as full-time education lengthened, so the time when young people started work was postponed for longer and longer. This created a lengthy period during which young people had an ambiguous status, which became thought of as a separate phase of the life cycle for the first time in history. During this adolescent phase, teenagers spent most of their time with other teenagers, and had weak ties to adults or adult institutions in conventional society. It can be argued, therefore, that the rise in crime in the period 1950–80 coincided with a weakening of conventional social bonds among young people.

The weakness of social control theory, as Caspi and Moffitt (1995) have pointed out, is that it does not explain why adolescents, when free from constraints, engage in offending rather than some other activity. 'Why don't unsupervised teens mow lawns for the elderly? Why don't youth weakly attached to their parents get together and do more algebra homework?' (ibid.: 500). An alternative explanation for adolescent offending is that it arises out of the autonomy wars associated with adolescent transitions. As developed by Caspi and Moffitt (ibid.) and Moffitt (1997), the argument is that maturity is a scarce resource for teenagers. Life-course persistent offenders appear to be mature, in the sense that they are relatively free from constraints, and therefore apparently autonomous; and many offending behaviours and associated activities, such as smoking, drinking, using drugs, staying out late, going to clubs and pubs, having sex, becoming pregnant, are obvious signs of maturity. For a time, therefore, adolescents mimic life-course persistent offenders as a method of gaining access to the scarce resource of maturity, and recognition of mature status. The whole point of these behaviours is that they are gestures of independence. When young people actually start to become more independent, they motive for engaging in them is removed, and they stop.

The most telling evidence in support of this idea shows that life-course persistent offenders tend to be isolated in childhood and adulthood, but have more contacts with peers during adolescence. This shows that a much broader spectrum of people will be influenced by serious offenders during adolescence than at any other stage of the life cycle. As set out in an earlier section, there is ample evidence that peers have a strong influence on offending. Also, relationships with others of the same age are more important and dominant in adolescence than at other stages, especially in the historical period since adolescence has become a clearly delimited status and stage in life. More specific evidence is needed, however, to demonstrate that peer influence is connected with change in offending in the adolescent years. This is provided by two longitudinal studies, which showed that individuals who started offending early continued to offend into adolescence with or without peer influence, whereas peer influence was decisive in explaining why certain individuals started offending in adolescence (Caspi *et al.* 1993; Simons *et al.* 1994).

CONCLUSION

The importance of the life course perspective in tackling the central issues in criminology can best be demonstrated by three examples of problems that remain to be solved. First, the large difference in rates of offending between males and females cannot be explained from what is currently known (but see Heidensohn, in Chapter 15 of this volume). Various longitudinal studies have now started to tackle the problem (Moffitt *et al.* 2001; McAra and Smith, forthcoming). The Edinburgh study findings at age twelve and thirteen suggested that the explanatory models that focus on teenage experiences apply to males and females in much the same way, but a substantial difference in offending remains after controlling for these variables. This fits with the findings of Moffit *et al.* (2001) from their literature review and analysis of the Dunedin Study. They concluded that the gender gap in offending arose because males are 'more likely to experience neuro-cognitive deficits, undercontrolled temperamental features, weak constraint (poor impulse control) and hyperactivity' and that these risks accounted for most of the sex difference in offending (ibid.: 7). There was little difference between males and females in the impact of adolescent developmental processes on offending, as also shown by the early Edinburgh study findings. Thus, in the terms of Moffitt's taxonomy, there was a substantial difference between the sexes in life-course persistent offending, but little difference in adolescence-limited offending. Substantial further developmental research is needed to refine and check these findings.

Secondly, there is limited understanding of the interactions between individual life histories and the communities and institutions in which they are located. Current analyses appear to show only small effects of neighbourhood characteristics as opposed to individual characteristics on crime rates. That seems to be in tension with what is known about rapid secular change in crime rates, and large differences between countries, which can only arise from social institutions and social structure. Also, analyses of the Pittsburgh study (Wikström 1998) suggest that neighbourhood influences may be quite different according to the problems ('risk factors') experienced by the individual adolescent.

Thirdly, it has proved extremely difficult to assess the effects of the criminal justice system on rates of crime. The most popular methods have involved building statistical models, on the pattern of those used by economists, in order to show how changes in the activity of the criminal justice system (arrests, convictions, sentences of imprisonment) are mathematically related to changes in the level of crime, after allowing for the effects of other variables. This approach has often failed to produce clear results. In order to make progress with the problem it will be important to describe the actual mechanisms that may link crime and punishment: for example, deterrence depends on potential offenders becoming aware of the risks they are taking. Developmental research is needed to show how direct and indirect knowledge of the activities of the criminal justice system influences offenders' decision making over the life course.

Selected further reading

For the general review of the topics covered in this chapter, see M.L. Benson, *Crime and the Life Course* (Los Angeles: Roxburg, 2002).

The best source for contemporary theoretical approaches to crime and the life course is T.P. Thornberry (ed.), *Advances in Criminological Theory, vol. 7: Developmental Theories of Crime and Delinquency*, 11–54 (New Brunswick and London: Transaction, 1977). This is a series of essays, each one covering one of the major theoretical traditions.

For a treatment of patterns of convictions over the life course (up to age forty), see K. Soothill, B. Francis, and R. Fligelsone, *Patterns of Offending Behaviour: A New Approach*, Home Office Research Findings 171. (London: Home Office, 2002). Full report at www.homeoffice.gov.uk/rds.

For a comprehensive review of the evidence on the effect of family factors on delinquency, see R. Loeber and M. Stouthamer-Loeber, 'Family Factors as correlates and predictors of juvenile conduct problems and delinquency', in M. Tonry and N. Morris (eds), *Crime and Justice: An Annual Review of Research*, vol. 7: 29–149 (Chicago: University of Chicago Press, 1986). Although this is not up-to-date, the main conclusions have not been substantially altered by more recent research.

For a succinct review of the evidence on genetic influences on antisocial behaviour, see G. Carey and D. Goldman, 'The Genetics of Antisocial Behaviour', in D. M. Stoff (ed.), *Handbook of Antisocial Behaviour*, 243–54 (New York: Wiley, 1997). For a more detailed treatment, see D.C. Rowe, *Biology and Crime* (Los Angeles: Roxburg, 2002). For a review of the influence of factors rooted in the central nervous system (whether or not inherited), see T.E. Moffitt, 'The Neuropsychology of Juvenile Delinquency: A Critical Review', in M. Tonry and N. Morris (eds), *Crime and Justice: An Annual Review of Research*, vol. 12, 99–169 (Chicago: University of Chicago Press, 1990).

For a conspectus of the voluminous output from the Cambridge Study, see D.P. Farrington, 'Key findings from the first 40 Years of the Cambridge Study in Delinquent Development', in T.P. Thornberry and M.D. Krohn (eds), *Taking Stock of Delinquency: An Overview of Findings from Contemporary Longitudinal Studies* (New York: Kluwer/Plenum, 2002).

Some of the most important findings from longitudinal research on crime in recent years are from the re-analysis of the earlier study in Boston by Sheldon and Eleanor Glueck. This work is brought together in an accessible way, and related to a developed theoretical framework, in R.J. Sampson and J.H. Laub, *Crime in the Making: Pathways and Turning Points through Life* (Cambridge, Mass: Harvard University Press, 1993).

Readers who are interested in analytical and empirical work on gender issues and offending should consult T.E. Moffitt, A. Caspi, M. Rutter, and P.A. Silva, *Sex Differences in Antisocial Behaviour*, (Cambridge: Cambridge University Press, 2001).

References

BANDURA, A. (1986), *Social Foundations of Thought and Action: A Social Cognitive Theory.* Englewood Cliffs, NJ: Prentice-Hall.

—— (1991), 'Social Cognitive Theory of Moral Thought and Action', in W.M. Kurtines and J.L. Gewirtz (eds), *Handbook of Moral Behaviour and Development, Vol I: Theory*, 45–103, Hillsdale, NJ: Lawrence Erlbaum.

—— (1997), *Self-Efficacy: The Exercise of Control* New York: W.H. Freeman and Co.

BANK, L. FORGATCH, M.S., PATTERSON, G.R., and FETROW, R.A. (1993), 'Parenting Practices of Single Mothers: Mediators of Negative Contextual Factors', *Journal of Marriage and the Family*, 55: 371–84.

BARCLAY, G.C., and TAVARES, C. (1999), *Digest 4*, London: Home Office Research and Statistics Directorate.

BLUMENSTEIN, A., COHEN, J., and FARRINGTON, D.P. (1988), 'Criminal Career Research: Its Value for Criminology', *Criminology*, 26: 1–35.

——, FARRINGTON, D.P., and MOITRA, S. (1985), 'Delinquency Careers: Innocents, Desisters, and Persisters', in M. Tonry and N. Morris (eds), *Crime and Justice: An Annual Review of Research*, vol. 6, 187–219, Chicago Ill.: University of Chicago Press.

——, COHEN, J., ROTH, J., and VISHER, C.A. (eds) (1986), *Criminal Careers and 'Career Criminals'*,

Vol 1. Report of the Panel on Research on Criminal Careers, Washington DC: National Research Council.

BOWLING, B. (1990), 'Conceptual and Methodological Problems in Measuring "Race" Differences in Delinquency: A Reply to Marianne Junger', *British Journal of Criminology*, 30: 483–92.

BRENNAN, P., MEDNICK, S., and JOHN, R. (1989), 'Specialization in Violence: Evidence of a Criminal Subgroup', *Criminology*, 27, 3: 437–53.

BRODY, G.H., STONEMAN, Z., FLOR, D., MCCRARY, C., HASTINGS, L., and CONYERS, O. (1994), 'Financial Resources, Parent Psychological Functioning, Parent Co-Caregiving, and Early Adolescent Competence in Rural Two-Parent African-American Families', *Child Development*, 65: 590–605.

BRONFENBRENNER, U. (1979), *The Ecology of Human Development: Experiments by Nature and Design*, Cambridge Mass.: Harvard University Press.

CAREY, G., and GOLDMAN, D. (1997), 'The Genetics of Antisocial Behaviour', in D.M. Stoff (ed.), *Handbook of Antisocial Behaviour*, 243–54, New York: Wiley.

CASPI, A., and MOFFITT, T. (1995), 'The Continuity of Maladaptive Behaviour: From Description to Understanding in the Study of Antisocial Behaviour', in D. Cicchetti and D. Cohen (eds),

Developmental Psychopathology, 2: 472–511, New York: Wiley.

——, LYNAM, D., MOFFITT, T.E., and SILVA, P.A. (1993), 'Unravelling Girls' Delinquency: Biological, Dispositional, and Contextual Contributions to Adolescent Misbehaviour', *Developmental Psychology*, 29: 19–30.

CERNKOVICH, S.A., GIORDANO, P.C., and PUGH, M.D. (1985), 'Chronic Offenders: The Missing Cases in Self-Report Delinquency Research', *The Journal of Criminal Law and Criminology*, 76, 3: 705–32.

CONGER, R.D., CONGER, K.J., ELDER, G.H., LORENZ, F.O., SIMONS, R.L., and WHITBECK, L.B. (1992), 'A Family Process Model of Economic Hardship and Adjustment of Early Adolescent Boys', *Child Development*, 63: 526–41.

——, ——, ——, ——, and —— (1993), 'Family Economic Stress and Adjustment of Early Adolescent Girls', *Developmental Psychology*, 29, 2: 206–19.

CRICK, N.R., and DODGE, K.A. (1994), 'A Review and Reformulation of Social Information-Processing Mechanisms in Children's Social Adjustment', *Psychological Bulletin* 115, 1: 74–101.

DEMBO, R., WILLIAMS, L., WOTHKE, W., SCHMEIDLER, J., GETREU, A., BERRY, E., and WISH, E. (1992), 'The Generality of Deviance: Replication of a Structural Model Among High-Risk Offenders', *Journal of Research in Crime and Delinquency*, 29, 2: 200–16.

DILALLA, L.F., and GOTTESMAN, I.I. (1989), 'Heterogeneity of Causes for Delinquency and Criminality: Lifespan Perspectives', *Development and Psychopathology*, 1: 339–49.

DISHION, T.J., and PATTERSON, G.R. (1997), 'The Timing and Severity of Antisocial Behaviour: Three Hypotheses within an Ecological Framework', in D. Stoff, J. Breiling, and J. Maser (eds), *Handbook of Antisocial Behaviour*, 205–17, New York: Wiley.

——, ——, and KAVANAGH, K.A. (1992), 'An Experimental Test of the Coercion Model: Linking Theory, Measurement, and Intervention', in J. McCord and R. Tremblay (eds), *Preventing Antisocial Behaviour*, 253–82, New York and London: Guilford Press.

DODGE, K.A. (1980), 'Social Cognition and Children's Aggressive Behaviour' *Child Development*, 51: 162–70.

——, PETTIT, G.S., and BATES, J.E. (1994), 'Socialization Mediators of the Relation between Socioeconomic Status and Child Conduct Problems', *Child Development*, 65: 649–65.

——, ——, ——, and VALENTE, E. (1995), 'Social Information-Processing Patterns Partially Mediate the Effect of Early Physical Abuse on Later Conduct Problems', *Journal of Abnormal Psychology*, 104, 4: 632–43.

—— and SCHARTZ, D. (1997), 'Social Information Processing Mechanisms in Aggressive Behaviour', in D.M. Stoff (ed.), *Handbook of Antisocial Behaviour*, 171–80, New York: Wiley.

DONOVAN, J.E., and JESSOR, R. (1985), 'Structure of Problem Behaviour in Adolescence and Young Adulthood', *Journal of Consulting and Clinical Psychology*, 53, 6: 890–904.

DUNFORD, F.W., and ELLIOTT, D.S. (1984), 'Identifying Career Offenders Using Self-Reported Data', *Journal of Research in Crime and Delinquency*, 21: 57–86.

EASTERLIN, R.A. (1968), *Population, Labor Force and Long Swings in Economic Growth: The American Experience*, New York: National Bureau of Economic Research.

EAVES, L.J., SILBERG, MEYER, J., MAES, H., SIMONOFF, E., PICKLES, A., RUTTER, M., TRUETT, T.R., and HEWITT, J.K. (1997), 'Genetics and Developmental Psychopathology: 2. The Main Effects of Gene and Environment on Behavioural Problems in the Virginia Twin Study of Adolescent Development', *Journal of Child Psychology and Psychiatry*, 38: 965–80.

ELLIOTT, D.S. (1994), 'Serious Violent Offenders: Onset, Developmental Course, and Termination—The American Society of Criminology 1993 Presidential Address', *Criminology*, 32, 1: 1–21.

——, AGETON, S.S., HUIZINGA, D., KNOWLES, B.A., and CANTER, R.J. (1983), *The Prevalence and Incidence of Delinquent Behavior: 1976–1980*, National Youth Survey Report No. 26, Boulder, Col.: Behavioral Research Institute.

ESBENSEN, F.-A., and HUIZINGA, D. (1993), 'Gangs, Drugs, and Delinquency in a Survey of Urban Youth', *Criminology*, 31, 4: 565–87.

FARRINGTON, D.P. (1973), 'Self-Reports of Deviant Behavior: Predictive and Stable?', *The Journal of Criminal Law and Criminology*, 64: 99–110.

—— (1977), 'The Effects of Public Labelling', *British Journal of Criminology*, 17: 122–35.

—— (1978), 'The Family Backgrounds of Aggressive Youths', in L.A. Hersove, M. Berger, and D. Shaffer (eds), *Aggression and Antisocial Behaviour in Childhood and Adolescence*, 73–93, Oxford: Pergamon.

—— (1979), 'Longitudinal Research on Crime and Delinquency', in N. Morris and M. Tonry (eds), *Crime and Justice: An Annual Review of Research*, Vol. 1, 289–348, Chicago, Ill.: University of Chicago Press.

—— (1983), 'Offending from 10 to 25 Years of Age', in K.T. Van Dusen and S.A. Mednick (eds), *Prospective Studies of Crime and Delinquency*, Boston: Kluwer-Nijhoff.

—— (1986), 'Age and Crime', in M. Tonry and N. Morris (eds), *Crime and Justice: An Annual Review of Research, Vol. 7*, 189–250, Chicago, Ill.: University of Chicago Press.

—— (1990), 'Age, Period, Cohort and Offending', in D.M. Gottfredson and R.V. Clarke (eds), *Policy and Theory in Criminal Justice*, 51–75, Aldershot: Avebury.

—— (1995), 'The Twelfth Jack Tizard Memorial Lecture: The Development of Offending and Antisocial Behaviour from Childhood: Key Findings from the Cambridge Study in Delinquent Development', *Journal of Child Psychology and Psychiatry*, 36: 929–64.

——, BARNES, G.C., and LAMBERT, S. (1996), 'The Concentration of Offending in Families', *Legal and Criminological Psychology*, 1: 47–63.

——, JOLLIFFE, D., LOEBER, R., STOUTHAMER-LOEBER, M., and KALB, L.M. (2001), 'The Concentration of Offenders in Families, and Family Criminality in the Prediction of Boys' Delinquency', *Journal of Adolescence*, 24: 579–96.

——, LOEBER, R., ELLIOTT, D.S. HAWKINS, J.D., KANDEL, D.B., KLEIN, M.W., McCORD, J., ROWE, D.C., and TREMBLAY, R.E. (1990), 'Advancing Knowledge About Delinquency and Crime', in B.B. Lahey and A.E. Kazdin (eds), *Advances in Clinical Child Psychology*, vol. 13, New York: Plenum.

——, OSBORN, S.G., and WEST, D.J. (1978), 'The Persistence of Labelling Effects', *British Journal of Criminology*, 18: 277–84.

——, SNYDER, H.N., and FINNEGAN, T.A. (1988), 'Specialization in Juvenile Court Careers', *Criminology*, 26, 3: 461–87.

—— and WEST, D.J. (1990), 'The Cambridge Study in Delinquent Development: A Long-term follow-up of 411 London Males', in H.-J. Kerner and G. Kaiser (eds), *Criminality: Personality, Behaviour, Life History*, 115–38, Berlin: Springer-Verlag.

FERGUSSON, D.M., HORWOOD, L.J., and LYNSKEY, M.T. (1993), 'The Effects of Conduct Disorder and Attention Deficit in Middle Childhood on Offending and Scholastic Ability at Age 13', *Jour-*

nal of Child Psychology and Psychiatry, 34, 6: 899–916.

——, LYNSKEY, M.T., and HORWOOD, L.J. (1996), 'Factors Associated with Continuity and Changes in Disruptive Behaviour Patterns', *Journal of Abnormal Child Psychology*, 24: 533–53.

GLUECK, S. and GLUECK, E. (1950), *Unravelling Juvenile Delinquency*, New York: The Commonwealth Fund.

GOTTFREDSON, M., and HIRSCHI, T. (1986), 'The True Value of Lambda Would Appear to be Zero: An Essay on Career Criminals, Criminal Careers, Selective Incapacitation, Cohort Studies, and Related Topics', *Criminology*, 24: 213–33.

—— and —— (1990), *A General Theory of Crime*. Stanford, CA: Stanford University Press.

HARRINGTON, V., and MAYHEW, P. (2001), *Mobile Phone Theft*, Home Office Research Study No. 235, London: Home Office Research, Development and Statistics Directorate.

HINSHAW, S.P. (1992), 'Externalizing Behaviour Problems and Academic Underachievement in Childhood and Adolescence: Causal Relationships and Underlying Mechanisms', *Psychological Bulletin*, 111, 1: 127–55.

HIRSCHI, T., and GOTTFREDSON, M. (1983), 'Age and the Explanation of Crime', *American Journal of Sociology*, 89: 552–84.

—— and —— (1994), 'The Generality of Deviance', in T. Hirschi and M.R. Gottfredson (eds), *The Generality of Deviance*, 1–22, New Brunswick and London: Transaction Publishers.

HUESMANN, L.R., ERON, L.D., LEFKOVITZ, M.M., and WALDER, L.D. (1984), 'Stability of Aggression over Time and Generations', *Developmental Psychology*, 20: 1120–34.

HUIZINGA, D. (1991), 'Assessing Violent Behavior with Self-Reports', in J.S. Milner (ed.), *Neuropsychology of Aggression*, 47–66, Boston: Kluwer.

—— and ELLIOTT, D.S. (1986), 'Reassessing the Reliability and Validity of Self-report Delinquency Measures', *Journal of Quantitative Criminology*, 2, 4: 293–327.

JUNGER, M. (1989), 'Discrepancies between police and self-report data for Dutch racial minorities', *British Journal of Criminology*, 29: 273–84.

KANDEL, D.B. (1978), 'Homophily, Selection, and Socialization in Adolescent Friendships', *American Journal of Sociology*, 84, 2: 427–36.

KEENAN, K., LOEBER, R., ZHANG, Q., STOUTHAMER-LOEBER, M., and VAN KAMMEN, W.B. (1995), 'The Influence of Deviant Peers on the Development of Boys' Disruptive and Delinquent

Behaviour: A Temporal Analysis', *Development and Psychopathology*, 7: 715–26.

KLEIN, M.W. (1984), 'Offence Specialization and Versatility Among Juveniles', *British Journal of Criminology*, 24, 2: 185–94.

KOLVIN, I., MILLER, F.J.W., FLEETING, M., and KOLVIN, P.A. (1988), 'Social and Parenting Factors Affecting Criminal-Offence Rates: Findings from the Newcastle Thousand Family Study (1947–1980)', *British Journal of Psychiatry*, 152: 80–90.

KRUEGER, R.F., CASPI, A., MOFFITT, T., and WHITE, J. (1996), 'Delay of Gratification, Psychopathology, and Personality: Is Low Self-Control Specific to Externalizing Problems?', *Journal of Personality*, 64: 107–29.

——, SCHMUTTE, P.S., CASPI, A., MOFFITT, T., CAMPBELL, K., and SILVA, P.A. (1994), 'Personality Traits Are Linked to Crime Among Men and Women: Evidence from a Birth Cohort', *Journal of Abnormal Psychology*, 103, 2: 328–38.

KUHN, T.F. (1962), *The Structure of Scientific Revolutions*, Chicago, Ill.: University of Chicago Press.

LARZELERE, R., and PATTERSON, G.R. (1990), 'Parental Management: Mediator of the Effect of Socioeconomic Status on Early Delinquency', *Criminology* 28, 2: 301–24.

LEBLANC, M., and GIRARD, S. (1997), 'The Generality of Deviance: Replication Over Two Decades With a Canadian Sample of Adjudicated Boys', *Canadian Journal of Criminology*: 171–83.

LEMERT, E. (1967), *Human Deviance, Social Problems and Social Control*, Englewood Cliffs, NJ: Prentice-Hall.

LERNER, R., CASTELLINO, D.R., PATTERSON, A.T., VILLARRUEL, F.A., and McKINNEY, M.H. (1995), 'Developmental Contextual Perspective on Parenting', in M.H. Bornstein, *Handbook of Parenting*, vol. 2, 285–309, Mahwah, NJ: Lawrence Erlbaum.

LEVY, F., HAY, D.A., McSTEPHEN, M., WOOD, C., and WALDMAN, I. (1997), 'Attention-Deficit Hyperactivity Disorder: A Category or a Continuum? Genetic Analysis of a Large-Scale Twin Study', *Journal of the American Academy of Child and Adolescent Psychiatry*, 36, 6: 737–44.

LOEBER, R., and DISHION, T.J. (1983), 'Early Predictors of Male Adolescent Delinquency: A Review', *Psychological Bulletin*, 94: 68–99.

——, FARRINGTON, D.P., STOUTHAMER-LOEBER, M., MOFFITT, T., and CASPI, A. (1998), 'The Development of Male Offending: Key Findings from the First Decade of the Pittsburgh Youth Study', *Studies on Crime and Crime Prevention*, 7, 2: 141–71.

—— and STOUTHAMER-LOEBER, M. (1986), 'Family Factors as Correlates and Predictors of Juvenile Conduct Problems and Delinquency', in M. Tonry and N. Morris (eds), *Crime and Justice: An Annual Review of Research*, vol. 7, 29–149, Chicago, Ill.: University of Chicago Press.

MAGNUSSON, D. (1987), 'Adult Delinquency in the Light of Conduct and Physiology at an Early Age': A Longitudinal Study', in D. Magnusson and A. Öhman (eds), *Psychopathology*, 221–34, Orlando, Fl.: Academic Press.

——, STATTIN, H., and DUNER, A. (1983), 'Aggression and Criminality in a Longitudinal Perspective', in K.T. Van Dusen and S.A. Mednick (eds), *Antecedents of Aggression and Antisocial Behaviour*, 277–301, Boston, Mass.: Kluwer-Nijhoff.

MATSUEDA, R.L., and HEIMER, K. (1997), 'A Symbolic Interactionist Theory of Role-Transitions, Role-Commitments, and Delinquency', in T.P. Thornberry (ed.), *Advances in Criminological Theory, vol. 7: Developmental Theories of Crime and Delinquency*, 163–213, New Brunswick and London: Transaction.

McARA, L., and SMITH, D.J. (forthcoming), 'How Different Are Girls? Testing the Need for a Gendered Theory of Criminal Offending'.

McGEE, L., and NEWCOMB, M.D. (1992), 'General Deviance Syndrome: Expanded Hierarchical Evaluations at Four Ages From Early Adolescence to Adulthood', *Journal of Consulting and Clinical Psychology*, 60, 5: 766–76.

MENARD, S., and ELLIOTT, D.S. (1994), 'Delinquent Bonding, Moral Beliefs, and Illegal Behaviour: A Three-Wave Panel Model', *Justice Quarterly*, 11, 2: 173–87.

MERTON, R.K. (1938), 'Social Structure and Anomie', *American Sociological Review*, 3, 672–82.

MILES, D.R., and CAREY, G. (1997), 'The Genetic and Environmental Architecture of Human Aggression', *Journal of Personality and Social Psychology*, 72: 207–17.

MISCHEL, W. (1983), 'Delay of Gratification as Process and as Person Variable in Development', in D. Magnusson and V.L. Allen (eds), *Human Development: An Interactional Perspective*: 149–65.

MOFFITT, T. (1990), 'Juvenile Delinquency and Attention Deficit Disorder: Boys' Developmental Trajectories from Age 3 to Age 15', *Child Development*, 61: 893–910.

Moffitt, T.E. (1993), ' "Life-course-persistent" and "Adolescence-limited" Antisocial Behaviour: A Developmental Taxonomy', *Psychological Review*, 100: 674–701.

—— (1997), 'Adolescence-Limited and Life-Course Persistent Offending: A Complementary Pair of Developmental Theories', in T.P. Thornberry (ed.), *Advances in Criminological Theory, vol. 7: Developmental Theories of Crime and Delinquency*, 11–54, New Brunswick and London: Transaction.

——, Caspi, A., Rutter, M., and Silva, P.A. (2001), *Sex Differences in Antisocial Behaviour: Conduct Disorder, Delinquency, and Violence in the Dunedin Longitudinal Study*, Cambridge: Cambridge University Press.

Nagin, D.S., and Farrington, D.P. (1992a), 'The Stability of Criminal Potential from Childhood to Adulthood', *Criminology*, 30, 2: 235–60.

—— and —— (1992b), 'The Onset and Persistence of Offending', *Criminology*, 30, 4: 501–23.

——, ——, and Moffitt, T. (1995), 'Life-course Trajectories of Different Types of Offenders', *Criminology*, 33, 1: 111–39.

—— and Land, K.C. (1993), 'Age, Criminal Careers, and Population Heterogeneity: Specification and Estimation of a Nonparametric, Mixed Poisson Model', *Criminology*, 31, 3: 327–62.

—— and Paternoster, R. (1991), 'On the Relationship of Past to Future Participation in Delinquency', *Criminology*, 29, 2: 163–89.

Olweus, D. (1979), 'Stability of Aggressive Reaction Patterns in Males: A Review', *Psychological Bulletin*, 86: 852–75.

Patterson, G.R. (1993), 'Orderly Change in a Stable World: The Antisocial Trait as a Chimera', *Journal of Consulting and Clinical Psychology*, 61, 6: 911–19.

——, DeBaryshe, B.D., and Ramsey, E. (1989), 'A Developmental Perspective on Antisocial Behaviour', *American Psychologist*, 44, 2: 329–35.

——, Reid, J.B., and Dishion, T.J.D. (1992), *Antisocial Boys*, Eugene, Or: Castalia Publishing Company.

Plomin, R., De Fries, J.C., McClearn, G.E., and Rutter, M. (1997), *Behavioural Genetics*, 3rd edn, New York: Freeman.

Pulkkinen, L. (1986), 'The Role of Impulse Control in the Development of Antisocial and Prosocial Behaviour', in D. Olweus, J. Block, and M. Radke-Yarrow (eds), *Development of Antisocial and Prosocial Behaviour*, 149–63, Orlando, Fl: Academic Press.

Quinton, D., Pickles, A., Maughan, B., and

Rutter, M. (1993), 'Partners, Peers, and Pathways: Assortative Pairing and Continuities in Conduct Disorder', *Development and Psychopathology*, 5: 763–83.

Reiss, A.J. (1988), 'Co-offending and Criminal Careers', in M. Tonry and N. Morris (eds), *Crime and Justice: A Review of Research*, vol. 10, 117–70, Chicago, Ill.: University of Chicago Press.

Robins, L.N. (1966), *Deviant Children Grown Up: A Sociological and Psychiatric Study of Sociopathic Personality*, Baltimore, Md: Williams and Wileus.

—— (1978), 'Sturdy Childhood Predictors of Adult Antisocial Behaviour: Replications from Longitudinal Studies', *Psychological Medicine*, 8: 611–22.

—— and Regier, D.A. (eds) (1991), *Psychiatric Disorders in America: The Epidemiological Catchment Area Study*, New York: Free Press.

Rowe, D.C., Woulbroun, E.J., and Gulley, B.L. (1994), 'Peers and Friends as Nonshared Environmental Influences', in E.M. Hetherington, D. Reiss, and R. Plomin (eds), *Separate Social Worlds of Siblings: The Impact of Nonshared Environment on Development*, 159–73, Hillsdale, NJ: Lawrence Erlbaum.

Rutter, M. (1989), 'Age as an Ambiguous Variable in Developmental Research: Some Epidemiological Considerations from Developmental Psychopathology', *International Journal of Behavioural Development*, 12: 1–24.

—— (1995), 'Causal Concepts and Their Testing', in M. Rutter and D.J. Smith (eds), *Psychosocial Disorders in Young People: Time Trends and Their Causes*, 7–34, Chichester: Wiley.

——, Giller, H., and Hagell, A. (1998), *Antisocial Behaviour by Young People*, Cambridge: Cambridge University Press.

—— and Smith, D.J. (eds), (1995), *Psychosocial Disorders in Young People: Time Trends and Their Causes*, Chichester: Wiley.

Sampson, R.J., and Laub, J.H. (1990), 'Crime and Deviance over the Life Course: The Salience of Adult Social Bonds', *American Sociological Review*, 55: 609–27.

—— and —— (1993), *Crime in the Making: Pathways and Turning Points through Life*, Cambridge, Mass.: Harvard University Press.

—— and —— (1997), 'A Life-Course Theory of Cumulative Disadvantage and the Stability of Delinquency', in T. Thornberry (ed.), *Developmental Theories in Crime and Delinquency: Advances in Theoretical Criminology*, vol. 7, New Brunswick, NJ: Transaction.

—— and LAURITSEN, J.L. (1997), 'Racial and Ethnic Disparities in Crime and Criminal Justice in the United States', in M. Tonry (ed.), *Ethnicity, Crime, and Immigration: Crime and Justice*, vol. 21, 311–74, Chicago, Ill.: University of Chicago Press.

——, RAUDENBUSH, S.W., and EARLS, F. (1997), 'Neighbourhoods and Violent Crime: A Multi-level Study of Collective Efficacy', *Science*, 277: 918–24.

SCARR, S. (1992), 'Developmental Theories for the 1990s: Development and Individual Differences', *Child Development*, 63: 1–19.

SHERMAN, D.K., IACONO, W.G., and McGUE, M. (1997), 'Attention-Deficit Hyperactivity Disorder Dimensions: A Twin Study of Inattention and Impulsivity-Hyperactivity', *Journal of the American Academy of Child and Adolescent Psychiatry*, 36, 6: 745–53.

SILBERG, J., RUTTER, M., MEYER, J., MAES, H., HEWITT, J., SIMONOFF, E., PICKLES, A., LOEBER, R., and EAVES, L. (1996), 'Genetic and Environmental Influences on the Covariation between Hyperactivity and Conduct Disturbance in Juvenile Twins', *Journal of Child Psychology and Psychiatry*, 37: 803–16.

SIMONS, R.L., WU, C., CONGER, R., and LORENZ, F. (1994), 'Two Routes to Delinquency: Differences Between Early and Late Starters in the Impact of Parenting and Deviant Peers', *Criminology*, 32: 247–76.

SMITH, D.J. (1997), 'Ethnic Origins, Crime, and Criminal Justice in England and Wales', in M. Tonry (ed.), *Ethnicity, Crime, and Immigration: Crime and Justice*, vol. 21, 101–82, Chicago, Ill.: University of Chicago Press.

—— (forthcoming), 'Adolescent Offending and Victimization: Two Sides of the Same Coin?'.

—— and McVIE, S. (forthcoming), 'Theory and Method in the Edinburgh Study of Youth Transitions and Crime', *British Journal of Criminology*.

—— and RUTTER, M. (1995), 'Time Trends in Psychosocial Disorders of Youth', in M. Rutter and D.J. Smith (eds), *Psychosocial Disorders in Young People: Time Trends and Their Causes*, 763–781, Chichester: Wiley.

SOOTHILL, K., FRANCIS, B., and FLIGELSONE, R. (2002), *Patterns of Offending Behaviour: A New Approach*, Home Office Research Findings No. 171. Full report at www.homeoffice.gov.uk/rds. London: Home Office.

SOUSSIGNAN, R., TREMBLAY, R.E., SCHALL, B., LAURENT, D., LARIVÉE, S., GAGNON, C., LEBLANC, M., and CHARLEBOIS, P. (1992), 'Behavioural and Cognitive Characteristics of Conduct Disordered-Hyperactive Boys from Age 6 to 11: A Multiple Informant Perspective', *Journal of Child Psychology and Psychiatry*, 33, 8: 1333–46.

STANDER, J., FARRINGTON, D.P., HILL, G., and ALTHAM, P.M.E. (1989), 'Markov Chain Analysis and Specialization in Criminal Careers', *British Journal of Criminology*, 29, 4: 317–35.

SYKES, G.M., and MATZA, D. (1957), 'Techniques of Neutralization: A Theory of Delinquency', *American Sociological Review*, 22: 664–70.

TAYLOR, E., CHADWICK, O., HEPTINSTALL, E., and DANCKAERTS, M. (1996), 'Hyperactivity and Conduct Problems as Risk Factors for Adolescent Development', *Journal of the American Academy of Child and Adolescent Psychiatry*, 35, 9: 1213–26.

THORNBERRY, T., and KROHN, M.D. (1997), 'Peers, Drug Use, and Delinquency', in D.M. Stoff (ed.), *Handbook of Antisocial Behaviour*, 218–33, New York: Wiley.

——, ——, LIZOTTE, A.J., and CHARD-WIERSCHEM, D. (1993), 'The Role of Juvenile Gangs in Facilitating Delinquent Behaviour', *Journal of Research in Crime and Delinquency*, 30, 1: 55–87.

——, LIZOTTE, A.J., KROHN, M.D., FARNWORTH, M., and JANG, J.S. (1994), 'Delinquent Peers, Beliefs, and Delinquent Behaviour: A Longitudinal Test of Interactional Theory', *Criminology*, 32, 1: 47–83.

TOLAN, P.H., and THOMAS, P. (1995), 'The Implications of Age of Onset for Delinquency Risk II: Longitudinal Data', *Journal of Abnormal Child Psychology*, 23, 2: 157–81.

TREMBLAY, R.E., MÂSSE, L.C., VITARO, F., and DOBKIN, P.L. (1995), 'The Impact of Friends' Deviant Behaviour on Early Onset of Delinquency: Longitudinal Data from 6 to 13 Years of Age', *Development and Psychopathology*, 7: 649–67.

WEST, D.J., and FARRINGTON, D.P. (1977), *Who Becomes Delinquent?*, London: Heinemann.

WHITE, J.L., MOFFITT, T.E., EARLS, F., ROBINS, L., and SILVA, P.A. (1990), 'How Early Can We Tell?: Predictors of Childhood Conduct Disorder and Adolescent Delinquency', *Criminology*, 28, 4: 507–33.

WIKSTRÖM, P.-O.H. (1998), 'Communities and crime', in M. Tonry (ed.) *The Oxford Handbook of Criminal Justice*, 269–301, New York: Oxford University Press.

WILSON, J.Q., and HERRNSTEIN, R. (1985), *Crime and Human Nature*, New York: Simon and Schuster.

WOLFGANG, M.E., FIGLIO, R.M., and SELLIN, T. (1972), *Delinquency in a Birth Cohort*, Chicago, Ill.: University of Chicago Press.

21

MENTALLY DISORDERED OFFENDERS, MENTAL HEALTH, AND CRIME

Jill Peay

INTRODUCTION

Mentally disordered offenders are, as Webb and Harris (1999: 2) observe, categorically awkward; being neither exclusively ill nor uncomplicatedly bad, such offenders 'totter between two not always compatible discourses of state intervention'. Are they offenders who have mental disorders, or people with mental disorders who have offended? Or both? When should we be treating illness and when punishing infractions? And where? Should such offenders be in penal institutions, in hospital, or in the community? This is a challenge faced alike by health and criminal justice personnel, and by criminologists. Can they agree on within whose remit mentally disordered offenders should fall? And if they could agree, is there any prospect of coherent legal reform given that the eminently sensibly recommendations of the Butler Committee (Butler 1975) have remained in limbo for over a quarter of a century?

While it is clear that mentally disordered offenders do not represent some single, easily identifiable group, not much else is straightforward about this field. This chapter charts a path through already muddied waters. It is perhaps unsurprising that as a synopsis, it embodies much of the incoherence and many of the mixed philosophies evident in the responses of the law and of practitioners, policy-makers, and the caring professions to 'mentally disordered offenders'. However, one theme recurs. If mentally disordered offenders are not a distinct group, to treat them as such for reasons of beneficence exposes them, in an era when the shift to risk-based sentencing dominates policy, to being dealt with more harshly. An alternative approach, the plurality model (Peay 1993) might provide some guide to a less discriminatory approach, since it takes as its starting point the notion that 'mentally disordered offenders' ought to be treated alike with 'ordered' offenders. This would not be to suggest that the latter model should simply embrace offenders with mental health problems, but rather that reform in this field needs to address issues both of culpability (where our mental condition defences are inadequate for properly distinguishing those who should be held responsible for their offending and those who should not) and capacity-based intervention. Thus, proportionality in sentencing, access to therapeutic regimes and crime reduction interventions, and questions of reparation ought to apply equally across the range of offenders, in whatever dietary mix is currently in vogue.

The chapter is divided into eight sections. The first reviews developments in policy and sets the context of conflicting themes. Questions of individual justice and the effectiveness of interventions, questions which rightly apply for all offenders, are writ large for those with mental disorder where the neutrality of an 'intervention' becomes imbued with the apparent beneficence of 'treatment'. The second section examines the concept of mentally disordered offenders: do such offenders constitute an isolated category meriting special provision, or do the issues this 'group' raise have wider implications for the study of criminology? The third addresses the problem of definition: what do the various stages of the criminal justice process include or exclude from the gamut of definitions applying to the 'mentally disordered offender'? Fourthly, are mentally disordered offenders a minority group? What is their incidence, their impact on the criminal justice system, and what are the mechanisms for diverting offenders outwith the penal system? Fifthly, mental disorder at trial. Section six examines the fundamental justification for separate provision, namely treatment. The section takes a critical look at evidence of the relationship between mental disorder and crime, and then focuses on a key problematic group—offenders suffering from psychopathic disorder—who straddle the ordered–disordered offending continuum. Here, controversial proposals for new sentences and services for 'dangerous people with severe personality disorder' ('DSPD') are pending. The seventh section tackles some hidden agendas—bifurcation, detention for protective purposes, due process in discharge and release mechanisms—and the eighth formulates some conclusions. Lastly, as with other chapters in this book, readers should be warned that the primary focus is upon developments in England and Wales, although literature from other countries is used to flesh out ideas and principles.

POLICY DEVELOPMENT IN ENGLAND AND WALES: A CONTEXT OF CONFLICTING THEMES

There can no longer be much pretence. Current policy in mental health and crime in England and Wales, as in many other western countries, is not dominated by humanitarian concerns; rather, it is permeated by perceptions and attributions of risk. Debates about the shift to a 'risk penality', reflecting conditions of late modernity, are now commonplace in the criminological literature (see, for example, Loader and Sparks, in Chapter 3 of this volume; Brown and Pratt 2000). Offenders with mental disorders are peculiarly 'at risk' of being perceived as posing an unquantifiable danger, and thus, peculiarly apt for the ubiquitous focus on risk management. As risk is transposed into danger, dangerous individuals are singled out for special attention, and the responsibility for preventing and managing risk is transferred to those professionals dealing with or caring for them (Douglas 1992). While previous editions of this *Handbook* have stressed the importance of Home Office Circular 66/90 which, in essence, encouraged the placement of mentally disordered offenders, wherever possible, into the care of health and personal social services, so that they should receive treatment not custody, it is perhaps not surprising that in a climate dominated by risk, therapeutic considerations no longer hold sway. Indeed, the impact of Circular 66/90 and its underlying themes have been leavened by a series of risk-infused policy developments.

What evidence is there of this shift in policy, and what has brought it about? Our approach to mentally disordered offenders has always been necessarily complex. On the one hand, the prevailing policy had appeared to adopt a broadly treatment-based approach. Thus, 'In making a hospital order the court is placing the patient in the hands of the doctors, foregoing [sic] any question of punishment and relinquishing from then onwards its own controls over them' (Butler Report 1975: para. 14.8). Punishment and protection were not overriding criteria; diversion and treatment were paramount.

This approach treated offenders who were mentally disordered primarily in terms of their mental disorder. While not wholly aproblematic, it did relegate questions of risk and re-offending to a lower order. In keeping with this, the report of the government's Expert Committee on the necessary scope of mental health legislation (Richardson 1999) would, with its emphasis on patient autonomy, non-discrimination, and issues of capacity, have taken mental health law generally in the direction of medical law (Fennell 2001). However, the government's contrary emphasis on risk management, the reduction of re-offending and, now, early intervention, rejected the approach of the Richardson Committee. Its White Paper (Department of Health/ Home Office 2000) took issues relating to the safety of the public as being of key importance. Indeed, the White Paper built on the proposals of the Home Office (1999) for new orders of indefinite detention and new services for dangerous people with severe personality disorder (DSPD). Thus, mental health law was to be pushed in the direction of 'penal law'.

These developments had been presaged by a number of warning signs. Questions of risk had always been present in the arrangements for discretionary life sentences for offenders of an 'unstable' character[1] who were in a 'mental state which makes them dangerous to the life or limb of members of the public'.[2] But risk also emerged in the Report on *Mentally Disturbed Offenders in the Prison System* (Home Office/DHSS 1987) where it was noted, in the context of transferring prisoners to hospital for treatment, that 'the response to the needs of individual mentally disturbed offenders has to take account of the legitimate expectation of the public that government agencies will take appropriate measures for its protection' (ibid.: para. 3.6). It was also evident in the arrangements under the Criminal Justice Act 1991; although proportionality in sentencing was the leading principle, with sentences being determined on the basis of offence seriousness and not lengthened on the grounds of deterrence or rehabilitation, there was a limited but important exception for violent and sexual offences, where 'longer than normal sentences' could be given if it was 'necessary to protect the public from serious harm' (s 2(2)(b)). As will be seen below, these

[1] *R v Hodgson* (1967) 52 Cr App R 113.
[2] *R v Wilkinson* (1983) 5 Cr App R (S) 105, at 109.

provisions have impacted disproportionately on mentally disordered offenders. Also, the provisions of s 2 of the Crime (Sentences) Act 1997 for automatic life sentences for a second serious offence, trump the court's discretion to impose certain kinds of therapeutic disposals on offenders found to be disordered at the point of sentence. The same Act also introduced the hospital and limitation direction, a hybrid order which permitted the courts to sentence those suffering from psychopathic disorder to a period of imprisonment, but to direct that they be admitted to a psychiatric hospital with the option of return to prison if treatment was either impossible or (less likely) highly and quickly effective. These legislative initiatives were contentious and at odds with over forty years of legal and psychiatric opinion (Eastman and Peay 1998). All in all, the developments illustrate a growing desire to maintain penal control over mentally disordered offenders.

This is, of course, only one manifestation of a wider trend towards greater repression (see Ashworth, and Loader and Sparks in Chapters 29 and 3 respectively of this volume). But for mentally disordered offenders the trend may have been unnecessarily fuelled by concerns about re-offending by former psychiatric patients. Such preoccupations were magnified by the introduction in 1994 of mandatory inquiries into homicides committed by those who had had contact with the specialist mental health services (Department of Health 1994; Peay 1996; Sheppard 1996). The spate of negative publicity the inquiries brought to psychiatric patients, services, and personnel (see, in respect of the last, Rumgay and Munroe 2001) did much to kindle an underlying public misconception of a relationship between mental disorder and violence.

It was particularly galling to those involved in treating the mentally disordered that such concerns persisted despite repeated demonstrations that 'Re-offending rates are in fact no higher than for any other class of offender' (Murray 1989: iii); that the trend was in the direction of mentally ill people committing fewer homicides than mentally ordered people (Taylor and Gunn 1999); and the fact that when psychiatric patients killed, they were much more likely to kill themselves than others (Appleby *et al.* 2001). However, there has been a small chink; in July 2001, the new Minister of State at the Health Department advised the Royal College of Psychiatrists that 'inquiries after homicide' were no longer to be 'mandatory'.[3]

In the light of all of this, it is not surprising that the policy context embodies both positive and negative messages. On the one hand, calls for diverting mentally disordered offenders from the damaging effects of the criminal justice system remain persistent. Equally, the increasing popularity of early intervention in the lives of offenders is consistent with a philosophy that 'treatment works'; people can be changed, diverted, distracted, or protected from inappropriate or damaging experiences. Yet on the negative side, there appears to be a real distrust of therapeutic disposals for some mentally disordered offenders.

Much of the confusion arises because of the tensions inherent across the continuum both of ordered–disordered behaviour and that of law-abiding–law-breaking behaviour. Notions of care and treatment are seen as appropriate for the seriously

---

[3] Health Minister Jacqui Smith at the RCP Conference, 2001: 'A Mind Odyssey: Science and Caring'.

disordered, provided this does not also arise in conjunction with offending of a worrying nature. Similarly, notions of protection and punishment are traditionally confined to serious offenders, again assuming an absence of obvious disorder. Yet these tensions are confounded where it is argued that disorder and offending exist side by side in one individual, or, more confusingly still, interact. Dilemmas are posed by the handling of those mentally disordered offenders isolated as meriting 'special' provision, whichever limb of the bifurcated policy (special care or special control) is adopted. Moreover, 'special' provision all too easily manifests itself in special discrimination (Campbell and Heginbotham 1991). Indeed, the discrimination and stigma faced by those with mental health problems is amplified when disorder and offending co-occur. As Porter (2001) observes:

Stigmatizing involves projecting onto an individual or group judgments about what is inferior, repugnant, or disgraceful. It translates disgust into the disgusting, apprehensions of danger into the dangerous. It is thus the creation of spoiled identity; first it singles out difference, next calls it inferiority, and finally blames those who are different for their outcomes.

Another conflict arises between welfarism and legalism. Gostin (1986: v) distinguishes the two approaches thus: legalism occurs 'where the law is used to wrap the patient in a network of substantive and procedural protections against unjustified loss of liberty and compulsory treatment'; whereas welfarism occurs where 'legal safeguards are replaced with professional discretion which is seen as allowing speedy access to treatment and care, unencumbered by a panoply of bureaucracy and procedures'.

Gostin argues that the Mental Health Act 1983, the Act which remains the key statutory provision in this field, achieves a balance between the two principles, retaining welfarism as established by the 1959 Mental Health Act, but enhancing safeguards for patients' rights in such areas as treatment without consent (the Act established the Mental Health Act Commission) and continued detention of offender patients (Mental Health Review Tribunals (MHRTs), the bodies that determine the necessity for continued detention under the Act, acquired the power to discharge restricted patients). Yet the two philosophies sit uneasily together. Thus, the ruling that a restricted patient was not entitled to an absolute discharge, even though there was no evidence of current mental disorder, on the basis that there was a liability to relapse, illustrates a philosophy for mentally disordered offenders of 'once ill, always ill'.[4] This is strikingly at odds with a criminal justice approach that has striven to deal with offenders on the basis of what they have done, rather than who they are. This impelled the criminal justice system to focus on the ideology of a just measure of punishment, in the recognition that offending behaviour may be no more than an adopted response to an environment which may or may not change, independent of any individual measure of pain. In stark contrast, mental health professionals are arguably more interested in the enduring features of individuals, placing the individual at the centre of the problem and thereby providing the justification for treatment. Ironically,

---

[4] *R v Merseyside MHRT and Another, ex p K* [1990] 1 All ER 694 (CA).

the future for both mental health and criminal justice professionals seems to lie in a shared future of risk prediction and greater penality where 'intervention' is perceived as not succeeding.

All of this now has also to be seen in the context of the Human Rights Act 1998. As will be discussed below, the European Convention on Human Rights (ECHR) has had a powerful influence on the relationship between the executive and the continuing detention of those with psychiatric disorders; an influence which has permeated out across discretionary decision-making for others than the mentally disordered. It is also the case that the ECHR is not a document which naturally lends itself to the protection of those with mental disorders. Indeed, it permits discrimination against those of 'unsound mind'. Yet, the first declaration of incompatibility under the Human Rights Act occurred in a case concerning an offender-patient detained in a psychiatric hospital (see the case of *H*, below). Perhaps this is mere coincidence. But perhaps it reflects the presence of conflicting tensions permeating the practices of all who work in this field, whether they are based in the police station or at the Court of Appeal.

MENTAL DISORDER AND OFFENDERS: A CASE FOR SPECIAL PROVISION?

Mentally disordered offenders are typically treated as an isolated topic, isolated often with gender, race, youth, and victims. This is unhelpful since mental disorder is not a fixed characteristic of an offender and victimology embraces the study of all of the former. What these topics do have in common is their 'inconvenience' for a criminology imbued with male, adult, mentally healthy, formerly non-victimized values. Yet the lessons to be learnt from how we deal conceptually, practically, and in principle with those deemed 'mentally disordered offenders' have as much to say about topics regarded as central to, or ranging across, the scope of criminology as they have to say about 'marginal' groups. Thus, mentally disordered offenders should not be seen as a Cinderella area.

Indeed, to argue for the existence of a discrete group of mentally disordered offenders would presuppose a category of mentally ordered offenders. This falsely comforting tendency is the same as that noted by Gilman (1988), that setting the sick apart sustains the fantasy that we are whole. The criminal law broadly adopts such an approach. For, while the mental element is an integral part of the definition of a crime, the law nonetheless assumes most mental elements are 'rational'. As Lord Devlin noted with reference to the insanity defence:

. . . it is reason which makes a man responsible to the law, reason and reason alone. It is reason which gives him sovereignty over animate and inanimate things. It is what distinguishes him from the animals, which emotional disorder does not; it is what makes him man; it is what makes him subject to the law. So it is fitting that nothing other than a defect of reason should give complete absolution [Smith and Hogan 1988: 200].

But such a clear-cut division is problematic. Even the reasonable man on the Clapham omnibus can experience a moment of madness if he alights at the Common. In turn, scientific advances in our understanding of the structure, functioning and chemistry of the brain have generated a more medical approach to some forms of offending (Hare 1996) and to calls for the law to recognize new neurological syndromes which may underlie offending behaviour (Lewis and Carpenter 1999). In the area of so-called normal offending, defences are frequently advanced or mitigation constructed which draw on elements of 'diminished responsibility', 'unthinking' behaviour, or uncontrolled responses to extreme social stress. Concepts of limited rationality will be familiar to criminologists. Yet few of these offenders would wish for the special treatment which may follow a finding of 'defect of reason'. Why not? Is it a recognition of the punishing aspects of such treatment? Or a desire not to be stigmatized along with those deemed mad (see, for example, Gardner and Macklem 2001, on the attractiveness of normal 'provocation' over 'abnormal' diminished responsibility)? As Porter (2001) observes: 'Criminalization may be less degrading than psychiatrization, and a psychiatric record may well be more scarring, more permanent, than a criminal. In taking his punishment the felon is at least credited with free will, and he thereby repays his debts to society'.

Or is it that we recognize that some level of disordered thinking ought to alleviate punishment, if not excuse it altogether? Thus, 'complete absolution' is a legal nicety. Mentally disordered offenders find themselves confined in hospitals, prisons, therapeutic regimes within prisons, and, most notably, within the remand population. The disorders that offenders present at court create opportunities for the defence and at mitigation, but lead to problems thereafter for those into whose care or custody these offenders are sent. Thus, mentally disordered offenders exist in one shape or form across the entire criminal justice system, and 'disorder' may be found to a greater or lesser extent—partly dependent on the incentives for its construction—throughout offending populations.

Accordingly, one theme which runs through this chapter concerns a plea that the component parts of the concept be disaggregated: mentally disordered offenders are first and foremost people; whether they may have offended or whether they may be disordered will be matters for individual resolution. Prioritization of one aspect (the mentally disordered element) of an individual's make-up readily leads to neglect of other, perhaps more pertinent, aspects. Mentally disordered people may have other needs which are arguably as important in respect of their special status within the criminal justice system. As the Reed Committee (1991: Overview, para. 7.ii) details, such categories may include: black and ethnic minority group members; women; the elderly; children and adolescents; sex offenders; substance misusers; people with personality (or psychopathic) disorders, or sensory disabilities, or brain damage, or learning disabilities. Equally, such offenders will manifest themselves amongst the homeless, amongst victims, and as witnesses to crime. It would be misleading to assume that there is any pure form of mentally disordered offender. Doing so risks negating the frequently reiterated need for flexibility within the mental health and criminal justice agencies; a flexibility which is required not only in respect of the movement of people between available resources, but also in the conceptualization of 'mentally disordered offending'. Without it, the gap between expectations and provision cannot be bridged.

THE PROBLEM OF DEFINITION

Hoggett (1996: 97) admirably details the interactions between the mentally disordered offender and the criminal justice system at all of its stages, noting that 'the fact that a person who is alleged to have committed a criminal offence may be mentally disordered can affect the normal processes of the law at several points'. These crisis points are sketched below. No attempt is made to replicate the detail of Hoggett's analysis, but some key themes emerge which reflect how an individual's mental state may affect prosecution, conviction, disposal, treatment, and release.

'Mental disorder' is itself problematic; indeed, it is a term of acute terminological inexactitude. Definitions of mental disorder act like a concertina, expanding and contracting in order to accommodate different client groups with little or no coherence. Their mismatch frequently results in uncertainties and anomalies. In order to illustrate the effects of this concertina, it is necessary to go into the statutory provisions in some detail. Those familiar with, and those who do not wish to become confused by, this legal exposition can read on to the next section.

The Mental Health Act 1983, s 1(2), defines mental disorder as 'mental illness, arrested or incomplete development of mind, psychopathic disorder *and any other disorder or disability of mind*' (emphasis added). Further definitions of severe mental impairment, mental impairment, and psychopathic disorder are provided. There is no definition of mental illness despite this being one of the key classifications under the Act. Psychopathic disorder is defined as 'a persistent disorder or disability of mind (whether or not including significant impairment of intelligence) which results in abnormally aggressive or seriously irresponsible conduct on the part of the person concerned'; regrettably this definition neither corresponds with psychiatric definitions of personality disorder, nor absolves itself of a tautological association with behaviour likely to be criminalized. The problems posed by psychopathic disorder are discussed further below, but it is worth noting here that forensic psychiatrists have been and remain deeply divided about whether psychopathic disorder should even be in the Mental Health Act: Cope's (1993) survey of forensic psychiatrists found 53 per cent in favour and 47 per cent against. The 1983 Act does make clear that a person may not be dealt with under the Act as suffering from mental disorder 'by reason only of promiscuity or other immoral conduct, sexual deviancy or dependence on alcohol or drugs'. Section 1(3) thus serves to count out from treatment under the Mental Health Act many of those in prison deemed by psychiatrists to be mentally disordered (see Singleton *et al.* 1998, below).

In addition to the catch-nearly-all phrase emphasized above, the 1983 Act may be conceived as having a dual hierarchy of mental disorder. The first tier encompasses mental illness and severe mental impairment; the second, psychopathic disorder and mental impairment. To invoke many of the sections of the 1983 Act in respect of this second tier (e.g., a hospital order under s 37; transfer from prison to hospital under s 47) it is necessary to satisfy an additional criterion that medical treatment in hospital be 'likely to alleviate or prevent a deterioration of' the individual's condition. Even though this treatability requirement has to be satisfied both at admission and by MHRTs considering discharge under s 72, for the latter minimal satisfaction of the criterion may be sufficient; indeed, the Privy Council has now held the detention of untreatable restricted patients on grounds of public safety *not* to be incompatible with Article 5(1)(e) of the ECHR.[5] The potential to confuse the role of clinicians and gaolers is evident.

Some alleged offenders may be diverted into hospital, with a civil admission constituting a real alternative to involvement with the criminal justice system. For admission under either s 2 (for assessment, twenty-eight days' duration) or s 4 (cases of emergency seventy-two hours' duration) the presence of mental disorder 'of a nature or degree which warrants detention of the patient in hospital' is sufficient. Similarly, s 136 (mentally disordered persons in a public place—removal to a place of safety) requires the person to appear to a constable to be suffering from mental disorder and to be in immediate need of care or control. All of these sections are accordingly broadly inclusive. Under s 3 (admission for treatment, six months' duration) the criteria are somewhat narrower; the patient must be suffering from one of the four categories above and, in the case of psychopathic disorder or mental impairment, the treatability criterion must be satisfied.

For hospital orders (a therapeutic post-conviction order enabling detention and treatment of the offender in a mental hospital), the criteria in respect of the definition of mental disorder are the same as in s 3 above, but the court must also be of the opinion under s 37(2)(b), 'having regard to all the circumstances including the nature of the offence and the character and antecedents of the offender, and to other available methods of dealing with him, that the most suitable method of disposing of the case is by means of an order under this section'. This makes medical evidence favouring a therapeutic disposal a necessary prerequisite, but not necessarily determinative. The courts may choose to punish or protect in the face of medical evidence, even given the additional option of attaching a restriction order under s 41 where 'necessary for the protection of the public from serious harm'. Indeed, a restriction order, which has the effect of taking away the doctor's power to discharge the offender-patient and leaving that decision in the hands of either the MHRT or the Home Secretary, can be made by the courts even where there is medical evidence that the offender is not regarded as dangerous.[6] The restriction order thus attaches limits to psychiatrists' control over the subsequent release of the patient and, with the exception of the MHRT's power to discharge mentioned above, places all control over the movements of the restriction order patient with the Home Secretary. In 1999 there

---

[5] See the Scottish cases of *Reid v Secretary of State for Scotland* [1999] 2 AC 413 (HL) and *Anderson, Reid and Doherty v The Scottish Ministers and the Advocate General for Scotland* (2001) Privy Council 15 October 2001.

[6] *R v Birch* (1989) 90 Cr App R 78.

were 745 hospital orders made under s 37(1) and (3), and a further 253 made with restrictions (Johnson and Taylor 2000); these figures have not changed markedly in recent years. However, some restriction orders are imposed unnecessarily (Street 1998), while most 'disordered' offenders do not receive a therapeutic 'hospital order' disposal, even though their culpability may be mitigated, if not absolved, by their mental state (see Ashworth and Gostin 1984; Verdun-Jones 1989).

Remand to hospital for treatment under s 36 requires mental illness or severe mental impairment, but curiously precludes those charged with murder; while s 35 remand to hospital for reports and s 38 interim hospital orders may be satisfied by the broader classifications of mental illness, severe mental impairment, mental impairment, or psychopathic disorder, with no treatability criterion.

For transfer from prison to hospital under s 47, for those serving sentences of imprisonment, there must be mental illness, severe mental impairment, mental impairment, or psychopathic disorder (with the last two satisfying the treatability criterion). But for other prisoners, for example remand prisoners, their transfer under s 48 demands both the first-tier classifications of mental illness or severe mental impairment, and that the prisoner be in 'urgent need' of medical treatment in hospital. Other routes into psychiatric care may follow a finding of 'unfit to plead' or where mental disorder provides a defence, for example, not guilty by reason of insanity, or a partial defence, for example, manslaughter by reason of diminished responsibility. Although not greatly used, both insanity verdicts and findings of 'unfit to plead' heavily feature offenders with diagnoses of schizophrenia, perhaps conforming best with lay notions of mental illness.

Within the prison system, an equally mixed population presents itself. The Reed Report (1991: para. 2.1) recognizes three groups of disordered offenders. First, those meeting the four narrow classifications under the 1983 Act and needing in-patient treatment; secondly, those falling within the International Classification of Diseases (WHO 1978) but not meeting Mental Health Act criteria or requiring in-patient treatment; and, thirdly, those 'who ask for the help of the caring agencies within the prison system'. Quite where alcohol and drug abuse falls is not clear. A similar confusion extends to mentally disordered offenders in the community. The Reed Report (1991: para. 1.6) recognizes three categories: alleged offenders for diversion into the health and social services and away from the criminal justice system; mentally disordered offenders discharged or diverted from hospital or prison; and non-offenders in the community who are vulnerable and may need assistance to prevent their offending. The third category would permit intervention for non-offenders predicted as likely to offend. In an era when notions of early intervention to prevent future offending (whether on the basis of social disadvantage or diagnostic category—the two latest being 'attention deficit hyperactivity disorder' amongst children and dangerous people with severe personality disorder) are rife, it is a definitional problem worth resolving. Moreover, where one recent study has shown particularly high levels of psychiatric disorder—including a prevalence of 28 per cent for conduct disorder— amongst adolescents in the care system (McCann et al. 1996), it is a problem of some urgency.

MENTALLY DISORDERED OFFENDERS:
A MINORITY GROUP?

This question may be addressed from a number of perspectives. First, there is the contribution mentally disordered offenders make to the totality of offending; secondly, the impact they have upon the criminal justice system; and, thirdly, the contribution they make to custodial populations. Parallels here may be made with the arguments about race and offending. Mental disorder may correlate with certain kinds of offending, but is rarely causative; yet there is a progressive concentration in the criminal justice system of those suffering from mental disorder (compare Singleton *et al.* 1998 with Meltzer *et al.* 1995). Similarly, selectivity is evident in the use of compulsion in the mental health system, with black people finding themselves subject to a greater use of coercion (see, for example, Boast and Chesterman 1995). Quite why this should be is not clear. However, both processes, of mental health and criminal justice, entail the exercise of discretion. Most offenders are neither convicted nor sentenced. Most of those with mental disorder are treated without the use of compulsion. Thus, the scope for selective inclusion of more visible offenders is obvious; combining notions of inept offending with the range of views held by the relevant 'gatekeepers' as to the needs of this problematic group will undoubtedly contribute to a highly skewed criminal justice 'output'. Earlier in the process it is difficult to disentangle the impact of various policies and diversion schemes; on the one hand they serve to filter offenders away from the formal process, while on the other hand net widening remains an issue. It is, however, important to note that surveys of incidence at the earliest stages will be an under-representation as the police, the Crown Prosecution Service (CPS), and the courts are likely to identify those with the most obvious symptomatology, while surveys of custodial populations will include those whose disorders have been exacerbated, or brought about, by the process of prosecution and punishment. Similarly, the regrettable tendency to remand into custody to obtain psychiatric reports will contribute to this concentration effect. Again, the tension between a desire to obtain treatment for the 'deserving' mentally disordered offender and protective concerns where that desire may be frustrated, plays itself out amongst a shifting population.

Although the arguments are complex the policy was clear. Wherever possible mentally disordered offenders were to be cared for and treated by health and social services rather than in the criminal justice system. Even if there had been no policy shift (see above), the numbers of disordered offenders still to be found within that system who could benefit under alternative regimes would belie it. Home Office Circular No 66/90, *Provision for Mentally Disordered Offenders*, had attempted to address this anomaly: by drawing attention to the relevant legal powers, by reinforcing the need to make best use of resources, and by discouraging prosecution where this was not required by the public interest. Where prosecution was necessary, Circular 66/90 stressed the importance of finding non-penal disposals wherever appropriate.

As will become evident below, however effective diversion schemes become, there will always be offenders with mental disorders in the penal system, either because of late onset of the disorder, or where the nature of the offending/disorder makes a penal disposal inevitable. Such offenders are supposedly not to be denied access to treatment. Accordingly, provision exists either for treatment within prison (on a voluntary basis),[7] or for transfer within or outwith the prison system. So, crudely put, the issues become those of numbers, identification, diversion, integration with custodial populations, and transfer to therapeutic regimes. At the start of the process, one is looking for a needle in a haystack; at the end, at remand populations being 'swamped' by those with unmet mental heath needs.

NUMBERS

The best epidemiological evidence from the United States indicates that major mental disorder accounts for at most 3 per cent of the violence in American society (Monahan 1992). However, the contribution that the mentally disordered make to the totality of offending would be almost impossible to estimate; like juvenile offenders, their offences are frequently highly visible, petty, and repeated. The great majority of mentally disordered offenders are to be found not on psychiatric wards but in local facilities supported by health, housing, and social services. Properly resourcing these facilities could have a major preventive impact. It is paradoxical, therefore, as Burney and Pearson (1995: 309) observe, that 'a court appearance may be the only way that their needs will become apparent'; yet that very involvement with the criminal justice system may constitute the reason why community services are denied to these individuals.

Developments in the mental health field have also mirrored those for 'normal' offenders, with greater reliance being placed on control by and punishment in the community. The Mental Health (Patients in the Community) Act 1995 constitutes one such initiative. It provides supervised after-care for patients who have been detained under the 1983 Act, and includes powers to require the patient to live at a specific address, to attend for medical treatment, and, most controversially, to convey patients to the appropriate places, including back to hospital.[8]

It is also paradoxical that the shift to community care, combined with the lack of reality of that care and support, brings more mentally disordered people into contact with the criminal justice system (NACRO 1993). Homelessness, the co-morbidity of alcohol, drug, and mental health problems, and the associated stress can all induce incidents leading to criminal charges. Burney and Pearson's (1995) report on a diversion scheme based at one Magistrates' court details how, although there may be only a small number of offenders in need of psychiatric hospitalization, there is a larger number of repeat petty offenders, and a third amorphous group of those sad and

---

[7] Even offenders certified as transferable under the 1983 Act cannot be treated on a compulsory basis under its provisions while still in prison.

[8] In essence, the debate has concerned the need to balance care and control. Doing so in the community is arguably more fraught than in an institutional setting. The ever-popular psychiatric probation orders attempt such a balance but, like guardianship orders, they lack any element of compulsory treatment. In the context of a power under the 1995 Act to take patients to hospital, where compulsory treatment can be administered, the need for the controversial 'community treatment order' remains unclear.

difficult people, where it is not clear whether or what type of intervention might be appropriate. Diversion accordingly becomes something of a logistical nightmare. Ideally, the problem requires the relevant personnel to be alive to the problem groups, having access to specialized services and permeability between service providers.

IDENTIFICATION

Despite the existence of diversion schemes at the police station and the introduction of the 'appropriate adult' scheme under the 1984 Police and Criminal Evidence Act (PACE)—whereby independent visitors attend police interviews to advise and protect vulnerable arrested persons—research consistently shows that the police fail to identify some of those in need of special services (Robertson *et al.* 1995; Gudjonsson *et al.* 1993). Palmer and Hart's (1996) study noted that relevant personnel lacked detailed knowledge of the provisions and had difficulties in identifying for whom the safeguards were intended, leading to inconsistent implementation. The lack of specialist mental health training amongst police surgeons, and the lack of training *per se* amongst 'appropriate adults', further undermined the safeguards' effectiveness. Their observation that the police were good at identifying those with overt symptoms but less so with others (despite what were the best of intentions), support the finding that the police are good at spotting schizophrenia but poor at clinical depression (Gudjonnson *et al.* 2001). As to disposal, Robertson *et al.* (1995) noted a degree of bifurcation; those identified with mental illness were four times as likely to be released without further action as other detainees, but slightly more likely to be charged where persistence or violence was involved. Vaughan *et al.*'s (2001) study notes that even police stations with diversion schemes fail to pick up, on average, 7 per cent of individuals who would be suitable for diversion, while inappropriately continuing to refer for diversion those who are not mentally disordered.

Then there is the risk of vulnerable individuals making false confessions. Laing (1995), reviewing the development of psychiatric assessment schemes at police stations, highlighted the vital role that solicitors have in identifying such vulnerable people. Whether the likelihood of false confessions has increased with the requirements in ss 34–36 of the Criminal Justice and Public Order Act 1994 (namely, to warn suspects that the failure to provide explanations may be held against them in court) is another reason why all parties at police stations need to be alive to the special needs of the mentally vulnerable.

Under PACE 1984, the presence *or suspicion* of mental disorder, as defined in the Mental Health Act 1983, should trigger all of the protections and additional rights to which the mentally vulnerable are entitled, including the right to have an appropriate adult present during questioning (Code C). Since psychopathic disorder falls within this definition, it would be interesting to know how frequently the police's definition of a 'psychopath' (a common enough epithet) impels them to adhere to these special protections. This may be another area where the mismatch between different agencies' expectations for, and definitions of, 'the mentally disordered' impedes the full protection to which that 'group' is entitled in law. Thus, where custody officers equate the presence of mental disorder with abnormal behaviour, they will be most likely to miss disorders such as depression and 'psychopathy'.[9] A failure to identify either the obscure or the obvious may contribute both to the risk of wrongful conviction and to the failure properly to divert vulnerable individuals to the services they require (Fennell 1994).

COURT ASSESSMENT AND DIVERSION SCHEMES

The burgeoning number of practical initiatives to identify and divert mentally disordered offenders at all stages from the police station to court sentence (Cavadino 1999), belies Burney and Pearson's (1995) argument that there is a relatively small number of mentally disordered offenders in need of psychiatric services passing through at any one point. Again, the problem of who gets counted in or out appears critical. As to the court diversion schemes, they take many forms, but all share the innovative and proactive approach of getting psychiatrist, CPS, mentally disordered alleged offender, and sentencer together. They aim to prevent offenders being remanded in custody for reports merely because they do not enjoy stable community ties or because of the absence of bail hostels;[10] ultimately, disposal into a custodial setting should be avoided where a therapeutic one would be more appropriate. Regrettably, as Cavadino (1999) points out, there is no requirement for the courts when making bail decisions to have regard to the effect of a remand in custody on the accused's mental health. Thus, the beneficent pressure is all one way.

In addition to the various diversion schemes, there are also formal powers under the 1983 Act to divert offenders into the hospital system. Sections 35 and 36 permitted remand to hospital for reports and treatment respectively; s 38 initiated interim hospital orders, to avoid the difficulty that could arise out of the 'once and for all' disposal to hospital under a s 37 hospital order. The interim order permits the court to 'hedge its bets'.[11] Although a punitive order should not follow where an offender responds to treatment under s 38 and is returned to court for sentence, a punitive approach may be adopted where it becomes apparent that no 'cure' is possible.

However, none of these orders has been frequently used.[12] In stark contrast, 5,569 psychiatric reports were carried out by prison medical officers following remand in 1989 (Fennell 1991). The possibility remains that courts continue to remand in

[9] This in turn would support the contention that psychopathic disorder is a label attached not in order to assist offenders, but subsequently to justify a more punitive or protective approach.

[10] The Reed Report (1991, Prison Advisory Group) recommended that magistrates' use of their powers to send an accused to prison solely for medical reports (regarded as wrong in principle and an unjustifiable use of the prison system) should be reviewed. Limiting these powers might result in an increase in magistrates' use of s 35, although clearly not all offenders would fit the required Mental Health Act classifications, nor would sufficiently secure provisions necessarily be available.

[11] This tendency will have been facilitated by the extension of the interim hospital order under the Crime (Sentences) Act from six to twelve months, arguably making redundant the introduction of the hospital and limitation direction (see Eastman and Peay 1998).

[12] Indeed, use of s 35 (remand to hospital for reports) has shown a marked decline over the last ten years (from 299 in 1989/90 to 198 in 1999/2000) whilst s 36 is barely used at all (18 orders in 1999/2000) (see Department of Health 2000). This may be because psychiatrists deem their twelve week maximum length as 'insufficient' for a proper forensic assessment.

custody for psychiatric and social reasons, rather than for reasons of public safety or the seriousness of offence as the denial of bail implies.

Should the mentally disordered be exempt from prosecution altogether? Some commentators believe that those with mental handicap should be prosecuted and held responsible where responsibility exists (Carson 1989). Others argue that defendants who have failed to seek psychiatric help when so advised, or who fail to take prescribed medication, should not then be able to rely upon their psychiatric condition as reducing their culpability (Mitchell 1999). The Code for Crown Prosecutors requires the CPS to consider a defendant's mental condition but notes, 'Crown Prosecutors must balance the desirability of diverting a defendant who is suffering from significant mental or physical ill health with the need to safeguard the general public'; disorder *per se* is not regarded as a sufficient basis for not proceeding (CPS 2000: para. 6.5g). Moreover, Home Office Circular 66/90 distinguishes in paragraph 6 those forms of mental disorder made worse by the institution of proceedings and those which come about by reason of instituting proceedings. Lastly, Robertson (1988) suggests that the presence of disorder may make prosecution more likely where a guilty plea is anticipated. Hence, in the decision to prosecute, the presence of mental disorder may act as a mitigating factor and pre-empt action, or it may act as an incentive to proceedings being taken. The public interest in ensuring that the offence will not be repeated needs to be weighed against that of the welfare of person in question.

Problems of due process also dog the diversion arena. Does the earlier involvement of psychiatrists inevitably favour welfarism over legalism? How is a balance to be achieved between the rights of the defendant and those of the victim (Laing 1999)? And, as Fennell notes (1991: 336–7), assuming an offender is prepared to be diverted, 'hospital authorities and local authorities have considerable discretion as to whether to accept responsibility for that person. If he is a persistent petty offender, or is potentially disruptive, he is unlikely to be afforded priority status in the queue for scarce resources'. With the drop at district level in in-patient beds for the adult mentally ill, from around 150,000 in the 1950s to approximately 63,000 in the early 1990s, and a reluctance by some to see offender-patients integrated with 'non-offenders', diversion and community care may have real limits to their ability to absorb all those whom the courts might wish so to allocate. Shaw *et al.* (2001) also note that of those diverted to inpatient psychiatric services, one in three had lost contact at twelve months follow-up, while of those referred to psychiatric community teams or outpatient clinics, less than a third attended for their first appointment. Maintaining supervision and contact with those in the community is inherently problematic, but this looks like a case of needles returning to the haystack.

PRISON POPULATIONS

In discussing remands to hospital while awaiting trial, Hoggett (1996: 108) provocatively asks whether it is worse to languish in hospital without trial, or in prison without treatment. This question has real force, given the extent of mental disorder within the prison population. Examination of this (i) details the range of disorders recognized by psychiatrists amongst an offending population; (ii) underlines the 'irrelevance' to many of these offenders of their mental disorder (since it has not resulted in their being subject to special provisions); and (iii) re-emphasizes the central point that offenders with mental disorder are not some minority group of only marginal concern.

Studies of the prevalence of mental disorder in prison populations have consistently found substantial levels of disorder. Amongst the sentenced male population, Gunn *et al.* (1991) found that 37 per cent had a diagnosable mental disorder. Brooke *et al.* (1996), looking at the remand population, found an incidence of 63 per cent, with 5 per cent suffering from psychosis. The 1997 national survey of psychiatric morbidity, looking at 3,000 prisoners across England and Wales (Singleton *et al.* 1998), found 7 per cent of sentenced men and 10 per cent of men on remand to have functional psychotic disorders. Of the five disorders surveyed in the research (personality disorder, psychosis, neurosis, alcohol misuse, and drug dependence), fewer than one in ten prisoners showed no evidence of any of these disorders.

Are these figures shocking in absolute terms? Yes. First, because the problem is in no sense new. Over twenty years earlier, Gunn *et al.* (1978) reported an incidence of 31 per cent with psychiatric disorders in the south-east prison population, of whom 2 per cent were psychotic. This high level of disorder (in its broad sense) but 'low' level of psychosis (the latter comparable with that in the community) is a common finding. Whether the increase over the last twenty years reflects more disorder or differential diagnostic practices is less clear; that it remains there at all to be diagnosed at these levels is the principal concern.

Secondly, the figures are shocking because of the incidence of suicide and self-harm in prison. Suicide in prison remains a persistent problem.[13] Taking their most rigorous measure—suicide attempts in the week prior to interview—Singleton *et al* (1998) note that 2 per cent of the male remand population reported attempting suicide (this is distinguished from para-suicide). One third of 'successful' prison suicides have a history of mental disturbance (Dooley 1990). In a highly unusual finding, the European Court of Human Rights found a breach of Article 3 ECHR (inhuman and degrading treatment) when a mentally ill prisoner was punished by segregation for an assault on prison hospital staff.[14] The prisoner committed suicide.

Thirdly, the prison population is projected to be 68,400 by March 2003 (Elkins *et al.* 2001). The June 2001 figures of 66,400 (ibid.) would, by extrapolation, mean a minimum of 4,648 prisoners with functional psychosis, prisoners certainly in need of treatment and probably in need of transfer to hospital. For even if services for people with personality, sexual, and substance misuse disorders were developed in prisons, and even with the new mental health 'in-reach' services to be provided by the NHS (Prison Service/NHS Executive 1999), transfer to hospital for the seriously mentally ill is the only current viable and humane option. Only in hospital can drugs be administered on a compulsory basis, victimization by other prisoners avoided, and unpredictable violence or incidents of self-harm be better controlled. Yet the available total of

[13] In 1999, there had been 84 deaths by 14 December, the highest per 100,000 for the previous six years (Narey 1999).

[14] *Keenan v UK, The Times*, 18 April 2001.

secure beds stood in 2001 at around 1,265 special hospital beds and 2,383 NHS secure places, with bed occupancy at around 90 per cent.[15] These figures fall manifestly short of the latent demand in the prison population.[16] There simply are not enough secure beds. In turn, the bed shortage goes against notions that mentally disordered offenders should be dealt with outwith custodial care, and in conditions of no greater security than is justified by the degree of danger they present to themselves and others.

However, considering the number and variety of hurdles that mentally disordered offenders have to jump in order not to be diverted from the prison population, the presence of some 4,648 seriously mentally ill people in prison suggests a number of additional hypotheses. First, these filters may fail either effectively to identify or, if identified, to divert these offenders into the hospital system. For example, Birmingham *et al.* (1996: 1523), in observing that fewer than a quarter of diagnosable mentally disordered remand prisoners were identified as such on initial screening at reception by the prison medical service, note: 'In a busy remand prison abnormal behaviour is often tolerated or perceived as a discipline problem and dealt with punitively, while the "quietly mad" are ignored.' Birmingham *et al.* (2000) argue that such routine mental health screening by doctors on reception should be abandoned in favour of a two-stage model. This would combine factors that identified the higher risk groups (namely, past history of psychiatric care, history of self-harm, a charge of homicide, and the prescription of anti-depressants prior to remand) with a thorough mental health assessment.

Secondly, the mismatch between the narrow criteria for Mental Health Act disposal at the point of sentence and the subsequent broad clinical diagnosis of disorder will substantially account for the finding of fewer than one in ten with no diagnosable disorder. The tautological relationship between personality disorder/drug/alcohol and sexual problems, and offending behaviour will also skew the figures. Many of these offenders could benefit from transfer to a therapeutic community like Grendon. However, even with the new Grendon-type prison at Marchington (see below), provision will fall short of demand.

Lastly, disagreements among doctors about treatability and the lack of suitable facilities for those suffering from personality disorder and sexual deviation will result in resort to prison by default. Treatment in hospital for some types of offender is simply not a probable outcome; difficult or violent behaviour will often discount a therapeutic disposal. While the courts may perceive a need for a psychiatric referral, this ultimately is not matched by those providing the services, who define their role in a more limited way. Where the courts cannot force doctors to accept patients for treatment, prison sweeps up.

Or perhaps the reality is as Shapland (1991: 2) notes: '[w]e shall always have mentally disordered offenders in what we are currently calling the penal system not

---

[15] See www.doh.gov.uk/hospital/. Secure hospital bed numbers kindly supplied by the Christine Holmes of the Department of Health.

[16] By the end of 1999 there were 1,193 restricted patients in the special hospitals, and 1,664 in other hospitals (Johnson and Taylor 2000). These figures reflect a relatively static special hospital total, but a doubling in the restricted population in regional and medium secure units over the ten years prior to 1999.

because of lack of facilities, but because of intrinsic contradictions in our ideas about mental disorder and its relation to offending'.

Although the sentencing of mentally disordered offenders is predicated on notions of diversion and treatment, there has always been the possibility of recourse to a penal disposal where there are elements of culpability (or predicted dangerousness) which require punishment (or control). Indeed, even where doctors are willing and able to treat an offender, the courts may still insist upon a penal sentence (see *Mortimer*, below).

TRANSFER TO HOSPITAL

The development of mental disorder *after* imprisonment, together with a persistent failure to identify all those needing treatment at an earlier stage, makes necessary some transfer mechanism. Transfer from prison to hospital, with or without a restriction direction, has a history plagued with problems. Again the basic premise is difficult to contest, namely that detention in prison is inappropriate for those whose mental disorder is sufficiently serious to justify transfer to hospital; yet the figures suggested that transfer was consistently under-used (Grounds 1991). Difficulties moving patients on from the special hospitals clearly results in fewer beds being available for transferred prisoners. Moreover, since offender-patients tend to remain in conditions of greater than necessary security for longer than is justifiable, and neither Regional Secure Units, nor local hospitals, nor the local authority can be made to accept a patient even if it is agreed that he or she is ready to proceed to a less secure environment, any log-jam effect is enhanced.[17] Problems with remission to prison where a patient is untreatable,[18] or is mentally ill and, having responded to medication in hospital, is predicted as being likely to refuse to continue with treatment in a prison environment where no compulsion can be used, can create further difficulties. Clearly, a policy of flexible transfer will succeed only where the psychiatric system is geared to meet increased demand: in the context of an under-provision of secure facilities, this looks unlikely.

Yet recent statistics (Johnson and Taylor 2000) show a significant and arguably welcome increase in the numbers of prisoners transferred from prison to hospital. For sentenced prisoners, there was a sustained increase in the numbers transferred[19] during the ten years prior to 1999; while for unsentenced prisoners, there was a massive increase, with thirty-eight prisoners transferred in 1985 and 464 in 1999.[20] However,

---

[17] Since the Home Secretary has the power to direct the admission of a prisoner without the agreement of the hospital managers, it makes the argument in favour of retaining clinicians' agreement under s 37(4) look less compelling.

[18] Although prisoner-patients with restricted status are transferred back from hospital to prison, the numbers are small by comparison. In 1999, 167 were returned to prison, while 742 prisoners—both sentenced and unsentenced—went from prison to hospital (Johnson and Taylor 2000).

[19] From 120 to 276 for those with a restriction direction.

[20] Indeed, increases in the numbers of transferred prisoners substantially account for the marked increase in the 'restricted' hospital population. While the courts' use of ss 37 or 41 has increased—from 170 in 1989 to 253 in 1999—110 of the latter were patients who had already been transferred as remand prisoners to hospital (see Johnson and Taylor 2000, as amended by a personal communication from Johnson).

do the increased numbers suggest greater flexibility in the use of transfer provisions *per se*, or a growing reluctance by the courts to use therapeutic disposals in the first instance? The question is hard to answer. Nevertheless, figures relating to overall court and prison disposals (Department of Health 2000) show a marked decrease in admissions (from 2,100 in 1994/95 to 1,600 in 1999/2000) and a decrease in the use of hospital orders (with or without restrictions) from 952 in 1989/90 to 669 in 1999/2000.[21] The study by Mackay and Machin (2000) broadly supports the notion of greater flexibility between prison and hospital.[22] However, since 63 per cent of their sample of patients transferred as remand prisoners had previously received in-patient psychiatric treatment, and the transfer process was initiated within 25 days of over half of them being remanded into custody, one question remains. Why is s 35 not used more?[23] If more of them were not sent to hospital by the courts because of a reluctance by practitioners to accept such remands on a twelve week maximum basis, the mismatch between principle and practice is lamentable.

Two aspects of transfer are noteworthy. First, as Grounds (1991) argues, transfer may be motivated by a desire to protect the public rather than by a wish to ensure that the patient receives the care needed. The use of transfer for prisoners reaching the end of their sentence would support this assertion, as does the drive to introduce new orders and services in respect of 'DSPD' (see below). Secondly, transferred patients are in a disadvantageous position. Although they would be detained on a notional hospital order once their prison sentence expired, in an era when automatic life sentences for a second serious offence will inevitably increase the numbers of prisoners on life sentences, it will also impact on the discharge arrangements for those transferred to hospital. Moreover, the use of hospital and limitation directions (a sentence of imprisonment with a direction that the offender be admitted to hospital) is, as Eastman and Peay (1998) feared, likely to be extended generally from those suffering from psychopathic disorder to those suffering from all mental disorders (Department of Health/Home Office 2000).[24] Such directions may yet prove attractive to a judiciary favouring concepts of 'punishment and public protection' and, if extended, will also impact on the mechanics and safeguards embodied in the current transfer arrangements.

As Fennell (1991: 333) concludes, 'it is likely that, despite current policies of diversion, significant numbers of mentally disordered offenders will remain in prisons, and therefore there is an urgent need to consider how a humane and therapeutic psychiatric service might be provided within the prison system'. And here is the nub of the problem; mentally disordered offenders cannot be neatly packaged and swept into the caring system, for, on a broad definition of the term, they make up some 90 per cent

[21] These figures are not directly comparable with Home Office Statistics (see Johnson and Taylor, above) and suggest that the decline is due primarily to a decrease in the popularity of the hospital order without restrictions.

[22] It is notable that while the absolute numbers of transferred remand prisoners has increased since the Mackay and Machin study (377 to 464), the proportions ultimately receiving a hospital disposal remain broadly constant at around 50 per cent; (updated figures kindly supplied by Steven Johnson).

[23] The figures on remand to hospital for reports are small, and declining (see DoH 2000, above).

[24] By 1999–2000, only two such orders had been made for patients suffering from psychopathic disorder (Department of Health 2000).

of the prison population (see Singleton *et al.* 1998, above). Thus, some means of offering effective 'treatment' (if not compulsory treatment) within prison will have to be considered.

Hence, the resurgence of a treatment movement within criminology. Although its genesis may lie equally in a disillusionment with just deserts and humane containment for what is evidently a 'damaged' population, the presence and extent of mentally disordered offenders in the prison population constitutes a compelling force. While the view was ominously expressed in 1991 by the Home Office that 'offenders are not given sentences of imprisonment by the courts for the purposes of ensuring their rehabilitation' (para. 1.28), attempts to reduce subsequent offending by specific groups have grown in scale and importance over the last few years, especially through the cognitive-behavioural programmes developed under the 'What Works' agenda (see Raynor, in Chapter 31 of this volume). Indeed, in the light of the Halliday Report (Halliday *et al.* 2001, see below and Ashworth, in Chapter 29 of this volume), with its emphasis on the contribution that sentencing can make to crime reduction through working with offenders under sentence—both during and after a period of imprisonment—it can be argued that 'rehabilitation' is firmly back in vogue, even if it appears in a new and more instrumental guise.

MENTAL DISORDER AT TRIAL

At trial the impact of the mentally disordered offender's mental state lacks any coherence. This is attributable to a number of factors. First, the law's ambivalent attitude towards those whom it would wish to hold responsible/culpable for their actions but for whom punishment is manifestly inappropriate. Separating the mad from the bad may be easy at the margins; it is not so easy for the bulk of offenders. Secondly, the criminal law has a wholly inconsistent approach to the relevance of mental disorder when determining what standard of behaviour ought to be met before culpability can be established. For example, mental disorder is irrelevant for the objective application of *Caldwell* recklessness,[25] but is relevant to the second objective limb of the test in duress.[26] Thus, the two models of the 'reasonable and prudent person' which these two legal tests employ to judge culpability are inconsistent. In respect of provocation, the previously conflicting judgments of the Court of Appeal and Privy Council[27] have now been resolved, if not reconciled, by the House of Lords:[28] mental disorder becomes a relevant factor for the jury in determining what standard of self-control is applicable to the defendant. However, this ruling has itself been characterized as confused and as 'inviting an evaluative free-for-all in which anything that induces sympathy by the same token helps to excuse, and in which little more than lip service

[25] *Elliot v C (a minor)* [1983] 1 WLR 939.

[26] *Bowen* [1996] Crim LR 577 (CA); see also Buchanan and Virgo (1999).

[27] See the Privy Council in *Luc* [1996] 3 WLR 45, and the Court of Appeal in, for example, *Campbell* [1997] 1 Cr App R 199, *Thornton* [1996] 1 WLR 1174, and *Ahluwalia* [1992] 4 All ER 889.

[28] *Smith (Morgan)* [2000] 3 WLR 654.

is paid to the all important objective (impersonal) standard of the reasonable person' (Gardner and Macklem 2001: 635). In short, superficial legal certainty seems to have been achieved at the expense of an underlying consistent and coherent application of the law. Thirdly, although the fluctuating conflict between the disciplines of psychiatry and law has resulted in law largely winning the battle over the grounds for conviction, psychiatry has been more influential in respect of the scope for and nature of disposal (Johnstone 1996). Moreover, it is evident that psychiatric and psychological evidence is increasingly prevalent and influential in criminal proceedings (Roberts 1996). This reflects the paradoxical reliance on a defendant's mental state where it might avoid culpability or mitigate sentence, but an avoidance of such 'labels' where it might increase the likelihood of 'undesirable' sentences. Lastly, it is a battle ground the perimeters and parameters of which have changed; the mandatory life sentence following a conviction for murder has had a significant impact on the evolution of the excusatory defences of diminished responsibility and now provocation, while diminished responsibility has also served to plug some of the gaps in the too narrowly drawn M'Naghten criteria (see below). Similarly, the relationship between provocation and self-defence serves to illustrate how conceptual notions of the responsible man can exclude women (through the inapplicability of the provocation test within traditional male/female interactions), leaving women more likely to be pathologized through resort to diminished responsibility (Wells 1994).

Some leavening of this selectivity has occurred both with the judgment in *Smith* (above) and with the partial recognition of two concepts necessary for 'battered woman syndrome' (BWS);[29] namely, cumulative provocation and the relegation of a time delay from a legal bar to a defence of provocation, to one where it is simply evidence of whether self-control was in fact lost suddenly. Even this, however, does not resolve the problem that BWS is not, as yet, a validated psychiatric syndrome (see Rix 2001).

The interaction of mental disorder, law, and trial processes is thus a fascinating area. Its continuing evolution will only be touched upon here in respect of four topics: unfit to plead (disorder at the point of trial); not guilty by reason of insanity (those 'M'Naghten Mad' at the time of the offence); infanticide (an exceptional charge for women); and diminished responsibility (a qualified defence to murder). Arguably, all four of these areas represent crisis points for legal theory, in that the consequences of a full application of the law would, or did, constitute intolerable outcomes for 'needy' individuals, attributable directly to the court's lack of discretion. Importation of psychiatric reasoning and the construction of concepts of responsibility have enabled offenders to be dealt with primarily on the basis of their medical condition rather than on the basis of their criminal behaviour. Hence, treatment for who they are, not for what they have done. Of course, the danger is that once deference to psychiatric notions is permitted, welfarism need no longer be tempered by legalism, and outcomes which challenge notions of justice can arise. Thus, psychiatry's role in

---

[29] BWS is a controversial psychiatric syndrome thought to arise in the context of prolonged cycles of violence, abuse, and humiliation, which is associated with a state of learned helplessness (i.e., a seeming inability to walk away from or deal with the abusive situation — until the eruption of violence by the battered woman).

managing and controlling offenders efficiently may even legitimize forms or length of confinement which could not be justified in purely legal-punitive terms.

UNFIT TO PLEAD

The Criminal Procedure (Insanity and Unfitness to Plead) Act 1991 (hereafter the '1991 Act') effected much-needed statutory reform both for those found unfit to plead at trial and for those contesting their guilt on grounds of insanity. The earlier Criminal Procedure (Insanity) Act 1964 included a mandatory disposal for those found 'unfit' or 'insane'; namely, indefinite confinement in a mental hospital. Counsel would not infrequently advise clients to avoid such outcomes by pleading guilty to offences they may not have committed or about which counsel could not be confident of securing a jury acquittal. Although the Mental Health Act 1983 had improved the theoretical position of these patients—in that they became entitled to be discharged by MHRTs where the presence of continuing disorder could not be established—use of the provisions remained minimal (Mackay 1991). Given their underlying humanitarian ethos, persistent under-usage of these orders was an indictment of the law. Although their grounds remain the same under the 1991 Act, the consequences that follow from such determinations have changed radically. The 1991 Act increases the court's disposal options to include:

— an admission order (equivalent to a hospital order);
— an admission order with restrictions (which may be indefinite or of fixed length);
— guardianship;
— a supervision and treatment order;
— absolute discharge.

For findings arising in respect of murder charges, the disposal remains mandatory; namely, the equivalent of a hospital order with indefinite restrictions.

As to their rationale, 'unfit to plead' provisions attempt to protect individuals from the ordeal of trial if their mental state might cause that trial to be unfair. The statute did not provide any specific test of unfitness, neither can one be equated with certifiability, for the legal criteria did not 'fit neatly with any diagnostic criteria' (Chiswick 1990: 174). The legal criteria for fitness, summarized recently in the case of *Friend*,[30] concern whether

the accused will be able to comprehend the course of the proceedings so as to make a proper defence. Whether he can understand and reply rationally to the indictment is obviously a relevant factor, but the jury must also consider whether he would be able to exercise his right to challenge jurors, understand the details of the evidence as it is given, instruct his legal advisers and give evidence himself if he so desires.

Psychiatrists will also take into account other criteria, such as whether the defendant

---

[30] [1997] 2 All ER 1012, at 1018; see also *R v Pritchard* (1836) 7 C & P 303.

can understand the consequences of the charge, or whether he or she would be able to control himself or herself during a trial (Mackay and Kearns 2000).

The 1991 Act requires unfitness to be determined by a jury on the evidence of two or more doctors. If the accused is found unfit, the trial will not proceed. However, a (new) jury will then consider, on the basis of such evidence adduced by the prosecution and by a person appointed by the court to put the case for the defence, whether the accused did the act or made the omission charged.[31] During this 'trial of the facts' there is no examination of the accused's intention. If the jury is satisfied that the *actus reus* is not made out, the accused is acquitted. If made out, the accused remains unfit, the court has access to the increased range of disposals. The provisions accordingly do not allow for the legal issues to remain in limbo; accused persons found to be unfit will either be acquitted and walk away from the court, or be found to have done the act or made the omission charged and be liable to 'therapeutic' intervention.[32]

In Mackay and Kearns's (2000) study of 110 disposals under the 1991 Act, 77 per cent received hospital disposals, with or without restrictions. While this might suggest that judges are still not making as great a use of the new flexible (non-hospital based) disposals as they might, Mackay and Kearns note that defendants found unfit to plead at trial are quite likely to be ill at the point of trial, and accordingly in need of hospital treatment. This contrasts with those pleading not guilty by reason of insanity, where the disorder has to have been present at the time of the offence but not at the time of trial. Here, over 50 per cent of disposals were non-hospital based (Mackay and Kearns 1999).

NOT GUILTY BY REASON OF INSANITY

For a verdict of not guilty by reason of insanity,[33] it must be established that the accused falls within the ambit of the M'Naghten Rules, their essence being that the accused:

at the time of the committing of the act . . . was labouring under such a defect of reason, from disease of the mind, as not to know the nature and quality of the act he was doing, or, if he did know it, that he did not know he was doing what was wrong [*M'Naghten's Case* (1843) 10 Cl & F 200, at 210].

The Rules provide a legal test of responsibility for the mentally disordered. Their emphasis on the accused's cognitive state, rather than on volition or conation, makes them problematic, in particular for psychiatrists. Moreover, insanity in the medical sense is not sufficient for the defence, and although mental disorder *per se* at the point

[31] See *AG's Reference (No. 3 of 1998)* [1999] 3 All ER 40; *Antoine* [1999] 3 WLR 1204.

[32] Difficulties nonetheless remain, as illustrated by the case of Szymon Serafinowicz, the first person (not) to be tried under the War Crimes Act 1991. Committed on murder charges, Serafinowicz was found unfit to plead by a jury who heard conflicting evidence as to his dementia before his trial commenced. Rather than moving to a 'trial of the facts', the Attorney General entered a plea of *nolle prosequi* permanently staying the proceedings.

[33] The defence applies both in the Crown Court and in summary trials: *R v Horseferry Road Magistrates' Court, ex p K* [1996] 3 All ER 733.

of the act alleged to constitute a crime is a prerequisite, what gets 'counted' legally as mental disorder would not necessarily be recognizable as such to psychiatrists.[34] It has been argued (Baker 1994) that incorporation of the ECHR via the Human Rights Act 1998 will remedy this indefensible anomaly. The Convention requires objective medical evidence of mental disorder before those of 'unsound mind' can be deprived of their liberty. Tellingly, *M'Naghten* has already been found incompatible with the European Convention in Jersey (Mackay and Gearty 2001), paving the way for similar reform in England and Wales.

Historically, the insanity defence has been used rarely (Dell 1983). Looking at cases over a fourteen-year period up to 1988, Mackay's (1990) research revealed that the verdict occurred primarily not in murder cases, but in other non-fatal offences against the person of an unprovoked nature. Curiously, given legal scholars' preference for the first limb of *M'Naghten* (did not know the nature or quality of the act), in well over half of the sample the second limb of the test (did not know that it was wrong) accounted for the verdicts. This may, of course, be partly attributable to the failure to distinguish between lack of knowledge of legal wrong (as required by law) and lack of knowledge of moral wrong (frequently a better fit with the facts of the sample). But, as Mackay notes (ibid.: 251), 'the general impression gained . . . was that the wrongness issue was being treated in a liberal fashion by all concerned, rather than in the strict manner regularly depicted by legal commentators' (see, e.g., Dell 1983; Verdun-Jones 1989).

In their study of forty-four insanity verdicts under the 1991 Act, Mackay and Kearns (1999) come to a similar conclusion; namely, that the question psychiatrists overwhelmingly addressed was: 'If the delusion that the defendant was experiencing at the time of the offence was in fact reality, then would the defendant's actions be morally justified?' As the authors note, this is not the narrow cognitive test of legal wrongness set by the M'Naghten Rules. In applying this interpretation the courts expand the Rules' scope. Moreover, despite the statute seemingly being clear, verdicts of not guilty by reason of insanity occurred where no jury was empanelled; indeed, in the majority of cases the insanity defence was not disputed by the prosecution.

A similar lack of fit between criminal law and criminal procedure where the defendant's mental state is at issue may be illustrated by one paradox raised by Mackay and Kearns (2000). In *Antoine*,[35] the House of Lords clarified that while a plea of diminished responsibility could not be relied upon during a trial of the facts for murder, the prosecution would nonetheless have to negative any arguable defences.[36] Thus, an individual suffering from epileptic automatism who is fit to plead but then found legally insane, will receive the special verdict (possibly a hospital order with indefinite restrictions). Yet the individual with the same condition who is unfit to

---

[34] For example, diabetic hyperglycaemia (*Hennessey* [1989] 2 All ER 9) and epilepsy (*Sullivan* [1984] AC 156).

[35] [1999] 3 WLR 1204.

[36] In *Antoine*, the House of Lords expressly also overruled *Egan* [1998] 1 Cr App R 121, which had problematically held that it was necessary for the prosecution to establish during any trial of the facts both that the defendant did the act charged and had the necessary *mens rea* or mental state at the time.

plead, and for whom the prosecution fail to negative an arguable defence during a trial of the facts, will receive a complete acquittal.

Lastly, whether the 1991 Act has significantly enhanced use of the 'unfit' and 'insanity' provisions remains unclear. The indications are that the insanity verdict remains a relatively rare outcome (Mackay and Kearns 1999), while 'unfit' findings have begun to rise as lawyers and psychiatrists have become more familiar with the workings of the 1991 Act (Mackay and Kearns 2000).[37] Since the implementation of the Crime (Sentences) Act 1997, with its mandatory sentencing provisions, it is likely that there will be further shift in the use of these orders, as a means of avoiding 'relevant' convictions.

INFANTICIDE

The Infanticide Act 1938 created a special category of offence under section 1(1), where a woman causes the death of her child aged under twelve months when her mind was 'disturbed by reason of not having fully recovered from the effect of giving birth to the child or by reason of the effect of lactation consequent upon the birth of the child'.

The provision enables the court to avoid the mandatory life sentence for murder and impose whatever penalty it thinks fit. Given that the homicide rate for children under the age of one year is greater than that for any other age group, it is curious that only twenty-seven homicides of children were classified as infanticide during the period 1982–89; manslaughter on grounds of diminished responsibility was the most common outcome in cases of child homicide (Wilczynski and Morris 1993). Since the defence of diminished responsibility encompasses a wider group of victims, including those aged over twelve months and the children of others, this is not wholly surprising. However, a charge of infanticide can provide a defence where a mother kills in circumstances of extreme stress arising out of, for example, poverty, social deprivation, failure of bonding, or otherwise being unable to cope with a new baby; such circumstances would not readily fall within the defence of diminished responsibility. Moreover, as there is no requirement on a charge of infanticide for causality between a woman's distressed condition and her actions in taking life (Maier-Katkin and Ogle 1993), it provides considerable scope for a psychiatric defence.

Although such usage may come dangerously close to making 'adverse social conditions a defence to child killing' (Smith and Hogan 1988: 363), the Criminal Law Revision Committee (1984: paras 103–6) wished to ratify this approach by extending the offence to cover stresses caused by 'circumstances consequent to the birth'. As Hoggett (1996: 114) questions, should such stresses amount to an excuse; and if so, why should they not apply to fathers as well, where provoked to kill by intolerable

---

[37] The Act came into force on 1 January 1992. Johnson and Taylor (2000) cite 28 'unfit' and 6 'insanity' based restriction orders for 1999, indicating some increase for the former but markedly little usage for the latter. These figures are somewhat misleading since they do not include the 'other disposals' permissible since the 1991 Act; indeed, the figures do not now appear to be collected in any consistent form. However, Mackay and Kearns, who have attempted to track the disposals' use nationally, similarly report 'unfit' provisions rising from 13 in 1990 to 33 in 1996, with insanity verdicts barely in double figures — 4 in 1990 and 13 in 1996.

circumstances but falling outside the current ambit of provocation?[38] Equally provocatively, in an era when the care of very young children is handed to au pairs, babysitters, and siblings, should such persons come within the ambit of infanticide?

DIMINISHED RESPONSIBILITY

The Homicide Act 1957, s 2(1), enabled a defendant to be found not guilty of murder, but guilty of manslaughter by reason of diminished responsibility, where the defendant could establish that:

he was suffering from such abnormality of mind (whether arising from a condition of arrested or retarded development of mind or any inherent causes or induced by disease or injury) as substantially impaired his mental responsibility for his acts and omissions in doing or being a party to the killing.

The abnormality test—'a state of mind so different from that of ordinary human beings that the reasonable man would term it abnormal'[39]—is sufficiently wide to include a gamut of disordered states, even if transient. It includes the failure to resist an impulse where, although the ability to resist was present, it was substantially less than that of an ordinary man and the offender could not, or could not without substantial difficulty, have resisted. Arguably, it has provided a psychiatrist's charter at trial. However, Mackay (1999) notes a recent reduction in the number of successful pleas, from sixty-eight in 1994 to forty-nine in 1996, while murder convictions rose in the same period. He argues that the decisions in the cases of *Sanderson* and *O'Connell*,[40] which provide judicial guidance on the meaning of 'inherent cause, disease and injury', may have made the defence less accessible, in particular to mercy killers. While a plea of diminished responsibility may be being looked at more sceptically by all concerned, its very presence suggests that it is possible to have degrees of responsibility. This raises a further difficulty. If there can be lesser degrees of responsibility, why should the defence be confined to murder?

Diminished responsibility, and the peculiar reliance on it by women who kill, should not be seen in isolation from the 'alternative' defences of provocation and self-defence. Broadly, the qualified defences of diminished responsibility and provocation are regarded in law as excuses—with the focus being on the actor—while self-defence is a justification and focuses on the act; where successful it provides a complete defence. Yet women in England and Wales make more use of 'psychiatric defences' such as diminished responsibility, while men resort to self-defence (Wells 1994) or lack of intent to kill. In turn, women are more likely to receive psychiatric disposals and men penal sentences. Pathologizing women via infanticide and diminished responsibility rather than utilizing self-defence—which leaves an offender with a normal response to abnormal circumstances rather than an abnormal response to

[38] In *R v Doughty* (1986) 83 Cr App R 319 the Court of Appeal held that a defence of provocation by a man based on a baby's persistent crying could properly be left to the jury.

[39] Lord Parker CJ in *R v Byrne* [1960] 2 QB 396, at 403.

[40] (1994) 98 Cr App R 325 and [1997] Crim LR 683, respectively

common circumstances (giving birth/woman battering)—may help to explain why although women are grossly outnumbered by men in the prison population, they are only outnumbered by men in the special hospitals at about a rate of 7:1.[41] Hence, gender rather than mental disorder may be the pre-eminent factor in determining special treatment.

MENTAL DISORDER, OFFENDING BEHAVIOUR, AND TREATMENT

Treatment is the fundamental justification for separate provision for mentally disordered people who have committed offences. But it is not readily clear what is meant by treatment, or what treatment is attempting to alter—the 'underlying disorder', the offending behaviour, or the link, if any, between the two? Or are our efforts really devoted largely to alleviating the distress and emotional problems offenders suffer, those either pre-existing or post-dating the offending? If it is the likelihood of criminal behaviour *per se*, the justification for treatment will not be confined to a 'mentally disordered' sub-group of offenders. Accordingly, an examination of the relationship between disorder and offending is critical. This leads into the final section on protection. Here, the argument is turned on its head: where mental disorder provides a basis not for a therapeutic disposal but for a lengthier custodial disposal than would be proportionate to the seriousness of the offence. Should there then be a compensatory right to treatment for that disorder?

WHAT IS THE RELATIONSHIP BETWEEN MENTAL DISORDER AND OFFENDING BEHAVIOUR?

As Prins (1990) has amply demonstrated, the relationship between mental abnormality and criminality is an uncertain one. Prins summarizes the principal psychiatric classifications of disorder and illustrates the forms of offending which may be more (or less) likely to be associated with them, concluding (ibid.: 256), 'Most psychiatric disorders are only very occasionally associated with criminality'. Prins also illustrates well the difficulties of establishing cause and effect in this troubled area: 'we are trying to make connections between very different phenomena, and these phenomena are the subject of much debate concerning both substance and definition' (ibid.: 247).

Another emphasis in the literature concerns the relationship between mental disorder and *violence* (Monahan 1992; Wesseley and Taylor 1991). The overwhelming correlates of violence are male gender, youth, lower socio-economic class, and the use/abuse of alcohol or drugs, and not the diagnosis of major mental disorder. However, the belief that mental disorder predisposes people to behave violently is widely held

---

[41] Patients detained on restriction orders (Johnson and Taylor 2000).

and enduring, resulting in discriminatory practices and attitudes towards those with mental disorder.[42] Thus,

certain mental disorders [are] characterized by some kind of confused, bizarre, agitated, threatening, frightened, panicked, paranoid or impulsive behaviour. That and the view that impulse (i.e. ideation) and action are interchangeable support the belief that all mental disorder must of necessity lead to inappropriate, anti-social or dangerous actions [Rubin 1972: 398].

The relationship has been highly problematic to research. However, available now are the results from the MacArthur study of mental disorder and violence (Monahan *et al.* 2001), a study based on 1,000 male and female acute admission civil patients from three sites in the United States. Patients were contacted up to five times in the community after discharge, and official data collected in relation to their histories and progress. In addition to this, there were extensive self-report data and interviews conducted with 'patient collaterals'—that is people nominated by the patient as being most familiar with their behaviour in the community. This methodologically rigorous study comes to a number of important conclusions, although the research is imbued with the familiar caveat that these relationships are complex. The authors counsel 'an interactional approach to violence risk assessment rather than one that relies on "main effects" that apply uniformly to all patients' (ibid.: 60). That said, their findings pose some challenging conclusions. With respect to criminological factors the authors observe, first, that men are no more likely to be violent than women over the course of a one-year follow-up, although the nature of their violence differs (this is consistent with other studies of mental disorder, but not with the criminological literature generally); secondly, that prior violence and criminality are strongly associated with post-discharge violence; thirdly, physical abuse as a child, but not sexual abuse, was associated with post-discharge violence; and neighbourhood disadvantage—in short, poverty—was significantly associated with violence. This finding helps us to understand why using individual level predictors of violence—for example, race—can be so misleading. For although African-American racial status was associated with violence (odds ratio = 2.7), this was halved when neighbourhood disadvantage was taken into account (odds ratio = 1.3), and in absolute terms the effect of 'poverty' was more significant (odds ratio = 1.7) (ibid.: 58–59). Thus, the authors conclude, 'violence by persons with mental disorders may be, in part, a function of the high-crime neighbourhoods in which they typically reside' (ibid.: 60). As the authors observe, this has implications for where we place half-way houses and other accommodation in the community for people with mental illness.

With respect to clinical factors, the presence of a *co-occurring diagnosis of substance abuse or dependence* was critical (a common finding, which has led to particular concerns about these so-called 'dual diagnosis' cases). More surprising was that a diagnosis of schizophrenia was associated with lower rates of violence than either a diagnosis of depression, or, more significantly, *personality disorder*. Curiously, although psychopathy was a strong predictor of violence, the predictive power of the

---

[42] For an excellent resource on mental disorder and stigma, see Crisp (2001).

Hare PCL:SV[43] derived from its 'antisocial behaviour' factor and not its 'emotional detachment' factor (the features more typically associated with those suffering from psychopathic disorder, see below). Notably, neither delusions, nor hallucinations, nor (controversially) command hallucinations[44] were associated with higher rates of violence (making prescient Monahan and Steadman's (1983) question as to why those with paranoid delusions should be any more or less likely to attack their tormentors than those who are in fact being tormented). Failure to support the previous findings that lack of control and associated violent behaviour may be a prerogative of the *currently actively psychotic* (Swanson *et al.* 1990; Link, Andrews, and Cullen 1992) conflicts with some dearly-held psychiatric notions. However, the authors point to the mediating factor of non-delusional suspiciousness, which may account for a tendency to interpret others' behaviour as hostile. Notably, even the relationship between violent thoughts and violence is not strong (although gaining an accurate measure of violent thoughts is inherently problematic), neither is that between anger and violence (although it was statistically significant).

While this litany of factors would seem, even using an interactional approach, to stack up against those with mental disorders, it is important to stress two matters. First, the complexity of the causes of violence amongst those with mental disorder (and, in all probability, of those without mental disorder) means that there will be no single solution to violence. Accordingly, any single treatment approach is likely to be of limited efficacy and predictions of future violence will remain extremely hazardous. Secondly, mental disorders 'in sharp contrast to alcohol and drug abuse—account for a minuscule proportion of the violence that afflicts American society' (Monahan 1997).

In contrast, merely weighing the contribution of Bluglass and Bowden's *Principles and Practice of Forensic Psychiatry* (1990) might lead one to conclude that there is no form of *criminal* behaviour without a psychiatric element, with chapters on everything from Amok to Sexual Asphyxia. Writing now, in the immediate aftermath of the terrorist attacks on the United States, the observation in earlier editions of the *Oxford Handbook* that it was regrettable that Bluglass and Bowden included nothing on Zealotry remains apt. Two UK journals—*Criminal Behaviour and Mental Health* and *The Journal of Forensic Psychiatry*—have also focused on the relationship between mental ill-health and criminal behaviour. Although I could not do justice to this body of knowledge, some general observations follow which are pertinent to this path of medicalized explanations.

First, offence categories amongst 'disordered offenders' mirror those of 'normal' populations, with the only differences being that the disordered populations are slightly less likely to be convicted of offences of violence and slightly more likely to have committed property offences. Popular images of axe-wielding maniacs are based on highly visible and intuitively attractive data, but are neither statistically sustainable nor replicable.[45]

---

[43] A screening version of the Hare Psychopathy Checklist (Hart *et al.* 1995).

[44] Hallucinations involving 'voices' instructing or compelling the recipient to carry out a particular act.

[45] Even the remand population (manifestly the most 'disordered' sub-sample: Singleton *et al.* 1998) exhibits strikingly high levels of self-harm (Dooley, 1990) and not violence against others. Of 64 prison suicides in 1996, 36 were on remand.

Secondly, the suggestion that many of the offending population have themselves been offended against constitutes another form of medicalized explanation of their behaviour. Undoubtedly, the level of disorder and disadvantage amongst the prison population testifies to the inadequacies of the average confined offending population, but it is, in essence, an index of social failure, not criminogenic predispositions. Disentangling correlation and causation is highly problematic. How, for example, can it be determined what the relevance of the victimization was to the individual, if observations are based on psychiatric contact with those who have offended? Why should physical but not sexual abuse be related to subsequent violence (see Monahan *et al.* 2001, above)? Offenders may be only too willing to have their behaviour treated as something 'uncontrollable' if there is an anticipated benefit of so doing. The scene is set: offenders are prepared to incorporate psychiatric explanations of their behaviour; victimization in one form or another is a common, if not universal, experience; psychiatrists are peculiarly reliant on what their clients tell them; offending is widespread. All of the ingredients are present to permit a re-structuring of experiences as explanations or excuses.

Or is the victim/offending relationship merely coincidental? The danger is twofold. Once criminologists start down this path it is hard to see where it ends. Are not all offences equally open to medicalization? Even seemingly comprehensible property offences may, especially where trivial items are involved, require some less readily accessible explanation than mere acquisitiveness. Secondly, a medicalized explanation precedes a medicalized solution. But if treatment is adopted and then fails, is the next step to throw away the key?

TREATMENT IN PRISON

In 1990 the Home Office observed, 'For most offenders, imprisonment has to be justified in terms of public protection, denunciation and retribution. Otherwise it can be an expensive way of making bad people worse' (para. 2.7). Since then, evidence-based treatment programmes, both in prison and in the community, have gained considerable momentum, under the general heading of the 'What Works' initiative (Home Office 2001). The latter has had a significant impact on the philosophy of imprisonment, even if the implementation of accredited programmes remains patchy. However, it is worth noting here that the focus has largely been on treating offending, rather than on mental disorder *per se*; problems inevitably remain with the programmes, including determining an acceptable measure of success. By the end of 2001, over 100 prisons were running such programmes, with five specific programmes in prisons and nine in the probation service having been accredited.[46] Cognitive behavioural programmes for sex offenders, offence-focused problem solving (the McGuire 'Think First' programme), substance abuse treatment programmes,

---

[46] Information kindly supplied by the What Works unit at the Prison Department, further to the above publication. These numbers are minimum numbers, first, because the accreditation programme has been gaining momentum since its inception, and partly because a number of sex offender accredited programmes pre-date the establishment of the Joint Accreditation Panel.

controlling and managing anger (CALM), and cognitive self-change programmes for violent offenders capture the flavour of these initiatives (see also Raynor, and Hollin in Chapters 31 and 5 respectively of this volume; Grubin 2001).

The pace of change has arguably already made outdated Crow's (2001: 116) observation that 'Rather than being a treatment, prison has become a place where treatment may occur', for clearly initiatives are underway. However, the extent to which treatment endeavours can be both sustained and effective remains questionable. Achieving effectiveness will be jeopardized by two enduring factors: prison overcrowding; and the use of short sentences. With four out of every five prisoners on sentences of less than twelve months, the potential for programme disruption remains acute. Moreover, if sentencers come to believe that imprisonment will secure access to beneficial treatment programmes for persistent offenders, 'ordered' offenders may find themselves at as great a risk as disordered offenders of therapeutic sentencing. Should imprisonment indeed acquire an image of anything other than 'the sentence of last resort', whatever good work might be achieved through accredited programmes is at risk of being overwhelmed by demand and the seemingly ever-present issues of overcrowding.

Emphasis is also shifting on to the importance of resettlement and providing through-care from prisons into the community via the probation service. Indeed, such joint working is likely to be the flavour of the future. While the 'through-care' approach has been applied, in particular, to sex offenders, its increasingly narrow focus on crime reduction is problematic. Grant (1999) sets this in the context of multi-agency working in the community, where pragmatic restraint rather than treatment *per se* is the objective. He argues that it is no easy task to support the health needs of less serious offenders while managing the risk they pose and the fear they engender in others because of their perceived potential for harm (for discussions of the expanding role of 'multi-agency public protection panels', which operate a combination of risk assessment, enhanced supervision, surveillance, and information sharing between various agencies, see Maguire *et al.* 2001; Kemshall and Maguire 2001). Such an approach will also involve criminal justice personnel in clinical decision-making (see Fennell and Yeates 2002).

The shift from broadly based rehabilitation to offence-specific crime reduction initiatives has also impacted on Grendon (psychiatric) Prison. Previously, the reduction of offending had not been the primary goal of its therapeutic community regime. However, with accreditation of the approach adopted in one of its main wings (under the 'What Works' criteria of the accreditation panel—see Raynor, in Chapter 31 of this volume), even Grendon has come within the thraldom of the crime reduction agenda. Genders and Player (1995), who conducted a major study of the therapeutic regime at Grendon in the pre-accreditation era, had noted that its rehabilitative ethos made prisoners address their offending behaviour as a means of preparing them for release, rather than striving for reformation *per se*. They observed that Grendon perceived crime neither as exclusively a function of personal pathology, nor as structurally caused; therapy was primarily a means of promoting the welfare of each inmate. The environment promoted individual responsibility and prevented 'a creeping and all-pervading dependency by prisoners on the prison authority' (Woolf 1991:

para. 14.13). Despite this potentially deviant history, there has been sufficient confidence in Grendon's (pre-accreditation) approach to difficult offenders (including those with personality disorders and sex offenders) for a second Grendon to be built. Curiously named Dovegate, this new prison is based near Uttoxeter.[47]

An inmate's therapeutic career, as charted by Genders and Player, takes some eighteen months to complete; any assessment of subsequent reconviction should thus be measured only against those who passed through all stages of the Grendon career. When such an approach is adopted (Cullen 1993) there are some limited but encouraging data to suggest that those rated 'successes' in therapy at Grendon have lower reconviction rates. All sorts of caveats need to be made about the validity of such data (Genders and Player 1995: 184–6); moreover, the authors remain cautious about the theoretical basis for a link between progress in therapy and future criminality. Any progress at Grendon represents only a small part of the prison experience; any change Grendon facilitates may have little or no bearing on an individual's subsequent social situation or structural position in society. Indeed, Gunn and Robertson's (1987) study had found *no* significant differences in reconviction rates in respect of either frequency or severity of offending for Grendon releases with a matched control group. Thus, Grendon's 'successes' may alter their behaviour only in respect of how they deal with problems, which may or may not have led them into criminal difficulties in the past. That may be a sufficient justification for the treatment endeavour, but it should not be confused with questions of re-offending, particularly in areas where offending is peculiarly intractable. To focus on measures of recidivism risks building into treatment programmes an element of self-destruct; or, as Player (1992) cautions, where the emphasis is on the unobtainable 'quick fix', the risk of a shift towards more Draconian methods of control remains.

Genders and Player (1995) also detail the incompatibilities between the demands of security and control and those of therapeutic endeavour. This is also a theme taken up by Crow (2001) in respect of the clash between therapeutic values and crime reduction measures. Where, for accreditation, the reduction of offending has to be the primary objective, treatment programmes may find themselves deficient in actual or committed volunteers if such programmes continue to emphasize sanctions (for example, having mandatory drug testing before entry into a programme). A similar theme applies to health care in prisons. Such health care is always likely to be problematic where 'the guiding doctrines of equity, autonomy and empowerment are . . . subordinated by the operational demands for security and control' Smith (2000: 350); despite this, recent developments have seen the acceptance of the principle of equivalence between prison health care and the NHS (as reviewed in Grounds 2000).[48]

Lastly, prison remains an inappropriate location for patients with psychotic dis-

---

[47] Grendon's record of success in controlling prisoners is, however, notable; there are few discipline problems with what is a highly problematic population. As Genders and Player (1995) point out, underpinning Grendon's success is the knowledge, by all concerned, that the rest of the prison system provides a very different form of containment.

[48] See also Woolf (1991).

orders. The inability to impose medication, together with the damning acceptance in *Knight v The Home Office*[49] that there may be 'circumstances in which the standard of care falls below that which would be expected in a psychiatric hospital without the prison authority being negligent', make this unarguable. Official reports continue to record the inadequacy of the care provided in prisons with, for example, HM Inspectorate of Prisons noting after a visit to Holloway that, of twenty-five in-patients in the health care centre fifteen 'were so ill that they should have been in an NHS facility as their health needs were far beyond the capacity of the staff on the ward' (2001: para. 2.109). And, most notably, the UK has now been found in violation of Article 2 of the ECHR—the right to life—following the killing of one mentally disordered man by another; both had been on remand and held in the same cell in Chelmsford Prison.[49A]

This minefield may be crudely summarized;

1. 'Treatment' may mean many different things—ranging from the administration of anti-psychotic medication to the acquisition of social survival skills. There may be a mismatch between health and criminal justice personnel in respect of the objectives of treatment.

2. If the relationship between the disorder and the offending behaviour is not primarily causal, there is less justification for excusing from punishment, and offenders should remain entitled to protection of their rights as offenders while not being denied access to treatment.

3. Even if there is some causal element, punishment for the partially responsible (and hence, partially guilty) can be combined with treatment, where requested.

4. Successful treatment for a disorder may have no bearing on future criminality; mentally disordered offenders should be accorded proportionality in the length of confinement; release should not be determined on the basis of predictions of future offending.

5. As Campbell and Heginbotham (1991: 135) argue, where an offender is treatable and there is some causal connection between the disorder and his or her offending behaviour, there may be less (or no) justification for continued detention after treatment.

6. In the existing context, the balance between jurisprudential logic, which may sanction punishment for the 'culpable' mentally disordered offender, and decades of a humanitarian response endorsing a commonsense preference for treatment rather than punishment, ought to be reversed in favour of the former only where treatment can be demonstrated to be wholly inappropriate.

PSYCHOPATHIC DISORDER

There is likely to be some association between disorders of personality and criminality, since the legal definition of psychopathic disorder under the 1983 Act includes

---

[49] [1990] 3 All ER 237.
[49A] *Paul and Audrey Edwards v The U.K.* Application No. 46477/99. Judgment 14 March 2002, Strasbourg.

the element that the disorder has resulted in 'abnormally aggressive or seriously irresponsible conduct'. In essence, it is a legal category defined by persistently violent behaviour.[50] But where the psychiatric profession employs clinical concepts of personality disorder, therapeutic and conceptual difficulties result (Grounds 1987). Confusion seems endemic. Some argue that the label 'psychopathic disorder' adds nothing to an understanding of the condition, and indeed doubt the very existence of an underlying medical condition. Others judge the label to be 'little more than a moral judgement masquerading as a clinical diagnosis' (Prins 1991: 119, citing Blackburn), while some recognize a disorder but doubt whether any psychiatric intervention could be successful. Yet others argue that an attempt should be made to continue to treat selected psychopathic offenders since the 'sheer range of psychopathology makes it more appropriate . . . to think of the psychopathic disorders rather than a single entity' (Coid 1989: 755).

What is psychopathy? Roth's definition (1990: 449) is noteworthy:

It comprises forms of egotism, immaturity, aggressiveness, low frustration tolerance and inability to learn from experience that places the individual at high risk of clashing with any community that depends upon cooperation and individual responsibility of its members for its continued existence. It has a characteristic sex distribution, age of onset, family history of similar symptoms and disorders and family constellations and influences that show a large measure of consistency in their course and outcome.

It is also important to stress that people suffering from 'psychopathic disorder' rarely find themselves subject to civil commitment, which might be expected if the disorder were genuinely problematic for the individual. Equally, it is not unimaginable that being ruthless, cold, uncaring, and egocentric may, in some walks of life, be beneficial.

From a criminological perspective, it is worth reiterating the findings of Monahan *et al.* (2001), above. Psychopathy, as measured by the Hare Psychopathy Check List, appears to have two dimensions: one relating to interpersonal and affective features (selfishness/callousness, etc.); and one to socially deviant behaviours (irresponsibility, anti-social behaviour, etc.). However, the relationship between psychopathy and violence (Hare 1999) appears, according to the Monahan *et al.* analysis (2001: 70), to be derived from the second dimension—the anti-social behaviour factor—and to tap personality traits associated with a consistent record of impulsive, irresponsible, anti-social acts. The underlying emotional pathology appears less important. If so, this would have obvious implications for the likelihood of success of any treatment regime.

Psychiatrists find themselves in a dilemma. The era of psychiatric optimism which preceded the 1959 Act has been replaced, particularly in respect of the treatment of aberrant behaviour, by an era of psychiatric pessimism. Psychiatrists are increasingly wary of being asked to 'treat' psychopathic offenders. Some of the resultant slack has been taken up by psychologists, but even their enthusiasm may wane if the treatment is really containment and control. Paradoxically, psychiatrists have found themselves

---

[50] The admission figures for 1999 of offenders suffering from psychopathic disorder given a restriction order indicate the infrequency with which the provisions are used (15 orders or 6 per cent of admissions) (Johnson and Taylor 2000).

criticized both for a failure to offer treatment to those they regard as untreatable, and for releasing those they deem successfully treated. In this context, their opposition to the introduction of a formal 'community treatment order', which would entail further responsibilities for them in respect of controlling offender-patients in the community, is hardly surprising.

DANGEROUS PEOPLE WITH SEVERE PERSONALITY DISORDER

All of the difficulties outlined above are typified in the government's DSPD initiative. This development (Home Office 1999; Department of Health/Home Office 2000) is the latest in a long line of legislative attempts to address the difficulties posed either by those with 'psychopathic disorder', or, in this case, by an ill-defined sub-set of them. While this group has been portrayed as having

high rates of depression, anxiety, illiteracy, poor relationships and loss of family ties, homelessness and unemployment. They have high rates of suicide and high rates of death by violent means. They have high rates of substance misuse. Their behaviour is often violent. Their behaviour is of immense distress to themselves and they are frequently in the position where they are asking for help and yet finding it very difficult to access suitable help [Home Office 1999: 34]

it is hard to resist the sense that the initiative stems not from concerns about treatment, justice, or due process, but explicitly from anxiety about re-offending by those 'prematurely' released from the hospital or prison system.[51]

The DSPD proposals have become, since the last edition of the *Handbook*, a prime focus for service development and legislative provision (see McAlinden 2001; Prins 2001; Fennell 2001). This sub-set of the personality disordered/psychopathically disordered is thought to number some 2,400 men (DoH/Home Office 2000: Part II, para. 1.5). A decision has still not been made as to exactly what form the order will take, or where these individuals (and not all of them will be offenders) will be contained. Or for how long. However, it is notable that the initiative seems to be focused on providing specialist facilities supported by new legislative powers in association with reform of the existing Mental Health Act. Are these programmes then to be outwith the traditional prison regime? This is not necessarily the case; cognitive behavioural programmes for 'psychopaths' in prison remain on the What Works agenda (see above). And, of the four DSPD pilot schemes, two are to be sited in prisons.[52] To what extent this reveals an emphasis on containment rather than treatment, or the tacit recognition that treatment may not be successful, is unclear.

The initiative does not bode well. It has shocked our North American counterparts, who have observed that even there such proposals had not been countenanced. Although a research programme has been initiated, there is a very strong sense that the legislation will proceed in advance of any firm research findings. This is not to be

---

[51] Other earlier initiatives in this field fell by the wayside, partly out of a recognition that these proposals might have led not to more control but to less (Peay 1988).

[52] At HMP Whitemoor and HMP Frankland. The two hospitals involved are Rampton and Broadmoor.

an evidence-based programme. And how, anyway, could it be? If there is no agreed definition, no clear diagnosis, no agreed treatment, no means of assessing when the predicted risk may have been reduced, and no obvious link between the alleged underlying condition and the behaviour, how could outcome measures be agreed upon and then evaluated? The potential for the demonization of this group and discrimination against them thereafter is self-evident.[53]

PROTECTIVE SENTENCING: PROCEDURAL SAFEGUARDS *v* TREATMENT

It will be recalled from the section on mental disorder at trial that reform in this area has been devoted primarily to increasing the court's sentencing options and not to addressing issues of prior culpability. This has a number of consequences for those who remain to be sentenced on a 'conventional' basis. Indeed, as Eastman and Peay (1999: 12) observe:

Mentally disordered offenders may thus be doubly disadvantaged; hardly any gain benefit from their disorder by securing an acquittal on grounds of insufficient responsibility, whilst few of those who are sentenced are treated solely as mentally disordered when they are sentenced. Of those few sent to hospital, many then attract mental disorder attributions about their future offending in subsequent consideration of their discharge, sometimes thereby unjustifiably extending their period in (therapeutic) detention.

Thus, the bulk of offenders remain to be sentenced with their mental disorder having little, if any, mitigating effect. But can the presence of mental disorder lead to disproportionately long sentences? Do paternalistic assumptions about the 'mental disorder' element, and protective-predictive ones about the offending element, leave prisoner-patients with more than their 'just' deserts?

It is first worth reiterating that, like all offenders, those with mental disorder are overwhelmingly not dangerous. However, some are. Arguments favouring limited special measures have their attractions, if only to deal with that small but worrying group about whom unsubstantiable fears of future offending abound; but their *quid pro quo* is that the preventive rationale should be tempered by procedural safeguards. Similarly, the arguments for bifurcation are inherently appealing, where diversion into humanitarian care protects offenders from damaging penal sentences. Yet the implications of these two propositions under our existing arrangements are that the route into confinement will affect both whether and what type of treatment will be given and the route out of confinement.

Concepts of dangerousness and its alleged association with mental disorder pepper the academic literature and the rhetoric of sentencing (Floud and Young 1981; Radzinowicz and Hood 1981; Peay 1982; Bottoms and Brownsword 1983; Prins 1986).

---

[53] See generally Chapter 6, 'Personality disorder, its nature, stigmatization, relationship to mental illness and its treatment possibilities' in Crisp (2001).

Academics and policy-makers have been fiercely divided both on predictive grounds—will it work?—and on questions of rights—should it be allowed to work? The argument embodies the distinction between statistical and legal-clinical decision-making; crudely put, the difference between risk factors associated with groups of people who have common characteristics (much of the risk prediction literature is of this nature) and the determination of whether any one individual within that group will be amongst those where risk is realized. These kinds of difficult decisions are faced regularly by courts, MHRTs, discretionary lifer panels, the parole board, and clinicians (see, for example, Peay 1989; Padfield and Liebling 2000; Hood and Shute 2000). The findings of research concerning such decision-making bodies are consistent: despite actuarial evidence that would support the release of patients and prisoners, attributions of risk are central, overvalued, and very difficult to refute. Yet one development should help to counter this general trend. The first declaration of incompatibility under the Human Rights Act 1998 may go some way to shifting the burden of proof on to those who maintain that risk is present; the case, of H,[54] concerned a patient detained in a special hospital on a restriction order.

Should offenders be entitled to a proportional measure of punishment? Walker (1996: 7) argues that there may be no such 'right' where offenders have forfeited the presumption of being harmless because they have *previously* attempted or caused harm to others. In these circumstances precautionary sentencing may be justifiable. But how is such precautionary sentencing to be limited? And are mentally disordered offenders at greater risk of imposition of such a sentence? Dworkin (1977) described the restraint and treatment of the 'dangerously insane' as an insult to their rights to dignity and liberty—an infringement that could be justified not where crime reduction might result, but only where the danger posed was 'vivid'. Bottoms and Brownsword (1983: 21) unpacked the concept of vivid danger into its elements of seriousness, temporality (that is frequency and immediacy), and certainty. Certainty was pivotal to precautionary sentencing, but even a high probability of future offending should become relevant only if the behaviour anticipated involved causing or attempting 'very serious violence'. Thus, the right to a proportional measure of punishment would yield a '*prima facie* right to release for the prisoner at the end of his normal term', and this would apply—in the absence of 'vivid danger'—equally to the alleged 'dangerous offender'. But at this point theory and practice diverge.

The leading principle of the Criminal Justice Act 1991 (which remains the key statutory provision, even though now consolidated in the Powers of Criminal Courts (Sentencing) Act 2000) is that custodial sentences should be commensurate with the seriousness of the offence. With the publication of the Halliday Report (Halliday *et al.* 2001) it is evident that that this philosophy is likely to be superseded by a new emphasis on crime reduction, risk management, reparation, and deterrence. Those deemed mentally disordered offenders are, under this proposed regime, likely to be in

[54] *R v Mental Health Review Tribunal, on the application of H* [2001] 3 WLR 512. *H* determined that under Articles 5(1) and 5(4) ECHR the tribunal would be required to be positively satisfied that all the criteria justifying the patient's detention in hospital for treatment continued to exist before refusing a patient's discharge.

triple, if not quadruple, jeopardy. Treatment for their underlying disorders, attempts to reduce independently their potential for crime through 'measures to change the way offenders think and behave' (ibid.: 1), and a deterrence philosophy which may impact even less successfully on offenders with mental disorders, are all likely to contribute to a greater than proportionate use of incapacitation with 'mentally disordered offenders'.

However, this would not be to assert that the 1991 Act did not impact differentially on those with mental disorders. Its principled emphasis on proportionality had always been subject to a number of practical exceptions. Most notable is s 2(2)(b), which permits courts to sentence 'where the offence is a violent or sexual offence, for such longer term (not exceeding that maximum) as in the opinion of the court is necessary to protect the public from serious harm from the offender'. The operation of s 2(2)(b) has been discussed elsewhere (Ashworth, in Chapter 29 of this volume; von Hirsch and Ashworth 1996), but the manner in which it bites on mentally disordered offenders is critical. Under the Act, medical reports are normally required where the court is considering passing a custodial sentence and the offender is or appears to be mentally disordered (s 4(1)). In *Fawcett*[55] the Court of Appeal held, 'if the danger is due to a mental or personality problem, the sentencing court should . . . always call for a medical report before passing sentence under section 2(2)(b), in order *to exclude a medical disposal*' (emphasis added).[56] The factors identified as assuming prominence in qualifying for a longer than normal sentence included irrational acts, unusual obsessions or delusions, a lack of remorse or unwillingness to accept medication, and any inability on the part of the offender to appreciate the consequences of his or her actions. All of these factors are more likely to be associated with those suffering from mental disorder. More worryingly, the Court observed that 'the fact that the defendant does have previous convictions need not necessarily itself be a qualifying factor, particularly where there is a mixture of minor offending, and some personality disorder, or other mental abnormalities'. Again, those with mental vulnerabilities seem to be peculiarly singled out as posing a risk.

Solomka (1996) has detailed how these provisions can lead to psychiatrists' reports, written for the decision concerning the appropriateness of a therapeutic disposal, being used instead to justify a longer than normal sentence. In his study of the first thirty-five Court of Appeal decisions under s 2(2)(b), he notes that twenty-two of them involved psychiatric evidence. Clearly, the potential for 'ratcheting-up' exists. The *appearance* of mental disorder to a lay audience leads to a request for a psychiatric report. If this report does not recommend a therapeutic disposal, it is, nonetheless, likely to make reference to a series of signs and symptoms which sentencers find worrying, leading to a longer than normal sentence. Here offenders neither acquire special rights to treatment, nor enjoy any of the (limited) procedural safeguards afforded to discretionary life sentence prisoners. As the medium for this process, psychiatrists should be aware of the ethical problems their involvement raises.

---

[55] (1995) 16 Cr App R (S) 55.

[56] Fawcett, sentenced to imprisonment, suffered from a personality disorder 'approaching psychopathic disorder'; her condition was thought to be unlikely to change.

Conceding the principle of preventive sentencing can create a number of further difficulties. First, protective imperatives can infect the way in which decisions are made about the release even of non-offenders amongst the detained psychiatric population; fears of future offending can lead to inappropriate denial of release (Peay 1989: 184). They can also lead to inappropriate transfer (Grounds 1990) and to offender-patients being detained in hospital for periods commensurate with their offence rather than on the basis of assessed recovery from their disorders (Dell and Robertson 1988).

There is also evidence that the Court of Appeal has been prepared to uphold a sentence of disproportionate length not falling within s 2(2)(b) where there was psychiatric evidence that the appellant had a persistent compulsion to kill his wife and children.[57] As attractive as the decision may appear on pragmatic safety grounds, where the legislative framework does not permit this, it is another manifestation of unjust dealings with the 'mentally disordered alleged dangerous would be offender'. Lastly, in *Fleming*[58] the Court of Appeal upheld a life sentence on a chronic paranoid schizophrenic, despite the availability of a bed in a special hospital, and despite the existing authority of *Howell*[59] to the effect that judges should not sentence offenders to imprisonment to avoid decisions about their release falling subsequently into the hands of an MHRT.[60] Protective confinement appears to be self-justifying and highly infectious.

The ambivalence felt towards offenders with mental disorders has also contributed to a significant shift in the manner in which automatic life sentences are imposed under the Crime (Sentences) Act 1997. At the time of the passage of the Act, it had been made clear that an offender's mental disorder would not constitute an 'exceptional circumstance'. What that inevitably meant was that offenders with mental disorder who committed a second serious offence could not avoid the imposition of an automatic life sentence, no matter how inadequate they might be or how preposterous was the 'seriousness' of their offending. This has recently been confirmed in *Newman*.[61] The Court of Appeal held that s 2 did trump any sentencing discretion under the Mental Health Act 1983 to impose a hospital order, and observed:

It is a matter for concern that a defendant so obviously and acutely suffering from mental illness should be ordered to prison and not to hospital. Even though, in practical terms, the difference between the two orders may lie less in the mode of treatment after sentence than in the procedures governing release and recall, we regret our inability to make what seems on the medical evidence the more appropriate order.

However, in the tranche of appeals in *R v Offen, McGilliard, McKeown, Okwuegbunam,*

---

[57] *Mortimer* [1996] Crim LR 836.

[58] (1995) 14 Cr App R (S) 151.

[59] (1985) 7 Cr App R (S) 360.

[60] In *Fairhurst* [1996] 1 Cr App R (S) 242, the Court of Appeal reiterated that if the offender qualified for a therapeutic disposal, such an order should be made. It was incorrect to impose life imprisonment simply to prevent the premature release of the offender by a MHRT.

[61] [2000] 2 Cr App R (S) 227.

S,[62] it was held by the Court of Appeal that the automatic life sentence was not intended by Parliament to apply in relation to someone who, taking account of all of the circumstances, did not create an unacceptable risk to the public. In *Offen* there were medical reports asserting that Offen was not a danger to the public; Offen suffered from schizophrenia and had robbed a building society in his slippers, but allowed himself to be deprived of the money by a woman who took his holdall from him. Offen's appeal succeeded. Whether this is attributable to his evident inadequacy, his relatively innocuous antecedents, the passage of the Human Rights Act, or mere adherence to statutory interpretation by the Court of Appeal is debatable. However, the use of negative attributions of risk, while to be welcomed as a way of out-manoeuvring the populist and unjust s 2, is a risky strategy where those with mental disorder are concerned. It is an approach that may yet backfire.

Spelling out the involvement of predictions of dangerousness is a first step in ensuring that such predictions are made with due regard to the rights of an offender not to be unjustifiably detained. A second necessary step is to ensure procedural fairness: the position of discretionary lifers has been somewhat improved by placing them on the same footing as restricted patients applying to MHRTs; equally though, all the problems which bedevil tribunals are likely to be replicated.[63] Even given a reversed burden of proof, offenders seeking their release on the ground of non-dangerousness will have an uphill struggle when doing so from conditions of security.

CONCLUSIONS

If the basic premise of this chapter is accepted—namely, that mentally disordered offenders are not, and should not be, treated as an isolated category—the conclusions that follow are of broader significance.

First, effort should be devoted to developing a pluralistic model of the criminal justice system. This has been discussed in detail elsewhere (Peay 1993). Piecemeal tinkering may provide solutions for the problems posed by specific offenders; it is insufficient as a basis for addressing problems across the ordered–disordered offending continuum. Equally, the temptation to problem solve by addressing only the back end of the process (namely, sentencing and disposal issues) distracts attention from the urgent need for the prior issues of culpability to be resolved on a fairer basis than is currently achieved.

Secondly, if the mentally disordered cannot effectively be identified and marginalized, diversion and transfer can never be the solution. Resource allocation needs to be across the board, not only in respect of a limited number of beds for potentially difficult offender-patients.

Thirdly, and stemming from this, it is unrealistic to confine treatment to hospital settings. Treatment in prison, and in community settings, needs full consideration.

---

[62] [2000] 1 WLR 253.
[63] See Peay (1989); Padfield and Leibling (2000).

The problem, of course, is the use of overt compulsion. What is clear is the need to think more carefully about the circumstances in which treatment will be offered, to whom, and what the consequences will be where it is deemed unwelcome, unsuccessful, or inappropriate. A pluralistic model would require the same limitations on intervention for all offenders, assuming they have the capacity to consent to treatment or undergo punishment. While adoption of a concurrent principle of proportionality would constitute a sound foundation for greater fairness between offenders, this seems less than likely in the current climate. Accordingly, if a risk-based/treatment approach is to be adopted, more thought needs to be given to the problematic aspects of multi-agency working where confidential 'health' information will seep into criminal justice agencies.

Fourthly, the justifications are many for singling out subsections of 'disordered offenders' for special treatment. But special treatment can readily become special control; to be seduced by the notion that risk can be managed through the containment of identifiable individuals is to allow discriminatory treatment for that group, while failing to tackle the roots of the problem. It is a false dawn.

Lastly, the failure to agree on a definition of what constitutes a mentally disordered offender, or to apply it consistently even if criteria could be agreed, is likely to result in there being a mismatch of expectations amongst the various personnel and agencies dealing with such offenders. As Watson and Grounds (1993) have observed, greater liaison combined with overcoming the boundaries between different parts of the criminal justice and health agencies will be insufficient while the discrepancy in expectations remains. Pursuing a pluralistic model may go some way to addressing these fundamental problems.

Selected further reading

The relationship between offenders with mental disorder and general mental health law and policy is reviewed both in Bartlett and Sandland (2000) and Eastman and Peay (1999), with the former being a more technical analysis. Singleton *et al.* (1998) detail the prevalence of mental disorder in the prison population, while Monahan *et al.* (2001) is the best analysis and critique of the problematic relationship between violence and mental disorder. Other edited collections, for example Brown and Pratt (2000) on dangerous offenders, Buchanan (2002) on community care, Hodgins and Muller-Isberner (2000) on clinical treatment and prevention, and Webb and Harris (1999) on the difficult issues of management, are all worth a look. Lastly, Peay (1998) is a collection of key articles reproduced from some other less accessible sources.

References

APPLEBY, L., SHAW, J., SHERRATT, J., and AMOS, T. (2001), *Safety First: Five-Year Report of the National Confidential Inquiry into Suicide and Homicide by People with Mental Illness*, London: Department of Health.

ASHWORTH, A., and GOSTIN, L. (1984), 'Mentally Disordered Offenders and the Sentencing Process', *Criminal Law Review*: 195–212.

BAKER, E. (1994), 'Human Rights, M'Naghten and the 1991 Act', *Criminal Law Review*: 84–92.

BARTLETT, P., and SANDLAND, R. (2000), *Mental*

Health Law: Policy and Practice, London: Blackstone Press.

BEAN, P. (2001), *Mental Disorder and Community Safety*, Basingstoke: Palgrave

BIRMINGHAM, L., MASON, D., and GRUBIN, D. (1996), 'Prevalence of Mental Disorder in Remand Prisoners: Consecutive Case Study', *British Medical Journal*, 313: 1521–4.

BIRMINGHAM, L., GRAY, J., MASON, D., and GRUBIN, D. (2000), 'Mental illness at reception into prison'. *Criminal Behaviour and Mental Health*, 10: 77–87.

BLUGLASS, R., and BOWDEN, P. (eds) (1990), *Principles and Practice of Forensic Psychiatry*, Edinburgh: Churchill Livingstone.

BOAST, N., and CHESTERMAN, P. (1995), 'Black People and Secure Psychiatric Facilities: Patterns of Processing and the Role of Stereotypes', *British Journal of Criminology*, 35: 218–35.

BOTTOMS, A., and BROWNSWORD, R. (1983), 'Dangerousness and Rights', in J.W. Hinton (ed.), *Dangerousness: Problems of Assessment and Prediction*, London: Allen and Unwin.

BROOKE, D., TAYLOR, C., GUNN, J., and MADEN, A. (1996), 'Point Prevalence of Mental Disorder in Unconvicted Male Prisoners in England and Wales', *British Medical Journal*, 313: 1524–7.

BROWN, M., and PRATT, J. (eds) (2000), *Dangerous Offenders: Punishment and Social Order*, London: Routledge.

BUCHANAN A. (ed.) (2002), *Community Care of the Mentally Disordered Offender*, Oxford: Oxford University Press.

—— and VIRGO, G. (1999), 'Duress and Mental Abnormality', *Criminal Law Review*: 517–31.

BURNEY, E., and PEARSON, G. (1995), 'Mentally Disordered Offenders: Finding a Focus for Diversion', *The Howard Journal*, 34: 291–313.

BUTLER, LORD (1975), *Report of the Committee on Mentally Abnormal Offenders*, Cmnd 6244, London: HMSO.

CAMPBELL, T., and HEGINBOTHAM, C. (1991), *Mental Illness: Prejudice, Discrimination and the Law*, Aldershot: Dartmouth.

CARSON, D. (1989), 'Prosecuting People with Mental Handicaps', *Criminal Law Review*: 87.

CAVADINO, P. (1999), 'Diverting Mentally Disordered Offenders from Custody', in D. Webb and R. Harris (eds), *Managing People Nobody Owns*, London: Routledge.

CHISWICK, D. (1990), 'Fitness to Stand Trial and Plead, Mutism and Deafness', in R. Bluglass and

P. Bowden (eds), *Principles and Practice of Forensic Psychiatry*, Edinburgh: Churchill Livingstone.

COID, J. (1989), 'Psychopathic Disorders', *Current Opinion in Psychiatry*, 2: 750–6.

COPE, R. (1993), 'A Survey of Forensic Psychiatrists' Views on Psychopathic Disorder', *Journal of Forensic Psychiatry*, 4: 215–35.

CRICHTON, J. (1999), 'Mental Disorder and Crime: coincidence, correlation and cause', *Journal of Forensic Psychiatry*, 10: 659–77.

CRIMINAL LAW REVISION COMMITTEE (1984), 15th Report, *Sexual Offences*, Cmnd 9213 London: HMSO.

CRISP, A. (ed.) (2001), *Every Family in the Land. Understanding prejudice and discrimination against people with mental illness*, London: Royal Society of Medicine. Internet publication at **www.stigma.org/everyfamily/**.

CROW, I. (2001), *The Treatment and Rehabilitation of Offenders*, London: Sage.

CROWN PROSECUTION SERVICE (2000), *Code for Crown Prosecutors*, London: CPS.

CULLEN, E. (1993), 'The Grendon Reconviction Study Part 1', *Prison Service Journal*, 90: 35–7.

DELL, S. (1983), 'Wanted: An Insanity Defence that can be Used', *Criminal Law Review*: 431.

—— and ROBERTSON, G. (1988), *Sentenced to Hospital: Offenders in Broadmoor*, Maudsley Monographs 32, London: Institute of Psychiatry.

DEPARTMENT OF HEALTH (1994), *Guidance on the Discharge of Mentally Disordered People and their Continuing Care in the Community*, NHS Executive HSG(94)27 and LASSL (94) 4: 10 May 1994.

—— (2000), *In-patients formally detained in hospitals under the Mental Health Act 1983 and other legislation, England: 1989–1990 to 1999–2000*, Bulletin 2000/19, London: Department of Health Statistics Division 2C.

—— / HOME OFFICE (2000), *Reforming the Mental Health Act: Part II High Risk Patients*, Cm 5016-II, London: The Stationery Office.

DOOLEY, E. (1990), 'Prison Suicide in England and Wales, 1972–87', *British Journal of Psychiatry*, 156: 40–5.

DOUGLAS, M. (1992), *Risk and Blame: Essays in Cultural Theory*, London: Routledge.

DUFF, P. (1997), 'Diversion from Prosecution into Psychiatric Care. Who Controls the Gates?', *British Journal of Criminology*, 37: 15–34.

DWORKIN, R. (1977), *Taking Rights Seriously*, London: Duckworth.

EASTMAN, N., and PEAY, J. (1998), 'Sentencing

Psychopaths: Is the "Hospital and Limitation Direction" an Ill-Considered Hybrid?', *Criminal Law Review*: 93–108.

—— and —— (eds) (1999), *Law Without Enforcement: Integrating Mental Health and Justice*, Oxford: Hart Publishing.

ELKINS, M., GRAY, C., and ROGERS, K. (2001), *Prison Population Brief: England and Wales: June 2001*: London: Home Office, Research Development Statistics.

FENNELL, P. (1991), 'Diversion of Mentally Disordered Offenders from Custody', *Criminal Law Review*: 333–48.

—— (1994), 'Mentally Disordered Suspects in the Criminal Justice System', *Journal of Law and Society*, 21: 57–71.

—— (2001), 'Reforming the Mental Health Act 1983: "Joined Up Compulsion"', *Journal of Mental Health Law*: 5–20.

—— and YEATES, V. (2002), 'To serve which master? Criminal justice policy, community care and the mentally disordered offender', in A. Buchanan (ed.), *Community Care of the Mentally Disordered Offender*, Oxford: Oxford University Press.

FLOUD, J., and YOUNG, W. (1981), *Dangerousness and Criminal Justice*, London: Heinemann.

GARDNER, J., and MACKLEM, T. (2001), 'Compassion without Respect? Nine Fallacies in *R v Smith*', *Criminal Law Review*: 623–35.

GENDERS, E., and PLAYER, E. (1995), *Grendon: A Study of a Therapeutic Prison*, Oxford: Clarendon Press.

GILMAN, S. (1988), *Disease and Representation. From Madness to AIDS*, Ithaca: Cornell University Press.

GOSTIN, L. (1986), *Mental Health Services — Law and Practice*, London: Shaw and Sons.

GRANT, D. (1999), 'Multi-agency risk management of mentally disordered sex offenders: a probation case study', in D. Webb and R. Harris (eds), *Managing People Nobody Owns*, London: Routledge.

GROUNDS, A. (1987), 'Detention of "Psychopathic Disorder Patients" in Special Hospitals: Critical Issues', *British Journal of Psychiatry*, 151: 474–8.

—— (1990), 'Transfers of Sentenced Prisoners to Hospital', *Criminal Law Review*: 544–51.

—— (1991), 'The Transfer of Sentenced Prisoners to Hospital 1960–1983', *British Journal of Criminology*, 31/1: 54–71.

—— (2000), 'The Future of Prison Health Care', *Journal of Forensic Psychiatry*, 11: 260–7.

GRUBIN, D. (2001), 'Editorial. Treatment for mentally disordered offenders', *Criminal Behaviour and Mental Health*, 11: S109-S112.

GUDJONSSON, G., HAYES, G., and ROWLANDS, P. (2001), 'Fitness to be interviewed and psychological vulnerability: the views of doctors, lawyers and police officers', *Journal of Forensic Psychiatry*, 11: 74–92.

GUNN, J., DELL, S., and WAY C. (1978), *Psychiatric Aspects of Imprisonment*, London: Academic Press.

—— , MADEN, A., and SWINTON, M. (1991), 'Treatment Needs of Prisoners with Psychiatric Disorders', *British Medical Journal*, 303: 338–41.

—— and ROBERTSON, G. (1987), 'A Ten Year Follow-up of Men Discharged from Grendon Prison', *British Journal of Psychiatry*, 151: 674–8.

HALLIDAY, J., FRENCH, C., and GOODWIN, C. (2001), *Making Punishments Work: Report of a Review of the Sentencing Framework for England and Wales*, London: Home Office.

HARE, R. (1996), 'Psychopathy: a clinical construct whose time has come', *Criminal Justice and Behaviour*, 23: 25–54.

—— (1999), 'Psychopathy as a risk factor for violence', *Psychiatric Quarterly*, 70: 181–97.

HART, S., COX, D., and HARE, R. (1995), *The Hare Psychopathy Checklist: Screening Version*, Toronto: Multi-Health Systems.

HM INSPECTORATE OF PRISONS (2001), *Report of an unannounced follow-up inspection of HM Prison Holloway 11–15 December 2000* (available on Home Office website).

HODGINS, S., and MULLER-ISBERNER, R. (eds) (2000), *Violence Crime and Mentally Disordered Offenders: Concepts and Methods for Effective Treatment and Prevention*, Chichester: Wiley.

HOGGETT, B. (1996), *Mental Health Law*, 4th edn, London: Sweet & Maxwell.

HOME OFFICE (1990), *Crime, Justice and Protecting the Public*, Cm 965, London: HMSO.

—— (1991), *Custody, Care and Justice*, London: HMSO.

—— (1999), *Managing Dangerous People with Severe Personality Disorder. Proposals for Policy Development*, London: Home Office.

—— (2001) *What Works: Second Report of the Joint Prison/Probation Service Accreditation Panel*, London: Home Office.

—— /DEPARTMENT OF HEALTH AND SOCIAL SECURITY (1987), *Report of the Interdepartmental Working Group of Home Office and*

DHSS Officials on Mentally Disturbed Offenders in the Prison System in England and Wales, London: Home Office/DHSS.

—— /DEPARTMENT OF HEALTH (1996), *Mentally Disordered Offenders—Sentencing and Discharge Arrangements*, a discussion paper on a proposed new power for the courts, London: Home Office.

HOOD, R., and SHUTE, S. (2000), *Parole decision-making: weighing the risk to the public*, Home Office Research Findings 144, London; Home Office, Research Development and Statistics Directorate.

JOHNSON, S., and TAYLOR, R. (2000), *Statistics of mentally disordered offenders 1999 England and Wales*, Statistical Bulletin 21/00, London: Home Office, Research Development and Statistics Directorate.

JOHNSTONE, G. (1996), 'From Experts in Responsibility to Advisers on Punishment: The Role of Psychiatrists in Penal Matters', Studies in Law, Hull: University of Hull Law School.

KEMSHALL, H., and MAGUIRE, M. (2001), 'Public Protection, Partnership and Risk Penality: The Multi-Agency Management of Sex and Violent Offenders', *Punishment and Society*, 3/2: 237–64.

LAING, J. (1995), 'The Mentally Disordered Suspect at the Police Station', *Criminal Law Review*: 371–81.

—— (1999), 'Diversion of Mentally Disordered Offenders: Victim and Offender Perspectives', *Criminal Law Review*: 805–19.

LINK, B., ANDREWS, H., and CULLEN, F. (1992), 'The Violent and Illegal Behaviour of Mental Patients Compared to Community Controls', *American Sociological Review*, 57: 275–92.

LEWIS, O., and CARPENTER, S. (1999), 'Episodic Dyscontrol and the English Criminal Law', *Journal of Mental Health Law*: 13–22.

MACKAY, R.D. (1990), 'Fact and Fiction about the Insanity Defence', *Criminal Law Review*: 247–55.

—— (1991), 'The Decline of Disability in Relation to the Trial', *Criminal Law Review*: 87–97.

—— (1995), *Mental Condition Defences in the Criminal Law*, Oxford: Clarendon Press.

—— (1999), 'The Abnormality of Mind Factor in Diminished Responsibility', *Criminal Law Review*: 117–25.

—— and GEARTY, C. (2001), 'On being Insane in Jersey—the case of Attorney General v Jason Prior', *Criminal Law Review*: 560–3.

—— and KEARNS, G. (1999), 'More Fact(s) about the Insanity Defence', *Criminal Law Review*: 714–25.

—— and —— (2000) 'An Upturn in Unfitness to Plead? Disability in Relation to Trial under the 1991 Act', *Criminal Law Review*: 532–46.

—— and MACHIN, D. (2000), 'The Operation of Section 48 of the Mental Health Act 1983: An Empirical Study of the Transfer of Remand Prisoners to Hospital', *British Journal of Criminology*, 40: 727–45.

McCANN, J.B., JAMES, A., WILSON, S., and DUNN, G. (1996), 'Prevalence of Psychiatric Disorders in Young People in the Care System', *British Medical Journal*, 313: 1529–30.

McALINDEN, A. (2001), 'Indeterminate Sentences for the Severely Personality Disordered', *Criminal Law Review*: 108–23.

MAGUIRE, M., KEMSHALL, H., NOAKS, L., SHARPE, K., and WINCUP, E. (2001), *Risk Management of Sexual and Violent Offenders: The Work of Public Protection Panels*, Police Research Series Paper 139, London: Home Office.

MAIER-KATKIN, D., and OGLE, R. (1993), 'A Rationale: for Infanticide Laws', *Criminal Law Review*: 903–14.

MELTZER, H., GILL, B., PETTICREW, M., and HINDS, K. (1995), *OPCS Surveys of Psychiatric Morbidity in Great Britain, Report 1: the prevalence of psychiatric morbidity among adults living in private households*, London: The Stationery Office.

MILLER, R.D. (1992), 'Economic Factors Leading to Diversion of the Mentally Disordered from the Civil to the Criminal Commitment Systems', *International Journal of Law and Psychiatry*, 15: 1–12.

MITCHELL, E.M. (1999), 'Madness and meta-responsibility: the culpable causation of mental disorder and the insanity defence', *Journal of Forensic Psychiatry*, 10: 597–622.

MONAHAN, J. (1992), 'Mental Disorder and Violent Behaviour. Perceptions and Evidence', *American Psychologist*, 47: 511–21.

—— and STEADMAN, H. (1983), 'Crime and Mental Disorder An Epidemiological Approach', in M. Tonry and N. Morris (eds), *Crime and Justice: An Annual Review of Research*, vol. 4, 145–89, Chicago, Ill.: University of Chicago Press.

——, STEADMAN, H., SILVER, E., APPELBAUM, P., ROBBINS, P., MULVEY, E., ROTH, L., GRISSO, T., and BANKS, S. (2001), *Rethinking risk assessment: The MacArthur study of mental disorder and violence*, New York: Oxford University Press.

MURRAY, D.J. (1989), *Review of Research on Re-offending of Mentally Disordered Offenders*, Research and Planning Unit Paper 55, London: Home Office.

NACRO (1993), *Mentally Disordered Offenders and Community Care*, Mental Health Advisory Committee Policy Paper No. 1, London: NACRO Publications.

NAREY, M. (1999) 'Reducing suicides "top priority" for Director General', *HM Prisons: News*, 14 December 1999.

PADFIELD, N., and LIEBLING, A. (2000), *An exploration of decision-making at discretionary lifer panels*, Home Office Research Study No. 213, London: Home Office, Research and Statistics Directorate.

PALMER, C., and HART, M. (1996), *A PACE in the Right Direction?*, Sheffield: Institute for the Study of the Legal Profession, Faculty of Law, University of Sheffield.

PEAY, J. (1982), 'Dangerousness—Ascription or Description?', in P. Feldman (ed.), *Developments in the Study of Criminal Behaviour. Volume 2: Violence*, Chichester: Wiley.

—— (1988), 'Offenders Suffering from Psychopathic Disorder: The Rise and Demise of a Consultation Document', *British Journal of Criminology*, 28: 67–81.

—— (1989), *Tribunals on Trial: A Study of Decision-Making Under the Mental Health Act 1983*, Oxford: Clarendon Press.

—— (1993), 'A Criminological Perspective', in W. Watson and A. Grounds (eds), *Mentally Disordered Offenders in an Era of Community Care*, Cambridge: Cambridge University Press.

—— (ed.) (1996), *Inquiries after Homicide*, London: Duckworth.

—— (ed.) (1998) *Criminal Justice and the Mentally Disordered*, Dartmouth; International Library Series.

PLAYER, E. (1992), 'Treatment for Sex Offenders: A Cautionary Note', *Prison Service Journal*, 85: 2–9.

PORTER, R. (2001), 'Is mental illness inevitably stigmatizing?', in A. Crisp (ed.), *Every Family in the Land. Understanding prejudice and discrimination against people with mental illness*, London: Royal Society of Medicine. Internet publication at www.stigma.org/everyfamily/.

PRINS, H. (1986), *Dangerous Behaviour, the Law and Mental Disorder*, London: Tavistock.

—— (1990), 'Mental Abnormality and Criminality —an Uncertain Relationship', *Medicine, Science and Law*, 30/3: 247–58.

—— (1991), 'Is Psychopathic Disorder a Useful Clinical Concept? A Perspective from England and Wales', *International Journal of Offender Therapy and Comparative Criminology*, 35/2: 119–25.

—— (2001), 'Offenders, Deviants or Patients—Comments on Part Two of the White Paper', *Journal of Mental Health Law*: 21–26.

PRISON SERVICE/NHS EXECUTIVE WORKING GROUP (1999), *Future Organisation of Prison Health Care*, London: Home Office/Department of Health.

RADZINOWICZ, L., and HOOD, R. (1981), 'A Dangerous Direction for Sentencing Reform', *Criminal Law Review*: 756–61.

REED REPORT (1991), *Review of Health and Social Services for Mentally Disordered Offenders and Others Requiring Similar Services*, London: Department of Health/ Home Office.

—— (1992), *Review of Health and Social Services for Mentally Disordered Offenders and Others Requiring Similar Services*, London: Department of Health/Home Office.

RICHARDSON, G. (1999), *Review of the Mental Health Act 1983*, Report of the Expert Committee, London: Department of Health.

RIX, K. (2001), '"Battered woman syndrome" and the defence of provocation: two women with something more in common', *Journal of Forensic Psychiatry*, 12: 131–49.

ROBERTS, P. (1996), 'Will you Stand Up in Court? On the Admissibility of Psychiatric and Psychological Evidence', *Journal of Forensic Psychiatry*, 7: 63–78.

ROBERTSON, G. (1988), 'Arrest patterns among mentally disordered offenders', *British Journal of Psychiatry*, 153: 313–16.

——, PEARSON, R., and GIBB, R. (1995), *The Mentally Disordered and the Police*, Research Findings No. 21, London: Home Office, Research and Statistics Department.

ROTH, M. (1990), 'Psychopathic (Sociopathic), Personality', in R. Bluglass and P. Bowden (eds), *Principles and Practice of Forensic Psychiatry*, Edinburgh: Churchill Livingstone.

RUBIN, D. (1972), 'Predictions of Dangerousness in Mentally Ill Criminals', *Archives of General Psychiatry*, 27: 397–407.

RUMGAY, J., and MUNROE, E. (2001), 'The Lion's Den: Professional Defences in the Treatment of

Dangerous Patients', *Journal of Forensic Psychiatry*: 357–78.

SHAPLAND, J. (1991), 'Where Do We Put Them? Coping with Mentally Disordered Offenders', Paper presented to the British Criminology Conference, York: July.

SHAW, J., TOMENSON, B., CREED, F., and PERRY, A. (2001), 'Loss of contact with psychiatric services in people diverted from the criminal justice system', *Journal of Forensic Psychiatry*, 12: 203–10.

SHEPPARD, D. (1996), *Learning the Lessons. Mental Health Inquiry Reports Published in England and Wales Between 1969–1996 and Their Recommendations for Improving Practice*, 2nd edn, London: Zito Trust.

SINGLETON, N., MELTZER, H., and GATWARD R. (1998), *Psychiatric morbidity among prisoners in England and Wales*, Office for National Statistics, London: The Stationery Office.

SMITH, C. (2000), ' "Healthy Prisons": A Contradiction in Terms?', *Howard Journal*, 39: 339–53.

SMITH, J.C., and HOGAN, B. (1988), *Criminal Law*, 6th edn, London: Butterworths.

SOLOMKA, B. (1996), 'The Role of Psychiatric Evidence in Passing "Longer than Normal" Sentences', *Journal of Forensic Psychiatry*, 7: 239–55.

STREET, R. (1998), *The Restricted Hospital Order: From Court to the Community*, Home Office Research Study No. 186, London: Home Office.

SWANSON, J., HOLZER, C., GANJU, V., and JONO, R. (1990), 'Violence and Psychiatric Disorder in the Community: Evidence from the Epidemiological Catchment Area Surveys', *Hospital and Community Psychiatry*, 41: 761–70.

TAYLOR, P., and GUNN, J. (1999), 'Homicides by people with mental illness: myth and reality', *British Journal of Psychiatry*, 174: 9–14.

TUMIM, S. (1990), *Suicide and Self Harm in Prison Service Establishments in England and Wales*, Report of a Review by Her Majesty's Chief Inspector of Prisons for England and Wales, Cm 1383, London: HMSO.

VAUGHAN, P., KELLY, M., and PULLEN, N. (2001), 'The working practices of the police in relation to mentally disordered offenders and diversion services', *Medicine, Science and the Law*, 41: 13–20.

VERDUN-JONES, S. (1989), 'Sentencing the Partly Mad and Partly Bad: The Case of the Hospital Order in England and Wales', *International Journal of Law and Psychiatry*, 12: 1–27.

VON HIRSCH, A., and ASHWORTH, A, (1996), 'Protective Sentencing under Section 2(2)(b): The Criteria for Dangerousness', *Criminal Law Review*: 175–83.

WALKER, N. (ed) (1996), *Dangerous People*, London: Blackstone Press.

WATSON, W., and GROUNDS, A. (eds) (1993), *Mentally Disordered Offenders in an Era of Community Care*, Cambridge: Cambridge University Press.

WEBB, D., and HARRIS, R. (eds) (1999), *Managing People Nobody Owns*, London: Routledge.

WELLS, C. (1994), 'Battered Woman Syndrome and Defences to Homicide: Where Now?', *Legal Studies*, 14: 266–76.

WESSELY, S., and TAYLOR. P. (1991), 'Madness and Crime: Criminology versus Psychiatry', *Criminal Behaviour and Mental Health*, 1: 193–228.

WILCZYNSKI, A., and MORRIS, A. (1993), 'Parents who Kill their Children', *Criminal Law Review*: 31–6.

WOOLF, LORD JUSTICE (1991), *Prison Disturbances April 1990*, Report of an Inquiry by the Rt Hon. Lord Justice Woolf (Parts I and II), and His Honour Judge Stephen Tumim (Part II), Cm 1456, London: HMSO.

WORLD HEALTH ORGANIZATION (1978), *Mental Disorders: Glossary and Guide to their Classification in accordance with the Ninth Revision of the International Classification of Diseases. Injuries and Causes of Death*, Geneva: WHO.

PART IV

FORMS OF CRIME

22

VIOLENT CRIME

Michael Levi with Mike Maguire

INTRODUCTION

Violent crime is a deeply emotive topic, and graphic illustrations of it abound on television and cinema screens and in newspapers, colouring the political and criminal justice responses not just to violence but to crime in general. Yet despite its prominence in both fiction and the news, the attention it has received from criminologists has been surprisingly patchy, focused mainly on a few specific forms of offending (in recent years, notably domestic and sexual violence) or on particular kinds of offender (especially, for writers with a psychological or psychiatric orientation, those who commit frequent or extreme acts of violence). It appears to be a self-evident category of behaviour, but there are disputes around whether or how far to include, for example, injuries caused through corporate negligence, or non-physical 'violence' such as threats and 'harassment'. There are also arguments about forms of violence claimed by some as 'justified' or 'ligitimate', such as that by security forces, or by 'freedom fighters'/'terrorists'. To arrive at a broad understanding of violent crime, we are obliged to do some careful 'unpicking'.

This chapter first explores some of the ways in which our perceptions of violence, and our attitudes towards its perpetrators, are moulded by a variety of social and cultural influences. We then look at evidence about how much violent crime of various kinds there may be, and at issues surrounding the risk of victimization and its distribution. This is followed by an examination of the different ways in which scholars from different disciplines—biology, socio-biology, psychology, psychiatry, and sociology—have tried to account for the existence, level, and forms of violent crimes. Recent trends and developments in attempts to control or reduce violence are also briefly reviewed. The principal focus of the empirical component will be on England and Wales, but we will include some comparative dimension.

What we place into the category of 'violent crime' makes a big difference to the range of behaviour we have to explain. Criminal statistics on violent crime in England and Wales consist of legal categories such as homicide and a variety of acts defined by the Offences Against the Person Act 1861: grievous bodily harm; wounding; plus supposedly less serious crimes such as assault and battery—the intentional or reckless application of force to the body.[1] The latter (often termed 'common assault'), which is

---

[1] A Home Office review identified over 70 different uses of the term 'assault' in law. The draft Offences

triable only at magistrates' courts, used to be excluded from the main 'notifiable crime' statistics, thereby keeping down the level of officially recorded 'violent crime'. However, common assault has been included since 1998, as have assault on a constable, stalking, and sexual and racial harassment (see Maguire, in Chapter 11 of this volume). 'Violent crime', then, is a slippery term which covers a huge and frequently changing range of heterogeneous physical and emotional behaviours, situations, and victim–offender relationships. It embraces, to take only a few examples:

1. terrorist bombings;

2. youth gangs fighting or intimidating each other, or residents or passers-by, in the streets, or in and around soccer grounds;

3. single and small group fights, usually same-sex and between acquaintances or strangers from similar backgrounds, in and around pubs and clubs;

4. violence (from homicide and rape to assaults involving minor physical injuries) against women in the home, most commonly by intimates;

5. street robberies in which items such as handbags, wallets, or—a key target since 1998—mobile phones are taken by threats or assault;

6. intimidation on the grounds of race or sex, both person-specific and general.

Wide though this conception of violent crime is, especially given the broad construction of intentionality and harm in the existing formulation, one could be more imaginative and include

7. deaths and injuries on the roads—in 2000, 3,409 people were killed and 38,155 seriously injured on British roads (DTLR 2001), with some 500 prosecutions for causing death or bodily harm; 9,200 for dangerous driving; 94,800 for careless driving and 1,202,300 for speeding offences; and 96,300 actions taken for the high risk offences of driving after consuming alcohol or taking drugs (Ayres and Hayward 2001); and

8. deaths and injuries following 'corporate crimes', such as breaches of health and safety regulations in factories and mines, or on offshore oil rigs, car ferries, and railways, or from *e coli* or other microbiological diseases resulting from breaches of public health legislation.[2] In 2000 in the UK, employees suffered 213 deaths

Against the Person Bill 1998—never put before Parliament to date—contained a set of relatively simple and straightforward new offences to replace the various existing offences of grievous and actual bodily harm and assault: intentional serious injury; reckless serious injury; intentional or reckless injury; and assault. This scales penalties according to a combination of motivation and outcome.

[2] In 1989, people in Britain stood a 100 times greater chance of being killed in the oil and gas industry, and a 12 times greater chance of being killed in the coal mining industry than they did from homicide (Royal Society 1992). We appreciate that this does little to reassure victims of homicide, but we ought to be clearer about such probabilities if we are interested in saving lives. Likewise, the understandable focus on dangerous driving by car 'thieves' should not blind us to the fact that vastly more people are killed and injured by those driving their own cars (whatever the ratio of sound to dangerous driving by car thieves and car owners of comparable ages respectively). The role of road and other engineering in reducing or increasing harm is important, though it may be inhibited by economies and by perspectives not focused on reducing harm. If avoidable deaths in the course of heavy industrial work have dropped markedly, largely due to the reduction of economic activity, serious illnesses from food poisoning increased seven-fold in the last fifteen years.

and 26,547 non-fatal major injuries; the self-employed suffered 78 deaths and 624 major injuries; and members of the public suffered 445 fatal and 20,202 non-fatal injuries connected with the workplace (HSE 2001). We have excluded here deaths and injuries from longer-term industrial diseases from asbestos and coal dust inhalation. 65,209 laboratory confirmed cases of food poisoning were attributed to the five most common bacterial pathogens, though it was not always clear whether these resulted from poor food handling by businesses or by consumers themselves, and no mortality data appear to be available (FSA 2001).[3] The Public Health Service Laboratory ascertained 86,528 cases of food poisoning in 2000 (compared with 14,253 in 1972).

The 'corporate crime' cases might be included in the 'violent crime' category on the grounds that though employers hardly ever *intend* harm, harms commonly result from paying 'piece-work', which encourages workers to take risks with their own welfare, or from economies such as poor rail track maintenance, the absence of automated devices to prevent train collisions, or from employing poor English speakers and untrained staff in roles (such as maritime work or food distribution, storage or preparation) where loss of life represents a real but infrequent risk. In that sense, they are not mere accidents but the result of a *process* of profit-maximizing self-centredness by corporations, which define as acceptable the levels of risk to themselves or others they (rationally or not) expect, or who (psychopathically?) do not think of themselves as producing risks for others.[4]

ATTITUDES TO VIOLENCE AND SOCIO-LEGAL CONSTRUCTIONS OF BLAME

How the police, courts, media, and different sections of the community respond to violence—and, indeed, what they construe as violent behaviour meriting a strong response—is shaped by a wide variety of individual, social, and cultural influences.

---

[3] According to the first Food Standards Agency survey, based on face-to-face interviews with 3,135 people across the UK between October and December 2000, over 80 per cent of people who had suffered from a food-borne illness did not report it to anyone; of those who did, most informed their GP rather than the suspect food outlet; 50 per cent of respondents had concerns over food hygiene in takeaways/fast-food outlets; 48 per cent felt 'confident' about current food safety measures, and 5 per cent 'very confident'.

[4] Prosecutions were a poor measure of harm in 2000; for example 692 businesses were prosecuted for food standards violations, mostly for severe and persistent violations of hygiene. It is easier to be fearless when the risk is taken by others, though often with financial and sometimes with penal consequences for the corporation in those countries that recognize the concept of corporate criminal liability. (Though this seldom involves homicide charges for the corporation or for any director personally: the only English corporate homicide prosecutions that have succeeded have been those in which the smallness of the firms has made it easier to prove that the person responsible was the 'directing mind' of the company (Wells 2001).) Due to business opposition and priority given to street crime issues, there has been a persistent lack of political motivation for reform of the law to facilitate prosecutions of corporate killing recommended by the Law Commission in 1998, despite media and victim criticism for failure to prosecute successfully after rail crashes; though in 2000, the Home Office included it in its proposals to reform the law of involuntary manslaughter.

Even so (and contrary to preconceptions on the part of conflict theorists), the results of surveys in western countries tend to show a high degree of consensus among people of different social classes in their ratings of the relative seriousness of property and violent offences, the latter consistently emerging as more serious (Levi and Jones 1985; O'Connell and Whelan 1996). Moreover, contrary to 'subculture of violence' theory (Wolfgang and Ferracuti 1967), people of colour have generally been found to be no more tolerant of violence than whites—though some British research has found that people of Afro-Caribbean origin were more tolerant than whites of violence between people who were acquainted (see Sparks, Genn, and Dodd 1977; Hough and Mayhew 1985). Analysing the 1984 British Crime Survey, Pease (1988) found almost perfect concord between people of different ages, sexes, and socio-economic group-ings in terms of their views on the seriousness of violence, including sexual crimes. Neither did it make any difference whether or not they had been victims of crime.

However, despite the well-tested methodology of such surveys, there may be socio-economic, ethnic, and gendered differences in what people *mean* by such ratings in context, particularly where justifiability and excusability are involved. For example, prior attitudes, as well as the rules of evidence and the way that interactions are represented in court, will influence whether a sexual assault is treated as a 'real rape' (Adler 1987; Lees 2002), or a homicide as murder or as an understandable response to long-term provocation. Ethnographic research emphasizes the subtlety of attitudes towards violence in context that cannot readily be captured in surveys.

Culture, then, shapes the conditions under which we attribute responsibility and blame to individuals whose acts result in harmful consequences. In mediated form, culture also has its effect on criminal law: thus, the Law Lords, later supported by the European Court of Human Rights, decided that adults could not lawfully consent beforehand to severe sado-masochistic sexual acts and that such acts constituted crime.[5] The law defines 'provocation' in homicide as requiring a *sudden and tempor-ary* loss of self-control by the killer, though many feminists argue that the experience of long-term abuse by some women who kill ought to be construed as excusable provocation; nevertheless, the courts have gradually shifted towards a looser construc-tion of loss of control.[6] By contrast with cross-gender partner violence, where assumptions about 'provocation' abound,[7] violence in public places may be mislead-

---

[5] See the 'Spanner' case, *R v Brown (Anthony) and others* [1994] 1 AC 212, later upheld in Europe in *Laskey v UK, The Times*, 20 February 1997 (ECHR); 24 EHRR 39.

[6] See *Thornton* [1982] Crim LR 54, *Ahluwalia* [1983] Crim LR 63, where the courts have ruled that delayed reaction to abuse makes the defence of provocation less plausible but not unarguable. The 'overcontrolled' males in Megargee's (1966) typology likewise are slow-burning 'explosives', so this phenomenon is not gender specific, though it may account for a larger proportion of killings by women. Historically the law, judges, and jurors have been more sympathetic to men who claim that sexual jealousy made them lose control than to women who kill in 'lukewarm blood'; but what level of irritation is acceptable to lead us to deem killings or woundings to be excusably provoked? Should the test of provocation be 'objectively' behavioural, or in the mind of the killer? If the latter, particularly, how do we test the claim?

[7] Including where race trumps gender, as in the acquittal of African American football star O.J. Simpson of murdering his blonde wife, where post-trial jury interviews revealed that black American women on the jury felt that his wife was a 'bitch' who deserved the prior beatings she had received (though they believed that Simpson had not killed her) (personal communication to Michael Levi; see also Dershowitz 1997).

ingly stereotyped as being a conflict between a guilty offender and an innocent victim, especially where there is an age or status difference, rather than—as discussed later— as being often an escalating, interactive process (Toch and Adams 1994; Toch and Karon 1992; Athens 1980).

Labels such as 'war criminal' and 'genocide' are usually applied against those out of power—though Serbia may be a rare exception. Equally, those who commit 'crimes of obedience' (Kelman and Hamilton 1989; Cohen 2000) define themselves, and are commonly defined in their culture, or at least, their narrower reference group, as 'loyal' rather than as being 'violent conspirators in a process of genocide'. Such a state of denial is commonplace in the murder of some 800,000 Tutsis in Rwanda during the 1990s (Gourevitch 2000)—more than the total UK homicides in the past two centuries—the millions killed in the Nazi Holocaust, and the killing of mostly inno- cent civilians in countless insurgency conflicts. How did so many Rwandans and Germans manage 'not to notice' that this genocide was going on, or manage not to view the dead or 'disappeared' as full humans, and thus avoid being, in their own eyes, blameworthy? In accounting for genocide, a socio-biologist might argue that 'not noticing' represents a personal survival-enhancing factor, while psychoanalysts and sociologists from the 'Frankfurt school' might stress the impact of authoritarian child-rearing with its stress on social conformity, plus the learned hatred of and contempt for particular ethnic, religious, or national categories of (non) person. There remain areas of intense dispute between genocide studies scholars and com- mentators (see, for example, Goldhagen 1997; Gourevitch 2000; Browning 2001; and Burleigh 2001). But in context, people tend not to regard all killings as being of equal seriousness: many Westerners (and certainly Americans) might rank the killing of American civilians by Al Qa'ida hi-jacked planes as more serious than the same number of innocent Afghan civilians killed by American 'carpet bombing' in 2001; the followers of *Jihad* might take the reverse view. The extension by some Protestant 'loyalists' in January 2002 of the concept of 'legitimate target' in Northern Ireland to postal workers and teachers is another illustration of the capacity of people to mould the boundaries of what they construe as acceptable violence, using subcultural justifi- cations.[8] Accounting for such shifts raises difficult issues of whether there can be an objective explanation, but popular accounts are inflected with views about justifi- ability: for instance, whether they refer to deficiencies of attachment, character dis- orders, socialized masculinity, or ideological principle. As in explaining any type of crime, some take seriously peoples' accounts of their motives, while others may disregard those accounts in favour of more 'objective' predictors.

Why does our conception of violent 'crime' take the form that it does? There are no ultimately satisfactory answers to this question, since there are few accounts that are sufficiently grounded in historical *process* to demonstrate why things turned out that way, and, moreover, historical processes themselves are not wholly determinate. Hall *et al.* (1978) and subsequent *marxisant* writers argue that intensified stories about 'mugging' during the 1970s formed part of a combined police and media attempt to associate 'the crime problem' with 'young blacks', with the objective of justifying

---

[8] The threat was withdrawn after protests developed, but their view of 'justifiable violence' remains elastic.

police repression in the interests of capitalist control (see also Bowling 1993). Others might reject the broad ideological rationale of such studies as over-theorized, but might accept that there are conscious or unconscious alliances between (a) police (to justify inner-city police operations); (b) crime reporters (to use cheap, voyeuristic articles and programmes which appeal to, and exacerbate, the already present underlying fears of the public in order to increase newspaper sales and viewing figures); and (c) some politicians, whether they have explicitly racist agendas or merely want to be seen to share the concerns of their constituents. (For reviews of the politics of crime journalism, see Schlesinger and Tumber 1994; Reiner in Chapter 12 of this volume.)

In the different context of health and safety 'violence', Pearce and Tombs (1992) and Slapper et al. (1999) argue that the reason this is not treated as 'real' violence is that corporate control over the political economy leads to its being marginalized in the interests of profit maximization. However, other advocates of corporate manslaughter prosecutions, such as Wells (2001), accept that there is (presumably inherently) something qualitatively different about unintended but reckless harms, even though the way we construct notions of 'reckless' and 'negligent' rather than malevolent is learned.[9] This intentionality issue is one which is central to many reactions to crime, including harmful driving: it could be argued that we over-inculpate street violence and under-inculpate corporate and motoring 'violence'. Lastly, in relation to violence against women, critics emphasize the benefits to patriarchal control of the mythology that women are somehow responsible for provoking male aggression (Dobash and Dobash 1992).

Cohen (1981, originally 1971) deployed the phrase 'moral panic' to point up the way in which campaigning groups amplified some social problems, using the media to whip up anxieties.[10] Moral entrepreneurship on violence issues is not restricted to the political right: feminists have tried to redress the traditional media and police neglect of violence against women and to shift the focus away from victim culpability in sex crime cases; with more success in changing police than in changing prosecutorial, judicial, or jury (i.e. public) responses (Gregory and Lees 1999; Hoyle 1998; Lees 2002).[11] In the realm of 'racial/racist assaults', also, difficulties have been experienced in translating changes in political and senior police agendas into the criminal justice arena (Bowling 1993; Bowling and Foster, in Chapter 27 of this volume).

[9] Though without the economic motivation for ignoring safety issues, similar arguments could be applied to the distinction many make between those car thieves who intentionally run down a car-owner or police officer 'because they were in the way', on the one hand, and those who drive their own cars recklessly or carelessly, on the other.

[10] A neglected feature of Cohen's work is that the initial fear of crime had a genuine basis in experience: indeed, there is a serious conceptual problem in whether we can ever discredit fears as 'irrational' and—if we can discredit some such fears—in how we can do so consistently. See also Young (1988).

[11] This difference may be understandable in that, in the post-MacPherson Report era (Phillips and Bowling, in Chapter 17 of this volume), police are now expected to take complaints as genuine ones, whereas juries have to be satisfied to the high standard of 'beyond reasonable doubt', and Crown Prosecutors have to conform to their Code which requires a reasonable prospect of conviction (see Sanders and Young, in Chapter 28 of this volume). This can cause serious difficulties, as in 2001 when the disgraced former MP Neil Hamilton and his wife were arrested in the glare of publicity for having allegedly taken part in the rape of a woman who identified them (and who has subsequently been arrested for related offences): they had a cast iron alibi, and there was severe criticism of the police for taking the complaint at face value.

But—setting terrorism aside—the tabloid media remain obsessed by allegedly *new* or newly 'threatening' crimes, such as 'rural violence' (often mistaking commuter dormitory towns and villages for rural areas—see Tuck 1989), violence in schools (especially by outsiders against children, or by pupils against teachers), road rage, mobile phone robbery, female gang violence, and 'paedophile' violence against children. Such panics can be triggered by individual incidents: for example, in 2001, one father killing another in a quarrel over their children's ice hockey game in the US led to debates about parental vicarious competitiveness and 'rink rage'. Pearson (1983) wrote of fifteen-year cycles of moral panic about youth since the Victorian era; but fuelled by the growth of the media and their constant need for audience-grabbing copy, the reinvention of the new appears to follow much shorter waves in the following decades. Thus, in addition to individual cases, it is the *rate of change* (or *perceived* rate of change) rather than absolute levels that is exciting to the media, though sometimes, tabloid newspapers such as the *Daily Mail* can *de*-amplify such panics, as they did over satanic abuse scares in the early 1990s.[12] In contrast to the US, the British media have generally supported weapons control policies such as, in 1996, the ban on handguns (following the killing of children at a primary school in Dunblane, Scotland) and on 'combat knives' (after the stabbing of headmaster Phillip Lawrence).[13] The hundreds of millions of pounds spent compensating gun-owners and gun vendors would have produced a better violence-reducing yield in another setting, yet the imperative to do something about dramatic, newsworthy crimes privileges such actions compared with the constant drip of male on male street (and prison) violence and male on female domestic violence, neither of which is 'new' or technologically soluble enough to merit campaigns. To the extent that the media drive political and policing responses—though the media usually claim that they merely *reflect* 'public opinion'—such coverage is consequential in practical terms (see Reiner's 'media-made crime' in Chapter 12 of this volume).

As Sparks, Genn, and Dodd (1977) observed, fear of crime may act as a surrogate for all sorts of disparate psychological and social phenomena: fear of getting old, poor health, social change (including ethnic and age mix), declining community, job insecurity, etc.[14] Support for the relationship between fear of crime (especially violence) and fear of social change can be found in Dowds and Ahrendt (1996). Instead of asking why do women and the elderly fear crime 'irrationally', why do we not ask why young men are so 'irrational' as to disregard the risks they face? However, neat though such an inversion is, such an approach to risk ignores the superior salience of the positive motivation to do the things that would have to be foregone by males to reduce the incidence of violence—companionship, heavy drinking, and the chance of

[12] It is arguable that the campaign of the *Daily Mail* and *Mail on Sunday* represented a defence of family autonomy against the state and its bureaucratic front-line, the social worker. But the demystification remains valid nonetheless.

[13] In his honour, the Home Office makes high-profile crime reduction Phillip Lawrence awards. One difference between the UK and the US is the power of the gun lobby there, and the ability of well-funded US campaigns to unseat politicians who favour gun control, in a political system where individual candidates mean more than party affiliation.

[14] Bannister and Fyfe (2001) and other contributors to the *Urban Studies* Special Issue on Fear and the City develop these themes.

finding a sexual partner, for example[15]—or, in the case of prostitutes, money and the avoidance of beating by 'their' pimp. In general, people are more fearful about risks over which they feel they have no control: an example is the greater concern about being killed or injured in public transport accidents than when driving (even taking into account the effect of seeing larger numbers injured or killed in any one public transport accident than in a private motoring one). This would make more under-standable the preoccupation of the public (as well as the media) with out-of-the-blue sexual or non-sexual attacks by strangers, even though the number of assaults by acquaintances is much higher.[16] (See Hough (1995), for a good empirical review of anxiety about crime; and Kershaw *et al.* 2001 for some trend and demographic data on concern about crime from the 2001 British Crime Survey.)

RISK OF VIOLENCE

Risk has become a central theme in social explanation and in discourse analysis. Indeed, some sociologists go as far as to regard it as a central organizing principle of late modern societies (Giddens 1990; Beck 1992; Bauman 1998). While some, follow-ing Beck, have explored new kinds of risks associated with technology (nuclear, gen-etic, etc.), others have focused on crime and responses to crime, identifying what has come to be known as a shift towards 'risk penality' (see, for example, Garland 1996; Ericson and Haggerty 1997; O'Malley 1998; Kemshall and Maguire 2001; and, in this volume, Hudson, and Sparks and Loader, in Chapters 8 and 3 respectively).

Current assessments of 'risk' in the crime field bear little resemblance to traditional calculations of mathematical probability (Royal Society 1992: 91). They are affected by factors such as the voluntariness, personal controllability, and familiarity of the criminal activity in question. Moreover, both the social attribution of harmfulness (deserving victims, dangerous offenders) and the demand for protection and incapacitation against particular crime risks are plainly refracted through (if not actually created by) vocal pressure groups, politicians, and the mass media. In making collective risk assessments on behalf of 'society'—for example, over police resource allocation—policy-makers implicitly or explicitly weight the opinions of powerful and less powerful groups as to which crimes are serious and should be dealt with

---

[15] We prefer the term 'incidence' to 'risk' here, because properly examined, the risk of street victimization should be a proportion of the occasions people go out: it is entirely possible that over-60s have a higher rate than young people of being mugged as a proportion of the times they go out, even though the proportion of over-60s who are mugged is much lower than the proportion of young people mugged.

[16] This does not mean automatically that the risk of being attacked by an acquaintance is higher. As a proportion of the number of times that one is plausibly at risk of being attacked, the ratio of attacks to opportunities may be higher for strangers than for acquaintances. In practice, operationalizing the concept of 'opportunities' here is far from easy, given the bizarre sorts of circumstances that can trigger sexual attacks. For example, if going shopping counts as an 'assault opportunity' for every stranger or acquaintance one passes, the chance of being attacked per 'person opportunity' falls to an extremely low level, even if a high proportion of women who lead an active night life are assaulted.

through the criminal justice process. Perceptions about the frequency of occurrence of specific crimes are also tied up with perceptions of their seriousness. For example, one American study discovered that, in estimating the risks of homicide and other forms of death, people tend to grossly overestimate risk in relation to the most vivid or imaginable events (Lichtenstein *et al.* 1978). More generally, Tversky and Kahnemann (1973) (see also Kahnemann *et al.* 1982) suggest that the easier it is to recall or imagine an event, the more likely we are to judge that it is risky or that it happens frequently. This perceptual process applies not only to crime victims, but also to police and parole decision-makers, whether dealing with violence or with any other type of crime. Mass media reportage serves as a substitute for direct experience—though research shows that people typically are active interpreters rather than passive consumers of what they see—and it is in this context that the impact of violence in the media must be considered. Thus, because dramatic crimes are more memorable, we are more frightened of them (and perhaps, though this does not logically follow, we are less frightened of more frequent but *less* dramatic crimes) than we 'need' to be.

Victimization probability data—in particular, those obtained through systematic methods of data collection from victims such as the British Crime Survey—can act to some extent as a counterweight to the most distorted media images—though, of course, they are themselves products of particular perceptions and definitions of violence, and should not be held up as the 'true picture' (Maguire, in Chapter 11 of this volume). They can be useful to illuminate:

1. the broad extent of different types of violent crime;

2. contemporary debates about who are the typical *sufferers* from violence—and especially those who are subject to multiple victimization, which has grown in importance as research has highlighted the disproportionate effects of crime on vulnerable populations and individuals (see Maguire, and Zedner, in Chapters 11 and 13 respectively of this volume);

3. possible trends in the level and types of violence over time; and

4. *explanations* of violence. For example, the frequency of violence and its social distribution, and their stability over time and place, tell us a great deal about the relative plausibility of biological/personality-based explanations for violent behaviour, on the one hand, or subcultural/cultural explanations, on the other. One might look for shifts in affluence, demographic composition, situational opportunity (e.g., more people drinking in public settings), substance abuse (e.g., crack cocaine and combination alcohol/drugs consumption) and styles of control to account for sudden fluctuations in 'real' violence rates. This, in turn, helps us to assess the justifications offered by politicians and police managers for their policies: though policies driven by popular appeal and/or retributivism may need no validation by research evidence of impact, we can only hope that rationality of input-outcome relationship imposes *some* constraints, at least on populist 'law 'n order' movements outside the United States (see Downes and Morgan, in Chapter 10 of this volume).

THE EXTENT OF VIOLENT CRIME

In this section, the principal features of risks of becoming a victim of violence are explored. We emphasize, however, that these 'objective risk' elements are also bound up in the routine activities of people of different ages, genders, and ethnicities, and these in turn are influenced by their judgements of the risk of crime alongside other life issues. Whatever the abstract risks, moreover, individual cases act as crystallizing points for public concern: examples (and note the late modern phenomenon of memorial websites to these cases) include the killing in 1993 of two-year-old James Bulger in Liverpool (**www.jamesbulger.co.uk**) and of eighteen-year-old Stephen Lawrence in London (see Philips and Bowling, in Chapter 17 of this volume); the stabbing to death in 1995 of head teacher Philip Lawrence (**www.homeoffice.gov.uk/lawrence.htm**); the school massacre at Dunblane, Scotland in 1996 (**www.dunblane.braveheart.com**); and the murder of eight-year-old Sarah Payne in 2000 (**www.sarahpayne.gotoo.com**). However, crime *statistics* are also a major battleground on which media, official, and local concern can be mobilized (Maguire, in Chapter 11 of this volume). For example, initially, the US National Study of the Incidence and Severity of Child Abuse and Neglect used an operational definition of 'child maltreatment' that did not specify how much harm was required before a case counted as maltreatment, and 30 per cent of all children were classed as victims—a figure repeated in countless media outlets across the United States. When a minimum degree of demonstrable harm was specified, the proportion dropped to 1 per cent (Burgdorf and Eldred 1978)! If the latter percentage had been reported initially, would child abuse have become such a major social issue?

Where the extent of 'violent crime' in general is concerned, the main official sources in England and Wales are the official totals of recorded offences published in *Criminal Statistics*, the annual Home Office compilation of data derived from police records, and the findings of the British Crime Survey (BCS), based on interviews with members of 40,000 households, which has recently moved to an annual cycle (see Kershaw *et al.* 2001). While both have important limitations, particularly in relation to violence between partners and acquaintances, they at least give us a broad picture of the numbers of people who are willing to report having been physically assaulted each year, and the levels of injuries they sustained. These figures can then be translated into 'risks' of being seriously assaulted, in comparison to, for example, being burgled, injured in a car accident, or whatever. However, as will become clear later, global figures of this kind can be seriously misleading.

More details on both recorded violence and BCS findings can be found in Maguire (Chapter 11, this volume), but it is worth setting out here the main statistics for 2000/2001. Over the twelve months of the financial year, the police officially recorded just over 600,000 offences of 'violence against person' (a mixture of offences ranging from homicide to common assault), to which can be added 95,000 robberies and 37,000 sexual offences. By contrast, the BCS produced estimates of 2,307,000 assaults and 276,000 robberies in 2000 (no estimate was made of sexual assaults, which tend to be grossly under-reported to interviewers): in other words, about four times the numbers of recorded offences.

High as these figures may sound, both sources indicate that violent offences make up only a minority of all known offences (about 25 per cent in the case of the BCS; under 15 per cent in the police figures). They also indicate that 'serious' assaults, judged in terms of levels of injury, are greatly outnumbered by cases resulting in only minor injury: *Criminal Statistics*, for example, puts the ratio of 'more serious' to 'less serious' offences at 1:20 (see Home Office 2001: Table 2.1). Translated into crude 'risk' figures, the BCS results suggest at first sight that about one in twenty-five adults is likely to fall victim to violent offences (and one in sixty to violence by a *stranger*) each year. Such figures, however, have little relevance at the individual level, as some people will fall victim several times, and the distribution of risk among different social groups is highly skewed (see below).

Comparative data on violent crime

Apart from looking at totals of recorded or BCS offences as above, one way of making judgements about the 'level of violence' in a particular society is to compare its crime figures with those of others. As Nelken (in Chapter 6 of this volume) indicates, this is by no means a straightforward task, owing to major cultural and legal differences in definitions and understandings of violent crime. The most commonly compared violence figures are therefore those on homicide, where these problems may be less serious (though they are certainly still present). Table 22.1 shows official homicide rates per 100,000 in several European cities between 1990 and 1994 (Barclay, personal communication), and between 1997–99 (Barclay *et al.* 2001). It indicates, for example, that London—which is perceived by many residents as having high rates of violence— is 'safer' in terms of the risk of homicide than many other cities: the rates in Amsterdam, Lisbon, Berlin, and Stockholm are consistently higher, though falling relatively in recent years.

Overall, there are modest but intriguing variations within Europe, whose average city homicide rate is 2.71 per 100,000 population, compared with 27.47 for Pretoria,

Table 22.1 Homicide rates per 100,000 population in selected European cities

City	1990	1991	1992	1993	1994	1997–99
London	2.5	2.5	2.4	2.2	2.3	2.36
Belfast	5.7	18.5	14.0	14.0	10.2	5.23
Edinburgh	2.7	1.8	2.1	2.5	2.0	2.15
Dublin	1.1	1.2	2.1	0.8	1.3	2.37
Amsterdam	8.2	3.7	7.1	6.9	8.4	5.37
Berlin	—	2.7	3.2	4.4	3.9	3.23
Brussels	—	3.4	3.5	3.1	3.7	2.67
Lisbon	—	4.0	4.8	4.5	5.6	1.99
Rome	2.9	2.1	1.6	1.5	1.6	1.22
Stockholm	3.7	3.4	3.8	5.4	—	2.67

9.38 for New York, and 50.82 for Washington DC—and much lower rates in Australia and New Zealand—over the similar 1997–99 period. These are hard to explain by economic, religious, ethnic, or other demographic criteria, although the exceptionally high rate in Amsterdam is probably related to its particular place in international drug markets (Belfast, of course, had the highest homicide rate of all, owing to terrorist activity at that time, though the lower rate in 1997–99 indicates the relative relaxation generated by the peace process).

THE DISTRIBUTION OF RISK: SOCIAL CLASS, RACE, GENDER, AND AGE

As already hinted, there are wide variations in the risk of violence between different social groups. The key factors appear to be social class (and area of residence), race, gender, and age—all of which, of course, interact. If one looks at single factors, one of the most significant is that of ethnic origin (Clancy et al. 2001). According to the BCS, Afro-Caribbean and Pakistani Britons are almost twice as likely to be assaulted as white Britons and Indian Britons. When one looks at threats—a category of crime that is often under-valued, but which can have a devastating impact on victims (Maguire and Corbett 1987)[17] and is exacerbated further by racist overtones—Asians are much more at risk than other groups (Fitzgerald and Hale 1996; see also Maung and Mirrlees-Black 1994). It is also likely that violence and threats against members of ethnic minorities are under-represented both in police statistics and BCS findings in comparison to those against white people.

According to the BCS, like most other sources of data on the subject, there are more male than female victims of violence. For example, one in twenty men reported being victimized in 2000, compared with one in thirty-three women (Kershaw et al. 2001: 63). However, there are probably many more female than male victims of repeat violence, especially of frequently repeated domestic violence.

The issue of the direction of domestic violence is not as clear-cut as might be thought by many readers. Research by Straus and Gelles (1990) in the US, based on two large national surveys exclusively on violence in the home, caused considerable argument when it appeared to show, first, as many male as female victims, and, secondly, that men are more likely than women to be victims of severe violence by their partner. The latter finding has not been replicated elsewhere, and most other surveys (both national and, especially, local) contradict the former too.[18] Even so, some BCS findings do support it. While data from standard BCS interviews show women as twice as likely as men to suffer domestic violence (e.g. Kershaw et al. 2001),

---

[17] A dramatic personal memory occurred in one of the authors' (ML's) childhood, when his father, an extermination camp survivor, came down one morning to find a swastika painted on the family's doorstep. No violence or threat needed to be 'offered'. Stalking, 'heavy breathing', or other telephonic threats to women can have a similar effect (Buck et al. 1995; Budd and Mattinson 2000), a fortiori when they appear to be systematic and personalized.

[18] For example, the American National Crime Survey found in 1993 that females reported seven times as many incidents of violence by partners (Craven 1996). Local surveys in Britain have found very high levels of domestic violence against women in inner city areas (see, for example, Mooney 1993; Jones et al. 1986).

a new, computerized *self-completion questionnaire* in the 1996 BCS produced the finding that equal proportions (4.2 per cent) of men and of women claimed to have been physically assaulted by a current or former partner in the last year (Mirrlees-Black 1999). This suggests that men are more likely to admit to such victimization when they do not have to answer questions face-to-face. Nevertheless, *threats* were found to be more common against women, and women were much more likely to have been injured, and to have suffered repeat victimization. The results of a repeat exercise in the 2001 BCS are not available at the time of writing, but will throw further light on this interesting issue.

It is worth noting, lastly, that the Straus and Gelles research was criticized (Dobash and Dobash 1992: chapter 9; Dobash *et al.* 1992) for failing to take account of:

1. the greater damage that men cause women than women cause men; and
2. the alleged difference between women's violence, which is provoked by genuine male threats, and men's violence, which is based on their power-control fantasies rather than on women's threats or 'unreasonable' taunting (see also Archer 1994).

Social class

The BCS indicates further significant differences in victimization rates by social class. However, this is much more marked in terms of the type of area or housing lived in, than in terms of the income of the individuals concerned. For example, private renters were found in the 2000 and 2001 surveys to be over three times more likely than owner-occupiers to be a victim of violence: this applied fairly evenly across all types of violent crime measured (Kershaw *et al.* 2001: 64). Again, adults living in council estates or in areas with a 'high level of physical disorder' were twice as likely to be victims as those in wealthy suburban areas or areas with low levels of disorder. Other research in the both the UK and the US has indicated strong social class differences in violence between spouses (Gelles 1998), rape by husbands (Painter 1991), and child abuse (Straus, Gelles, and Steinmetz 1980), as well as in violence outside the family (Weis 1989). Most violence, indeed, has been found to be both intra-class and intra-race, partly reflecting lifestyles in which males engage in honour contests or domestic oppression.

Homicide offers potentially the most valid *recorded* crime data set for ascertaining the social class of victims, but the Homicide Index does not provide information directly on social class: even so, the indications are that it largely involves people from lower-class backgrounds as both victims and offenders (Brookman, forthcoming). Both Australian (National Committee 1990; Polk 1994) and American (Greene and Wakefield 1979) studies indicate that homicide victims come disproportionately from the lower social classes; and since most homicides—*a fortiori* the 'family killings'—are 'cleared up' and are intra-class, it seems evident that it is the poor who are most likely to be injured and killed. This holds true not only of violence as conventionally defined but of the kinds of 'violence' which cause injury at work.[19]

---

[19] The latter is close to being a tautology: only those in consumer complaints departments would be likely to become victims of assault, for white-collar staff would seldom work on scaffolding, chop materials in workshops, etc.

Age

The 'lifestyle' approach to victimization relates risk to the patterns of living in which people engage (see Pease, in Chapter 26 of this volume). Young people are more at risk of becoming victims of any form of violence except spouse abuse, and this is related to the general patterns of life they lead, including the kinds of group drinking and quarrels in public places they get into (Tuck 1989; Mattinson 2001). Among males, 19 per cent of sixteen to twenty-four-year-olds interviewed by the BCS were assaulted at least once in 1999 or 2000—over three times as great a proportion as in any other age category. The equivalent figure for females aged sixteen to twenty-four was 9 per cent, more than twice the next highest female age group (twenty-five to forty-four). Victim surveys do not normally include juveniles, but those that do find that their victimization rates are only slightly lower than those of sixteen to nineteen-year-olds, even before the apparent boom in mobile phone robberies (Maung 1995; Anderson *et al.* 1990).

Occupation

In research, though far less so in theoretical analyses of masculinities which neglect it (Archer 1994; Collier 1998), increasing attention is being paid to the risks of violence among different occupational groups while at work, excepting the sort of 'corporate violence' risks discussed earlier. (As we argued earlier, the exclusion of workplace accident and avoidable industrial illness data from victimization surveys is under-standable, but reflects the conventional construction of violent crime.) Campaigns by social security officials against the removal of security screens from Job Centres, by teachers to make it easier to exclude 'violent pupils' and to prosecute violent parents and pupils, and by hospitals to exclude violent patients, demonstrate the emotive heat of work-related violence and the potential for disruption of public services. It is not always conceptually clear whether the best way of looking at these risks is in relation to the numbers of people doing a particular job, or in relation to the numbers of the people with whom they have to deal: ideally, one might want to look at assaults against 'street level bureaucrats' (police, teachers, social security officials, and social workers) as a ratio of their encounters with the public, allowing for jobs and time spent away from risky places and people.

The 2000 British Crime Survey estimated that there were almost 1.3 million incidents of 'violence' at work in England and Wales in 1999, roughly half of these being threats: the average was four assaults or threats per person assaulted or threatened (Budd 2001: 3). Put differently, in 1999, about 1.2 per cent of working adults were the victims of actual assaults, and a further 1.4 per cent had been threatened in the workplace. Budd (1999) illustrates the dangerousness of some workplaces, combining data from the 1994, 1996, and 1998 BCSs (see Table 22.2). Note that these categories relate to violence as understood in Home Office terms, excluding occupational health and safety risks, which are high in manual work (HSE 2001).

In terms of specific professions, the police had the highest annual risk of assault (25 per cent), followed by social workers and probation officers (9 per cent), publicans and bar staff (8 per cent), and nurses (5 per cent). Though the data indicate that policing risks have risen subsequently, earlier research suggested that the average risk

Table 22.2 Risks of assault and threats among selected professions

High Risk of Assaults	High Risk of Threats
Security and protective services (11.4 per cent)	Public transport (5.6 per cent)
Nurses (5.0 per cent)	Security and protective services (5.3 per cent)
Care workers (2.8 per cent)	Other health professionals (4.0 per cent)
Public transport (2.8 per cent)	Retail sales (3.5 per cent)
Catering/hotels/restaurants (2.6 per cent)	Nurses (3.1 per cent)
Other education and welfare (2.6 per cent)	Management and personnel (2.6 per cent)
Teachers (1.8 per cent)	Other education and welfare (2.3 per cent)
Retail sales (1.8 per cent)	Catering/hotels/restaurants (2 per cent)
Management and personnel (1.7 per cent)	Teachers (2 per cent)
Leisure/service providers (1.7 per cent)	Cashiers, bank managers, and money lenders (2 per cent)
Other health professionals (1.4 per cent)	Leisure/service providers (1.9 per cent)

of assaults against police officers—estimated by successive *Police Review* surveys at one in seven in 1988—differed only modestly from the average risks for men in the active police age group (Mayhew *et al.* 1989). This does not, of course, tell us what the relative severity patterns were in assaults on the police compared with other inter-male violence. As in other areas of violence, such physical risk data understate the impact of implicit and explicit threats, and the proportion of such threats or insults that lead to violent incidents is unknown.

CHANGES IN VIOLENT CRIME RATES

Lastly, is 'violence increasing', as the media constantly suggest? Does this matter; and, if so, to whom? Individual victims seldom feel better or worse because they would have stood a greater or lesser statistical chance of being beaten up or raped a year earlier, and their frightening experiences fill our newspapers and television news irrespective of how many of them there are. Nevertheless, the theme of social deterioration is an important one in general explanations, particularly since it is often asserted that 'in the good old days', when 'we had the death penalty and corporal punishment', there was less violent crime. In fact, the homicide rate today is thought to be roughly half what it was in the mid-seventeenth century, though the pattern of homicide is very different, being much more intra-familial now than then (Nuttall, personal communication). Gatrell (1980) has shown that the Victorian era did witness a significant fall in the level of violent crime (at least outside the home), and Gurr's review (1990) points to large American and English fluctuations within a general decline attributable to the 'civilizing process'. Eisner (2001) uses data from several European countries to suggest that a range of disciplinary arrangements in schooling, religious reform, and manufacturing promoted modern individualism and reduced individual-level violence.

According to both official statistics and victimization surveys, there was a substantial increase in violent crime between the early 1980s and the mid-1990s in England and Wales. British Crime Survey (BCS) data suggest that in the period from 1981 to 1995, domestic violence more than trebled; that acquaintance violence more than doubled; that stranger violence rose 12 per cent; and that 'mugging'—robberies and snatch thefts from the person—rose by more than half, mostly after 1991 (Mirrlees-Black *et al.* 1996). Thus, the public apparently had some reason to be more fearful, although the *degree* of their fear may have been made worse by their media-fuelled over-estimates of the chances of being assaulted, especially outside the home. However, in the period 1995–2000, the rate of BCS-recorded violence fell by more than a third, reducing the rate of victimization to its lowest since the early 1980s, when the surveys began. This trend is mirrored in Scotland (MVA Ltd 2000) and in the US (Rennison 2001), where the violent crime rate is the lowest since 1973, when American surveys began. The explanations for these changes in the late 1990s are not obvious.

The picture is complicated by the fact that violent offences recorded by the police have been moving in the opposite direction! Between 1998/9 and 2000/01, the official totals of offences of violence against the person rose significantly, from just over 500,000 to just over 600,000. About 70 per cent of this increase is accounted for by offences of 'common assault', 'assault on a constable', and 'harassment', all relatively minor offences prone to considerable variability in recording practice, but there were also increases in most of the more serious categories of offence. At present, then, it is difficult to reconcile or explain the two opposing trends—an excellent illustration of the need for extreme caution in drawing conclusions from any one set of official crime statistics (see Maguire, in Chapter 11 of this volume).

EXPLAINING VIOLENCE

Just as there is an array of forms of violence, so too is there a huge variety of approaches to explanation, from socio-biological through psychoanalytical and psychological to subcultural and other sociological theories which focus on hegemonic masculinity. As in other crimes, some of these differences represent not so much theoretical or empirical disagreements (though there are plenty of those) as differences in focus. Some scholars are interested in why this individual committed that crime against that person in those circumstances, whereas others want to account for why crime rates vary between those socio-economic or ethnic or age groups, or between men and women, or over time since the Middle Ages, and still others want to explain why violent careers follow the path that they do. The classical distinction in the psychological literature is between (a) instrumental, and (b) expressive violence (Megargee 1983). Instrumental violence might happen usually to obtain an economic benefit—from keeping other drugs dealers off one's territory or away from one's crime proceeds/drugs (Stelfox 1996); obtaining by robbery or threats money, credit cards, and resaleable goods such as mobile phones, laptops, and other portable products; or kidnapping for ransom, particularly in South-East Asia or Latin America. (For a particularly rich account of the last, see Marquez 1998.) Furthermore, especially where the state is weak, a reputation for violence *can be* economically functional, and thus 'rational', in obtaining 'consent' from persons blackmailed and to earn money as an arbiter of disputes between criminals or, where civil and/or criminal law is deemed unsatisfactory, as an arbiter of disputes between *non-criminals*: see, for example, the analysis of the Mafia by Reuter (1983) and Gambetta (1994). Indeed, where reputation is strong enough, there may be no need actually to hurt anyone, at least until violent competitors (such as Chechen, Colombian, or Russian gangs) come along. By contrast, expressive violence might be viewed as emotionally satisfying violence without economic gain: domestic violence or street fights would be the paradigmatic form. However, such a bifurcation of motive is far too crude, since:

1. many robbers also obtain a 'high' from the violence or threats they employ (Katz 1988), and gangsters may consider that "it is just business" when mutilating and/or murdering their victims, but actually they may be psychopathic or psychotic revellers in violence too; and

2. a reputation for 'irrational' behaviour can generate free domestic and sexual services from partners or other people in the local community, combined with the absence of complaint to the police, and therefore may also be instrumental.[20]

For reasons of space, we intend to devote little attention either to collective violence, though the presence of 'significant others' can act as a key trigger to the individual 'propensity' to behave aggressively—for example, to avoid loss of face in front of peers[21]—or to terrorism, despite the awesome destruction of people and property in the US on 11 September 2001, which led to more deaths than from homicides in the whole US that year.

The conceptual issue of 'what acts count as violence' does not cause too many difficulties for criminologists in practice *because they usually ignore it*. Much of the criminological literature on explaining violent crime takes as its field of enquiry the 'conventional' kinds of assault which dominate the 'offences against the person' recorded in *Criminal Statistics* (see Maguire, in Chapter 11 of this volume). A significant proportion of the psychological literature (and that by psychologically oriented criminologists) has a narrower focus on individuals who frequently assault others, or

---

[20] In days where manual work was much more common, it might have been handy for getting work, but even bouncers or club door staff (Hobbs *et al.* 2000) need to be able to exercise restraint in the context of controls over and sanctions for poor club management.

[21] The fear of losing face applies to police as well as to citizen responses. The mere fact that some people behave violently while others do not is not itself evidence of differential 'inner propensities' to violence; it can simply reflect different situational pressures, some of which—policing, housing, and family relationships, for example—may be consistent over time. See Waddington (1992) for an overview of collective violence.

on the more extreme kinds of violence, such as homicide and rape. Both approaches are perfectly defensible. Some people have a frankly psychotic or psychopathic view of the world and their relationship with it, and it seems appropriate in these extreme cases to take as the object of explanation 'why and in what respects are these people so different?' (see, for example, Hare 2001). Other violent offenders are closer to normal behaviour for their gender and age, and the appropriate focus is on social learning, situational interaction, cognitive processing, and opportunity factors. However, both approaches are also limited in terms of explaining violence in a wider sense, leaving out areas such as corporate violence and often not taking sufficient account of the gendered nature of much violence. Arguably, feminist literature attempts the greatest level of theorizing violence across the board: thus Campbell's classic (if empirically flawed in places) study *Goliath* gives us an impassioned analysis of the loss of meaning in *men*'s lives, which can account for their violence against each other as well as against women (Campbell 1993). However, feminist scholarship itself often neglects (i) those areas of corporate 'violence' which do not have female victims, and (ii) violence for gain such as robbery (though see Newburn and Stanko 1994).

Given the enormous heterogeneity of forms of violence discussed earlier this chapter, is it plausible that any one theory or theoretical paradigm can account for all these manifestations, or even serve as a common thread in all of them? As in the other areas of crime discussed in this volume (see particularly Chapter 2 by Rock), there is disagreement over what sort of explanation we are looking for. An explanation of why this person did that crime in a particular place and time (the criminologist's *whatsort-ofpersondunnit* allied to situational opportunity or routine activities models)? Literature on serial killers and rapists tends to take this form.[22] Alternatively, are we searching for an explanation of different *rates* of violence in different geographical areas or different countries, and/or over time? Or of different rates of victimization, by occupation, age, ethnicity, and gender (as discussed earlier); by locations; by weather; or by motivation? Different sorts of answers are required for different aims and levels of explanation, which partly explains why attention has been paid to such a variety of factors as autonomic nervous systems, circulating hormones (such as testosterone and corticosterone), food metabolization, electro-encephalogram readings, social and economic status (absolute, or by level of social inequality), gender, ethnicity, media coverage, and level of 'victim-precipitation' (i.e., the role of the victim in 'provoking' the violent incident).

One of the persistent difficulties with many approaches to explaining violence (and, for that matter, victimization risks) is that though they may lay down social

---

[22] It seldom explores, however, whether and/or why there are variations over time and between cultures in the frequency of the phenomenon, or even the psychopathology of suspects, except inasmuch as it helps to narrow down the range of plausible suspects. For a good review in this genre, see Holmes and Holmes (1996). For a deeply sceptical view of the social construction of serial homicide, see Jenkins (1994). Especially since the television series *Cracker*, there has been a vogue for books on profiling and about profilers (e.g. Canter 1995; Britton 1998, 2001).

indicators or 'marker variables'—some of which illuminate the dynamics of the phenomenon—they seldom generate anything close to a causal account which makes sense of *non*-violence as well as of violence. The accounts that come closest to helping us understand why this person committed that crime on that particular occasion are retrospective reviews; but the psychosexual conflicts which they reveal are much more common than violent behaviour, even if one takes into account opportunity variables. Those who write about violence understandably reflect their background disciplines, and although they mostly formally acknowledge that heredity, personality, family conflicts, cultural (including gendered) and situational factors all influence violent behaviour, it is the *relative* salience of these variables that produces a clear divide. We shall attempt to do justice to this multiplicity of perspectives, but given space constraints, we will reflect our biases by concentrating on the social interactionist and sociocultural explanations, while acknowledging that these too *over*predict levels of violence. Hence the importance of the data on the incidence and prevalence of violence which are presented in the first part of this review.

BIOLOGY, SOCIO-BIOLOGY AND VIOLENCE

Most work on the biology of violence concentrates on the physiology of the brain and how, in certain circumstances, it can lead to loss of self-control (Moir and Jessell 1995). Violence has also been associated with endogenous and exogenous physiological factors such as eating chocolate (Lester 1991), the menstrual cycle (Fishbein 1992), testosterone (Archer 1990) and the weather (Cheatwood 1995). It is fairly easy to make fun of the *general* value of the impact, for example, of chocolate on suicide and homicide (Lester 1991)—should we ban chocolate as well as guns?— but for some individuals, particular physiological triggers may apply under rare combinations of conditions that one may discover only after the violent incident. Brownmiller (1975) is one of the few feminists to argue that rape is the result of *biological drives* rather than being learned masculinity which is functional for male hegemony. The natural selection hypothesis that rape is a historical adaptation which substitutes for lawful access to reproductive mates is difficult to falsify, but many rapists do in fact enjoy access to consenting (or at least uncomplaining) females, and their generalized aggressiveness to people and to property suggests that 'the selfish gene' is not restricted to the desire to reproduce genetically. Classic methods following up the criminal records of monozygotic (identical) versus dizygotic (identical) versus dizygotic (identical) twins, whether separated or not, have been reviewed extensively. In the context of violence, some studies (Brennan *et al.* 1995; Mednick *et al.* 1987; Rowe 1990) have demonstrated substantial genetic effects; but they can hardly account for changes in violent crime rates in the same society over time, or for the frequency of violence among those who *sometimes* behave violently. Similar problems face those who would explain violence in terms of brain disorders or the metabolization of glucose (Eronen 1995; Moir and Jessell 1995; Raine 1993a, 1993b; Raine *et al.* 1994, 1995). The impact of hormonal factors, such as the post-pubertal adolescent 'testosterone rush', has been associated with the rise in aggression among boys, especially when combined with low frustration tolerance (Olweus 1987). This does at least provide some plausible account for age variation in aggression levels. Furthermore, such difficulties in explaining the *in*frequency of violent crime among 'the violent' also apply to sociological and social psychological/cognitive accounts, so they are not unique to biology and crime.

Even given a conventional view of what constitutes 'violent crime'—i.e., one which excludes genocide, war crimes, and corporate violence—controversy rages about the role of genetic factors. Wilson and Herrnstein (1985), Brennan *et al.* (1995), and Herrnstein (1995) argue that they *are* important, and that even the possession of an extra Y (male) chromosome is associated with violence. Some people behave violently for a long time in a variety of settings: although the manifestations of aggression vary, a child who is top of the distribution for aggression at age eight is likely to be near the top twenty years later. Psychological research has tended to focus upon the role of 'temperament', the origin of which is obscure but which seems to be a relatively stable phenomenon. Children who are extremely inhibited or uninhibited at twenty-one months are likely to be similarly classified at age seven. Farrington (1989, and in Chapter 19 of this volume) has argued that when they are children, violent offenders tend to be high on hyperactivity-impulsivity-attention deficit, tend to be restless and lacking in concentration, lack empathy (the ability to identify with others' feelings), and find it difficult to defer gratification. This may look like a caricature of the 'feckless poor' but is an *intra*-class discriminator of aggression levels. (See further Smith, in Chapter 20 of this volume.)

However, there are socio-biological approaches which are more dynamic and there-fore can accommodate changing violence rates. Burgess and Draper (1989) examine family violence in evolutionary terms, arguing that in certain conditions, child mal-treatment has a benefit in helping the fittest to survive: moreover, hostility towards stepchildren, for example, may be explicable in terms of our being prepared to act in a more hostile way towards people who share none of our genes,[23] while greater rates of violence against poor and 'physically challenged' children are understandable in rela-tion to competition for scarce resources and optimizing future individual repro-ductive potential.[24] (They explicitly state, however, that violence may currently be maladaptive.)

The analysis of homicide by Daly and Wilson (1988, 1994) explores the evolution-ary dimensions, including gender ones, which are understandable in terms of male attitudes of ownership of women, which have arisen from different evolutionary selection pressures on men and women which favour male risk-taking and female risk-avoidance. They stress that homicide predominantly occurs between individuals

[23] One might add that most so-called 'family violence' is committed by intimates who do not share the genes of their victims but rather are relatives by marriage.

[24] Natural selection arguments take into account epidemiological data but, like most functionalist explan-ations, tend towards the tautological. Selection operates at the level of the individual person, or even the individual gene, rather than in terms of 'reproducing the population': the latter is simply an aggregated consequence of individual selections. One problem posed for natural selection theory is the high prevalence of unrecorded incest. Another problem is how to account for variations in violence, such as the alleged increase in attacks upon 'disabled' people in Germany during the 1990s.

who are not related genetically; and that even when mothers kill, they normally are young ones who kill when they have a lot of time left to reproduce. Quite apart from the presence of alternative explanations, such as poverty and lack of social support for *some* young mothers, their theory requires the killers to believe that they will not be held accountable, since it is difficult to conceive further children while in most prisons. However, this is not to do justice to the general sophistication of their approach. For example, Daly and Wilson observe (1988: 128), partly caricaturing the stress on victim–offender interactions by Wolfgang (1958):

A seemingly minor affront is not merely a 'stimulus' to action, isolated in time and space. It must be understood within a larger social context of reputation, face, relative social status, and enduring relationships. Men are known by their fellows as 'the sort who can be pushed around' or 'the sort who won't take any shit', as guys whose girlfriends you can chat up with impunity or guys you don't want to mess with. In most social milieus, a man's reputation depends in part upon the maintenance of a credible threat of violence.

The difference between socio-biologists such as Daly and Wilson and social interactionists or ethnographers such as Bourgois (1996), lies more in their breadth of perspective and analysis of the *origins* of attitudes than in the situated accounts of behaviour. We may see that although *some* biologists, and especially physionomists, may be trapped in a static framework which obviously cannot account for the enormous variations in the extent of violence across societies and over time, the more sophisticated do take such variability into account, even though their analysis of the reasons behind such changes may be functionalist and teleological rather than genuine explanations.

PSYCHOANALYTICAL AND CLINICAL APPROACHES TO VIOLENCE

There is a self-evident quality in the proposition that people who commit especially vile acts have 'something wrong with them': the very abnormality of the *acts* makes it unsurprising that people should look for something abnormal about the *people* who performed them. There seem to be no family, social background or even situational factors that are unambiguously associated with violence, even homicide. Dobash *et al.* (2001) found that of all men currently serving sentences for homicide in Great Britain, just over a third of offenders came from broken homes and a quarter had a father who was violent to their mother. Almost three quarters had problems in school and a quarter had a conviction before age sixteen. Before sixteen, a quarter had problems with alcohol and one sixth had abused drugs: in adulthood, this proportion rose to half and a quarter respectively. A quarter had mental health problems and nearly two thirds were usually unemployed. In our view, though such statistical relationships tell us little about the psychodynamics of killers, one of the interesting things that may be inferred from them is the suprisingly large percentage that do *not* appear to come from a severely dysfunctional family or personal background. Doubtless some might query the empirical basis for self-reports or clinical notes on offenders' backgrounds: there remains a great deal of dispute over the role of sexual abuse in childhood as a cause of violence, since the concept of 'false memory syndrome' remains controversial (Pendergrast 1997).

Part of the difficulty lies in resolving what we expect from an explanation of violence. To the non-clinician, many accounts of 'the mind of the murderer' (for example, Guttmacher 1973, though not Malmquist 1995) amount to little more than a list of mental states and some *ex post facto* interpretation of how their family inter-actions might have generated those 'compulsions to kill', without any obvious reason as to why the crimes occurred at that time and not previously or against some other person, nor consideration of why similarly agonised individuals never kill or cause serious violence to others. Some killers and rapists appear quite normal most of the time, while others are obviously very disturbed and traumatized (Jefferson 1997). Gresswell and Hollin (1994) have provided a helpful typology of multiple murderers, breaking motivation into four areas:

1. visionary killers, who suffer from delusional beliefs about particular victims;

2. missionary killers, who have decided to rid society of certain types of people (such as prostitutes);

3. hedonistic or lust killers, who seek to remove the memory of humiliation by projecting rage on to their victims (found also by Hale 1994); and

4. power and control killers, who use killing as a form of domination.

However for some, this sort of motivational typology fails to illuminate the develop-ment of violent behaviour over time within the individual's life cycle. Brown (1991) argues that following stress, serial killers develop a taste for killing which relieves anxieties and is positively reinforced by the dissolution of anxiety, rather like other forms of addiction. This is compatible with the focus on the emotional 'high' that offenders get from sexual and other violence (Katz 1988), which can change the pattern of their violence (Canter 1995; Britton 1998, 2001).

Clinical psychologists tend to focus on the determinants of behaviour rather than on offenders' emotions. For example, acknowledging our very limited understanding of *why* some people turn out that way, Hare (2001: 27) asserts that 'the aggression and violence of the psychopath are instrumental, predatory and cold-blooded, and owe more to the nature of the individual than to the social and environmental forces that help to drive most other types of violence.' He seeks to develop a rigorous set of criteria into a 'psychopathy checklist' in which high scores are given to people who display lack of empathy, guilt or remorse and who use others only as tools for their own interests. People thus diagnosed have a significantly higher reconviction rate than people who score low: a situation made worse rather than better by the sort of therapeutic com-munity awareness regime sometimes recommended to increase empathy. Hare (1998) agrees that many people who receive high scores do not commit violent crimes or (by implication) any crimes: indeed, as classical psychiatric accounts also make clear, many would make successful captains of industry or politicians. So these are enhanced risk predictive factors rather than being either necessary or sufficient conditions for violent or any other crime. Moreover, despite the availability of such scientific constructs, psychopathy or 'anti-social personality disorder' has been and still can be treated as a rag-bag concept into which is dumped anyone who does not change their behaviour after punishments that would deter most of us (see Peay, Chapter 21 of this volume).

The episodic and non-recidivistic nature of most violent acts remains a difficulty for the general explanatory power of psychiatric and clinical psychological accounts, focusing as they do (understandably) upon the frequent and seriously violent acts. As Jones (2000: 43) concludes:

[I]t is not clear that any association between mental disorder and violent crime means that the offending occurred as a result of the disorder. The mental disorder may have been related to wider social problems which themselves precipitated the offending. Moreover, even where an association is apparent, it does not provide an explanation for the vast majority of violent crimes.

SOCIOCULTURAL AND SOCIAL PSYCHOLOGICAL EXPLANATIONS

We have grouped these explanations together because, although they spring from different academic traditions—sociology and social psychology—they are mutually consistent, the former being oriented towards culture, social structure, and stratification (Wolfgang 1958; Wolfgang and Ferracuti 1967; Curtis 1975; Scully 1990), the latter towards the more immediate cognitive and interpersonal dynamics that 'produce' the violent behaviour (Toch and Karon 1992; Frude 1989, 1994).

Psychological approaches to explaining individual-level violence have moved from the relatively crude frustration-aggression approach (later refined to suggest that frustration raises arousal which may be interpreted as anger), through social learning theory (Bandura 1973) in which aggression is learned vicariously through watching (though this too has been criticized for over-interpretation of play as aggression), to more cognitive and behavioural theories. Huessman and Eron (1989) argue that aggressive behaviour is largely controlled by programmes or 'scripts' about what events are likely to occur, how the person should react to the events, and what will result. These 'scripts' have been learned during the child's early development, and are retrieved from memory on the appropriate environmental cues. Children are likely to be influenced by parents' own cognitive processes, so people who are 'paranoid' and view the world as hostile reinforce the child's scripts. Such individual-level accounts emphasize the interactive nature of much violent behaviour, although the behavioural cues which 'trigger' the violent conduct may vary not only with the general cognitive state of that person, but also with the drugs, including alcohol and tranquillizers, that he or she has consumed. In research on non-sexual child abuse, for example, Frude (1989) notes that the child's behaviour may influence the aggression levels of the parent(s), and may also provide a less responsive feedback to parental discipline methods, though the negative attitudes of parents towards their children, as well as factors such as social isolation, poverty, etc., were salient to the risk of abuse. In his later exploration of marital violence, Frude (1994) reiterates the importance of interaction, stressing the salience of:

1. relationship dissatisfaction, which leads to more negative evaluation of the partner's behaviour and to anger;

2. the couple's power relationship, which can be exacerbated when the male has fewer resources than the female (Straus and Gelles 1990); and

3. the couple's conflict style. Violence is particularly common in relationships which have high 'ambient conflict', involving frequent rows and the absence of inhibitions in attacking the self-esteem of their partner.

The worse the self-esteem of the partner, the more likely it is that anger aggression will be generated in the process, and even the most ('objectively') mild behaviour can lead to violence, especially around sex and money.

Toch and Karon (1992) have usefully distinguished several types of violent offender: the 'self-image demonstrator', who uses violence to demonstrate toughness which he believes will be admired by his peers; the 'self-image defender', who tends to feel easily slighted or disparaged and will react to defend his ego; and the 'reputation defender', who acts as a member of a group to defend the values of the group when he or she believes them to be threatened. They all involve various methods of coping with fragile self-concepts: this may be class or status-group linked, in so far as those who are used to commanding social resources and respect may be less prone than poor whites or people of colour to having their self-image undermined. On the other hand, some high-status people expect respect and may react aggressively—for example, by firing staff or 'freezing' partners—when contradicted or thwarted: whether this ever comes to be defined as 'violence' or 'violent crime' depends upon what they do and how they do it.

There is much popular belief in the intergenerational aspect of child physical and sexual abuse; but even if the great majority of 'child abusers' were abused children, it would be possible that only a tiny proportion of abused children grow up to abuse their children. In the case of *non-sexual violence*, many abusing parents misperceive their children's culpability and treat the baby as if it were an adult who 'made a mess' *deliberately* (Frude 1989); however, some children are objectively more difficult to handle, cry more, and give less affection, thereby making a cycle of escalating violence more probable. Situational opportunity variables are also salient to baby battering; modern nuclear families are far more isolated than the extended families found in many Third World countries, where parents are seldom alone in the house. (Different considerations apply to physical punishment of older children, who are considered in many cultures, in extended or in nuclear families, to be properly blameworthy and 'reformable' by being beaten. Systematic incest patterns also are found in extended families.)

By contrast with the interactionists' social psychological accounts that focus on micro-level attempts to comprehend what goes on in relationships between the cognitive sets of assailants and the behaviour of the assaulted, sociological accounts concentrate on aggregate data sets and broad-scale cultural trends. One of the earliest comprehensive sociological attempts to explain violence was the 'subculture of violence' (Wolfgang and Ferracuti 1967). While not providing an account of why the supposed subculture developed in the first place, the authors revealed that many acts of violence arise from incidents that are trivial in origin—insult, curse, or a jostle—the significance of which is blown out of all proportion in poor neighbourhoods where self-esteem is low. A more micro-sociological successor to this approach is the 'lifestyle' theoretical paradigm, based on victimization survey research, which shows that offenders and victims of street violence not only belong to the same social, age, and gender groups—for example, schoolchildren (Aye Maung 1995); and two-thirds of those who attacked sixteen to twenty-four-year-olds were in the same age group (Davidoff and Greenhorn 1991)—but also that victims are likely to have criminal records not dissimilar to those of their assailants. (One of the important consequences of this is that under current legal interpretations—Miers 2001—unless the Criminal Injuries Compensation Authority deems it inappropriate, such victims are likely to be denied state compensation either on the grounds of their conduct at the time, or because of their prior criminal convictions, however blameless their behaviour on this occasion.)

Curtis (1975) later developed the 'subculture of violence' approach to account for the higher incidence of black than of white violence, arguing, *inter alia*, that black people were expected to have a lower 'boiling point' and that their identities were much more fragile precisely because of the racism and economic discrimination in the wider society—a point developed also by Blau and Blau (1982) and by Currie (1985).

Feminist critics express concern that the focus on social stratification evades the central issue about violent crime, which is that it is committed primarily by *men*. In England and Wales, for example, 89 per cent of all identified killers over the period 1995 to 1999 inclusive were male. Feminist theories of male violence against women stress the social construction of masculinity, violence, and sexuality in patriarchal society, the object of which is to reproduce and maintain men's relative status and authority over women (Hanmer *et al.* 1989; Scully 1990; Dobash *et al.* 1992; Newburn and Stanko 1994; Jefferson 1997). Wife-beating, for example, is seen as an interactive process in which—even discounting the effects of rosy retrospection on early stages of relationships—the women started out feeling loved and interpreted male possessive behaviour as a gesture of commitment; only later did this sense of possession escalate into paranoid violence at the least threat to the husband's control or 'patriarchal rights' (Dobash and Dobash 1979). However, such accounts are unsatisfactory in illuminating variations in violence against women over time or in different societies, and the shift to the more fluid 'masculinities' is an attempt to deal with this problem (Morgan 1987; Newburn and Stanko 1994; Messerschmidt 1993; and Jefferson 1997). Feminists are far from agreed upon the role of race and class, as contrasted with gender, in violent crime (Hanmer, Radford, and Stanko 1989), though Campbell and Muncer (1994), who argue that male and female aggression styles are very distinct, stress the importance of social status. However, although race and class factors are more pronounced in non-family than in spousal or parent-child violence, the data cited earlier indicate that theories based solely on gender seriously overpredict levels of violent crime both within and between societies.

Furthermore, those who are concerned mostly about the harms done to women by men risk sidelining the impact on other men, an unknown number of whom may *not* be willing participants in honour contests. Thus, in well over half (59 per cent) of all homicides in England and Wales in 1995–99, both offender and victim were male. This compares to 29 per cent of homicides involving a male suspect and female victim; almost 9 per cent involving a female as both offender and victim; and just over 3 per cent of homicides involving a female offender and male victim (Brookman, forthcoming). Whether or not men are biologically more aggressive than women, the level and manifestation of *machismo* is culturally variable. Thus Strong (1995), writing about the conditions of Colombian society that enabled major drugs traffickers such as Pablo Escobar to develop their power bases, discusses the role of the *sicarios*—young men on motorcycles who are willing to assassinate anyone for a few dollars, simply to prove themselves in a country where 'reputation' is crucial both for dignity and sexual display. This, plus 'turf wars', was why the homicide rate doubled between 1970 and 1980. Between 1980 and 1986, the homicide rate in the city of Medellin alone quadrupled to 2,000 killings (see further, Rubio 2001). In Colombia, as in many Latin American countries, male ego insecurity is extremely prevalent and leads to large numbers of 'honour contests' (Polk 1994).

Compared with Colombia, British representations of *machismo* (thankfully) are tame, although Campbell's (1993) journalistic account of the male British underclass has echoes of the following passage by Strong (1995: 157): 'The *sicarios* were characterized by their adoration for their mothers, their religious superstition and their relentless consumerism. In a world in which fathers were mostly dead, drunk, unemployed or simply absent, it was around the mothers that households hinged.'

Some features of social organization are not reflected in any of these macrocosmic accounts, but nevertheless appear to be significant in accounting for violence. Gartner (1990) has conducted some cross-national research in developed countries to see what factors best account for variation in homicide rates. She concludes that more micro-level research is required, but observes (1990: 102) that

Nations with greater material deprivation, more cultural heterogeneity, more family dissolution, higher female labor force participation, and greater exposure to official violence generally have higher homicide rates. . . . A disproportionate number of teens and young adults was not associated with higher homicide rates for any age group, among these 18 nations. . . . Female labor force participation may influence homicide by raising the motivations for female and child homicide, rather than by weakening controls.[25]

Braithwaite (1989) focuses likewise on economic inequality as a primary predictor of homicide rates, and this is implicated in the connections made between imperilled 'masculinities' and violence (Polk 1994). Links between unemployment and criminality are stronger for property crime than for violent crime (see Field 1990)—not least because of the link between having more money, going out and drinking more, and getting into fights (Tomsen 1997)—but more sophisticated sociological accounts might separate out the unemployed into those who are psychologically integrated into 'straight society' and those who see themselves as part of an 'underclass' (and are policed as if they were).

[25] For further research and commentary in this area, see Eisner 2001; Killias and Aebi 2000; LaFree and Drass 2001.

Accounting for rape

There is some controversy as to whether or not to account for rape separately from mainstream accounts of violence, especially violence towards women. Criminological (as opposed to psychological) explanations of rape are predominantly socio-cultural and social interactionist, arguing that rape reflects more general attitudes by men towards women in any particular society and that a substantial proportion of rapes arise from misinterpreted (to male advantage unless convicted) and unreciprocated seductions (Sanday 1981; Sorensen and White 1992; Scully 1990; White and Sorensen 1992). Felson (1993) argues that while most rapists *prefer* non-coercive strategies to obtain sex, subjectively defined sexual deprivation is their primary motivation, and rapists have high levels of both marital and extra-marital intercourse. Whether with women or (in prison) with men, they regard others as being there for their sexual gratification. These accounts are *social* psychological, but the role of individual psychopathology (or grossly mis-read 'sexual scripts') is important in some cases of 'blitz rapes' where there is no real interaction beforehand between offender and victim (see West 1983). It would be a caricature to assert that this is anything other than an awful parody of the bifurcation by men into 'good girls' and 'bad girls' that is more commonplace, since there is no evidence that a substantial proportion of men regard a woman merely walking in the street as parading her sexuality. In *some* societies, rape is directed towards women who display most independence (Sanday 1981), thereby attracting the functionalist 'explanation' that it occurs to keep all women subjugated (Brownmiller 1975). In Britain and the US it is committed primarily by young males attacking young females of similar background and ethnicity: based on official crime figures, almost two-thirds of rape victims and almost half of indecent assault victims knew their attacker previously, and two-thirds of rapes and half the indecent assaults took place at the home of the victim or suspect (Smith 1989; Watson 1996).[26]

Unless women are the target group for subjugation by those males who have little economic wealth to exchange for (relative) monogamy, or by wealthy men who do not fear the criminal law or for their social reputation, such a distribution of victims is hard to explain in terms of *collective* male interests.[27] There is insufficient detail to be able to describe most of these as 'date rapes', but the data support the argument that the explanation for most sexual violence must be sought in male misperceptions of females' attitudes towards them and/or in their beliefs that if they 'go too far' in such situations, the consequences will not be very serious. (See Chappell 1989.)

Rape is often part of a general tendency to use violence (Pollard 1994). Rapists may subscribe to rape mythology that if they continue despite female protestations, the

[26] We have counted 'no suspect' and 'unrecorded' as not acquainted, since one presumes that if someone has gone to the trouble of getting a sexual assault recorded, they would want to see an offender they could identify punished.

[27] Natural selection theorists would regard it as nonsensical to suggest that there could be a gene which generated behaviour which benefited a group as a whole. The high proportion of young females as victims, 'explained' by some socio-biologists as an attempt to maximize offenders' reproduction—though given female contraception, a more maladaptive response today—also owes much to their more active night life. Older women go out less, having responsibility for child-care under current gender roles. The situational opportunity factors are omitted from most socio-biological accounts (e.g., see Thornhill and Thornhill 1992).

women will enjoy the experience: to admit otherwise is to admit to themselves that they are unattractive, a conclusion that is all the more humiliating if one of their friends has had sex (or *claimed* to have had sex) with the woman. Herein may lie the true significance of Amir's (1971) controversial finding that a large percentage of rape victims had a 'bad reputation': men might find it harder to retreat from sex in those circumstances, as well as (incorrectly) feeling that there was no 'real harm' in indulging themselves with a 'spoiled female'. As for Amir's finding that 70 per cent of rapes are planned (ibid.) this has been misused to illustrate premeditation: his defin- ition of 'planned rape' is that it occurs when the offender rapes the victim in a place other than where they first met. So if a man met a woman in a bar, and went to either of their homes in the hope of voluntary sex, but raped her when she did not consent, this would constitute 'planned rape' on Amir's definition. Yet although many men are careless about women's feelings, there seems more reason to suppose that most rapes are unplanned but potentiated by 'cultures of masculinity'.

Based on interviews with American rapists, Scully (1990: 91) observes that rapists have nothing in their background to predict rape specifically, but rather are typical of non-white-collar felons. From the perspective of the rapists, almost no act—however brutal—is a 'real' rape and almost no man is a rapist. The key to justifying violence to others (and to themselves) is to make what was in fact rape appear ambivalent in terms of consent. Those who denied their rapes were prone to believe, or at least to assert, that women found them particularly desirable. Admitters, on the other hand, were much more aware of the emotional impact, and took satisfaction in the belief that their victims felt powerless, humiliated, or degraded. Neither group felt guilt or shame during or after the rape, nor did they feel empathy for their victims at the time. Indeed, the desire to dominate a woman is also a major component of rapists' sexual fantasies.

In short, at the risk of producing precisely the sort of list for which we criticized Guttmacher, rape can occur:

1. as a means of revenge and punishment;

2. as an afterthought or a bonus that offenders add to a burglary or robbery, as 'another thing to take';

3. as a male bonding activity in groups (especially in the aftermath of war, to their subjects' 'womenfolk'); and

4. to make a fantasy come true, to control and dominate impersonally (Scully 1990: 166).

The question of why most men who have chauvinistic attitudes and could rape do *not*, remains unresolved by any of the research literature. One could hypothesize that non- rapists fear more than rapists for their social reputations, for the expected future feelings of the prospective victim, or for the direct and indirect socio-economic consequences of arrest and conviction, but these concepts lack analytical specificity.

The culture of masculinity and violence involving the police

One special case of violent crime that illustrates the complexity of the psychological, socio-cultural, and routine activities issues that go into helping us to understand violence, is assaults either by or against the police. Comments from senior officers and politicians, and media reports of violent incidents, usually blame the public (or rather, some 'hooligan' section of the public which is hostile to the police). By contrast, in the specific area of violence in which police are hurt, early American research by Toch and Karon (1992) observed that many police victims of assault become so because they are personally insecure and wish to prove to themselves and others that they are 'Real Men' by daring others to defy them. (In societies such as the United States, such 'Desperately Seeking Challenges' can be a dangerous thing to do, since the *consequences* of the same displays of aggression can be readily more serious where guns and hunting knives are available.) This explanatory approach is also generalized to other contexts, such as inmate–inmate and inmate–officer violence in prison (Toch 1979: 272–3):

The term 'brawling' is used advisedly, because, as this man sees it, his conflicts with officers are 'fights'. In other words, they are disputes which are settled physically, as disputes must be settled among men. This view is partially shared and reinforced by the officers, who repeatedly describe in vivid detail the wrestling holds they deploy to neutralize the man . . . The man is said to have 'communication problems' and these are reciprocal . . . The central issue often appears to be that the man feels himself treated like a child, and that his version of *machismo* holds that no man must be ordered about by another man, and that it is demeaning and insulting to be told to do things, particularly when you have explained why you do not wish to do them or would have explained if you could have.

The issue of the man's reactions to uniforms does not necessarily enter the equation because the man sees encounters between himself and officers as personal, and perceives custodial instructions as originating in whims and expressions of disdain or disrespect. When the man feels disdained or disrespected in this way he reacts at the first available opportunity, which makes his behaviour unpredictable, because his reaction does not necessarily coincide with the move that originates the offense to which he reacts.

Those who defy the police might be expected to display similar reactions to other authority figures—such as teachers or employers—with similarly polarized interpretations of the *justifiability* of the demands by authority figures. To many people, including journalists, all such challenges are indicators of cultural disturbance or distorted thinking, but to others, they indicate a desire for personal autonomy which is being invaded by the powerful.

Another factor to consider in such violence is the traditional police subculture of masculinity (see, for example, Holdaway 1983), in which aggressive policing is encouraged, or at least may not be actively *dis*couraged. Adherents to this 'Dirty Harry' subculture believe—along with 'noble corruption' detectives who 'strengthen' evidence against those they 'know' to be guilty—that unless they act firmly, 'things will get out of hand', and they must especially clamp down on 'known troublemakers' in their area who set a bad example to others by demonstrating 'contempt of cop'. How do they know who the troublemakers are? Every police officer who joins an area has these individuals or families pointed out to him by supervisors, either in the police station or out on the beat. Other prime candidates are young 'ethnics', bikers, and other potential 'rowdies'. An alternative view is that in the great majority of cases of assault on police, members of the public who may be more generally anti-social and anti-authority become the worse for wear on drink and indulge in untrammelled violence which is generally unprovoked by any misconduct on the part of the police. In the minds of the beleaguered officers, the large amount of low-level verbal abuse and hostility to their presence in some licensed premises and city centres late at night makes it necessary to intervene to stop the area turning into a 'no-go' one. Whether or not police and public are right in believing that there is less respect for the police nowadays and that society is getting more violent, these beliefs impinge upon police anxieties about loss of control and can result in 'heavy-handed policing', particularly if:

1. their supervisory and senior officers encourage 'active' policing; and
2. the section of the public they are dealing with is seen as comprising 'criminal' and/or 'anti-police' types who belong to a 'subculture of violence'.

It is tempting to explain the rise in assaults against the police since the tranquil early 1950s in terms of the greater ease with which modern communications enable a police officer to get to the scene of the 'disturbance' while it is still in its upswing—a view with which some older police officers concur. However, this is to ignore the high assault rates in the period 1850–1927, when communications were also slow.

To the extent that assaults against the police *have* been increasing in recent years, this may also be because police legitimacy in the eyes of the public has diminished—which the police acknowledge has happened, but which they do not usually attribute to a general deterioration in *police* behaviour—and/or because the police have become less skilful in the handling of relations with the public (see *Which?* 1990; Skogan 1990; Reiner 2001). This process of desubordination to authority is a generalized feature which is implicated in assaults against a variety of personnel—police, prison officers, social workers, teachers—all of whom pose a threat to the desire for autonomy. This may be extended to others who threaten, or are expected, reasonably or unreasonably, to threaten in the future, the self-gratification of the offender. Looked at in this way, what may appear to be individual paranoia may be understood to have some sociocultural roots.

More generally, however, interviews with assailants and observation of police work support Toch and Karon's (1992) view that the way the police approach the public—such as appearing to pick on them, making them face humiliation in front of their friends or their girlfriends to whom they wish to present a *machismo* image,[28] or standing physically very close, thereby (a) winding them up psychologically, and (b) bringing themselves within ready head-butting range—is an important dimension in understanding assaults against the police (Christopher *et al.* 1989). Whatever the pleasure that individual officers obtain from violence (Katz 1988), changes in the nature of 'cop culture' or 'prison officer culture', as well as in officers' *perceptions* of being assaulted or killed themselves, may account for variations in violence by police and prison officers. Also relevant is Bernard's (1990) conclusion that a subculture of

---

[28] Research suggests that those who are convicted of assault against the police predominantly have friends present with them who believe that such assaults are justified (Christopher, Noaks, and Levi 1989).

angry aggression arises in conditions when serious social disadvantage is combined with individual social isolation.[29] Peer activity routines, once established, are likely to account for the immense social class and status group and gender variations in the prevalence of different forms of violence. The virtual abolition of opportunities for traditional unskilled labouring work has reduced the incentives for conformity, but those unacquainted with the role of socialization and ongoing social controls might be surprised that violence (and crime for gain) among the lowest social classes is so low, rather than that it is so high. On the other hand, it is clear that if assaults against the police were purely socially determined, the chances of officers patrolling a particular area or activity being assaulted would be roughly equal: yet some officers are assaulted more frequently than others, whatever jobs they are doing, suggesting that there are some personality and social skills dimensions in addition to wider issues of desubordination.

Specialization in violence

Are violent offenders specialists, and what do their criminal careers look like? Hare (2001) sees offence diversity as a normal part of the psychopath's generalized disregard for others' feelings and rights, but most violent offenders are not psychopaths, and *vice versa*. Because of the distortions generated by non-reporting and non-prosecution of family violence (and injuries in the workplace), criminal career data based on official statistics are prone to specific distortions. American research suggests that violent offenders have longer criminal careers and are less likely to stop in the early stage of their offending than are property criminals (Blumstein *et al.* 1986). The proportion of the population who account for different sorts of crime can change over time: the rate of violent offending by the cohort born in 1958 in Philadelphia exceeded that of the 1945 Philadelphia cohort by a factor of 3:1 for homicide, 1.7:1 for rape, and 2:1 for aggravated assault and burglary, and they were more likely than the 1945 cohort to be violent recidivists (Tracy, Wolfgang, and Figlio 1990: 276, 281). The 7.5 per cent of the 1958 cohort described as 'chronic offenders' accounted for 61 per cent of the homicides, 75 per cent of the rapes, 73 per cent of the robberies, and 65 per cent of the aggravated assaults: the 1945 'chronics' had committed an even higher proportion of *cleared up* violent crimes, presumably because violence was more widespread among the later group. But offending may be less concentrated and less repetitive in Britain, where other features of underclass desperation are milder.

Nearly all London offenders studied by Farrington were convicted of non-violent as well as violent crimes, and only a quarter of their crimes were violent. Essentially, although 70 per cent of violent offenders are convicted of only one violent offence, they are frequent general offenders who appear to turn to violence after property crime. In London, the majority of juvenile violent offenders did go on to commit adult violent offences (and those who did not committed *non*-violent offences as adults). Home Office (1989) data on the prospective and retrospective criminal careers of rapists suggest similar generalized offending. Of those convicted of rape in

1985, 55 per cent had previous convictions for theft and 43 per cent for burglary.[30] Just under half had previous convictions for one or more offences involving violence—a third of them for sexual offences, but only 3 per cent for rape. Looking forwards in time, of rapists convicted in 1951, 6 per cent were reconvicted of sex crimes by 1973, though those who did reoffend were just as dangerous a decade after their conviction as they had been earlier (Soothill, Jack, and Gibbens 1976). Of 264 people convicted of rape in 1972, 4.5 per cent had been reconvicted of rape by 1985[31] (Home Office 1989), and a review of Offenders Index data found that within five years of their first such conviction, 10 per cent of sexual offenders were reconvicted of a further sexual offence (Marshall 1997). Of those aged thirty or over who were discharged from prison in 1992 for rape and other serious sexual offences, none without convictions prior to their recent offence and only 1 per cent with prior convictions were reconvicted within two years (Kershaw *et al.* 1997a: 6).

A recent study of all persons currently in prison for homicide (Dobash *et al.* 2001) found that 38 per cent had at least one conviction for minor assault; 15 per cent for serious assault; and 9 per cent for serious sexual assault. Only 15 per cent had no prior conviction of any kind. Previous Home Office research found that of those convicted of homicide, only one in six had previous convictions for offences of violence against the person, sexual offences, or robbery. Of the 1,145 persons convicted between 1972 and 1990 who were released on licence from a life sentence for homicide, 3 per cent were reconvicted of a grave offence—i.e., one with a *maximum* of life imprisonment—within five years, and 1 per cent within two years. Within five years of release, 19 per cent were reconvicted of less serious offences: those without prior convictions before their imprisonment were only half as likely to be reconvicted afterwards (Kershaw *et al.* 1997a: 11).

Since the majority of offenders were not convicted of more than one violent offence, ideas such as 'careers of violence' are not very useful, at least outside the family context and, it is suggested, among some *extra*-familial paedophiles. Even within the family violence context, it is far from clear what proportion of men who have hit their wives do so again, let alone escalate the level of violence. Fagan's (1989) review of the cessation of family violence notes that three-quarters of spouse abusers stop following legal sanctions, but for how long they stop is uncertain, since the follow-up periods are not long. The shorter the time and less severe the battering, the more likely people are to stop beating (although it should be noted that in their replication of their original study, Sherman and Smith (1992) observe that this effect is found only for 'respectable' batterers). These findings of low recidivism for violence (see also Farrington, in Chapter 19 of this volume) have, or ought to have, important implications for those who believe in 'incapacitating the violent offender'.

---

[30] No statistics are kept, but in the UK, unlike the US, burglary-rape is rare.

[31] Over a quarter were reconvicted for violence within five years of discharge, 1 in 5 for theft and 1 in 6 for burglary: this supports the view that rape is part of a general profile of aggression, not all of it towards women. Altogether, 1 in 3 convicted of rape were reconvicted for some offence within two years and 54 per cent within five years of discharge. Even these percentages are lower than for offenders generally.

Situational factors and violence: the role of 'substance abuse'

Lastly, readers should be aware of one factor that is relevant to both cultural and biological/pharmacological accounts of violence. British Crime Survey data show that around a quarter of all incidents of stranger violence occur in pubs or clubs on weekend evenings (Mattinson 2001: 3); in over half stranger violence and a third of acquaintance violence incidents, victims described perpetrators as under the influence of alcohol.[32] (In a further 16 per cent of stranger and 22 per cent of acquaintance incidents, victims thought that perpetrators were under the influence of drugs.) Of male homicide offenders in British prisons, 38 per cent were described as drunk or very drunk at the time of the offence, while 14 per cent were using illegal drugs at the time (Dobash *et al.* 2001). Most people know others who behave much more aggressively when they have been drinking heavily or, more rarely, while under the influence of illegal drugs such as amphetamines or steroids. Though some violent offenders report that they choose to get 'tanked up' with alcohol to put themselves in an appropriate mood for the fight they desire anyway, i.e. it is an enjoyment enhancer as well as a disinhibitor, heavy drinking permeates almost every venue in which violence occurs.[33] However, it is very rare for such people to be violent every time that they consume those substances, so it cannot be said, for example, that the drink is a sufficient or even necessary explanation of their violence, even if one disregards powerful cross-cultural evidence that the relationship between substance use and aggression depends upon social norms and expectations (Collins 1989; Fagan 1990). Notwithstanding this, the opportunities for certain types of interaction offered by heavy alcohol use, combined with fragile self-respect of a kind that anyway would be threatened by a male or his female companion being 'looked at in a particular way' even when sober, implicate alcohol in the process of becoming violent.

Adolescents who drink or use drugs are more likely than those who do not to commit violent acts, though this may simply reflect the risk-taking mental set of those who also have their first sexual experiences early (Herrnstein 1995). Likewise, there is a positive correlation between (a) the severity and frequency of violent delinquency, and (b) the seriousness and frequency of drug-taking (Fagan 1990). American research indicates a positive relationship between alcohol use and violence against partners (Frieze and Browne 1989) and generally. British research indicates a strong relationship between crimes of violence and beer consumption (Field 1990), though this may be an artefact of street violence occurring where young people cluster and become embroiled in disputes when they leave drinking places (Tuck 1989, Ramsay 1996; Tomsen 1997; Deehan 1999). The impact of this can be mitigated by licensing policies, by pub and club management techniques, and by subtle policing (though the last may be easier to define afterwards than in advance). Drinking and drug-taking can be indulged in as trauma-less fun, but although some offenders are part of a peer culture in which 'handling it' without aggression is expected, frequent 'poly-substance

---

[32] The numbers were small, but Bennett's (2000) NEW-ADAM urine testing research revealed that of those arrested for assault, 61 per cent tested positive for illegal drugs and 32 per cent for alcohol.

[33] As Professor Al Reiss observed to ML (over a drink or two), when discussing the causes of violence: 'the explanation is booze, booze, booze'.

abusers' tend to be people with low self-esteem who find it difficult to confront problems in relationships. Common accompaniments are violence to self and to others, as well as generalised aggression. Collins (1989) observes that individuals with alcohol disorders frequently have other personality disorders, including crippling anxiety or sudden changes in relationships and mood.

As regards illicit substances, except in so far as there may be 'commercial' violence resulting from a desire to dominate drugs distribution or extort money from sellers, there is no evidence that the *pharmacological* effect of cannabis, hallucinogens, or opiates makes people violent, at least when taken alone: if anything, the reverse is true. There is a more plausible link between violence and amphetamines and solvents (and with steroids often associated with body-building), but, as with alcohol, demonstrating the causal link is confounded by the intervening personality variables. The effect of crack cocaine in increasing the risks of mental illness (one side-effect of which may be violence) is difficult to separate out from the need to get funds to obtain a 'fix', which can lead to robbery as well as to non-violent crimes for gain. A thoughtful overview by Fagan concludes (1990: 299) that:

intoxication affects cognitive processes that shape and interpret perceptions of both one's own physiology (i.e. expectancy) and the associated behavioral response. The cognitive processes themselves are influenced by cultural and situational factors that determine the norms, beliefs, and sanctions regarding behaviors following intoxication. . . . Propensity toward aggression reflects explanations regarding the use of personal power to resolve perceived conflicts.

RESPONSES TO VIOLENCE: RECENT TRENDS

As with any other type of crime, social and legal responses to crimes of violence vary widely over time and place, as penological thinking, priorities, and fashions change and as levels of public, media, and political concern rise or fall. There is no space here to cover the range of current responses to violence in any depth, and the *Handbook* already contains comprehensive reviews of developments in sentencing (Ashworth), offending behaviour programmes (Raynor, Hollin), multi-agency crime prevention measures (Pease), and the 'risk management' of 'dangerous' offenders (Peay; see also Hudson), which are all highly relevant to the issue. However, it is worth very briefly outlining some recent trends.

Over the past decade or so, violent crime (never long out of the headlines in any era) has been exceptionally high on the political agenda in England and Wales, and has been at the forefront of debates about penal policy. The 'headline' debates, and many of the legislative, policy, and practice changes which they have influenced, have been largely concerned with sentencing—in particular, 'tougher' and 'preventive' sentencing. However, other (and perhaps ultimately more 'effective') approaches have been developing in a quieter fashion.

SENTENCING AND POST-RELEASE CONTROL

The basic trend in the sentencing of violent offenders has been towards more and longer custodial sentences. This has been most conspicuous in the area of sexual crime: among all offenders sentenced for sexual offences, the percentage sentenced to immediate custody rose from 34 per cent in 1990 to 62 per cent in 2000 (Home Office 2001). Over the same period, the average length of custodial sentences for sexual offences in the Crown courts increased from thirty-seven to forty-one months. Indeed, among all the main offence groups, robbery (forty-seven months) and sex offences (forty-one months) attract the longest average sentences in the higher courts: by comparison, the average sentence in 2000 for burglary was twenty-two months, and for fraud and forgery it was fifteen months.

Averaging sentences in this way, however, conceals major differences in the sentencing of people at the top and bottom of the range. A trend towards 'bifurcation' (Bottoms 1977) has been evident for many years, whereby, in essence, long sentences get longer and short sentences get shorter. This has manifested itself in some very tough sentences, both for the more serious types of violence and for people considered 'dangerous' (Peay, in Chapter 21 of this volume). It has also had a significant impact on the size and structure of the prison population. By 2000, for example, 42 per cent of the entire sentenced prison population, and over four-fifths of the *long-term* prison population, were there for violence, including sexual violence (Elkins and Olagundaye 2001; for further discussion of this trend, see Morgan, in Chapter 30 of this volume). Such figures are particularly striking when one remembers that violent and sexual offences make up only about 15 per cent of officially recorded crime (Maguire, in Chapter 11 of this volume).

Long prison sentences for violence are often justified in terms of retribution and deterrence, but they have increasingly been aimed as much—if not more—at 'public protection' or (the more graphic American term) *'incapacitation'*. Indeed, this objective has been written into important statutes directed at both violent and sexual offending: notably the Criminal Justice Act 1991, which, despite enshrining 'just deserts' principles to limit sentence lengths for most types of offence, allowed much longer sentences for sexual and violent offenders on the grounds of public protection; and the Crime (Sentences) Act 1997, which introduced a mandatory life sentence on second conviction for a serious violent or sexual crime. This utilitarian approach to sentencing (which, perhaps tellingly, has hardly impacted upon responses to either corporate or motoring 'violence') has caused considerable argument and unease—at least among academics, who seem more troubled than politicians about justifications for punishment. The so-called 'dangerousness debate' has continued since the 1970s, mainly about the extent to which future serious offending by particular individuals can be predicted, and what accuracy of prediction would justify keeping people in custody to prevent future crimes (see, for example, Bottoms 1977; Floud and Young 1981; Morris and Miller 1985; Haapanen 1990; Monahan and Steadman 1994, 2001; see also Kemshall 2001; Peay, and Ashworth, in Chapters 21 and 29 respectively of this volume). As Morris and Miller (1985: 21) observe:

the societal decision, the moral decision, is . . . how to balance the risk of harm to society and the certain intrusion on the liberty of each member of the preventively detained group. At some level of predicted harms from the group, the intrusions on each individual's liberty may be justified.

Of course, we seldom have the opportunity of discovering what those incapacitated would have done had they been released, thereby making it difficult to test the validity of our expectancy rates.

In addition to sentences passed in court, statutory controls over sexual and violent offenders on completion of custodial sentences have also been tightened considerably. Since 1983, when the Home Secretary virtually applied a blanket veto on the early release of violent and sexual offenders serving over five years (see Maguire 1992), parole for such offenders has been greatly restricted. Moreover, once they are released, they are increasingly subject to risk assessment and 'risk management' (including police surveillance) by multi-agency 'public protection panels' (Maguire *et al.* 2001a; Kemshall and Maguire 2001, 2002). Sex offenders are also subject to extended license periods, as well as being placed on the sex offender register and obliged to notify the police of their whereabouts for a minimum of five years (Plotnikoff and Woolfson 2000); they can also be placed under a civil sex offender order, breach of which is a criminal offence carrying imprisonment for up to five years (Home Office, forthcoming).[34]

ALTERNATIVE APPROACHES

Not all recent developments have been based on the pessimistic view that violence reduction can be achieved only by 'incapacitating' known offenders – primarily by locking them away for lengthy periods. In particular, there has been a revival of belief in the effectiveness of 'correctional' methods, in the shape of structured programmes for offenders in prison or on probation. There has also been increasing experimentation with various forms of situational crime prevention, including efforts to 'design out' or 'manage' violence through altering 'risky' environments.

Offending behaviour programmes

As discussed in depth by both Raynor and Hollin in this volume (see Chapters 31 and 5 respectively), the 'What Works' initiative in England and Wales has produced a rapid increase in the use of 'offending behaviour programmes', most of them based on cognitive-behavioural approaches. These are tightly structured 'courses' in which tutors (in prisons and in probation offices) work through a sequence of modules intended essentially to teach offenders to avoid 'distorted thinking' and to improve their skills in handling social situations. Some of those designed specifically for

---

[34] The Sex Offenders Act 1997 established the arrangements for a Sex Offender Register, designed to keep track of the whereabouts of sex offenders for at least five years after their conviction or release from prison. To this was added the right of the police (under the Crime and Disorder Act 1998) to apply to the courts for a sex offender order. This was strengthened by Criminal Justice and Court Services Act 2000, which also formalized the responsibilities of public protection panels, officially extending their purview from sexual to other kinds of violent offenders.

violent offenders set out to teach them 'anger management' and self-control, although it is recognized that this approach is not appropriate for all: as discussed earlier, violent behaviour can also be highly instrumental and controlled (e.g., Megargee 1983; Polk 1994; Brookman 2000). The best programmes are now accredited by the Joint Prison/Probation Accreditation Panel, which also monitors the quality of their delivery (Home Office 2000): 'what works' research suggests that quality in both design and delivery is essential to effectiveness. Substantial claims have been made, based mainly on evidence from the United States, for the success of such programmes in reducing reconviction rates (see Raynor, in Chapter 31 of this volume), although there is less evidence about their impact on violence than on general offending.

Accredited programmes for sex offenders have a longer history than those for violent offenders, and are now widely run by the prison service. There is also more evidence of their effectiveness, although reconviction rates for sex offences are generally very low anyway, and it is difficult to identify significant changes brought about by 'treatment' (Beech et al. 1996; Hedderman and Sugg 1996; Friendship et al. 2001). In the case of domestic violence, too, there is some evidence that specially tailored programmes can make a difference, at least in the short term, to behaviour as well as to attitudes. Thus, only 33 per cent of men participating in one such Scottish programme had committed another violent act against their partner in twelve months, compared to 75 per cent who were dealt with by other sanctions. Further, only 7 per cent participating in the programmes, compared with 37 per cent of men dealt with in other ways, initiated five or more violent incidents during the follow-up period (Dobash et al. 1996; see also Dobash and Dobash 1992).

Crime reduction initiatives

Lastly, violent offending—particularly street robbery and alcohol-related offending in city centres—has been the target of innovative initiatives under the crime reduction programme, whereby efforts are made to identify and target specific 'hot spots' of violent behaviour and to 'manage' these through various forms of inter-agency cooperation.

For example, city centres have increasingly experienced huge influxes of young people on Friday and Saturday nights, to go 'clubbing' or engage in rounds of 'binge drinking'; so much so that Hobbs et al. (2000) refer to a whole new 'night time economy'. In some quite small central areas of major cities, the numbers on the streets or in licensed premises have been calculated at well over 100,000. These influxes are associated with a considerable degree of violence (though perhaps less than one might expect, given the presence of so many intoxicated people). A fair proportion of this violence involves altercations with 'bouncers' (Hobbs et al. ibid.), and much of the remainder arises through the escalation of minor arguments among people who have little or no previous record of violence – for example, while ordering drinks, trying to get taxis, and so on. These patterns suggest that some of the violence is preventable by means of altering or managing the environment. Indeed, there is mounting evidence that by, for example, better training of door staff and bar staff, better design of pubs and clubs, staggering of closing times, provision of late night transport, and so on, real reductions in the numbers of assaults can be achieved in particular 'hot-spots' (see, for example, Graham and Homel 1997; Deehan 1999; Maguire *et al.* 2001b). Such initiatives are not primarily about tough policing and threats of punishment, but involve strategic interventions instigated through partnerships between, for example, local councils, town planners, managers of licensed premises, police licensing officers, and taxi or bus companies.

In some ways, these initiatives are carrying forward the precise targeting approach to specific problems of violence that was pioneered earlier in response to football hooliganism, whereby opposing groups of fans were carefully segregated and their movements from train stations to football grounds, as well as their behaviour within grounds, were tightly controlled. However, most other situations which generate violence are not so spatially bounded as a football stadium (and the main routes to it), or confined to such easily identifiable groups as 'travelling fans'. In the context of the numerous licensed premises and networks of small streets in city centres, together with a more mixed population, much less reliance can be placed on policing tactics alone. There is thus a need for more flexible and less intrusive means of 'crowd control', and for the dispersal of methods of control away from the police to other key players.

CONCLUSIONS

Few of the accounts of violent crime examined in this review are mutually exclusive, though they may have been competing for theoretical and ideological primacy as models of how we should go about the task of explanation and over what the most serious forms of violence are. Much of the criminological progress during the 1980s and 1990s has been in refining our understanding of the risks of crime for different groups and the way that this relates to their lifestyles. Fuelled by feminist research and campaigns for action, fear of crime and the impact of crime on victims (see Zedner, in Chapter 13 of this volume) have been major growth areas.

By contrast with this focus on 'the victim', the causes of violence have received comparatively little criminological attention. This is not simply because victims are easier to get to, both physically and mentally, than are offenders, but also because the discovery of the victim has been a major area of criminal policy interest. It partly reflects also the greater theoretical simplicity of generating interesting facts about patterns of victimization than of explaining fundamentally why violence happens where and when it does, and not in other places at other times. We have stressed, perhaps *ad nauseam*, the enormous variation within that all too often simplified term 'violent crime', but one implication of this is that we may need different explanatory accounts for those who commit what everyone agrees are highly abnormal and unacceptable acts compared with those who behave in ways that are less condemned, or even are approved by people in their reference groups or subcultures. Lastly, there is behaviour—the varied forms of family violence—which occurs behind closed doors between 'repeat players', and which receives some special licence because of that.

'The ethos of masculinity' is one analytical thread that runs through much of the aetiological discussion (see, for example, Messerschmidt 1993, 1997; Polk 1994; Jefferson 1997; Brookman 2000 and forthcoming). Messerschmidt argues that men's resources for accomplishing masculinity vary with their class and race positions: this is consistent not just with his American data, but also with British and Australian data. Thus, one of the only arenas in which poor and ethnic minority groups can display masculinity is the world of violent gangs, whereas more affluent boys can find other areas in which to express themselves—including, later on in life, corporate aggression (see, e.g., Levi 1994).[35] As Polk (1994) argues, when overlaid with social class, it helps to account not just for 'typical' homicides but also for homicides for predatory gain and, as Kersten (1996) adds, for many sexual crimes too. But though the ever more subtly operationalized concept of *machismo* may be theoretically coherent, it is far from being theoretically complete, and its over-socialization component requires us to find other methods of accounting for, first, the non-violence of all males most of the time and, secondly, the non-violence of most males all of the time. As Jones (2000) notes, there is a deficient subjectivity and motivational component in the Messerschmidt models, and Collier (1998) critiques both the sex-gender distinction and hegemonic masculinity for their lack of clarity and Western ethnocentrism.

The personal and cultural dynamics of what constitutes a challenge 'requiring' a violent response have been explored by a variety of researchers, and have been accounted for largely in terms of sophisticated social learning theory, including expectations theory. Although it seems inappropriate to dignify with the term 'rational' the decision to head-butt a complete stranger because 'I didn't like the way he looked', and in some cases to do this fairly regularly to other strangers, much apparently 'mindless' violent behaviour is understandable in the context of the emotional need of offenders for respect. As implicit also in Bourgois's (1996) superb ethnography of crack use and dealing in an American *barrio*, this search for 'respect'—however illicit its forms—may have its psychodynamic roots in miserable (and/or misogynistic) family relationships and lack of 'men's work', but may also often have (to him, beneficial) consequences for that person's status and control within the family and/or peer group. Violence is more functional to those who practise it in poor neighbourhoods than in middle-class ones, where self-control is valued and aggression is more likely to be channelled into business competition, even though the latter may have unintended or uncared about consequences for worker, consumer, or environmental safety. Moreover, although there is a custodial compromise in prison, and even on the streets, which enables much aggressive display to go unpunished, those who are not deemed to be part of the 'dangerous classes' may enjoy their rugby or rowing club 'binges'; while the punier among the academicians parody delinquent gang members by 'trashing' the analytic abilities of their rivals, or fight for their friends' academic reputations. Each group has its own culturally approved outlets for aggression.[36]

---

[35] 'Masculinity' also offers an outlet for some young and poor women who want to show their rejection of their received roles (Messerschmidt 1997).

[36] Though personally, we would rather receive a bad academic review, however unmerited, than have our faces rearranged.

To conclude, this chapter has if nothing else demonstrated that 'violent crime' is a slippery and complex phenomenon, resistant to attempts at single or simple explanations. Societies and sectors of society vary over time in the extent to which aggressive behaviour of particular types is tolerated or approved. This has consequences for the extent to which we can regard violence as 'normal' and—given the regulating effect of subcultural approval—on the corresponding levels of offending. Violent behaviour has both instrumental and expressive functions, though the balance between these varies by type of crime, robbery being at the instrumental end of the axis, and hitting 'superiors' at work and spouses being at the expressive end. Particularly among the poor, the desire for some area in which to display dominion over others and gain 'respect' (or avoid lack of respect) appears to be common to many forms of violent behaviour. Fuelled by drink and/or drugs and by a lack of desire to avoid (or skill in avoiding) honour contests, violence between males becomes more likely. Pub managers and door staff can play a role too in mitigating or aggravating the level of honour contests between drinkers, or between drinkers and themselves. Some predatory individuals go out in search of people to attack, but however dangerous they are, these are the minority of assailants, rapists, and even killers. The fact that a substantial proportion of killers do *not* come from broken homes, have *not* had violent parents, were *not* unemployed at the time of the offence, or do not possess any of the other risk factors (Dobash *et al.* 2001) indicates the complex dynamics that go into the making of serious violence. British Crime Survey data show that over half of victims are assaulted by people they know, and acquaintance violence has been rising, while—despite many high-profile cases—stranger violence has not risen significantly since the early 1980s. Socio-cultural explanations overpredict violence, while personality-based explanations alone cannot account for the variations in violence over time and place. We now have a better understanding of the interplay between early family experiences, temperament, valuation by society, and situational factors in creating sets of violent behaviour that together constitute violent crime rates. But no existing clear theoretical model can make sense of all the data or account for all violent crime; neither should we expect to discover one that will.

Selected further reading

For general theoretical approaches to violent crime across the board, good sources are:

Archer, J. (ed.), *Male Violence*, London: Routledge.

Bernard, T. (1990), 'Angry Aggression among the "truly disadvantaged"', *Criminology*, 28(1): 73–93.

Jefferson, T., and Carlen, P. (eds) (1996), *Masculinities, Social Relations and Crime*, Special Issue of *British Journal of Criminology*, 36(2), articles by Jefferson and Kersten.

Journal of Social Issues (1992), Special Issue on comparative violence.

Newburn, T., and Stanko, B. (eds) (1994), *Just Boys Doing Business*, London: Routledge.

Polk, K. (1994), *When Men Kill: Scenarios of Masculine Violence*, Cambridge: Cambridge University Press.

For a slightly idiosyncratic, less 'academic' analysis of homicide, see Masters, B. (1997), *The Evil That Men Do*, London: Black Swan.

For a variety of interesting research studies that were not available when this chapter was completed but that will be available by the time of publication, see the studies conducted for the Economic & Social Research Council Violence Programme, currently hosted on **www1.rhbnc.ac.uk/sociopolitical-science/vrp/realhome.htm** or from ESRC.

For discussions of the new risk penality applied to violent crime, see Kemshall, H., and Maguire, M. (2001), 'Public Protection, Partnership and Risk Penality: The Multi-Agency Risk Management of Sexual and Violent Offenders', *Punishment and Society: The International Journal of Penology*, 5, 2: 237–64; and Monahan *et al.* (2001), *Rethinking Risk Assessment: The MacArthur Study of Mental Disorder and Violence*, New York: Oxford University Press.

For violence against children and women inside the home—which we are not seeing as a homogeneous category—see:

Dobash, R.E., and Dobash, R.D. (1992), *Women, Violence and Social Change*, London: Routledge.

Dobash, R.E., Dobash, R.D., Daly, M., and Wilson, M. (1992), 'The myth of sexual symmetry in marital violence', *Social Problems*, 39(1): 71–91.

Gelles, R. (1998), 'Family violence', in M. Tonry (ed.), *The Handbook of Crime and Punishment*, New York: Oxford University Press.

For a thoughtful review of the policing of domestic violence, see Hoyle, C. (1998), *Negotiating Domestic Violence—Police, Criminal Justice and Victims*, Oxford: Clarendon Press; and Sherman, L., and Smith, D. (1992), 'Crime, punishment, and stake in conformity: legal and informal control of domestic violence', *American Sociological Review*, 57: 680–90.

Sexual violence is well discussed in Felson, R. (1993), 'Sexual coercion: a social interactionist approach', in R. Felson and J. Tedeschi (eds), *Aggression and Violence: Social Interactionist Perspectives*, Washington, DC: American Psychological Association; and Scully, D. (1990), *Understanding Sexual Violence*, London: Harper Collins.

For a review of serial violence, see Holmes, R., and Holmes, S. (1996), *Profiling Violent Crimes: an Investigative Tool*, Thousand Oaks, Cal.: Sage.

References

ADLER, Z. (1987), *Rape on Trial*, London: Routledge.

AMIR, M. (1971), *Patterns in Forcible Rape*, Chicago, Ill.: University of Chicago Press.

ANDERSON, S., KINSEY, R., LOADER, I., and SMITH, C. (1990), *Cautionary Tales: a Study of Young People and Crime in Edinburgh*, Edinburgh: Centre for Criminology.

ARCHER, J. (1990), 'The influence of testosterone on human aggression', *British Journal of Psychology*, 82: 1–28.

—— (1994), 'Violence between men', in J. Archer (ed.), *Male Violence*, London: Routledge.

ASHWORTH, A. (1992), *Sentencing and Criminal Justice*, London: Weidenfeld and Nicolson.

ATHENS, L. (1980), *Violent Criminal Acts and Actors*, London: Routledge.

AYE MAUNG, N. (1995), *Young People, Victimisation and the Police*, Research Study No. 140, London: Home Office.

AYRES, M., and HAYWARD, P. (2001), *Motoring*

Offences and Breath Test Statistics, Home Office Statistical Bulletin, London: Home Office.

BANDURA, A. (1973), *Aggression: a Social Learning Analysis*, Englewood Cliffs, NJ: Prentice-Hall.

BANNISTER, J., and FYFE, N. (2001), 'Fear and the City', *Urban Studies*, 38(5/6): 807–13.

BARCLAY, G., TAVARES, C., and SIDDIQUE, A. (2001), *International Comparisons of Criminal Justice Statistics, 1999*, London: Home Office.

BAUMAN, Z. (1998), *Globalization*, Oxford: Polity Press.

BECK, U. (1992), *Risk Society*, London: Sage.

BEECH, A., FISHER, D., BECKETT, R., and FORDHAM, A. (1996), *Treating sex offenders in the community*, Home Office Research Bulletin 38, 21–26, London: Home Office.

BERGMAN, D. (1991), *Deaths at Work: Accidents or Corporate Crime*, London: Workers' Educational Association.

BERNARD, T. (1990), 'Angry Aggression among the "truly disadvantaged"', *Criminology*, 28(1): 73–93.

BLAU, J., and BLAU, P. (1982), 'The cost of inequality: metropolitan structure and violent crime', *American Sociological Review*, 47: 114–29.

BLUMSTEIN, A. (1996), 'Youth violence, guns, and illicit drugs markets', *National Institute of Justice Research Preview*, Washington, DC: US Department of Justice.

——, COHEN, J., ROTH, J., and VISHER, C. (1986), *Criminal Careers and 'Career Criminals'*, Washington, DC: National Academy Press.

BOTTOMS, A.E. (1977), 'Reflections on the Renaissance of Dangerousness', *Howard Journal*, 16(2): 70–96.

BOWLING, B. (1993), 'Racial harassment and the process of victimisation: conceptual and methodological implications for the local crime survey', *British Journal of Criminology*, 33: 231–250.

BOX, S. (1983), *Power, Crime, and Mystification*, London: Tavistock.

BOURGOIS, P. (1996), *In Search of Respect: Selling Crack in El Barrio*, Cambridge: Cambridge University Press.

BRAITHWAITE, J. (1989), *Crime, Shame, and Reintegration*, Cambridge: Cambridge University Press.

—— and BRAITHWAITE, V. (1980), 'The effects of income inequality and social democracy on homicide', *British Journal of Criminology*, 20: 45–53.

—— and PETTIT, P. (1990), *Not Just Deserts: a Republican Theory of Criminal Justice*, Oxford: Oxford University Press.

BRENNAN, P., MEDNICK, S., and VOLAVKA, J. (1995), 'Biomedical factors in Crime', in J. Wilson and J. Petersilia (eds), *Crime*, San Francisco: ICS Press.

BRITTON, P. (1998), *The Jigsaw Man*, London: Corgi.

—— (2001), *Picking up the Pieces*, London: Corgi.

BRODY, S., and TARLING, R. (1981), *Taking Offenders out of Circulation*, London: HMSO.

BROOKMAN, F. (2000), 'Dying for Control: Men, Murder and Sub-Lethal Violence', *British Criminology Conference: Selected Proceedings*, vol. 3. **www.lboro.ac.uk/departments/ss/bsc/bccsp/ vol03/Brookman.html**.

—— (forthcoming), 'Confrontational and Grudge Revenge Homicides in England and Wales', *The Australian and New Zealand Journal of Criminology*.

BROWN, J. (1991), 'The psychopathology of serial sexual homicide: a review of the possibilities', *American Journal of Forensic Psychiatry*, 12: 13–21.

BROWNING, C. (2001), *Ordinary Men*, London: Penguin.

BROWNMILLER, S. (1975), *Against Our Will*, Harmondsworth: Penguin.

BROWNSTEIN, H. (1996), *The Rise and Fall of a Violent Crime Wave: Crack Cocaine and the Social Construction of a Crime Problem*, New York: Harrow and Heston.

BUCK, W., CHATTERTON, M., and PEASE, K. (1995), *Obscene, threatening and other troublesome telephone calls to women in England and Wales, 1982–1992*, Research and Planning Unit Paper 92, London: Home Office.

BUDD, T. (1999), *Violence at Work: findings from the British Crime Survey*, London: Home Office.

—— (2001), *Violence at Work: New Findings from the 2000 British Crime Survey*, London: Health & Safety Executive and Home Office.

—— and Mattinson, J. (2000), *The Extent and Nature of Stalking: Findings from the 1998 British Crime Survey*, Home Office Research Study No. 210, London: Home Office.

BURGDORF, K., and ELDRED, C. (1978), *System of Operational Definitions*, Rockville, Md.: Westat.

BURGESS, R., and DRAPER, P. (1989), 'The explanation of family violence: the role of biological, behavioral, and cultural selection', in L. Ohlin and M. Tonry (eds), *Family Violence*, Chicago, Ill.: University of Chicago Press.

BURLEIGH, M. (2001), *The Third Reich: a New History*, London: Pan.

CAMPBELL, A., and MUNCER, S. (1994), 'Men and the meaning of violence', in J. Archer (ed.), *Male Violence*, London: Routledge.

CAMPBELL, B. (1993), *Goliath*, London: Methuen.

CANTER, D. (1995), *Chasing the Shadows*, London: Harper Collins.

—— and HERITAGE, R. (1990), 'A multivariate model of sexual offence behaviour: developments in "offender profiling"', *Journal of Forensic Psychiatry*, 1: 185–6.

CHAPPELL, D. (1989), 'Sexual criminal violence', in N. Wiener and M. Wolfgang (eds), *Pathways to Criminal Violence*, Newbury Park, Cal.: Sage.

——, GEIS, G., SCHAFER, S., and SIEGEL, L. (1977), 'A comparative study of forcible rape offenses known to the police in Boston and Los Angeles', in D. Chappell, R. Geis, and G. Geis (eds), *Forcible Rape*, New York; Columbia University Press.

CHEATWOOD, D. (1995), 'The effects of the weather on homicide', *Journal of Quantitative Criminology*, 11, 51–70.

CHRISTIE, N. (1981), *Limits to Pain*, Oxford: Martin Robertson.

CHRISTOPHER, S., NOAKS, L., and LEVI, M. (1989), *Assaults upon the Police: the Assailant's Perspective*, London: Home Office, unpublished.

CLANCY, A., HOUGH, M., AUST, R., and KERSHAW, C. (2001), *Ethnic Minorities' Experience of Crime and Policing: Findings from the 2000 British Crime Survey*, Findings 146, London: Home Office.

COHEN, S. (1981), *Folk Devils and Moral Panics*, 2nd edn, London: Paladin.

—— (2000), *States of Denial*, Cambridge: Polity Press.

COLLIER, R. (1998), *Masculinities, Crime and Criminology*, London: Sage.

COLLINS, J. (1989), 'Alcohol and interpersonal violence: less than meets the eye', in N. Weiner and M. Wolfgang (eds), *Pathways to Criminal Violence*, Newbury Park, Cal.: Sage.

COOK, P. and MOORE, M. (1995), 'Gun Control', in J. Wilson and J. Petersilia (eds), *Crime*, San Francisco: ICS Press.

CRAVEN, D. (1996), *Female Victims of Violent Crime: Select Findings*, Washington DC: US Department of Justice.

CURRIE, E. (1985), *Confronting Crime: an American Challenge*, New York: Pantheon Books.

CURTIS, L. (1975), *Violence, Race and Culture*, Lexington: Lexington Books.

DTLR (2001), *Road Casualties in Great Britain: Main Results 2000*, London: Department of Transport.

DALY, M., and WILSON, M. (1988), *Homicide*, New York: de Gruyter.

—— and —— (1994), 'Evolutionary psychology of male violence', in J. Archer (ed.), *Male Violence*, London: Routledge.

DAVIDOFF, L., and DOWDS, L. (1989), 'Recent trends in crimes of violence against the person in England and Wales', *Home Office Research Bulletin*, 27: 11–17.

—— and Greenhorn, M. (1991), 'Violent crime in England and Wales', paper presented at the British Criminology Conference, York.

DAVIES, A., and DALE, A. (1996), 'Locating the stranger rapist', *Medicine, Science and the Law*, 36: 146–56.

DEEHAN, A. (1999), *Alcohol and Crime: Taking Stock*, Crime Reduction Research Series Paper 3, London: Home Office.

DERSHOWITZ, A. (1997), *Reasonable Doubts: the Criminal Justice System and the O.J. Simpson Case*, New York: Touchstone

DOBASH, R.E., and DOBASH, R.D. (1979), *Violence against Wives*, New York: Free Press.

—— and —— (1992), *Women, Violence, and Social Change*, London: Routledge.

——, ——, CAVANAGH, K., and LEWIS, R. (1996), *Research Evaluation of Programmes for Violent Men*, Edinburgh: HMSO.

——, ——, ——, and —— (2001), *Homicide in Britain*, Research Bulletin No. 1, University of Manchester.

——, ——, DALY, M., and WILSON, M. (1992), 'The myth of sexual symmetry in marital violence', *Social Problems*, 39(1): 71–91.

DOWDS, L., and AHRENDT, D. (1996), 'Fear of Crime', in R. Jowell *et al.* (eds), *British Social Attitudes: the 12th Report*, Aldershot: Dartmouth.

EISNER, S. (2001), 'Modernization, self-control and lethal violence', *British Journal of Criminology*, 41: 618–638.

ELKINS, M., and OLAGUNDAYE, J. (2001), *The Prison Population in 2000: A Statistical Review*, Findings 154, London: Home Office.

ERICSON, R.V., and HAGGERTY, K.D. (1997), *Policing and the Risk Society*, Clarendon Studies in Criminology. Oxford: Oxford University Press.

ERONEN, M. (1995), 'Mental disorders and homicidal behavior in female subjects', *American Journal of Psychiatry*, 152: 1216–18.

ESRC (1998), *Taking Stock: What do We Know about Violence?*, Brunel University: Economic and Social Research Council Violence Programme.

FAGAN, J. (1989), 'Cessation of family violence: deterrence and dissuasion', in L. Ohlin and M. Tonry (eds), *Family Violence*, Chicago, Ill.: University of Chicago Press.

—— (1990), 'Intoxication and aggression', in M. Tonry and J. Wilson (eds), *Drugs and Crime*, Chicago, Ill.: University of Chicago Press.

FARRELL, G. (1992), 'Multiple victimisation: its extent and significance', *International Review of Victimology*, 2: 85–102.

FARRINGTON, D. (1989), 'Early predictors of adolescent aggression and adult violence', *Violence and Victims*, 4: 307–31.

—— (1991), 'Childhood aggression and adult violence: early precursors and later life outcomes', in D. Pepler and K. Rubin (eds), *The Development and Treatment of Childhood Aggression*, Hillsdale, NJ: Erlbaum.

—— and DOWDS, E. (1985), 'Disentangling criminal behaviour and police reaction', in D. Farrington and J. Gunn (eds), *Reactions to Crime: the public, the police, courts and prisons*, Chichester: John Wiley.

—— and LANGAN, P. (1992), 'Changes in crime and punishment in England and America in the 1980s', *Justice Quarterly*, 9(1): 5–31.

FELSON, R. (1993), 'Sexual coercion: a social interactionist approach', in R. Felson and J. Tedeschi (eds), *Aggression and Violence: Social Interactionist Perspectives*, Washington, DC: American Psychological Association.

FIELD, S. (1990), *Trends in Crime and Their Interpretation*, London: HMSO.

FISHBEIN, D. (1992), 'The psychobiology of female aggression', *Criminal Justice and Behaviour*, 19: 99–126.

FISCHHOFF, B. (1989), 'Risk: a guide to controversy', Appendix C in *Improving Risk Communication*, Washington DC: National Academy Press.

FITZGERALD, M., and HALE, C. (1996), *Ethnic Minorities, Victimisation and Racial Harassment*, Home Office Study No. 154, London: Home Office.

FLOUD, J., and YOUNG, W. (1981), *Dangerousness and Criminal Justice*, London: Heinemann.

FRIENDSHIP, C., BLUD, L., ERIKSON, M., TRAVERS, R., and THORNTON, D. (2001), *Cognitive-behavioural treatment for imprisoned offenders: an evaluation of H.M. Prison Services cognitive skills programmes*, Report to the Joint Prison/ Probation Accreditation Panel (mimeo).

FRIEZE, I., and BROWNE, A. (1989), 'Violence in marriage', in L. Ohlin and M. Tonry (eds), *Family Violence*, Chicago, Ill.: University of Chicago Press.

FRUDE, N. (1989), 'The physical abuse of children', in K. Howells and C. Hollin (eds), *Clinical Approaches to Violence*, Chichester: John Wiley.

—— (1994), 'Marital violence: an interactional perspective', in J. Archer (ed.), *Male Violence*, London: Routledge.

FSA (2001), *Annual Report, 2000*, www.food.gov.uk.

GAMBETTA, D. (1994), *The Sicilian Mafia*, Cambridge, Mass.: Harvard University Press.

GARLAND, D. (1995), 'Penal Modernism and Postmodernism', in T. Blomberg and S. Cohen (eds), *Punishment and Social Control*, New York: Aldine de Gruyter.

—— (1996), 'The Limits of the Sovereign State: Strategies of Crime Control in Contemporary Society', *British Journal of Criminology*, 36, 4: 445–71.

—— (2001), *Punishment and Control*. Oxford: Oxford University Press.

GAROFALO, J. (1987), 'Reassessing the lifestyle model of personal victimisation', in M. Gottfredson and T. Hirschi (eds), *Positive Criminology*, London: Sage.

GARTNER, R. (1990), 'The victims of homicide', *American Sociological Review*, 55(1): 92–107.

GATRELL, V. (1980), 'The decline of theft and violence in Victorian and Edwardian England', in V. Gatrell, B. Lenmna, and G. Parker (eds), *Crime and the Law: the Social History of Crime in Western Europe since 1500*, London: Europa Publications Ltd.

—— (1990), 'Crime, Authority, and the Policeman-State, 1750–1950', in F. Thompson (ed.), *The Cambridge Social History of Britain, 1750–1950*, Cambridge: Cambridge University Press.

GELLES, R. (1998), 'Family violence', in M. Tonry (ed.), *The Handbook of Crime and Punishment*, New York: Oxford University Press.

GENN, H. (1988), 'Multiple victimisation', in M. Maguire and J. Pointing (eds), *Victims of Crime: a New Deal?*, Milton Keynes: Open University Press.

GIDDENS, A. (1990), *The Consequences of Modernity*, Cambridge: Polity Press.

GOLDHAGEN, D. (1997), *Hitler's Willing Executioners*, London: Abacus.

GOUREVITCH, P. (2000), *We Wish to Inform You That Tomorrow We Will be Killed with Our Families*, London: Picador.

GRAHAM, K., and HOMEL, R. (1997), 'Creating Safer Bars', in M. Plant, E. Single, and T. Stockwell (eds), *Alcohol: Minimising the Harm—What Works?*, London: Free Association Books.

GREENE, E., and WAKEFIELD, R. (1979), 'Patterns of Middle and Upper Class homicide', *Journal of Criminal Law and Criminology*, 70(2): 172–81.

GREGORY, J., and LEES, S. (1999), *Policing Sexual Assault*, London: Routledge.

GRESSWELL, D., and HOLLIN, C. (1994), 'Multiple murder: a review', *British Journal of Criminology*, 34: 1–29.

GURR, T. (1990), 'Historical trends in violent crime: a critical review of the evidence', in N. Wiener, M. Zahn, and R. Sagi (eds), *Violence: Patterns, Causes, Public Policy*, San Diego, Cal.: Harcourt Brace Jovanovich.

GUTTMACHER, M. (1973), *The Mind of the Murderer*, New York: Farrar, Straus and Giroux.

HAAPANEN, R. (1990), *Selective Incapacitation and the Serious Offender*, New York: Springer-Verlag.

HALE, R. (1994), 'The role of humiliation and embarrassment in serial murder', *Psychology*, 31: 17–23.

HALL, S., CUTCHER, C., JEFFERSON, T., and ROBERTS, B. (1978), *Policing the Crisis*, London: Macmillan.

HANMER, J., RADFORD, J., and STANKO, E. (1989), *Women, Policing, and Male Violence: an International Perspective*, London: Routledge.

HARE, R. (1998), *Without Conscience: the disturbing world of the psychopaths amongst us*, New York: Guilford Press.

—— (2001), 'Psychopathy and risk for recidivism and violence', in N. Gray, J. Laing, and L. Noaks (eds), *Criminal Justice, Mental Health and the Politics of Risk*, 27–48, London: Cavendish.

HEDDERMAN, C., and SUGG, D. (1996), *Does Treating Sex Offenders Reduce Reoffending?*, Research Findings 45, London: Home Office.

HERRNSTEIN, R. (1995), 'Criminogenic traits', in J. Wilson and J. Petersilia (eds), *Crime*, San Francisco: ICS Press.

HOBBS, D., LISTER, S., HADFIELD, P., WINLOW, S. and HALL, S. (2000), 'Receiving shadows: governance and liminality in the night-time economy' *British Journal of Sociology* 51, 4: 682–700.

HOLDAWAY, S. (1983), *Inside the British Police*, Oxford: Basil Blackwell.

HOLMES, R., and HOLMES, S. (1996), *Profiling Violent Crimes: an Investigative Tool*, Thousand Oaks, Cal.: Sage.

HOME OFFICE (1989), *Statistics on Offences of Rape 1977–1987*, Statistical Bulletin 4/89, London: Home Office.

—— (2000), *First Report from the Joint Prison/ Probation Accreditation Panel*, London: Home Office

—— (2001), *Criminal Statistics in England and Wales 2000*, Cmnd 5312, London: Home Office.

—— (forthcoming), *Sex Offender Orders: A Preliminary Review of Policy and Practice*, London: Home Office.

HOUGH, M. (1995), *Anxiety about Crime: findings from the 1994 British Crime Survey*, Research Study 147, London: Home Office.

—— and MAYHEW, P. (1985), *Taking Account of Crime: Key Findings from the 1984 British Crime Survey*, London: HMSO.

HOYLE, C. (1998), *Negotiating Domestic Violence— Police, Criminal Justice and Victims*, Oxford: Clarendon Press.

HSE (2001), *Statistics, 2000/01*, London: Health and Safety Executive.

HUESSMAN, L., and ERON, L. (1989), 'Individual differences and the trait of aggression', *European Journal of Personality*, 3: 95–106.

JENKINS, P. (1994), *Using Murder: the Social Construction of Serial Homicide*, New York: de Gruyter.

JEFFERSON, T. (1997), 'Masculinities and Crimes', in M. Maguire, R. Morgan, and R. Reiner (eds), *The Oxford Handbook of Criminology*, 2nd edn, Oxford: Oxford University Press.

JOHNSON, A. (1980), 'On the prevalence of rape in the United States', *Signs*, 6: 136–46.

JONES, S. (2000), *Understanding Violent Crime*, Milton Keynes: Open University Books.

JONES, T., MACLEAN, B., and YOUNG, J. (1986), *The Islington Crime Survey: Crime, Victimization and Policing in Inner City London*, Aldershot: Gower.

KAHNEMANN, D., SLOVIC, P., and TVERSKY, A. (1982), *Judgment under Uncertainty: Heuristics and Biases*, Cambridge: Cambridge University Press.

KATZ, J. (1988), *The Seductions of Crime: the moral and sensual attractions of doing evil*, New York: Basic Books.

KELMAN, M.C., and HAMILTON, V.L. (1989), *Crimes of Obedience: Toward a social psychology of authority and responsibility*. New Haven and London: Yale University Press.

KEMSHALL, H. (2001), *Risk Assessment and Management of Known Sexual and Violent Offenders: A Review of Current Issues*, Police Research Series Paper 140, London: Home Office.

—— and MAGUIRE, M. (2001), 'Public Protection, Partnership and Risk Penality: The Multi-Agency Risk Management of Sexual and Violent Offenders', *Punishment and Society: The International Journal of Penology*, 5, 2: 237–64.

—— and —— (2002), 'Community Justice, Risk Management and the Role of Multi-Agency Public Protection Panels', *Journal of Community Justice*, 1.

KERSHAW, C., CHIVITE-MATTHEWS, N., THOMAS, C., and AUST, R. (2001), *The 2001 British Crime Survey*, Home Office Statistical Bulletin 18/01, London: Home Office.

—— DOWDESWELL, P., and GOODMAN, J. (1997a), *Life Licensees—Reconvictions and Recalls by the End of 1995: England and Wales*, London: Home Office.

——, ——, and —— (1997b), *Restricted Patients— Reconvictions and Recalls by the End of 1995: England and Wales*, London: Home Office.

KERSTEN, J. (1996), 'Culture, masculinities and violence against women', *British Journal of Criminology*, 36(3): 381–95.

KILLIAS, M., and AEBI, M. (2000), 'Crime trends in Europe from 1990 to 1996: how Europe illustrates the limits of the American experience', *European Journal on Criminal Policy and Research*, 8: 43–63.

LAFREE, G., and DRASS, K. (2001), *Are national crime trends converging? Evidence for homicide victimization rates, 1956 to 1994*, Paper presented at Law and Society Association Conference, Budapest.

LEES, S. (2002), *Carnal Knowledge*, London: The Women's Press.

LESTER, D. (1991), 'National consumption of chocolate and rates of personal violence (suicide and homicide)', *Journal of Orthomolecular Medicine*, 6: 81–82.

LEVI, M. (1994), 'Masculinities and white-collar crime', in T. Newburn and B. Stanko (eds), *Just Boys Doing Business*, London: Routledge.

—— and JONES, S. (1985), 'Public and Police Perceptions of Crime Seriousness in England and Wales', *British Journal of Criminology*, 25(3): 234–50.

LICHTENSTEIN, S., SLOVIC, P., FISCHHOFF, B., LAYMAN, M., and COMBS, B. (1978), 'Judged frequency of lethal events', *Journal of Experimental Psychology (Human Learning and Memory)*, 4: 551–78.

MAGUIRE, M. (1992), 'Parole', in E. Stockdale and S. Casale (eds), *Criminal Justice Under Stress*, London: Blackstone Press.

—— and CORBETT, C. (1987), *The Effects of Crime and the Work of Victim Support Schemes*, Aldershot: Gower.

——, KEMSHALL, H., NOAKS, L., WINCUP, E. (2001a), *Risk Management of Sexual and Violent Offenders: The work of Public Protection Panels*, Police Research Series Paper 139, London: Home Office.

——, MORGAN, R., and NETTLETON, H. (2001b), *Early Lessons from the Crime Reduction Programme: Tackling Alcohol Related Street Crime in Cardiff (TASC Project)*, Home Office Briefing Note 9/01.

MALMQUIST, C. (1995), *Homicide: a Psychiatric Perspective*, Washington, DC: American Psychiatric Press, Inc.

MARQUEZ, G. (1998), *News of a Kidnapping*, London: Penguin.

MARSHALL, P. (1997), *A Reconviction Study of HMP Grendon Therapeutic Community*, Research Findings No. 53, London: Home Office.

MATTINSON, J. (2001), *Stranger and Acquaintance Violence: Practice Messages from the British Crime Survey*, Briefing Note 7/01, London: Home Office.

—— and MIRRLEES-BLACK, C. (1994), *Racially Motivated Crime: a British Crime Survey analysis*, Research and Planning Unit Paper 82, London: Home Office.

MAYHEW, P., ELLIOTT, D., and DOWDS, L. (1989), *The 1988 British Crime Survey*, London: HMSO.

McGUIRE, J. (1995), *What Works: Reducing Reoffending*. London: Wiley.

McINTOSH, M. (1975), *The Organisation of Crime*, London: Macmillan.

MEDNICK, S., MOFFITT, T., and STACK, S. (1987), *The Causes of Crime: New Biological Approaches*, New York: Cambridge University Press.

MEGARGEE, E. (1966), 'Undercontrolled and overcontrolled personality types in extreme antisocial aggression', *Psychological Monographs*, 80: Whole No. 611.

—— (1983), 'Undercontrolled and overcontrolled personality types in extreme antisocial aggression', *Psychological Monographs*, 80 (3, whole No. 611).

MESSERSCHMIDT, J. (1993), *Masculinities and Crime*, Lanham, Md: Rowan and Littlefield.

—— (1997), *Crime as Structured Action*, Thousand Oaks, Cal.: Sage.

MESSNER, S., and GOLDEN, R. (1992), 'Racial inequality and racially disaggregated homicide rates: an assessment of alternative theoretical explanations', *Criminology*, 30(3): 421–37.

MIERS, D. (2001), 'Criminal Injuries Compensation; the new regime', *Journal of Personal Injury Law*, 4: 405–29.

MIETHE, T. (1984), 'Types of consensus in public evaluations of crime: an illustration of strategies for measuring "consensus"', *Journal of Criminal Law and Criminology*, 75(2): 459–73.

MIRRLEES-BLACK, C. (1995), 'Estimating the extent of domestic violence: findings from the 1992 BCS', *Home Office Research Bulletin*, 37: 1–10.

—— (1999), *Domestic Violence: Findings from a new British Crime Survey self-completion questionnaire*, Home Office Research Study No. 191, London: Home Office.

——, MAYHEW, P., and PERCY, A. (1996), *The 1996 British Crime Survey: England and Wales*, London: Home Office.

MOIR, A., and JESSEL, D. (1995), *A Mind to Crime: the Controversial Links between the Mind and Criminal Behaviour*, London: Michael Joseph.

MONAHAN, J., and STEADMAN, H.J. (1994), *Violence and Mental Disorder: Developments in Risk Assessment*, Chicago, Ill.: Chicago University Press.

——, ——, SILVER, E., APPELBAUM, P.S., CLARK ROBBINS, P., MULVEY, E.P., ROTH, L.H., GRISSO, T., and BANKS, S. (2001), *Rethinking Risk Assessment: The MacArthur Study of Mental Disorder and Violence*, New York: Oxford University Press.

MOONEY, J. (1993), *The Hidden Figure: Domestic Violence in North London*, London: Islington Council.

MORGAN, D. (1987), 'Masculinity and violence', in J. Hanmer and M. Maynard (eds), *Women, Violence, and Social Control*, London: Macmillan.

MORRIS, N., and MILLER, M. (1985), 'Predictions of dangerousness', in M. Tonry and N. Morris (eds), *Crime and Justice*, vol. 6, Chicago, Ill.: Chicago University Press.

MVA Ltd (2000), *The 2000 Scottish Crime Survey: First Results*, Edinburgh: Scottish Office.

NATIONAL COMMITTEE (1990), *Violence: Directions for Australia*, Canberra: Australian Institute of Criminology.

NATIONAL CRIME SURVEY (1986), *Teenage Victims: A National Crime Survey Report*, Washington: Government Printing Office.

NEWBURN, T., and STANKO, B. (eds) (1994), *Just Boys Doing Business*, London: Routledge.

NICHOLLS, T. (1991), 'Industrial injuries in British manufacturing industry and cyclical effects: continuities and discontinuities in industrial injury research', *Sociological Review*, 39(1): 131–9.

NORRIS, D. (1990), *Violence against Social Workers—The implications for practice*, London: Jessica Kingsley.

O'CONNELL, M., and WHELAN, A. (1996), 'Taking wrongs seriously: Public perceptions of crime seriousness', *British Journal of Criminology*, 36(2): 299–318.

O'MALLEY, P. (ed.) (1998), *Crime and the Risk Society*, Aldershot: Ashgate.

OLWEUS, D. (1987), 'Testosterone and adrenaline: aggression and antisocial behaviour in normal adolescent males', in S. Mednick, T. Moffitt, and S. Stack (eds), *The Causes of Crime: New Biological Approaches*, New York: Cambridge University Press.

PAINTER, K. (1991), *Wife Rape, Marriage and the Law*, Manchester: Manchester University.

—— and FARRINGTON, D. (1998), 'Marital violence in Great Britain and its relationship to marital and non-marital rape', *International Review of Victimology*, 5: 257–276.

PEARCE, F., and TOMBS, S. (1992), 'Realism and corporate crime', in R. Matthews and J. Young (eds), *Issues in Realist Criminology*, London: Sage.

PEARSON, G. (1983), *Hooligan*, London: Macmillan.

——, SAMPSON, A., BLAGG, H., STUBBS, P., and SMITH, D. (1989), 'Policing racism', in R. Morgan and D. Smith (eds), *Coming to Terms with Policing*, London: Routledge.

PEASE, K. (1988), *Crime Seriousness: findings from the British Crime Survey*, London: Home Office Research and Planning Unit.

PENDERGRAST, M. (1997), *Victims of Memory*, London: Harper Collins.

PLOTNIKOFF, J., and WOOLFSON, R. (2000), *Where are they now? An evaluation of sex offender registration in England and Wales*, Police Research Series, Paper 126, London: Home Office.

POLK, K. (1994), *When Men Kill: Scenarios of Masculine Violence*, Cambridge: Cambridge University Press.

POLLARD, P. (1994), 'Sexual violence against women: characteristics of typical perpetrators', in J. Archer (ed.), *Male Violence*, London: Routledge.

RADZINOWICZ, L. (ed.) (1957), *Sexual Offences*, London: Macmillan.

RAINE, A. (1993a), *The Psychopathology of Crime: Criminal Behaviour as a Clinical Disorder*, London: Academic Press.

—— (1993b), 'Features of borderline personality and violence', *Journal of Clinical Psychology*, 49: 277–81.

——, BUCHSBAUM, M., STANLEY, J., and LOTTENBERG, S. (1994), 'Selective reductions in prefrontal glucose metabolism in murderers', *Biological Psychiatry*, 36: 365–73.

——, —— and STODDARD, J. (1995), 'Glucose metabolism in murders: Response', *Biological Psychiatry*, 38: 342–3.

RAMSAY, M. (1996), 'The relationship between alcohol and crime', *Home Office Research Bulletin*, 38: 37–44.

REINER, R. (2000), *The Politics of the Police*, 3rd edn, Oxford: Oxford University Press.

—— (2001), *The Politics of the Police*, 3rd edn, Oxford: Oxford University Press.

RENNISON, C. (2001), *Criminal Victimization 2000: Changes 1999–2000 with Trends 1993–2000*, Washington, DC: Bureau of Justice Statistics.

REUTER, P. (1983), *Disorganized Crime*, Cambridge, Mass: MIT Press.

ROWE, D. (1990), 'Inherited dispositions toward learning delinquent and criminal behaviour', in L. Ellis and H. Hoffman (eds), *Crime in Biological, Social and Moral Contexts*, New York: Praeger.

ROYAL COMMISSION (1929), *Report*, Royal Commission on the Police 1929, London: HMSO.

ROYAL SOCIETY (1992), *Risk: Analysis, Perception, Management*, London: The Royal Society.

RUBIO, M. (2001), 'Homicide, kidnapping and armed conflict in Colombia', *Forum on Crime and Society*, 1(1): 55–68.

RUSSELL, D. (1984), *Sexual Exploitation*, Beverly Hills, Cal.: Sage.

SANDAY, P. (1981), 'The socio-cultural context of rape: a cross-cultural study', *Journal of Social Issues*, 37(4): 5–27.

SCHLESINGER, P., and TUMBER, H. (1994), *Reporting Crime*, Oxford: Clarendon Press.

SCULLY, D. (1990), *Understanding Sexual Violence*, London: Harper Collins.

SHEPHERD, J. (1990), 'Violent crime in Bristol: an accident and emergency department perspective', *British Journal of Criminology*, 30(3): 289–305.

SHERMAN, L., and SMITH, D. (1992), 'Crime, punishment, and stake in conformity: legal and informal control of domestic violence', *American Sociological Review*, 57: 680–90.

SKOGAN, W. (1990), *The Police and Public in England and Wales: A British Crime Survey Report*, London: HMSO.

SLAPPER, G., TOMBS, S., and MANSFIELD, M. (1999), *Corporate Crime*, London: Longman.

SMITH, L. (1989), *Concerns about Rape*, London: HMSO.

SOOTHILL, K., JACK, A., and GIBBENS, T. (1976), 'Rape: a 22 year cohort study', *Medicine, Science, and the Law*, 16(1): 62–69.

SORENSEN, S., and WHITE, J. (1992), 'Adult sexual assault: overview of research', *Journal of Social Issues*, 48: 1–8.

SPARKS, R. (1980), *Crime and Punishment*, unpublished paper presented at American Society of Criminology Conference, San Francisco.

——, GENN, H., and DODD, D. (1977), *Surveying Victims*, Chichester: John Wiley.

STANKO, B. (1990), *Everyday Violence*, London: Unwin Hyman.

STRAUS, M., and GELLES, R. (1990), 'How violent are American families? Estimates from the National Family Violence Survey and other studies', in M. Straus and R. Gelles (eds), *Physical Violence in American Families*, New Brunswick, NJ: Transaction.

——, ——, and STEINMETZ, S. (1980), *Behind Closed Doors*, New York: Anchor Press.

STRONG, S. (1995), *Whitewash: Pablo Escobar and the Cocaine Wars*, London: Pan.

THORNHILL, R., and THORNHILL, N. (1992), 'The evolutionary psychology of men's coercive sexuality', *Behavioural and Brain Sciences*, 15: 363–421.

TOCH, H. (1979), 'Perspectives on the offender', in H. Toch (ed.), *Psychology of Crime and Criminal Justice*, London: Holt, Rinehart and Winston.

—— and ADAMS, K. (1994), *The Disturbed Violent Offender*, Washington: American Psychological Association.

—— and KARON, B. (1992), *Violent Men: an Inquiry into the Psychology of Violence*, 2nd edn, Washington: American Psychological Association.

TOMBS, S. (1992), 'Safety, statistics, and business cycles: a response to Nichols', *The Sociological Review*, 40(1): 132–45.

TOMSEN, S. (1997), 'A Top Night: Social Protest, Masculinity and the Culture of Drinking Violence', *The British Journal of Criminology*, 37/1: 90–102.

TRACY, P., WOLFGANG, M., and FIGLIO, R. (1990), *Delinquency Careers in Two Birth Cohorts*, New York: Plenum Press.

TUCK, M. (1989), *Drinking and Disorder: a study of non-Metropolitan violence*, London: HMSO.

TVERSKY, A., and KAHNEMANN, D. (1973), 'Availability: a heuristic for judging frequency and probability', *Cognitive Psychology*, 4: 207–32.

VLEK, C., and STALLEN, P. (1981), 'Judging risks and benefits in the small and in the large', *Organizational Behaviour and Human Performance*, 28: 235–71.

VON HIRSCH, A. (1986), *Past or Future Crimes*, Manchester: Manchester University Press.

WADDINGTON, D. (1992), *Contemporary Issues in Public Disorder*, London: Routledge.

WALKLATE, S. (1990), *Victimology*, London: Unwin Hyman.

WALMSLEY, R. (1986), *Personal Violence*, London: HMSO.

WATSON, L. (1996), *Victims of Violent Crime Recorded by the Police England and Wales, 1990–1994*, London: Home Office.

WEIS, J. (1989), 'Family violence research methodology and design', in L. Ohlin and M. Tonry (eds), *Family Violence*, Chicago, Ill.: University of Chicago Press.

WELLS, C. (1993), *Corporations and Criminal Responsibility*, Oxford: Oxford University Press.

—— (2001), *Corporations and Criminal Responsibility*, 2nd edn, Oxford: Oxford University Press.

WEST, D. (1983), *Sexual Crimes and Confrontations*, Aldershot: Gower.

WHICH? (1990), 'The Police', *Which?*, May: 258–61.

WHITE, J., and SORENSEN, S. (1992), 'A sociocultural view of sexual assault: from discrepancy to diversity', *Journal of Social Issues*, 48: 187–95.

WILSON, J., and HERRNSTEIN, R. (1985), *Crime and Human Nature*, New York: Simon and Schuster.

WILSON, M., and DALY, M. (1992), 'Who kills whom in spouse killings: on the exceptional sex ratio of spousal homicides in the United States', *Criminology*, 30(2): 189–214.

WOLFGANG, M. (1958), *Patterns in Criminal Homicide*, Philadelphia, Pa.: University of Pennsylvania Press.

—— and FERRACUTI, F. (1967), *The Subculture of Violence*, London: Tavistock.

YOUNG, J. (1988), 'Risk of crime and fear of crime: a realist critique of survey-based assumptions', in M. Maguire and J. Pointing (eds), *Victims of Crime: a New Deal?*, Milton Keynes: Open University Press.

23

WHITE-COLLAR CRIME

David Nelken

INTRODUCTION

The media increasingly report cases of business or professional people caught out in serious offences, sometimes for behaviour which they did not expect to be treated as criminal, and for which it is often difficult to secure a conviction. Such Jekyll and Hyde contradiction between respectability and crime raises questions which are unlike those posed by other types of criminal behaviour. Why do they do it when they have so much to lose? How representative are they or their practices of other businessmen, or of business life in general? Is there one law for the rich and another for the poor?

One of the biggest difficulties in approaching this subject is to find a way of putting dramatic and newsworthy cases of business misbehaviour in to some sort of context and proportion. Study of the distribution and frequency of white-collar crimes is made problematic by the fact (not in itself unimportant) that, especially in the common law countries where the concept was first formulated, most white-collar crimes are not included in the official statistics which serve as the basis for debates about 'the crime problem'. The usual difficulties of interpreting the statistics of crime are greatly magnified here (Levi 1985). Falling back on the information recorded by specialized enforcement agencies (often not even made public) serves mainly as a source for describing methods of control rather than the misbehaviour being controlled. Neither can it be assumed that there is any uniformity in the meaning of data obtained in this way. A few agencies are reactive, and depend on complaints; others are proactive, but the level of enforcement is restricted by limited resources (in Britain factories are inspected for safety offences on average once every four years). Much regulation is geared to using prosecution as a last resort—thus the number of prosecuted offenders says little about the theoretical level of crime; conversely, the number of visits or warnings cannot be used as an index of the incidence of deliberate law breaking. There is a danger of double counting where the same behaviour is dealt with by different agencies, or where one firm has more sub-units than another. This also creates problems about defining recidivism—which were ignored by Sutherland in his pioneering study (Sutherland 1949). There are problems of classifying the date and location of some of these offences (a factor which often helps secure their immunity). Shifts in legislative mandates, and in the number, expertise, politics, and motivation of enforcers, make a treacherous basis for studies of changes in offending patterns over time. Lastly, supplementing official statistics with victim reports is difficult because the victims are often unaware of their victimization; and even where this is not the case, as in organizations subject to fraud, there is often unwillingness to admit to vulnerability (see Levi and Pithouse, forthcoming).

These difficulties mean that discussions of the subject in textbooks are often forced to rely unduly on newspaper reports or on the activities of crusading journalists (see, e.g., Coleman 1985; but see now Punch 1996). Obtaining information in this way complicates the task of assessing the accuracy, frequency, or representativeness of the cases reported. Are 'scandals' by definition unrepresentative of normal life, or should we rather see them, as Punch does, as occasions which expose *typical* practices and mechanisms of deviance—especially the way 'illicit solutions are found to managerial dilemmas' (Punch 1996)? What is clear is that newspapers, or those who feed them their stories, initiate crime control campaigns for reasons which may have little to do with the long-term trend in the misbehaviour at issue. It is therefore often hard to tell, here as elsewhere, whether business or financial crimes are increasing or are just more newsworthy, or to decide if apparent change is the result of an increase in a given kind of misbehaviour or more the consequence of a trend towards the use of formal and legal, rather than informal, means to deal with it.

Despite these problems there have been some useful studies drawing on agency records to survey the rate of corporate offending (Clinard and Yeager 1980), or even on court records to establish the type of offenders normally apprehended for what the authors call 'middle-class crimes' (Weisburd *et al.* 1991). What we know about white-collar crime also comes from interviews with enforcers as well as observation of their work (e.g., Carson 1970; Hawkins 1984; Hutter 1988, 1997; and cf. Nelken 1991); interviews with businessmen (e.g., Lane 1953; Braithwaite 1984); biographies of and retrospective accounts by offenders (e.g., Geis 1968); participant observation in offending organizations (e.g., Nelken 1983: chapter 2); experimental techniques such as those used by consumer organizations (Green 1990: chapter 2), as well as other sources (and for useful methodological hints on researching these type of offences, see Levi 1985).

Although most of the literature on white-collar crime is American, major contributions have been made by other English-language scholars such as Braithwaite, Carson, and Levi. The equivalent term for 'white-collar crime' is also widely found in other languages, and even used in foreign court proceedings. There are also interesting contributions, sometimes in foreign languages, which could serve as a useful starting point for comparative research (e.g., Tiedemann 1974; Cosson 1978; Magnusson 1985; Clarke 1990b; Delmas-Marty 1990; Zigler 1990; Van Duyne 1993; Passas and Nelken 1993; Savelsberg 1994). But the common use of the term can be misleading. Despite the similarities of modern industrialized economies, there are important differences in general and legal culture which affect the meaning of and response to white-collar crime (and its contrasting category of ordinary crime). These contrasts have not yet been sufficiently explored (see Nelken 1994a; Levi and Nelken 1996; Nelken 2000). In civil law countries such as Italy there are few of the special enforcement agencies used to deal with occupational offences found, for example, in America, Britain, and Australia. Instead, normal police forces, often spearheaded by specialized financial police, conduct investigations of economic crime, and business-men or politicians with white collars regularly see the inside of prisons (though few seem to stay there for long). American outrage over business misbehaviour may be connected to what Wright-Mills (1943/1963) saw as the small-town values of Ameri-can social reformers, as well as to a peculiar, American love–hate relationship with big businesses (are they the ultimate proof of capitalist success, or a threat to the market and to the individual?). In countries with a strong Catholic heritage the respectability attached to capitalist profit-making may be less secure than in Protestant countries (Ruggiero 1996).

Much of the literature on white-collar crime continues to be concerned to demon-strate the seriousness and diffuseness of such offending, and to show that its costs and damages dwarf those of conventional, or ordinary, crime (for a recent summary of attempts to measure the impact of white-collar crime, see Slapper and Tombs 1999: 37–41, 54–84). More than any other type of crime, white-collar offences are also attacked for undermining the basis of trust which holds society together (for example, by discrediting those in authority or positions of privelege who are supposed to be models of respectability). Colossal fines and settlements are imposed in cases of some financial crimes, for example, Michael Milken, the junk bond king, paid over $650 million in court-ordered restitution even before sentence. The collapse of the savings and loan institutions (similar to what in Britain are described as building societies) in the United States in the late 1980s, may end up costing a trillion dollars. This is many times the cost of the Marshall Plan or the Korean war; but the real impact is blunted because the costs are to be covered by a US government fifty-year loan (Pontell and Calavita 1993; Calavita *et al.* 1997; Zimring and Hawkins 1993). Contrary to what is supposed by some definitions (e.g., Edelhertz 1970), there is also no reason to exclude violence and death from the province of white-collar crime. There are a number of case studies which document this, even without going into more controversial but important calculations of the overall number of fatal accidents or diseases occurring at work which could have been prevented and prosecuted (Box 1983: 28ff; Hills 1988; Slapper 1991). Carson's study of the loss of life in the exploration for oil in the North Sea (confirmed by later events such as the blowing up of the Alpha oil rig in 1988 with the loss of 168 lives), for instance, showed that many lives could have been saved with rudimentary attention to safety considerations (Carson 1982). The devastating con-sequences of the nuclear disaster at Chernobyl, the chemical explosion at Bhopal, the suffering caused by the sale of the drug thalidomide, or the contraceptive known as the Dalkon shield, are other well-known examples.

Despite all this evidence, white-collar crimes are still subjected to very different interpretations. It might seem odd that sociologists, familiar with Durkheim's argu-ment that society considers dangerous those behaviours it responds to as criminal, rather than the other way round, should keep trying to prove that white-collar crime is really criminal simply because it causes great harm. The answer must be that they hope in this way to influence the social definition of such conduct. Debates over the causes and control of white-collar crime do connect to different political evaluations of the misdeeds of business or capitalism. Political conservatives tend to favour struc-tural explanations of business malpractice rather than personal guilt—thus changing places with liberals in comparison with their positions on ordinary crime (Zimring and Hawkins 1993). But even authors with very different political views argue that corporate crime requires 'a shift from a humanist to a structuralist problematic'— though they continue nonetheless to apply the criminal label to the behaviour which results from such a structural problematic (Slapper and Tombs 1999: 17)

SEVEN TYPES OF AMBIGUITY

Why is there still so much disagreement over white-collar crime? As with the equivo-cal designs produced by Gestalt psychologists, do we find it difficult to see 'the crim-inal' and 'the respectable person' in one and the same figure? Following Aubert (1952) I shall argue that ambiguity about the nature of white-collar crime and the best way of responding to it, forms an essential key to the topic and can be used to provide insights into this type of crime as well as the 'ordinary' crime to which it is contrasted. As the subject has become more established scholars have either tended to abandon Aubert's insight, or to concentrate on only one or two of the sources of ambiguity which will be considered here. They also tend to divide into those, on the one hand, who point to the ambiguous features of white-collar crime so as to explain and justify special treatment for this misbehaviour, and those, on the other hand, who claim that ambiguity is a socially constructed smoke-screen which ought to be dispelled. In this chapter I do not purport to settle the question of how far the features which sup-posedly make white-collar crime more ambiguous than ordinary crime are (merely) socially constructed. I shall, however, try to do something to clarify the uncertainties produced by the literature itself by offering a critical review both of those arguments which assert that ambiguity is intrinsic to the misbehaviour itself and of those which attempt to prove that white-collar crime is 'essentially' the same as ordinary crime but is transformed by the social reaction to it.

To provide a common thread to the following overview of what has been written about the definition of, causes of, and responses to white-collar crime, I shall seek to illustrate seven different sources of ambiguity which surround this topic. (I use the term 'ambiguity' loosely to embrace the various forms of equivocalness, uncertainty, and ambivalence referred to in and produced by discussions of the characteristics of white-collar crime.) The first ambiguities which I shall consider arise in trying to define what is meant by 'white-collar crime'. The ambiguous way the concept is used in the criminological literature means that it is not clear what range of crimes is being referred to. From the outset, Sutherland's concept has also been criticized for seeking to apply the crime label to behaviours whose definition as crime is legally or socio-logically controversial. The second set of ambiguities belongs more to discussions of the causes of white-collar crime. While many scholars try to apply the usual crimino-logical frameworks of explanation to this kind of offending, others have used the topic precisely so as to place these schemes in doubt. Ambiguity also surrounds discussions of the commission of these offences. Thus some writers stress the point that this type of offending behaviour takes place in a more respectable context than most other crimes, and that it is the product of more ambiguous intentions than is the case for ordinary crime. The third set of ambiguities derives from the regulation and handling of white-collar crime. White-collar crimes are often controlled in a different, and more ambivalent, way than ordinary crime, and it is controversial how far this reflects, reinforces, or even creates its ambiguity. The uncertain status of these crimes may also be seen to reflect a process of transition and social change in which the public is not yet ready for more outright criminalization of these behaviours. It is also argued that control of these offences is hampered by problems of competing values and social costs which do not arise in repressing ordinary crime.

I shall be taking these various ambiguities one by one, partly for purposes of exposition and partly because there are important differences amongst the sources and types of ambiguity. Taken as a whole, however, many of these ambiguities are mutually reinforcing and thus help to shape the perceived character of white-collar crime as a social phenomenon. If, for example, different and predominantly adminis-trative methods of enforcement are used in dealing with white-collar as opposed to ordinary crimes, this will shape public opinion concerning their relative seriousness. But at the same time, such (alleged) differences in public attitudes also serve as justifications offered by legislators and regulators for their different treatment of white-collar crimes. On the other hand, any given source of ambiguity may have implications under a number of different headings. For example, the fact that white-collar crimes generally take place in private settings represents a special feature of their causation which may facilitate their commission. This also serves as an impedi-ment to normal policing methods, which helps to explain the use of other forces and forms of enforcement. Lastly, the importance of respecting 'privacy' as a value also figures as an argument in policy debates over the appropriateness or otherwise of strengthening controls.

WHITE-COLLAR CRIME AS A CONTESTED CONCEPT

If Sutherland merited a Nobel prize, as Mannheim thought, for pioneering this field of study, he certainly did not deserve it for the clarity or serviceableness of his defin-ition. What, if anything, is there in common between the marketing of unsafe phar-maceuticals, the practice of insider trading, 'long-firm' fraud, computer crime, bank embezzlement, and fiddling at work? Though Sutherland claimed to be interested in reforming criminological theory, rather than changing society, the appeal of this topic, particularly through the 1970s and 1980s, was unquestionably linked to its progressive connotations and its implicit accusations of bias in the making and enforcing of criminal law (Yeager 1991). The apparent success of the label in finding public acceptance, while lacking a clear or agreed referent, may testify less to its coherence than to its capacity to name a supposed threat. Not all examples of white-collar crime are ambiguous (e.g., embezzlement), just as not all ambiguous deviance is white-collar crime. But considerable disagreement over the range of misbehaviour referred to, as well as doubts about the coherence of those behaviours it does include, makes the category as a whole rather ambiguous. And, peculiarly enough, those white-collar offences whose criminal character seems most unambiguous—such as bank embezzlement or (on some definitions) credit card fraud—are the ones least likely to illustrate the theoretical or policy-relevant features of white-collar crime in which Sutherland and his successors have been most interested.

We will not deal here with the intrinsic difficulties built into Sutherland's definition of white-collar crime as a crime committed by 'a person of high status in the course of his occupation' (1949: 9), a matter which was discussed in the first edition of this *Handbook* (Nelken 1994b: 361–3). But it is important to recognize that the problem of definition cannot just be put aside in order to get on with more interesting matters, because the solution found for this problem ultimately determines the findings of any investigation.

Green, in his textbook on *Occupational Crime* (1990), argues that white-collar crime should be seen as even more criminal than ordinary crime (likewise other recent USA textbooks such as Rosoff *et al.* 1998). Clarke (1990a), though considering much the same data, on the other hand, argues that 'business crime, however, in the sense in which it is used here, covers a much wider range of misconduct, which may be none the less damaging and otherwise undesirable, resulting from duress, incompetence, negligence, lack of training, lack of clarity in the rules, opportunism, technical infraction, or sheer muddle-headedness, rather than calculated deceit motivated by greed' (Clarke 1990a: 16).

Other more recent case studies of business misbehaviour also range widely, including activity from 'bandit banks' or stock market manipulation, to behaviour connected to nuclear and other accidents (Punch 1996). The common denominator here, in so far as there is one, is a focus on the way managers face up to the temptations and tensions inherent in their role.

At one extreme ambiguity is created by the attempt (particularly in the USA) to identify white-collar crime with the relatively humdrum crimes of the middle clases. Weisburd *et al.* (1991) try to put to the test the alleged relationship between white-collar crime and superior class background. Their findings are that 'contrary to the portrait generally presented we find a world of offending and offenders that is very close to the everyday lives of typical Americans' (ibid.: 184ff.). The majority of offenders 'do not necessitate nor do their defences rely upon elite social status'. The authors argue that small frauds are as normal a part of business context as street crimes are in poor communities, and conclude that 'the people we studied are the core American criminals whose ranks will grow as society becomes more middle class, as credit cards and credentialling grows, and television continues to hammer home the message of consumption'. The study is of great value in showing us that common crime and white-collar crime lie on a continuum, and in proposing (inductively) a new category of offending intermediate between common and corporate crime. But the definition of white-collar crime used in this work, based as it was on criminal convictions rather than administrative proceedings, and biased towards smaller-scale frauds (the crimes they selected included securities fraud and antitrust violations, bribery, embezzlement, mail fraud, tax fraud, false claims and accounting, and credit fraud), was almost bound to produce the picture of middle-class crime which the authors describe. Such work does not even merit a reference in a recent British textbook, which is entitled *Corporate Crime* so as to avoid the ambiguity associated with the term white-collar crime (Slapper and Tombs 1999).

At the opposite extreme there is also uncertainty about where to draw the line between white-collar crime and organized crime. As predicted in the first edition of this *Handbook* (Nelken 1994b), the overlap between these types of enterprise crime has become an important new focus of research (though one already anticipated in the theory of illegal enterprises put forward by Smith and others in the 1980s). Ruggiero, for example, claims that Sutherland created an unsatisfactory distinction between these two types of criminal behaviour (leaving only gangsters in the category of organized crime) which has wrongly been taken over by later criminologists. He argues that white-collar/organized crime should be seen as a normal rather than pathological aspect of business life, and its causes should be sought in wealth and power rather than greed as such. Organized crime, he insists, once we get away from ethnic stereotypes, involves the same flexible consumer-oriented behaviour which characterizes all successful business behaviour. Offering a wealth of examples of business-type crimes, Ruggiero argues that both white-collar and organized criminals use similar techniques, share the same illegal know-how, and share the same values— even if perpetrators come from different backgrounds. Their crimes are performed in or by organized structures, thrive on collusion, and normally enjoy the connivance of administrators and legislators (Ruggeiro 1996).

In part we may be witnessing real changes in the phenomena pointed to by these different criminological labels. In the first place, business crime may be taking on some of the characteristics of organized crime. As Reichman observes, 'insider trading as practiced in the 1980s is a form of crime that combines elements of the traditional categories of occupational and organizational crime' (Reichman 1992: 56). Likewise, traditional organized crime groups, such as the Mafia or the Camorra in Italy, or the Chinese or Taiwanese Triads, have become increasingly capitalistic in orientation and ethos (see, e.g., Arlachi 1985 on the Mafia and the Protestant ethic, or Gambetta's (1994) thesis of the Mafia as an industry of private protection). In Post-Communist countries which are without a recent history of capitalist markets, it may be indeed be artificial to draw a line between business and organized crime. More broadly, globalization may be leading to similar forms of structural integration of legitimate and illegitimate business activities, making regular collaboration between business and organized criminals both more possible and more necessary (Nelken 1997). An important topic for research is global tax avoidance and evasion, and the role of professionals such as lawyers and accountants on both sides of the fence as facilitators and enforcers.

On the other hand, this thesis should not be pushed too far. Claims concerning a symbiotic relationship between ordinary business, white-collar crime, and organized crime *presuppose* important differences rather than total overlap. Organized crime groups are able to gain legitimacy, respectability, protection, access, expertise, suppliers, customers, investment opportunities, or various other advantages from such relationships, and these benefits would be attenuated if the differences were to disappear. Both white-collar crime and organized crime cover such a continuum of activities that there will clearly be some that fall outside any attempt to categorize them together (think, on the one hand, of a small food shop breaking hygiene regulations, and, on the other, of a classical protection racket based on territorial domination). What is certainly true is that the distinction between these types of crime will vary according to the type of crime and the structure of the industry under consideration.

By common agreement, Sutherland's definition is not considered a helpful starting point for doing research into white-collar crime. Apart from its internal contradictions (for example, are we dealing with crimes committed for or against organizations?), changes in class structure, forms of business activity, organizational forms, and cultural valuations all threaten to undermine its empirical coherence. But what other definitions can be found which do not simply rely on selecting the most appropriate-seeming crimes from the official criminal statistics? One common inductive strategy is to start from the data produced by the non-police administrative agencies generally entrusted with dealing with business offences (especially in common law countries). This was the source of data used in the comprehensive Clinard and Yeager study which focused on various Federal regulatory bodies (Clinard and Yeager 1980). Non-police agencies in Britain include the Post Office, British Transport Police, Customs, water authorities, local government, Ministry of Agriculture, etc. (See Royal Commission 1980.) But though these agencies may have some enforcement practices in common it would be quite wrong to describe all the type of offenders they prosecute (many from poor backgrounds) as white-collar criminals.

Another strategy is to seek to develop typologies of different kinds of crime which fit under the general heading of 'white-collar crime'. Many writers work with subcategories such as crimes against the environment, crimes in the workplace, and economic crimes. The difficulty here is that the categories thus created are still likely to end up as containers for somewhat disparate behaviours. Green (1990) distinguishes organizational occupational crime, state authority occupational crime, professional occupational crime, etc. But these headings cannot pretend to be either theoretically defined, or even coherent classifications of types of crime. The offences considered as state crime range from bribe-taking to genocide; whilst the chapter on individual occupational crime—which is admitted to be a 'catch all' category—includes behaviours as different as employee theft and securities crimes. The drawbacks to inductivism are evident in the artificial distinctions which lead Green to discuss the crimes committed by bribe-givers in a different chapter from those of bribe-takers. Nonetheless, the range of crimes brought under the rubric of the white-collar crime concept continues to grow: Friedrichs (1996) devotes chapters to state corporate crime, enterprise crime, contrepreneurial crime, avocational crime, finance crime, and 'techno crime'.

There are also a variety of attempts to rethink Sutherland's concept in a more deductive fashion. Some of these are deliberately modest, such as Clarke's extended definition of business crime in terms of its distinguishing features (Clarke 1990a: chapter 3). In the rest of the book Clarke seeks to illustrate the applicability of his definition to a series of different areas of misbehaviour (and justifies a refusal to develop typologies partly on the somewhat odd grounds that opting for any one

typological scheme would exclude another which might be more appropriate for
other purposes). Despite the richness of his descriptions his approach can be criticized for already building in as part of his definition of business crime those controversial features of the social response which are less geared to prosecution than in the
case of ordinary crime. It is also unclear why the book is entitled *Business Crime* when
the thrust of the argument is intended to undermine this label.

Of greater value are the more ambitious efforts aimed at finding a key theoretical
variable which could produce a coherent focus for further research. Recent examples
(which go beyond the somewhat unimaginative 'crimes of the powerful', 'crimes of
the upperworld' or 'elite crimes') include Shapiro's focus on the increasing need to
trust agents and the consequent exposure to various forms of abuse of such trust in
which agents subordinate the interests of their principals to their own gain (Shapiro
1989). Coleman and others stress the importance of the growth of organizational
actors in what has been called the 'asymmetric society' (Gross 1980; Coleman 1992).
These approaches may include more or less than the offences that Sutherland covered:
Shapiro's proposal, for example, seems to be derived from her previous empirical
research interests in securities frauds and would not be applicable, say, to pollution
crimes; its focus on agents also lets principals off the hook. But such approaches
promise to be theoretically more productive than Sutherland's concept.

IS WHITE-COLLAR CRIME REALLY CRIME?

If there are basic uncertainties about what is being referred to when talking of white-
collar crime, there are also long-standing doubts whether or not all the misbehaviours
discussed under this rubric can be considered to count as crime. Most of the continuing controversy, as well as the stimulus, generated by this topic is due to the fact that it
appears to straddle the crucial boundary between criminal and non-criminal
behaviour. Since this is a well-aired problem, and the debates can be found in all the
readers on this subject (e.g., Geis 1968), I will confine myself to drawing out their
relevance to the issue of ambiguity. Many scholars have argued that the misbehaviours
discussed by Sutherland or his followers do not always satisfy the legal criteria for
crime; some even go so far as to insist on the necessity for a penal conviction at court
(e.g., Tappan 1947). It is, admittedly, ironic that Sutherland himself was unable to
publish the names of the companies whose administrative violations he described in
his book, because of his publisher's fears that he would then be exposed to claims of
libel for describing them as criminal (this was remedied only in the uncut version
published much later; Sutherland 1983). Restricting attention to those crimes found
in the ordinary criminal statistics, however, too easily robs the term of all its sense.
The results of following such a definition make it possible to argue that white-collar
crime is an otiose category and that white-collar criminals, like most ordinary criminals, are young, feckless, and unsuccessful (see Hirschi and Gottfredson 1987, 1989;
and the criticism by Steffensmeier 1989).

Others have made virtually the opposite attack, complaining that many white-collar crimes are merely technically criminal and are not socially considered on a par with ordinary crimes; hence they do not satisfy the requirements of a sociological definition of crime (see, e.g., Burgess 1950, criticizing Hartung 1950). While this is a more acute criticism, it tends to assume the unchanging circularity of social definitions and underestimates the potential for change (a process in which criminology can play a part).

The fact that such opposite criticisms can be raised is confirmation of the ambiguity of this concept—which is also reflected in the use of descriptions such as 'regulatory crimes' or 'mala prohibita'. Sutherland, and many later scholars, chose to include in their definition of white-collar crime not only misbehaviours with criminal penalties, but also those which carried only civil or administrative sanctions. This was done precisely so as not to invoke the question whether the choice of these different and generally lighter sanctions was justified (or only a sign of the political and economic power of the offenders involved). But it is only a small (if significant) step from this to argue for the inclusion in the category of white-collar crime of other types of harmful business behaviour which have succeeded (through much the same political and economic pressures) in avoiding being subject to any sanctions at all.

Must we use law to draw the line? One of the contributions made by the topic of white-collar crime to criminology lies in this very difficulty of assimilating all that Sutherland was getting at without breaking the boundaries of the discipline. Should the definition of crime adopted for sociological purposes be the same as that of the law? What are the dangers of tying criminology to a starting point defined by another em;politically conditioned—discipline? If we allow the political process to define what counts as crime, is this a politically conservative choice? Or is it just good tactics em;a way to avoid alienating the 'liberals' (as Box 1983 argues)? Leading writers insist that we must refer to the law because otherwise it would be impossible to decide who is to define what should count as business deviance (Coleman 1987). But this was exactly the decision that the labelling perspective tried to force criminologists to face. The topic of white-collar crime thus illustrates the possibility of divergence between legal, social, and political definitions of criminality—but in so doing it reminds us of the artificiality of all definitions of crime.

EXPLAINING THE CAUSES OF WHITE-COLLAR CRIME

Can white-collar crime be explained using the normal frameworks of criminological explanation? In previous editions I argued that the motives usually attributed to white-collar criminals (greed and power) were too often left unexplored and that more effort needed to be made to 'appreciate' the perspective of those engaged in white-collar crime, however politically distasteful this might be for some scholars (Nelken 1994b, 1997b). Some progress is being made. The insider stories which emerge from former participants, especially in the world of high finance, describe a sub-culture where the excitement for young men of living life in the fast lane is as important as the money benefits themselves (Portnoy 1997). Punch tries to get behind the 'surface solidity of the business organisation' so as to examine 'the fluctuating and even turbulent reality of managerial "backstage"' behaviour. In this 'world of power struggles, ideological debate, intense political rivalry, manipulation of information, and short term problem solving . . . managers emerge as something of amoral chameleons, buffeted by moral ambiguity and organizational uncertainty; they survive this "messy not to say dirty" environment by engaging in Michiavellian micropolitics' (Punch 1996). He finds that business studies students can get as indignant as the next person about the social and human costs of business misbehaviour. But once they are asked to role-play as managers having to make hard choices in risky situations, the same students regularly opt for 'macho', high-risk strategies. In the 'real world' of the organization the pressure 'to deliver the goods' or protect market share or just one's own career are potent motivations. And there are numerous ways of seeking to justify such behaviour as not really reprehensible.

More generally, however, the problem of *what* exactly needs to be explained continues to confuse the search for causes. Is white-collar crime conventional or unconventional behaviour for those who commit it? If it is conventional, why is so much effort put into keeping criminal activities secret even from other members of the same organization (Hirschi and Gottfredson 1987)? Where the explanatory approach adopted is to look for the individual motivations of what is taken to be clearly criminal behaviour, white-collar crime becomes just another test of standard theories of crime causation. Its novelty, if any, is tied to the emergence of new opportunities, for new groups, to commit old offences—for example, through the use of computers to carry out frauds. Where, instead, the issue becomes the criminogenic properties of business, of capitalism, or organizational behaviour in general, then the normative fabric of everyday business life seems placed in doubt and the actual evidence of white-collar crime seems to fall short of what would be possible.

These difficulties have not discouraged a series of attempts to explain the causes of white-collar crime, and there are even a number of good reviews of such work (see, e.g., Braithwaite 1985, who concludes, however, that 'only banal generalisations are possible', or Coleman 1987, who furnishes a (banal?) synthesis of existing work in terms of opportunity and motivation theory). I shall comment on explanations concerned with the whole area of white-collar crime. But, as already noted, the search for causes may be limited to typologies of crime, such as crimes by professional people, or even to specific offences. And obviously, where the topic is theoretically reformulated this will affect what needs to be explained. For Shapiro, for example, the study of white-collar crime belongs to the wider study of the maintenance and abuse of trust (see also Nelken 1994a; Friedrichs 1996). Attention should focus on the rising need to rely on agents and the consequent increased exposure to the risks of their malpractices. Trust is required in so far as it is difficult to tell when agents are putting their self-interests above those of their principals, especially as they tend to be the 'repeat players', and to act at a distance; but efforts to limit their discretion are self-defeating. To understand causation there therefore needs to be 'the marriage of a systematic understanding of the distribution of structural opportunities for trust abuse with an understanding of the conditions under which individual or organisational fiduciaries seize or ignore these illicit opportunities' (Shapiro 1989: 353).

The concept of white-collar crime was certainly not invented in order to provide comfort for standard approaches to causation in criminology. Sutherland hoped to use these misbehaviours as ammunition against the reigning tendency to explain crime in terms of individual or social pathology. By ridiculing the idea that businesses or businessmen could be said to misbehave because of their difficult childhoods, he intended to reform criminological theory and show that only his theory of 'differential association' could account for all forms of criminal behaviour. There is ample evidence of the diffusion of definitions favourable to white-collar forms of lawbreaking in business circles, whether these are based on loyalty to the firm, the alleged requirements of business life, or dislike of government regulation. But Sutherland's theory is nevertheless now regarded as flawed and superficial, and the search for a universal theory of crime has lost its attractions. Ironically, those who are most committed to the subject of white-collar crime are now under attack by criminologists who argue that there is no need for this special category of criminal behaviour precisely because it gets in the way of general explanations of the crime phenomenon (Hirschi and Gottfredson 1987; Gottfredson and Hirschi 1990: chapter 9).

Proponents both of 'strain' and of 'control' theories have tried to make sense of white-collar crime. Whatever his original focus may have been, most strain theories of corporate crime find their inspiration in Merton's concept of *anomie*. White-collar crimes can be seen, for example, as an 'innovative' response on the part of businesses (or particular roles such as middle management) to the strain of conforming to cultural prescriptions to maintain profits even in difficult circumstances (Passas 1990; Vaughan 1996; Slapper and Tombs 1999). The strain may be located in the business environment as such, in particular industries, or in particular firms. A classical study of the conditions under which the major car manufacturers in the USA constrain their car dealers to operate, showed the pressure put on dealers to cut corners if they wanted to survive economically (Leonard and Weber 1970); other situations may 'facilitate' rather than directly 'coerce' criminal solutions (Needleman and Needleman 1979). More could be made of these ideas (Nelken 1994c; Slapper and Tombs 1999).

Control theories, on the other hand, are premised on the initial question: why don't we all commit crimes when the temptations are so strong? The reply given is that most of us, the generally law-abiding, have too much invested in relationships and in legitimate society. The best way to rob a bank may indeed be to own one—or work in one—but, we assume, most of those in this position do not take advantage of it. This approach is a weak candidate for explaining white-collar crime because it finds it difficult to account for how middle-class criminals (and even most of those who find themselves in a position to embezzle) ever achieved their social positions in the first place. It also needs to show why they would be willing to risk their investment (Wheeler 1992). One neglected argument that is suggested here is based on the idea of 'over-investment'. The findings of Weisburd and his colleagues in their sample of middle-class criminals were that 'many of our offenders have the material goods associated with successful people but may barely be holding their financial selves together' (Weisburd *et al.* 1991: 65). This could be interpreted as meaning that such offenders are, if anything, so strongly tied to social expectations and obligations that they are even willing to offend to maintain their position (and so *anomie* and control theories meet up)! In any case, whatever its general bearing, more specific ingredients of control theory, such as the importance of 'neutralization' of social controls through the use of justifications (learned within or outside the company), are regularly adopted in explaining white-collar crime. Typical theoretical syntheses in textbooks dealing with white-collar crime in fact draw both on the 'strain' elements of capitalist competition and striving for business or individual success, and on the large possible variety of such 'techniques of neutralization' (see, e.g., Box 1983; Coleman 1987; Green 1990).

The labelling approach has, strangely, been comparatively neglected in the study of white-collar crime. One reason for this could be that criminologists here line up with those doing the labelling (see Katz 1980; Yeager 1991: chapter 1). There is of course the apparent paradox that it is the 'insiders' rather than the 'outsiders' who are being labelled—but the paradox normally disappears once the details of who is really affected become clearer. In any case, few would now want to deny the importance of legislative or other battles over the labelling of business misbehaviour. The perspective would seem peculiarly relevant given the relative recency of many laws regulating business, the sharp swings between political projects of regulation and deregulation, and the divergent views of different groups as to the appropriateness of criminaliza-tion. Some attention has been given to the success of techniques of 'non-labelling' or 'de-labelling' used by lawyers and accountants in diluting or avoiding the imposition of the criminal label, for example, in shaping the (mis)behaviour involved in some tax-avoidance schemes (McBarnet 1991; McBarnet and Whelan 1999). In my study of the social construction of landlord crime (Nelken 1983) I examined the process of criminal labelling and de-labelling in this area of business misbehaviour. I showed that those actually apprehended for landlord crime were small, immigrant landlords involved in disputes with their tenants (for similar findings for other white-collar crimes, see Hutter 1988; Croal 1989). With some effort it was possible to portray their self-help methods as criminal, but the malpractices characteristic of large business landlords stayed immune to criminalization because of their similarity to ordinary business behaviour—a 'limit' of the legal process which was, paradoxically, concealed by actually exaggerating the capacity of law to control such behaviour (Nelken 1983). White-collar crimes and the reaction to them seem, perhaps more than other crimes, to be subject to interrelated cycles of expansion and reform. The apparent growth of political corruption in the 1980s, followed by widespread crackdown in the 1990s, is a good example (Nelken and Levi 1996).

The attempt to explain white-collar crime within the 'normal science' approaches used in criminology shows itself not only in theories of causation, but also in the effort to follow the 'careers' of such criminals (Weisburd and Waring 2001). Many writers adopt a positivist search for the peculiar characteristics which distinguish offenders from non-offenders. Sutherland (1949, 1983) was keen to show the widespread nature of white-collar offences but also to identify the major culprits. He examined infringements of rules governing fair labour practices by General Motors and others, violations of rules against the restraint of trade, especially common in the major companies in the film industry, infringements of patents, and misrepresentation in advertising involving household names such as Bayer aspirin, Quaker Oats, Carnation milk, Phillips milk of magnesia, Hoover vacuum cleaners, and *Encyclopedia Britannica*. He particularly stressed the duration of some offences and the 'recidivism' of some of the companies concerned.

Clinard and Yeager (1980), in the most wide-ranging documentary study of corporate crime to date, examined all the federal administrative, civil, and criminal actions initiated in 1975 and 1976 by twenty-five federal agencies against 582 of America's largest corporations. The violations they examined were divided into non-compliance with agency regulations; environmental pollution; financial crimes, such as illegal payments or tax offences; labour discrimination, including unsafe working practices; manufacturing offences, such as the distribution of unsafe products; and unfair trading practices, including price-fixing arrangements. Going beyond Sutherland, they tried to control comparisons for the time available to commit offences and the different size of the companies they investigated. They found that three-fifths of their sample had charges brought against them in those years. While 13 per cent of the companies accounted for just over half the violations, large, medium, and small companies were all well represented amongst the violators. Where Sutherland had found the film, mercantile, and railroad industries particularly engaged in violations, Clinard and Yeager found their black sheep in the oil, pharmaceutical, and motor vehicle industries, which all had more than their proportional share of violations. The oil industry, for example, was involved in three-fifths of all serious violations, with twenty-two of twenty-eight oil-refining firms guilty of at least one violation in the period under consideration; car manufacturers were responsible in all for one-sixth of all the violations discovered and for a third of the manufacturing violations overall; pharmaceutical manufacturers accounted for one-tenth of all violations, and all seventeen companies were found to have committed at least one violation.

Some of Clinard and Yeager's findings were artefacts which resulted from using data which depended on the vagaries of regulatory regimes: the higher offending rates of diversified firms, for example, may simply mean that they were more exposed to different regulatory agencies (though the firms concerned may also have faced problems in maintaining oversight of their different operations). Their investigation produced some statistical support for the proposition that violations increased as financial performance became poorer; this was particularly marked for environmental and labour offences. On the other hand, firms with higher than average growth rates were more likely to have engaged in manufacturing violations. The authors admitted that the causal variables on which they concentrated—size, growth rate, diversification, and market power and resources—had only limited predictive power. Even the more confident of their claims concerning crime rates and economic performance have been questioned in the later literature (Braithwaite 1985). Their study was unable to allow for the complicating factor of why and when agencies choose to uncover violations, and has been criticized for taking agency records as the measure of corporate crime and for failing to see such behaviour as endemic to capitalism (Young 1981). A valuable study by Haines (1997) examines the way companies react after they have been involved in safety violations on the hypothesis that the same causes which explain violation would also account for what was done or not done afterwards to put things right. Her findings were that managers in larger companies were less likely to take a 'blinkered' view of what should be done to avoid recurrence and could afford to take a broader and longer-term approach to the problem of reconciling profit and safety.

A central debate amongst scholars of white-collar crime in fact concerns the extent to which corporate and business crime should be seen as an inevitable consequence of capitalism. Box (1983), in a Marxist-influenced application of Merton, argues that corporations are criminogenic because if legal means are blocked they will resort to illegal means so as to maintain or increase profitability. As and when necessary, they will use techniques aimed at competitors (e.g., industrial espionage or price fixing), at consumers (e.g., fraud or misleading advertising), or at the public at large (e.g., environmental pollution). Those recruited to work in corporations learn to justify such behaviour on the grounds that 'business is business' (cf. Pearce 1976; Punch 1996). This is particularly true for those who rise to the top and who then have a disproportionate influence over the ethos of their firms (although they generally take care not to be directly involved or informed of the illegal activities made necessary by their drive for profit). For those who subscribe to this theory businessmen comply with the law in so far as they see it enforced strictly (thereby denying competitive advantage to those who would break it). Where there are few effective controls, as in the third world, capitalism shows its true face, selling unsafe products, paying low wages, and exploiting the complaisance of poor and corrupt governments and regulators (see Slapper and Tombs 1999: chapter 7).

On the other hand, it is well to bear in mind some reservations about the idea that capitalism as such is criminogenic. If Merton's *anomie* theory is to be pressed this far it is at least necessary to go on to discuss the alternative, non-criminal modes of responding to 'strain', and (what Merton did not do) offer an explanation of when and why each mode is chosen. The argument appears to predict too much crime and makes it difficult to explain the relative stability of economic trade within and between nations, given the large number of economic transactions, the many opportunities for committing business crimes, the large gains to be made, and the relative unlikelihood of punishment. This theory also has difficulty in accounting for improvements in safety and increases in the quality of goods under capitalism. If it is somewhat oversimplified to argue that only a small proportion of businessmen are 'bad apples', it is not much more convincing to assume that all businesses act as 'amoral calculators' and would choose to offend but for the availability of serious sanctions (Pearce and Tombs 1990, 1991). The desires to continue in business and to maintain self-respect and the good will of fellow businessmen, go a long way to explaining reluctance to seize opportunities for a once-only windfall. Trading competitors (as well as organized consumer groups, unions, and others) can serve as a control on illicit behaviour for their own reasons. Law-abidingness can often be definitely in the competitive interests of companies. Braithwaite (1985) illustrates how American pharmaceutical companies able to obtain Federal Drug Administration authorization for their products are in this way guaranteed lucrative markets in countries which cannot afford their own expensive drug-testing facilities. It could be said that the clear evidence of exploitation and the sale of dangerous goods in third world countries reflects an anomalous situation which is at least partly the result of the excessive freedom of manoeuvre of powerful multinational companies who are not exposed to sufficient competition. On the other hand, we should not underestimate the role of state regulation in all this. Current pressures of globalization which may be leading to a 'de-coupling' of politics and economics both at home and abroad, could have dire consequences.

Marxist theory has no need to assume that all business crime will be tolerated. Many forms of business misbehaviour made into crimes may reflect changing forms of capitalism or inter-class conflict. At any given period, some corporate crimes, such as anti-trust offences, will not be in the interest of capitalism as a whole, so it is important to distinguish what is in the interests of capitalism from what suits particular capitalists. Even if the latter may succeed in blocking legislation or effective enforcement, at least in the short term, this does not prove that it is capitalism as such which requires the continuation of specific forms of misbehaviour. Moreover, capitalism is a set of practices and not just an important set of social actors. Practices may remain free from effective control even if the group concerned is not particularly economically powerful. Thus the relative immunity from control of abuses of the Rent Acts committed by private business landlords in Britain has been attributed less to their importance within the social structure and more to objective difficulties in controlling their behaviour without affecting normal commercial transactions (Nelken 1983). When professional criminals succeed in getting away with serious forms of business-related crime such as 'long-firm' fraud, it is implausible to say that this is in the interest of any capitalist group (Levi 1985). The same can be said of many of the large frauds perpertrated against companies or financial sectors by previously respected insiders.

We should not underestimate the fruitfulness of hypotheses based on the capacity of capitalism to generate business crime. But care needs to be taken in connecting macro and micro levels of explanation. All organizations, and not only the corporate form of trading, can be criminogenic in so far as they tend to reward achievement even at the expense of the outer environment (Kramer 1992). This would help to explain why public organizations such as the army, the police, or government bureaucracies also generate crime and corruption (these behaviours are increasingly being included in textbooks on white-collar crime). Likewise, the far from positive record of the former communist regimes in matters of worker safety, environmental pollution, or corruption cannot be blamed on the pressures of competition. Even in capitalist societies it is often the absence of market pressures which explains some types of business misbehaviours, such as the ease with which government subsidy programmes are diverted to improper uses (Passas and Nelken 1993; Nelken 2002).

WHITE-COLLAR CRIME IN ITS EVERYDAY SETTINGS

We have seen so far that there are, on the one hand, doubts about how far the same explanations will work for white-collar crime as for ordinary crime, and, on the other hand, risks of over-explanation in accounts which relate it too closely to ordinary business behaviour. For some commentators, however, the central issue concerns the extent to which white-collar crimes come about in similar ways to other criminal behaviour. Clarke's book on business crime, for example, argues strongly that these misbehaviours are typically 'less criminal' in their inception and motivation than much ordinary crime (Clarke 1990a). Whereas many textbook presentations of white-collar crime simply list a variety of dangerous behaviours in a way which emphasizes their harmful consequences and implies that these are incurred deliberately, or at least recklessly, Clarke attempts to recover their sense by putting them back into their everyday business context.

For Clarke there is a series of factors which distinguish the commission of business crimes. Their location in the midst of ordinary business and occupational activity both facilitates their achievement and helps to prevent their detection by colleagues and superiors as well as outside authorities. As compared to ordinary crimes such as burglary, the perpetrator has every justification to be present at the scene of the crime. Indeed, Clarke claims that unlike ordinary crimes, where a crucial clue is presence at the scene, with white-collar crimes the problem is to discover whether there has been an offence rather than to identify the culprit. Police or regulatory agencies are reluctant to enter private settings without invitation, and are often not called upon even where an offence has been committed. White-collar crimes are frequently what we could call 'complainantless crimes', and those who suffer the consequences of them cannot be relied upon to act as a reliable source of criminal intelligence. Clients of professionals are often unable to assess their performance—this is why they need to turn to them in the first place. Workers may simply be unaware of the risks to which they have been exposed; consumers will often not appreciate what they have lost; competitors will be unaware of collusive practices. The behaviour which constitutes white-collar crime is often indistinguishable on its surface from normal legal behaviour. For example, for fraud to be accomplished, it must obviously succeed in mimicking the appearance of legitimate transactions, and it is not unusual for those guilty of this crime to remain undetected for years or even a lifetime. Unlike all except 'victimless crimes' the involvement of the victim is apparently voluntary (though sometimes the result of the lure of easy money).

A further claim concerning the supposed distinctiveness of white-collar crime is virtually true by definition. The criminal aspects of the business or occupational activities under consideration are often *secondary* or *collateral* features, both in priority and in the succession of events, of an undertaking pursued for other, legitimate purposes. Criminal consequences, such as damage to the health of workers or to the environment, often come about either as a result of omissions, or because of financial pressures or unanticipated opportunities for gain; they are not inherent to the economic activity as such. Such criminality is difficult to recognize (in time) because of the narrow and constantly changing line between acceptable and unacceptable business behaviour. Even such essential features of outrightly crooked schemes as the deliberate withholding of payment to creditors may exist as practices in the legitimate world of business—for example, as a desperate manoeuvre by small businesses trying to survive on tight margins, or as a more cynical use of market strength by large enterprises exploiting the dependence on their patronage of small contractors. This makes it difficult for all concerned—creditors, regulators, and others—to tell whether, or at what point, the intention permanently to avoid payment was formed.

Ambiguity surrounds not only the goals of the activity in the midst of which white-collar crime is encountered, but also, it is argued, the degree of intentionality involved. There are certainly notorious cases of cold-blooded calculation, such as the way Ford went ahead with its dangerous design for the Ford Pinto rear engine because it estimated that the potential payment of damages would be less than the cost of recalling the cars (Dowie 1988), or the manner in which the P & O shipping company disregarded repeated requests for the installation of bow warning-lights to improve safety on their 'on-off' ferries (see Punch 1996; Slapper and Tombs 1999). But, it is claimed, these are the exceptions (and even these cases did not end in criminal convictions). More commonly it is difficult to distinguish malevolence from incompetence; and, as Clarke insists, in business and professional life, we are often more concerned about the harmful effects of the latter. Professionals are specifically valued for their competence rather than for their honesty as such (which is perhaps taken for granted); in large organizations and bureaucracies there is considerable scope for laziness or disinterest which may have tragic consequences. These points, it is said, are less true of ordinary crime.

On the other hand, many scholars insist that these aspects of the setting and commission of white-collar crimes mainly point to problems of detection and do not negate the essential similarities between these and ordinary crimes. Businesses involved in offending behaviour often do their best to organize so as to minimize the costs of their infractions (concealing compromising knowledge from directors, 'appointing vice presidents responsible for going to jail', etc.). Conversely, there are also occasions where enforcement against ordinary crime has to overcome similar difficulties of categorization. The difficulty of identifying the 'really' criminal cases is not unique to white-collar crime. The definition of 'dishonesty' in the English law of theft, for example, leaves it to the jury to decide whether the behaviour at issue demonstrates the requisite level of criminal intent in terms of what ordinary people would consider stealing to be: the business world would probably be capable of answering a similar question. Many ordinary crimes, such as assault, also fall on a continuum that runs from accidental to deliberate, but we do not let this place the appropriateness of criminal sanctions in doubt. Indeed, we take trouble to hold individuals responsible for the consequences of their assaults even when these exceed their intention or even their foresight. Much also depends on the 'time-frame' adopted for identifying the commission of an offence. For example, the conduct that causes a serious breach of health or safety standards may have been unintended at the time of the accident but deliberate when the choice was made not to install up-to-date but costly measures of prevention (Kelman 1981). Philosophical studies of when we choose to describe an action as voluntary or not assert that (because of the difficulty of defining what is meant by 'will') this is itself a way of indicating our evaluation of the actions in question rather than simply a description.

Like so much concerning the social definition of white-collar crime, the question of intention therefore easily lends itself to social construction. Much ambiguity, or, conversely, the provision of a cover of ostensible legality, is a contingent product of social processing. Thus accountants and barristers may use their professional skills to help businesses construct tax avoidance schemes which must then appear as anything but deliberate attempts to evade tax (McBarnet 1991; McBarnet and Whelan 1999). Even if a case reaches trial, defence lawyers work hard to redefine the misconduct as not having been deliberate (Mann 1985). White-collar criminals may even find that they have allies in the redefinition of their behaviour in those trying their misbehaviour. In the course of research into deviance by professionals I made a study of the (confidential) proceedings of English family practitioner tribunals, which deal with cases where dentists (and other professionals) are alleged not to have complied with their National Health contracts. Here everything is done to avoid the impression that potentially criminal behaviour is at issue even though, in cases where misconduct is proved, fixed withholdings from payment serve the function of fines. In one case, for example, a dentist admitted to 'fraud' in deliberately claiming for more work than he had done, only to find the tribunal members pleading with him to retract his admission (and claim inadvertence) so that they could retain jurisdiction.

While it is debatable how far the ambiguous aspects alleged to characterize the commission of white-collar crime are intrinsic features restricted to this type of misbehaviour, there are certainly some important cases where criminals deliberately exploit the appearance of legitimate business. In fact the overlap between white-collar crime and more clear-cut kinds of crime, such as organized crime, has so far been relatively neglected in comparison to the attention given to the boundary between white-collar crime and ordinary business behaviour. Professional or organized criminals may *create* ambiguity by fostering the impression of genuine business enterprises, if necessary by trading normally for an initial period. At other times they may penetrate legitimate companies, especially when these have fallen on hard times, and use them to launch purely criminal activities such as 'long-firm' frauds (Levi 1981). Organized criminal businesses may seek to monopolize the market for legitimate goods and services, such as public construction projects or waste-processing, beating their competitors with their lower marginal costs and using violence or corruption against competitors or those with the power to award lucrative contracts, as with Camorra enterprises in the Campania area of Italy and the activities of many of the cosche of the New Mafia (Arlachi 1985).

The division of labour between legitimate and illegitimate business can represent an attempt to disguise the criminal presuppositions of legal enterprises. Legitimate businesses may call upon the service of criminals for particular operations such as loan repayment, money laundering, or tax evasion (Block 1991: chapters 5 and 6). They may also take indirect advantage of the operation of international criminals. For example, major electrical companies apparently find it financially profitable to buy and resell (at the expense of other wholesalers) examples of their own products illegally smuggled on to the market (Van Duyne 1993). Legal enterprise may rely on organized criminals to supply a disciplined workforce, as in the New York construction industry (New York State Organized Crime Task Force 1988), or to get rid of industrial waste products in illegal ways so as to reduce their external costs of production (Szasz 1986). Conversely, organized criminals may call upon legitimate businesses, such as printers or supermarkets, in developing major frauds like those against the EEC agricultural subsidy programmes (Passas and Nelken 1993); such symbiosis is also essential for the purpose of recycling money earned in illegal activities. The steady growth in international and transnational trading—and the changing face of national and economic borders in Europe—is also leading to an increase in different types of criminals seeking to profit from the opportunities these changes offer them (Passas and Nelken 1993; Van Duyne 1993; Nelken 2002). Current research on white-collar crime is increasingly concerned with exploring the relationship between legal, semi-legal, and illegal economic activities—and such enquiry is likely to be intensified as regional groupings increasingly use harmonized crime control as a badge of identity. This requires giving attention to the comparative dimension, because the relationships between businessmen, professionals, and organized criminals vary in different countries and because many of these crimes have an international dimension which exploits differences between national legal systems (Ruggiero 1996; Nelken 1997a). Appreciation of the political and economic structures conducive to such operations requires the criminologist to be open to concepts pioneered in disciplines other than sociology, including ideas about clientilism in political science, legal and illegal monopolies in economics, and risk analysis in accounting and management science.

THE AMBIVALENT RESPONSE TO WHITE-COLLAR CRIME

The above discussion will have already illustrated various ways in which the control of white-collar crime can also play a part in its causation. Government and business may share similar imperatives which coincide to favour offending. Carson's description of the importance of 'speed' in the calculations of both the Treasury and the oil companies in the exploitation of North Sea oil, and the consequent sacrifice of ordinary safety standards, is an extreme example of such objective coincidence of interests (Carson 1981). The Bank of England may be caught between its duties as regulator of the banking system and its desire not to compromise the credibility of one of the major clearing banks (*Economist* 1992). But even where government and offenders are clearly opposed, weak regulatory regimes or moves towards deregulation may provide an incentive to offending. One common strategy which leads to increased crime is the combination of removing legal or informal constraints on a business sector with the simultaneous resort to (new) criminal penalties to be available as a last resort. Complex and changing regulatory regimes, especially those involving government payment schemes, may in themselves provide the opportunity for crime

(Calavita, Pontell, and Tillman 1997; Nelken 2002; Passas and Nelken 1993; Vaughan 1983).

The methods adopted in responding to white-collar crime play a particularly important part in shaping this type of behaviour, inasmuch as the difficulty of relying on complainants means that the accent must be put on prevention and proactive enforcement. In this way our information about these types of misbehaviour often tells us more about the theories and priorities of the controllers than anything else (for example, the belief that small firms are more likely than large ones to bend the rules will inevitably find confirmation in the statistics of violations discovered). New forms of enforcement contribute to the construction of ' "postmodern" policing' (Spalek 2001). When dealing with the type of offence which is seen to overlap with organized crime (such as international fraud or money laundering) the (often misleading) accounts of who is responsible for such activity which are put forward by enforcers have a large role in creating the type of policing then put in place (see Nelken 1997a).

But the main issue which needs to be discussed under this heading is the charge that the different enforcement methods used to respond to white-collar as compared to ordinary crimes reinforce their ambiguous status and indirectly contribute to their causation. Is the difference in handling the cause or consequence of the distinctiveness of white-collar crime? Many scholars stress the fact that white-collar crimes are difficult to detect and control. It is difficult to prove intention when dealing with decisions taken within an organization (and legal thinking has not yet caught up with the importance of organizations); trials are long and expensive; juries have problems in understanding the evidence in complex fraud cases; professional advisers acting for businessmen can delay or defeat prosecution. Extra powers for obtaining evidence given to the Department of Trade inspectors or the Serious Fraud Office go only some of the way to dealing with these difficulties, as the spectacular collapse of the famous Blue Arrow prosecutions, amongst others, demonstrates. A premium is therefore placed on achieving compliance without the need for prosecution (although this is used as a threat, the need actually to resort to it is seen as failure). It is considered still better to rely on self- regulation by an industry or by the business itself. But reliance on self-policing can easily lead to conflicts of interest. For example, banks find themselves both as potential participators in money laundering and as required to detect and deter it (Levi 1991a, 1991b).

Some scholars (such as Clarke 1990a, but here his views are more widely shared) argue that the way white-collar crimes are handled reflects the special circumstances of these offences. It makes sense to use compliance in the regulation of occupations because the offender can easily be found at his or her place of occupation and it is feasible to put repeated pressure on him. Violations of safety or pollution standards are difficult and costly to conceal. Even the apparently self-defeating practice of giving advance warning of inspection visits does not therefore lead to concealment of offending. The difficulty in other business offences, Clarke argues, is to identify the commission of an offence rather than find the offender. But even here offenders in organizations do tend to leave a 'paper trail' of their actions.

Different interpretations of the nature of white-collar crime lead to corresponding views concerning the best way to handle them. Clarke argues that an approach based on criminal prosecution is inappropriate for all but a few cases of business crime because complainants are mainly interested in recompense and go to the police only if all else fails; the criminal process polarizes the parties, involves delay, carries risks of failure, and, above all, does nothing to secure future improvement in the relevant working practices. Existing enforcement practices make more sense; suggestions for improvement should be based mainly on trying to internalize better methods of control within businesses themselves rather than increase prosecution (Stone 1975 is a classic discussion of this theme). But the opposite point of view is also well supported. Green summarizes an extensive American literature which offers various proposals for improving the effectiveness of prosecution against white-collar crimes (Green 1990: chapter 8; see also Groves and Newman 1986). The assumption behind much of this work is that business behaviour is in fact particularly well suited to the application of deterrent criminal sanctions. Offences ('it is alleged') are strictly instrumental and offenders have much to lose from prosecution; prison, if only it were to be used regularly, would be more potent than for ordinary criminals. The main problem in current practice is that of producing a level of fines sufficient actually to deter business. Solutions such as stock dilution, equity fining, or ceding shares to the state may all work, but in cases where there has been physical injury they may give the wrong message that everything can ultimately be paid for. Informal and formally initiated negative publicity is unlikely to put a firm out of business, but it can and does have collateral effects and may help to produce beneficial procedural changes within firms (Fisse and Braithwaite 1985). Green's discussion is thin on the questions which are central for Clarke, concerning the possible counter-productive effects of using the normal criminal process for white-collar crime. On the other hand, many of Clarke's arguments against the use of prosecution could also be made regarding ordinary crime—certainly the victim usually gains little from from the criminal process and seems rather used by the system to serve its own ends.

For many observers the difficulties of controlling white-collar crime, and the need to rely on compliance techniques, should rather be attributed to a lack of political will to provide the resources necessary for a full-blown prosecution approach. In Britain proportionally few policemen are assigned to the Fraud Squad; the prestige of such assignments is low and term of service short (Levi 1987). For the United States, Calavita and Pontell argue that the savings and loans crash was partly due to the lack of trained thrift examiners and the overloaded FBI agents directed to clear up the scandal (Calavita and Pontell 1992; Calavita *et al.* 1997). Even the famous and feared American Securities and Exchange Commission, according to Shapiro, is forced to choose between detection or enforcement and uses the criminal sanction only in around 11 per cent of its cases (Shapiro 1984).

The actual combination of objective difficulties and political priorities in decisions over prosecution is often concealed by ideologically-loaded communication. Much white-collar crime is subject to regulation under the heading of strict liability by which, in theory, even unintentional offending can be held criminally culpable. Criminal law textbooks and philosophic writers discuss whether or not this is justified by the difficulty of proving intention in complex, modern, industrial processes. However, investigations of the 'logic in use' of the inspectorates responsible (at least in common law countries) for some of the most important areas of social regulation, such as those concerning worker safety or environmental pollution, tell a different story. In practice, apart from cases in which accidents have taken place, breaches of rules will normally be subject to sanctions only if *mens rea*—and even recidivism—has been shown by a refusal to correct matters pointed out by the inspector in warning visits and letters (Carson 1970; Hawkins 1984, Hawkins and Thomas 1984; Hutter 1988, 1997). The inspectors involved in such enforcement activity refuse to see themselves as 'industrial policemen', seeing their role rather as one geared to advising and cajoling the majority of fundamentally law-abiding businessmen.

One consequence (perhaps even an intended one, see Carson 1974, 1980) of this difference between theory and practice is that the imposition of strict liability reduces the stigma associated with these offences so as to reinforce the impression that they represent behaviour which is merely 'mala prohibita' rather than 'mala in se'. Enforcement techniques which concentrate on consequences rather than intentions, by collapsing the distinction between incompetence and deliberateness, thus often end up diluting rather than extending criminal stigma. Recent efforts to convict corporations for crime, especially in the area of safety, have had some success. But it is too early to say whether this is changing the way such offences are perceived, or the likelihood of their repetition (Wells 1993; Slapper 1999). Larger social and cultural conditions and trends are at least as important: in Italy, employers found guilty of serious safety offences at work are regularly subject to sanctions in the ordinary courts, but Italy has one of the highest rates in Europe of what they refer to as 'white death'.

Difficulties of enforcement may often be exaggerated to conceal other decisions (or non-decisions) about responding to criminal behaviour by economically influential groups. In an important study, Carson argued convincingly that the causes of accidents on North Sea oil rigs were little different from those which lead to accidents in factories or construction (Carson 1981). The claim that the high level of injuries was due to the difficulty of regulating activities operating 'at the frontiers of technology' at hitherto untried depths of oil exploration at sea, was not supported by his careful examination of the relevant case-records. The crucial issue was the fact that the responsibility for ensuring compliance with the normal standards of safety had not been assigned to the factory inspectors of the Health and Safety inspectorate (here being seen in more heroic light than in Carson's earlier work) but to the Department of Energy. But since this was also the body responsible for encouraging oil exploration to proceed as fast as possible in the interests of the British balance of payments, there was an inevitable conflict of interests in which those of the weakest groups were sacrificed.

Since Sutherland, the subject of white-collar crime has also been the focus of attempts to prove that the rich and powerful are treated more favourably by the criminal justice system. Some caveats should be entered here. The main basis for the relative immunity of businessmen in the criminal process (at least in Anglo-American jurisdictions) derives from political choices regarding which behaviour to make criminal in the first place, and only to a lesser extent from the way their offences are categorized. Those effectively criminalized for business-related offences tend to be small businessmen, quite often from immigrant backgrounds (Nelken 1983; Croal 1989). It is thus a mistake to confuse the macro (legislative) and micro (enforcement) logics which keep criminality and respectability apart. Many of those working in the criminal justice system would actually be interested (and have an interest in) successful prosecutions of 'the powerful'. Thus apparently ineffective legislative outcomes are often best studied as a product of 'coherence without conspiracy' (Nelken 1983). This does not mean, of course, that there cannot also be more explicit cases of prejudice, and there have rightly been many attacks on alleged bias and injustice in the handling of white-collar crimes, from enforcement to trial and beyond. As with most accusations of bias, however, the difficulty is in ensuring that like is being compared with like.

A well-known debate over the alleged leniency involved in using 'compliance' methods for dealing with white-collar regulatory offences is that between Pearce and Tombs, on the one hand, and Hawkins on the other (Pearce and Tombs 1990, 1991; Hawkins 1990, 1991). Pearce and Tombs began by criticizing Hawkins's and other descriptions of the compliance approach, for giving the appearance of being persuaded by the 'logic in use' of those whose enforcement strategy they described. In this way, it was alleged, they (indirectly) confirmed an unfair status quo instead of supporting the adoption of stricter methods which could reduce the level of harm caused by such offences. Hawkins fiercely challenged this as a misreading of the role of interpretive sociology (which was not directed towards policy evaluation), but then went on to endorse the compliance strategy in general terms without necessarily agreeing with all its tactics or the level of severity of the sanctions applied. For their part, Pearce and Tombs recommended that prosecution should begin at an earlier stage; they favoured the imposition of (low) fines rather than simply warning notices and wanted there to be more use of other sanctions such as the withdrawal of licences. In his reply, Hawkins pointed out that very few of the violations noted in routine proactive enforcement do eventually turn out to be the cause of serious harm and that it is not possible to predict which will do so. In his view, unless Pearce and Tombs really want to cut back sharply on enforcement discretion, their proposals are unlikely to produce much change in current practice. And to insist on legal action each time a violation is revealed, as was tried for a time by the American OSHA mines authority, tends to be counter-productive in terms of alienating the good will of those being regulated. It also risks producing a political backlash leading to deregulation, as happened in the case of this agency.

As this summary suggests, this and similar debates fail to make progress mainly because the policy arguments of Hawkins and others like him assume as givens exactly those political realities which their critics would like to see changed (see now Slapper and Tombs 1997). A useful study which points to this moral is Cook's comparison of the harsh response to those suspected of social security fraud with that meeted out to those engaged in tax frauds of very similar kinds (Cook 1989). The very different treatment received by each group relates less to the practical possibilities of enforcement (more or less the same), or to fears of counter-productive effects from tougher penalties, but rather follows from a set of associated beliefs about the relative worth and importance of maintaining the good will of each set of offenders.

Some of the most fruitful proposals for strengthening the control of white-collar crime, which acknowledge the force of both sides of this debate, are those developed by Braithwaite on the basis of his research into the successes and failures of regulation in very different industries and businesses, such as drug manufacturing, coal mining, and nursing homes. He suggests that businesses (beyond a certain size) should be obliged by government to write a set of rules tailored to the unique contingencies of their firm. These rules should be submitted for comment and amendment to interest groups, including citizen groups. Firms should have their own internal compliance unit with statutory responsibility on the director to report cases of violation, and the function of government inspectors would be to audit and (if necessary) sanction the performance of this unit (see Braithwaite 1995; Hutter 1997; Haines 1997).

It might be thought that the study of bias in the prosecution and trial of white-collar crimes should be more straightforward than an evalution of the justifiability of its special style of enforcement; but even here there is no consensus. Analysis of the penalties meeted out for serious frauds in Britain, as compared to other types of crime, certainly suggests that these are the crimes which are the most rewarding (Levi 1991c). Shapiro, in her study of securities offenders in the USA, detected a tendency for higher status offenders to be less likely to receive criminal penalties instead of being dealt with by administrative and civil measures (Shapiro 1984, 1989). But in their more comprehensive American study, Weisburd et al. (even after double check-ing) found that higher status offenders were *more* likely to get prison sentences (Weisburd et al. 1991: 7). In their earlier study Wheeler et al., using a sample of pre-1980 American social enquiry reports and case files, showed that penalties for white-collar crimes depended on the normal criteria for other crimes: prior record, seriousness of crime, degree of involvement of offender, the nature of harm to the victim, etc. There was, however, some limited evidence of judges identifying with the offender more than in cases of ordinary crimes, especially if the latter involve personal violence (Wheeler et al. 1988). The authors left it open whether the judges were merely reproducing (unconsciously or deliberately) the biases of the wider population.

Instead of demanding that white-collar criminals be treated like ordinary criminals, we could argue the reverse (though this is rarely done). Why not apply the methods used for dealing with businessmen and professionals to ordinary criminals? Much of what purports to be regulation or self-regulation of white-collar crime is bogus or ineffectual, and deserves to be attacked as such. But there is also much to be learned from the variety of forms of regulation and self-regulation designed to reduce viola-tions without criminalizing the offender. Even if it would probably be impossible to model the handling of ordinary crime too closely on that used for businessmen, the differences are not always as great as made out. All non-police agencies—even when not dealing with powerful offenders—put the emphasis on recovering money rather than securing convictions (Royal Commission on Criminal Procedure 1980). The problem of apprehending and maintaining pressure on ordinary criminals (who are not linked to their place of work as white-collar criminals are) is not as great as it seems: the police do know just where to lay their hands on juvenile delinquents—and quite a few other criminal suspects. And white-collar criminals have even more resources than ordinary criminals for covering their tracks when it becomes necessary.

In a sense compliance does already get used with ordinary criminals; Pearce and Tombs (1991) mention police control of prostitution and gambling as an example of compliance methods. But they use this to show the danger of collusion and corruption in the use of such methods. The role of social work and diversion (before trial) and probation or other techniques of rehabilitation (after conviction) is a better example. The choice between co-operation or compulsion is repeatedly offered to ordinary criminals from the stage of pleading guilty to obtaining parole. A crucial difference, however, is that it is usually necessary for an offender accused of ordinary crime to suffer the stigma of a conviction *before* consideration is given to compliance, whereas the opposite is true for business offenders handled in this way. We may be tempted to believe that, beyond a certain point, enforcement against ordinary crime is geared precisely to maximizing stigma even at the expense of effectiveness.

Pearce and Tombs do seem correct in tracing the difference in approach to the (untested) assumption that businessmen are basically disposed to respond well to a compliance approach whereas ordinary criminals are presumed to require punishment. But they prefer the equally untested assumption that businessmen should be dealt with as 'amoral calculators'. The evidence from interviews, however, is that managers say that they do not, for the most part, think in deterrence terms because only unethical managers are seen to respond to deterrence. Interviewees do concede that this process can get out of control and that it is difficult to be ethical when not running at a profit (Simpson 1992; Yeager 1995). But they insist that 'reputable' managers 'cut corners' only to try to save the company; they may bend the rules but do not violate them and they do not act for personal gain. It is reasonable to conclude that practical considerations regarding effective enforcement provide insufficient justification for the extent of the present contrast between methods used for ordinary and business crimes. A considerable merit of Braithwaite's long-standing search for an effective as well as just approach to the control of all types of crime—what he calls 'reintegrative shaming' (Braithwaite 1989, 1995)—is that it builds in a series of attempts at compliance as a prelude to prosecution.

WHITE-COLLAR CRIME AS AN INDEX OF SOCIAL CHANGE

Whatever the reasons or justifications for the methods used to control white-collar crime, the ambivalence of the social response to this sort of behaviour is also related to wider social factors which have both objective and subjective dimensions. For Aubert (as well as for writers such as E.A. Ross, who anticipated Sutherland's ideas on this topic) the ambiguity of white-collar crimes reflected the objective fact that they were the index of important transitions in social structure. A good example of this phenomenon is the practice of 'insider trading' on the stock exchange and in other financial institutions, which has only relatively recently come to be penalized in Britain. Even now practioners can have difficulty in drawing the line between legal and illegal conduct (a problem exploited by defence lawyers) and can justify as good business the competitive testing of the limits of legality (Reichman 1992). As Clarke brilliantly puts it: 'It would have perplexed leading members of these institutions up to the end of the 1950s to be told that they were doing anything reprehensible in acting on such information. It was precisely because of the access to such information that one was part of the City, and one was part of the City in the clear expectation of making a considerable amount of money' (Clarke 1990a: 162). The crime of insider trading therefore nicely symbolizes the change from a time when there were only 'insiders' (see also Stanley 1992). The attacks on political corruption in the 1990s are a further example of white-collar crime as an index of changing social structure.

Ambiguity and ambivalence are inevitable results of situations in which previously legal behaviour has only recently been redefined, and this is exacerbated when the boundaries are changed in ways which are to some extent outside the control of the community being regulated. We could also extend Aubert's analysis by saying that social and legal definitions of crime may be out of joint either because public attitudes have not yet caught up with the legal recognition of important economic and social changes, or because the law has not yet recognized the seriousness of behaviour which causes public concern (in both cases these processes will be fanned, resisted, or mediated by interest and pressure groups). As a further complication we should note that economic and legal definitions will not always coincide (insider trading is still seen as economically useful by some economists). Conversely, at any given time there will be some practices which are quite legal but of dubious economic value, a current example being corporate raiding so as to bid up the price of a business and sell on at a profit. It is therefore not always easy to tell when the time has arrived at which certain business practices have lost all economic justification.

In their stimulating work on the savings and loans frauds, Calavita and Pontell discuss the economic justifications of the type of practices which were the subject of prosecutions during and after the period of Reaganite relaxation of economic controls in the 1980s (Calavita and Pontell 1992; Calavita *et al.* 1997). This period saw the breaking down of barriers between banks and other financial institutions, and a great increase in the scale and internationalization of financial transactions. Drawing on the idea of the French economist Allais, they argue that much of what is produced in what he calls the 'casino economy' is of illusory economic benefit. If, for example, it takes only $12 billion of commercial trade to generate $400 billion of foreign exchange transactions, the opportunities for manipulating money are far in excess of the goods to which they correspond. The system is kept going only by trust in the backing of these transactions, but an excess of confidence can equally bring about disaster if it allows the production of 'junk bonds' or helps sustain unsound financial institutions. They point to various characteristic abuses of this period, such as corporate takeovers, currency trading and futures trading, 'land flips', 'daisy chains' and other forms of property speculation, and the switching of loans to confuse auditors regarding actual assets. Emblematic for them was the accumulation of enormous uncollectable loans relying on federal deposit insurance which were at the heart of the massive 'savings and loans' losses.

An interesting question is how far the practices which Calavita and others describe (which they associate with finance capital as opposed to industrial capital) can be controlled severely without putting at risk jobs and economically sound activities. Much of what they describe, shorn of obvious abuses, may point to changes in what makes economic sense in a world where the costs of production increasingly favour countries other than the USA and Western Europe. It should also be noted that the savings and loans fiasco was as much the result of too generous government guarantees to bank investors, as it was of speculation and financial mismanagement. They themselves may be relying on an outdated model of industrial capitalism as the only proper conception of a functioning economy. This said, much white-collar and financial crime grows out of the opportunities to exploit objective changes in organizational forms of business trading (particularly marked in a period of increasing global competition) in ways which the law, especially national laws, are slow to deal with or incapable of catching in time. (See for example, Pearce and Snider 1995; Tombs 1995.) Other crimes are connected to the cycles of boom and bust which seem inherent in global capitalist expansion.

A more subjective source of ambivalence in the social response to white-collar crime is the assumption that there is less public concern about these behaviours—and therefore less support for severe sanctions, than is the case with more familiar street crimes—especially those involving violence (though this may be the result of existing methods of control). A series of studies has therefore sought to demonstrate that the public in fact ranks examples of these crimes quite severely as compared to ordinary crimes (see, e.g., Cullen *et al.* 1983; Green 1990: 47–57). Harsh attitudes towards such conduct, going well beyond the penalties actually meeted out, can be documented in cases of culpable disasters caused by white-collar offenders (Calavita *et al.* 1991). On the other hand, some other attempts to measure public attitudes to white-collar crime do reveal greater leniency in public attitudes (see, e.g., Goff and Nason-Clarke 1989). Much depends on the way questions about different crimes are phrased and the extent to which an effort is made to refer to the possible side-effects of the use of certain sanctions. But even if it were to be shown that there was greater public ambivalence towards white-collar crimes than towards ordinary crimes, writers such as Box would only regard this a further challenge 'to sensitize people to not seeing processes in which they are victimised as disasters or accidents' (Box 1983: 233).

THE COLLATERAL COSTS OF CONTROL

Many of the ambiguities discussed so far point to value conflicts and awkward policy dilemmas which are often cited as explaining, and even justifying, caution in seeking to curb white-collar crime. If risk-taking is really the motor of the capitalist economy then someone has to pay the price of the inevitable failures. The pursuit of greater health and safety (or even of greater bank transparency) has costs in terms of national and international competitiveness and jobs; it is not always easy to juggle competing pressures, and the interests of business and/or employment can be used to try to justify the acceptance of no more than a 'reasonable' level of safety or pollution. In

many areas of business crime enforcers are obliged to choose between going for
punishment (and stigmatization), or else achieving compliance or maximizing the
amount of revenue recovered. Other dilemmas are more particular. If we are worried
about money laundering, does this mean that we want to see banks become a crucial
part of the justice system? What about the rights to privacy and confidentiality (Levi
1991a, 1991b)?

But we should not be too quick to assume that such *post hoc* philosophical
dilemmas or justifications are the actual movers of political action. To explain the
social weight given to these conflicting values we also need to provide a sociology of
public policy choices. Starting from a Marxist perspective, Snider, for example, examines the dialectic between the state, business interests, pressure groups, public opinion
(etc.) in an attempt to explain the contrasting fate of different types of regulation
(Snider 1991; but see also the more hopeful analysis by Braithwaite 1995). She argues
that the resistance to effective implementation of legislation concerning health and
safety at work is explicable in terms of the fact that these laws are not in the interest of
business itself (except where they can be used by large businesses to beat off the
competition of smaller firms). Industry tends—with the collusion of the state—to
balance the safety of workers against the increased costs of production. The victims of
these crimes are diffuse, though not as diffuse as the victims of crimes against the
environment. Anti-trust legislation has more success because the state is interested in
bringing down its costs as a major purchaser from the private sector, and at least parts
of the business world are in favour of such laws. On the other hand, the monopolies
and cartels which already control many major markets provide firm resistance, and, of
less importance, unions may be ambivalent because of the threat to jobs which could
follow the break-up of large conglomerations. Insider trading and stock market fraud,
Snider claims, should encounter least resistance (as the success of the American Securities and Exchange Commission supposedly illustrates) because here the interests of
the state and business coincide. Business needs to be able to raise money on the stock
market, and government does not want to have to bail out defrauded investors. We
will be reminded of the political dimension of these policy dilemmas if we accept that
the control of ordinary crime may also have a number of negative side-effects—on the
offender, his family, and the community—which tend to be ignored when the crucial
criterion of policy choice is reduced to the need to continue business as usual.

The potential of criminology to contribute to shaping public policy concerning the
best way to regulate white-collar crime is likely to increase in importance, but it is
unlikely to be univocal in its recommendations. There will always be a need for
denouncing the 'crimes of the powerful' and their many illegal (as well as semi-legal
and legal) ways of causing harm. But practical experience as well as theoretical considerations would suggest that there are severe difficulties in using the criminal law to
control the groups most powerful within a given society. It is extremely difficult to get
laws passed which represent a real threat to current economic interests. And there is
always the danger that, in given political circumstances, tougher measures may have
counter-productive effects for victims or consumers in general. Yet we should not
assume that treating white-collar crime as crime, or trying to fit it into the usual
paradigm of criminological explanation, necessarily goes hand in hand with the belief

that we must use criminal sanctions to reduce the behaviour. Most of those who offer explanations which refer to capitalism or other structural factors of ordinary business life do, as it happens, also want to criminalize the offender (see, e.g., Box 1983). But there are many precedents for criminological explanations which do not indicate the individual offender as the key causal factor or the appropriate point of intervention (e.g., 'blocked opportunity' theories of juvenile delinquency). As Albert Cohen has argued, a sociological focus on crime in organizations may need to avoid seeking to assign blame in identifying the important links relevant to organizational outcomes (Cohen 1977). When and whether it is right or politic for law to attach criminal penalties to certain behaviours, and to seek to enforce such penalties even when this misses the underlying causes of such behaviour, is a question which goes beyond the scope of criminology. But it is certainly not a question confined to white-collar crimes, neither is it irrelevant to many more ordinary ones.

Selected further reading

An essential starting point for studying what was originally meant by the label of white-collar crime remains Edwin H. Sutherland, *White-collar Crime: The Uncut Version* (New Haven: Yale University Press, 1983). Useful overviews of the field include Steven Box, *Power, Crime and Mystification* (London: Tavistock, 1983); Michael Clarke, *Business Crime: It's Nature and Control* (Oxford: Polity Press, 1990); Hazel Croall, *White-collar Crime* (Milton Keynes: Open University Press, 1994); David Nelken (ed.) *White-collar Crime* (Aldershot; Dartmouth, 1994); David O. Friedrichs, *Trusted Criminals: White-collar Criminals in Contemporary Society* (Belmont: Wadsworth, 1996); and Gary Slapper and Steve Tombs, *Corporate Crime* (Harlow: Longman, 1999). The organization of the Slapper and Tombs volume—the most comprehensive recent UK text—roughly follows the expository order of this chapter. But the authors take a resolutely Marxist approach which links white-collar crime to the imperatives of capitalist social structure; and at the same time also wish to remove any ambiguity from the (capitalist) legal response to such behaviour. More detailed (mainly USA) case studies can be sampled in Kip Schlegel and David Weisburd (eds) *White-Collar Crime Reconsidered* (Boston: Northeastern University Press, 1992) and Michael Tonry and Albert Reiss Jnr (eds) *Beyond the Law: Crime in Complex Organizations* (Chicago: University of Chicago Press, 1993) and Maurice Punch, *Dirty Business: Exploring Corporate Misconduct* (London: Sage, 1996). On the response to the sort of white-collar crime which gets dealt with by the ordinary courts in Britain the best work is that by Mike Levi, *Regulating Fraud* (London: Tavistock, 1987) and Mike Levi and Andrew Pithouse, *Victims of White-Collar Crime* (Oxford: Oxford University Press forthcoming). An original and controversial approach to the increasingly important problem of the overlap between white-collar and organized crime is Vincenzo Ruggiero, *Organised Crime and Corporate Crime in Europe* (Aldershot: Dartmouth, 1996).

References

ARLACHI, P. (1985), *Mafia Business*, Oxford: Oxford University Press.

AUBERT, V. (1952), 'White-collar Crime and Social Structure' *American Journal of Sociology*, 58: 263–71.

BLOCK, A. (1991), *Perspectives on Organising Crime*, Boston/London: Kluwer.

BOX, S. (1983), *Power, Crime and Mystification*, London: Tavistock.

BRAITHWAITE, J. (1984), *Corporate Crime in the Pharmaceutical Industry*, London: Routledge and Kegan Paul.

—— (1985), 'White-collar crime', *Annual Review of Sociology*, 11: 1–25.

—— (1989), *Crime, Shame and Integration*, Cambridge: Cambridge University Press.

—— (1995), 'Corporate Crime and Republican Criminological Praxis', in F. Pearce and L. Snider (eds), *Corporate Crime*, 48–72, Toronto: University of Toronto Press.

BURGESS, E. (1950), 'Comment to Hartung', *American Journal of Sociology* 56: 25–34.

CALAVITA, K. *et al.* (1991), 'Dam Disasters and Durkheim', *International Journal of the Sociology of Law*, 19: 407–27.

—— and PONTELL, H. (1992), 'The Savings and Loans Crisis', in M. Erdmann and R. Lundman (eds) *Corporate and Governmental Deviance*, Oxford: Oxford University Press.

——, —— and TILLMAN, R. (1997), *Big Money Crime*, Berkeley: University of California Press.

CARSON, W.G. (1970), 'White-collar Crime and the Enforcement of Factory Legislation', *British Journal of Criminology*, 10: 383–98

—— (1974), 'Symbolic and instrumental dimensions of early factory legislation', in R. Hood (ed.) *Crime, Criminology and Public Policy*, 107–38, London: Heinemann.

—— (1980), 'The Institutionalisation of Ambiguity: The Early British Factory Acts', in G. Geis and E. Stotland (eds) *White-collar Crime: Theory and Research*, 142–73, London and New York: Sage.

—— (1981), *The Other Price of Britain's Oil*, Oxford: Martin Robertson.

COHEN, A.K. (1977), 'The Concept of Criminal Organisation', *British Journal of Criminology* 18: 97–111.

CLARKE, M. (1990a), *Business Crime: It's Nature and Control*, Oxford: Polity Press.

—— (1990b), 'The Control of Insurance Fraud: A Comparative View', *British Journal of Criminology*, 30: 1–23.

CLINARD, M., and YEAGER, P. (1980), *Corporate Crime*, New York: Free Press.

COLEMAN, J.W. (1985), *The Criminal Elite: The Sociology of White-Collar Crime*, New York: St Martins Press.

—— (1987), 'Toward an Integrated Theory of White-collar Crime', *American Journal of Sociology*, 93/2: 406–39.

—— (1992), 'The Asymmetric Society', in M. Erdmann and R. Lundman (eds) *Corporate and Governmental Deviance*, 95, Oxford: Oxford University Press.

COOK, D. (1989), *Rich Law, Poor Law*, Milton Keynes: Open University Press.

COSSON, J. (1978), *Les Industriels de la Fraude Fiscale*, Paris: Editions du Seuil.

CROALL, H. (1989), 'Who is the white-collar criminal?', *British Journal of Criminology*, 29: 157–74.

CULLEN, F. *et al.* (1983), 'Public Support for Punishing White-Collar Criminals', *Journal of Criminal Justice*, 11: 481–93.

DELMAS-MARTY, M. (1990), *Droit Pénal des Affaires*, Paris: Presses Universitaires de France.

DOWIE, M. (1988) 'Pinto Madness', in Stuart L. Hills (ed.) *Corporate Violence: Injury and Death for Profit*, Totowa, New Jersey: Rowman and Littlefield.

ECONOMIST (1992), 'The Blue Arrow Affair', 7 March: 23.

EDELHERTZ, H. (1970), *The Nature, Impact and Prosecution of White-Collar Crime*, Washington DC: US government Printing Press.

FISSE, B., and BRAITHWAITE, J. (1985), *The Impact of Publicity on Corporate Offenders*, Albany, NY: State University of New York Press.

FRIEDRICHS, D. (1996), *Trusted Criminals: White-collar Criminals in Contempory Society*, Belmont: Wadsworth.

GAMBETTA, D. (1994), *The Sicilian Mafia: An Industry of Private Protection*: Oxford: Oxford University Press.

GEIS, G. (1968), 'The Heavy Electrical Equipment Anti-Trust Cases of 1961', in G. Geis (ed.), *White-Collar Crime*, New York: Atherton Press.

GOFF, C., and NASON-CLARKE, N. (1989), 'The Seriousness of Crime in Fredericton, New Brunswick: Perceptions toward White-collar Crime', *Canadian Journal of Criminology*, 31: 19–34.

GOTTFREDSON, M., and HIRSCHI, T. (1990), *A General Theory of Crime*, Stanford, Cal.: Stanford University Press.

GREEN, G.S. (1990), *Occupational Crime*, Chicago: Nelson Hall.

GROSS, E. (1980), 'Organisational Structure and Organisational Crime', in G. Geis and E. Stotland (eds) *White-Collar Crime: Theory and Research*, New York: Sage.

GROVES,W.B., and NEWMAN, G. (eds) (1986), *Punishment and Privilege*, Albany, NY: Harrow and Heston.

HAINES, F. (1997), *Corporate Regulation: Beyond Punish or Persuade*, Oxford: Clarendon Press.

HARTUNG, F. (1950), 'White-collar Offences in the Wholesale Meat Industry in Detroit', *American Journal of Sociology*, 56: 25–34.

HAWKINS, K. (1984), *Environment and Enforcement: Regulation and the Social Definition of Pollution*, Oxford: Clarendon Press.

—— (1990), 'Compliance Strategy, Prosecution Policy and Aunt Sally: A Comment on Pearce and Tombs', *British Journal of Criminology*, 30: 444–66.

—— (1991), 'Enforcing Regulation: More of the same from Pearce and Tombs', *British Journal of Criminology*, 31: 427–30.

—— and THOMAS, J.M. (eds) (1984), *Enforcing Regulation*, Boston/ London: Kluwer.

HILLS, S.L. (ed.) (1988), *Corporate Violence: Injury and Death for Profit*, Totowa, NJ: Rowman and Littlefield.

HIRSCHI, T., and GOTTFREDSON, M. (1987), 'Causes of White-Collar Crime', *Criminology*, 25: 949–74.

—— and —— (1989), ' The Significance of White-Collar Crime for a General Theory of Crime', *Criminology*, 27: 359–72.

HUTTER, B. (1988), *The Reasonable Arm of the Law?* Oxford: Clarendon Press.

—— (1997), *Compliance: Regulation and the Environment*, Oxford: Clarendon Press.

KATZ, J. (1980), 'The Social Movement Against White-collar Crime', *Criminology Review Yearbook*: 161–84.

KELMAN, S. (1981), 'Substantive interpretation in the criminal law', 33 *Stanford Law Review*, 33: 591–673.

KRAMER, R.C. (1992), 'The Space Shuttle *Challenger* Explosion: A Case Study of State–Corporate Crime', in K. Schlegel and D. Weisburd, *White-Collar Crime Reconsidered*, 214–43, Boston: Northeastern University Press.

LANE, R. (1953), 'Why Businessmen Violate the Law', *Journal of Criminal Law, Criminology and Police Science* 44: 151–65.

LEONARD, W.N., and WEBER, M.G. (1970), 'Automakers and Dealers: A Study of Criminogenic Market Forces', *Law and Society Review*, 4: 407–24.

LEVI, M. (1981), *The Phantom Capitalists*, London: Gower Press.

—— (1985), 'A Criminological and Sociological Approach to Theories of and Research into Economic Crime', in D. Magnuson (ed.) *Economic Crime—Programs for Future Research*, Report No. 18: 32–72, Stockholm: National Council for Crime Prevention, Sweden.

—— (1987), *Regulating Fraud*, London: Tavistock.

—— (1991a), 'Pecunia Non Olet: Cleansing the Money Launderers from the Temple', in *Crime, Law and Social Change*, 16: 217–302.

—— (1991b), 'Regulating Money Laundering', *British Journal of Criminology* 31: 109–25.

—— (1991c), 'Fraudulent Justice? Sentencing the Business Criminal', in P. Carlen and D. Cook (eds), *Paying for Crime*, 86–108, Milton Keynes: Open University Press.

—— and NELKEN, D. (eds) (1996), *The Corruption of Politics and the Politics of Corruption*, special issue of the *Journal of Law and Society*, 23: 1.

—— and PITHOUSE, A. (forthcoming), *Victims of White-Collar Crime*, Oxford: Oxford University Press.

McBARNET, D. (1991) 'Whiter than White-collar Crime: Tax, Fraud Insurance and the Management of Stigma', *British Journal of Sociology*, 42: 323–44.

—— and WHELAN, C. (1999), *The One Eyed Javeline-Thrower*, London: Wiley.

MAGNUSSON, D. (ed.) (1985), *Economic Crime—Programs for Future Research*, Report No 18, Stockholm: National Council for Crime Prevention, Sweden.

MANN, M. (1985), *Defending White-collar Crime*, New Haven: Yale University Press.

NEEDLEMAN, M.L., and NEEDLEMAN, C. (1979), 'Organizational Crime: Two models of Crimogenisis', *Sociological Quarterly*, 20: 517–28.

NELKEN, D. (1983), *The Limits of the Legal Process: A Study of Landlords, Law and Crime*, London; Academic Press.

—— (1991), 'Why Punish ?', *Modern Law Review*, 53: 829–34.

—— (1994a), 'Whom can you Trust? The Future of

Comparative Criminology', in D. Nelken (ed.) *The Futures of Criminology*, 220–44, London; Sage.

—— (1994b), 'White-Collar Crime', in M. Maguire, R. Morgan and R. Reiner, (eds) *Oxford Handbook of Criminology*, 1st edn, 355–93, Oxford; Oxford University Press.

—— (ed.) (1994c), *White-collar Crime*, Aldershot: Dartmouth.

—— and LEVI, M. (1996), 'Introduction' to *The Corruption of Politics and the Politics of Corruption*, special issue of the *Journal of Law and Society*, 23/1: 1–17.

——(1997a), 'The Globalisation of Criminal Justice', in M. Freeman (ed.) *Law and Opinion at the End of the Century*, 251–79, Oxford; Oxford University Press.

—— (1997b), 'White-Collar Crime', in M. Maguire, R. Morgan, and R. Reiner (eds) *Oxford Handbook of Criminology*, 2nd edn, 891–924, Oxford.

—— (2000), 'Telling Difference', in D. Nelken (ed.) *Contrasting Criminal Justice*, 233–64, Aldershot: Dartmouth.

—— (2002), 'Corruption in the European Union', in M. Bull and J. Newell (eds), *Corruption and Scandal in Contemporary Politics*, London: Macmillan.

NEW YORK STATE ORGANIZED CRIME TASK FORCE (1988), *Corruption and Racketeering in the New York City Construction Industry*, New York; Cornell University Press.

PASSAS, N. (1990), 'Anomie and Corporate Deviance', *Contemporary Crises*, 14: 157–78.

—— and NELKEN, D. (1993), 'The thin line between legitimate and criminal enterprises: subsidy frauds in the European Community', in *Crime, Law and Social Change*, 19: 223–43.

PEARCE, F. (1976), *Crimes of the Powerful: Marxism, Crime and Deviance*, London: Pluto.

—— and TOMBS, S. (1990), 'Ideology, Hegemony and Empiricism: Compliance Theories of Regulation', *British Journal of Criminology*, 30: 423–43.

—— and —— (1991), 'Policing Corporate "Skid Rows"', *British Journal of Criminology*, 31: 415–26.

—— and SNIDER, L. (1995), 'Regulating Capitalism', in F. Pearce and L. Snider (eds) *Corporate Crime*, 19–48, Toronto: University of Toronto Press.

PONTELL, H.N., and CALAVITA, K. (1993), 'The Savings and Loan Industry', in M. Tonry and A. Reiss Jnr (eds), *Beyond the Law: Crime in Complex Organizations*, 203–47, Chicago: University of Chicago Press.

PORTNOY, F. (1997), *F.I.A.S.C.O: Blood in the Water on Wall Street*, London: Profile Books.

PUNCH, M. (1996), *Dirty Business: Exploring Corporate Misconduct*, London; Sage.

REICHMAN, N. (1992), 'Moving Backstage: Uncovering the Role of Compliance Practices in Shaping Regulatory Practices', in K. Schlegel and D. Weisburd, *White-Collar Crime Reconsidered*, 244–68, Boston; Northeastern University Press.

ROSOFF, S.M., PONTELL, H.N., and TILLMAN, R. (1998), *Profit Without Honour: White Collar Crime and the Looting of America*, Upper Saddle River, NJ: Prentice Hall.

RUGGIERO, V. (1996), *Organised Crime and Corporate Crime in Europe*, Aldershot: Dartmouth.

ROYAL COMMISSION ON CRIMINAL PROCEDURE (1980), *Prosecutions by Private Individuals and Non-Police Agencies*, Research Study No. 10, London: HMSO.

SAVELSBERG, J. (1994), *Constructing White-Collar Crime: Rationalities, Communication, Power*, Philadelphia, Pa: University of Pennsylvania Press.

SHAPIRO, S. (1984), *Wayward Capitalists*, New Haven: Yale University Press.

—— (1989), 'Collaring the Crime, not the Criminal: Reconsidering "White-Collar Crime"', *American Sociological Review*, 55: 346–65

SIMPSON, S.S. (1992), 'Corporate Crime Deterrence and Corporate Control Policies, Views from the Inside', in K. Schlegel and D. Weisburd, *White-Collar Crime Reconsidered*, 289–308, Boston: Northeastern University Press.

SLAPPER, G. (1999), *Blood in the Bank*, Aldershot: Dartmouth.

—— and TOMBS, S. (1999), *Corporate Crime*, Harlow: Longman.

SMITH, D.J. Jnr (1980), 'Paragons, Pariahs and Pirates: A Spectrum-Based Theory of Enterprise', *Crime and Delinquency* 26: 358–86.

SNIDER, L. (1991), 'The Regulatory Dance: Understanding Reform Processes in Corporate Crime', *International Journal of the Sociology of Law*, 19: 209–36.

SPALEK, P. (2001), 'Policing the UK Financial System: The Creation of the New Financial Services Authority and its Approach to Regulation', *International Journal of the Sociology of Law*, 29/1: 75–88.

STANLEY, C. (1992), 'Serious Money: Legitimation

of Deviancy in the Financial Markets', in *International Journal of the Sociology of Law*, 20: 43–60.

STEFFENSMEIER, D. (1989), 'On the Causes of White-collar Crime: An Assessment of Hirschi and Gottfredson's Claims', *Criminology* 27: 345–58.

STONE, C. (1975), *Where the Law Ends: The Social Control of Corporate Behaviour*, New York: Harper and Row.

SUTHERLAND, E.H. (1949), *White-collar Crime*, New York: Holt, Rinehart and Winston.

—— (1983), *White-collar Crime: the Uncut Version*, New Haven: Yale University Press.

SZASZ, D. (1986), 'Corporations, Organised Crime and the Disposal of Hazardous Waste: An Examination of the Making of a Criminogenic Regulatory Structure', *Criminology* 24: 1–27.

TAPPAN, P. (1947), 'Who is the Criminal?', *American Sociological Review*, 12: 96–102.

TIEDEMANN, K. (1974), 'Kriminologische und Kriminalistiche Aspekte der Subventionseschtei-chung', in H. Schafer (ed.), *Grundlagen der Kriminalistik, 13/1: Wirtschaftskriminalitat, Weissen-Kragen Kriminalitat*, Hamburg: Steinton.

TOMBS, S. (1995), 'Corporate Crime and new Organizational Forms', in F. Pearce and L. Snider (eds), *Corporate Crime*, 132–47, Toronto: University of Toronto Press.

VAN DUYNE, P. (1993), 'Organised Crime and Business Crime Enterprises in the Netherlands', in *Crime, Law and Social Change*, 19: 103–43.

VAUGHAN, D.E. (1983), *Controlling Unlawful Organizational Behaviour*, Chicago: University of Chicago Press.

—— (1996), *The Challenger Launch Decision*, Chicago: University of Chicago Press.

WEISBURD, D., WHEELER, S., WARING, E., and BODE, N. (1991), *Crimes of the Middle Classes: White-collar Offenders in the Federal Courts*, New Haven: Yale University Press.

—— and WARING, E.J. (2001), *White Collar Crime and Criminal Careers*, Cambridge: Cambridge University Press.

WELLS, C. (1993), *Corporations and Criminal Responsibility*, Oxford: Clarendon Press.

WHEELER S. (1992), 'The Problem of White-Collar Crime Motivation', in K. Schlegel and D. Weisburd, *White-Collar Crime Reconsidered*, 108–24, Boston: Northeastern University Press.

——, MANN, K., and SARAT, A. (1988), *Sitting in Judgement: The Sentencing of White-Collar Crimes*, New Haven: Yale University Press.

WRIGHT-MILLS, C. (1943/1963), 'The Professional Ideology of Social Pathologists', in C. Wright-Mills, *Power, Politics and People*, 525–52, New York: Oxford University Press.

YEAGER, P.C. (1991), *The Limits of Law: The Public Regulation of Private Pollution*, Cambridge: Cambridge University Press.

—— (1995), 'Management, Morality and Law, Organizational Forms and Ethical Deliberations', in F. Pearce and L. Snider (eds.), *Corporate Crime*, 147–68, Toronto: University of Toronto Press.

YOUNG, T.R. (1981), 'Corporate Crime: A Critique of the Clinard Report', *Contemporary Crises*, 5: 323–36.

ZIGLER, J. (1990), *La Suisse Lave Plus Blanc*, Amsterdam: Uitgeverij Balanss.

ZIMRING, F., and HAWKINS, G. (1993), 'Crime, Justice and the Savings and Loans Crisis', in M. Tonry and A. Reiss Jnr (eds), *Beyond the Law: Crime in Complex Organizations*, 247–92, Chicago: University of Chicago Press.

24

THE ORGANIZATION OF SERIOUS CRIMES

Michael Levi

INTRODUCTION

'Organized crime' has been a significant part of the popular discourse of American politicians and film-viewers since the 1920s, but it extended to European (and indeed global) politicians and police in the course of the 1990s and beyond (see, for example the United Nations Convention on Transnational Organized Crime 2000; Ruggiero 2000a; Sheptycki 2000). The aim of this chapter is to place both the organization of crimes—an intentional plural since the crimes are so diverse—and 'organized crime control' in perspective, and to guide readers through the competing accounts of 'the evidence'. I shall focus primarily on European, particularly British, research and thinking rather than on the more extensive American literature (or on the far less extensive and geographically patchy American research).[1] However, given that—as with legitimate products—many products (from drugs to counterfeit CDs) supplied by 'organized criminals' are grown and/or manufactured in far-distant parts of the world, it is difficult to sustain the nation state as a meaningful bounded unit of analysis for understanding the organized crime issue as a whole, even though most individuals involved in drug dealing, extortion, credit card fraud, armed robberies, sex work, etc. may not do any international business as part of their daily routines. This cross-border dimension—including complex multinational pressures for manpower movement and trade liberalization across national borders (Friman and Andreas 1999; Andreas 2000; Naylor 2002; Berdal and Serrano, forthcoming)—is what makes both organized crime and white-collar crime different from other crimes. It is hard to avoid discussing 'organized crime' as if it were a coherent common noun describing a well-understood set of arrangements to commit crime: this term indeed is part of the problem for critics. Precisely what is one attacking or defending? Is it the notion of a hierarchical organization dominating global activity (by analogy with Microsoft), or a set of giant firms competing but acting more or less in tandem (like the oil industry)? Or, as we will go on to see, are the arrangements to supply illegal goods and services

---

[1] I have tried not to overload this chapter with references, and apologize to colleagues who may reasonably consider that their work deserves inclusion. Those in search of more extensive organized crime bibliographies may find excellent ones in www.jus.unitn.it/transcrime and www.yorku.ca/nathanson/default.htm.

and to commit crimes for gain more like a network; in which case, why should we call 'it' 'organized crime'?

Definitional ambiguities do not seem to inhibit confident statements about the 'scale of the problem', which is always asserted to be 'growing' and often said to be using hi-tech methods, as if crossing borders by plane, motor vehicle, digital phone, or computer were not also done by businesspeople, professionals, and the general population, probably in greater proportions than criminals at work do. For example, given that *all* inter-bank transfers are transmitted by electronic means, it would be strange if that proportion of criminal money that is saved were *not* sent electronically; and though it is a fair point that the contents of the accounts can be transferred offshore by the time the police discover their existence and try to freeze them, precisely the same could be said since the invention of the telegraph, which enabled funds to be transferred trans-continentally in seconds rather than by steamship (Levi and Naylor 2000)! Using the crassest techniques, and ignoring the crucial question of how much criminals save from crime, huge figures are given for the volume of money laundering as if the patina of decimal point statistics or the use of a mathematical range made the guesses more scientific. Cleverer bureaucrats will cite authoritative institutions (as 'primary definers' of reality) such as the Financial Action Task Force (FATF), the UN, or the International Monetary Fund (IMF), to add credibility and to insulate themselves from responsibility for the 'data'. Thus, the FATF homepage (**www1.oecd/ fatf.com**) is telling us that it is dealing with a massive problem when it states, in 2001:

The International Monetary Fund, for example, has stated that the aggregate size of money laundering in the world could be somewhere between two and five per cent of the world's gross domestic product.

Using 1996 statistics, these percentages would indicate that money laundering ranged between US Dollar (USD) 590 billion and USD 1.5 trillion. The lower figure is roughly equivalent to the value of the total output of an economy the size of Spain.

This review will *not* argue either that organized crime is insignificant or that money laundering is small; but it is as well to take into account the huge sensationalist element in modern media treatment of these issues and, above all, that our images of organized crime are socially constructed, often relying on police images that themselves depend on the way in which intelligence and enforcement are organized and on more pervasive social mythologies about what sort of persons and what sort of behaviour constitute a 'threat to society'.[2] Suffice it to state here that to estimate how much money 'organized crime' launders from *market* offences, one must calculate how much drugs trafficking and sales and how much other vice there is, how much top criminals save (rather than spend on luxurious lifestyles and on bribes to law

---

[2] Sometimes, those policing agencies may underestimate the connections between criminals by failing to develop intelligence leads on networks. The methodology for assessing harm is usually implicit and inevitably has a subjective component. Furthermore, given the $40 billion or so collapse (despite bankrolling a large percentage of American congressmen) at the end of 2001 of the once seventh largest American corporation, Enron, accompanied by revelations of serious financial misstatements and shredding of documents by auditors Arthur Andersen, which plunged the unfortunate company pensionholders into penury while some directors offloaded their shares at a huge profit, it is tempting to ask which organized crime groups are doing more harm than Enron did.

enforcement personnel and politicians), and also what is a sensible threshold for understanding how much of these sales of illegal goods and services are 'organized' according to whatever definition of this exists in a given society, discussed below.

In this chapter, we will critically discuss legal and operational definitions of organized crime, and suggest more meaningful ways of thinking about them: how criminals organise themselves and how criminal markets work; how organized crime is controlled, not just by the police and customs authorities but also by a range of regulatory agencies and private sector firms; and finish with an appreciation of the importance of understanding the interrelationship between these crime control—criminal justice and prevention—methods and the ways in which criminals get together to commit serious crimes.

DEFINING ORGANIZED CRIME

ANALYTICAL ISSUES

In the US and in popular discourse, 'organized crime' is generally applied to describe a group of people who act together on a long-term basis to commit crimes for gain using the threat of violence: this is nicely encapsulated in *The Godfather* and *The Sopranos*, the former being a more macro and grandiose version than the latter, which is rooted much more in locale and more limited in ambition. Maltz (1976) proposed that 'organized crime' was identifiable by means of a list of distinguishing features, of which four were considered essential characteristics: violence; corruption; continuity; and variety in types of crime engaged in. However, though it might make sense to distinguish professional criminals from organized ones—the former by their skills; the latter by predatory power, including that over fellow criminals—there may be nothing at all disorganized about professional transnational financial criminals whose careers involve major frauds: they may find it simply convenient to side-step both (i) the moral panic and policing/intelligence resources surrounding organized crime, and (ii) the predatory and often ill-disciplined attentions of psychopathic gangsters, such as the Krays and Richardsons during the 1960s (Levi 1981).[3] Yet the term 'organized crime' is applied to denote not just a set of criminal *actors* but also a set of criminal *activities* (Cohen 1977): nowadays, these activities would include drugs trafficking; trafficking in people; extortion; kidnapping for profit; illegal toxic waste dumping (environmental crime); sophisticated credit card fraud; fraud against the European Union (EU); smuggling to evade excise tax on alcohol and tobacco; intellectual

---

[3] There may be other reasons for seeking to distinguish the sets of acts and actors, for example to diminish the spread of extraordinary powers used against organized crime to other areas of criminal law. However, it may not always work this way. Levi (1993) has pointed to the paradox in the way that tough investigative powers to discover the causes of corporate abuse or to retrieve assets for creditors can lead to fewer rights for those few white-collar 'offenders' who face criminal trials, though this differential is diminishing as the European Convention on Human Rights begins to generate procedural equivalence, even in Britain post-Human Rights Act. The attempts—albeit finally unsuccessfully—of the Guinness Four to get their convictions quashed are a case in point.

copyright theft (video and audio piracy and product counterfeiting); corruption to achieve these offences, etc.[4]

Cressey (1969), using the surveillance tapes and interviews with Joseph 'the Canary that Sang' Valachi, set out the official version of Italian-American Mafia as a line management, vertically integrated, and horizontally coordinated organization (though it was never clear how widely crime groups' 'license to operate' charges extended to burglaries, robberies, credit card frauds, etc.). However, few academics have been convinced by the Valachi Boss-Underboss-Soldier model as a portrait of organized crime in America. Although Jacobs *et al.* (1994) put up a spirited defence that LCN (La Cosa Nostra) organized crime families do exist in cities like New York (as confirmed by wiretap evidence as well as informants), analysts such as Reuter (1983), Reuter and Rubinstein (1978), and Smith (1980) have criticized heavily the general use of the term 'organized crime' on the grounds that it falsely implies a discontinuity between the 'organized criminal' and other criminals, and between organized criminals and the state, whereas studies of criminal markets and drugs/vice pricing data suggest otherwise. Work done in Italy and the United States particularly emphasizes the coalition between businesspeople, politicians, and crime groups in organizing crime against the public interest (Block and Chambliss 1981; Paoli 2002; Stille 1996; Woodiwiss 2001). However, this symbiotic model ignores the often unwanted parasitical and predatory crimes committed *against* business by crime groups, in which businesspeople get locked into a system of paying both to obtain services and contracts and to avoid active harm from regulators and enforcement personnel.

Moreover, one cannot assume that this coalition/conspiracy model applies everywhere: where it does not, organized crime is unlikely to flourish. Why, after all, should an organizational model of crime that applies to parts of Italy in some historical periods apply either to the north-eastern US or to the entire US; and even if it accurately depicts crime there, why should it apply throughout, or indeed in any part of, the UK, Germany, or Canada (Beare 1996)? (See Mack and Kerner 1975 for some early European scepticism on this point; and Hobbs 1997, 2001 for a view of 'the Firm' as rooted in and then uprooted from its English class and local environment that could not be more different from the Cressey model.) Even in Italy, there is a general consensus that while criminal organizations do exist, Mafia is more a method of patron/client relationships and extortion than it is a specific body 'in charge' of all serious criminality: see Arlacchi (1986, 1998); Gambetta (1994); Paoli (2002). Nevertheless, such critiques do not seem to have dented media or policy-makers' enthusiasms either for the term or for action against 'it', and this fear (or enthusiasm) has led to *legal* definitions that generate the boundaries of punishment both within nation states and, increasingly, outside them, as 'organized crime' becomes defined as a transnational threat requiring transnational action. This is important, because to the

---

[4] Politicians find it difficult to resist adding to the list of competencies of agencies charged with organized crime control. Following feminist, human rights, and media campaigns, trafficking of women rose to a high priority in the US and UN and, to a perhaps lesser extent, the EU. There are real concerns about whether some of this was just economic migration, despite low wage rates in host countries and the fact that many become sex workers and therefore part of the quasi-consensual crime market. Many may migrate voluntarily, but what proportion of them are then forced to work 'exploitatively' and by violence rather than from lack of job prospects for illegal immigrants is much disputed.

extent that organized criminals represent a set of people who are 'really dangerous' to the essential integrity of the state, and who trigger (especially in continental European legal systems) special investigative powers because of this threat, it would be helpful to know how special are their threats and what they constitute.

LEGAL DEFINITIONS

In domestic and international legal definitions, which bind countries to action, there is often a tension between (a) those who want the legislation to cover a wide set of circumstances to avoid the risk that any major criminal might 'get away with it', and (b) those who want the law to be quite tightly drawn to avoid the overreach of powers which might otherwise criminalize groups who are only a modest threat. This may be witnessed in the EU definitions (in the Joint Action of 1998) and in the UN Transnational Organized Crime Convention 2000, signed in Palermo after lengthy negotiation.

EU definitions of organized crime

In the EU, eleven characteristics of criminal organization—some core, others optional—are associated with the label of 'organized crime'. The EU definition (Adamoli *et al.* 1998: 8–9; Europol and the European Commission 2001: 42)—used not only for policy, but also for the annual reports on organized crime presented to the European Parliament—requires the presence of a minimum of six characteristics. The first four are mandatory criteria:

1. collaboration among more than two people;
2. extending over a prolonged or indefinite period (referring to stability and (potential) durability);
3. suspected of committing serious criminal offences, punishable by imprisonment for at least four years or a more serious penalty; and
4. the central goal of profit and/or power.

The remaining two (or more) must be drawn from the following optional criteria:

5. specialized division of labour among participants;
6. exercising measures of discipline and control;
7. employing violence or other means of intimidation;
8. employing commercial or business-like structures;
9. participating in money-laundering;
10. operational across national borders;
11. exerting influence over legitimate social institutions (polity, government, justice, economy).

It may be seen immediately that the optional criteria are easy to satisfy: what kinds of major profitable crimes do *not* entail money-laundering or some degree of specialization between participants (driving cars or trucks; visiting purchasers of stolen goods or illicit services; going to the bank)? Within the EU definition, provided that they work over a prolonged period of time—however long that is—'organized crime' can mean anything from major Italian syndicates in sharp suits or peasant garb, to three very menacing burglars with a window-cleaning business who differentiate by having one as look-out, another as burglar, and a third as money-launderer, and who sue every newspaper who suggests that their business is disreputable! Note, however, that the threat or commission of violence—seen as a necessary condition by Maltz (1976)—is merely an *optional* criterion for the EU. This at least opens the possibility of white-collar criminals also being organized criminals, though if one is pulling off multi-million Euro scams, how often does one have to commit crimes?[5]

US organized crime legislation

Congress enacted the Racketeer-Influence Corrupt Organizations Act (RICO) as Title IX of the Organized Crime Control Act of 1970 (Pub. L. 91–452, 84 Stat. 922), for the purpose of 'seek[ing] the eradication of organized crime in the United States' (at 923). Such crime was considered to be proliferating, and weakening the economy through undermining legitimate business. The available legislation at the time was considered to be too limited in scope and impact, so an offence that captured a sense of scale and continuity was developed that would be hard to avoid. A central unit in the US Department of Justice tries to ensure that the laws are not used against trivial gang activity, but they are used extensively against urban gangs who extort money and deal in drugs but fall well short of 'the Mafia'. RICO has been a model for diverse countries, including Canada and New Zealand. (See Jacobs 1999; Levi and Smith forthcoming.)

RICO has been used in most major American organized crime prosecutions since 1981. It is best seen as part of an array of techniques, including telephone tapping, official plea bargaining, structured sentence guidelines, and witness protection programmes, all aimed at dealing with criminal enterprise as a system rather than simply at incapacitating individuals.

The aim is to penalize persons who engage in a 'pattern of racketeering activity' or 'collection of an unlawful debt' that has a specified relationship to an 'enterprise'. A 'pattern' consists of two or more predicate offences from a list including extortion, theft, drugs, mail fraud, and securities fraud within a statutorily defined period. 'Enterprise' is defined to include any individual, partnership, corporate entity, and *any group of individuals associated in fact although not a legal entity*. This includes wholly illegal as well as legal businesses. Given the fluid nature of criminal associations, the definition of the term 'enterprise' can be a shifting one.

The prosecutor may allege within one RICO conspiracy numerous predicates against an individual defendant at different times, and perhaps in collaboration with different defendants. For that defendant to be convicted, at least two of those predicates need to be proven to the jury's satisfaction. The prosecution can introduce

---

[5] The lust for money and excitement fits slightly uncomfortably with notions of the 'rational criminal' developed by Cornish (1994), but rationality may apply more to the means than the ends of crime. This will be examined further at the end of this chapter.

a picture of a long term group engaged in perhaps a variety of criminal acts—some violent, some consensual, some predatory, and some involving fraud—perhaps related only by their connection with group members.

UN transnational organized crime convention

Similar flexibility is shown by the UN Transnational Organized Crime Convention. Article 2 of the Convention states:

(a) 'Organized criminal group' shall mean a structured group of three or more persons, existing for a period of time and acting in concert with the aim of committing one or more serious crimes or offences established in accordance with this Convention, in order to obtain, directly or indirectly, a financial or other material benefit;

(b) 'Serious crime' shall mean conduct constituting an offence punishable by a maximum deprivation of liberty of at least four years or a more serious penalty;

(c) 'Structured group' shall mean a group that is not randomly formed for the immediate commission of an offence and that does not need to have formally defined roles for its members, continuity of its membership or a developed structure;

The separate interpretative notes show the all-encompassing nature of the last term when they state that 'the term 'structured group' is to be used in a broad sense so as to include both groups with hierarchical or other elaborate structure and non-hierarchical groups where the roles of the members of the group need not be formally defined'.

To explain the need for an *international* instrument, the United Nations focuses on the need to regulate the *form* of crime as a global threat. Article 3(2) states that an offence is transnational in nature if:

(a) It is committed in more than one State;

(b) It is committed in one State but a substantial part of its preparation, planning, direction or control takes place in another State;

(c) It is committed in one State but involves an organized criminal group that engages in criminal activities in more than one State; or

(d) It is committed in one State but has substantial effects in another State.

By these criteria, for example, a group (of, say, Chinese or East European origin) which engages in 'skimming' credit card details with a small and inexpensive piece of software, and re-encoding them on to plastic cards to be used in another country, qualifies as a transnational organized crime group. Almost all drugs and fraud money-laundering, beyond simple self-laundering by placing funds in a local bank account, also qualifies. The scale of transnational financial crime correspondingly is very large.

RECONCEPTUALIZING ORGANIZED CRIME AS ENTERPRISE CRIME

The nature of 'organized crime' remains deeply contested terrain, at least in academic circles and in those countries who are worried about loss of civil liberties and foreign intrusion, and who demand more than merely rhetorical justification for repressive and surveillance measures. Analysing and dealing with 'organized crime' as both crimes and national security threats requires attention both to national and inter-national components. It is helpful to think of the tasks that need to be performed to commit serious crimes over a long period:

1. Obtain finance for crime.

2. Find people willing to commit crimes (though this may not always be necessary).

3. Obtain equipment and transportation necessary to commit the crimes.

4. Convert, where necessary, products of crime into money or other usable assets.

5. Find people and places able to store proceeds (and perhaps transmit and conceal their origin).

6. Neutralize law enforcement by technical skill, by corruption, and/or by legal arbitrage, using legal obstacles to enforcement operations and prosecutions which vary between states.

(These procedural elements can be broken down further into much more concrete steps, when analysing the dynamics of particular crimes: see Cornish 1994; Tremblay *et al.* 1994, 2001.)

All of these functional roles may exist within the boundaries of a state, but some may involve other states, which traditionally have their own sovereign legal rules and enforcement agencies with a mandate to deal with crimes that harm their *own* cit-izens, not the citizens of other polities.[6] States with a role in the production or supply of illegal commodities (drugs or people), or in the storing and laundering of proceeds of crime, can sometimes be said to be 'captured' by organized crime; while other 'collapsed states' (such as Afghanistan at times) are too weak and/or corrupted to deal with crime entrepreneurs and/or political rebels in their midst (Arquilla and Ronfeldt 2001; Mitsilegas 2000; Tilly 1985; Williams 2001; Zartman 1995). This makes 'State-Organized Crime' (Chambliss 1989) sometimes a more appropriate term[7] than mere

---

[6] The airplane attacks on New York and Washington on 11 September 2001 may have broadened concep-tions of the public and enforcement agencies on the limits of the national interest, but this proposition remains generally true.

[7] In mid-1998, the trial of senior politicians from the Spanish Gonzalez government and senior Civil Guard officials over atrocities committed as part of the 'war' against the Basque independence guerrillas, ETA, revealed extensive money-laundering in support of the assassinations of those believed to be ETA supporters. This meets all of the legal definitions of organized crime discussed later, though its adherents doubtless genuinely considered that they were doing it for the legitimate state. Likewise, there is scope for argument—as with corporate killing—about the extent to which there is formal high-level state approval for overseas or domestic intelligence collusion with 'organized criminals': ascertaining this is more difficult precisely because deniability strategies are built into such operations.

'organized crime', for the latter tends to focus us away from the role of political elites downwards towards the threat posed by some (usually alien) group of low-lifes and murky East European businesspeople: see Sterling (1991, 1994), Robinson (2002), and, for a more subtle account along the same lines, Jamieson (2000). In practice, the War on Drugs may be subordinated to wider foreign policy interests. For example, the role of intelligence agencies in covert military operations overseas, especially in support of anti-communist military regimes or guerrilla movements (regarding which assistance the American CIA is the best documented), has led to toleration of (or even active support for) some international suppliers and distributors of illegal drugs, provided they are deemed to assist in the War on Communism (see, for a particularly critical account, Woodiwiss 2001). This tolerance or *realpolitik* may be expected to reoccur in the context of the 'War on Terrorism' post-11 September 2001. Indeed, because 'its' manifestations are not obvious, and because of cynicism about any claim of 'threats to society' that suits the bureaucratic and personal interests of some police centralizers, international justice harmonizers, and intelligence agencies, some may be tempted to dismiss the existence of organized crime altogether (Hawkins 1969): but it is naive to discredit an argument simply on the basis that one distrusts the people who are making it (or to credit an argument simply because one does trust them). What is difficult is to work out what counts as 'adequate' evidence in relation to:

1. vertical integration, or how criminal behaviour is structured (e.g., hierarchical to loose networks);

2. horizontal integration, or the range of criminal behaviours that come under the umbrella of any group of criminals (fraud to drugs trafficking and distribution); and

3. how far up the political chain 'organized criminals' are to be found, not just in Colombia and Mexico.[8]

Those with access to highly classified material nevertheless may have *idées fixes* about 'organized crime', inadequate analytical skills or resources to carry out the sort of network analysis suggested by Coles (2001), or even may cynically use their mystique to get more powers and resources from over-credulous media and politicians. There is no obviously 'correct' view on these issues: if the organization of clandestine behaviour was so obvious, it would not be secret! But ethnographic and interview studies (Hobbs 2000, 2001; Pearson and Hobbs 2001; Rawlinson 2000; Wright *et al.* 1992); reviews of completed but not always prosecuted case files (Fijnaut *et al.* 1998; Van Duyne and Miranda 1999); and economic pricing analysis (Reuter 1983; Reuter and Kleiman 1986; Fiorentini and Peltzman 1995) can give us some clues

---

[8] Chambliss (1978) sub-titled his book on organized crime and corruption in the US 'From Petty Crooks to Presidents'. Jacobs *et al.* (1994) depict the war on organized crime in New York as the unravelling of the corruption of business and political elites by organized criminals: but this neglects the embrace of crime opportunities by venal elites. But the two accounts may not be inconsistent: gangsters may be a bulwark against labour activism and Communism, but they are not always useful to elites to help run the political economy. In Northern Italy, excessive racketeer demands for pay-offs from businesspeople led to the unravelling of tangentopoli (bribe city) by the investigating magistrates.

as to which accounts are more plausible. More importantly, there is reason why the organization of crime should be constant over time societies at any given moment. This is the very point stressed by McIntosh her account of modes of organization, shifting from *picaresque* banditry, routinized *craft* crime (like pick-pocketing of handkerchiefs in Victorian ti *project* crime (like major robberies and thefts such as Brinks Mat and the break-in by earth remover to attempt to steal valuable jewellery from the De Beers exhibition at the London Dome and to transport it away by speedboat) and *business* organization (such as the continuous supply of illegal goods and services). The organization of crime depends on the stage of historical development and also on the counter-measures to crime, which will be examined later in this chapter. The key thing is that those contemplating particular forms of crime find themselves in different situations, depending on the city, country, and their own embeddedness in concrete networks, criminal and elite.

Very few academics would defend the analytical utility of the term organized crime, with its crude binary organized/unorganized distinction which means that there is more variation *within* the category of organized than there is between organized and unorganized. Instead, many have shifted towards using the term 'enterprise crime', even though (or because) this shifts the focus away from the Russian Mafiya, Colombians, Albanians, and any other fearsome 'organized crime group' who 'menace our freedoms'. Van Duyne (1996) and Rawlinson (1998), for example, are severely critical of the kind of list of dangerous ethnic groups to be found (subsequent to their work) in the threat assessments of the US and UK authorities (NCIS 2001). (Though irrespective of whether they actually form large ethnic gangs or merely networks, criminals from such countries can be extremely violent and frightening to those who encounter them.) Coles (2001) opts for the term 'serious crime groups'.

Nevertheless, whatever academics and many thoughtful practitioners may think, the term 'organized crime' may have become so culturally and legally embedded that we cannot eliminate it, despite its manifest serious defects to anyone who wishes to think analytically. Like the psychiatrist's Rorschach blot, its attraction as well as its weakness is that one can read almost anything into it: do a media search typing in 'organized crime' to review this for yourself. But one can try to side-step it by using more meaningful categories wherever possible, to show how crimes for gain occur as part of a *system*, whether or not all those who participate form part of anything that could plausibly be termed a 'criminal organization'. The sorts of phenomena that commentators on organized crime might want to explain could include at least the following:

1. why types of crime are organized in particular ways;
2. why individual criminal careers develop in an 'organized'/'unorganized' way;
3. how (a) stable and (b) hierarchical are crime networks in particular places, and if they change, why do they do so?;
4. changes in social, business, and criminal justice reactions to organized crime;
5. the impact of organized crime on other forms of policing, and vice versa; and

6. the impact of social, prevention, and criminal justice reactions on individual offender learning and networking (including deterrence).

There is insufficient space to deal with all of these questions here, but they demonstrate how varied is the range of issues associated with organized crime, and also the range of academic areas encompassed by its study, including banking and market economics, political science, international relations, strategic studies, international law, media studies, social psychology, and sociology.

Naylor (2002) helpfully divides profit-driven crimes into three categories: predatory; market-based; and commercial.

Predatory crimes range from purse-snatching to ransom kidnapping to extortion, involving:

— redistribution of existing wealth from one party to another;

— wealth that was legally acquired by the original owner before being illegally taken;

— bilateral relations between victim and perpetrator(s);

— involuntary transfers which generally use stealth, but sometimes force (or its threat) or fraud;

— readily identifiable victims (individuals, institutions, or corporations);

— use of a non-business context, or a business front concocted purely to mislead;

— transfers which take place in cash or kind (physical goods, securities, or even information);

— losses which are simple to determine—the robbed or defrauded person, or institution, or corporation can point to specific money and property;

— no notion of fair market value for the property 'redistributed'; and

— an unambiguous morality—'the victim' has been wronged by 'the offender(s)'.[9]

Market-based crimes are most often associated with 'organized crime', and 'syndicated crime' from the Al Capone era onwards (McIntosh 1975). Dwight Smith (1980) termed market-based crimes 'enterprise crimes', but Naylor suggests that it may be more illuminating to analyse the process involved in the transfers than the business-like context. Market-based crimes involve:

— production and/or distribution of new goods and services;

— goods and services which are inherently illegal;

— multilateral exchanges involving producers, distributors, retailers, and money-managers on the supply side, and consumers on the demand side;

— covert commercial operations;

---

[9] Of course, Marxists, anarchists and other anti-capitalist protesters are unlikely to share the view that the morality of acquired or inherited wealth is so unambiguous (see Paul Rock and Jock Young, in Chapters 2 and 14 respectively of this volume). In *The Threepenny Opera* and *The Threepenny Novel*, Brecht's outlaw asks 'What is the robbing of a bank compared to the founding of a bank?'

— voluntary transfers;

— absence of self-defined victims;

— transfers which take place mainly in cash or bank instruments;

— an implicit notion of fair market value;

— ambiguity in moral condemnation, which anyway is less stable.

Otherwise legal goods (such as anabolic steroids and guns) with controlled availability which 'organized criminals' can exploit—for example, via official or unofficial involvement in pubs, clubs, and fitness centres—become traded in a relatively expensive *parallel* market. On the other hand (like stolen goods—see Sutton 1998), tax-evaded legal products such as alcohol and tobacco are available relatively cheaply through otherwise legitimate traders and local/pub networks. So too are low-stigma but illegal counterfeit products (unless they are sold fraudulently as the genuine full-price article).[10] Goods which are in themselves illegal—such as prohibited drugs—are traded in a black market.

Naylor's third category is *commercial* crimes committed by (rather than against, though offenders may well be victims too) otherwise legitimate entrepreneurs, investors, and corporations: these are discussed by Nelken (in Chapter 23 of this volume), so they will not be reviewed here.

THE NATURE OF ORGANIZED CRIME AND 'ITS' MARKETS

Most of the crimes and offender–victim relationships written about in the Oxford Handbook are set within the boundaries of the nation state, though crime-relevant issues such as unemployment are obviously affected by the global socio-economic context. It may be useful to distinguish here between what is required of a crime *trade* and what individual actors personally do. Hobbs (1998), for example, argues that most so-called organized criminals operate fairly locally; yet the activity of which they are a part can be global. Other countries exist as sources/transit routes for legal and illegal products to sell (tobacco, illegal drugs, illegal immigrants); as places to use or sell stolen goods (e.g., credit cards, cars/car parts); as places to create artificial paperwork for value-added tax and EU subsidy fraud; and as places to hide or launder proceeds of crime. Thus, especially for market offences, there is a need to comprehend crime within a wider cross-national context of crime opportunities (Van Duyne 1993, 1996). Despite the impact of modern horticulture on growing cannabis in the inclement weather of the UK, or of synthesizing drugs—making importation from outside Europe or even the UK unnecessary—some

---

[10] As Levi and Pithouse (forthcoming) argue, except when falsely claimed to have 'fallen off the back of a lorry', few purchasers of counterfeit goods are fooled into believing that goods are genuine—the prices are too low—but the growth of heavily advertised, branded 'must have' products, especially for youth, has created an artificial premium for genuine products and therefore a market incentive for counterfeiters.

element of cross border trade is inevitable, even if it is only the importation of seeds and precursor chemicals.

The Italian (or more precisely, Italian-American) model has embedded itself in popular culture, mediated through Hollywood. Yet all ethnographic accounts focus on a more complex set of patron/client relationships in which ethnic networks can sometimes supply a trust level that is as important for smoothly functioning crime as it is for commerce. Indeed, Reuter (1983 and subsequently) has suggested that the principal function of the Mafia is in contract enforcement, and that one should separate out the people and groups involved in the commission of crime from those involved in dispute settlement (for which role high information, and perhaps a reputation for extreme violence, is required). Similarly, Gambetta's (1994) book on the Sicilian Mafia, and Varese's (2001) book on the Russian Mafia, have suggested that the role of Mafia as 'enforcer' comes into play because of the absence of trust in normal underworld relationships, though its roots may lie in the particularities of Italian and Russian political history. These ethnographic studies, including interesting studies of Colombian (Zaich 2001) and Turkish (Bovenkerk and Yesilgöz 1998; Fijnaut *et al.* 1998) networks, as well as Hobbs's (1997, 2001) work in the UK, collectively demonstrate the subtle linkages between the organization of crime and the organization of ordinary social relations and work.

In brief, the accident of geography (where particular drugs can be easily produced, people want/need to emigrate, and direct supply routes), combined with the skill and contact set (including local corrupt contacts) and (variable) trust values that offenders bring to the table, have led a variety of ethnic groups to become involved in 'organized crime'. In the contemporary US, despite their growing involvement in securities fraud, there is hardly an Italian name in the FBI 'most wanted' list of targets (Reuter 1995). People of Cuban, Colombian, and Mexican origin have come to dominate the distribution of narcotics in the southern states, and other ethnic groups—Puerto-Rican, Japanese, Chinese (particularly Fukinese) (Chin 1996; Myers 1995), and Russian (Finckenauer and Waring 1999)—as well as white motor-cycle gangs, also are involved in organized crime in the US. So too are white, non-Italian origin Americans! Such groups make less use than previously of Italian-American Mafia dispute resolution services (including their former near monopoly of corrupt law enforcement and political contacts). Neither is there much vertical integration of organized crime groups, either in the US or Europe, even in drugs markets (Dorn *et al.* 1992, 1998; Pearson and Hobbs 2001; Ruggiero and South 1995; Paoli 2001): street-level criminals are normally independent of major crime syndicates, even where the latter do exist. As Block and Chambliss (1981) suggest, rather than being viewed as an alien group of outsiders coming in and perverting society, organized crime in America is best viewed as a set of shifting coalitions between groups of gangsters, businesspeople, politicians, and union leaders, normally local or regional in scope. Many of these participants have legitimate jobs and sources of income. Similar observations would apply in some Third World countries such as Mexico (Geopolitical Drug Dispatch 2001; Gomez-Cespedes 1999), where—pending modifications that may follow the defeat of the long-term PRI and the election of President Vicente Fox—a small élite have dominated the economy and political system and shared favours out among themselves though not always in harmony with *narco-trafficantes*. Ironically, the privatization of the economy in former Communist countries in the name of freedom enabled oligarchs—whether connected or not to organized crime groups—to buy former state assets for below their true value, and to buy up cheaply the shares given to the workers and public: privatization also provides easy avenues for money-laundering where the authorities and banks cannot afford to be too inquisitive about the source of the funds. (Though sensible criminals may not wish to leave their funds too long in countries with no depositor or investor protection schemes, or where a liquidator of a bank that goes bust might demand to know the beneficial ownership and origin of the funds before paying compensation.)

Among advanced industrial nations, the closest similarities to this 'political coalition' organizational model occur in Australia, where extensive narcotics, cargo theft, and labour racketeering rings with ties to state-level politicians and police were discovered during the 1970s and 1980s; and in Japan, where Yakuza and other racketeers specialize in vice and extortion, including *Sokaiya*—extortion by fear of embarrassment on the part of large corporations at their annual general meetings. Both of these illustrations, however, also suggest that the coalition—in which campaign funds also play an important role—is not entirely by consent: businesspeople would rather not pay the blackmail if they felt they had any realistic alternative. In Britain, by contrast, organized crime groups have not developed in this way, partly because of a more conservative social and political system (see Hobbs 1998), but principally because the supply and consumption of alcohol, gambling, and prostitution—and, for a while, opiates—remained legal but partly regulated. This reduces the profitability of supplying them criminally, though large profits can still be made by traffickers in women who make them work in near-slavery conditions in massage parlours, saunas and the like, in suburbia as well as in traditional red-light districts (for European research on trafficking in women, see Aronowitz 2001; Kelly and Regan 2001; Richard 2000; Vocks and Nijboer 2000). A host of ethnic groups are important—though far from exclusively so— in the supply of drugs to and via Britain (Dorn *et al.* 1992, 1998; Stelfox 1998; Pearson and Hobbs 2001). But except for narcotics importers and wholesalers, cargo thieves who work at airports, and local vice, protection, and pornography syndicates, the historic evidence suggests that British and German 'organized criminals' tend to be relatively short-term groups drawn together for specific projects, such as fraud and armed robbery, from a pool of long-term professional criminals on a within-force or regional basis: see McIntosh (1975) and Mack and Kerner (1975) for some early discussions along these lines, and Porter (1996) and the Phillips Report (1996) for later examples. As Stelfox (1999) acutely observes, most of the images of criminal organization generated by the police tend to reflect their own institutional organization, e.g., drugs squads. One may add that although the development of multi-crime type 'serious/major crime units' looks like it takes into account the complexity of criminal activities of crime networks, in practice such squads are dependent on where they can get human and technical intelligence from, and these may more likely come from the drugs than from the fraud arena. If the same criminal personnel are active in both types of crime, this may not matter (except in crime statistics); but if they are not then this advantages some groups—particularly specialist fraudsters—over others.

Instead of making routine comparisons with the US, it may be better to look at organized crime in Europe from its own set of economic and social landscapes in which organized crime *trade* takes place. As Van Duyne (1996) observes, Europe has a large diversity of economies, extensive economic regulations, many loosely controlled borders to cross, and relatively small jurisdictions. This means that the largest illegal profits for European crime entrepreneurs are to be gained in the drug market and in the area of organized business crime, with asymmetries in excise and value-added tax and the modest controls over fraud against the EU offering many opportunities. If the normal (licit) business nucleus in southern Italy, Turkey, or Pakistan is the extended family (Ianni and Reuss-Ianni 1972; Fijnaut *et al.* 1998), in northern Europe such socio-economic family units are much rarer and social bonds more restricted, for example, to people bound by loyalties of place (Hobbs 1997, 1998, 2001; Pearson and Hobbs 2001), though the very fracturing of the social fabric that has led to so much concern about social exclusion also paradoxically may inhibit *criminal* solidarity. The exceptions are the crime enterprises of minorities in Europe whose businesses are family matters, which should not be equated with impersonal 'syndicates' (Ianni 1974).

In order to make profits, those who offer illegal goods and services must advertise, if only to selected 'affinity groups' derived from other sources and activities. This generally means that in the long run, the police will come to know about the criminality too. To ensure freedom from the law, unless they can rely on police tolerance without a financial motivation, the criminals must therefore subvert the police and/or the courts, and this is a major reason for concern about the impact of organized crime. (Though, in reality, it is a side-effect of the prohibition of goods and services in popular demand, without which organized criminals would be operating in this area only as extorters from business.) In the Italian case, it seems clear that the state itself has at times in some sense collaborated with organized crime groups, though there is an unfortunate tendency to mix this up with the cosy corrupt deals between business-people and both national and Northern politicians, investigated mainly by the Milan magistrates to little final criminal justice outcome. But arguably, whatever the patron–client relationships with the 'professional politicians' that permeate Italian society, the Mafia (or Christian Democrat/Mafia) supremacy in the South probably required the tolerance of the US, which consistently has been more concerned about defeating Communism than about defeating organized crime (see Nelken 1996; della Porta and Pizzorno 1996; della Porta and Vanucci 1999; Stille 1996; Woodiwiss 2001). Alternatively, those crime entrepreneurs who are not confident about their abilities to subvert or sidestep the law might rationally choose to operate on a fairly small scale, in keeping with the illegality of the products, while the supply of criminal labour generates the total volume of product demanded by the market place. The result is a far more differentiated set of people and groups involved in supplying illegal goods and services than the organized crime imagery would lead us to expect (Paoli 2002). This applies even to the so-called Cali and Medellin drug 'cartels', where collaborative authority structures made it most unlikely that long-term price fixing could ever be accomplished (Thoumi 1995; Naylor 2002). Finally, Gambetta (1994) and Nelken (1997) suggest that the success of organized crime in Italy (and, one might further argue, in many parts of the former Soviet Union and Latin America) depends also on the more general lack of trust in society and between citizens and government. This imposes some limits on expansionism by serious crime groups, since when they come up against societies in which trust between citizens and governments/policing institutions operates well, Mafia-type organizations find an infertile soil in which to grow and—as far as we can tell—are unsuccessful in the long term, despite having substantial funds at their disposal. The importance of generating trust between citizens and government (sometimes where none has ever existed) is one reason why, if they want to succeed, attempts to combat organized crime in low-trust countries require more than a merely institutional focus on governance, i.e. more than whether their countries have something called an Independent Commission against Corruption and a panoply of intrusive surveillance and anti-laundering/asset forfeiture laws.

SKILLS AND PREREQUISITES FOR CRIME

In predatory acts such as robbery, violence or its threat is a key element, and professional robbers—whether of commercial premises (Gill 2001; Shover 1996) or of persons in the street—become highly skilled in its dramaturgy. In market offences, violence occurs mostly in disputes over territory, or over proceeds of crime stored in cash. In most Western societies, such violence is an artefact of the criminalization of popular goods and services; though elsewhere, extortion or 'protection' ('roof' in Eastern Europe) can take place where there is a weak state incapable of protecting all its people from such threats *and* where criminals (who can include police, or even senior politicians and officials) have the motivation and aptitude to make convincing threats. In all of these cases, violence is instrumental, but it can also be expressive of a need/wish to be shown 'respect' (Levi with Maguire, in Chapter 22 of this volume).

Despite the general social movement against corruption (Transparency International 2001; Pieth 1998/99; Anechiarico and Jacobs 1998), in profit-driven crime, corrupt payments are not central, because predatory crimes do not require them, while market offences give value to more or less voluntary purchasers (except for the addicted who really want to give up). However, corruption may occur either as a one-off, or as a regular payment to neutralize law enforcement, and in some societies, it may move from individual to group to systemic corruption (Sherman 1974; Punch 2000) from where, once established, 'good governance' campaigns will not generate ready change without an internal seismic shift, as happened in Indonesia and The Philippines.

Once the offences have occurred, an integral part of the crime process involves fencing (resale) of goods—where goods or traceable money have been obtained—and laundering those proceeds that have not been spent and need to be stored. Sutton (1998) has shown how stolen goods tend to be recycled through pubs and informal neighbourhood networks: one might add that this reduces local hostility to people otherwise depicted as dangers to 'society'. This focus on the embeddedness of crime within the local economy (see also Hobbs 2001; von Lampe 2001 and Ruggiero 2000b) may understate somewhat the use of supermarkets and local shops to sell (unaccounted for) produce from large hauls. In the 1970s, I interviewed someone who had stolen (without knowing its content) a truckload of yoghurt, which he would have had great difficulty in disposing of without it becoming spoiled, had he got that far: selling alcohol and tobacco smuggled in from the Continent is relatively easy, not just because there is a bigger market, but also because there are fewer storage problems and easy rationalizations for both sellers and purchasers that 'the amount of duty the government makes the punters pay is diabolical'.

As for money-laundering, this has been the subject of much nonsense and mystification. Laundering is the cleansing of funds so that they can be used in a way indistinguishable from legitimate money. What most people appear to mean by money-laundering is the hiding of funds in accounts somewhere outside of the *current* surveillance capabilities of enforcement agencies and/or professional inter- mediaries such as accountants, bankers, and lawyers who may have a legal duty to sensitize themselves to laundering typologies and to report suspicions or 'unusual' transactions to the authorities. If and when those official surveillance capabilities increase—as they did steadily during the 1990s, accelerating after the millennium, and especially after the plane-bomb attacks on New York and Washington on 11 September 2001—some funds that were just hidden become vulnerable to enforcement intervention and perhaps confiscation (Levi 2002). Those 'organized criminals'—the great majority, it appears (Shover 1996)—who make themselves popular with local car dealers, restaurateurs/publicans, and lovers by spending their money as they go along have no such problems (though they may be hit subsequently by proceeds of crime confiscation orders that they will never repay).

THE CONTROL OF ORGANIZED CRIME IN THE UK AND OTHER PARTS OF THE EU

As Justice and Home Affairs has become a key component of EU 'Third Pillar' activ- ities, and organized crime has ascended in importance as a political issue for the EU and the G-8 most powerful industrialized countries, it is no longer possible to see 'serious crime' policy in purely national terms. When drafting the provisions that gave the security services the mandate to deal with gangsters as well as more traditional security threats, Parliament avoided restrictive traps by referring to 'serious crime'. But the term 'organized crime' has an emotional kick which makes it easier to get resources and powers, and sociologists of crime control ought to study this labelling process in its own right. Thus, the 'threat of organized crime' and 'the invasion of the Russian Mafia' were and are used to persuade British politicians and others to set up and expand the National Criminal Intelligence Service (NCIS) and the National Crime Squad (NCS), assisted (though the former do not always see it that way) by the security services (MI5) and the security and intelligence services (MI6), publicly praised by the UK Foreign Secretary in April 1998 for their contribution to the fight against organized crime. Notwithstanding this, there are undercurrents of opposition among the *British police* to claims about how serious and widespread 'organized crime' is: many provincial police in many countries see the subject as a political (with both small and large 'p') mechanism for reallocating glamour and resources away from local policing by 'top slicing' their budgets.[11] Given that the Italian Mafia is the 'bogeyman' used in the organized crime debate as an example to be feared, it would be interesting to know whether this scepticism is equally true among provincial Italian police. British public views are unknown, but might be more concerned with local crime, perhaps failing to connect this with transnational crime.

In the wider European arena, there has been a flurry of anti-organized crime activity in the EU and the Council of Europe (a broader organization representing— as of 2002—forty-three states in Europe, but including all EU members). This has accelerated since the 1996 EU Dublin Summit (itself stimulated by the Irish government's response to the high-profile contract killing of crime journalist Veronica Guerin) and the 1999 Tampere Summit, with high-level multi-disciplinary groups seeking areas of cooperation, implementing a High-Level Joint Action Plan, and finally getting Europol off the ground constitutionally by 1999 (den Boer 2001).[12] Both the EU and the Council of Europe have extended their activities into EU applicant countries and others, training them in anti-laundering implementation, and ensuring as part of the *acquis communautaire* that legislation and some implementation machinery are in place before accession to the EU. Part of the 1998 Joint Action was a commitment to criminalize membership of criminal organizations—influenced by the Italian legislation, but harder to apply in less regimented settings—and tough action against criminal offshore finance centres. In the still wider international arena, the Financial Action Task Force (started only in 1989) and the UN have vied for activism and prestige in anti-laundering and crime prevention, especially on the drugs issue but later on all-crime anti-laundering measures, as the boundaries between proceeds of different types of crime become increasingly blurred. The arrival in the top UN Drug Control and Crime Prevention post in Vienna of Pino Arlacchi, a

[11] This comment is based on casual interviews with police in various European and North American jurisdictions over the past decade and a half: no claim is made about scientific representativeness of this sample, but it is such a common response that it makes a good working assumption. It is also true that corrupt law enforcement officials may deny the existence of organized crime to help cover up their own involvement; but this constitutes only a small proportion of the sceptics or 'deniers', especially in Europe and North America. The 'top slicing' refers particularly to the UK, where formal police funding is for individual constabularies and there is no centrally managed, national force: but conceptually, this is what happens in any system where 'high policing' is emphasized over the 'low policing' of ordinary local crime and public order.

[12] The establishment of Europol was agreed in the Maastricht Treaty on European Union of 7 February 1992. Based in The Hague, Europol started limited operations on 3 January 1994 in the form of the Europol Drugs Unit (EDU), adding other areas of criminality later. The Europol Convention was ratified by all member states and came into force on 1 October 1998. Europol commenced its full activities on 1 July 1999. Europol's current mandate is to support law enforcement activity against: drug trafficking; immigration networks; vehicle trafficking; trafficking in human beings, including child pornography; forgery of money (particularly the Euro) and other means of payment; trafficking in radioactive and nuclear substances; terrorism; and associated money-laundering activities. This applies where an organized criminal structure is involved and two or more member states are affected. The Europol mandate may be extended in the future to cover other forms of serious international organized crime, to the extent compatible with the Europol Convention and following unanimous agreement by the (EU) European Council.

sociologist-turned-politician Mafia expert,[13] placed organized crime at the top of the 1998 UN criminological agenda. This great political confluence has led to international pressure to harmonize the fight against organized crime, even if people do not always have a clear understanding of what 'it' is. The key point is that the UK might accuse Belgium or Germany (and vice versa) of not doing enough to help it deal with those components of its domestic crime problems that occur in Belgium or Germany, and they should therefore permit *for the UK's sake* covert policing tactics that they might not want for themselves.

CRIMINAL JUSTICE AND PREVENTION APPROACHES

There are two dimensions of shifts in approach to the control of organized crime in the UK and other European countries. The first relates to traditional criminal justice approaches, including:

1. substantive legislation, relating especially to money-laundering and proceeds of crime legislation (see Levi and Osofsky 1995; PIU 2000);

2. procedural laws involving mutual legal assistance (including the establishment of Eurojust, whose detached national prosecutors and investigative judges will be expected to facilitate urgent cases, and—in the aftermath of the terrorism attacks of 11 September 2001—the European arrest warrant that will free EU member states from the formalities of extradition); and

3. investigative resources, including the formation of specialist organizations such as NCIS, the NCS, and the National Hi-Tech Crime Unit (though not a national *fraud* squad, since fraud other than value-added tax and excise fraud—which hits government coffers directly—does not appear to be a policing priority: see Doig and Levi 2001; Levi and Pithouse, forthcoming).

There has been ongoing reform of anti-laundering and crime proceeds legislation around the world (Gilmore 1999; Stessens 2000), and greater policing (including customs and excise) involvement in financial investigation, still mainly in the drugs field but increasingly in excise tax fraud and (post-11 September 2001), terrorism. There has developed an Egmont Group of Financial Investigation Units (FIUs) world-wide, whose aim (not always realized in practice) is to facilitate inter-FIU enquiries across borders. Despite some inhibiting effect from the European Court of Human Rights and Data Protection Commissioners in some member states, the exchange of intelligence internationally and the depth of proactive surveillance—with the UK at the permissive extreme and Germany, because of its federal structure and data protection laws, at the other—have transformed the potential for intelligence-led policing (and disruption) of organized crime activity across borders. However, apart from questions of demand for illegal goods and services, one factor acting to obstruct the view of this Panopticon is limited resources. The historic tension between the local

[13] Professor Arlacchi left at the end of 2001 having decided not to seek a further term of office, following a storm of controversy about his management style and allegations of misconduct.

and the central has bedevilled policing since its inception in England and Wales (see Bowling and Foster, in Chapter 27 of this volume), and since the great majority of police chiefs expect to lose resources from any centralization, this gives them motivation to be sceptical about organized crime. Support for enhanced central policing was given by the report of the Home Affairs Committee (1995) on *Organized Crime*. Nevertheless, to mitigate suspicions that a 'British FBI' was being created, NCIS and the NCS have different Police Authorities (with some overlapping membership): NCIS is mandated to target 'core nominals' who, on the National Intelligence Model, are international and national offenders who represent a serious threat to society; while the NCS, other police services and HM Customs & Excise are tasked to take up the intelligence 'packages' that NCIS and their own intelligence departments have provided.

The other major plank of emerging activity is measures to *prevent* organized crime (Levi and Maguire 2001). The unpopularity of bankers, professionals and of drugs traffickers has enabled the state to obtain information for the interests of the state rather than the banks themselves about certain areas of financial services activity that otherwise might have been very difficult; and in this sense, the demonology of 'organized crime' has been very 'useful'. Likewise, in attempts to cut down on 'people trafficking', despite human rights issues still under appeal, lorry drivers have been fined heavily for carrying illegal migrants across the Channel, even when there was no evidence that the drivers knew that they had climbed on board through soft-sided canvas: this led large firms to introduce new technology for checking (by carbon dioxide levels) whether their trucks were stowaway-free. There has also been a focus on taking out drugs manufacturers and distributors in countries of origin, rather than waiting till they were close to the shores of the UK or other European countries.

There is no absolute demarcation between the above and criminal justice interventions: as countless European police officers have asserted to this author (not always based on evidence), repressive measures *are* preventive. Controls on money-laundering and asset confiscation/recovery, for instance, are intended to increase the probability of identification/conviction of organized criminals, to deprive them of the fruits of crime *and* to prevent their future harm by administrative and financial incapacitation. But there are other ways in which situational opportunity and designing out crime concepts are utilized to deal with crimes that are 'organized'.

Box 24.1 (which is adapted and extended from Schneider, forthcoming; see also Schneider 2001) represents the three main 'non-traditional' approaches to the prevention of organized crime that can be found at present. Like situational prevention techniques, this is a kind of 'natural history' classification of broad intervention methods, each of which may work by several mechanisms.

Community approaches

Traditional situational crime prevention neglects the area of community action, considering it as being too far from the proximal 'causes' of crime (Pease, in Chapter 26 of this volume). Nevertheless, in the arena of organized crime, community action has an impact on the pool of willing offenders, whether they are positively involved in crime, or are simply unwilling testifiers against offenders or passive assistants in the

Box 24.1 NON-TRADITIONAL APPROACHES TO ORGANIZED CRIME
PREVENTION

Community approaches	1. Community crime prevention
	2. Passive citizen participation: giving information about harms and risks, hotlines
	3. Active citizen participation: civic action groups
Regulatory, disruption and non-justice system approaches	4. Regulatory policies, programmes and agencies (domestic and foreign, including non-governmental organizations—NGOs—such as the IMF and World Bank as well as OECD/FATF)
	5. Routine and suspicious activity reporting by financial institutions and other bodies
	6. Tax policy and programmes
	7. Civil injunctions and other sanctions
	8. Military interventions
	9. Security and secret intelligence services
	10. Foreign policy and aid programmes (US 'certification' of countries as adequate/inadequate in their anti-drugs measures)
Private sector involvement	11. Individual companies
	12. Professional and industry associations
	13. Special private sector committees
	14. Anti-fraud and money-laundering software
	15. Private policing and forensic accounting

components of crime. Godson and Williams (1998: 34) discuss as an example of criminality prevention some social experiments in Palermo, where 25,000 children annually attend an educational program designed to change the cultural norms that allow the Mafia to flourish.[14] In Sicily, there have also developed local active citizen groups, though such anti-Mafia activism remains dangerous to those advocating it openly, and anger is hard to turn to constructive, long-term use.

Hicks (1998), in exploring the potential for a greater role of crime prevention strategies in tackling organized crime, stresses the linkages between unorganized property crime and more organized criminality because—especially when unemployed—drug

[14] While this would seem to be a good thing in itself, its effects in practice remain to be evaluated: these effects might take the form of greater willingness to pass information to the authorities (a shorter-term effect), or lesser willingness to assist or join Mafia-type associations in future (a much longer-term effect).

users require cash and crime is an important source of it.[15] Moreover, one of the most recent trends in urban property crime has been the organization of young offenders by adults to commit burglaries and car thefts (though one might counter that this phenomenon is hardly new: it goes back at least to the criminal careers of Jonathan Wilde and also Ikey Solomons—who was the model for Dickens' Fagin—and the Victorian rookeries). According to Hicks (1998: 334), the connection between unorganized and organized crime demands that preventive approaches, traditionally applied to the former, also be conceptualized to support local intervention to address the substructure of organized crime. However, it is worth noting that when applied to crop substitution for drugs and to employment alternatives to money-laundering, for example, the economic dimensions cannot sensibly be ignored by focusing simply on changing 'hearts and minds': setting aside the legal sanctions, crime is often more profitable than the alternative for individuals and even for countries.

Nevertheless, as a total concept in attacking organized crime, community crime prevention approaches are limited, because at some stage of the organized crime process—from financing through to laundering—other jurisdictions are likely to be involved which have less interest in crime suppression, unless they can be persuaded or forced to assist by some international action, including shaming and the threat of economic sanctions (see Blum *et al.* 1998; Levi 2002; Godson and Williams 1998; FATF 2000a, 2000b, 2001).

Regulatory, disruption, and non-criminal justice approaches

The second category in Box 24.1 covers a wide range of activities, which have in common the use of the powers of state agencies other than those whose main responsibility concerns law enforcement or criminal justice. One important aspect of this is the use of powers in the financial and tax areas, where in essence the focus of the attack is upon the financial assets of organized criminals rather than on criminal prosecution as such. (Tax evasion was the only charge feasible against Al Capone, but the use of tax prosecutions against gangsters has never been a feature of British criminal justice.) Thus, in the Irish Republic (Criminal Assets Bureau Act 1996) and the UK (Proceeds of Crime Bill 2001), as well as in the United States, *civil* law means and standards of proof are used to 'recover' for the state the assets deemed to be derived from crime, *irrespective of whether or not anyone is ever convicted or even prosecuted for those crimes.* The aim here is to undermine both the motivation of criminals to become 'top organisers' and their resources to be able to do so. This can be reinforced by extended powers to confiscate large cash sums inland that do not have a legitimate explanation, as contained in the Proceeds of Crime Bill 2001. A second, rather different, aspect is the use of the regulatory powers of local authorities, environmental and licensing agencies and the like, to disrupt the 'businesses' of organized criminals by making it more difficult for them to obtain necessary licences,

---

[15] There is a risk factor also not just in the need for cash, but also the susceptibility to blackmail of drug or 'hard porn' users working in the financial services industry should they fail to assist fraudsters and money launderers. There are plausible anecdotes about such cases, but it is not easy to unearth any concrete British examples. Such internal cooperation may also occur voluntarily, for example with disaffected staff or those going through personal crises.

find suitable premises, and so on. This can be seen in experiments in the Wallen 'red-light' district of Amsterdam, where tight controls are exercised over property owner-ship, with intensive reviews of intending and existing owners and their associates to 'keep organized crime out' (Levi and Maguire 2001). Civil injunctions have been used under US federal and state RICO laws to place corrupt unions and businesses under court-approved management and quite apart from high-profile arrests that may accompany the civil measures, this appears to have had an impact on this highly visible form of structured organized crime, measured, for example, by garbage dis-posal and fish market prices (Jacobs 1999; Levi and Smith, forthcoming), though there is less evidence of impact on other crime phenomena.

A major component of the regulatory efforts to prevent and detect organized crime relates to money-laundering. This term evokes images of sophisticated multi-national financial operations that transform proceeds of drugs trafficking into clean money. What was formerly a genteel, sovereign right of any nation to assure 'customer confidentiality', has become redefined pejoratively as unacceptable 'bank secrecy' that facilitates the drugs trade (Levi 1991). In this global risk management process, 'modern' areas of law enforcement have sought to combine targeting the suspected *person* (Maguire 2000) with targeting (or seeking to target) activities that might give rise to organized crime opportunities, such as international financial transfers and/or the conversion of large sums into foreign currencies. They have also tried to create an 'audit trail' for proceeds of crime by requiring all financial institutions to identify their customers. (Though this does not prevent gangsters and fraudsters from employing 'front men' to lend their names to accounts.)

The logic of controlling the crime proceeds money trail is that profit motivates crime, and because drugs and vice sales—certainly at street level—are (or are believed to be) in cash, the 'organizers' (to the extent that they exist) have to find some way of converting these funds into financial resources that appear to have legitimate origins. If they are prevented from doing so, their incentives to become major criminals are diminished, so there is both a general and a specific threshold preventive effect from anti-laundering efforts. These preventive effects can be reinforced by (i) requirements on financial and other 'risk-prone' institutions to report large cash and/or 'suspicious' transactions to specialized police or administrative financial intelligence units— the sort of 'responsibilization' process noted by Garland and other commentators on 'governance-at-a-distance' as a feature of late modern society (see Garland, in Chapter 1 of this volume and Levi 2002); and (ii) proceeds of crime confiscation or forfeiture laws that are intended to incapacitate both individuals and criminal organizations from accumulating substantial criminal capital and the socio-economic power that accrues from this. When Pablo Escobar offered to pay off the Colombian National Debt in exchange for not extraditing him to the US, we can safely say (if his offer was credible) that such socio-economic power exists; though the Colombian government, perhaps worried about US counter-measures, turned him down. Whether such socio-economic power is possessed by any 'organized criminal' in the UK or in any other EU country remains more doubtful, however (unless one takes the flexible approach to labelling corporations as organized criminals recommended by Ruggiero 1996).

An anti-laundering strategy requires a major global infrastructure of compatible legislation and mutual legal assistance, both for financial investigation and for proceeds of crime restraint and confiscation. However, the reason why this is in the second section of Box 24.1 rather than the first or third sections, is that these anti-laundering activities have become grafted on to the more conventional apparatuses of financial regulation administered by the Basle Committee of Banking Regulators and the International Monetary Fund, not always comfortably. The mode of governance selected for the spread of anti-laundering performance monitoring has been primarily mutual evaluation by peer countries within regional bodies and within the thirty-nine member Financial Action Task Force (FATF), set up in 1989 by the G-7 most industrialized countries. However in 2000, powerful FATF countries decided to penalise financially those (actually, non-member) countries who did not cooperate to their satisfaction, requiring financial institutions to take greater care (and slow down) when transacting business with countries that are publicly 'named and shamed': if the countries do not change, further sanctions are contemplated, and at the end of 2001, the tiny Pacific island of Nauru became the first to suffer these sanctions. This is an example of attempts to control globalization processes that facilitate crime, especially 'organized crime' and, latterly, terrorism. In so far as some preventive measures involve imposing costs on private sector interests, or even eliminating major chunks of profitability, there may be substantial political resistance, depending on the relative power of such interest groups in the localities concerned.[16] Without these pressures to conformity, there would remain a global (non) system of regulatory arbitrage—the ability to locate key operations where regulation is lightest, whether this lightness is based on lack of legal powers to invade banking or corporate secrecy, or is based on charisma, corruption, or economic power—of which criminals can take advantage *if* they have the discipline, knowledge and contacts.

Private sector involvement

Some of the private sector involvement has been discussed above, as it has been compelled by legal requirements placed on private sector institutions to play their part in crime opportunity reduction. An increasing number of banks have spent large sums—especially after the 11 September attacks—on fancy software to try to identify patterns of laundering electronically, mainly to avoid reputational risk and huge fines from regulators as well as possible jail sentences for designated money-laundering reporting officers. However, the choice of electronic methods results also from recognition that systems based on human awareness of customers cannot readily cope with the billions of transactions whizzing daily around the world without any staff seeing them. Furthermore, electronic systems offer some alternative intelligence to reduce the risks of corrupt staff turning a blind eye to particular customers' activities.

---

[16] In a Small Island Economy, an entrepreneur can exercise almost total domination, through charisma, corruption, or prospective economic damage should he or she withdraw. Where leading politicians personally have a large (declared or undeclared) stake in the interests affected, the difficulties of engineering change are most acute. In such cases, there may have to be incapacitation at the international level, as in the economic sanctions imposed by the US in their kingpins and other legislation which makes it an offence to transact business for particular individuals or even nation states such as Iraq or Libya.

Except for the sense that the world's economic system and its economic welfare is harmed by terrorist finance, few of these measures would be undertaken to enhance profitability, but there are other areas in which the private sector has invested in measures against organized crime because this threatens its core interests. Thus, the telecommunications industry, the payment card industry, the record and film industry, and the clothing industry have paid for small groups of investigators to carry out undercover operations and disrupt factories and key crime networks attacking their core interests. Much of this work is transnational, because factories in Bulgaria, China, Malaysia, Rumania, Russia, Taiwan, and Turkey may be churning out millions of CDs and DVDs or fake Levis that cut into the industries' profits and branding, even if many of the poorer cut-price purchasers would not have been able to buy the goods at full price. Moreover, quality counterfeit credit cards can be used to generate duplicate identities, leading to hundreds of millions of pounds in real losses to banks and merchants. Visa, MasterCard, and American Express also try to ensure that corrupt merchants are not allowed to open new accounts, at least within the same country. The reason why these measures are taken against *organized* crime rather than simply 'crime' is that well-organized operations (whether networks or hierarchical gangs) can do an enormous amount of economic damage very quickly. In a world of competitive profit-seeking, some individual companies will do more than the collective industry bodies, especially if they have advanced software. (For a detailed review of these issues, see Levi and Pithouse, forthcoming.)

EFFECTIVENESS OF ORGANIZED CRIME PREVENTION

The impact of anti-organized crime measures on *outcomes* remains insufficiently analysed, since there are little reliable data on the 'before' or 'after' (a) levels, or (b) organization of drugs and people trafficking, European Union fraud, etc. (Levi and Maguire 2001; Black *et al.* 2001). For example, the law enforcement agencies in EU and Council of Europe member countries are required to return annual counts of the number of organized crime groups, but, quite apart from quality monitoring issues, it is not obvious whether a reduction in the number is a good thing (less harm has been caused, or there is a lesser threat to society) or is a bad thing (it is an indicator of monopoly or oligopoly rather than of looser networking, and therefore a greater threat to society). Some approximations for illicit use can be made from self-report studies or from sophisticated techniques for estimating prevalence, but these do not explain or enable inferences to be made about how offending is *organized*. Very few countries or institutions will now accept strangers, or even established clients, bringing in briefcases full of cash—500 Euro notes offer the biggest amount of currency-per-square metre—without some plausible, legitimate explanation, so there is a commonsense effect on ease of cash laundering. (Though there is a corresponding negative effect on the ease with which overseas workers can send money quickly and easily back to their families.) However, there is no evidence that fewer drugs or trafficked women have become available as a result of the sorts of measures discussed above. In the private sector sphere, industry and public sector fraud data suggest some impact from data matching and from the coordination of data at an industry-wide level (Levi and Handley 1998; Levi and Pithouse, forthcoming).

Furthermore, despite exhortations, it is not always obvious how much policing has changed: despite some direct resource increase to NCIS and the NCS and institutional changes in the UK, for example, there has been little general police support for radical shifts in staff to financial investigation from equally prized and media-supported areas of crime and disorder. On the other hand, one of the advantages of moving away from a traditional criminal justice approach is that, once established, bureaucracies can become entrenched in 'law and order solutions' which obstruct alternative problem-solving approaches to complex social issues. Quite apart from the huge federal economic and privacy costs of the War on Drugs, many US state and local forces have become highly dependent on income from drugs-related Federal 'equitable sharing' and 'adoptive forfeiture', and there is some evidence of goal displacement there as enforcement agencies target forfeitable assets rather than just serious offenders (Blumensen and Nilsen 1998). This has not yet happened outside the US, partly because post-conviction reversal of the burden of proof typically yields modest results and crime proceeds income is not redirected fully towards the police (Freiberg and Fox 2001; Kilchling 2002). The measurement of changes in organized crime and the assessment of whether these are beneficial or not are in their infancy, quite apart from any ideological viewpoints about the desirability of policing the leisure habits of poor and rich alike.

ORGANIZED CRIME IN THE UK: NATURAL EVOLUTION OR RESPONSES TO CONTROL?

The explanation of how and why crime groups develop in the way that they do is important, but the argument here has been that a focus on what 'organized crime' is or is not doing is unilluminating because it imposes a false coherence on a diverse subject matter of people and activities. The organization of crimes results from the interaction of crime opportunities, offender and prospective offender skills and networks, and formal control efforts (whether through the criminal law, administrative law, or disruption). It is thus a *dynamic* process that evolves as offenders adapt (or fail to adapt) to their changing environment, including facilities offered by the legal commercial environment, such as container lorries and ships, car repair firms (Tremblay *et al.* 2001), payment card issuers and merchants (Levi 1998), and financial institutions. There are many cases where crime networks adapt to police preventive tactics even in the course of one series of frauds; and the losses of drugs or excise-evaded shipments constitute mainly opportunity costs from which higher members of crime groups develop counter-intelligence strategies or just accept risks and losses of (often female) 'mules'. If criminals fail to develop their technical skills or find people they need to add to their networks to commit crimes effectively, then evolution in crime prevention—stimulated by private and public sector cost-saving—and in technology may force them to desist from crime, or to resort to the *lumpenproletarian* crimes such as street robberies and thefts which cannot be eliminated by the spread of surveillance technology. In other words, there may be crime *type* displacement rather than geographical displacement of the same criminal activity.

Aggregate changes in routine activities, fashion, decriminalization and prevention technology—as well as in criminal networks—may produce changes or apparent changes in modes of 'organized criminality'. Former *Guardian* crime correspondent Duncan Campbell (1990: 1) starts one of his books on the changing face of professional crime by pointing to the shift in twenty-five years of two of the Great Train Robbers, 'from teams of organized criminals in overalls grabbing large bundles of Bank of England notes to quiet, besuited drug-dealers selling white powders from Latin America' . In principle, this shift could just as easily be a function of their age— they were simply too old to go around plausibly threatening people with shotguns— but it would be difficult to survive profitably in the drugs business without 'muscle' to protect oneself from people who would steal the drugs and/or the proceeds thereof. As with national 'defence' systems, this can easily escalate into more general rises in gun possession which—fuelled by the use as well as the economic value of crack cocaine— can generate higher rates of actual violent shootings. According to Campbell, the age of the gangster/family firm was replaced by the age of the robber, as cash in transit became the most rational means of by-passing improved safe technology and, allegedly with some assistance from corrupt elements in the Metropolitan Police, robbers were relatively free from arrest. However, the advent of supergrasses and the reduction in corruption ended this (for a while) in the early 1970s. As the Age of the Robber ended, the Age of the Dealer began.

Yet though there is much in this as a general trend—all the ethnographic, policing, and survey data point to the dramatic rise in the size of illegal drug markets—we should not be seduced by this periodization. There were twice as many robberies in the mid-1990s (before the theft of mobile phones drove up the robbery rate[17]) as in the mid-1980s, and considerably more than during the Age of the Robber. Although one might expect that the Age of the Fraudster represents the apotheosis of British organized crime, representing high profits and relatively low police interest and sentences, there appear to be cultural and skill barriers to entry into many areas of fraud which have inhibited this transformation for most predatory and market criminals. Several armed robbers turned to long-firm (bankruptcy) frauds as early as the late 1960s, and later to credit card fraud, social security fraud, and even to fraud against the European Union—either alongside or subsequent to drug dealing—but this move into the moderately upmarket areas of fraud has hardly dented those other types of crime, so arguably it is expansion rather than displacement. Some Russian crime syndicates (including wealthy businesspeople in the US) have shown the capacity to engage in vast international frauds (Van Duyne and Block 1994; Williams 2001), but so too have long-term Caribbean and Swiss residents operating businesses globally for decades without being defined as part of the 'organized crime problem'.

McIntosh (1975) more usefully and analytically distinguishes methods of

---

[17] Though little of this could be described as organized crime. There are sufficient lucrative scams in VAT and credit fraud involving easy-to-sell electronic products without resorting to playground robbery.

organizing crime in terms of the technological and policing barriers the particular crime confronts: where prevention precautions are high, organization shifts from routinized *craft* groups—pickpockets, and even safecrackers—to looser, perhaps even one-off, alliances between *project* criminals. (See Ekblom 1997, 2000, for a more general development of the interaction between control efforts and crime levels.) But this does not by itself tell us how the pre-existing social organization of criminals in its wider context shapes those factors, or how the organizational arrangements develop as a result of the efficiency and trust judgements made by criminal actors in a dynamic model.

An interview-based study of bankruptcy fraudsters found substantial variations in the organization of that form of crime during the 1960s and 1970s, but since the sixteenth century, fraudsters in particular have found cross-border crime attractive because it creates problems of legal jurisdiction, investigative cost, and practical interest by police, prosecutors, and even creditors themselves (Levi 1981). European Union harmonization and expansion does not itself make any difference to this, except (i) in providing new pretexts or 'storylines' for fraudsters to use to get credit or investment, and (ii) inasmuch as it changes the structures of control, e.g., reducing customs paperwork makes VAT evasion easier, or the UK's ratification of the European Convention on Mutual Assistance makes cooperation and conviction easier (see Passas and Nelken 1993).

There have been recent advances (see Coles 2001), but the lack of more than the most rudimentary research base on patterns of criminal relationships in most European countries—including the UK—means that academics have little information about how domestic criminals meet and decide what to do, let alone how and to what effect/lack of effect Euro-criminals meet. Major offenders do not advertise their services in the media, and apart from common holidays in Spain, marinas, and casinos, such contacts—mediated, no doubt due to language difficulties which British criminals may experience in more acute form than most—may often be tentative, hedged around with the problem of negotiating trust in an ambience in which betrayal (perhaps by an undercover agent, especially an American or British one) can have very serious consequence not just for freedom but also for retention of proceeds of crime. (Though clever regulatory arbitrage can put knowledge of variations in legal rules in European countries to good effect in frustrating successful prosecutions.) Most plausible is the notion that Euro-criminals are either crime entrepreneurs who already exploit international trade for the purposes of fraud and/or smuggling, or money-launderers who put their clients in touch with each other. Ruggiero (1996) has argued that both corporate and organized crime can be understood as variations on the same theme; but though there are cigarette companies that may at best fail to clamp down on the smuggling levels of their products in order to avoid other companies increasing their own market share at their expense, the Ruggiero view risks over-homogenizing both upperworld and underworld. Hobbs (1997) and Coles (2001) stress the importance to serious crime group activity in the UK of fluidity and brokerage roles—of temporary social arrangements—in putting people and skills together. Indeed, it is these connectors or 'nodes' rather than the most central or highest-ranking figures who may be the most crucial lubricants of serious crime (Jackson *et al.* 1996). The ιαρlu career development of some major criminals demonstrates that the rewards (and risks) of playing such a key entrepreneurial role can be very high (Barnes *et al.* 2000). Thus, while acknowledging the importance of missing data about the waxing and waning of relationships over time and place (Sparrow 1991; McAndrew 1999), Coles (2001: 586) argues:

It is possible to contemplate the situation where unsophisticated groups fail to use brokers and have no links to other groups; more sophisticated groups, particularly large and stable groups might employ a number of relatively static individuals as brokers; and, the most sophisticated, aggressively entrepreneurial groups would utilise a range of capable brokers operating themselves in chains of brokers. The identification of any varying usage of brokers in this way might provide an indication of the sophistication or degree of 'organization' of a criminal network.

The role of fences, criminal professionals (accountants, lawyers), money-launderers, and transportation firms may be important in facilitating networks, though they themselves may have to be 'brokered'. Such an intelligence methodology may bring increased risks for those upperworld members whose connections with the under-world may not previously have been noticed; but if neither the person nor the activity is part of the police and intelligence surveillance set, they may still remain safe from intervention (see Gill 2000).

Gradually (and see Sutton 1998, for a valuable analysis of this in relation to stolen property markets), criminologists have begun to see 'the causes of crime' as including an analysis of how crime is organized socially and technically. This fuses the neglected traditions of gang/subculture theory with situational opportunity theory, especially in its improved recent formulations (Clarke 1997; Clarke and Homel 1997), in showing how the forms of crime are shaped by the motivational and cultural environments in which they occur, which facilitate and/or inhibit the development of highly organized crime, whether or not accompanied by offender versatility. To understand how this is possible, we need to examine crime as a business process, requiring funding, technical skills, distribution mechanisms, and money-handling facilities. The larger the crim-inal business, the more likely it is that all these elements will be required, with the special business problem that what the participants are doing is illegal and, if caught and convicted, they—and their bankers or lawyers—could all go to jail for very long times as 'organized criminals'.

This chapter acknowledges that there are international groupings engaged in the commission of very serious social harms, though not all of them are labelled 'organ-ized criminals'. Despite the apocalyptic visions not only of the political right but also of sociologists such as Castells (1998), however, it seems far less likely that Chinese, Colombian, and Russian crime 'cartels' will dominate the West with their economic power than that there will be an increasing number of financial attacks on economic targets and a continuing devolved and networked supply of illegal goods and services, with some larger operators in countries where the evidential rules or the inefficiency/corruption of officials make proof of involvement too difficult. Though judgements of incidence and prevalence of threats may differ, there is general agreement that networked crime is more efficient than hierarchical 'planned centralism' for long-term criminal survival, at both national and transnational levels (Levi and Naylor 2000; Williams 2001). For criminals intending to stay in business for a long time, unless they are extraordinarily gifted and/or live in an extraordinarily corrupt haven, 'small (or at most medium-sized) is beautiful'. Furthermore, it appears that non-economic ties are the bedrock upon which is founded the longer-term stability and security of crime networks, only some of whose participants are full-time criminals. As the legal economy demonstrates, the mere fact that global markets exist does not mean that multinational conglomerates are the only, or even best suited, organizations able to supply criminal consumer needs. When the illegality of the activities imposes severe constraints on financing, recruitment, advertising, sales, and the collection and consolidation of funds, criminal growth may be inhibited. For all but those who simply want to develop a moral panic to get more powers and resources, what is important (for real-world crime control as well as academic understanding) is to appreciate the subtlety, complexity, and depth of field of the organization of crimes. In doing so, we should bear in mind that many different forms of organization can co-exist in parallel, and that to be an 'organized criminal' does not mean that one has to be a member of an 'organized crime syndicate'. Some offenders—whether or not they have powerful political connections—have access to considerable funds and the means of criminal production—weapons, people and reputation. Nevertheless, there is no Blofeld figure or SMERSH collective organizing 'crime' worldwide; rather, there are layers of different forms of enterprise criminal, some undertaking wholly illegal activities and others mixing the legal and illegal depending on contacts, trust, and assessment of risks from enforcement in particular national markets. Which of these we choose to call 'organized criminals' is a matter of judgement (and libel laws),[18] and we need to be clearer about which segments of the criminal market we are referring to before we can be sure we are discussing the same thing when we use the term 'organized crime'. It is for that reason that this chapter has been titled 'The Organization of Serious Crimes', which represents a more sensible starting point for research and policy, even if it lacks the punchy glamour of 'Organized Crime'.

[18] A fascinating insight into some of the problems of media commentary in the UK, contrasted with the US, is provided by the case of *Loutchansky v Times Newspapers Ltd and others* (QBD, 27 April 2001) [2001] All ER (D) 207. In that case, the judge found that *The Times* had libelled an Uzbekhi businessman in 1999 over reported links with Russian organized crime, despite media reports of the involvement of the Bank of New York in laundering the proceeds of criminal activity in Russia; media reports of suspicions about and investigations into serious crimes allegedly committed by Dr Loutchansky, which have resulted in his exclusion from various jurisdictions (including the UK); a statement by the then director of the CIA about the claimant's company, Nordex, being associated with Russian criminal activity; convictions of Dr Loutchansky by a Latvian court in 1983 for offences of dishonesty; and various reports in the media and the contents of reports by intelligence services. (Information provided to and by the author Jeffrey Robinson, (2002) was rejected as not meeting the test for a well-researched and reasonable foundation for the articles.) In *Loutchansky v Times Newspapers Ltd and others (No. 2)*, 5 December 2001, the Court of Appeal partially rejected the judge's conclusions, but in this and other cases (for example, involving the former Conservative Party Treasurer, Lord Ashcroft, and his corporate dealings in Belize), the perils of even suggesting that a prominent public figure is *suspected* of organized crime activities are plain.

Selected further reading

There are several sorts of approach to the study of organized crime and its control, spanning political science, international criminal law and international relations, social network analysis, socio-legal studies, etc.

Key works on the Italian Mafia and Mafia-type associations are Gambetta, D., *The Sicilian Mafia* (Cambridge, Mass: Harvard University Press, 1994); and Arlacchi, P., *Mafia Business: the Mafia Ethic and the Spirit of Capitalism* (London: Verso, 1986) (though this has been given a certain piquancy by criticism of Dr Arlacchi's governance style prior to his resignation as Executive Director of the UN Drugs and Crime Programme at the end of 2001). These Italian issues are nicely integrated into general organized crime literature in Paoli, L., 'The paradoxes of organized crime', *Crime, Law and Social Change*, 37: 51–97. A short historical overview that has never been bettered is McIntosh , M., *The Organization of Crime* (London: Macmillan, 1975)

The threat assessment issues are more clearly divided between those who consider that there is a serious threat from organized crime (whether in a hierarchical or a networked form) and those who are sceptical and see it as a loose market mechanism. Good sophisticated exemplars of the former may be found in Williams, P., 'Transnational criminal networks', in *Networks and Netwars: the Future of Terror, Crime and Militancy* Arquilla, J. and Ronfeldt, D. (eds) (Santa Monica, Cal.: RAND, 2001) (and in other publications in the journal *Transnational Organized Crime*). Good illustrations of the sceptical position may be found in Van Duyne, P. (1996), 'The Phantom and Threat of Organized Crime', *Crime, Law and Social Change*, 24: 341–77; and Naylor, R., *Wages of Crime: Black Markets, Illegal Finance, and the Underworld Economy* (New York: Cornell University Press, 2002) (and in other publications in *Crime, Law and Social Change* as well as in *Transnational Organized Crime*). A classic American sceptical empirical review is Reuter, P, *Disorganized crime: Illegal markets and the Mafia* (Cambridge, Mass.: MIT Press, 1983)

For those interested in the financial aspects of organized crime, good reviews may be found in Blum, J., Levi, M., Naylor, R.T., and Williams, P., *Financial Havens, Banking Secrecy and Money-Laundering* (New York, NY: United Nations Office for Drug Control and Crime Prevention, 1998); Van Duyne, P. (1998), 'Money-Laundering: Pavlov's Dog and Beyond', *The Howard Journal*, 37(4): 359–74; Levi, M. (2002), 'Money Laundering and its Regulation', *The Annals of the American Academy of Social and Political Science*, March; and in Naylor's *Wages of Crime* (above).

For British material on the organization of crime and networks, useful articles are: Coles, N. (2001), 'It's not *what* you know—it's *who* you know that counts: analysing serious crime groups as social networks', *British Journal of Criminology*, 41: 580–94; Hobbs, D. (1998), 'Going Down the Glocal: the local context of organised crime', *The Howard Journal*, 37, 4: 407–22; and Hobbs, D. (2001), 'The Firm: organizational logic and criminal culture on a shifting terrain', *British Journal of Criminology*, 41: 549–60.

For good drugs-focused work on organization of crime, see Dorn, N., Oette, L., and White, S. (1998), 'Drugs Importation and the Bifurcation of Risk: Capitalization, Cut Outs and Organized Crime', *British Journal of Criminology*, 38; 537–60; and Pearson, G., and Hobbs, D., *Middle Market Drug Distribution*, Home Office Research Study 227 (London: Home Office, 2001). For an illuminating journalistic account, see Barnes, T., Elias, R., and Walsh, P., *Cocky: The Rise and Fall of Curtis Warren Britain's Biggest Drug Baron* (London: Milo, 2000).

Those interested in the development of criminal techniques might find useful: Gill, M. (2001), 'The Craft of Robbers of Cash-in-transit Vans: Crime Facilitators and the Entrepreneurial Approach', *International Journal of the Sociology of Law*, 29: 277–91; Levi, M. (1998), 'Organising plastic fraud: enterprise criminals and the side-stepping of fraud prevention', *The Howard Journal*, 37(4): 423–38; and Tremblay, P., Talon, B., and Hurley, D. (2001), 'Body Switching and related adaptations in the resale of stolen vehicles', *British Journal of Criminology*, 41: 561–79.

Dutch criminology has generated some excellent criminological work, and a good overview in English is Fijnaut, C., Bovenkerk, F., Bruinsma, G., and van der Bunt, H., *Organised Crime in the Netherlands* (The Hague: Kluwer, 1998). For a more specialized study, see Zaich, D. (forthcoming), *Traquetos: Colombians involved in the cocaine business in the Netherlands* (The Hague: Kluwer). (Also available as PhD, University of Amsterdam, 2001.)

The policing of organized crime has been examined mostly in the context of drugs, but useful reviews include Sheptycki, J. *Issues in Transnational Policing* (London: Routledge, 2000)

A more overarching approach to organized crime prevention may be found in Schneider, S., with Beare, M. and Hill, J., *Alternative Approaches to Combating Transnational Crime* (Ottawa: Solicitor General Canada, November 1999) (**www.sgc.gc.ca/EPub/EPollist.htm**); and in Hicks, D.C. (1998), 'Thinking about Organized Crime Prevention', *Journal of Contemporary Criminal Justice*, 14(4): 325–51.

References

ADAMOLI, S., SAVONA, E., DI NICOLA, A., and ZOFFI, P. (1998), *Organised Crime around the World*, Helsinki: HEUNI.

ANDREAS, P. (2000), *Border Games: Policing the US-Mexico Divide*, New York: Cornell University Press.

ANECHIARICO, F., and JACOBS, J. (1998), *The Pursuit of Absolute Integrity*, Chicago, Ill.: University of Chicago Press.

ARLACCHI, P. (1986), *Mafia Business: the Mafia Ethic and the Spirit of Capitalism*, London: Verso.

—— (1998), 'Some observations on illegal markets', in V. Ruggiero, N. South, and I. Taylor (eds), *The New European Criminology*, London: Routledge.

ARONOWITZ, A. (2001), 'Smuggling and Trafficking in Human Beings: The Phenomenon, the Markets that Drive it and the Organisations that Promote it', *European Journal on Criminal Policy and Research*, 9(2): 163–95.

ARQUILLA, J., and RONFELDT, D. (2001), 'The advent of netwar (revisited)', in J. Arquilla and D. Ronfeldt (eds), *Networks and Netwars: the Future of Terror, Crime and Militancy*, Santa Monica, Cal.: Rand Corporation.

BARNES, T., ELIAS, R., and WALSH, P. (2000), *Cocky: The Rise and Fall of Curtis Warren Britain's Biggest Drug Baron*, London: Milo.

BEARE, M. (1996), *Criminal Conspiracies: Organized Crime in Canada*, Scarborough: Nelson Canada.

BERDAL, M., and SERRANO, M. (eds) (forthcoming), *Transnational Organized Crime: New Challenges to International Security*, Boulder: Lynne Rienner.

BLACK, C., VAN DER BEKEN, T., and DE RUYVER, B. (2000), *Measuring Organized Crime in Belgium*, Antwerp: Maklu.

BLOCK, A., and W. CHAMBLISS (1981), *Organizing Crime*, New York: Elsevier.

BLUM, J., LEVI, M., NAYLOR, R.T., and WILLIAMS, P. (1998), *Financial Havens, Banking Secrecy and Money-Laundering*, New York: United Nations Office for Drug Control and Crime Prevention.

BLUMENSON, E., and NILSEN, E. (1998), 'Policing for Profit: the drug war's hidden economic agenda', *University of Chicago Law Review*, 65(1): 35–114.

BOER DEN, M. (2001), 'The Fight against Organised Crime in Europe: A Comparative Perspective', *European Journal on Criminal Policy and Research*, 9(3)

BOVENKERK, F., and YESILGÖZ, Y. (1998), *De Maffia van Turkije*, Amsterdam: Meulenhoff.

CAMPBELL, D. (1990), *That was Business, This is Personal*, London: Secker and Warburg.

CASTELLS, M. (1998), *End Of Millennium*, Oxford: Blackwell Publishers.

CHAMBLISS, W. (1978), *On the Take: from Petty Crooks to Presidents*, Indiana: Indiana University Press.

—— (1989), 'State-Organized Crime—the American Society of Criminology, 1998 Presidential Address', *Criminology*, 27: 183–208.

CHIN, KO-LIN (1996), *Chinatown Gangs: Extortion, Enterprise, and Ethnicity*, New York: Oxford University Press.

CLARKE, R. (1997), 'Introduction', in R. Clarke (ed.), *Situational Crime Prevention: Successful Case Studies*, New York: Harrow and Heston.

—— and HOMEL, R. (1997), 'A revised classification of situational crime prevention techniques', in S. Lab (ed.), *Crime Prevention at a Cross-roads*, Cincinnati: Anderson.

COHEN, A.K. (1977), 'The concept of criminal organisation', *British Journal of Criminology*, 17: 97–111.

COLES, N. (2001), 'It's not *what* you know—it's *who* you know that counts: analysing serious crime groups as social networks', *British Journal of Criminology*, 41: 580–94.

CORNISH, D. (1994), 'The procedural analysis of offending and its relevance for situational prevention', in R. Clarke, (ed.), *Crime Prevention Studies*, Monsey: Criminal Justice Press.

CRESSEY, D.R. (1969), *Theft of the nation; the structure and operations of organized crime in America*, New York: Harper & Row.

DELLA PORTA, D., and PIZZORNO, A. (1996), 'The business politicians: Reflections from a study of political corruption', in M. Levi and D. Nelken (eds), *The Corruption of Politics and the Politics of Corruption*, *Journal of Law and Society*, 23: 73–94.

—— and VANNUCI, A. (1999), *Corrupt Exchanges*, New York: Aldine de Gruyter.

DOIG, A., and LEVI, M. (2001), 'New public management, old populism and the policing of fraud', *Public Policy and Administration*, 16(1): 91–113.

DORN, N., MURJI, K., and SOUTH, N. (1992) *Traffickers*, London: Routledge.

——, OETTE, L., and WHITE, S. (1998), 'Drugs Importation and the Bifurcation of Risk: Capitalization, Cut Outs and Organized Crime', *British Journal of Criminology*, 38: 537–60

EKBLOM, P. (1997), 'Gearing up against crime', *International Journal of Risk, Security and Crime Prevention*, 2: 249–65.

—— (2000), *Preventing Organised Crime: A Conceptual Framework*, presentation at Europol workshop on Organized Crime, The Hague, May 2000 (available from author).

EUROPOL and the EUROPEAN COMMISSION (2001), *Towards a European Strategy to Prevent Organised Crime*, Working Paper, Brussels: Europol and the European Commission.

FATF (2000a), 'Report on Non-Cooperative Countries and Territories' 14 February 2000, Paris: FATF.

—— (2000b), *Review to Identify Non-Cooperative Countries or Territories: Increasing the Worldwide Effectiveness of Anti-Money Laundering Measures* 22 June 2000, Paris: FATF.

—— (2001), *Review to Identify Non-Cooperative Countries or Territories: Increasing the Worldwide Effectiveness of Anti-Money Laundering Measures* 22 June 2001, Paris: FATF.

FIJNAUT, C., BOVENKERK, F., BRUINSMA, G., and VAN DER BUNT, H. (1998), *Organised Crime in the Netherlands*, The Hague: Kluwer.

—— and MARX, G. (eds), (1995), *Undercover: police surveillance in comparative perspective*, The Hague: Kluwer.

FINCKENAUER, J., and WARING, E. (1999), *Russian Mafia in America*, Boston: Northeastern University Press.

FIORENTINI, G., and PELTZMAN, S. (eds) (1995), *The Economics of Organised Crime*, Cambridge: Cambridge University Press.

FREIBERG, A., and FOX, R. (2001), 'Evaluating the effectiveness of Australia's confiscation laws', *Australia and New Zealand Journal of Criminology*, 1.

FRIMAN, R., and ANDREAS, P. (eds) (1999), *The Illicit Global Economy and State Power*, Lanham, Md: Rowman and Littlefield.

GAMBETTA, D. (1994), *The Sicilian Mafia*, Cambridge, Mass.: Harvard University Press.

GEOPOLITICAL DRUG DISPATCH (2001), Special issue of *Crime, Law and Social Change*.

GILL, M. (2001), 'The Craft of Robbers of Cash-in-transit Vans: Crime Facilitators and the Entrepreneurial Approach', *International Journal of the Sociology of Law*, 29: 277–91.

GILL, P. (2000), *Rounding Up the Usual Suspects?*, Aldershot: Ashgate.

GILMORE, W. (1999), *Dirty Money: The Evolution of Money Laundering Counter-Measures*, 2nd edn, Strasbourg: Council of Europe Publishing.

GODSON, R., and WILLIAMS, P. (1998), 'Strengthening Cooperation Against Transnational Crime: Elements of a Strategic Approach', paper presented at the International Conference on Responding to the Challenges of Transnational Crime, Courmayeur, Italy, 25–27 September.

GOMEZ-CESPEDES, A. (1999), 'Organized crime in Mexico', in F. Brookman, L. Noaks *et al.* (eds) *Qualitative Research in Criminology*, Brookfield, Vt: Ashgate.

HAWKINS. G. (1969), 'God and the Mafia', *The Public Interest*, 14: 24–51.

HICKS, D.C. (1998), 'Thinking About Organized Crime Prevention', *Journal of Contemporary Criminal Justice*, 14(4): 325–51.

HOBBS, D. (1997), 'Professional crime: change, continuity, and the enduring myth of the Underworld', *Sociology*, 31(1): 57–72.

—— (1998), 'Going Down the Glocal: the local context of organised crime', *The Howard Journal*, 37, 4: 407–22.

—— (2000), 'Researching Serious Crime', in R. D. King and E. Wincup (eds) (2000), *Doing Research on Crime and Justice*, Oxford: Oxford University Press.

—— (2001), 'The Firm: organizational logic and criminal culture on a shifting terrain', *British Journal of Criminology*, 41: 549–60.

HOME AFFAIRS COMMITTEE (1995), *Organised Crime*, London: HMSO.

IANNI, F.A., 'Authority, power and respect: the interplay of control systems in an organized crime "family"', in S. Rottenberg (ed.) (1974), *The economics of crime and punishment*, Washington DC: American Enterprise Institute for Public Policy Research.

—— and REUSS-IANNI, E. (1972), *A Family Business: Kinship and social control in organised crime*, London: Routledge & Kegan Paul.

JACKSON, J., HERBRINCK, J., and JANSEN, R. (1996), 'Examining criminal organisations: possible methodologies', *Transnational Organized Crime*, 2/4: 83–105.

JACOBS, J. (1999), *Gotham Unbound*, New York: New York University Press.

——, WORTHINGTON, J., and PANARELLA, C. (1994), *Busting the Mob*, New York: New York University Press.

JAMIESON, A. (2000), *The AntiMafia: Italy's Fight against Organized Crime*, London: Macmillan.

KELLY, L., and REGAN, L. (2000), *Stopping Traffic: Exploring the Extent of, and Responses to, Trafficking in Women for Sexual Exploitation in the UK*, Police Research Series Paper 125, London: Home Office.

KILCHLING, M. (ed.) (2002), *Die Praxis der Gewinnabschöpfung in Europa*, Freiburg in Breisgau: Kriminologische Forschungsberichte aus dem Max-Planck-Institut für ausländisches und internationales Strafrecht Band 99.

LEVI, M. (1981), *The Phantom Capitalists: the Organization and Control of Long-Firm Fraud*, Aldershot: Gower.

—— (1991), 'Regulating Money Laundering: the death of bank secrecy in the UK', *British Journal of Criminology*, 31(2): 109–25.

—— (1993), *The Investigation, Prosecution, and Trial of Serious Fraud*, Royal Commission on Criminal Justice Research Study No.14, London: HMSO.

—— (1998), 'Organising plastic fraud: enterprise criminals and the side-stepping of fraud prevention', *The Howard Journal*, 37(4): 423–38.

—— (2002), 'Money Laundering and its Regulation', *The Annals of the American Academy of Social and Political Science*, March.

—— and HANDLEY, J. (1998), *The Prevention of Plastic Fraud Revisited*, Home Office Research Study No. 184, London: Home Office.

—— and MAGUIRE, M. (2001), *The Identification, Development and Exchange of Good Practice for Reducing Organised Crime*, Report for Falcone Programme, European Commission, unpublished.

—— and NAYLOR, T. (2000), *Organised crime, the Organisation of Crime, and the Organisation of Business*, Essay for the Crime Foresight Panel, London: Department of Trade and Industry.

—— and OSOFSKY, L. (1995), *Investigating, seizing and confiscating the proceeds of crime*, Police Research Group Paper 61, London: Home Office.

—— and PITHOUSE, A. (forthcoming), *White-collar Crime and its Victims*, Oxford: Clarendon.

—— and SMITH, A. (forthcoming), *A Comparative Analysis of Organised Crime, Conspiracy Legislation and Practice and their Relevance to England and Wales*, Research Findings, London: Home Office.

McANDREW, D. (1999), 'The structural analysis of criminal networks', in D. Canter and L. Alison (eds), *The Social Psychology of Crime: Groups, Teams and Networks*, Aldershot: Ashgate.

McIntosh, M. (1975), *The Organisation of Crime*, London: Macmillan.

Mack, J., and Kerner, H. (1975), *The Crime Industry*, Lexington: Saxon House.

Maguire, M. (2000), 'Policing by risks and targets: some dimensions and implications of intelligence-led crime control', *Policing and Society*, 9: 315–36.

Maltz, M.D. (1976), 'On Defining Organised Crime: The Development of a Definition and a Typology', *Crime and Delinquency*, 22: 338–46.

Mitsilegas, V. (2000), *The reconceptualisation of security in the international arena and its legal impact: the case of measures against transnational organised crime*, unpublished PhD thesis, University of Leicester.

Myers, Willard H., III (1995), 'The Emerging Threat of Transnational Organized Crime From the East', *Crime, Law and Social Change*, 24(3), August: 181–222.

Naylor, R. (2002), *Wages of Crime: Black Markets, Illegal Finance, and the Underworld Economy*, New York: Cornell University Press.

NCIS (2001), *UK Threat Assessment, 2001*, London: NCIS.

Nelken, D. (1996), 'The judges and political corruption in Italy', in M. Levi and D. Nelken (eds), *The Corruption of Politics and the Politics of Corruption, Journal of Law and Society*, 23: 95–112.

—— (1997), 'The Globalization of crime and criminal justice: prospects and problems', in M. Freeman (ed.), *Law and Opinion at the end of the 20th Century*, 251–79, Oxford: Oxford University Press.

Paoli, L. (2001), *Illegal Drug Markets in Russia*, Freibourg: Max Planck Institut.

—— (2002), 'The paradoxes of organized crime', *Crime, Law and Social Change*, 37: 51–97.

Passas, N., and Nelken, D. (1993), 'The thin line between legitimate and criminal enterprises: subsidy frauds in the European Community', *Crime, Law and Social Change*, 3: 223–44.

Pearson, G., and Hobbs, D. (2001), *Middle Market Drug Distribution*, Home Office Research Study No. 227, London: Home Office.

PIU (2000), *Recovering the Proceeds of Crime*, London: Cabinet Office Performance and Innovation Unit.

Philips Report (1996), *Report of the Working Group on International, National and Cross-Border Crime*, London: Association of Chief Police Officers.

Pieth, M. (1998/99), 'The Harmonisation of Law against Economic Crime', *The European Journal of Law Reform*: 527 et seq.

Porter, M. (1996), *Tackling Cross Border Crime*, Crime Prevention and Prevention Series Paper 79, London: Police Research Group.

Punch, M. (2000), Police Corruption and its Prevention, *European Journal on Criminal Policy and Research*, 8(3): 301–24

Rawlinson, P. (1998), 'Mafia, media and myth: Representations of Russian organised crime', *Howard Journal of Criminal Justice*, 37(4): 346–58.

Rawlinson, P. (2000), 'Mafia, methodology and "Alien" Culture', in R. King and E. Wincup (eds), *The Oxford Handbook of Criminological Research Methods*, Oxford: Oxford University Press.

Reuter, P. (1983), *Disorganized crime: Illegal markets and the Mafia*, Cambridge, Mass.: MIT Press.

—— (1995), 'The decline of the American Mafia', *Public Interest*, 120: 89–99.

—— and Kleiman, M. (1986), 'Risks and Prices: An Economic Analysis of Drug Enforcement', in M. Tonry and N. Morris (eds), *Crime and Justice: A Review of Research*, vol. 7, Chicago, Ill: Chicago University Press.

—— and Rubinstein, J. (1978), 'Fact, Fancy, and Organized Crime', *The Public Interest*, 53: 45–68.

Richard, A. (2000), *International Trafficking in Women to the United States: A Contemporary Manifestation of Slavery and Organized Crime*, Washington, DC: United States Central Intelligence Agency.

Robinson, J. (2002), *The Merger: The International Conglomerate of Organized Crime*, London: Penguin.

Ruggiero, V. (1996), *Organized and Corporate Crime in Europe*, Aldershot: Dartmouth.

—— (2000a), 'Transnational Organized Crime: official and alternative fears', *International Journal of the Sociology of Law*, 28: 187–99.

—— (2000b), *Crime and Markets: Essays in Anti-Criminology*, Oxford: Clarendon Press.

—— and South, N. (1995), *Eurodrugs*, London: Routledge.

Schneider, S. (forthcoming), 'Alternative Approaches to Combating Organized Crime: A Conceptual Framework and Empirical Analysis', draft paper.

—— with Beare, M., and Hill, J. (2001), *Alterna-*

tive *Approaches to Combating Transnational Crime*, Ottawa: Solicitor General's Office.

SHEPTYCKI, J. (2000), *Issues in Transnational Policing*, London: Routledge.

SHERMAN, L. (1974), *Police Corruption: A Sociological Perspective*, Garden City, NJ: Doubleday.

SHOVER, N. (1986), *The Great Pretenders*, Boulder, Col.: Westview Press.

SMITH, D. (1980), 'Paragons, pariahs and pirates: a spectrum-based theory of enterprise', *Crime and Delinquency*, 26: 358–86.

SPARROW, M. (1991), 'The application of network analysis to criminal intelligence: an assessment of the prospects', *Social Networks*, 13: 251–74.

STELFOX, P. (1998), 'Policing the lower levels of organised crime', *Howard Journal of Criminal Justice*, 37(4): 335–438.

—— (1999), 'Transnational Organised Crime: A selected police perspective', unpublished paper presented at ESRC Seminar Series, Leicester.

STERLING, C. (1991), *The Mafia*, London: Grafton.

—— (1994), *Crime without Frontiers*, London: Warner.

STESSENS, G. (2000), *Money Laundering: an International Enforcement Model*, Cambridge: Cambridge University Press.

STILLE, A. (1996), *Excellent Cadavers*, London: Vintage.

SUTTON, M. (1998), *Handling stolen goods and theft: A market reduction approach*, Home Office Research Study No. 178, London: Home Office.

THOUMI, F. (1995), *Political Economy and Illegal Drugs in Colombia*, Boulder, Col.: Lynne Rienner.

TILLY, C. (1985), 'War making and State making as Organized Crime', in P. Evans, D. Reuschemeyer, and T. Skocpol (eds), *Bringing the State Back In*, Cambridge: Cambridge University Press.

TRANSPARENCY INTERNATIONAL (2001), *Global Corruption Report*, Berlin: Transparency International.

TREMBLAY, P., CLERMONT, Y., and CUSSON, M. (1994), 'Jockeys and joyriders: changing car theft opportunity structures', *British Journal of Criminology*, 34(3): 307–21.

——, TALON, B., and HURLEY, D. (2001), 'Body Switching and related adaptations in the resale of stolen vehicles', *British Journal of Criminology*, 41: 561–79.

VAN DUYNE, P. (1993), 'Organised Crime and Business-Crime Enterprises in the Netherlands', *Crime, Law and Social Change* 19: 103–42.

—— (1996), 'The Phantom and Threat of Organised Crime', *Crime, Law and Social Change*, 24: 341–77.

—— (1998), 'Money-Laundering: Pavlov's Dog and Beyond', *The Howard Journal*, 37(4): 359–74.

—— and BLOCK, A. (1994), 'Organized Cross Atlantic Crime', *Crime, Law and Social Change*, 22(2): 127–47.

—— and DE MIRANDA, H. (1999), 'The emperor's clothes of disclosure. Hot money and suspect disclosures', *Crime, Law and Social Change*, 3: 245–71.

VARESE, F. (2001), *The Russian Mafia*, Oxford: Oxford University Press.

VOCKS, J., and NIJBOER, J. (2000), 'The promised land: a study of trafficking in women from central and eastern Europe to the Netherlands', *European Journal on Criminal Policy and Research*, 8(3): 379–88.

von LAMPE, K. (2001) 'The Illegal Cigarette Market in Germany: A Case Study of Organized Crime', paper presented at the First Annual Meeting of the European Society of Criminology, Lausanne, Switzerland.

WILLIAMS, P. (2001), 'Transnational criminal networks', in J. Arquilla and D. Ronfeldt (eds). *Networks and Netwars: the Future of Terror, Crime and Militancy*, 61–97, Santa Monica, Cal.: RAND.

WOODIWISS, M. (2001), *Organized Crime and American Power: a History*, Toronto: University of Toronto Press.

WRIGHT, R., DECKER, S., REDFERN, A., and SMITH, D. (1992), 'A Snowball's Chance in Hell: Doing Fieldwork with Active Residential Burglars', *Journal of Research in Crime and Delinquency*, 29, 2: 148–61.

ZAICH, D. (forthcoming), *Traquetos: Colombians involved in the cocaine business in The Netherlands*, Amsterdam: Kluwer. (Also available as PhD, University of Amsterdam, 2001.)

ZARTMAN, W. (1995), *Collapsed States*, Boulder, Col.: Lynne Rienner.

25

DRUGS, ALCOHOL, AND CRIME[1]

Nigel South

INTRODUCTION

This chapter is concerned with illegal drugs and the most popular legal drug, alcohol. Illegal drugs are those designated as such according to various domestic laws and international agreements and treaties (McAllister 2000). In Britain the classification of illegal drugs is a tiered system reflecting official perceptions of their relative harmfulness. Thus Class A includes heroin and other strong opiates, cocaine, LSD, and ecstasy (MDMA); Class B includes amphetamines, barbiturates and cannabis, though in March 2002, the ACMD recommended that cannabis be re-scheduled as a Class C drug. This category also includes tranquillizers and some mild stimulants. Maximum penalties are highest for Class A, lowest for Class C.

In terms of general effects, alcohol and drugs such as tranquillizers and heroin have a depressant effect on the nervous system; while caffeine, amphetamines, cocaine, and tobacco are stimulants. Cannabis, LSD, and ecstasy distort perception; cannabis having a relaxing effect, LSD producing hallucinogenic effects, while ecstasy and similar drugs may produce restlessness and mild visual distortions with users feeling energized. However, in relation to all drug use—legal or illegal—actual behaviour and subjective experience will be strongly shaped by other influences, such as culture, context and expectations (Zinberg 1984), and, of course, strength (e.g., alcohol content) or relative purity versus adulteration.

This chapter reviews trends in drug and alcohol use; situates drug control in the British and global contexts; and discusses data and debates concerning drugs and alcohol, crime and criminal justice.

---

[1] This is a substantially revised version of the earlier chapters on drugs in the *Handbook*, and it omits some material found in these in order to accommodate updating and increased coverage of alcohol.

A REVIEW OF TRENDS IN DRUG AND ALCOHOL USE: 1950S TO 2001

Although most public and political attention tends to focus on illegal drugs as a source of social problems, this should not overshadow the significance of problems associated with legal drugs. For example, mass marketing and wide availability of prescribed and 'over the counter' pharmaceutical drugs, as well as solvents, may lead to misuse or dependency. Undoubtedly however, the Royal College of Psychiatrists (1986, 1987) was correct to call *alcohol* 'Our Favourite Drug'. Alcohol consumption today is far higher than in the post-war years of the mid-twentieth century. Increased consumption from the 1950s onward is probably related to increases in disposable income, changes in leisure patterns, the rise in social acceptability of female drinking, and the proliferation of outlets for sales and consumption. Concerns about alcohol and health (Alcohol Concern 2000) and young people's drinking behaviour are recurrent (Royal College of Physicians *et al.* 1995). The production of 'designer drinks', such as very strong 'white' ciders and fruit-flavoured alcoholic drinks ('alco-pops'; Roberts *et al.* 1999) targeted at the youth market, has contributed further to such concern (Parker *et al.* 1998: 54–55).

Mortality associated with tobacco and alcohol is considerably higher than deaths resulting from causes related to illegal drug misuse and complications. Deaths from the latter (mostly accidents) in 1998 are estimated at between 1,076 and 2,997 (ACMD 1999). Deaths from alcohol-specific diseases appear to have risen in the 1990s, from 3,565 in 1992 to 4,907 in 1997, and deaths where alcohol is 'a significant contributory cause' are estimated to be between 25,000 and 40,000 (Alcohol Concern 2000: 4).

However, such comparison should not be interpreted as clear support for the view that illegal drugs should be legalized because 'they cause less harm than legal drugs'. Instead, there is an argument for trying to minimize the harm associated with all forms of drug misuse (Taylor 1999: 85). The point is that legal drugs (even if restricted) are widely available, illegal drugs are not; the health-related consequences of widespread legal availability of presently illegal drugs are not known. Taylor (ibid.) remarks that 'a selective decriminalisation of certain drugs could be one dimension in a serious campaign of harm-reduction, not least in disrupting the process of production of "outsider cultures"' formed by those suffering disadvantage and social exclusion related to forms of substance misuse. However, Taylor also notes Currie's (1993: 68) conclusion, based on the US inner-city experience, that 'Proponents of full-scale deregulation of hard drugs . . . tend to gloss over the very real primary costs of hard drug use . . . and to exaggerate the degree to which the multiple pathologies surrounding drug use in America are an intended consequence of a "prohibitionist" regulatory policy.'

The legality of some drugs does not mean that they do not contribute to 'legal harms', i.e. crime. Drink and driving offences (including manslaughter deaths) and alcohol-related violence and social disturbance (Shepherd and Brickley 1996) result in costs to the community and to health and police services (Shepherd and Lisles 1998).

Both alcohol and tobacco, despite their legal status, are commodities which (more than ever) attract smuggling activity to profit from avoidance of taxation, as well as hijacking and theft.

A SHORT HISTORY OF DRUG USE TRENDS—1900S–1940S

Historically, illegal drug use has always crossed class boundaries. During the early years of the twentieth century and into the 1920s, drug users included: medical-professionals who had abused their access to opiates and other drugs; 'therapeutic addicts' of different class backgrounds who had become dependent during the course of pain-killing treatment with opiate-type drugs; working-class users of opiate-based patent medicines; and recreational users of illegal drugs. The last were relatively few in number, but included, for example, those on the bohemian fringes of high-society; opium-pipe smokers in the opium houses of the East London dock-lands; and in the West End, a small number of young, white, male criminals and female prostitutes who were using cocaine recreationally (Parssinen 1983: 216–7; Kohn 1992). However, while there was some considerable concern over drugs in this period (Kohn ibid.), evidence suggests that the extent of use was limited and, by the end of the 1920s, in decline.

In the inter-war years illegal drug use attracted little attention in the UK. However, subsequently, the paramount concern of nations at war was to secure drugs for med-ical purposes, and the entry of the USA into the Second World War brought unusual developments. The USA became a repository, producer, and supplier of pain-killing opiate-type drugs for the allied war effort and on the international scene played a coordinating role in the strategy of purchasing opium for allied stocks and denying such supply to the Axis powers (McAllister 2000: 147–9).

THE 1950S

During the early 1950s in Britain, both drug availability and official activity were minimal: 'The number of addicts known to the Home Office, most in medically related professions, remained low at between 300 and 400 . . . But prosecutions for the use of cannabis began to rise' (Berridge 1999: 281). By the late-1950s a drug sub-culture seemed to be emerging in the West End of London linked to bohemian and jazz cultures (Spear 1969; Tyler 1995: 169–70, 315–6). The availability of cannabis and of heroin in these circles moved the Ministry of Health to establish the 1958 Inter-Departmental Committee on Drug Addiction under Sir Russell Brain, reporting in 1961. In the USA, popular anxieties and legislative responses were rather more pronounced. Accounts of the new youth fashions of the 1950s and purported links between rock and roll, the mixing of black and white youth, communism, and drugs (Inciardi 1986: 103–104; Shapiro 1999) were seen as alarms about America's vulnerability not only to external threats, but also to subversion from within.

THE 1960S

Examining trends for the late 1950s, the 1961 Brain Committee reported that drug supply was 'almost negligible', and Britain was deemed to have no drug problem worth speaking of. However, the 1960 addict statistics had not been available for the Committee, and the number of addicts known to the Home Office was rising (Mott 1991: 78); and it continued to do so—from 454 in 1960 to 753 in 1964 (ibid.: 79). While these were extremely modest increases compared to developments just twenty years later, they suggested that a new trend was emerging.

The period of the 1960s is now culturally represented as one of post-war release, artistic innovation, anti-establishment sentiments, and alternative cultures (Shapiro 1999). In this context alarm about drugs was partly related to the emergence of new, young, working-class users of heroin and amphetamines. Middle-class youth also used heroin, but were particularly associated with images of a counter-culture—the 'hippy' life-style and drugs such as cannabis and LSD (Young 1971; Willis 1978)—but it should also be remembered that for most youth, the intoxicant most widely used was (and remains) alcohol.

For many official, medical, and other observers, the irresponsible prescribing of opiate drugs by a small minority of either gullible or profit-motivated private practitioners was the problem at the heart of a changing West-End drug scene (Ruggiero and South 1995: 19–23; Mott 1991; Leach 1991). The Brain Committee was re-convened in 1964 to report on changes occurring, and in 1965 recommended changes of considerable significance for the British response to serious drug use (Pearson 1991: 176–78).

FROM THE 1970S TO THE 1980S

Between 1973 and 1977, only 4,607 new 'addicts' came to official notice (Giggs 1991: 153). With regard to use of opiates then, much of the 1970s presented a picture of relative stability and localized concentration, predominantly in the London area. By the tail of the decade, however, there were signs of change, and the 1980s presented a profoundly different picture.

During the late 1970s, new sources of heroin were noted. Contrary to official perceptions that increasing availability was once again a sign of seepage from generous prescribing on to an illegal market, in fact a whole new era was opening. Political shifts in the Golden Crescent region of South West Asia (Iran, Pakistan, and Afghanistan) had opened new supply routes, with long-term implications for the global heroin market. These implications, and links between trafficking and other forms of international crime involving warlords in Afghanistan, and later criminal groups in the central Asian republics, received increasing attention from analysts from the late 1980s/early 1990s but, of course, since the 2001 terrorist attacks on the USA, will attract more sustained drug control efforts.

Cheap, high purity heroin was now becoming readily available and, with a tighter prescribing policy adopted by the new Drug Dependency Units (DDUs; see below), the new sources of availability stimulated the market. Of crucial importance was that the new heroin imports could be *smoked*, the prepared drug being heated and the smoke being inhaled ('Chasing the dragon'), snorted, or sniffed (Auld *et al.* 1986). These methods overcame the deep psychological barrier that injecting posed to many, and the mode of administration now seemed familiar and 'ordinary' (Mott 1991: 85–6). Glasgow and Edinburgh saw early and rapid increases in heroin use and, subsequently, high rates of HIV transmission between drug injectors and partners (Ditton and Speirits 1982; Robertson 1987). Other research in various areas of England confirmed a picture of the rapid spread of heroin use (Donoghoe *et al.* 1987; Giggs 1991; Parker *et al.* 1988; Pearson *et al.* 1986). 'Scoring smack' (Lewis *et al.* 1985) was not difficult in the new drug markets; further, it was of higher purity and cheaper in real terms than it had been four to five years before (Mott 1991: 87–88). Notifications of 'new addicts' increased (Giggs 1991: 153), and their spatial distribution around the country represented such an unanticipated spread that many commentators adopted an 'epidemic' analogy.

Based on available data (national statistics, local surveys, and Home Office addict notifications and applying a multiplier of five), estimates put the number of people in the UK dependent on opiates at some time in 1989 as between 74,000 and 112,000. The late 1980s also saw considerable official and popular concern over the 'crack' form of cocaine. For the end of the 1980s, data suggested that use of crack in Britain appeared to be quite limited, and crack represented less than a fifth of all cocaine seizures (Shapiro 1991: 40). That this situation changed considerably in just ten years is evident and discussed below.

Overall, at the end of the 1980s, heroin remained important, cocaine was increasing in availability but still of relatively minor concern, and the market was dominated by cannabis and amphetamine. However, in 1988, Acid House music had already heralded a whole new wave of dance-drug culture, bringing with it the return of LSD and new acquaintance with MDMA/ecstasy (Shapiro 1999).

THE 1990S AND INTO THE TWENTY-FIRST CENTURY

By the early 1990s, Britain had developed what remains a 'poly drug' culture. Of course, mixing drugs, purposeful selection for different effects, and/or use of alternatives to the preferred 'drug of choice' in times of scarcity, were not new phenomena. What was new was the integration into young people's drug cultures of an approach to available legal and illegal drugs as part of a pick 'n' mix culture embracing consumerism and hedonism (Davis and Ditton 1990; Parker *et al.* 1998; South 1999b). No longer is drug culture hidden away in a *sub*-culture; now it is argued to be a visible part of mainstream culture and 'normalized', if only in the sense that popular culture is full of images and knowing awareness about drugs (South 1999b). The ecstasy dance-culture proved distinctive, not least in involving relatively 'ordinary' people whose 'deviance' lay in being enthusiasts of dance and particular dance-drugs (Shapiro 1999; Hammersley *et al.* 2002).

PREVALENCE AND AVAILABILITY

A preoccupation of many studies has been with drug user careers and the question of 'when did drug (legal and illegal) use start'? To summarize, evidence suggests that teen (and early teen) years are significant; that for most young people, experimentation (and little more) with illegal drugs involves cannabis, amphetamine, and other Class 'B' drugs, and from the early 1990s onward, occasional to regular use of ecstasy and LSD (Class A); and that in the career of most drug users, 'escalation' to 'harder' drugs and long-term continuation of use is confined to a minority. Raistrick *et al.* (1999: 47) observe that 'as drug use has become prevalent among adolescents, it has ceased to be a simple matter clearly to separate out the role of alcohol from the role of other substances. Drug misusers tend to have misused alcohol under age, younger than their peers and prior to use of most or all illegal drugs'.

In the mid-1990s, Hough (1996: 10) reported that 'The British Crime Survey [BCS] . . . and the Four Cities Survey . . . suggest that around a third of people between 16 and 30 have taken illegal drugs at some time in their lives'. Results from the 2000 BCS indicate that 'about half of those aged 16 to 29 have tried an illicit drug in their lifetime', though more recent use is less common, and 'just over a fifth (21%) of young people aged 16 to 29 had used class A drugs in their lifetime' (Sharp *et al.* 2001: 1):

. . . divergent trends were found for the 16–19 year olds: their rate of overall drug use has fallen by a fifth from 34% in 1994 to 27% in 2000; cocaine use, however, has risen significantly from 1% in 1994 to 4% in 2000. Similarly, the proportion of 16-to-24-year-olds using cocaine in the last year rose significantly from 1% in 1994 to 5% in 2000. [ibid.: 1] . . . Ecstasy use (now 5%) has not changed significantly since 1996, but continues to be used by a cohort of those who were teenagers in the first part of the 1990s [ibid.: 4].

Clearly the major change in the 1990s was the increase in use of cocaine by young people in their twenties and below. Falling price (Corkery 2000; ISDD 1999) related to increased supply and hence easier availability, fashion and social acceptability (Boys *et al.* 2001), may all be part of the explanation for this development. From the early 1990s to 2000, most crack or cocaine users in Britain seemed to be poly-drug users (Shapiro 1991: 42; Ditton and Hammersley 1996), not using excessively and not developing heavy dependence (Druglink 1992: 6), but perhaps ill-informed about differences between cocaine and crack, and about risks, particularly taking cocaine and alcohol together (Boys *et al.* 2001).

The 2001 European School Survey Project on Alcohol and other Drugs (ESPAD 2001; Druglink 2001a) found that teenagers in Britain were more likely than their European counterparts to have tried alcohol, cannabis, or ecstasy. Fifteen to sixteen-year-olds were surveyed: 36% said they had taken cannabis, 8% amphetamines, 5% magic mushrooms, 3% cocaine, and almost 3% heroin. Such findings support the results of the large survey of cohorts of fourteen to sixteen-year-olds in north-west England by Parker *et al.* (1998), who have suggested that a pattern of 'normalization' of drug use is underway within the lifestyles and attitudes of those surveyed. Others (Shiner and Newburn 1997, 1999) find this a contentious and exaggerated conclusion. This emerging debate about 'normalization' or otherwise is one of tremendous significance, not least in its implications for drug laws and the planning and providing of services (South 1999b).

In the late 1980s and at the start of the 1990s, heroin availability was still high. Signs and predictions that its use was in decline were short-lived, and since the mid-1990s heroin use has seen a significant and continuing resurgence. Injection is still a major mode of administration, and this is a health concern. Injecting is a dangerous practice *per se*, and in the 1980s its association with the spread of HIV/AIDS was a key policy and practice issue. However, the new viral threat Hepatitis C is proving perhaps less easy to control, and yet has received far less media and health service attention (Finch *et al.* 1998; Wells 1998).

SOCIAL DIVISIONS AND SOCIAL EXCLUSION

Gender, drugs, and alcohol

Studies of women's use of drugs (legal or illegal) remain relatively rare compared to the volume of work focused on men (on links between sex- and drug-markets, see May *et al.* 1999 and Maher 1997; on women, alcohol, and drugs, McDonald 1994a, 1994b, Thom 1994, Hunt *et al.* 2000; also Ettorre 1992; Ettorre and Riska 1995; Taylor 1993; Erickson and Watson 1990; McConville 1991; Rosenbaum 1981). Henderson (1999: 38) discusses this continuing neglect in her study of young women and the ecstasy culture, observing that 'the state of the art of understanding gender and drug use . . . has changed surprisingly little' in the decades between the late-1970s and the end of the twentieth century:

A 1993 review of the literature found a similar picture: one based largely on the problematic end of the spectrum of women's drug use drawn from women contacted through drugs services (Taylor 1993). A picture which emphasised the exclusive role of men in introducing women to drug use; women's dependence on men to inject them to maintain their habit; women's desire to have babies to affirm their role as women and their irresponsibility as mothers; and their inevitable involvement in prostitution. No dramatic change since that time is to be found in published research . . . (Henderson 1999: 38)

It is no longer true that drug *use* is predominantly male to the extent that it has been in the past (Parker *et al.* 1998; Sharp *et al.* 2001). Drug *dealing* probably remains a mainly masculine territory, and there are familiar socio-cultural prejudices operating against women in the drugs economy which explain this (Ruggiero and South 1995: 138–41; Taylor 1993), but cultural and commercial aspects of drug markets may show signs of change (Hobbs 1997: 821). US research (Fagan 1994: 186; Maher 1997) indicates openings in cocaine and crack markets for women dealers, albeit with varying degrees of autonomy. Informal care and support for alcohol and drug misusers is generally provided by women, and as Henderson (1999: 38) notes: 'A concern with women's drug use as it affects others still appears to dominate the gender and drug use literature.'

Ethnicity

Drug use within ethnic minorities remains a story largely hidden from the record (Akhtar and South 2000; Pearson and Patel 1998). When the topic has received attention it has frequently been discussed in terms of 'the depiction of dangerous places defined by the linking of drugs, crime, race and violence' (Murji 1999: 49), a process that can sensationalize stories about drugs and minorities, 'racialize' certain forms of drug use and drug culture, and pathologize the places where 'the mugger' and the 'drug trafficker' are said to reside (ibid.: 50–61).

Survey data on this subject are not as reliable or comprehensive as we would like, despite the BCS adding 'booster samples' to recent surveys. As Murji (ibid.: 52) comments, 'Some surveys report that some ethnic or racial minority groups declare higher drug use. But other surveys have found the opposite'. Patel (1999: 18) remarks that

Surveys suggest that South Asians are less likely to use illicit drugs than their white counterparts, and very few South Asian drug users approach drug services. In contrast, qualitative research studies of perceptions, experiences and nature of drug use among Britain's South Asian communities suggest increasing levels of harmful drug use, particularly heroin, among South Asians (predominantly Pakistani and Bengali young men).

(see also Akhtar and South 2000; Webster 1996). Whittington (1999) describes how Vietnamese refugees settling in London had been introduced to heroin in refugee camps in Hong Kong and were now encountering crack-cocaine.

The 'Four Cities' (Leitner *et al.* 1993) study and data from the 1992 BCS suggested similar proportions of white and African-Caribbean drug use in the population (including cannabis), but whites were more likely to have used amphetamine or hallucinogens. The 2000 BCS suggests that 'in general, drug use is less prevalent in ethnic minority groups (all black groups, Indian and Pakistani/Bangladeshi) compared with whites' (Sharp *et al.* 2001: 3). 'Use in the last year' has increased for all sixteen to twenty nine-year-olds in all ethnic groups with the exception, according to the survey, of the Pakistani/Bangladeshi group (ibid.)—a finding at odds with Patel's remarks on the findings of qualitative work but consistent with his expectation of results from surveys. Tyler and others (1995: 203, 212–14; Pryce 1979; Oswald 1982) have reported on relationships between black populations and localized drug cultures, involving cannabis, heroin, and crack-cocaine; but again, research is very limited. Possession of cannabis by black youth and police 'stop and search' tactics were a background factor in several instances of inner-city unrest in the 1980s (Pearson 1991), and the manufacture and sale of 'crack' has been associated by the police and media with illegal Jamaican immigrants involved in 'Yardie' gangs (Bean 1993; Tyler 1995: 214–25; Murji 1999). In terms of *use* in the African-Caribbean community, cannabis is the favoured and most widely-used drug; and amidst the growth of heroin use across Britain in the 1980s, one striking feature was the relative absence of black users. Parker *et al.* (1998: 57) note that surveys of race and religion in relation to young people and alcohol use show relatively insignificant differences between the self-reported drinking of white and Afro-Caribbean youth but higher abstinence among young Muslims.

Prison and probation service statistics suggest that a high proportion of ethnic

minority individuals (compared to the white population) have come to the attention
of the criminal justice system for drug-related reasons. However, such statistics tell us
little or nothing about actual patterns of drug use. One reason that we know so little
about such use is because the counselling and advice services that can provide information about street-level use among white clients apparently remain unused by
minority clients. Ruggiero and South (1995: 116–9) have described the situation of
blacks in the drug-dealing economy as mirroring their secondary and exploited status
in the legitimate economy, but also pointed to both the practical research problems as
well as 'political correctness' which have inhibited further criminological research in
this area, problems which have not hampered or been detrimental to the rich history
of research on drug problems and minorities in the USA (e.g., Trimble *et al.* 1992).

Drugs, deprivation and social exclusion

High unemployment was a major social issue in the 1980s, and several studies examined hypothesized links between drug use and socio-economic conditions. Peck and
Plant (1986) found positive correlations between average annual unemployment statistics, cautions and convictions for drug offences, and notifications of users in treatment between 1970 and 1984. Pearson *et al.*'s (1986) study in the north of England
found that areas with a high concentration of use frequently exhibited very high rates
of unemployment, single-parent families, limited mobility, and other indices of social
disadvantage. The 'Four City' (Leitner *et al.* 1993) study incorporated 'booster group'
samples from measurably-deprived areas, but did not find significantly higher rates of
use compared to the main ('non-deprived') samples. Overall there seems to be some
correlation between drug use and high rates of deprivation. The 1998 ACMD report
on *Drug Misuse and the Environment* explicitly acknowledged that 'research points
strongly to a statistical association between deprivation and problematic drug use'
(ibid.: 3), and Foster (2000) revisited the site of a study undertaken ten years previously and found deterioration on most measures of deprivation and a parallel
increase in crime and drug use. However, there may also be inverse relationships.
Localities with high indices of deprivation may have low rates of use, while there are
socially-advantaged, middle-class areas with high rates of use. The 2000 BCS 'showed
consistently higher levels of drug use among 16–29s living in affluent urban areas.
Similar patterns are found for cocaine and Class A drugs. Heroin on the other hand, is
more common in less affluent areas' (Sharp *et al.* 2001: 3).

In the late 1990s the Labour administration developed a series of policy initiatives
aimed at reducing drug use and dealing by addressing social exclusion, improving the
living environment in run-down areas, and focusing on localities with concentrations
of long-term and high youth unemployment (MacGregor 1998: 190).

THE CONTROL OF DRUGS: BRITAIN AND THE GLOBAL CONTEXT

During the nineteenth century, opiate preparations were commonly marketed and widely used throughout Europe and North America (Berridge 1999), for example, as medicines and tonics, as an analgesic, as a sedative, as a remedy for cholera, and as children's 'quieteners'.[2] Apart from such therapeutic use, reports between the 1830s and 1860s describe the recreational use of opiates in factory districts, seaports, and the Fenlands (Parssinen 1983: 212), and the literature of the period indicates experimentation and familiarity with opium in literary and bohemian circles (Berridge and Edwards 1987: 49–61). However, the question of *control* was emerging.

The Industrial Revolution and other socio-economic developments promoted interest in the subject of public health, particularly in relation to the fitness of the urban working class. The common use of opiate preparations gave rise to some concern (although use for pleasure and pain relief among the middle class apparently received less disapproval and attention at this point; Berridge and Edwards 1987: 97–112, 49–61). A different provocation of public discussion about opiates was their common use as a means of sedating children—a practice which led to many cases of children dying of opium poisoning (Parssinen 1983: 207; Pearson 1991: 170). Additionally, from around the 1870s onward, sensational accounts of Chinese 'Opium Dens' in the Limehouse area of London's East End provided sinister stereotypes of corruption and alien culture, Oriental conspiracies, and clandestine organizations (Kohn 1992: 18–20). There was, of course, considerable hypocrisy in the promotion of such images.

Although in time, opium came to contribute to the economic development of China (Berridge 1999: xxvi), the country was originally an unwilling recipient of the drug. The original traffickers in the trade were the great colonial powers such as Britain and The Netherlands (McAllister 2000: 9–39). Britain had invested heavily in the export of opium from India to China, and engaged in two wars (1839–42 and 1856–58) to secure the future of the trade against Chinese opposition because it was so profitable. In light of this connection, it is perhaps less surprising to find that domestic control over opiate use in Britain had been so limited. Nonetheless, in the latter half of the century, moral opposition to Britain's opium trade was growing. Further, there was a shift in perception of opium use, from seeing it as an indulgence or habit to viewing it as a 'problem', classifiable in various ways by the new medical discourses (Berridge 1979, 1999). The 1868 Pharmacy Act removed morphine and opium derivatives from the shelves of general stores and gave pharmacists the monopoly of dispensing. Medical practitioners attempted, but failed, to bring the treatment and control of those dependent upon opium within the provisions of the 1888 Inebriates Act, already covering the voluntary detention of 'habitual drunkards'. Modest restrictions on supply developed, but control of *use* remained un-addressed by legislation. 'Insanity' certified to be the result of addiction could lead

---

[2] Such traditional patterns of use continue in many under-developed areas of the world.

to institutionalization and the 1890 Lunacy Act was sometimes applied, but only with the passing of the 1913 Mental Deficiency Act did legislation embrace 'any sedative, narcotic or stimulant drug' within the definition of an 'intoxicant' and thereby allow for the detention of 'moral imbeciles' in asylums or under the guardianship of another (Pearson 1991: 171).

As well as 'medical entrepreneurs', 'moral crusaders' were also active in seeking the introduction of new control measures. In 1874, the Society for the Suppression of the Opium Trade was formed, largely supported by Quaker campaigners, and subsequently securing Parliamentary support from the Radical wing of the Liberal party (Berridge and Edwards 1987: 176–80). In terms of political developments, the Report of the Royal Commission on Opium published in 1895 was something of a 'whitewash' (ibid.: 186–7), but the important *economic* development was that, even as moral and political debates waxed and waned, by the early 1880s the 'signs of decline in the importance of opium as an Indian revenue item were already visible' and 'by 1885, China was probably producing just as much opium as she imported. . . . In the 1890s, exports of Indian opium began to decline absolutely as well as relatively' (ibid.: 178). By 1906, it was neither a great act of moral conviction nor one incurring great financial loss, for a new Liberal government to commit Britain to phasing out opium exports from India to China.

By the early years of the twentieth century a polarity had emerged between the medical view of drug use as addictive or a 'disease', and a moral view of it as a vice to be controlled by law and punishment (Berridge 1979; Smart 1984). However, the concerns about vice that finally introduced the first real penal response to drug use in Britain, arose not as a result of peace-time lobbying but in the context of war-time emergency. During the early years of the First World War, Press and public were aroused by accounts of prostitution and cocaine posing a threat to the discipline of allied troops (Kohn 1992: 23–66). Similarly, concern about the productivity of war workers in the factories prompted calls for restriction of alcohol availability. In 1916, Regulation 40B of the Defence of the Realm Act (DORA), made possession of cocaine or opium a criminal offence except for professionals such as doctors, or where supplied on prescription (Kohn 1992: 44). DORA regulations also introduced licensing laws restricting opening times of public houses and regulating alcohol sales (relaxed only in the 1980s). Of course, alcohol controls had the greatest long-term impact for the majority of the public, but with regard to the cocaine 'threat', legal control was now exercised and unauthorized possession was criminalized. A significant step had been taken and the role of the Home Office was brought to centre stage in the control of drugs, both domestically (Tyler 1995: 312–13; Pearson 1991: 172; Berridge 1978: 293) and internationally (McAllister 2000).

Subsequently, various influences—such as the USA's push for prohibitionist policies, its increasing ambition to set the agenda for drug control (but not alcohol control, which members of the League of Nations had no interest in), and the peculiar de facto ratification of the 1912 Hague Convention on Opium through ratification of the post-war Versailles Treaty (Article 295) (Bruun *et al.* 1975: 12; McAllister 2000)— encouraged further government legislation in the form of the Dangerous Drugs Acts of 1920 and 1923. These confirmed possession of opiates and cocaine as illegal except where prescribed by a doctor. The Home Secretary gained powers to regulate the manufacture, distribution, and legitimate sale of these drugs, and policing practice and public perception reflected the new status of illegal drugs as a criminal matter (Parssinen 1983: 217; Pearson 1991: 172).

Problems relating to alcohol misuse or dependence have also been a source of moral, medical, and penal concern since the nineteenth century. Fines, imprisonment, or treatment programmes have been employed, and Johnstone (1996: 33–100) provides a valuable history of medical and penal approaches to 'the inebriate'. However, while control regarding opium and cocaine was now set on a path of increasing prohibition, control in relation to alcohol has largely been a story of increasing liberalization. DORA regulations were at first ignored and then lifted. The Licensing Act 1964 is now the main legislation defining where, when, and to whom alcohol can be sold, and laying out the system for discretionary granting of licences to sell alcohol to any person that the licensing magistrates think 'fit and proper.' (Alcohol Concern 2000). Since the 1980s, successive governments have relaxed controls on availability. A variety of laws have defined and specified responses to drunken behaviour, from the 1839 Metropolitan Police Act and the 1872 Licensing Act to the 1964 Act and subsequent amendments. Certain Acts are particularly concerned with public order and providing powers to police and others—for example, the Licensed Premises (Exclusion of Certain Persons) Act 1980, the Sporting Events (Control of Alcohol) Act 1985, the Confiscation of Alcohol (Young Persons) Act 1997—and, importantly, provisions of local by-laws can also be used to enforce prohibition of drinking in designated areas.

THE 'BRITISH SYSTEM' OF DRUG CONTROL

Following DORA and then the 1920 Act, the new Ministry of Health vied with the Home Office for authority over the formulation of subsequent regulations. For a few years, the Home Office made 'consistent attempts to impose a policy completely penal in direction' (Berridge 1984: 23). The response from the Ministry of Health and medical lobby was the 1924 Rolleston Committee, generally cited as the origin of the 'British system' of response to drugs. Chaired by Sir Humphrey Rolleston, President of the Royal College of Physicians, the 1926 Report of the Departmental Committee on Morphine and Heroin Addiction aimed to define the circumstances in which prescription was appropriate and the precautions to be taken to avoid the possibility of abuse (Ministry of Health 1926: 2; Tyler 1995: 313–4; Pearson 1991: 173). Hence, the Committee offered recommendations allowing for prescription of heroin and morphine to enable gradual withdrawal, or to 'maintain' a regulated supply to those judged unable to break their dependence or those whose lives would otherwise suffer serious disruption.

Given the influential view that this development represents a profoundly different path to that taken by the US, it is important to make two points. First, the view that Rolleston held of addicts was resolutely that they were 'middle class, middle aged, often from the medical profession and invariably an abuser of morphine. About five hundred such individuals existed nation-wide, and rather than representing a threat they were to be pitied' (Tyler 1995: 313); only as 'an afterthought' was passing consideration given to the existence of working-class use of opiate-based patent medicines (ibid.).

Secondly, the contention that it was the nature of the British response which avoided the creation of the criminal activity associated with the USA experience, can be challenged by looking at when such criminality actually emerged in the USA. As Parssinen (1983: 219) suggests:

Although the Harrison Act [of 1914] probably strengthened the connections between narcotics addiction and the urban underworld, these connections were firmly in place long before 1914. The increasingly hard-line American enforcement and treatment policy during the 1920s was less cause than effect of the emerging criminal-addict.

(See also Inciardi 1986: 16–17.) In other words, in terms of numbers of drug users, and the drugs–crime relationship, the British and US experiences were divergent already, ahead of the passing and subsequent interpretation of legislation.[3]

In Britain the drugs issue was receding in significance even as the Rolleston Committee deliberated: medical and recreational addiction was in decline. Press and public fascination persisted and sensational stories still made news (Kohn 1992); but, generally, such subcultures of use as had existed were fragile. Scarcity, related expense, and law enforcement efforts deterred both users and suppliers of cocaine and opiates. As Parssinen (1983: 220) argues, 'in Britain as in America, drug policy was less a cause than it was the effect of the addict population. Put simply, narcotic drug maintenance was accepted in Britain in the 1920s because the addict population was small, elderly and dying off'.

Various commentators (Smart 1984; Pearson 1991; Dorn and South 1992; Kohn 1992) agree that apparently dominant medical discourses of this time were in fact shadowed and influenced by strong moral and penal positions. Nonetheless, one reason for a general acceptance of the success of 'Rolleston' is that through the 1930s to the late 1950s, Britain did indeed experience no serious problems with illegal drugs. Policy was seen as a continuing success despite being, in the words of Downes's (1977: 89) famous assessment, 'little more than masterly inactivity in the face of ... an almost non-existent ... problem'. As Berridge and Edwards (1987: 254) observed, the contrast between the American and British experience had rather less to do with the triumph of the Rolleston philosophy than it had to do with the 'enormously different social conditions in the cities of the two countries—different patterns of poverty, urban decay, ethnic underprivilege and entrenched criminal organization'.

Despite such domestic calm, Britain was a signatory to a long string of control measures throughout the twentieth century, largely carried along by the momentum of international control initiatives (McAllister 2000). Virtually all of the significant drugs legislation passed in Britain between 1920 and 1964 represented less a response to any real domestic problem than a willingness to meet obligations set by

---

[3] How the 1914 Harrison Act was interpreted in its application is important. Initially set out as a taxation and regulatory code rather than a penal measure aimed at users, it was the practice of the US Treasury and decisions of the Supreme Court that changed the nature of the Act, contributing to conditions supporting expansion of the illegal drug market (Inciardi 1986: 14–15).

international treaties (Ruggiero and South 1995: 99–101). The 1960s, however, brought a change to this domestic scene. Nationally as well as internationally, drugs were a new social problem, associated with new challenges to society. In 1961, the UN Single Convention on Narcotic Drugs drew together provisions of nine previous treaties signed between 1912 (Hague Convention) and 1953, and extended control to cover the plants poppy, coca, and cannabis.

In Britain, in response to evidence of new patterns of drug availability, the Brain Committee was reconvened. Amphetamine was a new problem associated with new youth cultures, and the 1964 Drugs (Prevention of Misuse) Act was introduced to control possession, production, and supply (later adding control of LSD). In 1965, the Dangerous Drugs Act ratified the Single Convention and the Brain Committee published a new report. This was to lead to major legislation in the form of the Dangerous Drugs Act 1967. Prescribing was to continue, but general medical practitioners were to be more tightly controlled by regulations and were to 'notify' to the Home Office new addicts not previously in treatment. The aim was to intervene to prevent seepage of prescribed opiates (and similar drugs) into the illicit market. Specialist Drug Dependency Units or 'clinics' were opened from 1968, initially in and around London, as the centres of expertise in treatment of addiction. Henceforth, only their doctors could prescribe heroin and cocaine. However, general practitioners were not barred from prescribing other drugs for treatment of drug users, and there has been a long debate about the extent to which they are, can be, or should be involved in such specialist clinical work (Ford and Ryrie 1999; Gerada 2001).

In practice, the new clinics sought to break client dependence on street drugs by prescribing methadone as a 'substitute' drug, thought less attractive than heroin and suitable for detoxification or 'maintenance'. Thus medical *management* of addiction was endorsed, placing doctors in a role with responsibility for regulating supply and controlling the spread of dependence (Pearson 1991: 178–81; MacGregor 1999).

Debates aired around the dichotomies of 'soft' and 'hard' drugs, and 'users' and 'dealers', during the 1960s, were reflected in the distinction made by the 1971 Misuse of Drugs Act between offences of possession and supply. Drug users could be characterized as sad and weak types corrupted by drug dealers who were very bad types; the former needed counselling or treatment, the latter deserved the harshest punishment. Hence, despite the direction of liberalization followed in many legislative developments of these 'permissive' years, drugs received quite conservative treatment: even a call by the respectable Advisory Council on Drug Dependence (The Wootton Committee 1968) for relaxation of the law on cannabis, was dismissively rejected (Young 1971: 198–201).

The recent status of drug control as a 'war' on drugs can be traced to the mobilization in the USA of public and official sentiment against drugs by President Nixon (Inciardi 1986: 117–8). In the early 1970s, crime was ranked as pre-eminent among the problems facing US cities, with drugs close behind. It is perhaps unsurprising, then, that drug-related corruption in police services also caused alarm in these same years and prompted inquiries in New York and in London. In the 1980s President Reagan launched a renewed 'War on Drugs', and the coincidence of the conservative politics of the President and the new British Prime Minister, Mrs Thatcher, set the tone for the rhetoric—but not all of the practice—of drug control in that decade.

Drugs in Britain in the 1980s became a political and politicized issue, yet one attracting a political consensus that largely persists. Such consensus enabled the government to take the earlier proposals of the Howard League's Hodgson Committee (1984) and make provision for the recovery of the profits of crime, but without incorporating the Committee's liberal recommendations relating to sentencing. The far-reaching Drug Trafficking Offences Act 1986 (Dorn *et al.* 1992: chapter 10; Dorn and South 1991) was the result, and it set the precedent for subsequent and continually-evolving legislation targeting criminal organization and money-laundering, whether associated with drugs or terrorism.

The government's 'strategy document' *Tackling Drug Misuse* (first published 1985) proposed five fronts for action, largely organized around enforcement but including prevention and treatment. In the mid-1990s, the Conservative government introduced a further set of 'drugs strategies' for England, Scotland, Wales, and Northern Ireland, with some regional variation in emphasis. The England strategy, *Tackling Drugs Together* (1995), adopted a community crime prevention emphasis and established multi-agency Drug Action Teams to promote local initiatives. These elements were continued in the most recent national strategy produced by the post-1997 Labour government, *Tackling Drugs to Build a Better Britain* (HM Government 1998). This set four aims: '(i) to help young people resist drug misuse in order to achieve their full potential in society; (ii) to protect our communities from drug-related anti-social and criminal behaviour; (iii) to enable people with drug problems to overcome them and live healthy and crime-free lives; (iv) to stifle the availability of illegal drugs on our streets.' Law-enforcement and crime-reduction are central features of this agenda, but so too are aspirations to address social exclusion, community-oriented drugs prevention, and drug-related education and treatment. It is noteworthy that the strategy, and hence policy priorities and resources, focused on illegal drugs and not alcohol.

After Labour's re-election in 2001, the UK Anti-Drugs Coordination Unit, previously a cross-departmental body and based in the Cabinet Office, moved to the Home Office, while at the Department of Health, the new National Treatment Agency (NTA) started work. While this seemed to represent a return to traditional departmental divisions, the new Chief Executive of the NTA did suggest that a shared agenda would continue but be shaped by the national strategy: 'It is sound criminal justice policy to invest in drug treatment. At the same time, we have to look at the drugs strategy as a whole. It is just as important that putting more money into treatment will provide better health care for the user and address the public health agenda by continuing to support harm minimisation.' (Hayes 2001)

LAW ENFORCEMENT AND DRUGS PREVENTION: CRIMINAL JUSTICE AND MULTI-AGENCY INITIATIVES

The importance of intelligence-led policing, use of informants, and collation of data has long been recognized as the necessary strategy for drug law-enforcement (Dorn *et al.* 1992; Collison 1995). This has been reflected in the creation of a series of bodies, from the 1973 Central Drugs and Illegal Immigration Unit to the 1985 National Drugs Intelligence Unit (NDIU) (a joint Police and Customs Services' clearing-house for the collation and networking of information), superceded by the National Drugs Intelligence Unit and now the National Criminal Intelligence Service (NCIS). Following the 1996 Security Service Act, the Security Service (MI5) has contributed to operations against organized crime and drug trafficking. The roles of the Crown Prosecution Service and the Probation Service are discussed in Hough (1996: 23–25). In 2001, the latter was re-organized as a national service and now plays a key role in the national treatment system through administering the Drug Testing and Treatment Orders available to the courts.

Internationally, measures from the mid-1980s increased transnational mutual cooperation (Sheptycki 2000a, 2000b). In the future, Police, Customs, and Security Services liaison officers are likely to enhance their established roles in international anti-drugs and anti-terrorism operations. The European Union responded to the September 2001 attacks on the USA by proposing extensive new powers of cross-border investigation for Europol, effectively seeking to establish a European FBI. To date, this agency has largely acted as a clearing-house for intelligence about drugs and terrorism.

Arguably, given the volume of drugs now produced for the international market, modest improvement in enforcement effectiveness may make little difference to availability. For example, Makarenko (2001: 20) notes that data from the United Nations Drug Control Programme indicate:

Production of opium in Afghanistan increased 100% between 1988 and 1991. Between 1991 and 1999 production expanded from an estimated 2,000 tons to a record 4,600 tons. By the end of 1999 Afghanistan was said to produce 75% of the global supply of opium, from which 80% of global heroin was produced.

To increase enforcement effectiveness against this kind of supply requires some shift of prioritization away from the street and up the chain of supply.

Enforcement statistics

It is generally assumed that one measure of the 'impact' of enforcement is the detection of drugs as reflected in annual seizure statistics. This is, of course, a partial measure, but one upon which government, enforcement agencies, and media place great emphasis. In the past, years of high seizure have been greeted as either (a) a sign of increased success of enforcement efforts, and/or (b) a reflection of an increasing incoming volume of drugs requiring further enforcement resources. In recent years, Police and Customs have acknowledged that seizure statistics should be treated with caution: just one or two seizures of very large amounts can inflate the figures unrepresentatively; correspondingly, low seizure figures do not mean low importation or distribution, for many large consignments may have avoided detection. Generally, Customs and the Police of most countries are unlikely to feel able to claim much more than a 10–15 per cent interception rate.

Recent years have seen increased production and trafficking in heroin, cocaine, and cannabis, but generally seizures have fallen. Record seizures of heroin in several years

In the 1990s reportedly had no discernible effect on street price; and in 2001 the
National Criminal Intelligence Service estimated that up to 30 tonnes of heroin and
40 tonnes of cocaine had been smuggled into the UK in 2000, but that only 2 tonnes
of heroin and 3 tonnes of cocaine had been seized. Street prices for heroin and cocaine
had fallen and the average wholesale price for a kilo of heroin stood at an all-time low
(Druglink 2001b: 6). For cannabis, seizures fell from 80 tonnes between 1997 and
1998 to 42 tonnes in 2000, availability remains high and, again, the price has fallen.
Increasingly, the Home Office, Police and Customs are officially targeting Class A
drugs, and in some cases of cannabis possession (e.g., Lambeth, south London in
2001) police were piloting employment of formal warnings instead of arrests and
cautions.

Law enforcement statistics are therefore subject to severe limitations. They can
reflect only known detection, seizures, and convictions; drugs offences are rarely
reported in the same way as robberies or assault. At the street level of enforcement,
various police forces and strategy commentators have supported the idea of 'low level
policing' aimed at disrupting street markets (Dorn and Lee 1999), diverting users
from criminalization to counselling and treatment, and the consequent widespread
expansion of arrest-referral schemes via which offenders are encouraged to make use
of linked drugs agency services (Edmunds *et al.* 1999).

Sentencing

Data on national sentencing trends have become more widely available, but with
regard to drugs remain the subject of little critical scrutiny (Dorn *et al.* 1992: chapter
10, discussed the rising trend in penalties that commenced from the 1970s onward).
Briefly, this escalation developed as follows. In 1972, i.e. before the 1971 Misuse of
Drugs Act had come into effect, sentences were frequently of between six months' and
two years' duration. By 1976, when the Act had been in operation for three years, the
numbers of persons receiving a prison sentence had approximately doubled by comparison with 1972; and of these, the majority received sentences of between six
months and three years. From 1983 onwards, the courts could refer to guidelines
raising the tariff, subsequently amended upward as a result of *R v Bilinski* (Dorn *et al.*
1992: 185–6). In practice, sentences of ten years or more became common, following
the guidance set by the 1985 Controlled Drugs (Penalties) Act. Amendments and
subsequent legislation have reflected ever-increasing political prioritization of drugs/
crime as a social (but also electoral) issue. Overall, penalties relating to imprisonment
and asset seizure have risen for drug trafficking and related crime, but, as noted
below, new diversionary and treatment schemes have also been introduced for drug
users and related petty-crime offenders who come to court. The implementation of
the 1986 Drug Trafficking Offences Act meant that sentences could include asset
confiscation, although this proved a less effective tool than hoped despite allowing
the presumption that assets are the proceeds of trafficking unless the defendant can
prove otherwise. In a decision with serious implications for this kind of legislation, in
2000 the Scottish Criminal Court of Appeal held that the 1995 Proceeds of Crime
(Scotland) Act was unlawful because such a presumption violates the European Convention on Human Rights. In 2001–2002, £300,000 of money derived from assets

seized was channelled into a new Community Action on Drugs scheme, reflecting a long-argued-for principle of asset-seizure, that such funds should be used toward drug-prevention goals rather than being simply absorbed by the Treasury.

Since the mid-1980s, Home Office data on 'Offenders dealt with' show a consistent rise in the number of persons found guilty, cautioned, or 'dealt with by compounding' for drugs offences under the Misuse of Drugs Act. In 1998, the total number was 127,700, more than quadrupling since 1988. Ninety per cent of offences were for possession, and the majority related to cannabis; however, 'there was an increase of 77 per cent (to 14,780) in the number of heroin offenders in just one year from 1997 to 1998' (Drugscope 2000: 79). In 1992, over 65 per cent of the UK drug offender population were aged below twenty-four years, and 90 per cent were male. The same picture could be drawn at the end of the 1990s (ibid.).

Unsurprisingly, the proportion of offenders known to the criminal justice system who have some form of alcohol or illicit drug problem is significantly high: according to the Office of National Statistics (Singleton *et al.* 1999), 58 per cent of remand and 63 per cent of sentenced prisoners reported hazardous levels of drinking in the year prior to entering prison; 40 per cent of male and 47 per cent of female remand prisoners showed symptoms of severe dependence; 43 per cent of male and 42 per cent of female sentenced prisoners showed moderate to severe signs of dependence (Drugscope 2000: 79–80). Drug-testing of arrestees in eight sites across England and Wales found that 65 per cent tested positive for at least one illegal drug, 29 per cent for opiates and/or cocaine/crack (Bennett *et al.* 2001).

Conclusions about the impact of sentencing are difficult to draw. The little research available suggests that imprisonment may have little effect on drug or drug-related crime behaviour. Furthermore, prison is not generally an effective environment for reducing commitment to a drug-using lifestyle. Drugs are widely available in prisons and the sharing of injecting equipment makes risk of HIV/AIDS, or forms of hepatitis, a serious problem. Mandatory drug testing has probably encouraged a culture of use of drugs that are harder to detect, including a shift from cannabis to opiates.

Treatment, rehabilitation and diversion

The issue of *treatment* of drug and alcohol users by the medical system raises several key criminological questions, such as: what kinds of treatment are most efficacious in (a) reducing reliance on the illegal market for drug supply, and (b) reducing related criminal activity engaged in to generate funds for purchasing drugs? Treatment may be provided for under probation and court orders, in therapeutic communities, or prison settings (Hough 1996: 26–46, 51). However, as Jarvis and Parker (1990: 29) remarked over a decade ago, 'evidence of the efficacy of medical treatment, whatever form it might take, is neither plentiful nor conclusive'. The most significant reviews of efficacy since these remarks have probably been the National Treatment Outcomes Research Study and related 1996 Department of Health Task Force to Review the Effectiveness of Drug Treatment Services. MacGregor (1998: 192) notes that the latter 'concluded (rather surprisingly perhaps) that treatment works', but that in making this claim and justifying the role of treatment services, the Task Force 'aligned itself closely to the crime issue', arguing that 'drug misuse causes immense harm to individuals and to society' and presenting 'treatment as a less costly alternative to imprisonment and to benign neglect'.

One key underlying assumption of the practice of methadone maintenance for heroin users, has been that this will remove the need to resort to criminal activity and erode the profitability of the illegal market (Mott 1989: 32). Some significant studies have indicated that maintenance has little clear impact on criminal activity, though there is some evidence that methadone treatment can help to reduce acquisitive crime rates in areas of heroin-based drug markets and that 'tailored' or 'flexible' therapeutic programmes can be effective (Parker and Kirby 1996; Jarvis and Parker 1990: 32). The introduction of Drug Testing and Treatment Orders for use by the courts, as well as new specialist drug courts, may offer opportunities for innovation here. The outcome of such interventions will still face the problem of whether any success can be ascribed to the treatment *per se* or to personal biography and situation (for example, users feeling that they are 'growing out of drugs' or are weary of the life-style). In practice, the argument for flexibility is precisely about being able to draw users into treatment at the point where they feel willing or need to change.

In summary, studies are by no means unanimous in their conclusions about the impact of treatment upon drug-related crime behaviour. Broadly, Hough's (1996) review is optimistic about the prospects for effective interventions and impacts. By contrast, recent research (Bachus *et al.* 2000) concluded that reducing drug use does not necessarily reduce crime. The study followed-up former opiate addicts, 58 per cent of whom remained abstinent: 'A popular belief is that the end of an addiction career involves a concomitant abandonment of the criminal lifestyle. However, there was little evidence in our data to suggest this. In fact for many of the subjects quite the opposite was true.' Treatment, abstinence, and tailored programmes do seem to be able to improve social conditions and personal relationships, but they have had a poor record in improving labour market skills or housing, financial, and personal circumstances. Increasingly treatment, rehabilitation, and diversion schemes are incorporating opportunities for gaining vocational skills-training and qualifications (South *et al.* 2001).

In relation to serious alcohol misusers, Alcohol Concern (2000: 15) suggests that opportunities for treatment and prevention of re-offending are largely missed because of the absence of effective sentencing options (e.g. exclusion of alcohol from the Drug Testing and Treatment Orders and new drug courts). Many other problems here parallel those relevant to drugs, for example, the need for specialist services within prisons and improved support arrangements on release from prison.

The key concept and philosophy underpinning clinical and social work practice has undoubtedly been harm-minimization (Stimson 1998), an approach that aims to reduce health, legal, social, and financial harms associated with drug misuse. The concept first received 'official' endorsement in the pre-AIDS, 1984 ACMD *Prevention* report. Subsequently, although now somewhat de-emphasized, it was most evidently HIV/AIDS and the considerable impact this had on British drug policy that provided support for wide acceptance of harm-minimization. Syringe exchange schemes to draw injecting users into services, and provision of clean injecting equipment and harm-minimization advice, made major contributions to the containment of HIV/AIDS. Harm-minimization and new community partnerships placing stress on prevention have become the twin pillars of drugs-related health and social care service delivery since the late 1980s, and a major contribution to the success of such initiatives has been changes in policies adopted by the Police Service in many areas (MacGregor 1999; Dorn and Lee 1999).

DRUGS, ALCOHOL, AND CRIME

Decriminalization versus prohibition

The illegality of certain drugs obviously makes their possession, supply, or preparation and manufacture an offence. Cannabis is the key drug in the enforcement statistics, yet is clearly a recreational drug of choice for a significant population (Sharp *et al.* 2001) and argued to be relatively harmless compared to traditionally designated 'dangerous drugs' (Jacobson 1999). These points give rise to questions about whether the law is sensible, or whether legalisation or other options are desirable (Police Foundation 2000), a debate fuelled by campaigns for recognition of the therapeutic value of cannabis in alleviating some painful conditions (Grinspoon 1999). The wider debate about decriminalization or legalization of all or most drugs may gather further momentum in the twenty-first century.

Proponents (Nadelman 1989; Stevenson 1991; Graham 1991) argue that the costly, counter-productive, and unsuccessful efforts of law enforcement as a response to drug use suggest that legalization is a wiser alternative. It is suggested that availability would not mean unacceptable rises in use, and that taxation of legal supply would provide funds for educational, health, and counselling responses. Regulation would ensure purity levels and hence reduce health hazards caused by adulterants; and legal availability would remove the profit motive that drives the criminal market. Opponents (Inciardi and McBride 1989; Wilson 1990) argue that legalization *would* increase use, thereby increasing serious costs to society. The frequently cited example of *de facto* decriminalization of cannabis use—The Netherlands—has often been misunderstood, particularly by US prohibitionists. This is actually a case of a policy aimed at preserving 'market separation', keeping cannabis supply distinct from supply of drugs with an 'unacceptable risk' (Dorn 1992: 111); and in any case, in response to perceived abuses, The Netherlands government has introduced a series of restrictions on the cannabis café system in recent years (Horstink-Von Meyenfeldt 1996: 103–4).

Drugs and crime

Debates about the drugs/crime relationship generally follow one or other of the following propositions: 'criminal lifestyles may facilitate involvement with drugs'; or 'dependence on drugs then leads to criminal activity to pay for further drug use'. There are numerous elaborations on these themes, and Walters (1994) is a good example of an attempt to refine and expand such explanations drawing on theory from criminology, sociology, and psychology.

Typically, drug-related crime is non-violent and acquisitive, involving theft, shop-lifting, forgery, burglary, or prostitution. More serious drug-related crimes of violence, murder, large-scale trafficking, and money-laundering have been increasing in Britain—although still on a small scale by comparison with the USA. Hough (1996: 1) observed that 'the costs sustained by victims of drug-related crime are substantial: crimes committed by dependent heroin users alone may involve losses of between £58 million and £864 million annually'; and research by Parker and Bottomley (1996) suggested that crack-cocaine users may be spending £20k per year, and dependent heroin users £10k per year, deriving their income largely from acquisitive crime, although welfare benefits and legal work income also contributed. Others (Collison 1994, 1996; Parker 1996) noted a greater hedonistic attachment to a consumption-oriented lifestyle among young offenders using illegal drugs and/or alcohol, and that petty-crime was routinely engaged in for support.

'Involvement in criminal activity leads to drug use' Some studies provide evidence that heroin or other serious drug misusers would already have been involved in delinquent or criminal activities before they started using these drugs. The argument on this side is that: (a) involvement in deviant/criminal-oriented subcultures or groups would be likely to lead a person to encounter the availability of drugs sold within that culture; (b) they would have a deviant lifestyle which would accommodate deviant drug use with relative ease; and (c) while money from criminal activity might then pay for the drugs, it was not drug addiction or use *per se* which led to the perpetration of crime.

Work in this vein follows the classic New York study by Preble and Casey (1969), which emphasized that it is the activity and lifestyle surrounding drug use, as much as drug-taking itself, which are attractive to users. As described in this tradition of ethnographic research, the hustling, enterprising, dynamic life of the street user is quite the opposite of the stereotyped portrayal of the dazed and dozing junkie. In Scotland, studies by Hammersley *et al.* (1989) challenged the view that heroin use is a direct causal determinant of criminal activity: although the two are related, use of other drugs is also related to crime (an obvious but often neglected point); and furthermore, it is a prior history of criminality that is the more important determinant of crime frequency. Thus, considering teenage drug users' involvement in crime, they observe that 'explanations of delinquency are likely to be more relevant . . . than explanations invoking "drug addiction"' (Hammersley *et al.* 1990: 1592). Importantly, moderate heroin users were not significantly more criminal than cannabis and/or alcohol users.

'Involvement in drug use causes crime' Of course, other studies argue that there *is* a *causal* link, and that drug use (particularly of heroin) causes crime. Some crimes seem to have a clear relationship with drug use. In the early 1980s (and in the 1960s to a lesser extent) there was concern about break-ins to pharmacies with stocks of con-trolled drugs. Jarvis and Parker (1989) found that the criminal convictions of one group of heroin users doubled after they started using heroin regularly, and concluded that 'addiction leads to acquisitive crime'. There is a huge body of work supporting

this proposition, albeit principally from the USA. The evidence is convincing—but so too is the evidence from studies supporting the opposing proposition.

The simple resolution of this debate is to agree with Nurco *et al.* (1985: 101), who sensibly suggested that 'the long and continuing controversy over whether narcotic addicts commit crimes primarily to support their habits or whether addiction is merely one more manifestation of a deviant and criminal life-style seems pointless in view of the fact that addicts cannot be regarded as a homogeneous group'. (Hough (1996: 10–18) provides useful, further review of 'drugs and crime' studies, and many key articles are reprinted in South 1995: vol. 2.)

Drugs, crime, and drug markets

Diversity and sophistication of organization is evident in drug markets, albeit that the British market is best characterized in terms of 'disorganized crime' rather than images of 'Mafiosa' and 'Mr Bigs' (Ruggiero and South 1995; Dorn *et al.* 1992; Reuter 1983). Use of violence, of firearms, and of money-laundering has increased in various ways since the mid-1980s (Levi 1991; South 1992). Studies of the development of drug markets in heroin, cocaine/crack, cannabis, and ecstasy in the 1990s include Akhtar and South 2000; Bean 1993; Hobbs 1995; Parker *et al.* 1998; Ruggiero and South 1995. For some participants involved in large-scale trafficking/dealing, high rates of profit are achievable; although for users engaging in small-scale dealing and non-drug crimes, the returns per crime are probably small.

The picture of drug markets as fragmented, with a diversity of participants from highly successful entrepreneurs (Hobbs 1995) to petty-criminal users and dealers, often caught within the criminal justice system (Ruggiero and South 1995), has certain strategic implications. Enforcement efforts have increasingly employed intelligence sources to target the specific vulnerabilities of the different participants in drug markets. However, the globalized networking and interlocking of production, transport, finance, and distribution systems will receive greater enforcement and intelligence attention in the future. The drugs business may not be characterized by monopolistic control, but it does involve criminal cartels and conspiracies, which in turn may involve 'legitimate' actors such as state security agencies and corporations (Chambliss 1989; Levi 1991: 301) or nation states.

Alcohol and crime

Concerns about the relationship between alcohol and crime are not new. According to Lombroso (1911/1968: 95–96):

Alcohol . . . is a cause of crime, first because many commit crime in order to obtain drinks, further, because men sometimes seek in drink the courage necessary to commit crime, or an excuse for their misdeeds; again, because it is by the aid of drink that young men are drawn into crime; and because the drink shop is the place for meeting of accomplices, where they not only plan their crimes but squander their gains . . . it appears that alcoholism occurred oftenest in the case of those charged with assaults, sexual offences, and insurrections. Next came assassinations and homicide; and in the last rank those imprisoned for arson and theft, that is to say, crime against property.

As Collins (1982: xvi) observed, dominant opinions about the role of alcohol in criminal behaviour have probably changed little; more research may have been done, but the prisoners that Lombroso interviewed for his research have been followed by later generations of prisoners, asked similar questions, despite greater awareness of the problems inherent in generalizing from such respondent groups. However, conclusive findings remain elusive. The studies and debates concerning the extent to which alcohol consumption is responsible for certain forms of criminal behaviour are extensive but inconclusive (Raistrick *et al.* 1999; All Party Group on Alcohol Misuse 1995), and have some similarities and some dissimilarities with those concerning drugs and crime.

In terms of dissimilarities, it is alcohol rather more than illegal drugs that tends to be linked to aggression and violent crime, and hence, potentially, to crime with longer-term effects for victims and society (Alcohol Concern 2001; *Lancet* 1999). Estimates from the British Medical Association suggest that the offender or victim had been drinking in 65 per cent of murders, 75 per cent of stabbings, 70 per cent of beatings, and 50 per cent of fights or domestic assaults (ibid). Raistrick *et al.* (1999: 54) similarly note that

many perpetrators and victims of crimes of disorder or violence, including murder, as well as perpetrators of acquisitive crimes, such as burglary and theft, have alcohol in their blood at the time of the offence. . . . Furthermore, as with other drugs, heavier users of alcohol are more likely to have criminal records and to admit to criminal acts than are lighter users or abstainers.

Nonetheless, it remains the common conclusion of such research that the existence of a causal relationship between alcohol and violent crime is difficult to substantiate (Alcohol Concern 2001); furthermore, it can be argued that 'alcohol may be neither a necessary nor sufficient *cause* of crime, but may nonetheless *affect* crime' (Raistrick *et al.* 1999: 55; Collins 1982: 289). Research findings suggest that a variety of co-factors may play a significant role in alcohol-related aggression. As with illegal drug consumption, *belief* about how alcohol is 'supposed' to affect behaviour, *coupled* with the influences of immediate social context and wider culture, are as important for the behavioural outcome as the amount of alcohol consumed (Mott 1990: 25; Royal College of Psychiatrists 1986; Pearson 1992). A recent Home Office review of research concludes that situational and cultural variables may play a role in the relationship between alcohol and aggression, and that no direct pharmacological link between alcohol and violent behaviour is supported. More probably, alcohol influences the social and cognitive processes that may lead to aggression (Deehan 1999). Hence, socialization and cultural expectations, stereotypes and labelling, circumstances and significant others, all play their part in shaping people's identities as 'aggressive' and as 'drinkers' (Borrill and Stevens 1993). Such definitions change across time and cultures, and are also strongly influenced by positive and negative images of alcohol use in entertainment media and alcohol advertising. Masculinity, alcohol, and violence is a further complex relationship deserving more attention (Tomsen 1997; Taylor 1999: 85–86).

Alcohol may have a relationship with crime in other ways, for example:

intoxication may shift some people over the threshold from contemplating crime to committing it; . . . public disorder is commonly linked to open-air drinking by young people; . . . alcohol use can serve as a financial motive for crime; alcohol problems can produce a home environment conducive to anti-social behaviours; . . . drunk people may be amnesic regarding the negative consequences of their criminal actions, thus failing to learn from them; and alcohol intoxication can reduce inhibitions and judgement. (Raistrick *et al.* 1999: 55)

(See also Ramsay 1996; Hammersley *et al.* 1990.) Some of these factors may contribute to crimes in which there is a potential but unknown association with alcohol; in other words, there has been considerable research on alcohol and violence, sexual assault, and acquisitive crimes, but little on crimes such as 'fraud, tax evasion, smuggling, . . . and other white-collar crimes' and the influence of alcohol (Raistrick *et al.* 1999: 56).

Criminality of drinkers

Long-term, follow-up studies examining criminal careers and drinking careers suggest that 'criminality and alcohol abuse tend to run in parallel, as both have their peak incidence in young adults and tend to diminish with age' (d'Orban 1991: 298). Persistence of heavy drinking and petty-crime into mid-life characterizes 'habitual drunkenness offenders' (ibid.), and some studies show a disproportionately higher level of alcohol problems among arrestees and prisoners than found in the general population (Raistrick *et al.* 1999). The cautions about inferring causality still apply, however: d'Orban (1991: 296) observed that 'studies of offences of violence show that the majority of the offenders, the victims or both, had consumed alcohol prior to their offence'; but other commentators suggest that whatever the alcohol consumption levels of the offenders (be it higher or lower than average), consideration of their drinking 'must be related to specific criminal incidents' (Mott 1990: 25; also Murphy 1983; Myers 1982), and that where drinking and delinquency are 'functionally related, the drinking can be an antecedent to the commission of the delinquent act, or it can be a consequence of the crime' (McMurran and Hollin 1989: 386; also Cookson 1992).

Lastly, although detection and prosecution of drug-related driving offences have become an increased priority for traffic police in recent years, it has been road accidents and deaths related to drinking and driving that have attracted most attention from the police and community groups since the 1960s. Over the years, high-profile anti-drink driving campaigns, and tougher penalties and enforcement seem to have had some impact. Nonetheless, 'Despite a decline in road deaths between 1979 and 1993, there was also a rise in figures from 540 deaths in 1993 to 580 in 1996. In addition there was a rise in the total number of drink-drive injuries from 14,980 in 1993 to 17,040 in 1996'. (Alcohol Concern, Factsheet 10, 2001). Calls to reduce the 'drink-drive limit' further are often made.

CONCLUSIONS

There remains much that we do not know about alcohol and drug use, and about how such use ultimately relates to crime and criminality. As Raistrick *et al.* (1999: 47) note, 'it is not known why some substance misusers become dependent on one substance, such as alcohol, and others on another, such as heroin, while most avoid dependence and grow out of substance misuse, or grow into a relatively stable and controlled pattern of alcohol or other drug use as adults'. Similarly, despite improved evidence about the successes and failures of prevention, treatment, and criminal justice interventions, there is still a long way to go in improving our knowledge.

More importantly than ever, this need to improve our knowledge and under-standing applies not only to our domestic situation but also to the global context. The new anti-terrorism agenda of international law-enforcement embraces anti-drugs initiatives. Afghanistan and the central Asian republics were receiving more enforcement-intelligence and research interest before September 2001 (Makarenko 2001), but will receive even more now. In such a context, part of the agenda for a sane international drug control policy, as well as for the criminology of drugs, must be to take a more comparative approach and deepen our understanding of the production and use of intoxicants in non-Western societies. On the one hand, such work can inform anti-trafficking strategies, but on the other, it may also emphasize that identi-fying the 'villains versus the victims' is not an easy task (Macdonald 2001). A com-parative approach could also help to illuminate why 'international conventions and national laws can be inappropriate and ineffective in preventing traditional substance use' (Saxena 1995: 14) or tradition-based drug-crop cultivation. Lastly, knowing more about other societies can probably 'teach us much that is relevant to prevention in our own' (Gossop 1995: 16).

Selected further reading

Useful web sites with links to further sites are provided by Drugscope **www.drugscope.co.uk** and by Alcohol Concern **www.alcoholconcern.org.uk**. The Drugscope web site provides access to *Drugsearch*, an online drugs encyclopaedia. N. South (ed.), *Drugs: Cultures, Controls and Everyday Life* (London: Sage, 1999) includes essays covering up-to-date research and debates; N. South (ed.), *Drugs, Crime and Criminal Justice*, vols 1 and 2 (Aldershot: Dartmouth, 1995) reprint various classic and recent articles. A. Tyler, *Street Drugs* (London: Hodder and Stoughton, 1995) remains a good general overview, while P. Bean, *Drugs and Crime* (Cullompton, Devon: Willan, 2002) focuses on law enforcement and criminal justice debates.

On history, see W. McAllister, *Drug Diplomacy in the Twentieth Century* (London: Routledge, 2000) and the new edition of V. Berridge's classic text, *Opium and the People* (London: Free Association, 1999.)

The latest drug-related data from the BCS is usefully summarized in C. Sharp, P. Baker, C. Goulden, M. Ramsay and, A. Sondhi, *Drug Misuse Declared in 2000: Key Results from the British Crime Survey*, Findings 149 (London: Home Office, 2001).

References

ADVISORY COUNCIL ON MISUSE OF DRUGS (1984), *Prevention*, London: HMSO.

—— (1991), *Drug Misuse and the Criminal Justice System, Part 1*, London: HMSO.

—— (1994), *Drug Misuse and the Criminal Justice System, Part 2*, London: HMSO.

—— (1998), *Drug Misuse and the Environment: A Summary*, Supplement to *Druglink*, 13, 4.

—— (1999), *Reducing Drug Related Deaths*, London: The Stationery Office

AKHTAR, S., and SOUTH, N. (2000), 'Hidden from heroin's history: heroin use and dealing within an English Asian community', in M. Hough and M. Natarajan (eds), *International Drug Markets: From Research to Policy*, Crime Prevention Studies, vol. 11, New York: Criminal Justice Press.

ALCOHOL CONCERN (2000), *Britain's Ruin: meeting government objectives via a national alcohol strategy*, London: Alcohol Concern.

—— (2001), **www.alcoholconcern. org.uk/**.

ALL PARTY GROUP ON ALCOHOL MISUSE (1995), *Alcohol and Crime: Breaking the Link*, London: Alcohol Concern.

AULD, J., DORN, N. and SOUTH, N. (1986), 'Irregular Work, Irregular Pleasures: Heroin in the 1980s', in R. Matthews and J. Young (eds) *Confronting Crime*, London: Sage.

BACHUS, L., STRANG, J., and WATSON, P. (2000), 'Pathways to Abstinence: Two-Year Follow-up Data on 60 Abstinent Former Opiate Addicts', *European Addiction Research*, 6: 141–7.

BEAN, P. (1993), 'Cocaine and Crack: The Promotion of and Epidemic', in P. Bean (ed.), *Cocaine and Crack: Supply and Use*, Basingstoke: Macmillan.

BENNETT, T., HOLLOWAY, K., and WILLIAMS, T. (2001), 'Drug Use and Offending', *Findings*, 148, London: Home Office.

BERRIDGE, V. (1978), 'War Conditions and Narcotics Control: The Passing of the Defence of the Realm Act Regulation 40B', *Journal of Social Policy*, 7, 3: 285–304.

—— (1979), 'Morality and Medical Science: Concepts of Narcotic Addiction in Britain, 1820–1926', *Annals of Science*, 36: 67–85.

—— (1984), 'Drugs and social policy: the establishment of drug control in Britain, 1900–1930', *British Journal of Addiction*, 79: 1.

—— (1999), *Opium and the People*, rev. edn, London: Free Association.

—— and EDWARDS, G. (1987), *Opium and the People*, 2nd edn, New Haven, Conn: Yale University Press.

BORRILL, J., and STEVENS, D. (1993), 'Understanding human violence: the implications of social structure, gender, social perception and alcohol', *Criminal Behaviour and Mental Health*, 3: 129–41.

BOYS, A., DOBSON, J., MARSDEN, J., and STRANG, J. (2001), *Cocaine Trends: A Qualitative Study of Young People and Cocaine Use*, London: National Addiction Centre.

BRITISH MEDICAL ASSOCIATION (1986), *Young People and Alcohol*, London: British Medical Association.

BRUUN, K., PAN, L., and REXED, I. (1975), *The Gentlemen's Club: International Control of Drugs and Alcohol*, Chicago, Ill.: University of Chicago Press.

CHAMBLISS, W. (1989), 'State Organised Crime', *Criminology*, 27/2: 183–208.

COLLINS, J. (ed.) (1982), *Drinking and Crime: Perspectives on the Relationships between Alcohol Consumption and Criminal Behaviour*, London: Tavistock.

COLLISON, M. (1994), 'Drug offenders and criminal justice: careers, compulsion, commitment and penalty', *Crime, Law and Social Change*, 21: 49–71.

—— (1995), *Police, Drugs and Community*, London: Free Association.

—— (1996), 'In search of the high life: drugs, crime, masculinity and consumption', *British Journal of Criminology*, 36, 3: 428–44.

COOKSON, H. (1992), 'Alcohol use and offence type in young male offenders', *British Journal of Criminology*, 32: 352–60.

CORKERY, J. (2000), *Drug Seizure and Offender Statistics, UK, 1998*, Statistical Bulletin 3/00, London: Home Office.

CURRIE, E. (1993), 'Towards a policy on drugs', *Dissent* (Winter): 65–71.

DAVIS, J., and DITTON, J. (1990), 'The 1990s: Decade of the Stimulants?', *British Journal of Addiction*, 85: 811–13.

DEEHAN, A. (1999), *Alcohol and Crime: Taking Stock*, Policing and Crime Reduction Unit, London: Home Office.

Ditton, J., and Hammersley, R. (eds) (1996), A Very Greedy Drug: Cocaine in Context, Reading: Harwood.

—— and Speirits, K. (1982), 'The New Wave of Heroin Addiction in Britain', Sociology, 16/4: 595–8.

Donoghoe, M., Dorn, N., James, C., Jones, S., Ribbens, J., and South, N. (1987), 'How Families and Communities Respond to Heroin', in N. Dorn and N. South (eds) (1987), A Land Fit for Heroin?: Drug Policies, Prevention and Practice, London: Macmillan.

d'Orban, P. (1991), 'The Crimes Connection: Alcohol', in I. Glass (ed.), The International Handbook of Addiction Behaviour, London: Routledge.

Dorn, N. (1992), 'Clarifying Policy Options on Drug Trafficking: Harm Minimization is Distinct from Legalization', in E. Buning et al. (eds), Reduction of Drug Related Harm, London: Routledge.

——, Henderson, S., and South, N. (1992), AIDS: Women, Drugs and Social Care, London: Falmer Press.

—— and Lee, M. (1999), 'Drugs and policing in Europe', in N. South (ed.) (1999), Drugs: Cultures, Controls and Everyday Life, London: Sage.

——, Murji, K., and South, N, (1992), Traffickers: Drug Markets and Law Enforcement, London: Routledge.

—— and South, N. (eds) (1987), A Land Fit for Heroin?: Drug Policies, Prevention and Practice, London: Macmillan.

—— and —— (1991), 'Profits and Penalties: New Trends in Legislation and Law Enforcement Concerning Illegal Drugs', in D. Whynes and P. Bean (eds) (1991), Policing and Prescribing: The British System of Drug Control, London: Macmillan.

—— and —— (1992), 'The Power Behind Practice: Drug Control and Harm Minimisation in the Inter-Agency and Criminal Law Contexts', in J. Strang and M. Gossop (eds), Heroin Addiction and Drug Policy: the British System, Oxford: Oxford Medical Press

Downes, D. (1977), 'The Drug Addict as a Folk Devil', in P. Rock (ed.), Drugs and Politics, New Brunswick: Transaction.

Druglink (1992), 'Low Dependence and Use Typical of British Cocaine/Crack Users', Druglink, 7, 3: 6.

—— (2001a), 'The European School Survey Project', Druglink, 16, 2: 6.

—— (2001b), 'NCIS on Trafficking', Druglink 16, 5: 6.

Drugscope (2000), Drugs: Your Questions Answered—A Student Reader, London: Drugscope.

Edmunds, M., Hough, M., Turnbull, P., and May, T. (1999), Doing Justice to Treatment: Referring Offenders to Drug Services, DPAS paper 2, London: Home Office.

Erickson, P., and Watson, V. (1990), 'Women, Illicit Drugs and Crime', in L. Kozlowski et al. (eds), Research Advances in Alcohol and Drug Problems, vol. 10, 251–72, New York/London: Plenum Press.

ESPAD (2001), Report available at www.alcoholhealth.homepage.com/espad.htm

Ettorre, E. (1992), Women and Substance Use, London: Macmillan.

—— and Riska, E. (1995), Gendered Moods: Psychotropics and Society, London: Routledge.

Fagan, J. (1994), 'Women and drugs revisited: female participation in the cocaine economy', Journal of Drug Issues, 24, 2: 179–225.

Finch, E., Griffiths, P., and Farrell, M. (1998), 'HCV Policies—where do we go?', International Journal of Drug Policy, 9, 1: 1–2.

Ford, C., and Ryrie, I. (1999), 'Prescribing injectable methadone in general practice', International Journal of Drug Policy, 10, 1: 39–45.

Foster, J. (2000), 'Social Exclusion, Crime and Drugs', Drugs: Education, Prevention and Policy, 7, 4: 317–30.

Gerada, C. (2001), 'Times they are a'changing: doctoring drug users', Druglink, 16, 4: 23–25.

Giggs, J. (1991), 'The Epidemiology of Contemporary Drug Abuse', in D. Whynes and P. Bean (eds) (1991), Policing and Prescribing: The British System of Drug Control, London: Macmillan.

Gossop, M. (1995), 'Counting the Costs as well as the Benefits of Drug Control Laws', Addiction, 90: 16–17.

Graham, G. (1991), 'Criminalisation and Control', in D. Whynes and P. Bean (eds) (1991), Policing and Prescribing: The British System of Drug Control, London: Macmillan.

Grinspoon, L. (1999), 'Medical Marijuana in a Time of Prohibition', International Journal of Drug Policy, 10, 3: 145–56.

Hammersley, R., Forsyth, A., Morrison, V., and Davies, J. (1989), 'The Relationship between

Crime and Opioid Use', *British Journal of Addiction*, 84: 1029–44.

——, —— and LAVELLE, T. (1990), 'The Criminality of New Drug Users in Glasgow', *British Journal of Addiction*, 85: 1583–94.

——, KHAN, F., and DITTON, J. (2002), *Ecstasy and the Rise of the Chemical Generation*, London: Routledge.

HAYES, P. (2001), 'Driving up treatment standards: interview', *Access*, 4 (Drugs Prevention Advisory Service newsletter).

HENDERSON, S. (1999), 'Drugs and Culture: the Question of Gender', in N. South (ed.) (1999), *Drugs: Cultures, Controls and Everyday Life*, London: Sage.

HM GOVERNMENT (1998), *Tackling Drugs to Build a Better Britain*, London: Stationery Office.

HOBBS, D. (1995), *Bad Business: Professional Crime in Britain*, Oxford: Oxford University Press.

—— (1997), 'Criminal collaboration: youth gangs, subcultures, professional criminals, and organized crime', in M. Maguire, R. Morgan, and R. Reiner (eds), *The Oxford Handbook of Criminology*, 2nd edn, Oxford: Oxford University Press.

HORSTINK-VON MEYENFELDT, L. (1996), 'The Netherlands: Tightening Up of the Cafes Policy', in N. Dorn, J. Jepsen, and E. Savona (eds), *European Drug Policies and Enforcement*, London: Macmillan.

HOUGH, M. (1996), *Drugs Misuse and the Criminal Justice System: A Review of the Literature*, London: Home Office, Drugs Prevention Initiative.

HUNT, G., JOE-LAIDLER, K., and MACKENZIE, K. (2000), '"Chillin", Being Dogged and Getting Buzzed": Alcohol in the lives of female gang members', *Drugs: Education, Prevention and Policy*, 7, 4: 331–53.

INCIARDI, J. (1986), *The War on Drugs: Heroin, Cocaine and Public Policy*, Palo Alto, Cal.: Mayfield.

—— and MCBRIDE, D. (1989), 'Legalisation: A High Risk Alternative in the War on Drugs', *American Behavioural Scientist*, 32/3: 259–89.

INSTITUTE FOR THE STUDY OF DRUG DEPENDENCE (1999), 'Coke in the UK', *Druglink*, 14, 6: 4.

JACOBSON, M. (ed.) (1999), *Regulating Cannabis: Comparative Perspectives*, special issue, *International Journal of Drug Policy*, 10, 4.

JARVIS, G., and PARKER, H. (1989), 'Young Heroin Users and Crime', *British Journal of Criminology*, 29: 175–85.

—— and —— (1990), 'Can Medical Treatment Reduce Crime Amongst Young Heroin Users?', *Home Office Research Bulletin*, 28: 29–32.

JOHNSTONE, G. (1996), *Medical Concepts and Penal Policy*, London: Cavendish.

KOHN, M. (1992), *Dope Girls: The Birth of the British Drug Underground*, London: Lawrence and Wishart.

LANCET, THE (1999), 'Alcohol and Violence', *The Lancet*, vol. 336, 17 November: 1223–24.

LEACH, K. (1991), 'The Junkies' Doctors and the London Drug Scene in the 1960s: Some Remembered Fragments', in D. Whynes and P. Bean (eds), *Policing and Prescribing: The British System of Drug Control*, 35–39, London: Macmillan.

LEITNER, M., SHAPLAND, J., and WILES P. (1993), *Drug Usage and Drugs Prevention*, London: Home Office.

LEVI, M. (1991), 'Pecunia Non Olet: Cleansing the money-launderers from the Temple', *Crime, Law and Social Change*, 16: 217–302.

LEWIS, R., HARTNOL, R., BRYER, S., DAVIAUD, E., and MITCHESON, M. (1985), 'Scoring Smack: The Illicit Heroin Market in London, 1980–83', *British Journal of Addiction*, 80: 281–90.

LOMBROSO, C. (1968), *Crime: Its Causes and Remedies*, Montclair, NJ.: Patterson Smith, originally published 1911.

MACDONALD, D. (2001), 'Death, Destruction and Depression: Understanding Afghanistan', *Druglink*, 16, 5: 23–26.

MACGREGOR, S. (1998), 'Reluctant Partners: Trends in Approaches to Urban Drug-taking in Contemporary Britain', *Journal of Drug Issues*, 28, 1: 185–98.

—— (1999), 'Medicine, Custom or Moral Fibre: Policy Responses to Drug Misuse', in N. South (ed.), *Drugs: Cultures, Controls and Everyday Life*, London: Sage.

MAHER, L. (1997), *Sexed Work: Gender, Race and Resistance in a Brooklyn Drug Market*, Oxford: Clarendon Press.

MAKARENKO, T. (2001), 'Getting to Market', *Druglink*, 16, 5: 19–22.

MAY, T., EDMUNDS, M., and HOUGH, M. (1999), *Street Business: Links Between Sex and Drug Markets*, Crime Prevention Series Paper, London: Home Office Police Research Group.

MCALLISTER, W. (2000), *Drug Diplomacy in the Twentieth Century*, London: Routledge.

MCCONVILLE, B. (1991), *Women Under the Influence: Alcohol and its Impact*, London: Grafton.

McDonald, M. (ed.) (1994a), *Gender, Drink and Drugs*, Oxford: Berg.

—— (1994b), 'A Social-Anthropological View of Gender, Drink and Drugs', in M. McDonald (ed.), *Gender, Drink and Drugs*, Oxford: Berg.

McMurran, M., and Hollin, C. (1989), 'Drinking and Delinquency', *British Journal of Criminology*, 29/4: 386–93.

Ministry of Health (1926), *Report of the Departmental Committee on Morphine and Heroin Addiction*, London: HMSO.

Mott, J. (1989), 'Reducing Heroin Related Crime', *Home Office Research Unit Bulletin*, 26: 30–3.

—— (1990), 'Young People, Alcohol and Crime', *Home Office Research Bulletin* (Research and Statistics Department), 28: 24–28.

—— (1991), 'Crime and Heroin Use', in D. Whynes and P. Bean (eds), *Policing and Prescribing: The British System of Drug Control*, London: Macmillan.

Murji, K. (1999), 'White Lines: Culture, "Race" and Drugs', in N. South (ed.), *Drugs: Cultures, Controls and Everyday Life*, London: Sage.

Murphy, D. (1983), 'Alcohol and Crime', *Home Office Research and Planning Unit Research Bulletin*, 15: 8–11.

Myers, T. (1982), 'Alcohol and Violent Crime Re-examined', *British Journal of Addiction*, 77: 399–414.

Nadelman, E. (1989), 'Drug Prohibition in the United States: Costs, Consequences and Alternatives', *Science*, 245: 939–47.

Nurco, D., Ball, J., Shaffer, J., and Hanlon, T. (1985), 'The Criminality of Narcotic Addicts', *The Journal of Nervous and Mental Disease*, 173/2: 94–102.

Oswald, P. (1982), 'The Healing Herb?', *Youth in Society*, July, 68: 21–22.

Parker, H. (1996), 'Alcohol, persistent young offenders and criminological cul-de-sacs', *British Journal of Criminology*, 36, 2: 282–99.

——, Aldridge, J., and Measham, F. (1998), *Illegal Leisure: The Normalization of Adolescent Recreational Drug Use*, London: Routledge.

——, Bakx, K., and Newcombe, R. (1988), *Living with Heroin: The Impact of a Drugs 'Epidemic' on an English Community*, Milton Keynes: Open University Press.

—— and Bottomley, T. (1996), *Crack Cocaine and Drugs-Crime Careers*, R and SD Paper 34, London: Home Office.

—— and Kirby, P. (1996), *Methadone Maintenance and Crime Reduction on Merseyside*, London: Home Office, PRG.

—— and Measham, F. (1994), 'Pick 'n Mix: changing patterns of illicit drug use amongst 1990s adolescents', *Drugs: Education, Prevention and Policy*, 1, 1: 5–14.

Parssinen, T. (1983), *Secret Passions, Secret Remedies: Narcotic Drugs in British Society, 1820–1930*, Manchester: Manchester University Press.

Patel, K. (1999), 'Watching brief', *Druglink*, 14, 5: 18–19.

Pearson, G. (1987a), *The New Heroin Users*, Oxford: Basil Blackwell.

—— (1987b), 'Social Deprivation, Unemployment and Patterns of Heroin Use', in N. Dorn and N. South (eds), *A Land Fit for Heroin?: Drug Policies, Prevention and Practice*, London: Macmillan.

—— (1991), 'Drug Control Policies in Britain', in M. Tonry and J.Q. Wilson (eds), *Drugs and the Criminal Justice System, Crime and Justice*, 14: 167–227.

Pearson, G. (1992), 'The Role of Culture in the Drug Question', in G. Edwards, M. Lader and C. Drummond (eds), *The Nature of Alcohol and Drug Related Problems*, Oxford: Oxford University Press.

——, Gilman, M., and McIver, S. (1986), *Young People and Heroin: An Examination of Heroin Use in the North of England*, London: Health Education Council; Aldershot: Gower/Avebury.

—— and Patel, K. (1998), 'Drugs, Deprivation and Ethnicity: Outreach among Asian Drug Users in a Northern English City', *Journal of Drug Issues* 28, 1: 199–224.

Peck, D., and Plant, M. (1986), 'Unemployment and Illegal Drug Use: Concordant Evidence from a Prospective Study and National Trends', *British Medical Journal*, 293: 929–32.

Police Foundation (2000), *Drugs and the Law: Report of the Independent Inquiry*, London: Police Foundation.

Preble, E., and Casey, J. (1969), 'Taking Care of Business: The Heroin User's Life on the Street', *International Journal of the Addictions*, 4/1: 1–24.

Pryce, K. (1979), *Endless Pressure: A Study of West Indian Lifestyles in Bristol*, Harmondsworth: Penguin.

Raistrick, D., Hodgson, R., and Ritson, B. (eds) (1999), *Tackling Alcohol Together: The Evidence Base for a UK Alcohol Policy*, London: Free Association Books.

Ramsay, M. (1996), 'The relationship between

alcohol and crime', *Home Office Research and Statistics Directorate Research Bulletin*, 38: 37–44.

REUTER, P. (1983), *Disorganised Crime: Illegal Markets and the Mafia*, Cambridge, Mass.: MIT Press.

ROBERTS, C., BLAKEY, V., and TUDOR-SMITH, C. (1999), 'The Impact of "Alcopops" on Regular Drinking by Young People in Wales', *Drugs: Education, Prevention and Policy*, 6: 1.

ROBERTSON, J. (1987), *Heroin, AIDS and Society*, London: Hodder and Stoughton.

ROSENBAUM, M. (1981), *Women on Heroin*, New Brunswick, NJ: Rutgers University Press.

ROYAL COLLEGE OF PHYSICIANS AND BRITISH PAEDIATRIC ASSOCIATION (1995), *Alcohol and the Young*, London: Royal College of Physicians.

ROYAL COLLEGE OF PSYCHIATRISTS (1986), *Alcohol: Our Favourite Drug*, London: Tavistock.

—— (1987), *Drug Scenes: A Report on Drugs and Drug Dependence by the Royal College of Psychiatrists*, London: Gaskell.

RUGGIERO, V., and SOUTH, N. (1995), *Eurodrugs: Drug Use, Markets and Trafficking in Europe*, London: UCL.

SAXENA, S. (1995), 'A Stroke of Distinctive Colour', *Addiction*, 90: 13–14.

SHAPIRO, H. (1991), 'Contemporary Cocaine Use in Britain', in ISDD (ed.), *Drug Misuse in Britain*, London: ISDD.

—— (1999), 'Dances with Drugs', in N. South (ed.), *Drugs: Cultures, Controls and Everyday Life*, London: Sage.

SHARP, C., BAKER, P., GOULDEN, C., RAMSAY, M., and SONDHI, A. (2001), *Drug Misuse Declared in 2000: Key Results from the British Crime Survey*, Findings 149, London: Home Office.

SHEPHERD, J., and BRICKLEY, M. (1996), 'The relationship between alcohol intoxication, stressors and injury in urban violence', *British Journal of Criminology*, 36, 4: 546–66.

—— and LISLES, C. (1998), 'Towards Multi-Agency Violence Prevention and Victim Support', *British Journal of Criminology*, 38, 3: 351–70.

SHEPTYCKI, J. (ed.) (2000a), *Issues in Transnational Policing*, London: Routledge.

—— (2000b), 'The Drug War: Learning from the Paradigm Example of Transnational Policing', in J. Sheptycki (ed.), *Issues in Transnational Policing*, London: Routledge.

SHINER, M., and NEWBURN, T. (1997), 'Definitely, maybe not: The Normalisation of Recreational Drug Use amongst Young People', *Sociology*, 31, 3: 1–19.

—— and —— (1999), 'Taking Tea with Noel: The Place and Meaning of Drug Use in Everyday Life', in N. South (ed.), *Drugs: Cultures, Controls and Everyday Life*, London: Sage.

SINGLETON, N., FARREL, M., and MELTZER, H. (1999), *Substance Misuse among Prisoners in England and Wales*, London: Office of National Statistics.

SMART, C. (1984), 'Social Policy and Drug Addiction: A Critical Study of Policy Development', *British Journal of Addiction*, 79: 31–9.

SOUTH, N. (1992), 'Moving Murky Money: Drug Trafficking, Law Enforcement and the Pursuit of Criminal Profits', in D. Farrington and S. Walklate (eds), *Offenders and Victims: Theory and Policy*, 167–93, London: British Society of Criminology.

—— (ed.) (1995), *Drugs, Crime and Criminal Justice, vol. 1*, Aldershot: Dartmouth.

—— (ed.) (1999a), *Drugs: Cultures, Controls and Everyday Life*, London: Sage.

—— (1999b), 'Debating Drugs and Everyday Life', in N. South (ed.), *Drugs: Cultures, Controls and Everyday Life*, London: Sage.

——, AKHTAR, S., NIGHTINGALE, R., and STEWART, M. (2001), 'Idle Hands: The Role of Employment in Addiction Treatment', *Drug and Alcohol Findings*, 1, 6: 24–30.

SPEAR, B. (1969), 'The Growth of Heroin Addiction in the UK', *British Journal of Addiction*, 64: 245–55.

STEVENSON, R. (1991), 'The Economics of Drug Policy', in D. Whynes and P. Bean (eds), *Policing and Prescribing: The British System of Drug Control*, London: Macmillan.

STIMSON, G. (1998), 'Harm Reduction in Action: Putting Theory into Practice', *International Journal of Drug Policy*, 9, 6: 401–409.

TAYLOR, A. (1993), *Women Drug Users*, Oxford: Clarendon Press.

TAYLOR, I. (1999), *Crime in Context: A Critical Criminology of Market Societies*, Cambridge: Polity.

THOM, B. (1994), 'Women and Alcohol: The Emergence of a Risk Group', in M. MacDonald (ed.), *Gender, Drink and Drugs*, Oxford: Berg.

TOMSEN, S. (1997), 'A Top Night: Social Protest, Masculinity and the Culture of Drinking Violence', *British Journal of Criminology*, 37, 1: 90–102.

TRIMBLE, J. BOLEK, C. and NIEMCRYK, S. (1992), *Ethnic and Multicultural Drug Abuse*, New York: Howarth.

TYLER, A. (1995), *Street Drugs*, London: Hodder and Stoughton.

WALTERS, G. (1994), *Drugs and Crime in Lifestyle Perspective*, Thousand Oaks, Cal: Sage.

WEBSTER, C. (1996), 'Asian Young People and Drug Use', *Criminal Justice Matters*, 24: 11–12.

WELLS, P. (1998), 'HCV and IDUs: A Legacy for the Millennium', *International Journal of Drug Policy*, 9, 1: 63–9.

WHITTINGTON, D. (1999), 'Nang Tien Nan: Princess Opium in Deptford', *Druglink*, 14, 5: 13–14.

WHYNES, D., and BEAN, P. (1991), *Policing and Prescribing: The British System of Drug Control*, London: Macmillan.

WILLIS, P. (1978), *Profane Culture*, London: Routledge.

WILSON, J. (1990), 'Drugs and Crime', in M. Tonry and J.Q. Wilson (eds), *Drugs and Crime*, Chicago, Ill.: University of Chicago Press.

WOOTTON COMMITTEE (1968), *Cannabis: Report by the Advisory Committee on Drug Dependence*, London: HMSO.

YOUNG, J. (1971), *The Drugtakers: The Social Meaning of Drug Use*, London: Paladin.

ZINBERG, N. (1984), *Drug, Set and Setting: The Basis for Controlled Intoxicant Use*, New Haven: Yale University Press.

PART V
REACTIONS TO CRIME

PART V

REACTIONS TO CRIME

26

CRIME REDUCTION

Ken Pease

Crimes are those actions deemed so disturbing to citizens or disruptive to society as to justify state intervention. Such intervention takes the form of providing an infra-structure for detecting those responsible and subjecting them to the criminal justice process. Conflicts between citizens, which are not so serious as to justify state involvement, are dealt with under civil law. Murder is a crime in all countries. To the writer's knowledge, holding loud conversations on mobile phones is a crime in none. Anyone wishing to make someone stop having loud conversations on mobile phones would seek a remedy through civil law. What counts as a crime changes roughly in line with social values. In 1995, Thomas Hamilton entered Dunblane Primary School and shot dead seventeen small children and one teacher. In a wave of public revulsion following the massacre, the kinds of weapon used by Hamilton were prohibited by the Firearms (Amendment) Act 1997 (see Pease and Pease 1999). In 1981, a motion was put before Parliament to ban the early computer game 'Space Invaders' on the grounds that young people would become addicted to it, playing truant and stealing money to feed their habit (Mungo 1998). At the time of writing (November 2001) in England and Wales, the legal classification of cannabis has recently changed, and the status of blasphemy as a crime is under debate, along with incitement to religious hatred. Fifty years ago, sexual behaviour between adult men was prohibited; five hundred years ago witches were tried and executed. As the scope of the criminal law changes, so the scope of crime prevention changes with it.

Understanding one country's criminal law is difficult enough. Adding the inter-national dimension makes it worse. In Myanmar, unauthorized possession of a modem is a capital offence (Brekke 1998). The current 'war on terrorism' will high-light difficult issues about the thresholds of state oppression at which terrorists/criminals become freedom fighters/heroes, appealing to a higher loyalty. Criminal law tends to expand when a state feels under threat. The greater the perceived threat from terrorist weapons of mass destruction, the more criminal law will be enlarged, and with it the potential scope of crime prevention. Conventions on human rights and associated legislation represent attempts to hold a line against such trends (see Ignatieff 2001 for a detailed account of this).

Just as crime definitions vary with time and among nations, so the *diversity* of behaviour designated as criminal within any country at any time is immense. Crim-inal behaviour ranges from child abduction, through begging and bigamy, to conspir-acy (and we have only reached 'c' in the alphabet). Never forget that crimes are acts or omissions united only in their proscription by law. Given that crime encompasses so many different actions, and that the scope of crime changes with time, we should never seek universal, 'off-the-shelf' *techniques* of prevention. In many ways the concept of crime is like that of disease, comprising a range of conditions united only in a general judgement about their undesirability,[1] with new crimes/diseases emerging from time to time.

As if the variation in crime definitions across place and time were not enough, even the words used to describe attempts to stop crime vary. Traditionally in the UK, some police officers have carried the title 'crime prevention officers'. Reflecting this usage, in previous editions of the *Handbook*, the chapter corresponding to this one was titled 'Crime *Prevention*'. In recent years, the term 'crime *reduction*' has been favoured. This term features in government publications and on the Home Office web site.[2] The arrangements put in place to achieve the *prevention* or *reduction* of crime have the *community safety* officer at their heart. Stopping crime is thus referred to as *preventing* or *reducing* crime, or achieving *community safety*. In this chapter, the terms 'crime prevention' and 'crime reduction' will be used interchangeably, and 'community safety' will be avoided wherever possible as being a misnomer (see pages 963–964). Its origins in radical left politics as a way of seeking to wrest ownership of the crime problem from the police (see Hughes 2002) has been wholly successful, but a misnomer it remains.

TYPOLOGIES OF CRIME REDUCTION

Because of its role within the *Handbook*, this chapter starts with the assumption that the scope of the criminal law is provisionally accepted. Even within that limit, how can one start to get one's head around the prevention enterprise? To prevent or reduce something involves securing its non-occurrence. But many factors lead things not to happen. This section presents some of the frameworks, or typologies, which provide conceptual purchase on crime reduction, indicating possible points at which to intervene. Parallels with preventive medicine may help. In the classic case of cholera, the physician John Snow showed that the link between sufferers was the well from which they drew their drinking water (see Gilbert 1958; Tufte 1983). The condition phenylketonuria results from an interaction between a genetic condition and the kind of food ingested (Bellenir 2001). Disease may be thought of as a condition yielded by a range of interacting factors. Similarly, one can think about crime as a product of social conditions, genetic factors leading to criminality, and readily available opportunities to commit crime. All these suggest possibilities for blocking the path leading to the crime event.

Three broad perspectives on crime causation can be distinguished. They concentrate on structure, psyche, and circumstance respectively (the three Ss, at least if you

---

[1] This is not universal. Hallucinations interpreted as religious revelations illustrate the point.
[2] www.crimereduction.gov.uk

say them aloud). Structural views take prevention to be achievable only through economic and social change, especially by reducing inequality or levels of social exclusion. The second perspective sees crime as a product of the human psyche, seeking to change criminal inclination by deterrence, incapacitation, or reform. This view often has religious overtones. The final perspective, focusing on circumstance, contends that simple changes in the social and physical settings in which crime occurs can reduce crime.

Ask what should be done to reduce crime and you will get answers, most of which fall easily into one of the three categories. Some will advocate tackling the 'root causes of crime', typically deemed to include poverty, unemployment and poor housing (changes in structure). Some will point to inadequate parental discipline, or argue for compulsory service in the army, more severe sentencing, or personal mentoring (changes in psyche). Others will stress more CCTV, police patrols, and more secure homes and cars (changes in circumstance). These three perspectives on crime reduction are not mutually exclusive. Indeed, strong arguments can be mounted for a reduction programme coordinated across the categories. As a general rule, changes in circumstance can be achieved relatively quickly. One kind of shop theft involves removing a whole rack of clothes with one lunge, and running off. The reward this tactic yields can be easily reduced by alternating the direction of the hangers on the rack. A single lunge will no longer work. Alternating the direction of hangers does not take long. Changing an individual's inclination to steal clothes takes longer. Changing societal structures to reduce clothes theft takes even longer.

Arguments in favour of particular interventions presuppose that we are clear about what, precisely, drives the inclination to criminality. The difficulty of knowing what to change, with an eye to reducing crime in the medium and long term, is immense. For example, there now exists research suggesting that the availability of abortion may be a factor in crime rates two decades later, linking *ready availability* of abortion with *low rates of crime* (Donohue and Levitt 2000).[3] Parents who would prefer to have a pregnancy terminated *may* not be able (or inclined) to rear the resulting child with the wholehearted commitment of parents for whom the pregnancy was welcome. Risk-taking and impulsiveness, which may have yielded the unwanted pregnancy, are personality attributes also linked to criminality. In so far as these attributes may be inherited or learned from parents, criminality in the child may result. The wish for an abortion may be a rational response to the desperate social conditions in which a woman may find herself, which social conditions lead to a criminal career for children born into them. Is the availability of abortion a crime-reductive measure? How controversial advancing that argument would be! Yet it is only one of many examples of health, education, taxation, and other policies which may feed criminality. We had better hope that crime prevention by changing circumstances of the crime event works well, so that issues such as these are less central than they might otherwise be.

A simple way of thinking about crime reduction opportunities is offered by the 'problem analysis triangle', illustrated over. This is derived from routine activity theory and posits that all crimes require victims, offenders, and locations (Felson and

---

[3] This is also available at www.nber.org/papers/w8004

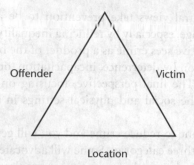

Clarke 1998). Removal of any of the elements prevents the crime. Crime may therefore be prevented by changing something about the offender, something about the
victim, or something about the location. Which is to be preferred depends on circumstances. In a pub (location), someone (offender) assaults someone else (victim) in an
argument about whose turn it was to be served. The offender could be banned, the
victim may choose to drink in another pub, or the licensee may be encouraged to
change bar arrangements or train staff so as to make such disputes less likely. Each
option could resolve the problem. The triangle is eagerly adopted by practitioners
seeking a way of breaking crime problems into their component parts.

The best-known means of classifying crime prevention was devised by Brantingham and Faust (1976). *Primary* prevention reduces crime opportunities without reference to characteristics of criminals or potential criminals. *Secondary* prevention
seeks to change people, typically those at high risk of embarking upon a criminal
career. *Tertiary* prevention works by the truncation of a criminal career, in length,
seriousness, or frequency of offending. The Brantingham and Faust classification was
later refined by van Dijk and De Waard (1991) and remains useful. In the UK, the
police tend to take the lead in primary prevention, youth services in secondary prevention, and correctional (prison and probation services) in tertiary prevention. The
recent emphasis on partnership working in crime prevention has blurred this division
of responsibility.

A more elaborate framework for theorizing about crime prevention has been
devised by Paul Ekblom (2000).[4] He sees his framework as a kind of 'universal story'
of the criminal event, a development of the routine activities theory of Marcus Felson
(3rd edn, 2002), in which an *offender* who is ready, willing, and able encounters, seeks
out or engineers a crime *situation* comprising a vulnerable and attractive *target*
of crime, in a favourable *environment* and in the absence of motivated and capable
preventers. A basic representation of Ekblom's framework is reproduced here as
Figure 26.1.

Centring on the crime event, Figure 26.1 distinguishes remote causes and immediate precursors. Ekblom then identifies eleven generic kinds of cause. These may be
primarily concerned with the situation which an offender encounters (the 'rays' to the
left of the figure, characteristics of the offender ('rays' to the right), or some combination of the two ('rays' in the middle). Each of the eleven rays may be thought of both

---

[4] See also www.crimereduction.gov.uk/cco.htm

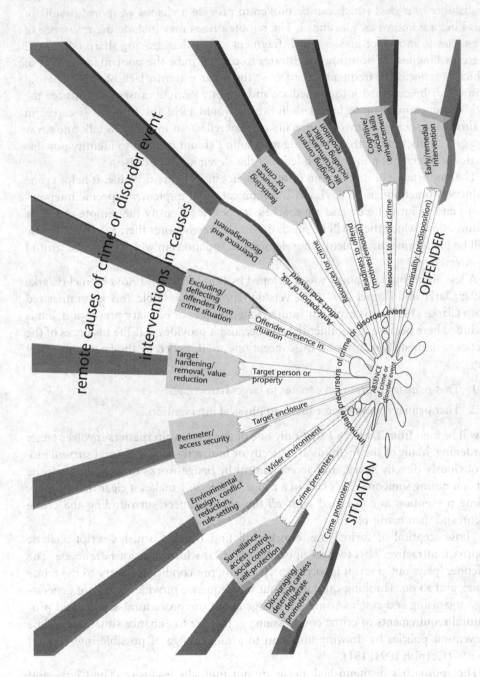

Fig. 26.1 Ekblom's *Conjunction of Criminal Opportunity* Framework

Labels in the figure:

remote causes of crime or disorder event

interventions in causes

OFFENDER

- Early/remedial intervention — Criminality (predisposition)
- Cognitive/social skills enhancement — Resources to avoid crime
- Changing current life circumstances including conflict resolution — Readiness to offend (motives/emotion)
- Restricting resources for crime — Resources for crime
- Deterrence and discouragement — Anticipation of risk, effort and reward
- Excluding/deflecting offenders from crime situation — Offender presence in situation

SITUATION

- Target hardening/removal, value reduction — Target person or property
- Perimeter/access security — Target enclosure
- Environmental design, conflict reduction, rule-setting — Wider environment
- Surveillance, access control, social control, self-protection — Crime preventers
- Discouraging/deterring careless or deliberate promoters — Crime promoters

ABSENCE of crime or disorder event

immediate precursors of crime or disorder event

as a remote cause and as an immediate precursor. For example, consider crime promoters. In a heated argument in a pub, the immediate precursor may involve the
availability of a glass which can be broken to provide a vicious weapon (assaults of
this kind are known as 'glassings'). The remote causes may include the resistance of
breweries to introduce glasses which fragment rather than leaving sharp edges, and
the unwillingness of licensing magistrates to control pubs the poor management of
which is reflected in frequent disorder. At the other extreme, lack of skills to avoid
crime may be classified into immediate and remote. Remote causes may include the
lack of educational or technical skills which would yield the offender a career in
mainstream society; immediate precursors may reflect an inability to talk one's way
out of a conflict rather than resorting to assault. Ekblom goes on to identify possible
tactics of intervention in respect of each of the eleven kinds of cause.

The importance of the Ekblom framework lies in its heuristic value. It helps crime
reduction practitioners to envisage, communicate, and implement specific interventions, and to integrate diverse approaches. It does not identify the remote causes of
crime, about which there will be much debate. It merely notes their existence. Its use
will lie predominantly in identifying elements of situations in which it may be fruitful
to intervene.

A less ambitious taxonomy was developed by Ron Clarke and Ross Homel (Clarke
1992; Clarke and Homel 1997). The version reproduced as Table 26.1 is summarized
from Clarke (1997). It is explicitly limited to techniques of primary prevention, but is
included here because it is influential and because it provides real-life instances of the
tactics described. Two common misconceptions are dispelled by the taxonomy. They
are:

1. That primary prevention equates to target hardening.

2. That primary prevention equates to physical intervention.

It will be seen from Table 26.1 that only one of the sixteen alternatives involves target
hardening. Many of the methods are directly or indirectly social. Natural surveillance
is obviously directly social, and access control by badge works only when someone
acts on noting someone else's lack of a badge.[5] Table 26.1 makes it clear that primary
crime prevention is concerned with *all* the circumstances surrounding the crime
event, and their manipulation.

Those sceptical of formal frameworks will find Derek Cornish's script analytic
approach attractive. This focuses upon the points at which decisions are made. The
offender 'plays out' a script involving preparation, pre-conditions, entry to the crime
scene, and so on. Thinking carefully about this sequence provides 'a way of generating, organising and systematising knowledge about the procedural aspects and procedural requirements of crime commission . . . helping to enhance situational crime
prevention policies by drawing attention to a fuller range of possible intervention
points' (Cornish 1994: 151).

The approaches distinguished above are not mutually exclusive. The Clarke and
Homel taxonomy, the problem triangle, the Brantingham and Faust classification,

---

[5] More precisely, is thought by intending offenders to be likely to act on the absence of a badge.

Table 26.1 The sixteen techniques of primary prevention

Increasing the Effort	Increasing the Risks	Reducing the Reward	Removing Excuses
Target Hardening	*Entry/exit Screening*	*Target Removal*	*Rule Setting*
Steering locks	Baggage screening	Keep car in garage	Customs declaration
Anti-robber screens	Merchandise tags	Removable car radio fascia	Hotel Registration
Access Control	*Formal Surveillance*	*Identify Property*	*Stimulating*
Entryphones	CCTV	Product serial numbers	Roadside speed displays
Computer Passwords	Automatic Number Plate Recognition	Vehicle licence plate	Drink-drive campaigns
Deflecting Offenders	*Employee Surveillance*	*Removing Inducements*	*Controlling*
Cul-de-sacs	Park wardens	Rapid repair of damaged property	Drinking age laws
Routing away fans at soccer matches	Club doormen	Removing graffiti	Parental controls on Internet
Controlling Means	*Natural Surveillance*	*Rule Setting*	*Facilitating Compliance*
Weapons availability	Street lighting	Tenancy agreements	Fine deduction from salary
Photographs on credit cards	Windows	Software copyright agreement before installation	Ample litter bins

and the Cornish script approach could all be reconciled with the Ekblom framework and each other, but the resulting figure would be fearsomely complicated.

The reader should now be familiar with common ways of thinking about crime reduction, and how to select from the repertoire of tactics which may be brought to bear upon crime problems, of which he or she may find some more useful or congenial than others. Readers particularly concerned with structural change will find least of interest, since all the classification schemes place this in the background. The routes whereby social structure may impact upon crime are so various as to defy simple classification, or have their effects through aspects of person or situation and are indirectly captured by that means. Classification is one thing: effectiveness is quite another. The next reasonable question concerns whether the classified tactics enjoy any success.

PRIMARY CRIME PREVENTION: DOES IT WORK?

Research attention to primary crime prevention in the United Kingdom can be dated precisely. It began in 1976. The event which signalled this new beginning was the publication of *Crime as Opportunity* (Mayhew *et al.* 1976). Obedience to rules had long been known to be heavily influenced by the specifics of the situations in which people found themselves. For example, apparently minor details of classroom or context determined which pupils cheated in tests (Hartshorne and May 1928). The insight was reinforced by research into patterns of suicide. The gas supply, formerly toxic town gas, was replaced by non-toxic natural gas. Thus the suicide method of preference no longer worked. The *total* number of suicides decreased. People chose not to kill themselves, rather than resort to a less favoured method. A similar decline in suicide resulted when US vehicle regulations on catalytic conversion were introduced. A favoured method of suicide (a hosepipe from the exhaust into the passenger compartment) thereby ceased to be available (see Clarke and Lester 1987; Clarke and Mayhew 1988). Taking one's life is an important decision. If even this can be affected by a change in presenting opportunities, how much more will the less critical decisions about whether to commit a burglary or a fraud be affected by the immediate environment? The *Crime as Opportunity* monograph demonstrated the efficacy of situational change in reducing crime. It included research on the prevention of car theft resulting from the introduction of steering column locks (Mayhew *et al.* 1976, 1979; Webb 1994). The compulsory fitting of such locks to all cars in West Germany led to a general reduction in car theft, sustained over the ensuing decade. The compulsory fitting of steering column locks in the UK was restricted to *new* vehicles. This, unsurprisingly, led to a reduction in the proportion of stolen cars which were new. Other work in the same tradition swiftly followed.

The literature demonstrating the effectiveness of primary prevention measures is now very extensive. Two volumes of separate 'successful case studies' have been published (Clarke 1992, 1997). Many other examples have been cited in earlier editions of the *Handbook*. It is no longer premature to claim that the vast bulk of well conceived and properly implemented primary prevention programmes achieve some success in crime reduction (see Poyner and Webb 1993). For instance, in their immense review of crime reduction programmes, Larry Sherman and his colleagues (1998) examine in turn all types of crime reductive effort. In one chapter John Eck considers those aspects of primary crime prevention concerned with the manipulation of aspects of place. He concludes in respect of the evaluations of such work as follows:

These evaluations are consistent with the hypothesis that opportunity blocking at places can prevent crime, at least under some circumstances. Ninety per cent of the evaluated interventions displayed evidence of crime reduction effects. Often these reductions were large. As we will see, these findings are consistent across a variety of evaluation designs, settings, and interventions [Eck 1998].

Of particular recent note has been the evaluation of Secured by Design (SBD) housing.[6] SBD offers crime prevention standards for buildings. Recent research suggests that levels of crime in SBD housing are some 30 per cent lower than in equivalent housing not built to SBD standards (Armitage 2000).

Demonstrating that primary prevention can work is only the beginning of the story. The follow-up question concerns how it can be deployed most efficiently. There are two, linked dangers:

1. The belief that anything that looks like primary prevention will work.

[6] www.securedbydesign.com/

2. The conclusion that because a measure works, the mechanism for how it works is a matter of common sense.

Stress was earlier laid on the fact that primary prevention was not reducible to target hardening, and that its mechanisms could be subtle. This is illustrated by the impact of street lighting on crime. Street lighting 'obviously' works via the enhancement of surveillance. Light should work by making the night brighter, allowing people to see each other better. Early studies counted *crimes in darkness* as a proportion *of total crime* to yield a measure of lighting effects on crime. However, lighting reduces crime in daytime too (Pease 1999)! The effect must thus be the result of some other changes; perhaps a greater pride in the local community; perhaps people come to know each other better because they spend more time outside their homes. Enhanced surveillance of ne'er-do-wells after dark is not the whole story, and perhaps not much of the story. Lighting provides a clear example of how subtlety of change can manifest itself in primary crime prevention. Kate Painter has carried out much of the research on lighting and crime. She, writing with David Farrington, suggests one causal pathway as '. . . improved lighting led to increased community pride, community cohesion and informal social control, which deterred potential offenders' (Painter and Farrington 1999: 116).

Interpreting primary prevention effects generally, as with the lighting example, feels like common sense. This neglects the *mechanism* through which prevention works. The importance of mechanism in evaluating interventions is increasingly recognized (see Pawson and Tilley 1994) but seldom fully reflected in how the work gets done. A recent review of the crime prevention literature, focusing on the point in time at which an effect seems to reveal itself, shows that in some 40 per cent of case studies reporting crime prevention success, the success seems to have occurred too soon to have been a product of the obvious situational change (Smith *et al.* 2002). In CCTV evaluations, the premature reduction of crime appears to be the norm.

Why do so many crime reduction initiatives work too quickly? There are many possible reasons, which are detailed by Smith *et al.* (ibid.). The most obvious mechanism involves publicity given to an initiative before it becomes operational. For example, Sallybanks (2000) shows that during a period of deployment of decoy vehicles[7] in Stockton-on-Tees, there was a modest reduction in vehicle theft. When the vehicles were withdrawn but the initiative was publicized, the reduction of vehicle theft, relative to surrounding areas, was much greater. Thus publicity seemed to work better than actually doing something. As with people in general, gossip and word of mouth are major features of offending groups. Manipulating these is a legitimate crime reduction tactic, so far woefully neglected.

Whatever the reason for anticipatory changes, understanding them should be a major research focus in the next decade. Identifying the 'active ingredients' in crime reduction is crucial. If we can understand the subtlety of these mechanisms, we can deploy them better, more cheaply, and hence more generally. For example, if publicity can make people think that any old Ford Escort they break into has a non-trivial possibility of being a police decoy vehicle, Escorts generally will be protected.

---

[7] Vehicles rigged to facilitate detection of those entering them illegally. Methods of achieving this can include tracking or camera systems, or physical restraint systems, whereby an intruder is unable to leave the vehicle.

Two major criticisms advanced against primary prevention concern displacement and sustainability. As time has passed and confidence in primary prevention has increased, the perceived importance of displacement has declined, and that of sustainability has increased. First, consider displacement:

There is little point in the policy-maker investing resources and effort into situational [crime] prevention if by doing so he merely shuffles crime from one area to the next but never reduces it. For this reason, the possibility of displacing crime by preventive intervention is a crucial issue for the policy maker [Heal and Laycock 1986: 123].

This 'crime shuffling' is what is conventionally meant by displacement. Displacement can induce a 'paralyzing extreme case pessimism' (Cornish and Clarke 1986). Hesseling (1994) reviewed all fifty-five published articles in which researchers specifically looked for evidence of displacement. He noted that 'critics of situational prevention . . . often state that the approach is useless because it only displaces crime to other places or times. Yet these critics tend to base their conclusions on ideological grounds rather than on the basis of sound empirical knowledge' (1994: 198).

A careful review of published studies (Hesseling ibid.) reveals that 'displacement is a possible, but not inevitable consequence of crime prevention. Further, if displacement does occur, it will be limited in size and scope. This conclusion is supported by other review studies on the topic' (ibid.: 219). Displacement is seldom likely to be anything like complete. The closest to complete displacement would be in respect of 'perpetrator displacement', whereby a crime opportunity is so compelling that the removal of any number of offenders will not prevent the crime. The obvious example concerns drug importation from a third world country, in which poverty generates an unlimited pool of volunteers to be 'mules'. More mundanely, offenders have limited 'travel to crime' ranges (see Wiles and Costello 1999). Other rational choice considerations also suggest that the extent of displacement will be limited (Cornish and Clarke 1987; Bouloukos and Farrell 1997).

In six of the studies he reviewed, Hesseling found diffusion of benefits, which is the opposite of displacement and involves crime *reduction* extending beyond the boundaries of an initiative. Where this has been looked for specifically, it has often been found (see Green 1995; Masuda 1992; Weisburd and Green 1995).

Sustainability is much more difficult for the crime reducer to dismiss (see Stockdale and Gresham 1998 for an example). There is a perverse incentive system whereby high crime rates attract central government money. Decreasing crime rates yield transitory praise followed by a conviction that there is not a problem any more, all too often followed by a resurgence of crime. The key to sustainability is to make people want to reduce crime. This requires a financial (or feel-good) dynamic whereby success in crime reduction is built upon because it brings benefits. Sustainability should be a matter of policy, not an example of the triumph of hope over experience. It is not surprising that sustainability is so little researched, since it requires evaluation periods well beyond those usual in crime evaluations. Attempts to make people or organizations want to reduce crime, and thus engineer sustainable crime reduction, will be discussed later (pages 966–970).

SECONDARY AND TERTIARY CRIME REDUCTION: DO THEY WORK?

The likelihood of embarking on or persisting in a criminal career is seen as a result of a combination of risk factors (such as criminal parents, health, and low intelligence) and protective factors (such as capable parents or non-delinquent peers). These terms are in common use (see Farrington 2000) and are central to understanding human development and crime. Secondary and tertiary prevention may be seen as attempts to reinforce protective factors, and reduce the impact of risk factors.[8] Farrington and Welsh (1999) identify four types of programme which are particularly successful in criminality reduction: parent education (in the context of home visiting); parent management training; child skills training; and pre-school intellectual enrichment programmes. In the best known study, health visits during pregnancy and the first two years of life were translated fifteen years later into fewer arrests of the mothers visited than of those receiving pre-natal visits only, or no visits at all (Olds *et al.* 1997). Children of mothers receiving pre-natal and/or post-natal home visits had less than half the number of arrests of those whose mothers received no visits (Olds *et al.* 1998). In the famous Perry pre-school intellectual enrichment programme, those experiencing the programme had, by the age of twenty-seven, been arrested only half as often as a comparable group (Schweinhart *et al.* 1993). Other studies also show the potential benefits of early intervention (for example Lally *et al.* 1998; Tremblay *et al.* 1995). 'Communities that Care' (CTC) is an important programme, which has not yet been fully evaluated. It seeks to counteract a wide range of adolescent problems, including crime and violence (Hawkins and Catalano 1992; Hawkins 1999). Its main focus is on family and school risk, and protective factors identified by research into individual development and offending.

As a generalization, the later in life an intervention is made, the more difficult it is to implement (see, for example, Harrell *et al.* 1997) and the less clearly beneficial the effects. Extrapolating, it is clear that tertiary prevention, whereby those already embarked upon criminal careers are targeted, has generally modest effects in relation to effort expended (see Andrews *et al.* 1990; Losel 1995). There is also a complicating factor. When someone has embarked upon a criminal career and is available for incapacitation (prison, or death where that penalty is available), programmes seeking to change him or her will be net generators of crime up to the point at which more crime is prevented by the change programme than is prevented by the incapacitation to which it was an alternative. Put simply, a programme which decreases the number of crimes per unit time committed by an offender by 10 per cent, but which increases the length of time he or she spends in the community by 20 per cent, will increase crime by 10 per cent.

There are UK government initiatives to enrich early life in ways which, among other things, are intended to impact upon crime. The most ambitious is 'Sure Start',

---

[8] Secondary crime prevention has close links with preventive medicine, given the close links between delinquency and ill-health (Junger, Stroebe, and van der Laan 2001).

which aims to 'work with parents-to-be, parents and children to promote the physical, intellectual and social development of babies and young children—particularly those who are disadvantaged—so that they can flourish at home and when they get to school, and thereby break the cycle of disadvantage for the current generation of young children'.[9] Specific projects express that aspiration.[10, 11]

STRUCTURAL CRIME PREVENTION

To this point, the crime reductive effects of changing situations and changing people have been rehearsed. Both of these are possible, to varying extents and with varying degrees of effort. The charge can be laid that these devices are the equivalent of walking south on a northbound aeroplane, with rates of crime fundamentally driven by social inequality, the prevailing economic system, differing degrees of material self-interest (see Halpern (2001), and so on. Most of these arguments are advanced else-where in this *Handbook*. The evidence suggests that there is ample scope for crime reduction within most social or economic arrangements. A parallel can be drawn with making policy more environment friendly. This is possible in the most resource prof-ligate countries of North America and the most resource protective countries of Northern Europe. At both ends of the spectrum of resource profligacy, the 'greening' of policy requires constant thought and adjustment of incentives for citizens and businesses, and becomes enmeshed in political discussions about the proper limits on the role of the state in free market economies. Short of widespread public disorder, crime considerations will never be powerful enough on their own to drive structural change—and that is arguably as it should be, there being more fundamental determinants of distributive justice (see Wiles and Pease 2001). Despite scepticism about the value of a lengthy discussion in this chapter of structural determinants of crime at the *national and global* level, some thought must be given to crime determination and the structure of *local* communities. 'In study after study, evidence emerges that crime prevention programs are more likely to take root, and more likely to work, in communities that need them the least' (Sherman *et al.* 1998: 38).

Community crime reduction refers to actions intended to change the social condi-tions believed to sustain crime. In a generally downbeat assessment of the efficacy (to date) of these change programmes, Tim Hope (1995a) opines that 'much of the effort to alter the structure of communities in order to reduce crime has not been noticeably successful or sustainable' (at 23). He concludes that '[c]ommunity approaches have foundered mostly because of insufficient understanding of social relations within residential areas and of how community crime careers are shaped by the wider urban market' (at 21). What is it about local communities which makes them crime-prone, and are these factors susceptible to change? A useful organizing

---

[9] www.surestart.gov.uk/home.cfm
[10] www.surestart.gov.uk/centreDetails.cfm?centre = 74
[11] www.surestart.gov.uk/centreDetails.cfm?centre = 157

concept is *neighbourhood collective efficacy*. This is compromised by concentrated disadvantage, immigration concentration, and residential instability. How does it feel to be in areas of high collective efficacy? Central to this experience are issues of informal social control, social cohesion, and trust. Statements with which people in areas of high collective efficacy agree include: 'People around here are willing to help their neighbours'; 'This is a close-knit neighbourhood'; and 'People in this neighbourhood can be trusted'. People in such areas feel more able to discipline neighbourhood children (Sampson *et al.* 1997a, 1997b; Sampson and Raudenbusch 1999). What can we do with our enriched understanding of the community variables associated with rates of crime? One (by no means the only possible) approach involves 'weed and seed'[12] or 'crackdown-consolidation' (Wright and Pease 1997) approaches to communities. An influential approach which centres upon the dissuasion of high-rate offenders from crime is that of Kennedy (1997). In the weed and seed approach, enforcement activities (weed) adjust power relations within a community so that collective efficacy (seed) has space in which to grow. The weed–seed metaphor is highly appropriate, given that fear of violence from powerful offenders within a community is a major disincentive to the expression of collective efficacy. The typically long period between arrest and conviction provides ample opportunity to intimidate those who might be witnesses against them.

The importance of intervention at the community level is reflected in evidence that community characteristics can override individual risk and protective factors. In her controversial but persuasive textbook about human development, Rich Harris (1998) concludes that the two most important determinants of a child's behaviour are parental genetics and choice of where to live. In another study of immense importance, it has been shown that where delinquency first manifests itself in adolescence (late onset), individual risk and protective factors are largely irrelevant. When living in the worst areas, even the best efforts of individual families have limited success (Wikström and Loeber 2000). Thus the proportions taking to crime in adolescence (late onset) do not differ according to risk/protective factor balance, being 38 per cent, 35 per cent, and 34 per cent for high protective, balanced, and high risk factors respectively in areas of disadvantaged public housing.

OVERALL, WHAT WORKS?

Manipulating situations can frequently have substantial crime reductive effects, many of which can be delivered in the short term. Manipulating early environment seems to have effects, including reduction of arrests, reduction in drug use, and other quality of life enhancements. There are thus good reasons beyond crime reduction for supporting early intervention programmes. According to the Wikström and Loeber (2000) research, in the worst environments, individual factors have less impact, being swamped by area quality. Put crudely, the limiting factor, the 'ceiling', on the

[12] www.ojp.usdoj.gov/eows/

effectiveness of primary prevention is criminal inclination and collective efficacy of the local community. That ceiling is generally (but not always) high enough to allow major changes to be achievable by primary prevention alone. The ceiling on the expression of criminal inclination is determined by presenting opportunities and collective efficacy in the local community.

Secondary and structural prevention does not require a crime reduction justification, just notions of fairness in the initial distribution of resources. People should not be raised in appalling communities, not because such communities may swamp family efforts to bring up children to 'fly straight', but because existence there is wretched. People should not be at the mercy of abusive or indifferent parents, not because that represents a risk factor for delinquency, but because it makes for misery. In short, the kind of enhancements to quality of life, which could be done in the name of crime reduction, could also be done in the name of fairness and humanity.

Summarizing the implications of the arguments above, an integrated programme of crime reduction, with a heavy primary prevention component, seems irresistibly persuasive. The movement towards an integrated programme will be facilitated by the beginning in October 2002 of a priority network funded by ESRC to advance this work.[13]

WHERE TO CONCENTRATE CRIME REDUCTION EFFORT: HOT SPOTS AND REPEAT VICTIMIZATION

An integrated programme of crime reduction would succeed. Where and when should preventive measures be deployed? One of the remarkable features of crime is the extent to which it is concentrated on particular areas, and on particular places and people within them. Some US communities have homicide rates twenty times higher than the national average (Sherman, Shaw, and Rogan 1995). Figure 26.2 illustrates the point by reference to the offence of robbery, with the unit of analysis being the local crime and disorder partnerships of England and Wales. These partnerships are ranked from lowest to highest rate of robbery per head of population. The period covered is March–September 2000. If all partnership areas suffered equal robbery rates, the curve would be a straight line. In fact it is very curved, with the thirty-two (out of 376) partnership areas at the right (those suffering highest robbery rates) accounting for half the robberies nationally. Within an area, this concentration reflects crime 'hot spots' (see Sherman *et al.* 1989; Sherman 1995; Bottoms and Wiles, in Chapter 18 of this *Handbook*). Looking for hot spots on the basis of time-limited data is often counter-productive (Townsley and Pease 2002), but since some locations have long careers as hot spots (Spelman 1995) intervention there makes good sense. Since police officers do not necessarily have good awareness of hot spot locations

[13] www.esrc.ac.uk/esrccontent/researchfunding/priority_networks_list.asp

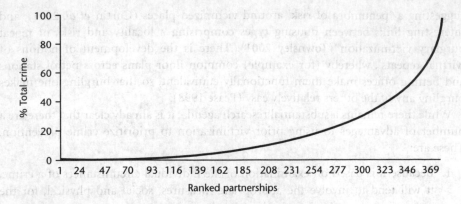

Fig. 26.2 Distribution of Robbery in England and Wales

(Ratcliffe and McCullagh 2001), identifying hot spots by mapping seems prudent, and crime mapping is perhaps *the* growth industry in criminology (see, for example, Weisburd and McEwen 1998; Harries 1999; Hirschfield and Bowers 2001; Murray *et al.* 2001).

At the level of the individual person, household, or business, concentration is known as repeat victimization (see Farrell and Pease 2001). Repeat victimization comes as no surprise. Domestic violence tends to be chronic, as does embezzlement, benefit and tax fraud, and some kinds of sexual offence, such as incest. For these offences, it is self-evident that preventing repeat crimes against the same target would prevent most crime. This is less self-evident for crime types like commercial burglary (see Mirrlees-Black and Ross 1995), where some 2 per cent of manufacturers suffer a quarter of the burglaries. The same pattern is found for burglaries (Shaw and Pease 2000), bank robberies (Matthews *et al.* 2001), and racial attacks (Sampson and Phillips 1992). When repeats happen, they tend to happen quickly. Given that the period of elevated risk is quite short, precautions to prevent repeats should be put in place quickly. Even if temporary, they will be worthwhile. The prevention of repeat victimization may prove a cost-efficient strategy of crime prevention generally, and features as such in the Police Reform White Paper published in December 2001 (Home Office 2001). Repeat victimization is linked to the 'broken windows' perspective (see Kelling and Coles 1996), whereby prompt repairs prevent or delay an area's decay and an individual building's re-victimization. The bulk of repeat offences against the same target are attributable to the same offender (Everson 2000), and these offenders tend to be more established in their criminal careers (Ashton *et al.* 1998; Gill and Pease 1998; Everson and Pease 2001). Offenders who return to the same place do so because there remain things of value, stolen goods will have been replaced, and the earlier crime(s) showed that there were no unpleasant surprises (Ashton *et al.* 1998). Farrell and Bouloukos (2001) show the rates of repetition internationally. Repeats may be thought of as existing at the level of individual person or household, or at that of streets, car parks, or indeed any unit of analysis which is small enough to be treated as a unit in crime reduction initiatives. How police forces were using repeat victimization in 1998 has been reviewed (Farrell *et al.* 2000b). There is evidence suggesting a 'penumbra of risk' around victimized places (Curtin *et al.* 2001), and interesting links between housing types comprising a locality and risks of repeat burglary victimization (Townsley 2001). There is the development of notions of 'virtual repeats', whereby (for example) common floor plans across petrol stations and betting offices make them functionally equivalent, so that burgling one makes burgling any of the others relatively easy (Pease 1998).

While there remains a substantial research agenda, it is already clear that there are a number of advantages to using prior victimization to prioritize crime prevention. These are:

1. Because it is based on examination of the individual circumstances of a crime, it will tend to involve the appropriate measures, social and physical, for the prevention of repeat victimization.

2. Preventing repeat victimization protects the most vulnerable social groups, without having to identify these groups, which can be socially divisive. Having been victimized represents the least contentious basis for allocating crime reductive resource.

3. Repeat victimization is highest, both absolutely and proportionately, in the most crime-ridden areas (Trickett *et al.* 1992), which are also the areas that suffer the most serious crime (Pease 1988). The prevention of repeat victimization thus automatically directs attention to the areas which need it most.

Besides its usefulness in scheduling crime prevention, repeat victimization highlights the way in which crime is depicted in official data. The conventional crime rate calculates the number of crime incidents per citizen or per household (incidence). This incorporates two elements: the number of people victimized (prevalence); and the number of times each victim is victimized (concentration). Separating these is crucial for crime reduction. To illustrate this, Farrell and Buckley (1999) examined an initiative against domestic violence. Reported crime incidence remained relatively constant. This masked an *increase* in the number of victims contacting the police (prevalence), but a *decrease* in the number of calls from each victim (concentration). These two changes offset each other, and if the initiative had been conventionally measured, it would have been judged a failure. In fact, the pattern is what would have been hoped for. Most victims of domestic violence do not report their victimization. When police service improves, more victims report, so prevalence increases. Since at least some get the help they need to prevent repetition, the number of calls per victim goes down. Hope (1995b) showed how important the separation of prevalence and concentration was in the understanding of crime trends at the small area level. Johnson *et al.* (2001) describe how to use data of this kind in evaluating crime reduction initiatives.

CRIME REDUCTION: THE INFRASTRUCTURE

Rates of crime have been declining since the mid-1990s. In 1997 a New Labour administration was elected, inheriting the crime decline, which has continued since that time, alongside a profound reorganization. The assumptions underpinning the new infrastructure are that crime reduction:

1. is possible by the manipulation of presenting opportunities, as well as by other means; and

2. is best done by relevant agencies operating in partnership.

Whether the current crime reduction strategy[14] is evidence-based, or whether confidence stems from the availability of large amounts of central government money to those who express confidence, is a matter for conjecture.[15] Whatever its basis, the question of whether it is possible to reduce crime has been replaced by that of how to engage people in collaborative enterprise to do it. At the time of writing in December 2001, such collaboration is emerging, patchily, between police and local authorities, but less so between these bodies, the private sector, and central government. The obstacles to partnership are deep-rooted, involving differences in culture and tradition between organizations thrown together as partners. How have arrangements to deliver crime reduction developed?

The Morgan Report (1991) advocated imposing a statutory responsibility upon local authorities for 'community safety'. This was realized by the Crime and Disorder Act 1998, which gave statutory responsibility to local crime and disorder reduction partnerships, comprising police and local authority acting jointly (an important refinement of the Morgan recommendations). The emphasis on partnership working derives from the recognition that the police do not control most of the *levers* which generate crime levels. For example, local authorities have powers in relation to the planning of new developments, tenancy agreements with those in social housing, and the operation of schools. These can be used to impact on crime opportunities. Partnerships are required by the legislation to prepare crime audits every three years, to consult with citizens, and to devise local strategies reflecting audits and consultation.[16]

Many things make a community unsafe. A community is unsafe whose citizens contract cholera through drinking water, food poisoning through salmonella in eggs, and whose children have their health compromised by heavy lorries passing through at high speed, leaving asthma-causing emissions in their wake. Vulnerability to crime is emphatically not the only way of being unsafe. Yet community safety appears to be a term reserved to reducing crime. Community safety was located in the Morgan

---

[14] www.homeoffice.gov.uk/crimprev/crsdoc.htm

[15] The writer thinks that the latter reason predominates. In the second edition of the *Handbook*, he was pessimistic about the future of primary crime prevention. That pessimism was misplaced. The most plausible reason for the turn-round was the ready availability of money to implement schemes with effects in the short term.

[16] www.audit-commission.gov.uk/comsafe/

Report within a crime context. Community safety, as legislated in the Crime and
Disorder Act 1998, is simply seen as a style of crime prevention, not a way of ranking
and dealing with dangers. Community safety finds itself within a Crime and Disorder
Act, whereas the argument set out above would mean that crime and disorder should
find itself, alongside other hazards, in a Community Safety Act! Does this matter? It
does, for many reasons, of which three will be listed (and see Wiles and Pease 2000 for
an elaboration of this argument):

1. *Risks* are never ranked across *reasons*. If children's safety is more often compromised by heavy traffic than local paedophiles, where will that judgement
   become evident? While community safety is locked into the vocabulary of crime
   reduction, the comparison will not be made.

2. *Community* safety is invoked rather than *individual* safety. Why? The word
   'community' invokes 'fluffiness' and a feeling of all being in this together—
   which in terms of crime risks we emphatically are not (see above, pages
   960–962). If the choice of phrase was deliberate, it was sinister. Community
   safety departs from the sum of individual safeties only if hazards are distributed
   unevenly. If each person's safety contributes equally to the safety of an entire
   community, community safety and individual safety are indistinguishable. If
   community safety is something other than the sum of individual safeties, this
   can be attained only by sacrificing the safety of some for the safety of others,
   with some small areas paying the crime dues for a town, the remainder of the
   town having crime levels held at a point associated with citizen feelings of safety.

3. Social policy has been 'criminalized', by placing crime at the heart of notions of
   community safety. This is eloquently expressed by Adam Crawford (2002: 233):
   'In the rush to promote crime prevention there is a need to be wary of requiring
   mainstream public services . . . to address social issues through the lens of crime
   and disorder . . . and in the process transforming and redefining their activity.
   The fear is that public issues may become marginalized except in so far as they
   are defined in terms of their criminogenic qualities'.

Be that as it may, the Crime and Disorder Act now lies at the heart of the crime
reduction enterprise. The key local agency for delivering community safety is identified as police and local authority acting jointly as the responsible authority. The chain
of community service responsibility is completed by Crime Reduction Directors,
operating regionally and linking local partnerships with the Home Office centrally.
These influential figures, largely recruited from the ranks of retired senior police
officers, are responsible for the distribution and monitoring of the substantial central
funding of local crime reduction initiatives. Diverse funds are drawn upon, most
recently a Partnership Development Fund to enable local bodies to become better
placed to use the money available prudently.

Local partnerships are required to undertake, in three-yearly cycles, crime and
disorder audits, public consultation, and the development of a reduction strategy.
This sequence is now in its second cycle. Partnerships have no shortage of advice,
the largest source in the UK being the Home Office crime reduction web site. This

comprises a 'knowledgebase', 'toolkits' (evaluated best practice), a discussion forum, strategy statement, and so on.[17] There are other websites of both British and North American origin also offering crime reduction advice.[18,19,20,21,22] Readers interested in crime and design should see Clare (2002) for Internet resources on that topic.

That the crime reduction agenda has moved from 'Does it Work?' to 'How can we make it work quickly and cheaply?' is clear from the infrastructure of support and advice for crime reduction. There are also subtle indicators, of which three will be mentioned.

COST–BENEFIT ANALYSIS

No one carries out cost–benefit analysis when benefit is impossible. Several cost–benefit analyses of crime reduction have recently appeared (Welsh and Farrington 1999, 2000; Farrell *et al.* 2000a; Roman and Farrell 2002), demonstrating confidence that some benefit may be gained. Researchers have included different types of programme costs and programme effects, and have used different methods for calculating monetary costs and benefits. There is a need for a standard how-to-do-it manual, which specifies a list of costs and benefits to be measured. Cost–benefit analysis has formed a major part of the Home Office's Crime Reduction Initiative of recent years. There exists within the Home Office's Research, Development and Statistics Directorate a group dedicated to this kind of work.

THE SETTING OF TARGETS

Setting targets for future crime levels is now an established Home Office practice. For example, there is a targeted reduction of 30 per cent in vehicle crime over the five-year period from 1999, and targets for domestic burglary and robbery have more recently been set. Sensible people and governments set targets only for things they think they can control.

THE INVOLVEMENT OF DESIGNERS

The design profession has recently become involved in crime reduction. Since the last edition of the *Handbook*, the Royal Society of Arts has introduced crime reduction to its student competitions.[23] These have included projects to make mobile phones less crime prone, student accommodation less liable to burglary, design of house entry points to facilitate secure delivery of goods ordered on-line, and bicycles less vulnerable to theft. The Design Council is engaged with a consortium of design schools to

[17] www.crimereduction.gov.uk
[18] www.usdoj.gov/cops/cp_resources/pubs_ppse/default.htm#Guide_series
[19] www.crimeprevention.rutgers.edu
[20] www.usdoj.gov/cops/cp_resources/pubs_ppse/default.htm
[21] www.preventingcrime.net/
[22] www.be-safe.org/
[23] www.rsa-sda.net/

incorporate crime-reductive considerations in industries in which such considerations have not hitherto been common.[24] Central Saint Martins Design School in
London has exhibited designs of chairs for pubs and cafes. These chairs have ingeni-
ous means of attaching bags, making them difficult to steal. The same School has
exhibited handbags resistant to common methods of theft.[25] This remarkable blossoming of interest would not have occurred had the zeitgeist been one in which crime
was not manipulable.

MAKING PEOPLE WANT TO REDUCE CRIME

The link between crime and change is best thought of as co-evolution, with species of
crime evolving in response to environmental change, and prospering or declining as
their ecological niche changes (see Ekblom and Tilley 2000). Predators rely on plentiful prey of a particular type, or on their capacity to prey on a variety of other
organisms. They rely on not becoming the prey of others ('bigger' criminals or law
enforcement). This metaphor has a long, albeit sparse, history (see Ogburn 1964).
Security measures have biological antecedents in some cases. The patent application
for barbed wire referred to it as the metal equivalent of a thorn hedge. Security devices
which advertise their presence are akin to the stripes on stinging insects, with biscuit
boxes posing as alarms having their parallel in hoverflies posing as wasps. The larva of
the Cinnabar moth is distinctively coloured. It is distasteful to birds. Each bird eats
one larva—and never another. The parallel here may be with Smart Water products,
which in one form sprays burglars with a uniquely identifiable dye, invisible except
under ultra-violet light. This places the offender unarguably at the crime scene. As
with the Cinnabar moth, it is the consequences of the first encounter which is
manipulated by Smart Water (Ekblom 1997, 2000; Farrell 1998).

Changing physical and social arrangements changes the supply of opportunities, to
which predators respond by changing their method of attack. Advantage is usually
temporary. Thus the key question concerns how to make people want to reduce crime
by responding promptly to changes in the point of attack. Change always presents
new crime opportunities. There are always three stages linking new products and new
ways of doing things with crime. They are:

1. Innovation without considering the crime consequences.

2. Reaping the crime harvest.

3. Retro-fitting a solution, usually partial.

This sequence has been common. The Penny Black postage stamp was introduced in
1840 and withdrawn in 1841. This is because it was cancelled by red franking ink,
which in 1840 was water-soluble, leading people to wash the franking ink off and

---

[24] www.design-council.org.uk/design/
[25] www.research.linst.ac.uk/dac

re-use the stamp. The Penny Black was replaced by the Penny Red, cancelled by black ink, which could not be washed off (see Pease 1997). Similar sequences are universally evident, most recently seen in mobile phones and laptop computers, where the manufacture of small, anonymous, valuable items, and the complexities surrounding numbers used for their identification, meant that they became a target for robbers and in thefts from cars. The magnetic stripe on credit cards was secure until thieves discovered techniques for 'skimming', where data from the stripe on one card is copied without the cardholder's knowledge and placed on another card. Skimming will remain common until the introduction of a new generation of 'smart' cards.

The sequence from innovation to retrofit highlights the importance of design in crime reduction, and makes it clear that few crime reductive tactics work forever; as the world changes, crime opportunities change. The constant factor necessary for sustainable crime reduction is the motive to 'go with the flow'; to understand changing opportunities for crime and to head them off or minimize their impact. For this reason, much recent concern has been devoted to *incentivizing* crime reduction, so that changes in criminal technique promptly motivate defensive changes in crime reduction.

Perhaps the most discussed aspect of the Crime and Disorder Act 1998 is its attempt to offer an incentive to local authorities to reduce crime. Section 17 (see Moss and Pease 1999; Moss 2001; Moss and Seddon 2001) requires each local body to 'exercise its functions with due regard to . . . the need to do all that it reasonably can to prevent crime and disorder in its area'. The underpinning notion of s 17 is that everyday decisions about the construction of homes or places of work, the provision of public transport, lighting, licensing of pubs and clubs and the running of schools, eviction arrangements for the unruly in social housing, are all implicated in the supply of criminal opportunities. This insertion of a crime reduction agenda into the fabric of local decision-making is perhaps the most important single recent development in the crime reduction infrastructure. Much of the impact of s 17 has been informal, during the normal interaction which partnerships are enjoined to undertake. Legal challenge to local authorities failing to discharge their responsibility under s 17 may take the form of claims for damages, or seeking judicial review of a decision.

The legislation underpinning the responsibility to take action to prevent crime may be s 17 of the Crime and Disorder Act, but there is scope for action under the Human Rights Act 1998, which was fully implemented as of 2 October 2000. The easiest scenario to envisage, by means of which to illustrate how s 17 (or its Human Rights Act equivalent) might work, is one in which a private housing development gains planning permission, despite being adjacent to a high-crime area and not being required to meet 'Secure by Design' standards. A householder in the new development, upon being burgled, may become angered by the terms on which planning permission was granted and apply for judicial review of the decision, or make a claim for damages against the local authority concerned.

There remains an anomaly in the scope of s 17 in the kind of planning case outlined above. The Crime and Disorder Act applies to local but not to central government. The case described above would go on appeal to the Planning Inspectorate, an arm of central government and thus not bound by s 17. The appeal would likely be upheld, as it recently was in a case concerning the extension of a club in Brighton. This arrangement is odd. It means that the local body makes a proper decision under the Act, which is then referred to an Inspectorate not bound by the same Act. All this happens at public expense. The Foresight Crime Reduction Panel (DTI 2000) recommended that s 17 should also apply to central government. This would have immense implications.

Like central government, the private sector is not legally required to consider the crime consequences of its actions and policies. The Institute for Public Policy Research, a think tank close to the UK government, will shortly be issuing an important report detailing how the principles of s 17 could be brought to bear upon the private sector. No one will spend long in the company of crime reduction practitioners without sharing their frustration about commercial practices which facilitate crime. Well-documented examples include distributing credit cards in ways which made fraud easy, and whose change led to year on year reductions in amounts lost through this crime type during the early 1990s. A second example is the reluctance to add photographs to cheque guarantee cards, despite evidence that such additions could lead to massive reductions in the fraudulent use of such cards (Knutsson and Kuhlhorn 1981). Some incentives are already applicable to commercial agencies. For example, the periodic publication by the Home Office of the Car Theft Index, which showed which makes and models of cars were most prone to theft, was intended to work by 'naming and shaming' makers of cars with poor perimeter security.[26] This led to laboratories at Thatcham testing the stealability of cars for the Association of British Insurers. Making stealability a factor in the insurance rating of new cars provides a financial incentive for making cars more secure.

The importance of s 17 is not that it will change the ways local authorities act (although it will), but that it represents a change of focus in the crime reduction enterprise, from those who suffer and perpetrate it, to 'third parties' (and to a much lesser extent repeat victims) who make it possible or easy. Foremost among these third parties are place managers. These include private landlords whose neglect of their property makes it easily burgled, or who allow it to be used for drug dealing. They include licensees, whose indifference to or poor management of their pub allows or facilitates assault or the fencing of stolen goods. They include the transport companies whose poorly lit stations and badly constructed bus shelters make sexual assault and criminal damage frequent.

Herman Goldstein's immense contribution to crime control has been the development of problem-oriented policing (see Goldstein 1990; Homel 1997; Scott 2001[27]). The essence of the Goldstein approach is that calls from the public for police service should be clustered into 'problems', which should then be addressed. Assaults in the same bar can have their common elements examined as a problem, perhaps susceptible to manipulation by the way in which the bar is run—hence the title of his approach. When the factors causing the clusters have been clarified, action is taken. Typically, those needing to take action are those listed above as third parties. Goldstein

[26] www.secureyourmotor.gov.uk/pages/car/ratecar.jsp
[27] www.usdoj.gov/cops/cp_resources/pubs_ppse/default.htm#Guide_series

(unpublished, see Scott 2001) has classified the means of 'shifting the ownership of crime prevention strategies' as follows, from least to most impactive on the third parties targeted:

- Educational programmes
- Straightforward informal requests
- Targeted confrontational requests
- Engaging another existing organization
- Pressing for the creation of a new organization to assume ownership
- Public shaming
- Withdrawing police service
- Charging a fee for police service
- Legislation mandating adoption of preventive action
- Bringing a civil claim.

Civil claims are a last resort, with many less oppressive tactics available earlier. That said, brevity requires some discussion of the option which will be least familiar as part of the crime reduction armoury, namely the use of civil remedies.

Unlike traditional criminal sanctions, civil remedies attempt to resolve underlying problems. Piecemeal initiatives along these lines are increasingly common. For example, a recent New York initiative used civil legislation originally designed for action against brothels as a means of targeting crack dens.

A private attorney . . . Filed a lawsuit against the property owner based on a 125-year-old state statute originally enacted to control 'bawdy houses' . . . The statute defined a nuisance property as any real property used for 'illegal trade, business or manufacture,' and outlined civil sanctions (up to a $5000 penalty) that a property owner could face if the owner 'does not in good faith diligently' move to evict the tenant . . . [T]he tenant was evicted, the house was sold, and the legal costs of the association were paid from the proceeds. The 'bawdy house' statute is now used in similar situations by the Manhattan District Attorney's Office [Mazerolle *et al.* 1998: 3].

In Oakland, California, a 'Beat Health' programme targeting landlords and housing, sewer, footpath, rodent infestation and the like 'decreased the level of drug dealing and improved . . . physical conditions . . . relative to efforts to affect drug dealing and physical decay in control sites targeted by uniformed police patrols' (Mazerolle *et al.* ibid.: 155).

The use of the civil law is not restricted to action against third parties. In the UK, injunctions and evictions by local authorities are among the civil remedies utilized (Morris 1998). One contentious provision of the 1998 Crime and Disorder Act is the introduction of the anti-social behaviour order (ASBO). Home Office guidance on ASBOs is self-explanatory:

The [ASBO] is a community based order akin to an injunction. It can be applied for by the police or local authority against an individual who acts in an anti-social manner—that is, a manner which causes harassment, alarm or distress to one or more people in a different household to the defendant. An order can be made against anyone who is at least 10 years old. . . . Applications for orders are made to the magistrates court acting in its civil capacity . . . Breach of an order, without reasonable excuse, is a criminal offence triable either way with a maximum penalty on indictment of 5 years in prison.[28]

Thus, although analogous to a civil injunction, breach of the ASBO is a crime. On the morning when this chapter was being revised (28 December 2001), the Radio 4 *Today* programme featured a scheme to reduce aggressive begging in Nottingham city centre, whereby warning letters were (when ignored) followed up by injunctions banning individual beggars from the city centre.

The section to this point has identified the emerging flavour of crime reduction as manipulating crime opportunities through the activity of third parties, notably place managers. This process will almost certainly continue, with particular emphasis coming to be placed on private sector obligations not to conduct business in ways which facilitate crime. This movement of crime reduction emphasis is in many ways analogous to the 'greening' of policy, wherein the behaviour of people and organizations is shaped to be less destructive of the environment.

WARNING VOICES

Towards the beginning of this chapter, its scope was restricted in the following sentence: 'Because of its role within the *Handbook*, this chapter starts with the assumption that the scope of the criminal law is provisionally accepted.' No apology is made for this restriction, but balance demands a brief account of the misgivings, which many scholars entertain, about the direction of policy. The Hughes *et al.* (2002) volume suggested as further reading provides a more thorough account of these, and is included primarily to provide the perspective lacking in this chapter. Another valuable source is provided by von Hirsch *et al.* (2001). The warning voices are not omitted because the writer thinks that their concerns are unanswerable. He thinks that there are adequate defences to most of the criticisms. The aspiration must be to develop a crime reduction agenda which is ethically grounded, and the warning voices must be heeded in pursuit of that aim.

The major misgivings may be summarized as follows:

PRIMARY PREVENTION PRECLUDES RELATIONSHIPS OF TRUST

The widespread deployment of primary prevention may be thought to bring with it the message that no one can be trusted. We would thus perceive ourselves as a society of strangers, without obligations to each other and to standards of decent behaviour. Late modern society is recognized to have substituted trust in individuals

---

[28] www.crimereduction.gov.uk/asbos5.htm

with trust in systems, and this trend would arguably be advanced by a primary prevention agenda.

MANAGING CRIME TENDS TO INTOLERANCE OF DIFFERENCE

The last decade has seen an attempt to reassert core social values. This has been influenced by the 'communitarian' writings of Amitai Etzioni (see Etzioni 1993; Hughes 1998). With the technicist infrastructure of crime reduction—audit processes, target-setting, and the other apparatus of managerialism—may come intolerance of difference, particularly in ethnically mixed urban communities beset by poverty. Intervention in family life there, for example, may be justified by the affirmation of core moral values, which a neo-liberal society has neglected, at the predictable cost in crime and disorder. While the Crime and Disorder Act 1998 requires community consultation as a safeguard against imposing inappropriate standards, how to access hard-to-reach sub-groups, and the purpose of consultation with them (and its feasibility of incorporation within a crime reduction strategy), remain unclear (McLaughlin 2002; Newburn 2002). The tension between maximum personal freedom and a stable society is very real, and is at the time of writing being rehearsed in the debate between freedom of religious expression balanced against the dangers of inflammatory religious education. The danger in treating crime reduction as a technical managerial issue carries with it the danger of overlooking legitimate variation in human behaviour, and by-passing the debate about tolerance of diversity in relation to the affirmation of central values. Measures such as ASBOs, where breach of a *civil* remedy is dealt with as a *crime*, give no comfort to people concerned about the restriction of legitimate diversity. Making crime reduction a technical rather than a moral issue means that government can think of itself as pragmatic rather than overbearing. Because crime reduction has so many facets, there is a danger of it being shaped and coopted as part of a right-wing law-and-order agenda (Crawford 1997; Gilling 1997). The criminalization of social policy alluded to earlier in the chapter could be perceived as one consequence of a process by which crime reduction, as practised, contributes to such an agenda.

CONCENTRATION ON THIRD PARTY RESPONSIBILITY FOR CRIME FACILITATES A DIVIDED, SURVEILLANCE SOCIETY

The trend towards crime reduction through action by third parties, rather than through formal policing, can lead to the exacerbation of social division (flight from the city of those who can afford to flee, creation of ethnically homogeneous areas, self-protection at the cost of community prevention). This is reflected in the existence and surveillance of mass private spaces, notably shopping malls, actively policed to exclude 'undesirables'. This brings with it the stigmatization of those excluded. People generally will have no right not to be observed, with allegedly intrusive effects on free speech and movement. This will be exacerbated by near future developments in which facial recognition software is hooked up to CCTV surveillance.

INCREASING INEQUALITY IN CRIME VICTIMIZATION AND VICTIM BLAME

In so far as the wealthy protect themselves against crime, some displacement may occur to those least able to reduce their own crime risks and poorly placed to benefit from state support. Throwing responsibility to prevent crime on citizens who suffer from it reduces the responsibility of the truly guilty and makes for victim blame. Less remarked by critics are the consequences of victim and third party oriented crime reduction strategies for cross-national injustice. If this same, domestic, cast of mind is brought to bear on global inequalities, it adds insult to the injury inflicted on third world countries used as cheap sources of supply for food and goods for first world consumption. The danger is of global moral blindness hidden behind domestic evidence-led prevention.

THE FUTURE OF CRIME REDUCTION

Much has been made of the way in which physical and social changes present crime opportunities. What futures will have what criminogenic consequences? Consideration of future crime patterns has been conspicuously absent from criminology. Most work about futures concerns the prediction not of crime, but of offender careers. An excellent book entitled *Prediction in Criminology* (Farrington and Tarling 1986) is exclusively about predicting crime careers. The keyword 'future' in searching criminology databases also throws up the occasional publication about the future of imprisonment and policing (see, for example, Morgan and Newburn's *The Future of Policing* (1997) and Bayley's *Police for the Future* (1994). If one searches the US National Institute of Justice web site, one finds many of the documents using the word 'future' to be concerned with DNA testing and the like, rather than developments in crime.

This tendency to focus on the future of criminality and responses to it, rather than on changes in crime itself, extends to fiction. The science fiction and fantasy literature concentrates upon the criminal justice process (see, for example, Olander and Greenfield 1977). The best-known science fiction work features Isaac Asimov's detective Elijah Bayley, and his robotic sidekick. Prediction of crime types and extents has thus been, for all practical purposes, not part of traditional criminology. The one book whose subtitle suggests that its contents should deal with future crime rather than future justice is *Visions for Change: Crime and Justice in the Twenty-First Century*. Unfortunately, this book (by Muraskin and Roberts 1996) does not fulfil the promise of its title.

Just as criminologists have by and large neglected the future, so futurologists have neglected crime. None of the books in the World Future Society's bookshop bears a title which suggests that it deals with crime (*Future Times* 1998). None of that Society's 'Sixty-Five Forecasts About Your Future Life' deals with crime (*The Futurist* 1998). Peter Cochrane is perhaps the UK's leading futurologist. His writing is unfailingly stimulating and shrewd. However, in his *108 Tips for Time Travellers* (Cochrane

1998), crime appears only twice in the index of the 227-page book: once in relation to encryption, and once about pornography.

In the light of the general neglect of the future, it is surprising and heartening that the Department of Trade and Industry included a Crime Reduction panel among the panels in its Foresight programme. The explicit purpose of the panel was to address possible changes in science and technology which would facilitate crime reduction. The trends which the panel foresaw (Foresight 2000a, 2000b) were:

1. New technology will allow individuals to commit crimes previously beyond their means (the 'empowered small agent').

2. Speed and globalization of criminal innovation may leave institutional responses, mainly nationally based, in a frantic attempt to keep up.

3. Proof of identity needs to become more sophisticated and general, since identity theft will proliferate as a means of self-enrichment and a cloak for violent and sexual crimes, and as a means of theft of services. Theft of services will become more important relative to theft of objects.

4. Crime will exploit the new electronic world. As a letter-writer to *Wired* magazine opined, 'A fool and his money are soon parted. The Internet just makes it quicker and easier'.

5. Location-aware and micro-chipped valuables will, in time, shrink the universe of stealable things.[29]

6. People may become increasingly the target of offenders thwarted in their pursuit of goods.

Their recommendations, flowing from the anticipations above but not relying on their accuracy for their relevance, were that:

1. a dedicated funding stream be established to focus science and technology attention on crime reduction;

2. a national e-crime strategy is established, for all levels of e-crime;

3. the wider impact of new technology on the criminal justice system is reviewed— including training, equipment, funding, coordination, and consistency—and action taken to address the issues identified;

4. thinking on crime reduction is incorporated into the mainstream of central government decision-making.

5. a programme is developed to address crime at all stages of a product's life cycle.

Space forbids the elaboration of all these recommendations, but recommendation 5. should perhaps be fleshed out to illustrate the approach. In essence, the

---

[29] Location awareness, of people and things, could revolutionize crime risks if deployed with purpose. The third generation of mobile phone technology will afford location awareness of people. Bluetooth and similar technologies will afford location awareness of objects. Failure to foresee the crime and crime reductive consequences of these developments would be a wasted opportunity.

recommendation aspires to create a culture of attack testing into product design and operation. It would involve:

- Identifying the roles of manufacturers, retailers, and consumers in developing secure products.
- Developing a voluntary standards system within manufacturing which would show that the 'criminogenic capacity' of a product had been addressed to diminish criminal misuse and 'stealability'.
- Detailing the contribution of the retailer, particularly the impact of e-commerce and home delivery on crime.
- Encouraging a climate of demand for secure products among consumers.
- Instituting an annual award for new products which have been designed with crime reduction in mind.

The Foresight crime panel will be wound up in mid-2002, but the thinking underpinning it, whereby reductive thinking permeates decision-making more completely, is certain to survive.

Selected further reading

Felson, M., *Crime and Everyday Life*, 3rd edn (London: Pine Forge, 2002) suggests why crime rises and falls, and suggests changes which may impact upon crime. The book is clear and enjoyable to read.

Hughes, G. , McLaughlin, E., and Muncie, J., *Crime Prevention and Community Safety: New Directions.* (London: Sage, 2002) is the textbook associated with the Open University's graduate course D863 on 'Community Safety, Crime Prevention and Social Control'. It deals more fully with the political and theoretical backdrop to community safety.

The 'Crime Reduction Papers' series published by the Home Office provides up-to-date original research on topics of current research interest in the field, and is an indispensable source, at **www.homeoffice.gov.uk/rds/crimreducpubs1.html.**

References

ANDREWS, D.A., ZINGER, I., HOGE, R.D., BONTA, J., GENDREAU, P., and CULLEN, F.T. (1990), 'Does Correctional Treatment Work? A Clinically Relevant and Psychologically Informed Meta-analysis', *Criminology*, 28: 369–404.

ARMITAGE, R. (2000), *An Evaluation of Secured by Design in Housing in West Yorkshire*, Briefing Note 7/00. London: Home Office.

ASHTON, J., SENIOR, B., and BROWN, I. (1998), 'Repeat Victimisation: Offender Accounts', *International Journal of Risk, Security and Crime Prevention*, 3: 269–80.

BAYLEY, D.H. (1994), *Police for the Future*, Oxford: Oxford University Press.

BELLENIR, K. (2001), *Genetic Disorders Sourcebook*, 2nd edn, Detroit: Omnigraphics.

BOULOUKOS, A.C., and FARRELL, G. (1997), 'On the Displacement of Repeat Victimisation', in G. Newman, R.V. Clarke and S.G. Shoham (eds), *Rational Choice and Situational Crime Prevention*, Aldershot: Dartmouth.

BRANTINGHAM, P.J., and FAUST, F.L. (1976), 'A Conceptual Model of Crime Prevention', *Crime and Delinquency*, 22: 130–46.

BREKKE, D. (1998), 'Aung Sang Suu Kyi Stares Down the Dictators', *Wired*, November: 128.

CLARE, L. (2002), 'Surfing the Crime Net: Investigating Crime and Design', *Crime Prevention and Community Safety: An International Journal*, 4: 65–71.

CLARKE R.V. (1992), *Situational Crime Prevention: Successful Case Studies*, New York: Harrow and Heston.

—— (1997), *Situational Crime Prevention: Successful Case Studies*, 2nd edn, New York: Harrow and Heston.

—— and LESTER, D. (1987), 'Toxicity of car exhausts and opportunity for suicide: comparison between Britain and the United States', *Journal of Epidemiology and Community Health*, 41: 114–20.

—— and MAYHEW, P. (1988), 'The British Gas Suicide Story and its Criminological Implications', in M. Tonry and N. Morris (eds), *Crime and Justice 10*, Chicago, Ill.: University of Chicago Press.

—— and HOMEL, R. (1997), 'A Revised Classification of Situational Crime Prevention Techniques', in S. Lab (ed.), *Crime Prevention at a Crossroads*, Nashville, Ky: Anderson.

COCHRANE, P. (1998), *108 Tips for Time Travellers*, London: Orion.

CORNISH, D.B. (1994), 'The Procedural Analysis of Offending and Its Relevance for Situational Prevention', in R.V. Clarke (ed.), *Crime Prevention Studies 3*, Monsey NY: Criminal Justice Press.

—— and CLARKE, R.V. (eds), (1986), *The Reasoning Criminal: Rational Choice Perspectives on Offending*, New York: Springer-Verlag.

—— and —— (1987), 'Understanding Crime Displacement: An Application of Rational Choice Theory', *Criminology*, 25: 933–47.

CRAWFORD, A. (1997), *The Local Governance of Crime: Appeals to Community and Partnerships*, Oxford: Clarendon Press.

—— (2002), 'The Growth of Crime Prevention in France as Contrasted with the English Experience', in G. Hughes, E. McLaughlin, and J. Muncie (eds), *Crime Prevention and Community Safety: New Directions*, London: Sage.

CURTIN, L., TILLEY, N., Owen, M., and PEASE, K. (2001), *Developing Crime Reduction Plans: Some Examples from the Reducing Burglary Initiative*, Crime Reduction Research Paper 7, London: Home Office.

DONOHUE, J.J. III, and LEVITT, S.D. (2000), *The Impact of Legalised Abortion on Crime*, Working Paper 8004, Cambridge, Mass: National Bureau of Economic Research.

DTI (2000), *Turning the Corner. Foresight Crime Prevention Panel Report*, London: DTI.

ECK, J. (1998), 'Preventing Crime at Places', in L.W. Sherman, D. Gottfredson, D. Mackenzie, J. Eck, P. Reuter, and S. Bushway, *Preventing Crime: What Works, What Doesn't, What's Promising*, Washington, DC: National Institute of Justice.

EKBLOM, P. (1997), 'Gearing up against crime: A dynamic framework to help designers keep up with the adaptive criminal in a changing world', *International Journal of Risk, Security and Crime Prevention*, 214: 249–65.

—— (2000), 'The conjunction of criminal opportunity—a tool for clear, joined-up thinking about community safety and crime reduction', in S. Ballintyne, K. Pease and V. McLaren (eds). *Secure foundations: issues in crime prevention, crime reduction and community safety*, London: IPPR.

—— and TILLEY, N. (2000), 'Going Equipped: Criminology, Situational Crime Prevention and the Resourceful Offender', *British Journal of Criminology*, 40: 376–398.

ETZIONI, A. (1993), *The Spirit of Community*, London: Fontana.

EVERSON, S. (2000), *Repeat Victims and Repeat Offenders*, unpublished PhD thesis, University of Huddersfield.

—— and PEASE, K. (2001), 'Crime Against the Same Person and Place: Detection Opportunity and Offender Targeting', in G. Farrell and K. Pease, *Repeat Victimisation*, Monsey, NY: Criminal Justice Press.

FARRELL, G. (1998), Smart Water and the Cinnabar Moth, *Information Security Bulletin*, 2: 25–32.

—— and BOULOUKOS, A.C. (2001), 'International Overview: A Cross-national Comparison of Rates of Repeat Victimization', in G. Farrell and K. Pease (eds), *Repeat Victimization*, Monsey, NY: Criminal Justice Press.

—— and BUCKLEY, A. (1999), 'Evaluation of a Police Domestic Violence Unit using Repeat Victimisation as Performance Indicator', *Howard Journal of Criminal Justice and Crime Prevention*, 38: 42–53.

—— CHAMARD, S., CLARK, K., and PEASE, K. (2000a), 'Towards an Economic Approach to Crime and its Prevention', in A.H. Clarke, N. Fielding and R. Witt (eds), *The Economic Dimensions of Crime*, New York: St Martins Press.

—— EDMUNDS, A., HOBBS, L., and LAYCOCK, G. (2000b) *RV Snapshot: UK Policing and Repeat Victimisation*, Crime Reduction Paper 5, London: Home Office.

—— and PEASE, K. (2001), *Repeat Victimization*. Monsey, NY: Criminal Justice Press.

FARRINGTON, D.P. (2000), 'Explaining and Preventing Crime: The Globalisation of Knowledge', *Criminology*, 38: 1–24.

—— and TARLING, R. (1986), *Prediction in Criminology*, London: HMSO.

—— and WELSH, B.C. (1999), 'Delinquency prevention using family-based interventions', *Children and Society*, 13: 287–303.

FELSON, M. (2002), *Crime and Everyday Life*, 3rd edn, London: Pine Forge.

—— and CLARKE, R.V. (1998), *Opportunity Makes the Thief: Practical Theory for Crime Prevention*, Police Research Series 98, London: Home Office.

FORESIGHT (2000a), *Just Around the Corner*, Report of the Crime Prevention Panel, London: Department of Trade and Industry.

—— (2000b), *Turning the Corner*, Report of the Crime Prevention Panel, London: Department of Trade and Industry.

FUTURE TIMES (1998), Bethesda: World Future Society, Summer.

FUTURIST (1998), Bethesda: World Future Society, June–July.

GILBERT, E.W. (1958), 'Pioneer Maps of Health and Disease in England', *Geographical Journal*, 124: 172–183.

GILL, M., and PEASE, K. (1998), 'Repeat Robbers: Are They Different?', in M. Gill (ed.), *Crime at Work: Increasing the Risk for Offenders*: Vol. 2, Leicester: Perpetuity Press.

GILLING, D. (1997), *Crime Prevention: Theory, Policy and Politics*, London: UCL Press.

GOLDSTEIN, H. (1990), *Problem-Oriented Policing*, Philadelphia: Temple University Press.

GREEN, L. (1995), 'Cleaning Up Drug Hot Spots in Oakland California: the Displacement and Diffusion Effects', *Justice Quarterly*, 12: 737–54.

HALPERN, D. (2001), 'Moral Values, Social Trust and Inequality: Can Values Explain Crime?' *British Journal of Criminology*, 41: 236–51.

HARRELL, A.V., CAVANAGH, S.E., HARMON, M.A., KOPER, C.S., and SRIDHARAN, S. (1997), *Impact of the Children at Risk Program: Comprehensive Final Report*. Washington, DC: The Urban Institute.

HARRIES, K. (1999), *Mapping Crime: Principle and Practice*, Washington, DC: National Institute of Justice.

HARTSHORNE, H., and MAY, M.A. (1928), *Studies in Deceit*, New York: Macmillan.

HAWKINS, J.D. (1999), 'Preventing Crime and Violence through Communities that Care', *European Journal of Criminal Policy and Research*, 7: 443–58.

—— and CATALANO, R.F. (1992), *Communities that Care*, San Francisco: Jossey-Bass.

HEAL, K., and LAYCOCK, G.K. (1986), *Situational Crime Prevention: From Theory into Practice*, London: HMSO.

HESSELING, R.B.P. (1994), 'Displacement: A Review of the Empirical Literature', in R.V. Clarke (ed.), *Crime Prevention Studies 3*, Monsey, NY: Willow Tree Press.

HIRSCHFIELD, A., and BOWERS, K. (2001), *Mapping and Analysing Crime Data*, London: Taylor & Francis.

HOME OFFICE (2001), *Policing a New Century: A Blueprint for Reform*, Cmnd. 5326, London: Home Office.

HOMEL, R. (1997), *Policing for Prevention: Reducing Crime, Public Intoxication and Injury*, Monsey, NY: Criminal Justice Press.

HOPE, T.J. (1995a), 'Community Crime Prevention', in M. Tonry and D.P. Farrington (eds), *Building a Safer Society*, Chicago, Ill.: University of Chicago Press.

—— (1995b), 'The Flux of Victimisation', *British Journal of Criminology*, 35: 327–42.

HUGHES, G. (1998), *Understanding Crime Prevention: Social Control, Risk and Late Modernity*, Buckingham: Open University Press.

—— (2002), 'Crime and Disorder Reduction Partnerships', in G. Hughes, E. McLaughlin and J. Muncie (eds), *Crime Prevention and Community Safety: New Directions*, London: Sage.

IGNATIEFF, M. (2001), *Human Rights as Politics and Idolatry*, Princeton: Princeton University Press.

JOHNSON, S.D., BOWERS, K.J., YOUNG, C., and HIRSCHFIELD, A.F.G. (2001), 'Uncovering the True Picture: Evaluating Crime Reduction Initiatives Using Disaggregate Crime Data', *Crime Prevention and Community Safety: An International Journal*, 3: 9–24.

JUNGER, M., STROEBE, W., and VAN DER LAAN, A.M. (2001), 'Delinquency, Health Behaviour and Health', *British Journal of Health Psychology*, 6: 103–20.

KELLING, G., and COLES, C.M. (1996), *Fixing Broken Windows. Restoring Order and Reducing Crime in Our Communities*, New York: Free Press.

KENNEDY, D.M. (1997), 'Pulling Levers: Chronic Offenders, High Crime Settings and a Theory of Prevention', *Valparaiso University Law Review*, 31: 449–84

KNUTSSON, J., and KUHLHORN, E. (1981), 'Macro-measures against crime: The Example of Cheque Forgeries', Information Bulletin No. 1, Stockholm: Swedish National Council for Crime Prevention. Reproduced in R.V. Clarke (ed.) (1992), *Situational Crime Prevention: Successful Case Studies*, New York: Harrow and Heston.

LALLY, J.R., MAGIONE, P.L., and HONIG, A.S. (1988), 'The Syracuse University Family Development Research Program: Long-range impact of an early intervention with low-income children and their families', in D. R. Powell (ed.), *Parent Education as Early Childhood Intervention: Emerging Directions in Theory, Research and Practice*, Norwood, NJ: Ablex.

LOSEL, F. (1995), 'Increasing Consensus in the Evaluation of Offender Rehabilitation? Lessons from Recent Research Syntheses', *Psychology, Crime and Law*, 2: 19–39.

MASUDA, B. (1992), 'Displacement vs Diffusion of Benefits and the Reduction of Inventory Losses in a Retail Environment', *Security Journal*, 3: 131–6.

MATTHEWS, R., PEASE, C., and PEASE, K. (2001), in G. Farrell and K. Pease (eds), *Repeat Victimisation*, Monsey, NY: Criminal Justice Press.

MAYHEW, P.M., CLARKE, R.V., and HOUGH, J.M. (1976), 'Steering Column Locks and Car Theft', in P.M. Mayhew, R.V. Clarke, A. Sturman and J.M. Hough (eds), *Crime as Opportunity*, Home Office Research Study 34, London: HMSO.

——, ——, ——, and WINCHESTER, S.W.C. (1979), 'Natural Surveillance and Vandalism in Telephone Kiosks', in P.M. Mayhew, R.V. Clarke, J.N. Burrows, J.M. Hough and S.W.C. Winchester (eds), *Crime in Public View*, Home Office Research Study 49, London: HMSO.

MAZEROLLE, L.G., and ROEHL, J. (1998), 'Civil Remedies and Crime Prevention: An Introduction', in L.G. Mazerolle and J. Roehl (eds), *Civil Remedies and Crime Prevention*, Monsey, NY: Criminal Justice Press.

——, ——, and KADLECK, C. (1998), 'Controlling Social Disorder Using Civil Remedies: Results from a Randomised Field Experiment in Oakland California', in L.G. Mazerolle and J. Roehl

(eds), *Civil Remedies and Crime Prevention*, Monsey, NY: Criminal Justice Press.

McLAUGHLIN, E. (2002), 'The Crisis of the Social and the Political Materialization of Community Safety', in G. Hughes, E. McLaughlin and J. Muncie (eds), *Crime Prevention and Community Safety: New Directions*, London: Sage.

MIRRLEES-BLACK, C., and ROSS, A. (1995), *Crime against Retail and Manufacturing Premises: Findings from the 1994 Commercial Victimisation Survey*, Home Office Research Study 146, London: HMSO.

MORGAN REPORT (1991), *Safer Communities: The Local Delivery of Crime Prevention through the partnership Approach*, London: Home Office.

MORGAN, R., and NEWBURN, T. (1997), *The Future of Policing*, Oxford: Clarendon.

MORRIS, S. (1998), 'A Case for Partnership: The Local Authority Landlord and the Local Police', in L.G. Mazerolle and J. Roehl (eds), *Civil Remedies and Crime Prevention*, Monsey, NY: Criminal Justice Press.

MOSS, K. (2001), 'Crime Prevention vs Planning: Section 17 of the Crime and Disorder Act 1998. Is it a Material Consideration?', *Crime Prevention and Community Safety: An International Journal*, 3(2): 43–8.

—— and PEASE, K. (1999), 'Crime and Disorder Act 1998: Section 17. A Wolf in Sheep's Clothing?', *Crime Prevention and Community Safety: An International Journal*, 1(4): 15–22.

—— and SEDDON, M. (2001), 'Crime Prevention and Planning: Searching for Common Sense in Disorder Legislation', *Crime Prevention and Community Safety: An International Journal*, 3(3): 25–31.

MUNGO, G. (1998), 'Technopanic', *Daily Telegraph Connected*, 29 October: 8–9.

MURASKIN, R., and ROBERTS, A.R. (1996), *Visions for Change: Crime and Justice in the Twenty-First Century*, New York: Prentice Hall.

MURRAY, A.T., McGUFFOG, I., WESTERN, J.S., and MULLINS, P. (2001), 'Exploratory Spatial Data Analysis Techniques for Examining Urban Crime', *British Journal of Criminology*, 41: 309–329.

NEWBURN, T. (2002), 'Community Safety and Policing', in G. Hughes, E. McLaughlin and J. Muncie, (eds), *Crime Prevention and Community Safety: New Directions*, London: Sage.

OGBURN, W.F. (1964), *On Culture and Social Change*, Chicago, Ill.: University of Chicago Press.

OLANDER, J.D., and GREENFIELD, H. (1977), *Criminal Justice through Science Fiction*, New York: Franklin-Watts.

OLDS, D.L., ECKENRODE, J., HENDERSON, C.R., KITZMAN, H., POWERS, J., COLE, R., SIDORA, K., MORRIS, P., PETTITT, L.M., and LUCKEY, D. (1997), 'Long-term effects of home visitation on material life course and child abuse and neglect: Fifteen year follow-up of a randomized trial', *Journal of the American Medical Association*, 278: 637–43.

—— HENDERSON, S.R., COLE, R., ECKENRODE, J., KITZMAN, H., LUCKEY, D., PETTITT, L., SIDORA, K., MORRIS, P., and POWERS, J. (1998), 'Long-term effects of nurse home visitation on children's criminal and antisocial behavior: 15-year follow-up of a randomized controlled trial', *Journal of the American Medical Association*, 280: 1238–44.

PAINTER, K., and FARRINGTON, D. (1999), 'Street Lighting and Crime: Diffusion of Benefits in the Stoke-on-Trent Project', in K. Painter and N. Tilley (eds), *Surveillance of Public Space: CCTV, Street Lighting and Crime Prevention*, Monsey, NY: Criminal Justice Press.

PAWSON, R., and TILLEY, N. (1994), *Realistic Evaluation*, London: Sage.

PEASE, K. (1988), *Judgements of Offence Seriousness: Evidence from the 1984 British Crime Survey*, Research and Planning Unit Paper 44, London: Home Office.

—— (1997), 'Predicting the Future: The Roles of Routine Activity and Rational Choice Theory', in G. Newman, R.V. Clarke and S.G. Shoham (eds), *Rational Choice and Situational Crime Prevention*, Aldershot: Avebury.

—— (1998), *Repeat Victimisation: Taking Stock*, Crime Detection and Prevention Paper 90, London: Home Office.

—— (1999), 'A Review of Street Lighting Evaluations: Crime Reduction Effects', in K. Painter and N. Tilley (eds), *Surveillance of Public Space: CCTV, Street Lighting and Crime Prevention*, Monsey, NY: Criminal Justice Press.

PEASE, C., and PEASE, K. (1999), 'Firearms Licensing: Facts in Danger of Neglect', *Crime Prevention and Community Safety: An International Journal*, 1: 55–65.

POYNER, B., and WEBB, B. (1993), 'What Works in Crime Prevention?', in R.V. Clarke (ed.), *Crime Prevention Studies I*, Monsey, NY: Criminal Justice Press.

RATCLIFFE, J.H., and McCULLAGH, M.J. (2001), 'Chasing Ghosts? Police Perceptions of High Crime Areas', *British Journal of Criminology*, 41: 330–41.

RICH HARRIS, J. (1998), *The Nurture Assumption*, London: Bloomsbury.

ROMAN, J., and FARRELL, G. (2002), 'Cost Benefit Analysis and Crime Prevention', in N. Tilley (ed.), *Analysis for Crime Prevention*, Monsey, NY: Criminal Justice Press.

SALLYBANKS, J. (2000), *Assessing the Police Use of Decoy Vehicles*, Police Research Series 137, London: Home Office.

SAMPSON, A., and PHILLIPS, C. (1992), *Multiple Victimisation: Racial Attacks on an East London Estate*, Crime Prevention Unit Paper 36, London: Home Office.

SAMPSON, R.J., and RAUDENBUSCH, S.W. (1999), 'Systematic Social Observation of Public Spaces: A New Look at Disorder in Urban Neighbourhoods', *American Journal of Sociology*, 105: 603–51.

—— ——, and EARLS, F. (1997a), 'Neighbourhoods and Violent Crime: A Multilevel Study of Collective Efficacy', *Science*, 277: 1–7.

—— ——, and EARLS, F. (1997b), *Neighbourhood Collective Efficacy—Does It Help Reduce Violence? Research Preview*, Washington, DC: National Institute of Justice.

SCHWEINHART, L.J., BARNES, H.V., and WEIKART, D.P. (1993), *Significant Benefits: The High/Scope Perry Preschool Study Through Age 27*, Ypsilanti, Michigan: High Scope Press.

SCOTT, M.S. (2001), *Problem-Oriented Policing: Reflections on the First Twenty Years*, www. usdoj.gov/cops/cp_resources/pubs_ppse/ default. htm#Guide_series.

SHAW, M., and PEASE, K. (2000), *Research on Repeat Victimisation in Scotland*, Edinburgh: Scottish Executive.

SHERMAN, L.W. (1995), 'Hot Spots of Crime and Criminal Careers of Place', in J.E. Eck and D. Weisburd (eds), *Crime and Place*, Monsey, NY: Willow Tree Press.

——, GARTIN, P., and BUERGER, M.E. (1989), 'Hot Spots of Predatory Crime: Routine Activities and the Criminology of Place', *Criminology*, 27: 27–55.

——, GOTTFREDSON, D., MACKENZIE, D., ECK, J., REUTER, P., and BUSHWAY, S. (1998), *Preventing Crime: What Works, What Doesn't, What's Promising*, Washington, DC: National Institute of Justice.

——, Shaw, J.W., and Rogan, D.P. (1995), *The Kansas City Gun Experiment: Research in Brief*, Washington, DC: National Institute of Justice.

Smith, M., Clarke, R.V., and Pease, K. (2002), 'Anticipatory Benefits in Crime Prevention', in N. Tilley (ed.), *Analysis for Crime Prevention*, Monsey, NY: Criminal Justice Press.

Spelman, W. (1995), 'Criminal Careers of Public Places', in J.E. Eck and D. Weisburd, (eds), *Crime and Place*, Monsey, NY: Willow Tree Press.

Stockdale, J., and Gresham, P.J. (1998), *Tackling Street Robbery: A Comparative Evaluation of Operation Eagle Eye*, Crime Detection and Prevention Paper 87, London: Home Office.

Townsley, M. (2001), *Spatial and Temporal Patterns of Burglary: Hot Spots and Repeat Victimisation in an Australian Police Division*, unpublished PhD, Griffith University, Brisbane, Australia.

—— and Pease, K. (2002), 'Winter in Bermuda and Summer in Alaska: Hot Spots, Crime and Climate', in N. Tilley (ed.), *Analysis for Crime Prevention*, Monsey, NY: Criminal Justice Press.

Tremblay, R.E., Piagini-Kurtz, L., Masse, L.C., Vitaro, F., and Phil, R.O. (1995), 'A bimodal preventive intervention for disruptive kindergarten boys: Its impact through mid-adolesence', *Journal of Consulting and Clinical Psychology*, 63: 560–68.

Trickett, A., Seymour, J., Osborn, D., and Pease, K. (1992), 'What is Different about High Crime Areas?', *British Journal of Criminology*, 32: 81–90.

Tufte, E.R. (1983), *The Visual Display of Quantitative Information*, Cheshire, Conn: Graphics Press.

van Dijk, J.J.M., and De Waard, J. (1991), 'A Two-dimensional Typology of Crime Prevention Projects: With a Bibliography', *Criminal Justice Abstracts*, 23: 483–503.

von Hirsch, A., Garland, D., and Wakefield, A. (eds) (2001), *Ethical and Social Perspectives on Situational Crime Prevention*, Oxford: Hart.

Webb, B. (1994), 'Steering Column Locks and Vehicle Theft: Evidence from Three Countries', in R.V. Clarke (ed.), *Crime Prevention Studies 2*, Monsey, NY: Willow Tree Press.

Weisburd, D., and Green, L. (1995), 'Policing Drug Hot Spots: the Jersey City Drug Market Analysis Experiment', *Justice Quarterly*, 12: 711–35.

—— and McEwen, T. (1998), *Crime Mapping and Crime Prevention*, Monsey, NY: Criminal Justice Press.

Welsh, B.C., and Farrington, D.P. (1999), 'Value for money? A review of the costs and benefits of situational crime prevention', *British Journal of Criminology*, 39: 345–68.

—— and —— (2000), 'Monetary costs and benefits of crime prevention programmes', in M. Tonry (ed.), *Crime and Justice 25*, Chicago, Ill.: University of Chicago Press.

Wikström, P.-O., and Loeber, R. (2000), 'Do disadvantaged neighborhoods cause well-adjusted children to become adolescent delinquents?', *Criminology*, 38: 1109–42.

Wiles, P., and Costello, A. (1999), *The Road to Nowhere: The Evidence for Travelling Criminals*, Home Office Research Study No. 207, London: Home Office.

—— and Pease, K. (2000), 'Crime Prevention and Community Safety: Tweedledum and Tweedledee?', in S. Ballintyne, K. Pease and V. McLaren (eds), *Secure foundations: issues in crime prevention, crime reduction and community safety*, London: IPPR.

—— and —— (2001), 'Distributive Justice', in R. Matthews and J. Pitts (eds), *Crime, Disorder and Community Safety: A New Agenda?*, London: Routledge

Wright, A., and Pease, K. (1997), 'Cracking down on Crime', *Policing Today*, 3: 34–36.

27

POLICING AND THE POLICE

Ben Bowling and Janet Foster

Situated at the gateway to the criminal justice process, the police have a major impact on what becomes defined as crime, which offences are prioritized, and which sections of the community are portrayed as 'dangerous' or 'troublesome'. The police are also sanctioned to use coercive force, and can intrude into the private lives of citizens in ways that would be 'exceptional, exceptionable or downright illegal if undertaken by anyone else' (Waddington 2000: 156).

Despite their powers and importance, the police came under sustained criminological scrutiny only in the 1960s, when concerns about civil rights in the United States prompted a number of pioneering studies on the role of discretion, the importance of policing processes, culture, and socialization (Westley 1970; Skolnick 1966, 1969; Reiss 1971; Bittner 1967; Wilson 1968). The development of police research in Britain coincided with the end of a perceived 'Golden Age of policing' that had been sustained by 'a myth based upon blind faith in authority and ignorance of actual police work at a time of relatively harmonious community relationships' (Downes and Morgan 1994: 221). Banton's (1964) pioneering study of policing in Scotland, for example, sought to explore what might be learnt from an organization that was 'working well' (cited in Reiner 1994a: 712). Subsequent British and American studies were far more critical, highlighting differential patterns of policing in terms of class, gender, age, and ethnicity (Cain 1973; Manning 1997; Van Maanen 1974; Hall *et al.* 1978; Reiner 1978; PSI 1983), and the processes involved in the police construction of cases against suspects and their influence upon subsequent stages of the criminal justice process (McCabe and Sutcliffe 1978; McConville, Sanders, and Leng 1991; Sanders and Young, in Chapter 28 of this volume).

In this chapter we seek to provide an overview of some of the key issues which have emerged from police research and public policy debates. We examine four central themes: what the police do and how well do they do it; the impact of changes in late modern society, and in particular globalization and privatization; theories of policing and their explanatory potential; and police governance and accountability. Before we discuss these, however, it is important to define policing and the police, and to highlight some key factors which provide a context for the discussion which follows.

POLICING AND THE POLICE: DEFINITIONS AND ISSUES

At first glance, it might seem that we all appreciate *who* the police are (people sanctioned by the state with powers to enforce the law and keep the peace) and *what* policing is (the types of activities they perform). However, as Reiner (2000a: 1) points out, there is a difference between 'this intuitive notion of what the police are' and what policing and police actually involves:

'Police' refers to a particular kind of social institution, while 'policing' implies a set of processes with specific social functions. 'Police' are not found in every society, and police organizations and personnel can have a variety of shifting forms. 'Policing', however, is arguably a necessity in any social order, which may be carried out by a number of different processes and institutional arrangements. A state-organized specialist 'police' organization of the modern kind is only one example of policing [Reiner 2000a: 1–2].

The police in liberal democracies have suffered a crisis in legitimacy in recent years (Bayley 1994; Morgan and Newburn 1997). The complexity and fragmentation of late modern society, rising expectations, the burgeoning of private policing, changing sources of trust, and the failure of state policing to tackle crime effectively, have all been factors (see Bottoms and Wiles 1996; Crawford 2000; Johnston 2000). Successive waves of public scandals in a number of countries since the late 1950s, involving a variety of recurrent themes—police corruption; miscarriages of justice; excessive use of force; and discrimination—have also played a pivotal role in undermining police legitimacy and public confidence.

Until recently, the police had themselves failed to understand that it is 'policing' rather than 'police' that is vital to social order. As Jacobs (1961: 41) famously observed, 'the public peace is . . . not kept by the police it is kept primarily by an intricate almost unconscious, network of voluntary controls and standards among the people themselves, and enforced by the people themselves'. Yet, a belief (perpetuated by the police) that policing was 'expert business', and an accompanying expectation that the police would *and* could control crime, contributed along with broader social changes (see Garland 2001; Jones and Newburn 2002) to weaken informal social control, and dashed public (and politicians') expectations when it became clear, as we discuss later, that there were serious questions about the police's capacity to tackle crime.

WHY DO WE NEED THE POLICE?

Locke, in his *Second Treatise of Civil Government* (1690), argued that human beings in a state of nature were prevented from enjoying basic rights—to life, liberty, and property—because of ignorance, powerlessness, insecurity, and arbitrary violence (cited in Kleinig 1996). In order to preserve these fundamental rights, Locke maintained that it was necessary to establish civil government, even though this involved relinquishing certain freedoms. Having established a legislature to make a 'known and settled Law', and a judiciary to apply it in individual cases, Locke argued that enforcement agencies were required to give it 'due execution'.

This justification for governmental authority—known as contract theory—is 'neat and persuasive': the exchange of complete freedom for some measure of protection by the state. It is not surprising, therefore, that this explanation dominates contemporary justifications for policing (Kleinig 1996). But contract theory does not tell the whole story or provide a complete justification, because policing is by definition ambiguous and complex in practice, with fundamental differences between law and its enactment and interpretation. Indeed the police, government, and governed are engaged in an inherently problematic relationship; one in which the police are in a contradictory position. They are sanctioned to protect us and are expected—and sometimes even *required*—to use coercion, deception, and intrusion in order to achieve the goals of a safe and peaceful society (Klockars 1980). But the use of these powers also has the capacity to induce fear and actually threaten our safety and security (Kleining 1996). Bittner (1970) argued that the capacity to use legitimate coercive force unites the 'bewildering miscellany of tasks' (Reiner 2000: 6) that the police are routinely called upon to perform, but it also helps to explain the controversies and moral dilemmas which are inherent in police work (Kleinig 1996; Klockars 1980).

While the policing function exists in most (if not all) societies, the form that it takes differs markedly across time and place (Brown and Heidensohn 2000; Mawby 1990, 1999; Reiner 2000a; Bayley and Shearing 2001). Sometimes the executive task has been the responsibility of many, while at others it has been vested in selected individuals formally organized and coordinated by the state (Kleinig 1996: 11). In Britain, Rawlings (2002) argues that policing passed through three stages, from its origins in communal self-policing in Anglo-Saxon Britain; the medieval period, dominated by the sovereignty of the feudal lord and king, with community-based systems, 'parish constables', bailiffs, justices of the peace, and the systems of the 'watch' and the 'hue and cry'; and the early modern period, where communities hired substitutes to take on policing duties, thus establishing a 'professional police'(Rawlings 2002). Greeted initially with hostility (Storch 1975), the modern police, who began with the creation of the Metropolitan Police in 1829, experienced a period of relative calm and legitimacy from the 1870s until the late 1950s (Newburn 1995: 43). However, from 1960 onwards, public confidence and legitimacy declined (Newburn 1995: 43; Reiner 2000a), and by 1979 policing had entered a 'late modern' phase where 'economic privatization', 'a rolling back of the state', globalization, the changing role of nation states, new public management, and different types of administration all become important trends (Johnston 2000: 69–71).

COMPETING MODELS OF POLICING

Although policing has some core features globally (Bayley 1985; Mawby 1999; Waddington 1999a: 3–4), the exact forms that it takes vary widely, even within particular localities. Modern British policing, for example, with its 'omnibus role'— incorporating 'crime prevention, detection, peace keeping, public order maintenance and the preservation of state security' (Reiner 1994a: 755)—emerges from several very different historical strands. The occupation of patrolling to prevent crime and apprehend offenders emerged from the functions of the medieval constable and watchmen, while 'riot control' emerged from the role of the military in suppressing disorderly crowds (Rawlings 2002; Vogler 1991). These differing traditions, and the ideologies and practices they have given rise to, represent continual tensions in policing.

While the social contract can be identified in most, if not all, democratic societies, the balance between the interests of security and liberty can be struck in a number of different ways (Kleinig 1996: 22–9). It is interesting, for example, that two dia-metrically opposed models of policing emerged in Britain during the late eighteenth century and early nineteenth century. Sir Robert Peel established the Metropolitan Police—the 'epitome of civil policing' (and what has become known as the 'liberal' model)—but also its antithesis, the Royal Irish Constabulary, which became the model for militarized and colonial forces around the world (Waddington 2000: 24–5; Mawby 1990).

These two models—expressed in Table 27.1 below as 'ideal types'—highlight how the ethos, management style, and tactics of the police are rooted either in principles of consensual, community-based policing, focusing on 'peace keeping' and conflict reso-lution, where the distance between the police and the policed is minimized; or in an authoritarian, 'military model', which prioritizes 'hard' paramilitary tactics and coercive, repressive, and 'distanced' policing (see Brewer 1991; Jones and Newburn 1996; Bowling *et al.* 2001).

'Ideal types', of course, oversimplify the complexities and variations of everyday policing practice which is frequently characterized by 'competing and conflicting goals' (Mastrofski 1999: 1). Even in liberal democracies, critical tensions exist between policing by consent (the 'liberal' model) and by coercion (the 'military' model), because police officers are 'under pressure to achieve results' but are 'constrained by the requirements of the rule of law in the methods they can use to reach their objectives' (Reiner 1994a: 733).

The legitimacy of the police, however, can be only maintained if policing structures and methods are 'perceived by important constituencies as the "right" way for the police to go about their business' (Mastrofski 1998: 168, citing Crank and Langworthy 1992). Ironically, although it is the state sanctioned use of force that characterizes the public police (Bittner 1974), their ability to solve problems without resorting to force is perceived to be a hallmark of good policing (see, for example, Bittner 1974; Muir 1977; Brodeur 1998; Bayley 1998; Reiner 2000a).

The importance given to the liberal or military models differs in the policing literature. Radical perspectives tend to focus attention on the use of repressive para-military tactics (e.g., Hall *et al.* 1978; Hall 1979; Jefferson and Grimshaw 1984; Jef-ferson 1990); conservative perspectives idealize the consensual basis for British policing (Critchley 1978; Ascoli 1979); and liberal approaches focus on the diverse and competing demands placed upon the police (Morgan and Newburn 1997; Reiner 1994b) where 'care' *and* 'control' are possible (see Stephens and Becker 1994).

With responsibility for high volume crime (such as burglary and theft), serious 'low volume' crimes (such as rape and murder), as well as disorder and neighbourhood

Table 27.1 Military versus liberal models of the police

	Military model	Liberal model
Tradition	Military/colonial/coercive	Civilian/communal/consensual
Values	Crime control, internal security, intelligence, suspicion, war on crime	Due process, human rights, trust, equity peace keeping, partnership
Goals	Crime fighting, suppression, intrusive forms of protection	Social peace keeping, community safety
Relationship with government	Directly controlled by central or local government; politically partisan and controlled by politicians	Insulated from political parties; governance is diffuse and decentralized
Source of legitimacy	Government, dominant political parties or ethnic groups	'Rule of law' and accountability to the community
Position of police officers	Police are crime control specialists. Isolated and separated from the community; a close-knit, distinct group of outsiders; 'policing by strangers'	Citizens in uniform. 'Police are the community, community are the police'; incorporates all sections of the community (including economically marginalized and ethnic minority communities)
Policing style	'Policing *against* people'. Covert, plain clothes, 'secret' or 'spy' policing methods (undercover, informers, agents, surveillance, and other proactive techniques), militaristic 'high profile' policing	'Policing *with* people'. Overt, visible policing methods (preventive patrol, reactive response to incidents, service role)
Techniques and equipment	Military weaponry (e.g. firearms, gas, water cannon, military vehicles), body armour	Minimal use of special equipment, largely unarmed
Use of force	Force used as a first resort. Maximal show of strength.	Force used as a last resort. Minimal force; 'winning by appearing to lose'
Role in crime prevention	Police are the thin blue line in a war against crime; criminals are the enemy; crime control achieved by social exclusion	Police and community are 'co-producers' of safety; crime prevention achieved by social inclusion
Role in maintaining public order	Order maintained by show of force and rapid deployment of special weapons and tactics	Order maintained by negotiation and 'pushing and shoving' methods
Also known as	Colonial model, divided societies model	Community model, civil model, democratic model

Sources: Brewer 1991; Kleinig 1996; Jones and Newburn 1996; Kraska 2001.

nuisances (such as riding bicycles on the pavement), and roles which now span the local and global, the police have a difficult job. Indeed, they 'are expected to achieve more than they can conceivably deliver' (Morgan and Newburn 1997: 151). In our contemporary world these demands are also influenced by broader social and economic changes.

There have been important transformations in what has become characterized as 'risk society' (Beck 1992), where 'an unduly selective focus on some features of modern life' has resulted in '[e]scalating fear and paranoia about risks' and generated 'demand for increasingly more sophisticated technologies of risk information' and particular types of risk management (Stenson and Sullivan 2001: 24–25). The police are at the heart of this 'knowledge management' (Ericson and Haggerty 1997). Newburn (2001) suggests that the consequences of fear and insecurity dominate late modern thinking, along with a number of social and economic factors outlined in Figure 27.1 below.

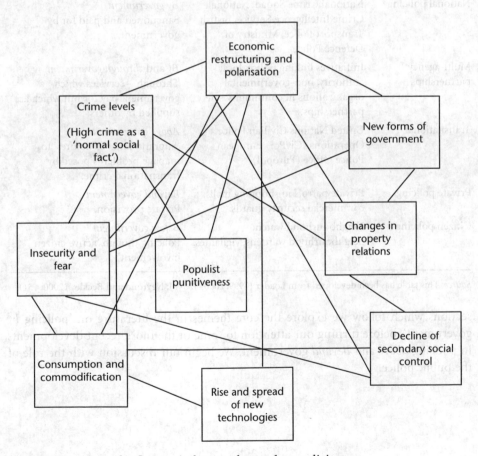

Fig. 27.1 Streams of influence in late modern urban policing

Source: Newburn 2001: 843. Reproduced by permission of Taylor & Francis Ltd, **www.tanf.co.uk/journals**.

These 'streams of influence' are also reflected in policing structures which are becoming increasingly complex, as Loader's (2000: 326–8) characterization of five distinct but co-existing levels of policing *by, through, above, beyond, and below* government demonstrates. These levels and the plurality of social institutions through which they are delivered are outlined in Table 27.2 below.

Although research on private and transnational policing is beginning to grow, the majority of police research to date has focused on the 'local' public police. In the

Table 27.2 Levels of policing and their relationship to government

Type of policing	Examples	Relationship to national government
Local police force	The 43 'Home Office' police forces of England and Wales; 8 in Scotland and the Police Service of Northern Ireland.	*By government* Paid for and provided by government employees.
National policing	National Crime Squad, National Crime Intelligence Service, British Transport Police, Ministry of Defence Police	*By government* Sanctioned and paid for by government.
Multi-agency partnerships	Initiatives linking police, local authority, non-governmental organizations in community safety partnerships.	*By* and *through government* Through—services which government pay for but which are supplied by others.
Transnational	United Nations Civilian Police Operations (CivPol) European Police Office (Europol).	*Above government* 'Supranational structures' to manage problems posed by transnational crime.
Private policing	Private patrols in shopping malls; commercial security guards.	*Beyond government* Private provision.
Citizen policing	Neighbourhood watch; neighbourhood wardens; vigilantes.	*Below government* Policing though 'active citizen involvement'.

Source: This table has been developed from Loader (1999, 2000: 326–8); Neyroud and Beckley (2000: 151).

sections which follow we explore the core themes in the literature on 'policing *by* government', before turning our attention to some of the more recent developments in policing *above* and *beyond* government. We begin our discussion with the role of the public police.

'POLICING BY GOVERNMENT': WHAT DO THE PUBLIC POLICE DO?

The public police often perform a broad range of roles (see Table 27.3) and 'are frequently the only 24-hour service agency available to respond to those in need' (Morgan and Newburn 1997: 79).

Table 27.3 The role of the public police

Functions	Mechanisms
Public reassurance	Visible patrol; contact with individuals and community organizations; effective crime investigation and emergency service.
Crime reduction	Visible patrol; targeted policing; proactive policing; effective crime investigation and emergency service.
Crime investigation	Reactive detective work to identify and arrest offenders and bring them to justice; proactive investigation.
Emergency service	Rapid response to disputes, disturbances, accidents, and emergencies.
Peace keeping	Routine negotiation and problem solving in a range of neighbourhood dispute and disorders.
Order maintenance	Controlling crowds at sporting events, entertainment, and demonstrations.
State security	Protection of public figures (politicians, royal family, diplomats), state buildings, covert policing of dissident organizations.

Sources: Morgan and Newburn (1997: 103); Neyroud and Beckley (2000: 19–36); Johnston (2000: 43). Discussions of the police role can also be found in Home Office (1993), HMIC (1999).

Despite the popularity of the 'crime-fighting' image (especially among police officers themselves), a great deal of police work is mundane. Indeed, police researchers frequently write about the consequences of officers' boredom and the proverbial 'quiet nights' where '*nothing* happened' (Smith and Gray 1983; Manning 1987; Van Maanen 1978; Foster 1989). Observational research also demonstrates that far less police time is spent in 'crime-related' activity than in providing a 'service' by, for example, calming disturbances, negotiating disputes, and responding to a wide range of accidents and emergencies (see Punch and Naylor 1973; Ekblom and Heal 1982; Skogan 1990; Shapland and Hobbs 1989).

Although the diversity of police tasks is well supported by research, some controversy exists about the *extent* of 'crime-related work', in part because it is so dependent on the definition of 'crime' (Mawby 2000: 107). Punch and Naylor, for example (1973), categorized 'domestics' as 'non-crime'. But Shapland and Vagg (1990) argue that 'many calls to the police that are not, at first sight, crime related, in fact concern "*potential* crime"' (Mawby 2000: 107). Other research suggests that crime-related police activity is much higher in particular locations (see, for example, Jones *et al.* 1986). It may be that the balance between 'service' and 'crime' functions differs across time and space (as did the latter in Punch and Naylor's original study). It is certainly the case that when police officers attend calls, they do not know what the outcome will be—classification comes after the event (see Morgan and Newburn 1997). In terms of our discussion here, what is important about this literature is that 'police work cannot accurately be encompassed by terms such as "law enforcement or crime control"' (Morgan and Newburn 1997: 81). Indeed Reiner (2000a: 112) concludes that 'most police work is neither social service nor law enforcement but order maintenance—the settlement of conflicts by means other than formal policing'. This raises some important ethical dilemmas in terms of accountability, equity, and fairness (see Reiner 2000a; Fielding 1995), and emphasizes the importance of policing strategies and police discretion (see Sanders and Young, in Chapter 28 of this volume).

It is ironic, given the proportion of time spent on 'service' or order maintenance roles, that these aspects of police work are devalued by the police themselves (Holdaway 1983; Smith 1983; McConville and Shepherd 1992; Fielding 1995; Waddington 1999b).

WHO DOES WHAT?

Although we often refer to 'the police' as if they were a singular entity, the diversity of different roles and functions within policing is important and deserves some discussion. Figure 27.2 below illustrates the range of different policing functions and the resources allocated to each of them. As we can see, more than 60 per cent of resources are consumed in foot or traffic patrol by uniformed officers, with the Criminal Investigation Department (CID) accounting for 15 per cent of the resources.

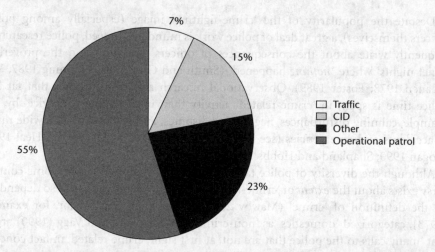

Fig. 27.2 Police resources; based on Audit Commission analysis of Home Office and HMIC data, 1994

Source: Audit Commission (1996), *Streetwise: Effective Police Patrol.*

Police patrol is popularly perceived to be the 'backbone' of policing, providing public reassurance and a general deterrent effect through visible 'omnipresence' (O.W. Wilson 1950). However, numerous studies suggest that despite its perceived importance, relatively few officers (approximately 5 per cent of the total police strength) are engaged in visible patrol at any one time (an average of one police officer for every 18,000 citizens) (Audit Commission 1996), and that patrol officers spend almost as much time in the police station (43 per cent) as on the streets (PA Consulting 2001). Even their time outside of the station is spent dealing with incidents and making enquiries as part of the 24-hour all-purpose emergency service (Morgan and Newburn 1997: 79). 'Foot patrol is a rarity' (PA Consulting 2001, paragraph V).

'Putting more officers on the street' is currently a central theme in political discourses about the police (see, for example, the White Paper: *Policing a New Century*). However, the connections between visible police presence and deterrence are not straightforward. One study, for example, estimated that a patrolling officer in London was likely to pass within 100 yards of a burglary in progress once every eight years, and even then might not know that the offence was occurring or be able to catch the offender (Clarke and Hough 1984: 6–7). It is not the numbers of police officers *per se* which is important, rather *how* police officers are deployed and their capabilities to perform their role.

Despite the significant role of the police in investigating suspected offences, arresting offenders, and initiating the criminal prosecution process (see Sanders and Young, in Chapter 28 of this volume), relatively little police research has focused on the CID (see Chaiken *et al.* 1977; Wilson 1978; Ericson 1981; Burrows and Tarling 1982; Hobbs 1988; Baldwin and Moloney 1992; Maguire and Norris 1992). The image of detective work portrayed in films and television is a far cry from the reality. Few crimes are cracked by *sleuthing* detectives, and a number of *causes célèbres* in the last twenty years have exposed investigative errors such as delays in discovering crucial items of evidence, failure to identify suspects, and the collapse of criminal prosecutions (Reiner 2000: 62–7). In the worst cases, investigative errors and malpractice led to wrongful convictions, for example, the Guildford Four, Birmingham Six, and Tottenham Three (Reiner 2000: 66; Rose 1996), and the failure to investigate properly and apprehend suspects as in the Lawrence case (Cathcart 1999; Macpherson 1999; Phillips and Bowling, in Chapter 17 of this volume).

In the following sections we discuss the core roles of the public police, something which has been a subject of on-going controversy since 'the inception of the "new" police' in 1829 (Newburn 1995: 55). We begin our discussion with two aspects of the order maintenance function—those based on developing good police/public relationships, informal resolution, and 'collaborative' and 'consultative' enterprise (Bennett 1994a)—and then their antithesis, paramilitary policing.

'Soft' policing—*with* people

It is widely acknowledged that good police/public relationships are vital to successful policing. Banton (1964: 165–6), for example, argued that without sustained public contact, officers would be unable to exercise their discretion appropriately, and would find themselves isolated, increasingly hostile, and unable to empathize with the public. Although it is highly questionable whether those who comprise 'police property' (Lee 1981)—the 'low-status, powerless groups' (Reiner 2000a: 93) such as the criminal, the homeless, the unemployed, those with alcohol and drug problems, and the socially excluded—have ever been sympathetically dealt with by police, or if there was ever a 'golden age' when police/public encounters were as harmonious as is often popularly believed (see Pearson 1983), changing police practices and broader societal changes have had an impact on the nature of police/public interactions and on expectations of the police.

The introduction of patrol cars in the late 1960s 'created an unprecedented gulf between police and public and . . . limited, or even removed, opportunity for day to day interaction' (Weatheritt 1986: 24). These changes, driven by the Home Office to enable wider coverage of police areas, alongside the introduction of personal radios, were intended to improve police response and quality of service (Holdaway 1983; Newburn 1995). But they had some very undesirable consequences, and were used within an action-oriented culture to 'maximize' police officers' excitement and narrow the nature of their contacts with the public (Holdaway 1983: 54–5, 135). Even '[t]he words used to characterise vehicle patrol—response, reaction and fire brigade policing' had 'negative connotations' (Weatheritt 1986: 24) which, as Reiner (2000a) notes, diminished the service elements of policing and established linkages between 'crime fighting' and technology. Interpersonal skills in police/public encounters, widely acknowledged to be important in dispute resolution, dwindled, and the need for 'democratic policing' to be 'concerned not only with the ends of crime control, but also with the means to achieve those ends' was diminished (Skolnick 1966, cited in Skolnick 1999: 6).

The urban riots that occurred in Britain in the early and mid-1980s, in which insensitive policing was perceived to play a pivotal role, were a profound indicator of just how problematic relationships between the police and some sections of society, particularly the most disenfranchised, had become (see Holdaway 1989; Scarman 1981; Benyon 1984; Bowling and Phillips 2002: 7–12). These disturbances had a profound impact on police sensibilities, and on public perceptions of the police too. Developing closer contacts and reducing the gulf between police and public in these areas became a priority, and community policing was seen as the antidote not only in Britain's inner cities, but also in other parts of the world where police legitimacy had been questioned and social divisions and discrimination were all too evident (see, for example, Mawby 1998 on Eastern Europe; Chan 1996, 1997 on Australia; Bowling et al. 2001).

Trojanowicz and Bucqueroux (1998) define community policing as a style which 'allows face-to-face contact with people in the same defined geographic area every day', in which officers should 'develop imaginative new ways to address the broad spectrum of concerns which exist in every community'. Their ten principles of community policing include: change; leadership; vision; partnership; problem-solving; equity; trust; empowerment; service, and accountability. These, of course, lie at the heart of consensual policing. Bayley and Shearing (1996: 604) suggest that community policing should be 'the organizing paradigm of public policing' and that it is a prerequisite for policing by consent, particularly in high-crime areas. This principle was also at the heart of the Patten Report (1999), where 'policing with the community' is cited as 'the core function' for the new Police Service of Northern Ireland (Recommendation 44: 23).

Evidence suggests that community policing can be transformative, changing officers' attitudes and approaches to their work (see Miller 1999; Skogan and Hartnett 1997: 246):

Evaluations find that a public hungry for attention has a great deal to tell police, and it is grateful for the opportunity to do so. When people see more police on foot or working out of a local substation, they feel less fearful. Officers have become committed to making community policing work, and where they have developed sustained cooperation with community groups and fostered self-help programs, they have witnessed declining levels of crime, social disorder and physical decay.

Research also suggests, however, that there are significant problems with community policing (see Skolnick and Bayley 1988; Bennett 1994a, 1994b; Fielding 1995; Trojanowicz and Bucqueroux 1998; Skogan and Hartnett 1997; Skogan *et al.* 1999), often because it has been inadequately defined, poorly implemented, and its impact not properly evaluated (Bennett 1994b). Community policing is also frequently used as a tactic rather than being the lever for fundamental reform of an entire police department (see Trojanowicz and Bucqueroux 1998; Bennett 1994a, 1994b; Miller 1999). Furthermore, in an occupation dominated by action, community policing, with its emphasis on problem-solving in the medium and longer term, developing closer links with communities and performing a broad range of policing tasks, often conflicts with the dominant values in policing culture (see Trojanowicz and Bucqueroux 1998; McConville and Shepherd 1992; Fielding 1995; Miller 1999; Skogan *et al.* 1999). As Skogan and Harnett (1997: 246) put it, 'the making-it-work stage primarily requires something that many cities have too little of—patience'.

Community policing has proved particularly difficult to implement in needy, high-crime environments, where 'participation in, and even sympathy for, community policing has been at low levels in neighbourhoods that need it most' (Skogan and Hartnett 1997: 238); and even those officers predisposed to community policing, often regard high-crime areas as requiring something 'harder' (see Miller 1999). In Britain, the leading advocate of community policing was the former Chief Constable of Devon and Cornwall (Alderson 1979), not an area typically associated with the kinds of problems of inner-city Liverpool or Brixton where the disorders in the 1980s occurred. This perhaps suggests that community policing is easiest to implement in the least problematic and needy areas.

'Community policing has been embraced as a buzzword, and the variety of activities associated with it seem to have little in common' (Skolnick and Bayley 1988: 4). This explains how some recent developments, popularly referred to as 'zero-tolerance', which is 'crime-oriented' and emphasizes 'law enforcement' (Bayley and Shearing 1996: 589), have also been referred to as 'community policing' (see Bratton 1997), despite 'zero tolerance' and some of its precepts being the antithesis of consensual policing. 'Zero tolerance', which involves routinely 'stopping the disorderly, unruly, and disturbing behaviour of people in public places, whether lawful or not'

(Bayley and Shearing 1996: 589) is perceived by some commentators and police officers to have a number of benefits. It 'reassures the public, demonstrating the limits for unacceptable behaviour', and is thought to 'reduce the incidence of more serious crime' (Wilson and Kelling 1982; Skogan 1990, Kelling and Coles 1996)' (Bayley and Shearing 1996: 589). Not surprisingly, 'zero tolerance' has generated considerable criticism in terms of its underlying philosophy, claims about its effectiveness (see Bowling 1999c; Karmen 2000), and its likely longer-term impact which may be counter-productive, reducing the legitimacy of the police and even increasing the likelihood of some future offending (Paternoster *et al.* 1997; Sherman 1998). The 'zero tolerance' debate also demonstrates how the ideal types of consensual 'soft' policing versus 'harder' more aggressive styles of policing can often be blurred in practice.

'Hard' order maintenance: policing against people

We mentioned earlier that the police find themselves in a contradictory role, aware that consensual policing is desirable but not always possible. 'Public order policing'— crowd control and responding to riot—is the example *par excellence*, where even in liberal democracies 'hard' paramilitary tactics are often adopted and the police come to symbolize the power of the state and governmental interests. Waddington (2000: 157) suggests that policing public order presents particular challenges to police legitimacy as both protesters and the police regard themselves to be 'morally' in the right: 'Thus a riot can be characterised as a battle between two groups (rioters and the police), both of whom are willing to use violence for what they each regard as "the common good". Protesters and pickets can, therefore, claim to be the moral equal of the police with a degree of success rarely achieved by criminals'.

Waddington (ibid. 159) suggests that 'public order policing is *not* the maintenance of order, but the maintenance of *a particular order*' (that of the State). This presents significant problems for the police, as they 'cannot shelter . . . behind the claim that they are merely enforcing the law. For if the law is itself unjust or sustains injustice, then enforcing it is tainted. Inevitably, this means defending the vested interests that are inherent within the established order and resisting the alternative order that protesters wish to establish'.

The demonstrations at the G8 summit in Genoa, Italy, in July 2001 highlighted the difficulties that can occur in these circumstances. Police cordoned off sections of the city, and deployed armed riot police and a range of paramilitary equipment. During the demonstration, a protester—Carlo Guiliani—wielding a fire-extinguisher was shot dead by the police, who then reversed over his body in their vehicle as they retreated in panic. Two hundred and fifty protesters and journalists were arrested, held without food for thirty-six hours, and many were abused and beaten in custody.[1] Yet initial reaction from government officials in Italy and Britain was to blame the protesters for the violence and to dismiss allegations of police brutality. Waddington (ibid. 163) sums up the problems with the police approach in this and other cases

[1] *Observer*, 29 July 2001; *Guardian*, 30 July 2001.

of public order, and once more highlights the contradictions which are inherent in policing:

Might is *not* right when it comes to the suppression of rioting. The police may 'win the battle' but lose the war if their actions are widely perceived as excessive. Whether or not rioters were actually motivated by a sense of injustice, if they can be portrayed in this light after the event, then it is *they* who become the victims. This illuminates the crucially import-ant fact, not only for public order policing but policing *per se*, that during a riot the police confront not an enemy, but fellow citizens.

Public order conflicts have also had a profound impact on police officers. For example, the 'riots' in some of Britain's inner cities in the late 1970s and early 1980s, generated fears within police ranks and led to pressures for paramilitary equipment to tackle this urban 'threat'. The Scarman Report—while criticizing the Metropolitan police for inflexibility and failing to achieve a balance between 'hard' and 'soft' policing—recommended expanding public order training and the acquisition of spe-cial equipment, such as armoured vehicles, water cannon, CS gas, and plastic bullets (Scarman 1981: paras 5.72–5.74). This led to the creation of a considerable para-military capacity within British police forces (Jefferson 1990) and presented a number of longer-term problems. The policing of the miners' dispute, for example, in the mid-1980s, and the violence on the picket lines relayed via our television screens, dented public confidence further (Waddington 1991). The depersonalizing image of officers in paramilitary uniforms with their faces hidden behind crash helmets, as well as the violence itself, led to ongoing debates about the impact of the dispute and the tactics police used (see Jefferson and Waddington debates (1987); Jefferson 1990; Waddington 1991). How can you negotiate and engage in conflict resolution when you cannot see another person's face?

In the complex debate about police roles which we mentioned earlier, Scarman (1981) concluded that, when keeping the peace and enforcing the law conflict, 'the maintenance of public tranquility comes first' (para. 4.57–8).

Our discussion of the 'soft' and 'hard' elements of policing has focused on the activity of uniformed officers. A discussion of policing functions would not be com-plete, however, without a discussion of crime management and crime investigation, and it is to these issues which we now turn.

DETECTIVES AND DETECTIVE PRACTICES

Although police work has traditionally been thought of as an intuitively learned 'craft' (Repetto 1978), developing police 'professionalism' and the adoption of a more 'sci-entific' approach to policing practice (e.g., Bayley and Bittner 1984) have recently gained impetus in the wake of high-profile miscarriages of justice and the need to keep pace with technological and scientific developments in crime investigation (Kleinig 1996: 35).

The early research on detective culture characterized the CID as a 'firm within a firm', where machismo and heavy drinking were prominent (Ericson 1981; Hobbs 1988; Rose 1996). Like their historical counterpart—the 'thief taker' (Rawlings 2002:

80–98)—detectives had a very close relationship (too close, many would argue) with the criminal underworld and its associated opportunities for corruption (Hobbs 1988; Dunnighan and Norris 1996a, 1996b, 1999).

Over the past two decades a range of structural changes have been introduced to protect suspects' rights and to improve investigation, including the Police and Criminal Evidence Act 1984 (PACE) and time-limited tenure in specific posts to reduce the potential for corruption. These changes are thought to have all but eliminated the 'old regime' of detectives (Rose 1996), and were intended to bring about a new era of professional, effective, and ethical investigation (Shepherd 1988; Maguire and Norris 1993). Optimists say a 'CID nouvelle'[2] is emerging, with better trained detectives, a more open management style and working environment, a more equal gender balance, and a more systematic approach to crime investigation. There is insufficient research at this stage to establish how prevalent or effective this 'new generation' of detectives might be, but at the moment the transition seems elusive. The Lawrence Inquiry found 'fundamental errors' and 'professional incompetence' in detective work and made wide-ranging recommendations for reform (Macpherson 1999: Recommendations 18–31), and a study conducted by the Home Office recently identified a 'growing shortage of senior investigating officers with the core investigative skills and abilities to perform their functions effectively' (Smith and Flanagan 2000: 1).

It is also worth reminding ourselves that while, as Punch (1985: 208) suggests, 'moral indignation' is always expressed when an organization is exposed for wrong-doing, the police remain 'fundamentally ambivalent about the ends and means of law enforcement'. As we discussed earlier, the police role is by definition larger than the police's ability to tackle it, and some writers suggest this generates inherent conflict and confusions about how to achieve the ends (see Goldstein 1975, for example), especially where officers perceive themselves to be under pressure from the media and the legal profession (Punch 1985). This situation generates a climate for deviance, and research consistently highlights that officers perceive themselves as forced 'to break the law in order to enforce it' (ibid.). Barker *et al.*'s (1994) research on the Los Angeles police aptly demonstrated this when 50 per cent of officers sampled felt that it was 'moderately acceptable to lie to get a bad guy off the streets' (see also Kappeller *et al.* 1994). Even within a climate of tighter legislative and procedural controls, therefore, it would be naive to assume that these kinds of processes do not continue to influence detective and other types of policing practice.

Proactive investigations

'Covert' or 'proactive' investigation uses informers, undercover police officers, and surveillance to produce an integrated 'intelligence led' approach (Maguire and John 1995; Maguire 2000; Heaton 2000). Based on the view that 'good quality intelligence is the life blood' of the modern police service (HMIC 1997a: 1), proactive investigation includes the systematic analysis of records of targeted suspects' movements, their financial dealings, and association with other suspected offenders. The approach also relies on recent innovations in technical surveillance, including the interception of

---

[2] A term coined by Peter Neyroud, Chief Constable Thames Valley Police (personal communication).

communications, planting of listening devices, video surveillance and tracking and tracing devices (Colvin and Noorlander 1998; Maguire 1998; Sheptycki 2000c).

Despite their growing role in crime investigation, there are serious ethical and other dilemmas about the use of informers (Maguire 2000; Innes 2000; Dunnighan and Norris 1996a and 1996b, 1999; Norris and Dunnighan 2000). While some informants are 'public spirited citizens' driven by a sense of civic responsibility, most of those who are useful to the police will be known offenders; indeed the most common occasion for recruiting an informer is while he or she is held in custody for an alleged offence (Dunnighan and Norris 1999; Innes 2000: 367–72). Informers may be motivated by revenge, competitive advantage, cash, and the possibilities for plea-bargaining (Collinson 1995; Innes 2000: 367). The 'participating' or 'tasked' informer, who continues to be involved in crime while in the pay of the police, is the most controversial (Norris and Dunnighan 2000).

Proactive policing has become increasingly popular as the perception has grown that the police are failing to meet their fundamental objective of reducing crime, as the anxieties about transnational crime have increased, and as managerialism has taken a hold on policing (Maguire 2000; Heaton 2000). Another powerful driver is the perceived 'pay-off' in cost–benefit terms. The Audit Commission (1993), for example, exhorted police managers to 'target the criminal not just the crime' on the basis of cost-effectiveness (see also HMIC 1997a: 2). However, its potential for crime reduction by incapacitating prolific offenders has been exaggerated (Heaton 2000), and the costs of recruiting and managing informers have been underestimated (Dunnighan and Norris 1999; Morgan and Newburn 1997; Innes 2000: 373–6).

Despite the proliferation of proactive policing, there has been virtually no public debate about the proper limits or framework for such activities (Maguire 2000). There may be no alternative to these techniques in certain cases. For example, the monitoring of international terrorist organizations (Marx 1988). But there are also concerns about the effectiveness, accountability, and fairness of such methods, and their effects on the privacy and rights of individuals who may be innocently caught up in surveillance operations (Maguire 2000; Colvin and Noorlander 1998).

It is also clear that proactive policing methods, and the technology which supports them, are developing faster than the framework of statutory and procedural controls (Maguire 2000; Colvin and Noorlander 1998). Until the Regulation of Investigatory Powers Act 1999, there were few controls on intelligence-led policing. The framework was patchy, inconsistent, and out-of-date, and did not provide adequate safeguards or remedies against abuse or misuse. Colvin and Noorlander (1998) identify a framework based on human rights jurisprudence and argue that the use of such practices should be bound by the principles of legality, necessity, proportionality, accountability, and remedy.

When the Regulation of Investigatory Powers Bill was introduced into Parliament in February 2000, the Home Secretary said: 'covert surveillance by police and other law enforcement officers is as old as policing itself; so too is the use of informants, agents and undercover officers' (Home Office Press Release 022/2000). This may be true, but these measures can diminish human rights to freedom and privacy at the expense of the demands of 'law and order' and the 'law enforcement agencies' (e.g., *Statewatch*, January 2000), and have the potential to undermine police legitimacy and destroy the social bases for trust (Marx 1988: 312). The historical literature highlights that undercover policing systems were resisted by many in Britain in the early nineteenth century on the ground that they were antithetical to notions of liberty (Emsley 1983). If, as Marx (1988: 312) argues, surveillance practices are a 'necessary evil', they must be used with great care.

Whether the legal formalization of covert policing powers will effectively regulate their use in practice remains to be seen. What is certain is that the 'police spies' model feared by opponents of the 'new police' in the 1820s and studiously avoided by Peel, now lies at the heart of government thinking about the future of some aspects of police work.

The preceding discussion has focused on the core police functions. We now turn to issues about how well the police perform those tasks.

HOW WELL DO THE POLICE PERFORM THEIR TASKS?

Public policing is an expensive business. In 2000/2001, the forty three forces of England and Wales had a budget of £7,370 million (Home Office 2001a), a figure that exceeded the combined costs of the courts, prisons, and the Probation Service (Home Office 1999). Despite gaining greater prominence in the late 1980s and 1990s, questions of police effectiveness have been a perennial concern since the 1950s (see Newburn 1995: 48). In this section we discuss whether the police can control crime, whether their effectiveness can be measured, and whether the vast sums invested in the police represent money well spent.

Do the police prevent crime?

The ability to prevent crime and disorder defines and justifies the existence of the public police in Britain. Peel saw 'the absence of crime and disorder' as the *key* goal of the London Metropolitan Police when it was introduced in 1829 (Lee 1901). Although the overwhelming public view of the police may be no more sophisticated than 'more police equals less crime', research in the 1970s and 1980s exploring the mechanisms through which the police could reduce crime (e.g., preventive patrol and crime investigation), began to suggest that the police might not be as central to crime prevention and control as might intuitively be thought (Clarke and Hough 1984; Pate *et al.* 1976; Kelling *et al.* 1974; Sherman and Berk 1995).

Studies suggested that crime was caused by factors—such as income inequality, poverty, and neighbourhood disorganization—that lay largely outside the control of the police (Downes and Morgan, Pease, Farrington, South, and Newburn, in Chapters 10, 26, 19, 25, and 16 respectively of this volume). The police therefore could logically play only a small part in crime control. This view was reinforced by a series of 'big science' police research studies in the USA, among them The Kansas City preventive patrol experiment (Kelling *et al.* 1974), which showed that crime rates, calls for service, and public satisfaction with the police were unaffected by doubling the police presence in a locality, leaving it the same, or removing the police presence all together. Further studies indicated that rapid response to crime calls (Pate *et al.* 1976) and detective work (Greenwood *et al.* 1977) had only a limited impact on crime rates. Home Office reviews of the relevant literature in the UK drew similar conclusions (Clarke and Hough 1984), and the view that 'nothing works' was underlined by rising levels of crime at a time of markedly increased police resources (Morgan and Newburn 1997).

In the mid-1990s, however, the picture began to change as part of a broader rediscovery of 'what works'. The established view that the police had little or no effect on recorded crime rates was challenged as crime reached a plateau in the UK, and began to drop sharply in some cities in the USA, most dramatically in New York (Bowling 1999b; Karmen 2001; Blumstein *et al.* 1999) where 'the major beneficiaries of the crime decline' were those living in high-crime communities (Skogan 1999: 3). Not surprisingly the police readily stepped in to take the credit, especially in New York, where these declines followed sizeable increases in police resources, 'smarter management', and new crime control tactics (Dennis *et al.* 1998; Silverman 1999; Bratton 1998; Karmen 2000; Bowling 1996, 1998, 1999b).

The relationship between declining crime rates and policing is complex, as recorded crime figures are fickle indicators and tend to reveal far more about the processes of recording crime than they do about its 'real extent', while changes in reporting practices can also make comparisons difficult (see Maguire 1997, and in Chapter 11 of this volume). However, it is also the case that a somewhat belated realization occurred that the proper management and targeting of police resources is better than unfocused patrol and 'fire fighting'. This led to a range of innovations in policing in the late 1990s that promised crime reduction, among them 'zero toler-ance', 'targeted hot-spots', and 'problem-oriented' and 'intelligence-led' policing. The conclusions drawn from recent reviews of the research evidence (e.g., Sherman *et al.* 1997; Jordan 1998; Waddington 1999: 4–12; Reiner 2000: 121–4) suggest that police impact on crime is still not compelling (see Table 27.4).

The most generous assessment is that some things work, in some places, under some conditions, particularly when social and economic factors are favourable. How-ever, substantial reductions in crime for long periods of time are difficult to achieve, because fashions in drug use and violent shifts in the shape and size of drug markets, economic downturn, and ethnic or political conflict, for example, can generate 'spikes' in crime rates, and are all outside the police's control (Bowling 1999a; Blumstein and Wallman 2000). The difficulty is in disentangling the effect of 'good police work' from changes in the economic and social context.

Measuring effectiveness

Measuring police effectiveness, as with the debate about police impact on crime, is not an easy task (Walker 1992; Coleman and Moynihan 1996; Maguire 1997). For many years, the 'clear-up rate', or proportion of cases in which a suspect was 'detected', was the standard measure of effectiveness. Clear-up rates for many offences declined during the 1980s and 1990s, and today vary from 90 per cent for homicide, 62 per cent for violence against the person, and 12 per cent for burglaries (Home Office 2001b: Table 2.8). The clear-up rate is a crude measure which offers no evaluation or insight into the *quality* of the investigative process.

Table 27.4 Police and crime reduction

Strategy	Underlying hypothesis	Effectiveness	Evidence
Increase police numbers	More police = less crime	Inconclusive	Kelling *et al.* (1974); Clarke and Hough (1984)
Random patrol	Deterrence through police omnipresence	Ineffective	Kelling *et al.* (1974); Audit Commission (1996)
Mandatory arrest	More arrests = less crime	Effective in some contexts, ineffective in others; can result in defiance	Sherman and Berk (1984); Sherman *et al.* (1992)
Community contact in general	More and better community contact = less crime	Inconclusive; can contribute to police legitimacy	Skolnick and Bayley (1988); Trojanowicz and Bucqueroux (1998); Fielding (1995)
Contact with young people	More and better contact with young people = less crime	Ineffective	Heal and Laycock (1987)
Rapid response	The faster the response to incidents = less crime	Inconclusive	Pate *et al.* (1976); Coupe and Griffiths (1996)
Intelligence-led policing	Target prolific offences or offenders, increased arrest rate = less crime	May be effective in some contexts	Audit Commission (1993); Stockdale and Gresham (1995, 1998); Maguire (2000); Innes (2000); Heaton (2000)

Directed patrol	Focus patrol on 'hot spots' and 'hot times' = less crime	Stockdale and Gresham (1998); May et al. (2000); Best et al. (2001)
Target repeat victims	Protecting victims = less crime	Forrester et al. (1988); Chenery et al. (1997); Phillips and Sampson (1998)
Multi-agency working	Partnership between police and other agencies = less crime	Weatheritt (1986); Bowling (1999a: 101–45); Crawford (1999); Hughes (1998)
Problem-oriented policing	Analysis of crime patterns, addressing underlying causes through solving problems = less crime	Goldstein (1990); Leigh et al. (1996)
Zero tolerance/aggressive order maintenance	Crackdowns on minor offences lead to reductions in more serious offences	Wilson and Kelling (1982); Kelling and Coles (1996); Bowling (1999a); Bratton (1997); Dennis (1997)
Proactive stop/search	Increases in use of stop and search powers = decrease in crime	Boydstun (1975); Wilson and Boland (1978); FitzGerald (1999); Miller, Bland, and Quinton (2000)
	May be effective in some contexts; ineffective in others (e.g. drugs)	
	Effective in some contexts; ineffective in others	
	Inconclusive	
	Inconclusive	
	Inconclusive; some support for 'broken windows' hypothesis but aggressive order maintenance can generate problems.	
	Inconclusive; limited effectiveness in some contexts; perceived as unfair; low ratio of stops to arrests; risks public disorder	

Sources: Jordan 1998; Sherman 1992a, 1993; Reiner 2000a: 121–4.

Research has established that the single most important determinant of whether a case will be solved is the information that the victim supplies to the police officer who is initially called for service (Greenwood 1980; Steer 1980; Maguire and Norris 1998). It is clear, therefore, that some offences are more easily 'detectable' (e.g., interpersonal violence) than others (e.g., burglary and criminal damage). Moreover, clear-up rates are notoriously malleable (Young 1991) and can be affected by recording practices and methods of detection, including the charging or cautioning of a suspect, or by 'secondary' means such as offences 'taken into consideration' by the courts. Differences in clear-up rates between divisions and police force areas are, therefore, just as likely to be the result of differences in 'crime mix', methods of clearance, and resource allocation as they are an indicator of investigative competence (Reiner 2000a: 118–21; Audit Commission 1996). Morgan and Newburn's (1997: 160) comment that 'There are no simple solutions to the crime and policing problems that confront us' seems equally apposite to the debates about measuring the effectiveness of police practice.

So how should we judge the police?

If, as the discussion above suggests, the police do not have much demonstrable impact on crime, and the measures used to assess their effectiveness are unhelpful, are there other ways in which we might assess the worth of our public police? Although it has been difficult to demonstrate the preventive potential of policing, there is a great deal of evidence that 'bad' policing can be counterproductive, contributing to increases in crime and undermining security. For example, oppressive policing tactics and those perceived as unduly harsh or unfair have triggered major public disorder (Scarman 1981), can undermine the legitimacy of government and voluntary compliance with the law (Tyler 1990; Paternoster et al. 1997), and engender defiance (Sherman 1993). Consequently, police leaders should be as concerned about 'figuring out who is doing a good job' as whether crime rates are going up or down (Mastrofski 1999: 4). This requires an examination of the *qualitative* experiences of those who come into contact with the police, and of the police's ability to resolve problems appropriately and professionally.

Mastrofski (1998) identifies six core factors which should be at the heart of policing: attentiveness; reliability; responsiveness; competence; manners; and fairness. Drawing on a wide range of evidence about encounters with the police, both as offenders and as victims, he suggests that the *way* the police behave is vitally important, especially in cases where there is no easy resolution of the problems encountered, or where the likelihood of apprehending a suspect is remote. 'When citizens are traumatized', for example, he argues, 'whatever else police might accomplish, it costs little to offer some measure of comfort' or to 'be responsive even when they deny a citizen's request, by explaining the denial' (Mastrofski ibid.: 2). However, research indicates that police officers can be rude, aggressive, and unresponsive, especially to those dismissed as 'dross' (Choongh 1997), who are 'disrespectful' (Reiss 1966; Parks et al. 1997), or who seek to challenge police authority. In the most recent sweep of the British Crime Survey, for example,

20 per cent of respondents reported being 'really annoyed' with the police (Clancy *et al.* 2001). When asked what had 'annoyed' them, 57 per cent of white respondents and 71 per cent of black respondents cited 'poor demeanour or manners' (ibid.: 77–8).

Despite the self-evident importance of professional policing, 'there is very little in the current police reform movement that promotes these ideals and that gives them the attention they deserve' (Mastrofski 1999: 4). In Britain, although the 'social disciplinary' nature of policing (Choongh 1997) remains strong, external pressures to encourage the police to look more closely at their practice and its discriminatory impact, and to develop a model of policing based on *need*, have recently been established (see Macpherson 1999, for example). This can most clearly be seen in debates concerning the policing of minority communities (see Phillips and Bowling, in Chapter 17 of this volume).

The recognition that the police cannot solve crime alone has, over the last two decades, promoted the growth of multi-agency partnerships to tackle crime and disorder. We discuss the notion of partnership, and the police role within it, below.

MULTI-AGENCY PARTNERSHIP AND POLICING

We noted earlier the fundamental difference between policing and *the* police. While the public police are an important criminal justice agency, they cannot (as we have seen) tackle crime or deliver community safety on their own. They require public support and coordination with a variety of different public sector agencies that often share similar (or identical) clients and problems. This is because crime is often interconnected with other social forces. For example, on high-crime housing estates, the problems of unemployment, crime, deprivation, low educational achievement, and poor housing often coexist (see Foster and Hope 1993; Hope and Foster 1992; Foster 2000). Despite its inherently 'multifaceted' quality, crime prevention was for decades 'ghettoized' and seen as a 'specialist' police function (Harvey *et al.* 1989; Crawford 1998a). In the last twenty years, however, the recognition that there are shared problems, and that solving them requires the involvement of more than one agency, led to the development of 'multi-agency' partnership working (Bowling 1999b: chapter 4; Crawford 1998, 1999).

The Morgan Report (Home Office 1991) was a key driver in contemporary partnership arrangements. This suggested the need to move away from narrow definitions of crime prevention (seen to imply a sole police role) and to focus instead on *community safety* (Hughes 1998: 81) The Report also recommended that local authorities should 'coordinate' and 'collaborate' with the police in delivering community safety. The Conservative government in power at the time the Report was published was deeply opposed to the notion of local authorities taking a key role, so it was not until a Labour administration was elected that Morgan's recommendations were finally implemented in the Crime and Disorder Act 1998, which made partnership between the police and local authorities mandatory (see Downes and Morgan, and Pease, in Chapters 10 and 26 respectively of this volume).

The police, for a variety of reasons, but many related to their can-do, action-oriented culture and a widely shared belief that they *should* be the lead agency on crime prevention, have often taken a very high-profile role in partnership working (Blagg *et al.* 1988; Sampson *et al.* 1988; Crawford 1998, 1999). To date the research suggests that while the philosophy of 'joined-up working' towards 'joint solutions' is widely accepted as desirable, a number of factors—including the growth and limitations of managerialism; single agency performance indicators; unresolved cultural differences between the different agencies; differing power relationships and priorities—mean that partnership often remains more 'rhetoric' than reality (Gilling 1997: 196; Crawford 1998a, 1998b; Hughes 1998). Gilling (2000: 135) argues that criminal justice is a 'fragmented, contradictory process' rather than a coordinated system, and 'there is no reason to assume that the absorption of even more agencies under the community safety umbrella will result in greater coordination'; instead, there is 'some logic in suggesting it might result in less'.

Despite its contradictions, the move from a focus on the police as the prime movers in crime prevention to joint agency working and greater emphasis on local communities and individuals taking responsibility for crime prevention, represents a fundamental shift in late modernity. As Crawford (2000: 202) notes:

The relationship between government and the governed is now one in which we are all reconfigured as 'partners' . . . . We are all now cast as 'partners against crime' in a new and corporate approach (Crawford 1994), involving a fundamental rearticulation of individual and group responsibilities and professional 'expertise', as well as state paternalism and monopoly of control. Where once we were told to leave it to the professionals', now we are enjoined to active participation in a 'self policing society'.

As Hughes (1998: 152) points out, these changes highlight 'the impossibility of adequately understanding the changing modes of crime prevention without a close and critical engagement with the wider politics of social order in late modernity'. Hughes's comments are equally apposite for the debates about policing *beyond* government which we discuss below.

'POLICING BEYOND GOVERNMENT'

Like the partnership agenda, 'policing *beyond* government' is fundamentally linked with broader political and social changes in late modern society (see, for example, Giddens 1990; Bottoms and Wiles 1996), particularly those related with risk (Beck 1992). Indeed Johnston (2000: 67) argues that 'the growth of private policing has to be considered within the context of late modern "mentalities"'. These have paved the way for a lucrative risk and security industry. In this section we begin by exploring the plurality of policing which takes place *beyond* government, and its implications.

Although private policing is relatively 'under-researched' (see Shearing and Stenning 1983; South 1988; Johnston 1992; Bayley and Shearing 1996; Jones and Newburn 1998; Johnston 2000 as exceptions), debates about privatization have tended to focus on whether authors are 'for or against' it 'rather than [on a] detailed analysis of the relationship *between* public and private provision' (Jones and Newburn 1995: 221, emphasis added). Furthermore, there is considerable controversy about how 'private' and 'public' provision should be defined, with important differences between the private security *industry* (that supplies security guards and crime prevention technology like alarms) and the private security *sector* (that encompasses a broader range, including 'body guards, private investigators, security consultants and in-house security' (Jones and Newburn 1995: 221; South 1988)). These differences highlight some important problems in assessing the size of the private security sector, as 'those doing the measuring rarely measure the same thing' and 'there is no agreed definition of what falls within the rubric of "private security"' (Jones and Newburn 1995). Not surprisingly perhaps, Johnston (1992: 43) characterized this situation as one with 'varying degrees of ambiguity, inconsistency, contradiction and confusion'.

Bayley and Shearing (2001: vii) argue that 'privatization' is not the most appropriate term to explain contemporary trends in policing because of the difficulties in distinguishing 'between public and private domains'. They suggest that 'multilateralization' is more appropriate for describing a situation with multiple providers, where '[w]ithout close scrutiny, it has become difficult to tell whether policing is being done by a government using sworn personnel, by a private security company using civilian employees, by a private company using public police, or by a government employing citizens' (Bayley and Shearing 2001: 15). This description is particularly apposite for North America, where 'commercial security personnel now outnumber public police . . . by a ratio of 2:1' (Johnston 2000: 71).

In Britain the picture is rather different. Using Census data as a guide to the numbers employed in the private security sector, Jones and Newburn (1998) illustrate that these activities were 'already well established in the immediate post war period' (Newburn 2001: 831); and that while the growth of the private security sector has been significant, the greatest growth was in the 1950s and 1960s. Furthermore, the *proportion* of those employed in private security vis–à-vis the public police has remained relatively constant (see Figure 27.3 below).

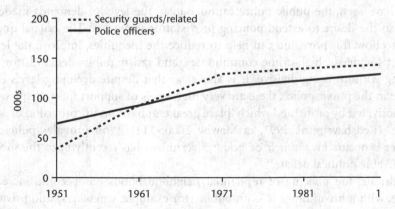

Fig. 27.3 Employment levels in 'Policing': Great Britain 1951–1991

Source: Jones and Newburn (1998: 96), based on Census data.

These findings not only highlight the importance of taking a wider historical perspective, but also suggest that 'current developments in policing' should not be 'interpreted as a sharp qualitative break with the past' because there are 'significant consistencies and continuities' (Jones and Newburn 2002: 129). Indeed, Jones and Newburn suggest that we should understand contemporary trends in policing not as fragmentation, but 'as part of a long-term process of formalization of social control' (ibid.: 129). Given the plethora of organizations and activities involved in policing 'beyond government', some authors suggest that 'security networks' (Shearing 1996; Johnston 2000a) is a more accurate and useful description than 'policing'.

Given our earlier discussion about the lack of proven effectiveness of the public police, should we be concerned about the growth of private provision—perhaps other service providers might do a better job? Loader (2000: 328–9) suggests that the key problems with policing beyond government are related to regulation and account-ability. Many of these changes have emerged without any significant public discussion (Bayley and Shearing 1996: 586), yet their implications are fundamental because 'if left unchecked', the plethora of policing functions we now see 'may give rise to a patchwork system of security which combines ineffectiveness (due to lack of coordination between the diverse elements) and injustice (due to inequities in the distribution of security and risk)' (Johnston 2000: 76). The ethics are also deeply questionable. As Bayley and Shearing (1996: 592–4) observe, although 'pluralizing of policing' can 'increase public safety':

The problem is that pluralizing under market auspices . . . does not improve security equally across society. It favours institutions and individuals that are well-to-do . . . [and] leads to the inequitable distribution of security along class lines. If public safety is considered a general responsibility of government, perhaps even a human right, then increased reliance on commercial private policing represents a growing injustice.

These are very important issues. However, it is equally the case that the public police currently and historically have reinforced class and race divisions (Choongh 1997; Morgan and Newburn 1997; Clancy et al. 2001; Bowling and Phillips 2002) and have frequently failed those communities in most need of their support. Furthermore, as we have seen, the public police cannot satisfy the level of demands made upon them, so the desire to extend policing provision is inevitable. The crucial questions relate to how this provision can help to reduce the inequities, improve the levels of support for needy, high-crime communities, and satisfy public demands for visible policing without being divisive. It is also clear that despite declining levels of con-fidence in the public police, there are very high levels of support for policing which is 'not motivated by profit' and which 'place great emphasis on the provision of a caring service' (Redshaw et al. 1997, in Mawby 2000: 114). Who provides policing and whether it occurs by, through, or below government has recently been the subject of considerable political debate.

In Britain the policing of residential neighbourhoods has become increasingly diverse, with a broad range of both public (for example, caretakers) and private (for example, security patrols) provision. These activities have been drawn together under the term 'Neighbourhood Warden Schemes' (Jacobson and Saville 1999: v). A recent evaluation suggested that 'warden schemes can help to address many of the problems faced by deprived neighbourhoods' and alongside other 'local crime prevention initiatives, can contribute to bringing down levels of crime and fear of crime' (Jacobson and Saville 1999: 31). These ideas have been endorsed by government in a White Paper, *Policing A New Century: A Blueprint for Reform* (2001). This outlines changes, including the creation of 'Community Support Officers', who will be employed by the public police and given powers to provide a visible patrolling function and tackle 'minor disorder and anti-social behaviour', with greater use being made of existing 'crime reduction activities e.g. traffic wardens, neighbourhood and street wardens and security staff, through an extended police family', 'accredited' by the police (ibid.: 4). Although such ideas are perhaps inevitably greeted by police officers as 'policing on the cheap', the Home Secretary regards them as 'a realistic hard headed approach to deploying and co-ordinating the people . . . who are already working in this area' (Blunkett 2001: 14).

Despite some very pessimistic predictions about the impact of policing *beyond* government, these recent changes suggest that in Britain, at least, a role for policing both *by* and *through* government is still thought to be important. Nevertheless, some commentators believe that the pressures we have outlined here may result in 'two tier policing' where the public police focus on intrusive methods of 'bandit catching' and paramilitary 'riot control', while crime prevention and 'community policing' becomes the preserve of local authorities, private security, and voluntary groups (e.g., Brogden and Shearing 1993; Loader 1997).

To date, the British police have continuously extended rather than limited their remit. The White Paper encourages this trend through the police providing accreditation and employing community support officers directly (this of course carries the danger that the police will select a narrower band of less representative people than external organizations). However these issues are resolved, or how extensive or otherwise the penetration of policing *beyond* government has become, it is certain that 'the connections between who authorizes policing, who provides it, and how it is done need to be studied. Not only may they not be independent of one another, but their distribution socially has enormous political implications for the future' (Bayley and Shearing 2001: 19).

GLOBALIZATION AND TRANSNATIONAL POLICE COOPERATION

To date, the focus of most research on crime and policing has been on the local. Recently, however, with the growing importance of globalization and the blurring of 'boundaries between domestic matters and global affairs' (Held *et al.* 1999: 8–16), policing *above* government is gaining prominence (Leishman *et al.* 1996: 9; Johnston 2000a: 18). Cross-border crimes—such as international terrorism, money-laundering, and trafficking in arms, drugs, and people—are high on the political agenda. These problems, emerging as capital and business internationalize and regulatory systems diminish (Bottoms and Wiles 1996; Sheptycki 1995; Rawlinson 1998; Johnston 2000a: 18–32), 'cannot be satisfactorily dealt with either by traditional military means or solely within a national framework' (Held *et al.* 1999: 8–16; House of Commons 1995; Sheptycki 1995; Hobbs 1997).

Transnational police cooperation has always existed through the exchange of ideas about 'new' policing systems (Miller 1977), international policing networks (Brown and Heidensohn 2000), the transfer of new technologies such as fingerprinting, forensic science, and computer databases (Sheptycki 1998b), and sharing information about wanted criminals. While policing is still largely embedded in nation states, shifts in the nature and scope of policing are occurring because of the 'transnationalisation of governance' (Sheptycki 2000a: 223). Alongside global economic structures (such as the IMF, WTO, and World Bank), and political structures (such as the UN, EU, and G8), a fledgling international legal system is emerging, including an international criminal court and an array of policing agencies which transcend the nation state (see Table 27.5).

The work of 'national security' and 'intelligence agencies'—such as MI5, MI6, Special Branch, and the Criminal Intelligence Agency (CIA), often referred to as 'high policing' agencies—was originally concerned solely with 'political crime' and the protection of the state itself (Brodeur 1983). Increasingly, however, it is also concerned with 'ordinary law crime' (Sheptycki 2000a: 9; Savage *et al.* 2000: 27). New agreements *between* governments have also been established to facilitate the exchange of information and create joint mechanisms for surveillance, investigation, and enforcement.

Private security corporations have operated internationally 'beyond government' for almost a century, growing rapidly since the 1970s (Johnston 2000a, 2000b). The big players in transnational private security are involved in a range of activities, including 'access control', drug testing and detection, intelligence, surveillance, under-cover operations, and providing private militias to support national police forces (Johnston 2000b). The implications of these developments, and the blurring of boundaries between private and public in the transnational realm, have barely begun to be understood (ibid.).

While the emphasis on transnational policing is important, the focus on the global has frequently led to neglect of 'variation between nation states' (Jones and Newburn 2002: 143; Bottoms and Wiles 1996). Cain (2000) suggests that people now act in ways that are 'indigenous-yet-globally-aware'. Thus contemporary police commanders are required to deliver local 'community safety' (to particular 'hotspots'), *and at the same time* to remain conscious of the impact of global forces on that locality. For example, the nature and extent of local drug markets are intrinsically linked to the transnational supply and distribution networks that feed them. *Operation Trident* in the Metropolitan Police, that targeted so-called 'Yardie' gangs, is a good illustration of the ways in which both global and local interact. It involved collaboration with police in Jamaica and New York as part of a *local* crime reduction strategy.

While the impact of globalization is felt all around us (Giddens 1990; Held *et al.* 1999), concerns have also been expressed about the exact nature, scope, and extent of the transnational crime problem (Hebenton and Thomas 1995). Although it may

Table 27.5 A typology of transnational policing

Type	Organizations	Functions
National policing agencies operating abroad (by government)	UK: National Crime Squad, National Crime Intelligence Service, MI6, MI5, Special Branch; UK Immigration Officers.	Police officers resident overseas engaged in 'bilateral' and 'multilateral' information exchange, mutual assistance.
	US: Central Intelligence Agency (CIA), Drugs Enforcement Agency (DEA), Federal Bureau of Investigation (FBI), National Security Agency (NSA).	DEA, for example, employs more than 200 agents in over 60 offices around the world.
Transnational and cross-border police cooperation arrangements (between governments)	European Council of Ministers intergovernmental framework (TREVI).	Set up in 1976 to combat terrorism, drugs, organized crime, nuclear security.
	Schengen Convention.	Agreement signed in 1985 to police frontier-free area in Benelux region, including border surveillance, right of 'hot pursuit' across borders; created Schengen Information System to share data on wanted persons and 'undesirable aliens'.
	European Police Office (Europol)	Formed in 1991 to facilitate intelligence exchange between law enforcement agencies in EU member states.
	United Nations Convention Against Transnational Organized Crime.	Signed in 2000 to promote cooperation to prevent and combat transnational organised crime. Facilitates the creation of 'joint investigative bodies' (art. 19).
International policing agencies (above government)	United Nations Security Police.	Protects UN buildings and employees, comprised of seconded police officers under central UN control.
	UN Civil Police Units (CivPol).	Part of UN peacekeeping operations. First employed in the Congo in 1960, now operational in six countries (largest in Kosovo), involves 4,720 officers from 45 countries.
	International Criminal Police Organization (INTERPOL).	Formed in 1923, acts as a global intelligence network between autonomous members; membership of 176 countries; not established by international treaty.

continued . . .

Table 27.5 continued

| *Private transnational policing (beyond government)* | Wells Fargo, Securitas, Pinkerton, Wakenhut, etc. | Uniformed private security guards in private buildings; airport security; employee vetting; securing intellectual property; surveillance and counter-surveillance. |
| | Military Professional Resources Inc.; Executive Outcomes; Sandline, etc. | Private militias employed to support public law enforcement agencies and private corporations. |

seem intuitively sensible that 'globally mobile robbers' need 'globally mobile cops' to pursue them, can we be sure that this does not constitute a 'moral panic' about a new international 'folk devil' (Sheptycki 1995)? The difficulty in quantifying 'global crime' also makes it hard to judge the effectiveness of attempts to reduce it, and to disentangle the impact of local, national and transnational arrangements (Hebenton and Thomas 1995). Given declining levels of public confidence in the police (BCS 2000) and the question mark over police effectiveness at a local level (where different specialisms within the *same* police force often fail to work co-operatively), what confidence should we have about the ability of the police to tackle cross-border crime, involving as it does cooperation between different cultures, languages, and legal traditions and frameworks (see Nadelman 1993)? While there is discussion about harmonizing systems, for example within the European Union, serious questions remain about whether coordination, cooperation, or integration of these systems is possible, or even desirable (Benyon *et al.* 1993; Hebenton and Thomas 1995; Anderson *et al.* 1995).

Ethical questions are also raised by transnational policing, especially because it more frequently involves intrusive techniques (McLaughlin 1992: 483) and more repressive styles of policing. These have the potential to undermine civil liberties, especially for those seen as an 'unwanted presence' in an insular and xenophobic social order. For example, the raft of new legislation in the UK, USA, and Australia on terrorism, security, and migration in the wake of the bombing of the twin towers in New York on 11 September 2001, focuses on asylum seekers, refugees, and other 'undesirable aliens', widening policing powers and intensifying 'immigration policing' (Weber and Bowling 2002).

There has been very little discussion about the mechanisms for accountability in transnational policing. The legal framework and systems for holding police commanders to account are under-developed, and few due process safeguards exist (Hebenton and Thomas 1995). Together with a general lack of transparency, we are forced to take on trust the expertise, efficiency, and effectiveness of transnational policing efforts, and the legality and integrity of such operations.

What form will transnational cooperation take in the future? In one scenario, local territorial police forces based on the Peelian model established in the nineteenth century will remain central to British policing, with transnational operations subservient and consequently short-term, patchy, and limited in scope. In another scenario (hastened by anxieties about international terrorism in the wake of the events of 11 September), we might see increasingly integrated regional policing agencies with an extra-territorial mandate, wide geographical mobility, an extensive intelligence capacity (combining international police and security services data-bases), and a full range of coercive and intrusive powers. In either scenario, trans-national policing needs to reduce the harms caused by organized crime across borders, but to do so in a way which protects fundamental human rights and freedoms (Sheptycki 2001).

THEORIZING POLICING IN PRACTICE

In the previous discussion we outlined some of the dominant trends in policing. Here we focus on the theories which seek to provide a framework for under-standing police work. These 'individual', 'legal-bureaucratic', 'cultural', and 'struc-tural' (Dixon 1997) theories are important because they help to explain how 'good policing' might be achieved, as well as explaining various aspects of police deviance and misconduct.

INDIVIDUAL ACCOUNTS

Individual theories see the problems of policing as the result of psychological weak-ness in police officers (Brogden et al. 1988: 11–29; Waddington 1999: 106–7). Often referred to as 'bad apple' theories, they suggest that organizational failures result from the actions of a small number of rogue police officers who are (variously) lazy, rude, unintelligent, intolerant, insensitive, brutal, authoritarian, sexist, racist, or corrupt (Brogden et al. ibid.: 11–29; Waddington ibid.: 106–7; Reiner 2000: 99–100). The 'bad' officers 'find their way (or are selectively recruited into) police work where they express their prejudices and crudeness' under the cloak of the law (Wilson 1968: 409, cited by Waddington ibid.: 107). The policy solutions to the problem of 'bad apples' include screening at recruitment, education, training, and more stringent disciplinary mechanisms (e.g., Scarman 1981; Sherman 1983; Chan 1997).

The bad apple thesis was a favoured explanation within the police organization for police mis-behaviour and police deviance. However, the recent recognition that both corruption (Newburn 1999; Williamson 2000) and racism (Macpherson 1999) are *institutionalized* highlights that while human agency, individual decision-making, and culpability are all important for understanding police work, indi-vidualist accounts are over-simplistic and tend to pay too little attention to the wider organizational, cultural, and structural context (Bowling and Phillips 2002: 155–62).

LEGALISTIC-BUREAUCRATIC ACCOUNTS

Based on legal and 'rational scientific' principles, these theories conceptualize the police organization as a 'machine' in which individual officers simply execute the law or policy directives (Grimshaw and Jefferson 1987: 6; Dixon 1997: 1–8). Police behaviour therefore can be understood by an analysis of administrative law, criminal law, criminal procedure, and other formal rules.

Legalistic-bureaucratic theories can readily be criticized for failing to differentiate between how organizations ideally *ought* to function rather than *how* they actually work in practice. This is particularly important in terms of policing, because individual police officers can exercise considerable discretion (Wilson 1968) and the relationship between laws and their enactment in practice is highly variable (see, for example, Quinton *et al.* 2000). Legalistic-bureaucratic theories are useful, however, in drawing attention to the structure of the police organization and the operation of the law; but they fail to explain why research consistently demonstrates that law and policy do not *determine* policing practice but only exert some influence in specific circumstances (Dixon 1997).

CULTURAL ACCOUNTS

From the very early studies of the police (Banton 1964; Van Maanen 1973, 1974; Rubinstein 1973), observational research identified the importance of police culture for understanding how the police saw their role and the ways in which they executed their duties (see Dixon 1997: 9). Reiner (2000a: 87) defines cop culture 'as a patterned set of understandings that help officers to cope with and adjust to the pressures and tensions confronting the police'. Many of the core characteristics of police culture are universal (Fielding 1994; Waddington 2000: 3–4), and some are directly connected with the nature of police work itself (Reiner 2000). In this section we examine: the nature of the culture; how it shapes and influences behaviour; and to what extent its more negative elements act as inhibitors for change.

Culture and behaviour

Most observational studies of police subcultures have focused on uniformed constables. This is partly because their work is the most visible (and perhaps easily observed), but also because their attitudes and behaviour most directly impact on police/public relationships and, unlike many public organizations, considerable discretion is exercised by officers at the most junior levels (J.Q. Wilson, 1968: 7).

Although most research on police culture suggests that it is a key element in explaining behaviour, the relationship is 'complex and context-driven' (Foster, forthcoming). A study conducted for the Policy Studies Institute (1983: iv, 109) in the 1980s, for example, suggested that despite 'prominent and pervasive' 'racialist language' and 'racial prejudice' in the police canteen, these attitudes did not influence police officers' interactions with minorities on the street. Research in the United States has drawn similar conclusions (see Black 1970; Sherman 1980, 1983; Waddington 1999a, 1999b). Waddington (1999b) suggests, on the basis of this and other evidence, that police culture acts as 'a palliative, rather than a guide to future action' (ibid.: 295), where talk about 'crime-fighting', action, and excitement involves 'telling it like it ain't' (ibid.: 299–300). Shearing and Ericson (1991) also highlight the importance of talk, but suggest that this *does* provide the backdrop to action and provides cues about how officers should behave.

Although it has been difficult to establish a *direct* transmission from words to actions, patterns of differential stop and search, and research on minorities' experiences of the police (see Bowling and Phillips 2002: 161–2; Phillips and Bowling, in Chapter 17 of this volume; Clancy *et al.* 2001) suggest that attitudes may well play a part in behaviour. As Holdaway and Barron (1997: 75–7) argue:

Although there may be an analytical distinction between the various forms of discourse about 'race' when officers talk within the police station and the ways in which they are enacted in their relationships with people from ethnic minorities, the occupational culture is not adequately analysed as discourse. It is both talk and action.

It seems that while differential enforcement according to class, ethnicity, and gender persists (Choongh 1997; Chan 1997), such practices 'are not articulated in simple or straightforward ways in all localities' (Walklate 2000: 235) or amongst all individuals. This also suggests that 'it is ... up to individuals to accommodate or resist' the influence of the culture (Chan 1996: 112). As Chan argues, 'a sound theory of police culture should recognise the interpretive and active role of officers in structuring their understanding of the organization and its environment' (ibid.).

The key characteristics of police culture which have been identified in the research are summarized in Table 27.6 below, along with the role these characteristics are seen to perform and the problems associated with them.

Although the features outlined in Table 27.6 have been found in numerous police studies over four decades, research also suggests that there are significant sub-cultural differences *within* police organizations according to *rank*, with distinctions between 'street cops' and 'management cops' (e.g. Ianni and Ianni 1983; Punch 1983; Manning 1997), and *role*, with distinctions between community officers and shift officers (e.g., Fielding 1995; McConville and Shepherd 1992) and between uniform and CID officers (Hobbs 1988; Young 1991; Ericson 1981). Culture also varies 'between forces, shaped by their differing "problems", "environments" and "the legacies of their histories"' (Reiner 2000: 86; Mulcahy 2000), and even in different police stations in the same force area (Foster 1989).

Cultural change

A number of recent studies in Australia, the United States, Britain, and South Africa all highlight that cultural change is possible precisely because the police are not immune to external pressures (see Chan 1996, 1997; Dixon 1997; Marks 1999; Miller 1999; Foster 1989, 2002). Chan (1997: 92–3), drawing on theories developed by Bourdieu and Sackmann, suggests that the key lies in being able to change '*the field*, that is, the social, economic, legal and political sites in which policing takes place' and 'the habitus' (the cultural knowledge).

Her study of the New South Wales Police in Australia, and their attempts to tackle

Table 27.6 Key characteristics of police culture

Characteristic	Explanation/Role	Problems
Sense of mission	Policing is 'not just as a job but the "preservation of a valued way of life and the protection of the weak against the predatory". Police officers are "the thin blue line" "safeguarding social order" ' (Reiner 2000: 89).	The sense of mission and 'moral imperative makes established practices much more resistant to reform than if they were merely self serving' (Reiner 2000: 89).
Thirst for action; or 'action orientation'	Much police work is mundane but the culture focuses on the challenge, excitement, and policing as 'a game of wits and skill' (Reiner 2000: 89).	The desire for action is reflected at all ranks and can lead to hasty rather than measured decisions. Focus on the immediate rather than the longer term (Foster, forthcoming).
Cynicism and pessimism	Police 'develop a hard skin of bitterness, seeing all social trends in apocalyptic terms, with the police as the beleaguered minority about to be overrun by the forces of barbarism' (Reiner 2000: 90).	Cynicism is a means whereby officers distance themselves from moral, psychological, and emotional stresses, and is ultimately self-destructive (Kleinig 1996: 79). Makes innovation and change difficult.
Suspicion	The job breeds an attitude of constant suspicion to look out for signs of trouble, potential danger, and clues to offences that cannot be switched off. Suspicion is regarded as 'healthy' (Reiner 2000: 91).	'While police suspiciousness and stereotyping are inescapable, the categories informing them reflect power in society . . . and reproduce a pattern of implicit discrimination' (Reiner 2000: 91).
Isolation and solidarity	Isolated from the community by the nature of the job; difficulty in mixing with civilians in their social life due to shift-work, erratic hours, and hostility from the public. Generates internal solidarity and the need to support and 'back-up' colleagues (Reiner 2000: 91–3).	Solidarity plays a role in masking minor and serious 'wrongdoings'; which are covered up by inappropriate loyalty the 'blue wall of silence'. Isolation/solidarity leads to a 'them' and 'us' mentality and dismissal of some groups as 'police property' or 'dross' (Choongh 1997).
Conservatism	The nature of the job and the recruits it attracts tend to be politically, morally, and socially conservative.	Intolerance, reluctance to change, belief in existing ways of doing things.

Table 27.6 continued

Machismo	A male dominated profession which represents policing as a 'hard', macho occupation, the preserve of 'real men' (Reiner 2000: 97–8; Waddington 1999).	Emphasis on 'aggressive, physical action; competition, preoccupation with the imagery of conflict. Exaggerated heterosexual orientations articulated in misogynistic and patriarchal attitudes (Brown and Heidensohn 2000; Fielding 1994: 47). Sexism and homophobia institutionalized in discrimination in recruitment and promotion (Brown 1998).
Racial prejudice	Suspiciousness, hostility, and prejudice towards ethnic minorities. Views and opinions often excused by suggestions that racism mirrors attitudes in society at large.	Like sexism, racism is institutionalized (Macpherson 1999). '[E]vidence of inappropriate language and behaviour by police officers' and the failure of supervisors to intervene to prevent it (HMIC 1997b, 1999).
Pragmatism	Policing is a practical occupation which demands 'common sense' (Crank 1998: 163), something thought to be 'crucial for survival on the street' (McNulty 1994, in Crank).	Policing is 'anti-theoretical' (Reiner 2000: 101) and action oriented. Focus on immediate and short-term-rather than longer term evidence-based approach (Sherman 1998).

Sources: Foster (forthcoming), based on summaries of culture in Reiner (2000a: 87–101).

endemic corruption and racism, highlights the possibilities for and barriers to change. During the 1980s attempts were made to rid the police department of corruption and to offer a more professional policing service to all members of the community, including aboriginal and Island people. Internal changes involving decentralization, changes to recruitment, training, and promotion, and the introduction of community policing and community crime prevention were implemented (Chan ibid.: 127). The reforms had a profound impact on corruption that was previously institutionalized. Officers became acutely aware that corruption would no longer be tolerated, and these internal changes, combined with external social and political factors, pressurised managers into providing the necessary resources and time for tackling the problems head-on. This was not the case with 'police racism or abuse of power'. Here changes were introduced through generalized crime prevention and community policing programmes, which were challenged by rank and file officers who continued to work in the way they had previously despite new structures (ibid.: 130), and who demonstrated 'a remarkable lack of concern' and knowledge about policies intended to address discriminatory police practice (ibid.: 124).

Chan's study highlights both the possibilities for change and the barriers to it. It also demonstrates, as have others (see, for example, Skolnick and Bayley 1986; Miller 1999; Schein 1992), how important leadership, continued vigilance (Sherman 1988), and the need to impact on officers at all levels of the organization are for achieving meaningful change. Recent concerns highlighted by MacPherson (1999), and a series of public scandals involving very senior British police officers, suggest that such leadership is currently in short supply (see Foster 2002).

The cultural model helps to explain how and why the police behave in particular ways in particular contexts. However, cultural studies rarely situate policing culture within a broader structural framework and it is to the theories which focus on these elements that we now turn.

STRUCTURAL ACCOUNTS

A number of theoretical approaches situate police work in its broader structural context.[3] Marxist theories, using evidence of abuse and discrimination at the hands of the police, focus on the ways in which policing impacts on the working class and other marginalized groups, setting this in a broader political, economic, and historical context (Hall *et al.* 1978; Scraton *et al.* 1987; Grimshaw and Jefferson 1987; Neocleus 2000). In its most simply stated form, Marxists suggest that economic class domination is reflected in laws and police enforcement, which thereby reproduce existing relations of exploitation (Grimshaw and Jefferson 1987). This paradigm can be criticized for being simplistic and 'reductive' (ibid.), because the processes which generate discrimination or exploitation are not simple and linear, but complex and contradictory.

Grimshaw and Jefferson (ibid.) suggest that what is needed is an approach that is 'faithful to the profane details of daily police work' observed in empirical studies, but which attempts to link these to the social system as a whole. They build on an analysis of the 'basic environmental features' of the police organization, such as its management, organizational structures, processes, policies and codes, the constraints of the law, and the prevailing political culture, to explain the working 'style' of police officers (J.Q. Wilson 1968). This approach requires cultural theories to be modified, because it suggests that law, managerial strategies, and constraints imposed by the community 'can affect at least some areas of police behaviour some of the time' (Grimshaw and Jefferson 1987: 10).

Contemporary structural theories retain the attention to underlying historical and social processes, and the recognition that social inequality is important in determining patterns of policing. Rather than assuming that policing in an unequal society will have a repressive effect, they urge an investigation of *how* inequality impacts on police work.

Each of the theories of police work described above has some utility in explaining police practice. Ultimately, however, we require a theory of police work that incorporates a number of these theoretical strands together with an understanding of the mechanisms of governance of the police and processes of policing reform.

---

[3] Dixon (1997: 20–48) identifies a number of variants of structural theories of policing, including those developed by Kinsey and Baldwin (1982), Jefferson and colleagues (Jefferson and Grimshaw 1984; Grimshaw and Jefferson 1987; Brogden *et al.* 1988), McBarnet (1983), and McConville, Sanders, and Leng (1991). Rather than attempting to draw out the nuances of each position, we attempt here to provide an overview of the thrust of structural theories of policing.

POLICE GOVERNANCE AND ACCOUNTABILITY: WHO POLICES THE POLICE?

In this section we explore three key issues: why accountability is important; what mechanisms exist to bring the police to account; and how effective such mechanisms are. All organizations, especially those that possess the power and authority to intervene in the private lives of citizens, must have mechanisms by which others can scrutinize their activities and deal with those who abuse the powers vested in them. Accountability is central to liberal or community-based models of policing (Kleinig 1996: 212). It involves a duty to *account* for actions taken, to *explain* them, and for the police to be 'cooperative' with an external, independent authority and ultimately with the wider community (Savage *et al.* 2000: 50). Police officers are employed to provide a service to the public, and it is important that this is not only lawful but also appropriate, relevant, accessible, and equitable (Bowling *et al.* 2001).

As we described earlier, contract theory dictates that we exchange some of our freedoms in return for protection from the state. It follows, therefore, that 'there is a moral onus on those who limit the freedom of others to provide a justification of that limitation' (Kleinig 1996: 13). Stella Rimmington (2001: xviii), the former Director-General of MI5, highlighted that there are crucial questions relating to 'how far . . . the state [should] intrude on citizens' privacy to ensure their safety' and how much the public should know. Rimmington argues that unnecessary secrecy is counter-productive, because it allows conspiracy theories to proliferate and undermines public confidence.

The British public police cannot operate under 'a cloak of secrecy'. The very *public* nature of police failings—in terms of bad practice, corruption, miscarriages of justice, and racism—has contributed to undermining public confidence and legitimacy in the police (Morgan and Newburn 1997; Reiner 2000a). Furthermore, the insular nature of the organizational culture, the discretion of front-line officers, the breadth of the police role, and the invisibility of most police decisions (McLaughlin and Murji 2001: 111) all render accountability very problematic indeed.

Despite some major legislative changes to the mechanisms of accountability in the last forty years, the public police in Britain have not exhibited either the openness or transparency required to scrutinize their work properly; have frequently failed to deal with wrong-doers (as the culture discourages officers from speaking out when they witness unprofessional, racist, or corrupt practice: Punch 1985; HMIC 1997/9); and have not engaged sufficiently in policing *with* people, to restore the confidence and trust of many sections of the public (particularly the young, the poor, and minority groups) (Macpherson 1999). While accountability is vital for controlling police powers and ensuring the effectiveness, efficiency, and fairness of policing, it is elusive (McLaughlin 1991, 1993; Morgan 1989; Reiner 2000a; Smith 2001). Furthermore, the plethora of activities taking place on the transnational stage and the plurality of public, semi-public, and private policing provision, render public scrutiny and democratic accountability very difficult indeed (Loader 1999: 333).

THE DIMENSIONS OF POLICE ACCOUNTABILITY

The history of police accountability in Britain has some similarities with other issues we have discussed in this chapter, in that continuities in the fundamental problems which arise from police accountability have persisted despite significant legislative changes over the last four decades, and none have achieved the kind of transparency and accountability that are desirable. This is not an easy task. Indeed, the contradictions and complexities which beset police work present considerable challenges in determining *how* and to *whom* the police should be accountable.

Conventional legal theorists argue that the police should be 'answerable to the law and the law alone' (Lord Denning 1968, cited by Jones and Newburn 1997: 13). This notion, enshrined in the doctrine of constabulary independence, reifies the law to a position where it 'stands above the narrowly political and partisan interests of a community and constitutes its ongoing collective public will' (Kleinig 1996: 213). Despite the frequency with which Lord Denning's judgment is quoted, there are significant problems with it (Lustgarten 1986; Jones and Newburn 1997: 3–4), not least because it leaves the police to make choices about *which laws* to uphold, *against whom*, and *by what means* (Brogden *et al.* 1988: 161). Many commentators argue that these decisions are *political* and that, as a matter of principle, they should be made by locally elected representatives not autonomous police officers (Greater London Council 1983; Lea and Young 1984; Kinsey, Lea, and Young 1986). Not surprisingly, therefore, legal accountability has been the subject of sustained criticism (Scarman 1981; McLaughlin 1994; Bowling 1999: 64–71; Macpherson 1999); and as Lustgarten (1986) argues, it is not whether the police are free to make decisions which is at issue, but the need to make them accountable for the decisions they take. There are also some good reasons why the desire for political control should be resisted. For example, politicians, bound by electoral cycles, often make short-term, ill-advised decisions frequently in response to media pressure (see, for example, Koch 1998; Foster 1999: 319–20).

Since 1964 a 'tripartite structure', comprising the Chief Constable, the Home Office, and the Police Authority (with locally elected councillors and magistrates (Lustgarten 1986; Reiner 2000a: 188–98)), has been the key accountability mechanism for England and Wales. Reiner (2000a: 189) characterized the relationship between the Chief Constable and the Police Authority in the 1964 tripartite arrangements as one where 'The police authorities paid the piper (or more precisely shared policing costs with central government) but did not call any tunes'. Differing power dynamics between the Police Authority and the Chief Constable, and an understandable reluctance on the part of those without specialist knowledge to make decisions about operational matters, may explain why, despite later changes with the introduction of the Police and Magistrates' Courts Act 1994 (which reduced the numbers of elected councillors, but added 'independent' members and made police authorities responsible for the efficiency and effectiveness of forces), power became 'concentrate[d] further in the hands of Chief Constables' (Jones and Newburn 1996: 205; see also Savage *et al.* 2000; Loveday 1996).

In recent years there has been a shift away from 'political' accountability to 'managerial' accountability (Jones and Newburn 1997; Savage *et al.* 2000). The Home Office, influenced by the Audit Commission, has been at the heart of these changes, increasing their influence by setting national policing objectives and key performance targets in a range of policing activities, as well as standardizing recruitment, equipment, and training (Savage *et al.* ibid.: 26–30). These changes have been widely interpreted as a process of centralization under the guise of administrative efficiency, effectiveness, and 'value for money' (ibid.: 30–7). Although managerial accountability appears to be a politically neutral and 'technical exercise' intended to measure performance (Jones and Newburn 1997: 15), it represents an important shift where public participation is seen in terms of consumers purchasing services, and responsiveness to elected bodies, direct participation, and equity have been de-emphasized.

The creation of national agencies that operate outside the tripartite arrangement (Johnston 2000a: 90–106; Reiner 2000a: 190–198)—for example, the National Crime Intelligence Service and the National Crime Squad—further constrains local decision-making processes (Savage *et al.* 2000: 205) and, alongside other changes, is seen as an indicator of 'creeping nationalisation' (Johnston 2000a). The increasingly 'mixed economy' of police work, and the blurring of boundaries between private and public provision, create new problems for the democratic accountability of the police.[4] Loader (1999: 337), for example, advocates the creation of 'policing commissions' to 'formulate policies and coordinate service delivery across the policing network, and to bring to democratic account the public, municipal, commercial and voluntary agencies that comprise it'.

COMMUNITY ACCOUNTABILITY

The formal mechanisms for police accountability described above have been widely criticized for not reflecting the demographic and social make-up of the communities they serve, and for adopting 'strongly pro-police orientations' (Weitzer 1995). The resulting 'democratic deficit' has long been recognized, as have its implications for policing diverse societies and the notion of 'policing by consent'[5] (Scarman 1981; Patten 1999: 22–39).

Since the 1980s, attempts have been made to increase the responsiveness of the police to ethnic minority communities, young people, and other socially excluded groups. However, the 'Police Community Consultative Groups' (PCCGs)[6] recommended by Scarman are widely viewed by police and public alike to be ineffective, unrepresentative, and to have neither 'the information nor independence to critically

---

4 The Private Security Industry Act 2001 creates the Security Industry Authority (SIA), a statutory regulatory system for the private security industry. The SIA will license individuals and companies concerned with guarding people and property, private investigations, and security consultants. It will review the operation and effectiveness of the private security industry, conduct inspections, and make recommendations to improve standards.

5 Scarman (1981) specifically cited a failure to consult and inform communities as a cause of the 1981 riots.

6 PCCGs or 'Scarman Committees' were formalized in s 106 of the Police and Criminal Evidence Act 1984, and consolidated in s 96 of the Police Act 1996 (see Keith 1988, 1993; Jones and Newburn 1997).

evaluate police proposals' (Loveday 2000: 218; Morgan 1989). Those who have attempted to use these as a vehicle for change have found their participation to be of 'marginal importance to the principal areas of police activity' (Commission for Racial Equality 1991: 30).

The 1998 Crime and Disorder Act requires local authorities and the police to consult with the public, including 'hard to reach' groups (see Jones and Newburn 1998, 2001; Phillips, forthcoming), and increasingly police authorities and other local bodies are using a broad range of new mechanisms and methods for such consultation. Although consultation is important if done well (which it often is not), it is not the same as accountability (Bridges 1982; Bayley and Shearing 1996: 91), and the deficit in legal and political accountability is unlikely to be redressed by the creation of new systems of 'consultation' (see Newburn and Jones 2002b).

COMPLAINTS AND CIVIL CLAIMS AGAINST THE POLICE

The police complaints process has been widely criticized, in part because it is difficult to have faith in a system where the police investigate themselves (Scarman 1981; Institute of Race Relations 1987; Brown 1987; Maguire 1991; House of Commons 1998). Currently, the Police Complaints Authority (PCA) 'supervises' police investigations of the most serious cases but has a very low substantiation rate. In the 1990s, for example, it was around 2 per cent and of the substantiated cases, one in five resulted in criminal or disciplinary hearings (Police Complaints Authority 2000). As Lustgarten (1986: 154) commented, '[e]ither those who do bother to complain are all liars, or there is something wrong with the system'.

Research has shown consistently that complainants whose cases are supervised by the PCA are rarely satisfied, although those complainants whose cases are not referred to the PCA are even less satisfied (Maguire and Corbett 1991; Brown 1997; House of Commons 1998; Waters and Brown 2000). Repeated sweeps of the British Social Attitudes Survey during the 1990s demonstrated almost unanimous support for an independent complaints authority (Tarling and Dowds 1997: 206), and in 2000 the government announced the creation of the Independent Police Complaints Commission (IPCC). This is intended to increase public confidence, accessibility, openness, and independence; to speed up the resolution of complaints; and to improve communication between police and complainants (Home Office 2000b).

The creation of an independent complaints process is a significant development. While it may increase public confidence, serious questions nonetheless remain about how effective it will be. Low rates of complaint substantiation are not only linked with the fact that police officers investigate other police, or because of the need to prove cases 'beyond reasonable doubt'. Many complaints are 'low visibility' with no independent witnesses, and often come down to the word of the complainant against the word of the police officer (Brown 1997). Even with a reduction in the standard of proof to 'the balance of probabilities' and with independent investigators, substantiation rates may not increase markedly (Reiner 2000a: 187). The experience from other countries suggests that many of the problems in investigating the police—such as the 'blue wall of silence' that covers up police misconduct (Kappeller *et al.* 1994), political interference (Manby 2000; Gordon 2001), a lack of skills among investigating officers, excessive workload, and insufficient resources (Melville 1999)—will not be solved by the introduction of a civilian element in complaint investigation (Goldsmith and Lewis 2000; Bowling *et al.* 2001).

Over the past two decades, the number and cost of civil actions (now called 'civil claims' following the Civil Procedure Rules 1998) against the police have increased dramatically. For example, in 1979, there were just seven cases against the Metropolitan Police and less than £2,000 damages paid (Institute of Race Relations 1987: 86). By 1996/7, the Metropolitan Police faced 1,000 threatened actions (Metropolitan Police 1997: 83), with damages amounting to nearly £4 million by 1999/2000 (Metropolitan Police 2000). While the civil courts clearly represent a more appealing route for individual complainants, it is questionable whether this can improve the fairness, effectiveness, and probity of the police service. It is likely too that recent restrictions on the extent of damages and reforms to the complaints system may reduce the growth of civil claims (Dixon and Smith 1998: 438; Reiner 2000: 188).

WHERE DO WE GO FROM HERE?

Although the existing frameworks for accountability have been inadequate, in Northern Ireland The Patten Commission recently put accountability at the centre of its proposals for reforming the police, suggesting that it 'should run through the bloodstream of the whole body of a police service and is at least as much a matter of the culture and ethos of the service as it is of . . . institutional mechanisms' (Patten 1999: para. 5.4). Patten recommended the creation of a powerful local body with elected and independent members from the local community, which can call for reports and hold local commanders to account, and require them to explain and justify their practices (ibid.: 22–39). In addition to strengthening mechanisms of legal and democratic accountability, Patten wanted policy making and service delivery to be transparent and open to public scrutiny, with 'the presumption that everything should be available for public scrutiny unless it is in the public interest—not the police interest—to hold it back' (ibid.: Recommendation 37; see also Bowling 1999a: xxii; Macpherson 1999: Recommendation 5; Neyroud and Beckley 2000: 217).

It remains to be seen whether the laudable aims of Patten are realized in practice, but the aspirations are important and clear—accountability and transparency need to be at the centre of policing, because without them the public cannot have confidence in the police.

CONCLUSION

Although 'the dominant academic discourse appears currently to privilege change over continuity' (Newburn 2001: 844), it is clear that both are important in understanding the recent trends in policing outlined in this chapter. On the one hand change seems to be everywhere, manifested in shifting patterns of crime, rapidly advancing technologies, privatization, and globalization; yet on the other hand the policing mandate to control crime, preserve public tranquillity, investigate reported offences, and go to the aid of those who call for help, has changed little in the 170 years since the birth of the 'new police'. The basic policing skills of negotiation and persuasion, the resources of intrusion and coercion, and the debates about police effectiveness and accountability have barely changed either, and are no less controversial today than they were in the 1820s.

The neo-liberal project of 'rolling back' the welfare state and increasing the 'responsibilization' of citizens has not led to less expenditure on public policing or the criminal justice system more broadly (see Garland 2001). On the contrary, the markets for public and private policing have expanded dramatically in the past two decades. Are the problems we face so severe that they justify the billions invested in public and private policing? Is the money spent in ways that will make us safer and feel more secure? The pessimists believe that the pluralization of policing is socially divisive, with the rich (who often 'need' it least) being able to secure their sense of safety at the expense of the poor (Bayley and Shearing 1996). However, pluralization need not be negative *per se*. It could have a liberating effect by altering firmly established and perhaps anachronistic structures (see Johnston 2000: 78). David Wall (1999), for example, suggests that 'it is likely that chief officers will emerge more as directors of local, or regional, police services rather than chief executives of large police organisations, particularly if the new private forms of policing become regulated by central police policy' (Wall 1999: 27). If the joint statutory responsibility for crime reduction on police and local authorities established by the 1998 Crime and Disorder Act is taken to its full extent, we could see multi-disciplinary, area-based problem-solving teams, working out of combined offices of public service (integrating housing, health, social services, and policing), perhaps even directed by non-police personnel. Private patrols (run by citizens, local councils, or the private sector) may well become the most visible form of 'policing' presence on the streets (see Morgan and Newburn 1997). Should we fear policing *through*, *below*, and *beyond* government? Perhaps not if it is capable of addressing the problems so often dismissed as 'rubbish' by the public police, and if it provides a decent service for the poor and needy in high-crime areas. Our fears perhaps lie in the elusive quality of accountability and in a firmly established belief that while the public police fail us in numerous respects, at least they are the devil we know. Furthermore, in a world characterized by a lack of trust (see Crawford 2000), relying on semi-public and private organizations is problematic when they are run for profit or private interest and are not embued with a sense of mission, authority, mythology, and history as the British public police are. This still, despite all their problems, gives the public police a head start.

Changes will continue to occur in policing: the question is whether we are able to control and shape them in ways which will encourage respect, equity, and a higher quality of service. Mastrofski (1999: 9) argues that at 'a time when aspirations about what the police might become are running high . . . we should take advantage of these times to promote a style of policing that gives the people what they want. . . . If we want our police to serve us right, then we are obliged to illuminate, articulate and continuously reinforce what it means to police for people'.

A crucial part of 'policing for people' involves recognizing the position of the police at the gateway to the criminal justice system. It can be argued that the entire criminal justice process—and its ability to 'do justice', to deter or reform offenders, and protect the public—is dependent on good police work. One way to enhance the effectiveness of the gate-keeping function would be to develop new principles of investigative practice, changing from ones that have historically worked 'for the prosecution', to create a '*public* investigation service' based on a broader 'search for the truth' and rooted in strong ethical principles of probity and fairness.

Whether the police will become more open, democratic, and focused on policing *for people*, or increasingly detached, militaristic, and policing *against people*, is open to debate (DeMichelle and Kraska 2001). On the one hand, the rise of community policing, the developments of multi-agency partnerships, changing loci of responsibility, new developments in police accountability—such as the implementation of an independent complaints system, the Human Rights Act 1998, the Race Relations (Amendment) Act 2000, and the Freedom of Information Act 2000—together with a new willingness to take account of research findings, suggest that openness, accountability, and accessibility of policing to the public will increase. On the other hand, a raft of recent legislation, including the Criminal Justice and Public Order Act 1994, the Crime and Disorder Act 1998, the Regulation of Investigatory Powers Act 2000, and the Terrorism Act 2001, has extended *policing* powers, and the sphere of police influence, in new and unwelcome directions (Gilling 2000: 136). These shifts mirror a greater separation of public policing functions at the national and transnational level, which has been established without any significant public discussion.

In less than half a century, academic research on the police has developed from a small handful of books and articles to a vast and rapidly growing literature. The boundaries of police research have grown far beyond the studies of uniformed patrol that characterized the early years, and new generations of researchers are seeking to capture both the diversity and complexity of the policing field. While the sheer breadth of policing has taxed the minds of police leaders and researchers alike, we can draw both comfort and disappointment from the sense that continuities are as apparent as change. Future overviews of this field will probably have to map an even more detailed and complex terrain than we have explored here. However, to interpret this complexity we must also keep the historical developments of *policing* in mind, because '[c]onstructions of the past are fundamental to understandings of the present and visions of the future' (Mulcahy 2000: 68).

Selected further reading

The standard text, now in its third edition, is *The Politics of the Police* by Robert Reiner (Oxford: Oxford University Press, 2000a); and shorter overviews by the same author can be found in 'Police Research', in *Doing Research on Crime and Justice*, edited by Roy King and

Emma Wincup (Oxford: Oxford University Press, 2000b), and 'Policing and the Police' in the second edition of *The Oxford Handbook of Criminology* (1997). Other useful introductions include *Policing Britain* by Les Johnston (London: Longman, 2000), *Policing Citizens* by P.A.J. Waddington (London: UCL Press, 1999), *The Future of Policing* by Rod Morgan and Tim Newburn (Oxford: Oxford University Press, 1997), and *What Everyone in Britain Should Know About the Police* by David Wilson, John Ashton, and Douglas Sharp (London: Blackstone Press, 2001). Recent edited collections include Robert Reiner's two volume compendium *Policing* (Aldershot: Dartmouth, 1996), *Policing Futures* by P. Francis, P. Davies and V. Jupp (eds) (London: Macmillan, 1997), and *Core Issues in Policing* by Frank Leishman, Barry Loveday, and Steve Savage (2nd edn, London: Longman, 1999).

Readers interested in police history should consult *Policing: A Short History* by Phillip Rawlings (Cullompton, Devon: Willan, 2002), or *The English Police* by Clive Emsley (2nd edn, London: Longman, 1996); while theoretical perspectives can be found in *The Ethics of Policing* by John Kleinig (Cambridge: Cambridge University Press, 1996), *Interpreting Policework* by Jefferson and Grimshaw (London: Unwin, 1987), *Law in Policing* by David Dixon (Oxford: Oxford University Press, 1997), and *Changing Police Culture* by Janet Chan (Cambridge: Cambridge University Press, 1997). The police role as gatekeepers to the criminal justice process is examined in *The Criminal Process* by Andrew Ashworth (2nd edn, Oxford: Oxford University Press, 1998) and in 'From Suspect to Trial' by Sanders and Young (in Chapter 28 of this volume), while recent studies of covert, 'intelligence-led' policing are the subject of a special issue of *Policing and Society* (9(4): 311–434, 2000). Recent research on privatization and transnationalization of policing is examined in *Private Security and Public Policing* by Trevor Jones and Tim Newburn (Oxford: Oxford University Press, 1998), and in *Issues in Transnational Policing* by James Sheptycki (ed.) (London: Routledge 2000).

References

ALDERSON, J. (1979), *Policing Freedom*, Plymouth: McDonald and Evans.

ANDERSON, M., DEN BOER, M., CULLEN, P., WILLMORE, W., RAAB, C., and WALKER, N. (1995), *Policing the European Union: Theory, Law and Practice*, Oxford: Oxford University Press.

ASCOLI, D. (1979), *The Queen's Peace*, London: Hamish Hamilton.

ASHWORTH, A. (1998), *The Criminal Process*, 2nd edn, Oxford: Oxford University Press.

ASSOCIATION OF CHIEF POLICE OFFICERS (1996), *Towards 2000: A Crime Prevention Strategy for the New Millennium*, Lancaster: ACPO.

AUDIT COMMISSION (1993), *Helping with Enquiries: Tackling Crime Effectively*, London: HMSO.

—— (1996), *Streetwise: Effective Police Patrol*, London: HMSO.

BALDWIN, J., and MOLONEY, T. (1992), *Supervision of Police Investigations in Serious Criminal Cases*, Royal Commission on Criminal Justice Research Study No. 4, London: HMSO.

BANTON, M (1964), *The Policeman in the Community*, London: Tavistock.

BARKER, T., FRIERY, R., and CARTER, D. (1994), 'After LA. Would your local police lie?' in Barker, T., and Carter, D. (eds), *Police Deviance*, Cincinnati: Anderson Publishing.

BAYLEY, D. (1985), *Patterns of Policing: A Comparative International Analysis*, New Brunswick, NJ: Rutgers University Press.

—— (1994), *Police for the Future*, New York: Oxford University Press.

—— (1998), *What Works in Policing?*, New York: Oxford University Press.

—— and BITTNER, E. (1984), 'Learning the Skills of Policing', *Law and Contemporary Problems*, 47: 35–60. (Reprinted in Reiner 1996: II.)

—— and SHEARING, C. (1996), 'The Future of Policing', *Law and Society Review*, 30/3: 586–606.

—— and —— (2001), *The New Structure of Policing*, Washington, DC: National Institute of Justice.

BECK, U. (1992), *Risk Society*, London: Sage.

BENNETT, T. (1994a), 'Recent Developments in Community Policing', in S. Becker and M. Stephens (eds), *Police Force, Police Service*, London: Macmillan.

—— (1994b), 'Community Policing on the Ground: Developments in Britain', in D.P. Rosenbaum (ed.), *The Challenge of Community Policing: Testing the Premises*, Thousand Oaks, Cal.: Sage.

BENYON, J. (ed.) (1984), *Scarman and After*, Oxford: Pergamon.

——, TURNBULL, L., WILLIS, A., WOODWARD, R., and BECK, A. (1993), *Police Cooperation in Europe: An Investigation*, Leicester: University of Leicester Centre for the Study of Public Order.

BEST, D., STRANG, J., BESWICK, T., and GOSSOP, M. (2001), 'Assessment of a Concentrated, High-Profile Police Operation: No Discernible Impact on Drug Availability, Price or Purity', *British Journal of Criminology*, 41: 4, Autumn: 738–45.

BIGO, D. (2000), 'Liaison Officers in Europe: New Officers in the European Security Field', in J.W.E. Sheptycki (ed.), *Issues in Transnational Policing*, London: Routledge.

BITTNER, E. (1967), 'The Police on Skid Row: A Study in Peacekeeping', *American Sociological Review*, 32.

—— (1970), *The Functions of the Police in Modern Society*, Chevy Chase, Md: National Institute of Mental Health.

—— (1974), 'Florence Nightingale in Pursuit of Willie Sutton: A Theory of the Police', in H. Jacob (ed.), *The Potential for Reform Of Criminal Justice*, Beverly Hills, Cal: Sage.

BLACK, D. (1970), 'Production of Crime Rates', *American Sociological Review*, 35: 733–48. (Reprinted in Reiner 1996: I.)

BLAGG, H., PEARSON, G., SAMPSON, S., SMITH, D., and STUBBS, P. (1988), 'Inter-agency Cooperation: Rhetoric or Reality', in T. Hope and M. Shaw (eds), *Communities and Crime Reduction*, London: HMSO.

BLUMSTEIN, A., and WALLMAN, A. (2000), *The Crime Drop in America*, Cambridge: Cambridge University Press.

BLUNKETT, D. (2001), *Policing for the 21st Century*, Speech by the Home Secretary to the Police Superintendents' Conference, 11 September.

BOTTOMS, A.E., and WILES, P. (1996), 'Understanding Crime Prevention in late Modern Societies', in T. Bennett (ed.), *Preventing Crime and Disorder: Targeting Strategies and Responsibilities*, Cambridge: Institute of Criminology Cropwood Series.

BOWLING, B. (1996), 'Cracking Down on Crime in New York City', *Criminal Justice Matters*, 25, Autumn.

—— (1998), Review of N. Dennis (ed.), 'Zero Tolerance: Policing a Free Society', *British Journal of Criminology*, 38: 2, 318–21.

—— (1999a), *Violent Racism: Victimisation, Policing and Social Context*, Oxford: Clarendon Press.

—— (1999b), 'Arresting the Abuse of Police Power: Stop and Search in "Post-Lawrence" London', *Diversity-onLine*, **www.diversity-onLine.org**.

—— (1999c), 'The Rise and Fall of New York Murder', *British Journal of Criminology*, 39/4: 531–54.

—— and PHILLIPS, C. (2002), *Racism, Crime and Justice*, London: Longman.

——, ——, CAMPBELL, A., and DOCKING, M. (2001), *Policing and human rights: eliminating discrimination, xenophobia, intolerance and the abuse of power from policework*, Geneva: United Nations Research Institute for Social Development.

BOYDSTUN, J.E. (1975), *San Diego Field Interrogation Study: Final Report*, Washington, DC: Police Foundation.

BRATTON, W. (1997), 'Crime is Down in New York: Blame the Police', in N. Dennis (ed.), *Zero Tolerance: Policing a Free Society*, London: Institute for Economic Affairs.

—— (1998), *Turnaround: How America's Top Cop Reversed the Crime Epidemic*, New York: Random House.

BREWER, J.D. (1991), 'Policing in Divided Societies: Theorising a Type of Policing', *Policing and Society*, 1/3: 179–91.

BRIDGES, L. (1982), *Racial Attacks*, Legal Action Group Bulletin, January.

BRODEUR, J.-P. (1983), 'High Policing and Low Policing: Remarks about the Policing of Political Activities', *Social Problems*, 30, 5: 507–20.

—— (1998), *How to Recognise Good Policing*, Thousand Oaks, Cal.: Sage

—— (2000), 'Transnational Policing and Human Rights: A Case Study', in J.W.E. Sheptycki (ed.) (2000), *Issues in Transnational Policing*, London: Routledge.

BROGDEN, M., and SHEARING, C. (1993), *Policing for a New South Africa*, London: Routledge.

——, JEFFERSON, T., and WALKLATE, S. (1988), *Introducing Policework*, London: Unwin.

BROWN, D. (1987), *The Police Complaints Procedure: A Survey of Complainants' Views*, London: HMSO.

BROWN, J. (1997), 'Equal Opportunities and the Police in England and Wales: Past, Present and Future Possibilities', in P. Francis, P. Davies, and V. Jupp (eds), *Policing Futures: the Police, Law Enforcement and the 21st Century*, Basingstoke: Macmillan.

—— and Heidensohn, F. (2000), *Gender and Policing*, Basingstoke: Macmillan.

BURKE, R.H. (1998), *Zero Tolerance Policing*, Leicester: Perpetuity Press.

BURROWS, J., and TARLING, R. (1982), *Clearing up Crime*, London: Home Office Research.

CAIN, M. (1973), *Society and the Policeman's Role*, London: RKP.

—— (2000), 'Orientalism, occidentalism and the sociology of crime', *British Journal of Criminology*, 40, 2: 239–60.

CATHCART, B. (1999). *The Case of Stephen Lawrence*, London: Viking.

CHAIKEN, J., GREENWOOD, P., and PETERSILIA, J. (1977), 'The Criminal Investigation Process: A Summary Report', reprinted as 'The Rand Study of Detectives', in C. Klockars and S. Matrofski (eds), *Thinking about Crime*, London: McGraw-Hill, 170–87.

CHAN, J. (1996), 'Changing Police Culture', *British Journal of Criminology*, 36/1: 109–34.

—— (1997), *Changing Police Culture: Policing in a Multicultural Society*, Cambridge: Cambridge University Press.

CHENERY, S., HOLT, J., and PEASE, K. (1997), *Biting Back II: Reducing Repeat Victimisation in Huddersfield*, Police Research Group, CDPS Paper 82, London: Home Office.

CHOONGH, S. (1997), *Policing as Social Discipline*, Oxford: Oxford University Press.

CHRISTIE, N. (1994), *Crime Control as Industry: Towards Gulags Western Style*, 2nd edn, London: Routledge.

CLANCY, A., HOUGH, M., AUST, R., and KERSHAW, C. (2001), *Crime, Policing and Justice: The Experiences of Ethnic Minorities. Findings from the 2000 British Crime Survey*, London: Home Office.

CLARKE, R., and HOUGH, M. (1984), *Crime and Police Effectiveness*, London: Home Office Research Unit.

COLEMAN, C., and MOYNIHAN, J. (1996), *Understanding Crime Data*, Buckingham: Open University Press.

COLINSON, M. (1995), *Police, Drugs and Community*, London: Free Association Books.

COLVIN, M., and NOORLANDER, P. (1998), *Under Surveillance: Covert Policing and Human Rights Standards*, London: Justice.

COMMISSION FOR RACIAL EQUALITY (1991), *The Point of Order: A Study of Consultative Arrangements under Section 106 of the Police and Criminal Evidence Act*, London: Commission for Racial Equality.

COUPE, T., and GRIFFITHS, M. (1996), *Solving Residential Burglary*, Police Research Group Paper 77, London: Home Office.

CRANK, J.P. (1998), *Understanding Police Culture*, Cincinatti, Oh: Anderson Publishing.

—— and LANGWORTHY, R. (1992), 'An Institutional Perspective of Policing', *Journal of Criminal Law and Criminology*, 83, 2: 338–63.

CRAWFORD, A. (1997), *The Local Governance of Crime: Appeals to Community and Partnerships*, Oxford: Clarendon Press.

—— (1998a), *Crime Prevention and Community Safety: Politics, Policies and Practices*, Harlow: Addison Wesley Longman.

—— (1998b), 'Community Safety and the Quest for Security: Holding Back the Dynamics of Social Exclusion', *Policy Studies*, 19, (3/4): 237–53.

—— (1999), 'Questioning Appeals to Community within Crime Prevention and Control', *European Journal on Criminal Policy and Research*, 7(4) 509–30.

—— (2000), 'Situational Crime Prevention, Urban Governance and Trust Relations', in A. von Hirsch, D. Garland, and A. Wakefield (eds), *Ethical and Social Perspectives on Situational Crime Prevention*, Oxford: Hart Publishing.

—— and JONES, M. (1995), 'Inter-agency cooperation and community based crime prevention: some reflections on the work of Pearson and colleagues', *British Journal of Criminology*, 35, 1.

CRITCHLEY, T.A. (1978), *A History of Police in England and Wales*, 2nd edn, London: Constable (1st edn, 1967).

DeMICHELE, M., and KRASKA, P. (2001), 'Community Policing in Battle Garb: A Paradox or Coherent Strategy', in P. Kraska (ed.), *Militarizing the American Criminal Justice System: The Changing Roles of the Armed Forces and the Police*, Boston: Northeastern University Press.

DENNIS, N. (ed.) (1997), *Zero Tolerance: Policing a Free Society*, London: IEA Health and Welfare Unit.

—— (ed.) (1998), *Zero Tolerance: Policing a Free Society*, 2nd edn, London: Institute of Economic Affairs.

DIXON, B., and SMITH, G. (1998), 'Laying Down the Law: The Police, the Courts and Legal Accountability', *International Journal of the Sociology of Law*, 26: 419–35.

DIXON, D. (1997), *Law in Policing: Legal Regulation and Police Practices*, Oxford: Oxford University Press.

DOWNES, D., and Morgan, R. (1994), '"Hostages to Fortune"? The Politics of Law and Order in Postwar Britain', in M. Maguire, R. Morgan, and R. Reiner (eds), *The Oxford Handbook of Criminology*, 1st edn, Oxford: Oxford University Press.

DUNHILL, C. (ed.) (1989), *The Boys in Blue: Women's Challenge to Policing*, London: Virago.

DUNNIGHAN, C., and NORRIS, C. (1996a), 'A risky business: the recruitment and running of informers by English police officers', *Police Studies*, 19, 2.

—— and —— (1996b), 'The Nark's Game', *New Law Journal*, 146: 402–404, 456–57.

—— and —— (1999), 'The Detective, the Snout and the Audit Commission: The Real Cost of Using Informants', *Howard Journal of Criminal Justice*, 38/1: 67–86.

EKBLOM, P., and HEAL, K. (1982), *The Police Response to Calls from the Public*, Home Office Research and Planning Paper 9, London: Home Office.

EMSLEY, C. (1983), *Policing and Its Context 1750–1870*, London: Macmillan.

—— (1996), *The English Police*, 2nd edn, London: Longman.

ERICSON, R., and HAGGERTY, K. (1997), *Policing Risk Society*, Oxford: Oxford University Press.

ERICSON, R.V. (1981), *Making Crime: A Study of Detective Work*, Toronto: Butterworth.

FIELD, S., and PESLER, C. (eds) (1998), *Invading the Private: state Accountability and New Investigative Methods in Europe*, Aldershot: Ashgate.

FIELDING, N. (1988), *Joining Forces*, London: Routledge.

—— (1994a), 'Cop Canteen Culture', in T. Newburn and E.A. Stanko (eds), *Just Boys Doing Business: Men, Masculinity and Crime*, London: Routledge.

—— (1994b), 'The Organisational and Occupational Troubles of Community Police', *Policing and Society*, 4/3: 305–22.

—— (1995), *Community Policing*, Oxford: Oxford University Press.

FIJNAUT, C., and MARX, G. (eds) (1996), *Undercover: Police Surveillance in Comparative Perspective*, The Hague: Kluwer.

FITZGERALD, M. (1999), *Report into Stop and Search*, London: Metropolitan Police.

FLYGHED, J. (2001), 'Normalisation of the Exceptional', Paper presented to *The Crime Prevention, Safety, Security and Democracy Conference*, Gothenburg, 7 December, 2001.

FORRESTER, D., CHATTERTON, M., and PEASE, K. (1988), *The Kirkholt Burglary Prevention Project*, Crime Prevention Unit Paper 13, London: Home Office.

FOSTER, J. (1989), 'Two Stations: An Ethnographic Study of Policing in the Inner City', in D. Downes (ed.), *Crime and the City*, London: Macmillan.

—— (1999), *Docklands: cultures in conflict, worlds in collision*, London: UCL Press.

—— (2000), 'Social Exclusion, Crime and Drugs', *Drugs: Education, Prevention and Policy*, 7, 4: 317–30.

—— (2002), '"People Pieces": The Neglected but Essential Elements of Community Crime Prevention', in G. Hughes and A. Edwards (eds), *Community Crime Prevention*, Cullompton, Devon: Willan Publishing.

—— and Hope, T. (1993), *Housing, Community and Crime: The Impact of the Priority Estates Project*, Home Office Research Study No. 131, London: HMSO.

FOUCAULT, M. (1977), *Discipline and Punish*, Harmondsworth: Penguin/New York: Pantheon.

GARLAND, D. (2001), *The Culture of Control: Crime and Social Order in Contemporary Society*, Oxford: Oxford University Press.

GIDDENS, A. (1990), *The Consequences of Modernity*, Cambridge: Polity Press.

GILLING, D. (1997), *Crime Prevention: Theory, Practice and Politics*, London: UCL Press.

—— (2000), 'Policing, Crime Prevention and Partnerships', in F. Leishman, B. Loveday, and S. Savage (eds), *Core Issues in Policing*, 2nd edn, Harlow: Pearson Education.

GILROY, P., and SIM, J. (1987), 'Law, Order and the state of the Left', in P. Scraton (ed.), *Law, Order and the Authoritarian State*, Milton Keynes: Open University Press.

GOLDSMITH, A., and LEWIS, C. (eds), (2000), *Civilian Oversight of Policing*, Oxford: Hart.

GOLDSTEIN, H. (1975), *Police Corruption: A perspective on its nature and control*, Washington, DC: Police Foundation.

—— (1990), *Problem-Oriented Policing*, New York: McGraw-Hill.

GORDON, D. (2001), 'Democratic Consolidation and Community Policing: Conflicting Imperatives in South Africa', *Policing and Society*, 11, 2: 121–50.

GRAEF, R. (1989), *Talking Blues: The Police in Their Own Words*, London: Collins Harvill.

GREATER LONDON COUNCIL (1983), *A New Police Authority for London: A Consultation Paper on Democratic Control of the Police in London*, GLC Police Committee Discussion Paper No. 1, London: Greater London Council.

GREENWOOD, P. (1980), 'The Rand Study of Criminal Investigation', in R. Clarke and J. Hough (eds), *The Effectiveness of Policing*, 35–43, Aldershot: Gower.

——, CHAIKEN, J., and PETERSILIA, J. (1977), *The Criminal Investigation Process* (a Rand Corporation Research Study), Lexington, Mass.

GREGORY, J., and LEES, S. (1999), *Policing Sexual Assault*, London: Routledge.

GRIMSHAW, R., and JEFFERSON, T. (1987), *Interpreting Policework*, London: Unwin.

HALL, S. (1979), *Drifting into a Law and Order Society*, London: Cobden Trust.

——, CRITCHER, C ., JEFFERSON, T., CLARKE, J., and ROBERTS, B. (1978), *Policing the Crisis: Mugging, the State and Law and Order*, London: Macmillan.

HARVEY, L., GRIMSHAW, P., and PEASE, K. (1989), 'Crime Prevention Delivery: The Work of CPOs', in R. Morgan and D. Smith (eds), *Coming to Terms with Policing*, London: Routledge.

HEAL, K., and LAYCOCK, G. (1987), *Preventing Juvenile Crime: The Staffordshire Experience*, Police Research Group Crime Prevention Unit Series Paper 8, London: Home Office.

HEATON, R. (2000), 'The Prospects for Intelligence-Led Policing: Some Historical and Quantitative Considerations', *Policing and Society*, 9/4: 337–56.

HEBENTON, B., and THOMAS, T. (1995), *Policing Europe: Co-Operation, Conflict and Control*, London: Macmillan.

HELD, D., MCGREW, A., GOLDBLATT, D., and PERRATON, J. (1999), *Global Transformations: politics, economics and culture*, Cambridge: Polity Press.

HER MAJESTY'S INSPECTORATE OF CONSTABULARY (1997a), *Policing with Intelligence: Criminal Intelligence—A Thematic Inspection on Good Practice*, London: Home Office.

—— (1997b), *Winning the Race*, London: Home Office.

—— (1999), *Winning the Race Revisited*, London: Home Office.

HOBBS, D. (1988), *Doing the Business: Entrepreneurship, the Working Class and Detectives in the East End of London*, Oxford: Oxford University Press.

—— (1997), 'Criminal Collaboration: Youth Gangs, Subcultures, Professional Criminals, and Organised Crime', in M. Maguire, R. Morgan, and R. Reiner (eds), *The Oxford Handbook of Criminology*, 2nd edn, Oxford: Oxford University Press.

HOLDAWAY, S. (1983), *Inside the British Police*, Oxford: Basil Blackwell.

—— (1989), 'Discovering Structure: Studies of the British Police Occupational Culture', in M. Weatheritt (ed.), *Police Research: Some Future Prospects*, Aldershot: Avebury.

—— (1996), *The Racialisation of British Policing*, London: Macmillan.

—— and BARRON, A. (1997), *Resigners? The experience of Black and Asian Police Officers*, Basingstoke: Macmillan.

HOME OFFICE (1991), *Safer Communities: The Local Delivery of Crime Prevention Through the Partnership Approach*, London: Home Office.

—— (1993), *Police Reform: A Police Service for the Twenty-First Century*, Cm. 2281, London: HMSO.

—— (1999), *Information on the Criminal Justice System in England and Wales: Digest 4*, ed. G.C. Barclay and C. Tavares, London: Home Office Research, Development and Statistics Directorate.

—— (2000a), *Complaints Against the Police: a Consultation Paper*, www.homeoffice.gov.uk.

—— (2000b), *Complaints Against the Police: Framework for a New System*, www.homeoffice.gov.uk.

—— (2000c), *Operation of Certain Police Powers Under PACE*, Statistical Bulletin 9/00, London: Home Office Research, Development and Statistics Directorate.

—— (2001a), *The Police Grant Report (England and Wales) 2001/2. Report by the Secretary of state for the Home Department under s 46 of the Police Act 1996*, London: House of Commons. www.homeoffice.gov.uk/pcrg/pg0102.html.

—— (2001b), *Criminal Statistics 2000*, London:

Stationery Office. **www.archive.official-documents.co.uk**.

HOPE, T., and FOSTER, J. (1992), 'Conflicting forces changing the dynamics of crime and community on "problem" estates', *British Journal of Criminology*, 32(4): 488–503.

HOUSE OF COMMONS HOME AFFAIRS COMMITTEE (1995), *Organised Crime*, London: HMSO.

—— (1997) 'Police Disciplinary and Complaints Procedures', *First Report*, HC 258, London: HMSO.

—— (1998), *Police Disciplinary and Complaints Procedures*, London: The Stationery Office.

HOYLE, C. (1998), *Negotiating Domestic Violence: Police, Criminal Justice and Victims*, Oxford: Oxford University Press.

HUGHES, G. (1998), *Understanding Crime Prevention: Social Control, Risk and Late Modernity*, Buckingham: Open University Press.

IANNI, E.R., and IANNI, R. (1983), 'Street Cops and Management Cops: The Two Cultures of Policing', in M. Punch (ed.), *Control in the Police Organization*, Cambridge, Mass.: MIT Press.

INNES, M. (1999a), '"An Iron Fist in an Iron Glove?" The Zero Tolerance Policing Debate' *Howard Journal of Criminal Justice*, 38/4: 397–410.

—— (1999b), 'Policing Change and Changing Policing', *Policing and Society*, 9/3: 287–308.

—— (1999c), 'The Media as an Investigative Response in Murder Enquiries', *British Journal of Criminology*, 39/2: 268–85.

—— (1999d), *Investigating Murder: The Police Response to Criminal Homicide*, PhD thesis, London: London School of Economics.

—— (2000), 'Professionalising the Role of the Police Informant: The British Experience', *Policing and Society*, 9/4: 357–84.

INSTITUTE OF RACE RELATIONS (1979), *Police Against Black People: Evidence Submitted to the Royal Commission on Criminal Procedure*, London: Institute of Race Relations.

—— (1987), *Policing Against Black People*, London: Institute of Race Relations.

JACOBS, J. (1961), *The Death and Life of Great American Cities*, New York: Vintage.

JACOBSON, J., and Saville, E. (1999), *Neighbourhood Warden Schemes*, London: Home Office.

JEFFERSON, T. (1987), 'Beyond Paramilitarism', *British Journal of Criminology* 27, 1.

—— (1990), *The Case against Paramilitary Policing*, Milton Keynes: Open University Press.

—— and GRIMSHAW, R. (1984), *Controlling the Constable: Police Accountability in England and Wales*, London: Muller.

JOHNSTON, L. (1992), *The Rebirth of Private Policing*, London: Routledge.

—— (2000a), *Policing Britain: Risk, Security and Governance*, London: Longman.

—— (2000b), 'Private Policing: problems and prospects', in F. Leishman, B. Loveday & S. Savage (eds), *Core Issues in Policing*, 2nd edn, Harlow: Pearson Education.

JONES, T. (1986), *The Islington Crime Survey: crime, victimisation and policing in inner-city London*, Aldershot: Gower.

—— and NEWBURN, T. (1995), *How Big is the Private Security Sector? Policing and Society*, 221–232.

—— and —— (1996), *Policing and disaffected communities: a review of the literature*, a Report to the Standing Advisory Committee on Human Rights, London: Policy Studies Institute.

—— and —— (1997), *Policing After the Act*, London: Policy Studies Institute.

—— and —— (1998), *Private Security and Public Policing*, Oxford: Oxford University Press.

—— and —— (2002), 'The Transformation of Policing? Understanding Current Trends in Policing Systems', *British Journal of Criminology*, 42 129–46.

——, —— and SMITH, D.J. (1994), *Democracy and Policing*, London: PSI.

JORDAN, P. (1998), 'Effective Policing Strategies for Reducing Crime', in C. Nuttall, P. Goldblatt, and C. Lewis (eds), *Reducing Offending*, Home Office Research Study 187, London: Home Office.

KAPPELLER, V.E., SLUDER, R.D., and ALPERT, P. (1994), *Forces of Deviance: Understanding the dark side of policing*, Prospect Heights Ill.: Waveland Press.

KARMEN, A. (2000), *New York Murder Mystery: The True Story Behind the Crime Crash of the 1990s*, New York: New York University Press.

KEITH, M. (1988), 'Squaring Circles?: Consultation and "Inner City" Policing', *New Community*, 15, 1: 63–77.

—— (1993), *Race, Riots and Policing: Lore and Disorder in a Multi-Racist Society*. London: UCL Press.

KELLING, G., and COLES, C. (1997), *Fixing Broken Windows: Restoring Order and Reducing Crime in Our Communities*, New York: Free Press.

——, PATE, A., DIECKMAN, D., and BROWN, C. (1974), *The Kansas City Preventive Patrol*

Experiment: Technical Report, Washington, DC: Police Foundation.

KERSHAW, C., BUDD, T., KINSHOTT, G., MAYHEW, P., and MYHILL, A. (2000), *The 2000 British Crime Survey (England and Wales)*, Home Office Statistical Bulletin, 18/00, London: Home Office.

KINSEY, R., and BALDWIN, R. (1982), *Police Powers and Politics*, London: Quartet.

——, LEA, J., and YOUNG, J. (1986), *Losing The Fight Against Crime*, Oxford: Blackwell.

KLEINIG, J. (1996), *The Ethics of Policing*, Cambridge: Cambridge University Press.

KLOCKARS, C. (1980), 'The Dirty Harry Problem', *The Annals*, 452 (November): 33–47.

KOCH, B. (1998), *The Politics of Crime Prevention*, Aldershot: Ashgate.

KPMG (2000), *Feasibility of an Independent System for Investigating Complaints Against the Police*, Police Research Series Paper No. 124, London: Home Office Policing and Reducing Crime Unit.

KRASKA, P. (ed.) (2001), *Militarising the American Criminal Justice System*, New York: New York University Press.

LAWRENCE, R.G. (2000), *The Politics of Force: Media and the Construction of Police Brutality*, Berkeley, Cal.: University of California Press.

LEA, J., and YOUNG, J. (1984), *What is to be Done About Law and Order?*, Harmondsworth: Penguin.

LEE, J.A. (1981), 'Some Structural Aspects of Police Deviance in Relations with Minority Groups', in C. Shearing (ed.), *Organizational Police Deviance*, Toronto: Butterworth.

LEE, M. (1901), *A History of Police in England*, London: Methuen.

LEIGH, A., READ, T., and TILLEY, N. (1996), *Problem-Oriented Policing: Brit Pop*, Police Research Group Paper 75, London: Home Office.

LOADER, I. (1997), 'Private security and the demand for protection in contemporary Britain', *Policing and Society*, 7: 43–62.

—— (1999), 'Consumer Culture and the Commodification of Policing and Security', *Sociology*, 33(2): 373–92.

—— (2000), 'Plural Policing and Democratic Governance', *Social and Legal Studies*, 9: 3, 323–45.

LOCKE, J. (1690), *Second Treatise of Civil Government*, cited in J. Kleinig (1996) *The Ethics of Policing*, 12–14, 281n, Cambridge: Cambridge University Press.

LOVEDAY, B. (1996), 'Crime at the Core?', in F. Leishman, B. Loveday, and S. Savage (eds), *Core Issues in Policing*, Harlow, Essex: Longman.

LUSTGARTEN, L. (1986), *The Governance of the Police*, London: Sweet & Maxwell.

MCARDLE, A., and ERZEN, T. (2000), *Zero Tolerance: Quality of Life and the New Police Brutality in New York City*, New York: New York University Press.

MCBARNET, D. (1981), *Conviction*, London: Macmillan.

MCCABE, S., and SUTCLIFFE, F. (1978), *Defining Crime*, Oxford: Basil Blackwell.

MCCONVILLE, M., SANDERS, A., and LENG, R. (1991), *The Case for the Prosecution: Police Suspects and the Construction of Criminality*, London: Routledge.

—— and SHEPHERD, D. (1992), *Watching Police, Watching Communities*, London: Routledge.

MCLAUGHLIN, E. (1991), 'Police Accountability and Black People', in E. Cashmore and E. McLaughlin, *Out of Order? Policing Black People*, London: Routledge.

—— (1992), 'The Democratic Deficit: European Unity and the Accountability of the British Police', *British Journal of Criminology*, 32/4: 473–87.

—— (1994), *Community, Policing and Accountability*, Aldershot: Avebury.

—— and MURJI, K. (1998), 'Resistance Through Representation: "Storylines", Advertising and Police Federation Campaigns', *Policing and Society*, 8/4: 367–99.

—— and —— (2001), 'Lost connections and new directions: neo liberalism, new public managerialism, and the "modernization" of the British police', in K. Stenson and R. Sullivan (eds), *Crime, Risk and Justice*, Cullompton, Devon: Willan.

MACPHERSON, SIR WILLIAM (1999), *The Stephen Lawrence Inquiry, Report of an Inquiry by Sir William Macpherson of Cluny*. Cm 4262–1. London: HMSO.

MAGUIRE, M. (1991), 'Complaints against the Police: The British Experience', in A. Goldsmith (ed.), *Complaints against the Police: The Trend to External Review*, Oxford: Oxford University Press.

—— (1997), 'Crime Statistics, Patterns and Trends: Changing Perceptions and their Implications', in M. Maguire, R. Morgan, and R. Reiner (eds), *The Oxford Handbook of Criminology* 2nd edn, Oxford: Oxford University Press.

—— (1998), 'Restraining Big Brother? The

Regulation of Surveillance in England and Wales', in C. Norris, G. Armstrong, and J. Moran (eds), *Surveillance, Closed Circuit Television and Social Control*, Aldershot: Ashgate.

—— (2000), 'Policing by Risks and Targets: Some Dimensions and Implications of Intelligence-Led Social Control', *Policing and Society*, 9/4: 315–37.

—— and Corbett, C. (1991), *A Study of the Police Complaints System*, London: PACE.

—— and John, T. (1995), *Intelligence, Surveillance and Informants: Integrated Approaches*, Crime Detection and Prevention Series Paper 64, London: Home Office.

—— and Norris, C. (1992), *The Conduct and Supervision of Criminal Investigations*, Royal Commission on Criminal Justice Research Report 5, London: Her Majesty's Stationery Office.

Manby, B. (2000), 'The South African Independent Complaints Directorate', in A. Goldsmith and C. Lewis (eds), *Civilian Oversight of Policing*, Oxford: Hart.

Manning, P. (1997), *Police Work*, 2nd edn, Prospect Heights, Ill.: Waveland Press.

—— (1977), *Police Work: the social organization of policing*, Cambridge; London: MIT Press.

Marks, M. (1999), 'Changing Dilemmas and the Dilemmas of Change: Transforming the Public Order Police Unit in Durban', *Policing and Society*, 9: 2, 157–181.

Marx, G. (1988), *Undercover: Police Surveillance in America*, Berkeley, Cal.: University of California Press.

Mastrofski, S.D. (1998), 'Community Policing and Police Organisation Structure', in *How to Recognise Good Policing: Problem and Issues*, London: Sage.

—— (1999), *Policing for People*, Washington, DC: Police Foundation.

Mawby, R.I. (1990), *Comparative Policing Issues: The British and American Experience in Comparative Perspective*, London: Routledge/Unwin.

—— (1999), *Policing Across the World: Issues for the Twenty-First Century*, London: UCL Press.

—— (2000), 'Core Policing: The Seductive Myth', in F. Leishman, B. Loveday, and S. Savage (eds), *Core Issues in Policing*, 2nd edn, Harlow: Pearson Education.

May, T., Harocopos, A., Turnbull, P., and Hough, M. (2000), *Serving Up: The Impact of Low-Level Police Enforcement on Drug Markets*, Police Research Series Paper 133, London: Home Office.

Melville, N. (1999), *The Taming of the Blue: Regulating Police Misconduct in South Africa*, Pretoria: Human Sciences Research Council.

Metropolitan Police (1997), *Annual Report*, London: Metropolitan Police.

—— (2000), *Annual Report*, London: Metropolitan Police.

Miller, J., Bland, N., and Quinton, P. (2000), *The Impact of Stops and Searches on Crime and the Community*, Police Research Series Paper 127, London: Home Office.

Miller, S. (1999), *Gender and Community Policing*, Boston: North Eastern University Press.

Miller, W. (1977), *Cops and Bobbies* 2nd edn, Columbus, Oh.: Ohio State University Press.

Morgan, R. (1989), 'Policing by Consent: Legitimating the Doctrine', in R. Morgan and D. Smith (eds), *Coming to Terms with Policing*, London: Routledge.

—— and Newburn, T. (1997), *The Future of Policing*, Oxford: Oxford University Press.

Muir, K.W., Jr (1977), *Police: Streetcorner Politicians*, Chicago: Chicago University Press.

Mulcahy, A. (2000), 'Policing History: The Official Discourse and Organizational Memory of the Royal Ulster Constabulary', *British Journal of Criminology*, 40, 1: 68–87.

Nadelmann, E. (1993), *Cops Across Borders: The Internationalization of US Criminal Law Enforcement*, University Park, Pa: Pennsylvania State University Press.

—— (1996), 'The DEA in Europe', in C. Fijnaut and G. Marx (eds) *Undercover: Police Surveillance in Comparative Perspective*, The Hague: Kluwer.

Neocleus, M. (2000), *The Fabrication of Social Order: A Critical Theory of Police Power*, London: Pluto.

Newburn, T. (1995), *Crime and Criminal Justice Policy*, London: Longman.

—— (1999), *Understanding and preventing police corruption: Lessons from the literature*, Police Research Series Paper 110, London: Home Office.

—— (2001), 'The Commodification of Policing: Security Networks in the Late Modern City', *Urban Studies*, 38, 5–6: 829–48.

—— and Jones, T. (2002) *Consultation by crime and disorder partnerships*, Police Research Series 158. London: Home Office.

NEYROUD, P., and BECKLEY, A. (2001), *Policing, ethics and human rights*, Cullompton, Devon: Willan.

NORRIS, C., and DUNNIGHAN, C. (2000), 'Subterranean Blues: Conflict as an Unintended Consequence of the Police Use of Informers', *Policing and Society*, 9/4: 385–412.

PA CONSULTING (2001), *Diary of a Police Officer*, Police Research Series Paper 149, London: Home Office

PARKS, R., MASTROFSKI, S., ALBERT, J., REISS, A.J. Jr, WORDEN, R., TERRILL, W., DEJONG, C., and SNIPES, J. (1997), *Indianapolis project on policing neighbourhoods: A study of the police and community*, Report to the Indianapolis Police Department and the National Institute of Justice, Bloomington, Indiana: Indiana University

PATE, T., FERRAR, A., BOWERS, R.A., and LORENCE, J. (1976), *Police Response Time: Its Determinants and Directs*, Washington, DC: Police Foundation.

PATERNOSTER, R., BRAME, R., BACHMAN, R., and SHERMAN, L. (1997), 'Do fair procedures matter? The effect of procedural justice on spouse assault', *Law and Society Review*, 31, 1: 163–204.

PATTEN, C. (1999), *A new beginning: policing in Northern Ireland: the report of the Independent Commission on Policing for Northern Ireland*, London: Stationery Office. **www.belfast.org.uk/report.htm**

PEARSON, G. (1983), *Hooligan: A History of Respectable Fears*, London: Macmillan.

PHILLIPS, C., and SAMPSON, A. (1998), 'Preventing Repeated Victimisation: An Action Research Project', *British Journal of Criminology*, 38, 1, Winter: 124–44.

POLICE COMPLAINTS AUTHORITY (2000), *Annual Report* London: Police Complaints Authority.

POLICY STUDIES INSTITUTE (1983), *Police and People in London*: i, D.J. Smith, *A Survey of Londoners*; ii, S. Small, *A Group of Young Black People*; iii, D.J. Smith, *A Survey of Police Officers*; iv, D.J. Smith and J. Gray, *The Police in Action*, London: Policy Studies Institute.

PUNCH, M. (ed.) (1983), *Control in the Police Organisation*, Cambridge, Mass.: MIT Press.

—— (1985), *Conduct Unbecoming: The Social Construction of Police Deviance and Control*, London: Tavistock.

—— (1996), *Dirty Business: Exploring Corporate Misconduct*, London: Sage.

—— and NAYLOR, T. (1973), 'The Police: A Social Service' *New Society*, 24: 358–61. (Reprinted in Reiner 1996a: I.)

QUINTON, P., BLAND, N., and MILLER, J. (2000), *Police Stops, Decision-making and Practice*, Police Research Series, London: Home Office, Policing and Reducing Crime Unit.

RAWLINGS, P. (2002), *Policing: A Short History*, Cullompton, Devon: Willan.

RAWLINSON, P. (1998), 'Russian organised crime: moving beyond ideology', in V. Ruggiero, N. South, and I. Taylor (eds), *The New European Criminology: Crime and Social Order in Europe*. London: Routledge.

REDSHAW, J., MAWBY, A.I., and BUNT, P. (1997), 'Evaluating Core Policing in Britain: The Views of Police and Consumers', *International Journal of the Sociology of Law*, 25: 282–301.

REINER, R. (1978), *The Blue-Coated Worker*, Cambridge: Cambridge University Press.

—— (1992a), 'Police Research in the United Kingdom: A Critical Review', in N. Morris and M. Tonry (eds), *Modern Policing*, Chicago, Ill.: Chicago University Press.

—— (1992b), 'Policing a Postmodern Society', *Modern Law Review*, 55/6: 761–81.

—— (1994a), 'Policing and the Police', in M. Maguire, R. Morgan, and R. Reiner (eds), *The Oxford Handbook of Criminology*, Oxford: Clarendon Press.

—— (1994b), 'The Dialectics of Dixon: The Changing Image of the TV Cop', in M. Stephens and S. Becker (eds), *Police Force, Police Service*, London: Macmillan.

—— (ed.) (1996), *Policing Volumes I and II*, Dartmouth: Aldershot.

—— (2000a), *The Politics of the Police*, 3rd edn, Oxford: Oxford University Press.

—— (2000b), 'Police Research', in R. King and E. Wincup (eds), *Doing Research on Crime and Justice*, Oxford: Oxford University Press.

—— (2000c), 'Crime and Control in Britain', *Sociology*, 34/1:71–94.

—— and LEIGH, L. (1994), *Police Power*, in C. McCrudden and G. Chambers (eds), *Individual Rights and the Law in Britain*, 69–108, Oxford: Oxford University Press.

—— and SPENCER, S. (eds) (1987), *Accountable Policing: Effectiveness, Empowerment and Equity*. London: Institute for Public Policy Research.

REISS, A.J., Jr (1971), *The Police and the Public*, New Haven, Conn.: Yale University Press.

REPETTO, T. (1978), 'The Detective Task: state of the Art, Science, Craft?', *Police Studies*, No. 3 (September), Reprinted in A.S. Blumberg and

E. Neiderhoffer (eds) (1985), *The Ambivalent Force: Perspectives On the Police*, London: Holt, Reinhart and Winston.

RHODES, R. (1997), *Understanding Governance: Policy Networks, Governance, Reflexivity and Accountability*, Buckingham: Open University Press.

RIMMINGTON, S. (2000), *Open Secret*, London: Hutchinson.

ROSE, D. (1996), *In the Name of the Law: The Collapse of Criminal Justice*, London: Vintage.

RUBINSTEIN, J. (1973), *City Police*, New York: Ballantine.

RUGGIERO, V., SOUTH, N., and TAYLOR, I. (1998), *The New European Criminology; Crime and Social Order in Europe*, London: Routledge.

SAMPSON, A., STUBBS, P., SMITH, D., PEARSON, G., and BLAGG, H. (1988), 'Crime, localities and the multi-agency approach', *British Journal of Criminology*, 28, 4, Autumn.

SAMPSON, F., and DE SILVA, N. (2001), *Police Conduct, Complaints and Efficiency*, London: Blackstone Press.

SAVAGE, S., CHARMAN, S., and COPE, S. (2000), *Policing and the Power of Persuasion: The Changing Role of the Association of Chief Police Officers*, London: Blackstone Press.

SCARMAN, LORD (1981), *The Scarman Report: The Brixton Disorders*, London: HMSO. Cmnd 8427. (Reprinted Harmondsworth: Penguin, 1982, and with a new introduction, 1996.)

SCHEIN, E. (1996), *Organizational Culture and Leadership*, San Francisco: Jossey Boss.

SCRATON, P. (ed.) (1987), *Law, Order and the Authoritarian State*, Milton Keynes: Open University Press.

SHAPLAND, J., and HOBBS, D. (1989), 'Policing on the Ground', in R. Morgan and D. Smith (eds), *Coming to Terms with Policing*, London: Routledge.

—— and VAGG, J. (1990), *Policing the Public*, London: Routledge.

SHEARING, C., and ERICSON, R. (1991), 'Culture as Figurative Action', *British Journal of Sociology*, 42/4: 481–506.

—— and STENNING, P. (1983), 'Modern private security: Its growth and implications', in M. Tonry and N. Morris (eds), *Crime and Justice: An Annual Review of Research*, 193–246, Chicago, Ill.: University of Chicago Press.

SHEPTYCKI, J. (1993), *Innovations in Policing Domestic Violence*, Aldershot: Avebury.

—— (1995), 'Transnational Policing and the Makings of a Postmodern State', *British Journal of Criminology*, 35, 4: 613–35.

—— (1998a), 'Policing, Post-modernism and Transnationalisation', *British Journal of Criminology*, 38/3: 485–503.

—— (1998b), 'The Global Cops Cometh', *British Journal of Sociology*, 49/1: 57–74.

—— (2000a), *Issues in Transnational Policing*, London: Routledge.

—— (2000b), 'Surveillance, Closed Circuit Television and Social Control', *Policing and Society*, 9: 429–34.

—— (2000c), 'Policing and Human Rights: An Introduction', *Policing and Society*, 10/1: 1–10.

—— (2001), *Accountability Across the Policing Field: Towards a general cartography of accountability for post-modern policing*, Paper presented to Workshop on Democratic Control of Policing and Security Sector Reform, Geneva Centre for the Democratic Control of Armed Forces, Geneva, 1–2 November.

SHERMAN, L. (1978), *Scandal and Reform: Controlling Police Corruption*, Berkeley, Cal.: University of California Press.

—— (1980), 'Causes of Police Behaviour: The Current State of Quantitative Research', *Journal of Research in Crime and Delinquency*, 17/1: 69–99. (Reprinted in Reiner 1996a: II.)

—— (1983), 'After the Riots: Police and Minorities in the US 1970–1980', in N. Glazer and K. Young (eds), *Ethnic Pluralism and Public Policy*, London: Heinemann.

—— (1992), 'Attacking Crime: Police and Crime Control', in M. Tonry and N. Morris (eds), *Modern Policing*, Chicago, Ill.: Chicago University Press.

—— (1993), 'Defiance, deterrence and irrelevance: a theory of the criminal sanction', *Journal of Research in Crime and Delinquency*, 30, 4: 445–73.

—— (1998), *Evidence-Based Policing*, Washington, DC: The Police Foundation.

—— and BERK, R.A. (1984), 'The Specific Deterrent Effects of Arrest for Domestic Assault', *American Sociological Review*, 49: 261–72.

SHERMAN, L. et al. (1997), *Preventing Crime: What works, what doesn't, what's promising*, Office of Justice Programs Research Report, Washington, DC: US Department of Justice.

——, SCHMIDT, J., ROGAN, D.P., SMITH, D.A., GARTIN, P.R. COHEN, E.G., COLLINS, D.J., and

BACICH, A.R. (1992), 'The Variable Effects of Arrest of Criminal Careers: The Milwauke Domestic Violence Experiment', *Journal of Criminal Law and Criminology*, 83, 1, Spring: 137–69).

SIBLEY, D. (1995), *Geographies of Exclusion*, London: Routledge.

SILVERMAN, E. (1999), *NYPD Battles Crime: Innovative Strategies in Policing*, Boston: Northerastern University Press.

SKOGAN, W. (1990), *Disorder and Decline: Crime and the Spiral of Decay in American Neighbourhoods*, New York: Free Press.

—— and HARTNETT, S. (1997), *Community Policing, Chicago Style*, Oxford: Oxford University Press.

——, ——, DuBois, J., COMEY, J., KAISER, M., and LOVIG, J. (1999), *On the Beat: Police and Community Problem Solving*, Colorado: Westview Press.

SKOLNICK, J. (1966), *Justice without Trial*, New York: Wiley.

—— (1969), *The Politics of Protest*, New York: Bantam.

—— (1999), *On Democratic Policing*, Washington DC: Police Foundation.

—— and BAYLEY, D.B. (1988), *Community Policing: Issues and Practices around the World*, Washington, DC: National Institute of Justice.

SMITH, D.J., and GRAY, J. (1985), *Police and People in London*, Aldershot: Gower.

SMITH, G. (1997), 'The DPP and Prosecutions of Police Officers', *New Law Journal*, 147/6804: 1180.

—— (2000), *Managing Police Misconduct: Reform of the Discipline Process and Unresolved Accountability Issues*, Paper presented to European Group for the Study of Deviance and Social Control Conference, University of Wales, Bangor, 25–27 April.

—— (2001), 'Police Complaints and Criminal Prosecutions', *Modern Law Review*, 64, 3: 372.

SMITH, N., and FLANAGAN, C. (2000), *The effective detective: identifying the skills of an effective SIO*, Police Research Series; Paper 122, London: Home Office.

SOUTH, N. (1988), *Policing for Profit*, London: Sage.

STEER, D. (1980), *Uncovering Crime*, Royal Commission on Criminal Procedure Research Study 7, London: HMSO.

STENSON, K., and SULLIVAN, R. (2001), *Crime, Risk and Justice: The politics of crime control in liberal democracies*, Cullompton, Devon: Willan Publishing.

STEPHENS, M., and BECKER, S. (1994), *Police Force, Police Service*, London: Macmillan.

STOCKDALE, J., and GRESHAM, P. (1995), *Combating Burglary: An Evaluation of Three Strategies*, Police Research Group Crime Detection and Prevention Series Paper 59, London: Home Office.

—— and —— (1998), *Tackling Street Robbery: A Comparative Evaluation of Operational Eagle Eye*, Police Research Group Crime Detection and Prevention Series Paper 87, London: Home Office.

STORCH, R. (1975), 'The Plague of Blue Locusts: Police Reform and Popular Resistance in Northern England 1840–57', *International Review of Social History*, 20: 61–90.

TARLING, R., and DOWDS, L. (1997), 'Crime and Punishment', in Jowell, *et al.*, *British Social Attitudes*, London: National Statistics.

TAYLOR, I. (1999), *Crime in Context: A Critical Criminology of Market Societies*, Cambridge: Polity Press.

TROJANOWICZ, R., and BUCQUEROUX, B. (1998), *Community Policing*, Cincinnati, Oh.: Anderson Publishing.

TYLER, T. (1990), *Why People Obey the Law*, London: Yale University Press.

UNITED NATIONS (2000), *United Nations Convention Against Transnational Organised Crime*, New York: United Nations.

VAN MAANEN, J. (1973), 'Observations on the making of policeman', *Human Organisation*: 32.

—— (1974), 'Working the Street', in H. Jacob (ed.), *The Potential for Reform of Criminal Justice*, Beverley Hills, Cal.: Sage.

—— (1978), 'Watching the Watchers', in P. Manning and J. Van Maanen (eds), *Policing*, Santa Monica, Cal.: Goodyear.

VOGLER, R. (1991), *Reading the Riot Act*, Milton Keynes: Open University Press.

WADDINGTON, P.A.J. (1987), 'Towards Paramilitarism: Dilemmas in Policing Civil Disorder', *British Journal of Criminology*, 27, 1: 37–46.

—— (1991), *The Strong Arm of the Law*, Oxford: Oxford University Press.

—— (1999a), *Policing Citizens*, London: UCL Press.

—— (1999b), 'Police (Canteen), Sub-Culture: An Appreciation', *British Journal of Criminology*, 39/2: 286–308.

—— (2000), 'Public Order Policing: citizenship and moral ambiguity', in F. Leishman, B. Loveday and

S. Savage (eds), *Core Issues in Policing*, 2nd edn, Harlow: Pearson.

WALKER, M. (1992), 'Do We Need a Clear Up Rate?', *Policing and Society*, 2/4.

WALKLATE, S. (2000), 'Reflections on "New Labour" or "Back to the Future"?', *Criminal Justice Matters*, 38: 7–8.

WALL, D. (1999), 'The Organisation of Police 1829–2000' in M. Stallion and D. Wall, *The British Police: Police Forces and Chief Officers 1829–2000*, Bramshill, Hampshire: The Police History Society.

WATERS, I., and BROWN, K. (2000), 'Police Complaints and the Complainants' Experience', *British Journal of Criminology* 40, 4, Autumn: 617–38.

WEATHERITT, M. (ed) (1986), *Innovations in Policing*, London: Croom Helm.

WEBER, L., and BOWLING, B. (2002), 'The Policing of Immigration in the New World Disorder', in P. Scraton (ed), *Beyond 11 September: An Anthology of Dissent*, London: Pluto.

WERTHMAN, C., and PILIAVIN, I. (1967), 'Gang Members and the Police', in D. Bordua (ed.), *The Police*, New York: Wiley.

WESTLEY, W. (1970), *Violence and the Police*, Cambridge, Mass.: MIT Press.

WILLIAMSON, T. (2000), 'Policing: the changing criminal justice context—twenty-five years of missed opportunities', in F. Leishman, *et al.*, *Core Issues in Policing*, Harlow: Pearson Education.

WILSON, D., ASHTON, J., and SHARP, D. (2001), *What Everyone in Britain Should Know about the Police*, London: Blackstone Press.

WILSON, J.Q. (1968), *Varieties of Police Behavior*, Cambridge, Mass.: Harvard University Press.

—— (1978), *The Investigators*, New York: Basic Books.

—— and BOLAND, B. (1978), 'The Effects of the Police on Crime', *Law and Society Review*, 12/3: 367–90.

—— and KELLING, G. (1982), 'Broken Windows: The Police and Neighbourhood Safety', *Atlantic Monthly*, March: 29–38. (Reprinted in Reiner 1996: I.)

WILSON, O.W. (1950), *Police Administration*, New York: McGraw Hill.

YOUNG, J. (1999), *The Exclusive Society: Social Exclusion, Crime and Difference in Late Modernity*, London: Sage.

YOUNG, M. (1991), *An Inside Job: Policing and Police Culture in Britain*, Oxford: Oxford University Press.

28

FROM SUSPECT TO TRIAL

Andrew Sanders and Richard Young

This chapter looks critically at the use of legal powers, including prosecution, in the criminal justice system of England and Wales. The principles underlying different criminal justice systems vary according to history, culture, and ideology. The adversary principle is an important characteristic of the English System, of other common law systems such as those of Australia, Canada, and the United States, and of many 'hybrid' systems such as in Scotland. Thus much of what follows draws upon what we know of, and what applies to, these other systems, although the focus is domestic.

First, we look at different models of criminal justice, including the 'new' Human Rights approach and 'inclusion' and 'exclusion' approaches, in order to highlight the tensions between the different aims of the system. Then we look at police decisions 'on the street' (primarily to stop/search and to arrest). Here, and throughout the chapter, we contrast the 'law in the books' with the way law enforcement bodies actually enforce the law, and examine policies and practice to see which criminal justice aims are given priority. Discussion of the most important aspects of police station detention, including police questioning, the right of silence, and access to legal advice, follows. We then look at police decisions to prosecute, caution, or take no action, along with the role of the Crown Prosecution Service (CPS). The pre-trial process, including bail and plea bargaining, is then examined. Although we do not look at trials as such, the main processes in most cases are covered here as the overwhelming majority of prosecutions are settled by guilty pleas or (more rarely) are dropped by the CPS.

Most police actions and court cases are in all likelihood unproblematic. Inevitably, though, this chapter highlights the problems—for it is little consolation to someone who is constantly stop-searched, or to an innocent person who is found guilty, that their experience is unusual and that the system usually works well. We therefore have a section that looks at how the system deals with injustice, police malpractice in particular. Lastly, in the Conclusion we draw the threads together and try to identify the main operating aims of the criminal justice system. Here, and elsewhere, we look not only at how particular parts of the system (or 'process' as some commentators prefer, on the grounds that the agencies are too uncoordinated to constitute a 'system') work, but also contrast the police with other enforcement agencies. This contrast reveals a lot about fairness, inclusion, and exclusion in criminal justice.

MODELS OF CRIMINAL JUSTICE

The adversary principle is often characterized as embodying the search for 'proof' rather than 'truth' (Damaska 1973). The search for 'truth' is usually said to be embodied in 'civil law' systems (such as the French), which are 'inquisitorial'. It would be nice if 'proof' and 'truth' were synonymous and sought with equal vigour, as one of Britain's leading Chief Constables has advocated (Pollard 1996); but, using the 'due process' and 'crime control' models developed by Packer (1968), we will see that this is unrealistic.

'Due process' values prioritize civil liberties in order to secure the maximal acquittal of the innocent, risking acquittal of many guilty people. 'Crime control' values prioritize the conviction of the guilty, risking the conviction of some (fewer) innocents and infringement of the liberties of some citizens to achieve the system's goals. Due process-based systems tightly control the actions and effects of crime control agencies, while crime control-based systems, with their concern for convictions, do not. No system can correspond exactly with either model (just as no system is entirely adversarial or entirely inquisitorial), but in most systems the values of one or the other model appear to predominate.

As soon as the police challenge any individual whom they have any reason to suspect, an adversarial relationship is formed. In Britain, this triggers due process protections, such as the caution against self-incrimination and the requirement of 'reasonable' suspicion for the exercise of coercive powers. On arrest the suspect is generally taken to a police station and detained. This triggers further due process protections, such as a right of access to lawyers and others, as civil liberties are further eroded by lengthy detention, interrogation, search of the suspect's home, fingerprinting, and so forth. In order to charge, further evidence is required and further protections are provided—the CPS to vet the case, and legal aid to prepare a defence. In order to convict there must be yet more evidence. So, due process requirements become more stringent at each stage, in parallel with the increased coerciveness of suspicion, accusation, and trial. Suspects may be believed to be guilty by the police— and may indeed be guilty 'in truth'—but in the absence of sufficient evidence (i.e., sufficient proof) due process requires that they be exonerated. At the final stage proof need not be absolute but only 'beyond reasonable doubt'. Legal guilt and actual guilt are therefore not synonymous. Even in a due process system there will occasionally be legally guilty persons who are not 'actually' guilty, and many actually guilty persons who are not legally guilty. This means that all systems will produce some cases like the infamous 'miscarriage' cases of the last twenty-five years: the Birmingham Six, Guildford Four, Bridgewater Four, West Midlands Police Serious Crime Squad cases, and so forth. Whether or not these are evidence of system failure depends on how often they occur, why they occur, and whether there are adequate systems of review and appeal.

One difference between the different models lies in their methods of discovery of the truth and their degrees of success. Doubts about, for instance, the way each side in the adversarial trial guards 'its' evidence lead critics to argue for more 'transparency' in the pursuit of truth (Pollard 1996), while doubts about the impartiality of inquisitorial systems reveal different ways in which the truth can be obscured (Hodgson 2001). Similarly, doubts about police efficiency and propriety on the part of advocates of due process lead them to argue for the process of legal proof; while advocates of crime control argue that court processes and legal protections obstruct truth discovery.

Despite the clarification provided by Packer's models, their value is limited. In particular, they do not attempt to prescribe what the goals of the criminal process should be. Ashworth makes such an attempt by developing a framework of ethical principles derived from the European Convention on Human Rights (ECHR) (Ashworth 1998). This is valuable, particularly now that the Human Rights Act 1998 makes the ECHR applicable to all areas of UK law, but it creates as many problems as it solves. For example, Ashworth's principles include rights for victims ('to respect' and 'to compensation') that are major lacunae in Packer's models, but little guidance is provided on how to reconcile these rights with those of suspects and defendants when conflicts occur. Other rights are reformulations of key due process principles. Many of them are vague, such as 'to be treated fairly and without discrimination' and 'reasonable grounds for arrest and detention'. Those that are precise, such as the 'right of innocent persons not to be convicted', are not absolute but may be undercut by the kinds of considerations one finds in the crime control model.

Another promising framework is that of social integration and exclusion. Faulkner (1996) characterizes the 'exclusion' approach as one whereby 'crime is to be prevented by efficiency of detection, certainty of conviction and severity of punishment. . . . "criminals" are to be seen as an "enemy" to be defeated and humiliated, in a "war" in which the police are seen as the "front line".' He contrasts this with Locke's view, that 'the end of law is not to abolish or restrain but to preserve and enlarge freedom'. On this inclusionary approach, 'authority will not be respected if it is simply imposed: it has to be accountable and it has to be legitimate. . . . solutions to the problem of crime have to be sought by inclusion within the community itself' (ibid.: 6). This position is compatible with those forms of 'restorative justice' that emphasize the need to bring together all the 'stakeholders' in an offence (including the victim) in order to discuss how the harm caused to material, psychological, and relational interests can be repaired, although the relationship between adversarial structures and restorative justice remains problematic (see Zedner, in Chapter 13 of this volume; Morris and Maxwell 2001). The inclusion/exclusion model has now been fleshed out by several analysts (for example, Young 1999; Garland 2001), and the difficulties in reorienting the system towards inclusion have been recognized, both in general (Faulkner 2001) and in relation to specific issues such as victims (Sanders 2002). It offers more than the other models discussed, for the inclusion approach combines the comprehensiveness of the human rights model with a clear sense of purpose.

We have put this sense of purpose at the centre of our own 'freedom model' (Sanders and Young 2000). It starts from the recognition that the criminal process involves many conflicting values, aims, and interests, such as: convicting the guilty; protecting the innocent from wrongful conviction; protecting human rights by guarding against arbitrary or oppressive treatment; protecting victims; maintaining order;

securing public confidence in, and cooperation with, policing and prosecution; and achieving these goals without disproportionate cost and consequent harm to other public services. While politicians like to pretend that these goals are all equally achievable, the reality is that choices have to be made over which are to have priority, and such choices inevitably express a particular philosophical standpoint. The standpoint we prefer establishes the promotion of freedom as the overriding purpose of the criminal justice system in a liberal democracy. All of the various interests and goals of the criminal justice system can be seen as connected to this underlying goal. Prosecution is not a valuable activity in itself. Rather, prosecutions are brought in the hope that the punishment or treatment consequent upon conviction will reduce the propensity of offenders to commit crime, and in the expectation that censuring wrongdoing will reinforce everyone else's law-abiding instincts and habits. Either way, the freedom of past and potential future victims should be enhanced through having their fear of crime reduced. Similarly, we expect prosecutors to respect the rights of suspects and defendants not because protection is a goal in itself, but rather in order to promote their freedom. And prosecutions are brought as one method of upholding order not because an orderly society is desirable in and of itself, but rather because a degree of order is needed to enable individuals and communities to pursue their own ends. While the various interests described will still come into conflict, at least under this model we keep in focus the ultimate aim of the system and can opt for compromises that are likely to maximize overall freedom. This is not a crude form of utilitarianism, for it does not oppose a 'human rights' approach to criminal justice. It does, however, suggest that human rights could be better secured if we adopted the language of freedom rather than, or at least as a supplement to, that of rights. We might, for example, more effectively convince the police to respect defendants' rights if we highlight how those rights do not constrain but rather facilitate the achievement of the ultimate criminal justice goal of promoting freedom. It also suggests that the human rights perspective will be of little assistance in resolving many of the dilemmas that arise in the criminal justice system, for many of the most morally troubling aspects of that system operate primarily to the detriment of social groups and communities rather than to particular individuals. 'Freedom' is, of course, a deeply contestable notion that means very different things within different political traditions. Our use of the term 'freedom' is deliberately loose and unspecific, because we concentrate attention here on the need for change instead of getting bogged down regarding exactly what that change should be, although we are more prescriptive elsewhere.

POLICE DECISIONS 'ON THE STREET'

The due process origins of our system can be seen in the fact that, in the first decades after the establishment of the police, sufficient evidence to prosecute was needed before street powers could be exercised. Stop-and-search powers did not exist, and arrested persons were taken directly before the magistrates, who decided whether to prosecute. In theory, then, police investigation had to take place *before* arrest, although in reality many people used to be held by the police without formal arrest (supposedly 'helping the police with their enquiries'). Arrests are now often made to *facilitate* investigation, bringing the formal rules into line with a crime control reality. The current legal position is now somewhere between the crime control and due process polarities. Both stop-and-search and arrest without judicial warrant are allowed for most 'normal' crimes (theft, burglary, serious assaults, sexual offences, drugs offences, public order offences, possession of offensive weapons, etc.), and the police are periodically given more powers for more offences.

The Police and Criminal Evidence Act (PACE), in 1984, provided the first nation-wide stop-and-search powers. They were extended in relation to certain types of knife by the Criminal Justice Act 1988, extended further by the Criminal Justice and Public Order Act in 1994, extended yet again in the Prevention of Terrorism (Additional Powers) Act 1996, and likely to be extended in relation to terrorism again in the wake of the terrorist attack on New York and Washington on 11 September 2001. The police must have 'reasonable suspicion' in order to exercise most arrest and stop-search powers. The Code of Practice on stop-and-search issued by the Home Office under the authority of PACE states that 'there must be some objective basis' for the sus-picion (para. 1.6), which 'can never be supported on the basis of personal factors alone' (para. 1.7). The 'objective' factors envisaged (which apply equally to arrest) include 'information received', someone 'acting covertly or warily', and someone 'carrying a certain type of article at an unusual time or in a place' where there have been relevant crimes recently (para. 1.6) Other important recent stop-search powers do not require reasonable suspicion, such as the power to stop-search for weapons created under s 60 of the Criminal Justice and Public Order Act 1994 and extended by subsequent legislation (see generally Sanders and Young 2000: chapters 2 and 3).

DISCRETION

Discretion is at the root of criminal justice practice. Police officers necessarily exercise discretion in deciding whether to stop and search and arrest. Some people look less 'suspicious' than others, and multitudes of actual or likely offences have to be priori-tized. Minor offenders (prostitutes, unlicensed street traders, and so forth) are often simply ignored (Smith and Gray 1983). Arrest is less frequent than informal action, even for relatively serious violence (Clarkson *et al.* 1994; Hoyle 1998). Similarly, when officers are able to be proactive (as compared to their usual reactive mode) they have to use discretion about in which offences or offenders to invest scarce time. Discretion is also created as a consequence of the way offences are defined. Most offences require *mens rea* (a 'guilty mind') that, broadly, amounts to intent or advertent recklessness. Thus breaking someone's leg by tripping him or her up would be a crime if done deliberately, but not if done accidentally. A police officer could make an arrest if he or she reasonably suspected the former, but not if he or she suspected the latter. However, since *mens rea* is so difficult to assess, officers have ample scope to arrest or not according to their preference. So, stop-and-search and arrest decisions are con-strained only loosely by law: the powers themselves, based on reasonable suspicion, are ill-defined and subjective, the offences for which the powers are exercised are similarly ill-defined, and the police set their own priorities.

There are four levels at which discretion is structured, none of which have much to do with the law. First, there are general policing goals. To say that a prime function of the police is to maintain order, control crime, and catch criminals may be trite, but it identifies a fundamental conflict between policing goals and the due process model. In so far as that model is an obstacle course, it can only get in the way of policing goals. To expect the police to abide by due process standards voluntarily—without coercion through 'inhibitory' rules—is therefore unrealistic. The second level is force policy. In the United States, in particular, this can vary considerably from locality to locality (Meehan 1993). Another example, as we write this, is the controversy surrounding cannabis: the Metropolitan Police, but not other forces, have now virtually decriminalized simple possession. Then there is 'cop culture' (see Chan 1996; Bowling and Foster, in Chapter 27 of this volume). Its elements of sexism and racism, and its stereotyping of people and groups of certain types (on 'rough' estates, with certain lifestyles, etc.), affect the way officers view society. Take the Code of Practice's reference to 'wary' actions and what is normal for certain 'times and places'. How one views these matters depends on prevailing culture and individual officers' own ways of mediating that culture. The last level, then, is that of the individual. Police officers are not representative of the population. They tend to be disproportionately white, male, and conservative. The homogeneity of this group, coupled with police training and socialization processes, enables 'cop culture' to be easily reproduced (Reiner 2000: especially chapter 3).

PATTERNS OF BIAS AND POLICE WORKING RULES

Research has found that the weak constraints imposed on discretion by law allow considerable scope for bias in policing. Prior to the implementation of PACE in the mid-1980s, study after study produced similar findings (e.g., Stevens and Willis 1979; Tuck and Southgate 1981; Field and Southgate 1982; Smith and Gray 1983; Willis 1983). Smith and Gray, for example, found that there was no 'reasonable suspicion' in one-third of all stops which they observed; and Willis found that stop-and-search was often based on the suspects' 'movements'. 'This category', Willis remarked, 'covered stops on grounds which police officers find it hard to specify.' This would be consistent with the crime control model if officers relied on intangible but reliable 'instinct' or 'experience', but the arrest rate (which was generally low, at perhaps 10 per cent of all stops) was particularly low in the 'movements' cases. However, as stop-and-search is useful for intelligence-gathering (McConville et al. 1991; Miller et al. 2000: 44–45), a low arrest rate is not inconsistent with crime control goals. It certainly appears that due process standards, even the minimal requirements of 'reasonable suspicion', were rarely adhered to. These findings are consistent with research in the United States (see, for instance, Tonry 1995; Geller and Toch 1996; and, generally, Reiner 2000) which has similar rules on stop-and-search and arrest. Stops were often based on classic stereotypes leading to patterns of bias on lines of class, gender, and race.

The introduction of PACE in the mid-1980s was intended to make some difference.

For although PACE gave more, not less, power to the police, it also incorporated more controls than there were before. These include requirements to tell suspects why they are being arrested or stop-searched, and to make records of the incident. However, stop-and-search and arrest decisions are of intrinsically low visibility (Goldstein 1960). Thus written records can be constructed after the event (McConville *et al.* 1991: chapter 5). No longer are the reasons for stops recorded as 'movements', but the actual reasons could be unchanged. As one officer put it to McConville *et al.* (ibid.), he would stop a suspect 'instinctively and then think about how he would satisfy a disinterested third party' (field notes). This suggests that the Code has altered the way officers *account* for their exercise of discretion, but not the way they *actually* exercise it. Accounts of incidents can correspond as much with legal expectations as with the reality of the incidents (Scott and Lyman 1968; Ericson 1981). Thus officers are aware that the precise way in which forms are completed may either help or hinder the public making a complaint about their actions (Bland *et al.* 2000: 73). It is hardly realistic to expect an officer to record on his stop-search form that his reason for exercising a power was that he had come across a 'Rastafarian out at night', yet we know that such reasoning does take place (see below). On the other hand, at least the requirement to record has the *potential* to focus officers' minds on the limits of their legal powers, and some officers do claim that this has an influence on them (ibid.: 71–72). However, when scrutiny of forms reveals the reasons for searches to be some-times recorded in such vague terms as 'drugs search', 'info received', and 'acting furtively' (ibid.: 44), the extent to which there has been a genuine shift in police reasoning remains open to question. Moreover, few stops are recorded at all. But this is only a breach of PACE if PACE powers are actually exercised (that is, if the stop is not consensual) and if there is a search or arrest (Sanders and Young 2000: chapter 2).

Research has not found the control and accountability mechanisms in PACE to have achieved their intended effects. Norris *et al.* (1992) observed 272 stops in one London borough, of which 28 per cent were of black people despite only 10 per cent of the local population being black, and this over-representation of black people is continued at the arrest stage (Hillyard and Gordon 1999). The problem with most research is that it compares stop-search or arrest statistics for a particular area with the composition of the resident population for that same area. But MVA and Miller (2000) found that over half of the available pedestrian population resided outside of the five police areas in which they were studying stop-search practices. They argued that when statistics on recorded stops and searches are compared with the population 'available' to be stopped and searched (i.e., those who use public places when and where stops take place), no general pattern of bias against those from ethnic minor-ities was evident. The most consistently over-represented group in the stop-search statistics relative to the proportion in the available population was young males.

Although the method used in this study represents an advance on those which make simplistic comparisons between stop-search patterns and resident populations, it would be a mistake to place too much weight on the finding of no general pattern of bias against ethnic minorities. This study was conducted shortly after the publication of the Stephen Lawrence Inquiry Report (Macpherson 1999). This Inquiry sought to discover what went wrong in the investigation into the death of a young black man. It concluded that the failure to prosecute anyone successfully was, in part, because of institutionalized racism in the police. The Report ranged more widely than just this investigation, looking at the general problem of police–ethnic minority relations, and highlighted the damaging effect of stop-search practices on ethnic minority confidence in the police. Moreover, the five study sites were all involved in piloting a recommendation of that Report (which was that all stops and all searches should be recorded, whether consensual or not). This may have made the police more circumspect about carrying out stops and searches of blacks and Asians, or at least in making records of such searches when they were carried out. Indeed, a separate study by Bland *et al.* (2000) found evidence of substantial under-recording of both stops and searches during the pilot period. As the MVA and Miller (2000) study was based on *recorded* stop-searches, the possibility that it underestimated the actual rates of ethnic minority stops and searches is obvious. In addition, the study did not examine (i) whether ethnic minorities suffered more often than did whites from stops and searches that were not legally justified (i.e., no reasonable suspicion); (ii) whether the use of stop-search powers resulted in an arrest (i.e., whites may have been less often drawn further into the system); (iii) and whether the use of stop-search powers was accompanied by differing degrees of respectful treatment according to the colour of the suspect's skin. Lastly, and as the authors rightly acknowledge, the study does not controvert the fundamental point that black and Asian people are over-represented in the stop-search figures relative to their presence in the overall population, and that this remains 'an important indicator of the actual experience of different ethnic groups within police force areas' (ibid.: 88). Black people, Brown concluded in a review of PACE research, are more likely to be stopped than white people or Asians, more likely to be repeatedly stopped, more likely (if stopped) to be searched, and more likely to be arrested (1997: chapters 2 and 4; see also Phillips and Bowling, in Chapter 17 of this volume). The research by Bland *et al.* (2000) confirmed that the manner in which the police exercise their powers is a crucial determinant of whether their actions were regarded as legitimate: 'It's not what they say, it's how they say it' (ibid.: 87). Offensive and racist language was particularly resented. One Pakistani young adult described his interaction as follows: '. . . their exact words were, yeah (and I've got witnesses because I was with two other people, yeah) was: "Don't fuck me about right, and I won't fuck you about, where have you got your drugs?"' (ibid.: 83). Black people were far less likely than Asian or white people to report any positive experiences of respectful treatment by the police.

Stop-search is a crude instrument of crime control. Although more stops lead to more arrests, the proportion of stops that lead to arrest decreases as the number of stops rises. This predictable consequence of the crime control approach can be observed in most years since 1986, as the number of recorded stops has increased tenfold since 1986 yet the proportion leading to arrest declined from 17 per cent in 1984 to less than 11 per cent in 1997/8 (Sanders and Young 2000: chapter 2). In other words, it is rare for police suspicions to be borne out by evidence on which to base an arrest. Searches where there is no legal requirement of reasonable suspicion (such as voluntary searches, and those carried out under s 60 of the Criminal Justice and Public Order Act 1994) are even more 'inefficient', with about a 1:20 chance that they will lead to an arrest (Miller *et al.* 2000: 39). While s 60 was 'sold' politically as a way of tackling serious violent crime, in practice it has become a useful police resource in responding to low-level disorder where no other power exists. Thus one officer said that he used s 60 for 'Anyone causing trouble really—but people who aren't worth pulling [arresting] 'cause they haven't done enough' (Quinton *et al.* 2000: 50). Over-all, it has been estimated that the various types of searches conducted by the police in 1997 reduced the number of crimes susceptible to this tactic by just 0.2 per cent (Miller *et al.* 2000: 28).

McConville *et al.* (1991) identify several 'working rules' which structure police decision-making. The first is 'previous' (i.e., being known to the police). As an arrest-ing officer told McConville *et al.*: 'When you get to know an area, and see a villain about at 2.00 a.m. in the morning, you will always stop him to see what he is about' (ibid.: 24). The second concerns disorder and police authority. Dealing with disorder is a prime police task. Although Shapland and Vagg (1988) found that the police do not usually arrest when they intervene in disorderly incidents, arrests are usual if the disorder does not cease, even when it is trivial and only the police are involved (Brown and Ellis 1994). This is in part because of the challenge thereby presented to police authority, even if no specific charge fits the facts. Other working rules include con-sideration of types of victims and their wishes, 'information received', and workload. But perhaps the most important working rule is 'suspiciousness'. This entails the suspect being 'out of the ordinary' or 'uncooperative', or keeping the wrong company, or its being 'just a matter of instinct' on the officer's part, 'something undefinable' (all these phrases are from officers quoted in McConville *et al.* 1991: 26–8). A study carried out in the wake of the Stephen Lawrence Inquiry confirmed the continuing purchase of all of these working rules (Quinton *et al.* 2000: 19–52).

Such rules have a differential impact according to such social dimensions as ethnicity, class, age, and gender. For example, the relatively high degree of exclusion from 'normal employment' experienced by black people and Asians means that they more often work unsociable hours (as mini-cab drivers, postal workers, fast-food deliverers, factory shift workers, etc.). When going to and from work it is their experi-ence that they are particularly likely to become the focus of police suspicion (Stone and Pettigrew 2000: 27) because of the following working rule: 'Late night/early morning. Why are they out? People aren't usually out at that time' (Quinton *et al.* 2000: 30). Similarly, the working rule which holds that people who 'won't look you in the eye' merit a stop causes problems for those ethnic minority groups who regard meeting someone's eye as disrespectful (ibid.: 27). While the police regard youths as inherently suspicious, their presence in certain locations and at certain times is regarded as especially incongruous, as in the following examples drawn from interviews with police officers: 'Early morning—teenagers walking around—I want to know why'; 'Secluded spots—couples go there but if, say, four youths [I'll] have a chat and then check for the grounds' (ibid. 2000: 19). Incongruity is precisely the kind of consideration against which the Code of Practice (referred to above) cautions the police in its attempt to identify 'objective' factors which would satisfy a third party.

Dixon *et al.* (1989) argue that non-adherence to due process standards is not so much wilful failure by police officers as the failure of due process standards to meet the reality of policing. Policing is about the creative use of experience in crime control. The development, and diminution, of suspicion is a dynamic process. It cannot, they argue, be reduced to compartmentalized legalistic steps dependent on precisely measured levels of evidence. Police working rules gel with cop culture, stressing the importance of 'facing down' challenges to authority, investigating the incongruous, picking on 'known criminals', and so forth, far more than with PACE. This is not to say that, under certain conditions, changes in formal rules are completely ineffective. Hoyle's (1998) study of domestic violence assessed the impact of a Home Office Circular which encouraged arrest wherever there was evidence of an offence. Arrests rose significantly as a result, although not to the extent that full adherence to the Circular would have produced. The perception by 'cop culture' of domestic assaults as 'rubbish' can, it seems, be overcome, albeit not entirely. As Chan (1996) argues, police culture is not independent of societal pressures and legal rules. Whether or not, and the way in which, practices and rules correspond is always an empirical matter. So, Hoyle found that, in the enthusiasm of police officers to implement this new policy, many arrests took place on inadequate evidence: a classic example of legal rules being overridden by non-legal concerns. It will be harder, however, to change police practice in the direction of *less* frequent use of their power, or more frequent *compliance with safeguards*, as can be seen by the minimal impact of the high-profile Macpherson Report (1999) on street-level policing (see the earlier discussion). The pilot project mentioned earlier did not even require the police to record the 'frequent informal' stops, where 'known criminals' or 'informants' were stopped by the police for the purpose of gathering 'criminal intelligence', because officers had objected that such recording might 'impact on their working practices' (Bland *et al.* 2000: 14–15). This no doubt helps explain why those members of the public in the pilot sites who reported being stopped and searched repeatedly, sometimes in the course of just one day, were almost never given records of these encounters.

STOP-SEARCH AND ARREST: INCLUSIONARY OR EXCLUSIONARY?

Arrests usually follow information from, and complaints by, victims or witnesses (Shapland and Vagg 1988; Reiss 1971; Steer 1980), although the late 1990s saw a revival of proactive policing (see later). If relatively few arrests are proactive, does discretion, and the patterns of bias that are reflected by it, play only a minor part in determining the shape of the official suspect population? McConville *et al.* (1991) argue that most of the studies cited above are based on indictable offences, missing out the summary offences (such as public order, prostitution, drunkenness, etc.) in which police initiative is more pronounced. Also, the issue is less who is influenced by stereotyping as whether the initiator, whoever he or she is, is so influenced. Store detectives stereotype (Cameron 1964; Murphy 1986), and doubtless 'ordinary' members of the public do too. Further, citizen initiation rarely takes the form of citizen arrest. More usually it is simply the transmission of rather sketchy—and sometimes downright unreliable—information to the police (Quinton *et al.* 2000: 31–3). That information has to be sifted, evaluated, and acted upon (or not) by the police. The British Crime Survey has repeatedly shown that the police record only about half of all the crime reported to them (Kershaw *et al.* 2000). McConville *et al.* (1991: 2) provide several examples where, even when the police did act upon complaints (for instance, by an ex-lodger and by a restaurateur), the way in which they acted, whether or not to arrest, was decided according to the working rules discussed earlier; and Sanders *et al.* (1997) provide further examples. In other words, police discretion and the exercise of judgement are still operative even when arrests are citizen-initiated. The same is true of information from informants, on which the police increasingly depend (Maguire and Norris 1992; Field and Pelser 1998). Information from the public is one resource among many which the police use in exercising discretion on the street according to their own priorities, and so the community is harnessed by the police in an inclusionary way, but only where doing so is consistent with police working rules.

The increased formal powers of stop-search and arrest given to the police since the mid-1980s, together with the ability of the police to stop-search and arrest largely when they want to on the basis of broad, intangible suspicion, led to the increased use of this intrusive activity throughout the late 1980s and 1990s. Other new laws, such as s 5 of the Public Order Act 1986, provided arrest powers for trivial offences that the police use extensively to bolster their authority (Brown and Ellis 1994). Young males, especially from poor and minority sections of the community, bear the brunt of all this power (Meehan 1993; Brown 1997: chapters 2 and 4; Loader 1996). They feel—with some justification—discriminated against, and the consequent social unrest creates a vicious spiral of yet more policing and more unrest (Scarman 1981; Keith 1993; Macpherson 1999). The police sometimes use arrest powers to stamp their authority on challengers, often without any intention of prosecuting (Choongh 1997). In these circumstances, the poor and underprivileged are treated dismissively as part of, and in order to emphasize, their exclusion from normal standards of protection (Young 1991). If our 'freedom' approach underlay the criminal justice system, arrest and stop-search powers would be used very differently and with restraint.

DETENTION IN THE POLICE STATION

We have already noted that only in relatively recent years has the law moved in a crime control direction by allowing interference in the liberty of the citizen in the absence of sufficient evidence to prosecute. This movement was initially unplanned, *ad hoc*, and imprecise, giving rise to legal 'fudges' like 'helping police with their enquiries'. The Royal Commission on Criminal Procedure (RCCP) (1981) was therefore urged, on the one hand, to prohibit pre-charge detention (the due process position) and on the other to extend it (the crime control position). The Royal Commission decided that pre-charge detention should be reduced and allowed only when it was 'necessary'. In this and other ways the Royal Commission attempted to satisfy both due-process and crime-control lobbies. Although the Royal Commission on Criminal Justice (RCCJ) (1993) also claimed to balance due process and crime control considerations, many critics argue that it was actually captured by the 'crime control' lobby, a remarkable outcome in light of the fact that it was set up in the wake of a spectacular series of miscarriages (McConville and Bridges 1994; Field and Thomas 1994; Young and Sanders 1994). However, because the RCCJ did not attempt to re-think criminal justice in any fundamental way, the implementation of (most of) its recommendations did not alter the overall shape of the system. At the time of writing, the Auld Report is likely to bring about more significant change.

DETENTION WITHOUT CHARGE

In line with the Royal Commission's (1981) recommendations, PACE 1984 provides that anyone at a police station should either be free to leave at will, or be under arrest (s 29). If the latter, there are clear time limits on how long a suspect can be held: normally twenty-four hours, but in exceptional cases up to thirty-six hours, or even ninety-six hours with the leave of the magistrates (ss 41–44). On arrest, all suspects, except in exceptional cases, should be taken directly to a police station (s 30). It is then for the 'custody officer' (the old 'station sergeant', with an enhanced role and training) to decide whether or not the suspect should be detained. There are only two grounds for detention: (i) in order to charge the suspect; or (ii), where there is insufficient evidence to charge, in order to secure that extra evidence. But detention for the latter ground is allowed only where it is *necessary* for that purpose (s 37), and only for as long as it is necessary; senior officers are supposed periodically to review detention to ascertain this.

The aims of these provisions should be clear. Being either arrested or free to go was designed to eliminate the travesty of 'helping the police with their enquiries'. Clear time limits were designed to ensure that both suspects and police knew what their respective rights and powers were, and to ensure that suspects were not intimidated by the prospect of indefinite detention. And immediate transit to a police station, where a custody officer then becomes responsible for the suspect (and then, only when detention is 'necessary'), was designed to ensure that suspects did not remain in the hands of officers who might mistreat them.

However, many of the RCCP's hopes have not been fulfilled. Although 'independent' custody officers have to complete 'custody sheets' on all suspects that record the particulars of their detention, and so forth, this 'evidence' is written by the police against whom this is supposed to be a protection for suspects—like records of stop-and-search. It is not surprising to find that 'helping with enquiries' has not been eliminated, detention is hardly ever refused, and detention is continued for as long as investigating officers wish (subject to the time limits in PACE) by custody officers in the same, routinized way that it is authorized in the first place (McConville *et al.* 1991; Dixon *et al.* 1990; Phillips and Brown 1998).

ACCESS TO LEGAL ADVICE

The most striking due process provision of PACE 1984 is the provision, in ss 58–59, of free legal advice to all suspects who request it. Information about this unambiguous right has to be provided by the custody officer to the suspect. Advice may be delayed in exceptional cases but not denied outright. Custody records state whether or not suspects were informed of their rights, whether or not suspects requested advice, and what (if anything) happened then. Request rates have now risen to around 40 per cent, and actual advice rates to around 34 per cent (Bucke and Brown 1997). This is a massive increase over the pre-PACE situation, but it is still lower than one might have expected. Why should nearly two out of three people reject an entirely free service? Why do over one out of ten requests fail?

The research (summarized by Sanders and Young 2000: 214–40; and by Brown 1997: chapter 6) shows, first, that some suspects do not request advice because they are not informed (wholly or partly) of their rights. Secondly, some suspects' requests are denied, ignored, or simply not acted upon, custody records recording only some of these malpractices. This underlines the point made earlier about police-created records. Thirdly, the police often use 'ploys' to attempt to dissuade suspects from seeking advice and to persuade them to cancel their requests. These ploys range from the incomprehensible reading of rights to scare stories, such as 'You'll have to wait in the cells until the solicitor gets here'.

The problem does not lie wholly with the police. Many suspects have negative attitudes towards solicitors, which is not surprising, given their level of service. Advice is frequently provided by telephone rather than in person, in many cases solicitors do not attend interrogations, and when they do they are usually passive. Legal aid lawyers have a generally non-adversarial stance and take their lead from the police. They routinely allow the police to use overbearing tactics, such that in one notorious case the suspect's lawyer had not objected to intimidation that the Court of Appeal condemned without hesitation (this was the Cardiff Three case, discussed by Sanders and Young 2000: 292–3). Sometimes defence lawyers are actually sought by the police to put their case to recalcitrant suspects. McConville et al. (1994: 8) found one firm, which specialized in criminal work, advising—over the telephone—'Tell the truth, son, you won't go far wrong on that advice.' The net result is that the possibility of help from a solicitor is one thing among many that suspects must weigh up when detained. Belatedly, police station legal advice and assistance is now regulated more rigorously, but the effect of this is undermined by changes to the right of silence (discussed below and, in detail, in Sanders and Young 2000: 233–40).

POLICE INTERROGATION

Interrogation has assumed ever greater importance in police investigation over the years. Nearly half of all detained suspects are interrogated. In part this is because, as we have seen, investigation now usually takes place after, rather than before, arrest. It is also a product of the *mens rea* requirements of substantive criminal law. It is usually necessary to prove that the suspect intended the offences or was reckless. Since these are features of the suspect's mental state, the best evidence is a confession. Even when other ways of securing evidence are available, interrogation often serves as a 'short cut' and produces information about other offences and other offenders (Softley 1980). The due process insistence on the prosecution proving their own case originally prohibited non-consensual interrogation, but this changed in 1912 when the

Judges' Rules first allowed interrogation before charge. Confessions were invalid if secured 'involuntarily' or 'oppressively', but the 1981 RCCP questioned how meaningful it was to talk of confessions given in conditions of involuntary detention being 'voluntary'. The PACE Code of Practice on Detention and Questioning sets out basic standards for interrogation (the provision of proper heating, ventilation, breaks, access to solicitors and others, and so forth), but also states that a police officer is 'entitled to question any person from whom he thinks useful information can be obtained. . . . A person's declaration that he is unwilling to reply does not alter this entitlement' (Note 1B). So, police officers may attempt to persuade suspects to change their minds and to hold them, subject to the time limits, for as long as that takes. To understand just how coercive this is, it is necessary to appreciate how detention is experienced by suspects. Newburn and Hayman (2002: 97) note that for the seventy-three detainees they interviewed, 'time passed exceedingly slowly in the cells'. Given the importance attached by most suspects to the shortest detention possible (Brown and Larcombe 1992), and recent changes to the right of silence (see below), the pressures on suspects to speak are considerable (also see Hillyard 1993; Choongh 1997).

How is evidence of guilt secured? First, there are those many suspects who simply and speedily acquiesce, against whom there would often be plenty of evidence anyway (Moston and Williamson 1992). Secondly, many suspects are susceptible to 'deals' (confessions in exchange for favours or reduced charges): 'They always want to deal. When they're arrested they're immediately in the game of damage limitation' (CID officer, quoted by Maguire and Norris 1992: 5). Then there are those who are intimidated by their situation, by being held against their will in 'police territory' where the environment is deliberately denuded of psychological supports (Driver 1968; Holdaway 1983; Walkley 1987), by being in fear of spending the night in the cells (Sanders *et al.* 1989), or by the employment of any number of 'tactics' against them (Evans 1992; McConville *et al.* 1994). Such tactics include offering inducements such as bail, claiming that there is overwhelming evidence against the suspect, using custodial conditions such as return to the cells, and so forth. The effectiveness of the last tactic is related to the nature of the typical police cell. Thus Newburn and Hayman (2002) noted that:

Many detainees are reluctant either to sit or lie because they feel uncomfortable about the level of cleanliness. . . . The [integral] toilets have no separate seat and the top surfaces are badly discoloured. They have no lids and the cells sometimes smell fetid. Toilet paper is provided on request, but in limited amounts because of fears that a detainee will attempt to block the system. There is no hand basin and drinking water has to be requested.

The fact that detainees could be observed while going to the toilet was a further humiliation, felt particularly keenly by women, Muslims, and others from cultures that place particular emphasis on bodily privacy. If a tactic does not work in the initial interrogation, twenty-four hours (or more) thus allow ample time for the suspect to be psychologically 'softened up' for further interrogation. Evans (1992: 49) found a strong statistical association between the use of tactics and confessions.

Extreme tactics are now unacceptable in formal interrogations since such sessions are tape-recorded. This gives rise to a fourth way of securing confession: through informal interrogation. The extent of this is controversial but its existence is not. Informal interrogation occurs on the way to the police station (the 'scenic route': Evans and Ferguson 1991; Maguire and Norris 1992: 5); before and after formal interrogations (Sanders *et al.* 1989; McConville *et al.* 1991: 4, 7; McConville 1992); and in the cells under the guise of 'welfare visits' (Dixon *et al.* 1990). Custody records are supposed to record the precise times at which interviews begin and end, but this does not prevent officers having 'a little chat to get things straight before I switch on the tape' (Evans and Ferguson 1991; see also Evans 1992: 36; McConville 1992). It is precisely on confessions allegedly made 'informally' (but not repeated 'formally') that so many appeals have turned. To the extent that 'tactics' are now used less frequently in formal interrogations than they were before PACE, it is likely that they are now simply being used more under 'low visibility' conditions (Maguire and Norris 1992). Research by Brown and Larcombe (1992) and Moston and Stephenson (1993), although methodologically flawed (Sanders and Young 2000: 299–300), found that officers admitted to a considerable amount of informal interviewing. The low visibility of informal interviews provides the opportunity to officers to 'gild the lily' (Holdaway 1983). As one officer told Maguire and Norris (1992: 46–7), there was nothing to prevent him from distorting the contents of informal conversations 'if I was dishonest'.

Coercion may occur too, in both informal and formal interrogations. This is inevitable under English law, for the job of the police interrogator is to elicit answers even from suspects who have declared a refusal to provide answers—in other words, to change their minds. Tactics are designed to do this, and not all tactics are of the 'carrot' variety: 'Sometimes it's necessary to shout at people . . . you have to keep up the pressure' (detective, quoted by McConville *et al.* 1991: 4). Even interrogation practices which would be innocuous to most people are coercive to vulnerable people (Gudjonsson and MacKeith 1982; Littlechild 1995). Procedures for identifying, and making allowances for, vulnerable people in police custody are inadequate (Laing 1995, 1999; Palmer 1996; Bucke and Brown 1997; Phillips and Brown 1998). And even supposedly non-vulnerable people often make 'coerced-passive' confessions (McConville *et al.* 1991: 4) as a result of leading questions (defended by Walkley 1987) and legal-closure questions (Irving 1985). Thus suspects get trapped into accepting they have 'stolen' when they in fact would put it in a different, exculpatory way (see also Sanders *et al.* 1989: 7; Evans 1992).

Lastly, there are false confessions. Gudjonsson and MacKeith (1988) discuss various types of false confession arising from coercion, but coercion is not always necessary. Questioning taking the form of a supported direct accusation (i.e., an accusation with details of the crime itself) can lead to internalization by suggestible suspects whose subsequent 'confessions' will contain only the details provided by the police themselves (Moston 1992). While vulnerable suspects figure particularly among cases of false confession (Littlechild 1995), many people who are apparently robust are vulnerable to police tactics and the sheer fear of being cut off and confined for a period of time beyond their own control. As one of the authors of a false confession in the 'Kerry Babies' case put it, 'I didn't think my mind was my own' (O'Mahony 1992).

While false confessions arising from disorientation are doubtless rare, falsity can be a matter of interpretation and degree. McConville *et al.* argue that interrogation is a process of construction whereby facts are made and not discovered. An example is given by Maguire and Norris (1992: 4), who report a CID sergeant saying that he had been taught to induce people found carrying knives to say that they were for their own protection. This, unknown to the suspect, constitutes admission of the crime of carrying an 'offensive weapon'. This type of confession, with elements of falsity arising from the process of case construction, is doubtless far more common than 'false confessions', yet equally likely to lead to wrongful convictions.

While the police do not actively seek false confessions, McConville *et al.* argue that their adversarial role inevitably leads to the crime control value that this is a price worth paying. This view contrasts with that of Moston (1992), who argues that police failure to verify confessions and avoid leading questions is simply a matter of technical competence, a failure of training, and the decision to adopt adversarial styles. Inquisitorial styles, going under labels such as 'investigative interviewing' or 'ethical interviewing', were advocated in the early 1990s by the Home Office and the police, as well as by academics such as Moston. However, it appears from Cherryman and Bull's (2000) summary of the literature that there has been little research on the use and impact of these new interview styles, suggesting that they are little used. Solutions such as these, along with technical solutions, such as better training or video-recording (Baldwin and Bedward 1991), imply a bureaucratic explanation for false confessions and coercion. They presuppose that due process is achievable in interrogation. McConville *et al.* argue that the search for 'better' or more 'objective' interrogation is naive, because the job of the police is to build a case, not to identify verifiable facts. Miscarriages of justice arising from coercion and false confessions would be more effectively reduced by preventing confession evidence forming the sole basis of convictions, and by providing the defence with the same resources as are provided to the prosecution, than by trying to change interrogation practices.

THE RIGHT OF SILENCE

Over half of all suspects who are interrogated either confess, or make incriminating statements to the police (see, for the most recent research, Bucke *et al.* 2000). We have seen that the police have various methods of securing confessions, but these do not always work; and they work with varying success according to a wide range of factors, in particular, offence severity, prior legal advice, and strength of evidence (Moston and Stephenson 1992). Evans (1992) also found age and criminal record to be significant. When suspects exercise their 'right to remain silent', are the police unjustifiably impeded? The answer turns principally on three things: (i) what, precisely, 'silence' means in this context; (ii) what the association is between silence and outcome; and (iii) in what ways the police are obstructed by silence (although there are of course arguments of principle as well as practical policy at stake: Easton 1998). Only 2–4 per cent of suspects in the post-PACE studies exercise absolute silence, although a further 5 per cent or so simply make flat denials; while 8–15 per cent answer some questions and not others, and some suspects are silent at the start but then answer questions later (or vice versa). So accurate estimates of the extent of silence are near impossible, and studies which simply count the number of interviews in which questions were not answered at some point can be misleading. Following analysis of these 'counting' problems, Leng (1992) found a 'true' silence rate of 4.5 per cent. He found that in only a small percentage of 'no further actions' or acquittals was silence exercised, and that these outcomes rarely seemed to be a product of silence. Moston and Williamson (1990) also found little association between silence and charge, plea, or verdict. Leng found that 'ambush' defences (not disclosed until trial) were rare. When they were used, they were unsuccessful. Most acquittals were the result of unforeseen, but not unforeseeable, defences—sometimes they mirrored exculpatory statements to which the police would not listen in interrogation.

The RCCJ examined this evidence, concluding that the right to silence should be retained, as abolition would benefit the police in few cases and would put pressure on innocent people instead of experienced criminals. Despite this, the government changed the law in line with the changes it had already made in Northern Ireland. The Criminal Justice and Public Order Act 1994 now provides that, when someone relies in court on a fact which he or she could have been reasonably expected to mention when questioned by the police, the court can draw an adverse inference from this silence. Similarly, courts can draw adverse inferences from failures to answer questions in court. Exactly what inferences a court should draw from silence is a matter of debate. The law is still being developed by the English and European courts, and is likely to remain a matter of great difficulty for lawyers, police officers, and judges for some time to come. Consequently, these changes have been castigated on pragmatic (for example, Birch 1999) as well as principled grounds (for example, Belloni and Hodgson 2000). Despite Article 6(2) of the ECHR proclaiming that 'Everyone . . . shall be presumed innocent until proved guilty according to law', the European Court of Human Rights has accepted the lawfulness, with caveats, of these provisions (Sanders and Young 2000: 251–68). As might be expected, the effect of the new provisions is to lower the use of the right of silence, probably because lawyers, who were becoming more adversarial in the early to mid-1990s, became more circumspect again about advising silence. Thus Bucke et al. (2000) estimate silence and confessions in the late 1990s at around the rates found in the 1980s.

A SEA CHANGE IN THE NATURE OF DETENTION?

Rather than leading to less pre-charge detention, the RCCP's scheme (enacted in PACE 1984) led to more. The formalization of pre-charge procedures was intended to protect suspects, and it doubtless does so to some extent. But its unintended consequence has been to lead to more arrests (fewer suspects being held in limbo), more police station interrogation (instead of interviews at home), and the rushing (in some cases) of the charging process to beat the time limits. Despite PACE, detention can still be lengthy and intimidating, access to lawyers can be obstructed and is often of little value (particularly now that the right of silence has been further restricted), and the police have learnt to substitute psychological pressure for physical pressure. On the broader impact of PACE on policing, researchers have reached different conclusions.

As part of a critique of *The Case for the Prosecution* (McConville *et al.* 1991), Dixon divides criminal justice researchers into two main camps: the 'sea change theorists' who argue that PACE has significantly obstructed the police and enhanced protections for suspects; and 'new left pessimists' who argue that the changes are largely cosmetic. Dixon places his own work between these camps, arguing that whether legal rules change police practices 'depends on what kind of rules and what kind of culture, what kind of reform and when' (1992: 536). This seems to us to be an indisputable sociological truth with which few researchers would disagree, but it does not resolve the argument about the significance of the changes (for debate about *The Case for the Prosecution*, see Duff 1998; McConville *et al.* 1997; Smith 1997, 1998; various articles in Noaks *et al.* 1995; see also Maguire 2002, for a view similar to that of Dixon).

It seems that PACE has changed practices, but largely by *shifting* the unwanted behaviour instead of eradicating or even reducing it. Thus there is little violence now, but there is more use of other tactics and pressures, and confessions purportedly given in 'informal' interrogations are still admissible. The PACE framework is like the post-*Miranda* approach in the United States, where interrogation has similarly shifted from physical to psychological strategies. As Leo puts it, 'The law has also empowered the police to create more specialised and seemingly more effective interrogation strategies . . . they can lie, they can cajole, and they can manipulate' (1994: 116). The new rules and constraints that are implicitly relied upon by Dixon are access to lawyers, tape-recording of interrogation, custody records, and the general supervisory role of the custody officer. As we have seen—and as Dixon (1991) partially acknowledges himself—these developments hardly represent a 'sea change' in policing.

Sanders and Young (1994) argue that PACE only appears to provide a 'balance' between due process and crime control because we now unquestioningly accept the right of the police to use coercive powers. But why, they ask, do suspects not want to wait for a lawyer, for instance, to come to the station? Why are so many people so vulnerable that PACE has to establish elaborate codes and protections? Why do suspects 'voluntarily' answer police questions? Only because they are in the police station against their will in the first place. So, for example, most suspects do want lawyers, but the desire to get out of the station quickly is stronger (Brown and Larcombe 1992). And why is police station legal work so poor so often? Again, largely because the police have the power to create the forces that so shape it. Solicitors send unqualified staff, give telephone advice, or miss interrogations largely because of all the time they would otherwise waste. But it is the police who control the time-frame (Sanders 1996a). And the legal 'trading' which undermines adversarialism is forced on to lawyers—who, it has to be admitted, usually need little persuading—because the police are in control. Once the police are given the right to detain, the rule of law is jeopardized, due process is made unviable, and human rights norms are tested to their limit. Thus, Sanders and Young argue, PACE does not merely 'balance' rights and powers poorly, but, in providing the right to detain in such broad circumstances, it cedes most practical power to the police. The 'sea change', if there has been one, has been in favour of the police.

Why do we put up with this? Sanders and Young (2000: 128–9) argue that it is because it is not 'we' who bear the brunt of these powers. Most people who are stopped, searched, arrested, detained, and interrogated are young, working-class men, especially in ethnic minorities. The treatment they are given is frequently humiliating—and deliberately so (Young 1991; Choongh 1997). Opinion-formers, lawyers, and legislators, on the other hand (older, middle-class, white men in the main), are very rarely subjected to such exclusionary processes. It is true that over one-third of men will have been convicted of at least one non-motoring offence before they reach the age of forty, which means that many more than this will have been stopped, arrested, and/or reported for motoring offences. But the way in which police power is exercised and its frequency are as important as outcome (Tyler 1990), and this bears down far more heavily on the poor than on the wealthy. Of course some middle-class people are roughly treated and some poor people are not. But the contrast between the integrated and the excluded is as striking in the field of criminal justice as in other fields of social policy. Arguably, major advances in liberty are only ever secured in the United Kingdom when the middle classes are threatened. If so, we can expect this divided society to manifest these exclusionary processes for a long time to come, and for 'freedom' in the sense we use it here to be given little weight by policy-makers and practitioners.

PROSECUTION AND DIVERSION

When the police were first established they gradually took over responsibility for prosecution in the absence of any specific or exclusive prosecution powers or controls over their discretion. As arrest turned into a tool for (rather than the culmination of) investigation, pre-charge detention arose and the police developed various non-prosecution dispositions. There are now well over a million police prosecutions per year, but around one in four suspects are released from pre-charge detention with no further action (NFA), and many suspects are cautioned. As many juveniles are cautioned as are prosecuted. Many other agencies also prosecute. These include the Inland Revenue (IR), Department of Social Security (DSS), Health and Safety Inspectorate, Customs and Excise, and so forth (Slapper 2001). Although these agencies follow a diversity of policies and procedures, they all share a propensity not to prosecute (Sanders 1996b: Part IV; Slapper and Tombs 1999: chapter 8). The DSS is the most prosecution-minded of the non-police agencies. The DSS mounted 8,090 prosecutions in 1986–7, compared to the IR's 459 in the same year (Cook 1989: 7), despite the far greater number of tax offences. These agencies NFA and caution far more often than they prosecute (Sanders 1985a), attempting to secure compliance with the law and/or to secure financial compensation primarily through informal negotiation. Whether their approach is so different from that of the police because the offences with which they deal are viewed differently by 'society', or whether the causal effect is in the other direction, is not clear (see Nelken, in Chapter 23 of this volume). However, it is clear that even the treatment of people who are unlawfully killed is completely different: non-police agencies virtually never ask the police to consider prosecuting for manslaughter in circumstances where this would be viable and, arguably, desirable (Slapper 1999). Thus arrest does not necessarily lead to prosecution, prosecution need not be the normal response to suspected crime, and the specific charge prosecuted is an entirely discretionary matter (see generally Sanders 1996b).

NO FURTHER ACTION (NFA)

The NFA rate has risen greatly over the years, especially since the introduction of PACE (Hillyard and Gordon 1999). This is consistent with the 'new left pessimist' argument that PACE reflects and reproduces a 'crime control' trend. Police officers decide both whether to arrest and whether to charge, and they make release decisions themselves on the basis of their own criteria and on evidence collected and evaluated by them.

McConville *et al.* (1991: 6) found that many arrests were a result of pressure from the public. If the police arrested reluctantly the outcome was often NFA, usually after consultation with the victim, regardless of the strength of evidence. Other reasons for NFA in cases where the police did find (or could have found) evidence include the doing of 'deals' with suspects, especially informants. And just as prosecution is sometimes used to protect the police against allegations of malpractice (Wilcox 1972), so in some circumstances NFA prevents the airing in public of events about which the police prefer to keep quiet (McConville *et al.* 1991: 111). Some NFAs, of course, are simply cases in which the police would have liked to prosecute had they had more evidence. The obstacle here is rarely physical or legal, but simply one of resources. The police rarely seek evidence other than from eye-witnesses, the victim, and the suspect himself. They could often investigate further but choose not to (Leng 1992). Cases are a product of police work, and so the absence of a case is also a police product. On the other hand, many NFAs are a product of purely speculative arrests (McConville *et al.* 1991: 2). Often the police accept that the suspect did not commit the offence, or that there is no evidence: for instance, where the police 'trawl' local people with relevant previous convictions simply to eliminate them from a major rape enquiry; where suspects are arrested so that they can be held pending their questioning as witnesses; and where *all* inhabitants of, and visitors to, a building where there has been a drugs raid are arrested, even though the building consists of several self-contained flats (Leng 1992).

Further, arrest and detention are not always geared to prosecution. If the police arrest in furtherance of the 'assertion of authority' working rule, for instance, the arrestee may be detained in order to be humbled. The exercise of power is sometimes used to intimidate sections of the population such as the Irish (Hillyard 1993) or other ethnic minorities (Choongh 1997). NFAs would have been anticipated even at the moment of arrest. In these types of case, and in many of those discussed earlier, no due process standards, substantive or procedural, are adhered to.

POLICE DIVERSION

Although the ratio of prosecutions to cautions is about 3:1, this reflects a massive increase in the cautioning of both adults and juveniles since the 1970s. The Royal Commission on Criminal Procedure (1981: Table 23.4) noted considerable variations in cautioning rates among police forces that could not be explained solely by offence variations (Sanders 1985b). The Home Office responded in 1985 with new guidelines that established clearer criteria for prosecution and caution: offence seriousness, previous convictions, dramatic mitigating circumstances, wishes of the victim, and so forth. However, both inter-force and intra-force disparity continued (Wilkinson and Evans 1990), because of the procedural arrangements for prosecution and caution (discussed below) and the guidelines themselves.

The guidelines are vague (how serious an offence or record?; what kinds of personal circumstance should be taken into account?), manipulable (the police themselves sometimes influence the wishes of victims), and non-prioritized (are victims' wishes, suspects' circumstances, or offence seriousness to predominate?). New guidelines were produced in 1990 and again in 1994, and cautioning for youths was put on a statutory basis by the Crime and Disorder Act 1998. As intended, the 1994 and 1998 changes reversed the trend of increasing cautions (see Newburn, in Chapter 16 of this volume). Diversion is none the less encouraged in many cases which would once have been prosecuted, because it is cheaper than prosecution and because it is thought to avoid stigmatizing offenders. Drawing on labelling theory (e.g., Becker 1963), it was generally accepted in the 1980s and early 1990s that prosecution and punishment can exaggerate criminal self-identity. The 1990 caution guidelines exhorted cautioning as 'reducing the risk that [offenders] will re-offend' (Home Office 1990: para. 5). Thus 'courts should only be used as a last resort, particularly for juveniles and young adults' (ibid.: para. 7). Now the Crime and Disorder Act specifies that a maximum of two cautions (save in exceptional circumstances) can be offered to youths (in the form of 'reprimands' for minor offences, or 'warnings' for more serious or repeat offending). Warnings are supposed to be accompanied by 'action plans' drawn up by the multi-agency Youth Offender Teams created under the 1998 Act, and the emphasis is now on 'early intervention' and 'nipping crime in the bud', although cost-reduction and stigma-avoidance aims have not been entirely dispensed with.

The various objectives of cautioning would be undermined if cautions, reprimands, and warnings were used in cases that would not otherwise be prosecuted. The 1990 guidelines warned against such 'net-widening' (ibid.: para. 3). This occurs when cautions are used as alternatives to NFA rather than to prosecution, although it is difficult to assess how widespread this is (Cohen 1985; Duff 1993). Secondly, preconditions for caution are set out: that there is sufficient evidence to prosecute, and that the suspect admits the offence and accepts the caution (the requirement of consent was removed in the case of youths by the 1998 Act). But Sanders (1988a) found that these preconditions were often ignored. Indeed, some suspects were cautioned precisely *because* there was insufficient evidence to prosecute. McConville *et al.* (1991: chapter 7), and Evans and Ferguson (1991) found that little had changed in more recent years. Over 20 per cent of the juveniles cautioned in the latter study, for instance, made no clear admission. The low-visibility nature of caution decisions also enables the police to use cautions as bargaining tools with suspects who would normally be prosecuted (McConville *et al.* 1991: 6).

Both on the street and in the station, rules have little effect on police behaviour unless they are both enforceable and enforced (neither applying to cautioning), or coincide with police working rules. These controls often do not coincide, for cautioning can serve crime control objectives. Cohen's original (1985) 'net widening' thesis was that less obviously coercive measures (the whole spectrum of 'community' policing and 'community' dispositions) were developing in order to exercise more control over the suspect population. The police want to have on record suspects who are not prosecuted, and for these purposes legalistic questions of evidence and admission are trivial distractions. On this argument due process is subordinated to crime control in the practice of cautioning. Similarly, ostensibly cautionable cases are often prosecuted where this serves policing objectives; and the interests of the victim, whether opposed to those of the suspect or not, are also sometimes subordinated to those of the police (Hoyle 1998; Sanders *et al.* 1997). Cohen also warned of 'mesh-thinning', that those drawn into the net would find themselves subjected to greater levels of unaccountable intrusion in their lives, and this is certainly one way in which the changes brought about by the 1998–1999 legislation can be conceptualized. It is worth noting, for example, that defence lawyers are not represented on Youth Offender Teams, and are discouraged from attending Young Offender Panels. This not only saves the government money, but also increases the risk of low-level miscarriages of justice and disproportionate punishment, all in the name of benign-sounding 'early intervention'.

The patterns of bias identified in street policing (race, class, and so forth) may also be evident in prosecution and diversion decisions. This has certainly appeared to be so with juvenile decisions (Evans 1992; Fitzgerald 1993; Lee 1995), and may be true with adults too (Sanders 1985a). But the greater class bias is between police-enforced and other crime. Despite variations in the use of police cautioning the overwhelming pattern is, in adult cases, the use of prosecution instead of caution. Both the police and other types of agency have near-absolute discretion. The police (dealing with mainly working-class crime) use it one way, while most other agencies (dealing with mainly middle-class crime) use it in another. Indeed, non-police agencies that deal with poor people behave much more like the police than like the IR or HSE (Walker and Wall 1997; Pantazis and Gordon 1997). It is difficult to see how this can be justified in terms of offence seriousness, previous criminality, and so forth (Sanders 1985a; Cook 1989), except, perhaps, in terms of a narrowly defined 'efficiency' (Hutter 1988). Thus the dispositions of both police and non-police agencies serve to further the different working rules of those different agencies. And the stigmatizing and exclusionary process of prosecution is used routinely against the poor but rarely against the wealthy.

POLICE CHARGING

In most cases the police now decide, following arrest, whether or not to charge. The usual threshold used to be a *prima facie* case. This, the RCCP believed, led to many acquittals, and it recommended the more stringent criterion of 'a reasonable prospect of conviction'. Sanders (1985b) found that by no means all cases even passed the *prima facie* threshold. More recently, McConville *et al.* (1991: chapter 6) found the same in relation to the new threshold, as did research done for the RCCJ (Block *et al.* 1993). McConville *et al.* (1991) argue that the police continue to follow their working rules when making charge decisions, and follow American and English writers (such as Bittner 1967; and Chatterton 1976) in arguing that the charge, like stop-and-search, arrest, interrogation, and caution, is a resource for the police as much as it is an end in itself. Decisions to charge cases that are weak and to fail to charge cases that are strong are inconsistent and incomprehensible only in terms of the official guidelines. They are perfectly rational in terms of police working rules. This increases the acquittal rate, but convictions are only one dimension on the crime-control scale. Acquisition of information (through interrogation which is then justified by charge), assertion of authority, or protection of an officer against whom a complaint is expected are all reasons which McConville *et al.* (1991) found officers gave for charging with little or no regard for the rules. One might add to the list, contrary to McConville *et al.*'s expectations, the charging of suspected offenders against vulnerable victims (Sanders *et al.* 1997).

Unlike cautions, which are usually decided by inspectors or more senior officers, charges are a matter for the arresting officer and custody officer. Very rarely do custody officers caution or NFA when the arresting officer wants a prosecution, or vice versa, for custody officers are in a weak position in enquiring into evidential strength. If they try to evaluate an arresting officer's evidence they have only one source of information on which to draw (apart from the suspect)—that same arresting officer. McConville *et al.* found that, as one custody officer put it, 'I would go along with what the arresting officers have to say'. As an arresting officer said: 'Perhaps by the book . . . 'The custody officer will decide' sort of thing, but in practice it's different. He trusts your judgement' (McConville *et al.* 1991: 119–20). Cop culture prevents the suspect from rising high in the hierarchy of credibility: 'I accept that [the officer's] got no cause to be telling lies and the other chap has' (ibid.: 119). Arresting officers can, in other words, 'construct' their cases to achieve the results they want, and may even 'gild the lily' in the process (Ericson 1981; Holdaway 1983). Case construction involves selection, interpretation, and creation of facts. Cases are usually constructed deliberately to appear strong, in accordance with adversarial principles. Since the system is concerned more with legal truth than with actual truth, the police are also more concerned with the former, sometimes 'creating' facts which bear little relation to any reality which the suspect might recognize (McBarnet 1981). This is simply a continuation of processes revealed in studies of interrogation and other policing practices. It follows that, just as officers can often secure cautions when NFA would be more in keeping with the rules, so they can often secure charges when cautions would be more appropriate (and vice versa).

THE CROWN PROSECUTION SERVICE

The RCCP realized that the police, left to their own devices, would not consistently apply the guidelines on evidential sufficiency and cautioning. To secure consistency, and to counterbalance extra police powers, it recommended establishing the Crown Prosecution Service (CPS). Apart from organizational and accountability matters with which we shall not be concerned here (on which see Sanders and Young 2000: 377–82), the government followed the Royal Commission's recommendations in the Prosecution of Offences Act 1985 and built the CPS around the pre-existing system. The police continue to charge, summons, caution, and NFA, as before. Once charged or summonsed, however, the accused becomes the responsibility of the CPS, which decides whether to continue the prosecution. The CPS is headed by the Director of Public Prosecutions (DPP), whose office had previously been responsible for national prosecutions of particular importance and for the prosecution of police officers. The Code for Crown Prosecutors provides guidance on prosecution decisions in almost identical terms to that discussed before on evidential sufficiency and cautionability, so that poor police decisions can be corrected by the CPS.

McConville *et al.* (1991) found that the CPS rarely dropped cases that were evidentially weak, and that when it did so this was usually on the initiative of the police and/ or only after several court appearances. There were three main reasons for this: policy (the furtherance of police working rules, shared by both prosecutors and police officers); the chance of a freak conviction (because verdicts are so hard to predict); and guilty pleas (just because a case is evidentially weak it does not follow that the defendant will contest the case; weak cases are continued in the often correct expectation of a guilty plea). If the CPS is passive in relation to weak cases where case failure is a measure of institutional efficiency, it is not surprising to discover that it is even more passive in relation to cautionable cases. McConville *et al.* (ibid.) found no cases at all being dropped on this ground alone, despite many similar cases being cautioned by the police. Again, where police working rules point to prosecution, the CPS is reluctant to stop the case (Gelsthorpe and Giller 1990). In more recent years there has been a significant rise in discontinuances, particularly on evidential grounds. However, many 'public interest' discontinuances are of trivial cases, and are made on cost grounds. That there is scope for far more diversion by the CPS has been confirmed by Crisp *et al.* (1994), who found that cases which went through experimental 'Public Interest Case Assessment' (PICA) schemes were far more likely to be discontinued than normal. Despite this, many cases that were assessed as cautionable were not discontinued and yet received nominal penalties. McConville *et al.*'s argument that the police and CPS insist on prosecuting when they have extraneous reasons for so doing would appear to hold firm. Similarly, Cretney and Davis (1996) and Sanders *et al.* (1997) found that the police and CPS prosecuted weak cases involving victims of domestic violence and vulnerable victims because they believed in the guilt of the suspect, ignoring the probability that problems concerning the victims' testimony would lead to acquittal.

Recent research has shown that ethnic minority defendants have their cases disproportionately discontinued by the CPS *and* dismissed in court (Mhlanga 2000).

This suggests that the CPS counters some of the race bias produced by the police discussed earlier in this chapter, but not all. The CPS is in a structurally weak position to carry out its ostensible aims primarily because of police case construction. The CPS reviews the quality of police cases on the basis of evidence provided solely by the police. This is like the problem of written records, where those who are being evaluated write their own reports. Cases being prosecuted are usually presented as prosecutable; the facts to support this are selected, and those that do not support it are ignored, hidden, or undermined. Thus weaknesses or cautionable factors, whether known by the police or not, often emerge only in or after trial (Leng 1992).

This situation is exacerbated when the CPS relies on police summaries, which are very selective indeed (Baldwin and Bedward 1991). The CPS had long realized this and, as part of its striving for independence, managed, some ten years after its establishment, virtually to eradicate the use of summaries. No sooner had this been achieved when a Home Office Report (Narey 1997) led to relatively simple magistrates' court cases being 'fast-tracked'. In these cases, where a guilty plea is often taken the day after arrest, there is often no time for the CPS to see a full police file. This has set everything back again. Moodie and Tombs (1982) and Duff (1997) in Scotland, and Gelsthorpe and Giller (1990) in England cite prosecutors who agree that the police present them only with what seems relevant to them as prosecutors (as distinct from neutral intermediaries). Similarly, when the police seek advice from the CPS, they can obtain the advice they want by carefully selecting the information they present (Sanders *et al.* 1997). This is why PICA schemes (see above), which present prosecutors with information from non-police sources, lead to increased numbers of discontinuances.

That the CPS is primarily a police prosecution agency is hardly surprising in an adversarial system, but it does suggest that suspects cannot rely on the CPS, as presently constituted, to protect them. Prosecutors could become adequate reviewers of either evidence or public interest only if placed in an entirely different structural relationship with the police. This would require fundamental changes in the adversarial system, and might well then be unsuccessful, if the evidence we have of continental systems is anything to go by (Hodgson 2001). It would be better to strengthen the position of the defence in the adversarial system, but the political will to achieve this is singularly lacking. Indeed, the turn of the century saw three changes in the crime control direction: the 'Narey' reforms mentioned earlier, the 'co-location' of police and CPS to process less serious cases more efficiently (returning to some of the pre-CPS methods of working); and the creation of a 'Criminal Defence' service, including a 'Public Defender' service on US lines (discussed in detail in Sanders and Young 2000: 380–2, 499–505, 538–40).

PRE-TRIAL PROCESSES

POLICE BAIL

After charge, the custody officer decides whether to release on bail or to hold the suspect in custody pending the next magistrates' court hearing (usually the next morning). Detention is allowed only if the suspect's real name and address cannot be ascertained, if he is unlikely to appear in court to answer the charge, if he is likely to interfere with witnesses or further police investigations, or if he is likely to commit further significant crimes. While this is consistent with the ECHR, the case law of the European Court of Human Rights provides that refusal of bail for any of these reasons must be based on evidence, not speculation. However, like much human rights-speak, this is both unrealistic and inconsistent with the crime control elements of English law and practice. For example, most of these provisions require custody officers to predict what might happen if suspects were released—in other words, to speculate. Further, custody officers have to rely on what investigating officers say, and what little may be known about the suspect's previous record of appearing in court, offending on bail, and so forth. Also, suspects cannot prove that they would not have done something wrong had they been given the opportunity to do it. Thus decisions are taken quickly on the basis of inadequate information; although decisions are taken by theoretically independent custody officers to protect suspects from the partisanship of arresting/investigating officers, most of the information used will come from the very officers against whom protection is provided; and assessment of the quality of decision-making is almost impossible. So the initial bail/custody decision is entirely for the police, without real accountability, and surely contrary to the spirit of the ECHR.

Bail gives the police a powerful bargaining tool in interrogation. Although they should not offer 'inducements' (of which bail is one), this is a recognized interrogation 'tactic' (Irving 1980): 'They [the police] said if I cough I'll get bail; if not then I'll be in court tomorrow' (McConville and Hodgson 1992: 79). The opportunity for informal 'chats' discussed above ensures that such negotiations need never take place in front of tape recorders or solicitors, and most suspects know (or think they know) that they can make deals on these lines. For bail bargaining is 'all part of the relationship' (detective, quoted in McConville et al. 1991: 63). The building of relationships is a vital working rule, and, like other working rules, cannot simply be legislated away (Maguire and Norris 1992). The power of the police to deny bail is enhanced by the suspect's fear of being held overnight and by the failure of many solicitors to attend the station and, when they do, to stay long. Implicit bargaining over bail leading to 'voluntary' confessions is part of the differential power relationship between officer and suspect which leads suspects 'voluntarily' to agree to many similar things like stop-and-search, attendance at the station, search of premises, and so forth. However, victims also sometimes have an interest in whether alleged offenders secure bail, or the terms on which they get bail. Victims of violence, for example, may want a 'no contact' condition. Courts have for many years been able to grant conditional, as well as unconditional, bail (see later). The police were given the power to set conditions in the mid-1990s because it was believed that the police were refusing bail to some suspects in order to encourage the court to set conditions which the police (often justifiably) thought were appropriate. The result has been an increase in the percentage of defendants being granted bail (now around 80 per cent). No changes in the rate of offending while on bail are discernible as a result of this increase in bail (Bucke and Brown 1997; Raine and Willson 1997).

COURT BAIL

Defendants who are granted police bail are not thereafter remanded in custody unless circumstances change. When defendants are not granted police bail, court bail may or may not be opposed by the police (through the CPS), and may or may not be requested by the defendant (usually through a solicitor). The CPS does not always oppose bail when the police asks it to, though when it does not it almost invariably asks for conditions to be attached (Morgan 1996). Not surprisingly, magistrates usually reach the same conclusions as the police and CPS, for they consider similar criteria and similar information (Hucklesby 1996). However, a magistrate, like a custody officer, has 'to come to a decision on the basis of probabilities and not certainties' (Hailsham, quoted in Zander 1988: 241). As with police bail decisions, this is at odds with the spirit of the human rights approach to which the UK supposedly adheres, and probably the letter of the law as well (Burrow 2000).

Courts have considerable scope for the exercise of discretion and judgement, leading to disparity between different courts (Hucklesby 1996; Paterson and Whitaker 1994, 1995). Overall, about 11–13 per cent of magistrates' cases (100,000) are denied bail each year. Though a small (but rising) percentage of all cases, remand prisoners form a substantial percentage of people in prison, greatly contributing to overcrowding and the huge cost of criminal justice (see Morgan, in Chapter 30 of this volume). Most hearings seem to take less than ten minutes (Doherty and East 1985). This shocked Lord Woolf (1991), and reflects the limited information that is usually provided (Hucklesby 1996). When information from more diverse sources is presented, bail is less frequently opposed by the CPS and more frequently granted. Bail information schemes, organized by local probation services, lead to the release of higher proportions of defendants than normal, demonstrating the partial (i.e., adversarial) approach of the police and the over-cautious approach of many courts. Mair and Lloyd (1996), in an appraisal of bail information schemes, estimate that by 1996 these schemes covered over 190 magistrates' courts and thirty-eight prison establishments. As with diversion from prosecution, these schemes show the potential in the CPS for more independence if independent information is provided to it.

A suspect's remand in custody can obstruct defence work (including preparation of bail applications). Thus defendants remanded in custody are, all other things being equal, more likely to be convicted and, if convicted, to be given custodial sentences than those granted bail. But since not all defendants remanded in custody are convicted and given custodial sentences, some defendants who are legally innocent are held in custody, and some whose offence or circumstances do not warrant custodial sentences are also held in custody before sentence. Thus in 1998, 36 per cent of defendants in custody in the magistrates' courts received non-custodial penalties, and a further 22 per cent were acquitted. On the other hand, 10–17 per cent of all persons released on bail commit an offence while at liberty (Hucklesby and Marshall 2000; Morgan and Henderson 1998). Clearly magistrates have inadequate information on which to make confident decisions, yet the stakes are high. Offending on bail is undesirable; yet so, in a supposedly due process-based system, is pre-trial imprisonment of some seven to ten weeks when so many remanded defendants are not subsequently jailed. Magistrates seem to cope by over-using conditions when they do grant bail (Hucklesby 1994), and by developing an 'unquestioning culture' whereby information from the CPS is seen as factual but information from the defence is seen as partial. Magistrates even sometimes refer to prosecutors as 'our solicitor' (Hucklesby 1996: 218–19, 224). Despite all this, the two post-1997 Labour governments have followed the lead of the early to mid-1990s Conservative governments in introducing ever-more Draconian anti-bail laws. Although these are likely to have little practical effect, as the ECHR does provide a safety net, they further legitimize crime control policy, practice, and rhetoric (Sanders and Young 2000: 528–30).

GUILTY PLEAS

Of those defendants whose cases proceed to a hearing, the overwhelming majority— around 60 per cent in the Crown Court and 94 per cent in the magistrates' courts— either plead guilty or fail to appear and are found guilty in their absence (Sanders and Young 2000: 396). Why do so many defendants give up their right to put the prosecution to proof? The nature of the legal profession, both its solicitor branch (McConville *et al.* 1994; Mulcahy 1994) and the Bar (Baldwin and McConville 1977; Morison and Leith 1992), is a major explanatory factor, although Sanders and Young (2000, 1994) argue that it is the wider system and wider society that shapes legal attitudes and practices (see also McConville and Mirsky 1988). What is beyond doubt is that, in both the United Kingdom and United States, police and prosecutorial pre-trial practices are geared in large part to securing guilty pleas. Confessions are particularly important, for it is difficult for suspects to contest, in court, the guilt that they admitted to the police earlier. Confessions, then, guarantee guilty pleas in all cases except those in which the prosecution are unable to establish (if challenged on the point by the defence) that the confession was not obtained through oppression, or as a result of something said or done that rendered the confession likely to be unreliable. This is less difficult than it sounds given that the police generally interview in pairs, which means that the circumstances in which a confession is made are not simply *one* person's word against another's. For as long as the law permits conviction on the basis of uncorroborated confession alone, the police will inevitably seek confessions without corroboration. The potential for police law-breaking (to secure confessions) and for false confessions (unverified by corroborative evidence but produced under pressure) is clear.

Defendants are encouraged to plead guilty through bargaining. Explicit plea bargaining over sentence with the judge is not permitted. However, courts are now urged by the Criminal Justice and Public Order Act 1994 (s 48) to 'take into account' guilty pleas, which they had done in practice for many years anyway. The 'sentence discount' is around 25–30 per cent, and plea sometimes determines not just the length but also the type of sentence. However, since no offences other than murder have fixed sentences in Britain, the difference between reducing sentence for a guilty plea and raising it for a not guilty plea is largely presentational. There has been some attempt to research the precise effect of guilty pleas on sentences, but the results are inconclusive (see discussion in Sanders and Young 2000: chapter 7; or research by Flood-Page and Mackie 1998, and by Henham 1999, 2000). Bargaining also takes place over the seriousness of the charge and over venue, for cases that are kept in the lower courts are generally sentenced more lightly, and courts have pre-trial reviews which aim, among other things, to promote plea bargaining.

We have seen that defence lawyers often fail to attend interrogations, sending to suspects the due process message that it is the court, not police questioning, which is important (Sanders et al. 1989). However, this facilitates crime-control practices at the police station, and hence confessions, leaving little for the defence lawyer to do in court other than to mitigate on a guilty plea and to bargain. Baldwin, in a study of pre-trial reviews, showed that defence lawyers frequently provide information to the prosecution which they need not, agree not to press their case when it might succeed, and agree to 'lean on' or 'pressure' their clients, or 'beat them over the head'. This is the message of other English research too (e.g., McConville et al. 1991, 1994). The result is a remarkably high guilty plea rate, achieved with the cooperation of the legal defence community. Inevitably, some innocent people plead guilty: over 10 per cent of guilty pleaders in the Crown Court claim to be innocent; in a similar number of cases the CPS believes that there would have been a reasonable chance of acquittal; and in around half of these cases—some 1,400 each year—claims of innocence are believed by the defendants' barristers (Zander and Henderson 1993).

We have seen that many defendants are jailed wrongly under the bail system and that many people are convicted wrongly under the guilty plea system. The more likely one is to be innocent, the more powerful are the pressures to plead guilty—one will be more fearful of custody, hence more likely to confess in exchange for bail, and weak cases are given greater sentence discounts than are strong cases. The RCCJ accepted the risk of the innocent sometimes pleading guilty because of 'the benefits to the system . . . of encouraging those who are in fact guilty to plead guilty' (1993: 111), although it underestimated the risks on scandalously thin grounds (McConville and Mirsky 1994). Moreover, the production of confessions and guilty pleas hides the absence of legal grounds in many cases for arrest, detention, and prosecution; this encourages 'fishing expeditions' by the police, which impact not only on the legally guilty (whether factually so or not) but also on those held without charge (or prosecuted and acquitted) who should never have been deprived of their liberty without reasonable suspicion in the first place (McBarnet 1981; McConville et al. 1991; McConville and Mirsky 1992, 1995). Lastly, the system has discriminatory effects: since black defendants contest their cases more often than do white defendants, they get heavier sentences (Hood 1992). Yet the pressures to plead guilty are increasing rather than decreasing. Less serious cases are now 'fast-tracked', which includes pressure to finish the case at the first hearing—almost inevitably, by guilty plea. This 'Narey' reform gives little time to the police (to prepare a file, so the evidence will not always be complete), to the CPS (to consider that evidence), and to the defence lawyer, if there is one (to consider what plea to advise) (Bridges 1999). And at the time of writing, the government appears determined to abolish the defendant's right to opt for jury trial in cases of medium seriousness, even though Parliament rejected its first attempt to do this. One effect of this would be to force many cases that currently go to the Crown Court to stay in the magistrates' courts. Since the conviction rate in the latter is higher than that in the former, this will increase the pressure to plead guilty while doing little about the causes of the problem ostensibly responsible for the reform: cases in which defendants opt for contested Crown Court trials but which 'collapse' before trial. Bridges argues that this happens largely when the CPS agrees to reduce charges only at the last minute, and that many more relatively trivial cases go to Crown Court because magistrates send them there than because defendants 'play the system' (Bridges et al. 1999; Bridges 2000).

REVIEWING INJUSTICE

Criminal justice systems, like any human systems, need reviewing mechanisms, for some degree of fallibility is inevitable. There are four types of mechanisms: preventive; punitive; compensatory; and restitutionary. They can operate in relation to two types of injustice: abuse of power; and wrongful conviction. Preventive mechanisms were envisaged by the RCCP as a necessary counterweight to the extra powers it wished to grant to the police and which became PACE. They include custody officer reviews of detention, and the review function of the CPS. We have seen that these are of little value in this respect. The jury could be seen as a review mechanism of more importance because of their independence. Thus juries sometimes acquit on grounds of 'equity' (i.e., in the face of strict legal rules) because they believe that the police or state have behaved oppressively. But we should not exaggerate the role of the jury. As we have seen, enormous efforts are made to avoid jury trial, by securing trials in magistrates' courts and/or guilty pleas. Little more than 1 per cent of defendants are tried by jury in the United Kingdom, and even in these cases the judge is enormously influential (Sanders and Young 2000: 570–78; Winter 2002). And while juries sometimes prevent wrongful conviction, they cannot prevent any of the many abuses of power documented earlier—such as stop/search, detention, and remand in custody— and the extent to which they deter such oppressive behaviour must be slight given the tiny proportion of cases they handle.

The other main preventive mechanism in respect of wrongful convictions is the exclusion in court of unlawfully obtained evidence. Only unreliable or oppressively obtained confession evidence is automatically excluded. Trial courts have discretion to hear unfairly obtained evidence, e.g., from unlawful stops, police-car interrogations, and after denial of access to a solicitor. The working rules used by courts to decide what to allow are difficult to determine. Although the courts exclude more evidence now than was the case before PACE, and do so more often than critics expected, in many cases where the right to legal advice is obstructed the decision to allow the evidence is upheld (Hunter 1994; Sharpe 1998). Neither courts nor Parliament adopt the American 'fruit of the forbidden tree' doctrine that is the hallmark of due process. Instead the emphasis is on the probative value of evidence, however it was obtained (up to a point): the crime control doctrine. Like jury trials, the exclusion of evidence can help only the small minority of defendants who contest their cases. However, there is a punitive element here too. In so far as evidence is *sometimes* excluded because it was obtained unfairly or oppressively, the police are punished in a round-about way for their abuse of power, especially if an acquittal results. It is arguable that the most powerful influence on police interrogation practices, making them adopt less overtly intimidatory tactics, is the trend towards exclusion of evidence (Sanders and Young 2000: 703–24).

There are three other punitive mechanisms available, all concerned with the abuse of power rather than with wrongful convictions. The first is the complaints and discipline procedure. Despite the introduction of the 'civilian' Police Complaints Authority (PCA) in 1985, very few complaints are substantiated. In 1998/9, a typical year, only 745 complaints were substantiated—8.1 per cent of the complaints which were investigated, but only 2.3 per cent of those initially made (Cotton and Povey 1999). The difference in these figures is because of withdrawn complaints, something that often happens because of police pressure (Maguire and Corbett 1991). There are three possible explanations for the low level of substantiation: that most complaints are unjustified; that most police investigations (and PCA scrutiny) are biased; and that evidence of malpractice cannot be obtained in most cases. The first two explanations are doubtless partially true. Regarding bias, the discrediting process discussed by Box and Russell (1975) in relation to the pre-PCA system is unaffected by changes in the structure of supervision, for all complaints are still investigated by the police them-selves. The PCA is in the same position as is the CPS vis-à-vis investigating police officers. Rather than reinvestigate, the PCA simply peruses a carefully constructed document. Most complainants interviewed by Maguire and Corbett thought 'that the PCA was on the side of the police' (1991: 176), and this is reiterated in more recent general opinion surveys (Harrison and Cuneen 2000).

The complaints system fails all due process tests (openness, not allowing officials to be judges in their own cause, giving all parties a fair hearing, and so forth) and fails to deter the police from crime control practices in general and law-breaking in particular, as even the RCCJ acknowledged. Like the rest of the system, black and working-class people seem to bear the brunt of its failings. This should be surprising only if we see incidents that give rise to complaints as the products of pathological 'bad apples'. If they are on the contrary regarded as normal reflections of policing practice (Goldsmith 1991), both the behaviour complained of and the closing of ranks preventing a high proportion of substantiation, are to be expected (Irving and Dunnighan 1993). Moreover, as in other contexts, officers do not see the 'black letter' of the law as the dividing line between acceptable and unacceptable behaviour. As Maguire (1992) notes, police investigators probably do not consciously try to exonerate officers who 'overstep the mark', but 'the mark' is not a clear or unchanging line. It depends on the circumstances at the time, the police working rules being pursued, and the characteristics of the complainant. Eventually, most of this has become accepted by government and the police themselves, especially in the wake of the Stephen Lawrence scandal of the late 1990s in which the Establishment finally admitted both that the police are 'institutionally racist' and that, as a result, ethnic minorities are thereby unjustly treated. Some changes were made to the system in 1999, but the whole system is due to be overhauled (Home Office 2000). Whether change will be cosmetic, as in the past, or more radical, remains to be seen (Sanders and Young 2000: 683–703). Doubtless the 'civilian' element of the system will be increased, but, as the experience of other countries shows, this is no panacea (Goldsmith and Lewis 2000).

It is not surprising to find that many people are deterred from complaining and instead prosecute or sue the police. Prosecutions are rare for obvious reasons, not least because few types of police malpractice are actually criminal; however, prosecutions were brought (unsuccessfully) against some of the officers in the Birmingham Six case. Prosecutions are occasionally initiated by the DPP following invocation of the complaints procedure, but this happened in only thirty eight cases in 1998–9 (Cotton and Povey 1999). Increasingly, aggrieved complainants or relatives of people who die in police custody are challenging DPP decisions to not prosecute police and prison officers (or to prosecute on relatively trivial charges), sometimes successfully. This suggests that the DPP is over-cautious in deciding not to prosecute, in contrast to cases where the police are the complainants and the socially marginalized are the accused (where companies are the accused, even where there are deaths, there is a similar reluctance to lay serious charges) (Slapper 1999; Burton 2001). Punitive damages can be awarded in civil proceedings, and juries are becoming increasingly outraged at police behaviour. In a notable case in 1996 (some four years after being punched, kicked, racially abused, and illegally detained for ninety minutes), Kenneth Hsu was awarded £220,000 in punitive damages. Significantly, and typically, the officers remained unpunished and undisciplined, and in 1997 the Court of Appeal stated that the maximum sum that could be awarded for abuse of police power was £50,000. Hsu's damages were reduced to £35,000. However, the Court rejected the police case that the complaint mechanism was the appropriate way of dealing with malpractice and that therefore no punitive damages should be awarded at all (Dixon and Smith 1998). Proceedings are expensive, lengthy, and difficult to win, but civil claims nonetheless increased in number throughout the 1980s and 1990s, indicating the inadequacy of the other available remedies. Wrongful arrest and false imprisonment are traditional claims in tort, but PACE created no new torts or crimes. Thus the 'right' to a lawyer is not a real right, for there is no court action available to enforce it or to seek compensation for its denial. The same is true of most unlawful interrogation (Sanders 1988b), the caution guidelines, and the Code for Crown Prosecutors. It seems that it is more important to protect property, reputation, and tranquillity than it is to protect the civil liberties of 'police property'. Unlike the complaints system, court-based remedies are open and complainant-driven, as distinct from being police-driven, but their disadvantages render them equally ineffective in preventing or punishing miscarriages of justice.

The final review mechanism is restitutionary, i.e. returning suspects and defendants to the position they were in before being abused or wrongfully convicted. This is impossible in relation to the abuse of power, but wrongful convictions can be overturned by the appeal courts. Again, though, this channel is blocked to the majority who plead guilty unless the plea was not made freely. As with police powers, a formalistic notion of 'free will' is adopted by the courts, which ignores the real-life pressures to plea bargain. Of not guilty pleaders in the magistrates' courts, about 7 per cent appeal against conviction, of whom fewer than one-third succeed. Only about 4 per cent of not guilty pleaders in the Crown Court manage to appeal, of whom fewer than half succeed (Sanders and Young 2000: 619, 634). These figures reflect the enormous obstacles put in the way of defendants who want to appeal. The Court of Appeal justifies these rules by claiming deference to the jury, but it is quite happy to interfere with jury verdicts in respect of the quantum of damages for victims of police malpractice. The Criminal Cases Review Commission, an independent body set up under the Criminal Appeals Act 1995, has a remit of investigating cases in which appeal procedures are exhausted, referring back to the appellate courts those in which miscarriages are suspected to have occurred. However, it suffers many of the same structural flaws as the PCA, so too much should not be expected of it, and the Court of Appeal will remain a hurdle (Walker and Starmer 1999).

CONCLUSION

Criminal justice continually evolves in response to new ideas, new pressures, new scandals, and deeper socio-economic and political changes (Garland 2001). No system corresponds exactly with any one theoretical model, and there are always gaps between rhetoric, rules, and reality. Thus we have seen a largely due process-based rhetoric, rules which (often incoherently) combine both crime control and due process, and a largely crime control reality. Even in court the presumption of innocence is compromised by the erosion of the right of silence, the guilty plea system, and bail systems whereby most decisions are made on the basis of police information.

The gap between many legal rules and the working rules of the police shows that the law appears to exert little moral force on the police. If legal rules were enforced rigorously it is not clear whether crime would be less well controlled. It depends on how successful the police (and associated agencies) are in establishing actual guilt and innocence. The infamous miscarriages of justice of the last twenty years raise serious doubts about this, as do the less dramatic findings of research on unsuccessful stops, NFAs in the police station, questionable cautioning decisions, and the failure of cases in court. Just because due process is a suspect-oriented way of establishing 'truth', it does not follow that it is a less effective one. As it is, law-breaking by the police and lesser failures of due process are tolerated by a system which fails to punish and deter the police, or to compensate most victims of those practices. It is argued by some (such as Maguire 2002) that changes to legal rules can radically change police practices rather than simply do so at the margin. These critics point to an apparent effect of PACE on changes in interrogations, leading to 'ethical interviewing', less informal interviewing, fewer confessions, and a drop in convictions. Early indications do suggest that there is some truth in this. However, the effect is, first, seen in the speedy response of government to erode the right of silence, thus returning to the police their eroded interrogation power; and, secondly, to displace crime control activity to another part of the system. Proactive policing—including the use of informants, surveillance, and bugging—is an increasingly important part of the police armoury. This is even less controllable and of less visibility than interrogation (Colvin 1998; Sanders and Young 2000: 737–41; for a European perspective, see Field and Pelser 1998; for an American perspective, see Marx 1988). Whether the crime control reality of criminal justice is primarily a product of bureaucratic pressures or societal structures remains an open question, but the results are clear. Patterns of bias on the street, particularly concerning class and race, are reproduced throughout the system, so that in the prisons black and working-class people in particular are grossly over-represented.

Cynicism about criminal justice abounds. The complaints system lacks credibility. Police rule-breaking is not regarded as deviant. The police discipline 'toe rags' without judicial authority or oversight. Lawyers treat their clients with disdain. Suspects are not a sub-set of the wider criminal population; rather, criminals are a sub-set of the wider (official) suspect population. How closely this relates to the 'actually guilty' population must remain a matter of speculation, but any close relationship could well be coincidental. For we suggest that the criminal justice system is not geared solely to detecting and punishing criminal activity. It—and its modern arm, the police—has always been at least as concerned with high-level politics and low-level disorder; that is, with the control of the less powerful. It follows that, contrary to the rhetoric of the crime control model, the interests of victims (especially less powerful victims) are furthered where this fits in with broader working rules, but not necessarily otherwise (Roach 1999, Garland 2001). This is certainly the implication of Gregory and Lees' (1996) research, which found a high attrition rate in sexual assault cases (on the treatment of victims in general by the criminal justice system, and the limited effectiveness of ostensibly victim-oriented reforms, see Zedner, in Chapter 13 of this volume; Sanders and Young 2000: 741–5). The social integration and exclusion approach should, in future, help us to understand these processes more than any other model, for according to this approach the system prioritizes authority and control over the less powerful—above justice, the Rule of Law, and the interests of victims—for victims can be the victims of exclusionary criminal justice practices as much as of criminal practices (Sanders 2002).

Prospects for change depend in part on one's view of the reasons for the failure of criminal justice to live up to its rhetoric. Bureaucratic explanations, which focus on the values of particular institutions, produce more optimistic scenarios than do societal ones. They also depend on the impact of changes to criminal justice processes, about which we know too little. There has been an explosion of criminal justice research in the last twenty years, but most of it is 'top-down', trying to solve the system's problems; very little has been 'bottom-up', asking what it feels like for suspects and defendants. Research should pay more attention to the experiences of suspects, to the lessons to be drawn from Northern Ireland, and to the linking of theoretical, policy, and empirical questions (Hudson 1993). When it has done this—notable examples are those of Hillyard 1993; Carlen 1996; Loader 1996; Choongh 1997—the results are illuminating.

Only rarely is the fundamental question 'why prosecute?' asked in relation to the police. Prosecution often does too much and too little: in many cases it does too much by stigmatizing offenders and driving a wedge between them and their victims; and it does too little to protect victims from re-offending. In other cases it does too much by putting the victim through the ordeal of the court process and too little by allowing a plea bargain, discontinuance, or acquittal which minimizes the harm done to the victim. For victims and defendants alike, a reintegrative approach would be more effective and less alienating than the punitive, dichotomous approach embodied in prosecution. Since victims are generally less punitive than the tabloid media would have us believe, this might be widely welcomed. So there is scope for the development of cautioning schemes and more extensive restorative 'caution-plus' initiatives under which offenders, victims, and their respective 'supporters' come together to discuss the harm caused by an offence and how this might be repaired (see Zedner, in Chapter 13 of this volume). Traditional police cautioning is sometimes used in a far from 'welfarist' way. Lee (1995) describes many cautioning processes as 'degradation ceremonies', her accounts of which sound similar to the accounts of the humiliation of 'toe rags' in the custody room provided by Choongh (1997) and the non-prosecution processes of the DSS (Cook 1989). We do not know how typical are Lee's findings, or those of Choongh, because too few people care about how suspects and defendants are treated to fund the research that would enable us to find out. The early findings on 'restorative cautioning' indicate significant and welcome shifts in police practice, but also raise concerns that a traditional police agenda may dominate restorative encounters, leaving offenders and victims almost as marginalized as before in some cases (Young and Goold 1999; Young 2001). This fits with our argument that prosecution processes and many diversionary processes are currently exclusionary. The question 'why prosecute?' is a question that could be asked only from an inclusionary perspective. The question is at least implicitly asked in one sphere of criminal justice: 'white-collar' law enforcement. Here, inclusionary policies are adopted by non-police agencies. They avoid prosecution and the other trappings of crime control such as arrest, detention, oppressive interrogation, and so forth. Instead they use techniques of 'compliance'. It is hardly credible that these differences are the product of bureaucratic pressures or accident. Present practice reflects processes of inclusion for 'white-collar criminals' and processes of exclusion for the poor, deprived, and powerless. This is a society in which some of the most damaging criminals are treated in the most humane ways, while those who are arguably society's victims are treated as society's enemies so that, in time, they live up to their labels. It remains to be seen whether the recent enthusiasm for restorative justice will result in more inclusionary, freedom-enhancing ways of responding to street-level crime, or simply create new sites for unaccountable extensions of state power wielded to exclusionary ends.

Selected further reading

There are now several texts on criminal justice, many of which cover sentencing and penal policy as well as the earlier stages discussed in this chapter. Most take either a 'legal' or a 'social policy' approach. Two texts which integrate legal and sociological material, and which do not discuss sentencing and penal policy, are A. Ashworth, *The Criminal Process*, 2nd edn (Oxford: Oxford University Press, 1998) and A. Sanders and R. Young, *Criminal Justice*, 2nd edn (London: Butterworths, 2000). These books utilize contrasting theoretical frameworks, as explained in the opening section of this chapter. A good socio-legal combination of text and original materials, which also includes a detailed sentencing section, is M. Wasik, T. Gibbons, and M. Redmayne, *Criminal Justice* (London: Longman, 1999). For a detailed legal treatment, see K. Lidstone and C. Palmer, *The Investigation of Crime—A Guide to Police Powers*, 2nd edn, (London: Butterworths, 1996).

Among the edited collections, N. Lacey (ed.), *Criminal Justice* (Oxford: Oxford University Press, 1994) provides a very broad selection of previously published articles and book extracts. C. Walker and K. Starmer (eds), *Miscarriages of Justice: A Review of Justice in Error* (London: Blackstone Press, 1999) take miscarriages of justice as their theme. All the chapters are written for the volume but summarize the salient issues arising from the main stages of the pre-trial and trial process. R. Young and D. Wall's *Access to Criminal Justice* (London: Blackstone Press, 1996) also contains specially written chapters, but they are focused on legal aid and the legal profession. The newest collection is M. McConville and G. Wilson (eds), *The Handbook of the Criminal Justice Process* (Oxford: Oxford University Press, 2002), which also contains specially written chapters on all aspects of the system.

Among the monographs in this area of work, D. McBarnet, *Conviction* (London: Macmillan, 1981) is still well worth reading for its analysis of the relationship between legal rules and the reality of the criminal justice system. Lawyers receive critical scrutiny from M. McConville, J. Hodgson, L. Bridges, and A. Pavlovic, *Standing Accused* (Oxford: Oxford University Press, 1994). Recent high-quality monographs which blend theory with strong empirical analysis include I. Loader, *Youth, Policing and Democracy* (Basingstoke: Macmillan Press, 1996), C. Hoyle, *Negotiating Domestic Violence* (Oxford: Clarendon, 1998), and S. Choongh, *Policing as Social Discipline* (Oxford: Clarendon, 1997). For the international state of the art in restorative justice, see A. Morris, and G. Maxwell, (eds), *Restorative Justice for Juveniles* (Oxford: Hart, 2001). The Royal Commission on Criminal Justice, which reported in 1993, came in for a considerable amount of critical scrutiny. Two edited collections are by M. McConville and L. Bridges (eds), *Criminal Justice in Crisis* (Aldershot: Edward Elgar, 1994) and S. Field and P. Thomas (eds), *Justice and Efficiency?* (Oxford: Blackwell, 1994).

References

ASHWORTH, A. (1991), 'Videotaping in Police Stations', *New Law Journal*, 141: 1512–16.

—— (1998), *The Criminal Process*, 2nd edn, Oxford: Oxford University Press.

BALDWIN, J., and BEDWARD, J. (1991), 'Summarizing Tape Recordings of Police Interviewing', *Criminal Law Review*: 671–9.

—— and McCONVILLE, M. (1977), *Negotiated Justice*, Oxford: Martin Robertson.

BECKER, H. (1963), *Outsiders: Studies in the Sociology of Deviance*, New York: Free Press.

BELLONI, F., and HODGSON, J. (2000), *Criminal Injustice*, Basingstoke: Macmillan.

BIRCH, D. (1999), 'Suffering in Silence?', *Criminal Law Review*: 769–88.

BITTNER, E. (1967), 'The Police on Skid-Row: A Study of Peace-keeping', *American Sociological Review*, 32: 699–715.

BLAND, N., MILLER, J., and QUINTON, P. (2000) *Upping the PACE? An evaluation of the recommendations of the Stephen Lawrence Inquiry on stops and searches*, Police Research Series Paper 128, London: Home Office.

BLOCK, B., CORBETT, C., and PEAY, J. (1993), *Ordered and Directed Acquittals in the Crown Court*, London: HMSO.

BOX, S., and RUSSELL, K., (1975), 'The Politics of Discreditability: Disarming Complaints Against the Police', *Sociological Review*, 23: 315–46.

BRIDGES, L. (1999), 'False Starts and Unrealistic Expectations', *Legal Action*, 6 October: 6.

—— (2000), 'Taking Liberties', *Legal Action*, 6 July: 8.

——, CHOONGH, S., and McCONVILLE, M. (1999), *Ethnic Minority Defendants and the Right to Jury Trial*, London: CRE.

BROWN, D. (1997), *PACE Ten Years On: A Review of the Research*, Home Office Research Study No. 155, London: HMSO.

—— and ELLIS, T. (1994), *Policing Low Level Disorder*, Home Office Research Study No. 135, London: HMSO.

—— and LARCOMBE, K. (1992), 'Changing the Code: Police Detention under the Revised PACE Codes of Practice', Home Office Research Study No. 129, London: HMSO.

BUCKE, T., and BROWN, D. (1997), *In Police Custody: Police Powers and Suspects' Rights under the Revised PACE Codes of Practice*, Home Office Research Study No. 174, London: HMSO.

—— STREET, R., and BROWN, D. (2000), *The Right of Silence: The Impact of the CJPO 1994*, Home Office Research Study No. 199, London: HMSO.

BURROW, J. (2000), 'Bail and the Human Rights Act 1998', *New Law Journal*, 150: 677–84.

BURTON, M. (2001), 'Reviewing CPS Decisions not to Prosecute', *Criminal Law Review*: 374.

CAMERON, M. (1964), *The Booster and the Snitch*, New York: Free Press.

CARLEN, P. (1996), *Jigsaw: A Political Criminology of Youth Homelessness*, Buckingham: Open University Press.

CHAN, J. (1996), 'Changing Police Culture', *British Journal of Criminology*, 36: 109–34.

CHATTERTON, N. (1976), 'Police in Social Control', in J. King (ed.), *Control without Custody*, Cambridge: Institute of Criminology.

CHERRYMAN, J., and BULL, R. (2000), 'Reflections on Investigative Interviewing', in F. Leishman, B. Loveday, and S. Savage, (2000), *Core Issues in Policing*, London and New York: Longman.

CHOONGH, S. (1997), *Policing as Social Discipline*, Oxford: Clarendon Press.

CLARKSON, C., CRETNEY, A., DAVIES, G., and SHEPHERD, J. (1994), 'Criminalising Assault', *British Journal of Criminology*, 34: 15–29.

COHEN, S. (1985), *Visions of Social Control*, Cambridge: Cambridge University Press.

COLVIN, M. (1998), *Under Surveillance—Covert Policing and Human Rights Standards*, London: JUSTICE.

COOK, D. (1989), *Rich Law, Poor Law*, Milton Keynes: Open University Press.

COTTON, J., and POVEY, D. (1999), *Police Complaints and Discipline, 1998–9*, Statistical Bulletin 17/99, London: Home Office.

CRETNEY, A., and DAVIS, G (1996), 'Prosecuting Domestic Assault', *Criminal Law Review*: 162–74.

CRISP, D., WHITTAKER, C., and HARIS, J. (1994), *Public Interest Case Assessment Schemes*, Home Office Research Study No. 138, London: HMSO.

DAMASKA, E. (1973), 'Evidentiary Barriers to Conviction and Two Models of Criminal Procedure: A Comparative Study', *University of Pennsylvania Law Review*, 121: 506–89.

DIXON, B., and SMITH, G. (1998), 'Laying Down the Law: The Police, the Courts and Legal Accountability', *International Journal of the Sociology of Law*, 26: 419.

DIXON, D., (1991), 'Common Sense, Legal Advice, and the Right of Silence', *Public Law*: 233–54.

—— (1992), 'Legal Regulation and Policing Practice', *Social and Legal Studies*, 1: 515.

——, BOTTOMLEY, A., COLEMAN, C., GILL, M., and WALL, D. (1989), 'Reality and Rules in the Construction and Regulation of Police Suspicion', *International Journal of the Sociology of Law*, 17: 185–206.

——, ——, ——, and ——, (1990), 'Safeguarding the Rights of Suspects in Police Custody', *Policing and Society*, 1: 115–40.

DOHERTY, M., and EAST, R. (1985), 'Bail Decisions in Magistrates' Courts', *British Journal of Criminology*, 25: 251–66.

DRIVER, P. (1968), 'Confessions and the Social Psychology of Coercion', *Harvard Law Review*, 82: 42–61.

DUFF, P. (1993), 'The Prosecutor Fine and Social Control', *British Journal of Criminology*, 33: 481–503.

—— (1997), 'Diversion from Prosecution into Psychiatric Care', *British Journal of Criminology*, 37: 15–34.

—— (1998), 'Crime Control, Due Process and "The Case for the Prosecution"', *British Journal of Criminology*, 38: 611–15.

EASTON, S. (1998), *The Case for the Right of Silence*, Aldershot: Ashgate.

ERICSON, R. (1981), *Making Crime*, London: Butterworths.

EVANS, R. (1992), 'The Conduct of Police Interviews with Juveniles', Royal Commission on Criminal Justice, Research Study No. 8, London: HMSO.

—— and FERGUSON, T. (1991), *Comparing Different Juvenile Cautioning Systems in One Police Force*, London: Home Office, unpublished report.

FAULKNER, D. (1996), *Darkness and Light*, London: Howard League.

—— (2001), *Crime, State and Citizen: A Field Full of Folk*, Winchester: Waterside Press.

FIELD, S., and PELSER, C. (1998), *Invading the Private: State Accountability and New Investigative Methods in Europe*, Aldershot: Dartmouth.

—— and SOUTHGATE, P. (1982), *Public Disorder*, Home Office Research Study No. 72, London: HMSO.

—— and THOMAS, P. (eds) (1994), *Justice and Efficiency?*, Oxford: Blackwell.

FITZGERALD, M. (1993), 'Ethnic Minorities and the Criminal Justice System', Royal Commission on Criminal Justice, Research Study No. 20, London: HMSO.

FLOOD-PAGE, C., and MACKIE, A. (1998), *Sentencing Practice: an Examination of Decisions in Magistrates Courts and the Crown Court in the mid-1990s*, Home Office Research Study No. 180, London: Home Office.

GARLAND, D. (2001), *The Culture of Control*, Oxford: Oxford University Press.

GELLER, W., and TOCH, H., (eds) (1996), *Police Violence*, New Haven, Conn.: Yale University Press.

GELSTHORPE, L., and GILLER, H. (1990), 'More Justice for Juveniles: Does More Mean Better?', *Criminal Law Review*, 153–64.

GOLDSMITH, A., (ed.) (1991), *Complaints against the Police: A Comparative Study*, Oxford: Oxford University Press.

GOLDSMITH, A., and LEWIS, C. (ed.) (2000), *Civilian Oversight of Policing: Governance, Democracy and Human Rights*, Oxford: Hart.

GOLDSTEIN, J. (1960), 'Police Discretion not to Invoke the Criminal Process: Low Visibility Decisions in the Administration of Justice', *Yale Law Journal*, 69: 543.

GREGORY, J., and LEES, S. (1996), 'Attrition in Rape and Sexual Assault Cases', *British Journal of Criminology*, 36: 1–17.

GUDJONSSON, G., and MacKEITH, J. (1982), 'False Confessions', in A. Trankell (ed.), *Reconstructing the Past*. Deventer: Kluwer.

—— and—— (1988), 'Retracted Confessions: Legal, Psychological and Psychiatric Aspects', *Medicine, Science, and the Law*, 28: 187–94.

HARRISON, J., and CUNEEN, M. (2000), *An Independent Police Complaints Commission* London: Liberty.

HENHAM, R. (1999), 'Bargain Justice or Justice Denied? Sentence Discounts and the Criminal Process', *Modern Law Review*, 63: 515.

—— (2000), 'Reconciling Process and Policy: Sentence Discounts in the Magistrates' Courts', *Criminal Law Review*: 436–51.

HILLYARD, P. (1993), *Suspect Community*, London: Pluto.

—— and GORDON, D. (1999), 'Arresting Statistics: The Drift to Informal Justice in England and Wales', *Journal of Law and Society*, 26: 502–22.

HODGSON, J. (2001), 'The Police, the Prosecutor and the Juge d'Instruction: Judicial Supervision in France, Theory and Practice', *British Journal of Criminology* 41: 342–61.

HOLDAWAY, S. (1983), *Inside the British Police*, Oxford: Blackwell.

HOME OFFICE (1990), *The Cautioning of Offenders*, Circular No. 59/1990, London: Home Office.

—— (2000), *Complaints Against the Police—A Consultation Paper*, London: Home Office.

HOOD, R. (1992), *Race and Sentencing*, Oxford: Oxford University Press.

HOYLE, C. (1998), *Negotiating Domestic Violence*, Oxford: Clarendon Press.

HUCKLESBY, A. (1994), 'The Use and Abuse of Conditional Bail', *Howard Journal*, 33: 258.

—— (1996), 'Bail or Jail', *Journal of Law and Society*, 23: 213–33.

—— and MARSHALL, E. (2000), 'Tackling Offending on Bail', *Howard Journal*, 39: 150–70.

HUDSON, B. (1993), *Racism and Criminology*, London: Sage.

HUNTER, M. (1994), 'Judicial discretion: s. 78 in practice', *Criminal Law Review*: 558.

HUTTER, B. (1988), *The Reasonable Arm of the Law? The Law Enforcement Procedures of Environmental Health Officers*, Oxford: Oxford University Press.

IRVING, B. (1980), *Police Interrogation: A Study of Current Practice*, London: HMSO.

—— (1985), 'Research Into Policy Won't Go', in E. Alves and J. Shapland (eds), *Legislation for Policing Today: The PACE Act*, Leicester: Leicester University Press.

—— and DUNNIGHAN, C. (1993), 'Human Factors in the Quality Control of CID Investigations', Royal Commission on Criminal Justice, Research Study No. 21, London: HMSO.

KEITH, M. (1993), *Race, Riots and Policing*, London: UCL Press.

KERSHAW, C., KINSHOTT, G., MATTINSON, J., MAYHEW, P., and MYHILL, A. (2000), *The 2000 British Crime Survey*, Home Office Statistical Bulletin, Issue 18/00, London: Home Office.

LAING, J. (1995), 'The Mentally Disordered Suspect at the Police Station', *Criminal Law Review*: 371.

—— (1999), *Care or Custody? Mentally Disordered Offenders in the Criminal Justice System*, Oxford: Oxford University Press.

LEE, M. (1995), 'Pre-court Diversion and Youth Justice', in L. Noaks (ed.) (1995), *Contemporary Issues in Criminology*, Cardiff: University of Wales Press.

LENG, R. (1992), 'The Right to Silence in Police Interrogation', RCCJ Research Study No. 10, London: HMSO.

LEO, R. (1994), 'Police Interrogation and Social Control', *Social and Legal Studies*, 3: 93.

LITTLECHILD, B. (1995), 'Re-assessing the Role of the Appropriate Adult', *Criminal Law Review*: 540.

LOADER, I. (1996), *Youth, Policing and Democracy*, Basingstoke: Macmillan Press.

MACPHERSON, SIR WILLIAM (1999), *The Stephen Lawrence Inquiry*, Cm 4262-I, London: Stationery Office.

MCBARNET, D. (1981), *Conviction*, London: Macmillan.

MCCONVILLE, M. (1992), 'Videotaping Interrogations: Police Behaviour on and off Camera', *Criminal Law Review*: 522–48.

—— and BRIDGES, L. (eds) (1994), *Criminal Justice in Crisis*, Aldershot: Edward Elgar.

—— and HODGSON, J. (1992), 'Custodial Legal Advice and the Right to Silence', RCCJ Research Study No. 16, London: HMSO.

——, ——, BRIDGES, L., and PAVLOVIC, A. (1994), *Standing Accused*, Oxford: Oxford University Press.

—— and MIRSKY, C. (1988), 'The State, the Legal Profession, and the Defence of the Poor', *Journal of Law and Society*, 15: 342–60.

—— and —— (1992), 'What's in the Closet: The Plea Bargaining Skeletons', *New Law Journal*, 142: 1373–81.

—— and —— (1994), 'Re-defining and Structuring Guilt in Systemic Terms', in M. McConville and L. Bridges (eds), *Criminal Justice in Crisis*, Aldershot: Edward Elgar.

—— and —— (1995), 'The Rise of Guilty Pleas', *Journal of Law and Society*, 22: 443–74.

——, SANDERS, A., and LENG, R. (1991), *The Case for the Prosecution*, London: Routledge.

——, ——, and —— (1997), 'Descriptive or Critical Sociology', *British Journal of Criminology*, 37: 347–58.

MAGUIRE, M. (1992), 'Complaints against the Police: Where Now?', unpublished paper.

—— (2002), 'Regulating the police station: the case of the Police and Criminal Evidence Act 1984', in M. McConville and G. Wilson (eds), *The Handbook of the Criminal Justice Process*, Oxford: Oxford University Press.

—— and CORBETT, C. (1991), *A Study of the Police Complaints System*, London: HMSO.

—— and NORRIS, C. (1992), *The Conduct and Supervision of Criminal Investigations*, RCCJ Research Study No. 5, London: HMSO.

MAIR, G., and LLOYD, C. (1996), 'Policy and Progress in the Development of Bail Schemes in England and Wales', in F. Paterson (ed.), *Understanding Bail in Britain*, London: HMSO.

MARX, G. (1988), *Undercover: Police Surveillance in America*, Berkeley, Cal.: University of California Press.

MEEHAN, A. (1993), 'Internal Police Records and the Control of Juveniles', *British Journal of Criminology*, 33: 504–24.

MHLANGA, B. (2000), *Race and the CPS*, London: Stationery Office.

MILLER, J., BLAND, N., and QUINTON, P. (2000), *The Impact of Stops and Searches on Crime and the Community*, Police Research Series Paper 127, London: Home Office.

MOODIE, S., and TOMBS, J. (1982), *Prosecution in the Public Interest*, Edinburgh: Edinburgh University Press.

MORGAN, P. (1996), 'Bail in England and Wales: Understanding the Operation of Bail', in F. Paterson (ed.), *Understanding Bail in Britain*, London: HMSO.

—— and HENDERSON, P. (1998), *Remand Decisions and Offending on Bail*, Home Office Research Study No. 184, London: Home Office.

MORISON, J., and LEITH, P. (1992), *The Barrister's World*, Oxford: Oxford University Press.

MORRIS, A., and MAXWELL, G. (eds), (2001), *Restorative Justice for Juveniles*, Oxford: Hart.

MOSTON, S. (1992), 'Police Questioning Techniques in Tape Recorded Interviews with Criminal Suspects', *Policing and Society*, 3.

—— and STEPHENSON, G. (1993), 'The Questioning and Interviewing of Suspects outside the Police Station', Royal Commission on Criminal Justice, Research Study No. 22, London: HMSO.

——, ——, and WILLIAMSON, T. (1992), 'The Effects of Case Characteristics on Suspect Behaviour during Police Questioning', *British Journal of Criminology*, 32: 23–40.

—— and WILLIAMSON, T. (1990), 'The Extent of Silence in Police Interviews', in S. Greer and R. Morgan (eds), *The Right to Silence*, Centre for Criminal Justice, Bristol: University of Bristol.

MULCAHY, A. (1994), 'The Justifications of Justice', *British Journal of Criminology*, 34: 411–30.

MURPHY, D. (1986), *Customers and Thieves*, Farnborough: Gower.

MVA and MILLER, J. (2000), *Profiling Populations Available for Stops and Searches*, Police Research Series Paper 131, London: Home Office.

NAREY, M. (1997), *Review of Delay in the Criminal Justice System*, London: Home Office.

NEWBURN, T., and HAYMAN, S. (2002), *Policing, Surveillance and Social Control*, Cullompton, Devon: Willan.

NOAKS, L. (ed.) (1995), *Contemporary Issues in Criminology*, Cardiff: University of Wales Press.

NORRIS, C. *et al.* (1992), 'Black and Blue: an Analysis of the Influence of Race on Being Stopped by the Police', *British Journal of Sociology*, 43: 207.

O'MAHONEY, P. (1992), 'The Kerry Babies Case: Towards a Social Psychological Analysis', *Irish Journal of Psychology*, 13: 223.

PACKER, H. (1968), *The Limits of the Criminal Sanction*, Stanford, Cal.: Stanford University Press.

PALMER, C. (1996), 'Still Vulnerable After All These Years', *Criminal Law Review*: 633–44.

PANTAZIS, C., and GORDON, D. (1997), 'TV Licence Evasion and the Criminalisation of Female Poverty', *Howard Journal of Criminal Justice*, 36: 170.

PATERSON, F., and WHITAKER, C. (1994), *Operating Bail*, Edinburgh: HMSO.

—— and —— (1995), 'Criminal Justice Cultures: Negotiating Bail and Remand', in L. Noaks (ed.), *Contemporary Issues in Criminology*, Cardiff: University of Wales Press.

PHILLIPS, C., and BROWN, D. (1998), *Entry into the Criminal Justice System*, Home Office Research Study No. 185, London: Home Office.

POLLARD, C. (1996), 'Public Safety, Accountability and the Courts', *Criminal Law Review*: 152–61.

QUINTON, P., BLAND, N., and MILLER, J. (2000), *Police Stops, Decision-making and Practice*, Police Research Series Paper 130, London: Home Office.

RAINE, J., and WILLSON, M. (1997), 'Police Bail with Conditions', *British Journal of Criminology*, 37: 593–607.

REINER, R. (2000), *The Politics of the Police*, 3rd edn, Oxford: Oxford University Press.

REISS, A. (1971), *The Police and the Public*, New Haven, Conn.: Yale University Press.

ROACH, K. (1999), *Due Process and Victim's Rights*, Toronto, Toronto University Press.

ROYAL COMMISSION ON CRIMINAL JUSTICE (1993), *Report*, London: HMSO.

ROYAL COMMISSION ON CRIMINAL PROCEDURE (1981), *Report*, London: HMSO.

SANDERS, A. (1985a), 'Class Bias in Prosecutions', *Howard Journal of Criminal Justice*, 24: 176–99.

—— (1985b), 'Prosecution Decisions and the Attorney-General's Guidelines', *Criminal Law Review*: 4–19.

—— (1988a), 'The Limits to Diversion from Prosecution', *British Journal of Criminology*, 28: 513–32.

—— (1988b), 'Rights, Remedies and the PACE Act', *Criminal Law Review*: 802–12.

—— (1996a), 'Access to Justice in the Police Station', in R. Young and D. Wall (eds), *Access to Criminal Justice*, London: Blackstone Press.

—— (ed.) (1996b), *Prosecutions in Common Law Jurisdictions*, Aldershot: Dartmouth.

—— (2002), 'Victim Participation in Criminal Justice and Social Exclusion', in C. Hoyle and R. Young (eds), *New Visions of Crime Victims*, Oxford: Hart.

——, BRIDGES, L., MULVANEY, A., and CROZIER, G. (1989), *Advice and Assistance at Police Stations and the 24 Hour Duty Solicitor Scheme*, London: Lord Chancellor's Department.

——, CREATON, J., BIRD, S., and WEBER, L. (1997), *Victims with Learning Disabilities: Negotiating the Criminal Justice System*, Occasional Paper No. 17, Oxford: Centre for Criminological Research.

—— and YOUNG, R. (1994), 'The Rule of Law, Due Process and Pre-trial Criminal Justice', *Current Legal Problems*, 47: 125–56.

—— and —— (2000), *Criminal Justice*, 2nd edn, London: Butterworths.

SCARMAN, LORD (1981), *The Scarman Report: The Brixton Disorders*, London: HMSO.

SCOTT, M., and LYMAN, S. (1968), 'Accounts', *American Sociological Review*, 33: 46–62.

SHAPLAND, J., and VAGG, J. (1988), *Policing by the Public*, London: Routledge.

SHARPE, S. (1998), *Judicial Discretion and Criminal Investigation*, London: Sweet & Maxwell.

SLAPPER, G. (1999), *Blood in the Bank: Social and Legal Aspects of Death at Work*, Aldershot: Ashgate.

—— (2001), *Organisational Prosecutions*, Aldershot: Ashgate.

—— and TOMBS, S. (1999), *Corporate Crime*, Harlow: Longman.

SMITH, D. (1997), 'Case Construction and the Goals of the Criminal Process', *British Journal of Criminology*, 37: 319–46.

—— (1998), 'Reform or Moral Outrage', *British Journal of Criminology*, 38: 616–22.

—— and GRAY, J. (1983), *Police and People in London*, Aldershot: Gower.

SOFTLEY, P. (1980), *Police Interrogation: An Observational Study in Four Police Stations*, London: HMSO.

STEER, J. (1980), *Uncovering Crime: The Police Role*, London: HMSO.

STEVENS, P., and WILLIS, C. (1979), *Race, Crime, and Arrests*, Home Office Research Study No. 58, London: HMSO.

STONE, V., and PETTIGREW, N. (2000), *The Views of the Public on Stops and Searches*, Police Research Series Paper 129, London: Home Office.

TONRY, M. (1995), *Malign Neglect: Race, Crime and Punishment in America*, New York: Oxford University Press.

TUCK, M., and SOUTHGATE, P. (1981), *Ethnic Minorities, Crime and Policing*, Home Office Research Study No. 70, London: HMSO.

TYLER, R.T. (1990), *Why Do People Obey the Law?*, New Haven, Conn., and London: Yale University Press.

WALKER, C., and STARMER, K. (1999) (eds), *Miscarriages of Justice*, London: Blackstone Press.

—— and WALL, D. (1997), 'Imprisoning the Poor: TV Licence Evaders and the Criminal Justice System', *Criminal Law Review*: 173–86.

WALKLEY, J. (1987), *Police Interrogation*, Police Review, London: HMSO.

WILCOX, A. (1972), *The Decision to Prosecute*, London: Butterworths.

WILKINSON, C., and EVANS, R. (1990), 'Police Cautioning of Juveniles: The Impact of Home Office Circular 14/1985', *Criminal Law Review*: 165–76.

WILLIS, C. (1983), *The Use, Effectiveness, and Impact of Police Stop and Search Powers*, Research and Planning Unit Paper No. 15, London: Home Office.

WINTER, J. (2002), 'The truth will out? Judicial summings up in the trials of Rose West and Myra Hindley', *Social and Legal Studies* (forthcoming).

WOOLF, LORD JUSTICE (1991), 'Prison Disturbances April 1990', Report of an Inquiry by The Rt Hon. Lord Justice Woolf (Parts I and II) and His Honour Judge Stephen Tumim (Part II), Cm 1456, London: HMSO.

YOUNG, J. (1999), *The Exclusive Society*, London: Sage.

YOUNG M. (1991), *An Inside Job*, Oxford: Oxford University Press.

YOUNG, R. (2001), 'Just Cops Doing "Shameful" Business: Police-Led Restorative Justice and the Lessons of Research', in A. Morris and G.

Maxwell (eds), *Restorative Justice for Juveniles*, Oxford: Hart.

—— and GOOLD, B. (1999), 'Restorative Police Cautioning in Aylesbury: From Degrading to Reintegrative Shaming Ceremonies?', *Criminal Law Review*: 126–38.

—— and SANDERS, A. (1994), 'The Royal Commission on Criminal Justice: A confidence trick?', *Oxford Journal of Legal Studies*, 14: 435–48.

ZANDER, M. (1988), *Cases and Materials on the English Legal System*, London: Weidenfeld.

—— and HENDERSON, P. (1993), *Crown Court Study*, Royal Commission on Criminal Justice, Research Study No. 19, London: HMSO.

29

SENTENCING

Andrew Ashworth

The passing of a sentence on an offender is probably the most public face of the criminal justice process. This chapter discusses several aspects of the sentencing decision. It begins by pointing to the growing politicization of sentencing policy, a trend which threatens to marginalize principled and empirically-based arguments about sentencing. The chapter does not follow that trend. It turns next to examine the various rationales for sentencing. There is then detailed discussion, in turn, of sentencing procedures, of custodial sentencing, and of non-custodial sentencing. In conclusion, possible directions for the reform of sentencing are considered.

SENTENCING AND POLITICS

The 1990s witnessed a sharp rise in the politicization of sentencing policy. As Downes and Morgan show (in Chapter 10 of this volume), the bipartisan approach to criminal policy was eroded in the late 1970s. The 1979 general election was won partly on a 'law and order' ticket. In the late 1980s, however, as the then government became more assured of its position, the opportunity was taken (under Douglas Hurd as Home Secretary) to create policies aimed at greater consistency and rationality in sentencing. When the Criminal Justice Act 1991 became law, there was little opposition in Parliament to its principal thrust, and no significant adverse comment in the newspapers (Windlesham 1993). The judges and some magistrates, however, objected to the fettering of the discretion they had previously enjoyed, objections which gained some strength from the abysmal drafting of parts of the 1991 Act. Their campaign was soon taken up more widely, and in 1993, a year of heightened media interest in law and order, the government brought forward legislation which abandoned some key pillars of the 1991 Act. The appointment of Michael Howard as Home Secretary brought 'law and order' to the very centre of party politics: he proclaimed that 'prison works', and introduced a range of measures including curtailment of the right of silence and major changes to the law on disclosure of evidence. A populist sentencing policy soon came to be thought politically advantageous for both major parties, with Howard leading the way and challenging the then Opposition to disagree, at peril of being called 'soft on crime'. When Howard proposed the introduction of mandatory sentences, the Labour Party did not oppose them, and it was largely left to the Lord

Chief Justice, other senior judges, and some bishops to force amendments in the House of Lords (see Dunbar and Langdon 1998; Ashworth 2001).

Under New Labour there has been a bewildering mixture of policies. Crime prevention has been a priority, and this has led to various rehabilitative initiatives ('accredited programmes') in the prisons and in the community. Some restorative elements have been introduced into youth justice, and for dealing with adults in some areas. At the same time, there is an abiding strain of severity, apparent both in the use of custody in the youth justice system and in the targeting of repeat offenders. Little official discontent has been expressed about the rising prison population (from 42,000 in early 1993 to 61,000 in 1997 and 70,000 in 2002): discussions about reducing the prison population, frequent in the 1980s, are rarely heard. The Halliday Report (2001) contains no thrust in that direction, and responds to the government's concerns about persistent offenders by proposing a presumption of greater severity for all recidivists.

RATIONALES FOR SENTENCING

The events of recent years can only sharpen interest in examining the justifications for sentencing in general and for particular sentencing policies. When a court passes sentence, it authorizes the use of state coercion against a person for committing an offence. The sanction may take the form of some deprivation, restriction, or positive obligation. Deprivations and obligations are fairly widespread in social contexts—e.g., duties to pay taxes, to complete various forms, etc. But when imposed as a sentence, there is the added element of condemnation, labelling, or censure of the offender for what has been done. In view of the direct personal and indirect social effects this can have, it calls for justification.

Much writing about the rationales of sentencing has focused on one or more particular justifications. In order to unravel punishment as a social institution, however, and to understand the tensions inherent in any given 'system', there is benefit in identifying the main thrusts of the several approaches. Among the issues to be considered are the behavioural and the political premises of each approach, its empirical claims, and its practical influence.

DESERT OR RETRIBUTIVE THEORIES

Retributive theories of punishment have a long history, including the writings of Kant and Hegel. In their modern guise as the desert approach, they came to prominence in the 1970s, to some extent propelled by the alleged excesses and failures of rehabilitative ideals (von Hirsch 1976; Bottoms and Preston 1980). Punishment is justified as the morally appropriate response to crime: those who commit offences deserve punishment, it is claimed, and the amount of punishment should be proportionate to the degree of wrongdoing. The justification for the institution of punishment also incorporates the consequentialist element of underlying general deterrence: without the restraining effect of a system of state punishment, anarchy might well ensue (see von Hirsch 1993). Some, notably Duff (2000), tie further consequentialist aims into a fundamentally retributivist justification, arguing that punishment ought not only to communicate justified censure but also thereby to persuade offenders to repentance, self-reform, and reconciliation. The behavioural premise of desert is that individuals are responsible and predominantly rational decision-makers. The political premise is that all individuals are entitled to equal respect and dignity: an offender deserves punishment, but does not forfeit all rights on conviction, and has a right not to be punished disproportionately to the crime committed.

Proportionality is the key concept in desert theory (cf. the critique by Bottoms 1998). Cardinal proportionality is concerned with the magnitude of the penalty, requiring that it not be out of proportion to the gravity of the conduct: five years' imprisonment for shoplifting would clearly breach that, as would a small penalty for a very serious offence. Social conventions and cultural traditions tend to determine the 'anchoring points' of the punishment scale, i.e. the contrasting levels at which sentences are set in different national or historical contexts (cf. Downes 1988 on The Netherlands and England at that time; Graham 1990 on Germany), although these conventions can change for various reasons. Ordinal proportionality concerns the ranking of the relative seriousness of different offences. In practice, much depends here on the evaluation of conduct, especially by sentencers, and on social assumptions about traditional or 'real' crime (e.g., street crime) compared with new types of offence (e.g., commercial fraud, pollution). In theory, ordinal proportionality requires the creation of a scale of values which can be used to assess the gravity of each type of offence: culpability, together with aggravating and mitigating factors, must then be assimilated into the scale. This task, which is vital to any approach in which proportionality plays a part, makes considerable demands on theory (see von Hirsch and Jareborg 1991; Ashworth 2000a: chapter 4); some would say that decisions on relative offence-seriousness can never be more than contingent judgements which bear the marks of the prevailing power structure.

DETERRENCE THEORIES

Deterrence theories regard the prevention of further offences through a deterrent strategy as the rationale for punishing. As an exercise of state power, sentencing can be justified only by its consequences. The quantum of the sentence depends on the type of deterrent theory. There is little modern literature on individual deterrence, which sees the deterrence of further offences by the particular offender as the measure of punishment. A first offender may require little or no punishment. A recidivist might be thought to require an escalation of penalties. The seriousness of the offence becomes less important than the prevention of repetition. Traces of this approach can certainly be detected in the treatment of persistent offenders in modern sentencing practice, including the mandatory and minimum sentences introduced in 1997 and the proposals of the Halliday Report (2001).

More attention has been devoted to general deterrence, which involves calculating the penalty on the basis of what might be expected to deter others from committing a similar offence. Major utilitarian writers such as Bentham (1789; cf. Walker 1991) and economic theorists such as Posner (1985) develop the notion of setting penalties at levels sufficient to outweigh the likely benefits of offending. The behavioural premise is that of responsible and predominantly rational, calculating individuals— a premise that criminologists may call into question. The political premise is that the greatest good of the greatest number represents the supreme value, and that the individual counts only for one: it may therefore be justifiable to punish one person severely in order to deter others effectively, thereby overriding the claims of proportionality. Satisfactory empirical evidence of the effect of deterrent sentencing on individual behaviour is difficult to obtain. Among other things, it is necessary to demonstrate that people are aware of the level of likely sentences; and that they desist from offending largely because of that sentence level and not for other reasons. A recent analysis of the general deterrence research by von Hirsch, Bottoms, Burney, and Wikström (1999) found that there is some evidence of a link between the *certainty* of punishment and crime rates, but considerably weaker evidence of a link between the *severity* of sentences and crime rates. This distinction is particularly important when marginal deterrence is the issue, i.e. not whether the threat of punishment deters (which it often does), but whether the threat of greater punishment would have greater deterrent effect. The authors discuss reasons why the commonsense belief that greater punishment would deter more cannot be accepted without substantial qualifications: it is heavily dependent on the context.

REHABILITATIVE SENTENCING

Sentencing aimed at the reformation of the offender's lawbreaking tendencies has a lengthy history, being evident in the early days of probation and of borstal institutions. The rationale here is to prevent further offending by the individual through the strategy of rehabilitation, which may involve therapy, counselling, intervention in the family, cognitive-behavioural programmes, skills training, etc. Still a leading rationale in many European countries, it reached its zenith in the United States in the 1960s, declined spectacularly in the 1970s, and then began to regain ground in the 1990s (see von Hirsch and Ashworth 1998: chapter 1). A humanitarian desire to provide help for those with obvious behavioural problems has ensured that various treatment programmes continue to be developed. The key issue is the effectiveness of various interventions, and there is a long-running debate about the concept and the measurement of effectiveness (e.g. Lloyd *et al.* 1994). The true position is probably that certain rehabilitative programmes are likely to work for some types of offender in some circumstances. The recent 'What Works?' movement has rekindled interest in various programmes for behaviour modification, with the development of 'accredited' programmes in prisons and as part of community sentences (see McGuire 1995; Vennard and Hedderman 1998).

The behavioural premise of rehabilitative theory is that some or many criminal offences are to a significant extent determined by social pressures, psychological difficulties, or situational problems of various kinds. The new drug treatment and testing order is a particular example of this; more generally, the links with positivist criminology are strong. The political premise is that offenders are seen as unable to cope in certain situations and as in need of help from experts, and therefore (perhaps) as less than fully responsible individuals. The rehabilitative approach indicates that sentences should be tailored to the needs of the particular offenders: in so far as this needs-based approach places no limits on the extent of the intervention, it conflicts with the idea of a right not to be punished disproportionately. Its focus instead is upon the processes of diagnosis, treatment, and the completion of accredited programmes. 'Diagnostic' tools such as the pre-sentence report are seen as essential to this approach to sentencing.

INCAPACITATIVE SENTENCING

The incapacitative approach is to identify offenders or groups of offenders who are likely to do such harm in the future that special protective measures (usually in the form of lengthy incarceration) should be taken against them. The discretionary sentence of life imprisonment has been used increasingly for this purpose, and the Criminal Justice Act 1991 authorized courts to go beyond proportionate sentences and to impose 'public protection' sentences for violent and sexual offenders who are considered likely to do serious harm (von Hirsch and Ashworth 1996). There was also an element of incapacitative reasoning behind the mandatory sentences of life imprisonment for second serious sexual or violent offences introduced by the Crime (Sentences) Act 1997.

The incapacitative approach has no behavioural premise. It is neither linked with any particular causes of offending nor dependent on changing the behaviour of offenders: it looks chiefly to the protection of potential victims. The political premise is often presented as utilitarian, justifying incapacitation by reference to the greater aggregate social benefit. It is sometimes said that in these cases the rights of potential victims are being preferred to the rights of the offenders. This notion of a conflict of rights attracted some discussion in the Floud Report, which also found that predictions of 'dangerousness' tended to be wrong more often than not (Floud and Young 1981); rather different analyses of the conflict of rights can be found in Bottoms and Brownsword (1982) and Wood (1988). The repeatedly-confirmed fallibility of predictive judgments (e.g., Brody and Tarling 1981; Monahan *et al.* 2001) calls into question the justification for any lengthening of sentences on grounds of public protection, and yet the political pressure to have some form(s) of incapacitative sentence available to the courts has been felt in most countries. If this is the reality of penal politics then there is surely a strong case for procedural safeguards to ensure that the predictive judgments are open to thorough challenge. None of the dangerousness provisions introduced by the 1991 Act and the Crime (Sentences) Act 1997 meet this requirement, since a court may pass such sentences without a medical report. Recent proposals for the special incarceration of certain 'dangerous' citizens, first proposed in the Dangerous People with Severe Personality Disorder Bill 1999 but not yet enacted, are open to many procedural and substantive objections: see McAlinden (2001); and Peay, in Chapter 21 of this volume.

RESTORATIVE AND REPARATIVE THEORIES

These are not regarded as theories of punishment. Rather, their argument is that sentences should move away from punishment of the offender towards restitution and reparation, aimed at restoring the harm done to the victim and to the community: see Zedner, in Chapter 13 of this volume. At the core of most restorative theories lies an emphasis on the significance of stakeholders in the offence (not just the state and the offender, but also the victim and the community), on the importance of process (bringing the stakeholders together in order to decide on the response to the offence), and on restorative goals (usually some form of reparation to the victim and 'restoration' of the community, and often extending to rehabilitation and reintegration of the offender). There are many variations of restorative justice in different countries, some established in law and others at an experimental stage, and an assessment cannot be given here (see Braithwaite 1999; Johnstone 2001; and Zedner, above). They are often based on a behavioural premise similar to rehabilitation for the offender, and also on the premise that the processes help to restore the victim; their political premise is that the response to an offence should not be dictated by the state but determined by all the interested parties, placing compensation and restoration ahead of mere punishment of the offender, and encouraging maximum participation in the processes so as to bring about social reintegration.

There are other victim-oriented initiatives which are not restorative but may be reparative in their goal. One that is widespread in both European and common law countries is to allow victims to submit a 'victim impact statement' to the court, detailing the effects of the crime from their point of view. Experiments with such statements have been conducted in England and, despite misgivings expressed in the report (Hoyle *et al.* 1998), Victim Personal Statements may now be submitted to all sentencing courts. It is debatable whether this change is either appropriate in principle or desirable in practice (cf. Erez 1999 with Sanders *et al.* 2001). In some countries the statement may also include the victim's opinion on the appropriate sentence, a development which raises deep questions about crimes as public and/or private wrongs (see Ashworth 1993; Ashworth 2000a: 317–21).

SOCIAL THEORIES

There has been a resurgence of writings which emphasize the social and political context of sentencing (see Duff and Garland 1994: chapter 1). Important in this respect are Garland's (1990) analysis of the theoretical underpinnings of historical trends in punishment, and Hudson's arguments (1987, 1993) in favour of a shift towards a more supportive social policy as the principal response to the problem of crime. Those who have been influenced by Hart's distinction (1968) between the general justifying aim of punishment (in his view, utilitarian or deterrent) and the principles for distribution of punishment (in his view, retribution or desert) should consider the challenge to this dichotomy in Lacey's work (1988). She argues that both these issues raise questions of individual autonomy and of collective welfare, and that, rather than denying it, we should address this conflict and strive to ensure that neither value is sacrificed entirely at either stage. In developing this view she explores the political values involved in state punishment and argues for a clearer view of the social function of punishing.

The political philosophy underlying the work of Braithwaite and Pettit (1990) is what they term republicanism, at the heart of which lies the concept of dominion. Its essence is liberty, not in the sense of simple freedom from constraint by others, but more in the form of a status of guaranteed protection from certain kinds of interference, based on a political compromise in which each citizen has participated. This leads them to propose that sentences should increase the dominion of victims with the least loss of dominion to the offenders punished. They gesture towards (vague) upper limits on severity, but not lower limits, and their view is that the censuring function of the criminal justice system can and should so far as possible be fulfilled by means other than punishment. Since dominion lays emphasis on reassuring citizens about the prospect of liberty, it might require long preventive sentences based on deterrence or incapacitation. There is thus no recognition of an individual's right not to be punished more than is proportionate to the seriousness of the crime: all depends on what will advance overall dominion, which might happen to be more or less in any individual case than the 'deserved' punishment (see further the debate in von Hirsch and Ashworth 1998: chapter 7).

APPRAISING THE RATIONALES

One of the aims of the Criminal Justice Act 1991 was to depart from the previous vagueness over sentencing aims—the 'cafeteria' system of sentencing—and to promote some clarity. Desert was installed as the primary rationale, except for the relatively rare cases where the conditions for imposing an incapacitative sentence for 'public protection' were met. Deterrence was not to be used to justify a disproportionately severe sentence. Rehabilitative considerations would be important when choosing among community orders of a similar severity, and would also serve as a justification for supervision after early release from custody. Compensation orders have priority over fines and not over custody. This legal framework was hardly conflict-free, but it established some parameters. However, the Lord Chief Justice quickly reinstated general deterrence as an aim in certain cases (*Cunningham* (1993) 14 Cr App R (S) 444); and Parliament has subsequently introduced mandatory and minimum sentences which have deterrence and incapacitation as their aims.

These developments make clear the socio-political basis for much sentencing policy. The above summary of several rationales, necessarily brief and omitting much of their richness, has referred to the behavioural and theoretical bases of each one. Doubts were expressed earlier about the efficacy of strategies of individual deterrence, general deterrence, and rehabilitation and incapacitation. In respect of the last two it may be possible to refine techniques for identifying suitable targets, but it is also important to note that the object of discussion is *marginal* preventive effects. Thus a sentencing system based on desert is likely to deter and incapacitate to a certain degree, and so the proponents of deterrent or incapacitative theories must seek to justify the search for extra increments of prevention, by reference to evidence of likely

success and the types of measure which must be adopted in order t
success. Given the absence of significant empirical evidence supporting
(cf. Walker and Padfield 1996: chapters 7, 22), the objective of m
mandatory and minimum sentences is chiefly the political survival o

Even if there were satisfactory evidence of efficacy, however, there ɪ-
about the rights involved in punishment—notably, those of victims and of offenders.
The victim's right to receive compensation from the offender is surely undoubted, but
in what circumstances should it give way to the offender's interest in not being utterly
impoverished for months or years to come? Should victims be allowed to express
an opinion on sentence to the court; or would this be unfair, subjecting offenders to
the varying attitudes (vindictive, sympathetic) of different victims? Should the state
continue to dominate punishment, or ought victims and communities to take
responsibility (cf. Gardner 1998 with MacCormick and Garland 1998)? What rights
should be accorded to offenders? Deterrence theory seems to regard individual
offenders as mere units in the overall calculation of social benefit; incapacitative
theory overrides the right not to be punished more than is proportionate to the
offence in certain situations, the definition of which is contentious; and rehabilitative
theory has often failed to recognize any such general right, especially when invoked in
support of indeterminate sentences. It may therefore be seen as a strength of desert
theory that it limits punishment to what is proportionate and proposes criteria for
determining proportionality. Some limits on state power out of respect for the rights
of the offender are proposed in the republicanism of Braithwaite and Pettit (1990)
and the communitarianism of Lacey (1988), although neither book works out the
detailed implications.

The choice of one or more rationales for punishment has no necessary connection
with the level of punitiveness in a sentencing system. The argument that desert theory
leads to harsh penalties is not sustainable on an international comparison (cf. Tonry
1996, chapter 1, with von Hirsch 1993, chapter 10). Indeed, many desert theorists have
argued throughout for lower severity levels. Desert theory has never established itself
in England and Wales, because the judges reintroduced deterrence as a legitimate
objective almost as soon as the 1991 Act came into force, and the government followed
suit subsequently (Ashworth 2001). The Halliday Report (2001) purports to reinforce
proportionality as the leading principle, but only by corrupting its definition so as to
include both proportionality to the seriousness of the offence and proportionality to
the seriousness of the offender's criminal history. The latter proposition is inconsistent
with most versions of desert theory, and cuts away one of its restraining pillars in
favour of a barely-concealed deterrent and incapacitative strategy.

THE MECHANICS OF SENTENCING

In this part of the chapter some basic elements of the law and practice of sentencing
are set out. The various stages of a criminal case are discussed, together with the
procedures which surround the sentencing stage itself.

THE SELECTION OF CASES FOR SENTENCE

It is a commonplace that the courts pass sentence for only a small proportion of the crimes committed in any one year. Findings from the 1997 British Crime Survey suggest that only some 45 per cent of offences committed are reported. Police recording practices reduce that figure, so that only 24 per cent of all offences are recorded as such. Since only one-fifth of these offences are 'cleared up' (i.e. traced to an offender) by the police, the figure is further reduced to just over 5 per cent of offences committed. By no means all those offences which are cleared up result in the taking of official action, perhaps because the suspected offender is too young, perhaps because the evidence is not sufficiently strong. This reduces to 3 per cent of all crimes the numbers proceeded with (Home Office 1999: 29). Overall about one-third of offenders are cautioned rather than prosecuted: that leaves 2 per cent of all offences in any one year which result in convictions and court sentences (see further Maguire, in Chapter 11 of this volume). This is not to suggest that sentencing is unimportant, for it may be thought to have a social or symbolic importance considerably in excess of the small proportion of crimes dealt with. But it does suggest the need for caution in assessing the crime-preventive effects of sentencing. Those theoretical rationales which look to the social consequences of sentencing may overestimate its potential for altering general patterns of behaviour.

   The selection of cases for sentence is not merely a quantitative filtering process. There are also various filters of a qualitative kind, some formal, some informal. The role of the regulatory agencies is significant: the Health and Safety Executive, the Environment Agency, and various other regulatory bodies do not record all breaches of the law as crimes (see, for example, Hawkins and Thomas 1984; Hutter 1997). These and other agencies, such as the Inland Revenue and the Customs and Excise, also have various means of enforcing compliance without resort to prosecution, such as warning notices or the 'compounding' of evaded tax and duty. For those offences reported to the police, decisions are formally regulated by National Standards. The low visibility of crucial decisions (whether to warn an offender informally, or to take no further action, or to administer a formal caution, or to prosecute) leaves the police with ample leeway to advance their own working priorities above the concerns of the formal guidelines (see Sanders and Young, in Chapter 28 of this volume). Where the police decide to prosecute, the Crown Prosecution Service (CPS) has the power to drop the case if the evidence is insufficiently strong, or if it is not in the public interest to proceed. The Code for Crown Prosecutors (4th edn, 2000) contains guidance on this decision and on choice of charge, which may in turn determine the level of court in which the case is heard (see below). At the stage of plea the true extent of negotiations is not known, but there is no shortage of empirical evidence that negotiation is a familiar part of justice in magistrates' courts (Baldwin 1985) and in the Crown Court (Riley and Vennard 1988). That this issue continues to cause concern is shown by the recent formulation of new 'guidelines' on 'the acceptance of pleas' (Attorney-General 2001), and the Auld Review of the Criminal Courts (2001) recommends graduated sentence discounts for early pleas of guilty.

   In summary, therefore, the offences for which the courts have to pass sentence are both quantitatively and qualitatively different from what might be described as the social reality of crime. The courts see only a small percentage of cases. Even if it may be assumed that these are generally the more serious offences, how they are presented in court may be shaped as much by the working practices and priorities of the police, prosecutors, and defence lawyers as by any objective conception of 'the facts of the case' (see also Sanders and Young, in Chapter 28 of this volume).

CROWN COURT AND MAGISTRATES' COURTS

Of the two levels of criminal court in England and Wales, the Crown Court deals with the more serious cases and the magistrates' courts with the less serious. The Crown Court sits as a trial court with judge and jury. Some two-thirds of Crown Court cases involve a guilty plea, and these are dealt with by judge alone, since juries have no part in sentencing. The most serious Crown Court cases are taken by a High Court judge on circuit, but the majority of cases are taken by a Circuit Judge (full-time), or by a Recorder or Assistant Recorder (part-time). The magistrates' courts are organized on a local basis: there are some 30,000 lay magistrates in England and Wales, and they usually sit in benches of three, advised by a justices' clerk. Typically a lay magistrate will sit in court one day a fortnight. There are also around 100 full-time district judges (formerly known as stipendiary magistrates), together with some who sit part-time. District judges are professionally qualified appointees, and they tend to be assigned the longer or more difficult cases. They used to sit mostly in metropolitan areas, but recently the number of appointees has increased (Morgan and Russell 2000). Radical changes to the above system are proposed by the Auld Review of the Criminal Courts (2001), notably the introduction of a new, unified criminal court, the insertion of a new middle tier of courts (the District Division) between the Crown Division and the Magistrates' Division, the staffing of the District Division by a district judge and two magistrates (with powers to pass sentences up to two years), and a consequent reduction in the availability of trial by jury.

If the Auld Report is implemented, defendants will not be able to determine the level of court in which their case is heard. In the present system, three categories of offence must be distinguished. Indictable-only offences are the most serious group, and may be dealt with only in the Crown Court. Summary-only offences are the least serious group, and may be dealt with only in the magistrates' courts. Between them lies the category of offences triable either way. These are offences of intermediate gravity, which will generally be tried in a magistrates' court unless either the defendant elects to be committed for Crown Court trial (an absolute right), or the magistrates decide that the case should be committed to the Crown Court. In 1996 Parliament introduced a new procedure of 'plea before venue', to ensure that defendants who intend to plead guilty at the Crown Court have the opportunity to be sentenced by magistrates if they thought fit. This resulted in a fall in committals to the Crown Court from around 20 per cent of all indictable offences in the mid-1990s to 15 per cent in 1999, with corresponding reductions in Crown Court waiting times.

Hand in hand with this continued transfer of business from Crown Court to magistrates' courts has been a movement to relieve magistrates' courts of many traffic cases by enabling the police to issue fixed penalty notices. Thus in 1999 some 77,000 defendants were tried in the Crown Court, some 1.9 million people were prosecuted in the magistrates' courts, and a further 7 million fixed penalty notices were issued.

MAXIMUM SENTENCES

Apart from a few common law offences which have no fixed maximum (e.g., manslaughter, conspiracy to outrage public decency), Parliament has generally provided the maximum sentence for each offence. Much statutory consolidation of criminal offences was completed in the mid-nineteenth century, and there have been several reforms of the criminal law in the last thirty years. As a result, maxima have been set at different times, in different social circumstances, and without any overall plan. Indeed, the statutory maxima set in the nineteenth century were much influenced by the traditional periods of transportation (Thomas 1978; Radzinowicz and Hood 1990: chapter 15).

Many had hoped that the Advisory Council on the Penal System would be able to improve the coherence of the system, but in its 1978 Report on *Sentences of Imprisonment: a Review of Maximum Penalties* it declined to revise the various statutory maxima, regarding the task as too controversial. Parliament therefore continues to assign and revise maximum penalties on a piecemeal basis: a recent example is provided by the various maxima for the racially aggravated crimes introduced by the Crime and Disorder Act 1998, which led the Court of Appeal to lay down guidelines in *Kelly and Donnelly* [2001] Crim LR 411.

THE RANGE OF AVAILABLE SENTENCES

Beneath the maximum penalty for the offence, the court usually has a wide discretion to choose among alternatives. In England and Wales the range of alternatives is wider than in most other jurisdictions, but before they are considered two general points should be noted. First, the tradition is to create maximum penalties in terms either of a period of custody, or an amount or level of fine: no offences have been assigned a community sentence as the maximum penalty. Secondly, since the mid-1960s there has been a tendency to enact broadly-defined offences with relatively high maximum penalties: for example, in England and Wales there is a single offence of theft with a maximum of seven years' imprisonment, whereas in many other European countries there are grades of theft with separate maxima. The English approach leaves sentencers with much greater discretion (see Thomas 1974).

At the lowest level, the range of available sentences begins with absolute and conditional discharges, and binding over. Fines come next, and a compensation order should be considered in every case involving death, injury, loss, or damage. At the next level come community sentences, of which there is a growing list (see below). Then come suspended sentences of imprisonment, and imprisonment itself. For offenders under the age of twenty-one, the custodial sentence takes the form of detention in a young offender institution; suspended sentences are unavailable; and attendance centre orders can be made. All these forms of sentence are discussed further below. There are separate orders for young offenders (see Chapter 16 of this volume) and for mentally disordered offenders (see Chapter 21 of this volume).

The many changes in sentencing law in the 1990s led to increasing confusion, and in 2000 Parliament consolidated most of the law in the Powers of Criminal Courts (Sentencing) Act. This statute brings together relevant provisions from previous legislation such as the Criminal Justice Act 1991, the Crime (Sentences) Act 1997, and the Crime and Disorder Act 1998. However, some of its provisions have already been overtaken by other statutes, such as the Criminal Justice and Court Services Act 2000.

DISCRETION IN SENTENCING

Alleged inconsistencies in sentencing have been a frequent cause for concern. This might seem an obvious consequence of the expanse of discretion left by fairly high maximum penalties and the wide range of available sentences. But there is a paradox here. Many sentencers seem to place more emphasis on the restrictions on 'their' discretion than on the choices that remain. Judges have been critical of the various limits which Parliament places on their powers, and of the duties imposed upon them. Courts are now under an obligation to consider making a compensation order in every case of death, injury, loss, or damage; and in drug trafficking cases a court is required to follow the prescribed statutory procedure for confiscation of the offender's assets—a procedure soon to be extended to all serious crimes by the (proposed) Proceeds of Crime Act 2002. Even before these restrictions began to appear in the 1980s, judges expressed themselves as having little choice in the sentences they passed: 'the least possible sentence I can pass . . .', 'I have no alternative but to . . .' (Oxford Pilot Study 1984: 53–54). To some extent this terminology may reflect the constraints imposed by Court of Appeal decisions, but it is more likely that it reflects self-generated constraints which stem from the attitudes and beliefs of the sentencer.

The paradox is that, despite these feelings of constraint, the sentencer's discretion is considerable in legal terms. The Criminal Justice Act 1991 sought to impose a new structure and new restrictions, but it left considerable room for judicial discretion in the length of custodial sentences, in the decision to impose custody or not, and among the various community orders. Magistrates' courts have upper limits on their powers (generally, six months' imprisonment), but otherwise the choice among alternatives is little affected by Court of Appeal decisions (of which few are relevant). Just as Hood (1962) showed that some benches are 'probation-minded' and others are not, so Tarling (1979) demonstrated that among the thirty courts he surveyed the use of probation varied between 1 and 12 per cent, suspended sentences between 4 and 16 per cent, fines between 46 and 76 per cent, and so on. Significant elements of these variations remained after account had been taken of the different 'mix' of offences coming before the courts (Tarling *et al.* 1985). As Hood found in his study of motoring cases (1972), membership of a particular bench tends to be a major determinant of a magistrate's approach to sentencing. The influence of magistrates' clerks, who generally undertake the initial training of new magistrates, may be considerable (Darbyshire 1999).

During the last decade the *Magistrates' Courts Sentencing Guidelines* (most recent edition 2000) have been used quite widely, but they are not legally binding. There are undoubtedly some spheres in which the power of local traditions, or certain justices' clerks and district judges, continues to be felt. Variations are also to be found in the Crown Court: following their survey of sentencing in both levels of courts in the mid-1990s, Flood-Page and Mackie (1998) found that 'attempts to predict sentences on the basis of case factors were not particularly successful,' indicating wide differences in the way that community sentences, in particular, were used. Findings of this kind lie behind the proposal in the Halliday Report (2001) for the introduction of comprehensive sentencing guidelines for all courts.

While discretion is important to enable sentencers to take account of the wide and varying range of factors that might be relevant, it does leave decision-making open to irrelevant influences (see Galligan 1986; Hawkins 1992). For example, Hood's 1992 study showed that at some courts black offenders are significantly more likely to receive custody than similarly situated white offenders. Hedderman and Gelsthorpe (1997) found detailed variations in the sentencing of men and women that cannot be explained by case factors, and show that sentencers' attitudes may explain why women are fined less frequently and given certain community sentences more frequently than men. Judges tend to argue strongly against any curtailment of 'their' discretion—an argument raised loudly against the mandatory and minimum sentences introduced in 1997—but rarely acknowledge the risks of discrimination, individual idiosyncrasy, and other irrelevant influences which accompany discretion that is not well structured or well monitored (see Hudson 1998).

INFORMATION ABOUT THE OFFENCE

Courts depend for their information on what they hear or what they are told. Since over 90 per cent of cases in magistrates' courts and around two-thirds of cases in the Crown Court are pleas of guilty, the information is usually constructed for the court by the prosecutor or others. The main source of information about the offence is likely to be the statement of facts which the prosecutor reads out. It will usually have been compiled by the police, and the way in which it describes or omits certain factors may reflect a particular view of the offence, or perhaps a 'charge-bargain' struck with the police (see Sanders and Young, in Chapter 28 of this volume; McConville *et al.* 1991: chapter 7). Sometimes the statement of facts may have been reconstructed, wholly or in part, by the prosecuting lawyer as a result of a change of plea or other negotiations: in *Beswick* [1996] Crim LR 62, it was held that the judge can require a '*Newton* hearing' (see below) if not satisfied that the facts as stated are true. In addition to the prosecution statement of facts, the court may gather further information about the offence from the defence plea in mitigation, and perhaps from a pre-sentence report. Any account of 'the facts' is likely to be selective, determined to some extent by the compiler's preconceptions. It is likely that judges and magistrates will be influenced by the selections made by those who inform them, as well as by their own preconceptions.

The prosecution's account of the facts may be disputed by the defence. In a trial there is usually an opportunity to resolve these matters, but this is not always so: some facts relevant to sentencing are irrelevant to criminal guilt. The greatest difficulty arises where the defendant pleads guilty but only on the basis of a more favourable version of the facts than the prosecution present. The courts have developed a procedure for resolving most such issues by means of a pre-sentence hearing, known as a 'Newton hearing' (after the leading case of Newton (1982) 4 Cr App R (S) 388), at which evidence is presented and witnesses may be heard. There is now a wealth of case law on the situations in which a 'Newton hearing' is necessary and on the procedures to be followed, but there remains a need for an authoritative commitment to the same evidentiary protections for the defendant as apply at the trial itself (Ashworth 2000a: chapter 11). The outcome can have a considerable effect on the length of a custodial sentence, and proper safeguards should therefore be insisted upon.

INFORMATION ABOUT THE OFFENDER

The court may obtain information about the offender from at least five sources: the police antecedents statement; the defence plea in mitigation; a pre-sentence report; a medical report; and the offender's own appearance in court.

The contents of the *antecedents statement* are regulated by a 1998 Practice Direction from the Lord Chief Justice. They are compiled by the police from the Police National Computer, and should always contain personal details and information about previous convictions and previous cautions. The purpose of a *defence plea in mitigation* is to show the offender and offence in the best light. In practice, it appears that a realistic recognition of any aggravating factors may improve the credibility of what is said in mitigation (Shapland 1981: chapter 5).

The purpose of a *pre-sentence report* is to assist the sentencer by providing information and analysis of offence, offender, and related matters. The form of the report is now regulated by National Standards for the Supervision of Offenders in the Community (2000): the four substantive sections of a report are to be titled 'offence analysis'; 'offender analysis'; 'risk to the public of re-offending'; and 'conclusions'. That last section should build upon the previous findings so as to make 'a clear and realistic proposal for sentence designed to protect the public and reduce re-offending, including for custody where this is necessary'. Any proposal for a community sentence should indicate the most appropriate form, and the available programmes which would meet the offender's perceived needs.

A *psychiatric report* is relatively rare, but a court may decide to call for one, and is obliged to obtain one before passing a custodial sentence if the defendant is or appears to be mentally disordered (see further Peay, in Chapter 21 of this volume). The impact of *the offender's own appearance* and demeanour in court is difficult to gauge, but judges recognize that they take account of it and tend to feel that sentencing would be even more difficult if they did not see the offender in person (Cooke 1987: 58; Oxford Pilot Study 1984: chapter 3). This fifth source of influence serves to demonstrate that the impact of the reports, etc., received by a court may be mediated by the attitudes of the sentencer (Shapland 1987).

REPRESENTATIONS ON SENTENCE

Some of what is said by an advocate making a defence plea in mitigation will bear directly on the sentence. It is well established that counsel has a duty to prevent the judge from passing an unlawful sentence by drawing the judge's attention to the relevant authority. Beyond that, it will usually be appropriate for counsel to remind the judge of any relevant sentencing guidelines, but it is still not always thought acceptable for counsel to cite other Court of Appeal decisions. If, as proposed in the Halliday Report (2001), there is a movement towards comprehensive sentencing guidelines, it is likely that these will become the focus of defence counsel's arguments on sentence.

The English tradition is that the prosecutor plays no part in sentencing, in the sense that no sentence is 'asked for' or recommended. It is sometimes assumed that such a practice would lead to higher sentences, although this has not been the outcome in The Netherlands, where prosecutors recommend sentences and judges rarely exceed the recommendation (Van Duyne 1987: 144–5).

APPEALS AGAINST SENTENCE

A person who is sentenced in a magistrates' court may appeal to the Crown Court. The appeal is usually heard by a judge sitting with two magistrates, and it takes the form of a re-hearing. The Crown Court is then empowered to pass any sentence which the magistrates' court could have imposed, whether more severe or more lenient than the original sentence. The possibility of a more severe sentence tends to discourage appeals. Fewer than 1 per cent of offenders appeal, mostly those who have been sentenced to custody.[1] Where there is a disputed point of law, the defendant may appeal to the Divisional Court by means of case stated or for judicial review.

A person sentenced in the Crown Court may appeal to the Court of Appeal (Criminal Division) on a point of law. Otherwise an offender may apply for leave to appeal against sentence to the Court of Appeal. Applications for leave to appeal are parcelled out to individual High Court judges: little is known about how these decisions are made. If an offender is granted leave to appeal, the Court will hear submissions, usually from defence counsel only, and increasingly including reference to other decided cases. The Court may substitute any sentence which is not more severe than the original sentence. Around 8 per cent of defendants sentenced in the Crown Court appeal, and about one-fifth of those appeals succeed.[2]

There is no prosecution appeal against sentence in England and Wales. Such appeals exist in several other European and Commonwealth countries, but the closest approximation in English law is the power of the Attorney-General to refer to the

---

[1] *Criminal Statistics 1999: Table 6.7.*
[2] ibid.

Court of Appeal cases in which the sentence is thought to be unduly lenient. The power, introduced by the Criminal Justice Act 1988, is now exercised in some seventy cases per year. The Court of Appeal may increase the sentence if it is found to have been so lenient as to fall outside the normal range for the offence, but any increase should take account of the 'double jeopardy' factor arising from offenders' uncertainty as to their fate (Shute 1999). These decisions also contribute to the corpus of sentencing guidance for lower courts.

THE SENTENCING ADVISORY PANEL

The Crime and Disorder Act 1998 added a new institution to English sentencing, the Sentencing Advisory Panel. Its main function is to formulate guidelines on sentencing and to submit them as advice to the Court of Appeal. The Court is not bound to adopt the Panel's advice: it declined to adopt the advice on environmental offences (in *R v Milford Haven Port Authority* [2000] 2 Cr App R (S) 423); adopted its advice on racially aggravated offences in modified form (*R v Kelly and Donnelly* [2001] Crim LR 411); and adopted its advice substantially on opium offences (*R v Mashaollahi* [2001] 1 Cr App R (S) 96) and on handling stolen goods (*R v Webbe* [2001] Crim LR 666).

The Panel must respond to a reference from the Court of Appeal (e.g., opium offences) or from the Home Secretary (e.g., environmental offences), and may itself decide to formulate guidelines on a particular offence (e.g., racially aggravated offences, handling stolen goods). It is required to take account of sentencing statistics and the cost and effectiveness of penal measures. It must consult both the public and an approved list of organizations, and issues a Consultation Paper for this purpose on **www.sentencing-advisory-panel.gov.uk**. The Panel has a much broader membership than the Court of Appeal, including three academics, three judges, three lay members with no criminal justice background, and others experienced in policing, probation, prisons, and magistrates' courts. It is a part-time body and its future is uncertain, following the recommendation in the Halliday Report (2001) in favour of comprehensive sentencing guidelines. Who should undertake the enormous task of formulating those guidelines? Should the consultation process required of the Panel be adopted by any new body?

ENGLISH SENTENCING PROCEDURES

From this brief review, three main themes emerge. First, it is evident that other actors, apart from judges and magistrates, exert considerable influence on the sentencing process. Not only do the police and prosecutors select and shape the cases which come to court, but they (together with probation officers and defence lawyers) provide the courts with information which they have selected and constructed. There may also be suggestions, implicit or sometimes explicit, as to sentence. Secondly, what courts may receive in terms of information about the offence and the offender, and representations on sentence, is governed mostly by court practice and judicial decisions. Apart from pre-sentence reports, there is little legislative intervention in the field. The judges themselves have developed '*Newton* hearings'. They could equally develop or modify other practices. And thirdly, there are several points at which the approach or attitude of the sentencer may be influential. Thus, despite the growth of legislation on sentencing, there remains considerable room for different approaches to be taken by particular judges or particular benches of magistrates. More research and analysis of the decision-making of sentencers is needed, to discover to what extent legal or other factors actually determine judicial sentencing.

CUSTODIAL SENTENCING

THE EVOLUTION OF A 'TARIFF'

Maximum sentences are generally high, and English law has only one mandatory minimum sentence,[3] and three minimum sentences introduced by the Crime (Sentences) Act 1997. Consequently most day-to-day sentencing practices are little affected by legislative constraints. For Crown Court sentencing some normal ranges or starting points have developed, often termed 'the going rate' by judges and 'the tariff' by others. Historically the idea of 'normal' sentences can be traced back at least as far as the 'Memorandum of Normal Punishments' drawn up by Lord Alverstone, the Lord Chief Justice, in 1901 (Thomas 1978; Radzinowicz and Hood 1990: 755–8). Since 1907 the Court of Criminal Appeal, and since 1966 its successor the Court of Appeal (Criminal Division), has adjusted and altered aspects of the tariff. Increased reporting of Court of Appeal decisions on sentencing has assisted the concretization of sentencing principles, and the publication of the first edition of Dr David Thomas's *Principles of Sentencing* (1970) was a landmark in the development of a common law of sentencing. In more recent years it has become normal practice for Court of Appeal judgments to refer to previous decisions.

It remains true, however, that the bulk of Court of Appeal decisions deal with fairly severe and long sentences, while relatively few decisions have a direct bearing on day-to-day sentencing in the Crown Court for the majority of offences, which tend to be thefts, burglaries, deceptions, and handling stolen goods. Here, the 'going rate' stems largely from court practice. There appears to be less sense of a 'going rate' for offences which attract non-custodial sentences. For lower courts the Magistrates' Association took the initiative in 1989 in promulgating its own sentencing guidelines, in an effort to fill the vacuum created by the lack of guidance from other quarters, and their successors are the Magistrates' Courts Sentencing Guidelines 2000.

STATUTORY RESTRICTIONS ON CUSTODIAL SENTENCES

One of the supposed aims of the Criminal Justice Act 1991 was to reduce the use of custodial sentences for low and medium range offences, and to replace them with community sentences. This did not happen: as the Halliday Report (2001) records,

---

[3] Twelve months' disqualification from driving on conviction for drunk driving.

sentences of under twelve months increased by 67 per cent between 1989 and 1999, from 27,000 to 45,000. The increase was greatest in the shortest sentences: sentences under three months went up by 167 per cent in that period, and those of three to six months by 89 per cent. It is therefore apparent that the provision in the 1991 Act, stating that a court should not impose custody unless the offence was 'so serious that only such a sentence could be justified' (now s 80, Powers of Criminal Courts (Sentencing) Act 2000), has had limited effect. For several years the courts interpreted this to mean that custody should not be imposed unless 'it would make right-thinking members of the public, knowing all the facts, feel that justice had not been done by the passing of any sentence other than a custodial one': *Cox* (1993) 96 Cr App R 452, at 455. This malleable test provided no real guidance, and it was removed by the Lord Chief Justice in *Howells* [1999] 1 Cr App R (S) 335. However, Lord Bingham then gave no further guidance, other than to say that there is no 'bright line' between custodial and non-custodial cases. More recently his successor, Lord Woolf, has urged judges and magistrates not to add to overcrowding in the prisons, and has advocated the greater use of community sentences for non-violent crimes: *Kefford, The Times*, 7 March 2002.

PROPORTIONALITY AND THE COURT OF APPEAL

A conventional 'going rate' for many offences has developed over the years, shaped and assisted by judgments of the Court of Appeal. The logic of the upper echelons of the tariff was considered by Lord Justice Lawton in his judgment in *Turner* (1975) 61 Cr App R 67, at 89–91. He started from the assumption that it would be absurd if an offender could receive a longer sentence for armed robbery than for murder itself. So he estimated the number of years that a murderer without mitigating circumstances could expect to spend in prison, and then ranged the sentences for other serious offences just beneath that. He took the period for the murderer as fifteen years in prison, equivalent to a determinate sentence of twenty-two years (less the one-third remission which obtained in 1975). Just beneath this notional twenty-two years he placed a number of 'wholly abnormal' offences, such as political kidnapping and bomb attacks. He then held that armed robbery should be placed at the next level down, yielding around eighteen years for the two offences in that case. This scheme continues to apply more or less to the upper end of the 'tariff', but the lower reaches are less well settled.

The Court of Appeal's greatest achievement in exercising its function of structuring discretion has been the formulation of 'guideline judgments'. Lord Lane, the Lord Chief Justice in the 1980s, would occasionally take a particular case and, rather than giving a judgment on the facts alone, would construct a judgment dealing with sentencing for all the main varieties of that particular crime. The first of these was in the case of *Aramah* (1982) 4 Cr App R (S) 407, where guidance was given on sentencing levels for the whole gamut of drugs offences, from large-scale trafficking down to possession of small amounts for individual use. This judgment was subsequently revised (in *Aroyewumi* (1995) 16 Cr App R (S) 211) so that its guidance is calibrated according to weight and purity level rather than estimates of 'street value', and parallel guidance for 'ecstasy' cases was given in *Warren and Beeley* [1996] 1 Cr App R (S) 233). A much-discussed guideline judgment is that in *Billam* (1986) 8 Cr App R (S) 48, on rape. The Lord Chief Justice established two starting points, of five years' and eight years' imprisonment, according to the presence or absence of certain factors. He went on to enumerate eight aggravating factors, three mitigating factors, and certain factors which courts should not take into account. The judgment has subsequently been extended to deal with cases of rape of a wife or former partner (in *W* (1993) 14 Cr App R (S) 256). However, the *Billam* guideline judgment says little about the relative effect to be given to the various aggravating factors, a failure which impairs its contribution to sentencing consistency (see Ranyard *et al.* 1994).

Guideline judgments are intended by the Lord Chief Justice to be binding on judges and magistrates, and it seems that they are so regarded. This method of guidance seems to have caused less judicial opposition than the systems in certain American states (see section below on 'International Patterns in Sentencing Reform'), probably because it has been developed *by* judges *for* judges, and because the guidance is in the familiar narrative form of a judgment. One advantage of guideline judgments is that they cover most manifestations of a particular crime at once, and produce more coherence than a series of separate judgments in different cases. There have, however, been three major disadvantages in the way they have been developed in this country: that there is no explicit linking of the separate punishment scales they establish; that relatively few such judgments have been delivered, covering only a small number of crimes; and that they have been formulated by the Court of Appeal, with its restricted membership and restricted perspectives. The creation of the Sentencing Advisory Panel addresses the last criticism directly, and its work has also begun to lead to an increase in guideline judgments. But it seems clear from the Halliday Report (2001) that there will be a move towards a rapid expansion in the number of sentencing guidelines. This will require the Panel or another body to address the first criticism directly, and to perform the task which has been studiously avoided over the years— that is, to try to shape all the guidelines into a coherent hierarchy of comparative severity.

AGGRAVATION AND MITIGATION

When courts are determining the seriousness of an offence, they should have regard to its aggravating and mitigating features. Flood-Page and Mackie (1998: 77) found that custody is significantly more likely in Crown Court cases where there is a breach of trust, the victim is elderly, or the offender is a ringleader, or the offence was planned, or a weapon was used, and there are Court of Appeal judgments supporting all these aggravating factors (see Ashworth 2000a: chapter 5.3). Among the mitigating factors recognized by the courts are various forms of reduced culpability (e.g., mental disturbance, financial pressures) and a good previous record. Courts also give mitigating effect to various factors that have no bearing on the offence or the offender's culpability—the collateral impact of the sentence on others, an act of heroism by the offender, the payment of compensation to the victim, or the giving of information to the police about other offenders (ibid.: chapter 5.5).

A frequent aggravating factor is a bad criminal record. The common law principle was that of progressive loss of mitigation: a first offender received substantial mitigation, which would be lost after the second or third conviction, but it would not be right to 'sentence on the record' and to impose a penalty disproportionate to the seriousness of the offence committed (ibid.: chapter 6). This principle appears to have succumbed to a silent eclipse during the 1990s: the Criminal Justice Act 1993 was taken by many sentencers as permitting them to sentence 'on the record' (as the statistics in Appendix 3 of the Halliday Report 2001 show), and the Court of Appeal has made no pronouncement on the subject since 1992. Sentences for repeat offenders have drifted upwards. The Halliday Report (2001) proposes that this movement should be strengthened, by providing sentencing guidelines which clearly indicate higher levels of sentence as the offender's previous convictions become more numerous or more serious. This policy seems to be based on deterrent and incapacitative claims which have not been substantiated, but it is one to which the government appears strongly committed. It remains to be seen whether the result will be the imprisonment of minor offenders for long periods, as with many previous initiatives on 'persistent offenders'.

Perhaps the most substantial mitigating factor is the plea of guilty, which can prompt a discount of up to one-third off the sentence: *Buffrey* (1993) 14 Cr App R (S) 511. In 1994 Parliament confirmed the importance of this discount by enacting a specific statutory requirement, as part of its strategy to persuade more defendants to plead guilty at an earlier stage (rather than on the morning of the trial, which wastes resources and inconveniences victims and witnesses). This requirement, now found in s 152 of the Powers of Criminal Courts (Sentencing) Act 2000, makes it clear that courts should give a graduated discount, according to the stage at which the guilty plea was entered. The *Magistrates' Courts Sentencing Guidelines* state: 'for a timely guilty plea allow a discount of about a third.' The annual volumes of Criminal Statistics (Tables 7C and 7D) show the guilty plea rates and average Crown Court sentences for different types of crime, although in practice there are considerable local divergences (Henham 1999; cf. Darbyshire 2000). Substantial discounts place enormous pressure on defendants to forgo the right to trial which goes with the presumption of innocence. Where defendants are advised that the discount may make the difference between a custodial and a non-custodial sentence, the risk of innocent people pleading guilty is particularly high.

MANDATORY AND MINIMUM SENTENCES

The introduction of mandatory and minimum sentences in 1997 followed a fierce battle between the Home Secretary and the senior judiciary. The government argued that such sentences would have deterrent and incapacitative effects. The judiciary pointed to low detection rates as undermining those effects, and also to the injustice of having to pass such sentences in inappropriate cases (see Dunbar and Langdon 1998: chapter 10; Ashworth 2001). These counter-arguments, together with the unpromising American evidence (Tonry 1996: chapter 5), had only limited effects. The Crime (Sentences) Act 1997 introduced the first mandatory and minimum sentences since the mandatory sentence of life imprisonment for murder, which has been the object of constant criticism (see Windlesham 1993: chapter 7; Windlesham 1996: chapter 9). However, each of the three new sentences (for details, see Henham 1998) is now much more flexible than was originally planned.

First, the mandatory sentence of life imprisonment for a second serious offence can be avoided only if the court finds 'exceptional circumstances'. This was intended to be interpreted narrowly: this is what the Court of Appeal did in *Kelly* [1999] 2 Cr App R (S) 176, and it subsequently found itself upholding life sentences in some manifestly inappropriate cases (such as *Buckland* [2000] Crim LR 308). Then the Human Rights Act 1998 came into force, and Lord Woolf CJ was able to hold, in *Offen (No. 2)* [2001] 1 Cr App R (S) 372, that the law would be inconsistent with the European Convention on Human Rights unless courts find 'exceptional circumstances' whenever there is insufficient evidence that the offender constitutes a significant danger to the public. This enables courts to avoid manifest injustice: it dilutes the law's mandatory force, although it remains a provision based on 'dangerousness'.

Secondly, a court is required to impose a minimum sentence of seven years for the third Class A drug trafficking offence, unless it would be 'unjust to do so in all the circumstances'. In fact most such offenders would receive at least seven years anyway, and therefore this minimum prescription has impinged little on sentencing practice.

Thirdly, a court is required to impose a minimum sentence of three years for the third domestic burglary conviction, so long as the offender is aged at least eighteen and each burglary was committed after the previous conviction for burglary. The law was brought into force in December 1999, and few burglars have yet brought themselves within the terms of the statute. In the coming years many offenders are likely to satisfy the conditions, and therefore attention will turn to two other aspects of the law. One is that, where there is a guilty plea, a court may reduce the minimum by 20 per cent: the thirty-six months minimum thus becomes just over twenty-eight months for most guilty pleaders. The other is that a court is not bound to impose the minimum it if would be 'unjust to do so in all the circumstances'. It is not yet clear how the courts will interpret this, but defence lawyers will urge them to use this exception wherever there is a significant mitigating factor.

'PUBLIC PROTECTION' SENTENCES

Although the 1991 Act was based on proportionate sentencing, it created one exception to that principle. Where a court is dealing with a sexual or violent offender, s 2(2)(b), now s 80(2)(b) of the 2000 Act, permits it to impose a longer than proportionate sentence (though within the statutory maximum) if that is 'necessary to protect the public from serious harm from the offender'. The Act defines the key terms, but does not require a court to consider a psychiatric report before imposing such a sentence. The Court of Appeal has developed some guidance on how this power should be exercised: it has quashed several longer than proportionate sentences, particularly where there was insufficient evidence that the offender would do 'serious harm' (e.g., *Thornton* [2000] 2 Cr App R (S) 47); but on other occasions has upheld such sentences on rather speculative reasoning (see von Hirsch and Ashworth 1996).

The Crime and Disorder Act 1998 introduced a further form of 'public protection' sentence, the extended sentence (now s 85 of the 2000 Act). An extended sentence is made up of two periods: the custodial term, which may be either a proportionate sentence or a longer-than-normal sentence under the provisions just considered; and the extension period, which is a period of extended licence in the community. The overall aim is to ensure that certain offenders (particularly sex offenders) receive lengthier supervision on release from custody, but both forms of 'public protection' sentence rest on contestable judgements about dangerousness.

CUSTODIAL SENTENCES AND EXECUTIVE RELEASE

One aspect of sentencing which is open to much public misunderstanding is the meaning of custodial sentences in terms of the time served. The system has changed several times in the last two decades, and seems likely to change again. Before the Criminal Justice Act 1991, the general principle was that every prisoner would have one-third deducted ('remission') from the sentence on starting a custodial sentence. From 1968, release on parole for part or all of the middle one-third of the sentence became possible too. The government made several changes to the effects of remission and parole during the 1980s, and the Carlisle Committee (1988) responded to judicial disquiet by proposing a new system.

This was implemented, more or less, by the Criminal Justice Act 1991. Remission was abolished. Parole was replaced by two systems of early release. All those serving terms of under four years are conditionally released after one-half, subject to serving the unexpired balance if they are convicted of another offence which was committed during the second half of the full sentence. Additionally, those serving between one and four years are subject to supervision on licence until the three-quarters point in their sentence. A system of discretionary conditional release was introduced for those serving four years and over, who may be so released after one-half of their sentence. Those not considered suitable for discretionary release are conditionally released after two-thirds of their sentence, and are then subject to supervision until the three-quarters point. Thus, while sentencing decisions may be based on proportionality, release decisions are based on risk. The risk assessments made by the Parole Board have been shown to be unduly conservative in many cases (Hood and Shute 2000).

One result of the 1991 Act was that every part of a custodial sentence counts for something. Conditional release means that the possibility of return to custody remains until the last day of the sentence pronounced in court. However, the Halliday Report (2001) raises concerns about the absence of compulsory supervision for those serving sentences under twelve months, and wishes to see supervision until the end of the nominal sentence for all offenders. The Report therefore proposes two new regimes to enhance supervision, support, and 'risk management' in the community. A new sentence of 'custody plus' would be introduced instead of sentences under twelve months: it would prescribe up to three months in custody, plus between six and nine months of supervision, with the possibility of recall to custody. For offenders sentenced to twelve months or longer, there would still be release after one-half, but the licence and supervision would continue until the end of the sentence. It is unclear how the courts would react to this reduction of their sentencing range for non-serious offenders: unless they accept its spirit, various forms of adaptive sentencing behaviour could emerge to undermine the scheme.

REVIEW OF POLICY AND PRACTICE

Two of the principal purposes of the 1991 Act were to install proportionality as the leading sentencing principle and to replace many shorter custodial sentences with demanding community sentences. Neither of these goals was achieved. Senior judges torpedoed the proportionality principle by reinstating deterrence as a sentencing rationale (in *Cunningham* (1993) 15 Cr App R (S) 444). The use of short prison sentences went up and up, as indeed did the use and length of prison sentences generally during the 1990s. We have seen that the prison population rose steeply from 42,000 in early 1993 to 58,000 in December 1996, and to 70,000 in early 2002 (for further analysis of imprisonment rates and international comparisons, see Morgan, in Chapter 30 of this volume). The judiciary and the magistracy tend to explain this as a response to what they regard as the climate of opinion in society, fuelled largely by political and media rhetoric rather than by carefully constructed opinion surveys. Thus Lord Bingham, when Lord Chief Justice, admitted that 'since 1993 the use of custody has increased very sharply, in response (it would seem) to certain highly publicised crimes, legislation, ministerial speeches and intense media pressure': *Brewster* [1998] 1 Cr App R (S) 181, at 184. In fact legislation had played only a small part. The courts used their discretion to increase the use of custody, not wishing to appear out of touch with the clamour of politicians and the media. Yet it is well known that the basis for this clamour does not lie in a well-founded public concern. There is strong evidence of widespread public misunderstanding about sentencing levels (Hough and Roberts 1998), and politicians and the media have generally seemed content to trade on this misunderstanding by calling for tougher sentences. Efforts to inform the public and to persuade the media towards greater responsibility have been few.

While it may thus be said that significant numbers of politicians, sentencers, and the media appear to agree about increased resort to imprisonment, this alliance breaks down when it comes to the question of method. Most judges categorically reject the need for mandatory sentences of any kind, and call for trust to be reposed in their discretion to impose the appropriate sentence for each individual case. This debate will be taken up again in the concluding part of the chapter, but it is relevant here to note that discretion has its disadvantages as well as its advantages. It is a good thing to avoid mechanical sentencing and rigid controls which prevent courts from taking account of particular factors in individual cases. But it is undesirable to allow different approaches that amount to discrimination on grounds of race (Hood 1992) or gender (Hedderman and Gelsthorpe 1997), or individual judges to pursue their own policies, or local courts to follow local traditions. And, most of all, since it was the judges and magistrates themselves who brought about the steep rise in custodial sentencing in the 1990s, there are deep questions about why and when sentence levels should be adjusted upwards or downwards by the collective exercise of discretion.

NON-CUSTODIAL SENTENCING

Thus far the focus has been on custodial sentencing, chiefly in the Crown Court. But the figures for 2000 show that, combining the numbers in magistrates' courts and the Crown Court, some 77 per cent of indictable offenders were dealt with by non-custodial sentences.

The scheme of the Criminal Justice Act 1991 is that the different forms of sentence should be regarded as a kind of pyramid, with courts requiring good reasons to move up from one stage to the next. At the lowest level come absolute and conditional discharges. At the next level come fines. Then a court may take the step up to a community sentence only if it is satisfied that the offence is serious enough to warrant this. And the step from community sentence to custody should be taken only if the court is of the opinion that the offence is so serious that only a custodial sentence can be justified.

There are relatively few Court of Appeal guidelines which include non-custodial measures in their ranges of sentences, but the *Magistrates' Courts Sentencing Guidelines*, last revised in 2000, have fines and community sentences as guidelines sentences for several types of less serious offence.

Table 29.1 Males aged 21 and over sentenced for indictable offences: percentage use of different sentences

	1975	1980	1985	1990	1995	2000
Discharge	9	7	9	13	15	13
Fine	55	52	43	43	34	28
Probation	6	5	7	7	11	11
Community Service	1	4	7	7	11	9
Combination Order	—	—	—	—	3	3
Suspended Imprisonment	13	12	12	10	1	1
Immediate Imprisonment	16	17	17	17	24	30
Total numbers sentenced	170,000	200,300	211,700	188,400	178,400	184,700

DISCHARGES

The least order a court can make on conviction is an absolute discharge. Such orders are usually reserved for cases of very low culpability, or where the offender is seriously ill, or where the court thinks the prosecution should not have been brought (Wasik 1985). A conviction followed by a discharge does not rank as a conviction for any other purposes. The same applies to a conditional discharge: however, the condition is that the offender is not convicted of another offence within a specified period (up to three years), and if there is such a conviction, the offender is liable also to be re-sentenced for the original crime. Conditional discharges are quite widely used,

Table 29.2 Females aged 21 and over sentenced for indictable offences: percentage use of different sentences

	1975	1980	1985	1990	1995	2000
Discharge	21	18	23	32	30	24
Fine	58	52	41	32	26	22
Probation	13	15	18	18	20	22
Community Service	0	2	3	4	7	8
Combination Order	—	—	—	—	3	3
Suspended Imprisonment	5	7	8	8	2	2
Immediate Imprisonment	3	4	6	6	10	16
Total numbers sentenced	39,600	43,300	38,400	30,500	26,800	33,600

amounting to some 13 per cent of adult male indictable offenders in 2000 and 24 per cent of adult female indictable offenders. Their use had increased considerably in the early 1990s, during the turmoil following the introduction of 'unit fines' and other changes under the 1991 Act, but levels are now returning to those of the late 1980s. Courts also have various powers to 'bind over' offenders, an order much used in some courts and little used in others.

FINES

Although the fine remains a much-used sentence, even for indictable offences, it has declined significantly in proportionate use in recent years—from 55 per cent in 1975 to 28 per cent in 2000 for adult males, and from 58 per cent to 22 per cent for adult females. The decline, often attributed to courts being reluctant to fine unemployed offenders or feeling it inappropriate to fine them small amounts, now suggests that courts are deliberately choosing more restrictive community sentences, and thus that levels of punitiveness have been ratcheted upwards.

In the 1991 Act the government attempted to revive the use of the fine and to increase its fairness by introducing 'unit fines' into magistrates' courts. This approach, modelled on the 'day fines' much used in other European countries, requires a considered separation of the seriousness of the offence (worth x units) from the offender's ability to pay (£y per unit). Unit fines were resisted by some courts, and sections of the media attacked them for relating the size of the fine to the means of offenders rather than to the offence. This was the very purpose of unit fines—to equalize the impact of fines on people of different means—but the government failed to defend the new approach and instead responded by abolishing the entire system of unit fines in the Criminal Justice Act 1993, returning to the broad principle that courts should take account of the financial circumstances of each offender. Courts are now relatively unfettered by legal requirements in calculating the amounts of fines.

A survey in 1996 found that while 83 per cent of areas used the Magistrates'

Association's guidelines, or a modified version of them, the remaining 17 per cent of areas used a form of unit fine. The research also found that courts using unit fines were more consistent and that they drew clearer distinctions in fine levels according to the incomes of offenders, whereas other courts often made little distinction between those on low and medium incomes (Charman *et al.* 1996). These findings suggest that a general exhortation to take account of the means of offenders is less effective than the more structured unit fine approach.

Great strides have been made, however, towards acceptance of the principle that someone whose offence was only adjudged serious enough for a fine should not be sent to prison for non-payment. The Crime (Sentences) Act 1997 introduced two alternatives to the use of custody for fine defaulters—short community service orders and curfew orders (with the further alternative of an attendance centre order if the offender is under twenty-five). Since then, the use of imprisonment for fine default has declined dramatically: whereas in 1994 almost 24,000 fine defaulters were committed to prison, the number was little over 5,000 by 1998. On 31 July 2001, there were thirty-three fine defaulters in prison.

COMPENSATION ORDERS

Although there were miscellaneous powers beforehand, the present compensation order was introduced in 1972. In 1982 courts were allowed to use it as the sole order in a case, and courts were required to give priority to a compensation order over a fine if the offender had limited means. Since 1988 courts have been required to consider making a compensation order in every case involving death, injury, loss, or damage, or to give reasons if no order is made. Notwithstanding this, the frequency of compensation orders has continued to decline over the last decade. In 1989 nearly 22,000 violent offenders were ordered to pay compensation by magistrates' courts, whereas in 1999 the figure was less than 10,000; in the Crown Court the number of orders in cases of violence halved from 4,700 to 2,300 over the same period. The decline may reflect the increased used of custody. In magistrates' courts the figure represented 43 per cent of all those sentenced in cases of violence in 1999; a higher proportion of cases of robbery (45 per cent, but rarely sentenced in magistrates' courts) and of criminal damage (51 per cent) resulted in compensation orders.

The contribution of compensation orders to greater justice for victims is important, but possibly more at a symbolic level than in terms of actual recompense for large numbers of victims: see further Zedner, in Chapter 13 of this volume. To some extent this is because compensatory principles inevitably come into conflict with other sentencing principles: for example, although compensation orders have priority over fines, the amount of a compensation order must still be reduced so as to be within the means of the offender. To some extent it is simply that few victims have the opportunity of receiving money from this source, because the offender must be detected, prosecuted, convicted, and in funds before a court can make a compensation order. It remains to be seen whether the arrival of elements of restorative justice, and the introduction of the reparation order, result in more victims receiving some compensation from their offenders.

COMMUNITY SENTENCES

In the 1980s and before, sentences such as probation and community service were officially described as alternatives to custody. This terminology did not assist in persuading courts to use them instead of custody, largely because they were not believed to be true alternatives. The 1991 Act introduced the term 'community sentence', emphasizing the demanding nature of 'punishment in the community' and the restrictions on liberty involved (see Brownlee 1998; Bottoms *et al.* 2001). The Act's scheme is that a court should not impose any community sentence unless satisfied that the offence is serious enough to warrant it: this is intended to convey the greater severity of community penalties as compared with discharges and fines. If the court decides that the case is serious enough, it should ensure that the community order or orders (a) are the most suitable for the offender, and (b) impose restrictions on liberty which are commensurate with the seriousness of the offence (Criminal Justice Act 1991, s 6). This scheme is designed to ensure that community sentences are proportionate, while allowing some room for choices among types of community sentence so as to reflect the perceived needs of the offender (Rex 1998). In most such cases a 'pre-sentence report' (see above) will have been prepared by the Probation Service to 'assist' the court.

The theory and practice of community sentences are discussed by Raynor in Chapter 31 of this volume, and so only a brief outline of the legal framework will be given here. That legal framework was changed in two major ways in 2000: first, all the statutory provisions were consolidated by the Powers of Criminal Courts (Sentencing) Act 2000; secondly, the names of some sentences were changed by the Criminal Justice and Court Services Act 2000. In addition, the government issued a new version of National Standards for Supervision in the Community in 2000.

A *community rehabilitation order* (formerly, probation order) may be for between six months and three years. The basic order requires supervision by a probation officer, and the obligations are set out in the National Standards. Five additional requirements are available to courts: residence; specified activities; attendance at a probation centre; mental treatment; or treatment for drug or alcohol dependency. Between 1990 and 2000 the use of community rehabilitation orders increased from 7 to 11 per cent of adult male offenders, and from 18 to 22 per cent for adult females. Some three-quarters of orders are completed satisfactorily.

A *community punishment order* (formerly, community service order) may be for between 40 and 240 hours, requiring the performance of unpaid work during leisure hours. Again, the National Standards set out various obligations. Between 1990 and 2000 the use of community punishment orders increased from 7 to 9 per cent of adult male offenders, and from 4 to 8 per cent for adult females. Some three-quarters of orders are completed satisfactorily.

A *community punishment and rehabilitation order* (formerly, combination order) may consist of 40 to 100 hours' community punishment combined with one to three years of community rehabilitation, with or without additional requirements. Introduced in 1992, such orders accounted for some 3 per cent of sentenced adult males and females in 2000. Although they are the most severe of community penalties, in

2000 the vast majority (16,000) were imposed by magistrates' courts rather than by the Crown Court (3,200).

A *curfew order* is intended to restrict an offender's movements for between two and twelve hours per day for up to six months. A curfew order may be (and usually is) combined with electronic monitoring. Although this is now available in all areas of the country, courts have been slow to make use of the power: in 2000 only 2,600 such orders were imposed.

A *drug treatment and testing order* is now available, following pilot schemes in 1999. The order, lasting between six months and three years, may be made where the court is satisfied that the offender is a regular drug user who requires and is willing to accept treatment. The order provides not only for treatment but also for regular testing of the offender for drugs, and for review of the order's progress by a court.

In relation to young offenders, there are two more forms of community sentence that are available: the supervision order, which may be regarded as a 'junior' alternative to the probation order for less mature youngsters; and the attendance centre order, which is available for offenders aged fourteen to twenty. The Crime and Disorder Act 1998 also introduced reparation orders for young offenders. For discussion of the new framework for youth justice, see Newburn in Chapter 16 of this volume.

SUSPENDED SENTENCES

A sentence of imprisonment of two years or less may be suspended for a period of up to two years. If the offender is convicted of another offence committed during the operational period, the court must activate the suspended sentence in addition to the sentence for the new crime, unless it is 'unjust to do so'. Suspended sentences did not succeed in lowering the prison population following their introduction in 1967. Research showed that courts sometimes defied the law by imposing suspended sentences when immediate imprisonment would not be justifiable, and by imposing longer sentences when suspending (Bottoms 1981; Moxon 1988: 34–8). Although the suspended sentence is meant to be the most severe of non-custodial measures, it seems that many courts and offenders regard it as a 'let-off'. Suspended sentences were abolished for offenders under twenty-one in 1982, and abolition has clearly been contemplated for adults. The 1991 Act retained them in restricted form: a court may impose a suspended only sentence if immediate custody is justified and if there are 'exceptional circumstances' in favour of suspension. The Court of Appeal has confirmed that the term 'exceptional' must be interpreted restrictively, although it has wavered occasionally (Campbell 1995), and the figures show that suspended sentences are now passed much less frequently: whereas in the late 1980s they accounted for some 10 per cent of adult indictable sentences, from 1993 onwards the proportion has been 1 per cent of adult male offenders and 2 per cent of adult female offenders. If a court does suspend, it must consider adding a fine or compensation order, to give the sentence an immediate sting.

REVIEW OF POLICY AND PRACTICE

To what extent did the 1991 Act's concept of 'punishment in the community' succeed in expanding the numbers dealt with non-custodially and reducing the numbers sentenced to custody? If one compares the figures for 1990 and 2000, the proportionate use of community sentences increased in magistrates' courts from 20 to 31 per cent, and in the Crown Court from 25 to 26 per cent (the latter having peaked at 33 per cent in 1994). However, in the same period the proportionate use of immediate custody increased in magistrates' courts from 4.4 to 14 per cent, and in the Crown Court from 43.2 to 63.9 per cent. It seems to follow that, if the rise in community sentences has not been at the expense of custodial sentences, it must have been at the expense of lesser measures. Thus we have seen that, although the proportion of discharges has not declined, the use of the fine is much lower. It is apparent that the emasculation of the suspended sentence by the 1991 Act has contributed to the rise in both custody and community sentences, although it is not clear in what proportions.

As has happened on many occasions in the past, when new non-custodial measures have been introduced in the hope that some offenders will be diverted from custody, the result appears to have been a form of net-widening, with the new non-custodial measures being applied to offenders who would previously have received a lesser form of sentence. This demonstrates some of the difficulties of ensuring that sentencing policy follows the intended penal policy. In relation to community sentences and other non-custodial measures, the Court of Appeal makes hardly any contribution in terms of guidance, and so the legislation stands virtually alone.

However, there may be some force in an alternative explanation. In the late 1980s and early 1990s there was a significant rise in the proportionate use of police cautions for indictable offences, both for adult males (from 7 per cent in 1985 to 26 per cent in 1995) and for adult females (from 19 to 44 per cent). The percentages had declined slightly by 2000 (to 20 for men and 34 for women), but the total numbers sentenced for indictable offences have still declined in recent years, as Tables 29.1 and 29.2 show. The higher cautioning rate may mean that many less serious offenders who would have been sentenced in the 1980s do not now come to court at all. The ones that do come to court are the most serious, and it would hardly be surprising if a higher proportion of severe sentences (imprisonment, community sentences) resulted. As Tables 29.1 and 29.2 demonstrate, this analysis is not a complete fit, since the rise in the proportionate use of discharges since 1985 goes against it (if minor offenders are being cautioned, there ought to be fewer discharges). But, in other respects, this argument may have some explanatory force, in addition to net-widening and to the rising tide of punitiveness in recent years.

Since these changes occurred at a time when the community sentences were made tougher and more demanding, some of Cohen's early work has become pertinent again. His 1979 warnings of increased social control through net-widening, blurring, and the thinning of the mesh were questioned by Bottoms (1983), who showed that it was the fine rather than surveillance-based measures which increased in the 1970s. But the last two decades have seen the decline of the fine and the rise of custody and community sentences. Cohen's thesis is thus rekindled (Cohen 1985), and the 1991

Act's reliance on punishment in the community—even to the extent of legislating for electronic surveillance—established its continued relevance. On one view this is the inevitable price for any element of progress in a society whose political system is much affected by punitive lobbies: the greater use of non-custodial sanctions can only be bought by making them tougher, and also perhaps by continuing to imprison certain groups of offenders for extremely long periods.

Further legislation is now anticipated in the wake of the Halliday Report (2001). The proposal is for a single 'community punishment order', made up of whatever ingredients the court believes to be appropriate in view of the offender's needs, but within overall bounds set by proportionality. Pre-sentence reports would be important in suggesting programmes suitable for the offender, whether work, supervision, curfew, drug treatment, or any combination thereof. There would be 'sentence review courts' to assess progress and to deal with breaches, which would often attract custody. Much of this proposed system appears rehabilitative in motivation, but with a strongly punitive underpinning for those who fail to meet expectations.

SENTENCING REFORM

INTERNATIONAL PATTERNS IN SENTENCING REFORM

Recent years have seen major sentencing reforms in several countries, and proposals for reform in many others (see further Clarkson and Morgan 1995; Tonry and Hatlestad 1997; Tonry and Frase 2001). Most attention has been focused on the various 'guideline systems' in the United States. Minnesota, Oregon, and other states have introduced guidelines which indicate sentence ranges according to the type of offence and the criminal history of the offender, and which attempt to shape sentencing practice in certain ways. Usually there is a permanent Sentencing Commission to monitor practice, and often there is appellate review to determine the propriety of judicial departures from the guidelines (cf. von Hirsch 1995 with Frase 1995; Tonry 1996; Reitz 2001). Since 1987 there have been guidelines for federal sentencing, issued by the United States Sentencing Commission, which also monitors practice. These guidelines are inherently more complex, and also have to incorporate several mandatory minimum sentences introduced by Congress. Critics point to the absence of clear rationales, the difficulties of applying them, their subservience to previous practice, and their lack of concern for rising prison populations (Doob 1995; Tonry 1996). However, the creation and extension of mandatory minimum penalties for certain crimes seems to be a greater political concern than the shortcomings of the federal sentencing guidelines (Windlesham 1996: Part III).

Closer to the approach taken in the English reforms of 1991 are the systems introduced in Finland in 1976 and in Sweden in 1989. The Finnish statute introduced proportionality-based sentencing, and has given rise to a progressive reduction in the use of custodial sentences (Lappi-Seppala 2001). The Swedish statute states the aims and principles of sentencing, requiring the court to assess the 'penal value' (i.e., seriousness) of the offence and giving **guidance** on aggravating and mitigating factors. It leaves the courts to interpret and apply the rules to particular cases, and provides for appellate review (Jareborg 1995). In other European countries there has been less emphasis on the renewal of sentencing frameworks, despite the encouragement given by the Council of Europe (1993). In several countries there is evidence of strong increases in the use of imprisonment for certain types of crime (Ashworth 2000b), partly in response to Europe-wide initiatives against drug-trafficking, money-laundering, etc.

The Australian states continue to experience a maelstrom of sentencing reforms (Freiberg 2001). In Victoria the Sentencing Act 1991 introduced a fairly comprehensive rationalization of sentencing, including a 'truth in sentencing' provision which required judges to adjust their sentences downwards to ensure that the abolition of remission did not result in longer effective sentences. Two years and a change of government later, however, Victoria also experienced 'law and order' legislation which raised sentences for serious sexual and violent offenders (Freiberg 2001). The Victorian statute was adopted also in Queensland, whereas in New South Wales the courts have played a major role, by formulating and publicizing sentencing guideline judgments in an attempt to allay public concerns about sentence levels, an approach eschewed by the courts in Western Australia (see Morgan and Murray 1999).

One particularly innovative approach may be found much closer to home, however. This is the Sentencing Information System in Scotland, using a database consisting of all High Court sentences passed in recent years. The aim of the system is to enable a sentencing judge to enter on a computer certain key features of a case to be sentenced, and the computer then gives details of sentences passed in cases with similar features. The system is not a reform of sentencing, as such, but its use is likely to generate greater mutual awareness among sentencers and greater consistency of approach (Hutton 1999). For that reason it is strongly commended in the Auld Report (2001) for introduction in England and Wales.

FURTHER REFORMS IN ENGLAND AND WALES

The 1990s were such a decade of turmoil in English sentencing that many sentencers would now prefer to see a period of calm, with little further legislative change. The judiciary undoubtedly contributed positively to the sentencing debate in the 1990s, by continuing to develop the use of sentencing guidelines and by pointing out the weakness of the deterrent and incapacitative arguments used to support the introduction of mandatory and minimum sentences in 1997. But the judiciary also had some negative effects, through its refusal to accept the framework of the 1991 Act, its ready resort to deterrent reasoning (in contrast to its criticism of the government for making unwarranted assumptions about marginal deterrence: Ashworth 2001), its failure to give a lead on reducing custody for non-serious offenders, and its continued refusal to permit full research into the working practices of Crown Court sentencers (cf. the Oxford Pilot Study 1984). Moreover, the courts themselves raised their use of imprisonment steeply during the 1990s, albeit under pressure from politicians and the media to do so.

It could also be said that the Court of Appeal failed to adopt the guidelines approach when confronted with the types of offence most frequently coming up for sentence—theft, burglary, deception, and handling stolen goods. The creation of the Sentencing Advisory Panel appears to be tackling that desideratum, by advising the Court of Appeal to issue guidelines in a number of those areas—the Panel's advice on sentencing for handling has already been adopted by the Court, and the Panel will shortly bring out further advice on sentencing for burglary. However, it is clear that the method of working that the Panel is required to adopt, notably the fairly lengthy consultation process, is likely to impair its ability to generate large numbers of guidelines in a few years. The Panel's task is chiefly that of bringing increased structure into the realm of sentencing discretion, thereby increasing predictability, transparency, and accountability in sentencing decisions.

However, there are other issues such as levels of punitiveness, and it should be recalled that it was largely the courts' decision to raise sentencing levels in the 1990s. The power struggle between the judiciary and politicians in the 1990s seems to have concerned, at bottom, the preservation of judicial sentencing discretion. The judges undermined the 1991 Act by refusing to accept proportionality as the principal aim of sentencing and reintroducing deterrence; the judges and the government agreed in 1993 on the need to abolish the unit fine and to re-state the law on the relevance of previous convictions; but the judges clashed with the government in 1997 over the proposals to introduce mandatory and mandatory minimum sentences—a battle won by the judges, as we saw above, by forcing late amendments in Parliament (Ashworth 2001) and subsequently by using the Human Rights Act to open up the exceptions to the automatic life sentence.

If the preservation of maximum discretion is the factor which generates the greatest show of judicial power, what is the likely reception of the Halliday Report's proposals for a comprehensive system of sentence guidelines? The Report puts forward a variety of possible models for formulating the guidelines and then promulgating them. There can be no doubt that the work of formulation will be an immense task, if it really is intended to cover the Crown Court, the magistrates' courts, youth courts, and the new level of courts proposed in the Auld Report (2001). The judicial response will be determined to some extent by the degree of their involvement in the final formulation and in the promulgation of the guidelines. At present the Sentencing Advisory Panel proposes guidelines which the Court of Appeal may accept, modify, or even reject. It seems unlikely that the government intends the Court to have the third option; but if it does not, the Court (and higher judiciary) is unlikely to have the 'ownership' of the guidelines which may be a necessary condition of its support for the endeavour. That might lead to the kind of adaptive behaviour that undermined the 1991 Act. Much may also turn on the extent to which the new guidelines are binding. This depends on whether they specify starting points and/or ranges of sentence, and how tightly they seek to restrict the ability of courts to move upwards and downwards from the guidelines. The Halliday Report's proposal of graduated ranges, according to the seriousness of the offender's criminal record, might be taken to indicate a fairly restrictive approach. While Halliday's discussion of previous convictions makes it clear that courts must be free to take a qualitative approach to previous record—whether the offences are different in kind, whether there has been a trouble-free gap, etc.—the proposed framework of stepped responses to re-offending suggests a doubtful reliance on individual deterrence and incapacitation, propped up unconvincingly with references to rehabilitation (e.g., Halliday 2001: 13).

If there are to be major sentencing reforms in the wake of the Halliday Report, it is imperative that there should be careful monitoring of the effect of the guidelines. This will rekindle the debate about research into sentencing, particularly in the Crown Court. At present there is little reliable evidence about how judges approach their task in sentencing: a comparison with the amount of research into police behaviour (see Bowling and Foster, in Chapter 27 of this volume) shows how little is known about how sentencing decisions are actually approached and taken. However, it remains important not to see all these matters as technical issues about the sentencing process itself. They must not be separated from the impact that the sentencing system has, and the orders which the courts impose on convicted offenders. Thus the Halliday Report proposes that there should be a revival in the use of fines—but does not discuss the potential for discrimination against the poor, or the danger of adverse media coverage of the kind that undermined unit fines. The Halliday Report proposes to make community sentences more credible by drawing the courts more into a regular review of progress, but fails to attend to the danger that greater expectations will lead to more breaches and then to more custody. The Halliday Report proposes a new form of 'custody plus' to replace short prison terms, but fails to embrace any wider principle of restraint in the use of custodial sentences. Indeed, even among those critical of the soaring use of prison in this country, there is little evidence of a 'replacement discourse' that will challenge the prevailing pro-prison culture among politicians and the media. Thus, despite the efforts to introduce standards of predictability, consistency, and accountability into sentencing, it remains unlikely that the trend towards greater repression will be reversed.

Selected further reading

From the considerable literature on sentencing and related issues, a dozen works may be selected for further reading. An excellent overview of the sociology of punishment may be found in David Garland, *Punishment in Modern Society* (Oxford: Oxford University Press, 1990). Wider readings on rationales for sentencing may be found in A. von Hirsch and A. Ashworth (eds), *Principled Sentencing: Readings in Theory and Policy* (2nd edn, Oxford: Hart Publishing, 1998), R.A. Duff and D. Garland (eds), *A Reader on Punishment* (Oxford: Oxford University Press, 1994), together with the edited works by M. Matravers (ed.), *Punishment and Political Theory* (Oxford: Hart Publishing, 1999) and A. Ashworth and M. Wasik (eds), *Fundamentals of Sentencing Theory* (Oxford: Oxford University Press, 1998). Three influential monographs on sentencing theory are N. Lacey, *State Punishment* (London: Routledge, 1988), A. von Hirsch, *Censure and Sanctions* (Oxford: Oxford University Press, 1993), and R.A. Duff, *Punishment, Communication and Community* (New York: Oxford University Press, 2001).

Three current texts can be recommended for further details of English sentencing law and practice: M. Wasik, *Emmins on Sentencing* (4th edn, London: Blackstone Press, 2001);

A. Ashworth, *Sentencing and Criminal Justice* (3rd edn, London: Butterworths, 2000); and N. Walker and N. Padfield, *Sentencing: Theory, Law and Practice* (2nd edn, London: Butterworths, 1996). Helpful readings may be found in the relevant chapters of M. Wasik, T. Gibbons, and M. Redmayne, *Criminal Justice: Text and Materials* (London: Longman, 1999), and of N. Padfield, *Text and Materials on the Criminal Justice Process* (2nd edn, London: Butterworths, 2000). Large-scale research studies on sentencing may be found in C. Flood-Page and A. Mackie, *Sentencing Practice: an examination of decisions in magistrates' courts and the Crown Court in the mid-1990s*, Home Office Research Study No. 180 (London: Home Office, 1998), and R. Hood, *Race and Sentencing* (Oxford: Oxford University Press, 1992). Good, short discussions of sentencing may be found in M. Cavadino and J. Dignan, *The Penal System* (3rd edn, London: Sage 2002), chapter 4; and in D. Faulkner, *Crime, State and Citizen* (Winchester: Waterside Press, 2001), chapter 12.

References

ADVISORY COUNCIL ON THE PENAL SYSTEM (1978), *Sentences of Imprisonment: a Review of Maximum Penalties* London: HMSO.

ASHWORTH, A. (1993), 'Victim Impact Statements and Sentencing', *Criminal Law Review*: 498–509.

—— (2000a), *Sentencing and Criminal Justice*, 3rd edn, London: Butterworths.

—— (2000b), 'Sentencing', in C. Nuttall (ed.), *Crime and Criminal Justice in Europe*, Strasbourg: Council of Europe.

—— (2001), 'The Decline of English Sentencing', in M. Tonry and R. Frase (eds), *Sentencing and Sanctions in Western Countries*, New York: Oxford University Press.

ATTORNEY-GENERAL (2001), *Guidelines on the Acceptance of Pleas*, 1 Cr App R 425.

AULD, LORD JUSTICE (2001), *Review of the Criminal Courts*, London: The Stationery Office.

BALDWIN, J. (1985), *Pre-Trial Justice in Magistrates' Courts*, Oxford: Oxford University Press.

BENTHAM, J. (1789), *Principles of Morals and Legislation*, London.

BOND, R.A., and LEMON, N. (1979), 'Changes in Magistrates' Attitudes during the First Year on the Bench', in D. Farrington, K. Hawkins and S. Lloyd-Bostock (eds), *Psychology, Law and Legal Processes*, London: Macmillan.

BOTTOMS, A.E. (1981), 'The Suspended Sentence in England, 1967–78', *British Journal of Criminology*, 21: 1–25.

—— (1983), 'Neglected Features of Contemporary Penal Systems', in D. Garland and P. Young (eds), *The Power to Punish*, 166–202, London: Heinemann.

—— (1995), 'The Philosophy and Politics of Punishment and Sentencing', in C. Clarkson and R. Morgan (eds), *The Politics of Sentencing Reform*, Oxford: Oxford University Press.

—— (1998), 'Five Puzzles in von Hirsch's Theory of Punishment', in A. Ashworth and M. Wasik (eds), *Fundamentals of Sentencing Theory*, Oxford: Oxford University Press.

—— and BROWNSWORD, R. (1982), 'The Dangerousness Debate after the Floud Report', *British Journal of Criminology*, 22: 229.

——, GELSTHORPE, L., and REX, S. (eds) (2001), *Community Penalties: change and challenges*, Cullompton, Devon: Willan Publishing.

—— and PRESTON, R.H. (eds) (1980), *The Coming Penal Crisis*, Edinburgh: Scottish Academic Press.

BRAITHWAITE, J. (1999), 'Restorative Justice: Assessing Optimistic and Pessimistic Accounts', in M. Tonry (ed.), *Crime and Justice: a Review of Research*, 25: 1.

—— and PETTIT, P. (1990), *Not Just Deserts*, Oxford: Oxford University Press.

BRODY, S.R., and TARLING, R. (1981), *Taking Offenders out of Circulation*, Home Office Research Study No. 64, London: HMSO.

BROWNLEE, I. (1998), *Community Punishment: a Critical Introduction*, London: Longman.

CAMPBELL, J.Q. (1995), 'A Sentencer's Lament on the Imminent Death of the Suspended Sentence', *Criminal Law Review*: 293–95.

CARLISLE, LORD (1988), *The Parole System in England and Wales*, Report of the Review Committee, London: HMSO.

CHARMAN, E., GIBSON, B., HONESS, T., and MORGAN, R. (1996), *Fine Impositions and Enforcement following the Criminal Justice Act 1993*, Research Findings 36, London: Home Office.

CLARKSON, C., and MORGAN, R. (eds), (1995), *The Politics of Sentencing Reform*, Oxford: Oxford University Press.

COHEN, S. (1979), 'The Punitive City', *Contemporary Crises*, 3: 339–63.

—— (1985), *Visions of Social Control*, New York: Plenum.

COOKE, R.K. (1987), 'The Practical Problems of the Sentencer', in D. Pennington and S. Lloyd-Bostock (eds), *The Psychology of Sentencing*, Oxford: Centre for Socio-Legal Studies.

COUNCIL of EUROPE (1993), *Consistency in Sentencing*, Recommendation No. R(92) 17, Strasbourg: Council of Europe Press.

DARBYSHIRE, P. (1999), 'A Comment on the Powers of Magistrates' Clerks', *Criminal Law Review*: 377–86.

—— (2000), 'The Mischief of Plea Bargaining and Sentencing Rewards', *Criminal Law Review*: 894–910.

DOOB, A. (1995), 'The United States Sentencing Commission Guidelines: If you don't know where you are going, you might not get there', in C. Clarkson and R. Morgan (eds), *The Politics of Sentencing*, Oxford: Oxford University Press.

DOWNES, D. (1988), *Contrasts in Tolerance*, Oxford: Oxford University Press.

DUFF, A., and GARLAND, D. (eds), (1994), *A Reader on Punishment*, Oxford: Oxford University Press.

DUFF, R.A. (2000), *Punishment, Communication and Community*, New York: Oxford University Press.

DUNBAR, I., and LANGDON, A. (1998), *Tough Justice: Sentencing and Penal Policies in the 1990s*, London: Blackstone Press.

EREZ, E. (1999), 'Who's Afraid of the Big, Bad Victim', *Criminal Law Review*, 545–56.

FLOOD-PAGE, C., and MACKIE, A. (1998), *Sentencing Practice: an examination of decisions in magistrates' courts and the Crown Court in the mid-1990s*, Home Office Research Study No. 180, London: Home Office.

FLOUD, J., and YOUNG, W. (1981), *Dangerousness and Criminal Justice*, London: Heinemann.

FRASE, R. (1995), 'Sentencing Guidelines in Minnesota and other American states: A Progress Report', in C. Clarkson and R. Morgan (eds), *The*

Politics of Sentencing Reform, Oxford: Oxford University Press.

FREIBERG, A. (2001a), 'Three Strikes and You're Out—It's Not Cricket: Colonization and Resistance in Australian Sentencing', in M. Tonry and R. Frase (eds), *Sentencing and Sanctions in Western Countries*, New York: Oxford University Press.

GALLIGAN, D. (1986), *Discretionary Powers*, Oxford: Oxford University Press.

GARDNER, J. (1998), 'Punishment—in Proportion and in Perspective', in A. Ashworth and M. Wasik (eds), *Fundamentals of Sentencing Theory*, Oxford: Oxford University Press.

GARLAND, D. (1990), *Punishment and Modern Society*, Oxford: Oxford University Press.

GRAHAM, D. (1990), 'Decarceration in the Federal Republic of Germany', *British Journal of Criminology*, 30: 150–70.

HALLIDAY REPORT (2001), *Making Punishments Work: Report of a Review of the Sentencing Framework*, London: Home Office.

HART, H.L.A. (1968), *Punishment and Responsibility*, Oxford: Oxford University Press.

HAWKINS, K. (ed.) (1992), *Discretion*, Oxford: Oxford University Press.

—— and THOMAS, J. (eds) (1984), *Enforcing Regulation*. Boston: Kluwer-Nijhoff.

HEDDERMAN, C., and GELSTHORPE, L. (1997), *Understanding the Sentencing of Women*, Home Office Research Study No. 170, London: Home Office.

HENHAM, R. (1998), 'Making Sense of the Crime (Sentences) Act 1997', *Modern Law Review*, 61: 223.

—— (1999), 'Bargain Justice or Justice Denied? Sentence Discounts and the Criminal Process', *Modern Law Review*, 62: 515.

HOME OFFICE (1990), *Crime, Justice and Protecting the Public*, London: HMSO.

—— (1994), *Monitoring of the Criminal Justice Acts 1991–1993—Results from a Special Data Collection Exercise*, Statistical Bulletin 20/94, London: Home Office.

—— (1999), *Digest 4: Information on the Criminal Justice System in England and Wales*, London: Home Office.

—— (2000), *National Standards for the Supervision of Offenders in the Community*, 3rd edn, London: Home Office.

HOOD, R. (1962), *Sentencing in Magistrates' Courts*, London: Tavistock.

—— (1972), *Sentencing the Motoring Offender*, London: Heinemann.

—— (1992), *Race and Sentencing*, Oxford: Oxford University Press.

—— and SHUTE, S. (2000), *The Parole System at Work*, Home Office Research Study No. 202, London: Home Office.

HOYLE, C., CAPE, E., MORGAN, R., and SANDERS, A. (1998), *Evaluation of the 'One Stop Shop' and Victim Statement Pilot Projects*, London: Home Office.

HOUGH, M. and ROBERTS, J.V. (1998), *Attitudes to Punishment: Findings from the British Crime Survey*, Home Office Research Study No. 179, London: Home Office.

HUDSON, B. (1987), *Justice through Punishment: a Critique of the Justice Model of Corrections*, London: Macmillan.

—— (1993), *Penal Policy and Social Justice*, London: Macmillan.

—— (1998), 'Doing Justice to Difference', in A. Ashworth and M. Wasik (eds), *Fundamentals of Sentencing Theory*, Oxford: Oxford University Press.

HUTTER, B. (1997), *Compliance: Regulation and Environment*, Oxford: Oxford University Press.

HUTTON, N. (1999), 'Sentencing in Scotland', in P. Duff and N. Hutton (eds), *Criminal Justice in Scotland*, Aldershot: Ashgate.

JAREBORG, N. (1995), 'The Swedish Sentencing Reform', in C. Clarkson and R. Morgan (eds), *The Politics of Sentencing Reform*, Oxford: Oxford University Press.

JOHNSTONE, G. (2001), *Restorative Justice*, Cullompton, Devon: Willan Publishing.

JUDICIAL STUDIES BOARD (1995), *Report, 1992–95*, London: HMSO.

LACEY, N. (1988), *State Punishment*, London: Routledge.

LAPPI-SEPPALA, T. (2001), 'Sentencing and Punishment in Finland: The Decline of the Repressive Ideal', in M. Tonry and R. Frase (eds), *Sentencing and Sanction Systems in Western Countries*, New York: Oxford University Press.

LLOYD, C., MAIR, G., and HOUGH, M. (1994), *Explaining Reconviction Rates: a critical analysis*, Home Office Research Study No. 135 London: HMSO.

MacCORMICK, N., and GARLAND, D. (1998), 'Sovereign States and Vengeful Victims: the Problem of the Right to Punish', in A. Ashworth and M. Wasik (eds), *Fundamentals of Sentencing Theory*, Oxford: Oxford University Press.

McALINDEN, A. (2001), 'Indeterminate Sentences for the Severely Personality Disordered', *Criminal Law Review*, 108–23.

McCONVILLE, M., SANDERS, A., and LENG, R. (1991), *The Case for the Prosecution*, London: Routledge.

McGUIRE, J. (ed.) (1995), *What Works?*, London: Sage.

MONAHAN, J. *et al.* (2001), *Rethinking Risk Assessment: the MacArthur study of mental disorder and violence*, New York: Oxford University Press.

MORGAN, N., and MURRAY, B. (1999), 'What's in a Name? Guideline Judgments in Australia', *Criminal Law Journal*, 23: 90.

MORGAN, R., and RUSSELL, N. (2000), *The Judiciary in the Magistrates' Courts*, London: Home Office and LCD Paper 66.

MOXON, D. (1988), *Sentencing Practice in the Crown Court*, Home Office Research Study No. 103, London: HMSO.

MUNRO, C. (1992), 'Judicial Independence and Judicial Functions', in C. Munro and M. Wasik (eds), *Sentencing, Judicial Discretion and Judicial Training*, London: Sweet & Maxwell.

OXFORD PILOT STUDY (1984), *Sentencing in the Crown Court*, by A. Ashworth, E. Genders, G. Mansfield, J. Peay, and E. Player. Oxford: Centre for Criminological Research.

PENNINGTON, D., and LLOYD-BOSTOCK, S. (eds) (1987), *The Psychology of Sentencing*, Oxford: Centre for Socio-Legal Studies.

POSNER, R. (1985), 'An Economic Theory of the Criminal Law', *Columbia Law Review*, 85: 1193–1231.

RADZINOWICZ, SIR L., and HOOD, R. (1990), *The Emergence of Penal Policy in Victorian and Edwardian England*, Oxford: Oxford University Press.

RANYARD, R., HEBENTON, B., and PEASE, K. (1994), 'An Analysis of a Guideline Case as applied to the Offence of Rape', *Howard Journal of Criminal Justice*, 33: 203.

REITZ, K. (2001), 'The Disassembly and Reassembly of US Sentencing Practice', in M. Tonry and R. Frase (eds), *Sentencing and Sanction Systems in Western Countries*, New York: Oxford University Press.

REX, S. (1998), 'Applying Desert Principles to Community Sentences: Lessons from two Criminal Justice Acts', *Criminal Law Review*: 381.

RILEY, D., and VENNARD, J. (1988), *Triable-Either-Way Cases: Crown Court or Magistrates' Court*,

Home Office Research Study No. 98, London: HMSO.

SANDERS, A. (1985), 'Class Bias in Prosecutions', *Howard Journal*, 24: 176–99.

——, HOYLE, C., MORGAN, R., and CAPE, E. (2001), 'Victim Impact Statements: Don't Work, Can't Work', *Criminal Law Review*, 447–58.

SHAPLAND, J. (1981), *Between Conviction and Sentence*, London: Routledge.

—— (1987), 'Who Controls Sentencing? Influences on the Sentencer', in D. Pennington and S. Lloyd-Bostock (eds), *The Psychology of Sentencing*, Oxford: Centre for Socio-Legal Studies.

SHUTE, S. (1999), 'Who Passes Unduly Lenient Sentences?', *Criminal Law Review*: 603.

TARLING, R. (1979), *Sentencing Practice in Magistrates' Courts*, Home Office Research Study No. 56, London: HMSO.

——, MOXON, D., and JONES, P. (1985), 'Sentencing of Adults and Juveniles in Magistrates' Courts', in D. Moxon (ed.), *Managing Criminal Justice*, London: HMSO.

THOMAS, D.A. (1970), *Principles of Sentencing*, London: Heinemann.

—— (1974), 'The Control of Discretion in the Administration of Criminal Justice', in R. Hood (ed.), *Crime, Criminology and Public Policy*, London: Heinemann.

—— (1978), *The Penal Equation*, Cambridge: Institute of Criminology.

TONRY, M. (1996), *Sentencing Matters*, New York: Oxford University Press.

—— and FRASE, R. (eds) (2001), *Sentencing and Sanctions in Western Countries*, New York: Oxford University Press.

—— and HATLESTAD, K. (eds) (1997), *Sentencing Reform in Overcrowded Times*, New York: Oxford University Press.

VAN DUYNE, P. (1987), 'Simple Decision-Making', in D. Pennington and S. Lloyd-Bostock (eds), *The*

Psychology of Sentencing, Oxford: Centre for Socio-Legal Studies.

VENNARD, J., and HEDDERMAN, C. (1998), 'Effective Interventions with Offenders', in C. Nuttall (ed.), *Reducing Offending*, Home Office Research Study 187, London: Home Office.

VON HIRSCH, A. (1976), *Doing Justice*, New York: Hill and Wang.

—— (1993), *Censure and Sanctions*, Oxford: Oxford University Press.

—— (1995), 'Proportionality and Parsimony in American Sentencing Guidelines: the Minnesota and Oregon Standards', in C. Clarkson and R. Morgan (eds), *The Politics of Sentencing Reform*, Oxford: Oxford University Press.

—— and ASHWORTH, A. (eds) (1998), *Principled Sentencing: Readings in Theory and Policy*, 2nd edn, Oxford: Hart Publishing.

—— and —— (1996), 'Protective Sentencing under section 2(2)(b): the Criteria for Dangerousness', *Criminal Law Review*: 175–83.

——, BOTTOMS, A.E., BURNEY, E., and WIKSTRÖM, P.-O. (1999), *Criminal Deterrence: an Analysis of Recent Research*, Oxford: Hart Publishing.

—— and JAREBORG, N. (1991), 'Gauging Criminal Harm: a Living Standard Analysis', *Oxford Journal of Legal Studies*, 11: 1–38.

WALKER, N. (1991), *Why Punish?*, Oxford: Oxford University Press.

—— and PADFIELD, N. (1996), *Sentencing: Theory, Law and Practice*, 2nd edn, London: Butterworths.

WASIK, M. (1985), 'The Grant of an Absolute Discharge', *Oxford Journal of Legal Studies*, 5: 211.

WINDLESHAM, LORD (1993), *Responses to Crime: volume 2*, Oxford: Oxford University Press.

—— (1996), *Responses to Crime: volume 3*, Oxford: Oxford University Press.

WOOD, D. (1988), 'Dangerous Offenders and the Morality of Protective Sentencing', *Criminal Law Review*: 424–33.

30

IMPRISONMENT

A BRIEF HISTORY, THE CONTEMPORARY SCENE, AND LIKELY PROSPECTS

Rod Morgan

SETTING THE SCENE

The existence of prisons and the use of imprisonment are almost universal, and raise issues far beyond the few buildings and the small minority of the population they house. They concern the nature and integrity of the state and the society on whose behalf it purports to act. This chapter will be able to sketch only a few of these questions, and that almost entirely in relation to Britain. However, a good deal of the literature on which the chapter draws is more broadly based and from time to time international comparisons will be made, particularly with respect to our closer ties with Europe (see Sim *et al.* 1995). The aim is to examine six questions: What are the social forces associated with the emergence and use of imprisonment? What are the purposes of imprisonment, and what objectives should prison administrators set themselves? What is the character of the prison population and how is it changing? How are prisons organized and made accountable? How do the dynamics of prison life—that is, the sociology of the prison—affect objectives? And how might prisons change in the near future?

RECENT DEVELOPMENTS AND PENAL MODERNISM

In 2001 two major policy review reports were published in England and Wales—a review of sentencing, the Halliday Report (Home Office 2001a), and a review of the criminal courts, the Auld Report (2001). Both represent part of New Labour's *Modernising Government* project and both, if implemented either in whole or part, have potentially far-reaching implications for the size and nature of the prison population in England and Wales. The Halliday Report proposes that: prior convictions should count as a specific aggravating factor in sentencing; all custodial sentences should involve offenders being subject to supervision until the expiry of the sentence, with the possibility of recall to prison; and more flexible 'custody plus' sentences of less than twelve months be introduced. The Auld Report proposes that the criminal courts be vertically integrated and a new, middle, third tier created, in which the tribunal for imprisonable cases of moderate seriousness, comprise lay magistrates sitting along-side district judges. Though Halliday calls for the Court of Appeal, or a new judicial body, to provide new sentencing guidelines, his proposals make it more likely that sentences for prolific offenders will be longer and that many more released prisoners will be recalled to prison for failing to meet obligations placed on them during the longer community supervision portion of their sentences. The Auld proposals may reduce court delay but also imply a considerable reduction in the number of jury trials, most likely a lower acquittal rate, and probably greater reliance by sentencers on custodial sentences (see Rex and Tonry 2002).

At the time of writing (autumn 2001) it is too early to say which parts of this agenda will be adopted and, if adopted, what the consequences will be for prison numbers. However, there are certain straws in the wind. Neither of the New Labour Home Secretaries since the General Election of 1997 has employed the vigorous 'prison works' mantra of their Conservative predecessor, Michael Howard. But they have given greater emphasis to New Labour's 'tough on crime' undertaking than to the other part of the equation, 'tough on the causes of crime'. When taxed with the fact that the incarceration rate in England and Wales is almost the highest in Western Europe, they have typically responded with the argument that to take this as a policy starting point is the equivalent of looking through the wrong end of a telescope. The discussion should begin with an analysis of crime. If that analysis points to the need to protect the public from serious crime either by locking up more offenders, or by locking up dangerous or prolific offenders for longer, then so be it. The *sotto voce* message reflected in this is that imprisonment plays a central strategic role in the management of crime—and, thus, in that sense, prison works.

We appear now to inhabit a period characterized by what some writers have termed new penology (Feeley and Simon 1992) or penal modernism (Garland 2001) in which, though differences remain, the principal political parties have re-established a degree of consensus (see Downes and Morgan, in Chapter 10 of this volume). The responsibilities of the state appear to be undergoing a process of redefinition and delimitation. The new consensus includes the following propositions. Mundane crime has become part of our daily lives. We—the citizenry and the local state rather than the state—must take responsibility for managing and preventing it. One function of the criminal justice system is to back up these grass-roots controls by applying an array of swift, economical, and effective sanctions (mostly financial, but also surveil-lance and supervision where necessary) so that rational *homo criminologus* behaves according to a predictable calculus. Imprisonment has some role to play in this, but it is a minor, diminishing, back-up role (for contempt or fine default, for example). The principal focus of the state, however, is to be on serious crime and repeat, prolific, or dangerous offenders from whom the public expects, and has a right, to be protected. These offenders are to be targeted by the police, their past behaviour and future risk are to be systematically assessed by the Probation Service, the courts are to impose sentences proportionate to their offending careers, and their sentences are to be applied so as to safeguard the public. Public opinion and victims's views are to be

privileged, and every effort is to be made by the penal agencies to *correct* the criminogenic *deficits* which underlie these chronic or dangerous offenders' behaviour. This
means that they may forfeit the right to be presumed safe, they may have their liberties
restored only if they have satisfied the correctional authorities that the risk they pose
is now minimal, they may be subject, when given back their liberty, to a continuing
obligation to report their whereabouts to the authorities, and they may be returned to
custody if they breach contractual obligations imposed on them in the community
until the expiry of their sentences.

This twin-track crime prevention approach—dividing offenders into two groups,
the first normal, run-of-the-mill, rational, routine, and relatively harmless; and the
second abnormal, serious, dispositionally pathological, and dangerous—has been
termed bifurcation (Bottoms 1977). The assumption is that the public will better
tolerate having the great proportion of normal offenders in their midst if really bad
ones are taken out. This is of course a conceptual model. The criminal justice policies
actually pursued do not neatly conform to the model. Reality is more nuanced and
contradictory. Nevertheless, in the account that follows we shall repeatedly encounter
reflections of this bifurcated approach. Though the boundary between the two offending populations—the normal and harmless and the abnormal and dangerous—
ideally coincides broadly with the boundary between custodial and non-custodial
responses, in fact nothing is so well defined in practice. Quite apart from the fact that
imprisonment functions as a back-up for non-custodial sentences, resources within
prisons are limited, and there is less than perfect agreement as to who needs to be in
prison and what the criminogenic status of many prisoners is. This strategic argument
is fundamentally political because, though sentencing in particular cases is the
responsibility of the courts, the legislative framework and the climate of opinion
within which sentencers make their case-by-case decisions are determined principally
by politicians. If that be so, what are the likely prospects for the size of the prison
population?

There are currently just over 68,000 persons in prison in England and Wales, 6,000
in Scotland and 1,200 in Northern Ireland. In the case of England of Wales, this is a
few thousand more than three years ago, but the current plateau stands in marked
contrast to the trend up to 1997–8 and it is by no means certain that it will be
maintained. Having risen modestly during the 1980s, the prison population peaked at
around 50,000 in 1988–9 then declined to around 45,000 in the period 1990–93. It
then rose dramatically to 62,000 by the time of the 1997 General Election. Had the
Conservatives won that Election, the prospects were that this growth would have
continued. In 1996 the Conservatives set out their strategy for dealing with crime in a
White Paper, *Protecting the Public* (Home Office 1996), and subsequently in the Crime
(Sentences) Act 1997. Had those plans been implemented they would have added an
estimated 10,800 to the number of offenders in custody (ibid.: para. 13.8). But the
incoming Labour administration adopted only some of the Conservatives's measures.
Minimum custodial sentences for certain offences (notably third-time burglary convictions) were introduced, but release on licence (parole) was not abolished; and in
early 1999 the Labour government introduced a Home Detention Curfew scheme
whereby short-and medium-term prisoners (serving up to four years) became eligible

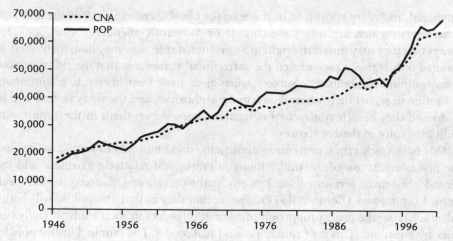

Fig. 30.1 Certified Normal Accommodation (CNA) and Average Prison Population (POP) 1946–2001

Source: Based on *Prison Statistics England and Wales 1999*, Fig. 1.3 (Home Office 2001c).

for release up to sixty days early subject to an electronically monitored curfew, if they satisfied a risk assessment and had an address to go to: the impact of this early release scheme was to reduce the prison population by almost 2,000 (see Dodgson *et al.* 2001). Thus though the prison population continued to soar during Labour's first year in office, it has since been more stable.

If the current custody rate and sentence lengths are maintained, we should expect to see only a modest growth in prison numbers to 2008. This modest growth will reflect both the estimated reduction and growth consequences of changes in criminal justice procedures and legislative provisions already enacted (see Gray and Elkins 2001). But the adoption of the Halliday and/or Auld proposals may radically change the picture.

IMPRISONMENT 1945 TO 2001

During the period 1945–85 the prison system in England and Wales suffered escalating overcrowding. There was virtually no overcrowding in the 1950s, but it reached 10–15 per cent by the 1980s. There then began the largest prison building programme since the middle of the nineteenth century. Between 1980 and 1996 twenty-one new prisons were opened providing 11,285 additional places. A further 7,500 places were created by developing existing prisons. These additions represented an almost 50 per cent increase in capacity. The total number of prison places and prisoners came briefly into equilibrium during 1993. By spring 1994, however, the surge in prison numbers brought a return to system overcrowding, which, despite the addition of on average two new prisons and the construction of extra accommodation at existing sites annually, has continued ever since. Further, because some spare capacity must always be reserved, and because there is always a mismatch between the geographical location of prisoners and available places, many individual prisons are seriously crowded. At the close of 2001 about a dozen of the 137 prisons were overcrowded by 30 or more per cent.

This massive expansion is costing a great deal of money. About £13 billion is currently spent on 'law and order services' of which 16 per cent, or £2.1 billion, goes on prisons, not far short of the 19 per cent spent on legal aid, criminal injuries compensation and Victim Support, the magistrates's courts and the Crown Court, and the Probation Service combined. This translates to £27,566 per prisoner per annum, or £530 per week. About 110,000 individuals are committed annually to prison or to young offender institutions (YOIs). Just over 43,000 full-time equivalent staff, about 31,000 of them uniformed prison officers, are employed to make sure that they stay there, an overall prisoner to staff ratio of 1.5:1 (Prison Service 2001).

This is a far cry from the situation fifty years ago. In 1946 there were about forty prisons, approximately 15,000 prisoners, and around 2,000 staff: a prisoner to staff ratio of 7.5:1 (Home Office 1947). It is true that the big Victorian prisons which still form the hub of the system today would be recognizable to a prisoner from that period. But only just. The external layouts and galleried wings remain much the same; but the grounds have been in-filled with modern gate-lodges, visiting centres, education blocks, workshops, gymnasia, and new accommodation wings. The cells are equipped today with lavatories and sinks: slopping-out has gone. Pastel colours have replaced the drab painted walls of green, cream, and brown. Fitted cell furniture has replaced the stark, iron beds. Moreover, the majority of prisoners are now accommodated in modern, purpose-built establishments constructed since the 1950s on green-field sites, many of them replacing the converted houses and war-time camps that were taken over for use as prisons in the immediate post-war period.

The social character of prison life has also changed dramatically. There are no longer rows of convicts hand-sewing mailbags in silence. The flogging triangles and bread and water dietary punishments have been abolished, and the shabby, ill-fitting serge uniforms of grey and brown have gone. When they are not alone, locked into their better-appointed cells, or milling about in groups on the landings and in the recreational areas, prisoners are now more likely to be engaged in literacy programmes, occupational training, and a variety of offence-focused courses, shod in their own trainers. Nevertheless, though prisoners now have more creature comforts, may use the telephone, and can see their families more often in more civilized environments, these gains have to be set against new psychological pressures and insecurities that have not diminished the pains of imprisonment. For some prisoners these pains prove unbearable.

First, most contemporary prisoners are in custody for longer than their predecessors. Though imprisonment was used proportionately more often by the courts in the 1940s, the sentences were typically short compared to now, though there has been a dramatic increase in the number of short prison sentences in the last ten years. In 1945, fewer than 5 per cent of offenders sentenced to immediate imprisonment were given eighteen months or more, life sentences were rare, and prisoners serving determinate sentences over ten years almost unknown. Of the daily average sentenced population, fewer than 7 per cent were serving four years or more. Today, 21 per cent of all prison sentences are for more than eighteen months, almost half the average daily population of sentenced prisoners are serving four years or more, and the number serving a life sentence, or a determinate sentence of ten years or more, is such that at any one time there are approximately 7,000 of them (Home Office 2001c: Table 1.3).

Secondly, prisoners now are subject to security measures unknown or scarcely developed half a century ago—prison perimeters made virtually impenetrable by multiple-high-tech barriers, landings and stairwells draped with wire mesh, CCTV, electronic locking systems, intensive staff surveillance, strip searches, and random compulsory drug testing. Moreover, the amount of time many prisoners now spend out of their cells is modest compared to that which was taken for granted in most training prisons thirty years ago. Communal activities, like eating in dining halls, for example, are today considered too risky an arrangement to be generally viable.

Thirdly, it seems certain, though these matters are difficult to assess, that prisons have become less orderly and safe. Concerted acts of prisoner indiscipline used to be rare (Fox 1952: 160) and staff industrial action unheard of. In the 1980s, culminating in the Strangeways and associated riots of 1990, prison disturbances became commonplace, and managing prison officers was for a period a more difficult task for prison administrators than managing prisoners. The litany of serious industrial disputes and prisoner disorders in the 1970s and 1980s led to two major inquiries—the May Committee in 1978–79 and the judicial inquiry conducted by Lord Justice Woolf in 1990–91—the reports of which have become landmarks for analysts of prisons policy. Fear has become a significant feature of much prison life (King and McDermott 1995: chapter 3). By the early 1990s both hard and soft drugs were freely available in many prisons—a trend which the Prison Service seems now to be reversing (Edgar and O'Donnell 1998)—with all the predictably violent and intimidating consequences (Seddon 1996; Home Affairs Committee 1999: paras 26–8). More than 3,000 prisoners are segregated for their own protection, either under Rule 43 or in the twenty-four vulnerable prisoner units (VPUs) scattered around the country. The number of recorded assaults on both staff and prisoners has greatly increased, and in 1999 a record ninety-one prisoners committed suicide (Home Office 2001c: Table 7.20).

THE DAY-TO-DAY POLITICS OF IMPRISONMENT

The result is that prisons are seldom out of the news. It may be several years since a major riot or high security escape rocked the system. But robustly independent, critical Chief Inspectors of Prisons have repeatedly identified 'appalling' or 'unhealthy' prisons in their treatment of and conditions for prisoners, so much so that they have wondered what further they could do (see, for example, the preface to the report on Birmingham Prison (HMCIP 2000a)). Prisons are: costly; all too often overcrowded, in spite of the huge prison building programme; a constant management headache, and apparently difficult places in which to maintain a positive regime momentum (Laming Report 2000); a conspicuous failure in terms of the subsequent behaviour of those committed to them (about three-quarters of all young offenders and just over half of all adults are reconvicted within two years of release (Home Office 2000a: chapter 9)); and of marginal value in terms of public protection, because so small a proportion of those responsible for offences are caught, convicted, and imprisoned (estimated as 0.3 per cent—see Home Office 1999a: 29).

All of this means that there is perennial debate about the purpose and value of imprisonment. What constitutes a sensible rate of imprisonment? Though international comparisons are fraught with difficulty (Pease 1994), England, Wales, and Scotland, though somewhat surprisingly not Northern Ireland, rely on the use of imprisonment to an extent greater than practically all other countries in Western Europe. In 1999, 125 persons were incarcerated per 100,000 population in England and Wales, compared to 95 in Germany, 89 in France and Italy, 75 in The Netherlands, and 59 in Sweden (Home Office 2000a: Table 1.19). There are other countries with far higher incarceration rates—the USA, China, and most countries in Eastern Europe, for example—but these countries have markedly different serious crime rates, histories, or political cultures. They do not make comfortable penal bedfellows.

Should we, as some politicians and judges argue, be relatively unconcerned about the size of our prison population and focus rather on the serious crime against which the courts have a duty to protect the public by locking up more offenders for longer? And if locking up more offenders means that conditions in prisons are less than ideal, should we conclude that this is no more than prisoners deserve? Or does the prison, as others argue, reflect a punitively British obsession, and a largely chimerical crime control device, the use of which we could significantly reduce without risk to anyone? Should we regard poor prison conditions as a bar to our claims to be civilized and a misuse of state power against vulnerable and disadvantaged minorities? What, after all, should prisons be like: dark, deterrent statements of the consequences of committing crime; training camps in citizenship; human warehouses; or protective, therapeutic communities for damaged and sometimes dangerous offenders?

THE EMERGENCE OF THE MODERN PRISON AND THE USE OF IMPRISONMENT

Prisons, as mere places of confinement, have existed since time immemorial. Yet prisons as we know them today—places to which offenders are sent as a punishment, there also to be worked on and changed—are a product of the industrial age. The modern prison emerged slowly in Northern Europe from the sixteenth century onwards, but it was not until the late eighteenth and early nineteenth century that the idea came to fruition. The gaols that John Howard travelled up and down the country visiting and laboriously recording in the 1770s were mostly small and seldom purpose-built. They were rooms in ancient city gateways, stables behind the keeper's house, or cellars within town halls. Only in the major cities were there prisons built for the purpose, and here the inhabitants were typically herded together, little subject to regulation save in the exploitative interests of their custodians (Howard 1784).

When opened in 1842, Pentonville Prison, dubbed the 'Model Prison', represented the scale of the transformation: over 500 identical cells in each of which a prisoner was separately to live in silence according to a routine meticulously regulated by a uniformed staff employed by the state. The modern prison, and its institutional counterpart—the workhouse for the indigent poor, the asylum for the insane, the reformatory for wayward youth, and the penitentiary for fallen women—reflected what Foucault (1967: chapter 2) has termed 'the great confinement', and emerged alongside the factory (Melossi and Pavarini 1981). They were social and architectural counterparts. In the factories labour was rationalized for the purposes of more efficient production. In the new institutions of confinement those unproductive sections of the labour force were differentiated, segregated, and disciplined. John Howard's proposals for the better regulation of the insanitary and morally corrupting gaols of the eighteenth century were the corollary of the managerial revolution being wrought in Richard Arkwright's mill at Cromford and Josiah Wedgwood's factory at Etruria. Over each of their model buildings, both actually and metaphorically, was placed a clock according to the hands of which everything was now done (McGowan 1995).

Prisons have historically had three uses: *custodial*, *coercive*, and *punitive*. Though imprisonment was used from medieval times as a punishment, it was generally for minor offences (Pugh 1970). Its primary legal function was custodial or coercive. Accused persons were held awaiting 'gaol delivery' (the arrival of travelling courts), or following conviction pending execution of sentence, generally an assault on the body or death, carried out in a public place. To this was later added imprisonment pending transportation to the colonies. The coercive function of imprisonment was almost entirely for civil debt. The modern prison emerged as its function changed from being primarily custodial-coercive to punitive (Radzinowicz and Hood 1990)—a transformation dramatically illustrated in the opening pages of Foucault's seminal study *Discipline and Punish: the Birth of the Prison* (1977), where the grotesquely brutal execution of a regicide in 1757 Paris is juxtaposed with the clockwork precision of a totally regulated daily regime at a Paris reformatory half a century later. For Foucault the modern prison, with its mechanisms of total surveillance, represented a new form of knowledge and power, irrespective of the interests that power served. Between 1750 and 1850, throughout most of Europe, imprisonment became the principal punishment for serious crime—*carceral* rather than *corporal* punishment, addressing the soul (or the mind) rather than the body (or the outward reputation)—judicial torture was formally abolished (Peters 1996), and the death penalty, henceforth carried out within prisons rather than in public, was reserved for only the most heinous crimes (Spierenburg 1984).

During the nineteenth century this transformation was mostly represented as a vital sub-plot in the Whig version of history as progress: the triumph of reason over superstition, civilization over barbarism. John Howard, Elizabeth Fry, and other penal reformers were depicted in hagiographic terms, Enlightenment saviours whose efforts ushered in humanity. Some Victorian observers, for example Charles Dickens, had their doubts, discovering in the reformed prisons new torments systematically imposed in the name of the people (Collins 1962; see also Mayhew and Binny 1862), a phenomenon which in the twentieth century became devastatingly apparent with the rise of the totalitarian state, the re-emergence of torture, and the mass incarcerations of the concentration camps, gulags, and Soviet and Chinese resocialization centres (see Stern 1998).

Attention naturally turned to the origins of those mechanisms which twentieth-century states were manifestly using to oppress their citizens. Rusche and Kirchheimer (1968), pioneering Marxist theorists in the realm of penal studies, argued that it was not punishment that needed to be explained but specific and concrete *forms of punishment*. Particular penalties, they argued, could be linked to particular modes of production and labour market conditions. When labour was cheap and plentiful, penalties were careless of human life and health. When labour became more valuable, the penal system responded to the economic imperatives of the day: transportation was developed to serve the interests of imperialism; the Houses of Correction were designed to make productive use of the recalcitrant poor; and 'less eligibility', the utilitarian doctrine that convicted prisoners are morally less deserving than the least well-off persons enjoying their freedom in the community, and should therefore not enjoy a life-style and facilities superior or equal to those enjoyed outside the prisons and workhouses, was an ancillary discipline for the labour market beyond the walls. In a similar vein it has since been argued that the proportionate use of imprisonment has declined in most jurisdictions with the growth of the welfare state and onset of fiscal crisis (Scull 1977). The development of electronic surveillance has added another consideration. Why keep large numbers of offenders expensively incarcerated if less eligibility can be assured through carefully graduated transfer payments from which deductions can easily be made, or incapacitation achieved through electronic tagging?

Rusche and Kirchheimer's economic determinism was crude, and their analysis did not exactly fit the facts. But their work stimulated a wealth of scholarship, such that today there is a rich historical penal policy literature on which students may draw. A more nuanced account has emerged of historical and contemporary 'penality', that is, our ideas about and practices of imprisonment (Garland and Young 1983), and how it varies between countries and over time (see the collection of essays in Morris and Rothman 1995). The eighteenth-century penal reformers *were* nearly all motivated by religious faith, pursuing what they perceived to be an humanitarian mission. There *was* a growing revulsion against public corporal and capital punishment which, the evidence suggests, was also counter-productive in that it often served to inflame rather than subdue the mob. Imprisonment comprised both a vivid and a subtle symbolic message. The reformed prisons, monolithically built in rusticated stone, generally sited in the new working-class districts of the expanding urban centres, represented the growing power of the state. Whereas the transaction between the public executioner and the hapless offender appeared personal and arbitrary, the mysterious prison represented impersonal regularity, orderliness, and certainty. In the age of liberty it was particularly apt that those who breached the social contract should lose their freedom. Prison sentences were meted out, proportionate to the gravity of the offence, and were served, at least in theory, in a perfectly regulated environment where all were stripped of their external identities and treated equally (see Ignatieff 1978; McConville 1981).

The multi-faceted appeal of the prison and imprisonment, then and now, emphasises that imprisonment, like punishment generally, needs to be understood from a variety of angles, as: a technical means to an end; a coercive relationship; an instrument of class domination; a form of power; and an expression of collective moral feeling ritually expressed (for reviews of the sociological literature, see Garland 1990; Cavadino and Dignan 2002). To the extent that imprisonment serves different social functions, this suggests that attempts to change the degree to which imprisonment is used are unlikely to succeed simply by proclaiming the utilitarian shortcomings of the enterprise.

All developed societies, whatever their ideological pretensions, employ imprisonment as their principal penalty for serious crime. Everyone claims to support the use of imprisonment only as a last resort. Yet the rate at which imprisonment is used varies greatly over time and between jurisdictions (Rutherford 1984; Christie 1994). These variations cannot fully be explained by crime rates, changing fashions in the philosophy of punishment, demographic factors, levels of economic activity, or public policy considerations; though factors subsumed by these headings—unemployment or the supply of prison places, for example—have undoubtedly influenced the rate of imprisonment in some countries in some periods (Zimring and Hawkins 1991). The use of imprisonment is a complex issue (see, for example, Downes 1988 and 1997 for examinations of penal policy in The Netherlands). Yet the rate of imprisonment is not beyond government control. It is ultimately a matter of political choice.

THE MISSION: THE PURPOSE OF IMPRISONMENT

THE LEGAL FUNCTIONS OF IMPRISONMENT

The most fundamental way of answering the question 'What are prisons for?' is to distinguish the three legal functions—*custodial*, *coercive*, and *punitive*—we have already identified.

Suspects refused bail and detained before trial, or convicted but not yet sentenced (generally awaiting medical or pre-sentence reports), are held in custody for no other reason than to ensure that the course of justice proceeds to its conclusion and that everyone concerned is protected against the likelihood of harm in the interim. A small number of non-criminal prisoners—detained under the Immigration Act, for example—are held in prisons pending completion of enquiries or execution of an administrative decision. There is no justification for holding such prisoners in conditions more oppressive than is warranted by the fact of custody itself, either because they are not eligible for punishment (the unconvicted are subject to the presumption of innocence) or, if convicted, because the court has not yet determined that loss of liberty is the appropriate sentence.

Offenders held coercively—nowadays almost entirely fine defaulters—are kept in prison for as long as they fail to comply with a court order that they pay a financial penalty enforced by the court. As soon as they pay, or once the custodial period in lieu of payment is served, they are released. In this case the prison, the loss of liberty, and possibly also the conditions in custody, are used to pressurize the offender into conforming.

Lastly, there are persons held punitively—nowadays the great majority—as a sanction for offences of which they stand convicted. Since the abolition of the death penalty in 1965 imprisonment has been the most serious penalty the courts can impose in Britain. The punishment of imprisonment for sentenced prisoners might comprise both loss of liberty and harsh living conditions in the name of 'less eligibility' (see above) or deterrence. Today prison administrators generally disavow such purposes, reiterating Paterson's famous dictum that offenders are sent to prison 'as a punishment, not for punishment' (Ruck 1951: 23). However, it is difficult to square conditions and practices in many prisons with this disavowal, and 'less eligibility' remains a potent political (if not administrative) imperative (Garland 1990); an imperative given a new spur by the last Conservative Home Secretary, Michael Howard's stipulation that prison conditions be 'austere' (Sparks 1996). Remand prisoners, in spite of the presumption of innocence, tend, both in Britain and elsewhere, to be viewed by prison staff as sentenced prisoners in waiting (Fox 1952: 286): their living conditions are generally among the worst to be found in the system (King and Morgan 1976; Morgan 1993), as true in Scotland (Scottish Executive 2000) as in England and Wales (HMCIP 2000a).

A distinction needs to be drawn between the sentencers' purposes and prison managers' objectives. The two should ideally be consistent and spring from the same principles. But they are not the same and, prior to the Human Rights Act 1998, sentencers were not required to spell out the rationale for their decisions. Whatever justifications sentencers have for using imprisonment (see Ashworth, in Chapter 29 of this volume), prison administrators have practically to manage prisons with regard to the welfare of staff as well as prisoners. What, then, inspires the daily management practice of the Prison Service?

THE LEGAL FRAMEWORK

The work of the Prison Service is framed by the Prison Act 1952 which: lays down the general duties of the prison authorities; defines what a prison is; and, most importantly, empowers the Minister to make Rules for the management of prisons (s 47(1)). The Rules are exercisable by statutory instrument and have recently been substantially revised (SI 1999/728), though the core rules regarding purpose remain the same as those dating from 1964 (see Loucks and Plotnikoff 1993): 'The purpose of the training and treatment of convicted prisoners shall be to encourage and assist them to lead a good and useful life' (rule 3); 'Order and discipline shall be maintained with firmness, but with no more restriction than is required for safe custody and well ordered community life' (rule 6). The treatment of prisoners shall also promote 'self-respect' and the development of 'personal responsibility'. However, the rules have always been unspecific about what prisoners should be provided with in terms of conditions and access to facilities. This tendency has now been entrenched by rule 8: there shall 'be established at every prison systems of privileges ... appropriate to the classes of prisoners there'. The privileges may include time out of cell and in association with other prisoners greater than that normally permitted (rule 8(2)). Further, the system may include arrangements whereby privileges are granted 'to prisoners only in so far as they have met, and for so long as they continue to meet, specified standards in their behaviour and their performance in work or other activities' (rule 8(3)). To emphasize the meaning of the terminology, though the arrangements for granting privileges shall include 'a requirement that the prisoner be given reasons for any decision adverse to him', nothing in Rule 8 'shall be taken to confer on a prisoner any *entitlement* to any *privilege*' (emphasis added). Which is to say, the rules do not confer *rights*.

The new Rules endorse the operational reality and legal position *status quo ante*. They remain ungenerous in their provisions, are seldom specific, and, even when specific, generally grant prison managers extensive discretion as to whether facilities will be provided (Richardson 1993). They make clear what the courts had previously held, namely, that breaches of the Rules do not provide the basis for a claim for breach of statutory duty and do not vest prisoners with any special rights (*Hague v Deputy Governor of Parkhurst Prison* [1991] 3 All ER 733, confirming *Arbon v Anderson* [1943] KB 252).[1] The question at issue, therefore, is whether the arguments which raged in the 1980s about the relative merits of competing formulations to summarize the proper aims of prisons management—'treatment and training' (rule 1 in the 1964 Prison Rules), 'positive custody' (the May Committee (1979) formula), or 'humane containment' (the King and Morgan (1980) basic standards and prisoners' rights-inspired proposal)—have been made irrelevant as a result of subsequent managerialist initiatives. The official answer to that question is possibly to be found in the fact that the new 1999 Prison Rules figured not at all in the annual reports of the Prison Service for 1998–9 and 1999–2000: the emphasis is entirely on Home Office and Prison Service management objectives and performance indicators.

THE MANAGERIAL FRAMEWORK

Posted at the entrance of all Prison Service establishments is a *Statement of Purpose*:

Her Majesty's Prison Service serves the public by keeping in custody those convicted by the courts. Our duty is to look after them with humanity and to help them lead law abiding and useful lives in custody and after release.

This *Statement*, with its references to security, basic standards, and rehabilitation, is backed up by an increasingly complex set of interrelated Home Office, Criminal Justice Service, and Prison Service 'aims', 'objectives', 'public service agreements' (PSAs), 'targets' and 'key performance indicators' (KPIs).

The problems associated with management frameworks of this kind include: getting to grips with those aspects of performance not easily measured; developing an array of performance measures to ensure that inbalances of effort do not result from

---

[1] For detailed reviews of the degree to which the courts, both domestic and European, have generally intervened in prison life, see Creighton and King 1996; Feldman 2002; Livingstone and Owen 1999.

Box 30.1 BASED ON THE LATEST STATEMENT OF PRISON SERVICE
AIMS, OBJECTIVES, AND PRINCIPLES

THE HOME OFFICE STATEMENT OF PURPOSE:

'*To build a safe, just and tolerant society in which the rights and responsibilities of individuals, families and communities are properly balanced and the protection and security of the public are maintained.*'

CRIMINAL JUSTICE SYSTEM OBJECTIVES:

- To reduce crime and the fear of crime and their social and economic costs.
- To dispense justice fairly and efficiently and promote the rule of law.

HOME OFFICE AIM 4—HM PRISON SERVICE AIM

'*Effective execution of the sentences of the courts so as to reduce re-offending and protect the public.*'

HM PRISON SERVICE OBJECTIVES

- *Protect the public by holding those committed by the courts in a safe, decent and healthy environment.*
- *Reduce crime by providing constructive regimes which address offending behaviour, improve educational and work skills and promote law abiding behaviour in custody and after release.*

HM PRISON SERVICE PRINCIPLES

- *Deal fairly, openly and humanely with prisoners and all others who come into contact with us.*
- *Encourage prisoners to address offending behaviour and respect others.*
- *Value and support each other's contribution.*
- *Promote equality of opportunity for all and combat discrimation wherever it occurs.*
- *Work constructively with criminal justice agencies and other organisations.*
- *Obtain best value from the resources available.*

Source: Prison Service (2001): 9.

staff skewing their performance to satisfy that which is easily measured; focusing on *outputs* rather than *outcomes*; not stifling professionalism and local initiative by exerting excessively centralized control; and not sapping staff morale and energy with too great a burden of bureaucratic compliance and formal inspection processes. There are always ethical lucunae and operational dilemmas built into the deceptively clearest of plans. Two illustrations will suffice to make the point.

The Aim—'Effective execution of the sentences of the courts so as to reduce re-offending and protect the public' (see Box 30.1)—contains two potentially conflicting elements, *security* and giving prisoners sufficient *responsibility* effectively to test their resolve not to commit offences or engage in behaviour associated with their offending (use of drugs, for example). Escapes are relatively easy to measure, though even here things are not straightforward. KPI escapes are 'those where the escapee is not recaptured within 15 minutes, or is recaptured earlier but not before committing one or more criminal offences other than the offence of escape itself' (Prison Service 2000a: 30). Absconds (from home leave, for example) are not accounted escapes, a positive decision because absconds could absolutely be prevented by never granting home leave. The point is this. Security, humanity, and rehabilitation need to be kept in balance and proportion. Thus the Prison Service currently has three KPIs relating to escapes, one for the highest security category of prisoners, one for all escapes from prisons, and one for escapes from prison escorts, including those to and from court-houses. However, there is arguably insufficient performance measurement of what the Chief Inspector and Director General respectively call *humanity* and *decency*. Has security been too much emphasized? Absconds may not count as escapes, but are there now too few home leaves and outside work placements (see HMCIP/Probation 2001: para. 6.35) and too many prisoners in security categories not granted home leaves and outside work placements?

Likewise, the current Home Office PSA aims to reduce the rate of reconvictions of all offenders subject to custodial and community penalties by 5 per cent by 2004 (Prison Service 2000b: 43). The Prison Service has set itself targets to: deliver 'What Works' offending programmes (see Raynor, in Chapter 31 of this volume), educational and vocational courses, and associated qualifications; randomly drug test prisoners; and create living units in which residents sign voluntary drug testing compacts (see Prison Service 2001: 10–11). Most people would consider these programmes worthwhile. Nevertheless they concern *outputs* rather than *outcomes*. It remains to be seen whether rolling out such programmes on a mass scale will reduce the overall rate of reconvictions, or drive out one-to-one and non-accredited work important for the development of some individuals or for staff–prisoner relationships generally. The debate about overall prison regime and decision-making standards will continue.

THE WOOLF REPORT AND THE STANDARDS DEBATE

In his Report on the 1990 disturbances, Lord Woolf found merit in the Prison Service's *Statement of Purpose*, but he added two vital caveats. He was critical of the absence of any reference to justice and he did not agree that the *statement* adequately covered the unconvicted and unsentenced (Woolf 1991: paras 10.16–10.64).

Woolf's use of the term 'justice' was arguably too broad (see Morgan 1992), but it tied together sentencing and prisons policy. He maintained that when the Prison Service says it 'serves the public' it does so by more than simply keeping in custody those committed by the courts: it does so best by furthering the objectives of the criminal justice system by preventing crime. That means, *inter alia:* looking after prisoners with humanity; safeguarding prisoners' 'civil rights which are not taken away expressly or by necessary implication' (*Raymond v Honey* [1983] 1 AC 1, cited by Woolf, at para. 14.289; minimizing 'the negative effects of imprisonment which make re-offending more likely'; ensuring 'that life in prisons . . . [is] as close to life outside as the demands of imprisonment permit'; as well as providing opportunities for training and rehabilitation (para. 10.29). This did not mean 'a return to . . . the treatment model' (para. 10.34) because imprisonment is not justified for reformative purposes, neither is 'being a criminal . . . a creative condition'. But if prisoners are released 'in an embittered and disaffected state' then the criminal justice objective of preventing re-offending is undone (paras 14.8–14.9).

If the Prison Service contains [the] prisoner in conditions which are inhumane or degrading . . . then a punishment of imprisonment which was justly imposed will result in injustice . . . it is the Prison Service's duty to look after prisoners with humanity. If it fulfils this duty, the Prison Service is partly achieving what the Court must be taken to have intended when it passed a sentence of imprisonment.' (para. 10.19)

Which is to say that Woolf assumed that Paterson's dictum (see above) had come into its own as a statement of what sentencers use prisons for. He was also endorsing the Prison Department view that: 'Imprisonment itself . . . is the punishment inflicted by law and no further available hardship should be imposed on a prisoner except by way of formal disciplinary action' (Home Office 1984: para. 108).

In order that basic living conditions be addressed, Woolf favoured an interlocking hierarchy of 'contracts' or 'compacts'—between the Chief Executive of the Service and the Minister, between area managers and governors, between governors and officers, and between governors and prisoners—setting out resources and facilities to be provided for a stated prison population. This would permit, in the case of prisoners, 'legitimate expectations' to be generated (Woolf Report 1991: para. 12.129), which 'could provide a platform for an application for judicial review' were those expectations unreasonably not met (ibid.: para. 12.123). The contracts should not be drawn up in such a way that they would give prisoners private rights leading to awards of damages if breached. But the contracts might lead, Woolf hoped, to the promulgation of aspirational standards, to a system of accrediting prisons for having achieved those standards (as happens in the USA), and, eventually, to the incorporation of those standards in a new set of Prison Rules. Furthermore, Woolf recommended that prisoners be given reasons, in writing if they reasonably request it, 'for any decision which materially and adversely affects them' (ibid.: paras 14.300, 14.307).

Woolf's recommendation is hazily reflected in the new rule 8(4), which, as we have seen, requires that reasons be given to prisoners having privileges withdrawn. However, this is some distance from the proposition that prisoners have 'legitimate expectations' capable of judicial review, a prospect which some critics (Richardson 1993b) in any case considered a 'notoriously flexible' doctrine. And it is certainly a far cry from the aspirations of earlier critics seeking legally enforceable minimum standards (Casale 1984; Gostin and Staunton 1985; Casale and Plotnikoff 1989, 1990).

The Prison Service has not ignored the standards debate, but the steps so far taken have been modest. First, Woolf's 'contracts' have subtly been turned, through the 'national framework for incentives and earned privileges' (IEPs) (Prison Service 1996: 26–7), and as some commentators warned was likely (Casale 1993), into mechanisms for exerting greater paternalistic control *over* prisoners rather than establishing minimum standards and rights for *their* protection (for an evaluation of the IEP scheme, see Liebling *et al.* 1997, 1999). These are the arrangements legitimated by rule 8. Secondly, though the Prison Service has developed a set of *Standards* which 'conform to current legislation' are 'achievable and affordable across the Service', are 'measurable and auditable', and which 'communicate clearly and succinctly what the Prison Service *aims* to deliver and why' (emphasis added), such *Standards* keep 'prescriptive elements to the minimum required to achieve consistent delivery of Service' and they 'do not change the legal rights of individuals nor do they imply additional rights or entitlements' (Prison Service 2000c). Neither do the current *Standards* incorporate any minimum standards for untried and unsentenced prisoners beyond those meagre provisions in the Prison Rules (HMCIP 2000a: 22).

Thus prisoners can still be and are transferred in large numbers, without explanation, to prisons relatively distant from their homes in order better to distribute prisoner numbers within the prison estate, or as an administrative control measure. Prisoners still have no entitlement to be given reasons either for their initial or for subsequent security classification, a decision which critically affects the quality of their lives. And Woolf's key proposal to prevent overcrowding and thereby safeguard basic living conditions—that there be introduced a prison rule that no prison hold more prisoners than 3 per cent above its certified normal accommodation (CNA), except temporarily, or following the laying by the Minister of an authorizing certificate before both Houses of Parliament (Woolf Report: paras 11.141–11.142)—was initially rejected (Home Office 1991: para 6.13) and has not subsequently been resurrected.

As a result, many prisons continue to be severely overcrowded and the case for having legally enforceable, detailed living standards remains as strong as ever. However, as we shall see, the process of contracting out the management of prisons and, in relation to juvenile prisoners, the fact that the Prison Service has become the contractor-supplier of custodial places for the Youth Justice Board (YJB), are keeping the question of what custodial standards should apply to the fore.

WHO ARE THE PRISONERS?

Prisoners are overwhelmingly young, male, socially and economically disadvantaged, repetitive property offenders. Prisoners from socially privileged backgrounds attract disproportionate media attention largely because of their rarity. Prisons are a feature and hazard of working-class life. Only governors have traditionally been 'gentlemen', and invariably their reminiscences betray their identification with that strange animal, the 'toff' prisoner thrust into an alien underclass world (see Priestley 1989: 40; Blake 1927: chapter 6; Clayton 1958: chapter 8). Most prisoners, moreover, are transient, even if a high proportion return again and again: the staff, typically, spend much more of their lives in prison than their charges. A growing minority of prisoners, however, are forced to make the prison their long-term home. Indeed, a few seem destined to remain incarcerated until they die.

THE GROWTH IN THE LONG-TERM PRISON POPULATION

It is important to distinguish prison 'receptions' and the 'average daily population' (ADP). The overwhelming majority of prisoners are in prison for a matter of days, weeks, or months rather than years. Remand prisoners are in custody for on average less than two months. Eighty per cent of sentenced prisoners are released within twelve months.[2] The ADP figures tell a different story, however. At any one time 30 per cent of remand prisoners have been in custody for more than three months, and long-term adult prisoners dominate prisons both numerically and, more importantly, culturally: 47 per cent of the ADP are serving sentences of four or more years.

The contrast between prison receptions and the ADP has progressively become more marked as 'bifurcation' (see above) has been pursued at all decision-making levels.

First are the changes in sentencing. In spite of the increase in recorded crime, the proportionate use of custody gradually declined until the 1980s, then fluctuated, then, since the early 1990s, increased markedly: between 1989 and 1999 it rose from 17 to 25 per cent. The greater part of this recent increase has comprised very short sentences: the number of sentences of six months or less has more than doubled (see Home Office 2001a: Appendix 2). There has also been a dramatic increase in the number of prisoners sentenced to very long sentences. In 1965, the year that the death penalty was abolished, eighty-eight prisoners were received with sentences of ten years or more, including life: 862 such prisoners were received in 2000.

The increase in the number of long-term prison receptions has been matched by an increase in the proportion of their sentences served in prison. In 1985 the average time served by life sentence prisoners released on licence was 10.7 years: in 1999/2000 it was around 14 years. Both murderers (for whom the life sentence is mandatory) and discretionary life-sentence prisoners are generally now required to remain longer in prison before being conditionally released. Moreover, bifurcation has characterized executive release policy across the whole range of sentences. The shorter the sentence, the smaller the proportion of the sentence the prisoner is required to serve in prison (see Home Office 2000a: Table 4.11).

These trends have transformed the character of the ADP. Long-term prisoners now preoccupy prison administrators because long-term prisoners dominate life in most training prisons (see Figure 30.2).

---

[2] All figures, unless otherwise stated, are taken from the annual *Prison Statistics*, the most recent of which were published in 2001 (Home Office 2001c). For a a general review of prison statistics, see Morgan (1995).

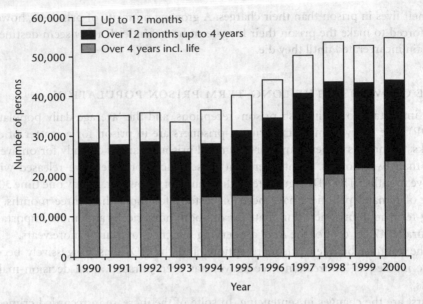

Fig. 30.2 Sentenced population by length of sentence 1990–2000
Source: Home Office (2001c), Fig. 1.5.

PAROLE

Part of the explanation for these population trends lies in the introduction in 1967 of parole (superimposed on an existing policy, which had been in existence since 1940, of one-third automatic remission for good conduct on all determinate sentences) and its development since. After a cautious beginning, when parole was seen very much as a privilege to be earned by prisoners who had reached a 'recognisable peak in their training' (Home Office 1965), executive release was gradually liberalized (see Carlisle Report 1988; Maguire 1992). Following initiatives by two Home Secretaries, Roy Jenkins in 1974 and Leon Brittan in 1983, an increasing proportion of short- and medium-sentence prisoners received parole almost routinely. Indeed, after 1987 all prisoners serving sentences of twelve months or less were automatically released without assessment at the halfway point in their sentences. In the case of Leon Brittan's initiative, however, this liberalization at the lower end of the sentence range was balanced by a much tougher policy for certain categories of longer term prisoner, a policy which was highly controversial because it effectively involved Ministers making sentencing decisions. It was announced that: parole would not normally be granted at all to prisoners serving over five years for violent offences or drug-trafficking; ministers would set a minimum tariff period to be served by life sentence prisoners, dependent on the circumstances of their offence; and special categories of lifer—those convicted for the murder of police or prison officers, the sexual or sadistic murder of children, murder by firearms in the course of robbery, or murder in the furtherance of terrorism—would not normally be released until they had served at least twenty years.

The policy of Ministers setting a minimum tariff period to 'meet the interests of deterrence and retribution' was modified in 1987 in the case of discretionary life sentences (following *R v Secretary of State for the Home Department, ex p Handscombe* (1991) *The Times*, 4 March), such that the recommendations of the judiciary were strictly adhered to. In the case of mandatory life sentences for murder, however, Ministers, typically Junior Ministers, continued to determine the tariff to be served and, as evidence given to a House of Lords Select Committee showed, they typically altered upwards the tariffs recommended by trial judges and the Lord Chief Justice (House of Lords 1989). Since 1994 (following *R v Secretary of State for the Home Department, ex p Doody* [1994] 1 AC 531, HL) mandatory lifers have had the right to know the minimum period the judge thought they should serve, any alteration in the tariff set, and the reasons for all such decisions, and, the right to make representations. It has become apparent that sometimes Ministers have increased the tariff recommended by the judge by as much as ten years (Creighton and King 1996: chapter 10). Even when the tariff has been served, lifers may not be released on the basis that they present a continued risk to the public or, most controversially, to maintain public confidence in the criminal justice system. In what is undoubtedly the most famous case in which this consideration arises—that of Myra Hindley—it arguably amounts to sentencing by the tabloid press. Successive Home Secretaries have announced that they will never authorize Hindley's release, or that of a handful of other convicted murderers (twenty-three of them in 1999—see HMCIP/Probation 1999: para. 9.6). These decisions are not binding on successors, but in a tough 'law and order' climate they undoubtedly make more liberal decisions in the future less likely.

In 1987–8 the parole system was thoroughly reviewed by the Carlisle Committee, whose recommendations were, with certain important exceptions, adopted in the Criminal Justice Act 1991. The current system provides for: automatic conditional release at the halfway point of sentences under four years; Parole Board responsibility for release decisions for prisoners serving determinate sentences of between four and fifteen years, the threshold for release being the halfway point in sentences, with conditional release up to the three-quarter point; and continued involvement of the Home Secretary in release decisions of sentences of fifteen years or more, though the Brittan rules have been abolished (for an evaluation of the new automatic conditional release system, see Cavadino and Dignan 2002: chapter 7). If the Halliday proposals are adopted most determinate sentence prisoners will be released at the half-way point in their sentences, the decision resting with review courts. The Parole Board would then deal only with life sentences and violent and sexual offenders presenting a risk of serious harm, subject to a new 'special' sentence—a further form of bifurcation (Home Office 2001a: chapter 4).

The benefits of having a parole system are contested. In 1997 the Conservative government made statutory provision for its abolition. It wished to promote 'honesty in sentencing' , by which was meant that sentences announced in court would more or less equate with those actually served in prison (Home Office 1996; Conservative Party 2001: 12). But it is difficult to see why such a policy would either be more honest—when judges pass sentences of imprisonment they simultaneously announce what this means in terms of parole eligibility—or serve the public interest. The absence of parole would provide prisoners with little or no incentive to engage in offence-focused and other programmes while in prison, would reduce or extinguish their close supervision following release, and would mean the continued incarceration of the overwhelming majority (96 per cent) of prisoners who do not currently engage in offending behaviour—or at least offending behaviour that is detected—while on parole (Parole Board 2000: 18). The evidence suggests that the Parole Board is rather risk aversive (Hood and Shute 2000; Padfield and Leibling 2000). Looked at solely in terms of prisoners reoffending while subject to licence, parole works.

GENDERED PRISONS AND THE GROWTH IN THE NUMBER OF WOMEN PRISONERS

Prisoners are overwhelmingly male—92 per cent of all receptions and 94 per cent of the ADP. Moreover, since it has long been the policy for women to be housed in institutions used exclusively for women (though some remand prisons accommodate males and females in separate wings), and because, until relatively recently, prison officers were employed exclusively to work with prisoners of the same sex, prisons are heavily gendered institutions. This has influenced the differential regimes thought appropriate for male and female prisoners, the nature of the relationships between prisoners and staff, the character of the activities provided, the relative use of drugs, disciplinary measures, and so on (for accounts of the history of women's imprisonment, see Dobash *et al.* 1986; Zedner 1994, 1995). The tendency has been to label women prisoners as mad or sad rather than bad, and the activities organized for them have traditionally been geared to the roles of mother and homemaker rather than the labour market (Carlen 1983). Thus the only major local prison to have been rebuilt this century—Holloway, the largest prison for women—was redesigned to operate on medically-oriented therapeutic lines (Casale 1989; Rock 1996), an approach considered particularly appropriate for women, but marginalized for men, as evidenced by the failure, until 2001, to replicate, despite its evident success, the experimental therapeutic prison at Grendon Underwood (Genders and Player 1994; Marshall 1997). The latest survey evidence suggests that most work provided for women prisoners continues to comprise menial, unskilled maintenance tasks, little integrated with their training (Hamlyn and Lewis 2000).

The staffing gender profile of prisons is changing, however. By 2001, 17 per cent of prison officers were female, and in all prisons a growing proportion of officers were of the opposite sex to their charges (for a breakdown, by establishment, see Leibling and Price 2001: Appendix A).

The female prison population is in several respects different from that of the male population. It is not clear that women, all other things being equal, are more likely to receive a custodial sentence, but the differences between the men and women in custody nevertheless raise important questions of justice. First, 21 per cent of the female ADP comprises remands compared to 17 per cent for men, this in spite of the fact that the average remand period for women is significantly shorter (thirty-six compared to forty-nine days in 2000). The principal explanation for the disparity is that a far lower proportion of female than male custodial remands—36 compared to

48 per cent—do not subsequently receive a custodial sentence. This prompts the question as to whether so many women need have been remanded in custody. Sentenced women prisoners also differ from men. They are typically older, serving shorter sentences, less recidivist, and less likely to have committed sexual, violent, or robbery offences. They are also substantially less likely to be reconvicted, a consideration reflected in their higher release rate under the Home Detention Curfew scheme (see HMCIP/Probation 2001: para. 7.12). Some writers, notably Carlen (1990; Carlen and Tchaikovsky 1996), argue that these differences in the male and female prison populations mean that the imprisonment of women is *different* from that of men and indicate that, despite their relatively small number, there is a powerful case for there being substantially fewer. In fact the opposite is occurring, and the rate of increase is dramatic. At the end of 2001 there were over 4,000 women in prison, a 150 per cent increase over ten years compared to a 40 per cent increase for men. Precisely why the female prison population has risen so dramatically is not well understood, though one factor is the growth in the number of female foreign nationals convicted of drug trafficking (see below).

Nineteen out of the 137 Prison Service establishments currently house women. Most of these accommodate women only. There is a fundamental dilemma. Approximately two-thirds of women prisoners have at least one child below the age of eighteen, but whereas the children of male prisoners are mostly looked after by wives or partners (Dodd and Hunter 1992), those of women prisoners tend to be cared for by grandmothers or friends (Caddle and Crisp 1997). The highest priority for many women prisoners is (not surprisingly) to be in a prison close to home so as to be able to see their children and other family members regularly (HMCIP 1997a: 12–15). Because there are relatively few prisons for women, they tend to be a greater average distance from prisoners' homes. Nevertheless, the Prisons Inspectorate has concluded that the sharing of sites with men does not benefit women. *Equality* of provision for women should not mean the *same* provision as for men. Their needs are different.

A 1997 thematic review by the Prisons Inspectorate of *Women in Prison* led to improvements in the provisions for women, not least because there is now an Area Manager for the women's estate and a Women's Policy Group at HQ (HMCIP 2001b). Moreover, the government is sufficiently concerned about the growth in women prisoners to have announced a *Strategy for Women Offenders* with a view to reducing prisoner numbers (Home Office 2001d; see also Heidensohn, in Chapter 15 of this volume).

ETHNICITY, NATIONALITY, AND IMPRISONMENT

Nineteen per cent of male prisoners and 25 per cent of female prisoners are members of ethnic minorities, two-thirds of them Afro-Caribbean. If foreign nationals and children under sixteen years are excluded from the analysis, black residents are imprisoned at roughly eight times the rate of white residents—a difference greater than in the USA—whereas persons of South Asian origin are incarcerated at roughly the same rate as whites. Further, within these groups there are significant differences,

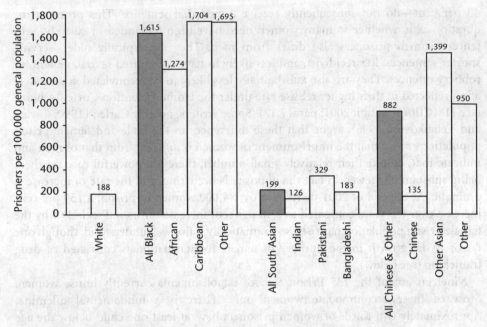

British nationals, males aged 15–64, females aged 15–54

Fig. 30.3 Incarceration rates ethnic group 2000

Source: Home Office (2001c), Fig. 6.6.

persons of Caribbean origin being incarcerated at a rate much higher than persons of African origin, and people of Pakistani origin being incarcerated at a rate approaching two or three times as high as persons of Bangladeshi and Indian origin respectively (see Figure 30.3).

These data enable the reasons for over-representation to be examined more closely. Nationality is one factor. Over 5,500 prisoners, or 9 per cent of the prison population, comprise foreign nationals, a rising tide noted throughout Europe (Tomashevski 1994). A significant proportion of these foreign prisoners are not normally resident in Britain. Whereas only 3 per cent of white prisoners are foreign nationals, the proportions of black, South Asian, and Chinese prisoners are 25, 29, and 50 per cent respectively. Moreover, a significantly higher proportion of women prisoners are foreign nationals (15 per cent) than are men (8 per cent), and half of these foreign women are African or Afro-Caribbean, a large proportion of them sentenced for drugs offences: these are the drug 'mules' apprehended at ports of entry (Green 1991). Another factor is the relative youth of the ethnic minorities compared to the white population: thus the over-representation is greatest among young adult prisoners. Lastly, the ethnic minorities are most over-represented among the remand population—a feature which has attracted much critical attention (see Hood 1992; Fitzgerald and Marshall 1996)—and among sentenced prisoners their offence and sentence profile is different from the white population. Within all the ethnic minority groups, male and female, foreign nationals and British, the proportion of drug offenders is significantly higher than that of whites. Drug offences, particularly trafficking, attract longer than average sentences, and this explains part of the general over-representation.

THE YOUNG BUT AGEING PRISON POPULATION

Imprisonment is experienced largely by the young. Twenty seven per cent of unsentenced receptions, and 23 per cent of sentenced receptions, are under twenty-one years of age. Of adult sentenced prisoner receptions, 52 per cent are under thirty years of age. Prisoners in their twenties dominate life in most prisons. This is not surprising. Crime, or at least the sort of crime that leads to conviction, is largely the activity of adolescents and young adults, and sentences of imprisonment are generally imposed on repeat offenders: two-thirds of the offenders sentenced to immediate custody have three or more previous convictions, over a quarter have eleven or more. The modal age of male prisoners received under sentence is twenty-eight, that for women one year higher. Nevertheless the prison population is ageing. The long-term trend, substantially reversed in the 1990s, has been a reduction in the number of very young prisoners and growth in the number of middle aged and even elderly prisoners. Younger prisoners tend to have shorter sentences. In 1989 some 41 per cent of the sentenced ADP was under twenty-five years and approximately 15 per cent was aged forty years or more; in 2000 the proportions were 32 and 19 per cent. There are now over 1,150 prisoners at any one time over sixty years of age, many of them serving long sentences.

The period since 1945 has witnessed the use of several differently titled custodial sentences for prisoners under twenty-one—immediate imprisonment, borstal training, detention in a detention centre, and youth custody—but all were replaced by detention in a YOI by the Criminal Justice Act 1988, for which sentence the minimum age was raised in 1991 from fourteen to fifteen years. This simplification was thrown into reverse by the Crime and Disorder Act 1998 which introduced the detention and training order (DTO) for juveniles, a sentence which can be served in a Prison Service YOI (currently 2,850 places), or one of the local authority secure centres (250 places for offenders), or one of three contracted-out Secure Training Centres (125 places). The YOIs nevertheless continue to be called YOIs, and most are occupied *both* by juveniles serving DTO sentences *and* by young adults (eighteen to twenty year-olds), albeit in increasingly segregated units. The government has issued a Consultation Paper regarding the custody of young adults (Home Office 1999b), but has yet to decide whether separate institutional arrangements should be made for them. On the basis that the transition to full adult male independence extends beyond the age of twenty (see Graham and Bowling 1995), there are advocates (NACRO 2001) for male prisoners aged eighteen to twenty-four being housed and provided for separate from older prisoners.

Given these changes and the current uncertainty regarding the status of young adults, the only sensible way to consider the use of custody for young offenders is to aggregate all sentences for persons under twenty-one years. The results of this exercise

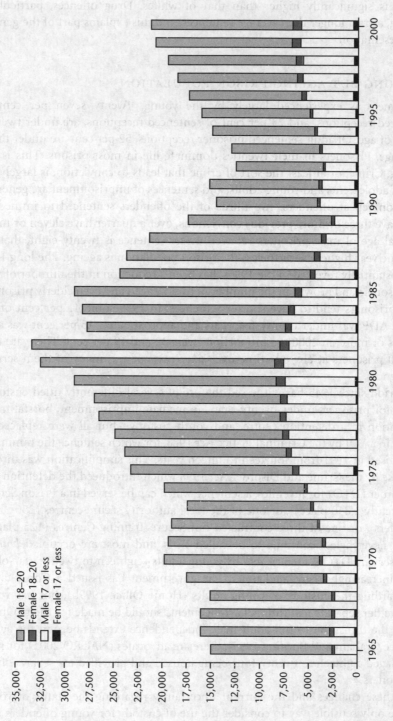

Fig. 30.4 Males and females under 21 serving immediate custodial sentences in Prison Service establishments

are depicted in Figure 30.5. Though the number of young offender receptions has risen since 1993, thereby tracking the upward trend in the use of custody for adults, nevertheless the number of offenders under twenty-one sentenced to an immediate custodial sentence remains only three-fifths of what it was in the early 1980s, and is now at about the same level it was thirty years ago.

The number of juveniles held on remand has also risen in recent years, though remanding in custody of fourteen-year-old boys ceased in 1992. The government has said it is committed to ending remands in prison of fifteen- and sixteen-year-old boys (girls of this age are already excluded), a commitment prompted by the furore over the suicide of two fifteen-year-old boys in local prisons in 1990 and 1991. Since then all sense of urgency appears to have evaporated. Five hundred and twenty-one fifteen-year-olds were remanded in custody in 1999, and juveniles comprised some 8 per cent of all remands in custody. The Prisons Inspectorate has found that a 'significant minority of these young people are even more isolated, victimised and disturbed' than their adult counterparts (HMCIP 2000a: 25).

A MORE INTRACTABLE PRISON POPULATION?

It is difficult to evaluate the extent to which prisoners are more intractable today than once they were. The proportion of sentenced receptions who have been convicted of crimes of violence (including sexual offences and robbery) is, at 21 per cent, less than it was ten years ago. Moreover, the limited data available suggest that the prison population is not significantly more recidivist today (see Home Office 2001a: Table 4.2). However, because sentences are now longer—particularly those for violent offences—and parole is less readily given for longer sentences, a substantially higher proportion of the sentenced ADP has been convicted of offences of violence—44 per cent in 2000, compared to 30 per cent in 1980 (see Figure 30.5). There has also been a gradual build up of prisoners—those convicted of drug-related offences, for

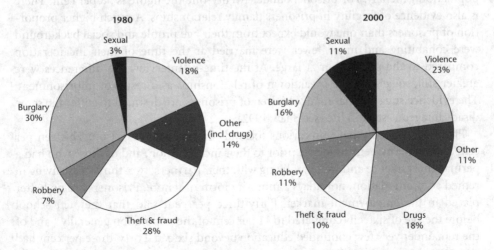

Fig. 30.5 Adult male average daily prison population by offence type 1980–2000

example—who fall outside the definition of violent offenders, but many of whom may be more inured to violence.

These prison population features, combined with the fact that an increasing proportion of prisoners have little or no prospect of early release, and prisoners generally are subject to an increased security quotient, may be the explanation for the fact that, until the early 1990s, major prison disturbances and prisoner disciplinary proceedings became more common. The current picture is more complex, with conflicting indices of orderliness. There has not been a major disorder since that at Wymott in 1993. However, despite the fact that the number of assaults on staff or prisoners has been adopted as a Service Performance Indicator (PI)—and thus might be expected to be recorded more parsimoniously—the overall number of recorded assaults has stayed at much the same rate (Prison Service 2000a: Annexe 2) and the recorded incidence of violence per head of population in male YOIs has more than doubled in the last ten years (Home Office 2000a: Table 8.3). It appears that certain types of prisons have become less orderly, and others more so. Leibling (2001) has convincingly argued, for example, that the dispersal prisons are now safer and more orderly than at any time in their history.

PRISONERS' SOCIO-ECONOMIC CHARACTER AND PERSONAL RELATIONSHIPS

The prison population is socially and economically disadvantaged relative to the population generally. A survey of prisoners conducted in 1991 on behalf of the Home Office (Walmsley *et al.* 1992) shows that prisoners are disproportionately working class (83 per cent of male prisoners are from manual, partly skilled, or unskilled groups, compared to 55 per cent of the population generally) and exhibit telling indicators of social stress. An implausibly high proportion, 23 per cent, report having been in local authority care below the age of sixteen (this may have more to do with prisoners' contact with social services when children) compared to 2 per cent for the population generally. For prisoners under twenty-one the figure is 38 per cent. There is also evidence of fragility in prisoners' family relationships. A much higher proportion of prisoners than one would expect from their age profile and social background were cohabiting and many fewer were married at the time of their incarceration compared to the population at large. At the time of interview the differences were greater still, suggesting the breakdown of relationships as a result of imprisonment. The evidence suggests that many children of prisoners are destined to suffer the same disadvantageous start in life (see Shaw 1992).

Prisoners generally have precarious toeholds on life outside prison. Thirteen per cent had no permanent residence prior to their incarceration, and of those who had a permanent residence and were not living with their partners, two-thirds were living in rented accommodation, nowadays a minority form of tenure. Prisoners are no better placed in the employment market. Forty-three per cent said that they left school before the age of sixteen (compared to 11 per cent of the population generally), and of the remainder very few continued education beyond sixteen. Forty-three per cent had no education qualification whatsoever (many of these prisoners are functionally illiterate) and only 8 per cent had qualifications beyond GCSE. They have low levels of literacy, numeracy, and educational attainment. A recent basic skills survey of prisoners estimated that 60–70 per cent of prisoners have literacy and numeracy levels so low that they are ineligible for 96 per cent of jobs (Prison Service 1999: 6–7). Unsurprisingly, therefore, the 1991 survey found that one-third of prisoners were unemployed before their imprisonment, two-fifths of those under twenty-five, almost three times as many as one would expect to find in the population generally.

PRISONERS' MENTAL HEALTH

The mental health of prisoners has been a perennial cause for concern, and several epidemiological studies (Gunn *et al.* 1991; Dell *et al.* 1991) have been undertaken to assess their levels of morbidity. The most recent data (Singleton *et al.* 1998) indicate that 10 per cent of male and 20 per cent of female prisoners have been mental hospital patients at some point prior to their incarceration, and that very high proportions of all prisoner groups—78 per cent of male remands, 64 per cent of sentenced males, and 50 per cent of sentenced females—have some form of personality disorder, of which, not surprisingly, anti-social disorders are the most prevalent. Psychoses are strikingly common. Whereas an estimated 0.4 per cent of the general population are psychotic, 7 per cent of the male sentenced population are. At 10 per cent and 14 per cent respectively, the figures for male remand and female prisoners are even higher.

Proportionately three times as many male prisoners display high scores for neurotic symptoms as in the population generally. The figures for women are worse. The most severe of the neurotic conditions measured is the *depressive episode*. It is found in 2.1 per cent of the general population. But among prisoners the proportions are 17 and 21 per cent of male and female remands; and 8 per cent and 15 per cent of male and female sentenced prisoners. Thoughts of suicide among prisoners are relatively commonplace, particularly among remand prisoners. Forty six per cent of male remands report having thought of suicide at some stage of their lives, 35 per cent in the last year and 12 per cent in the week prior to interview. Twenty seven per cent report that they have actually attempted to kill themselves at some point, 2 per cent in the week prior to interview. Once again the figures for women are even higher: a quarter of women remand prisoners report having tried to kill themselves in the year prior to interview.

Very high proportions of prisoners are abusers of all categories of drugs. Fifty eight per cent of male remands, 63 per cent of sentenced males, and more than one-third of all female prisoners have engaged in hazardous drinking prior to their imprisonment. The overwhelming majority of all prisoners have used cannabis at some stage. However, whereas use of cannabis is also widespread in the general population, use of heroin is not. Between one-third and one-half of prisoners in different categories have used heroin. Poly-drug use is the norm. Two-fifths of all women prisoners, for example, have injected drugs at some stage in their lives and between two-fifths and one half of prisoners in all categories report having been dependent on one drug or another during the year prior to their incarceration. Prisoners convicted of property offences have above average rates of drug dependence.

The overall picture of the prison population is therefore one of multiple depriv-ation, social stress and co-morbidity. As a group prisoners are seriously disadvantaged before their imprisonment and their social marginality is heightened by their incarceration. If the personal inadequacy of many prisoners compounds their vulner-ability, it is essential that we turn to an age-old question: *Quis custodies custodiet?* Who guards the guards?

ORGANIZATION, PRIVATIZATION, AND ACCOUNTABILITY

Prisoners stand condemned legally, are judged deficient morally, and are of little account politically. They are drawn disproportionately from the ranks of the power-less. Prisons are relatively 'total institutions' (Goffmann 1968). The essence of imprisonment is loss of liberty, and it is all too easy for prison systems to adopt secretive and restrictive policies, ostensibly in fulfilment of their mandate. When prisoners protest, their pleas are often not heard or, when heard, not listened to. Winston Churchill was surely correct when he maintained, in a much-quoted passage, that 'the mood and temper of the public in regard to the treatment of crime and criminals is one of the most unfailing tests of the civilisation of any country' (*HC Debates*, col. 1354, 20 July 1910). To ensure that prisoners are not ill-treated, we have to know what is done to them in our collective name.

LEGAL AND MANAGERIAL ACCOUNTABILITY

Since1877, when they were brought wholly under central government control, prisons in England and Wales have been the financial and administrative responsibility of the Home Secretary. Until 1962 this was via the Prison Commission, and subsequently the Prison Department, a department within the Home Office and renamed the Prison Service in the mid-1980s. In 1992 the Service became a government executive agency. It is headed by a Director General, and it operates within a Framework Agreement, which takes into account, as we have seen, Home Office aims and objectives, and the Prison Act 1952. The key policy and management bodies are the Correctional Services Strategy Board (CSSB), chaired by the Prisons and Probation Minister, and the Prison Service Management Board (PSMB), chaired by the Director General. As far as institutions are concerned, the key operational line of management accountability is the twelve geographical areas into which most of the 137 prisons and YOIs are grouped, each headed by an Area Manager, plus three cross-cutting functional groups, one for juveniles (under eighteeens), one for most institutions for women, and one for the eight high-security prisons.

This management structure is the latest of many designed to address two perennial tensions: that between Ministers and senior prison executives; and that between the out-stations—the individual prisons—and headquarters. Both tensions have been the subject of frequent analyses and endless organizational changes. In 1995, in the wake of high-profile escapes, the Director General, Derek Lewis, was sacked. The inquiry report into the escapes (Learmont 1995) showed the extent of day-to-day interference by the Minister, though the inquiry team failed, or was unwilling, to make the connection between this factor and the management ills and low morale of the Service, a shortcoming which Mr Lewis's account (1997) sought to remedy. Given the importance which Woolf (1991: Section 12) attached to there being a clear agreement between Ministers and the Director General, this dismal saga was disappointing.

The current management arrangement acknowledges that Ministers need and wish to be involved in setting strategic policy. Whether the new structure better ensures that they do *not* involve themselves in *day-to-day operational* policy is an issue difficult to determine, though the current Director General has said that the arrangement has brought 'clarity and focus to the line management chain' and given the Service 'added confidence' that the aims and objectives of the Service are integrated with those of the criminal justice system generally (Prison Service 2000a: 14).

The new structure embodies three commitments. First, Prison Service area organization is co-terminous with that of other criminal justice agencies. This should make for better inter-agency planning and partnership working for such issues as the resettlement of prisoners. Secondly, the existence of a Director of High Security Prisons, as well as a Director of Security, underlines the importance the Service attaches to ensuring that the management of high security risk prisoners does not go awry: the Service is determined that there will be no repetition of the security failures of 1994–5. Thirdly, the appointment of an Area Manager specifically to manage prisons for women is an acknowledgement that the needs of women are different from those of men. The residual question is whether the current organizational structure adequately acknowledges the particular needs of juvenile and young adult prisoners, arguably a relatively neglected population given the critical importance of their development (see NACRO 2001). The care of male juveniles is subject to two lines of management accountability (to the functional *and* geographical area managers) and there is some confusion regarding the position of young women.

The Prison Service is required to produce an annual report for the Minister to lay before Parliament, and this is supplemented by the annual *Prison Statistics* produced by the Home Office. The Service also publishes annually a *Corporate and Business Plan*. These and other documents are available on the Prison Service web site (details at the end of the chapter), and there has been much progress in the accountability of the Service as a result of these developments. Until recently, for example, no Service publication provided details about facilities and arrangements (about such matters as visits, for example), a gap which an ex-prisoner remedied by independently producing *The Prisons Handbook* (latest edition Leech and Cheney 2001).

Today there is an informative entry for each prison on the Service web site. However, the greater information provided about some aspects of policy and performance in the increasingly glossy *Annual Report*—better financial accounts, performance data by establishment by PSA target, etc.—is offset by the provision of less or inadequate information about other matters. For example, the list of establishments in the Annual Report no longer indicates what special facilities are provided in each

(Vulnerable Prisoner Units (VPUs), Special Security Units (SSUs), and so on): the external analyst cannot easily establish how the overall estate is being used. No breakdown is provided of the number of prisoners by security category. *Prison Statistics* no longer report prisoner adjudications for disciplinary offences by establishment. Moreover, some aspects of policy are reported in so limited a manner that it arguably serves to obfuscate the degree to which progress is being made. For example, the staff at every prison are required to carry out random drug tests of their population. The published results suggest great success—the proportion of random tests proving positive having been halved from 24 per cent in 1996 to 12 per cent in 2000 (Prison Service 2001: 10). What is not reported, however, is how many random drug tests there are, and how many additional *targeted* tests are carried out of prisoners suspected of having taken drugs. If *random* and *targeted* drug tests are aggregated the number proving positive has declined by only 22 per cent,[3] a decline more in keeping with the more modest reduction in the number of prisoners per head of population adjudicated for drugs offences (see Home Office 2001c: Table 8.5).

THE PRISON ESTATE

Many British prisons provide imaginative prisoner programmes delivered by committed staff in physical settings which are arguably among the best in Europe (for an overview of European prison systems, see Van Zyl Smit and Dunkel 1991, 2001). Most are modern, uncrowded, have good facilities, and are not prone to major disorder. There is a dark side, however. Some prisons are old, overcrowded, ill-resourced, and uncaring. Until recently, many of them were also insanitary and grossly overcrowded. In 1980 the then Director General of the Prison Department described the prison conditions in some of the institutions as an 'affront to civilised society' (Home Office 1981: 2). These were the 'bricks of shame' about which Stern (1997) wrote. In 2001, Martin Narey, the present Director General, commended his prison governors for their overwhelmingly 'magnificent' response to the increasing demands made on them. But he also said that he could no longer tolerate apologizing for the 'litany of failure', 'moral neglect' and 'degradation' in some establishments (Narey 2001). How was this institutional legacy established and allowed to remain?

There are two main types of institutions. First, the local prisons and remand centres. Their primary task is to receive prisoners from and deliver prisoners to the courts, and to assess and allocate those serving sentences sufficiently long for it to be thought sensible that they be allocated. Second are the prisons to which sentenced prisoners are allocated, the YOIs and the adult *training* prisons. The latter are further subdivided into closed and open institutions. This sub-division reflects a prisoner security classification and the level of security which institutions are able to provide. All prisoners are security classified A, B, C, or D according to a

---

[3] Figures provided in personal communication by the Prison Service HQ. In 1996/7 there were 56,647 random and 18,743 targeted drug tests, of which 13,821 and 7,791 respectively were positive. In 2000/1 there were 51,474 random and 37,212 targeted drug tests, of which 6,382 and 10,568 respectively were positive.

basic scheme adopted in 1966 on the recommendation of Lord Mountbatten (1966), following his investigation of notorious breaches of security. Category A prisoners, who Mountbatten envisaged would comprise no more than 120, but who now comprise approximately 700 (HMCIP/Probation 1999: para. 9.3), are those 'whose escape would constitute a danger to the public, the police or the security of the state'. Category D prisoners are those suitable for open conditions, that is, those who may be trusted not to abscond. Category B and C prisoners are those required to be held in closed conditions providing more or less security. Trial and remand prisoners are, with the exception of a few provisionally categorized as A, all assumed to be Category B.

The allocation of sentenced Category A prisoners has been the subject of long-running controversy (King and Elliott 1977; King and Morgan 1980). Mountbatten recommended that they be confined to a single, purpose-built fortress, but on the recommendation of the Radzinowicz Committee (ACPS 1968), it was decided that they should be dispersed among a few high-security prisons, the majority of whose occupants would be Category B or even C. In fact Category A prisoners have never been wholly accommodated in the so-called 'dispersal prisons'—pre-existing high-security units were retained and others developed—and the dispersal policy has been subtly modified so that there is now less dispersal than Radzinowicz envisaged (Home Office 1984; Prison Service 1991; Leibling 2001). There are currently five Category A dispersal prisons.

It is increasingly common for institutions to have multiple functions. This is an important development which, in the light of Woolf's recommendation that there be developed 'community prisons' (1991: paras 11.49–11.68), is likely to become more common. It has become more difficult, therefore, to delineate the numbers and characteristics of different types of institutions. Moreover, it is a feature of penal institutions that their titles and functions change rather more frequently than their facilities and culture.

Of the 137 institutions it is possible to generalize as follows. A quarter of the estate comprises Victorian, generally radial, prisons. Most of them fulfil a role similar to that they had over a century ago. They are local prisons in major cities or county towns, formerly city or county gaols. A few—like Dartmoor, Parkhurst, and Portland—occupy isolated sites, a legacy of their former role as government centres for convicts awaiting transportation. Many of the open prisons and YOIs are former military camps, residential institutions, or country houses, but most now incorporate more recently added accommodation blocks. This means that the overwhelming majority of prisons, more than three-fifths of them, are entirely or mostly purpose-built since the 1950s.

This pattern of capital investment reflected the Prison Service's historical commitment to 'treatment and training'. Until the 1990s nearly all the new building went into the 'training' sector for adults or youths. The training prisons also got the lion's share of other resources and were largely protected from overcrowding which was concentrated, as a matter of policy, in the local prisons. Here, in treatment and training terms, nothing much was expected to happen (a tradition which to some extent continues—see HMCIP/Probation 2001: para. 10.17). In the local prisons were

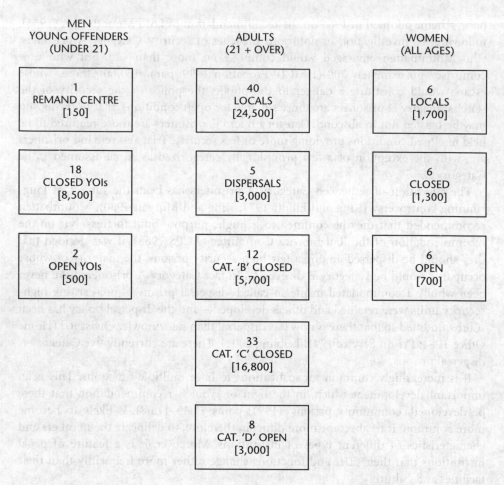

Fig. 30.6 The Prison Estate (as at the close of 2001: all figures are approximate)

concentrated the prisoners excluded from the noble mission: the untried and unsentenced; prisoners serving short sentences, for whom there was said to be insufficient time to achieve anything; and the seriously recalcitrant, judged to be beyond the training pale. The local prisons became 'penal dustbins', as the governor of Wormwood Scrubs described his prison in a letter to *The Times* in 1982, for those prisoners with whom the training prisons could not cope, the 'inappropriately allocated' (see Woolf Report 1991: paras 12.221–12.263).

The consequence is that those prisoners who on any criterion should be given the least oppressive conditions, typically experienced the most impoverished regimes, and vice versa. In successive reports the Chief Inspector of Prisons chronicled: the 'degrading' and 'insanitary' accommodation; the slopping-out procedures; the 'enforced idleness'; the prolonged, daily cellular confinement; the miserable visiting rooms; and the general absence of facilities (for particularly graphic examples, see HMCIP 1988, 1990a, 1993). The untried were the 'forgotten people' (HMCIP 1989; para. 4.30), held in 'completely insupportable' conditions (Home Affairs Committee 1981: para. 54), 'the worst . . . the prison system has to offer' (Stern 1987: 33). Most damningly, the Council of Europe Committee for the Prevention of Torture concluded in 1990 that conditions in Brixton, Leeds, and Wandsworth Prisons—all three Victorian local prisons—amounted to 'inhuman and degrading' treatment (Council of Europe 1991; for commentary see Morgan and Evans 1994; Evans and Morgan 1998: 243–5). The phrase could not have been used lightly: it suggested that the conditions might be held to breach Article 3 of the European Convention for the Protection of Human Rights and Fundamental Freedoms, let alone comply with Prison Rule requirements regarding the encouragement of useful lives, self-respect, and a sense of personal responsibility. It was in response to these conditions that the pressure for minimum standards in the 1980s was mounted.

INSPECTION AND COMPLAINTS

Part of the case for establishing a code of standards for prisoners' living conditions is that the effectiveness of all grievance ventilation and accountability mechanisms depends on there being a rudder by which overseers can steer. The ability to be accountable *to* someone depends on knowing what one is accountable *for*.

Every prison in England and Wales is served by a board of visitors, a body of lay volunteers appointed by the Secretary of state. The boards have two functions: inspecting prison conditions; and hearing prisoner grievances. Until April 1992 they had a third function: undertaking disciplinary hearings of more serious charges. The last was long held by critics to be incompatible with the first and second and the principal reason why the boards' 'watchdog' role was so poorly developed (Prior Report 1985). This criticism, plus evidence that there remained major shortcomings in the quality of justice dispensed by boards, led to the recommendation that boards no longer be involved in disciplinary proceedings (Woolf Report 1991: paras 14.363– 14.435). But it is not clear that boards have become more willing publicly to criticize conditions or staff, and their credibility with prisoners appears not to have greatly improved (Worrall 1995). The most recent review of boards found that: they have no real existence in the general management structure of the Prison Service ('no duty is laid on governors to deal with them; no obligation on Area Managers to respond to matters they raise'); members feel that nobody listens to them; and many prison staff feel that board members need to 'get real' in interpreting their role (Lloyd 2001: 13–14). It is not yet clear whether the recommendations that boards change their function to 'Satisfy themselves as to the decent and just treatment of prisoners and to the range and quality of the programmes preparing them for release', change their name to 'monitoring panel' or 'independent monitors', be co-located, with HM Inspectorate of Prisons and the Prison and Probation Ombudsman, be served by a secretariat outwith the Prison Service and Home Office, will be implemented. But it is difficult to see that this amended, but nevertheless very broad, remit will lead to boards being more effective in the future than they have been in the past.

There has been a prisons inspectorate, outwith the Prison Service, though part of the Home Office, since 1981. The establishment of HMCIP was recommended by the May Committee (1979: 92–6) and represents that Committee's only lasting achievement (see Morgan 1985). The Inspectorate's reports are published and, under the leadership of successive Chief Inspectors (notably Judge Steven Tumim 1987–1995 and Sir David 'Rambo' Ramsbotham 1995–2001), HMCIP has established a reputation for conspicuous independence. HMCIP is charged with reporting to the Minister 'on the treatment of prisoners and conditions in prison' (Prison Act 1952, s 5a(3)), and does so by undertaking: regular inspections of prisons (each is fully inspected every five years, though the Youth Justice Board requires that YOIs housing juveniles be inspected annually); thematic reviews of aspects of policy (these have recently included reports on women prisoners (1997a), young prisoners (1997b), CSCs (2000b), suicide (1999a), lifers (HMCIP/Probation 1999), remand prisoners (2000a), and resettlement (HMCIP/Probation 2001)); and by occasionally investigating major incidents. The Chief Inspector's critiques invariably attract publicity, but they have sometimes lacked policy impact because it was not always clear by what standards they concluded that provisions were 'impoverished', 'degrading', 'unacceptable', and so on. Further, by falling out with Home Office Ministers or senior Prison Service administrators, Chief Inspectors have sometimes lost the cooperation of policy-makers. On the occasions when the Chief Inspector's criteria and solutions have been precise, as in his unequivocal denunciation of 'slopping out' (HMCIP 1989) or advocacy of separate line management accountability for women's establishments (HMCIP 1997a, 2001b), the impact has been considerable.

In July 2001, as his last act, Sir David Ramsbotham published in an annexe to his *Annual Report* more than 100 pages of 'Expectations: criteria for assessing the treatment and conditions for prisoners'. These standards are designed to guide inspectors when assessing the quality of what the Prison Service provides and ensure that they make 'accurate and consistent judgements'. The majority of the criteria—and the terminology is significant, for seldom are the criteria expressed as specific standards (see conclusion)—are said to be in 'harmony with existing Prison Service policies' (HMCIP 2001c: Annex 7, 1). Whether the latter is indeed the case, or whether the criteria stretch what the Service provides, is a topic likely henceforth to be closely considered by lawyers as well as Prison Service administrators.

It was partly lack of precision, and thus accountability, which robbed the prisoner complaints system of credibility with prisoners and which, *inter alia*, led Woolf to conclude that there was an absence of justice in prisons. Prisoners have always been able to complain about any aspect of their custody to their board of visitors, to their governor, or to the Secretary of state, by way of petition. But the system lacked the straightforwardness, expedition, effectiveness, and independence which Woolf argued any satisfactory grievance ventilation system should have (para. 14.309). A new integrated grievance system was already being introduced when Woolf conducted his inquiry, but he, like previous commentators, considered there should be an independent 'complaints adjudicator' at the apex of the internal system (paras 14.326–14.362). This independent element has since been introduced in the form of a Prisons Ombudsman, the first of whom was appointed and began receiving complaints in 1994.

The first Ombudsman, Sir Peter Woodhead, had vigorously to assert himself in the face of ambiguities and lacunae in his brief and obstacles placed in the way of his investigations (see Prison Ombudsman 1996: paras 2.1–2.25). However, though the Ombudsman's office and terms of reference have still not been placed on a statutory footing, they have been greatly extended (not least, in 2001, to the Probation Service), and the appointment as Ombudsman in 1999 of Stephen Shaw, formerly Director of the Prison Reform Trust, confirmed the status of the office as a truly independent part of the accountability landscape.

The Prison Ombudsman is not restricted, as his title implies, to matters of mal-administration. He may consider the merits of decisions, including disciplinary awards and the clinical judgements of prison doctors, and his remit covers both state-run and contracted-out prisons. Further, it is clear that the Ombudsman has forged good collaborative relationships with the Inspectorate and the management of the Prison Service (Prison Ombudsman 2001a: 3) so as better to get to grips with ill-treatment when a pattern emerges. In 2000, for example, the Ombudsman passed a dossier of complaints from prisoners at Birmingham Prison to the Director General, and it is notable that both he (Narey 2001) and the Chief Inspector of Prisons sub-sequently lent substance to his concerns: the former did not share the Birmingham Board of Visitors' confidence that prisoners had *not* been physically abused, and the latter found a high proportion of prisoners alleging staff assault and the Board of Visitors to be less than scrupulously independent in dealing with prisoner complaints (HMCIP 2001a: para. 3.80).

The number of complaints received by the Ombudsman has steadily increased, as has the proportion (just under two-fifths) found to be eligible. Prisoners must first exhaust the internal complaints avenues, and the efficiency of these have recently been improved. The largest category of investigated prisoner complaints are about adjudi-cations, followed by alleged damage to or loss of property, security categorization decisions, transfers, etc., though complaints about living conditions—87 per cent of which are found to be ineligible—are the most commonly received. This points to issues which we have touched on earlier and which the Ombudsman is proactively following up. Young prisoners, for example, including young prisoners in institutions about which HMCIP has been particularly critical, are much less likely to complain to the Ombudsman than adults, and long-term high-security prisoners are much more likely to complain than their short-term low-security counterparts. This pattern is to some extent unavoidable: adults have more confidence and long-termers will not be deterred by delay. But the Ombudsman is pursuing a number of initiatives (surgeries, more user-friendly publicity for use in YOIs (Prison Ombudsman 2001b), etc.) to make his services more accessible to less advantaged or motivated prisoners. The Ombudsman currently upholds just under a third of the complaints he receives, and only rarely are his findings and recommendations *not* accepted by the Director General.

CONTRACTING OUT

Privatization, or contracting out, was by far the most controversial prisons develop-ment of the 1990s (for general reviews of competing arguments, see Logan 1990; Shichor 1995). The privatized management of prisons has been vigorously opposed in

principle on the grounds that the administration of state punishment is fundamentally a state responsibility, and because it is wrong to derive financial profit from
it. A pragmatic long-term objection is that the growth of privatized prisons represents
an investment stake by the shrinking military-industrial complex in the burgeoning
crime-control complex, an investment which will create a vested commercial interest
in the expanded use of imprisonment. The huge growth of the prison and gaol
population in the United States, which is now in excess of two million, or approaching
700 per 1,000 population (almost six times the rate in the UK), is taken by some to be
the spectre to which privatization might contribute (Christie 1994; Donziger 1995).
Most of the argument about privatization has concerned day-to-day accountability,
however.

The Criminal Justice Act 1991, the terms of which have since been extended to all
prisons, including those in Scotland, provides that for every contracted-out prison a
'controller', a Crown servant, is appointed to oversee the running of the prison and
ensure compliance with the Prison Rules and the specific terms of the contract. The
'prison custody officers' and the 'director' appointed by the contractor must be
approved, and though they have the power to search prisoners and their visitors they
do not have formal disciplinary powers. These are vested in the controller, who in
practice is a governor grade employee of the Prison Service with an office within the
contracted-out prison. Thus, it is argued by some, contracted-out prisons are *more
accountable* than state-run prisons (Harding 1997). The state has in no sense relin-
quished its responsibilities. And, in addition to the general legal framework, the
contract is a backdoor means of delivering the higher standards which cannot be
enforced in state-run establishments. Moreover, the contracting out of particular
services within prisons—employment, education and training, the provision of food,
laundry, medical services, and so on—arguably represents the 'normalization' of
prison regimes for which many critics have long pressed. It is doubtful whether
privatization reflects the demise of the rehabilitative ideal and acceptance that
prisoners can as easily be warehoused by the private sector as the state (Beyens and
Snacken 1996: 241). Indeed the early English evidence, which may not be replicated in
other jurisdictions, is that contracts have been used to breathe life back into the
rehabilitative ideal and stimulate cross-fertilization of practice between state and
privately-managed institutions.

The deeply-felt antagonisms over privatization—not least among the prison staff
associations who have vigorously opposed it, but from whose senior ranks the
security industry has easily recruited its directors—have stimulated a process of disinformation and selective reporting which has made objective appraisal difficult. The
government pursued privatization primarily to tackle restrictive staff practices, and
thus high costs, in a state-run system not reputed for its innovative or effective
management. By this test the success of the initiative does not rest only on the relative
unit costs of contracted-out compared to state-run institutions—costs that for various reasons are difficult to compare—but rather in the degree to which practices in
state-run prisons are transformed by the threat of privatization and the need to tender
against contractor-competitors. What is clear is that the small contracted-out sector is
cheaper per prisoner, though not per baseline CNA place (Park 2000), and, after some

early difficulties, is setting some high standards—as the House of Commons Home Affairs Committee (1997) and successive inspection reports from the Chief Inspector testify (see, for example, HMCIP 1998a, 1998b, 1999b)—though not always, and in all respects, higher standards than those achieved in equivalent state-run prisons (James *et al.* 1997; Park 2000).

This raises the question as to whether privatization takes a step further an increasingly segmented prison system, with higher or lower standards prevailing in different institutions depending on whether they are local or training, state-run or contracted-out. To the extent that contracting out is now being used as a general managerial device to galvanize change—the Director General has informed the prison staff associations that institutions identified as 'failing' will be given six months to improve, and in the event of their not coming up with an acceptable action plan, or failing to implement it, will be contracted out (see, for example, the Director General's response to the highly critical inspection report on Feltham YOI in July 2001 (HMCIP 2001e)—then privatization should leverage greater conformity to common standards.

CONTRACTING IN

Custodial provisions for juveniles have since April 2000 been subject to the direction of the Youth Justice Board (YJB) which acts as the purchaser for services provided by the Prison Service. The Service Level Agreement between the YJB and the Prison Service specifies substantially enhanced regimes than were provided previously or elsewhere in Prison Service establishments. Though all the YOIs accommodating juveniles have so far been subject to interim 'variation orders', allowing for standards lower than those specified in the SLA, the improvements have already been favourably noted by the Prisons Inspectorate (see, for example, successive reports on YOI Brinsford in HMCIP 2001f and 2001g). Compliance with the SLA is ensured by YJB Monitors, who operate in a manner similar to Prison Service Controllers in contracted-out establishments, though less intensively. They visit each contracting-in YOI at least once a month and have unrestricted access.

The improvements for juveniles have thrown into sharp relief the dismal provision for young adults who, in the majority of YOIs, share inadequately resourced sites. The 2001 report on Feltham provides the most glaring example to date. The Chief Inspector found considerable improvement in the conditions for juveniles, but described those for young adults as 'digraceful' and 'unsafe' (HMCIP 2001e). The government has said that it wishes to build on the experience of the youth justice system to achieve similar improvements for all categories of offenders, and has indicated that eighteen to twenty-year-olds will be the early target (Home Office 2001b: paras 2.9–10; Labour Party 2001: 32). It is not yet clear how this is to be done, but it is apparent that contracting in, like contracting out, has knock-on operational consequences for the standards debate.

SPECIAL UNITS

The Prison Service has become preoccupied (as have other systems in Europe—see Van Zyl Smit and Dunkel 1991; Muncie and Sparks 1991) with the control of a relatively small number of long-term, 'dangerous' or 'disruptive' prisoners (see Bottoms and Light 1987) and with the protection of other prisoners in danger. Thirty years ago there was no talk of dangerous prisoners and no maximum-security accommodation in the system. Now there are more than 3,000 places in the five dispersal prisons and the five Close Supervision Centres (CSCs) at two further closed prisons. There are important distinctions to be made here. Prisoners who are a *security* risk are not necessarily a *control* problem. Some prisoners who have the personal capacity and external organizational backing to escape from relatively secure prisons—international drugs racketeers, for example—are often model prisoners. Other prisoners who represent a significant danger to the public—some sex offenders, for example—are also often model prisoners; and though they do not generally have the capacity to escape, they are at risk of attack from fellow prisoners and must generally be held in the VPUs. Some other prisoners, not necessarily those serving the longest sentences, are a control problem. A very few prisoners are both a security and a control risk.

Prior to their transfer to Northern Ireland, or release as part of the Good Friday Peace Agreement, there were established three Special Security Units (SSUs), mostly for IRA terrorists. It was the escape of six Category A 'exceptional risk' prisoners from one such unit, at Whitemoor Prison in September 1994 (Woodcock Report 1994), which triggered the train of events eventually leading to the sacking of the Director General. The SSUs have now been closed, though some of the facilities are currently being used for witness protection. The CSCs remain, however.

The establishment of special prisoner statuses and units poses problems for procedural and substantive justice and accountability. It complicates the question of standards and upsets the balance of incentives and disincentives for good behaviour (Home Office 1984). Model prisoners may, in King and Elliott's phrase (1977), be held in an 'electronic coffin' if considered a security threat (for reviews of the history and operation of the SSUs, see Walmesley 1989, and Bottomley and Hay 1991), or suffer an impoverished regime in segregation if they are repeatedly attacked by fellow prisoners (Priestley 1981; Prison Reform Trust 1990). Conversely, special units can absorb such disproportionate resources, and afford so many privileges, that the envy and opposition of the Service is excited: it may be said that the occupants are being rewarded for their bad behaviour.[4] Special control units are also extremely difficult to staff and thus expensive to run. How to create conditions within which security *and* order can be achieved with respect to long-term, uncooperative prisoners, yet establish a ladder of opportunity whereby those prisoners will wish to be recategorized and transferred to less secure conditions, is one of the most difficult management issues

---

[4] The most famous example of the marginalization of a special unit concerned the Barlinnie Prison Special Unit, Glasgow (see Boyle 1977, 1984; Coyle 1987; Cooke 1989). In England, Grendon Underwood Prison, which provides a psychiatrically-oriented therapeutic regime, has to some extent suffered the same process (see Genders and Player 1994).

confronting the Prison Service (Home Office 1984; Dunbar 1985; Scottish Prison Service 1990).

The CSCs, which operate under Prison Rule 46, providing for a prisoner's removal from association in the interests of good and discipline, are encountering precisely these problems. In 2001 the five centres provided places for up to forty-eight prisoners with a history of seriously disruptive and aggressive behaviour. Of the forty-one prisoners accommodated in 1999: all were serving ten years or more; the majority were lifers, two with whole-life tariffs; five had been convicted of killing while in prison, one on more than one occasion; nearly all were Category A; most were severely personality disordered, though falling outside the scope of the Mental Health Act diagnostically or with respect to treatability; and all had spent long periods in dispersal prison segregation units prior to their transfer. Four of the centres were designed with progression in mind, while one was reserved for seriously disturbed prisoners presenting risks likely to preclude their early return to mainstream conditions. Both the Prisons Inspectorate and independent evaluators have come to similar conclusions about the operation of the CSCs. The units have generally not succeeded in getting prisoners to return satisfactorily to normal conditions (Clare and Bottomley 2001: chapter 2). The progressive ideal assumes the prisoners' capacity for dispassionate decision making which is not characteristic of personality disordered individuals whose belief systems are highly emotionally charged, distorted and self-fulfilling (HMCIP 2000b: para. 5.1). The conditions in one centre, at Woodhill Prison, designed for persistently uncooperative prisoners, were 'unacceptably' more restrictive than those found in dispersal prison segregation units and were in breach of the Prison Rules (ibid.: paras 2.25 and 5.2). On those few occasions when each prisoner was individually allowed out of his cell he was attended by five prison officers dressed in full riot gear. Thus all contact by prisoners with staff was literally with 'helmeted figures' (ibid.: para. 2.24), a regime which, if precedent is any guide, the Council of Europe Torture Committee (CPT) would say ran the risk of degenerating into inhuman and degrading treatment (Morgan and Evans 2001: chapter 6, the CPT made an inspection visit to Woodhill in 2001, though the report is not yet published). There is undoubtedly a need for small specialist units for difficult prisoners, but the regimes within them need arguably to be more flexible in response to more sophisticated psychiatrically-informed appraisals of prisoner needs (HMCIP 2000b: chapter 5; Clare and Bottomley 2001: chapter 8). There also needs to be more human interaction between staff and prisoners, a recommendation which leads us to the question of the social dynamics of prison life.

THE SOCIOLOGY OF PRISONS

Prisons represent the power of the state ultimately to coerce. Order within prisons may in the last resort depend on the use of force by staff. Yet disorder is not the norm of prison life. As in any other social setting, order in prisons is negotiated (McDermott and King 1988; Leibling and Price 2001). The negotiation is not between equals. But it is for the most part achieved with the grudging consent of prisoners, who invariably far outnumber the prison officers who guard them. The 105,000 offences against the prison disciplinary code that are formally punished each year belie the fact that staff and prisoners generally coexist harmoniously: frictions are for the most part resolved through more subtle accommodations, including the use of what the Prison Officers' Association once described as the 'alternative disciplinary system' (1984: 2). What counts as order within prisons?

The sociological literature on prisons points to the existence of a prison culture—a set of attitudes and a way of doing things—in which both prisoners and prison officers have roles. This literature is largely American and mostly based on studies of long-term prisoners in relatively high-security prisons. It is questionable to what extent that literature applies to Britain. Few social scientists have been permitted to set up their anthropological huts on British prison landings; and though a good deal can be learnt about life in prison from the autobiographical accounts of prisoners, few prisoners have written analytically about the minutiae of daily life. Prison staff, retired or serving, have contributed even less to the literature.[5]

To the extent that prisons exhibit a specific culture there has been a long-standing debate as to whether it is of primarily *indigenous* or *imported* origin. The indigenous approach is represented by Sykes's classic account of the *Society of Captives* (1958) and Goffmann's seminal discussion of *Asylums* (1968). Both writers stress the distinctiveness of prison life. Prisons, because of their encompassing character, are 'total institutions', and prisoners are relatively shut off from the world at large. The prison has been seen as a more or less closed social system in which it is the task of one group of persons, the prison officers, to manage or process another group, the prisoners. Sykes's focus is on the 'pains of imprisonment'—the various deprivations that living in prisons involves—while Goffmann's stress is on the dynamics of mortification—the transformation of the self—that results from entering a 'people-processing' institution. In both accounts the prisoner is described as being under psychological assault, with the usual supports for and expressions of personal identity—possessions, control over personal appearance, autonomy of movement, personal privacy, security, and so on—being greatly diminished. Prisoners may develop individualistic responses to these stresses, responses ranging from escape attempts or playing the role of the barrack-room lawyer, to psychological withdrawal or intensive auto-didacticism. However, for Sykes the distinctive aspect of the prison culture—largely, though not entirely, its emphasis on prisoner solidarity against staff—represents a functional response to these social and psychological assaults: a means by which the rejected can reject their rejectors (McCorkle and Korn 1954) and thus maintain a degree of self-esteem. According to this view, the more that prisoners adopt a cohesive stance, the more the pains of imprisonment can be mitigated for everyone.

This process points to a paradox. Some of the relative deprivations of prison life are the result of staff attempts to maintain external security and internal order. Yet the pains of imprisonment stimulate a solidaristic counter-culture subversive of official

---

[5] For a bibliography of valuable prison research writings and prisoner and staff biographies, see the previous edition of this chapter (Morgan 1997), especially footnote 7.

objectives. Thus the apparently total power of staff is compromised by their need to reach an accommodation with their charges in order that routine tasks may be accomplished. In this way, whatever purposes prisons officially pursue are in practice undermined by the daily reality of the negotiated settlements which take place between officers and prisoners. This suggests that in reality prisons are unlikely to be about the pursuit of noble missions: they are ultimately more about practical survival in settings which, because inherently coercive, have extreme potential for instability and disorder. In the case of the uniformed staff, the essence of a good day is one in which the routines are accomplished professionally without trouble, including the need to use unnecessary force (for illustrations, see Leibling and Price 2001: chapters 5 and 6).

The problem with indigenous accounts of prison culture is that they fail to provide an explanation of change, other than the sort of minor shifts from crisis to equilibrium which might occur within a closed system. They do not explain the more fundamental changes in operational policy and prisoner response which have taken place in British prisons since 1945, or, more dramatically, which occurred in American prison systems in the wake of the black civil rights movement in the 1960s. Thus, by contrast, importation theorists stress the connection between relationships within prisons and those outside—for example, changes in political expectations, the legitimacy of authority and legal culture (see Jacobs' (1977) classic study of Stateville Prison, Illinois). Importationists also highlight the degree to which the cultural norms to which prisoners subscribe, and the individual roles they adopt in prison, are extensions of subcultures of which they are a part before being incarcerated (Irwin and Cressey 1962; Irwin 1970). According to this approach, the prison culture is not peculiar to prison; it is both a microcosm of the wider society and a sort of career continuation of the criminal culture of the streets from which a high proportion of prisoners are drawn. Thus Irwin and Cressey identify a 'thief subculture' outside prison which stresses group loyalty and toughness. To the extent that there is group solidarity between *some* prisoners within prison, this 'convict' or 'prisoner' subculture is both an extension of that street culture *and* an adaption in response to the contingencies of life inside.

Indigenous and importationist perspectives are nowadays generally seen as complementary (Jacobs 1979). Moreover, whatever is to be learnt from the American literature, British (and, indeed, most Western European) prisons are unlikely to exhibit the same cultural patterns as in the USA. There has hitherto not, for example, been sophisticated organized crime in Britain as found in the USA; neither, with one or two notable exceptions, have criminal street gangs regularly employing life-threatening violence been a prominent feature of British crime, and thus their influence has not been greatly felt in prisons. Further, maximum-security prisons of the kind widely employed for the mainstream prison population in some US states (King 1999), have only recently become part of the English system, and even today only a tiny minority of the prison population is housed in such conditions. Lastly, though British society is riven by deeply ingrained class differences and racial divides, Britain is nevertheless culturally a relatively homogeneous society. With the exception of Northern Ireland (McEvoy 2001), there are not the deep cleavages which in the

USA have historically separated the African-American from the white population and, in more recent times, the Hispanic from the English-speaking community. These cleavages have fatally dominated parts of the American prison scene (Colvin 1992; Wacquant 2001) to an extent largely unknown in Britain and, indeed, most of Western Europe. Mathieson's (1965) classic study of a Norwegian prison failed to reveal much in the way of prisoner solidarity. Prisoners were relatively weak and isolated; they were vulnerable to the discretionary favours which the staff were in a position to distribute.

The British 'sociology of prisons' literature has emphasized the complexity and varied quality of prison communities: researchers, critical of stereotypical portrayals of staff and prisoners, have argued that both groups adapt to the particular circum-stances in which they find themselves. Total institutions may be characterized by social relations and 'ways of doing things' that are different from those prevailing in the world outside, but prisons nevertheless differ a good deal along all the regime dimensions that Goffmann provisionally identified (see Jones and Cornes 1977: chapter 4; King and McDermott 1989). Further, it is clear that the regime which different groups of prisoners experience differ considerably within prisons (King and Morgan 1976: chapter 3). Thus, while prisoners' responses to custody may owe much to their previous institutional and criminal careers and political affiliations (McEvoy 2001), they are also shaped by the length of their sentences (see, e.g., Sapsford 1983, on life-sentence prisoners), the physical restrictions to which they are subject (see Cohen and Taylor 1972, on a high-security unit), and whatever opportunities and facilities (or lack of them) are provided (King and Elliot 1977; Sparks *et al.* 1996; Leibling *et al.* 1997).

It is also evident from the limited literature on prison staff that the background characteristics of prison officers have changed a good deal in recent years, as have their working conditions. Officers now, as in the past, generally join the Service in their late twenties or thirties, after a spell in other occupations. But whereas the majority used to be recruited from the regular armed forces (Morris and Morris 1963: chapter 4; Jones and Cornes 1977: chapter 7), this is seldom the case today. Thirty years ago few prison officers had any educational qualifications. Today the indelibly working-class culture of the majority, shaped now by previous experience of manual and clerical work rather than military discipline, is blended with a sizeable minority of recruits with 'A' levels or degrees (26 per cent in 1985—see Marsh *et al.* 1985: Table 3.6) seeking advancement within an integrated career structure (Leibling and Price 2001: chapter 2). Moreover, the simple world of the 'gentleman' governors and prison 'screws' of the 1940s and 1950s has been complicated by the employment of women in all institutions and at all levels, and the importation of specialists who, in the 1960s and 1970s at least, took on the majority of the plum 'treatment and training' tasks— education, social work, and the various therapies with which the Service flirted (Thomas 1972: chapter 9). Prison officers typically spend a far higher proportion of their lives in prison than do their charges. They also have a culture, shaped by their previous experience and the increasingly complicated managerial context within which they operate (Leibling and Price 2001: chapter 8). The living conditions of prisoners are the working conditions of prison officers.

In criminal career terms, indigenous and importationist factors may reinforce each other. Clemmer (1940), a pioneer American analyst of the prison community, wrote of the process of 'prisonization', the gradual, destructive socialization of prisoners into the norms of prison life which makes it difficult for them successfully to adapt to a law-abiding life outside, thereby possibly deepening criminality. The idea of prisonization, which most researchers have rejected on the grounds that it posits too mechanical and linear a process, bears a close resemblance to the idea of institution-alization, a syndrome which analysts of mental hospitals have employed to describe the adjustment, with pathological consequences, of patients to stultifying regimes. Most of the prison studies identify a minority of prisoners whose reaction to custody is one of extreme social withdrawal, prisoners who know how to 'do time' passively 'behind their doors', typically 'old lags' imprisoned on many previous occasions and resistant to more open regimes and extended association (see Morris and Morris 1963: 172–3; King and Elliott 1977: 241–4).

To the extent that there is a prisoner culture it is plausible to see it as the product of utilitarian responses which different groups of prisoners, depending on their background, reputation, offence, and length of sentence, make to the pressures and opportunities arising out of captivity. There may be an informal code of not 'grassing' to staff, but there is also as much rivalry and emnity in prisons as there is camaraderie (Morris and Morris 1963: 168). Moreover, there are plenty of ways in which prisoners can and do inform staff about those prisoners whose behaviour they may wish to control, either for reasons of power play or simply to prevent a breakdown in the orderliness which most prisoners and staff have a vested interest in preserving. All the British studies emphasize with Sykes that one of the worst aspects of prison life is having to live with other prisoners. This may be because fellow prisoners are 'dirty in their personal habits, socially unpleasant or guilty of crimes which other prisoners regard as revolting' (Morris and Morris 1963: 168–9); or because of a lack of privacy within a highly restricted physical space (Cohen and Taylor 1972: 80–1); or because of the discomforting strategies which colleagues adopt to cope with whatever time they have to serve (King and Elliott 1977: chapter 8); or for reasons of racial prejudice (Genders and Player 1989) or political attachment (McEvoy 2001).

There are moral and power hierarchies within prisons. One of the reasons why most prisoners are keen that order, however tenuous, should be maintained is that disturbances provide opportunities to settle scores and confirm moral hierarchies (see Woolf 1991: section 3). It is doubtful that British prisoner communities can be characterized in class analogy terms in which the gangsters constitute a ruling class and the sex offenders (or 'nonces') a lumpenproletariat (Genders and Player 1994). The categories 'gangster' and 'sex offender' are problematic and subject to subtle qualifications relating to the nature of a prisoner's original offence and the reputation he or she establishes within prison (Cohen and Taylor 1972: chapter 3). Nevertheless, it is clear that certain categories of sex offenders, particularly those who have com-mitted offences against children, are anathematized, and that established professional criminals who have experienced prison before, are older, and are doing longer than average sentences, tend within training prisons to be the 'top men' (King and Elliot 1977: 254–6). But social prominence within prisons is a complex matter. Whereas Irwin's professional Californian thieves were allegedly oriented to the outside world,

King and Elliot's 'top men' had as few outside contacts as their 'retreatists'. Nor were they heavily involved in power cliques and the culture of barter in contraband goods. On the contrary, their reputation enabled them to secure good positions (attractive cell locations and valued jobs) and non-interference from prisoners and staff alike. They were able to do their 'bird' in relative peace and security. The prisoners prominent in 'jailing' activities—regarded by the 'top men' as 'hotheads', 'tearaways', and 'Borstal boys'—were on the whole younger, shorter-sentence prisoners whose criminal careers were disorganized (ibid.: 250–2).

Power structures within prisons vary a good deal according to the nature of the prison (there has, for example, been virtually no research attention given to the predatory behaviour which, according to HMCIP, dominates many young offender and low-security adult institutions—see HMCIP 2001e and 2001g for two recent examples) and depend less on a rigid class structure and rather more on a fluid pattern of competing groups based on ethnic and regional affinities as well as prior friendships and 'business' interests (Sparks *et al.* 1996: chapter 5). There is not one prisoner world but many (Rock 1996: 39–41), and they are shifting. This conclusion makes comprehensible the fact that attempts at predicting where trouble will occur and who will spark it off, or participate in incidents once they have started, have borne little fruit. Ditchfield's review (1990) of the literature on disturbances and control in prisons found little evidence that the likelihood of incidents could straightforwardly be related to such factors as overcrowding, architectural design, or prisoner facilities, though changes, both positive and negative, which destabilized power structures and relationships increased the likelihood of disorder (see also Adams 1992: chapters 5–7). Moreover, attempts by prison psychologists to identify prisoners likely to be control problems, or to find common features among those prisoners identified by governors as control problems and transferred to special units, have not been conspicuously successful (see Williams and Longley 1987; and a critical review by King and McDermott 1990). Neither, despite references by senior prison administrators to disorder-prone 'toxic mixes' in their reviews of some recent prison disorders (see HMCIP 1987 on disturbances at Wymott and Northeye in 1986; also Ditchfield 1990: chapter 4), was the Woolf Inquiry able to identify a pattern among the prisoners prominent in the 1990 disturbances. There was, as Woolf concluded, 'no single cause of the riots and no simple solution or action which will prevent rioting' (1991: para. 9.23). Nor was there any basis on which prisoners could be categorized for 'control' as opposed to 'security' purposes (ibid.: paras 9.43–9.50). The fact 'that a prisoner who creates control problems in one prison, may behave with complete propriety in another' (ibid.: para. 9.48) suggested to Woolf that more attention needed to be paid to the quality of relationships between prisoners and staff, to the nature of regimes, to procedural justice, and to day-to-day fairness (ibid.: section 9).

This is in line with what analysts of the prison community have long maintained: namely, that 'order' and 'control' are not synonymous (Young 1987). Given his broader insight, it is unfortunate, therefore, that Woolf employed 'control' rather than 'order' in his troika of objectives—'security', 'control' , and 'justice'—to be kept in balance (ibid.: paras 9.19–9.23; for commentary, see Morgan 1992). Control measures may be designed to achieve order, but they tend often to produce the reverse outcome.

This is the essence of King and McDermott's (1990) critical analysis of the use of transfers to control 'troublesome' prisoners, and Sparks *et al.*'s (1996) comparison of staff–prisoner dynamics in two dispersal prisons.

There are three lessons to be drawn from this research. First, though there are undoubtedly a few prisoners whose response to most penal situation's is so disruptive or aggressive—the extreme case being prisoners who have killed within prison—that they must for a time be placed in special units, attention needs most to be paid to trouble-generating *situations* and *procedures* rather than to the relatively illusive 'disruptive' population. Removal of 'troublesome' prisoners is seldom a solution. Such labelled prisoners often go on to confirm their labels (Boyle's autobiographical accounts (1977; 1984) are object lessons in this process) and the situation within which their troublesome behaviour was first identified typically generates further trouble. Secondly, it is the regime experienced by the 'mainstream' population which has crucially to be got right. It is there that trouble sporadically occurs, and the proliferation of special units disrupts the ladder of incentives and disincentives on which the stability and fairness of the whole system ultimately rests. Thirdly, positive relationships between prisoners and basic-grade prison officers are critical to the quality of prisoners' lives. This suggests, to take the crime-preventive analogy adopted by Sparks *et al.* (1996), that benefits are likely to flow from adopting a 'social' rather than 'situational' control strategy, in effect what Dunbar (1985) termed 'dynamic security'. This involves devising 'active' regimes for 'healthy' prisons for prisoners, in which prison officers are positively involved *with* prisoners in the delivery of programmes, services, and facilities between which prisoners may exercise a degree of responsible choice. The same lessons are implicit in the developing literature on suicide prevention in prison (Lloyd 1990). There are a few prisoners who recognizably feel so suicidal that they can be identified and focused measures adopted to prevent them taking their own lives (Prison Service 1992; Liebling 1992). The latter should not involve segregation in an environment within which suicide is made physically impossible: by definition, 'strip cells' of the sort that used regularly to be employed can only deepen the slough of despond. But a high proportion of prison suicides are not predictable; they occur more or less randomly within the mainstream population. The solution is to enhance the quality of life for *all* prisoners (HMCIP 1990b).

FUTURE PROSPECTS

This review ends where it began. The future trajectory of the prison population is uncertain. Home Office projections are little to be relied on. This is because, first, it is unclear to what extent the recommendations of two recently published reports, one reviewing sentencing (Home Office 2001a) and the other the structure and processes of the criminal court system (Auld 2001), are to be implemented. Secondly, in June 2001 New Labour was elected to a second term of office, and there are indications that the new team of Home Office Ministers is considering changes in policy direction.

Given these population uncertainties, what other aspects of current prisons policy are likely to change?

It is a feature of the tough language with which the government likes to clothe its penal policy (see Downes and Morgan, in Chapter 10 of this volume) that the gentle terms *aftercare* and *throughcare* have been replaced by the neutral term of *resettlement*, though the last arguably focuses on the desired outcome of reintegration of prisoners into the community as well as on the processes which allegedly further that outcome. But whatever term is used, the evidence suggests that there is almost an inverse relationship between the extent of prisoner resettlement needs and the degree to which they are addressed. Shorter-term prisoners—the overwhelming majority (more than four fifths of sentenced prisoners are, when remand and current executive release provisions are acted on, released within twelve months of their sentence being passed)—typically have multiple socio-economic and offence-related problems. For most prisoners and their families release is surrounded by profound problems of adjustment (Light 1993; King and McDermott 1995: chapter 6). Most offenders are released from prison without a job to go to and remain unemployed for a long time (NACRO 1999; Simon 1999: chapter 6). A high proportion face considerable financial difficulties, lack accommodation, and encounter early problems of substance abuse (NACRO 1993; King and McDermott 1995; Simon and Corbett 1996; Hagell *et al.* 1995). And not surprisingly, offenders with multiple social problems of this nature are more likely to be reconvicted (Crow *et al.* 1989; Simon and Corbett 1996; Hough 1996; May 1999).

The shorter the sentence from which they are released, the higher the proportion of released prisoners in every age group that is reconvicted (Home Office 2001c: Table 9.3). And yet prisoners serving sentences of twelve months or less are not subject to sentence planning, are not supervised when automatically released at the half-way point and, unless high risk of harm is identified, which is seldom, have little or no priority with the Probation Service. There is an absence of effective joint working between the Prison and Probation Services for resettlement purposes with longer-term prisoners as well (HMCIP/Probation 2001), but at least those prisoners serving longer sentences are subject to individual assessment and reporting requirements preparatory to their cases being considered by the Parole Board.

This argument can be taken further. The available evidence suggests that if the benefits of the largely cognitive behavioural 'What Works' programmes (see Raynor, in Chapter 31 of this volume) are to have long-term impact, they need to be backed up with interventions designed to assist prisoners with their domestic circumstances (family relationships, housing, employment, finance, alcohol and drugs, etc.—for reviews, see Haines 1990; Sampson and Laub 1993). The best results appear to be obtained through practical, active, participatory methods (Andrews 1995), and these appear to be the sort of methods being pursued at three designated *resettlement* prisons and a number of other resettlement units. In May 2000 one of these resettlement prisons, Blantyre House, was subject to an extraordinary and unprecedented night-time raid by officers from other establishments searching for drugs and evidence of criminal activity. Practically nothing was found, though the governor was removed from his post. The House of Commons Home Affairs Committee looked into the incident and came to very critical conclusions: neither the raid nor its conduct was justified (Home Affairs Committee 2000). Two pieces of evidence brought before the Committee are worth noting. First, that Blantyre House appeared to be successful in reducing the rate of reconvictions following release (though to what degree this was attributable to the selection of prisoners taken as opposed to the regime was unclear). Secondly, the Deputy Chief Inspector of Prisons told the Committee that, in his opinion, senior Prison Service staff perceived themselves to be judged more in terms of escapes than re-offending rates following release (ibid.: 29).

This suggests that the balance currently struck between security and rehabilitative and resettlement considerations may, in the wake of the security scandals of the mid-1990s, have been skewed unduly towards security. Within the next five years the Prison Service is likely to be taxed with evidence about the *outcome* of re-offending rather than the current large range of *outputs.* Preventing the escape of high-risk, high-security prisoners will clearly remain a priority. But the principal purpose of imprisonment, as the Woolf Report emphasized, is to support the criminal justice system in reducing the incidence of crime. At present the Prison Service's operational targets are focused on outputs—reducing escapes, delivering accredited educational, vocational and offending behaviour programmes, improving prison health care, and achieving productivity gains and cash savings (Prison Service 2001). Several of these targets are based on the evidence-based hypothesis that reduced offending post-release will be the result. But it is one thing to find that programmes are effective when applied by skilled and committed group leaders, in ideal circumstances, with carefully targeted subjects, who are prepared for the exercise and provided with follow-up support both prior to and following release. It is quite another thing to find that reduced re-convictions result when such programmes are generally rolled out. At the time of writing resettlement pilot programmes are being evaluated, and their number will almost certainly be expanded. But the proof of the government's investment strategy for prisons will only really be tested when data are routinely published linking the delivery of improved regimes, offence-focused programmes, supportive resettlement frameworks, and subsequent offending.

Selected further reading

Discussions of imprisonment ideally take place within the broader context of the debate on the philosophy and sociology of punishment. Nigel Walker's *Why Punish?* (Oxford: Oxford University Press, 1991) is an excellent introduction to the former; and David Garland's *Punishment and Modern Society* (Oxford: Oxford University Press, 1990) is a masterly overview of the major theorists who have explored the latter.

The current organization of imprisonment is heavily influenced by past practice. Michael Ignatieff's *A Just Measure of Pain* (London: Macmillan, 1978) provides an inspirational account of the emergence of imprisonment as the principal penalty for serious crime at the end of the eighteenth century; and *The Oxford History of the Prison* (edited by Norval Morris and David Rothman, New York: Oxford University Press, 1996) comprises a fine collection of essays by leading historians on the international origins and use of imprisonment.

As far as the contemporary use and organization of imprisonment is concerned, there is no substitute for becoming familiar with the Annual Report of the Prison Service on the work of the Service, and with the Home Office Research and Statistics Department's annual volume of *Prison Statistics*. To access these and many other documents (the reports of the Prisons Inspectorate and Prison Ombudsman, for example), the Home Office web site (**www.homeoffice.gov.uk**) is essential. The web sites of the Prison Reform Trust (**www.prisonreformtrust.org.uk**), NACRO (**www.nacro.org.uk**) and the Kings College Centre of Criminal Justice Studies (**www.kcl.ac.uk/depsta/rel/ccjs/events.htm**) are also very useful.

As far as introductory texts are concerned, Michael Cavadino's and James Dignan's *The Penal System: An Introduction* (3rd edn, London: Sage, 2002) and Roger Mathews' *Doing Time: An Introduction to the Sociology of Imprisonment* (Basingstoke: Macmillan, 1999) are the best available. A scholarly analysis of the recent, vitally important history of imprisonment in Northern Ireland is provided by Kieran McEvoy's *Paramilitary Imprisonment in Northern Ireland: Resistance, Management and Release* (Oxford: Oxford University Press, 2001).

Imprisonment is ultimately an experience which only those who have been incarcerated can adequately relate. Victor Serge's *Men in Prison* (London: Gollancz, 1970), Rod Caird's *A Good and Useful Life* (London: Hart-Davies, 1977), Jimmy Boyle's *A Sense of Freedom* (London: Canongate, 1977), and Audrey Peckham's *A Woman in Custody* (London: Fontana, 1985) are among the best contemporary accounts.

References

ADAMS, R. (1992), *Prison Riots in Britain and the USA*, New York: St Martins Press.

ADVISORY COUNCIL ON THE PENAL SYSTEM (1968), *The Regime for Long-Term Prisoners in Conditions of Maximum Security* (Radzinowicz Report), London: HMSO.

ANDREWS, D.A. (1995), 'The psychology of criminal conduct and effective treatment', in J. McGuire (ed.), *What Works? Reducing Offending*, Chichester: Wiley.

AULD REPORT (2001), *Review of the Criminal Courts of England and Wales: Report by the Right Honourable Lord Justice Auld*, London: Stationery Office.

BEYENS, K., and SNACKEN S. (1996), 'Prison privatization: an international perspective', in R. Matthews and P. Francis (eds), *Prisons 2000: an International Perspective on the Current State of and Future of Imprisonment*, Basingstoke: Macmillan.

BLAKE, W. (1927), *QUOD*, London: Hodder and Stoughton.

BOTTOMLEY, A.K., and HAY, W. (eds) (1991), *Special Units for Difficult Prisoners*, Hull: Centre for Criminology and Criminal Justice.

——, JAMES, A., CLARE, E., and LIEBLING, A. (1997), *Monitoring and Evaluation of Wolds Remand Prison*, Home Office Research and Planning Unit, London: Home Office.

BOTTOMLEY, K. (1995), *CRC Special Units: A General Assessment*, London: Home Office Research and Planning Unit.

BOTTOMS, A.E. (1977), 'Reflections of the Renaissance of Dangerousness', *Howard Journal*, 16/2: 70–76.

—— and LIGHT, R. (1987), *Problems of Long-term Imprisonment*, Aldershot: Gower.

BOYLE, J. (1977), *A Sense of Freedom*, Edinburgh: Canongate.

—— (1984), *The Pain of Confinement: Prison Diaries*, Edinburgh: Canongate.

CADDLE, D., and CRISP, D. (1997), *Mothers in Prison*, Research Findings 38, London: Home Office.

CARLEN, P. (1983), *Women's Imprisonment*, London: Routledge.

—— (1990), *Alternatives to Women's Imprisonment*, Milton Keynes: Open University Press.

—— and TCHAIKOVSKY, C. (1996), 'Women's imprisonment in England and Wales at the end of the twentieth century, realities and utopias', in R. Matthews and P. Francis (eds), *Prisons 2000: an International Perspective on the Current State and Future of Imprisonment*, Basingstoke: Macmillan.

CARLISLE REPORT (1988), *The Parole System in England and Wales: Report of the Review Committee*, Cm. 532, London: HMSO.

CASALE, S. (1984), *Minimum Standards for Prison Establishments*, London: NACRO.

—— (1989), *Women Inside: The Experience of Women Remand Prisoners in Holloway*, London: Civil Liberties Trust.

—— (1993), 'Conditions and standards', in E. Player and M. Jenkins, (eds), *Prisons After Woolf: reform through riot*, London: Routledge.

—— and PLOTNIKOFF, J. (1989), *Minimum Standards for Prisons: A Programme of Change*, London: NACRO.

—— and —— (1990), *Regimes for Remand Prisoners*, London: Prison Reform Trust.

CAVADINO, M., and DIGNAN, J. (2002), *The Penal System: An Introduction*, 3rd edn, London: Sage.

CHRISTIE, N. (1994), *Crime Control as Industry: Towards Gulags, Western Style*, London: Routledge.

CLARE, E., and BOTTOMLEY, K. (2001), *Evaluation of Close Supervision Centres*, Research Study 219, London: Home Office.

CLAYTON, G.F. (1958), *The Wall is Strong: The Life of a Prison Governor*, London: John Long.

CLEMMER, D. (1940), *The Prison Community*, New York: Holt, Rinehart and Winston.

COHEN, S., and TAYLOR, L. (1972), *Psychological Survival*, Harmondsworth: Penguin.

COLLINS, P. (1962), *Dickens and Crime*, Basingstoke: Macmillan.

COLVIN, M. (1992), *The Penitentiary in Crisis: From Accommodation to Riot in New Mexico*, Albany: State University of New York Press.

CONSERVATIVE PARTY (2001), *Time for Common Sense*, London: Conservative Party.

COOKE, D.J. (1989), 'Containing Violent Prisoners: An Analysis of the Barlinnie Special Unit', *British Journal of Criminology*, 29.1: 129–43.

COUNCIL OF EUROPE (1991), *Report to the United Kingdom Government on the Visit to the United Kingdom Carried Out by the European Committee for the Prevention of Torture and Inhuman or Degrading Treatment or Punishment from 29 June 1990 to 10 August 1990*, Strasbourg: Council of Europe.

COYLE, A. (1987), 'The Scottish Experience with Small Units', in A.E. Bottoms and R. Light (eds), *Problems of Long-term Imprisonment*, Aldershot: Gower.

—— (1994), *The Prisons We Deserve*, London: HarperCollins.

CREIGHTON, S., and KING, V. (1996), *Prisoners and the Law*, London: Butterworths.

CROW, I., RICHARDSON, C., RIDDINGTON, C., and SIMON, F. (1989), *Unemployment, Crime and Offenders*, London: Routledge.

DELL, S., GROUNDS, A., JAMES, K., and ROBERTSON, G. (1991), *Mentally Disordered Remanded Prisoners: Report to the Home Office*, Cambridge: University of Cambridge.

DITCHFIELD, J. (1990), *Control in Prisons: A Review of the Literature*, Home Office Research Study No. 118, London: HMSO.

DOBASH, R., DOBASH, R., and GUTTERIDGE S. (1986), *The Imprisonment of Women*, Oxford: Blackwell.

DODD, T., and HUNTER, P. (1992), *The National Prisoner Survey 1991: A Report to the Home Office of a Study of Prisoners in England and Wales Carried Out by the Social Survey Division of OCPS*, London: HMSO.

DODGSON, K., GOODWIN, P., HOWARD, P., LLEWELLYN-THOMAS, S., MORTIMER, E., RUSSELL, N., and WEINER, N. (2001), *Electronic monitoring of released prisoners: an evaluation of the Home Detention Curfew Scheme*, Research Study 222, London: Home Office.

DONZIGER, S.R. (1995), *The Real War on Crime: the Report of the National Criminal Justice Commission*, New York: HarperCollins.

DOWNES, D. (1988), *Contrasts in Tolerance: Post-War Penal Policy in the Netherlands and England and Wales*, Oxford: Oxford University Press.

—— (1997), 'The buckling of the shields: Dutch penal policy 1985–1995', in N. South and R. Weiss (eds), *International Prison Systems*, Reading: Gordon and Breach.

DUNBAR, I. (1985), *A Sense of Direction*, London: Prison Service.

EDGAR, K., and O'DONNELL, I. (1998), *Mandatory drug testing in prisons: the relationship between MDT and the level and nature of drug misuse*, Research Study 189, London: Home Office.

EVANS, M., and MORGAN, R. (1998), *Preventing Torture: A Study of the European Convention for the Prevention of Torture and Inhuman or Degrading Treatment or Punishment*, Oxford: Oxford University Press.

Feeley, M., and Simon, J. (1992) 'The New Penology: Notes on the emerging strategy of corrections and its implications', *Criminology*, 30, 4: 449–74.

Feldman, D. (2002), *Civil Liberties and Human Rights in England and Wales*, 2nd edn, Oxford: Oxford University Press.

Fitzgerald, M., and Marshall, P. (1996), 'Ethnic minorities in British prisons: some research implications', in R. Matthews and P. Francis (eds) *Prisons 2000: An International Perspective on the Current State and Future of Imprisonment*, Basingstoke: Macmillan.

Foucault, M. (1967), *Madness and Civilisation*, London: Tavistock.

—— (1977), *Discipline and Punish: The Birth of the Prison*, London: Allen Lane.

Fox, L. (1952), *The English Prison and Borstal System*, London: Routledge.

Garland, D. (1990), *Punishment and Modern Society: A Study in Social Theory*, Oxford: Oxford University Press.

—— (2001), *The Culture of Control: Crime and Social Order in Contemporary Society*, Oxford: Oxford University Press.

—— and Young, P. (1983), 'Towards a Social Analysis of Penality', in D. Garland and P. Young (eds), *The Power to Punish*, London: Heinemann.

Genders, E., and Player, E. (1989), *Race Relations in Prison*, Oxford: Clarendon Press.

—— and —— (1994), *Grendon: A Study of a Therapeutic Prison*, Oxford: Clarendon Press.

Goffmann, E. (1968), 'The Characteristics of Total Institutions', in *Asylums*, Harmondsworth: Penguin.

Gostin, L., and Staunton, M. (1985), 'The Case for Prison Standards: Conditions of Confinement, Segregation and Medical Treatment', in M. Maguire, J. Vagg, and R. Morgan (eds), *Accountability and Prisons: Opening Up a Closed World*, London: Tavistock.

Graham, J., and Bowling, B. (1995), *Young People and Crime*, Research Study 145, London: Home Office.

Gray, C., and Elkins, M. (2001), *Projections of Long Term Trends in the Prison Population to 2008: England and Wales*, Statistical Bulletin 8/01, London: Home Office.

Green, P. (1991), *Drug Couriers*, London: Prison Reform Trust.

Gunn, J., Maden, A., and Swinton, M. (1991), *Mentally Disordered Prisoners*, London: Institute of Psychiatry.

Hagell, A., Newburn, T., and Rowlingson, K. (1995), *Financial Difficulties on Release from Prison*, London: Policy Studies Institute.

Haines, K. (1990), *After-Care Services for Released Prisoners: a Review of the Literature*, London: Home Office.

Hamlyn, B., and Lewis, D. (2000), *Women Prisoners: a survey of their work and training experiences in custody and on release*, Research Study 208, London: Home Office.

Harding, R.W. (1997), *Private Prisons and Public Accountability*, Buckinghan: Open University Press.

Her Majesty's Chief Inspector of Prisons (1987), *Report of an Inquiry into the Disturbances in Prison Service Establishments in England between 29 April and 2 May 1986*, HC 42, London: HMSO.

—— (1988), *HM Remand Centre Risley*, London: Home Office.

—— (1989), *Prison Sanitation*, London: Home Office.

—— (1990a), *HM Prison Brixton*, London: Home Office.

—— (1990b), *Suicide and Self-Harm in Prison Service Establishments in England and Wales*, Cm. 1383, London: HMSO.

—— (1993), *HM Prison Cardiff*, London: Home Office.

—— (1996), *Annual Report, April 1995—March 1996*, London: HMSO.

—— (1997a), *Women in Prison: A Thematic Review*, London: Home Office.

—— (1997b), *Young Prisoners: A Thematic Review*, London: Home Office.

—— (1998a), *HM Blakenhurst*, London: Home Office.

—— (1998b), *HM Wolds*, London: Home Office.

—— (1999a), *Suicide is Everyone's Concern: A Thematic Review*, London: Home Office.

—— (1999b), *HM Altcourse*, London: Home Office.

—— (2000a), *Unjust Deserts: A Thematic Review of the Treatment and Conditions for Unsentenced Prisoners in England and Wales*, London: Home Office.

—— (2000b), *Inspection of Close Supervision Centres, August–September 1999*, London: Home Office.

—— (2001a), *HM Prison Birmingham*, London: Home Office.

—— (2001b), *Follow-up to Women in Prison: A Thematic Review*, London: Home Office.

—— (2001c), *Annual Report 1999–2000*, London: Home Office.

—— (2001d), *Young Offender Institutions*, London: Home Office.

—— (2001e), *HM YOI and Remand Centre Feltham*, London: Home Office.

—— (2001f), *HM YOI Brinsford (inspection June 2000)*, London: Home Office.

—— (2001g), *HM YOI Brinsford (inspection May 2001)*, London: Home Office.

—— (2001h), *HM YOI Stoke Heath*, London: Home Office.

HMCIP/PROBATION (1999), *Lifers: A Joint Thematic Review by HM Inspectorates of Prison and Probation*. London: Home Office.

—— (2001), *Through the Prison Gate: A Joint Thematic Review by HM Inspectorates of Prison and Probation*, London: Home Office.

HOME AFFAIRS COMMITTEE, HOUSE OF COMMONS (1981), *The Prison Service*, vol. 1, HC 412, 1980/1, London: HMSO.

—— (1997), *The Management of the Prison Service (Public and Private)*, London: HMSO.

—— (1999), *Drugs and Prisons*, vol 1, 363-I, 1998–99, London: HMSO.

—— (2000), *Blantyre House Prison*, Session 1999–2000, London: HMSO.

HOME OFFICE (1947), *Report of the Commissioners of Prison and Directors of Convict Prisons for the Year 1946*, Cmd. 7271, London: HMSO.

—— (1965), *The Adult Offender*, Cmnd 2852, London: HMSO.

—— (1981), *Annual Report of the Work of the Prison Department 1980*, Cmnd 8228, London: HMSO.

—— (1984), *Managing the Long-term Prison System: The Report of the Control Review Committee*, London: HMSO.

—— (1990), *Crime, Justice and Protecting the Public*, Cmnd 965, London: HMSO.

—— (1991), *Custody, Care and Justice: The Way Ahead for the Prison Service in England and Wales*, Cmnd 1647, London: HMSO.

—— (1996), *Protecting the Public: The Government's Strategy on Crime in England and Wales*, Cmnd 3190, London: Home Office.

—— (1999a), *Digest 4: Information on the Criminal Justice System in England and Wales*, London: Home Office.

—— (1999b), *Detention in a YOI for 18–20 year olds—A Consultation Paper*, London: Home Office.

—— (2001a) (Halliday Report), *Making Punishments Work. Report of a Review of the Sentencing Framework for England and Wales*, London: Home Office.

—— (2001b), *Criminal Justice: the Way Ahead*, Cmnd 5074, London: Home Office.

—— (2001c), *Prison Statistics England and Wales 1999*, Cmnd 5250, London: Home Office.

—— (2001d), *The Government's Strategy for Women Offenders: Consultation Report*, London: Home Office.

HOOD, R. (1992), *Race and Sentencing: A Study in the Crown Court*, Oxford: Clarendon Press.

—— and SHUTE, S. (2000), *The Parole System at Work: a study of risk based decision-making*, Research Study 202, London: Home Office.

HOUGH, M. (1996), *Drug Misuse and the Criminal Justice System: a review of the literature*, CDPU Paper 15, London: Home Office.

HOWARD, J. (1784), *The State of the Prisons in England and Wales with Preliminary Observations, and an Account of some Foreign Prisons and Hospitals*, 3rd edn, Warrington.

IGNATIEFF, M. (1978), *A Just Measure of Pain*, London: Macmillan.

IRWIN, J. (1970), *The Felon*, Englewood Cliffs, NJ: Prentice-Hall.

—— and CRESSEY, D. (1962), 'Thieves, Convicts and the Inmate Culture', *Social Problems*, 10/92: 145–55.

JACOBS, J. (1977), *Stateville: The Penitentiary in Mass Society*, Chicago, Ill.: University of Chicago Press.

—— (1979), 'Race Relations and the Prisoner Sub-Culture', in N. Morris and M. Tonry (eds), *Crime and Justice: An Annual Review of Research*, vol. 1, Chicago, Ill.: University of Chicago Press.

—— (1980), 'The Prisoners' Rights Movement and its Impacts, 1960–1980', in N. Morris and M. Tonry (eds), *Crime and Justice: An Annual Review of Research*, vol. 2., Chicago, Ill.: University of Chicago Press.

JAMES, A.L., BOTTOMLEY, A.K., CLARE, E., and LIEBLING, A. (1997), *Privatizing Prisons: Rhetoric and Reality*, London: Sage.

JONES, H., and CORNES, P. (1977), *Open Prisons*, London: Routledge.

KING, R.D. (1999), 'The rise and rise of supermax: an American solution in search of a problem', *Punishment and Society*, 1, 2, 163–86.

—— and Elliott, K. (1977), *Albany: Birth of a Prison—End of an Era*, London: Routledge.

—— and McDermott, K. (1989), 'British Prisons 1970–1987: The Ever-Deepening Crisis', *British Journal of Criminology*, 29: 107–28.

—— and —— (1990), 'My Geranium is Subversive: Some Notes on the Management of Trouble in Prisons', *British Journal of Sociology*, 41: 445–71.

—— and —— (1995), *The State of Our Prisons*, Oxford: Clarendon Press.

King, R., and Morgan, R. (1976), *A Taste of Prison: Custodial Conditions for Trial and Remand Prisoners*. London: Routledge.

—— (1980), *The Future of the Prison System*, Aldershot: Gower.

Labour Party (2001), *Ambitions for Britain: Labour's Manifesto 2001*, London: Labour Party.

Laming, Lord (Laming Report) (2000), *Modernising the Management of the Prison Service: An independent report by the Targeted Performance Initiative Working Group*, London: Communications Directorate, Home Office.

Learmont Report (1995), *Review of Prison Service Security in England and Wales and the Escape from Parkhurst Prison on Tuesday 3rd January 1995*, Cm 3020, London: HMSO.

Leech, M., and Cheney, D. (2001), *The Prisons Handbook*, Winchester: Waterside Press.

Lewis, D. (1997), *Hidden Agendas*, London: Hamish Hamilton.

Liebling, A. (1992), *Suicides in Prison*, London: Routledge.

—— (2001), 'A "liberal regime within a secure perimeter?": dispersal prisons and penal practice in the late 20th century', a Paper delivered at a Radzinowicz Commemorative Symposium, Institute of Criminology, University of Cambridge, March.

——, Muir, G., Rose, G., and Bottoms, A. (1997), *An Evaluation of Incentives and Earned Privileges: report for the Home Office*, Cambridge: Institute of Criminology.

——, ——, —— and —— (1999), *Incentives and earned privileges—an evaluation*, Research Findings 87, London: Home Office.

—— and Price, D. (2001), *The Prison Officer*, London: Prison Service Journal.

Livingstone, S., and Owen, T. (1999), *Prison Law*, 2nd edn, Oxford: Oxford University Press.

Lloyd, C. (1990), *Suicide and Self-Injury in Prison: A Literature Review*, Research Study 115, London: HMSO.

Lloyd, Sir P. (2001), *Review of the Boards of Visitors: A Report of the Working Group*, London: Home Office.

Logan, C.H.(1990), *Private Prisons: Pros and Cons*, New York: Oxford University Press.

Loucks, N., and Plotnikoff, J. (1993), *Prison Rules: A Working Guide*, London: Prison Reform Trust.

McConville, S. (1981), *A History of English Prison Administration*, vol. 1: 1750–1877, London: Routledge.

McCorkle, L., and Korn. R. (1954), 'Resocialisation within the Walls', *Annals of the American Academy of Political and Social Science*, 293: 88–98.

McDermott, C., and King, R.D. (1988) 'Mind Games: Where the Action is in Prisons', *British Journal of Criminology*, 28, 3: 357–77.

McEvoy, K. (2001), *Paramilitary Imprisonment in Northern Ireland: Resistance, Management and Release*, Oxford: Oxford University Press.

McGowan, R. (1995), 'The Well-Ordered Prison: England 1780–1865', in N. Morris and D. Rothman (eds), *The Oxford History of the Prison*, New York: Oxford University Press.

Maguire, M. (1992), 'Parole', in E. Stockdale and C. Casale (eds), *Criminal Justice under Stress*, London: Blackstone Press.

Marsh, A., Dobbs, J., Mont, J., and White, A. (1985), *Staff Attitudes in the Prison Service*, London: HMSO.

Marshall, P. (1997), *A Reconviction Study of HMP Grendon Therapeutic Community*, Research Findings 53, London: Home Office.

Mathieson, T. (1965), *The Defences of the Weak*, London: Tavistock.

May, C. (1999), *Explaining Reconviction following a Community Sentence: the role of social factors*, Research Study 192, London: Home Office.

May Committee (1979), *Report of the Committee of Inquiry into the United Kingdom Prison Services*, Cmnd 7673, London: HMSO.

Mayhew, H., and Binny, J. (1862), *The Criminal Prisons of London and Scenes of Prison Life*, London: Charles Griffin.

Melossi, D., and Pavarini, M. (1981), *The Prison and the Factory: The Origins of the Penitentiary*, Basingstoke: Macmillan.

Morgan, R. (1985), 'Her Majesty's Inspectorate of Prisons', in M. Maguire, J. Vagg, and R. Morgan (eds), *Accountability and Prisons: Opening Up a Closed World*, 106–23, London: Tavistock.

—— (1992), 'Following Woolf: The Prospects for Prisons Policy', *Journal of Law and Society*, 19: 231–50.

—— (1993), 'An Awkward Anomaly: Remand Prisoners', in E. Player and M. Jenkins (eds), *Prisons After Woolf : reform through riot*, London: Routledge.

—— (1995), 'Prison', in M. Walker, (ed.), *Interpreting Crime Statistics*, Oxford: Clarendon Press.

—— (1997), 'Imprisonment: Current Concerns and a Brief History since 1945', in M. Maguire, R. Morgan, and R. Reiner (eds), *The Oxford Handbook of Criminology*, 2nd edn, Oxford: Oxford University Press.

—— and EVANS, M. (1994), 'Inspecting Prisons: the view from Strasbourg', in R.D. King and M. Maguire (eds), *Prisons in Context*, Oxford: Clarendon Press.

—— and —— (2001), *Combating Torture in Europe: The Work and Standards of the European Committee for the Prevention of Torture*, Strasbourg: Council of Europe.

MORRIS, N., and ROTHMAN, D.J. (eds) (1995), *The Oxford History of the Prison*, New York: Oxford University Press.

MORRIS, T., and MORRIS, P. (1963), *Pentonville: A Sociological Study of an English Prison*, London: Routledge.

MOUNTBATTEN REPORT (1966), *Report of the Inquiry into Prison Escapes and Security*, Cmnd 3175, London: HMSO.

MUNCIE, J., and SPARKS, R. (1991), 'Expansion and Contraction in European Penal Systems', in J. Muncie and R. Sparks (eds), *Imprisonment: European Perspectives*, London: Harvester Wheatsheaf.

NACRO (1993), *Opening the Doors: The Resettlement of Prisoners in the Community*, London: NACRO.

—— (1999), *Going Straight to Work*, London: NACRO.

—— (2001), *Young Adult Offenders: a period of transition*, London: NACRO.

NAREY, M. (2001) *Speech to the Governors' Annual Conference*, London: Prison Service.

PADFIELD, N., and LIEBLING, A. (2000), *An Exploration of Decision-making at Discretionary Lifer Panels*, Research Study 213, London: Home Office.

PARK, I. (2000), *Review of Comparative Costs and Performance of Privately and Publicly Operated Prisons 1998–99*, Statistical Bulletin 6/00, London: Home Office.

PAROLE BOARD (2000), *Annual Report and Accounts of the Parole Board 1999–2000*, London: Stationery Office.

PEASE, K. (1994), 'Cross-national imprisonment rates: limitations of method and possible conclusions', in R.D. King and M. Maguire (eds), *Prisons in Context*, Oxford: Clarendon Press.

PETERS, E. (1996), *Torture*, 2nd edn, Pennsylvania: University of Pennsylvania Press.

PRIESTLEY, P. (1981), *Community of Scapegoats*, Oxford: Pergamon Press.

—— (1989), *Jail Journeys: The English Prison Experience 1918–1980*, London: Routledge.

PRIOR REPORT (1985), *Report on the Departmental Committee on the Prison Disciplinary System*, London: HMSO.

PRISON OFFICERS' ASSOCIATION (1984), *The Prison Disciplinary System: Submissions to the Home Office Departmental Committee on the Prison Disciplinary System*, London: Prison Officers' Association.

PRISON OMBUDSMAN (1996), *Annual Report 1995*, London: Prison Ombudsman.

—— (2001a), *Independent Investigation of Prisoners' Complaints: Annual Report 2000–2001*, London: Prison Ombudsman.

—— (2001b), *Listening to Young Prisoners: a review of complaints procedures in Young Offender Institutions*, London: Prisons Ombudsman.

PRISON REFORM TRUST (1990), *Sex Offenders in Prison*, London: Prison Reform Trust.

PRISON SERVICE (1991), *The Control Review Committee 1984: Implementation of the Committee's Recommendations*, Directorate of Custody, London: Home Office/Prison Service.

—— (1992), *Caring for Prisoners at Risk of Suicide and Self-Injury: The Way Forward*, London: Prison Service.

—— (1996), *Corporate Plan 1996–9*, London: Prison Service.

—— (1999), *Prison Service: Annual Report and Accounts, April 1998 to March 1999*, London: Prison Service.

—— (2000a), *Prison Service: Annual Report and Accounts, April 1999 to March 2000*, HC 622, London: Prison Service.

—— (2000b), *Prison Service: Corporate Plan 2001–2002 to 2003–2004, Business Plan 2001–2002*, London: Prison Service.

—— (2000c), *HM Prison Service Performance Standards Manual*, London: Prison Service

—— (2001) *Prison Service: Annual Report and Accounts, April 2000 to March 2001*, HC 29, London: Prison Service.

PUGH, R.B. (1970), *Imprisonment in Mediaeval England*, Cambridge: Cambridge University Press.

RADZINOWICZ, L., and HOOD, R. (1990), *The Emergence of Penal Policy in Victorian and Edwardian England*, Oxford: Clarendon Press.

REX, S., and TONRY, M. (eds) (2002), *Reform and Punishment: the Future of Sentencing and Sanctions*, Cullompton, Devon: Willan.

RICHARDSON, G. (1985), *Law, Custody and Process: Prisoners and Patients*, London: Hodder and Stoughton.

—— (1993), 'From Rights to Expectations', in E. Player and M. Jenkins (eds), *Prisons After Woolf*, London: Routledge.

ROCK, P. (1996), *Reconstructing a Women's Prison: The Holloway Redevelopment Project*. Oxford: Clarendon Press.

RUCK, S.K. (ed.) (1951), *Paterson on Prisons: Prisoners and Patients*, London: Hodder and Stoughton.

RUSCHE, G., and KIRCHHEIMER, O. (1968), *Punishment and Social Structure*, New York: Columbia University Press.

RUTHERFORD, A. (1984), *Prisons and the Process of Justice*, Oxford: Oxford University Press.

SAMPSON, R.J., and LAUB, J.H. (1993), *Crime in the Making: Pathways and Turning Points through Life*, Cambridge, Mass.: Harvard University Press.

SAPSFORD, R. (1983), *Life Sentence Prisoners*, Milton Keynes: Open University Press.

SCOTTISH EXECUTIVE (2000), *A Review of Conditions for Remand Prisoners in Scotland at the End of the 20th Century* (HM Chief Inspector of Prisons, Scotland, thematic report), Edinburgh: Scottish Executive.

SCOTTISH PRISON SERVICE (1990), *Opportunity and Responsibility*, Edinburgh: Scottish Prison Service.

SCULL, A. (1977), *Decarceration: Community Treatment and the Deviant*, Englewood Cliffs, NJ: Prentice-Hall.

SEDDON, T. (1996), 'Drug Control in Prisons', *Howard Journal*, 35: 327–35.

SHAW, R. (ed.) (1992), *Prisoners' Children: What are the Issues?*, London: Routledge.

SHICHOR, D. (1995), *Punishment for Profit: Private Prisons—Public Concerns*, Thousand Oaks, Cal.. Sage.

SIM, J. (1990), *Medical Power in Prisons: the Prison Medical Service in England 1774–1989*, Buckingham: Open University Press.

——, RUGGIERO, V., and RYAN, M. (1995), 'Punishment in Europe: Perceptions and Commonalities', in V. Ruggiero, M. Ryan, and J. Sim (eds), *Western European Penal Systems: A Critical Analysis*, London: Sage.

SIMON, F. (1999), *Prisoners' Work and Vocational Training*, London: Routledge.

—— and CORBETT, C. (1996), *An Evaluation of Prison Work and Training*, London: Home Office.

SINGLETON, N., MELTZER, H., and GATWARD, R. (1998), *Psychiatric Morbidity among Prisoners in England and Wales*, London: Stationery Office.

SPARKS, R. (1994), 'Can prisons be legitimate? Penal politics, privatization, and the timeliness of an old idea', in R.D. King and M. Maguire (eds), *Prisons in Context*, Oxford: Clarendon Press.

—— (1996), 'Penal "Austerity": The Doctrine of Less Eligibility Reborn?', in R. Matthews and P. Francis (eds), *Prisons 2000: An International Perspective on the Current State and Future of Imprisonment*, Basingstoke: Macmillan.

——, BOTTOMS, A.E., and HAY, W. (1996), *Prisons and the Problem of Order*, Oxford: Clarendon Press.

SPIERENBERG, P. (1984), *The Spectacle of Suffering: Executions and the Evolution of Repression, from a Pre-industrial Metropolis to the European Experience*, Cambridge: Cambridge University Press.

STERN V. (1997), *Bricks of Shame: Britain's Prisons*, Harmondsworth: Penguin.

—— (1998), *A Sin Against the Future: Imprisonment in the World*, Harmondsworth: Penguin.

SYKES, G. (1958), *The Society of Captives*, Princeton: Princeton University Press.

THOMAS, J.E. (1972), *The English Prison Officer Since 1850*, London: Routledge.

TOMASHEVSKI, K. (1994), *Foreigners in Prison*, Helsinki: European Institute for Crime Prevention and Control.

VAN ZYL SMIT, D., and DUNKEL, F. (eds), (1991), *Imprisonment Today and Tomorrow: International Perspective on Prisoners' Rights and Prison Conditions*, 1st edn, Deventer: Kluwer.

—— and —— (2001), *Imprisonment Today and Tomorrow: International Perspective on Prisoners'*

Rights and Prison Conditions, 2nd edn, Deventer: Kluwer.

WALMESLEY, R. (1989), *Special Security Units*, Research Unit Study No. 109, London: HMSO.

——, HOWARD, L., and WHITE, S. (1992), *The National Prison Survey 1991: Main Findings*, Research Study 128, London: HMSO.

WACQUANT, L. (2001), 'Deadly Symbiosis: when ghetto and prison meet and merge', *Punishment and Society*, 3, 1: 95–133.

WILLIAMS, M., and LONGLEY, D. (1987), 'Identifying Control-Problem Prisoners in Dispersal Prisons', in A.E. Bottoms and R. Light (eds), *Problems of Long-term Imprisonment*, Aldershot: Gower.

WOODCOCK REPORT (1994), *Report of the Enquiry into the Escape of Six Prisoners from the Special Security Unit at Whitemoor Prison, Cambridgeshire, on Friday 9th September 1994*, Cm. 2741, London: HMSO.

WOOLF REPORT (1991), *Prison Disturbances April 1990: Report of an Inquiry by the Rt Hon. Lord Justice Woolf (Part I and II) and His Honour Judge Stephen Tumin (Part II)*, Cm. 1456, London: HMSO.

WORRALL, A. (1994), *Have You Got a Minute?*, London: Prison Reform Trust.

YOUNG, P. (1987), 'The Concept of Social Control and its Relevance to the Prisons Debate', in A.E. Bottoms and R. Light (eds), *Problems of Long-term Imprisonment*, 97–114, Aldershot: Gower.

ZEDNER, L. (1994), *Women, Crime and Custody in Victorian England*, Oxford: Clarendon Press.

—— (1995), 'Wayward sisters', in N. Morris and D. Rothman (eds), *The Oxford History of the Prison*, New York: Oxford University Press.

ZIMRING, F.E., and HAWKINS, G. (1991), *The Scale of Imprisonment*, Chicago, Ill.: Chicago University Press.

31

COMMUNITY PENALTIES
PROBATION, PUNISHMENT, AND 'WHAT WORKS'

Peter Raynor

INTRODUCTION: CATCHING THE SLIPPERY FISH

The title of this chapter is imprecise, reflecting the contested and imprecise nature of the concept of 'community penalties'. The term is widely used and we think we know what it means, but it would not be easy to explain to somebody unfamiliar with the history and sentencing tradition in which it belongs. For example, 'community penalty' is not normally used simply to describe forms of punishment imposed in the community, or outside prison. If this were its usual meaning, most discussions of community penalties would probably be about fines, since these are the most widely used non-custodial punishment. Instead, we find that most discussions of community penalties are actually about probation, a penalty which allows the offender to retain his or her liberty by complying with the requirements of a court order and being supervised by an appropriately authorized official employed by, or acting on behalf of, a probation service.

In recent years such discussions have also included community service orders (a rather different kind of penalty involving indirect reparation supervised by probation services) and other forms of supervisory penalty such as electronically monitored curfew orders, which are not necessarily supervised by probation services. On the other hand, discussions of community penalties often exclude a large proportion of the offenders actually supervised by probation services (at least in Britain) because their original sentences are custodial, and they are being supervised under a form of licence or conditional release. And in case this is not confusing enough, the term 'probation order', understood and recognized throughout the English-speaking world and beyond, has been abolished in England and Wales by the Criminal Justice and Court Services Act 2000, to be replaced by the 'community rehabilitation order'. Similarly, the community service order became the 'community punishment order', the combination of probation and community service became a 'community punishment and rehabilitation order', and the Probation Service itself nearly became the Community Punishment and Rehabilitation Service until it was realised that only a small error in word order would result in the particularly undignified acronym

CRAPS. These rather fatuous acts of political relabelling are part of a much larger shift, not confined to England and Wales, in the politics of penal policy and the consequent perceptions of the role of probation services; this will be discussed more fully below, but here it serves to illustrate the continuing fluidity and contested nature of the concept of a 'community penalty', and its dependence on changing social and political environments.

One attempt to clarify the concept, at least for England and Wales, was made by the 1991 Criminal Justice Act, which defined a number of 'community sentences' which could be imposed if an offence was 'serious enough', but not 'so serious' that only a custodial sentence could be justified. Broadly speaking the framework established in the 1991 Act still applies, although modified by later legislation which weakened the principle that the severity of sentencing should primarily reflect the seriousness of the current offence. Other legislation has introduced new 'community sentences' (or, as outlined above, has confusingly renamed those which already existed). What 'community sentences' in the 1991 Act had in common was that offenders subject to them were in the community rather than in custody but were required to comply with various requirements as to their behaviour, and this compliance was to be monitored, supervised, and enforced if necessary by prosecution for non-compliance. The detailed requirements and characteristics of different 'community sentences' are discussed further below, but what the legislation quite neatly does is to group together a set of related sentencing options, mainly for adults, which have a number of characteristics in common. These include giving offenders an opportunity to demonstrate that they can avoid further offending, and holding them accountable through a supervision process which combines monitoring with encouragement and assistance—the mixture of supervision and help which, as we shall see, has been probation's preferred style since very early in its evolution. Thus 'community sentences' are usually not purely punitive (like a fine), neither are they based on coercive restriction of liberty like a prison; instead they rely on the cooperation of offenders in accepting the requirements of a court order, and often on the capacity of supervisors to negotiate, motivate, and persuade. So although there are some difficulties inherent in the 1991 concept of a community sentence, and in particular some problems in reconciling the pursuit of rehabilitative community sentencing with the Act's emphasis on proportionality (Raynor 1997), expediency suggests its use to define the territory of this chapter.

This chapter, then, is mainly about 'community sentences', mainly but not exclusively about Britain (particularly England and Wales), and mainly about adults, though some mention will be made of some similar orders for juvenile offenders and occasionally of those aspects of post-custodial supervision which resemble community sentences. (It should also be noted in this connection that the sentencing framework of the 1991 Act is currently under review (Halliday 2001), and that some of the proposed changes will further erode the distinction between custodial and 'community' sentences. Some possible implications of this are discussed later.) The chapter briefly describes the current variety of community sentences and their use in sentencing, and outlines the changes in the functions and perception of probation services which have led up to the current pattern of work. In particular the emergence of new evidence of effectiveness, and its adoption to support evidence-based practice or 'What Works', is having a profound and controversial impact on the world of community sentencing. This chapter seeks to document the development, implementation, and consequences so far of 'What Works' in British probation practice. The final parts of the chapter are concerned with other issues in current research on community penalties and look towards some of the dilemmas and opportunities which the future may present.

CURRENT COMMUNITY PENALTIES IN ENGLAND AND WALES

The community sentences available at the time of writing for adults (sixteen and over) in England and Wales are:

1. *Community rehabilitation orders* (the former probation orders), which require an offender to keep in contact with the Probation Service and cooperate with arrangements made for his supervision, which can include participation in programmes. Other requirements can be included by the court, such as residential requirements, attendance at specified activities or a 'probation centre', treatment for mental illness or addictions, curfew or exclusion requirements, and abstinence from drugs. These orders can be made for up to three years, though shorter periods are normal, and like all community sentences they are subject to enforcement proceedings if offenders do not comply with their requirements. This normally means that the Probation Service initiates a prosecution for breach of the order, which if proved can lead to various sentences but is often dealt with by imprisonment.

2. *Community punishment orders* (the former community service orders), which require an offender to perform, under Probation Service supervision (directly or indirectly through other organizations), a set number of hours of unpaid work for the benefit of the community. The required hours can range from forty to 240.

3. *Community punishment and rehabilitation orders* (the former 'combination order', a less than transparent title), which combine the requirements of a community punishment order (up to 100 hours) with those of a community rehabilitation order.

4. *Drug treatment and testing orders*, which require offenders to undergo treatment in relation to drug problems, supported by regular tests to detect illicit drug use and reviewed at intervals by the court. These orders are normally managed on behalf of the Probation Service by specialist drug treatment agencies working in partnership with the Service, and failure to comply or positive drug tests can lead to breach action. DTTOs, as they are known, are a recent innovation now

being implemented nationally after broadly encouraging findings from pilot projects (Turnbull *et al.* 2000).

5. One of the less used adult community sentences is the *curfew order*, requiring an offender to stay at a particular location between particular hours; these can range from two to twelve in any one day, and the order as a whole cannot last more than six months. Such orders can involve electronic monitoring, discussed later in the chapter, and have been slow in attracting the support of probation staff and sentencers.

6. Also available for some offenders (aged twenty-one or over, and only if sentenced in the Crown Court) is the *suspended sentence supervision order*, something of a survival from earlier legislation which requires an offender to be supervised during all or part of the period of suspension of a suspended prison sentence (these are usually suspended for two years).

Community sentences for juveniles include the long-established supervision order, which places a young offender (aged from ten to under eighteen) under the supervision of, normally, a local authority social worker for up to three years. Again a range of additional requirements is available, and enforcement is possible in the event of breach, though this has never been the focus of so much attention here as it has in the case of adult offenders. More recently a number of new orders have been created, some of which are still being piloted and evaluated. Not all of these are strictly 'community sentences' as described by the 1991 Act, but they are similar in spirit, including: a reparation order requiring up to twenty-four hours of reparative activity to benefit the community or, with consent, the victim; a parenting order, requiring the parents of offenders to attend parenting classes for three months, with the option of a further discretionary period; and an action plan order, requiring a young offender to comply with a three-month action plan drawn up by an inter-agency team to address his or her difficulties.

According to the most recent figures (National Probation Service 2001; Home Office 2001), the Service is responsible for supervising well over 200,000 offenders at any one time, including about 61,000 on community rehabilitation orders, 46,000 on community punishment orders, 29,000 on community punishment and rehabilitation orders and 7,000 on money payment supervision orders (which place a fined offender under supervision until the fine is paid). Another 80,000 are subject to statutory supervision on release from prisons and other custodial establishments, but only about 25,000 of these are actually being supervised in the community. All young offenders sentenced to custodial sentences and all adult prisoners sentenced to twelve months or more are subject to some form of supervision after release, for periods ranging from a few months following a short sentence to life following release from a life sentence. These forms of post-custodial supervision are not 'community sentences' but are increasingly seen as an integral part of a single sentence served partly in custody and partly in the community (Maguire and Raynor 1997), an idea which is developed further in the government's current review of sentencing policy (Halliday 2001). A recent Probation Circular provides a summary of how some of these figures have changed over twenty years: the number of court orders supervised at any one time rose from 84,420 at the end of 1980 to around 130,000 in 2000 (Probation Circular 148/2001).

Community penalties similar to the main options outlined above are also available in Scotland. Probation and community service orders retain their original titles there, but are not supervised by officers of a probation service, which has not existed in Scotland since 1969; instead they are normally the responsibility of criminal justice specialists working in social work departments of local authorities.

Elsewhere in Europe many countries have some form of probation (Hamai *et al.* 1995), and the idea of community penalties is spreading to Eastern European countries where the levels of imprisonment inherited from former authoritarian regimes are seen as no longer necessary or affordable (for example, Jones 2001). Similar developments are under way in the developing world in an attempt to control or reverse growth in prison numbers. There the most favoured option seems sometimes to be community service, which has been successfully introduced in several African jurisdictions without the need for a large, professionalized probation service (Stern 1998). Ironically, the increasing popularity of probation and community service throughout the world has coincided with a period in Britain when they have often struggled for political approval and support.

COMMUNITY PENALTIES IN A CHANGING PENAL LANDSCAPE: THE ERAS OF 'TREATMENT' AND 'DIVERSION'

The history of community penalties has been shaped by changing ideas of the purposes of criminal justice and of the functions and effects of penal sanctions. Through most of their history community penalties have also been the subjects of research, but because the vast majority of such research has been funded by government it has often been shaped by taken-for-granted policy assumptions. This section aims to trace the interaction of policy and research in community penalties up to and through the era of 'nothing works'. It illustrates how research, funded mainly by government, has often been more a product or reflection of current policy than an influence on it.

ORIGINS OF PROBATION

Probation has its origins in local court practices in the early nineteenth century, whereby young offenders or those guilty of minor offences could be discharged or bound over if a suitable person offered to take responsibility for supervising their future conduct. In 1876 the Church of England Temperance Society, helped (according to tradition) by five shillings from the printer Frederick Rainer of Hertford, began to maintain an active presence in some city police courts in order to promote the moral reform of offenders and abstention from alcohol. Sentencers developed the practice of seeking information from the missionaries about offenders and placing some of them under informal supervision in lieu of other punishment if they seemed likely to reform. This was an opportunity to 'prove' themselves: hence the term 'probation', a proof or test.

A similar system, rooted in missionary work, charitable endeavour, and the temperance movement, had developed in parts of the United States from the 1840s, and seems first to have been formalized in the legal guise of supervision by an officer of the court in Massachusetts in 1869. Developments there were eagerly studied by penal reformers campaigning for a probation law in Britain. Their efforts bore fruit in 1907 in the Probation of Offenders Act, but several more decades were to elapse before probation services everywhere in Britain were provided by salaried public officials rather than by a mixed workforce of professionals and missionaries. This early period is described by McWilliams, in his seminal series of articles on the history of probation (McWilliams 1983, 1985, 1986, 1987), as concerned with saving souls, but it also played a part in the emergence of what Garland has called the 'penal-welfare' complex (Garland 1985). More recent historical work by Vanstone (2001) has documented other influences on some of the court-based missionaries and early probation officers, including interest in eugenics and in Lombrosian theories about the constitutional inferiority of criminals. A marked theoretical eclecticism has been a feature of the probation service throughout its history. However, by the time that serious research on probation began to be undertaken the emerging professional service had found itself a new theory: like the rest of social work, it had adopted a psychosocial theory strongly influenced by psychoanalytic ideas about the unconscious and defence mechanisms (see Richmond 1917 for a pre-Freudian model of diagnostic social work, and Hollis 1964 for a more developed and psychoanalytically influenced version).

THE 'TREATMENT MODEL' AND CASEWORK

The new theory co-opted the old term 'casework' (which in its original usage by the Charity Organization Society meant simply 'work on cases') and changed its meaning to denote a process of therapeutic work in which the offender's needs and motivations, characteristically hidden behind a 'presenting problem', could be revealed through a process of insight facilitated by a relationship with a probation officer (see, for example, Monger 1964). The fact that psychotherapeutic relationships were intended to be voluntary whereas the probation officer could prosecute his 'client' for not cooperating was an apparent inconsistency, and a source of concern for those inclined to redefine probation as psychotherapy. However, as Foren and Bailey (1968) explained, those who were helped to gain increased insight would then realize that they would have volunteered if they had understood their own needs properly, and so the relationship was really voluntary in a kind of retrospective way, even if this was not apparent at the time. This principle was concretely illustrated by Hunt (1964) in an article in the *British Journal of Delinquency* which contained a letter from a young man in Borstal (a young offenders' custodial institution) thanking the probation officer who sent him there, on the grounds that it was what he really needed all along. The evident convenience of such theories kept them going for several decades, consolidating what McWilliams called probation's diagnostic era. In Harris's words, probation had moved 'from a theologically to a psychiatrically driven discourse' (Harris 1994: 34). Armed with such theories, the Probation Service could take its place alongside other useful but paternalistic agencies as a small but significant part of the post-war Welfare State.

During the next four decades, from the 1950s to the 1980s, probation was to undergo at least two further periods of rethinking and reformulation, each with major implications for the questions addressed by probation research. Early British studies of the effects of probation, such as Wilkins (1958) and Radzinowicz (1958), were clearly located within what subsequently became known as the 'treatment model': in Radzinowicz's formulation, probation was 'a form of social service preventing further crime by a readjustment of the culprit', and the studies were designed to measure whether this readjustment had been successfully achieved. They investigated reconviction, assumed to be a surrogate measure of reoffending. These two studies were methodologically different, since Radzinowicz documented subsequent offending without comparing it with those subject to other sentences while Wilkins used a comparison group; perhaps not surprisingly, they also came to rather different conclusions about effectiveness, with more negative conclusions in Wilkins's study. However, from the point of view of this chapter it is more interesting to consider where they directed their attention and where they did not. In line with the 'treatment' model, they looked for effects on offenders' subsequent behaviour; they were not interested in criminal justice system issues such as impacts on sentencing, 'market shares', or the tariff level of those supervised. ('Tariff level' in this context refers to the severity of sentence an offender might expect if not on probation: prison is high in the sentencing 'tariff', fines are low.) They also appeared to have little interest in the methods used: probation is regarded as a method in itself, and the package is not unwrapped to see what lies inside. The research agenda was confined to the claims of the treatment model and circumscribed by contemporary assumptions about what probation was for, though Wilkins did at least raise the important question of whether probation's effects were measurably better than those of other disposals.

Soon after this the Home Office launched an ambitious programme of research aimed at classifying probationers and their problems empirically, leading to large and interesting studies such as Davies (1969) and eventually to a focus on what probation officers actually did in response to these problems (Davies 1974). A significant emerging concern was that probation as psychosocial casework aspired, at least in the textbooks, to a focus on emotional problems (particularly 'underlying' ones) while probationers clearly had many social and environmental difficulties which probation officers addressed to varying degrees. Often, according to Davies, there was not much evidence of resulting change. The agenda was still 'treatment', but anxieties were emerging about the fit between the treatment provided and actual needs. The Probation Service, of course, could claim that caseloads were too high to allow it to show what it could achieve given better resources, and the eventual response to this was a controlled experiment. The IMPACT study ('Intensive Matched Probation and After-Care Treatment') randomly allocated probationers to normal or 'intensive' caseloads, and compared both the work done and the subsequent offending in these two groups—a classic research design for testing 'treatment'.

The results of the study (Folkard *et al.* 1976) were remarkably little discussed in the Probation Service but had a significant effect on the research agenda. The probationers in the experimental small caseloads did receive more attention; the nature of the attention was left to the officers, and could mostly be summarized as more of what they would normally do. The overall results were 'small non-significant differences in reconviction in favour of the control cases', and no confirmation that more probation 'treatment' produced better (or any) effects. The one significant exception was that 'the only experimental cases that apparently do much better are those which have been rated as having low criminal tendencies and which perceive themselves as having many problems', a fairly small group and arguably rather untypical of offenders in general, but broadly resembling offenders who showed positive results in some other studies (Shaw 1974; Adams 1961; Palmer 1974). One possible interpretation is that the typical content of probation in the 'treatment' era could be helpful to those who were distressed, anxious to change, and not particularly criminal. This prefigured later findings about the limited relevance of relationship-based counselling to work with persistent offenders, but the overall conclusion had to be seen as a negative verdict on probation as a general-purpose 'treatment' for crime. Most of the 'culprits' were not being 'readjusted', and the Home Office began to turn its research attention elsewhere. As the Home Office was (and still is) the dominant player in the funding and management of research on the penal system in Britain, this was to have decisive effects on the next decade of British probation research.

'NOTHING WORKS' AND 'ALTERNATIVES TO CUSTODY'

By the end of the 1970s the 'treatment model' was being strongly criticized on a number of empirical and ethical grounds. Empirically, studies of the effectiveness of penal sanctions of all kinds had produced generally discouraging results, and while this was not true of all studies, the general impression that 'nothing works' was reinforced by journalistic summaries (Martinson 1974) and by the overall conclusions of wide-ranging research reviews (Lipton *et al.* 1975; Brody 1976). These findings also gained strength from what were essentially moral or philosophical arguments against 'treatment', such as that it objectified or dehumanized its subjects, or that it rested on unsubstantiated claims of superior professional wisdom (Bottoms and McWilliams 1979). Legal scholars were increasingly questioning whether unreliable predictions about future behaviour should continue to influence sentencing and argued instead for proportionate 'justice' based on the seriousness of the offence (Hood 1974; von Hirsch 1976).

Meanwhile, researchers on juvenile justice following the 'treatment'-oriented Children and Young Persons Act 1969 were beginning to document unintended adverse consequences, such as increased incarceration following the failure of community-based supervision to prevent further offending (Thorpe *et al.* 1980). It began to appear that young offenders, like their older counterparts, might actually benefit from proportionate 'tariff' sentencing which did not aim to do them good but would at least avoid the excesses of over-ambitious compulsory 'treatment'. If the emphasis of the 1970s had been on doing good, without much success in demonstrating that good was being done, the 1980s were to be about avoiding harm, in particular by reducing unnecessary incarceration. This seemed a more achievable aim, and one which might commend itself on the grounds of economy even to communities or politicians who were not in sympathy with the underlying humanitarian aim. So began the era of 'alternatives to custody': probation was to be a non-custodial penalty aiming to increase its market share and reduce imprisonment, rather than a 'treatment' aiming to change people.

Elsewhere, and particularly across the Atlantic, some similar processes were at work, but the more pluralistic research environment allowed the continuation of some research which ran counter to the received orthodoxies of the time. The 1975 research review by Lipton, Martinson, and Wilks (which prompted Martinson's headline-grabbing 'nothing works' article of 1974) did not in fact reach uniformly negative conclusions about the studies it examined, and later re-examinations of the same studies (for example by Thornton 1987) found a number of positive results. Other reviews also began to point to more encouraging conclusions: for example, Blackburn (1980) reviewed a more recent group of studies than those covered by Lipton, Martinson, and Wilks, and found that while few studies met rigorous methodological standards, those which did meet them showed reductions in recidivism. In Canada, Gendreau and Ross identified a number of studies with positive outcomes and reviewed them as 'bibliotherapy for cynics' (Gendreau and Ross 1980), an early example of the many positive contributions Canadian researchers were to make to the literature of effective rehabilitation. Perhaps most surprisingly, Martinson himself published a reappraisal of his earlier conclusion that 'nothing works' (Martinson 1979), arguing that this view was simply incorrect.

The debate which seemed largely closed in Britain continued in other countries, with positive findings emerging from Europe (for an early example, see Berntsen and Christiansen 1965) as well as from North America. Even in Britain, some studies showed positive results: for example, enhanced input from prison welfare officers prior to release led, in a well-designed study, to lower reconvictions than in a randomly allocated control group (Shaw 1974), and probation hostels with firm but caring wardens showed less reoffending among their residents than other hostels (Sinclair 1971). Shaw's study in particular prefigured current concerns about the 'resettlement' of prisoners. However, these results were seen as anomalous and did little, in Britain, to dent the 'nothing works' consensus.

The apparently conclusive demise of 'treatment' produced not only a major shift in policy-makers' views of what probation might realistically achieve, but also a corresponding shift in focus for the questions asked by evaluative researchers. The influence of early juvenile justice system studies (such as Thorpe *et al.* 1980) has been mentioned already. These studies paid detailed attention to patterns of decision-making in the juvenile courts in an attempt to measure how the activities of social workers were reducing or increasing incarceration, but showed little interest in the content of supervision or the subsequent behaviour of offenders: the guiding assumption seemed to be that post-custodial reconviction rates for juveniles were already so high that any likely outcome of a community-based project would be an improvement. The Home Office itself had already begun to undertake studies guided by a similar set of assumptions about what it was interesting to measure: as well as early work on police cautions, which addressed system issues such as net-widening (Ditchfield 1976), a substantial programme of evaluative work on the new community service order had been developing in parallel with the final stages of the probation research programme.

Community service, introduced by the 1972 Criminal Justice Act, was initially implemented on an experimental basis in a number of pilot areas, and the associated Home Office research was primarily concerned with whether it was feasible to implement it; whether courts were using it; and how far it was being used for offenders who would otherwise be sent to prison (Pease *et al.* 1977; Pease and McWilliams 1980). In other words, the community service research agenda was about effects on systems rather than people, and a complete departure from the 'treatment' agenda. This departure was so complete that the decision to extend community service to all probation areas was taken before effects on reoffending had been assessed, and issues such as the kinds of help needed or received by offenders and its effects on their behaviour were not addressed until a much later Scottish study (McIvor 1992). Community service was intended to influence sentencers rather than offenders, and the research conformed closely to these priorities. Other more rehabilitation-oriented innovations, such as the day training centres, received far less official research attention (Vanstone and Raynor 1981). Although activities such as social enquiry reports (reports to sentencers by probation officers about offenders prior to sentence, now known as pre-sentence reports) continued to attract interest (Thorpe 1979), government-sponsored research on the effectiveness of probation virtually ceased after IMPACT. One of the few exceptions to this was a short study of probation day centres (Mair 1988), which revealingly pointed out that 'it is difficult to assess the success of centres in preventing reoffending; there is little monitoring of the centres in this respect and the main aim of the centres is to provide an alternative to custody'.

The dominance of new post-treatment, system-centred aims was underlined by the publication in 1984 of a *Statement of National Objectives and Priorities* for probation services in England and Wales (Home Office 1984). This document, the first attempt at a national statement of the Probation Service's purpose, was clearly informed by the intention to develop community-based supervision in such a way as to reduce custodial sentencing. Social enquiry reports were to be a high priority 'where the court may be prepared to divert an offender from what would otherwise be a custodial sentence', and probation and community service orders were desirable 'especially in cases where custodial sentences would otherwise be imposed'. After-care of prisoners, presumed to have no diversionary impact, was allocated a lower place in the order of priorities. Nothing was said about the content or methods of supervision.

REOPENING THE EFFECTIVENESS DEBATE

For the Probation Service itself matters were not so simple. Community service seemed to be a marketing success, but the market share of probation orders had been falling through most of the 1970s. Probation orders which could be seen as a credible disposal for more serious offenders would need to offer more demanding and, if possible, effective programmes of supervision. The 1982 Criminal Justice Act encouraged the inclusion of additional requirements in probation orders to facilitate special programmes, but new, larger packages needed more content. Juvenile justice specialists were already developing intensive Intermediate Treatment (that is, programmes of supervised activity undertaken as part of a supervision order) with often quite sophisticated programme content (e.g., Denman 1982), and probation services began to follow suit with various forms of enhanced probation, despite the reservations of some of their staff (Drakeford 1983). Occasionally these involved an almost bizarre degree of emphasis on control and discipline (Kent Probation and After-Care Service 1981), but more often they looked for content which seemed likely to be useful to offenders and was intended to reduce their offending. Among these piecemeal and often unevaluated developments, a few projects took research seriously enough to involve local academics in what became a new style of evaluative study.

Such local projects were typically concerned both with 'market shares' and with impacts on offending, and the combination of modest scale and locally-based research allowed for adequate follow-up of both sentencing trends and the behaviour of offenders. Two studies in particular, carried out during the 1980s and published towards the end of the decade (Raynor 1988; Roberts 1989), were able to address some of the issues about effectiveness which had almost vanished from the national research agenda, and in both cases some diversion from custody and some impact on reconviction could be reasonably convincingly demonstrated. One of the studies (Raynor 1988) was also able to document changes in offenders' self-perceived problems and suggested a link between these and subsequent reductions in offending. The findings and implications of both these studies are discussed further below. As researchers increasingly moved away from the assumption that 'nothing works' the government began to outline an enhanced 'centre stage' role for the Probation Service in the new policy proposals which were leading towards the 1991 Criminal Justice Act, and the prospects for a more effective and rehabilitative approach to probation began to look brighter than they had for some time.

The first stirrings of a new optimism about rehabilitation were beginning to be felt in the Prison Service as well as in the Probation Service: for example, people became aware of Canadian experiments in running prison-based cognitive skills programmes. So, paradoxically, probation services were suddenly discouraged by Home Office officials from using the language of 'alternatives to custody': community sentences and prisons were no longer to be in competition but were targeting different levels of seriousness. Also the two services were meant to be cooperating in new forms of throughcare for prisoners (Maguire and Raynor 1997), which would not be helped if one service continued to define its mission as saving people from the other. In practice, the 1991 Act turned out to be genuinely decarcerative, securing unprecedented reductions in the use of custodial sentences during the few months of 1992 and 1993 in which it was allowed to operate as intended before politicians shifted their stance and repealed key sections of it. However, the decisive shift away from the language of 'alternatives to custody' turned out to be one of the more enduring legacies of the 1991 Act, to the extent that much of what was learned from successful diversionary research and practice in the 1980s is seldom discussed.

This is a mistake, partly because successes in this field are not so common that we can afford to ignore them, and partly because there are practical lessons to learn or re-learn from them. The first lesson is that diversion was not abandoned because it failed: on the contrary, among juveniles in particular it succeeded quite well, with very substantial reductions in custodial sentencing and the almost complete disappearance of residential care for juvenile offenders during the 1980s (Smith 1995). Although concentrating too exclusively on diversion may involve doing too little about some persistent offenders, in its own terms the policy of 'alternatives to custody' for juvenile offenders succeeded until public and political opinion in the 1990s began to favour a more punitive approach and the numbers of juvenile offenders in custody began to rise again.

Among adults, community penalties in the 1980s successfully moved 'up-tariff' to accommodate a riskier and more heavily convicted group of offenders: by 1989 only 14 per cent of community service orders were being made on first offenders, but by 1999, with diversion from custody no longer a policy priority and with probation services financed according to the number of people they supervised, the figure had drifted back to 42 per cent, with probation and combination orders showing similar trends (Raynor 1998a), in spite of evidence that for first offenders a fine is much less likely to be followed by reconviction than a probation order (Walker *et al.* 1981). It is not surprising that this recent drift towards a less criminal community sentence population has coincided with a growth in imprisonment and a reduction in the use of fines.

Neither is it the case, as some have argued, that the creation of 'alternatives to custody' *necessarily* has the unintended effect of increased recruitment to the custodial part of the system. Several commentators, most notably Cohen (1985), have argued that the creation of less severe sentencing options often serves simply to draw more people into the net of social control measures ('net-widening') and that this exposes them to more severe sanctions when lower-tariff measures 'fail' (a process known in youth justice circles as 'tariff escalation'). Worries of this kind accompanied, for example, the introduction of specific requirements in probation orders intended to operate as 'alternatives to custody' (Drakeford 1983). Were probationers being 'set up to fail' by over-demanding requirements which would lead to custodial sentences on breach? (Similar concerns are expressed currently about the stringent approach to enforcement of community sentences demanded by Home Office National Standards, and are discussed further near the end of this chapter.) Such concerns, particularly about net-widening, were not groundless: for example, juvenile justice researchers in the late 1970s found that virtually all custodial sentences passed on juvenile offenders were recommended by social workers (Thorpe *et al.* 1980) and that supervision orders on first offenders could, if breached, lead to a custodial sentence much earlier in the offending career than would otherwise have been expected. Much was also made of the finding that suspended prison sentences appeared to have led to an increase in the prison population rather than a reduction (Bottoms 1980). The reason seemed to be that sentencers were passing suspended prison sentences in cases where they would not otherwise have sentenced custodially, and when some offenders re-offended the resulting custodial sentence was lengthened by the addition of the suspended term, leading to a substantially longer first custodial sentence than they might otherwise have expected.

However, there was not much other evidence of a general tendency towards tariff escalation. (The case of suspended sentences is special, in that the court is *required* to sentence custodially on breach except in very narrowly defined exceptional circumstances.) Studies of successful 'alternative' projects emphasized appropriate targeting to ensure that only those genuinely at risk of custodial sentences became involved, and appropriate enforcement strategies, agreed with the courts, to ensure that the outcome of enforcement action would be a return to the project in as many cases as possible. For example, seven out of ten breach cases in one successful project (Raynor 1988) resulted in returns to the project rather than custodial sentences, despite the 'high-tariff' nature of the offenders concerned. In short, the unintended outcomes identified by Cohen can happen, but can also be avoided by conscious attention to targeting, to appropriate proposals in reports to sentencers, and to influencing decision-making in local criminal justice systems.

Given such safeguards, the existence of additional sentencing options can be advantageous, and appropriate targeting is quite feasible: for instance, it appeared to be achieved in several early 'intensive probation' experiments (Mair *et al.* 1994) which recruited offenders clearly at risk of custodial sentences. Early studies of community service also found that 45–50 per cent of such orders appeared to be made instead of prison (Pease *et al.* 1977). Even in a generally punitive climate, local criminal justice systems have some relative autonomy and good results are possible. Unfortunately the determinism of Cohen's account may have contributed to the resistance shown by some probation officers to the inclusion and enforcement of additional requirements in probation orders. However, the evidence of the 1980s indicates that given good information and a systematic approach, community sentences can successfully be used on a considerable scale where otherwise custodial sentences would be passed. It is to be hoped that these aspects of effective practice have not been completely forgotten as the rhetoric of 'alternatives to custody' has been abandoned.

One of the other lessons to be learned appears to be that although some researchers would clearly like it to do so, research does not seem to influence policy or practice in a direct and simple way. Research which fits, augments, or provides a rationale for the policy climate of the time will often achieve a degree of prominence and influence for that reason, while research of comparable or sometimes greater merit and rigour which does not 'fit' in the same way will attract less attention. Sometimes it comes into its own when the climate changes, or sometimes it is doomed to become part of a marginal critique outside the mainstream of thinking. Much research funding, particularly government funding of criminal justice research, concentrates on finding answers to questions identified as important by policy-makers; these are often to do with effective implementation of a policy line which has already been decided rather than asking whether the policy itself is right. Findings which are not clear-cut and lend themselves to a number of interpretations are likely to receive the interpretation which fits the culture of the times: for example, studies once read as evidence that 'nothing worked' can be reinterpreted as evidence that 'some things do work' as readers' expectations and background assumptions change.

Yet another salutary lesson for probation researchers was that they could simply be ignored. In 1993, as part of an unprecedented package of populist 'Law and Order' initiatives, the recently appointed Conservative Home Secretary Michael Howard announced that 'prison works'. Before long he was proposing a series of changes to the Probation Service which were intended to constitute a definitive break with its former 'social work' identity. These included the abolition of training places for probation officers on university-based social work courses, a policy backed up by a remarkable campaign of media disinformation (see Aldridge and Eadie 1997) and a rigged review by civil servants (Dews and Watts 1994). Other proposals included threats of extensive privatization, and 'fast track' recruitment of redundant military personnel who, it was claimed, would not require much training since they already knew about discipline and 'handling men'. (At least one appointment of a senior naval officer to a probation management post did actually occur: Jeffrey Collins, who had commanded a nuclear submarine before gaining senior administrative experience in the Ministry of Defence, was appointed as Chief Officer of the West Glamorgan Probation Service in 1995, and proved to be a very effective and innovative Chief Officer until prevented from continuing his probation career by the reorganization of probation areas in 2001. Ironically, he did not at all resemble the stereotypes invoked by Michael Howard.)

One surprising feature of Howard's ideologically-motivated assault was that it had not come much earlier. Margaret Thatcher's Conservative governments of 1979–1992 had shown a consistent neo-liberal hostility to the Welfare State and welfare professionals, often portraying them as self-interested, expensive, and ineffective (for a representative example of the anti-social work writing of the time, see Brewer and Lait 1980); but probation officers, although mildly criticized in the build-up to the 1991 Criminal Justice Act, had on the whole been protected by the fact that they were essential to the policies of the Home Secretaries who preceded Michael Howard (for example Douglas Hurd, now president of the Prison Reform Trust). In the end it was perhaps inevitable that the next Conservative government, headed by John Major and consistently unpopular, should seek to recover its electoral standing by taking a populist stance. Although the government was ousted in 1997, its criminal justice policies have had profound consequences for the prison population, rising almost continuously since Michael Howard's 1993 speech, and for the Probation Service, which needed urgently to find a new mission around which to build a case for survival. The new mission became the 'What Works' movement that most of the remainder of this chapter will describe.

COMMUNITY PENALTIES AND CRIME REDUCTION:
THE REDISCOVERY OF REHABILITATION

Although the most famous exponent of 'nothing works', Robert Martinson, came from the United States, his views were never universally accepted there. Indeed, the study on which his original article was based had itself reached more measured and qualified conclusions, including some moderately positive findings about some projects. For example, both casework and counselling were found to have produced some positive results with offenders in some circumstances, even though their overall impact was small:

... to the degree that casework and individual counselling provided to offenders in the community is directed towards their immediate problems, it may be associated with reduction in recidivism rates. Unless this counselling leads to solution of problems such as housing, finances, jobs or illness which have high priority for offenders, it is unlikely to have any impact upon future criminal behaviour. (Lipton *et al.* 1975: 572)

Ironically the 'nothing works' doctrine was more dominant in Britain. One consequence of this was that practitioners had to find their own sources of optimism and belief in what they were doing, and the 'nothing works' era actually became a period of creativity and enthusiasm in the development of new methods and approaches. These were often not evaluated and depended on the enthusiasm of a few officers, but within this pluralistic approach to practice can be found the fore-runners of modern evidence-based approaches (Vanstone 2000). For example, the first attempts in Britain to introduce principles based on learning theory into mainstream probation practice came about through the work of two psychologists, James McGuire and Philip Priestley, who were to play a major role in the development of evidence-based practice. During the mid-1970s they offered courses to probation officers on methods they published in a handbook of 'social skills and personal problem solving' (Priestley *et al.* 1978), and were also involved in the implementation of the methods in probation day centres and prisons. The methods used were based on 'life skills' and problem-solving techniques which were increasingly being taught by clinical psychologists to their patients or clients, and many of them were already in use in a Canadian project for unemployed young people called Saskatchewan Newstart.

Later, when evaluation of the work in prisons indicated little effect on subsequent offending except among violent offenders, Priestley and McGuire developed and taught an approach based more specifically on the analysis and modification of offending behaviour (Priestley *et al.* 1984; McGuire and Priestley 1985). However, official encouragement was lukewarm and, as described above, probation services in the 1980s were mainly seen as providing alternatives to custody. A brief official flirtation with emerging ideas about effective rehabilitation occurred during the preparation of the 1991 Criminal Justice Act, but strong government endorsement of an evidence-based rehabilitative approach had to await the election of a new Labour government in 1997. By then, significant strands of evidence had emerged in Britain and elsewhere to support the methods and techniques of a new model of rehabilitation.

Summarizing research in a limited space always carries the risk of simplifying, and of omitting important caveats and reservations. However, it seems useful at this point to indicate what have been the main research influences on the current developments in community sentencing which have come to be known as 'What Works', if only in order to encourage readers to go and look at the research for themselves. Other summaries are also available, for example in Home Office publications issued to support the Probation Service's development strategy (Chapman and Hough 1998; McGuire 2000). Basically those studies which have influenced developments in the UK, and in some cases throughout the English-speaking world, fall into three groups, all of which have produced some significant outputs during the late 1980s and 1990s.

PSYCHOLOGICAL APPROACHES

The first group of studies and approaches to rehabilitation comprises the work of psychological criminologists, many of them Canadian, who have emphasized the role of social learning and of thinking or cognition in the development and maintenance of offending. A feature of the environment in which this work has developed is that a number of key individuals have combined significant academic or research contributions with experience as practitioners within the criminal justice system, in a way which has always proved difficult in Britain (examples are Don Andrews, Jim Bonta, Paul Gendreau, Frank Porporino, Liz Fabiano, Robert Ross). A clear statement of a social learning approach to offending is provided by, among others, Andrews and Bonta's textbook *The Psychology of Criminal Conduct* (1998). This sets out an integrated theory of offending which connects social disadvantage, personality traits, thinking styles, and social strategies into a model of how offending occurs and continues (see also Farrington, in Chapter 19 of this volume). For example, adverse social factors such as poverty and lack of opportunities can make it difficult for parents to provide a consistent and supportive environment for children. Personality characteristics such as impulsiveness or risk-seeking, perhaps reinforced by peer expectations, are likely to limit the benefits gained from formal education, while exposure to illegitimate opportunities and positive peer support for delinquency will make offending an attractive option. Add to this poor social skills and problem-solving abilities, perhaps due to rigid thinking, lack of awareness of alternatives, and difficulty in appreciating or taking into account the views and needs of others, and offending becomes likely; add a strong possibility of getting away with the offence, or alternatively a penal response which stigmatizes and excludes without addressing any of these problems, and continued offending becomes more likely. Some of these 'risk factors' are 'static', meaning they have already happened and cannot now be changed (for example, a pattern of offending in the past), while others are, at least in principle, 'dynamic' or potentially subject to change (such as current attitudes, beliefs, behaviour, and opportunities).

This kind of model also suggests a process of intervention based on trying to change risk factors which are accessible and likely to make a difference: for example, habits of thinking ('cognition') and patterns of behaviour which can be altered to bring about better results for the individual. The process of change is often seen primarily as the acquisition of new skills. Such approaches are also consistent with the style of work advocated by McGuire and Priestley in Britain, but a particularly influential development in Canada and elsewhere was the idea of a 'programme' which put together a series of planned and sequential learning opportunities into a cumulative sequence, covering an appropriate curriculum of skills and allowing plenty of opportunity to reinforce learning through structured practice (often over-looked by UK practitioners of 'social skills' approaches in probation—see Hudson 1988). Robert Ross, for example, after carrying out research which identified a focus on thinking as a common feature of many successful interventions with offenders (Ross and Fabiano 1985), developed a programme called 'Reasoning and Rehabilita-tion' which systematically adopted a cognitive-behavioural focus (Ross et al. 1986) and was to exercise a widespread influence on work with offenders both in prisons and in the community. The influence of this programme is discussed further in the later part of this chapter.

META-ANALYSIS AND RESEARCH REVIEWS

The second major strand of research which helped to revive rehabilitation as a feasible goal in criminal justice was a series of research reviews which tried to pull together the findings of what was by now a substantial body of research in order to draw out general lessons about what approaches were likely to be effective. Some of these were carried out at the request of governments and were traditional narrative reviews which summarized a number of studies and pointed to shared or important findings: for example, McLaren (1992) in New Zealand and McIvor (1990) in Scotland. The latter was a particularly impressive piece of work and was destined to influence developments throughout Britain. In general, the narrative research reviews of this period found more studies with positive outcomes than had been available to earlier reviewers such as Lipton et al. (1975).

In addition to this traditional style of review, researchers and practitioners were also beginning to benefit from the new statistical technique of meta-analysis, which combines the results from a number of studies by coding them to a common frame-work and applying a common measure of 'effect size', i.e. the extent to which out-comes for 'treated' groups differ from those for control groups or (in some studies) matched comparison groups. These methods have been criticized (for example by Mair 1995): coding a range of rather different studies to a common framework can introduce some distortions, and since not all studies record the same variables, some findings may in reality be based on fairly small numbers because few studies have looked at the particular variables concerned even though thousands of cases may be covered by the meta-analysis as a whole. Equally, the evidence-base for the meta-analysis will reflect the subjects available for the original research, and we need to avoid over-confidence in drawing conclusions about adults from meta-analyses in which most of the studies have involved juveniles, or conclusions about female or ethnic minority populations from groups of studies which are mainly about white males.

Different meta-analyses apply different selection criteria, different search techniques, and sometimes slightly different standards of methodological rigour in choosing what studies to include, and there are also at least three different ways of calculating an effect size in use in the literature. However, there seems little room for doubt that meta-analysis has greatly increased our capacity to draw general conclusions by aggregating findings from a number of smaller studies, some of which might carry little weight on their own. Two major meta-analyses in particular have had a large influence on our current understanding of effective practice with offenders, one carried out by Andrews and his colleagues in Canada (Andrews *et al.* 1990), which famously launched the principles of Risk, Need, and Responsivity (explained further below), and one by Lipsey in the United States (Lipsey 1992). Others (such as Izzo and Ross 1990) have also made significant contributions, while some researchers have begun to address the problem of groups which are under-represented in the research (for example, Dowden and Andrews 1999).

EVALUATIONS OF STRUCTURED PROGRAMMES

The third major strand of research that prepared the way for the 'What Works' movement of the 1990s, was a small group of studies which provided reasonably convincing evidence for reductions in reconviction among fairly high-risk probationers who had, as part of their probation orders, participated in structured programmes of various kinds designed to address their offending. Such studies were a rarity in Britain after a decade of discouragement, but a few researchers had not completely accepted the 'nothing works' agenda and had the opportunity to carry out evaluative studies with local probation services. Two studies which have already been mentioned in this chapter were published in the late 1980s and showed positive results. The first of these (Raynor 1988), carried out in South Wales, showed a group of young adult male probationers achieving a reconviction rate some 13 per cent below comparable offenders sentenced to custody, as well as reporting a reduction in social and personal problems. There was also evidence that the project had reduced the use of custodial sentences by local courts. The second study (Roberts 1989), carried out in Hereford and Worcester, also showed substantial reductions in offending by young adult probationers, including not only reductions in the number offending but also reductions in the frequency of offending by those who did offend. Around the same time, those who actually looked at research from other countries (not a widespread habit in British probation at the time) could study the first comparative evaluation of the Reasoning and Rehabilitation programme (Ross *et al.* 1988) which showed particularly encouraging results. Other research, such as the evaluations of American experiments with 'Intensive Supervision', also contained lessons for those who were interested in effectiveness (for example, Petersilia 1990), although the overall results were less encouraging.

Taken together these various strands of research carried an encouraging message: far from nothing working, it appeared that appropriate forms of supervision were capable of delivering reductions in offending of between 10 and 20 per cent, or even more in some cases. Conversely, the wrong kind of supervision could do harm. The research pointed to a number of characteristics of effective supervision, which are listed in slightly different ways by different authorities but cover the same ground, and may be summarized as follows. In the present state of our knowledge, it appears likely that the more effective programmes are those which:

1. Target high-risk offenders who are otherwise likely to continue to offend, rather than low-risk offenders who may gain little benefit or be harmed. (This is Andrews' 'Risk Principle', nowadays usually interpreted as guidance to target a medium-to-high range, as the very highest-risk offenders are likely to be unresponsive except perhaps to very high levels of intervention beyond what one programme is likely to provide. 'Risk' here refers to risk of reconviction rather than to dangerousness.)

2. Focus on criminogenic need, i.e. those characteristics or circumstances of offenders which have contributed to their offending (equivalent to 'dynamic risk factors'; this is Andrews' 'Need Principle').

3. Are highly structured, making clear and explicit demands and following a logical sequence determined by their learning goals.

4. Use a directive working approach, so that participants know what they are meant to be doing.

5. Use broadly cognitive-behavioural methods, to provide opportunities to learn new thinking and behaviour. (This kind of multi-modal, skills-oriented focus is likely to offer a learning style accessible to many offenders, and therefore to help to satisfy Andrews' 'Responsivity' principle that programmes must promote the engagement and involvement of offenders by using an appropriate learning style and delivery.)

6. Are best located in the community (though this does not mean they are ineffective in prison).

7. Have programme integrity, i.e. are delivered as intended, with procedures to ensure this (for further explanation, see Hollin 1995).

8. Have committed and effective management.

9. Have appropriately trained staff who believe they can be effective.

10. Have adequate resources for continuity.

11. Have integral evaluation and feedback, ideally involving external researchers.

IMPLEMENTING 'WHAT WORKS': ACHIEVEMENTS AND PROBLEMS SO FAR

The first fully evaluated attempt in England and Wales to apply these principles to a programme for offenders supervised by the Probation Service was started in the (then) Mid-Glamorgan Probation Service in South Wales in 1990, under the leadership of the late David Sutton as Chief Probation Officer. It was known as Straight

Thinking On Probation, or STOP, a version of Ross's Reasoning and Rehabilitation (R & R) programme. The R & R programme included modules on problem solving, social skills, management of emotions, negotiation skills, critical reasoning, creative thinking, and values enhancement. In Mid-Glamorgan these were delivered over thirty-five two-hour sessions. The evaluation study's findings concerning the programme's impact on offenders have been widely discussed in Britain, largely because of the shortage of other comparable studies at the time. As a consequence, the results have often been quoted as lending support to cognitive-behavioural methods of supervision, and their impact may even appear disproportionate for what are in reality fairly modest outcomes from a local study carried out with small numbers (fifty-nine programme completers, and 655 offenders altogether including comparison groups), little research funding, and, at the beginning, very little official encouragement at national level.

For a full account of the findings, readers should refer to Raynor and Vanstone (1996, 1997) and Raynor (1998b). Overall, a fair summary of the findings of the STOP evaluation is that there was some evidence of fairly short-term reductions in offending (35 per cent of programme completers were reconvicted in a year, compared to a predicted rate of 42 per cent; in contrast, a custodially sentenced comparison group with the same predicted reconviction rate showed that 49 per cent were reconvicted within a year of release). There were also more persistent reductions in more serious offending among those who completed the programme. These were associated with reported changes in attitudes, thinking, and behaviour consistent with the rationale of a cognitive-behavioural programme. On the whole, STOP appeared to offer a more effective and constructive sentencing option than other likely sentences for this group of relatively serious and persistent offenders. However, the findings also pointed to a need to improve the matching of offenders to the programme and the proportion completing it: some programme members were clearly selected on a tariff basis, being at high risk of a custodial sentence, rather than on the basis of assessed needs appropriate to the programme. Most importantly, the study pointed to a need to reinforce what was learned during the programme by appropriate follow-up during the remainder of the period of supervision.

While this and other local experiments were proceeding, managers, practitioners, and researchers who were interested in the practical implications of new ideas about effective practice were organizing an annual series of 'What Works' conferences to disseminate the new ideas. A number of papers from the first three of these were eventually published in 1995 as a very influential collection edited by James McGuire. A conference organized by Colin Roberts at Green College, Oxford, also helped to promote the new approaches, and in 1993 the Home Office organized a conference in Bath, followed by another conference in London in 1995 on 'Managing What Works'. This was followed by a circular encouraging (or requiring) probation services to adopt effective methods and promising follow-up action by the independent Probation Inspectorate (although, as many pointed out at the time, the relevant evidence base for Britain was at that stage quite small).

Involvement of the Inspectorate, and of the then Chief Inspector Graham Smith, proved to be an essential catalyst in taking forward the 'What Works' agenda (or, as it was known at first, the Effective Practice Initiative). Instead of a simple inspection, a research exercise was set up involving a detailed survey of probation areas by Andrew Underdown, a senior probation manager who was already closely involved in issues around effective practice. The results, eventually published in 1998 (Underdown 1998), were an eye-opener: of the 267 programmes which probation areas claimed they were running based on effective practice principles, evidence of effectiveness based on reasonably convincing evaluation was available only for four (one of which was not actually included in the responses to the initial survey). One of these was the Mid-Glamorgan STOP programme; the others were in London, where John Wilkinson played an important role in programme evaluation (Wilkinson 1997, 1998).

These very poor results pointed to the need for a centrally-managed initiative to introduce more effective forms of supervision, and the election in 1997 of a new government committed to evidence-based public policy created a climate in which political support could be gained for such an initiative. The Home Office's Probation Unit worked closely with the Inspectorate to develop what was now the What Works initiative; good publications were issued to promote awareness (Chapman and Hough 1998; McGuire 2000) and a number of promising programmes were identified for piloting and evaluation as 'pathfinder' programmes, with support in due course from the government's Crime Reduction Programme. The Pathfinders included several cognitive-behavioural programmes (one of them designed by James McGuire, and another being a revised version of Reasoning and Rehabilitation), but also included work on basic skills (improving literacy and numeracy to improve chances of employment), pro-social approaches to supervision in community service, and a number of joint projects run by probation services with prisons and in some cases voluntary organizations, working on the resettlement of short-term prisoners after release. Evaluations of the Pathfinders are incomplete at the time of writing, but some encouraging interim findings are beginning to emerge (for example, Hatcher and McGuire 2001).

In the meantime a new probation service was taking shape, to come formally into existence as the National Probation Service for England and Wales in April 2001, replacing the old, separate area probation services and explicitly committed to public protection and crime reduction. Instead of fifty-four separate probation services, each responsible to and employed by a local Probation Committee consisting largely of local magistrates, the new National Probation Service is a single organization run by a Director with a substantial central staff located in the Home Office (the National Probation Directorate). Some local influence is still provided by the forty-two Area Boards, each employing the staff in its own area (apart from the area's Chief Officer, who is appointed by the Home Secretary and is a member of the Area Board), but policy is now made at the centre and implemented through a national management structure. This includes 'regional managers' employed by the National Directorate rather than by the Boards in their region. The new areas are coterminous with police, court, and Crown Prosecution Service areas in order to facilitate multi-agency working in the criminal justice system (though they do not coincide with local authorities or with Youth Offending

Teams), and board members are chosen on the basis of relevant expertise, with much less representation of sentencers than on the old Committees. The new Service has an annual budget of about £500 million (roughly 4 per cent of overall spending on the criminal justice system) and a staff of around 13,000, of whom about half are probation officers.

This new structure emerged from a substantial review of prison and probation services (Home Office 1998) which, among other possibilities, considered merging prisons and probation into a single correctional service, but eventually concluded that this would be a step too far. The main aim of the changes was to create an organization which could be more effectively managed and directed from the centre, so that central policy initiatives could be implemented without local priorities or variations leading to the kind of uneven implementation documented by Underdown (1998). Detailed national policies and targets are now published (National Probation Service 2001) incorporating 'stretch objectives' designed to produce change, and performance is closely monitored. All this represents a considerable transformation over a very short period of time, and the new organization will need to address the problem of how to maintain a sense of involvement among those groups which have less influence in the new structure than they had in the past. These groups include the magistrates who pass most of the community sentences, and some of the Service's own staff (the response of the Probation Officers' Association to the What Works agenda is discussed later in the chapter).

As these structural changes were taking effect, the roll-out of accredited programmes was continued well beyond the original 'pathfinder' pilots, with a very ambitious training programme and a new management structure involving programme managers and treatment managers to ensure the implementation and integrity of the 'What Works' initiatives. In particular, much was learned from developments in the Prison Service which, although starting later than the Probation Service, had put in place a well managed and well monitored range of cognitive-behavioural programmes aimed originally at the treatment of sex offenders, and later expanded to include general offending programmes (including Reasoning and Rehabilitation). A particular feature of the prison programmes was rigorous and continuing evaluation (see, for example, Beech *et al.* 1998; Friendship *et al.* 2001).

While probation services were struggling with a variety of unevaluated local initiatives, the Prison Service had developed a quality assurance system based on an Accreditation Panel with international expert membership to ensure that only programmes with a convincing evidence-base were used, with a comprehensive audit system to inspect the delivery of programmes and ensure integrity. Many hundreds of offenders had passed through programmes supported by this system. After some debate, the Home Office decided to adopt similar systems to support the emerging curriculum of programmes in the Probation Service. A Joint Prisons and Probation Accreditation Panel was formed in 1999, with a number of new members and the inclusion of experts on probation matters (Joint Prisons and Probation Accreditation Panel 2000). From being unable in 1997 to point to more than a handful of evaluated effective initiatives, the Probation Service had been transformed within a few years into an organization able to offer quality-controlled programmes throughout England and Wales, in what is believed to be the largest initiative in evidence-based corrections to be undertaken anywhere in the world.

RISKS, NEEDS, AND EFFECTIVE CASE MANAGEMENT

The STOP evaluation and other studies (such as Burnett 1996) indicated the importance of assessment, targeting, and overall case management. If offenders were to be influenced, this would be the outcome of the whole period of supervision, of which the programme was a part, rather than simply of the programme itself. Also, attention was needed to the practical difficulties and social stresses faced by offenders during supervision: often these were not addressed by programmes, which concentrated on teaching problem-solving skills for long-term benefit rather than on assistance with immediate problems. Nevertheless, offenders overwhelmed by difficulties of coping and survival in the community were less likely to attend and complete their programmes; others needed targeted attention to problems such as substance abuse which limited their ability to benefit from other opportunities. In prisons, programmes could be delivered within a fairly stable but understimulating environment, and attendance and completion rates were good; programmes in the community faced more obstacles and more competition for the offender's attention.

All this pointed to the need for a thought-out case management process based on careful assessment of risks and needs. Case management is still the subject of ongoing Home Office research to identify possible models, but it is clear that completion rates for community-based programmes vary from area to area and are often very low. Although the Jersey Probation Service achieved 100 per cent completion in a Reasoning and Rehabilitation programme in 1999 (Raynor and Miles 2001), this is quite exceptional, and mainland probation areas are nowhere near achieving this, often having only a minority of starters actually completing. The original STOP completion rate of 75 per cent looks good by current standards, and much remains to be done to bring case management up to the level of efficacy which now seems achievable in programmes. However, one area in which a good deal of learning has taken place during the 1990s is on the subject of risk assessment.

RISK, DANGER, AND PREDICTION

Probation services in England and Wales have only recently begun to use standardized instruments for the assessment of 'risk' and 'need'. Less than a decade ago this practice was almost unknown in the United Kingdom, and its recent growth has been associated particularly with the use of the two instruments which were the focus of a recent Home Office study (Raynor *et al.* 2000)—the Level of Service Inventory Revised (Andrew and Bonta 1995), or LSI-R, developed in Canada; and the Assessment, Case Management and Evaluation instrument (ACE) developed by the Probation Studies Unit in England (Roberts *et al.* 1996). The underlying principles are now so widely accepted that the Home Office is developing a comprehensive assessment instrument intended for use in all prisons and probation services (OASys Project Team 1999) to underpin the wider 'What Works' initiative (Home Office 1999).

The background to these developments is the requirement that probation officers should routinely undertake assessments of the 'risk' presented by the offenders with whom they came into contact. This was first embodied in the National Standards issued in 1992, and repeated with greater emphasis when the Standards were revised in 1995 (Home Office 1992, 1995). However, there were no widely accepted methods of doing this other than relying on the judgement of individual probation officers. No doubt the Probation Service was to some extent reflecting the wider preoccupation with 'risk' which social theorists (for example Beck 1992) were identifying as a particular feature of late modern societies, but the Service also had concrete and specific reasons of its own to be concerned about risk as its role in the criminal justice system changed. An inspection of work with potentially dangerous offenders led to considerable concern about how consistently risk assessment was carried out in such cases (HM Inspectorate of Probation 1995), and a large amount of development and training activity began to be undertaken around issues of 'risk' (see Kemshall 1996), both in the sense of risk of reconviction and in the rather different sense of danger of serious harm.

At the same time Home Office researchers were developing another approach to risk, which was based on using information about offenders' criminal records to provide a quantified estimate of the probability of further offences within a given period (Copas 1992). This approach was regarded both as a contribution to risk assessment and as an aid to evaluative research, since it allowed researchers to calculate expected reconviction rates for groups of offenders subjected to particular sentences or forms of supervision and to compare these with the rates actually achieved (see, for example, Raynor and Vanstone 1994; Lloyd *et al.* 1994). It eventually led to the development of the very effective 'static' predictor OGRS, the Offender Group Reconviction Scale, and the astonishing comment by the National Association of Probation Officers that 'the chances of the reconviction of an offender was [sic] based on factors such as: job prospects, education, stable housing and personal relationships, likely misuse of drugs or alcohol, criminal associates, mental health and good quality rehabilitative work, not square roots and algebra' (NAPO 1995: 1).

Meanwhile the growing interest in effective and evidence-based probation practice led to a desire for methods of measuring the effectiveness of supervision through questionnaires or assessments administered at the beginning and end of periods of supervision, rather than waiting typically two or three years for the completion of a reconviction study. This led some services to rely heavily on psychometric tests and psychological expertise to measure intermediate targets of supervision, i.e. targets of change which were believed to contribute to lower offending (for example, McGuire *et al.* 1995), while others were interested particularly in attitudes and problems associated with offending, and a new instrument, CRIME-Pics, was developed for this purpose (Frude *et al.* 1994). The Home Office itself supported research on a simple 'needs assessment' instrument (Aubrey and Hough 1997). All these developments indicated the need for a comprehensive approach, and risk/needs assessment seemed the most likely candidate.

RISK AND NEED ASSESSMENT

Risk/need assessment, based on the assessment of criminogenic needs or 'dynamic' risk factors, has been described as a 'third generation' method of risk prediction (Bonta 1996), with the first generation represented by the individual judgement of practitioners and the second by actuarial methods based solely on static factors such as criminal history. 'Dynamic' risk factors, as explained earlier in the chapter, are in principle alterable, while 'static' risk factors are historical characteristics which are not reversible. An opportunity to test this approach was provided by the evaluation of LSI-R and ACE in England and Wales (Raynor *et al.* 2000). This produced a number of findings which support the feasibility of the risk/needs approach and which are helping to inform the development of the Home Office's own instrument OASys. For example, both LSI-R and ACE predict reconviction at far better than chance levels, and LSI-R in particular performs almost as well as the latest version of the Home Office's static predictor OGRS. Both also provide assessments of need and, most importantly, both are capable of functioning as 'risk-related change measures': in other words, their repeated administration can show changes in scores which are actually reflected in changes in the rate of reconviction. People whose risk/needs scores decrease during supervision have a lowered risk of reconviction compared to their starting point. Moreover, the use of such instruments for repeated assessments can help to document the impact of supervision on the criminogenic needs of offenders, and helps to show what probation officers are achieving.

To sum up, the 1990s were a period of fundamental transformation in our understanding of how offenders could be supervised successfully in the community. Key components of an effective approach, which at the beginning of the decade were the focus of interest for only a few researchers and practitioners, were by its end part of an officially recognized and endorsed strategy, underpinned by some serious research (not yet enough) and prompting a considerable reorganization of the process of supervising offenders. These components included effective programmes, cognitive/ behavioural approaches, accreditation, risk and need assessment, case management, and a commitment to research.

METHODS AND MESSAGES: SOME MORE SELECTIONS FROM THE RESEARCH AGENDA

In this section I aim simply to remind readers that there is an important and worthwhile probation research agenda beyond effective programmes, but still connected with the overall theme of 'What Works'. Some probation staff appear unaware of a 'What Works' agenda beyond programmes: for example, the 2001 AGM of the National Association of Probation Officers adopted the following resolution:

This AGM believes that the politics of Accredited Programmes are totally unacceptable . . .
[accredited programmes] fit with a simplistic model of offending that isolates individual
behaviour from its social, economic and political context . . .
This AGM believes that Accredited Programmes utilise a medical model which labels
people who commit offences . . . This AGM demands that NAPO Officers and Officials
lead the political fight against Accredited Programmes [and] issue guidance to all
members deconstructing the flawed, outdated, conservative philosophy of accredited
programmes . . . (NAPO 2001a: 13)

This kind of reaction shows a degree of misunderstanding, but also illustrates how
some staff continue to believe that any concentration on individual attitudes, beliefs,
or characteristics is a denial of the social and environmental contribution to
offending. If offenders are understood by some officers simply as victims of society,
and assessment of individual characteristics is misconstrued as a form of individual
blaming, it becomes difficult for them to engage with an evidence-based agenda
concerned with the social learning processes of becoming or ceasing to be an offender.

Other, more reasoned criticisms of the way the 'What Works' agenda has been
implemented (for example, Merrington and Stanley 2000) point to the speed of the
national roll-out of accredited programmes, its centrally directed and top-down
nature, and the fact that we are still waiting for most of the evidence of the success
of the 'Pathfinder' pilot projects. Clearly the Probation Service had to take advantage of government funding when it was attainable, but the consequent stresses and
challenges for staff need to be addressed. Some other aspects of recent and current
research help to point to areas in which work is likely to be needed if the full potential
of the evidence-based approach is to be realized.

For example, unlike the early research cited above, recent research on community
service (now renamed 'community punishment') has begun to concentrate on its
effects upon participants, not simply on its impact upon sentencing (for a recent,
well-controlled European study, see Killias *et al.* 2000). Indications that the most
positive impact on offenders is achieved when tasks are pro-social and constructive
(McIvor 1992) and offenders' own difficulties are not ignored (McIvor 1991) has
helped to stimulate a widespread interest in pro-social approaches to supervision (Rex
and Matravers 1998) and in Trotter's Australian research which showed that
pro-social styles of supervision were associated with better outcomes for offenders
(Trotter 1993, 2000). The positive contribution of supervisors' personal skills to the
case management process, always in fact recognized by programme designers, is given
added weight by such research: the 'What Works' agenda is not about deskilling
practitioners.

Many other areas of practice and research have shown significant development in
the last few years. Space forbids a review of them all, and I select only a few which
seem to me to be among the more interesting and important. First, electronic monitoring or 'tagging' has moved further into the acceptable mainstream of supervision
methods. Originating in a probation requirement based on an American judge's
reading of a 'Spiderman' comic, it has moved far beyond the early research (Mair
and Nee 1990) which documented its technical shortcomings and the reluctance
of sentencers to use it. More recent trials have seen more use and better reliability

(Sugg *et al.* 2001), and have seemed particularly effective when used to facilitate the early release of prisoners (Mortimer 2001). Tagging in Britain has involved the private sector much more than the (initially hostile) Probation Service (Whitfield 1997), although in Sweden extensive trials have suggested that electronic monitoring works best when used as part of an overall probation supervision package rather than when used, as in Britain, mainly on its own (van der Laan 1999). On the other hand, recent evaluation in Canada (Bonta *et al.* 2000: 61) suggests that 'electronic monitoring added little to more traditional forms of community control'. (The Spiderman-based requirement in a probation order continues an American tradition of imaginative requirements: in one reported case a pickpocket was required to fit metal plates to the heels and toes of his shoes like a tap-dancer so that he could no longer sneak up silently on his victims (Jaffe 1979).) Other particularly promising areas of current research on community penalties include provision for substance misusing offenders, where we have good grounds to expect useful reductions in drug misuse and related acquisitive crime (Hough 1996; Turnbull *et al.* 2000) when probation services work in partnership with specialist agencies.

Lastly, there is a group of promising research topics which aim to address how probation services are seen and understood, and the consequences of this for the offenders they supervise. Most of these offenders are shown in numerous studies to suffer from many social disadvantages, sometimes reinforced by the consequences of their offending (see, among many other sources, Stewart *et al.* 1994; Maguire *et al.* 1996; Davis *et al.* 1997; Mair and May 1997; May 1999; Maguire *et al.* 2000; Raynor *et al.* 2000). To take just a few examples, they are likely to be disadvantaged in relation to income, employment, accommodation, health, educational attainment, family stability (with an over-representation of people brought up in the care of local authorities), and substance abuse (identified by May 1999 as one of the strongest predictors of failure on a community sentence). When asked (for example by Bailey and Ward 1992, or Rex 1996) about their experiences of supervision, they generally express positive views about their probation officers, particularly if the officers are good and understanding listeners, are honest and straightforward about their role, and show concern by helping in practical ways. A few studies have tried to elicit what offenders believe they have learned during supervision, and some very clear examples are provided by programme completers of strategies they have learned and used to cope with problems or temptations to offend (for examples, see Raynor and Vanstone 1997).

Interest in public responses to probation is less well represented in the research, though only 23 per cent of survey respondents rated them in 2000 as doing 'a good job' (down from 26 per cent in 1998: Mirrlees-Black 2001). In contrast, sentencers' responses to social enquiry reports and pre-sentence reports were a frequent focus of research in the past (including Perry's famous content analysis which found that the only items covered by *all* reports were the offender's name and age (Perry 1974)) but have been less investigated in recent years, apart from a study of Crown Court reports which showed that the more thorough and better written reports were more likely to have a beneficial impact on sentencing (Gelsthorpe and Raynor 1995). Continuing attention to this interesting topic has suffered from the lower priority attached to influencing sentencing patterns since 'alternatives to custody' went out of fashion.

Another promising recent theme of research has been how the attitudes of offenders and the public, and particularly offenders' compliance with supervision requirements, might be influenced by a focus on the perceived legitimacy of proba- tion activities. In the United States a 'Reinventing Probation Council' has been trying to apply the lessons of public surveys which indicate a public demand for protection, but also for sentences which are constructive and restorative in character (Reinventing Probation Council 2000), while a focus on legitimacy and compliance is being pur- sued in Britain particularly by Bottoms and his colleagues (Bottoms 2001; Rex and Matravers 1998). Also involved in any discussion of legitimacy (which is centrally concerned with fairness, respect for rights, and the justifiable use of authority) must be the Probation Service's response to diversity: how is it seen by, and how success- fully does it serve, members of ethnic and other minorities? How far does the 'What Works' movement reflect its origins in research on (mainly) white male offenders? A substantial amount of current research is seeking to address these questions; their urgency is underlined by a recent inspection identifying a number of areas of probation work in which ethnic minorities are disadvantaged (HM Inspectorate of Probation 2000).

Lastly in this section, it is worth pointing to enforcement of community sentences as an area requiring further research. Probation services are criticized for failing to maintain expected standards of enforcement, and reports of inspections frequently comment on this; however, they are also expected to increase the proportion of offenders who complete programmes of supervision, which may prove difficult to achieve if large numbers are prosecuted for relatively minor breaches of requirements (Ellis 2000). Some recent research suggests that enforcement action short of breach has positive effects on offenders' behaviour (May and Wadwell 2001), but the details are unclear and more research is needed. In the meantime, it appears that enforcement of community penalties may be less important to other criminal justice agencies: latest reports suggest that unexecuted warrants for breach of community penalties, increasingly handled by civilian fines enforcement officers, are piling up, and some probation services may be asked to cancel them if they remain unexecuted for a year (NAPO 2001b). The time is surely ripe for a new look at enforcement based not on what politicians think will sound good, but on what it achieves, which should be to support effective supervision rather than to frustrate it.

THE FUTURE OF COMMUNITY PENALTIES

Community penalties clearly have a future: they are such an important part of our sentencing system that it is not possible to imagine their disappearance under any reasonably probable or foreseeable set of criminal justice policies. That does not mean we can expect all, or even most, of their features to continue as they are; change has occurred with unprecedented speed over the last few years and shows few signs of slowing down, despite the clear strains involved for organizations and practitioners. Some aspects of future policy and practice can be regarded as probable, based on extrapolation of firmly established current trends, while some are no more than possible, depending on the unknown outcomes of current processes or experiments.

Some of the clear candidates for inclusion in the 'probable' future are information technology, monitoring, and standardization. Although the development of the online case management system CRAMS has been fraught with expensive procurement problems, other systems are being developed and rolled out piecemeal which will eventually be part of an integrated system. The offender assessment system OASys is being made available to services during 2002 after a longer-than-planned development process, and although it is initially for use in a paper version only, it is guaranteed to generate demand for the eventual online version if only because the paper version is fairly cumbersome. 'Integrated Accredited Programme Software' is also approaching general availability and, when fully online, will greatly facilitate both tracking of offenders through programmes and auditing of the programmes' delivery and effectiveness. The same software which helps probation staff to monitor offenders can be used, when it is part of a national system, to monitor the work of probation services. In addition we can expect to see more use of electronic monitoring, including perhaps the tracking tag capable of following an offender's movements and the use of voice recognition software to verify the identity of offenders checking in by telephone. Another probable consequence of the increasing use of larger information flows to support processes such as audit (HM Inspectorate of Probation 2001) and resource allocation will be greater standardization of policies and practices, and a higher degree of compliance with National Standards and any other performance indicators that are linked to funding.

Another feature of future probation services is likely to be a continuing emphasis on risk. Probation services have become increasingly conscious of their role in supervising (together where possible with other agencies) the potentially violent offender or the predatory sex offender (Kemshall and Maguire 2001), and further developments may be anticipated here: for example, intensive surveillance schemes in collaboration with the police (Walton 2001). The problem of what to offer to the 'high risk, low needs' offender is likely to receive more attention, and this is one of the areas in which electronic monitoring may have a contribution to make. One further consequence of this is likely to be an increase in 'bifurcation', or the provision of very different levels and kinds of services according to the assessed dangerousness of the offender. Partly this reflects the 'risk principle', but it is also the characteristic response to an increasing focus on dangerousness (Bottoms 1977).

Two other recent trends seem to have every prospect of becoming still more firmly established. One is the continuing extension of the 'What Works' agenda beyond programmes and community punishment orders to consider effective case management, pro-social approaches to supervision, and improved opportunities of access to 'protective factors' or social resources such as education, training, employment, accommodation, assistance with substance abuse problems, and health care. The approaches to resettlement currently being developed for people released from short-term prison sentences are often concerned with problems that many offenders face whether or not recently released from prison, and although the term 'resettlement needs' suggests needs which are particularly characteristic of those who have recently been removed from the community, they can more usefully be thought of as 'social integration' needs or 'inclusion' needs. If unmet, they can often frustrate even a quite determined attempt to avoid reoffending.

The other clear candidate for inclusion in the 'probable' category is increasing differentiation and specialization in the Probation Service itself, together with an increasing amount of service delivery by staff who are not probation officers. New roles are increasingly underpinned by competency specifications, selection, assessment, and specialist training. These are increasingly organized into a comprehensive framework by the Criminal Justice National Training Organization (CJNTO 2001), including vocational qualifications which can potentially be shared with staff of other criminal justice services. The probation officer is no longer a semi-autonomous generalist attempting a range of roles and tasks on the basis of a broad qualification and experience; instead, he or she is deployed by management in a particular service delivery niche, and will often not be a qualified probation officer but a staff member of some other grade who has received specific training for the particular role. The consequences for industrial relations and human resources policy of a situation where people of very different grades and pay can find themselves doing the same work, or even in a supervisory relationship which reverses the normal grade seniority, have yet to be explored and confronted, but they will need to be.

KEY VARIABLES: RESEARCH AND POLITICS

Moving from probable to possible future scenarios, much will depend on two factors which are currently difficult to predict: first, the outcomes of evaluation of the current wave of 'What Works' initiatives; and secondly, the politics of law and order. Considering these in turn, the large-scale roll-out of accredited programmes to the Probation Service is not due to produce clear evidence of its effectiveness or ineffectiveness for some time. The reconviction studies which will form the final and most conclusive stage of evaluation of the original 'Pathfinder' pilot schemes will not report until 2003, and evaluation of initiatives rolled out since the Pathfinders will appear a good deal later. However, there are a number of reasons why these evaluations might not prove quite so critical in determining the future of probation as many people would naturally suppose. Obviously a clear set of negative results would lead to considerable problems, but the more likely scenario of mixed and some unclear results would probably not lead to huge changes in policy, provided that the political climate remains broadly similar to today's. Findings will probably not need to be uniformly or strongly positive to justify the continuation of projects or programmes. It will be possible to argue that the evaluations reflect early or underdeveloped practice (particularly in the assessment of offenders, an acknowledged area of difficulty pending the introduction of new methods such as OASys), or that early implementation problems meant that evaluations were not based on best practice (a clear feature, for example, of some of the 'resettlement' Pathfinder projects (Lewis *et al.* 2001)).

More importantly, public and political commitment to 'What Works' creates a climate in which even limited positive findings can carry a good deal of weight, in contrast to the near invisibility of even quite substantial positive findings during the 'nothing works' era. The target which has been set for the Probation and Prison Services of a 5 per cent reduction in re-offending by offenders under their supervision presents considerable problems of measurement. In addition, the Probation Service performance indicator related to this target concentrates on the numbers of offenders completing accredited programmes rather than on direct measurement of crime reduction (Probation Circular 92/2000). In sum, there are a number of reasons to believe that even a moderate amount of good news from the evaluations currently in progress would be seen as broad justification for the continuation of current policies, particularly as the focus of recent political statements has been more on community safety than on crime reduction. This will tend to direct scrutiny towards the effectiveness of other criminal justice agencies such as the police. Implementation of the recent sentencing review (Halliday 2001) will also tend to consolidate the position and role of probation services by substantially increasing the number of people under their supervision. This is likely to happen regardless of whether there is any trend to decrease the use of custodial sentences, since the new proposals for 'custody plus' involve a compulsory period of post-release supervision for almost all short-sentence prisoners.

In such a system the Probation Service may well find itself simply so central to the process of managing offenders, and so well integrated into the penal process, that it cannot easily be subjected to the kind of political attack which it experienced during the early 1990s. However, being a big player in the system does not guarantee influence and friendly policies: in the 1980s the Prison Service was a very big player, but policy was driven by the attempt to find alternatives to custody, since prisons were widely perceived as failing. A better scenario for probation would follow from a very positive set of evaluation findings, which would greatly increase the Service's capacity to influence policies and events.

In addition to the unpredictable results of current evaluations, the second (and probably greater) risk factor for the future of community penalties must be the political climate. As Garland has pointed out, late modern criminal justice policies are subject to frequent and sometimes extreme changes of direction (Garland 1996) as politicians seek support from anxious populations through media-friendly gestures. The Conservative Home Secretary Michael Howard's 'prison works' speech of 1993 was just such a gesture, which had profound consequences for the Probation Service and for the principles of the 1991 Criminal Justice Act. Nobody can rule out the possibility of similar populist stunts in the future, and a continuing search for eye-catching initiatives by New Labour politicians has already been responsible for unhelpful tinkering such as changing the familiar names of the former probation and community service orders. Two factors, however, seem likely to offer some protection for community penalties: one is the strong survival instinct of senior probation managers, which historically has allowed them to embrace a wide and varied range of political and technocratic initiatives; the other is the improbability of a sustained campaign against community sentences as long as they remain a relatively cheap sentencing option for many thousands of offenders every year.

One further way in which probation services might seek to strengthen their political position and their perceived legitimacy might be to learn something from the politicians, and to find their own ways of seeking a greater degree of public support. Probation services always risk being seen as primarily existing for the benefit of the offender rather than serving the community as a whole. A probation service which could show communities how they gain from the rehabilitation of offenders would itself gain significantly in influence and in perceived legitimacy. One implication of this would be that instead of rehabilitative programmes being seen primarily as a benefit to offenders, and therefore arguably unfair to those facing similar difficulties who have not offended, probation services should try to present rehabilitation as work that offenders undertake as a consequence of a crime: work which is directed to changing their own behaviour and attitudes in a more pro-social direction, to the advantage of the communities in which they live. A rehabilitative penalty can reflect the interests and values of the wider community, and perhaps equip offenders with skills to maintain themselves more effectively and to contribute more to society. The notion of rehabilitation as offenders working to rehabilitate themselves may be better aligned with community values, and more consistent with restorative principles, than the notion of offenders simply receiving help. It would also probably be more constructive than the attempt to improve public confidence by ever more rigorous approaches to enforcement.

A concrete way to embody these principles in practice (explored further in Raynor 2001) might be to seek to include an explicitly reparative element in a wider range of community sentences, perhaps with some community involvement, or involvement where appropriate of victims, in determining what the reparative content should be. The central point is to demonstrate that rehabilitation is itself fundamentally restorative and benefits the community as well as the offender. A probation service which could consistently achieve this shift in public perception would be a significant contributor to criminal justice policy and practice, promoting not only crime reduction but also the belief that communities can engage constructively with the problems caused by crime. However, this kind of speculation lies outside the scope of this chapter, except to illustrate the possibility that probation services may continue to explore their undoubted potential to develop some qualitatively different responses to offending: penalties which differ from other sentences not only in degree but also in kind, building on human capacities for cooperation, sympathy, and inclusion rather than hostility and division.

Selected further reading

General texts on community penalties or the work of probation services quickly go out of date. Current edited collections include David Ward and Malcolm Lacey's *Probation: Working for Justice*, first published in 1995 (London: Whiting and Birch) and about to emerge in a substantially updated edition, and an excellent collection of conference papers edited by Anthony Bottoms, Loraine Gelsthorpe, and Susan Rex, *Community Penalties: Change and Challenges* (Cullompton: Willan, 2001). Among other general texts, see Ian Brownlee's *Community Punishment* (Harlow: Longman, 1998) and, for a critical account, Ann Worrall's *Punishment in the Community* (Harlow: Longman, 1997). *Effective Probation Practice* by

Peter Raynor, David Smith, and Maurice Vanstone (Basingstoke: Macmillan 1994) is widely used but partly outdated. A new general text is Raynor and Vanstone's *Understanding Community Penalties* (Buckingham: Open University Press, forthcoming), some of which is based on an expanded version of this chapter.

On the history and development of Britain's probation services, see Dorothy Bochel's *Probation and After-Care: its development in England and Wales* (Edinburgh: Scottish Academic Press, 1976), which is a sound descriptive account of early developments, and Bill McWilliams' series of *Howard Journal* articles (McWilliams 1983, 1985, 1986, 1987) which provided a 'history of ideas' in probation up to the mid-1980s. Maurice Vanstone's recent historical research (Vanstone 2001) is still being prepared for publication, but some of it has informed the historical discussion in *Understanding Community Penalties*.

Other useful texts and articles on particular aspects of Probation Service practice include Chris Trotter's *Working with Involuntary Clients* (London: Sage, 1999), and Anthony Bottoms and Andy Stelman's excellent *Social Inquiry Reports* (Aldershot: Wildwood House, 1988). Community service orders (now community punishment orders) were well covered in their early days by texts such as Ken Pease and Bill McWilliams' edited collection *Community Service by Order* (Edinburgh: Scottish Academic Press, 1980) and, more recently, by Gill McIvor's Scottish evaluative study *Sentenced to Serve* (Aldershot: Avebury, 1992).

Through-care and after-care of prisoners are addressed by Brian Williams in *Work with Prisoners* (Birmingham: Venture, 1991) and in some recent research (for example, Maguire and Raynor 1997; Maguire *et al.* 2000). Brian Williams has also written about the Probation Service's new responsibilities in relation to victims of crime in *Working with the Victims of Crime* (London: Jessica Kingsley, 1999). On the emerging area of risk, Hazel Kemshall's *Risk in Probation Practice* (Aldershot: Ashgate, 1998) is useful, as are a number of articles (for example, Robinson 1999; Kemshall and Maguire 2001).

Lastly, the recent literature on 'What Works' includes two excellent edited collections, one from Britain and one from America: James McGuire's *What Works: Reducing Reoffending* (Chichester: Wiley, 1995); and Alan Harland's *Choosing Correctional Options that Work* (Thousand Oaks, Cal.: Sage, 1996). The Home Office has published Tim Chapman and Michael Hough's *Evidence-Based Practice* (London: Home Office, 1998) and James McGuire's *Cognitive-Behavioural Approaches* (London: Home Office, 2000). The crucial transition from evaluated pilot to general application is explored in the recent collection edited by Gary Bernfeld, David Farrington and Alan Leschied, *Offender Rehabilitation in Practice* (Chichester: Wiley, 2001), and readers interested in keeping up with the latest results of the 'Pathfinder' evaluations are advised to pay regular visits to the Home Office web site.

References

ADAMS, S. (1961), 'Interaction between individual interview therapy and treatment amenability in older youth authority wards', in *Inquiries Concerning Kinds of Treatment for Kinds of Offenders*, 27–44, Sacramento, Cal.: California Board of Corrections.

ALDRIDGE, M., and EADIE, C. (1997), 'Manufacturing an Issue: the Case of Probation Officer Training', *Critical Social Policy*, 17: 111–24.

ANDREWS, D.A., and BONTA, J. (1995), *The Level of Service Inventory-Revised Manual*, Toronto: Multi-Health Systems Inc.

—— and —— (1998), *The Psychology of Criminal Conduct*, Cincinnati, Oh.: Anderson.

ANDREWS, D.A., ZINGER, I., HOGE, R.D., BONTA, J., GENDREAU, P., and CULLEN, F.T. (1990), 'Does Correctional Treatment Work? A Clinically Relevant and Psychologically Informed Meta-Analysis', *Criminology*, 28: 369–404.

AUBREY, R., and HOUGH, M. (1997), *Assessing Offenders' Needs: assessment scales for the Probation Service*, Research Study 166, London: Home Office.

BAILEY, R., and WARD, D. (1992), *Probation Supervision: Attitudes to Formalised Helping*, Belfast: Probation Board for Northern Ireland.

BECK, U. (1992), *Risk Society: Towards a New Modernity*, London: Sage.

BEECH, A., FISHER, D., and BECKETT, R. (1998), *STEP 3: an Evaluation of the Prison Sex Offender Treatment Programme*, London: Home Office.

BERNTSEN, K., and CHRISTIANSEN, K. (1965), 'A resocialization experiment with short-term offenders', *Scandinavian Studies in Criminology*, 1: 35–54.

BLACKBURN, R. (1980), *Still not working? A look at recent outcomes in offender rehabilitation*, Paper presented at the Scottish Branch of the British Psychological Society Conference on Deviance, University of Stirling.

BONTA, J. (1996), 'Risk-needs assessment and treatment', in A. Harland (ed.), *Choosing Correctional Options that Work*, 18–32, London: Sage.

——, WALLACE-CAPRETTA, S., and ROONEY, J. (2000), 'Can Electronic Monitoring Make a Difference? An evaluation of 3 Canadian programmes', *Crime and Delinquency*, 46: 61–75.

BOTTOMS, A.E. (1977), 'Reflections on the Renaissance of Dangerousness', *Howard Journal*, 16: 70–96.

—— (1980), *The Suspended Sentence after Ten Years*, Leeds: Centre for Social Work and Applied Social Studies, University of Leeds.

—— (2001), 'Compliance and community penalties', in A. Bottoms, L. Gelsthorpe, and S. Rex (eds), *Community Penalties: Change and Challenges*, Cullompton, Devon: Willan.

—— and McWILLIAMS, W. (1979), 'A non-treatment paradigm for probation practice', *British Journal of Social Work*, 9: 159–202.

BREWER, C., and LAIT, J. (1980), *Can Social Work Survive?*, London: Temple Smith.

BRODY, S.R. (1976), *The Effectiveness of Sentencing*, London: HMSO.

BURNETT, R. (1996), *Fitting Supervision to Offenders: assessment and allocation decisions in the Probation Service*, Research Study 169, London: Home Office.

CHAPMAN, T., and HOUGH, M. (1998), *Evidence-Based Practice*, London: Home Office.

CJNTO (2001), *Annual Report 2000–2001*, London: Community Justice National Training Organization.

COHEN, S. (1985), *Visions of Social Control*, Cambridge: Polity.

COPAS, J.B. (1992), *Statistical analysis for a risk of reconviction predictor*, Report to the Home Office, University of Warwick: unpublished.

DAVIES, M. (1969), *Probationers in their Social Environment*, Research Study 2, London: HMSO.

—— (1974), *Social Work in the Environment*, Research Study 21, London: HMSO.

DAVIS, G., CADDICK, B., LYON, K., DOLING, L., HASLER, J., WEBSTER, A., REED, M., and FORD, K. (1997), *Addressing the literacy needs of offenders under probation supervision*, Research Study 169, London: Home Office.

DENMAN, G. (1982), *Intensive Intermediate Treatment with Juvenile Offenders: a Handbook of Assessment and Groupwork Practice*, Lancaster: Centre of Youth, Crime and Community, Lancaster University.

DEWS, V., and WATTS, J. (1994), *Review of Probation Officer Recruitment and Training*, London: Home Office.

DITCHFIELD, J. (1976), *Police Cautioning in England and Wales*, Home Office Research Study 37, London: HMSO.

DOWDEN, C., and ANDREWS, D. (1999), 'What Works for Female Offenders: a Meta-Analytic Review', *Crime and Delinquency*, 45, 4: 438–52.

DRAKEFORD, M. (1983), 'Probation: containment or liberty?', *Probation Journal* 30: 7–10.

ELLIS, T. (2000), 'Enforcement Policy and Practice: Evidence-Based or Rhetoric-Based?', *Criminal Justice Matters*, 39: 6–8.

FOLKARD, M.S., SMITH, D.E., and SMITH, D.D. (1976), *IMPACT. Intensive Matched Probation and After-Care Treatment. Volume II. The results of the experiment*, Home Office Research Study 36, London: HMSO.

FOREN, R., and BAILEY, R. (1968) *Authority in Social Casework*, Oxford: Pergamon Press.

FRIENDSHIP, C., BLUD, L., ERIKSON, M., TRAVERS, R., and THORNTON, D. (2001), *Cognitive-behavioural treatment for imprisoned offenders: an evaluation of HM Prison Service's cognitive skills programmes.* Report to the Joint Prison/ Probation Accreditation Panel.

FRUDE, N., HONESS, T., and MAGUIRE, M. (1994), *CRIME-PICS II Manual*, Cardiff: Michael and Associates.

GARLAND, D. (1985), *Punishment and Welfare: A History of Penal Strategies*, Aldershot: Gower.

—— (1996), 'The Limits of the Sovereign state: Strategies of Crime Control in Contemporary Society', *British Journal of Criminology*, 36: 445–71.

GELSTHORPE, L., and RAYNOR, P. (1995), 'Quality and effectiveness in probation officers' reports to sentencers', *British Journal of Criminology*, 35: 188–200.

GENDREAU, P., and ROSS, R. (1980), 'Effective correctional treatment: bibliotherapy for cynics', in R. Ross and P. Gendreau (eds), *Effective Correctional Treatment*, Toronto: Butterworths.

HALLIDAY, J. (2001), *Making Punishments Work*, London: Home Office.

HAMAI, K., HARRIS, R., VILLE, R., HOUGH, M., and ZVEKIC, U. (1995), *Probation Round the World: a Comparative Study*, London: Routledge.

HARRIS, R. (1994), 'Continuity and Change: Probation and Politics in Contemporary Britain', *International Journal of Offender Therapy and Comparative Criminology*, 38: 33–45.

HATCHER, R., and McGUIRE, J. (2001), *Report on the Psychometric Evaluation of the Think-First Programme in Community Settings*, Liverpool: University of Liverpool Department of Clinical Psychology.

HER MAJESTY'S INSPECTORATE OF PROBATION (1995), *Dealing with Dangerous People: the Probation Service and Public Protection*, London: Home Office.

—— (2000), *Towards Race Equality*, London: Home Office.

—— (2001), *Performance Standards Manual for the Delivery of Accredited Group Work Programmes*, London: HMIP.

HOLLIN, C. (1995), 'The meaning and implications of programme integrity', in J. McGuire (ed.), *What Works: Reducing Reoffending*, Chichester: Wiley.

HOLLIS, F. (1964), *Casework: a Psychosocial Therapy*, New York: Random House.

HOME OFFICE (1984), *Probation Service in England and Wales: Statement of National Objectives and Priorities*, London: Home Office.

—— (1992), *National Standards for the Supervision of Offenders in the Community*, London: Home Office.

—— (1995), *National Standards for the Supervision of Offenders in the Community*, London: Home Office.

—— (1998), *Joining Forces to Protect the Public*, London: Home Office.

—— (1999), *What Works: reducing re-offending: evidence-based practice*, London: Home Office.

—— (2001), *Probation Statistics England and Wales 1999*, London: Home Office.

HOOD, R. (1974), *Tolerance and the Tariff*, London: NACRO.

HOUGH, M. (1996), *Drugs Misuse and the Criminal Justice System: a review of the literature*, London: Drugs Prevention Initiative, Home Office.

HUDSON, B. (1988), 'Social skills training in practice', *Probation Journal*, 35: 85–91.

HUNT, A.W. (1964), 'Enforcement in probation casework', *British Journal of Delinquency*, 4: 239–52.

IZZO, R., and ROSS, R. (1990), 'Meta-analysis of rehabilitation programs for juvenile delinquents', *Criminal Justice and Behaviour*, 17: 134–42.

JAFFE, H. (1979), 'Probation with a Flair', *Federal Probation*, 43: 25–36.

JOINT PRISON/PROBATION ACCREDITATION PANEL (2000), *First Report from the Joint Prison/ Probation Accreditation Panel*, London: Home Office.

JONES, K. (2001), 'Probation in Romania', *Probation Journal*, 48: 269–79.

KEMSHALL, H. (1996), *Reviewing Risk: A review of research on the assessment of risk and dangerousness: implications for policy and practice in the Probation Service*, Birmingham: Report to the Home Office Research and Statistics Directorate.

—— and MAGUIRE, M. (2001), 'Public protection, partnership and risk penality: the multi-agency risk management of sexual and violent offenders', *Punishment and Society*, 3: 237–64.

KENT PROBATION AND AFTER-CARE SERVICE (1981), 'Probation Control Unit: a community-based experiment in intensive supervision', in *Annual Report on the Work of the Medway Centre*, Maidstone: Kent Probation and After-Care Service.

KILLIAS, M., AEBI, M., and RIBEAUD, D. (2000), 'Does Community Service Rehabilitate Better than Short-Term Imprisonment? Results of a controlled experiment', *Howard Journal*, 39: 40–57.

LEWIS, S., MAGUIRE, M., RAYBOULD, S., RAYNOR, P., RIX, A., VANSTONE, M., and VENNARD, J. (2001), *Evaluation of Crime Reduction Programme Pathfinder Projects: Resettlement of Short-Term Prisoners*, Interim Report to Home Office, unpublished.

LIPSEY, M. (1992), 'Juvenile delinquency treatment: a meta-analytic enquiry into the variability of effects', in T. Cook, H. Cooper, D.S. Cordray, H. Hartmann, L.V. Hedges, R.L. Light, T.A. Louis, and F. Mosteller (eds), *Meta-Analysis for Explanation: a case-book*, 83–127, New York: Russell Sage.

LIPTON, D., MARTINSON, R., and WILKS, J. (1975), *The Effectiveness of Correctional Treatment*, New York: Praeger.

LLOYD, C., MAIR, G., and HOUGH, M. (1994), *Explaining Reconviction Rates: a critical analysis*, London: HMSO.

MAGUIRE, M., PERROUD, B., and RAYNOR, P. (1996), *Automatic Conditional Release: the first two years*, Research Study 156, London, Home Office.

——, and RAYNOR, P. (1997), 'The Revival of Throughcare: Rhetoric and Reality in Automatic Conditional Release', *British Journal of Criminology*, 37, 1: 1–14.

——, ——, VANSTONE, M., and KYNCH, J. (2000), 'Voluntary After-Care and the Probation Service: a case of diminishing responsibility', *Howard Journal of Criminal Justice*, 39: 234–48.

MAIR, G. (1988), *Probation Day Centres*, Home Office Research Study 100, London: HMSO.

—— (1995), 'Standing at the Crossroads: What Works in Community Penalties', *Managing What Works Conference Programme*, London: Home Office.

——, LLOYD, C., NEE, C., and SIBBITT, R. (1994) *Intensive Probation in England and Wales: an evaluation*, London: HMSO.

—— and MAY, C. (1997), *Offenders on Probation*, Research Study 167, London: Home Office.

—— and NEE, C. (1990), *Electronic Monitoring: the trials and their results*, Home Office Research Study 120, London: HMSO.

MARTINSON, R. (1974), 'What works? Questions and answers about prison reform', *The Public Interest*, 35: 22–54.

—— (1979), 'New findings, new views: a note of caution regarding sentencing reform', *Hofstra Law Review*, (7): 243–58

MAY, C. (1999), *Explaining Reconviction Following a Community Sentence: the role of social factors*, Home Office Research Study 192, London: Home Office.

—— and WADWELL, J. (2001), *Enforcing Community Penalties: the relationship between enforcement and reconviction*, Research Findings 155, London: Home Office.

McGUIRE, J. (ed.) (1995), *What Works: Reducing Reoffending*, Chichester: Wiley.

—— (2000), *Cognitive-Behavioural Approaches*, London: Home Office.

——, BROOMFIELD, D., ROBINSON, C., and ROWSON, B. (1995), 'Short-term impact of probation programs: an evaluative study', *International Journal of Offender Therapy and Comparative Criminology*, 39: 23–42.

—— and PRIESTLEY, P. (1985), *Offending Behaviour: skills and stratagems for going straight*, London: Batsford.

McIVOR, G. (1990), *Sanctions for Serious or Persistent Offenders*, Stirling: Social Work Research Centre.

—— (1991), 'Social Work Intervention in Community Service', *British Journal of Social Work*, 21: 591–610.

—— (1992), *Sentenced to Serve*, Aldershot: Avebury.

McLAREN, K. (1992), *Reducing Reoffending: What Works Now?*, Wellington, NZ: Department of Justice.

McWILLIAMS, W. (1983), 'The Mission to the English Police Courts 1876–1936', *Howard Journal*, 22: 129–47.

—— (1985), 'The Mission Transformed: Professionalisation of Probation Between the Wars', *Howard Journal*, 24: 257–74.

—— (1986), 'The English Probation System and the Diagnostic Ideal', *Howard Journal*, 25: 241–60.

—— (1987), 'Probation, Pragmatism and Policy', *Howard Journal*, 26: 97–121.

MERRINGTON, S., and STANLEY, S. (2000), 'Doubts about the What Works Initiative', *Probation Journal*, 47: 272–5.

MIRRLEES-BLACK, C. (2001), *Confidence in the Criminal Justice System: findings from the 2000 British Crime Survey*, Research Findings 137, London: Home Office.

MONGER, M. (1964), *Casework in Probation*, London: Butterworth.

MORTIMER, E. (2001), *Electronic Monitoring of Released Prisoners: an evaluation of the Home Detention Curfew scheme*, Research Findings 139, London: Home Office.

NATIONAL ASSOCIATION OF PROBATION OFFICERS (1995), 'New Reconviction Scale', *NAPO News* 72: 1.

—— (2001a), 'AGM Resolutions 2001', *NAPO News*, 134: 10–15.

—— (2001b), 'Unexecuted Warrants', *NAPO News*, 135: 1.

NATIONAL PROBATION SERVICE (2001), *A New Choreography*, London: Home Office.

OASYS PROJECT TEAM (1999), *The Offender Assessment System (OASys) Manual*, London: Home Office.

PALMER, T. (1974), 'The Youth Authority's Community Treatment Project', *Federal Probation*, 38: 3–14.

—— (1975), 'Martinson revisited', *Journal of Research in Crime and Delinquency*, 12: 133–52.

PEASE, K., and McWILLIAMS, W. (eds) (1980), *Community Service by Order*, Edinburgh: Scottish Academic Press.

——, BILLINGHAM, S., and EARNSHAW, I. (1977), *Community Service Assessed in 1976*, Home Office Research Study No. 39, London: HMSO.

PERRY, F. (1974), *Information for the Court*, Cambridge: Institute of Criminology.

PETERSILIA, J. (1990), 'Conditions that permit intensive supervision programmes to survive', *Crime and Delinquency*, 36: 126–45.

PRIESTLEY, P., McGUIRE, J., FLEGG, D., HEMSLEY, V., and WELHAM, D. (1978), *Social Skills and Personal Problem Solving: A Handbook of Methods*, London: Tavistock.

——, ——, ——, ——, ——, and BARNITT, R. (1984), *Social Skills in Prisons and in the Community*, London: Routledge and Kegan Paul.

RADZINOWICZ, L. (ed.) (1958), *The Results of Probation*, A Report of the Cambridge Department of Criminal Science, London: Macmillan.

RAYNOR, P. (1988), *Probation as an Alternative to Custody*, Aldershot: Avebury.

—— (1997), 'Some observations on rehabilitation and justice', *Howard Journal*, 36: 248–62.

—— (1998a), 'Reading Probation Statistics: a Critical Comment', *VISTA* 3: 181–5.

—— (1998b), 'Attitudes, social problems and reconvictions in the STOP probation experiment', *Howard Journal*, 37: 1–15.

—— (2001), 'Community penalties and social integration: "community" as solution and as problem', in A. Bottoms, L. Gelsthorpe, and S. Rex (eds), *Community Penalties: Change and Challenges*, Cullompton, Devon: Willan.

——, KYNCH, J., ROBERTS, C., and MERRINGTON, M. (2000), *Risk and Need Assessment In Probation Services: an Evaluation*, Research Study 211, London: Home Office.

—— and MILES, M. (2001), *Risks, Needs and Reoffending: evaluating the impact of community sentences in Jersey*, Report to the Jersey Probation Service, Swansea: University of Wales, Swansea, and Cognitive Centre Foundation.

—— and VANSTONE, M. (1994), *Straight Thinking on Probation: third interim evaluation report: reconvictions within 12 months*, Bridgend: Mid-Glamorgan Probation Service.

—— and —— (1996), 'Reasoning and Rehabilitation in Britain: the results of the Straight Thinking On Probation (STOP) programme', *International Journal of Offender Therapy and Comparative Criminology*, 40: 272–84.

—— and —— (1997), *Straight Thinking On Probation (STOP): The Mid Glamorgan Experiment. Probation Studies Unit Report No. 4*, Oxford: University of Oxford Centre for Criminological Research.

REINVENTING PROBATION COUNCIL (2000), *Transforming Probation through Leadership: the Broken Windows Model*, Internet publication, New York: Manhattan Institute.

REX, S. (1996), *Perceptions of Probation in a Context of Just Deserts*, PhD thesis, University of Cambridge.

—— and MATRAVERS, A. (eds) (1998), *Pro-Social Modelling and Legitimacy*, Cambridge: Institute of Criminology.

RICHMOND, M. (1917), *Social Diagnosis*, New York: Russell Sage Foundation.

ROBERTS, C. (1989), *Hereford and Worcester Probation Service Young Offender Project: first evaluation report*, Oxford: Department of Social and Administrative Studies.

——, BURNETT, R., KIRBY, A., and HAMILL, H. (1996), *A System for Evaluating Probation Practice*, Probation Studies Unit Report 1, Oxford: Centre for Criminological Research.

ROBINSON, G. (1999), 'Risk Management and Rehabilitation in the Probation Service: Collision and Collusion', *Howard Journal*, 38: 421–33.

—— (2001), 'Power, knowledge and What Works in probation', *Howard Journal*, 40: 235–54.

ROSS, R.R., and FABIANO, E.A. (1985), *Time to Think: a cognitive model of delinquency prevention and offender rehabilitation*, Johnson City, Tenn: Institute of Social Sciences and Arts.

——, —— and Ewles, C.D. (1988), 'Reasoning and rehabilitation', *International Journal of Offender Therapy and Comparative Criminology*, 32: 29–35.

——, —— and Ross, R.D. (1986), *Reasoning and Rehabilitation: a handbook for teaching cognitive skills*, Ottawa: University of Ottawa.

Shaw, M. (1974), *Social Work in Prison*, London: HMSO.

Sinclair, I. (1971), *Hostels for Probationers*, Home Office Research Study 6, London: HMSO.

Smith, D. (1985), *Criminology for Social Work*, Basingstoke: Macmillan.

Stern, V. (1998), *A Sin Against the Future: Imprisonment in the World*, Harmondsworth: Penguin.

Stewart, J., Smith, D., Stewart, G., and Fullwood C. (1994), *Understanding Offending Behaviour*, Harlow: Longman.

Sugg, D., Moore, L., and Howard, P. (2001), *Electronic monitoring and offending behaviour—reconviction results for the second year of trials of curfew orders*, Research Findings 141, London: Home Office.

Thornton, D. (1987), 'Treatment effects on recidivism: a reappraisal of the nothing works doctrine', in B. McGurk, D. Thornton, and M. Williams (eds), *Applying Psychology to Imprisonment: Theory and Practice*, London: HMSO.

Thorpe, D.H., Smith, D., Green, C.J., and Paley, J. (1980), *Out of Care*, London: Allen & Unwin.

Thorpe, J. (1979), *Social Inquiry Reports: a survey*, Home Office Research Study 48, London: HMSO.

Trotter, C. (1993), *The Supervision of Offenders—What Works? A Study Undertaken in Community Based Corrections*, Victoria: Social Work Department, Monash University and the Victoria Department of Justice, Melbourne.

—— (2000), 'Social work education, pro-social modelling and effective probation practice', *Probation Journal*, 47: 256–61.

Turnbull, P., McSweeney, T., Webster, R., Edmunds, M., and Hough, M. (2000), *Drug Treatment and Testing Orders: final evaluation report*, Research Study 212, London: Home Office.

Underdown, A. (1998), *Strategies for Effective Supervision: Report of the HMIP What Works Project*, London: Home Office.

van der Laan, P. (1999), 'Electronic Monitoring in Europe: outcomes from experiments in England and Wales, the Netherlands and Sweden', *Bulletin of the Conference Permanente Européenne de la Probation*, 13: 8–10.

Vanstone, M. (2000), 'Cognitive-behavioural work with offenders in the UK: a history of influential endeavour', *Howard Journal*, 39, 2: 171–83.

—— (2001), *Making Sense of Probation: a History of Professional Discourse*, PhD thesis, University of Wales.

—— and Raynor, P. (1981), 'Diversion from prison—a partial success and a missed opportunity', *Probation Journal*, 28: 85–9.

von Hirsch, A. (1976), *Doing Justice*, New York: Hill and Wang.

Walker, N., Farrington, D., and Tucker, G. (1981), 'Reconviction rates of adult males after different sentences', *British Journal of Criminology*, 21: 357–60.

Walton, D. (2001), 'When the Carrot Meets the Stick', *What Works*, 6: 6.

Whitfield, D. (1997), *Tackling the Tag*, Winchester: Waterside.

Wilkins, L.T. (1958), 'A small comparative study of the results of probation', *British Journal of Delinquency*, 8: 201–9.

Wilkinson, J. (1997), 'The Impact of Ilderton Motor Project on Motor Vehicle Crime and Offending', *British Journal of Criminology*, 37: 568–81.

—— (1998), *Developing the evidence-base for probation programmes*, PhD thesis, University of Surrey.

INDEX